NATIONAL INDEX
of AMERICAN IMPRINTS
THROUGH 1800
THE SHORT-TITLE EVANS

NATIONAL INDEX
of AMERICAN IMPRINTS
THROUGH 1800
THE SHORT-TITLE EVANS

Volume Two: N-Z

CLIFFORD K. SHIPTON

JAMES E. MOONEY

AMERICAN ANTIQUARIAN SOCIETY
and BARRE PUBLISHERS · 1969

SYMBOLS AND SOURCES

AAS	American Antiquarian Society, Worcester, Mass.
AB	Association of the Bar of the City of New York, N. Y.
ABHS	American Baptist Historical Society, Rochester, N. Y.
AHTS	Andover Harvard Theological Library, Cambridge, Mass.
	Albany Institute, Albany, N. Y.
	American Bible Society, New York, N. Y.
	American Geographical Society, New York, N. Y.
	Amherst College, Amherst, Mass.
ANTS	Andover Newton Theological Seminary, Newton Center, Mass.
APS	American Philosophical Society, Philadelphia, Pa.
	Archives Nationales, Paris, France
	Archivo General des Indias, Seville, Spain
	Archivo Nacional, Havana, Cuba
	Attleborough Public Library, Attleborough, Mass.
BA	Boston Athenaeum, Boston, Mass.
Ball	Miss Elisabeth Ball, Muncie, Indiana
Bancroft	Bancroft Library, University of California, Berkeley, Calif.
	Bennington Museum, Bennington, Vt.
BM	British Museum, London, England.
BMFA	Museum of Fine Arts, Boston, Mass.
BML	Boston Medical Library, Boston, Mass. (Now Francis L. Countway Library)
BN	Bibliothèque Nationale, Paris, France
BODL	Bodleian Library, Oxford, England
	Boston College, Chestnut Hill, Mass.
	Boston University, Boston, Mass.
	Bostonian Society, Boston, Mass.
Bowe	Forrest Bowe, New York, N. Y.
BPL	Boston Public Library, Boston, Mass.
	Brattleborough Public Library, Brattleborough, Vt.
	Brooklyn Public Library, Brooklyn, N. Y.

BrU	Brown University, Providence, R. I.
	Burton Collection, Detroit Public Library, Detroit, Mich.
Butterfield	Roger Butterfield, New York, N. Y.
	California, University of, Berkeley, Calif.
	Cambridge University, Cambridge, England
	Carnegie Institute of Technology, Pittsburgh, Pa.
Carson	Mrs. Joseph Carson, Philadelphia, Pa.
	Central College, Pella, Iowa
	Chatham Historical Society, Chatham, N. J.
	Christ Church College, Oxford, England
CHS	Connecticut Historical Society, Hartford, Conn.
	Cincinnati Historical Society, Cincinnati, Ohio (formerly Ohio Historical and Philosophical Society, q. v.)
CL&CLA	Congregational Library, 14 Beacon St., Boston, Mass.
CLS	Charleston Library Society, Charleston, S. C.
Coleman	George P. Coleman, Williamsburg, Va.
	Colgate-Rochester Divinity School, Rochester, N. Y.
	College of Charleston Library, Charleston, S. C.
	College of Physicians Library, Philadelphia, Pa.
	Collegiate Reformed Church of New York, New York, N. Y.
	Colonial Williamsburg, Inc., Williamsburg, Va.
	Cornell University, Ithaca, N. Y.
Countway	Francis A. Countway Library, Boston, Mass. (formerly Boston Medical Library)
	Crozer Theological Seminary, Chester, Pa.
CSL	Connecticut State Library, Hartford, Conn.
CU	Columbia University, New York, N. Y.
CVHS	Connecticut Valley Historical Society, Springfield, Mass.
DC	Dartmouth College, Hanover, N. H.
	Dedham Historical Society, Dedham, Mass.
Deering	Joseph G. Deering, Saco, Maine (collection sold to Newberry Library, Chicago, Ill., in 1967).
	Delaware Historical Society, Wilmington, Del.
	Delaware Public Archives Commission Library, Dover, Del.
	Delaware State Library (all holdings now in Delaware

	Public Archives Commission Library, Dover, Del.)
DeRGL	Wymberly Jones DeRenne Georgia Library, Savannah, Ga. (now at University of Georgia Libraries, Athens, Ga.)
	Detroit Public Library, Detroit, Mich.
	Drew University, Madison, N. J.
	Duke University Library, Durham, N. C.
duPont	Henry F. duPont, Winterthur, Del.
	East Hampton Free Library, East Hampton, N. Y.
	Eden Theological Seminary, Webster Groves, Mo.
	Edinburgh University, Edinburgh, Scotland
EI	Essex Institute, Salem, Mass.
EPFL	Enoch Pratt Free Library, Baltimore, Md.
Finney	Theodore M. Finney, University of Pittsburgh, Pittsburgh, Pa.
Fisher	Samuel H. Fisher, Litchfield, Conn.
FL	Friends Historical Library, Swarthmore College, Swarthmore, Pa.
	Fort Worth Library, Fort Worth, Tex.
	Furman University, Greenville, S. C.
Gaines	Pierce W. Gaines, Fairfield, Conn.
	Garrett Biblical Institute, Evanston, Ill.
	Garrett, John Work, Library, Evergreen House Foundation, Baltimore, Md.
GHS	Georgia Historical Society, Savannah, Ga.
Gimbel	Colonel Richard Gimbel, Yale University Library, New Haven, Conn.
	Glasgow University, Glasgow, Scotland
Graff	Everett D. Graff, Winnetka, Ill. (collection now at Newberry Library, Chicago, Ill.)
Greenaway	Emerson Greenaway, Free Library of Philadelphia, Philadelphia, Pa.
Greenwood	Mrs. Arthur M. Greenwood, Marlborough, Mass.
Griffin	Gillett Griffin Collection, Princeton University Library, Princeton, N. J.

GrL	Grosvenor Library, Buffalo & Erie County Public Library, Buffalo, N. Y.
GSL	Georgia State Library, Atlanta, Ga.
GSP	German Society of Pennsylvania, Philadelphia, Pa.
GTS	General Theological Seminary of the Protestant Episcopal Church in the United States, New York, N. Y.
GU	Georgetown University Library, Washington, D. C.
	Hartford County Bar Association, Hartford, Conn.
	Hartford Seminary Foundation, Case Memorial Library, Hartford, Conn.
	Haverford College, Haverford, Pa.
	Haverhill Historical Society, Haverhill, Mass.
	Haverhill Public Library, Haverhill, Mass.
HC	Harvard University, Cambridge, Mass.
HEH	Henry E. Huntington Library and Art Gallery, San Marino, Calif.
	Historical Foundation of the Presbyterian and Reformed Churches, Montreat, N. C.
HML	Harvard Medical Library. (now Francis A. Countway Library, Boston, Mass.)
HPL	Hartford Public Library, Hartford, Conn.
	Howard-Tilton Memorial Library, Tulane University, New Orleans, La.
HSP	Historical Society of Pennsylvania, Philadelphia, Pa.
	Hunterian Museum, University of Glasgow, Glasgow, Scotland
	Illinois, University of, Urbana, Ill.
	Indiana, University of, Bloomington, Ind.
	Iowa Masonic Library, Cedar Rapids, Ia.
JCB	John Carter Brown Library, Providence, R. I.
JH	Johns Hopkins University, Baltimore, Md.
	Jones Memorial Library, Lynchburg, Va.
	Juniata College, Huntingdon, Pa.

	Kansas City Public Library, Kansas City, Mo.
	Kansas, University of, Lawrence, Kansas
KySL	Kentucky State Library, Frankfort, Ky.
KyU	Kentucky, University of, Lexington, Ky.
	Lambeth Palace Library, Lambeth, London S. E. 1, England
	Lancaster County Historical Society, Lancaster, Pa.
	Lane Medical Library, San Francisco, Calif.
LCP	Library Company of Philadelphia, Philadelphia, Pa.
LHS	Litchfield Historical Society, Litchfield, Conn.
LIHS	Long Island Historical Society, Brooklyn, N. Y.
LOC	Library of Congress, Washington, D. C.
	Louisville Free Public Library, Louisville, Ky.
	Louisville Law College, Louisville, Ky.
	Lunenburg Historical Society, Lunenburg, Mass.
	Lutheran Theological Seminary, Philadelphia, Pa.
MA	Massachusetts Archives, State Library, Boston, Mass.
	Marywood College, Scranton, Pa.
MdDL	Maryland Diocesan Library, Baltimore, Md.
MdFM	Masonic Temple, Baltimore, Md.
MdHS	Maryland Historical Society, Baltimore, Md.
MdNL	U. S. Naval Academy Library, Annapolis, Md.
MdSL	Maryland State Library, Annapolis, Md.
MeHS	Maine Historical Society, Portland, Me.
	Memorial Hall Museum, Deerfield, Mass.
	Meriden Gravure Co., Meriden, Conn.
MFM	Massachusetts Grand Lodge, F. & A. M. Library, Boston, Mass.
MHS	Massachusetts Historical Society, Boston, Mass.
	Miami University, Oxford, Ohio
	Michigan, University of, Ann Arbor, Mich.
MissAr	Mississippi Dept. of Archives & History, Jackson, Miss.
	Moravian Archives, Winston-Salem, N. C.
	Moravian Church Archives, Bethlehem, Pa.
	Moravian Historical Society, Nazareth, Pa.
MSL	State Library of Massachusetts, Boston, Mass.

Museum of the City of New York, New York, N. Y.

NA	National Archives, Washington, D. C.
NCA	North Carolina Archives, Raleigh, N. C.
NCHC	North Carolina Historical Commission, Raleigh, N. C.
NCSCL	North Carolina Supreme Court Library, Raleigh, N. C.
NCSL	North Carolina State Library, Raleigh, N. C.
NCU	North Carolina, University of, Chapel Hill, N. C.
NEHGS	New England Historic Genealogical Society, Boston, Mass.
NHHS	New Hampshire Historical Society, Concord, N. H.
NHS	Newport Historical Society, Newport, R. I.
NHSL	New Hampshire State Library, Concord, N. H.
NJHS	New Jersey Historical Society, Newark, N. J.
NJSL	New Jersey State Library, Trenton, N. J.
NL	Newberry Library, Chicago, Ill.
NLM	National Library of Medicine, Bethesda, Md.
	New York State Historical Asso. Library, Cooperstown, N. Y.
	Northern Michigan College of Education, Marquette, Mich.
	Notre Dame, University of, South Bend, Indiana
NYAM	Metropolitan Museum of Art, New York, N. Y.
NYBA	Association of the Bar of the City of New York, New York, N. Y.
NYFM	Masonic Grand Lodge Library, New York, N. Y.
NYHS	New-York Historical Society, New York, N. Y.
NYLI	New York Law Institute, New York, N. Y.
NYPL	New York Public Library, New York, N. Y.
NYSL	New York State Library, Albany, N. Y.
NYSOC	New York Society Library, New York, N. Y.
	Oberlin College Library, Oberlin, Ohio
OH&PS	Ohio Historical and Philosophical Society, (now Cincinnati Historical Society, Cincinnati, Ohio)
	Peabody Historical Society, Peabody, Mass.
	Peabody Institute, Baltimore, Md. (now incorporated in the Enoch·Pratt Free Library).

	Pennsylvania State University, University Park, Pa.
Pequot	Pequot Library, Yale University Library, New Haven, Conn.
PFM	Grand Lodge Library, Philadelphia, Pa.
	Pittsburgh, University of, Pittsburgh, Pa.
	Pittsburgh-Xenia Theological Seminary, Pittsburgh, Pa.
PLYM	Library of the Pilgrim Society, Plymouth, Mass.
	Pocumtuck Valley Memorial Asso., Deerfield, Mass.
PPL	Free Library of Philadelphia, Philadelphia, Pa.
	Presbyterian Historical Society, Philadelphia, Pa.
PRO	Public Record Office, London, England
	Providence Town Papers, Providence, R. I.
PrPL	Providence Public Library, Providence, R. I.
PrU	Princeton University, Princeton, N. J.
PSL	Pennsylvania State Library, Harrisburg, Pa.
PTS	Princeton Theological Seminary Library, Princeton, N. J.
PU	Pennsylvania, University of, Philadelphia, Pa.
QL	Friends Reference Library, Friends House, Euston Road, N. W. 1, London, England
RF	Rosenbach Foundation, Philadelphia, Pa.
	Richmond, University of, Richmond, Va.
RIHS	Rhode Island Historical Society, Providence, R. I.
RIMS	Rhode Island Medical Society, Providence, R. I.
RISL	Rhode Island State Library, Providence, R. I.
	Rochester, University of, Rochester, N. Y.
RU	Rutgers University, New Brunswick, N. J.
	Sacred Heart Seminary, Detroit, Mich.
	Saint John's College, Annapolis, Md.
SCHS	South Carolina Historical Society, Charleston, S. C.
	Schwenkfelder Library, Pennsburg, Pa.
SCU	South Carolina, University of, Columbia, S. C.
	Shelburne Museum, Shelburne, Vt.
	Sheldon Museum, Middlebury, Vt.
	Sibley Music Library, Rochester, N. Y.
	Smithtown Public Library, Smithtown, N. Y.

	Sondley Reference Library, Asheville, N. C.
	Stadtbibliothek, Frankfurt-am-Main, Germany
	Stanford University, Stanford, Calif.
Stark	Lewis M. Stark, New York Public Library, New York, N. Y.
Streeter	Thomas W. Streeter collection, dispersed at Parke-Bernet Auctions, 1968-69.
	Supreme Council, Library of the, Washington, D. C.
Swan	Bradford F. Swan, Providence, R. I.
	Swarthmore College, Swarthmore, Pa.
	Toledo Museum of Art, Toledo, Ohio
	Trenton Public Library, Trenton, N. J.
	Trinity College, Hartford, Conn.
	Tufts University, Medford, Mass.
	Tulane University, New Orleans, La.
	Union College, Hamilton, N. Y.
	United States Dept. of Agriculture, Washington, D. C.
	Universalist Historical Society, Boston, Mass.
UOChi	Chicago, University of, Chicago, Illinois
UOCol	Colorado, University of, Boulder, Colorado
UOMi	Michigan, University of, Ann Arbor, Mich.
UOP	Pennsylvania, University of, Philadelphia, Pa.
UTS	Union Theological Seminary, New York, N. Y.
VaBH	Virginia Baptist Historical Association, University of Richmond, Richmond, Va.
VaHS	Virginia Historical Society, Richmond, Va.
VaSL	Virginia State Library, Richmond, Va.
	Vassar College, Poughkeepsie, N. Y.
VaU	Virginia, University of, Charlottesville, Va.
VtHS	Vermont Historical Society, Montpelier, Vt.
VtSL	Vermont State Library, Montpelier, Vt.
VtU	Vermont, University of, Burlington, Vt.
	Wake Forest College, Winston-Salem, N. C.
	Warren Public Library, Warren, Mass.

WC	Williams College, Williamstown, Mass.
Welch	d'Alté A. Welch, Cleveland Hts., Ohio
	Wesleyan University, Middletown, Conn.
	West Bridgewater High School, West Bridgewater, Mass.
	Westerly Public Library, Westerly, Rhode Island
	Wilmington Institute Free Library, Wilmington, Del.
Winterthur	Winterthur Museum, Winterthur, Del.
WisHS	Wisconsin Historical Society, Madison, Wis.
WL	Watkinson Library, Trinity College, Hartford, Conn.
WLC	William L. Clements Library, Ann Arbor, Mich.
	Woodstock College, Woodstock, Md.
	Worcester Art Museum, Worcester, Mass.
WRHS	Western Reserve Historical Society, Cleveland, Ohio
	Yale Medical Library, New Haven, Conn.
YC	Yale University, New Haven, Conn.
YHS	York County Historical Society, York, Pa.
	Zion Research Library, Brookline, Mass.

READEX MICROPRINT LOCATIONS

Partial List

T HE FOLLOWING INSTITUTIONS hold in their collections the Readex Microprint Corporation's edition of *Early American Imprints, 1639-1800,* edited by Clifford K. Shipton of the American Antiquarian Society. This edition reproduced in Microprint the full text of every edition of every book, pamphlet, and broadside printed between 1639 and 1800 in the area that is now the United States. There are other institutions whose permission to be included in this list was not given in time for inclusion.

Alabama   Auburn University, Auburn
University of Alabama, Huntsville
University of Alabama, University

Arizona   Arizona State University, Tempe
North Arizona University, Flagstaff
University of Arizona, Tucson

Arkansas   University of Arkansas, Fayetteville

California   Claremont College, Pomona
Fresno State College
Long Beach State College
Pacific School of Religion, Berkeley
San Diego State College
San Fernando Valley State College, Northridge
San Francisco Public Library
University of California at Davis
University of California at Goleta
University of California at Irvine
University of California at La Jolla
University of California at Riverside
University of California at San Jose
University of California at Santa Barbara

	University of California at Santa Cruz
	University of San Francisco
	University of Santa Clara
	University of Southern California, Los Angeles
Colorado	Denver Public Library
	University of Colorado, Boulder
Connecticut	Connecticut College for Women, New London
	Connecticut Historical Society, Hartford
	Fairfield University, Fairfield
	University of Connecticut, Storrs
	Wesleyan University, Middletown
Delaware	University of Delaware, Newark
District of Columbia	Georgetown University
	Library of Congress
Florida	Florida State University, Tallahassee
	Miami Public Library
	University of Florida, Gainesville
	University of South Florida, Tampa
	University of West Florida, Pensacola
Georgia	University of Georgia, Athens
	West Georgia College, Carrollton
Hawaii	University of Hawaii, Honolulu
Idaho	University of Idaho, Moscow
Illinois	Center for Research Libraries, Chicago
	Illinois State University, Normal
	McCormick Theological Seminary, Chicago
	Newberry Library, Chicago
	Northern Illinois University, DeKalb

Northwestern University, Evanston
Southern Illinois University, Carbondale
Southern Illinois University, Edwardsville
University of Illinois, Urbana

Indiana   Ball State University, Muncie
                 Indiana State University, Terre Haute
                 Purdue University, Lafayette

Iowa   Iowa State University, Ames

Kansas   Kansas City Public Library
                 Kansas State University, Manhattan
                 University of Kansas, Lawrence

Kentucky   University of Kentucky, Lexington
                 Western Kentucky University, Bowling Green

Louisiana   Louisiana State University, Baton Rouge
                 Tulane University, New Orleans

Maine   Bangor Public Library

Maryland   Enoch Pratt Free Library, Baltimore
                 Johns Hopkins University, Baltimore
                 University of Maryland, College Park

Massachusetts   American Antiquarian Society, Worcester
                 Boston Public Library
                 Boston University
                 Brandeis University, Waltham
                 Clark University, Worcester
                 Hampshire Interlibrary Center, Amherst
                 Harvard College, Cambridge
                 Massachusetts Historical Society, Boston
                 Northeastern University, Boston

Michigan	Michigan State University, East Lansing
	Oakland University, Rochester
	University of Detroit
	University of Michigan, Ann Arbor
Minnesota	University of Minnesota, Minneapolis
Mississippi	University of Southern Mississippi, Hattiesburg
	University of Mississippi, University
Missouri	University of Missouri, Columbia
	University of Missouri, Saint Louis
Montana	Montana State University, Bozeman
Nebraska	University of Nebraska, Lincoln
Nevada	University of Nevada, Reno
New Hampshire	Dartmouth College, Hanover
	University of New Hampshire, Durham
New Jersey	Fairleigh Dickinson University, Rutherford
	Princeton University, Princeton
	Rutgers University, New Brunswick
New Mexico	Eastern New Mexico University, Portales
New York	Brooklyn Public Library
	C. W. Post College, Greenville
	City College of New York
	Colgate University, Hamilton
	Columbia University, New York
	Cornell University, Ithaca
	New York Historical Society
	New York Public Library
	New York State Library, Albany

Queens College, Flushing
State University College at Brockport
State University College at Buffalo
State University College at Cortland
State University College at Potsdam
State University College at Stonybrook
Syracuse University
United States Military Academy, West Point
University of Rochester
Vassar College, Poughkeepsie

North
Carolina

Appalachian State University, Boone
Duke University, Durham
East Carolina University, Greenville
South East Baptist Theological Seminary, Wake Forest
University of North Carolina, Charlotte

Ohio

Cleveland Public Library
Kent State University
Miami University, Oxford
Ohio State University, Columbus
Ohio University, Athens
University of Toledo
Youngstown State University

Oklahoma

Oklahoma State University, Stillwater

Oregon

Southern Oregon College, Portland
University of Oregon, Eugene
University of Portland

Pennsylvania

American Philosophical Society, Philadelphia
California State College
East Stroudsburg State College
Edinboro State College
Free Library of Philadelphia
Geneva College, Beaver Falls

Indiana University
Library Company of Philadelphia
Mansfield State College
Pennsylvania State Library, Harrisburg
Pennsylvania State University, University Park
State College at Kutztown
University of Pittsburgh
Ursinus College, Collegeville
West Chester State College

Rhode Island	Brown University, Providence
South Carolina	University of South Carolina, Columbia
Tennessee	East Tennessee State University, Johnson City
	Joint University Libraries, Nashville
	Memphis State University
	Middle Tennessee State University, Murfreesboro
	University of Tennessee at Chattanooga
	University of Tennessee at Knoxville
Texas	Baylor University, Waco
	Fort Worth Public Library
	North Texas State College, Denton
	Rice University, Houston
	Southwest Texas State College, San Marcos
	University of Texas, Austin
Utah	Brigham Young University, Provo
	University of Utah, Salt Lake City
	Utah State University, Logan
Vermont	University of Vermont, Burlington
Virginia	College of William and Mary, Williamsburg
	Virginia State Library, Richmond
	University of Virginia, Charlottesville

Washington	Central Washington State College, Ellensburg
	Eastern Washington State College, Cheney
	University of Washington, Seattle
West Virginia	West Virginia University, Morgantown
Wisconsin	Milwaukee Public Library
	Wisconsin State Historical Society, Madison
Wyoming	University of Wyoming, Laramie
Australia	Commonwealth National Library, Canberra
	Monash University
	University of Sydney
Canada	McGill University, Montreal
	Montreal Library
	National Library, Ottawa
	University of Alberta, Edmonton
	University of British Columbia, Vancouver
	University of New Brunswick, Fredericton
	University of Toronto
	University of Western Ontario, London
Germany	Free Library of Berlin
	University of Germany
Great Britain	British Museum
Sweden	University of Uppsala

NATIONAL INDEX
of AMERICAN IMPRINTS
THROUGH 1800
THE SHORT-TITLE EVANS

N

Nachdenken über mich Selbst [by
Johann Caspar Lavater, 1741-1801].
Lancaster, 1788. 43 pp.
HSP copy.   21195

Nachempfindungen . . . den 7ten October,
1793 [by Justus Heinrich Christian
Helmuth, 1745-1825].
[Philadelphia, 1793.] 4 pp.
LCP copy.   46777

Nachklang zum Gesäng.
Ephrata, 1755. 112 pp.
HSP copy.   7496

Nadere Trouwhartige Waarschouwinge.
New York, 1763. vii, 56 pp.
LCP copy.   9451

Nadir, William, pseud.
Mercurius Nov-Anglicanus: or an
Almanack . . . 1743.
Boston, Rogers & Fowle, 1743. [24] pp.
(Attributed to William Douglass,
1691-1752.)
AAS copy.   4935

[Nadir, William, pseud.
1744. Mercurius Nov Anglicanus, or an
Almanack.
Boston, Rogers & Fowle. [24] pp.]
(Assumed from the sequence.)   5168

[Nadir, William, pseud.
Mercurius Nov-Anglicanus: or an
Almanack . . . 1745.
Boston, Rogers & Fowle. [24] pp.]
(Assumed by Evans from the sequence;
not adv. in newspapers.)   5380

[Nadir, William, pseud.
1746. Mercuricus Nov-Anglicanus, or an
Almanack.
Boston, Rogers & Fowle. [24] pp.]
(Assumed by Evans from the sequence.
Not adv.)   5575

Nadir, William, pseud.
Mercurius Nov-Anglicanus: or an
Almanack . . . 1747.
Boston, Rogers & Fowle, 1747.
[16] pp.
AAS copy.   5763

[Nadir, William, pseud.
1748. Mercurius Nov-Anglicanus, or an
Almanack . . .
Boston, Rogers & Fowle.]
(No copy found.)   5935

Nailor, Patrick.
Fresh and Most Interesting Intelligence:
Extract of a Letter from Patrick Nailor.
Printed at P. Hassenclever's Iron Works
[Baltimore? 1791?] Broadside.
EPFL copy.   46174

Nails Fastened [by Cotton Mather,
1663-1728].
Boston, Edwards, 1726. [2], 22 pp.
AAS copy.   2773

Nalton, James, 1600-1662.
(D. N. B.)
The Nature and Necessity.
Boston, Kneeland & Green, 1741.
36 pp.
AAS copy.   4757

Names of the Subscribers [to Churchill's
Poems] [by James Rivington, 1724-1802].
[New York? 1768?] lvi pp.
AAS copy.   41875

Nancrede, Paul Joseph Guérard de,
1760-1841.
L'Abeille Françoise.
Boston, Belknap & Young, 1792. 352, v,
3 pp.
AAS copy.   24566

Nancrede, Paul Joseph Guérard de,
1760-1841.
Books: - Importation of May, 1798.
Boston, 1798. 84 pp.
AAS copy.   34165

Nancrede, Paul Joseph Guérard de,
1760-1841.
Books Published by Joseph Nancrede.
[Boston, 1797?] [4] pp.
LOC copy.   48186

Nancrede, Paul Joseph Guérard de,
1760-1841.
Boston, February 5, 1799. Proposals for
Publishing . . . the History of the
Destruction of the Helvetian Union.
[Boston, 1799.] Broadside.
RIHS copy.   35855

Nancrede, Paul Joseph Guérard de,
1760-1841.
Joseph Nancrede's Catalogue of Books.
[Boston, Nancrede, 1796.] [2],
46 pp.
AAS copy.   30833

Nancrede, Paul Joseph Guérard de,
1760-1841.
Prospectus du Courier des Deux Mondes.
[Boston? 179?]
(Not available for reproduction.)
EI copy.   45783

Naogra Andeliga Wisor [by Andrew
Rudman, 1668-1708].
[Philadelphia, Jansen, 1700?] 8 pp.
JCB copy.   39368

Napoleon I, Emperor of the French,
1769-1821.
Military Journal . . . from Egypt into
Syria.
Baltimore, Warner & Hanna, 1800.
46 pp.
MdHS copy.   38024

Narragansett Proprietors.
Advertisement. Forasmuch as by His
Majesty's Gracious Care, his Immediate
Government. . . . Boston, June 9th, 1686.
[Boston, 1686.] Broadside.
MHS copy.   39229

Narragansett Proprietors.
An Advertisement. Whereas, the Lands of
Narragansett, and Niantick
Countryes. . . . Boston, July 30, 1678.
[Boston, 1678?] Broadside.
PRO copy.   39203

Narragansett Proprietors.
To the Honourable the Committee.
Boston, 1708. [2] pp.
AAS ph. copy.   39472

A Narrative. &c. The Following late
Transactions. . . . [by John Bowman, fl.
1798].
[Charleston, S. C.], Young, [1798].
16 pp.
NYPL copy.   33447

Narrative of a late Expendition against
the Indians [by Hugh Henry
Brackenridge, 1748-1816].

Andover, Mass., Ames & Parker,
[1798?], 46 pp.
AAS copy.   35689

Narrative of a late Expedition against the
Indians [by Hugh Henry Brackenridge,
1748-1816].
Andover, Ames & Parker, [1798?].
46 pp.
AAS copy.   48378

A Narrative of a new and Unusual
American Imprisonment [by Francis
Makemie, 1658-1708].
[New York], 1707. [4], 47 pp.
AAS copy.   1300

A Narrative of a new and Unusual
American Imprisonment [by Francis
Makemie, 1658-1708].
New York, Gaine, 1755. [12], 52 pp.
AAS copy.   7455

A Narrative of the Captivity . . . of
Benjamin Gilbert [by William Walton,
1740-1824].
Philadelphia, Crukshank, 1784. 96 pp.
AAS copy.   18497

A Narrative of the Capture of Certain
Americans, at Westmoreland [by Moses
Van Campen, b. 1757].
Hartford, [1780?]. Front., 24 pp.
LOC copy.   17218

A Narrative of the Capture of Certain
Americans at Westmoreland [by Moses Van
Campen, b. 1757].
New London, 1784. 16 pp.
MHS copy.   18850

[A Narrative of the Excursion and
Ravages of the King's Troops . . . the
Nineteenth of April, 1775.
Boston, 1779.]
(Authority Sabin 51804; improbable.)
                                   16380

A Narrative of the Extraordinary
Adventures of Four Russian Sailors [by
Petr Ludovik Le Roy, 1699-1774].
Norwich, Trumbull, 1785. 16 pp.
AAS copy.   44709

A Narrative of the Extraordinary Case of
George Lukins.
Philadelphia, Hall, 1792. 19 pp.
AAS copy.   24485

[A Narrative of the Extraordinary Case of
George Lukins.
Stockbridge, Andrews, 1794. 16 pp.]
(Imprint assumed by Evans from adv.
"Just Published, and for sale at the
Printing-Office," Andrews' Western Star,
July 1, 1794.)   27239

A Narrative of the Late Massacres [by
Benjamin Franklin, 1706-1790].
[Philadelphia], 1764. 31 pp.
NYPL copy.   9667

A Narrative of the Life and Adventures of
Venture [by Venture Smith, 1729?-1805].
New London, Holt, 1798. 32 pp.
CHS copy.   34560

A Narrative of the Life of William Beadle
[by Stephen Mix Mitchell, 1743-1835].
Hartford, Webster, 1783. 24 pp.
AAS copy.   17828

[A Narrative of the Life of William

Beadle [by Stephen Mix Mitchell, 1743-1835].
Bennington, Haswell, 1794.] 47 pp.
(The only known copy is defective.)
NYHS copy.   26629

A Narrative of the Life of William Beadle [by Stephen Mix Mitchell, 1743-1835].
Windsor, Vt., Spooner, 1795. 24 pp.
AAS copy.   28246

[A Narrative of the life of Zilpha Smith, alias Sylva Wood.
Providence, Wheeler, 1798.]
(Alden 1567; no copy known.)   48519

Narrative of the Loss of the Ship Hercules [by Benjamin Stout].
New York, Chevalier, [1798?]. liii, 113 pp.
AAS copy.   32886

Narrative of the Loss of the Ship Hercules [by Benjamin Stout].
Hudson, [N. Y.], Stoddard, 1800. 118 pp.
AAS copy.   38571

Narrative of the Loss of the Ship Hercules [by Benjamin Stout].
New Bedford, Shearman, 1800. 124 pp.
AAS copy.   38570

A Narrative of the Miseries of New-England [by Increase Mather, 1639-1723].
Boston, 1688. 8 pp.
BPL copy.   450

A Narrative of the Miseries of New-England [by Increase Mather, 1639-1723].
Boston, 1775. 8 pp.
NYPL copy.   14252

The Narrative of the most Dreadful Tempest, Hurricane, or Earthquake in Holland . . . the 22 of July last. . . .
Cambridge, [Mass.], Green for Ratcliffe, 1674. 8 pp.
MHS copy.   39187

A Narrative of the Planting [by Joshua Scottow, 1618-1698].
Boston, 1694. [4], 75, [1] pp.
AAS copy.   709

A Narrative of the Proceedings of Sir Edmond Andros.
[Boston?] 1691. 12 pp.
(Signed by William Stoughton [1631-1701] and others. See note under Sabin 92350.)
BA copy.   572

A Narrative of the Proceedings of the Black People [by Absalom Jones].
Philadelphia, Woodward, 1794. 28 pp.
LCP copy.   27170

A Narrative of the Proceedings of Those Ministers of the County of Hampshire.
Boston, 1736. [4], 93, [1] pp.
BA copy.   4044

A Narrative of the Treatment Coll.
Bayard Received.
[New York, 1702.] 6 pp.
PRO copy.   1079

[A Narrative Relating to the Fund.
Cambridge, 1674.]
(No copy known. Title from Evans 337.)   194

Narratives of a Late Expedition [by Hugh Henry Brackenridge, 1748-1816].
Philadelphia, Bailey, 1773 (i. e., 1783). 38 pp.
(See Vail 684 and Blanck, I, 263.)
University of Pittsburgh copy.   17993

Nash, Joseph.
An Elegy Occasioned by the Death of . . . Doct. Thomas Hastings, of Hatfield . . . April 14, 1728.
n.p., n.d. Broadside.
(19th century printing.)
BPL copy.   39895

Nash, Joseph.
An Elegy upon the much Lamented Decease of . . . Solomon Stoddard . . . February 11th . . . 1729.

[Boston, 1729.] Broadside.
BPL copy.   39923

Nash, Judah, 1728-1805.
A Discourse, Delivered at the Funeral of Mrs. Anna Kendall.
Springfield, Weld, 1792. 13 pp.
AAS copy.   24567

Naskov, Peder Zacharlaesen, 1635-1695.
The Articles of Faith.
New York, 1754. [2], ii, ii, [2], 314, 30, [2] pp., irreg.
AAS copy.   7262

Nassy, David de Isaac Cohen, 1747-1806.
Observations on the Cause.
Philadelphia, Parker for Carey, 1793. 26 pp.
AAS copy.   25855

Nassy, David de Isaac Cohen, 1747-1806.
Observations sur la Cause.
Philadelphia, Parker for Carey, 1793. 48 pp.
AAS copy.   25854

[Nathan, John.
An Almanack, for the Year . . . 1747.
New York, Zenger.]
(Adv. N. Y. Weekly Journal, Oct. 13, 1746.)   5814

[Nathan, John.
An Almanack for the Year . . . 1748.
New York, Zenger.]
("Just Published," N. Y. Weekly Journal, Oct. 5, 1747.)   6014

Nathan, John.
An Almanack, for the Year . . . 1749.
New York, Zenger. [24] pp.
HEH copy.   6197

[Nathan, John.
An Almanack for the Year . . . 1750.
New York, Zenger. [24] pp.]
(Title from Hildeburn.)   6374

[Nathan, John.
An Almanack, for the Year . . . 1751.
New York, Zenger.]
(From adv. "An Almanack," N. Y. Weekly Journal, Feb. 4, 1750/1.)   6556

Nathan ben Saddi, pseud.
(See D. N. B. under Robert Dodsley.)
The Chronicle of the Kings of England.
Newport, 1744. 56 pp.
(The unique copy is imperfect.)
LOC copy.   5378

[Nathan ben Saddi, psued.
(See D. N. B. under Robert Dodsley.)
The Chronicle of the Kings of England.
Boston, Fowle and Draper, 1758. 100 pp.]
(No copy of this edition could be found.)   8112

Nathan ben Saddi, pseud.
(See D. N. B. under Robert Dodsley.)
The Chronicle of the Kings of England.
Boston, Fowle and Draper, 1759. 79, [1] pp.
AAS copy.   8340

Nathan ben Saddi, pseud.
(See D. N. B. under Robert Dodsley.)
The Chronicle of the Kings of England.
Norwich, 1773. 87 pp.
MHS copy.   12755

Nathan ben Saddi, pseud.
The Chronicle of the Kings of England.
Philadelphia, Bell and Towne, 1774. 119 pp.
HSP copy.   13253

[Nathan ben Saddi, pseud.
The Chronicle of the Kings of England.
Lancaster, 1775.]
(Adv. Pa. Journal, Feb. 8, 1775.)   14008

[Nathan ben Saddi, pseud.
The Chronicle of the Kings of England.
Philadelphia, 1775.]
(Adv. Pa. Evening-Post, July 11, 1775.)   14009

Nathan ben Saddi, pseud.
The Chronicles of the Kings of England.

Worcester, Thomas, 1795. 196 pp.
AAS copy.   28579

Nathan ben Saddi, pseud.
The Chronicles of the Kings of England.
New York, Buel for Davis, 1797. 119 pp.
Watkinson Library copy.   32059

Nathan Ben Salomon, pseud.
An Astronomical Diary or Almanack, for . . . 1786.
New Haven, Meigs, Bowen & Dana.
[24] pp., 1 map.
(The map which is found in some copies is an overrun from Morse's Geography, 18615.)
AAS copy.   19108

National Credit and Character by John Beale Bordley, 1727-1804].
Philadelphia, Humphreys, 1790. 4 pp.
LCP copy.   45834

The Natural History of Four Footed Beasts. By Tommy Trip.
Hudson, N. Y., Stoddard, 1795. 158, [2] pp.
PPL copy.   29656

The Natural Principles of Liberty [by David Hoar].
Boston, Edes, 1782. [2], ii, 12 pp.
AAS copy.   17559

[Die Naturalisationsform Derjenigen.
Germantown, 1761.]
(Title from Seidensticker.)   8936

The Nature and Design of Christianity [by William Law, 1686-1761].
Philadelphia, Bradford, 1744. 34 pp., irreg.
HSP copy.   5511

The Nature and Design of Christianity [by William Law, 1686-1761].
Germantown, 1756. 16 pp.
AAS copy.   7814

The Nature and Design of Christianity. . . . Ninth Edition [by William Law, 1686-1761].
Providence, Carter, 1792. 16 pp.
AAS copy.   25013

The Nature and Extent of Parliamentary Power [by William Hicks].
New York, Holt, 1768. 40 pp.
LOC copy.   10986

The Nature and Extent of Parliamentary Power [by William Hicks].
Philadelphia, 1768. xvi, 32 pp.
NYPL copy.   10985

The Nature and Extent of the Redemption [by Ebenezer Punderson, 1705-1764].
New Haven, 1758. 16 pp.
YC copy.   8245

The Nature and Importance of Oaths and Juries.
New York, 1747. [24] pp.
NYPL copy.   6015

The Nature, Certainty, and Evidence of true Christianity [by Sarah (Haggar) Osborn, 1714-1796].
Newport, [R.I.], Hall, 1754 (i.e. 1764?). 15 pp.
RIHS copy.   41478

The Nature, Certainty and Evidence of true Christianity [by Sarah (Haggar) Osborn, 1714-1796].
Boston, Kneeland, 1755. 15 pp.
AAS copy.   7523

The Nature, Certainty, and Evidence of True Christianity [by Sarah (Haggar) Osborn, 1714-1796].
Danbury, Douglas for Crawford, [1793]. 23 pp.
NYPL copy.   25949

The Nature, Certainty and Evidence of True Christianity [by Sarah (Haggar) Osborn, 1714-1796].
Providence, Carter, 1793. 15 pp.
AAS copy.   25950

Nautical Songster or Seaman's
Companion.
Baltimore, Keatinge, 1798. 64 pp., frontis.
LOC copy.34167

Naval Engagements, in the West-Indies.
From the Pennsylvania Packet.
Philadelphia, May 18.
Baltimore, [1782]. Broadside.
MdHS copy.17611

Nazro, John.
John Nazro, at his Shop, the Corner of
Queen-Street. . . .
[Boston, 1770?] Broadside.
BPL copy.42131

Nazro, John.
Public Auction. . . . Worcester, April
18th, 1800.
[Worcester], Mower & Greenleaf, [1800].
Broadside.
AAS copy.39148

Ne Kesukod Jehovah Kessehtunkup [by
Cotton Mather, 1663-1728].
Boston, 1707. [2], 36, 36, 2, 2 pp.
AAS copy.1313

Neal, James Armstrong, 1774-1808.
An Essay on the Education . . . of the
Female.
Philadelphia, Johnson, 1795. v, [3],
37 pp.
AAS copy.29135

[Neal, Moses Leavitt], 1766-1829.
(Harvard College records.)
The Presbyteriad. With Notes.
n.p., 1797. 12 pp.
(This is apparently the item described by
Evans from Bragg's adv.)
AAS copy.32516

[Neal, Moses Leavitt, 1766-1829.
The Presbyteriad. With Notes.
Rutland, Vt., Williams & Fay, 1797.
("Is Published, and for sale at this office"
Rutland Herald, July 24, 1797. Probably
a ghost of 32516, q.v.)32517

Neale, Samuel, 1729-1792.
Some Account of the Life and Religious
Exercises of Mary Neale.
Philadelphia, Crukshank, 1796. 118 pp.
AAS copy.30834

Necessaries; Best Product of Land[by
John Beale Bordley, 1727-1804].
Philadelphia, Humphreys, 1776. 17,
[2] pp.
LCP copy.14896

Necessary Admonitions [by Cotton
Mather, 1663-1728].
Boston, 1702. [2], 34 pp.
AAS copy.1072

[Necessary Directions to Live an Holy
Life.
Boston, Rogers for Eliot, 1740. 24 pp.]
(Title from Haven.)4565

Necessary Truth: or Seasonable
Considerations [by Samuel Smith,
1720-1776].
Philadelphia, 1748. 16 pp.
HSP copy.6241

The Necessity and Divine Excellency [by
Samuel Fothergill, 1715-1772].
Philadelphia, Crukshank, 1780.
148 pp.
AAS copy.16777

The Necessity and Divine Excellency. . . .
Second Edition [by Samuel Fothergill,
1715-1772].
Philadelphia, Crukshank, 1783.
148 pp.
AAS copy.17932

The Necessity of a Well Experienced
Souldier [by John Richardson,
1647-1696].
Cambridge, 1679. [2], 15 pp.
BPL copy.276

[The Necessity of an Established Church
in any State.
Williamsburg, Dixon & Hunter, 1777.]
("Just Published," Dixon & Hunter's Va.
Gazette, 1777.)15448

The Necessity of Brotherly Love [by
Edmund March, c.1704-1791].
Boston, Fowle & Draper, 1762. 36 pp.
(Signatured with 9196, q.v.)9169

The Necessity of Reformation [by
Increase Mather, 1639-1723].
Boston, 1679. [8], 15 pp.
AAS copy.263

The Necessity of Repealing the American
Stamp-Act.
Boston, Edes & Gill, 1766. 31 pp.
AAS copy.10402

Necker, Jacques, 1732-1804.
Of the Importance of Religious Opinions.
Philadelphia, Carey & Stewart, 1791. 2,
263, [1] pp.
AAS copy.23588

Necker, Jacques, 1732-1804.
Of the Importance of Religious Opinions.
Boston, Hall, for Thomas & Andrews,
etc., 1796. 230, [2] pp.
AAS copy.30835

[Nederduitsche Almanack voor het Jaar
1742.
New York.]
(Adv. N. Y. Weekly Journal, Nov. 9, 1741.)
4758

[Nederduitsche Almanacke vor het Jaar
1743.
New York.]
(Assumed from the adv. of Dutch
almanacs in N. Y. Weekly Journal, Nov.
22, 1742.)5012

[Nederduitsche Almanacke voor het Jaar,
1744.
New York.]
(Assumed by Evans from the sequence.)
5251

[Nederduytsche Almanacke voor het Jarr
1745.
New York.]
(Adv. New York Evening Post, Dec. 17,
1744.)5441

[Nederduytsche Almanacke voor het Jaar
1746.
New York.]
(Adv. N. Y. Evening Post, Nov. 18, 1745.)
5647

[Nederduytsche Almanacke voor het Jaar
1747.
New York, DeForeest.]
(Adv. N. Y. Evening Post, Dec. 29, 1746.)
5815

[Nederduytsche Almanacke voor het Jaar
1748.
New York, DeForeest.]
(Dutch almanac adv. N. Y. Evening
Post, Dec. 29, 1746.)6016

[Nederduytsche Almanacke vor het Jaar,
1749.
New York, De Foreest.]
(Both De Foreest and Zenger advertised
Dutch almanack.)6198

[Nederduytsche Almanacke voor het Jaar
1750.
New York, De Foreest.]
(Adv. N. Y. Evening Post, Jan. 15, 1750.)
6375

[Nederduytsche Almanacke voor het Jaar
1751.
New York, De Foreest.]
(No copy found.)6557

[Nederduytsche Almanacke voor het Jaar,
1752.
New York, De Foreest.]
(From adv. for Dutch Almanacs.)6723

[Nederduytsche Almanacke voor het Jaar
1753.
New York, De Foreest.]
(Assumed from a ref. to Dutch almanacs.)
6891

Nederlandsch Hervormde Kerk. Classis
van Amsterdam.
A Letter from the Reverend Classis . . . to
the . . . Ministers . . . of New-York and
New-Jersey.

New York, Holt, 1766. [4], 21 pp.
NYPL ph. copy.41645

[Neele, E. J.
A Map of the Country between Albermarle
Sound, and Lake Erie.
Philadelphia, Prichard & Hall. 1788.]
(The unique copy listed by Evans was of
the London ed.)21277

The Negro Boy. Sung by Mr. Tyler [by
George Colman, 1762-1836].
New York, Carr, [1796]. [2] pp.
AAS copy.30243

The Negro Christianized [by Cotton
Mather, 1663-1728].
Boston, 1706. [2], 46 pp.
BPL copy.1262

[Negro Slavery Defended by the Word of
God. By Philanthropos.
[New York? 1798.]]
(No origin of this entry is known.)34370

A Neighbour's Tears [by Benjamin
Thompson, 1642-1714].
[Boston, 1710.] Broadside.
MHS copy.1489

[Neill, Hugh, c. 1725-1781.
(Weis, Colonial Clergy Del.)
The Doctrine of Water Baptism.
Philadelphia, Steuart, 1761.]
("This Day is Published," Pa. Gazette.)
8937

Neilson, William, fl. 1769.
To the Public. . . . New-York, Dec. 23,
1769.
[New York, 1769.] 6 pp.
LCP copy.11350

Neisser, George, 1715-1784.
Aufrichtige Nachricht ans Publicum.
Philadelphia, Franklin, 1742. 18 pp.
HSP copy.5013

Nelson, D., fl. 1800.
An Investigation of that False . . . Thomas
Paine.
[Lancaster, Pa., 1800.] 192 pp.
AAS copy.38028

Nelson, John, 1707-1774.
(J. Nelson, Journals, 1809 ed.)
The Case of John Nelson. . . . Third
Edition.
Wilmington, Del., 1771. 32 pp.
HSP copy.12134

Nelson, John, 1738?-1766.
A Letter to the Protestant-Dissenters.
Salem, 1771. 121 pp.
AAS copy.12135

Nelson, John, 1738?-1766.
A Letter to the Protestant-Dissenters. . . .
Second Salem Edition.
Salem, 1772. 111 pp.
AAS copy.12470

Nelson, John, 1738?-1766.
A Letter to the Protestant-Dissenters. . . .
Second American Edition.
Newburyport, March, 1797. 209 pp.
HC copy.32518

Nelson, John, 1738?-1766.
A Letter to the Protestant-Dissenters.
Newburyport, March, 1798. 209 pp.
AAS copy.34168

[Nelson, William], 1760-1813, supposed
author.
An Enquiry whether the Act of Congress
. . . Generally Called the Sedition Bill. . . .
Richmond, Va., Pleasants, 1798.
15 pp.
AAS copy.34375

Nelson's Charleston Directory . . . for . . .
1801.
Charleston, [S. C.], Nelson, 125 pp.
(The unique copy is imperfect.)
CLS copy.38029

Netherlands. Treaties, etc.
By the United States in Congress
Assembled: a Proclamation. Whereas in
Pursuance. . . . [Jan. 23, 1783.]
[Philadelphia, 1783.] [2] pp.
AAS copy.18231

Netley Abbey: a Gothic Story. In Two
Volumes.
Philadelphia, for Dobson, etc., 1796. [4],
108; [4], 104 pp.
LCP copy. 30836

[Netly Abbey, a Gothic Story.
Baltimore, 1796.]
("This day published," Md. Journal, Aug.
23, 1796.) 47840

The Nets of Salvation [by Cotton Mather,
1663-1728].
Boston, 1704. 56 pp.
JCB copy. 1176

Ein neu Trauer-Lied. . . .
MDCCLXXXIII.
n. p., n. d. Broadside.
AAS copy. 18041

Ein Neu Trauer-Lied, wie man
Vernommen von einem Menschen.
n.p., 1783. Broadside.
NYHS copy. 44409

Ein Neu Trauer-Lied.
[Carlisle, Pa.], Hohman, [1785].
Broadside.
HSP copy. 44731

[Neu-Eingerichteter Americanischer
Geschichts-Kalender, auf das Jahr . . .
1747.
Philadelphia, Armbrüster.]
(Hildeburn 982.) 5816

[Neu-Eingerichteter Americanischer
Geschichts-Kalender, auf das Jahr 1748.
Philadelphia, Franklin & Boehm, 1747.]
(Curtis 364; Hildeburn 1023; no copy
known.) 40433

[Neu-Eingerichteter Americanischer
Geschichts-Calender, auf das Jahr . . .
1748.
Philadelphia, Armbruester.]
(Seidensticker, p. 29.) 6017

Neu-Eingerichteter Americanischer
Geschichts-Calender, auf das Jahr. . . .
1749.
Philadelphia, Armbruster.
(The only copy located is imperfect.)
AAS copy. 6199

Neu-Eingerichteter Americanischer
Geschichts-Calender. Auf das Jahr . . .
1750.
Philadelphia, Franklin & Boehm. [36] pp.
(The only copy located is imperfect.)
HSP copy. 6376

[Neu-Eingerichteter Americanische
Geschichts-Calender, auf das Jahr, 1751.
Philadelphia, Franklin & Boehm.]
(No copy found.) 6558

Neu-Eingerichteter Americanischer
Geschichts-Calender, auf das Jahr 1752.
Philadelphia, Franklin. [40] pp.
GSP copy. 6724

[Neu-Eingerichteter Americanische
Geschichts-Calender, auf das Jahr 1753.
Philadelphia, Franklin.]
(Assumed from the sequence.) 6892

Neu-Eingerichteter Americanischer
Geschichts-Calender-auf das Jahr . . .
1754.
Philadelphia, Armbruester. [36] pp.
(The only copy located is incomplete.)
PrU copy. 7069

Neu-Eingerichteter Americanischer
Geschichts-Calender, auf das Jahr 1755.
Philadelphia, Franklin & Armbruester.
(The only copy found is stained and
imperfect.)
AAS copy. 7263

Neu-Eingerichteter Americanischer
Geschichts-Calender, auf das Jahr 1756.
Philadelphia, Franklin & Armbruester.
[44] pp.
(The only copy located is mutilated.)
AAS copy. 7497

[Neu-Eingerichteter Americanischer
Geschichts-Calender, auf das Jahr 1757.
Philadelphia, Franklin & Armbruster.]
(Assumed by Hildeburn from the
sequence.) 7725

[Neu-Eingerichteter Americanischer
Geschichts-Calender, auf das Jahr 1758.
Philadelphia, Franklin & Armbruester.]
(Assumed by Hildeburn from the
sequence.) 7962

[Neu-Eingerichteter Americanischer
Geschichts Calender, auf das Jahr 1759.
Philadelphia, Armbruester.]
(Hildeburn 1594.) 8198

Neu-Eingerichteter Americanischer
Geschichts und Haus Calender, auf das
Jahr . . . 1760.
Philadelphia, Müller. [36] pp.
AAS copy. 8425

[Neu-Eingerichteter Americanischer
Geschichts-und Haus-Calender. Auf das
Jahr 1761.
Philadelphia, Miller.]
(Evans' expansion of Hildeburn 1688.)
8677

[Neu-Eingerichteter Americanischer
Geschichts-und Haus-Calender. Auf das
Jahr 1762.
Philadelphia.]
(No copy located.) 8938

[Neu-Eingerichteter Americanischer
Geschichts-und Haus-Calender, auf das
Jahr 1765.
Philadelphia, Armbruester.]
(Assumed from the sequence.) 9746

[Neu-Eingerichteter Amerikanischer
Geschichts-und Haus-Calender, auf das
Jahr 1766.
Philadelphia, Armbruester.]
(No copy located.) 10083

[Neu-Eingerichteter Americanischer
Geschichts-und Haus-Calender, auf das
Jahr 1767.
Philadelphia, Armbruester.]
(Assumed by Hildeburn from the
sequence.) 10403

Neu-Eingerichteter Americanischer Stadt
und Land Calender, auf das Jahr . . . 1763.
Philadelphia, Armbruester and
Hasselbach. [48] pp.
(No complete copy found.)
AAS copy. 9198

Neu-Eingerichteter Americanischer Stadt
und Land Calender, auf das Jahr . . . 1764.
Philadelphia, Armbruester. [38] pp.
(No complete copy located.)
AAS copy. 9452

Neu-Eingerichteter Americanischer Stadt
und Land Calender, auf das Jahr . . . 1768.
Philadelphia, Armbruester. [38] pp.
HSP copy. 10697

Neu Eingerichtes ABC Buchstabir-und
Lese-Büchlin . . . Herausgegeben in Jahr
1743.
Philadelphia, 1760. 44 pp.
HSP copy. 41146

Neu-Eingerichtetes Gesang-Buch.
Germantown, 1762. xxiii, [3], 760, [40]
pp.
AAS copy. 9266

Neu-Eingerichtetes Schul-Büchlein.
Philadelphia, Cist, 1789. [4], 92 pp.
LOC copy. 21982

Neu-Vermehrt-und Vollständiges
Gesang-Buch. . . . Zweyte Auflage.
Germantown, 1763. front., [2], 208, [2],
536, [10], 24, 82, [1] pp.
HSP copy. 9495

Neu-Vermehrt-und Vollstaendiges
Gesang-Buch. . . . Dritte Auflage.
Germantown, 1772. Front., [2], 208, [2],
404, [8], 18, 66 (i.e. 60) pp.
AAS copy. 12534

Neu-Vermehrtes Gesaeng der Einsamen
Turtel-Taube.
Ephrata, 1762. [6], 329, [3] pp.
(The only copy located lacks four pages at
the end.)
AAS copy. 9062

[Die Neue Acte Enthaltend.
Germantown, 1753.]
(Title from adv.) 7070

Der Neue Allgemein Nützliche
Volks-Calender, auf das Jahr Christi 1801.
Lancaster, Pa., Hütter. [40] pp.
LOC copy. 38030

Eine Neue Anrede an die Deutschen.
[Philadelphia, 1764.] [4] pp.
HSP copy. 9747

Eine Neue Charte und Sinnliche
Abbildung.
[Baltimore, 1795.] [2] pp.
AAS copy. 29136

Das Neue Deutsche A.B.C.-und
Büchstabir-Buchlein.
Frederick Town, Md., Bartgis, 1795.
[38] pp.
PPL copy. 29137

Der Neue Gemeinnützige
Landwirthschafts Calender auf das Jahr
. . . 1788.
Lancaster, Stiemer, Albrecht & Lohn.
[38] pp.
AAS copy. 20538

[Der Neue Gemeinnützige
Landwirthschaft Calender.
Auf das Jahr . . . 1788.
Lancaster, Albrecht & Lahn.]
(A ghost of 20538.) 21278

[Der Neue Gemeinnützige
Landwirthschafts Calender, auf das Jahr
. . . 1788 [Zweyte Auflage].
Lancaster, Steimer, Albrecht & Lahn.]
(No means of identifying copies of the 2nd
ed. is known.) 20539

Der Neue Gemeinnützige
Landwirthschaft Calender, auf das jahr
. . . 1789.
Lancaster, Albrecht & Lahn. [34] pp.
AAS copy. 21279

Der Neue, Gemeinnützige
Landwirthschafts Calender, auf das Jahr
. . . 1790.
Lancaster, Albrecht & Lahn. [44] pp.
(Composite copy.) 21981

Der Neue Gemeinnützige
Landwirthschafts Calender, auf das Jahr
. . . 1791.
Lancaster, Albrecht. [42] pp.
AAS copy. 22687

Der Neue, Gemeinnützige
Landwirthschafts Calender, auf das Jahr
. . . 1792.
Lancaster, Albrecht, [44] pp.
AAS copy. 23589

Der Neue, Gemeinnützige
Landwirthschafts Calender, auf das Jahr
. . . 1793.
Lancaster, Albrecht, [42] pp.
AAS copy. 24569

Der Neue, Gemeinnützige
Landwirthschafts Calender, auf das Jahr
. . . 1794.
Lancaster, Albrecht. [44] pp.
AAS copy. 25857

Der Neue, Gemeinnützige
Landwirthschafts Calender, auf das Jahr
. . . 1795.
Lancaster, Albrecht. [44] pp.
AAS copy. 27358

Der Neue, Gemeinnützige
Landwirthschafts Calender, auf das Jahr
. . . 1796.
Lancaster, Albrecht. [44] pp.
AAS copy. 29138

Der Neue, Gemeinnützige
Landwirthschafts Calendar, auf das Jahr
. . . 1797.
Lancaster, Pa., Albrecht. [46] pp.
AAS copy. 30837

Der Neue, Gemeinnützige
Landwirthschafts Calender, auf das Jahr
. . . 1798.
Lancaster, La., Albrecht. [44] pp.
AAS copy. 32519

Der Neue Gemeinnützige
Landwirthschafts Calender, auf das Jahr
. . . 1799.
Lancaster, Pa., Albrecht. [42] pp.
AAS copy. 34169

Der Neue, Gemeinnützige
Landwirthschafts Calender, auf das Jahr
. . . 1800.
Lancaster, Pa., Albrecht. [44] pp.
AAS copy. 35858

Der Neue, Gemeinnützige
Landwirthschafts Calender, auf das Jahr
. . . 1801.
Lancaster, Pa., Albrecht. [44] pp.
AAS copy. 38031

Der Neue Hoch Deutsche Americanische
Calender, auf das Jahr Christi, 1791.
Chestnut Hill, Saur. [40] pp.
HSP copy. 22688

Der Neue Hoch Deutsche Americanische
Calendar, auf das Jahr . . . 1792.
Chestnut Hill, Saur. [40] pp.
WLC copy. 23590

Der Neue Hoch Deutsche Americanische
Calender, auf das Jahr . . . 1793.
Chestnut Hill, Saur. [46] pp.
WLC copy. 24570

Der Neue Hoch Deutsche Americanische
Calender, auf das Jahr Christi, 1794.
Chestnuthill, Saur. [44] pp.
LOC copy. 25858

Der Neue Hoch Deutsche Americanische
Calender, auf das Jahr Christi, 1795.
Philadelphia, Saur. [40] pp., 1 plate.
LCP copy. 27359

Der Neue Hoch Deutsche Americanische
Calender, auf das Jahr . . . 1796.
Baltimore, Saur. [32] pp.
AAS copy. 29139

Der Neue Hoch Deutsche Americanische
Calender, auf das Jahr Christi 1797.
Baltimore, Saur for Kramer, etc.
[40] pp.
LOC copy. 30838

Der Neue Hoch-Deutsche Americanische
Calender, auf das Jahr Christi 1798.
Baltimore, Saur. [40] pp.
NYPL copy. 32520

Der Neue Hoch-Deutsche Americanische
Calender auf das Jahr Christi 1799.
Baltimore, Saur. [40] pp.
(No perfect copy located.)
Carnegie Library, Pittsburgh, copy. 34170

Der Neue Hoch-Deutsche Americanische
Calender, auf das Jahr Christi 1800.
Baltimore, Saur. [40] pp.
HSP copy. 35859

Der Neue Hoch Deutsche Americanische
Calender, auf das Jahr Christi 1801.
Baltimore, Saur. [42] pp.
AAS copy. 38032

Der Neue Nord-Americanische Stadt und
Land Calender, auf das Jahr . . . 1797.
Hagerstown, Gruber. [28] pp.
LCP copy. 47841

Der Neue Nord-Americanische Stadt und
Land Calender, auf das Jahr . . . 1798.
Hagerstown, Md., Gruber. [32] pp.
LCP copy. 32521

Der Neue Nord-Americanische Stadt und
Land Calender auf . . . 1799.
Hagerstown, [Md.], Gruber. [28] pp.
(The only known copy is imperfect.)
EPFL copy. 34171

Der Neue Nord-Americanische Stadt und
Land Calender, auf das Jahr Christi 1800.
Hagerstown, Md., Gruber. [40] pp.
NYPL copy. 35860

Der Neue Nord-Americanische Stadt und
Land Calender, auf das Jahr 1801.
Hagerstown, Gruber. [32] pp.
(No copy located.) 38033

Das Neue und Verbesserte Gesangbuch.
See

Reformed Church in the United States.
35861

Der Neue, Verbessert-und Zuverlässige
Americanische Calender auf das 1777ste
Jahr.
Philadelphia, Miller. [44] pp.
AAS copy. 14897

Der Neue, Verbessert-und Zuverlässige
Americanische Calender auf das 1778ste
Jahr.
Philadelphia, Miller. [40] pp.
(The unique copy is imperfect.)
AAS copy. 15449

Der Neue, Verbesserte-und Zuverlassige
Americanische Calender, auf das 1783ste
Jahr Christi.
Philadelphia, Crukshank. [38] pp.
LOC copy. 17612

Der Neue, Verbessert und Zuverlässige
Americanische Calender, auf das 1783 ste
Jahr Christi.
Philadelphia, Cossart. [40] pp.
(The only copy located is imperfect.)
AAS copy. 44226

Der Neue, Verbessert-und Zuverlässige
Americanische Calender, auf das 1785 ste
Jahr Christi.
Philadelphia, Crukshank. [40] pp.
(No perfect copy located.)
AAS copy. 44561

Der Neue, Verbesserte und Zuverlässige
Americanische Calender, auf das 1786 ste
Jahr Christi.
Philadelphia, Crukshank. [38] pp.
AAS copy. 44732

[Neuer, Ernfahrner, Amerikanischer
Haus-und Stall-Arzt.
Frederick Town, Md., Bartgis, 1796.
("Zu haben, beym dutzend und einzein
stück bey Matthias Bartgis," adv. in
Federal Gazette, June 21, 1796.) 30842

Neuer Hauswirthafts Calender, auf das
Gnadenreiche Jahr . . . 1798.
Reading, Pa., Jungman. [44] pp.
AAS copy. 32525

Neuer Hauswirthschafts Calender, auf das
Gnadenreiche Jahr . . . 1799.
Reading, Pa., Jungmann. [44] pp.
AAS copy. 34175

Neuer Hausswirthschafts Calender, auf
. . . 1800.
Reading, Pa., Jungmann. [44] pp.
AAS copy. 35863

Neuer Hauswirthschafts Calender, auf
das Gnadenreiche Jahr . . . 1801.
Reading, [Pa.], Jungmann & Bruckmann.
[44] pp.
HSP copy. 38037

Neuer Hauswirthschafts Calender, auf das
Jahr . . . 1799.
Philadelphia, Schweitzer. [40] pp.
(No perfect copy located.)
AAS copy. 34174

Neuer Hauswirthschafts Calender, auf das
Jahr . . . 1800.
Philadelphia, Schweitzer. [40] pp.
AAS copy. 35864

Neuer Hauswirthschafts Calender, auf das
Jahr . . . 1801.
Philadelphia, Schweitzer. [40] pp.
LCP copy. 38038

Neuer Erfahrner Americanischer
Haus-und Stallarzt.
Frederick Town, Bartgis, 1794. [15], 84,
36, [4] pp.
AAS copy. 27362

Ein Neuer Schlauspiel durch die Herren
Egalite.
[Philadelphia, 1795.] Broadside.
LOC copy. 29163

Der Neueste, Verbessert-und
Zuverlässige Americanische Calender
auf das 1763ste Jahr.
Philadelphia, Miller. [40] pp.
(Only known copy is imperfect.)
HSP copy. 9199

Der Neueste, Verbessert-und
Zuverlässige Americanische Calender,
auf das 1764ste Jahr.
Philadelphia, Miller. [48] pp.
HSP copy. 9453

Der Neueste, Verbesserte-und
Zuverlässige Americanische Calender
auf das 1765ste Jahr.
Philadelphia, Miller, [1746].
[36] pp.
HSP copy. 9748

Der Neueste, Verbessert-und
Zuverlässige Americanische Calender
auf das 1766ste Jahr.
Philadelphia, Miller. [42] pp.
HSP copy. 10084

Der Neuste, Verbessert-und
Zuverlässige Americanische Calender
auf das 1767ste Jahr.
Philadelphia, Miller. [40] pp.
LOC copy. 10404

[Der Neuste, Verbessert-und
Zuverlässige Americanische Calender
auf das 1767ste Jahr. . . . Zweyte Auflage.
Philadelphia, Miller. [40] pp.]
(No copy located has words "Zweyte
Auflage.") 10405

[Der Neuste, Verbessert-und
Zuverlässige Americanische Calender
auf das 1767ste Jahr. . . . Dritte Auflage.
Philadelphia, Miller. [40] pp.]
(Adv. in Woechentliche Phil. Stattsbote,
Jan. 26, 1767.) 10406

Der Neueste, Verbessert-und
Zuverlässige Americanische Calender
auf das 1768ste Jahr.
Philadelphia, Miller. [40] pp.
HSP copy. 10698

[Der Neueste, Verbessert-und
Zuverlaessige Americanische Calender auf
das 1769ste Jahr.
Philadelphia, Miller.]
(Assumed from the sequence.) 10987

Der Neueste, Verbessert-und
Zuverlässige Americanische Calender
auf das 1770ste Jahr.
Philadelphia, Miller. [44] pp.
LOC copy. 11351

Der Neueste, Verbessert-und
Zuverlaessige Americanische Calender auf
das 1771ste Jahr.
Philadelphia, Miller. [44] pp.
AAS copy. 11754

Der Neueste, Verbessert-und
Zuverlaessige Americanische Calendar
auf das 1772ste Jahr.
Philadelphia, Miller. [52] pp.
AAS copy. 12136

Der Neueste, Verbessert-und
Zuverlaessige Americanische Calender auf
das 1773ste Jahr.
Philadelphia, Miller, [48] pp.
LOC copy. 12471

Der Neueste, Verbessert-und
Zuverlässige Americanische Calender
auf das 1774ste Jahr.
Philadelphia, Miller. [44] pp.
(The only copy located is imperfect.)
AAS copy. 12876

Der Neueste, Verbesserte-und
Zuverlässige Americanische Calender.
Auf das 1775ste Jahr.
Philadelphia, Miller. [48] pp.
HSP copy. 13451

Der Neueste, Verbessert-und
Zuverlässige Americanische Calender
auf das 1776ste Jahr.
Philadelphia, Miller. [52] pp.
AAS copy. 14270

Neufville, John de.
Boston, September 5, 1785. Whereas I. . . .
[Boston, 1785.] Broadside.
LOC copy. 19109

Der Neugestellte, Verbessert-und
Zuverlässige Americanische Calender
auf das 1779ste Jahr.

Philadelphia, Miller. [36] pp.
AAS copy.   15920

Der Neugestellete und Verbesserte
Americanische Staats-Calender auf das
1780ste Jahr.
[Philadelphia, Miller. [32] pp.
AAS copy.   16381

Neujahrs-Verse, des Herumträgers der
Neuen Unpartheyischen Läncaster
Zeitung, den 1sten Januar, 1792.
[Lancaster, 1792.] Broadside.   46512

Neujahrs-Verse des Herumträgers der
Philadelphischen Correspondenz. Den.
1sten Januar, 1782.
[Philadelphia, 1782.] Broadside.
HSP copy.   17546

Neujahrs-Verse des Herumträgers des
Philadelphischen Correspondenz. Den
1sten Januar, 1783.
[Philadelphia, 1783.] Broadside.
HSP copy.   17944

[Neujahrs-Verse des Herumträgers der
Philadelphische Correspondenz. Den
1sten Januar, 1784.
[Philadelphia, 1784. Broadside.]
(Entry from Hildeburn.)   18494

[Nevill, Samuel], 1697?-1764.
(Whitehead, Judicial Hist. N. J., pp.
393-394.)
The History of North-America.
Woodbridge, 1761.]
(Evans assumed a reprint from the New
American Magazine, but none has been
found.)   8939

[Neville, Henry, 1620-1694.
The Isle of Pines.
Cambrige, 1668.]
(No copy known. See G. P. Winship,
Cambridge Press, pp. 286-287.)   127

A New Academy of Compliments.
Worcester, 1795. pp. [7], [10]- 144.
AAS copy.   29145

A New Academy of Compliments.
[New York?], Gomez, [1799?]. 144 pp.,
front.
NYHS copy.   48941

The New American Almanac for . . . 1783.
Fredericktown, Bartgis. [32] pp.
AAS copy.   44227

[The New American Mock-Bird.
New York, Gaine, 1761.]
(See Ford, Gaine, I, 107.)   8940

New American Spelling Book [by Isaiah
Thomas, 1749-1831].
Worcester, Thomas, 1785. 144 pp.
AAS copy.   19271

New Amphitheatre. This Evening,
January 6th, 1795 . . . Horsemanship.
[New York, 1795.] Broadside.
NYPL copy.   47500

[A New and Complete Guide to the
English Tongue.
Philadelphia, Franklin, 1740.]
(Adv. Pa. Gazette, July 31, 1740.)   4566

A New and Compleat Introduction to the
Grounds and Rules of Music [by Daniel
Bayley, d. 1792].
Newburyport (Boston), Emerson, 1764.
[6], 25, [4] pp., 23 plates.
(No copy found with the imprint given by
Evans.)
AAS copy.   9598

A New and Concise History of the
Revolution in France.
Philadelphia, Hoff & Derrick, 1794. pp.
[i]-iv, [9]-164; 1 plate.
AAS copy.   27364

[New and Old Principles of Trade
Compared.
Philadelphia, Dobson, 1788.]
(Entry from an adv. for the London ed.)   21281

[A New and Select Collection of the Best
English, Scots and Irish Songs.

New York, Rivington, 1780.]
("This day Published," Royal Gazette,
June 17, 1780.)   16874

[New and True Aegyptian Fortune Teller.
Boston, Fowle, 1753. 22 + pp.]
(Title from adv. Only known copy
defective.)
AAS copy.   7101

The New and True Egyptian Fortune-
Teller.
[Boston], the Printing-Office in
Marlborough Street, MDCCLXXIV.
23 pp.
BPL copy.   42640

A New and True Relation, of a Little Girl
in . . . Simsbury . . . Bewitch'd, in March
1763.
Boston, 1766. Broadside.
AAS ph. copy.   41646

[A New and Valuable Collection of
Religious Poems.
Bennington, 1786.]
(McCorison 117; no copy known.)   44925

New-Ark Land and Cash Lottery, in New
Castle.
[Philadelphia, 1771.] Broadside.
LCP copy.   12138

New-Ark Lottery.
Christiana Bridge, March 23, 1771. . . .
[Philadelphia, 1771.] Broadside.
LCP copy.   12137

A New Ballad upon a New Occasion.
[Philadelphia, 1771.] Broadside.
BPL facsim. copy.   42255

The New Baltimore Directory, and
Annual Register; for 1800 and 1801.
[Baltimore], Warner & Hanna, [1800].
104, 50, [1] pp.
MdHS copy.   38040

New Bedford, Mass.
Hymn, Ode, and Dirge, to be Sung at New
Bedford, the 22d of February, 1800.
[New Bedford, 1800.] Broadside.
HEH copy.   38041

[New Bedford, Mass. Social School.
Regulations for the Government. . . .
November 25th, 1798.
New Bedford, Spooner, 1799. 14 pp.]
(Entry from Sabin 52498.)   35866

A New Book for Children to Learn in [by
Stephen.Crisp, 1628-1692].
Newport, Southwick, 1769. 96 pp.
(The only known copy is defective.)
RIHS copy.   41925

[The New Book of Knowledge.
Boston, Fowle, 1762. 172 pp.]
(See Nicholas, Isaiah Thomas, p. 39.) 9200

The New Book of Knowledge.
Boston, Barclay, 1767. 172 pp.
(The only known copy is imperfect.)
AAS copy.   41739

The New Book of Knowledge.
Boston, Fowle, [1767 ?]. front.,
172 pp.
(No copy found with imprint assumed by
Evans from an adv. AAS and MHS have
Barclay imprints. Printed by Thomas
when working for Fowle.)
AAS copy.   10699

[The New Book of Knowledge.
Boston, Thomas, 1772. 150 pp.]
(Adv. Mass. Spy, Dec. 31, 1772.)   12472

New Brunswick Church Lottery.
A List of the Numbers that Came up
Prizes in the. . . . Drawn April, 1749.
n.p., [1749]. Broadside.
HSP copy.   40507

New Castle County, Del. Poor-House.
Ordinances, Rules and Bye-laws for the
Poor-House.
Wilmington, Adams, 1791. Broadside.
LOC copy.   23594

New-Castle, February 6, 1772. Scheme of
a Lottery.

[Philadelphia, 1772.] Broadside.
LCP copy.   12473

New-Castle Lottery.
Christiana Bridge, July 13, 1771.
[Philadelphia, 1771.] Broadside.
LCP copy.   12140

New-Castle Lottery.
New-Castle, June 15, 1771.
[Philadelphia, 1771.] Broadside.
LCP copy.   12139

New-Castle Lottery.
New-Castle Lottery . . . for Raising the
Sum . . . towards . . . a Presbyterian
Church, in . . . Philadelphia.
[Philadelphia, 1772.] Broadside.
HSP copy.   42356

A New Collection of Country Dances, for
the Use of Dancing Assemblies: in the
Year 1797.
Leominster, Mass., 1799. 12 pp.
AAS copy.   35867

A New Collection of Hymns and Spiritual
Songs, from Various Authors.
Wrentham, Mass., Heaton, 1795.
46 pp.
AAS copy.   47501

A New Collection of Hymns, on Various
Subjects.
Newport, Southwick, 1773. 56 pp.
BrU copy.   42466

A New Collection of Verses Applied to
the First of November, A. D. 1765.
New Haven, [1765]. 24 pp.
BrU copy.   10085

[The New Complete American Letter
Writer.
Philadelphia, Spotswood, 1789.]
(Entry from advs.)   21985

[A New Complete Guide to the English
Tongue.
New York, 1745.]
(Title from Hildeburn.)   5648

The New Complete Letter Writer: or, The
Art of Correspondence.
Worcester, Thomas, 1791. 271 pp.
AAS copy.   23327

The New Complete Letter Writer; or, The
Art of Correspondence.
Boston, Thomas & Andrews, 1794.
252 pp.
AAS copy.   27365

The New Complete Letter Writer; or, The
Art of Correspondence.
Boston, Etheridge for Brewer, etc., 1798.
228 pp.
AAS copy.   34177

The New, Complete Letter Writer; or, The
Art of Correspondence.
New York, Tiebout, 1800. [2], 82 pp.
(No perfect copy located.)
AAS copy.   38042

A New Display of the United States.
New Haven, Doolittle, 1799. Broadside.
MHS copy.   35868

[A New Drawing Book, from the Best
Masters.
Philadelphia, Cobbett, 1796.]
(Imprint assumed by Evans from adv.
"This Day is Published," Gazette of the
U.S., Aug. 27, 1796.)   30844

[The New Duty of Man.
New York, Rivington, 1781.]
("A new edition this day published and
sold by the Printer," Royal Gazette, Nov.
10, 1781.)   17243

New England (Colony) Laws, Statutes,
etc., 1687.
[Order for the Constable to Bring in the
Rates.
Boston, Pierce, 1687.] Broadside.
(Known from Pierce's bill.)   39241

New England (Colony) Laws, Statutes,
etc., 1687.
[Order for the Rate of a Penny a Pound.

Boston, Pierce, 1687.] Broadside.
(Known by Pierce's bill.)   39243

New England (Colony) Laws, Statutes,
etc., 1687.
[Orders for the Price of Grain.
Boston, Pierce, 1687.] Broadside.
(Known from Pierce's bill.)   39242

New England (Colony) President, 1686.
By the President and Council. . . . 8th Day
of June . . . 1686.
Boston, 1686. Broadside.
CSL copy.   410

New England (Colony) President, 1686.
By the President . . . Published the 10th of
June, 1686. [Courts.].
[Boston, 1686.] pp. 3-10.
MHS facsimile copy.   39233

New England (Colony) President, 1686.
A Proclamation . . . against the
Governour and Company of the
Massachusetts Bay . . . May 25, 1686.
[Boston, 1686.] Broadside.
(No copy located.)   39234

New England (Colony) President, 1686.
A Proclamation. . . . 28th Day of May . . .
1686.
Boston, [1686.] Broadside.
HC copy.   409

New England (Colony) President, 1686.
A Proclamation. [Marriage. May 29,
1686.]
Boston, Pierce, [1686]. Broadside.
MHS copy.   411

New England (Colony) President, 1686.
. . . The Speech of the Honourable Joseph
Dudley . . . May 17 1686.
Boston, Pierce for Phillips, 1686. 4 pp.
PRO copy.   39235

New England (Colony) President, 1686.
[Thanksgiving proclamation, Nov. 1686.
Boston, 1686.] Broadside.
(Known from Pierce's bill for printing.)   39236

New England (Colony) President, 1688.
By his Excellency. A Proclamation. . . .
[January 10, 1688].
Boston, [1688]. Broadside.
MHS copy.   449

New England (Colony) President, 1688.
By His Excellency, a Proclamation
Commanding the Setting at Liberty His
Majesty's Subjects lately Taken by the
Indians [Dated Oct. 20, 1688].
Boston, Pierce, [1688]. Broadside.
PRO copy.   39246

New England (Colony) President, 1689.
By His Excellency a Proclamation.
Whereas His Majesty . . . the Sixteenth
Day of October . . . Invasion from Holland
[Dated January 10, 1688].
Boston, Pierce, [1689]. Broadside.
MHS copy.   39261

New England (Colony) Receiver General,
1688.
John Usher, Esq.; Receiver General of
His Majesty's Revenues . . . to the . . .
Select-Men of the Town [Blank] . . . July
1688].
[Boston? 1688.] Broadside.
NYHS copy.   39247

The New-England Almanack for. . . . 1686
[by Samuel Danforth, 1666-1727].
Cambridge, 1685. [16] pp.
AAS copy.   403

The New-England Almanack for. . . . 1686
[by Samuel Danforth, 1666-1727].
Cambridge, 1686. [16] pp.
MHS copy.   404

The New-England Almanack . . . for . . .
1777. . . . By Edmund Freebetter [by
Nathan Daboll, 1750-1818].
New London, Green. [24] pp.
AAS copy.   14724

The New-England Almanack for . . . 1778
[by Nathan Daboll, 1750-1818].

Hartford, Patten. [24] pp.
AAS copy.   15281

The New-England Almanack . . . for . . .
1783 [by Nathan Daboll, 1750-1818].
New London, Green. [24] pp.
AAS copy.   17507

The New-England Almanack . . . for . . .
1783. . . . By Isaac Bickerstaff [by
Benjamin West, 1730-1813].
Providence, Carter, [24] pp.
AAS copy.   17795

The New-England Almanack, for 1786, by
Isaac Bickerstaff [by Benjamin
West, 1730-1813].
Hartford, Elisha Babcock. [24] pp.
CHS copy.   44651

The New-England Almanack . . . for . . .
1798. . . . By Isaac Bickerstaff [by
Benjamin West, 1730-1813].
Providence, Carter & Wilkinson.
[24] pp.
AAS copy.   33201

The New-England Almanack . . . for . . .
1800. . . . By Isaac Bickerstaff [by
Benjamin West, 1730-1813].
Providence, R. I., Carter. [24] pp.
AAS copy.   36700

The New-England Almanack . . . for . . .
1801. . . . By Isaac Bickerstaff [by
Benjamin West, 1730-1813].
Providence, R. I., Carter. [24] pp.
AAS copy.   36962

New England Bravery. Being a full . . .
Account of the taking of . . . Louisburg
. . . June, 1745.
Boston, at the Heart and Crown, [174-?]
(No copy located.)   40184

[The New-England Calendar and
Ephemeris for 1801.
Newport, Farnsworth for Richardson,
1800.]
(Alden 1652; no copy known.)   49119

The New-England Callendar: or
Almanack, for . . . 1793. . . . By Richard
Astrologer.
Boston, Coverly. [24] pp.
AAS copy.   24743

[The New-England Callendar; or
Almanack . . . 1794.
Boston, Coverly. [24] pp.]
(The only reported copy cannot be
located.)   26081

[The New-England Callendar: or
Almanack, for . . . 1795. By Richard
Astrologer.
Boston, Coverly. [24] pp.]
(Assumed by Evans from the fact that
there was a 1794 ed.)   27620

. . . The New-England Diary, Or,
Almanack for . . . 1722 [by Nathan
Bowen, 1697-1776].
Boston, 1722. [16] pp.
AAS copy.   2205

. . . . The New-England Diary, or
Almanack for . . . 1723 [by Nathan
Bowen, 1697-1776].
Boston, Green for Belknap, 1723.
[16] pp.
AAS copy.   2322

. . . . The New-England Diary, or,
Almanack for . . . 1724. [By Nathan
Bowen, 1697-1776].
Boston, Green, 1724. [16] pp.
AAS copy.   2415

. . . . The New-England Diary, or
Almanack for . . . 1725 [by Nathan
Bowen, 1697-1776].
Boston, Franklin, 1725. [16] pp.
AAS copy.   39821

. . . . The New-England Diary, or,
Almanack for . . . 1725 [by Nathan
Bowen, 1697-1776].
Boston, Green, 1725. [24] pp.
AAS copy.   2506

. . . The New-England Diary, or,
Almanack for . . . 1726 [by Nathan

Bowen, 1697-1776].
Boston, Green, 1726. [16] pp.
AAS copy.   2611

. . . . The New-England Diary, or,
Almanack for . . . 1726 [by Nathan
Bowen, 1697-1776].
Boston, 1726. [16] pp.]
(Evans evidently saw a copy which
differed from 2611 in the bookseller's
imprint.)   2612

. . . . The New-England Diary, or,
Almanack for . . . 1727 [by Nathan
Bowen, 1697-1776].
Boston, Green, 1727. [16] pp.
AAS copy.   2732

. . . . The New-England Diary, or,
Almanack for . . . . 1728 [by Nathan
Bowen, 1697-1776].
Boston, Green, 1728. [16] pp.
AAS copy.   2845

. . . . The New-England Diary, or,
Almanack for . . . 1729 [by Nathan
Bowen, 1697-1776].
Boston, Green, 1729. [16] pp.
AAS copy.   2995

. . . . The New-England Diary: or,
Almanack for . . . 1731 [by Nathan
Bowen, 1697-1766].
Boston, Green, 1731. [16] pp.
AAS copy.   3258

. . . . The New-England Diary, or,
Almanack, for . . . 1732, [by Nathan
Bowen, 1697-1776].
Boston, Green, 1732. [16] pp.
AAS copy.   3395

. . . . The New-England Diary, or,
Almanack, for . . . 1733 [by Nathan
Bowen, 1697-1776].
Boston, Green, 1733. [16] pp.
AAS copy.   3508

. . . . The New-England Diary, or,
Almanack, for . . . 1734 [by Nathan
Bowen, 1697-1776].
Boston, 1734. [16] pp.
AAS copy.   3632

. . . . The New-England Diary: or,
Almanack, for . . . 1735 [by Nathan
Bowen, 1697-1776].
Boston, Fleet, 1735. [16] pp.
AAS copy.   3755

. . . . The New-England Diary: Or,
Almanack, for . . . 1736 [by Nathan
Bowen, 1697-1776].
Boston, Fleet, 1736. [16] pp.
AAS copy.   3877

. . . . The New-England Diary: or,
Almanack, for . . . 1737 [by Nathan
Bowen, 1697-1776].
Boston, Fleet, 1736. [16] pp.
AAS copy.   3995

[. . . . The New-England Diary: or,
Almanack, for . . . 1738 [by Nathan
Bowen, 1697-1776].
Boston, Fleet, 1738. [16] pp.]
(Assumed by Evans from the sequence.)   4126

New-England Freemen [by John
Oxenbridge, 1609-1674].
[Cambridge], 1673. [6], 48 pp.
AAS copy.   181

The New-England Harmony, Containing a
Set of Excellent Psalm Tunes.
Boston, Fleeming, 1771.
(Known only by this tp.)
AAS copy.   42256

The N. England Kalendar, 1703. Or an
Almanack for . . . 1703.
Boston, B. Green & Allen, 1703.
[16] pp.
AAS copy.   39401

The N. England Kalendar, 1704. Or an
Almanack for . . . 1704.
Boston, B. Green & Allen for Buttolph,
1704. [16] pp.
(The unique original cannot be
reproduced.)   39412

The N. England Kalendar, 1704. Or an
Almanack for . . . 1704.
Boston, B. Green & Allen for Phillips,
1704. [16] pp.
AAS copy.   39413

The N. England Kalender, 1705. Or an,
Almanack for . . . 1705.
Boston, B. Green for Buttolph, 1705. [16]
pp.
AAS copy.   39429

The N. England Kalendar, 1705. Or, an,
Almanack for . . . 1705.
Boston, B. Green for Phillips, 1705. [16]
pp.
(But for imprint identical with 39429,
q. v.)   39430

The N. England Kalendar, 1706. Or An
Almanack for . . . 1706.
Boston, B. Green for Buttolph, 1706.
[16] pp.
AAS copy.   39441

The N. England Kalendar, 1706. Or, an
Almanack for . . . 1706.
Boston, B. Green for Phillips, 1706.
[16] pp.
(For the text see 39441.)
AAS copy.   39442

The New England Memorandum-Book.
Boston, M'Alpine & Fleeming, 1765.
[120] pp.
AAS copy.   10086

New England Mississippi Land Company.
Articles of Association and Agreement.
[Boston, 1797?] 7 pp.
DeRGL copy.   48187

New England Mississippi Land Company.
Articles of Association . . . March 12,
1798.
[Boston, 1798.] 9 pp.
AAS copy.   34178

New England Mississippi Land Company.
To the President of the United States. The
Subscribers. . . .
[Boston, 1798.] 19 pp.
DeRGL copy.   34179

New-England Persecutors Mauled [by
Thomas Maule, 1645-1724].
[New York, 1697.] iv, 62 pp.
JCB copy.   801

[The New-England Primer.
Boston, 1689?]
(There is no record of the printing of this
first edition, and no copy has survived.)
                                             494

[The New-England Primer Enlarged.
Boston, 1691.]
(Title from adv. in Evans 574.)   573

The New-England Primer Enlarged.
Boston, Kneeland and Green, 1727.
[80] pp.
(The unique copy is imperfect.)
NYPL copy.   2927

The New-England Primer Enlarged.
Boston, Kneeland & Green, 1735.
[80] pp.
HEH copy.   3934

The New-England Primer Enlarged.
Boston, Fleet, 1737. [80] pp.
(The only copy located is badly defective.)
WL copy.   4167

The New-England Primer Enlarged.
Boston, Fleet, 1738. [80] pp.
HEH copy.   4280

The New-England Primer Improved with
Additions.
Boston, Rogers & Fowle, 1746.
[80] pp.
HEH copy.   5817

The New-England Primer Further
Improved.
Boston, Rogers & Fowle, 1749.
[80] pp.
(The present location of this is unknown.)
                                             40508

The New-England Primer Further
Improved.
Boston, for the Booksellers, 1750.
[80] pp.
(No copy located.)   40553

The New-England Primer Improved.
Boston, J. Green, 1750. [80] pp.
YC (Pequot) copy.   40554

The New-England Primre Improved.
New York, 1750. [96] pp.
HEH copy.   6726

[The New-England Primer Enlarged.
Boston, Fleet, 1751.]
(Mentioned by Isaiah Thomas.)   6725

The New-England Primer Enlarged.
Boston, Kneeland & Green, 1752.
[80] pp.
AAS copy.   40629

The New-England Primer Further
Improved.
Boston, 1754.
(Owned by E. M. Kidder, 1922.)   40703

The New-England Primer Enlarged.
Germantown, 1754. [78] pp.
HEH copy.   7264

The New-England Primer Improved.
Boston, Printed for the Booksellers, 1756,
[26+].
(Known only by this fragment.)
AAS copy.   40854

[The New-England Primer Enlarged.
Boston, Fowle & Mecom, 1757.]
(Title from I. Thomas.)   7963

[The New-England Primer Enlarged.
Philadelphia, 1757.]
(Adv. Pa. Gazette, Jan. 16, 1757.)   7964

The New-England Primer Enlarged.
Philadelphia, Franklin & Hall, 1760.
[52] pp.
(The only reported copy cannot be
located.)   41147

The New-England Primer.
[Boston, Kneeland for Winter, 1761.]
[80] pp.
(The only copy located is imperfect.)
CU copy.   8941

The New-England Primer Improved.
Boston, Adams, 1762. [80] pp.
HEH copy.   9201

The New-England Primer Enlarged.
Boston, Fleet, 1763. [64] pp.
(Bought by Geo. D. Smith; unlocated.)
                                             9454

The New-England Primer Improved.
Boston, Wharton & Bowes, 1764.
[80] pp.
HEH copy.   41465

The New-England Primer Enlarged.
Germantown, Sower, 1764. 10+pp.
(Heartman 20; no copy located.)   41466

The New-England Primer Enlarged.
Philadelphia, Franklin & Hall, 1764. [78]
pp.
(Heartman 19; no copy located.)   41467

[The New-England Primer Improved.
Boston, White, 1766. [80] pp.]
(Neither known copy could be filmed.)
                                             10407

The New-England Primer Improved.
Boston, M'Alpine, 1767. [80] pp.
HEH copy.   10700

The New-England Primer Improved.
Boston, Perkins, 1767. [80] pp.
HEH copy.   41740

The New-England Primer Improved.
Boston, Barclay, 1768. [80] pp.
CHS copy.   10990

The New-England Primer Improved.
Boston, Kneeland & Adams for Leverett,
1768.
(Owned by Samuel A. Green in 1904.)
                                             41852

The New-England Primer Improved.
Boston, Perkins, 1768. [80] pp.
HEH copy.   10989

The New-England Primer Improved.
Boston, Boyles, 1770. [80] pp.
(Copy attributed to Woburn Public
Library, but could not be confirmed.)
                                             11755

The New-England Primer Enlarged.
Boston, Fleets, 1770. [80] pp.
(No perfect copy located.)
AAS copy.   42132

The New-England Primer Improved.
Boston, M'Alpine, 1770. [80] pp.
WL copy.   11756

The New-England Primer Improved.
Boston, Perkins, 1770. [80] pp.
Pequot Library (Yale) copy.   11757

[The New-England Primer Improved.
Germantown, 1770.]
(Wickersham's Hist. Ed. Pa.)   11758

[The New-England Primer Improved.
Philadelphia, Bell for Aitken, 1770.]
(Aitken's waste book.)   11759

The New-England Primer Improved.
Salem, Halls, [1770]. [80] pp.
(The only known copy cannot be
reproduced.)   42037

The New-England Primer Improved.
Boston, 1771. [80] pp.
HC copy.   12143

The New-England Primer Improved.
Boston, Kneeland & Adams, 1771.
Front., [80] pp.
PL copy.   12142

The New-England Primer Improved.
Boston, Leverett, 1771. Front., [80] pp.
PL copy.   12144

[The New-England Primer Improved.
Boston, Perkins, 1771. [80] pp.]
(Copy formerly owned by George D.
Smith.)   12145

The New-England Primer Improved.
Boston, Perkins, 1771. [80] pp.
(No copy located.)   42258

The New-England Primer Enlarged.
Germantown, [Pa.], Sower, 1771.
[79] pp.
PPL copy.   42257

The New-England Primer Enlarged.
Philadelphia, Hall & Sellers, 1771.
[80] pp.
HSP copy.   12141

The New-England Primer Improved.
Boston, Perkins, 1772. [80] pp.
BPL copy.   12474

The New-England Primer Improved.
Boston, Ellison, 1773. [80] pp.
LOC copy.   12877

The New-England Primer Improved.
Boston, Perkins, [1773]. [80] pp.
AAS copy.   42467

The New-England Primer Enlarged.
Philadelphia, Hall & Sellers, 1773.
[80] pp.
HEH copy.   42468

The New-England Primer Improved.
Boston, Boyle, 1774. [80] pp.
Pequot Library (Yale) copy.   13452

[The New-England Primer Improved.
Norwich, 1774.]
(Entry from Evans; source unlocated.)
                                              13453

[The New-England Primmer.
Baltimore, 1775.]
(The Source of Evans' entry is unknown.)
                                              14273

The New-England Primer Improved.
Providence, 1775. [80] pp.
NYPL copy.   14272

The New-England Primer Improved.
Providence, Carter, 1775. [72] pp.
(Only this fragment could be located.)
AAS copy.   42888

The New-England Primer Improved.
Boston, Draper and Boyle, 1777. [80] pp.
BPL copy.   15450

[The New-England Primer Improved.
Hartford, Patten, 1777. [80] pp.]
(The unique copy could not be
reproduced.)   15451

[The New-England Primer Enlarged.
Philadelphia, Aitken, 1777.]
(Sold at American Art, Anderson, sale
4372 (Feb. 1938), No. 314.)   15452

The New-England Primer Improved.
Boston, 1779. [64] pp.
AAS copy.   16382

The New-England Primer Improved.
Boston, Coverly, 1779. [80] pp.
(The only recorded copy has disappeared.)
                                             43662

The New-England Primer, Enlarged.
Boston, Fleets, [1779]. [96] pp.
LOC copy.   16875

[The New-England Primer Enlarged.
Philadelphia, Crukshank, 1779.]
(Adv. in Dec., 1779.)   16385

[The New-England Primer Enlarged.
Philadelphia, Hall & Sellers, 1779.]
(Adv. Pa. Gazette, Jan., 1779; title
uncertain.)   16383

[The New-England Primer Enlarged.
Philadelphia, Steiner & Cist, 1779.]
(Adv. Pa. Gazette, Jan. 5, 1779.)   16384

The New-England Primer (Enlarged and
much Improved).
Philadelphia, Spotswood and Seddon,
[178-]. [80] pp.
LCP copy.   43749

[The New-England Primer, Improved.
Trenton, 1780.]
(Origin of entry an adv. "New-England
Primers to be sold by the Thousand" in
New-Jersey Gazette, Sept. 6, 1780.) 16876

The New-England Primer. For the More
Easy Attaining the true Reading of
English.
Philadelphia, Aitken, 1780. [48] pp.
(Copy not located.)   43843

[The New-England Primer Improved.
[Boston?], 1781. [80] pp.]
(Sold at George D. Smith sale, 1904.)
                                             17245

The New-England Primer. Improved.
Boston, M'Dougall, 1781. 72 pp.
WL copy.   17244

The New-England Primer Improved.
Hartford, Hudson & Goodwin, 1781.
[80] pp.
CHS copy.   17246

[The New-England Primer Improved.
Hartford, Webster, 1781.]
(Adv. Conn. Courant, Apr. 17, 1781.)
                                             17247

[The New-England Primer Improved.
Philadelphia, Bradford & Hall, 1781.]
(Adv. Pa. Journal, June 13, 1781.) 17248

The New-England Primer, Improved.
Boston, Coverly, 1782. [80] pp.
BA copy.   17613

[The New-England Primer Improved.
Chatham, 1782.]
(Entry from Nelson, who questioned it.)
                                             17614

The New-England Primer Improved.
Exeter, N. H., 1782. [80] pp.
(The only known copy is imperfect.)
AAS copy.   44228

The New-England Primer.
Philadelphia, Cist, 1782. [80] pp.

(The present location of this copy is
unknown.)   44229

The New-England Primer Improved.
Providence, Carter, 1782. [80] pp.
(No complete copy located.)
AAS copy.   19428

[The New-England Primer Improved.
Providence, Wheeler, 1782.]
(A ghost of 22697, q. v.)   17615

The New-England Primer, Improved.
Hartford, Hudson & Goodwin, 1783.
[80] pp.
CSL copy.   44410

The New England Primer (Enlarged and
much Improved).
Philadelphia, Crukshank, 1783. 80 pp.
(No copy located.)   44411

The New-England Primer Improved.
Boston, 1784. [64] pp.
PPL copy.   18620

The New-England Primer Improved.
Boston, Edes & Sons, 1784. [80] pp.
(Only sample pages could be reproduced.)
YC copy.   44562

The New-England Primer, or the First
Step to the True Reading of the English
Tongue.
Boston, Warden and Russell, 1784.
[78?] pp.
(The only known copy is imperfect.)
HC copy.   44563

The New-England Primer Improved.
Salem, Hall, 1784. [80] pp.
AAS copy.   18621

The New-England Primer Improved.
Hartford, Patten, 1785. [80] pp.
(The only known copy is imperfect.)
AAS copy.   44733

The New-England Primer, Improved.
New London, Green, 1785. [80] pp.
(The only known copy is imperfect.)
AAS copy.   44734

The New-England Primer Improved.
Plymouth, Coverly, 1785. [64] pp.
(Heartman 79; no copy located.)   44735

The New-England Primer, Improved.
Providence, Carter, 1785. [80] pp.
(This copy is imperfect.)
AAS copy.   44736

The New-England Primer Improved.
Providence, Wheeler, [c. 1785]. [80] pp.
HEH copy.   22697

The New-England Primer, Improved.
Middletown, 1786. [80] pp.
AAS copy.   19814

The New-England Primer, Improved.
Norwich, Trumbull, 1786. [64] pp.
HEH copy.   44926

[The New-England Primer Improved.
Philadelphia, Spotswood, 1786.]
("Sold by W. Spotswood," Pa. Herald,
July 12, 1786.)   19815

The New-England Primer Improved.
Plymouth, 1786. [64] pp.
Gillett G. Griffin copy.   19816

The New-England Primer Improved.
Boston, the booksellers, 1787. [64] pp.
(This copy is imperfect.)
BPL copy.   45106

The New-England Primer Enlarged.
Boston: Printed by E. Draper, and Sold
by the Book-Sellers, [1787]. [80] pp.
(This is apparently the ed. recorded by
Evans from an adv.)
AAS copy.   20542

[The New-England Primer Enlarged.
Boston, Draper for West, [1787].
[80] pp.
(Offered for sale; present location
unknown.)   20543

[The New-England Primer Enlarged.

Boston, Draper for White, [1787].
[80] pp.]
(Offered for sale: present location
uknown.)   20544

[The New-England Primer Improved.
New York, Campbell, 1787.]
(From an adv.)   20545

[The New-England Primer, Amended
and Improved.
Philadelphia, Crukshank, 1787. [80] pp.]
(This item is described by Evans from
an adv. The unique copy is at present
unavailable.)   20546

The New-England Primer, Improved.
Springfield, Mass., Russell & Webster,
[1787]. [80] pp.
AAS copy.   45107

The New-England Primer Enlarged.
Boston, Draper for White, 1788. [80] pp.
HEH copy.   45304

The New-England Primer Improved.
Hartford, Hudson & Goodwin, 1788.
[80] pp.
(Too fragile to copy.)   45305

The New-England Primer, Improved.
Hartford, N. Petten [!], 1788.
[80] pp.
CHS copy.   45306

The New-England Primer Improved.
New York, Loudon, 1788. 72 pp.
(Only known copy is imperfect.)
PPL copy.   45307

The New-England Primer Enlarged.
Boston, Draper for West, 1789.
[80] pp.
(Heartmen 98; no copy located.)   45523

The New-England Primer Enlarged.
Boston, Draper for White, 1789.
[80] pp.
(Only the tp. could be reproduced.)
YC (Pequot) copy.   45524

The New-England Primer.
Boston, White & Cambridge, 1789.
[64] pp.
LOC copy.   21986

[The New-England Primer, Amended and
Improved.
Hartford, Babcock, 1789.]
("Just Published at Hartford," Middlesex
Gazette, Jan. 17, 1789.)   21989

[The New-England Primer Improved.
Hartford, Babcock, 1789.]
(This entry apparently came from an adv.
for 21989.)   21987

The New-England Primer Improved.
New Haven, Abel Morse, 1789. 72 pp.
AAS copy.   45526

The New-England Primer Improved.
New Haven, A. Morse, 1789. [72] pp.
(But for imprint identical with 45526, q. v.
for text.)
AAS copy.   45527

The New-England Primer, Amended [by
Noah Webster, 1758-1843].
New York, Patterson, 1789. [72] pp.
CHS copy.   45746

[The New-England Primer, much
Improved.
Philadelphia, M'Culloch, 1789.]
(Entry from advs.)   21990

The New-England Primer Improved.
Portsmouth, Melcher, [1789].
[64] pp.
HEH copy.   21988

The New-England Primer Improved.
Boston, Folsom, [179?] [64] pp.
HEH copy.   45784

The New-England Primer Improved.
Boston, Bumstead, 1790. [64] pp.
HEH copy.   22695

The New-England Primer Enlarged.

Boston, Draper for White, 1790.
[80] pp.
(The only known copy could not be
reproduced.)
NYPL copy.   45917

The New-England Primer, Or, an Easy
and Pleasant Guide.
Boston, White & Cambridge, 1790.
[64] pp.
(No copy available for reproduction.)
    45918

The New England Primer, for the More
Easy Attaining the True Reading of
English.
Lancaster, [Pa.], Bailey, 1790.
[64] pp.
(The only known copy is imperfect.)
AAS copy.   45919

The New-England Primer, Enlarged.
Newburyport, Mycall, [1790].
[80] pp.
AAS copy.   22692

The New-England Primer, Enlarged.
Newburyport, Mycall for Boyle, [1790].
[80] pp.
AAS copy.   22694

The New-England Primer, Enlarged.
Newburyport, Mycall for Thomas, [1790].
[80] pp.
AAS copy.   22693

[The New-England Primer, much
Improved.
Philadelphia, M'Culloch for Campbell,
1790.]
(Imprint assumed from advs.)   22696

[The New-England Primer, (Enlarged and
Improved).
Baltimore, Graham, 1791.]
("In the Press," Md. Journal, Aug. 12,
1791.)   23597

The New-England Primer Improved.
Boston, Bumstead for West, 1791.
[62] pp.
LOC copy.   23595

The New-England Primer Improved.
Boston, Coverly, 1791. [64] pp.
AAS copy.   23596

The New-England Primer Enlarged.
Boston, Draper for Dabney in Salem,
1791. [64] pp.
(The only known copy is not available
for reproduction.)
EI copy.   46228

The New-England Primer, Improved.
Middletown, [Ct.], Woodward, 1791.
[80] pp.
(The only known copy lacks the last leaf.)
AAS copy.   46229

The New-England Primer Improved.
New York, Campbell, 1791. 70 pp.
(The only known copy lacks the half title.)
AAS copy.   46230

The New-England Primer (Enlarged and
much Improved).
Philadelphia, B. Johnson, 1791.
[78] pp.
HEH copy.   46231

The New-England Primer, Improved.
Boston, Loring, 1792. [64] pp.
(Copy cannot be reproduced.)   46513

The New-England Primer, Improved.
Hartford, Patten, 1792. [64] pp.
(The only known copy cannot be
reproduced.)
YC (Pequot) copy.   46514

[The New-England Primer Improved.
Hudson, Stoddard, 1792?]
(From an adv., apparently for copies of
the Hartford ed., for which see Vol. 15.)
    24573

The New-England Primer, Improved.
Litchfield, Collier & Buel, 1792. 29 pp.
(No copy located.)   46515

The New England Primer Improved.

Middletown, Woodward, 1792. [80] pp.
(No copy located.)   46516

The New-England Primer; much
Improved.
Philadelphia, Johnston & Justice for
Campbell, [1792]. 36 leaves.
(Rosenbach: Ch 162; present location
unknown.)   46517

The New-England Primer, Improved.
Boston, Coverly for Blake, 1793.
[56] pp.
HC copy.   25864

[The Good old Genuine New-England
Primer.
Catskill Landing. Croswell, 1793.]
(Title and imprint assumed by Evans from
Croswell's advs.)   25865

[The New-England Primer, Amended.
Hartford, Babcock for Babcock, 1793?]
(Imprint assumed by Evans from adv.
"Just Published, and for sale at this
Office," in American Mercury, Dec. 23,
1793.)   25866

The New-England Primer.
Hartford, Babcock, 1793. 80 pp.
(Copy cannot be reproduced.)   46829

The New-England Primer, Improved.
Middletown, Woodward, 1793.
[80] pp.
HEH copy.   25867

The New-England Primer, Improved.
Concord, [Mass], Coverly, 1794.
[62] pp.
AAS copy.   47121

The New-England Primer, Improved.
Litchfield, Collier & Buel, 1794.
[58] pp.
(The only known copy is imperfect.)
AAS copy.   27366

[The New England Primer Improved.
New Brunswick, N. J., Blauvelt, 1794.]
(Imprint assumed by Evans from advs.)
    27367

The New-England Primer, Improved.
New London, T.C. Green, 1794.
[78 +] pp.
(The only recorded copy is imperfect.)
AAS copy.   47122

The New England Primer Improved.
New York, Forman for MacGill, 1794.
64 pp.
LOC copy.   27368

The New-England Primer, with the
Shorter Catechism.
Wilmington, Brynberg & Andrews, 1794.
72 pp.
(Only known copy is imperfect.)
d'Alté A. Welch facsim. copy.   47123

The New-England Primer, Improved.
Amherst, N. H., Coverly, 1795.
[64] pp.
AAS copy.   29146

The New-England Primer, Enlarged.
Boston, for the Booksellers, 1795.
[64] pp.
AAS copy.   47503

[The New-England Primer Improved.
Boston, Bumstead for Boyle, [1795].
[60] pp.
(Imprint assumed by Evans from Boyle's
adv.)   29147

The New-England Primer Improved.
Boston, Bumstead for West, [1795]. [60]
pp.
(Because of the condition of the unique
copy only the tp. can be reproduced.)
NYPL copy.   29148

The New-England Primer Enlarged.
Boston, Fleet, 1795. [64] pp.
BPL copy.   29149

The New-England Primer Enlarged.
Boston, Fleet, 1795. [96] pp.
(Not located, 1968.)   47502

The New-England Primer, Enlarged.

Boston, Hall, [1795]. [64] pp.
(No copy of this ed. could be located.)
    29150

The New England Primer, Enlarged.
Boston, Hall, "Sold by him, and at the
several Booksellers in town," [1795].
[64] pp.
AAS copy.   29151

The New-England Primer, or, an Easy and
Pleasant Guide.
Boston, White, [1795?]. [64] pp.
AAS copy.   29152

The New England Primer, Improved.
Elizabethtown, Kollock, 1795. 68 pp.
(Present location unknown.)   47504

The New-England Primer, Improved.
Hartford, Hudson & Goodwin, 1795.
[79] pp.
AAS copy.   29153

[The New-England Primer Improved.
Hudson, Stoddard, 1795.]
(Imprint assumed by Evans from
Stoddard's adv.)   29154

The New-England Primer, Improved.
New London, Springer for Green, 1795.
[80] pp.
AAS copy.   29155

The New-England Primer, Improved.
New London, Springer for Trumbull,
1795. [80] pp.
AAS copy.   29156

The New-England Primer Improved.
New York, Reid, 1795. 68 pp.
HC copy.   29157

[The New-England Primer, Enlarged.
Newfield, Beach & Jones, 1795.]
(Imprint assumed by Evans from adv.
"For sale" in Am. Telegraph, July 15,
1795.)   29158

The New-England Primer, Enlarged.
Norwich, Conn., Hubbard, [1795]. [64]
pp.
AAS copy.   29159

The New-England Primmer: Improved.
Norwich; Sterry, 1795. [66 +] pp.
CHS copy.   47505

The New-England Primer Improved.
Portsmouth, Melcher, [1795].
[72] pp.
(The unique copy is imperfect.)
Trinity College (Watkinson) copy.   29160

The New-England Primer; Improved.
Springfield, Mass., Gray, 1795.
[64] pp.
AAS copy.   34187

[The New-England Primer.
Boston, Blake, 1796.]
(Imprint assumed by Evans from Blake's
advs.)   30846

The New-England Primer Enlarged.
Boston, T. Fleet, 1796. [48] pp.
(The only known copy is imperfect.)
AAS copy.   47842

The New-England Primer Enlarged.
Boston, T. Fleet for West, [1796].
(Known only by this fragment.)
AAS copy.   47843

The New-England Primer, Improved.
Boston, White, [1796]. [64] pp.
(The one recorded copy is not now to be
located.)   30845

[The New-England Primer.
Carlisle, Pa., Kline for Loudon, 1796.]
(Imprint assumed by Evans from adv. in
the Gazette, Apr. 13, 1796.)   34184

The New-England Primer: much
Improved.
Germantown, 1796. [80] pp.
UOP copy.   30847

The New-England Primer; much
Improved.
Germantown, 1796. [20] pp.

(Heartman 127; present location
unknown.)   47844

The New England Primer, much Enlarged.
Lancaster, Pa., Dickson, 1796. [80] pp.
(The only copy reported lacks two
leaves.)
AAS copy.   30848

[The New-England Primer.
New York, Harrison, 1796. [80] pp.]
(Imprint assumed by Evans from
Harrison's adv.)   34186

[The New-England Primer.
Newburyport, Blunt, 1796.]
(Imprint assumed by Evans from Blunt's
adv.)   30849

[The New-England Primer Amended and
Improved; by the Author of the
Grammatical Institute.
Hartford, E. Babcock for J. Babcock,
1797.]
(Imprint assumed by Evans from adv.
"For sale at this Office," Am. Mercury,
May 6, 1797.)   32527

[The New England Primer (Enlarged
and Much Improved).
Philadelphia, Cist, 1796. [76] pp.]
(Apparently a ghost of 32530.)   32529

The New-England Primer, for the More
Easy Attaining the True Reading of
English.
New York, Harrisson, 1797. [71] pp.
(The unique copy is imperfect.)
LOC copy.   32528

The New-England Primer; Much
Improved.
Philadelphia, Dobson, 1797. [72] pp.
AAS copy.   32530

[The New-England Primer, or an Easy
and Pleasant Guide to the Art of
Reading.
Wilmington, Del., Brynberg, 1797.]
(Imprint assumed by Evans from
Brynberg's adv.)   32531

[The New-England Primer, Improved.
Baltimore, Pechin, 1798?] 72 pp.
(No perfect copy located. Evans
assumed imprint from adv. in Telegraphe
and Daily Advertiser, Apr. 12, 1798.)
AAS copy.   34181

The New-England Primer Improved.
Baltimore, Pechin for Thomas, Andrews
& Butler, [1798?]. 72 pp.
d'Alté A. Welch copy.   48520

The New-England Primer Enlarged.
Boston, Draper for White, 1798. [77] pp.
HC copy.   34183

The New-England Primer, Improved.
Boston, Loring, [1798]. [62] pp.
CHS copy.   48521

[The New-England Primer.
Boston, White, [1798]. [96] pp.]
(A ghost of the 1789 ed.)   34182

[The New-England Primer Amended.
Hartford, Ct., Babcock, 1798.]
(Imprint assumed by Evans from
Babcock's adv.)   34180

The New-England Primer, Improved.
Litchfield, Collier, 1798. [72] pp.
(Trumbull: Second Supplement 2868; no
copy located.)   48522

The New-England Primer Improved.
New London, S. Green for J.W. Green,
[1798]. [72] pp.
(Trumbull: Supplement 2443; no copy
located.)   48523

The New-England Primer, Improved.
Suffield, Ct., Farnsworths, 1798. [80] pp.
(The only copy located is very imperfect.)
HEH copy.   34188

The New-England Primer, Improved.
Suffield, Ct., Farnsworths for Cookes,
1798. [80] pp.
CHS copy.   34189

The New-England Primer, Improved.

Suffield, Ct., Gray & Allis for Davies,
1798. [64] pp.
(Anderson auction cat. 2190 (1927),
item 200.)   34190

The New-England Primer.
Albany, N. Y., Thomas, Andrews &
Penniman, 1799. [70] pp.
PPL copy.   35877

The New-England Primer Enlarged.
Boston, Draper for White, 1799. [80] pp.
(The copy formerly in the Stone coll.
cannot now be located.)   35870

The New-England Primer Improved.
Hartford, Ct., Patten, 1799. [62] pp.
(There was a copy in the Stone
collection.)   35871

The New-England Primmer Improved.
New York, Judah, 1799. 72 pp.
AAS copy.   35872

The New-England Primer; much
Improved.
Philadelphia, Dobson, 1799. [72] pp.
YC (Pequot) copy.   35876

The New-England Primer Improved.
Suffield, Ct., Gray for Patten, 1799.
[48] pp.
(No copy could be reproduced.)   35874

[The New-England Primer Improved.
New York, Swords, 1799.]
(Heartman No. 176.)   35875

The New England Primmer; Improved.
Norwich, Ct., Sterry, 1799. [70] pp.
CHS copy.   35873

The New-England Primer, Improved.
Hartford, Ct., Babcock, 1800. 64 pp.
AAS copy.   38047

The New-England Primer, Improved.
Hartford, Ct., Hudson & Goodwin, 1800.
[80] pp.
CHS copy.   38044

The New England Primmer Improved.
New York, Jansen, 1800. 70 pp.
(The only recorded copy is imperfect.)
AAS copy.   38045

The New-England Primer Enlarged.
Newport, R. I., Farnsworth, 1800.
[72] pp.
RIHS copy.   38043

[The New England Primmer Improved.
Windham, Ct., Byrne, 1800. [72] pp.]
(Entry from Bates.)   38046

New-England's Ebenezer.
Boston, Gray, 1745. Broadside.
(No copy located.)   40383

New-England's Misery.
Boston, Fowle & Draper, 1758. 15,
[1] pp.
AAS copy.   8201

[New-England's Misery.
Boston, 1768. 24 pp.]
(Despite the pagination, which is from
Haven, this appears to be a ghost of the
HC copy of 8201.)   10988

New-England's Spirit of Persecution [by
George Keith, 1638-1716].
[New York], 1693. [2], 38 pp.
(See Eames. First Year. p. 9.)
AAS copy.   642

The New Entertaining Philadelphia
Jest-Book.
Philadelphia, Woodhouse, 1790.
100 pp.
(The only copy recorded is imperfect.)
AAS copy.   22799

[The New Entertaining Philadelphia
Jest-Book.
Philadelphia, Woodhouse, 1791.]
(Evans' entry from adv. in 23440 for
"Books published by W. Woodhouse.")   23598

A New Entertainment, by Messrs
L'Égalité.

[Philadelphia, 1795.] Broadside.
LOC copy.   29161

A New Epilogue to Cato. Spoken at a late
Performance [by Jonathan Mitchell
Sewall, 1748-1808].
n. p., [1777]. [2] pp.
AAS copy.   43372

The New Exercise of Firelocks and
Bayonets.
New London, 1717. [4], 27, [1] pp.
YC copy.   1914

The New Federal Primer.
Wilmington, [Del.], Brynberg & Andrews,
1796. 71 pp.
NYPL copy.   32120

The New Federal Primer, or, An Easy and
Pleasant Guide to the Art of Reading.
Wilmington, Brynberg & Andrews, 1796.
72 pp.
(Copy cannot be filmed.)   47845

New Game of Cards; or, a Pack of Cards
Changed into a Perpetual Almanack.
Boston, [1761]. 8 pp.
(Seen by J. H. Trumbull.)   8942

The New Game of Cards: or, a Pack of
Cards Chang'd into a Compleat and
Perpetual Almanack.
New London, [1785?] 8 pp.
YC copy.   19110

The New Game of Cards: or, a Pack of
Cards Chang'd into a Compleat and
Perpetual Almanack.
Windham, [1792]. 11 pp.
AAS copy.   24576

The New Game of Cards, or, a Pack of
Cards Changed into a Compleat and
Perpetual Almanack.
Northampton, [Mass.], 1797. 8 pp.
AAS copy.   48188

The New Game of Cards.
Northampton, Mass., 1799. 8 pp.
AAS copy.   35878

[The New Gardener's Calendar.
New London, Holt, 1798.]
(Imprint assumed by Evans from adv.
"For sale at this office" in The Bee, May
9, 1798.)   34191

A New General Chart of the West
Indies. . . . Examined. . . . By Osgood
Carleton.
Boston, Norman, Dec. 28, 1789. Map.
AAS copy.   22698

A New Gift for Children.
Boston, Fowle, [1750?]. 30 pp., printed
covers.
HEH copy.   40555

A New Gift for Children. . . . Fourth
Edition.
Boston, Fowle & Draper, 1762. Front., 34
pp.
PPL copy.   9202

New Hampshire (Colony) General Court,
1776.
Colony of New Hampshire. By the
Council and Assembly. A Proclamation
[Fast, Apr. 18. Dated Mar. 15, 1776].
Portsmouth, [1776]. Broadside.
MHS copy.   14903

New Hampshire (Colony) General Court,
1776.
Colony of New Hampshire. By the
Council and Assembly, a Proclamation
[Plan of Government. Mar. 19, 1776].
Portsmouth, [1776]. Broadside.
AAS ph. copy.   14902

New Hampshire (Colony) Governor, 1699.
His Excellency, the Earl of Bellomont's
Speech to the General Assembly . . .
August 7 1699.
Boston, Green and Allen, 1699. 2 pp.
PRO copy.   39348

New Hampshire (Colony) Governor, 1745.
By His Excellency Benning Wentworth . . .
A Proclamation. Whereas I have. . . .
[Feb. 2, 1744/5].

[Boston, 1745.] Broadside.
LOC copy.   40384

New Hampshire (Colony) Governor, 1745.
By His Excellency Benning Wentworth.
. . . A Proclamation. Whereas the General
Assembly . . . French Settlements. . . .
[Feb. 2, 1744.]
[Boston, 1745.] Broadside.
MHS copy.   40385

New Hampshire (Colony) Governor, 1746.
By His Excellency Benning Wentworth,
Esq. . . . A Proclamation. Whereas His
Majesty has been . . . Pleased to Order . . .
Troops. . . . [June 5, 1746.]
Boston, Fleet, [1746]. Broadside.
MHS copy.   40414

New Hampshire (Colony) Governor, 1750.
. . . By His Excellency Benning
Wentworth. . . . A Proclamation for a
General Thanksgiving [Nov. 25. Dated
Nov. 16, 1750].
[Portsmouth? 1750.] Broadside.
LOC copy.   40556

New Hampshire (Colony) Governor, 1752.
. . . The Message of His Excellency
Benning Wentworth. . . . January 4th,
1752.
[Boston, 1753.] Broadside.
NHSL copy.   7071

New Hampshire (Colony) Governor, 1757.
. . . By . . . Benning Wentworth. . . . A
Proclamation for a General Thanksgiving
[Nov. 16, 1756 (i.e. 1757)].
[Portsmouth, 1757] Broadside.
(No copy located.)   40923

New Hampshire (Colony) Governor, 1757.
. . . By His Excellency Benning
Wentworth. . . . A Proclamation. His
Excellency . . . [for Raising 350 men]. . . .
February 28th, 1757.
[Portsmouth? 1757.] Broadside.
LOC copy.   40924

New Hampshire (Colony) Governor, 1758.
By . . . Benning Wentworth. . . . A
Proclamation. Forasmuch as our
Dependance. . . . [March 28, 1758.]
Portsmouth, Fowle, 1758. Broadside.
LOC copy.   40992

New Hampshire (Colony) Governor, 1758.
By His Excellency Benning Wentworth.
. . . A Proclamation. His Majesty Having
Nothing more at Heart. . . . [Apr. 1,
1758.]
Portsmouth, Fowle, 1758. Broadside.
LOC copy.   40993

New Hampshire (Colony) Governor, 1759.
By His Excellency Benning Wentworth.
. . . A Proclamation for a General
Thanksgiving [Nov. 10. Dated Nov. 4,
1759].
Portsmouth, Fowle, [1759]. Broadside.
NHHS copy.   41063

New Hampshire (Colony) Governor, 1760.
By His Excellency Benning Wentworth.
. . . A Brief. The Great God having
Permitted a Fire . . . Boston . . . April 8,
1760.
Portsmouth, Fowle, 1760. Broadside.
MHS copy.   41148

New Hampshire (Colony) Governor, 1760.
By His Excellency Benning Wentworth.
. . . I Have therefore Thought fit
[Thanksgiving Mar. 13. Dated Feb. 28,
1760].
Portsmouth, Fowle, [1760]. Broadside.
LOC copy.   41149

New Hampshire (Colony) Governor, 1761.
By His Excellency Benning Wentworth.
. . . A Proclamation. Almighty God
having. . . . [Nov. 24, 1761.]
Portsmouth, Fowle, [1761]. Broadside.
LOC copy.   41225

New Hampshire (Colony) Governor, 1762.
George the Third . . . to Our Trusty and
Well-beloved Theodore Atkinson . . .
[Feb. 8, 1762.]
[Portsmouth, 1762.] Broadside.
LOC copy.   41288

New Hampshire (Colony) Governor, 1763.

By His Excellency Benning Wentworth . . . a
Proclamation for a General Thanksgiving
[Aug. 11. Dated July 28, 1763].
[Portsmouth, 1763.] Broadside.
LOC copy.   41400

New Hampshire (Colony) Governor, 1763.
By His Excellency Benning Wentworth . . .
a Proclamation, for a General
Thanksgiving [Nov. 24. Dated Nov. 9,
1763].
Portsmouth, Fowle, [1763]. Broadside.
LOC copy.   41401

New Hampshire (Colony) Governor, 1764.
By His Excellency Benning Wentworth.
. . . A Proclamation for a General Fast [Apr.
20. Dated Mar. 31, 1764]. . . .
Portsmouth, Fowle, [1764]. Broadside.
NHHS copy.   41468

New Hampshire (Colony) Governor, 1764.
By His Excellency Benning Wentworth . . .
A Proclamation for a General
Thanksgiving [Nov. 8, 1764. Dated Oct.
29, 1764]. . . .
[Portsmouth, 1764.] Broadside.
NHHS copy.   41469

New Hampshire (Colony) Governor, 1764.
By His Excellency Benning Wentworth.
. . . A Proclamation, Whereas His Honor
Cadwallader Colden. . . . 13th Day of
March, 1764.
Portsmouth, Fowle, [1764]. Broadside.
AAS ph. copy.   41470

New Hampshire (Colony) Governor, 1765.
By His Excellency Benning Wentworth.
. . . A Proclamation for a General Fast
[Apr. 5. Dated Mar. 14, 1765].
Portsmouth, D. Fowle, 1765. Broadside.
NHHS copy.   41570

New Hampshire (Colony) Governor, 1765.
By His Excellency Benning Wentworth.
. . . A Proclamation for a General
Thanksgiving [Nov. 14. Dated Oct. 29,
1765].
Portsmouth, D. and R. Fowle, [1765].
Broadside.
AAS copy.   41571

New Hampshire (Colony) Governor, 1766.
By His Excellency John Wentworth. . . . A
Proclamation [Fast, May 21. Dated May
6, 1766].
Portsmouth, [1766]. Broadside.
MHS copy.   10410

New Hampshire (Colony) Governor, 1767.
By His Excellency John Wentworth. . . . A
Proclamation [Thanksgiving, Nov. 19.
Dated Nov. 3, 1767].
Portsmouth, 1767. Broadside.
MHS copy.   10701

New Hampshire (Colony) Governor, 1768.
By His Excellency John Wentworth. . . . A
Proclamation [Fast, Apr. 14. Dated Mar.
15, 1768].
Portsmouth, [1768]. Broadside.
MHS copy.   10992

New Hampshire (Colony) Governor, 1768.
By His Excellency John Wentworth. . . . A
Proclamation [Thanksgiving, Nov. 24,
Dated Oct. 26, 1768].
Portsmouth, [1768]. Broadside.
MHS copy.   10993

New Hampshire (Colony) Governor, 1769.
By His Excellency John Wentworth. . . . A
Proclamation [Coin. Mar. 2, 1769].
Portsmouth, Fowles, [1769]. Broadside.
NHSL copy.   11352

New Hampshire (Colony) Governor, 1769.
By His Excellency John Wentworth. . . . A
Proclamation [Fast, Apr. 6. Dated Mar.
20, 1769].
Portsmouth, 1769. Broadside.
MHS copy.   11353

New Hampshire (Colony) Governor, 1769.
By His Excellency John Wentworth. . . . A
Proclamation [Thanksgiving, Nov. 23.
Dated Oct. 25, 1769].
[Portsmouth, 1769.] Broadside.
MHS copy.   11354

New Hampshire (Colony) Governor, 1770.
By His Excellency John Wentworth. . . . A

Proclamation [Fast, Apr. 5. Dated Mar.
19, 1770].
[Portsmouth, 1770.] Broadside.
MHS copy.   11760

New Hampshire (Colony) Governor, 1770.
. . . By His Excellency John Wentworth.
. . . A Proclamation for a General
Thanksgiving [Dec. 6. Dated Nov. 6,
1770].
[Portsmouth, 1770.] Broadside.
NHHS copy.   42133

New Hampshire (Colony) Governor, 1771.
By His Excellency John Wentworth. . . . A
Proclamation [Fast, Apr. 18. Dated Mar.
23, 1771].
[Portsmouth, 1771.] Broadside.
MHS copy.   12147

New Hampshire (Colony) Governor, 1771.
By His Excellency John Wentworth. . . . A
Proclamation [Thanksgiving, Nov. 21.
Dated Oct. 30, 1771].
[Portsmouth, 1771.] Broadside.
MHS copy.   12148

New Hampshire (Colony) Governor, 1772.
By His Excellency John Wentworth. . . . A
Proclamation [Fast, Apr. 2. Dated Mar.
13, 1772].
[Portsmouth, 1772.] Broadside.
MHS copy.   12475

New Hampshire (Colony) Governor, 1772.
By His Excellency John Wentworth. . . . A
Proclamation [Thanksgiving, Dec. 3.
Dated Nov. 3, 1772].
[Portsmouth, 1772.] Broadside.
MHS copy.   12476

New Hampshire (Colony) Governor, 1773.
By His Excellency John Wentworth. . . . A
Proclamation [Fast, Apr. 15. Dated Mar.
19, 1773].
[Portsmouth, 1773.] Broadside.
MHS copy.   12878

New Hampshire (Colony) Governor, 1773.
By His Excellency John Wentworth. . . . A
Proclamation [Thanksgiving, Nov. 25.
Dated Nov. 3, 1773].
[Portsmouth, 1773.] Broadside.
MHS copy.   12879

New Hampshire (Colony) Governor, 1774.
. . . By His Excellency John Wentworth.
. . . A Proclamation [Fast, Apr. 14, Dated
Mar. 10, 1774].
[Portsmouth, 1774.] Broadside.
LOC copy.   13454

[New Hampshire (Colony) Governor,
1774.
. . . By His Excellency John Wentworth.
. . . A Proclamation [Fast, July 14, 1774].
[Portsmouth, 1774.] Broadside.
(The unique copy could not be located.)
                                             13455

New Hampshire (Colony) Governor, 1774.
. . . By His Excellency John Wentworth.
. . . A Proclamation [Thanksgiving, Nov.
24. Dated Nov. 1, 1774].
[Portsmouth, 1774.] Broadside.
AAS copy.   13456

New Hampshire (Colony) Governor, 1774.
. . . A Proclamation by the Governor.
Whereas Several Bodies of Men did . . .
the 14th . . . Attack . . . His Majesty's
Castle. . . .
[Portsmouth, 1774.] Broadside.
NHHS ph. copy.   42642

New Hampshire (Colony) Governor, 1775.
. . . By the Governor. A Proclamation
[Fast, Apr. 27. Dated Mar. 24, 1775].
[Portsmouth, 1775.] Broadside.
MHS copy.   14274

New Hampshire (Colony) House Journals,
1745.
A Journal of the House of Representatives
[Jan. 24, 1744/5, to May 3, 1745].
Boston, Bushell, Allen, & Green, 1745.
[2], 45 pp.
AAS copy.   5649

New Hampshire (Colony) House Journals,
1762.
Journal of the General Assembly [Jan. 19
Feb. 4, 1762].

Portsmouth, [1762]. [2], 13 pp.
MSL copy. 9203

New Hampshire (Colony) House Journals,
1767.
. . . The Journal of the House [July 1-Oct.
3, 1767].
[Portsmouth, 1767.] 31 pp.
AAS copy. 41741

New Hampshire (Colony) House Journals,
1768.
. . . The Journal of the House of
Representatives [July 1, 1767 - Mar. 24,
1768].
[Portsmouth, 1768.] 60 pp.
LOC copy. 10991

New Hampshire (Colony) House Journals,
1769.
A Journal of the House [May 17,
1768-Apr. 4, 1769].
Portsmouth, Fowles, 1769. [2], 63-124.
LOC copy. 41977

New Hampshire (Colony) House of
Representatives, 1699.
The Answer of the House . . . to . . . the
Earl of Bellomont's Speech. . . . August 7.
1699.
Boston, Green and Allen, 1699.
Broadside.
PRO copy. 39349

New Hampshire (Colony) House of
Representatives, 1699.
A Congratulatory Address of the House.
Boston, Green and Allen, 1699.
Broadside.
PRO copy. 39350

New Hampshire (Colony) House of
Representatives, 1738.
Appendix (A). To the King's most
Excellent Majesty. . . . Boston, June 9
1738.
[Boston, 1738.] 4 pp.
LOC copy. 40149

New Hampshire (Colony) House of
Representatives, 1761.
Province of New-Hampshire. In the
House of Representatives, January 28,
1761. [Tax].
[Portsmouth, 1761.] Broadside.
NHHS copy. 8944

New Hampshire (Colony) House of
Representatives, 1773.
. . . January 14, 1773. In the House of
Representatives. Whereas . . . a Province
Tax. . . .
[Portsmouth, 1773.] 2 pp.
NHHS copy. 42470

New Hampshire (Colony) House of
Representatives, 1774.
Whereas the American Continental
Congress. . . . Nov. 30, 1774.
[Portsmouth, 1774.] Broadside.
NHHS copy. 42643

New Hampshire (Colony) House of
Representatives, 1774.
Whereas the Colonies in General, upon
this Continent. . . .
[Portsmouth? 1774?] Broadside.
AAS copy. 42644

[New Hampshire (Colony) Laws,
Statutes, etc., 1706.
Acts and Laws Passed by the General
Court.
Boston, 1706. 130 pp.]
(This is a ghost of the 1716 edition, Evans
1842.) 1271

New Hampshire (Colony) Laws, Statutes,
etc., 1716.
Acts and Laws.
Boston, 1716. [2], iv, 60 pp.
HC-L copy. 1842

[New Hampshire (Colony) Laws,
Statutes, etc., 1726.
Acts and Laws.
Boston, Green for Russel, 1726. [2], 7,
171 pp.]
(A ghost arising from the fact that when in
1885 the Acts of 1716 with supplements
through 1726 were reprinted, the last date
was placed on the title-page.) 2784

New Hampshire (Colony) Laws, Statutes,
etc., 1759.
[An Act Levying 1000 Men].
Portsmouth, 1759. 4 pp.
AAS copy. 8427

New Hampshire (Colony) Laws, Statutes,
etc., 1760.
An Act . . . Feb. 9th, 1760 . . . for the
Better Regulating High Days.
[Portsmouth, 1760.] 4 pp.
(Whittemore 41; no copy located.) 41150

New Hampshire (Colony) Laws, Statutes,
etc., 1760.
An Act for Regulating the
Admeasurement of Lumber. . . . Pass'd
the 33d year of Geo. 2.
[Portsmouth, 1760.] 4 pp.
AAS copy. 41151

New Hampshire (Colony) Laws, Statutes,
etc., 1761.
Acts and Laws.
Portsmouth, 1761 (-66). [2], xii,
252 pp.
AAS copy. 8943

New Hampshire (Colony) Laws, Statutes,
etc., 1761.
. . . January 28th. 1761. Whereas by the
Change of Circumstances . . . the Province
Tax. . . .
n. p., [1761]. Broadside.
AAS ph. copy. 41226

New Hampshire (Colony) Laws, Statutes,
etc., 1771.
Acts and Laws.
Portsmouth, 1771. [2], 6, 8, 5, [1], iv, 286,
[1], 51, [1], xiii pp.
AAS copy. 12146

New Hampshire (Colony) Provincial
Convention, 1775.
. . . To the Select-Men of the [blank] of
[blank]. Gentlemen, As we were
Appointed [to call a convention at Exeter,
May 17]. . . .
[Portsmouth? 1775.] Broadside.
NHHS copy. 42889

New Hampshire (Colony) Provincial
Congress, 1774.
. . . To the Selectmen of the [blank] . . .
Convention . . . at Exeter, the 17th Day of
May next.
[Portsmouth, 1774.] Broadside.
LOC copy. 42641

New Hampshire (Colony) Provincial
Congress, 1775.
In Congress at Exeter, November 16th,
1775. Voted, that the Committee. . . .
[Exeter? 1775.] Broadside.
NHHS copy. 42890

New Hampshire (Colony) Provincial
Congress, 1775.
. . . In the Congress at Exeter, the 4th Day
of November, 1775. Voted. . . .
[Exeter? 1775.] Broadside.
NHHS copy. 42891

New Hampshire (Colony) Provincial
Congress, 1775.
In Congress at Exeter, December 27th,
1775. Whereas a Vote. . . .
[Exeter? 1775?] Broadside.
NHHS copy. 42892

New Hampshire (Colony) Provincial
Congress, 1775.
In Provincial Congress, Exeter, June 2,
1775. To the Inhabitants. . . .
[Exeter? 1775.] Broadside.
NHHS copy. 42893

New Hampshire (Colony) Provincial
Congress, 1775.
In Provincial Congress, New Hampshire,
August 25th, 1775. Whereas it is
Necessary.
[Exeter? 1775.] Broadside.
NHHS copy. 42894

New Hampshire (Colony) Session Laws,
1699.
Acts and Laws [Aug. 7, 1699 +].
Boston, 1699. 10 pp.
HSP copy. 882

New Hampshire (Colony) Session Laws,
1718.
Acts and Laws [May 13, 1718 +].
Boston, 1718. pp. 61-131, iv.
AAS copy. 1985

New Hampshire (Colony) Session Laws,
1719.
Acts and Laws [May 2, 1719 +].
Boston, 1719. pp. 133-156.
AAS copy. 2057

New Hampshire (Colony) Session Laws,
1721.
Acts and Laws [Apr. 18, 1721 +].
Boston, 1722. pp. 157-163.
NYPL copy. 2269

New Hampshire (Colony) Session Laws,
1754.
. . . An Act for Preventing and
Suppressing Riots. . . . Published 23d
April 1754.
n.p., n.d. 9 pp.
AAS copy. 40704

[New Hampshire (Colony) Session Laws,
1766.
Laws Publish'd the 27th June, 1765.
Portsmouth, 1766. 4, 8 pp.]
(These are parts of 8945, q.v.) 10409

[New Hampshire (Colony) Session Laws,
1766.
Acts and Laws [- Jan. 23, 1766].
Portsmouth, 1766. pp. ?-252.]
(This is the concluding part of 8943, q.v.) 10408

New Hampshire (Colony) Temporary
Laws, 1761.
Temporary Acts and Laws [Oct. 16, 1759 -
Mar. 18, 1768].
Portsmouth, 1761 (-68). [2], 49 pp.
NHSL copy. 8945

New Hampshire (Colony) Temporary
Laws, 1768.
. . . An Act in Addition. . . .
Portsmouth, 1768. pp. 29-49.
AAS copy. 10994

New Hampshire (Colony) Temporary
Laws, 1773.
[Temporary Laws . . .] of
New-Hampshire [Dec. 23, 1771 - Feb. 12,
1774].
[Portsmouth, 1773 - 74.] pp. 53-72.
(Grosvenor Lib. Buffalo has
pp. 1-72, i-xii but only located 1969.)
AAS copy. 12880

New Hampshire (Colony) Treasurer, 1760.
. . . To the Select-men of [blank] . . . for
the Current Year 1760.
[Portsmouth, 1760.] [2] pp.
NHHS copy. 41152

New Hampshire (Colony) Treasurer, 1762.
. . . To the Selectmen of [blank] . . . for
. . . 1762.
[Portsmouth, 1762.] Broadside.
NHHS copy. 41289

New Hampshire (Colony) Treasurer, 1763.
Treasurer's Warrant. . . . To the Select-
men of [blank] . . . for the year Current,
A.D. 1763.
[Portsmouth, Fowle, 1763.] Broadside.
LOC copy. 41402

New Hampshire (Colony) Treasurer, 1764,
Treasurer's Warrant. . . . To the
Selectmen of [blank] . . . for . . . 1764.
[Portsmouth, 1764.] Broadside.
AAS copy. 41471

New Hampshire (Colony) Treasurer, 1769.
. . . George Jaffrey. . . . To the Selectmen
[Blank] May [blank] 1769.
[Portsmouth, 1769.] Broadside.
NHHS copy. 41978

New Hampshire (Colony) Treasurer, 1772.
. . . George Jaffrey, Esq: Treasurer. . . .
To the Selectmen of [blank]. . . . The
[blank] Day of July . . . 177 [blank].
[Portsmouth, 1772?] Broadside.
NHHS copy. 42357

New Hampshire. Board of Commissioners
on Valuation.

The Board of Commissioners Appointed
. . . in Pursuance of an Act of Congress
Passed on the 9th Day of July, 1798.
[Exeter, 1798.] Broadside.
NYPL copy.   34192

New Hampshire. Commissioners, 1791.
. . . Exeter, August 17, 1791. The
Commissioners. . . .
[Exeter, 1791. 8 pp.
LOC copy.   46233

New Hampshire. Committee of Safety,
1776.
. . . In Committee of Safety, April 12,
1776. In Order to Carry. . . .
[Portsmouth, 1776.] Broadside.
AAS copy.   14904

New Hampshire. Committee of Safety,
1778.
State of New Hampshire. In Committee of
Safety, March 27th, 1778. Ordered, That
the Following Proclamation of the . . .
Continental Congress [Fast, Apr. 22].
Exeter, 1778. Broadside.
MHS copy.   16118

New Hampshire. Committee of Safety,
1779.
. . . Exeter, September 24th, 1779.
Whereas General Washington Lately
Wrote. . . .
[Exeter, 1779.] Broadside.
NHHS copy.   43663

New Hampshire. Committee of Safety,
1779.
. . . In Committee of Safety, April 10th
1779. Ordered, That the Following
Proclamation [Continental Fast].
Exeter, 1779. Broadside.
AAS copy.   16553

[New Hampshire. Committee of Safety,
1779.
. . . In Committee. Proclamation
[Continental Thanksgiving, Dec. 9, 1779].
Exeter, 1779. Broadside.]
(Assumed by Evans from 16553.)   16556

New Hampshire. Committee of Safety,
1779.
In Congress, June 29, 1779 [Continental
loan]. . . . In Committee of Safety, Exeter,
July 30 1779.
Exeter, 1779. Broadside.
LOC copy.   16578

New Hampshire. Committee of Safety,
1779.
A List of the Soldiers who have Deserted
from the three New Hampshire
Battalions, in the Continental Service. . . .
July 23, 1779.
[Exeter, 1779.] Broadside.
AAS copy.   43664

New Hampshire. Committee of Safety,
1780.
. . . In Committee of Safety, Exeter, April
14th, 1780.
Whereas [Continental Fast, Apr. 26].
Exeter, 1780. Broadside.
LOC copy.   17014

New Hampshire. Committee of Safety,
1780.
. . . Public Dispatches. . . . April 8, 1780.
[Exeter, 1780.] Broadside.
NYPL copy.   16881

New Hampshire. Committee of Safety,
Apr. 14, 1781.
. . . In Committee of Safety, April 14,
1781. . . . Proclamation [Continental Fast,
May 3].
[Exeter, 1783.] Broadside.
MHS copy.   17387

New Hampshire. Committee of Safety,
1782.
. . . In Committee of Safety, April 12th,
1782. . . . A Proclamation . . . done by the
United States in Congress. . . . [Mar. 19,
1782.]
Exeter, 1782. Broadside.
(No copy located.)   44230

New Hampshire. Committee of Safety,
1782.
. . . In Committee of Safety, Exeter,
November 1, 1782.

Ordered [Continental Thanksgiving. Nov.
28].
Exeter, [1782]. Broadside.
MHS copy.   17763

New Hampshire. Committee of Safety,
1783.
. . . In Committee of Safety, April 16,
1783. A Proclamation, Whereas the Form
of Government. . . .
Exeter, [1783]. Broadside.
HC copy.   18044

New Hampshire. Committee of Safety,
1783.
. . . In Committee of Safety, Exeter, Nov.
14, 1783. Whereas the Honorable
Continental Congress [Thanksgiving,
Dec. 11].
Exeter, 1783. Broadside.
AAS copy.   18248

New Hampshire. Constitution, 1783.
A Constitution, Containing a Bill of
Rights.
Portsmouth, 1783. 47 pp.
AAS copy.   18043

New Hampshire. Constitution, 1792.
The Constitution of New Hampshire.
Concord, Hough, 1792. 70 pp.
AAS copy.   24580

New Hampshire. Constitution, 1792.
The Constitution . . . as Altered . . .
M.DCC.XCII.
Concord, Hough, [1792]. 59 pp.
AAS copy.   25871

New Hampshire. Constitution, 1797.
The Constitution . . . as Altered and
Amended.
Concord, Hough, [1796]. 59 pp.
JCB copy.   30850

New Hampshire. Constitutional
Convention, 1779.
A Declaration of Rights. . . . June 5th,
1779.
Exeter, 1779. [2] pp.
AAS copy.   16386

New Hampshire. Constitutional
Convention, 1781.
An Address of the Convention.
Portsmouth and Exeter, 1781. 63,
[1] pp.
AAS copy.   17249

New Hampshire. Constitutional
Convention, 1782.
An Address of the Convention.
Exeter, 1782. 63 pp.
AAS copy.   17616

New Hampshire. Constitutional
Convention, 1783.
An Address of the Convention . . . June
1783.
Portsmouth, 1783. 8 pp.
HC copy.   18042

New Hampshire. Convention, 1792.
Articles in Addition to and Amendment
of the Constitution of the State.
Dover, Ladd, 1792. 31 pp.
NYPL copy.   24577

New Hampshire. Convention, 1792.
Articles in Addition to and Amendment
of the Constitution.
Dover, Ladd, 1792. 31 pp.
(Sabin 52802; present location unknown.)
                                    46518

New Hampshire. Convention, 1792.
Articles in Addition to and Amendment
of the Constitution of the State.
Exeter, Ranlet, 1792. 33, [2] pp.
AAS copy.   24578

New Hampshire. Council, 1778.
A Proclamation. . . . Thanksgiving [Dec.
30; dated Dec. 18, 1778].
Exeter, Fowle, 1778. Broadside.
NYPL ph. copy.   43502

[New Hampshire. Court of Common
Pleas, 1780.
. . . The Government and People, of the
State of New-Hampshire, ss. To the

Sheriff of the County of. . . .
[Exeter, 1780.] Broadside.]
(The unique copy could not be located.)
                                    16878

New Hampshire. General Court, 1776.
State of New-Hampshire. A Proclamation
for a Public Fast [Oct. 10. Dated Sept. 12,
1776].
Exeter, [1776]. Broadside.
MHS copy.   14906

New Hampshire. General Court, 1776.
State of New Hampshire. A Proclamation
[Thanksgiving, Nov. 21. Dated Oct. 19,
1776].
Exeter, 1776. Broadside.
MHS copy.   14907

New Hampshire. General Court, 1777.
State of New Hampshire. By the Council
and House of Representatives. A
Proclamation [Fast, Jan. 29. Dated Jan.
15, 1777].
Exeter, 1777. Broadside.
AAS copy.   15453

New Hampshire. General Court, 1777.
State of New Hampshire. By the Council
and House of Representatives. A
Proclamation [Fast, Apr. 24. Dated Mar.
27, 1777].
Exeter, 1777. Broadside.
MHS copy.   15454

New Hampshire. General Court, 1777.
State of New-Hampshire. By the Council
and House of Representatives. A
Proclamation [Fast, Aug. 7. Dated July
19, 1777].
[Exeter, 1777.] Broadside.
MHS copy.   15455

New Hampshire. General Court, 1777.
State of New-Hampshire. A Proclamation
[Thanksgiving, Dec. 4. Dated Nov. 17,
1777].
Exeter, 1777. Broadside.
LOC copy.   15456

New Hampshire. General Court, 1777.
State of New-Hampshire. The Council and
Assembly. . . . Proclamation [Continental
Thanksgiving, Dec. 18].
Exeter, 1777. Broadside.
LOC copy.   15680

New Hampshire. General Court, 1778.
A Proclamation [Continental
Thanksgiving. Dec. 30]. . . . In the House
of Representatives, December 18th.
1778. . . . In Council, December 18th, 1778.
Exeter, 1778. Broadside.
MHS copy.   16135

New Hampshire. General Court, 1778.
State of New-Hampshire. By the Council
and House of Representatives, a
Proclamation [Fast, Apr. 16. Dated Mar.
11, 1778].
Exeter, 1778. Broadside.
AAS copy.   15921

New Hampshire. General Court, 1778.
State of New Hampshire. In the House of
Representatives, February 17th, 1778.
Voted, That one . . . Militia. . . . In
Council . . . Concurred.
[Exeter, 1778.] Broadside.
AAS ph. copy.   43503

New Hampshire. General Court, 1779.
. . . By the Council and House of
Representatives. A Proclamation [Fast,
Apr. 29. Dated Mar. 19, 1779].
Exeter, 1779. Broadside.
AAS copy.   16387

New Hampshire. General Court, 1779.
. . . The Government and People . . . to
the Selectmen of [blank]. . . . October 25,
1779.
[Exeter, 1779.] Broadside.
NHHS copy.   43665

New Hampshire. General Court, 1779.
. . . In the House of Representatives,
June 17th, 1779. Voted that the Address
from the Continental Congress. . . . In
Council, June 18, 1779.
[Exeter, 1779]. 2 pp.
BPL copy.   16638

New Hampshire. General Court, 1779.
... In the House of Representatives,
December 28th, 1779. Where it has been. ...
In Council the same Day.
[Exeter, 1779.] Broadside.
LOC copy. 16390

New Hampshire. General Court, 1779.
... A Proclamation for a Public Fast
[Apr. 22, 1779].
[Exeter, 1779.] Broadside.
NHHS copy. 16388

New Hampshire. General Court, 1780.
... The Government and People of the
said State. To the Selectmen of [blank]
... Greeting ... Portsmouth, October 20,
1780.
[Exeter, 1780.] Broadside.
NHHS copy. 43844

New Hampshire. General Court, 1780.
A Proclamation [Thanksgiving, Dec.
7]. ... In the House of Representatives,
November 11, 1780.
[Exeter, 1780.] Broadside.
LOC copy. 17018

New Hampshire. General Court, 1783.
... In the House of Representatives,
June 20th, 1783. An Address to the
People. ...
Exeter, 1783. Broadside.
AAS copy. 18046

New Hampshire. General Court, 1783.
... In the House of Representatives, June
20th, 1783.
The Committee on the Recommendations
of Congress. ... In Council June 20th,
1783.
Exeter, 1783. Broadside.
NYPL copy. 18047

New Hampshire. General Court, 1784.
... A Proclamation for a Public Fast
[Apr. 22, 1784].
[Exeter, 1784.] Broadside.
LOC copy. 18626

New Hampshire. General Court, 1784.
... To the Selectmen of [blank]. ...
Greeting. You are hereby Required
[election warrant]. ... Concord, January,
1784.
[Exeter? 1784.] Broadside.
NHHS copy. 44565

New Hampshire. General Court, 1786.
... In the House of Representatives,
March 3d, 1786. Resolved, That the
Selectmen. ...
Portsmouth, Fowle, 1786. Broadside.
LOC copy. 19822

New Hampshire. General Court, 1786.
... The Following Plan was laid before a
Committee of both Branches ... on the
14th day of September.
Exeter, [1786]. Broadside.
AAS copy. 19823

New Hampshire. General Court. House
of Representatives, 1778.
State of New-Hampshire. In the House of
Representatives, January 2d, 1778
[Resolution].
Exeter, [1778]. Broadside.
NYPL copy. 15922

[New Hampshire. General Court. House
of Representatives, 1779.
... The Committee of both Houses
[Taxes]. ... In the House of
Representatives, Nov. 16, 1779.
[Exeter, 1779.] Broadside.]
(The unique copy could not be located.)
16389

New Hampshire. General Court. House of
Representatives, 1779.
... Nov. 8, 1779. Voted that the
Proclamation for a General
Thanksgiving. ...
[Exeter, 1779.] Broadside.
(The one recorded copy cannot now be
located.) 43666

New Hampshire. General Court. House of
Representatives, 1781.
... In the House of Representatives,
August 24th, 1781. The Committee to
Consider ... Continental Soldiers.

[Exeter, 1781.] Broadside.
(The one recorded copy cannot be
located.) 44004

New Hampshire. General Court. House of
Representatives, 1798.
... In the House of Representatives,
December 26th, 1798. Resolved, that the
Senators and Representatives ... be ...
Requested [to Obtain Amendments to the
Constitution].
[Portsmouth, 1799.] [2] pp.
RISL copy. 35885

New Hampshire. Governor, 1789.
By His Excellency John Sullivan. ... A
Proclamation for a General Thanksgiving
[Nov. 6, dated Sept. 28, 1789].
Exeter, Ranlet, [1789]. Broadside.
NHHS copy. 45530

New Hampshire. Governor, 1793.
By His Excellency Josiah Bartlett. ... A
Proclamation for a Day of Public Fasting
[dated Feb. 9, 1793]. ...
Portsmouth, Melcher, 1793. Broadside.
NYPL ph. copy. 46830

New Hampshire. Governor, 1794.
By His Excellency John Taylor
Gilman. ... A Proclamation for a Public
Thanksgiving [Sept. 29, 1794.]
Portsmouth, Melcher, 1794. Broadside.
LOC copy. 47124

New Hampshire. Governor, 1794.
By His Excellency Josiah Bartlett, Esq.
... A Proclamation for a Day of Public
Fasting [Mar. 27. Dated Feb. 6, 1794].
n.p., [1794]. Broadside.
AAS copy. 47125

New Hampshire. Governor, 1794.
... To the Selectmen of. ... Pursuant to
an Act of this State, Passed June 21st,
1792. ... Given ... this 29th Day of
September, One Thousand Seven Hundred
and Ninety-Four.
Portsmouth, Melcher, 1794. Broadside.
NHHS copy. 27377

New Hampshire. Governor, 1795.
By His Excellency John Taylor
Gilman. ... A Proclamation. ... A Day
of Public Fasting [Apr. 2. Dated Jan. 13,
1795].
[Concord? 1795] Broadside.
AAS copy. 47506

[New Hampshire. Governor, 1795.
By His Excellency John T. Gilman. ... A
Proclamation for a Public Thanksgiving
[Nov. 12. Dated Oct. 12, 1795].
Exeter, Ranlet, 1795. Broadside.]
(No broadside printing located.) 29164

New Hampshire. Governor, 1796.
By His Excellency John Taylor
Gilman. ... A Proclamation ... Fasting
[Apr. 7. Dated Feb. 24, 1796.]
Exeter, Ranlet, 1796. Broadside.
(The only reported copy could not be
located.) 30854

[New Hampshire. Governor, 1796.
... By the Governor. A Proclamation for
a Public Thanksgiving [Nov. 17. Dated
Oct. 17, 1796].
Exeter, Ranlet, 1796. Broadside.]
(No copy located.) 30855

New Hampshire. Governor, 1796.
... To the Selectmen of [blank]
Greeting. ... You are hereby Required to
... Warn a Meeting ... on the First
Monday of November.
Exeter, Ranlet, [1796]. Broadside.
NYPL ph. copy. 47846

[New Hampshire. Governor, 1800.
... By the Governor. A Proclamation ...
a Day of Humiliation [Apr. 24. Dated
Mar. 20, 1800].
n.p., n.d. Broadside.]
(Entry from Evans' note.) 38055

New Hampshire. Governor, 1800.
... By the Governor. A Proclamation ...
A Day of Public Thanksgiving [Nov. 13.
Dated Oct. 6, 1800].
n.p., n.d. Broadside.
(Entry from Evans note.) 38054

New Hampshire. House Journals, 1784.
A Journal of the Proceedings of the ...
House of Representatives [June 2 - 15,
1784].
Portsmouth, 1784. 26 pp.
AAS copy. 18624

New Hampshire. House Journals, 1784.
A Journal of the Proceedings of the. ..
House of Representatives ... October
[1784].
[Exeter, 1784.] pp. [27], 54, 57-68.
NYPL copy. 44566

New Hampshire. House Journals, 1785.
A Journal of the Proceedings of the ...
House of Representatives [Feb. 9 - 24,
1785].
Portsmouth, Gerrish, 1785.
pp. 69-104.
AAS copy. 44738

New Hampshire. House Journals, 1785.
A Journal of the Proceedings of the ...
House of Representatives [June 1 - 24,
1785].
Portsmouth, Gerrish, 1785. 54 pp.
AAS copy. 44739

New Hampshire. House Journals, 1785.
A Journal of the Proceedings of the ...
House of Representatives [Oct. 19 - Nov.
10, 1785].
[Portsmouth], Gerrish, [1786?].
pp. 55-97.
AAS copy. 44927

New Hampshire. House Journals, 1786.
... A Journal of the Proceedings of the
... House of Representatives [Feb. 1 -
Mar. 4, 1786].
Portsmouth, Fowle, [1786].
pp. [99] - 170.
AAS copy. 19818

New Hampshire. House Journals, 1786.
A Journal of the Proceedings of the ...
House of Representatives [June 7 - 27,
1786].
Portsmouth, Osborne, 1787. 78 pp.
AAS copy. 19819

New Hampshire. House Journals, 1786.
A Journal of the Proceedings of the ...
House of Representatives [Sept. 6 - 23,
1786].
[Portsmouth, 1787.] pp. 81-116.
AAS copy. 19820

New Hampshire. House Journals, 1786.
A Journal of the Proceedings of the ...
House of Representatives [Dec. 13, 1786 -
Jan. 18. 1787].
[Portsmouth, 1787.] pp. 119-190.
AAS copy. 20550

New Hampshire. House Journals, 1787.
A Journal of the Proceedings of the ...
House of Representatives [June 6-30,
1787].
Portsmouth, Osborne, 1787. 70 pp.
AAS copy. 20551

New Hampshire. House Journals, 1787.
A Journal of the Proceedings of the ...
House of Representatives [Sept. 12-29,
1787].
[Portsmouth, 1787.] pp. [71]-117.
AAS copy. 20552

New Hampshire. House Journals, 1786.
A Journal of the Proceedings of the ...
Senate [June 7-27, 1786].
Portsmouth, Melcher, 1787. 48 pp.
AAS copy. 20553

New Hampshire. House Journals, 1787.
A Journal of the Proceedings of the ...
House of Representatives [Dec. 5-15,
1787].
Portsmouth, Osborne, [1788].
pp. [119]-138.
AAS copy. 21283

New Hampshire. House Journals, 1788.
A Journal of the Proceedings of the ...
House of Representatives [Jan. 23 - Feb.
13, 1788].
Portsmouth, Osborne, 1788.
pp. [139]-197.
AAS copy. 21284

New Hampshire. House Journals, 1788.

A Journal of the Proceedings of the . . .
House of Representatives [June 4-18,
1788].
Portsmouth, Osborne, 1788. 56 pp.
AAS copy.   21285

New Hampshire. House Journals, 1788.
A Journal of the Proceedings of the . . .
House of Representatives [Nov. 5-13,
1788].
[Portsmouth, 1788.] pp. [57]-83.
AAS copy.   21286

New Hampshire. House Journals, 1788.
A Journal of the Proceedings of the . . .
House of Representatives, [Dec. 24, 1788 -
Feb. 7, 1789].
[Portsmouth, 1789.] pp. [85]-226.
AAS copy.   21944

New Hampshire. House Journals, 1789.
A Journal of the Proceedings of the House
of Representatives [June 3 - 19, 1789].
Portsmouth, Osborne, 1789. 64 pp.
AAS copy.   21995

New Hampshire. House Journals, 1789.
A Journal of the Proceedings of the . . .
House of Representatives [Dec. 23, 1789 -
Jan. 26, 1790].
Portsmouth, Osborne, 1790. 97 pp.
AAS copy.   22699

New Hampshire. House Journals, 1790.
A Journal of the Proceedings of the . . .
House of Representatives [June 2 - 19,
1790].
Portsmouth, Osborne, 1790. 82 pp.
AAS copy.   22700

New Hampshire. House Journals, 1791.
A Journal of the Proceedings of the . . .
House of Representatives [Jan. 5 - Feb.
18, 1791].
Portsmouth, Melcher, 1791. 175 pp.
AAS copy.   23599

New Hampshire. House Journals, 1791.
A Journal of the Proceedings of the Hon.
House of Representatives . . . at Concord.
June, 1791.
Portsmouth, Melcher, 1791. 96 pp.
AAS copy.   46234

New Hampshire. House Journals, 1791.
A Journal of the Proceedings of the Hon.
House of Representatives [Nov. 31, 1791 -
Jan. 6, 1792].
Portsmouth, Melcher, 1792. 151 pp.
AAS copy.   24581

New Hampshire. House Journals, 1792.
A Journal of the Proceedings of the Hon.
House of Representatives [June 1 - 22,
1792].
Portsmouth, Melcher, 1792. 88 pp.
AAS copy.   24582

New Hampshire. House Journals, 1792.
A Journal of the Proceedings of the Hon.
House of Representatives [Nov. 21 - Dec.
28, 1792].
Portsmouth, Melcher, 1793. 143 pp.
AAS copy.   25872

New Hampshire. House Journals, 1793.
A Journal of the Proceedings of the Hon.
House of Representatives [June 1-21,
1793].
Portsmouth, Melcher, 1793. 109 pp.
AAS copy.   25873

New Hampshire. House Journals, 1793.
A Journal of the Proceedings of the Hon.
House of Representatives [Dec. 25, 1793 -
Feb. 22, 1794].
Portsmouth, Melcher, 1794. 220 pp.
AAS copy.   27371

New Hampshire. House Journals, 1794.
A Journal of the Proceedings of the Hon.
House of Representatives [June 4 - 21,
1794].
Portsmouth, Melcher, 1794. 107 pp.
AAS copy.   27373

New Hampshire. House Journals, 1794.
A Journal of the Proceedings of the Hon.
House of Representatives [Dec. 16, 1794 -
Jan. 16, 1795].
(No copy with a tp. could be located.)
HC copy.   29165

New Hampshire. House Journals, 1795.
A Journal of the Proceedings of the Hon.
House of Representatives [Dec. 2, 1795 -
Jan. 1, 1796].
Portsmouth, Melcher, 1796. 152 pp.
AAS copy.   47847

New Hampshire. House Journals, 1796.
A Journal of the Proceedings of the Hon.
House of Representatives [June 1 - 17,
1796].
Portsmouth, Melcher, 1796. 90 pp.
AAS copy.   30851

New Hampshire. House Journals, 1796.
A Journal of the Proceedings of the Hon.
House of Representatives [Nov. 23 - Dec.
15, 1796].
Portsmouth, Melcher, 1797. 141 pp.
LOC copy.   32533

New Hampshire. House Journals, 1797.
A Journal of the Proceedings of the Hon.
House of Representatives [June 7 - 22,
1797.]
Portsmouth, Melcher, 1797. 96 pp.
AAS copy.   32534

New Hampshire. House Journals, 1797.
A Journal of the Proceedings of the Hon.
House of Representatives [Nov. 22-Dec.
21, 1797].
Portsmouth, Melcher, 1798. 127 pp.
NYPL copy.   34193

New Hampshire. House Journals, 1798.
A Journal of the Proceedings of the . . .
House of Representatives [June 6-20,
1798].
Portsmouth, Melcher, 1798. 76 pp.
AAS copy.   34195

New Hampshire. House Journals, 1798.
A Journal of the Proceedings of the Hon.
House of Representatives [Nov. 21-Dec.
28, 1798].
Portsmouth, Melcher, 1799. 93 pp.
AAS copy.   35879

New Hampshire. House Journals, 1799.
A Journal of the Proceedings of the Hon.
House [June 5-15, 1799.]
Portsmouth, Melcher, 1799. 78 pp.
AAS copy.   35880

New Hampshire. House Journals, 1799.
A Journal of the Proceedings of the . . .
House of Representatives [Dec. 4 - 31,
1799].
Portsmouth, Melcher, 1800. 106 pp.
AAS copy.   38048

New Hampshire. House Journals, 1800.
A Journal of the Proceedings of the House
[June 4-16, 1800].
Portsmouth, Melcher, 1800. 71 pp.
AAS copy.   38051

New Hampshire. Laws, Statutes, etc.,
1776.
Exeter, July 4, 1776. . . . Voted that Three
Hundred Hand Bills. . . . In Council,
Eodem die, Read and Concurred.
Exeter, [1776]. Broadside.
NHHS copy.   43094

New Hampshire. Laws, Statutes, etc.,
1776.
In Congress at Exeter, January 5th, 1776.
We the Members. . . . In the House of
Representatives, September 19, 1776.
Portsmouth, Fowle, [1776]. 2 pp.
LOC copy.   14901

New Hampshire. Laws, Statutes, etc.,
1777.
. . . Exeter, January 14th, 1777. Whereas
Orders. . . . Bounty.
[Exeter? 1777.] Broadside.
NHHS copy.   43301

New Hampshire. Laws, Statutes, etc.,
1777.
. . . In the House of Representatives, June
7th, 1777.
Voted, that all Military Officers. . . . In
Council . . . Read and concurred.
NHHS copy.   43300

New Hampshire. Laws, Statutes, etc.,
1777.
. . . Whereas . . . Taxes . . . March 31,
1777.

[Exeter? 1777.] Broadside.
NHHS copy.   43299

New Hampshire. Laws, Statutes, etc.,
1778.
. . . In the House of Representatives,
February 26th, 1778. Whereas the Present
Situation. . . . Taxes. . . . [Dated Mar. 4,
1778].
Exeter, [1778]. Broadside.
NHHS copy.   43504

New Hampshire. Laws, Statutes, etc.,
1778.
State of New-Hampshire. . . . An Act to
Prevent the Return . . . of Certain
Persons. . . . November 19, 1778.
Exeter, 1778. Broadside.
LOC copy.   15923

New Hampshire. Laws, Statutes, etc.,
1779.
. . . An Act to Prevent Monopoly of
Corn. . . . April 3, 1779.
[Exeter? 1772.] Broadside.
AAS copy.   43667

New Hampshire. Laws, Statutes, etc.,
1780.
. . . An Act for Raising Eleven Thousand
. . . Weight of Beef.
[Exeter, 1780.] [2] pp.
BPL copy.   16880

New Hampshire. Laws, Statutes, etc.,
1780.
. . . An Act for Raising Six Hundred Men
[June 16, 1780].
[Exeter, 1780.] Broadside.
NYPL copy.   16879

New Hampshire. Laws, Statutes, etc.,
1780.
. . . An Act to Prevent the Transportation
of live Cattle . . . out of this State. . . .
Passed April 29th, 1780.
[Exeter? 1780.] [2] pp.
AAS copy.   43845

New Hampshire. Laws, Statutes, etc.,
1780.
Acts and Laws of the State of
New-Hampshire.
Exeter, 1780. 295 pp., irreg.
Composite copy.   16877

New Hampshire. Laws, Statutes, etc.,
1781.
. . . An Act for Impowering the
Sheriff. . . . November 28th, 1781.
[Exeter, 1781.] Broadside.
LOC copy.   17251

New Hampshire. Laws, Statutes, etc.,
1781.
. . . An Act for Making Gold and Silver a
Tender for all Debts. . . . Passed Sept. 1,
1781.
[Exeter? 1781.] Broadside.
HEH copy.   44006

New Hampshire. Laws, Statutes, etc.,
1781.
. . . An Act for Raising the sum of One
Hundred and Twenty Thousand
Pounds. . . . In Council, January 27th,
1781.
[Exeter, 1781.] Broadside.
AAS copy.   17252

New Hampshire. Laws, Statutes, etc.,
1781.
. . . An Act for Supplying the Continental
Army.
[Exeter, 1781.] 4 pp.
NYPL copy.   17253

New Hampshire. Laws, Statutes, etc.,
1781.
. . . An Act for the Raising & Compleating
. . . January 12th, 1781.
[Exeter, 1781.] [2] pp.
LOC copy.   44007

New Hampshire. Laws, Statutes, etc.,
1781.
. . . An Act in Addition to, and an
Alteration of an Act Passed [Jan. 12,
1781] . . . Entitled An Act for Raising and
Compleating this State's Quota.
[Exeter, 1781.] Broadside.
LOC copy.   17254

New Hampshire. Laws, Statutes, etc.,
1781.
. . . An Act in Addition to two Several
Acts . . . Raising and Filling up this
State's Quota. . . . In Council, June 27th,
1781.
[Exeter, 1781.] Broadside.
LOC copy.   17255

New Hampshire. Laws, Statutes, etc.,
1781.
. . . An Act to Ascertain the Time for the
old Continental Bills. . . . In Council, June
30, 1781.
[Exeter, 1781.] Broadside.
LOC copy.   17256

New Hampshire. Laws, Statutes, etc.,
1781.
. . . Exeter, November 22, 1781. Pursuant
to an Order of the General Court. . . .
Exeter, [1781]. Broadside.
NHHS copy.   44001

New Hampshire. Laws, Statutes, etc.,
1781.
. . . In the House of Representatives, April
5, 1781. Whereas [Constitutional
Convention. Dated Apr. 6, 1781].
[Exeter, 1781.] Broadside.
LOC copy.   17250

New Hampshire. Laws, Statutes, etc.,
1781.
. . . In the House of Representatives, July
3, 1781. The Committee to Form a
Table. . . . In Council . . . Read and
Concurred.
[Exeter, 1781.] Broadside.
NHHS copy.   44003

New Hampshire. Laws, Statutes, etc.,
1781.
. . . In the House of Representatives:
November 20th, 1781. Resolved, That the
Several Towns. . . . In Council, November
21st.
[Exeter, 1781.] Broadside.
Lewis M. Stark copy.   44005

New Hampshire. Laws, Statutes, etc.,
1782.
. . . An Act for Raising and Compleating
this State's Quota. . . . March 21st, 1782.
Exeter, [1782]. 3 pp.
(Copy not located.)
LOC copy.   44231

New Hampshire. Laws, Statutes, etc.,
1782.
. . . In the House of Representatives, June
13th, 1782. Resolved, That the Time of
Returning. . . .
[Exeter, 1782.] Broadside.
(No copy located.)   44232

New Hampshire. Laws, Statutes, etc.,
1783.
. . . The Committee to Consider . . . future
Taxes. . . . In Council, February 21,
1783. . . . M. Weare.
[Exeter, 1783.] Broadside.
NHHS copy.   44412

New Hampshire. Laws, Statutes, etc.,
1783.
. . . In the House of Representatives,
February 27th, 1783. Whereas, by the
Various Accounts. . . .
[Exeter, 1783.] Broadside.
HC copy.   18045

New Hampshire. Laws, Statutes, etc.,
1783.
. . . In the House of Representatives, June
21st, 1783. Voted, That an Order Issue to
the Selectmen. . . .
[Exeter, 1783.] Broadside.
LOC copy.   18048

New Hampshire. Laws, Statutes, etc.,
1784.
. . . In Senate, June 15, 1784. Resolved,
that the Soldiers. . . . M. Weare,
President.
Exeter, Melcher & Osborne, 1784.
Broadside.
MHS copy.   44567

New Hampshire. Laws, Statutes, etc.,
1787.
An Act for Forming and Regulating the
Militia.

Portsmouth, Gerrish, 1787. 14 pp.
NHHS copy.   20547

New Hampshire. Laws, Statutes, etc.,
1788.
. . . An Act, for Carrying into Effect an
Ordinance of Congress. . . . November 12,
1788.
[Portsmouth, 1788.] [2] pp.
AAS copy.   45309

New Hampshire. Laws, Statutes, etc.,
1788.
. . . The Committee to Consider what
Method Shall be Adopted for Taking a
new Valuation. . . . February 5, 1788.
[Portsmouth, 1788.] Broadside.
NYPL copy.   21291

New Hampshire. Laws, Statutes, etc.,
1789.
. . . An Act, for the Better Observation of
the Lord's Day. . . . Feb. 2d, 1789.
[Exeter, 1789.] 4 pp.
AAS copy.   45531

New Hampshire. Laws, Statutes, etc.,
1789.
The Committee Appointed to Re-examine
and Cast the Votes. . . . In Senate,
January 2, 1789 . . . Concurred.
[Exeter? 1789.] Broadside.
NHHS ph. copy.   45529

New Hampshire. Laws, Statutes, etc.,
1789.
The Perpetual Laws.
Portsmouth, Melcher, 1789. pp. [6],
[9]-256.
AAS copy.   21997

New Hampshire. Laws, Statutes, etc.,
1790.
. . . An Act Directing the Mode of
Choosing Representatives. . . . June 17,
1790.
[Exeter, 1790.] Broadside.
LOC copy.   22704

New Hampshire. Laws, Statutes, etc.,
1791.
. . . An Act in Addition to an Act,
entitled, "An Act to Establish an
Equitable Method of making Rates. . . . "
. . . December 28, 1791. . . . Enacted.
Portsmouth, Osbornes, [1791].
[2] pp.
AAS copy.   46235

New Hampshire. Laws, Statutes, etc.,
1791.
. . . An Act in Addition to . . . An Act for
Regulating Schools.
[Portsmouth, 1791.] Broadside.
HSP copy.   46232

New Hampshire. Laws, Statutes, etc.,
1791.
. . . In Senate, June 13, 1791. Resolved,
That the Selectmen. . . . In the House of
Representatives, June 15, 1791.
[Portsmouth, 1791.] Broadside.
JCB copy.   23602

New Hampshire. Laws, Statutes, etc.,
1791.
. . . In the House of Representatives,
December 29, 1791. Whereas a Resolve
Passed the General Court, June 13th,
1791. . . . In Senate, December 30, 1791.
Portsmouth, Osbornes, [1791]. Broadside.
JCB copy.   23603

[New Hampshire. Laws, Statutes, etc.,
1792.
. . . An Act Directing the Mode of
Ballotting.
[Portsmouth, 1792.] Broadside.]
(No printing in broadside form located.)
                                             25869

New Hampshire. Laws, Statutes, etc.,
1792.
. . . An Act Directing the Mode of
Ballotting. . . . June 21, 1792.
[Portsmouth, 1792.] Broadside.
NHHS copy.   46520

New Hampshire. Laws, Statutes, etc.,
1792.
. . . An Act to Establish a Bank. . . . In
Senate, January 3, 1792.

[Portsmouth, 1792.] [2] pp.
JCB copy.   24587

[New Hampshire. Laws, Statutes, etc.,
1792.
Additions to the Militia Laws. December
28, 1792.
Portsmouth, 1793.]
(Apparently this entry is a ghost of the
printing in the N. H. Gazette. Mar. 26,
1793.)   25870

[New Hampshire. Laws, Statutes, etc.,
1792.
. . . In the House of Representatives,
December the Eleventh, A.D. 1792.
Resolved, That the Selectmen . . . take an
Inventory. . . . In Senate, December 17th,
1792.
[Portsmouth, 1792.] Broadside.]
(No copy located.)   25878

New Hampshire. Laws, Statutes, etc.,
1792.
. . . In the House of Representatives,
December the 11th, A.D. 1792. . . .
Inventory. . . . In Senate, December
17th. . . .
[Portsmouth, 1792.] Broadside.
NHHS copy.   46519

New Hampshire. Laws, Statutes, etc.,
1792.
The Laws of the State of New-Hampshire.
Portsmouth, Melcher, 1792. 396 pp.
AAS copy.   24585

New Hampshire. Laws, Statutes, etc.,
1797.
The Laws of the State of New-Hampshire.
Portsmouth, Melcher, 1797. 492 pp.
AAS copy.   32536

New Hampshire. Laws, Statutes, etc.,
1799.
. . . An Act to Authorize Samuel Blodget,
Esquire, to set up a Lottery.
[Portsmouth? 1799.] Broadside.
BPL copy.   35887

New Hampshire. Laws, Statutes, etc.,
1799.
. . . An Act to Incorporate Samuel Blodget
. . . Cutting a Canal by Amoskeag
Falls. . . . Approved December 24th, 1798.
[Portsmouth, 1799?] 3 pp.
(Not located, 1968.)   48942

[New Hampshire. Laws, Statutes, etc.,
1799.
. . . An Act to Incorporate . . . the Third
Turnpike Road. . . . Approved, December
27.
[Portsmouth? 1799.] Broadside.]
(No copy of the broadside printing
reported in the NUC could be located.)
                                             35888

New Hampshire. Laws, Statutes, etc.,
1799.
. . . In the House of Representatives, Dec.
10, 1799. Whereas the Constitution of this
State. . . . Approved Dec. 13, 1799.
[Portsmouth, 1799.] Broadside.
LOC copy.   35886

New Hampshire. President, 1781.
. . . The Government and People of said
State. To the Selectmen of [blank]. . . .
Taxes. . . . Dated Exeter, the 27th Day of
January, 1781.
[Exeter, 1781.] Broadside.
NHHS copy.   44002

[New Hampshire. President, 1782.
. . . A Proclamation, Adopting a
Constitution. . . . January 12, 1782.
Exeter, [1782]. Broadside.]
(No copy located.)   17617

New Hampshire. President, 1782.
. . . A Proclamation. Whereas a Number
of Towns. . . . January 12, 1782.
Exeter, 1782. Broadside.
LOC copy.   17618

New Hampshire. President, 1784.
. . . A Proclamation for a General
Thanksgiving [Dec. 2. Dated Nov. 2,
1784].
[Exeter, 1784.] Broadside.
LOC copy.   18627

New Hampshire. President, 1784.
. . . A Proclamation. Whereas, by the
Constitution [Nov. 24, 1784]. . . .
[Exeter, 1784.] Broadside.
NHHS copy.   44564

New Hampshire. President, 1785.
By His Excellency John Langdon . . . A
Proclamation for a General Thanksgiving
[Nov. 24. Dated Oct. 21, 1785].
Portsmouth, Melcher & Osborne, 1785.
Broadside.
MHS copy.   19116

New Hampshire. President, 1785.
. . . By His Excellency Mishech Weare . . .
a Proclamation for a Public Fast [Apr.
14. Dated Mar. 18, 1785].
Portsmouth, [1785]. Broadside.
AAS copy.   19115

New Hampshire. President, 1785.
State of New-Hampshire. To [Justices of
the Peace] Greeting. . . .
[Exeter], Melcher & Osborne, 1785.
Broadside.
LOC copy.   44737

New Hampshire. President, 1786.
By His Excellency John Langdon . . . a
Proclamation for a day of Public Fasting
[Apr. 6. Dated Feb. 21, 1786].
Portsmouth, Gerrish, 1786. Broadside.
MHS copy.   19824

New Hampshire. President, 1786.
By His Excellency John Sullivan. . . . A
Proclamation for a General Thanksgiving
[Nov. 23. Dated Sept. 26, 1786].
Exeter, [1786]. Broadside.
MHS copy.   19825

New Hampshire. President, 1788.
By His Excellency John Langdon. . . . A
Proclamation for a General Thanksgiving
[Nov. 29, Dated Oct. 10, 1788].
[Portsmouth, 1788.] Broadside.
NHHS copy.   45308

New Hampshire. President, 1789.
By His Excellency John Pickering. . . . A
Proclamation for a General Fast [Apr. 2,
dated Feb. 21, 1789].
Exeter, Lamson & Ranlet, [1789].
Broadside.
NHHS copy.   45528

New Hampshire. President, 1790.
By His Excellency Josiah Bartlett. . . . A
Proclamation for a Public Thanksgiving
[Nov. 25. Dated Oct. 13, 1790].
Exeter, Ranlet, [1790]. Broadside.
DC copy.   45920

New Hampshire. President, 1790.
. . . By His Excellency the President. . . .
A Proclamation for a General Fast [April
15, dated Feb. 23, 1790].
Exeter, Lamson, [1790]. Broadside.
NHHS copy.   45921

[New Hampshire. President, 1792.
By His Excellency Josiah Bartlett. . . . A
Proclamation for a Public Thanksgiving
[Nov. 15. Dated Sept. 1, 1792].
Exeter, Ranlet. Broadside.]
(No copy of a broadside printing located.)
                                                24579

New Hampshire. Provincial Congress,
1775.
In Provincial Congress, Exeter, June 6,
1775. . . .
[Exeter, 1775.] Broadside.
AAS copy.   14275

[New Hampshire. Provincial Congress,
1775.
In Provincial Congress, Exeter [Fast, July
20, 1775].
Exeter, 1775. Broadside.]
(Source of this Evans entry unknown.)
                                                14276

New Hampshire. Provincial Congress,
1775.
In Congress, Exeter, Nov. 4, 1775. A
Proclamation [Thanksgiving, Nov. 30].
[Exeter, 1775.] Broadside.
MHS copy.   14277

New Hampshire. Provincial Congress,
1776.

In Congress at Exeter, January 5th, 1776.
We the Members. . . .
[Portsmouth, 1776.] 2 pp.
JCB copy.   43095

New Hampshire. Senate Journals, 1784.
. . . The Journals of the Senate [June 2 -
15, 1784].
Exeter, 1784. 19 pp.
AAS copy.   18625

New Hampshire. Senate Journals, 1784.
. . . Present in the Senate [Oct. 20, 1784 -
Feb. 25, 1785].
[Portsmouth], Melcher & Osborne, 1785.
pp. 21-67.
NYPL copy.   19114

New Hampshire. Senate Journals, 1785.
At a Session of the General Court . . .
October . . . 1785.
Portsmouth, Fowle, [1785].
pp. 31-50.
AAS copy.   44741

New Hampshire. Senate Journals, 1785.
A Journal of the Proceedings of the . . .
Senate [June 1-23, 1785].
Portsmouth, Gerrish, 1785. 29 pp.
AAS copy.   44740

New Hampshire. Senate Journals, 1786.
A Journal of the Proceedings of the . . .
Senate [Feb. 1 - Nov. 4, 1786].
[Portsmouth], Gerrish, [1786]. pp. [51] -
79.
AAS copy.   19821

New Hampshire. Senate Journals, 1786.
A Journal of the Proceedings of the . . .
Senate [Sept. 6-23, 1786].
Portsmouth, Melcher, 1787. 24 pp.
AAS copy.   20554

New Hampshire. Senate Journals, 1786.
A Journal of the Proceedings of the . . .
Senate [Dec. 13, 1786 - Jan. 18, 1787].
Portsmouth, Melcher, 1787. 52 pp.
AAS copy.   20555

New Hampshire. Senate Journals, 1787.
A Journal of the Proceedings of the . . .
Senate [June 6-30, 1787].
Portsmouth, Melcher, 1787. 51 pp.
AAS copy.   20556

New Hampshire. Senate Journals, 1787.
A Journal of the Proceedings of the . . .
Senate [Sept. 12-29, 1787].
Portsmouth, Melcher, 1787. 31 pp.
AAS copy.   20557

New Hampshire. Senate Journals, 1787.
A Journal of the Proceedings of the . . .
Senate [Dec. 5-15, 1787].
Portsmouth, Melcher, 1788. 16 pp.
NYPL copy.   21287

New Hampshire. Senate Journals, 1788.
A Journal of the Proceedings of the
Senate [Jan. 23 - Feb. 13, 1788].
Portsmouth, Melcher, 1788. 38 pp.
AAS copy.   21288

New Hampshire. Senate Journals, 1788.
A Journal of the Proceedings of the . . .
Senate [June 4-18, 1788].
Portsmouth, Melcher, 1788. 43 pp.
AAS copy.   21289

New Hampshire. Senate Journals, 1788.
A Journal of the Proceedings of the
Senate [Nov. 5-13, 1788].
Portsmouth, Melcher, 1788. 21 pp.
AAS copy.   21290

New Hampshire. Senate Journals, 1788.
A Journal of the Proceedings of the . . .
Senate [Dec. 24, 1788-Feb. 7, 1789].
Portsmouth, Melcher, 1789. 75 pp., irreg.
AAS copy.   21992

New Hampshire. Senate Journals, 1789.
A Journal of the Proceedings of the . . .
Senate [June 3-19, 1789].
Portsmouth, Melcher, 1789. 45 pp.
AAS copy.   21993

New Hampshire. Senate Journals, 1789.
A Journal of the Proceedings of the . . .
Senate [Dec. 23, 1789-Jan. 26, 1790].
Portsmouth, Melcher, 1790. 69 pp.
AAS copy.   22701

New Hampshire. Senate Journals, 1790.
A Journal of the Proceedings of the . . .
Senate [June 2-19, 1790].
Concord, Hough, 1790. 51 pp.
AAS copy.   22702

New Hampshire. Senate Journals, 1791.
A Journal of the Proceedings of the . . .
Senate [Jan. 5-Feb. 18, 1791].
Portsmouth, Melcher, 1791. 85 pp.
AAS copy.   23600

New Hampshire. Senate Journals, 1791.
A Journal of the Proceedings of the . . .
Senate [June 1-15, 1791].
Portsmouth, Melcher, 1791. 48 pp.
AAS copy.   23601

New Hampshire. Senate Journals, 1791.
A Journal of the Proceedings of the . . .
Senate [Nov. 30, 1791-Jan. 6, 1792].
71 pp.
AAS copy.   24583

New Hampshire. Senate Journals, 1792.
A Journal of the Proceedings of the . . .
Senate [June 6-22, 1792].
Portsmouth, Melcher, 1792. 47 pp.
AAS copy.   24584

New Hampshire. Senate Journals, 1792.
A Journal of the Proceedings of the . . .
Senate [Nov. 21-Dec. 28, 1792].
Portsmouth, Melcher, 1793. 67 pp.
AAS copy.   25874

New Hampshire. Senate Journals, 1793.
A Journal of the Proceedings of the . . .
Senate [June 5-21, 1793].
Portsmouth, Melcher, 1793. 53 pp.
AAS copy.   25875

New Hampshire. Senate Journals, 1793.
A Journal of the Proceedings of the . . .
Senate [Dec. 23, 1793-Feb. 22, 1794].
Portsmouth, Melcher, 1794. 95 pp.
AAS copy.   27372

New Hampshire. Senate Journals, 1794.
A Journal of the Proceedings of the . . .
Senate [June 4-21, 1794].
Portsmouth, Melcher, 1794. 59 pp
AAS copy.   27374

New Hampshire. Senate Journals, 1794.
A Journal of the Proceedings of the . . .
Senate [Dec. 16, 1794-Jan. 16, 1795].
Portsmouth, Melcher, 1795. 72 pp.
LOC copy.   29166

New Hampshire. Senate Journals, 1795.
A Journal of the Proceedings of the . . .
Senate [June 1-18, 1795].
Portsmouth, Melcher, 1795. 54 pp.
AAS copy.   29167

New Hampshire. Senate Journals, 1795.
A Journal of the Proceedings of the . . .
Senate [Dec. 2, 1795-Jan. 1, 1796].
Portsmouth, Melcher, 1796. 72 pp.
AAS copy.   47848

New Hampshire. Senate Journals, 1796.
A Journal of the Proceedings of the . . .
Senate [June 1-17, 1796].
Portsmouth, Melcher, 1796. 57 pp.
AAS copy.   47849

New Hampshire. Senate Journals, 1796.
. . . A Journal of the Proceedings of the
. . . Senate [Nov. 23-Dec. 16, 1796].
Portsmouth, Melcher, 1797. 89 pp.
AAS copy.   32532

New Hampshire. Senate Journals, 1797.
A Journal of the Proceedings of the . . .
Senate [June 7-22, 1797].
Portsmouth, Melcher, 1797. 58 pp.
AAS copy.   48189

New Hampshire. Senate Journals, 1797.
A Journal of the Proceedings of the . . .
Senate [Nov. 22-Dec. 21, 1797].
Portsmouth, Melcher, 1798. 80 pp.
AAS copy.   34194

New Hampshire. Senate Journals, 1798.
A Journal of the Proceedings of the . . .
Senate [June 6-20, 1798].
Portsmouth, Melcher, 1798. 48 pp.
AAS copy.   34196

New Hampshire. Senate Journals, 1798.

A Journal of the Proceedings of the . . .
Senate [Nov. 21-Dec. 28, 1798].
Portsmouth, Melcher, 1799. 72 pp.
AAS copy.   35881

New Hampshire. Senate Journals, 1799.
A Journal of the Proceedings of the . . .
Senate [June 5-15, 1799].
Portsmouth, Melcher, 1799. 47 pp.
AAS copy.   35882

New Hampshire. Senate Journals, 1799.
A Journal of the Proceedings of the . . .
Senate [Dec. 4-31, 1799].
Portsmouth, Melcher, 1800. 57
(i.e. 67) pp.
AAS copy.   38049

New Hampshire. Senate Journals, 1800.
A Journal of the Proceedings of the . . .
Senate [June 4-16, 1800].
Portsmouth, Melcher, 1800. 48 pp.
AAS copy.   38050

New Hampshire. Session Laws, 1776.
. . . An Act for Encouraging the Fixing
out of Armed Vessels [June Session].
Exeter, 1776. pp. 19-42.
Composite copy.   14900

New Hampshire. Session Laws, 1776.
Acts and Laws [Mar. Session].
Exeter, 1776. pp. 3-18.
NHSL copy.   14899

New Hampshire. Session Laws, 1777.
. . . An Act, for Regulating the Choice of
County Treasurer.
Portsmouth, 1777. pp. 47-54.
AAS ph. copy.   43303

New Hampshire. Session Laws, 1777.
. . . An Act for Regulating the Prices.
Exeter, 1777. pp. 43-46.
AAS ph. copy.   43302

New Hampshire. Session Laws, 1777.
. . . An Act, in Addition to an Act . . .
Regulating the Prices.
Exeter, 1777. pp. 55-58.
HC copy.   43304

New Hampshire. Session Laws, 1777.
. . . An Act to Prevent the Desertion of
Soldiers.
[Exeter? 1777.] pp. 59-86.
AAS ph. copy.   43305

New Hampshire. Session Laws, 1778.
. . . An Act [Mar. 14-Dec. 26, 1778].
[Exeter? 1778]. pp. 87-104.
HC copy.   43506

New Hampshire. Session Laws, 1782.
[Acts passed Sept. 14, 1782 to Mar. 1,
1783.]
[Exeter, 1783.] pp. 297-304.
AAS copy.   44413

New Hampshire. Session Laws, 1783.
. . . An Act [Oct., 1783-Apr., 1784].
[Portsmouth, 1784.] pp. 305-322.
AAS copy.   18622

New Hampshire. Session Laws, 1784.
. . . An Act [June, 1784].
Exeter, 1784. pp. 323-330.
AAS copy.   18623

New Hampshire. Session Laws, 1784.
. . . An Act to Invest the United States
[Nov. 5-11, 1784].
[Exeter], Melcher & Osborne, 1785.
pp. 331-336.
AAS copy.   19111

New Hampshire. Session Laws, 1785.
. . . An Act to Establish a Seal [Feb. 12-
24, 1785].
[Exeter], Melcher & Osborne, 1785.
pp. 337-344.
AAS copy.   19112

New Hampshire. Session Laws, 1785.
. . . An Act Directing . . . the
Appointment . . . of Petit-Jurors [June
17-Nov. 10, 1785].
[Portsmouth], Gerrish, [1785].
pp. 345-371.
AAS copy.   19113

[New Hampshire. Session Laws, 1785.
Acts and Laws [June 17-Nov. 10, 1785].

[Portsmouth], Gerrish, [1786].
pp. 345-371.]
(A duplicate of 19113, q. v.)   19817

New Hampshire. Session Laws, 1786.
. . . An Act for the Opening . . . a High-
Way from Dartmouth-College [Feb. 13,
1786-Jan. 18, 1787].
[Portsmouth, 1787.] pp. 373-350 (i.e.,
440)
AAS copy.   20548

New Hampshire. Session Laws, 1787.
. . . An Act . . . Concerning the
Maintenance of the Poor [June 19-Sept.
28, 1787].
[Portsmouth, 1787.] pp. 351 (441)-460.
AAS copy.   20549

New Hampshire. Session Laws, 1788.
An Act [Feb. 2-June 18, 1788].
[Portsmouth, 1788.] pp. 461-471.
AAS copy.   21282

New Hampshire. Session Laws, 1788.
. . . An Act to Prevent the Spreading of
the Small Pox [Nov. 11, 1788-Feb. 7,
1789].
[Portsmouth, 1789.] pp. 473-452
(i.e. 552).
AAS copy.   21991

New Hampshire. Session Laws, 1789.
The Acts and Laws [June 3-19, 1789].
Exeter, Ranlet, [1789]. pp. [2], 247-252.
AAS copy.   21996

New Hampshire. Session Laws, 1789.
The Public Acts and Laws [Dec. 23,
1789-Jan. 26, 1790].
Exeter, Ranlet, 1790. pp. [253]-263.
AAS copy.   22703

New Hampshire. Session Laws, 1792.
The Laws . . . Passed at . . . Dover, June,
1792.
Portsmouth, Melcher, 1792. pp. [2],
397-422.
AAS copy.   24586

New Hampshire. Session Laws, 1792.
The Laws . . . Passed at . . . Exeter,
November, 1792.
Portsmouth, Melcher, 1793. pp. [2],
423-451.
AAS copy.   25876

New Hampshire. Session Laws, 1793.
The Laws . . . Passed at . . . Concord,
June 1793.
Portsmouth, Melcher, 1793. pp. [2],
453-456.
AAS copy.   25877

New Hampshire. Session Laws, 1793.
The Laws . . . Passed at . . . Exeter . . .
December 1793.
Portsmouth, Melcher, 1794.
pp. [459]-481.
AAS copy.   27375

New Hampshire, Session Laws, 1794.
The Laws . . . Passed at . . . Amherst,
June, 1794.
Portsmouth, Melcher, 1794. pp. [2],
483-496, 498-505.
AAS copy.   27376

New Hampshire. Session Laws, 1794.
The Laws . . . Passed at . . . Concord,
December, 1794.
Portsmouth, Melcher, 1795.
pp. [506]-521.
AAS copy.   29168

New Hampshire. Session Laws, 1795.
The Laws . . . Passed at . . . Hanover,
June, 1795.
Portsmouth, Melcher, 1795.
pp. [522]-527.
AAS copy.   29169

New Hampshire. Session Laws, 1796.
Laws Passed . . . Concord Session, 1796.
[Portsmouth? 1796]. 7 pp.
(Not located, 1968.)   47850

New Hampshire. Session Laws, 1796.
The Laws . . . Passed at . . . Concord
. . . December, 1795.
Portsmouth, Melcher, 1796. pp. [2],
530-535.
AAS copy.   30852

New Hampshire. Session Laws, 1796.
The Laws . . . Passed at . . . Exeter,
June, 1796.
Portsmouth, Melcher, 1796. pp. [2],
538-550.
AAS copy.   30853

New Hampshire. Session Laws, 1796.
The Laws . . . Passed at . . . Concord,
December, 1796.
Portsmouth, N. H., Melcher, 1797. 22 pp.
AAS copy.   32535

New Hampshire. Session Laws, 1797.
The Laws . . . Passed at . . . Concord,
June, 1797.
Portsmouth, N. H., Melcher, 1797.
pp. [491]-498.
AAS copy.   32537

New Hampshire. Session Laws, 1797.
The Laws . . . Passed at . . . Portsmouth,
November, 1797.
Portsmouth, Melcher, 1797. pp. [2],
499-512.
(Copy is imperfect.)
NYPL copy.   48190

New Hampshire. Session Laws, 1798.
The Laws . . . Passed at . . . Concord,
December, 1798.
Portsmouth, Melcher, 1799. pp. [4],
[517]-530.
AAS copy.   35883

New Hampshire. Session Laws, 1798.
The Laws . . . Passed at . . . Hopkinton.
June, 1798.
Portsmouth, N.H., Melcher, 1798.
pp. [4], 515-516.
AAS copy.   48524

New Hampshire. Session Laws, 1799.
The Laws . . . Passed at . . . Concord,
June, 1799.
Portsmouth, Melcher, 1799. pp. [4],
531-541.
AAS copy.   35884

New Hampshire. Session Laws, 1799.
The Laws . . . Passed at . . . Exeter,
December, 1799.
Portsmouth, Melcher, 1800. pp. [4],
542-561.
AAS copy.   38052

New Hampshire. Session Laws, 1800.
The Laws . . . Passed at . . . Concord,
June, 1800.
Portsmouth, Melcher, 1800. pp. [4],
562-565.
AAS copy.   38053

New Hampshire. Treasurer, 1776.
. . . Nicholas Gilman. . . . To the
Selectmen of [blank] in said State. . . .
September, A.D. 1776.
[Exeter? 1776.] Broadside.
DC copy.   43096

New Hampshire. Treasurer, 1781.
. . . Nicholas Gilman, Esquire, Treasurer
. . . to the Selectmen [Assessment. Feb.
21, 1781].
[Exeter, 1781.] Broadside.
LOC copy.   17257

New Hampshire. Treasurer, 1784.
. . . John Taylor Gilman. . . . To the
Selectmen of [blank] Greeting. . . .
[June 30, 1784.]
Exeter, Melcher & Osborne, 1784.
Broadside.
DC copy.   44568

New Hampshire. Treasurer, 1785.
. . . John Taylor Gilman. . . . To the
Selectmen of [blank] Greeting [Mar. 25,
1785].
[Exeter], Melcher & Osborne, 1785.
Broadside.
LOC copy.   44742

New Hampshire. Treasurer, 1786.
Treasury-Office . . . John Taylor Gilman
. . . To the Selectmen of [blank]
Greeting. . . [Dated Mar. 1786.]
Portsmouth, Melcher, 1786. Broadside.
DC copy.   44928

New Hampshire. Treasurer, 1786.
Treasury-Office . . . John Taylor Gilman
. . . . To the Selectmen of [blank]

Greeting. . . . [Dated Sept. 1786].
Exeter, Lamson & Ranlet, [1786].
Broadside.
DC copy.   44929

New Hampshire, Treasurer, 1790.
. . . William Gardner, Treasurer . . . to
the Selectmen of [blank] Greeting
[March, 1790].
[Exeter? 1790.] Broadside.
DC copy.   45922

The Newhampshire & Vermont Almanac,
for . . . 1795.
Concord, N.H., Russell & Davis. [24] pp.
(The only copy located lacks a leaf.)
AAS copy.   27379

[The Newhampshire & Vermont Almanac
for 1795.
Hanover, N.H., Dunham.]
(Imprint assumed by Evans from adv.
"for Sale at this Office" in The Eagle,
Jan. 12, 1795.)   27380

The New-Hampshire Diary; or Almanack:
for . . . 1797.
Exeter, Ranlet. [40] pp.
AAS copy.   30857

New Hampshire Medical Society.
The Charter of the. . . .
Exeter, Ranlet, 1792. 35 pp.
JCB copy.   24588

New Hampshire Medical Society.
Laws of the Eastern District.
Exeter, Ranlet, 1799. 8 pp.
AAS copy.   35891

The New Hampshire Register, with an
Almanack for . . . 1796.
Exeter, Ranlet, 1795. [84] pp., printed
wraps.
AAS copy.   29386

New Haven.
Bye Laws of the City of New-Haven.
New Haven, Greens, 1790. 16 pp.
HC copy.   22708

New Haven, Charter.
The Charter, of the City of New-Haven.
New Haven, Green, [1784]. 16 pp.
NYPL copy.   18630

New Haven. Merchants.
To the Public. A Number of Merchants,
Traders, and Others in New-Haven. . . .
Illicit Trade. . . . August 31st, 1781.
[New Haven, 1781.] Broadside.
CHS copy.   44008

New Haven. Selectmen.
New-Haven, March 11, 1774. At a
Meeting of the Select-Men. . . .
[New Haven, 1774.] Broadside.
NYPL ph. copy.   42645

New Haven. Selectmen.
[Hand bill regarding yellow fever.
New Haven, 1794.] Broadside.
(No copy located.)   27383

[New Haven. United Congregational
Society.
An Ecclesiastical Council Convened . . .
May 19th, 1795.
[New Haven, 1795.] Broadside.]
(No copy located.)   28465

New Haven Bridge Lottery.
A List of the Fortunate Numbers in the
First Class.
[New Haven? 1781.] Broadside.
NYHS copy.   44009

New Haven Bridge Lottery.
New-Haven Lottery, for Building a
Bridge over East-River. Class First . . .
Second Class . . . July 31, 1780.
[New Haven, 1780.] Broadside.
CHS copy.   43846

New Haven County Medical Association,
New Haven.
Cases and Observations by the. . . .
New Haven, Meigs, 1788. 86 pp.
NYHS copy.   21296

New-Haven, May 20. On the Evening of
. . . the 12th instant . . . Departed this Life
. . . Ezra Stiles.

n. p., [1795]. Broadside.
AAS copy.   47507

New Haven. Mechanic Library Society.
The Constitution and Bye-Laws of the. . . .
New Haven, Morse, 1793. pp. [1]-7, [3],
11-17.
YC copy.   46831

New-Haven, September 2, 1772. A Short
Account of Moses Paul . . . this Day to be
Executed.
[New Haven, 1772.] Broadside.
NYHS copy.   42358

[The New-Haven Sheet Almanack for
1787.
New-Haven, Meigs & Dana.]
(Adv. New-Haven Gazette, Jan. 12, 1787.)
                                                  44930

A New Hieroglyphical Bible.
Boston, Norman, [1796?]. [2], 144 pp; 1
folding plate.
AAS copy.   26651

A New History of a True Book in Verse.
[Newburyport], March, [1802].
12 pp.
(Adv. in Newburyport Herald, May 14,
1802, as just published.)
AAS copy.   32543

A New History of the Grecian States [by W.
D. Cooper].
Lansingburgh, N. Y., Tiffany for Spencer,
1794. 140, [4] pp., 6 plates.
AAS copy.   26819

The New History of the Trojan Wars.
Philadelphia, Carey, 1794. 108 pp., irreg.
AAS copy.   27384

The New Holyday Present; or, The
Child's Plaything.
Boston, Folsom, 1798. 30 pp.
Vassar College Library copy.   34198

[New Husbandry to New-England.
Philadelphia, 1692.]
(Advertised on last leaf of Evans 608.) 626

[The New Impenetrable Secret.
Philadelphia, Rice, 1786.]
("This day is Published," Pa. Eve. Herald,
Jan. 4, 1786. An importation.)   19832

[New Instructions for the German Flute.
New York, Rivington, 1778.]
(Adv. Rivington's Royal Gazette, Aug.,
1778.)   15925

The New Instructive History of Miss
Patty Proud.
Hartford, Ct., Babcock, 1800. 31 pp.
YC copy.   38061

The New Instructive History of Miss
Patty Proud.
New Haven, Sidney's Press, 1800. 31 pp.
HSP copy.   38060

[A New Introduction to Reading: or a
Collection of Easy Lessons.
Philadelphia, Rice, 1793?]
(Imprint assumed by Evans from advs.)
                                                  26119

[A New Introduction to Reading: or a
Collection of Easy Lessons.
Philadelphia, Rice, 1794.]
(Imprint assumed by Evans from advs.)
                                                  27663

[A New Introduction to Reading: or A
Collection of Easy Lessons. . . . Third
Edition.
Philadelphia, Rices, 1795.]
(Imprint assumed by Evans from Rice
adv.)   29455

[A New Introduction to Reading: or A
Collection of Easy Lessons. . . . Fourth
Edition.
Philadelphia, Rices, 1795.]
(Imprint assumed by Evans from Rice
adv.)   29456

A New Introduction to Reading: or, a
Collection of Easy Lessons. . . . Fifth
Edition.

Philadelphia, Rices, 1796. viii,
328 pp.
PSL copy.   31146

[A New Introduction to Reading. . . .
Fourth edition.
Baltimore, Townsend, 1797.]
("Just published," Federal Gazette, Feb.
18, 1797.)   48191

New Jersey (Colony).
A Brief of the Claim, on the Part of the
Province. . . . September 28, 1769.
[New York, 1769.] 44 pp.
LOC copy.   11356

New Jersey (Colony).
The Grants, Concessions, and Original
Constitutions of the Province.
Philadelphia, Bradford, [1758]. [4], 763
pp.
AAS copy.   8205

New Jersey (Colony) Boundary
Commission, 1769.
To the Honourable, / the / Commissioners
/ . . . for Ascertaining . . . the Boundary,
or Partiti-/ on Line between . . . New
York, and Nova Cae/ sarea. [Dated July
18, 1769].
[New York, 1769.] 9 pp.
NYPL copy.   42011

New Jersey (Colony) Boundary
Commission, 1769.
To/ the Honourable,/ the/ Commissioners/
. . . for Ascertaining the Boundary, or
Partition / Line, between . . . New-York,
and Nova-Caesarea [Dated July 18, 1769].
[New York, 1769.] 9 pp.
NYPL ph. copy.   42012

New Jersey (Colony) Chancery Court,
1771.
A Bill in the Chancery of New-Jersey, at
the Suit of Priscilla Bland. . . .
[Burlington], 1771. 25 pp.
NYPL copy.   12159

New Jersey (Colony) Council, 1739.
To His Excellency Lewis Morris. . . . The
Humble Address of His Majesty's
Council.
[New York], Zenger, 1739. 4 pp.
NJSL copy.   4394

New Jersey (Colony) Council, 1744.
To His Excellency Lewis Morris. . . . The
Humble Representation of His Majesty's
Council.
[Philadelphia, 1744.] 8 pp.
NYPL copy.   5443

New Jersey (Colony) Council, 1775.
A Message to the Governor. . . . Dec. 4,
1775.
[Burlington, 1775.] Broadside.
NYPL copy.   42895

New Jersey (Colony) Council, 1775.
To His Excellency William Franklin. . . .
The Humble Address of His Majesty's
Council. . . . Nov. 25, 1775.
[Burlington, 1775.] [2] pp.
LCP copy.   14286

New Jersey (Colony) General Assembly,
1707.
A Remonstrance of the Assembly.
[New York, 1707.] 8 pp.
HEH copy.   1325

New Jersey (Colony) General Assembly,
1710.
The Humble Representation of the
General Assembly.
New York, 1710. 13 pp.
NYHS copy.   1477

New Jersey (Colony) General Assembly,
1721.
Speeches and Addresses [Feb. 28, 1721
+].
[Philadelphia, 1721.] 32 pp.
NYPL copy.   2270

New Jersey (Colony) General Assembly,
1722.
Speeches and Addresses during the Sitting
of the Assembly.
[New York, Bradford, 1722.] 16 pp.
(The one recorded copy could not be
located.)   2366

New Jersey (Colony) General Assembly, 1736.
A Copy of the Petition of the President [Mar. 19, 1735/6.]
[New York, 1736.] 4 pp.
NYPL copy.   4046

New Jersey (Colony) General Assembly, 1739.
To His Excellency Lewis Morris . . . The Humble Address of the Representatives.
[New York], Zenger, [1739]. 3 pp.
NJSL copy.   4395

New Jersey (Colony) General Assembly, 1740.
A Bill . . . Entitled, An Act to Establish two Trading Companies.
Philadelphia, Franklin, 1740. 14 pp.
(No copy located.)   40204

New Jersey (Colony) General Assembly, 1772.
Extracts from the Minutes and Proceedings of the Assembly . . . September 1772.
Burlington, [1772]. 32 pp.
LOC copy.   12478

New Jersey (Colony) General Assembly, 1775.
To His Excellency William Franklin. . . . The Humble Address of the Representatives. . . . Nov. 29, 1775.
[Burlington, 1775.] [2] pp.
LCP copy.   14287

New Jersey (Colony) General Assembly. House of Representatives, 1707.
The Reply of the House of Representatives.
[New York, 1707.] 12 pp.
NYPL copy.   1326

New Jersey (Colony) General Assembly Journals, 1710.
A Journal of the Votes of the General Assembly [Dec. 1710 - July, 1711].
[New York, 1711.] 40, 5 pp.
NYPL copy.   1520

New Jersey (Colony) General Assembly Journals, 1716.
Journal of the Votes of the House of Representatives [Apr. - May, 1716].
New York, 1716. 20 pp.
(The journals of the other sessions of 1716 are not known in printed form.)
NJSL copy.   1844

New Jersey (Colony) General Assembly Journals, 1716.
Journal of the Votes of the House of Representatives [Nov. 27, 1716 +].
[New York, 1717.] 28 pp.
NJSL copy.   1917

New Jersey (Colony) General Assembly Journals, 1718.
A Journal of the Votes of the General Assembly [May 27 - Oct. 16, 1718].
New York, 1718. 8 pp.
(The unique copy is incomplete.)
PRO copy.   1987

[New Jersey (Colony) General Assembly Journals, 1719.
Votes of the General Assembly [Jan. 13 Mar. 28, 1719].
New York, Bradford, 1719.]
(Probably not printed.)   2059

New Jersey (Colony) General Assembly Journals, 1727.
Journal of the Votes and Proceedings of the General Assembly [Dec. 9, 1727 +].
[New York, 1727.] 14 pp.
NYPL copy.   2929

New Jersey (Colony) General Assembly Journals, 1730.
A Journal of the Votes of the General Assembly [May 7 - July 8, 1730].
[New York, 1730.] 60 pp.
PRO copy.   3327

[New Jersey (Colony) General Assembly Journals, 1731.
The Votes and Proceedings of the General Assembly.
New York, 1731.]
(The Assembly was not sitting July 8, 1730 to May 1732.)   3452

[New Jersey (Colony) General Assembly Journals, 1732.
The Votes and Proceedings of the General Assembly.
Philadelphia, 1732.]
(Assumed by Evans; no copy found.) 3580

New Jersey (Colony) General Assembly Journals, 1733.
The Votes and Proceedings of the General Assembly [Apr. 26, 1733 +].
[Philadelphia, 1733.]. 41 pp.
(No copy located.)   40026

[New Jersey (Colony) General Assembly Journals, 1734.
The Votes and Proceedings of the General Assembly [1734].
Philadelphia, 1734.]
(There was no session of the General Assembly in 1734.)   3802

[New Jersey (Colony) General Assembly Journals, 1735.
The Votes and Proceedings of the General Assembly.
Philadelphia, 1735.]
(There was no session in 1735.)   3936

[New Jersey (Colony) General Assembly Journals, 1736.
The Votes and Proceedings of the General Assembly [1736].
Philadelphia, 1736.]
(There was no session of the Assembly this year.)   4047

[New Jersey (Colony) General Assembly Journals, 1737.
The Votes and Proceedings of the General Assembly.
Philadelphia, 1737.]
(There was no session of the General Assembly in 1737.)   4169

New Jersey (Colony) General Assembly Journals, 1738.
The Votes and Proceedings of the General Assembly [Oct. 27, 1738 - Mar. 15, 1738/9].
[New York, 1738] 68 pp., irreg.
NJSL copy.   4283

[New Jersey (Colony) General Assembly Journals, 1739.
The Votes and Proceedings of the General Assembly.
New York, 1739.]
(There was no session of the General Assembly in 1739.)   4396

New Jersey (Colony) General Assembly Journals, 1740.
The Votes and Proceedings of the General Assembly [April 10, 1740 +].
Philadelphia, Franklin, 1740. 92 pp.
NYPL copy.   4569

New Jersey (Colony) General Assembly Journals, 1741.
The Votes and Proceedings of the General Assembly [Oct. 2, 1741 +].
Philadelphia, Franklin, 1741. 46 pp.
NYPL copy.   4760

New Jersey (Colony) General Assembly Journals, 1742.
Extracts from the Minutes [Oct. 16, 1742 +].
[Philadelphia], 1743. 56 pp.
NYPL copy.   5253

New Jersey (Colony) General Assembly Journals, 1742.
The Minutes and Votes of the House [Oct. 16, 1742 +].
Philadelphia, Franklin, 1742. 41 pp.
NYPL copy.   5015

New Jersey (Colony) General Assembly Journals, 1743.
The Votes and Proceedings [Oct. 10, 1743 +].
Philadelphia, Bradford, 1743. 77 pp.
(No copy available.)   40312

New Jersey (Colony) General Assembly Journals, 1744.
The Votes and Proceedings of the General Assembly [June 22, 1744 +].
Philadelphia, Bradford, 1744. 28 pp.
NYPL copy.   5444

New Jersey (Colony) General Assembly Journals, 1744.
The Votes and Proceedings of the General Assembly [Aug. 18-25, 1744].
Philadelphia, Bradford, 1744. 10 pp.
NJSL copy.   5445

New Jersey (Colony) General Assembly Journals, 1744.
The Votes and Proceedings of the General Assembly [Oct. 4-Dec. 8, 1744].
Philadelphia, Bradford, 1744. 125 pp.
(No complete copy found.)
NJSL copy.   5446

New Jersey (Colony) General Assembly Journals, 1745.
The Votes and Proceedings of the General Assembly [Apr. 4-Aug. 24, 1745].
Philadelphia, W. Bradford, 1745. 73 pp.
NYPL copy.   5650

New Jersey (Colony) General Assembly Journals, 1745.
The Votes and Proceedings of the General Assembly [Sept. 24-Oct. 28, 1745].
Philadelphia, W. Bradford, 1745. 26 pp.
NYPL copy.   5651

New Jersey (Colony) General Assembly Journals, 1746.
The Votes and Proceedings of the General Assembly [Feb. 26, 1745/6-May 8, 1746].
Philadelphia, Bradford, 1746. 46 pp.
NYPL copy.   5820

New Jersey (Colony) General Assembly Journals, 1746.
The Votes and Proceedings of the General Assembly [May 9-June 28, 1746].
Philadelphia, Bradford, 1746. 23 pp.
NYPL copy.   5821

New Jersey (Colony) General Assembly Journals, 1746.
Votes and Proceedings of the General Assembly [Oct. 9-Nov. 1, 1746].
[Philadelphia, 1746.] pp. 25-38.
PRO copy.   5822

New Jersey (Colony) General Assembly Journals, 1747.
Votes of the General Assembly [May 4-9, 1747].
Philadelphia, Bradford, 1747. pp. 39-46.
NYPL copy.   6018

New Jersey (Colony) General Assembly Journals, 1747.
The Votes and Proceedings of the General Assembly [Aug. 20-25, 1747].
Philadelphia, Bradford, 1747. 11 pp.
PRO copy.   6019

New Jersey (Colony) General Assembly Journals, 1747.
Votes of the General Assembly [Nov. 17, 1747-Feb. 18, 1747/8].
Philadelphia, Bradford, 1747. pp. 13-108.
(No complete copy found.)
NYPL copy.   6020

New Jersey (Colony) General Assembly Journals, 1748.
The Votes and Proceedings of the General Assembly [July 6-Dec. 16, 1748].
Philadelphia, Bradford, 1748. 60 pp.
NYPL copy.   6201

New Jersey (Colony) General Assembly Journals, 1749.
The Votes and Proceedings of the General Assembly [Feb. 20, 1748/9-Oct. 20, 1749].
Philadelphia, Bradford, 1749. 90 pp.
NYPL copy.   6379

New Jersey (Colony) General Assembly Journals, 1750.
The Votes and Proceedings of the General Assembly [Feb. 13-27, 1749/50].
Philadelphia, Bradford, 1750. 18 pp.
PRO copy.   6560

New Jersey (Colony) General Assembly
Journals, 1750.
The Votes and Proceedings of the
General Assembly [Sept. 20-Oct. 8,
1750].
Philadelphia, Bradford, [1750]. 18 pp.
PRO copy.   6561

New Jersey (Colony) General Assembly
Journals, 1751.
The Votes and Proceedings of the
General Assembly [Jan. 24-Feb. 22,
1750/1].
Philadelphia, Bradford, [1751]. 58 pp.
PRO copy.   6562

New Jersey (Colony) General Assembly
Journals, 1751.
The Votes and Proceedings of the
General Assembly [May 20-June 7,
1751].
Philadelphia, Bradford, [1751]. 25 pp.
PRO copy.   6729

New Jersey (Colony) General Assembly
Journals, 1751.
The Votes and Proceedings of the
General Assembly [Sept. 10-Oct. 23,
1751].
Philadelphia, Bradford, [1751]. 48 pp.
PRO copy.   6730

New Jersey (Colony) General Assembly
Journals, 1752.
The Votes and Proceedings of the
General Assembly [Jan. 25-Feb. 12,
1751/2].
Philadelphia, Bradford, [1752]. 22 pp.
PRO copy.   6731

New Jersey (Colony) General Assembly
Journals, 1752.
The Votes and Proceedings of the
General Assembly [Dec. 14-22, 1752].
Philadelphia, Bradford, [1752]. 12 pp.
PRO copy.   6895

New Jersey (Colony) General Assembly
Journals, 1753.
The Votes and Proceedings of the
General Assembly [May 16-June 8,
1753].
Philadelphia, Bradford, [1753]. 52 pp.
PRO copy.   7073

New Jersey (Colony) General Assembly
Journals, 1754.
The Votes and Proceedings of the
General Assembly [Apr. 17-June 21,
1754].
Philadelphia, Bradford, 1754. 39 pp.
NJSL copy.   7266

New Jersey (Colony) General Assembly
Journals, 1754.
The Votes and Proceedings of the
General Assembly [Oct. 1-21, 1754].
Philadelphia, Bradford, 1754. 27 pp.
NJSL copy.   7267

New Jersey (Colony) General Assembly
Journals, 1755.
The Votes and Proceedings of the
General Assembly [Feb. 24-Mar. 3,
1755].
Philadelphia, Bradford, 1755. 13 pp.
NJSL copy.   7503

New Jersey (Colony) General Assembly
Journals, 1755.
The Votes and Proceedings of the
General Assembly [Apr. 7-26, 1755].
[Philadelphia, Bradford, 1755.] 22 pp.
NJSL copy.   7504

New Jersey (Colony) General Assembly
Journals, 1755.
The Votes and Proceedings of the
General Assembly [July 31-Aug. 20,
1755].
Philadelphia, Bradford, 1755. 33 pp.
NJSL copy.   7505

New Jersey (Colony) General Assembly
Journals, 1755.
The Votes and Proceedings of the
General Assembly [Nov. 12-14,
1755].
Philadelphia, Bradford, 1755. 9 pp.
NJSL copy.   7506

New Jersey (Colony) General Assembly
Journals, 1755.

The Votes and Proceedings of the
General Assembly [Dec. 15-24, 1755].
Philadelphia, Bradford, 1755. 20 pp.
NJSL copy.   7507

New Jersey (Colony) General Assembly
Journals, 1756.
Votes and Proceedings of the General
Assembly [Mar. 9-16, 1756].
Philadelphia, Bradford, 1756. 14 pp.
PRO copy.   7730

New Jersey (Colony) General Assembly
Journals, 1756.
Votes and Proceedings of the General
Assembly [May 20-June 2, 1756].
Woodbridge, Parker, 1756. 21 pp.
PRO copy.   7731

New Jersey (Colony) General Assembly
Journals, 1756.
Votes and Proceedings of the General
Assembly [July 22-27, 1756].
Woodbridge, 1756. 11 pp.
NJSL copy.   7732

New Jersey (Colony) General Assembly
Journals, 1756.
Votes and Proceedings of the General
Assembly [Oct. 12-15, 1756].
Woodbridge, 1756. 7 pp.
NJSL copy.   7733

New Jersey (Colony) General Assembly
Journals, 1756.
Votes and Proceedings of the General
Assembly [Dec. 17-24, 1756].
Woodbridge, 1756. 8 pp.
NJSL copy.   7734

New Jersey (Colony) General Assembly
Journals, 1757.
The Votes and Proceedings of the
General Assembly [Mar. 15-31,
1757].
Woodbridge, 1757. 27 pp.
NJSL copy.   7970

New Jersey (Colony) General Assembly
Journals, 1757.
The Votes and Proceedings of the
General Assembly [May 24-June 3,
1757].
Woodbridge, 1757. 19 pp.
NJSL copy.   7971

New Jersey (Colony) General Assembly
Journals, 1757.
The Votes and Proceedings of the
General Assembly [Aug. 19-Sept. 13,
1757].
Woodbridge, 1757. 17 pp.
NJSL copy.   7972

New Jersey (Colony) General Assembly
Journals, 1757.
Votes and Proceedings of the General
Assembly [Oct. 10-22, 1757].
Woodbridge, 1757. 15 pp.
NJSL copy.   7973

New Jersey (Colony) General Assembly
Journals, 1758.
The Votes and Proceedings of the General
Assembly [Mar. 23 - Apr. 18, 1758].
Woodbridge, 1758. 28 pp.
NJSL copy.   8206

New Jersey (Colony) General Assembly
Journals, 1758.
The Votes and Proceedings of the General
Assembly [July 25 - Aug. 12, 1758].
Woodbridge, 1758. 38 pp.
NJSL copy.   8207

New Jersey (Colony) General Assembly
Journals, 1759.
The Votes and Proceedings of the General
Assembly [Mar. 8-17, 1759].
Woodbridge, 1759. 23 pp.
NJSL copy.   8429

New Jersey (Colony) General Assembly
Journals, 1760.
The Votes and Proceedings of the General
Assembly [Mar. 11-26, 1760].
Woodbridge, 1760. 15 pp.
NJSL copy.   8681

New Jersey (Colony) General Assembly
Journals, 1760.
The Votes and Proceedings of the General
Assembly [Oct. 29 - Dec. 5, 1760].

Woodbridge, 1760. 67 pp.
NJSL copy.   8682

[New Jersey (Colony) General Assembly
Journals, 1760.
The Votes and Proceedings of the General
Assembly . . . the 24th of January,
1760-61.]
(The Assembly was not in session at this
time.)   8948

New Jersey (Colony) General Assembly
Journals, 1761.
The Votes and Proceedings of the General
Assembly [Mar. 27 - Apr. 7, 1761].
Woodbridge, 1761. 19 pp.
NJSL copy.   8949

New Jersey (Colony) General Assembly
Journals, 1761.
Votes and Proceedings of the General
Assembly [July 4-8, 1761].
Woodbridge, 1761. 8 pp.
NJSL copy.   8950

New Jersey (Colony) General Assembly
Journals, 1761.
Votes and Proceedings of the General
Assembly [Nov. 30 - Dec. 12, 1761].
Woodbridge, 1761. 28 pp.
NJSL copy.   8951

New Jersey (Colony) General Assembly
Journals, 1762.
The Votes and Proceedings of the General
Assembly [Mar. 3-10, 1762].
Woodbridge, Parker, 1762. 20 pp.
NJSL copy.   9205

New Jersey (Colony) General Assembly
Journals, 1762.
The Votes and Proceedings of the General
Assembly [Apr. 26-28, 1762].
Woodbridge, 1762. 8 pp.
NJSL copy.   9206

New Jersey (Colony) General Assembly
Journals, 1762.
Votes and Proceedings of the General
Assembly [Sept. 14-25, 1762].
Woodbridge, 1762. 24 pp.
NJSL copy.   9207

New Jersey (Colony) General Assembly
Journals, 1763.
The Votes and Proceedings of the
General Assembly [May 25 - June 3,
1763].
Woodbridge, 1763. 27 pp.
NJSL copy.   9456

New Jersey (Colony) General Assembly
Journals, 1763.
The Votes and Proceedings of the General
Assembly [Nov. 15 - Dec. 7, 1763].
Woodbridge, 1764. 38 pp.
NJSL copy.   9750

New Jersey (Colony) General Assembly
Journals, 1764.
The Votes and Proceedings of the General
Assembly [Feb. 14-23, 1764].
Woodbridge, 1764. 22 pp.
NJSL copy.   9751

New Jersey (Colony) General Assembly
Journals, 1765.
The Votes and Proceedings of the General
Assembly [May 21 - June 20, 1765].
Burlington, 1765. 74 pp.
NJSL copy.   10088

New Jersey (Colony) General Assembly
Journals, 1765.
The Votes and Proceedings of the General
Assembly. . . . Twelfth Session of the
Twentieth Assembly [Nov. 26-30, 1765].
Woodbridge, Parker, 1765. 11 pp.
NJSL copy.   10089

New Jersey (Colony) General Assembly
Journals, 1766.
The Votes and Proceedings of the General
Assembly. . . . The Thirteenth Session of
the Twentieth Assembly [June 11-28,
1766].
Woodbridge, Parker, 1766. 54 pp.
NJSL copy.   10413

New Jersey (Colony) General Assembly
Journals, 1767.
Votes and Proceedings of the General
Assembly. . . . The Fourteenth Session of

New Jersey (Colony) Laws, Statutes, etc.,
1724.
An Ordinance for Regulating and
Establishing Fees [May 1, 1724].
[New York, 1724.] 7 pp.
NYPL copy.   2568

New Jersey (Colony) Laws, Statutes, etc.,
1724.
An Ordinance for Regulating &
Establishing fees within this His Majesty's
Province [Nov. 26, 1724].
[New York], 1724. 14 pp.
NYPL copy.   2567

New Jersey (Colony) Laws, Statutes, etc.,
1724.
An Ordinance for Regulating Courts of
Judicature.
New York, W. Bradford, 1724. 10 pp.
NYHS copy.   39816

New Jersey (Colony) Laws, Statutes, etc.,
1725.
An Ordinance for Regulating Courts.
New York, 1725. 9 pp.
NYHS copy.   2683

[New Jersey (Colony) Laws, Statutes, etc.,
1727.
An Ordinance for Regulating and
Establishing Fees.
New York, [1727]. 6 pp.]
(The unique copy could not be found.)
      2930

New Jersey (Colony) Laws, Statutes, etc.,
1728.
An Ordinance for Regulating Courts.
[New York, Bradford, 1728]. 5 pp.
NYHS copy.   39896

New Jersey (Colony) Laws, Statutes, etc.,
1732.
The Acts of the General Assembly.
Philadelphia, Bradfords, 1732. [14], 281
pp.
NJSL copy.   3578

New Jersey (Colony) Laws, Statutes, etc.,
1742.
[Body of the Laws of the Province of New
Jersey.
Philadelphia, 1742.]
(Sabin 53076; no copy located.)   40281

New Jersey (Colony) Laws, Statutes, etc.,
1748.
. . . February 18, 1747. . . . The Following
Act was Passed.
Philadelphia, Bradford, [1748]. 18 pp.
(No copy available for reproduction.)
      40471

New Jersey (Colony) Laws, Statutes, etc.,
1752.
The Acts of the General Assembly.
[Philadelphia], Bradford, 1752. [4], 507
pp.
AAS copy.   6893

[New Jersey (Colony) Laws, Statutes, etc.,
1753.
An Ordinance for Regulating and
Establishing the Fees . . . November 23,
1753.
Woodbridge, 1755. 6 pp.]
(No copy found.)   7502

New Jersey (Colony) Laws, Statutes, etc.,
1757.
At a Session of the General Assembly. . . .
A Supplementary Act [Militia. May 24,
1757].
Woodbridge, [1757]. 18 pp.
LOC copy.   7969

New Jersey (Colony) Laws, Statutes, etc.,
1759.
An Act for the further Preservation of
Timber. . . . Published the Seventeenth of
March, 1759.
[Woodbridge? 1759.] Broadside.
Reproduced from Am. Art Assoc. cat.,
Apr. 5-7, 1916, item 789.   41064

New Jersey (Colony) Laws, Statutes, etc.,
1761.
The Acts of the General Assembly. . . .
Volume the Second.
Woodbridge, 1761. [4], x, [2], 401, [1],
56, [1], 64 pp.
(The final leaves called for by Evans are a

separate item bound into the NYPL
copy.)
AAS copy.   8947

[New York (Colony) Laws, Statutes, etc.,
1772.
An Act [Militia].
New York, 1772.]
(Adv. N. Y. Mercury, 1078.)   12483

New Jersey (Colony) Laws, Statutes, etc.,
1773.
A Supplement to the Act, Intituled, "An
Act for Running . . . the Line. . . ."
[Burlington, 1773.] Broadside.
LOC ph. copy.   42471

New Jersey (Colony) Lieutenant
Governor, 1709.
By the Honourable Richard
Indgoldsby. . . . A Proclamation
[volunteers]. . . . Burlington . . . the 30th
Day of June . . . 1709.
[New York? 1709.] Broadside.
NYHS copy.   39493

New Jersey (Colony) Proprietors
See
Board of General Proprietors

New Jersey (Colony) Session Laws, 1703.
At a General Assembly [Nov. 8, 1703 +].
New York, 1703. 4 pp.
HSP copy.   1136

New Jersey (Colony) Session Laws, 1704.
An Act for Raising a Revenue [Dec.,
1704].
[New York, 1704.] 20 pp.
HSP copy.   1184

New Jersey (Colony) Session Laws, 1709.
Acts Passed by the General Assembly . . .
in January, 1709.
[New York, 1710]. pp. 28-38, irreg.
NYPL copy.   1476

New Jersey (Colony) Session Laws, 1710.
Acts of the General Assembly [Jan., 1710
+].
[New York, 1711.] 39-58 pp.
NYPL copy.   1519

New Jersey (Colony) Session Laws, 1716.
Acts Passed by the General Assembly
[Jan. 1716].
[New York, 1716-17.] pp. 61-78.
NYPL copy.   1916

New Jersey (Colony) Session Laws, 1718.
Acts Passed at a General Assembly
[1718].
[New York, 1718.] [13] pp.
HSP copy.   1986

New Jersey (Colony) Session Laws, 1718.
Acts Passed by the General Assembly
[Apr. 1718].
[New York, W. Bradford, 1720.]
pp. 79-115.
NYPL copy.   39729

New Jersey (Colony) Session Laws, 1719.
An Act for Running [Mar. 27, 1719 +].
[New York, 1719.] pp. 95-123.
NYHS copy.   2058

New Jersey (Colony) Session Laws, 1722.
An Act for the Support of the
Government [May 5, 1722].
[New York, 1722.] pp. 123-145.
HSP copy.   2365

New Jersey (Colony) Session Laws, 1723.
. . . At a Session of the General Assembly
[Nov. 30, 1723].
New York, W. Bradford, 1723. 32 pp.
NYHS copy.   39798

New Jersey (Colony) Session Laws, 1723.
. . . At a Session of the General Assembly
. . . Acts [Nov. 30, 1723 +].
Perth-Amboy, 1723. 33, [4] pp.
NYPL photostat copy.   2463

New Jersey (Colony) Session Laws, 1725.
. . . At a Sessions of the General Assembly
[Aug. 23, 1725 +].
New York, 1725. pp. [2], 117-136, 23-24,
NYPL copy.   2682

New Jersey (Colony) Session Laws, 1727.
Acts and Laws [Dec. 9, 1727 +].

Burlington, Keimer, 1728. 51, [2] pp.
NJSL copy.   3071

New Jersey (Colony) Session Laws, 1730.
Acts and Laws [May 7, 1730 +].
Philadelphia, Bradford, 1730. 39,
[1] pp.
NJSL copy.   3326

New Jersey (Colony) Session Laws, 1732.
An Act the Better to Enable.
[Philadelphia, 1732.] pp. 283-299, [4].
(No perfect copy could be located.)
NJSL copy.   3579

New Jersey (Colony) Session Laws, 1733.
At a General Assembly [Aug. 16, 1733 +].
Philadelphia, Franklin, 1733. pp. [2],
301-343, [1].
NJSL copy.   3693

New Jersey (Colony) Session Laws, 1735.
[Acts of Assembly, Sept. 1735].
Philadelphia, Franklin, 1735. pp. [2],
347-366.
(No complete copy could be located.)
NJSL copy.   3801

New Jersey (Colony) Session Laws, 1738.
. . . At a General Assembly [Nov. 13,
1738 +].
Philadelphia, Franklin, 1739. pp. [2],
369-395, [1].
NJSL copy.   4392

New Jersey (Colony) Session Laws, 1740.
. . . At a General Assembly [Apr. 10,
1740+].
Philadelphia, Bradford, 1740. [2],
397-433, [2] pp.
NJSL copy.   4568

New Jersey (Colony) Session Laws, 1741.
At a General Assembly [Oct. 2, 1741 +].
Philadelphia, Franklin, 1742. [2],
17 pp.
NJSL copy.   5014

New Jersey (Colony) Session Laws, 1743.
At a General Assembly [Oct. 10, 1743 +].
Philadelphia, Franklin, 1743. pp. [2],
21-61.
NJSL copy.   5252

New Jersey (Colony) Session Laws, 1746.
At a General Assembly [May 8, 1746 +].
Philadelphia, Franklin, 1746. 14 pp.
NJSL copy.   5818

New Jersey (Colony) Session Laws, 1746.
At a General Assembly [June 28, 1746].
Philadelphia, Franklin, 1746. 22 pp.
NJSL copy.   5819

New Jersey (Colony) Session Laws, 1748.
At a General Assembly [Feb. 18,
1747/8 +].
Philadelphia, Bradford, [1750]. 18 pp.
NJSL copy.   6559

New Jersey (Colony) Session Laws, 1748.
Acts and Laws [Oct. 10, 1743 - Aug. 10,
1748].
Philadelphia, Bradford, 1749. 56, [1] pp.
NJSL copy.   6377

New Jersey (Colony) Session Laws, 1748.
At a General Assembly [Nov. 17, 1747 +].
Philadelphia, Franklin, 1748. 53,
[1] pp.
NJSL copy.   6200

New Jersey (Colony) Session Laws, 1749.
Acts and Laws [Feb. 20, 1748/9 +].
Philadelphia, Bradford, 1749. 11,
[1] pp.
NJSL copy.   6378

New Jersey (Colony) Session Laws, 1751.
At a General Assembly [May 20 - June 6,
1751].
Philadelphia, Bradford, [1751].
15 pp.
NJSL copy.   6727

New Jersey (Colony) Session Laws, 1751.
At a General Assembly [Sept. - Oct.
1751].
Philadelphia, Bradford, [1751].
21 pp.
NJSL copy.   6728

New Jersey (Colony) Session Laws, 1752.

At a Session of the General Assembly
[Jan. 25 - Feb. 12, 1752].
Philadelphia, Bradford, [1752].
27 pp.
NJSL copy.   6894

New Jersey (Colony) Session Laws, 1753.
At a General Assembly [May 16 - June 8,
1753].
Philadelphia, Bradford, [1753]. 59, [1]
pp., 2 leaves folded.
NJSL copy.   7072

New Jersey (Colony) Session Laws, 1754.
At a Session of the General Assembly
[Apr. 17 - June 21, 1754].
Philadelphia, Bradford, [1754]. 36 pp.
NJSL copy.   7265

New York (Colony) Session Laws, 1754.
. . . At a Session of the General Assembly
[Aug. 20, 1754 - Feb. 19, 1755].
New York, Parker, 1755. 100, [1] pp.
MHS copy.   7510

New Jersey (Colony) Session Laws, 1755.
At a Session of General Assembly [Feb.
20 - Mar. 3, 1755].
Philadelphia, Bradford, [1755]. 8 pp.
NJSL copy.   7498

New Jersey (Colony) Session Laws, 1755.
At Two Sessions of General Assembly
[Apr. 7-26, 1755].
Philadelphia, Bradford, [1755].
24 pp.
NJSL copy.   7499

New Jersey (Colony) Session Laws, 1755.
At a Session of the General Assembly
[Aug. 1-20, 1755].
Philadelphia, Bradford, [1755]. 64 pp.
NJSL copy.   7500

New Jersey (Colony) Session Laws, 1755.
At a Session of General Assembly [Dec.
16, 1755 +].
Philadelphia, Bradford, [1755]. 17 pp.
NJSL copy.   7501

New Jersey (Colony) Session Laws, 1756.
At a Session of General Assembly [Mar.
16, 1756].
Philadelphia, Bradford, [1756]. 12 pp.
NJSL copy.   7727

New Jersey (Colony) Session Laws, 1756.
At a Session of the General Assembly [May
20-June 2, 1756].
Philadelphia, Bradford, [1756]. 78 pp.
NJSL copy.   7728

New Jersey (Colony) Session Laws, 1756.
At a Session of the General Assembly
[Dec. 17-24, 1756].
Philadelphia, Bradford, [1756]. 5 pp.
NJSL copy.   7729

New Jersey (Colony) Session Laws, 1757.
At a Session of General Assembly [Mar.
15-31, 1757].
Philadelphia, Bradford, [1757]. 52 pp.
(Best copy available.)
NYPL copy.   7966

New Jersey (Colony) Session Laws, 1757.
At a Session of General Assembly [May,
1757].
Philadelphia, Bradford, [1757].
27 pp.
NJSL copy.   7967

New Jersey (Colony) Session Laws, 1757.
At a Session of General Assembly [Oct.
1757].
Philadelphia, Bradford, [1757].
30 pp.
NJSL copy.   7968

New Jersey (Colony) Session Laws, 1758.
At a Session of General Assembly [Apr.
4, 1758 +].
Philadelphia, Bradford, [1758]. 28 pp.
NJSL copy.   8203

New Jersey (Colony) Session Laws, 1758.
. . . At a Session [Aug. 12, 1758 +].
Woodbridge, Parker, 1758. 60 pp.
PRO copy.   40995

New Jersey (Colony) Session Laws, 1758.
At a Session of General Assembly [Apr.
15, 1758 +].

Philadelphia, Bradford, [1758]. 8 pp.
NJSL copy.   8204

New Jersey (Colony) Session Laws, 1761.
. . . At a Session of General Assembly . . .
July . . . 1761.
Woodbridge, Parker, 1761. 11 pp.
(Humphrey 57; no copy located.)   41228

New Jersey (Colony) Session Laws, 1761.
. . . At a Session of the General Assembly
[Oct. 27-Dec. 5, 1761].
Woodbridge, Parker, 1761. 80 pp.
(Humphrey 55; no copy located.)   41229

New Jersey (Colony) Session Laws, 1761.
. . . At a Session of the General Assembly
[Nov. 5-Dec. 12, 1761]. . . .
Woodbridge, Parker, 1761. 20 pp.
(Humphrey 58; no copy located.)   41230

New Jersey (Colony) Session Laws, 1762.
. . . At a Session of General Assembly . . .
April 26, 1762.
Woodbridge, Parker, 1762. 4 pp.
NYPL copy.   41290

New Jersey (Colony) Session Laws, 1766.
. . . At a Session of General Assembly. . . .
The Twelfth Session of the Twentieth
Assembly [June 11-28, 1766].
Woodbridge, Parker, 1766. 50, [1] pp.
NJSL copy.   10412

New Jersey (Colony) Session Laws, 1767.
. . . At a Session of the General Assembly.
The Fourteenth Session of the Twentieth
Assembly [June 9-24, 1767].
Woodbridge, Parker, 1767. 30 pp.
NJSL copy.   10703

New Jersey (Colony) Session Laws, 1768.
. . . At a Session of the General
Assembly. . . . The Fifteenth Session of
the Twentieth Assembly [Apr. 12-May 10,
1768].
Woodbridge, Parker, 1768. 60 pp.
NJSL copy.   10996

New Jersey (Colony) Session Laws, 1769.
. . . At a Session of the General
Assembly. . . . The First Session of the
Twenty-First Assembly [Oct. 10-Dec. 6,
1769].
Burlington, Parker, 1770. 123,
[1] pp.
NJSL copy.   11762

New Jersey (Colony) Session Laws, 1770.
. . . At a Session of the General Assembly.
. . . The Second Session of the Twenty-
First Assembly [Mar. 14-27, 1770].
Woodbridge, Parker, 1770. 23, [1] pp.
NJSL copy.   11763

New Jersey (Colony) Session Laws, 1770.
. . . At a Session begun at Perth-Amboy.
. . . The Third Session of the Twenty-First
Assembly [Sept. 26-Oct. 27, 1770].
Burlington, Collins, 1770. 28, [1] pp.
NJSL copy.   11764

New Jersey (Colony) Session Laws, 1771.
. . . At a Session. . . . The Fourth Session
of the Twenty-First Assembly [Apr.
17-Dec. 21, 1771].
Burlington, Collins, 1771. 74,
[1] pp.
NJSL copy.   12150

New Jersey (Colony) Session Laws, 1772.
. . . At a Session began at Perth-Amboy
. . . [Aug. 19-Sept. 26, 1772]. Being the
First Session of the Twenty-Second
Assembly.
Burlington, Collins, 1772. 67, [1] pp.
(Only located copy is imperfect.)
NJHS copy.   42360

New Jersey (Colony) Session Laws, 1774.
. . . At a Session. . . . The Second Session
of the Twenty-Second Assembly [Nov. 19,
1773-Mar. 11, 1774].
Burlington, Collins, 1774. 160,
[2] pp.
NJSL copy.   13458

New Jersey (Colony) Session Laws, 1775.
At a Session began at Perth-Amboy. . . .
Being the Third Session of the
Twenty-Second Assembly [Jan. 11 - Feb.
13, 1775].

Burlington, Collins, 1775. 28 pp.
NJSL copy.   14280

New Jersey (Colony) Session Laws, 1775.
. . . At a Session Began at Burlington . . .
November 15, 1775. . . . The Fourth
Session of the Twenty-Second Assembly.
Burlington, Collins, 1775. 20, [1] pp.
NJSL copy.   14281

New Jersey (Colony) Surveyor General,
1747.
General Instructions . . . to the Deputy
Surveyors of the Eastern Division of
New-Jersey.
[Philadelphia? 1747.] 5, [1] pp.
HSP copy.   40434

New Jersey (Colony) Surveyor General,
1747.
General Instructions . . . to the Deputy
Surveyors of the Western Division of
New-Jersey.
[Philadelphia? 1747.] 5, [1] pp.
HSP copy.   40435

New Jersey (Colony) Treasurer, 1773.
A Bill in the Chancery . . . against
Archibald Kennedy.
Burlington, Collins, 1773. 11 pp.
NYPL copy.   42472

New Jersey (Colony) Treaties, etc., 1756.
A Treaty between the Government of
New-Jersey and the Indians [Jan. 8-9,
1756].
Philadelphia, Bradford, [1756]. 11 pp.
NYPL copy.   7688

[New Jersey (Colony) Treaties, etc., 1758.
At a Conference held in the Great
Meeting-House at Crosswicks . . .
February, 1758.
[Woodbridge, 1758.] 5 pp.]
(No copy located.)   8154

New Jersey (Colony) Treaties, etc., 1758.
The Minutes of a Treaty held at Easton
. . . in October, 1758.
Woodbridge, 1758. 35 pp.
LOC copy.   8157

New Jersey. Adjutant-General's Office.
Trenton, December 22, 1794. Division
Orders.
[Trenton, 1794.] Broadside.
Rutgers University copy.   27388

New Jersey. Citizens, 1794.
To the Honourable the Senate and House
of Representatives of the United States
. . . the Petition. . . .
n. p., [1794]. Broadside.
(Not located, 1968.)   47126

New Jersey. Commissioners to Erect
Bridges.
Contract for Erecting Bridges. . . . April
22, 1791.
[Elizabethtown, 1791.] Broadside.
NYHS copy.   23626

New Jersey. Constitution, 1776.
Constitution of New-Jersey.
Burlington, 1776. 12 pp.
NJHS copy.   14912

New Jersey. Convention, 1776.
In Convention . . . at Brunswick, August
11, 1776. . . .
[Burlington, 1776.] [2] pp.
LCP copy.   43097

New Jersey. Convention, 1776.
Journal of the Votes and Proceedings.
Burlington, 1776. 150 pp.
NYPL copy.   14914

New Jersey. Convention, 1787.
Minutes of the Convention . . . Holden at
Trenton the 11th Day of December, 1787.
Trenton, 1788. 31 pp.
NYPL copy.   21302

New Jersey. Court of Chancery.
The Evidence in a Cause Depending in the
Court of Chancery.
Trenton, Croft, 1799. 136 pp., 1 folding
table.
(Also entered as 36396, q. v.)   35897

New Jersey. General Assembly Journals,
1776.

Votes and Proceedings of the General
Assembly [Aug. 27, 1776 - June 7, 1777].
[Burlington, 1777.] 148 pp.
NJSL copy.   15466

New Jersey. General Assembly Journals,
1777.
Votes and Proceedings of the General
Assembly [Aug. 27-Oct. 11, 1777].
Trenton, 1779. pp. [4], 153-206.
LOC copy.   16398

New Jersey. General Assembly Journals,
1777.
Votes and Proceedings of the General
Assembly [Oct. 28, 1777 - Oct. 8, 1778].
Trenton, 1779. 204 pp.
LOC copy.   16399

New Jersey. General Assembly Journals,
1778.
Votes and Proceedings of the General
Assembly [Oct. 27-Dec. 12, 1778].
Trenton, 1779. 64 pp.
NYPL copy.   16400

New Jersey. General Assembly Journals,
1779.
Votes and Proceedings of the General
Assembly [Apr. 20-June 12, 1779].
Trenton, 1779. pp. [4], 69-156.
NYPL copy.   16401

New Jersey. General Assembly Journals,
1779.
Votes and Proceedings of the General
Assembly [Sept. 15-Oct. 7, 1779].
Trenton, 1779. pp. [4], 161-208.
NYPL copy.   16402

New Jersey. General Assembly Journals,
1779.
Votes and Proceedings of the General
Assembly. . . . First Sitting of the Fourth
Assembly [Oct. 26 - Dec. 26, 1779].
Trenton, 1780. 112 pp.
NYPL copy.   16891

New Jersey. General Assembly Journals,
1780.
[Minutes and proceedings of the joint
meeting of the Council and General
Assembly, June 17, 1780 - Dec. 20, 1783.
Trenton? 1783?] pp. 41-60.
(Not located 1967.)
NJSL copy.   44414

New Jersey. General Assembly Journals,
1780.
Votes and Proceedings of the General
Assembly [Feb. 16 - Mar. 21, 1780].
Trenton, 1780. pp. [4], 115-182.
NYPL copy.   16892

New Jersey. General Assembly Journals,
1780.
Votes and Proceedings of the General
Assembly [May 10 - June 19, 1780].
Trenton, 1780. pp. [2], 185-252.
NYPL copy.   16893

New Jersey. General Assembly Journals,
1780.
Votes and Proceedings of the General
Assembly [Sept. 13 - Oct. 7, 1780].
Trenton, 1780. pp. [2], 255-299.
NYPL copy.   16894

New Jersey. General Assembly Journals,
1780.
Votes and Proceedings of the Fifth
General Assembly [Oct. 24 - 27, 1780].
Trenton, 1780. 8 pp.
NYPL copy.   16895

New Jersey. General Assembly Journals,
1780.
Votes and Proceedings of the General
Assembly [Oct. 28 - Nov. 3, 1780].
Trenton, [1780]. pp. 9-16.
NYPL copy.   16896

New Jersey. General Assembly Journals,
1780.
Votes and Proceedings of the General
Assembly [Nov. 4 - 10, 1780].
Trenton, [1780]. pp. 17-24.
NYPL copy.   16897

New Jersey. General Assembly Journals,
1780.
Votes and Proceedings of the General
Assembly [Nov. 11-17, 1780].

Trenton, [1780]. pp. 25-31.
NYPL copy.   16898

New Jersey. General Assembly Journals,
1780.
Votes and Proceedings of the General
Assembly [Nov. 18 - 24, 1780].
[Trenton, 1780.] pp. 33-40.
NYPL copy.   16899

New Jersey. General Assembly Journals,
1780.
Votes and Proceedings of the General
Assembly [Nov. 25 - Dec. 1, 1780].
[Trenton, 1780]. pp. 41-47.
NYPL copy.   16900

New Jersey. General Assembly Journals,
1780.
Votes and Proceedings of the General
Assembly [Dec. 2 - 8, 1780].
Trenton, [1780]. pp. 48-52.
NYPL copy.   16901

New Jersey. General Assembly Journals,
1780.
Votes and Proceedings of the General
Assembly [Dec. 9-15, 1780].
[Trenton, 1780.] pp. 53-60.
NYPL copy.   16902

New Jersey, General Assembly Journals,
1780.
Votes and Proceedings of the General
Assembly. [Dec. 16, 1780 - Jan. 9, 1781].
[Trenton, 1781]. pp. 61-108.
NYPL copy.   17264

New Jersey. General Assembly Journals,
1781.
Votes and Proceedings of the Fifth
General Assembly. . . . Second Sitting
[May 15 - June 28, 1781].
Trenton, 1781. 101, [1] pp.
NYPL copy.   17265

New Jersey. General Assembly Journals,
1781.
Votes and Proceedings of the Fifth
General Assembly. . . . Third Sitting
[Sept. 19 - Oct. 6, 1781].
Trenton, 1781. 34 pp.
NYPL copy.   17266

New Jersey. General Assembly Journals,
1781.,
Votes and Proceedings of the General
Assembly [Oct. 23 - Dec. 29, 1781].
Trenton, 1782. 81 pp.
NYPL copy.   17625

New Jersey. General Assembly Journals,
1782.
Votes and Proceedings of the General
Assembly [May 15 - June 24, 1782].
Trenton, 1782. 50 pp.
NYPL copy.   17626

New Jersey. General Assembly Journals,
1782.
Votes and Proceedings of the General
Assembly [Sept. 18 - Oct. 5, 1782].
Trenton, 1782. 24 pp.
NYPL copy.   17627

New Jersey. General Assembly Journals,
1782.
Votes and Proceedings of the Seventh
General Assembly. . . . First Sitting [Oct.
22-Dec. 26, 1782].
Trenton, 1783. 89 pp.
NYPL copy.   18054

New Jersey. General Assembly Journals,
1783.
Votes and Proceedings of the Seventh
General Assembly. . . . Second Sitting
[May 15-June 19, 1783].
Trenton, 1783. pp. [2], 93-150.
NYPL copy.   18055

New Jersey. General Assembly Journals,
1783.
Votes and Proceedings of the Eighth
General Assembly. . . . First Sitting [Oct.
28 - Dec. 24, 1783].
Trenton, 1784. 90 pp.
NYPL copy.   18638

New Jersey. General Assembly Journals,
1784.
Votes and Proceedings of the General

Assembly. . . . Second Sitting. [Aug. 5
Sept. 2, 1784].
New Brunswick, 1784. pp. [2], 93 - 146.
NYPL copy.   18639

New Jersey. General Assembly Journals,
1784.
Votes and Proceedings of the Ninth
General Assembly. . . . First Sitting [Oct.
26 - Dec. 24, 1784].
Trenton, 1784. 101 pp.
NYPL copy.   19124

New Jersey. General Assembly Journals,
1785.
Votes and Proceedings of the Tenth
General Assembly. . . . First Sitting [Oct.
25 - Nov. 29, 1785].
Trenton, 1785. 83 pp.
NYPL copy.   19125

New Jersey. General Assembly Journals,
1786.
Votes and Proceedings of the Tenth
General Assembly. . . . Second Sitting
[Feb. 15 - Mar. 24, 1786].
Trenton, 1786. 87 pp.
NYPL copy.   19839

New Jersey. General Assembly Journals,
1786.
Votes and Proceedings of the Tenth
General Assembly. . . . Third Sitting.
[May 17 - June 2, 1786].
Elizabethtown, 1786. 31 pp.
NYPL copy.   19840

New Jersey. General Assembly Journals,
1786.
Votes and Proceedings of the Eleventh
General Assembly. . . . First Sitting [Oct.
24-Nov. 24, 1786].
Trenton, 1786. 76 pp.
NYPL copy.   19841

New Jersey. General Assembly Journals,
1787.
Votes and Proceedings of the General
Assembly [May 16 - June 7, 1787].
Trenton, 1787. 44 pp.
NYPL copy.   20568

New Jersey. General Assembly Journals,
1787.
Votes and Proceedings of the Twelfth
General Assembly [Oct. 23 - Nov. 6,
1787].
Trenton, 1787. 66 pp.
NYPL copy.   20569

New Jersey. General Assembly Journals,
1788.
Votes and Proceedings of the Twelfth
General Assembly. . . . Second Sitting
[Aug. 2 - Sept. 9, 1788].
Trenton, Collins, 1788. 33 pp.
NYPL copy.   21303

New Jersey. General Assembly Journals,
1788.
Votes and Proceedings of the Thirteenth
General Assembly. . . . First Sitting [Oct.
28 - Dec. 1, 1788].
Trenton, Collins, 1788. 103 pp.
NYPL copy.   21304

New Jersey. General Assembly Journals,
1789.
Votes and Proceedings [Oct. 27 - Dec. 1,
1789.]
New Brunswick, Blauvelt, 1789. 111 pp.
NJSL copy.   22714

New Jersey. General Assembly Journals,
1790.
Votes and Proceedings of the Fourteenth
General Assembly. . . . Second Sitting
[May 18-June 12, 1794].
Burlington, 1790. 71 pp.
(Not located 1967.)
NJSL copy.   45923

New Jersey. General Assembly Journals,
1791.
Votes and Proceedings of the Sixteenth
General Assembly. . . . First Sitting [Oct.
25 - Nov. 25, 1791].
Burlington, Neale, 1791. 91 pp.
NJSL copy.   23611

New Jersey. General Assembly Journals,
1792.

Votes and Proceedings of the Sixteenth
General Assembly. . . . Second Sitting
[May 15 - June 2, 1792]. 45 pp.
NJSL copy.   24594

New Jersey. General Assembly Journals,
1792.
Votes and Proceedings of the Seventeenth
General Assembly. . . . First Sitting [Oct.
23 - Nov. 30, 1792].
Trenton, Collins, 1793. 98 pp.
NJSL copy.   25888

New Jersey. General Assembly Journals,
1793.
Votes and Proceedings of the Seventeenth
General Assembly. . . . Second Sitting
[May 15 - June 6, 1793].
Trenton, Day & Hopkins, 1793. pp. [99]
149.
NJSL copy.   25889

New Jersey. General Assembly Journals,
1793.
Votes and Proceedings of the Eighteenth
General Assembly. . . . Being the First
[-Third] Sitting [Oct. 22, 1793-June 20,
1794].
Burlington, Neale, 1794. 134, 17 pp., 1
folded table.
(No copy available, 1969.)   27390

New Jersey. General Assembly Journals,
1794.
Votes and Proceedings of the Nineteenth
General Assembly. . . . Being the First
[-Second] Sitting [Oct. 28, 1794-Mar. 19,
1795].
Elizabethtown, Kollock, [1795]. 104,
75 pp.
NJSL copy.   29176

New Jersey. General Assembly Journals,
1795.
Votes and Proceedings of the Twentieth
General Assembly. . . . Being the First
Sitting [Oct. 27 - Nov. 25, 1795].
Trenton, Collins, 1795. 86 pp.
NJSL copy.   29177

New Jersey. General Assembly Journals,
1796.
Votes and Proceedings of the Twentieth
General Assembly. . . . Second Sitting
[Feb. 3 - Mar. 18, 1796].
Trenton, Collins, 1796. 66 pp.
(Not located, 1968.)   47851

New Jersey. General Assembly Journals,
1796.
Votes and Proceedings of the
Twenty-First General Assembly. . . . First
Sitting [Oct. 25-Nov. 17, 1796].
Trenton, Day, 1796. 95 pp.
(Not located, 1968.)   47852

New Jersey. General Assembly Journals,
1797.
Votes and Proceedings of the
Twenty-First General Assembly. . . .
Being the Second Sitting [Jan. 25 - Mar.
10, 1797].
Trenton, Day, 1797. 72 pp.
LOC copy.   32546

New Jersey. General Assembly Journals,
1797.
Votes and Proceedings of the
Twenty-Second General Assembly. . . .
Being the First Sitting [Oct. 24-Nov. 10,
1797].
Trenton, Day, 1797. 73 pp.
(Not located, 1968.)   48192

New Jersey. General Assembly Journals,
1798.
Votes and Proceedings of the
Twenty-Second General Assembly. . . .
Being the Second Sitting. [Jan. 17 - Mar.
16, 1798.]
Trenton, Day, 1798. 76 pp.
LCP copy.   34202

New Jersey. General Assembly Journals,
1798.
Votes and Proceedings of the Twenty-Third
General Assembly. . . . Being the First
Sitting [Oct. 23 - Nov. 8, 1798].
Trenton, Day, 1798. 64 pp., fold. table.
(Not located, 1968.)   48525

New Jersey. General Assembly Journals,
1799.

Votes and Proceedings of the
Twenty-Third General Assembly. . . .
Being the Second Sitting [Jan. 16 - Feb.
21, 1799].
Trenton, Sherman, Mershon & Thomas
for Day, 1799. 63 pp.
LCP copy.   35902

New Jersey. General Assembly Journals,
1799.
Votes and Proceedings of the
Twenty-Third General Assembly . . .
Being the Third Sitting [May 21 - June 13,
1799].
Trenton, Sherman, Mershon & Thomas
for Day, 1799. 44 pp.
LCP copy.   35903

New Jersey. General Assembly Journals,
1799.
Votes and Proceedings of the
Twenty-Fourth General Assembly [Oct.
22 - Nov. 21, 1799].
Trenton, Craft, [1799]. 100 pp.
LCP copy.   35904

New Jersey. General Assembly Journals,
1800.
Votes and Proceedings of the
Twenty-Fifth General Assembly. . . .
Being the First Sitting [Oct. 28 - Nov. 20,
1800.]
Trenton, Sherman, Mershon & Thomas,
1800. 88 pp.
NJSL copy.   38065

New Jersey, Governor, 1776.
Burlington Nov. 1776. Sir, General
Howe. . . .
[Burlington, 1776.] Broadside.
LOC copy.   14916

New Jersey. Governor, 1777.
By His Excellency, William Livingston.
. . . A Proclamation. Whereas by a Certain
Act. . . . [Aug. 14, 1777.]
LOC copy.   43306

New Jersey. Governor, 1777.
By His Excellency William Livingston. . . .
A Proclamation [Traitors. Feb. 5, 1777].
[Burlington, 1777.] Broadside.
NYHS copy.   15462

New Jersey. Governor, 1777.
Speech of His Excellency William
Livingston . . . to the . . . Council, and the
General Assembly. . . . 25th February,
1777.
[Burlington, 1777.] [4] pp.
LCP copy.   15464

New Jersey. Governor, 1777.
To the Officers and Soldiers. . . . Geo.
Washington. . . . Wil. Livingston. . . .
Nov. 23, 1777.
[Burlington, 1777.] Broadside.
HSP copy.   15465

New Jersey. Governor, 1778.
Lancaster, June 11, 1778. Extracts from
. . . Governor Livingston's Message. . . .
May 29, 1778.
Lancaster, Dunlap, [1778]. Broadside.
LOC copy.   43507

New Jersey. Governor, 1783.
By His Excellency William Livingston . . .
Proclamation. Whereas the United
States. . . . [Nov. 11, 1783.]
Trenton, Collins, [1783]. Broadside.
HEH copy.   44415

New Jersey. Governor, 1789.
By His Excellency William Livingston. . . .
Proclamation [Thanksgiving, Nov. 26].
[Trenton], Collins, [1789.] Broadside.
NJHS copy.   45532

[New Jersey. Governor, 1795.
By His Excellency, Richard Howell . . .
Proclamation . . . Thanksgiving [Nov. 25.
Dated Nov. 10, 1795].
Trenton, Day, 1795. Broadside.]
(No broadside printing located.)   29174

New Jersey. Laws, Statutes, etc., 1776.
Acts of the General Assembly . . . from
. . . 1702, to . . . 1776.
Burlington, 1776. viii, 493, [1], 6, 6, 4, 4,
3, [1], 15 pp.
AAS copy.   14911

New Jersey. Laws, Statutes, etc., 1776.
An Ordinance for Regulating the Militia
. . . October, 1775.
Burlington, 1776. 35 pp.
HEH copy.   14917

New Jersey. Laws, Statutes, etc., 1777.
[An Act for purchasing clothing, passed
Nov. 27, 1777.]
n. p., 1777.]
(Sabin 53142; no copy known.)   43307

New Jersey. Laws, Statutes, etc., 1777.
An Act for the Better Regulating the
Militia.
[Burlington, 1777.] 14 pp.
LCP copy.   15458

New Jersey. Laws, Statutes, etc., 1778.
An Act for Recovering Arrears of Certain
Taxes. . . . December 7, 1778.
n.p., [1778]. Broadside.
(No copy located.)   43508

New Jersey. Laws, Statutes, etc., 1778.
. . . An Act for Taking Charge of . . . Real
Estate. . . . [Dated Apr. 18, 1778.]
[Trenton, 1778.] [4] pp.
HEH copy.   43509

New Jersey. Laws, Statutes, etc., 1779.
. . . An Act for Procuring Provisions for
the Use of the Army.
[Trenton? 1779.] [2] pp.
NYPL copy.   43668

New Jersey. Laws, Statutes, etc., 1779.
. . . An Act to Procure a Supply of
Flour. . . . Sept. 27, 1779.
[Trenton, 1779.] Broadside.
CHS copy.   43669

New Jersey. Laws, Statutes, etc., 1780.
. . . An Act for Compleating the Quota of
Troops. . . . March 11, 1780.
[Trenton, 1780.] Broadside.
LOC copy.   43848

New Jersey. Laws, Statutes, etc., 1780.
. . . An Act for Completing and Keeping
up the Quota. . . . December 26, 1780.
[Trenton, 1780.] [2] pp.
LOC copy.   43847

New Jersey. Laws, Statutes, etc., 1780.
. . . An Act for Procuring Provisions for
the Use of the Army.
[Trenton, 1780.] Broadside.
(No copy located.)   43849

New Jersey. Laws, Statutes, etc., 1780.
. . . An Act to Compleat the Three
Regiments. . . . June 14th, 1780.
Trenton, Collins, [1780]. Broadside.
LOC copy.   43850

New Jersey. Laws, Statutes, etc., 1780.
. . . An Act to Raise and Embody . . . Six
Hundred and Twenty-Four Men.
[Trenton, 1780.] [2] pp.
(The only known copy is imperfect.)
LOC copy.   43851

New Jersey. Laws, Statutes, etc., 1780.
. . . A Supplemental Act to the Act,
Intituled, An Act for Procuring
Provisions. . . . March 18, 1780.
[Trenton, 1780.] 2 pp.
LOC copy.   43852

New Jersey. Laws, Statutes, etc., 1784.
Acts of the Council and General
Assembly.
Trenton, 1784. x, 389, [1], 28, 4, 4,
30 pp.
AAS copy.   18632

New Jersey. Laws, Statutes, etc., 1787.
An Act for Laying an Excise on Sundry
Articles. . . . June 4, 1787.
[Trenton, 1787.] 8 pp.
(No copy could be reproduced.)   45108

[New Jersey. Laws, Statutes, etc., 1790.
An Act to Ascertain the Sums to be
Raised . . . for . . . 1790.
New Brunswick, Blauvelt, 1790.]
(The origin of this entry is unknown.)
                                          22709

[New Jersey. Laws, Statutes, etc., 1791.
An Act Incorporating the Society for
Establishing Useful Manufactures. Passed

at Trenton, 22d November, 1791.
Burlington, Neale, 1791.|
(Entry from an adv.)   23609

New Jersey. Laws, Statutes, etc., 1794.
. . . An Act more Effectually to Prevent
the Waste of Timber. . . . June 13, 1783.
[Trenton, 1794.] Broadside.
(Not located, 1968.)   47127

New Jersey. Laws, Statutes, etc., 1794.
. . . An Act to Alter the Mode of
Collecting Militia Fines. . . . June 20,
1794.
[Trenton, 1794.] Broadside.
(The only known copy is imperfect.)
NYPL copy.   47128

New Jersey. Laws, Statutes, etc., 1794.
. . . An Act to Authorize the Commander
in Chief. . . . June 20, 1794.
[Trenton, 1794.] 4 pp.
LOC copy.   47129

New Jersey. Laws, Statutes, etc., 1794.
[An Act to prevent the cutting of Timber
on unlocated lands, passed Feb. 10, 1784.
Trenton, 1794. Broadside.]
(Morsch 237; no copy known.)   47130

New Jersey. Laws, Statutes, etc., 1794.
. . . An Additional Supplement to an Act,
Intitled, "An Act for Regulating Roads
and Bridges." . . . Passed . . . February 21,
1794.
[Trenton, 1794.] 4 pp.
NYPL copy.   27386

New Jersey. Laws, Statutes, etc., 1794.
Laws for Regulating the Militia.
Philadelphia, Cist, 1794. 39 pp.
HEH copy.   47131

New Jersey. Laws, Statutes, etc., 1796.
. . . A Bill, Intitled, An Act Concerning
Sheriffs.
[Trenton? 1796?] 16 pp.
(Not located, 1968.)   47853

New Jersey. Laws, Statutes, etc., 1797.
An Additional Supplement to an Act . . .
for . . . the Militia [Mar. 9, 1797.]
[Trenton, 1797.] 23 pp.
HEH copy.   48193

New Jersey. Laws, Statutes, etc., 1798.
An Act . . . Authorizing Justices of the
Peace. . . .
Morristown, Mann, 1798. [2], 23 pp.
HEH copy.   48526

New Jersey. Laws, Statutes, etc., 1798.
. . . An Act Incorporating the Inhabitants
of Townships. . . . February 21, 1798.
[Trenton, 1798.] 14 pp.
(The unique copy is mislaid.)   34200

New Jersey. Laws, Statutes, etc., 1798.
. . . An Act, Respecting Slaves. . . . Passed
at Trenton, March 14, 1798.
Trenton, Croft, [1798]. 16 pp.
NYPL copy.   34201

New Jersey. Laws, Statutes, etc., 1798.
. . . An Act to Incorporate the Chosen
Freeholders.
[Trenton, 1798.] pp. 270-279.
CU-L copy.   48527

New Jersey. Laws, Statutes, etc., 1799.
An Act for the Regulation of the Militia.
Trenton, Sherman, Mershon & Thomas,
1799. 48 pp.
NYPL copy.   35893

New Jersey. Laws, Statutes, etc., 1799.
. . . An Act, to Regulate the Practice of
the Courts of Law.
[Trenton? 1799.] 16 pp.
NYHS copy.   35901

New Jersey. Laws, Statutes, etc., 1800.
Laws of the State of New Jersey.
New Brunswick, Blauvelt, 1800. [2], xxi,
[1], 455, [33] pp.
AAS copy.   38064

New Jersey. Laws, Statutes, etc., 1800.
Laws of the State of New-Jersey.
Newark, Day, 1800. [2], 455, [1], xxi,
[1], 2, 46, [1] pp.
AAS copy.   38063

New Jersey. Legislative Council Journals,
1776.
A Journal of the Proceedings [Aug. 27,
1776 - June 7, 1777].
Burlington, Collins, 1777. 95 pp.
NYHS copy.   43308

New Jersey. Legislative Council Journals,
1777.
Journal of the Proceedings of the
Legislative Council [Sept. 3 - Oct. 11,
1777].
Burlington, Collins, 1777. pp. [97] - 126.
NJSL copy.   15463

New Jersey. Legislative Council Journals,
1777.
Journal of the Proceedings of the
Legislative Council [Sept. 3 - Oct. 11,
1777].
Trenton, 1779. pp. [4], 101-126.
LOC copy.   16396

New Jersey. Legislative Council Journals,
1777.
Journal of the Proceedings of the
Legislative-Council [Oct. 28, 1777 - Oct. 8,
1778].
Trenton, 1779. 114 pp.
LOC copy.   16397

New Jersey. Legislative Council Journals,
1778.
A Journal of the Proceedings of the
Legislative-Council . . . Third Session
[Oct. 27, 1778 - Oct. 9, 1779].
Trenton, 1780. 106 pp.
NYPL copy.   16887

New Jersey. Legislative Council Journals,
1779.
A Journal of the Proceedings of the
Legislative Council. . . . First [and
Second] Sitting of the Fourth Session
[Oct. 26, 1779 - Mar. 21, 1780].
Trenton, 1780. 73 pp.
NYPL copy.   16888

New Jersey. Legislative Council Journals,
1780.
A Journal and Proceedings of the
Legislative-Council. . . . Third and Fourth
Sitting of the Fourth Session [May 10 -
Oct. 7, 1780].
Trenton, 1780. pp. [2], 77-126.
NYPL copy.   16889

New Jersey. Legislative Council Journals,
1780.
A Journal of the Proceedings of the
Legislative-Council. . . . First Sitting of
the Fifth Session [Oct. 24, 1780-Jan. 9,
1781].
Trenton, 1781. 70, [1] pp.
NYPL copy.   17262

New Jersey. Legislative Council Journals,
1781.
A Journal of the Proceedings of the
Legislative-Council. . . . Second, and
Third Sittings of the Fifth Session [May
15 - Oct. 6, 1781.].
Trenton, 1781. 50 pp.
NYPL copy.   17263

New Jersey. Legislative Council Journals,
1781.
Journal of the Proceedings of the
Legislative-Council. . . . First Sitting of
the Sixth Session [Oct. 23-Dec. 29, 1781].
Trenton, 1782. 37 pp.
NYPL copy.   17623

New Jersey. Legislative Council Journals,
1782.
A Journal of the Proceedings of the
Legislative-Council. . . . Second and Third
Sittings of the Sixth Session [May 15-Oct.
5, 1782].
Trenton, 1782. 39 pp.
NYPL copy.   17624

New Jersey. Legislative Council Journals,
1782.
A Journal of the Proceedings of the
Legislative-Council. . . . First Sitting of
the Seventh Session [Oct. 22-Dec. 26,
1782].
Trenton, 1783. 38 pp.
NYPL copy.   18052

New Jersey. Legislative Council Journals,
1783.

Journal of the Proceedings of the
Legislative-Council. . . . Second Sitting of
the Seventh Session [May 15-June 19,
1783].
Trenton, 1783. pp. [2], 41-69.
NYPL copy.   18053

New Jersey. Legislative Council Journals,
1783.
Journal of the Proceedings of the
Legislative-Council. . . . First Sitting of
the Eighth Session [Oct. 28 - Dec. 24,
1783].
Trenton, 1784. 60 pp.
NYPL copy.   18636

New Jersey. Legislative Council Journals,
1784.
Journal of the Proceedings of the
Legislative Council. . . . Second Sitting of
the Eighth Session.
[Aug. 5 - Sept. 2, 1784].
Trenton, 1784. 26 pp.
NYPL copy.   18637

New Jersey. Legislative Council Journals,
1784.
Journal of the Proceedings of the
Legislative Council. . . . First Sitting of
the Ninth Session [Oct. 27 - Dec. 21,
1784].
Trenton, 1785. 53 pp.
NYPL copy.   19122

New Jersey. Legislative Council Journals,
1785.
Journal of the Proceedings of the
Legislative - Council. . . . First Sitting of
the Tenth Session [Oct. 25 - Nov. 29,
1785].
Trenton, 1785. 37 pp.
NYPL copy.   19123

New Jersey. Legislative Council Journals,
1786.
Journal of the Proceedings of the
Legislative-Council. . . . Second Sitting of
the Tenth Session [Feb. 15-Mar. 24,
1786].
Trenton, 1786. 48 pp.
NYPL copy.   19836

New Jersey. Legislative Council Journals,
1786.
Journal of the Proceedings of the
Legislative-Council. . . . Third Sitting of
the Tenth Session [May 17 - June 2,
1786].
Trenton, 1786. 16 pp.
NYPL copy.   19837

New Jersey. Legislative Council Journals,
1786.
Journal of the Proceedings of the
Legislative-Council. . . . First Sitting of
the Eleventh Session.
Trenton, 1786. 36 pp.
NYPL copy.   19838

New Jersey, Legislative Council Journals,
1787.
Journal of the Proceedings of the
Legislative-Council . . . Second Sitting of
the Eleventh Session [May 16 - June 7,
1787].
Trenton, 1787. 26 pp.
NYPL copy.   20566

New Jersey. Legislative Council Journals,
1787.
Journal of the Proceedings of the
Legislative-Council. . . . [Oct. 23 - Nov. 7,
1787].
Trenton, 1787. 26 pp.
NYPL copy.   20567

New Jersey. Legislative Council Journals,
1788.
Journal of the Proceedings of the
Legislative-Council. . . . Second Sitting of
the Twelfth Session.
Trenton, 1788. 18 pp.
NYPL copy.   21300

New Jersey. Legislative Council Journals,
1788.
Journal of the Proceedings of the
Legislative-Council [Oct. 28 - Dec. 1,
1788].
Trenton, Collins, 1788. 35 pp.
NYPL copy.   21301

New Jersey. Legislative Council Journals, 1789.
A Journal of the Proceedings of the Legislative Council [Oct. 27 - Dec. 1, 1789].
New Brunswick. Blauvelt, 1789.
43 pp.
NYPL copy.   22004

New Jersey. Legislative Council Journals, 1790.
Journal and Proceedings [May 18-June 12, 1790].
New Brusnwick, Blauvelt, 1790. 33 pp.
(The Evans entry is garbled.)
LOC copy.   22712

New Jersey. Legislative Council Journals, 1790.
A Journal of the Proceedings [Oct. 26 - Nov. 26, 1790.]
Burlington, Neale & Lawrence, 1790.
39 pp.
NJSL copy.   22713

New Jersey. Legislative Council Journals, 1791.
A Journal of the Proceedings of the Legislative-Council [Oct. 25 - Nov. 25, 1791].
Burlington, Neale, 1791. 30 pp.
NJSL copy.   23610

New Jersey. Legislative Council Journals, 1792.
Journal and Proceedings of the Legislative-Council [May 15 - June 2, 1792].
Burlington, Neale, 1792. 24 pp.
NYPL copy.   24593

New Jersey. Legislative Council Journals, 1792.
Journal of the Proceedings of the Legislative Council. . . . The First Sitting [and second] of the Seventeenth Session [Oct. 23, 1792 - June 6, 1793].
Trenton, Collins, 1793. 40, 23 pp.
NJSL copy.   25887

New Jersey. Legislative Council Journals, 1793.
Journal of the Proceedings of the Legislative-Council. . . . Being the First and Second Sittings of the Eighteenth Session [Oct. 22, 1793 - Feb. 21, 1794].
Trenton, Day, 1794. 48 pp.
NYPL copy.   27389

New Jersey. Legislative Council Journals, 1794.
Journal of the Proceedings of the Legislative-Council. . . . Being the First [-Second] Sitting of the Nineteenth Session [Oct. 28, 1794-Mar. 19, 1795].
Trenton, Collins, 1795. 36, 48 pp.
NJSL copy.   29175

New Jersey. Legislative Council Journals, 1794.
Journal of the Proceedings of the Legislative-Council. . . . Being the Third Sitting of the Eighteenth Session [June 11-20, 1794].
Trenton, Collins, 1795. 12 pp.
LCP copy.   47508

New Jersey. Legislative Council Journals, 1795.
Journal of the Proceedings of the Legislative-Council . . . being the First and Second Sittings of the Twentieth Session [Oct. 27, 1795 - Mar. 18, 1796].
Trenton, Day, 1796. [2], 69 pp.
(Evans assumed the title from a defective copy.)
NYPL copy.   30862

New Jersey. Legislative Council Journals, 1797.
Journal of the Proceedings of the Legislative-Council. . . . Being the First and Second Sittings of the Twenty-First Session [Oct. 25, 1796 - Mar. 3, 1797].
Trenton, Day, 1797. pp. 87-93.
(Not located, 1968.)   48194

New Jersey. Legislative Council Journals, 1798.
Journal of the Proceedings of the Legislative-Council. . . . Being the First and Second Sittings of the Twenty-Second Session [Oct. 24, 1797 +].

Trenton, Day, 1798. 83 pp.
(Best available copy lacks title page.)
LCP copy.   48528

New Jersey. Legislative Council Journals, 1798.
Journal of the Proceedings of the Legislative-Council. . . . Being the First and Second Sittings of the Twenty-Third Session [Oct. 23, 1798 - Feb. 21, 1799.]
Trenton, Day, 1799. 56 pp.
LCP copy.   35898

New Jersey. Legislative Council Journals, 1799.
Journal of the Proceedings of the Legislative-Council. . . . Being the Third Sitting of the Twenty-Third Session [May 21 - June 13, 1799].
Trenton, Sherman, Mershon & Thomas for Day, 1799. 42 pp.
LCP copy.   35899

New Jersey. Legislative Council Journals, 1799.
Journal of the Proceedings of the Legislative-Council. . . . Being the First Sitting of the Twenty-Fourth Session [Oct. 22 - Nov. 21, 1799].
Trenton, Sherman, Mershon & Thomas, 1799. 47 pp.
LCP copy.   35900

New Jersey. Legislature, 1779.
Gentlemen, the Legislative Council and General Assembly . . . by Leave. . . .
September 29, 1779.
[Trenton, 1779.] Broadside.
HEH copy.   43670

New Jersey. Legislature, 1798.
. . . A Bill, Intitled, "An Act Constituting Courts for the Trial of Small Causes."
[Trenton, 1798.] 15 pp.
NYPL copy.   48529

New Jersey. Legislature, 1798.
. . . A Bill, Intitled, "An Act Granting Relief . . . against Collusive Judgments. . . ."
[Trenton, 1798]. 4 pp.
NYPL copy.   48530

New Jersey. Legislature, 1798.
. . . A Bill, intituled, "An Act making Provision for Carrying into Effect the Act for the Punishment of Crime. . . ."
[Trenton, 1798.] 7 pp.
(Morsch 390; no copy known.)   48531

New Jersey. Legislature, 1798.
. . . A Bill, intitled, "An Act Making Provision for Working . . . the Highways. . . ."
[Trenton, 1798.] 6 pp.
(Copy is imperfect.)
NYPL copy.   48532

New Jersey. Legislature. Journals, 1776.
Minutes and Proceedings of the Council and General Assembly in Joint Meeting [Aug. 30, 1776 - May, 1780].
Trenton, 1780. 34 pp.
LOC copy.   16890

New Jersey. Militia, 1796.
Brigade Orders. August 1st, 1796.
n.p., [1796]. Broadside.
(Not located, 1968.)   47854

New Jersey. Provincial Congress, 1775.
Extracts from the Journal of Proceedings.
Burlington, 1775. [2], 42 pp.
NYPL copy.   14282

New Jersey. Provincial Congress, 1775.
In Provincial Congress, at Trenton, New-Jersey, June 3, 1775.
New York, Holt, [1775]. 2 pp.
NYPL copy.   14283

New Jersey. Provincial Congress, 1775.
Journal of the Votes and Proceedings . . . in . . . October, 1775.
Burlington, 1775. 78, [1] pp.
NYPL copy.   14284

New Jersey. Provincial Congress, 1776.
In Provincial Congress, New-Jersey, Burlington, June 16, 1776. . . . Five Battalions.

[Burlington, 1776.] Broadside.
NJHS copy.   43098

New Jersey. Provincial Congress, 1776.
Journal of the Votes and Proceedings [Jan. 31 - Mar. 2, 1776.].
New York, Anderson, 1776. 146, [1] pp.
LOC copy.   14913

New Jersey. Session Laws, 1776.
Acts of the General Assembly [Sept. 13, 1776 - Mar. 17, 1777].
Burlington, 1777. x, 48 pp.
LOC copy.   15459

New Jersey. Session Laws, 1777.
Acts of the General Assembly [May 12 - June 7, 1777].
Burlington, 1777. pp. [2], 51-80.
LOC copy.   15460

New Jersey. Session Laws, 1777.
Acts of the General Assembly [Sept. 20 - Oct. 11, 1777].
Burlington, 1777. pp. 81-128.
LOC copy.   15461

New Jersey. Session Laws, 1777.
Acts of the General Assembly [Nov. 25 - Dec. 12, 1777].
Burlington, 1778. 24, [2] pp.
NYPL copy.   15926

New Jersey. Session Laws, 1778.
Acts of the General Assembly [Feb. 21 - Apr. 18, 1778].
Trenton, 1778. pp. 27-84.
NYPL copy.   15927

New Jersey. Session Laws, 1778.
Acts of the General Assembly [June 17 - 22, 1778].
[Trenton, 1778.] pp. 85-91.
NYPL copy.   15928

New Jersey. Session Laws, 1778.
Acts of the General Assembly [Sept. 24 - Oct. 8, 1778].
Trenton, 1778. pp. 93-109.
NYPL copy.   15929

New Jersey. Session Laws, 1778.
Acts of the General Assembly [Nov. 20 - Dec. 12, 1778].
Trenton, 1779. 45, [1] pp.
NYPL copy.   16393

New Jersey. Session Laws, 1779.
Acts of the General Assembly [May 22 - June 12, 1779].
Trenton, 1779. pp. 47-124.
NYPL copy.   16394

New Jersey. Session Laws, 1779.
Acts of the General Assembly [Sept. 27 - Oct. 7, 1779].
Trenton, 1779. pp. 125-139, [1] pp.
NYPL copy.   16395

New Jersey. Session Laws, 1779.
Acts of the General Assembly. . . . First Sitting of the Fourth Assembly [Oct. 26 - Dec. 25, 1779].
Trenton, 1780. 54 pp.
NYPL copy.   16883

New Jersey. Session Laws, 1780.
Acts of the General Assembly [Feb. 26 - Mar., 1780].
Trenton, 1780. pp. 56-76, [1].
LOC copy.   16884

New Jersey. Session Laws, 1780.
Acts of the General Assembly [May 24 - June 19, 1780].
Trenton, 1780. pp. 79-126.
LOC copy.   16885

New Jersey. Session Laws, 1780.
Acts of the General Assembly [Sept. 29 - Oct. 7, 1780].
Trenton, 1780. pp. 127-139, [1].
LOC copy.   16886

New Jersey. Session Laws, 1781.
Acts of the Fifth General Assembly [Nov. 15, 1780 - Jan. 9, 1781].
Trenton, 1781. 67 pp.
NYPL copy.   17259

New Jersey. Session Laws, 1781.
Acts of the Fifth General Assembly. . . .

The Second Sitting [May 24 - June 28,
1781].
Trenton, 1781. pp. 69-118, [1].
NYPL copy.   17260

New Jersey. Session Laws, 1781.
Acts of the Fifth General Assembly....
Third Sitting [Sept. 21 - Oct. 6, 1781].
Trenton, 1781. pp. 119-136.
NYPL copy.   17261

New Jersey. Session Laws, 1781.
Acts of the Sixth General Assembly....
Third Sitting [Sept. 18 - Oct. 5, 1782].
Trenton, Collins, 1782. pp. [115] - 126.
NJSL copy.   17622

New Jersey. Session Laws, 1781.
Acts of the Sixth General Assembly....
First Sitting [Nov. 2 - Dec. 29, 1781].
Trenton, 1782. 61 pp.
NYPL copy.   17620

New Jersey. Session Laws, 1782.
Acts of the Sixth General Assembly....
Second Sitting [May 27 - June 24, 1782].
Trenton, 1782. pp. 63-114.
NYPL copy.   17621

New Jersey. Session Laws, 1782.
Acts of the Seventh General
Assembly.... First Sitting.
[Nov. 6-Dec. 26, 1782].
Trenton, 1783. 28 pp.
NYPL copy.   18050

New Jersey. Session Laws, 1783.
Acts of the Seventh General
Assembly.... Second Sitting [May 27 -
June 19, 1783].
Trenton, 1783. pp. 29-76, [1].
NYPL copy.   18051

New Jersey. Session Laws, 1783.
Acts of the Eighth General Assembly
[Nov. 11 - Dec. 24, 1783].
Trenton, 1784. 72, [1] pp.
NYPL copy.   18633

New Jersey. Session Laws, 1784.
Acts of the Eighth General Assembly....
Second Sitting [Aug., 30 - Sept. 2, 1784].
Trenton, 1784. pp. [2], 75-121,
[1].
NYPL copy.   18634

New Jersey. Session Laws, 1784.
Acts of the Ninth General Assembly....
First Sitting [Nov. 4 - Dec. 24, 1784].
Trenton, 1784. pp. 123-186, [1].
NYPL copy.   18635

New Jersey. Session Laws, 1785.
Acts of the Tenth General Assembly....
The First Sitting [Nov. 5 - 29, 1785].
Trenton, 1785. pp. 189-230. [1].
NYPL copy.   19121

New Jersey. Session Laws, 1786.
Acts of the Tenth General Assembly....
Second Sitting [Feb. 20 - Mar. 23, 1786].
Trenton, 1786. pp. [233] - 288,
[1].
NYPL copy.   19833

New Jersey. Session Laws, 1786.
Acts of the Tenth General Assembly....
Third Sitting [May 26 - June 2, 1786].
Trenton, 1786. pp. [291] - 334.
NYPL copy.   19834

New Jersey. Session Laws, 1786.
Acts of the Eleventh General
Assembly.... First Sitting [Nov. 2 - 24,
1786].
Trenton, 1786. pp. [335] - 383,
[1].
NYPL copy.   19835

New Jersey. Session Laws, 1787.
Acts of the Eleventh General
Assembly.... Being the Second Sitting
[May 24 - June 7, 1787].
Trenton, 1787. pp. 385-435, [1].
NYPL copy.   20564

New Jersey. Session Laws, 1787.
Acts of the Twelfth General Assembly
[Oct. 30 - Nov. 6, 1787].
Trenton, 1787. pp. 437-452.
NYPL copy.   20565

New Jersey. Session Laws, 1788.

Acts of the Twelfth General
Assembly.... Second Sitting.
Trenton, 1788. pp. [453]-470.
NYPL copy.   21298

New Jersey. Session Laws, 1788.
Acts of the Thirteenth General
Assembly.... First Sitting.
Trenton, Collins, 1788. pp. [471]-514, [1].
NYPL copy.   21299

New Jersey. Session Laws, 1789.
Acts of the Fourteenth General Assembly
[Nov. 7 - Dec. 1, 1789].
New Brunswick, Blauvelt, 1789. pp. [2],
515-579.
NYPL copy.   22003

New Jersey. Session Laws, 1790.
Acts of the Fourteenth General
Assembly.... Second Sitting [May 25 -
June 12, 1790].
New Brunswick, Blauvelt, 1790. pp.
[581]-657.
NYPL copy.   22710

New Jersey. Session Laws, 1790.
Acts of the Fifteenth General
Assembly.... First Sitting [Nov. 8-26,
1790].
Burlington, Neale & Lawrence, 1790. pp.
[659]-716.
NYPL copy.   22711

New Jersey. Session Laws, 1791.
Acts of the Sixteenth General
Assembly.... First Sitting [Nov. 5-25,
1791].
Burlington, Neale, 1791. pp. [2], 720-763,
[1].
NYPL copy.   23608

New Jersey. Session Laws, 1792.
Acts of the Sixteenth General
Assembly.... Second Sitting [May 18 -
June 2, 1792].
Burlington, Neale, 1792. pp. [764]-814,
[1].
NYPL copy.   24591

New Jersey. Session Laws, 1792.
Acts of the Seventeenth General
Assembly.... First Sitting [Oct. 31 -
Nov. 30, 1792].
Trenton, Collins, 1792. pp. [781]-829, [1].
NYPL copy.   24592

New Jersey. Session Laws, 1793.
Acts of the Seventeenth General
Assembly.... Being the Second Sitting
[May 21 - June 6, 1793].
Trenton, Collins, 1793. pp. [831] - 870,
[2] pp.
NYPL copy.   25886

New Jersey. Session Laws, 1793.
Acts of the Eighteenth General
Assembly.... Being the First and Second
Sittings [Oct. 22, 1793 - Feb. 21, 1794].
Trenton, Collins, 1794. pp. [873]-914.
HC copy.   27385

New Jersey. Session Laws, 1794.
Acts of the Eighteenth General
Assembly.... Being the Third Sitting
[June 1794].
Trenton, Day, 1794. pp. [915]-922.
NYPL photocopy.   27387

New Jersey. Session Laws, 1794.
Acts of the Nineteenth General
Assembly.... Being the First [-Second]
Sitting [Oct. 28, 1794-Mar. 19, 1795].
Trenton, Day, 1795. pp. [923]-1081.
NJSL copy.   29172

New Jersey. Session Laws, 1795.
Acts of the Twentieth General
Assembly.... Being the First Sitting
[Oct. 27 - Nov. 25, 1795].
Trenton, Day, 1795. 21 pp.
LOC copy.   29173

New Jersey. Session Laws, 1796.
Acts of the Twentieth General
Assembly.... Being the Second Sitting
[Feb. 1796].
Trenton, Day, 1796. pp. [23]-114.
LOC copy.   30860

New Jersey. Session Laws, 1796.
Acts of the Twenty-First General

Assembly.... Being the First Sitting
[Oct. 1796].
Trenton, Day, 1796. pp. [115]-125, [1].
LOC copy.   30861

New Jersey. Session Laws, 1797.
Acts of the Twenty-First General
Assembly.... Being the Second Sitting
[Jan., 1797].
Trenton, Day, 1797. pp. [127]-138.
LOC copy.   32544

New Jersey. Session Laws, 1797.
Acts of the Twenty-Second General
Assembly.... Being the First Sitting
[Oct., 1797].
Trenton, Day, 1797. pp. [239]-256, ix, [1].
LOC copy.   32545

New Jersey. Session Laws, 1797.
Acts of the Twenty-Second General
Assembly.... Being the Second Sitting
[Oct. 1797].
Trenton, Day, 1798. Pp. [257]-412.
LOC copy.   34199

New Jersey. Session Laws, 1798.
Acts of the Twenty-Third General
Assembly.... Being the First Sitting.
Trenton, Craft, 1798. pp. [2], 415-421.
(Not located, 1968.)   48533

New Jersey. Session Laws, 1798.
Acts of the Twenty-Third General
Assembly.... Being the Second Sitting
[Oct., 1798].
Trenton, Craft, 1799. pp. [2], 425-510.
HEH copy.   35894

New Jersey. Session Laws, 1799.
Acts of the Twenty-Third General
Assembly.... Being the Third Sitting
[May, 1799].
Trenton, Croft, 1799. pp. [511]-637.
HEH copy.   35895

New Jersey. Session Laws, 1799.
Acts of the Twenty-Fourth General
Assembly [Oct., 1799].
Trenton, Sherman, Mershon & Thomas,
1799. pp. [639]-663.
NYPL copy.   35896

New Jersey. Session Laws, 1800.
Acts of the Twenty-Fifth General
Assembly.... Being the First Sitting
[Oct., 1800].
Trenton, Sherman, Mershon & Thomas,
1800. 29, [2] pp.
LCP copy.   38062

New Jersey. Supreme Court.
Cases Adjudged in the Supreme Court ...
Relative to the Manumission of Negroes.
Burlington, Neale, 1794. 32 pp.
LCP copy.   27391

The New-Jersey Almanack ... for ...
1768.
New York, Parker. [32] pp.
(The only known copies are imperfect.)
AAS copy.   10798

The New-Jersey Almanack for ... 1769.
New York, Parker. [22] pp.
(The only copy located apparently lacks
the final leaf.)
AAS copy.   11109

The New-Jersey and New-York Almanac,
for ... 1800.
Newark, Day for Davis. [36] pp.
(Also entered as 36302, q. v.)   35905

The New-Jersey and Pennsylvania
Almanac, for ... 1793.
Burlington, Neale. [48] pp.
AAS copy.   46521

The New-Jersey and Pennsylvania
Almanac, for ... 1796.
Trenton, Day. [36] pp.
NJSL copy.   29178

The New-Jersey and Pennsylvania
Almanac, for ... 1797.
Trenton, Day. [40] pp.
LOC copy.   30865

The New-Jersey and Pennsylvania
Almanac, for ... 1798.
Trenton, N. J., Day. [40] pp.
AAS copy.   32833

The New-Jersey and Pennsylvania
Almanac, for . . . 1800.
Trenton, Sherman, Mershon & Thomas.
[36] pp.
(Also entered as 36305, q. v.)   35906

The New-Jersey and Pennsylvania
Almanac, for . . . 1801.
Trenton, Sherman, Mershon & Thomas.
[36] pp.
(Also entered as 38498, q.v.)   38066

New Jersey, College of
See
Princeton University

New-Jersey Harmony: being the Best
Selection of Psalm Tunes.
Philadelphia, M'Culloch, 1797. 80 pp.
NYPL copy.   32547

New Jersey Infantry. Union Brigade.
Proceedings . . . on the Death of General
Washington.
[New York], Lang's Press, 1800.
36 pp.
AAS copy.   38686

The New-Jersey, Pennsylvania and
Maryland Almanac, for . . . 1796.
Philadelphia, Jacob Johnson. [36] pp.
AAS copy.   47509

The New-Jersey, Pennsylvania, Delaware,
Maryland and Virginia Almanac . . . for
. . . 1790.
Baltimore, Adams [1789]. [48] pp.
(No perfect copy located.)
MdHS copy.   22007

The New-Jersey, Pennsylvania, Delaware,
Maryland and Virginia Almanac . . . for
. . . 1791.
Baltimore, Adams. [48] pp.
AAS copy.   22716

The New-Jersey, Pennsylvania, Delaware,
Maryland and Virginia Almanac . . . for
. . . 1792.
Baltimore, Adams. [36] pp.
(The only copy located is imperfect.)
AAS copy.   23613

The New-Jersey, Pennsylvania, Delaware,
Maryland and Virginia Almanac. . . . For
. . . 1793.
Baltimore, Adams. [36] pp.
MdHS copy.   24596

The New-Jersey Pocket Almanack for . . .
1781.
Trenton, Collins. [24] pp.
Trenton Public Library copy.   17011

New-Jersey Pocket Almanack, for . . .
1782.
Trenton, Collins. [24] pp.
Rutgers University copy.   17381

New-Jersey Pocket Almanack, for . . . 1783.
Trenton, Collins. [24] pp.
AAS copy.   44233

[The New-Jersey Pocket Almanac for
1800.
New Brunswick, N. J., Blauvelt.]
(Title and imprint assumed by Evans.)
   35214

New-Jersey Society for Promoting the
Abolition of Slavery.
The Constitution of. . . . [Four lines
from] Declaration of Independence.
Burlington, Neale, 1793. 14 pp.
LCP copy.   25890

New-Jersey Society for Promoting the
Abolition of Slavery.
The Constitution of the. . . . [Three lines
from] Declaration of Independence.
Burlington, Neale, 1793. 16 pp.
AAS copy.   25891

New Jerusalem Church.
A Catechism for the Use of the New
Church.
Philadelphia, Bailey, 1791. 12 pp.
AAS copy.   46236

New Jerusalem Church. Liturgy and
Ritual.
The Liturgy of the New Church. . . .
Fourth Edition.

Baltimore, Adams, 1792. 342, [2] pp.
AAS copy.   24599

The New Ladies' Memorandum-Book, for
. . . M.DCC.XCIV.
Boston, Thomas & Andrews, etc. 156+
pp., 3 plates.
(This is apparently the item described by
Evans from a Carter adv. The unique copy
is imperfect.)
AAS copy.   27191

A New Liberty Song, Composed at the
Camp at Prospect Hill, August, 1775.
Salem, [Mass.], Russell, [1775].
Broadside.
BPL copy.   42897

New London, Ct. Presbyterian Church.
Funeral Eulogy and Oration.
New London, Ct., Green, 1800. 17, [1] pp.
(Also entered as 37666, q. v.)   38070

New London, Ct. Selectmen.
At a Meeting of the Authority, Selectmen,
&c. . . .
[New London, 1777.] Broadside.
CHS copy.   43309

New London, Ct. Selectmen.
. . . April 1, 1778. Agreeable to an Act . . .
Regulating the Prices. . . .
[New London, 1778.] Broadside.
CHS copy.   43510

[New-London Price Current. Friday,
April 14, 1786.
New London, 1786.]
(Entry from an adv.)   19846

The New Manual and Platoon Exercise
[by Edward Harvey, adjutant-general].
New York, 1769. 19 pp.
JCB copy.   11288

[A New Manual Exercise [by William
Blakeney, 1672-1761].
New York, Gaine, 1759.]
(Known only from ph. of tp. formerly in
LOC.)   8300

[A New Map of South-Carolina and Parts
Adjacent.
Charleston, 1786.]
("Just Published," Columbian Herald,
Mar. 23, 1786. Probably separates of the
map in 19211, q.v.)   19847

[A New Map of that Part of
Massachusetts State which Includes the
Proposed Canal.
Boston, 1795.]
(No copy found.)   29183

A New Map of the Harbour of New York.
[New York, Bradford, 1735]. 12 x 11
inches.
HEH copy.   3922

The New Massachusetts Liberty Song.
[Boston, 1770] Broadside.
HSP copy.   42135

[New Memorandum, Addressed to all
Real Lovers of Liberty.
New York, 1768.]
(Sabin 53273, from an adv.)   11000

[New Memorandum Book. Third Edition.
New York, 1750. [104] pp.]
(Entry from Sabin.)   6563

A New Method of Ejectment . . .
Especially in N. C-r-l-na.
Charleston, [176-?]. Broadside.
NYPL copy.   41103

[A New Method of Keeping Bill-Books
Adapted for the Ease and Convenience of
Merchants.
Philadelphia, Campbell, 1797.]
(Entry from the copyright notice.)   32549

[New Milford, Conn. Union Library.
Constitution and By-laws of the. . . .
[Danbury, 1796.] 16 pp.]
(The origin of this entry is unknown.)
   30868

New news from Robinson Cruso's Island,
in a Letter to a Gentleman at Portsmouth.
Cruso's Island [Boston], 1720. 8 pp.

(See Brinley Cat., 1440.)
BPL copy.   2153

A New Offer to the Lovers of Religion
and Learning [by Cotton Mather,
1663-1728].
[Boston, 1714?] 16 pp.
(For the date see T. J. Holmes, Cotton
Mather, II, 729-730.)
AAS copy.   1468

The New Pennsylvania Almanac, for . . .
1787.
Pennsylvania, Bailey and Steele.
[40] pp.
(The only copy located lacks the final
leaf.)
AAS copy.   19848

The New Pennsylvania Almanac, for . . .
1792.
Philadelphia, Campbell. [32] pp.
NYPL copy.   46237

[A New Pennsylvania Primer [by John
Simmons, fl. 1794].
Philadelphia, 1794.]
(Entry from the copyright notice.)   27704

The New Pennsylvania Spelling-Book.
Norristown, [Pa.], Sower, 1799. 156 pp.
LCP copy.   35910

A New Pilgrims Progress.
Boston, 1760. 24+ pp.
(The only known copy is imperfect.)
JCB copy.   41154

The New Pleasing Instructor.
Boston, Thomas & Andrews, etc., 1799.
323 pp.
AAS copy.   35911

New Plymouth (Colony).
A Declaration of the Warrantable
Grounds.
Boston, Greenleaf, 1773. 24 pp.
AAS copy.   12885

New Plymouth (Colony) General Court,
1690.
An Address Presented to the King,
August 7th, 1689.
Boston, 1690. Broadside.
MHS copy.   543

New Plymouth (Colony) Laws, Statutes,
etc., 1672.
The Book of the General Laws.
Cambridge, 1672. 47, [8] pp.
MHS copy.   171

New Plymouth (Colony) Laws, Statutes,
etc., 1685.
The Book of the General Laws.
Boston, 1685. [6], 75, [9] pp.
MHS copy.   397

[New Pocket Almanack or, Repository
for 1795.
New York, Durell.]
("Just Published, and for sale, by Durell,"
Ev. Post, Mar. 16, 1795.)   29184

The New President's March.
New York, Hewitt, [1799?]. 1 leaf.
LOC copy.   35638

The New President's March [with]
Washington's March.
[Philadelphia], B. Carr, [1796].
Broadside.
(Apparently the item described in the adv.
from which Evans made his entry.)
HEH copy.   31554

A New Primer.
Norwich, Trumbull for Spencer of East
Greenwich, 1776. [64] pp.
JCB copy.   43099

A New Primer, or Little Boy and Girls
Spelling Book.
Springfield, [Mass.], [1786].
[80] pp.
AAS copy.   44931

The New Primer, or Little Boy and Girls
Spelling Book [by Robert Ross,
1726-1799].
Boston, Edes, 1788. [96?] pp.
(The unique copy is imperfect.)
BPL copy.   21437

A New Primmer or Methodical Directions
[by Franz Daniel Pastorius, 1651-1719].
New York [1698]. 88 pp.
Friends' House copy.　　　　　851

A New Privateering Song: Concluding
with some Remarks upon the Cruelty . . .
upon our poor Prisoners.
n.p., [1777?] Broadside.
NYPL copy.　　　　　43310

A New Proclamation! By Thomas
Gage. . . . [by John Trumbull, 1750-1831].
[Hartford, 1775.] 8 pp.
LOC copy.　　　　　14526

[The New Recruit, or the Gallant
Volunteer. A Song.
Philadelphia, 1779.]
(Adv. Pa. Gazette, Feb. 10, 1779.)　　16405

The New Robinson Crusoe [by Joachim
Heinrich Campe, 1746-1818].
Boston, Thomas & Andrews, 1790. Front.,
270 pp.
AAS copy.　　　　　22389

The New Robinson Crusoe. . . . In two
volumes [by Joachim Heinrich Campe,
1746-1818].
Philadelphia, Woodhouse, 1792. 172: 163,
[1] pp.
AAS copy.　　　　　24171

The New Robinson Crusoe [by Joachim
Heinrich Campe, 1746-1818].
Hartford, Ct., Babcock, 1800. 108 pp.
AAS copy.　　　　　38071

A New Scene Interesting to the Citizens
[by Alexander Martin, 1740-1807].
[Philadelphia], Bache, 1798. 12 pp.
LOC copy.　　　　　34050

A New Scene Interesting to the Citizens
[by Alexander Martin, 1740-1807].
Philadelphia, [Bache for] Condie, 1798. 8
pp.
BrU copy.　　　　　34051

New Sentiments, Different from any yet
Published, upon . . . Universal Salvation.
Providence, Wheeler, 1786. 64 pp.
AAS copy.　　　　　44932

New Sentiments, Different from any yet
Published, upon . . . Universal Salvation.
Providence, Wheeler, 1786. 68 pp.
(For the 64 p. ed. see Alden 1033.)
LOC copy.　　　　　19452

New Sermons to Asses [by James Murray,
1732-1782].
Philadelphia, Sparhawk, 1774. 94 pp.
AAS copy.　　　　　13450

A New Set of Geographical Cards, for the
Agreeable Improvement of Gentlemen.
[Philadelphia, 1786.] [63] cards.
LOC copy.　　　　　44933

A New Song, About Miss Ketty.
[Philadelphia, 1765.] Broadside.
HSP copy.　　　　　10092

A New Song, Address'd to the Sons of
Liberty . . . Particularly to the . . .
Ninety-Two of Boston.
[Boston, 1768.] Broadside.
HSP copy.　　　　　41853

[The New Song Book being Miss
Ashmore's Favorite Collection.
Boston, McAlpine, 1771.]
(Adv. Boston Evening Post, Nov. 25,
1771.)　　　　　11969

A New Song, Called the Gaspee.
Providence, [1772?] Broadside.
(The only known copy is imperfect.)
RIHS copy.　　　　　42361

A New Song, in High Vogue in
Northampton County.
[Philadelphia], 1771. Broadside.
LCP copy.　　　　　12153

New Song, My Dearest Life, were you my
Wife . . .
n.p., n.d. Broadside.
CHS copy.　　　　　49120

A New Song, on the Alteration of the
Stile.
n.p., [1752?]. Broadside.
AAS copy.　　　　　40630

A New Song, on the Repeal of the
Stamp-Act.
[Philadelphia, 1766.] Broadside.
LCP copy.　　　　　10415

A New Song Suitable to the Season.
[Philadelphia, 1765.] [2] pp.
LCP copy.　　　　　10093

A New Song. To the Tune of Hearts of
Oak [by John Dickinson, 1732-1808].
[Philadelphia, 1768.] Broadside.
LCP copy.　　　　　10880

A New Song. To the Tune of the British
Grenadiers [by Jonathan Mitchell Sewall,
1748-1808].
n.p., [1776]. Broadside.
HSP copy.　　　　　14918

[A new song, witty and satirical.
Baltimore, 1798.]
("This day published," Mar. 8, 1798.)　48534

A New System of Chemistry.
Philadelphia, Dobson, 1800. [2], 364 pp.
AAS copy.　　　　　38072

A New System of Military Discipline
Founded upon Principle [by Richard
Lambart, 6th earl of Cavan, d. 1774].
Philadelphia, Aitken, 1776. 267,
[1] pp.
AAS copy.　　　　　14815

A New System of Philosophy; or, the
Newtonean Hypothesis Examined.
Poughkeepsie, 1783. [3], 19 pp.
HC copy.　　　　　18058

A New Th[anksgiving] Song . . . The
Glorious Conquest of Canada.
Boston, at the New Printing-Office,
[1760]. Broadside.
AAS copy.　　　　　41155

A New Touch on the Times.
[Salem? 1778?] Broadside.
(Copy not located.)　　　　　43511
|
A New Touch on the Times. Well
Adapted to the Distressing Situation of
every Sea-Port Town.
n.p., [1779.] Broadside.
NYHS copy.　　　　　43671

The New Town and Country Almanac, for
. . . 1796 [by Abraham Shoemaker].
New York, Shoemaker. [48] pp.
AAS copy.　　　　　29505

The New Trade Directory for New-York,
Anno 1800.
New York, [1799]. xii, 192.
HEH copy.　　　　　35913

The New Trade Directory for New-York
Anno 1800.
New York, [1800?]. xii, 192 pp.
(Aslo entered as 35913, q. v.)　　　38073

The New Trade Directory, for
Philadelphia, Anno 1800.
Philadelphia, Way & Groff, 1799. [2], xii,
216 pp.
APS copy.　　　　　35914

[The New Union.
[Boston?, 1795.] Broadside.]
(The origin of this entry is unknown.)　29185

The New Universal Letter-Writer.
Philadelphia, Hogan, 1800. front., pp.
[i]-vii, [13]-254, [4].
AAS copy.　　　　　38074

The New Vade Mecum; or, Young Clerk's
Magazine [by Thomas Spencer,
1752-1840].
Lansingburgh, Tiffany for Spencer, 1794.
346 pp.
AAS copy.　　　　　27728

A New Virginia Almanack, for . . . 1787.
Richmond, Allen. [50] pp.
LOC copy.　　　　　19849

New Yankee Doodle Sung with Great
Applause at the Theatre.
New York, Hewitt, etc., [1798]. [4] pp.
HEH copy.　　　　　48535

[New Yankee Doodle. Tough Times.
n.p., 1798.]
(Evans' entry constructed from advs.)　35064

The New Year. From the Carrier of the
Newburyport Herald, &c., to his
Generous Customers.
[Newburyport, 1799.] Broadside.
(No copy located.)　　　　　35965

A New Year. The Carrier of the Mirrour,
to his Customers. . . . January, 1795.
[Concord, 1795.] Broadside.
(Not located, 1968.)　　　　　47510

New-Year Addresses! January 1, 1793.
[Providence Gazette]. Now our
Grandams Earth. . . .
[Providence, 1793.] Broadside.
(See Alden 1321.)
RIHS copy.　　　　　26049

[New-Year Verses, Addressed to tne
Patrons of the Baltimore Daily
Repository. . . . January 2, 1792.
[Baltimore, 1792.] Broadside.]
(The unique copy is at present mislaid.)　24068

New-Year Verses, by the Carrier of the
Gazette. Ladies and Gentlemen. . . . [Jan.
1, 1800] [by William Gerrish].
[Providence, R. I., Carter, 1800.]
Broadside.
RIHS copy.　　　　　38346

[New-Year Verses of the Carriers of the
American Weekly Mercury.
Philadelphia, Bradford, 1743.]
(Assumed by Hildeburn from the custom.)　5115

[New-Year Verses of the Carriers of the
American Weekly Mercury.
Philadelphia, Warner & Bradford, 1744.
Broadside.]
(Assumed from the sequence.)　　5329

[New-Year Verses of the Carriers of the
American Weekly Mercury.
Philadelphia, Bradford, 1745.]
(Title from Hildeburn; no copy located.)　5530

[New-Year Verses of the Carriers of the
American Weekly Mercury.
Philadelphia, C. Bradford. 1746.]
(Hildeburn 984.)　　　　　5730

[New-Year Verses of the Carriers of the
Freeman's Journal.
Philadelphia, 1782.]
(Assumed from the sequence.)　　17539

[New-Year Verses of the Carriers of the
Independent Gazetteer, Jan. 1, 1784.
Philadelphia 1784. Broadside.]
(Assumed from the custom.)　　18536

[New-Year Verses of the Carriers of the
New-York Gazette.
New York, Parker, 1750.]
(Hildeburn listed this item as seen.)　6575

[New-Year Verses of the Carriers of the
Pennsylvania Chronicle.
Philadelphia, Goddard, 1768. Broadside.]
(Assumed from the sequence.)　　11029

[New-Year Verses of the Carriers of the
Pennsylvania Chronicle.
Philadelphia, Goddard, 1769. Broadside.]
(Assumed from the sequence.)　　11405

[New-Year Verses of the Carriers of the
Pennsylvania Chronicle.
Philadelphia, Goddard, 1770.]
(Assumed by Hildeburn from the
sequence.)　　　　　11805

[New-Year Verses of the Carriers of the
Pennsylvania Chronicle, Jan. 1, 1771.
Philadelphia, 1771.]
(Assumed by Hildeburn from the
sequence.)　　　　　12181

[New-Year Verses of the Carriers of the

Pennsylvania Chronicle.
Philadelphia, 1772.]
(Assumed by Hildeburn from the
sequence.)   12509

[New-Year Verses of the Carriers of the
Pennsylvania Chronicle.
Philadelphia, 1773.]
(Assumed by Hildeburn from the
sequence.)   12926

[New-Year Verses of the Carriers of the
Pennsylvania Chronicle, Jan. 1, 1774.
Philadelphia, 1774. Broadside.]
(Assumed by Hildeburn from the
sequence.)   13527

[New-Year Verses of the Carriers of the
Pennsylvania Evening Post.
Philadelphia, 1776.]
(Assumed by Hildeburn.)   15002

[New-Year Verses of the Carriers of the
Pennsylvania Evening-Post.
Philadelphia, 1779. Broadside.]
(Assumed by Hildeburn from the
sequence.)   16452

[New-Year Verses of the Carriers of the
Pennsylvania Evening Post.
Philadelphia, 1782.]
(Assumed from the sequence.)   17666

New-Year Verses, for those who Carry
the Pennsylvania Gazette to the
Customers. January 1, 1785.
[Philadelphia, 1785.] Broadside.
AAS copy.   44743

[New-Year Verses of the Carriers of the
Pennsylvania Gazette.
Philadelphia, Franklin, 1744. Broadside].
(Hildeburn.)   5476

[New-Year Verses of the Carriers of the
Pennsylvania Gazette.
Philadelphia, 1745.]
(Hildeburn 940.)   5673

[New-Year Verses of the Carriers of the
Pennsylvania Gazette.
Philadelphia, Franklin, 1746. Broadside.]
(No copy located.)   5850

[New-Year Verses of the Carriers of the
Pennsylvania Gazette.
Philadelphia, Franklin, 1747. Broadside.]
(Hildeburn 1024.)   6046

New-Year Verses of the Carriers or
Printer's Boys, who Carries the
Pennsylvania Gazette. . . . 1748.
[Philadelphia, Franklin, 1748.]
Broadside.
AAS copy.   6216

New-Year Verses of the Carriers or
Printer's Boys, who Carries the
Pennsylvania Gazette. . . . MDCCXLIX.
[Philadelphia, Franklin & Hall, 1749.]
Broadside.
AAS copy.   6400

[New-Year Verses of the Carriers of the
Pennsylvania Gazette.
Philadelphia, Franklin & Hall, 1750.]
(Hildeburn 1190.)   6585

[New-Year Verses of the Carriers of the
Pennsylvania Gazette.
Philadelphia, Franklin & Hall, 1751.]
(Hildeburn, 1229.)   6750

The New-Year Verses of the Printers Lad,
who Carries the Pennsylvania Gazette. . . .
MDCCLII.
[Philadelphia, Franklin & Hall, 1752.]
Broadside.
AAS copy.   6910

[New-Year Verses of the Carriers of the
Pennsylvania Gazette.
Philadelphia, Franklin & Hall, 1753.]
(Assumed by Hildeburn.)   7088

[New-Year Verses of the Carriers of the
Pennsylvania Gazette.
Philadelphia, Franklin & Hall, 1754.]
(Assumed from the sequence.)   7289

The New-Year Verses of the Printers
Lads, who Carry the Pennsylvania Gazette
. . . for 1755.

[Philadelphia, 1755.] Broadside.
LCP copy.   7534

The New-Year Verses of the Printers
Lads, who carry the Pennsylvania
Gazette. . . . For 1756.
[Philadelphia, 1756.] Broadside.
LCP copy.   7759

[The New-Year Verses of the Printers
Boys, who Carry about the Pennsylvania
Gazette.
[Philadelphia, 1757.] Broadside.
(Entry from Hildeburn.)   8000

[The New-Year Verses of the Printers
Lads, who Carry the Pennsylvania
Gazette.
Philadelphia, 1758. Broadside.]
(Hildeburn 1598.)   8232

The New-Year Verses of the Printers
Lads, who Carry about the Pennsylvania
Gazette.
[Philadelphia, 1759.] Broadside.
LCP copy.   8462

The New-Year Verses, of the Printers
Lads, who Carry about the Pennsylvania
Gazette. . . . January 1, 1760.
[Philadelphia, 1760.] Broadside.
LCP copy.   8709

[New-Year Verses of the Carriers of the
Pennsylvania Gazette.
Philadelphia, Franklin & Hall, 1761.]
(Assumed by Hildeburn from the
sequence.)   8974

[New-Year Verses of the Carriers of the
Pennsylvania Gazette.
Philadelphia, Franklin & Hall, 1762.]
(Assumed by Hildeburn from the
sequence.)   9234

[New-Year Verses of the Carriers of the
Pennsylvania Gazette.
Philadelphia, Franklin & Hall, 1763.]
(Assumed by Hildeburn from the
sequence.)   9479

The New-Year Verses, of the Printers
Lads, who Carry about the Pennsylvania
Gazette. . . . January 1, 1764.
[Philadelphia, 1764.] Broadside.
LCP copy.   9789

The New-Year Verses, of the Printers
Lads, who Carry about the Pennsylvania
Gazette . . . January 1, 1765.
[Philadelphia, 1765.] Broadside.
LCP copy.   10126

[The New-Year Verses, of the Printers
Lads, who Carry about the Pennsylvania
Gazette . . . January 1, 1766.
[Philadelphia, 1766.] Broadside.]
(The unique copy is mislaid.)   10447

The New-Year Verses, of the Printers
Lads, who Carry the Pennsylvania
Gazette. . . . January 1, 1767.
[Philadelphia, 1767.] Broadside.
LCP copy.   10732

The New-Year Verses, of the Printers
Lads, who Carry about the Pennsylvania
Gazette. . . . January, 1769.
[Philadelphia, 1769.] Broadside.
LCP copy.   11407

The New-Year Verses, of the Printers
Lads, who Carry about the Pennsylvania
Gazette. . . . January, 1770.
[Philadelphia, 1770.] Broadside.
LCP copy.   11807

The New-Year Verses, of the Printers
Lads, who Carry about the Pennsylvania
Gazette. . . . January, 1771.
[Philadelphia, 1771.] Broadside.
LCP copy.   12183

The New-Year Verses, of the Printers
Lads, who Carry about the Pennsylvania
Gazette. . . . January, 1772.
[Philadelphia, 1772.] Broadside.
(Bound into the HC file of the Pa. Gazette
is a carriers' address headed "The
News-Boy's Verses to his Customers,
January 1, 1772.")
LCP copy.   12511

The New-Year Verses, of the Printers
Lads, who Carry about the Pennsylvania
Gazette. . . . January, 1773.
[Philadelphia, 1773.] Broadside.
LCP copy.   12928

[New-Year Verses of the Carriers of the
Pennsylvania Gazette, Jan. 1, 1774.
Philadelphia, 1774. Broadside.]
(Assumed by Hildeburn from the
sequence.)   13529

[New-Year Verses of the Carriers of the
Pennsylvania Gazette.
Philadelphia, 1775. Broadside.]
(Assumed by Hildeburn from the
sequence.)   14376

[New-Year Verses of the Carriers of the
Pennsylvania Gazette.
Philadelphia, 1776.]
(Assumed by Hildeburn.)   15004

[New-Year Verses of the Carriers of the
Pennsylvania Gazette.
Philadelphia, 1779. Broadside.]
(Assumed by Hildeburn from the
sequence.)   16454

[New-Year Verses of the Carriers of the
Pennsylvania Gazette.
Philadelphia, 1780.]
(Assumed from the sequence.)   16939

The New-Year Verses of the Printers
Lads, who Carry the Pennsylvania
Gazette. . . . January 1, 1781.
[Philadelphia, 1781.] Broadside.
NYPL copy.   17302

The New-Year Verses of the Printers
Lads, who Carry the Pennsylvania
Gazette. . . . January 1, 1782.
[Philadelphia, 1782.] Broadside.
NYPL copy.   17668

The New-Year Verses of the Printers
Lads, who Carry about the Pennsylvania
Gazette . . . January 1, 1783.
[Philadelphia, 1783.] Broadside.
NYPL copy.   44416

New-Year Verses, for those who Carry
the Pennsylvania Gazette. . . . January 1,
1784 [by Philip Morin Freneau,
1752-1832].
[Philadelphia, 1784.] Broadside.
LCP copy.   18717

New-Year Verses, of those who Carry the
Pennsylvania Gazette . . . January 1, 1790.
Philadelphia, Hall & Sellers, [1790].
Broadside.
NYHS copy.   45925

[New-Year Verses of the Carriers of the
Pennsylvania Journal.
Philadelphia, 1745.]
(Hildeburn 941.)   5675

The New-Year's Verses of the . . .
Pennsylvania Journal. . . . January 1,
1746.
[Philadelphia, 1746.] Broadside.
HSP copy.   5852

[New-Year Verses of the Carriers of the
Pennsylvania Journal.
Philadelphia, Bradford, 1747. Broadside.]
(Hildeburn 1025.)   6048

[New-Year Verses of the Carriers of the
Pennsylvania Journal.
Philadelphia, Bradford, 1748. Broadside.]
(Hildeburn 1087.)   6218

[New-Year Verses of the Carriers of the
Pennsylvania Journal.
Philadelphia, Bradford, 1749. Broadside.]
(Hildeburn 1145.)   6402

[New-Year Verses of the Carriers of the
Pennsylvania Journal.
Philadelphia, Bradford, 1750.]
(Hildeburn 1191.)   6587

[New-Year Verses of the Carriers of the
Pennsylvania Journal.
Philadelphia, Bradford, 1751.]
(Hildeburn 1230.)   6752

[New-Year Verses of the Carriers of the
Pennsylvania Journal.

Philadelphia, Bradford, 1752. |
(Hildeburn 1270.)　　　　6912

[New-Year Verses of the Carriers of the
Pennsylvania Journal.
Philadelphia, Bradford, 1753. |
(Assumed by Hildeburn.)　　　　7090

[New-Year Verses of the Carriers of the
Pennsylvania Journal.
Philadelphia, Bradford, 1754. |
(Assumed from the sequence.)　　　　7291

[New-Year Verses of the Carriers of the
Pennsylvania Journal.
Philadelphia, Bradford, 1755. |
(Assumed from sequence.)　　　　7536

[New-Year Verses of the Carriers of the
Pennsylvania Journal.
Philadelphia, Bradford, 1756. |
(Assumed by Hildeburn from the
sequence.)　　　　7761

[New-Year Verses of the Carriers of the
Pennsylvania Journal.
Philadelphia, Bradford, 1757. |
(Assumed by Hildeburn from the
sequence.)　　　　8002

[New-Year Verses of the Carriers of the
Pennsylvania Journal.
Philadelphia, Bradford, 1758. |
(Hildeburn 1599.)　　　　8234

[New-Year Verses of the Carriers of the
Pennsylvania Journal.
Philadelphia, Bradford, 1759. |
(Hildeburn 1637.)　　　　8464

[New-Year Verses of the Carriers of the
Pennsylvania Journal.
Philadelphia, Bradford, 1760. |
(Assumed by Hildeburn.)　　　　8711

[New-Year Verses of the Carriers of the
Pennsylvania Journal.
Philadelphia, Bradford, 1761. |
(Assumed by Hildeburn from the
sequence.)　　　　8976

[New-Year Verses of the Carriers of the
Pennsylvania Journal.
Philadelphia, Bradford, 1762. |
(Assumed by Hildeburn from the
sequence.)　　　　9236

[New-Year Verses of the Carriers of the
Pennsylvania Journal.
Philadelphia, Bradford, 1763. |
(Assumed by Hildeburn from the
sequence.)　　　　9481

[New-York Verses of the Carriers of the
Pennsylvania Journal.
Philadelphia, Bradford, 1764. |
(Assumed by Hildeburn from the
sequence.)　　　　9791

[New-Year Verses of the Carriers of the
Pennsylvania Journal, January 1, 1765.
Philadelphia, 1765. Broadside. |
(Assumed from the sequence.)　　　　10128

The New-Year Verses of the Printer's
Lads, who Carry the Pennsylvania Journal
. . . January 1, 1766.
[Philadelphia, 1766. | Broadside.
HSP copy.　　　　10449

[New-Year Verses of the Carriers of the
Pennsylvania Journal.
Philadelphia, 1767. |
(No copy found.)　　　　10734

[New-Year Verses of the Carriers of the
Pennsylvania Journal.
Philadelphia, Bradfords, 1768.
Broadside. |
(Assumed from the sequence.)　　　　11033

[New-Year Verses of the Carriers of the
Pennsylvania Journal.
Philadelphia, Bradfords, 1769.
Broadside. |
(Assumed from the sequence.)　　　　11409

[New-Year Verses of the Carriers of the
Pennsylvania Journal.
Philadelphia, Bradfords, 1770. |
(Assumed by Hildeburn from the
sequence.)　　　　11809

[New-Year Verses of the Carriers of the
Pennsylvania Journal, Jan. 1, 1771.
Philadelphia, 1771. |
(Assumed by Hildeburn from the
sequence.)　　　　12185

[New-Year Verses of the Carriers of the
Pennsylvania Journal.
Philadelphia, 1772. |
(Assumed by Hildeburn from the
sequence.)　　　　12513

[New-Year Verses of the Carriers of the
Pennsylvania Journal.
Philadelphia, Bradfords, 1773.
Broadside. |
(The unique copy is mislaid.)　　　　12930

The New-Year's Verses of those who
Carry the Pennsylvania Journal. . . .
January 1, 1774.
[Philadelphia, 1774. | Broadside.
HSP copy.　　　　13531

New-Year's Verses of those who Carry
the Pennsylvania Journal. . . . January,
1775.
[Philadelphia, 1775. | Broadside.
HSP copy.　　　　14378

[New-Year Verses of the Carriers of the
Pennsylvania Journal.
Philadelphia, 1776. |
(Assumed by Hildeburn.)　　　　15006

[New-Year Verses of the Carriers of the
Pennsylvania Journal.
Philadelphia, 1779. Broadside. |
(Assumed by Hildeburn from the
sequence.)　　　　16456

[New-Year Verses of the Carriers of the
Pennsylvania Journal.
Philadelphia, 1780. |
(Assumed from the sequence.)　　　　16941

[New-Year Verses of the Carriers of the
Pennsylvania Journal.
[Philadelphia, 1781. | Broadside. |
(Assumed from the sequence.)　　　　17304

[New-Year Verses of the Carriers of the
Pennsylvania Journal.
Philadelphia, 1782. Broadside. |
(Assumed from the sequence.)　　　　17670

[New-Year Verses of the Carriers of the
Pennsylvania Journal.
Philadelphia, 1783. Broadside. |
(Assumed from the sequence.)　　　　18131

[New-Year Verses of the Carriers of the
Pennsylvania Journal, Jan. 1, 1784.
Philadelphia, 1784. Broadside. |
(Assumed from the custom.)　　　　18719

[New-Year Verses of the Carriers of the
Pennsylvania Ledger.
Philadelphia, 1776. |
(Assumed by Hildeburn.)　　　　15008

[New-Year Verses of the Carriers of the
Pennsylvania Packet.
Philadelphia, 1772. |
(Assumed by Hildeburn from the
sequence.)　　　　12515

[New-Year Verses of the Carriers of the
Pennsylvania Packet.
Philadelphia, Dunlap, 1773. |
(Assumed by Hildeburn from the
sequence.)　　　　12932

[The New-Year Verses, of the Printer's
Lads, who Carry the Pennsylvania Packet.
. . . January 1st, 1774.
[Philadelphia, 1774. | Broadside. |
(Entry from Hildeburn.)　　　　13262

[The New-Year Verses, of those who
Carry the Pennsylvania Packet . . .
January, 1775.
Philadelphia, 1775. Broadside. |
(Assumed from the custom.)　　　　14018

[New-Year Verses of the Carriers of the
Pennsylvania Packet.
Philadelphia, 1776. |
(Assumed by Hildeburn.)　　　　14745

[New-Year Verses of the Carriers of the
Pennsylvania Packet.
Lancaster, 1778. |

(Assumed by Hildeburn from the
sequence.)　　　　15987

[New-Year Verses of the Carriers of the
Pennsylvania Packet.
Philadelphia, 1779. Broadside. |
(Assumed by Hildeburn from the
sequence.)　　　　16458

[New-Year Verses of the Carriers of the
Pennsylvania Packet.
Philadelphia, 1780. |
(Assumed from the sequence.)　　　　16943

[New-Year Verses of the Carriers of the
Pennsylvania Packet.
[Philadelphia, 1781. | Broadside. |
(Assumed from the sequence.)　　　　17306

[New-Year Verses of the Carriers of the
Pennsylvania Packet.
Philadelphia, 1782. Broadside. |
(Assumed from the custom.)　　　　17672

[New Year Verses of the Carriers of the
Pennsylvania Packet.
Philadelphia, 1783. Broadside.
(Assumed from the sequence.)　　　　18133

[New-Year Verses of the Carriers of the
Pennsylvania Packet, Jan. 1, 1784.
Philadelphia, 1784. Broadside. |
(Assumed from the custom.)　　　　18723

The New-Year Verses, of the Flying
Mercuries . . . who carry the Maryland
Journal. . . . January 1, 1787.
[Baltimore, 1787. | Broadside.
EPFL copy.　　　　45109

[New Year Verses of the Weekly Post-
Boy.
New York, 1744.
(No copy found.)　　　　5467

New-Year Verses, of those who carry the
Pennsylvania Gazette . . . January 1, 1790.
[Philadelphia, Hall & Sellers, 1790. |
Broadside.
NYHS copy.　　　　45925

New-Year Verses, or Circular Epistle
from the Carrier to the Patrons of the
Minerva January 1 1796.
[Dedham, Mass., 1796. | Broadside.
(Not located, 1968.)　　　　47855

A New Year Well-begun | by Cotton Mather,
1663-1728 |.
New London, 1719. [4], 29, [1] pp.
AAS copy.　　　　2044

A New-Year's Address, from the Carrier
of the Newport Herald.
[Newport, 1789. | Broadside.
NJHS copy.　　　　45533

A New-Year's Address, to the Customers,
of the Boston Gazette, &c. for January
1765.
[Boston, 1765. | Broadside.
HSP copy.　　　　41573

A New-Year's Address, which the Carrier
of the Boston News-Letter, &c. humbly
Presents. . . . January, 1765.
[Boston, 1765. | Broadside.
HSP copy.　　　　41574

A New-Years Address, which your
Obedient Servant the Young Shaver
Humbly Presents to all his Generous
Customers.
n. p., [1767? | Broadside.
HSP copy.　　　　41854

New-Year's Day, 1768. The News Boy's
Verses who Carries the Boston
Evening-Post.
[Boston, 1768. | Broadside.
HSP copy.　　　　41855

A New Year's Gift for Children.
Boston, Fowle, [1754?]. Broadside.
AAS copy.　　　　40529

A New-Year's Gift, or A Brief Account
. . . of the Lord's Supper.
Philadelphia, Bradford, 1748. viii, 26 pp.
HEH copy.　　　　40472

A New-Year's Gift to the Democrats | by
William Cobbett, 1762-1835 |.

Philadelphia, Bradford, 1796. 71,
[1] pp.
AAS copy.   30215

Second Edition. A New Year's Gift to the
Democrats [by William Cobbett,
1762-1835].
Philadelphia, Bradford, 1796. 71 pp.
AAS copy.   30216

A New Year's Gift to the Democrats. . . .
By Peter Porcupine. . . . Third Edition [by
William Cobbett, 1762-1835].
Philadelphia, Cobbett, 1798. 71 pp.
AAS copy.   33527

A New-Years Gift, Written a few Years
ago by a Young Woman.
Concord, Hough and Russell, 1792.
8 pp.
LOC copy.   25894

A New-Years Present from the Lad that
Carries the Boston News-Letter . . .
January 1, 1761.
[Boston, 1761.] Broadside.
HSP copy.   41231

A New-Year's Verse. New Joys Arise. . . .
Haverhill, January 1, 1795. [for the
carrier of the Guardian of Freedom].
[Haverhill, 1795.] Broadside.
MHS copy.   28780

New Year's Verses Addressed to the
Customers of the Freeman's Journal. . . .
January 8th, 1783 [by Philip Freneau,
1752-1832].
[Philadelphia, 1783.] Broadside.
LOC copy.   17937

New-Year's Verses, Addressed to the
Customers of the Massachusetts-Gazette.
[Boston, 1773?] Broadside.
HSP copy.   42469

New-Year's Verses. Addressed to the
Customers of the Newport Mercury by the
Printer's Boys.
[Newport, 1769.] Broadside.
NHS copy.   41980

New-Year's Verses, Addressed to the
Customers of the Newport Mercury . . .
January 1, 1770.
[Newport, 1770.] Broadside.
NHS copy.   42137

New-Year's Verses, Addressed to the
Friends and Patrons of the Maryland
Journal. . . . January 1, 1794.
[Baltimore, 1794.] Broadside.
EPFL copy.   47133

New Year's Verses, Addressed to the
Kind Customers of the Massachusetts
Gazette.
[Boston, 1774?] Broadside.
HSP copy.   42647

New Year's Verses, Addressed to the kind
Customers of the Pennsylvania Evening
Post. . . . January 1, 1778.
[Philadelphia, 1778.] Broadside.
LCP copy.   15980

New-Year's Verses, Addressed to the
Patrons of the Baltimore Daily
Intelligencer. . . . January 1, 1794.
[Baltimore, 1794.] Broadside.
(Not located 1967.)
EPFL copy.   47132

New Year's Verses, for 1786; Addressed
to the Customers of the Columbian
Herald [by Philip Morin Freneau,
1752-1832].
[Charleston, 1786.] Broadside.
NYHS copy.   44889

New-Year's Verses for 1791; Respectfully
Inscribed to the . . . Patrons of the
Maryland Gazette.
[Baltimore, 1791.] Broadside.
EPFL copy.   46238

[New Year's Verses. For the Connecticut
Courant, January 1, 1795 [by Lemuel
Hopkins, 1750-1801].
Hartford, Hudson & Goodwin, 1795.]
(Known from the reprint in 28855.) 28472

New-Year's Verses for the Lad who

Carries the Connecticut Gazette. . . . A.D.
1767.
[New Haven, 1767.] Broadside.
HSP copy.   41742

[New-Year's Verses, for the Lad who
Carries the Evening Post.
[Philadelphia, 1780.] Broadside.]
(Only reported copy not to be found.)
     16937

New Year's Verses for the Lads that Carry
the Daily Advertiser. . . . January 1, 1789.
[Charleston, 1789.] Broadside.
NYPL copy.   45534

New-Year's Verses for the Printer's Lads
who Carry the Evening Post.
[Philadelphia, 1781.] Broadside.
AAS copy.   17300

New-Year's Verses, of the Printer's Boys,
who Carry About the South-Carolina
Gazette. . . . January 1, 1767.
[Charleston, 1767.] Broadside.
HSP copy.   41743

New-Year's Verses of Those who Deliver
the Pennsylvania Ledger. . . . January 1,
1778.
[Philadelphia, 1778.] Broadside.
LCP copy.   15984

New-Year Verses, Humbly Addressed to
the Patrons of the Morning Post. . . .
January 1, 1792.
[New York, 1792.] Broadside.
NYHS copy.   46522

New-Year Verses of the Carrier of the
Gazette. . . . Providence, January 1, 1798.
[Providence, 1798.] Broadside.
RIHS copy.   48536

A New-Year's Warning. Another Year has
Roll'd its Round. . . . January 1, 1795.
[Providence, 1795.] Broadside.
(Not located, 1968.)   47511

A New-Year's Wish. A Happy Year to my
Generous Customers. . . . Boston, January
1, 1764.
[Boston, 1764.] Broadside.
HSP copy.   41474

A New Year's Wish. Europa still Partakes
the Joys of Peace. . . . 1765.
n. p., n. d. Broadside.
HSP copy.   41575

A New-Year's Wish for the Public, for the
Year 1769.
(From the Carrier of the Boston-Gazette,
&c.)
[Boston, 1769.] Broadside.
HSP copy.   41981

A New-Year's Wish, for the Year 1770. By
the Carrier of The Boston Chronicle.
[Boston, 1770.] Broadside.
HSP copy.   42138

A New Year's Wish, from the Baker's
Boy. . . . Boston, January 1, 1768.
[Boston, 1768.] Broadside.
HSP copy.   41856

A New-Year's Wish from the Baker's Lad.
. . . Boston, January, 1769.
[Boston, 1769.] Broadside.
HSP copy.   41982

New-Year's Wish from the Carrier of the
Boston Post-Boy, &c.
[Boston, 1766.] Broadside.
HSP copy.   41647

A New-Year's Wish, from the Carrier of
the Post-Boy and Advertiser. To Scenes
of Blood. . . .
[Boston, 1784?] Broadside.
(The one recorded copy cannot be
located.)   44570

A New Year's Wish, from the Carrier of
the Post-Boy & Advertiser . . . . Boston,
January 1, 1762.
[Boston, 1762.] Broadside.
HSP copy.   41293

A New Year's Wish from the Carrier of
the Post-Boy & Advertiser.

[Boston, 1767.] Broadside.
HSP copy.   41744

A New Year's Wish, from the Carrier of
the Post Boy and Advertiser.
[Boston, 1768.] Broadside.
HSP copy.   41857

A New-Year's Wish, from the Farrier's Lad.
. . . Boston, January, 1769.
[Boston, 1769.] Broadside.
HSP copy.   41983

A New Year's Wish, from the Lad, who
Carries the Post-Boy & Advertiser. . . .
Boston, January 1, 1760.
[Boston, 1760.] Broadside.
HSP copy.   41232

A New-Year's Wish. My Honour'd
Patrons . . . Your Humble Farrier.
[Boston, 1768.] Broadside.
HSP copy.   41858

A New-Year's Wish My Kind Benefactors.
. . . January, 1795.
n. p., [1795]. Broadside.
NYHS copy.   47511a

[The New-Year's Wish of the Carrier of
the Philadelphia Federal Gazette, Jan. 1,
1789.
Philadelphia, 1789. Broadside.]
(No copy located.)   21817

[The New-Year's Wish of the Post who
Carries the Western-Star.
[Stockbridge, Andrews, 1791.]
Broadside.]
(Broadside printing assumed by Evans.)
     23992

A New-Years Wish, Once more my
Friends I do Appear. . . .
n.p., [1767?] Broadside.
HSP copy.   41745

A New-Year's Wish. This Year's Begun. . . .
[Boston, 1768.] Broadside.
HSP copy.   41859

New York (City)
New York (Colony)
New York (County)
New York (State) official headings
Institutions and titles in one alphabet.

New York (City).
. . . Be it Remembered, that . . . in the
Year . . . One Thousand Seven Hundred
and Ninety-Six. . . .
[New York, 1796.] Broadside.
LOC copy.   47856

New York (City).
The Citizens of New York are Informed.
. . . March 27, 1786.
[New York, 1786] Broadside.
LOC copy.   44934

New York (City).
A Copy of the Poll List [Jan. 23-27, 1769].
[New York, 1769.] [4], 43 pp.
LCP copy.   11374

New York (City).
To His Excellency William Tryon. . . . The
Humble Address of the Mayor . . .
[February 22, 1774].
[New York, 1774.] [2] pp.
PRO copy.   13470

[New York (City) Cabinet and Chair
Makers.
The Journeymen Cabinet and
Chair-Maker's New-York Book of Prices.
New York, 1796.]
(The origin of this entry is unknown.)
     30880

New York (City) Chamber of Commerce.
Bye-laws, Resolutions and Orders . . .
May 10th, 1796.
New York, M'Lean, 1796. 12 pp.
YC copy.   30881

New York (City) Chamber of Commerce.
Gentlemen, The Interest of the
Landholder. . . .
[New York, 1785.] Broadside.
NYPL copy.   19136

New York (City) Chamber of Commerce.
. . . New-York, March 1, 1785. Upon a
Motion. . . .
[New York, 1785.] Broadside.
CHS copy.   44744

New York (City) Chamber of Commerce.
I. That the Members . . . shall meet. . . .
[New York, 1795.] Broadside.
NYSL copy.   47512

[New York (City) Chamber of
Commerce.
Rules and Regulations of the. . . .
[New York, 1795.] Broadside.]
(No copy located.)   29198

New York (City) Chamber of Commerce.
To the Farmers and Traders. . . . April
7, 1792.
[New York, 1792.] Broadside.
LOC copy.   46523

New York (City) Charters.
The Charter of the City of New York.
[New York, 1694.] 10 pp.
HEH copy.   706

New York (City) Charters.
The Charter and the Several Laws.
New York, 1719. [2], 11, 24 pp.
HEH copy.   2161

New York (City) Charters.
The Charter of the City of New-York.
New York, 1735. 52 pp.
AAS copy.   3942

New York (City) Charters.
The Charter of the City of New-York.
New York, Weyman, 1765. 50 pp.
AAS copy.   10100

New York (City) Charter, 1774.
The Charter of the City of New York.
New York, Gaine, 1774. 52 pp.
NYPL copy.   13471

[New York (City) Charters.
The Charter of the City of New York.
New York, Loudon, 1776.]
(Origin of entry unknown.)   14939

New York (City) Church of Christ.
Proceedings in the Constitution of the
Church of Christ in Fair-Street.
New York, Swords, 1795. 12 pp.
LOC copy.   29199

New York (City) Citizens, 1775.
New-York, April 28, 1775. To the Publick
At a Meeting. . . .
[New York, 1775.] Broadside.
LOC copy.   42908

New York (City) Citizens, 1784.
At a Meeting of a Number of Inhabitants
at Cape's Tavern . . . the Twenty-Third
Instant. . . .
New York, Loudon, [1784?]. Broadside.
NYPL ph. copy.   44571

New York (City) Citizens, 1786.
The Citizens of New-York are Informed.
. . . March 27, 1786.
[New York, 1786.] Broadside.
LOC copy.   44934

New York (City) Citizens, 1789.
At a Meeting of a Respectable Number
of Freeholders . . . The 9th of March,
1789.
[New York, 1789.] 12 pp.
HEH copy.   45535

New York (City) Commissioners of the
Alms-House.
. . . At a Common Council held . . . the
15th Day of January, 1798.
[New York, 1798?] Broadside.
(Best copy available.)
NYHS copy.   48537

New York (City) Commissioners of the
Alms-House.
At a Meeting . . . the First of February,
1796. . . .
New York, Forman, [1796]. Broadside.
(Not located, 1968.)   47857

New York (City) Committee Appointed
to Prevent the Introduction and

Spreading of Infectious Diseases.
Health Committee . . . Fevers . . . West-
India Islands. . . . April 3, 1795.
[New York, 1795.] Broadside.
(Not located, 1968.)   47513

New York (City) Committee for Drawing
Constitutional Resolves, 1774.
To the Inhabitants of the City and
County of New-York. The Committee.
. . . July 23, 1774.
[New York, 1774.] Broadside.
LOC copy.   13662

New York (City) Committee of
Arrangements for Washington
Observation.
(From the Office of the Daily
Advertiser. The Following Interesting
Description, is from the Committee . . .
January 4.)
[New York, 1800.] Broadside.
LOC copy.   38097

New York (City) Committee of
Correspondence, 1774.
Advertisement. . . . 5th July, 1774.
[New York, 1774.] Broadside.
NYHS copy.   13094

New York (City) Committee of
Correspondence, 1774.
At a Meeting at the Exchange, 16th
May, 1774.
[New York, 1774.] Broadside.
NYHS copy.   13125

New York (City) Committee of
Correspondence, 1774.
Committee Chambers, July 13, 1774.
The Public are. . . .
[New York, 1774.] Broadside.
LOC copy.   13478

New York (City) Committee of
Correspondence, 1774.
Committee Chambers, July 18, 1774.
Proceedings. . . .
[New York, 1774.] Broadside.
LOC copy.   13479

New York (City) Committee of
Correspondence, 1774.
Committee-Chambers, July 25, 1774.
Proceedings. . . .
[New York, 1774.] Broadside.
LOC copy.   13481

New York (City) Committee of
Correspondence, 1774.
Committee Chambers, Sept. 30, 1774.
6 o'Clock. . . .
[New York, 1774.] Broadside.
LOC copy.   13482

New York (City) Committee of
Correspondence, 1774.
A Committee of Twenty-Five.
[New York, 1774.] Broadside.
NYHS copy.   13474

New York (City) Committee of
Correspondence, 1774.
Extract of the Proceedings of the
Committee. . . . July 8th, 1774.
[New York, 1774.] Broadside.
NYHS copy.   13476

New York (City) Committee of
Correspondence, 1774.
New-York. Committee-Chamber. 7th
July, 1774.
[New York, 1774.] Broadside.
NYHS copy.   13475

New York (City) Committee of
Correspondence, 1774.
New-York, July 29, 1774. Gentlemen,
We should have Answered your
Letter. . . .
[New York, 1774.] Broadside.
NYPL copy.   42648

New York (City) Committee of
Correspondence, 1774.
Notice. The Committee Appointed. . . .
[blank] 1774.
[New York, 1774.] Broadside.
NYHS copy.   42650

New York (City). Committee of
Correspondence, 1774.

On Tuesday the 19th day of July, 1774,
the Inhabitants. . . .
[New York, 1774.] Broadside.
LCP copy.   13480

New York (City) Committee of
Correspondence, 1774.
Proceedings . . . July 13, 1774.
[New York, 1774.] Broadside.
NYHS copy.   13477

New York (City) Committee of
Correspondence, 1774.
To the Inhabitants of the City and
County of New-York. . . . July 5, 1774.
[New York, 1774.] Broadside.
AAS ph. copy.   42651

New York (City) Committee of
Correspondence, 1775.
To the Public. By the Following Letters
. . . Rembrancer, New York, January 18,
1775.
[New York, 1775.] 2 pp.
NYPL copy.   14314

New York (City) Committee of Health.
Names of Persons who have Died in New
York of the Yellow Fever, from the 29th
of July to the beginning of November,
1795.
New York, 1795. [2], 26 pp.
AAS copy.   29196

New York (City) Committee of Health.
Record of Death, or an Accurate List, of
. . . our Fellow Citizens, who have Fallen
Victims to the Late Fever.
[New York], Hill, [1799]. 14 pp.
NY Academy of Medicine copy.   35942

New York (City) Committee of
Inspection, 1775.
In Committee of Inspection and
Observations, February 5th, 1775.
[New York, 1775.] Broadside.
NYPL copy.   14316

New York (City) Committee of
Mechanicks, 1774.
Advertisement. . . . July 6, 1774.
[New York, 1774.] Broadside.
NYHS copy.   13093

New York (City) Committee of
Mechanicks, 1774.
New-York, November 18, 1774.
The Mechanicks of this City are Earnestly
Requested to Meet. . . .
[New York, 1774.] Broadside.
NYHS copy.   13435

New York (City) Committee of
Observation, 1775.
Committee-Chamber, New-York, April
26, 1775.
[New York, 1775.] Broadside.
LOC copy.   14321

New York (City) Committee of
Observation, 1775.
Committee-Chamber, New-York, April
28, 1775. Gentlemen. . . .
[New York, 1775.] Broadside.
LOC copy.   14323

New York (City) Committee of
Observation, 1775.
Committee-Chamber, New-York, April
29, 1775. Extract. . . .
[New York, 1775.] Broadside.
NYHS copy.   14324

New York (City) Committee of
Observation, 1775.
Committee-Chamber, New-York, 1st.
May, 1775. Whereas. . . .
[New York, 1775.] Broadside.
LOC copy.   14326

New York (City) Committee of
Observation, 1775.
Committee-Chamber, New-York, May,
1775. Resolved. . . .
[New York, 1775.] Broadside.
LOC copy.   14327

New York (City) Committee of
Observation, 1775.
Committee Chamber, New-York, May 12,
1775. Whereas. . . .

[New York, 1775.] Broadside.
LOC copy.   14328

New York (City) Committee of
Observation, 1775.
Committee Chamber, New-York,
November 3, 1775. Whereas. . . .
[New York, 1775.] Broadside.
LOC copy.   14335

New York (City) Committee of
Observation, 1775.
The Following Extracts from the
Proceedings. . . . March 9, 1775.
[New York, 1775.] 2 pp.
NYPL copy.   14318

New York (City) Committee of
Observation, 1775.
The Following Persons were Mentioned.
. . . April 28, 1775.
[New York, 1775.] Broadside.
(A facsimile; original not located.)
AAS copy.   42898

New York (City) Committee of
Observation, 1775.
General Committee, May 1, 1775.
[New York, 1775.] Broadside.
LOC copy.   14325

New York (City) Committee of
Observation, 1775.
New-York, Committee-Chamber, May 15,
1775. Resolved. . . .
[New York, 1775.] Broadside.
LOC copy.   14329

New York (City) Committee of
Observation, 1775.
New-York, Committee-Chamber, 29th
May, 1775. Whereas. . . .
[New York, 1775.] Broadside.
LOC copy.   14330

New York (City) Committee of
Observation, 1775.
New-York, Committee-Chamber, 5th
June, 1775. Resolved. . . .
[New York, 1775.] Broadside.
LOC copy.   14331

New York (City) Committee of
Observation, 1775.
New-York, Committee-Chamber,
Wednesday, 26th April, 1775.
[New York, 1775.] Broadside.
NYPL copy.   14322

New York (City) Committee of
Observation, 1775.
New-York, 16th March, 1775. Gentlemen,
The Late Congress Having Deemed it
Expedient. . . .
[New York, 1775.] Broadside.
NYHS copy.   14319

New York (City) Committee of
Observation, 1775.
To the Respectable Inhabitants. . . . 29th
March, 1775.
[New York, 1775.] Broadside.
LOC copy.   14320

New York (City) Committee of
Observation, 1775.
Whereas a Report. . . . 4th Aug. 1775.
[New York, 1775.] Broadside.
LOC copy.   14333

New York (City). Committee on the
Observation of Washington's Death.
Funeral Procession. New-York
Regulations, Relative to the Procession
for Rendering Funeral Honors to . . .
Washington. . . . 29th Dec. '99.
[New York, 1799.] Broadside.
(The one recorded copy is mislaid.) 35937

New York (City). Committee on
Observation of Washington's Death.
Order of the Funeral Procession the 31st
of December, 1799. . . . New-York,
December 29, 1799.
[New York, 1799.] Broadside.
HSP copy.   35940

New York (City) Committee to Promote
Frugality.
The Committee Appointed . . . the 29th of
December Last . . . do Report. . . .

[New York, 1768.] [2] pp.
AAS copy.   11008

New York (City) Committee to Promote
Frugality.
New-York, February 2, 1768. This
Evening. . . .
[New York, 1768.] Broadside.
NYPL copy.   11009

New York (City) Common Council, 1693.
To His Excellency Benjamin Fletcher. . . .
The Humble Address of the Mayor. . . .
New York, 1693. Broadside.
PRO copy.   677

New York (City) Common Council, 1788.
Supplement to the Daily Advertiser . . .
November 10, 1788. . . . An Account of
Cash Paid.
[New York, 1788.] Broadside.
AAS copy.   45310

New York (City) Common Council, 1799.
At a Common Council held on Monday
the 21st Day of January, 1799-the
Following Report [on Pestilential
Diseases] was Read.
[New York, 1799.] Broadside.
(Apparently the unique original was lost
in the Albany fire.)   35936

New York (City) Common Council, 1799.
Proceedings of the Corporation of
New-York, on Supplying the City with . . .
Water.
[New York], Furman, 1799. 29 pp.
NYPL copy.   35941

New York (City) Common Council, 1800.
. . . At a Common Council held on
Monday the 28th Day of April 1800. . . .
The Cartmen. . . .
[New York, 1800.] Broadside.
NYHS copy.   38096

New York (City) Constables, 1773.
City of New York, ss. Personally
Appeared, Moses Sherwood. . . . Sworn
before me, this 7th Day of October, 1773.
[New York, 1773.] Broadside.
NYPL ph. copy.   42473

New York (City) Convention of Delegates
and Churches, 1785.
Extracts of the Proceedings. . . . May 19th,
1800.
[New York, 1800.] 4 pp.
AAS copy.   37392

New York (City) Dealers in Public Funds.
At a Meeting of the Dealers in the Public
Funds in the City of New-York, . . . on the
21st September, 1791.
[New York], Childs & Swaine, [1791].
Broadside.
NYHS copy.   46212

New York (City) Election Prox, 1769.
Philip Livingston, Peter Van Brugh
Livingston. . . .
[New York, 1769.] Broadside.
LOC copy.   41984

New York (City) Election Prox, 1774.
To the Inhabitants of the City and County
of New-York My Friends and
Fellow-Citizens. . . . July 5, 1774.
[New York, 1775.] Broadside.
NYHS copy.   42652

New York (City) Election Prox, 1789.
The Federal Mechanic Ticket. Robert
Yates, Esq., Governor.
[New York, 1789?] Broadside.
NYHS copy.   45536

New York (City) Election Prox, 1791.
Let Every True Whig read this with
Attention.
[New York, 1791.] Broadside.
NYHS copy.   46239

New York (City) First Baptist Church.
The Covenant of the First Baptist Church.
[New York, 1762.] 8 pp.
WL copy.   9215

New York (City) First Presbyterian
Church.
The Address of the Trustees.

[New York, 1790.] Broadside.
NYHS copy.   45926

New York (City) First Universalist
Church.
United Christian Friends. Hymns for the
Use of the Society . . . with the
Constitution.
New York, Tiebout, 1797. 144 pp.
(See Papers B.S.A., XXXVII, 77. The
unique copy could not be reproduced.)
                                               32949

New York (City) Grand Jury, 1744.
To His Excellency George Clinton. . . . 24
April, 1744.
[New York, 1744.] Broadside.
PRO copy.   5460

[New York (City) Hand-in-Hand Fire
Company.
Rules and Orders . . . November, 1780.
New York, Gaine, 1782. 8 pp.]
(The only copy recorded could not be
located.)   17634

New York (City). Heart-in-Hand Fire
Company.
Rules and Orders to be Observed . . .
January, 1781.
New York, Rivington, 1781. 11 pp., 2
leaves.
JCB copy.   44010

New York (City) Heart-in-Hand Fire Co.
Rules and Orders to be Observed.
New York, Loudon, 1784. 12 pp.
NYHS copy.   44572

New York (City) Hospital.
Charter for Establishing an Hospital. . . .
13th July, 1771.
New York, Gaine, 1771. 12 pp.
JCB copy.   12161

New York (City) Independent Company
of Free Citizens.
New York, [blank] 1775. Sir, the
Independent Company of Free Citizens
. . . are to meet at [blank] o'clock in the
Brick-Meeting Yard.
[New York, 1775.] Broadside.
LOC copy.   42899

New York (City) Library.
A Catalogue of the Library belonging to
the Corporation.
New York, Holt, 1766. 48 pp.
HEH copy.   41648

New York (City) Mayor, 1770.
To the Inhabitants . . . of this City.
Whereas. . . . Jan. 22, 1770.
[New York, 1770.] Broadside.
NYHS copy.   11776

New York (City) Mayor, 1772.
New-York, 18th January, 1772. To the
Inhabitants. . . .
[New York, 1772.] Broadside.
NYPL copy.   12486

New York (City) Mayor, 1775.
Copy of the Address left with His
Excellency, Gov. Tryon, the 3d of July,
1775 . . . with the Governor's Answer . . .
the 7th of the same month.
[New York, 1775.] [8] pp.
NYHS copy.   14296

New York (City) Mayor, 1797.
List of Foremen of the Respective Classes
of Cartmen. . . . December 1, 1797.
[New York, 1797.] Broadside.
LOC copy.   32563

New York (City) Mechanics, 1774.
New-York, November 13, 1774. The
Mechanicks of this City, are Earnestly
Requested to meet. . . .
[New York, 1774.] Broadside.
NYHS copy.   42653

New York (City) Merchants, 1734.
New York, June 3, 1734. On Tuesday last
Several of the Principal Merchants. . . .
New York, W. Bradford, 1734. Broadside.
LOC ph. copy.   40057

New York (City) Merchants, 1765.
A Patriotic Advertisement. City of
New-York, October 31, 1765. At a
General Meeting of the Merchants.

[New York, 1765.] Broadside.
LCP copy.   41576

New York (City) Merchants, 1769.
New-York [blank] Gentlemen, Boston
and this Place, having Considered. . . .
[New York, 1769.] Broadside.
(Am. Art Assoc. Cat. 3381, Jan. 14, 1931,
item 253.)   41985

New York (City) Merchants, 1774.
To the Public. An Advertisement having
Appeared . . . the merchants to Meet . . .
May 18, 1774.
[New York, 1774.] Broadside.
LOC copy.   42654

New York (City) Merchants, 1778.
New York, November 25, 1778. At a late
Meeting. . . .
[New York, 1778.] 3 pp.
(Only this facsim. of the 1st page located.)
NYPL copy.   43512

New York (City) Merchants, 1778.
To their Excellencies the Earl of Carlisle,
Sir Henry Clinton, and William Eden. . . .
[New York? 1778?] [3] pp.
NYHS copy.   43513

New York (City) New-York Library,
1754.
A List of the Subscribers to the. . . .
[New York, 1754.] Broadside.
NYPL copy.   40706

New York (City) New-York Library,
1754.
Whereas a Publick Library would be very
Useful. . . . April 2d, 1754.
[New York, 1754.] Broadside.
NYPL copy.   40707

[New York (City) Ordinances, etc., 1695.
Laws and Ordinances.
New York, 1695.]
(No copy found.)   736

[New York (City) Ordinances, etc., 1695.
An Ordinance . . . for Building a Battery.
New York, 1695.]
(No copy found. Mentioned in Common
Council minutes.)   737

[New York (City) Ordinances, etc., 1699.
Notice of the Ferry Lease.
New York, 1699.]
(Title from Hildeburn, N. Y.)   890

[New York (City) Ordinances, etc., 1699.
Regulations of the Market.
New York, 1699.]
(Title from Hildeburn, N. Y.)   891

New York (City) Ordinances, etc., 1700.
An Ordinance [Impost. Sept. 24, 1700].
[New York, 1700.] [2] pp.
PRO copy.   1015

New York (City) Ordinances, etc., 1703.
An Ordinance . . . Dry Cask [Feb. 5].
New York, 1703. Broadside.
HEH copy.   1141

New York (City) Ordinances, etc., 1707.
Several Laws. . . . [Mar. 28, 1707].
New York, 1707. 18 pp.
NYPL copy.   1328

[New York (City) Ordinances, etc., 1720.
City of New-York. On the First day of
December. . . .
[New York, 1720.] 24 pp.]
(A part of 2161.)   2162

New York (City) Ordinances, etc., 1731.
. . . A Law for Regulating Negroes and
Slaves in the Night Time.
[New York, 1731.] Broadside.
NYPL copy.   39975

New York (City) Ordinances, etc., 1731.
Laws, Orders, & Ordinances [Nov. 18,
1731].
New York, 1731. 32, [2] pp.
HEH copy.   3458

New York (City Ordinances, etc., 1734.
. . . A Law for Preserving the Fish in
Fresh-Water Pond.
[New York, 1734.] p. 48.
HEH copy.   40055

New York (City) Ordinances, etc., 1735.
A Law for the Better Regulating . . . the
Publick Markets.
New York, Bradford, 1735. pp. 49-44 (i. e.
54).
HEH copy.   40078

New York (City) Ordinances, etc., 1738.
A Law for Regulating and Declaring the
Duty of Fire-Men [Sept. 19, 1738].
[New York, 1738.] pp. 56-58.
NYPL copy.   4288

[New York (City) Ordinances etc., 1749.
The Carmen's Law.
New York, Parker, 1749.]
(Title from adv.)   6387

New York (City) Ordinances, etc., 1749.
Laws, Statutes, Ordinances, and
Constitutions.
[New York], 1749. 79, [1] pp.
NYPL copy.   6388

[New York (City) Ordinances, etc., 1754.
A Law for Regulating Carts and Car-Men.
New York, Parker & Weyman, 1754.]
(From an adv.)   7278

New York (City) Ordinances, etc., 1763.
Laws, Statutes, Ordinances, and
Constitutions.
[New York], Holt, 1763. [1], 108, [2] pp.
AAS copy.   9463

New York (City) Ordinances etc., 1774.
A Law for the Better Regulating of the
Publick Markets. . . . Aug. 11, 1774.
[New York, 1774.] Broadside.
NYPL copy.   13472

New York (City) Ordinances, etc., 1774.
Laws, Statutes, Ordinances and
Constitutions.
New York, Gaine, 1774. [1], 136, [4] pp.
NYPL copy.   13473

[New York (City) Ordinances, etc. 1784.
Laws, Statutes, Ordinances and
Constitutions. . . .
New York, Gaine, 1784.]
(Apparently a ghost of the 1786 ed.)   18651

New York (City) Ordinances, etc., 1785.
Ordinances, Rules and Bye-laws, for the
. . . Alms-House.
New York, Loudon, [1785?] Broadside.
NYPL copy.   44745

New York (City) Ordinances, etc., 1786.
The Laws and Ordinances.
New York, Loudons, 1786. 29, 44 pp.
NYSL copy.   19855

New York (City) Ordinances, etc., 1793.
Laws and Ordinances. . . . Published the
Tenth day of May, 1793.
New York, Gaine, 1793. 51, [2], 79, [4],
96 pp.
AAS copy.   25907

New York (City) Ordinances, etc., 1794.
. . . A Law to Regulate Carts. . . . this
Twenty-Eight Day of July, 1794.
[New York, 1794.] Broadside.
LOC copy.   27401

New York (City) Ordinances, etc., 1797.
. . . At a Common Council . . . the 9th Day
of November, 1797. . . . A Law to
Regulate Carts and Cartmen.
[New York, 1797.] Broadside.
LOC copy.   32561

New York (City) Ordinances, etc., 1797.
Laws and Ordinances. . . . Published the
First Day of May, 1797.
New York, Forman, 1797. 67, [1] pp.
AAS copy.   32562

New York (City) Ordinances, etc., 1799.
Laws and Ordinances. . . . Published the
29th Day of April, 1799.
[New York], Furman, [1799]. 70,
[1] pp.
NYSoc. copy.   35938

New York (City) Ordinances, etc., 1799.
Laws and Ordinances. . . . Published the
29th Day of April, 1799. . . . Second
Edition.
[New York], Furman, [1799]. 47, [1] pp.
NYSoc. copy.   35939

New York (City) Reformed Dutch
Church, 1774.
A Collection of the Psalms and Hymn
Tunes, used by the. . . .
New York, Hodge & Shober, 1774. [7],
54, 54, [3] pp.
HEH copy.   42655

New York (City) St. George's Chapel.
An Hymn to be Sung by the Episcopal
Charity Children . . . November 30, 1800.
[New York], Ming & Young, [1800].
Broadside.
HC copy.   38100

New York (City) St. Paul's Church.
Sacred Music to be Performed . . . the 31st
December, 1799.
[New York, 1799.] Broadside.
AAS copy.   35951

New York (City) Second Baptist Church.
The Second Baptist Church . . . to the
Warrick Association met at Bedford,
October 15, 1793.
[New York, 1793.] 4 pp.
NYSL copy.   25913

[New York (City) Society Library.
Additional Catalogue of Books belonging
to the. . . .
New York, Swords, 1797.]
(No copy located.)   32569

New York (City) Society Library.
A Catalogue of the Books Belonging
to. . . .
New York, Gaine, [1758]. 20, 3 pp.
NYSOC copy.   8217

New York (City) Society of
Non-Episcopal Churches, 1769.
Whereas it is of the Utmost Importance
for the . . . Denominations . . . not
belonging to the Church . . . to Unite
to form a Society of Non-Episcopal
Churches.
[New York, 1769.] 4 pp.
JCB copy.   41986

New York (City) Sons of Liberty.
At a Meeting of the true Sons of Liberty,
in the City of New-York, July 27, 1774.
[New York, 1774.] Broadside.
AAS ph. copy.   13126

New York (City) Tammany Museum.
Tammany Museum, belonging to
Gardiner Baker.
New York, Harrisson, [1799?] Broadside.
MHS copy.   48943

New York (City) Tammany Society.
American Museum. . . . June 1, 1791.
[New York], Swords, [1791]. Broadside.
NYPL copy.   23619

New York (City) Tax Collector.
To the Inhabitants [Tax on Houses, Act
of Congress, July 14, 1798].
[New York, 1798.] Broadside.
LOC copy.   34222

New York (City) Theater, 1750.
New York, March 1750. By His
Excellency's Permission; at the Theatre in
Nassau-Street, on Monday Evening next
. . . The Orphan.
[New York, 1750.] Broadside.
(The only known copy is imperfect.)
HC copy.   40557

New York (City) Theater, 1752.
For the Benefit of Mrs. Upton . . . at the
Theatre in Nassau-Street . . . will be
Acted Venice Preserv'd.
[Feb. 20, 1752].
[New York, 1752.] Broadside.
NYPL facsim. copy.   40631

New York (City) Theater, 1753.
For the Benefit of the Poor. . . . December
20, 1753.
[New York, 1753.] Broadside.
NYPL ph. copy.   40660

New York (City) Theater, 1753.
New-York, November 12, 1753. By a
Company of Comedians.
[New York, 1753.] Broadside.
Reproduced from Odell.   7077

New York (City) Theater, 1782.

New-York, Theatre, 1782. General
Account.
[New York, 1782.] Broadside.
NYHS copy.   17635

New York (City) Theater, 1787.
John Street Theatre. By the Old American
Company. . . . 20th of March.
[New York, 1787.] Broadside.
(No copy located.)   45110

New York (City) Theater, 1787.
New York, February 17, 1787. . . . By the
Old American Company. . . . The
Gamester.
[New York, 1787.] Broadside.
LOC copy.   45111

New York (City) Theater, 1787.
New York, March 17, 1787. . . . By the
Old American Company. . . . Much Ado
About Nothing.
[New York, 1787.] Broadside.
(Reproduced from Amer. Art Assoc. cat.,
Dec. 6-7, 1921, item 214.)   45112

[New York (City) Theater, 1790.
New-York, May 18, 1790. Mrs. Johnson's
Benefit.
[New York, 1790.] Broadside.]
(The copy reported by Evans could not be
located.)   22722

New York (City) Theater, 1791.
New-York, December 17, 1791.
[New York, 1791.] Broadside.
NYPL copy.   23620

New York (City) Theater, 1792.
New York, February 11th, 1792. . . . By
the Old American Company. . . . He
Would Be a Soldier.
[New York, 1792.] Broadside.
(Not located, 1968.)   46525

New York (City) Theater, 1792.
New-York, April 14th, 1792 . . . Mrs.
Gray's Night. . . . The Beaux Stratagem.
[New York, 1792.] Broadside.
NYHS copy.   46524

New York (City) Theater, 1793.
New-York, June 13, 1793. Theatre.
[New York, 1793.] Broadside.
NYHS copy.   25916

[New York (City) Theater, 1794.
By the Old American Company. . . .
January 8, 1794.
[New York, 1794.] Broadside.]
(No copy located.)   27407

New York (City) Theater, 1794.
New York, April 1, 1794. . . . By the Old
American Company.
[New York, 1794.] Broadside.
(Not located, 1968.)   47134

New York (City) Theater, 1795.
Benefit of Mr. Hallam, jun. On Monday
Evening, the 25th of May.
[New York, 1795.] Broadside.
HEH copy.   47514

New York (City) Theater, 1795.
. . . Benefit of Mr. Humphreys.
[New York, 1795.] Broadside.
(Only known copy is imperfect.)
HEH copy.   47515

New York (City) Theater, 1795.
Mr. Carr's Night. On Wednesday Evening,
the 22d of April.
[New York, 1795.] Broadside.
HEH copy.   47516

New York (City) Theater, 1796.
New York, February 27, 1796. Theatre.
By the Old American Company.
[New York, 1796.] Broadside.
NYPL copy.   47858

New York (City) Theatre, 1796.
New-York, March 7, 1796. Theatre. . . .
The Deserted Daughter.
[New York, 1796.] Broadside.
(Not located, 1968.)   47859

New York (City) Theater, 1796.
New-York, May 18, 1796. Mrs. Johnson's
Benefit.
[New York, 1796.] Broadside.
(Not located, 1968.)   47860

New York (City) Theater, 1796.
New-York, September 26, 1796. Theatre.
On Wednesday Evening. . . .
[New York, 1796.] Broadside.
(Not located, 1968.)   47861

New York (City) Theater, 1797.
New-York, October 2, 1797. New Theatre.
. . . The Way to Get Married.
[New York, 1797.] Broadside.
NYPL facsim. copy.   48195

New York (City) Theater, 1798.
New-York, May 14, 1798. For the Benefit
of Mr. Milns.
[New York, 1798.] Broadside.
NYPL facsim. copy.   48538

New York (City) Trinity Church.
April 14, 1789. Church Wardens.
[New York, 1789.] Broadside.
NYHS copy.   45537

[New York (City) Trinity Church.
At a Meeting of the Corporation of. . . .
The 18th day of May, 1784.
[New York, 1784.] [2] pp.]
(Ford, I, 155; no copy located.)   18652

New York (City) Trinity Church.
The Charter of Trinity Church.
[New York, 1788.] 33 pp.
AAS copy.   21321

New York (City) Trinity Church.
Church Wardens. Hon James Duane.
[New York, 1789.] Broadside.
NYHS copy.   45537

New York (City) Trinity Church.
Church Wardens. James Duane, Robert
Watts.
[New York, 1791.] Broadside.
NYHS copy.   23621

New York (City) Trinity Church.
An Hymn, to be Sung by the Children . . .
the 3d December, 1775.
[New York, 1775.] Broadside.
NYHS copy.   42900

New York (City) Trinity Church.
Notice is hereby Given . . . Lots of
Ground. . . . May 23, 1787.
New York, M'Lean, [1787]. Broadside.
NYPL copy.   45113

New York (City) Trinity Church
On Sunday the 1st of August, will be
Sung. . . .
[New York, 1790.] Broadside.
NYHS copy.   45927

New York (City) Vestrymen, 1747.
A Guide to Vestrymen.
New York, Parker, 1747. 38, [2] pp.
HSP copy.   5960

New York (Colony).
An Argument Delivered on the Part of
New-York, at the Hearing before His
Majesty's Commissioners.
[New York?], 1769. 47, [31] pp.
NYPL copy.   11373

[New York (Colony).
This Indenture Made . . . [1762] Between
Colonel John Henry Lydius. . . .
[New York, 1762.] Broadside.]
(Hasse 832; not now to be located.)   9212

New York (Colony) Attorney General,
1729.
The Attorney General on Reading the
Votes of the 19th of June last.
[New York, 1729.] 3 pp.
PRO copy.   3195

New York (Colony) Commission on
Massachusetts Boundary.
A Journal of the Proceedings of the
Commissaries of New-York, at a Congress
with the Commissaries of the
Massachusetts-Bay.
[New York, 1767]. 19, [1] pp.
NYHS copy.   10706

New York (Colony) Committee of Safety,
1775.
In Committee of Safety . . . the [blank]
Day of [blank] 1775. To [blank]
Greeting. . . .

[New York, 1775.] Broadside.
NYHS copy.   42901

New York (Colony) Committee of Safety,
1775.
In the Committee of Safety . . . July 13,
1775. Whereas. . . .
[New York, 1775.] Broadside.
LOC copy.   14315

New York (Colony) Council, 1693.
A Catalogue of Fees.
New York, 1693. 11 pp.
NYPL copy.   673

New York (Colony) Council, 1698.
An Account of the Proceedings [May 8,
1698].
New York, 1698. 6 pp.
LCP copy.   834

New York (Colony) Council, 1709.
By the Honourable Col. Francis
Nicholson. . . . A Proclamation. Whereas
Her Majesty. . . . New-York, May 26 1709.
New York, Bradford, 1709. Broadside.
NYPL copy.   39484

New York (Colony) Council, 1720.
By the Honourable Peter Schuyler. . . . A
Proclamation [Adjournment. Apr. 21,
1720].
[New York, 1720.] Broadside.
NYSL copy.   2157

New York (Colony) Council, 1727.
At a Council Held at Fort George . . .
November 25, 1727.
[New York, 1727.] 15 pp.
AAS copy.   2932

New York (Colony) Council, 1734.
At a Council held at Fort-George in
New-York on the 5th of November, 1734.
. . . Large Tracts . . . Land.
New York, W. Bradford, 1734. 3 pp.
NYHS copy.   40056

New York (Colony) Council, 1734.
The Report of the Committee of His
Majesty's Council [Letter. Feb. 1,
1733/4].
New York, 1734. 11 pp.
NJHS copy.   3816

New York (Colony) Council, 1734.
To His Excellency William Cosby. . . .
The Humble Address of His Majesty's
Council [Nov. 28, 1734].
New York, Bradford, 1734. 2 pp.
PRO copy.   3818

New York (Colony) Council, 1735.
At a Council held at Fort George [June
12, 1735. +].
[New York, 1735.] 3 pp.
PRO copy.   3938

New York (Colony) Council, 1736.
By the Honourable George Clarke. . . . A
Proclamation [Death of Cosby, Mar. 10,
1735/6].
New York, Bradford, 1735 [/6].
Broadside.
NYPL copy.   4049

New York (Colony) Council, 1736.
By the Honourable George Clarke. . . . A
Proclamation [Adjournment. Mar. 18,
1735/6].
New York, Bradford, 1735 [/6].
Broadside.
NYPL copy.   4050

New York (Colony) Council, 1736.
By the Honourable George Clarke. . . . A
Proclamation [Adjournment. Sept. 15,
1736].
New York, 1736. Broadside.
NYPL copy.   4051

[New York (Colony) Council, 1736.
By the Honourable George Clarke. . . . A
Proclamation [Rip Van Dam. Oct. 1,
1736].
New York, 1736. Broadside.]
(The unique copy could not be located.)
    4052

New York (Colony) Council, 1737.
To the Honourable George Clarke . . . the
Humble Address of His Majesty's
Council.

New York, Bradford, 1737. 3 pp.
NYHS copy.   4177

[New York (Colony) Council, 1740.
To the Honourable George Clarke . . . the
Humble Address of the . . . Council.
[New York, 1740.] Broadside.]
(The unique copy was lost in the Albany
fire.)   4578

New York (Colony) Council, 1741.
An Order of Council [Custom-House.
Jan. 19, 1741].
New York, 1740 [/1]. Broadside.
PRO copy.   4769

New York (Colony) Council, 1744.
To His Excellency the Honourable George
Clinton. . . . The Humble Address [Mar.
13, 1744].
[New York, 1744.] Broadside.
PRO copy.   5459

New York (Colony) Council, 1744.
To His Excellency the Honourable George
Clinton. . . . The Humble Address of the
Council [Apr. 25, 1744].
[New York, 1744.] Broadside.
PRO copy.   5461

New York (Colony) Council, 1745.
To His Excellency the Honourable George
Clinton . . . the Humble Address of His
Majesty's Council [June 26, 1745].
[New York, 1745.] Broadside.
PRO copy.   5660

[New York (Colony) Council, 1746.
To His Excellency . . . George Clinton.
. . . The Humble Representation of the
Council.
New York, 1746.]
(No copy found.)   5834

New York (Colony) Council, 1749.
To His Excellency the Honourable George
Clinton . . . The Humble Address of . . .
His Majesty's Council [June 30, 1749].
[New York, 1749.] Broadside.
PRO copy.   6385

[New York (Colony) Council, 1751.
To His Excellency the Honourable George
Clinton. . . . The Humble Address of His
Majesty's Council [Oct. 9, 1751].
[New York, 1751.] Broadside.]
(The unique copy was lost in the Albany
fire.)   6736

New York (Colony) Council, 1751.
To His Excellency the Honourable George
Clinton. . . . The Humble Address of His
Majesty's Council [Nov. 23, 1751].
[New York, 1751.] 4 pp.
NYSL copy.   6737

New York (Colony) Council, 1753.
To His Excellency the Honourable George
Clinton. . . . The Humble Address of His
Majesty's Council [May 31, 1753].
[New York, 1753.] 2 pp.
(Unique copy lost in Albany fire.)   7076

New York (Colony) Council, 1754.
To the Honourable James De Lancey. . . .
The Humble Address of His Majesty's
Council [Apr. 11, 1754].
[New York, 1754.] Broadside.
PRO copy.   7274

New York (Colony) Council, 1754.
To the Honourable James De Lancey. . . .
The Humble Address of the Council
[Aug. 22, 1754].
[New York, 1754.] Broadside.
PRO copy.   7275

New York (Colony) Council, 1754.
Two Reports of a Committee of His
Majesty's Council [Boundary].
New York, Parker, 1754. 22 pp.
LOC copy.   7276

New York (Colony) Council, 1755.
To His Excellency Sir Charles Hardy. . . .
The Humble Address of the Council
[Sept. 6, 1755].
[New York, 1755.] Broadside.
NYSL copy.   7513

New York (Colony) Council, 1755.
To His Excellency Sir Charles Hardy. . . .

The Humble Address of the Council [Dec.
4, 1755].
[New York, 1755.] 2 pp.
PRO copy.   7514

New York (Colony) Council, 1756.
To His Excellency Sir Charles Hardy. . . .
The Humble Address of the Council
[Sept. 25, 1756].
[New York, 1756.] 2 pp.
PRO copy.   7740

New York (Colony) Council, 1757.
To His Excellency Sir Charles Hardy. . . .
The Humble Address of the Council [Feb.
17, 1757].
[New York, 1757.] 2 pp.
PRO copy.   7977

New York (Colony) Council, 1758.
By the Honourable Cadwallader Colden.
. . . a Proclamation . . . [The Winchester.
Dated Aug. 20, 1760].
[New York, 1760.] Broadside.
NYHS copy.   41158

New York (Colony) Council, 1758.
To the Honourable James De Lancey . . .
the Humble Address of the Council [Nov.
24, 1758].
[New York, 1758.] Broadside.
PRO copy.   8215

New York (Colony) Council, 1759.
To the Honourable James De Lancey . . .
The Humble Address of the Council [Dec.
8, 1759].
[New York, 1759.] Broadside.
PRO copy.   8438

New York (Colony) Council, 1760.
By the Honourable Cadwallader Colden.
. . . A Proclamation. Whereas it has
Pleased Almighty God. . . .
[Thanksgiving, Oct. 23, dated Oct.
1, 1760.]
[New York, 1760.] Broadside.
HSP copy.   41157

New York (Colony) Governor, 1760.
. . . A Proclamation [Oct. 1, 1760].
[New York, Weyman, 1760.] Broadside.
(Also entered as 41157, q. v.)   41159

New York (Colony) Council, 1760.
To the Honourable Cadwallader Colden.
. . . The Humble Address of the Council
[Oct. 28, 1760].
[New York, 1760.] 2 pp.
PRO copy.   8689

New York (Colony) Council, 1761.
To the Honourable Cadwallader Colden
. . . the Humble Address of the Council
[Sept. 3, 1761].
[New York, 1761.] Broadside.
PRO copy.   8957

New York (Colony) Council, 1764.
To the Honourable Calwallader Colden.
. . . The Humble Address of the Council
[Sept. 5, 1764].
[New York, 1764.] Broadside.
PRO copy.   9759

[New York (Colony) Council, 1765.
To His Excellency Sir Henry Moore. . . .
The Humble Address of the Council
[Nov. 22, 1765].
[New York, 1765.] Broadside.]
(Unique copy lost in the Albany fire.)   10098

New York (Colony) Council, 1766.
To his Excellency Sir Henry Moore. . . .
The Humble Address of the Council [June
14, 1766].
[New York, 1766.] Broadside.
PRO copy.   10422

[New York (Colony) Council, 1767.
To His Excellency Sir Henry Moore. . . .
The Humble Address of the Council . . .
May 28, 1767.
[New York, 1767.] Broadside.]
(Unique copy lost in the Albany fire.)   10709

[New York (Colony) Council, 1767.
To His Excellency Sir Henry Moore. . . .
The Humble Address of the Council. . . .
November 20, 1767.

[New York, 1767.] Broadside.]
(Unique copy lost in the Albany fire.)   10711

New York (Colony) Council, 1768.
To His Excellency Sir Henry Moore . . .
the Humble Address of the Council [Nov.
1, 1768].
[New York, 1768.] Broadside.
PRO copy.   11004

New York (Colony) Council, 1769.
To the Honourable Cadwallader Colden.
. . . The Humble Address of the Council
[Nov. 25, 1769].
[New York, 1769.] Broadside.
PRO copy.   11369

New York (Colony) Council, 1773.
To His Excellency William Tryon. . . . The
Humble Address of the Council [Jan. 8,
1773].
[New York, 1773.] Broadside.
LOC copy.   12891

New York (Colony) Council, 1774.
To His Excellency William Tryon. . . . The
Humble Address of the Council . . .
[January 13, 1774.]
[New York, 1774.] [2] pp.
PRO copy.   13468

New York (Colony) Council, 1775.
To the Honorable Cadwallader Colden.
. . . The Humble Address of His Majesty's
Council. . . . Jan. 18, 1775.
[New York, 1775.] Broadside.
LOC copy.   14294

[New York (Colony) Council Journals,
1725.
Extracts from the Minutes of the Council.
[New York, 1725.] 34 pp.]
(De Puy thought this a ghost of 2698.)   2685

New York (Colony) Election Prox, 1775.
The Following are the Names of the
Gentlemen Nominated, as Deputies . . .
for whom the Friends of Liberty. . . .
[New York, 1775.] Broadside.
NYPL copy.   42902

New York (Colony) General Assembly,
1698.
The Remonstrance of Several of the
Representatives.
New York, Bradford, 1698. 4 pp.
PRO copy.   846

New York (Colony) General Assembly,
1698.
To the Kings most Excellent Majesty.
[New York, 1698.] Broadside.
PRO copy.   847

New York (Colony) General Assembly,
1700.
Some Queries Sent up to His Excellency.
[New York, 1700.] 2 pp.
PRO copy.   944

New York (Colony) General Assembly,
1722.
To His Excellency William Burnet . . . The
Humble Address of the General Assembly
[June 14, 1722].
[New York, 1722.] Broadside.
PRO copy.   2377

New York (Colony) General Assembly,
1726.
To His Excellency William Burnet [Sept. 29,
1726].
[New York, 1726.] 2 pp.
PRO copy.   2790

New York (Colony) General Assembly,
1734.
To His Excellency William Cosby. . . . The
Humble Address of the General-
Assembly.
New York, Bradford, 1734. 2 pp.
PRO copy.   3817

New York (Colony) General Assembly,
1737.
To the Honourable George Clarke. . . .
The Humble Address of the General
Assembly.
[New York, 1737]. 6 pp.
NYPL copy.   4178

New York (Colony) General Assembly,
1739.
To the Honourable George Clarke . . . the
Humble Address of the General
Assembly. . . . 1739.
[New York, 1739.] Broadside.
PRO copy.   4405

New York (Colony) General Assembly,
1741.
To the Honourable George Clarke
[Address of the Assembly. Apr. 24, 1741].
[New York, 1741.] 5 pp.
PRO copy.   4771

New York (Colony) General Assembly,
1741.
To the Honourable George Clarke
[Address of the Assembly. Sept. 30,
1741].
New York, Bradford, 1741. 6 pp.
PRO copy.   4772

New York (Colony) General Assembly,
1745.
To His Excellency the Honourable George
Clinton . . . the Humble Address of the
General Assembly [June 27, 1745].
[New York, 1745.] Broadside.
PRO copy.   5661

[New York (Colony) General Assembly,
1747.
A Representation of the General
Assembly . . . to His Excellency the
Governor.
New York, 1747.]
(No copy found.)   6032

[New York (Colony) General Assembly,
1749.
To His Excellency the Honourable George
Clinton [Address of the General
Assembly, June 30, 1749].
[New York, 1749.] Broadside.]
(Hasse 754; not now to be found.)   6386

[New York (Colony) General Assembly,
1754.
Votes of the General Assembly [Trustees,
College].
New York, Parker and Weyman, 1754. 12
pp.]
(See BSA, XLIV, 322.)   7277

New York (Colony) General Assembly,
1758.
To the Honourable James De Lancey. . . .
The Humble Address of the General
Assembly [Nov. 23, 1758].
[New York, 1758.] Broadside.
PRO copy.   8216

New York (Colony) General Assembly,
1766.
To His Excellency Sir Henry Moore. . . .
The Humble Address of the General
Assembly [June 16, 1766].
[New York, 1766.] Broadside.
PRO copy.   10423

New York (Colony) General Assembly,
1767.
To His Excellency Sir Henry Moore. . . .
The Humble Address of the General
Assembly. . . . the 3rd June, 1767.
[New York, 1767.] Broadside.
PRO copy.   10710

New York (Colony) General Assembly,
1768.
To His Excellency Sir Henry Moore. . . .
The Humble Address of the General
Assembly [Nov. 3, 1768].
[New York, 1768.] Broadside.
PRO copy.   11005

New York (Colony) General Assembly,
1769.
The Managers on the Part of New-York
[July 26, 1769].
[New York, 1769.] Broadside.
LCP copy.   11372

New York (Colony) General Assembly,
1769.
To the Honourable Cadwallader Colden.
. . . The Humble Address of the General
Assembly [Nov. 29, 1769].
[New York, 1769.] Broadside.
PRO copy.   11370

New York (Colony) General Assembly,
1769.
To the Honourable His Majesty's
Commissioners for Settling the
Partition-line, between the Colonies of
New-York, and New-Jersey [July 18,
1769].
[New York, 1769.] 4 pp.
LCP copy.   11371

New York (Colony) General Assembly,
1773.
A Narrative of the Proceedings
Subsequent to the Royal Adjudication.
New York, Holt, 1773. 28, [66] pp.
AAS copy.   12889

New York (Colony) General Assembly,
1773.
A State of the Right of the Colony of
New-York, with Respect to its Eastern
Boundary.
New York, Gaine, 1773. 28 pp.
AAS copy.   12888

New York (Colony) General Assembly,
1775.
Extracts of the Votes and Proceedings . . .
January 28, 1775. . . . To the Public . . .
31st January, 1775.
[New York, 1775.] [2] pp.
CHS copy.   42903

New York (Colony) General Assembly,
1775.
To the King's Most Excellent Majesty.
The Humble Petition of the General
Assembly. . . . The 25th Day of March,
1775.
[New York, 1775.] 11 pp.
NYPL copy.   14295

New York (Colony) General Assembly.
House of Representatives, 1700.
To His Excellency [Address. July
29, 1700].
New York, Bradford, 1700. Broadside.
PRO copy.   945

New York (Colony) General Assembly
Journals, 1691.
Journal of the Votes and Proceedings of
the General Assembly. . . . Vol. I [Apr. 9,
1691 - Sept. 27, 1743].
New York, Gaine, 1764. iv, 840, [2] pp.,
irreg.
AAS copy.   9756

New York (Colony) General Assembly
Journals, 1695.
A Journal of the House [June 20, 1695 +].
New York, Bradford, 1695. [2], 20 pp.
PRO copy.   735

[New York (Colony) General Assembly
Journals, 1696.
Votes and Proceedings of the Assembly.
New York, 1696.]
(Apparently a ghost of 757 and 758.)   772

New York (Colony) General Assembly
Journals, 1697.
Votes of the House of Representatives
[Mar. 25 - 27, 1697].
[New York, 1697.] pp. 70-73.
NYSL copy.   810

New York (Colony) General Assembly
Journals, 1698.
Votes of the House. . . . 21 Mart. 1698.
[New York, 1698.] 6 + pp.
(Only reported copy defective.)
NYPL photostat copy.   848

New York (Colony) General Assembly
Journals, 1698.
Votes of the House [May 19 - June 14,
1698].
[New York, 1698.] 12 pp.
PRO copy.   849

New York (Colony) General Assembly
Journals, 1701.
The Votes of the House [Aug. 19 - Oct.
18, 1701].
[New York, 1701.] 38 pp.
PRO copy.   1014

New York (Colony) General Assembly
Journals, 1702.
The Votes of the House [Oct. 20 - Nov.
27, 1702].

New York, 1702. 20 pp.
PRO copy.   1092

New York (Colony) General Assembly
Journals, 1702.
A Journal of the Votes of the General
Assembly [Oct. 20, 1702 +].
[New York, 1708.] 78 pp.
AAS copy.   1368

New York (Colony) General Assembly
Journals, 1709.
A Journal of the Votes of the General
Assembly [1709].
New York, 1709. 40 pp.
NYPL copy.   1424

New York (Colony) General Assembly
Journals, 1710.
A Journal of the Votes of the General
Assembly [Sept. 1 - Nov. 24, 1710].
New York, Bradford, 1710. 31 pp., irreg.
PRO copy.   1479

New York (Colony) General Assembly
Journal, 1711.
A Journal of the Votes [Oct.-Nov. 1711].
[New York, 1711.] 22 pp.
PRO copy.   1524

New York (Colony) General Assembly
Journals, 1712.
A Journal of the Votes of the General
Assembly [Apr. 30-Dec. 10, 1712].
New York, Bradford, 1712. 18, 17 pp.
PRO copy.   1576

[New York (Colony) General Assembly
Journals, 1713.
A Journal of the Votes of the General
Assembly.
New York, 1713.]
(Apparently a ghost of 1637 and 1638, or
of the Ms. Journal.)   1640

[New York (Colony) General Assembly
Journals, 1714.
A Journal of the Votes of the General
Assembly [Mar. 22, 1714 +].
New York, 1714.]
(Perhaps not printed.)   1707

New York (Colony) General Assembly
Journals, 1715.
A Journal of the Votes of the General
Assembly [May 3 - July 21, 1715].
[New York, 1715.] 20 pp.
(The unique copy is not now to be found.)
                                                       1774

[New York (Colony) General Assembly
Journals, 1716.
A Journal of the Votes of the General
Assembly.
New York, 1716.]
(Perhaps not printed.)   1847

New York (Colony) General Assembly
Journals, 1717.
Votes of the General Assembly [Apr. 9, -
May 28, 1717].
[New York, 1717.] 17 pp.
PRO copy.   1919

New York (Colony) General Assembly
Journals, 1718.
A Journal of the Votes of the General
Assembly [May 27 - June 24, 1718].
[New York, 1718.] 8 + pp.
PRO copy.   1991

[New York (Colony) General Assembly
Journals, 1719.
A Journal of the Votes of the General
Assembly.
New York, 1719.]
(Not known in printed form.)   2064

New York (Colony) General Assembly
Journals, 1720.
The Votes of the General Assembly [Oct.
13,-Nov. 19, 1720].
[New York, 1720.] 34 pp.
PRO copy.   2160

New York (Colony) General Assembly
Journals, 1721.
The Votes of the General Assembly [May,
1721 +].
[New York, 1721.] 37 pp.
PRO copy.   2280

New York (Colony) General Assembly
Journals, 1722.
The Votes of the General Assembly [June
1, 1722 +].
[New York, 1722.] 27 pp., irreg.
(No perfect copy is known.)
NYPL copy.   2378

New York (Colony) General Assembly
Journals, 1722.
The Votes of the General Assembly [Oct.
16, 1722 +].
[New York, 1722.] 12 pp.
(The unique copy is defective.)
NYPL copy.   2379

New York (Colony) General Assembly
Journals, 1723.
The Votes of the General Assembly [May
8-July 6, 1723].
[New York, 1723.] 26 pp.
PRO copy.   2470

New York (Colony) General Assembly
Journals, 1724.
The Votes of the General Assembly [May
12, 1724 +].
[New York, 1724.] 28 pp.
PRO copy.   2572

New York (Colony) General Assembly
Journals, 1725.
Numb. I. The Votes of the General
Assembly [Aug. 31, 1725 +].
New York, 1725. 38 pp.
PRO copy.   2687

New York (Colony) General Assembly
Journals, 1726.
The Votes of the General Assembly [Apr.
5,-June 17, 1726].
New York, 1726. 37 pp.
NYPL copy.   2791

New York (Colony) General Assembly
Journals, 1726.
A Journal of the Votes . . . of the General
Assembly [Sept. 27, 1726 +].
[New York, 1726.] 26 pp.
PRO copy.   2792

New York (Colony) General Assembly
Journals, 1727.
. . . The Votes of the General Assembly
[Sept. 30, 1727 +].
New York, 1727. 28 pp.
PRO copy.   2935

New York (Colony) General Assembly
Journals, 1728.
. . . A Journal of the Votes & Proceedings
of the General Assembly [July 23, 1728
+].
[New York], Bradford, [1728]. 37 pp.
PRO copy.   3074

New York (Colony) General Assembly
Journals, 1729.
. . . A Journal of the Votes & Proceedings
of the General Assembly [May 13,
1729 +].
[New York], Bradford, [1729]. 36 pp.
PRO copy.   3196

New York (Colony) General Assembly
Journals, 1730.
. . . A Journal of the Votes and
Proceedings of the General Assembly
[Aug. 25, 1730 +].
[New York, 1730.] 34 pp.
PRO copy.   3332

New York (Colony) General Assembly
Journals, 1731.
A Journal of the Votes and Proceedings of
the General Assembly [Aug. 25 - Sept. 31,
1731].
[New York, 1731.] 21 pp., irreg.
PRO copy.   3456

New York (Colony) General Assembly
Journals, 1732.
A Journal of the Votes and Proceedings of
the General Assembly [Aug. 9, 1732 +].
New York, 1732. 44 pp.
(All known copies are defective.)
NYPL copy.   3583

New York (Colony) General Assembly
Journals, 1733.
. . . A Journal of the Votes and
Proceedings of the General Assembly
[Oct. 15, 1733 +].

[New York], Bradford, [1733.]
12 pp.
PRO copy.   3698

New York (Colony) General Assembly
Journals, 1734.
A Journal of the Votes and Proceedings of
the General Assembly [Apr. 25, 1734 +].
New York, 1734. 36 pp.
NYPL copy.   3814

New York (Colony) General Assembly
Journals, 1734.
A Journal of the Votes and Proceedings of
the General Assembly [Oct. 2, 1734].
New York, 1734. 20 (i.e. 30) pp.
(Pagination irregular.)
NYHS copy.   3815

New York (Colony) General Assembly
Journals, 1735.
A Journal of the Votes and Proceedings of
the General Assembly [Oct. 16, 1735 +].
New York, 1735. 22 pp.
NYPL copy.   3941

New York (Colony) General Assembly
Journals, 1736.
A Journal of the Votes and Proceedings of
the General Assembly [Oct. 13, 1736 +].
New York, 1736. 16 pp.
NYPL copy.   4053

New York (Colony) General Assembly
Journals, 1737.
A Journal of the Votes and Proceedings of
the General Assembly [Apr. 5, 1737 +].
[New York, 1737.] 15 pp.
NYHS copy.   4173

New York (Colony) General Assembly
Journals, 1737.
A Journal of the Votes and Proceedings of
the General Assembly [June 15, 1737 +].
[New York, 1737.] 107 pp.
NYPL copy.   4174

New York (Colony) General Assembly
Journals, 1738.
. . . A Journal of the Votes and
Proceedings of the General Assembly
[Apr. 4, 1738 +].
[New York, 1738.] 35 pp.
PRO copy.   4286

New York (Colony) General Assembly
Journals, 1739.
Journal of the Votes and Proceedings of
the General Assembly [Mar. 27, 1739 +].
[New York, 1739.] 16 pp.
NYHS copy.   4402

New York (Colony) General Assembly
Journals, 1739.
Journal of the Votes and Proceedings of
the General Assembly [Aug. 29, 1739 +].
New York, 1739. 51 pp.
NYHS copy.   4403

New York (Colony) General Assembly
Journals, 1740.
Votes and Proceedings of the General
Assembly [May 23, 1740]
New York, 1740. Broadside.
NYHS copy.   4573

New York (Colony) General Assembly
Journals, 1740.
Journal of the Votes and Proceedings of
the General Assembly [June 30, 1740 +].
New York, 1740. 3, 4 pp.
NYHS copy.   4574

New York (Colony) General Assembly
Journals, 1740.
Journal of the Votes and Proceedings of
the General Assembly [Sept. 11, 1740 +].
[New York, 1740.] 34 pp.   4575

New York (Colony) General Assembly
Journals, 1741.
Journal of the Votes and Proceedings of
the General Assembly [Apr. 14, 1741 +].
New York, 1741. 29 pp.
PRO copy.   4766

New York (Colony) General Assembly
Journals, 1741.
Journal of the Votes and Proceedings of
the General Assembly [Sept. 15 - 17,
1741].
New York, 1741, 4 pp.
PRO copy.   4767

New York (Colony) General Assembly
Journals, 1741.
Journal of the Votes and Proceedings of
the General Assembly [Sept. 15-Nov. 27,
1741].
New York, 1741. 47 pp.
NYHS copy.   4768

New York (Colony) General Assembly
Journals, 1742.
Journal of the Votes and Proceedings of
the General Assembly [Mar. 16, 1742 +].
New York, 1742. 9 pp.
PRO copy.   5021

New York (Colony) General Assembly
Journals, 1742.
Journal of the Votes and Proceedings of
the General Assembly [Apr. 19-30, 1742.]
New York, Bradford, 1743. 8 pp.
PRO copy.   5258

New York (Colony) General Assembly
Journals, 1742.
Journal of the Votes and Proceedings of
the General Assembly [Aug. 3, 1742 +].
New York, 1742. 14 pp.
PRO copy.   5022

New York (Colony) General Assembly
Journals, 1743.
Journal of the Votes and Proceedings of
the General Assembly [Nov. 8, 1743 +].
New York, 1743. 45 pp.
PRO copy.   5259

New York (Colony) General Assembly,
Journals, 1743-1765.
Journal of the Votes and Proceedings of
the General Assembly. . . . 1743 . . . 1765.
Vol. II.
New York, Gaine, 1766. [2], 811, [1], viii
pp.
AAS copy.   10418

New York (Colony) General Assembly
Journals, 1744.
Votes and Proceedings of the General
Assembly [Apr. 17, 1744 +].
[New York], Parker, [1744]. 26 pp.
PRO copy.   5453

New York (Colony) General Assembly
Journals, 1744.
Votes and Proceedings of the General
Assembly [July 17, 1744 +].
New York, Parker, 1744. 59 pp.
PRO copy.   5454

New York (Colony) General Assembly
Journals, 1744.
Votes and Proceedings of the General
Assembly [Nov. 6, 1744, to May 14,
1745].
[New York, 1745.] 38, 2 pp.
HSP copy.   5657

New York (Colony) General Assembly
Journals, 1745.
Votes of the General Assembly [June 25
to July 6, 1745].
New York, 1745. 20 pp.
HSP copy.   5658

New York (Colony) General Assembly
Journals, 1745.
Votes of the General Assembly [Aug. 6 to
Dec. 24, 1745].
New York, 1745. 52 pp.
HSP copy.   5659

[New York (Colony) General Assembly
Journals, 1746.
Votes of the General Assembly [Jan. 7 -
May 3, 1746].
New York, 1746. pp. 53-101.]
(The only known copy seems to have been
destroyed in the Albany fire. There are
reprints, however.   5835

New York (Colony) General Assembly.
Journals, 1746.
Votes and Proceedings of the General
Assembly [June 3 - July 15, 1746].
New York, 1746. 28 pp.
PRO copy.   5836

New York (Colony) General Assembly
Journals, 1746.
Votes and Proceedings of the General
Assembly [July 29 - Dec. 6, 1746].
[New York, 1746.] 41 pp.
PRO copy.   5837

[New York (Colony) General Assembly
Journals, 1747.
Journal of the Votes and Proceedings of
the General Assembly [Mar. 24 - Sept. 22,
1747].
New York, 1747. 58 pp.]
(Probably lost in Albany fire of 1911.)
6029

[New York (Colony) General Assembly
Journals, 1747.
Votes and Proceedings of the General
Assembly [Sept. 29 - Nov. 25, 1747].
[New York, 1747.] 64 pp.]
(Apparently lost in Albany fire of 1911.)
6030

New York (Colony) General Assembly.
Journals, 1748.
A Journal of the Votes and Proceedings of
the General Assembly [Feb. 12,
1747/8-Nov. 12, 1748].
New York, 1747/8. 96 pp.
PRO copy.   6206

New York (Colony) General Assembly
Journals, 1749.
Votes and Proceedings of the General
Assembly [June 27 - Aug. 4, 1749].
[New York, 1749.] 28 pp.
PRO copy.   6382

[New York (Colony) General Assembly
Journals, 1750.
Journal of the Votes and Proceedings of
the General Assembly [Sept. 4 - Nov. 24,
1750].
New York, 1750.]
(Unique copy lost in Albany fire.)   6569

New York (Colony) General Assembly
Journals, 1751.
Votes and Proceedings of the General
Assembly [Oct. 1 - Nov. 25, 1751].
New York, 1751. 47 pp.
HSP copy.   6735

New York (Colony) General Assembly
Journals, 1752.
Votes and Proceedings of the General
Assembly [Oct. 24 - Nov. 11, 1752].
New York, Parker, 1752. 21 pp.
PRO copy.   6896

New York (Colony) General Assembly
Journals, 1753.
Votes and Proceedings of the General
Assembly [May 30 - July 4, 1753].
[New York], Parker, [1753]. pp. 1-4,
[1]-2, 5-42.
PRO copy.   7074

New York (Colony) General Assembly
Journals, 1757.
Votes and Proceedings of the General
Assembly [Feb. 15-26, 1757].
[New York, 1757.] 14 pp.
LOC copy.   7979

New York (Colony) General Assembly
Journals, 1757.
Votes and Proceedings of the General
Assembly [Dec. 6-24, 1757].
[New York, 1757.] 20 pp.
PRO copy.   7980

New York (Colony) General Assembly
Journals, 1759.
[Votes and Proceedings of the General
Assembly Jan. 31-Mar. 7, 1759.
New York, Weyman, 1759.] 38 pp.
(The only copy located lacks tp.)
PRO copy. CO 5/1216-1.   8439

New York (Colony) General Assembly
Journals, 1759.
Votes and Proceedings of the General
Assembly [June 26 - July 3, 1759].
[New York], Weyman, [1759.] pp. 39-44.
PRO copy. CO 5/1216-1.   8440

New York (Colony) General Assembly
Journals, 1759.
Votes and Proceedings of the General
Assembly [Oct. 17 - 18, 1759].
[New York, Weyman, [1759]. pp. 45-48.
PRO copy. CO 5/1216-1.   8441

New York (Colony) General Assembly
Journals, 1759.
Votes and Proceedings of the General
Assembly [Dec. 4 - 24, 1759].

[New York], Weyman, [1759].
pp. 53-56, 63-80.
PRO copy. CO 5/1216-1.   8442

New York (Colony) General Assembly
Journals, 1760.
Votes and Proceedings of the General
Assembly [Mar. 11 - June 10, 1760].
[New York], Weyman, [1760].
pp. [81]-131.
PRO copy.   8690

New York (Colony) General Assembly
Journals, 1760.
Votes and Proceedings of the General
Assembly [Oct. 21-31, 1760].
[New York, 1760.] 16 + pp.
(The only copy located is imperfect.)
PRO copy.   8691

New York (Colony) General Assembly
Journals, 1763.
Votes and Proceedings of the General
Assembly [Nov. 8 - Dec. 20, 1763].
[New York], Weyman, [1763]. 47 pp.
(C. O. 5/1217.)
PRO copy.   9462

New York (Colony) General Assembly
Journals, 1764.
Votes and Proceedings of the General
Assembly [Apr. 17-21, 1764].
[New York], Weyman, [1764]. 9 pp.
PRO copy.   9760

New York (Colony) General Assembly
Journals, 1765.
Votes and Proceedings of the General
Assembly [Nov. 12-13, 1765].
[New York], Weyman, [1765].
Broadside.
PRO copy.   10099

New York (Colony) General Assembly
Journals, 1766.
Journal of the General Assembly [June
11, 1766-Dec. 19, 1766].
[New York], Weyman, [1766]. 24, 46 pp.
PRO copy. C. O. 5/1217   10419

[New York (Colony) General Assembly.
Journals, 1767.
Journal of the Votes and Proceedings of
the General Assembly [Nov. 17, 1767 -
Feb. 6, 1768].
New York, Weyman [and Gaine], [1768].
92 pp.]
(Described by Evans and Ford but not
now to be located.)   11006

[New York (Colony) General Assembly.
Journal, 1768.
Votes and Proceedings of the General
Assembly [Oct. 27-Nov. 30, 1768].
[New York], Gaine, [1768]. 38 pp.]
(This is the first part of 11364, q.v.)   11007

New York (Colony) General Assembly.
Journal, 1768.
Journal of the Votes and Proceedings of
the General Assembly [Oct. 27, 1768 -
Jan. 2, 1769].
New York, Gaine, 1769. 80 pp.
NYPL copy.   11364

New York (Colony) General Assembly.
Journal, 1769.
Journal of the Votes and Proceedings of
the General Assembly [Apr. 4-May 20,
1769].
New York, Gaine, 1769. 88 pp., irreg.
LOC copy.   11365

[New York (Colony) General Assembly.
Journal, 1769.
Journal of the Votes and Proceedings of
the General Assembly [Nov. 21 - Dec. 30,
1769].
[New York], Gaine, [1769] 64 pp.]
(A duplicate of 11774, q.v.)   11366

New York (Colony) General Assembly
Journal, 1769.
Journal of the Votes and Proceedings of
the General Assembly [Nov. 21, 1769 -
Jan. 27, 1770].
New York, Gaine, 1770. 120 pp.
(The unique copy is imperfect.)
LOC copy.   11774

New York (Colony) General Assembly
Journal, 1770.
Journal of the Votes and Proceedings of

the General Assembly [Dec. 11,
1770-Mar. 4, 1771].
New York, Gaine, 1771. 88 pp.
AAS copy.   12158

New York (Colony). General Assembly
Journal, 1772.
Journal of the Votes and Proceedings
[Jan. 7 - Mar. 24, 1772.]
New York, Gaine, 1772. 118 pp.
HSP copy.   12484

New York (Colony) General Assembly
Journal, 1773.
Journal of the Votes and Proceedings of
the General Assembly.
New York, Gaine, 1773. 120 pp.
AAS copy.   12887

New York (Colony) General Assembly
Journal, 1774.
Journal of the Votes and Proceedings of
the General Assembly [Jan. 6 - 18, 1774].
New York, Gaine, 1774. 14 pp.
NYPL copy.   13462

New York (Colony) General Assembly
Journal, 1774.
[Journal of the General Assembly of
New-York, Mar. 10-15, 1774.]
[New York, 1774.] pp. 91-98.
NYPL copy.   13465

New York (Colony) General Assembly,
1774.
To His Excellency William Tryon. . . . The
Humble Address of the General Assembly
. . . [January 18, 1774.]
[New York, 1774.] [2] pp.
PRO copy.   13469

New York (Colony) General Assembly
Journal, 1774.
Votes and Proceedings of the General
Assembly [Jan. 19 - 29, 1774].
[New York, 1774.] pp. 15-30.
NYPL copy.   13463

New York (Colony) General Assembly
Journal, 1774.
Votes and Proceedings of the General
Assembly [Jan. 31-Mar. 9, 1774].
[New York, 1774.] pp. 31-90.
NYPL copy.   13464

New York (Colony) General Assembly
Journal, 1774.
Votes and Proceedings of the General
Assembly [Mar. 16 - 18, 1774].
[New York, 1774.] pp. 99-105.
NYPL copy.   13466

New York (Colony) General Assembly
Journal, 1775.
Journal of the Votes and Proceedings of
the General Assembly [Jan. 10 - Apr. 3,
1775].
New York, Gaine, 1775. [4], 131 pp.
LOC copy.   14291

New York (Colony) Governor, 1665.
The Conditions for New-Planters.
[Cambridge, 1665.] Broadside.
MHS copy.   98

New York (Colony) Governor, 1693.
By His Excellency Benjamin Fletcher. . . .
A Proclamation [Swearing, Apr. 29, 1693].
LOC copy.   668

New York (Colony) Governor, 1693.
Benjamin Fletcher, Captain General. . . .
To all Officers and Ministers. . . . 8th Day
of June.
New York, 1693. Broadside.
(The copy with the four-line title is that in
the APS; that with the five-line title is in
the NYSL.)   669

New York. (Colony) Governor, 1693.
Benjamin Fletcher, Capiteyn Generael.
. . . 8ste Dag van Juny.
New York, 1693. Broadside.
Collegiate Reformed Dutch Church copy.
670

New York (Colony) Governor, 1693.
Benjamin Fletcher, Captain General. . .
To all Officers and Ministers. . . . 8th Day
of June.
New York, 1693. Broadside.
(Four-line title. Reproduced with 669.)
APS copy.   39304

New York (Colony) Governor, 1693.
By His Excellency Benjamin Fletcher. . . .
A Proclamation [Assembly Dissolved,
July 27, 1693].
New York, 1693. Broadside.
PRO copy.   671

New York (Colony) Governor, 1693.
By His Excellency, Benjamin Fletcher. . . .
A Proclamation [War, Aug. 25, 1693].
New York, 1693. Broadside.
(The original was destroyed in the Albany
fire; reproduced from a reprint.)
NYPL copy.   672

New York (Colony) Governor, 1693.
By His Excellency Benjamin Fletcher. . . .
A Proclamation [Connecticut. Nov. 8,
1693].
New York, 1693. Broadside.
LOC copy.   675

New York (Colony) Governor, 1693.
By His Excellency Benjamin Fletcher. . . .
A Proclamation [Deserters, Nov. 13,
1693].
New York, 1693. Broadside.
NYSL copy.   676

New York (Colony) Governor, 1695.
By His Excellency Benjamin Fletcher. . . .
A Proclamation [Dissolution. Apr. 22,
1695].
New York, 1695. Broadside.
NYSL copy.   733

New York (Colony) Governor, 1695.
By His Excellency Benjamin Fletcher. . . .
A Proclamation [French Privateers. June
6, 1695].
New York, 1695. Broadside.
NYSL copy.   734

New York (Colony) Governor, 1696.
By His Excellency Benjamin Fletcher. . . .
A Proclamation [King William, Jan. 9,
1695/6].
[New York, 1696.] Broadside.
NYPL ph. copy.   759

New York (Colony) Governor, 1696.
By His Excellency Benjamin Fletcher. . . .
A Proclamation [Deserters. Feb. 27,
1695/6].
New York, 1695 [1696]. Broadside.
NYSL copy.   761

New York (Colony) Governor, 1696.
By His Excellency Benjamin Fletcher. . . .
A Proclamation [Fast, Mar. 27. Dated
Feb. 27, 1695/6.]
New York, 1695 [1696]. Broadside.
NYSL copy.   760

New York (Colony) Governor, 1696.
By His Excellency Coll. Benjamin
Fletcher. . . . Proclamation [Bounty. Apr.
21, 1696].
New York, 1696. Broadside.
NYSL copy.   762

New York (Colony) Governor, 1696.
By His Excellency Coll. Benjamin
Fletcher. . . . A Proclamation
[Conspiracy. May 21, 1696].
New York, 1696. Broadside.
NYSL copy.   764

New York (Colony) Governor, 1696.
By His Excellency Coll. Benjamin
Fletcher. . . . A Proclamation [Embargo.
June 11, 1696].
New York, 1696. Broadside.
NYSL copy.   765

New York (Colony) Governor, 1696.
By His Excellency Coll. Benjamin
Fletcher. . . . A Proclamation [Exports.
July 2, 1696].
New York, 1696. Broadside.
NYSL copy.   766

New York (Colony) Governor, 1696.
By His Excellency Coll. Benjamin
Fletcher. . . . A Proclamation [Frontiers.
May 11, 1696].
New York, 1696. Broadside.
NYSL copy.   763

New York (Colony) Governor, 1696.
By His Excellency Coll. Benjamin
Fletcher. . . . A Proclamation [Fuzileers.
Aug. 1, 1696].

New York, 1696. Broadside.
NYSL copy.   767

New York (Colony) Governor, 1696.
By His Excellency Coll. Benjamin
Fletcher. . . . A Proclamation [French.
Aug. 2, 1696].
New York, 1696. Broadside.
NYSL copy.   768

New York (Colony) Governor, 1696.
By His Excellency Coll. Benjamin
Fletcher. . . . A Proclamation
[Adjournment. Sept. 12, 1696].
New York, 1696. Broadside.
NYSL copy.   770

New York (Colony) Governor, 1696.
By His Excellency Coll. Benjamin
Fletcher. . . . A Proclamation [Deserters.
Sept. 12, 1696].
New York, 1696. Broadside.
NYSL copy.   769

New York (Colony) Governor, 1696.
By His Excellency Coll. Benjamin
Fletcher. . . . A Proclamation
[Transportation, Sept. 12, 1696].
New York, 1696. Broadside.
NYPL copy.   771

New York (Colony) Governor, 1696.
The Speech of . . . Coll. Benjamin
Fletcher. . . . To the Assembly the 7th Day
of April, 1696.
[New York, 1696.] 3 pp.
LOC ph. copy.   39320

New York (Colony) Governor, 1697.
By His Excellency Coll. Benjamin
Fletcher. . . . A Proclamation.
[Thanksgiving, Apr. 22. Dated Mar. 25,
1697].
New York, 1607. Broadside.
NYSL copy.   804

[New York (Colony) Governor, 1697.
By His Excellency Collonel Benjamin
Fletcher. . . . A Proclamation [Rye, Apr.
15, 1697].
New York, 1697. Broadside.]
(Lost in Albany fire.)   805

New York (Colony) Governor, 1697.
By His Excellency Collonel Benjamin
Fletcher. . . . A Proclamation. [Exports.
May 31, 1697].
New York, 1697. Broadside.
NYSL copy.   806

New York (Colony) Governor, 1697.
By His Excellency Collonel Benjamin
Fletcher. . . . A Proclamation [Bounty.
June 4, 1697].
New York, 1697. Broadside.
NYSL copy.   807

New York (Colony) Governor, 1697.
By His Excellency Collonel Benjamin
Fletcher. . . . A Proclamation.
[Prorogation, Oct. 21, 1697].
New York, 1697. Broadside.
NYSL copy.   808

New York (Colony) Governor, 1697.
By His Excellency Collonel Benjamin
Fletcher. . . . A Proclamation [Deserters.
Nov. 4, 1697].
New York, 1697. Broadside.
NYSL copy.   809

[New York (Colony) Governor, 1698.
By His Excellency Collonel Benjamin
Fletcher. . . . A Proclamation. [Peace,
Feb. 26, 1697/8].
New York, 1698. Broadside.]
(Lost in Albany fire.)   836

New York (Colony) Governor, 1698.
By His Excellency Collonel Benjamin
Fletcher. . . . Proclamation
[Thanksgiving, Mar. 10. Dated Feb. 26,
1697/8].
New York, 1698. Broadside.
NYSL copy.   835

New York (Colony) Governor, 1698.
By His Excellency Richard Earle of
Bellomont. . . . A Proclamation
[Commissions. Apr. 2, 1698].
New York, 1698. Broadside.
PRO copy.   837

New York (Colony) Governor, 1698.
By His Excellency Richard Earl of
Bellomont. . . . A Proclamation
[Dissolution, Apr. 2, 1698].
New York, 1698. Broadside.
NYSL copy.   838

New York (Colony) Governor, 1698.
By His Excellency Richard Earl of
Bellomont. . . . A Proclamation
[Profanity. Apr. 2, 1698].
New York, Bradford, 1698. Broadside.
PRO copy.   839

New York (Colony) Governor, 1698.
By His Excellency Richard Earl of
Bellomont. . . . A Proclamation.
[Elections. Apr. 7, 1698].
New York, 1698. Broadside.
NYSL copy.   840

New York (Colony) Governor, 1698.
His Excellency, the Earl of Bellomont his
Speech to the Representatives . . . the 19th
of May, 1698.
New York, 1698. 3 pp.
LCP copy.   845

New York (Colony) Governor, 1698.
By His Excellency Richard Earl of
Bellomont. . . . A Proclamation [Pyrates.
May 9, 1698].
New York, Bradford, 1698. Broadside.
PRO copy.   842

New York (Colony) Governor, 1698.
By His Excellency Richard Earl of
Bellomont. . . . A Proclamation
[Perth-Amboy. May 24, 1698].
New York, Bradford, 1698. Broadside.
PRO copy.   841

New York (Colony) Governor, 1698.
By His Excellency Richard Earl of
Bellomont. . . . A Proclamation [Fast,
Oct. 26. Dated Oct. 6, 1698].
New York, Bradford, [1698]. Broadside.
PRO copy.   843

New York (Colony) Governor, 1698.
By His Excellency Richard Earl of
Bellomont. . . . A Proclamation [Oath.
Nov. 23, 1698].
New York, 1698. Broadside.
NYSL copy.   844

New York (Colony) Governor, 1698.
By His Excellency Richard Earl of
Bellomont . . . a Proclamation. Whereas
the Acts . . . [Jan. 19, 1698].
New York, Bradford, 1698. Broadside.
LOC ph. copy.   39331

[New York (Colony) Governor, 1699.
By His Excellency Richard Earl of
Bellomont. . . . A Proclamation [Gold and
Silver Smiths, Mar. 16, 1699].
New York, 1699. Broadside.]
(Lost in Albany fire.)   884

New York (Colony) Governor, 1699.
By His Excellency Richard Earl of
Bellomont. . . . A Proclamation [Darien,
May 15, 1699].
New York, 1699. [2] pp.
PRO copy.   885

New York (Colony) Governor, 1699.
His Excellency, the Earl of Bellomont his
Speech [Mar. 21, 1699].
Nw York, 1699. 3 pp.
PRO copy.   888

New York (Colony) Governor, 1700.
By His Excellency Richard Earl of
Bellomont. . . . A Proclamation [Pyrates.
July 26, 1700].
New York, Bradford, 1700. Broadside.
PRO copy.   942

New York (Colony) Governor, 1700.
His Excellency the Earl of Bellomont's
Speech [July 2, 1700].
[New York, 1700.] Broadside.
PRO copy.   943

New York (Colony) Governor, 1702.
By His Excellency Edward Lord
Cornbury. A Proclamation [Officers. May
3, 1702].
New York, 1702. Broadside.
NYSL copy.   1083

New York (Colony) Governor, 1702.
By His Excellency Edward Lord Cornbury
. . . A Proclamation [Officers. May 3,
1702].
New York, Bradford, 1702. Broadside.
PRO copy.   1084

New York (Colony) Governor, 1702.
By His Excellency Edward Lord Cornbury
. . . A Proclamation [Thomas Weaver,
Sept. 8, 1702].
New York, Bradford, [1702]. Broadside.
PRO copy.   1085

New York (Colony) Governor, 1702.
By His Excellency Edward Lord Cornbury
. . . A Proclamation [Assembly. Sept. 17,
1702].
New York, Bradford, [1702]. Broadside.
PRO copy.   1086

New York (Colony) Governor, 1702.
By His Excellency Edward Lord
Cornbury. . . . A Proclamation [Court.
Sept. 17, 1702].
New York, Bradford, [1702]. Broadside.
PRO copy.   1087

New York (Colony) Governor, 1702.
By His Excellency Edward Lord
Cornbury. A Proclamation [Immorality.
Sept. 17, 1702].
New York, Bradford, [1702]. Broadside.
PRO copy.   1088

New York (Colony) Governor, 1702.
By His Excellency Edward Lord
Cornbury. . . . A Proclamation [Lime
Burning. Sept. 17, 1702].
New York, Bradford, [1702]. Broadside.
PRO copy.   1089

New York (Colony) Governor, 1702.
By His Excellency Edward Lord
Cornbury. . . . A Proclamation [Fast.
Dated Sept. 17, 1702].
New York, Bradford, [1702]. Broadside.
PRO copy.   1090

New York (Colony) Governor, 1702.
An Ordinance of His Excellency Edward
Lord Cornbury . . . High Court of
Chancery [June 12, 1702].
New York, Bradford, 1702. Broadside.
PRO copy.   1091

New York (Colony) Governor, 1703.
By His Excellency Edward Viscount
Cornbury. . . . A Proclamation [Ill
affected persons. Nov. 4, 1703].
New York, 1703. Broadside.
NYHS copy.   1140

New York (Colony) Governor, 1704.
By His Excellency Edward Viscount
Cornbury . . . A Proclamation . . .
Quit-rents [June 17, 1704].
New York, Bradford, 1704. Broadside.
JCB copy.   39414

New York (Colony) Governor, 1704.
An Ordinance [Supreme Court. Apr. 3,
1704].
New York, 1704. [2], 2 pp.
NYPL copy.   1188

New York (Colony) Governor, 1704.
An Ordinance of His Excellency [Court of
Chancery. Nov. 7, 1704].
[New York, 1704.] 5 pp.
NYPL copy.   1189

New York (Colony) Governor, 1705.
An Ordinance of His Excellency
[Privateers. Apr. 14, 1705].
[New York, 1705.] 4 pp.
NYPL copy.   1227

New York (Colony) Governor, 1706.
By His Excellency Edward Viscount
Cornbury. . . . A Proclamation [Byerly.
Feb. 6, 1706].
[New York, 1706.] Broadside.
PRO copy.   1274

[New York (Colony) Governor, 1707.
An Order to the Justices of the Peace.
New York, 1707.]
(Title from Hildeburn. Apparently this
ghost had its origin in an adv. for the
Conductor Generalis in the Leeds'
almanac for 1715.)   1327

New York (Colony) Governor, 1710.
An Ordinance for Regulating and
Establishing Fees.
[New York, 1710.] [12] pp.
NYPL copy.   1481

New York (Colony) Governor, 1710.
An Ordinance for Regulating &
Establishing Fees.
[New York, 1710.] 20 pp.
AAS copy.   1482

New York (Colony) Governor, 1711.
By His Excellency Robert Hunter. . . . A
Proclamation [Lord's Day. Jan. 12, 1711].
[New York, 1711.] Broadside.
NYHS copy.   1523

New York (Colony) Governor, 1712.
His Excellency's Speech [Sept. 17, 1712].
[New York, 1712.] pp. 3-4.
PRO copy.   1575

New York (Colony) Governor, 1713.
His Excellency's Speech [May 27, 1713].
New York, Bradford, 1713. 2 pp.
PRO copy.   1639

New York (Colony) Governor, 1713.
To all whom These Presents may Concern.
New York, W. Bradford, 1713. 7 pp.
NYHS copy.   39580

New York (Colony) Governor, 1713.
To All whom these Presents may Concern.
New York, W. Bradford, 1713. 8 pp.
NYPL copy.   1641

New York (Colony) Governor, 1715.
By his Excellency . . . Sitting of the
Supream Court [Oct. 20, 1715].
[New York, 1715.] [3] pp.
NYHS copy.   1772

New York (Colony) Governor, 1715.
His Excellencys Speech . . . the 3d day of
May, 1715.
[New York, 1715.] 2 pp.
PRO copy.   1773

New York (Colony) Governor, 1716.
His Excellency's Speech . . . the 5 June,
1716.
New York, Bradford, 1716. 2 pp.
PRO copy.   1846

New York (Colony) Governor, 1718.
By His Excellency Robert Hunter. . . . A
Proclamation [Pirates. Oct. 9, 1718].
[New York, 1718.] Broadside.
NYSL copy.   1990

New York (Colony) Governor, 1719.
His Excellency Brigadier Hunter's Speech
made to the General Assembly [June 24,
1719].
[New York, 1719.] [2] pp.
PrU copy.   39712

New York (Colony) Governor, 1720.
By His Excellency William Burnet. . . . A
Proclamation [Adjournment. Sept. 29,
1720].
New York, 1720. Broadside.
NYSL copy.   2158

New York (Colony) Governor, 1720.
His Excellency's Speech to the General
Assembly [Oct. 13, 1720].
[New York, 1720.] 3 pp.
NJSL copy.   2159

[New York (Colony) Governor, 1721.
By His Excellency William Burnet. . . .
Proclamation [Adjournment. Jan. 27,
1721].
New York, 1721. Broadside.]
(The unique copy was lost in the Albany
fire.)   2274

[New York (Colony) Governor, 1721.
By His Excellency William Burnet. . . . A
Proclamation. . . . [Adjournment, Feb. 13,
1720/1].
[New York, 1721.] Broadside.
NYSL copy.   2156

[New York (Colony) Governor, 1721.
By His Excellency William Burnett. . . .
Proclamation [Adjournment. Feb. 22,
1721].
New York, 1721. Broadside.]

(The unique copy was lost in the Albany
fire.)   2275

New York (Colony) Governor, 1721.
By His Excellency William Burnett . . .
Proclamation [Adjournment. Mar. 30,
1721.]
[New York, 1721.] Broadside.
NYSL copy.   2277

New York (Colony) Governor, 1721.
By His Excellency William Burnet . . .
Proclamation [Adjournment. Nov. 4,
1721].
New York, 1721. Broadside.
NYSL copy.   2279

New York (Colony) Governor, 1721.
By His Excellency William Burnet. . . . A
Proclamation. . . . Lewis Morris [Feb. 13,
1720/1].
[New York, 1721.] Broadside.
NYSL copy.   2155

New York (Colony) Governor, 1721.
By His Excellency William Burnet. . . .
Ordinance [Court. July 6, 1721].
[New York, 1721.] Broadside.
NYSL copy.   2278

[New York (Colony) Governor, 1721.
By His Excellency William Burnet . . .
Ordinance [Courts. Mar. 3, 1721].
[New York, 1721.] Broadside.]
(The unique copy was lost in the Albany
fire.)   2276

[New York (Colony) Governor, 1722.
By His Excellency William Burnet. . . .
Proclamation [Adjournment. Apr. 2,
1722].
New York, 1722. Broadside.]
(The unique copy was lost in the Albany
fire.)   2367

[New York (Colony) Governor, 1722.
By His Excellency William Burnet. . . .
Proclamation [Prorogation. Apr. 30,
1722].
New York, 1722. Broadside.]
(The unique copy was burned in the
Albany fire.)   2368

New York (Colony) Governor, 1722.
His Excellency's Speech to the General
Assembly . . . May 31, 1722.
[New York, 1722.] 2 pp.
NYPL copy.   2369

New York (Colony) Governor, 1723.
His Excellency's Speech to the General
Assembly [May 14, 1723].
[New York, 1723.] 2 pp.
PRO copy.   2467

[New York (Colony) Governor, 1724.
By His Excellency William Burnet. . . .
Proclamation [Merchants. Feb. 11, 1724].
[New York, 1724.] Broadside.]
(Unique NYSL copy burned.)   2570

New York (Colony) Governor, 1724.
His Excellency's Speech to the General
Assembly . . . the 15th of May, 1724.
[New York, 1724.] 2 pp.
NYPL copy.   2571

New York (Colony) Governor, 1725.
His Excellency's Speech to the General
Assembly . . . [Sept. 15, 1725].
[New York, 1725.] 2 pp.
NYPL copy.   2686

New York (Colony) Governor, 1726.
By His Excellency William Burnet. . . . A
Proclamation [Assembly. Aug. 10, 1726].
New York, 1726. Broadside.
(The unique copy was lost in the Albany
fire.)   2788

New York (Colony) Governor, 1726.
His Excellency's Speech to the General
Assembly [Sept. 27, 1726.]
[New York, 1726.] 2 pp.
PRO copy.   2789

New York (Colony) Governor, 1727.
His Excellency's Speech to the General
Assembly . . . September 30, 1727.
[New York, 1727.] 2 pp.
NYPL copy.   2934

New York (Colony) Governor, 1728.

His Excellency's Speech to the General
Assembly . . . the 23rd of July, 1728.
New York, 1728. 2 pp.
NYPL copy.   3073

[New York (Colony) Governor, 1731.
His Excellency's Speech to the Council
and General Assembly [Aug. 25, 1731].
New York, 1731.]
(Ordered printed.)   3455

[New York (Colony) Governor, 1732.
His Excellency's Speech to the Council
and House.
New York, 1732.]
(Ordered printed, Assembly Journal, I,
633.)   3582

[New York (Colony) Governor, 1733.
His Excellency's Speech to the Council
and House.
New York, 1733.]
(Ordered printed Assembly Journal, I,
649.)   3697

New York (Colony) Governor, 1734.
By His Excellency William Cosby. . . . A
Proclamation [Scandalous Songs. [Nov.
6, 1734].
[New York, 1734.] Broadside.
NYPL copy.   3809

New York (Colony) Governor, 1734.
By His Excellency William Cosby. . . . A
Proclamation [Seditous Reflections. Nov.
6, 1734].
[New York, 1734.] Broadside.
NYPL copy.   3810

New York (Colony) Governor, 1734.
His Excellency's Speech to the General
Assembly . . . April 25, 1734.
New York, Bradford, 1734. 3 pp.
PRO copy.   3813

New York (Colony) Governor, 1734.
The Account Stated, in Respect to the
Province.
New York, 1734. 3 pp.
NYPL copy.   3803

[New York (Colony) Governor, 1735.
His Excellency's Speech to the General
Assembly [Opening of Session].
New York, 1735.]
(Ordered printed by the Assembly.)   3939

[New York (Colony) Governor, 1735.
His Excellency's Speech to the General
Assembly [Revenue].
New York, 1735.]
(Ordered printed by the Assembly.)   3940

New York (Colony) Governor, 1743.
His Excellency's Speech to the General
Assembly [Sept. 17, 1743].
New York, Bradford, 1743. Broadside.
PRO copy.   5256

New York (Colony) Governor, 1743.
His Excellency's Speech to the General
Assembly [Nov. 8, 1743].
New York, Bradford, 1743. [2] pp.
PRO copy.   5257

New York (Colony) Governor, 1744.
By His Excellency the Honourable George
Clinton. . . . A Proclamation [Ratan. Feb.
1, 1744].
[New York, 1744.] Broadside.
NYSL copy.   5450

New York (Colony) Governor, 1744.
By His Excellency the Honourable George
Clinton. . . . A Proclamation [Thompson.
May 16, 1744].
[New York, 1744.] Broadside.
PRO copy.   5451

New York (Colony) Governor, 1744.
By His Excellency the Honourable George
Clinton. . . . A Proclamation [War. May
21, 1744].
[New York, 1744.] Broadside.
PRO copy.   5452

[New York (Colony) Governor, 1744.
His Excellency's Speech at the Dissolution
of the General Assembly [Nov. 25, 1744].
[New York, 1744.] 4 pp.
(Hasse 664; could not be located.)   5458

New York (Colony) Governor, 1744.

Speech of His Excellency the Honourable
George Clinton. . . . To the Council . . .
the 12th of March, 1744.
[New York, 1744.] 4 pp.
PRO copy.   5455

New York (Colony) Governor, 1744.
Speech of His Excellency George Clinton.
. . . To the General Assembly . . . the 17th
April, 1744.
New York, Parker, 1744. 2 pp.
PRO copy.   5456

New York (Colony) Governor, 1744.
Speech of His Excellency the Honourable
George Clinton. . . . To the General
Assembly . . . the 18th of July, 1744.
[New York, 1744.] 2 pp.
PRO copy.   5457

New York (Colony) Governor, 1745.
By His Excellency, the Honourable
George Clinton. . . . A Proclamation,
Prohibiting all Traffick. . . . [Sept. 5,
1745.]
[New York, 1745.] Broadside.
NYHS copy.   40386

New York (Colony) Governor, 1745.
His Excellency's Speech, at the
Dissolution of the General Assembly . . .
May 14, 1745.
[New York, 1745.] 2 pp.
HSP copy.   5655

New York (Colony) Governor, 1745.
His Excellency's Speech to the Council
and General Assembly [June, 25, 1745].
[New York, 1745.] 2 pp.
HSP copy.   5656

[New York (Colony) Governor, 1746.
By His Excellency . . . George Clinton. . . .
A Proclamation [Jan. 20, 1745/6].
New York, Parker, 1746. Broadside.]
(No copy found.)   5828

[New York (Colony) Governor, 1746.
By His Excellency . . . George Clinton. . . .
A Proclamation [Desertions. Feb. 3,
1745/6].
New York, Parker, 1746. Broadside.]
(No copy found.)   5829

[New York (Colony) Governor, 1746.
By His Excellency . . . George Clinton. . . .
A Proclamation [June 7, 1746].
New York, Parker, 1746. Broadside.]
(No copy found.)   5830

New York (Colony) Governor, 1746.
By His Excellency . . . George Clinton. . . .
A Proclamation [Thanksgiving. July 15,
1746].
[New York, 1746.] Broadside.
NYSL copy.   5831

New York (Colony) Governor, 1746.
His Excellency's Speech to the Council
and General Assembly [June 6, 1746].
[New York, 1746.] [2] pp.
PRO copy.   5832

[New York (Colony) Governor, 1746.
His Excellency's Speech to the Council
and General Assembly [June 9, 1746].
New York, 1746. Broadside.]
(No copy located.)   5833

[New York (Colony) Governor, 1747.
By His Excellency the Honourable George
Clinton. . . . A Proclamation [Dated Apr.
30, 1747].
[New York, 1747.] Broadside.]
(No copy found.)   6025

New York (Colony) Governor, 1747.
By His Excellency the Honourable George
Clinton . . . to Joseph Robinson [Nov. 4,
1747].
[New York, 1747.] Broadside.
PRO copy.   6026

New York (Colony) Governor, 1747.
His Excellency's Speech to the Council
and General Assembly [Feb. 12, 1747].
[New York, 1747.] 2 pp.
PRO copy.   6027

New York (Colony) Governor, 1747.
His Excellency's Speech to the Council
and General Assembly [Mar. 25, 1747].

[New York, 1747.] 2 pp.
PRO copy.   6028

New York (Colony) Governor, 1747.
A Message from His Excellency . . .
George Clinton . . . to the General
Assembly [Oct. 13, 1747].
[New York,1747.] [4] pp.
PRO copy.   6031

[New York (Colony) Governor, 1748.
By His Excellency . . . George Clinton. . . .
A Proclamation [Peace. Oct. 4, 1748].
New York, 1748. Broadside.]
(No copy found.)   6204

New York (Colony) Governor, 1748.
His Excellency's Speech to the Council
and General Assembly [Oct. 14, 1748].
[New York, 1748.] 4 pp.
PRO copy.   6205

[New York (Colony) Governor, 1749.
By His Excellency the Honourable George
Clinton. . . . A Proclamation
[Prorogation. Dated Feb. 28, 1748/9].
New York, 1749. Broadside.]
(No copy found.)   6380

[New York (Colony) Governor, 1749.
By His Excellency the Honourable George
Clinton . . . A Proclamation [Prorogation.
Dated Apr. 29, 1749].
New York, 1749. Broadside.]
(No copy found.)   6381

New York (Colony) Governor, 1749.
His Excellency's Speech to the Council
and General Assembly [June 28, 1749].
[New York, 1749.] [2] pp.
PRO copy.   6383

New York (Colony) Governor, 1749.
His Excellency's Speech to the General
Assembly [Aug. 4, 1749].
[New York, 1749.] 4 pp.
PRO copy.   6384

[New York (Colony) Governor, 1750.
By His Excellency the Honourable George
Clinton. . . . A Proclamation [Dated Jan.
6, 1749/50].
[New York, 1750.] Broadside.
(No copy found.)   6566

New York (Colony) Governor, 1750.
By His Excellency the Honourable George
Clinton. . . . A Proclamation [Indian
Traders. June 29, 1750].
[New York, 1750.] Broadside.
NYSL copy.   6567

New York (Colony) Governor, 1750.
By His Excellency the Honourable George
Clinton. . . . A Proclamation
[Prorogation. Dated July 21, 1750].
[New York, 1750.] Broadside.
NYSL copy.   6568

New York (Colony) Governor, 1750.
The Speech of His Excellency . . . George
Clinton . . . to the Council and General
Assembly [Sept. 4, 1750.].
[New York, 1750.] 2 pp.
PRO copy.   6570

New York (Colony) Governor, 1750.
To His Excellency the Honourable George
Clinton . . . the Humble Address of . . .
His Majesty's Council [Sept. 6, 1750].
[New York, 1750.] Broadside.
PRO copy.   6571

New York (Colony) Governor, 1751.
By His Excellency the Honourable George
Clinton. . . . A Proclamation [Order in
Council, Apr. 24. Dated Oct. 25, 1751].
[New York, 1751.] Broadside.
(Unique copy lost in Albany fire.)   6734

New York (Colony) Governor, 1753.
By His Excellency the Honourable George
Clinton. . . . A Proclamation. Whereas
Several Incroachments . . .
[New York, 1753.] Broadside.
NYHS copy.   40661

New York (Colony) Governor, 1755.
By the Honourable James DeLancey . . .
A Proclamation. Whereas Several
Desertions. . . . [May 13, 1755.]
[New York, 1755.] Broadside.
LOC copy.   40787

New York (Colony) Governor, 1755.
The Speech of His Excellency Sir Charles
Hardy [Dec. 3, 1755].
[New York, 1755.] 2 pp.
NYSL copy.   7512

[New York (Colony) Governor, 1756.
By His Excellency Sir Charles Hardy....
you are Hereby Empowered ... to Inlist
Voluntiers [Fort George, 1756].
[New York, 1756.] 4 pp.]
(Unique copy cannot be located.)   7737

New York (Colony) Governor, 1756.
The Speech of His Excellency Sir Charles
Hardy [Sept. 24, 1756].
[New York, 1756.] 4 pp.
(The only copy available is in poor
condition.)
NYSL copy.   7739

New York (Colony) Governor, 1757.
By the Honourable James De Lancey....
A Proclamation [Deserters. Dated Fort
George, July 1, 1757].
[New York, 1757.] Broadside.
NYSL copy.   7975

New York (Colony) Governor, 1757.
By His Excellency Sir Charles Hardy
[Recruiting. Dated Fort George, 1757].
[New York, 1757.] Broadside.
NYSL copy.   7974

New York (Colony) Governor, 1757.
The Speech of His Excellency Sir Charles
Hardy ... to the Council [Feb. 16, 1757].
[New York, 1757.] 2 pp.
PRO copy.   7976

[New York (Colony) Governor, 1762.
Speech of His Excellency Robert
Monckton ... to the Council and General
Assembly, November 16, 1762.
New York, 1762.]
(From an adv.)   9214

New York (Colony) Governor, 1763.
By the Honourable Cadwallader Colden.
... To [blank] You are hereby
Authorized.... [blank] December, 1763.
[New York, 1763.] [2] pp.
LOC copy.   41404

[New York (Colony) Governor, 1765.
By His Excellency Sir Henry Moore....
A Proclamation [Dated Nov. 13, 1765].
[New York, 1765.] Broadside.]
(Unique copy lost in the Albany fire.)   10094

[New York (Colony) Governor, 1765.
By His Excellency Sir Henry Moore....
A Proclamation [Dated Dec. 2, 1765].
[New York], Weyman, [1765].
Broadside.]
(Unique copy lost in the Albany fire.)   10095

[New York (Colony) Governor, 1765.
The Speech of His Excellency Sir Henry
Moore [Nov. 19, 1765].
[New York, 1765.] Broadside.]
(Unique copy lost in the Albany fire.)   10097

New York (Colony) Governor, 1766.
By His Excellency Sir Henry Moore....
A Proclamation.... High Treason
[Dated June 20, 1766].
[New York, 1766.] Broadside.
PRO copy.   10416

[New York (Colony) Governor, 1766.
By His Excellency Sir Henry Moore....
A Proclamation [Schuyler. July 3, 1766].
[New York, 1766.] Broadside.]
(Unique copy lost in the Albany fire.)   10417

New York (Colony) Governor, 1766.
The Speech of His Excellency Sir Henry
Moore ... to the Council and General
Assembly [June 12, 1766].
[New York, 1766.] Broadside.
PRO copy.   10420

[New York (Colony) Governor, 1766.
The Speech of His Excellency Sir Henry
Moore ... to the Council and General
Assembly [Nov. 10, 1766].
[New York, 1766.] Broadside.]

(Unique copy lost in the Albany fire.)   10421

New York (Colony) Governor, 1767.
The Speech of His Excellency Sir Henry
Moore ... to the Council, and General
Assembly ... May 27. 1767.
[New York, 1767.] 2 pp.
PRO copy.   10707

[New York (Colony) Governor, 1767.
The Speech of His Excellency Sir Henry
Moore ... to the Council and General
Assembly ... November 18, 1767.
[New York, 1767.] 2 pp.]
(Unique copy lost in the Albany fire.)   10708

New York (Colony) Governor, 1768.
By His Excellency Sir Henry Moore....
A Proclamation [Riot, Nov. 14. Dated
Nov. 19, 1768].
[New York, 1768.] Broadside.
LCP copy.   11002

New York (Colony) Governor, 1768.
The Speech of His Excellency Sir Henry
Moore ... to His Majesty's Council ...
on the 28th of October, 1768.
[New York, 1768.] [2] pp.
PRO copy.   11003

New York (Colony) Governor, 1769.
The Speech of His Excellency Sir Henry
Moore ... to His Majesty's Council ...
the 4th of April, 1769.
[New York, 1769]. Broadside.
PRO copy.   11367

New York (Colony) Governor, 1770.
By His Excellency the Right Honourable
John, Earl of Dunmore.... A
Proclamation [Nov. 1, 1770].
[New York, Gaine, 1770.] Broadside.
PRO copy.   11773

New York (Colony) Governor, 1770.
The Speech of His Excellency ... John,
Earl of Dunmore ... the 11th of
December, 1770.
[New York, 1770.] Broadside.
PRO copy.   11775

New York (Colony) Governor, 1771.
By His Excellency ... John, Earl of
Dunmore .... A Proclamation [Repeal,
Mar. 4, 1771].
[New York, 1771.] Broadside.
Rutgers University copy.   12155

New York (Colony) Governor, 1771.
By His Excellency William Tryon....
A Proclamation [Aug. 17, 1771].
[New York, 1771.] Broadside.
PRO copy.   12156

New York (Colony) Governor, 1771.
By His Excellency William Tryon.... A
Proclamation [Boundary. Dec. 11, 1771].
[New York, 1771.] Broadside.
PRO copy.   12157

New York (Colony) Governor, 1773.
The Speech of His Excellency William
Tryon ... the 6th of January, 1773.
[New York, Gaine, 1773.] [2] pp.
NYHS copy.   12890

[New York (Colony) Governor, 1774.
By His Excellency William Tryon.... A
Proclamation [Outrages. Dated 1774].
[New York, 1774.] Broadside.]
(Apparently not printed.)   13461

New York (Colony) Governor, 1775.
By His Excellency William Tryon.... A
Proclamation [Suppression of Rebellion.
Nov. 14, 1775].
[New York, 1775.] Broadside.
LOC copy.   14078

New York (Colony) Governor, 1775.
Letters which Lately Passed between His
Excellency Governor Tryon, and
Whitehead Hicks....
New York, Rivington, 1775. 8 pp.
NYPL ph. copy.   42904

New York (Colony) Governor, 1775.
New-York, December 6, 1775. ... To the
Inhabitants of the Colony of New-York
[Dated Dec. 4, 1775].

[New York, 1775.] Broadside.
PRO copy.   14297

New York (Colony) Governor, 1775.
Ship Dutchess of Gordon, off New-York,
18th Dec. 1775....
[New York, 1775.] Broadside.
LOC copy.   14298

New York (Colony) Governor, 1776.
By His Excellency William Tryon.... A
Proclamation [Dissolving the Assembly.
Jan. 2, 1776].
[New York, 1776.] Broadside.
NYHS copy.   14919

New York (Colony) Governor, 1776.
To the Inhabitants of the Colony of
New-York. ... 16th March, 1776.
[New York, 1776.] 7 pp.
PRO copy.   14920

New York (Colony) Governor, 1778.
By His Excellency William Tryon.... A
Proclamation.... Pardons.... [Dated
Dec. 24, 1778.]
[New York? 1778.] [3] pp.
NYPL ph. copy.   43514

New York (Colony) Governor, 1779.
By His Excellency William Tryon....
Convinced by Experience ... Impressing.
... [Mar. 8, 1779.]
[New York, 1779.] Broadside.
NYPL ph. copy.   43672

New York (Colony) Governor, 1780.
By His Excellency James Robertson....
A Proclamation. The King having been
Graciously Pleased.... [Apr. 15, 1780].
[New York], Rivington, [1780].
Broadside.
AAS copy.   43854

New York (Colony) Governor, 1783.
By His Excellency James Robertson....
A Proclamation [Thanksgiving, Jan. 23.
Dated Jan. 14, 1783].
[New York, 1783.] Broadside.
HSP copy.   17963

New York (Colony) House of
Representatives, 1699.
To His Excellency Richard Earl of
Bellomont.... The Humble Petition....
15 May, 1699.
[New York, 1699.] 3 pp.
NYPL copy.   39351

New York (Colony) Laws, Statutes, etc.,
1691.
... By His Excellency the Governor and
Council, and House of Representatives.
... April 17, 1691.... Resolved. Jacob
Leisler. ...
[n. p., 1691.] Broadside.
MHS ph copy.   39293

New York (Colony) Laws, Statutes, etc.,
1692.
An Act for Granting to their Majesties the
Rate. ... November the 12th, 1692.
[New York, 1693.] 4 pp.
NYPL copy.   665

New York (Colony) Laws, Statutes, etc.,
1692.
... An Act for Restraining and Punishing
Privateers and Pyrates.
[New York, 1693.] 3 pp.
NYPL copy.   663

New York (Colony) Laws, Statutes, etc.,
1692.
... An Act for Restraining and Punishing
Privateers and Pyrates [Sept. 10, 1692].
[New York, 1693.] 3 pp.
HEH copy.   664

New York (Colony) Laws, Statutes, etc.,
1693.
... An Act for Raising Six Thousand
Pounds [Apr. 10, 1693].
New York, 1693. [6] pp.
NYPL copy.   667

New York (Colony) Laws, Statutes, etc.,
1693.
... An Act Passed the 12th of September
1693, for Settling a Minister. ...
[New York, 1693.] 4 pp.
MHS ph copy.   39305

New York (Colony) Laws, Statutes, etc.,
1693.
An Act Passed the 12th of September,
1693. . . . April 12 1695. A Petition of the
Church-Wardens.
[New York, 1695.] 4 pp.
PRO copy.   39316

New York (Colony) Laws, Statutes, etc.,
1694.
. . . An Act for Raising Six Thousand
Pounds [Apr. 10, 1694].
New York, 1693. [6] pp.
HEH copy.   666

New York (Colony) Laws, Statutes, etc.,
1699.
An Ordinance . . . for the Ease . . . of each
. . . city.
[New York, 1699.] 4 pp.
(The HEH has two variant issues.)
NYPL copy.   889

New York (Colony) Laws, Statutes, etc.,
1699.
An Ordinance . . . for the Establishing
Courts of Judicature . . . [May 15, 1699].
[New York, 1699.] 4 pp.
HEH copy.   39352

New York (Colony) Laws, Statutes, etc.,
1701.
An Ordinance for Erecting . . . a High
Court of Chancery [Aug. 28, 1701].
New York, Bradford, 1701. Broadside.
PRO copy.   1013

[New York (Colony) Laws, Statutes, etc.,
1703.
An Act Declaring the Illegality of the
Proceedings.
New York, 1703. [2] pp.]
(No copy of a separate of this Act has
been found. The text is pp. 210-211 of
1137.)   1138

New York (Colony) Laws, Statutes, etc.,
1703.
An Act for the Levying and Collecting the
Sum.
[New York, 1703.] 5 pp.
NYPL ph. copy, incomplete.   1139

New York (Colony) Laws, Statutes, etc.,
1705.
An Act for Defraying the Common . . .
Charges.
[New York, 1705.] Broadside.
NYPL copy.   1226

New York (Colony) Laws, Statutes, etc.,
1705.
. . . An Act for the Better Establishment
of . . . the Minister of the City of
New-York.
[New York? 1705?] 6 pp., irreg.
NYHS copy.   39431

New York (Colony) Laws, Statutes, etc.,
1709.
An Act for Laying an Excise on all
Liquors.
[New York, 1709]. 4 pp.
NYPL copy.   1416

New York (Colony) Laws, Statutes, etc.,
1709.
An Act for Levying Four Thousand
Pounds.
[New York, 1709.] 4 pp.
NYPL copy.   1418

New York (Colony) Laws, Statutes, etc.,
1709.
An Act for Regulating and Establishing
Fees.
[New York, 1709.] 13 pp.
PRO copy.   1414

[New York (Colony) Laws, Statutes, etc.,
1709.
. . . An Act for the Assignment to the
Lady Lovelace.
New York, Bradford, 1709. [1] pp.]
(No such separate printing located. See p.
113 of 1423.)   39494

New York (Colony) Laws, Statutes, etc.,
1709.
An Act for the Currency of Bills of Credit.
[New York, 1709.] 3 pp.
NYPL copy.   1417

New York (Colony) Laws, Statutes, etc.,
1709.
An Act to Detach Four Hundred.
[New York, 1709.] 4 pp.
NYPL copy.   1415

[New York (Colony) Laws, Statutes, etc.,
1709.
Acts of the General Assembly Relating to
Trinity.
New York, 1709.]
(Ordered printed by Trinity Church,
vestry minutes, Nov. 24, 1709.)   1419

New York (Colony) Laws, Statutes, etc.,
1710.
The Laws, of Her Majesties Colony
[1691-1709].
New York, 1710. [4], 72, [12], 73-76,
89-96, 4, 101-114, 13, 78, 40 pp.
(This includes items separately listed as
1367, 1414, and 1418. No complete copy
could be found.)
HSP copy.   1480

[New York (Colony) Laws, Statutes, etc.,
1710.
An Ordinance for Regulating and
Establishing Fees [Oct. 19, 1710].
New York, 1752. 8 pp.]
(No copy of a 1752 ed. found.)   6898

New York (Colony) Laws, Statutes, etc.,
1713.
The Laws, of Her Majesties Colony [Apr.
9, 1691 +].
New York, 1713. [5], 253 pp. irreg.
NYBA copy.   1636

New York (Colony) Laws, Statutes, etc.,
1715.
. . . An Act Passed . . . in July, 1715 . . .
Declaring . . . all Persons of Forreign
Birth . . . Naturalized.
[New York, 1715.] 6 pp.
NYHS copy.   39632

New York (Colony) Laws, Statutes, etc.,
1716.
An Ordinance for Regulating &
Establishing Fees [Oct. 19, 1716].
[New York, 1716.] 20 pp.
HSP copy.   1848

[New York (Colony) Laws, Statutes, etc.,
1719.
By Order of the Government.
New-York, 1719.]
(See Hist. Mag. V (1861), 347.)   2063

New York (Colony) Laws, Statutes, etc.,
1719.
The Laws [Apr. 9, 1691 +].
New York, 1719. [12], 324, pp., irreg.
NYHS copy.   2065

New York (Colony) Laws, Statutes, etc.,
1720.
By the Honourable Peter Schuyler . . . an
Ordinance [Mar. 3, 1719/20].
[New York, 1719/20.] Broadside.
NYSL copy.   2062

[New York (Colony) Laws, Statutes, etc.,
1721.
An Act for Settling the Militia. . . . July
27, 1721.
New York, 1721.]
(Adv. at end of 2271.)   2272

[New York (Colony) Laws, Statutes, etc.,
1721.
An Act for the Better Clearing . . .
High-ways [July 27, 1721].
New York, 1721.]
(Adv. at end of 2271.)   2273

[New York (Colony) Laws, Statutes, etc.,
1722.
. . . The Following Act was Past in the
Ninth Year of His Majesty's Reign, 1722.
New York, 1722. pp. 317-319.]
(Printed in 1726 as a part of 2785, q.v.)   2370

New York (Colony) Laws, Statutes, etc.,
1722.
An Ordinance for Regulating and
Establishing fees for the Court of
Admiralty [July 16, 1722].
[New York, 1722.] 4 pp.
NYPL copy.   2376

New York (Colony) Laws, Statutes, etc.,
1723.
An Ordinance for the Regulating and
Establishing the Fees [Aug. 22, 1723].
[New York, 1723.] [4] pp.
AAS copy.   2468

New York (Colony) Laws, Statutes, etc.,
1723.
An Ordinance for Regulating the
Recording of Deeds [Aug. 22, 1723].
[New York, 1723.] [2] pp.
AAS copy.   2469

New York (Colony) Laws, Statutes, etc.,
1724.
. . . An Act for Settling and Regulating the
Militia.
[New York, W. Bradford, 1724.] pp.
269-146 [sic].
HEH copy.   39817

New York (Colony) Laws, Statutes, etc.,
1725.
Acts of Assembly Passed in the Province
of New-York, from 1691 to 1725.
New York, 1726. [10], 319 pp., irreg.
AAS copy.   2785

New York (Colony) Laws, Statutes, etc.,
1725.
The Thirteenth Sessions of the Second
Assembly. . . . An Act Appointing
Commissioners.
[New York, 1725.] 7 pp.
AB copy.   2684

New York (Colony) Laws, Statutes, etc.,
1727.
An Ordinance for Establishing the
Remedies for Abuses in the Practice of
Law [Mar. 2, 1727].
New York, 1728. 6 pp.
NYPL copy.   3075

New York (Colony) Laws, Statutes, etc.,
1728.
An Ordinance for Regulating and
Establishing Fees [Feb. 28, 1727/8].
New York, [1728]. 4 pp.
PRO copy.   3076

New York (Colony) Laws, Statutes, etc.,
1729.
. . . An Act for the Better Clearing . . .
Highroads in the City and County of
Albany.
[New York, 1729.] pp. 401-407.
(The one recorded copy cannot now be
located.)   39924

New York (Colony) Laws, Statutes, etc.,
1730.
An Act to Revive and Enforce an Act
[Oct. 1730].
New York, 1730. 37, [1] pp.
HSP copy.   3330

[New York (Colony) Laws, Statutes, etc.,
1731.
George the Second [Letters Patent. June
8, 1731].
[New York, 1731.] 8 pp.]
(The unique copy could not be found.)   3454

[New York (Colony) Laws, Statutes, etc.,
1731.
An Ordinance for Holding a Court [Feb.
4, 1731].
[New York, 1731.] [2] pp.]
(The unique copy could not be found.)   3457

[New York (Colony) Laws, Statutes, etc.,
1733.
An Ordinance for the Running . . . the
Partition Lines between the Counties
[Aug. 29, 1733].
[New York, 1733.] 3 pp.]
(Lost in the Albany fire.)   3699

New York (Colony) Laws, Statutes, etc.,
1737.
An Ordinance for Appointing the Times
and Places for Holding the Annual Circuit
Courts.
New York, Zenger, 1737. 2 pp.
NYSL copy.   40125

New York (Colony) Laws, Statutes, etc.,
1741

. . . An Act for the Better Fortifying of
this Colony. . . . Published the 13th Day of
June 1741.
[New York, William Bradford, 1741.]
11 pp.
NYSL copy.   40250

New York (Colony) Laws, Statutes, etc.,
1741.
. . . An Act for the more Equal Keeping
Military Watches.
New York, Bradford, 1741. 3 pp.
NYSL copy.   40251

New York (Colony) Laws, Statutes, etc.,
1742.
. . . An Act to Apply the Sum of . . . for
Repairing Fort-George [May 22, 1742].
New York, William Bradford, 1742. pp.
8-11.
NYSL copy.   40282

New York (Colony) Laws, Statutes, etc.,
1743.
Acts Passed in the Sixteenth Year of His
Majesty's Reign, 1743.
[New York, Bradford, 1743.] 4 pp.
(No copy available, 1969.)   40314

[New York (Colony) Laws, Statutes, etc.,
1744.
An Act of the General Assembly for
Settling and Better Regulation of the
Militia.
New York, 1744.]
(Adv. in N. Y. Weekly Post-Boy.)   5448

[New York (Colony) Laws, Statutes, etc.,
1744.
An Act of the General Assembly for the
Relief of Insolvent Debtors.
New York, 1744.]
(Adv. in N. Y. Weekly Post-Boy.)   5449

New York (Colony) Laws, Statutes, etc.,
1746.
An Act for Raising a Supply of Forty
Thousand Pounds.
[New York, 1746.] pp. 5-20.
(This is the second part of 5824, q.v.) 5826

New York (Colony) Laws, Statutes, etc.,
1746.
An Act to let to Farm the Excise.
[New York, 1746.] pp. 21-47.
(This is the third part of 5824, q.v.)   5827

New York (Colony) Laws, Statutes, etc.,
1746.
An Act to Prevent the Exportation of
Provisions.
[New York, 1746.] [4] pp.
(This is the first part of 5824, q.v.)   5825

[New York (Colony) Laws, Statutes, etc.,
1750.
An Act to Prevent the Exportation of
Unmerchantable Flour.
New York, Parker, 1750.]
(From printer's adv.)   6564

[New York (Colony) Laws, Statutes, etc.,
1750.
An Act to Regulate the Guaging of Rum.
New York, Parker, 1750.]
(From printer's adv.)   6565

New York (Colony) Laws, Statutes, etc.,
1752.
Laws of New-York, from the Year 1691,
to 1751.
New York, 1752. [8], iii, 488, [1] pp.
(No copy found with pagination given by
Evans.)
AAS copy.   6897

New York (Colony) Laws, Statutes, etc.,
1754.
An Act for Paying Five Thousand Pounds
[Aug. 29, 1754].
[New York, 1754.] Broadside.
NYSL copy.   7272

[New York (Colony) Laws, Statutes, etc.,
1754.
The Act of the Assembly to Regulate the
Militia.
New York, Parker & Weyman, 1754.]
(From an adv.)   7269

[New York (Colony) Laws, Statutes, etc.,
1754.
An Act to Impower Justices of the Peace.

New York, Parker & Weyman, 1754.]
(From an adv.)   7270

[New York (Colony) Laws, Statutes, etc.,
1754.
An Act to Regulate the Collecting the
Duty.
New York, Parker & Weyman, 1754.]
(From an adv.)   7271

New York (Colony) Laws, Statutes, etc.,
1755.
An Act to Restrain the Sending of
Provisions to Cape-Breton [Feb. 19,
1755].
[New York, 1755.] Broadside.
LOC copy.   7509

[New York (Colony) Laws, Statutes, etc.,
1756.
The Militia Act.
New York, Parker & Weyman, 1756.]
(From an adv.)   7736

New York (Colony) Laws, Statutes, etc.,
1758.
Extract of an Act [Troops. Mar. 24,
1758].
New York, Parker & Weyman, 1758. [2], 17
pp.
NYPL copy.   8211

[New York (Colony) Laws, Statutes, etc.,
1758.
The Militia Act.
New York, Gaine, 1758.]
(Adv. N. Y. Mercury, No. 295.)   8218

New York (Colony) Laws, Statutes, etc.,
1759.
Chap. VI. An Act for Emitting Bills of
Credit.
New York, Weyman, [1759]. pp. 23-28.
PRO copy.   8432

New York (Colony) Laws, Statutes, etc.,
1759.
Extract of An Act of the
General-Assembly [for Raising One
Hundred Thousand Pounds, Mar. 7,
1759].
New York, Weyman, [1759]. [2],
18 pp.
MHS copy.   8435

[New York (Colony) Laws, Statutes, etc.,
1760.
An Act for the Better Regulation of
Seamen.
New York, Weyman, 1760.]
(From an adv.)   8686

New York (Colony) Laws, Statutes, etc.,
1760.
Extract of an Act. . . . Levying . . . Two
Thousand Six Hundred and Eighty
Effective Men.
New York, Weyman, [1760]. 16 pp.
NYHS copy.   41160

New York (Colony) Laws, Statutes, etc.,
1761.
An Act . . . for Raising . . . Seventeen
Hundred and Eighty Seven Effective Men.
New York, Weyman, [1761]. 16 pp.
NYHS copy.   41233

New York (Colony) Laws, Statutes, etc.,
1762.
Laws of New York [Nov. 11, 1752-May
22, 1762].
New York, Weyman, 1762. [8], 268 pp.
AAS copy.   9213

New York (Colony) Laws, Statutes, etc.,
1769.
An Act to Impower Justices. . . . the 20th
May, 1769.
[New York, 1769.] 12 pp.
NYPL copy.   11358

New York (Colony) Laws, Statutes, etc.,
1772.
At a Session of the General Assembly
[Mar. 12, 1772. Five Pound Act.]
New York, Gaine, 1772. 16 pp.
NYPL copy.   12482

New York (Colony) Laws, Statutes, etc.,
1774.
Laws of New-York, from the year 1691, to
1773.

New York, Gaine, 1774. 2 vol. pp. [1]-iv,
1-420; [4], 421-835, [1].
AAS copy.   13467

New York (Colony) Lieutenant Governor,
1699.
By the Honourable John Nanfan. . . . A
Proclamation [Gillam. Aug. 29, 1699].
[New York, 1699.] Broadside.
PRO copy.   886

New York (Colony) Lieutenant Governor,
1699.
By the Honourable John Nanfan. . . . A
Proclamation [Pine Trees. Sept. 22,
1699].
New York, Bradford, 1699. Broadside.
PRO copy.   887

New York (Colony) Lieutenant Governor,
1701.
By the Honourable John Nanfan. . . . A
Proclamation [Conspiracy. Jan. 24, 1701].
New York, 1701. Broadside.
NYSL copy.   1002

New York (Colony) Lieutenant Governor,
1701.
By the Honourable John Nanfan
[Commissions. Jan. 29, 1701].
New York, 1701. Broadside.
NYSL copy.   1003

New York (Colony) Lieutenant Governor,
1701.
By the Honourable John Nanfan. . . . A
Proclamation [Prorogation. Dated Mar.
2, 1701].
New York, 1701. Broadside.
NYSL copy.   1004

New York (Colony) Lieutenant Governor,
1701.
By the Honourable John Nanfan. . . . A
Proclamation [Libels. Mar. 10, 1701].
New York, 1701. Broadside.
NYSL copy.   1005

[New York (Colony) Lieutenant
Governor, 1701.
By the Honourable John Nanfan. . . . A
Proclamation [Agreement, Nov. 23, 1686;
dated May 30, 1701].
New York, 1701. Broadside.]
(Apparently the unique copy was lost in
the Albany fire.)   1006

[New York (Colony) Lieutenant
Governor, 1701.
By the Honourable John Nanfan. . . . A
Proclamation [Chancery. June 1, 1701].
New York, 1701. Broadside.]
(Apparently the unique copy was lost in
the Albany fire.)   1009

New York (Colony) Lieutenant Governor,
1701.
By the Honourable John Nanfan. . . . A
Proclamation [Death of Bellomont. June
1, 1701].
New York, Bradford, 1701. Broadside.
PRO copy.   1008

[New York (Colony) Lieutenant
Governor, 1701.
By the Honourable John Nanfan. . . . A
Proclamation [Peace. June 1, 1701].
New York, 1701. Broadside.]
(Apparently the unique copy was lost in
the Albany fire.)   1007

New York (Colony) Lieutenant Governor,
1701.
By the Honourable John Nanfan. . . . A
Proclamation [Dissolution. June 1, 1701].
New York, 1701. Broadside.
PRO copy.   1010

[New York (Colony) Lieutenant
Governor, 1701.
By the Honourable John Nanfan. . . . A
Proclamation [Prorogation. July 18,
1701].
New York, 1701. Broadside.]
(Apparently the unique copy was lost in
the Albany fire.)   1011

New York (Colony) Lieutenant Governor,
1701.
By the Honourable John Nanfan. . . . A
Proclamation [Algiers. Aug. 19, 1701].
New York, Bradford, 1701. Broadside.
PRO copy.   1012

New York (Colony) Lieutenant Governor, 1702.
By the Honourable John Nanfan. . . . A Proclamation [Attendance. Mar. 20, 1702].
New York, 1702. Broadside.
NYSL copy.   1081

New York (Colony) Lieutenant Governor, 1702.
By the Honourable John Nanfan. . . . A Proclamation [Gallows. Mar. 29. 1702].
New York, 1702. Broadside.
NYSL copy.   1082

[New York (Colony) Lieutenant Governor, 1737.
By the Honourable George Clarke . . . A Proclamation [Prorogation. Mar. 29, 1737].
New York, 1737. Broadside.]
(The unique copy was lost in the Albany fire.)   4171

New York (Colony) Lieutenant Governor, 1737.
The Honourable Lieutenant Governor. . . . His Speech [Apr. 5, 1737].
New York, 1737. 3 pp.
NYPL copy.   4172

New York (Colony) Lieutenant Governor, 1737.
The Speech of the Honourable George Clarke [June 16, 1737].
[New York, 1737.] [2] pp.
NYPL copy.   4175

New York (Colony) Lieutenant Governor, 1737.
The Speech of the Honourable George Clarke [Sept. 2, 1737].
[New York, 1737.] 2 pp.
NYPL copy.   4176

New York (Colony) Lieutenant Governor, 1738.
His Honour the Lieutenant Governor His Speech [Dissolution. Oct. 20, 1738].
New York, Bradford, 1738. 2 pp.
PRO copy.   4285

New York (Colony) Lieutenant Governor, 1738.
The Speech of the Honourable George Clarke [Sept. 5, 1738].
New York, Zenger, 1738. [2] pp.
PRO copy.   4287

New York (Colony) Lieutenant Governor, 1739.
The Honourable George Clarke. . . . His Speech to the General Assembly [Mar. 27, 1739].
[New York, 1739.] 3 pp.
PRO copy.   4401

New York (Colony) Lieutenant Governor, 1739.
The Speech of the Honourable George Clarke. . . . To the General Assembly [Oct. 3, 1739].
New York, Bradford, 1739. Broadside.
PRO copy.   4404

New York (Colony) Lieutenant Governor, 1740.
By the Honourable George Clarke. . . . A Proclamation [Foreign Coins. Dec. 2, 1740].
New York, Bradford, 1740. Broadside.
PRO copy.   4572

[New York (Colony) Lieutenant Governor, 1740.
By the Honourable George Clarke. . . . A Proclamation [Apr. 15, 1740].
New York, 1740. Broadside.]
(The unique copy was lost in the Albany fire.)   4571

New York (Colony) Lieutenant Governor, 1740.
The Speech of the Honourable George Clarke. . . . To the General Assembly . . . the 30th June, 1740.
New York, Bradford, 1740. Broadside.
PRO copy.   4576

[New York (Colony) Lieutenant Governor, 1740.
The Speech of the Honourable George Clarke. . . . To the General Assembly. . . .

September 10, 1740.
New York, 1740].
(Ordered printed, Assembly Journal, I, 778.)   4577

[New York (Colony) Lieutenant Governor, 1741.
By the Honourable George Clarke. . . . A Proclamation [Conspiracy. June 19, 1741].
New York, 1741. Broadside.]
(The unique copy cannot be located.) 4763

New York (Colony) Lieutenant Governor, 1741.
By the Honourable George Clarke. . . . A Proclamation [Inlistment. Sept. 8, 1741].
New York, Bradford, 1741. Broadside.
PRO copy.   4764

New York (Colony) Lieutenant Governor, 1741.
His Honour the Lieut. Governour's Speech to the General Assembly [Apr. 15, 1741].
[New York, 1741.] 4 pp.
PRO copy.   4765

New York (Colony) Lieutenant Governor, 1741.
The Speech of the Honourable George Clarke [Sept. 17, 1741].
[New York, 1741.] Broadside.
PRO copy.   4770

New York (Colony) Lieutenant Governor, 1742.
His Honour the Lieutenant Governour His Speech . . . the Fifteenth of October, 1742.
[New York, 1742.] Broadside.
PRO copy.   5020

New York (Colony) Lieutenant Governor, 1742.
His Honour the Lieutenant Governour's Speech to the General Assembly [Apr. 22, 1742].
[New York, 1742.] Broadside.
PRO copy.   5018

New York (Colony) Lieutenant Governor, 1742.
His Honour the Lieutenant Governour His Speech to the General Assembly [Oct. 13, 1742].
[New York, 1742.] Broadside.
PRO copy.   5019

New York (Colony) Lieutenant Governor, 1753.
The Speech of the Honourable James De Lancey [Oct. 31, 1753].
[New York, 1753.] 2 pp.
PRO copy.   7075

New York (Colony) Lieutenant Governor, 1754.
The Speech of the Honourable James De Lancey [Apr. 9, 1754].
[New York, 1754.] 3 pp.
PRO copy.   7273

New York (Colony) Lieutenant Governor, 1755.
By the Honourable James De Lancey. . . . A Proclamation [Incroachments. Apr. 2, 1755].
[New York, 1755.] Broadside.
NYHS copy.   7511

New York (Colony) Lieutenant Governor, 1757.
By the Honourable James DeLancey. . . . A Proclamation. Whereas it appears . . . Livingston Manor. . . . [June 8, 1757].
[New York, 1757.] Broadside.
NYPL facsim. copy.   40926

New York (Colony) Lieutenant Governor, 1757.
By the Honourable James De Lancey. . . . A Proclamation. Whereas it Hath Pleased Almighty God. . . . a Day of Prayer and Fasting [July 13. Dated June 21, 1757].
[New York, 1757.] Broadside.
HSP copy.   40925

New York (Colony) Lieutenant Governor, 1758.
By the Honourable James De Lancey. . . . A Proclamation [Military Bounty. Mar. 25, 1758].

[New York, 1758.] Broadside.
LOC copy.   8210

New York (Colony) Lieutenant Governor, 1758.
By the Honourable James De Lancey. . . . A Proclamation. Whereas our only Refuge . . . [setting May 12 as a Day of Fasting. Dated Apr. 14, 1758].
[New York, 1758.] Broadside.
HSP copy.   40996

New York (Colony) Lieutenant Governor, 1758.
The Speech of the Honourable James De Lancey . . . to the Council [Mar. 10, 1758].
[New York, 1758.] 3 pp.
PRO copy.   8213

New York (Colony) Lieutenant Governor, 1758.
The Speech of the Honourable James Delancy . . . to the Council [Nov. 21, 1758].
[New York, 1758.] 2 pp.
PRO copy.   8214

New York (Colony) Lieutenant Governor, 1759.
By the Honourable James De Lancey [Supply of £100,000. Dated Fort George, 1759].
[New York, 1759.] Broadside.
NYSL copy.   8433

New York (Colony) Lieutenant Governor, 1759.
By the Honourable James De Lancey. . . . A Proclamation [Thanksgiving, Nov. 22. Dated Nov. 1, 1759].
[New York, 1759.] Broadside.
PRO copy.   8434

New York (Colony) Lieutenant Governor, 1759.
The Speech of the Honourable James De Lancey. . . . To the Council [Dated Feb. 1, 1759].
[New York, 1759.] 3 pp.
PRO copy.   8436

New York (Colony) Lieutenant Governor, 1759.
The Speech of the Honourable James De Lancey . . . to the Council [Dated Dec. 6, 1759].
[New York, 1759.] 2 pp.
PRO copy.   8437

New York (Colony) Lieutenant Governor, 1760.
By the Honourable James De Lancy . . . You are to Repair to the County of [blank]. . . . [blank] Day of [blank] 1760.
[New York, 1760] Broadside.
NYHS copy.   41161

[New York (Colony) Lieutenant Governor, 1761.
Speech of the Honourable Cadwallader Colden . . . to the Council and General Assembly . . . March 11, 1761.
New York, 1761.]
(From an adv.)   8954

New York (Colony) Lieutenant Governor, 1761.
The Speech of the Honourable Cadwallader Colden . . . to the Council and General Assembly [Sept. 2, 1761].
[New York, 1761.] 2 pp.
PRO copy.   8955

[New York (Colony) Lieutenant Governor, 1761.
Speech of the Honourable Cadwallader Colden . . . to the Council and General Assembly . . . September 25, 1761.
New York, 1761.]
(From an adv.)   8956

New York (Colony) Lieutenant Governor, 1762.
By the Honourable Cadwallader Colden. . . . A Proclamation [Indians. Dated Feb. 17, 1762].
[New York, 1762.] Broadside.
PRO copy.   9210

New York (Colony) Lieutenant Governor, 1762.
By the Honorable Cadwallader Colden.

. . . A Proclamation [Fast, May 7. Dated
Apr. 15, 1762].
[New York, 1762.] Broadside.
NYHS copy.   9211

New York (Colony) Lieutenant Governor,
1762.
By the Honourable Cadwallader Colden
. . . Recruiting Officers. . . . [May 21,
1762.]
[New York, 1762.] Broadside.
NYHS copy.   41295

New York (Colony) Lieutenant-Governor,
1762.
By the Honourable Cadwallader Colden.
. . . A Proclamation. Whereas it
Appearing that Certain Persons
. . . Robert Livingston, Jr. . . . [Dated
March 31, 1762.]
[New York, 1762.] Broadside.
NYHS copy.   41294

New York (Colony) Lieutenant Governor,
1763.
By the Honourable Cadwallader Colden.
. . . A Proclamation [Lands. Dec. 28,
1763].
[New York, 1763.] Broadside.
PRO copy.   9460

New York (Colony) Lieutenant Governor,
1763.
By the Honourable Cadwallader Colden.
. . . A Proclamation [Royal Proclamation.
Dec. 1, 1763].
[New York, 1763.] Broadside.
(Unique copy lost in the Albany fire.) 9459

[New York (Colony) Lieutenant
Governor, 1763.
Speech of the Honourable Cadwallader
Colden . . . to the Council . . . November
9, 1763.
New York, 1763.]
(From an adv.)   9461

New York (Colony) Lieutenant Governor,
1764.
By the Honourable Cadwallader Colden.
. . . Greetings [Table of Fees. Dated
1764].
[New York, 1764.] Broadside.
PRO copy.   9754

New York (Colony) Lieutenant Governor,
1764.
By the Honourable Cadwallader Colden.
. . . A Proclamation [Indian Trade. Dated
Dec. 8, 1764].
[New York, 1764.] Broadside.
PRO copy.   9755

[New York (Colony) Lieutenant
Governor, 1764.
Speech of the Honourable Cadwallader
Colden . . . to the Council . . . April 19,
1764.]
(From an adv.)   9757

New York (Colony) Lieutenant Governor,
1764.
The Speech of the Honourable
Cadwallader Colden [Dated Sept. 5,
1764].
[New York, 1764.] Broadside.
PRO copy.   9758

New York (Colony) Lieutenant Governor,
1765.
The Lieutenant Governor Declares he will
do Nothing in Relation to the Stamps
[Nov. 2, 1765].
[New York, 1765.] Broadside.
NYHS copy.   10096

[New York (Colony) Lieutenant
Governor, 1769.
By the Honourable Cadwallader Colden.
. . . A Proclamation [Dec. 12, 1769].
[New York, 1769.] Broadside.]
(Hasse 893; not now to be located) 11361

New York (Colony) Lieutenant Governor,
1769.
By the Honourable Cadwallader Colden.
. . . A Proclamation. . . . Whereas a
Certain Seditious and Libelous Paper.
. . . [Dec. 20, 1769].
[New York, 1769.] Broadside.
LOC copy.   11362

New York (Colony) Lieutenant Governor,
1769.
By the Honourable Cadwallader Colden.
. . . A Proclamation. Whereas a Certain
Seditious Paper. . . . [Dec. 20, 1769].
[New York, 1769.] Broadside.
LOC copy.   11363

New York (Colony) Lieutenant Governor,
1775.
The Speech of . . . Cadwallader Colden
. . . January 13, 1775.
[New York, 1775.] Broadside.
LOC copy.   14293

New York (Colony) Lieutenant Governor,
1769.
The Speech of the Honourable
Cadwallader Colden . . . to His Majesty's
Council . . . the 22d of November, 1769.
[New York, 1769.] [2] pp.
LOC copy.   11368

New York (Colony) President, 1736.
The President and Commander in Chief.
His Speech [Oct. 14, 1736].
[New York, 1736.] 3 pp.
NYPL copy.   4054

New York (Colony) President, 1760.
Speech of the Honourable Cadwallader
Colden [Oct. 22, 1760].
[New York, 1760.] 2 pp.
PRO copy.   8688

New York (Colony) President, 1761.
By the Honourable Cadwallader Colden.
. . . A Proclamation [Lydius. Feb. 18,
1761].
[New York, 1761.] Broadside.
PRO copy.   8953

New York (Colony) President, 1761.
Whereas it Hath Pleased Almighty God to
Call . . . George the Second [Jan. 17,
1761].
[New York, 1761.] Broadside.
PRO copy.   8958

New York (Colony) Provincial Congress,
1775.
Committee Chamber, New-York, August
22, 1775.
[New York, 1775.] Broadside.
NYHS copy.   14334

New York (Colony) Provincial Congress,
1775.
Le Congrès de la Colonie de la
Nouvelle-York Assemblé, le 25 de Mai
1775.
[New York, 1775.] Broadside.
NYHS copy.   14302

New York (Colony) Provincial Congress,
1775.
The Provincial Congress at their Meeting.
. . . Apr. 22, 1775.
[New York, 1775.] Broadside.
LOC copy.   14416

New York (Colony) Provincial Congress,
1775.
In Provincial Congress. New-York, May
29, 1775. You will see. . . .
[New York], Holt, [1775]. Broadside.
NYHS copy.   14299

New York (Colony) Provincial Congress,
1775.
In Provincial Congress, New-York, May
31, 1775. Resolved. . . .
[New York], Holt, [1775]. Broadside.
NYHS copy.   14300

New York (Colony) Provincial Congress,
1775.
In Provincial Congress, New-York, June
2, 1775. Friends. . . .
[New York, 1775.] Broadside.
NYHS copy.   14301

New York (Colony) Provincial Congress,
1775.
In Provincial Congress, New-York, June
3, 1775. Whereas. . . .
[New York], Holt, [1775]. Broadside.
LOC copy.   14303

New York (Colony) Provincial Congress,
1775.
In Provincial Congress, New-York, June
7, 1775. Resolved. . . .

[New York], Holt, [1775]. Broadside.
NYHS copy.   14304

New York (Colony) Provincial Congress,
1775.
In Provincial Congress. New-York, July 7,
1775. Whereas. . . .
[New York], Holt, [1775]. Broadside.
NYHS copy.   14306

New York (Colony) Provincial Congress,
1775.
In Provincial Congress. August 8, 1775.
Resolved. . . .
[New York, 1775.] Broadside.
NYHS copy.   14308

New York (Colony) Provincial Congress,
1775.
In Provincial Congress, New-York,
August 29th, 1775. Whereas. . . .
[New York, 1775.] Broadside.
NYHS copy.   14310

New York (Colony) Provincial
Congress, 1775.
In Provincial Congress, New-York,
September 1, 1775. Whereas. . . .
New York, Holt, 1775. 4 pp.
NYHS copy.   14311

New York (Colony) Provincial Congress,
1775.
In Provincial Congress, New-York,
October, 1775. Sir. . . .
[New York, 1775.] Broadside.
NYHS copy.   14312

New York (Colony) Provincial Congress,
1775.
In Provincial Congress, New-York,
December 12, 1775. Whereas. . . .
[New York, 1775.] Broadside.
NYHS copy.   14313

New York (Colony) Provincial Congress,
1775.
In Provincial Congress, New-York, Dec.
13, 1775. Whereas the Congress. . . .
[New York, 1775.] Broadside.
NYHS copy.   42905

New York (Colony) Provincial Congress,
1775.
Instructions for the Inlisting of Men. . . .
June . . . 1775.
[New York, 1775.] Broadside.
NYPL copy.   14305

New York (Colony) Provincial Congress,
1775.
Instructions for the Inlisting of Men. . . .
June 1775.
[New York, 1775.] Broadside.
NYHS copy.   42906

New York (Colony) Provincial Congress,
1775.
Rules and Orders for Regulating the
Militia. . . . August 22, 1775.
New York, Holt, 1775. 12 pp.
NYPL copy.   14309

New York (Colony) Provincial Congress,
1775.
State of the Four Regiments Raised in the
Colony of New-York. . . . August 4, 1775.
[New York, 1775.] Broadside.
NYHS copy.   14307

New York (Colony) Provincial Congress,
1775.
The Provincial Congress . . . have
Thought Proper that an Ox should be
Roasted. . . . April 22, 1775.
[New York, 1775.] Broadside.
(The one recorded copy cannot be
located.)   42907

New York (Colony) Receiver General,
1752.
New-York, May 22, 1752. Advertisement.
All Persons Indebted to His Majesty for
Quit-Rent of Land, in the County of
Albany. . . .
[New York? 1752.] Broadside.
NYHS copy.   40632

New York (Colony) Secretary, 1693.
An Account of Several Passages.
New York, 1693. 8 pp.
JCB copy.   674

New York (Colony) Session Laws, 1691.
The Laws & Acts [Apr. 9, 1691 - Sept. 12, 1693].
New York, 1694. [4], 84 pp.
(The pagination given by Evans includes his item 673.)
NYPL copy.   703

New York (Colony) Session Laws, 1694.
Laws & Acts [Mar. 24, 1693/4].
[New York, 1694.] pp. 85-92.
Rosenbach Foundation copy.   704

New York (Colony) Session Laws, 1694.
The Fourth Assembly, Second Sessions [Oct. 4, 1694 +].
[New York, 1694.] [4] pp.
NYPL copy.   705

New York (Colony) Session Laws, 1695.
The Fifth Assembly, First Sessions [June 20 - July 4, 1695].
New York, 1695. pp. 101-106.
NYPL copy.   731

New York (Colony) Session Laws, 1695.
The Sixth Assembly, First Sessions [Oct. 1-26, 1695].
[New York, 1695.] pp. [107] - 113.
NYPL copy.   732

New York (Colony) Session Laws, 1696.
The Fifth Assembly, Third Sessions [Mar. 25 - Apr. 24, 1696].
New York, 1696. [10] pp.
NYPL copy.   757

New York (Colony) Session Laws, 1696.
Acts made the 5th Assembly, 4th Session [Oct. 15 - Nov. 3, 1696].
[New York, 1696.] [6] pp.
HEH copy.   758

New York (Colony) Session Laws, 1697.
Acts Made the 5th Assembly, 5th Sessions [March, 1697].
[New York, 1697.] [5] pp.
NYPL copy.   803

New York (Colony) Session Laws, 1698.
Acts Made the 7th Assembly & 7th Sessions [Mar. 2, 1698 - May 16, 1699].
New York, 1699. pp. 119-150.
NYPL copy.   883

New York (Colony) Session Laws, 1700.
The 2d Sessions of the Seventh Assembly [July 29, 1700 +].
[New York, 1700.] pp. 151-155.
NYPL copy.   940

New York (Colony) Session Laws, 1700.
Acts Passed the 7th Assembly and 3d Sessions [Oct. 1 - Nov. 2, 1700].
[New York, 1700.] pp. [155]-196 [i.e. 164].
NYPL copy.   941

New York (Colony) Session Laws, 1701.
Acts Made the 7th Assembly & 3d. Sessions [Aug. 13 - Oct. 18, 1701].
[New York, 1701.] pp. 157-176.
HSP copy.   1001

New York (Colony) Session Laws, 1702.
Acts Passed by the First Sessions [Oct. 20, 1702 +].
[New York, 1702.] 177-202 pp.
NYPL copy.   1080

New York (Colony) Session Laws, 1703.
Acts Passed the 2d Sessions [Apr. 13, 1703 +].
[New York, 1703.] pp. 203-228.
HSP copy.   1137

New York (Colony) Session Laws, 1704.
Acts Passed the 4d Sessions [Apr. 13, 1704 +].
[New York, 1704.] pp. 229-238.
NYPL copy.   1187

New York (Colony) Session Laws, 1705.
Acts Passed the 5th Sessions [June 13, 1705 +].
[New York, 1705.] pp. 223-239.
NYPL copy.   1225

New York (Colony) Session Laws, 1706.
Acts Passed the 6th Sessions [June 29, 1706 +].
[New York, 1706.] [2] pp.
HSP copy.   1272

New York (Colony) Session Laws, 1706.
Acts Passed the 7th Session [Sept. 27, 1706 +].
[New York, 1706.] [6] pp.
NYPL copy.   1273

New York (Colony) Session Laws, 1708.
Acts Passed ... in September and October ... 1708.
[New York, 1708.] [12] pp.
NYPL copy.   1367

New York (Colony) Session Laws, 1709.
... An Act for Levying Divers Sums.
[New York, 1709.] pp. 89-96.
NYSL copy.   1420

New York (Colony) Session Laws, 1709.
Acts Passed by the General Assembly ... in May ... 1709.
[New York, 1709.] 4 pp.
NYPL copy.   1413

[New York (Colony) Session Laws, 1709.
Anno Regni Octavo Annae Reginae [Bills of Credit].
[New York, 1709.] pp. 101-112].
(A defective copy of 1422.)   1421

New York (Colony) Session Laws, 1709.
... An Act for the Currency of Bills of Credit.
New York, 1709. pp. 101-113, irreg.
NYSL copy.   1422

New York (Colony) Session Laws, 1709.
... An Act to Repeal an Act [Robt. Livingston].
[New York, 1709.] pp. 113-114.
NYSL copy.   1423

New York (Colony) Session Laws, 1710.
Acts Passed ... in October & November, 1710.
[New York, 1710.] pp. 115-128, irreg.
PRO copy.   1478

New York (Colony) Session Laws, 1711.
Acts Passed by the General Assembly [July-Aug. 1711].
[New York, 1711.] pp. 133-144.
HEH copy.   1521

New York (Colony) Session Laws, 1711.
An Act Passed ... in July, 1711 [Canada expedition].
[New York, 1711.] pp. 129-131, irreg.
PRO copy.   1522

New York (Colony) Session Laws, 1711.
Acts Passed ... in October and November, 1711.
[New York, 1711.] pp. 145-150.
HEH copy.   39534

New York (Colony) Session Laws, 1712.
Acts Passed by the General Assembly [June-Dec. 1712].
[New York, 1712.] pp. 151-[167] irreg.
NYBA copy.   1574

New York (Colony) Session Laws, 1713.
Acts Passed by the General Assembly [July, 1713].
[New York, 1713.] pp. 168-169.
NYPL copy.   1637

New York (Colony) Session Laws, 1713.
Acts Passed by the General Assembly [Oct. 1713].
[New York, 1713.] pp. 170-182.
NYPL copy.   1638

New York (Colony) Session Laws, 1714.
Acts Passed by the General Assembly [June-July, 1714].
[New York, 1714.] pp. 183-206.
NYPL copy.   1706

New York (Colony) Session Laws, 1714.
An Act Passed ... the Fourth Day of September, 1714.
New York, 1715. pp. 239-280, irreg.
HSP copy.   1771

New York (Colony) Session Laws, 1715.
Acts Passed by the General Assembly ... in July, 1715.
[New York, 1715.] pp. 207-238.
NYPL copy.   1770

New York (Colony) Session Laws, 1716.

Acts Passed by the General Assembly. ... 1716.
[New York, 1716.] pp. 239-245 (i.e. 253).
HSP copy.   1845

New York (Colony) Session Laws, 1717.
Acts Passed by the General Assembly [May - Nov. 1717].
[New York, 1717.] pp. 246-302.
NYHS copy.   1918

New York (Colony) Session Laws, 1718.
... Acts Passed [July 3, 1718].
[New York, 1718.] pp. 303-306.
NYPL copy.   1988

New York (Colony) Session Laws, 1718.
... Acts Passed [Oct. 16, 1718].
[New York, 1718.] pp. 307-310.
NYHS copy.   1989

New York (Colony) Session Laws, 1719.
... Acts Passed by the General Assembly [Apr., 1719].
[New York, 1719.] pp. 311-324.
NYHS copy.   2060

New York (Colony) Session Laws, 1719.
Acts Passed by the General Assembly [June 24, 1719 +].
New York, 1719. pp. 349-351.
AB copy.   2061

New York (Colony) Session Laws, 1720.
Acts Passed by the General Assembly [Nov. 1720].
[New York, 1720.] pp. 325-348.
AB copy.   2154

New York (Colony) Session Laws, 1721.
Acts Passed by the General Assembly [July 27, 1721 +].
[New York, 1721.] pp. [353-390.]
PRO copy.   2271

New York (Colony) Session Laws, 1722.
Acts Passed by the General Assembly ... in July, 1722.
[New York, 1722.] pp. 391-401.
AB copy.   2371

New York (Colony) Session Laws, 1722.
Acts Passed by the General Assembly ... in November, 1722.
[New York, 1722.] pp. 403-406.
PRO copy.   2372

New York (Colony) Session Laws, 1722.
An Act for Raising the sum of Five Hundred Pounds to Encourage and Promote a Trade with the ... Indians.
[New York, 1722.] pp. 407-416.
PRO copy.   2373

New York (Colony) Session Laws, 1722.
... An Act for the Payment of the Representatives.
[New York, 1722.] pp. 417-418.
PRO copy.   2374

New York (Colony) Session Laws, 1722.
... An Act for Paying Gerrit van Horne.
[New York, 1722.] pp. 419-422.
PRO copy.   2375

New York (Colony) Session Laws, 1723.
... At a Session of the General Assembly [May 8, 1723 +].
New York, 1723. pp. [2], 423-446.
(The only copy available is in bad condition.)
HSP copy.   2466

New York (Colony) Session Laws, 1724.
Acts Passed by the General Assembly ... in July, 1724.
[New York, 1724.] pp. 261-316.
NYPL copy.   2569

New York (Colony) Session Laws, 1726.
... At a Sessions of the General Assembly [June 17, 1726 +].
New York, 1726. [2], 46 pp.
NYPL copy.   2786

New York (Colony) Session Laws, 1726.
Laws or Acts [June 1726 +].
[New York, 1730]. pp. [2], 320-348.
NYPL copy.   3328

New York (Colony) Session Laws, 1726.
... At a Session of the General Assembly [Sept. 24, 1726 +].

New York, 1726. [2], 36 pp.
PRO copy. 2787

New York (Colony) Session Laws, 1727.
Acts Passed by the General Assembly . . .
November, 1727.
[New York, 1727.] 36 pp.
HSP copy. 2931

New York (Colony) Session Laws, 1728.
Acts Passed by the General Assembly . . .
in the Second Year of His Majesty
George II.
[New York, 1728.] 55 pp.
PRO copy. 3072

New York (Colony) Session Laws, 1729.
. . . Acts Passed by the General Assembly
. . . in . . . 1729.
[New York, 1729.] 48 pp.
PRO copy. 3194

New York (Colony) Session Laws, 1730.
Acts Passed by the General Assembly . . .
October 1730.
[New York, 1730.] pp. 348-373.
NYPL copy. 3329

New York (Colony) Session Laws, 1730.
More Acts Passed in the Year 1730.
[New York, 1730.] pp. 374-377.
NYPL copy. 3331

New York (Colony) Session Laws, 1731.
Acts Passed by the General Assembly . . .
In September, 1731.
[New York, 1731.] pp. 374-399.
NYPL copy. 3453

New York (Colony) Session Laws, 1732.
At a Session of the General Assembly. . . .
Acts [Oct. 14, 1732 +].
New York, 1732. pp. [2], 344-403.
NYPL copy. 3851

New York (Colony) Session Laws, 1733.
Acts Passed by the General Assembly . . .
in . . . 1733. An Act for the Further
Continuing. . . .
[New York, 1733.] pp. 405-411.
AB copy. 3694

New York (Colony) Session Laws, 1733.
Acts Passed by the General-Assembly . . .
in . . . 1733. An Act to Prevent. . . .
[New York, 1733.] pp. 405-408.
NYPL copy. 3695

New York (Colony) Session Laws, 1734.
An Act for Regulating the Rates to be
taken for Ships.
[New York, 1734.] pp. 427-428.
NYHS copy. 3806

New York (Colony) Session Laws, 1734.
An Act to Lay a Duty on Empty-Cask.
[New York, 1734.] pp. 455-462.
NYPL copy. 3808

New York (Colony) Session Laws, 1734.
Acts Passed by the General Assembly . . .
1734.
An Act to lay a Duty of Tonnage of
Vessels.
[New York, 1734.] pp. 413-421.
NYPL copy. 3805

New York (Colony) Session Laws, 1734.
Acts Passed by the General-Assembly . . .
1734. An Act to lay a Duty of Tonnage on
the Vessels.
[New York], 1734. pp. 413-426.
(Pagination irregular.)
NYHS copy. 3804

New York (Colony) Session Laws, 1734.
Acts Passed by the General Assembly . . .
Nov. 1734.
[New York, 1734.] pp. 427-454.
NYPL copy. 3807

New York (Colony) Session Laws, 1735.
Acts Passed by the General Assembly . . .
in November 1735.
[New York, 1735.] pp. 427-834 (i.e. 438).
NYPL copy. 3937

New York (Colony) Session Laws, 1736.
Acts Passed by the General Assembly . . .
November, 1736.
[New York, 1736.] pp. 439-454.
NYPL copy. 4048

New York (Colony) Session Laws, 1737.
At a General Assembly [June 15, 1737 +].
New York, 1738. [2], 100, [1] pp.
NYHS copy. 4284

New York (Colony) Session Laws, 1737.
Acts Passed by the General Assembly . . .
in October 1737.
New York, 1737. pp. 454-457. 4170

New York (Colony) Session Laws, 1739.
. . . An Act to Regulate the Militia.
New York, Bradford, 1739. 10 pp.
PRO copy. 4397

New York (Colony) Session Laws, 1739.
Acts Passed in October and November,
1739.
New York, 1739. 10 pp.
NYHS copy. 4398

New York (Colony) Session Laws, 1739.
. . . An Act for Compleating and Building
the Fortifications.
[New York, 1739.] pp. 11-53.
PRO copy. 4399

New York (Colony) Session Laws, 1739.
. . . Acts Passed . . . in April 1739.
New York, Bradford, 1739. [3] pp.
(Gotshall 278; no copy located.) 40172

New York (Colony) Session Laws, 1739.
The Thirteenth [Third] Session of the
Second Asembly. . . . An Act Appointing
Commissioners to Farm the Excise.
[New York, 1739.] 7 pp.
(The unique copy cannot at present be
located.) 4400

[New York (Colony) Session Laws, 1740.
An Act for Transporting and Victualing
of Volunteers.
New York, 1740. 41 pp.]
(No copy located.) 4570

New York (Colony) Session Laws, 1740.
. . . At a Sessions of the General Assembly
[Sept. 11, 1740 +].
New York, Bradford, 1741. [2], 60 pp.,
irreg.
NYSL copy. 4761

New York (Colony) Session Laws, 1741.
At a Sessions of General Assembly [Sept.
15, 1741 +].
New York, 1741. 44 pp.
NYHS copy. 4762

New York (Colony) Session Laws, 1742.
Acts Passed in the Fifteenth Year of His
Majesty's Reign [May 22, 1742 +].
[New York, 1742.] 9 pp.
NYHS copy. 5016

New York (Colony) Session Laws, 1742.
Acts Passed by the General Assembly
[Nov. 1742].
New York, 1742. 35 pp.
NYHS copy. 5017

New York (Colony) Session Laws, 1743.
At a General Assembly [Nov. 8, 1743 +].
New York, 1743. 42 pp.
NYHS copy. 5255

New York (Colony) Session Laws, 1744.
At a General Assembly [July 17, 1744 +].
New York, 1744. 57, [1] pp.
NYHS copy. 5447

New York (Colony) Session Laws, 1745.
Acts of the General Asembly . . . Passed
in the Eighteenth Year of His Majesty's
Reign.
New York, 1745. 4 pp.
NYHS copy. 5652

New York (Colony) Session Laws, 1745.
At a General Assembly [June 25, 1745 +].
New York, 1745. 61, [1] pp.
NYHS copy. 5823

New York (Colony) Session Laws, 1745.
Chap. I. An Act for the Paying of Five
Thousand Pounds towards the Expedition
Carrying on against Cape Breton.
[New York, 1745.] 8 pp.
(This is the first part of 5823, q.v.) 5653

New York (Colony) Session Laws, 1745.

Chap. III. An Act to Let to Farm the
Excise.
[New York, 1745.] pp. 9-40.
(This is the second part of 5823, q.v.) 5654

New York (Colony) Session Laws, 1746.
At a General Assembly [June 3, 1746 +].
New York, 1746. 47, [1] pp.
NYHS copy. 5824

New York (Colony) Session Laws, 1748.
. . . At a Session of the General Assembly
[Feb. 12, 1747/8 - Apr. 9, 1748.].
New York, Parker, 1747. 39, [1] pp.
PRO copy. 6202

[New York (Colony) Session Laws, 1748.
At a Session of the General Assembly
[Sept. - Nov. 1748].
New York, 1748.]
(It is not likely that the laws of this
session were printed.) 6203

[New York (Colony) Session Laws, 1751.
At a Session of the General Assembly
[May - June, 1751].
New York, 1751.]
(There were no laws passed this session.)
6732

New York (Colony) Session Lws, 1751.
At a Session of the General Assembly
[Oct. 1 - Nov. 25, 1751].
New York, 1751. 30, [1] pp.
NYPL copy. 6733

[New York (Colony) Session Laws, 1754.
Acts of the last Session of the General
Assembly.
New York, Parker & Weyman, 1754.]
(Unique NYSL copy unlocated.) 7268

New York (Colony) Session Laws, 1755.
[At a Session of the General Assembly,
Dec. 2, 1755 +.]
New York, Parker & Weyman, 1756.
pp. 3-65.
MHS copy. 7735

New York (Colony) Session Laws, 1756.
At a Session of the General Assembly
[Sept. 21, 1756 - Dec. 1, 1756].
New York, Parker & Weyman, 1757. pp.
[1]-41, [1], 3-15, [1], 3-22.
MHS copy. 8209

New York (Colony) Session Laws, 1757.
. . . At a Session of the General Assembly
[Feb. 15, 1757-Dec. 16, 1758].
New York, Parker, 1759. [2], 66, [1] pp.
MHS copy. 8431

New York (Colony) Session Laws, 1759.
[At a Session of the General Assembly,
Jan. - Dec. 1759.]
New York, Weyman, 1759. 53 pp.
MHS copy. 8687

New York (Colony) Session Laws, 1762.
. . . Chap. CCLX. . . . Pass'd the 11th
December, 1762.
[New York, 1762.] pp. 269-308.
LOC copy. 41296

New York (Colony) Session Laws, 1764.
. . . The Twenty-First Assembly. Fourth
Sessions.
New York, Weyman, 1764. pp. 309-353
(i.e. 357).
LOC copy. 41475

New York (Colony) Session Laws, 1764.
. . . Chap. CCCXVI. . . . Pass'd the 20th of
October, 1764.
[New York, Weyman, 1764.] pp. 359-407.
LOC copy. 41476

New York (Colony) Session Laws, 1765.
. . . The Twenty-First Assembly [Dec. 23,
1765].
New York, Weyman, [1765]. pp. 409-440.
LOC copy. 41577

New York (Colony) Session Laws, 1766.
. . . The Twenty-First Assembly [July 3,
1766].
New York, Weyman, [1766]. pp. 441-444.
LOC copy. 41649

New York (Colony) Session Laws, 1766.
. . . Chap. CCCLXXVIII. . . . [passed
Dec. 19, 1766-June 6, 1767].

[New York, 1767.] pp. 445-469.
LOC copy.   41746

New York (Colony) Session Laws, 1767.
Chap. CCCCI, Dec. 21, 1767 +].
[New York, Gaine, 1768.] pp. 471-568.
LOC copy.   11001

New York (Colony) Session Laws, 1768.
Chap. CCCCXXXIV. December 31,
1768 +].
New York, Gaine, 1769. pp. 569-605, [1].
LOC copy.   11359

New York (Colony) Session Laws, 1769.
Chap. CCCCLXIV. An Act. . . .
New York, Gaine, 1769. pp. 607-637, [1].
NYSL copy.   11360

New York (Colony) Session Laws, 1769.
Chap. CCCCLXXXIV [Nov. 31, 1769 +].
New York, Gaine, pp. 639-728, [2].
LOC copy.   11772

New York (Colony) Session Laws, 1771.
Chap. DXLIV. An Act. . . .
New York, Gaine, 1771. 731-822 pp.
AAS copy.   12154

New York (Colony) Session Laws, 1772.
. . . Chap. DLXXVIII. An Act. . . .
New York, Gaine, 1772. pp. 823-949, [2].
AAS copy.   12481

New York (Colony) Session Laws, 1773.
Chap. MDLXXIII. An Act. . . .
New York, Gaine, 1773. 105, [2] pp.
LOC copy.   12886

New York (Colony) Session Laws, 1774.
Volume III. The Twenty-Ninth Assembly.
Sixth Session.
New York, Gaine, 1774. 79, [1] pp.
AAS copy.   13460

New York (Colony) Session Laws, 1775.
The Thirtieth Assembly. Seventh Session.
New York, Gaine, 1775. pp. 81-202, [2].
AAS copy.   14292

New York (Colony) Supreme Court, 1717.
A Writ Issu'd . . . to the Justices . . . of
Jamaica.
[New York?] 7 pp.
NYHS copy.   39668

New York (Colony) Treaties, etc., 1694.
An Account of the Treaty . . . [with the]
Five Nations.
New York, 1694. 39 pp.
BM copy.   702

New York (Colony) Treaties, etc., 1746.
A Treaty, between His Excellency . . .
George Clinton. . . . And the Six . . .
Nations. . . . Albany . . . August . . . 1746.
New York, 1746. 23 pp.
NYPL copy.   5791

New York (Colony) Treaties, etc., 1757.
Proceedings and Treaty with the
Shawanese, Nanticokes, and Mohikander
Indians.
New York, Parker & Weyman, 1757.
14 pp.
MHS copy.   7925

[New York (Colony) Treaties, etc., 1757.
Proceedings and Treaty with the
Shawanese, Nanticokes, and Mohikander
Indians.
Boston, 1757.]
(Entry from Sabin 65, 759 and Winsor,
Nar. and Crit. Hist., V, 581.)   7926

New York (County) Grand Jury, 1713.
To His Excellency Robert Hunter. . . . The
Humble Address of the Grand-Jury [May
5, 1713].
[New York, 1713.] 2 pp.
PRO copy.   1642

[New York (County) Militia.
A Statement, Explanatory of the
Resignation of the Officers.
New York, Loudon, 1795.]
(For a corrected entry see 32568.)   29203

New York (County) Sheriff, 1769.
New-York, January 6, 1769.
Advertisement, for Summoning the
Freeholders . . . of New York, to . . . Elect

four Representatives to . . . the next
General Assembly.
[New York, 1769.] Broadside.
NYHS copy.   41987

New York (State) Adjutant General.
Adjutant General's Office. July 20, 1798.
General Orders. . . . Aug. 19, 1798.
Albany, Websters, [1798.] Broadside.
NYSL copy.   48539

New York (State) Adjutant-General.
The Adjutant-General's Report.
[Albany? 1799?] 28 pp.
NYHS copy.   48944

New York (State) Adjutant General's
Office, 1790.
Extracts from the Regulations for the . . .
Militia.
Albany, Websters, 1790. 29 pp.
(Best copy available.)
NYSL copy.   45928

New York (State) Agent for Military
Stores.
In Pursuance of a Law Passed by the State
of New-York, Dated . . . 6th of March,
1778, Impowering me to Export . . .
Flour. . . .
n.p., [1778]. Broadside.
Mass. Archives copy.   43475

New York (State) Assembly Journals,
1777.
The Votes and Proceedings of the
Assembly . . . at their First Session [Sept.
10-20, 1777].
Kingston, Holt, 1777. 16 pp.
NYSL copy.   15478

New York (State) Assembly Journals,
1777.
A.D. 1777. George Clinton, Esq.,
Governor [Sept. 22, 1777 - Apr. 4, 1778].
[Poughkeepsie, 1778.] pp. 17-109.
NYSL copy.   15932

New York. Assembly Journals, 1778.
Journal of the Assembly [June 22 - 30,
1778].
[Poughkeepsie, 1778.] pp. 111-125.
NYSL copy.   15933

New York (State) Assembly Journals,
1778.
The Votes and Proceedings of the
Assembly [Oct. 1, 1778 - Mar. 16, 1779].
Poughkeepsie, 1779. 107 pp.
NYPL copy.   16408

New York (State) Assembly Journals,
1779.
The Votes and Proceedings of the
Assembly [Aug. 9 - Oct. 25, 1779].
Fishkill, 1779. 86 pp.
NYPL copy.   16409

New York (State) Assembly Journals,
1780.
The Votes and Proceedings of the
Assembly [Jan. 27 - Mar. 14, 1780.]
[Fishkill, Loudon, 1780.] pp. [87]-156.
NYPL copy.   43853

New York (State) Assembly Journals,
1780.
Votes and Proceedings of the Assembly
[Sept. 7, 1780 - June 30, 1781].
[Poughkeepsie, 1781.] 43, [23] pp.
NYHS copy.   16907

New York (State) Assembly Journals,
1781.
Votes and Proceedings of the Assembly
. . . October 24th [-Nov. 23d, 1781].
[Poughkeepsie, 1781?] 47 pp.
(No perfect copy located.)
NYSL copy.   44011

New York (State) Assembly Journals,
1784.
Votes and Proceedings of the Assembly
[Oct. 4 - Nov. 29, 1784].
[New York, 1784.] pp. 3-79.
(No copy with title page located.)
NYSL copy.   18649

New York (State) Assembly Journals,
1784.
Journal of the Eighth Assembly . . .
Seventh Session [Jan. 21 - May 12, 1784].

New York, Holt, 1784. 168 pp.
NYHS copy.   18648

New York (State) Assembly Journals,
1785.
Journal of the Assembly. . . . Second
Meeting of the Eighth Session [Jan.
27-Apr. 27, 1785].
New York, Loudon, 1785. 183 pp.
AAS copy.   19131

New York (State) Assembly Journals,
1786.
Journal of the Assembly. . . . First
Meeting of the Ninth Session [Jan. 12 -
May 5, 1786].
New York, Loudons, 1786. 176 pp.
AAS copy.   19852

New York (State) Assembly Journals,
1787.
Journal of the Assembly . . . Tenth
Session [Jan. 12 - Apr. 21, 1787].
New York, Loudons, 1787. 179 pp.
NYPL copy.   20576

New York (State) Assembly Journals,
1788.
Journal of the Assembly [Jan. 9 - Mar. 22,
1788].
Poughkeepsie, 1788. 144 pp., irreg.
AAS copy.   21314

New York (State) Assembly Journals,
1788.
Journal of the Assembly . . . at their
Twelfth Session. [Dec. 11, 1788 - Mar. 2,
1789].
Albany, Loudons, 1788 (1789). pp. 163,
[1].
NYSL copy.   22008

New York (State) Assembly Journals,
1789.
Journal of the Assembly . . . Thirteenth
Session [July 6-16, 1789].
New York, Loudons, 1789. 27 pp.
LOC copy.   22009

New York (State) Assembly Journals,
1790.
Journal of the House of Assembly. . . .
Second Meeting of the Thirteenth Session
[Jan. 13 - Apr. 6, 1790].
New York, Childs & Swaine, 1790. 118 pp.
NYPL copy.   22718

New York (State) Assembly Journals,
1791.
Journal of the House of Assembly. . . .
Fourteenth Session [Jan. 5 - Mar. 24,
1791].
New York, Childs & Swaine, 1791. 128 pp.
NYPL copy.   23615

New York (State) Assembly Journals,
1792.
Journal of the Assembly. . . . Fifteenth
Session [Jan. 4 - Apr. 12, 1792].
New York, Childs & Swaine, 1792. 207 pp.
AAS copy.   24600

New York (State) Assembly Journals,
1792.
Journal of the Assembly. . . . Sixteenth
Session [Nov. 6, 1792 - Mar. 12, 1793].
New York, Childs & Swaine, 1792. 247 pp.
AAS copy.   25900

New York (State) Assembly Journals,
1794.
Journal of the Assembly . . . Seventeenth
Session [Jan. 7 - Mar. 27, 1794].
Albany, Websters for Childs & Swaine,
1794. 180 pp.
NYHS copy.   27397

New York (State) Assembly Journals,
1795.
Extract from the Journals . . . March 19,
1795.
[New York? 1795.] Broadside.
(Not located, 1968.)   47517

[New York (State) Assembly Journals,
1795.
Journal of the Assembly. . . . Eighteenth
Session [Jan. 6 - Apr. 9, 1795].]
New York, Childs, 1795. 148 pp.]
(Apparently the first part of 29187, q. v.)
     29186

New York (State) Assembly Journals, 1795.
Journal of the Assembly . . . Eighteenth Session. [Jan. 6 - Apr. 9, 1795].
New York, Childs, 1795. 182, [3] pp.
NYHS copy.   29187

New York (State) Assembly Journals, 1796.
Journal of the Assembly. . . . Nineteenth Session [Jan. 6, 1796 +].
New York, Childs, 1796. 193, [12] pp.
NYPL copy.   47862

New York (State) Assembly Journals, 1796.
Journal of the Assembly . . . Twentieth Session [Nov. 1, 1796 - Apr. 3, 1797].
Albany, Websters for Morton, [1797]. 218 pp., 1 folding table.
NYSL copy.   32553

New York (State) Assembly Journals, 1798.
Journal of the Assembly . . . Twenty-First Session [Jan. 2-Apr. 6, 1798].
Albany, Andrews, [1798]. 339, [1] pp.
NYPL copy.   34210

New York (State) Assembly Journals, 1798.
Journal of the Assembly . . .
Twenty-Second Session [Aug. 9 - 27, 1798].
Albany, Andrews, [1798]. 39 pp.
LOC copy.   34212

New York (State) Assembly Journals, 1799.
Journal of the Assembly . . .
Twenty-Second Session, Second Meeting [Jan. 2 - Apr. 3, 1799].
Albany, Andrews, [1799]. 293 pp.
NYHS copy.   35924

New York (State) Assembly Journals, 1800.
Journal of the Assembly . . . Twenty-Third Session [Jan. 28 - Apr. 8, 1800].
Albany, Andrews, [1800]. 299, [4] pp.
NYPL copy.   38084

[New York (State) Census, 1790.
A Census of the Electors and Inhabitants . . . Taken . . . 1790.
[New York], Childs & Swaine, [1790?].
Broadside.]
(Correctly entered under 23614.)   22717

New York (State) Census, 1790.
A Census of the Electors and Inhabitants in the State of New-York, Taken in the Year 1790.
[New York], Childs & Swaine, [1791].
Broadside.
NYHS copy.   23614

New York (State) Census, 1795.
A General Account of the Number of Electors.
[New York? 1795?] [2] pp.
(Not located 1968).   47518

[New York (State) Census, 1800.
Census of the State of New York, for 1800.]
(Described by Sabin (53576) as in NYSL before the fire.)   38077

New York (State) Chamber of Commerce of the State of New York.
Bye-Laws, Resolutions and Orders, Adopted . . . September 18, 1787.
New York, Gaine, 1787. 14 pp.
AAS copy.   20579

New York (State) Commission Respecting the Jurisdiction of New York and Massachusetts.
An Instrument Agreed upon between the Commissioners . . . of New-York and Massachusetts.
New York, Loudons, 1787. 12 pp.
LOC copy.   20575

New York (State) Commissioners for Erecting State Prisons.
To the Honorable the Legislature [Jan. 13, 1798]. . . .
[Albany], Andrews, [1798]. Broadside.
HC copy.   48540

New York (State) Commissioners of Forfeiture.
By the Commissioners . . . of the Eastern District. . . . July 27, 1786.
[Albany, 1786.] Broadside.
NYHS copy.   44935

New York (State) Committee of Safety, 1776.
Committee Chamber. New-York, January 10, 1776. Whereas the Business. . . .
[New York, 1776.] Broadside.
NYHS copy.   14924

New York (State) Committee of Safety, 1776.
Committee of Safety, New-York, January 27, 1776. Instructions. . . .
[New York, 1776.] Broadside.
LOC copy.   14925

New York (State) Committee of Safety, 1776.
Committee-Chamber, New-York, April 9, 1776. Whereas. . . .
[New York, 1776.] Broadside.
NYPL copy.   14926

New York (State) Committee of Safety, 1776.
Committee-Chamber, New-York, April 13th, 1776. The Following Persons. . . .
[New York, 1776.] Broadside.
NYHS copy.   14927

[New York (State) Committee of Safety, 1776.
Essays upon the Making of Salt-Petre.
New York, Loudon, 1776. 22 pp.]
(A defective copy of 14930.)   14929

New York (State) Committee of Safety, 1776.
Essays upon the Making of Salt-Petre.
New York, Loudon, 1776. 39 pp.
LOC copy.   14930

New York (State) Committee of Safety, 1776.
. . . Fish-Kills, Oct. 9, 1776. Resolved, That . . . Coarse Woolen Cloth. . . .
[Fishkill, 1776.] Broadside.
NYSL copy.   43100

New York (State) Committee of Safety, 1776.
Gentlemen, Although a Certain Day is Fixed for the Session of Congress . . . the First of February. . . .
[New York, 1776.] Broadside.
NYHS copy.   43101

New York (State) Committee of Safety, 1776.
In Committee of Safety, for the State of New-York.
Fish-Kills, Nov. 7, 1776 [Passes].
[Fishkill, 1776.] Broadside.
NYHS copy.   14928

New York (State) Committee of Safety, 1776.
. . . January 27, 1776. Instructions to the Colonels.
[New York, 1776.] Broadside.
NYHS copy.   43102

New York (State) Committee of Safety, 1776.
. . . Nov. 12, 1776. Resolved, that Notice is Given. . . .
[Fishkill, 1776.] Broadside.
LOC copy.   43103

New York (State) Committee of Safety, 1776.
Sir, By Virtue of the Authority Vested in Us. . . .
[Fishkill, 1776.] Broadside.
(No copy located.)   43104

New York (State) Committee of Safety, 1776.
To the Inhabitants of the Colony of New-York. . . . Jan. 9, 1776.
New York, Holt, [1776]. 8 pp.
AAS copy.   43105

New York (State) Committee of Safety, 1777.
. . . Fish-Kill, Jan. 6, Whereas it Appears . . . that Fines. . . .

[Fishkill? 1777.] Broadside.
NYHS copy.   43315

New York (State) Committee of Safety, 1777.
. . . Fish-Kill, Jan. 22, 1777. Several Matters. . . .
[Fishkill, 1777.] Broadside.
(The only copy located is in very poor condition.)
NYSL copy.   43316

New York (State) Committee of Safety, 1777.
. . . Kingston, March 1, 1777. Resolved, That the Several Towns. . . .
[Fishkill, 1777.] Broadside.
NYPL copy.   15476

New York (State) Committee to Explore Western Waters.
The Report of a Committee, Appointed to Explore. . . .
Albany, Barber & Southwick, 1792. 24 pp.
NYPL copy.   24604

New York (State) Comptroller's Office, 1798.
Statement of the Funds . . . in the Year 1797.
Albany, Andrews, 1798. 16 pp.
AAS copy.   34218

New York (State) Comptroller's Office, 1798.
To the Honourable the Legislature. . . .
August 15, 1798.
[Albany, 1798.] [3] pp.
NYHS copy.   48541

New York (State) Comptroller's Office, 1799.
Forms and Directions for the Assessors. . . . 20th April, 1799.
[Albany, 1799.] [3] pp.
NYSL copy.   35922

New York (State) Constitution, 1777.
The Constitution of the State of New-York.
Fishkill, 1777. 33 pp.
AAS copy.   15472

New York (State) Constitution, 1777.
The Constitution of the State of New-York.
Fishkill, 1777. 34 pp.
NYPL copy.   15473

New York (State) Constitution, 1777.
The Constitution of the State of New York.
Philadelphia, Styner & Cist, 1777. 32 pp.
AAS copy.   15474

New York (State) Constitution, 1783.
The Constitution of the State of New-York.
New York, Loudon, 1783. 43 pp.
NYPL copy.   18059

New York (State) Constitution, 1785.
The Constitution of the State of New-York.
New York, Holt, 1785. 48 pp.
(The only copy located could not be reproduced.)   19130

New York (State) Constitutional Convention, 1788.
The Debates and Proceedings of the. . . .
New York, Childs, 1788. [2], 144 pp.
AAS copy.   21310

[New York (State) Constitutional Convention, 1788.
In Convention, at Poughkeepsie . . . July 26, 1788.
Poughkeepsie, 1788.]
(No copy located.)   21312

New York (State) Constitutional Convention, 1788.
Journal of the Convention . . . at Poughkeepsie.
Poughkeepsie, [1788]. 86 pp.
NYPL copy.   21313

New York (State) Convention, 1776.
An Address of the Convention of the Representatives.
Fishkill, 1776. 19 pp.
AAS copy.   14921

[New York (State) Convention, 1776.
An Address of the Convention of the
Representatives.
Fishkill, [1776]. 19 pp.]
(The BPL copy described by Evans was
not a nd. ed., but a copy of 14921 cropped
like that here reproduced.) 14922

New York (State) Convention, 1776.
An Address of the Convention of the
Representatives.
Norwich, Green & Spooner, [1777].
16 pp.
("Just published": New London Gazette,
Jan. 24, 1777.)
AAS copy. 14923

New York (State) Convention, 1776.
In Convention of the Representatives of
the State. . . . September 21, 1776.
[Fishkill, 1776.] Broadside.
LOC copy. 43106

New York (State) Convention, 1776.
In Convention of the Representatives of
the State of New-York, October 2, 1776.
[Rangers].
Fishkill, [1776]. 12 pp.
LOC copy. 14932

New York (State) Convention, 1776.
In Convention of the Representatives of
the State of New-York. September 21,
1776. Whereas. . . .
[Fishkill, 1776.] Broadside.
AAS copy. 14931

New York (State) Convention, 1776-1777.
Fish-Kill, December 23, 1776. An Address
of the Convention.
[Annapolis, 1777.] [4] pp.
(The only recorded copy could not be
located.) 43311

New York (State) Convention, 1776-1777.
In Convention of the Representatives of
the State of New-York, at Kingston,
March 7, 1777. Whereas. . . .
[Fishkill, 1777.] Broadside.
AAS copy. 43312

New York (State) Convention,
1776-1777.
In Convention of the Representatives of
the State . . . April 1, 1777.
[Fishkill, 1777.] Broadside.
NYHS copy. 43313

New York (State) Convention,
1776-1777.
In Convention of the Representatives of
the State . . . May 5, 1777.
[Fishkill, 1777.] Broadside.
NYPL copy. 43314

New York (State) Convention, 1777.
Aanspraak van de Vergadering. . . .
Decem. 23, 1776.
Fishkill, 1777. 24 pp.
NYPL copy. 15470

New York (State) Convention, 1777.
An Address of the Convention.
Baltimore, 1777. 15 pp.
JCB copy. 15469

New York (State) Convention, 1777.
An Address of the Convention.
Philadelphia, Dunlap, 1777. 12 pp.
LCP copy. 15468

New York (State) Convention, 1777.
A Declaration . . . Passed May 10, 1777.
[Fishkill, 1777]. Broadside.
NYPL copy. 15475

New York (State) Convention, 1777.
An Ordinance of the Convention . . . for
. . . Establishing the Government.
Fishkill, 1777. 12 pp.
NYPL copy. 15477

New York (State) Convention, 1777.
Zuschrift aus der Versammlung.
Philadelphia, Steiner & Cist, 1777. 21 pp.
LCP copy. 15471

New York (State) Council of Safety,
1777.
In Council of Safety, for the State of
New York, July 30, 1777, a Proclamation
. . . George Clinton.

Kingston, Holt, [1777]. Broadside.
NYPL ph. copy. 43317

New York (State) Council of Safety,
1777.
In Council of Safety for the State of
New York, Kingston, July 31, 1777.
Whereas. . . .
Kingston, Holt, [1777]. Broadside.
NYSL copy. 43318

New York (State) Council of Safety,
1777.
In Council of Safety for the State of New-
York, Marbletown, Nov. 11, 1777.
Whereas. . . .
[Fishkill, 1777.] Broadside.
NYSL copy. 43320

New York (State) Council of Safety,
1777.
. . . Kingston, August 13, 1777. Whereas
. . . The Act of Grace. . . .
Kingston, Holt, [1777]. Broadside.
NYHS copy. 43319

New York (State) Court of Impeachment
and Errors, 1790.
. . . Peter Servis and Others,
respondents. . . .
[New York], Greenleaf, [1790?].
Broadside.
NYHS copy. 45929

New York (State) Courts.
Rules of the Supreme Court. . . . To
which are Added, the Circuit Courts.
Albany, Websters, 1799. 38 pp.
HC copy. 35931

New York (State) Election Prox, 1795.
Albany, February 23, 1795.
Gentlemen. . . .
[Albany, 1795.] Broadside.
NYHS copy. 47519

New York (State) Election Prox, 1796.
To the Electors of the Sothern District.
. . . April 19, 1796.
[New York, 1796.] Broadside.
NYSL copy. 47863

New York (State) Election Prox, 1799.
In Committee Albany, 8th April, 1799.
[Albany, 1799.] Broadside.
(Same as 48893, q. v.)
NYHS copy. 48945

New York (State) General Assembly,
1788.
. . . In Assembly, January 31st, 1788.
Whereas the United States. . . . In
Assembly, February 1st, 1788. . . . An
Extract from the Minutes.
[New York, 1788.] Broadside.
NYSL copy. 45311

New York (State) General Assembly
Journals, 1780.
Votes and Proceedings of the Assembly
[May 25-July 2, 1780].
[Poughkeepsie, 1783.] pp. [157]-192.
NYHS copy. 44417

New York (State) General Assembly
Journals, 1780.
Votes and Proceedings of the Assembly
[Sept. 7-Oct. 10, 1780].
[Poughkeepsie, 1783.] 43 pp.
NYHS copy. 44418

New York (State) General Assembly
Journals, 1781.
Votes and Proceedings of the Assembly
[June 16-July 1, 1781].
[Poughkeepsie, 1783.] [23] pp.
NYHS copy. 44419

New York (State) General Assembly
Journals, 1782.
Votes and Proceedings of the Assembly.
. . . February 21st [-Apr. 14, 1782].
[Poughkeepsie, 1782.] pp. [49]-100
(i.e. 104).
HEH copy. 44234

New York (State) General Assembly
Journals, 1782.
Votes and Proceedings of the Assembly
. . . July 11th [-25th, 1782].
[Poughkeepsie, 1782.] pp. [105]-122
(sic 128).
NYSOC copy. 44235

New York (State) General Assembly
Journals, 1783.
Votes and Proceedings of the Assembly
. . . 27th January, 1783 [-Mar. 28, 1783].
[Poughkeepsie, 1783.] pp. [97]-179.
NYHS copy. 44420

New York (State) Governor, 1777.
By His Excellency George Clinton. . . . A
Proclamation. . . . The Honourable the
Congress [Dec. 15, 1777].
[Fishkill, 1777.] Broadside.
(The only known copy is imperfect.)
NYSL copy. 43321

New York (State) Governor, 1778.
By His Excellency George Clinton. . . .
Proclamation [Controverted Lands. Oct.
31, 1778].
Poughkeepsie, [1778]. Broadside.
LOC copy. 15931

[New York (State) Governor, 1779.
By His Excellency George Clinton. . . . A
Proclamation [Disaffected Persons. Feb.
23, 1778].
Poughkeepsie, 1778. Broadside.]
(No copy located.) 16406

New York (State) Governor, 1780.
. . . Head-Quarters, Poughkeepsie,
November 1780. General Orders.
[Poughkeepsie, 1780.] Broadside.
HC copy. 43855

New York (State) Governor, 1781.
By His Excellency George Clinton . . .
Proclamation The Appointment of
Delegates. . . . September 6th, 1781.
Poughkeepsie, 1781. Broadside.
BPL copy. 44012

New York (State) Governor, 1781.
. . . Head-Quarters, Poughkeepsie, July
1st, 1781. General Orders.
[Poughkeepsie, 1781.] Broadside.
NYHS copy. 44013

New York (State) Governor, 1782.
General Orders. Poughkeepsie, 25th
March, 1782.
[Poughkeepsie, 1782.] Broadside.
NYSL copy. 44236

New York (State) Governor, 1784.
New-York, October 18, 1784. The
Speech of . . . the Governor.
[New York], Holt, [1784]. Broadside.
NYHS copy. 44573

New York (State) Governor, 1787.
By His Excellency George Clinton. . . . A
Proclamation [Shays' Rebellion. Dated
Feb. 24, 1787].
New York, Loudons, [1787]. Broadside.
NYPL copy. 45114

New York (State) Governor, 1788.
By His Excellency George Clinton. . . . A
Proclamation. Whereas the Senate. . . .
John Livingston. . . . [Mar. 1, 1788.]
Poughkeepsie, Power, [1788]. Broadside.
NYPL copy. 45312

New York (State) Governor, 1792.
Proclamation by His Excellency George
Clinton . . . to . . . apprehend . . . John
Ryer. . . . This Twenty-fourth Day of
May, 1792.
[New York, 1792.] Broadside.
LOC copy. 25906

New York (State) Governor, 1793.
By George Clinton. . . . A Proclamation.
Whereas a Proclamation of the President.
. . . [May 9, 1793].
[New York, 1793.] Broadside.
Albany Institute copy. 46834

New York (State) Governor, 1793.
A Proclamation. Whereas by the Statute
entitled "An Act to Prevent bringing in
Infectious Distempers. . . ."
[New York, 1793.] Broadside.
NYHS copy. 46835

New York (State) Governor, 1798.
By His Excellency John Jay. . . . A
Proclamation. Whereas it is the Duty
[Mar. 1, 1798].
[Albany? 1798] Broadside.
WLC copy. 48542

New York (State) Governor, 1798.
Governor's Speech. Gentlemen of the
Senate and Assembly.... August 9th,
1798.
[Albany], Andrews, [1798]. [2] pp.
NYPL copy.   48543

New York (State) Governor, 1798.
Speech of His Excellency John Jay ... to
the Two Houses of the Legislature ...
January 2d, 1798.
Albany, Websters, [1798]. [3] pp.
NYPL copy.   34217

New York (State) Governor, 1799.
Gentlemen, I now Lay before you an
Authenticated Copy of an Act.... 25th
February, 1799.
[Albany, 1799.] Broadside.
(Apparently the unique original was lost
in the Albany fire.)   35923

New York (State) Governor, 1799.
... In Senate. January 12, 1799. The
Following Message from His
Excellency....
[Albany], Andrews, [1799]. [4] pp.
NYSL copy.   35932

[New York (State) Governor, 1799.
Message from Governor Jay, of the 12th
January, 1799.
[Albany, 1799.] 4 pp.]
(A description of 35932, q. v.)   35928

New York (State) Governor, 1800.
By His Excellency John Jay.... A
Proclamation [Presidential Electors]. ...
7th November 1800.
n.p., n.d. Broadside.
NYSL copy.   38076

New York (State) Governor, 1800.
Gentlemen. I herewith lay before you a
Report. ... February 17, 1800.
[Albany, 1800.] 16 pp.
NYPL copy.   38082

New York (State) Governor, 1800.
Gentlemen of the Senate and Assembly.
The Great Importance of the
Business. ... November 1, 1800.
[Albany, 1800.] [2] pp.
(No copy located.)   38082a

New York (State) Inspectors of the
State-Prisons.
The Inspectors ... Report. ... First
Month 1798.
[Albany], Andrews, [1798]. [3] pp.
(Copy not located.)   48544

New York (State) Inspectors of the
State-Prisons.
To the Representatives.... Render ...
their Annual Account.
[Albany, 1800.] 5 pp., 3 folded tables.
NYHS copy.   38094

New York (State) Laws, Statutes, etc.,
1778.
... An Act for Raising Monies. ...
Passed the 28th of March, 1778.
Poughkeepsie, Holt, [1778]. [2] pp.
MHS copy.   43515

[New York (State) Laws, Statutes, etc.,
1778.
An Act for Regulating the Militia ...
Passed ... April 3, 1778.
Poughkeepsie, [1778]. 19 pp.]
(The only copy located could not be
reproduced.)   15937

New York (State) Laws, Statutes, etc.,
1778.
State of New-York, An Act for
Completing the Five Continental
Battalions.
[Poughkeepsie, 1778]. [2] pp.
LOC copy.   15935

New York (State) Laws, Statutes, etc.,
1778.
State of New-York, An Act for Regulating
Impresses.
Poughkeepsie, [1778]. 2 pp.
LOC copy.   15936

New York (State) Laws, Statutes, etc.,
1779.
... An Act to Amend an Act for
Regulating Impresses.

Poughkeepsie, [1779]. Broadside.
LOC copy.   16407

New York (State) Laws, Statutes, etc.,
1780.
An Act for Regulating the Militia ...
Passed ... in the Third Session.
Poughkeepsie, Holt, 1780. 26 pp.
NYHS copy.   43856

[New York (State) Laws, Statutes, etc.,
1780.
An Act to Procure Supplies. ... June
24th, 1780.
[Poughkeepsie, 1780.] 4 pp.]
(No copy located.)   16905

[New York (State) Laws, Statutes, etc.,
1780.
An Act to Raise Troops [Sept. 29, 1780].
[Poughkeepsie, 1780. Broadside.]
(No copy located.)   16906

New York (State) Laws, Statutes, etc.,
1782.
... An Act for Pardoning Certain
Offenses. ... Passed 14th of April, 1782.
[Poughkeepsie, 1782.] 3 pp.
LOC copy.   17632

New York (State) Laws, Statutes, etc.,
1782.
Laws of the State of New-York,
Commencing with the First Session ...
after the Declaration of Independency.
Poughkeepsie, 1782. [2], vi, 255 pp.
NYPL copy.   17630

New York (State) Laws, Statutes, etc.,
1783.
Haerlem, November 21, 1783. ... An Act
to Provide for the Temporary
Government.
New York, Loudon, [1783]. Broadside.
JCB copy.   44421

New York (State) Laws, Statutes, etc.,
1784.
An Act Imposing Duties. ... Passed the
22d Day of March, 1784.
[New York, 1784.] Broadside.
LCP copy.   44574

New York (State) Laws, Statutes, etc.,
1784.
... An Act to Compel the Payment of the
Arrears of Taxes ... Passed November
26th, 1784.
New York, Holt, [1784]. 4 pp.
NYPL copy.   18643

New York (State) Laws, Statutes, etc.,
1784.
An Act to Preserve the Freedom ... of
this State. ... Passed May 12th, 1784.
New York, Loudon, [1784]. [2] pp.
LOC copy.   18642

[New York (State) Laws, Statutes, etc.,
1784.
Laws of the State of New York [1777 -
Mar. 27, 1783].
Poughkeepsie, 1782. pp. [2], vi, [1], iii,
3-400].
(This Evans entry duplicates 17630, 17631,
18060, and 18646.)   18645

[New York (State) Laws, Statutes, etc.,
1785.
An Act for Regulating the Fees. ...
Passed the 18th of April, 1785.
New York, Loudon, 1785.]
(Sabin 53445, apparently from NYSL copy
now lost.)   19129

New York (State) Laws, Statutes, etc.,
1785.
An Act to Facilitate the Settlement of the
Waste and Unappropriated Lands. ...
Passed the 11th of April, 1785.
[New York, 1785.] Broadside.
NYPL copy.   19128

New York (State) Laws, Statutes, etc.,
1785.
The Ten Pound Act.
Albany, 1785. 16 pp.
NYPL copy.   19134

New York (State) Laws, Statutes, etc.,
1786.
An Act to Regulate the Militia ... Passed
the 4th of April, 1786.

New York, Loudons, [1786]. 24 pp.
LOC copy.   19851

New York (State) Laws, Statutes, etc.,
1786.
Chap. LXVII. An Act for the Speedy Sale
of the Unappropriated Lands.
[New York], Loudons, [1786]. 8 pp.
NYPL copy.   19850

New York (State) Laws, Statutes, etc.,
1787.
An Act for Regulating Elections. ...
Tenth Session.
New York, Loudons, [1787]. 22, [1] pp.
NYPL copy.   20572

New York (State) Laws, Statutes, etc.,
1787.
An Act for the more Speedy Recovery of
Debts.
New York, Loudons, [1787]. 8 pp.
NYPL copy.   20573

New York (State) Laws, Statutes, etc.,
1787.
Act to Amend an Act, Entitled An Act to
Regulate the Militia.
Albany, 1787. 4 pp.
(Perhaps issued only affixed to 21318.)
LOC copy.   20574

New York (State) Laws, Statutes, etc.,
1787.
[The ten pound act, enacted Apr. 7, 1787.
Albany, 1787.]
(The only reported copy was lost in the
NYSL fire.)   45115

[New York (State) Laws, Statutes, etc.,
1788.
An Act for Giving Relief in Cases of
Insolvency.
New York, 1788.]
("To-morrow will be Published," N. Y.
Packet, Apr. 4, 1788.)   21306

[New York (State) Laws, Statutes, etc.,
1788.
An Act for the Better Settlement and
Relief of the Poor.
New York, 1788.]
("This day is published," N. Y. Packet,
July 18, 1788.)   21307

New York (State) Laws, Statutes, etc.,
1788.
An Act, to Regulate the Exportation of
Flax-seed.
New York, Greenleaf, [1788]. Broadside.
NYPL copy.   21308

[New York (State) Laws, Statutes, etc.,
1788.
The Import Laws ... Passed the 11th of
March, 1788.
New York, 1788.]
("This day published," N. Y. Journal,
Apr. 24, 1788.)   21311

[New York (State) Laws, Statutes, etc.,
1788.
Mercantile Laws of the State of New
York.
New York, 1788.]
("Tomorrow will be published," N. Y.
Journal, Apr. 3, 1788.)   21317

New York (State) Laws, Statutes, etc.,
1788.
The Militia Act ... April ... 1786.
Hudson, [1788]. 24 pp.
LOC copy.   21318

New York (State) Laws, Statutes, etc.,
1789.
An Act, Directing the Times, Places and
Manner of Electing Representatives.
Albany, Loudons, 1789. [2] pp.
NYSL copy.   45538

New York (State) Laws, Statutes, etc.,
1789.
An Act for Regulating the Fees of the
Several Officers. ... Passed the 18th of
February, 1789.
[New York, 1789.] 29 pp.
NYHS copy.   22016

[New York (State) Laws, Statutes, 1789.
The Law for Regulating the Fees.
Albany, Websters, 1789.]

("This day Published," Albany Gazette,
Aug. 13, 1789.)   22015

New York (State) Laws, Statutes, etc.,
1789.
Laws of the State of New-York . . .
Since the Revolution.
New York, Gaine, 1789. 2 vol. [4], 336,
[12], xii, [1]; [2], 471, [18] pp.
AAS copy.   22012

[New York (State) Laws, Statutes, etc.,
1789.
The Ten Pound Act.
Albany, Websters, 1789.]
("This day published," Albany Gazette,
June 11, 1789.)   22017

New York (State) Laws, Statutes, etc.,
1790.
An Act for Taking a Census. . . . Passed
the 18th February, 1790.
New York, Childs & Swaine, 1790.
[2] pp.
AAS copy.   45930

New York. Laws, Statutes, etc., 1791.
. . . In Senate, 16th, February, 1791. . . .
An Act for Apportioning the
Representation. . . . Passed the 7th
February, 1791.
[New York], Childs & Swaine, [1791].
Broadside.
NYSL copy.   46240

New York (State) Laws, Statutes, etc.,
1792.
. . . An Act for Establishing and
Opening Lock Navigations . . . Passed
the 30th of March, 1792.
[New York], Childs & Swaine, 1792.
4 pp.
NYPL copy.   46526

[New York (State) Laws, Statutes, etc.,
1792.
An Act to Incorporate the Society of
Mechanics and Tradesmen of the City of
New-York. . . . Passed the 14th of
March, 1792.
New York, Loudon, [1792]. 11 pp.]
(No copy of a separate printing of this
Act by Loudon has been located.
Apparently a ghost of 24609.)   24608

New York (State) Laws, Statutes, etc.,
1792.
. . . In Senate, March 21st, 1792.
Resolved, That the Secretary of State. . . .
[New York], Childs & Swaine, 1792.
4 pp.
(Not located, 1968.)   46527

New York (State) Laws, Statutes, etc.,
1792.
Laws of the State of New-York. . . . In
Two Volumes.
New York, Greenleaf, 1792. [4], 511;
[4], 521, [15] pp.
AAS copy.   24602

New York (State) Laws, Statutes, etc.,
1792.
State of New York, In Senate, March
21st, 1792. Resolved . . . That the
Secretary of State. . . .
[New York], Childs & Swaine, 1792.
4 pp.
(Not located, 1968.)   46527

[New York (State) Laws, Statutes, etc.,
1793.
An Act to Organize the Militia.
Albany, 1792.]
("For sale at Webster's Printing-Office,"
Albany Gazette Aug. 5, 1793. In Albany
Institute catalogue of 1855.)   25896

New York (State) Laws, Statutes, etc.,
1793.
An Act, to Organize the Militia.
New York, Childs & Swaine, 1793.
15 pp.
LOC copy.   25897

[New York (State) Laws, Statutes, etc.,
1793.
The Militia Law.
Hudson, Stoddard, 1793.]
(Imprint assumed by Evans from
Stoddard's advs.)   25898

[New York (State) Laws, Statutes, etc.,
1793.
The Road Act.
Lansingburgh, Wands, 1793.]
(Imprint assumed by Evans from Wands'
advs.)   25899

[New York (State) Laws, Statutes, etc.,
1794.
The Fee-Bill.
Albany, Websters, 1794.]
(No copy located.)   27396

New York (State) Laws, Statutes, etc.,
1794.
The Ten Pound Act, enacted April 17,
1787.
Albany, Websters, 1794. 24 pp.
(Not located, 1968.)   47135

[New York (State) Laws, Statutes, etc.,
1795.
The Poor Act.
Albany, Websters, 1795.]
(Not adv. with other Acts.)   29191

[New York (State) Laws, Statutes, etc.,
1795.
The School Law.
Albany, Webster, 1795.]
(Not adv. with other Acts.)   29192

New York (State) Laws, Statutes, etc.,
1795.
The Ten Pound Act.
Albany, Websters, [1795]. 23, [1] pp.
NYPL copy.   29193

[New York (State) Laws, Statutes, etc.,
1795.
The Ten Pound Act.
Hudson, Stoddard, 1795.]
(Imprint assumed by Evans from
Stoddard adv.)   29194

New York (State) Laws, Statutes, etc.,
1795.
The Ten Pound Act.
Lansingburgh, Tiffany, 1795. 24 pp.
(The Troy imprint was assumed by
Evans from adv. "Just published, by
Silvester Tiffany" in The Recorder, Aug.
4, 1795.)
Williams College copy.   29195

New York (State) Laws, Statutes, etc.,
1796.
The Following is a Copy of an Act of
Assembly of our Neighbours of Newyork.
. . . An Act to Prevent Intrusions. . . .
11th March, 1796.
n. p., [1796?]. Broadside.
AAS copy.   47864

[New York (State) Laws, Statutes, etc.,
1796.
The Militia Act. With Latest
Amendments.
Poughkeepsie, 1796.]
(Imprint assumed by Evans from adv.
"For sale by N. Power" in Poughkeepsie
Journal, May 25, 1796.)   30877

[New York (State) Laws, Statutes, etc.,
1796.
The Ten Pound Act. With the
Amendment.
Poughkeepsie, Power, 1796.]
(Imprint assumed by Evans from adv.
"For sale by N. Power" in Poughkeepsie
Journal, June 8, 1796.)   30878

New York (State) Laws, Statutes, etc.,
1797.
Laws of the State of New-York. . . .
Volume III.
New York, Greenleaf, 1797. pp. [4],
[1]-98, [3], 99-100, [1]-8, 107-160,
[159]-258, [3], [259]-354, [2], [355]-525.
NYHS copy.   32555

[New York (State) Laws, Statutes, etc.,
1797.
The New Road Law.
Albany, Barber & Southwick, 1797.]
(Imprint assumed by Evans from adv.
"For sale by Barber & Southwick" in
Albany Register, passim. Probably a
ghost of 32557, q. v.)   32558

[New York (State) Laws, Statutes, etc.,
1797.
The Road Act.

New York, Greenleaf, 1797.]
(Imprint assumed by Evans from
Greenleaf's adv.)   32560

New York (State) Laws, Statutes, etc.,
1797.
The Road-Act Passed into a Law . . .
March 21, 1797.
Albany, Websters, [1797]. 20 pp.
NYHS copy.   32557

[New York (State) Laws, Statutes, etc.,
1797.
The Road Act. To which is Added,
Extracts from the School Act.
Cooperstown, Phinney, 1797.]
("Just Published, and for sale at this
Office" Otsego Herald, May 11, 1797.)
     32559

New York (State) Laws, Statutes, etc.,
1798.
An Act for the Benefit of Insolvent
Debtors.
[Albany], Andrews, [1798]. 16 pp.
JCB copy.   34205

New York (State) Laws, Statutes, etc.,
1798.
An Act for the Benefit of Insolvent
Debtors.
[New York], Hopkins, [1798].
16 pp.
JCB copy.   34206

[New York (State) Laws, Statutes, etc.,
1798.
An Act to Amend an Act Entitled An Act
to Regulate Highways.
Albany, Andrews, 1798.]
(For sale at the Albany Book Store,
Centinel, May 4, 1798.)   34207

[New York (State) Laws, Statutes, etc.,
1798.
An Index to the Laws of the 20th and 21st
Session.
Albany, Andrews, 1798]
("Will shortly be published," Centinel,
June 1, 1798; "For sale," ibid, June 19.
This is probably the "Contents" of
34215, q. v.)   34209

New York (State) Laws, Statutes, etc.,
1798.
Laws of the State of New York. . . . In
Three Volumes. Volume I. Second
Edition.
New York, Greenleaf, 1798. [4], 507 pp.
AAS copy.   34214

New York (State) Laws, Statutes, etc.,
1798.
Laws of the State of New-York. . . .
Volume II. Second Edition.
New York, Greenleaf, 1798. [2],
520 pp.
LOC copy.   48545

New York (State) Laws, Statutes, etc.,
1799.
An Act for Regulating . . . the Militia.
n.p.; [1799?]. 80 pp.
NYHS copy.   48946

New York (State) Laws, Statutes, etc.,
1799.
An Act for the Assessment and Collection
of Taxes.
[Albany], Andrews, 1799. 28 pp.
NYPL copy.   35916

New York (State) Laws, Statutes, etc.,
1799.
An Act for the Benefit of Insolvent
Debtors.
[Albany, Andrews, 1799?] 15 pp.
NYHS copy.   48947

[New York (State) Laws, Statutes, etc.,
1799.
An Act to Amend an Act Entitled an Act
for Regulating Elections.
Albany, Andrews, 1799. [2] pp.]
(Apparently seen by Evans.)   35918

[New York (State) Laws, Statutes, etc.,
1799.
An Act to Organize the Militia of the
State.
Poughkeepsie, Power and Southwick,
1799. 22 pp.]

(Apparently seen by Evans before the
Albany Fire.)   35919

New York (State) Laws, Statutes, etc.,
1799.
An Act to Raise a Sum of Money for the
Use of this State. . . . Passed the 3d of
April, 1799.
[Albany? 1799.] Broadside.
NYSL copy.   35920

New York (State) Laws, Statutes, etc.,
1799.
Collection of Penal Laws.
New York, Collins, 1799. 40 pp.
HPL copy.   35921

New York (State) Laws, Statutes, etc.,
1799.
The Militia Act. . . . Also, Two Other
Acts.
Albany, Websters, 1799. 36 pp.
NYPL copy.   35929

New York (State) Laws, Statutes, etc.,
1800.
Collection of Acts Concerning the
Recovery of Debts.
New York, Hopkins, 1800. 28 pp.
JCB copy.   38078

New York (State) Laws, Statutes, etc.,
1800.
Laws of the State of New-York. . . .
Volume III.
Albany, Websters, 1800. [4], 605 pp.
NYHS copy.   38086

New York (State) Laws, Statutes, etc.,
1800.
Titles of the Laws Passed by the
Legislature . . . at their Twenty-Third
Session.
[Albany, 1800.] Broadside.
(The one recorded copy is mislaid.) 38093

[New York (State) Legislature, 1781.
An Address of the Legislature [Mar. 15,
1781].
Fishkill, 1781. 12 pp.]
(No copy located.)   17269

New York (State) Legislature, 1782.
State of New-York, No. 1. Albany, ss.
John Edgar, late of Detroit. . . .
Poughkeepsie, [1782]. [2] pp.
AAS copy.   17633

[New York (State) Legislature, 1793.
Examinations Relative to the Committee
who Canvassed the Votes for Governor,
Lieutenant Governor, and Senators,
November 30, 1792, - February 23, 1793.
New York, 1792. 16 sheets.]
(No copy located.)   25905

New York (State) Legislature, 1793.
A List of the Names of Persons to whom
Military Patents have Issued.
[New York], Childs & Swaine, 1793. 25
pp.
AAS copy.   25904

New York (State) Legislature, 1798.
An Act tc Incorporate the Inhabitants of
. . . Schenectady . . . February 9th, 1798.
Albany, Websters, [1798]. 14 pp.
NYSL copy.   34208

New York (State) Legislature, 1798.
Albany, February 16, 1798. Connecticut
Gore.
[Albany, 1798.] Broadside.
LOC copy.   34219

New York (State) Legislature, 1800.
An Act, Authorizing the Comptroller to
Correct Certain Errors.
[Albany, 1800.] Broadside.
NYPL ph. copy.   38075

New York (State) Legislature, 1800.
Titles of the Laws Passed by the . . .
Twenty-Third Session.
[Albany, 1800.] Broadside.
NN ph. copy.   38093

New York (State) Legislature. Assembly,
1798.
Members of the House of Assembly. . . .
January 2, 1798.
[Albany], Websters, [1798]. Broadside.
(No copy located.)   48546

New York (State) Legislature. Assembly,
1798.
Rules and Orders.
[Albany], Andrews, [1798]. Broadside.
HC copy.   48547

New York (State) Legislature. Assembly.
1800.
Members of the House of Assembly. . . .
February 3, 1800.
[Albany], Andrews, [1800]. Broadside.
NYHS copy.   38089

[New York (State) Legislature.
Committee on Filling Battalions.
Resolve of Committee on Filling
Battalions.
[Poughkeepsie, 1778.] Broadside.]
(No copy located.)   15934

New York (State) Legislature. Senate,
1781.
The Votes and Proceedings of the Senate
. . . October [10 - Nov. 23, 1781].
Poughkeepsie, 1782. 35 pp.
(Not available.)   44237

New York (State) Legislature. Senate.
1794.
. . . In Senate, January 10, 1794. Resolved
. . . that the Printer. . . .
[Boston, 1794.] Broadside.
(The only known copy is imperfect.)
(Not located, 1968.)   47126

New York (State) Legislature. Senate.
1796.
. . . In Senate, February 10, 1796.
Resolved, That the Report of the Western
Inland Lock Navigation Companies, be
forthwith Printed.
[New York], Robins, [1796]. Broadside.
NYPL copy.   31622

New York (State) Legislature. Senate.
1798.
. . . In Senate, August 17th, 1798. Ordered,
That Mr. Foote. . . .
[Albany], Andrews, [1798]. Broadside.
(Not located, 1968.)   48548

New York (State) Legislature. Senate,
1798.
Members Composing the Senate. . . .
January 2d, 1798.
[Albany], Websters, [1798]. Broadside.
(No copy located.)   48549

New York (State) Legislature. Senate,
1799.
Members Composing the Senate. . . .
January, 1799.
[Albany, 1799.] Broadside.
NYHS copy.   35927

New York (State) Legislature. Senate.
1800.
. . . In Senate, March 15th, 1800. Mr.
Spencer. . . .
[Albany, 1800.] [4] pp.
NYPL copy.   38091

New York (State) Legislature. Senate.
1800.
. . . In Senate, 28th January, 1800. Mr.
President. . . .
[Albany, 1800.] 7 pp.
NYPL ph. copy.   38090

New York (State) Legislature. Senate.
1800.
. . . In Senate March 22d, 1800. . . .
Returns Received from the Adjutant
General.
[Albany, 1800.] Broadside.
(No copy located.)   38092

New York (State) Legislature. Senate.
1800.
Members Composing the Senate. . . . Nov.
4, 1800.
[Albany, 1800.] Broadside.
NYPL copy.   38088

New York (State) Prison Dept.
Report of the Inspectors of the
State-Prison. . . . [1st month, 15, 1799.]
Albany, Andrews, [1799]. 8 pp., 3 folded
leaves.
NYPL copy.   35930

[New York (State) Provincial Congress,
1776.

In Provincial Congress, New-York, March
4th, 1776. Resolved. . . .
[New York, 1776.] Broadside.]
(The unique copy could not be
reproduced.)   14933

New York (State) Provincial Congress,
1776.
In Provincial Congress, New-York, May
31, 1776. Whereas. . . .
[New York, 1776.] Broadside.
NYHS copy.   14934

New York (State) Provincial Congress,
1776.
In Provincial Congress, New-York, June
7, 1776. Your Committee. . . .
New York, Loudon, 1776. 12 pp.
NYPL copy.   14935

New York (State) Provincial Congress,
1776.
In Provincial Congress, New-York, June
13, 1776. Whereas. . . .
[New York, 1776.] Broadside.
NYHS copy.   14936

New York (State) Provincial Congress,
1776.
In Provincial Congress, New-York, June
20, 1776 [Disarming].
[New York, 1776.] Broadside.
NYHS copy.   14937

New York (State) Provincial Congress,
1776.
Resolutions . . . for the Encouragement of
Manufactures. . . .
New York, Holt, 1776. 7 pp.
LOC copy.   14938

New York (State) Secretary of State, 1796.
A General Account of the Number of
Electors.
[Albany? 1796.] [4] pp.
(Not located, 1968.)   47865

New York (State) Senate Journals, 1777.
Votes and Proceedings of the Senate
[Sept. 9, 1777 - Mar. 17, 1779].
Fishkill, 1777. 216 pp.
NYPL copy.   15480

New York (State) Senate Journals, 1777.
Votes and Proceedings of the Senate
[Sept. 9, 1777 - Mar. 17, 1779].
Kingston, 1777. 216 pp.
NYSL copy.   15479

New York (State) Senate Journals, 1779.
Votes and Proceedings [Aug. 24, 1779 -
Mar. 14, 1780].
Fishkill, Loudon, 1779. 107 pp.
NYHS copy.   43673

New York (State) Senate Journals, 1780.
Votes and Proceedings of the Senate
[May 23-July 2, 1780].
[Poughkeepsie, 1783.] pp. [109]-134.
NYHS copy.   44422

New York (State) Senate Journals, 1780.
Votes and Proceedings of the Senate
[Sept. 7-Oct. 10, 1780].
[Poughkeepsie, 1783.] pp. [3]-34.
NYHS copy.   44423

New York (State) Senate Journals, 1781.
Votes and Proceedings of the Senate [Jan.
31-July 1, 1781].
[Poughkeepsie, 1783.] pp. [35]-114.
NYHS copy.   44424

New York (State) Senate Journals, 1782.
Votes and Proceedings of the Senate . . .
Feb. 23 [-Apr. 14, 1782].
[Poughkeepsie, 1782.] pp. [37]-77.
NYSL copy.   44238

New York (State) Senate Journals, 1782.
Votes and Proceedings of the Senate [July
3 - 25, 1782].
[Poughkeepsie, 1782.] pp. [79] - 96.
NYSL copy.   44239

New York (State) Senate Journals, 1783.
Votes and Proceedings of the Senate [Jan.
27-Mar. 28, 1783].
[Poughkeepsie, 1783.] pp. [97]-165.
NYHS copy.   44425

New York (State) Senate Journals, 1784.
Journal of the Senate . . . Seventh Session

[Jan. 6 - May 12, 1784].
New York, Holt, 1784. 147 pp.
AAS copy.   18644

New York (State) Senate Journals, 1784.
Votes and Proceedings of the Senate [Oct. 18-Nov. 29, 1784.]
[New York, 1784.] pp. 3 - 42.
NYPL copy.   18650

New York (State) Senate Journals, 1785.
Journal of the Senate. . . . Second Meeting of the Eighth Session [Jan. 24 - Apr. 27, 1785].
New York, Loudon, 1785. 109 pp.
AAS copy.   19132

New York (State) Senate Journals, 1786.
Journal of the Senate. . . . First Meeting of the Ninth Session [Jan. 16 - May 5, 1786].
New York, Loudons, 1786. 104 pp.
AAS copy.   19853

New York (State) Senate Journals, 1787.
Journal of the Senate. . . . Tenth Session [Jan. 12 - Apr. 21, 1787].
New York, Loudons, 1787. 103 pp.
AAS copy.   20577

New York (State) Senate Journals, 1788.
Journal of the Senate [Jan. 11 - Mar. 22, 1788].
Poughkeepsie, 1788. 78 pp.
AAS copy.   21315

New York (State) Senate Journals, 1788.
Journal of the Senate . . . Twelfth Session [Dec. 11, 1788 - Mar. 3, 1789].
Albany, Loudons, 1789. 88 pp.
AAS copy.   22010

New York (State) Senate Journals, 1789.
Journal of the Senate . . . Thirteenth Session [July 6 - 16, 1789].
New York, Loudons, 1789. 18 pp.
NYPL copy.   22011

New York (State) Senate Journals, 1790.
Journal of the Senate. . . . Second Meeting of the Thirteenth Session [Jan. 12 - Apr. 6, 1790].
New York, Childs & Swaine, 1790. 56 pp.
NYPL copy.   22719

New York (State) Senate Journals, 1791.
Journal of the Senate. . . . Fourteenth Session [Jan. 5 - Mar. 24, 1791].
New York, Childs & Swaine, 1791. 68 pp.
AAS copy.   23616

New York (State) Senate Journals, 1792.
Journal of the Senate. . . . Fifteenth Session [Jan. 5 - Apr. 12, 1792].
New York, Childs & Swaine, 1792. 89 pp.
NYPL copy.   24601

New York (State) Senate Journals, 1792.
Journal of the Senate. . . . Sixteenth Session [Nov. 6, 1792 - Mar. 12, 1793].
New York, Childs & Swaine, 1792. 117 pp.
NYPL copy.   25901

New York (State) Senate Journals, 1792.
. . . November 20th, 1792. Please to give the following Extracts from the Journal . . . a Place in your Paper.
[New York, 1792.] Broadside.
NYHS copy.   46528

New York (State) Senate Journals, 1794.
Journal of the Senate. . . . Seventeenth Session [Jan. 7-Mar. 27, 1794].
Albany, Websters for Childs & Swaine, 1794. 84 pp., irreg.
NYHS copy.   27398

New York (State) Senate Journals, 1795.
Journal of the Senate. . . . Eighteenth Session [Jan. 20 - Apr. 9, 1795].
New York, Childs, 1795. 90 pp.
NYHS copy.   29188

New York (State) Sentate Journals, 1796.
Journal of the Senate. . . . Nineteenth Session [Jan. 6-Apr. 11, 1796].
New York, Childs, 1796. 110 pp.
NYPL copy.   30871

New York (State) Senate Journals, 1796.
Journal of the Senate . . . Twentieth Session [Nov. 1, 1796 - Apr. 3, 1797].
Albany, Websters for Morton [1797]. 138 pp.
NYSL copy.   32554

New York (State) Senate Journals, 1798.
Journal of the Senate . . . Twenty-First Session [Jan. 2 - Apr. 6, 1798].
Albany, Andrews, [1798]. 144 pp.
NYPL copy.   34211

New York (State) Senate Journals, 1798.
Journal of the Senate . . . Twenty-Second Session [Aug. 9 - 27, 1798].
Albany, Andrews, [1798]. 26 pp.
AAS copy.   34213

New York (State) Senate Journals, 1799.
Journal of the Senate . . . Twenty-Second Session, Second Meeting [Jan. 2 - Apr. 3, 1799].
Albany, Andrews, [1799]. 129 pp.
AAS copy.   35925

New York (State) Senate Journals, 1800.
Journal of the Senate . . . 23rd Session [Jan. 28 - Apr. 8, 1800.]
Albany, Andrews, [1800]. [2], 131 pp.
NYHS copy.   38085

New York (State) Session Laws, 1782.
Laws . . . Passed . . . in the First Meeting of the Sixth Session [July 12-25, 1782].
[Poughkeepsie, 1782.] pp. 257-268.
AAS copy.   17631

New York (State) Session Laws, 1783.
Laws of the State of New York [Feb. 14 - Mar. 27, 1783].
[Poughkeepsie, 1783.] pp. 269-300.
AAS copy.   18060

New York (State) Session Laws, 1784.
Laws of the State of New York. . . .
Seventh Session [Feb. 12 - May 12, 1784].
New York, Holt, 1784. pp. [1], iii, 3-127.
AAS copy.   18646

New York (State) Session Laws, 1784.
Laws of the State of New York, Passed at the First Meeting of the Eighth Session [Oct. 4 - Nov. 29, 1784].
New York, Holt, 1784. 34 pp.
AAS copy.   18647

New York (State) Session Laws, 1785.
Laws . . . Passed by the Legislature . . . at this last Meeting of the Eighth Session [Feb. 15 - Apr. 27, 1785].
New York, Loudon, 1785. 104 pp.
AAS copy.   19133

New York (State) Session Laws, 1786.
Laws . . . Passed . . . Ninth Session [Jan. 31 - May 5, 1786].
New York, Loudons, 1786. 137 pp.
AAS copy.   19854

New York. Session Laws, 1787.
Laws of the State of New York . . . Tenth Session [Jan. 26-Apr. 21, 1787].
New York, Loudons, 1787. 212, [2] pp.
AAS copy.   20578

New York (State) Session Laws, 1788.
Laws of the State . . . Eleventh Session.
New York, Loudons, 1788. 223 pp.
LOC copy.   21316

New York (State) Session Laws, 1789.
Laws of the State of New-York . . . Twelfth Session [Jan. 5 - Mar. 3, 1789].
New York, Loudons, 1789. 81 pp.
AAS copy.   22013

New York (State) Session Laws, 1789.
Laws of the State of New-York . . . First Meeting of the Thirteenth Session [July 14-16, 1789].
New York, Loudons, 1789. 3 pp.
NYPL copy.   22014

New York (State) Session Laws, 1789.
Laws of the State. . . . Volume the Third [July 14, 1789 - Apr. 6, 1790].
New York, Childs & Swaine, 1790. [2], 48 pp.
NYPL copy.   22720

New York (State) Session Laws, 1791.
Laws. . . . Fourteenth Session [Jan. 18 - Mar. 24, 1791].
New York, Childs & Swaine, 1791. 38, [2] pp.
NYPL copy.   23617

New York (State) Session Laws, 1792.
Laws. . . . Fifteenth Session [Jan. 12 - Apr. 12, 1792].
New York, Childs & Swaine, 1792. 74, [2] pp.
NYPL copy.   24603

New York (State) Session Laws, 1792.
Laws. . . . Sixteenth Session [Nov. 19, 1792 - Mar. 12, 1793].
New York, Childs & Swaine, 1793. 63, [1] pp.
NYPL copy.   25902

New York (State) Session Laws, 1792.
Sixteenth Session of the Laws . . . (Greenleaf's Edition.) Number I - Volume III.
New York, Greenleaf, 1793. 100 pp., printed wraps.
AAS copy.   25903

[New York (State) Session Laws, 1792.
Sixteenth Session of the Laws. . . . (Greenleaf's Edition.) Number 1.-Volume III.
New York, Greenleaf, 1793. [2], 100, [2] pp.]
(A duplicate of 25903, q. v.)   30872

[New York (State) Session Laws, 1794.
Seventeenth Session, of the Laws. . . . (Greenleaf's Edition.) Number II.-Volume III.
New York, Greenleaf, 1794. pp. [2], 101-158.]
(Evans assumed the Greenleaf from the sequence of the pagination, but no copy has been located with this imprint.) 30873

New York (State) Session Laws, 1794.
Laws. . . . Seventeenth Session [Jan. 8 - Mar. 27, 1794].
New York, Childs & Swaine, 1794. 36, [2] pp.
NYHS copy.   27399

New York (State) Session Laws, 1795.
Laws. . . . Eighteenth Session [Jan. 29 - Apr. 9, 1795].
New York, Childs, 1795. 55, [2] pp.
NYHS copy.   29189

New York (State) Session Laws, 1795.
Eighteenth Session of the Laws [Jan. 29-Apr. 9, 1795]. . . . No. III of Vol. III.
New York, Greenleaf, 1795. Cover title, pp. 159-258, [3].
Composite copy.   29190

[New York (State) Session Laws, 1795.
Eighteenth Session, of the Laws. . . . (Greenleaf's Edition.) Number III. - Volume III.
New York, Greenleaf, 1795. pp. [2], 159-258, [3].]
(A duplicate of 29190, q. v.)   30874

New York (State) Session Laws, 1796.
Nineteenth Session, of the Laws. . . . (Greenleaf's Edition.) Number iv-Volume III.
New York, Greenleaf, 1796. pp. [259]-354, [2], printed wraps.
AAS copy.   30875

New York (State) Session Laws, 1796.
Laws. . . . Nineteenth Session [Jan. 9 - Apr. 11, 1796].
New York, Childs, 1796. 54, [2], pp.
NYHS copy.   30876

New York (State) Session Laws, 1797.
Laws . . . Twentieth Session [Jan., 1797].
New York, Robins, 1797. 340 (i.e. 240), [4] pp.
LOC copy.   32556

New York (State) Session Laws, 1798.
Laws of the State of New York . . . Twenty-First Session [Jan. 8 - Apr. 6, 1798].
Albany, Andrews for Thomas, Andrews & Penniman, 1798. pp. [241]-535, [6].
AAS copy.   34215

New York (State) Session Laws, 1798.
Laws of the State of New-York . . .
Twenty-Second Session [Aug., 1798].
Albany, Andrews, 1798. pp. [537]-552.
LOC copy.   34216

New York (State) Session Laws, 1799.
Laws . . . Twenty-Second Meeting [Jan. 2
- Apr. 3, 1799].
Albany, Andrews, 1799. [553]-844,
[4] pp.
NYPL copy.   35926

New York (State) Session Laws, 1800.
Laws of the State of New-York . . .
Twenty-Third Session . . . January, 1800.
Albany, Andrews, 1800. 294, [8] pp.
NYPL copy.   38087

[New York (State) Superintendent of the
Onondaga Salt Springs.
Annual Report of the Superintendent of
the . . . 1798.
Albany, 1798.]
(Entry from Sabin 57362, note.)   34272

New York (State) Superintendent of the
Onondaga Salt Springs.
To the Representatives. . . . March 1st,
1800.
[Albany, 1800.] [4] pp., 3 folded tables.
(No copy located.)   38095

New York (State) Supreme Court.
Rules Respecting the Admission of
Attornies . . . the 28th Day of October,
1797.
[New York, 1797.] Broadside.
HC copy.   48196

New York (State) Surveyor General.
Gentlemen, By an Act of the
Legislature. . . . 20th May, 1797.
[Albany, 1797.] Broadside.
HC copy.   48197

New York (State) Treasurer, 1800.
Dr. The State of New-York in Account
Current with Robert McClallen,
Treasurer. . . . January the 8th, 1800.
[Albany, 1800.] 3 pp.
NYSL copy.   38081

The New-York Almanack. For . . . 1745
[by J. Gale].
New York, De Foreest. [24] pp.
LIHS copy.   5402

[The New-York Almanack for the Year
. . . 1746.
New York.]
(Adv. N. Y. Evening Post, Jan. 13, 1746.)
                                      5662

The New-York Almanack for . . . 1747 [by
J. Gale].
New York, De Foreest. [24] pp.
LIHS copy.   5778

[The New-York Almanack for . . . 1749
[by J. Gale].
New York, De Foreest.]
(Adv. N. Y. Post, Dec. 26, 1748.)   6147

New-York and Country Almanack for . . .
1776.
New York, Shober & Loudon. [38] pp.
AAS copy.   14344

New-York, April 23, 1777. Song for St.
George's Day.
[New York, 1777.] Broadside.
NYHS copy.   43322

New-York, April 29, 1775. A General
Association. . . .
[New York, 1775.] Broadside.
NYHS copy.   14339

[New-York, August 2, 1793. Grand Naval
Combat . . . 1st, August 1793.
[New York, 1793.] Broadside.]
(No copy located.)   25917

New-York, August 23, 1774. Sir, As the
Collection. . . .
[New York, 1774.] [2] pp.
LOC copy.   13766

New-York City Lottery.
Scheme of a Lottery. . . . March 6, 1790.
[New York, 1790.] Broadside.
NYHS copy.   22721

New York Committee Appointed to
Prevent the Introduction and Spreading of
Infectious Diseases.
As it is a Point Agreed on by all
Writers. . . . September 30, 1793.
[New York, 1793.] Broadside.
NYHS copy.   46832

New York Committee Appointed to
Prevent the Introduction and Spreading of
Infectious Diseases.
To the Inhabitants of the State of New
York. . . . September 30, 1793.
[New York, 1793.] Broadside.
(Not located, 1968.)   46833

. . . The New-York Connecticut, & New
Jersey Almanack . . . for . . . 1799 [by
Andrew Beers, 1749-1824].
New York, Reid. [36] pp.
AAS copy.   33390

New-York, December 23, 1773. On
Tuesday Night Arrived in this City. . . .
[New York, 1773.] Broadside. folio ed.
NYHS copy.   12913

New-York, Dec. 13, 1776. To the
Public. . . . Camillus.
[New York], M'Donald & Cameron,
[1776]. Broadside.
NYHS copy.   43107

The New-York Directory . . . for . . . 1789.
New York, Hodge, Allen & Campbell,
1789. 144 pp., 1 map.
AAS copy.   22021

The New-York Directory, and Register,
for . . . 1790.
New York, Hodge, Allen & Campbell,
1790. 144 pp., 1 plan.
NYHS copy.   22724

New-York Dispensary, New York.
Charter and Ordinances of the. . . .
New York, Hopkins, Webb & Co., 1797.
30 pp.
NYHS copy.   32566

New York Dispensary, New York.
Charter, By-laws . . . of the. . . .
New York, 1795. 35, [1] pp.
(The only copy recorded cannot now be
found.)   29200

New York Dispensary, New York.
Rules of the City Dispensary. . . .
February 1, 1791.
[New York], Greenleaf, [1791]. 16 pp.
AAS copy.   46241

New York Dispensary, New York.
Rules of the City Dispensary. . . .
February 12, 1795.
New York, Greenleaf, [1795]. 16 pp.
NYHS copy.   29201

New-York. Every Friend to the
Americans. . . .
[Philadelphia? 1774.] [2] pp.
NYHS copy.   13488

New-York, February 27th, 1770.
Forasmuch as it is Manifest, that there is
a . . . Pernicious Conspiracy.
[New York, 1770.] 2 pp.
JCB copy.   42136

New-York Friars' Tontine.
Constitution . . . Instituted . . . the third
day of March, 1792.
New York, M'Lean, 1792. 15 pp.
NYPL copy.   24607

New York Hospital.
Charter. . . . Granted . . . the 13th July,
1771.
New York, Gaine, 1794. 24 pp.
(Pp. 25-34 were printed in 1797. See the
supplement to Evans.)
NLM copy.   27406

New-York Hospital.
No. 1. Charity Extended to All.
[New York, 1797.] [4] pp.
HC copy.   48198

New-York Insurance Company.
An Act to Incorporate the Stockholders of
the. . . . (Passed 2d April, 1798.).
New York, Oram, 1798. 15 pp.
NYHS copy.   34226

New-York Insurance Company.
Articles of Association of the. . . .
New York, Childs, 1796. 20 pp.
NYPL copy.   30884

New York, January 1, 1774. On
Thursday. . . .
New York, Holt, [1774]. Broadside.
NYPL copy.   13487

New-York, January 4, 1769. To the
Freeholders. . . .
[New York, 1769.] Broadside.
LOC copy.   11375

New-York, January 5, 1770.
Advertisement.
[New York, 1770.] Broadside.
NYHS copy.   11778

New-York, January 6, 1769.
Advertisement, for Summoning the
Freeholders and Freemen, of the City and
County of New-York.
[New York, 1769.] Broadside.
NYHS copy.   11136

New-York, January 6th, 1769. Whereas. . . .
[New York, 1769.] Broadside.
LCP copy.   11376

New-York, January 8. All the real Friends
of Liberty. . . .
[New York, 1770.] Broadside.
LOC copy.   11779

New-York, January 9, 1769.
The Freeholders. . . .
[New York, 1769.] Broadside.
LOC copy.   11377

New-York, January 17, 1769.
Advertisement.
[New York, 1769.] Broadside.
LCP copy.   11378

New-York Journal and Weekly Register.
New Year's Verse, for 1790. . . . January
1, 1790.
[New York, 1790.] Broadside.
NYHS copy.   45931

New-York, July 1769.
Mr. Printer, I send you the Inclosed Copy
of a Printed Circular Letter. . . .
[New York, 1769.] Broadside.
NYHS copy.   41988

New-York, July 1, 1776.
By the Arrival of Capt. Williams. . . .
[New York, 1776.] Broadside.
LOC copy.   14942

New-York, July 7, 1769.
At this Alarming Crisis.
[New York, 1769.] Broadside.
LCP copy.   11379

New-York, July 20th, 1769.
Advertisement.
[New York, 1769.] Broadside.
LOC copy.   11380

New-York, July 25, 1774.
Extract of a Letter.
[New York, 1774.] Broadside.
LOC copy.   13493

New-York, June 12, 1770.
Advertisement. Whereas an Act. . . .
[New York, 1770.] Broadside.
LCP copy.   11784

New-York, June 12, 1770.
Advertisement. Whereas a Number of
Persons. . . .
[New York, 1770.] Broadside.
LCP copy.   11783

New-York, June 22, 1774.
Whereas. . . .
[New York, 1774.] Broadside.
LOC copy.   13492

[New-York, June 24th, 1775.
Last Night. . . .
[New York], Holt, 1775. Broadside.]
(Only known copy mislaid.)   14342

New York Lying-In Hospital.
See.
Society of the Lying-In Hospital.

New-York, March 1, 1790.
Brown's Self-Interpreting Folio Family
Bible.
[New York, 1790.] [4] pp.
NYHS copy.　　　　　　　　　　45840

New-York, March 8, 1768.
To the Worthy Freeholders.
[New York, 1768.] Broadside.
LCP copy.　　　　　　　　　　11091

New-York, March 24, 1789. Gentlemen,
You will Receive, with this. . . .
[New York, 1789.] Broadside.
NYHS copy.　　　　　　　　　　45539

New-York, May 1, 1775. To the Regular
Soldiery. . . .
[New York, 1775.] 3 pp.
LOC copy.　　　　　　　　　　14340

New-York, May 8, 1775. Extract. . . .
New York, Anderson, [1775]. Broadside.
NYPL copy.　　　　　　　　　　14341

New-York, May 11, 1774. The
Mechanicks. . . .
[New York, 1774.] Broadside.
LOC copy.　　　　　　　　　　13490

New-York, May 17, 1770. Advertisement.
[New York, 1770.] Broadside.
LCP copy.　　　　　　　　　　11780

New-York, May 20, 1766.
Joy to America!
[New York, 1766.] Broadside.
NYHS copy.　　　　　　　　　　10347

New-York, May 31st, 1770.
Advertisement.
[New York, 1770.] Broadside.
LCP copy.　　　　　　　　　　11782

New-York Missionary Society.
The Address and Constitution of the. . . .
New York, Swords, 1796. 19 pp.
AAS copy.　　　　　　　　　　30883

New-York Missionary Society.
Thoughts on the Plan for Social Prayer.
New York, T. & J. Swords, 1797. 10 pp.
CHS copy.　　　　　　　　　　48199

New York. Mutual Assurance Company.
A Sketch of the rates.
[New York], M'Leans [1788]. Broadside.
NYHS copy.　　　　　　　　　　45303

New-York, November 5, 1773.
To the Friends of Liberty.
[New York, 1773.] Broadside.
NYHS copy.　　　　　　　　　　12711

New-York, Nov. 24, 1783. The Committee
Appointed to Conduct . . . Receiving . . .
General Clinton and General Washington.
New York, Loudon, [1783]. Broadside.
WLC facsim. copy.　　　　　　　44426

New-York, October 1, 1774.
To the Publick. We the Subscribers having
been Appointed as a Committee, by a
Considerable Number of the
Inhabitants. . . .
[New York, 1774.] Broadside.
NYPL copy.　　　　　　　　　　13484

New-York, October 18, 1776.
To the Public. . . . Camillus.
[New York], printed in Water Street,
[1776]. Broadside.
NYPL ph. copy.　　　　　　　　43108

[The New-York Pocket Almanack for the
Year 1755 [by Theophilus Grew, - 1759].
New York, Gaine, 1754.]
("Wednesday Morning next will be
published," N. Y. Mercury, Nov. 4, 1754.)
　　　　　　　　　　　　　　7206

[The New-York Pocket Almanack for . . .
1756.
New York, Gaine, 36 pp.]
(Adv. N. Y. Mercury, No. 279.)　　7427

[The New-York Pocket Almanack for
1757. By Poor Tom. Philo.
New York, Gaine.]
("Just published," N. Y. Mercury, Nov.
29, 1756.)　　　　　　　　　　7678

[The New-York Pocket Almanack, for the

Year 1758 [by Theophilus Grew,-1759].
New York, Gaine.]
(Adv. N. Y. Mercury.)　　　　　7907

The New-York Pocket Almanack, for the
Year 1759 [by Theophilus Grew, -1759].
New York, Gaine, [1758]. [48] pp., front.
HSP copy.　　　　　　　　　　8144

New York Poor Lottery.
A List of the Fortunate Numbers . . . the
15th of May, 1782.
[New York, 1782.] Broadside.
AAS copy.　　　　　　　　　　17642

New-York Poor Lottery.
New-York, March 27, 1779. A List of the
Fortunate Numbers in the . . . Lottery,
1779.
[New York, 1779.] Broadside.
LOC copy.　　　　　　　　　　43674

New-York Preserved, or the Plot
Discovered.
[New York, 1788.] Broadside.
LOC copy.　　　　　　　　　　21329

[The New-York Primmer, Enlarged.
New York, 1746.]
(Adv. N. Y. Evening Post, Dec. 8, 1746.)
　　　　　　　　　　　　　　5838

[The New-York Primmer, Enlarged.
New York, De Foreest, 1747.]
("Just published," N. Y. Evening Post,
Sept. 7, 1747.)　　　　　　　　6033

[The New-York Primmer, Enlarged.
New York, De Foreest, 1750.]
("To be sold by the Printer hereof,"
N. Y. Evening Post, Mar. 19, 1750.)
　　　　　　　　　　　　　　6572

[The New-York Reviewers Reviewed.
New London, Green, 1795.]
(The origin of this entry has not been
found.)　　　　　　　　　　29209

[The New-York Royal Sheet Almanack
for 1759.
New York, Gaine. Broadside.]
(Adv. N. Y. Mercury, No. 339.)　　8241

[The New-York Royal Sheet Almanack
for 1760.
New York, Gaine. Broadside.]
(Adv. N. Y. Mercury, No. 339.)　　8472

[The New-York Royal Sheet Almanack
for 1761.
New York, Gaine. Broadside.]
(Assumed by Evans from the sequence;
not adv.)　　　　　　　　　　8717

[The New-York Royal Sheet Almanack
for 1762.
New York, Gaine. Broadside.]
(Assumed by Evans from the sequence.)
　　　　　　　　　　　　　　8985

[The New-York Royal Sheet Almanack
for . . . 1763.
New York, Gaine. Broadside.]
(Adv. N. Y. Mercury, Jan. 3, 1763.)　9244

[The New-York Royal Sheet Almanack
for 1764.
New York, Gaine. Broadside.]
(Assumed by Evans from the sequence.)
　　　　　　　　　　　　　　9490

[The New-York Royal Sheet Almanack
for 1765.
New York, Gaine. Broadside.]
(Assumed by Evans from the sequence.)
　　　　　　　　　　　　　　9800

[The New-York Royal Sheet Almanack
for . . . 1766.
New York, Gaine. Broadside.]
(Assumed by Evans from the sequence.)
　　　　　　　　　　　　　　10144

[The New-York Royal Sheet Almanack
for 1767.
New York, Gaine. Broadside.]
(Assumed by Evans from the sequence.)
　　　　　　　　　　　　　　10467

New York, Saturday, July 15, 1780.
The Admiral Having Requested a
Number of Seamen Volunteers. . . .

[New York? 1780.] Broadside.
JCB copy.　　　　　　　　　　43857

New-York, Sept. 15, 1773.
To the Corporation. . . .
[New York, 1773.] Broadside.
NYHS copy.　　　　　　　　　　12893

New-York, September 18, 1769.
Advertisement.
[New York, 1769.] Broadside.
LOC copy.　　　　　　　　　　11381

New-York, September 28, 1774.
To the Public. An Application Having
Been Made. . . .
[New York, 1774.] Broadside.
NYHS copy.　　　　　　　　　　42656

New-York, September 28, 1774.
To the Public. An Application having
been Made.
[New York, 1774.] Broadside.
NYHS copy.　　　　　　　　　　13667

[New York. Sir, As Civil and Religious
Liberty. . . .
[New York, 1774.] 2 pp.]
(The unique copy is mislaid.)　　13494

New York Society for Promoting
Christian Knowledge and Piety.
The Constitution of the. . . .
New York, Loudon & Brower, 1794.
12 pp.
AAS copy.　　　　　　　　　　27409

New-York Society for Promoting the
Manumission of Slaves.
The Constitution of the. . . .
New York, Hopkins, Webb & Co., 1796.
19 pp.
WLC copy.　　　　　　　　　　30885

New York Society for the Information
and Assistance of Persons Emigrating
from Foreign Countries.
From Reviewing. . . . 30th June, 1794.
[New York, 1794.] Broadside.
JCB copy.　　　　　　　　　　27408

New York Society Library.
The Charter, and Bye-Laws, of. . . .
New York, Gaine, 1773. 35 pp.
LOC copy.　　　　　　　　　　12895

New York Society Library.
The Charter, Bye-Laws. . . .
New York, Gaine, 1789. 80 pp.
AAS copy.　　　　　　　　　　22018

New York Society Library.
The Charter, Bye-laws, and Names of the
Members . . . with a Catalogue of the
Books.
New York, Swords, 1793. 99 pp.
AAS copy.　　　　　　　　　　25915

New York Society Library.
Continuation of the Catalogue.
[New York, 1791 ?]. pp. [81]-108.
AAS copy.　　　　　　　　　　23618

[New York Society Library.
A Farther Continuation of the Catalogue
of Books belonging to the New-York
Society Library.
New York, Swords, 1792. 100 pp.]
(Evans' entry was apparently made from
an announcement of the publication of
24610.)　　　　　　　　　　24611

New York Society Library.
A Farther Continuation of the Catalogue
Belonging to the New-York Society
Library.
New York, Swords, 1792. pp. [107]-127,
[4].
NYPL copy.　　　　　　　　　　24610

New York Society Library.
A Supplementary Catalogue.
New York, Swords, 1800. 46, [2] pp.
AAS copy.　　　　　　　　　　38099

New-York, Sunday 23d April, 1775.
The Following. . . .
[New York, 1775.] [2] pp.
LOC copy.　　　　　　　　　　14337

New-York Tammanial Tontine
Association.
Plan of the. . . .

New York, Childs & Swaine, 1792.
12 pp.
NYHS copy.   24612

New-York. The Following Dialogue. . . .
May 20, 1774.
[New York, 1774.] 2 pp.
NYHS copy.   13489

New-York, Tuesday, April 25, 1775.
This day, about Noon, Arrived a Second
Express.
[New York], Holt, [1775]. Broadside.
(In the Wilmerding collection was a copy
with the heading incorrectly dated "April
24.")
Reproduced from Henkels cat. 809, sup.
                                              14338

New-York, 12th of April, 1788.
Friends and Countrymen. . . .
[New York, 1788.] Broadside.
NYHS copy.   45313

New-York, 24th January, 1793.
Sir, A Number of Gentlemen. . . .
[New York, 1793.] Broadside.
(Not located, 1968.)   46836

New York Washington Military Society.
The Constitution and Bye-Laws of the. . . .
New York, Davis, 1796. 12 pp.
NYPL copy.   30887

New-York Washington Military Society.
The Constitution and Bye-Laws of the.
. . . 22d. May 1798.
New York, Tiebout, 1798. 14 pp.
LOC copy.   34227

[New-York, Wednesday, May 18, 1774.
To the Publick. . . .
[New York, 1774.] Broadside.]
(No copy can be located.)   13491

Newark, N.J. Board of Trustees.
Take Notice. The Trustees of the Town.
. . . May 26, 1789.
[Newark, 1789.] Broadside.
NJHS copy.   45540

Newark, N. J. Newark Fire Association.
Articles of Association.
Newark, N. J., Dodge, 1797. 24 pp.
NYHS copy.   32574

Newark Academy Lottery.
Scheme of the Newark Academy Lottery.
. . . July 3, 1793.
[Newark? 1793.] Broadside.
NJHS copy.   46837

Newark, New-Jersey, January 1, 1794.
Proposals for . . . the United States
Magazine.
[New York, 1794.] Broadside.
(Not located, 1968.)   47137

Newark Stocking Manufactory.
. . . A Number of Journeymen Stocking
Makers are Wanted. . . . June 5, 1792.
[Newark, 1792.] Broadside.
NYHS copy.   24617

Newbern, N. C. Committee of
Correspondence, 1775.
At a Meeting of the Committee for the
County of Craven and Town of Newbern,
on the 4th Day of March, 1775.
[Newbern, 1775.] Broadside.
PRO copy.   42909

Newbern, N. C. Committee of
Correspondence, 1775.
Proceedings of the Committee. . . . May
31, 1775. Circular Letter.
[Newbern, N. C., 1775.] 4 pp.
Moravian Archives, Winston-Salem, copy.
                                              42910

[Newbern, N. C. Convention, 1774.
Journal of the Convention met at
Newbern, in August, 1774.]
(There is no evidence that the journal
was printed.)   13497

Newbern, N. C. Convention, 1774.
Newbern, August 9, 1774. To the
Freeholders of Craven County.
[Newbern, 1774.] Broadside.
PRO copy.   42657

Newbern, N. C. Theater, 1797.

Newbern Theatre. Dr. Llewellyn
Lechmere Wall . . . will on . . . the 16th
of May, 1797. . . .
[Newbern, 1797.] Broadside.
Colonial Williamsburg copy.   48200

Newbern, N.C. Theater, 1797.
New Theatre, Newbern. This Evening . . .
March the 31st, 1797. . . .
[Newbern, 1797.] Broadside.
Colonial Williamsburg copy.   48201

Newbern, N.C. Theater, 1797.
To All Lovers of Wit . . . 13th of May,
1797.
[Newbern, 1797.] Broadside.
Colonial Williamsburg copy.   48202

[Newberry, John], 1713-1767.
Newberry's History of the World.
Philadelphia, Spotswood, 1786.]
(A ghost of a London ed.)   19863

Newberry's History of the World [by
John Newberry, 1713-1767].
Philadelphia, Spotswood, 1786.]
(A ghost of a London ed.)   19863

Newbury, Mass. Committee of Safety,
1777.
In Pursuance of an Act . . . Prices. . . .
Newburyport, Mycall, 1777. Broadside.
                                              15484

Newbury, Mass. Fire Society.
These Presents Witness. . . . 8th Day of
December . . . 1761.
[Newburyport? 1761.] Broadside.
EI copy.   41234

Newburyport, Mass. Assessors.
Town of Newburyport, [blank] Day of
[blank] To [blank] You are hereby
Notified. . . .
[Newburyport, 179?]. Broadside.
AAS copy.   45785

Newburyport. Assessors, 1792.
To the Assessors of Newburyport. . . .
The First Day of May, 1792.
[Newburyport, 1792.] Tax return form.
AAS copy.   46529

Newburyport, Mass. Committee for
Paying a Tribute to Washington.
Arrangements made for Paying a Tribute
of Public Respect. . . . December 31,
1799.
[Newburyport], Blunt, [1799].
Broadside.
AAS copy.   48948

Newburyport, Mass. Fire Society.
These Presents Witneseth. . . . [Dated
Feb. 23, 1767.]
[Boston? 1767.] Broadside.
AAS copy.   41747

Newburyport, Mass. First Church.
Sacred Concert. . . . June 11, 1800.
n. p., n. d. Broadside.
NYHS copy.   38108

Newburyport, Mass. Ordinances, etc.,
1797.
Bye-laws of Newburyport. . . . July, 1797.
[Newburyport, 1797.] Broadside.
LOC copy.   48203

Newburyport, Mass. Relief Fire Society.
Articles and Regulations.
[Newburyport, 1775.] [8] pp.
MHS copy.   14347

Newburyport, Mass. Relief Fire Society.
Articles and Regulations. . . . 1800,
June.
[Newburyport, 1800.] 8 pp.
AAS copy.   49121

Newburyport, Mass. Second Presbyterian
Church.
This Bible, was Presented to the Pulpit of
the . . . on the 1st of January, 1800.
[Newburyport, 1800.] Broadside.
AAS copy.   49122

Newburyport, Mass. Selectmen, 1777.
In Pursuance of an Act . . . Prices.
Newburyport, Mycall, 1777. Broadside.
AAS copy.   43323

Newburyport, Mass. Selectmen, 1778.

. . . Gentlemen. The Inhabitants . . . have
Adverted to the Constitution. . . .
[Salem? 1778.] Broadside.
MHS copy.   43516

Newburyport, October 28, 1789. . . .
Order of Procession.
[Newburyport, Mycall, 1789.] Broadside.
AAS copy.   45541

Newburyport, Sept. 3, 1790.
The Author of the following. . . .
[Newburyport? 1790.] Broadside.
(No copy available for reproduction.)
                                              45932

Newburyport, Sept. 3, 1794.
The Second Number of the Times.
[Newburyport, 1794.] Broadside.
AAS copy.   47138

Newcastle County, Del.
. . . In August Session, 1778. Ordered by
the Court, that all Keepers of Public
Houses. . . .
Wilmington, Adams, [1778]. Broadside.
(No copy located.)   43517

Newcastle County, Del.
List of Rates, for Innkeepers . . . as
Settled by the . . . Court . . . May
Sessions [1797].
Newcastle, S. & J. Adams, [1797].
Broadside.
(Not located, 1968.)   48204

Newcomb, Richard English, 1770-1849.
An Oration, Spoken at Greenfield.
Greenfield, Mass., Dickman, 1799. 15 pp.
JCB copy.   35966

Newell, Abel, 1730-1813.
(Weis, Colonial Clergy N. E.)
Good Men.
Hartford, 1768. [2], 49 pp.
AAS copy.   11014

Newell, Jonathan, 1749-1830.
A Sermon, Preached at Stow, on the 16th
of May, 1783.
Boston, Gill, 1784. 27 pp.
AAS copy.   18658

Newfield, Ct.
Act of Incorporation . . . And the
Ordinances.
[Newfield], Beach, [1800]. 16 pp.
HEH copy.   38111

Newland, Jeremiah.
Verses Occasioned by the Earthquakes in
. . . November, 1755.
[Boston, 1755.] Broadside.
MHS copy.   40788

Newman, H[enry], 1670-1743.
(D. A. B.)
Non Cessant Anni. . . . Harvard's
Ephemeris. . . . 1690.
Cambridge, 1690. [16] pp.
MHS copy.   544

Newman, Henry, 1670-1743.
(D. A. B.)
Ut Fluctus. . . . An Almanack. . . . For . . .
1691.
Boston, 1691. [25] pp.
MHS copy.   574

Newman, John, fl. 1791.
A Treatise, on Schirrus Tumours.
Boston, 1791. 8 pp.
Cornell Univ. Library copy.   23627

Newman, John, fl. 1796.
The Columbian Calendar, or
New-England Almanack for . . . 1797.
Dedham, Minerva Press for Heaton. [24]
pp.
LOC copy.   30894

Newman, John, fl. 1796.
The Columbian Calendar, or
New-England Almanack for . . . 1797.
Dedham, Minerva Press. [24] pp.
AAS copy.   47866

Newnan, John, fl. 1793.
An Inaugural Dissertation on General
Dropsy.
Philadelphia, Hall, 1793. 31 pp.
AAS copy.   25922

Newport, R. I.
Town Tax. . . . May 18, 1791.
[Newport, 1791.] Broadside.
Newport Hist. Soc. copy.   23628

Newport, R. I. Artillery Company.
The Charter and Regulations of the. . . .
Warren, Phillips, 1793. 19 pp.
NHS copy.   46838

Newport, R. I. Engine Company Number
V.
Newport Engine Company, Number V.
Whereas. . . .
Newport, Farnsworths, 1799. Broadside.
(The unique copy cannot be reproduced.)
  35967

Newport, R. I. First Congregational
Church.
First Congregational Meeting-house
Lottery. . . . June 24, 1800.
n.p., n.d. Broadside.
RIHS copy.   38112

Newport, R. I. Hand-in-Hand Fire-Club.
. . . These Presents to Witness. . . . [Dec. 30,
1749.]
[Newport, 1750.] Broadside.
NHS copy.   40558

[Newport, R. I. Hand-in-Hand
Fire-Club.]
These Presents Witnesses. . . . Reprinted
in October, 1750.
[Newport, 1750.] Broadside.
NYHS copy.   40559

Newport, R. I. Hand-in-Hand Fire Club.
These Presents Witnesses. . . . [Sept. 26,
1752.]
[Newport, 1752?] Broadside.
RIHS copy.   40633

Newport, R. I. Hand-in-Hand Fire Club.
These Presents Witness, that We the
Subscribers. . . . May, 1770.
[Newport], 1770. Broadside.
NHS copy.   42139

Newport, R. I. Marine Society.
[Charter and by-laws.
Newport, 1786.]
(Alden 1046, no copy known.)   44936

Newport, R. I. Marine Society.
Charter of the Marine Society.
Newport, Edes, [c. 1790]. 5 pp.
RIHS copy.   45933

Newport, R. I. Marine Society.
Laws of the Marine Society. . . . Instituted
at Newport, Dec. 5, A. D. 1752.
Newport, Barber, 1799. 16 pp.
(The only known copy is badly defective.)
NHS copy.   35968

Newport, R. I. Redwood Library.
Laws of the Redwood-Library Company.
Newport, 1764. 7, [1] 28 pp.
AAS copy.   9764

Newport, R. I. Star Fire Society.
Articles of the. . . . The Ninth Day of
June, 1785.
[Newport, 1785.] Broadside.
NHS copy.   44746

Newport, R. I. Star Fire Society.
S.F.S. Articles . . . Revised the 23d Day of
March, 1796.
Newport, Barber, 1796. 9 pp.
NHS copy.   30896

Newport, R.I. Theater, 1793.
[This evening will be presented Barnaby
Buttle.
Newport, 1793.] Broadside.
(Alden 1315a; only known copy
mutilated.)
RIHS copy.   46839

Newport, R.I. Theatre, 1794.
(For the Benefit of the Unfortunate
Americans . . . in Algiers). . . . May 29.
[Newport, 1794.] Broadside.
NHS copy.   47139

Newport, R. I. Theater, 1800.
. . . Mr. Villiers' Night. . . . October 6,
1800.
n.p., n.d. Broadside.
LOC copy.   38114

Newport, R. I. Town Meeting, 1767.
At a Town-Meeting Called . . . November
26, 1767.
Newport, 1767. Broadside.
JCB copy.   10716

Newport, R. I. Town Meeting, 1774.
Colony of Rhode-Island, &c. At a Town
Meeting . . . the 12th day of January,
1774. . . .
[Newport, 1774.] Broadside.
NYPL copy.   13498

Newport, R.I. Trinity Church.
An Address Presented to the Rev. James
Sayre.
Newport, 1789. 6 pp.
AAS copy.   22130

Newport Trinity Church Lottery.
. . . The General Assembly. . . . March 12,
1791.
[Newport, 1791.] Broadside.
NHS copy.   46242

Newport, R.I. United Fire Club.
Articles . . . Instituted February 6, 1783.
[Newport, 1783.] Broadside.
JCB copy.   44427

The Newport Almanac, for . . . 1800.
Newport, R. I., Farnsworth. [24] pp.
RIHS copy.   35969

The Newport Almanac, for . . . 1801.
Newport, R. I., Farnsworth. [24] pp.
AAS copy.   38115

Newport, April 17, 1783.
Proposals for Printing . . . An Inquiry
Concerning the Future Punishment.
[Newport? 1783.] Broadside.
(Better entered as 44460.)   44428

Newport, April 17, 1783.
Proposals for Printing . . . An Inquiry
Concerning the Future Punishment [by
Solomon Southwick, 1731-1797].
[Newport, Southwick, 1783]. Broadside.
NYHS copy.   44460

Newport Association of Mechanics and
Manufactures.
The Charter, Constitution and Bye-laws
of the. . . .
Newport, Barber, [1792]. vi, 24 pp.
AAS copy.   24618

Newport, Aug. 3, 1796. Francis Malbone,
Esq. one of our Representatives. . . .
[Newport, 1796.] Broadside.
NHS copy.   47867

Newport Guards.
The Charter and By-Laws of the. . . .
Newport, Southwick, 1794. 23, [1] pp.
RIHS copy.   47140

Newport Insurance Company.
. . . An Act to Incorporate the. . . .
Newport, Farnsworths, [1799]. 10 pp.
AAS copy.   35970

Newport Long-Wharf, Hotel and Public
School Lottery.
. . . By Authority of the Legislature. . . .
March 20th, 1795.
Warren, R. I., Phillips, [1795].
Broadside.
NHS copy.   47520

Newport, May 15, 1782.
By the Arrival of the Eastern Post. . . .
[Newport, R. I., 1782.] Broadside.
LOC ph. copy.   44240

Newport Mercury. The Reduction of
Quebec. [Supplement to no. 69].
Newport, 1759. Broadside.
(Anderson Galleries sale May 2-3, 1934,
item 357.)   41066

Newport, October 25, 1781.
Glorious Intelligence.
New London, Green, [1781]. Broadside.
MHS copy.   44014

[Newport, October 25, 1781.]
Yesterday Afternoon Arrived . . . Capt.
Lovett. . . .
Newport, 1781.] Broadside.
(Alden 861; no copy known.)   44015

Newport, October 27, 1783.
By the Brig ----, Captain Coffin. . . .
[Newport], Barber, [1783]. Broadside.
RIHS copy.   44429

Newport (Rhode-Island) October 9, 1786.
. . . The following Draught of an Act. . . .
[Newport], Southwick & Barber, [1786].
[2] pp.
AAS ph. copy.   44937

The News-Boy, who now Carries the
New-Hampshire Gazette, Presents his
Compliments of . . . 1767.
[Portsmouth, 1767.] Broadside.
AAS copy.   41748

[News-Boy's Address, or, The Last
Words and Dying Speech of Citizen
Ninety-Four [Middlesex Gazette].
Middletown, Woodward, 1795.
Broadside.]
(No copy of a broadside printing has been
located.)   29079

[The News-boy's Address to his
Customers.
[Hartford, 1790.] Broadside.]
(Known by reprints in Mass. Centinel,
Jan. 23, 1790, etc.)   22429

The Newsboys Address to the Generous
Subscribers of Wood's Newark Gazette
. . . January 1, 1794.
[Newark, 1794.] Broadside.
(Not located, 1968.)   47141

The News-Boy's Address, to the Patrons
of the Albany Centinel, January 1, 1799.
[Albany, 1799.] Broadside.
LOC copy.   35089

The News-Boys Address to the Patrons
of the New-Jersey State Gazette, January
1, 1799.
[Trenton, 1799.] Broadside.
(The one recorded copy is mislaid.)
  35909

The News-Boy's Address to the Patrons
of the State Gazette. . . . January 1,
1799.
[Trenton, 1799.] Broadside.
(The only reported copy is mislaid.)
  36361

[The News-Boy's Address to the Readers
of the American Mercury.
Hartford, Babcock, 1795. Broadside.]
(No copy located.)   28177

The News-Boy's Address, to the Readers
of the American Mercury.
[Hartford, 1798.] Broadside.
NYHS copy.   48550

The News-Boys Address to the
Subscribers of the Lansingburgh
Recorder. . . . January 1, 1795.
[Lansingburgh, 1795.] Broadside.
(Not located, 1968.)   47521

[The Newsboys Annual Address to the
Esteemed Patrons of the Norwich-Packet.
[Norwich, 1799.] Broadside.]
(Adv. Ritter Hopson Galleries, sale no.
14, Nov. 24, 1931, Item 165.)   35996

The News-Boy's Christmas and New-
Year's Verses. . . . To the Gentlemen
and Ladies to whom he Carries the
Boston Evening-Post. . . . December 31,
1764.
[Boston, Fleets, 1764.] Broadside.
HSP copy.   41477

The News-Boy's New-Year Jingle, for
1798.
[Litchfield, 1798.] Broadside.
NYHS copy.   48551

[The Newsboy's New Year's Address,
The Mirror.
Concord, N. H., 1799. Broadside.]
(No copy located.)   35824

The News-Boy's Verses, for January 1,
1765. . . . The New-York Gazette.
[New York, 1765.] Broadside.
LOC copy.   41578

The News-Boy's Verses, for January 1st,
1788; Respectfully Inscribed to the . . .

Patrons of the Maryland Gazette.
[Baltimore, 1788.] Broadside.
NYPL copy.   21231

The News-Boy's Verses, for January 1,
1790. . . . of the Maryland Gazette.
[Baltimore, 1790.] Broadside.
(Also entered as 45542, q. v.)   45934

The News-boys' Verses, for January 1,
1790; respectfully Inscribed to the . . .
Patrons of the Maryland Gazette.
[Baltimore, 1789.] Broadside.
EPFL copy.   45542

The News-Boys Verses, for New-Year's
Day, 1763. . . . The Thursday New-York
Gazette.
[New York, 1762.] Broadside.
NYPL copy.   9217

News. By a Letter from a Member of
Congress. . . . Nov. 1, 1777.
Lancaster, [1777]. [2] pp.
APS copy.   15486

The News-Carrier's Address [Georgetown
Weekly Ledger] . . . for January 1, 1792.
[Georgetown, 1792.] Broadside.
LOC copy.   46530

News Carrier's Address to his Customers.
For January 1, 1797.
n. p., [1797]. Broadside.
NYHS copy.   48205

The News-Carrier's Address to his
Customers.
Hartford, January 1, 1783.
[Hartford, 1783.] Broadside.
AAS copy.   44430

The News-Carriers Address to his
Customers. Hartford, January 1, 1784.
[Hartford, 1784.] Broadside.
NYHS copy.   44575

The News-Carrier's Address to his
Customers. Hartford, January 1, 1785.
[Hartford, 1785.] Broadside.
JCB copy.   44747

The News-Carriers Address to his
Customers. January 1st, 1782.
n.p., [1782]. Broadside.
NYHS copy.   44241

The News-Carrier's Address to the
Patrons of the Centinel. . . . January 1,
1800.
[Newark, N. J., 1800.] Broadside.
NJHS copy.   37114

The News Carrier's Address to the
Subscribers of the George-Town Weekly
Ledger. For January 1, 1792.
[Georgetown, 1791.] Broadside.
LOC copy.   46243

The News-Carriers' Address to the
Subscribers to the Burlington Advertiser.
January 1, 1791.
[Burlington, 1791.] Broadside.
NYPL copy.   23240

The News-Carrier's Verses to the
Subscriber of the Mail. . . . January 1st,
1793.
[New York, 1793.] Broadside.
NYHS copy.   46840

News From Robinson Cruso's Island:
with an Appendix Relating to Mr. Cook's
Late Pamphlet.
Boston, 1720. 11 pp.
BPL copy.   39730

News from the Liberty-Pole. . . . Dec. 29,
1769.
[New York, 1769.] Broadside.
NYPL copy.   11387

News from the Moon. A Review of the
State of the British Nation [by Daniel
Defoe, 1661?-1731].
[Boston, 1721.] 8 pp.
NYPL copy.   2281

News from the Moon. Containing a Brief
Account of the . . . Inhabitants [by
Daniel Defoe, 1661?-1731].
Boston, 1772. 16 pp.
AAS copy.   12491

[The News Lad's Address to the Readers
of the Connecticut Courant. . . . January
1, 1792.
Hartford, 1792.] Broadside.]
(No copy located.)   24222

News of a Strumpet Co-Habiting in the
Wilderness [by Daniel Leeds, 1652-1720].
[New York], 1701. 26 pp.
(The Evans title is incorrect. See Merwin
catalogue 487 (Dec. 5, 1912), No. 181.
The Attribution of authorship is based on
the author's ms. signature on the unique
copy.)
HEH copy.   982

Newton, John, 1725-1807.
Apologia.
New York, Hodge, Allen & Campbell,
1789. 144 pp.
AAS copy.   22028

[Newton, John], 1725-1807.
An Authentic Narrative of some
Remarkable and Interesting Particulars in
the Life of Mr. Newton.
[Philadelphia], 1783. 103 pp.
HSP copy.   17973

Newton, John, 1725-1807.
An Authentic Narrative.
Philadelphia, Young, 1795. [4], 103 pp.
AAS copy.   28813

Newton, John, 1725-1807.
An Authentic Narrative.
New York, W. A. Davis for C. Davis,
1796. [4], 248 pp., 1 plate.
AAS copy.   30898

[Newton, John], 1725-1807.
Cardiphonia. . . . Fifth Edition. In Two
Volumes.
Philadelphia, Young, 1792. pp. [1]-307;
[2], [1]-4, [2], [5]-312.
AAS copy.   24620

[Newton, John], 1725-1807.
Cardiphonia. . . . Sixth Edition. In Two
Volumes.
Philadelphia, Young, 1795. 307; 312 pp.
AAS copy.   29212

Newton, John, 1725-1807.
A Letter, on the Doctrines of Election.
Martinsburg, Willis, [1796?] 8 pp.
(Present location unknown.)   47868

Newton, John, 1725-1807.
Letters and Sermons. . . . In Six
Volumes. Vol. I [-III].
Philadelphia, Young, 1795. [6], 372; [2],
307; [2], 312 pp.
(The first volume was also published with
the title "Letters Originally Published.")
AAS copy.   29213

Newton, John, 1725-1807.
Letters and Sermons. . . . In Six
Volumes. Vol. VI.
Philadelphia, Young, 1792. [2], 348,
[4] pp.
AAS copy.   24622

Newton, John, 1725-1807.
Letters and Sermons. . . . In Six
Volumes. Vol. IV [-VI].
Philadelphia, Young, 1795-96. [2], viii,
340; xviii, 320; [2], 348 pp.
(This is a revision of the entry made by
Evans who did not describe accurately
the set which he saw.)
AAS copy.   30899

Newton, John, 1725-1807.
Letters and Sermons. . . . Vol. IV [and
VII].
Philadelphia, Young, 1795. [2], 340; [4],
336 pp.
(Evans described incorrectly the copies
which he saw. All reported copies of Vol.
VII lack pp. 13-48.)
AAS copy.   29214

Newton, John, 1725-1807.
Letters and Sermons. . . . Vol. IX.
Philadelphia, Young, 1795. [12], 336,
[37] pp.
AAS copy.   29215

Newton, John, 1725-1807.
Letters and Sermons. . . . In Six
Volumes. Vol. VI-[VIII].

Philadelphia, Young, 1796. pp. [2], [i]-
348; [4], [i]-12, 49-336, [i]-vi, [1]-31,
[11]; [4], [i]-xi, [21], [1]-335.
(Sets differ in the order of the binding of
the parts.)
AAS copy.   32580

Newton, John, 1725-1807.
Letters, Originally Published.
Philadelphia, M'Culloch for Young, 1788.
[4], 403, [11] pp.
AAS copy.   21332

Newton, John, 1725-1807.
Letters, Originally Published. . . .
Philadelphia, Young, 1792. [4], 372 pp.
AAS copy.   24621

Newton, John, 1725-1807.
Letters to a Wife.
New York, Campbell, 1794. [4], 281,
3 pp.
AAS copy.   27415

Newton, John, 1725-1807.
Letters to a Wife.
Whitehall, Pa., Young, 1797. pp. [2],
[i]-12, 49-336, [i]-vi, [1]-31, [11].
(This differs only in imprint from vol. 7
of 32580, q.v.)
AAS copy.   32581

Newton, John, 1725-1807.
A Monument to the Praise of the Lord's
Goodness.
Philadelphia, Lang & Ustick for Rogers,
1796. pp. [i]-viii, [7]-30.
AAS copy.   30900

[Newton, John], 1725-1807.
Olney Hymns, in Three Books.
New York, 1787.]
(Apparently a ghost of a later ed.)   20588

[Newton, John], 1725-1807.
Olney Hymns. . . . Sixth Edition.
New York, Hodge, Allen & Campbell,
1790. 348 pp.
AAS copy.   22734

Newton, John, 1725-1807.
Olney Hymns, in Three Books.
Philadelphia, Young, 1791. 348 pp.
LOC copy.   23631

Newton, John, 1725-1807.
Olney Hymns.
Burlington, Neale, 1795. 348, [12] pp.
AAS copy.   29216

Newton, John, 1725-1807.
A Review of Ecclesiastical History.
Whitehall, [Pa.], Young, 1797. xviii,
320 pp.
LCP copy.   48206

Newton, John, 1725-1807.
Verses . . . on his Marriage.
New York, Davis, 1796. 12 pp.
(Heartman Sale 281, No. 915.)   30901

Newton, John, 1725-1807.
A View of Ecclesiastical History.
Boston, Bumstead, [1798?]. xviii, 320 pp.
AAS copy.   34234

Newton, Roger, 1737-1816.
A Discourse, Delivered on the
Anniversary of American Independence.
Greenfield, Mass., Dickinson, 1797.
21 pp.
AAS copy.   32582

Newton, Thomas, bp., 1704-1782.
Dissertations on the Prophecies. . . . In
two Volumes. . . . Eighth Edition.
Elizabethtown, 1787. pp. [24], [22]-412;
[44], [41]-439, [1].
AAS copy.   20589

Newton, Thomas, bp., 1704-1782.
Dissertations on the Prophecies. . . . In
Two Volumes.
New York, Durell, 1794. pp. [24], [21]-
412; [24], [41]-439.
AAS copy.   27417

Newton, Thomas, bp., 1704-1782.
Dissertations on the Prophecies. . . . In
Two Volumes.
New York, Swords for Allen, 1794. xv,
[i], 266; xvii, [1], 284, [22] pp.
AAS copy.   27416

Newton, Thomas, bp., 1704-1782.
Dissertations on the Prophecies.
Northampton, Mass., Butler, 1796. [8],
591 pp.
AAS copy. 30902

Newton, N. H. Baptist Church.
A Confession of Faith.
Exeter, Ranlet for Peak, 1796. 16 pp.
AAS copy. 30903

Newton Library Society.
Constitution of the. . . .
[Newton, Mass? 1799?] 8 pp.
WLC copy. 48949

Nicetas [by Cotton Mather, 1663-1728].
Boston, 1705. 44 pp.
NYPL copy. 1218

Nicholas, George, 1754-1799.
Correspondence between George Nicholas
. . . and . . . Robert G. Harper.
Lexington, Ky., Bradford, 1799. 26,
viii pp.
Newberry Library copy. 35972

Nicholas, George, 1754-1799.
A Letter from George Nicholas.
Lexington, Ky., Bradford, 1798. 42 pp.
AAS copy. 34235

Nicholas, George, 1754-1799.
A Letter from George Nicholas, of
Kentucky, to his Friend in Virginia.
Philadelphia, Carey, 1799. 39 pp.
AAS copy. 35973

Nicholas, George, 1754-1799.
To the Citizens of Kentucky. . . . October
15, 1798.
[Lexington? 1798.] 42 pp.
HEH copy. 48552

Nicholas, George, 1754-1799.
To the Freemen of Kentucky. . . . March
30th, 1799.
[Lexington, Ky., 1799.] Broadside.
LOC copy. 35974

[Nicholas, Robert Carter], 1728-1780.
(LOC card.)
Considerations on the Present State of
Virginia Examined.
[Williamsburg], 1774. 43 pp.
NYPL copy. 13500

[Nicholls, William, fl. 1781.
Advertisement. . . . Feb. 2, 1781.
Philadelphia, Aitken, 1781.]
(Entry from Aitken's accounts.) 17276

[Nichols, Francis, fl. 1795-1820.
A Compendious View of Natural
Philosophy.
Boston? 1795.]
(Entry from copyright notice.) 29217

Nichols, Francis, fl. 1795-1820.
A Treatise of Practical Arithmetic.
Boston, Manning & Loring for West,
1797. 103 pp.
AAS copy. 32583

Nichols, James, 1748-1829.
(Dexter, III, 425-427.)
A Sermon, Delivered at Manchester . . .
the 27th of December, 1785.
Bennington, Haswell & Russell, 1786.
21 pp.
(Signatured to 19450.)
WLC copy. 44938

Nichols, Thomas, fl. 1791.
Hymns, and Anthems.
Albany, Websters, 1793. 204 pp.
LOC copy. 46841

[Nichols, Thomas, fl. 1791.
Hymns and Divine Songs.
Providence, Wheeler, 1791. 200 pp.]
(The origin of this entry is unknown.)
23632

[Nichols, Thomas, fl. 1791.
Poverty and Riches.
Bennington, Haswell, 1796.]
(Haswell's records indicate 1000 copies
were printed. Adv. Vt. Gazette, Apr. 13,
1796.) 30905

[Nicholson, John, 1760?-1800.
(D. A. B.)

Address and Representation. . . . January
24, 1787.
[Philadelphia, 1787.] Broadside.]
(No copy located.) 20590

Nicholson, John, 1760?-1800.
Address to the People of Pennsylvania.
Philadelphia, Bailey, 1790. 68 pp.
LOC copy. 22735

[Nicholson, John], 1760?-1800.
A View of the Proposed Constitution of
the United States.
Philadelphia, Aitken, 1787. 37 pp.
BA copy. 20591

[Nicholson, Joseph Hopper], 1770-1817.
To the Printer of the Maryland
Herald, &c.
[Easton? 1792.] 24 pp.
JCB copy. 29646

Nicholson, Thomas, 1715-1780.
(Southern Hist. Assoc., Pubs, IV,
pp. 172-186.)
An Answer to the Layman's Treatise.
Williamsburg, 1757. vi, 49, [1] pp.
HC copy. 7983

Nicholson, Thomas, 1715-1780.
An Epistle to Friends in Great Britain.
[Newbern, 1762.] 4 pp.
NYPL copy. 9221

Nicholson, William, 1753-1815.
An Introduction to Natural Philosophy.
. . . Third Edition.
Philadelphia, Dobson, 1788. 2 vol.
292 pp., 19 plates; pp. [8], 293-570, [8],
and 6 plates.
AAS copy. 21333

Nicholson, William, 1753-1815.
An Introduction to Natural Philosophy.
. . . In Two Volumes. Vol. II.
Philadelphia, Dobson, 1793. viii, 366,
[10] pp., plates.
(No. vol. I of this ed. is known.)
AAS copy. 46842

Nicholson, William, 1753-1815.
An Introduction to Natural Philosophy.
. . . In Two Volumes.
Philadelphia, Dobson, 1795. xx, 359,
[8] pp., 19 plates; viii, 366, [10] pp.,
6 plates.
AAS copy. 29218

Die Nichtigkeit der Welt [by William
Law, 1686-1761].
Germantown, 1744. 30 pp.
PSL copy. 5512

Nickerson, Ansell, defendant.
The Following Circumstances Relating to
the Famous. . . .
[Boston? 1773?] Broadside.
HSP copy. 42475

Nicola, Lewis, 1717-1807.
The Divinity of Jesus Christ.
Philadelphia, Oswald, 1791. 81, [2] pp.
LOC copy. 23633

[Nicola, Lewis], 1717-1807.
A Treatise of Military Exercise,
Calculated for the Use of the Americans.
Philadelphia, Styner & Cist, 1776. viii,
91, [1] pp., 9 plates.
AAS copy. 14947

Nicolai, Valentin, d. 1799.
A Favorite Sonata (1.) By Niccolai.
[Philadelphia], Willig, [1796]. 7 pp.
NYPL copy. 30904

[Nicoll, Benjamin.]
A Brief Vindication of the Proceedings of
the Trusties.
New York, Gaine, 1754. 12 pp.
NYPL copy. 7282

[Nicoll, B.]
A Wonderful Dream.
[New York, 1770.] 2 pp.
NYPL copy. 11791

[Niessen, Gertrude Dericks.
A Paper.
Philadelphia, 1700.]
(Hildeburn, I, 35.) 946

The Nightingale. A Collection of the
Most Elegant Songs.
Amherst, [N.H.], Preston, 1797. 40 pp.
(The only known copy is imperfect.)
AAS copy. 48207

The Nightingale. An Essay [by Cotton
Mather, 1663-1728].
Boston, Green, 1724. [4], 19 pp.
AAS copy. 2556

The Nightingale of Liberty.
New York, Harrisson, 1797. 83 pp.,
1 plate.
LOC copy. 32584

[The Nightingale; or Charms of Melody.
Baltimore, Keatinge, 1798.]
(Imprint assumed by Evans from adv.
"New publications," Telegraphe, Aug.
15, 1798.) 34237

The Nightingale; or Rural Songster.
Dedham, [Mass.], Mann, 1800. 125,
[3] pp.
AAS copy. 49123

[The Nightingale; or, Songster's
Companion.
Philadelphia, Woodhouse, 1791.]
(Evans' entry is from an adv. in 23440:
"Books published by W. Woodhouse.")
23634

[Niles, Aaron.]
A Controversy between the Four
Elements.
Norwich, 1775. 20 pp.
CHS copy. 13890

[Niles, Nathaniel], 1741-1828.
The American Hero. Made on the Battle
of Bunker-Hill.
n. p., [1775?]. Broadside.
HEH copy. 42911

Niles, Nathaniel, 1741-1828.
The American Hero.
Norwich, 1775. [2] pp.
(Usually found bound with 13149-51.)
AAS copy. 14349

Niles, Nathaniel, 1741-1828.
(Weis, Colonial Clergy N. E.)
A Descant on Sinful Pleasure.
Norwich, 1774. 33 pp.
NYPL copy. 13501

Niles, Nathaniel, 1741-1828.
The Perfection of God.
Norwich, Green & Spooner, 1778. 55 pp.
NYPL copy. 15941

Niles, Nathaniel, 1741-1828.
The Perfection of God.
Elizabethtown, Kollock, 1791. 40 pp.
AAS copy. 23635

Niles, Nathaniel, 1741-1828.
(Weis, Colonial Clergy N. E.)
The Remembrance of Christ.
Boston, Kneeland, 1773. 42 pp.
AAS copy. 12900

Niles, Nathaniel, 1741-1828.
Secret Prayer.
Boston, Kneeland, 1773. 82 pp.
AAS copy. 12901

Niles, Nathaniel, 1741-1828.
The Substance of two Sermons.
Norwich, Trumbull, 1779. 40 pp.
NYPL copy. 16414

Niles, Nathaniel, 1741-1828.
Two Discourses on Liberty.
Newburyport, 1774. 60 pp.
AAS copy. 13502

Niles, Nathaniel, 1741-1828.
Two Discourses, on I John.
Newport, 1773. 55 pp.
AAS copy. 12902

[Niles, Samuel, 1674-1762.
(Sibley, IV, 485-491.)
A Brief and Plain Essay.
New London, 1745. [6], 34 pp.]
(A ghost of 6037 arising from the date of
its subject matter.) 5666

Niles, Samuel, 1674-1762.
(Sibley, IV, 485-491.)

A Brief and Plain Essay.
New London, 1747. [6], 34 pp.
NYPL copy.   6037

Niles, Samuel, 1674-1762.
A Pressing Memorial. . . . Braintree,
June 23, 1761.
[Boston, 1761.] 4 pp.
BPL copy.   41235

Niles, Samuel, 1674-1762.
Tristitiae Ecclesiarum.
Boston, Draper, 1745. 21, 5 pp., irreg.
(The pagination given by Evans follows
the BA copy which contains pages
inserted from the American Magazine.)
AAS copy.   5667

Niles, Samuel, 1674-1762.
(Sibley, IV, 485-491.)
The True Scripture-Doctrine of Original
Sin.
Boston, Kneeland, 1757. [6], 320 pp.
AAS copy.   7984

Niles, Samuel, 1674-1762.
(Sibley, IV, 485-491.)
A Vindication.
Boston, Kneeland, 1752. [2], 120 pp.
AAS copy.   6902

Niles, Samuel, 1743-1814.
The Vanity of Man Considered.
Boston, Fleets, 1800. 23 pp.
AAS copy.   38117

Niles, Sands.
Some Short Remarks . . . on Baptism.
New London, [1788]. 27 pp.
ABHS copy.   21334

Nips, Jack, pseud.
The Yankee Spy [by John Leland,
1754-1841].
Boston, Asplund, [1794]. 20, 4 pp.
AAS copy.   27215

Nisbet, Charles, 1736-1804.
An Address to the Students of Dickinson
College.
Carlisle, [1786]. 16 pp.
BA copy.   19865

Nisbet, Charles, 1736-1804.
The Usefulness and Importance of
Human Learning.
Carlisle, [1786]. 32 pp.
BA copy.   19866

[Nisbet, Richard.
The Capacity of Negroes.
Baltimore, Rice, 1792?]
(Entry from adv., apparently for London
ed.)   24623

Nisbet, Richard.
Numbers of Poetry - Serious and Comic.
. . . No. 1. The Simple, soft Leylock.
[n. p., 1799.] 4 pp.
(The one reported copy is mislaid.)   35975

Nisbet, Richard.
. . . No. II. The Fruits of Sermon-
Hunting.
[n. p., 1799.] 16 pp.
(The only reported copy is mislaid.)   35976

[Nisbet, Richard.]
Slavery not Forbidden by Scripture.
Philadelphia, 1773. [2], iii, [1], 30 pp.
AAS copy.   12903

[Nisbet, Richard.
The Source of Virtue.
Baltimore, Rice, 1792?]
(Entry from an adv., apparently for
Philadelphia ed.)   24624

Nixon, Rev. William.
Analogical-Vocabulary.
Philadelphia, Carey, 1792. 28 pp.
SCHS copy.   24625

[Nixon, Rev. William.
An Easy Introduction to the Latin
Prosody.
Charleston, 1790. 16 pp.]
(Origin of this entry unknown.)   22736

Nixon, Rev. William.
Prosody made Easy.
Philadelphia, Spotswood for Gaine,

Wright, etc., 1786. xvi, (i.e., xiii), [3],
36 pp.
AAS copy.   19867

Nixon, Rev. William.
Specimen of a Plan.
Charleston, Bowen, 1789. [2], 26, [1] pp.
AAS copy.   22029

No Mercer! No Man for Congress who
Disregards the Instructions. . . .
September 28, 1792.
[Annapolis? 1792.] Broadside.
LOC copy.   46531

No Placeman, Pensioners, Ministerial
Hirelings. . . . An Honest Free-Holder of
West-Chester County.
[New York, 1775.] Broadside.
NYPL copy.   14400

No Placemen, Pensioners, Ministerial
Hirelings. . . . An Honest Free-Holder of
King's County.
[New York, 1775.] [2] pp.
LOC copy.   14401

No Placemen, Pensioners, Ministerial
Hirelings. . . . Phileleutheros. New-York,
13th March, 1775.
[New York, 1775.] Broadside.
NYPL copy.   14399

No Provincial Convention. Let Us Act
for Ourselves.
[Philadelphia, 1776.] Broadside.
LOC copy.   43109

No Provincial Convention. Let us
Choose. . . .
[New York, 1775.] Broadside.
NYPL copy.   14350

No Song, no Supper: a Comic Opera.
. . . Third American Edition [by Prince
Hoare, 1755-1834].
New York, Harrison, 1793. 36 pp.,
1 plate.
(Evans' entry was from an adv.)
AAS copy.   25611

No Song no Supper: An Opera. . . .
Second Philadelphia Edition [by Prince
Hoare, 1755-1834].
Philadelphia, Carey, 1793. 32, [3] pp.
AAS copy.   25612

No Song No Supper [by Prince Hoare,
1755-1834].
Boston, Blake, 1794. 29 pp.
AAS copy.   27125

No Stamped Paper to be had [Nov. 7,
1765].
[Philadelphia, 1765.] Broadside.
(This is the Pa. Gazette for Nov. 7,
1765.)
AAS copy.   10106

No Standing Army in the British
Colonies. . . .
New York, Holt, 1775. 18 pp.
LOC copy.   14351

Noble, Job.
An Alarm Sounded.
Philadelphia, 1740. 19 pp.
HSP copy.   4581

Noble, Oliver, 1734-1792.
The Knowledge, or well Grounded Hope.
Newburyport, 1781. 40 pp.
AAS copy.   17277

Noble, Oliver, 1734-1792.
(Weis, Colonial Clergy N. E.)
Preaching Christ.
Salem, 1771. 32 pp.
AAS copy.   12167

Noble, Oliver, 1734-1792.
(Weis, Colonial Clergy N. E.)
Regular and Skilful Music.
Boston, Mills & Hicks for Bayley, 1774.
46 pp.
AAS copy.   13503

Noble, Oliver, 1734-1792.
(Weis, Colonial Clergy N. E.)
Some Strictures.
Newburyport, 1775. 31, [1] pp.
AAS copy.   14352

Noble, William.
A Terror to some Lawyers.
[Philadelphia?], 1749.
(Only these ph. can now be located.)
                                             40509

The Noble Slaves [by Penelope Aubin, fl.
1721-1729].
New Haven, Bunce, 1798. 216 pp.
CHS copy.   48342

The Noble Slaves [by Penelope Aubin, fl.
1721-1729].
New York, Tiebout, 1800. 139 pp.
AAS copy.   36861

The Noble Slaves.
New York, Tiebout, 1800. 139 pp.
(Also entered as 36861, q. v.)   38118

Nobles, John.
November 18th, 1793. These are the
Predictions of. . . .
[Boston ? 1793.] Broadside.
AAS copy.   25924

[Noch Mehr Zeugnusse der Wahrheit.
Germantown, 1747.]
(See Reichmann 89.)   6038

Noel, Garrat, fl. 1733-1762.
A Catalogue of Books in History. . . .
New York, Gaine, 1755. 24 pp.
BPL copy.   7519

Noel, Garrat, fl. 1733-1762.
A Catalogue of Books.
New York, Gaine, 1762. 36 pp.
LOC copy.   9222

[Noel, Garrat, fl. 1733-1762.
Catalogue of Books.
New York, 1767. 23 + pp.]
("Now publishing," N. Y. Gazette, Aug.
3, 1767.)   10718

[Noel, Garrat, fl. 1733-1762.
A Short Introduction to the Spanish
Language.
New York, Parker, 1751.]
(From bookseller's adv.)   6741

Noel, Garrat, & Co.
A Catalogue of Books.
New York, Gaine, 1759. 18 + pp.
(The only copy located is imperfect.)
LOC copy.   8447

Noel & Hazard, publishers.
A Catalogue of Books, sold by. . . .
New York, Inslee & Car, 1771. 40 pp.
CHS copy.   12168

Nomenclatura Brevis Anglo-Latino [by
Francis Gregory, 1625-1707].
Boston, Draper for Edwards and Foster,
1735. [4], 88 pp.
AAS copy.   3910

Nomenclatura Brevis Anglo-Latino [by
Francis Gregory, 1625-1707].
Boston, Fowle for Edwards, 1752. [4],
88 pp.
AAS copy.   6850

Nomenclatura Brevis [by Francis
Gregory, 1625-1707.]
Boston, the Printing-Office in Hanover
St., 1773. 83 pp.
(The only known copy is imperfect.)
BPL copy.   42448

La Nomenclature Anglaise.
Philadelphia, Bradford, 1794. [2], 78 pp.
AAS copy.   27418

None but Christ [by Clement Cotton].
Boston, Kneeland for Henchman, 1723.
[2], viii, 73 pp.
AAS copy.   2426

Norcom, James, 1778-1850.
An Inaugural Thesis on Jaundice.
Philadelphia, Carey, [1799]. 49, [1] pp.
AAS copy.   35977

Norcot, John,-1676.
(McAlpin cat., III, 731.)
Baptism Discovered Plainly.
Boston, Fleet, 1723. [8], 39 pp.
AAS copy.   2472

Norcot, John,-1676.

(McAlpine cat., III, 731.)
Baptism Discovered Plainly. . . . Fifth
Edition.
[Boston or London], 1747. [8], 39 pp.
AAS copy. 6039

Norcot, John, -1676.
(McAlpine cat., III, 731.)
Baptism Discovered. . . . Fifth Edition.
Philadelphia, Steuart, 1764. 47, [1] pp.
LOC copy. 9766

Norcot, John, d. 1676.
Baptism Discovered. . . . Twentieth
Edition.
Bennington, Haswell & Russell, 1785.
36 pp.
(The only known copy is imperfect.)
VtSL copy. 44748

Norcot, John, d. 1676.
Baptism Discovered.
Mount Holly, N. J., Ustick, 1799. [2],
52 pp.
LCP copy. 35978

[Norcot, John, d. 1676.
Baptism Discovered.
Mount Holly, N. J., Ustick for M'Gown,
[1799]. [2], 52 pp.]
(The only recorded copy of this variant is
lost.) 35979

[Norfolk Circulating Library.
Catalogue of the Books in the. . . .
Norfolk, Willett & Connor, 1796.]
("Now in press," Norfolk Herald, Dec. 5,
1795; "Published this day," ibid. Jan. 9,
1796.) 31068

[Norfolk County, Mass. Convention,
1775.
At a Meeting of the Delegates from each
Town. . . .
Watertown, 1775. Broadside.]
(A ghost of 13646. There was no Norfolk
County, Mass., at this time.) 14353

Norfolk, Va., Charters.
Copy of the Charter of Norfolk Borough.
Norfolk, Willett & O'Connor, 1797.
16 pp.
VaSL copy. 32588

[Norman, John, 1748-1817.
An Almanack for . . . 1780.
Philadelphia, Norman. Broadside.]
(The origin of this entry is unknown.) 16415

[Norman, John], 1748-1817.
The American Pilot.
Boston, Norman, 1791. 12 charts.
HC copy. 23637

Norman, John, 1748-1817.
The American Pilot.
Boston, Norman, 1792. [4] pp., 11 maps.
(Copy not located.) 46532

Norman, John, 1748-1817.
The American Pilot.
Boston, Norman, 1794. [3] pp., maps.
(Evans took his title from the copyright
entry and assumed the date of imprint.)
LOC copy. 25925

[Norman, John, 1748-1817.
The American Pilot.
Boston, Norman, 1798. 6 pp., 9 maps.]
(No such ed. located.) 34239

[Norman, John], 1748-1817.
The American Pilot.
Boston, Norman, 1798. [6] pp., 11 maps.
LOC copy. 48553

Norman, John, 1748-1817.
Boston, May 5th, 1785. . . . An Accurate
Map of the Four New England States.
[Boston, 1785.] Broadside.
MHS copy. 44749

[Norman, John, 1748-1817.
Map of the United States of America.
Boston, Norman, 1791. 6 sheets.]
("Just Published," Boston Gazette, Feb.
28, 1791.) 23638

Norman, John, 1748-1817.
A New Map of the New-England States.
[Boston, 1785.]

(No copy located would reproduce
legibly.) 19144

Norman, White & Freeman, publishers,
Boston.
Proposals for Printing by Subscription,
the Boston Magazine.
[Boston, 1784.] Broadside.
LOC copy. 44576

Norris, Edward, 1584-1659.
(S. E. Morison, Founding of Harvard,
p. 392.)
A Short Catechisme.
Cambridge, 1649. 30, [2] pp.
(See Harvard Library Bulletin, XIII,
25-28.)
Lambeth Palace Library copy. 24

[Norris, Isaac], 1671-1735.
(D. A. B.)
Friendly Advice to the Inhabitants of
Pensilvania.
[Philadelphia, 1710.] 3 pp.
JCB copy. 1483

[Norris, Isaac], 1671-1735.
(D. A. B.)
Friendly Advice to the Inhabitants of
Pensilvania.
[Philadelphia, 1728.] 3 pp.
HSP copy. 3078

[Norris, Isaac], 1671-1735.
(D. A. B.)
The Speech Delivered from the Bench . . .
the 11 day of September, 1727.
[Philadelphia, 1727.] 3, [1] pp.
JCB copy. 2937

Norristown, Pa. Library Company.
The Act of Incorporation . . . of the. . . .
Philadelphia, Ormrod, 1799. 22 pp.
HSP copy. 35982

North, Edward Washington, d. 1843.
An Inaugural Dissertation.
Philadelphia, Woodward, 1797. [2],
37 pp.
AAS copy. 32592

North, Frederick North, baron,
1732-1792.
The Speech of the Right Hon. Lord
North.
Baltimore, [1778]. 16 pp.
LCP copy. 15942

The North-American Calendar: or, the
Rhode-Island Almanack, for . . . 1786 [by
Benjamin West, 1730-1813].
Providence, Wheeler. [24] pp.
(The AAS has two issues.)
AAS copy. 19377

The North-American Calendar: or, the
Rhode-Island Almanack, for . . . 1788 [by
Benjamin West, 1730-1813].
Providence, Wheeler. [24] pp.
AAS copy. 20881

North American Land Company.
Plan of Association of the. . . .
Philadelphia, Aitken, 1795. 25 pp., 1
folded leaf.
AAS copy. 29220

The North American Pocket Almanack,
for . . . 1790.
Wilmington, Brynberg & Andrews.
[32] pp.
AAS copy. 45543

A North Britain Extraordinary. . . . Third
Edition [by Tobias George Smollett,
1721-1771].
Philadelphia, Dunlap, 1769. 50 pp.
AAS copy. 11471

North Carolina (Colony) Convention,
1775.
. . . At a Convention . . . at Newbern the
6th Day of April, 1773. . . . Having Found
Ourselves under the Necessity of
Withdrawing. . . .
[Newbern, 1775.] Broadside.
NCU copy. 42912

North Carolina (Colony) Convention,
1775.
. . . At a General Meeting of the
Delegates [Apr. 3-7, 1775]. . . .

[Newbern, 1775.] 4 pp.
NCU copy. 42913

North Carolina (Colony) Council, 1759.
To His Excellency Arthur Dobbs. . . .
The Humble Address of the Council.
n. p., [1759] Broadside.
WLC copy. 41067

North Carolina (Colony) Council, 1767.
To His Excellency William Tryon . . .
the Humble Address of His Majesty's
Council.
[Newbern, 1767.] Broadside.
PRO copy. 41749

North Carolina (Colony) General
Assembly, 1748.
. . . A Table of the Number of Taxables
in this Province from . . . 1748.
n. p., [176-?] [2] pp.
MHS copy. 41104

North Carolina (Colony) General
Assembly, 1754.
A Draught of an Act Proposed . . . for
Establishing a Paper Credit.
Newbern, Davis, 1754. [2], 14 pp.
PRO copy. 40708

North Carolina (Colony) General
Assembly, 1759.
To His Excellency Arthus Dobbs. . . .
The Humble Address of the Assembly.
n. p., [1759] Broadside.
WLC copy. 41068

North Carolina (Colony) General
Assembly. House of Burgesses, 1767.
To His Excellency William Tryon . . . the
Humble Address of the House of
Assembly.
[Newbern, 1767.] 2 pp.
PRO copy. 41750

North Carolina (Colony) Governor, 1754.
A Message from His Excellency Arthur
Dobbs [Plan of Union. Dec. 12, 1754].
[Newbern, 1754.] 4 pp.
LOC copy. 7284

North Carolina (Colony) Governor, 1757.
. . . His Excellency Arthur Dobbs. . . . A
Proclamation, Whereas . . . James
Murray and John Rutherford [Dec. 5,
1757.]
[Newbern, 1757.] Broadside.
PRO copy. 40927

North Carolina (Colony) Governor, 1758.
. . . By His Excellency Arthur Dobbs. . . .
A Proclamation. Whereas the Enormity
of our Sins [setting June 7 as a Fast Day,
dated Apr. 29, 1758].
[Newbern, 1758.] Broadside.
PRO copy. 40997

North Carolina (Colony) Governor, 1759.
The Speech of . . . Arthur Dobbs . . . the
8th Day of May, 1759.
n. p., [1759]. Broadside.
WLC copy. 41069

North Carolina (Colony) Governor, 1767.
The Speech of His Excellency . . . to the
General Assembly [Dec. 5, 1767].
[Newbern, 1767.] 3 pp.
PRO copy. 41751

North Carolina (Colony) Governor, 1768.
. . . A Proclamation. Whereas Complaints
[of exorbitant fees. Dated July 21, 1768].
[Newbern, 1768.] Broadside.
PRO copy. 41860

North Carolina (Colony) Governor, 1769.
The Speech of His Excellency William
Tryon . . . to the General Assembly [Oct.
23, 1769].
[Newbern, 1769.] 3 pp.
PRO copy. 41989

North Carolina (Colony) Governor, 1774.
Advertisement. Whereas it Appears that
many Persons. . . May 3, 1774.
[Newbern, 1774.] Broadside.
NCU copy. 42658

North Carolina (Colony) Governor, 1775.
. . . By His Excellency Josiah Martin. . . .
A Proclamation. Whereas his Majesty.
. . . [dated Feb. 10, 1775.]

[Newbern, 1775.] Broadside.
PRO copy.   42914

North Carolina (Colony) Governor, 1775.
. . . By His Excellency Josiah Martin. . . .
A Proclamation. Whereas . . . sundry Ill-
disposed Persons [June 16, 1775.]
[Newbern, 1775.] Broadside.
PRO copy.   42915

North Carolina (Colony) Governor, 1776.
North-Carolina, St. By His Excellency
Josiah Martin. . . . A Proclamation
[Martial Law. Apr. 7, 1776].
[Newbern, 1776.] Broadside.
LOC copy.   14949

North Carolina (Colony) Grand Jury.
[Presentment to Suppress the Insurgents.
Newburn, 1771.]
(McMurtrie, N. C., 64; no copy known.)
   42260

North Carolina (Colony) House Journals,
1746.
The Journal of the House [June 12, 1746-
Sept. 26, 1749].
Newbern, Davis, 1749. 14 pp.
PRO copy.   40510

North Carolina (Colony) House Journals,
1750.
The Journal of the House of Burgesses
[July 5-10, 1750].
[Newbern, 1750.] 4 pp.
PRO copy.   40560

North Carolina (Colony) House Journals,
1751.
The Journal of the House of Burgesses
[Sept. 26-Oct. 12, 1751.]
[Newbern, 1751.] pp. 3-20.
PRO copy.   40598

North Carolina (Colony) House Journals,
1752.
A Journal of the House. . . . Being the
Eleventh Session [Mar. 31-Apr. 15,
1752].
Newbern, Davis, 1753. 16 pp.
PRO copy.   40662

North Carolina (Colony) House Journals,
1753.
The Journal of the House [Mar. 28-Apr.
12, 1753].
[Newbern, 1753.] pp. 3-18.
PRO copy.   40663

North Carolina (Colony) House Journals,
1754.
The Journal of the House. . . . Being the
Thirteenth Session [Feb. 19-Mar. 9,
1754].
Newbern, Davis, 1754. 16 pp.
PRO copy.   40709

North Carolina (Colony) House Journals,
1754.
[The Journal of the House, Dec. 13,
1754-Jan. 15, 1755.]
Newbern, Davis, 1755.] pp. [3]-14+.
(The only known copy is imperfect.)
PRO copy.   40789

North Carolina (Colony) House Journals,
1762.
The Journal of the House of Assembly
[Apr. 13-29, 1762+].
[Newbern, 1762.] 28 pp.
PRO copy.   41297

[North Carolina (Colony) House
Journals, 1762.
The Journal of the House of Assembly
[Nov. 3-Dec. 11, 1762.]
Newbern, 1762 or 1763.]
(Ordered printed.)   9470

[North Carolina (Colony) House
Journals, 1764.
Laws and Journals of January, February,
and March Sessions, 1764.
Newbern, Davis, 1764.]
(Printing mentioned in Colonial Records,
VII, 334.)   9768

North Carolina (Colony) House Journals,
1764.
The Journal of the House . . . at
Wilmington [Feb. 3, 1764-May 3, 1765]
. . . being the Third Session.

Newbern, Davis, 1766. 18 pp.
NCU copy.   41651

North Carolina (Colony) House Journals,
1766.
[Journal of the House, Nov. 20-24, 1766.
Newbern, 1766?] pp. 37-44.
(Known only by this fragment.)
LOC copy.   41652

North Carolina (Colony) House Journals,
1769.
The Journal of the House [Oct. 23-Nov.
6, 1769]. . . . Being the First Session.
[Newbern, 1769.] 20 pp.
Moravian Archives, Salem, N. C., copy.
   41990

North Carolina (Colony) House Journals,
1770:
The Journal of the House [Dec. 5, 1770-
Jan. 26, 1771.]
[Newbern, 1771.] 74 pp., irreg.
NCU copy.   42261

North Carolina (Colony) House Journals,
1770.
The Journal of the House [Dec. 5,
1770?].
Newbern, 1771.] 27+ pp.
(No complete copy of this ed. is known.)
Moravian Archives, Salem, N.C., copy.
   42262

North Carolina (Colony) House Journals,
1773.
The Journal of the House [Jan. 23-Mar.
6, 1773].
[Newbern, 1773.] 67 pp.
Moravian Archives, Winston-Salem,
copy.   42476

North Carolina (Colony) House Journals,
1773.
The Journals of the House [Dec. 4-21,
1773].
Newbern, Davis, 1773. 8+ pp.
(The only known copy is imperfect.)
Moravian Archives, Winston-Salem,
copy.   42477

North Carolina (Colony) House Journals,
1774.
[The journal, Mar. 2-25, 1774.]
Newbern, 1774.] 49 pp.
(Known only by this fragment.)
Moravian Archives, Winston-Salem copy.
   42659

North Carolina (Colony) Laws, Statutes,
etc., 1751.
A Collection of all the Public Acts.
Newbern, 1751. [4], xii, [2], 353, 8 pp.
NYPL copy.   6742

North Carolina (Colony) Laws, Statutes,
etc., 1752.
A Collection of all the Public Acts.
Newbern, 1752. [4], xii, [2], 371, [2] pp.
LOC copy.   6903

North Carolina (Colony) Laws, Statutes,
etc., 1755.
An Act, for the Erecting . . . Wachovia,
into a Distinct Parish.
[Newbern, 1755?] Broadside.
NcU copy.   40790

[North Carolina (Colony) Laws, Statutes,
etc., 1763.
An Act for the more Effectual Observing
of the Queen's Peace.
Newbern, 1763.]
(Ordered printed.)   9469

North Carolina (Colony) Laws, Statutes,
etc., 1764.
A Collection of all the Acts of Assembly
. . . Since . . . 1751.
Newbern, 1764. [4], 386, [8] pp.
NCU copy.   9767

North Carolina (Colony) Laws, Statutes,
etc., 1765.
A Collection of all the Acts . . . now in
Force. . . . Vol. I [-II].
Newbern, Davis, 1765. xvi, 176; 393, [21]
pp.
NCU copy.   41580

North Carolina (Colony) Laws, Statutes,
etc., 1770.
[An Act for Authorizing Presbyterian

Ministers to Solemnize Matrimony.
Newbern, 1770.]
(No copy known.)   42140

North Carolina (Colony) Laws, Statutes,
etc., 1773.
A Complete Revisal of all the Acts of
Assembly.
Newbern, 1773. [6], x, 566, [9] pp.
NCU copy.   12904

North Carolina (Colony) Provincial
Congress, 1775.
The Journal of the Proceedings of the
Provincial Congress. . . . Held . . . the 20th
Day of August, 1775.
Newbern, 1775. 40 pp.
LOC copy.   14354

North Carolina (Colony) Session Laws,
1753.
Acts of the Assembly [Mar. 27, 1753 +].
Newbern, 1753. pp. 373-384.
LOC copy.   7080

North Carolina (Colony) Session Laws,
1754.
. . . At a General Assembly [Feb. 19, 1754
+].
[Newbern, 1754.] pp. 385-410.
PRO copy.   7283

North Carolina (Colony) Session Laws,
1754.
. . . At a General Assembly [Dec. 12, 1754
+].
[Newbern, 1755.]. pp. 3-63, [1].
PRO copy.   7520

North Carolina (Colony) Session Laws,
1755.
. . . At a General Assembly [Sept. 25,
1755 +].
[Newbern, 1755.] 30 pp.
PRO copy.   7521

North Carolina (Colony) Session Laws,
1756.
. . . At a General Assembly [Sept. 30,
1756 +].
[Newbern, 1756.] 38 pp.
PRO copy.   7743

North Carolina (Colony) Session Laws,
1757.
. . . At a General Assembly [May 16, 1757
+].
[Newbern, 1757.] 5 pp.
PRO copy.   7985

North Carolina (Colony) Session Laws,
1757.
. . . At a General Assembly [Nov. 21, 1757
+].
[Newbern, 1757.] 15 pp.
PRO copy.   7986

North Carolina (Colony) Session Laws,
1758.
. . . At a General Assembly [Apr. 28, 1758
+].
[Newbern, 1758.] 8 pp.
PRO copy.   8221

North Carolina (Colony) Session Laws,
1758.
. . . At a General Assembly [Nov. 23, 1758
+].
[Newbern, 1758.] 31 pp.
PRO copy.   8222

North Carolina (Colony) Session Laws,
1759.
. . . At a General Assembly [May 8, 1759
+].
[Newbern, 1759.] 3 pp.
PRO copy.   8448

North Carolina (Colony) Session Laws,
1759.
. . . At a General Assembly [Nov. 20, 1759
+].
[Newbern, 1760.] 19 pp.
PRO copy.   8695

North Carolina (Colony) Session Laws,
1760.
. . . At an Assembly [Apr. 24, 1760 +].
[Newbern, 1760.] 32 pp.
PRO copy.   8696

North Carolina (Colony) Session Laws,
1760.

... At an Assembly [May 26, 1760 +].
[Newbern, 1760.] 14 pp.
PRO copy.   8697

North Carolina (Colony) Session Laws,
1760.
... At an Assembly [June 26, 1760 +].
[Newbern, 1760.] 7 pp.
PRO copy.   8698

[North Carolina (Colony) Session Laws,
1760.
At an Assembly [Nov. 1760 +].
[Newbern, 1760.]
(No copy known.)   8699

North Carolina (Colony) Session Laws,
1762.
... At an Assembly, begun . . . the Third
Day of November [1762].
[Newbern, 1762.] 28 + pp.
(The only known copy is imperfect.)
NCU copy.   41298

North Carolina (Colony) Session Laws,
1764.
At an Assembly [Feb. 3, 1764 +].
Wilmington, N. C., Steuart, 1764. [2],
28 pp.
(The unique copy is incomplete.)
NCUcopy.   9769

North Carolina (Colony) Session Laws,
1765.
... At an Assembly [May 3, 1765 +].
Wilmington, N. C., Steuart, 1765. pp. [2],
29-33.
Moravian Archives (Winston-Salem) copy.
                                                   10107

North Carolina (Colony) Session Laws,
1766.
... At an Assembly . . . Newbern [Nov. 3,
1766]: being the First Session.
[Newbern, Davis, 1766.]
pp. 395-438.
NCU copy.   41653

North Carolina (Colony) Session Laws,
1770.
[Laws of North Carolina.
n.p., 1770.] pp. 29-64.
(No copy located.)   42141

North Carolina (Colony) Session Laws,
1774.
The Acts of Assembly [Mar. 2, 1774 +].
Newbern, 1774. pp. [2], 567-612.
NCU copy.   13504

North Carolina. Comptroller, 1786.
Abstract of the Army Accounts
[1784-1786].
n.p., [1786?] 224 pp.
NCU copy.   44939

North Carolina. Constitution, 1779.
The Constitution . . . of North-Carolina.
Philadelphia, Bailey, 1779. 16 pp.
HSP copy.   16419

North Carolina. Constitution, 1788.
A Declaration of Rights, made by the
Representatives of the Freemen.
[Newbern, Hodge & Blanchard, [1788]. 4
pp.
(The only copy located is imperfect.)
NCU copy.   20593

North Carolina. Constitutional
Convention, 1788.
... In Convention, August 1, 1788.
Resolved, That a Declaration of
Rights. . . .
[Hillsborough? 1788.] [4] pp.
LOC copy.   21341

North Carolina. Constitutional
Convention, 1788.
The Journal of the Convention of
North-Carolina.
[Hillsborough, 1788.] 10, 16 pp.
NCU copy.   21337

North Carolina. Convention, 1788.
Proceedings and Debates.
Edenton, Hodge & Wills, 1789. 280 pp.
AAS copy.   22037

North Carolina. Convention, 1789.
... In Convention, November 23, 1789.
Resolved, Unanimously. . . .

[Edenton, 1789.] Broadside.
AAS ph copy.   22039

North Carolina. Convention, 1789.
Journal of the Convention. . . . At
Fayetteville.
Edenton, Hodge & Wills, [1790].
16 pp.
NCHC copy.   22738

North Carolina. Convention, 1789.
The Ratification of the Constitution. . . .
November 21, 1789.
[Edenton, 1789?] 27 pp.
NYPL copy.   45544

[North Carolina. General Assembly,
1783.
A Bill Concerning the Poor.
[Newbern? 1783?] [2] pp.]
(Probably printed c. 1820.)   44432

North Carolina. General Assembly, 1786.
Dr. State of New-Hampshire.
Newbern, Arnett & Hodge, [1786].
20 pp.
LOC copy.   19871

North Carolina. General Assembly, 1795.
A Bill to Authorize the Secretary to Issue
Grants for Military Lands.
[Halifax, 1795.] Broadside.
NC-Ar copy.   47522

North Carolina. General Assembly
Journals, 1785.
The Journals of the General Assembly
[Nov. 19-Dec. 29, 1786]. [2], 44, 52 pp.
LOC copy.   19869

[North Carolina. Governor, 1784.
... By His Excellency Alexander Martin.
. . . a Proclamation [Peace of Paris].
Newbern, [1784]. Broadside.]
(Entry from Weeks.)   18821

North Carolina. Governor, 1793.
... By His Excellency Richard Dobbs
Spaight. . . . A Pestilential Fever [Sept.
28, 1793]. . . .
[Newbern, 1793.] Broadside.
N. C. Archives copy.   46843

North Carolina. House Journals, 1778.
The Journal of the House [Apr. 14-May
2, 1778]. . . . First Session.
[Newbern, 1778.] 36 + pp.
(The only known copy is imperfect.)
LOC copy.   43518

North Carolina. House Journals, 1778.
The Journal of the House [Aug. 8-19,
1778]. . . . Second Session.
[Newbern, 1778.] 24 + pp.
(The only known copy is imperfect.)
NCU copy.   43519

North Carolina. House Journals, 1779.
The Journal of the House . . . May . . .
1779.
[Newbern, 1779.] 33 pp.
LOC copy.   43675

North Carolina. House Journals, 1783.
The Journal of the House . . . [Apr. 18-
May 17, 1783].
Halifax, Davis, [1783]. 67 pp.
(No copy available.)   44431

North Carolina. House Journals, 1784.
The Journal of the House . . . begun the
Nineteenth Day of April.
Halifax, Davis, 1784. 71 pp.
LOC copy.   44577

North Carolina. House Journals, 1786.
The Journal of the House of Commons
[Nov. 18, 1786-Jan. 6, 1787].
[Newbern, 1787.] 80, 8, [16] pp.
LOC copy.   20594

North Carolina. House Journals, 1787.
The Journal of the House of Commons
[Nov. 19-Dec. 22, 1787].
Newbern, [1788]. 56 pp., 4 tables.
LOC copy.   21338

North Carolina. House Journals, 1788.
Journal of the House of Commons [Nov.
3-Dec. 6, 1788].
Edenton, Hodge & Wills, [1789]. 56,
[12] pp.
LOC copy.   22034

North Carolina. House Journals, 1789.
Journal of the House of Commons [Nov.
2-Dec. 22, 1789].
Edenton, Hodge & Wills, [1790]. 71,
9 pp.
LOC copy.   22739

North Carolina. House Journals, 1790.
Journal of the House of Commons. . . .
November . . . Session.
Edenton, Hodge & Wills, 1791. 91 pp.
LOC copy.   23639

North Carolina. House Journals, 1791.
Journal of the House of Commons [Dec.
5-Jan. 20, 1792].
Edenton, Hodge & Wills, [1792]. 66 pp.
NCSL copy.   24628

North Carolina. House Journals, 1792.
Journal of the House [Nov. 15, 1792-
Jan. 1, 1793].
Edenton, Hodge & Wills, [1793]. 63 pp.
NCSL copy.   25926

North Carolina. House Journals, 1793.
Journal of the House . . . [Dec. 2, 1793-
Jan. 11, 1794].
Halifax, Hodge & Wills, [1794]. 67 pp.
NCSL copy.   27420

North Carolina. House Jorrnals, 1794.
Journal of the House [July 7-19, 1794].
[Newbern, Martin, 1794]. 11, [1] pp.
LOC copy.   27421

North Carolina. House Journals, 1794.
Journal of the House of Commons [Dec.
30, 1794-Feb. 7, 1795].
Edenton, Hodge & Wills, [1795]. 60 pp.
NCSL copy.   29222

North Carolina. House Journals, 1795.
[Journal of the House . . . November-
December Session, 1795.
Edenton, 1796?]. 57 pp.
(The only copy reported lacks the tp.)
NCSL copy.   30910

North Carolina. House Journals, 1796.
Journal of the House [Nov. 21-Dec. 24,
1796].
Edenton, Hodge & Wills, [1797]. 54 pp.
NYPL copy.   32593

North Carolina. House Journals, 1796.
Journal of the House. . . . [Nov. 21-Dec.
24, 1796].
Edenton, Hodge & Wills, [1797]. 54 pp.
(Also entered as 32593, q. v.)   34240

North Carolina. House Journals, 1797.
Journal of the House . . . [Nov. 20-Dec.
23, 1797].
Halifax, Hodge, [1798]. 56 pp.
N.C. Supreme Court Library.   34242

North Carolina. House Journals, 1798.
Journal of the House of Commons. . . .
[Nov. 19-Dec. 24, 1798.]
[Wilmington, Hall, 1798.] 80 pp.
N.C. Supreme Court Library copy.   34244

North Carolina. House Journals, 1799.
Journal of the House of Commons [Nov.
18-Dec. 23, 1799.]
Raleigh, Hodge & Boylan, [1800]. 68 pp.
LOC copy.   38123

North Carolina. Laws, Statutes, etc.,
1777.
An Act for Confiscating the Property.
. . . December 28, 1777.
[Newbern, 1777.] Broadside.
LOC ph. copy.   43324

North Carolina. Laws, Statutes, etc.,
1777.
An Act for Confiscating the Property of
All . . . as are Inimical to the United
States. . . . December 28, 1777.
[Newbern, 1778.] Broadside.
PRO copy.   43520

[North Carolina. Laws, Statutes, etc.,
1777.
A Complete Revisal of all the Acts of
Assembly.
Newbern, 1777.]
(No 1777 ed. could be located.)   15488

[North Carolina. Laws, Statutes, etc.,
1778.

An Act for Raising Men [Apr. 27, 1778].
[Newbern, 1778.] 2 pp.
(Title from Weeks, No. 45.)　　　　　　15945

North Carolina. Laws, Statutes, etc.,
1787.
... An Act for Appointing Deputies ...
to ... Philadelphia. ... In General
Assembly, January 6, 1787.
[Newbern, 1787.] Broadside.
AAS ph. copy.　　　　　　　　　　　45116

[North Carolina. Laws, Statutes, etc.,
1789.
Regulations for the Exercise and
Discipline of the Cavalry of Halifax
District.
Edenton, Hodge & Wills, 1789.]
(Adv. in State Gazette of N.C., Oct. 15,
1789.)　　　　　　　　　　　　　　22038

North Carolina. Laws, Statutes, etc.,
1791.
Laws of the State. ... By James Iredell.
Edenton, Hodge & Wills, 1791. [4], 712,
xxi, [3] pp.
AAS copy.　　　　　　　　　　　　23641

North Carolina. Laws, Statutes, etc.,
1792.
A Collection of the Statutes of the
Parliament of England in Force in ...
North Carolina.
Newbern, 1792. xxvi, 424, [3] pp.
AAS copy.　　　　　　　　　　　　24627

North Carolina. Laws, Statutes, etc.,
1794.
A Collection of the Private Acts ...
from ... 1715.
Newbern, Martin, 1794. [6], 249, [3] pp.
NCSL copy.　　　　　　　　　　　　27419

North Carolina. Laws, Statutes, etc., 1795.
An Act to Authorize the Secretary to
Issue Grants for Military Lands.
[Halifax, 1795?] Broadside.
(Not located, 1968.)　　　　　　　　47523

North Carolina. Laws, Statutes, etc., 1795.
The Acts of the General Assembly ...
1791 ... 1794.
Newbern, Martin, 1795. [4], 181, [6] pp.,
1 folded table.
NYHS. copy.　　　　　　　　　　　29221

[North Carolina. Laws, Statutes, etc.,
1796.
A Collection of the Statutes of the
Parliament of England in force in ...
North Carolina.
Newbern, Martin, 1796.]
(Apparently a ghost of 24627.)　　　　30909

[North Carolina. Laws, Statutes, etc.,
1799.
The Militia Laws.
Salisbury, 1799.]
("This day is published," North-Carolina
Mercury, June 27, 1799.)　　　　　　35985

North Carolina. Laws, Statutes, etc., 1800.
Index to the Appendix.
n.p., n.d. 8 pp.
(This is the index to 23641 and
supplement.)
AAS copy.　　　　　　　　　　　　38122

North Carolina. Militia, 1781.
Rules and Regulations. ... 25th
September, 1781.
[Wilmington? 1781.] Broadside.
(The one recorded copy cannot now be
located.)　　　　　　　　　　　　44016

North Carolina. Provincial Congress,
1776.
The Journal of the Proceedings [Apr. 4,
1776 +].
Newbern, 1776. 45 pp.
Composite.　　　　　　　　　　　14948

North Carolina. Provincial Congress,
1777.
The Journal of the Proceedings.
Newbern, 1777. 84 pp.
(No complete or legible copy located.)
Composite copy.　　　　　　　　　15489

North Carolina. Senate Journals, 1784.
The Journal of the Senate. ... Begun ...
the Nineteenth Day of April.

Halifax, Davis, 1784. 52 pp.
LOC copy.　　　　　　　　　　　44578

North Carolina. Senate Journals, 1786.
The Journal of the Senate [Nov. 20, 1786 -
Jan. 6, 1787].
[Newbern, 1787.] 76 pp.
LOC copy.　　　　　　　　　　　20595

North Carolina. Senate Journals, 1787.
The Journal of the Senate [Nov. 19 - Dec.
21, 1787].
Newbern, Hodge & Wills, [1788].
51 pp.
LOC copy.　　　　　　　　　　　21339

North Carolina. Senate Journals, 1788.
Journal of the Senate [Nov. 3 - Dec. 6,
1788].
Edenton, Hodge & Wills, [1789].
41 pp.
LOC copy.　　　　　　　　　　　22035

North Carolina. Senate Journals, 1789.
Journal of the Senate [Nov. 2 - Dec. 22,
1789].
[Edenton, 1790.] 52 pp.
LOC copy.　　　　　　　　　　　22740

North Carolina. Senate Journals, 1790.
Journal of the Senate [Nov. 2 - Dec. 15,
1790.]
Edenton, Hodge & Wills, [1791].
60 pp.
NYPL copy.　　　　　　　　　　　23640

North Carolina. Senate Journals, 1791.
Journal of the Senate [Dec. 5, 1791 - Jan.
19, 1792].
[Edenton, 1792.] 48 pp.
NCSL copy.　　　　　　　　　　　24629

North Carolina. Senate Journals, 1792
Journal of the Senate [Nov. 15, 1792 -
Jan. 1, 1793.]
Edenton, Hodge & Wills, [1793]. 50
[2] pp.
NCSL copy.　　　　　　　　　　　25927

North Carolina. Senate Journals, 1793.
Journal of the Senate [Dec. 2, 1793 - Jan.
11, 1794].
Halifax, Hodge & Wills, [1794].
49 pp.
NCSL copy.　　　　　　　　　　　27422

North Carolina. Senate Journals, 1794.
Journal of the Senate [July 7 - 19, 1794].
Newbern, Martin, [1794]. 10 pp.
LOC copy.　　　　　　　　　　　27423

North Carolina. Senate Journals, 1794.
Journal of the Senate [Dec. 30, 1794-Feb.
7, 1795].
Edenton, Hodge & Wills, [1795].
48 pp.
NCSL copy.　　　　　　　　　　　29223

North Carolina. Senate Journals, 1795.
[Journal of the Senate ...
November-December Session, 1795.
Edenton, 1796?] 46 pp.
(The only copy reported lacks the tp.)
NCSL copy.　　　　　　　　　　　30911

North Carolina. Senate Journals, 1796.
Journal of the Senate [Nov. 21-Dec. 25,
1796].
Edenton, Hodge & Wills, [1797].
47 pp.
NYPL copy.　　　　　　　　　　　32594

North Carolina. Senate Journals, 1796.
Journal of the Senate. ... [Nov. 21-Dec.
25, 1796.]
Edenton, Hodge & Wills, [1797].
47 pp.
(Also entered as 32594, q. v.)　　　　34241

North Carolina. Senate Journals, 1797.
Journal of the Senate. ... [Nov. 20-Dec.
23, 1797.]
Halifax, Hodge, [1798]. 44 pp.
N.C. Supreme Court Library.　　　　34243

North Carolina. Senate Journals, 1798.
Journal of the Senate. ... [Nov. 19-Dec.
24, 1798.]
Wilmington, Hall, [1798]. 79 pp.
N. C. Supreme Court Library.　　　　34245

North Carolina. Senate Journals, 1799.

Journal of the Senate [Nov. 18- Dec. 23,
1799.]
[Raleigh, Hodge & Boylan, 1800.]
60 pp.
N. C. Supreme Court Lib., Raleigh, copy.
　　　　　　　　　　　　　　　　38124

North Carolina. Session Laws, 1777.
Acts of Assembly [Apr. 8, 1777 +].
[Newbern, 1777.] 38 pp.
NCU copy.　　　　　　　　　　　15487

North Carolina. Session Laws, 1777.
The Acts of Assembly [Nov. 15, 1777 +].
Newbern, 1778. 84 pp.
NCU copy.　　　　　　　　　　　15943

North Carolina. Session Laws, 1778.
[Acts of Assembly [Apr. 14, 1778+].
Newbern, 1778.] 20 pp.
(All known copies lack the title page.)
NCU copy.　　　　　　　　　　　15944

North Carolina. Session Laws, 1778.
... Acts of Assembly [Aug. 8, 1778 +].
[Newbern, 1778.] 4 pp.
NCU copy.　　　　　　　　　　　15946

North Carolina. Session Laws, 1779.
... Acts of Assembly [Jan. 19, 1779+].
[Newbern, 1779.] 38 pp.
NCU copy.　　　　　　　　　　　16416

North Carolina. Session Laws, 1779.
The Acts of Assembly [May 3, 1779+].
[Newbern, 1779.] 4 pp.
NCU copy.　　　　　　　　　　　16417

North Carolina. Session Laws, 1779.
Acts of Assembly [Oct. 18, 1779+].
[Newbern, 1779.] 34 pp.
NCU copy.　　　　　　　　　　　16418

North Carolina. Session Laws, 1780.
Acts of Assembly [Apr. 17, 1780 +].
[Newbern, 1780.] 16 pp.
NCU copy.　　　　　　　　　　　16913

North Carolina. Session Laws, 1780.
Acts of Assembly [Sept. 5, 1780 +].
[Newbern, 1780.] 11 pp.
NCU copy.　　　　　　　　　　　16914

North Carolina. Session Laws, 1781.
Acts of Assembly [Jan. 18, 1781 +].
[n.p., n.d.] 16, [4] pp.
NCU copy.　　　　　　　　　　　17278

North Carolina. Session Laws, 1781.
Acts of Assembly [June, 1781].
[n.p., n.d.] 16, [4] pp.
NCU copy.　　　　　　　　　　　17279

North Carolina. Session Laws, 1782.
Acts of Assembly [Apr. 13, 1782+].
Halifax [1782]. 56 pp.
NCU copy.　　　　　　　　　　　17644

North Carolina. Session Laws, 1783.
Acts of Assembly [Apr. 18, 1783+].
Halifax, [1783.] 50 pp.
NCU copy.　　　　　　　　　　　18069

North Carolina. Session Laws, 1784.
Acts of Assembly [Apr. 19, 1784+].
Halifax, [1784]. 92, [2] pp.
NCU copy.　　　　　　　　　　　18660

North Carolina. Session Laws, 1784.
Acts of Assembly [Oct. 22, 1784+].
Newburn, [1784]. [2], 64 pp.
NCU copy.　　　　　　　　　　　18661

North Carolina. Session Laws, 1785.
The Laws ... Passed ... December, 1785.
Newbern, 1786. [2], 38 (sic 42) pp.
NCU copy.　　　　　　　　　　　19870

North Carolina. Session Laws, 1786.
The Laws of North-Carolina [Nov. 18,
1786 - Jan. 6, 1787.]
Fayetteville, [1787]. 55, [1] pp.
NCU copy.　　　　　　　　　　　20596

North Carolina. Session Laws, 1787.
The Laws of North-Carolina [Nov. 18 -
Dec. 22, 1787].
Newbern, Hodge & Wills, [1788]. 30,
[2] pp.
NCU copy.　　　　　　　　　　　21340

North Carolina. Session Laws, 1788.

Laws of North-Carolina [Nov. 3 - Dec. 4, 1788].
Edenton, Hodge & Wills, [1789]. 27, [1] pp.
NCU copy.   22036

North Carolina. Session Laws, 1789.
Laws of North-Carolina [Nov. 2 - Dec. 22, 1789].
Edenton, Hodge & Wills, [1790]. 57, [1] pp.
LOC copy.   22741

North Carolina. Session Laws, 1790.
Laws of North-Carolina [Nov. 1 - Dec. 15, 1790].
Edenton, Hodge & Wills, [1790?]. 28 pp.
NCU copy.   23642

North Carolina. Session Laws, 1791.
. . . At a General Assembly . . . at Newbern . . . December [1791].
Edenton, Hodge & Wills, [1791]. 32, [2] pp.
(Not located, 1968.)   46244

North Carolina. Session Laws, 1791.
Laws of North-Carolina [Dec. 5, 1791 - Jan. 19, 1792].
[Edenton, 1792.] pp. 713-732.
NCU copy.   24630

North Carolina. Session Laws, 1792.
Laws of North-Carolina [Nov. 15-Dec. 31, 1792].
Halifax, Hodge & Wills, [1793]. 42 pp.
NCSL copy.   25928

North Carolina. Session Laws, 1793.
Laws of North-Carolina [Dec. 2, 1793-Jan. 11, 1794].
Edenton, Hodge & Wills, [1794]. 34, [1] pp.
NYPL copy.   27424

North Carolina. Session Laws, 1794.
Laws of North Carolina [July 7 - 18, 1794].
Newbern, Martin, [1794]. 9, [1] pp.
LOC copy.   27425

North Carolina. Session Laws, 1794.
Laws of North Carolina [July 7-18, 1794.]
Newbern, Martin, [1794]. 9, [1] pp.
HC-L copy.   47142

North Carolina. Session Laws, 1794.
Laws of North-Carolina [Dec. 30, 1794-Feb. 7, 1795].
Halifax, Hodge & Wills, [1795]. 39, [1] pp.
NCSL copy.   29224

North Carolina. Session Laws, 1794.
Laws of North-Carolina [Dec. 30, 1794-Feb. 7, 1795].
Halifax, Hodge & Wills, [1795]. 39, [1] pp.
HC-L copy.   47524

North Carolina. Session Laws, 1795.
Laws of North-Carolina [Nov. 2 - Dec. 9, 1795].
Edenton, Hodge & Wills, [1796]. 31, [1] pp.
NCSL copy.   30912

North Carolina. Session Laws, 1796.
Laws of North-Carolina [Nov. 21 - Dec. 25, 1796].
[Edenton, 1797.] 45 pp., irreg.
NYPL copy.   32595

North Carolina. Session Laws, 1796.
Laws of North-Carolina [Nov. 21 - Dec. 25, 1796].
Halifax, Hodge & Wills, [1797]. 68 pp.
LOC copy.   32596

North Carolina. Session Laws, 1797.
Laws of North-Carolina [Nov. 20-Dec. 23, 1797].
Halifax, Hodge, [1798]. 25 pp.
N.C. Supreme Court Library.   34246

North Carolina. Session Laws, 1798.
Laws of North-Carolina [Nov. 19-Dec. 24, 1798].
[Wilmington, 1799.] 27 pp.
(This ed. is the supplement to 23641.)
AAS copy.   35984

North Carolina. Session Laws, 1798.

Laws of North-Carolina. [Nov. 19-Dec. 24, 1798.]
Wilmington, Hall, [1798]. 58 pp.
N.C. Supreme Court Library.   34247

North Carolina. Session Laws, 1799.
Laws of North-Carolina [Nov. 18-Dec. 23, 1799].
n. p., n. d. 20 pp.
(This is the supplement to 23641.)
AAS copy.   38126

North Carolina. Session Laws, 1799.
Laws of North-Carolina [Nov. 18 - Dec. 23, 1799].
[Raleigh], Hodge & Boylan, [1800]. 41, [3] pp.
NCU copy.   38125

North Carolina. Treasurer, 1788.
An Account of the Monies Received . . . 1787.
[Newbern, 1788.] 12 pp.
LOC copy.   21336

North Carolina. University.
Laws of the University . . . December, 1799.
Raleigh, Gales, 1800. 24 pp.
NCU copy.   38130

[The North-Carolina Almanack for 1769.
Williamsburg, Va., Rind, 1768.]
("Just published," Va. Gazette, Aug. 25, 1768.)   41861

[The North-Carolina Almanac, for . . . 1791.
Fayetteville, Roulstone? for Sibley.]
(Adv. N. C. Chronicle, Oct. 4, 1790.)
                                        22742

[North-Carolina almanac for 1792.
Newbern, Martin, 1791.]
(McMurtrie North Carolina 171. No copy known.)   46245

The North-Carolina Almanack, for . . . 1797.
Newbern, Martin, [1796]. [36] pp.
(Not located, 1968.)   47869

The North-Carolina Almanack for . . . 1799.
Newbern, Osborn. 38 pp.
(The only copy recorded is imperfect.)
NCU copy.   34248

The North-Carolina Almanac, for . . . 1799.
Salisbury, Coupee. [40] pp.
LOC copy.   34249

[The North-Carolina Almanack, for . . . 1801.
Salisbury, Coupee.] [44] pp.
(The only known copy lacks tp.)
(Too fragile to copy.)   49124

North Carolina. A Table of the Numbers of Taxables [by John Burgwyn, 1731-1803].
n. p., [1770?] [2] folding tables.
MHS copy.   42072

North-Kingstown Academy.
Charter of the. . . . In General Assembly, June Session, A. D. 1800.
n.p., n. d. 8 pp.
AAS copy.   38383

Northampton, Mass. First Church, Ecclesiastical Council, 1742.
A Copy of the Resolves of the Council . . . May 11, 1742.
Boston, Kneeland & Green, 1742. 6 pp.
LOC copy.   40283

Northampton, Mass. First Church, Ecclesiastical Council, 1750.
The Result of a Council of Nine Churches met at Northampton, June 22, 1750.
[Boston, 1750.] 8 pp.
AAS copy.   6577

Northampton Co., Pa.
Sale of a Forfeited Estate. . . . Christian Hook. . . . September 16th, 1788.
Philadelphia, Aitken, [1788]. Broadside.
LOC copy.   45314

Northern Inland Lock Navigation Co.
The Northern Inland Lock Navigation

Company, will purchase. . . . October 10th, 1792.
Albany, Websters, [1792]. Broadside.
(The only known copy is mislaid.)   24634

Northern Inland Lock Navigation Co.
A Report of the Committee . . . to Examine Hudsons River.
[New York], Durell, [1792]. 20 pp.
AAS copy.   24635

A Northern Light.
Troy, N. Y., Moffitt, 1800. 101, iii, [2] pp.
(Also mentioned as 36775, q. v.)   38133

A Northern Light; or A New Index to the Bible [by Matthew Adgate].
Albany, N. Y., Barber & Southwick, 1800. 108 pp.]
(Entry from Evans.)   36776

A Northern Light; or a New Index to the Bible [by Matthew Adgate].
Troy, N. Y., Moffitt, 1800. 101, iii, [2] pp.
AAS copy.   36775

Northern Missionary Society in the State of New York.
The Constitution of the. . . .
Schenectady, Wyckoff, 1797. 19 pp.
AAS copy.   32601

Northwest Territory, U. S. House Journals, 1799.
Journal of the House. . . . First Session . . . 1799.
Cincinnati, Carpenter & Findlay, 1800. 211 pp.
OH&PS copy.   38134

Northwest Territory, U.S. House Journals, 1800.
Journal of the House . . . Second Session of the First General Assembly.
Chillicothe, Winship & Willis, 1800. 131 pp.
AAS copy.   38135

Northwest Territory, U. S. Laws, Statutes, etc., 1796.
Laws of the Territory.
Cincinnati, Maxwell, 1796. 225 pp.
LOC copy.   30916

[Northwest Territoy, U. S. Laws, Statutes, etc., 1796.
A Table of the Variations in the Laws.
Cincinnati, Freeman, 1796.]
(The adv. quoted by Evans has not been located.)   30917

Northwest Territory, U. S. Laws, Statutes, etc., 1799.
Laws . . . Passed at the First Session of the General Assembly . . . also Certain Laws Enacted by the Governor.
Cincinnati, Carpenter & Findlay, 1800. 280 pp.
WRHS copy.   38137

[Northwest Territory, U. S. Laws, Statutes, etc., 1799.
The Militia Law. Act of December 13, 1799.
Cincinnati, 1800.]
(Adv. Western Spy. May 28, 1800.)   38138

Northwest Territory, U. S. Legislative Council Journals, 1799.
Journal of the Legislative Council [Sept. 16, 1799 +].
Cincinnati, Carpenter & Findlay, [1799]. [1], 103 pp.
OH & PS copy.   35994

Northwest Territory, U. S. Legislative Council Journals, 1800.
Journal of the Legislative Council. . . . Second Session . . . November . . . 1800.
Chillicothe, Winship & Willis, 1800. 77 pp.
OH&PS copy.   38136

Northwest Territory, U.S. Session Laws, 1788.
Laws Passed in the Territory [July 1788 - Dec. 31, 1791].
Philadelphia, Childs & Swaine, 1792. 68, [2] pp.
LOC copy.   24633

Northwest Territory, U. S. Session Laws, 1794.

Laws Passed . . . from July to December.
Philadelphia, Childs & Swaine, 1794. 74,
[2] pp.
JCB copy.   27428

Northwest Territory, U. S. Session Laws,
1798.
Laws of the Territory . . . April . . . 1798.
Cincinnati, Freeman, 1798. 32 pp.
NYPL copy.   34257

Norton, Elijah.
Fools in their Folly.
Litchfield, 1785. 24 pp.
Robert L. Fisher copy.   19147

Norton, Elijah.
The Impossibility of Sinners' Coming.
Suffield, Ct., Farnsworths, 1798.
48 pp.
AAS copy.   34258

Norton, Elijah.
Methodism Examined.
Windsor, Spooner, 1791. 24 pp.
AAS copy.   23645

Norton, Elijah.
Salvation for All Men.
Windsor, Spooner, 1794. 23 pp.
VtSL copy.   27429

Norton, John, 1606-1663.
(D. A. B.)
A Brief Catechisme.
Cambridge, 1660. 22 pp.
(Only known copies are defective.)
NYPL copy.   63

[Norton, John, 1606-1663.
(D. A. B.)
Brief Catechisme.
Cambridge, 1666.]
(Mentioned by T. Prince. No copy
known.)   110

Norton, John, 1606-1663.
(S. E. Morison, Founding, p. 392.)
The Heart of N-England Rent.
Cambridge, 1659. [2], 58 pp.
AAS copy.   56

Norton, John, 1606-1663.
(S. E. Morison, Founding, p. 392.)
Three Choice and Profitable Sermons.
Cambridge, 1664. [6], 38 pp.
AAS copy.   90

Norton, John, 1651-1716.
(Sibley, II, 394-396.)
An Essay Tending to Promote
Reformation.
Boston, 1708. [2], 29 pp.
AAS copy.   1369

Norton, John, 1716-1778.
(Dexter, I 587-588.)
The Redeemed Captive.
Boston, 1748. 40 pp.
AAS copy.   6211

Norton, Noah U.
An Oration . . . Delivered at Southington,
March 7, 1791.
Danbury, Douglas & Ely, 1791. 12 pp.
CHS copy.   23646

Norwich, Ct. Charter.
The Charter, of the City of Norwich. . . .
May, 1784.
Norwich, Trumbull, 1784. 16 pp.
BA copy.   18663

Norwich, Ct. Convention, Sept. 8, 1774.
At a Meeting of Delegates of the Towns in
the Counties of New-London.
Norwich, Spooner, [1774]. Broadside.
AAS copy.   42660

Norwich, Ct. Franklin Library Co.
The Constitution of the. . . .
Norwich, Trumbull, 1794. 8 pp.
AAS copy.   27430

Norwich, Ct. Ordinances, etc. 1780.
At a Town-Meeting, held . . . the
Twenty-Fourth Day of June . . . Voted . . .
that a Committee of Fifty. . . .
[Norwich? 1780?] Broadside.
JCB copy.   43858

Norwich, Ct. Selectmen, 1778.

An Account of the Prices of Articles as
Stated. . . . March, 1778.
[Norwich], Green & Spooner, [1778]. [2]
pp.
CHS copy.   43521

[Norwich, Ct. Town Meeting, 1779.
At an Adjourned Town Meeting. . . . Mar.
29, 1779.
[Norwich, 1779.] Broadside.]
(The origin of the entry is unknown.)
                                             16420

Norwich, Ct. Town Warrant, 1796.
To Mr. Benjamin Tracy. By Virtue of a
Special Statute. . . . 24th of Oct. 1796.
[Norwich, 1796.] Broadside.
CHS copy.   47870

Norwich, August 26. The Following
Interesting Intelligence.
Norwich, Trumbull, [1779]. Broadside.
NYPL ph. copy.   43676

[Norwich Mutual Assurance Company.
Insurance Policy of the. . . .
Norwich, Ct., Hubbard, 1798. Broadside.]
(No copy located.)   34259

A Nosegay, for the Young Men [by James
Carey, d. 1801].
Philadelphia, [1796]. 16 pp.
LOC copy.   33494

A Nosegay for the Young Men. . . . By
Thomas Griendbif [by James Carey, d.
1801].
Philadelphia (New York), [1798]. 16 pp.
(Apparently a ghost of 33494.)   33495

Nosum Nosorum.
Philadelphia, 1762. 8 pp.
HSP copy.   9223

The Note-Maker Noted.
[Philadelphia], 1743. 31 pp.
LCP copy.   5263

[Notes and Observations upon the Votes
of the House of Assembly of the Colony of
New-Jersey . . . the 16th of October, 1742.
[New York?], 1743.]
(Sabin 55952, but apparently a ghost.)
                                              5264

Notes of a Few Decisions in the Superior
Courts of . . . North Carolina [Francois
Xavier Martin, 1764-1846].
Newbern, Martin, 1797. [8], 78, 83, [8]
pp.
HC-L copy.   48173

Notes on Farming.
New York, 1787. 38 pp.
AAS copy.   20599

Notes on the Establishment of a Money
Unit [by Thomas Jefferson, Pres. U. S.,
1743-1826].
[Annapolis, 1784.] 14 pp.
LOC copy.   18541

Notes on the Finances of the State of
South-Carolina [by Henry William
Desaussure, 1763-1839].
Charleston, Young, [1799]. xii, 32 pp., 3
tables.
AAS copy.   35977

Notes on the Slave Trade [by Anthony
Benezet, 1713-1784].
[Philadelphia, 1781.] 8 pp.
AAS copy.   17095

[Notes on the Two Reports from the
Committee of the Honourable House of
Assembly of Jamaica.
Philadelphia, 1794.]
(Imprint assumed by Evans from advs. for
London printing.)   27432

Notes upon Luke xvii. 30.
Boston, 1800. 23 pp.
AAS copy.   38140

Notes upon Scripture Texts.
Boston, 1798. 24 pp.
BA copy.   34261

[Noth und Hülfsbüchlein für
Bauersleute.
Philadelphia, Neal & Kammerer, 1796.]
(Entry from Seidensticker, p. 145.)   30920

Notice is hereby Given to the
Surveyor-General . . . of the Several
Districts within the last Indian Purchase.
. . . May 17, 1785.
[Philadelphia, 1785.] Broadside.
BPL copy.   44750

Notice. The Citizens of New-York, who
are Determined to Support the
Constitution. . . . April 21, 1796.
[New York, 1796.] Broadside.
(Not located, 1968.)   47871

Nott, Eliphalet, 1773-1866.
Federal Money.
Cooperstown, Phinney, 1797. [6] pp.
Union College Library copy.   32603

Nott, Samuel, 1754-1852.
A Funeral Oration, upon the Death of
Samuel Gurley.
New Haven, [1778]. 15 pp.
AAS copy.   15949

Nott, Samuel, 1754-1852.
A Sermon, Delivered at the Ordination of
the Rev. Oliver Ayer.
Stockbridge, Andrews, 1793. 24 pp.
AAS copy.   25932

Nott, Samuel, 1754-1852.
A Sermon, Preached at the Interment of
. . . Joseph Hunt.
Norwich, Trumbull, 1786. 36 pp.
AAS copy.   19874

Nourse, G.
The History of the Independents.
Frankfort, Ky., Hunter & Beaumont,
1799. 12 pp.
University of Chicago copy.   35998

Nova Scotia. Governor, 1759.
. . . By his Excellency Charles Lawrence.
. . . A Proclamation. Whereas since the
Issuing . . . [Dated Jan. 11, 1759.]
Boston, J. Draper, 1759. Broadside.
MHS copy.   41070

Nova Scotia. House of Assembly, 1775.
Extract from the Votes of the House.
Boston, Draper, 1775. 13 pp.
AAS copy.   14357

Novion, Citoyen de, pseud.
The Altar of Baal Thrown Down [by
James Sullivan, 1744-1808].
Boston, Adams & Larkin, 1795. 31 pp.
AAS copy.   29585

Novion, Citoyen de, pseud.
The Altar of Baal Thrown Down [by
James Sullivan, 1744-1808]. [2nd Issue,
without halftitle and tailpiece.]
Boston, Adams & Larkin, 1795. 31 pp.
NYPL copy.   29586

Novion, Citoyen de, pseud.
The Altar of Baal Thrown Down [by
James Sullivan, 1744-1808].
Philadelphia, 1795. 32 pp.
LCP copy.   29587

Novion, Citoyen de, pseud.
The Altar of Baal Thrown Down [by
James Sullivan, 1744-1808].
Stockbridge, Andrews, 1795. 28 pp.
AAS copy.   29588

Now in Press, and next Week will be
Published. . . . The True Art of Every
Kind of Wine and Spirits.
[Philadelphia, 1771.] Broadside.
LCP copy.   12170

Now in the Press, and will be Speedily
Published, The Life and Adventures of a
Certain Quaker.
[Philadelphia, 1766.] Broadside.
LCP copy.   10433

Nowell, Alexander, 1645-1672.
(Sibley, II, 148-149.)
MDCLXV. An Almanack.
Cambridge, 1665. [16] pp.
AAS copy.   104

[Nowell, Samuel], 1634-1688.
(Sibley, I, 335-352.)
Abraham in Arms.
Boston, 1678. [4], 19 pp.
AAS copy.   256

Noxon, Thomas.
Mr. Noxon's Observations.
New York, 1732. Broadside.
NYPL copy.   3585

Noyes, Belcher, 1709-1785.
Advertisement.... Pursuant to a
Warrant.... Boston, November 13th, 1751.
[Boston, 1751.] Broadside.
MHS copy.   40599

Noyes, Belcher, 1709-1785.
To be Sold, one Moiety or half part of the
Island of Roanoke.... Boston, May 26th,
1740.
[Boston, 1740.] Broadside.
Duke Univ. copy.   40207

[Noyes, Belcher], 1746-1791.
(Sibley, VIII, 239.)
The Rudiments of Latin Syntax and
Prosody.
Salem, Hall, 1783. 51 pp.
AAS copy.   18072

[Noyes, James, 1608-1656.
A Short Catechism.
Cambridge, 1641.]
(Probably not printed at this time.)   7

Noyes, James, 1608-1656.
(S. E. Morison, Founding, pp. 392-393.)
A Short Catechism.
Cambridge, 1661. 16 pp.
AAS copy.   67

[Noyes, James, 1608-1656.
(S. E. Morison, Founding, pp. 392-393.)
A Short Catechism.
Boston, 1676. 15 pp.]
(Known only from the Addenda to S. F.
Haven's list, 1874.)   222

Noyes, James, 1608-1656.
(S. E. Morison, Founding, pp. 392-393.)
A Short Catechism.
Boston, 1694. 15 pp.
AAS copy.   707

Noyes, James, 1608-1656.
(S. E. Morison, Founding, pp. 392-393.)
A Short Catechism.
Boston, 1714. 15 pp.
NYPL copy.   1708

Noyes, James, 1608-1656.
A Short Catechism.
Newburyport, Barrett & March, 1797. 13
pp.
(No perfect copy located.)
BPL copy.   32604

Noyes, James. 1778-1799.
An Astronomical Diary or Almanack, for
... 1797.
Dover, N.H. [24] pp.
LOC copy.   30921

Noyes, James, 1778-1799.
The Federal Arithmetic.
Exeter, Ranlet, 1797. 128 pp.
AAS copy.   32605

Noyes, James, 1778-1799.
Ladd's Pocket Almanack, for ... 1794.
... To which is Annexed, The
New-Hampshire Register.
Dover, Ladd. [84] pp.
NL copy.   25934

Noyes, James, 1778-1799.
The New-Hampshire and Massachusetts,
Pocket Almanack, for ... 1794.
[Dover], New Hampshire. [24] pp.
(Evans' entry was from advs.)
AAS copy.   25933

Noyes, Moses, 1643-1729.
A Sermon, Delivered by the Rev. Mr.
N-o-y-e-s.
Vermont, 1785. 8 pp.
AAS copy.   19149

Noyes, Nathaniel, 1735-1810.
A Dialogue between Paimen and Agamos.

Newburyport, Mycall, 1792. 16 pp.
AAS copy.   24637

Noyes, Nathaniel, 1735-1810.
Man on Probation for the World to Come.
Newburyport, Barrett, 1797. 19 pp.
BA copy.   32606

Noyes, Nathaniel, 1735-1810.
A Sermon Preached at South-Hampton
December 2, 1784.
Newburyport, Mycall, 1785. 23 pp.
AAS copy.   19150

Noyes, Nicholas, 1647-1717.
May 28th, 1706. To my Worthy Friend,
Mr. James Bayley.... A Poem.
[Boston, 1707.] Broadside.
BPL copy.   39456

Noyes, Nicholas, 1647-1717.
(Sibley, II, 239-246.)
New-Englands Duty and Interest.
Boston, 1698. [12], 99 pp.
AAS copy.   850

Noyes, Nicholas, 1647-1717.
Upon the Much Lamented Death of ...
Mrs. Mary Gerrish ... November 17th,
1710.
[Boston, 1710.] Broadside.
BPL copy.   39515

[Noyes, Oliver], 1675-1721.
(Sibley, IV, 260-264.)
A Letter from a Gentleman, Containing
some Remarks.
Boston, Kneeland for Boone, Gray, and
Edwards, 1720. 15 pp.
LOC copy.   2163

Noyes, Thomas, 1769-1837.
A Discourse Delivered at Fitchburg.
Leominster, Mass., Prentiss, 1797. 22 pp.
AAS copy.   32607

Eine Nuetzliche Anweisung.
Germantown, 1751. [4], 288, [4], 288, [4]
pp.
NYPL copy.   6777

Eine Nuetzliche Anweisung.
Germantown, 1762. [4], 287, [4] pp.
(A duplicate of 9264, q.v.)   9224

Eine Nuetzliche Anweisung [by
Christopher Sower, 1721-1784].
Germantown, 1762. [2], 287, [5] pp.
AAS copy.   9264

Eine Nuetzliche Anweisung.... Dritte
Auflage [by Christopher Sower,
1721-1784].
Germantown, 1772. [8], 262 pp.
AAS copy.   12552

Eine Nützliche Anweisung.... Vierte
und Vermehrte Auflage [by Christopher
Sower, 1721-1784].
Germantown, Leibert, 1792. [4], 282 pp.
AAS copy.   24771

Nugae Canorae; Consisting of a few
Minor Poems [by Richard Beresford,
1755-1803].
Charleston, S. C., Young, 1797. 28 pp.
AAS copy.   31802

Nugent, Henry Paul.
Mr. Nugent's Vindication.
[Albany, N. Y.], 1799. v, 40 pp.
AAS copy.   35999

[A Number of citizens of the fourth
district.
Hagerstown? 1800?]
(Minick 618; no copy known.)   49125

A Number of Englishmen have heretofore
Arrived in this Province....
[Philadelphia, 1772.] Broadside.
NYPL copy.   42362

A Number of the Subscribers....
September 17, 1770.

[Philadelphia, 1770.] Broadside.
LOC copy.   11793

(No. 1) A Circular Letter from a
Philadelphian.
Philadelphia, [1789]. Broadside.
(No copy located.)   45545

No. 3. The Dougliad. On Liberty.
[New York, 1770.] 4 pp.
LCP copy.   11638

(No. 33, Smith-Street.) To the Inhabitants
of New-York.... May 13, 1790 [by William
Rollinson, 1762-1842].
[New York, 1790.] Broadside.
NYHS copy.   22857

Nun will Ich Valediceren.
[New York, 1769.] Broadside.
LCP copy.   11389

Nunc Dimittis briefly Descanted on [by
Cotton Mather, 1663-1728].
Boston, 1709. [6], 42, 8 pp.
AAS copy.   1405

Nurse, John.
John Nurse, Carrier of the Essex Gazette
... 1774.
[Salem, 1774.] Broadside.
EI copy.   13271

[Nurse Truelove's Christmas Box....
First Worcester Edition.
Worcester, Thomas, 1786. 27 pp.]
(No copy of the first ed. is known.) 20030

Nurse Truelove's Christmas Box.
Hartford, Patten, 1789. 26+ pp.
(The only known copy is imperfect.)
CHS copy.   45546

Nurse Truelove's Christmas Box....
Second Worcester Edition.
Worcester, Thomas, 1789. 27, [5] pp.
AAS copy.   22188

[Nurse Truelove's Christmas Box.
Boston, Hall, 1794? 32 pp.?]
(Known only by this fragment.)
AAS copy.   47143

Nurse Truelove's Christmas Box.
Boston, Hall, 1795. 26 pp.
(The only copy reported cannot now be
found.)   29658

Nurse Truelove's Christmas Box....
Third Worcester Edition.
Worcester, Thomas, Son & Thomas, 1796.
29, [1] pp., printed wrappers.
AAS copy.   31317

Nurse Truelove's New-Year's Gift....
First Worcester Edition.
Worcester, Thomas, 1786. 58, [6] pp.
AAS copy.   20033

Nurse Truelove's New-Year's Gift.
Plymouth, [Mass.], Coverly, 1787. 32 pp.
AAS copy.   45117

[Nurse Truelove's New-Year's Gift.
Boston, Hall, 1793.]
Lunenberg Hist. Soc. copy.   26284

Nurse Truelove's New Year's Gift....
Second Worcester Edition.
Worcester, Thomas, 1794. 58, [4] pp.
(The only copy located is defective.)
AAS copy.   27820

Nurse Truelove's New-Year's Gift.
[Boston, Hall, 1796.] 58, [5] pp.
(No perfect copy known.)
AAS copy.   47872

Nurse Truelove's New Year's Gift....
Third Worcester Edition.
Worcester, Thomas, 1800. 61 pp.
d'Alté A. Welch copy.   49126

Nutzliche gegen Nachricht.
[New York, 1769.] Broadside.
LCP copy.   11390

O

O Come away my Soldier Bonny [by
William Shield, 1748-1829].
Philadelphia, Willig, [1798]. [2] pp.
AAS copy.   34262

O Dear What can the Matter Be. A
Favorite Song or Duett.
Philadelphia, Carr [1793]. [2] pp.
(Evans' entry from advs.)
NYPL copy.   25936

[O Had it Been my Happy Lot.
Boston, von Hagen, 1798.]
(Imprint assumed by Evans from von
Hagen's adv.)   34263

O! Justitia. A Complete Trial.
[Philadelphia, 1765.] 16 pp.
LCP copy.   10110

O Liberty, thou Goddess Heavenly
Bright.
[New York, 1732.] 3 pp.
NYPL copy.   3595

[Oakes, Urian], 1631-1681.
(Sibley, I, 173-185.)
. . . An Almanack . . . for . . . 1650.
Cambridge, 1650. 16 pp.
(The unique copy lacks the final leaf.)
HEH copy.   32

[Oakes, Urian], 1631-1681.
(Sibley, I, 173-185.)
An Elegie upon . . . Thomas Shepard.
Cambridge, 1677. 16 pp.
BrU copy.   240

Oakes, Urian, 1631-1681.
(D. A. B.)
New-England Pleaded With.
Cambridge, 1673. [6], 64 pp.
AAS copy.   180

Oakes, Urian, 1631-1681.
(Sibley, I, 173-185.)
A Seasonable Discourse.
Cambridge, 1682. [6], 23 (i.e. 33) pp.
AAS copy.   325

Oakes, Urian, 1631-1681.
The Soveraign Efficacy.
Boston, Sewall, 1682. [6], 40, [1] pp.
MHS copy.   326

Oakes, Urian, 1631-1681.
(Sibley, I, 173-185.)
The Unconquerable.
Cambridge, 1674. [6], 40 pp.
AAS copy.   195

Oaths Appointed to be Taken Instead of
the Oaths of Allegiance.
[Boston, 1699?] Broadside.
HEH copy.   39353

Obadiah Palmer . . . Against Jacobus van
Cortland . . . in Cancellaria Novae
Eborac.
[New York, 1727.] 58 pp.
AAS copy.   2940

O'Beirne, Thomas Lewis, 1748-1823.
A Sermon Preached at St. Paul's, New-
York.
New York, Gaine, 1776. 20 pp.
BA copy.   14952

O'Beirne, Thomas Lewis, 1748-1823.
A Sermon, Preached at St. Paul's, New
York, September 22, 1776.
[New York, 1776.] 15 pp.
NYPL copy.   43110

O'Beirne, Thomas Lewis, 1748-1823.
A Sermon Preached at St. Paul's, New-
York, September 22, 1776.
New York, Gaine, 1776. 20 pp.
BA copy.   43111

Objections to the Bank of Credit [by
Paul Dudley, 1675-1751].
Boston, 1714. 32 pp.
AAS copy.   1675

O'Brien, Matthew, fl. 1800.
Charity Sermon.
Philadelphia, Carey, 1800. 21 pp.
(The only recorded copy is now mislaid.)
                                             38141

Observanda [by Cotton Mather, 1663-
1728].
Boston, 1695. 56 pp.
AAS copy.   726

Observations and Prognostications on the
Urine.
n.p., 1782. [4], 33, [6] pp.
LOC copy.   44242

Observations and Propositions for an
Accommodation between Great Britain
and her Colonies. . . . 10th Oct. 1768.
[New York? 1768.] 3 pp.
AAS copy.   41862

Observations and Remarks on the Putrid
Malignant Sore-Throat [by Hall Jackson,
1739-1797].
Portsmouth, Melcher, 1786. 28 pp.
AAS copy.   19732

Observations Concerning the Funding
System of Pennsylvania.
Philadelphia, Aitken, 1789. 16 pp.
AAS copy.   22042

Observations Leading to a Fair
Examination [by Richard Henry Lee,
1732-1794].
[New York], 1777 (1787). 40 pp.
AAS copy.   20454

Observations Leading to a Fair
Examination [by Richard Henry Lee,
1732-1794].
[New York], 1787. 40 pp.
AAS copy.   20455

Observations Leading to a Fair
Examination [by Richard Henry Lee,
1732-1794].
[New York]. Re-Printed by Order of a
Society of Gentlemen, 1787. 40 pp.
AAS copy.   20456

Observations Occasioned by Writings
against Alterations.
Portsmouth, Osbornes, 1792. 23 pp.
AAS copy.   24638

Observations on a late Epitaph.
Philadelphia, Armbruster, [1764]. 8 pp.
LCP copy.   9772

Observations on a late Pamphlet,
Entituled, "Considerations upon the
Society . . . of the Cincinnati."
Philadelphia, Bell, 1783. 28, [4] pp.
AAS copy.   18073

Observation on a late Pamphlet
Entituled, "Considerations on the Society
. . . of the Cincinnati."
Hartford, Hudson & Goodwin, 1784.
18 pp.
AAS copy.   18665

Observations on a late Pamphlet entitled
"Considerations on the . . . Cincinnati."
Hartford, Webster, 1784. 22 pp.
CHS copy.   44579

Observations, on a Letter from George
Nicholas of Kentucky.
Cincinnati, Freeman, 1799. 46 pp.
OH & PS copy.   36000

[Observations on a Pamphlet, Published
in Philadelphia.
Baltimore, 1788.]
("Now in press," Wheeler 479a.)   45315

Observations on a Variety of Subjects,
Literary, Moral and Religious [by Jacob
Duché, 1738-1798].
Philadelphia, Bell, 1774. x, 241, [1] pp.
(Except for title-page, the same as 13258,
q. v. for text.)
LOC copy.   13259

Observations on a Variety of Subjects,
Literary, Moral and Religious [by Jacob
Duché, 1738-1798].
Philadelphia, Dunlap, 1774. x, 241,
[1] pp.
AAS copy.   13258

Observations on Accidental Fires.
New York, Oram for Swords and Belden,
1797. 40 pp.
NYPL copy.   32608

[Observations on African Slavery.
New Haven, 1784.]
("Just Published," New Haven Gazette,
Nov. 18, 1784.)   18666

[Observations on, and a Reply to a Card
[by William Crane, M.D.].
Boston, England, 1795. 22 pp.]   28500

Observations on Conventions [by William
Pitt Smith, 1760-1796].
New York, Harrisson, 1793. 13 pp.
MHS copy.   26176

Observations on Dr. Mackrill's History of
the Yellow Fever.
Baltimore, Hayes, 1796. 60 pp.
NLM copy.   30922

Observations on 1st. the Chronology of
Scripture. . . .
New York, Greenleaf, 1795. 141 pp.
AAS copy.   29230

Observations on Free Masonry [by
Abigail (Blodget) Stickney Lyon,
1751-1808].
Worcester, Mass., 1798. 14 pp.
AAS copy.   34027

Observations on Government, Including
some Animadversions on Mr. Adams's
Defence [by John Stevens, 1749-1838].
New York, Ross, 1787. 56 pp.
(Usually assigned to William Livingston, but
the draft in Stevens' hand is at the Stevens
Institute.)
LCP copy.   20465

Observations on Mr. Buckminster's
Sermon [by Daniel Humphreys?,
1740-1827].
Portsmouth, N. H., Peirce, 1796. 23 pp.
AAS copy.   30606

Observations, on Mr. Justice Livingston's
Address. . . . Dec. 6, 1769.
[New York, 1769.] 4 pp.
LOC copy.   11391

[Observations on Novel-Reading.
Philadelphia, Dobson, 1792?]
(Entry from an adv.)   24639

Observations on Samuel Shepard's Three
Letters [by Moses Brown, 1738-1836].
Providence, Carter, 1793. 23 pp.
AAS copy.   25233

Observations on Several Acts of
Parliament.
[Boston], Edes & Gill, 1769. [2], 24 pp.
AAS copy.   11392

[Observations on Several Acts of
Parliament.
Boston, Edes & Gill, 1769. 24 pp.]
(Apparently this is a ghost of 11392.)
     11393

[Observations on the Act for Granting
Excise on Wine.
Boston, [1720].]
(Adv. Boston Gazette, May 23, 1720.)
     2164

Observations on the Agriculture,
Manufacture and Commerce of the United
States [by Tench Coxe, 1755-1824].
New York, Childs & Swaine, 1789. 102 pp.
AAS copy.   21774

Observations on the Alien & Sedition
Laws of the United States.
Washington, Pa., Colerick, 1799.
43 pp.
AAS copy.   36001

Observations on the Angina Maligna [by
John Kearsley, d. 1777].
Philadelphia, Bradfords, 1769. 7 pp.
Library of the College of Physicians,
Philadelphia, copy.   11449

Observations on the Articles of
Confederation of the Thirteen United
States of America, Entered into in July,
1778.
New York, Loudons, [1787]. 16 pp.
LCP copy.   20600

Observations on the Commerce of Spain.
Philadelphia, Carey, 1800. pp. [i]-vii, [4],
[9]-63, 1 folded table.
APS copy.   38142

Observations on the Commerce of the
American States [by John Baker Holroyd,
1st Earl of Sheffield, 1735-1821].
Philadelphia, Bell, 1783. [2], 77 pp.
LOC copy.   17975

Observations on the Commerce of the
American States [by John Baker Holroyd,
1st Earl of Sheffield, 1735-1821].
Philadelphia, Bell, 1783. [2], 77,
[1] pp.
AAS copy.   17976

Observations on the Doctrines [by John
Tucker, 1719-1792].
Boston, Edes & Gill, 1757. 70 pp.
AAS copy.   8050

Observations on the Emigration of Dr.
Joseph Priestly [by William Cobbett,
1763-1835].
New York, 1794. 40 pp.
HC copy.   26778

Observations on the Emigration of Dr.
William Priestley [by William Cobbett,
1763-1835].
Philadelphia, Bradford, 1794.
(Adv. as "This day published" in Gazette
of the U.S., July 25, 1794, but all located
copies are the London reprint.)   26777

Observations on the Emigration of Dr.
Joseph Priestley, and on the Several
Addresses. . . . Third Edition [by William
Cobbett, 1763-1835].
Philadelphia, Bradford, 1795. 88 pp.
AAS copy.   28439

Observations on the Emigration of Dr.
Joseph Priestley: to which is Added, a
Comprehensive Story [by William Cobbett,
1763-1835].
[Philadelphia], Folwell, [1795].
88 pp.
NL copy.   28440

Observations on the Emigration of Dr.
Joseph Priestley [by William Cobbett,
1763-1835].
Philadelphia, Bradford, 1796. 64 pp.
AAS copy.   30217

Bradford's Fourth Edition. Observations
on the Emigration of Dr. Joseph Priestley
[by William Cobbett, 1763-1835].
Philadelphia, Bradford, 1796. 88 pp.
AAS copy.   30218

Observations on the Fourth and Fifth
Articles of the Preliminaries for a Peace
[by Meriwether Smith].
Richmond, Dixon & Holt, [1783].
28 pp.
JCB copy.   44454

Observations on the Importance of the
Northern Colonies [by Archibald
Kennedy, 1685-1763].
New York, 1750. [4], 36 pp.
AAS copy.   6524

Observations on the Influence of the
Moon.
Philadelphia, Folwell, 1798. 24 pp.
AAS copy.   34264

Observations on the Inslaving, Importing
and Purchasing of Negroes [by Anthony
Benezet, 1713-1784].
Germantown, 1759. 15 pp.
HSP copy.   8298

Observations on the Inslaving. . . . Second
Edition [by Anthony Benezet, 1713-1784].
Germantown, 1760. 16 pp.
AAS copy.   8542

Observations on the Justicative Memorial
[by Pierre Auguste Caron de
Beaumarchais, 1732-1799].
Philadelphia, Bailey, 1781. 129 pp.
AAS copy.   17093

Observations on the Late and Present
Conduct of the French [by William Clark,
1709-1760].
Boston, Kneeland, 1755. [8], iv, 47, [1],
15 pp.
AAS copy.   7389

Observations on the Late Law for
Regulating the Nightly Watch. . . .
January 10, 1771.
[Philadelphia, 1771.] Broadside.
LCP copy.   12171

Observations on the late Popular
Measures [by John Drinker].
Philadelphia, 1774. 24 pp.
LOC copy.   13179

Observations on the Nature and Use of
Paper-Credit [by William Barton,
1755?-1817].
Philadelphia, Aitken, 1781. 40 pp.
AAS copy.   17091

Observations on the New Constitution,
and on the Federal and State Conventions
[by Mercy (Otis) Warren, 1728-1814].
[Boston, 1788.] 19 pp.
AAS copy.   21111

Observations on the New Constitution and
on the Federal and State Conventions [by
Mercy (Otis) Warren, 1728-1814].
New York, 1788. 22 pp.
AAS copy.   21112

Observations on the Peculiar Case of the
Whig Merchant [by Nathaniel Hazard].
New York, 1785. 31 pp.
(The authority for authorship is the
inscription in the hand of John Trumbull
in this copy.)
WLC copy.   19151

Observations on the Pernicious Practice
of the Law [by Benjamin Austin,
1752-1820].
Boston, Adams & Nourse, 1786. 52 pp.
AAS copy.   19481

Observations on the Present Situation of
Landed Property in America.
[New York?], 1792. 3 pp.
NYHS copy.   24640

Observations on the Present State of

Religion in Maryland [by William Duke,
1757-1840].
Baltimore, Adams, 1795. 53 pp.
JCB copy.   28593

[Observations on the Proposed Bill,
Entitled, "An Act to Declare. . . ."
Easton, Pa., Cowan, 1794. 43 pp.]
(Entry from Sabin 56554.)   27433

Observations on the Proposed
Constitution for the United States of
America.
New York, 1788. 126 pp.
NYPL copy.   21344

Observations on the Proposed State Road.
. . . to Lake Erie [by Charles Williamson,
1757-1808].
Boston, Swords, 1800. 18 pp., 1 folded
map.
NYHS copy.   39109

Observations on the Proposed State Road.
New York, Swords, 1800. 18 pp., folded
map.
(Also entered as 39109, q. v.)   38143

Observations on the Propriety of Fixing.
. . . [by Thomas Hartley, 1748-1800].
[New York], 1789. 11 pp.
LCP copy.   21878

[Observations on the Public Fast,
December 12, 1766.
Newport, 1766.]
(A ghost of 10346, q.v.)   10434

Observations on the Reasons Given by
Mr. Hamilton's Advisers [by Lewis
Morris, 1671-1746].
[New York], 1736.] 11 pp.
LOC copy.   4057

Observations on the Reasons, Lately
Published, for the Malicious Combination
[Jan. 16, 1769].
[New York, 1769.] 3 pp.
NYPL copy.   11394

Observations on the Reconciliation of
Great-Britain and the Colonies [by Jacob
Green, 1722-1790].
New York, Holt, 1776. 16 pp.
LOC copy.   14790

Observations: on the Reconciliation of
Great-Britain, and the Colonies [by Jacob
Green, 1722-1790].
Philadelphia, Bell, 1776. 40 pp.
AAS copy.   14791

Observations on the Reflections of . . .
Edmund Burke [by Mrs. Catharine
(Sawbridge) Macauley Graham,
1731-1791].
Boston, Thomas & Andrews, 1791. 39 pp.
AAS copy.   23517

Observations on the Reverend Pastor of
Roxbury's Thanksgiving Discourse [by
Harrison Gray, 1711?-1794].
Boston, 1775. 8 pp.
AAS copy.   14358

Observations on the Right of Jurisdiction
Claimed by the States of New-York and
New-Hampshire.
Danvers, 1778. 15 pp.
AAS copy.   15950

Observations on the River Potomack [by
Tobias Lear, 1762-1816].
New York, Loudons, 1793. 29 pp.
AAS copy.   25711

Observations on the River Potomack [by
Tobias Lear, 1762-1816].
New York, Loudon & Brower, 1794. 30
pp., 1 folded plan.
AAS copy.   27209

Observations on the Slavery of the
Negroes, in the Southern States.
New York, Ross, 1785. 23 pp.
JCB copy.   44751

Observations on the Slaves. . . .
Philadelphia, August 14, 1777.
[Philadelphia], Styner & Cist, [1777]. [2]
pp.
HSP copy.   15239

Observations on the Whale-Fishery [by
Thomas Jefferson, pres. U. S., 1743-
1826].
[New York, 1788.] 18 pp.
BA copy.   21345

[Observations on two Campaigns against
the Cherokee Indians, in 1760 and 1761.
By Philopatrios.
Charleston, 1762. 88, [1] pp.]
(A ghost of 9243, q.v.)   9242

Observations on Universal Salvation.
New Haven, Morse, 1790. 24 pp.
AAS copy.   22746

[Observations upon Beauty.
Philadelphia, 1747.]
(Adv. Pa. Journal, Apr. 2, 1747.)   6040

Observations upon the Effects [by George
Walton, 1740-1804].
Philadelphia, Aitken, 1781. 10 pp., 1
folded leaf.
AAS copy.   17419

[Observations upon the New Divinity, as
it is Called.
Bennington, Haswell, 1793.]
(Imprint assumed by Evans from adv.
"For sale at the Printing-Office," Vt.
Gazette, Dec. 13, 1793. A ghost of 25478.)
                                    25935

Observations upon the Present
Government of Pennsylvania [by
Benjamin Rush, 1745-1813].
Philadelphia, Steiner & Cist, 1777. 24 pp.
JCB copy.   15589

Observations upon the Proposed Plan of
Federal Government [by James Monroe?,
pres. U. S., 1758-1831].
Petersburg, 1788. 64, [2] pp.
(For authorship see Wyatt, Petersburg
Imprints.)
VaHS copy.   21264

[The Observator Observed.
Boston, 1733.]
("Just Published," Weekly Rehearsal, Jan.
1, 1733.)   3705

The Observator's Trip to America.
[Philadelphia], 1726. 45 pp.
HSP copy.   2794

The Observer, extra. Friday, April 15,
1785. Exertion or Ruin.
[Boston, 1785.] Broadside.
MHS copy.   44752

[The Observer Observed.
Boston, 1733.]
("Last Week was published . . . in Answer to
. . . The Observator Observed," Weekly
Rehearsal, Jan. 15, 1733.)   3706

Occasional Essays on the Yellow Fever.
Philadelphia, Ormrod, 1800. 42 pp.
AAS copy.   38145

Occasional Ode, for February 22, 1800.
n. p., n. d. Broadside.
BA copy.   38146

Occasional Ode, for the 17th of June,
1786.
[Boston, 1786]. Broadside.
BPL copy.   19875a

An Occasional Paper, Containing the
most Important . . . Advices. Newport . . .
Nov. 6, 1775.
[Newport, 1775.] Broadside.
NHS copy.   42916

The Occasionalist.
[New York, 1768.] [4] pp.
LOC copy.   11017

Occom, Samson, 1723-1792.
A Choice Collection of Hymns.
New London, 1774. 119 pp.
MHS copy.   13507

[Occom, Samson, 1723-1792.
A Choice Collection of Hymns. . . .
Second Edition.
New London, 1784. 111 pp.]
(There is said to have been a 1783 ed, as
well, but no copies have been found.)
                                    18667

Occom, Samson, 1723-1792.
A Choice Collection of Hymns. . . .
Second Edition.
New London, 1785. 112 pp.
CSL copy.   19152

Occom, Samson, 1723-1792.
A Choice Collection of Hymns. . . . Third
Edition.
Hudson, [N. Y.], Stoddard, 1787.
109 pp.
AAS copy.   45118

Occom, Samson, 1723-1792.
A Choice Collection of Hymns. . . . Third
Edition.
New London, Greens, 1792. 112 pp.
HEH copy.   24641

Occom, Samson, 1723-1792.
Mr. Occom's Address to his Indian
Brethren, on the Day that Moses Paul . . .
was Executed . . . the 2nd of September,
1772.
n. p., n. d. Broadside.
AAS copy.   42362a

Occom, Samson, 1723-1792.
Mr. Occom's Address to his Indian
Brethren . . . 2d of September, 1772.
Boston and Newburyport, [1773].
Broadside.
NYPL photostat copy.   12911

[Occom, Samson, 1723-1792.
A Sermon at the Execution of Moses Paul.
New Haven, 1788.]
(A ghost of this London printing.)
DC copy.   45316

Occom, Samson, 1723-1792.
A Sermon Preached at the Execution of
Moses Paul.
New Haven, [1772]. 32 pp.
AAS copy.   12494

Occom, Samson, 1723-1792.
A Sermon, Preached at the Execution of
Moses Paul.
New London, [1772]. 23, [1] pp.
AAS copy.   12493

Occom, Samson, 1723-1792.
A Sermon Preached at the Execution of
Moses Paul. . . . Third Edition.
New London, 1772. 23, [1] pp.
AAS copy.   12495

Occom, Samson, 1723-1792.
A Sermon Preached at the Execution of
Moses Paul. . . . Fourth Edition.
New London, 1772 (1773). 23,
[1] pp.
AAS copy.   12496

Occom, Samson, 1723-1792.
A Sermon Preached at the Execution of
Moses Paul.
Boston, Boyles, 1773. 22, [2] pp.
AAS copy.   12908

Occom, Samson, 1723-1792.
A Sermon, Preached at the Execution of
Moses Paul.
Boston, Boyles, next door to the Three
Doves, 1773. 31, [1] pp.
(The AAS has a variant with the imprint
reading "Boyles, in Marlborough-Street.")
AAS copy.   42478

Occom, Samson, 1723-1792.
A Sermon, Preached at the Execution of
Moses Paul.
Boston, R. Draper, 1773. 31, [1] pp.
(An imprint variant of 42478, q.v. for
text.)
HEH copy.   42479

Occom, Samson, 1723-1792.
A Sermon Preached at the Execution of
Moses Paul.
Boston, Draper and Boyles, 1773. 31,
[1] pp.
AAS copy.   12907

Occom, Samson, 1723-1792.
A Sermon, Preached at the Execution of
Moses Paul.
Hartford, [1773]. 24 pp.
AAS copy.   12909

Occom, Samson, 1723-1792.

A Sermon, Preached at the Execution of
Moses Paul.
Salem, 1773. 31 pp.
AAS copy.   12910

Occom, Samson, 1723-1792.
A Sermon Preached at the Execution of
Moses Paul. . . . Ninth Edition.
Boston, Hunter, 1774. 24 pp.
AAS copy.   13508

Occurrences of the Times.
[Boston, 1789.] 23 pp.
AAS copy.   22043

O'Connor, Arthur, 1763-1852.
Address to the Free Electors of . . .
Antrim.
Philadelphia, Snowden & M'Corkle, 1797.
12 pp.
LOC copy.   32610

[O'Connor, John, ed.
Anecdotes of the Reign of Louis the
XVIth.
New York, Childs, [1785]. 202 pp.]
(A Duplicate of 20601, q. v.)   19153

O'Connor, John, ed.
Anecdotes of the Reign of Lewis the
XVIth.
New York, Childs, [1787]. 202 pp.
AAS copy.   20601

[O'Connor's Geographical Cards.
Augusta, Ga., Smith, 1793.]
(Imprint assumed by Evans from Smith's
advs.)   25937

Octob. 20, 1740. My Lords [by Sir George
Thomas, bart., 1695?-1774].
[Philadelphia, 1740.] 8 pp.
HSP copy.   4613

Ode, Anniversary - June 2, 1794.
[Boston, 1794.] Broadside.
HSP copy.   27434

Ode for Election-Day, 1792.
n.p., [1792]. Broadside.
CHS copy.   46533

Ode for the Federal Procession [by
Samuel Low, b. 1765].
[New York, 1788.] Broadside.
AAS ph. copy.   45284

An Ode for the 4th of July 1788 [by
Francis Hopkinson, 1737-1791].
[Philadelphia, 1788.] Broadside.
AAS ph. copy.   21151

[An Ode, for the Thanksgiving Day. By
Titus Antigallicus.
Boston, Fleet, 1749.]
(Title from printer's adv.)   6277

Ode for the 23d of October, 1792.
n.p.n.d., [1792]. Broadside.
AAS copy.   24642

An Ode for the Year 1770.
From the Carrier of the Boston-Gazette,
&c.
[Boston, 1770.] Broadside.
HSP copy.   42142

An Ode in Honor of the Pennsylvania
Militia.
Albany, N. Y., 1800. 10 pp.
(Also entered as 37031, q. v.)   38147

Ode on Ends; or the Boy's Address who
Carries the American Mercury. Hartford,
January 1, 1799.
[Hartford, 1799.] Broadside.
NYHS copy.   36004

Ode on the Birth-Day of the President.
. . . 1796.
[Philadelphia, 1796.] Broadside.
LCP copy.   30924

Ode, on the Late Glorious Sucesses [by
Nathaniel Evans, 1742-1767].
Philadelphia, Dunlap, 1762. 14 pp.
MHS copy.   9113

Ode on the New-Year, 1753 [by William
Smith, 1727-1803].
New York, Parker, [1753?]. 16 pp.
HEH copy.   40670

Ode on the New Year 1774.
Delivered by Hugh Duncan one of the
Carriers of Rivington's New-York
Gazeteer.
[New York, 1774.] Broadside.
NYPL copy.   42661

Ode Performed at the First Church of the
Universalists.
[Boston, 1800.] Broadside.
(Also entered as 37008, q. v.)   38148

Ode Sacred to Masonry [by Anthony
Haswell, 1756-1816].
[Bennington, 1793.] Broadside.
AAS copy.   46775

An Ode set to Music, Consecrated to . . .
George Whitefield . . . September 30th,
1770.
[Boston, 1770.] Broadside.
MHS copy.   11794

Ode, Sung at the Feast of St. John, June
24, 1795. To a new Tune.
n.p., [1795]. Broadside.
AAS copy.   29232

Ode, Sung at the Feast of St. John, June
24, 1795. Tune - Attick Fire.
n.p., [1795]. Broadside.
AAS copy.   29234

Ode, Sung at the Feast of St. John, June
24, 1795. Tune - Rule Britannia.
n.p., [1795]. Broadside.
AAS copy.   29233

An Ode, Sung at the Lecture of the
Congregational Charitable Society, in
Boston, on the 12th of February, 1795. By
Mr. Rea. [by James Sullivan, 1744-1808].
[Boston, 1795.] Broadside.
MHS copy.   29590

Ode to be Sung on the Arrival of the
President [by Samuel Low, b. 1765].
[New York, 1789.] Broadside.
NYHS copy.   45505

Ode to the President of the United States
on his Arrival at Boston [by Oliver
Holden, 1765-1831].
[Boston, 1789.] Broadside.
AAS copy.   45496

Ode to Washington, and Days of Absence.
. . . October 24th, 1789.
Boston, [1789]. Broadside.
(Not located 1967.)
BrU copy.   45547

[Odell, Jonathan], 1737-1818, supposed
author.
On Spring. . . .
Philadelphia, 1788. Broadside.
UOP copy.   45317

Odes for the Fourth of July, 1796.
[Providence, 1796.] Broadside.
RIHS copy.   30925

Odiorne, Thomas, 1769-1851.
The Progress of Refinement.
Boston, Young & Etheridge, 1792. 176 pp.,
1 plate.
AAS copy.   24643

Odlin, John, 1681-1754.
(Sibley, V, 168-172.)
Christian Courage Necessary.
Boston, Green, 1727. [4], ii, 22 pp.
AAS copy.   2939

Odlin, John, 1681-1754.
(Sibley, V, 168-172.)
Doing Righteousness.
Boston, Kneeland & Green, 1742. [2], ii,
25 pp.
BA copy.   5025

O'Donnel, Charles, d. 1797.
The Life and Confession of. . . .
Lancaster, Dicksons, 1798. 14 pp.
(Best available copy.)
NYHS copy.   48554

The Oeconomy of Human Life.
See Robert Dodsley, 1703-1764.
The Oeconomy of Love [by John
Armstrong, 1709-1779].
Philadelphia, Mentz, 1772. 24 pp.
AAS copy.   12313

Of Commerce and Luxury.
Philadelphia, Lang, 1791. iv, 51 pp.,
printed cover.
AAS copy.   23648

[Number 1. Of the Christian Art of
Teaching.
Hanover, N. H., Dunham, 1795.]
("Just out of the Press," Eagle, Mar. 22,
1795.)   29235

[The Office, Duty and Authority of
Sheriffs.
Philadelphia, 1721.]
(Title from Hildeburn; apparently issued
only as the second part of 2327, q.v.) 2282

Official Account of a Glorious Victory.
Baltimore.
[Baltimore, 1798.] Broadside.
JCB copy.   33814

An Official Account of the Situation of
that Part of Louisiana, which lies between
the mouth of the Missouri and New
Madrid.
Lexington, Ky., Bradford, [1796]. 8 pp.
LOC copy.   32387

Official Intelligence from Virginia.
Providence, November 8, 1781.
Providence, Carter, [1781]. Broadside.
RIHS copy.   44017

[Ogden, David], 1707-1798.
The Claim of the Inhabitants of the Town
of Newark.
Woodbridge, 1766. 14 pp.
JCB copy.   10435

Ogden, David, 1707-1798.
To the Several Persons. . . . February 20,
1767.
[Woodbridge, 1767.] 7 pp.
PrU copy.   10720

Ogden, David Bazard, 1775-1849.
An Oration Delivered on the Fourth of
July, 1798.
Newark, N. J., Halsey, 1798. 12 pp.
NYHS copy.   34266

Ogden, John Cosens, 1751-1800.
An Address Delivered at the Opening of
Portsmouth Academy.
Portsmouth, Osborne, 1791. 35 pp.
AAS copy.   23649

[Ogden, John Cosens], 1751-1800.
An Appeal to the Candid, upon the
Present State of Religion and Politics in
Connecticut.
[Stockbridge? 1799?] 23,
(i.e. 24) pp.
NYHS copy.   34267

Ogden, John Cosens, 1751-1800.
An Excursion into Bethlehem.
Philadelphia, Cist, 1800. [2], 167,
[1] pp.
AAS copy.   38149

Ogden, John Cosens, 1751-1800.
The Female Guide.
Concord, Hough, 1793. 50 pp.
(The unique copy is imperfect.)
NHHS copy.   25938

[Ogden, John Cosens], 1751-1800.
Friendly Remarks to the People of
Connecticut.
[Litchfield, Ct.], 1799. 42 pp.
AAS copy.   36005

Ogden, John Cosens, 1751-1800.
Letters. . . .
Boston, Thomas & Andrews, 1791. 60 pp.
AAS copy.   23650

Ogden, John Cosens, 1751-1800.
A Sermon Delivered before His
Excellency.
Concord, Hough, 1790. 24 pp.
AAS copy.   22747

Ogden, John Cosens, 1751-1800.
A Sermon Preached before the Columbian
Lodge.
Portsmouth, Melcher, 1791. 23, [1] pp.
AAS copy.   23651

Ogden, John Cosens, 1751-1800.

A Sermon upon Peace, Charity, and
Toleration.
Philadelphia, Carey, 1800. 23,
[1] pp.
AAS copy.   38150

[Ogden, John Cosens], 1751-1800.
A Short History of Late Ecclesiastical
Oppressions in New-England and
Vermont.
Richmond, Vt., Lyon, 1799. 19 pp.
AAS copy.   36006

[Ogden, John Cosens], 1751-1800.
A Tour, through Upper and Lower
Canada.
Litchfield, Ct., 1799. 119 pp.
AAS copy.   36007

Ogden, John Cosens, 1751-1800.
A Tour through Upper and Lower
Canada. . . . Second Edition.
Wilmington, Del., Bonsal & Niles, 1800.
117 pp.
AAS copy.   38151

[Ogden, John Cosens], 1751-1800.
A View of the Calvinistic Clubs in the
United States.
[Litchfield, Ct., 1799?] 23 pp.
AAS copy.   36008

[Ogden, John Cosens], 1751-1800.
A View of the New England Illuminati.
Philadelphia, Carey, 1799. 20 pp.
APS copy.   36009

[Ogden, John Cosens], 1751-1800.
A View of the New-England Illuminati.
. . . Second Edition.
Philadelphia, Carey, 1799. 20 pp.
AAS copy.   36010

Ogden, Samuel, 1746-1810.
A Plain Narrative of a Certain Dispute
between the Earl of Stirling and. . . .
n.p., 1775. [2], 56 pp.
APS copy.   42917

Ogden, Uzal, 1744-1822.
An Address to those Persons at
Elizabeth-Town.
New York, M'Lean, 1785. 43 pp.
AAS copy.   19154

Ogden, Uzal, 1744-1822.
Antidote to Deism. . . . In Two Volumes.
Newark, N. J., Woods, 1795. pp. [i]-
xxiv, [13] - 327; [i] - xxii, [13] - 342.
AAS copy.   29237

Ogden, Uzal, 1744-1822.
Four Sermons, on Important Subjects.
Elizabethtown, 1788. 78 pp.
LOC copy.   21347

Ogden Uzal, 1744-1822.
A Letter from the Rev. . . .
[Newark, N.J., 1798.] 7 pp.
NYHS copy.   34268

[Ogden, Uzal], 1744-1822.
A Letter to Major General Alexander
Hamilton.
New York, Hopkins, 1800. 32 pp.
AAS copy.   38152

[Ogden, Uzal], 1744-1822.
A Letter to Maj. Gen. Alexander
Hamilton.
Salem, Mass., Cushing, 1800. 28,
[1] pp.
AAS copy.   38153

[Ogden, Uzal], 1744-1822.
Regeneration, A Sermon.
Chatham, 1783.]
("Just Published, and to be sold by the
Printer hereof" N. J. Journal, Jan. 29,
1783.)   18074

Ogden, Uzal, 1744-1822.
A Sermon Delivered at Morris-Town.
New York, M'Lean, 1785. 47 pp.
AAS copy.   19155

Ogden, Uzal, 1744-1822.
A Sermon Delivered at Roxbury . . .
March 19, 1781.
Chatham, N. J., 1781. 17 pp.
BA copy.   17281

Ogden, Uzal, 1744-1822.

A Sermon, Delivered in Saint Peter's
Church . . . May 16, 1786.
New York, Loudons, 1786. 31 pp.
HC copy.   19876

Ogden, Uzal, 1744-1822.
A Sermon on Practical Religion. . . .
Number I.
Chatham, N. J., [1779]. 26 pp.
PrU copy.   16422

Ogden, Uzal, 1744-1822.
A Sermon on Practical Religion. . . .
Number II.
Chatham, 1780. 42, [2] pp.
BA copy.   16423

Ogden, Uzal, 1744-1822.
A Sermon on Practical Religion. . . .
Number III.
Chatham, 1782. vi, 46 pp.
BA copy.   17646

Ogden, Uzal, 1744-1822.
The Theological Preceptor.
New York, Holt, 1772. xii, 259 pp.
AAS copy.   12497

Ogden, Uzal, 1744-1822.
Two Discourses, Occasioned by the Death
of . . . Washington.
Newark, N. J., Day, 1800. frontis.,
46 pp.
AAS copy.   38154

Ogden, Uzal, 1744-1822.
Two Discourses, Occasioned by the Death
of . . . Washington. . . . Second Edition.
Philadelphia, Maxwell for Dickins, 1800.
40 pp.
LCP copy.   38155

Ogilvie, James, 1760-1820.
A Speech Delivered in Essex County.
Richmond, Va., Jones & Dixon, 1798.
12 pp.
LOC copy.   34269

Ogilvie, John, 1733-1813.
(D. N. B.)
Providence, an Allegorical Poem.
Boston, Mein, 1766. 180 pp.
AAS copy.   10436

[Ogilvie, John, 1733-1813.
(D. N. B.)
Providence. An Allegorical Poem.
Philadelphia, Bell, 1774.]
(Adv. Pa. Gazette, May 18, 1774.)   13509

Ogleby, Richard.
Nebuchadnezzar, a Full-bred Dray Horse,
will Stand. . . . March 19, 1790.
Baltimore, Goddard & Angell, [1790].
Broadside.
LOC copy.   45935

Oh the Moment was Sad [by Samuel
Arnold, 1740-1802].
New York, Hewitt, [1798?] Broadside.
NYPL copy.   48341

O'Hara, Kane, 1714-1782.
Midas. A Burletta.
Boston, Belknap & Hall for Blake and
Clap, [1794]. 24 pp.
AAS copy.   27435

O'Hara, Kane, 1714-1782.
Songs, Duetts, Trios, etc., in The Two
Misers.
[Philadelphia], Wrigley & Berriman,
1794. 12 pp.
LCP copy.   27436

Ohio Company, 1786-1795.
Articles of Agreement Entered into.
[Newport, 1788.] 4 pp.
RIHS copy.   21348

Ohio Company, 1786-1795.
Articles of an Association.
Worcester, Thomas, 1786. 12 pp.
AAS copy.   19877

Ohio Company, 1786-1795.
Articles of an Association.
New York, Loudons, 1787. 45 pp.
HC copy.   20605

Ohio Company, 1786-1795.
At a Meeting of the Directors and

Agents of the Ohio Company . . .
March 5, 1788.
[Providence, 1788.] 4 pp.
JCB copy.   21349

Ohio Company, 1786-1795.
At a Meeting of the Directors and Agents
of the Ohio Company . . . the 21st of
November.
[Worcester, 1787.] 4 pp.
AAS copy.   20603

Ohio Company, 1786-1795.
At a Meeting . . . at Hartford . . . the
5th Day of July, A.D. 1792.
[Hartford? 1792.] Broadside.
JCB copy.   46534

Ohio Company, 1786-1795.
August 29th, 1787. At a Meeting of the
Directors. . . .
[Worcester, 1787.] Broadside.
AAS copy.   20602

Ohio Company, 1786-1795.
The Contract of the Ohio Company . . .
October 27, 1787.
[New York ? 1787.] 4 pp.
AAS copy.   20604

[Ohio Company, 1786-1795.
To the Honorable the Senate and House.
. . . The Memorial and Petition of the
. . . Directors of the Ohio Company. . . .
March 2d, 1792.
[Philadelphia, 1792.] 4 pp.]
(No copy located.)   26369

[The Ohio Navigator.
Washington, Ky., 1798.]
(See McMurtie, Ky. Imprints, p. 55.)
                                            33915

[The Ohio Navigator. . . . Second
Edition.
Washington, Ky., 1798.]
(See McMurtie, Ky. Imprints, p. 57.)
                                            33916

O'Keeffe, John, 1747-1833.
The Agreeable Surprise.
New York, Morton, and Berry & Rogers,
1786. 38, [1] pp.
AAS copy.   19878

O'Keeffe, John, 1747-1833.
The Agreeable Surprise.
Philadelphia, Carey, 1793. 32 pp.
(Because of the binding only the tp can
be reproduced.)
NYPL copy.   25939

O'Keeffe, John, 1747-1833.
The Agreeable Surprise.
Boston, Belknap & Hall for Blake and
Clap, 1794. 33 pp.
AAS copy.   27437

O'Keeffe, John, 1747-1833.
The Dead Alive.
New York, Hodge, Allen & Campbell,
1789. 46, [2] pp.
AAS copy.   22044

O'Keeffe, John, 1747-1833.
The Farmer. . . . First American Edition.
Philadelphia, Carey, 1792. 40 pp.
NYPL copy.   24644

O'Keeffe, John, 1747-1833.
The Farmer: a Comic Opera.
Boston, Belknap & Hall for Blake and
Clap, 1794. 35 pp.
AAS copy.   27439

O'Keeffe, John, 1747-1833.
The Highland Reel.
New York, Harrisson, 1794. 72 pp.
AAS copy.   27441

O'Keeffe, John, 1747-1833.
The Highland Reel.
Philadelphia, Story, [1794]. 55 pp.
AAS copy.   27442

O'Keeffe, John, 1747-1833.
The Highland Reel.
Boston, Blakes, 1797. 68, [3] pp.
(No copy reported has the imprint given
by Evans.)
AAS copy.   32611

O'Keeffe, John, 1747-1833.

The Highland Reel: a Comic Opera.
Boston, Blakes, 1797. 68, [3] pp.
HEH copy.   48208

[O'Keeffe, John, 1747-1833.
Life's Vagaries. A Comedy.
Philadelphia, 1795.]
(Imprint assumed by Evans from adv.)
                                            29238

[O'Keeffe, John, 1747-1833.
London Hermit. . . . A Comedy.
Philadelphia, 1795.]
(Imprint assumed by Evans from adv.)
                                            29239

[O'Keeffe, John, 1747-1833.
The New Highland Laddie.
Philadelphia, 1794.]
(Adv. in newspapers in May.)   27443

O'Keeffe, John, 1747-1833.
Patrick in Prussia.
Philadelphia, Story, [1789]. 34 pp.
LCP copy.   22045

O'Keeffe, John, 1747-1833.
Patrick in Prussia.
Philadelphia, Taylor, 1791. 39 pp.
AAS copy.   23652

[O'Keeffe, John, 1747-1833.
The Poor Soldier.
New York, 1787.]
(Assumed by Evans from the fact that
plays performed were often reprinted.)
                                            20608

O'Keeffe, John, 1747-1833.
The Poor Soldier.
Philadelphia, [Story], 1787. 29 pp.
AAS copy.   20606

O'Keeffe, John, 1747-1833.
The Poor Soldier.
Philadelphia, Seddon & Spotswood, 1787.
34, [2] pp.
BPL copy.   20607

[O'Keeffe, John, 1747-1833.
The Poor Soldier. A Comic Opera.
Philadelphia, Spotswood, 1790.]
(Entry from adv. for "New books,
American editions," Pa. Gazette, Sept.
22, 1790.)   22748

O'Keeffe, John, 1747-1833.
The Poor Soldier: a Comic Opera.
Philadelphia, Taylor, 1791. 32 pp.
AAS copy.   46246

[O'Keeffe, John, 1747-1833.
The Poor Soldier.
Boston, Blake, [1794].]
("Just Published, and for Sale,"
Columbian Centinel, May 31, 1794.)
                                            27445

[O'Keeffe, John, 1747-1833.
The Prisoner at Large.
Philadelphia, Story, 1790.]
("Will be published Wednesday next,"
Independent Gazatteer, Jan. 6, 1790.)
                                            22750

O'Keeffe, John, 1747-1833.
The Prisoner at Large.
Philadelphia, Taylor, 1791. 35 pp.
AAS copy.   23653

[O'Keeffe, John, 1747-1833.
The Quaker; a Comic Opera.
Boston, Edes & Etheridge for Blake and
Clap, 1794. 32 pp.]
(The author was Charles Dibdin, under
whose name it is entered as 26880.) 27449

O'Keeffe, John, 1747-1833.
Songs, Duets, etc. in The Poor Soldier.
New York, Berry & Rogers, [1790]. 24
pp.
HSP copy.   22749

O'Keeffe, John, 1747-1833.
The Songs in the Castle of Andalusia.
Philadelphia, Carey, 1794. 12 pp.
LCP copy.   27438

O'Keeffe, John, 1747-1833.
Songs in the Comic Opera, Called, The
Son-in-Law.
Philadelphia, Carey, 12 pp.
WLC copy.   27446

O'Keeffe, John, 1747-1833.
Songs in the Highland Reel.
[Philadelphia], Carey, 1794. 19 pp.
AAS copy.   27444

O'Keeffe, John, 1747-1833.
Songs of The Farmer.
Philadelphia, Carey, 1794. 12 pp.
LCP copy.   27440

[O'Keeffe, John, 1747-1833.
Wild Oats.
New York, Harrison, 1793.]
(Imprint assumed by Evans from
Harrison's advs., apparently for 25940.)
    25941

O'Keeffe, John, 1747-1833.
Wild Oats.
New York, Swords, 1793. 67 pp., 1 plate.
WLC copy.   25940

O'Keeffe, John, 1747-1833.
Wild Oats.
Philadelphia, Carey, 1793. 66, [2] pp.
AAS copy.   25942

O'Keeffe, John, 1747-1833.
The World in a Village.
New York, Swords for Berry, Rogers &
Berry, 1794. 87, [1] pp.
AAS copy.   27447

[O'Keeffe, John], 1747-1833.
The Young Quaker, a Comedy.
Philadelphia, Bradford, 1794. 62,
[2] pp.
AAS copy.   27448

[O'Kelly, James], 1735-1826.
The Author's Apology for Protesting
against the Methodist Episcopal
Government.
Richmond, Dixon, 1798. 120 pp.
Garrett Biblical Institute, Evanston, copy.
    48555

[O'Kelly, James, 1735-1826.
Essay on Negro Slavery.
Philadelphia, 1784.]
(Sabin 57097.)   18668

[O'Kelly, John.
The Preceptor's Guide.
Georgia, 1798.]
(Proposed, but apparently not printed.)
    34270

Okely, Francis, 1719?-1794.
The Disjointed Watch.
Baltimore, Sower, 1795. [10] pp.
NYPL copy.   29240

Olcott, Bulkley, 1733-1793.
Brotherly-Love.
Westminster, Vt., 1782. 15 pp.
AAS copy.   17647

Olcott, Bulkley, 1733-1793.
Rightiousness and Peace.
Windsor, 1783. 16 pp.
CHS copy.   18075

The Old Bachelor's Masterpiece.
Fairhaven, Vt., Spooner, 1797. 47 pp.
AAS copy.   32612

[The Old Bachelor's Reasons for
Celibacy.
Norwich, Trumbull, 1794.]
(Imprint assumed by Evans from adv.
"Just Published at this office," Norwich
Packet, May 22, 1794.)   27450

Old England's Triumph. Sung at the
Second Anniversary Meeting of the Sons
of St. George, in New-York, April 23d,
1771.
[New York, 1771.] Broadside.
AAS copy.   42263

The Old English Baron [by Clara Reeve,
1729-1807].
Philadelphia, Stewart & Cochran, 1797.
213, [3] pp.
AAS copy.   32742

Old Ireland's Misery at an End. Or, The
English Empire in the Brazils Restored.
Newport, [R. I.], [1752?]. 8+pp.
(The only known copy is imperfect.)
AAS copy.   40634

Old Ireland's Misery at an End.
Boston, [1752]. 8 pp.
AAS copy.   6904

Old Mens Tears [by Joshua Scottow,
1618-1698].
Boston, 1691. [6], 23, [1] pp.
BA copy.   576

Old Mens Tears [by Joshua Scottow,
1618-1693].
Boston, 1715. 58 pp.
(The only copy located is badly defective.)
BPL copy.   1779

Old Men's Tears [by Joshua Scottow,
1618-1693].
Boston, Gray, 1733. [4], 20 pp.
AAS copy.   3604

Old Men's Tears [by Joshua Scottow,
1618-1693].
New London, 1769. 22 pp.
AAS copy.   11457

The Old Path.
Portsmouth, 1765. 4 pp.
MHS copy.   10111

The Old Pathes Restored [by Cotton
Mather, 1663-1728].
Boston, 1711. [2], 24 pp.
YC copy.   1509

The Old Principles of New England [by
Cotton Mather, 1663-1728].
[Boston, 1700?] 16 pp.
AAS copy.   929

Oldys, Francis, pseud.
The Life of Thomas Paine. . . . [by
George Chalmers, 1742-1825].
Boston, Manning & Loring for West, 1796.
40 pp.
MHS copy.   30178

O'Leary, Arthur, 1729-1802.
An Essay on Toleration.
Philadelphia, Kline & Reynolds, 1785. pp.
[11], [3]-70, [2].
NYPL copy.   19156

Oliphant, James, 1734-1818.
A Sacramental Catechism. . . . Fifth
Edition.
Philadelphia, Young, 1788. 156 pp.
LCP copy.   45318

[Oliphant, James, 1734-1818.
A Sacramental Catechism.
Philadelphia, Young, 1791.]
(Entry from adv. in 23178 for "American
editions, to be sold.")   23654

The Olive-Branch! Baltimore, February 5.
Yesterday Arrived. . . .
Baltimore, [1783]. Broadside.
MdHS copy.   18076

Oliver, Andrew, 1731-1799.
(D. A. B.)
An Essay on Comets.
Salem, 1772. [6], vi, 87 pp., folded plate.
AAS copy.   12498

Oliver, John, of London.
A Present to be Given to Teeming Women.
Boston, 1694. 12, [130] pp.
NYAM copy.   708

[Oliver, Peter], 1713-1791.
(Sibley, VIII, 737-763.)
A Poem Sacred to the Memory of Mrs.
Abigail Conant.
New London, 1759. 7 pp.
AAS copy.   8323

[Oliver, Peter], 1713-1791.
(Sibley, VIII, 737-763.)
A Poem Sacred to the Memory of the
Honorable Josiah Willard.
Boston, Green & Russel, 1757. 16 pp.
AAS copy.   7988

Oliver, Peter, 1713-1791.
(Sibley, VIII, 737-763.)
A Speech Delivered in the New
Court-House.
Boston, Fowle, 1750. [2], 12 pp.
(A part of 6605, q.v.)   6578

[Oliver, Peter, 1767-1831?

The Adopted Son. A Comedy in Five
Acts.
Boston, 1798.]
(Entry from the copyright.)   34271

Oliver, Thomas Fitch, 1757-1797.
(Sprague, V, 383-384.)
A Discourse, Delivered at the Episcopal
Church in Providence.
Providence, Carter, [1784]. 16 pp.
AAS copy.   18669

Olivers, Thomas, 1725-1799.
A Hymn to the God of Abraham. . . .
Sixth Edition.
Philadelphia, Miller, 1773. 8 pp.
HSP copy.   42480

Olney Hymns. . . . Sixth Edition [by John
Newton, 1725-1807].
New York, Hodge, Allen & Campbell,
1790. 348 pp.
AAS copy.   22734

Omar Khayyam.
Consolation from Homar.
Newburyport, Blunt, 1794.
(Better entered under Smith, William,
1754-1821)   29241

[On Equality. By an Officer of the
Commonwealth.
Philadelphia, 1793.]
(The origin of this entry has not been
found.)   25943

On Friendship.
[Hartford]. Hudson & Goodwin, [1779?].
Broadside.
CHS copy.   43677

[On General Wayne's Taking Strong Point.
A Song.
Philadelphia, Towne, 1779.]
(Hildeburn 3923; apparently from an
unlocated adv. in the Pa. Evening Post.)
    16424

On Joseph's Making Himself Known to
his Brethren.
Boston, 1797. Broadside.
AAS copy.   32613

On Joseph's Making Himself Known to
his Brethren.
[Boston? 1797?] Broadside.
AAS copy.   48209

On Monies, Coins, Weights, and Measures
[by John Beale Bordley, 1727-1804].
Philadelphia, Humphreys, 1789. [2], 25,
[1] pp.
AAS copy.   21698

On Philemon Robbins . . . who died, a
Member of Yale-College, Sept. 6th, A.D.
1756.
[New Haven? 1756.] Broadside.
CHS copy.   40858

On Saturday next will be Performed, by a
Society of Ladies and Gentlemen, at
Faneuil-Hall, the Tragedy of Zara. [Sept.
1775].
[Boston, 1775.] Broadside.
MHS copy.   13841

On Spring. . . . [by Jonathan Odell,
1737-1818, supposed author].
Philadelphia, 1788. Broadside.
UOP copy.   45317

On the Conqueror of America shut up in
Boston [by Philip Morin Freneau,
1752-1832].
[New York, 1775.]
(1775 printing assumed from topical
nature.)   14042

On the Dark Day, May Nineteenth, 1780.
[Boston? 1780.] Broadside.
AAS copy.   43859

On the Dark Day May 19th 1780.
n. p., [1780]. Broadside.
AAS copy.   43860

On the Death of Beulah Worfield, who
Departed this Life September 26, 1776.
n. p., [1776?]. Broadside.
AAS copy.   43112

On the Death of Five Young Men who

was Murthered, March 5th, 1770.
[Boston? 1770.] Broadside.
NYHS copy.   42143

[On the Death of Polly Goold.
[Boston], Russell, [1797]. Broadside.]
(The one recorded copy cannot now be
located.)   32614

On the Death of General Washington.
n. p., n. d. Broadside.
HEH copy.   38157

On the Death of the Reverend Benjamin
Colman [by Joseph Seccombe,
1706-1760].
Boston, Rogers & Fowle, [1748]. 8 pp.
("This day is Published," Ind. Adv., Feb.
29, 1748.)
AAS copy.   5937

On the Decrees, or, The Arminian
Attacked.
Poughkeepsie, Woods, 1798. 19 pp.
NYPL copy.   48556

On the Evacuation of Boston by the
British Troops, March 17th, 1776.
n. p., [1776]. Broadside.
Bostonian Soc. copy.   43113

On the Landing of the Troops in Boston,
1758.
[Boston], Sold at the Printing-Office in
Newbury-Street, [1758]. Broadside.
AAS copy.   40998

On the Much Lamented Death of . . .
Noadiah Russell [by Nathaniel Collins,
1677-1756].
[New London, 1714.] Broadside.
YC copy.   1670

On the New-Year, 1773.
To all Worthy Customers of the New
Hampshire Gazette.
[Portsmouth, 1773.] Broadside.
NYHS copy.   42481

On the Prisons of Philadelphia [by
François Alexander Frédéric, duc de la
Rochefoucauld Liancourt, 1747-1827].
Philadelphia, Moreau de Saint-Méry,
1796. 46 pp.
AAS copy.   30674

On the Reverend Mr. Gilbert Tennent's
Powerful and Successful Preaching in
Boston.
[Boston, 1741.] Broadside.
MHS copy.   40252

On this Day of Renown, All Joys Shower
Down. . . . April 23, 1779.
[New York, 1779.] Broadside.
NYHS copy.   43678

On Tuesday Night Arrived in this City
[Dec. 23, 1773].
[New York, 1773.] Broadside. 4 to. ed.
NYHS copy.   12912

On Tuesday the 28th Inst. will be sold by
Public Vendue, at the House of Madam
Fitzpatrick in Roxbury. . . . May 23, 1793.
[Boston, 1793.] Broadside.
MHS copy.   25487

Onania; or, the Heinous Sin [10th ed.].
Boston, Phillips, 1724. [4], iv, 64 pp.
AAS copy.   2573

[Onania, or the Heinous Sin of Self-Pollu-
tion. . . . Tenth Edition.
Boston, 1726. 70 pp.]
(Title from Haven, probably reflecting an
adv. for the London edition of that year.)
                                           2795

Onania: or the Heinous sin.
Boston, Kneeland & Green, 1742. [1], 2,
55 pp.
(A copy was sold by Heartman, Nov. 27,
1926.)   5026

Once more - for the - Liberties of the Peo-
ple. . . . April 2, 1788.
[New York, 1788.] Broadside.
LOC copy.   21350

One Kind Kiss. A Favorite Song. Composed by Dr. [George K.] Jackson [by
James Oswald, 1711-1769].

Printed at Carr's Musical Repositories,
[1796]. [2] pp.
AAS copy.   30931

One Story Good till the Other is Heard.
. . . New York, 27th April, 1800.
n. p., n. d. Broadside.
NYHS copy.   38156

One Thousand Valuable Secrets.
Philadelphia, [Woodward] for Davies and
Stephens, 1795. xxxvi, 377 pp.
AAS copy.   29242

. . . Onesimus; or, The Run-away Servant.
Philadelphia, Johnsons, 1800. 36 pp.
AAS copy.   37167

The Only Sure Guide to the English
Tongue.
see
Perry, William   36011

The Opinion of One [by Charles Chauncy,
1705-1787].
Boston, Green & Russell, 1758. 28 pp.
AAS copy.   8100

Opinions Respecting the Commercial Intercourse. . . . [by James Bowdoin, 1752-
1811].
Boston, Hall, 1797. 61, [1] pp.
AAS copy.   31857

Oppression. A Poem. By an American.
Boston, 1765. [2], 21 pp.
AAS copy.   10112

Oppression. A Poem. By an American.
New York, Gaine, 1765. 20 pp.
AAS copy.   10113

Oppression: a Poem. Or, New-England's
Lamentation.
[Boston, 1777.] Broadside.
(For date see Winslow, Am. Broadside
Verse, p. 188.)
NYHS copy.   10114

The Oracle of Liberty [by Caesar Augus-
tus Rodney, 1772-1824].
Philadelphia, Hall, [1791]. 39 pp.
NYPL copy.   23742

Oracles of Reason [by Josiah Sherman,
1729-1789].
Litchfield, [1787]. 40 pp.
VtU copy.   20706

Oratio [by Nicolaus Ludwig Zinzendorf,
1700-1760].
[Philadelphia, 1742.] 4 pp.]
(Neither of the two copies recorded could
be located.)   5107

[An Oration Commemorative of Ameri-
can Independence Intended to have been
Delivered at Lexington on the Fourth Day
of July, 1798.
[Boston? 1798] [2] pp.]
(No copy located.   34277

An Oration, Commemorative of the Dec-
laration of American Independence.
Philadelphia, Young, 1794. 16 pp.
AAS copy.   27453

An Oration; Delivered at Portsmouth,
New-Hampshire, on the Fourth of July
[by Jonathan Mitchell Sewall, 1748-1808].
Portsmouth, Osborne, 1788. 23 pp.
AAS copy.   21456

[An Oration Delivered at Washington,
Pennsylvania, on the General Fast, May
9th, 1798.
Washington, Pa., 1798.]
(Entry from a newspaper reference.) 34278

[An Oration Delivered March Fifth, 1773
[by Benjamin Church, 1734-1776].
Boston, 1785. 14 pp.]
(A part of 18997, q. v.)   18955

An Oration, in Memory of the Virtues of
. . . Washington.
New York, Davises for Arden, 1800.
23 pp.
AAS copy.   38162

An Oration, on the Beauties of Liberty
[by John Allen, fl. 1764].
Boston, Kneeland & Davis, 1773. 31 pp.

(The AAS has another issue without the
note on p. 31.)
AAS copy.   13015

An Oration, upon the Beauties of Liberty.
[Half title:] The Second Edition
Corrected [by John Allen, fl. 1764].
Boston, Kneeland & Davis, 1773. 31 pp.
AAS copy.   13016

An Oration on the Beauties of Liberty.
. . . Fourth Edition [by John Allen, fl.
1764].
Boston, Russell, 1773. 80 pp.
AAS copy.   13018

An Oration, upon the Beauties of Liberty.
. . . The Third Edition Corrected [by John
Allen, fl. 1764].
New London, 1773. 23 pp.
AAS copy.   13017

An Oration on the Beauties of Liberty.
. . . Fifth Edition [by John Allen, fl.
1764].
Hartford, 1774. 40 pp.
(No perfect copy of this ed. located.)
CHS copy.   13627

An Oration, upon the Beauties of Liberty
[by John Allen, fl. 1764].
Wilmington, Del., 1775. 21 pp.
NYPL copy.   14457

An Oration, Prepared for Delivery before
the Inhabitants of Charleston. . . . the 27th
May, 1788.
[Charleston], Bowen, 1788. 12 pp.
LCP copy.   45319

[An Oration, Pronounced at Concord, the
4th of July, 1794.
Amherst, N.H., Coverly, 1794.]
(A ghost of 27172, q.v.)   27454

An Oration, Pronounced at Hanover, New
Hampshire, January 9, 1800.
Hanover, N. H., Davis, 1800. 17 pp.
(Also entered as 39141, q. v.)   38163

An Oration, Written at the Request of the
Young Men of Boston. . . . Second Edition
[by Robert Treat Paine, 1773-1811].
Boston, Russell, 1799. 30 pp.
AAS copy.   36032

Orations Delivered at the Request of the
Inhabitants of the Town of Boston.
Boston, Edes, [1785]. 200 pp.
AAS copy.   18997

Order of Divine Service in the North
Dutch Church.
[Albany, 1800.] Broadside.
(Also entered as 36785, q. v.)   38164

Order of Performances, at the Old South
Meeting-House, February 22, 1800.
[Boston, 1800.] Broadside.
(Also entered as 37010, q. v.)   38165

Order of Performances. Instrumental
Dirge.
[Boston, 1800.] Broadside.
(Also entered as 36999, q. v.)   38166

Order of Procession.
Philadelphia, Bradford, [1799].
Broadside.
(Not located, 1968.)   48950

Order of Procession, for November 4,
1786.
Philadelphia, Oswald, [1786]. Broadside.
HSP copy.   19915

Order of Procession for the Funeral of the
Late Governor Sumner.
[Boston, 1799.] Broadside.
(Also entered as 35793, q. v.)   36017

Order of Procession, in Honor of the
Constitution of the United States. . . . The
23d July.
[New York, 1788.] Broadside.
AAS ph. copy.   45320

Order of Procession, in Honor of the
Establishment of the Constitution of the
United States . . . the 4th of July, 1788.
Philadelphia, Hall & Sellers, [1788].
Broadside.
AAS copy.   21386

Order of Procession, to be Observed on
the Arrival of the President.
[Providence], Carter, [1790]. Broadside.
HEH copy.   45936

[Order of Procession] to be Observed on
the Arrival of the President. . . .
Providence, August 17, 1790. Broadside.
RIHS copy.   22824

Order of the Exhibition of the Fire-works,
on . . . the First of December, 1783.
[New York], State Printing Office, 1783.
Broadside.
NYPL copy.   44434

Order of the Funeral Procession, to be
Had at Trenton.
n. p., [1800]. Broadside.
(Also entered as 38667, q. v.)   38167

The Oriental Moralist, see Arabian
Nights.   31743

The Origin of Evil, An Elegy [by Royall
Tyler, 1757-1826].
Printed in the Year 1793. 8 pp.
AAS copy.   26290

The Origin of the American Contest with
Great-Britain [by Daniel Leonard,
1740-1829].
New York, Rivington, 1775. [2], 86 pp.
LOC copy.   14158

The Origin of the Whale bone-petticoat.
Boston, 1714. 8 pp.
BM copy.   1709

An Original Essay on Animal Motion [by
Henry Wilkins, 1767-1847].
Philadelphia, 1792. 33 pp.
LCP copy.   25036

The Original Letters of Ferdinand and
Elizabeth [by John Davis, 1774-1854].
New York, 1798. 144 pp.
AAS copy.   33607

Original Poems, on Various Occasions. By
a Lady [by Frances Maria (Madan)
Cowper].
Philadelphia, Young, 1793. 111, [1] pp.
AAS copy.   25353

The Original Rights of Mankind [by
Increase Mather, 1639-1723].
Boston, 1722. [6], 22 pp.
(Probably not by Mather. See Holmes,
Increase Mather, II, 645-646.)
AAS copy.   2346

The Original Steam-Boat [by John Fitch,
1743-1798].
Philadelphia, Poulson, 1788.·34 pp.
NYPL copy.   21093

Ormond [Charles Brockden Brown,
1771-1810].
New York, Forman for Caritat, 1799. 338
pp.
AAS copy.   35245

Ormond ou le Témoin Sécret [by
Charles Brockden Brown, 1771-1810].
New York, Caritat, 1799.
(The only recorded copy is not to be
located.)   35246

Ormsby, John, d. 1734.
The Last Speech and Dying Words of . . .
Executed . . . the 17th of October, 1734.
Boston, T. Fleet, 1734. Broadside.
BPL copy.   40058

Orr, Benjamin, 1772-1828.
An Oration, Delivered at Bedford, N. H.
Amherst, N. H., Preston, 1800. 16 pp.
AAS copy.   38169

Orr, Hector, 1770-1855.
A History of Free Masonry.
Boston, Etheridge, 1798. 32 pp.
AAS copy.   34280

Orr, William, 1766-1797.
The Trial of William Orr.
Philadelphia, Carey for Douglas, 1798. 20
pp.
NYHS copy.   34281

[Orton, Job, 1717-1783.
(D. N. B.)

Discourses to the Aged.
Boston, 1774.]
(Entry from Haven.)   13510

Orton, Job, 1717-1783.
Letters to a Young Clergyman.
Boston, Manning & Loring for White,
1794. 120 pp.
AAS copy.   27455

Orton, Job, 1717-1783.
Memoirs of . . . Philip Doddridge, D.D.
London (Boston), 1766. 265, [3] pp.
AAS copy.   41654

[Orton, Job, 1717-1783.
Memoirs of . . . Philip Doddridge.
Philadelphia, Bell, 1774.]
(Adv. Pa. Gazette, May 18, 1774.)   13511

Osborn, Benjamin, 1751-1818.
Conformity to Truth.
Bennington, 1788. 24 pp.
AAS copy.   21351

Osborn, Samuel, 1685-1774.
(Weis, Colonial Clergy N.E.)
The Case and Complaint.
Boston, 1743. 29, [1] pp.
AAS copy.   5265

[Osborn, Sarah (Haggar)], 1714-1796.
The Nature, Certainty, and Evidence of
true Christianity.
Newport, [R. I.], Hall, 1754 (i.e. 1764?).
15 pp.
RIHS copy.   41478

[Osborn, Sarah (Haggar)], 1714-1796.
The Nature, Certainty and Evidence of
True Christianity.
Boston, Kneeland, 1755. 15 pp.
AAS copy.   7523

[Osborn, Sarah (Haggar)], 1714-1796.
The Nature, Certainty, and Evidence of
True Christianity.
Danbury, Douglas for Crawford, [1793].
23 pp.
NYPL copy.   25949

[Osborn, Sarah (Haggar)], 1714-1796.
The Nature, Certainty and Evidence of
True Christianity.
Providence, Carter, 1793. 15 pp.
AAS copy.   25950

[Osborn, Selleck, 1783-1826.
An Oration, Delivered at Newburgh.
Newburgh, 1798.]
(Sabin 57756; no copy located.)   34282

Osborne, George Jerry, d. 1800.
The Poetical Miscellany; Containing a
Collection of the Most Valuable Pieces.
. . . First American Edition.
Newburyport, Osborne, 1793. [8],
203 pp.
AAS copy.   26014

[Osborne, George Jerry], 1761-1800.
Printing-Office Portsmouth, January
1, 1791. Proposals for Printing by
Subscription. . . . .
[Portsmouth, 1791.] Broadside.
AAS copy.   46247

Osborne, Henry.
An English Grammar.
Charleston, Burd & Boden, [1785].
[66] pp.
(Not found 1967.)
RF copy.   44753

Osborne's New-Hampshire Register: with
an Almanack, for . . . 1787.
Portsmouth, Osborne. [42] pp.
NHHS copy.   19879

Osborne's New-Hampshire Register: with
an Almanack for . . . 1788.
Portsmouth, Osborne. [49] pp.
AAS copy.   20609

Osborne's New-Hampshire Register: with
an Almanack, for . . . 1789.
Portsmouth, Osborne. [58] pp.
AAS copy.   21352

Osgood, David, 1747-1822.
A Conclusive Argument for the Truth of
the Gospel.

Newburyport, March, 1799. 32 pp.
AAS copy.   36019

[Osgood, David], 1747-1822.
The Devil let Loose.
Boston, Hall, 1799. 16 pp.
AAS copy.   36020

Osgood, David, 1747-1822.
A Discourse Delivered December 29,
1799.
Boston, Hall, 1800. 19 pp.
Pierce W. Gaines copy.   49127

Osgood, David, 1747-1822.
A Discourse, Delivered December 29,
1799.
Boston, Hall, 1800. 40 pp.
BA copy.   38170

Osgood, David, 1747-1822.
A Discourse Delivered February 19th,
1795.
Boston, Hall, 1795. 30 pp.
AAS copy.   29246

[Osgood, David, 1747-1822.
A Discourse Delivered February 19, 1795.
. . . Second Edition.
Boston, Hall, 1795. 30 pp.
(A ghost of 29251 arising from Evans'
confusion of advs.)   29247

[Osgood, David, 1747-1822.
A Discourse Delivered February 19, 1795.
. . . Third Edition.
Boston, Hall, 1795. 30 pp.]
(Entry taken by Evans from advs. for what
appears to be 29252.)   29248

Osgood, David, 1747-1822.
A Discourse Delivered February 19th,
1795.
Litchfield, Collier & Buel, [1795].
24 pp.
AAS copy.   29249

Osgood, David, 1747-1822.
A Discourse Delivered on the Day of
Annual Thanksgiving, November 19, 1795.
Boston, Hall, 1795. 32 pp.
AAS copy.   29250

Osgood, David, 1747-1822.
Reflections on the Goodness of God.
Boston, Fleet, 1784. 35 pp.
AAS copy.   18670

Osgood, David, 1747-1822.
St. Paul's Example.
Boston, Belknap & Hall, 1793. 32 pp.
AAS copy.   25952

Osgood, David, 1747-1822.
A Sermon, Preached at the Request of the
Ancient and Honourable Artillery
Company.
Boston, Russell, 1788. 20 pp.
AAS copy.   21353

Osgood, David, 1747-1822.
The Signal Advantages Derived. . . .
Boston, Hall, 1798. 32 pp.
AAS copy.   34283

Osgood, David, 1747-1822.
Some Facts Evincive. . . .
Boston, Hall, 1798. 27 pp.
AAS copy.   34284

Osgood, David, 1747-1822.
The Uncertainty of Life.
Boston, Hall, 1797. 22 pp.
AAS copy.   32621

Osgood, David, 1747-1822.
The Unsearchable Riches of Christ.
Boston, Draper, 1785. 28, [1] pp.
AAS copy.   19157

Osgood, David, 1747-1822.
The Wonderful Works of God.
Boston, Hall, 1794. 29 pp.
AAS copy.   27456

Osgood, David, 1747-1822.
The Wonderful Works of God. . . . Second
Edition.
Boston, Hall, 1794. 29 pp.
AAS copy.   27457

Osgood, David, 1747-1822.
The Wonderful Works of God.

Albany, Websters, 1795. 24 pp.
AAS copy.   29251

Osgood, David, 1747-1822.
The Wonderful Works of God. . . . Third
Edition.
Boston, Hill, 1795. 29 pp.
AAS copy.   29252

Osgood, David, 1747-1822.
The Wonderful Works of God.
Newburyport, Blunt & March, 1795.
24 pp.
AAS copy.   29253

[Osgood, David, 1747-1822.
The Wonderful Works of God.
Philadelphia, 1795. 31 pp.]
(Entry from Sabin 57776. All reported
copies are E 29255.)   29254

Osgood, David, 1747-1822.
The Wonderful Works of God.
Stockbridge, Andrews, 1795. 30 pp.
AAS copy.   29255

Osgood, John, 1711-1773.
(Sibley, IX, 319-323.)
A Letter of Prudent Advice.
Savannah, [1774]. iv, 11 pp.
NYHS copy.   10115

Osgood, Joseph.
An Almanack, for . . . 1801.
Boston, White. [24] pp.
AAS copy.   38171

Osgood, Joseph.
An Almanack, for . . . 1801.
Portsmouth, Treadwell. [24] pp.
(Too fragile to copy.)   49128

Osgood, Joseph.
The Town and Country Almanack, for . . .
1796.
Boston, White. [24] pp.
AAS copy.   47525

Osgood, Nathan.
An Oration, Delivered at Rutland.
Rutland, Vt., Williams, 1799. 16,
[1] pp.
VtU copy.   36021

[Osgood, Samuel], 1748-1813.
Remarks on the Book of Daniel.
New York, Greenleaf, 1794. [2], 503, [2]
pp.
AAS copy.   26663

Osterwald, Jean Frédéric, 1663-1747.
A Compendium of Christian Theology.
Hartford, Patten, 1788. 400, [1] pp.
AAS copy.   21354

Osterwald, Jean Frédéric, 1663-1747.
Practical Observations.
Trenton, N. J., Collins, 1791. [156] pp.
Free Public Library of Trenton copy.   23656

[Oswald, Eleazer], 1755-1795.
Letters of Franklin, on the Conduct of the
Executive.
Philadelphia, Oswald, 1795. 56 pp.
AAS copy.   29256

Oswald, Eleazer, 1755-1795, defendant.
The Case of the Commonwealth against
Eleazer Oswald.
Philadelphia, Spotswood, 1788. 16 pp.
AAS copy.   21363

[Oswald, James], 1711-1769.
One Kind Kiss. A Favorite Song.
Composed by Dr. [George K.] Jackson.
Printed at Carr's Musical Repositories,
[1796]. [2] pp.
AAS copy.   30931

The Other Side of the Question [by Philip
Livingston, 1716-1778].
New York, Rivington, 1774. 29, [2] pp.
AAS copy.   13381

Otis, Cushing, 1768-1837.
An Oration, Pronounced at Scituate.
Boston, Manning & Loring, [1800].
16 pp.
AAS copy.   38172

Otis, Harrison Gray, 1765-1848.
Letter . . . to . . . William Heath.

Boston, Russell, 1798. 30 pp.
AAS copy.   34285

Otis, Harrison Gray, 1765-1848.
An Oration Delivered July 4, 1788.
Boston, Russell, 1788. 23 pp.
AAS copy.   21355

[Otis, James], 1725-1783.
Brief Remarks on the Defence of the
Halifax Libel.
Boston, Edes & Gill, 1765. 40 pp.
AAS copy.   10116

Otis, James, 1725-1783.
The Rights of the British Colonies.
Boston, Edes & Gill, 1764. 80 pp.
AAS copy.   9773

[Otis, James], 1725-1783.
The Rudiments of Latin Prosody.
Boston, Mecom, 1760. 60, 72 pp.
AAS copy.   8701

[Otis, James], 1725-1783.
A Vindication of the British Colonies.
Boston, Edes & Gill, 1765. 32 pp.
AAS copy.   10117

Otis, James, 1725-1783.
A Vindication of the Conduct of the
House.
Boston, Edes & Gill, 1762. 53 pp.
AAS copy.   9225

[Ottawa Council, 1791.
Minutes of Debates in Council on the
Banks of the Ottawa . . . November, 1791.
Philadelphia, Young, 1792.]
(Same as 24647, q.v.)   25653

Ottawa Council, 1791.
Minutes of Debates in Council on the
Banks of the Ottawa River . . . November,
1791.
Philadelphia, Young, 1792. [2], 22 pp.
LCP copy.   24647

Otterbein, Georg Gottfried, 1731-1800.
Lesebuch für Deutsche Schulkinder.
Philadelphia, Cist, 1795. [2], xii, 221 pp.
AAS copy.   29258

[Otterbein, Johann Daniel], 1736-1804.
Jesus und de Kraft Seines Bluts.
Lancaster, 1790. 232 pp.
AAS copy.   22752

[Otterbein, Philip William, 1726-1813.
(D. A. B.)
Die Heilbringende Menschwerdung.
Germantown, 1763. 15 pp.]
(Entry from Seidensticker.)   9471

[Otto, Henrich.]
Eine Grausame Geschichte . . . Aprils,
1785.
[Philadelphia? 1785?] Broadside.
LOC copy.   44754

Otto, Henrich.
Eine Unerhörte that von einem
mörder.
[Philadelphia? 1785?] Broadside.
(Not found 1967.)
RF copy.   44755

Otto, Johann Heinrich
Ein Geistlich Lied.
[Philadelphia, 1772.] Broadside.
HSP copy.   12499

Otto, John Conrad, 1774-1844.
An Inaugural Essay on Epilepsy.
Philadelphia, Lang & Ustick, 1796.
55 pp.
AAS copy.   30934

Ottolenghe, Joseph.
Directions for Breeding Silk-Worms.
Philadelphia, Crukshank, 1771. 8 pp.
HSP copy.   12172

Ouâbi [by Sarah Wentworth (Apthorp)
Morton, 1759-1846].
Boston, Thomas & Andrews, 1790. Front.,
51, [1] pp.
AAS copy.   22684

Oudenaarde, Hendrick.
An Expostulatory Letter.
New York, 1766. 16 pp.
HEH copy.   10437

Oudenaarde, Hendrick.
Seven Letters.
New York, 1766. 16 pp.
HEH copy.   10438

Oulton, Walley Chamberlain, 1770?-1820?
The Wonderful Story-Teller.
Boston, Bumstead for Thomas &
Andrews, etc., 1797. 321, [3] pp.
AAS copy.   32623

[Our Country is our Ship. A new Patriotic
Song.
Boston, von Hagen, 1798.]
(Imprint assumed by Evans from von
Hagen's adv.)   34287

Outlines of a Plan for the Establishment
of a Mint. . . . August 22, 1785.
Philadelphia, Cist, [1785]. [4] pp.
LOC copy.   44756

Out-Lines. Say, Great M'Milkman. . . .
[New York, 1770.] Broadsie.
LCP copy.   11795

An Overture Presented to the Reverend
Synod [by John Thomson, - 1753].
[Philadelphia], 1729. 32 pp.
BPL copy.   3223

Ovidius Naso, Publius.
Ovid's Art of Love.
New York, Campbell, 1795. 216 pp.
AAS copy.   47526

Ovidius Naso, Publius.
P. Ovidii Nasonis Metamorphoseon.
Philadelphia, Spotswood, 1790. iv, [40],
328 pp.
AAS copy.   22753

[Owen, Charles], - 1746.
(D. N. B.)
Plain Reasons, I. For Dissenting. . . .
Eighteenth Edition.
Boston, Hancock, 1725. [4], 40 pp.
AAS copy.   2721

Owen, John, 1616-1683.
The Death of Death. . . . First American
Edition.
Carlisle, Kline, 1792. 320 pp.
AAS copy.   24648

Owen, John, 1616-1683.
(D. N. B.)
Eshcol. . . . Seventh Edition.
Boston, Green for Gookin, 1744. 6, 86,
[2] pp.
AAS copy.   5468

Owen, John, 1616-1683.
Eshcol. . . . Eighth Edition.
Boston, Thomas for Hawes, [1771]. 58,
[1] pp.
("This day was published," Mass. Spy,
Dec. 19, 1771.)
AAS copy.   12500

Owen, John, 1616-1683.
The Nature, Power, Deceit . . . of . . . Sin.
Philadelphia, Young, 1793. pp [i]-viii,
[13]-279, [1].
AAS copy.   25953

[Owen, John, schoolmaster.
The Youth's Instructor.
Philadelphia, Chattin, 1753.]
(Adv. Pa. Journal, Feb. 26, 1754.)   7082

[Oxenbridge, John], 1609-1674.
(Magnalia, Bk. 3, Pt. 4, Ch. 6.)
New-England Freemen.
[Cambridge], 1673. [6], 48 pp.
AAS copy.   181

Oxenbridge, John, 1609-1674.
A Quickening Word.
Cambridge, 1670, 21 pp.
NYPL copy.   152

[Oxford County, Me.
Petition to the Senate and House of
Representatives of Massachusetts. . . .
June 12th, 1797.
[Augusta, 1797.] [3] pp.]
(No copy located.)   32624

The Oxfordshire Tragedy.
Worcester, 1787. 8 pp.
AAS copy.   20610

P

Paaneah, Zaphnath, pseud.
The Two Covenants Fairly Described: or,
Believers Baptism Vindicated.
New London, 1784. 16 pp.
YC copy.   18672

A Pacificatory Letter about Psalmody.
Boston, Franklin for Eliot, 1724. 16 pp.
(Evans' attribution to Cotton Mather is
most improbable on grounds of style and
content.)
AAS copy.   2457

A Pack of Cards Chang'd into a Compleat
Almanac and Prayer-Book.
Boston, Back-Street, [1751?] 8 pp.
AAS copy.   40530

A Pack of Cards Changed into a Complete
Almanack. . . . Tenth Edition.
Worcester, 1785. 10, [1] pp.
AAS copy.   19158

A Pack of Cards Changed into a Compleat
Almanac and Prayer-Book.
Boston, at the Printing-Office in
Marlborough Street, [1786?]. 4 leaves.
(Not found 1967.)
RF copy.   44940

A Pack of Cards Changed into a Complete
Almanack, and Prayer-Book. . . . Eleventh
Edition.
Norwich, 1789. 6 leaves.
(No copy located.)   45548

A Pack of Cards Changed into a Compleat
Almanac. . . .
[Boston], in Marlborough St., [1790?]. 8
pp.
LOC copy.   45937

A Pack of Cards Changed into a Complete
Almanack, and Prayer Book. . . . Eleventh
Edition.
Stockbridge, 1792. 8 pp.
(The only known copy is imperfect.)
AAS copy.   46535

A Pack of Cards Changed into a Complete
Almanack. . . . Twelfth Edition.
Stoningtonport, Ct., 1800. 14,
[1] pp.
AAS copy.   38174

Packard, Asa, 1758-1843.
A Sermon, Preached at Surry.
Walpole, N. H., Carlisle, 1796. 30 pp.
AAS copy.   30935

[Packard, Hezekiah], 1761-1849.
A Catechism, Containing the First
Principles of our Religious and Social
Duties. . . . By Arminius Calvinus.
Boston, Hall, 1795. 32 pp.
AAS copy.   28385

Packard, Hezekiah, 1761-1849.
A Catechism.
Boston, Hall, 1796. 84 pp.
AAS copy.   30936

Packard, Hezekiah, 1761-1849.
Federal Republicanism.
Boston, Russell, 1799. 35, [1] pp.
AAS copy.   36023

[Packard, Hezekiah], 1761-1849.
Packard's Catechism.
Amherst, N. H., Preston, 1798.]
(Imprint assumed by Evans from adv.
"May be had at Doct. Preston's . . . and at
the Printing Office," Village Messenger,
May 5, 1798.)   34288

Packard, Hezekiah, 1761-1849.
The Plea of Patriotism.
Boston, Greenough, 1795. 24 pp.
AAS copy.   29260

Packard, Hezekiah, 1761-1849.
The Rational Method of Preaching.
Newburyport, Blunt, 1797. 36 pp.
AAS copy.   32625

Packard, Hezekiah, 1761-1849.
A Sermon at the Funeral of Miss Polly
Varnum.
Amherst, N. H., Preston, 1798. 19 pp.
AAS copy.   34289

Packard, Hezekiah, 1761-1849.
A Sermon Preached on the Death of Miss
Sibyl Richardson.
Amherst, N. H., Preston, 1799. 28 pp.
AAS copy.   36024

[Packer, Joseph Bill.
A Journal of the Life and Travels of. . . .
Albany, 1773. 15 pp.]
(Entry from imprint of 12915 as given by
Sabin.)   12914

Packer, Joseph Bill.
[A Journal of the Life and Travels of. . . .
Hartford, 1773.] 15 pp.
(The only located copy is imperfect.
Imprint from Sabin.)
HC copy.   12915

Ein Päcklein von diesem Pulver thut
man in ein Peint.
[Frederick, Md., 1794.] Broadside.
WLC copy.   47144

Paddy's Resource: being a Select
Collection of Original and Modern
Patriotic Songs.
Philadelphia, Stephens, 1796. 72 pp.
(The unique copy lacks several pages.)
LOC copy.   30937

Paddy's Resource, Being a Select
Collection of Original and Modern
Patriotic Songs.
New York, Wilson, 1798. [4], 48 pp.
(No perfect copy located.)
AAS copy.   34290

Padlin, Benjamin.
Ein Ernstliche Ermahnung.
Germantown, Sauer, 1738. Broadside.
HSP copy.   4292

The Padlock: a Comic Opera [by Isaac
Bickerstaffe, d. 1812?]
Boston, Spotswood, 1795. 31, [4] pp.
LCP copy.   28296

Paedagogium, Nazareth, Pa.
Regulations of the . . . Boarding School.
[Philadelphia, 1785?] 2, [1] pp.
NYPL copy.   44757

Paftillo, Henry, 1726-1801.
A Geographical Catechism.
Halifax, N. C., Hodge, 1796. 62 pp.
NCU copy.   30963

Page, John, 1744-1808.
An Address to the Citizens of . . . York.
[Philadelphia, 1797.] 32 pp.
(Imprint dated from 32623.)
HSP copy.   30938

Page, John, 1744-1808.
An Address to the Citizens of . . . York.
[Philadelphia, 1797.] 40 pp.
AAS copy.   32626

Page, John, 1744-1808.
An Address to the Citizens of . . . York.
[Philadellhia, 1799?] 40 pp.
(Also entered as 32626, q. v.)   36026

Page, John, 1744-1808.
An Address to the Freeholders of
Gloucester.
Richmond, Va., Dixon, 1799. 44 pp.
AAS copy.   36027

Page, John, 1744-1808.
To the Citizens of Accomack. . . .
November 16, 1798.
[Richmond, 1798.] Broadside.
LOC copy.   34291

Page, Thomas, d. 1813.
(Lawrence, New Hampshire Churches, p.
548.)
A Sermon, on the Nature of Divine
Government.
Concord, N. H., Hough, 1793. 36 pp., 2
folding plates.
AAS copy.   25954

Paige, Reed, 1764-1816.
(Chapman, Dartmouth Alumni, p. 42.)
A Sermon, Delivered at the Ordination of
Jabez P. Fisher.
Amherst, N. H., Cushing, 1796. 48 pp.
AAS copy.   30939

Pain, Philip, d. 1668.
Daily Meditations.
Cambridge, 1668. [4], 16, [2] pp.
HEH copy.   128

Pain, Philip, d. 1668?
Daily Meditations.
Cambridge, 1670. [3], 16, [2] pp.
MHS copy.   153

Pain, Philip, d. 1688?
[Daily Meditations.
Boston, 1682.] 16, [5] pp.
(The only known copy is defective.)
NYPL copy.   327

Pain, William, 1730?-1790?
The Builder's Pocket Treasure.
Boston, Norman, 1794. iv, 20 pp., 55
plates.
(Misdated by Evans who assumed the
imprint from Norman's adv.)
NYHS copy.   25955

Pain, William, 1730?-1790?
The Carpenter's Pocket Directory.
Philadelphia, Dobelbower and Thackera,
1797. [28] pp., 25 plates.
Columbia Univ. copy.   32627

Pain, William, 1730?-1790?
The Practical Builder. . . . Fourth Edition.
Boston, Norman, 1792. 8 pp., 83 plates.
AAS copy.   25956

Pain, William, 1730?-1790?
The Practical House Carpenter.
Boston, Norman, 1796. 16, 7, [1] pp., 146
plates.
AAS copy.   30940

Pain, William, 1730?-1790?
The Practical House Carpenter.
Philadelphia, Dobson, 1797. v, [30] pp.,
146 (i.e. 147) plates.
AAS copy.   32628

Paine, Clement, 1769-1849.
An Oration on Masonry.

Charleston, S. C., Freneau & Paine, 1799.
14 pp.
AAS copy.   36028

[Paine, Robert Treat], 1731-1814.
The Art of Making Common Salt.
Boston, Gill, 1776. 15 pp., plate.
AAS copy.   14652

[Paine, Robert Treat], 1731-1814.
The Art of Making Common Salt.
Philadelphia, Aitken, 1776. 7 pp., plate.
(For authorship see A.A.S., Proc., XXIX,
212-213.)
AAS copy.   14651

Paine, Robert Treat, 1773-1811.
Adams and Liberty, a new Patriotic Song.
Baltimore, Hanna & Greene for Thomas,
Andrews & Butler and Cotton, [1798].
7 pp.
MdHS copy.   48559

[Paine, Robert Treat], 1773-1811.
Adams and Liberty; together with Hail
Columbia, and the American Sailor.
[Boston? 1798?] Broadside.
AAS copy.   34295

Paine, Robert Treat, 1773-1811.
Adams and Liberty, the Boston Patriotic
Song.
[Boston, Thomas & Andrews, 1798.] 2 pp.
AAS copy.   34293

[Paine, Robert Treat], 1773-1811.
Adams and Liberty. The Boston Patriot's
Song. Tune - - "Anacreon in Heaven."
Boston, White, [1798]. Broadside.
AAS ph. copy.   34296

[Paine, Robert Treat], 1773-1811.
Adams and Liberty. A Patriotic Song.
Concord, N.H., Hough, 1798. Broadside.]
(No copy of such an ed. located.)   34297

[Paine, Robert Treat], 1773-1811.
Adams and Liberty.
New York, Gilfert, [1798?]. Broadside,
and 2 leaves.
(Best copy available.)
HEH copy.   48557

Paine, Robert Treat, 1773-1811.
Adams and Liberty. The Boston Patriotic
Song [nine-line verses, with music.]
[Portsmouth, N. H., 1798.] 2 pp.
BrU copy.   34298

Paine, Robert Treat, 1773-1811.
Adams and Liberty. Written by Thomas
Paine, A.M.
Salem, Mass., [1798]. Broadside.
EI copy.   34299

[Paine, Robert Treat], 1773-1811.
Adams and Liberty. Ye Sons of Columbia.
[Worcester? 1798.] Broadside.
AAS copy.   48558

Paine, Robert Treat, 1773-1811.
Adams and Liberty. The Boston Patriotic
Song. . . . Second Edition.
[Boston, Thomas & Andrews for] Linley
& Moore, [1799?]. 2 pp.
LOC copy.   34294

Paine, Robert Treat, 1773-1811.
Adams and Liberty. The Boston Patriotic
Song. Written by Thomas Paine, A. M.
Third Edition Corrected.
Boston, Von Hagen, [1800]. [2] pp.
BPL copy.   38177

[Paine, Robert Treat], 1773-1811.
Adams & Washington. A New Patriotic
Song.
Boston, von Hagen, [1798]. [2] pp.
AAS copy.   34300

Paine, Robert Treat, 1773-1811.
Boston, September [blank] 1794. Sir, The
Editor of the Federal Orrery. . . .
[Boston, 1794.] Broadside.
JCB copy.   47145

[Paine, Robert Treat], 1773-1811.
The Carrier of the Federal Orrery. Prsnts
his Kind Customers the Following
Customary Ode. . . . January 1, 1796.
[Boston, 1796.] Broadisde.
AAS copy.   30409

[Paine, Robert Treat, 1773-1811.
Dedicatory Address; Spoken by Mr.
Hodgkinson, October 29, 1798.
Boston, 1798.]
(No copy located.)   34301

Paine, Robert Treat, 1773-1811.
An Eulogy on the Life of General George
Washington.
Newburyport, Blunt, 1800. 22 pp.
AAS copy.   38178

Paine, Robert Treat, 1773-1811.
An Eulogy on the Life of General George
Washington.
Richmond, Va., Pace, [1800]. Broadside.
VaU copy.   38179

Paine, Robert Treat, 1773-1811.
The Green Mountain Farmer; a New
Patriotic Song.
Boston, Linley & Moore, [1798]. [2] pp.
AAS copy.   34302

Paine, Robert Treat, 1773-1811.
The Invention of Letters. . . . By Thomas
Paine.
Boston, 1795. 15 pp.
AAS copy.   29270

Paine, Robert Treat, 1773-1811.
The Invention of Letters. . . . By Thomas
Paine, A.M. The Second Edition.
Boston, Martin, 1795. 16 pp.
AAS copy.   29271

Paine, Robert Treat, 1773-1811.
An Oration, Written at the Request of the
Young Men of Boston.
Boston, Russell, 1799. 30 pp.
AAS copy.   36030

[Paine, Robert Treat], 1773-1811.
An Oration, Written at the Request of the
Young Men of Boston. . . . Second
Edition.
Boston, Russell, 1799. 30 pp.
AAS copy.   36032

Paine, Robert Treat, 1773-1811.
An Oration, Written at the Request of the
Young Men of Boston.
Suffield, Ct., Gray, 1799. 16 pp.
AAS copy.   36031

[Paine, Robert Treat, 1773-1811.
The Prize Prologue . . . January, 1794.
Boston, 1794.]
(No copy located.)   27467

Paine, Robert Treat, 1773-1811.
The Ruling Passion.
Boston, Manning & Loring, 1797. 32 pp.
AAS copy.   32634

[Paine, Robert Treat, 1773-1811.
Thomas Paine, To the Friends of Liberty.
. . . September 1, 1794.
Boston, 1794. Broadside.]
(No copy located.)   27468

Paine, Robert Treat, 1773-1811.
To Arms Columbia.
Boston, von Hagen for Gilfert, [1799].
[2] pp.
AAS copy.   36033

Paine, Seth, 1766-1801.
An Eulogy, on General George
Washington.
Charleston, S. C., Freneau & Paine, 1800.
[2], 28 pp.
AAS copy.   38176

Paine, Solomon, 1698-1754.
A Short View of the Difference. . . .
Newport, [R. I.], Franklin, 1752. 13, [2],
74 pp.
AAS copy.   40635

Paine, Thomas, pseud.
Tom Paine's Jests.
Philadelphia, Carey, 1794. 65, [7] pp.
AAS copy.   27469

Paine, Thomas, pseud.
Tom Paine's Jests.
Philadelphia, Carey, 1796. 72 pp.
AAS copy.   30952

Paine, Thomas, 1694-1757.
. . . An Almanack, for . . . 1718.

Boston, Crump, 1718. [16] pp.
AAS copy.   1920

Paine, Thomas, 1694-1757.
. . . An Almanack, for . . . 1719.
Boston, Fleet, 1719. [16] pp.
AAS copy.   1992

[Paine, Thomas], 1694-1757.
(Sibley, VI, 201-207.)
A Discourse Shewing.
Boston, Franklin for Henchman, 1721. 16
pp.
LOC copy.   2283

Paine, Thomas, 1694-1757.
(Sibley, VI, 201-207.)
The Doctrine of Earthquakes.
Boston, Henchman, 1738. 87 pp.
MHS copy.   3079

Paine, Thomas, 1694-1757.
(Sibley, VI, 201-207.)
The Doctrine of Original Sin.
Boston, Green for Henchman, 1724. [2],
ii, 23 pp.
AAS copy.   2574

Paine, Thomas, 1694-1757.
(Sibley, VI, 201-207.)
Gospel-Light.
Boston, Henchman, 1731. [4], 51 pp.
AAS copy.   3460

Paine, Thomas, 1694-1757.
(Sibley, VI, 201-207.)
Of the Evidence.
Boston, Kneeland and Green, 1732. [2],
27, [3], 7, [1] pp.
HC copy.   3586

Paine, Thomas, 1694-1757.
(Sibley, VI, 201-207.)
The Pastoral Charge.
Boston, Green for Henchman, 1720. [4],
ii, 42 pp.
AAS copy.   2165

Paine, Thomas, 1694-1757.
The Temporal Safety.
Boston, Kneeland and Green for Gerrish,
1732. [2], 19 pp.
AAS copy.   3587

Paine, Thomas, 1737-1809.
The Age of Reason.
Boston, Hall, 1794. 58 pp.
AAS copy.   27458

[Paine, Thomas, 1737-1809.
The Age of Reason.
Hartford, Babcock, 1794.]
(Imprint assumed by Evans from adv.
"Just Published, and selling at this
Office," Am. Mercury, Sept. 8, 1794.)   27459

Paine, Thomas, 1737-1809.
The Age of Reason.
New York, Birdsall & Hyers, 1794.
69 pp.
(Only known copy is tightly bound and
imperfect.)
JCB copy.   47147

Paine, Thomas, 1737-1809.
The Age of Reason. . . . Second American
Edition.
New York, Forman for Fellows, 1794.
[2], 84 pp.
AAS copy.   27461

Paine, Thomas, 1737-1809.
The Age of Reason.
New York, printed for J. Fellows, 1794. 69
pp.
(Not located, 1968.)   47146

Paine, Thomas, 1737-1809.
The Age of Reason.
New York, Swords for Fellows, 1794.
[1]-192, 191-202.
BA copy.   27460

Paine, Thomas, 1737-1809.
The Age of Reason.
Philadelphia, 1794. 196 pp.
AAS copy.   27462

[Paine, Thomas, 1737-1809.
The Age of Reason.
Worcester, Thomas, 1794. 116 pp.]
(The authority for such an ed. is the note

in Lincoln, Bib. Worcester, 2nd ed.,
p. 51.) 27463

Paine, Thomas, 1737-1809.
The Age of Reason. . . . To which is
Added an Examination of the Work, by
Gilbert Wakefield.
Worcester, Thomas, 1794. 158 pp.
AAS copy. 27464

[Paine, Thomas, 1737-1809.
The Age of Reason. . . . Third American
Edition.
New York, Swords for Fellows, 1795.]
(Assumed by Evans from the fact that
there was a 6th ed.) 29261

[Paine, Thomas, 1737-1809.
The Age of Reason. . . . Fourth American
Edition.
New York, Swords for Fellows, 1795.]
(Assumed by Evans from the fact that
there was a 6th ed.) 29262

[Paine, Thomas, 1737-1809.
The Age of Reason. . . . Fifth American
Edition.
New York, Swords for Fellows, 1795.]
(Assumed by Evans from the fact that
there was a 6th ed.) 29263

Paine, Thomas, 1737-1809.
The Age of Reason. . . . Sixth American
Edition.
New York, Forman for Fellows & Adam,
1795. 96 pp.
AAS copy. 29264

Paine, Thomas, 1737-1809.
The Age of Reason. Part the Second.
[Paris], "Printed for the Author," 1795.
viii, 143 pp.
(This is apparently the ed. described by
Evans. For the place of printing, see
Conway, Paine, IV, 13-16.)
AAS copy. 29267

[Paine, Thomas, 1737-1809.
The Age of Reason. . . . To which is
Added, An Abstract of a Work . . . by M.
Lequinio.
New York, 1795.]
(Apparently a garbled title resulting from
an adv.) 29266

Paine, Thomas, 1737-1809.
The Age of Reason. . . . Seventh
American Edition.
New York, Forman, 1795. 96 pp., 1 plate.
LOC copy. 29265

Paine, Thomas, 1737-1809.
The Age of Reason.
Philadelphia, Folwell, 1795. 82,
[1] pp.
LCP copy. 47527

Paine, Thomas, 1737-1809.
The Age of Reason. . . . Part the Second.
New York, Mott & Lyon for Fellows &
Adam and Reid, 1796. 199, [2] pp.
AAS copy. 30941

Paine, Thomas, 1737-1809.
The Age of Reason. Part the Second.
[Philadelphia], 1796. vii, [1],
100 pp.
AAS copy. 30942

Paine, Thomas, 1737-1809.
Agrarian Justice, Opposed to Agrarian
Laws.
Albany, Barber & Southwick, 1797. 31,
[1] pp.
NYSL copy. 48210

Paine, Thomas, 1737-1809.
Agrarian Justice.
Baltimore, Keatinge, 1797. 34 pp.
(Issued with and without adv. matter at
end.)
AAS copy. 32629

Paine, Thomas, 1737-1809.
Agrarian Justice.
Philadelphia, Folwell for Bache, [1797].
32 pp.
AAS copy. 32630

[Paine, Thomas], 1737-1809.
The American Crisis. (No. 1)
[Boston], Sold opposite the Court-House,

Queen-Street, [1776]. Broadside.
MHS copy. 43114

[Paine, Thomas], 1737-1809.
The American Crisis. Number 1.
Norwich, Trumbull, [1776]. 11 pp.
JCB copy. 43115

[Paine, Thomas], 1737-1809.
The American Crisis. Number I. . . .
[Philadelphia, 1776.] 8 pp.
(There are three eds. See Gimbel.)
HSP copy. 14953

[Paine, Thomas], 1737-1809.
No. II. The American Crisis.
[Fishkill, 1777]. pp. 9-24.
HEH copy. 43327

[Paine, Thomas], 1737-1809.
The American Crisis. Number II. By the
Author of Common Sense.
Philadelphia, Styner & Cist, [1777].
pp. 9-24.
NYPL copy. 15493

[Paine, Thomas], 1737-1809.
No. III. The American Crisis.
[Fishkill, 1777.] pp. [25]-54,
[1] pp.
HEH copy. 43328

[Paine, Thomas], 1737-1809.
The American Crisis. Number III. By the
Author of Common Sense.
Philadelphia, Styner & Cist, [1777]. pp.
[25]-56.
NYPL copy. 15494

[Paine, Thomas], 1737-1809.
No. IV. The American Crisis.
[Fishkill, 1777]. pp. [57]-60.
NYHS copy. 43329

[Paine, Thomas], 1737-1809.
The Crisis. Number IV. By the Author of
Common Sense.
Philadelphia, Steiner & Cist, [1777]. pp.
[57]-60.
HSP copy. 15495

[Paine, Thomas], 1737-1809.
The American Crisis. Number V.
Hartford, 1778. 32 pp.
AAS copy. 15952

[Paine, Thomas], 1737-1809.
The American Crisis. Number V.
Lancaster, 1778. pp. [3], 64-88.
AAS copy. 15951

[Paine, Thomas], 1737-1809.
The American Crisis. Number V.
New Haven, 1778. 32 pp.
AAS copy. 15953

[Paine, Thomas], 1737-1809.
The American Crisis. Number VI.
Philadelphia, Dunlap, 1778.]
(Announced in the Pa. Gazette of June
13,1778, but apparently not printed in
America at this time.) 15954

[Paine, Thomas], 1737-1809.
The American Crisis. Number VII.
Philadelphia, Dunlap, 1778.]
(Not printed in America at this time.)
15955

[Paine, Thomas, 1737-1809.
The American Crisis Number X. On the
King of England's Speech. . . . March 5,
1782.
Philadelphia, 1782.]
(No separate printing at this time has
been located.) 17648

[Paine, Thomas, 1737-1809.
The American Crisis Number XI. On the
Present State of News. . . . May 22, 1782.
(No separate printing made at this time
has been located.) 17649

[Paine, Thomas, 1737-1809.
The American Crisis Number XII. To the
Earl of Shelburne. Philadelphia, 1782.]
(No separate printing made at this time
has been located.) 17650

[Paine, Thomas, 1737-1809.
The American Crisis. Number XIII.
Thoughts on this Peace. . . . April 19,
1783.]

(This edition was assumed by Evans.)
18077

Paine, Thomas, 1737-1809.
Common Sense; Addressed to the
Inhabitants of America.
n. p., Printed for the perusal of the
inhabitants of the Thirteen United
Colonies, 1776. 44 pp.
LCP copy. 43122

[Paine, Thomas], 1737-1809.
Common Sense; Addressed to the
Inhabitants of America.
Boston, Edes & Gill and Fleets, 1776. [4],
44 pp.
AAS copy. 14955

[Paine, Thomas], 1737-1809.
Common Sense; Addressed to the
Inhabitants of America.
Hartford, Watson, [1776]. 59 pp.
(The only recorded copy is defective.)
AAS copy. 43116

[Paine, Thomas], 1737-1809.
Common Sense; Addressed to the
Inhabitants of America. . . . Fourth
Edition.
Lancaster, [1776]. 63 pp.
LOC copy. 14960

[Paine, Thomas], 1737-1809.
Common Sense, Addressed to the
Inhabitants of America.
New York, Anderson, [1776]. [4], 56 pp.
AAS copy. 14956

[Paine, Thomas], 1737-1809.
Common Sense, Addressed to the
Inhabitants of America.
Newburyport, [1776]. 61, [1] pp.
AAS copy. 14961

[Paine, Thomas], 1737-1809.
Common Sense; Addressed to the
Inhabitants of America.
Newburyport, [Mycall] for Phillips of
Andover, [1776]. 61, [1] pp.
AAS copy. 43117

[Paine, Thomas], 1737-1809.
Common Sense; Addressed to the
Inhabitants of America.
Newport, 1776. pp. [4], 16, [2], 31, [1],
[32]-70, [1].
PrPL copy. 14965

[Paine, Thomas], 1737-1809.
Common Sense; Addressed to the
Inhabitants of America.
Newport, Southwick, 1776. [4],
16 pp.
AAS copy. 43118

[Paine, Thomas], 1737-1809.
Common Sense; Addressed to the
Inhabitants of America.
Norwich, Spooner and Green, 1776.
56 pp.
AAS copy. 14957

[Paine, Thomas], 1737-1809.
Common Sense; Addressed to the
Inhabitants of America.
Norwich, Spooner for Green of New
London, [1776]. 64 pp.
AAS copy. 43119

[Paine, Thomas], 1737-1809.
Common Sense; Addressed to the
Inhabitants of America.
Philadelphia, Bell, 1776. [4], 79,
[1] pp.
AAS copy. 14954

[Paine, Thomas], 1737-1809.
Common Sense; with the Whole Appendix.
Philadelphia, Bell, 1776. pp. [8], [1]-79.
[4], 82-147, [6], 6-16.
AAS copy. 14966

[Paine, Thomas], 1737-1809.
Common Sense: Addressed to the
Inhabitants of America.
Philadelphia, Bell, 1776. [4], 77 pp.
AAS copy. 43120

[Paine, Thomas], 1737-1809.
Common Sense; Addressed to the
Inhabitants of America. . . . Second
Edition.
Philadelphia, Bell, 1776. pp. [4], 1-79,

[6], 82-147, [1].
AAS copy.   14964

[Paine, Thomas], 1737-1809.
Common Sense; Addressed to the
Inhabitants of America.
Philadelphia, Bradfords, [1776]. [6], 50
pp.
(There are two eds. and two variants of
each. See Gimbel.)
AAS copy.   14959

[Paine, Thomas], 1737-1809.
Common Sense; Addressed to the
Inhabitants of America.
Philadelphia, Bradfords, 1776. 99 pp.
AAS copy.   43121

[Paine, Thomas], 1737-1809.
Common Sense: Addressed to the
Inhabitants of America. . . . Sixth Edition.
Providence, 1776. 44, [2] pp.
AAS copy.   14958

[Paine, Thomas], 1737-1809.
Common Sense: Addressed to the
Inhabitants of America. . . . Tenth
Edition.
Providence, Carter, 1776. 33 pp.
AAS copy.   43123

[Paine, Thomas], 1737-1809.
Common Sense; Addressed to the
Inhabitants of America.
Salem, Russell, 1776. 28 pp.
AAS copy.   14962

[Paine, Thomas], 1737-1809.
Common Sense; Addressed to the
Inhabitants of America.
Albany, Websters, 1791. 60 pp.
AAS copy.   23657

Paine, Thomas, 1737-1809.
Common Sense.
Philadelphia, Bradfords, 1791. 99 pp.
AAS copy.   23658

[Paine, Thomas], 1737-1809.
The Crisis Extraordinary.
Philadelphia, "Sold by William Harris at his
Store," [1780]. 16 pp.
NYPL copy.   16918

[Paine, Thomas], 1737-1809.
The Crisis Extraordinary.
Philadelphia, "Sold by William Harris in
Second-Street," [1780]. 16 pp.
AAS copy.   16919

[Paine, Thomas], 1737-1809.
The Crisis. Number IV. By the Author of
Common Sense.
Philadelphia, Steiner & Cist, [1777]. pp.
[57]-60.
HSP copy.   15495

[Paine, Thomas], 1737-1809.
The Crisis. Number VIII.
Philadelphia, 1780.]
(Separate printing assumed by Evans.)
                                             16916

[Paine, Thomas], 1737-1809.
The Crisis. Number IX.
Philadelphia, 1780.]
(Separate printing assumed by Evans.)
                                             16917

Paine, Thomas, 1737-1809.
The Decline and Fall of the English
System of Finance.
New York, Mott & Lyon for Fellows,
1796. 56 pp.
AAS copy.   30943

Paine, Thomas, 1737-1809.
The Decline & Fall of the English System
of Finance. . . . Second American Edition.
New York, Davis for Fellows, 1796. 58,
[1] pp.
AAS copy.   30944

Paine, Thomas, 1737-1809.
The Decline and Fall of the English
System of Finance.
Philadelphia, Campbell, 1796. 27,
[1] pp.
AAS copy.   30947

[Paine, Thomas], 1737-1809.
The Decline and Fall of the English
System of Finance.

Philadelphia, Campbell, 1796. 58, [1] pp.]
(No copy could be located with such
pagination.)   30948

Paine, Thomas, 1737-1809.
The Decline and Fall of the English
System of Finance.
Philadelphia, Page for Bache, 1796. pp.
[2], [1]-33, [2], 34-40.
AAS copy.   30945

Paine, Thomas, 1737-1809.
Dissertation on First Principles of
Government.
Philadelphia, Conrad, 1795. 41 pp.
AAS copy.   29268

Paine, Thomas, 1737-1809.
Dissertations on Government.
Philadelphia, Cist for Hall & Sellers and
Prichard, 1786. [4], 53 pp.
AAS copy.   ,19880

Paine, Thomas, 1737-1809.
Dissertation on the First-Principles of
Government.
Carlisle, Pa., Steel, 1796. 36 pp.
JCB copy.   30949

Paine, Thomas, 1737-1809.
Examination of the Passages in the New
Testament.
New York, [1807]. 56 pp.
(Misdated 1795 by Evans.)
AAS copy.   29269

[Paine, Thomas], 1737-1809.
The First Principles of Government.
New York, Fellows, 1796.]
(Imprint assumed by Evans from adv.)
                                             30950

[Paine, Thomas], 1737-1809.
Gesunde Vernunft.
Philadelphia, Steiner & Cist, 1776. viii, 70
pp.
NYPL copy.   14963

Paine, Thomas, 1737-1809.
Letter Addressed to the Abbe Raynal.
Boston, Edes, 1782. 70 pp.
AAS copy.   17653

Paine, Thomas, 1737-1809.
Letter Addressed to the Abbe Raynal.
Philadelphia, Steiner for Aitken, 1782.
[4], 77 pp.
AAS copy.   17651

[Paine, Thomas], 1737-1809.
Letter Addressed to the Abbe Raynal. . . .
Second Edition.
Philadelphia, Steiner for Aitken, 1782.
[4], 77 pp.]
(There was a 2nd ed., but no means is
known of distinguishing copies of it.)
                                             17652

[Paine, Thomas], 1737-1809.
Letter Addressed to the Abbe Raynal.
Trenton, 1782.]
(Entry from an adv.)   17654

Paine, Thomas, 1737-1809.
Letter Addressed to the Addressers.
New York, Greenleaf, 1793. [2],
38 pp.
AAS copy.   25957

Paine, Thomas, 1737-1809.
Letter Addressed to the Addressers.
Philadelphia, Rice, 1793. 43, [4] pp.
LCP copy.   25958

Paine, Thomas, 1737-1809.
A Letter from Mr. Paine to Mr. Secretary
Dundas.
New York, Loudon, [1792]. 16 pp.
LOC copy.   24649

Paine, Thomas, 1737-1809.
Letter to George Washington.
Philadelphia, Bache, 1796. [2], 76, [1] pp.
AAS copy.   30951

Paine, Thomas, 1737-1809.
Thomas Paine's Letter to George
Washington. . . . [July 30th, 1796.]
Baltimore, 1797. 36 pp.
HC copy.   32631

Paine, Thomas, 1737-1809.
A Letter to the Hon. Thomas Erskine.

Newburgh, N. Y., Denniston, [1797].
48 pp.
HEH copy.   32632

Paine, Thomas, 1737-1809.
Letter to the People of France.
New York, 1798. 28 pp.
LCP copy.   34292

[Paine, Thomas], 1737-1809.
The Liberty Tree. A song.
Philadelphia, 1779.]
(Adv. Pa. Evening Post, Feb. 10, 1779.)
                                             16323

Paine, Thomas, 1737-1809.
Prospects on the War, and Paper
Currency.
Baltimore, Adams for Fisher & Cole,
1794. 37, [11] pp.
NYHS copy.   27465

[Paine, Thomas], 1737-1809.
Public Good, Being an Examination into
the Claim of Virginia.
Philadelphia, Dunlap, 1780. 38 pp.
AAS copy.   16920

Paine, Thomas, 1737-1809.
Rights of Man.
Baltimore, Graham, 1791. 88 pp.
AAS copy.   23659

Paine, Thomas, 1737-1809.
Rights of Man.
Bennington, 1791. 87 pp.
AAS copy.   23660

Paine, Thomas, 1737-1809.
Rights of Man. . . . Third Edition.
Boston, Thomas & Andrews, 1791. 79 pp.
AAS copy.   23661

Paine, Thomas, 1737-1809.
Rights of Man. . . . Fourth American
Edition.
Boston, Thomas & Andrews, 1791. 79 pp.
AAS copy.   23662

Paine, Thomas, 1737-1809.
Rights of Man.
Carlisle, Kline, 1791. 93 pp.
AAS copy.   23663

Paine, Thomas, 1737-1809.
Rights of Man. . . . Second Edition.
Philadelphia, Smith, 1791. 105 pp.
AAS copy.   23664

Paine, Thomas, 1737-1809.
Rights of Man. . . . Second Philadelphia
Edition.
Philadelphia, Smith, 1791. [4], 100 pp.
LOC copy.   23665

Paine, Thomas, 1737-1809.
Rights of Man: Part the First.
New York, Berry, Rogers & Berry, 1742
(1792). 76 pp.
BrU copy.   24650

Paine, Thomas, 1737-1809.
Rights of Man. Part the First [-Second].
Boston, Fleets, 1793. 87 pp.
JCB copy.   25959

[Paine, Thomas], 1737-1809.
Rights of Man. Part the Second.
Baltimore, Graham, 1792?]
(Imprint assumed by Evans from an adv.)
                                             24655

Paine, Thomas, 1737-1809.
Rights of Man. Part the Second.
Albany, Websters, 1792. 90, 10 pp.
AAS copy.   25960

Paine, Thomas, 1737-1809.
Rights of Man. Part the Second.
Boston, Fleets, 1792. ix, [1], 108 pp.
AAS copy.   24652

Paine, Thomas, 1737-1809.
Rights of Man. Part the Second.
Carlisle, Kline, 1792. 100 pp.
(The title given by Evans was assumed
from an adv.)
AAS copy.   24656

[Paine, Thomas], 1737-1809.
Rights of Man. Part the Second.
New London, Green, 1792?]
(Imprint assumed by Evans from adv. "To

be sold by" Green in Conn. Gazette, Aug.
30, 1792.)   24657

Paine, Thomas, 1737-1809.
Rights of Man. Part the Second.
New York, Gaine, 1792. 88 pp.
NYPL copy.   24651

Paine, Thomas, 1737-1809.
Rights of Man. Part the Second.
Philadelphia, Rice and Smith, 1792. 120
pp.
NYPL copy.   24653

Paine, Thomas, 1737-1809.
Rights of Man. Part the Second. . . .
Second Philadelphia Edition.
Philadelphia, Rice and Smith, 1792. 96 pp.
AAS copy.   24654

Paine, Thomas, 1737-1809.
Rights of Man: Part the Second.
New York, Berry, Rogers & Berry, 1793.
87, [1] pp.
AAS copy.   25961

Paine, Thomas, 1737-1809.
Rights of Man. Part the Second.
Albany, Websters, 1794. 96, 10 pp.
NYSL copy.   47148

Paine, Thomas, 1737-1809.
The Rights of Man. For the Use and
Benefit of all Mankind.
Philadelphia, 1797. iv, 56 pp.
BM copy.   32767

Paine, Thomas, 1737-1809.
The Rights of Man, for the Benefit of All
Mankind.
Philadelphia, Webster, 1797. iv, 56 pp.
Pierce W. Gaines copy.   48211

Paine, Thomas, 1737-1809.
Speech of Thomas Paine . . . July 7, 1795.
Philadelphia, Page for Bache, 1796.
(This is the 2nd part of 30945, q. v.)   30946

[Paine, Thomas, 1737-1809.
A Supernumary Crisis. Number XIV. To
Sir Guy Carleton. . . . May 31, 1783.
Philadelphia, 1783.]
(This edition was assumed by Evans.)
          18078

[Paine, Thomas, 1737-1809.
A Supernumary Crisis. Number XV. To
the People of America. . . . September 9,
1793.
New York, 1793.]
(This edition was assumed by Evans.)
          18079

Paine, Thomas, 1737-1809.
To the Public . . . December 28, 1778. . . .
By the Goddess of Plain Truth.
[Philadelphia, 1778.] Broadside.
HSP copy.   43522

Paine, Thomas, 1737-1809.
The Works of. . . . In Two Volumes.
Philadelphia, Carey, 1797. vi, [2], 391,
[1]; [8], 368, 148 pp.
(Issued also with 33157 bound at the end.)
AAS copy.   32633

Paine, Thomas, 1737-1809.
The Writings of Thomas Paine.
Albany, Websters, [1792]. xii, 124; 90, 60;
10, 186; 41; 70; 24 pp.
LOC copy.   24658

Paine, Thomas, 1737-1809.
The Writings of Thomas Paine.
Albany, Websters, [1792]. [517] pp.
HEH copy.   46536

Paine, Thomas, 1737-1809.
The Writings of. . . .
Albany, Websters, [1794?]. pp. [i]-xii,
[1]-60, [2], [1]-186, [1]-41, [4], vi-vii,
[1], [9]-70, [2], [1]-24, [1]-124, [1]-90,
[1]-10.
(Other copies have different eds. of some
of the pamphlets.)
AAS copy.   27466

Paine, Thomas, 1737-1809.
The Writings of. . . .
Albany, Websters for Webster & Steel,
etc., 1794.

(An imprint variant of 27466, q. v. for
text.)
AAS copy.   47149

Paine, Thomas, 1737-1809, defendant.
The Trial of Thomas Paine.
Boston, Thomas & Andrews, 1793. 43 pp.
AAS copy.   26280

Paine, Thomas, 1737-1809, defendant.
The Trial of Thomas Paine.
Philadelphia, Parker, 1793. 28 pp.
LCP copy.   26281

Paine, Thomas, 1773-1811.
See
Paine, Robert Treat, 1773-1811.

[Paine detected [by John Henderson,
1755-1841].
Natchez, Marschalk, 1799.] ii, 53 pp.
(Copy cannot be reproduced.)   48876

Paisiello, Giovanii, 1741-1816.
Recitativo e Rondo.
Filadelfia, Trisobio, [1797]. 8 pp.
(Not located, 1968.)   48212

[Paisiello, Giovanni], 1773-1836.
How Can I Forget.
New York & Philadelphia, B. Carr,
[1796]. [2] pp.
AAS copy.   47873

Paley, William, 1743-1805.
The Principles of Moral and Political
Philosophy. . . . Seventh Edition.
Philadelphia, Dobson, 1788. [2], 499, [1]
pp.
AAS copy.   21356

Paley, William, 1743-1805.
The Principles of Moral and Political
Philosophy.
Philadelphia, Dobson, 1794. 618, [2] pp.
AAS copy.   27470

Paley, William, 1743-1805.
The Principles of Moral and Political
Philosophy.
Boston, Etheridge for White, etc., 1795.
pp. [i]-xvii, [3], [23]-490.
AAS copy.   29272

Paley, William, 1743-1805.
A View of the Evidences of Christianity.
Boston, Manning & Loring for Hall, etc.,
1795. pp. [i]-iv, [4], [13]-387.
AAS copy.   29273

Paley, William, 1743-1805.
A View of the Evidences of Christianity.
Philadelphia, Dobson, 1795. xii, 443 pp.
AAS copy.   29274

[Palisot de Beauvois, Ambroise Marie.
Catalogue Raisonne du Museum de Mr. C.
W. Peale.
Philadelphia, 1800.]
(Sabin 4211 is the only authority for an
ed. with this imprint.)   36915

The Palladium of Conscience.
Philadelphia, Bell, 1773. [5], 119, [1], xii,
155, [1] pp.
(Some copies have a general title dated
1774. See Evans' note.)
AAS copy.   13154

Palladium of Knowledge.
See also
Young, William P.

Palladium of Knowledge: or, the Carolina
and Georgia Almanac, for . . . 1797.
Charleston, Young. [50] pp.
AAS copy.   31682

Palladium of Knowledge: or, the Carolina
and Georgia Almanac, for. . . . 1798.
Charleston, Young. [48] pp.
AAS copy.   33256

Palmer, Elihu, 1764-1806.
An Enquiry Relative to the . . . Human
Species.
New York, Crookes, 1797. 35 pp.
AAS copy.   32635

Palmer, Elihu, 1764-1806.
The Political Happiness of Nations.
[New York, 1800.] 23 pp.
AAS copy.   38181

Palmer, Herbert, 1601-1647.
(D. N. B.)
Memorials of Godliness.
Boston, 1713. [2], ii, 36, [2], ii, 28, [2],
ii, 18 pp.
HC copy.   1643

Palmer, John, schoolmaster at Bath.
The Haunted Cavern.
Baltimore, Pechin for Keatinge, 1796. 127
pp.
(Evans guessed at the printer from
Keatinge's adv.)
AAS copy.   30953

Palmer, John, schoolmaster at Bath.
The Haunted Cavern.
Bennington, Haswell, 1796. 197 pp., 1
plate.
(The frontispiece here reproduced is from
the LOC copy.)
VtU copy.   30954

[Palmer, John, 1729-1790.
Free Thoughts on the Inconsistency of
Conforming.
Boston, White, 1787.]
("To be sold," Ind. Chronicle, Feb. 15,
1787; ghost of a London ed.)   20613

[Palmer, John, 1729-1790.
Observations in Defence of the Liberty of
Man.
Boston, White, 1787.]
("To be sold," Ind. Chronicle, Feb. 15,
1787; ghost of a London ed.)   20614

Palmer, Joseph, & Co.
Sperma-ceti Candles Warranted Pure.
[Boston, 1770?] Broadside.
MHS copy.   42144

[Palmer, Robert F.
The Prodigal Reformed. By a Virginia
Farmer.
Richmond? 1796.]
(Entry from copyright notice.)   30955

Palmer, Stephen, 1766-1821.
A Sermon, Delivered at Rowley.
Dedham, Heatons, 1797. 35 pp.
AAS copy.   32636

Palmer, Stephen, 1766-1821.
A Sermon, Occasioned by the Death of
Calvin Whiting.
Boston, Etheridge, 1795. 19 pp.
AAS copy.   29275

Palmer, Stephen, 1766-1821.
A Sermon, Occasioned by the Death of
Mr. Jeremiah Fuller.
Dedham, Mass., Mann & Adams, 1798. 27
pp.
AAS copy.   34304

[Palmer, Thomas.
Serious Address to Unbaptized
Christians.
New York, 1750.]
(From Hildeburn.)   6579

[A Pamphlet for the information of
merchants concerned in export.
Baltimore, Hayes, 1798.]
("Just published," Federal Gazette, Jan.
13, 1798.)   48560

Panca, Sancho, pseud.
Advertisement! To the Several Printers in
Hartford, New-Haven, New-London and
Norwich. . . . March 19.
n. p., [178-?]. Broadside.
CHS copy.   43750

A Panegyrick, By Strephon.
Philadelphia, Dunlap, 1762. 11 pp.
LCP copy.   9280

[Panther, Abraham, pseud.
An Account of a Beautiful Young Lady.
Middletown, 1787.]
("To be had at this office," Middlesex
Gazette, May 21, 1787.)   20615

[Panther, Abraham, pseud.
A Surprising Narrative of a Young
Woman.
New York, [1787]. 9 pp.
(Sabin 93981; no copy located.)   20616

Panther, Abraham, pseud.

A Very Surprising Narrative. . . . Fifth
Edition.
New York, [1790]. 11 pp.
WisHS copy.   45938

[Panther, Abraham]
A Very surprising narrative of a young
woman, third edition.
Springfield, 1794.]
(Vail: Old Frontier 997; no copy known.)
          47151

[Panther, Abraham]
A Very Surprising Narrative of a Young
Woman. . . . Second Windsor Edition.
[Windsor], Spooner, 1794. 12 pp.
AAS copy.   47150

Panther, Abraham, pseud.
A Very Surprising Narrative.
Windsor, Spooner, 1794. 11 pp.
(Evans assumed the title from advs. The
unique copy is defective.)
Wis. Hist. Soc. copy.   27471

[Panther, Abraham, pseud.
A Surprising Narrative. . . . Second Windsor
Edition.
Windsor, Spooner, 1795.]
(Apparently a ghost of 27471 arising from
an adv.)   29276

Panther, Abraham, pseud.
A Very Surprising Narrative.
Greenfield, Mass., 1796. 10 pp.
AAS copy.   30956

Panther, Abraham, pseud.
A Very Surprising Narrative. . . . Third
Windsor Edition.
[Windsor, Vt.], Spooner, 1796. 11 pp.
HEH copy.   30957

[Panther, Abraham, pseud.
A Very Surprising Narrative.
Putney, Vt., 1797. 12 pp.
(Imprint assumed by Evans from adv.
"For sale at this office," The Argus, Mar.
30, 1797.)   32637

Panther, Abraham, pseud.
A Surprising Narrative of a Young
Woman.
Rutland, Vt., Fay, 1797.
(Dawson's Book Shop cat. 177 (1943), No.
143.)   32638

Panther, Abraham, pseud.
A Very Surprising Narrative.
Augusta, Me., [1798]. 12 pp.
Deering copy.   34305

Panther, Abraham, pseud.
A Surprising Narrative.
Fryeburgh, Me., 1799. 8 pp.
AAS copy.   36036

Panther, Abraham, pseud.
A Surprising Narrative.
Leominster, Mass., Prentiss for
Whitcomb, [1799]. 12 pp.
AAS copy.   36035

Panther, Abraham, pseud.
A Very Surprising Narrative.
Bennington, Vt., Collier & Stockwell,
1800. 12 pp.
NYSL copy.   38183

Panther, Abraham, pseud.
A Very Surprising Narrative.
Brookfield, Mass., 1800. 12 pp.
AAS copy.   38182

[A Paper Concerning some Disturbances
in Christ-Church.
Philadelphia, 1745.]
(Answered in Am. Weekly Mercury, Apr.
4, 1745.)   5669

[A Paper Containing Exceptions against
some Things in the Present Mode of
Administering . . . the Lord's Supper.
Lancaster, 1747. 17 pp.]
(Unique copy at NYSL not located.) 6056

Papers Relating to an Act of the Assembly
[by Cadwallader Colden, 1688-1776].
New York, 1724. [2], 24 pp., map.
NYPL copy.   2512

Papers Respecting Intrusions by
Connecticut Claimants.

[Philadelphia], Hall & Sellers, [1797?] 6
pp.
(The only known copy is imperfect.)
NYPL copy.   48213

Papers Respecting Intrusions by
Connecticut Claimants.
[Philadelphia], Hall & Sellers, 1796. 24
pp.
LCP copy.   30958

[The Papist's Curses.
Philadelphia? 1743.]
("Just published," Pa. Journal, Nov. 3,
1743.)   5266

Par sa Legereté.
[Philadelphia, 1798?] Broadside.
HEH copy.   48561

. . . . The Parable of the Labourers in the
Vineyard.
Philadelphia, Johnsons, 1800. 36 pp.
AAS copy.   37130

The Parable of the One Talent,
Expounded.
n.p., n.d. Broadside.
CHS copy.   49129

Paradise Regain'd. . . . Dec. 18, 1770.
[New York, 1770.] 3 pp.
NYPL copy.   11849

Die Paradisische Aloe [by Samuel Lutz,
1674-1750].
Germantown, 1770. 303, [1] pp.
AAS copy.   11706

Paradisisches Wunder-Spiel [by Johann
Conrad Beissel, 1690-1768].
Ephrata, 1754. [1], 212, [1] pp.
AAS copy.   7147

Paradisisches Wunder-Spiel [by Johann
Conrad Beissel, 1690-1768].
Ephrata, 1766. 9, [2], 472, [6] pp.
(The AAS copy in a contemporary
binding lacks the Foreword and the Index.
These are added from the HSP copy.)
Composite copy.   10239

A Paraphrase on Eight Chapters of the
Prophet Isaiah [by Simeon Strong,
1735-1805].
Worcester, Thomas, 1795. 41 pp.
AAS copy.   28284

A Paraphrase, on part, of the Oeconomy
of Human Life [by James Bowdoin,
1726-1790].
Boston, 1759. [6], 88 pp.
AAS copy.   8307

A Paraphrase on Some Parts of the Book
of Job [by Richard Devens, 1749-1835].
Boston, Hall, 1795. 39 pp.
AAS copy.   28273

A Paraphrase on the Second Epistle of
John, the Round-head.
[Boston? 1775?] Broadside.
(The only known copy is imperfect.)
BPL copy.   42918

A Paraphrastical Exposition [by John
Philly].
[New York], 1693. 8 pp.
(See Eames, First Year, p. 10.)
NYPL copy.   680

Parental Wishes and Charges [by Cotton
Mather, 1663-1728].
Boston, 1705. 60 pp.
VaU copy.   1219

A Parent's Advice for his Family.
New London, Greens, 1792. 24 pp.
AAS copy.   24659

The Parent's Best Gift: Containing the
Church Catechism.
New York, Harrisson, 1796. 23 pp.
AAS copy.   47874

[Parent's Gift.
Boston, 1741.]
("Just Published," Boston Evening Post,
May 18, 1741.)   4775

Pariset, Nicholas.
The American Trooper's Pocket
Companion.

Trenton, 1793. 45 pp.
HC copy.   25962

Parish, Elijah, 1762-1825.
The Excellence of the Gospel.
Newburyport, March, 1798. 28 pp.
AAS copy.   34306

Parish, Elijah, 1762-1825.
An Oration, Delivered at Byfield,
February 22d, 1800.
Newburyport, March, [1800]. 32 pp.
AAS copy.   38184

Parish, Elijah, 1762-1825.
An Oration Delivered at Byfield, July 4,
1799.
Newburyport, March, [1799]. 18 pp.
AAS copy.   36037

Parish, Elijah, 1762-1825.
An Oration Delivered at Byfield July 4,
1799. . . . Second Edition.
Newburyport, March, [1799]. 14 pp.
AAS copy.   36038

Parish, Elijah, 1762-1825.
A Sermon, Occasioned by the Death of
. . . John Cleaveland.
Newburyport, March, [1799].
28 pp.
AAS copy.   36039

Parish, Elijah, 1762-1825.
A Sermon, Preached at the Ordination of
. . . Ariel Parish.
Salem, Cushing, 1792. 40 pp.
AAS copy.   24660

The Parishioner, Having Studied the
Point [by Ebenezer Devotion, 1714-1771].
[Hartford], 1769. 24 pp.
BA copy.   11237

Park, Sir James Allan, 1763-1838.
A System of the Law of Marine
Insurances.
Philadelphia, Crukshank, 1789. xvi, [8],
xliv, 530, [45] pp.
AAS copy.   22048

Park, Sir James Allan, 1763-1838.
A System of the Law of Marine
Insurances. . . . Second American . . .
Edition.
Boston, Thomas & Andrews, etc., 1799.
xxvii, [1], liv, 516 (i.e. 570) pp.
AAS copy.   36040

Park, Sir James Allan, 1763-1838.
Appendix to a System of the Law of
Marine Insurance.
Boston, Thomas & Andrews, for D. West
and J. West, 1800. [40] pp., irregularly
numbered.
(Also issued as part of 38187, q. v.) 38185

Park, Sir James Allan, 1763-1838.
A System of the Law of Marine
Insurances. . . . Third American, from the
Latest English Ed.
Boston, Thomas & Andrews for D. West
and J. West, 1800. xxvii, [1], liv, 516
(i.e. 570) pp.
(Issued with revised tp. as 38187, q. v.)
          38186

Park, Sir James Allan, 1763-1838.
A System of the Law of Marine
Insurances. . . . Third American, from the
Third English Edition. . . . An Appendix.
Boston, Thomas & Andrews for D. West
and J. West, 1800, xxvii, [1], liv, 516
(i.e. 570), [40] (irregularly numbered) pp.
AAS copy.   38187

Park, Joseph, 1705-1777.
(Sibley, VII, 415-421.)
God Visiting and Avenging.
New London, 1761. 39, 23 pp.
YC copy.   8962

[Park, Joseph, 1705-1777.
A Sermon Delivered in the
Congregational Church in Preston.
New London, 1761.]
(Perhaps not printed.)   8963

Park, Mungo, 1771-1806.
Travels, in the Interior Districts of Africa.
New York, Tiebout, 1800. 354, [2], 86 pp.,
1 map.
AAS copy.   38189

Park, Mungo, 1771-1806.
Travels in the Interior Districts of Africa.
Philadelphia, Humphreys, 1800. 484 pp., 1
map.
AAS copy.   38188

Park, Thomas, 1766-1844.
An Oration: Delivered in the
College-Hall.
Providence, Wheeler, [1788]. 16 pp.
AAS copy.   21357

Parker, Benjamin, 1718-1789.
The Difficulties, Duties and
Encouragements.
Portsmouth, 1759. 33 pp.
AAS copy.   8450

Parker, Benjamin, 1718-1789.
(Sibley, X.)
The Excellent Spirit.
Salem, 1774. 19 pp.
AAS copy.   13512

Parker, Daniel, 1669-1728.
A Perswasive to make a Publick
Confession.
Boston, Henchman, 1730. [4], 19 pp.
BPL copy.   3334

Parker, Daniel, 1669-1728.
(D. Parker, Perswasive, preface.)
A Perswasive.
Salem, 1770. 24 pp.
AAS copy.   11796

Parker, Isaac, 1768-1830.
An Oration, Delivered at Castine, July 4,
1796.
Boston, Hall, 1796. 15 pp.
LOC copy.   30959

Parker, Isaac, 1768-1830.
An Oration on the Sublime Virtues.
Portland, Me., Jenks, [1800]. 24 pp.
AAS copy.   38190

Parker, Isaiah, 1752-1848.
A Funeral Discourse . . . Josiah Bowles.
Boston, Parker, 1800. 21 pp.
AAS copy.   38191

Parker, James, 1714?-1770.
An Appeal to the Publick of
New-York. . . . February 23, 1759.
[Woodbridge, Parker, 1759.] [2] pp.
LCP copy.   41071

Parker, James, 1714?-1770.
(D. A. B.)
Conductor Generalis.
Woodbridge, Parker, for Hall, 1764. xvi, 592
pp.
(The NYPL copy described by Evans
could not be reproduced. NJHS has a
Parker for Holt issue.)
AAS copy.   9775

Parker, James, 1714?-1770.
Conductor Generalis.
Woodbridge, [N. J.], Parker for Holt,
1764. xvi, 592 pp.
(An imprint variant of 9775, q. v.)   41479

[Parker, James, 1714?-1770.
The Conductor Generalis.
New York, Parker, 1767.]
("Lately publish'd and to be sold by
James Parker," N. Y. Gazette: or Weekly
Post-Boy, Feb. 5, 1767.)   10721

[Parker, James, 1714?-1770.
The Conductor Generalis.
New York, Gaine, 1790.]
("Just published," N. Y. Journal, Apr. 22,
1790.)   22754

Parker, James, 1714?-1770.
The Conductor Generalis.
Philadelphia, Campbell, 1792. xv, [1], 464
pp.
AAS copy.   24661

Parker, James, 1714?-1770.
The Conductor Generalis.
Albany, Websters, 1794. 467, [1] pp.
AAS copy.   27472

Parker, James, 1714?-1770.
An Humble Address to the Publick. . . .
May 30, 1766.
[New York, 1766]. [2] pp.
APS copy.   41655

Parker, James, 1714?-1770.
Proposals for Printing by Subscription, a
Journal of the Proceedings . . . of the
Conspiracy. . . . July 16, 1742.
[New York, 1742.] 2 pp.
NYHS copy.   40285

Parker, James, 1714?-1770.
Showing the Unreasonableness of the . . .
Stamp-Duty.
[New York, Parker, 1759.] 4 pp.
LCP copy.   41042

Parker, Richard (d. 1797), defendant.
The Trial of. . . . Taken in Short Hand
. . . by Job Sibly.
Boston, Etheridge for Clap, 1797,
60 pp.
AAS copy.   32837

Parker, Richard, (d. 1797), defendant.
The Tryal, Last Dying Words, Speech and
Confession of. . . .
[New York: 1797?] Broadside.
NYHS copy.   48214

Parker, Samuel, bp., 1744-1804.
A Sermon, Preached before His Honor
the Lieutenant-Governor.
Boston, Adams, 1793. 42 pp.
AAS copy.   25963

Parkhurst, Jabez.
An Oration, Delivered on the Fourth of
July, 1798.
Newark, N. J., Pennington & Dodge, 1798.
12 pp.
NYHS copy.   34308

Parkinson, Richard, 1748-1815.
The Experienced Farmer. . . . In Two
Volumes.
Philadelphia, Cist, 1799. xx, 275; [2], 292
pp.
AAS copy.   36041

Parkman, Ebenezer, 1703-1782.
(Sibley, VI, 511-527.)
The Love of Christ.
Boston, Fowle & Draper for Winter; 1761.
37 pp.
AAS copy.   8965

Parkman, Ebenezer, 1703-1782.
(Sibley, VI, 511-527.)
Reformers and Intercessors.
Boston, Kneeland, 1757. [6], 44 pp.
AAS copy.   7989

[Parkman, Ebenezer], 1703-1782.
Zebulun Advised.
Newport, 1738. [2], 6, iv, 80,
[1] pp.
JCB copy.   4293

Parks, Daniel.
Parks, Carrier of the Centinel, begs
Permission [Jan. 1, 1787]. . . .
[Boston, 1787.] Broadside.
AAS copy.   45119

Parkyns, G. I.
No. 1. Sketches of Select American
Scenery.
Philadelphia, Ormrod, 1799. [6] pp., 2
plates.
JCB copy.   48951

Parkyns, G. I.
Proposals for Engraving in Aquatinta,
four Select Views.
n.p., [179?]. Broadside.
LOC ph. copy.   45786

Parkyns, G. I.
Proposals for Publishing . . . a Series of
Views.
[Philadelphia, 1799.] Broadside.
JCB copy.   48952

[The Parlour Preacher: a Pack of Cards
for all Who are Determined to Win
Christ.
Newburyport, March, 1798.]
(Entry assumed by Evans from adv. "Just
Published" in Herald, Oct. 23, 1798.)
                                                   34309

Parks, William, d. 1750.
Advertisement to the Reader. In the 237th
page. . . .
[Annapolis, Parks, 1727.] Broadside.
MdHS copy.   39870

[Parnell, Thomas], 1679-1718.
(D. N. B.)
The Hermit. A Poem.
[Germantown, 1756.] 8 pp.
(Imprint based on comparison with Sower
printing of 1756.)
AAS copy.   7084

Parnell, Thomas, 1679-1718.
The Hermit, a Poem.
New Haven, 1784. 14 pp.
NYPL copy.   18673

[Parnell, Thomas], 1679-1718.
The Hermit, A Poem.
Boston, Griffith, 1786.]
("This Day Published, and to be Sold, at
James D. Griffith's Office," Continental
Journal, Oct. 19, 1786.)   19881

[Parnell, Thomas], 1679-1718.
The Hermit; or The Justice of Divine
Providence Represented.
Salem, [1793]. Broadside.
NYHS copy.   25601

Parnell, Thomas, 1679-1718.
A Vision.
New York, Parker, 1762. 10 pp.
LOC copy.   41299

[The Parody Parodized, or the
Massachusetts Song of Liberty.
Boston, 1768.] Broadside.
(Ford 1456; Duyckinck, I, 452.)   41863

[Parrington, John Rivington.
A Map and Description of the State of
Tennessee.
Knoxville, 1798.]
(Projected in Register for Aug. 14, 1798.)
                                                   34310

Parsons, Benjamin, 1769-1857.
An Oration, Delivered at Chesterfield.
Northampton, Mass., Butler, 1800.
16 pp.
AAS copy.   38192

Parsons, David, 1749-1823.
The Duty of a People to Pray.
Northampton, Butler, 1795. 28 pp.
AAS copy.   29277

Parsons, David, 1749-1823.
A Sermon, Preached before His
Excellency.
Boston, Adams & Nourse, [1788].
46 pp.
AAS copy.   21360

Parsons, Jesse.
The American Ephemeris . . . for . . .
1757.
New York, Parker & Weyman.
[24] pp.
AAS copy.   7745

Parsons, Jesse.
The American Ephemeris; or, an
Almanack for . . . 1759.
New Haven, Parker. [16] pp.
AAS copy.   40999

Parsons, Jesse.
A Pocket Almanack, for . . . 1755.
New York, De Foreest. [24] pp.
NYHS copy.   40710

[Parsons, Jonathan], 1705-1776.
(Dexter, I, 388-393.)
Communion of Faith Essential.
Salem, 1770. 11 pp.
AAS copy.   11797

Parsons, Jonathan, 1705-1776.
(Dexter, I, 388-393.)
The Connection.
Boston, Green & Russell, 1759. 31 pp.
AAS copy.   8451

Parsons, Jonathan, 1705-1776.
(Dexter, I, 388-393.)
The Doctrine of Justification.
Boston, Bayley, 1748. [4], 95 pp.
AAS copy.   6213

Parsons, Jonathan, 1705-1776.
(Dexter, I, 388-393.)
Freedom from Civil and Ecclesiastical
Slavery.
Newburyport, [1774]. 19 pp., irreg.
AAS copy.   13513

Parsons, Jonathan, 1705-1776.
(Dexter, I, 388-393.)
A Funeral Sermon . . . of Ebenezer Little.
Salem, 1768. 26 pp.
AAS copy.　　　　　　　　11020

Parsons, Jonathan, 1705-1776.
(Dexter, I, 388-393.)
Good News from a Far Country.
Portsmouth, 1756. viii, 168 pp.
AAS copy.　　　　　　　　7746

Parsons, Jonathan, 1705-1776.
(Dexter, I, 388-393.)
Infant Baptism.
Boston, M'Alpine & Fleming, 1765.
65 pp.
AAS copy.　　　　　　　　10119

Parsons, Jonathan, 1705-1776.
(Dexter, I, 388-393.)
Infant Baptism. . . . Second Edition.
Boston, M'Alpine, 1767. 142 pp.
AAS copy.　　　　　　　　10722

Parsons, Jonathan, 1705-1776.
(Dexter, I, 388-393.)
Manna Gathered in the Morning.
Boston, Fowle, 1751. 37, [2] pp.
AAS copy.　　　　　　　　6743

Parsons, Jonathan, 1705-1776.
(Dexter, I, 388-393.)
A Needful Caution.
New London, 1742. [4], 71 pp.
CHS copy.　　　　　　　　5027

Parsons, Jonathan, 1705-1776.
(Dexter, I, 388-393.)
A Rejoinder to the Reverend Mr. Robert
Abercrombie's late Remarks.
Boston, Green & Russell, 1758. 27 pp.
AAS copy.　　　　　　　　8224

Parsons, Jonathan, 1705-1776.
Sixty Sermons on Various Subjects. . . .
Volume I.
Newburyport, 1779. [2], lxvi, 625,
vii pp.
AAS copy.　　　　　　　　16425

Parsons, Jonathan, 1705-1776.
Sixty Sermons.
Newburyport, 1780. 855, ix, [2] pp.
AAS copy.　　　　　　　　16921

Parsons, Jonathan, 1705-1776.
To Live is Christ.
Portsmouth, [1770]. 44 pp.
AAS copy.　　　　　　　　11798

Parsons, Jonathan, 1705-1776.
Wisdom Justified.
Boston, Rogers & Fowle for Procter, 1742.
[4], viii, 5-54 pp.
AAS copy.　　　　　　　　5028

Parsons, Jonathan, 1735-1784.
A Consideration of some Unconstitutional
Measures.
Newburyport, 1784. 24 pp.
AAS copy.　　　　　　　　18674

Parsons, Joseph, 1671-1740.
(Sibley, IV, 366-369.)
The Validity of Presbyterian Ordination.
Boston, Kneeland and Green, 1733. [4],
27 pp.
JCB copy.　　　　　　　　3708

Parsons, Joseph, 1702-1765.
(Sibley, VI, 393-396.)
Christians.
Boston, Rogers & Fowle for Eliot, 1744.
30 pp.
AAS copy.　　　　　　　　5469

Parsons, Joseph, 1702-1765.
(Sibley, VI, 393-396.)
A Minister's Care.
Boston, Rogers for Eliot, 1741. 30 pp.
AAS copy.　　　　　　　　4776

Parsons, Joseph, 1702-1765.
Religion Recommended.
Boston, Green for Henchman and
Edwards, 1744. 30 pp.
AAS copy.　　　　　　　　5470

Parsons, Joseph, 1702-1765.
(Sibley, VI, 393-396.)
A Sermon Preach'd in the Audience of
His Excellency.

Boston, Draper, 1759. 35 pp.
AAS copy.　　　　　　　　8452

Parsons, Joseph, 1702-1765.
Two Discourses.
Boston, Draper, 1759. 37 pp.
AAS copy.　　　　　　　　8453

Parsons, Moses, 1716-1783.
(Sibley, X.)
The Character of Able Ministers.
Salem, 1773. 38 pp.
AAS copy.　　　　　　　　12916

Parsons, Moses, 1716-1783.
(Sibley, X.)
The Ministers of Christ.
Boston, Drapers, 1766. 36 pp.
AAS copy.　　　　　　　　10439

Parsons, Moses, 1716-1783.
(Sibley, X.)
A Sermon Preached at Cambridge.
Boston, Edes & Gill, 1772. 43 pp.
AAS copy.　　　　　　　　12502

Part of an Exposition of Paul's Journey
[by Andrew Croswell, 1709-1785].
Boston, Kneeland & Adams, 1768.
11 pp.
AAS copy.　　　　　　　　10870

Part of an Exposition of Paul's
Journey. . . . Second Edition [by Andrew
Croswell, 1709-1785].
Boston, Kneeland & Adams, 1768. 11, [1],
6 pp.
AAS copy.　　　　　　　　10871

A Particular Account of the Insurrection
of the Negroes of St. Domingo. . . . Third
Edition.
[London, 1792.] 32 pp.
(Evans assumed American printing from
advs.)
NYPL copy.　　　　　　　　24675

A Particular Account of the Insurrection
of the Negroes of St. Domingo. . . .
Fourth Edition.
[London, 1792.] 32 pp.
NYPL copy.　　　　　　　　24766

A Particular Account of the most
Barbarous and Horrid Massacre. . . .
March 5, 1770.
[Boston? 1770.] Broadside.
AAS copy.　　　　　　　　42145

A Particular Account of the most
Barbarous and Horrid Massacre. . . .
March 5, 1770.
[Boston], Boyles, 1770. Broadside.
LCP copy.　　　　　　　　42146

A Particular Plain and Brief Memorative
Account [by John Brown, 1696-1742].
Boston, Fleet for Gerrish, 1726. [2], 70,
[2] pp.
(Signatured with 2733, q.v.)　　　　2734

Particulars of the late Melancholy and
Shocking Tragedy . . . June 17th, 1773.
[Boston, 1773.] Broadside.
NYHS copy.　　　　　　　　12918

Partnership for Circulating Bills or Notes
Founded on Land-Security.
Advertisement. . . . Boston, October 16,
1714.
[Boston, 1714.] Broadside.
BA copy.　　　　　　　　39602

Partridge, Copernicus, pseud.
The New-England Calendar: or, the
Boston Almanack, for . . . 1786. . . . [by
Benjamin West, 1730-1813].
Boston, Battelle. [24] pp.
AAS copy.　　　　　　　　19376

Partridge, Copernicus, pseud.
The North-American Calendar: or, The
Rhode-Island Almanack, for . . . 1784.
Providence, Wheeler. [24?] pp.
(Alden 977; no copy located.)　　　44580

Partridge, Copernicus, pseud.
The North-American Calendar: or, the
Rhode-Island Almanack, for . . . 1786. . . .
Second Edition [by Benjamin West,
1730-1813].
Providence, Wheeler, [24] pp.
AAS copy.　　　　　　　　19378

[Partridge, John, pseud.
Merlinus Liberatus: Being an Almanack
for 1733.
Boston, 1732.]
(Title from Haven, probably from a
bookseller's adv. for the well-known
London almanac.)　　　　　　　　3588

Partridge, John, 1644-1715.
(D. N. B.)
Monthly Observations.
Boston, 1692. 16 pp.
MHS copy.　　　　　　　　627

Party-Spirit Exposed [by Donald Fraser,
1755?-1820].
New York, Kirk, 1799. 24 pp.
NYSL copy.　　　　　　　　35501

Pascalis-Ouvière, Félix, 1750?-1832.
An Account of the Contagious Epidemic
Yellow Fever.
Philadelphia, Snowden & M'Corkle, 1798.
viii, 180 pp., 1 plate.
LCP copy.　　　　　　　　34311

[Pascalis-Ouvière, Félix], 1750?-1832.
Medico-Chymical Dissertations.
Philadelphia, Snowden & McCorkle, 1796.
41, [3] pp.
AAS copy.　　　　　　　　30960

Pasquin, Anthony, pseud.
A Dirge, or Sepulchral Service.
[Boston, 1800.] 4 pp.
(Also entered as 39106, q. v.)　　　38193

Pastoral Desires [by Cotton Mather,
1663-1728].
Boston, Green for Boone, 1712. [2], 116.
BPL copy.　　　　　　　　1554

A Pastoral Letter, from a Minister in the
Country [by Ashbell Green, 1762-1848].
Philadelphia, Ormrod, 1799. 12 pp.
LCP copy.　　　　　　　　35563

A Pastoral Letter, to Families. . . . Third
Impression [by Cotton Mather,
1663-1728].
Boston, Green for Gerrish, 1721. [2],
24 pp.
BPL copy.　　　　　　　　2249

A Pastoral Letter to the English Captives
[by Cotton Mather, 1663-1728].
Boston, 1698. 16 pp.
HC copy.　　　　　　　　830

A Pastoral Visit to the Afflicted.
[Boston, 1737.] [2], 13 pp.
AAS copy.　　　　　　　　4181

A Pastoral Visit, to the Afflicted.
Keene, N. H., Sturtevant, 1796. 12 pp.
AAS copy.　　　　　　　　30961

Pastorius, Franz Daniel, 1651-1719.
(D. A. B.)
Henry Bernhard Koster.
New York, 1697. 15 pp.
(Only reported copy of the original was in
the "Bevan-Naish Library, Birmingham,
England." Reproduced from a
photographic facsimile at the HSP.)　811

[Pastorius, Franz Daniel], 1651-1719.
A New Primmer or Methodical
Directions.
New York, [1698]. 88 pp.
Friends' House copy.　　　　　　　851

[Patent for the Oblong, or Equivalent
Lands.
New York, 1731.]
(A ghost of 3454.)　　　　　　　3461

A Patern of Christian Education [by
Francois de Salignac de la Mothe
Fénelon, 1651-1715].
Germantown, 1756. 16 pp.
AAS copy.　　　　　　　　7655

[Paterson, William], 1658-1719.
(D. N. B.)
An Abstract of a Letter.
Boston, 1699. 2, 4 pp.
AAS copy.　　　　　　　　892

Paterson, William, 1658-1719.
Observations of a Person of Eminence.
Boston, 1699. 76 pp.
JCB copy.　　　　　　　　893

NATIONAL INDEX OF AMERICAN IMPRINTS

Paterson, William, 1745-1806.
The Charge of Judge Paterson to the Jury.
Philadelphia, Smith, 1796. 41,
[2] pp.
AAS copy. 30962

Pateshall, Richard, 1714-1768.
(Sibley, IX, 558-560.)
Pride Humbled.
Boston, Draper, 1745. 12 pp.
AAS copy. 5670

The Path to Happiness.
Newark, N. J., Pennington & Dodge for
Davis, 1798. 92; 38; 22 pp.
AAS copy. 34312

The Path to Riches [by James Sullivan,
1744-1808].
Boston, Edes for Thomas & Andrews,
1792. 77 pp.
AAS copy. 24829

Pathetic History of the Plague [by Daniel
Defoe, 1661-1731].
Charlestown, White, [1795]. 15,
[1] pp.
(Evans assumed the imprint.)
AAS copy. 28551

The Paths of Virtue Delineated [by
Samuel Richardson, 1689-1761].
Philadelphia, Woodhouse, 1791. 135 pp.
1 plate.
Philadelphia Free Library copy. 23740

The Paths of Virtue Delineated; or, The
History . . . of . . . Clarissa Harlowe [by
Samuel Richardson, 1689-1761].
Cooperstown, Phinney, 1795. 154,
[1] pp.
(Title and imprint assumed by Evans from
adv.)
AAS copy. 29414

The Paths of Virtue Exemplified in the
Lives of Eminent Men and Women.
Philadelphia, Lawrence, 1792. 167 pp.
AAS copy. 46537

The Patriot, a Poem.
Charlestown, Mass., 1798. 24 pp.
LCP copy. 34313

The Patriot Chief. A tragedy [by Peter
Markoe, 1753-1792].
Philadelphia, Prichard, 1784. [4],
70 pp.
JCB copy. 18571

The Patriot, with an Act of Parliament.
Boston, 1714. 4 pp.
(The unique copy is mislaid.) 1711

Patriotic Medley, being a Choice
Collection of . . . Songs.
New York, Johnkin, 1800. 208,
[7] pp.
NL copy. 38195

[The Patriotic Songster for July 4th, 1798.
Baltimore, Sower for Thomas, Andrews &
Butler, 1798.]
(Imprint assumed by Evans from adv.)
34314

Patriotischen Gesellschaft der
Philadelphia.
Die Artikel der. . . .
Philadelphia, Miller, [1772]. Broadside.
LCP copy. 12525

The Patriots of North-America.
New York, 1775. iv, 47, [1] pp.
NYPL copy. 14359

Patten, Thomas, 1714-1790.
(D. N. B.)
The Christian Apology. . . . Third Edition.
New Haven, 1757. 30 pp.
LOC copy. 7990

Patten, William, 1738-1775.
(Weis, Colonial Clergy N. E.)
The Death of Men of Virtue.
Hartford, 1772. 25 pp.
AAS copy. 12503

Patten, William, 1738-1775.
(Weis, Colonial Clergy N. E.)·
A Discourse Delivered at Hallifax.

Boston, Kneeland for Leverett, 1766.
22 pp.
AAS copy. 10440

Patten, William, 1738-1775.
(Weis, Colonial Clergy N. E.)
The Vanity of Man.
Hartford, 1771. 28 pp.
CHS copy. 12173

Patten, William, 1763-1839.
Christianity the True Theology.
Warren, R. I., Phillips, 1795. 177,
[3] pp.
AAS copy. 29279

Patten, William, 1763-1839.
Directions with Regard to the
Improvement.
New London, [1784]. 22 pp.
AAS copy. 18675

Patten, William, 1763-1839.
A Discourse, Delivered in the 2d
Congregational Church, Newport,
December 29th, 1799. Occasioned by the
Death of . . . Washington.
Newport, R. I., Barber, 1800. 19 pp.
(Issued under common halftitle with
38196, q. v.) 38197

Patten, William, 1763-1839.
A Discourse, Delivered in the 2d
Congregational Church, Newport, the
Sabbath Succeeding the Interment of
Doctor Isaac Senter.
Newport, R. I., Barber, 1800. 12,
iv, 19 pp.
AAS copy. 38196

Patten, William, 1763-1839.
A Discourse Occasioned by the Death of
. . . President Stiles.
Exeter, Ranlet for Woodbridge, 1795.
16 pp.
AAS copy. 29280

Patten, William, 1763-1839.
On the Inhumanity of the Slave-Trade.
Providence, Carter, 1793. 14 pp.
AAS copy. 25964

Patterson, Mrs.
The Unfortunate Lovers.
New Haven, Read & Morse, 1799.
23 pp.
AAS copy. 36045

Patterson, Mrs.
The Unfortunate Lovers.
Springfield, Mass., Ashley, 1800.
23 pp.
AAS copy. 38198

[Patterson, Robert, 1743-1824.
Table of Latitude and Departure.
Philadelphia, 1797.]
(Imprint assumed by Evans from adv.)
32639

Patterson, Robert, 1743-1824.
A New Table of Latitude and Departure.
[Philadelphia], Stewart & Cochran, 1794.
30, (i.e. 36) pp.
HSP copy. 47152

Pattillo, Henry, 1726-1801.
Sermons, &c.
Wilmington, Del., 1788. 295,
[1] pp.
AAS copy. 21361

Paul, Jeremiah.
A Collection of Copies for Writing.
Philadelphia, Budd & Bartram, 1798. 54
pp.
(The only copy located is imperfect.)
Marian S. Carson copy. 34315

Paul, William.
A Treatise on Prayer.
West Springfield, [Mass.], Gray, [1797?].
44 +pp.
(The only known copy is imperfect.)
AAS copy. 48215

Pauvre Madelon [by George Colman,
1762-1836].
New York, Gilfert, 177 Broadway,
[1798]. [2] pp.
NYPL copy. 33536

Pawlet, Vt. Library.

Constitution and Catalogue of. . . .
Bennington, Haswell, 1799. [10] pp.
AAS copy. 36046

[Pawtucket cannon factory 5 December
1798.
Providence, 1798.] Broadside.
(Alden 1568; no copy known.) 48562

The Paxton Boys, a Farce.
[Philadelphia], 1764. 16 pp.
NYPL copy. 9776

[The Paxton Boys, a Farce.
[Philadelphia, 1764?] 8 pp.]
(Apparently Evans was describing a
defective copy of another ed.) 9778

The Paxton Boys, a Farce. . . . Second
Edition.
Philadelphia, Armbruster, 1764. 16 pp.,
folding plate.
LCP copy. 9777

The Paxton Expedition [by Henry
Dawkins, fl. 1735-1780].
[Philadelphia], 1764.] Broadside.
LCP copy. 9627

Payne, John, fl. 1800.
A New and Complete System of Universal
Geography. . . . In Four Volumes. Vol. I.
New York, Low, 1798. xlviii, 518, [11]
pp., 10 folding plates.
AAS copy. 34316

Payne, John, fl. 1800.
New and Complete System of Universal
Geography. . . . In Four Volumes. Vol. II
[-III].
New York, Low, 1800. 578, [12]; 710, [8]
pp., plates and folding maps.
AAS copy. 38199

Payne, John, fl. 1800.
New and Complete System of Universal
Geography. . . . Vol. IV.
New York, Low, 1799. [2], 525, [1], 36,
[4], 17, [11] pp., 22 maps.
AAS copy. 36047

Payne, William, fl. 1756.
Mr. Payne's Game of Draughts.
New York, 1799. 32 pp.
(The only copy reported was formerly in
the possession of the University Place
Book Shop.) 36048

Payne and Hearn's Book Store, Savannah.
A Catalogue of Books to be Sold.
[Savannah, 1790.] Broadside.
LOC copy. 22755

Payne & Inches, firm.
Messieurs Payne & Inches. In the Evening
Post. . . . March 15th, 1770.
[Boston, 1770.] 8 pp.
AAS copy. 42147

Payson, Edward, 1657-1732.
(Sibley, II, 514-518.)
Pious Heart-Elations.
Boston, Green for Phillips, 1728. [6], 23,
[1] pp.
AAS copy. 3080

Payson, John P., fl. 1800.
Masonic Oration Delivered . . . at
Deerfield.
Portsmouth, N. H., Melcher, [1800].
20 pp.
NYHS copy. 38200

Payson, Phillips, 1705-1778.
(Sibley, VII, 421-424.)
A Professing People.
Boston, Kneeland & Green for Eliot, 1741.
[4], ii, 49 pp.
AAS copy. 4777

Payson, Phillips, 1736-1801.
(Weis, Colonial Clergy N. E.)
A Memorial of Lexington Battle.
Boston, Edes, 1782. 24 pp.
AAS copy. 17655

Payson, Phillips, 1736-1801.
A Sermon, Delivered at Chelsea, January
14, 1800.
Charlestown, Mass., Etheridge, 1800. 15
pp.
AAS copy. 38201

Payson, Phillips, 1736-1801.
(Weis, Colonial Clergy N. E.)
A Sermon Preached at the Ordination of
. . . John Payson.
Boston, Draper, 1768. 27 pp.
AAS copy.   11021

Payson, Phillips, 1736-1801.
(Weis, Colonial Clergy N. E.)
A Sermon Preach'd at the Ordination of
. . . Samuel Payson.
Boston, Fleet, 1762. 27 pp.
AAS copy.   9226

Payson, Phillips, 1736-1801.
A Sermon Preached at the Ordination of
. . . Seth Payson.
Boston, Fleets, 1783. 30 pp.
AAS copy.   18080

Payson, Phillips, 1736-1801.
(Weis, Colonial Clergy N. E.)
A Sermon Preached before the Honorable
Council.
Boston, Gill, 1778. 39 pp.
AAS copy.   15956

Payson, Seth, 1758-1820.
Ministers Christ's Ambassadors.
Worcester, Thomas, 1791. 32 pp.
AAS copy.   23666

Payson, Seth, 1758-1820.
A Sermon, at the Consecration of the
Social Lodge.
Amherst, N. H., Preston, 1800.
16 pp.
AAS copy.   38202

Payson, Seth, 1758-1820.
A Sermon, Delivered at the Ordination of
. . . Joseph Brown.
Dover, N. H., Bragg, 1796. 24 pp.
AAS copy.   30965

Payson, Seth, 1758-1820.
A Sermon Preached at Concord.
Portsmouth, N. H., Melcher, 1799.
23 pp.
AAS copy.   36049

Peabody, Oliver, 1698-1752.
An Essay to Revive . . . Military
Exercises.
Boston, Fleet for Eliot and Phillips, 1732.
45 pp.
AAS copy.   3589

Peabody, Oliver, 1698-1752.
(Sibley, VI, 529-534.)
The Foundations.
Boston, Fowle for Eliot, 1742. 52 pp.
AAS copy.   5029

Peabody, Oliver, 1698-1752.
(Sibley, VI, 529-534.)
That Ministers are to Seperate Men.
Boston, Kneeland & Green, 1736. [4], ii,
26 pp.
AAS copy.   4058

Peabody, Stephen, 1741-1819.
A Sermon, Delivered at Concord.
Concord, N. H., Hough, 1797. 23 pp.
AAS copy.   32640

Peabody, Stephen, 1741-1819.
A Sermon, Delivered at the Ordination of
. . . Josiah Webster.
Haverhill, Mass., Moore, [1799].
35 pp.
AAS copy.   36050

Peace. Salem, February 21, 1783. By
Captain John Osgood. . . .
[Salem, 1783.] Broadside.
MHS copy.   44435

[Peacock, Lucy], fl. 1786-1816.
Visit for a Week.
Philadelphia, Ormrod Conrad, 1796.
[4], 275, [1] pp., 1 plate.
AAS copy.   30966

Peak, John, 1761-1842.
A New Collection of Hymns. . . . Third
Windsor Edition.
Windsor, Spooner, 1793. 35 pp.
AAS copy.   25965

Peak, John, 1761-1842.
A Sermon, Preached at the Ordination of
. . . William Batchelder.

Exeter, Ranlet, 1797. 28 pp.
AAS copy.   32641

Peake, Thomas, 1771-1838.
Cases Determined at Nisi Prius, in the
Court of King's Bench.
Hartford, Hudson & Goodwin, [1795?] iv,
241, [36] pp.
JCB copy.   47528

Peale, Charles Willson, 1741-1827.
A Descriptive Catalogue of Mr. Peale's
Exhibition of Perspective Views.
Philadelphia, Bailey, [1786]. Broadside.
APS copy.   44941

Peale, Charles Willson, 1741-1827.
Discourse, Introductory to a Course of
Lectures.
Philadelphia, Poulson, 1800. 50 pp., 5
folding plates.
AAS copy.   38203

Peale, Charles Willson, 1741-1827.
An Essay on Building Wooden Bridges.
Philadelphia, Bailey, 1797. 16 pp., 6
plates.
LCP copy.   32642

Peale, Charles Willson, 1741-1827.
An Historical Catalogue of Peales'
Collection of Paintings.
Philadelphia, Folwell, 1795. 20 pp.
AAS copy.   29281

Peale, Charles Willson, 1741-1827.
Introduction to a Course of Lectures.
Philadelphia, Baileys, 1800. 28 pp.
AAS copy.   38204

Peale, Charles Willson, 1741-1827.
A Scientific and Descriptive Catalogue of
Peale's Museum.
Philadelphia, Smith, 1796. [1], xii, 44 pp.,
printed cover.
AAS copy.   30967

[Peale, Charles Willson, 1741-1827.
Shades, or Profiles, of the President.
Charleston, 1791.]
(Entry from advs. for one of the several
prints of Washington by Peale.)   23667

Pearce, William.
Amidst the Illusions. From Hartford
Bridge.
Philadelphia, etc., Carrs, [1796].
[2] pp.
AAS copy.   30969

[Pearce, William.]
The Cheering Rosary. . . . Composed by
Mr. Shield.
Philadelphia, Carr, [1793]. [2] pp.
LOC copy.   25966

[Pearce, William.]
The Heaving of the Lead. A Favorite Sea
Song. Composed by Mr. Shield.
Philadelphia, Carr, [1793]. [2] pp.
AAS copy.   25967

[Pearce, Zachary], 1690-1774.
(D. N. B.)
A Letter to the Clergy of the Church of
England.
Boston, Green and Kneeland, 1722.
23 pp.
AAS copy.   2380

Pearl, Stephen.
To the Candid Public. Having Received
Information. . . . Rutland, October
15, 1792.
[Rutland? 1792.] Broadside.
AAS copy.   46538

Pearsall, Richard, 1698-1762.
(D. N. B.)
The Power and Pleasure. . . . Second
Edition.
Boston, Kneeland and Bromfield, 1755.
[2], xx, [2], 130, [2] pp.
AAS copy.   7524

Pearse, Edward, 1633?-1674?
The Best Match. . . . Tenth Edition.
Boston, Green for Buttolph, 1708.
204 pp.
AAS copy.   39470

Pearse, Edward, 1633?-1674?
(D. N. B.)

The Great Concern. . . . Twenty-First
Edition.
Boston, Green for Eliot and Boone, 1705.
[6], 182 pp.
MHS copy.   1228

Pearse, Edward, 1633?-1674?
(D. N. B.)
The Great Concern.
Boston, 1711. [4], 188 pp.
AAS copy.   1525

Pearson, William, 1768-1795.
(Harvard College Records.)
A Dissertation on the Mixed Fever.
[Boston, 1789.] [4], 12 pp.
AAS copy.   22049

Pease, Seth, 1764-1819.
A Map of the Connecticut Western
Reserve.
New Haven, Doolittle, 1798. Map.
JCB copy.   34317

Peck, Abiezer.
On the Proceedings of the English and
French in North-America. . . . Rehoboth,
Feb. 2, 1756.
n.p., n.d. 3 pp.
NHS copy.   40859

Peck, Abiezer.
On the Valiant New-England General. . . .
Rehoboth, April 5, 1756.
n.p., n.d. Broadside.
MHS copy.   40860

[Peck, Jabez], 1761-1791.
Columbia and Britannia.
New London, 1787. 63 pp.
UOP copy.   19922

[Peck, Jedidiah].
The Political Wars of Otsego.
Cooperstown, Phinney, 1796. 122, [4] pp.
BA copy.   30968

Peck, John, 1735-1812.
(Desc. of Joseph Peck, pp. 43, 50-1.)
A Description of the Last Judgment. . . .
Second Edition.
Boston, Russell, 1773. 31, [1] pp.
AAS copy.   12919

[Peck, John], 1735-1812.
Facts and Calculations Respecting the
Population and Territory of the United
States.
[Boston, 1799.] 7, [1] pp.
AAS copy.   36051

Peck, William Dandridge, 1763-1822.
Natural History of the Slug Worm.
Boston, Young & Minns, 1799. 14 pp., 1
plate.
AAS copy.   36052

Peckham, Thomas.
To the Members of the Hon. General
Assembly of the State of
Rhode-Island. . . . May 3d, 1791.
[Newport, 1791.] Broadside.
RIHS copy.   46248

[Peddle, Mrs.].
Rudiments of Taste, in a Series of Letters.
Philadelphia, Spotswood, 1790. iv,
140 pp.
AAS copy.   22756

[Peddle, Mrs.]
Rudiments of Taste.
Chambersburg, Pa., Dover & Harper for
Carey, 1797. 52 pp.
AAS copy.   32643

[Peddle, Mrs.]
Rudiments of Taste, in a Series of Letters.
Litchfield, Ct., Collier, [1799].
142 pp.
YC copy.   36053

[Pede, Dr.
The Door of Salvation.
Boston, Gray and Butler, 1730.
16 pp.]
(Title from Haven.)   3335

Pede, Dr.
The Door of Salvation Opened.
Boston, Butler, 1734. 22, [2] pp.
AAS copy.   40059

Pede, Dr.
The Door of Salvation Opened.
Boston, Rogers & Fowle, 1741. 15,
[1] pp.
MHS copy.   4778

Peden, Alexander, 1626?-1686.
The Lord's Trumpet Sounding.
Newburyport, Walker, 1798. 42 pp.
AAS copy.   34318

Peden, Alexander, 1626?-1686.
The Life and Prophecies of the Reverend
Mr. . . .
Newburyport, Walker, 1798. 57 pp.
(Not located, 1968.)   48563

A Peep into the Antifederal Club.
New York, Aug. 16, 1793. Cartoon.
AAS copy.   25968

Peirce, Charles, 1770-1851.
Valuable Medicines, Just Received. . . .
Oct. 11, 1800.
[Portsmouth, 1800.] Broadside.
MHS copy.   38310

[Peirce, James], 1673-1726.
(D.N.B.)
A Caveat against the New Sect of
Anabaptists.
Boston, Fleet for Eliot, 1724. 40 pp.
(Attributed also to John Withers and
Hubert Stogdon.)
AAS copy.   2575

[Peirce, James, 1673-1726.
(D. N. B.)
The Curse Causeless. . . . Fifth Edition.
Boston, Love, 1728. 30 pp.]
(Assumed by Evans from the sequence of
editions.)   3081

Peirce, James, 1673-1726.
The Curse Causeless. . . . Sixth Edition.
Boston, Love, 1728. 30 pp.
AAS copy.   3082

[Peirce, James, 1673-1726.
(D. N. B.)
Y Dull & Fedyddio.
Philadelphia, 1730. 80 + pp.]
(There is supposed to be a copy at The
Free Library, Cardiff, Wales, but
inquiries concerning it were not
answered.)   3336

Peirce, John, comp.
The New American Spelling-Book. . . .
Sixth Edition.
Philadelphia, Crukshank, 1793. [6],
198 pp.
LCP copy.   46844

[Peirce, John, comp.
The New American Spelling Book
Improved.
Philadelphia, Crukshank, 1795.]
(Entry from copyright notice.)   29282

[Peirce, John, comp.
The New American Spelling-Book. . . .
Second Edition.
Philadelphia, Crukshank, 1796.]
(Imprint assumed by Evans.)   30970

Peirce, John, comp.
The New American Spelling-Book. . . .
Third Edition.
Philadelphia, Crukshank, 1797. iv,
200 pp.
(The only copy located is imperfect.)
Columbia University (Plimpton) copy.
                                             32644

Peirce, John, comp.
The New American Spelling-Book
Improved. . . . Fourth Revised Edition.
Philadelphia, Crukshank, 1799. [4],
200 pp.
(The only copy recorded could not be
reproduced.)   36054

Peirce, John, comp.
The New, American Spelling-Book. . . .
Fifth Revised Edition.
Philadelphia, Crukshanks, 1800. [4],
200 pp.
(The only copy located is imperfect.)
AAS copy.   38205

Peirce, John, comp.
The New American Spelling-Book. . . .

Seventh Edition.
Wilmington, Del., Brynberg, 1800. [6],
198 pp.
(The only recorded copy cannot be
reproduced.)   38206

Peirce, Joseph.
Joseph Peirce, at his Shop. . . .
[Boston], Mills & Hicks, [1773?].
Broadside.
BPL copy.   42482

Peirce, Levi, No. 20, Cornhill, Boston,
Imports and has for Sale. . . .
[Boston], Young & Minns, [1796?].
Broadside.
EI copy.   47875

Peirce, Nathanael, fl. 1752.
An Account of the Great Dangers.
Boston, Edes & Gill, 1756. 20 pp.
AAS copy.   7747

Peirce, Proctor, 1768-1821.
An Eulogy, Pronounced on the 22d of
February.
Greenfield, Mass., Dickman, 1800.
16 pp.
BrU copy.   38207

[Peirce, William, - 1641.
An Almanac.
Cambridge, 1639.]
(No copy known.)   2

Peirson, Abraham, 1608-1678.
(D. N. B.)
Some Helps for the Indians.
Cambridge, 1658. 67 pp.
(Probably printed in 1659. The BM copy
has a variant title-page.)
NYPL copy.   52

Peirson, Abraham, 1608-1678.
Some Helps for the Indians. . . . Examined
. . . by . . . John Scot.
Cambridge, 1658. 67 pp.
(Only the title-page, which was printed in
England, differs from Evans 52.)
BM copy.   53

Pejepscott Proprietors, 1764.
. . . To the Proprietors. . . . Boston, Dec.
23, 1764.
[Boston, 1764.] Broadside.
AAS copy.   41480

Pelham, William, 1759-1827.
At Pelham's Book Store and Circulating
Library. . . .
[Boston, 1796.] Broadside.
MHS copy.   30971

Pelissier, Victor.
Washington and Independence. A Favorite
Patriotic Song.
New York, Gilfert, [1798?]. [2] pp.
(This is apparently the item which Evans
described from von Hagen's adv.)
AAS copy.   34959

Pelosi, Vincent M.
Philadelphia [blank] 1791. At the Request
of Several Merchants. . . .
[Philadelphia, 1791.] Broadside.
JCB copy.   46249

Pemberton, Ebenezer, 1672-1717.
(Sibley, IV, 107-113.)
Advice to a Son.
London, 1705. [2], 25 pp.
(The Boston edition described by Evans is
a ghost arising from a bookseller's adv.)
AAS copy.   1229

[Pemberton, Ebenezer], 1672-1717.
(Sibley, IV, 107-113.)
A Brief Account of the State of the
Province.
Boston, Crump for Phillips, 1717.
8 pp.
(For authorship see Holmes, Cotton
Mather, I, 101.)
AAS copy.   1896

Pemberton, Ebenezer, 1672-1717.
(Sibley, IV, 107-112.)
A Christian Fixed in his Post.
Boston, 1704. [4], 39 pp.
AAS copy.   1190

Pemberton, Ebenezer, 1672-1717.
(Sibley, IV, 107-113.)

The Divine Original and Dignity of
Government.
Boston, 1710. [2], 106 pp.
AAS copy.   1484

Pemberton, Ebenezer, 1672-1717.
(Sibley, IV, 107-113.)
A Funeral Sermon on . . . Samuel Willard.
Boston, 1707. [16], 80, [2], 14 pp.
AAS copy.   1329

[Pemberton, Ebenezer, 1672-1717.
(Sibley, IV, 107-113.)
Massachusetts Artillery Election Sermon.
Boston, 1709.]
(Pemberton preached the sermon on this
occasion, but there is no evidence that it
was ever printed.)   1427

Pemberton, Ebenezer, 1672-1717.
(Sibley, IV, 107-113.)
A Sermon Preached in the Audience.
Boston, 1706. [2], 35, [1] pp.
(The title given by Evans is that under
which this sermon is reprinted in
Pemberton's collected works.)
AAS copy.   1275

Pemberton, Ebenezer, 1672-1717.
(Sibley, IV, 107-113.)
The Souldier Defended.
Boston, 1701. [2], 42, [1] pp.
AAS copy.   1016

Pemberton, Ebenezer, 1672-1717.
(Sibley, IV, 107-113.)
A True Servant of his Generation.
Boston, 1712. [2], 32 pp.
AAS copy.   1577

Pemberton, Ebenezer, 1705-1777.
(Sibley, VI, 535-546.)
All Power in Heaven.
Boston, Fowle, 1756. [4], iv, 30,
[1] pp.
AAS copy.   7748

Pemberton, Ebenezer, 1705-1777.
(Sibley, VI, 535-546.)
The Duty of Committing our Souls.
Boston, Rogers & Fowle, 1743. 41 pp.
LOC copy.   5267

Pemberton, Ebenezer, 1705-1777.
(Sibley, VI, 535-546.)
Heaven the Residence of the Saints.
Boston, Kneeland for Edwards, 1770.
31 pp.
AAS copy.   11799

Pemberton, Ebenezer, 1705-1777.
(Sibley, VI, 535-546.)
The Knowledge of Christ.
New London, 1741. [4], 28,
[2] pp.
AAS copy.   4779

Pemberton, Ebenezer, 1705-1777.
Practical Discourses.
Boston, Fleet for Henchman, 1741. [6],
199 pp.
AAS copy.   4780

Pemberton, Ebenezer, 1705-1777.
(Sibley, VI, 535-546.)
Salvation by Grace.
Boston, Fleets, 1774. iv, 143 pp.
AAS copy.   13514

Pemberton, Ebenezer, 1705-1777.
(Sibley, VI, 535-546.)
A Sermon Delivered at the Presbyterian
Church.
New York, 1746. 22 pp.
AHTS copy.   5842

Pemberton, Ebenezer, 1705-1777.
(Sibley, VI, 535-546.)
A Sermon Preached at the Ordination of
. . . Isaac Story.
Salem, 1771. 27 pp.
AAS copy.   12174

Pemberton, Ebenezer, 1705-1777.
(Sibley, VI, 535-546.)
A Sermon Preach'd at the Ordination . . .
Walter Wilmot.
Boston, Draper for Henchman, 1738. [4],
38 pp.
AAS copy.   4294

Pemberton, Ebenezer, 1705-1777.

A Sermon Preached at the Presbyterian
Church.
New York, Parker, 1743. 32 pp.
NYPL copy.   5268

Pemberton, Ebenezer, 1705-1777.
(Sibley, VI, 535-546.)
A Sermon, Preach'd before the
Commission.
New York, 1735. 21 pp.
MHS copy.   3945

Pemberton, Ebenezer, 1705-1777.
(Sibley, VI, 535-546.)
A Sermon Preach'd in New-Ark.
Boston, Rogers & Fowle for Pemberton,
1744. [4], iv, 39 pp.
AAS copy.   5471

Pemberton, Ebenezer, 1705-1777.
(Sibley, VI, 535-546.)
A Sermon Preached in the Audience of
the Honourable His Majesty's Council.
Boston, Draper, 1757. 32 pp.
AAS copy.   7991

Pemberton, Ebenezer, 1705-1777.
A Sermon Preached to the Ancient and
Honourable Artillery Company.
Boston, Edes & Gill, 1756. 22 pp.
AAS copy.   7749

Pemberton, Ebenezer, 1705-1777.
Sermons on Several Subjects.
Boston, Fleet for Henchman, 1738. [6],
94 pp.
AAS copy.   4295

Pemberton, Israel, 1715-1779.
An Address to the Inhabitants of
Pennsylvania.
[Philadelphia], Bell, 1777. 36 pp.
JCB copy.   43330

Pemberton, Israel, & Son, Philadelphia.
Copy of Part of a Letter . . . to David
Barclay. . . . Philadelphia, the 1st of the 3d
m. 1740.
[Philadelphia, Franklin, 1741.]
Broadside.
LOC copy.   40253

Pemberton, Thomas, 1728-1807.
An Historical Journal of the American
War.
Boston, Hall, 1793. [2], 206 pp.
NYHS copy.   46845

[Pemberton, Thomas], 1728-1807.
An Historical Journal of the American
War.
Boston, Belknap, 1795. [2], 206 pp.
AAS copy.   29283

Pembroke, Mass. Town Clerk, 1774.
A List of the Training Soldiers in the
First Military Foot Company . . . October
the 17, ad 1774.
[Pembroke, 1774.] [3] pp.
LCP copy.   42662

Pembroke, N. H. Consociated Church.
A Plan of Union . . . June - 1797.
Concord, N. H., Hough, 1798. 8 pp.
BA copy.   34319

Pender, Thomas, fl. 1728.
The Divinity of the Scriptures.
New York, 1728. 32 pp.
BM copy.   3083

Pendleton, Edmund, 1721-1803.
An Address . . . on the Present State of
our Country.
Boston, Edes, 1799. 20 pp.
AAS copy.   36055

Penhallow, Samuel, 1665-1726.
(D. A. B.)
The History of the Wars of New-England.
Boston, Fleet for Gerrish and Henchman,
1726. [2], iv, [2], 134, [1] pp.
AAS copy.   2796

Penington, John, 1768-1793.
Chemical and Economical Essays.
Philadelphia, James, 1790. iv, [2], 200 pp.
AAS copy.   22757

Penington, John, 1768-1793.
An Inaugural Dissertation.
Philadelphia, James, 1790. 30 pp.
AAS copy.   22758

[Penman's Repository. Text, Round and
Running Hand Copies.
New York, 1797.]
(Title from adv.)   32481

[Penn, Hannah (Callowhill), c. 1670-1727.
(Pound, Penns of Pennsylvania.)
Letter to Sir William Keith. Dated, London,
26th of 3d. month, 1724.
[Philadelphia, 1726?] 4 pp.]
(Apparently a ghost of 2576 arising from
Hildeburn's entry.)   2797

Penn, Hannah (Callowhill), c. 1670-1727.
(Pound, Penns of Pennsylvania.)
London, 26th of the 3d Month, 1724.
[Philadelphia, 1724.] 4 pp.
NYPL copy.   2576

[Penn, James], 1727-1800.
The Farmer's Daughter of Essex.
Hartford, Babcock, 1797. 143 pp.
AAS copy.   32107

[Penn, James], 1727-1800.
The Farmer's Daughter of Essex.
New London, Springer, 1797.]
(Imprint assumed by Evans from adv.
"This Day Printed," Weekly Oracle, Aug.
13, 1797.)   32108

[Penn, James], 1727-1800.
The Farmer's Daughter of Essex.
New York, Mott, 1798. 96 pp.
AAS copy.   34320

[Penn, James], 1727-1800.
The Farmer's Daughter of Essex.
New York, Tiebout, 1798. 96 pp.
(An imprint of 34320, q. v. for text.)
AAS copy.   48564

[Penn, James], 1727-1800.
The Farmer's Daughter, of Essex.
[Leominster, Mass?], Whitcomb,
[1800?] 18 pp.
AAS copy.   49130

Penn, John, 1760-1834.
Philadelphia, 15th May, 1783. Inventory
of the Furniture and Goods of . . . John
Penn.
[Philadelphia], Dunlap & Claypoole,
[1788]. Broadside.
HSP copy.   21362

Penn, William, 1644-1718.
Argumentum ad Hominem.
Philadelphia, 1775. 28 pp.
LOC copy.   14360

[Penn, William], 1644-1718.
The Excellent Priviledge.
[Philadelphia, 1687.] [8], 63 pp.
FL copy.   433

Penn, William, 1644-1718.
Extract from the Writings of. . . .
Providence, 1767. 28 pp.
RIHS copy.   10723

Penn, William, 1644-1718.
Forderung der Christenheit.
Philadelphia, Cist, 1791. pp. [12],
[3]-119.
AAS copy.   23669

Penn, William, 1644-1718.
Fruits of a Father's Love. . . .
Philadelphia, Bradford, 1727.
[96] pp.
(The unique copy at the PPL is too tightly
bound to admit of the reproduction of the
text. There are many other editions.)
PPL copy.   2941

Penn, William, 1644-1718.
Fruits of a Father's Love. . . . Sixth
Edition.
Philadelphia, Crukshank, 1776. 60 pp.
PSL copy.   43124

[Penn, William, 1644-1718.
Fruits of a Father's Love. . . . Seventh
Edition.
Philadelphia, Crukshank, 1787.
60 pp.]
(Entry from an adv.)   20617

Penn, William, 1644-1718.
Fruits of a Father's Love. . . . Seventh
Edition.

Philadelphia, Crukshank, 1788. 60 pp.
LCP copy.   45321

Penn, William, 1644-1718.
Fruits of a Father's Love. . . . Eighth
Edition.
Philadelphia, Johnson, 1792. 86 pp.
AAS copy.   24662

Penn, William, 1644-1718.
Fruits of Solitude. . . . Tenth Edition.
Philadelphia, Johnson, 1792. xi, [9], 166
pp.
AAS copy.   24663

Penn, William, 1644-1718.
Fruits of Solitude. . . . Eleventh Edition.
Philadelphia, Johnson, 1794. 133, [1], 64,
[6] pp.
AAS copy.   27473

[Penn, William, 1644-1718.
A Key Opening a Way.
Philadelphia, 1717.]
(See Hildeburn 143.)   1922

Penn, William, 1644-1718.
A Letter from William Penn, to his Wife.
Lancaster, Busher, 1785. 16 pp.
LCP copy.   44758

[Penn, William], 1644-1718.
More Fruits of Solitude.
Newport, 1748. [6], 108, [2] pp.
(The Newport Hist. Soc. has an edition
with a Preface instead of an
Introduction.)
AAS copy.   6393

Penn, William, 1644-1718.
No Cross, no Crown. . . . Seventh Edition.
Boston, Rogers & Fowle, 1747. [24]; 287;
[5], 184, [4] pp.
AAS copy.   6041

[Penn, William, 1644-1718.
No Cross, No Crown.
Boston, Fowle, 1751. 470 pp.]
(Title from Sabin; no copy located.) 6744

Penn, William, 1644-1718.
No Cross, No Crown.
Philadelphia, Crukshank, 1789.
358 pp.
AAS copy.   22050

Penn, William, 1644-1718.
No Cross, No Crown.
Philadelphia, Johnson, 1796.
358 pp.
AAS copy.   30972

Penn, William, 1644-1718.
No Cross, No Crown.
Philadelphia, Johnsons, 1797.
358 pp.
AAS copy.   32645

Penn, William, 1644-1718.
Primitive Christianity Revived.
Philadelphia, Crukshank, 1783. [2], 66, iv,
98, [2] pp.
AAS copy.   18081

[Penn, William, 1644-1718.
Some Fruits of Solitude.
Philadelphia, Chattin, 1754.]
("Books printed and Sold by James
Chattin," Pa. Gazette, Oct. 17, 1754.) 7285

[Penn, William], 1644-1718.
Some Fruits of Solitude. . . . Eighth
Edition.
Newport, 1749. [12], 158, [7] pp.
AAS copy.   6392

Penn, William, 1644-1718.
Tender Counsel and Advice. . . . Fifth
Edition.
Philadelphia, Story, 1783. 49 pp.
AAS copy.   18082

Penn, William, 1644-1718.
. . . To the Children of Light.
[Philadelphia? 1776?] 4 pp.
BPL copy.   43125

[Penn, William], 1644-1718.
To the Children of Light in this
Generation. It being Recommended to
Friends. . . .
[Philadelphia, 1776.] 4 pp.
NYPL copy.   14968

[Pennington, Edward, 1726-1796.
A Description of Pennsbury Manor.
[Philadelphia, 1767.] Broadside.]
(Unique copy mislaid.)
10724

Pennsylvania (Colony).
Directions for Manouvres . . . the
Fourteenth of November, 1775.
[Philadelphia, 1775.] Broadside.
HSP copy.
14366

Pennsylvania (Colony).
To the King's Most Excellent Majesty in
Council, The Representation and Petition
of . . . Freeholders and Inhabitants of . . .
Pennsylvania. . . .
[Philadelphia, 1764.] 2 pp.
LOC copy.
9786

Pennsylvania (Colony).
To the King's Most Excellent Majesty in
Council, The Petition of the Freeholders
and Inhabitants of . . . Pennsylvania.
Philadelphia, Franklin & Hall, 1764.
2 pp.
UOP copy.
9785

[Pennsylvania (Colony) Charters.
The Frame of Government.
Philadelphia, 1689.]
(The copy described as Hildeburn 16
cannot now be found. For English editions
see Wing.)
496

Pennsylvania (Colony) Charters.
The Charter of . . . October 28, 1701.
Philadelphia, 1625 [i.e. 1725]. 8 pp.
LCP copy.
2690

Pennsylvania (Colony) Charters.
A Collection of Charters.
Philadelphia, Franklin, 1740. [2],
46 pp.
HSP copy.
4583

Pennsylvania (Colony) Charters.
The Charters of the Province of
Pennsylvania and City of Philadelphia.
Philadelphia, Franklin, 1741. 30 pp.
(The one recorded copy cannot be
located.)
40254

Pennsylvania (Colony) Charters.
The Charter of Privileges.
Philadelphia, Franklin, 1741. 8 pp.
UOP copy.
4782

Pennsylvania (Colony) Charters.
Der Neue Charter.
Germantown, 1743. 55 pp.
HSP copy.
5271

Pennsylvania (Colony) Citizens, 1764.
. . . An Seine Königliche Mäjestat, in
Dero Rath. Die Bitteschrift der
Erbleheuleute . . . der Provinz
Pennsylvanien.
[Philadelphia, 1764.] Broadside.
NYPL ph. copy.
41481

Pennsylvania (Colony) Citizens, 1764.
To the King's Most Excellent Majesty in
Council.
[Philadelphia, 1764.]. 2 pp.
(Has also been entered as 9785, q.v.)
UOP copy.
41482

[Pennsylvania (Colony) Collector of the
Excise, 1734.
Advertisement of the Collector of the
Excise.
Philadelphia, 1734. Broadside.]
(Ordered printed by the Assembly.) 3821

Pennsylvania (Colony) Commissioners of
Property, 1712.
Advertisement. Whereas the Proprietor
William Penn. . . .
[Philadelphia, 1712.] Broadside.
APS copy.
1580

Pennsylvania (Colony) Commissioners of
Property, 1722.
The Swedes Petition to the House of
Representatives.
Philadelphia, 1722. 8 pp.
HSP copy.
2383

Pennsylvania (Colony) Commissioners of
Property, 1757.
Philadelphia, January 24, 1757.
Advertisement [Quitrents.].

Philadelphia, 1757.] Broadside.
HSP copy.
7828

Pennsylvania (Colony) Committee of
Safety, 1775.
Rules of Establishing Rank.
[Philadelphia, 1775.] 12 pp.
LOC copy.
14369

Pennsylvania (Colony) Convention, 1774.
Resolution . . . July 15, 1774.
[Philadelphia, 1774.] pp. [1]-8, v-vi,
9-126.
(The only known copy cannot be
reproduced.)
42663

Pennsylvania (Colony) Convention, 1775.
Proceedings of the Convention . . .
January 23, 1775.
Philadelphia, Bradfords, 1775. [2],
10 pp.
AAS copy.
14367

Pennsylvania (Colony) Council, 1742.
At a Council held at Philadelphia, May
17th, 1742.
[Philadelphia, 1742.] 12 pp.
HSP copy.
5031

Pennsylvania (Colony) Council, 1771.
By the Honourable James Hamilton. . . .
A Proclamation. Whereas a Number of
Persons [July 10, 1771]. . . .
Philadelphia, Hall & Sellers, 1771.
Broadside.
JCB copy.
42264

Pennsylvania (Colony) Council, 1771.
By the Honourable James Hamilton. . . .
A Proclamation, Whereas the Honourable
John Penn [May 6, 1771]. . . .
Philadelphia, Hall & Sellers, 1771.
Broadside.
LOC copy.
42265

Pennsylvania (Colony) Court of Oyer and
Terminer (Philadelphia Co.)
The Latter Part of the Charge [Sept. 24,
1733].
[Philadelphia, 1733.] 3 pp.
UOP copy.
3711

Pennsylvania (Colony) Election Prox,
1772.
Assembly. John Dickenson. . . . October 1,
1772.
[Philadelphia, 1772.] Broadside.
HSP copy.
42363

Pennsylvania (Colony) General Assembly,
1742.
The Assembly's Answer to Two Messages
from the Governor, of the 17th and 23
instant.
[Philadelphia, Franklin, 1742.] 3 pp.
HSP copy.
40284

Pennsylvania (Colony) General Assembly,
1743.
A Bill for the Better Regulating the
Nightly Watch.
Philadelphia, Franklin, 1743. 11 pp.
HSP copy.
5270

Pennsylvania (Colony) General Assembly,
1764.
Resolves of the Assembly . . . March 24,
1764.
[Philadelphia, 1764.] Broadside.
HSP copy.
41483

Pennsylvania (Colony) General Assembly,
1765.
Weil am 18ten Jetztaufenden
Septembers. . . .
Philadelphia, Miller, [1765].
[2] pp.
AAS copy.
41581

Pennsylvania (Colony) General Assembly.
House of Representatives, 1728.
Copies of some Original Papers [Apr. 20,
1728 +].
[Philadelphia, 1728.] [4] pp.
HSP copy.
3084

Pennsylvania (Colony) General Assembly.
House of Representatives, 1728.
To the Honourable Patrick Gordon. . . .
The Representation of the Assembly.
Philadelphia, Bradford, [1728].
10 pp.
LOC copy.
3089

Pennsylvania (Colony) General Assembly.
House of Representatives, 1728.
The Two Following Depositions were laid
before the House the Ninth Day of
August, 1728.
[Philadelphia, 1728.] [2] pp.
LCP copy.
3090

Pennsylvania (Colony) General Assembly.
House of Representatives, 1729.
To the Honourable Patrick Gordon. . . .
The Humble Address of the
Representatitves [Mar. 29, 1729].
[Philadelphia, 1729.] Broadside.
HSP copy.
3203

Pennsylvania (Colony) General Assembly.
House of Representatives, 1742.
A Message to the Governor from the
Assembly [Dated 27 3 mo. 1742].
[Philadelphia, 1742.] 4 pp.
AAS copy.
5034

Pennsylvania (Colony) Governor, 1701.
The Governour's Speech to the Assembly
[Sept. 15, 1701].
Philadelphia, 1701. [2] pp.
HSP copy.
1017

Pennsylvania (Colony) Governor, 1720.
. . . By William Keith. . . . A
Proclamation [Robert Moore, Nov. 5,
1720].
[Philadelphia, 1720.] Broadside.
HSP copy.
2166

Pennsylvania (Colony) Governor, 1722.
By William Keith. . . . A Proclamation.
. . . Robert Moore [Nov. 5, 1722].
[Philadelphia], A. Bradford, [1722].
Broadside.
HSP copy.
39774

Pennsylvania (Colony) Governor, 1724.
By Sir William Keith. . . . Proclamation
[Lands. May 15th. 1724].
[Philadelphia, 1724.] Broadside.
HSP copy.
2577

Pennsylvania (Colony) Governor, 1725.
The Speech of Sir William Keith [Jan. 5,
1724/5].
Philadelphia, 1725. [2] pp.
NYPL copy.
2695

Pennsylvania (Colony) Governor, 1729.
The Governour's Message to the House
[Mar. 25, 1729.
[Philadelphia, 1729.] [2] pp.
HSP copy.
3199

Pennsylvania (Colony) Governor, 1746.
By the Honourable George Thomas. . . . A
Proclamation [Culloden. Dated July 14,
1746].
Philadelphia, Franklin. Broadside.
HSP copy.
5847

Pennsylvania (Colony) Governor, 1758.
By the Honourable William Denny, Esq. . . .
A Proclamation. Whereas Constant
Experience. . . . [Sept. 22, 1758.]
Philadelphia, Franklin & Hall, 1758.
Broadside.
LOC copy.
41000

Pennsylvania (Colony) Governor, 1766.
By the Honourable John Penn. . . . A
Proclamation [Indian Lands. Sept. 23,
1766].
Philadelphia, Hall & Sellers, [1766].
Broadside.
HSP copy.
10444

Pennsylvania (Colony) Governor, 1770.
By the Honourable John Penn. . . . A
Proclamation. Whereas a Number of
Persons. . . . [June 28, 1770.]
Philadelphia, Hall & Sellers, 1770.
Broadside.
LOC copy.
42148

Pennsylvania (Colony) Governor, 1770.
By the Honourable John Penn. . . . A
Proclamation. Whereas Information hath
been made . . . [Oct. 1, 1770.]
Philadelphia, Hall & Sellers, 1770.
Broadside.
(No copy located.)
42149

Pennsylvania (Colony) Governor, 1770.
By the Honourable John Penn. . . . A
Proclamation. Whereas it Appears. . . .

[Oct. 3, 1770.]
Philadelphia, Hall & Sellers, 1770.
Broadside.
LOC copy.   42150

Pennsylvania (Colony) Governor, 1771.
By the Honourable John Penn. . . . A
Proclamation. Whereas the Honourable
[continuance of officers]. . . . [Dated May
6, 1771.]
Philadelphia, Hall & Sellers, 1771.
Broadside.
LOC copy.   42266

Pennsylvania (Colony) Governor, 1772.
By the Honourable Richard Penn. . . . A
Proclamation. Whereas I have Received
. . . . [June 22, 1772.]
Philadelphia, Hall & Sellers, 1772.
Broadside.
LOC copy.   42364

Pennsylvania (Colony) Governor, 1773.
By the Honourable John Penn. . . . A
Proclamation [Settlers. Sept. 20, 1773].
Philadelphia, Hall & Sellers, 1773.
Broadside.
HSP copy.   12922

Pennsylvania (Colony) Governor, 1774.
By the Honourable John Penn . . . a
Proclamation [Connecticut Settlers.
Dated, Feb. 28, 1774].
Philadelphia, Hall & Sellers, 1774.
Broadside.
LOC copy.   13518

Pennsylvania (Colony) Governor, 1774.
By the Honourable John Penn . . . a
Proclamation [Lord Dunmore. Dated,
Oct. 12, 1774].
Philadelphia, Hall & Sellers, 1774.
Broadside.
HSP copy.   13521

Pennsylvania (Colony) Governor, 1774.
By the Honourable John Penn . . . a
Proclamation [Maryland Boundary.
Dated, Sept. 15, 1774].
Philadelphia, Hall & Sellers, 1774.
Broadside.
HSP copy.   13520

Pennsylvania (Colony) Governor, 1774.
By the Honourable John Penn . . . a
Proclamation [Maryland Line. Nov. 2,
1774].
Philadelphia, Hall & Sellers, 1774.
Broadside.
HSP copy.   13522

Pennsylvania (Colony) Governor, 1774.
By the Honourable John Penn . . . a
Proclamation [Reward. Dated, July 28,
1774].
Philadelphia, Hall & Sellers, [1774].
Broadside.
HSP copy.   13519

Pennsylvania (Colony) Governor, 1775.
By the Honourable John Penn . . . a
Proclamation [Boundaries, Apr. 8, 1775].
Philadelphia, Hall & Sellers, [1775].
Broadside.
LOC copy.   14365

Pennsylvania (Colony) House Journals,
1682.
Votes and Proceedings of the House of
Representatives. . . . Volume the First.
[Dec. 4, 1682 +].
Philadelphia, Franklin & Hall, 1752.
xxxviii, 164, xxxix, [2], viii, 187 pp.
HSP copy.   6908

Pennsylvania (Colony) House Journals,
1707.
Votes and Proceedings of the House of
Representatives. . . . Volume the Second
[Oct. 14, 1707 - June 16, 1726].
Philadelphia, Franklin & Hall, 1753. [2],
494 pp.
HSP copy.   7086

Pennsylvania (Colony) House Journals,
1724.
A Journal of the Votes and Proceedings of
the Representatives. . . . Anno Domini,
1724.
Philadelphia, Mary Rose, [1725]. 12 pp.,
irreg.
HSP copy.   2691

Pennsylvania (Colony) House Journals,
1724.
A Journal of the Votes and Proceedings
of the . . . Representatives [Oct. 14, 1724
+].
Philadelphia, Bradford, 1725. vi, 42 pp.
irreg.
HSP copy.   2693

Pennsylvania (Colony) House Journals,
1725.
A Journal of the Votes and Proceedings of
the . . . Representatives [Feb. 1, 1724/5
+].
Philadelphia, Bradford, 1725. 42 pp.
APS copy.   2692

[Pennsylvania (Colony) House Journals,
1725.
A Journal of the Votes and Proceedings of
the Representatives [Oct. 14, 1725 +].
[Philadelphia], Keimer, [1725]. 4 pp.]
(This is a duplicate of the first part of
2800, q.v.)   2694

Pennsylvania (Colony) House Journals,
1725.
A Journal of the Votes and Proceedings of
the Representatives [Oct. 14, 1725 - Aug.
6, 1726.]
[Philadelphia, Keimer, 1726.] 50 pp.
APS copy.   2800

Pennsylvania (Colony) House Journals,
1726.
A Journal of the Votes and Proceedings of
the House. . . . Anno Domini 1726.
Philadelphia, Bradford, [1726]. 16 pp.
(This is the first part of 2943, q.v.)   2799

Pennsylvania (Colony) House Journals,
1726.
A Journal of the Votes and Proceedings
of the House. . . . Anno Domini 1726.
[Philadelphia, Bradford, 1727.]
38 pp.
HSP copy.   2943

Pennsylvania (Colony) House Journals,
1726.
Votes and Proceedings [Vol. III. Oct. 14,
1726 +].
Philadelphia, Franklin & Hall, 1754.
591 pp.
NYPL copy.   7286

Pennsylvania (Colony) House Journals,
1727.
A Journal of the Votes and Proceedings of
the House of Representatives [Oct. 14,
1727 +].
Philadelphia, Bradford, [1728].
22 pp.
LOC copy.   3185

Pennsylvania (Colony) House Journals,
1728.
A Journal of the Votes and Proceedings
of the House. . . . Anno Domini, 1728.
[Philadelphia, 1729.] 60 pp.
HSP copy.   3200

Pennsylvania (Colony) House Journals,
1729.
Votes and Proceedings of the House [Oct.
14, 1729 +].
Philadelphia, Franklin and Meredith,
1730. 38 pp.
HSP copy.   3341

Pennsylvania (Colony) House Journals,
1730.
The Votes and Proceedings of the House
of Representatives [Oct. 14, 1730 +].
Philadelphia, Franklin and Meredith,
1731. 80 pp.
(No copy of the first part of this Journal is
known.)
HSP copy.   3463

Pennsylvania (Colony) House Journals,
1731.
Votes and Proceedings of the House of
Representatives [Oct. 14, 1731 +].
Philadelphia, Franklin, 1731. 36 pp.
HSP copy.   3464

Pennsylvania (Colony) House Journals,
1732.
Votes and Proceedings of the House of
Representatives [Oct. 14, 1732 - Mar. 24,
1732/3.]

Philadelphia, Franklin, 1732. 14 pp.
HSP copy.   3592

[Pennsylvania (Colony) House Journals,
1733.
Votes and Proceedings of the House of
Representatives [Aug. 6-11. 1733].
Philadelphia, 1733.]
(The Votes for this session have not been
found.)   3712

Pennsylvania (Colony) House Journals,
1733.
Votes and Proceedings of the House [Oct.
14, 1733 +].
Philadelphia, Franklin, 1734. 61, [1] pp.
(The unique copy is incomplete.)
HSP copy.   3825

Pennsylvania (Colony) House Journals,
1734.
Votes and Proceedings of the House [Oct.
14, 1734 +].
Philadelphia, Franklin, 1734. 30 + pp.
(The unique copy is incomplete.)
HSP copy.   3826

[Pennsylvania (Colony) House Journals,
1735.
The Votes and Proceedings of the House
of Representatives.
Philadelphia, Franklin, 1735.]
(Probably not printed.)   3948

Pennsylvania (Colony) House Journals,
1736.
Votes of the House of Representatives
[Feb. 18-20, 1735/6].
[Philadelphia, Franklin, 1736.] pp. 57-71.
NYPL copy.   4062

Pennsylvania (Colony) House Journals,
1737.
Votes and Proceedings of the House of
Representatives [Oct. 14, 1737 +].
Philadelphia, Franklin, 1737. 36 pp.
HSP copy.   4184

Pennsylvania (Colony) House Journals,
1738.
Votes and Proceedings of the House of
Representatives [Oct. 13, 1738 +].
Philadelphia, Franklin, 1738. 60, [2] pp.
HSP copy.   4299

Pennsylvania (Colony) House Journals,
1739.
Votes and Proceedings of the House of
Representatives [Oct. 15, 1739 +].
Philadelphia, Franklin, 1739. 131,
[1] pp.
NYPL copy.   4411

Pennsylvania (Colony) House Journals,
1740.
Votes and Proceedings of the House of
Representatives [Oct. 14, 1740 +].
Philadelphia, Franklin, 1741. 33,
[1] pp.
HSP copy.   4784

Pennsylvania (Colony) House Journals,
1741.
Votes and Proceedings of the House of
Representatives [Oct. 14, 1741 +].
Philadelphia, Franklin, 1741. 92 pp.
HSP copy.   4785

Pennsylvania (Colony) House Journals,
1742.
Votes and Proceedings of the House of
Representatives [Oct. 14, 1742 +].
Philadelphia, Franklin, 1743. 114 pp.
UOP copy.   5272

Pennsylvania (Colony) House Journals,
1743.
Votes and Proceedings of the House of
Representatives [Oct. 14, 1743 to Aug. 11,
1744].
Philadelphia, Franklin, 1744. 54 pp.
HSP copy.   5474

Pennsylvania (Colony) House Journals,
1744.
Votes and Proceedings of the House of
Representatives [Oct. 14, 1744, to Sept. 7,
1745].
Philadelphia, Franklin, 1745. 54 pp.
UOP copy.   5671

Pennsylvania (Colony) House Journals,
1744.

Votes and Proceedings of the House of Representatives [Oct. 15, 1744 +].
Volume the Fourth.
Philadelphia, Miller, 1774. [2], 856 pp.
LCP copy.   13525

Pennsylvania (Colony) House Journals, 1745.
Votes and Proceedings of the House of Representatives [Oct. 14, 1745 - Aug. 23, 1746].
Philadelphia, Franklin, 1746. 59 pp.
HSP copy.   5848

Pennsylvania (Colony) House Journals, 1746.
Votes and Proceedings of the House of Representatives [Oct. 14, 1746 - Aug. 26, 1747].
Philadelphia, Franklin, 1747. 36, [1] pp.
NYPL copy.   6044

Pennsylvania (Colony) House Journals, 1747.
Votes and Proceedings of the House of Representatives [Oct. 14, 1747 - Sept. 3, 1748].
Philadelphia, Franklin, 1748. 55, [1] pp.
UOP copy.   6214

Pennsylvania (Colony) House Journals, 1748.
Votes and Proceedings of the House of Representatives [Oct. 14, 1748 - Aug. 19, 1749].
Philadelphia, Franklin, 1749. 57, [1] pp.
HSP copy.   6398

Pennsylvania (Colony) House Journals, 1749.
Votes and Proceedings of the House of Representatives [Oct. 14, 1749 - June 18, 1750].
Philadelphia, Franklin, 1750. 77, [1] pp.
HSP copy.   6583

Pennsylvania (Colony) House Journals, 1750.
Votes and Proceedings of the House of Representatives [Oct. 14, 1750 +].
Philadelphia, Franklin, 1751. 94, [2] pp.
UOP copy.   6748

Pennsylvania (Colony) House Journals, 1751.
Votes and Proceedings of the House of Representatives. . . . [Oct. 14, 1751-Aug. 22, 1752].
Philadelphia, Franklin, 1752. 62 pp.
(The one recorded copy cannot be located.)   40636

Pennsylvania (Colony) House Journals, 1752.
Votes and Proceedings of the House of Representatives [Oct. 14, 1752 - Sept. 11, 1753].
Philadelphia, Franklin, 1753. 52 pp.
HSP copy.   7085

Pennsylvania (Colony) House Journals, 1753.
Votes and Proceedings [Oct. 15, 1753 - Aug. 17, 1754].
Philadelphia, Franklin, 1754. 78, [1] pp.
HSP copy.   7287

Pennsylvania (Colony) House Journals, 1754.
Votes and Proceedings of the House of Representatives [Oct. 14, 1754 +].
Philadelphia, Franklin, 1755. 187, [1], 4 pp.
HSP copy.   7532

Pennsylvania (Colony) House Journals, 1755.
Votes and Proceedings of the House of Representatives [Oct. 14, 1755 - Sept. 24, 1756].
Philadelphia, Franklin, 1756. 174, iii, 4, 4 pp.
LCP copy.   7757

Pennsylvania (Colony) House Journals, 1756.

Votes and Proceedings of the House of Representatives [Oct. 14, 1756 - Sept. 30, 1757.]
Philadelphia, Franklin, 1757. 168, [1], 12 pp.
LCP copy.   7998

Pennsylvania (Colony) House Journals, 1757.
Votes and Proceedings of the House of Representatives [Oct. 14, 1757 - Sept. 30, 1758].
Philadelphia, Franklin, 1758. 122 pp.
HSP copy.   8230

Pennsylvania (Colony) House Journals, 1758.
Votes and Proceedings of the House of Representatives [Oct. 14, 1758 - Sept. 30, 1759].
Philadelphia, Franklin, 1759. 111, [1] pp.
HSP copy.   8460

Pennsylvania (Colony) House Journals, 1758.
Votes and Proceedings of the House of Representatives [Oct. 14, 1758 +]
Volume the Fifth.
Philadelphia, Miller, 1775. [2], 560 pp.
LOC copy.   14372

Pennsylvania (Colony) House Journals, 1759.
Votes and Proceedings of the House of Representatives [Oct. 15, 1759 - Sept. 27, 1760].
Philadelphia, Franklin, 1760. 58, [1] pp.
LOC copy.   8707

Pennsylvania (Colony) House Journals, 1760.
Votes and Proceedings of the House of Representatives [Oct. 14, 1760 - Sept. 26, 1761].
[Philadelphia, 1761.] 80 pp.
LCP copy.   8971

Pennsylvania (Colony) House Journals, 1761.
Votes and Proceedings of the House of Representatives [Oct. 14, 1761 - Sept. 25, 1763].
Philadelphia, Franklin, 1762. 58, [1] pp.
HSP copy.   9232

Pennsylvania (Colony) House Journals, 1762.
Votes and Proceedings of the House of Representatives [Oct. 14, 1762 - Sept. 30, 1763].
Philadelphia, Franklin, 1763. 67, [1] pp.
LCP copy.   9477

Pennsylvania (Colony) House Journals, 1763.
Votes and Proceedings of the House of Representatives [Oct. 14, 1763 +].
Philadelphia, Franklin & Hall, 1764. 113 pp.
HSP copy.   9787

Pennsylvania (Colony) House Journals, 1764.
Votes and Proceedings of the House of Representatives [Oct. 15, 1764-Sept. 21, 1765].
Philadelphia, Franklin & Hall, 1765. 72, [1] pp.
LCP copy.   10124

Pennsylvania (Colony) House Journals, 1765.
Votes and Proceedings of the House of Representatives [Oct. 14, 1765 - Sept. 20, 1766].
Philadelphia, Hall & Sellers, 1766. 79, [1] pp.
LOC copy.   10445

Pennsylvania (Colony) House Journals, 1766.
Votes and Proceedings of the House of Representatives [Oct. 14, 1766 - Sept. 26, 1767].
Philadelphia, Goddard, 1767. 86 pp.
(No Hall & Sellers ed. could be found.)
LOC copy.   10729

Pennsylvania (Colony) House Journals, 1767.
Votes and Proceedings of the House of Representatives. . . . Beginning the Fourteenth day of October, 1767. Volume the Sixth.
Philadelphia, Miller, 1776. [2], [2], 766, [2] pp.
HSP copy.   15000

Pennsylvania (Colony) House Journals, 1767.
Votes and Proceedings of the House of Representatives [Oct. 14, 1767 - Sept. 24, 1768].
Philadelphia, Goddard, 1768. 137 pp.
LOC copy.   11027

Pennsylvania (Colony) House Journals, 1768.
Votes and Proceedings of the House of Representatives [Oct. 14, 1768 - Sept. 30, 1769].
Philadelphia, Goddard, 1769. 109 pp.
HSP copy.   11403

Pennsylvania (Colony) House Journals, 1769.
Votes and Proceedings of the House of Representatives [Oct. 14, 1769 +].
Philadelphia, Miller, 1769. pp. [2], 113-201.
HSP copy.   11803

Pennsylvania (Colony) House Journals, 1770.
Votes and Proceedings of the House of Representatives [Oct. 14, 1770 - Sept. 25, 1771].
Philadelphia, Miller, 1771. pp. [2], 205-300.
LCP copy.   12179

Pennsylvania (Colony) House Journals, 1771.
Votes and Proceedings of the House of Representatives [Oct. 14, 1771 - Sept. 19, 1772].
Philadelphia, Miller, 1772. pp. [2], 303-412.
HSP copy.   12507

Pennsylvania (Colony) House Journals, 1772.
Votes and Proceedings of the House of Representatives [Oct. 14, 1772 - Sept. 28, 1773].
Philadelphia, Miller, 1773. pp. [2], 415-498.
HSP copy.   12923

Pennsylvania (Colony) House Journals, 1773.
Votes of the House of Representatives [Jan. 4 - Feb. 26, 1773].
Philadelphia, Miller, [1773]. 41 pp.
HSP copy.   12924

Pennsylvania (Colony) House Journals, 1773.
Votes and Proceedings of the House of Representatives [Oct. 14, 1773 - Sept. 29, 1774].
Philadelphia, Miller, 1774. pp. [2], 501-578.
LCP copy.   13523

Pennsylvania (Colony) House Journals, 1774.
Votes of the House of Representatives [Dec. 29, 1773 - Dec. 29, 1774].
[Philadelphia, 1774.] pp. 19-74.
HSP copy.   13524

Pennsylvania (Colony) House Journals, 1774.
Votes and Proceedings of the House of Representatives [Oct. 14, 1774 - Sept. 30, 1775].
Philadelphia, Miller, 1775. pp. [2], 581-682.
HSP copy.   14373

Pennsylvania (Colony) House Journals, 1775.
Votes of the House of Representatives [Feb. 20 - Nov. 25, 1775].
Philadelphia, Miller, [1775]. pp. 75-172.
HSP copy.   14371

Pennsylvania (Colony) House Journals, 1776.

Votes of the House of Representatives
[Feb. 12-June 15, 1776].
Philadelphia, Miller, [1776].
pp. 173-265.
HSP copy. 14999

Pennsylvania (Colony) Land Office, 1765.
Land-Office, 17th of June, 1765.
[Philadelphia, 1765.] Broadside.
LOC copy. 10123

Pennsylvania (Colony) Laws, Statutes,
etc., 1693.
. . . An Act for Granting to King
William. . . .
[New York, 1693.] 4 pp.
NYPL copy. 678

Pennsylvania (Colony) Laws, Statutes,
etc., 1701.
An Abstract or Abridgment of the Laws.
Philadelphia, 1701. [4], 43 pp.
HSP copy. 1018

Pennsylvania (Colony) Laws, Statutes,
etc., 1705.
. . . An Act for the Better Proportioning
the Rates of Money.
[Philadelphia, 1705.] Broadside.
LOC copy. 39432

[Pennsylvania (Colony) Laws, Statutes,
etc., 1712.
Acts of the General Assembly.
Philadelphia, 1712.]
(See Hildeburn 117.) 1579

Pennsylvania (Colony) Laws, Statutes,
etc., 1714.
The Laws of the Province of
Pennsylvania.
Philadelphia, 1714. [4], 184 pp., irreg.
NYPL copy. 1712

Pennsylvania (Colony) Laws, Statutes,
etc., 1717.
An Act Passed in a General Assembly
[Oct. 14, 1717].
Philadelphia, 1718. 6 pp.
NYPL copy. 1993

Pennsylvania (Colony) Laws, Statutes,
etc., 1719.
An Act Passed in the General Assembly
[Apr. 25, 1719].
Philadelphia, 1719. [10] pp.
NYPL copy. 2066

Pennsylvania (Colony) Laws, Statutes,
etc., 1721.
An Act for Preventing Accidents [Aug.
26, 1721].
[Philadelphia, 1730?].
HSP copy. 3337

Pennsylvania (Colony) Laws, Statutes,
etc., 1722.
An Act [Free Society of Traders. Mar. 22,
1722].
Philadelphia, 1723. 14 pp.
NYPL copy. 2473

Pennsylvania (Colony) Laws, Statutes,
etc., 1728.
The Laws of the Province of
Pennsylvania: now in Force.
Philadelphia, Bradford, 1728. [6],
352 pp.
NYPL copy. 3086

Pennsylvania (Colony) Laws, Statutes,
etc., 1730.
. . . An Act for the Better Enabling Divers
Inhabitants . . . to hold Lands.
Philadelphia, Franklin & Meredith, 1730.
6 pp.
NYPL ph. copy. 39958

Pennsylvania (Colony) Laws, Statutes,
etc., 1734.
At a General Assembly [Poor Laws, Mar.
17, 1734].
Philadelphia, Franklin, 1734. 24 pp.
NYPL copy. 3947

Pennsylvania (Colony) Laws, Statutes,
etc., 1739.
. . . At a General Assembly. . . . May,
1739. . . . An Act for the Better Enabling
. . . Trade.
Philadelphia, Franklin, 1739. 7 pp.
APS copy. 40173

Pennsylvania (Colony) Laws, Statutes,
etc., 1739.
The Bill for the Better Raising of Money.
[Philadelphia], 1739. [2], 16 pp.
HSP copy. 4409

Pennsylvania (Colony) Laws, Statutes,
etc., 1742.
The Charters of the Province of
Pensilvania.
Philadelphia, Franklin, 1742. 30, 562, iv,
24, xi pp.
AAS copy. 5033

[Pennsylvania (Colony) Laws, Statutes,
etc., 1746.
An Act for the more Effectual
Suppressing Profane Cursing.
Philadelphia, 1746. Broadside.]
(Adv. Pa. Gazette, Jan. 19, 1746.) 5843

Pennsylvania (Colony) Laws, Statutes,
etc., 1753.
Eine im Herbst 26sten Jahrs . . . Georgs
des Zweiten . . . Gemachte Acte oder
Landisgesetz. . . .
Germantown, Sauer, 1753. 24 pp.
JCB copy. 40664

Pennsylvania (Colony) Laws, Statutes,
etc., 1755.
An Act for Granting Sixty Thousand
Pounds [Nov. 27, 1755].
[Philadelphia? 1755]. 3, [1] pp.
HSP copy. 7531

Pennsylvania (Colony) Laws, Statutes,
etc., 1755.
A Bill, Intitled, An Act for Raising Fifty
Thousand Pounds.
[Philadelphia, 1755.] 4 pp.
YC copy. 7530

Pennsylvania (Colony) Laws, Statutes,
etc., 1756.
An Act for . . . Military Purposes.
[Philadelphia, 1756.] 3, [1] pp.
HSP copy. 40861

[Pennsylvania (Colony) Laws, Statutes,
etc., 1756.
Oath to be Administered to all such
Persons as Enter into the King's Service.
[Philadelphia, 1756.] Broadside.]
(Hildeburn 4630.) 7756

Pennsylvania (Colony) Laws, Statutes,
etc., 1757.
An Act for Forming and Regulating the
Militia [Mar. 1757].
[Philadelphia, 1757.] 12 pp.
(The only copy reported could not be
located.) 7997

[Pennsylvania (Colony) Laws, Statutes,
etc., 1759.
An Act [£100,000. Feb. 5, 1759 +].
Philadelphia, Franklin, 1759. [2], 45 pp.]
(Sabin 59781.) 8458

Pennsylvania (Colony) Laws, Statutes,
etc., 1760.
A Collection of the Laws of the
Province. . . . Vol. II.
Philadelphia, Miller, 1760. [2], xii, 464
pp.
HSP copy. 8706

Pennsylvania (Colony) Laws, Statutes,
etc., 1762.
The Charters and Acts of Assembly
[Folio Edition].
Philadelphia, Miller, 1762. [2], 21, [1], 4,
164; [2], iii, [1], 116, [2], 18, 32 pp.
AAS copy. 9227

Pennsylvania (Colony) Laws, Statutes,
etc., 1762.
The Charters and Acts of Assembly
[Octavo Edition].
Philadelphia, Miller, 1762. 2 vol. [4], 82,
16, 653, [1] [2], xii, 464, [2], 71, 127 pp.
Composite copy. 9228

Pennsylvania (Colony) Laws, Statutes,
etc., 1764.
. . . An Act for Preventing Tumults.
[Philadelphia, 1764?]. 4 pp.
HSP copy. 9782

Pennsylvania (Colony) Laws, Statutes,
etc., 1766.
An Act for the Better Employment.

[Philadelphia, 1766.] 4 pp.
UOP copy. 10441

Pennsylvania (Colony) Laws, Statutes,
etc., 1768.
An Act to Remove the Persons now
Settled. . . .
[Philadelphia, 1768.] Broadside.
HSP copy. 41865

Pennsylvania (Colony) Laws, Statutes,
etc., 1770.
An Act for Incorporating the Society for
the Relief of Poor . . . Masters of
Ships. . . . Passed February 24, 1770.
[Philadelphia, 1700.] 8 pp.
HEH copy. 42151

Pennsylvania (Colony) Laws, Statutes,
etc., 1771.
An Act for Preventing Tumults. . . .
February 9, 1771.
[Philadelphia, 1771.] Broadside.
MHS copy. 42267

Pennsylvania (Colony) Laws, Statutes,
etc., 1771.
An Act for the Relief of the Poor.
Philadelphia, Hall & Sellers, 1771.
[2], 30 pp.
HSP copy. 12175

[Pennsylvania (Colony) Laws, Statutes,
etc., 1772.
An Act [Dog Damages.]
Philadelphia, 1772.]
(Adv. Pa. Gazette, June 4, 1772.) 12504

Pennsylvania (Colony) Laws, Statutes,
etc., 1774.
An Act for Preventing Tumults. . . .
January 22, 1774.
[Philadelphia, 1774.] Broadside.
LOC ph. copy. 42664

Pennsylvania (Colony) Laws, Statutes,
etc., 1775.
The Acts of Assembly.
Philadelphia, Hall & Sellers, 1775. xxi,
[1], 536, 22, [12], 3 pp.
AAS copy. 14364

[Pennsylvania (Colony) Laws, Statutes,
etc., 1775.
Resolutions Directing the Mode of
Levying Taxes.
Philadelphia, Miller, 1775.]
(Ordered printed by the Assembly.) 14368

Pennsylvania (Colony) Lieutenant
Governor, 1704.
By the Honourable Collonel John
Evans. . . . Proclamation [Immorality.
Oct. 9, 1704].
[Philadelphia, 1704.] Broadside.
HSP copy. 1191

Pennsylvania (Colony) Lieutenant
Governor, 1726.
The Speech of the Honourable Patrick
Gordon [Aug. 2, 1726].
Philadelphia, Bradford, [1726]. 4 pp.
HSP copy. 2802

Pennsylvania (Colony) Lieutenant
Governor, 1726.
Proclamation. By the Honourable Patrick
Gordon [Riots. Oct. 4, 1726].
Philadelphia, Bradford, 1726. Broadside.
HSP copy. 2801

Pennsylvania (Colony) Lieutenant
Governor, 1726.
The Speech of the Honourable Patrick
Gordon [Nov. 22, 1726].
Philadelphia, Bradford, [1726]. 4 pp.
LOC copy. 2803

Pennsylvania (Colony) Lieutenant
Governor, 1728.
By the Honourable Patrick Gordon. . . . A
Proclamation [Indians. May 16, 1728].
Philadelphia, Bradford, 2728 [sic].
Broadside.
HSP copy. 3087

Pennsylvania (Colony) Lieutenant
Governor, 1728.
The Speech of the Honourable Patrick
Gordon. . . . December 17th, 1728.
Philadelphia, Bradford, 1728. [4] pp.
HSP copy. 3088

Pennsylvania (Colony) Lieutenant
Governor, 1729.
By the Honourable Patrick Gordon . . . a
Proclamation [Disorderly Persons. Mar.
31, 1729].
Philadelphia, Bradford, 1729. Broadside.
LOC copy.   3201

Pennsylvania (Colony) Lieutenant
Governor, 1729.
The Speech of the Honourable Patrick
Gordon . . . April the 2d, 1729.
Philadelphia, Bradford, 1729. [2] pp.
HSP copy.   3202

Pennsylvania (Colony) Lieutenant
Governor, 1730.
The Speech of the Honourable Patrick
Gordon [Jan. 13, 1729/30].
Philadelphia, Franklin and Meredith,
[1730]. [2] pp.
HSP copy.   3340

Pennsylvania (Colony) Lieutenant
Governor, 1738.
By the Honourable George Thomas . . . a
Proclamation . . . Disorders. . . . Aug. 29,
1738.
[Philadelphia, Franklin, 1738.]
Broadside.
(Curtis 121.)   40150

Pennsylvania (Colony) Lieutenant
Governor, 1738.
The Speech of the Honourable George
Thomas. . . . To the Representatives. . . .
August 8, 1738.
Philadelphia, Franklin, 1738. [3] pp.
HSP copy.   4298

[Pennsylvania (Colony) Lieutenant
Governor, 1741.
By the Honourable George Thomas
[Recruiting. Sept. 28, 1741].
Philadelphia, Franklin, 1741. Broadside.]
(Title from Hildeburn.)   4781

Pennsylvania (Colony) Lieutenant
Governor, 1742.
By the Honourable George Thomas, Esq.
. . . A Proclamation [Settlers. Oct. 5,
1742].
[Philadelphia, 1742.] Broadside.
LOC copy.   5032

Pennsylvania (Colony) Lieutenant
Governor, 1744.
By the Honourable George Thomas. . . . A
Proclamation [War. June 11, 1744].
[Philadelphia, 1744.] Broadside.
HSP copy.   5473

Pennsylvania (Colony) Lieutenant
Governor, 1746.
By the Honourable George Thomas. . . . A
Proclamation. His Grace the Duke of
Newcastle [troops for Canada. . . . June
9, 1746].
Philadelphia, Franklin, [1746].
Broadside.
BPL copy.   40415

Pennsylvania (Colony) Lieutenant
Governor, 1747.
[Proclamation for a General Fast, 1747.
Philadelphia, Franklin, 1747.] Broadside.
(Curtis 369; no copy known.)   40436

Pennsylvania (Colony) Lieutenant
Governor, 1749.
By the Honourable James Hamilton . . . A
Proclamation [Indian Lands. July 18,
1749].
Philadelphia, Franklin, [1749].
Broadside.
HSP copy.   6396

Pennsylvania (Colony) Lieutenant
Governor, 1749.
By the Honourable James Hamilton . . . A
Proclamation [Liquor. Aug. 11, 1749].
Philadelphia, Franklin, [1747].
Broadside.
HSP copy.   6397

Pennsylvania (Colony) Lieutenant
Governor, 1750.
By the Honourable James Hamilton. . . .
A Proclamation [Iron Works.Aug. 16,
1750].
Philadelphia, Franklin, 1750. Broadside.
HSP copy.   6582

[Pennsylvania (Colony) Lieutenant
Governor, 1751.
By the Honourable James Hamilton. . . .
A Proclamation.
Philadelphia, Franklin, 1751. Broadside.]
(Title from Sabin.)   6747

Pennsylvania (Colony) Lieutenant
Governor, 1755.
By the Honourable Robert Hunter
Morris. . . . A Proclamation. Whereas
[Fast, June 19. Dated June 6, 1755]. . . .
Philadelphia, Franklin & Hall, 1755.
Broadside.
LCP copy.   40791

Pennsylvania (Colony) Lieutenant
Governor, 1756.
By the Honourable Robert Hunter
Morris. . . . A Proclamation [Delaware
Indians. Apr. 14, 1756].
Philadelphia, Franklin & Hall, 1756.
Broadside.
HSP copy.   7754

Pennsylvania (Colony) Lieutenant
Governor, 1756.
By the Honourable Robert Hunter
Morris. . . . A Proclamation [Delaware
Indians. June 3, 1756].
Philadelphia, Franklin & Hall, 1756.
Broadside.
NYPL copy.   7755

[Pennsylvania (Colony) Lieutenant
Governor, 1758.
By the Honorable William Denny, Esq.
. . . An Advertisement [Indians. July
5, 1758].
[Philadelphia, 1758.] Broadside.]
(No copy found.)   8229

Pennsylvania (Colony) Lieutenant
Governor, 1761.
By the Honourable James Hamilton. . . .
A Proclamation [Bounties. Mar. 17,
1761].
Philadelphia, Franklin & Hall, [1761].
Broadside.
HSP copy.   8969

[Pennsylvania (Colony) Lieutenant
Governor, 1761.
By the Honourable James Hamilton. . . .
A Proclamation [Settlers. Feb. 20, 1761].
Philadelphia, Franklin & Hall, 1761.
Broadside.]
(The unique copy is mislaid.)   8970

Pennsylvania (Colony) Lieutenant
Governor, 1763.
By the Honourable John Penn . . . A
Proclamation, Whereas I have Received
Information [Dec. 22, 1763]. . . .
Philadelphia, Franklin & Hall, [1763].
Broadside.
LOC copy.   41405

Pennsylvania (Colony) Lieutenant
Governor, 1764.
By the Honourable John Penn. . . . A
Proclamation [Paxton Boys. Jan. 2, 1764].
Philadelphia, Franklin & Hall, [1764].
Broadside.
NYPL copy.   9783

Pennsylvania (Colony) Lieutenant
Governor, 1764.
By the Honourable John Penn. . . . A
Proclamation [Scalps. July 7, 1764].
Philadelphia, Franklin & Hall, [1764].
Broadside.
NYPL copy.   9784

Pennsylvania (Colony) Lieutenant
Governor, 1765.
By the Honourable John Penn. . . . A
Proclamation. Whereas his Majesty [trade
with the Indians. Dated June 4, 1765].
Philadelphia, Franklin & Hall, [1765].
Broadside.
UOP copy.   41582

Pennsylvania (Colony) Lieutenant
Governor, 1765.
By the Honorable John Penn. . . .
Whereas [blank] Prayed my Licence to
Trade with the [blank] Indians. . . .
[blank] 1765.
[Philadelphia, 1765.] Broadside.
BPL copy.   41583

Pennsylvania (Colony) Lieutenant

Governor, 1768.
By the Honourable John Penn. . . . A
Proclamation [Robbery. Aug. 6, 1768].
Philadelphia, Hall & Sellers, [1768].
Broadside.
HSP copy.   11025

Pennsylvania (Colony) Lieutenant
Governor, 1768.
By the Honourable John Penn. . . . A
Proclamation [Squatters Feb. 24, 1768].
Philadelphia, Hall & Sellers, [1768].
Broadside.
LOC copy.   11026

Pennsylvania (Colony) Lieutenant
Governor, 1768.
By the Honourable John Penn. . . . A
Proclamation [Stump. Mar. 16, 1768].
Philadelphia, Hall & Sellers, 1768.
Broadside.
LOC copy.   11024

Pennsylvania (Colony) Lieutenant
Governor, 1768.
By the Honorable John Penn. . . . A
Proclamation. Whereas it Appears by a
Deposition. . . . [Jan. 19, 1768.]
Philadelphia, Hall & Sellers, 1768.
Broadside.
LOC copy.   41864

Pennsylvania (Colony) Lieutenant
Governor, 1769.
By the Honourable John Penn. . . . A
Proclamation. Whereas an Act of the
General Assembly [Oct. 7, 1769]. . . .
Philadelphia, Hall and Sellers, 1769.
Broadside.
LOC copy.   41991

Pennsylvania (Colony) Lieutenant
Governor, 1769.
By the Honourable John Penn. . . . A
Proclamation [Wyoming. May 16, 1769].
Philadelphia, Hall & Sellers, 1769.
Broadside.
LOC copy.   11402

Pennsylvania (Colony) Lieutenant
Governor, 1771.
By the Honourable John Penn. . . . A
Proclamation [Reward. Feb. 9, 1771].
Philadelphia, Hall & Sellers, 1771.
Broadside.
MHS copy.   12178

[Pennsylvania (Colony) President, 1736.
By the Honourable the President . . . A
Proclamation [Invasion].
Philadelphia, Franklin, [1736].
Broadside.]
(No copy could be located.)   4060

[Pennsylvania (Colony) President, 1737.
By the Honourable James Logan. . . . A
Proclamation [against Trading with the
Spanish].
Philadelphia, Franklin, 1737. 1 leaf.]
(Hildeburn 560.)   4183

[Pennsylvania (Colony) President, 1747.
By the President and Council. . . . A
Proclamation [Fast, Jan. 7, 1747/8].
Philadelphia, Franklin, 1747. Broadside.]
(See Hildeburn 1033.)   6043

Pennsylvania (Colony) President, 1748.
By the Honourable the President and
Council. . . . A Proclamation. Whereas
Divers Insults. . . . [Apr. 11, 1748.]
Philadelphia, Franklin, [1748].
Broadside.
BPL copy.   40473

Pennsylvania (Colony) Proprietor, 1699.
By the Proprietary . . . A Proclamation
[Pirates. 23 day 10 mo. 1699].
Philadelphia, 1699. Broadside.
APS copy.   894

[Pennsylvania (Colony) Proprietor, 1703.
Advertisement for Proprietary Quit Rents.
Philadelphia, 1703. Broadside.]
(Hildeburn, Pa.)   1142

Pennsylvania (Colony) Proprietor, 1735.
Scheme of a Lottery for One Hundred
Thousand Acres of Land in . . .
Pennsylvania. . . . July 12, 1735.
[Philadelphia, 1735.] 4 pp.
HSP copy.   40081

Pennsylvania (Colony) Proprietor, 1738.
By the Proprietaries of Pennsylvania
[Quit-Rents. Nov. 23, 1738].
[Philadelphia, 1738.] Broadside.
HSP copy.   4297

Pennsylvania (Colony) Proprietor, 1739.
By the Proprietaries of Pennsylvania
[Quit-rents. June 25, 1739].
[Philadelphia, 1793.] Broadside.
HSP copy.   4410

[Pennsylvania (Colony) Proprietor, 1741.
Notice is Hereby Given [Lands. Sept. 21,
1741].
[Philadelphia, 1741.] Broadside.]
(Title from Hildeburn.)   4783

[Pennsylvania (Colony) Proprietor, 1742.
Advertisement [Quit rents. 12/12/1742].
Philadelphia, Franklin, 1742. 1 leaf.]
(Hildeburn 741. One of a series issued
annually by the quit rent commissioners.)
                                         5030

Pennsylvania (Colony) Proprietor, 1761.
[Advertisement Jan. 29, 1761.
Philadelphia, 1761. [2] pp.]
(Hildeburn 4641.)   8780

[Pennsylvania (Colony) Proprietor, 1763.
Land Office, Philadelphia, March 10,
1763.
[Philadelphia, 1763.] Broadside.]
(The unique copy is mislaid.)   9476

Pennsylvania (Colony) Receiver-General,
1734.
Advertisement. . . . James Steel,
Receiver-General. [Sept. 5, 1734].
[Philadelphia, 1734.] Broadside.
HSP copy.   3822

Pennsylvania (Colony) Receiver-General,
1735.
Advertisement. . . . Philad. Dec. 24 1735.
[Philadelphia, 1735.] Broadside.
NYPL facsim. copy.   40079

[Pennsylvania (Colony) Session Laws,
1712.
Acts and Laws [Oct., 1712 - Mar., 1713].
Philadelphia, 1713.]
(Assumed by Hildeburn.)   1644

Pennsylvania (Colony) Session Laws,
1715.
The Acts and Laws [May 28, 1715 +].
Philadelphia, 1715. pp. [4], 101-152,
253-274.
NYPL copy.   1775

Pennsylvania (Colony) Session Laws,
1715.
The Laws of the Province . . . Passed . . .
1715, 1717, and 1718.
Philadelphia, 1718. pp. [2], 275-289, [34],
325-352.
HSP copy.   1994

Pennsylvania (Colony) Session Laws,
1720.
Acts of the Province [Feb. 25, 1720 +].
Philadelphia, Bradford, 1721. 12 pp.
LCP copy.   2284

Pennsylvania (Colony) Session Laws,
1720.
Acts of the Province [Aug. 26, 1720 +].
Philadelphia, Bradford, 1721. pp. [2],
13-30.
LCP copy.   2285

Pennsylvania (Colony) Session Laws,
1722.
Acts of the Province [May 22, 1722 +].
Philadelphia, 1722. pp. [2], 33-90.
NYPL copy.   2381

Pennsylvania (Colony) Session Laws,
1723.
Acts Passed [Oct. 14, 1722 +].
Philadelphia, Bradford, 1723. 47 pp.
HSP copy.   2474

Pennsylvania (Colony) Session Laws,
1723.
Acts Passed [Dec. 12, 1723 +].
Philadelphia, Bradford, 1723. 28 pp.
LCP copy.   2475

Pennsylvania (Colony) Session Laws,
1724.

Acts [Oct. 14, 1724 +].
Philadelphia, 1725. 32 pp.
HSP copy.   2689

Pennsylvania (Colony) Session Laws,
1726.
Acts [Oct. 14, 1725 +].
Philadelphia, Bradford, 1726. 28 pp.
HSP copy.   2798

[Pennsylvania (Colony) Session Laws,
1726.
Acts. [October 14, 1726 + .]
Philadelphia, 1727. 2 pp.]
(A ghost; no acts passed.)   2942

Pennsylvania (Colony) Session Laws,
1729.
Acts Passed in the General Assembly
[Aug. 11, 1729 +].
Philadelphia, Bradford, 1729. pp. [2],
353-387.
NYPL copy.   3198

Pennsylvania (Colony) Session Laws,
1729.
At a General Assembly . . . [Oct. 14, 1729
+].
Philadelphia, Franklin and Meredith,
1730. 48 pp.
NYPL copy.   3338

Pennsylvania (Colony) Session Laws,
1730.
At a General Assembly [Jan. 12, 1729/30
+].
Philadelphia, Franklin, 1734. 34 pp.
UOP copy.   3824

Pennsylvania (Colony) Session Laws,
1730.
At a General Assembly [Aug. 3, 1730 +].
Philadelphia, Franklin and Meredith,
1730. pp. [2], 51-57.
LOC copy.   3339

Pennsylvania (Colony) Session Laws,
1731.
At a General Assembly [Jan. 4, 1730/31
+].
Philadelphia, Franklin and Meredith, 1730
(1731). pp. [2], 61-89.
HSP copy.   3462

Pennsylvania (Colony) Session Laws,
1732.
At a General Assembly [Jan. 10, 1731/2
+].
Philadelphia, Franklin, 1731 (1732). pp.
[2], 93-95.
HSP copy.   3590

Pennsylvania (Colony) Session Laws,
1732.
At a General Assembly of the Province
[July 31, 1732 +].
Philadelphia, Franklin, 1732. pp. [2],
99-102.
HSP copy.   3591

Pennsylvania (Colony) Session Laws,
1733.
At a General Assembly [Dec. 17,1733
+].
Philadelphia, Franklin, 1733. pp. [2],
105-128.
NYPL copy.   3709

Pennsylvania (Colony) Session Laws,
1734.
At a General Assembly [Aug. 12, 1734
+].
Philadelphia, Franklin, 1734. pp. [2],
131-133.
UOP copy.   3823

Pennsylvania (Colony) Session Laws,
1735.
At a General Assembly [Mar. 17,
1734/5 +].
Philadelphia, Franklin, 1734 (1735). pp.
[2], 137-154.
HSP copy.   3946

Pennsylvania (Colony) Session Laws,
1736.
At a General Assembly [Jan. 12, 1735/6
+].
Philadelphia, Franklin, 1736. pp. [2],
157-169.
NYPL copy.   4059

Pennsylvania (Colony) Session Laws,
1738.
At a General Assembly [Aug. 7, 1738 +].
Philadelphia, Franklin, 1738. pp. [2],
173-189.
HSP copy.   4296

Pennsylvania (Colony) Session Laws,
1739.
At a General Assembly [May 1, 1739 +].
Philadelphia, Franklin, 1739. pp. [2],
193-228, [1] pp.
NYPL copy.   4408

[Pennsylvania (Colony) Session Laws,
1743.
Acts of Assembly. February, 1742, 3.
Philadelphia, 1743.]
(Probably printed only in 5033.)   5269

Pennsylvania (Colony) Session Laws,
1744.
. . . At a General Assembly [May, 1744].
Philadelphia, Franklin, 1744. 22 pp.
HSP copy.   5472

Pennsylvania (Colony) Session Laws,
1745.
At a General Assembly [Mar. 7, 1745 +].
Philadelphia, Franklin, 1746. pp. [2],
25-59.
HSP copy.   5845

Pennsylvania (Colony) Session Laws,
1746.
. . . At a General Assembly [June 9, 1746
+].
Philadelphia, Franklin, 1746. pp. [2], 61,
64-9.
HSP copy.   5846

Pennsylvania (Colony) Session Laws,
1746.
At a General Assembly [Oct. 15, 1744 +].
Philadelphia, Franklin, 1746. pp. [2],
xxv-xxvi.
HSP copy.   5844

Pennsylvania (Colony) Session Laws,
1747.
. . . At a General Assembly [May 3, 1747
+].
Philadelphia, Franklin, 1747. iv pp.
HSP copy.   6042

Pennsylvania (Colony) Session Laws,
1749.
. . . At a General Assembly [Jan. 2, 1748/9
+].
Philadelphia, Franklin, 1749. pp. [2],
73-88.
HSP copy.   6394

Pennsylvania (Colony) Session Laws,
1749.
. . . At a General Assembly [Aug. 7,
1749 +].
Philadelphia, Franklin, 1749. 19 pp.
(Curtis 408; no copy located.)   40511

Pennsylvania (Colony) Session Laws,
1749.
. . . At a General Assembly [Aug. 7, 1749
+].
Philadelphia, Franklin, 1749. pp. [2],
91-105.
HSP copy.   6395

Pennsylvania (Colony) Session Laws,
1750.
. . . At a General Assembly [Jan. 1,
1749/50 +].
Philadelphia, Franklin, 1750. pp. [2],
107-119.
HSP copy.   6580

Pennsylvania (Colony) Session Laws,
1750.
. . . At a General Assembly [Aug. 6, 1750
+].
Philadelphia, Franklin, 1750. pp. [2],
123-125.
HSP copy.   6581

Pennsylvania (Colony) Session Laws,
1751.
. . . At a General Assembly [Jan. 7,
1750/1].
Philadelphia, Franklin, 1751. pp. [2],
129-151.
HSP copy.   6745

Pennsylvania (Colony) Session Laws, 1751.
. . . At a General Assembly [May 6, 1751 +].
Philadelphia, Franklin, 1751. pp. [2], 155-158.
HSP copy. 6746

Pennsylvania (Colony) Session Laws, 1751.
At a General Assembly [Aug. 6, 1751 +].
Philadelphia, Franklin, 1752. pp. [clix]-clxi.
LCP copy. 6905

Pennsylvania (Colony) Session Laws, 1752.
. . . At a General Assembly [Feb. 3, 1752 +].
Philadelphia, Franklin, 1752. pp. [2], 161-184.
HSP copy. 6906

Pennsylvania (Colony) Session Laws, 1752.
. . . At a General Assembly [Aug. 10, 1752 +].
Philadelphia, Franklin, 1752. pp. [2], 187-208.
HSP copy. 6907

Pennsylvania (Colony) Session Laws, 1755.
. . . At a General Assembly [Mar. 17, 1755 +].
Philadelphia, Franklin, 1755. pp. [2], 211-214.
HSP copy. 7525

Pennsylvania (Colony) Session Laws, 1755.
. . . At a General Assembly [June 13, 1755 +].
Philadelphia, Franklin, 1755. pp. [2], 217-222.
HSP copy. 7526

Pennsylvania (Colony) Session Laws, 1755.
. . . At a General Assembly [July 23, 1755 +].
Philadelphia, Franklin, 1755. pp. [2], 225-235.
HSP copy. 7527

Pennsylvania (Colony) Session Laws, 1755.
. . . At a General Assembly [Sept. 15, 1755 +].
Philadelphia, Franklin, 1755. pp. [2], 239.
HSP copy. 7528

Pennsylvania (Colony) Session Laws, 1755.
. . . At a General Assembly [Oct. 14, 1755 +].
Philadelphia, Franklin, 1755. pp. [2], 243-260.
HSP copy. 7529

Pennsylvania (Colony) Session Laws, 1756.
. . . At a General Assembly [Feb. 3, 1756 +].
Philadelphia, Franklin, 1756. pp. [2], 263-266.
HSP copy. 7750

Pennsylvania (Colony) Session Laws, 1756.
. . . At a General Assembly [Apr. 5, 1756 +].
Philadelphia, Franklin, 1756. pp. [2], 269-270.
HSP copy. 7751

Pennsylvania (Colony) Session Laws, 1756.
. . . At a General Assembly [May 10, 1756 +].
Philadelphia, Franklin, 1756. pp. [2], 273-274.
HSP copy. 7752

Pennsylvania (Colony) Session Laws, 1756.
. . . At a General Assembly [Aug. 16, 1756 +].
Philadelphia, Franklin, 1756. pp. [2], 277-316.
HSP copy. 7753

Pennsylvania (Colony) Session Laws, 1756.
At a General Assembly [Nov. 4, 1756 +].
Philadelphia, Franklin, 1757. pp. [2], 319-321.
HSP copy. 7992

Pennsylvania (Colony) Session Laws, 1756.
At a General Assembly [Nov. 22, 1756 +].
Philadelphia, Franklin, 1757. pp. [2], 325-334.
HSP copy. 7993

Philadelphia, Franklin, 1757. pp. [2], 325-334.
HSP copy. 7993

Pennsylvania (Colony) Session Laws, 1757.
At a General Assembly [Jan. 3, 1757 +].
Philadelphia, Franklin, 1757. pp. [2], 337-344.
LOC copy. 7994

Pennsylvania (Colony) Session Laws, 1757.
At a General Assembly [Jan. 31, 1757 +].
Philadelphia, Franklin, 1757. pp. [2], 347-361.
LOC copy. 7995

Pennsylvania (Colony) Session Laws, 1757.
At a General Assembly [May 30, 1757 +].
Philadelphia, Franklin, 1757. pp. [2], 365-372.
LOC copy. 7996

Pennsylvania (Colony) Session Laws, 1757.
. . . At a General Assembly [Oct. 14, 1757 +].
Philadelphia, Franklin, 1758. pp. [2], 375-390.
HSP copy. 8225

Pennsylvania (Colony) Session Laws, 1758.
. . . At a General Assembly [Jan. 2, 1758 +].
Philadelphia, Franklin, 1758. pp. [2], 393-407.
UOP copy. 8226

Pennsylvania (Colony) Session Laws, 1758.
. . . An Act [Apr. 1758].
[Philadelphia, 1758.] pp. 409-427.
UOP copy. 8227

Pennsylvania (Colony) Session Laws, 1758.
. . . At a General Assembly [Sept. 4, 1758 +].
Philadelphia, Franklin, 1758. pp. [2], 431-436.
HSP copy. 8228

Pennsylvania (Colony) Session Laws, 1759.
. . . At a General Assembly [Feb. 5, 1759 +].
Philadelphia, Franklin, 1759. pp. [2], 439-483.
HSP copy. 8454

Pennsylvania (Colony) Session Laws, 1759.
. . . At a General Assembly [May 21, 1759 +].
Philadelphia, Franklin, 1759. pp. [2], 487-513.
HSP copy. 8455

Pennsylvania (Colony) Session Laws, 1759.
. . . At a General Assembly [Sept. 10, 1759 +].
Philadelphia, Franklin, 1759. pp. [2], 517-526.
HSP copy. 8456

Pennsylvania (Colony) Session Laws, 1759.
. . . At a General Assembly [Nov. 20, 1759 +].
Philadelphia, Franklin, 1759. pp. [2], 529-530.
HSP copy. 8457

Pennsylvania (Colony) Session Laws, 1760.
At a General Assembly [Feb. 11, 1760 +].
Philadelphia, Franklin, 1760. 45 pp.
NYPL copy. 8705

Pennsylvania (Colony) Session Laws, 1760.
At a General Assembly [Oct. 14, 1760 +].
Philadelphia, Franklin, 1761. pp. [2], 49-98.
NYPL copy. 8966

Pennsylvania (Colony) Session Laws, 1761.
At a General Assembly [Apr. 23, 1761].
Philadelphia, Franklin, 1761. pp. [2], 101-103.
NYPL copy. 8967

Pennsylvania (Colony) Session Laws, 1761.
At a General Assembly [Sept. 26, 1761 +].
Philadelphia, Franklin, 1761. pp. [2], 107-125.
NYPL copy. 8968

Pennsylvania (Colony) Session Laws, 1762.
At a General Assembly [Feb. 16, 1762 +].
Philadelphia, Franklin, 1762. pp. [2], 129-183.
NYPL copy. 9229

Pennsylvania (Colony) Session Laws, 1762.
At a General Assembly [Mar. 26, 1762 +].
Philadelphia, Franklin, 1762. pp. [2], 187-211.
NYPL copy. 9230

Pennsylvania (Colony) Session Laws, 1762.
At a General Assembly [May 3, 1762 +].
Philadelphia, Franklin, 1762. pp. [2], 215-220.
NYPL copy. 9231

Pennsylvania (Colony) Session Laws, 1763.
At a General Assembly [Mar. 4, 1763 +].
Philadelphia, Franklin, 1763. pp. [2], 223-276.
NYPL copy. 9472

Pennsylvania (Colony) Session Laws, 1763.
At a General Assembly [July 8, 1763 +].
Philadelphia, Franklin, 1763. pp. [2], 279-286.
NYPL copy. 9473

Pennsylvania (Colony) Session Laws, 1763.
At a General Assembly [Sept. 30, 1763 +].
Philadelphia, Franklin, 1763. pp. [2], 289-296.
NYPL copy. 9474

Pennsylvania (Colony) Session Laws, 1763.
At a General Assembly [Oct. 22, 1763 +].
Philadelphia, Franklin, 1763. pp. [2], 299-311.
NYPL copy. 9475

Pennsylvania (Colony) Session Laws, 1764.
At a General Assembly [Mar. 24, 1764 +].
Philadelphia, Franklin, 1764. pp. [2], 315-330.
NYPL copy. 9779

Pennsylvania (Colony) Session Laws, 1764.
At a General Assembly [May 30, 1764 +].
Philadelphia, Franklin, 1764. pp. [2], 333-358.
NYPL copy. 9780

Pennsylvania (Colony) Session Laws, 1764.
At a General Assembly [Sept. 22, 1764 +].

Philadelphia, Franklin, 1764. pp. [2],
361-369.
NYPL copy.   9781

Pennsylvania (Colony) Session Laws,
1765.
At a General Assembly [Feb. 15,
1765 +].
Philadelphia, Franklin, 1765. pp. [2],
373-410.
NYPL copy.   10120

Pennsylvania (Colony) Session Laws,
1765.
At a General Assembly [May 18,
1765 +].
Philadelphia, Franklin, 1765. pp. [2],
413-428.
NYPL copy.   10121

Pennsylvania (Colony) Session Laws,
1765.
At a General Assembly [Sept. 21, 1765.]
Philadelphia, Franklin, 1765. pp. [2],
431-448.
NYPL copy.   10122

Pennsylvania (Colony) Session Laws,
1766.
At a General Assembly [Oct. 14, 1765 -
Feb. 8, 1766].
Philadelphia, Hall, 1766. pp. [2], 451-485.
NYPL copy.   10442

Pennsylvania (Colony) Session Laws,
1766.
At a General Assembly [Sept. 20,
1766 +].
Philadelphia, Hall & Sellers, 1766. pp.
[2], 489-498.
NYPL copy.   10443

Pennsylvania (Colony) Session Laws,
1767.
At a General Assembly [Oct., 1766 - Jan.,
1767].
Philadelphia, Hall & Sellers, 1767. pp.
[2], 501-538.
HSP copy.   10725

Pennsylvania (Colony) Session Laws,
1767.
At a General Assembly [May 20,
1767 +].
Philadelphia, Goddard, 1767. pp. [2],
541-583, [1].
HSP copy.   10726

Pennsylvania (Colony) Session Laws,
1767.
. . . At a General Assembly [Sept. 26,
1767 +].
Philadelphia, Goddard, 1767. pp. [2],
587-594.
HSP copy.   10727

Pennsylvania (Colony) Session Laws,
1767.
At a General Assembly [Sept. 26,
1767 +].
Philadelphia, Hall & Sellers, 1767. pp. [2],
587-593.
HSP copy.   10728

Pennsylvania (Colony) Session Laws,
1768.
. . . At a General Assembly [Feb. 20, 1768
+].
Philadelphia, Hall & Sellers, 1768. pp.
[2], 597-636.
HSP copy.   11022

Pennsylvania (Colony) Session Laws,
1768.
. . . At a General Assembly [Feb. 20, 1768
+].
Philadelphia, Goddard, 1768. 44, [1] pp.
HSP copy.   11023

Pennsylvania (Colony) Session Laws,
1769.
. . . At a General Assembly [Feb. 18, 1769
+].
Philadelphia, Hall & Sellers, 1769. pp.
[2], 639-737, [1].
HSP copy.   11396

Pennsylvania (Colony) Session Laws,
1769.
At a General Assembly [Feb. 18,
1769 +].
Philadelphia, Miller, 1769. 101 pp.
HSP copy.   11399

Pennsylvania (Colony) Session Laws,
1769.
. . . At a General Assembly [May 27,
1769 +].
Philadelphia, Hall & Sellers, 1769. pp.
[2], 741-744.
HSP copy.   11397

Pennsylvania (Colony) Session Laws,
1769.
At a General Assembly [May 27,
1769 +].
Philadelphia, Miller, 1769. pp. [2],
105-108, [1].
HSP copy.   11400

Pennsylvania (Colony) Session Laws,
1769.
At a General Assembly [Sept. 30, 1769
+].
Philadelphia, Goddard, 1769. pp. [2],
113-120.
HSP copy.   11401

Pennsylvania (Colony) Session Laws,
1769.
. . . At a General Assembly [Sept. 30,
1769 +].
Philadelphia, Hall & Sellers, 1769.
pp. [2], 747-754.
HSP copy.   11398

Pennsylvania (Colony) Session Laws,
1769.
At a General Assembly [Oct. 14, 1769
+].
Philadelphia, Hall & Sellers, 1770.
34 pp.
HSP copy.   11800

Pennsylvania (Colony) Session Laws,
1770.
At a General Assembly [May 16,
1770 +].
Philadelphia, Hall & Sellers, 1770. pp.
[2], 37-38.
HSP copy.   11801

Pennsylvania (Colony) Session Laws,
1770.
At a General Assembly [Sept. 29,
1770 +].
Philadelphia, Hall & Sellers, 1770. pp.
[2], 41-50.
HSP copy.   11802

Pennsylvania (Colony) Session Laws,
1771.
. . . At a General Assembly [Mar. 9,
1771].
Philadelphia, Hall & Sellers, 1771. pp.
[2], 53-153, [1].
HSP copy.   12176

Pennsylvania (Colony) Session Laws,
1771.
. . . At a General Assembly [Oct. 19, 1771
+].
Philadelphia, Hall & Sellers, 1771. pp.
[2], 157-165.
HSP copy.   12177

Pennsylvania (Colony) Session Laws,
1772.
At a General Assembly [Oct. 14, 1771
+].
Philadelphia, Hall & Sellers, 1772. pp.
[2], 169-286, 2.
NYPL copy.   12505

Pennsylvania (Colony) Session Laws,
1772.
. . . At a General Assembly [Sept. 19,
1772 +].
Philadelphia, Hall & Sellers, 1772. pp.
[2], 289-290.
HC-L copy.   12506

Pennsylvania (Colony) Session Laws,
1773.
. . . At a General Assembly [Feb. 26, 1773
+].
Philadelphia, Hall & Sellers, 1773. pp.
[2], 293-355, [1].
HSP copy.   12920

Pennsylvania (Colony) Session Laws,
1773.
. . . At a General Assembly [Sept. 28,
1773 +].
Philadelphia, Hall & Sellers, 1773. pp.
[357]-365.
HC-L copy.   12921

Pennsylvania (Colony) Session Laws,
1773.
At a General Assembly [Oct. 14,
1773 +].
Philadelphia, Hall & Sellers, 1774. pp.
[2], 367-407. [1].
HSP copy.   13515

Pennsylvania (Colony) Session Laws,
1774.
. . . An Act for Lending. . . . July 23, 1774.
[Philadelphia, 1774.] pp. 409-411.
HSP copy.   13516

[Pennsylvania (Colony) Session Laws,
1774.
At a General Assembly [Sept. 29, 1774
+].
Philadelphia, Hall & Sellers, 1774. pp.
[2], 413-36.]
(Apparently these pages were not printed.)
                                         13517

Pennsylvania (Colony) Session Laws,
1775.
. . . At a General Assembly [Mar. 18,
1775 +].
Philadelphia, Hall & Sellers, 1775. pp.
[2], 439-464.
HSP copy.   14361

[Pennsylvania (Colony) Session Laws,
1775.
At a General Assembly . . . June, 1775.
Philadelphia, 1775.]
(Apparently not printed.)   14362

[Pennsylvania (Colony) Session Laws,
1775.
At a General Assembly . . . September,
1775.
Philadelphia, 1775.]
(Apparently not printed.)   14363

Pennsylvania (Colony) Supreme Court.
Extract aus der Registratur der
Supreem-Court.
[Philadelphia, 1743.] 4 pp.
(Evans entry was from adv. in
Geschicht-Schreiber, Aug. 16, 1743.)
LOC copy.   5175

Pennsylvania (Colony) Treaties, etc., 1722.
The Particulars of an Indian Treaty at
Conestogoe.
Philadelphia, Bradford, [1722]. 8 pp.
HEH copy.   2342

Pennsylvania (Colony) Treaties, etc., 1722.
A Treaty of Peace and Friendship.
Philadelphia, 1722. 8 pp.
BM copy.   2343

Pennsylvania (Colony) Treaties, etc., 1728.
Two Indian Treaties the one Held at
Conestogoe in May 1728.
Philadelphia, Bradford, [1728].
16 pp.
LCP copy.   3041

Pennsylvania (Colony) Treaties, etc., 1736.
A Treaty of Friendship held with the
Chiefs of the Six Nations, at Philadelphia,
in September . . . 1736.
Philadelphia, Franklin, 1737. 14 pp.
UOP copy.   4146

Pennsylvania (Colony) Treaties, etc., 1742.
The Treaty held with the Indians of the
Six Nations, at Philadelphia in July, 1742.
Philadelphia, Franklin, 1743. 25 pp.
NYPL copy.   5216

[Pennsylvania (Colony) Treaties, etc.,
1744.
Council with the Indians at Philadelphia,
in August, 1744.
Philadelphia, Franklin, 1744. 16 pp.]
(A ghost of 5474 arising from an imperfect
copy at LCP.)   5415

Pennsylvania (Colony) Treaties, etc., 1747.
A Treaty between . . . Pennsylvania, and
the Indians of Ohio, held at Philadelphia,
Nov. 13, 1747.
Philadelphia, Franklin, 1748. 8 pp.
NYPL copy.   6168

Pennsylvania (Colony) Treaties, etc., 1748.
A Treaty held by Commissioners . . . with
some Chiefs of the Six Nations at Ohio
. . . in . . . July, 1748.

Philadelphia, Franklin, 1748. [4],
10 pp.
UOP copy.   6169

Pennsylvania (Colony) Treaties, etc., 1753.
A Treaty held with the Ohio Indians, at
Carlisle, in October, 1753.
Philadelphia, Franklin & Hall, 1753.
12 pp.
(The MHS has a 10 p. ed. without
imprint.)
HSP copy.   7026

Pennsylvania (Colony) Treaties, etc., 1756.
Der Inhalt von den Verschiedenen
Conferentzen.
Philadelphia and Germantown, 1757.
55 pp.
HSP copy.   7924

Pennsylvania (Colony) Treaties, etc., 1756.
Minutes of Conference, held with the
Indians, at Easton, in . . . July and
November, 1756.
Philadelphia, Franklin & Hall, 1757.
32 pp.
HSP copy.   7923

Pennsylvania (Colony) Treaties, etc., 1757.
Der Inhalt von den Verschiedenen
Conferentzen . . . zu Easton.
Germantown, 1757. 36 pp.
NYPL copy.   7922

Pennsylvania (Colony) Treaties, etc., 1757.
Minutes of the Conferences, held with the
Indians, at Easton, in . . . July, and
August, 1757.
Philadelphia, Franklin & Hall, 1757.
24 pp.
NYPL copy.   7921

Pennsylvania (Colony) Treaties, etc., 1757.
Minutes of a Conference, held with the
Indians, at Harris's Ferry.
Philadelphia, Franklin & Hall, 1757.
22 pp.
NYPL copy.   7920

Pennsylvania (Colony) Treaties, etc., 1758.
Minutes of Conferences, held at Easton, in
October, 1758.
Philadelphia, Franklin & Hall, 1758.
31 pp.
NYPL copy.   8156

Pennsylvania (Colony) Treaties, etc., 1758.
Minutes of Conferences, Held at Easton,
in October, 1758.
Philadelphia, Franklin & Hall, 1759.
31 pp.
UOP copy.   8377

Pennsylvania (Colony) Treaties, etc., 1761.
Minutes of Conferences, held at Easton, in
August, 1761.
Philadelphia, Franklin & Hall, 1761.
18 pp.
HSP copy.   8887

Pennsylvania (Colony) Treaties, etc., 1762.
Minutes of Conferences, Held at
Lancaster, In August, 1762.
Philadelphia, Franklin & Hall, 1763.
36 pp.
UOP copy.   9412

Pennsylvania (Colony) University.
An Exercise Containing a Dialogue and
Two Odes, Performed at the
Commencement . . . June 5th, 1770.
Philadelphia, Crukshank & Collins,
[1770]. 8 pp.
UOP copy.   42152

Pennsylvania (Colony) University. Alumni
Catalogue, 1762.
Viris Praecellentissimis, Thomas
Penn. . . . Catalogus Eorum qui . . . in
Collegio Philadelphiensi Missi Fuerunt.
[Philadelphia], Miller, [1762]. Broadside.
(No copy located.)   41317

Pennsylvania. Adjutant-General's Office,
1779.
For the use of the Militia of Pennsylvania.
An Abstract of a System of Military
Discipline; Framed by . . . Baron Steuben.
Philadelphia, Bailey, 1779. 38 pp.
LCP copy.   16629

[Pennsylvania. Army 1776.

Chester, March 23, 1776. All such
Soldiers. . . .
Philadelphia, Dunlap, [1776]. Broadside.]
(No copy located.)   14972

[Pennsylvania. Army, 1777.
General Orders. Philadelphia, April 16,
1777.
[Philadelphia, 1777.] Broadside.]
(No copy located.)   15515

[Pennsylvania. Army, 1777.
General Return of Philadelphia Troops,
June 2, 1777.]
(From Aitken's records.)   15516

Pennsylvania. Army, 1777.
Head Quarters, York, August 23, 1777.
[Lancaster, 1777.] Broadside.
NYPL copy.   15517

Pennsylvania. Board of War, 1777.
Pennsylvania War Office, April 13th, 1777
[Henry Fisher].
[Philadelphia], Dunlap, [1777].
Broadside.
HSP copy.   15541

Pennsylvania Board of War, 1777.
Pennsylvania War Office, May 2d. 1777.
To the Public. . . .
Philadelphia. Dunlap, [1777]. Broadside.
LCP copy.   15544

Pennsylvania. Board of War, 1777.
Pennsylvania War-Office, Philadelphia,
April 17th, 1777. . . . Provisions.
[Philadelphia], Dunlap, [1777].
Broadside.
LCP copy.   15542

Pennsylvania. Board of War, 1777.
Pennsylvania War Office, Philadelphia, May
2d, 1777. Application. . . .
Philadelphia, Dunlap, [1777]. Broadside.
LCP copy.   15543

Pennsylvania. Board of Wardens for the
Port of Philadelphia, 1785.
. . . Wardens Office . . . 30th April, 1785.
Extract of an Act. . . .
[Philadelphia], Hall & Sellers, [1785].
Broadside.
LOC copy.   44759

Pennsylvania. Citizens, 1780.
To the Representatives . . . in General
Assembly met, The Representation and
Petition of the Subscribers. . . . For the
"Gradual Abolition of Slavery."
[Philadelphia, 1780.] Broadside.
Col. Richard Gimbel copy.   43861

Pennsylvania. Citizens, 1785.
To the Honourable the Representatives
. . . the Subscribers . . . Affected by the
. . . Fisheries on the River Schuylkill.
[Philadelphia, 1785.] [3] pp.
(No copy located.)   44760

Pennsylvania. Citizens, 1790.
Memorial of the Public Creditors who are
Citizens of . . . Pennsylvania.
Philadelphia, Poulson, 1790. 28 pp.
LCP copy.   45939

Pennsylvania. Collector of the Revenue,
1795.
S.S. (Form of an Application for a
License to work a Snuff Mill.) . . . The
First Day of April 1795.
[Philadelphia, 1795.] Broadside.
AAS copy.   29286

Pennsylvania. Commission to Explore the
Delaware, etc.
Copy of a Report from Reading
Howell. . . .
Philadelphia, Bailey, 1791. 33 pp.
LCP copy.   23678

Pennsylvania. Commission to View and
Explore the Rivers Susquehanna and
Juniata, etc.
Reports of Sundry Commissioners
Appointed. . . .
Philadelphia, Bailey, 1791. 27 pp.
LCP copy.   23679

Pennsylvania. Commissioners, 1781.
Gentlemen, Agreeable to a late Act . . .
Passed the 25th of June, 1781. . . .

[Philadelphia, 1781.] Broadside.
(No copy located.)   44018

Pennsylvania. Committee of Safety, 1776.
Extracts from the Votes of the House . . .
Containing Rules . . . of the Military
Association.
Philadelphia, Bradfords, [1776].
20 pp.
NYPL copy.   14976

Pennsylvania. Comptroller-General, 1783.
State of the Accounts of Andrew
Kachline.
Philadelphia, Aitken, 1783. 14 pp.
AAS copy.   18102

Pennsylvania. Comptroller-General, 1783.
A State of the Accounts of Archibald
Thompson.
Philadelphia, Hall & Sellers, 1783. [2], 41
pp.
HSP copy.   18123

Pennsylvania. Comptroller-General, 1783.
State of the Accounts of Benjamin
Brannon.
[Philadelphia, 1783.] 3 pp.
HSP copy.   18107

Pennsylvania. Comptroller-General, 1783.
State of the Accounts of Col. George
Smith.
Philadelphia, Bailey, 1783. 72 pp.
HSP copy.   18122

Pennsylvania. Comptroller-General, 1783.
State of the Accounts of Jacob Engle.
Philadelphia, Dunlap, 1783. [2], 128 pp.
JCB copy.   18120

Pennsylvania. Comptroller-General, 1783.
State of the Accounts of Jacob Morgan
. . . 1777 . . . 1780.
Philadelphia, Aitken, 1783. 54 pp.
LOC copy.   18099

Pennsylvania. Comptroller-General, 1783.
A State of the Accounts of John Gill.
Philadelphia, Dunlap, 1783. [2], 17 pp.
AAS copy.   18101

Pennsylvania. Comptroller-General, 1783.
State of the Accounts of John Hay.
Philadelphia, Aitken, 1783. 12 pp.
AAS copy.   18125

Pennsylvania. Comptroller-General, 1783.
State of the Accounts of John Lacey.
Philadelphia, Aitken, 1783. 20 pp.
HSP copy.   18104

Pennsylvania. Comptroller-General, 1783.
State of the Accounts of Joseph Hart.
Philadelphia, Aitken, 1783. 24 pp.
AAS copy.   18103

Pennsylvania. Comptroller-General, 1783.
State of the Accounts of Lewis Gronow.
Philadelphia, Aitken, 1783. 22 pp.
AAS copy.   18108

Pennsylvania. Comptroller-General, 1783.
State of the Accounts of Peter Richards.
[Philadelphia, 1783.] 8 pp.
HSP copy.   18121

Pennsylvania. Comptroller-General, 1783.
State of the Accounts of Robert Smith.
Philadelphia, Aitken, 1783. 12 pp.
HSP copy.   18110

Pennsylvania. Comptroller-General, 1783.
A State of the Accounts of Samuel
Dewees.
Philadelphia, Dunlap, 1783. [2],
23 pp.
AAS copy.   18119

Pennsylvania. Comptroller-General, 1783.
State of the Accounts of the Collectors of
Excise, for Berks County.
Philadelphia, Aitken, 1783. 7 pp.
AAS copy.   18100

Pennsylvania. Comptroller-General, 1783.
State of the Accounts of the Collector of
the Excise, for Chester County.
Philadelphia, Bailey, 1783. 4 pp.
AAS copy.   18106

Pennsylvania. Comptroller-General, 1783.
State of the Accounts of the Collectors of

Excise, for Cumberland County.
Philadelphia, Bailey, 1783. 7 pp.
AAS copy. 18111

Pennsylvania. Comptroller-General, 1783.
State of the Accounts of the Collectors of
Excise, for Lancaster County.
Philadelphia, Hall & Sellers, 1783.
11 pp.
AAS copy. 18112

Pennsylvania. Comptroller-General, 1783.
State of the Accounts of the Collectors of
Excise for Northampton County.
Philadelphia, Dunlap, 1783. [2],
12 pp.
AAS copy. 18115

Pennsylvania. Comptroller-General, 1783.
State of the Accounts of the Collectors of
Excise for the Counties of Bedford,
Northumberland, Westmoreland and
Washington.
Philadelphia, Bailey, 1783. 4 pp.
AAS copy. 18098

Pennsylvania. Comptroller-General, 1783.
State of the Accounts of the Collectors of
Excise for York County.
Philadelphia, Aitken, 1783. 8 pp.
AAS copy. 18124

Pennsylvania. Comptroller-General, 1783.
State of the Accounts of the Hon. George
Wall.
Philadelphia, Aitken, 1783. 34 pp.
HSP copy. 18105

Pennsylvania. Comptroller-General, 1783.
State of the Accounts of the late
Lieutenant and Sub-Lieutenants of
Lancaster County [Mar. 1777 - Feb. 15,
1780].
Philadelphia, Dunlap, 1783. [2], 77, [1]
pp.
HSP copy. 18113

Pennsylvania. Comptroller-General, 1783.
State of the Accounts of the late
Lieutenant and Sub-Lieutenants of
Northampton County.
[Philadelphia], Hall & Sellers, [1783]. 40
pp.
HSP copy. 18116

Pennsylvania. Comptroller-General, 1783.
State of the Accounts, of the Lieutenant
and Sub-Lieutenants of Lancaster County
[Mar., 1781 - Jan., 1782].
Philadelphia, Bradford, 1783. [101] pp.
(Evans' entry is from the caption.)
AAS copy. 18114

Pennsylvania. Comptroller-General, 1783.
State of the Accounts of Thomas Levis.
Philadelphia, Aitken, 1783. 11 pp.
HSP copy. 18109

Pennsylvania. Comptroller-General, 1783.
State of the Accounts of Wm. Antes.
[Philadelphia, 1783.] 17 pp.
AAS copy. 18117

Pennsylvania. Comptroller-General, 1783.
A State of the Accounts of William Coats.
Philadelphia, Aitken, 1783. [2], 28 pp.
HSP copy. 18118

Pennsylvania. Comptroller-General, 1784.
Accounts of Pennsylvania. Volume I.
[Philadelphia, 1784.] [4], 237, 16, 25, 18,
4, 6, 11, 11, 8, 7, 7, 7, 6, 12, 4, 4, 165, 17
pp.
AAS copy. 18676

Pennsylvania. Comptroller-General, 1784.
A Brief View of the Accounts of the
Treasury.
Philadelphia, Hall & Sellers, 1784.
237 pp.
AAS copy. 18679

Pennsylvania. Comptroller-General, 1784.
State of the Accounts of Adam Orth, Esq.
Late Sub-Lieutenant of Lancaster
County. . . . 1778, to . . . 1780.
Philadelphia, Bailey, 1784. 23 pp.
AAS copy. 18704

Pennsylvania. Comptroller-General, 1784.
State of the Accounts of Andrew Boyd,
Esq. A Sub-Lieutenant of Chester County.
From March 1777, to March 1780.

Philadelphia, Bailey, 1774 (1784).
12 pp.
HSP copy. 18698

Pennsylvania. Comptroller-General, 1784.
State of the Accounts of Col. Samuel
Hunter, Lieutenant of Northumberland
County. . . . 1777, to . . . 1784.
Philadelphia, Bailey, 1774 (1784). 13, [1]
pp.
AAS copy. 18706

Pennsylvania. Comptroller-General, 1784.
State of the Accounts of Conrad Foos,
Collector of the Excise, Berks County . . .
1781, to . . . 1783.
Philadelphia, Aitken, 1784. 6 pp.
AAS copy. 18695

Pennsylvania. Comptroller-General, 1784.
State of the Accounts of Edward
Bartholomew, Collector of Excise for . . .
Philadelphia.
Philadelphia, Bailey, 1774 (1784).
25 pp.
AAS copy. 18708

Pennsylvania. Comptroller-General, 1784.
State of the Accounts of Jacob Barnitz
Esquire, Collector of Excise, York County
. . . 1782, to . . . 1784.
Philadelphia, Aitken, 1784. 8 pp.
AAS copy. 18712

Pennsylvania. Comptroller-General, 1784.
State of the Accounts of Jesse Jones, Esq.
Late Collector of Excise for Northampton
County.
Philadelphia, Bailey, 1784. 4 pp.
AAS copy. 18705

Pennsylvania. Comptroller-General, 1784.
State of the Accounts of John Buchanan
Esquire, Collector of Excise, Cumberland
County . . . 1783.
Philadelphia, Aitken, 1784. 7 pp.
AAS copy. 18702

Pennsylvania. Comptroller-General, 1784.
State of the Accounts of Joshua
Anderson, Esq., late Sub-Lieutenant of
Bucks County. From March 1780, to April
1783.
Philadelphia, Bailey, 1774 (1784).
38 pp.
HSP copy. 18697

Pennsylvania. Comptroller-General, 1784.
State of the Accounts of Samuel
Cunningham, Esq; late Collector of Excise
for Chester County. . . . 1782, to . . . 1783.
Philadelphia, Bailey, 1784. 6 pp.
AAS copy. 18699

Pennsylvania. Comptroller-General, 1784.
State of the Accounts of the Collectors of
Excise, for Bucks County . . . 1776 . . . to
. . . 1783.
Philadelphia, Bailey, 1784. 18 pp.
AAS copy. 18696

Pennsylvania. Comptroller-General, 1784.
State of the Accounts of the Lieutenant
and Sub-Lieutenants of Chester
County. . . . 1780, to . . . 1783.
Philadelphia, 1774 (1784). 88 pp.
HSP copy. 18701

Pennsylvania. Comptroller-General, 1784.
State of the Accounts of the Lieutenant
and Sub-Lieutenants of Cumberland
County.
Philadelphia, Bailey, 1774 (1784).
67 pp.
LCP copy. 44581

Pennsylvania. Comptroller-General, 1784.
State of the Accounts of the Lieutenant
and Sub-Lieutenants of the City of
Philadelphia. . . . 1777, to . . . 1783.
Philadelphia, Bailey, 1784. 165 pp.
AAS copy. 18707

Pennsylvania. Comptroller-General, 1784.
State of the Accounts of the Lieutenant &
Sub-Lieutenants of Westmoreland
County. . . . 1777 to . . . 1783.
Philadelphia, Bailey, 1774 (1784).
18 pp.
HSP copy. 18711

Pennsylvania. Comptroller-General Office,
1784.

State of the Accounts of the Lieutenants &
Sub Lieutenants of York County.
Philadelphia, Bailey, 1784. 56 pp.
AAS copy. 44582

Pennsylvania. Comptroller-General, 1784.
State of the Accounts of the
Sub-Lieutenants of Washington County
. . . 1781 . . . to . . . 1783.
Philadelphia, Bailey, 1784. 8 pp.
LOC copy. 18710

Pennsylvania. Comptroller-General, 1784.
State of the Accounts of Thomas
Strawbridge, Esq. Late Sub-Lieutenant of
Chester County. . . . 1777, to . . . 1778.
Philadelphia, Bailey, 1784. 7 pp.
HSP copy. 18700

Pennsylvania. Comptroller-General, 1784.
State of the Accounts of William Crispin,
Esq. Late Collector of Excise for . . .
Philadelphia.
Philadelphia, Bailey, 1774 (1784).
16 pp.
AAS copy. 18709

Pennsylvania. Comptroller-General, 1784.
State of the Accounts of William Hay,
Esq. Collector of Excise for Lancaster
County. . . . 1782, to . . . 1783.
Philadelphia, Bailey, 1774 (1784).
11 pp.
AAS copy. 18703

Pennsylvania. Comptroller-General, 1785.
State of the Accounts of Andrew Forrest
. . . 26th of September, 1786.
Philadelphia, Aitken, 1787. 5 pp.
NYPL copy. 45123

Pennsylvania. Comptroller-General, 1785.
State of the Accounts of Andrew
Kachline, Esq. Sub-Lieutenant of Bucks
County. . . . 1777, to . . . 1780.
Philadelphia, Bailey, 1785. 24 pp.
AAS copy. 19168

Pennsylvania. Comptroller-General, 1785.
State of the Accounts of Edward
Bartholomew, Esq. Collector of Excise for
. . . Philadelphia.
Philadelphia, Bailey, 1785. 27 pp.
AAS copy. 19182

Pennsylvania. Comptroller-General, 1785.
Statement of the Accounts of Edward
Cook. . . . Westmoreland County . . . to
1st June 1784.
Philadelphia, Steele, 1785. 4 pp.
LCP copy. 44761

Pennsylvania. Comptroller-General, 1785.
State of the Accounts of George Graff,
Esq. Collector of Excise, Lancaster
County.
Philadelphia, Steele, 1785. 6 pp.
AAS copy. 19178

Pennsylvania. Comptroller-General, 1785.
State of the Accounts of George Graff,
Esq. Collector of Excise, Northampton
County.
Philadelphia, Steele, 1785. 7 pp.
NYPL copy. 19180

Pennsylvania. Comptroller-General, 1785.
State of the Accounts of Gerardus
Wynkoop . . . of Bucks County. . . . to 21st
Nov. 1784.
Philadelphia, Steele, 1785. 9 pp.
LOC copy. 44762

Pennsylvania. Comptroller-General, 1785.
State of the Accounts of Jacob Barnitz,
Esq. Collector of Excise, York County.
Philadelphia, Steele, 1785. 6 pp.
AAS copy. 19184

Pennsylvania. Comptroller-General, 1785.
State of the Accounts of James Marshall,
Esq. Lieutenant of Washington County.
Philadelphia, Steele, 1785. 3 pp.
AAS copy. 44763

Pennsylvania. Comptroller-General, 1785.
State of the Accounts of James Rose,
Esquire, Lieutenant of the County of
Lancaster, from . . . the 21st August, 1785.
Philadelphia, Aitken, 1785. 4 pp.
HSP copy. 19179

Pennsylvania. Comptroller-General, 1785.

State of the Accounts of John Buchanan, Esquire, Collector of Excise. Cumberland County, from . . . 1783, to . . . 1785.
Philadelphia, Steele, 1785. 3 pp.
NYPL copy.　　　　　　　　　　19173

Pennsylvania. Comptroller-General, 1785. State of the Accounts of John Christie, Esq. Collector of Excise, Chester County. . . . 1783, to . . . 1784.
Philadelphia, Steele, 1785. 6 pp.
AAS copy.　　　　　　　　　　19172

Pennsylvania, Comptroller-General, 1785. State of the Accounts of Joseph Hart, Esq. Late Lieutenant of Bucks County, from . . . March . . . to November, 1783.
Philadelphia, Steele, 1785. 11 pp.
HSP copy.　　　　　　　　　　19167

Pennsylvania. Comptroller-General, 1785. State of the Accounts of Joseph Kirkbride . . . Lieutenant of Bucks County . . . to March 1780.
Philadelphia, Aitken, 1785. 16 pp.
AAS copy.　　　　　　　　　　19169

Pennsylvania. Comptroller-General, 1785. State of the Accounts of Joshua Elder, Esquire, late Sub-Lieutenant of Lancaster County.
Philadelphia, Aitken, 1785. 12 pp.
HSP copy.　　　　　　　　　　19177

Pennsylvania. Comptroller-General, 1785. State of the Accounts of Nicholas Brosius, Esq; Collector of Excise, Berks County . . . 1783, to . . . 1784.
Philadelphia, Steele, 1785. 7 pp.
LOC copy.　　　　　　　　　　19166

Pennsylvania. Comptroller-General, 1785. State of the Accounts of Robert Smith . . . Chester County . . . to 1st of April, 1785.
Philadelphia, Steele, 1785. 4 pp.
LCP copy.　　　　　　　　　　44764

Pennsylvania. Comptroller-General, 1785. State of the Accounts of Robert Wilson . . . of Chester County . . . to the 11th August 1779.
Philadelphia, Bailey, 1785. 4 pp.
LCP copy.　　　　　　　　　　44765

Pennsylvania. Comptroller-General, 1785. State of the Accounts of the Lieutenant . . . of Lancaster County 1780 to . . . 1781.
Philadelphia, Aitken, 1785. 46 pp.
NYPL copy.　　　　　　　　　　19175

Pennsylvania. Comptroller-General, 1785. State of the Accounts of the Lieutenant . . . of Lancaster County; to the 20th of April, 1783.
Philadelphia, Aitken, 1785. 48 pp.
AAS copy.　　　　　　　　　　19176

Pennsylvania. Comptroller-General, 1785. State of the Accounts of the Sub-Lieutenants of Lancaster County . . . to the 20th of March 1780.
Philadelphia, Aitken, 1785. 7 pp.
HSP copy.　　　　　　　　　　19174

Pennsylvania. Comptroller-General, 1785. State of the Accounts of the Treasury . . . from . . . 1782 . . . to 1785.
Philadelphia, Aitken, 1785. 135 pp.
AAS copy.　　　　　　　　　　19165

Pennsylvania. Comptroller-General, 1785. State of the Accounts of Thomas Armor, Esq. Collector of Excise, York County. . . . to 28th January, 1783.
Philadelphia, Steele, 1785. 6 pp.
AAS copy.　　　　　　　　　　44766

Pennsylvania. Comptroller-General, 1785. State of the Accounts of Thomas Cheney, Esq.; Sub-Lieutenant of Chester County. . . . 1777, to March, 1780.
Philadelphia, Bailey, 1785. 12 pp.
HSP copy.　　　　　　　　　　19171

Pennsylvania. Comptroller-General, 1785. State of the Accounts of Walter Clarke & William Murray, Esqrs. Sub-Lieutenants of Northumberland County.
Philadelphia, Aitken, 1785. 4 pp.
AAS copy.　　　　　　　　　　19181

Pennsylvania. Comptroller-General, 1785.

State of the Accounts of William Henry, Esquire, Lieutenant of . . . Philadelphia.
Philadelphia, Aitken, 1785. 16 pp.
AAS copy.　　　　　　　　　　19183

Pennsylvania. Comptroller-General, 1785. State of the Accounts of William M'Henry, Esq. Late Sub-Lieutenant of Bucks County. . . . 1781 . . . 1783.
Philadelphia, Aitken, 1785. 8 pp.
AAS copy.　　　　　　　　　　19170

Pennsylvania. Comptroller-General, 1785. State of the Accounts of William Scott . . . of York County . . . to 1st of November, 1784.
Philadelphia, Steele, 1785. 6 pp.
LCP copy.　　　　　　　　　　44767

Pennsylvania. Comptroller-General, 1786. State of the Accounts of Adam Hubley . . . Lancaster County.
Philadelphia, Aitken, 1786. 7 (i.e. 3) pp.
HSP copy.　　　　　　　　　　19895

Pennsylvania. Comptroller-General, 1786. State of the Accounts of Edward Bartholomew . . . Collector of Excise, Philadelphia City and County . . . 1785.
Philadelphia, Aitken, 1786. 23 pp.
HSP copy.　　　　　　　　　　19901

Pennsylvania. Comptroller-General, 1786. State of the Accounts of George Graff . . . Collector of Excise, Lancaster County . . . 1784 . . . 1785.
Philadelphia, Aitken, 1786. 9 pp.
AAS copy.　　　　　　　　　　19894

Pennsylvania. Comptroller-General, 1786. State of the Accounts of George Graff . . . Collector of Excise, Northampton County . . . 1784 . . . 1785.
Philadelphia, Aitken, 1786. 5 pp.
NYPL copy.　　　　　　　　　　19899

Pennsylvania. Comptroller-General, 1786. State of the Accounts of Gerardus Wyncoop . . . Bucks County . . . till the 21st of November, 1785.
Philadelphia, Aitken, 1786. 6 pp.
AAS copy.　　　　　　　　　　44942

Pennsylvania. Comptroller-General, 1786. State of the Accounts of Jacob Auld . . . Collector of Excise . . . County of Montgomery . . . 1784 . . . 1786.
Philadelphia, Aitken, 1786. 5 pp.
NYPL copy.　　　　　　　　　　19898

Pennsylvania. Comptroller-General, 1786. State of the Accounts of Jacob Barnitz . . . Collector of Excise, for the County of York . . . 1785.
Philadelphia, Aitken, 1786. 6 pp.
AAS copy.　　　　　　　　　　19903

Pennsylvania. Comptroller-General, 1786. State of the Accounts of John Christie . . . for the County of Chester.
Philadelphia, Aitken, 1786. 5 pp.
AAS copy.　　　　　　　　　　44943

Pennsylvania. Comptroller-General, 1786. State of the Accounts of John Nixon . . . 1775 . . . 1776 . . . as Treasurer of the Committee of Safety.
Philadelphia, Aitken, 1786. 56 pp.
AAS copy.　　　　　　　　　　19891

Pennsylvania. Comptroller-General's Office, 1786. State of the Accounts of John M. Nesbitt.
Philadelphia, Aitken, 1786. 138 pp.
LCP copy.　　　　　　　　　　44948

Pennsylvania. Comptroller-General, 1786. State of the Accounts of Nicholas Brosius, Esquire, Collector of Excise, of Berks County . . . 1784 . . . 1785.
Philadelphia, Aitken, 1786. 4 pp.
HSP copy.　　　　　　　　　　19892

Pennsylania. Comptroller-General, 1786. State of the Accounts of Samuel Adams. Esquire, Collector of Excise, for the County of Fayette . . . 1783 . . . 1785.
Philadelphia, Aitken, 1786. 3 pp.
NYPL copy.　　　　　　　　　　19893

Pennsylvania. Comptroller-General, 1786. State of the Accounts of Samuel Turbett . . . Collector for the County of

Lancaster: from the Time of his Appointment until the 24th of February, 1786.
Philadelphia, Aitken, 1786. 4 pp.
HSP copy.　　　　　　　　　　19896

Pennsylvania. Comptroller-General, 1786. State of the Accounts of Samuel Turbett . . . Collector of Excise, for the County of Lancaster; from the 25th February, till 21st Sept. 1786.
Philadelphia, Aitken, 1786. 9 pp.
LOC copy.　　　　　　　　　　19897

Pennsylvania. Comptroller-General, 1786. State of the Account of Thomas Urie. . . . of . . . Bedford County . . . till 17th October, 1775.
Philadelphia, Aitken, 1786. [2],
1 pp.
AAS copy.　　　　　　　　　　44944

[Pennsylania. Comptroller-General, 1786. State of the Accounts of William Graham . . . Collector of Excise, for the Counties of Westmoreland, Washington, and Fayette . . . 1785 . . . 1786.
Philadelphia, Aitken, 1786. 3 pp.]
(No copy located.)　　　　　　　19902

[Pennsylvania. Comptroller-General, 1786. State of the Accounts of William Webb . . . Pay Master of late Navy Board of Pennsylvania [Mar. - Sept., 1777].
Philadelphia, Aitken, 1786. 36 pp.]
(No copy located.)　　　　　　　19890

Pennsylvania. Comptroller General, 1786. State of the Account of William Wilson . . . Collector of Excise. Northumberland County . . . 1783.
Philadelphia, Aitken, 1786. 3 pp.
AAS copy.　　　　　　　　　　19900

Pennsylvania. Comptroller-General, 1786. . . . A View of the Debts and Expences of the Commonwealth of Pennsylvania . . . 1786.
[Philadelphia], Aitken, [1786].
25 pp.
AAS copy.　　　　　　　　　　19904

Pennsylvania. Comptroller-General, 1787. Account of the Taxes of Bucks County.
Philadelphia, Aitken, 1787. 102 pp.
AAS copy.　　　　　　　　　　20634

Pennsylvania. Comptroller-General, 1787. State of the Account of Edw. Bartholomew, Esq. Collection of Excise for . . . Philadelphia . . . 1786.
Philadelphia, Aitken, 1787. 25 pp.
NYPL copy.　　　　　　　　　　20635

Pennsylvania. Comptroller General's Office, 1787. State of the Account of Gerardus Wyncoop . . . Collector of Excise. Bucks County . . . until . . . October 26th, 1786.
Philadelphia, Aitken, 1787. 6 pp.
LCP copy.　　　　　　　　　　45120

Pennsylvania. Comptroller-General, 1787. State of the Account of Henry Miller and Michael Hahn . . . York County.
Philadelphia, Aitken, 1787. 6 pp.
LOC copy.　　　　　　　　　　45121

Pennsylvania. Comptroller-General, 1787. State of the Acounts of John M'Clellan . . . of York County . . . the 1st of November, 1786.
Philadelphia, Aitken, 1787. 6 pp.
LCP copy.　　　　　　　　　　45125

Pennsylvania. Comptroller-General, 1787. State of the Accounts of James Pettigrew . . . of Northampton County . . . till 20th June, 1786.
Philadelphia, Aitken, 1787. 6 pp.
LOC copy.　　　　　　　　　　45124

Pennsylvania. Comptroller-General, 1787. State of the Accounts of John M'Clellan . . . of York County . . . the 1st of November, 1786.
Philadelphia, Aitken, 1787. 6 pp.
LCP copy.　　　　　　　　　　45125

Pennsylvania. Comptroller-General, 1787.

State of the Accounts of Samuel Rhea . . .
of Northampton County . . . June 1st,
1781.
Philadelphia, Aitken, 1787. 9 pp.
LCP copy.   45126

Pennsylvania. Comptroller-General, 1788.
State of the Account of John M'Clellan
. . . 1st August 1787.
Philadelphia, Aitken, 1788. 7 pp.
LOC copy.   45322

Pennsylvania. Comptroller-General, 1788.
State of the Account of Peter Burkholder,
Esq., late Sub-lieutenant of Northampton
County . . . 1st April, 1783.
Philadelphia, Aitken, 1788. 8 pp.
JCB copy.   45326

Pennsylvania. Comptroller-General, 1788.
State of the Account of the Taxes in
Lancaster County.
Philadelphia, Aitken, 1788. 83 pp.
LCP copy.   45323

Pennsylvania. Comptroller-General, 1788.
State of the Accounts of Jacob Auld, Esq.
Collector of the Excise, Montgomery
County . . . September, 1787.
Philadelphia, Aitken, 1788. 7 pp.
NYPL copy.   45324

Pennsylvania. Comptroller-General, 1788.
State of the Accounts of James
Pettigrew. . . . 20th June, 1786.
Philadelphia, Bailey, 1788. 5 pp.
LOC copy.   45325

Pennsylvania. Comptroller-General, 1789.
State of the Account of Alexander Hunter,
Esq. Collector of Excise for
Northumberland County . . . the 10th
August 1785.
Philadelphia, Bailey, 1789. 6 pp.
PSL copy.   45549

Pennsylvania. Comptroller-General, 1789.
State of the Account of John Forsyth . . .
York County . . . till the 1st of August,
1788.
Philadelphia, Bailey, 1789. 7 pp.
AAS copy.   45550

Pennsylvania. Comptroller General, 1790.
The Account of John Forsyth, Esquire,
Collector of Excise, for York County . . .
1st October, 1789.
Philadelphia, Bailey, 1790. 7 pp.
AAS copy.   45940

Pennsylvania. Comptroller-General, 1790.
Account of the Taxes of Chester County.
Philadelphia, Bailey, 1790. 17 pp.
AAS copy.   22771

Pennsylvania. Comptroller-General, 1790.
Accounts of the Taxes of Chester County.
Philadelphia, Bailey, 1790. 35 pp.
LCP copy.   45941

Pennsylvania. Comptroller-General, 1790.
Accounts of the Taxes of Huntingdon
County.
Philadelphia, Oswald, 1790. 4 pp.
NYPL copy.   22775

Pennsylvania. Comptroller-General, 1790.
David Rittenhouse; Esq. late Treasurer,
Account of Balances . . . December 17th,
1790.
[Philadelphia, 1790.] [2] pp.
HSP copy.   45942

Pennsylvania. Comptroller-General, 1790.
State of the Account of Andrew Forrest.
Philadelphia, Bailey, 1790. 5 pp.
NYPL copy.   22772

Pennsylvania. Comptroller-General, 1790.
State of the Account of Jacob Auld.
Philadelphia, Bailey, 1790. 9 pp.
NYPL copy.   22776

Pennsylvania. Comptroller-General, 1790.
State of the Account of David Rittenhouse
. . . 1786 . . . 1787.
Philadelphia, Bailey, 1790. [64] pp.
NYPL copy.   22769

Pennsylvania. Comptroller-General, 1790.
State of the Account of the Taxes of
Northampton County.

Philadelphia, Bailey, 1790. [88] pp.
NYPL copy.   22777

Pennsylvania. Comptroller-General, 1790.
State of the Account of the Taxes of
Washington County.
Philadelphia, Bailey, 1790. 6 pp.
NYPL copy.   22778

Pennsylvania. Comptroller-General, 1790.
State of the Account of William Harney,
Esq. Collector. . . . for Bucks. . . . til
March 28th, 1789.
Philadelphia, Bailey, 1790. 4 pp.
HC copy.   45944

Pennsylvania. Comptroller-General, 1790.
State of the Accounts of Christopher
Derring . . . of . . . Northumberland
County . . . until May 31st, 1789.
Philadelphia, Aitken, 1790. 4 pp.
AAS copy.   45945

Pennsylvania. Comptroller-General, 1790.
State of the Accounts of David
Rittenhouse. . . . 1785 . . . 1786.
Philadelphia, Oswald, 1790. 52 pp.
NYPL copy.   22768

Pennsylvania. Comptroller-General, 1790.
State of the Accounts of David
Rittenhouse . . . from 1st January till
November, 1787. Including his
Continental and State Money.
Philadelphia, Aitken, 1790. 70 pp.
NYPL copy.   22770

Pennsylvania. Comptroller-General, 1790.
State of the Accounts of Ephraim Douglas
. . . Treasurer of Fayette County,
1785-1790.
Philadelphia, Aitken, 1790. 5 pp.
University of Pittsburgh copy.   22773

Pennsylvania. Comptroller General, 1790.
State of the Accounts of Excise, Bedford
County.
Philadelphia, Aitken, 1790. 6 pp.
AAS copy.   45946

Pennsylvania. Comptroller-General, 1790.
State of the Accounts of Excise for
Cumberland County . . . June, 1789.
Philadelphia, Bailey, 1790. 4 pp.
LOC copy.   45947

Pennsylvania. Comptroller-General, 1790.
State of the Accounts of George Clingan.
Philadelphia, Aitken, 1790. 12 pp.
AAS copy.   22774

Pennsylvania. Comptroller-General, 1790.
State of the Accounts of Jacob Krug . . .
Collector for Lancaster County . . . 15th
February, 1790.
Philadelphia, Aitken, 1790. 8 pp.
LCP copy.   45948

Pennsylvania. Comptroller-General, 1790.
State of the Accounts of James Pettigrew,
Esq., Collector for Northampton County
. . . till June 20, 1788.
Philadelphia, Bailey, 1790. 10 pp.
LCP copy.   45949

Pennsylvania. Comptroller-General, 1790.
State of the Accounts of John Baker . . .
Treasurer of . . . Philadelphia. . . . 1st of
December, 1789.
Philadelphia, Bailey, 1790. 31 pp.
U. of Pittsburgh copy.   45950

Pennsylvania. Comptroller-General, 1790.
State of the Accounts of John Thorne,
Esq., Collector . . . for Dauphin County
. . . 24th September, 1789.
Philadelphia, Aitken, 1790. 8 pp.
LCP copy.   45951

Pennsylvania. Comptroller-General, 1790.
State of the Accounts of Joseph Chapman,
Esq., Treasurer of Chester County . . . 7th
January, 1790.
Philadelphia, Aitken, 1790. 13 pp.
LCP copy.   45952

Pennsylvania. Comptroller General, 1790.
State of the Accounts of Stephen Duncan,
Esq. Treasurer of Cumberland County . . .
1789.
Philadelphia, Bailey, 1790. 42 pp.
LCP copy.   45953

Pennsylvania. Comptroller-General, 1790.
State of the Accounts of the Taxes of
Northumberland County.
Philadelphia, Bailey, 1790. 38 pp.
PSL copy.   45955

Pennsylvania. Comptroller-General, 1790.
State of the Accounts of the Taxes of
Montgomery County. . . . December, 1789.
Philadelphia, Oswald, 1790. 30 pp.
LCP copy.   45954

Pennsylvania. Comptroller-General, 1790.
State of the Accounts of William Perry
. . . Treasurer of Westmoreland County,
till 20th March, 1788.
Philadelphia, Aitken, 1790. 17 pp.
LCP copy.   45956

Pennsylvania. Comptroller-General, 1791.
State of the Accounts of David
Rittenhouse, Esq. Treasurer of
Pennsylvania, For the Year 1788.
Philadelphia, Aitken, 1791. 56 pp.
NYPL copy.   23680

Pennsylvania. Comptroller-General, 1791.
State of the Accounts of David
Rittenhouse, Esq. Treasurer of
Pennsylvania, from September 1788, till
September 1st, 1789.
Philadelphia, Aitken, 1791. 84 pp.
NYPL copy.   23681

Pennsylvania. Comptroller-General, 1791.
State of the Accounts of John Craig . . .
Collector of Excise, Northampton County.
Philadelphia, Aitken, 1791. 5 pp.
NYPL copy.   46250

Pennsylvania. Comptroller General, 1791.
State of the Accounts of the Taxes, of
Berks County, from, 1776 till 1790.
Philadelphia, Aitken, 1791. 36 pp.
University of Pittsburgh copy.   23682

Pennsylvania. Comptroller General, 1791.
State of the Accounts of the Taxes, of
York County.
Philadelphia, Aitken, 1791. 45 pp.
AAS copy.   23683

Pennsylvania. Comptroller-General, 1794.
The Following Letter . . . Directed to the
Speaker, was Read in the House . . . on
the 9th January, 1794.
[Philadelphia, 1794.] 2 pp.
HSP copy.   27485

Pennsylvania. Comptroller-General, 1799.
Report of the Arrears of Taxes due from
the Several Counties.
Philadelphia, Poulson, 1799. 8 pp.
LCP copy.   36067

Pennsylvania. Comptroller-General, 1800.
Report of the Comptroller-General.
Lancaster, Hamilton, 1800. 6 pp.
(Also bound with 38215, q.v.)   38221

Pennsylvania. Conference of Committees,
1776.
Extracts from the Proceedings of the
Provincial Conference of Committees . . .
June 18, 1776.
Philadelphia, Styner & Cist, [1776].
6 pp.
LCP copy.   14975

Pennsylvania. Conference of Committees,
1776.
Proceedings of the Provincial Conference
of Committees [June 18 - 25, 1776].
Philadelphia, Bradfords, [1776]. 31 pp.
LOC copy.   14974

Pennsylvania. Constitution, 1776.
The Constitution of the Common-Wealth.
Philadelphia, Dunlap, 1776. 32 pp.
AAS copy.   14979

Pennsylvania. Constitution, 1776.
The Constitution of the Common-Wealth.
Philadelphia, Dunlap, 1777. pp. [6], 3-18.
AAS copy.   15512

Pennsylvania. Constitution, 1776.
The Constitution of the Common-Wealth.
Philadelphia, Bailey, 1781. 67 pp.
AAS copy.   17285

Pennsylvania. Constitution, 1776.
The Constitution of the Commonwealth.

Philadelphia, Bailey, 1784. 64 pp.
AAS copy.   18680

Pennsylvania. Constitution, 1776.
Die Regierungsverfassung.
Philadelphia, Bailey, 1784. 47 pp.
AAS copy.   18690

Pennsylvania. Constitution, 1776.
Die Regierungsverfassung.
Philadelphia, Steiner, 1784. 49 pp.
NYPL copy.   18691

Pennsylvania. Constitution, 1776.
The Constitution of the Commonwealth.
Philadelphia, Humphreys, 1786. 16 pp.
AAS copy.   19883

Pennsylvania. Constitution, 1784.
We, the People of the Commonwealth of
Pennsylvania Ordain. . . .
[Philadelphia, 1784.] 3 pp.
(No copy located.)   44583

Pennsylvania. Constitution, 1789.
We the People of the Commonwealth. . . .
[Philadelphia], Poulson, [1789].
[3] pp.
NYHS copy.   45551

Pennsylvania. Constitution, 1790.
The Constitution of the Commonwealth.
Philadelphia, Poulson, 1790. 29 pp.
AAS copy.   22759

Pennsylvania. Constitution, 1790.
The Constitution of the Commonwealth
. . . as Altered and Amended.
Philadelphia, Poulson, 1790. 28 pp.
NYPL copy.   22760

Pennsylvania. Constitution, 1790.
Die Regierungsverfassung der Republik
Pennsylvanien.
Germantown, Billmeyer, 1790. 28 pp.
LOC copy.   45957

Pennsylvania. Constitution, 1790.
Der Regierungsverfassung der Republik
Pennsylvanien.
Philadelphia, Steiner, 1790. [2], 20, [2]
pp.
LOC copy.   22761

Pennsylvania. Convention, 1776.
An Essay of a Declaration of Rights.
[Philadelphia, 1776.] Broadside.
HSP copy.   14984

Pennsylvania. Convention, 1776.
Kurze Anzeigen von dem Verfahren der
Convention . . . Gehalten zu Philadelphia,
den Fünfzehnten tag July, 1776.
Philadelphia, Miller, 1776. 67 pp.
HSP copy.   14978

Pennsylvania. Convention, 1776.
In Convention for the State of
Pennsylvania. Friday, August 9, 1776. On
Motion. . . .
[Philadelphia, 1776.] Broadside.
LCP copy.   14980

Pennsylvania. Convention, 1776.
In Convention for the State of
Pennsylvania. Friday, August 16, 1776
[Deserters].
[Philadelphia, 1776.] Broadside.
LCP copy.   14982

Pennsylvania. Convention, 1776.
In Convention for the State of
Pennsylvania. Philadelphia, August 13,
1776.
[Philadelphia, 1776.] Broadside.
LCP copy.   43126

Pennsylvania. Convention, 1776.
In Convention for the State of
Pennsylvania. Saturday, August 10, 1776
[Seven Resolutions].
[Philadelphia, 1776.] Broadside.
LCP copy.   14981

Pennsylvania. Convention, 1776.
In Convention for the State of
Pennsylvania. Thursday, September 26,
1776 [Election].
Philadelphia, Steiner & Cist, [1776].
Broadside.
LCP copy.   14983

Pennsylvania. Convention, 1776.

Minutes of the Proceedings of the
Convention . . . held at Philadelphia, the
Fifteenth day of July, 1776.
Philadelphia, Miller, 1776. 67 pp.
HSP copy.   14977

Pennsylvania. Convention, 1776.
The Proposed Plan or Frame of
Government.
[Philadelphia, 1776.] 12 pp.
HSP copy.   14993

Pennsylvania. Convention, 1776.
To the Several Committees of
Correspondence. . . . July 19, 1776.
[Philadelphia.] [2] pp.
(No copy located.)   43127

Pennsylvania. Convention, 1787.
The Address and Reasons of Dissent of
the Minority of the Convention of the
State of Pennsylvania, to their
Constituents.
[Boston, Powars, 1787.] 22, [1] pp.
AAS copy.   20619

Pennsylvania. Convention, 1787.
The Address and Reasons of Dissent of
the Minority of the Convention of the
State of Pennsylvania to their
Constituents.
Hudson, [1787]. [4] pp.
AAS copy.   20620

Pennsylvania. Convention, 1787.
The Address and Reasons of Dissent of
the Minority of the Convention of the
State of Pennsylvania, to their
Constituents. . . . December 12, 1787.
Philadelphia, Oswald, 1787. [3] pp.
AAS copy.   20618

[Pennsylvania. Convention, 1787.
The Address & Reasons of Dissent of the
Minority of the Convention of the State of
Pennsylvania, to their Constituents.
Richmond, Davis, 1787.]
(No copy located.)   20621

[Pennsylvania. Convention, 1787.
Debates of the Convention . . . on the
Constitution.
Philadelphia, James, 1787. 147, [4] pp.]
(A ghost of 21365 arising from Evans' use
of copyright date as date of imprint.)   20625

Pennsylvania. Convention, 1787.
Debates of the Convention.
Philadelphia, James, 1788. 147, [4] pp.
AAS copy.   21365

Pennsylvania. Convention, 1787.
Minutes of the Convention . . . Taking
into Consideration the Constitution
Framed by the late Foederal Convention.
Philadelphia, Hall & Sellers, 1787.
28 pp.
HC copy.   20630

Pennsylvania. Convention, 1787.
Tagebuch der Convention der Republik.
Philadelphia, Steiner, 1788. 38 pp.
APS copy.   21372

Pennsylvania. Convention, 1789.
Minutes of the Convention.
Philadelphia, Poulson, 1789. 146 pp.
AAS copy.   22764

Pennsylvania. Convention, 1790.
Minutes of the Grand Committee.
Philadelphia, Poulson, [1790]. 101 pp.
AAS copy.   22766

Pennsylvania. Convention, 1790.
Minutes of the Second Session of the
Convention.
[Philadelphia, 1790.] pp. [147]-222.
AAS copy.   22765

Pennsylvania. Council, 1780.
In Council, Philadelphia, June 1, 1780.
Sir, The Continental Army. . . .
[Philadelphia, 1780.] Broadside.
HSP copy.   43862

Pennsylvania. Council, 1781.
Council-Chamber, Philadelphia, [blank]
1781. Instructions for Recruiting a Corps
of Rifle Men. . . . July 14th, 1781.
[Philadelphia, 1781.] Broadside.
NYHS copy.   44023

Pennsylvania. Council, 1781.
In Council. Philadelphia, January 26th,
1781. Whereas the Militia Law. . . .
[Philadelphia, 1781.] Broadside.
HSP copy.   44021

Pennsylvania. Council, 1781.
In Council, Philadelphia, February 15,
1781. Resolved, That the Several . . .
Recruits. . . .
[Philadelphia, 1781.] Broadside.
LOC copy.   44019

Pennsylvania. Council, 1781.
In Council, Philadelphia, June 15, 1781.
Whereas the Honourable the Continental
Congress. . . .
[Philadelphia], Bailey, [1781]. Broadside.
HSP copy.   44022

Pennsylvania. Council, 1781.
Im Rath. Philadelphia, den 26sten Jenner,
1781.
[Philadelphia, 1781.] Broadside.
HSP copy.   44020

Pennsylvania. Council, 1781.
To the Commissioners and Assessors of
the County of [blank], Gentlemen. . . .
June 30th, 1781.
[Philadelphia, 1781.] Broadside.
(No copy located.)   44024

Pennsylvania. Council of Censors, 1783.
Journal of the Council of Censors [Nov.
10, 1783 - Sept. 25, 1784].
Philadelphia, Hall & Sellers, 1783.
179 pp.
HSP copy.   18093

Pennsylvania. Council of Censors, 1784.
An Address of the Council of Censors to
the Freemen of Pennsylvania.
[Philadelphia], Hall & Sellers, [1784].
Broadside.
HSP copy.   18677

Pennsylvania. Council of Censors, 1784.
. . . In the Council of Censors, Friday,
September 24th, 1784 P.M. The Draught
of an Address. . . .
Philadelphia, Bailey, [1784]. [2] pp.
LOC copy.   18694

Pennsylvania. Council of Censors, 1784.
A Report of the Committee of the Council
of Censors.
Philadelphia, Bailey, 1784. 27 pp.
LOC copy.   18693

Pennsylvania. Council of Censors, 1784.
Report of the Committee of the Council
of Censors. . . . Published by their Order.
Philadelphia, Bailey, 1784. 15 pp.
LOC copy.   18692

Pennsylvania. Council of Censors, 1784.
Tagbuch des Raths der Censoren.
Philadelphia, Steiner, 1784. 147 pp.
HC copy.   18713

Pennsylvania. Council of Censors, 1784.
To the Freemen of Pennsylvania
[Minority Report].
[Philadelphia, 1784.] 12 pp.
HSP copy.   18715

Pennsylvania. Council of Safety, 1776.
In Council of Safety, Philadelphia,
November 16th, 1776. Sir, The Fleet. . . .
[Philadelphia, 1776.] Broadside.
LOC copy.   43130

Pennsylvania. Council of Safety, 1776.
In Council of Safety, Philadelphia,
December 2, 1776. Sir, The Army. . . .
[Philadelphia, 1776.] Broadside.
LOC copy.   43131

Pennsylvania. Council of Safety, 1776.
In Council of Safety, December 5, 1776.
Resolved, That Messieurs Robert
Baily. . . .
Philadelphia, Dunlap, [1776]. Broadside.
LOC copy.   43129

Pennsylvania. Council of Safety, 1776.
In Council of Safety, Philadelphia,
December 7, 1776. Whereas the Safety
. . . .
[Philadelphia], Dunlap, [1776].
Broadside.
HSP copy.   43132

Pennsylvania. Council of Safety, 1776.
In Congress, December 9, 1776. Whereas
General Washington. . . . In Council of
Safety . . . December 9, 1776.
[Philadelphia, 1776.] Broadside.
LOC copy.   43128

[Pennsylvania. Council of Safety, 1777.
In Congress, December 17, 1776. . . . In
Council of Safety, Philadelphia, January
1, 1777.
Philadelphia, Dunlap, [1777]. Broadside.]
(No copy located.)   15651

[Pennsylvania. Council of Safety, 1777.
In Council of Safety. Philadelphia,
January 1, 1777. To the Public. . . .
[Philadelphia, 1777.] Broadside.]
(No copy located. Assumed by Evans from
15521.)   15520

[Pennsylvania. Council of Safety, 1777.
Im Sicherheits-Rath. Philadelphia den
Ersten Januar 1777.
[Philadelphia, 1777.] Broadside.]
(No copy located.)   15521

Pennsylvania. Council of Safety, 1777.
In Council of Safety. Philadelphia,
January 22, 1777.
Resolved, That Colonel Melcher. . . .
[Philadelphia, 1777.] Broadside.
LCP copy.   15522

Pennsylvania. Council of Safety, 1777.
In Council of Safety. Philadelphia,
January 22, 1777.
[Philadelphia, 1777.] Broadside.
LCP copy.   15523

[Pennsylvania. Council of Safety, 1777.
In Council of Safety. March 11, 1777
[Cleaning Houses].
[Philadelphia, 1777.] Broadside.]
(Entry from Aitken accounts.)   15524

Pennsylvania. Council of Safety, 1777.
In Council. Philadelphia, April 9, 1777.
To the People of Pennsylvania. . . .
[Philadelphia], Steiner & Cist, [1777].
Broadside.
HSP copy.   15525

Pennsylvania. Council of Safety, 1777.
Sir, The Opinion which General
Washington. . . . April 16, 1777.
[Philadelphia, 1777.] Broadside.
NYHS copy.   43335

Pennsylvania. Council of Safety, 1777.
In Council, June 13, 1777. Major General
Mifflin. . . . To [blank] Lieutenant of the
County of [blank].
[Philadelphia? 1777.] Broadside.
(No copy located.)   43331

Pennsylvania. Council of Safety, 1777.
In Council. Philadelphia, July 9, 1777. . . .
Billeting.
[Philadelphia, 1777.] Broadside.
LCP copy.   15526

Pennsylvania. Council of Safety, 1777.
In Council. Philadelphia, 28th July, 1777.
[Philadelphia, 1777.] Broadside.
LCP copy.   15527

Pennsylvania. Council of Safety, 1777.
In Council, Philadelphia, July 31, 1777.
Sir, I wrote. . . .
[Philadelphia, 1777.] Broadside.
NYHS copy.   43334

Pennsylvania. Council of Safety, 1777.
In Council. Philadelphia, September 4,
1777.
[Philadelphia], Steiner & Cist, [1777].
Broadside.
LCP copy.   15528

[Pennsylvania. Council of Safety, 1777.
By the Council of Safety . . . a
Proclamation [Invasion. Oct. 17, 1777].
[Lancaster], 1777. Broadside.]
(No copy could be located.)   15511

Pennsylvania. Council of Safety, 1777.
In Council of Safety. Lancaster, 21st
October, 1777. Whereas Divers. . . .
[Confiscation].
Lancaster, [1777]. [2] pp.
LOC copy.   15529

Pennsylvania. Council of Safety, 1777.
To the Inhabitants of Pennsylvania. . . .
23d October, 1777.
Lancaster, Bailey, [1777]. Broadside.
LOC copy.   43336

Pennsylvania. Council of Safety, 1777.
In Council of Safety. Lancaster, 25th
October, 1777. An Ordinance . . . for
Appointing . . . Sub-Lieutenants.
Lancaster, Bailey, [1777]. Broadside.
LOC copy.   43332

Pennsylvania. Council of Safety, 1777.
In Council of Safety. Lancaster, 25th
October, 1777. An Ordinance for the
more Effectual Levying . . .
Lancaster, Bailey, [1777]. Broadside.
LOC copy.   43333

[Pennsylvania. Council of Safety, 1777.
In Council of Safety. Lancaster,
November 7, 1777.
A Proclamation [Liquors].
Lancaster, [1777]. Broadside.]
(Ordered published.)   15531

[Pennsylvania. Council of Safety, 1777.
In Council of Safety. Lancaster,
November 7, 1777.
A Proclamation [Provisions].
Lancaster, [1777]. Broadside.]
(Ordered published.)   15530

Pennsylvania. Council of Safety, 1778.
In Council Lancaster, May 29, 1778.
Instructions to the Agents.
Lancaster, Bailey, [1778]. [2] pp.
APS copy.   43523

Pennsylvania. Council of Safety, 1778.
In Council. Philadelphia, July 9th, 1778.
Sir, As it is of Great Importance. . . .
[Philadelphia, 1778.] Broadside.
NYHS copy.   43524

Pennsylvania. Court of Admiralty.
Judgements in the Admiralty of
Pennsylvania.
Philadelphia, Dobson & Lang, 1789. 131
pp.
AAS copy.   22053

Pennsylvania. Courts, 1792.
Rules and Orders, for Regulating the
Practice of the County Court of Common
Pleas.
Lancaster, Bailey & Dickson, 1792.
11 pp.
AAS copy.   46539

Pennsylvania. Courts, 1800.
Rules, Established for Regulating the
Practice of the Supreme and Circuit
Courts.
[Whitehall, 1800.] 24 pp.
LOC copy.   38223

Pennsylvania. General Assembly, 1776.
In Assembly, December 12, 1776
[Bounties].
[Philadelphia], Dunlap, [1776.]
Broadside.
LCP copy.   14986

[Pennsylvania. General Assembly, 1776.
In der Assembly, den 12ten December
1776 [Bounties].
[Philadelphia, 1776.] Broadside.]
(Seidensticker assumed a German ed. of
14986.)   14987

Pennsylvania. General Assembly, 1776.
In Assembly, December 24, 1776.
Resolved, That the Following
Address. . . .
[Philadelphia, 1776.] Broadside.
HSP copy.   14988

Pennsylvania. General Assembly, 1776.
In Assembly, Thursday, December 5, 1776
P.M. On Motion, Resolved
Unanimously. . . .
[Philadelphia], Dunlap, [1776].
Broadside.
LCP copy.   14985

Pennsylvania. General Assembly, 1776.
A Proposed Ordinance . . . Declaring
what Shall be Treason.
Philadelphia, Styner & Cist, [1776].
Broadside.
LCP copy.   14992

Pennsylvania. General Assembly, 1777.
I do hereby Certify . . . the 13th day of
June, A.D. 1777.
[Philadelphia], Dunlap, [1777].
Broadside.
LOC copy.   15519

Pennsylvania. General Assembly, 1777.
In General Assembly for the Common
Wealth of Pennsylvania. Tuesday, June
17, 1777. P.M. An Act. . . . Printed for
Public Consideration.
Philadelphia, Dunlap, [1777]. Broadside.
LCP copy.   15535

Pennsylvania. General Assembly, 1777.
In General Assembly, for the State of
Pennsylvania. Thursday, June 12, 1777.
P.M. On Motion, Resolved. . . .
[Philadelphia], Dunlap, [1777].
Broadside.
LCP copy.   15534

Pennsylvania. General Assembly, 1777.
In General Assembly, Friday, June 6,
1777. The Bill Intitled. . . .
[Philadelphia], Dunlap, [1777]. 2 pp.
LCP copy.   15533

Pennsylvania. General Assembly, 1777.
In General Assembly. Monday, September
15, 1777. A.M. An Act. . . . Printed for
Public Consideration.
Philadelphia, Steiner & Cist, [1777].
Broadside.
LCP copy.   15536

Pennsylvania. General Assembly, 1777.
In General Assembly. Thursday, June 5th,
1777. . . . A Supplement to the Act,
Entituled, An Act for Amending the
Several Acts. . . .
[Philadelphia], Steiner & Cist, [1777]. 8
pp.
HSP copy.   15532

Pennsylvania. General Assembly, 1778.
In der General Assembly von
Pennsylvania, Samstag [convention, June,
1779].
Philadelphia, Steiner & Cist, [1778].
Broadside.
(No copy located.)   43525

Pennsylvania. General Assembly, 1778.
In General Assembly of Pennsylvania,
Saturday, November 28, 1778
[Constitutional convention].
Philadelphia, Dunlap [1778]. Broadside.
HSP copy.   43526

Pennsylvania. General Assembly, 1779.
In General Assembly, of Pennsylvania,
Thursday, April 1, 1779. An Act for the
Regulation of the Markets. . . .
[Philadelphia, 1779.] Broadside.
LCP copy.   16445

Pennsylvania. General Assembly, 1779.
In General Assembly, Saturday, February
13, 1779. . . . An Act to Raise the
Supplies. . . .
Philadelphia, Dunlap, [1779]. [3] pp.
MHS copy.   16444

Pennsylvania. General Assembly, 1779.
Report of the Committee of the Assembly,
on the state of the Public Accounts, 1777
and 1778.
Philadelphia, Dunlap, [1779]. 67 pp.
LCP copy.   16449

Pennsylvania. General Assembly, 1779.
Supplement to the Lancaster Mercury,
No. 26. . . . "An Act for Supplying the
Army. . . ."
[Philadelphia, 1779.] [2] pp.
HSP copy.   43679

Pennsylvania. General Assembly, 1780.
. . . In General Assembly, Thursday,
September 21, 1780. . . . An Act for
Establishing a Land-Office.
[Philadelphia], Dunlap, [1780].
[3] pp.
NYPL copy.   16922

[Pennsylvania. General Assembly, 1780.
. . . In General Assembly, Thursday,
September 21, 1780. On Motion, Ordered,
That the Bill. . . .

[Philadelphia], Dunlap, [1780].
3 pp.]
(A ghost of 16922, q. v.)   43863

Pennsylvania. General Assembly, 1782.
. . . In General Assembly, Tuesday,
February 26, 1782. . . . Plan for
Establishing a National Bank. . . . May 28,
1801.
[Philadelphia], Hall & Sellers, [1782].
Broadside.
LCP copy.   44243

Pennsylvania. General Assembly, 1782.
Report of the Committee of Assembly, on
the state of the Public Accounts . . . for
. . . 1801.
[Philadelphia], Dunlap, [1802].
51 pp.
(No copy located.)   44244

Pennsylvania. General Assembly, 1783.
In Assembly, Tuesday, December 2d, 1783
[Celebration of Peace].
[Philadelphia, 1783.] Broadside.
LOC copy.   18092

Pennsylvania. General Assembly, 1783.
. . . In General Assembly, Saturday,
February 1, 1783. The Bill entituled "An
Act for Extending the Provision. . . ."
Ordered to be Transcribed.
[Philadelphia], Hall & Sellers, [1783].
[2] pp.
HSP copy.   44436

Pennsylvania. General Assembly, 1784.
. . . In General Assembly. Monday,
September 27, 1784. The Bill entitled "A
Further Supplement to the Test Laws"
was Read the Second Time.
[Philadelphia, 1784.] Broadside.
HSP copy.   44584

Pennsylvania. General Assembly, 1784.
. . . In General Assembly. Tuesday, March
16, 1784. A.M. The Bill entitled "An Act
for Opening the Land-Office" was Read
the Second Time.
[Philadelphia], Bradford, [1784].
4 pp.
LCP copy.   44585

Pennsylvania. General Assembly, 1784.
To the Citizens of Pennsylvania. . . .
September 29, 1784.
[Philadelphia], Hall & Sellers, [1784].
Broadside.
LOC copy.   18714

Pennsylvania. General Assembly, 1786.
. . . April 6, 1786. The Bill Entitled, An
Act for Incorporating the City of
Philadelphia.
Philadelphia, Bradford, [1786]. 14 pp.
APS copy.   44945

Pennsylvania. General Assembly, 1786.
Debates and Proceedings . . . on the . . .
Charter of the Bank.
Philadelphia, Carey and Seddon &
Pritchard, 1786. [4], 132 pp.
AAS copy.   19884

Pennsylvania. General Assembly, 1787.
. . . Wednesday, Nov. 14, A.M. The Bill,
entitled, "An Act . . . Bridge over the
River Schuylkill. . . ."
[Philadelphia, 1787.] Broadside.
HSP copy.   45127

Pennsylvania. General Assembly, 1787.
. . . Wednesday, Nov. 14 . . . 1787. The
Bill, entitled, "An Act . . . Bridge over the
River Schuylkill. . . ."
[Philadelphia, 1787.] Broadside.
(No copy located.)   45128

Pennsylvania. General Assembly, 1788.
. . . Thursday, March 27, A.M. 1788. The
Bill, entitled, "A Further Act for Quieting
. . . Wyoming. . . ."
Philadelphia, Bradford, [1788]. 3 pp.
HSP copy.   45327

Pennsylvania. General Assembly, 1789.
. . . The Bill. . . . An Act to Incorporate
the City of Philadelphia.
[Philadelphia], Stewart, 1789. 11 pp.
LOC copy.   22052

Pennsylvania. General Assembly, 1789.
. . . In General Assembly, Tuesday, March

24th, 1789. . . . Extract from the Minutes.
Philadelphia, Hall & Sellers, [1789].
Broadside.
HSP copy.   45552

Pennsylvania. General Assembly, 1789.
. . . In General Assembly, Tuesday,
September 15, 1789. A.M. The Report of
the Committee of the Whole.
Philadelphia, Hall & Sellers, [1789].
Broadside.
NYHS copy.   45553

Pennsylvania. General Assembly, 179?
An Act for more Effectually Securing the
Trade Peace and Safety.
[Philadelphia], Poulson, [179?]. 4 pp.
LOC copy.   45787

Pennsylvania. General Assembly, 1791.
In General Assembly, Monday, March 7,
1791, Read the First Time. . . .
[Philadelphia, 1791.] 2 pp.
LOC copy.   23672

Pennsylvania. General Assembly, 1791.
In General Assembly, Saturday, March
26, 1791, Read the First Time. . . .
[Philadelphia, 1791.] 2 pp.
LOC copy.   23673

Pennsylvania. General Assembly, 1791.
In General Assembly, Tuesday, March 29,
1791, Read the First Time. . . .
Philadelphia, Bradford, [1791]. 3 pp.
LOC copy.   23674

Pennsylvania. General Assembly, 1793.
In General Assembly, Monday, March 25,
1793. An Act for the Better Preventing of
Crimes.
Philadelphia, Bradford, [1793].
10 pp.
NYPL copy.   46846

Pennsylvania. General Assembly, 1793.
In General Assembly, Saturday,
December 21, 1793. A Supplement to the
Act . . . Promoting the Cultivation of
Vines.
Philadelphia, Bradford, [1793]. 2 pp.
AAS copy.   46847

Pennsylvania. General Assembly, 1794.
An Act for the Improvement of the
Wissahickon Road.
[Philadelphia], Poulson, [1794].
8 pp.
HSP copy.   27475

Pennsylvania. General Assembly, 1794.
. . . An Act for the More Effectually
Securing the Trade. . . .
[Philadelphia], Poulson, [1784?].
4 pp.
(Not located, 1968.)   47153

Pennsylvania. General Assembly, 1794.
An Act to Exonerate the late
Proprietaries from the Payment of Certain
Taxes.
[Philadelphia, 1794.] 2 pp.
AAS copy.   47154

Pennsylvania. General Assembly, 1794.
An Act to Prevent the Damages which
may Happen by Firing of Woods.
[Philadelphia], Poulson, [1794].
3 pp.
AAS copy.   47155

Pennsylvania. General Assembly, 1794.
An Act to Repeal an Act entitled "An Act
for Erecting a Loan-Office. . . ."
[Philadelphia], Poulson, [1794]. 2 pp.
AAS copy.   47156

Pennsylvania. General Assembly, 1794.
In General Assembly, Friday, February
21, 1794. An Act for the Relief of Grizel
Robinson.
[Philadelphia, 1794.] 3 pp.
AAS copy.   47157

Pennsylvania. General Assembly, 1794.
In General Assembly, Friday, January 17,
1794. An Act to Provide for the Safe
Keeping of the Records.
[Philadelphia, 1794.] 2 pp.
AAS copy.   47158

Pennsylvania. General Assembly, 1794.
In General Assembly, Monday, February

17, 1794. An Act to Prevent the Damages
which may Happen by Firing of Woods.
[Philadelphia, 1794.] 3 pp.
AAS copy.   47159

Pennsylvania. General Assembly, 1794.
In General Assembly, Monday, February
17, 1794. An Act to Prevent the Damages
which May Happen by Firing of Woods.
[Philadelphia, 1794.] 3 pp.
HSP copy.   27479

Pennsylvania. General Assembly, 1794.
In General Assembly, Monday, January
20, 1794. An Act for the Relief of Blackall
William Ball.
Philadelphia, Bradford, [1794].
Broadside.
AAS copy.   47160

Pennsylvania. General Assembly, 1794.
In General Assembly, Monday, March 24,
1794. An Act to Regulate the Practice of
Physic and Surgery.
Philadelphia, Bradford, [1794]. 4 pp.
College of Physicians copy.   47161

Pennsylvania. General Assembly, 1794.
In General Assembly, Saturday, February
15, 1794. An Act to Authorise the
Admission of Certain Persons as
Witnesses.
[Philadelphia, 1794.] Broadside.
AAS copy.   47162

Pennsylvania. General Assembly, 1794.
In General Assembly, Saturday, February
22, 1794. An Act for the Prevention of
Vice.
Philadelphia, Bradford, [1794]. 13 pp.
NYPL copy.   47163

Pennsylvania. General Assembly, 1794.
In General Assembly, Saturday, February
22, 1794. An Act to Incorporate the . . .
Insurance Company of North America.
Philadelphia, Bradford, [1794]. 10 pp.
JCB copy.   47164

Pennsylvania. General Assembly, 1794.
In General Assembly, Tuesday, January
21, 1794. An Act to Regulate the
Exportation of Pot and Pearl Ash.
Philadelphia, Bradford, [1794]. 6 pp.
AAS copy.   47165

Pennsylvania. General Assembly, 1794.
In General Assembly, Tuesday, March 25,
1794. An Act for the Better Preventing of
Crimes.
Philadelphia, Bradford, [1794]. 10 pp.
NYPL copy.   47166

Pennsylvania. General Assembly, 1794.
. . . In General Assembly. Wednesday,
December 17, 1794. A Supplement to the
Act intituled an "Act for the Regulation
of Bankruptcy. . . ."
[Philadelphia], Humphreys, [1794]. 2 pp.
AAS copy.   47168

Pennsylvania. General Assembly, 1794.
A Supplement to the Act entitled "An Act
to Enable the Governor . . . to
Incorporate a Company for Opening a
Canal . . . on Brandywine Creek.
[Philadelphia], Poulson, [1794]. 2 pp.
AAS copy.   47169

Pennsylvania. General Assembly, 1795.
. . . An Act Relative to Donation Lands.
[Philadelphia], Poulson, [1795]. 5 pp.
(The only known copy is defective.)
AAS copy.   47529

Pennsylvania. General Assembly, 1795.
. . . An Act to Amend an Act entitled "An
Act to Regulate the Trials. . . ."
[Philadelphia], Poulson, [1795]. 2 pp.
AAS copy.   47530

Pennsylvania. General Assembly, 1795.
An Act to Erect an Additional Election
District in Washington County.
[Philadelphia], Poulson, [1795].
Broadside.
AAS copy.   47531

Pennsylvania. General Assembly, 1795.
. . . An Act to Erect the Township of
Heidelberg . . . into a Separate Election
District.

[Philadelphia], Poulson, [1795].
Broadside.
AAS copy.   47532

Pennsylvania. General Assembly, 1795.
. . . An Act to Establish [the Permanent]
Seat of the Government.
[Philadelphia], Poulson, [1795]. 3 pp.
(The only known copy is imperfect.)
AAS copy.   47533

Pennsylvania. General Assembly, 1795.
[Act to incorporate the Wissahickon Toll
Road.
Philadelphia, 1795? 6+pp.]
(The one recorded copy cannot be
located.)   47534

Pennsylvania. General Assembly, 1795.
. . . An Act to Supply the Deficiencies in
Former Appropriations.
[Philadelphia], Poulson, [1795].
2 pp.
AAS copy.   47535

Pennsylvania. General Assembly, 1795.
No. XXXIX. In General Assembly,
Tuesday, February 10, 1795. An Act for
the Relief of Anne Russel.
[Philadelphia], Humphreys, [1795].
2 pp.
AAS copy.   47536

Pennsylvania. General Assembly, 1795.
No. XLIV. In General Assembly.
Tuesday, February 17, 1795. An Act
Declaring Lacoming Creek a Highway.
[Philadelphia], Humphreys, [1795].
Broadside.
(The only known copy is imperfect.)
AAS copy.   47537

Pennsylvania. General Assembly, 1795.
No. XLIX. In General Assembly.
Saturday, February 28, 1795. An Act for
Reviving Suits.
[Philadelphia], Humphreys, [1795].
[2] pp.
AAS copy.   47538

Pennsylvania. General Assembly, 1795.
No. LIII. In General Assembly. Tuesday,
March 3, 1795. An Act for the Relief of
John Kline.
[Philadelphia], Humphreys, [1795].
2 pp.
AAS copy.   47539

Pennsylvania. General Assembly, 1795.
No. LIX. In General Assembly. Friday,
March 6, 1795. An Act to Alter Certain
Election Districts.
[Philadelphia], Humphreys, [1795].
2 pp.
AAS copy.   47540

Pennsylvania. General Assembly, 1795.
No. LX. In General Assembly. Friday,
March 6, 1795. An Act to Repeal . . . "An
Act for Raising . . . Money. . . ."
[Philadelphia], Humphreys, [1795].
Broadside.
AAS copy.   47541

Pennsylvania. General Assembly. 1795.
No. LXX. In General Assembly. Monday,
March 16, 1795. An Act to Reimburse the
Guardians.
[Philadelphia, Humphreys, 1795.]
Broadside.
AAS copy.   47542

Pennsylvania. General Assembly, 1795.
No. LXXV. In General Assembly.
Thursday, March 19, 1795. An Act to
Establish the Permanent Seat of the
Government.
[Philadelphia], Humphreys, [1795].
3 pp.
AAS copy.   47543

Pennsylvania. General Assembly, 1795.
No. LXXVII. In General Assembly.
Thursday, March 19, 1795. An Act to
Erect the Townships of Cocalico and
Elizabeth.
[Philadelphia], Humphreys, [1795].
Broadside.
AAS copy.   47544

Pennsylvania. General Assembly, 1795.
No. LXXXIV. In General Assembly.
Monday, March 23, 1795. A Supplement

to Laws for Preventing the Exportation of
Flour.
[Philadelphia], Humphreys, [1795].
2 pp.
AAS copy.   47545

Pennsylvania. General Assembly, 1795.
No. XC. In General Assembly. Wednesday,
March 25, 1795. An Act for Erecting Part
of the County of Northumberland. . . .
[Philadelphia], Humphreys, [1795].
4 pp.
AAS copy.   47546

Pennsylvania. General Assembly, 1795.
. . . A Supplement to an Act entitled An
Act Making Provision for . . . Orphan
Children.
[Philadelphia], Poulson, [1795].
Broadside.
AAS copy.   47547

Pennsylvania. General Assembly, 1795.
. . . A Supplement [to] the Act entitled
"An Act to Appoint Trustees. . . ."
[Philadelphia], Poulson, [1795].
Broadside.
(The only known copy is imperfect.)
AAS copy.   47548

Pennsylvania. General Assembly, 1797.
. . . An Act to Provide for the Instruction
of Youth.
[Philadelphia], Poulson, 1797. 12 pp.
AAS copy.   32647

Pennsylvania. General Assembly, 1797.
No. XXXVIII. In General Assembly.
Friday, January 27, 1797. An Act for
Affording Relief to Persons who have
Paid Money into the Land Office.
[Philadelphia], Bradford, [1797].
4 pp.
(Best copy available.)
LCP copy.   48216

Pennsylvania. General Assembly, 1797.
No. XLV. In General Assembly . . .
February 8, 1797. An Act to Establish a
System of Bankruptcy.
[Philadelphia, 1797.] 39 pp.
(No copy located.)   32650

Pennsylvania. General Assembly, 1797.
No. LXXV. In General Assembly Friday
March 3, 1797. An Act to Prevent and
Punish. . . .
[Philadelphia, 1797.] 16 pp.
(Too fragile to copy.)   48217

Pennsylvania. General Assembly, 1798.
No. LV. In General Assembly. Tuesday,
February 6, 1798. An Act to Provide for
Unsatisfied Warrants.
[Philadelphia, 1798.] 2 pp.
(Best copy available.)
LCP copy.   48565

Pennsylvania. General Assembly, 1800.
Report. The Committee to whom was
Referred the Statements of the
Comptroller-General. . . . March 8, 1800.
[Lancaster, 1800.] 2 pp.
LCP copy.   49131

Pennsylvania. General Assembly,
Committee of Ways and Means, 1785.
Plan of a Report of the Committee.
[Philadelphia, 1785.] 14 pp.
NYPL copy.   19163

Pennsylvania. General Assembly.
Committee on Ways and Means, 1792.
Report of the Committee.
[Philadelphia], Bailey & Lang, [1792]. 6
pp.
LCP copy.   46540

Pennsylvania. General Assembly.
Committee on the Complaint of George
Logan.
Report of the Committee Appointed to
Enquire. . . .
Lancaster, Baileys, [1800]. 56 pp.
LCP copy.   38220

Pennsylvania. General Assembly.
Committee on the State of Public
Accounts, 1779.
Philadelphia, Dunlap, [1779]. 39 pp.
HSP copy.   16450

Pennsylvania. General Assembly.

Committee on the State of Public
Accounts, 1781.
Report of the Committee [for 1780].
[Philadelphia], Dunlap, [1781]. 46 pp.
HSP copy.   17296

Pennsylvania. General Assembly. House
of Representatives, 1777.
In General Assembly . . . June 17, 1777.
The House Resumed. . . .
[Philadelphia, 1777.] [4] pp.
LCP copy.   43337

Pennsylvania. General Assembly. House
of Representatives, 1791.
In the House . . . September 20, 1791, read
the First Time, An Act to Provide for
Compleating the Repairs of the
Wharf. . . ."
[Philadelphia, 1791.] Broadside.
LCP copy.   46251

Pennsylvania. General Assembly. House
of Representatives, 1795.
A List of Members of the House.
[Philadelphia], Bailey, [1795]. Broadside.
HSP copy.   29292

Pennsylvania. General Assembly. House
of Representatives, 1799.
The Dissent of the Minority . . .
December, 1798.
[Philadelphia, 1799.] 8 pp.
AAS copy.   36060

Pennsylvania. General Assembly, Senate,
1795.
. . . Report of a Special Committee on Bill
Q. A Supplement to the Act entitled "An
Act to Incorporate . . . Southwark."
[Philadelphia], Poulson, [1795].
Broadside.
AAS copy.   47549

Pennsylvania. General Assembly. Senate,
1797.
The Names and Places of Abode of the
Members and Officers.
[Philadelphia], Poulson, [1797].
Broadside.
AAS copy.   32656

Pennsylvania. General Assembly Journals,
1776.
Journals and Proceedings of the General
Assembly [Nov. 28, 1776 - Oct. 13, 1777].
Philadelphia, Dunlap, 1777. 100 pp.
LCP copy.   15538

Pennsylvania. General Assembly Journals,
1777.
Minutes of the General Assembly. . . .
[Sept. 31-Oct. 13, 1777].
Lancaster, Bailey, [1777]. pp. [85] - 100.
LCP copy.   43338

Pennsylvania. General Assembly Journals,
1777.
Minutes of the Second General Assembly
[Oct. 27, 1777 +].
Lancaster, 1778. 116 pp.
LCP copy.   15973

Pennsylvania. General Assembly Journals,
1778.
Minutes of the Third General Assembly
[Oct. 26, 1778 +].
Philadelphia, Dunlap, 1778. 154 pp.
LCP copy.   15974

Pennsylvania. General Assembly Journals,
1779.
Minutes of the First Session, of the
Fourth General Assembly [Oct. 25, 1779 -
Sept. 23, 1780].
[Philadelphia, 1779.] pp. 154-298.
LCP copy.   16447

Pennsylvania. General Assembly Journals,
1780.
Minutes of the First Sitting of the Fifth
General Assembly [Oct. 23, 1780].
Philadelphia, Dunlap, [1780].
pp. 301-357.
LCP copy.   16934

Pennsylvania. General Assembly Journals,
1781.
Minutes of the Second Sitting [Feb. 6 -
Apr. 10, 1781].
[Philadelphia, 1781.] pp. 359-434.
LCP copy.   17292

Pennsylvania. General Assembly Journals, 1781.
Minutes of the Third Sitting of the Fifth General Assembly [May 24 - June 26, 1781].
[Philadelphia, 1781.] pp. 435-473.
LCP copy.   17293

Pennsylvania. General Assembly Journals, 1781.
Minutes of the Fourth Sitting of the Fifth General Assembly [Sept. 4 - Oct. 2, 1781].
[Philadelphia, 1781.] pp. 475-496.
LCP copy.   17294

Pennsylvania. General Assembly Journals, 1781.
Minutes of the First [-Third] Session, of the Sixth General Assembly [Oct. 22, 1781 - Sept. 20, 1782.]
Philadelphia, Dunlap, 1781. pp. [497] - 712.
LCP copy.   17295

Pennsylvania. General Assembly Journals, 1782.
Minutes of the First Session, of the Seventh General Assembly [Oct. 28, 1782 - Sept. 26, 1783].
Philadelphia, Dunlap, [1782]. pp. [2], 715-968.
HSP copy.   17663

Pennsylvania. General Assembly Journals, 1783.
Minutes of the First [-Third] Session of the Eighth General Assembly [Oct. 27, 1783 - Sept. 29, 1784].
Philadelphia, Hall & Sellers, 1783. 361, 3 pp.
HSP copy.   18097

Pennsylvania. General Assembly Journals, 1784.
Minutes of the First [-Third] Session of the Ninth General Assembly [Oct. 25, 1784 - Sept. 23, 1785].
Philadelphia, Bailey, 1784. 402 pp.
HSP copy.   18684

Pennsylvania. General Assembly Journals, 1785.
Minutes of the Second Session of the Ninth General Assembly [Feb. 1 - Sept. 23, 1785].
[Philadelphia, 1785.] pp. 105-402.
PSL copy.   19162

Pennsylvania. General Assembly Journals, 1786.
Minutes of the First [-Third] Session of the Tenth General Assembly [Oct. 24, 1785 - Sept. 27, 1786].
Philadelphia, Hall & Sellers, 1785. 336, 2 pp.
PSL copy.   19888

Pennsylvania. General Assembly Journals, 1786.
Minutes of the First Session of the Eleventh General Assembly [Oct. 23-Dec. 30, 1786].
[Philadelphia, 1786.] 114 pp.
LCP copy.   44947

[Pennsylvania. General Assembly Journals, 1786.
Tagebuch der General Assembly [1786 - 1787].
Germantown, 1786.]
(Printing assumed by Seidensticker from the sequence.)   19889

Pennsylvania. General Assembly Journals, 1787.
Minutes of the Second Session of the Eleventh General Assembly . . . February. . . .
Philadelphia, Hall & Sellers, [1787]. pp. [115]-198.
LCP copy.   45129

Pennsylvania. General Assembly Journals, 1787.
Minutes of the Third Session of the Eleventh General Assembly . . . September. . . .
Philadelphia, Hall & Sellers, [1787]. pp. [199]-250.
LCP copy.   45130

Pennsylvania. General Assembly Journals, 1787.

Minutes of the First Session of the Twelfth General Assembly. . . . October. . . .
Philadelphia, Hall & Sellers, 1787. 97 pp.
LCP copy.   45131

Pennsylvania. General Assembly Journals, 1787.
Proceedings and Debates of the General Assembly. . . . Volume the First [Sept. 4-29, 1787].
Philadelphia, Humphreys, 1787. 143 pp.
AAS copy.   20631

Pennsylvania. General Assembly Journals, 1787.
Proceedings and Debates of the General Assembly. . . . Volume the Second [Oct. 22 - Nov. 29, 1787].
Philadelphia, James, 1787. [2], 189, [2] pp.
AAS copy.   20632

[Pennsylvania. General Assembly Journals, 1787.
Tagebuch der General Assembly . . . 1787-1788.
Germantown, 1788.]
(Entry apparently from advs. in the Germantauner Zeitung for 21370-1.) 21373

Pennsylvania. General Assembly Journals, 1788.
Minutes of the Second Session of the Twelfth General Assembly . . . February 19. . . .
Philadelphia, Hall & Sellers, [1788]. pp. [99]-199.
LCP copy.   45328

Pennsylvania. General Assembly Journals, 1788.
Minutes of the Third Session of the Twelfth General Assembly . . . September. . . .
Philadelphia, Hall & Sellers, [1788]. pp. [201]-280.
LCP copy.   45329

Pennsylvania. General Assembly Journals, 1788.
Minutes of the First Session of the Thirteenth General Assembly.
Philadelphia, Hall & Sellers, 1788. 49 pp.
LCP copy.   45330

Pennsylvania. General Assembly Journals, 1788.
Proceedings and Debates of the General Assembly. . . . Volume the Third [Feb. 19 - Mar. 29, 1788].
Philadelphia, 1788. [2], 234 pp.
AAS copy.   21370

Pennsylvania. General Assembly Journals, 1788.
Debates of the General Assembly. . . . Volume the Fourth [Sept. 2 - Oct. 4, 1788].
Philadelphia, 1788. 348 pp.
AAS copy.   21371

[Pennsylvania. General Assembly Journals, 1788.
Tagebuch der General Assembly . . . 1788-1789.
Germantown, Billmeyer, 1789.]
(Assumed by Seidensticker from the sequence.)   22056

Pennsylvania. General Assembly Journals, 1789.
Minutes of the Thirteenth General Assembly . . . Second Session.
Philadelphia, Hall & Sellers, [1789]. pp. [51]-205.
LCP copy.   45554

Pennsylvania. General Assembly Journals, 1789.
Minutes of the Thirteenth General Assembly . . . Third Session.
Philadelphia, Hall & Sellers, [1789]. pp. [207]-306.
LCP copy.   45555

Pennsylvania. General Assembly Journals, 1789.
Minutes of the First Session of the Fourteenth General Assembly [Oct. 26 +].

Philadelphia, Hall & Sellers, 1789. 113, [1] pp.
LCP copy.   45556

Pennsylvania. General Assembly Journals, 1790.
Minutes of the Second Session of the Fourteenth General Assembly [Feb. 2 - Apr. 6, 1790].
[Philadelphia, 1790.] pp. [113]-281.
LCP copy.   45958

Pennsylvania. General Assembly Journals, 1790.
Minutes of the Third Session of the Fourteenth General Assembly [Aug. 24-Sept. 3, 1790].
[Philadelphia, 1790.] pp. [283]-302.
LCP copy.   45959

[Pennsylvania. General Assembly Journals, 1790.
Tagebuch der General Assembly, 1789-1790.
Germantown, Billmeyer, 1790.]
(Entry from Seidensticker, p. 126.) 22779

Pennsylvania. General Assembly Journals, 1791.
Tagebuch der Ersten Sitzung des Zweyten Hauses.
Germantown, Billmeyer, 1791. 327, [1], 33 pp.
German Society of Pennsylvania copy.
                                             23684

Pennsylvania. Governor, 1781.
Proposals made to the Non-Commissioned Officers and Soldiers of the Pennsylvania Line . . . January 7, 1781.
n.p., [1781]. Broadside.
LOC copy.   44034

Pennsylvania. Governor, 1791.
. . . By Thomas Mifflin . . . a Proclamation [election. Dated Nov. 14, 1791].
Philadelphia, Hall & Sellers, [1791].
Broadside.
HSP copy.   46252

Pennsylvania. Governor, 1791.
. . . By Thomas Mifflin. . . . A Proclamation [election of Sheriffs. Dated Nov. 14, 1791.]
Philadelphia, Hall & Sellers, [1791].
Broadside.
LCP copy.   46253

Pennsylvania. Governor, 1791.
. . . By Thomas Mifflin. . . . A Proclamation [Elizabeth Reeves. Aug. 22, 1792].
[Philadelphia, Dunlap, 1792.] Broadside.
(No copy located.)   24672

Pennsylvania. Governor, 1793.
. . . By Thomas Mifflin, Governor. . . . A Proclamation, Appointing a Day of General Humiliation [Dec. 12. Dated Nov. 14, 1793].
Philadelphia, Oswald, [1793]. Broadside.
HSP copy.   25976

Pennsylvania. Governor, 1794.
. . . By Thomas Mifflin. . . . A Proclamation. Whereas it Appears [August 7, 1794].
[Philadelphia, 1794]. Broadside.
LOC copy.   47170

Pennsylvania. Governor, 1794.
Sir, In the Present State of our National Affairs. . . .
[Philadelphia, 1794.] [2] pp.
HSP copy.   27487

Pennsylvania. Governor, 1800.
Erläuterde Bemerkungen über Seiner Excellenz Thomas McKean. . . . Addresse an Beide Hauser.
Lancaster, Hutter, 1800. 16 pp.
(No copy could be located.)   38209

Pennsylvania. Governor, 1800.
. . . Governor's Message. . . . November 21, 1800.
Lancaster, Hamilton, 1800. 4 pp.
NYPL copy.   38217

Pennsylvania. Governor, 1800.
The Inaugural Address of Thomas M'Kean . . . with their Answers.

Lancaster, Dicksons, [1800]. 16 pp.
NYPL copy.   38210

Pennsylvania. High Court of Errors and
Appeals, 1785.
The Resolutions of the High Court . . . In
the Cause of Silas Talbot.
Philadelphia, Bradford, 1785. 8, 16 pp.
NYPL copy.   19164

Pennsylvania. House Journals, 1776.
Journals of the House of
Representatives. . . . Volume the First
[Nov. 28, 1776 - Oct. 2, 1781].
Philadelphia, Dunlap, 1782. [2], 698,
[1] pp.
AAS copy.   17658

Pennsylvania. House Journals, 1790.
Journal of the First Session of the House
of Representatives [Dec. 7, 1790 - Apr. 13,
1791].
Philadelphia, Hall & Sellers, 1790. pp.
[2], [i]-xii, [3]-433.
PSL copy.   23675

[Pennsylvania. House Journals, 1790.
Tagebuch der Ersten Sitzung des Zweyten
Hauses [Dec. 6, 1790 +].
Germantown, Billmeyer, [1792]. 327, 33
pp.]
(The origin of this entry is unknown.)
     24668

Pennsylvania. House Journals, 1791.
Journal of the First Session of the Second
House [Dec. 6, 1791 - Apr. 10, 1792].
Philadelphia, Bailey & Lang, 1791 (1792).
327, [34] pp.
PSL copy.   24667

Pennsylvania. House Journals, 1791.
Journal of the Second Session of the
House of Representatives [Aug. 23 - Sept.
30, 1791].
[Philadelphia], Hall & Sellers, 1791. pp.
[435]-573, [1]-20, [1]-5.
PSL copy.   23676

[Pennsylvania. House Journals, 1791.
Tagebuch des Dritten Hauses. . . .
1791-1792.
Germantown, Billmeyer, 1792.]
(Entry from Seidensticker, who appears to
have been misled by German-language
advs. of the English ed.)   24669

Pennsylvania. House Journals, 1792.
Journal of the First Session of the Third
House [Dec. 4, 1792 - Apr. 11, 1793].
Philadelphia, Bailey & Lang, 1792. 386,
[22], [23] pp.
LCP copy.   25974

Pennsylvania. House Journals, 1793.
Journal of the Second Session of the Third
House [Aug. 27-Sept. 5].
Philadelphia, Bailey, [1793]. 35, [22] pp.
(Not located, 1968.)   46848

Pennsylvania. House Journals, 1793.
Journal of the First Session of the Fourth
House [Dec. 3, 1793 - Apr. 22, 1794].
Philadelphia, 1794. 417, [37] pp.
LCP copy.   27480

[Pennsylvania. House Journals, 1793.
Tagbuch des Vierten Hauses der
Repräsentanten . . . 1793-1794.
Germantown, Billmeyer, 1794.]
(Entry assumed by Seidensticker from a
German-language adv. of the English ed.)
     27481

[Pennsylvania. House Journals, 1794.
Tagebuch des Fünften Hauses der
Repräsentanten. . . . 1794-1795.
Germantown, Billmeyer, 1795.]
(Evans entry from Seidensticker, p. 141.)
     29288

Pennsylvania. House Journals, 1794.
Journal of the House of Representatives
[Dec. 2, 1794-Apr. 20, 1795].
Philadelphia, Hall & Sellers, 1795. 433,
[1], 8, 18 pp.
LCP copy.   29287

Pennsylvania. House Journals, 1795.
Journal of the First Session of the Sixth
House [Dec. 1, 1795 - Apr. 4, 1796].
Philadelphia, Baileys, 1795. 487 pp.
AAS copy.   30978

[Pennsylvania. House Journals, 1795.
Tagebuch des Sechsten Houses . . .
1795-1796.
Philadelphia, Steiner & Kammerer, 1796.]
(Entry taken by Evans from
Seidensticker.)   30979

Pennsylvania. House Journals, 1796.
Journal of the First Session of the Seventh
House [Dec. 6, 1796 - Apr. 5, 1797].
Philadelphia, Hall & Sellers, 1797. 440, 10,
16 pp.
AAS copy.   32651

[Pennsylvania. House Journals, 1796.
Tagebuch des Siebenten Haus der
Repräsentanten . . . 1796-1797.
Philadelphia, Steiner und Kammerer,
1797.]
(Apparently a ghost arising from a
German-language adv. for 32651.)   32652

Pennsylvania. House Journals, 1797.
Journal of the Second Session of the
Seventh House [Aug. 28-29, 1797].
Philadelphia, Hall & Sellers, 1797. 18 pp.
LCP copy.   48218

Pennsylvania. House Journals, 1797.
Journal of the First Session of the Eighth
House [Dec. 5, 1797-April 5, 1798].
Philadelphia, Bailey, 1797. 398, [2], 62,
19 pp.
AAS copy.   34326

[Pennsylvania. House Journals, 1797.
Tagebuch des Achten Hauses.
Lancaster, Pa., Albrecht, 1798.]
(No copy located.)   34328

[Pennsylvania. House Journals, 1797.
Tagebuch des Achten Hauses.
Lancaster, Pa., Albrecht & Lahn, 1798.]
(Assumed by Evans from what appears to
be a German-language adv. for the
English ed.)   34327

Pennsylvania. House Journals, 1798.
Journal of the First Sessions of the Ninth
House [Dec. 4, 1798 - Apr. 11, 1799].
Philadelphia, Hall & Sellers, 1799. [2],
488, 61, [1], 17, [1], 8 pp.
AAS copy.   36062

Pennsylvania. House Journals, 1799.
Journal of the First Session of the Tenth
House [Dec. 3, 1799 - Mar. 17, 1800].
Lancaster, Baileys, 1799. 439, [1], 59, [1],
18 pp.
AAS copy.   38212

Pennsylvania. House Journals, 1800.
Journal of the First Session of the
Eleventh House [Nov. 5, 1800-Feb. 27,
1801].
Lancaster, Bailey, 1800. [2], 474, 67, [1],
21, [1], 6 pp.
LCP copy.   38213

Pennsylvania. Indian Commissioners,
1787.
State of the Accounts of the. . . .
Philadelphia, Aitkens, 1787. 11 pp.
NYPL copy.   45132

Pennsylvania. Land Office.
. . . Sept. 13, 1800. The First Day of
October. . . .
n.p., n.d. Broadside.
LOC copy.   38216

Pennsylvania. Laws, Statutes, etc., 1776.
An Act, Directing the Mode and Time of
Electing Justices of the Peace.
[Philadelphia, 1776.] 3 pp.
LCP copy.   14969

Pennsylvania. Laws, Statutes, etc., 1776.
An Ordinance for Rendering the Burthen
of Associators . . . Equal.
[Philadelphia, 1776.] [3] pp.
HSP copy.   14989

Pennsylvania. Laws, Statutes, etc., 1776.
An Ordinance for the Appointment of
Justices of the Peace.
Philadelphia, Dunlap, [1776]. Broadside.
LCP copy.   14990

Pennsylvania. Laws, Statutes, etc., 1776.
An Ordinance of the State of
Pennsylvania, Declaring what Shall be
Treason.

Philadelphia, Styner & Cist, [1776].
Broadside.
LCP copy.   14991

Pennsylvania. Laws, Statutes, etc., 1776.
Regiments-Verfassung von Pennsylvanien.
[Philadelphia, 1776.] 16 pp.
HSP copy.   14996

[Pennsylvania. Laws, Statutes, etc., 1776.
Resolutions Directing the Mode of
Levying Taxes on Non-Asssociators.
Philadelphia, Miller, 1776.]
(Apparently a ghost of 14989.)   14994

[Pennsylvania. Laws, Statutes, etc., 1776.
Rules and Articles for the Government of
the Pennsylvania Forces.
Philadelphia, Miller, 1776.]
(English printing assumed by Hildeburn
from 14996.)   14995

[Pennsylvania. Laws, Statutes, etc., 1776.
Rules and Regulations for the Better
Government of the Military Associations.
Philadelphia, 1776.]
(Adv. Pa. Staatsbote, June 11, 1776.)
     14997

[Pennsylvania. Laws, Statutes, etc., 1776.
Rules and Regulations [in German] for
the Better Government of the Military
Associations.
Philadelphia, 1776.]
(Probably a ghost of 14996.)   14998

Pennsylvania. Laws, Statutes, etc., 1777.
An Act Obliging the Male White Inhabitants
. . . to Give . . . Allegiance.
Philadelphia, Dunlap, [1777]. 7 pp.
JCB copy.   43339

Pennsylvania. Laws, Statutes, etc., 1777.
An Act to Discourage Desertion. . . .
February 20, 1777.
[Philadelphia, 1777.] Broadside.
LCP copy.   15502

Pennsylvania. Laws, Statutes, etc., 1777.
An Act to Regulate the Militia.
Philadelphia, Dunlap, 1777. 32 pp.
NYPL copy.   15503

Pennsylvania. Laws, Statutes, etc., 1777.
Eine Acte zur Anordnung der Militz.
Philadelphia, Steiner & Cist, 1777.
28 pp.
LCP copy.   15504

Pennsylvania. Laws, Statutes, etc., 1777.
A Supplement to the Act, Intitled, "An
Act to Regulate the Militia."
[Philadelphia], Dunlap, [1777].
Broadside.
LCP copy.   15506

Pennsylvania. Laws, Statutes, etc., 1777.
A Supplement to the Act Intitled "An Act
to Regulate the Militia."
[Philadelphia], Dunlap, 1777.] 4 pp.
LCP copy.   15505

Pennsylvania. Laws, Statutes, etc., 1778.
An Act for Raising a Regiment of Horse.
[Philadelphia, 1778?] Broadside.
HSP copy.   43527

Pennsylvania. Laws, Statutes, etc., 1778.
An Act for the Regulation of Waggons [Jan.
2, 1778].
[Lancaster, 1778.] [2] pp.
LCP copy.   15957

Pennsylvania. Laws, Statutes, etc., 1778.
An Act to Prevent Forestalling [Jan. 2,
1778].
[Lancaster, 1778.] [2] pp.
APS copy.   15958

Pennsylvania. Laws, Statutes, etc., 1778.
An Act to Prohibit for a Limited Time the
Making of Whiskey.
Philadelphia, Dunlap, [1778]. Broadside.
HSP copy.   43528

Pennsylvania. Laws, Statutes, etc., 1778.
A Farther Supplement to the Act Entitled
"An Act to Regulate the Militia. . . ."
Lancaster, Dunlap, 1778. 8 pp.
(No copy located.)   43529

Pennsylvania. Laws, Statutes, etc., 1778.
A Further Supplement to the Act Intitled,

"An Act Directing the Mode. . . ."
Philadelphia, Dunlap, [1778]. Broadside.
LCP copy.   15959

Pennsylvania. Laws, Statutes, etc., 1778.
A Further Supplement to the Act Entitled,
"An Act to Regulate the Militia. . . ."
Lancaster, Dunlap, 1778. 8 pp.
LCP copy.   15960

[Pennsylvania. Laws, Statutes, etc., 1778.
In der General Assembly . . . den 28ten
November, 1778 [Resolution on
Convention].
Philadelphia, Steiner & Cist, [1778].
Broadside.]
(Ordered printed.)   15966

Pennsylvania. Laws, Statutes, etc., 1778.
In General Assembly . . . December 3,
1778. . . . An Act to Establish and
Regulate Vendues.
[Philadelphia, 1778.] Broadside.
LCP copy.   15967

Pennsylvania. Laws, Statutes, etc., 1778.
In General Assembly . . . November 28,
1778 [Resolution on Convention].
Philadelphia, Dunlap, [1778]. Broadside.
LCP copy.   15965

Pennsylvania. Laws, Statutes, etc., 1778.
In General Assembly . . . September 4,
1778. . . . A Further Supplement to the
Act Entitled, "An Act for the Regulation
of Waggons."
Philadelphia, Dunlap, [1778]. Broadside.
LCP copy.   15962

Pennsylvania. Laws, Statutes, etc., 1778.
In General Assembly . . . September 7,
1778. A Supplement to the Act Intitled,
"An Act for the Further Security. . . ."
[Philadelphia, 1778.] Broadside.
LCP copy.   15963

Pennsylvania. Laws, Statutes, etc., 1778.
In the General Assembly . . . September 1,
1778. An Act for the Recovery of the
Duties on Negroes.
[Philadelphia, 1778.] Broadside.
LCP copy.   15961

Pennsylvania. Laws, Statutes, etc., 1778.
A Supplement to the Act Intitled, "An
Act for the Further Security. . . ."
Philadelphia, Dunlap, [1778]. Broadside.
LCP copy.   15964

Pennsylvania. Laws, Statutes, etc., 1779.
An Act to Appoint a Representation for
the City of Philadelphia.
Philadelphia, Dunlap, [1779]. Broadside.
LCP copy.   16426

Pennsylvania. Laws, Statutes, etc., 1779.
The Acts of the General Assembly . . .
since . . . the Fourth Day of July, A.D.
1776.
Philadelphia, Dunlap, 1779. [72] pp.
HEH copy.   16427

Pennsylvania. Laws, Statutes, etc., 1779.
General Militia Orders. Philadelphia,
October 27, 1779.
Philadelphia, Bailey, [1779]. 2 pp.
HSP copy.   16438

[Pennsylvania. Laws, Statutes, etc., 1779.
Instructions to the Agents for Forfeited
Estates.
Philadelphia, Bailey, [1779]. Broadside.]
(No copy located.)   16446

Pennsylvania. Laws, Statutes, etc., 1780.
An Act for Confirming and Amending the
Charter of the German Lutheran
Congregation in . . . Philadelphia. [Mar.
3, 1780.]
[Philadelphia, 1780.] Broadside.
HSP copy.   43864

[Pennsylvania. Laws, Statutes, etc., 1780.
An Act for Procuring an Immediate
Supply [June 1, 1780].
[Philadelphia, 1780.] Broadside.]
(No copy of a broadside printing located.)
                                                   16923

Pennsylvania. Laws, Statutes, etc., 1780.
An Act for the Regulation of the Militia.
[Philadelphia, 1780.] 20 pp.
HC copy.   16924

[Pennsylvania. Laws, Statutes, etc., 1781.
. . . An Act Directing the Mode of
Adjusting . . . Debts [Jan. 1, 1777 - Mar.
1, 1781].
[Philadelphia, 1781.] Broadside.]
(Described from a copy formerly in
private hands.)   17297

Pennsylvania. Laws, Statutes, etc., 1781.
. . . An Act for Recruiting the
Pennsylvania Line. . . . Enacted [June 25,
1781].
[Philadelphia, 1781.] [2] pp.
HSP copy.   44026

[Pennsylvania. Laws, Statutes, etc., 1781.
An Act for the gradual abolition of
slavery.
Philadelphia, 1781? 16 pp.]
(Taylor 285; no copy located.)   44027

Pennsylvania. Laws, Statutes, etc., 1781.
. . . An Act for the Repeal of so much of
the Laws of this Commonwealth as make
the Continental Bills of Credit . . . Legal
Tender.
[Philadelphia, 1781.] [2] pp.
HSP copy.   17298

Pennsylvania. Laws, Statutes, etc., 1781.
. . . An Act to Raise Effective Supplies
[dated June 21, 1781].
[Philadelphia, 1781.] [3] pp.
NYPL copy.   44028

Pennsylvania. Laws, Statutes, etc., 1781.
The Acts of the General Assembly.
Philadelphia, Bailey, 1781. [4], xxxi, [1],
528, [1], viii pp.
(But for imprint, the same as 17656, q. v.
for text.)
AAS copy.   44029

Pennsylvania. Laws, Statutes, etc., 1781.
Postscript to the Pennsylvania Packet. . . .
In General Assembly, Thursday, June 14,
1781.
[Philadelphia, 1781. [2] pp.
LOC copy.   44030

Pennsylvania. Laws, Statutes, etc., 1782.
The Acts of the General Assembly.
Philadelphia, Bailey, 1782. [4], xxxi, [1],
527, [1], viii pp.
AAS copy.   17656

Pennsylvania. Laws, Statutes, etc., 1784.
. . . An Act for Opening the Land-Office.
[Philadelphia, 1784.] 4 pp.
LCP copy.   44586

Pennsylvania. Laws, Statutes, etc., 1784.
An Act 1784 for the further Regulation of
the Port of Philadelphia. . . . [Apr. 1,
1784.]
[Philadelphia, 1784.] 8 pp.
(No copy located.)   44587

Pennsylvania. Laws, Statutes, etc., 1784.
. . . An Act to Remedy the Defects of the
several Acts . . . Regulating the Election
of the Justices.
[Philadelphia, 1784.] 8 pp.
LCP copy.   44588

Pennsylvania. Laws, Statutes, etc., 1785.
An Act to Regulate the Elections.
Philadelphia, Bradford, 1785. 22 pp.
LCP copy.   19159

Pennsylvania. Laws, Statutes, etc., 1786.
Abstract of the Laws . . . Relative to
Excise.
Philadelphia, Aitken, 1786. 60 pp.
AAS copy.   19882

Pennsylvania. Laws, Statutes, etc., 1786.
In General Assembly, December 26th,
1785. Resolved, That all Officers. . . .
Philadelphia, Carey, 1786. Broadside.
LCP copy.   44946

Pennsylvania. Laws, Statutes, etc., 1787.
An Act for the Regulation of Bankruptcy
[amended Mar. 15, 1787].
[Philadelphia? 1787?] 15 pp.
JCB copy.   45133

Pennsylvania. Laws, Statutes, etc., 1787.
A Supplement to the Bankrupt Law and
Import Law.
Philadelphia, Bradford, [1787]. 12 pp.
LCP copy.   45134

Pennsylvania. Laws, Statutes, etc., 1788.
An Act, Relating to the Meadows, in
Kingsessing.
Philadelphia, James, 1788. 13 pp.
LCP copy.   45331

Pennsylvania. Laws, Statutes, etc., 1788.
. . . An Act to Explain and Amend . . .
"An Act for the Gradual Abolition of
Slavery". . . . [Mar. 29, 1788.]
Philadelphia, Bradford, [1788].
Broadside.
NYHS copy.   45332

Pennsylvania. Laws, Statutes, etc., 1788.
. . . An Act to Incorporate the Society for
Propagating. . . .
[Philadelphia, 1788.] 4 pp.
(Issued as the 2d part of 45363, q. v.)   45333

[Pennsylvania. Laws, Statutes, etc., 1789.
An Act for Incorporating . . . Saint
George's Church.
Philadelphia, Neall, 1789. 7 pp.]
(A ghost of a much later printing.)   45557

Pennsylvania. Laws, Statutes, etc., 1789.
An Act for Vesting in James Rumsey.
[Philadelphia, 1789.] [3] pp.
JCB copy.   22051

Pennsylvania. Laws, Statutes, etc., 1790.
Acte Donnant Pouvoir aux Aubains . . . le
. . . Onze de Fevrier.
Philadelphia, Bache, [1790]. Broadside.
LOC copy.   45960

Pennsylvania. Laws, Statutes, etc., 1792.
An Act, for Incorporating the Society,
Formed for the Relief of Poor, Aged and
Infirm Masters of Ships.
Philadelphia, Stewart & Cochran, 1792. 35
pp.
NYHS copy.   24664

Pennsylvania. Laws, Statutes, etc., 1792.
An Act . . . for Making an Artificial Road
from the City of Philadelphia to . . .
Lancaster.
[Philadelphia, 1792.] 13 pp.
HSP copy.   24665

Pennsylvania. Laws, Statutes, etc., 1792.
Act of the Legislature of Pennsylvania of
Third April 1792 and Opinions thereon.
[Philadelphia, 1796.] 16 pp.
AAS copy.   30975

Pennsylvania. Laws, Statutes, etc., 1793.
An Act for the Regulation of the Militia.
Philadelphia, Oswald, 1793. 16 pp.
LCP copy.   25969

Pennsylvania. Laws, Statutes, etc., 1793.
Eine Acte zur Einrichtung der Militz.
Philadelphia, Cist, 1793. 31 pp.
LOC copy.   25971

[Pennsylvania. Laws, Statutes, etc., 1793.
The Militia Law.
Carlisle, Kline, 1793.]
(Imprint assumed by Evans from adv.
"Just published" in Kline's Gazette, July
3, 1793.)   25970

[Pennsylvania. Laws, Statutes, etc., 1794.
An Act for Establishing an Health-Office.
[Philadelphia, 1794.] 33 pp.]
(No copy of a separate printing located.)
                                                   27474

Pennsylvania. Laws, Statutes, etc., 1794.
Collection of the Penal Laws.
Philadelphia, Poulson, 1794. 56 pp.
AAS copy.   27478

Pennsylvania. Laws, Statutes, etc., 1794.
Laws . . . Regulating the General
Elections.
Philadelphia, Poulson, 1794. 55 pp.
LOC copy.   47171

Pennsylvania. Laws, Statutes, etc., 1795.
An Act for Establishing an Health
Office. . . . Approved April 17, 1795.
[Philadelphia? 1795?] 44 pp.
AAS copy.   47550

Pennsylvania. Laws, Statutes, etc., 1795.
An Act to Enable the . . . Philadelphia
and Lancaster Turnpike Road to Increase
the Width. . . .

[Philadelphia, 1795.] Broadside.
HSP copy. 47551

Pennsylvania. Laws, Statutes, etc., 1795.
. . . An Act to Enable the President . . . of
the Schuylkill and Susquehanna
Navigation . . . to Raise by . . .
Lottery. . . . Approved, April 17th, 1795.
[Philadelphia], Poulson, [1795].
2 pp.
LCP copy. 47554

Pennsylvania. Laws, Statutes, etc., 1795.
Laws. . . . [Dec. 7, 1790 - Apr. 20, 1795].
Published . . . by Alexander James Dallas.
Vol. III.
Philadelphia, Hall & Sellers, 1795. [6],
xxxix, [1], 793, [1], v, [1], [39] pp.
AAS copy. 29291

Pennsylvania. Laws, Statutes, etc., 1796.
An Act for the Government and
Regulation of Seamen.
Philadelphia, Young, [1796]. Broadside.
HSP copy. 47876

Pennsylvania. Laws, Statutes, etc., 1796.
A Compilation of the Laws of the State
. . . Relative to the Poor, from the Year
1700, to 1795. Published for the Guardians
of the Poor.
Philadelphia, Poulson, 1796. [2], 112, 10
pp.
LCP copy. 30977

Pennsylvania. Laws, Statutes, etc., 1797.
Laws of the Commonwealth. . . . Vol. I.
Philadelphia, Hall & Sellers, 1797. [4],
913, [1], 64, iv, [22] pp.
AAS copy. 32655

Pennsylvania. Laws, Statutes, etc., 1798.
An Act . . . and a Patent to Incorporate a
Company for Erecting a Permanent
Bridge over the River Schuylkill.
Philadelphia, Fenno, [1798]. 21 pp.
MHS copy. 34321

Pennsylvania. Laws, Statutes, etc., 1798.
An Act to Enable the Governor . . . to
Incorporate a Company for the Purpose of
Improving the Navigation of the River
Lehigh.
[Philadelphia, 1798.] 15 pp.
APS copy. 34322

Pennsylvania. Laws, Statutes, etc., 1798.
A Compilation of the Health-Laws of the
State.
Philadelphia, Poulson, 1798. 56 pp.
AAS copy. 34324

Pennsylvania. Laws, Statutes, etc., 1798.
A Further Supplement to the Act Entitled
"An Act for Making an Artificial Road
from . . . Philadelphia to . . .
Lancaster. . . . Approved, April 4th, 1798.
[Philadelphia, 1798.] Broadside.
HSP copy. 34325

Pennsylvania. Laws, Statutes, etc., 1798.
Laws of the Commonwealth. . . . Vol. II.
Philadelphia, Hall & Sellers, 1798. [4], ix,
[1], 817, iii, [33] pp.
(Some copies have imprint date 1793.)
AAS copy. 34331

Pennsylvania. Laws, Statutes, etc., 1799.
An Act for Establishing an Health Office.
Philadelphia, 1799. 28 pp.
AAS copy. 36056

Pennsylvania. Laws, Statutes, etc., 1799.
An Act for the Regulation of the Militia
. . . Approved April 9, 1799.
[Harrisburg? 1799.] 62 pp.
University of Chicago copy. 36057

Pennsylvania. Laws, Statutes, etc., 1799.
An Act to Extend . . . an Artificial Road
. . . to . . . Lancaster.
[Philadelphia, 1799.] Broadside.
HSP copy. 48953

Pennsylvania. Laws, Statutes, etc., 1799.
An Act, to Regulate the General
Elections.
Philadelphia, Baileys, 1799. 40 pp.
HSP copy. 36058

Pennsylvania. Laws, Statutes, etc., 1799.
Extract from the Election Law of
Pennsylvania, 1799.

[Philadelphia? 1799.] Broadside.
LOC copy. 36061

Pennsylvania. Loan Office, 1787.
Philadelphia, June 30, 1787. . . . Trustees
of the General Loan Office. . . .
Philadelphia, Cist, [1787]. Broadside.
(No copy located.) 45135

Pennsylvania. Militia, 1775.
Orders, Thursday, July 27, 1775. The
Light Infantry Company.
[Philadelphia, 1775.] Broadside.
LOC copy. 42887

Pennsylvania. Militia, 1794.
Roll Designating the Quota. . . . 19th Day
of May, 1794.
[Philadelphia? 1794]. Broadside.
(No copy located.) 47172

Pennsylvania. Navy Board, 1777.
Day and Night Signals.
Philadelphia, Bradfords, 1777. 17 leaves.
HSP copy. 15513

Pennsylvania. President, 1779.
By His Excellency Joseph Reed . . . and
the Supreme Executive Council. . . . A
Proclamation [Fort Wilson Rioters, Oct.
6, 1779].
[Philadelphia], Hall & Sellers, 1779.
Broadside.
LCP copy. 16435

Pennsylvania. President, 1779.
By His Excellency Joseph Reed . . . and
the Supreme Executive Council . . . a
Proclamation [Va. Boundary, Dec. 28,
1779].
[Philadelphia], Hall & Sellers, 1779.
Broadside.
LCP copy. 16437

Pennsylvania. President, 1779.
By His Excellency the President, and
Council . . . a Proclamation . . . Cruel and
Inveterate Enemies. . . . April 2, 1779.
[Philadelphia], Hall & Sellers, 1779.
Broadside.
HSP copy. 16431

[Pennsylvania. President, 1779.
By His Excellency the President, and
Council . . . a Proclamation [Fast, May 1.
Dated, Apr. 16, 1779].
[Philadelphia], Hall & Sellers, 1779.
Broadside.]
(No copy located.) 16432

Pennsylvania. President, 1779.
A Proclamation. By His Excellency
Joseph Reed . . . and the Supreme
Executive Council [Embargo, Apr. 30,
1779].
[Philadelphia], Hall & Sellers, 1779.
Broadside.
LCP copy. 16433

Pennsylvania. President, 1779.
A Proclamation by His Excellency Joseph
Reed . . . and the Supreme Executive
Council [Treason, June 22, 1779].
[Philadelphia], Hall & Sellers, 1779.
Broadside.
LCP copy. 16434

Pennsylvania. President, 1780.
By His Excellency Joseph Reed. . . . A
Proclamation [Ill-Disposed Persons. Apr.
16, 1780].
[Philadelphia], Hall & Sellers, 1780.
Broadside.
LCP copy. 16926

Pennsylvania. President, 1780.
By His Excellency Joseph Reed. . . . A
Proclamation [Savages. Apr. 22, 1780].
[Philadelphia, 1780.] Broadside.
LCP copy. 16925

[Pennsylvania. President, 1780.
By His Excellency Joseph Reed. . . . A
Proclamation [State Finances. Dec. 23,
1780].
Philadelphia, Dunlap, [1780]. Broadside.]
(No broadside printing located.) 16927

Pennsylvania. President, 1780.
By His Excellency Joseph Reed. . . . A
Proclamation. To all Justices of the Peace
[July 25, 1780]. . . .

[Philadelphia, 1780.] Broadside.
LOC copy. 43865

Pennsylvania. President, 1780.
By His Excellency Joseph Reed . . . A
Proclamation. Whereas Divers of the
Inhabitants. . . . [Mar. 25, 1780.]
[Philadelphia], Hall & Sellers, 1780.
Broadside.
LOC copy. 43866

Pennsylvania. President, 1781.
By His Excellency Joseph Reed . . . a
Proclamation [Bills of Credit. May 11,
1781].
[Philadelphia], Hall & Sellers, [1781].
Broadside.
LCP copy. 17283

Pennsylvania. President, 1781.
By His Excellency Joseph Reed . . . a
Proclamation [Spurious Coins. July 14,
1781].
[Philadelphia], Bailey, [1781]. Broadside.
LCP copy. 17284

Pennsylvania. President, 1782.
. . . By the President and Supreme
Executive Council . . . a Proclamation
[Suppression of Vice. Nov. 20, 1782].
[Philadelphia], Bailey, [1782]. Broadside.
AAS copy. 17664

Pennsylvania. President, 1783.
. . . By the President and the Supreme
Executive Council. . . . A Proclamation
[Cessation of Arms. Apr. 16, 1783].
[Philadelphia, Bailey, 1783]. Broadside.
LCP copy. 18086

Pennsylvania. President, 1783.
. . . By the President and Supreme
Executive Council . . . A Proclamation
[Connecticut Boundary. Jan. 6, 1783].
[Philadelphia], Bailey, [1783]. Broadside.
AAS copy. 18084

Pennsylvania. President, 1783.
. . . By the President and the Supreme
Executive Council . . . A Proclamation
[Continental Thanksgiving, Dec. 1783.
Dated Oct. 30, 1783.].
[Philadelphia, Bailey, 1783]. Broadside.
LCP copy. 18089

Pennsylvania. President, 1783.
. . . By the President and Supreme
Executive Council . . . a Proclamation
[Molineaux Murder. July 24, 1783].
[Philadelphia, Bailey, 1783]. Broadside.
LCP copy. 18087

Pennsylvania. President, 1783.
. . . By the President and the Supreme
Executive Council. . . . a Proclamation
[Reward for Robbers. July 26, 1783].
[Philadelphia, Bailey, 1783]. Broadside.
LCP copy. 18088

Pennsylvania. President, 1783.
. . . By the President and Supreme
Executive Council. . . . A Proclamation
[Spurious British Half-Pence. Aug. 13,
1783].
[Philadelphia, Bailey, 1783]. Broadside.
LCP copy. 18091

Pennsylvania. President, 1783.
. . . By the President and Supreme
Executive Council . . . A Proclamation
[Susquehannah Land. July 31, 1783].
[Philadelphia], Bailey, [1783]. Broadside.
LCP copy. 18090

Pennsylvania. President, 1783.
. . . By the President and the Supreme
Executive Council . . . a Proclamation
[Virginia Boundary. Mar. 26, 1783].
[Philadelphia], Bailey, [1783]. Broadside.
LCP copy. 18085

Pennsylvania. President, 1783.
By the President and the Supreme
Executive Council . . . a Proclamation.
Whereas by an Act [Sept. 13, 1783].
[Philadelphia], Bailey, [1783]. Broadside.
LCP copy. 44437

Pennsylvania. President, 1784.
. . . By the President and the Supreme
Executive Council. . . . A Proclamation
[Buoys. May 31, 1784].

[Philadelphia, 1784.] Broadside.
LOC copy.   18688

Pennsylvania. President, 1784.
. . . By the President and the Supreme
Executive Council. . . . A Proclamation
[Murder of Richard Marple. Mar. 24,
1784].
[Philadelphia, 1784.] Broadside.
LOC copy.   18686

[Pennsylvania. President, 1784.
. . . By the President and Supreme
Executive Council. . . . A Proclamation
[Murder of Samuel Dean. Mar. 24, 1784].
[Philadelphia, 1784.] Broadside.]
(No copy located.)   18685

[Pennsylvania. President, 1784.
By the President and the Supreme
Executive Council . . . a Proclamation
[Peace of Paris. January 22, 1784].
[Philadelphia, 1784.] Broadside.]
(No copy located.)   18822

Pennsylvania. President, 1784.
. . . By the President and the Supreme
Executive Council . . . a Proclamation
[Robbery of Thomas Leaming, May 12.
Dated May 15, 1784].
[Philadelphia, 1784.] Broadside.
LOC copy.   18687

Pennsylvania. President, 1784.
. . . By the President and the Supreme
Executive Council . . . A Proclamation.
Whereas [Wyoming Oct. 5, 1784].
[Philadelphia, 1784.] Broadside.
LCP copy.   44590

Pennsylvania. President, 1784.
By the President and the Supreme
Executive Council . . . a Proclamation.
Whereas by Dispositions . . . [de
Longchamps June 4, 1784]. . . .
[Philadelphia, 1784.] Broadside.
LCP copy.   44589

Pennsylvania. President, 1787.
. . . By the President and Supreme
Executive Council. . . . A Proclamation
. . . Riot. . . . November 12, 1787.
NYPL ph. copy.   20624

Pennsylvania. President, 1787.
By the President and Supreme Executive
Council. . . . A Proclamation [Shays. Mar.
10, 1787].
[Philadelphia, 1787.] Broadside.
MHS copy.   20623

Pennsylvania. Register General, 1789.
Statement of the Public Accounts . . . to
the Thirtieth of September, 1789.
[Philadelphia? 1789.] 7 pp.
(Not located.)
LCP copy.   45558

Pennsylvania. Register General, 1790.
Report of the . . . to the . . . Committee of
Ways and Means.
Philadelphia, Hall & Sellers, 1790.
NYPL ph (tp. only) copy.   45961

Pennsylvania. Register General, 1795.
Report . . . of . . . the Finances of
Pennsylvania, for the Year MDCCXCIV.
Philadelphia, Poulson, [1795]. 19 pp.
AAS copy.   29293

Pennsylvania. Register General, 1796.
Report . . . of the Finances of
Pennsylvania, for the Year M,DCC,XCV.
Philadelphia, Baileys, [1796]. 19, [1], 12
pp.
AAS copy.   30981

Pennsylvania. Register-General, 1796.
Report . . . of the Finances of
Pennsylvania, for the Year 1795.
Philadelphia, Poulson, [1796]. 19 pp.
LCP copy.   30982

Pennsylvania. Register General, 1797.
Report of . . . the Finances of
Pennsylvania, for the Year 1796.
Philadelphia, Poulson, 1797. 19 pp.
(This is the printing made for inclusion
with the Senate Journals. For the Hall &
Sellers ed., see the House Journals,
32651.)
LCP copy.   32657

Pennsylvania. Register General, 1798.
Report . . . for the Year 1797.
Philadelphia, Poulson, 1798. 19 pp.
LCP copy.   34334

Pennsylvania. Register-General, 1798.
(Appendix.) Report . . . of Finances . . .
for . . . M, DCC, XCVII.
Philadelphia, F. & R. Bailey, [1798]. 19
pp.
LCP copy.   48566

Pennsylvania. Register-General, 1798.
Report . . . of the Finances of . . .
Pennsylvania, for . . . 1798.
Philadelphia, Poulson, 1799. 17 pp.
LCP copy.   36068

Pennsylvania, Register General, 1799.
Report . . . of the Finances of . . .
Pennsylvania, for the Year 1799.
Lancaster, Hamilton, 1800. 19 (i.e. 17) pp.
(Also issued bound with 28214, q. v.)
                                            38222

Pennsylvania. Receiver General, 1800.
The Receiver-General most Respectfully
begs leave to Submit. . . . January 6th,
1800.
[Lancaster, 1800.] 3 pp.
LCP copy.   49132

Pennsylvania. Register-General, 1800.
Mein Herr, In Befolgung . . . 13ten
Jenner, 1800.
[Philadelphia ? 1800.] Broadside.
HSP copy.   36064

Pennsylvania. Secretary of the
Commonwealth, 1794.
Gentlemen, The Governor Having
Received Information, that a . . . Cruel
Outrage. . . . 25th July, 1794.
[Philadelphia, 1794.] [4] pp.
(Copy not available.)   47173

Pennsylvania. Secretary of the
Commonwealth, 1798.
Letter . . . Relative to the Late Malignant
Fever.
Philadelphia, Bradfords, 1798. 16 pp.
AAS copy.   34332

Pennsylvania. Senate Journals, 1790.
Journal of the Senate [Dec. 7, 1790 - Sept.
30, 1791].
Philadelphia, Poulson, [1791]. 355 pp.
LOC copy.   23677

[Pennsylvania. Senate Journals, 1790.
Tagebuch des Senats, 1790-1791.
Germantown, Billmeyer, 1791.]
(Entry from Seidensticker who was
sometimes misled by German language
advs. for English eds.)   23685

Pennsylvania. Senate Journals, 1791.
Journals of the Senate [Dec. 6, 1791 -
Apr. 10, 1792].
Philadelphia, Poulson, [1791]. 266 pp.
LOC copy.   24670

[Pennsylvania. Senate Journals, 1791.
Tagebuch des Senats. . . . 1791-1792.
Germantown, Billmeyer, 1792.]
(Entry from Seidensticker, who was
apparently misled by German-language
advs. for 24670.)   24671

Pennsylvania. Senate Journals, 1792.
Journal of the Senate [Dec. 4, 1792 - Sept.
5, 1793].
Philadelphia, Poulson, [1793]. 308 pp.
LCP copy.   25975

Pennsylvania. Senate Journals, 1793.
Journal of the Senate. . . . Volume IV
[Dec. 3, 1793 - Apr. 22, 1794].
Philadelphia, Poulson, [1794]. 252 pp.
LCP copy.   27482

[Pennsylvania. Senate Journals, 1793.
Tagebuch des Senats . . . 1793 - 1794.
Germantown, Billmeyer, 1794.]
(Entry assumed by Seidensticker from a
German-language adv. of the English ed.)
                                            27486

Pennsylvania. Senate Journals, 1794.
Journal of the Senate [Sept. 1-23, 1794].
Philadelphia, Poulson, [1794]. pp. 253-304.
LCP copy.   27483

Pennsylvania. Senate Journals, 1794.
Journal of the Proceedings of the Senate
. . . when Sitting for the Purpose of Trying
an Impeachment.
Philadelphia, Poulson, [1794]. 18 pp.
LCP copy.   27484

Pennsylvania. Senate Journals, 1794.
Journal of the Senate. . . . Volume V
[Dec. 2, 1794-Apr. 20, 1795].
Philadelphia, Poulson, [1795]. 289 pp.
LCP copy.   29289

Pennsylvania. Senate Journals, 1794.
Tagebuch des Senate. . . . [Dec. 20, 1794 -
Apr. 20, 1795].
Germantown, Billmeyer, [1795]. 289 pp.
LOC copy.   29290

Pennsylvania. Senate Journals, 1795.
Journal of the Senate. . . . Volume VI
[Dec. 1, 1795-Apr. 4, 1796].
Philadelphia, Poulson, [1796].
249 pp.
                                            30980

Pennsylvania. Senate Journals, 1796.
Journal of the Senate [Dec. 6, 1796 - Aug.
29, 1797].
Philadelphia, Poulson, 1796. 319 pp.
LCP copy.   32653

[Pennsylvania. Senate Journals, 1796.
Tagebuch des Senats. . . . 1796-1797.
Germantown, Billmeyer, 1797.]
(Apparently a ghost of 32653 arising from
a German-language adv.)   32654

Pennsylvania. Senate Journals, 1797.
Journal of the Senate [Dec. 5, 1797-Apr.
5, 1798].
Philadelphia, Poulson, 1797. 278 pp.
LCP copy.   34329

[Pennsylvania. Senate Journals, 1797.
Tagebuch des Senats. . . . 1797-1798.
Germantown, Billmeyer, 1798.]
(Assumed by Seidensticker, apparently
from a German-language adv. for the
English ed.)   34330

Pennsylvania. Senate Journals, 1798.
Journal of the Senate. . . . Volume IX
[Dec. 4, 1798 - Apr. 11, 1799].
Philadelphia, Poulson, 1798. 371, 8, 61, 17
pp.
LCP copy.   36063

[Pennsylvania. Senate Journals, 1798.
Tagebuch des Senate. . . . 1798-1799.
Germantown, Billmeyer, 1799.]
(Ordered printed by the Senate.)   36069

Pennsylvania. Senate Journals, 1799.
Journal of the Senate. . . . Volume X
[Dec. 3, 1799 +].
Lancaster, Hamilton, [1800]. 281, [1], 19,
[1], 59 pp.
                                            38214

[Pennsylvania. Senate Journals, 1800.
Journal des Senates [Nov. 15, 1800?].
Lancaster, Albrecht, 1800.]
(Reported in 1955, but not to be found in
1964.)   38211

Pennsylvania. Senate Journals, 1800.
Journal of the Senate. . . . Volume XI
[Nov. 5, 1800 +].
Lancaster, Hamilton, 1800. 356, 66, 6, 21
pp.
LCP copy.   38215

[Pennsylvania. Session Laws, 1776.
At a General Assembly [Feb. 12 - June
15, 1776].
Philadelphia, Hall & Sellers, 1776. [2]
pp.
(No acts were passed so only the title-page
was printed. The unique copy is mislaid.)
                                            14973

Pennsylvania. Session Laws, 1776.
Laws Enacted [Nov. 28, 1776 +].
Philadelphia, Dunlap, 1777. [2], 48, [1]
pp.
HSP copy.   15539

Pennsylvania. Session Laws, 1777.
Laws Enacted [May 12, 1777 +].
Lancaster, 1777. pp. [2], 51-65, [2].
HSP copy.   15540

Pennsylvania. Session Laws, 1777.
Laws Enacted in the Second General
Assembly [Oct. 7, 1777 +].
Lancaster, 1778. pp. [2], 71-100.
HSP copy.   15968

Pennsylvania. Session Laws, 1778.
Laws Enacted in the Second Sitting of the
Second General Assembly [Feb. 18,
1778].
[Lancaster, 1778.] pp. 101-132.
HSP copy.   15969

Pennsylvania. Session Laws, 1778.
Laws Enacted in the Third Sitting of the
Second General Assembly [May 13,
1778].
[Lancaster, 1778.] pp. 133-136.
HSP copy.   15970

Pennsylvania. Session Laws, 1778.
Laws Enacted in the Fourth Sitting of the
Second General Assembly [Aug. 4,
1778 +].
[Philadelphia, 1778.] pp. 137-164.
HSP copy.   15971

Pennsylvania. Session Laws, 1778.
Laws Enacted at the Third General
Assembly [Oct. 26, 1778 +].
Philadelphia, Dunlap, 1778. pp. [2],
167-177, [1].
HSP copy.   15972

Pennsylvania. Session Laws, 1779.
Laws Enacted in the Second Sitting of the
Third General Assembly [Feb. 1, 1779 +].
[Philadelphia, 1779.] pp. 177-228.
LOC copy.   16428

Pennsylvania. Session Laws, 1779.
Laws Enacted in the Third Sitting of the
Third General Assembly [Aug. 30,
1779 +].
[Philadelphia, 1779.] pp. 229-260.
LOC copy.   16429

Pennsylvania. Session Laws, 1779.
Laws Enacted in the First Sitting of the
Fourth General Assembly [Oct. 25,
1779 +].
[Philadelphia, 1779.] pp. 261-280, [2].
LOC copy   16430

Pennsylvania. Session Laws, 1780.
Laws Enacted in the Second Sitting of the
Fourth General Assembly [Jan. 19,
1780 +].
[Philadelphia, 1780.] pp. 283-365, [1].
NYPL copy.   16930

Pennsylvania. Session Laws, 1780.
Laws Enacted in the Third Sitting of the
Fourth General Assembly [May 10, 1780
+].
[Philadelphia], Dunlap, [1780]. pp.
367-384.
NYPL copy.   16931

Pennsylvania. Session Laws, 1780.
Laws Enacted in the Fourth Sitting of the
Fourth General Assembly [Sept. 1, 1780].
[Philadelphia], Dunlap, [1780]. pp.
385-394, [1].
NYPL copy.   16932

Pennsylvania. Session Laws, 1780.
Laws of the First Sitting of the Fifth
General Assembly [Oct. 23, 1780 +].
[Philadelphia], Dunlap, [1780]. pp.
397-417, [1].
LOC copy.   16933

Pennsylvania. Session Laws, 1781.
Laws Enacted in the Second Sitting of the
Fifth General Assembly [Feb. 6, 1781 +].
[Philadelphia], Dunlap, [1781]. pp.
395-432, [2].
LOC copy.   17289

Pennsylvania. Session Laws, 1781.
Laws Enacted in the Third Sitting of the
Fifth General Assembly [May 24, 1781].
[Philadelphia, 1781.] pp. 459-476.
LOC copy.   17290

Pennsylvania. Session Laws, 1781.
Laws Enacted in the Fourth Sitting, of the
Fifth General Assembly [Sept. 4, 1781 +].
[Philadelphia, 1781.] pp. 477-488.
LOC copy.   17291

Pennsylvania. Session Laws, 1781.

Laws Enacted in the Sixth General
Assembly. . . . Vol. II [Oct. 22, 1781 +].
Philadelphia, Hall & Sellers, 1782.
8 pp.
LOC copy.   17659

Pennsylvania. Session Laws, 1782.
Laws Enacted in the Second Sitting of the
Sixth General Assembly [Feb. 11, 1782
+].
Philadelphia, Hall & Sellers, 1782. pp.
9-81, [2].
LOC copy.   17660

Pennsylvania. Session Laws, 1782.
Laws Enacted in the Third Sitting of the
Sixth General Assembly [Aug. 1, 1782 +].
Philadelphia, Hall & Sellers, 1782. pp.
85-110, [2].
LOC copy.   17661

Pennsylvania. Session Laws, 1782.
Laws Enacted in the Seventh General
Assembly [Oct. 28, 1782 +].
Philadelphia, Hall & Sellers, 1782. pp.
[2], 115-126.
LOC copy.   17662

Pennsylvania. Session Laws, 1783.
Laws Enacted in the Second Sitting of the
Seventh General Assembly [Jan. 15,
1783 +].
[Philadelphia], Hall & Sellers, [1783], pp.
127-184.
LOC copy.   18094

Pennsylvania. Session Laws, 1783.
Laws Enacted in the Third Sitting of the
Seventh General Assembly [Aug. 14,
1783 +].
[Philadelphia, 1783.] pp. 185-254, [2].
LOC copy.   18095

Pennsylvania. Session Laws, 1783.
Laws Enacted in the First Sitting of the
Eighth General Assembly [Oct. 27,
1783 +].
[Philadelphia], Bradford, [1783]. pp.
255-270, [2].
LOC copy.   18096

Pennsylvania. Session Laws, 1784.
Laws Enacted in the Second Sitting of the
Eighth General Assembly [Jan. 13,
1784 +].
Philadelphia, Bradford, [1784]. pp.
271-368, iii.
NYPL copy.   18681

Pennsylvania. Session Laws, 1784.
Laws Enacted in the Third Sitting of the
Eighth General Assembly [July 20, 1784
+].
[Philadelphia], Bradford, [1784]. pp.
371-399, [2], [1]-3.
LOC copy.   18682

Pennsylvania, Session Laws, 1784.
Laws Enacted in the First Sitting of the
Ninth General Assembly [Oct. 25, 1784
+].
[Philadelphia], Bradford, [1784]. pp.
401-415, [1].
NYPL copy.   18683

Pennsylvania. Session Laws, 1785.
Laws Enacted in the Second Sitting of the
Ninth General Assembly [Feb. 1 - Apr. 8,
1785].
Philadelphia, Bradford, [1785]. pp.
417-587, i-iv.
LOC copy.   19160

Pennsylvania. Session Laws, 1785.
Laws Enacted in the Third Sitting of the
Ninth General Assembly [Aug. 23 - Sept.
23, 1785].
Philadelphia, Bradford, [1785]. pp.
589-704, i-iii.
LOC copy.   19161

Pennsylvania. Session Laws, 1785.
Laws Enacted at the First Sitting of the
Tenth General Assembly [Oct. 24, 1785 -
Dec. 24, 1785].
Philadelphia, Bradford, [1786]. 8, [1] pp.
LOC copy.   19885

Pennsylvania. Session Laws, 1786.
Laws Enacted in the Second Sitting of the
Tenth General Assembly [Feb. 21 - Apr.
8, 1786].

Philadelphia, Bradford, [1786]. pp. 9-87,
[1], 1-4.
LOC copy.   19886

Pennsylvania. Session Laws, 1786.
Laws Enacted in the Third Sitting of the
Tenth General Assembly [Aug. 22 - Sept.
27, 1786].
Philadelphia, Bradford, [1786]. pp.
[89]-179, [3].
LOC copy.   19887

Pennsylvania. Session Laws, 1786.
Laws Enacted in the First Sitting of the
Eleventh General Assembly [Oct. 23 -
Dec. 30, 1786].
[Philadelphia, 1787.] pp. 181-194, [2].
LOC copy.   20626

Pennsylvania. Session Laws, 1787.
Laws Enacted in the Second Sitting of the
Eleventh General Assembly [Feb. 20 -
Mar. 29, 1787].
[Philadelphia, 1787.] pp. 195-313, iv.
LOC copy.   20627

Pennsylvania. Session Laws, 1787.
Laws Enacted in the Third Sitting of the
Eleventh General Assembly [Sept. 4 - 29,
1787].
Philadelphia, Bradford, [1787]. pp.
315-400, ii.
LOC copy.   20628

Pennsylvania. Session Laws, 1787.
Laws Enacted in the First Sitting of the
Twelfth General Assembly [Oct. 22 - Nov.
27, 1787].
Philadelphia, Bradford, [1787]. pp.
401-404, [2].
LOC copy.   20629

Pennsylvania. Session Laws, 1788.
Laws Enacted in the Second Sitting of the
Twelfth General Assembly [Feb. 19 -
Mar. 29, 1788].
[Philadelphia, 1788.] pp. [404]-454, [2].
NYPL copy.   21366

Pennsylvania. Session Laws, 1788.
Laws Enacted in the Third Sitting of the
Twelfth General Assembly [Sept. 2 - Oct.
4, 1788].
[Philadelphia, 1788.] pp. [455]-537, [2].
NYPL copy.   21367

Pennsylvania. Session Laws, 1788.
Laws Enacted in the First Sitting of the
Thirteenth General Assembly [Oct. 27 -
Nov. 22, 1788].
Philadelphia, Bradford, [1788]. 7, [1] pp.
LOC copy.   21368

Pennsylvania. Session Laws, 1789.
Laws of the Thirteenth General Assembly
. . . Second Sitting [Feb. 3 - Mar. 28,
1789].
Philadelphia, Bradford, [1789]. pp. [9] -
104 (i.e., 108).
LCP copy.   22054

Pennsylvania. Session Laws, 1789.
Laws of the Thirteenth General Assembly
. . . Third Sitting [Aug. 18 - Sept. 30,
1789].
[Philadelphia, 1789.] pp. [105] - 203, [3].
LCP copy.   22055

Pennsylvania. Session Laws, 1789.
Laws of the Fourteenth General Assembly
. . . First Sitting [Oct. 26 - Dec. 9, 1789].
[Philadelphia, 1790.] pp. [205]-232, [2].
HSP copy.   22762

Pennsylvania. Session Laws, 1789.
Laws of the Fourteenth General Assembly
. . . Second Sitting [Feb. 2 - Apr. 6, 1790].
Philadelphia, Bradford, [1790]. pp. [233]
- 317.
HSP copy.   22763

Pennsylvania. Session Laws, 1790.
Acts of the General Assembly [Dec. 7,
1790 - Apr. 13, 1791].
Philadelphia, Hall & Sellers, 1791. xxxix,
108 pp.
LOC copy.   23670

Pennsylvania. Session Laws, 1791.
Acts of the General Assembly [Aug. 23 -
Sept. 30, 1791].

Philadelphia, Hall & Sellers, 1791. pp.
[2], [111]-174.
LOC copy.   23671

Pennsylvania. Session Laws, 1791.
Acts of the General Assembly [Dec. 6,
1792 (i.e. 1791) - Apr. 10, 1792].
Philadelphia, Hall & Sellers, 1792. pp.
[175]-289.
LOC copy.   24666

Pennsylvania. Session Laws, 1792.
Acts of the General Assembly [Dec. 4,
1792 - Apr. 11, 1793].
Philadelphia, Hall & Sellers, 1793. pp.
[291]-442.
LOC copy.   25972

Pennsylvania. Session Laws, 1793.
Acts of the General Assembly [Aug. 27 -
Sept. 5, 1793].
Philadelphia, Hall & Sellers, 1793. pp.
[443]-450, [1].
LOC copy.   25973

Pennsylvania. Session Laws, 1793.
Acts of the General Assembly [Dec. 3,
1793-Mar. 31, 1794].
Philadelphia, Hall & Sellers, 1794. pp.
[2], 455-623.
LOC copy.   27476

Pennsylvania. Session Laws, 1794.
Acts of the General Assembly [Sept. 1 -
23, 1794].
Philadelphia, Hall & Sellers, 1794. pp.
[2], 627-644, [1] pp.
LOC copy.   27477

Pennsylvania. Session Laws, 1794.
Acts of the General Assembly [Dec. 2,
1794 - Feb. 25, 1795].
Philadelphia, Hall & Sellers, 1795. pp.
[647] - 793, i - v, [39].
LOC copy.   29285

Pennsylvania. Session Laws, 1795.
Acts of the General Assembly [Dec. 1-23,
1795].
Philadelphia, Hall & Sellers, 1796. [2], 89
pp.
AAS copy.   30976

Pennsylvania. Session Laws, 1796.
Acts of the General Assembly [Dec. 6,
1796 - Feb. 14, 1797].
Philadelphia, Hall & Sellers, 1797. pp.
[91]-182.
AAS copy.   32648

Pennsylvania. Session Laws, 1797.
Acts of the General Assembly [Aug. 28 -
29, 1797].
Philadelphia, Hall & Sellers, 1797. pp.
[183] - 186.
AAS copy.   32649

Pennsylvania. Session Laws, 1798.
Acts of the General Assembly [Feb.
24-Apr. 5, 1798].
Philadelphia, Hall & Sellers, 1798. pp.
[187]-316.
AAS copy.   34323

Pennsylvania. Session Laws, 1798.
Acts of the General Assembly [Dec. 4,
1798 - Apr. 11, 1799].
Philadelphia, Hall & Sellers, 1799. pp.
[317] - 527.
AAS copy.   36059

Pennsylvania. Session Laws, 1799.
Acts of the General Assembly [Dec. 3,
1799 - Mar. 15, 1800].
Lancaster, Baileys, 1800. pp. [529]-622
(i.e. 621).
AAS copy.   38208

Pennsylvania. Supreme Court.
Rules and Orders for Regulating the
Practice of. . . .
Philadelphia, 1788. 29 pp.
(Evans' entry is apparently a ghost of
this.)
AAS copy.   20633

Pennsylvania. Supreme Executive
Council, 1777.
By the Supreme Executive Council. . . . A
Proclamation [Fast, Apr. 3. Dated Mar.
7, 1777].
[Philadelphia, 1777.] Broadside.
LCP copy.   15509

Pennsylvania. Supreme Executive
Council, 1777.
By the Supreme Executive Council . . . a
Proclamation [Invasion. Sept. 10, 1777].
Philadelphia, Steiner & Cist, [1777].
Broadside.
LCP copy.   15510

Pennsylvania. Supreme Executive
Council, 1778.
. . . By the Supreme Executive Council.
Proclamation [Fast, Dec. 30. Dated Nov.
26, 1778].
Philadelphia, Dunlap, [1778]. Broadside.
HSP copy.   15978

Pennsylvania. Supreme Executive
Council, 1778.
Pennsylvania, ss. A Proclamation
[Attainted Persons. May 8, 1778].
Lancaster, [1778]. [2] pp.
LCP copy.   15975

Pennsylvania. Supreme Executive
Council, 1778.
Pennsylvania ss. A Proclamation
[Surrender. Dated May 21, 1778].
Lancaster, [1778]. Broadside.
LCP copy.   15976

Pennsylvania. Supreme Executive
Council, 1778.
Pennsylvania, ss. A Proclamation
[Surrender. Dated Oct. 30, 1778].
Philadelphia, Dunlap, [1778]. Broadside.
LCP copy.   15977

Pennsylvania. Supreme Executive
Council, 1779.
In Council. Philadelphia, February 3d,
1779. This Board [Gen. Arnold].
Philadelphia, Bailey, [1779]. Broadside.
MHS copy.   16439

Pennsylvania. Supreme Executive
Council, 1779.
In Council. Philadelphia, July 8, 1779.
Whereas it is. . . .
Philadelphia, Bailey, [1779]. Broadside.
LCP copy.   16441

Pennsylvania. Supreme Executive
Council, 1779.
In Council. Philadelphia, May 28th, 1779.
Whereas it has been. . . .
Philadelphia, Dunlap, [1779]. Broadside.
LCP copy.   16440

Pennsylvania. Supreme Executive
Council, 1779.
In Council. Philadelphia, October 13,
1779. [Militia].
[Philadelphia, 1779.] Broadside.
LCP copy.   16442

Pennsylvania. Supreme Executive
Council, 1779.
In Council. Philadelphia, October 26,
1779. To the Merchants. . . .
Philadelphia, Bailey, 1779. 6, [2] pp.
HSP copy.   16443

Pennsylvania. Supreme Executive
Council, 1779.
Proceedings . . . in the Case of Major
General Arnold.
[Philadelphia], Hall & Sellers, 1779. 11
pp.
LOC copy.   16448

Pennsylvania. Supreme Executive
Council, 1780.
An Address . . . to the Inhabitants of
Pennsylvania. . . . Council Chamber,
August 7, 1780.
[Philadelphia, 1780.] Broadside.
LOC copy.   43867

Pennsylvania. Supreme Executive
Council, 1780.
In Council. January 3, 1780. Instructions
to the Lieutenants.
[Philadelphia, 1780.] Broadside.
LOC copy.   16928

[Pennsylvania. Supreme Executive
Council, 1780.
In Council, Philadelphia June 1, 1780. Sir,
The Continental Army. . . .
[Philadelphia, 1780.] Broadside.]
(Vote not located in broadside form.)
                                         16929

Pennsylvania. Supreme Executive
Council, 1780.
To the Merchants and Traders of the City
of Philadelphia.
[Philadelphia, 1780?] Broadside.
(No copy located.)   43868

Pennsylvania. Supreme Executive
Council, 1781.
Arrangement of the Pennsylvania Line,
January 17, 1781.
Philadelphia, Bailey, [1781]. 15 pp.
AAS copy.   17282

Pennsylvania. Supreme Executive
Council, 1781.
In Council, May 4, 1781 [Rate of
Exchange].
[Philadelphia], Bailey, [1781]. Broadside.
LCP copy.   17288

Pennsylvania. Supreme Executive
Council, 1781.
In Council, Philadelphia, February 15,
1781. [Recruits].
[Philadelphia], Bailey, [1781]. Broadside.
LOC copy.   17286

Pennsylvania. Supreme Executive
Council, 1781.
In Council, Philadelphia. March 10, 1781
[Recruiting Bounties].
[Philadelphia], Bailey, [1781]. Broadside.
HSP copy.   17287

[Pennsylvania. Supreme Executive
Council, 1782.
In the Name and by the Authority of the
Freemen. . . .
[Philadelphia, 1782.] Broadside.]
(No copy located.)   17657

[Pennsylvania. Supreme Executive
Council, 1784.
At a Meeting at the Council Chamber,
15th September, 1784.
[Philadelphia, 1784.] Broadside.
(Hildeburn 4423; no copy located.) 18678

Pennsylvania. Supreme Executive
Council, 1786.
State of the Accounts of Fees, Received
by the Secretary of the Supreme Executive
Council. . . . 1786 . . . 1790.
Philadelphia. Oswald, 1790. 11 pp.
(The only copy located could not be
filmed.)   22767

Pennsylvania. Supreme Executive
Council, 1787.
. . . A Proclamation. . . . Patents from
Virginia [dated Sept. 26, 1787].
[Philadelphia], Bailey, [1787]. Broadside.
(No copy located.)   45136

Pennsylvania. Supreme Executive
Council, 1788.
. . . By the Vice-President and the
Supreme Executive Council. . . . A
Proclamation. . . . Timothy Pickering.
[Philadelphia? 1788.] Broadside.
JCB copy.   45335

Pennsylvania. Supreme Executive
Council, 1790.
. . . Met at Philadelphia, the 18th of
December, 1790. . . .
[Philadelphia, 1790.] Broadside.
HSP copy.   45962

Pennsylvania. Supreme Executive
Council, 1791.
The Supreme Executive Council met at
Philadelphia.
[Philadelphia, 1791.] Broadside.
HSP copy.   46256

Pennsylvania. Treasurer, 1791.
Balance Account. David Rittenhouse,
Esq., late Treasurer.
[Philadelphia, 1791?] [3] pp.
HSP copy.   46254

Pennsylvania. Treasurer, 1791.
List of Deliquent [sic.] Collectors. . . .
March 28th, 1791.
Carlisle, Kline & Reynolds, [1791].
Broadside.
HSP copy.   46255

Pennsylvania. Treasury Dept., 1787.
A State of the Finances of the
Commonwealth. . . . November 7th, 1787.

Philadelphia, Hall & Sellers, [1787]. 11 pp.
MHS copy.   45137

Pennsylvania. Treasury Dept., 1795.
Accounts of the Treasury . . . from the First of January to the Thirty-First of December [1795].
Philadelphia, Baileys, [1796]. 12 pp.
(This is signatured to 30981 q. v.)   30973

Pennsylvania. Treasury Dept., 1795.
Accounts of the Treasury.
Philadelphia, Hall & Sellers, 1795. 8 pp.
LOC copy.   47552

Pennsylvania. Treasury Dept., 1795.
Accounts of the Treasury of Pennsylvania, from the First of January to the Thirty-First of December, [1795].
Philadelphia, Poulson, [1796]. 12 pp.
LCP copy.   30974

Pennsylvania. Treasury Dept., 1796.
Accounts of the Treasury . . . from the First of January to the Thirty-First of December [1796].
Philadelphia, Poulson, 1797. 12 pp.
LCP copy.   32646

Pennsylvania. Treasury Dept., 1797.
(Appendix.) Receipts and Expenditures in the Treasury . . . 1797.
Philadelphia, F. & R. Bailey, 1798. 62 pp.
LCP copy.   48567

Pennsylvania. Treasury Dept., 1797.
Receipts and Expenditures in the Treasury. . . . 1797.
Philadelphia, Poulson, 1798. 62 pp.
LCP copy.   34333

Pennsylvania. Treasury Dept., 1798.
Receipts and Expenditures in the Treasury of Pennsylvania, from the First of January to the Thirty-First of December, 1798.
Philadelphia, Poulson, 1799. 61 pp.
AAS copy.   36066

Pennsylvania. Treasury Dept., 1799.
Receipts and Expenditures . . . from the First of January to the Thirty-First of December, 1799.
Lancaster, Hamilton, 1800. 59 pp.
LCP copy.   38218

Pennsylvania. Treasury Dept., 1800.
Receipts and Expenditures. . . . from the First of January to the Twenty-Ninth of November, 1800.
Lancaster, Hamilton, 1800. 66 pp.
(Also issued as the second part of 38215, q. v.)   38219

Pennsylvania. University.
Account of the Commencement in the College of Philadelphia, May 17, 1775.
[Philadelphia, 1775.] 15 pp.
UOP copy.   14395

Pennsylvania. University.
An Exercise, Containing a Dialogue and Ode. . . . May 18th, 1762.
Philadelphia, Dunlap, 1762. 8 pp.
HSP copy.   9108

Pennsylvania. University.
An Exercise, Containing a Dialogue and Ode. . . . May 17th, 1763.
Philadelphia, Steuart, 1763. 8 pp.
LCP copy.   9484

Pennsylvania. University.
An Exercise, containing a Dialogue and Ode. . . . November 17, 1767.
Philadelphia, Goddard, [1767]. 8 pp.
HSP copy.   10594

Pennsylvania. University.
An Exercise; Containing a Dialogue and Two Odes. . . . May 17th, 1775.
Philadelphia, Crukshank, 1775. 8 pp.
LCP copy.   14396

Pennsylvania. University.
An Exercise, Performed at the Public Commencement . . . July 17, 1790.
Philadelphia, Young, 1790. 11 pp.
UOP copy.   22798

Pennsylvania. University.
Four Dissertations.

Philadelphia, Bradfords, 1766. x, viii, 12, [2], 112 pp.
AAS copy.   10400

Pennsylvania. University.
General Heads and Plan of a Course of Lectures . . . in the College of Philadelphia, 1778.
[Philadelphia, 1778.] [2] pp.
NYPL copy.   15994

Pennsylvania. University.
Morning Prayer.
[Philadelphia], Dunlap, [1780]. 10 leaves.
LCP copy.   16935

Pennsylvania. University.
The Plan of a Performance of Solemn Musick.
[Philadelphia, 1765.] 4 pp.
LCP copy.   10140

Pennsylvania. University.
The Report of the Committee for the Arrangement of the Schools.
Philadelphia, Smith, 1795. 32 pp.
APS copy.   47555

Pennsylvania. University.
Rules for the Good Government. . . . August 4, 1784.
Philadelphia, Bailey, [1784]. Broadside.
UOP copy.   44608

Pennsylvania. University. Charters.
Additional Charter of the College, Academy, and Charity School of Philadelphia.
Philadelphia, Franklin & Hall, 1755. [2], 13 pp.
HSP copy.   7540

Pennsylvania. University. Theses, 1761.
Viris Praecellentissimis, Thomae Penn.
[Philadelphia], Dunlap, [1761]. Broadside.
UOP copy.   8981

Pennsylvania. University. Theses, 1762.
Viris Praecellentissimis, Thomae Penn.
[Philadelphia], Miller, [1762]. Broadside.
HSP copy.   9239

Pennsylvania. University. Theses, 1763.
Viris Praecellentissimis, Thomae Penn.
[Philadelphia], Miller, [1763]. Broadside.
UOP copy.   9485

[Pennsylvania. Vice-President, 1779.
By the Honorable George Bryan . . . and the Supreme Executive Council
[Embargo. Oct. 11, 1779].
Philadelphia, Hall & Sellers, 1779. Broadside.]
(No copy located.)   16436

Pennsylvania. Vice-President, 1785.
. . . By the Vice-President and the Supreme Executive Council. . . . A Proclamation [Timothy Pickering].
[Philadelphia? 1785?] Broadside.
JCB copy.   44768

Pennsylvania: a Poem [by Jacob Duch, 1738-1798].
Philadelphia, Franklin & Hall, 1756. 11 pp.
LCP copy.   7648

The Pennsylvania Almanack . . . for . . . 1787. . . . By Mark Time.
Philadelphia, Oswald. [40] pp.
(Evans assumed the title from an adv.)
BM copy.   20023

The Pennsylvania Almanac, for . . . 1788.
Pennsylvania, F. Bailey, J. Steele, etc. [38] pp.
(Only known copy is imperfect.)
WisHS copy.   45138

The Pennsylvania Almanack, for . . . 1788.
Philadelphia, Oswald. [40] pp.
AAS copy.   20751

The Pennsylvania Almanack, for . . . 1789.
Philadelphia, Bailey, etc. [40] pp.
AAS copy.   21374

The Pennsylvania Almanac, for . . . 1790.
Pennsylvania, Bailey, etc. [40] pp.
AAS copy.   22058

The Pennsylvania Almanac, for . . . 1801.
Philadelphia, Baileys. [36] pp.
HSP copy.   38225

Pennsylvania Cavalry. Associated Independent Philadelphia Troop of Volunteer Greens.
Articles, or By-laws for the Government of the. . . .
Philadelphia, Tuckniss, 1798. 8, [2] pp.
LCP copy.   34351

Pennsylvania Cavalry. Second Troop of Philadelphia Horse.
Bye-Laws and Regulations for the. . . .
[Philadelphia], Folwell, [1795]. Broadside.
HSP copy.   29317

The Pennsylvania, Delaware, Maryland, and Virginia Almanack . . . for 1782 [by Andrew Ellicott, 1754-1820].
Baltimore, Goddard, for Smith in Fredericktown. [48] pp.
(No complete copy located.)
JCB copy.   17145

The Pennsylvania Delaware, Maryland, and Virginia Almanack . . . for . . . 1783 [by Andrew Ellicott, 1754-1820].
Baltimore, Goddard, for Richards and Smith. [48] pp.
AAS copy.   17527

The Pennsylvania, Delaware, Maryland and Virginia Almanack . . . for . . . 1784 [by Andrew Ellicott, 1754-1820].
Baltimore, Goddard for Richards [1783]. [48] pp.
LOC copy.   17920

The Pennsylvania, Delaware, Maryland and Virginia Almanack . . . for . . . 1786.
Baltimore, Goddard. [40] pp.
(Better entered as 18999, q. v.)   44769

The Pennsylvania, Delaware, Maryland, and Virginia Almanack . . . for . . . 1788 [by Benjamin Workman].
Baltimore, Goddard, [48] pp.
MdHS copy.   20898

The Pennsylvania, Delaware, Maryland, and Virginia Almanack . . . for . . . 1789 [by Benjamin Workman].
Baltimore, Goddard. [48] pp.
MdHS copy.   21619

The Pennsylvania, Delaware, Maryland and Virginia Almanack . . . for . . . 1790 [by Benjamin Workman].
Baltimore, Goddard & Angell. [48] pp.
LOC copy.   22294

The Pennsylvania, Delaware, Maryland, and Virginia Almanack . . . for . . . 1791 [by Benjamin Workman].
Baltimore, Goddard and Angell. 46 pp.
AAS copy.   23094

Pennsylvania Land Company.
Plan of Association . . . Established March 1797.
Philadelphia, Aitken, 1797. 15 pp.
(No copy could be located with the pp. given by Evans.)
LOC copy.   32660

Pennsylvania Land Company.
A Schedule of the Property of the. . . .
[Philadelphia? 1797?] 12 pp.
NYHS copy.   48220

Pennsylvania Land Company.
Statement of the Incumbrances.
n.p., [1797]. 3 pp.
(Not located, 1968.)   48221

[Pennsylvania Land Company.
The Subscribers, Proprietors. . . . June 7, 1796.
[Philadelphia, 1796.] Broadside.
(No copy located.)   30988

[The Pennsylvania, Maryland, and Virginia Almanack, for . . . 1793.
Fredericktown, Bartgis.]
("Just published," Bartgis's Md. Gazette, Nov. 6, 1792.)   24676

[The Pennsylvania, Maryland, and Virginia almanac for 1794.

Fredericktown, Bartgis.]
(Minick 132; no copy known.)　　46849

[The Pennsylvania, Maryland and
Virginia Almanack, for . . . 1797.
Fredericktown, Md. Bartgis.]
("Just published," Bartgis's Federal
Gazette, Dec. 22, 1796.)　　47877

[The Pennsylvania, Maryland, and
Virginia Almanack, for . . . 1798.
Frederickstown, Md., Bartgis.]
("Just published," Bartgis's Federal
Gazette, Dec. 6, 1797.)　　32662

[The Pennsylvania, Maryland, and
Virginia Almanack, for 1799.
Frederick, Md., Bartgis.]
("Just published," Federal Gazette, June
19, 1799.)　　48954

[The Pennsylvania, Maryland and
Virginia Almanack, for 1800.
Frederick, Md., Bartgis.]
("Just in the press," Federal Gazette,
Sept. 11, 1799.)　　36075

The Pennsylvania, New-Jersey, Delaware,
Maryland and Virginia Almanac, for . . .
1799.
Philadelphia. [24] pp.
HSP copy.　　48568

The Pennsylvania, New-Jersey, Delaware,
Maryland and Virginia Almanac, for . . .
1799.
Philadelphia, Stewart. [40] pp.
AAS copy.　　34631

The Pennsylvania, New-Jersey, Delaware,
Maryland and Virginia Almanac, for . . .
1800.
Philadelphia, Stewart. [40] pp.
AAS copy.　　36076

The Pennsylvania, New-Jersey, Delaware,
Maryland and Virginia Almanac, for . . .
1801.
Philadelphia, Stewart. [40] pp.
AAS copy.　　38227

[The Pennsylvania Pocket Almanack for
. . . 1760.
Philadelphia, Bradford.]
(Hildeburn 1640.)　　8465

The Pennsylvania Pocket Almanack, for
. . . 1761.
Philadelphia, Bradford, [24] pp.
LOC copy.　　8712

The Pennsylvania Pocket Almanack, for
. . . 1762.
Philadelphia, Bradford. [48] pp.
(The unique copy is badly stained.)
HSP copy.　　8977

[The Pennsylvania Pocket Almanack, for
. . . 1763.
Philadelphia, Bradford.]
(Adv. Pa. Journal, Dec. 23, 1762.)　　9237

[The Pennsylvania Pocket Almanack, for
. . . 1764.
Philadelphia, Bradford.]
(Adv. Pa. Journal, Dec. 29, 1763.)　　9482

The Pennsylvania Pocket Almanack, for
. . . 1765.
Philadelphia, Bradford. [24] pp.
LOC copy.　　9792

The Pennsylvania Pocket Almanack for
. . . 1766.
Philadelphia, Bradford, [1765]. [28] pp.
AAS copy.　　10129

The Pennsylvania Pocket Almanack for
. . . 1767.
Philadelphia, Bradfords. [24] pp.
LOC copy.　　10450

[The Pennsylvania Pocket Almanack for
. . . 1768.
Philadelphia, Bradfords.]
(Assumed by Hildeburn from the
sequence.)　　10735

The Pennsylvania Pocket Almanack for
. . . 1769.
Philadelphia, Bradfords. [26] pp.
AAS copy.　　11034

The Pennsylvania Pocket Almanack for
. . . 1770.
Philadelphia, Bradfords. [28] pp.
AAS copy.　　11410

The Pennsylvania Pocket Almanack for
. . . 1771.
Philadelphia, Bradfords. [32] pp.
AAS copy.　　11810

[The Pennsylvania Pocket Almanack for
. . . 1772.
Philadelphia, Bradfords.]
(Adv. Pa. Journal, Jan. 2, 1772.)　　12187

The Pennsylvania Pocket Almanack, for
. . . 1773.
Philadelphia, Bradfords. [36] pp.
HSP copy.　　12516

The Pennsylvania Pocket Almanack, for
. . . 1774.
Philadelphia, Bradfords. [32] pp.
LOC copy.　　12933

[The Pennsylvania Pocket Almanack for
. . . 1775.
Philadelphia, Bradfords.]
(Assumed by Hildeburn from the
sequence.)　　13532

[The Pennsylvania Pocket Almanack for
. . . 1776.
Philadelphia, Bradfords.]
(Assumed from the sequence by
Hildeburn.)　　14381

[The Pennsylvania Pocket Almanack for
. . . 1777.
Philadelphia, Bradfords.]
(Assumed by Hildeburn from the
sequence.)　　15010

[The Pennsylvania Pocket Almanack for
. . . 1779.
Philadelphia, Bradfords.]
(Assumed from the sequence.)　　15988

[The Pennsylvania Pocket Almanack for
. . . 1780.
Philadelphia, Bradford.]
(Hildeburn 3928.)　　16459

The Pennsylvania Pocket Almanac, for
. . . 1781.
Philadelphia, Bradford. [24] pp.
LOC copy.　　16944

[The Pennsylvania Pocket Almanack for
. . . 1782.
Philadelphia, Bradford & Hall.]
(Assumed from the sequence.)　　17307

[The Pennsylvania Pocket Almanack for
. . . 1783.
Philadelphia, Bradford.]
(Adv. Pa. Packet, Nov. 23, 1782.)　　17673

The Pennsylvania Pocket Almanack, for
. . . 1784.
Philadelphia, Bradford. [24] pp.
(The only copy located is incomplete.)
LOC copy.　　18134

[The Pennsylvania Pocket Almanack for
. . . 1785.
Philadelphia, Bradford.]
(Adv. Pa. Journal, Jan. 24, 1785.)　　18724

[The Pennsylvania Pocket Almanack for
. . . 1786.
Philadelphia, Bradford.]
(Assumed from the sequence.)　　19190

[The Pennsylvania Pocket Almanack for
. . . 1787.
Philadelphia, Bradford.]
(Assumed by Evans from the sequence.)
　　19910

[The Pennsylvania Pocket Almanac for
. . . 1791.
Philadelphia, Bailey.]
(Entry assumed from advs. for pocket
almanacs.)　　22785

The Pennsylvania Pocket Almanac, for
. . . 1791.
Philadelphia, Lang for Campbell.
[24] pp.
(No better copy available.)
LCP copy.　　45963

[Pennsylvania Pocket Almanac, for . . .
1792.
Philadelphia, Bailey.]
(Entry assumed by Evans from advs. for
pocket almanacs.)　　23690

[The Pennsylvania Primer . . . for the Use
of Country Schools.
Lancaster, 1755.]
(Adv. in 7388.)　　7537

[Pennsylvania Property Company.
Plan of Association of the. . . .
Philadelphia, 1795. 12 pp.]
(a ghost of the 1797 ed.)　　29296

Pennsylvania Property Company.
Plan of Association of the. . . .
Philadelphia, Aitken, 1797. 16, 12 pp.
LCP copy.　　32661

A Pennsylvania Sailor's Letters [by John
Macpherson, c. 1726-1792].
Philadelphia, 1771. 64 pp.
LCP copy.　　12107

The Pennsylvania Sheet Almanac for . . .
1789.
Philadelphia, Towne. Broadside.
HSP copy.　　45336

Pennsylvania Society for Mechanical
Improvements and Philosophical
Inquiries.
The Constitution and Fundamental Rules
of the. . . .
[Philadelphia, 179?]. Broadside.
NYPL ph. copy.　　45788

Pennsylvania Society for Promoting the
Abolition of Slavery.
An Address . . . B. Franklin, President.
[Philadelphia, Francis Bailey, 1789] 2 pp.
NYHS copy.　　45559

Pennsylvania Society for Promoting the
Abolition of Slavery.
An Address from the Pennsylvania
Abolition Society to the Free Black
People.
Philadelphia, Ormrod, 1800. 8 pp.
NL copy.　　38229

Pennsylvania Society for Promoting the
Abolition of Slavery.
An Address . . . B. Franklin, President.
[Philadelphia, Francis Bailey, 1789]. 2 pp.
NYHS copy.　　45559

Pennsylvania Society for Promoting the
Abolition of Slavery.
Constitution and Act of Incorporation of
the. . . .
Philadelphia, Ormrod, 1800. 53 pp.
AAS copy.　　38228

Pennsylvania Society for Promoting the
Abolition of Slavery.
The Constitution of the. . . .
Philadelphia, James, 1787. 15 pp
AAS copy.　　20636

Pennsylvania Society for Promoting the
Abolition of Slavery.
The Constitution of the. . . .
Philadelphia, Bailey, 1788. 29 pp.
NYPL copy.　　21381

Pennsylvania Society for Promoting the
Abolition of Slavery.
Remarks on the Slave Trade, Extracted
from the American Museum, for May,
1789.
[Philadelphia, 1789. Broadside.
(No copy located.)　　45560

Pennsylvania Society for Promoting the
Abolition of Slavery.
Rules for the Regulation of the Society for
the Relief of Free Negroes.
Philadelphia, Crukshank, 1784. [2], 16 pp.
LCP copy.　　18786

[Pennsylvania Society for Promoting the
Abolition of Slavery.
Rules for the Regulation of the. . . .
Philadelphia, Poulson, 1789.]
(No such ed. has been located.)　　22057

Pennsylvania Society for Promoting the
Abolition of Slavery. Committee for
Improving the Condition of Free Blacks.
Address of the Committee.

Philadelphia, Ormrod, 1800. 8 pp.
APS copy. 38247

Pennsylvania Society for the
Encouragement of Manufactures.
The Plan of the Pennsylvania Society. . . .
Philadelphia, Aitken, 1787. 12 pp.
BA copy. 20637

The Pennsylvania State Trials. . . . Vol. I
[by Edmund Hogan, ed.].
Philadelphia, Bailey, 1794. xii, 776 pp.
AAS copy. 27132

Pennsylvanischer Kalender, auf das
1796ste Jahr Christi.
Ephrata, Mayer. [40] pp.
AAS copy. 29297

Pennsylvanischer Calender, auf das
1797ste Jahr Christi.
York, Mäyer. [44] pp.
AAS copy. 47878

Pennsylvanischer Calender. Auf das
1797ste Jahr Christi.
York, Mayer. [44] pp.
HSP copy. 30989

Pennsylvanischer Calender auf das 1798ste
Jahr Christi.
York, Mäyer. [44] pp.
AAS copy. 48222

[Pennsylvanischer Kalender. Auf das
1798ste Jahr Christi.
Ephrata, Mayer, 1797. [42] pp.]
(Only this imperfect copy was located.)
AAS copy. 32665

Pennsylvanischer Kalender, auf das
1799ste Jahr Christi.
York, Pa., Mayer. [44] pp.
LOC copy. 34340

Pennsylvanischer Calender, auf das
1800ste Jahr Christi.
York, Mayer. [40] pp.
AAS copy. 36077

A Penny's Worth of Wit.
n.p., [179?]. Broadside.
CHS copy. 45789

The Pennyworth of Wit.
[Boston.] Sold at the Bible & Heart, in
Cornhill, [1796]. Broadside.
BPL copy. 30990

A Penny Worth of Wit.
Hudson, N.Y., [1796]. 8 pp.
AAS copy. 30991

Pennyless, Peter, pseud.
Sentimental Lucubrations.
Philadelphia, Gibbons, 1793. 168 pp.
AAS copy. 25980

The People the Best Governors: or A Plan
of Government Founded on the Just
Principles. . . .
n.p., [1776]. 13 pp.
HEH copy. 43134

Pepper, Henry.
Juvenile Essays.
Philadelphia, Folwell, [1798]. 75, [1] pp.
AAS copy. 34341

Percival, Thomas, 1740-1804.
A Father's Instructions.
Philadelphia, Dobson, 1788. 238, [10] pp.
AAS copy. 21382

Percival, Thomas, 1740-1804.
A Father's Instructions . . . Ninth Edition.
Philadelphia, Dobson, 1797. xii, 219 pp.
AAS copy. 32666

Percival, Thomas, 1740-1804.
A Father's Instructions. . . . Ninth
Edition.
Richmond, Va., Pritchard, 1800. xii, 219
pp.
AAS copy. 38232

Percival, Thomas, 1740-1804.
Moral and Literary Dissertations.
Philadelphia, Dobson, 1798. pp. [i]-xii,
[1]-204, [203]-204, [1].
AAS copy. 34342

Percy, John.

The Schedule Referred to in these Letters
Patent. . . . March 1, A.D. 1800.
n.p., [1800]. Broadside.
NYPL copy. 49133

[Percy, John], 1749-1797.
The Captive.
New York, Moller, [1797]. [2] pp.
LOC copy. 48223

Perkins, Daniel.
An Oration, Pronounced before the
Western Star Lodge, in Bridgewater.
Whitestown, [N.Y.], M'Lean, 1797.
16 pp.
NYSL copy. 48224

Perkins, Elijah, 1767-1806.
An Inaugural Dissertation on Universal
Dropsy.
[Philadelphia], Stewart, 1791. 43,
[1] pp.
AAS copy. 23691

Perkins, Elisha, 1741-1799.
Certificates of the Efficacy of Doctor
Perkins's Patent Metallic Instruments.
New London, Green, [1796]. 16 pp.
AAS copy. 47879

Perkins, Elisha, 1741-1799.
Certificates of the Efficacy of Doctor
Perkins's Patent Metallic Instruments.
Newburyport, Blunt, [1797]. 24 pp.
NLM copy. 32669

[Perkins, Elisha, 1741-1799.
Evidences of the Efficacy of Doctor
Perkins's Patent Metallic Instruments.
New Haven, 1797.]
(This entry was apparently an error.)
32667

Perkins, Elisha, 1741-1799.
Evidences of the Efficacy of Doctor
Perkins's Patent Metallic Instruments.
New London, Green, [1797]. 32 pp.
AAS copy. 32668

Perkins, Elisha, 1741-1799.
Evidences of the Efficacy of Doctor
Perkins's Patent Metallic Instruments.
Philadelphia, Folwell, [1797]. 36 pp.
AAS copy. 32670

Perkins, Elisha, 1741-1799.
Evidences of the Efficacy of Doctor
Perkins's Patent Metallic Instruments.
Richmond, Dixon, [1797]. 40 pp.
HEH copy. 48225

Perkins, Elisha, 1741-1799.
To all People to whom these Presents
shall come. . . .
[Philadelphia? 1796?] Broadside.
LCP copy. 47880

[Perkins, John], 1698-1781.
(A. A. S., Proc., 1956.)
An Essay on the Agitations of the Sea.
Boston, Mecom, 1761. 40 pp.
NYPL copy. 8851

[Perkins, John], 1698-1781.
(Am. Antiq. Soc., Proc., Oct. 1956.)
Theory of Agency.
Boston, Perkins, 1771. 43 pp.
AAS copy. 12188

[Perkins, John], 1698-1781.
(A.A.S., Proc., Oct. 1956.) Thoughts on
Agency.
New Haven, 1765. pp. [2], 5-27.
AAS copy. 10130

[Perkins, John], 1698-1781.
(A. A. S., Proc., Oct. 1956.)
The True Nature and Cause of the
Tails of Comets.
Boston, Edes & Gill, 1772. 8 pp.
AAS copy. 12517

Perkins, Joseph, 1772-1803.
An Oration on Eloquence.
Boston, Weld & Greenough, 1794.
8 pp
JCB copy. 27490

Perkins, Joseph, 1772-1803.
An Oration upon Genius.
Boston, Manning & Loring for Nancrede,
1797. 22 pp.
AAS copy. 32671

Perkins, Nathan, 1748-1838.
A Discourse, at the Ordination of . . .
Calvin Chapin.
Hartford, Hudson & Goodwin, 1794.
38 pp.
AAS copy. 27491

Perkins, Nathan, 1748-1838.
A Discourse, Delivered at the Ordination
of . . . William F. Miller.
Hartford, Babcock, 1792. 22 pp.
AAS copy. 24678

[Perkins, Nathan], 1748-1838.
Letters of Gratitude, to the Connecticut
Pleader.
Hartford, 1781. 76 pp.
(Authorship on authority of Trumbull.)
AAS copy. 17085

[Perkins, Nathan], 1748-1838.
The Reprimander, Reprimanded.
Hartford, 1781. 16 pp.
NYPL copy. 17086

Perkins, Nathan, 1748-1838.
A Sermon, Delivered at the Ordination of
. . . Hezekiah N. Woodruff.
New London, 1790. 30 pp.
AAS copy. 22786

Perkins, Nathan, 1748-1838.
A Sermon Occasioned by the Unhappy
Death of Mr. Lloyd.
Hartford, Hudson & Goodwin, 1780.
19 pp.
CHS copy. 16945

Perkins, Nathan, 1748-1838.
A Sermon, Preached at the Installation of
. . . Solomon Wolcott.
Hartford, Hudson & Goodwin, [1786.] 39
pp.
NYPL copy. 19911

Perkins, Nathan, 1748-1838.
A Sermon, Preached to the Soldiers.
Hartford, [1775]. 15 pp.
AAS copy. 14382

Perkins, Nathan, 1748-1838.
Twenty-Four Discourses.
Hartford, Hudson & Goodwin, 1795.
519 pp.
AAS copy. 29298

Perkins, Nathan, 1748-1838.
Two Discourses . . . on . . . the Christian's
Hope.
Hartford, Ct., Hudson & Goodwin, 1800.
62 pp.
AAS copy. 38233

Perkins, William, 1558-1602.
(D. N. B.)
The Foundation of Christian Religion.
Boston, 1682. [8], 39, [1] pp.
AAS copy. 328

The Pernicious Practice of
Dram-Drinking [by Stephen Hales,
1677-1761].
Woodbridge, [N.J.], Parker, MCCLIX.
[2], 8 pp.
NYPL copy. 41036

[A Perpetual Almanack.
Richmond, Davis, 1790.]
(The origin of the entry is unknown.)
22787

A Perpetual Almanack: shewing, the
Prime, Epact, Cycle of the Sun.
Newport, Franklin, [1730?]. Broadside.
RIHS copy. 39959

The Perplexity of Poverty.
Concord, [N.H.], 1792. 15 pp.
AAS copy. 46541

Perquimans County, N.C. Convention.
Advertisement. Perquimans County, Feb.
11, 1775. The Respective Counties . . . are
Requested to Elect Delegates . . . to meet
at . . . Newbern . . . the 3rd Day of April
next.
[Newbern, 1775.] Broadside.
PRO copy. 42761

[Perrault, Charles], 1628-1703.
Cinderella or the Little Glass Slipper.
Litchfield, Collier, [1800?]. 29 pp.
(Copy cannot be reproduced.) 49134

Perrault, Charles, 1628-1703.
Fairy Tales, or the Histories of Past
Times.
Haverhill, 1794. 83 pp.
(This is the item described by Evans from
an adv.)
EI copy.   29299

[Perrault, Charles], 1628-1703.
Fairy Tales, or Histories of Past Times.
New York, Harrisson, 1798. 107 pp.
(The only known copy is imperfect.)
d'Alté A. Welch copy.   48569

[Perrault, Charles], 1628-1703.
Little Red Riding Hood, the Fairy.
Philadelphia, M'Culloch, 1797. 31 pp.
d'Alté A. Welch copy.   48226

[Perrault, Charles, 1628-1703.
A New History of Blue Beard.
Hartford, Ct., Babcock, 1800.]
(Bates 2450.)   38059

Perrin, Jean Baptiste, fl. 1786.
The Elements of French Conversation.
Philadelphia, Bradford, 1794. [4], 163,
[1] pp.
AAS copy.   27492

[Perrin, Jean Baptiste, fl. 1786.
Entertaining and Instructive Exercises.
New York, Duyckinck, 1800. 384 pp.]
(No copy of such an ed. could be located.)
     38234

Perrin, Jean Baptiste, fl. 1786.
A Grammar of the French Tongue.
Philadelphia, Styner & Cist, 1779. xii, [2],
320 pp.
AAS copy.   16461

Perrin, Jean Baptiste, fl. 1786.
A Grammar of the French Tongue. . . .
Ninth Edition.
Philadelphia, for Young, Carey, etc., 1794.
pp. [i]-viii, [1]-368, [1], x-xii, [4].
AAS copy.   27493

Perrin, Jean Baptiste, fl. 1786.
A Grammar of the French Tongue. . . .
Tenth Edition.
New York, Davises for Duyckinck, etc.,
1799. xii, 358 pp.
BA copy.   36081

Perrin, Jean Baptiste, fl. 1786.
A Grammar of the French Tongue. . . .
Tenth Edition.
New York, Davises for Duyckinck, etc.,
1800. xii, 358 pp.
LCP copy.   38235

Perrin, Jean Baptiste, fl. 1786.
Instructive and Entertaining Exercises.
Philadelphia, Cist, 1781. v, [1], 216 pp.
AAS copy.   17308

Perrin, Jean Baptiste, fl. 1786.
The Practice of the French Pronunciation.
Philadelphia, Steiner & Cist, 1780. iv, 108
pp.
AAS copy.   16946

Perry, David, 1746-1817.
A Short View, and Defence.
Danbury, Ct., Ely & Nichols, 1796. 20 pp.
BA copy.   30992

Perry, Edward,-1695.
(F. W. Brown, Ancestors of Oliver Hazard
Perry, pp., 1-9.)
A Memorable Account.
[Philadelphia], 1726. [2], iii, 3, 86 pp.
YC copy.   3205

[Perry, Edward - 1695.
A Memorable Account. . . . Second
Edition.
Philadelphia, Keimer, 1729.]
(Adv. Pa. Gazette Aug. 3, 1729.)   3206

Perry, Eliakim, Jr.
The Vermont Almanack, for . . . 1785.
Bennington, Haswell & Russell. [24] pp.
AAS copy.   18725

Perry, Joseph, 1728-1793.
An Astronomical Diary; or Almanack, for
. . . 1772.
New Haven, Greens. [28] pp.
AAS copy.   42268

Perry, Joseph, 1728-1793.
An Astronomical Diary, or Almanack, for
. . . 1773.
New Haven, Greens. [28] pp.
YC copy.   42365

Perry, Joseph, 1728-1793.
(Cothren, Ancient Woodbury, p. 666;
Perry's Astronomical Diary for 1772,
p. [2].)
An Astronomical Diary, or Almanack, for
. . . 1774.
New Haven, Greens. [28] pp.
AAS copy.   12934

Perry, Joseph, 1728-1793.
An Astronomical Diary, or Almanack, for
. . . 1775.
New Haven, Greens. [20] pp.
AAS copy.   42665

Perry, Joseph, 1728-1793.
An Astronomical Diary, or Almanack, for
. . . 1784.
New Haven, Greens. [16] pp.
(The only known copy is imperfect.)
CHS copy.   44438

Perry, Joseph, 1731-1783.
(Weis, Colonial Clergy N. E.)
The Character and Reward of the
Faithful.
Hartford, 1770. 24 pp.
AAS copy.   11811

Perry, Joseph, 1731-1783.
(Weis, Colonial Clergy N. E.)
The Character of Moses.
Hartford, [1767]. 28 pp.
AAS copy.   10736

[Perry, Joseph], 1731-1783.
Died at East-Windsor, the 28th of August,
1778 . . . Mrs. Sarah Perry.
[n.p., 1778.] Broadside.
(From reproduction in Groton Hist. Ser.,
II, 455.)   43530

Perry, Joseph, 1731-1783.
(Weis, Colonial Clergy N. E.)
A Sermon Preached before the General
Assembly.
Hartford, 1775. 23 pp.
AAS copy.   14383

Perry, Philo, 1752-1798.
A Sermon, Delivered at Danbury.
Danbury, [Ct.], Douglas & Ely, 1791. 20
pp.
AAS copy.   46257

Perry, Philo, 1752-1798.
A Sermon Delivered at New-Milford.
Danbury, Douglas & Ely, 1793. 23 pp.
CHS copy.   46850

Perry, R.
A Poem, on the Destruction of Sodom.
Middletown, Woodward, [1790]. [16] pp.
CHS copy.   22788

Perry, William, of Kelso, Scotland.
The Only sure Guide to the English
Tongue. . . . Eighth Edition.
Worcester, Thomas, 1785. 180 pp.
HC copy.   19191

Perry, William, of Kelso, Scotland.
The Only Sure Guide to the English
Tongue. . . . Second Worcester Edition.
Worcester, Thomas, 1786. 180 pp.
AAS copy.   19912

Perry, William, of Kelso, Scotland.
The Only Sure Guide to the English
Tongue.
Boston, Coverly, 1788. 180 pp.
BPL copy.   21384

Perry, William, of Kelso, Scotland.
The Only Sure Guide to the English
Tongue. . . . Third Worcester Edition.
Worcester, Thomas, for Hall, etc., 1788.
180 pp.
AAS copy.   21383

Perry, William, of Kelso, Scotland.
The Only Sure Guide to the English
Tongue. . . . Fourth Worcester Edition.
Worcester, Thomas, 1789. 180 pp.
AAS copy.   22063

Perry, William, of Kelso, Scotland.

The Only Sure Guide to the English
Tongue.
Brookfield, Merriam, [179?]. 180 pp.
LOC copy.   45790

[Perry, William, of Kelso, Scotland.
The Only Sure Guide to the English
Tongue.
Boston, Coverly for Thomas, 1790.]
(No copy located.)   22789

Perry, William, of Kelso, Scotland.
The Only Sure Guide to the English
Tongue. . . . Fifth Worcester Edition.
Worcester, Thomas, 1790. 180 pp.
AAS copy.   22790

Perry, William, of Kelso, Scotland.
The Only Sure Guide to the English
Tongue. . . . Sixth Worcester Edition.
Worcester, Thomas & Worcester, 1792.
180 pp.
AAS copy.   24679

Perry, William, of Kelso, Scotland.
The Only Sure Guide to the English
Tongue. . . . Seventh Worcester Edition.
Worcester, Thomas, 1793. 180 pp.
JCB copy.   25981

Perry, William, of Kelso, Scotland.
The Only Sure Guide to the English
Tongue. . . . Hall's Second Boston
Edition.
Boston, Hall for D. West, 1794. 180 pp.
PrU copy.   47174

Perry, William, of Kelso, Scotland.
The Only Sure Guide to the English
Tongue. . . . Eighth Worcester Edition.
Worcester, Thomas, 1794. 180 pp.
AAS copy.   27494

Perry, William, of Kelso, Scotland.
The Only Sure Guide to the English
Tongue. . . . Ninth Worcester Edition.
Worcester, Thomas, 1794. 180 pp.
(An imprint variant of 27494, q. v. for
text.)
PrU copy.   47175

[Perry, William, of Kelso, Scotland.
The Only Sure Guide to the English
Tongue . . . Ninth Worcester Edition.
Worcester, Thomas for West, Larkin, etc.,
1795. 180 pp., 1 plate.]
(No copy of such an ed. known.)   29301

Perry, William, of Kelso, Scotland.
The Only Sure Guide to the English
Tongue. . . . Tenth Worcester Edition.
Worcester, Thomas, 1797. 180 pp.
EI copy.   32672

Perry, William, of Kelso, Scotland.
The Only Sure Guide to the English
Tongue. . . . Eleventh Worcester Edition.
Worcester, Thomas for Thomas &
Andrews, 1798. 180 pp.
AAS copy.   34343

Perry, William, of Kelso, Scotland.
The Only Sure Guide to the English
Tongue. . . . Hall's Seventh Boston
Edition.
Boston, Hall, 1799. 180 pp.
BMFA copy.   36083

Perry, William, of Kelso, Scotland.
The Only Sure Guide to the English
Tongue. . . . Twelfth Worcester Edition.
Worcester, Thomas for Thomas &
Andrews, 1799. 180 pp.
EI copy.   36082

Perry, William, of Kelso, Scotland.
The Royal Standard English
Dictionary. . . . First American Edition.
Worcester, Thomas, 1788. [4], 596.
AAS copy.   21385

Perry, William, of Kelso, Scotland.
The Royal Standard English
Dictionary. . . . Second American
Worcester Edition.
Worcester, Thomas, 1793. [4], 596 pp.
AAS copy.   25982

Perry, William, of Kelso, Scotland.
The Royal Standard English
Dictionary. . . . Third Worcester Edition.

Worcester, Worcester for Thomas, 1794.
[4], 596 pp.
AAS copy.   27495

Perry, William, of Kelso, Scotland.
The Royal Standard English
Dictionary. . . . Fourth American
Worcester Edition.
Worcester, Worcester for Thomas, etc.,
1796. [4], 596.
AAS copy.   30993

Perry, William, of Kelso, Scotland.
The Royal Standard English
Dictionary. . . . Fifth American Edition.
Boston, Thomas & Andrews, 1800. [4],
596 pp.
AAS copy.   38236

Preseverance. A Poem [by John Gill,
1697-1771].
Boston, Thomas, 1773. 13 pp.
NYPL copy.   42444

Personal Slavery Established.
Philadelphia, Dunlap, 1773. 26 pp.
AAS copy.   12935

Personel, Francis Burdett, 1747-1773.
An Authentic & Particular Account of the
Life of. . . .
New Haven, [1773]. 23 pp.
CHS copy.   42483

Personel, Francis Burdett, 1747-1773.
An Authentic and Particular Account of
the Life of. . . .
New York, 1773. 23 pp.
NYHS copy.   12936

Perth Amboy, N. J. Charters.
An Act for Incorporating the Free Port of
Perth-Amboy.
Trenton, 1785. 26 pp.
HEH copy.   19120

Perth Amboy, N.J. Citizens.
To the Legislative-Council . . . Presented
the 27th Day of January, 1798.
[Trenton, 1798.] Broadside.
(Morsch 386; no copy located.)   48570

Perth-Amboy, N.J. Proprietors.
Advertisement, Perth-Amboy, September
17, 1745. Whereas. . . .
[New York, Zenger, 1745.] Broadside.
NYHS copy.   40357

Peters, Hugh, 1598-1660.
A Dying Fathers last Legacy.
Boston, Green for Eliot, 1717. front., [2],
ii, 92 pp.
AAS copy.   1923

Peters, Hugh, 1598-1660.
Dying Father's last Legacy.
Boston, B. Green for Gerrish, 1717. front.,
[2], ii, 92 pp.
(But for imprint identical to 1923, q. v.)
                                                 39669

Peters, Phillis (Wheatley).
see
Wheatley, Phillis, afterward Phillis Peters.

Peters, Richard. 1704-1771.
Lancaster, May 30th, 1755. To the
Inhabitants of the County of Berks.
[Lancaster, Pa., 1755.] Broadside.
AAS facsim. copy.   40792

Peters, Richard.
Philadelphia, January 29, 1761.
Advertisement.
[Philadelphia, 1761.] Broadside.
HSP copy.   41236

Peters, Richard, 1704-1776.
(Sprague, V, 88-91.)
A Sermon on Education.
Philadelphia, Franklin & Hall, 1751. vii,
[1], 48, 8 pp.
HSP copy.   6754

Peters, Richard, 1704-1776.
(Sprague, V, 88-91.)
A Sermon, Preached in the New Lutheran
Church.
Philadelphia, Dunlap, 1769. 37 pp.
AAS copy.   11412

Peters, Richard, 1704-1776.
(Sprague, V, 88-91.)

The Two Last Sermons.
Philadelphia, Franklin, 1737. xxii, 29 pp.
(No complete copy could be located.)
LCP copy.   4186

Peters, Richard, 1744-1828.
Agricultural Enquiries.
Philadelpha, Cist and Markland, 1797.
[2], 111, [3] pp.
AAS copy.   32673

[Peters, Richard], 1744-1828.
Dialogue, &c, For the Commencement.
[Philadelphia, 1765.] 4 pp.
AAS copy.   10131

[Peters, Samuel Andrew], 1735-1826.
Reasons why Mr. Byles left New-London.
[New London], 1768. 12 pp.
AAS copy.   11035

[Petersburg Church lottery.
Petersburg, 1791.]
(Wyatt 8e; no copy known.)   46258

Petersburg, Va. Theater.
The Petersburg Theatre. On Wednesday
Evening, November 13, 1799, will be
Presented . . . The Child of Nature.
[Petersburg, Va., 1799.] Broadside.
NYHS copy.   36084

[A Petition and Remonstrance to the
President and Congress of the United
States.
[Philadelphia? 1791.] Broadside.]
(For a better entry see 27496.)   23692

A Petition and Remonstrance to the
President and Congress.
[Philadelphia? 1794.] Broadside.
NYPL copy.   27496

A Petition for a Contribution in Order to
Relieve a Distressed Prisoner.
[Worcester, 1786.] Broadside.
AAS copy.   19914

[Petition of Sundry Inhabitants to the
Speaker and Member of the General
Assembly of . . . New York . . . 17th
February, 1772.
[New York, 1772.] 4 pp.]
(No copy located.)   12485

A Petition to His Majesty, King George
the Third [Lands. Nov., 1766].
[Hartford, 1766.] [2], 5 pp.
VtSL copy.   10451

[Petition to the General Assembly of
Connecticut Respecting Susquehannah
Matters. . . . March 30, 1774.
np., nd. Broadside.]
(Obviously a descriptive title, this item
has not been identified.)   13213

A Petition to the Honourable the
Committee of Safety for the Colony of
New-York. We the Subscribers. . . .
[New York, 1775.] Broadside.
LOC copy.   14384

Petition to the Senate and House of
Representatives of the United States.
[Philadelphia], Poulson, [1800?].
8 pp.
HSP copy.   49135

The Petitions and Memorials of the
Proprietors of West and East-Jersey.
New York, Kollock, [1785]. 96 pp.,
1 map.
LOC copy.   19126

Petitpierre, Ferdinand Oliver, 1722-1790.
Thoughts on the Divine Goodness.
Hartford, Babcock, 1794. 288 pp.
AAS copy.   27497

Pettey's Island Lottery, for Effects to the
Full Value of 10,000 Dollars.
[Philadelphia, 1761.] Broadside.
LCP copy.   8979

Pettibone, Augustus, 1766-1847.
An Oration, Pronounced at Norfolk.
Litchfield, Ct., Collier, 1798. 16 pp.
CHS copy.   34344

Pettie's Island Cash Lottery. For
Raising. . . .

[Philadelphia, 1772.] Broadside.
LCP copy.   12519

Pettie's Island Cash Lottery, in Three
Classes. . . . March 1, 1773. [Glass
Manufacture].
[Philadelphia, 1773.] Broadside.
LCP copy.   12938

Pettie's Island Cash Lottery.
January 17, 1774. Supplement to the
American Flint Glass Manufactory.
[Philadelphia, 1774.] Broadside.
LCP copy.   13533

Pettie's Island and Cash Lottery.
Advertisement. For the Satisfaction of the
Adventurers. . . .
[Philadelphia, 1771.] Broadside.
LCP copy.   12191

Pettie's-Island Land and Cash Lottery.
For Disposing of Sundry Houses. . . .
October 9, 1772.
[Philadelphia, 1772.] Broadside.
LCP copy.   12520

Pettie's Island Land and Cash Lottery. To
be Drawn. . . . The Drawing shall begin on
Monday, the Twenty-First day of
October. . . .
[Philadelphia, 1771.] Broadside.
LCP copy.   12192

Pettie's Island Land and Cash Lottery. To
be Drawn. . . . The Drawing will begin as
soon as the Tickets are Disposed of. . . .
[Philadelphia, 1771.] Broadside.
LCP copy.   12190

Pettie's Island Land and Cash Lottery, to
be Drawn. . . . the First Day of July, 1771.
[Philadelphia, 1771.] Broadside.
LCP copy.   12189

Pettie's-Island Lottery, for Disposing of a
Great Variety of Curious Pictures.
[Philadelphia, 1772.] Broadside.
LCP copy.   12521

Pettie's Island Lottery.
A List of the Numbers, that Came up
Prizes in the Pettie's Island Jewellery and
Plate Lottery.
[Philadelphia, 1772.] Broadside.
LCP copy.   42366

[Pettit, Charles], 1736-1806.
An Impartial Review of the Rise and
Progress of the Controversy.
Philadelphia, Ormrod, 1800. 50 pp.
AAS copy.   38239

Petty, John.
To the Public. Annapolis, August 18,
1788.
[Annapolis, 1788.] [2] pp.
MdHS copy.   45338

Petty, John.
To the Public. Annapolis, July 1, 1788.
[Annapolis, 1788.] Broadside.
MdHS copy.   45337

[Petyt, George].
Lex Parliamentaria.
New York and Philadelphia, 1716. [6], 184
pp.
AAS copy.   1850

Peyton, V.J.
Les Elemens de la Langue Angloise.
Philadelphia, Wrigley & Berriman for
Carey, 1794. 158 pp.
(The AAS has another copy with the
Preface reset.)
AAS copy.   27498

[Peyton, V. J.
The Elements of the English Language.
Philadelphia, Carey, 1792?]
(Imprint assumed by Evans from adv.)
                                                 24680

Pfeiffer, George, 1769-1804.
An Eulogium to . . . Washington.
Natchez, Stokes, 1800. 38 pp.; printed
wraps.
MFM copy.   38240

Pfeiffer, George, 1769-1804.
An Inaugural Dissertation on the Gout.

Philadelphia, Dobson, 1791. 50 pp.
AAS copy.   23693

Pharmacopoeia Simpliciorum [by
William Brown, 1748-1792].
Philadelphia, Steiner & Cist, 1778. 32 pp.
LCP copy.   15750

Philadelphia.
The Constitution and Ordinances of the
City.
Philadelphia, Hall & Sellers, 1790. xxxii,
87 pp.
NYHS copy.   22791

Philadelphia.
The Freeholders and other Electors, in the
City of Philadelphia, in the Northern
Liberties, and District of Southwark, are
Requested to Attend at ten. . . . November
11, 1774.
[Philadelphia, 1774.] Broadside.
LCP copy.   13537

Philadelphia.
Order of the Procession.
Philadelphia, Poulson, [1793?].
Broadside.
LCP copy.   46851

Philadelphia. African Methodist
Episcopal Church.
Articles of Association of the. . . .
Philadelphia, Ormrod, 1799. 21 pp.
LCP copy.   36095

Philadelphia. Amicable Fire Company.
The Amicable Fire Company are
Requested to Meet. . . . January 26, 1778.
[Philadelphia, 1778.] Broadside.
LCP copy.   15992

Philadelphia. Assembly of Colonial
Refugees.
Proces Verbaux de l'Assemblée Tenue
par les Colons Refugies.
Philadelphia, Parent, [1795]. 7 pp.
(Not located 1967.)
JCB copy.   47556

Philadelphia. Bank of Pennsylvania.
An Act to Incorporate. . . . 12th August,
1793.
[Philadelphia, 1793.] 32 pp.
(Not located.)   25989

Philadelphia. Baptist Church, 1767.
An Account of the Burials and Baptized
in the Baptist Church . . . from December
25, 1766, to December 25, 1767.
[Philadelphia, 1767.] Broadside.
LCP copy.   10737

[Philadelphia. Baptist Church, 1769.
An Account of the Burials and Baptisms
in the Baptist Church, December 25, 1768,
to December 29, 1769.
[Philadelphia, 1769.] Broadside.]
(Assumed from the sequence.)   11413

[Philadelphia. Baptist Church, 1770.
An Account of the Burials and Baptisms
in the Baptist Church, from December 25,
1769, to December 25, 1770.]
(Assumed by Hildeburn from the
sequence.)   11818

[Philadelphia. Baptist Church, 1771.
An Account of the Burials and Baptisms
in the Baptist Church.
Philadelphia, 1771.]
(Assumed by Hildeburn from the
sequence.)   12193

[Philadelphia. Baptist Church, 1773.
An Account of the Baptisms and Burials
in the Baptist Church.
Philadelphia, 1773.]
(Assumed by Hildeburn from the
sequence.)   12949

[Philadelphia. Baptist Church, 1774.
An Account of the Burials and Baptisms
in the Baptist Church.
Philadelphia, 1774.]
(Assumed by Hildeburn from the
sequence.)   13540

[Philadelphia. Baptist Church, 1775.
An Account of the Burials and Baptisms
in the Baptist Church.
Philadelphia, 1775. Broadside.]
(Assumed by Hildeburn.)   14387

Philadelphia. Board of Health.
Health-Office, Port of Philadelphia, June
30, 1795. . . .
[Philadelphia, 1795.] [2] pp.
HSP copy.   29304

Philadelphia. Cabinet and Chair Makers.
The Philadelphia Cabinet &
Chair-Makers' Book of Prices. Instituted
March 4th, 1796.
Philadelphia, Richard Folwell, 1796.
28 pp.
HSP copy.   30999

Philadelphia. Christ Church, 1737.
An Account of the Births and Burials . . .
to December 24, 1737.
[Philadelphia, 1737.] Broadside.
HEH copy.   48126

Philadelphia. Christ Church, 1746.
An Account of the Births and Burials in
Christ-Church Parish . . . from December
24, 1746, to December 24, 1747.
[Philadelphia, 1747.] Broadside.
LCP copy.   6050

Philadelphia. Christ-Church, 1747.
An Account of the Births and Burials in
Christ-Church Parish . . . December 24,
1747, to December 24, 1748.
[Philadelphia, 1748.] Broadside.
LCP copy.   6220

[Philadelphia. Christ Church, 1748.
An Account of the Births and Burials in
Christ-Church Parish . . . from December
24, 1748, to December 24, 1749.
Philadelphia, 1749. Broadside.]
(Hildeburn 1115.)   6404

[Philadelphia. Christ Church, 1750.
An Account of the Births and Burials in
Christ-Church Parish . . . from December
24, 1749, to December 24, 1750.
Philadelphia, 1750. Broadside.]
(Hildeburn 1168.)   6589

Philadelphia. Christ Church, 1751.
An Account of Births and Burials in
Christ-Church Parish . . . from December
24, 1750, to December 24, 1751.
[Philadelphia. 1751.] Broadside.
LOC copy.   6755

Philadelphia, Christ Church, 1752.
An Account of the Births and Burials in
Christ-Church Parish . . . from December
24, 1751, to December 24, 1752.
[Philadelphia, 1752.] Broadside.
LOC copy.   6914

Philadelphia. Christ Church, 1753.
An Account of the Births and Burials in
Christ-Church Parish . . . from December
24, 1752, to December 24, 1753.
[Philadelphia, 1753.] Broadside.
LCP copy.   7092

Philadelphia. Christ Church, 1754.
An Account of the Births and Burials in
Christ-Church Parish . . . from December
24, 1753, to December 24, 1754.
[Philadelphia, 1754.] Broadside.
LCP copy.   7293

Philadelphia. Christ Church, 1755.
An Account of the Births and Burials in
Christ-Church Parish . . . from December
24, 1754, to December 24, 1755.
[Philadelphia, 1755.] Broadside.
LCP copy.   7539

Philadelphia. Christ Church, 1756.
An Account of the Births and Burials in
Christ-Church Parish . . . from December
24, 1755, to December 24, 1756.
[Philadelphia, 1756.] Broadside.
LCP copy.   7763

Philadelphia. Christ Church, 1757.
An Account of the Births and Burials in
Christ-Church Parish . . . from December
24, 1756, to December 24, 1757.
[Philadelphia, 1757.] Broadside.
LCP copy.   8004

Philadelphia. Christ Church, 1758.
An Account of the Births and Burials in
Christ-Church Parish . . . December 24,
1757, to December 24, 1758.
[Philadelphia, 1758.] Broadside.
LCP copy.   8236

[Philadelphia Christ Church, 1759.
An Account of the Births and Burials in
Christ-Church Parish . . . from December
24, 1758, to December 24, 1759.
Philadelphia, 1759.]
(Assumed by Hildeburn from the
sequence.)   8467

Philadelphia. Christ Church, 1760.
An Account of the Births and Burials in
Christ-Church Parish . . . from December
24, 1759, to December 24, 1760.
[Philadelphia, 1760.] Broadside.
LCP copy.   8714

Philadelphia. Christ Church, 1761.
An Account of the Births and Burials in
Christ-Church Parish . . . from December
25, 1760, to December 25, 1761.
[Philadelphia, 1761.] Broadside.
LCP copy.   8980

Philadelphia. Christ Church, 1762.
An Account of the Births and Burials in
Christ-Church Parish . . . from December
25, 1761, to December 25, 1762.
[Philadelphia, 1762.] Broadside.
LCP copy.   9238

Philadelphia. Christ Church, 1763.
An Account of the Births and Burials in
St. Peter's and Christ-Church Parish . . .
from Dec. 25, 1762, to December 25, 1763.
[Philadelphia, 1763.] Broadside.
LCP copy.   9483

Philadelphia. Christ Church, 1764.
An Account of the Births and Burials in
St. Peter's and Christ-Church Parish . . .
from December 25, 1763, to December 25,
1764.
[Philadelphia, 1764.] Broadside.
LCP copy.   9793

Philadelphia. Christ Church, 1765.
An Account of the Births and Burials in
Christ-Church and St. Peter's Parish . . .
from December 25, 1764, to December 25,
1765.
[Philadelphia, 1765.] Broadside.
HSP copy.   10136

Philadelphia. Christ Church, 1766.
An Account of the Births and Burials in
Christ-Church Parish . . . from December
25, 1765, to December 25, 1766.
[Philadelphia, 1766.] Broadside.
LCP copy.   10452

Philadelphia. Christ Church, 1767.
An Account of the Births and Burials in
the United Churches of Christ-Church and
St. Peter's . . . from December 25, 1766, to
December 25, 1767.
[Philadelphia, 1767.] Broadside.
LCP copy.   10738

Philadelphia. Christ Church, 1767.
Chapter VIII, Of the Rules of the United
Episcopal Churches.
[Philadelphia, 1767.] Broadside.
HSP copy.   41753

Philadelphia. Christ Church, 1768.
An Account of the Births and Burials in
the United Churches of Christ-Church and
St. Peter's . . . from December 25, 1767, to
December 25, 1768.
[Philadelphia, 1768.] Broadside.
LCP copy.   11036

Philadelphia. Christ Church, 1769.
An Account of the Births and Burials in
the United Churches of Christ-Church and
St. Peter's . . . from December 25, 1768, to
December 25, 1769.
[Philadelphia, 1769.] Broadside.
LCP copy.   11414

Philadelphia. Christ Church, 1770.
An Account of the Births and Burials in
the United Churches of Christ-Church and
St. Peter's . . . from December 25, 1769, to
December 25, 1770.
[Philadelphia, 1770.] Broadside.
LCP copy.   11819

Philadelphia. Christ Church, 1771.
An Account of the Births and Burials in
the United Churches of Christ-Church and
St. Peter's . . . from New-Year's Day,
1771, to New-Year's Day, 1772.

[Philadelphia, 1772.] Broadside.
LCP copy.   12522

Philadelphia. Christ Church, 1772.
An Account of the Births and Burials in
The United Churches of Christ-Church and
St. Peter's . . . from December 25, 1771, to
December 25, 1772.
[Philadelphia, 1772.] Broadside.
LCP copy.   12524

Philadelphia. Christ Church, 1772.
By Charles Wilson, Sexton of the Baptist
Church. . . . An Account of the Births and
Burials in the United Churches of Christ
Church and St. Peters . . . from
New-Year's Day, 1771, to New-Year's
Day, 1772.
[Philadelphia], Evitt, [1772]. Broadside.
LCP copy.   12523

Philadelphia. Christ Church, 1773.
An Account of the Births and Burials in
the United Churches of Christ-Church and
St. Peter's . . . from December 25, 1772, to
December 25, 1773.
[Philadelphia, 1773.] Broadside.
LCP copy.   12950

Philadelphia. Christ Church, 1774.
An Account of the Births and Burials in
the United Congregations of
Christ-Church and St. Peters . . . from
December 25, 1773, to December 25, 1774.
[Philadelphia, 1774.] Broadside.
LCP copy.   13541

Philadelphia. Christ Church, 1775.
An Account of the Births and Burials in
the United Churches of Christ-Church and
St Peter's . . . from December 25, 1774,
to December 25, 1775.
[Philadelphia, 1775.] Broadside.
LCP copy.   14388

[Philadelphia. Christ Church, 1777.
An Account of the Births and Burials in
Christ Church and St. Peters.
Philadelphia, 1777. Broadside.]
(Assumed from the sequence.)   15552

[Philadelphia. Christ Church, 1778.
An Account of the Births and Burials in
the United Churches of Christ Church and
St. Peter's.
Philadelphia, 1778. Broadside.]
(Assumed by Hildeburn from the
sequence.)   15993

[Philadelphia. Christ Church, 1779.
An Account of the Births and Burials in
the United Churches of Christ-Church and
St. Peter's.
Philadelphia, 1779. Broadside.]
(Assumed by Hildeburn from the
sequence.)   16476

[Philadelphia. Christ Church, 1780.
An Account of the Births and Burials in
the United Churches of Christ Church and
St. Peter's.
[Philadelphia, 1780.] Broadside.]
(Assumed from the sequence.)   16947

[Philadelphia. Christ Church, 1781.
An Account of the Births and Burials in
the United Churches of Christ Church and
St. Peter's.
[Philadelphia, 1781.] Broadside.]
(Assumed from the sequence.)   17311

Philadelphia. Christ Church, 1782.
An Account of Births and Burials in the
United Churches of Christ Church and St.
Peter's . . . from December 25, 1781, to
December 25, 1782.
[Philadelphia, 1782.] Broadside.
LCP copy.   17675

[Philadelphia. Christ Church, 1783.
An Account of the Births and Burials in
the United Churches of Christ Church and
St. Peter's.
Philadelphia, 1783. Broadside.]
(Assumed from the sequence.)   18137

[Philadelphia. Christ Church, 1784.
An Account of the Births and Burials in
the United Churches of Christ-Church and
St. Peter's.
[Philadelphia, 1784.] Broadside.]
(Assumed by Hildeburn from the
sequence.)   18728

[Philadelphia. Christ Church, 1785.
An Account of the Births and Burials in
the United Churches of Christ-Church and
St. Peter's.
Philadelphia, 1785.]
(Assumed from the sequence.)   19192

Philadelphia. Christ Church, 1785.
At a Meeting of the Congregations of
Christ Church and St. Peter's . . . on . . .
the 15th August, 1785.
[Philadelphia], Hall & Sellers, [1785].
Broadside.
HSP copy.   44770

[Philadelphia. Christ Church, 1786.
An Account of the Births and Burials in
the United Churches of Christ-Church and
St. Peter's.
[Philadelphia, 1786.] Broadside.]
(Assumed from the sequence.)   19916

[Philadelphia. Christ Church, 1787.
An Account of the Births and Burials in
the United Churches of Christ-Church and
St. Peters.
Philadelphia, 1787. Broadside.]
(Assumed by Evans from the Sequence.)   20643

[Philadelphia. Christ Church, 1788.
An Account of the Births and Burials in
the United Churches of Christ-Church and
St. Peter's.
Philadelphia, 1788. Broadside.]
(Assumed by Evans from the sequence.)   21387

[Philadelphia. Christ Church, 1789.
An Account of the Births and Burials in
the United Churches of Christ-Church and
St. Peter's.
[Philadelphia, 1789.] Broadside.
(Assumed by Evans from the sequence.)   22065

[Philadelphia. Christ Church, 1790.
An Account of the Births and Burials in
the United Churches of Christ-Church and
St. Peter's, from December 24, 1789, to
December 24, 1790.
[Philadelphia, 1790.] Broadside.]
(Assumed by Evans from the sequence.)   22793

[Philadelphia. Christ Church, 1791.
An Account of the Births and Burials in
the United Churches of Christ Church and
St. Peter's, from December 24, 1790, to
December 24, 1791.
[Philadelphia, 1791.] Broadside.]
(No copy located.)   23696

Philadelphia. Christ Church, 1792.
An Account of the Births and Burials in
the United Churches of Christ Church and
St. Peter's . . . from December 25, 1791, to
December 25, 1792.
[Philadelphia, 1792.] Broadside.
LCP copy.   24686

Philadelphia. Christ Church, 1793.
Mortality. . . . An Account of the
Baptisms and Burials in the United
Churches of Christ Church and St. Peter's
. . . from December 25, 1792 to December
25, 1793.
[Philadelphia, 1793.] Broadside.
LCP copy.   25991

Philadelphia. Christ Church, 1794.
Mortality. . . . An Account of the Births
and Burials in the United Churches of
Christ-Church and St. Peter's . . . from
December 25, 1793. to December 25, 1794.
[Philadelphia], Ormrod & Conrad,
[1794]. Broadside.
LCP copy.   27504

Philadelphia. Christ Church, 1795.
Mortality. . . . An Account of the
Baptisms and Burials in the United
Churches of Christ-Church and St. Peter's
. . . from December 25, 1794 to December
25, 1795.
[Philadelphia], Ormrod & Conrad [1795].
Broadside.
LCP copy.   29309

Philadelphia. Christ Church, 1796.
Mortality. An Account of the Baptisms
and Burials in the United Churches of
Christ-Church and St. Peter's . . . from

December 25, 1795, to December 25, 1796.
[Philadelphia], Ormrod & Conrad,
[1796]. Broadside.
AAS copy.   30998

Philadelphia. Christ Church, 1797.
Mortality. An Account of the Baptisms
and Burials in the United Churches of
Christ-Church and St. Peter's. . . . From
December 25, 1796, to December 25, 1797.
[Philadelphia], Ormrod & Conrad,
[1797]. Broadside.
LCP copy.   32679

Philadelphia. Christ Church, 1798.
Mortality. An Account of the Baptisms
and Burials in the United Churches of
Christ-Church and St. Peter's. . . . From
December 25, 1797, to December 25, 1798.
[Philadelphia], Ormrod, [1798].
Broadside.
LCP copy.   34354

Philadelphia. Christ Church, 1799.
Mortality. An Account of the Baptisms
and Burials in the United Churches of
Christ Church and St. Peter's. . . . From
December 25, 1798, to Dec. 25, 1799.
[Philadelphia], Ormrod, [1799].
Broadside.
LCP copy.   36097

Philadelphia. Churches, 1775.
An Account of the Baptisms and Burial in
all the Churches and Meetings in
Philadelphia. From Dec. 25, 1774, to
December 25, 1775.
[Philadelphia, 1775.] Broadside.
LCP copy.   14391

Philadelphia. Churches, 1800.
Mortality. Account of the Baptisms and
Burials in the United Churches of Christ
Church and St. Peter's. . . . Also . . .
Baptisms . . . in Various Congregations
. . . from Dec. 25, 1799 to Dec. 25, 1800.
[Philadelphia], Ormrod. Broadside.
LCP copy.   38245

Philadelphia. Citizens, 1770.
Philadelphia, Thursday, Sept. 27, 1770. . . .
[Philadelphia, 1770.] Broadside.
AAS ph. copy.   42153

Philadelphia. Citizens, 1774.
At a Very Large . . . Meeting . . . June 18,
1774. . . .
[Philadelphia, 1774.] Broadside.
HSP copy.   42666

Philadelphia. Citizens, 1776.
At a Meeting, held at the Philosophical
Society-Hall, on Thursday Evening,
October 17th, 1776.
[Philadelphia, 1776.] [2] pp.
LCP copy.   15018

Philadelphia. Citizens, 1776.
At a Meeting of a Number of the Citizens
of Philadelphia, in the Philosophical
Society-Hall, the 8th of November, 1776.
[Philadelphia, 1776.] Broadside.
HSP copy.   15020

Philadelphia. Citizens, 1776.
At a Meeting of a Number of the Citizens
of Philadelphia, at the Philosophical
Society's Hall, November the 2d. . . .
[Philadelphia, 1776.] Broadside.
HSP copy.   15019

Philadelphia. Citizens, 1776.
Bey Einer Versammlung einer Anzahl
Philadelphischer Bürger, Gehalten . . .
den 8ten November, 1776.
[Philadelphia, 1776.] Broadside.
LOC copy.   43135

Philadelphia. Citizens, 1779.
At a General Meeting of the Citizens of
Philadelphia, and parts Adjacent . . . the
25th of May 1779.
Philadelphia, Bailey, [1779]. Broadside.
LCP copy.   16463

Philadelphia. Citizens, 1784.
To the Honorable the Representatives . . .
the Petition . . . to Extend the Arch over
the Common Sewer.
[Philadelphia, 1784.] Broadside.
LOC copy.   44591

Philadelphia. Citizens, 1792.

Circular. Philadelphia, August 3d, 1792.
Sir, By the Enclosed. . . .
[Philadelphia, 1792.] Broadside.
HSP copy.   46542

Philadelphia. Citizens, 1792.
Extract from the Minutes of . . . a General
Meeting . . . the 30th of July, 1792.
[Philadelphia, 1792.] Broadside.
HSP copy.   46543

[Philadelphia. Citizens, 1793.
Copy of a Petition now Circulating.
[Philadelphia, 1793.] Broadside.
(The one copy reported could not be
located.)   25988

[Philadelphia. Citizens, 1795.
Town-Meeting. - Treaty. Citizens!
Assemble at the State-House . . . the 23d
instant.
[Philadelphia, 1795.] Broadside.]
(No copy located.)   29306

Philadelphia. Citizens, 1798.
At a Meeting of a Number of the Citizens
of Philadelphia . . . for the Purpose of
Nominating. . . .
[Philadelphia, 1798.] Broadside.
HSP copy.   48571

Philadelphia. Clergy.
The Address and Petition of a Number of
the Clergy.
Philadelphia, Young, 1793. 16 pp.
AAS copy.   25986

[Philadelphia. Clock and Watchmakers.
A List of Articles with their Prices. . . .
Philadelphia, 1795.]
(No copy located.)   29310

Philadelphia. Committee Appointed to
Examine into the Title of the Corporation
to the North East Public Square.
. . . Report. . . . February 4th, 1797.
[Philadelphia], Poulson, [1797].
[2] pp.
HSP copy.   32675

Philadelphia. Committee for Enquiring
into the State of Trade, 1779.
Whereas the Rapid and Alarming
Depreciation of the Currency. . . .
Philadelphia, Bailey, [1779]. Broadside.
LCP copy.   16474

Philadelphia. Committee for the City and
Liberties, 1779.
Committee for the City and Liberties of
Philadelphia [Election Ticket].
[Philadelphia, 1779.] Broadside.
LCP copy.   16464

Philadelphia. Committee of
Correspondence, 1774.
Committee Chamber, December 6,
1774. . . .
[Philadelphia, 1774.] Broadside.
LCP copy.   13538

Philadelphia. Committee of
Correspondence, 1774.
In Committee, December 14, 1774.
[Philadelphia, 1774.] Broadside.
LCP copy.   13539

Philadelphia. Committee of
Correspondence, 1799.
An Address to the Freemen of
Pennsylvania.
Germantown, Poulson, 1799. 24 pp.
AAS copy.   35081

Philadelphia. Committee of
Correspondence, 1799.
Eine Addresse an die Freyen Leute.
Philadelphia, Cist, 1799. 24 pp.
AAS copy.   35082

Philadelphia. Committee of Inspection,
1776.
Committee Chamber, Philadelphia, May
18, 1776. . . .
[Philadelphia, 1776.] Broadside.
LCP copy.   15014

Philadelphia. Committee of Inspection,
1776.
In Committee Chamber, May 16,
1776. . . .
[Philadelphia, 1776.] Broadside.
LCP copy.   15013

Philadelphia. Committee of Inspection,
1776.
In Committee, of Inspection and
Observation, February 5th, 1776. . . .
[Philadelphia, 1776.] Broadside.
LCP copy.   15011

Philadelphia. Committee of Inspection,
1776.
List of the Sub-Committees. . . . February
26, 1776.
[Philadelphia, 1776.] Broadside.
LCP copy.   15012

Philadelphia. Committee of Inspection,
1776.
Philadelphia, May 21, 1776. Gentlemen,
We have. . . .
[Philadelphia, 1776.] [2] pp.
HSP copy.   43136

Philadelphia. Committee of Safety, 1776.
Philadelphia, September 2, 1776. In
Compliance with the Resolves of
Convention. . . .
Philadelphia, Snyder & Cist, [1776].
Broadside.
(Taylor 34. No copy located.)   43137

Philadelphia. Committee of Safety, 1776.
The Process for Extracting and Refining
Salt-Petre.
Philadelphia, Bradfords, 1776. 8 pp.
HSP copy.   14827

Philadelphia. Committee of the City and
Liberties, 1779.
The Address of the Committee of the City
and Liberties of Philadelphia, to their
Fellow-Citizens throughout the United
States.
Philadelphia, Bailey, [1779]. Broadside.
LCP copy.   16462

[Philadelphia. Committee on Peace
Celebration, 1783.
The Committee Appointed to Confer with
Council. . . .
[Philadelphia, 1783.] 2 pp.]
(No copy located.)   18135

Philadelphia. Committee on Prices, 1779.
Committee-Room. May 28, 1779.
Resolved. . . .
Philadelphia, Bailey, [1779]. Broadside.
LCP copy.   16465

Philadelphia. Committee on Prices, 1779.
Committee-Room. May 31st, 1779.
Notice. . . .
[Philadelphia, Bailey, [1779]. Broadside.
LCP copy.   16466

Philadelphia. Committee on Prices, 1779.
Committee Room, June 10, 1779. Whereas
Sundry. . . .
[Philadelphia, 1779.] Broadside.
LCP copy.   16467

Philadelphia. Committee on Prices, 1779.
Committee Room, June 18, 1779. At a
Meeting. . . .
Philadelphia, Bailey, [1779]. Broadside.
LCP copy.   16468

Philadelphia. Committee on Prices, 1779.
Committee-Room, June 26, 1779.
Agreeable. . . .
Philadelphia, Bailey, [1779]. Broadside.
LCP copy.   16469

Philadelphia. Committee on Prices, 1779.
In Committee, July 14, 1779. Resolved,
That the Plan. . . .
Philadelphia, Bradford, [1779].
Broadside.
MHS copy.   16470

Philadelphia. Committee to aid Boston,
1774.
Sir, You are Desired to Attend a Special
Meeting of the Committee . . . at the
Carpenter's Hall.
[Philadelphia, 1774.] Broadside.
LCP copy.   13536

Philadelphia. Committee to aid Boston,
1774.
Sir, You are Desired to Attend a Special
Meeting of the Committee at the
Philosophical Society Hall.
[Philadelphia, 1774.] Broadside.
LCP copy.   13535

Philadelphia. Committee to Attend to and
Alleviate the Sufferings of the Afflicted
with the Malignant Fever.
Minutes of the Proceedings of the
Committee, Appointed on the 14th
September, 1793.
Philadelphia, Aitken for Crukshank,
Young & Dobson, 1794. [2], 223 pp.
NLM copy.   27501

Philadelphia. Common Council
Committee on the City Debts and
Expenditures.
. . . Report of the. . . . Feb. 15, 1798.
[Philadelphia], Poulson, 1798. 12 pp.
NYPL copy.   34349

Philadelphia. Constables.
To be Sold, by Public Vendue . . . the 27th
of February. . . .
[Philadelphia], Patterson & Cochran,
[1799]. Broadside.
(The only located copy was not available
for reproduction.)   36092

Philadelphia. Constitutional Society.
To the Citizens of Pennsylvania. . . .
[Philadelphia, 1780.] Broadside.
LCP copy.   16949

Philadelphia. Cordwainers.
A List of the Prices of Boots and
Shoes. . . . 8th November, 1790.
[Philadelphia, 1790.] Broadside.
LCP copy.   45964

Philadelphia. Council of Safety, 1776.
In Council of Safety. Philadelphia,
October 14, 1776. . . .
[Philadelphia, 1776.] Broadside.
APS copy.   15017

Philadelphia. Council of Safety, 1776.
In Council of Safety, Philadelphia,
November 14th, 1776. . . .
[Philadelphia], Dunlap, [1776].
Broadside.
HSP copy.   15021

Philadelphia. Council of Safety, 1776.
In Council of Safety, November 27, 1776.
To the Freemen. . . .
[Philadelphia, 1776.] Broadside.
LCP copy.   15022

[Philadelphia. Council of Safety, 1776.
In Council of Safety, Philadelphia,
December 2, 1776. Resolved. . . .
Philadelphia, Miller, [1776]. Broadside.]
(No copy located.)   15023

Philadelphia. Council of Safety, 1776.
In Council of Safety, December 3,
1776. . . .
Philadelphia, Dunlap, [1776]. Broadside.
LCP copy.   15024

Philadelphia. Council of Safety, 1776.
In the Council of Safety, Philadelphia,
December 8, 1776. Sir. . . .
[Philadelphia, 1776.] Broadside.
HSP copy.   15025

Philadelphia. Council of Safety, 1776.
In Council of Safety, Philadelphia,
December 13, 1776 [Israel Putnam].
[Philadelphia], Dunlap, [1776].
Broadside.
LCP copy.   15026

Philadelphia. Council of Safety, 1776.
In Council of Safety, Philadelphia,
December 23, 1776. Friends. . . .
[Philadelphia], Dunlap, [1776].
Broadside.
HSP copy.   15027

Philadelphia. Councils. Joint Committee
on the Schuylkill Bridge and Ferry.
A Communication from the. . . . July 30th,
1798.
Philadelphia, 1798. 7, [1] pp.
NYPL copy.   34348

Philadelphia. Councils. Joint Committee
on Water Supply.
Report of the. . . .
Philadelphia, Poulson, 1798. 12 pp.
AAS copy. ,   34350

Philadelphia. Councils. Joint Committee
on Water Supply.
Report of the Joint Committee.

Philadelphia, Poulson, 1799. 7 pp.
HSP copy.   36089

Philadelphia. Councils. Joint Committee
on Water Supply.
Report to the Select and Common Council
on the 24th of November, 1799. . . .
Philadelphia, Poulson, 1799. 44 pp.
AAS copy.   36091

Philadelphia. Councils. Joint Committee
to Estimate Sums Necessary to Meet
Expenses of the Current Year.
Report of the. . . .
Philadelphia, Poulson, 1799. 20 pp.
LCP copy.   36090

Philadelphia. County Prison. Board of
Inspectors.
Directions for the Inspectors. . . . 26th
February, 1792.
[Philadelphia, 1792.] Broadside.
NYHS copy.   24683

Philadelphia. County Prison. Board of
Inspectors.
Rules, Orders, and Regulations. . . . 26th
February, 1792.
Philadelphia, Humphreys, [1792].
Broadside.
NYHS copy.   24684

Philadelphia. Dispensary for Medical
Relief.
Plan of the Philadelphia Dispensary.
[Philadelphia, 1787.] 8 pp.
MHS copy.   19917

Philadelphia. Dispensary for Medical
Relief.
To the Attending Physician. . . . I
Recommend [blank]. . . .
[Philadelphia, 1797.] Broadside.
UOP copy.   48228

Philadelphia. Election Prox, 1774.
Committee. 1 John Dickinson. . . .
[Philadelphia, 1774.] Broadside.
LCP copy.   42667

Philadelphia. Election Prox, 1774.
Committee. 1 Thomas Mifflin. . . .
[Philadelphia, 1774.] Broadside.
LCP copy.   42668

Philadelphia. Election Prox, 1775.
Committee for the City of Philadelphia,
District of Southwark and Northern
Liberties. Dr. Franklin.
[Philadelphia, 1775.] Broadside.
LCP copy.   42920

Philadelphia. Election Prox, 1775.
Committee, for the City of Philadelphia
and Northern Liberties, to be and
Continue until the 16th Day of February,
A.D. 1776.
[Philadelphia, 1775.] Broadside.
LCP copy.   14385

Philadelphia. Election Prox, 1775.
Committee for the City of Philadelphia
and the Northern Liberties. To Continue
for Six Months.
[Philadelphia, 1775.] Broadside.
LCP copy.   42919

Philadelphia. Election Prox, 1776.
Committee for the City of Philadelphia, to
be and Continue until the Sixteenth Day
of August, A.D., 1776.
[Philadelphia, 1776.] Broadside.
LCP copy.   43138

Philadelphia. English Presbyterian
Society.
To all Charitably Disposed Persons. . . .
The Petition. . . . December 28, 1749/50.
[Philadelphia, 1749.] Broadside.
BPL copy.   40512

Philadelphia. Evangelical Lutheran
Church.
Die Spuren der Güte Gottes.
Germantown, Billmeyer, 1791. 36 pp.
APS copy.   23697

Philadelphia.
Evangelische-Lutheranischen Gemeine.
Die Grundregeln der Gesellschaft.
Philadelphia, Steiner u Kämmerer, 1795.
12 pp.
HC copy.   28642

Philadelphia. Fire Companies.
Return of the Several Fire Companies. . . .
Philadelphia, Poulson, [1799]. Broadside.
JCB copy.   36099

Philadelphia. First Baptist Church, 1781.
An Address . . . to their Sister Churches.
Philadelphia, Aitken, 1781. 16 pp.
AAS copy.   17310

Philadelphia. First Troop of Cavalry.
Bye-Laws of the First Troop of
Philadelphia Cavalry.
[Philadelphia, 1798.] 12 pp.
LCP copy.   48572

Philadelphia. First Unitarian Church.
Constitutional Rules of the. . . . 28th of
August, 1796.
Philadelphia, Gales, 1796. 7 pp.
LCP copy.   31003

Philadelphia. Friendly Association.
To William Denny. . . . The Address of
the Trustees.
[Philadelphia, 1757.] 4 pp.
NYPL copy.   8005

Philadelphia. Friends Library.
Catalogue of Books in. . . .
[Philadelphia, Crukshank, 1795.] 32 pp.
AAS copy.   29312

Philadelphia. Friendship Fire Company.
Articles . . . Instituted in the Year, 1796.
[Philadelphia]. Aitken, [1796].
Broadside.
HSP copy.   31000

Philadelphia. Friendship Fire Company.
Articles and By-Laws of the. . . .
Philadelphia, Poulson, 1800. [12] pp.
HSP copy.   38248

Philadelphia. Friendship Fire Company.
Bye-Laws of the. . . .
Philadelphia, Poulson, 1795. 12 pp.
LCP copy.   29313

Philadelphia. Friendship Fire Company.
. . . A Meeting . . . will be held. . . . Nov.
20th, 1797.
[Philadelphia], Poulson, [1797].
Broadside.
LCP copy.   48229

Philadelphia. Grand Jury, 1718.
To the Honourable William Keith. . . .
The Grand Jury.
Philadelphia, 1718. Broadside.
HSP copy.   1995

Philadelphia. Grand Jury, 1726.
To the Honourable Patrick Gordon. . . .
The Humble Address of the
Grand-Jury. . . . July 8, 1726.
[Philadelphia], Bradford, [1726].
Broadside.
HSP copy.   2805

Philadelphia. Guardians for the Relief and
Employment of the Poor.
A Compilation of the Poor Laws . . . 1700,
to 1788.
Philadelphia, Poulson, 1788. 95 pp.
LCP copy.   21364

Philadelphia. Hibernia Fire Company.
Articles of the. . . .
[Philadelphia, 1786.] Broadside.
HSP copy.   19918

Philadelphia. Library Company.
Be it Remembered, in Honor of the
Philadelphian Youth. . . .
[Philadelphia, Poulson, 1789.] Broadside.
LCP copy.   45504

[Philadelphia. Library Company.
Catalogue of the Library Company of
Philadelphia.
Philadelphia, Franklin, 1733. Broadside.]
(Ordered printed, but no copy found.)
                                                 3714

[Philadelphia. Library Company.
Catalogue of the Library Company.
Philadelphia, 1735. Broadside.]
(Ordered printed, but no copy found.)
                                                 3950

Philadelphia. Library Company.
A Catalogue of Books.

Philadelphia, Franklin, 1741. 55, [1] pp.
AAS copy.   4787

Philadelphia. Library Company.
A Catalogue of Books.
Philadelphia, Bradford, 1765. 68 pp.
HSP copy.   10137

Philadelphia. Library Company.
A Catalogue of the Books.
Philadelphia, Poulson, 1789. xl, 406,
[1] pp.
AAS copy.   22066

Philadelphia. Library Company.
Supplement to the Catalogue of Books.
Philadelphia, Poulson, 1793. 38 pp.
AAS copy.   25995

Philadelphia. Library Company.
Second Supplement to the Catalogue of
Books.
Philadelphia, Poulson, 1794. 34 pp.
AAS copy.   27509

Philadelphia. Library Company.
Third Supplement to the Catalogue of
Books.
Philadelphia, Poulson, 1796. 38 pp.
AAS copy.   31001

Philadelphia. Library Company.
Fourth Supplement to the Catalogue of
Books.
Philadelphia, Poulson, 1798. 40, 8 pp.
LCP copy.   34357

Philadelphia. Library Company.
Fifth Supplement to the Catalogue of
Books.
Philadelphia, Poulson, 1799. 32 pp.
LCP copy.   36100

Philadelphia. Library Company.
The Charter of the Library Company.
Philadelphia, Franklin, 1746. 8, 15, 28, [4]
pp.
UOP copy.   5853

Philadelphia. Library Company.
The Charter, Laws, and Catalogue of the
Books.
Philadelphia, Franklin & Hall, 1757. 23,
132 pp.
HSP copy.   8006

Philadelphia. Library Company.
The Charter, Laws, and Catalogue.
Philadelphia, Franklin & Hall, 1764 26,
150 pp.
AAS copy.   9794

Philadelphia. Library Company.
The Charter, Laws, and Catalogue of. . . .
Philadelphia, Crukshank, 1770. 38, [316]
pp.
AAS copy.   11820

Philadelphia. Library Company.
Many Members. . . . October 4th, 1771.
[Philadelphia, 1771.] Broadside.
LCP copy.   12194

Philadelphia. Library Company.
The Second Part of the Catalogue.
Philadelphia, Aitken, 1775. 67 pp.
HSP copy.   14392

Philadelphia. Library Company.
Whereas a Law was Passed . . . Enabling the
Directors . . . to Admit the Members of
the Union Library Company. . . . 1769.
[Philadelphia, 1769.] Broadside.
UOP copy.   41975

Philadelphia. Library Company.
You are hereby Notified, that a General
Meeting of the Library Company . . . is to
be held . . . the 3rd August. . . . July 21,
1741.
[Philadelphia, Franklin, 1741.]
Broadside.
LCP copy.   40255

Philadelphia. Lieutenant, 1777.
All the Male White Inhabitants
Residing. . . . April 23, 1777.
[Philadelphia, 1777.] Broadside.
LCP copy.   15508

Philadelphia. Linen Manufactory.
A Number of the Inhabitants of this
City. . . .

[Philadelphia, 1765.] 2 pp.
LCP copy.   10134

Philadelphia. Linen Manufactory.
Whereas the Number of Poor in and
around this City. . . .
[Philadelphia, 1764.] 2 pp.
LCP copy.   9870

Philadelphia. Loganian Library.
Catalogus Bibliothecae Loganianae.
Philadelphia, Miller, 1760. [2], 116 pp.
AAS copy.   8715

Philadelphia. Loganian Library.
Catalogue of the Books belonging to
the. . . .
Philadelphia, Poulson, 1795. 220 pp.
AAS copy.   29314

Philadelphia. Lottery Accounts.
Philadelphia, Franklin & Hall, 1752. 16
pp.
(Curtis 494. No copy located.)   40638

Philadelphia. Mayor, 1726.
To the Honourable Patrick Gordon. . . .
The Address of the Mayor [July 16,
1726].
Philadelphia, Bradford, [1726]. [2] pp.
HSP copy.   2804

Philadelphia. Mayor, 1765.
City of Philadelphia. By the Mayor . . .
and the Commissioners for Paving. . . .
March, 1765.
[Philadelphia, 1765.] Broadside.
LCP copy.   10132

Philadelphia. Merchants, 1765.
The Merchants and Traders of the City
. . . Taking into Consideration . . .
North-American Commerce. . . .
[Philadelphia, 1765.] Broadside.
LCP copy.   41584

Philadelphia. Merchants, 1794.
For the Information of the Merchants.
The Committee having been Notified. . . .
Nov. 8, 1794.
[Philadelphia, 1794.] Broadside.
CHS copy.   47176

Philadelphia. Merchants, 1794.
-From Thomas Fitzsimons to the
Secretary of State. . . . 7th November,
1794.
[Philadelphia, 1794.] [2] pp.
CHS copy.   47177

Philadelphia. Militia Legion.
Legionary Orders. December 28th,
2799 [!].
[Philadelphia, 1799.] Broadside.
LOC copy.   36105

Philadelphia. Militia Legion.
Legionary Orders. The Militia Legion. . . .
Dec. 24th, 1799.
[Philadelphia, 1799.] Broadside.
LOC copy.   36106

Philadelphia. New Theatre.
At a General Meeting of the Subscribers
to the . . . 25th of June, 1795.
[Philadelphia, 1795.] Broadside.
HSP copy.   29315

Philadelphia. New Theatre.
. . . Resolutions and Articles of
Agreement.
[Philadelphia, 1799.] 16 pp.
HSP copy.   36103

Philadelphia. Ordinances, etc., 1745.
An Ordinance for Establishing a Market
in the District of Southwark.
[Philadelphia], Humphreys, [1745?].
Broadside.
(No copy could be located.)   40387

Philadelphia. Ordinances, etc., 1790.
By the Mayor, Aldermen, and Citizens . . .
an Ordinance for the Regulation of the
Drivers of Carriages.
Philadelphia, James & Johnson, [1790].
Broadside.
HSP copy.   45965

Philadelphia. Ordinances, etc., 1790.
By the Mayor, Aldermen, and
Citizens. . . . An Ordinance for the
Suppression of Nuisances. . . .

[Philadelphia, 1790.] Broadside.
(The only reported copy cannot be
located.)   45966

Philadelphia. Ordinances, etc., 1794.
An Ordinance for the Suppression of
Nuisances . . . within the District of
Southwark [Sept. 22, 1794].
[Philadelphia, 1794.] Broadside.
HSP copy.   27502

Philadelphia. Ordinances, etc., 1794.
Carters, Porters, and Others. . . . 22d Day
of September, 1794.
[Philadelphia, 1794.] Broadside.
HSP copy.   47178

Philadelphia. Ordinances, etc., 1794.
A Supplement to an Ordinance, Passed
the 22 Day of September, 1794, for
Regulating the Cording of Wood.
[Philadelphia, 1794.] Broadside.
HSP copy.   47179

Philadelphia. Ordinances, etc., 1796.
. . . An Ordinance to Prevent the Erection
of Wooden Buildings. . . . The Sixth Day
of June . . . One Thousand Seven Hundred
and Ninety-Six.
[Philadelphia, 1796.] Broadside.
HSP copy.   30995

Philadelphia. Ordinances, etc., 1798.
The Ordinances of the City of
Philadelphia.
Philadelphia, Poulson, 1798. 166 pp.
AAS copy.   34347

Philadelphia. Ordinances, etc., 1799.
An Ordinance for Raising Supplies, and
making Appropriations, for . . . 1799.
Philadelphia, Poulson, 1799. 7 pp.
LCP copy.   48955

Philadelphia. Ordinances, etc., 1799.
An Ordinance . . . for Supplying the City
. . . with Wholesome Water.
Philadelphia, Poulson, 1799. 7 pp.
LCP copy.   36087

Philadelphia. Ordinances, etc., 1800.
The Ordinances . . . and the Several
Supplements.
Philadelphia, Poulson, 1800. 46 pp.
LCP copy.   38242

Philadelphia. Ordinances, etc., 1800.
The Ordinances . . . and the Several
Supplements.
Philadelphia, Poulson, 1800. pp. [1]-46,
[2], 47-70.
AAS copy.   38243

Philadelphia. Overseers of the Poor, 1779.
Philadelphia, March 13, 1779. Mr. . . . Sir,
You are Returned one of the Overseers of
the Poor. . . .
[Philadelphia, 1779.] Broadside.
LCP copy.   16473

Philadelphia. Pennsylvania Hospital.
The Committee, Appointed to Prepare an
Account of the Monies Received from the
Legislature . . . Report. . . . 12 mo. 18th,
1797.
[Philadelphia], Fenno, [1797]. Broadside.
AAS copy.   32680

Philadelphia. Pennsylvania Hospital.
The Committee Appointed to Prepare an
Account of the Monies Received from the
Legislature. . . . Report . . .
Twelfth-Month 22d, 1800.
Philadelphia, Poulson, [1800]. Broadside.
(No copy could be located.)   38250

Philadelphia. Pennsylvania Hospital.
Continuation of the Account of the
Pennsylvania Hospital [May 1, 1754 -
May 5, 1761].
Philadelphia, Franklin & Hall, 1761. pp.
[2], 41-77.
UOP copy.   8972

Philadelphia. Pennsylvania Hospital.
Rules Agreed to by the Managers [Jan.
23, 1752].
[Philadelphia, 1752.] [2] pp.
(The only recorded copy could not be
located.)   40637

Philadelphia, Pennsylvania Hospital.

State of the Accounts of the. . . . 4th
Month, 1800.
[Philadelphia], Claypoole, [1800].
Broadside.
AAS copy.   38251

Philadelphia. Pennsylvania Hospital.
To the Senate and House of
Representatives.
Philadelphia, Poulson, 1799. 7 pp.
AAS copy.   36104

Philadelphia. Pennsylvania Hospital.
To the Senate and House of
Representatives. . . . 12th Month, 28th,
1797.
[Philadelphia, 1797.] [2] pp.
LCP copy.   48219

Philadelphia. Pennsylvania Hospital.
Library.
A Catalogue of the Books Belonging to
. . .
Philadelphia, Poulson, 1790. 35 pp.
JCB copy.   22795

Philadelphia. Pennsylvania Hospital.
Library.
A Catalogue of the Books Belonging to
the. . . .
Philadelphia, Poulson, 1790. 78 pp.
LCP copy.   27510

Philadelphia. Philadelphia Fire Company.
Articles and Bye-Laws . . . List of
Members.
Philadelphia, 1800. 24 pp.
(No copy could be located.)   38252

Philadelphia. Post Office, 1788.
. . . January 1st, 1778. Establishment of
the Posts and Post Coaches for . . .
1788. . . .
[Philadelphia, 1788.] Broadside.
APS copy.   45339

Philadelphia. Post Office, 1789.
. . . Philadelphia, January 1st, 1789.
Establishment of the Post Coaches, for
. . . 1789. . . .
[Philadelphia, 1789?] Broadside.
APS copy.   45561

Philadelphia. Post Office, 1790.
. . . December 30th, 1790. Establishment
of the Mails for . . . 1791. . . .
Philadelphia, Brown, [1790]. Broadside.
APS copy.   45967

Philadelphia. Post Office, 1793.
Post-Office, Philadelphia. January 1st,
1793. Establishment of the Mails.
Philadelphia, Cist, [1793]. Broadside.
(Not located, 1968.)   46852

Philadelphia. Post Office, 1796.
Post-Office, Philadelphia, 19th September,
1796. Establishment of the Mails. . . .
[Philadelphia, 1796.] Broadside.
LOC copy.   47881

Philadelphia. Post Office, 1797.
Post-Office, Philadelphia, 30th March,
1797. . . .
[Philadelphia, 1797.] Broadside.
LOC copy.   48230

[Philadelphia. Post Office, 1798.
Post-Office, Philadelphia, 22d May, 1798.
Establishment of the Mails. . . .
[Philadelphia, 1798.] [Broadside.]
(No copy located.)   34358

Philadelphia. Public Schools.
Rules for the Good Government . . . of.
. . . 12 Mo. 10, 1795.
[Philadelphia, 1795.] Broadside.
HSP copy.   29305

Philadelphia. Publick Academy.
Constitutions of the Publick Academy.
[Philadelphia, 1749.] 4 pp.
UOP copy.   6405

Philadelphia. Reliance Fire Company.
Articles of the. . . .
[Philadelphia, 1786.] Broadside.
HSP copy.   19919

Philadelphia. St. Andrew's Society.
Rules for the St. Andrew's Society.

Philadelphia, Franklin & Hall, 1751. 16 pp.
LCP copy.   6756

Philadelphia. St. James's Church, 1762.
And this Stone which I have set as a Pillar. . . .
Philadelphia, Miller, [1762.] Broadside.
LCP copy.   41300

Philadelphia. St. Mary's Church, 1779.
M. . . . Vous êtes prié de la part du Ministre Plenipotentiare. . . .
Philadelphia, Bailey, [1779]. Broadside.
LCP copy.   16475

Philadelphia. St. Paul's Church.
An Account of the Births and Burials in St. Paul's Church in Philadelphia, from December 25, 1771, to December 25, 1772.
[Philadelphia, 1772.] Broadside.
LCP copy.   12526

[Philadelphia. St. Paul's Church.
An Account of the Births and Burials in St. Paul's Church.
Philadelphia, 1773.]
(Assumed by Hildeburn from the sequence.)   12952

Philadelphia. St. Paul's Church, 1774.
An Account of the Births and Burials in St. Paul's Church . . . from December 25, 1773, to December 25, 1774.
[Philadelphia, 1774.] Broadside.
LCP copy.   13542

[Philadelphia. St. Paul's Church, 1775.
An Account of the Births and Burials in St. Paul's Church.
Philadelphia, 1775. Broadside.]
(Assumed by Hildeburn.)   14389

Philadelphia. St. Paul's Church, 1794.
Articles of Agreement, &c.
Philadelphia, Poulson, 1794. 16 pp.
NYPL copy.   27511

[Philadelphia. St. Paul's Church, 1798.
Articles of Agreement, &c.
Philadelphia, Ormrod, 1798. 16 pp.]
(Sabin 61481; no copy located.)   34359

Philadelphia. St. Thomas's African Church.
Constitution and Rules.
Philadelphia, Woodward, 1797. 8 pp.
LCP copy.   48231

Philadelphia. Second City Troop of Horse.
Articles, or By-laws, for the. . . .
Philadelphia, Tuckniss, 1799. 7 pp.
HSP copy.   36109

Philadelphia. Second Presbyterian Church, 1767.
An Account of the Burials in the Second Presbyterian Church . . . from December 25, 1766, to December 25, 1767.
[Philadelphia, 1767.] Broadside.
LCP copy.   10739

Philadelphia. Second Presbyterian Church, 1768.
An Account of the Burials of the Second Presbyterian Church . . . from December 25, 1767, to December 25, 1768.
[Philadelphia, 1768.] Broadside.
LCP copy.   11037

[Philadelphia. Second Presbyterian Church, 1769.
An Account of the Burials in the Second Presbyterian Church, December 25, 1768, to December 25, 1769.
Philadelphia, 1769. Broadside.]
(Assumed by Hildeburn from the sequence.)   11417

[Philadelphia. Second Presbyterian Church, 1770.
An Account of the Burials in the Second Presbyterian Church, to December 25, 1770.
Philadelphia, 1770. Broadside.]
(Assumed by Hildeburn from the sequence.)   11822

[Philadelphia. Second Presbyterian Church, 1771.
An Account of the Burials in the. . . .
Philadelphia, 1771.]

(Assumed by Hildeburn from the sequence.)   12196

[Philadelphia. Second Presbyterian Church, 1772.
An Account of the Burials in. . . .
Philadelphia, 1772. Broadside.]
(Assumed by Hildeburn from the sequence.)   12527

[Philadelphia. Second Presbyterian Church, 1773.
An Account of the Burials in the Second Presbyterian Church.
Philadelphia, 1773.]
(Assumed by Hildeburn from the sequence.)   12953

[Philadelphia. Second Presbyterian Church, 1774.
An Account of the Burials in the Second Presbyterian Church.
Philadelphia, 1774.]
(Assumed by Hildeburn from the sequence.)   13543

[Philadelphia. Second Presbyterian Church, 1775.
An Account of the Burials in the Second Presbyterian Church.
Philadelphia, 1775. Broadside.]
(Assumed by Hildeburn.)   14390

Philadelphia. Select Council, 1790.
Rules and Orders for the Regulation of the. . . .
[Philadelphia, 1790.] 3 pp.
LCP copy.   45968

Philadelphia. Select Council, 1796.
Report of a Committee of the. . . . Read November 10th, 1796.
Philadelphia, Poulson, 1796. 24 pp.
LCP copy.   30996

Philadelphia. Sheriff, 1776.
Advertisement. In Pursuance of a Writ [Election, Mar. 2. Dated Feb. 28, 1776].
[Philadelphia, 1776.] Broadside.
LCP copy.   14970

Philadelphia. Sheriff, 1776.
Kundmachung Zufolge [Election, Mar. 2. Dated Feb. 28, 1776].
[Philadelphia, 1776.] Broadside.
LCP copy.   14971

Philadelphia. Sheriff, 1788.
Philadelphia, August 21, 1788. By Virtue of a Writ. . . .
Philadelphia, Cist, [1788]. Broadside.
LCP copy.   45340

Philadelphia. Sheriff, 1791.
By Virtue of Several Writs of Venditioni. . . .
Philadelphia, Hall & Sellers, [1791].
Broadside.
HSP copy.   46259

Philadelphia. Sheriff, 1791.
Philadelphia, October 26, 1791. By Virtue of a Writ. . . .
[Philadelphia, 1791.] Broadside.
NYPL copy.   46260

Philadelphia. Sheriff, 1796.
Philadelphia, June 27, 1796. By Virtue of a Writ. . . .
[Philadelphia, 1796.] Broadside.
LCP copy.   47882

Philadelphia. Society of Friends.
To our Fellow Citizens. . . . The 15th of the 11th Month, 1799.
[Philadelphia, 1799.] 3 pp.
(Also entered as 35522, q. v.)   36110

Philadelphia. Society of Victuallers.
Rules and Orders of the. . . . Novbmeer [!] 7, 1793.
Philadelphia, Sweitzer, 1798. 21 pp.
LCP copy.   48573

Philadelphia. Tanners, Curriers, and Cordwainers.
To the Inhabitants of Pennsylvania [July 11, 1779].
[Philadelphia, 1779.] 2 pp.
LCP copy.   16547

Philadelphia. Theater, 1754.

For the Benefit of Miss Hallam [June 10, 1754].
[Philadelphia, 1754.] Broadside.
HSP copy.   7294

[Philadelphia. Theater, 1767.
By Authority. By the American Company [Apr. 7].
[Philadelphia, 1767.] Broadside.]
(No copy located.)   10573

Philadelphia. Theater, 1770.
This Evening March 27th, will be Presented . . . David and Goliah.
[Philadelphia, 1770?] Broadside.
NYPL ph. copy.   42039

Philadelphia. Theater, 1778.
For the Benefit of the Widows and Orphans of the Army.
On [Jan. 19, 1778]. . . .
Philadelphia, Humphreys, [1778].
Broadside.
NYPL copy.   15995

Philadelphia. Theater, 1778.
On Friday next the First day of May. . . .
Philadelphia, Humphreys, [1778].
Broadside.
LCP copy.   16010

Philadelphia. Theater, 1778.
On Friday next, the Tenth day of April. . . .
Philadelphia, Humphreys, [1778].
Broadside.
LCP copy.   16005

Philadelphia. Theater, 1778.
On Friday next, the Twenty-Fourth day of April. . . .
Philadelphia, Humphreys, [1778].
Broadside.
LCP copy.   16009

Philadelphia. Theater, 1778.
On Monday next, the Thirteenth day of April. . . .
Philadelphia, Humphreys, [1778].
Broadside.
LCP copy.   16007

Philadelphia. Theater, 1778.
On Monday Next, the Thirtieth day of March. . . .
Philadelphia, Humphreys, [1778].
Broadside.
LCP copy.   16004

Philadelphia. Theater, 1778.
On Monday, the Ninth day of March. . . .
Philadelphia, Humphreys, [1778].
Broadside.
LCP copy.   16000

Philadelphia. Theater, 1778.
On Monday, the Second day of March. . . .
Philadelphia, Humphreys, [1778].
Broadside.
LCP copy.   15998

Philadelphia. Theater, 1778.
On Monday, the Sixteenth Day of March at the Theatre in Southwark. . . . The Inconstant. To which will be Added . . . Lethe. . . .
Philadelphia, Humphreys, [1778].
Broadside.
LCP copy.   16001

Philadelphia. Theater, 1778.
On Monday, the Sixteenth Day of March, at the Theatre in Southwark. . . . The Inconstant. To which will be Added, The Mock Doctor. . . .
Philadelphia, Humphreys, [1778].
Broadside.
LCP copy.   16002

Philadelphia. Theater, 1778.
On Monday, the Sixteenth Instant . . .
Philadelphia, Humphreys, [1778].
Broadside.
LCP copy.   15997

Philadelphia. Theater, 1778.
On Monday, the Twenty-Sixth Instant [January]. . . .
Philadelphia, Humphreys, [1778].
Broadside.
LCP copy.   15996

Philadelphia. Theater, 1778.

On Wednesday next, the Sixth day of
May. . . .
Philadelphia, Humphreys, [1778].
Broadside.
LCP copy.   16011

Philadelphia. Theater, 1778.
On Wednesday, the Twenty-Fifth day of
March. . . .
Philadelphia, Humphreys, [1778].
Broadside.
LCP copy.   16003

Philadelphia. Theater, 1778.
Saturday, February 28, 1778. Theatre. For
very Particular Reasons, the Play,
Advertised for Monday next, must be
Postponed. . . .
Philadelphia, Humphreys, [1778].
Broadside.
LCP copy.   15999

Philadelphia. Theater, 1778.
Theatre. On Account of the Indisposition
of one of the Actresses. . . . April 8th,
1778.
[Philadelphia], Humphreys, [1778].
Broadside.
LCP copy.   16006

Philadelphia. Theater, 1778.
Theatre. This week being Passion week.
. . . April 12, 1778.
[Philadelphia, 1778.] Broadside.
LCP copy.   16008

Philadelphia. Theater, 1792.
By Authority. By the Old American
Company . . . December 17. . . . The Road
to Ruin.
[Philadelphia, 1792.] Broadside.
LCP copy.   46544

[Philadelphia. Theater, 1795.
Play Bill of the Dramatist, Given at the
New Theatre, October 26, 1795.
Philadelphia, 1795. Broadside.]
(No copy located.)   29316

[Philadelphia. Theater, 1796.
Playbill of Richard III at New Theater,
Aug. 31, 1796.
Philadelphia, 1796. Broadside.]
(The source of this entry has not been
found.)   31002

Philadelphia. Theater, 1799.
The Last Night. Mr. Reinagle's Benefit.
On Saturday Evening, May 25th. . . .
[Philadelphia, 1799.] Broadside.
LOC copy.   36101

Philadelphia. Theater, 1799.
New Theatre. On Wednesday Evening,
Feb. 27, will be Presented. . . .
[Philadelphia, 1799.] Broadside.
NYPL copy.   36102

Philadelphia. Town Meeting, 1779.
Proceedings of the General Town-Meeting
[July 26-27, 1779].
Philadelphia, Bailey, 1779. 26 pp.
LCP copy.   16472

Philadelphia, Union Fire Company.
Articles of the. . . .
[Philadelphia, 1794.] Broadside.
HSP copy.   47180

Philadelphia. Union Library Company.
A Catalogue of Books.
Philadelphia, Chattin, 1754. 53 pp., irreg.
LCP copy.   7295

Philadelphia. Union Library Company.
A Catalogue of Books.
Philadelphia, Miller, 1765. xxiv, 40 pp.
HSP copy.   10139

Philadelphia. Volunteer Company of
Artillery and Infantry.
Orders. For Wednesday, February 22,
1792.
[Philadelphia, 1792.] Broadside.
(Not located, 1968.)   46545

Philadelphia. Wardens Office, 1784.
. . . February 1, 1784. . . . Whereas by an
Act . . . to Prevent Infectious Diseases.
. . .
[Philadelphia, 1784.] Broadside.
UOP copy.   44592

Philadelphia. Young Ladies' Academy.
The Rise and Progress of the. . . .
Philadelphia, Stewart & Cochran, 1794.
119 pp.
NYPL copy.   27514

Philadelphia. Zion German Evangelical
Lutheran Church.
Arrangement of the Music . . . December
26, 1799.
[Philadelphia, 1799.] 6 pp.
AAS copy.   36111

Philadelphia. Zion German Lutheran
Church.
Klagen uber den Tod des General
Washingtons.
[Philadelphia, 1800.] [4] pp.
(Also entered as 37603, q. v.)   38260

[Philadelphia. Zion's Church.
Lob und Ambetung . . . am 10 October
1790.
Germantown, Billmeyer, 1790.]
(Entry from Seidensticker, p. 126.)   22797

Philadelphia County.
In Pursuance of a Writ to me Directed.
. . .
[Philadelphia, 1777.] Broadside.
LCP copy.   15537

Philadelphia Co., Pa. Collector of Excise.
State of the Accounts of William Crispin
. . . July 1, 1781, to July 1, 1782.
Philadelphia, Bradford, 1783. [10] pp.
LCP copy.   44439

Philadelphia Co., Pa. Recorder.
. . . Information Relative to the Title of
the Corporation to the North-East
Public-Square . . . April, 1797.
[Philadelphia], Poulson, June 13, 1797. 2
pp.
AAS ph. copy.   48227

Philadelphia Co., Pa. Sheriff's Office.
Philadelphia, March 4, 1799. By Virtue of
a Writ. . . . Jonathan Penrose.
[Philadelphia, Humphreys, [1799].
Broadside.
NYHS copy.   36080

Philadelphia Co., Pa. Sheriff's Office.
Philadelphia, May 15, 1789. By Virtue of a
Writ of Levari Facias . . . the 2d Day of
June next.
Philadelphia, Cist, [1789]. Broadside.
HSP copy.   45562

Philadelphia Co., Pa. Sheriff's Office.
Philadelphia, September 22, 1785. On
Monday . . . Public Sale. . . .
[Philadelphia, 1785.] Broadside.
AAS copy.   44771

Philadelphia Co., Pa. Sheriff's Office.
Public Notice. . . . Of the . . . Election. . . .
September 26, 1799.
[Philadelphia], Carey, [1799]. Broadside.
HSP copy.   36088

Philadelphia Academy.
Prayers, for the Use of the Philadelphia
Academy.
Philadelphia, Franklin & Hall, 1753. 20
pp.
UOP copy.   7093

The Philadelphia Almanack for . . . 1778.
[Philadelphia.] [20] pp., map.
HSP copy.   15553

[Philadelphia, April 14, 1780. . . . Slow
and Sure.
Philadelphia, 1780. Broadside.]
(Known from the reward offered for the
author.)   16950

Philadelphia, April 24, 1775. An Express.
. . .
[Philadelphia], Bradfords, [1775].
Broadside.
MdHS copy.   14397

Philadelphia. April 25th, 1775.
An Express Arrived at Five O'clock this
Evening. . . .
Lancaster, [1775]. Broadside.
NYPL copy.   14026

Philadelphia, April 26, 1775. Wednesday.

[Philadelphia], Dunlap, [1775].
Broadside.
LCP copy.   14398

Philadelphia, August, 1783.
[Philadelphia, 1783.] Broadside.
HSP copy.   18136

Philadelphia, August 9, 1798. By Virtue of
a Writ of Fieri Facias. . . .
[Philadelphia], Humphreys, [1798].
Broadside.
LOC copy.   48575

Philadelphia, August 22, 1777. By an
Express. — Annapolis, August 25, 1777.
The Governor is Informed. . . .
[Annapolis, 1777.] Broadside.
MdHS copy.   43341

[Philadelphia Contributionship.
An Act for Incorporating the Society. . . .
Philadelphia, 1768. 8 pp.]
(The copy described by Evans was printed
c. 1810.)   11038

Philadelphia. December [blank] 1798. Sir,
the late Distress. . . .
[Philadelphia, 1798.] Broadside.
JCB copy.   48576

Philadelphia, December 12th, 1796. . . .
The Convention of the different Abolition
Societies. . . .
[Philadelphia, 1796.] Broadside.
LOC copy.   47883

Philadelphia den 19ten May 1766.
Wo des Verdachters Netz . . .
[Philadelphia, 1766.] Broadside.
HSP copy.   10454

The Philadelphia Directory.
See
Stafford, Cornelius William.   36112

The Philadelphia Directory, for 1800.
[Philadelphia], Woodward, 1800. 151,
[1], 80 pp.
(Also entered as 38549, q. v.)   38262

Philadelphia Dispensary for the Medical
Relief of the Poor.
Rules of the Philadelphia Dispensary. . . .
August 1st, 1789.
[Philadelphia, 1789.] 11 pp.
LOC copy.   45563

Philadelphia, February 8, 1781. This
Morning Arrived from the Southward. . . .
[Philadelphia], Claypool, [1781].
Broadside.
JCB copy.   44032

Philadelphia, 15th May, 1788. Inventory
of the Furniture and Goods of . . . John
Penn.
[Philadelphia], Dunlap & Claypoole,
[1788]. Broadside.
(The only known copy is mutilated.)
HSP copy.   45341

Philadelphia. 1st February, 1785. At the
Particular Request of Mr. George Meade.
. . .
[Philadelphia, 1785.] Broadside.
(The one recorded copy could not be
located.)   44772

Philadelphia, January 6. 1734/5.
Advertisement.
[Philadelphia, 1735.] Broadside.
HSP copy.   3862

Philadelphia, January 16, 1776.
Williamsburg (Virginia) Jan. 6. Extract of
a Letter from Col. Howe.
[Philadelphia], Dunlap, [1776].
Broadside.
AAS copy.   43139

Philadelphia, January 22, 1781.
Extract of a Letter from Trenton, Dated
January 20, 1781.
[Philadelphia, 1781.] Broadside.
LOC copy.   17151

Philadelphia. January 31, 1797.
Sir, I Have Noticed that One of the
Objects. . . .
[Philadelphia, 1797?] Broadside.
AAS copy.   32684

The Philadelphia Jockey Club.
[Philadelphia], 1795. 23 pp.
AAS copy.   29638

Philadelphia, July 12, 1770. The
Inhabitants of the City of New-York. . . .
[Philadelphia, 1770.] Broadside.
LOC copy.   11817

Philadelphia, July 20, 1776.
By an Express Arrived Yesterday from
South Carolina.
[Philadelphia, 1776.] Broadside.
NYHS copy.   14671

Philadelphia, July 20, 1776.
By Express. . . . Extract of a Letter from
Fort Johnson, South-Carolina.
[Philadelphia, 1776.] Broadside.
NYHS copy.   43140

Philadelphia, July 24, 1769.
Eight Dollars Reward. . . .
[Philadelphia, 1769.] Broadside.
HSP copy.   11484

Philadelphia, July 29, 1780.
To the Public. . . .
[Philadelphia], Dunlap, [1780].
Broadside.
LCP copy.   16990

Philadelphia, June 7, 1775.
The Committee last Evening. . . .
[Philadelphia, 1775.] Broadside.
LCP copy.   14386

Philadelphia, June 18, 1777.
Sir, You are Desired to take Notice, that
you are Rated in the Tax on
Non-associators.
[Philadelphia, 1777.] Broadside.
LCP copy.   43340

Philadelphia, June [24] 1773.
You are Earnestly Requested to Meet. . . .
[Philadelphia, 1773.] Broadside.
LCP copy.   12948

Philadelphia, March 20, 1798.
Dear Sir, After Fourteen Days. . . .
[Philadelphia, 1798.] Broadside.
(Copy not located, 1968.)   48574

Philadelphia, March 31, 1781.
Intelligence from the Southward.
[Philadelphia], Claypoole, [1781].
Broadside.
HSP copy.   17195

Philadelphia, May 4. (Reprinted in
New-York.) Yesterday. . . .
[New York, 1774.] [2] pp.
NYHS copy.   42669

Philadelphia, May 6, 1783.
1 o'clock, P. M. A Gentleman. . . .
[Philadelphia], Claypoole, [1783].
Broadside.
LOC copy.   18138

Philadelphia, May 7, 1741.
Extract of a Letter from one of the
Officers, who went from this Place, Dated,
Before Carthagena, April 3, 1741.
[Philadelphia, 1741.] Broadside.
AAS copy.   40256

Philadelphia, May 19, 1766.
To the Printers [by Samuel Garrigues].
[Philadelphia, 1766.] Broadside.
(The unique copy is mislaid.)   10308

Philadelphia, May 20.
At a Meeting, at the Statehouse. . . .
[Philadelphia, 1776.] Broadside.
LCP copy.   15015

Philadelphia, May 22, 1770.
The Tradesmen, Artificers and Other
Inhabitants. . . .
[Philadelphia, 1770.] Broadside.
LCP copy.   11897

Philadelphia, May 25, 1782.
A Gentleman from the Eastward. . . .
Philadelphia, Hall & Sellers, [1782].
Broadside.
LOC copy.   44245

Philadelphia, May 27th, 1799.
Sir, Deeply Interested in the Approaching
Election. . . .

[Philadelphia, 1799.] Broadside.
LCP copy.   48956

Philadelphia Medical Society.
The Act of Incorporation and Laws of
the. . . .
Philadelphia, Johnston & Justice, 1793. 16
pp.
MHS copy.   25996

[Philadelphia Medical Society.
Act of Incorporation, and Laws of the.
. . .
Philadelphia, 1797.]
(No such ed. located.)   32681

Philadelphia Medical Society.
The Act of Incorporation and Laws of
the. . . .
Philadelphia, Carey, 1800. 23 pp.
AAS copy.   38253

Philadelphia, Monday, December 27,
1773. The Unanimity, Spirit and
Zeal. . . .
[Philadelphia, 1773.] Broadside.
LOC copy.   12945

The Philadelphia Newest Almanack for
. . . 1775.
Philadelphia, Aitken. [44] pp.
LOC copy.   13648

The Philadelphia Newest Almanack for
. . . 1776.
Philadelphia, Aitken. 48 pp.
MHS copy.   14482

Philadelphia, 9th of December, 1773.
By the Medium of a Curious Numerical
Machine. . . .
[Philadelphia, 1773.] Broadside.
LCP copy.   12703

Philadelphia, November 7, 1765.
At a General Meeting of the Merchants
and Traders.
[Philadelphia, 1765.] Broadside.
LCP copy.   10133

The Philadelphia Pocket Almanack for
. . . 1779.
[Philadelphia, 1778.]
HSP copy.   16012

[The Philadelphia Pocket Companion for
the German Flute.
Philadelphia, Carr, 1794.]
("This day is Published," Dunlap's Daily
Amer. Adv., Apr. 28, 1794.)   27516

. . . The Philadelphia Pocket Companion
for the Guitar or Clarinett. . . . Vol. I for
1794.
[Philadelphia], Carr, [1794]. 40 pp.
AAS copy.   27517

Philadelphia (Saturday) June 18, 1774.
The Inhabitants of the City . . . are
Desired. . . .
[Philadelphia, 1774.] Broadside.
HSP copy.   42670

Philadelphia, Saturday, July 30, 1748.
The Freemen. . . .
[Philadelphia, 1768.] Broadside.
LCP copy.   10906

Philadelphia, September 1st. 1774.
This is true Liberty. . . .
[Philadelphia, 1774.] Broadside.
LCP copy.   13545

Philadelphia, September 6th, 1790.
Gentlemen, Permit us. . . .
[Philadelphia? 1790.] Broadside.
HSP copy.   45969

Philadelphia, September 14th, 1790.
Sir, You are Particularly Requested. . . .
[Philadelphia, 1790.] Broadside.
NYPL copy.   45970

Philadelphia, September 21, 1779.
The Mote Point of Finance.
[Philadelphia, 1779.] Broadside.
LCP copy.   16224

Philadelphia, Sept. 22, 1779.
Taxation Royal Tyranny. . . .
[Philadelphia, 1779.] Broadside.
LCP copy.   16541

Philadelphia, September 23, 1773. . . .
Pettie's-Island Cash Lottery.
[Philadelphia, 1773.] Broadside.
LCP copy.   12937

Philadelphia Society for Alleviating the
Miseries of Public Prisons.
At a Quarterly Meeting . . . held . . . April
14th, 1788.
[Philadelphia, 1788.] Broadside.
AAS copy.   21388

Philadelphia Society for Alleviating the
Miseries of Public Prisons.
Extracts and Remarks.
Philadelphia, Poulson, [1790]. 23 pp.
AAS copy.   22796

Philadelphia Society for Alleviating the
Miseries of Public Prisons.
On Tuesday, the 8th day of May, 1787. . . .
Constitution. . . .
[Philadelphia, 1787.] 4 pp.
AAS copy.   20644

Philadelphia Society for Promoting
Agriculture.
An Address, from the Philadelphia
Society.
[Philadelphia], 1785. 20 pp.
AAS copy.   19193

Philadelphia Society for Promoting
Agriculture.
Laws of the. . . .
Philadelphia, Hall & Sellers, 1785. 8 pp.
AAS copy.   44773

Philadelphia Society for Promoting
Agriculture.
Laws of the Philadelphia Society . . . with
the Premiums Proposed, February 5, 1788.
[Philadelphia], 1788. 24 pp.
LOC copy.   21389

Philadelphia Society for Promoting
Agriculture.
Laws of the. . . .
[Philadelphia], 1789. 23 pp.
LCP copy.   22067

Philadelphia Society for Promoting
Agriculture.
Outlines of a Plan, for Establishing a
State Society of Agriculture.
Philadelphia, Cist, 1794. [2], 11 pp.
AAS copy.   27512

Philadelphia Society for the Information
and Assistance of Persons Emigrating
from Foreign Countries.
The Act of Incorporation, Constitution
and By-laws of the. . . .
Philadelphia, Gales, 1797. 72 pp.
AAS copy.   48232

Philadelphia, Thursday, Sept. 27, 1770.
Many Respectable Freeholders.
[Philadelphia, 1770.] Broadside.
LOC copy.   11880

Philadelphia, Wednesday, November 6,
1765.
Your Attendance at the Court-House. . . .
[Philadelphia, 1765.] Broadside.
LCP copy.   10135

The Philadelphiad; or, new Pictures of the
City.
Philadelphia, Kline & Reynolds, 1784. 2
vol. 83; 59, [1] pp.
HSP copy.   18730

Philander and Rosabella.
New London, [c. 1783]. Broadside.
AAS copy.   44440

Philanthropic Company. Warren, R.I.
By-laws for the Regulation of the. . . .
Warren, Phillips, 1795. 16 pp.
Bradford Swan copy.   47557

Philanthropic Lottery.
A List of all those Numbers which were
Drawn.
[Boston, 1800.] [16] pp.
AAS copy.   38266

[Philanthropic Lottery, by Act of
Legislature of Vermont . . . for the Benefit
of . . . Mr. Hawkins.

[Burlington? 1798.] Broadside.]
(No copy of such a handbill has been
found; the tickets are known.)   33861

Phillips, Caleb.
[New Method of Shorthand.
Boston, 1727.]
(Adv. Boston News-Letter, Dec. 14, 1727.)
                                     39871

Phillips, Catherine, 1726-1794.
Memoirs of the Life of. . . .
Philadelphia, Budd & Bartram for
Johnson, 1798. 384 pp.
AAS copy.   34371

Phillips, Catharine (Payton), 1727-1794.
Reasons why the People Called Quakers
Cannot so Fully Unite with the
Methodists.
Philadelphia, Lawrence, 1792. 20 pp.
LCP copy.   46546

Phillips, John, of Charleston, S.C.
An Appeal to Matter of Fact.
New York, Kirk, 1798. 31, [1] pp.
AAS copy.   34372

Phillips, John, of Charleston, S. C.
Familiar Dialogues on Dancing.
New York, Kirk, 1798. 39 pp.
AAS copy.   34373

Phillips, John, of Charleston, S. C.
A Narrative Shewing Why. . . .
Charleston, M'Iver, 1796. 36 pp.
AAS copy.   31007

Phillips, John, of Charleston, S. C.
A Short Treatise on Divine Prescience.
New York, 1798. 49 pp.
AAS copy.   34374

Phillips, John, 1770-1823.
An Oration, Pronounced July 4th, 1794.
Boston, Edes, 1794. 19 pp.
AAS copy.   27520

Phillips, Samuel, 1690-1771.
Advice to a Child.
Boston, Phillips, 1729. [2], iv, 138 pp.
HC copy.   3207

Phillips, Samuel, 1690-1771.
(Sibley, V, 432-440.)
Children well Imployed.
Boston, Kneeland & Green for
Henchman, 1739. [4], vi, 109 pp.
AAS copy.   4413

Phillips, Samuel, 1690-1771.
(Sibley, V, 432-440.)
An Elegy upon the Deaths of . . . Nicholas
Noyes . . . and . . . George Curwin.
[Boston, 1717.] 8 pp.
AAS copy.   1924

Phillips, Samuel, 1690-1771.
(Sibley, V, 432-440.)
The Gospel Doctrine.
Boston, Kneeland & Adams, 1766. 62 pp.
AAS copy.   10456

Phillips, Samuel, 1690-1771.
(Sibley, V, 432-440.)
Gospel-Ministers.
Boston, Kneeland, 1752. [4], 31 pp.
AAS copy.   6915

Phillips, Samuel, 1690-1771.
(Sibley, V, 432-440.)
The History of Our Lord.
Boston, Kneeland & Green for
Henchman, 1738. [4], iv, 60, [3] pp.
LOC copy.   4301

Phillips, Samuel, 1690-1771.
(Sibley, V, 432-440.)
The Living Water.
Boston, Kneeland for Henchman, 1750.
[4], 28 pp.
AAS copy.   6592

Phillips, Samuel, 1690-1771.
(Sibley, V, 432-440.)
The Necessity of God's Drawing.
Boston, Kneeland, 1753. [4], 30 pp.
AAS copy.   7094

Phillips, Samuel, 1690-1771.
The Orthodox Christian.

Boston, Kneeland and Green for
Henchman, 1738. [4], viii, 135, [7] pp.
(No perfect copy was available for
filming.)
AAS copy.   4302

Phillips, Samuel, 1690-1771.
Political Rulers.
Boston, Draper, 1750. [4], 59 pp.
AAS copy.   6593

Phillips, Samuel, 1690-1771.
Preaching Peace.
Boston, Kneeland for Phillips, 1753. [4],
42 pp.
AAS copy.   7095

Phillips, Samuel, 1690-1771.
(Sibley, V, 432-440.)
Seasonable Advice.
Boston, Kneeland, 1761. [4], xi, [1], 86
pp.
AAS copy.   8982

Phillips, Samuel, 1690-1771.
A Serious Address.
Boston, Kneeland, 1763. viii, 103, [1] pp.
HC copy.   9488

Phillips, Samuel, 1690-1771.
(Sibley, V, 432-440.)
The Sin of Suicide.
Boston, Kneeland & Adams, 1767. 48 pp.
AAS copy.   10740

Phillips, Samuel, 1690-1771.
The Sinner's Refusal.
Boston, Kneeland, 1753. [4], 29 pp.
AAS copy.   7096

Phillips, Samuel, 1690-1771.
(Sibley, V, 432-440.)
Soldiers Counselled.
Boston, Fleet for Phillips, 1741. 53 pp.
AAS copy.   4788

Phillips, Samuel, 1690-1771.
(Sibley, V, 432-440.)
Three Plain Practical Discourses.
Boston, Phillips, 1728. [2], vi, 226, [1] pp.
AAS copy.   3091

Phillips, Samuel, 1690-1771.
(Sibley, V, 432-440.)
Wisdom, an Essential Requisite.
Boston, Kneeland, 1759. [4], 50 pp.
AAS copy.   8468

Phillips, Samuel, 1690-1771.
A Word in Season.
Boston, Kneeland and Green for Phillips,
1727. [2], viii, 213, [5] pp.
AAS copy.   2944

[Phillips, Teresia Constantia, 1709-1765.
(D. N. B.)
A Letter Humbly Address'd to the . . .
Earl of Chesterfield.
New York, Parker, 1751.]
(From bookseller's adv.)   6722

Phillips's United States Diary, or an
Almanack, for . . . 1793.
Warren, R. I., Phillips. [22] pp.
RIHS copy.   24689

Second Edition. Phillips's United States
Diary, or Almanack, for . . . 1793.
Warren, R. I., Phillips. [22] pp.
(Copies differ as to back matter.)
LOC copy.   24690

Phillips's United States Diary, or an
Almanack, for . . . 1794.
Warren, Phillips. [24] pp.
AAS copy.   25999

Phillips's United States Diary; or an
Almanack for . . . 1795.
Warren, R. I., Phillips. [24] pp.
AAS copy.   27521

Phillips's United States Diary; or an
Almanack, for . . . 1796.
Warren, R. I., Phillips. [24] pp.
AAS copy.   29321

Phillips's United States Diary; or an
Almanack, for . . . 1797.
Warren, R. I., Phillips. [24] pp.
AAS copy.   31008

Phillips's United States Diary; or an
Almanack, for . . . 1798.
Warren, R. I., Phillips. [24] pp.
AAS copy.   32689

Philological Society, New York.
The Constitution of the. . . .
New York, Harrisson & Purdy, 1788.
7 pp.
LOC copy.   21320

Philological Society, Philadelphia.
The Constitution, Laws and Rules of the.

Philadelphia, Woodward, 1794. 13 pp.
HEH copy.   47181

[Philomela; with the Notes for Morning
Prayer.
Boston, 1720. 110 pp.]
(A ghost arising from Havens' description
of a mangled copy of 2562, q.v.)   2167

Philo's Essex Almanack, for . . . 1770.
Salem, Hall. [24] pp.
AAS copy.   11283

Philosophic Solitude, [by William
Livingston, 1723-1790].
New York, 1747. [2], 44 pp.
AAS copy.   5986

Philosophic Solitude, [by William
Livingston, 1723-1790].
Boston, Mecom, 1762. 46 pp.
AAS copy.   9160

Philosophic Solitude. . . . Third Edition
[by William Livingston, 1723-1790].
New York, Holt, [1769]. 40 pp.
LOC copy.   11315

Philosophic Solitude: or, the Choice of a
Rural Life [by William Livingston,
1723-1790].
Trenton, 1782. 28 pp.
AAS copy.   17574

The Philosophical Dictionary, for the
Pocket [by François Marie Arouet de
Voltaire, 1694-1778].
Catskill, Croswell for Fellows and
Duyckinck, 1796.[10], 336 pp.
AAS copy.   31518

Phipps, Joseph, 1708-1787.
Abhandlungen über die Natur.
Philadelphia, Cist, 1786. [2], 63 pp.
(The pagination given by Evans includes
19523, q.v.)
AAS copy.   19923

Phipps, Joseph, 1708-1787.
An Address to the Youth of Norwich.
New York, Durell, 1794. 16 pp.
AAS copy.   27522

Phipps, Joseph, 1708-1787.
Dissertations on the Nature and Effect of
Christian Baptism.
New York, Ross, 1786. 52, 32 pp.
AAS copy.   19924

Phipps, Joseph, 1708-1787.
The Doctrine of Baptisms, &c.
[Philadelphia, 1786.] [2], 59, [1]; 32 pp.
AAS copy.   19925

Phipps, Joseph, 1708-1787.
The Original, and Present State of Man.
Philadelphia, Crukshank, 1783. [4],
209 pp.
AAS copy.   18139

Phipps, Joseph, 1708-1787.
The Original and Present State of Man.
New York, Ross, 1788. [4], 230 pp.
AAS copy.   21391

Phipps, Joseph, 1708-1787.
The Original and Present State of Man.
Trenton, Collins, 1793. [4], 228 pp.
AAS copy.   26000

Phips, William, 1720-1798.
(Weis, Colonial Clergy N. E.)
A Breach in Jerusalem's Walls.
Boston, Draper, 1761. 28, [1] pp.
AAS copy.   8983

Phoenomenon. That Beautiful Full
Blooded Stallion. . . . March 28, 1798.

[Portsmouth], Melcher, [1798].
Broadside.
LOC copy. 48577

A Physical Enquiry into the Origin and
Causes of the Pestilential Fevers.
New York, Tiebout for Jansen, 1798.
32 pp.
LOC copy. 34377

Pia Desideria [by Cotton Mather,
1663-1728].
Boston, Kneeland for Gerrish, 1722. [2],
22 pp.
BM copy. 2358

Piccinni, Niccolo, 1728-1800.
Overture La Buona Figliuola.
[Philadelphia], Willig, [1796]. 2 pp.
NYPL copy. 31009

Piccinni, Niccolo, 1728-1800.
Overture. La Schiava.
[Philadelphia, 1789.] [2] pp.
(Evans' description was based on an adv.)
HC copy. 22069

[Pickering, George], 1769-1846.
Methodism Delineated.
Norwich, Trumbull, 1795. 12 pp.
CHS copy. 29259

Pickering, Theophilus, 1700-1747.
(Sibley, VI, 331-336.)
A Bad Omen to the Churches.
Boston, Rogers & Fowle, 1747. 12 pp.
AAS copy. 6051

[Pickering, Theophilus], 1700-1747.
(Sibley, VI, 331-336.)
The Chebacco Narrative.
Boston, Kneeland & Green, 1738. 20 pp.]
(This tract was by John Cleaveland and
was printed in 1748. See Sprague, I,
458-461. It is more accurately listed as
6113, q.v.) 4303

Pickering, Theophilus, 1700-1747.
(Sibley, VI, 331-336.)
Mr. Pickering's Letter to Mr. Whitefield.
Boston, Rogers & Fowle, 1745. 8 pp.
AAS copy. 5676

Pickering, Theophilus, 1700-1747.
(Sibley, VI, 331-336.)
The Rev. Mr. Pickering's Letters.
Boston, Fleet, 1742. 20 pp.
AAS copy. 5037

Pickering, Theophilus, 1700-1747.
A Supplement to a Piece Lately Printed.
Boston, Rogers & Fowle, 1747. 4 pp.
HC copy. 6052

Pickering, Timothy, 1745-1829.
An Easy Plan of Discipline for a Militia.
Salem, Halls, 1775. 28, 169, 2, [1] pp., 14
plates.
BA copy. 14404

Pickering, Timothy, 1745-1829.
An Easy Plan of Discipline for a Militia.
. . . Second Edition.
Boston, Hall, 1776. 24, 154, 2 pp., 12
plates.
AAS copy. 43141

Pickering, Timothy, 1745-1829.
From Timothy Pickering, to P. Johnson,
Esq. . . . Sept. 29, 1798.
[Trenton, Day, 1798.] Broadside.
EI copy. 34378

Pickman, Benjamin, 1763-1843.
An Oration, Pronounced, February 22,
1797.
Salem, Cushing, 1797. 22 pp.
AAS copy. 32691

Pictet, Benedict, 1655-1724.
[The Affections of the Mind.
Williamsburg? 1769?] 52 pp.
(The only known copy lacks tp.)
AAS copy. 41992

The Picture Exhibition.
Albany, Websters, 1790. Broadside.
NYPL copy. 45971

Picture Exhibition, or, The Ladder to
Learning. . . . First Worcester Edition.
Worcester, Thomas, 1798. 30, [1] pp.
d'Alté A. Welch, ph. copy. 48578

Pictures of Seventy-Two Beasts & Birds.
Boston, Hall, 1796. 118 pp.
(The only copy known is imperfect.)
AAS copy. 47884

Pidgin, William, 1772-1848.
Great Plainness Necessary.
Newburyport, Blunt, 1799. 28 pp.
LOC copy. 36116

Pierce, John, 1773-1849.
A Eulogy on George Washington.
Boston, Manning & Loring, 1800. 24, 24
pp.
AAS copy. 38267

Pierce, John, 1773-1849.
On the Mystery of Godliness.
Dedham, Mass., Mann & Adams, 1798. 22
pp.
AAS copy. 34379

Pierce, William, 1740-1789.
An Oration, Delivered at Christ Church.
Savannah, Johnston, 1788. [2], 17 pp.
BA copy. 21393

Pierpont, James, 1660-1714.
(Sibley, III, 222-230.)
Sundry False Hopes of Heaven.
Boston, 1712. [2], xxiv, 46 pp.
AAS copy. 1581

Piers, Henry.
A Sermon Preached (in part).
New York, Holt, 1766. 34 pp.
AAS copy. 10459

[Pierson, Abraham, 1641-1707.
(Sibley, II, 253-258.)
Connecticut Election Sermon.
Boston, 1700.]
(There is no reason to think that this
sermon was ever printed.) 947

Pierson, John, 1690-1770.
Christ the Son of God.
Boston, Fowle, 1751. 29, [1] pp.
AAS copy. 6759

Pierson, John, 1690-1770.
A Discourse on the Nature.
Woodbridge, 1765. [2], 23 pp.
LOC copy. 10141

Pierson, John, 1690-1770.
(Dexter, I, 103-105.)
The Faithful Minister.
New York, 1748. 24 pp.
AAS copy. 6221

[Pierson, John, 1690-1770.
(Dexter, I, 103-105.)
A Sermon Preached at the Ordination of
the Rev. Aaron Burr, January 25, 1737, 8.
New York? 1738.]
(Listed among Pierson's works by Dexter,
but it was probably not published.) 4304

Pierson, Josiah G.
New Invented Washing-mill. . . . October
6, 1792.
[New York], Greenleaf, [1792].
Broadside.
LOC copy. 46547

Piety Demanded [by Cotton Mather,
1663-1728].
Boston, Fleet & Crump for Henchman,
1716. 36 pp.
Bodleian copy. 39653

Pigot, George, fl. 1722-1738.
(Weis, Colonial Clergy N. E.)
A Vindication.
Boston, Fleet for Phillips, 1731. 25, [1],
41, [1] pp.
AAS copy. 3466

[Pigott, Charles], d. 1794.
An Abridgment of "The Jockey Club."
Boston, Manning & Loring, 1795. 144, [2]
pp.
AAS copy. 29322

[Pigott, Charles], d. 1794.
The Female Jockey Club.
New York, Greenleaf, Fellows and
Wayland, 1794. [4], 270 pp.
AAS copy. 27523

[Pigott, Charles], d. 1794.
The Jockey Club.

New York, Greenleaf, 1793. 205 pp.
AAS copy. 26001

Pigott, Charles, d. 1794.
A Political Dictionary.
New York, Greenleaf, 1796. 198 pp.
AAS copy. 31011

Pike, James, 1703-1792.
(Sibley, VII, 550-553.)
Gospel-Ministers.
Boston, Fowle, 1751. 31 pp.
AAS copy. 6760

Pike, Joseph, c.1657-1729.
(Joseph Smith, Friends' Books, II, 422.)
An Epistle to the National Meeting.
Philadelphia, Franklin & Hall, 1757. 23
pp.
HSP copy. 8008

Pike, Nicholas, 1743-1819.
Abridgment of the New and Complete
System of Arithmetick.
Newburyport, Mycall for Thomas, 1793.
371 pp.
AAS copy. 26002

Pike, Nicolas, 1743-1819.
Abridgment of the New and Complete
System of Arithmetick.
Worcester, Thomas, [1793]. 371 pp.
(A tp. variant of 26002, q.v. for text.)
AAS copy. 46853

Pike, Nicholas, 1743-1819.
Abridgment of the New and Complete
System of Arithmetick. . . . Second
Edition.
Worcester, Isaiah Thomas for Thomas &
Andrews in Boston, and Thomas &
Carlisle in Walpole, 1795. 348 pp.
(AAS has a var. imprint including the
names of West and Larkin.)
AAS copy. 29324

Pike, Nicholas, 1743-1819.
Abridgment of the New and Complete
System of Arithmetick. . . . Second
Edition.
Worcester, Isaiah Thomas for Thomas &
Andrews, West, and Larkin, 1795. 348 pp.
(An imprint variant of 29324, q. v. for
text.)
AAS copy. 47558

Pike, Nicholas, 1743-1819.
A New and Complete System of
Arithmetic.
Newburyport, 1788. 512, [1] pp.
AAS copy. 21394

Pike, Nicolas, 1743-1819.
A New and Complete System of
Arithmetic. . . . Second Edition.
Worcester, Mass., Worcester for Thomas,
etc., 1797. 516 pp.
AAS copy. 32692

Pike, Nicholas, 1743-1819.
The New Complete System of Arithmetic.
. . . Abridged. . . . Third Edition.
Worcester, Mass., Worcester for Thomas,
etc., 1798. 352 pp.
AAS copy. 34380

[Pike, Samuel, 1717?-1773.
(D. N. B.)
An Epistolary Correspondence.
[Boston, 1759.] 96 pp.]
(A ghost of the London, 1760 ed. arising
from a defective copy.) 8469

Pike, Samuel, 1717?-1773.
A Letter Wrote by Mr. Samuel Pike.
Portsmouth, [1766]. 6 pp.
MHS copy. 10460

Pike, Samuel, 1717?-1773.
(D. N. B.)
Mr. Pike's Present Thoughts.
Boston, Mein & Fleeming, 1768. 31 pp.
AAS copy. 11044

[Pike, Samuel], 1717?-1773.
A Plain and Full Account of the Christian
Practices.
Boston, Fowle for Butler, 1766. 28 pp.
AAS copy. 10461

[Pike, Samuel, 1717?-1773.
A Plain and Full Account.
Danbury, Ct., Ely & Nichols, 1796.]

(Imprint assumed by Evans from adv.
"For Sale at this Office," Farmers
Chronicle, May 23, 1796.)   31012

Pike, Samuel, 1717?-1773.
Religious Cases of Conscience.
Philadelphia, Campbell, 1794. viii, 527 pp.
AAS copy.   27524

Pike, Samuel, 1717?-1773.
Religious Cases of Conscience.
Philadelphia, Campbell, 1800. viii, 527 pp.
AAS copy.   38268

[Pike, Samuel], 1717?-1773.
(D. N. B.)
Simple Truth Vindicated.
Boston, Kneeland & Adams, 1771. 72 pp.
AAS copy.   12198

Pike, Samuel, 1717?-1773.
Some Important Cases of Conscience. . . .
Vol. II.
Boston, Fowle & Draper and Green &
Russell, 1759. [2], 166 pp.
AAS copy.   8470

Pike, Samuel, 1717?-1773.
Some Important Cases of Conscience. . . .
Third Edition.
Boston, Green & Russell, 1757. [8], 138,
[2] pp.
AAS copy.   8009

Pike, Samuel, 1717?-1773.
(D. N. B.)
Some Important Cases of Conscience. . . .
Fourth Edition.
Boston, Fowle & Draper and Green &
Russell, 1760. [8], 136 pp.
AAS copy.   8716

[Pike, Samuel, 1717?-1773.
(D. N. B.)
Some Important Cases of Conscience.
Philadelphia, Bradford, 1762. 2 vol.]
(Adv. Pa. Journal, Nov. 22, 1764.)   9798

Pilkington, Mary (Hopkins), 1766-1839.
A Mirror for the Female Sex.
Hartford, Hudson & Goodwin for O. & I.
Cooke, 1799. xxiv, 211, [1] pp.
AAS copy.   36117

[Pilkington, Mary (Hopkins)], 1766-1839.
Tales of the Hermitage.
Philadelphia, Maxwell for Thackara, 1800.
158 pp.
(No perfect copy located.)
EI copy.   38269

A Pill for Porcupine [by James Carey, d.
1801].
Philadelphia, 1796. 83 pp.
AAS copy.   30155

A Pill for the Committee of
Non-Importation. . . . October 1, 1769.
[New York, 1769.] 2 pp.
NYHS copy.   11395

Pillars of Salt [by Cotton Mather,
1663-1728].
Boston, 1699. 111, [1] pp.
AAS copy.   877

Pills for the Delegates. . . . September 5,
1774.
New York, Rivington, 1775. 32 pp.
LOC copy.   14094

Pillsbury, Edmund, 1738-1816.
The Law and the Gospel.
Portsmouth, N. H., Peirce, 1799. 37 pp.
(The one copy reported cannot now be
located.)   36118

Pilmore, Joseph, 1734?-1825.
An Address on the Importance of Female
Education.
Philadelphia, 1788. 14, [2] pp.
LCP copy.   21395

Pilmore, Joseph, 1734?-1825.
The Blessings of Peace.
New York, Buel, 1794. 32 pp.
AAS copy.   27525

Pilmore, Joseph, 1734?-1825.
The Renovation of Man.
Philadelphia, Johnston & Justice, 1792. 23
pp.
AAS copy.   24692

Pilmore, Joseph, 1734?-1825.
A Sermon, Preached in St. Pauls Church
Philadelphia . . . 27th, December, 1786.
New York, Durell, 1793. 24 pp.
NYHS copy.   26003

Pilmore, Joseph, 1734?-1825.
A Sermon, Preached in St. Paul's Church,
Philadelphia. . . . 27th December, 1786.
Philadelphia, Oswald, 1787. 23 pp.
(Evans' title comes from an adv.)
AAS copy.   20647

Pilsbury, Amos.
The United States' Sacred Harmony.
Boston, Thomas & Andrews, 1799. 224 pp.
AAS copy.   36119

[Pinchard, Mrs.
The Blind Child.
Worcester, Thomas, 1787.]
(From a newspaper adv., apparently for
some other title.)   20648

[Pinchard, Mrs.
The Blind Child.
New York, Berry, Rogers & Berry, 1792?]
(Imprint assumed by Evans from list of
"New Publications" in N.Y. Diary, Oct.
9, 1792.)   24693

[Pinchard, Mrs.
The Blind Child.
Philadelphia, Spotswood, 1792?]
(Imprint assumed by Evans from
Spotswood adv.)   24694

[Pinchard, Mrs.]
The Blind Child.
Philadelphia, Spotswood and Rice, 1793.
192 pp., 1 plate.
(No perfect copy of this ed. located.)
AAS copy.   26004

[Pinchard, Mrs.]
The Blind Child.
Boston, Spotswood, 1795. 191, [1], pp., 1
plate.
AAS copy.   29325

[Pinchard, Mrs.]
The Blind Child.
Philadelphia, H. & P. Rice and J. Rice,
1795. 191, [1] pp.
AAS copy.   47559

[Pinchard, Mrs.]
The Blind Child.
Worcester, Thomas, 1796. 190 pp.; 1 plate.
AAS copy.   31013

[Pinchard, Mrs.]
Dramatic Dialogues, for the Use of Young
Persons.
Boston, Spotswood, 1798. [4], 42, [2], 50,
95, [1], 38, 45, [1], 22, 28 pp., 6 plates.
AAS copy.   34381

[Pinchard, Mrs.]
The Little Trifler.
Boston, Spotswood, 1798. 95 pp., 1 plate.
AAS copy.   34005

[Pinchard, Mrs.]
The Two Cousins.
Boston, Etheridge, 1796. 142 pp., 1 plate.
AAS copy.   31014

[Pinchard, Mrs.]
The Two Cousins.
New York, Tiebout, 1799. 130 pp.
(The only copy located is imperfect.)
AAS copy.   36120

Pinckney, Charles, 1757-1824.
Case of Jonathan Robbins.
Baltimore, Warner & Hanna, 1799. 36 pp.,
irreg.
AAS copy.   36121

Pinckney, Charles, 1757-1824.
Charleston, July 24, 1798. Dear Sir. . . .
[Charleston, S. C., 1798.] Broadside.
LOC copy.   35382

Pinckney, Charles, 1757-1824.
Mr. Charles Pinckney's Speech, in Answer
to Mr. Jay . . . August 16, 1786.
[New York, 1786.] [4] pp.
LOC copy.   19926

Pinckney, Charles, 1757-1824.
(D. A. B.)

Observations on the Plan of Government.
. . . By Mr. Charles Pinckney.
New York, Childs, [1787]. 27 pp.
LOC copy.   20649

Pinckney, Charles, 1757-1824.
(D. A. B.)
Observations on the Plan of Government.
. . . By the Hon. Charles Pinckney.
New York, Childs, [1787]. 27 pp.
AAS copy.   20650

Pinckney, Charles, 1757-1824.
Speeches . . . in Congress.
[Philadelphia], 1800. [4], iii, [1], 135 pp.
AAS copy.   38270

Pinckney, Charles, 1757-1824.
Three Letters, Addressed to the People.
Charleston, S. C., Cox, 1799. [2], 69 pp.
AAS copy.   36122

[Pinckney, Charles, 1757-1824.
Three Letters, Addressed to the People.
. . . to which is Added, an Appendix.
Charleston, S. C., 1799. [4], 69 pp.]
(A ghost, being a composite of 36122 and
36124.)   36123

Pinckney, Charles, 1757-1824.
Three Letters, Written, and Originally
Published. . . .
Philadelphia, 1799. [2], 65 pp.
AAS copy.   36124

[Pindar, Paul, pseud.
Justice Progressive.
Boston, Edes, 1795.]
("Now in Press," Boston Gazette, Oct. 12,
1795.)   29326

Pindar, Peter, pseud.
Hair Powder: a Plaintive Epistle . . . [by
John Wolcot, 1738-1819].
New York, Smith, 1795. [2], 20, [1] pp.
AAS copy.   29915

Pindar, Peter, Esq., pseud.
Instructions to a Celebrated Laureat. . . .
The Eighth Edition [by John Wolcot,
1738-1819].
New York, 1788. 27 pp.
NYPL copy.   21615

Pindariana; or Peter's Portfolio [by John
Wolcot, 1738-1819].
Philadelphia, Bache, 1794. x, 242 pp.
AAS copy.   28119

[Pinkham, Paul.
A Chart of George's Bank.
Newburyport, Blunt, 1797.]
(Evans' entry was from the copyright
entry.)   32693

Pinkham, Paul.
A Chart of Nantucket-Shoals.
Boston, Norman, 1791. Map.
BPL copy.   23700

Pinkney, John, fl. 1774-1776.
Williamsburg, Friday Evening, Eight
O'Clock. Our Paper was Entirely
Prepared. . . .
[Williamsburg, Pinkney, [1775].
Broadside.
(No copy located.)   42921

[Pinkney, William], 1764-1822.
A Few Remarks on Mr. Hamilton's Late
Letter.
Baltimore, Warner & Hanna, 1800. 24 pp.
AAS copy.   38271

Pinkney, William, 1764-1822.
Speech . . . in the House of Delegates . . .
November, 1789.
Philadelphia, Crukshank, 1790. 22 pp.
AAS copy.   22800

Pintard, John Marsden.
To Timothy Pickering. . . . 15th Nov.
1799.
[New York, 1800?] pp. [1]-28, 25-35.
LOC copy.   38272

The Pious Guide to Prayer and Devotion.
Georgetown, Doyle, 1792. iv, [8], 282 pp.,
2 folding tables.
Georgetown University copy.   24695

The Pious Man's Directions.
Boston, Edwards, 1729. [2], 2, 103 pp.

(The only reported copy is imperfect.)
AAS copy.   3208

Pious Remains of a Young Gentleman [by
Samuel Byles, 1743-1764].
Boston, Draper, 1764. 12 pp.
BPL copy.   9610

[Pitcher, Nathaniel], 1685-1723.
Words of Consolation to Mr. Robert
Stetson. . . . November 7th, 1718.
[Boston, 1718.] Broadside.
EI copy.   39689

Pitchero-Threnodia.
Boston, Green, 1724. [4], 11, [1] pp.
(See Sibley, V, 237.)
AAS copy.   2579

Pitkin, Timothy, 1727-1812.
(Weis, Colonial Clergy N. E.)
A Sermon Delivered at Litchfield.
Hartford, [1768]. 18 pp.
(The only known copy is incomplete.)
CSL copy.   11045

Pitkin, Timothy, 1766-1847.
A Sermon, Preached at New-Cambridge
. . . February 12th, 1789.
Hartford, Hudson & Goodwin, 1790. 20
pp.
AAS copy.   22801

Pitt, C. I.
The Poor Blind Girl. . . . Music by V. de
Cleve.
New York, Gilfert, [1798]. [2] pp.
AAS copy.   34383

Pitt, William, 1st Earl of Chatham,
1708-1778.
An Authentic Copy of Lord Chatham's
Proposed Bill.
Annapolis, 1775. 16 pp.
NL copy.   14076

Pitt, William, 1st Earl of Chatham,
1708-1778.
Des Hoch-Edlen Grafen von Chatham
Rede . . . den 20sten Jenner, 1775.
Philadelphia, Miller, 1775. 16 pp.
HSP copy.   14407

Pitt, William, 1st Earl of Chatham,
1708-1778.
Mr. Pitt's Speech [Stamp Act].
[New York, 1766.] Broadside.
LOC copy.   10462

Pitt, William, 1st Earl of Chatham,
1708-1778.
The Speech of Lord C. . . .m, (Mr. P--t)
London, Dec. 6.
n. p., [1770?] Broadside.
AAS copy.   42154

Pitt, William, 1st Earl of Chatham,
1708-1778.
[Speech, Jan. 20, 1775, on removing
troops.
Newbern, 1775.]
(Adv. N. C. Gazette, June 30, 1775.) 42922

Pitt, William, 1st Earl of Chatham,
1708-1778.
The Speech of . . . the Earl of Chatham
. . . the 17th June, 1774.
[Boston, 1774.] [2] pp.
MHS copy.   42671

Pitt, William, 1st Earl of Chatham,
1708-1778.
The Speech of the Right Honorable the
Earl of Chatham . . . Jan. 20, 1775.
[Newport, 1775]. 14 pp.
(Adv. Newport Mercury, May 8, 1775.)
NYPL copy.   14406

Pitt, William, 1st Earl of Chatham,
1708-1778.
The Speech, of the Right Honorable the
Earl of Chatham . . . January 20th, 1775.
Philadelphia, Dunlap, 1775. 16 pp.
AAS copy.   14405

Pitt, William, 1759-1806.
Speech of . . . in the House of Commons
. . . February 3, 1800.
New York, Furman, 1800. 68 pp.
AAS copy.   38273

The Pittsburg Almanac . . . for . . . 1788.

Pittsburgh, Scull & Boyd. [40] pp.
AAS copy.   20652

The Pittsburgh Almanack, for . . . 1801.
[Pittsburgh, Cramer]. [34] pp.
(The only recorded copy is imperfect.)
AAS copy.   38274

[Pity the Sorrows of a Poor Old Man.
Philadelphia, Carr, 1793.]
(Adv. by Carr in Dec., 1793.)   26006

A Plain Account of the Ordinance of
Baptism. . . . Third Edition.
Boston, Kneeland & Adams for Freeman,
1771. 75, 6 (5) pp.
AAS copy.   12199

A Plain Account of the Ordinance of
Baptism. . . . First Ballston Edition.
Ballston, Childs, 1798. 84 pp.
JCB copy.   34385

A Plain Almanack, for . . . 1782.
Philadelphia, Crukshank. [36] pp.
AAS copy.   17313

A Plain Almanack, for . . . 1783.
Philadelphia, Crukshank. [36] pp.
AAS copy.   17677

A Plain Almanack, for . . . 1784.
Philadelphia, Crukshank. [36] pp.
AAS copy.   18140

[A Plain Almanack for . . . 1785.
Philadelphia, Crukshank.]
(Hildeburn 4537).   18733

A Plain and Brief Rehersal [by Joseph
Seccombe, 1706-1760.]
Boston, Kneeland and Green, 1740. [4],
ii, 23, [1] pp.
AAS copy.   4595

A Plain and Earnest Address from a
Minister [by Jeremy Belknap, 1744-1798].
Salem, 1771. 26 pp.
LOC copy.   11980

A Plain and Full Account of the Christian
Practices [by Samuel Pike, 1717?-1773].
Boston, Fowle for Butler, 1766. 28 pp.
AAS copy.   10461

A Plain and Serious Address to the
Inhabitants of the Massachusetts
Province.
[Boston, 1747?] Broadside.
MHS copy.   40437

A Plain Answer from a Gentleman in
Queen's County to a Familiar Letter from
a Citizen of New-York. . . . [Aug. 21,
1750.]
[New York? 1750.] 2 pp.
NYPL ph. copy.   40561

The Plain Case Stated of Old.
Boston, [1688]. Broadside.
MHS copy.   453

The Plain Dealer; Numb. I [by Hugh
Williamson, 1735-1819].
Philadelphia, Steuart, [1764]. 16 pp.
NYHS copy.   9876

The Plain Dealer: Numb. II [by Hugh
Williamson, 1735-1819].
Philadelphia, 1764. 16 pp.
NYPL copy.   9877

The Plain Dealer: or, a few Remarks upon
Quaker-Politicks [by Hugh Williamson,
1735-1819].
Philadelphia, 1764. 19 pp.
NYPL copy.   9875

The Plain Dealer: or, Remarks on Quaker
Politics. . . . Numb. III [by Hugh
Williamson, 1735-1819].
Philadelphia, 1764. 24 pp.
NYPL copy.   9878

Plain Discourse for Little Children. . . .
Seventh Edition.
Boston, 1765. 38 pp.
MHS copy.   10142

Plain Facts: being an Examination into
the Rights of Indian Nations [by Samuel
Wharton, 1732-1800].

Philadelphia, Aitken, 1781. 164,
[1] pp.
MHS copy.   17437

A Plain Narrative of the Proceedings
which Caused the Separation of a Number
of Aggrieved Brethren from the Second
Church in Ipswich.
Boston, Kneeland & Green, 1747. 16 pp.
(Perhaps drawn for the Aggrieved
Brethren by John Cleaveland.)
AAS copy.   5920

The Plain Path to Christian Perfection
[by Johannes Tauler, 1290-1361].
Philadelphia, Crukshank, 1772. xi, [1],
124, 16 pp.
AAS copy.   12530

The Plain Path to Christian Perfection
[by Johannes Tauler, 1290-1361].
Philadelphia, Crukshank, 1780. xi, [1], 91
pp.
AAS copy.   16953

The Plain Path-way to Heaven.
Boston, [1788]. 12 pp.
AAS copy.   21620

[The Plain Planter and Farmer's Family
Assistant.
Wilmington, Del., Adams, 1788.]
(Entry from an adv.)   21397

Plain Psalmody, or Supplementary Music.
Boston, Thomas & Andrews, 1800. 71,
[1] pp.
AAS copy.   38276

Plain Reasons, I. For Dissenting. . . .
Eighteenth Edition [by Charles Owen,
1746].
Boston, Hancock, 1725. [4], 40 pp.
AAS copy.   2721

A Plain Scriptural Description of Jesus
Christ.
Newport, [R. I.], Franklin, 1754.
8 pp.
AAS copy.   40711

Plain Sense: or, The History of Henry
Villars. . . . In two Volumes.
Philadelphia, Carey, 1799. 211, [6]; 246,
[6] pp.
HC copy.   36127

A Plain Sermon for Little Children. . . .
[Third Edition].
[New Haven, Parker, 1761.] 42 + pp.
(The unique copy is imperfect.)
CHS copy.   8984

A Plain Short Catechism [by George
Keith, 1638-1716].
Philadelphia, 1690. [6], 48 pp.
QL copy.   514

Plain Truth, Addressed to the Inhabitants
of America [by James Chalmers,
1727-1806].
Philadelphia, Bell, 1776. pp. [i]-96, [8],
[97]-135.
HEH copy.   43000

Plain Truth, Addressed to the Inhabitants
of America [by James Chalmers,
1727-1806].
Philadelphia, Bell, 1776. pp. [1]-96, [8],
[97]-135, [3].
NL copy.   43002

Plain Truth; Addressed to the Inhabitants
of America [by James Chalmers,
1727-1806].
Philadelphia, Bell, 1776. pp. [3]-64, 57-64,
73-96, [9], 98-136.
AAS copy.   43001

Plain Truth; Addressed to the Inhabitants
of America [by James Chalmers,
1727-1806].
Philadelphia, Bell, 1776. [8], 84,
[2] pp.
AAS copy.   15088

Plain Truth; Addressed to the Inhabitants
of America [by James Chalmers,
1727-1806].
Philadelphia, Bell, 1776. 136 pp., irreg.
(For variants see R. Gimbell, Thomas
Paine, pp. 116 ff.)
AAS copy.   15089

Plain Truth: Addressed to the People of
Virginia . . . February 1799-By a Citizen
of Westmoreland [by Henry Lee,
1756-1818].
[Richmond? 1799.] 56 pp.
HEH copy.   35723

Plain Truth: Addressed to the People of
Virginia.
[Richmond? 1799.] 56 pp.
(Also entered as 35723, q. v.)   36128

Plain Truth: or, Serious Considerations
[by Benjamin Franklin, 1706-1790].
[Philadelphia, Franklin], 1747. 22 pp.
MHS copy.   5948

Plain Truth: or, Serious Considerations
[Second Edition] [by Benjamin Franklin,
1706-1790].
[Philadelphia, Franklin], 1747. 22,
[2] pp.
(The text which duplicates 5948 is
omitted.)
MHS copy.   5949

Plain Truths in a Few Words.
[New York, 1768.] Broadside.
LCP copy.   11046

[Plan de Vente de Trois Cent Mille Acres
. . . Situées dans les Comtés de
Northumberland et de Huntingdon dans
l'Etat de Pennsylvanie.
Philadelphia (Paris?), 1794.]
(The copy reported by Evans cannot now
be located.)   27527

A Plan for a School on an Establishment
Similar to that at Ackworth [by Owen
Biddle, 1737-1799].
Philadelphia, Crukshank, 1790. 52 pp.
AAS copy.   22361

The Plan for Correspondence and
Friendly Intercourse.
[New York, 1800.] 4 pp.
AAS copy.   38277

Plan for Establishing a General Marine
Society.
Philadelphia, Fenno, 1798. 32 pp.
AAS copy.   33944

The Plan for Establishing a new American
Post-Office. . . . April 30, 1774.
[Boston, 1774.] Broadside.
MHS copy.   42672

[A Plan for Liquidating Certain Debts of
the State of Pennsylvania.
[Philadelphia, 1780?] 6 pp.]
(See Sabin 60393 and Hildeburn 3775.)
                                             16954

. . . A Plan for Liquidating Certain Debts
of the State of Pennsylvania ["Second
Edition."]
[Philadelphia], Aitken, [1785?]. 6 pp.
LOC copy.   44774

A Plan for the Establishment of Public
Schools [by Benjamin Rush, 1745-1813].
Philadelphia, Dobson, 1786. 36 pp.
BA copy.   19974

[A Plan for the Maintenance of the
Ministers in New-England.
Boston, 1724.]
(Title from Haven; apparently a ghost of
2529.)   2580

A Plan for the More Effectual Instruction
of Children and Youth. . . . December 3,
1800.
New Haven, Ct., Read & Morse, 1800. 8
pp.
CL copy.   38278

A Plan for the Payment of the National
Debt, by Means of a National Bank.
Philadelphia, 1785. 16 pp.
LCP copy.   44775

A Plan for the Payment of the National
Debt, by means of a National Bank.
[New York, 1787.] 13 pp.
LOC copy.   20653

[A Plan for the Payment of the National
Debt, by means of a National Bank.
New York, Greenleaf, [1787]. [15] pp.]
(Sabin 63278.)   20654

Plan of an Association in Honor of Jesus
Christ.
Baltimore, Hayes, 1794. 12 pp.
(Minick 197; no copy located.)   47182

A Plan of Consociation, Adopted . . . by a
Convention of Churches in Windham
County, November, 1800.
Windham, Ct., Byrne, 1800. 16 pp.
(Also entered as 39121, q. v.)   38280

A Plan of Exercise for the Militia of the
Colony of Connecticut [by William
Windham, 1717-1761].
New Haven, 1772. 60 pp.
HEH copy.   12623

A Plan of Exercise for the Militia of the
Colony of Connecticut [by William
Windham, 1717-1761].
New London, 1772. 72 pp.
LOC copy.   12624

A Plan of Exercise, for the Militia of
the Province of the Massachusetts-Bay [by
William Windham, 1717-1761].
Boston, Draper, 1768. [2], 104 pp.
(Reissued in 1770 with a dated half-title
and an Appendix, pp. 105-106. The AAS
copy has these.)
AAS copy.   11121

A Plan of Exercise, for the Militia of the
Province of the Massachusetts-Bay [Third
Edition], [by William Windham,
1717-1761].
Boston, Draper, 1771. [4], 104 pp.
AAS copy.   12290

A Plan of Exercise, for the Militia of the
Province of the Massachusetts-Bay [by
William Windham, 1717-1761].
Boston, Draper, 1772. [2], 104 pp.
LOC copy.   12622

A Plan of Exercise, for the Militia of the
Province of Massachusetts-Bay [by
William Windham, 1717-1761].
Boston, 1774. [4], 104 pp.
LOC copy.   13777

A Plan of the Attack of Fort Sullivan the
key of Charlestown . . . on the 28th of
June 1776.
Philadelphia, Humphreys, Styner & Cist,
[1776]. Map.
HEH copy.   43142

Plan of the Book Auction to be the First
of July Next. . . . Savannah, May 19, 1791.
[Savannah, 1791.] Broadside.
LOC copy.   23702

Plan of the City of Washington [by
Andrew Ellicott, 1754-1820].
New York, Reid, Wayland & Smith, 1795.
map.
HEH copy.   47413

Plan of the French Invasion of England
and Ireland, &c. . . . April 16, 1798.
Philadelphia, Carey, [1798]. Broadside.
LOC copy.   48580

The Plan of the Invasion of England and
Ireland.
Philadelphia, Carey, [1798]. Broadside.
LOC copy.   33753

[Plan of the review for July 4, 1795.
Baltimore, 1795.]
(Minick 247; no copy known.)   47560

[Plan of the review for October 29, 1795.
Baltimore, 1795.]
(Minick 248; no copy known.)   47561

A Plan of Union by Admitting
Representatives from the American
Colonies . . . into the British Parliament.
[Philadelphia, 1770?] 3 pp.
LCP copy.   42155

A Plan. More Effectual Religious
Instruction of Children and Youth.
Stockbridge, 1800. 6 pp.
(The only reported copy is mislaid.)   38279

[Plant, Thomas.]
Joyful News for America.
[Philadelphia, 1766.] Broadside.

(The HSP has another printing with the
author's name.)
HSP copy.   10464

[Plant, Thomas.]
Joyful News to America, a Poem.
[Philadelphia], 1766. 8 pp.
FL copy.   10465

Platt, Jonas, 1769-1834.
To the People of Oneida County. . . .
October 1st, 1800.
[Utica, 1800.] 23 pp.
NYPL copy.   38281

Plattes, Gabriel, fl. 1638.
A Discovery of Subterranean Treasure.
Philadelphia, Bell, 1784. 37, [3] pp.
AAS copy.   18732

Plattes, Gabriel, fl. 1638.
A Discovery of Subterranean Treasure.
Philadelphia, 1792. 24 pp.
AAS copy.   24697

Playfair, William, 1759-1823.
The History of Jacobinism . . . Vol. I
[-II].
Philadelphia, Cobbett, 1796. pp. [1]-30,
[2], [35]-385; [1]-301, [48].
AAS copy.   31016

A Plea before the Ecclesiastical Council at
Stockbridge [by Joseph Huntington,
1735-1794].
Boston, Coverly & Hodge, 1782. 130 pp.
AAS copy.   17561

A Plea before the Venerable Ecclesiastical
Council at Stockbridge [by Joseph
Huntington, 1735-1794].
Norwich, Trumbull, 1780. 36 pp.
AAS copy.   16805

A Plea before the Venerable Ecclesiastical
Council at Stockbridge [by Joseph
Huntington, 1735-1794].
Norwich, Trumbull, 1780. 46 pp.
NYPL copy.   16806

A Plea for Literature [by Richard
Beresford, 1755-1803].
Charleston, Harrison & Bowen, 1793. [4],
119 pp.
LOC copy.   25162

[A Plea for Pure and Undefiled Religion.
Addressed to Col. James Gardner.
New York, 1742.]
(Title from Haven.)   5038

A Plea for the Ministers of New-England
[by Jabez Fitch, 1672-1746].
Boston, Gerrish, 1724. [2], 14 pp.
AAS copy.   2529

A Plea for the Ministers of the Gospel.
Boston, 1706. [2], 29 pp.
(See T. J. Holmes, Increase Mather, II,
646-648.)
AAS copy.   1276

A Plea for the Poor and Distressed.
Boston, 1754. 14 pp.
AAS copy.   7296

A Plea for the Poor Soldiers [by Pelatiah
Webster, 1726-1795].
New Haven, 1790. 33 pp.
BA copy.   23061

A Plea for the Poor Soldiers [by Pelatiah
Webster, 1726-1795].
Philadelphia, Bailey, 1790. 39 pp.
AAS copy.   23060

[A Plea for Truth, in Opposition to
Arminian Doctrines.
Boston, Kneeland & Green, 1739?]
("Just Published," New England Weekly
Journal, July 10, 1739.)   4414

The Plea of Erin, or the Case of the
Natives of Ireland in the United States.
Philadelphia, office of the Freeman's
Journal, [1798]. [4] pp.
LOC copy.   48581

The Plea of the Colonies [by Hugh
Williamson, 1735-1819].
Philadelphia, Bell, 1777. Front., [8], 38,
[2] pp.
NYPL copy.   15713

The Pleasant and Profitable Companion.
Boston, Edwards and Foster, 1733. [2],
176 pp., front.
AAS copy.   40027

[The Pleasant Art of Money Catching.
Boston, Fowle, 1753.]
(From an adv.)   7097

[Pleasant History of the Fryar and Boy.
Keene, Blake, 1793. 14 pp.]
(No copy located.)   26007

Pleasant Stories and Lessons for Children.
Fairhaven, Spooner, 1797. 30, [1] pp.
(Not located, 1968.)   48233

[Pleasants, Mrs.
Mrs. Pleasant's Story Book.
Philadelphia, Hogan, 1798.]
(Imprint assumed by Evans from adv.
"Just Published, and for sale by David
Hogan," in 33357.)   34386

The Pleasing History of Pamela [by
Samuel Richardson, 1689-1761].
Boston, Hall, [1793?]. 96 pp.
AAS copy.   26088

Pleasing Incitements to Wisdom and
Virtue.
Philadelphia, Humphreys, 1800. iv, [2],
120 pp.
AAS copy.   38282

The Pleasing Instructor, or Entertaining
Moralist [by Ann (Fisher) Slack,
1719-1778].
Boston, Bumstead for B. Larkin & E.
Larkin, and D. West, 1795. 312, [3] pp.
AAS copy.   29518

[The Pleasing Songster; or Festive
Companion.
Philadelphia, 1795.]
(Entry apparently from an adv.)   29328

The Pleasures of Memory [by Samuel
Rogers, 1763-1855].
Boston, Manning & Loring, 1795. [4], 124
pp., 4 plates.
AAS copy.   29426

[Pleyel, Ignaz Joseph], 1757-1831.
Come Blushing Rose.
[New York], Willig, [c. 1794]. Broadside.
AAS copy.   47183

Pleyel, Ignaz Joseph, 1757-1831.
Henry's Cottage Maid.
New York, Gilfert, [1796]. 1 leaf.
AAS copy.   31017

Pleyel, Ignaz Joseph, 1757-1831.
Pleyel's German Hymn, with variations.
New York, Erben, [1800?]. 4 pp.
WLC copy.   49136

[Pleyel, Ignaz Joseph, 1757-1831.
Twelve Duets for 2 Clarinets.
New York, Harrison, 1794.]
(Imprint assumed by Evans from
Harrison's advs. "for sale.")   27528

The Plot. By way of a Burlesk.
[Philadelphia], 1764. Broadside.
(Printed on the same sheet with 9581.)
LCP copy.   9799

The Plot Discovered, Communicated by a
Letter. . . . March 15, 1775.
[New York? 1775.] Broadside.
NYHS copy.   14408

[Plot of the Seven Ranges of Townships
. . . N.W. of the River Ohio.
Philadelphia, Carey, 1796.]
(Entry from the copyright notice.)   30918

[Plowden, Charles], 1743-1821.
A Short Account of the Establishment of
the New See of Baltimore.
Philadelphia, Carey, Stewart & Co., 1791.
20 pp.
Georgetown University copy.   23703

Plowden, Francis Peter, 1749-1829.
A Short History of the British Empire,
from May, 1792 to the Close of the Year
1793.
Philadelphia, Carey, 1794. pp. [2], [1]-16,
25-261, [3].
AAS copy.   27529

A Plowman's Complaint [by Seth
Brooks].
Philadelphia, 1767. vii, 27 pp.
LCP copy.   10570

Plummer, Jonathan, 1761-1819.
(D. A. B.)
An Address to Miss Katherine
Wigglesworth. . . . October 16, 1792.
[Newburyport, 1792.] Broadside.
AAS copy.   24698

Plummer, Jonathan, 1761-1819.
The Awful Malignant Fever at
Newburyport, in the Year 1796.
[Newburyport], Printed and sold by the
Author, [1796]. Broadside.
AAS copy.   31018

Plummer, Jonathan, 1761-1819.
Dying Confession of Pomp . . . the 6th of
August, 1795.
[Newburyport], Plummer, [1795].
Broadside.
EI copy.   29329

Plummer, Jonathan, 1761-1819.
Elegy on the Death of the Rev. Mr. John
Murray.
[Newburyport, 1793.] Broadside.
AAS copy.   26008

[Plummer, Jonathan, 1761-1819.
Funeral Dirge.
[Newburyport, 1793?]. Broadside]
(Assumed by Evans from an adv.)   26009

Plummer, Jonathan, 1761-1819.
Newburyport, July 23, 1794. On Saturday
last. . . .
[Newburyport, 1794.] Broadside.
LOC copy.   27530

[Plummer, Jonathan, 1761-1819.
Plummer's Declaration of War with the
Fair Ladies.
[Newburyport, Mycall, 1793.] Broadside.]
(Described from a copy in private hands;
present location unknown.)   26010

Plummer, Jonathan, 1761-1819.
[A Sketch of the History of the Life . . .
of. . . .
Newburyport, Blunt & March, 1795.]
240+pp.
(The only recorded copy lacks Part I and
several other pages.)
EI copy.   29330

[Plummer, Jonathan, 1761-1819.
To Sir Timothy Dexter, on his Returning
to Newburyport.
Newburyport, Barrett, 1797. Broadside.]
(No copy located.)   32695

Plummer, Jonathan, 1761-1819.
To the Inhabitants of Newburyport.
Friends and Fellow-Candidates. . . .
[Newburyport, 1793.] Broadside.
NYHS copy.   26011

[Plumptre, Anne], 1760-1818.
Antoinette Percival.
Philadelphia, Carey, 1800. 234 pp.
AAS copy.   38283

Plymouth Company, 1749-1816.
Advertisement. The Proprietors. . . . May
9th, 1759.
[Boston, 1759.] Broadside.
MHS copy.   41051

Plymouth Company, 1749-1816.
Advertisement. The Proprietors of the
Kennebunk Purchase. . . . February 16,
1760.
[Boston, 1760]. Broadside.
BPL copy.   41162

Plymouth Company, 1749-1816.
Advertisement. The Proprietors of the
Kennebeck Purchase. . . . 20th February,
1761.
[Boston, 1761.] Broadside.
AAS copy.   41237

Plymouth Company, 1749-1816.
Advertisement. The Proprietors of the
Kennebeck Purchase. . . . Boston, May 18,
1763.
[Boston, 1763.] Broadside.
AAS copy.   41407

Plymouth Company, 1749-1816.
Advertisement. This is to Notify all the
Proprietors. . . . [Sept. 1, 1752.]
[Boston, 1752.] Broadside.
AAS copy.   40639

Plymouth Company, 1749-1816.
Advertisement. Whereas by some late
Advertisements. . . . By Order of the
Proprietors. . . . Boston, May 1, 1751.
[Boston, 1751.] Broadside.
AAS copy.   40600

Plymouth Company, 1749-1816.
Advertisement. Whereas the Plymouth
Proprietors. . . . Boston, March 7, 1750.
[Boston, 1750.] Broadside.
AAS copy.   40562

Plymouth Company, 1749-1816.
Advertisement. Whereas the Proprietors
of the Kennebeck Purchase. . . . Jan. 2,
1754.
[Boston, 1754.] Broadside.
AAS copy.   40712

Plymouth Company, 1749-1816.
At a Meeting of the Proprietors of the
Kenebeck Purchase . . . on the 12th of
January, 1753. . . .
[Boston, 1753.] Broadside.
AAS copy.   40665

Plymouth Company, 1749-1816.
A Defence of the Remarks of the
Plymouth Company.
Boston, 1753. [2], 50 pp.
AAS copy.   6988

Plymouth Company, 1749-1816.
Forasmuch as there have been many
Disputes. . . .
[Boston, 1753?] 3 pp.
AAS copy.   40666

Plymouth Company, 1749-1816.
Forasmuch as there have been many
Disputes. . . .
[Boston, 1753?] 4 pp.
AAS copy.   40667

Plymouth Company, 1749-1816.
A Patent for Plymouth in New-England.
Boston, Draper, 1751. [2], 19, [1] pp.
AAS copy.   6761

[Plymouth Company], 1749-1816.
Remarks on the Plan . . . of January 4th
1753.
[Boston, 1753.] 8 pp.
AAS copy.   7098

Plymouth Company, 1749-1816.
To all to whom this Presents Shall Come,
Greeting . . . to Have and to Hold. . . .
[Boston? 175-]. [2] pp.
AAS copy.   40531

Plymouth Company, 1749-1816,
defendants.
The Proprietors Holding under Lake &
Clark, Plaintiffs, against Proprietors from
Plymouth Colony, Defendants.
[Boston? 1757?] 7 pp.
AAS copy.   40928

Plymouth, Mass.
Festival of the Sons of the Pilgrims. Ode
for the 22d of December. . . . 1800.
n. p., n. d. Broadside.
MHS copy.   38284

[The Pocket Almanack for the Year 1748.
New York, Parker.]
("Just published, and to be sold by the
Printer hereof," N. Y. Gazette, Nov. 23,
1747.)   6053

[The Pocket Almanack for the Year,
1749.
New York, Parker.]
(Title from printer's adv.)   6222

A Pocket Almanack, for . . . 1770.
Philadelphia, Dunlap. [32] pp.
AAS copy.   11522

A Pocket Almanack for . . . 1779.
Boston, Fleets. [54] pp.
AAS copy.   15794

A Pocket Almanack for . . . 1780.

Boston, Fleets. [68] pp.
AAS copy.   16274

A Pocket Almanack for ... 1781....
Calculated for ... Massachusetts.
Boston, Fleets. [64] pp.
AAS copy.   16774

A Pocket Almanack for ... 1782.
Boston, Fleets. [84] pp.
AAS copy.   17154

A Pocket Almanack for ... 1783.
Boston, Fleets. [24], 72 pp.
AAS copy.   17534

A Pocket Almanack for ... 1784.
Boston, Fleets. [24], 80 pp.
AAS copy.   17929

A Pocket Almanack for ... 1785.
Boston, Fleets. [24], 84 pp.
AAS copy.   18469

A Pocket Almanack for ... 1786.
Boston, Fleets. [24], 114, [1] pp.
AAS copy.   19006

A Pocket Almanack for ... 1787.
Boston, Fleets. [20], 112 pp.
AAS copy.   19649

[A Pocket Almanac, for 1791.
Philadelphia, M'Culloch.]
(Entry from an adv. for pocket almanacs.)
    22803

A Pocket Almanack for ... 1794.
Boston, Fleets. [20], 148 pp.
AAS copy.   25488

A Pocket Almanack for ... 1795.
Boston, Fleets. [20], 148 pp.
AAS copy.   26977

A Pocket Almanack for ... 1796.
Boston, Fleets. [20], 148 pp.
AAS copy.   28680

A Pocket Almanack for ... 1796....
Second Edition.
Boston, Fleet. [20], 148 pp.
(The words "Second Edition" occur at the
head of p. 1, leaf [11].)
NYPL copy.   28681

[A Pocket Book for the German Flute.
New York, Rivington, 1778.]
(Adv. Rivington's Royal Gazette, July,
1778.)   16014

[A Pocket Book for the Guitar.
New York, Rivington, 1778.]
(Adv. in Rivington's Royal Gazette, July,
1778.)   16015

[A Pocket Book for the Violin.
New York, Rivington, 1778.]
(Adv. in Rivington's Royal Gazette, July,
1778.)   16016

A Pocket Commentary of the First
Settling of New-Jersey.
New York, Parker, 1759. 19, [1] pp.
NYPL copy.   8369

The Pocket Gazetteer: or, a Description
of all the Principal Cities and Towns, in
the United States.
Walpole, N. H., 1795. 40 pp., 1 table.
AAS copy.   29331

A Pocket Hymn Book, Designed as a
Constant Companion for the Pious. ...
Fifth Edition.
New York, Ross, 1786. 224, [8] pp.
AAS copy.   44949

A Pocket Hymn Book, Designed as
Constant Companion for the Pious. ...
Eighth Edition.
Philadelphia, Prichard & Hall, 1788. 257,
[1] pp.
AAS copy.   45342

A Pocket Hymn Book, Designed as a
Constant Companion for the Pious. ...
Ninth Edition.
Philadelphia, James, 1788. 257, [2] pp.
AAS copy.   21254

A Pocket Hymn-Book, Designed as a
Constant Companion for the Pious. ...

Eleventh Edition.
Philadelphia, Pritchard & Hall for
Dickins, 1790. pp. [1]-v, [1], 5-276, [10].
(The imprint given by Evans was assumed
from an adv. The only known copy is
incomplete.)
AAS copy.   22667

A Pocket Hymn Book, Designed as a
Constant Companion for the Pious.
Eighth Edition.
Wilmington, [Del.], Andrews, Craig &
Brynberg, 1790. 276, [10] pp.
(The only recorded copy cannot now be
located.)   45972

A Pocket Hymn-Book, Designed as a
Constant Companion for the Pious. ...
Twelfth Edition.
New York, Durell, 1791. 276, [10] pp.
LOC copy.   23567

A Pocket Hymn-Book, Designed as a
Constant Companion for the Pious. ...
Thirteenth Edition.
Philadelphia, Hall for Dickins, 1791. pp.
[i]-v, [1], [5]-285, [11] pp.
AAS copy.   23566

[A Pocket Hymn-Book, Designed as a
Constant Companion for the Pious. ...
Thirteenth Edition.
Philadelphia, Hall, 1792.]
(Entry apparently from an adv. for 23566.)
    24545

A Pocket Hymn-Book, Designed as
Constant Companion for the Pious. ...
Fifteenth Edition.
Philadelphia, Hall for Dickins, 1792. 285,
[13] pp.
UTS copy.   25809

[A Pocket Hymn-Book, Designed as a
Constant Companion for the Pious. ...
Sixteenth Edition.
Philadelphia, Hall for Dickins, 1793. 300
pp.]
(No copy of a 16th ed. located.)   25810

A Pocket Hymn-Book, Designed as a
Constant Companion for the Pious. ...
Seventeenth Edition.
Philadelphia, Hall for Dickins, 1793. 285,
[11] pp.
(Evans assumed the imprint from advs.
The only copy located is imperfect.)
AAS copy.   27315

[A Pocket Hymn-Book, Designed as a
Constant Companion for the Pious. ...
Eighteenth Edition.
Philadelphia, Hall for Dickins, 1794.]
(Assumed by Evans from the sequence of
eds.)   27316

[A Pocket Hymn-Book, Designed as a
Constant Companion for the Pious. ...
Nineteenth Edition.
Philadelphia, Tuckniss for Dickins, 1795.]
(Imprint assumed by Evans from adv. in
28549.)   29073

A Pocket Hymn-Book, Designed as a
Constant Companion for the Pious. ...
Twentieth Edition.
Philadelphia, Tuckniss for Dickins, 1795.
[2], 285, [13] pp.
AAS copy.   29074

A Pocket Hymn-Book Designed as a
Constant Companion for the Pious. ...
Twenty-First Edition.
Philadelphia, Tuckniss for Dickins, 1796.
[2], 285, [13] pp.
AAS copy.   30788

A Pocket Hymn-Book Designed as a
Constant Companion for the Pious. ...
Twenty-First Edition.
Philadelphia, Tuckniss for Dickins, 1797.
[2], 285, [13] pp.
AAS copy.   32474

A Pocket Hymn-Book, Designed as a
Constant Companion for the Pious. ...
Twenty-Second Edition.
Philadelphia, Tuckniss for Dickins, 1798.
[2], 285, [13] pp.
LOC copy.   34104

A Pocket Hymn-Book, Designed as a
Constant Companion for the Pious. ...

Twenty-Third Edition.
Philadelphia, Tuckniss for Cooper, 1800.
ii, 285, [10], 6, [2] pp.
AAS copy.   38285

[A Pocket Memorandum Book, or Daily
Journal for ... 1785.
Philadelphia, Crukshank. [132] pp.]
(Copy seen by Evans not now to be
located.)   18734

The Pocket Miscellany. In Prose and
Verse.
Philadelphia, Carey, 1798. [2], 282 pp.
AAS copy.   34387

Poellnitz, Frederick Carl Hans Bruno,
baron von, 1734-1801.
(Henry P. Johnston, Little Acorns.)
Essay on Agriculture.
New York, Childs & Swain, 1790. 24 pp.,
4 folded plates.
AAS copy.   22805

A Poem, Addressed to a Young Lady [by
Henry Hulton, d. 1790].
Boston, Green & Russell, 1773. 33 pp.
AAS copy.   I-1688

A Poem, Addressed to the Armies of the
United States [by David Humphreys,
1752-1818].
New Haven, 1780. 16 pp.
AAS copy.   16801

A Poem, Called Edwin and Emma [by
David Mallet, 1705?-1765].
Boston, 1764. 8 pp.
AAS copy.   9649

A Poem, Commemorative of Goffe,
Whaley, & Dixwell.
Boston, Hall, 1793. 28 pp.
AAS copy.   25998

A Poem Composed July 4, 1783, being a
Day of General Rejoicing.
n.p., [1783]. Broadside.
NYPL ph. copy.   44441

A Poem, Containing two Letters [by
Hendricus Dow, 1761-1814].
New Haven, 1799. 11 pp.
HEH copy.   35422

A Poem Dedicated to ... Urian Oakes
[by Cotton Mather, 1663-1728].
Boston, 1682. [4], 16 pp.
BrU copy.   319

A Poem, Descriptive of the Terrible Fire
... the Twenty-First of April, 1787.
[Boston], at the Printing-Office in
Essex-Street, [1787]. Broadside.
JCB copy.   45140

A Poem, Descriptive of the Terrible Fire
... in Boston ... April 21, 1787.
[Boston], at the Office next Liberty-Pole,
[1787]. Broadside.
MHS copy.   45139

A Poem in Memory of that Pious Servant
and Faithful Minister ... Isaac Cushman.
[Boston, 1732.] Broadside.
BPL copy.   40001

A Poem, in Memory of the (Never to be
Forgotten) Fifth of March, 1770.
[Boston], Printed and Sold next to the
Writing-School, in Queen-Street, [1770?]
Broadside.
MHS copy.   42156

[A Poem in Seven Parts; Containing
Reflections upon a Farewell.
Boston, 1774.]
(Entry from Haven.)   13549

A Poem, in two Cantos. ... By ... Simon
Spunkey [by Samuel Chipman,
1763-1839].
Vergennes, Vt., Chipman, 1799.]
(Entry from copyright and advs.)   35479

A Poem. In two Letters [by Hendricus
Dow, 1761-1814].
Newfield, 1795. 11 pp.
YC copy.   28587

A Poem. In two Letters [by Hendricus
Dow, 1761-1814].

Worcester, 1795. 12 pp.
AAS copy.   28588

A Poem, in two Letters. Argument [by
Hendricus Dow, 1761-1814].
Brattleborough, 1799. 11 pp.
HEH copy.   35421

A Poem Occasioned by a Funeral Essay
on Governor Law.
[New London], 1754. 8 pp.
WL copy.   7298

A Poem, Occasioned by Hearing the late
Reverend George Whitefield Preach.
[Boston, 1771?] Broadside.
BPL copy.   13548

A Poem Occasioned by the Death of . . .
Jonathan Law [by John Hubbard,
1703-1773].
[New London], 1751. [4], 8 pp.
AAS copy.   6651

A Poem Occasion'd by the late Powerful
and Awakening Preaching of . . . Gilbert
Tennent.
[Boston, 1741?] Broadside.
MHS copy.   40257

A Poem Occasioned by the late Sudden
and Awful Death, of a Young Woman . . .
July 14th, 1771.
Medford, [Mass.], 1771. Broadside.
MHS copy.   42269

Poem Occasioned by the most Shocking
and Cruel Murder that ever was
Represented on the Stage.
[Hartford, 1782.] Broadside.
WLC copy.   44246

A Poem Occasioned by the Spreading in
this Province the Result of a
Consociation.
Boston, Rogers & Fowle, 1742. [7] pp.
LOC copy.   5039

A Poem, Occasioned by the Sudden and
Surprising Death of Mr. Asa Burt . . . the
28th of January, 1774.
Hartford, [1774]. Broadside.
CHS copy.   42673

[A Poem on Death.
Boston, Russell, 1793.]
(Evans assumed the imprint from an adv.)
                                             26012

A Poem on Divine Revelation [by Hugh
Henry Brackenridge, 1748-1816].
Philadelphia, Aitken, 1774. [6], 22 (i.e.
23) pp.
AAS copy.   13172

A Poem, on Religious Ignorance [by
Chapman Whitcomb, 1765-1833].
n. p., for the Purchaser, 1795. Broadside.
AAS copy.   47682

A Poem, on Religious Ignorance [by
Chapman Whitcomb, 1765-1833].
Boston, 1795. 4 pp.
AAS copy.   29332

A Poem, on Religious Ignorance, Pride
and Avarice [by Chapman Whitcomb,
1765-1833].
[Leominster, Mass.? 1800?] Broadside.
AAS copy.   49191

A Poem, on the Death of Deacon William
Barns [by James Potter, fl. 1769].
Hartford, 1769. 15 pp.
WL copy.   11422

A Poem, on the Death of Deacon William
Brown, of Groton.
Norwich, Conn., Trumbull, 1794.
CHS copy.   27531

Poem on the Death of Dr. Abraham
Howe.
Worcester, [1779]. Broadside.
AAS copy.   19429

A Poem. On the Execution of Samuel
Frost . . . October 31, 1793.
[Worcester, Thomas ? 1793.] Broadside.
AAS copy.   26013

A Poem, on the Execution of William
Shaw . . . December 13th, 1770 [by

William Carpenter, fl. 1770].
[Hartford, 1771.] Broadside.
HSP copy.   12200

A Poem, on the Joyful News of the Rev.
Mr. Whitefield's Visit to Boston.
Boston, 1754. Broadside.
HEH copy.   40713

A Poem on the late Distress of the Town
of Boston [by Elisha Rich, 1740-1804?].
Chelmsford, 1776. Broadside.
AAS copy.   15061

A Poem on the President's Farewell
Address.
Philadelphia, Ormrod, [1800]. 8 pp.
(Also entered as 37644, q. v.)   38286

A Poem on the President's Farewell
Address. . . . Second Edition [by St. John
Honeywood, 1763-1798].
Philadelphia, Ormrod & Conrad, [1800].
8 pp.
BPL copy.   37644

A Poem on the Rebuke of God's Hand in
the . . . Fire in . . . Boston [by Andrew
Johonnot].
Boston, Draper, 1760. Broadside.
(See Winslow, Am. Broadside Verse, p.
70.)
W. H. Whitmore copy.   8595

A Poem on the Rise and Progress of
Moor's Indian Charity School [by Levi
Frisbie, 1748-1806].
(Weis, Colonial Clergy N. E.)
[Hartford, 1771.] 8 pp.
(Apparently printed only as part of 12284,
q. v.)   12051

A Poem on the Rising Glory of America
[by Philip Morin Freneau, 1752-1832].
Philadelphia, Crukshank for Aitken, 1772.
27, [1] pp.
AAS copy.   12398

A Poem, on the Unsuccessful Measures,
Taken by the British Army [by Ezekiel
Kellogg, 1732-1785].
Printed 1782. 16 pp.
AAS copy.   44208

A Poem on the Untimely Deaths of the
Unfortunate Mr. Rufus Randall and Mr.
Hopkins Hudson.
[Providence? 1798?] Broadside.
(The only known copy is imperfect.)
(Not located, 1968.)   48582

A Poem on Visiting the Academy of
Philadelphia [by William Smith,
1727-1803].
Philadelphia, 1753. 16 pp.
BA copy.   7122

[A Poem on Winter, Printed for the
Benefit of a Poor Child.
Williamsburg? 1769?]
(Adv. Rind's Va. Gazette, Feb. 16, 1769.
"Lately published."   41993

A Poem. One God There is.
Medford, [Mass.], 1771. Broadside.
MHS copy.   42270

A Poem on the Rising Glory of America
[by Philip Morin Freneau, 1752-1832].
Philadelphia, Crukshank for Aitken, 1772.
27, [1] pp.
AAS copy.   12398

A Poem Presented to His Excellency
William Burnet.
[Boston, 1728.] [2], 5 pp.
BPL copy.   3092

A Poem Sacred to the Memory of James
Wolfe [by Thomas Young, 1732-1777].
New Haven, [1761]. 19 pp.
(Dated from adv. in Conn. Gazette, Sept.
12, 1761.)
LOC copy.   8471

A Poem Sacred to the Memory of Mrs.
Abigail Conant [by Peter Oliver,
1713-1791].
New London, 1759. 7 pp.
AAS copy.   8323

A Poem Sacred to the Memory of the
Honorable Josiah Willard [by Peter

Oliver, 1713-1791].
Boston, Green & Russell, 1757. 16 pp.
AAS copy.   7988

A Poem, Spoken Extempore, by a Young
Lady, on Hearing the Guns . . . of
York-Town.
[Boston], Russell, [1782]. Broadside.
AAS copy.   44247

[A Poem upon the Death of Mrs. Martha
Chandler.
[Boston, 1737.] Broadside.]
(Title from Haven.)   4187

A Poem upon the Deaths, and in Memory
of . . . Isaac Cushman . . . and Dr. Caleb
Loring.
[Boston, 1733?] Broadside.
BPL copy.   40028

A Poem, upon the Present Times, with a
Brief and Humble Address.
[New Haven? 1775.] Broadside.
NYPL copy.   14403

The Poem which the Committee of the
Town. . . . [by James Allen, 1739-1808].
Boston, Russell, 1772. 30 pp.
(For difference between the two issues,
see Sibley XIV, under James Allen.)
AAS copy.   12301

A Poem, Wrote upon the Execution of a
Man . . . at Fairfield for Burglary, the
First Day of March . . . 1769.
n. p., [1769]. Broadside.
CHS copy.   41994

Poems, Occasioned by Several
Circumstances [by Wheeler Case, d.
1793].
New Haven, 1778. 28 pp.
HC copy.   15754

Poems, Occasioned by Several
Circumstances. . . . Second Edition [by
Wheeler Case, d. 1793].
New Haven, 1788 (i.e. 1778). 24 pp.
WL copy.   15755

The Poems of Arouet [by Joseph Brown
Ladd, 1764-1786].
Charleston, Bowen & Markland, 1786. xvi,
128 pp.
AAS copy.   19747

Poems, on Different Subjects: Calculated
to Improve and Edify Young Christians.
Albany, Websters, [1790?] 12 pp.
BrU copy.   45973

Poems on Several Occasions. Quod si non.
. . . By a Gentleman of Virginia.
Williamsburg, 1736. 30 pp.
BA copy.   4066

Poems, on Several Occasions, Written in
Pennsylvania [by William Moore Smith,
1759-1821].
Philadelphia, Story, 1786. 141, [3] pp.
AAS copy.   19994

Poems on Several Occurrences. . . . Fifth
Edition [by Wheeler Case, d. 1793.]
Chatham, 1779. 24 pp.
(The only copy of this ed. located is badly
stained.)
LOC copy.   16218

Poems on Several Occurrences [by
Wheeler Case, d. 1793].
Philadelphia, Bailey, 1779.]
(Entry from an unlocated adv.)   16219

Poems on Several Occurrences in the
Present Grand Struggle. . . . Fourth
Edition [by Wheeler Case, d. 1793].
Trenton, 1779. 24 pp.
(No legible copy could be found.)
AAS copy.   16217

Poems, on Various Subjects. Written by a
Youth.
Hartford, Hudson & Goodwin, 1781. 24
pp.
AAS copy.   17314

Poems. The Conflagration [by Mather
Byles, 1707-1788].
Boston, Fowle, [1755]. 8 pp.
AAS copy.   7376

Poems upon Several Occasions.
Boston, 1779. 16 pp.
AAS copy.   16479

Poems, upon Several Sermons [by Jane
Dunlap, fl. 1771].
Boston, 1771. [2], 19, [1] pp.
AAS copy.   12031

[Poetic Miscellany, on Subjects Moral and
Religious.
Portsmouth, N. H., Peirce, 1798.]
(A duplicate of 33856, q. v.)   34388

A Poetical Description of Song Birds. . . .
First Worcester Edition.
Worcester, Thomas, 1788. 88 pp.
NYPL copy.   21399

A Poetical Discription of the Present
Oppressions [by Dominick Cornyn].
Reading, Pa., Schneider, 1798. [2], 33,
[1] pp.
LOC copy.   33572

A Poetical Epistle to His Excellency
George Washington [by Charles Henry
Wharton, 1748-1833].
Annapolis, 1779. 24 pp.]
(Apparently this ed. is a ghost.)   16677

A Poetical Epistle to His Excellency
George Washington [by Charles Henry
Wharton, 1748-1833].
Philadelphia, Kline, 1781. 10 pp.
LCP copy.   17435

A Poetical Epistle to His Excellency
George Washington [by Charles Henry
Wharton, 1748-1833].
Providence, 1781. Front., 24 pp.
AAS copy.   17436

A Poetical Epistle, to His Excellency
George Washington [by Charles Henry
Wharton, 1748-1833].
Springfield, 1782. 18 pp.
AAS copy.   17801

A Poetical Epistle to the Enslaved
Africans.
Philadelphia, Crukshank, 1790. 24 pp.
AAS copy.   22806

The Poetical Flower Basket. . . . First
American Edition.
Worcester, Thomas, 1799. 71 pp.
AAS copy.   36129

The Poetical Nosegay; or the Swindler
James Geo. Semple Revived in . . . Hugh
Workman.
n. p., 1800. [10], 20+ pp.
(The only reported copy is imperfect.)
NYPL copy.   38291

Poetical Remarks upon the Fight at the
Boston Light-House [by Elisha Rich,
1740-1804?].
[Chelmsford, 1775.] Broadside.
(This copy may be cropped.)
AAS copy.   14427

[A Poetical Sermon, Occasioned by a
Disappointment in Love.
Newport, Edes, 1787.]
("This day published," Newport Herald,
Mar. 29, 1787.)   20655

The Poetical Wanderer [by John Blair
Linn, 1777-1804].
New York, Forman, 1796. 112, [6] pp.
AAS copy.   30696

The Poetical Works of Peter Pindar [by
John Wolcot, 1738-1819].
Philadelphia, Spotswood, 1789. ix, [1],
314 pp.
AAS copy.   22288

The Poetical Works of Peter Pindar [by
John Wolcot, 1738-1819].
Newburyport, Mycall for Boyle, [1790?].
viii, 314 pp.
AAS copy.   23087

The Poetical Works of Peter Pindar. . . .
Vol. II [by John Wolcot, 1738-1819].
Philadelphia, Spotswood and Rice, 1790.
pp. [191]-402.
AAS copy.   23088

The Poetical Works of Peter Pindar. . . .

Vol. I [-II] [by John Wolcot,
1738-1819].
Philadelphia, Spotswood & Rice, 1792.
viii, 307, [1]; iv, 324 pp.
AAS copy.   25052

Poivre, Pierre, 1719-1786.
Travels of a Philosopher.
Augusta, Me., Edes, 1797. 94 pp.
AAS copy.   32696

Pole, Edward.
Military Laboratory, at No. 34, Dock
Street . . . where Owners . . . of Armed
Vessels may be Supplied. . . .
[Philadelphia], Aitken, [1789].
Broadside.
LOC copy.   45521

Pole, Edward, & Co., Philadelphia.
Sales at Auction of Horses & Carriages.
. . . April 24, 1799.
Philadelphia, Aitken, [1799]. Broadside.
HSP copy.   36098

A Polemic Essay [by Noah Worcester,
1758-1837].
Newark, [N. J.], Pennington & Dodge,
1799. 42 pp.
NYHS copy.   36739

The Polite Lady; or, A Course of Female
Education.
Philadelphia, Carey, 1798. 271, [5] pp.
AAS copy.   34389

[The Polite Philosopher [by James
Forrester].
Philadelphia, Dunlap, 1758.]
(From an adv.)   8125

The Polite Philosopher. . . . Fifteenth
Edition [by James Forrester].
New York, Parker & Weyman, 1758. iv,
44 pp.
AAS copy.   8124

The Polite Philosopher. . . . Ninth Edition
[by James Forrester].
Philadelphia, Bradford & Hall, 1781.
54 pp.
AAS copy.   17155

The Polite Philosopher [by James
Forrester].
Boston, Norman, 1787. xv, 38 pp.
(The advs. call for a frontispiece, but
there is none in this copy in the original
binding.)
AAS copy.   20363

[A Political Address, Lately Delivered in
Kentucky.]
("Just received, and for sale, October 1,
1798.")   34390

The Political Censor, or Monthly Review
[for March 1796] [by William Cobbett,
1762-1835].
Philadelphia, Davies, 1796. pp. [i]-vi, [2],
[7]-70, printed wraps.
AAS copy.   30219

The Political Censor, or Monthly Review
[for March 1796]. . . . Second Edition [by
William Cobbett, 1762-1835].
Philadelphia, Cobbett, 1796. 70 pp.
AAS copy.   30220

The Political Censor, or Monthly Review
[for April, 1796] [by William Cobbett,
1762-1835].
Philadelphia, Davies, 1796. pp. [69]-169, 1
plate.
AAS copy.   30221

The Political Censor, or Monthly Review
[for May, 1796] [by William Cobbett,
1762-1835].
Philadelphia, Davies, 1796. pp. [170]-239,
1 plate.
AAS copy.   30223

The Political Censor, or Monthly Review
[for May, 1796].
Second Edition [by William Cobbett,
1762-1835].
Philadelphia, Cobbett, 1796. pp.
[169]-240.
JCB copy.   30224

The Political Censor; or Review [for

September, 1796] [by William Cobbett,
1762-1835].
Philadelphia, Cobbett, 1796. 79, [1] pp.
AAS copy.   30225

A Political Creed for the Day.
[New York, 1768.] Broadside.
AAS copy.   11047

[A Political Creed for the Day.
[New York, 1769.] Broadside.]
(The unique copy could not be located.)
                                             11420

A Political Creed. I believe that the
Proceedings of the Senate. . . .
[Lexington? 1798.] Broadside.
LOC copy.   48583

Political Curiosities Including An
Account of the State of Political Affairs in
Europe.
Philadelphia, Lee, [1796]. [2], 23, [1];
10, 23, [1]; 19, [1]; 8; 8; 8; 15, [1]; 16;
16; 16; 12; 4; 8; 8; 8; 16; 4; 8.
(Lee made up these tract volumes of
anything, including odd signatures, which
he happened to have at hand.)
AAS copy.   31010

Political Debates.
Paris (Philadelphia?), 1766. [2], 18 pp.
HSP copy.   10466

The Political Duenna [by Israel Pottinger,
fl. 1759-1761].
Philadelphia, Bell, 1778. 56 pp.
AAS copy.   16017

The Political Establishments of the
United States.
Philadelphia, Bell, 1784. 28 pp.
AAS copy.   18735

The Political Green-House, for the Year
1798.
Hartford, Ct., Hudson & Goodwin,
[1799]. 24 pp.
AAS copy.   36133

The Political Grinder; A Poetic Satire.
Boston, [1800]. 12 pp.
NYHS copy.   38288

The Political Massacre. . . . By James
Quicksilver [by James Philip Puglia].
Philadelphia, Moreau de St. Mery, 1796.
29, [2] pp.
LCP copy.   31066

Political Miscellany. Containing: I
Observations. . . .
New York, Forman, 1793. 31 pp.
AAS copy.   26015

Political Observations [by James
Madison, pres. U. S., 1751-1836].
[Philadelphia, 1795.] 24 pp.
HSP copy.   29017

Political Opinions, Particularly
Respecting the Seat of Federal Empire.
n. p., 1789. 72 pp.
LOC copy.   22072

Political Papers, Addressed to the
Advocates for a Congressional Revenue
[by Abraham Yates, 1724-1796].
New York, Kollock, 1786. 20 pp.
NYPL copy.   20168

The Political Progress of Britain [by
James Thomson Callender, 1758-1803].
Philadelphia, Wrigley & Berriman, 1794.
80 pp.
AAS copy.   26725

The Political Progress of Britain [by
James Thomson Callender, 1758-1803].
Philadelphia, Callender, [1795]. pp. [1]-4,
[3]-71.
AAS copy.   28380

The Political Progress of Britain. . . . Part
First. Third Edition [by James Thomson
Callender, 1758-1803].
Philadelphia, Folwell, 1795. 120 pp.
AAS copy.   28379

The Political Progress of Britain. . . . Part
Second [by James Thomson Callender,
1758-1803].

Philadelphia, Folwell for Rivington, 1795.
96 pp.
AAS copy.   28381

The Political Reformer: or a Proposed
Plan of Reformations.
Philadelphia, Woodward, 1797. 73 pp.
BA copy.   31909

Political Schemes and Calculations [by
Alexander Contee Hanson, 1749-1806].
Annapolis, Greens, 1784. vi, 38 pp.
JCB copy.   18517

Political Truth: or Animadversions on the
Past and Present [by Edmund Randolph,
1753-1813].
Philadelphia, Smith, 1796. 44 pp.
AAS copy.   31072

The Political Wars of Otsego [by Jedidiah
Peck].
Cooperstown, Phinney, 1796. 122, [4] pp.
BA copy.   30968

The Politician Out-Witted [by Samuel
Low, b. 1765].
New York, Ross, 1789. 71 pp.
AAS copy.   21926

The Politicians: or, A State of Things [by
John Murdock, 1748-1834].
Philadelphia, 1798. 37 pp.
AAS copy.   34160

The Politicks and Views of a Certain
Party [by William Laughton Smith,
1758-1812].
n.p., 1792. 36 pp.
AAS copy.   24801

Pollen, Thomas, fl. 1721-1760.
The Duty of Defending our Countrymen
Recommended.
Newport, Franklin, 1758. 9 pp.
RIHS copy.   41001

Pollen, Thomas, fl. 1721-1760.
(Weis, Colonial Clergy N. E.)
The Principal Marks of True Patriotism.
Newport, 1758. 10 pp.
RIHS copy.   8239

Pollen, Thomas, fl. 1721-1760.
(Weis, Col, Clergy N. E.)
Sermon Preached in Trinity Church.
Newport, 1755. 13 pp.
AAS copy.   7542

Pollen, Thomas, fl. 1721-1760.
Universal Love.
Boston, Green & Russell for Leverett,
1758. 19 pp.
AAS copy.   8240

Pollock, Carlisle.
I Request the Favour. . . . 7th April, 1785.
[New York, 1785.] Broadside.
NYHS copy.   44776

[Polly Cherry.
Philadelphia, Young, Stewart &
M'Culloch, 1786.]
("Just Published," Pa. Gazette, June 7,
1786.)   19930

Polwhele, Richard, 1760-1838.
The Unsex'd Females.
New York, Cobbett, 1800. pp. [i]-vi,
[3]-68.
AAS copy.   38293

Pomeroy, Jonathan Law, 1768-1836.
The Folly of Denying a God.
Northampton, Mass., Butler, 1800. 45 pp.
AAS copy.   38294

Pomeroy, Jonathan Law, 1768-1836.
Religion a Security against Death.
Northampton, Mass., Butler, 1800. 28 pp.
AAS copy.   38295

Pomeroy, Josiah.
Doctor Pomeroy's Affidavit.
n.p., [1792]. Broadside.
Albany Institute copy.   46548

Pomeroy, Zadock, 1774-1804.
Sign of the Indian Queen. . . . June, 1799.
[Boston, 1799.] Broadside
AAS copy.   36135

Pomfret, John, 1667-1702.
(D. N. B.)
Poems. . . . Eleventh Edition.
Boston, Fowle, 1751. viii, 136 pp.
AAS copy.   6762

Pomfret, John, 1667-1702.
Poems upon Several Occasions. . . .
Twelfth Edition.
New York, Gaine, 1785. vi, 98, iv, 12,
10, [2] pp.
AAS copy.   19195

Pomfret, John, 1667-1702.
Poems upon Several Occasions.
Philadelphia, Hall, 1791. 158, [1] pp.
AAS copy.   23705

[Pomfret, John, 1667-1702.
Poems upon Several Occasions.
New York, Gaine, 1792?]
(Imprint assumed by Evans from Gaine
advs.)   24700

Pomfret, John, 1667-1702.
Poems upon Several Occasions.
Boston, Etheridge, 1794. 158, [1] pp.
AAS copy.   27532

[Pomfret, John, 1667-1702.
The Poetical Works of. . . .
Philadelphia, 1795.]
(Imprint assumed by Evans from advs.)
                                                   29334

[Pommereul, Francois Rene Jean, baron
de], 1745-1823.
Campaign of General Buonaparte in
Italy.
New York, 1798. 304 pp.
AAS copy.   34393

Pomp, John Nicholas, 1734-1819.
(Weis, Clergy of the Middle Colonies.)
Kurzgefasste Prüfungen.
Philadelphia, Miller, 1774. xvi, 200 pp.
AAS copy.   13550

Pool,
Mr. Pool, the First American that Ever
Exhibited . . . Horsemanship. . . .
August 23, 1786.
Providence, Carter, [1786]. Broadside.
RIHS copy.   44950

Poor, John, 1752-1829.
A Collection of Psalms and Hymns.
Philadelphia, M'Culloch, 1794. 48 pp.
AAS copy.   27533

The Poor Man's Advice to his Poor
Neighbours.
New-York, 1774. 19 pp.
AAS copy.   13551

The Poor Man's Wealth Described, in an
Epitome of a Contented Mind.
Printed and sold in New-London,
[c. 1770]. Broadside.
CHS copy.   49137

The Poor Orphans Legacy.
Philadelphia, Franklin, 1734. 39 + pp.
(No complete copy is known.)
LOC copy.   3828

The Poor Orphans Legacy.
Richmond, Dixon, 1792. 32 pp.
(Not located, 1968.)   46549

Poor Richard Improved: being an
Almanack . . . for . . . 1798.
Philadelphia, Hall & Sellers. [44] pp.
HSP copy.   48234

[Poor Richard Revived: being the
Farmers' Diary; or the Albany Almanac
. . . for . . . 1793.
Albany, Barber & Southwick. [32] pp.]
(A ghost of 26083 arising from an adv.)
                                                   26082

Poor Richard Revived: being the
Farmer's Diary; or, Barber &
Southwick's Albany Almanac, for . . .
1794.
Albany, Barber & Southwick. [32] pp.
(The only copy located is imperfect.)
AAS copy.   26083

Poor Richard Revived: being the
Farmer's Diary; or, Barber &

Southwick's Albany Almanac, for . . .
1795.
Albany, Barber & Southwick. [36] pp.
AAS copy.   27621

Poor Richard Revived: being the
Farmers Diary; or, Barber & Southwick's
Albany Almanack; for . . . 1796.
Albany, Barber & Southwick. [36] pp.
AAS copy.   29409

Poor Richard Revived: being the
Farmers Diary; or, Barber & Southwick's
Albany Almanack; for . . . 1797.
Albany, Barber & Southwick. 36 pp.
NYPL copy.   31099

Poor Richard Revived: or, Barber &
Southwick's Almanack: for . . . 1798.
Albany, Barber & Southwick. [42] pp.
HC copy.   32762

Poor Richard Revived: or, Barber &
Southwick's Almanack for . . . 1799.
Albany, N. Y., Barber & Southwick.
[40] pp.
AAS copy.   34462

[Poor Richard Revived: or, Barber &
Southwick's Almanack, for . . . 1799.
Albany, N. Y., Barber & Southwick.
[40] pp.]
(Also entered as 34462, q. v.)   36136

Poor Richard Revived: or, Barber &
Southwick's Almanack for . . . 1800.
Albany, N. Y., Barber & Southwick.
[36] pp.
Grosvenor Library copy.   36137

Poor Richard Revived: or, The Albany
Almanack: for . . . 1801.
Albany, N. Y., Barber. [36] pp.
AAS copy.   38296

Poor Richard, 1744, An Almanack . . .
by Richard Saunders [by Benjamin
Franklin, 1706-1790].
Philadelphia, Franklin. [24] pp.
AAS copy.   40304

Poor Richard's Almanack, for . . . 1784.
New York, Morton & Horner, [1783].
[32] pp.
NYHS copy.   44442

Poor Richard's Rhode-Island Almanack
for . . . 1789.
[Newport], Edes. [24] pp.
AAS copy.   21400

[Poor Robin Almanack . . . for . . .
1790.
Georgetown, Fierer.]
(See Goff, Georgetown.)   22808

Poor Robin's Almanack for 1742.
Philadelphia, Bradford.
(The only copy located is imperfect.)
LOC copy.   4789

[Poor Robin's Almanack for 1743.
Philadelphia, Bradford.]
(Was not adv. as usual this year.)   5040

[Poor Robin's Almanack, for the . . .
Year 1744.
Philadelphia, Bradford.] [30] pp.
(The only copy found is imperfect.)
LOC copy.   5276

[Poor Robin's Almanack for 1745.
Philadelphia, Bradford.] [24] pp.
(The only copy located is defective.)
LOC copy.   5479

[Poor Robin's Almanack for 1746.
Philadelphia.]
("Lately published," Pa. Gazette, Nov.
28, 1745.)   5677

[Poor Robin's Almanack for the Year,
1747.
Philadelphia, Bradford.]
(Adv. Pa. Journal, June 6, 1746/7.)   5854

[Poor Robin's Almanack for the Year,
1748.
Philadelphia, Bradford.]
(Adv. Pa. Journal, Dec. 8, 1747.)   6054

[Poor Robin's Almanack for the Year
1750.

Philadelphia, Bradford.]
(Hildeburn 1148.)   6407

[Poor Robin's Spare Hours . . . Almanack
for 1749.
Philadelphia, Bradford. [32] pp.]
(Adv. Pa. Journal, Nov. 24, 1748.)   6223

Poor Robin's Spare Hours . . . a Diary, or
Almanack, for . . . 1751.
Philadelphia, Bradford. [32] pp.
(No complete copy found.)
AAS copy.   6594

[Poor Robin's Almanack for the Year
1752.
Philadelphia, Bradford.] 22 pp.
(No perfect copy found.)
NYPL copy.   6763

[Poor Robin's Almanack for the Year
1753.
Philadelphia, Bradford.]
(Hildeburn 1274.)   6916

[Poor Robin's Spare Hours . . . for 1754.
Philadelphia, Bradford. [32] pp.]
(The only copy located is badly defective.)
AAS copy.   7099

Poor Robin's Spare Hours . . . Almanack,
. . for . . . 1755.
Philadelphia, Bradford. [32] pp.
LOC copy.   7299

[Poor Robin's Almanack for the Year
1756.
Philadelphia, Bradford.]
(No copy located.)   7543

[Poor Robin's Almanack for the Year
1757.
Philadelphia, Bradford.]
(Adv. Pa. Journal, Dec. 2, 1756.)   7766

Poor Robin's Spare Hours . . . for 1758.
Philadelphia, Bradford. [28] pp.
(The only copy located is imperfect.
Evans' title came from adv. in Pa.
Journal, Oct. 20, 1757.)
AAS copy.   8010

[Poor Robin's Almanack for . . . 1771.
Philadelphia, Evitt.]
(Adv. Pa. Gazette, Sept. 30, 1770.) 11825

[Poor Robin's Almanack for . . . 1772.
Philadelphia, Evitt.]
(Adv. Pa. Journal, Oct. 17, 1771.)   12201

[Poor Robin's Almanack for 1786.
Fredericktown, Bartgis.]
("Just published," Md. Chronicle, Jan. 18,
1786.)   44777

Poor Robin's Almanack for . . . 1787.
Fredericktown, Bartgis. [32] pp.
PrU copy.   44951

[Poor Robin's Almanack, for . . . 1788.
Fredericktown, Bartgis.]
("Just published," Maryland Chronicle,
Aug. 29, 1787.)   20656

[Poor Robin's House Almanac, for . . .
1790.
Philadelphia, M'Culloch.]
(Entry from an adv.)   22074

Poor Robin's Almanac, for . . . 1791.
Philadelphia, M'Culloch. [24] pp.
(The only copy located is imperfect.)
LCP copy.   45974

Poor Robin's Almanac, for . . . 1792.
Philadelphia, M'Culloch. [36] pp.
AAS copy.   23706

[Poor Robin's Almanack for . . . 1793.
Philadelphia.]
(Assumed by Evans from the sequence.)
                                     24701

Poor Robin's Almanac, for . . . 1795.
Philadelphia, M'Culloch. [36] pp.
AAS copy.   27534

Poor Robin's Almanac for . . . 1799 [by
Joshua Sharp].
Philadelphia, M'Culloch. [32] pp.
AAS copy.   34535

Poor Tom's Almanack for . . . 1789.

Philadelphia, Clark. [32] pp.
AAS copy.   45343

Poor Will's Almanack, for . . . 1774.
Philadelphia, Crukshank. [36] pp.
HSP copy.   12649

Poor Will's Almanack, for . . . 1775 [by
William Andrews, fl. 1750].
Philadelphia, Crukshank. [36] pp.
AAS copy.   13116

Poor Will's Almanack for . . . 1776 [by
William Andrews, fl. 1750].
Philadelphia, Crukshank. [32] pp.
AAS copy.   13813

Poor Will's Almanack, for . . . 1777 [by
William Andrews, fl. 1750].
Philadelphia, Crukshank. [36] pp.
HSP copy.   14648

Poor Will's Almanack, for . . . 1778 [by
William Andrews, fl. 1750].
Philadelphia, Crukshank. [36] pp.
AAS copy.   15237

Poor Will's Almanack, for . . . 1779 [by
William Andrews, fl. 1750].
Philadelphia, Crukshank. [36] pp.
AAS copy.   15722

Poor Will's Almanack, for . . . 1780 [by
William Andrews, fl. 1750].
Philadelphia, Crukshank. [36] pp.
AAS copy.   16190

Poor Will's Almanack, for . . . 1781 [by
William Andrews, fl. 1750].
Philadelphia, Crukshank. [36] pp.
AAS copy.   16699

Poor Will's Almanack, for . . . 1782 [by
William Andrews, fl. 1750].
Philadelphia, Crukshank. [36] pp.
AAS copy.   17081

Poor Will's Almanack, for . . . 1783 [by
William Andrews, fl. 1750].
Philadelphia, Crukshank. [36] pp.
AAS copy.   17459

Poor Will's Almanack, for . . . 1784 [by
William Andrews, fl. 1750].
Philadelphia, Crukshank. [36] pp.
AAS copy.   17818

Poor Will's Almanack, for . . . 1785 [by
William Andrews, fl. 1750].
Philadelphia, Crukshank. [44] pp.
AAS copy.   18331

Poor Will's Almanack, for . . . 1786 [by
William Andrews, fl. 1750].
Philadelphia, Crukshank. [36] pp.
AAS copy.   18913

Poor Will's Almanack, for . . . 1787 [by
William Waring, d. 1793].
Philadelphia, Crukshank. [44] pp.
AAS copy.   20120

Poor Will's Almanack for . . . 1795 [by
William Waring, pseud.].
Philadelphia, Crukshank. [44] pp.
HSP copy.   28023

Poor Will's Almanack, for . . . 1796.
Philadelphia, Crukshank. [44] pp.
AAS copy.   29335

Poor Will's Almanack, for . . . 1797.
Philadelphia, Crukshank. [36] pp.
AAS copy.   31021

Poor Will's Almanack, for . . . 1798.
Philadelphia, Crukshanks. [36] pp.
AAS copy.   32699

Poor Will's Almanack for . . . 1799.
Philadelphia, Crukshanks. [36] pp.
AAS copy.   34396

Poor Will's Almanack for . . . 1800.
Philadelphia, Crukshanks. [36] pp.
AAS copy.   36139

Poor Will's Almanack, for . . . 1801.
Philadelphia, Crukshanks. [36] pp.
AAS copy.   38297

Poor Will's Pocket Almanac, for . . . 1770
[by William Andrews, fl. 1750].

Philadelphia, Crukshank. [32] pp.
(Evans' description came from the
defective LOC copy.)
AAS copy.   11154

Poor Will's Pocket Almanack, for . .
1771 [by William Andrews, fl. 1750].
Philadelphia, Crukshank. [36] pp.
AAS copy.   11553

Poor Will's Pocket Almanack, for . . .
1773 [by William Andrews, fl. 1750].
Philadelphia, Crukshank. [36] pp.
LOC copy.   12312

Poor Will's Pocket Almanack, for . . .
1774 [by William Andrews, fl. 1750].
Philadelphia, Crukshank. [32] pp.
AAS copy.   12650

Poor Will's Pocket Almanack, for . . .
1775 [by William Andrews, fl. 1750].
Philadelphia, Crukshank. [48] pp.
LOC copy.   13117

Poor Will's Pocket Almanack, for . . .
1776 [by William Andrews, fl. 1750].
Philadelphia, Crukshank. [48] pp.
AAS copy.   13814

Poor Will's Pocket Almanack, for . . .
1777 [by William Andrews, fl. 1750].
Philadelphia, Crukshank, opposite the
butcher's shambles. [24] pp.   14650

Poor Will's Pocket Almanack, for . . .
1777 [by William Andrews, fl. 1750].
Philadelphia, Crukshank, opposite the
Presbyterian Meeting House. [24] pp.
AAS copy.   14649

Poor Will's Pocket Almanack, for . . .
1778 [by William Andrews, fl. 1750].
Philadelphia, Crukshank. [24] pp.
AAS copy.   15238

Poor Will's Pocket Almanack, for . . .
1779 [by William Andrews, fl. 1750].
Philadelphia, Crukshank. [24] pp.
AAS copy.   15723

Poor Will's Pocket Almanack, for . . .
1780 [by William Andrews, fl. 1750].
Philadelphia, Crukshank. [24] pp.
AAS copy.   16191

Poor Will's Pocket Almanack for . . . 1781
[by William Andrews, fl. 1750].
Philadelphia, Crukshank. [24] pp.
AAS copy.   16700

Poor Will's Pocket Almanack, for . . .
1782 [by William Andrews, fl. 1750].
Philadelphia, Crukshank. [24] pp.
AAS copy.   17082

Poor Will's Pocket Almanack, for . . .
1783 [by William Andrews, fl. 1750].
Philadelphia, Crukshank. [24] pp.
AAS copy.   17460

Poor Will's Pocket Almanack, for . . .
1784 [by William Andrews, fl. 1750].
Philadelphia, Crukshank. [24] pp.
AAS copy.   17819

Poor Will's Pocket Almanack, for . . .
1785 [by William Andrews, fl. 1750].
Philadelphia, Crukshank. [24] pp.
AAS copy.   18332

Poor Will's Pocket Almanack, for . . .
1786 [by William Andrews, fl. 1750].
Philadelphia, Crukshank. [32] pp.
AAS copy.   18914

Poor Will's Pocket Almanack, for . . .
1787 [by William Waring, d. 1793].
Philadelphia, Crukshank. [32] pp.
AAS copy.   20121

Poor Will's Pocket Almanack, for . . .
1788 [by William Waring, d. 1793].
Philadelphia, Crukshank. [32] pp.
AAS copy.   20854

Poor Will's Pocket Almanack, for . . .
1789 [by William Waring, d. 1793].
Philadelphia, Crukshank. [32] pp.
AAS copy.   21571

Poor Will's Pocket Almanack, for . . .

1790 [by William Waring, d. 1793].
Philadelphia, Crukshank. [40] pp.
AAS copy.   22240

Poor Will's Pocket Almanack, for . . .
1791 [by William Waring, d. 1793].
Philadelphia, Crukshank. [40] pp.
AAS copy.   23033

Poor Will's Pocket Almanack, for . . .
1792 [by William Waring, d. 1793].
Philadelphia, Crukshank. [44] pp.
AAS copy.   23957

Poor Will's Pocket Almanack, for . . .
1793 [by William Waring, d. 1793].
Philadelphia, Crukshank. [42] pp.
AAS copy.   24982

Poor Will's Pocket Almanack, for . . .
1795 [by William Waring, pseud.].
Philadelphia, Crukshank. [48] pp.
AAS copy.   28024

Poor Will's Pocket Almanack, for . . .
1796.
Philadelphia, Crukshank. [48] pp.
AAS copy.   29336

Poor Will's Pocket Almanack, for . . .
1797.
Philadelphia, Crukshank. [38] pp.
AAS copy.   31022

Poor Will's Pocket Almanack, for . . .
1798.
Philadelphia, Crukshanks. [48] pp.
AAS copy.   32700

Poor Will's Pocket Almanack, for . . .
1799.
Philadelphia, Crukshanks. [48] pp.
AAS copy.   34397

Poor Will's Pocket Almanack, for . . .
1800.
Philadelphia, Crukshanks. [48] pp.
AAS copy.   36140

Poor Will's Pocket Almanack, for . . .
1801.
Philadelphia, Crukshanks. [48] pp.
AAS copy.   38298

Pope, Alexander, 1688-1744.
An Essay on Man.
Philadelphia, Bradford, 1747. 51 pp.
NYPL copy.   6055

[Pope, Alexander, 1688-1744.
An Essay on Man.
Philadelphia, Bradford, 1748.]
(Adv. Pa. Journal, Aug. 4, 1748.)   6224

Pope, Alexander, 1688-1744.
An Essay on Man.
Philadelphia, Dunlap, for Noel, 1760. 68
pp., 1 plate.
(NYPL copy has the imprint as given by
Evans but lacks plate.)
UOP copy.   8718

Pope, Alexander, 1688-1744.
An Essay on Man.
Providence, McDougall, 1776. viii, 48 pp.
RIHS copy.   43143

Pope, Alexander, 1688-1744.
An Essay on Man.
Philadelphia, Crukshank, 1778. [8], 38,
[5] pp.
LCP copy.   16018

Pope, Alexander, 1688-1744.
An Essay on Man.
Newbury, Mycall for Coverly of Boston,
1780. 55 pp.
AAS copy.   16955

[Pope, Alexander, 1688-1744.
An Essay on Man.
Providence, 1780.]
(Adv. Am. Journal, June 7, 1780.)   16956

Pope, Alexander, 1688-1744.
An Essay on Man.
Bennington, 1785. 43 pp.
VtU copy.   19197

Pope, Alexander, 1688-1744.
An Essay on Man.
New York, Gaine, 1786. 46, [2] pp.
AAS copy.   19931

Pope, Alexander, 1688-1744.
An Essay on Man.
Boston, Fleets, 1787. [6], 48, [2] pp.
AAS copy.   45141

Pope, Alexander, 1688-1744.
An Essay on Man.
Hartford, Patten, 1787. 52 pp.   20657

[Pope, Alexander, 1688-1744.
An Essay on Man.
Philadelphia, Dobson, 1787. 48 pp.]
(No such ed. located.)   45142

Pope, Alexander, 1688-1744.
An Essay on Man.
Philadelphia, Spotswood, 1788. [2], 42 pp.
AAS copy.   45344

[Pope, Alexander, 1688-1744.
Essay on Man.
Philadelphia, Spotswood, 1789.]
(From an adv. of books for sale.)   22075

Pope, Alexander, 1688-1744.
An Essay on Man.
Concord, [N.H.], Hough, 1790. 52 pp.
AAS copy.   45975

Pope, Alexander, 1688-1744.
An Essay on Man.
Lansingburgh, Babcock & Hickok, 1790.
viii, 44 pp.
AAS copy.   22809

Pope, Alexander, 1688-1744.
An Essay on Man.
Worcester, Thomas, 1790. 48 pp.
AAS copy.   22810

[Pope, Alexander, 1688-1744.
An Essay on Man.
New London, Greens, 1791.]
(Entry from an adv.)   23707

Pope, Alexander, 1688-1744.
An Essay on Man.
Boston, Folsom, 1792. 65, [4] pp.
AAS copy.   24703

Pope, Alexander, 1688-1744.
An Essay on Man.
Philadelphia, Dobson, 1792. 48 pp.
NYPL copy.   24702

[Pope, Alexander, 1688-1744.
An Essay on Man.
Concord, N. H., Hough, 1793.]
(Imprint assumed by Evans from Hough's
advs.)   26018

[Pope, Alexander, 1688-1744.
An Essay on Man.
Hartford, Babcock, 1793.]
(Imprint assumed by Evans from adv.
"Just published, and for sale at this
Office," Am. Mercury, Dec. 23, 1793.)
    26017

Pope, Alexander, 1688-1744.
An Essay on Man.
Boston, Hall, 1794. 59, [1] pp.
JCB copy.   27535

Pope, Alexander, 1688-1744.
An Essay on Man.
Exeter, [N. H.], Odiorne, 1794. 63 pp.
AAS copy.   47184

Pope, Alexander, 1688-1744.
An Essay on Man.
Greenfield, Dickman, 1795. 47 pp.
(The only copy located is imperfect.)
Pocumtuck Valley Memorial Association
Library copy.   29338

[Pope, Alexander, 1688-1744.
An Essay on Man.
Keene, N. H., Blake, 1795.]
(Imprint assumed by Evans from Blake's
adv.)   29339

Pope, Alexander, 1688-1744.
An Essay on Man.
Wrentham, Mass., Heaton, 1795. 48 pp.
JCB copy.   29337

[Pope, Alexander, 1688-1744.
An Essay on Man.
Litchfield, Ct., Collier & Buck, 1796.]
("Is ready for sale at this office,"
Litchfield Monitor, Apr. 13, 1796.)   31023

Pope, Alexander, 1688-1744.
An Essay on Man.
New York, Tiebout for Duyckinck and
Mesier, 1796. 104, [1] pp.
AAS copy.   31024

Pope, Alexander, 1688-1744.
An Essay on Man.
Providence, R. I., Carter & Wilkinson,
1796. 72 pp.
AAS copy.   31025

Pope, Alexander, 1688-1744.
An Essay on Man.
Worcester, Thomas, 1796. 44 pp.
AAS copy.   31026

Pope, Alexander, 1688-1744.
An Essay on Man.
Fairhaven, Vt., Spooner, 1797. 47 pp.
VtHS copy.   32701

Pope, Alexander, 1688-1744.
An Essay on Man.
Worcester, Thomas, Son & Thomas, 1797.
59 pp.
AAS copy.   32702

Pope, Alexander, 1688-1744.
An Essay on Man.
Peacham, Vt., Farley & Goss, 1798. 44 pp.
HC copy.   34398

Pope, Alexander, 1688-1744.
An Essay on Man.
Boston, Hall, 1800. 60 pp.
AAS copy.   38299

Pope, Alexander, 1688-1744.
An Essay on Man.
Salem, [Mass.], J. Cushing for T. C.
Cushing, 1800. vii, [1], 43+ pp.
(The unique copy lacks the appended
matter called for on the tp.)
EI copy.   38300

Pope, Alexander, 1688-1744.
A Select Collection of Poems.
New London, Ct., Springer, 1796. 132 pp.
AAS copy.   31027

Pope, Amos, 1771-1837.
An Astronomical Diary or Almanack, for
. . . 1792.
Boston, Folsom. [24] pp.
AAS copy.   23708

Pope, Amos, 1771-1837.
An Astronomical Diary: or Almanack, for
. . . 1793.
Boston, Folsom. [24] pp.
AAS copy.   24704

Pope, Amos, 1771-1837.
An Astronomical Diary: or Almanack, for
. . . 1794.
Boston, Folsom. [40] pp.
AAS copy.   26019

Pope, Amos, 1771-1837.
Pope's Almanack, for . . . 1794.
Boston, Folsom. [40] pp.
AAS copy.   26020

Pope, Amos, 1771-1837.
Pope's Almanack, for . . . 1795.
Boston, Folsom. [40] pp.
AAS copy.   27536

[Pope, Amos, 1771-1837.
Pope's Almanack for . . . 1796.
Boston, Folsom.]
(Entry from Nichols, Mass. Almanacs,
which is apparently in error.)   29340

Pope, Amos, 1771-1837.
Pope's Massachusetts, Rhode-Island,
Connecticut, New-Hampshire and
Vermont Almanac, for . . . 1797.
Boston, Folsom. [24] pp.
LOC copy.   31028

Pope, John, fl. 1793.
Cancers. The Following is a small
Specimen. . . . Feb. 6. 1793.
[Boston, 1793.] Broadside.
AAS copy.   26021

Pope, John, fl. 1793.
Certificates of Cures in Cancerous Cases.
Providence, R. I., Wheeler, 1800. 38 pp.
BrU copy.   38342

Pope, John, 1770-1845.
[To the Citizens of the Electoral District
Composed of the Counties of Nelson and
Jefferson. . . . October 31st, 1800.
Broadside.]
(McMurtrie, Kentucky, 134.)   38301

Pope, John, 1770-1845.
A Tour through the Southern and Western
Territories.
Richmond, Dixon, 1792. 104 pp.
(The H. V. Jones copy had a leaf of
errata.)
JCB copy.   24705

Pope, Joseph, 1745-1826.
The Loss of Christian Friends.
Worcester, Mass., Worcester, 1797. 23 pp.
AAS copy.   32703

Pope, Nathaniel, d. 1809.
A Speech, Delivered . . . the 17th Day of
October, 1798.
Richmond, [Va.], Jones, 1800. 37 pp.
HEH copy.   38302

Popish Cruelty Displayed.
Boston, Fleet, [1753]. 24 pp.
AAS copy.   7100

Popish Cruelty Displayed: being a Full
and True Account of the Massacre . . . in
Ireland.
Portsmouth, Fowle, 1757. 24 pp.
(No copy located.)   40929

Popish Hierarchy Suppressed.
Springfield, Mass., Stebbins, 1798. 55 pp.
AAS copy.   33462

The Porcupine, alias the Hedge-Hog.
Boston, Edes, 1784. [2], ii, 43, [1], vi, [2]
pp., 3 plates.
AAS copy.   18774

The Porcupine, alias the Hedge-hog.
Canaan, Phinney, 1795. 48 pp.
(Present location unknown.)   47562

Porcupine's Political Censor, for
November, 1796 [by William Cobbett,
1762-1835].
Philadelphia, Cobbett, 1796. 78 pp.
AAS copy.   30226

Porcupine's Political Censor, for
December, 1796 [by William Cobbett,
1762-1835].
Philadelphia, Cobbett, [1796]. 47, [1], 18,
[5] pp.
AAS copy.   30227

Porcupine's Political Censor, for
December, 1796. . . . Second Edition [by
William Cobbett, 1762-1835].
Philadelphia, Cobbett, [1796]. 64 pp., 1
plate.
LCP copy.   30228

Porcupine's Political Censor, for Jan.
1797 [by William Cobbett, 1762-1835].
Philadelphia, Cobbett, [1797]. 51 pp.
AAS copy.   31946

Porcupine's Political Censor, for March,
1797 [by William Cobbett, 1762-1835].
Philadelphia, Cobbett, [1797]. pp. [2],
53-123.
AAS copy.   31947

Porcupine's Works. Vol. II [by William
Cobbett, 1762-1835].
Philadelphia, Cobbett, 1796. pp. [6],
[37]-104; [2], [105]-169; [2], [173]-240;
23; 56; 79; [1]; 18; 64, 1 plate.
(Copies differ as to the pamphlets bound
up at the end.)
NYPL copy.   30233

Port of Charles-Town in South-Carolina,
November 1, 1736.
An Account of Sundry Goods Imported
[1724-1735].
PRO copy.   4079

Port-Road Lottery.
From the United States Chronicle. . . .
March 9th, 1791.
[Providence], Wheeler, [1791].
Broadside.
JCB copy.   46261

Port Royal, Messieurs de.

The Royal Convert.
Boston, D. & J. Kneeland, 1761. 95 pp.
AAS copy.   41238

Port Royal, Messieurs de.
The Royal Convert.
Boston, Hall, 1794. 68, [1] pp.
AAS copy.   27537

Port Royal, Messieurs de.
The Royal Convert. . . . First Exeter
Edition.
Exeter, N. H., Ranlet, 1796. 96 pp.
AAS copy.   31029

Porter, Augustus, 1769-1864.
A Map of Messrs. Gorham & Phelps's
Purchase, now the County of Ontario in
the State of New York.
[New Haven? 1795?]. Map.
(The unique original at the Ontario
County Hist. Soc. is too dark to
reproduce.)   29341

Porter, David, 1761-1851.
Two Discourses.
Hudson, N. Y., Stoddard, 1800. 33 pp.
BA copy.   38304

Porter, Eliphalet, 1758-1833.
A Discourse, Delivered at Brookline.
Boston, Russell, 1798. 36 pp.
AAS copy.   34401

Porter, Eliphalet, 1758-1833.
A Discourse, Delivered before the
Roxbury Charitable Society.
Boston, Hall, 1795. 22 pp.
AAS copy.   29342

Porter, Eliphalet, 1758-1833.
An Eulogy on George Washington.
Boston, Manning & Loring, [1800]. 22,
[2], 22 pp.
AAS copy.   38305

Porter, Eliphalet, 1758-1833.
A Sermon. Delivered to the First
Religious Society in Roxbury, December
11, 1783.
Boston, Adams & Nourse, 1784. 24 pp.
AAS copy.   18736

Porter, Eliphalet, 1758-1833.
A Sermon, Delivered to the First
Religious Society in Roxbury, June 16,
1799.
Boston, Young & Minns, 1799. 27 pp.
AAS copy.   36142

Porter, Huntington, 1755-1844.
A Discourse on Resignation to the Divine
Will.
Portsmouth, Melcher, 1792. pp. [3]-21.
AAS copy.   46550

Porter, Huntington, 1755-1844.
A Discourse on Sympathy.
Portsmouth, Peirce, 1794. 19 pp.
(A part of 26708, q. v.)   27538

Porter, Huntington, 1755-1844.
A Funeral Discourse Delivered at Rye.
Portsmouth, N. H., Peirce, 1800. 18 pp.
AAS copy.   38306

Porter, John, 1716-1802.
(Sibley, X.)
The Absurdity and Blasphemy.
Boston, 1750. [4], 30, [1] pp.
AAS copy.   6595

Porter, John, 1716-1802.
(Sibley, X)
The Evangelical Plan.
Boston, M'Alpine, 1769. 52 pp.
NYPL copy.   11421

Porter, John, 1716-1802.
(Sibley, X)
Superlative Love.
Boston, Rogers & Fowle, 1748. 36, [2] pp.
AAS copy.   6225

Porter, John, 1716-1802.
Superlative Love to Christ.
Newburyport, Mycall, 1789. 32 pp.
AAS copy.   45564

Porter, John, 1716-1802.
(Sibley, X.)
A Vindication of a Sermon.

Boston, Kneeland, 1751. [4], 64 pp.
AAS copy.   6764

Porter, Nathaniel, 1745-1837.
A Discourse on the Death of . . .
Washington.
Portsmouth, N. H., Melcher, 1800. 23 pp.
AAS copy.   38307

[Porter, Nathaniel, 1745-1837.
The Friendly Monitor.
Concord, N. H., Davis, 1798.]
("For sale at this Office," The Mirror,
Oct. 22, 1798.)   34402

Porter, Robert, 1768-1848.
An Oration . . . July 4th, 1791.
Philadelphia, Dobson, 1791. 23 pp.
WLC copy.   23709

Porter, Samuel, 1709-1758.
(Sibley, VIII, 769-772.)
A Sermon Preach'd at Douglass.
Boston, Rogers & Fowle, 1748. 23 pp.
AAS copy.   6226

Porter, Samuel, 1709-1758.
(Sibley, VIII, 769-772.)
A Sermon Preached at the Ordination of
. . . Joseph Perry.
Boston, Draper, 1755. 30 pp.
AAS copy.   7544

Porter, Samuel, 1760-1825.
An Address to the Rev. John Jamison.
Hagerstown, Herbert, 1794. 24 pp.
(The only copy located is imperfect.)
HSP copy.   47185

Porter, Samuel, 1760-1825.
A Discourse on the Decrees of God.
Pittsburgh, [1793]. 67, [1] pp.
HEH copy.   26023

Porter, Mrs. Sarah.
The Royal Penitent.
Concord, Hough, 1791. 19 pp.
MHS copy.   23710

Porter, Mrs. Sarah.
The Royal Penitent.
Newburyport, Osborne, [1793]. 21, [1]
pp.
AAS copy.   26024

Porteus, Beilby, 1731-1808.
Death. . . . Fourth Edition.
Philadelphia, Bell for Woodhouse, 1773.
20 pp.
AAS copy.   12958

Porteus, Beilby, 1731-1808.
Death. . . . Sixth Edition.
Boston, Mills & Hicks for Cox & Berry,
1773. 15, [1] pp.
BA copy.   12959

Porteus, Beilby, 1731-1808.
Death; a Poetical Essay.
Boston, M'Dougall, 1780. 15 pp.
HC copy.   16957

Porteus, Beilby, 1731-1808.
A Review of the Life of . . . Archbishop
Secker.
New York, Gaine, 1773. [4], iii, [1],
lxviii pp.
AAS copy.   12960

Porteus, Beilby, 1731-1808.
A Summary of the Principal Evidences.
. . . Third Edition.
Charlestown, Mass., Etheridge for
Larkins, 1800. 159 pp.
AAS copy.   38308

Portland, Me., Convention, 1786.
Proceedings of the Convention, held at
Portland, September 6, 1786.
[Portland? 1786.] Broadside.
MHS copy.   44952

[Portland, Me. Convention, 1794.
Address to the People of Maine on
Separation from Massachusetts, of the
Convention . . . at Portland on the Third
Wednesday of June, 1794.
[Portland, 1794.] 7 pp.]
(The Evans entry is a garbling of
Williamson 140, Williamson 6080, and an
1819 tract in the Bowdoin College
Library. For the text see the Debates,

Resolutions . . . of the Convention of . . .
1819, Portland 1820, pp. 296-297.)   27539

Portland, Me. Convention, 1795.
Address of a Convention of Delegates.
Portland, Wait, [1795]. 31 pp.
AAS copy.   29343

A Portrait. Behold! The Barrator.
[New York, 1768.] [2] pp.
LCP copy.   11048

Port-Royal Company.
Advertisement. Whereas at the Instance
and Request of Divers Gentlemen and
Merchants, the Governour and Council
. . . have . . . Accepted the Propositions of
the . . . Gentlemen . . . to settle . . . an
Officer and Garrison at Port-Royal. . . .
June 5th, 1691.
[Boston? 1691.] Broadside.
MA copy.   39282

Portsmouth, N. H.
Portsmouth Resolves Respecting Tea. . . .
Decemb. 16th, 1773.
[Portsmouth, 1773.] Broadside.
BPL copy.   12961

Portsmouth, N. H. Committee of
Correspondence, 1774.
Gentlemen, we Presume you are not
Unacquainted. . . .
[Portsmouth, 1774.] Broadside.
(No copy located.)   42674

Portsmouth, N.H. Friendly Fire Society,
1795.
Friendly Fire Society, Established at
Portsmouth. . . . November, 1795.
[Portsmouth], Melcher, [1795].
Broadside.
AAS copy.   47553

Portsmouth, N. H. Ordinances, etc.
By-laws . . . Passed . . . March 25th, 1795.
Portsmouth, Melcher, 1795. 13 pp.
NYHS copy.   29344

Portsmouth, N.H. Selectmen.
. . . At a Meeting. . . . May 1st, 1800.
n. p., n. d. Broadside.
AAS copy.   38309

Portsmouth, N.H. Town Meeting, Oct. 1,
1779.
Regulation of Sundry Articles.
[Portsmouth, 1779.] Broadside.
MA copy.   43681

Portsmouth, January 1st, 1768. To the
Customers of the New-Hampshire
Gazette.
[Portsmouth, N. H., Fowles, 1768.
Broadside.
NYHS copy.   41821

Post, Jotham, 1771-1817.
An Inaugural Dissertation.
New York, Swords, 1793. 29 pp.
AAS copy.   26028

Postscript. Being a Short Answer [by
William Douglas, 1691-1752].
[Boston, Franklin, 1722.] 8 pp.
HC copy.   2333

Post-Script, in 1732.
[Boston, 1734.] 8 pp.
HC copy.   3840

The Postscript. Sir. . . . Deadham, 1720
[by John Valentine, d. 1724].
[Boston, 1720.] 3 pp.
LOC copy.   39732

[Postscript, to a Discourse [by William
Douglass], 1691-1752.
Boston, Kneeland & Green, 1740.]
(pp. 49-62 of 4530, q.v.)   4531

Postscript to Abuses [by William
Douglass, 1691-1752].
[Boston, Franklin, 1722.] 8 pp.
HC copy.   2333

Postscript to the Boston News-Letter,
August 25 1768.
[Boston, 1768.] Broadside.
AAS copy.   41866

Postscript to the Connecticut Journal.

[New Haven, 1776.] Broadside.
NYPL copy.   14717

Postscript to the Pennsylvania Gazette. . . .
December 24, 1773.
[Philadelphia, 1773.] Broadside.
BPL copy.   42484

Postscript to the Pennsylvania Gazette of
May 2, 1778. York-Town, May 4. On
Saturday last Simeon Deane. . . .
[York], Hall & Sellers, [1778].
Broadside.
BPL copy.   43584

[Pote, Jeremy.
A Narrative Containing Strictures on the
Life of. . . .
Portland, 1798.]
("Just Published. . . . Printed and for sale
at the Office of the Eastern Herald,"
ibid., Sept. 10, 1798.)   34405

The Potent Enemies of America [by
Anthony Benezet, 1713-1784].
Philadelphia, Crukshank, [1774]. [2], 48,
83, 16, 16 pp.
LOC copy.   13146

The Potent Enemies of America Laid
Open.
Philadelphia, Crukshank, [1774]. [2], 48,
83 pp.
HEH copy.   42675

Potomack Company.
Great Falls, July 2, 1799. Entrusted as we
are. . . .
[Georgetown, 1799.] Broadside.
LOC copy.   36144

The Potomak Almanac . . . for . . . 1793.
Georgetown, Doyle. [40] pp.
LOC copy.   24706

Potter, Elam, 1742-1794.
The Author's Account of his Conversion.
Boston, Kneeland, 1772. 16 pp.
YC copy.   12531

Potter, Elam, 1742-1794.
The River of God.
New London, Greens, 1793. 15 pp.
AAS copy.   26030

Potter, Elam, 1742-1794.
A Second Warning to America.
Hartford, [1777]. 13 pp.
YC copy.   15555

Potter, Elam, 1742-1794.
(Weis, Colonial Clergy N. E.)
Two Sermons on the Amiableness of Jesus
Christ.
Boston, Draper, 1771. viii, 26 pp.
AAS copy.   12202

Potter, Elam, 1742-1794.
Two Sermons to Young People.
Boston, Draper, 1771. [2], vi, 20 pp.
AAS copy.   12203

Potter, Elam, 1742-1794.
A Warning to America.
Hartford, Watson, 1777. 8 pp.
YC copy.   43342

Potter, Isaiah, 1746-1817.
The Young Men are Dead!
Hanover, N.H., True, 1798. 16 pp.
AAS copy.   34407

[Potter, James], fl. 1769.
A Poem, on the Death of Deacon William
Barns.
Hartford, 1769. 15 pp.
WL copy.   11422

Potter, James, fl. 1781.
An Oration, on the Rise and Progress of
Physic in America.
Hartford, Hudson & Goodwin, 1781. 16
pp.
BA copy.   17315

Potter, John, 1734?-1804?
The Words of the Wise.
Philadelphia, Crukshank, 1790. 75 pp.
AAS copy.   45976

Potter, Lyman, 1748-1827.
A Sermon, Preached before the General
Assembly . . . October 11, 1787.

Windsor, 1788. 23 pp.
VtU copy.   21401

Potter, Nathaniel, -1768.
(Weis, Colonial Clergy N. E.)
A Discourse on Jeremiah.
Boston, Edes & Gill, 1758. 27 pp.
AAS copy.   8243

Potter, Nathaniel, 1770-1843.
An Essay on the Medicinal Properties . . .
of Arsenic.
Philadelphia, Woodward, 1796. [6], 64 pp.
NLM copy.   31031

[Pottinger, Israel], fl. 1759-1761.
The Political Duenna.
Philadelphia, Bell, 1778. 56 pp.
AAS copy.   16017

Potts, John, fl. 1762.
Confusion is Fallen.
Philadelphia, 1762. 96, [4] pp.
AAS copy.   9245

[Potts, John, fl. 1799.
A Plain and Concise Table . . . of the
Duties.
Petersburg, Va., 1799.]
(Entry from copyright registration.) 36146

Potts, Jonathan, 1745-1781.
Dissertatio Medica Inauguralis.
Philadelphia, Dunlap, 1771. vii, [1], 37
pp.
NYPL copy.   12204

Poughkeepsie, N. Y.
State of New-York. Instructions Proposed
for the Consideration of the Inhabitants of
Poughkeepsie Precinct. . . . July 24th,
1779.
[Poughkeepsie, 1779.] Broadside.
NYHS copy.   43682

Poulson's Town and Country Almanac, for
. . . 1793. [by William Waring, d. 1793].
Philadelphia, Poulson. [40] pp.
LOC copy.   24983

Poulson's Town and Country Almanac,
for . . . 1793. . . . Second Edition [by
William Waring, d. 1793].
Philadelphia, Poulson. [40] pp.
AAS copy.   46666

Poulson's Town and Country Almanac,
for . . . 1795 [by Abraham Shoemaker].
Philadelphia, Poulson. [44] pp.
AAS copy.   27699

Poulson's Town and Country Almanac, for
. . . 1796 [by Abraham Shoemaker].
Philadelphia, Poulson. [48] pp.
AAS copy.   29506

Poulson's Town and Country Almanac,
for . . . 1797 [by Abraham Shoemaker].
Philadelphia, Poulson. [48] pp.
AAS copy.   31189

Poulson's Town and Country Almanac,
for . . . 1798 [by Abraham Shoemaker].
Philadelphia, Poulson. [48] pp.
AAS copy.   32834

Poulson's Town and Country Almanac,
for . . . 1799 [by Abraham Shoemaker].
Philadelphia, Poulson. [48] pp.
AAS copy.   34544

Poulson's Town and Country Almanac,
for . . . 1800.
Philadelphia, Poulson. [48] pp.
AAS copy.   36148

Poulson's Town and Country Almanac,
for . . . 1801.
Philadelphia, Poulson. [48] pp.
AAS copy.   38315

The Pourtraiture of a Good Man [by
Cotton Mather, 1663-1728].
Boston, 1702. 34, [1] pp.
AAS copy.   1073

[Powell, Thomas.
The Writing Master's Assistant.
Philadelphia ? 1764.]
(Adv. Pa. Gazette, July 10, 1764.)   9801

Power, Alexander, fl. 1790.
Copy of a Petition. . . . June 10, 1790.

[Philadelphia, 1790.] 12 pp.
LOC copy.   22813

Power, Nicholas.
Books and Stationery.
[Poughkeepsie, 1795.] Broadside.
(Not located, 1968.)   47563

The Power and Grandeur of Great-
Britain.
New York, Parker, 1768. 24 pp.
AAS copy.   11049

The Power and Grandeur of Great-
Britain.
Philadelphia, Goddard, 1768. 22 pp.
AAS copy.   11050

Power of Delusion! The Following
Account . . . from the Columbian
Magazine, for 1788. . . .
n. p., [1788?] Broadside.
(No copy available for reproduction.)
                                                             43545

The Power of Grace Illustrated [by - Van
Lier].
Philadelphia, Neale & Kammerer for
Condie, 1796. 142 pp.
(An imprint variant of 30194, q. v. for
text.)
AAS copy.   48001

The Power of Grace Illustrated [by -
Van Lier].
Philadelphia, Neale & Kammerer for
Denoon, 1796. 142 pp.
AAS copy.   30194

The Power of Grace Illustrated [by -
Van Lier].
Philadelphia, Neale & Kammerer, 1796.
'42 pp.
(An imprint variant of 30194, q. v. for
text.)
AAS copy.   48000

The Power of Grace Illustrated [by -
Van Lier].
Philadelphia, for Denoon, 1796. 142 pp.
(An imprint variant of 30194, q. v. for
text.)   47999

The Power of Religion on the Mind [by
Lindley Murray, 1745-1826].
Philadelphia, Crukshank, 1790. 144 pp.
AAS copy.   22686

The Power of Religion on the Mind [by
Lindley Murray, 1745-1826].
Philadelphia, Crukshank, 1793. 144 pp.
AAS copy.   25853

The Power of Religion on the Mind [by
Lindley Murray, 1745-1826].
New Brunswick, N. J., Blauvelt, 1795.
112 pp.
(Because of the condition of the only
copy located, it could not be reproduced.)
NYPL copy.   29132

The Power of Religion on the Mind. . . .
Seventh Edition [by Lindley Murray,
1745-1826].
New Bedford, Shearman, 1799. viii,
232 pp.
AAS copy.   35853

The Power of Sympathy [by William
Hill Brown, 1766-1793].
Boston, Thomas, 1789. Front., 138;
158 pp.
AAS copy.   21979

Powers, Peter, 1728-1800.
(Weis, Colonial Clergy N. E.)
The Espousing of Souls to Christ.
Portsmouth, 1765. 27 pp.
NHHS copy.   10146

Powers, Peter, 1728-1800.
(Weis, Colonial Clergy N. E.)
Heaven Ready for the Saints.
Boston, Kneeland, 1773. 31 pp.
AAS copy.   12962

Powers, Peter, 1728-1800.
A Humble Enquiry.
Newburyport, Blunt & March, 1796.
44 pp.
AAS copy.   31033

Powers, Peter, 1728-1800.

Jesus Christ the true King.
Newburyport, 1778. 40 pp.
VtSL copy.   16019

Powers, Peter, 1728-1800.
Tyranny and Toryism Exposed.
Westminster, Vt., 1781. 16 pp.
(In the NHHS copy the first word is
spelled "Tyrany.")
AAS copy.   17316

Powers, Thomas, 1776-1796.
The Dying Speech of. . . .
Haverhill, N. H., [1796]. Broadside.
NHHS copy.   31034

[Powers, Thomas, 1776-1796.
The Last Words . . . of . . . Executed . . .
the 28th July.
Windsor, Vt., Spooner, 1796.]
(Imprint assumed by Evans from
Spooner's advs.)   31035

[Powers, Thomas, 1776-1796.
The Narrative and Confession of. . . .
Hanover, N. H., Dunham & True, 1796.]
(Title and imprint assumed by Evans
from advs.)   31036

Powers, Thomas, 1776-1796.
The Narrative and Confession of. . . .
Norwich, Ct., 1796. 12 pp.
LOC copy.   31037

[Pownall, Mary Ann], 1751-1796.
Jemmy of the Glen.
Baltimore, Carr, 1798. [2] pp.
LOC copy.   34409

Pownall, Mary Ann, 1751-1796.
Mrs. Pownall's Address.
Philadelphia, Story, [1793]. [6], 28,
[2] pp.
NYPL copy.   26032

Pownall, Mary Ann, 1751-1796.
Six Songs for the Harpsichord.
New York, Pownall and Hewitt, [1794].
[1], 19 pp.
(Evans' title came from the advs. See
Sonneck-Upton, p. 48.)
NYPL (Shapiro) copy.   27542

[Pownall, Thomas], 1722-1805.
Considerations towards a General Plan
of Measures for the English Provinces.
New York, Parker & Weyman, 1756.
15 pp.
LCP copy.   7641

[Pownall, Thomas], 1722-1805.
March 5th, 1770. Mr. S-----r. I did. . . .
[Boston? 1770?] 10 pp.
MHS copy.   42157

[Pownall, Thomas], 1722-1805.
Proposals for Securing the Friendship of
the Five Nations.
New York, Parker & Weyman, 1756.
14 pp., table.
LCP copy.   7767

Pownall, Thomas, 1722-1805.
The Speech of Th-m-s P-wn-ll.
[Boston, 1769.] 16 pp.
AAS copy.   11423

[Pownall, Thomas, 1722-1805.
The Speech of Th-m-s P-wn-ll. . . . Second
Edition.
Boston, 1769. 16 pp.]
(Assumed by Evans from Sabin's
reference to a 4th ed.)   11424

[Pownall, Thomas, 1722-1805.
The Speech of Th-m-s P-wn-ll. . . . Third
Edition.
Boston, 1769. 16 pp.]
(Assumed by Evans from Sabin's
reference to a 4th ed.)   11425

[Pownall, Thomas, 1722-1805.
The Speech of Th-m-s P-wn-ll. . . . Fourth
Edition.
Boston, 1769. 16 pp.]
(Entry from Sabin's reference to an
unlocated. 4th ed., n.d., n.p.)   11426

[Poydras, Julien de Lallande], 1746-1824.
Epitre a Don Bernard de Galvez.
New Orleans, Boudousquié, 1777. [4] pp.
NYPL copy.   43344

[Poydras, Julien de Lallande], 1746-1824.
Le Dieu et les Nayades.
New Orleans, Boudousquié, 1777.
[4] pp.
NYPL copy.   43343

Poyntell, William, 1756-1811.
Just Published . . . Zion Besieg'd &
Attack'd 1787.
[Philadelphia, 1787.] Broadside.
LCP copy.   45143

Practical Exercises in Grammar,
Punctuation and Rhetoric.
Exeter, Ranlet, 1799. 24 pp.
AAS copy.   36149

[A Practical Question Piously Resolved.
Boston, 1682. 9 pp.]
(No copy known. Title from the addenda
to the S. F. Haven list.)   329

Practice of Piety. . . . [53 ed.] [by Lewis
Bayly, bp. of Bangor, d. 1631].
Boston, 1716. [8], 419, [1] pp.]
(A ghost of 1944, q.v.)   1797

The Practice of Piety. [53rd ed.] [by
Lewis Bayly, d. 1631].
Boston, Green for Eliot and Henchman,
1718. [12], 419, [1] pp.
AAS copy.   1944

Praise out of the Mouths of Babes.
Boston, 1709. 24 pp.
AAS copy.   1428

Praise out of the Mouth of Babes.
Boston, Foster, 1741. 23, [1] pp., irreg.
(The AAS has a copy with the imprint of
Rogers and Fowle.)
BM copy.   4790

[Pratt, Charles, Earl Camden, 1714-1794.
Lord Camden's Opinion of Connecticut's
Claim to the Wyoming Valley, May 1,
1769.
n.p., n.d., [1769]. Broadside.]
(No copy in broadside form has been
found.)   11427

Pratt, Peter, - 1730.
(The Rogerenes, pp. 209, 216, 321-322.)
The Prey Taken from the Strong.
New London, 1725. [4], viii, 69, [1] pp.
AAS copy.   2696

[Pratt, Samuel Jackson], 1749-1814.
Emma Corbett. . . . By Courtney
Melmoth.
Philadelphia, Bell, 1782. 48, 48, 48 pp.
LOC copy.   17678

[Pratt, Samuel Jackson], 1749-1814.
Emma Corbett. . . . The First [- Third]
Volume.
Philadelphia, Bell, 1783. 48; 48, 48 pp.
AAS copy.   44443

[Pratt, Samuel Jackson], 1749-1814.
Emma Corbett. . . . Sixth Edition.
Newburyport, [1786]. 239; 227, [1] pp.
AAS copy.   19933

[Pratt, Samuel Jackson], 1749-1814.
Emma Corbett. . . . By Courtney
Melmoth.
Philadelphia, Young & M'Culloch, 1786.
2 vol.]
(Entry from an adv.)   19932

[Pratt, Samuel Jackson], 1749-1814.
The Pupil of Pleasure. . . . By Courtney
Melmoth.
Philadelphia, Bell, 1778. [2], 154; 157, [1]
pp.
HSP copy.   16020

[Pratt, Samuel Jackson], 1749-1814.
The Pupil of Pleasure. By Courtney
Melmoth. . . . Vol. I [-II].
Boston, M'Dougall, 1780. 168; 168 pp.
AAS copy.   43869

[Pratt, Samuel Jackson], 1749-1814.
The Sublime and Beautiful. . . .. By
Courtney Melmoth.
New York, Tiebout & O'Brien for Davis
& Mitchell, 1795. 247, [5] pp.
AAS copy.   29348

A Prayer Book, for the Use of Families.
Portsmouth, N. H., Peirce, 1799. 72 pp.

(Reproduced as 36125, q.v.)
AAS copy.   36150

The Prayer of Agur [by Samuel
Fothergill, 1715-1772].
Philadelphia, Hall & Sellers, 1768.
43 pp.
AAS copy.   10899

The Prayer of Agur [by Samuel
Fothergill, 1715-1772].
Newport, 1773. 34 pp.
AAS copy.   12769

Prayers, A Prayer for the Courts of
Justice [by Samuel Seabury, 1729-1796].
n.p., [1795?] [4] pp.
Pierce W. Gaines copy.   47595

[Prayers. Thanksgivings, and
Meditations.
Haverhill, Mass., Edes, 1795.]
(Imprint assumed by Evans from Edes'
adv.)   31038

Precepts for Christian Practice [by
Edward Reyner, 1600-1668].
Cambridge, 1668. [6], 34 pp.
(Mass. Hist. Soc., Preceedings, XLVI,
259.)
AAS copy.   116

The Precipitate Choice.
Boston, Edes, 1783. 140 pp.
AAS copy.   18142

Precis de la Revolution de
Saint-Domingue.
Philadelphia, Parent, 1795. viii, 232 pp.
JCB copy.   29349

A Precise Journal of General Wayne's
Last Campaign.
Hagertown, Gruber, 1795. 36 pp.
AAS copy.   47564

Predestination Consistent with General
Liberty [by Samuel Harker, fl.
1749-1763].
New York, Parker, 1761. [2], 118 pp.
AAS copy.   8874

. . . Predictions for the Year 1783.
[Boston], the Printing-Office in Essex
Street, [1783]. Broadside.
JCB copy.   44444

Eine Predigt, über die Worte Jacobus.
Philadelphia, Saur, 1794. 39 pp.
LOC copy.   27543

Eine Predigt, über I. Joh. Cap. 2, V. 28
zum Abschied . . . den 6ten October, 1793.
Reading, Jungmann & Gruber, 1793.
(Nolan p. 26; present location unknown.)
    46854

[De Predik-Beurten der Piedikanten.
New York, De Foreest, 1751.]
("Daar is nu Weder Gedruckt," New-York
Evening-Post, June 24, 1751.)   6765

[Prefontaine, Peter Papin de.
A Direct Guide to the French Language.
Philadelphia, 1757.]
(Proposals in Pa. Gazette, Oct. 28, 1756;
apparently not printed.)   8011

Preiss, Johannes.
Geistlich u. Andächtige Lieder.
[Germantown, 1753.] 16, 8 pp.
HSP copy.   40668

Prentice, Caleb, 1746-1803.
A Sermon, Delivered before Mount
Moriah Lodge.
Leominster, Mass., Prentiss, 5799 (1799).
16 pp.
AAS copy.   36151

Prentice, Caleb, 1746-1803.
A Sermon Preached at the Instalment of
. . . Elias Hull.
Newburyport, Blunt, 1799. 22 pp.
AAS copy.   36152

Prentice, Caleb, 1746-1803.
A Sermon, Preached at the Instalment of
. . . Joseph Willard.
Worcester, Thomas, 1786. 48 pp.
AAS copy.   19934

Prentice, Caleb, 1746-1803.

The Truth and Faithfulness of God.
Boston, Hall, 1791. 30 pp.
AAS copy.   23713

Prentice, John, 1682-1748.
(Sibley, IV, 529-532.)
Christ's Compassion.
Boston, Kneeland and Green, 1731.
[4], 27 (i.e. 31) pp.
(Issued under common half-title with
3479, q.v.)   3468

Prentice, John, 1682-1748.
King Jehoshaphat's Charge.
Boston, Kneeland and Green for
Henchman, 1731. [4], 25, [1] pp.
AAS copy.   3469

Prentice, John, 1682-1748.
(Sibley, IV, 529-532.)
Pure and Undefiled Religion.
Boston, Kneeland for Henchman, 1735.
[4], 28 pp.
AAS copy.   3952

Prentice, Thomas, 1702-1782.
(Sibley, VIII, 81-89.)
The Believer's Triumph.
Boston, Edes & Gill, 1755. [4], 26,
[2] pp.
AAS copy.   7545

[Prentice, Thomas], 1702-1782.
(Sibley, VIII, 81-89.)
A Letter to the Reverend Andrew
Croswell.
Boston, Russell, 1771. 42, [1] pp.
AAS copy.   12205

Prentice, Thomas, 1702-1782.
(Sibley, VIII, 81-89.)
Observations Moral and Religious.
Boston, Kneeland for Henchman, 1756.
[4], 24 pp.
AAS copy.   7768

Prentice, Thomas, 1702-1782.
(Sibley, VIII, 81-89.)
The Vanity of Zeal.
Boston, Rogers & Fowle, 1748. 27 pp.
AAS copy.   6227

Prentice, Thomas, 1702-1782.
(Sibley, VIII, 81-89.)
When the People.
Boston, Rogers & Fowle, 1745. 39 pp.
AAS copy.   5679

Prentiss, Caleb.
See
Prentice, Caleb.   36153

Prentiss, Charles, 1774-1820.
A Collection of Fugitive Essays.
Leominster, Mass., 1797. 204 pp.
AAS copy.   32708

[Prentiss, John, perfumer.
The Compleat Toilet or Ladies
Companion.
New York, 1794.]
(Entry from copyright record.)   27544

Prentiss, Thomas, 1747-1814.
A Discourse Delivered at Medfield . . .
July 4, 1799.
Dedham, Mass., Mann, 1799. 22 pp.
AAS copy.   36154

Prentiss, Thomas, 1747-1814.
(Weis, Colonial Clergy N. E.)
The Great Duty.
Boston, Fleets, 1773. 23 pp.
AAS copy.   12963

Prentiss, Thomas, 1747-1814.
A Sermon, Delivered at the Ordination
of . . . Thomas Mason.
Brattleborough, Smead, 1799. 24 pp.
AHTS copy.   36155

Prentiss, Thomas, 1747-1814.
A Sermon, Preached at Norton, July 3,
1793.
Boston, Hall, 1793. 30 pp.
AAS copy.   26033

Prentiss, Thomas, 1747-1814.
A Sermon, Preached at the Ordination of
. . . Henry Wight.
Providence, Wheeler, [1785]. 26 pp.
AAS copy.   19198

[Prentiss, Thomas Mellen, 1773-1823.
The Maine Spelling Book.
Augusta, 1799. 132 pp.]
(Williamson 8298. "Portland, Jan. 1799.
New Publication, Now in Press,"
Kennebeck Intelligencer, Feb. 9, 1799.)
    36157

Prentiss, Thomas Mellen, 1773-1823.
The Maine Spelling Book.
Leominster, Mass., Prentisses, 1799.
123 pp.
HC copy.   36156

A Preparatory Sheet, Occasioned by the
Author's being Ask'd . . . Shall all that
have never Heard of Jesus Christ, be
Eternally Damned?
[Boston? 1689?] 8 pp.
MHS copy.   39269

[Presbyter, John, pseud.
Some Observations made in Defence of
the Leag'd Character.
New London, 1737?]
(No copy found. See pp. 16-17 in 4190.)
    4188

The Presbyteriad. With Notes [by Moses
Leavitt Neal, 1766-1829].
n. p., 1797. 12 pp.
(This is apparently the item described by
Evans from Bragg's adv.)
AAS copy.   32516

Presbyterian Church in the U.S.A.
Associated Presbyteries.
See
Associated Presbyteries.   31040

Presbyterian Church in the U.S.A.
Constitution.
The Constitution of the. . . .
Philadelphia, Bradford, 1789. [8],
215 pp.
AAS copy.   22079

Presbyterian Church in the U.S.A.
Constitution.
The Constitution of the Presbyterian
Church.
Philadelphia, Bradford, 1792. [8],
215 pp.
AAS copy.   24711

Presbyterian Church in the U.S.A.
Constitution.
The Constitution of the. . . .
Philadelphia, Aitken, 1797. vii, [1],
470 pp.
AAS copy.   32711

Presbyterian Church in the U.S.A.
General Assembly, 1789.
Acts and Proceedings . . . in . . . 1789.
Philadelphia, Bailey, 1789. 8 pp.
LOC copy.   22078

Presbyterian Church in the U.S.A.
General Assembly, 1790-1791.
Acts and Proceedings.
Philadelphia, Aitken, 1791. 24 pp.
AAS copy.   23714

Presbyterian Church in the U.S.A.
General Assembly, 1792.
Acts and Proceedings.
Philadelphia, Aitken, 1792. 14 pp.
AAS copy.   24710

Presbyterian Church in the U.S.A.
General Assembly 1793.
Acts and Proceedings . . . 1793.
Philadelphia, Aitken, 1793. 13 pp.
AAS copy.   26034

Presbyterian Church in the U.S.A.
General Assembly, 1794.
Acts and Proceedings . . . 1794.
Philadelphia, Aitken, 1794. 32 pp.
AAS copy.   27547

Presbyterian Church in the U.S.A.
General Assembly, 1795-1796.
Acts and Proceedings of . . . 1795 &
1796.
Philadelphia, Smith, 1796. 17 pp.
AAS copy.   31041

Presbyterian Church in the U.S.A.
General Assembly, 1797.
Acts and Proceedings. . . . May 18, 1797.

Philadelphia, Woodward, 1797. 8 pp.
AAS copy.   32710

Presbyterian Church in the U.S.A.
General Assembly, 1798.
Acts and Proceedings. . . . May 17th, 1798.
Philadelphia, Smith, 1798. 16, xii,
[4] pp.
AAS copy.   34410

Presbyterian Church in the U.S.A.
General Assembly, 1799.
Acts and Proceedings . . . May 16th, 1799.
Philadelphia, Woodward, 1799. 24 pp.
AAS copy.   36159

Presbyterian Church in the U.S.A. General
Assembly, 1800.
Acts and Proceedings. . . . 1800.
Philadelphia, Aitken, 1800. 18 pp.
AAS copy.   38318

Presbyterian Church in the U.S.A.
Presbytery of Boston, 1756.
A Fair Narrative.
Boston, Fowle, 1756. 43 pp.
AAS copy.   7720

Presbyterian Church in the U.S.A.
Presbytery of Charleston.
Pastoral Letter . . . to the Churches.
Charleston, S. C., Timothy, 1799. [2], 14
pp.
HEH copy.   36158

Presbyterian Church in the U.S.A.
Presbytery of Kentucky.
A Narrative of Mr. Adam Rankin's Trial.
Lexington, Maxwell, 1793. 41 pp.
(Evans assumed the imprint from that of
27591.)
Presb. Hist. Soc. copy.   27545

Presbyterian Church in the U.S.A.
Presbytery of Lexington, Va.
A Pastoral Letter, from the Presbytery.
n.p., [179?]. 7 pp.
AAS copy.   45791

Presbyterian Church in the U.S.A.
Presbytery of New-Brunswick, 1743.
A Declaration of the Presbyteries of
New-Brunswick and New-Castle . . . May
26th, 1743.
Philadelphia, Bradford, 1743. [2],
13 pp.
YC copy.   5277

Presbyterian Church in the U.S.A.
Presbytery of New Brunswick, 1800.
Rules Established by the. . . . April 23d,
1800.
New Brunswick, N. J., Blauvelt, 1800. 30
pp.
AAS copy.   38317

Presbyterian Church in the U.S.A.
Presbytery of Newcastle, 1754.
A Warning of the Presbytery of New-Castle.
Lancaster, 1754. 55 pp.
(The unique copy at LOC could not be
filmed.)   7300

Presbyterian Church in the U.S.A.
Presbytery of Newcastle, 1784.
An Address from the Presbytery of
New-Castle. . . . August 11, 1784.
Wilmington, 1785. 62 pp.
AAS copy.   19199

Presbyterian Church in the U.S.A.
Presbytery of Pennsylvania, 1774.
Act of the Associate Presbytery. . . . The
Seventh day of November, One Thousand
Seven Hundred and Seventy-Four.
Philadelphia, Aitken. 4 pp.
AAS copy.   13552

Presbyterian Church in the U.S.A.
Presbytery of Pennsylvania, 1778.
A Solemn Warning by the Associated
Presbytery.
Lancaster, [1778]. 27 pp.
LCP copy.   16021

Presbyterian Church in the U.S.A.
Presbytery of Pennsylvania, 1785.
Formula of Question . . . Agreed to at
Pequea, April 13, 1785.
[Philadelphia? 1786?] 4 pp.
(The unique original will not be
reproduced.)   44953

Presbyterian Church in the U.S.A.
Presbytery of Pennsylvania, 1786.
An Acknowledgment of Sins . . . April 20,
1786.
Philadelphia, 1786. 33, [1] pp.
JCB copy.   19479

Presbyterian Church in the U.S.A.
Presbytery of Pennsylvania, 1786.
An Act . . . Concerning the Connexion of . . .
with the Associate Synod of Edinburgh.
Philadelphia, Young & M'Culloch, [1786].
4 pp.
HSP copy.   19478

Presbyterian Church in the U. S. A.
Presbytery of Pennsylvania, 1786.
A Brief Vindication . . . June 2, 1786.
[Philadelphia, 1786.] 12 pp.
JCB copy.   19480

[Presbyterian Church in the U.S.A.
Presbytery of Transylvania.
Extracts from the Minutes . . . Relative to
James Moore's Trials.
Lexington, Ky., Stewart, 1796.]
(Adv. Stewart's Kentucky Herald, Oct. 18,
1796.)   31039

Presbyterian Church in the U.S.A. Synod
of New-York and Pennsylvania, 1758.
The Plan of Union. . . . Agreed upon May
29th, 1758.
Philadelphia, Dunlap, [1758]. [2], 13, [1]
pp.
HEH copy.   41002

Presbyterian Church in U.S.A. Synod of
New York and Pennsylvania, 1766.
A Pastoral Letter.
[New York, Gaine, 1766]. 8 pp.
HEH copy.   10469

[Presbyterian Church in the U.S.A. Synod
of New York and Philadelphia, 1735.
An Extract of the Minutes of the
Commission.
Philadelphia, Bradford, 1735. 13 pp.]
(The unique copy could not be found.)
    3951

Presbyterian Church in the U. S. A. Synod
of New York and Philadelphia, 1769.
An Account of the Annual Contribution
. . . as Returned . . . 20th May, 1769.
[Philadelphia? 1769.] 6, [1] pp.
LOC copy.   11428

Presbyterian Church in the U.S.A. Synod
of New York and Philadelphia, 1775.
An Address of the Presbyterian
Ministers. . . . 10th Day of July, 1775.
Philadelphia, 1775. 8 pp.
LOC copy.   14411

Presbyterian Church in the U.S.A. Synod
of New York and Philadelphia, 1775.
A Pastoral Letter . . . June 29, 1775.
New York, Shober & Loudon, 1775. 8 pp.
LOC copy.   14410

Presbyterian Church in the U. S. A. Synod
of New York and Philadelphia, 1783.
A Pastoral Letter . . . May 24, 1783.
Philadelphia, Bailey, [1783]. Broadside.
LOC copy.   44445

Presbyterian Church in the U. S. A. Synod
of New York and Philadelphia, 1786.
A Draught of a Plan of Government.
Philadelphia, Bailey, 1786. 47 pp.
HEH copy.   19935

Presbyterian Church in the U.S.A. Synod
of New York and Philadelphia, 1787.
A Draught of the Form of Government.
New York, Loudons, 1787. 143 pp.
LOC copy.   20658

Presbyterian Church in the U. S. A. Synod
of New York and Philadelphia, 1788.
Acts and Proceedings of the Synod of
New-York and Philadelphia, A.D. 1787, &
1788.
Philadelphia, Bailey, 1788. 8 pp.
LOC copy.   21402

Presbyterian Church in the U. S. A. Synod
of New York and Philadelphia, 1788.
A List of the Presbyteries, Ministers,
Probationers, and Congregations.
Philadelphia, Bailey, 1788. 12 pp.
LOC copy.   21403

Presbyterian Church in the U. S. A. Synod
of the Carolinas.
A Pastoral Letter.
Fayetteville, Sibley & Howard, 1790. 44
pp.
(Evans, taking his entry from the adv. in
the N.C. Gazette, Apr. 1, 1790, assumed
that this was a publication of the
Episcopal Church.)
AAS copy.   22820

[Prescott, Benjamin], 1687-1777.
(Sibley, V, 485-491.)
A Letter Relating to the Divisions in the
First Church in Salem.
Boston, Fleet, [1734]. 15 pp.
AAS copy.   3829

[Prescott, Benjamin], 1687-1777.
(Sibley, V, 485-491.)
A Letter to a Friend, Relating to the
Differences in the First Church in Salem.
Boston, Fleet, 1735. 31 pp.
AAS copy.   3953

Prescott, Benjamin, 1687-1777.
(Sibley, V, 485-491.)
A Letter to the Reverend Mr. George
Whitefield.
Boston, Gookin, 1745. 16 pp.
AAS copy.   5680

Prescott, Benjamin, 1687-1777.
(Sibley, V, 485-491.)
A Letter to the Reverend Mr. Joshua Gee.
Boston, Green, Bushell & Allen for Eliot,
1743. 28 pp.
AAS copy.   5278

Prescott, Benjamin, 1687-1777.
(Sibley, V, 485-491.)
Mr. Prescot's Examination of Certain
Remarks.
Boston, Henchman, 1735. 58, [1] pp.
AAS copy.   3954

[Prescott, Robert], 1725-1816.
(D. N. B.)
A Letter from a Veteran.
America (New York), 1774. 19, [1] pp.
AAS copy.   13554

The Present Alarming Crisis. . . .
New-York, May 30, 1770.
Advertisement.
[New York, 1770.] Broadside.
LCP copy.   11781

A Present for an Apprentice [by John
Barnard, 1685-1764].
Boston, Rogers & Fowle, 1747. 83 pp.
AAS copy.   5904

A Present for an Apprentice. . . . Fourth
Edition [by John Barnard, 1685-1764].
Philadelphia, Franklin & Hall, 1749. 103,
[4] pp.
LCP copy.   6282

A Present for an Apprentice [by Sir John
Barnard, 1685-1764].
Philadelphia, Crukshank for Williamson,
1774. 83 pp.
AAS copy.   13133

A Present for an Apprentice [by Sir John
Barnard, 1685-1764].
Philadelphia, Dobson, 1788. 80, [8] pp.
AAS copy.   20953

A Present for an Apprentice [by Sir John
Barnard, 1685-1764].
Albany, N. Y., Fry, 1798. pp. [8],
[13]-160.
AAS copy.   33375

A Present for an Apprentice [by Sir John
Barnard, 1685-1765].
Philadelphia, Cist, 1800. [8], 112 pp.
AAS copy.   36895

[Present for Misses.
Worcester, Thomas, 1794.]
(Imprint assumed from Thomas' advs.)
    27548

A Present from a Farr Countrey [by
Cotton Mather, 1663-1728].
Boston, Green and Allen for Perry, 1698.
53, [1] pp.
AAS copy.   39330

The Present Melancholy Circumstances.

Boston, for Gray and Edwards, 1719. 16 pp.
MHS copy.   2067

The Present Situation of Affairs in North-America.
A Poem.
[Philadelphia, 1775.] 8 pp.
LCP copy.   14412

The Present State of America, &c.
Philadelphia, 1789. 8 pp.
JCB copy.   22080

The Present State of Medical Learning [by Samuel Latham Mitchill, 1764-1831].
New York, Swords, 1797. 16 pp.
LCP copy.   32488

The Present State of New-England [by John Palmer, 1650-1700].
[Boston, 1689.] 44 pp.
LOC copy.   495

The Present State of North-America [by Ellis Huske, 1700-1755].
(A.A.S. cat.)
Boston, D. & Z. Fowle, 1755. [2], 64, [1] pp.
AAS copy.   7434

The Present State of North-America. . . .
Second Edition [by Ellis Huske, 1700-1755].
Boston, D. & Z. Fowle, 1755. [2], 64, [1] pp.
AAS copy.   40755

The Present State of the Colony of Connecticut [by Benjamin Gale, 1715-1790].
[New London], 1755. [2], 21 pp.
AAS copy.   7423

The Present State of the Controversy [by Ethan Allen, 1738-1789].
Hartford, Hudson & Goodwin, 1782. 16 pp.
HC copy.   17452

The Present State of the New-English Affairs [by Increase Mather, 1639-1723].
Boston, 1689. Broadside.
AAS copy.   492

A Present to Children.
New London, Green, 1783. 16 pp.
YC copy.   44446

A Present to Children. Consisting of Several New Divine Hymns and Moral Songs.
New London, Green, [1783]. [16] pp.
(No copy available for reproduction.)   44248

[A Present to Children. Consisting of Several New Divine Hymns and Moral Songs.
Norwich, Trumbull, 1791.]
("Just Published, at this Office," Norwich Packet, June 6, 1791.)   23715

A Present to Children.
Norwich, Bushnell, 1792. 14, [1] pp.
YC copy.   46551

A Present to Children.
Norwich, Hubbard, 1794. [16] pp.
LOC copy.   47186

A Present to Children. Consisting of Several new Divine Hymns, Moral Songs & Entertaining Stories.
[Leominster, Mass.], Whitcomb, [1800?]. 12 pp.
AAS copy.   49138

A Present to the Unprejudiced.
Newfield, Conn., Beach & Jones, 1795. 42 pp.
(The only copy located is imperfect.)
AAS copy.   29350

The Present Way [by Elihu Hall, 1714-1784].
New London, 1749. [2], 74 pp.
NYPL copy.   6328

A Preservative against the Doctrine of Fate.
Boston, Fowle & Thomas, 1770. 31 pp.
AAS copy.   11826

President II. Being Observations on the late Official Address of George Washington.
Baltimore, 1796. 16 pp.
(Best copy available.)
EPFL copy.   47885

President II. Being Observations on the Late Official Address of George Washington.
Newark, N.J., Dodge, 1796. 16 pp.
NYPL copy.   31043

President II. Being Observations on the Late Official Address of George Washington.
[Philadelphia], 1796. 16 pp.
LCP copy.   31042

Presidents March [by Philip Phile, d. 1793].
New York, Gilfert, [1796?]. 1 leaf.
JCB copy.   31044

The President's March. A New Federal Song [by Joseph Hopkinson, 1770-1842].
Philadelphia, Willig, [1798]. [2] pp.
LOC copy.   33902

Preston, Francis, 1765-1835.
Address to the People.
Philadelphia, 1796. 29 pp.
LOC copy.   31045

Preston, Samuel.
A Charge Delivered to the Grand Jury.
Easton, Pa., Longcope, 1800. 22 pp.
HSP copy.   38321

Preston, William, 1753-1807.
Death of Louis, the Sixteenth.
Philadelphia, Story, 1794. [2], 70 pp.
LOC copy.   27549

Preston, William, 1753-1807.
Louis the Sixteenth . . . Third Edition.
New York, Swords, 1794. 64 pp.
AAS copy.   27550

The Pretensions of Thomas Jefferson [by William Loughton Smith, 1758-1812].
United States (Philadelphia), 1796. 64 pp.
AAS copy.   31212

The Pretensions of Thomas Jefferson. . . .
Part the Second [by William Loughton Smith, 1758-1812].
United States (Philadelphia), 1796. [2], 42 pp.
AAS copy.   31213

[A Pretty Book for Children; or, an Easy Guide to the English Tongue.
New York, Gaine, 1762.]
(See Ford, Gaine, I, 108.)   9247

[A Pretty Play-Thing for Children of all Denominations.
New York, Gaine, 1775.]
(Adv. in 15227.)   14413

[A Pretty Plaything for Children of all Denominations.
New York, Gaine, 1785.]
(Adv. in 19195.)   19200

[A Pretty Plaything for Children of all Denominations.
Philadelphia, Spotswood, 1786.]
(Entry from an adv. for imported books in Pa. Herald, July 12, 1786.)   19936

A Pretty Play-Thing [sic], for Children of all Denominations.
Philadelphia, B. Johnson, 1794. 62+ pp.
(No perfect copy known.)
AAS copy.   47187

[Price, Isaac, fl. 1797.
The Jersey Man's Common Sense.
Morristown, Cooper, 1798.]
(Entry from Nelson, who dates it 1797.)   34411

[Price, Jonathan.
A Chart of the Sea Coasts . . . of North-Carolina.
Newbern, Martin, 1796. Map.]
(Entry from the copyright application.)   31046

[Price, Jonathan.]
A Description of Occacock Inlet.
Newbern, Martin, 1795. [2], 8 pp., 1+ map.
N. C. Archives copy.   29351

[Price, Jonathan.
A Map of the State of North-Carolina.
Newbern, Martin, 1796. Map.]
(Entry from copyright notice.)   31047

Price, Laurence, 1628-1680.
A Key to open Heaven's Gate.
Worcester, 1787. 8 pp.
AAS copy.   20659

Price, Lawrence, 1628-1680.
A Key to Open Heaven's Gate.
Springfield, Mass., Ashley, 1800. 10 pp.
NYPL copy.   49139

Price, Nathaniel, defendant.
The Trial of. . . . May 1797.
New York, Weedg, [1797]. 8 pp.
NYHS copy.   32712

Price, Richard, 1723-1791.
Additional Observations.
Philadelphia, Hall & Sellers, 1778. x, 122 pp., 1 folded leaf.
AAS copy.   16022

Price, Richard, 1723-1791.
A Discourse on the Love of our Country.
Boston, Powars, 1790. 40 pp.
AAS copy.   22814

Price, Richard, 1723-1791.
The General Introduction.
Philadelphia, Hall & Sellers, 1778. [2], xiv, [1] pp.
AAS copy.   16023

[Price, Richard, 1723- 791.
The General Introduction.
Philadelphia, Hall & Sellers, 1778. 27 pp.]
(Entry from Sabin. No copy with such pagination found.)   16024

Price, Richard, 1723-1791.
Observations on the Importance of the American Revolution.
Boston, Powars & Willis, 1784. 87, [1] pp.
AAS copy.   18739

Price, Richard, 1723-1791.
Observations on the Importance of the American Revolution.
Bennington, 1785. 84 pp.
(The only reported copy is imperfect.)
AAS copy.   19204

Price, Richard, 1723-1791.
Observations on the Importance of the American Revolution.
Hartford, Barlow & Babcock, 1785. 60 pp.
AAS copy.   44778

Price, Richard, 1723-1791.
Observations on the Importance of the American Revolution.
New Haven, 1785. 87, [1] pp.
AAS copy.   19201

Price, Richard, 1723-1791.
Observations on the Importance of the American Revolution.
Philadelphia, Carey for Spotswood & Rice and Seddon, 1785. [2], 60, [2] pp.
AAS copy.   44779

Price, Richard, 1723-1791.
Observations on the Importance of the American Revolution. . . . Second Edition.
Philadelphia, Carey for Spotswood, Rice and Seddon, 1785. [2], 60, [2] pp.
HC copy.   19202

Price, Richard, 1723-1791.
Observations on the Importance of the American Revolution.
Trenton, 1785. 87, [1] pp.
AAS copy.   19203

[Price, Richard, 1723-1791.
Observations on the Importance of the American Revolution.
Charleston, Bowen & Markland, 1786.]
(Entry from booksellers' adv.)   19937

Price, Richard, 1723-1791.

Observations on the Nature of Civil
Liberty.
Boston, Fleets, [1776]. 71 pp.
AAS copy.   15032

Price, Richard, 1723-1791.
Observations on the Nature of Civil
Liberty.
Charleston, 1776. [8]. 104 pp.
LOC copy.   15034

Price, Richard, 1723-1791.
Observations on the Nature of Civil
Liberty.
New York, Loudon, 1776. 107 pp.
AAS copy.   15033

Price, Richard, 1723-1791.
Observations on the Nature of Civil
Liberty.
Philadelphia, Dunlap, [1776]. 61 (i.e.
71) pp.
AAS copy.   15030

Price, Richard, 1723-1791.
Observations on the Nature of Civil
Liberty.
Philadelphia, Dunlap, 1776. 71 pp.
AAS copy.   15031

Price, Richard, 1723-1791.
Sermons on the Security and Happiness.
Philadelphia, Dobson, 1788. 222 pp.
AAS copy.   21404

Price, Richard, 1723-1791.
Sermons on the Security and Happiness of
a Virtuous Course.
Boston, Weld & Greenough for West, 1794.
270. [1] pp.
AAS copy.   27551

Price, Roger, 1696?-1762.
(Sprague, V, 69-75.)
A Funeral Sermon . . . John Jekyll.
[Boston], 1733. [4], 19 pp.
AAS copy.   3716

Price, Roger, 1696?-1762.
(Sprague, V, 69-75.)
A Sermon Preach'd at the King's Chappel.
Boston, Kneeland & Green, 1738. [4], 19
pp.
AAS copy.   4305

Prices Current: - Charleston [blank] 1784.
[Charleston, 1784.] Broadside.
JCB copy.   44593

Prices Current. Charleston [by Rogers &
Barker, Charleston, S. C.].
[Charleston, 1795.] Broadside.
JCB copy.   29427

Prichard, Samuel.
Masonry Dissected. . . . Re-printed . . .
M,DCC,XLIX.
[Newport? 1750?] 32 pp.
(The only recorded copy could not be
located.)   40563

Prichard & Hall, Philadelphia.
Proposals for Printing by Subscription, A
Geographical . . . History of America.
[Philadelphia, 1787.] 4 pp.
LCP copy.   45147

Prideaux, Humphrey, 1648-1724.
The History of . . . Mahomet.
Philadelphia, Stewart & Cochran, 1796.
126 pp.
AAS copy.   31048

Prideaux, Humphrey, 1648-1724.
The True Nature of Imposture.
Fairhaven, Vt., Lyon, 1798. 108, 84 pp.
Composite copy.   34412

Priestcraft Defended. . . . Sixth Edition
[by John MacGowan, 1726-1780].
Philadelphia, Bradfords, 1769. v, 25 pp.
LOC copy.   11320

Priestcraft Defended. . . . Seventh Edition
[by John MacGowan, 1726-1780].
Boston, Edes & Gill, 1769. 24 pp.
LOC copy.   11321

Priestcraft Defended. . . . Twelfth Edition
[by John MacGowan, 1726-1780].
Newport, 1770. 36 pp.
AAS copy.   11711

Priestcraft Defended. . . . Tenth Edition
[by John MacGowan, 1726-1780].
Boston, Edes & Gill, 1771. 24 pp.
AAS copy.   12104

Priestcraft Defended. . . . Thirteenth
Edition [by John MacGowan, 1726-1780].
New Haven, [1773]. 32 pp.]
(Evans had the date 1771 from Haven and
Brinley 6180, but adv. "just published" in
New London Gazette, Aug. 6, 1773. The
AAS has a 1773 12th ed.)   12105

Priestcraft Defended. . . . Twelfth Edition
[by John MacGowan, 1726-1780].
New London, Greens, 1773. 24 pp.
AAS copy.   42460

[Priestcraft Defended. . . . Nineteenth
Edition [by John MacGowan, 1726-1780].
Litchfield, Collier, [1791]. 30 pp.]
(The origin of this entry is unknown.)   23526

Priestcraft Defended. . . . Eleventh
Edition [by John MacGowan, 1726-1780].
Baltimore, Edwards, 1792. 23 pp.
HEH copy.   24492

Priestcraft Defended. . . . Seventh Edition
[by John MacGowan, 1726-1780].
Boston, Folsom, 1793. 24 pp.
AAS copy.   25744

[Priestley, Joseph], 1733-1804.
An Address to Protestant Dissenters of all
Denominations.
Boston, Fleets, 1774. 16 pp.
AAS copy.   13555

[Priestley, Joseph], 1733-1804.
An Address to Protestant Dissenters of all
Denominations.
Philadelphia, Humphreys, 1774. 24 pp.
AAS copy.   13556

[Priestley, Joseph], 1733-1804.
An Address to Protestant Dissenters of all
Denominations.
Wilmington, Del., 1774.]
(Adv. Pa. Packet, Sept. 26, 1774.)   13557

Priestley, Joseph, 1733-1804.
An Address to the Unitarian
Congregation at Philadelphia.
Philadelphia, Gales, 1797. 24 pp.
LCP copy.   32713

Priestley, Joseph, 1733-1804.
An Appeal to the Serious and Candid.
Philadelphia, Bell, 1784. 57, [1] pp.
AAS copy.   18741

Priestley, Joseph, 1733-1804.
An Appeal to the Serious and Candid.
Philadelphia, Dobson, 1794. [2], vi, 52 pp.
AAS copy.   27552

Priestley, Joseph, 1733-1804.
The Case of Poor Emigrants.
Philadelphia, Gales for Birch, 1797. 32 pp.
LCP copy.   32714

Priestley, Joseph, 1733-1804.
A Comparison of the Institutions.
Northumberland, Pa., Kennedy, 1799.
xxvii, [1], 428, [8] pp.
AAS copy.   36160

Priestley, Joseph, 1733-1804.
Considerations on the Doctrine of
Philogiston.
Philadelphia, Dobson, 1796. 39 pp.
LCP copy.   31049

Priestley, Joseph, 1733-1804.
A Continuation of the Letters to the
Philosophers.
Northumberland-Town, Kennedy, 1794.
vii, [1], 96 pp.
AAS copy.   27558

Priestley, Joseph, 1733-1804.
A Continuation of the Letters.
Salem, Cushing, 1795. 72 pp.
AAS copy.   29352

Priestley, Joseph, 1733-1804.
A Description of a New Chart of History.
New Haven, Doolittle, 1792. 91, [4] pp., 1
chart.
AAS copy.   24713

Priestley, Joseph, 1733-1804.
Discourses on the Evidence of Revealed
Religion. . . . Second Edition.
Boston, Spotswood, 1795. 275, [1] pp.
AAS copy.   29353

Priestley, Joseph, 1733-1804.
Discourses, Relating to . . . Revealed
Religion.
Philadelphia, Dobson, 1796.]
(No copy located has the imprint given by
Evans.)   31050

Priestley, Joseph, 1733-1804.
Discourses Relating to . . . Revealed
Religion.
Philadelphia, Thompson, 1796. xx, [2],
426 pp.
AAS copy.   31051

Priestley, Joseph, 1733-1804.
Discourses Relating to the Evidences of
Revealed Religion. . . . Vol. II.
Philadelphia, Dobson, 1797. xi, [3], 474,
[2] pp., errata slip.
AAS copy.   32715

Priestley, Joseph, 1733-1804.
The Doctrine of Phlogiston Established.
Northumberland, [Pa.], Kennedy, 1800.
xv, 90, [2] pp.
LCP copy.   49140

Priestley, Joseph, 1733-1804.
Ecclesiastical History. Dr. Priestly having
Continued. . . . 22nd February, 1797.
[Philadelphia, 1797.] Broadside.
AAS copy.   32716

[Priestley, Joseph], 1733-1804.
Extracts from a Catechism.
Boston, Hall, 1798. 22 pp.
AAS copy.   34413

Priestley, Joseph, 1733-1804.
Extracts from Dr. Priestley's Catechism.
Salem, Hall, 1785. 12 pp.
AAS copy.   19206

Priestley, Joseph, 1733-1804.
Extracts from Doctor Priestley's
Catechism.
Boston, Hall, [1787]. 12 pp.
JCB copy.   45144

Priestley, Joseph, 1733-1804.
Extracts from Doctor Priestley's
Catechism.
Salem, Cushing, 1793. 12 pp.
(No better copy exists.)
AAS ph. copy.   46855

Priestley, Joseph, 1733-1804.
Extracts from Doctor Priestley's
Catechism.
Salem, Carlton, 1796. 12 pp.
AAS copy.   31052

Priestley, Joseph, 1733-1804.
A Familiar Illustration.
Philadelphia, Dobson, 1794. pp. [2],
[i]-iv, [1], [7]-72.
AAS copy.   27553

Priestley, Joseph, 1733-1804.
A General View.
Philadelphia, Dobson, 1794. 24 pp.
AAS copy.   27554

Priestley, Joseph, 1733-1804.
A General View of the Arguments for the
Unity of God.
New York, Robertson, 1796. 26 pp.
(Evans guessed at the imprint from
Fellows' adv. "New Publications, for
sale" in 30944.)   31053

Priestley, Joseph, 1733-1804.
An History of the Corruptions of
Christianity, in Two Volumes.
Boston, Spotswood, 1797. xii, 245, [2];
316 pp.
AAS copy.   32717

Priestley, Joseph, 1733-1804.
Letters to a Philosophical Unbeliever.
Philadelphia, Dobson, 1795. 86 pp.
LCP copy.   29354

Priestley, Joseph, 1733-1804.
Letters to Mr. Volney.
Philadelphia, Dobson, 1797. 28 pp.
AAS copy.   32718

Priestley, Joseph, 1733-1804.
Letters to the Inhabitants of
Northumberland. . . . Part I.
Northumberland, [Pa.], Kennedy, 1799.
[4], 48 pp.
LCP copy.   36161

Priestley, Joseph, 1733-1804.
Letters to the Inhabitants of
Northumberland. . . . Part II.
Northumberland, Pa., Kennedy, 1799. 42,
[1] pp.
AAS copy.   36162

[Priestley, Joseph, 1733-1804.
Letters to the Inhabitants of
Northumberland.
Philadelphia, Bioren, 1800. v, [1], 96 pp.]
(No such edition located.)   38322

Priestley, Joseph, 1733-1804.
Letters to the Jews.
New York, Harrison for Gomez, 1794. 131
pp.
AAS copy.   27555

Priestley, Joseph, 1733-1804.
Letters to the Philosophers.
Boston, Hall, 1793. 30 pp.
AAS copy.   26035

Priestley, Joseph, 1733-1804.
Letters to the Philosophers.
New York, Loudon & Brower, 1794. [2],
26 pp.
AAS copy.   27556

Priestley, Joseph, 1733-1804.
Letters Addressed to the Philosophers.
Philadelphia, Dobson, 1794. [2], ii, 80,
[8] pp.
AAS copy.   27557

Priestley, Joseph, 1733-1804.
Letters to the Right Honourable Edmund
Burke.
New York, Gaine, 1791. vi, 73, [1] pp.
AAS copy.   23716

Priestley, Joseph, 1733-1804.
Miscellaneous Observations Relating to
Education.
New London, Springer for T.C. Green, S.
Green, and Trumbull, 1796. x, 102, [2] pp.
AAS copy.   31054

Priestley, Joseph, 1733-1804.
Observations on the Doctrine of
Phlogiston.
Philadelphia, Dobson, 1797. 38 pp.
NLM copy.   32719

Priestley, Joseph, 1733-1804.
Observations on the Increase of Infidelity.
Northumberland, Penn., Kennedy, 1795.
xiii, [3], 83, [2] pp.
AAS copy.   29355

Priestley, Joseph, 1733-1804.
Observations on the Increase of
Infidelity. . . . Third Edition.
Philadelphia, Dobson, 1797. xxvi, 179 pp.
AAS copy.   32721

Priestley, Joseph, 1733-1804.
An Outline of the Evidences of Revealed
Religion.
Philadelphia, Dobson, 1797. viii, 30, [2]
pp.
AAS copy.   32722

Priestley, Joseph, 1733-1804.
Réflexions sur la Doctrine du
Phlogistique.
Philadelphia, Moreau de St. Mery, 1797.
[4], 96 pp.
NLM copy.   32720

Priestley, Joseph, 1733-1804.
Two Sermons.
Philadelphia, Dobson, 1794. 106, [6] pp.
AAS copy.   27559

Priestley, Joseph, 1733-1804.
Unitarianism Explained and Defended.
Philadelphia, Thompson, 1796. viii, 32 pp.
AAS copy.   31055

Priestley, Timothy, 1734-1814.
The Christian's Looking-Glass.
Newburyport, Osborne, 1793. 90, [1] pp.
AAS copy.   26036

Priestley, Timothy, 1734-1814.
The Christian's Looking Glass.
Concord, Mass., Coverly, 1794. 89, [1] pp.
AAS copy.   27560

Priestley, Timothy, 1734-1814.
The Christian's Looking Glass. . . . Part
the Second.
Newburyport, Blunt, 1794. [2], 102 pp.
JCB copy.   27561

Priestley, Timothy, 1734-1814.
Family Exercises.
Newburyport, Blunt & March, 1795. 37
pp.
AAS copy.   29356

The Priests Lips [by Joseph Haynes,
1715-1801].
Portsmouth, Fowle, 1760. 78, [2], 17 pp.
AAS copy.   8617

Prima Morum & Pietatis Praecepta.
Philadelphia, Aitken, 1776. 34 pp.
HSP copy.   15035

Prime, Benjamin Youngs, 1733-1791.
Columbia's Glory.
New York, Greenleaf, 1791. vi, 42 pp.
AAS copy.   23717

[Prime, Benjamin Youngs], 1733-1791.
(D.A.B.)
An Excellent new Song, for the Sons of
Liberty.
[New York], Holt, [1769]. Broadside.
Copy attributed to Smithtown (N. Y.)
Public Library, but could not be
confirmed.   11429

[Prime, Benjamin Youngs], 1733-1791.
The Unfortunate Hero; a Pindaric Ode.
New York, Parker & Weyman, 1758.
15 pp.
HEH copy.   41003

Prime, Ebenezer, 1700-1779.
The Importance of the Divine Presence.
New York, Parker, [1759. [2], 64, [1] pp.
YC copy.   8473

Prime, Ebenezer, 1700-1779.
(Dexter, I, 192-194.)
Mr. Prime's two Ordination Sermons.
New York, Gaine, 1758. [2], 74, 63 pp.
AAS copy.   8244

Prime, Ebenezer, 1700-1779.
A Sermon Preached in Oysterbay,
February 27. 1743/4.
New York, Parker, 1744. 95 pp.
NYHS copy.   5480

[A Primer.
Philadelphia, Franklin & Hall, 1764.]
(Assumed by Evans from references to
primers in the Franklin accounts.)   9802

[A Primer.
Philadelphia, Franklin & Hall, 1765.]
(Mentioned in Franklin's accounts.) 10147

[A Primer.
Philadelphia, Walters & Norman, 1779.]
(Adv. Pa. Evening Post, June 23, 1779.)
                                             16480

[A Primer, Containing a most Easy Way
to Attain. . . . In a Catechism Compailed by
the Assembly of Divines.
Annapolis? 1729?]
(Wroth 56. No copy known.)   39925

[A Primer for the Colony of Connecticut.
New London, 1715.]
(Adv. in Evans 1769.)   1776

A Primer: or, An Easy and Pleasant
Guide to the Art of Reading.
Salem, [Mass.], Dabney & Cushing,
[1790]. [32] pp.
AAS copy.   45977

[A Primer or Catechism, set forth
Agreeable to the Book of
Common-Prayer.
Annapolis? Parks? 1729?]
(Wroth 57. No copy known.)   39926

A Primmer for Children. Or, An
Introduction to the true Reading of
English. . . . (13th, Edit.)
New London, Green, 1744.

(Known only by the tp.)
AAS copy.   40347

Prince, John, 1751-1836.
A Discourse, Delivered at Salem.
Salem, Cushing, 1798. 44 pp.
AAS copy.   34414

Prince, John, 1751-1836.
A Discourse, Delivered at Salem. . . .
Second Edition.
Salem, Cushing, 1798. [4], 30 pp.
AAS copy.   34415

[Prince, John, 1751-1836.
A Discourse, Delivered at Salem. . . .
Third Edition.
Salem, Cushing, 1798. 30 pp.]
(No copy of a "Third Edition" located.)
                                             34416

Prince, John, 1751-1836.
Part of a Discourse Delivered on the 29th
of December.
Salem, Mass., Cushing, [1800].
24 pp.
AAS copy.   38323

[Prince, Nathan], 1698-1748.
(Sibley, VI, 268-279.)
An Answer to Lesley.
[Boston, 1724.] 28, 12 pp.
(The unique copy could not be found.)
                                             2581

Prince, Nathan, 1698-1748.
(Sibley, VI, 268-279.)
The Constitution and Government of
Harvard College.
[Boston, 1743.] 43 pp.
("Just published," Boston News-Letter,
Jan. 13, 1743.)
AAS copy.   5041

Prince, Nathan, 1698-1748.
The Constitution and Government of
Harvard College.
[Boston, 1743.] 27 pp.
BPL copy.   5042

[Prince, Nathan], 1698-1748.
(Sibley, VI, 268-279.)
An Essay to Solve the Difficulties.
Boston, Kneeland & Green, 1734. [2], 30
pp.
AAS copy.   3830

Prince, Thomas, 1687-1758.
(Sibley, V, 341-368.)
An Account of a Strange Appearance.
Boston, 1719. [2], 13 pp.
BA copy.   2068

Prince, Thomas, 1687-1758.
(Sibley, V, 341-368.)
Annals of New England. . . . Vol. II.
Numb. 1.
Boston, Kneeland and Leverett, [1755].
[2], 32, [2] pp.
AAS copy.   7301

Prince, Thomas, 1687-1758.
(Sibley, V, 341-368.)
Annals of New-England. . . . Vol. II,
Numb. 2.
Boston, Edes & Gill for Kneeland and
Leverett, [1755]. pp. [2], 33-64, [2].
AAS copy.   7546

Prince, Thomas, 1687-1758.
Annals of New-England. . . . Vol. II.
Numb. 3.
Boston, Edes & Gill for Kneeland and
Leverett, [1755]. pp. [2], 65-96, [2] pp.
AAS copy.   7547

Prince, Thomas, 1687-1758.
Be Followers.
Boston, Edes & Gill for Henchman, 1755.
[4], 27 pp.
AAS copy.   7548

Prince, Thomas, 1687-1758.
Boston, April 10, 1729. Reverend Sir, The
New-England Chronology. . . .
[Boston, 1729.] Broadside.
NYHS copy.   39927

Prince, Thomas, 1687-1758.
Boston, Feb. 20, 1728/9. Reverend Sir,
The New England Chronology. . . .
[Boston, 1729.] Broadside.

(The only known copy cannot be located.)
39928

[Prince, Thomas], 1687-1758.
Carmen Miserabile. . . . For . . . Jonathan
Marsh.
[Boston, 1708.] Broadside.
(The only known copy is imperfect.)
BA copy.   39471

Prince, Thomas, 1687-1758.
(Sibley, V, 341-368.)
The Case of Heman Considered.
Boston, Kneeland, 1756. [4], 33, [2] pp.
AAS copy.   7769

Prince, Thomas, 1687-1758.
The Character of Caleb.
Boston, Kneeland, 1756. [4], 30 pp.
(Issued separately with a half-title and
without it but bound under a joint
half-title with 7790, q.v.)   7770

Prince, Thomas, 1687-1758.
(Sibley, V, 341-368.)
Christ Abolishing Death.
Boston, Draper for Henchman, 1736. [2],
41, [3], ii, 6 pp.
AAS copy.   4067

Prince, Thomas, 1687-1758.
A Chronological History of New-England.
Boston, Kneeland & Green, 1736. [10], xi,
[1], 20, 104, [2], 254 pp.
AAS copy.   4068

Prince, Thomas, 1687-1758.
(Sibley, V, 341-368.)
Civil Rulers Raised up.
Boston, Gerrish, 1728. [4], 24 pp.
AAS copy.   3093

Prince, Thomas, 1687-1758.
The Departure of Elijah.
Boston, Henchman, 1728. [4], 26 pp.
AAS copy.   3094

Prince, Thomas, 1687-1758.
Dying Exercises of Mrs. Deborah Prince.
Newburyport, 1789. 59 pp.
AAS copy.   22082

Prince, Thomas, 1687-1758.
(Sibley, V, 341-368.)
The Dying Prayer.
Boston, Kneeland and Green for Gerrish,
1732. [4], 26 pp.
AAS copy.   3596

Prince, Thomas, 1687-1758,
(Sibley, V, 341-368.)
Earthquakes the Works of God.
Boston, Henchman, 1727. [6], 45, [3] pp.
AAS copy.   2945

Prince, Thomas, 1687-1758.
Earthquakes the Works of God. . . . Second
Edition.
Boston, Henchman, 1727. [6], 45, [3] pp.
AAS copy.   2946

Prince, Thomas, 1687-1758.
Earthquakes the Works of God.
Boston, Fowle, 1755. 23, [1] pp.
(The AAS has another issue lacking the
adv. on the last leaf.)
AAS copy.   7549

Prince, Thomas, 1687-1758.
(Sibley, V, 341-368.)
Extract of a Sermon Preach'd at the South
Church.
Boston, 1774. 15 pp.
HC copy.   13558

Prince, Thomas, 1687-1758.
Extract of a Sermon.
Watertown, 1776. 15 pp.
AAS copy.   15036

Prince, Thomas, 1687-1758.
(Sibley, V, 341-368.)
Extraordinary Events.
Boston, Henchman, 1745. 35 pp.
AAS copy.   5681

Prince, Thomas, 1687-1758.
(Sibley, V, 341-368.)
Extraordinary Events. . . . Second Edition.
Boston, Henchman, 1747. 35 pp.
AAS copy.   6057

Prince, Thomas, 1687-1758.

The Faithful Servant.
Boston, Kneeland and Green for
Henchman, 1732. [8], 35, [3], 24, [4], 4
pp.
AAS copy.   3597

Prince, Thomas, 1687-1758.
(Sibley, V, 341-368.)
The Fulness of Life.
Boston, Kneeland & Green, 1748. 24 pp.
AAS copy.   6228

Prince, Thomas, 1687-1758.
A Funeral Sermon on the Reverend Mr.
Nathanael Williams.
Boston, Kneeland & Green, 1738, [2], 30
pp.
AAS copy.   4306

Prince, Thomas, 1687-1758.
(Sibley, V, 341-368.)
God Brings to the Desired Haven.
Boston, 1717. [4], iii, [1], 32 pp.
MHS copy.   1925

Prince, Thomas, 1687-1758.
(Sibley, V, 341-368.)
God Destroyeth the Hope of Man!
Boston, Kneeland for Henchman, 1751.
[4], 34 pp.
AAS copy.   6766

Prince, Thomas, 1687-1758.
The Grace and Death.
Boston, Gerrish, 1728. [4], 23 pp.
AAS copy.   3095

Prince, Thomas, 1687-1758.
An Improvement of the Doctrine of
Earthquakes.
Boston, Fowle, 1755. 16 pp.
(The AAS has another leaf without the
adv. on verso of title.)
AAS copy.   7550

Prince, Thomas, 1687-1758.
It being Earnestly Desired. . . . in the
Christian History. . . .
Boston, [1743]. 1 leaf.
AAS copy.   40316

Prince, Thomas, 1687-1758.
Morning Health.
Boston, Henchman, 1727. [6], 26, [2] pp.
AAS copy.   2947

Prince, Thomas, 1687-1758.
Morning Health. . . . Second Edition.
Boston, Henchman, 1727. [8], 37, [2] pp.
LOC copy.   2948

Prince, Thomas, 1687-1758.
(Sibley, V, 341-368.)
The Natural and Moral Government.
Boston, Kneeland & Green, 1749. [6],
40 pp.
AAS copy.   6408

[Prince, Thomas, 1687-1758.
(Sibley, V, 341-368.)
The Natural and Moral Government.
Boston, Kneeland & Green, 1750. [6],
40 pp.]
(A ghost of 6408.)   6596

Prince, Thomas, 1687-1758.
(Sibley, V, 341-368.)
The People of New-England.
Boston, Green for Henchman, 1730. [4],
48, [3] pp.
AAS copy.   3343

Prince, Thomas, 1687-1758.
(Sibley, V, 341-368.)
The Pious Cry.
Boston, Rand, 1746. 38 pp.
AAS copy.   5855

Prince, Thomas, 1687-1758.
(Sibley, V, 341-368.)
Precious in the Sight of the Lord.
Boston, Kneeland & Green, 1735. [4], 26,
[1] pp.
AAS copy.   3955

Prince, Thomas, 1687-1758.
The Salvations of God in 1746.
Boston, Henchman, 1746. 35 pp.
AAS copy.   5856

Prince, Thomas, 1687-1758.
A Sermon at the Publick Lecture in
Boston.

Boston, Green, 1730. [4], 36, 4 pp.
AAS copy.   3344

Prince, Thomas, 1687-1758.
A Sermon Delivered at the South Church.
Boston, Henchman and Kneeland &
Green, 1746. 38, [1] pp.
AAS copy.   5857

Prince, Thomas, 1687-1758.
(Sibley, V, 341-368.)
A Sermon Delivered by Thomas Prince.
Boston, Franklin for Gerrish, 1718. [8],
76, [4], 15 pp.
(The AAS has two copies with variant
settings of the last page of the
Dedication.)
AAS copy.   1996

Prince, Thomas, 1687-1758.
A Sermon on the Sorrowful Occasion of
the Death of . . . King George.
Boston, Henchman, 1727. [4], 27 pp.
AAS copy.   2949

Prince, Thomas, 1687-1758.
(Sibley, V, 341-368.)
The Sovereign God.
Boston, Rogers & Fowle for Rand, 1744.
40 pp.
AAS copy.   5481

[Prince Thomas], 1687-1758.
(Sibley, V, 341-368.)
The Vade Mecum for America.
Boston, Kneeland and Green for
Henchman and Hancock, 1731. [2], iv,
[2], 220 pp.
AAS copy.   3470

[Prince, Thomas], 1687-1758.
The Vade Mecum for America.
Boston, Kneeland and Green for
Henchman, 1732. [2], iv, [2], 220 pp.
AAS copy.   3598

Prince, Thomas, 1687-1758.
Young Abel Dead.
Boston, Henchman, 1732. [2], 24, [4], 4
pp.
(Signatured with 3597, q.v.)   3599

Prince, William, 1766-1842.
A Catalogue of Fruit-Trees. . . .
New-York, March 10, 1799.
[New York], Gaine, [1799]. Broadside.
MHS copy.   35955

Prince, William, 1766-1842.
To be Sold, by William Prince, at
Flushing-Landing . . . a Large Collection,
as follows, of Fruit Trees and Shrubs.
New York, Gaine, 1790. Broadside.
LOC copy.   22816

Prince, William, 1766-1842.
To be sold, by William Prince, at
Flushing-Landing, a Large Collection of
Fruit Trees, as follows. . . .
New York, Gaine, 1771.
LCP copy.   12206

Prince George's County is so very
Large. . . .
[Annapolis, 1748.] Broadside.
MdHS copy.   40474

The Prince of Brittany: an Historical
Novel.
New York, Harrison, 1798. [2], 144 pp.
Peabody Inst., Baltimore, copy.   34417

The Princely Convert. A Faithful Relation
of an Happy Conversion [by Cotton
Mather, ed., 1663-1728].
Boston, 1722. [2], 13 pp.]
AAS copy.   2385

Princeton University.
Laws of the College of New-Jersey . . .
April 1794.
Trenton, Collins, 1794. 38 pp.
AAS copy.   27392

Princeton University. Alumni Catalogue,
1770.
Catalogus. Eorum qui . . . Laurea . . .
Donati sunt ab anno 1748, ad annum 1770.
Philadelphia, Bradfords, 1770. Broadside.
PrU copy.   11770

Princeton University. Alumni Catalogue,
1773.

Catalogus eorum . . . Laurea alicujus
Gradus Donati sunt ab Anno 1748, ad
Annum 1773.
Philadelphia, Bradfords, [1773].
Broadside.
JCB copy.   12883

[Princeton University. Alumni Catalogue,
1786.
Catalogus Collegii Neo-Caesariensis.
Princeton, 1786. 12 pp.]
(The unique copy seen by Evans is
mislaid.)   19842

Princeton University. Alumni Catalogue,
1787.
Catalogus Collegii Neo-Caesarensis.
Princeton, Tod, 1787. 12 pp.
(Copy not available for reproduction.)
                                              45145

Princeton University. Alumni Catalogue,
1789.
Catalogus Collegii Naeo-Caesariensis.
Trenton, Collins, 1789. 16 pp.
AAS copy.   22005

Princeton University. Alumni Catalogue,
1792.
Catalogus Collegii Naeo-Caesariensis.
Trenton, Collins, 1792. 16 pp.
MHS copy.   24595

Princeton University. Alumni Catalogue,
1794.
Catalogus Collegii Naeo Caesariensis.
Trenton, Collins, 1794. 15 pp.
AAS copy.   47188

Princeton University. Alumni Catalogue,
1797.
Catalogus Collegii Naeo-Caesariensis.
Trenton, Day, 1797. 16 pp.
AAS copy.   48235

Princeton University. Alumni Catalogue,
1800.
Catalogus Collegii Naeso-Caesariensis.
Trenton, [N. J.], Sherman, Mershon &
Thomas, 1800. 16 pp.
PrU copy.   37203

Princeton University. Library.
A Catalogue of Books in the Library.
Woodbridge, 1760. 36 pp.
AAS copy.   8683

Princeton University. President.
(Circular.) Princeton, 179-. Sir, As
Complaints have Sometimes. . . .
[Trenton, 1796.] Broadside.
LOC copy.   30863

Princeton University. Theses, 1760.
Viro Praeclarissimo. . . . MDCCLX.
[Philadelphia], Steuart, 1760. Broadside.
LCP copy.   8684

Princeton University. Theses, 1762.
Viro Perhonorifico.
[Woodbridge], 1762. Broadside.
PrU copy.   9208

Princeton University. Trustees.
A General Account of the Rise and State
of the College.
New York, Parker, 1752. 8 pp.
PrU copy.   40640

Princeton University. Trustees.
To His Excellency Jonathan Belcher. . . .
An Address. . . . Sept. 24, 1755.
[New York? 1755.] Broadside.
NYPL ph. copy.   40793

Princeton University. Trustees.
To the Honourable the
Legislative-Council and General
Assembly. . . . February 9, 1796.
[Trenton, 1796.] Broadside.
LCP copy.   30864

The Principles of the Christian Religion
[by Philip Doddridge, 1702-1751]
Worcester, Thomas, 1799. 30, [1] pp.
AAS copy.   35415

The Principles of the Christian Religion.
Worcester, Mass., Thomas, 1799. 30,
[1] pp.
(Also entered as 35415, q. v.)   36163

The Principles of the Protestant Religion
Maintained.
Boston, Pierce, 1690. [10], 156 pp.
AAS copy.   502

Prindle, Chauncey, 1753-1833.
A Discourse, Delivered in Christ's Church
in Watertown on Friday, March 3, 1797.
Litchfield, Ct., Collier, [1797]. 30 pp.
JCB copy.   32723

Prindle, Joseph.
An Astronomical Diary; or, an Almanack
for . . . 1760.
New Haven, Parker. [16] pp.
(The unique copy is mislaid.)   8474

[Pringle, John], 1707-1802.
(D. N. B.)
The Life of General James Wolfe.
Boston, 1760. 36 pp.
AAS copy.   8702

[Pringle, John], 1707-1802.
The Life of General James Wolfe.
Portsmouth, 1760. 24 pp.
AHTS copy.   8703

Pringle, John Julius, 1753-1843.
An Oration, Delivered in St. Philip's
Church.
Charleston, S. C., Young, 1800. [2], 37
pp.
AAS copy.   38326

Printing-Office, in Hanover-Square,
January 1, 1769.
The Printer's Lads who Carry about the
New-York Gazette. . . .
[New York, 1769.] Broadside.
AAS copy.   41995

Printing-Office in Newbury-port. . . .
March 22d, 1786.
Proposals for Publishing A Complete
System of Arithmetic . . . by Nicholas
Pike.
[Newburyport, 1786.] Broadside.
LOC copy.   44954

Printing-Office Portsmouth, January 1,
1791. Proposals for Printing by
Subscription [by George Jerry Osborne,
1761-1800].
[Portsmouth, 1791.] Broadside.
AAS copy.   46247

Prioleau, Philip Gendron, d. 1814.
An Inaugural Dissertation.
Philadelphia, Bioren, 1798. 72 pp.
AAS copy.   34418

Prior, Rev. Mr.
A Funeral Sermon . . . on . . . Christiana
Lane.
Baltimore, S. & J. Adams, 1792. 12 pp.
AAS copy.   46552

Prior, Matthew, 1664-1721.
The Turtle and Sparrow.
Newburyport, Osborne, 1793. 23, [1] pp.
AAS copy.   26037

Prior, Thomas, 1682?-1751.
(D. N. B.)
The Authentick Narrative of the Success
of Tarwater.
Boston, Rogers & Fowle, 1749. 80 pp.
AAS copy.   6409

Prior, Thomas, 1682?-1751.
An Authentic Narrative of the Success of
Tarwater.
Providence, Carter, 1793. 75, [5] pp.
AAS copy.   26038

Prior, William, fl. 1738.
A Charge Delivered at the Ordination . . .
at Bridport. . . . Third Edition.
Boston, Bushell & Green for Gookin,
1748. 66, [1] pp.
AAS copy.   6229

Le Prise du Morne du Baton Rouge
New Orleans, Boudousquié, 1779.
(McMurtrie: New Orleans 30. no copy
located.)   43683

[The Prisoner's Magazine.
Boston, Russell, 1789.]
(Russell adv. the 4th issue of this serial;
no indication of imprint.)   22083

Des Prisons de Philadelphie [by François
Alexandre Frédéric, duc de la
Rochefoucauld Liancourt, 1747-1827].
Philadelphia, Moreau de Saint-Méry,
1796. 44 pp.
NYPL copy.   30673

[Pritchard, William, fl. 1782-1809.
Catalogue of a Collection of Books to be
sold October 24, 1788.
Philadelphia, 1788.]
(Adv. Pa. Packet, Oct. 24, 1788.)   21406

[Pritchard, William, fl. 1782-1809.
Catalogue of a Collection of Modern
Books. . . . November 17, 1787.
Philadelphia, Oswald, 1787.]
["Catalogues may be had," Ind. Gazette,
Nov. 17, 1787.)   20661

[Pritchard, William, fl. 1782-1809.
Catalogue of a Gentleman's Library . . .
will be sold, April 3d, 1789.
Philadelphia, 1789.]
(Adv. Pa. Packet Apr. 2, 1789.)   22081

[Pritchard, William, fl. 1782-1809.
Catalogue of a Sale of Books, by Auction
[Mar. 18, 1790.]
(Adv. Pa. Packet, Mar. 17, 1790.)   22815

Pritchard, William, fl. 1782-1809.
A Catalogue of a Scarce and Valuable
Collection of Books.
[Philadelphia, 1785.] [4], 43 pp.
NYPL copy.   19205

[Pritchard, William, fl. 1782-1809.
A Catalogue of a very Valuable and
Scarce Catalogue of Books.
Philadelphia, 1784.]
(Adv. in Freeman's Journal, June 9, 1784.)
                                              18740

[Pritchard, William, fl. 1782-1809.
A Catalogue of Ancient and Modern
Books for 1787.
Philadelphia, Oswald for Pritchard,
[1787]. 32, 8 pp.
University of Pittsburgh copy.   20660

[Pritchard, William, fl. 1782-1809.
Catalogue of Books by Auction . . .
December 6, 1786.
Philadelphia, Oswald, 1786.]
(Adv. Pa. Packet, Dec., 1786.)   19938

[Pritchard, William, fl. 1782-1809.
Catalogue of the Circulating Library
of. . . . Philadelphia, 1783.]
(Adv. Freeman's Journal, Oct. 1, 1783.)
                                              18143

[Pritchard, William, fl. 1782-1809.
Catalogue of two Extensive Libraries. . . .
November 28 . . . 1787.
Philadelphia, Oswald, 1787.]
(Adv. Pa. Packet, Nov. 28, 1787, etc.)
                                              20662

[Pritchard, William, fl. 1782-1809.
Literature. . . . Sale of Books by Auction
. . . February 13, 1792.
Philadelphia, Pritchard, 1792.]
(Entry apparently from an adv.)   24712

[Pritchard, William, fl. 1782-1809.
Pritchard's Auction Room. December 8th.
Philadelphia, Oswald, 1787.]
(Adv. Pa. Packet, Dec, 8, 1787, etc.) 20663

[Pritchard, William, fl. 1782-1809.
Pritchard's Auction Room, next Door to
the Post Office. . . .
Philadelphia, Oswald, 1787.]
(Adv. Pa. Packet, Dec. 17, 1787, etc.)
                                              20664

Pritchard, William, fl. 1782-1809.
William Prichard's Catalogue of Books,
&c.
[Philadelphia, Oswald for Prichard,
1788.] 22 pp.
JCB copy.   21405

Private Meetings Animated & Regulated
[by Cotton Mather, 1663-1728].
Boston, 1706. 23 pp.
WL copy.   1263

[The Private Tutor for Little Masters and
Misses.

New York, Gaine, 1762.]
(See Ford, Gaine, I, 108.)   9248

Private Vertue and Public Spirit
Display'd.
Boston, Kneeland, 1751. 20 pp.
AAS copy.   6767

Pro Bono [Publico] Ascot-Heath, Second
Meeting. . . . May 8th, 1781.
[New York], Robertson, [1781].
Broadside.
(The only recorded copy is imperfect.)
AAS copy.   44033

The Probation Odes of Jonathan Pindar
[by St. George Tucker, 1752-1827].
Philadelphia, Balch, 1796. [2], 103 pp.
LCP copy.   31320

Proceedings at a Numerous Meeting of
the Citizens of New-York. . . . December
17th, 1773.
[New York], Holt, [1773.] Broadside.
NYHS copy.   12894

Proceedings in Different Parts of
Virginia, on the Subject of the late
Conduct of the General Government.
n. p., [1798]. [2] pp.
LOC copy.   48584

Proceedings in the Case of Francis
Johnston.
Lancaster, Pa., Baileys, 1799. 27 pp.
(Also entered as 36065, q. v.)   36164

The Proceedings of some Members of the
Assembly, at Philadelphia, April 1728.
Vindicated.
[Philadelphia, 1728.] [4] pp.
HSP copy.   3096

The Proceedings of the Committee
Appointed to Examine into the
Importation of Goods . . . in February,
1770.
Annapolis, 1770. [4], xii, 27 pp.
LOC copy.   11720

The Proceedings of the Court-Martial on
the Trial of Admiral Byng [by Charles
Ferne, 1742-1794].
Boston, Green & Russell and Draper,
1757. 28 pp.
(The pagination given by Evans includes
7865.)
AAS copy.   7892

Procès Verbal de Célébration de la
fête du 25 Thermidor.
Philadelphia, Parent, [1794]. 8 pp.
JCB copy.   47189

Proces Verbal de la Fete qui a eu lieu le 2
Pluvoise.
Philadelphia, Parent, [1795?] 7 pp.
JCB copy.   47565

The Procession, with the Standard of
Faction.
[New York, 1770.] 4 pp.
LCP copy.   11827

[The Prodigal Daughter; or the
Disobedient Lady Reclaimed.
Boston, Fleet, 1736.]
(Adv. Boston Evening Post, May 31,
1736.)   4069

[The Prodigal Daughter.]
Boston, The New Printing-Office, over
against the Old Brick Meetin [1758].
[6] pp.
(Known only by this fragment.)
AAS copy.   41004

The Prodigal Daughter; being a Strange
and Wonder Relation of a Young Lady of
Bristol.
Boston, Printed and Sold in Back-Street,
[1767?]. 15 pp.
(The known copies are defective.)
AAS copy.   41754

The Prodigal Daughter: or a Strange and
Wonderful Relation.
Boston, printed at the Heart and Crown,
[1768?]. 8 + pp.
(No perfect copy located.)
PrU copy.   41867

The Prodigal Daughter. Or, a Strange and
Wonderful Relation.
Providence, [1768?]. 16 pp.
AAS copy.   41868

The Prodigal Daughter: or, a Strange and
Wonderful Relation.
Boston, [T. Fleet], [1769?]. 16 pp.
Emerson Greenaway copy.   41996

The Prodigal Daughter: or, a Strange and
Wonderful Relation.
Newport, 1770. 16 pp.
RIHS copy.   42158

The Prodigal Daughter; or a Strange and
Wonderful Relation.
Boston, Thomas, [1772?]. 15, [1] pp.
(Anderson cat. 1485 (Apr. 1, 1920), Item
796, describes a Ms. copy with authorship
attributed to "Rev. Mr. Williams.")
AAS copy.   12532

The Prodigal Daughter: or, A Strange and
Wonderful Relation.
Danvers, Russell, [1776?]. 16 pp.
PrU copy.   43144

The Prodigal Daughter: or, A Strange and
Wonderful Relation.
Boston, at the Bible and Heart, [1780?]
16 pp.
AAS copy.   43751

The Prodigal Daughter, or a Strange and
Wonderful Relation.
Worcester, Mass., 1787. 12 pp.
AAS copy.   45146

The Prodigal Daughter: or, a Strange and
Wonderful Relation.
[Boston], at the Bible & Heart, [179?]. 16
pp.
(No perfect copy known.)
d'Alté A. Welch copy.   45804

The Prodigal Daughter.
Boston, Russell, 1790. 16 pp.
BPL copy.   45978

The Prodigal Daughter; or, a Strange and
Wonderful Relation.
Boston, Russell, 1794. 16 pp.
AAS copy.   27563

The Prodigal Daughter: or, a Strange and
Wonderful Relation.
Boston, Bible & Heart, [1795]. 12+ pp.
(The only known copy is imperfect.)
d'Alté A. Welch copy.   47566

[The Prodigal Daughter.
Windsor, c. 1795.]
(McCorison 352; no copy known.)   47567

The Prodigal Daughter: or, The
Disobedient Lady Reclaimed.
Boston, Russell's Office, 1797. 16 pp.
AAS copy.   48236

The Prodigal Daughter, or a Strange and
Wonderful Relation.
Hartford, Ct., 1799. 12 pp.
AAS copy.   36166

The Prodigal Daughter, or a Strange and
Wonderful Relation.
New York, 1799. 8 pp.
JCB copy.   36167

[The Prodigal Daughters.
Stockbridge, Andrews, 1790.]
("Just re-published," Western Star, Aug.
10, 1790.)   22817

. . . Profit and Loss: an Elegy upon . . .
Mrs. Mary Gerrish [by John Danforth,
1660-1730].
[Boston, 1710.] Broadside.
BA copy.   39502

The Progress of Dulness [by John
Trumbull, 1750-1831].
[New Haven], 1772. 26 pp.
HC copy.   12585

The Progress of Dulness, Part First. . . .
Second Edition [by John Trumbull,
1750-1831].
[New Haven], 1773. 20 pp.
AAS copy.   13050

The Progress of Dulness, Part Second [by

John Trumbull, 1750-1831].
[New Haven], 1773. 27, [1] pp.
AAS copy.   13051

The Progress of Dulness. Part Third [by
John Trumbull, 1750-1831].
New Haven, 1773. 28 pp.
AAS copy.   13052

The Progress of Dulness [by John
Trumbull, 1750-1831].
Exeter, Ranlet, 1794. 72 pp.
AAS copy.   27822

The Progress of Science. A Poem [by
Samuel Dexter, 1761-1816].
[Boston], 1780. 10 pp.
AAS copy.   16759

Progress of Truth and Genius . . . the
Boy's Address who Carries the American
Mercury. . . . Hartford, January 1, 1800.
[Hartford, 1800.] Broadside.
NYHS copy.   36818

A Project for the Emission of an Hundred
Thousand Pounds [by Edward
Wigglesworth, 1693-1765].
Boston, Kneeland for Edwards, 1720. 16
pp.
AAS copy.   2168

A Projection for Erecting a Bank of
Credit.
[Boston], 1714. 22 pp.
(Apparently issued as a part of Evans
1685, q.v.)   1713

The Prompter; or, a Commentary on
Common Sayings.
See
Webster, Noah.   38329

The Prompter: to which is Added The
Whistle [by Noah Webster, 1758-1843].
Burlington, N.J., Neale, 1792. 50 pp.
Rutgers University copy.   25007

The Prompter; or, a Commentary on
Common Sayings [by Noah Webster,
1758-1843].
New York, Campbell, 1795. 108 pp.
AAS copy.   47677

The Prompter [by Noah Webster,
1758-1843].
n. p., 1798. 88 pp.
(No copy located.)   48755

A Prophecy, Lately Discovered; in which
are Predicted many Great and Terrible
Events.
[Philadelphia], 1763. 14 pp.
LCP copy.   9491

A Prophecy, or a Warning to all Sinners.
[Philadelphia, 1765.] Broadside.
HSP copy.   10148

The Prophet Nathan; or, Plain Friend.
Hudson, 1788. 30 pp.
LOC copy.   21407

Prophetic Conjectures on the French
Revolution.
Baltimore, Hayes for Richards, 1794. [2],
63, [1] pp.
EPFL copy.   47190

Prophetic Conjectures on the French
Revolution. . . . Third Edition.
Northampton, Butler, 1794. 96 pp.
(Not available, 1968.)   47191

Prophetic Conjectures on the French
Revolution.
Philadelphia, Young, 1794. 84 pp.
AAS copy.   27564

Prophetic Conjectures on the French
Revolution. . . . Second Edition.
Philadelphia, Young, 1794. 96 pp.
AAS copy.   27565

Prophetische Muthmassungen.
Philadelphia, Saur, 1794. [2], 88 pp.
AAS copy.   27566

The Prophet's Disguise, or Baptist's
Complaint.
Baltimore, Edwards, 1794. 55, [2] pp.
(Not located, 1968.)   47192

A Proposal for an Evangelical Treasury
[by Cotton Mather, 1663-1728].
[Boston, 1725.] 3 pp.
HC copy.   2671

Proposal, for Printing by Subscription, in
One Volume Octavo, Gospel News [by
Young & Minns, Boston].
[Boston, Young & Minns, 1794.]
Broadside.
AAS copy.   47333

A Proposal for Promoting Useful
Knowledge [by Benjamin Franklin,
1706-1790].
[Philadelphia, 1743.] [2] pp.
LOC copy.   5190

Proposal for Publishing by Subscription,
More Wonders [by William Carlton,
1771?-1805].
[Salem, 1796?]. Broadside.
EI copy.   47747

A Proposal to Supply the Trade with a
Medium of Exchange.
Boston, Edwards, 1737. [1], xi, pp.
BPL copy.   4189

Proposals for a Bank. . . . Providence,
September 6, 1791.
[Providence, 1791.] Broadside.
NHS copy.   46262

Proposals for a Subscription to Build a
Cathedral Church at Baltimore.
[Baltimore], Pechin, [1795]. 3 leaves.
(Parsons 137; no copy located.)   47568

Proposals for a Tobacco-Law, in the
Province of Maryland.
Annapolis, 1726. 21 pp.
NYHS copy.   2806

Proposals for Carrying on a Manufacture
in the Town of Boston.
[Boston, 1768.] [2] pp.
AAS ph. copy.   10828

Proposals, for Erecting and Encouraging a
new Manufactory.
[New York, 1770.] Broadside.
LCP copy.   11555

Proposals for Establishing a Circulating
Library, in Baltimore-Town.
[Baltimore, 1773.] Broadside.
MdHS copy.   12964

Proposals for Establishing an Association
for Working Mines.
Philadelphia, Smith, 1796. 22 pp.
LOC copy.   47886

Proposals for Printing by Subscription, a
Magazine entitled the Christian Herald,
or the Union Magazine.
[New York? 1795?] Broadside.
(Not located, 1968.)   47569

Proposals for Printing by Subscription
"Psalterium Americanum" [by Cotton
Mather, 1663-1728].
[Boston, 1718.] 7 pp.
BPL copy.   1904

Proposals for Printing by Subscription,
The Conquest of Canaan [by Timothy
Dwight, 1752-1817].
n.p., [1775]. Broadside.
AAS copy.   42808

[Proposals for Printing by Subscription
the Gentlemen and Ladies Military Closet
Furniture.
New York, Gaine, 1759.]
(Offered in N. Y. Mercury, Apr. 9, 1759.)
                                             8475

Proposals for Printing by Subscription the
History of Adjutant Trowel [by Samuel
Waterhouse].
[Boston, 1766.] 8 pp.
BA copy.   10519

Proposals for Printing by Subscription.
The History of . . . Sir Thomas Brazen [by
Samuel Waterhouse].
[Boston], 1760. 18, [1] pp.
AAS copy.   8763

Proposals for Printing by Subscription . . .
the Journal of . . . Job Scott [by Isaac

Collins, 1746-1817].
[New York, Collins, 1797.] Broadside.
HSP copy.   48091

Proposals for Printing by Subscription,
the Second Edition of "A Voyage to the
South Sea. . . ."
[Philadelphia, 1756.] Broadside.
HSP copy.   7771

Proposals for Printing by Subscription,
The Vision of Columbus.
[New York? 1787?] Broadside.
NYHS copy.   45148

Proposals for Publishing . . . a
Dissertation on Gravitation. . . . May 12,
1791.
[Baltimore, 1791.] Broadside.
LCP copy.   46263

Proposals for Publishing a Periodical . . .
entitled The American Library or
Universal Magazine.
[Philadelphia, 1796.] Broadside.
(Not located, 1968.)   47887

Proposals for Securing the Friendship of
the Five Nations [by Thomas Pownall,
1722-1805].
New York, Parker & Weyman, 1756.
14 pp., table.
LCP copy.   7767

[Proposals for the Opening of an
Insurance Office against Fires.
Charleston, S. C., 1732.]
(McMurtrie, S. C. Imprints, 6.)   40002

Proposals for the Preservation of Religion
[by Cotton Mather, 1663-1728].
[Boston, 1702.] 4 pp.
BPL copy.   1093

Proposals for the Speedy Settlement of the
Waste and Unappropriated Lands [by
Christopher Colles, 1738? - 1816].
New York, Loudon, 1785. 14 pp.
AAS copy.   18960

Proposals for Traffick and Commerce.
[New York], 1718. 24 pp.
NYHS copy.   1942

Proposals Offered to Consideration [Mar.
1, 1733].
[Boston, 1733.] 4 pp.
AAS ph. copy.   3717

Proposals Relating to the Education of
Youth in Pensilvania [by Benjamin
Franklin, 1706-1790].
Philadelphia, 1749. 32 pp.
AAS copy.   6321

Proposals to Amend and Perfect the
Policy of the Government.
[Baltimore], 1782. 36 pp.
APS copy.   17679

Proposals to Prevent Scalping, &c.
New York, Parker & Weyman, 1755. 8 pp.
LCP copy.   7551

Propositions made by the Sachems.
Boston, 1690. 12 pp.
MHS copy.   545

Propositions Respecting the Coinage of
Gold, Silver, and Copper.
[Philadelphia, 1791.] 12 pp.
LOC copy.   23906

Proprietors of the Kennebec Bridge.
Extracts from the Act of Incorporation
and By-laws of the. . . .
Hallowell, Edes, 1796. 16 pp.
MeHS copy.   30004

Proprietors of the Locks and Canals on
Merrimac River.
By-laws . . . Passed August 8, 1792.
Newburyport, Mycall, 1792. 14 pp.
MHS copy.   24715

Proprietors of the Locks and Canals on
the Merrimac River.
To the Inhabitants of the Town. . . .
October 29, 1794.
[Newburyport, 1794.] Broadside.
AAS copy.   27567

The Prospect before Us
See
Callender, James Thomson.   38330

A Prospect from the Congress-Gallery [by
William Cobbett, 1762-1835].
Philadelphia, Bradford, 1796. pp. [i]-iv,
[1]-12, 17-68, printed wraps.
AAS copy.   30229

A Prospect from the
Congress-Gallery. . . . Second Edition [by
William Cobbett, 1762-1835].
Philadelphia, Bradford, 1796. iv, 64 pp.
AAS copy.   30230

Prospect Hill. Bunker's Hill.
[Watertown, 1775?] [2] pp.
(Presumably printed on the back of a
handbill printed in England.)
MHS copy.   14414

A Prospective View of Death . . . the Trial
. . . of Levi Ames. . . . Sept. 10, 1773.
Boston, Russell, [1773]. Broadside.
AAS copy.   42485

Prospectus of a New Weekly Paper. . . .
The Port Folio [by Joseph Dennie,
1768-1812].
[Philadelphia, 1800.] Broadside.
HSP copy.   49059

Prospectus of a New Weekly Paper. . . .
The Port Folio [by Joseph Dennie,
1768-1812].
[Philadelphia, 1800.] [6] pp.
AAS copy.   49060

A Protest Entered into by Nine Patriotic
Members of the House of Lords . . . the 3d
of December 1774.
New York, Anderson, [1775]. 2 pp.
LOC copy.   14090

The Protest of Divers of the Inhabitants
of the Province [May 20, 1776].
[Philadelphia, 1776.] Broadside.
LCP copy.   15016

A Protest Presented to the House of
Assembly . . . Concerning the Sending Mr.
Franklin . . . to . . . Great-Britain. . . .
Oct. 26, 1764.
[Philadelphia, Bradford, 1764.]
Broadside.
HSP copy.   41484

[Protestant Episcopal Church in the U. S.
A., 1784.
At a Convention . . . held in New-York,
October 6th and 7th 1784.
[New York, 1784.] Broadside.]
(No copy of this printing located.) 18744

[Protestant Episcopal Church in the U. S.
A., 1784.
The Body now Assembled. . . .
[New York, 1784.] Broadside.]
(No copy of this printing located.) 18745

[Protestant Episcopal Church in the
U.S.A., 1794.
Constitution of the. . . .
Boston, 1794.]
(Entry from Sabin 66135.)   27579

Protestant Episcopal Church in the U. S.
A. Book of Common Prayer.
The Book of Common Prayer.
Philadelphia, Hall & Sellers, 1786. [363],
8 pp.
AAS copy.   19940

Protestant Episcopal Church in the
U.S.A. Book of Common Prayer.
Occasional Offices . . . taken from the
Book of Common Prayer.
Philadelphia, Hall & Sellers, 1790. [61]
pp.
LCP copy.   45979

Protestant Episcopal Church in the U. S.
A. Book of Common Prayer.
The Book of Common Prayer.
Philadelphia, Hall & Sellers, 1790. [327]
pp.
AAS copy.   22821

Protestant Episcopal Church in the U. S.
A. Book of Common Prayer.
The Book of Common Prayer.

Philadelphia, Hall & Sellers, 1791. [292],
221, [3] pp.
AAS copy.   23721

Protestant Episcopal Church in the
U.S.A. Book of Common Prayer.
The Book of Common Prayer.
New York, Gaine, 1793. [376], 171, [5]
pp. 12 mo.
AAS copy.   26042

Protestant Episcopal Church in the
U.S.A. Book of Common Prayer.
The Book of Common Prayer.
New York, Gaine, 1793. [424], 204, [3]
pp.
AAS copy.   26043

Protestant Episcopal Church in the
U.S.A. Book of Common Prayer.
The Book of Common Prayer.
Boston, Manning & Loring for Thomas &
Andrews, 1794. [396], 244, [4] pp.
AAS copy.   27575

Protestant Episcopal Church in the
U.S.A. Book of Common Prayer.
The Book of Common Prayer.
New York, Gaine, 1794. [324], 74, [2] pp.
AAS copy.   27576

Protestant Episcopal Church in the
U.S.A. Book of Common Prayer.
The Book of Common Prayer.
New York, Gaine, 1794. [324], 171, [5]
pp.
AAS copy.   27577

[Protestant Episcopal Church in the
U.S.A. Book of Common Prayer.
The Book of Common Prayer.
Philadelphia, Hall & Sellers, 1794.]
(Imprint assumed by Evans from "for sale
by" advs.)   27578

Protestant Episcopal Church in the
U.S.A. Book of Common Prayer.
The Book of Common Prayer.
New York, Gaine, 1795. [194] pp.
AAS copy.   29362

Protestant Episcopal Church in the
U.S.A. Book of Common Prayer.
The Book of Common Prayer.
Philadelphia, Young & Ormrod, 1795.
[366], 171 pp.
AAS copy.   29363

Protestant Episcopal Church in the
U.S.A. Book of Common Prayer.
Morning and Evening Prayer.
Portsmouth, N. H., Peirce, 1795. 215 pp.
AAS copy.   29365

Protestant Episcopal Church in the
U.S.A. Book of Common Prayer.
The Book of Common Prayer.
New York, Allen, 1797. [186], 168, [2]
pp.
AAS copy.   32727

Protestant Episcopal Church in the
U.S.A. Book of Common Prayer.
The Book of Common Prayer.
New York, Gaine, 1798. [356], 171, [5]
pp.
AAS copy.   34420

[Protestant Episcopal Church in the
U.S.A. Book of Common Prayer.
The Book of Common Prayer.
Charleston, S. C., Young, 1799. [368] pp.]
(No such edition located.)   36175

Protestant Episcopal Church in the
U.S.A. Book of Common Prayer.
The Book of Common Prayer.
Boston, Thomas & Andrews for I.
Thomas, etc., 1800. [378], 70, [2] pp.
AAS copy.   38334

Protestant Episcopal Church in the
U.S.A. Book of Common Prayer.
The Book of Common Prayer.
New York, Davises for Duyckinck and
Arden, 1800. [368], 217, [3] pp.
AAS copy.   38335

Protestant Episcopal Church in the
U.S.A. Book of Common Prayer.
The Book of Common Prayer.

Philadelphia, Hall & Sellers, 1800. [363]
pp.
LCP copy.   38336

Protestant Episcopal Church in the
U.S.A. Book of Common Prayer.
The Book of Common Prayer.
Wilmington [Del.], Brynberg, 1800.
[370], 26, [2] pp.
(No perfect copy located.)
HEH copy.   38337

Protestant Episcopal Church in the U. S.
A. Catechism.
A Catechism from the Book of Common
Prayer.
Philadelphia, Poulson, 1792. 8 pp.
AAS copy.   24721

Protestant Episcopal Church in the
U.S.A. Catechism.
The Protestant Episcopal Church
Catechism.
New York, Davis, 1795. 29 pp., 1 plate.
HC copy.   29366

Protestant Episcopal Church in the
U.S.A. Catechism.
Protestant Episcopal Church Catechism.
Johnstown, N. Y., Dockstader, 1797. 32+
pp.
(The only recorded copy is apparently
imperfect at the end.)
NYHS copy.   32728

Protestant Episcopal Church in the
U.S.A. Catechism.
The Catechism of the Protestant
Episcopal Church.
Philadelphia, Ormrod, 1799. 8 pp.
LCP copy.   36176

Protestant Episcopal Church in the
U.S.A. Catechism.
The Catechism of the Protestant
Episcopal Church.
Philadelphia, Ormrod, 1800. 17 pp.
LCP copy.   38338

Protestant Episcopal Church in the
U.S.A. Connecticut (Diocese), 1785.
The Address of the Episcopal Clergy.
New Haven, [1785]. 8, 18, 15, 5 pp.
AAS copy.   19207

Protestant Episcopal Church in the
U.S.A. Connecticut (Diocese), 1789.
Proposals for Instituting an Episcopal
Academy. . . . January 16th, 1789.
[New Haven, 1789.] Broadside.
CHS copy.   45565

Protestant Episcopal Church in the
U.S.A. Connecticut (Diocese), 1792.
The Constitution . . . Agreed upon. . . .
June 6, 1792.
[New Haven, 1792.] Broadside.
NYHS copy.   46553

Protestant Episcopal Church in the
U.S.A. Connecticut (Diocese), 1792.
Journal of the Proceedings of the Bishop,
Clergy, and Laity . . . in their Conventions
Held in June, 1792, 1793, 1794 and 1795.
Newfield, Conn., Beach & Jones, 1795. 16
pp.
(Evans assumed title and imprint from an
adv.)
AAS copy.   29358

[Protestant Episcopal Church in the U. S.
A. Constitution.
Constitution of the Protestant Episcopal
Church.
Philadelphia, 1791.]
(From an adv.)   23722

Protestant Episcopal Church in the U. S.
A. Constitution.
The Constitution and Canons . . . together
with the Ecclesiastical Constitution for
. . . Massachusetts.
Boston, Fleets, 1800. 46 pp.
AAS copy.   38332

Protestant Episcopal Church in the U. S.
A. Delaware (Diocese), 1791.
Journal of the Proceedings . . . December,
1791.
New York, Gaine, 1791. 14 pp.
AAS copy.   23718

[Protestant Episcopal Church in the

U.S.A. Delaware (Diocese), 1792.
Journal of the Proceedings of a
Convention. . . . 1792.
New York, Gaine, 1792?]
(Source of entry unknown; apparently a
ghost.)   24716

Protestant Episcopal Church in the
U.S.A. General Convention, 1785.
Journal of a Convention.
Philadelphia, Hall & Sellers, 1785. [2], 18
pp.
AAS copy.   19209

Protestant Episcopal Church in the U. S.
A. General Convention, 1786
(Wilmington). Journal of a Convention
. . . at Wilmington.
Philadelphia, Crukshank [1786]. 22 pp.
AAS copy.   19942

Protestant Episcopal Church in the
U.S.A. General Convention, 1786
(Philadelphia).
Journal of a Convention . . . in . . .
Philadelphia.
Philadelphia, Hall & Sellers, 1786. 18 pp.
AAS copy.   19941

Protestant Episcopal Church in the
U.S.A. General Convention, 1789.
Journal . . . July 28th to August 8th, 1789.
Philadelphia, Hall & Sellers, 1789. 31 pp.
AAS copy.   22084

Protestant Episcopal Church in the U. S.
A. General Convention, 1789.
Journal of the Proceedings of the Bishops.
Philadelphia, Hall & Sellers, 1790. 43 pp.
AAS copy.   22822

Protestant Episcopal Church in the U. S.
A. General Convention, 1792.
Journal of the Proceedings of the Bishop.
New York, Gaine, 1792. 35 pp.
AAS copy.   24722

Protestant Episcopal Church in the
U.S.A. General Convention, 1795.
Journal of the Proceedings . . . in . . .
Philadelphia . . . September 8, to . . . Sept.
18, 1795.
Philadelphia, Ormrod and Conrad, 1795.
44 pp.
AAS copy.   29364

Protestant Episcopal Church in the
U.S.A. General Convention, 1799.
Journal of the Proceedings . . . in . . .
Philadelphia, 1799.
Philadelphia, Ormrod, 1799. 80 pp.
AAS copy.   36177

Protestant Episcopal Church in the
U.S.A. General Convention, 1792.
Committee on Missions.
To the Members of the Protestant
Episcopal Church. . . . April 22, 1793.
[Philadelphia, 1793.] 7 pp.
AAS copy.   26046

[Protestant Episcopal Church in the
U.S.A. Liturgy and Ritual.
The Form and Manner of Making . . .
Bishops.
New York, Gaine, 1793. 42 pp.]
(No copy located.)   26044

Protestant Episcopal Church in the
U.S.A. Liturgy and Ritual.
Tables of Lessons of Holy Scripture.
[Philadelphia? 1790?] [60] pp.
JCB copy.   45980

Protestant Episcopal Church in the
U.S.A. Liturgy and Ritual.
Tables of Lessons of Holy Scripture.
[Boston, Thomas & Andrews, 1792.]
[68] pp.
(See note in Evans, IX, 139.)
AAS copy.   26045

Protestant Episcopal Church in the U. S.
A. Maryland (Diocese) 1784.
An Address to the Members. . . .
Published . . . June 22d, 1784.
Baltimore, Goddard, 1784. 35 pp.
AAS copy.   18742

Protestant Episcopal Church in the
U.S.A. Maryland (Diocese), 1784.
At a Convention . . . at Chester . . .
October 1784.

[Baltimore, 1784.] Broadside.
LCP copy.   44594

Protestant Episcopal Church in the
U.S.A. Maryland (Diocese), 1788.
At a Meeting . . . at Baltimore, May 29,
1788.
[Baltimore, 1788.] 7 pp.
AAS copy.   45346

Protestant Episcopal Church in the
U.S.A. Maryland (Diocese), 1789.
Journal of a Convention . . . in . . .
Baltimore . . . June 5th, 1789.
Baltimore, Goddard, 1789. 22 pp.
MdDL copy.   45566

Protestant Episcopal Church in the
U.S.A. Maryland (Diocese), 1790.
Journal of the Proceedings . . . at Easton
. . . May [1790].
Wilmington, [Del.], Andrews, Craig &
Brynberg, 1790. 39 pp.
AAS copy.   45981

Protestant Episcopal Church in the U. S.
A. Maryland (Diocese), 1791.
Journal of the Proceedings . . . June 16, to
. . . 18, 1791.
Baltimore, Goddard & Angell, 1791. 15
pp.
AAS copy.   23719

Protestant Episcopal Church in the
U.S.A. Maryland (Diocese), 1792.
Journal of the Proceedings . . . May 31 . . .
June 2, 1792.
Baltimore, Goddard & Angell, 1729.
19 pp.
AAS copy.   24717

Protestant Episcopal Church in the
U.S.A. Maryland (Diocese), 1793.
Journal of the Proceedings of a
Convention. . . . 1793.
Baltimore, Angell, 1793. 28 pp.
NYPL copy.   26039

Protestant Episcopal Church in the
U.S.A. Maryland (Diocese), 1794.
The Convention . . . to the Vestries . . .
June 14, 1794.
[Baltimore, 1794.] 8 pp.
AAS copy.   27569

Protestant Episcopal Church in the
U.S.A. Maryland (Diocese), 1794.
Journal . . . of a Convention . . . in
Baltimore . . . June 12th, to . . . June 14.
Baltimore, Edwards, 1794. 17 pp.
AAS copy.   27568

Protestant Episcopal Church in the
U.S.A. Maryland (Diocese), 1795.
Journal of a Convention . . . in
Baltimore-Town . . . May . . . 1795.
Baltimore, Edwards & Allen, 1795. 15 pp.
AAS copy.   47570

Protestant Episcopal Church in the
U.S.A. Maryland (Diocese), 1797.
Journal of a Convention . . . at Easton . . .
May . . . 1796.
Baltimore, Hayes, 1797. 24 pp.
AAS copy.   48237

Protestant Episcopal Church in the
U.S.A. Maryland (Diocese), 1798.
Journal of a Convention . . . in Baltimore.
Baltimore, Sower, 1798. 12 pp.
AAS copy.   48585

Protestant Episcopal Church in the
U.S.A. Maryland (Diocese), 1799.
Journal of a Convention . . . at Easton.
Easton, Md., Cowan, 1799. 8 pp.
AAS copy.   36171

Protestant Episcopal Church in the
U.S.A. Maryland (Diocese), 1800.
Journal of a Convention . . . at Baltimore
. . . 1800.
n.p., n.d. 12 pp.
MdHS copy.   38331

Protestant Episcopal Church in the U. S.
A. Massachusetts (Diocese), 1790.
At a Convention of Clergy and
Lay-Deputies. . . .
Newburyport, Mycall, [1790]. Broadside.
AAS copy.   22818

Protestant Episcopal Church in the

U.S.A. Massachusetts (Diocese), 1790.
Ecclesiastical Constitution . . . Approved
. . . at Salem, Mass., Oct . . . 1790.
[Salem? 1790.] Broadside.
(No copy available for reproduction.)
     45982

[Protestant Episcopal Church in the U. S.
A. Massachusetts (Diocese), 1792.
Journal of the Proceedings of a
Convention.
Boston, 1792?]
(Apparently not printed at this time.)
     24718

Protestant Episcopal Church in the U. S.
A. New Jersey (Diocese), 1787.
Proceedings of the Convention . . . in . . .
New Jersey.
Trenton, 1787. 31 pp.
AAS copy.   20666

Protestant Episcopal Church in the
U.S.A., New Jersey (Diocese), 1788.
Proceedings of the Fifth Convention . . .
June, 1788.
[Trenton, 1788.] pp. [2], 44-48.
(There is a troublesome facsimile on
modern paper.)
PrU copy.   21408

Protestant Episcopal Church in the
U.S.A. New Jersey (Diocese) 1789.
Proceedings of the Sixth Convention . . .
Elizabeth-Town . . . June 1789.
n.p., n.d. pp. 51-57.
(No contemporary printing could be
located; this is the 1890 ed.)
AAS copy.   45567

Protestant Episcopal Church in the
U.S.A. New Jersey (Diocese), 1790.
Proceedings of a Convention . . . in
Trenton, June . . . 1790.
Trenton, Collins, 1790. 22 pp.
(Only this reprint of 1905 located.)
AAS copy.   45983

Protestant Episcopal Church in the U. S.
A. New Jersey (Diocese), 1791.
Proceedings of a Convention . . . in
Newark.
Newark, Woods, 1791. 15 pp.
LOC copy.   23720

[Protestant Episcopal Church in the
U.S.A. New Jersey (Diocese), 1792.
Proceedings of a Convention, 1792.
Newark, Woods, 1792.]
(A ghost of 26040, q. v.)   24719

Protestant Episcopal Church in the
U.S.A. New Jersey (Diocese), 1792.
Proceedings of a Convention . . . in . . .
New-Brunswick . . . June, 1792.
New Brunswick, Arnett & Blauvelt, 1793.
pp. [22]-29.
AAS copy.   26040

Protestant Episcopal Church in the
U.S.A. New Jersey (Diocese), 1793.
Proceedings of a Convention . . . in . . .
Burlington . . . June, 1793.
Burlington, Neale, 1793. pp. [30]-44.
AAS copy.   26041

Protestant Episcopal Church in the
U.S.A. New Jersey (Diocese), 1794.
Proceedings of a Convention . . . in . . .
Perth-Amboy . . . June, 1794.
Elizabethtown, 1794. pp. [46]-53.
AAS copy.   27570

Protestant Episcopal Church in the
U.S.A. New Jersey (Diocese), 1795.
Proceedings of the Convention . . . in . . .
Shrewsbury, on the Third and Fourth
Days of June, 1795.
Newark, N. J., Woods, 1795. pp. [54]-61.
AAS copy.   29359

Protestant Episcopal Church in the
U.S.A. New Jersey (Diocese), 1796.
Proceedings of a Convention . . . at
Elizabeth-Town . . . June, 1796.
Elizabethtown, Kollock, 1796. pp. [62]-81.
(A copy of the 1880 reprint is reproduced,
because no copy of the original printing
could be located.)   31057

Protestant Episcopal Church in the
U.S.A. New Jersey (Diocese), 1797.
Proceedings of a Convention . . . at

Trenton, the Seventh of June, 1797.
Philadelphia, Ormrod & Conrad, 1797. pp.
[81]-89, [3], [1]-15.
AAS copy.   32725

Protestant Episcopal Church in the
U.S.A. New Jersey (Diocese), 1798.
Proceedings of a Convention. . . . At
Newark.
Newark, N. J., Halsey, 1798. 12 pp.
AAS copy.   34419

Protestant Episcopal Church in the
U.S.A. New Jersey (Diocese), 1799.
Proceedings of a Convention . . . at
New-Brunswick . . . June, 1799.
Newark, N. J., Halsey, 1799. 8 pp.
AAS copy.   36172

Protestant Episcopal Church in the
U.S.A. New Jersey (Diocese), 1799.
Proceedings of a Special Convention . . .
Perth-Amboy . . . Oct. 1799.
Elizabethtown, Kollock, 1799. 16 pp.
AAS copy.   36173

Protestant Episcopal Church in the
U.S.A. New Jersey (Diocese), 1800.
Proceedings of a Convention . . . at
Burlington.
Trenton, N. J., Craft, 1800. 8 pp.
AAS copy.   38333

Protestant Episcopal Church in the
U.S.A. New York (Diocese), 1785.
Proceedings of the Convention . . . held in
the city of New-York . . . June 22d, 1785.
New York, Gaine, 1787. 24 pp.
AAS copy.   20667

Protestant Episcopal Church in the U. S.
A. New York (Diocese), 1787.
Journal of the Convention . . . November
6th, 1787 . . . October 13th, 1791.
New York, Gaine, 1792. 32 pp.
AAS copy.   24720

Protestant Episcopal Church in the
U.S.A. New York (Diocese), 1792.
Journal of . . . a Convention . . . in Trinity
Church, in the City of New-York . . . 1792.
New York, Gaine, 1794. 8 pp.
NYHS copy.   27571

Protestant Episcopal Church in the
U.S.A. New York (Diocese), 1793.
Journal of . . . a Convention . . . in Trinity
Church, in the City of New-York . . . 1793.
New York, Gaine, 1794. 8 pp.
AAS copy.   27572

Protestant Episcopal Church in the
U.S.A. New York (Diocese), 1794.
Journal of . . . a Convention . . . in Trinity
Church, in the City of New-York . . . 1794.
New York, Gaine, 1794. 8 pp.
AAS copy.   27573

Protestant Episcopal Church in the
U.S.A. New York (Diocese), 1796.
Journal of the Proceedings . . . in Trinity
Church.
New York, Gaine, 1796. 12 pp.
NYSoc. copy.   31058

Protestant Episcopal Church in the
U.S.A. New York (Diocese), 1797.
Journal of . . . a Convention . . . in Trinity
Church, in the City of New York . . . One
Thousand Seven Hundred and
Ninety-Seven.
New York, Gaine, 1797. 7, [1] pp.
AAS copy.   32726

Protestant Episcopal Church in the
U.S.A. North Carolina (Diocese). 1793.
Circular. Dearly Beloved. . . . the 21st Day
of November, 1793.
[Edenton? 1793.] Broadside.
N. C. Archives copy.   46856

Protestant Episcopal Church in the U.S.A.
Pennsylvania (Diocese), 1784.
At a Meeting . . . in Philadelphia on . . .
25th day of May, 1784.
[Philadelphia, 1784.] Broadside.
HSP copy.   18743

Protestant Episcopal Church in the
U.S.A. Pennsylvania (Diocese) 1785.
An Act of Association of the Clergy and
Congregations.

[Philadelphia, 1785] 3 pp.
NYHS copy.   44780

Protestant Episcopal Church in the U. S.
A. Pennsylvania (Diocese), 1790.
Journal of the Meetings. . . .
Philadelphia, Hall & Sellers, 1790. 26 pp.
AAS copy.   22819

Protestant Episcopal Church in the
U.S.A. Pennsylvania (Diocese), 1791.
Journals of Five Conventions . . . 1791 . . .
1795.
Philadelphia, Ormrod & Conrad, 1795. 31
pp.
AAS copy.   29360

[Protestant Episcopal Church in the
U.S.A. Pennsylvania (Diocese), 1794.
Minutes of the Proceedings of a
Convention.
Philadelphia, 1794.]
(An error by Evans.)   27574

Protestant Episcopal Church in the
U.S.A. Pennsylvania (Diocese), 1795.
An Act of Association of the Clergy and
Congregation.
[Philadelphia? 1795?] 3 pp.
(Not located, 1968.)   47571

Protestant Episcopal Church in the
U.S.A. Pennsylvania (Diocese) 1795.
Canons of the . . . Church, in . . .
Pennsylvania.
Philadelphia, Ormrod & Conrad, 1795. 7
pp.
AAS copy.   47572

Protestant Episcopal Church in the
U.S.A. Pennsylvania (Diocese) 1796.
Journal of the Twelfth [Fourteenth]
Convention. . . . 1796 [-1798].
[Philadelphia, 1798?] [10] pp.
AAS copy.   48586

Protestant Episcopal Church in the
U.S.A. Pennsylvania (Diocese), 1799.
Journal of the Fifteenth [-Seventeenth]
Convention . . . 1799 . . . 1800.
[Philadelphia, 1800.] [4], [4] pp.
AAS copy.   36174

Protestant Episcopal Church in the
U.S.A. Vermont (Diocese) 1791.
Minutes, &c. at a Convention . . . in
Sandgate, February 23, 1791.
[Bennington? 1791.] 8 pp.
(The only known copy is imperfect.)
NYHS copy.   46264

Protestant Episcopal Church in the
U.S.A. Vermont (Diocese), 1795.
A True Copy of the Proceedings of John
A. Graham.
Boston, Young & Minns, 1795. 56 pp.
AAS copy.   29361

Protestant Episcopal Church in the
U.S.A. Virginia (Diocese), 1785.
Journal of a Convention . . . in . . .
Richmond . . . May 18, 1785.
Richmond, Dixon & Holt, 1785. 23 pp.
NYPL copy.   44781

Protestant Episcopal Church in the
U.S.A., Virginia (Diocese), 1786.
Journal of a Convention . . . May, 1786.
Richmond, Nicolson, [1786]. 16 pp.
NYPL copy.   44955

Protestant Episcopal Church in the
U.S.A. Virginia (Diocese), 1787.
Journal of a Convention . . . in Richmond,
May 16, 1787.
Richmond, Nicolson, 1787. 9 pp.
NYPL copy.   45149

Protestant Episcopal Church in the
U.S.A. Virginia (Diocese), 1789.
Journal of a Convention . . . in . . .
Richmond . . . May . . . 1789.
Richmond, Nicolson, [1789]. 14 pp.
NYPL copy.   45568

Protestant Episcopal Church in the
U.S.A. Virginia (Diocese), 1791.
Journal of a Convention . . . in . . .
Richmond . . . May . . . 1791.
Richmond, Nicolson, [1791]. 16 pp.
NYPL copy.   46265

Protestant Episcopal Church in the
U.S.A. Virginia (Diocese), 1792.

Journal of a Convention . . . in . . .
Richmond, May 3, 1792.
Richmond, Nicolson, [1792]. 8 pp.
NYPL copy.   46554

Protestant Episcopal Church in the U. S.
A. Virginia (Diocese), 1793.
Journal of a Convention. . . . Richmond,
May 2, 1793.
Richmond, Va., Nicolson, [1793]. 31, [1],
16, [1] pp.
AAS copy.   46857

Protestant Episcopal Church in the
U.S.A. Virginia (Diocese), 1794.
Journal of a Convention . . . in . . .
Richmond, May 6, 1794.
Richmond, Nicolson, [1794]. 8 pp.
NYPL copy.   47193

Protestant Episcopal Church in the
U.S.A. Virginia (Diocese), 1799.
Journal of a Convention . . . in . . .
Richmond, May 7, 1799.
Richmond, Nicholson, [1799]. 16 pp.
NYPL copy.   36178

The Protestant Tutor [by Benjamin
Harris, fl. 1673-1720].
Boston, 1685. [19], 10 pp.
AAS copy.   387

A Protestant's Resolution.
Boston, Gookin, 1746. [2], 44 pp.
BA copy.   5858

Protestation gegen die Bestellung.
[Philadelphia, Miller, 1764.] Broadside.
HSP copy.   9803

A Protestation of the Members of the
Protestant Lutheran and Reformed
Religion.
[Philadelphia, 1742.] Broadside.
HSP copy.   5043

A Protestation Presented to the Synod of
Philadelphia, June 1. 1741.
Philadelphia, Franklin, 1741. 16 pp.
AAS copy.   4704

[A Protestation Presented to the Synod of
Philadelphia, May 29, 1742.
Philadelphia, 1742. 10 pp.]
(Title from Sabin.)   4932

Protestations des Colons Patriotes de
Saint-Domingue, Refugies a Philadelphia.
[Philadelphia, 1794]. 4 pp.
JCB copy.   27665

Proud, Robert, 1728-1813.
The History of Pennsylvania. . . . Volume
I.
Philadelphia, Poulson, 1797. 508 pp., 1
plate.
AAS copy.   32729

Proud, Robert, 1728-1813.
The History of Pennsylvania. . . . Volume
II.
Philadelphia, Poulson, 1798. 373, [1], 146
pp., 1 map.
AAS copy.   34421

Proudfit, Alexander Moncrief, 1770-1843.
The Importance of Family Religion.
Salem, N. Y., Dodd, 1799. 23 pp.
AAS copy.   36179

Proudfit, Alexander Moncrief, 1770-1843.
A Sermon, Preached before the Northern
Missionary Society.
Albany, N. Y., 1798. 38, [1] pp.
AAS copy.   34422

Proudfit, Jacob.
Dissertatio Medica Inauguralis.
Philadelphia, Aitkens, 1790. 29 pp.
LCP copy.   22823

[Prout, Timothy, 1721-1782.
(Sibley, XI.)
Diana's Shrines Turned into Ready
Money.
New York, 1773. 23 pp.
AAS copy.   12965

Providence, R.I., Amicable Fire Society.
Articles of the. . . .
Providence, Carter, [1783]. Broadside.
AAS copy.   44782

[Providence, R. I. Association of
Mechanicks.
To the Hon. General Assembly, June. The
Memorial of the Providence Association.
Newport, Farnsworth, 1799.]
(Apparently an incorrect entry for 35434,
q. v.)   36181

Providence, R. I. Baptist Church.
Scheme of a Lottery. . . . June 25, 1774.
Providence, [1774]. Broadside.
JCB copy.   13559

Providence, R. I. Beneficent
Congregational Church.
A Short Catechism.
Providence, Wheeler, 1798. 36 pp.
AAS copy.   34424

Providence, R. I. Benevolent
Congregational Society.
The Act of Incorporation.
Providence, 1771. [8], 14, [1] pp.
AAS copy.   12207

Providence, R. I. Cathedral of St. John.
The Act of Incorporation of. . . .
Providence, Carter & Wilkinson, 1795. vii,
[1], 12 pp.
RIHS copy.   29368

Providence, R.I. Clergy.
A Friendly Address to the Inhabitants.
. . . December 19, 1794.
[Providence], Wheeler, [1794].
Broadside.
RIHS copy.   47194

Providence, R. I. Committee of
Correspondence, 1779.
Providence, July 26, 1779. Sir: By the
Annexed Vote. . . .
Providence, Carter, [1779.] Broadside.
RIHS copy.   43684

Providence, R. I. Convention, 1776-1777.
Extract from the Minutes of the
Committees.
n.p., [1777]. 10 pp.
MHS copy.   43346

Providence, R. I. Convention, 1796.
At a Convention of Delegates from Eight
Towns . . . August, 1796.
[Providence, 1796.] [2] pp.
RIHS copy.   31061

Providence, R. I. First Baptist Church.
To all Persons to whom these Presents
shall come. . . .
[Providence, c. 1777.] Form.
AAS copy.   42040

Providence, R. I. House Carpenters.
Rules for House-Carpenters Work.
Providence, Carter & Wilkinson, 1796. 29,
[3] pp.
HEH copy.   31062

Providence, R. I. King's Chapel.
This Evening, the Tenth of December . . .
the New Organ. . . .
[Providence, 1771.] Broadside.
JCB copy.   42271

Providence, R. I., Library.
Catalogue of all the Books, Belonging
to. . . .
Providence, 1768. 24 pp.
JCB copy.   11051

Providence, R. I., Marine Society.
Charter, Laws, &, of the. . . .
Providence, R. I., Wheeler, 1799. 22 pp.
AAS copy.   36183

Providence, R. I. Meeting of Committees,
1796.
Providence, July 27, 1796. Gentlemen, At
a Meeting. . . .
[Providence, 1796.] Broadside.
RIHS copy.   31060

Providence, R. I. Merchants, 1767.
Providence, December 2, 1767. Luxury
and Extravagance . . . we will not . . .
Import. . . .
[Providence, 1767.] Broadside.
RIHS copy.   41755

Providence, R.I. Merchants, 1793.
Wharfage and Storage of Goods . . . to be
in Force from November 9, 1793.

[Providence, 1793.] Broadside.
BrU copy. 26047

Providence, R. I. Ordinances, etc., 1799.
At a Town-Council. . . . An Act to Prevent
the Spreading of the Small-Pox.
[Providence, 1799.] Broadside.
JCB copy. 36180

Providence, R. I. Parsonage Lottery.
Scheme of a Lottery. . . . Providence,
November 5, 1771.
[Providence], Carter, [1771]. Broadside.
RIHS copy. 42272

Providence, R. I. St. John's Lodge.
Providence, November, 1796. Brother. . . .
[Providence, 1796.] Broadside.
JCB copy. 31063

Providence, R. I. School Committee.
At a Meeting . . . the 16th of January, A.
D. 1786.
[Providence], Carter, [1786]. Broadside.
JCB copy. 19943

Providence, R.I. Sheriff, 1782.
One Hundred Pounds Reward, Escaped
last Night . . . William Prentice . . .
September 7. 1782.
[Providence, 1782.] Broadside.
(Not located 1967.)
Town Papers, Providence City Hall, copy.
44249

Providence, R. I. Theater, 1762.
[A play bill
Providence, Goddard, 1762.] Broadside.
(See Alden 265.) 41301

Providence, R. I., Theater, 1795.
New Theatre, Providence. On Wednesday
Evening, September 16th. . . .
[Providence, 1795.] Broadside.
RIHS copy. 29370

Providence, R. I. Theater, 1796.
By Desire of the . . . Masons . . . June 24,
1796, will be Presented . . . The
Benevolent Hebrew.
[Providence, Wheeler, [1796]. Broadside.
RIHS copy. 47888

Providence, R. I. Town Meeting, 1771.
At a Town-Meeting . . . the Committee
. . . in Case of Fire. . . . April 17, 1771.
[Providence], Carter, [1771]. Broadside.
(Alden 469; no copy located.) 42273

Providence, R. I. Town Meeting, 1779.
Providence, July 3, 1779. At a Meeting of
the Freemen [on Currency].
Providence, Carter, [1779]. Broadside.
AAS copy. 19430

Providence, R. I. Town Meeting, 1796.
At a General Assembly of the State of
Rhode-Island. . . . June 18, A.D. 1796. . . .
At a Town-Meeting on the Twenty-
Ninth. . . .
[Providence], Wheeler, [1796]. Broadside.
AAS copy. 31095

Providence, R. I. Town Meeting, 1796.
(Circular) Providence, June 29th, 1796.
Gentlemen. . . .
Providence, Wheeler, [1796]. Broadside.
RIHS copy. 31059

Providence, R. I. Treasurer.
Schedule of the Expenses of the Town . . .
from August 1, 1799 to August 1, 1800.
[Providence], Carter, [1800]. Broadside.
RIHS copy. 38339

Providence, R. I. United Fire Society.
The Constitution . . . formed in
Providence, March 2d, 1786.
[Providence], Wheeler, [1786]. Broadside.
AAS copy. 44956

Providence, R. I. Washington Insurance Co.
Charter of the. . . .
[Providence], Wheeler, 1800. 12 pp.
(Also entered as 38344, q.v.) 39016

Providence Country, R. I. Sheriff.
Two Hundred Silver Dollars Reward . . .
Broke Goal . . . George Haswell. . . .
Nov. 19, 1780.
Providence, Carter, [1780]. Broadside.
(No copy located.) 43870

Providence, April 2, 1794. By last
Evening's Mail. . . .
Providence, Carter & Wilkinson, [1794].
Broadside.
RIHS copy. 27583

Providence, April 13th, 1799. Sir, you
have Probably been Informed. . . .
[Providence, 1799.] Broadside.
RIHS copy. 35250

Providence Assembly.
Rules for the Providence Assembly . . .
1792.
[Providence, 1792.] Broadside.
RIHS copy. 24723

Providence Asserted and Adored [by
Cotton Mather, 1663-1728].
Boston, 1718.]
(Mentioned by C. Mather, S. Mather, and
Prince.) 1979

Providence Association of Mechanics and
Manufacturers.
The Charter, Constitution and Bye-laws
of. . . .
Providence, Wheeler, [1789]. 28 pp.
AAS copy. 22085

Providence Association of Mechanics and
Manufacturers.
The Charter, Article of Agreement. . . .
Providence, R. I., Wheeler, 1798. 40 pp.
AAS copy. 34423

Providence Bank.
Constitution of the Bank.
[Providence], Carter, [1791]. Broadside.
RIHS copy. 23723

Providence Bank.
Rules Observed at the Bank. . . . October
13, 1791.
[Providence], Carter, [1791]. Broadside.
RIHS copy. 23724

Providence Beacon. The Town of
Providence to the Inhabitants of the
Towns Adjacent. . . . August 10, 1775.
[Providence, 1775.] Broadside.
NYHS ph. copy. 42923

Providence, February 20, 1781. This
Afternoon an Express. . . .
[Providence, Carter, 1781.] Broadside.
AAS copy. 44035

Providence Insurance Company.
Charter of the. . . .
Providence, R. I., Wheeler, 1799. 10 pp.
RIHS copy. 36182

Providence, January 1, 1783. The
Following . . . Account . . . of the late
Cruel Murder. . . .
Providence, Wheeler, [1783]. Broadside.
AAS copy. 19431

Providence, January 5, 1777. Fresh
Advices from the Westward.
Providence, Carter, [1777].
Broadside.
AAS copy. 43345

Providence, July 20. Extract of a Letter
from Newport, Dated July 18.
[Providence, 1782.] Broadside.
AAS ph. copy. 44250

Providence, March 31, 1790. Gentlemen,
No Prox. . . .
[Providence, 1790.] Broadside.
RIHS copy. 22825

[Providence, Monday, May 31, 1790.
Saturday Night, at 11 o'clock, an Express
Arrived. . . .
[Providence, 1790.] Broadside.]
(Ghost of 22847.) 22846

Providence Mutual Fire Insurance Co.
The Constitution, or Deed of Settlement,
of the. . . .
[Providence, R. I.], Carter, [1800]. 15
pp.
BrU copy. 38343

Providence, November 13, 1800. Sir, the
Importance of the Approaching Town
Meeting. . . .
[Providence, R. I., 1800.] Broadside.
JCB copy. 38348

Providence, October 25, 1781. Three
o'Clock, P.M. This Moment an
Express. . . .
Providence, Carter, [1781]. Broadside.
MHS copy. 44036

Providence, Saturday Afternoon, April 11,
1789. Gentlemen, I have in Vain used
Every Means. . . .
[Providence? 1789.] Broadside.
(No copy located.) 45569

Providence Society for Abolishing the
Slave-Trade.
Constitution of the. . . .
[Providence, 1789.] Broadside.
RIHS copy. 45570

Providence Society for Abolishing the
Slave-Trade.
Constitution of a Society.
Providence, Carter, 1789. 19 pp.
AAS copy. 22114

Providence Street Lottery.
List of the Fortunate Numbers in the
Third Class. . . . June 8th, 1795.
[Providence, 1795.] Broadside.
RIHS copy. 47573

The Prowess of the Whig Club [by
William Goddard, 1740-1817].
Baltimore, [1777]. 16, 4, 4 pp.
(This copy shows the author's revisions.)
AAS copy. 15315

[Proyart, Liévain Bonaventure],
1743-1808.
The Life of John Mary Decalogne.
Baltimore, Warner & Hanna, 1799. 178,
[1] pp.
MdHS copy. 35390

Prudden, Nehemiah, 1750-1815.
A Sermon, Delivered at East-Windsor,
June 24, 1795.
Hartford, Hudson & Goodwin, 1795.
19 pp.
Iowa Masonic Library (Cedar Rapids)
copy. 29371

[Prussia.
The Prussian Exercise.
New York, Gaine, 1757.]
("To be sold at the Bible and Crown. . . .
A neat Edition of," N. Y. Mercury, Oct.
10, 1757.) 8013

[Prussia.
The Prussian (Short) Exercise.
New York, Parker & Weyman, 1757.]
(Title from an adv.) 8012

Prussia. Treaties, etc.
Treaty of Amity and Commerce between
. . . the King of Prussia, and the United
States. . . . Printed by Order of the Senate.
Philadelphia, Way & Groff, 1799. 19 pp.
LOC copy. 36597

Prussia. Treaties, etc., 1800.
Traité d'Amitié et de Commerce, entre
Sa Majesté le Roi de Prusse, et les États
Unis.
[Washington? 1800.] [1], 19 pp.
LOC copy. 38910

A Psalm of Thanksgiving . . . the 30th of
March, 1766 [by Francis Hopkinson,
1737-1791].
[Philadelphia, 1766.] Broadside.
LCP copy. 10335

[Ein Psalm zum Grossen Sabbath.
Friedensthal bei Bethlehem, 1767. 4 pp.]
(Title from Seidensticker.) 10746

Psalmodia Germanica [by Johann
Christian Jacobi, 1670-1750].
New York, Gaine, 1756. vi, 279, [10] pp.
LOC copy. 7772

The Psalms of David, Imitated.
See Watts, Isaac, 1674-1748.

Psalms, Hymns and Spiritual Songs. . . .
Philadelphia, Dobson, 1792. [2], 222, [2],
viii pp.
HSP copy. 46555

Public Expressions of Grief, for the Death
of . . . Washington, at Dorchester.
[Charlestown, Mass., 1800.] pp. [1]-6

[3]-22, [2], [1]-16, [1]-30.
(Also entered as 37332, q. v.)   38349

Public Good, Being an Examination into
the Claim of Virginia [by Thomas Paine,
1737-1809].
Philadelphia, Dunlap, 1780. 38 pp.
AAS copy.   16920

Public Notice. Friday the Fourth Day of
November next, is the Day Appointed by
Law, for the People to . . . Choose . . .
Electors . . . of a President . . . of the
United States. . . . Extract of a Letter
from Thomas Paine.
[Philadelphia, 1796.] Broadside.
HSP copy.   30983

Public Notice. Friday the Fourth of
November next, is the Day Appointed by
Law, for the People to . . . Choose . . .
Electors . . . of a President. . . . Citizens of
Pennsylvania!
[Philadelphia, 1796.] Broadside.
HSP copy.   30984

Public Notice is hereby Given that a
General Inoculation is to take Place.
Richmond, 1794. Broadside.
(Heartman cat. 287, no. 182. Present
location unknown.)   47195

. . . Publick Occurrences.
Boston, 1690. [3] pp.
(This and other serials will be reproduced
in a supplementary microprint project.)   546

[Puckle, James], 1667?-1724.
The Club: or, A Grey Cap.
Philadelphia, Bailey, 1795. 198 pp.
AAS copy.   29372

[Puckle, James], 1667?-1724.
A Grey-Cap for a Green-Head.
Philadelphia, Longcope, 1798. pp. [8],
[13]-159.
AAS copy.   34426

Pugh, Ellis, 1656-1718.
(D. A. B.)
Annerch ir Cymru.
Philadelphia, 1721. ix, 111 pp.
WLC copy.   2286

Pugh, Ellis, 1656-1718.
(D. A. B.)
A Salutation to the Britains.
Philadelphia, Keimer for Davies, 1727. xv,
[1], 222 pp.
AAS copy.   2950

[Puglia, James Philip.]
The Blue Shop. . . . By James Quicksilver.
Philadelphia, Moreau de St. Méry, 1796.
52 pp.
NYPL copy.   31065

Puglia, James Philip.
El Desengaño del Hombre.
Philadelphia, Bailey, 1794. x, 113, xvii,
[1] pp.
LOC copy.   27584

[Puglia, James Philip.
The Disappointment. . . . By James
Quicksilver.
Philadelphia, 1797.]
(No copy located.)   32731

Puglia, James Philip.
The Federal Politician.
Philadelphia, Bailey, 1795. 284 (i.e.,
244) pp.
AAS copy.   29373

[Puglia, James Philip.]
The Political Massacre. . . . By James
Quicksilver.
Philadelphia, Moreau de St. Méry, 1796.
29, [2] pp.
LCP copy.   31066

Puglia, James Philip.
A Short Extract.
Philadelphia, Johnston & Justice, 1793.
16 pp.
AAS copy.   26050

[Punderson, Ebenezer], 1705-1764.
The Nature and Extent of the
Redemption.
New Haven, 1758. 16 pp.
YC copy.   8245

[Purcell, Henry], d. 1802.
Strictures on the Love of Power in the
Prelacy.
Charleston, Young, 1795. 68 pp.
LOC copy.   29374

Purcell, Joseph.
A Map of the States of Virginia North
Carolina South Carolina and Georgia. . . .
[New Haven, 1788.] Map.
HC copy.   21412

[Purdon, John, d. 1835.
Advertisement.
Philadelphia, 1784.]
(From Aitken's accounts.)   18747

Purdon, John, d. 1835.
At the Ninth House above the
Drawbridge. . . . November, 1789.
Philadelphia, Humphreys, [1789].
Broadside.
HSP copy.   45571

[Purdon, John, d. 1835.
A Leisure Hour; or, a Series of Poetical
Letters.
Philadelphia, 1794.]
(Imprint assumed from adv. "Just
Published" in Gazette of the U.S., Aug. 6,
1794.)   27585

The Pure Nazarite [by Cotton Mather,
1663-1728].
Boston, Fleet for Phillips, 1723. [4], 19
pp.
AAS copy.   2458

Purport of a Letter on Sheep. Written in
Maryland, March the 30th, 1789 [by John
Beale Bordley, 1727-1804].
[Philadelphia, 1789.] 6 pp.
AAS copy.   21699

Pursuits of Literature. A Satirical Poem
[by Thomas James Mathias, 1754?-1835].
Philadelphia, Maxwell, 1800. 481 pp.
(Except for the imprint, identical with
37939, q. v. for text.)   37938

Pursuits of Literature. A Satirical Poem
[by Thomas James Mathias, 1754?-1835].
Philadelphia, Maxwell for Dickins, 1800.
481, [7] pp.
(The AAS has a var. with imprint on p.
371 and different adv. at end.)
AAS copy.   37939

Pursuits of Literature. A Satirical Poem
[by Thomas James Mathias, 1754?-1835].
Philadelphia, Maxwell for Nancrede,
Dickins & Ormrod, 1800. 481 pp.
(For text see 37939.)
AAS copy.   37940

[Purves, James, 1734-1795.
Humble Attempt to Investigate and
Defend the Scripture.
Philadelphia, Dobson, 1788.]
(Entry from an adv.)   21413

Purves, James, 1734-1795.
Observations on Doctor Priestley's
Doctrines.
Philadelphia, Pritchard, 1797. 244 pp.
AAS copy.   32732

Purviance, Samuel Dinsmore, 1774-1806.
To the Freemen of Fayetteville
District. . . . July 1, 1800.
Raleigh, Gales, [1800]. Broadside.
NCU copy.   38351

Pusey, Caleb, 1650-1727.
(Penn. Mag. of Hist., LII, 295.)
The Bomb Search'd and Found.
Philadelphia, 1705. 76 pp.
LOC copy.   1230

Pusey, Caleb, 1650-1727.
Daniel Leeds, Justly Rebuked.
Philadelphia, 1702. [6], 28 pp.
(Only a poor copy is available for

reproduction.)
HSP copy.   1094

[Pusey, Caleb], 1650-1727.
(Penn. Mag. of Hist., LII, 295.)
False News from Gath Rejected.
[Philadelphia, 1704.] Broadside.
NYPL ph. copy.   1192

[Pusey, Caleb], 1650-1727.
(Penn. Mag. of Hist., LII, 295.)
George Keith once more Brought to the
Test.
Philadelphia, [1703]. [8], 32 pp.
FL copy.   1143

Pusey, Caleb, 1650-1727.
Proteus Ecclesiasticus.
Philadelphia, [1703]. [6], 60, 28, 4, [2]
pp.
HSP copy.   1144

[Pusey, Caleb], 1650-1727.
(Penn. Mag. of Hist., LII, 295.)
Satan's Harbinger.
Philadelphia, 1700. [3], 114, [1] pp.
HSP copy.   948

Pusey, Caleb, 1650-1727.
Some Brief Observations.
Philadelphia, 1706. [4], 28 pp.
Swarthmore College, Dept. Recs. Yearly
Meeting copy.   1277

[Pusey, Caleb], 1650-1727.
Some Remarks upon a late Pamphlet.
[Philadelphia, 1705.] 40 pp.
LOC copy.   1231

Putnam, Aaron, 1733-1813.
A Sermon, upon the Being of God.
New London, Ct., Green, 1798. 16 pp.
AAS copy.   34427

Putnam, Aaron, 1733-1813.
(Weis, Colonial Clergy N. E.)
The Work of a Gospel Minister.
Boston, Edes & Gill, 1763. 30 pp.
AAS copy.   9493

Putnam, Archelaus, 1743-1800.
To the Public. The Dispute. . . . April 9th,
1774.
[Salem, 1774.] [2] pp.
AAS copy.   42676

[The Puzzling-cap; being a Choice
Collection of Riddles.
Worcester, Thomas, 1787.]
(From an adv., Title uncertain.)   20460

The Puzzling Cap.
Boston, Coverly, 1792. 32 pp.
AAS copy.   25195

The Puzzling Cap; a Choice Collection of
Riddles.
New York, Durell for Jansen, 1800. 31 pp.
(The only known copy is imperfect. An
imprint variant, Durell for Law, is also in
Welch collection.)
d'Alté A. Welch copy.   49141

The Puzzling Cap; a Choice Collection of
Riddles.
New York, Durrell for Law, 1800. 31 pp.
(An imprint variant of S49141, q. v.)
d'Alté A. Welch copy.   49141a

[Pye, Henry James], 1745-1813.
The Democrat; or Intrigues and
Adventures of Jean Le Noir. . . . In Two
Volumes.
New York, Rivington, 1795. xii, 136; [4],
162 pp.
AAS copy.   29375

[Pye, Henry James, 1745-1813.
The Siege of Meaux. A Tragedy.
Philadelphia, 1795.]
(Imprint assumed by Evans from adv.)   29376

[Pyron du Martre, Antoine].
Models of Letters, in French and English.
Philadelphia, Bradford, 1795. ix, [3], 219
pp.
AAS copy.   29377

Q

The Quaker; a Comic Opera [by Charles Dibdin, 1745-1814].
Boston, Edes & Etheridge for Blake and Clap, 1794. 32 pp.
AAS copy.   26880

The Quaker Unmask'd; or, Plain Truth [by David James Dove, 1692?-1769].
Philadelphia, 1764. 15 pp.
NYPL copy.   9646

The Quaker Unmask'd; or Plain Truth. . . . Second Edition [by David James Dove, 1692?-1769].
Philadelphia, Steuart, 1764. 16 pp.
NYPL copy.   9647

The Quaker Vindicated; or, Observations on a late Pamphlet.
[Philadelphia], 1764. 16 pp.
JCB copy.   9805

The Quakers Assisting, to Preserve the Lives of the Indians, in the Barracks, vindicated; Shewing. . . . Number II.
Philadelphia, 1764. 12 pp.
LCP copy.   9807

The Quakers Assisting to Preserve the Lives of the Indians in the Barracks, Vindicated and Proved.
Philadelphia, Armbruster, 1764. 16 pp.
HSP copy.   9806

The Quakers Grace . . . Sixth, Tenth Month, 1765.
[Philadelphia, 1765.] Broadside.
LCP copy.   10150

Quarll, Philip, pseud.
The English Hermit.
Hartford, Ct., Babcock, 1799. 95, [1] pp.
(Also entered as 35203, q. v.)   36187

Queens County, N.Y. Citizens.
To the Right Honorable Richard, Lord Viscount Howe. . . . The Humble Representation . . . of the . . . Inhabitants. . . .
[New York], Printed [by Macdonald & Cameron] in Water-Street, [1776].
Broadside.
HC (Matt B. Jones) copy.   43145

Queen's County, N.Y. Loyalists.
We, Freeholders and Inhabitants of Queen's County. . . . December 6, 1775.
[New York, 1775.] Broadside.
NYHS copy.   42924

Queries, Addressed to Robert Lemmon. . . . October 22, 1779 [by Luther Martin, 1744-1826].
Baltimore [1779]. [2] pp.
MdHS copy.   16331

Queries Humbly Offered to the Freeholders in the County of Westchester.
[New York, 1750 ?] Broadside.
NYPL copy.   6597

Queries Respecting the Introduction, Progress and Abolition of Slavery in Massachusetts. . . . Feb. 17, 1795 [by Jeremy Belknap, 1744-1798].
[Boston, 1795.] Broadside.
MHS copy.   28257

Queries, to the Voters of Baltimore County. . . . January - 1789.
[Baltimore, 1789.] Broadside.
LOC copy.   22087

Queries to the Whigs of Maryland.
Baltimore, 1779.] Broadside.
MdHS copy.   16482

The Querist, No. 1.
To the Freeholders and Freemen, of the City and County of New-York. The Querist, No. 1.
[New York, 1769.] 2 pp.
LCP copy.   11431

The Querist, No. 2.
To the Freeholders and Freemen, of the City and County of New-York. The Querist, No. II.
[New York, 1769.] 2 pp.
LCP copy.   11432

The Querist: or, a Letter to a Member of the General Assembly [by William Livingston, 1723-1790].
[New York], 1754. 14 pp.
LOC copy.   7228

The Querists, or, an Extract of Sundry Passages.
Boston, Fleet, 1740. [4], vi, 29 pp.
AAS copy.   4587

The Querists, or, an Extract of Sundry Passages.
Philadelphia, 1740. 32 pp.
HSP copy.   4586

The Querists: or an Extract of Sundry Passages Taken out of Mr. Whitefield's Printed Sermons.
Charleston, 1741. 32 pp.
(The date given by Evans was his reading of the imprint on this copy.)
BM copy.   7302

[The Querists, or an Extract of Sundry Passages.
Philadelphia, Franklin, 1741.]
(The copies located were 4792.)   4791

The Querists, Part III.
Philadelphia, Franklin, 1741. 150 pp.
AAS copy.   4792

The Querists, the Rev. Mr. Whitefield's Answer.
New York, 1740. 160 pp.
HC copy.   4588

Question: Are we Obliged in this Government of the Massachusetts, by Charter.
[Boston, 1729.] ii pp.
NYPL copy.   3209

[Questions & Answers, to the Prophetic Numbers of Daniel & John.
Boston, Greene & Russell and Edes & Gill, 1759. 16 pp.]
(A ghost of 8351.)   41072

Questions to be Put to the Electors.
[Philadelphia], Ormrod, [1798?]
Broadside.
HSP copy.   48587

Quick, John, 1636-1706.
(D. N. B.)
The Young Mans Claim.
Boston, 1700. [2], 92 pp.
MHS copy.   949

Quick, John, 1636-1706.
The Young Man's Claim. . . . Fourth Edition.
Boston, Gerrish, 1725. [2], viii, 22 pp.
MHS copy.   39836

Quick, John, 1636-1706.
The Young Man's Claim. . . . Fifth Edition.
Boston, Gerrish, 1728. [4], viii, 22 pp.
BPL copy.   3097

Quick, John, 1636-1706.
(D. N. B.)
The Young Man's Claim.
Boston, Kneeland & Green, 1741. viii, 26 + pp.
(The only copy located is imperfect.)
BA copy.   4793

[Quick, John, 1636-1706.
(D. N. B.)
The Young Man's Claim.
Boston, Kneeland & Green, 1746.]
(Title from Haven.)   5859

The Quickened Soul [by Cotton Mather, 1663-1728].
Boston, Green, 1720. [2], 30 pp.
MHS copy.   2141

Quicksilver, James, pseud.
The Blue Shop [by James Philip Puglia].
Philadelphia, Moreau de St. Mery, 1796. 52 pp.
NYPL copy.   31065

Quicksilver, James, pseud.
The Political Massacre [by James Philip Puglia].
Philadelphia, Moreau de St. Mery, 1796. 29, [2] pp.
LCP copy.   31066

Quinby, Josiah, b. 1693.
Copy of the First Letter . . . sent to the Dutch Church.
New York, 1733.
(A supplement to the N. Y. Gazette, Jan. 28, 1733/4.)
NYPL ph. copy.   3718

Quinby, Josiah, 1693-.
A Short History of a Long Journey.
New York, 1740. 61 pp.
Composite copy.   4589

Quince, Peter.
See
Story, Isaac   36188

Quincy, Edmund, 1703-1788.
(Sibley, VII, 106-116.)
A Treatise of Hemp-Husbandry.
Boston, Green & Russell, 1765. 32, [2] pp.
AAS copy.   10151

Quincy, Josiah, 1709-1774.
A Letter to the Inhabitants of Braintree. . . . August 22, 1754.
[Boston, 1754.] 7 pp.
(The only known copy could not be reproduced.)   40714

Quincy, Josiah, 1744-1775.
Observations on the Act of Parliament.
Boston, Edes & Gill, 1774. [2], 82 pp.
AAS copy.   13561

Quincy, Josiah, 1744-1775.
Observations on the Act of Parliament.
Philadelphia, Sparhawk, 1774. 60 pp.
AAS copy.   13562

Quincy, Josiah, 1772-1864.
An Oration, Pronounced, July 4, 1798.
Boston, Russell, 1798. 31 pp.
AAS copy.   34429

Quincy, Josiah, 1772-1864.

An Oration, Pronounced, July 4, 1798. . . .
Second Edition.
Boston, Russell, 1798. 31 pp.
AAS copy.   34430

Quincy, Josiah, 1772-1864.
An Oration, Pronounced July 4, 1798.

Philadelphia, 1798. 21 pp.
AAS copy.   34431

Quincy, Samuel, fl. 1730-1749.
(Weis, Colonial Clergy Ga.)
Twenty Sermons.

Boston, Draper, 1750. [20], 370, [1] pp.
AAS copy.   6598

[Quincy, Samuel], 1734-1789.
A Monody Inscribed to Benjamin Church.
[Boston, 1768.] 7 pp.
BA copy.   10855

R

[Rabaut Saint-Étienne, Jean Paul, 1743-1793.
An Address to the People of England.
Boston, Howel for Larkin, 1791.]
(Entry from an adv.)   23726

Rabaut Saint-Étienne, Jean Paul, 1743-1793.
The History of the Revolution of France.
New York, Greenleaf for Greenleaf & Fellows, 1794. 2 vol. 346, [2] pp. 2 plates; 478 pp., 2 plates.
AAS copy.   27586

[Racine, Jean, 1639-1699.
The Distrest Mother.
New York, Gaine, 1761.]
(Adv. N. Y. Mercury, July 20, 1761. See BSA, XXXV, 160.)   8986

Radcliffe, Ann (Ward), 1764-1823.
The Castles of Athlin and Dunbayne.
Philadelphia, Bradford, 1796. 260, [2] pp.
AAS copy.   31067

[Radcliffe, Ann (Ward), 1764-1823.
The Castles of Athlin and Dunbayne.
Boston, West, 1797.]
(Imprint assumed by Evans from adv. "Also for sale" in 32068.)   32733

[Radcliffe, Ann (Ward), 1764-1823.
The Italian.
Boston, Etheridge, 1797.]
(Proposed by apparently not published.)
                                        32734

Radcliffe, Ann (Ward), 1764-1823.
The Italian. . . . In Two Volumes.
Mount Pleasant, N. J., Durell for Magill, etc., 1797. 293; 291 pp.
AAS copy.   32735

[Radcliffe, Ann (Ward), 1764-1823.
The Italian.
New York, Greenleaf, 1797. 2 vol.]
(Imprint assumed by Evans from Greenleaf's adv.)   32736

[Radcliffe, Ann (Ward), 1764-1823.
The Italian.
Philadelphia, Carey, 1797.]
(Imprint assumed by Evans from Carey's adv.)   32737

Radcliffe, Ann (Ward), 1764-1823.
The Italian. . . . In Two Volumes.
Philadelphia, [Folwell] for Rices and Campbell, 1797. ix, [1], 302; 363, [1] pp.
Composite copy.   32738

Radcliffe, Ann (Ward), 1764-1823.
The Mysteries of Udolpho. . . . In Three Volumes.
Boston, Etheridge for White, Spotswood, Thomas & Andrews, etc., 1795. 224; 224; 232 pp.
(Evans assumed a Worcester imprint from Thomas' ad. "Just published" in Mass. Spy, Oct. 13, 1795.)
AAS copy.   29378

Radcliffe, Ann (Ward), 1764-1823.
The Mysteries of Udolpho. . . . In Three Volumes.
Philadelphia, Rices, 1800. 253; 251; 266 pp.
PPL copy.   38352

Radcliffe, Ann (Ward), 1764-1823.
The Romance of the Forest. . . . In Two Volumes.
Boston, Etheridge for Larkin, Spotswood,

Thomas & Andrews, etc., 1795. 156; 168 pp.
AAS copy.   29379

Radcliffe, Ann (Ward), 1764-1823.
The Romance of the Forest. . . . In Two Volumes.
Philadelphia, Bradford, 1795. 218; 236 pp.
AAS copy.   29380

Radcliffe, Ann (Ward), 1764-1823.
A Sicilian Romance.
Philadelphia, for H. & P. Rice, and for J. Rice, Baltimore, 1795. 230, [2] pp.
AAS copy.   29381

Raguet, Claudius Paul.
Catalogue of French, and other Books.
[Philadelphia, 1790.] 8 pp.
AAS copy.   45984

[A Rake Exhibited [by Samuel Bartholomew, 1762-1842].
Fairhaven, Spooner, 1796. 80 pp.]
(McCorison 380; no copy known.)   47720

Ralling, John.
Miscellaneous Sketches.
Newburyport, Barrett, 1796. 24 pp.
BrU copy.   31069

[Ralling, John ?]
Miscellanies, viz. . . .
Philadelphia, M'Culloch, 1790. 24 pp.
AAS copy.   22827

Ralling, John.
A Short Essay: on Scriptural Instructions.
Philadelphia, 1800. 22, [1] pp.
LCP copy.   38354

A Rallying Point for All True Friends to their Country.
[Charleston, S. C., 1800.] 16 pp.
(Also reproduced as 38506, q. v.)   38355

The Rambler. In Four Volumes [by Samuel Johnson, 1709-1784].
New York, Campbell, 1800. 309, 296; 309; 254, [28] pp.
(This is a reissue of the London ed. of 1791 with American tps., one of which is reproduced.)
NYPL copy.   37710

The Rambler.
New York, Campbell, 1800. 4 vol.
(Also entered as 37710, q. v.)   38356

[Ramsay, Allan, 1685-1758.
(D. N. B.)
The Gentle Shepherd.
New York, Parker, 1750.]
(From printer's adv.)   6599

[Ramsay, Allan, 1685-1758.
The Gentle Shepherd.
Philadelphia, Aitken, 1771.]
(Entry probably from an adv.)   12209

Ramsay, Allan, 1685-1758.
The Gentle Shepherd.
n. p., 1788. 60 pp.
AAS copy.   45347

Ramsay, Allan, 1685-1758.
The Gentle Shepherd.
Philadelphia, Campbell, 1795. 72 pp.
AAS copy.   29382

Ramsay, Allan, 1685-1758.
The Gentle Shepherd.
Philadelphia, Stewart, 1798. 72, [4] pp.
AAS copy.   34432

Ramsay, Andrew Michael, 1686-1743.
The Travels of Cyrus. . . . Tenth Edition.
— First American.
Burlington, N.J., 1793. xx, 352 pp.
AAS copy.   26052

Ramsay, Andrew Michael, 1686-1743.
The Travels of Cyrus.
Boston, Manning & Loring for Hall, etc., 1795. 308 pp.
AAS copy.   29383

Ramsay, Andrew Michael, 1686-1743.
Les Voyages de Cyrus.
Philadelphia, Ormrod & Conrad for Rivington, 1796. 2 vol. [2], [2], 4, 4, 147, 147; [4], [4], 97, [2], 73, 73 pp.
AAS copy.   31070

[Ramsay, David], 1749-1815.
An Address to the Freemen of South Carolina.
Charleston, Bowen, [1788]. 12 pp.
LOC copy.   21414

[Ramsay, David], 1749-1815.
A Dissertation on the Manner of Acquiring the Character and Privileges of a Citizen.
n. p., 1789. 8 pp.
AAS copy.   22088

Ramsay, David, 1749-1815.
A Dissertation on the Means of Preserving Health in Charleston.
Charleston, Markland & McIver, 1790. 32 pp.
HC copy.   22828

Ramsay, David, 1749-1815.
The History of the American Revolution.
Philadelphia, Aitken, 1789. vi, 359; iv, 360 pp.
AAS copy.   22090

Ramsay, David, 1749-1815.
The History of the Revolution of South-Carolina.
Trenton, 1785. 2 vol. xx, 453 pp., 1 map; xx, 574 pp., 4 maps.
AAS copy.   19211

Ramsay, David, 1749-1815.
Observations on the Decision of the House.
New York, Hodge, Allen & Campbell, 1789. 16 pp.
AAS copy.   22089

Ramsay, David, 1749-1815.
An Oration, Delivered . . . the Fourth of July, 1794.
Charleston, Young, [1794]. 22 pp.
AAS copy.   27590

Ramsay, David, 1749-1815.
An Oration on the Advantages of American Independence.
Charleston, 1778. [6], 21 pp.
HC copy.   16026

Ramsay, David, 1749-1815.
An Oration on the Advantages of American Independence.
Charleston, S. C., Cox, 1800. [4], 28 pp.
MHS copy.   38357

Ramsay, David, 1749-1815.
An Oration on the Death of . . . Washington.
Charleston, S. C., Young, 1800. [4], 30 pp.
AAS copy.   38358

Ramsay, David, 1749-1815.
A Sketch of . . . South-Carolina.
Charleston, Young, 1796. [4], 30 pp., 3
tables.
AAS copy.   31071

Rand, William, 1700-1779.
(Sibley, VI, 549-553.)
Gospel-Ministers.
Boston, Green & Russell, 1757. 23 pp.
AAS copy.   8014

[Rand, William], 1700-1779.
(Sibley, VI, 549-553.)
The Late Religious Commotions.
Boston, Green, Bushell & Allen for Fleet,
1743. [4], 20, 40 pp.
(For authorship see BSA, XLV, 131.)
AAS copy.   5150

Rand, William, 1700-1779.
(Sibley, VI, 549-553.)
The Minister's Duty.
Boston, Kneeland & Green, 1739. 30 pp.
AAS copy.   4415

Rand, William, 1700-1779.
(Sibley, VI, 549-553.)
Ministers Exhorted.
Boston, Rogers & Fowle, 1749. 24 pp.
AAS copy.   6410

Rand, William, 1700-1779.
(Sibley, VI, 549-553.)
Ministers Must Preach Christ.
Boston, Kneeland & Green, 1736. [4], 17
pp.
AAS copy.   4070

Rand, William, 1700-1779.
(Sibley, VI, 549-553.)
The Ministers of Christ.
Boston, Fleet for Henchman, 1741.
27 pp.
AAS copy.   4794

Rand, William, 1700-1779.
Ministers Should have a Sincere and
Ardent Love.
Boston, Fleet, 1742. 24 pp.
AAS copy.   5044

Rand, William, 1700-1779.
(Sibley, VI, 549-553.)
The Superiour Dignity.
Boston, Draper, 1756. 23 pp.
AAS copy.   7773

[Randall, John, fl. 1764.
(D. N. B.)
The Semi-Virgilian Husbandry.
Philadelphia, Bradford, 1764.]
(Adv. Pa. Journal, Apr. 26, 1764.)   9808

[Randall, Joseph, fl. 1747.
A Brief Account of the . . . Quakers.
New York, Ross, 1788.]
(From an adv., apparently for a London
ed.)   21415

Randall, Thomas, 1711-1780.
(Hew Scott, Fasti Ecclesiae Scoticanae.)
Whereas a Report Prevails in this City. . . .
[New York, 1769.] Broadside.
LCP copy.   11433

[Randolph, Edmund], 1753-1813.
Germanicus.
[Philadelphia, 1794.] 77, [1] pp.
LCP copy.   27597

Randolph, Edmund, 1753-1813.
A Letter of His Excellency Edmund
Randolph. . . . October 10, 1787.
[Richmond, 1787.] 16 pp.
NYPL copy.   20669

Randolph, Edmund, 1753-1813.
(D. A. B.)
An Oration in Commemoration of the
Founders of William and Mary College.
Williamsburg, Rind, 1771. 12 pp.
LOC copy.   12210

[Randolph, Edmund], 1753-1813.
Political Truth: or Animadversions on the
Past and Present.
Philadelphia, Smith, 1796. 44 pp.
AAS copy.   31072

[Randolph, Edmund], 1753-1813.
A Vindication of Mr. Randolph's
Resignation.

Philadelphia, Smith, 1795. 103, [2] pp.
AAS copy.   29384

[Randolph, Edmund], 1753-1813.
A Vindication of Mr. Randolph's
Resignation.
Philadelphia, Smith, 1795. 103 pp.
AAS copy.   29385

Randolph, John, 1693-1737.
The Speech of Sir John Randolph, upon
his being Elected Speaker. . . . Printed by
Order of the House.
Williamsburg, Parks, 1734. [4] pp.
PRO copy.   40060

[Randolph, John], 1727-1784, supposed
author.
Considerations on the Present State of
Virginia.
[Williamsburg], 1774. 24 pp.
PRO copy.   42677

[Randolph, John?], 1727?-1784.
An Intercepted Original Letter from
General Washington. . . . June 24, 1776.
[Philadelphia, 1777.] Broadside.
LCP copy.   15557

Randolph, John, 1727?-1784.
A Treatise of Gardening. By a Native of
this State.
Richmond, Nicolson, 1793.
(See Sabin 96739.)   26275

[Randolph, Peyton?], c. 1721-1775.
A Letter to a Gentleman in London, from
Virginia.
Williamsburg, 1759. 28 pp.
(Authorship also attributed to Landon
Carter.)
BA copy.   8476

Rankin, Adam, 1755-1824.
A Process in the Transilvania Presbytery.
Lexington, Maxwell & Cooch, [1793]. 96
pp.
LOC copy.   46858

Rankin, Adam, 1755-1827.
A Reply to a Narrative of Mr. Adam
Rankin's Trial.
Lexington, Bradford, 1794. 71 pp.
LOC copy.   27598

Ranlet, Henry, 1763?-1807.
The Gentleman's Pocket Almanack, for
. . . 1798. To which is Added a Register of
New-Hampshire.
Exeter, Ranlet, 108, [1] pp.
(Also entered as 32009, q.v.)   32739

[Ranlet, Henry, 1763?-1807.
The Youth's Instructor or Spelling Book.
Exeter, Ranlet, 1792.]
("Just Published, By the printer hereof,"
Newhampshire Gazetteer, Oct. 26, 1792.)   24726

[Ranlet, Henry, 1763?-1807.
The Youth's Instructor or Spelling
Book. . . . Second Edition.
Exeter, Ranlet, 1794.]
(Imprint assumed by Evans from advs.)   27599

Ranlet's New-Hampshire and
Massachusetts Almanack, for . . . 1799.
Exeter, Ranlet, 1798. [24] pp.
AAS copy.   34433

[Rapin-Thoyras, Paul de], 1661-1725.
A Dissertation on the Rise, Progress . . .
and Characters . . . of the Whigs and
Tories.
(Bib. Soc. Am., Papers, XXXV, 161.)
Boston, Greenleaf, 1773. 71, [1] pp.
AAS copy.   12753

Rare Observations: or, Some Remarks
[by Samuel Hopkins, 1721-1803].
Providence, Carter, 1770. 76 pp.
AAS copy.   42111

[Raseau, Beauvais de.
Indigorier.
Charleston, 1776.]
(No such ed. located.)   15040

[Raspe, Rudolph Erich], 1737-1794.
Gulliver Revived. . . . Fourth Edition.
Norfolk, M'Lean, 1787. iv, 139 pp.

(The only known copy is imperfect.)
JCB copy.   45150

[The Rates of Porterage and Carriage,
&c. to any Parts of the City.
Philadelphia, Humphreys, 1774.
Broadside.]
(Adv. Pa. Gazette, Jan. 19, 1774.)   13563

Rathbun, Daniel.
A Letter from Daniel Rathbun.
n.p., [1785?]. 120 pp.
AAS copy.   44783

Rathbun, Daniel.
A Letter from Daniel Rathbun.
Springfield, 1785. 128 pp.
AAS copy.   19212

Rathbun, Reuben.
Reasons Offered for Leaving the Shakers.
Pittsfield, Mass., Smith, 1800. 28 pp.
BrA copy.   38359

Rathbun, Valentine Wightman, b. 1724.
An Account of the Matter.
Providence, Wheeler, 1781. 23 pp.
LOC copy.   17318

Rathbun, Valentine Wightman, b. 1724.
A Brief Account of a Religious Scheme
. . . Called Shaking Quakers.
Worcester, 1782. 36 pp.
AAS copy.   17681

[Rathbun, Valentine Wightman, b. 1724.
Some Brief Hints. . . . Second Edition.
Hartford, 1781. 27 pp.]
(The only recorded copy of this ed. was
sold at the Brinley sale.)   17319

Rathbun, Valentine Wightman, b. 1724.
Some Brief Hints.
Boston, Edes, 1781. 24 pp.
AAS copy.   17320

Rathbun, Valentine Wightman, b. 1724.
Some Brief Hints.
Norwich, Trumbull, 1781. 24 pp.
AAS copy.   17321

Rathbun, Valentine Wightman, b. 1724.
Some Brief Hints of a Religious Scheme.
Boston, Edes, 1782. 24 pp.
AAS copy.   17682

Rathbun, Valentine Wightman, b. 1724.
Some Brief Hints of a Religious Scheme.
Salem, Hall, 1782. 23 pp.
AAS copy.   17683

Rathbun, Valentine Wightman, b. 1724.
Some Brief Hints of a Religious Scheme.
New York, 1783. 36 pp.
AAS copy.   18145

The Ratifications of the new Foederal
Constitution.
Richmond, Davis, 1788. [4], 32 pp.
AAS copy.   21529

Ratio Disciplinae Fratrum [by Cotton
Mather, 1663-1728].
Boston, Gerrish, 1726. [2], iv, 10, 207, [3]
pp.
AAS copy.   2775

Ratzer, Bernard.
To His Excellency Sir Henry Moore. . . .
This Plan of the City of New York.
[New York, 1769.]
HC copy.   11434

Ravara, Joseph.
A Statement of Facts. . . .
Philadelphia, Dobson, 1793. 21 pp.
LCP copy.   26053

[Rawle, Francis], 1662-1727.
(D. A. B.)
A Just Rebuke to a Dialogue betwixt
Simon and Timothy.
Philadelphia, Keimer, 1726. 31, [1] pp.
HSP copy.   2807

[Rawle, Francis], 1662-1727.
(D. A. B.)
Some Remedies Proposed.
[Philadelphia], 1721. 20 pp.
LCP copy.   2287

[Rawle, Francis], 1662-1727.
Ways and Means.

Philadelphia, Keimer, 1725. 65, [7] pp.
Composite copy.   2697

Rawlet, John, 1642-1686.
The Christian Monitor. . . . Twenty-Fifth
Edition.
Boston, Cox, 1733. [2], 62, [8] pp.
YC copy.   3719

[Rawlet, John, 1642-1686.
(D. N. B.)
The Christian Monitor. . . . Twenty-Sixth
Edition.
Boston, Gookin, 1743.]
("Just Published," Boston Gazette, Nov.
15, 1743, and in 5289.)   5279

[Rawson, Edward?], 1615-1693.
The Revolution in New England Justified.
Boston [i.e. London], 1691. [6], 48 pp.
NYPL copy.   575

[Rawson, Edward?], 1615-1693.
The Revolution in New England Justified.
Boston, Thomas, 1773. 59 pp.
AAS copy.   12973

Rawson, Grindall, 1659-1715.
(Sibley, III, 159-168.)
Miles Christianus.
Boston, 1703. [2], 52 pp.
AAS copy.   1145

Rawson, Grindall, 1659-1715.
(Sibley, III, 159-168.)
The Necessity of a Speedy and Thorough
Reformation.
Boston, 1709. [2], 40 pp.
AAS copy.   1429

Rawson, Jonathan, 1759-1794.
A Compendium of Military Duty.
Dover, N.H., Ladd for West and Larkin,
1793. 305 pp.
AAS copy.   26054

[Rawson, Jonathan, 1759-1794.
The Instructor Generalis . . . for all Town,
Parish and County Officers.
Dover, N.H., Ladd, 1793.]
(Imprint assumed by Evans from
copyright entry.)   26055

[Ray, James, fl. 1745.
The Acts of the Rebels.
New York, Parker, 1747.]
("Lately published in New-York," Pa.
Gazette, Feb. 24, 1746/7.)   6058

[Ray, James, fl. 1745.
The Acts of the Rebels.
Philadelphia, Franklin, 1747.]
(Adv. Pa. Gazette, Apr. 23, 1747.) 6059

[Ray, James, fl. 1745.
The Acts of the Rebels. . . . Sixth Edition.
Philadelphia, Franklin, 1747.]
(Adv. Pa. Gazette, Apr. 23, 1747.) 6060

[Ray, James, fl. 1745.
The Lamentations of Charles.
Boston, Fleet, 1747.]
("This Day is published," Boston Evening
Post, Mar. 16, 1747.)   6061

Ray, Nicholas.
The Importance of the Colonies.
New York, Holt, 1766. [4], 16 pp.
LOC copy.   10471

Raymond, Gershom.
In what Only True Religion Consist's. . . .
Fairfield, [Ct.], Forgue & Bulkeley, 1788.
[2], 16 pp.
CHS copy.   45348

[Raynal, Guillaume Thomas François,
1713-1796.
The Revolution of America.
Boston, 1781.]
(Sabin 68104. Apparently from an adv. for
London ed.)   17322

[Raynal, Guillaume Thomas François,
1713-1796.
The Revolution of America.
New York, Rivington, 1781.]
("This Day is Published," Royal Gazette,
Aug. 25, 1781.)   17323

Raynal, Guillaume Thomas François,
1713-1796.
The Revolution of America.

Norwich, Trumbull, 1782. 94 pp.
AAS copy.   17686

Raynal, Guillaume Thomas François,
1713-1796.
The Revolution of America.
Philadelphia, Bell, 1782. 72 pp.
AAS copy.   17684

Raynal, Guillaume Thomas François,
1713-1796.
The Revolution of America. . . . Second
Edition.
Philadelpphia, Bell, 1782. 72 pp.
AAS copy.   17685

Raynal, Guillaume Thomas Francois,
1713-1796.
The Revolution of America.
Salem, Hall, 1782. vii, [1], 92 pp.
AAS copy.   17687

Raynal, Guillaume Thomas François,
1713-1796.
The Revolution of America.
Hudson, Stoddard, 1792. 124 pp.
AAS copy.   24728

[Raynal, Guillaume Thomas François],
1713-1796.
The Sentiments of a Foreigner, on the
Disputes.
Philadelphia, Humphreys, 1775. 27, [1]
pp.
AAS copy.   14417

Read, Charles, 1715-1774.
(L. O. C.)
Copy of a Letter from Charles Read.
Philadelphia, Steuart, 1764. 8 pp.
NYPL copy.   9809

[Read, Charles, 1715-1774.
Copy of a Letter from Charles Read. . . .
Second Edition.
Philadelphia, Steuart, 1764. 8 pp.]
(Assumed from the fact that there was a
3rd ed.)   9810

Read, Charles, 1715-1774.
Copy of a Letter from Charles Read. . . .
Third Edition.
Philadelphia, Steuart, 1764. 8 pp.
NYHS copy.   9811

Read, Collinson, 1751-1815.
Lancaster, January 6, 1800. Sir, A Bill.
. . .
[Lancaster, Pa., 1800.] 1 leaf.
UOP copy.   38360

Read, Collinson, 1751-1815.
Precedents in the Office of a Justice of
Peace.
Philadelphia, Hall & Sellers, 1794. [4], 63,
[1], 33, [1] pp., errata slip.
AAS copy.   27600

Read, Daniel, 1757-1841.
The American Singing Book.
New Haven, 1785. 72, [1] pp.
WLC copy.   19213

Read, Daniel, 1757-1841.
The American Singing Book. . . . Second
Edition.
New Haven, 1786. 72, [2] pp.
(The only copy located is imperfect.)
BPL copy.   44957

Read, Daniel, 1757-1841.
The American Singing Book . . . to which
is Added a Supplement. . . . Third
Edition.
New Haven, 1787. 72, [3], 16 pp.
YC copy.   20673

[Read, Daniel, 1757-1841.
The American Singing-Book. . . . Second
Edition.
New Haven, Read, 1788.]
(Entry from an adv. in the Conn. Journal,
Jan. 2, 1788, but perhaps for the
remainder of 19213.)   21416

[Read, Daniel, 1757-1841.
The American Singing Book. . . . Third
Edition.
New Haven, 1792?]
(Imprint assumed by Evans from
copyright notice, "May be had," Conn.
Journal, Nov. 7, 1792.)   24729

Read, Daniel, 1757-1841.
The American Singing-Book. . . . Fourth
Edition.
New Haven, [1793]. 72, [4], 16 pp.
MHS copy.   26056

[Read, Daniel, 1757-1841.
The American Singing Book. . . . Fifth
Edition.
New Haven, 1795.]
(No copy of a 5th ed. located. Evans
constructed his entry from advs. which
give no clue as to ed., date, or imprint.)
                                   29388

Read, Daniel, 1757-1841.
The Columbian Harmonist. No. 1.
New Haven, Atwell, [1793]. 39, [1] pp.
AAS copy.   26057

Read, Daniel, 1757-1841.
The Columbian Harmonist. No. 1 [-3].
New Haven, [1795?]. 111, [9] pp.
(The sequence of editions as indicated by
pagination suggests that this is the 1795
printing.)
AAS copy.   29389

Read, Daniel, 1757-1841.
The Columbian Harmonist, No. 2
Containing First: a Plain and Concise
Introduction.
New Haven, [1794]. 39, [1] pp.
(Evans' entry was from the copyright
notice.)
AAS copy.   29390

Read, Daniel, 1757-1841.
The Columbian Harmonist. No. III.
Containing, a Collection of Anthems.
New Haven, [1795]. 39, [1] pp.
AAS copy.   29391

[Read, Daniel, 1757-1841.
An Introduction to Psalmody.
New Haven, 1790.]
("Just published," Conn. Journal, Mar.
17, 1790.)   22829

[Read, Daniel, 1757-1841.
An Introduction to Psalmody, or the
Child's Instruction in Vocal Music.
New Haven, 1795.]
(Apparently a ghost of 22829, Evans'
being from advs. which gave no clue as to
imprint.)   29392

Read, John, 1680-1749.
(Sibley, IV, 369-378.)
A Latin Grammar.
Boston, Kneeland & Green, 1736. [2], 34,
20 pp.
AAS copy.   4071

Read, John K., 1746-1805.
Commemorative Oration, Delivered on
the 22d of February, 1800.
[Norfolk, Va.], Jordan, [1800]. 15 pp.
LOC copy.   38361

Read, John K., 1746-1805.
(Blanton, Medicine in Va. in 18th Cent.,
p. 344.)
The New Ahiman Rezon.
Richmond, Dixon, 1791. xvi, [6], 9, [1],
241, [1] pp.
AAS copy.   23727

Reading Philip, 1720-1778.
(Weis, Col. Clergy Del.)
The Protestant's Danger.
Philadelphia, Franklin & Hall, 1755. 28
pp.
HSP copy.   7552

Reading, Pa. Theater, 1797.
Reading Theater (under the Direction of
Mr. M'Grath) . . . February 7.
[Reading, 1797.] Broadside.
(Present location unknown.)   48238

Reading, Pa. Theater, 1798.
Reading Theatre. . . . The Moral and
Historical Play of George Barnwell.
[Reading, 1798.] Broadside.
(No copy located. Reproduced from a
cut.)   34435

Reading made Easy, in some Scripture
Instructions for Children.
Philadelphia, Dunlap, 1765. [2], 78 pp.
JCB copy.   41585

[Reading Made Easy, or Child's Instructor.
Philadelphia, Spotswood, 1786.]
(Ghost of a London ed. Adv. in Pa. Herald, July 12, 1786.)   19946

[Reading Made Easy; or Child's Toy and Pretty Plaything.
Boston, Spotswood, 1795.]
(Imprint assumed by Evans from Spotswood's adv.)   29393

Reading no Preaching [by Roderick Mackenzie, fl. 1797].
Boston, Edes & Gill, 1757. 28 pp.
(Authorship from Halkett & Laing.)
AAS copy.   8015

Reading no Preaching [by Roderick Mackenzie, fl. 1797].
Philadelphia, Steuart, [1761]. 24 pp.
LOC copy.   8907

Reading no Preaching [by Roderick Mackenzie, fl. 1797].
Norwich, Ct., Hubbard, 1797. 24 pp.
AAS copy.   32408

The Ready Reckoner, or the Trader's Sure Guide [by Daniel Fenning].
Reading, Johnson, 1789. 195 pp.
AAS copy.   21822

The Ready Reckoner or Trader's Sure Guide [by Daniel Fenning].
Philadelphia, Johnson, 1794. 195 pp.
AAS copy.   26968

The Ready Reckoner [by Daniel Fenning].
York, Pa., Myer, 1797. 191 pp.
(No perfect copy could be located.)
AAS copy.   32127

The Ready Reckoner, or, Trader's Useful Assistant [by Daniel Fenning].
York, Pa., Myer for Carey, 1798. 191 pp.
AAS copy.   33730

The Real Advantages which Ministers and People may Enjoy [by Noah Welles, 1718-1776].
[New Haven], 1762. 47 pp.
AAS copy.   9302

A Real Treasure for the Pious Mind.
Hartford, Babcock, 1797. 96 pp.
AAS copy.   32741

A Real Treasure for the Pious Mind. . . .
Second Edition.
Hartford, Ct., Babcock, 1799. 96 pp.
AAS copy.   36191

[Real Union of Christ and His Church [by William Cudworth].
Boston, 1764?]
(The source of this entry has not been found.)   9626

[Reason against Coition.
Philadelphia, Armbruester, 1750.]
(Adv. Pa. Gazette, May 10, 1750.)   6600

. . . Reason and Faith [by Joshua Hezekiah DeCordova, 1720-1797].
Philadelphia, Bailey, 1791. pp. [i]-xii, [9]-183.
AAS copy.   23728

Reason Satisfied: and Faith Established [by Cotton Mather, 1663-1728].
Boston, 1712. 47 pp.
AAS copy.   1555

The Reasonableness of, Regular Singing [by Thomas Symmes, 1678-1725].
Boston, Green for Gerrish, 1720. [2], 22 pp.
AAS copy.   2183

Reasons against any of His Majesty's Council Voting, or Using Their Influence in the Ensuing Election.
[New York, 1769.] Broadside.
LOC copy.   11435

Reasons against the Renewal of the Sugar Act.
Boston, Leverett, 1764. 19 pp.
   9812

[Reasons for Adhering to our Platform.
[Boston, 1732.] 10 pp.]
(This title is the second part of 3854 and 3855. The "reprint" described by Evans was a separated part.)   3600

Reasons for Adhering to our Platform.
[Boston, 1734.] 10, [2], 15 pp.
(This item is the second and third parts of 3854, q.v.)   3831

Reasons for Repealing the Act of the Legislative of Pennsylvania, of September 13, 1785 [by Pelatiah Webster, 1726-1795].
Philadelphia, Oswald, 1786. 8 pp.
AAS copy.   20130

Reasons for the Indictment.
[London, 1680.] Broadside.
(See W. C. Ford, Mass. Broadsides.)
MHS copy.   294

Reasons for the Necessity of Silent Waiting [by Mary (Brotherton) Brook, 1726?-1782].
Philadelphia, Crukshank, 1780. 32 pp.
AAS copy.   16724

Reasons for the Present Glorious Combination of the Dissenters in this City.
[New York, 1769.] Broadside.
NYPL copy.   11436

[Reasons for Writing that False, Malicious. . . .
New York, 1740.]
(Title taken by Hildeburn from an adv.)   4590

Reasons in Support of an Opinion Offered to the Public Respecting the Votes of Otsego County.
New York, Swords, 1792. 30 pp.
AAS copy.   24730

Reasons why Mr. Byles left New-London [by Samuel Andrew Peters, 1735-1826].
[New London], 1768. 12 pp.
AAS copy.   11035

Reasons why the British Colonies in America, Should not be Charged with Internal Taxes [by Thomas Fitch, 1700-1774].
New Haven, 1764. 39 pp.
AAS copy.   9658

The Rebels Reward: or, English Courage Display'd . . . at Norrigiwock.
Boston, J. Franklin, 1724. Broadside.
HEH copy.   39818

The Recantation; being an Anticipated Valedictory Address [by Donald Fraser, 1755?-1820].
New York, 1797. 15 pp.
AAS copy.   32153

The Recantation: being an Anticipated Valedictory Address [by Donald Fraser, 1755?-1820].
Reprinted in North-Carolina, 1797. 13 pp.
NYPL copy.   48118

The Recantations of Jacob Fowle . . . and Thomas Lewis. In Committee of Safety . . . May 2, 1775.
Salem, Russell, [1775]. [2] pp.
AAS copy.   42925

The Recantations of Robert Hooper, John Pedrick . . . Cambridge, May 4, 1775.
[Boston], Printed and sold in Queen Street, [1775]. Broadside.
MHS copy.   42926

The Recantations of Robert Hooper, John Pedrick. . . . May 4, 1775.
Salem, Russell, [1775]. Broadside.
AAS copy.   42927

A Receipt to Make a Speech. By J. G., Esquire
[Philadelphia, 1766.] Broadside.
LCP copy.   10472

Recovery from Sickness. . . . Fourth Edition [by Michaiah Towgood, 1700-1792].
Boston, Fleets, 1768. 34, [1] pp.
AAS copy.   11905

Recovery from Sickness. . . . Fifth Edition [by Michaiah Towgood, 1700-1792].
Portsmouth, Peirce, 1794. 43 pp.
LOC copy.   27809

Red and Black; or The Fates of Faro, a Serious Drama.
Philadelphia, Woodward, 1796.
(Only recorded appearance in Am. Art. Assoc. cat., Jan. 21-2, 1926, No. 19.)   31075

[Rede, Carteret.
Token for Youth.
Boston, Foster, 1741.]
("Just published," Boston Evening Post, Apr. 6, 1741.)   4795

[Rede, Mrs. Sarah].
A Token for Youth. . . . Twenty-Fifth Edition.
Boston, 1727.]
(Adv. Boston News-Letter, Feb. 9, 1727.)   2886

[Rede, Mrs. Sarah.]
A Token for Youth. . . . Twenty-Fifth Edition.
Boston, 1729. [1], iii, 32 pp.
(The only known copy is imperfect.)
AAS copy.   39929

Rede, Mrs. Sarah.
A Token for Youth. . . . Twenty-Seventh Edition.
Boston, Kneeland, 1766. 24 pp.
AAS copy.   10473

The Redeemer's Work.
Albany, [N. Y.], Websters, [1791?]. 12 pp.
AAS copy.   46266

Redfield, Levi, 1745-1838.
A Succinct Account.
Brattleborough, Vt., Smead, 1798. 12 pp.
HEH copy.   34436

Redfield, Levi, 1745-1838.
A True Account of some Memorable Events.
Norwich, [Ct.], for White, [1799]. 24 pp.
AAS copy.   48957

[Redfield, Nathan.
A Treatise on Surveying.
Hartford? 1796.]
(Entry from the copyright notice.)   31076

Redick, John.
A Detection.
Baltimore, [1765]. 48 pp.
(The unique original could not be located so a reprint is reproduced.)   10152

[Redman, John, 1722-1808.
(D. A. B.)
A Defence of Inoculation.
Philadelphia, 1759.]
(No copy found.)   8477

Reed, Abner, 1771-1866.
The First Step to Learning.
East Windsor, Ct., Pratt, 1800. 60 pp.
(The only copy located lacks the tp. but has the preface dated April, 1799.)
CHS copy.   38362

Reed, Abner, 1771-1866.
The First Step to Learning. . . . Second Edition.
East Windsor, Ct., Pratt, 1800. 60 pp.
AAS copy.   38363

Reed, Jesse.
A Sermon, on the Religion of Moses.
Greenfield, Dickman, 1793. 23 pp.
AAS copy.   26062

Reed, John, fl. 1774-1785.
An Explanation of the Map of the City.
Philadelphia, Brooks, 1774. 24, [8], 23, [9] pp.
AAS copy.   13564

Reed, John, 1751-1831.
A Sermon, Preached December 12, 1787.
Boston, Freeman, 1788. 31 pp.
AAS copy.   21417

Reed, John, 1751-1831.
A Sermon, Preached October 19, 1792.
Dover, N. H., Ladd, 1793. 33 pp.
AAS copy.   26063

[Reed, Joseph, 1723-1787.
The Register Office.
Philadelphia, Steuart, 1762.]
(Pa. Journal, Dec. 29, 1762.) 9250

Reed, Joseph, 1741-1785.
The Following Paper. . . . Jan. 15, 1781.
Philadelphia, Bailey, [1781]. Broadside.
AAS copy. 17324

Reed, Joseph, 1741-1785.
Joseph Reed, Defendant, vs. John Reid.
[Philadelphia, 1768?] 28 pp.
HSP copy. 11053

Reed, Joseph, 1741-1785.
Philadelphia, January 27, 1781. My late
Engagements of a Public Nature. . . .
[Philadelphia, 1781.] Broadside.
HSP copy. 17325

[Reed, Joseph], 1741-1785.
Remarks on a late Publication in the
Independent Gazetteer.
Philadelphia, Bailey, 1783. 72, [1] pp.
AAS copy. 18147

[Reed, Joseph], 1741-1785.
Remarks on a late Publication in the
Independent Gazetteer. . . . Second
Edition.
Philadelphia, Bailey, 1783. 56? pp.]
(The recorded copies turned out to be the
1863 reprint.) 18148

[Reed, Joseph], 1741-1785.
Remarks on Governor Johnstone's
Speech.
Philadelphia, Bailey, 1779. 61 pp.
AAS copy. 16483

Rees, Thomas, stenographer.
A New System of Stenography.
Philadelphia, Humphreys, 1800. 14 pp., 2
plates.
AAS copy. 38364

Reese, Thomas, 1742-1796.
An Essay on the Influence of Religion.
Charleston, Markland & M'Iver, 1788. 87
pp.
BA copy. 21418

Reese, Thomas, 1742-1796.
Steadfastness in Religion.
Philadelphia, Young, 1793. 36 pp.
HEH copy. 46859

[Reeve, Clara], 1729-1807.
The Old English Baron.
Philadelphia, Stewart & Cochran, 1797.
213, [3] pp.
AAS copy. 32742

[Reeve, John, 1608-1658.
A Transcendent Spiritual Treatise. . . .
Second American Edition.
New London, Springer for Walden, 1797.
38 pp.]
("This day printed," Weekly Oracle, Aug.
12, 1797.) 32743

[Reeve, William], 1757-1815.
The Galley Slave.
Philadelphia, Carr, [1794]. [2] pp.
AAS copy. 47196

Reeve, William, 1757-1815.
[The Galley slave: a ballad.
Walnut Hills, Miss., Marschalk, 1798?]
(McMurtrie: Mississippi 1; no copy
known.) 48588

[Reeve, William], 1757-1815.
When Seated with Sal.
Philadelphia, Shaw, 1795.]
(Imprint assumed by Evans from Shaw's
advs.) 28504

[Reeve, William], 1757-1815.
When Seated with Sal.
Philadelphia, etc., Carr, [1795].
[2] pp.
AAS copy. 28503

[Reeve, William], 1757-1815.
The Witch.
New York, Gilfert, [1797]. [2] pp.
AAS copy. 48239

Reflections of a few Friends of the
Country. . . .

Philadelphia, 1776. 48 pp.
LCP copy. 15041

Reflections of a Saint.
Boston, J. Kneeland, 1772. 8 pp.
AAS copy. 42368

Reflections of a Saint.
Norwich, [Ct.], Green & Spooner,
[1773]. 8 pp.
AAS copy. 42486

[Reflections of a Saint, under a View of
the Presence of . . . God.
Norwich, Green & Spooner, [1774?]
8 pp.]
(No copy located.) 42678

[Reflections on a Wonderful Comet.
Concord, N.H., Russell, 1793.]
(Evans assumed the imprint from adv.
"To be sold" in 25274.) 26064

[Reflections on Courtship and Marriage
[by Benjamin Franklin, 1706-1790].
New York, 1746.]
(Title from adv., probably for copies of
5772.) 5773

Reflections on Courtship and Marriage
[by Benjamin Franklin, 1706-1790].
Philadelphia, Franklin, 1746. vii, 68 pp.
HSP copy. 5772

[Reflections on Courtship and Marriage.
. . . Third Edition [by Benjamin Franklin,
1706-1790].
Philadelphia, Dunlap, 1758.]
(Adv. Pa. Gazette, Feb. 23, 1758.) 8132

Reflections on Courtship and Marriage
[by Benjamin Franklin, 1706-1790].
Harrisburgh, Allen & Wyeth, 1793. vi, 95,
[1] pp.
NYPL copy. 25501

Reflections on Gov. Hopkins's
Vindication. . . . April 17, 1762.
[Newport, 1762.] 4 pp.
RIHS copy. 41302

Reflections on Love.
n. p., 1800. 12 pp.
AAS copy. 38365

Reflections on Monroe's View [by Uriah
Tracy, 1755-1807].
[Philadelphia, 1798.] 88 pp.
AAS copy. 34675

[Reflections on Taxes: the Principles
whereof are Essentially Applicable.
Wilmington, Del., Adams, 1794.]
("Just published by the Printers hereof,"
Delaware & Eastern-Shore Advertiser,
May 31, 1794.) 27601

Reflections on the Evil Consequences of
Tea Drinking.
n. p., 1760. 24 pp.
(No copy located.) 41869

Reflections on the Inconsistency of Man.
New York, Buel, 1796. 27 pp.
NYHS copy. 31077

[Reflections on the Policy and Necessity
of Encouraging the Commerce. . . .
Richmond, [1785]. 16 pp.]
(A ghost of 20036. q. v.) 19214

Reflections on the Policy and Necessity of
Encouraging the Commerce . . . of the
United States [by St. George Tucker,
1752-1827].
New York, Loudons, 1786. 16 pp.
LCP copy. 20036

Reflections on the Present State
Government of Virginia.
[Richmond?], 1793. 34 pp.
NYPL copy. 46860

Reflections on the Present State of the
Province of Massachusetts Bay.
Boston, Eliot and Henchman, 1720.
22 pp.
AAS copy. 2169

Reflections on the Proposition to
Communicate, by a Navigable Canal, the
Waters of Chesapeake with those of
Delaware Bay [by James Carroll].

Annapolis, Green, [1797]. 50 pp.
APS copy. 32744

Reflections upon Reflections: or more
news from Robinson Crusoes Island.
[Boston], 1720. [2], 14 pp.
(Attributed by Evans to Elisha Cooke,
1678-1737.)
BPL copy. 2111

Reflexiones sobre el Comercia de
España.
Philadelphia, Carey, 1799. 90, [2] pp., 1
folded table.
JCB copy. 36192

[Reflexions on the Present Combination
of the American Colonies.
New York, Gaine, 1778.]
(Entry from a Gaine adv.) 16027

Reflexions on the State of the Union [by
Tench Coxe, 1755-1824].
Philadelphia, Carey, 1792. 38 pp.
AAS copy. 24230

Reformed Church in America.
Acts and Proceedings of the General
Synod of the Reformed Dutch Church . . .
June 6, 1797.
New York, Forman, 1797. 14 pp.
Central College, Pella, Iowa, copy. 32745

Reformed Church in America.
A Collection of the Psalm and Hymn
Tunes, used by the Reformed Protestant
Dutch Church . . . of New York.
New York, Hodge & Shober, 1774. [8],
54, [2] pp.
(The one recorded copy could not be
located.) 42679

[Reformed Church in America.
The Constitution of the Dutch Church.
New Brunswick, Blauvelt, 1794.]
(Entry from advs., apparently for copies
of 26065.) 27602

Reformed Church in America.
The Constitution of the Reformed Dutch
Church, in the United States.
New York, Durell, 1793. xii, 354 pp.
AAS copy. 26065

Reformed Church in America.
Den Nederduytse Gereformeerde
Kerkenfaden . . . den 6 October, 1761.
[Philadelphia? 1761.] Broadside.
NYPL ph. copy. 41239

Reformed Church in America.
The Psalms of David. . . . For the Use of
the Reformed Dutch Church in America.
Albany, [N.Y.], Websters, 1791. 515, [3]
pp.
AAS copy. 46267

Reformed Church in America.
The Psalms of David. . . . For the Use of
the Reformed Dutch Church in North
America.
New Brunswick, N. J., Blauvelt, 1798. xii,
348 pp.
(For the 1797 Catechism which Evans
includes as part of this entry, see 32242.)
AAS copy. 33412

[Reformed Church in America.
The Whole Book of Forms.
New York, 1748. 216 pp.]
("Just published," N. Y. Evening-Post,
Sept. 5, 1748.) 6230

Reformed Church in America. General
Synod.
Acts and Proceedings of . . . 1800.
New York, Forman, [1800]. 40 pp.
AAS copy. 38366

Reformed Church in America. General
Synod.
Proceedings of the Meeting . . . October,
1771.
New York, M'Lean, [1785]. 24 pp.
JCB copy. 19215

Reformed Church in the United States.
Bekanmachung. Wir Vorsteher. . . .
[Philadelphia, 1743.] Broadside.
JCB copy. 5280

Reformed Church in the United States.

Catechismus, oder Kurtzer Unterricht
Christlicher Lehre.
Chestnut-Hill, [Pa.], 1763. 94, [1] pp.
PPL copy.   41408

Reformed Church in the United States.
Kern Alter und Neuer.
Germantown, 1752. 562, [10], 123 pp.
AAS copy.   6917

Reformed Church in the United States.
Kirchen-Formularien der
Evangelisch-Reformirten Gemeinen.
Germantown, Pa., Billmeyer, 1798. 60 pp.
AAS copy.   33701

Reformed Church in the United States.
Das Neue und Verbesserte Gesang-Buch.
Philadelphia, Steiner & Kammerer and H.
Kammerer, 1797. [6], 148, [8], 585, [43]
pp., 1 plate.
AAS copy.   32100

Reformed Church in the United States.
Das Neue und Verbesserte Gesangbuch.
Germantown, Billmeyer, 1799. [6], 148,
[8], 585, [9], 26 pp.
AAS copy.   35453

Reformed Church in the United States.
Neu-Vermehrt und Volktaendiges
Gesang-Buch.
Germantown, 1753. front., [2], 214,
[2] pp.
AAS copy.   7102

Reformed Church in the United States.
Neu-vermehrt-und Vollständiges
Gesang-Buch. . . . Vierte Auflage.
Philadelphia, Baisch, 1774. 190, [2], 480,
[12], 24, 72 pp.
AAS copy.   13565

Reformed Church in the United States.
Das Neue Verbesserte Gesangbuch.
Germantown, Billmeyer, 1799. [4], 148,
[8], 585, [9], 26 pp.
(Also entered as 35453, q. v.)   36193

Reformed Church of Scotland. Presbytery.
The Constitution of the
Associate-Reformed Synod in America
Considered.
Philadelphia, Young & M'Culloch, 1787.
24 pp.
AAS copy.   20207

Reformed Dutch Church in the United
States,
See
Reformed Church in America.

The Reformed German Church Lottery.
. . . April 13, 1772.
[New York, 1772.] Broadside.
LCP copy.   12535

Regeln und Articuls zu Besserer
Regierung.
Philadelphia, Franklin & Armbruester,
1757. [2], 40, [1] pp.
LOC copy.   8016

The Register of New Hampshire, with an
Almanack, for . . . 1795.
Exeter, Stearns & Winslow, 1795. [84] pp.
AAS copy.   27740

A Regulator for Crazy Will's Death-
Watch.
[New Haven? 1761.] 5 pp.
LOC copy.   8988

Reiche, Charles Christopher.
Fifteen Discourses.
Philadelphia, James & Johnson, 1791. [8],
180 pp.
AAS copy.   23729

[Reid, James, d. 1777.
(Weis, Colonial Clergy N. E.)
A Sermon Recommending Public Schools.
Newbern, 1763.]
(Ordered printed.)   9496

[Reid, Thomas, 1710-1796.
Essays on the Intellectual and Active
Powers of Man.
Philadelphia, Young, 1792? 2 vol.]
(Imprint assumed by Evans from adv.)
        24731

Reid, Thomas, 1710-1796.

Essays on the Intellectual and Active
Powers of Man.
Philadelphia, Young, 1793. 2 vol. pp.
[1]-xiv, [17]-590; [1]-604.
AAS copy.   26066

Reid, Thomas, 1739-1802.
An Essay on the Nature and Cure of . . .
Consumption.
Philadelphia, Crukshank, 1785. xi, [1], 89
pp.
AAS copy.   19216

Reinagle, Alexander, composer,
1756-1809.
America, Commerce & Freedom [by
Susanna (Haswell) Rowson, 1762-1824].
Philadelphia, Carr, [1794]. [2] pp.
NYPL copy.   27647

Reinagle, Alexander, 1756-1809.
Chorus sung before Gen. Washington. . . .
Apr. 21st, 1789.
Philadelphia, Rice, [1789]. [2], 4 pp.
LOC copy.   22093

[Reinagle, Alexander, 1756-1809.
A Collection of Favorite Songs.
Philadelphia, 1788.]
(The only copy recorded cannot be
located.)   21420

Reinagle, Alexander, 1756-1809.
A Collection, of Favorite Songs.
Philadelphia, Reinagle, [1789?]. [2], 22
pp.
LOC copy.   45572

Reinagle, Alexander, 1756-1809.
A Collection of Favorite Songs.
Philadelphia, Reinagle and Aitken,
[1789]. 20 pp.
UOP copy.   22095

Reinagle, Alexander, 1756-1809.
Federal March . . . the 4th of July, 1788.
[Philadelphia, 1788.] Broadside.
LOC copy.   21421

[Reinagle, Alexander], 1756-1809.
Indian March.
Philadelphia, Hupfeld, [c.1797].
Broadside.
NL copy.   48240

[Reinagle, Alexander, 1756-1809.
The Music of the Historical Play of
Columbus.
Philadelphia, 1799.]
(See Sonneck-Upton, p. 80.)   36194

Reinagle, Alexander, 1756-1809.
My Soul is Thine Sweet Norah.
[Philadelphia, 1789.] [2] pp.
NYPL copy.   22096

Reinagle, Alexander, 1756-1809.
A Select Collection of the most Favorite
Scots Tunes.
Philadelphia, [1787]. [2], 28 pp.
BPL copy.   20674

Reinagle, Alexander, 1756-1809.
A Sonata, sung by a Number of Young
Girls . . . April 21, 1789.
[Trenton, 1789.] Broadside.
LCP copy.   22094

Reinagle, Alexander, 1756-1809.
Tantivy Hark Forward Huzza.
Philadelphia, Reinagle and Aitken,
[1789]. [2] pp.
LOC copy.   22097

Reinagle, Alexander, 1756-1809.
'Tis not the Bloom on Damons Cheek.
Philadelphia, Reinagle, [1789]. 3 pp.
NYPL copy.   22098

Reinagle, Alexander, 1756-1809.
Twelve Favorite Pieces.
Philadelphia, Reinagle, [1789?]. [2], 24
pp.
LOC copy.   45573

Reinholdt, George Christoph, fl.
1763-1793.
George Christoph Reinholdt, Buchbinder.
. . .
[Philadelphia, 1773.] Broadside.
LCP copy.   12971

Eine Reise Nach Jerusalem. . . . [by

Nathaniel Crouch, 1632?-1725?].
Lancaster, Albrecht, 1792. 72 pp.
AAS copy.   46418

Reitz, Johann Heinrich, 1655-1720.
Das Fürbilde.
Lancaster, 1788. [12], 167 pp.
AAS copy.   21422

The Relapse.
[Boston, 1754.] 4 pp.
AAS copy.   7303

Relation de l'Anniversaire de la
Fédération du 14 Juillet 1789, Celebrée
. . . 14 Juillet 1795.
Charleston, Béleurgey, 1795. 4 pp.
JCB copy.   47574

Relation de la Sortie de l'Escadre
Française . . . 16 Mars, 1781.
[Newport, R.I., Imprimerie Royale de
l'Escadre, 1781?] 4 pp.
AAS copy.   44037

[A Relation of a Remarkable Providence,
which fell out at the Time of the Great
Earthquake at Jamaica.
Philadelphia, Chattin, 1755.]
(Adv. Pa. Journal, Nov. 27, 1755.)   7553

A Relation of the Fearful State of Francis
Spira [by Nathaniel Bacon, 1593-1660].
Wilmington, Del., Brynberg for
Thompson, [1796]. 57 pp.
Wilmington Institute Free Library copy.
        30012

A Relation of the Fearful Estate of
Francis Spira [by Nathaniel Bacon,
1593-1660].
Hartford, Ct., Babcock, 1798. 47 pp.
AAS copy.   33356

A Relation of the Fearful State of Francis
Spira [by Nathaniel Bacon, 1593-1660].
Philadelphia, Hogan, 1798. 107,
[1] pp.
AAS copy.   33357

A Relation of the Opposition which some
Baptist People met with [by John Bolles,
1677-1767].
[n.p., 1761.] 24 pp.
NYHS copy.   8802

Rélation, ou Journal des Opérations du
Corps Français [by Jean Baptiste
Donatien de Vimeur, Comte de,
1725-1807].
Philadelphia, Hampton, [1781]. 15 pp.
National Archives, Paris, copy.   44051

[Relf, Samuel], 1776-1823.
Infidelity, or the Victims of Sentiment.
Philadelphia, Woodward, 1797. 190,
[2] pp.
AAS copy.   32746

[Relfe, John], 1763-c. 1837.
Mary's Dream, or Sandy's Ghost.
Philadelphia, Carr, [1793]. [2] pp.
LOC copy.   26067

Reliance Property Company.
Constitution of the . . . June, 1799.
Baltimore, Hayes, 1799. [1], 12 pp.
HSP copy.   36195

Relief Society, Boston.
Rules and Orders of the . . . Instituted . . .
March 5th . . . 1773.
[Boston], Boyles, [1773]. Broadside.
BPL copy.   42487

The Religion of an Oath [by Cotton
Mather, 1663-1728].
Boston, Green for Henchman, 1719. [2],
30 pp.
AAS copy.   2045

The Religion of Jesus Christ the only True
Religion [7th ed.] [by Charles Leslie,
1650-1722].
Boston, Fleet for Checkley, 1719. [2], xii,
51, 7 pp.
AAS copy.   2029

Religion of the Ancient Brachmans.
Philadelphia, Chattin, 1752. 24 pp.
AAS copy.   6918

The Religion of the Closet [by Cotton
Mather, 1663-1728].
[Boston, 1705.] 42 pp.
(The only known copy is defective.)
MHS copy.   1220

The Religion of the Closet. . . . Second
Edition [by Cotton Mather, 1663-1728].
Boston, 1706. 42, [2] pp.
LOC copy.   1264

The Religion of the Cross [by Cotton
Mather, 1663-1728].
Boston, 1714. [4], 47, [1] pp.
AAS copy.   1697

Religious Courtship: being Historical
Discourse [by Daniel Defoe, 1661?-1731].
New York, Durell, 1793. 282 pp.
AAS copy.   25384

Religious Courtship: being Historical
Discourses [by Daniel Defoe,
1661?-1731].
Boston, Thomas & Andrews, 1794.
246 pp.
AAS copy.   26862

Religious Courtship: being Historical
Discourses [by Daniel Defoe,
1661?-1731].
New York, Duyckinck, 1794. 282 pp.
NYPL copy.   26863

Religious Courtship: being Historical
Discourses [by Daniel Defoe,
1661?-1731].
New York, Harrisson, 1794. 143 pp.
(The only known copy lacks pp. 11-14.)
AAS copy.   47025

Religious Courtship [by Daniel Defoe,
1661?-1731].
Wilmington, Del., Johnson, 1796.
303 pp.
(Pp. 265-274 omitted in pagination.)
AAS copy.   30326

The Religious Imposter Unmask'd; a
Satirical Poem.
Charleston, 1795. 50 (i.e., 52) pp.
JCB copy.   29395

Religious Instructions for Children,
Seventeenth Edition.
Philadelphia, Crukshank for Dickins,
1791. 72 pp.
AAS copy.   46268

The Religious Marriner [by Cotton
Mather, 1663-1728].
Boston, 1700. 40 pp.
MHS copy.   932

The Religious Tradesman, or, Plain and
Serious Hints [by Richard Steele,
1629-1692].
Newburyport, [1780]. 180 pp.
AAS copy.   16999

Religious Societies [by Cotton Mather,
1663-1728].
Boston, Kneeland for Phillips, 1724. [4],
8, 19 pp.
BA copy.   2558

The Religious Trader.
New York, Hodge & Shober for Loudon,
1773. 156 pp.
NYPL copy.   12972

The Religious Tradesman, or, Plain and
Serious Hints [by Richard Steele,
1629-1692].
Newburyport, Mycall for Titcomb &
Sawyer, [1790]. 180 pp.
(A duplicate of 16999, q. v.)   22831

[Relly, James, 1722?-1778.
Christian Hymns.
Boston, 1774.]
(Entry apparently from an adv. for
London ed.)   13566

Relly, James, 1722?-1778.
Christian Hymns.
Burlington, 1776. pp. [2], iv, 3-236, [8]
pp.
HC copy.   15042

Relly, James, 1722?-1778.
Christian Hymns.

Portsmouth, 1782. pp. [2], i-iv, 3-241, [1].
LOC copy.   17688

[Relly, James, 1722?-1778.
Christian Hymns.
Portsmouth, 1789.]
(From an adv., apparently for a remainder
of 17688.)   22099

Relly, James, 1722?-1778.
[Christian Hymns.
Fairhaven, Vt., Spooner, 1796?]. 40, 47
pp.
(The only known copy is imperfect.)
AAS copy.   47889

[Relly, James, 1722?-1778.
Hymns used in the Universal Churches.
Boston, Larkin, 1791.]
("Just published, and to be sold by B.
Larkin," Columbian Centinel, June 11,
1791.)   23730

Relly, James, 1722?-1778.
The Salt of the Sacrifice.
Concord, [N.H.], Russell, 1793. viii, 112
pp.
AAS copy.   46861

[Relly, James], 1722?-1778.
A Short Specimen of Apostolick
Preaching.
Burlington, Collins, 1773. 19 pp.
HEH copy.   42488

Relly, James, 1722?-1778.
Union.
Boston, White & Adams, 1779. xx, 72 pp.
AAS copy.   16484

Relly, James, 1722?-1778.
Union: or, A treatise of Consanguinity.
Boston, Edes for Larkin, [178-?] xxxiv,
174 pp.
LOC copy.   43752

Relly, James, 1722?-1778.
Union.
Providence, Carter, 1782. xvi, 75 pp.
AAS copy.   17689

Relly, James, 1722?-1778.
Union.
Boston, Edes, 1791. xxxiv, 174 pp.
AAS copy.   46269

Relly, James, 1722?-1778.
Union.
Boston, Edes for Larkin, [1791]. xxxiv,
174 pp.
(But for imprint identical with 46269, q. v.
for text.)
AAS copy.   46270

Relly, John.
Written on Hearing of the Much-
Lamented Death of . . . George
Whitefield.
Philadelphia, Dunlap, [1770?] Broadside.
BPL copy.   42159

The Remainder of the Observations
Promised in the Mercury.
[Philadelphia, 1735.] 4 pp.
LCP copy.   3956

A Remark on the Disputes and
Contentions in this Province [by
Theodorus Frelinghuysen, 1723-1761?].
New York, Gaine, 1755. 12 pp.
(For authorship see BSA, XLIV, 327-329.)
NYHS copy.   7456

A Remarkable Account, of a Young Lady
of Fortune.
Boston, Fowle, 1753. 16 pp.
MHS copy.   7103

A Remarkable Account of Guy, who, by
Strange Enterprizes in War. . . .
Windsor, Vt., Spooner, 1792. 11 pp.
BA copy.   46556

A Remarkable and Surprising Account of
the Abandoned Life . . . and Comfortable
Death of Fanny Sidney.
Troy, 1799. 8 pp.
NYPL copy.   36196

Remarkable Curiosities.
n. p., [1794]. 16 pp.
AAS copy.   47197

[A Remarkable Dream; Turned into
Verse.
Boston, Kneeland & Green, 1736.]
(Adv. Boston News-Letter, Sept. 23,
1736.)   4072

Remarkable Dreams, &c. or. Thoughts
from the Visions of the Night.
Printed in the year 1800. 36 pp.
AAS copy.   49142

The Remarkable History of Augi.
Worcester, Thomas, 1796. 31 pp.
AAS copy.   31080

The Remarkable History of Augi. . . .
Second Worcester Edition.
Worcester, Thomas, 1799. 31 pp.
AAS copy.   36197

The Remarkable History of Miss Villars
[by William Rufus Chetwood, d. 1766].
Norwich, Trumbull, 1793. 24 pp.
AAS copy.   25294

The Remarkable History of Miss Villars
[by William Rufus Chetwood, d. 1766].
Keene, Sturtevant, 1795. 16+ pp.
(The only recorded copy is incomplete.)
JCB copy.   28415

The Remarkable History of Miss Villars
[by William Rufus Chetwood, d. 1766].
Keene, N.H., Sturtevant, 1795. 17 pp.
(No perfect copy known.)
AAS copy.   47383

The Remarkable History of Tom Jones.
. . . First Worcester Edition [by Henry
Fielding, 1707-1754].
Worcester, Thomas, 1787. 31 pp.
AAS copy.   20356

The Remarkable History of Tom Jones
[by Henry Fielding, 1707-1754].
Boston, Hall, 1791. 28, [2] pp.
AAS copy.   46166

The Remarkable History of Tom Jones
[by Henry Fielding, 1707-1754].
Boston, Hall, 1794. 28, [3] pp.
(Present location unknown.)   47042

The Remarkable History of Tom Jones.
. . . Third Worcester Edition [by Henry
Fielding, 1707-1754].
Worcester, Mass., Thomas, 1794. 31 pp.
AAS copy.   47043

The Remarkable History of Tom Jones
[by Henry Fielding, 1707-1754].
Salem, Mass., "Printed and sold at Faust's
Head, Essex Street," 1799. 29 pp.
AAS copy.   36198

The Remarkable History of Tom Jones.
. . . Fourth Worcester Edition [by Henry
Fielding, 1707-1754].
Worcester, Thomas, 1799. 28, [3] pp.
AAS copy.   35482

A Remarkable Narrative of an Expedition
against the Indians [by Hugh Henry
Brackenridge, 1748-1816].
[Leominster, Mass.], Whitcomb,
[1799?] 23, [1] pp.
HEH copy.   48810

A Remarkable Narrative of the Captivity
and Escape of Mrs. Frances Scott.
Newburyport, Parker & Robinson,
[1799]. 15 pp.
(No perfect copy located.)
AAS copy.   36199

A Remarkable Narrative of the Captivity
and Escape of Mrs. Frances Scott.
[Leominster, Mass?], Whitcomb, [1800?].
16 pp.
AAS copy.   49143

Remarkable Occurrences.
[Philadelphia, 1765.] [4] pp.
(This is the Pa. Gazette for Nov. 14,
1765.)
AAS copy.   10153

[Remarkable Prophecy, Found Engraved
on a Stone.
Portsmouth, N. H., Peirce, 1798.]
(Imprint assumed by Evans from adv. "To
be sold," Oracle of the Day, Sept. 29,
1798.)   34438

A Remrkable Prophecy Supposed to have
been laid Six Hundred Years under a
Stone in Paris.
Boston, White, 1798. 11 pp.
(Not located, 1968.) 48589

A Remarkable Prophecy. The Following
was Handed in. . . .
Exeter, Ranlet, 1794. 11 pp.
LOC copy. 27603

A Remarkable Prophecy (The Following
was Handed in Print. . . .)
Portsmouth, 1794. 8 pp.
(The title given by Evans is from the
advs.)
AAS copy. 27604

A Remarkable Relation. You Parents that
have Children Dear. . . .
Hartford, 1772. Broadside.
AAS copy. 42369

Remarks, &c. on some late Laws Passed
in New-York. . . . Bennington, April 15th,
1774.
n. p., [1774]. Broadside.
MHS ph. copy. 42680

Remarks Occasioned by the Late Conduct
of Mr. Washington.
Philadelphia, Bache, 1797. [iv], 84 pp.
AAS copy. 31759

Remarks on a late Pamphlet Entitled
Plain Truth.
Philadelphia, Dunlap, 1776. 31 pp.
AAS copy. 14735

[Remarks on a late Pamphlet Entitled,
"Some Considerations, on the
Consequences of the French Settling
Colonies on the Mississippi."
Boston, 1720.]
(Prince Ms. and Sabin 69394.) 2170

Remarks on a late Pamphlet, Intitled,
"The Opinion. . . ." [by Peter Clark,
1694-1768].
Boston, Edes & Gill, 1758, 43, [1] pp.
AAS copy. 8102

Remarks on a late Performance, Sign'd A
Freeman of the Colony. . . . [Dated:]
March 22, 1762.
[Newport, R. I., 1762.] 3 pp.
AAS copy. 41303

Remarks on a late Piece, Intitled, "A Fair
Narrative. . . ." [By Robert Abercrombie,
1712-1780].
Boston, Edes & Gill for McAlpine, 1757.
64 pp.
AAS copy. 7826

Remarks on a late Publication in the
Independent Gazetteer [by Joseph Reed,
1741-1785].
Philadelphia, Bailey, 1783. 72, [1] pp.
AAS copy. 18147

[Remarks on a late Publication in the
Independent Gazetteer. . . . Second
Edition [by Joseph Reed, 1741-1785].
Philadelphia, Bailey, 1783. 56? pp.]
(The recorded copies turned out to be the
1863 reprint.) 18148

Remarks on a Pamphlet, Entitled, "A
Dissertation on the Political Union. . . .
[by Roger Sherman, 1721-1793].
[New Haven], 1784. 43 pp.
AAS copy. 18782

Remarks on a Pamphlet, Entitled,
"Considerations on the Bank of
North-America."
Philadelphia, Steele, 1785. 16 pp.
HC copy. 19217

Remarks on a Second Publication of B.
Henry Latrobe.
[Philadelphia, 1797.] 7 pp.
(The second part of 35399, q. v.) 36200

Remarks on Dr. Gale's Letter [by
Eliphalet Dyer, 1721-1807].
[Hartford], 1769. 27 pp.
AAS copy. 11243

Remarks on Dr. Mayhew's Incidental
Reflections [by Arthur Browne,
1699-1773].

Portsmouth, 1763. 31 pp.
AAS copy. 9357

Remarks on Governor Johnstone's Speech
[by Joseph Reed, 1741-1785].
Philadelphia, Bailey, 1779. 61 pp.
AAS copy. 16483

[Remarks on Several Passages of Mr.
Whitefield's Sermons.
Philadelphia, 1740.]
(Adv. Pa. Gazette, Oct. 16, 1740.) 4591

Remarks on Sir William Keith's
Vindication [by James Logan, 1674-1751].
Philadelphia, Bradford, 1726. 24 + pp.
(The unique copy is imperfect.)
HSP copy. 2808

Remarks on Some Contents of a Letter
Relating to the Divisions of the First
Church in Salem.
Boston, Fleet, 1735. 16 pp.
(In re authorship see Sibley, VII, 462.)
AAS copy. 3880

Remarks on Some Points of Doctrine [by
John Chipman?, 1691-1775].
Boston, Kneeland & Green, 1746. 44 pp.
AAS copy. 5890

Remarks on the Address of Sixteen
Members of the Assembly of Pennsylvania
[by Pelatiah Webster, 1726-1795].
Philadelphia, Oswald, 1787. 28 pp.
AAS copy. 20871

Remarks on the American Universal
Geography [by James Freeman,
1759-1835].
Boston, Belknap & Hall, 1793. 61, [1] pp.
AAS copy. 25510

Remarks on the Assertions of the Author
of the Memoirs of Jacobinsim Respecting
. . . Swedenborg.
Philadelphia, Ormrod, 1800. 37 pp.
(Also entered as 37197, q. v.) 38367

Remarks on the Bill of Rights [by James
Hay, fl. 1796].
n. p., 1796. 35 pp.
LOC copy. 47801

Remarks on the Book of Daniel [by
Samuel Osgood, 1748-1813].
New York, Greenleaf, 1794. [2], 503, [2]
pp.
AAS copy. 26663

Remarks on the Doings of a Convention
held at Cornish [by Thomas Fessenden,
1739-1813].
Westminster, 1782. 35 pp.
AAS copy. 17533

Remarks on the Insidious Letter of the
Gallic Despots.
By Peter Porcupine [by William Cobbett,
1762-1835].
[Philadelphia, 1798.] Broadside.
AAS copy. 33529

[Remarks on the Introduction to Rev.
Charles Inglis' Essay on Infant Baptism.
New York, 1769.]
(Haven says that there was a N. Y.
reprint.) 11437

Remarks on the Jacobiniad [by John
Sylvester John Gardiner, 1765-1830].
Boston, Wild & Greenough, 1795. 54 pp.,
6 plates.
AAS copy. 28726

Remarks on the Jacobiniad. . . . Part
Second [by John Sylvester John Gardiner,
1765-1830].
Boston, 1798. pp. [i]-xi, [1], [9]-56.
AAS copy. 33779

Remarks on the late Printed Answer to
Colonel Choate's Reasons [by John
Choate, 1697-1765].
Boston, Edes & Gill, 1761. 43 pp.
AAS copy. 8814

Remarks on the late Proceedings of some
Members of the Assembly at Philadelphia:
April, 1728.
[Philadelphia, 1728.] [4] pp.
HSP copy. 3098

Remarks on the Letter Addressed to Two
Great Men [by William Burke, -1798].
Boston, Mecom, [1761]. 40 pp.
("This day published," Boston
News-Letter, Jan. 22, 1761.)
AAS copy. 8751

Remarks on the Manufacturing of Maple
Sugar.
Philadelphia, James & Johnson, 1790. 24
pp.
JCB copy. 22832

[Remarks on the Manufacturing of Maple
Sugar.
Albany, Websters, 1791.]
("This day printed and now selling at
Webster's Printing-Office," Albany
Gazette, Feb. 24, 1791.) 23732

Remarks on the Manufacturing of Maple
Sugar.
New York, Morton, 1791. 23 pp.
JCB copy. 23731

Remarks on the Nature and bad Effects of
Spirituous Liquors [by Anthony Benezet,
1713-1784].
[Philadelphia, 1775.] 12 pp.
AAS copy. 13831

Remarks on the Organization and
Constitutional Powers of the Council of
Appointment.
Albany, N. Y., Barber & Southwick, 1799.
15 pp.
NYHS copy. 36201

[Remarks on the Pamphlet, Entitled, The
Folly of Reason.
New London, Green, 1795.]
(The origin of this entry is unknown.)
29396

Remarks on the Plan . . . of January 4th
1753 [Plymouth Company, 1749-1816].
[Boston, 1753.] 8 pp.
AAS copy. 7098

Remarks on the Preface of a Pamphlet
Published by John Presbyter [by Andrew
Le Mercier, 1692-1763].
[Boston, 1737.] 17 pp.
(Authorship from contemporary ms. note
in MHS copy.)
AAS copy. 4190

Remarks on the Proceedings of the
Episcopal Conventions for Forming an
American Constitution [by Bailey
Bartlett, 1750-1830].
Boston, Hall, 1786. 8 pp.
AAS copy. 19495

Remarks on the Proposed Plan of a
Federal Government [by Alexander
Contee Hanson, 1749-1806].
Annapolis, Green, [1788]. 42 pp.
AAS copy. 21131

Remarks on the Proposed Plan of an
Emission of Paper [by Alexander Contee
Hanson, 1749-1806].
Annapolis, Green, [1787]. 43 pp.
AAS copy. 20403

Remarks on the Quaker Unmask'd.
Philadelphia, Morris, [1764]. 8 pp.
HSP copy. 9813

Remarks on the Report of the Secretary of
the Treasury to the House of
Representatives.
n.p., 1790. 31 pp.
NYPL copy. 22833

Remarks on the Result of an Ecclesiastical
Council, which met at Dorchester [by
Jonathan? Bowman, 1704-1775].
Boston, Boyle, 1774. 39 pp.
AAS copy. 13171

Remarks on the Rev. Mr. Cooper's
Objections.
[Boston, 1743.] 8 pp.
MHS copy. 4947

Remarks on the Rev. Mr. Cooper's
Objections. . . . Second Edition.
[Boston, 1743.] 8 pp.
AAS copy. 4948

Remarks on the Rev. Mr. Cooper's

Objections. . . . Third Edition.
Boston, 1743. 8 pp.
AAS copy.   4949

Remarks on the Rev. Mr. Joshua Gee's
Letter.
[Boston, 1743.] 7 pp.
(Adv. Boston News-Letter, July 28, 1743.)
AAS copy.   5392

Remarks on the Treaty of Amity,
Navigation, and Commerce.
Philadelphia, Tuckniss for Carey, 1796. 36
pp.
AAS copy.   30255

Remarks on Zenger's Trial [by Jonathan
Blenman, of Barbados].
[Philadelphia, 1737.] 71 pp.
(See Hildeburn 551.)
HSP copy.   4118

Remarks on Zenger's Tryal [by Jonathan
Blenman].
New York, Gaine, 1770. 60 pp.
LOC copy.   11573

Remarks. The Common Rates of Land
Carriage. . . . Philadelphia, January 20,
1772.
[Philadelphia, 1772.] Broadside, maps.
LCP copy.   42370

Remarks upon a Discourse Preached
December 15th 1774 [by Henry Barry?,
1750-1822].
[New York, 1775.] 11 pp.
AAS copy.   13825

Remarks upon a Late Paper of
Instructions, Calculated for the Meridian
of Four Counties . . . of New York.
New York, Holt, 1770. [2], 22 pp.
Chapin Library, Williams College, copy.
                                             42160

Remarks upon a Message, Sent by the
Upper to the Lower House of the
Assembly of Maryland, 1762.
[Philadelphia?], 1763 (1764). 71 pp.
(See Wroth, Maryland, p. 221.)
NYPL copy.   9497

Remarks upon a Pamphlet [by Jonathan
Dickinson, 1688-1747].
Philadelphia, Bradford, 1735. [2], 32 pp.
MHS copy.   3897

Remarks upon the Advice of the
Freeholders, & c.
[Philadelphia, 1727.] 4 pp.
NYPL copy.   2951

Remarks upon The Delineated
Presbyterian.
Philadelphia, Armbruster, 1764. 8 pp.
HSP copy.   9814

Remarks upon the Resolves of the New
Committee. . . . July 22, 1774.
[New York, 1774.] Broadside.
NYPL copy.   13244

The Remarks, which the Author [by
Nicolaus Ludwig Zinzendorf, 1700-1760].
Philadelphia, 1742. 24 pp.
NYPL copy.   5108

A Rememberable Account, of the Death
of Stephen Fisk, of Brinfield.
n.p., [1785?]. Broadside.
NYPL copy.   44784

A Remembrance of Former Times [by
William Jameson?].
Boston, 1697. 32 pp.
AAS copy.   784

Remer Lottery.
Scheme of a Lottery . . . November 3,
1769.
[New York, 1769.] Broadside.
LCP copy.   41997

Remington, E [lizabeth?]
A Short Account of Three Men . . . Killed
by Lightning.
New London, Green, 1767. Broadside.
PrU copy.   41756

Remington, E[lizabeth?].
A Short Account of Three Young Men.
. . . Aug. 26, 1766.

[New London, 1767?]. Broadside.
NYHS copy.   10747

Remington, James, pseud.
The Last Words, Dying Speech, and
Confession of J--s R--g--n . . . on the
Thirteenth day of April, 1775.
[New York, 1775.] Broadside.
NYPL copy.   14041

Remmele, John.
The Design and Nature of Atonement.
Windsor, 1786. 42 pp.
VtU copy.   19948

Remmey, John.
An Account of the Present State of Egypt.
New York, Davises for Reid, 1799. pp.
[4], [9]-107, [1]; 2 folding maps.
AAS copy.   36202

A Remonstrance; By David Marin Ben
Jesse [Dated Nov. 4, 1754], [by
Theodorus Frelinghuysen, 1723-1761?].
[New York], 1755. [2], 14 pp.
(For authorship see BSA, XLIV, 327-329.)
HEH copy.   7457

Renatus [by Cotton Mather, 1663-1728].
Boston, Gerrish, 1725. 34 pp.
MHS copy.   2672

Renault & Verger, firm.
Prospectus of an Allegorical Picture, of
the Triumph of Liberty. . . . December 1,
1796.
[Philadelphia? 1796.] Broadside.
(Not located 1967.)
JCB copy.   47890

Renault & Verger, firm.
Sir, Conscious of your Taste for Arts. . . .
[New York, 1796.] Broadside.
JCB copy.   47891

[A Renewal of the Covenants . . . at
Middle Octorars . . . November 11, 1743.
Philadelphia, Franklin & Hall, 1748.] [2],
104 pp. (Ms. tp.)
HSP copy.   40475

Reparation Lottery.
. . . Class the First. Scheme . . . October
31, 1792.
[Windsor? 1793.] Broadside.
AAS ph. copy.   46862

Repeated Admonitions [by Cotton
Mather, 1663-1728].
Boston, Fleet, 1725. [2], iii, 19 pp.
(For the text see E2673.)
VaU copy.   39835

Repeated Warnings [by Cotton Mather,
1663-1728].
Boston, 1712. [2], 33, [1] pp.
YC copy.   1556

Repent and be Converted [by Samuel
Fothergill, 1715-1772].
Philadelphia, Crukshank, 1778. 31 pp.
HSP copy.   15796

A Reply to a Letter from a Gentleman in
New-York to his Friend in Brunswick.
[New York], 1750. 8 pp.
HEH copy.   6618

A Reply to a Pamphlet, Entitled,
Considerations on the Society or Order of
Cincinnati, &c.
Annapolis, [1783]. 30 pp.
HC copy.   18149

A Reply to a Pamphlet, Entitled, The
Answer of the Friend in the West [by
Benjamin Gale, 1715-1790].
[New London], 1755. 63 pp.
LOC copy.   7424

A Reply to Alexander Hamilton's Letter
Concerning . . . John Adams.
New York, Nichols, 1800. 16, 4 pp.
NYPL copy.   38370

A Reply to An Address to the Author of a
Pamphlet, Entitled, A Candid
Examination [by Joseph Galloway,
1731?-1803].
New York, Rivington, 1775. 42 pp.
NYPL ph. copy.   14060

A Reply to An Address to the Roman

Catholics of the United States [by Charles
Henry Wharton, 1748-1833].
Philadelphia, Cist, 1785. 97, [1], 9, [1]
pp.
AAS copy.   19382

A Reply to an Address: Written by the
Great I [by Clark Brown, 1771-1817].
[Worcester], Spy Printing-Office, 1798.
16 pp.
BA copy.   34439

A Reply to Col. Clap's Vindication.
[Boston], 1760. 24 pp.
AAS copy.   8719

A Reply to Sir Henry Clinton's Narrative.
New York, Sower, Morton, & Horner for
Berry & Rogers, 1783. [2], 48 pp.
AAS copy.   18208

A Reply to some Remarks on a Letter to a
Gentleman.
[Boston, 1731.] 16 pp.
AAS copy.   3471

A Reply to the Church of England
Planter's First Letter [by Bennett Allen,
1737-1782 +].
Annapolis, 1770. 22 pp.
MdHS copy.   11830

A Reply to the Church of England
Planter's First Letter [by Bennett Allen,
1737-1782 +].
Annapolis, Green, 1770. 16 pp.
MdHS copy.   42052

A Reply to the False Reasoning in the
"Age of Reason" [by Miers Fisher,
1748-1819].
Philadelphia, Tuckniss, 1796. 40 pp.
AAS copy.   30423

A Reply to the Objections made against
Taking the Small Pox. . . . Third
Impression [by William Cooper, 1694-
1743].
Boston, Gerrish and Phillips, 1730. [4],
iv, 14, [2] pp.
AAS copy.   3270

Réponse a la Lettre Circulaire de
Monsieur Dn. Martin Novarro, Intendant.
. . . Du 29 Aout, 1780.
[New Orleans], Boudousquie, 1780. [2]
pp.
(McMurtrie: New Orleans 31b. Present
location unknown.)   43871

Report of an Action for a Libel, Brought
by Dr. Benjamin Rush.
Philadelphia, Woodward, 1800. [70] pp.
(Also entered as 37103, q. v.)   38371

A Report of the Case between Field and
Harrison [by George Wythe, 1726-1806].
Richmond, Nicolson, 1796. 32 pp.
VaSL copy.   31667

[Report of the Case] Between Joseph
Wilkins . . . and John Taylor [by George
Wythe, 1726-1806].
[Richmond, 1796.] 30, [1] pp.
LOC copy.   31670

[Report of the Case] Between, William
Fowler and Susanna his Wife, Plaintiffs
and Lucy Saunders [by George Wythe,
1726-1806].
[Richmond, 1796.] 28 pp.
LOC copy.   31668

[Report of the Case] Between William
Yates and Sarah his Wife . . . and
Abraham Salle. . . . [by George Wythe,
1726-1806].
[Richmond, 1796.] 30, [1] pp.
LOC copy.   31671

[Report of the Case of] Love against
Donelson and Hodgson [by George
Wythe, 1726-1806].
[Richmond, 1796.] 34 pp.
LOC copy.   31669

Reports of Committee in Congress to
whom were Referred Certain Memorials
. . . Concerning the Alien and Sedition
Laws. . . . Also an Answer of the
Massachusetts Legislature.
Richmond, Va., Nicolson, 1799. 20 pp.
(Also entered as 36573, q. v.)   36205

The Representation and Petition of Divers
Religious Denominations of the City of
Philadelphia to the Legislature.
Philadelphia, Aitken, 1798. 16 pp.
LCP copy.   34335

A Representation of Facts, Relative to the
Conduct of Daniel Moore.
Charleston, 1767. 43 pp.
(The pagination given by Evans comes
from the Sabin entry.)
BM copy.   10748

A Representation of the Figures Exhibited
and Paraded through the Streets of
Philadelphia [Sept. 30, 1780].
[Philadelphia, 1780.] Broadside.
Williams College copy.   16959

Representative for the 7th Congress.
Thomas Noyes, of Westerly.
n. p., n. d. Broadside.
BrU copy.   38374

Representative Reform Association.
An Address to the People of
South-Carolina.
Charleston, Young, 1794. pp. [2], [i]-vi,
[3]-42.
JCB copy.   26784

The Reprimander, Reprimanded [by
Nathan Perkins, 1748-1838].
Hartford, 1781. 16 pp.
NYPL copy.   17086

The Reprobate's Reward, or, A
Looking-glass for Disobedient Children.
Philadelphia, 1793. 8 pp.
NYPL copy.   46863

The Reprobate's Reward.
Philadelphia, 1798. 8 pp.
(Not located, 1968.)   48590

The Republican Calendar for . . . 1800.
Washington, Pa., Israel. [36] pp.
AAS copy.   36207

Republican Party, 1792-1828.
See
Democratic Party.

Republican Prayers.
New York, 1796. [24] pp.
Forrest Bowe copy.   47892

Republican Society of South Carolina.
Charleston, [blank] August, 1793. Fellow
Citizens. . . .
[Charleston, 1793.] [2] pp.
JCB copy.   46864

Der Republikanische Calender, auf das
1779ste Jahr.
Lancaster, Cossart. [40] pp.
NYPL copy.   16029

Der Republikanische Calender auf das
1780ste Jahr Christi.
Lancaster, Cossart, 1779. [36] pp.
Lancaster County Hist. Soc. copy.   16485

Der Republikanische Calender auf das
1781ste Jahr.
Lancaster, Cossart. [40] pp.
(The only copy located is defective.)
AAS copy.   16960

Der Republikanische Calender, auf das
1782ste Jahr Christi.
Lancaster, Cossart. [32] pp.
(The only copy located lacks a leaf.)
AAS copy.   17326

[Der Republikanische Calender auf das
1783ste Jahr Christi.
Philadelphia, Cossart.]
(Adv. Freeman's Journal, Oct. 2, 1782.)
                                             17690

The Request [by Gerard Vogler].
New York and Philadelphia, B. Carr;
Baltimore, J. Carr, [1796]. Broadside.
AAS copy.   48008

A Residence in France [by Helen Maria
Williams, 1762-1827].
Elizabethtown, N. J., Kollock for Davis,
1798. 517 pp.
AAS copy.   35030

Resignation. In Two Parts [by Edward
Young, 1683-1765].
Philadelphia, Bradford, 1764. 74 pp.
AAS copy.   9888

Resignation, a Poem [by Edward Young,
1683-1765].
Philadelphia, Bailey, 1795. 88 pp.
AAS copy.   29938

The Resolutions of Congress, of the 18th
of April, 1783. . . . By a Republican.
New York, Carroll & Patterson, 1787. 68
pp.
AAS copy.   20783

The Resolved Christian [by Cotton
Mather, 1663-1728].
Boston, 1700. [8], 128 pp.
(This is Evans 487 reissued with a new
title-page.)
JCB copy.   933

The Resort of Piety [by Cotton Mather,
1663-1728].
Boston, 1716. 47 pp.
JCB copy.   1830

Restitutus [by Cotton Mather, 1663-1728].
Boston, Gerrish, 1727. [4], 54 pp.
AAS copy.   2917

The Resurrection of Laurent Ricci [by
Claude Florent Bouchard de la Poterie, b.
1751].
Philadelphia, 1789. 28 pp.
AAS copy.   21706

Retort, Dick, pseud.
Tit for Tat; or, A Purge for a Pill [by
William Cobbett, 1763-1835].
Philadelphia, [1796]. 34, 25 pp.
LOC copy.   30314

The Returned Captive. A Poem.
Hudson, 1787. 60 pp.
BrU copy.   20676

[The Returned Captive. A Poem.
Philadelphia, Dobson, 1787.]
("This Day is Published, and Sold by
Thomas Dobson, " Pa. Mercury, July 6,
1787.)   20677

The Returned Captive, a Poem.
Northampton, Mass., Wright, 1800. 50 pp.
AAS copy.   38381

The Returned Captive a Poem. Founded
on a Fact.
Norwich, Trumbull, 1790. 56 pp.
CHS copy.   22834

A Revealed Knowledge of the Prophecies
and Times, Particularly of the Present
Time [by Richard Brothers, 1757-1824].
Philadelphia, Bailey, 1795. 72 pp.
AAS copy.   28358

A Revealed Knowledge of the Prophecies
and Times, Particularly of the Present
Time [by Richard Brothers, 1757-1824].
Philadelphia, Campbell, 1795. 139 pp.
AAS copy.   28359

The Revelation of Nature [by John
Stewart, 1749-1822].
New York, Mott & Lyon, [1796]. xxxix,
[1], 104 pp.
AAS copy.   31238

Revere, Paul, 1733-1815.
The Bloody Massacre Perpetrated.
Boston, Revere, [1770]. Engraving.
AAS composite copy.   42161

Reverend Mr. [blank] Sir. It Having
Pleased the Great Head of the Church.
. . . New-Haven December 5th. 1794.
[Norwich? 1794.] [4] pp.
CHS copy.   47198

Rev. Mr. [blank] Sir, We have Taken the
Liberty. . . . Sept. 1794.
[Norwich, 1794]. [2] pp.
CHS copy.   47199

The Reverend Mr. Smith Vindicated [by
William Smith, 1727-1803].
[Philadelphia, 1756.] [2] pp.
LCP copy.   7793

The Review. It was a Saying. . . .

[Boston, 1754.] 8 pp.
BA copy.   7304

Review of the Administration of the
Government of the United States . . .
Since the Year Ninety-Three.
Boston, Russell, 1797. 87 pp.
AAS copy.   33066

A Review of the Constitution Proposed by
the late Convention.
Philadelphia, Smith & Prange, 1787. 39
pp.
PSL copy.   20678

A Review of the Military Operations in
North-America [by William Smith,
1728-1793].
New York, Robertsons, 1770. 170 pp.
AAS copy.   11701

A Review of the Question, In whom has
the Constitution Vested the Treaty
Power?
Philadelphia, Smith, 1796. 35, [1] pp.
LCP copy.   31086

A Review of the Rector Detected [by
John Camm, 1718-1779.].
Williamsburg, 1764. 29 pp.
NYPL copy.   9612

A Review of the Revenue System [by
William Findley, 1741?-1821].
Philadelphia, Dobson, 1794. [2], ii, 130
pp.
AAS copy.   26973

A Revisal of the Intreagues of the
Triumvirate.
[Philadelphia, 1729?] 4 pp.
LCP copy.   3210

The Revolution in France [by Noah
Webster, 1758-1843].
New York, Bunce, 1794. 72 pp.
AAS copy.   28053

The Revolution in New England Justified
[by Edward Rawson? 1615-1693].
Boston [i.e. London], 1691. [6], 48 pp.
NYPL copy.   575

The Revolution in New England Justified
[by Edward Rawson? 1615-1693].
Boston, Thomas, 1773. 59 pp.
AAS copy.   12973

Revolutionary Justice [by baron Honore
Riouffe, 1764-1813].
Philadelphia, Folwell for Davies, [1796].
180 pp.
AAS copy.   31106

The Reward of Avarice: or, Abdalla and
the Iron Candlestick.
Hartford, Babcock, 1798. 29, [2] pp.
(Not located, 1968.)   48591

[Reyner, Edward], 1600-1668.
(D. N. B.)
Precepts for Christian Practice.
Cambridge, 1668. [6], 34 pp.
(Mass. Hist. Soc., Proceedings, XLVI,
259.)
AAS copy.   116

[Reyner, Edward], 1600-1668.
(D. N. B.)
The Rule of a new Creature.
Boston, 1682. 15 pp.
(Mass. Hist. Soc., Proceedings, XLVI,
259.)
PPL copy.   333

Reynolds, Frederic, 1764-1841.
The Dramatist.
New York, Swords for Reid, 1793. 60 pp.,
1 plate.
AAS copy.   26070

Reynolds, Frederic, 1764-1841.
How to Grow Rich: a Comedy.
Philadelphia, Smith, 1794. 48 pp.
AAS copy.   27606

[Reynolds, John], 1667-1727.
(D. N. B.)
A Compassionate Address to the
Christian World.
Boston, Phillips, [1730]. [2], 108, [1], ii,
4 pp.
AAS copy.   3345

Reynolds, Peter, 1700-1768.
The Kingdom is the Lord's.
New London, 1757. 51 pp.
AAS copy.   8017

Reynolds, Thomas, 1667?-1727.
(D. N. B.)
Practical Religion Exemplify'd.
Boston, 1713. [10], 109 pp.
AAS copy.   1645

A Rhapsody. A Poem.
New York, Hodge, Allen & Campbell,
1789. 19 pp.
BrU copy.   22100

Rhea, John, fl. 1765.
John Rhea Desires to Return his Thanks.
. . . February 18, 1772.
[Philadelphia, 1772.] Broadside.
LCP copy.   12536

Rhees, Morgan John, 1760-1804.
The Altar of Peace.
Philadelphia, Conrad, 1798. 15 pp.
AAS copy.   34441

[Rhees, Morgan John], 1760-1804.
Letters on Liberty and Slavery. . . .
Second Edition.
New York, Wilson, 1798. 24 pp.
LCP copy.   34442

Rhees, Morgan John, 1760-1804.
An Oration, Delivered at Greenville.
Philadelphia, Lang & Ustick, 1795. 7 pp.
JCB copy.   29399

Rhetoric and Poetry [by Robert Dodsley,
1703-1764].
Boston, Thomas & Andrews, 1796. 59 pp.
AAS copy.   30360

[Rhoads, Asa.
An American Spelling-Book.
New York, 1798.]
(Entry from the copyright application.)
                                                   34443

Rhode Island (Colony) Charters.
The Charter Granted by His Majesty King
Charles.
Boston, Allen for Boone, 1719. [2], 8 pp.
NYPL copy.   2070

Rhode Island (Colony) Charters.
The Charter Granted by His Majesty.
Newport, 1744. 15 pp.
(Issued to be prefixed to 5683, q.v.)   5484

[Rhode Island (Colony) Charters.
The Charter Granted by His Majesty.
Newport, 1744. 15, [15] pp.]
(No copy as described by Evans could be
found; apparently a ghost of 5683.)   5483

Rhode Island (Colony) Charters.
The Charter, Granted by . . . Charles II.
Newport, Hall, 1767. 15 pp.
(Reproduced as the first part of 10749.)
                                                   41757

Rhode Island (Colony) Deputy Governor,
1775.
[By the honourable Nicholas Cooke, Esq.
. . . A Proclamation for a day of
thanksgiving, Nov. 16, 1775.
Providence, Carter, 1775.] Broadside.
(No copy known.)   42928

Rhode Island (Colony) Deputy Governor,
1775.
[By the honourable Nicholas Cooke, Esq.
. . . A proclamation for a public fast,
dated June 22, 1775.
Providence, Carter, 1775.]
(Alden 613A; no copy known.)   42929

Rhode Island (Colony) Election Prox.,
1744.
Richard Ward, Esq.; Gov. Samuel Clarke.
[Newport, 1744?] Broadside.
RIHS copy.   40348

Rhode Island (Colony) Election Prox,
1758.
Hon. Stephen Hopkins, Esq.; Gov. Hon.
John Gardner, Esq; Dept. Gov. . . .
[Newport, 1758?] Broadside.
RIHS copy.   41006

Rhode Island (Colony) Election Prox,
1763.

Honorable Samuel Ward, Esq., Governor.
. . .
[Newport? 1763?] Broadside.
RIHS copy.   41409

Rhode Island (Colony) Election Prox,
1764.
Honorable Stephen Hopkins. . . .
[Newport, 1764.] Broadside.
RIHS copy.   41485

Rhode Island (Colony) Election Prox,
1767.
Seekers of Peace. . . .
[Newport? 1767?] Broadside.
JCB copy.   41758

Rhode Island (Colony) Election Prox,
1769.
American Liberty. Honourable Joseph
Wanton. . . .
[Providence? 1769?] Broadside.
RIHS copy.   41998

Rhode Island (Colony) Election Prox,
1773.
Colony of Rhode-Island, 1773. The
Honorable Joseph Wanton. . . . Darius
Sessions. . . .
[Newport? 1773.] Broadside.
RIHS copy.   42489

Rhode Island (Colony) Election Prox,
1773.
The Honourable Joseph Wanton, Esq; Gov.
. . . Darius Sessions, Esq; Dept. Gov. . . .
[Newport, 1773.] Broadside.
RIHS copy.   42490

Rhode Island (Colony) Election Prox,
1773.
The Honorable Joseph Wanton, Esq;
Governor. . . . Darius Sessions Esq; Dept.
Governor. . . .
[Newport? 1773.] Broadside.
RIHS copy.   42490a

Rhode Island (Colony) Election Prox,
1774.
Colony of Rhode Island, 1774. The
Honorable Joseph Wanton.
[Newport? 1774.] Broadside.
RIHS copy.   42681

Rhode Island (Colony) Election Prox,
1774.
For the Privilege of Trials by Juries . . .
[Providence? 1774.] Broadside.
RIHS copy.   42682

Rhode Island (Colony) Election Prox,
1774.
. . . The Honorable Joseph Wanton, Esq;
Gov. . . .
[Newport? 1774.] Broadside.
(Also entered as 42682.)   42683

Rhode Island (Colony) Election Prox,
1775.
Liberty, and no Tories. The Honorable
William Greene. . . .
[Providence? 1775.] Broadside.
RIHS copy.   42930

Rhode Island (Colony) Electors, 1774.
We, a Part of the Electors . . . of Rhode
Island.
[Providence? 1774.] Broadside.
RIHS copy.   42684

Rhode Island (Colony) General Assembly
1721.
A Vindication of the Governour and
Government.
[Boston, 1721.] 12 pp.
PRO copy.   39750

Rhode Island (Colony) General Assembly,
1768.
A Summary of the Amount of the
Estimation of the Colony. . . . May 6th,
1768.
[Newport, Southwick, 1768.] Broadside.
AAS copy.   41872

Rhode Island (Colony). General
Assembly. Grand Committee.
[The Following is a List of all the Deeds
. . . now in the Grand Committee's Office
. . . County of King's County.
Newport, 1761.] Broadside.
(Alden 230.)   41240

Rhode Island (Colony). General
Assembly. Grand Committee.
[The Following is a List of all the Deeds
. . . now in the Grand Committee's Office
. . . County of Providence.
Newport, 1761?] Broadside.
(Alden 231.)   41242

Rhode Island (Colony). General
Assembly. Grand Committee.
The Following is a List of all the
Mortgage Deeds . . . now in the Grand
Committee's Office . . . County of Kent.
[Newport, 1761.] Broadside.
(The only known copy is imperfect.)
RIHS copy.   41241

Rhode Island (Colony) Governor, 1736.
[A Proclamation for Apprehending
Nathaniel Shelton.
Newport, Franklin, 1736?] Broadside.
(Alden 37.)   40102

Rhode Island (Colony) Governor, 1739.
[A Proclamation in Regard to
Counterfeiting.
Newport, 1739. Broadside?]
(Alden 52.)   40174

Rhode Island (Colony) Governor, 1742.
By the Honourable Richard Ward. . . . A
Proclamation [Obadiah Mors. May 27,
1742].
[Newport, 1742.] Broadside.
JCB copy.   5045

Rhode Island (Colony) Governor, 1746.
By the Honourable William Greene. . . . A
Proclamation [Canada. June 4, 1746].
[Newport, 1746.] Broadside.
RIHS copy.   5860

Rhode Island (Colony) Governor, 1751.
By the Honourable William Green . . . the
Death of Frederick, Prince of Wales. . . .
[June 19, 1751.]
[Newport, 1751.] Broadside.
RIHS copy.   40601

Rhode Island (Colony) Governor, 1751.
[Proclamations on creating Prince
George, Prince of Wales.
Newport, 1751. Broadside.]
(Alden 106; no copy known.)   40602

Rhode Island (Colony) Governor, 1755.
An Account of the People in the Colony.
. . . December 24th, 1755.
n. p., [1755?]. Broadside.
RIHS copy.   40794

Rhode Island (Colony) Governor, 1756.
By the Honorable Stephen Hopkins. . . . A
Proclamation [Fast, May 20. Dated May
12, 1756].
RIHS copy.   7784

Rhode Island (Colony) Governor, 1757.
[By the Honourable Stephen Hopkins. . . .
A Proclamation . . . for Raising . . . 450
Men.
Newport, 1757. Broadside.]
(Alden 180. No copy known.)   40931

Rhode Island (Colony) Governor, 1758.
[Proclamation calling for the Enlistment
of 1000 men.
Newport, Franklin, 1758, Broadside.]
(Payment authorized Aug. 22, No copy
known.)   41007

Rhode Island (Colony) Governor, 1758.
[Proclamation commanding deserters to
give themselves up.
Newport, Franklin, 1758. Broadside.]
(Alden 200; no copy known.)   41008

Rhode Island (Colony) Governor, 1758.
[Proclamation laying an embargo.
Newport, Franklin, 1758, Broadside.]
(Alden 201; no copy known.)   41009

Rhode Island (Colony) Governor, 1759.
By the Honorable Stephen Hopkins . . . A
Proclamation.
It Having Pleased . . . [Nov. 2, 1759].
[Newport, 1759.] Broadside.
RIHS copy.   41073

Rhode Island (Colony) Governor, 1760.
By the Honorable Stephen Hopkins. . . . A
Proclamation for a General Thanksgiving
[Nov. 20. Dated Nov. 5, 1760].

[Newport, 1760.] Broadside.
RIHS copy. 41164

Rhode Island (Colony) Governor, 1760.
[Proclamation Prohibiting Trading with the French.
Newport, 1760.]
(Alden 220.) 41165

Rhode Island (Colony) Governor, 1760.
[Proclamation regarding Boston fire.
Newport, 1760.]
(Alden 221.) 41166

Rhode Island (Colony) Governor, 1762.
By the Honourable Samuel Ward. . . . A
Proclamation. Almighty God . . . A Day
of Public Worship and Thanksgiving
[Nov. 18. Dated Nov. 5, 1762].
Providence, Goddard, [1762]. Broadside.
AAS copy. 41304

Rhode Island (Colony) Governor, 1762.
[By the Honourable Samuel Ward. A
Proclamation prohibiting the exportations
of provisions.
Newport, 1762.]
(Alden 252.) 41305

Rhode Island (Colony) Governor, 1763.
By the Honorable Stephen Hopkins, Esq.
. . . A Proclamation. . . . A Day of Public
Thanksgiving [Aug. 25. Dated Aug. 8,
1763]. . . .
[Providence, Goddard, [1763]. Broadside.
RIHS copy. 41410

Rhode Island (Colony) Governor, 1765.
By the Honourable Samuel Ward. . . . A
Proclamation. The General Assembly . . .
Having Appointed [Nov. 28] . . .
Thanksgiving. . . . [Dated Nov. 11, 1765.]
Newport, Hall, [1765]. Broadside.
AAS copy. 41586

Rhode Island (Colony) Governor, 1766.
By the Honourable Samuel Ward. . . . A
Proclamation [Thanksgiving, June 26.
Dated June 16, 1766].
[Newport, 1766.] Broadside.
RIHS copy. 10480

Rhode Island (Colony) Governor, 1767.
By the Honorable Stephen Hopkins. . . . A
Proclamation. Whereas the General
Assembly. . . . [June 15, 1767.]
Newport, Hall [1767]. Broadside.
Westerly Public Library copy. 41759

Rhode Island (Colony) Governor, 1768.
[By the Honourable Josias Lyndon. . . . A
Proclamation . . . for Apprehending
Melchisedeck Kinsman.
Newport, Southwick, 1768.]
(Alden 390; no copy known.) 41873

Rhode Island (Colony) Governor, 1769.
[By the Honourable Josias Lyndon. . . . a
Proclamation . . . Relating the Seizure of
a Sloop. . . .
Newport, Southwick, 1769.] Broadside.
(Alden 418; no copy known.) 41999

Rhode Island (Colony) Governor, 1770.
[By the Honourable Joseph Wanton, a
proclamation for the apprehension of
certain criminals, Nov. 7, 1770.
Providence, Carter, 1778.] Broadside.
(No copy known.) 42162

Rhode Island (Colony) Governor, 1772.
By the Honorable Joseph Wanton. . . . A
Proclamation. Whereas on Tuesday. . . .
[Dated June 12, 1772.]
[Newport, 1772.] Broadside.
RISL copy. 42371

Rhode Island (Colony) Governor, 1774.
. . . By the Honorable Joseph Wanton. . . . A
Proclamation [Fast, June 30. Dated June
20, 1774].
[Newport, 1774.] Broadside.
NYPL copy. 13573

Rhode Island (Colony) Governor, 1774.
[A Proclamation for Apprehending
Daniel Wilson.
Providence, Carter, 1774.] Broadside.
(Alden 551; no copy known.) 42685

Rhode Island (Colony) Laws, Statutes,
etc., 1719.
Acts and Laws.

Boston, 1179 (1719). [2], 102, [3] pp.
NYPL copy. 2069

Rhode Island (Colony) Laws, Statutes,
etc., 1729.
[An Act Relating to the Small Pox.
Newport, 1729.]
(Alden 12. No copy known.) 39930

Rhode Island (Colony) Laws, Statutes,
etc., 1730.
The Charter. . . . Acts and Laws.
Newport, 1730. [2], 12, [2], 210 pp.
AAS copy. 3346

[Rhode Island (Colony) Laws, Statutes,
etc., 1730.
The Charter. . . . Acts and Laws.
Newport, 1730. [2], 12, [12], [2], 243
pp.]
(In this item Evans describes one of the
copies of 3346 which has pp. 211-243 of
the supplement bound in. For these pages
see 4191.) 3347

Rhode Island (Colony) Laws, Statutes,
etc., 1744.
The Charter Granted by His Majesty King
Charles II.
Newport, 1744. 15, [18], 308 pp.
(The Charter was printed to accompany
the 1745 ed. of the Acts and Laws with
which it is here reproduced.)
AAS copy. 5683

Rhode Island (Colony) Laws, Statutes,
etc., 1752.
[An Act to Prevent the Small-pox.
Newport, Franklin, 1752.]
(Alden 127; no copy known.) 40641

Rhode Island (Colony) Laws, Statutes,
etc., 1752.
Acts and Laws. . . . From Anno 1745, to
Anno 1752.
Newport, Franklin, 1752. [8], 110 pp.
AAS copy. 6919

[Rhode Island (Colony) Laws, Statutes,
etc., 1753.
A Bill to Prevent Disorderly Houses.
Newport, 1753.]
(No copy found.) 7110

Rhode Island (Colony) Laws, Statutes,
etc., 1754.
. . . An Act for Assessing . . . a Tax of
Thirty-Five Thousand Pounds.
[Newport, 1754.] 3 pp.
RIHS copy. 40715

Rhode Island (Colony) Laws, Statutes,
etc., 1754.
An Act for the Relief of Insolvent
Debtors.
[Newport, 1754.] 5 pp.
BrU copy. 40716

Rhode Island (Colony) Laws, Statutes,
etc., 1755.
November 1, 1755. To the House of
Magistrates. . . .
[Newport, 1755.] 2 pp.
BrU copy. 40795

Rhode Island (Colony) Laws, Statutes,
etc., 1757.
. . . An Act for Assessing . . . a Rate or
Tax of Four Thousand Pounds.
[Newport, 1757.] 3 pp.
BrU copy. 40933

Rhode Island (Colony) Laws, Statutes,
etc., 1757.
. . . An Act for Proportioning the Rate . . .
Upon the Several Towns.
[Newport, Franklin, 1757.] 2 pp.
BrU copy. 40932

Rhode Island (Colony) Laws, Statutes,
etc., 1757.
. . . An Act for Raising One Sixth Part of
the Militia.
[Newport, 1757.] 4 pp.
RIHS copy. 40934

Rhode Island (Colony) Laws, Statutes,
etc., 1757.
. . . An Act for Supplying the General
Treasury.
[Newport, 1757.] 3 pp.
BrU copy. 40935

Rhode Island (Colony) Laws, Statutes,
etc., 1757.
[. . . An Act for Taking a True Account of
all Rateable Estates.
Newport, Franklin, 1757.] 4? pp.
(Alden 186. No copy located.) 40936

Rhode Island (Colony) Laws, Statutes,
etc., 1757.
[. . . An Act for the more speedy payment
of the charges of the late expedition.
Newport, 1757.]
(Alden 191; no copy known.) 40937

Rhode Island (Colony) Laws, Statutes,
etc., 1757.
At the General Assembly . . . November
[1756]. . . . A Rate or Tax of Four
Thousand Pounds. . . .
[Newport, 1757.] 5 pp.
(The only copy located is imperfect.)
BrU copy. 40930

Rhode Island (Colony) Laws, Statutes,
etc., 1758.
. . . An Act for Assessing and Levying . . .
a Rate . . . of Six Thousand Pounds.
[Newport, 1758.] 2 pp.
RIHS copy. 41010

Rhode Island (Colony) Laws, Statutes,
etc., 1759.
. . . An Act Apportioning . . . the Rate or
Tax . . . [June 11, 1759].
[Newport, 1759.] 2 pp.
RIHS copy. 41074

Rhode Island (Colony) Laws, Statutes,
etc., 1759.
An Act for Vesting and Distributing
Intestate Estates.
[Newport, 1759.] 2 pp.
JCB copy. 8483

Rhode Island (Colony) Laws, Statutes,
etc., 1760.
[An Act for a rate of £15,547. June
Session, 1760.
Newport, 1760.] Broadside.
(Alden 227.) 41167

Rhode Island (Colony) Laws, Statutes,
etc., 1761.
. . . An Act for Apportioning . . . the Rate
of Tax [Oct. 19, 1761].
[Newport, 1761.] [3] pp.
RIHS copy. 41243

Rhode Island (Colony) Laws, Statutes,
etc., 1761.
[An Act for inquiring into the value of
rateable estates.
Newport, 1761.] Broadside?
(Alden 240.) 41244

Rhode Island (Colony) Laws, Statutes,
etc., 1762.
. . . An Act for Supplying the General
Treasury. . . . Published . . . the Thirtieth
of September, 1762.
[Newport, 1762.] 3 pp.
RIHS copy. 41306

Rhode Island (Colony) Laws, Statutes,
etc., 1762.
An Act, in Addition to an Act . . .
Providing in Case of Fire . . . in the Town
of Newport.
[Newport, 1762.] [2] pp.
RISL copy. 41307

Rhode Island (Colony) Laws, Statutes,
etc., 1762.
[An Act in addition to several Acts,
regulating the manner of admitting
freemen.
Newport, Franklin & Hall, 1762. 4? pp.]
(Alden 263.) 41308

Rhode Island (Colony) Laws, Statutes,
etc., 1763.
An Act Declaring what is . . . Lawful
Money.
Newport, [1763]. 4 pp.
RIHS copy. 9503

Rhode Island (Colony) Laws, Statutes,
etc., 1763.
. . . An Act for Assessing . . . a Rate or
Tax of Twelve Thousand Pounds.
Newport, Hall, [1763]. 3 pp.
RIHS copy. 41411

Rhode Island (Colony) Laws, Statutes,
etc., 1764.
... An Act for Assessing ... a Rate or
Tax of Twelve Thousand Pounds.
Newport, Hall, [1764]. 3 pp.
RIHS copy.   41486

Rhode Island (Colony) Laws, Statutes,
etc., 1764.
... An Act for the Establishment of a
college.
Newport, [1764]. 8 pp.
AAS copy.   9823

Rhode Island (Colony) Laws, Statutes,
etc., 1765.
... An Act for Assessing ... a Rate or
Tax of Twelve Thousand Four Hundred
and Sixty-Eight Pounds.
Newport, Hall, [1765]. [3] pp.
RIHS copy.   41587

Rhode Island (Colony) Laws, Statutes,
etc., 1767.
[An act for assessing a tax of six thousand
pounds.
Newport, Hall, 1767.]
(No copy known)   41760

Rhode Island (Colony) Laws, Statutes,
etc., 1767.
... An Act for Making a Just Estimate.
[Newport, 1767.] 4 pp.
BrU copy.   41761

Rhode Island (Colony) Laws, Statutes,
etc., 1767.
The Charter, Granted by His Majesty.
Newport, 1767. 15, [1], 272, [1] pp.
(The 46 p. index called for by Evans was
printed later.)
AAS copy.   10749

Rhode Island (Colony) Laws, Statutes,
etc., 1768.
The Table [to the Laws of 1767].
[Newport, Southwick, 1768.] 46 pp.
RISL copy.   41874

Rhode Island (Colony) Laws, Statutes,
etc., 1769.
[An Act for the Relief of Insolvent
Debtors.
Newport, Southwick, 1769.]
(Alden 424; no copy known.)   42000

Rhode Island (Colony). Laws, Statutes,
etc., 1769.
At the General Assembly. . . . An Act
[Tax. May, 1769].
[Newport, 1769.] 3 pp.
JCB copy.   11443

Rhode Island (Colony) Laws, Statutes,
etc., 1770.
... An Act for Assessing ... a Rate or
Tax of Twelve Thousand Pounds.
[Newport 1770.] 4 pp.
BrU copy.   42163

Rhode Island (Colony) Laws, Statutes,
etc., 1771.
... An Act for Assessing ... a Rate or
Tax of Twelve Thousand Pounds.
[Newport, 1771.] 4 pp.
RIHS copy.   42274

Rhode Island (Colony) Laws, Statutes,
etc., 1772.
... An Act for Assessing ... a Rate of
Tax of Twelve Thousand Pounds.
[Newport, 1772.] 4 pp.
RIHS copy.   42372

Rhode Island (Colony) Laws, Statutes,
etc., 1772.
Acts and Laws. . . . Since the Revision in
June, 1767.
Newport, 1772. 41 pp.
AAS copy.   12537

Rhode Island (Colony) Laws, Statutes,
etc., 1773.
... An Act for Assessing ... a Rate or
Tax of Four Thousand Pounds.
[Newport, Southwick, 1773.] 3 pp.
RIHS copy.   42491

Rhode Island (Colony) Laws, Statutes,
etc., 1774.
... An Act for Assessing ... a Tax of
Four Thousand Pounds.

[Newport, 1774.] 3 pp.
RIHS copy.   42686

Rhode Island (Colony) Laws, Statutes,
etc., 1774.
At the General Assembly ... December
[1774]. . . . Whereas the Hon. Stephen
Hopkins ... made Report of ... a
Memorial to the Inhabitants of the British
Colonies in America. . . .
[Newport, Southwick, 1774.] Broadside.
AAS copy.   42687

Rhode Island (Colony) Laws, Statutes,
etc., 1774.
The Following is the Account of the
Number of Inhabitants. . . .
Newport, [1774]. Broadside.
JCB copy.   13572

Rhode Island (Colony) Laws, Statutes,
etc., 1774.
[Voted that the number of families and
persons in the colony be taken.
Newport, 1744.]
(Printer's record, no copy known.)   42688

Rhode Island (Colony) Laws, Statutes,
etc., 1775.
[An act for enlisting one fourth part of
the militia as minute-men.
Providence, Carter, 1775.] Broadside.
(Alden 620A; no copy known.)   42931

Rhode Island (Colony) Laws, Statutes,
etc., 1775.
[Voted and resolved, that messieurs Jabez
Champlin. . . .
Providence, Carter, 1775.] Broadside.
(Alden 620B; no copy known.)   42932

Rhode Island (Colony) Militia, 1775.
Rules and Regulations for the
Rhode-Island Army.
Newport, Southwick, 1775. 16 pp.
RIHS copy.   42933

Rhode Island (Colony) Second Bank.
Mortgage Deeds Laid by in the Office,
without Bonds.
[Newport, 1750.] 16 pp.
RIHS copy.   40564

Rhode Island (Colony) Secretary, 1751.
Newport, June 19th. 1751. . . . In
Obedience to an Act of the General
Assembly.
[Newport, 1751.] 6 pp.
AAS copy.   6773

Rhode Island (Colony) Session Laws,
1730.
Laws, Made and Passed [May, 1730 +].
[Newport, 1737,] pp. 211-283.
NYPL copy.   4191

Rhode Island (Colony) Session Laws,
1747.
At the General Assembly [Oct. 1747].
[Newport, 1747.] 6 pp.
Facsimile reproduction.   6062

Rhode Island (Colony) Session Laws,
1748.
At the General Assembly [Feb. 1747/8].
[Newport, 1748.] 12 pp.
AAS copy.   40476

Rhode Island (Colony) Session Laws,
1748.
At a General Assembly [May 3 - July 27,
1748].
[Newport, 1748.] 23 pp.
JCB copy.   6231

Rhode Island (Colony) Session Laws,
1748.
At the General Assembly ... October
[1748].
[Newport, 1748.] pp. 37-44.
Bongartz facsim. copy.   40477

Rhode Island (Colony) Session Laws,
1749.
At the General Assembly [Jan. 1749].
[Newport, 1749.] 45-61 pp.
Bongartz facsim. copy.   40513

Rhode Island (Colony) Session Laws,
1749.
At a General Assembly [May 2, 1749-
Feb., 1750].

[Newport, 1749-50.] 76 pp.
JCB copy.   6411

Rhode Island (Colony) Session Laws,
1750.
At the General Assembly [May 1750].
[Newport, 1750.] 18 pp.
AAS copy.   40565

Rhode Island (Colony) Session Laws,
1750.
At the General Assembly [June 1750].
[Newport, 1750.] pp. 19-32.
AAS copy.   40566

Rhode Island (Colony) Session Laws,
1750.
At a General Assembly [Aug. 1750].
[Newport, 1750.] pp. 33-60.
AAS copy.   40567

Rhode Island (Colony) Session Laws,
1750.
At the General Assembly [December,
1750].
[Newport, 1751.] pp. 60 (i.e. 61) - 70.
AAS copy.   40603

Rhode Island (Colony) Session Laws,
1751.
At the General Assembly [Mar. 1751].
[Newport, 1751.] pp. 71-97.
AAS copy.   40604

Rhode Island (Colony) Session Laws,
1751.
At a General Assembly [Apr. 30, 1751].
[Newport, 1751.] pp. 5.
AAS copy.   6768

Rhode Island (Colony) Session Laws,
1751.
At the General Assembly [May, 1751].
[Newport, 1751.] pp. 6-16.
AAS copy.   6769

Rhode Island (Colony) Session Laws,
1751.
At the General Assembly [June, 1751].
[Newport, 1751.] pp. 17-30.
AAS copy.   6770

Rhode Island (Colony) Session Laws,
1751.
At the General Assembly [Aug. 26,
1751 +].
[Newport, 1751.] pp. 31-46.
AAS copy.   6771

Rhode Island (Colony) Session Laws,
1751.
At the General Assembly [Nov. 6,
1751 +].
[Newport, 1751.] pp. 47-55.
AAS copy.   6772

Rhode Island (Colony) Session Laws,
1752.
At the General Assembly [Feb. 1752].
[Newport, 1752.] pp. 57-69.
AAS copy.   6920

Rhode Island (Colony) Session Laws,
1752.
At the General Assembly [May 5,
1752 +].
[Newport, 1752.] 4 pp.
AAS copy.   6921

Rhode Island (Colony) Session Laws,
1752.
At the General Assembly [May 11, 1752].
[Newport, 1752.] pp. 5-20.
AAS copy.   6922

Rhode Island (Colony) Session Laws,
1752.
At the General Assembly [June 1, 1752
+].
[Newport, 1752.] pp. 21-38.
AAS copy.   6923

Rhode Island (Colony) Session Laws,
1752.
At the General Assembly [Aug. 1752].
[Newport, 1752.] pp. 39-55.
AAS copy.   6924

Rhode Island (Colony) Session Laws,
1752.
At the General Assembly [Oct. 1752].
[Newport, 1752.] pp. 57-67.
AAS copy.   6925

Rhode Island (Colony) Session Laws, 1753.
At a General Assembly [Feb. 1753].
[Newport, 1753.] pp. 69-84.
AAS copy.   7104

Rhode Island (Colony) Session Laws, 1753.
At the General Assembly [May 1, 1753.].
[Newport, 1753.] 4 pp.
AAS copy.   7105

Rhode Island (Colony) Session Laws, 1753.
At the General Assembly [May 10, 1753].
[Newport, 1753.] pp. 5-16.
AAS copy.   7106

Rhode Island (Colony) Session Laws, 1753.
At the General Assembly [June, 1753].
[Newport, 1753.] pp. 17-25.
Bongartz facsimile.   7107

Rhode Island (Colony) Session Laws, 1753.
At the General Assembly [Aug. 1753].
[Newport, 1753.] pp. 26-35.
AAS copy.   7108

Rhode Island (Colony) Session Laws, 1753.
At the General Assembly [Oct. 1753.].
[Newport, 1753.] pp. 36-47.
AAS copy.   7109

Rhode Island (Colony) Session Laws, 1754.
At the General Assembly [Feb. 1754].
[Newport, 1754.] pp. 48-55.
Bongartz facsimile copy.   7305

Rhode Island (Colony) Session Laws, 1754.
At the General Assembly [Apr. 1754].
[Newport, 1754.] 20 pp.
AAS copy.   7306

Rhode Island (Colony) Session Laws, 1754.
At the General Assembly [June 1754].
[Newport, 1754.] pp. 21-38.
AAS copy.   7307

Rhode Island (Colony) Session Laws, 1754.
At the General Assembly [Aug. 1754].
[Newport, 1754.] pp. 39-49.
AAS copy.   7308

Rhode Island (Colony) Session Laws, 1754.
At the General Assembly [Oct. 1754].
[Newport, 1754.] pp. 51-59.
AAS copy.   7309

Rhode Island (Colony) Session Laws, 1755.
At the General Assembly [Jan. 1, 1755 +].
[Newport, 1755.] pp. 61-66.
Bongartz facsimile copy.   7554

Rhode Island (Colony) Session Laws, 1755.
At the General Assembly [Feb. 1755 +].
[Newport, 1755.] pp. 66-82.
Bongartz facsimile copy.   7555

Rhode Island (Colony) Session Laws, 1755.
At the General Assembly [Mar. 6, 1755 +].
[Newport, 1755.] pp. 83-90.
AAS copy.   7556

Rhode Island (Colony) Session Laws, 1755.
At the General Assembly [May 6, 1755 +].
[Newport, 1755.] 5 pp.
AAS copy.   7557

Rhode Island (Colony) Session Laws, 1755.
At the General Assembly [May 7, 1755 +].
[Newport, 1755.] pp. 6-21.
AAS copy.   7558

Rhode Island (Colony) Session Laws, 1755.

At the General Assembly [June, 1755 +].
[Newport, 1755.] pp. 23-30.
AAS copy.   7559

Rhode Island (Colony) Session Laws, 1755.
At the General Assembly [Aug. 11, 1755 +].
[Newport, 1755.] pp. 31-44.
AAS copy.   7560

Rhode Island (Colony) Session Laws, 1755.
At the General Assembly [Sept. 8, 1755 +].
[Newport, 1755.] pp. 45-54.
AAS copy.   7561

Rhode Island (Colony) Session Laws, 1755.
At the General Assembly [Oct. 1755 +].
[Newport, 1755.] pp. 45-54.
AAS copy.   7562

Rhode Island (Colony) Session Laws, 1755.
At the General Assembly [Dec. 22, 1755 +].
[Newport, 1755.] pp. 55-60.
AAS copy.   7563

Rhode Island (Colony) Session Laws, 1756.
At the General Assembly [Feb. 1756].
[Newport, 1756.] pp. 61-79.
AAS copy.   7774

Rhode Island (Colony) Session Laws, 1756.
At the General Assembly [May 4, 1756 +].
[Newport, 1756.] 4 pp.
Bongartz facsimile copy.   7775

Rhode Island (Colony) Session Laws, 1756.
At a General Assembly [May, 1756].
[Newport, 1756.] pp. 5-18.
AAS copy.   7776

Rhode Island (Colony) Session Laws, 1756.
At the General Assembly [June 18-21, 1756].
[Newport, 1756.] pp. 19-33.
Bongartz facsimile copy.   7777

Rhode Island (Colony) Session Laws, 1756.
At the General Assembly [June 22 - July 2, 1756].
[Newport, 1756.] pp. 35-42.
AAS copy.   7778

Rhode Island (Colony) Session Laws, 1756.
At the General Assembly [Aug. 1756].
[Newport, 1756.] pp. 43-56.
AAS copy.   7779

Rhode Island (Colony) Session Laws, 1756.
At the General Assembly [Sept. 6, 1756 +].
[Newport, 1756.] pp. 57-70.
AAS copy.   7780

Rhode Island (Colony) Session Laws, 1756.
At the general Assembly [Oct. 14, 1756].
[Newport, 1756.] pp. 71-78.
AAS copy.   7781

Rhode Island (Colony) Session Laws, 1756.
At the General Assembly [Oct. 1756].
[Newport, 1756.] pp. 79-87.
AAS copy.   7782

Rhode Island (Colony) Session Laws, 1756.
At the General Assembly [Nov. 1756].
[Newport, 1756.] pp. 88-107.
AAS copy.   7783

Rhode Island (Colony) Session Laws, 1757.
At the General Assembly [Jan. 10, 1757 +].
[Newport, 1757.] pp. 108-118.
AAS copy.   8018

Rhode Island (Colony) Session Laws, 1757.

At the General Assembly [Jan. 26, 1757 +].
[Newport, 1757.] pp. 119-122.
AAS copy.   8019

Rhode Island (Colony Session Laws, 1757.
At the General Assembly [Feb. 1, 1757 +].
[Newport, 1757.] pp. 123-140.
AAS copy.   8020

Rhode Island (Colony) Session Laws, 1757.
At the General Assembly [Mar. 14, 1757 +].
[Newport, 1757.] pp. 141-163.
Bongartz facsimile copy.   8021

Rhode Island (Colony) Session Laws, 1757.
At the General Assembly [May 3, 1757 +].
[Newport, 1757.] 5 pp.
AAS copy.   8022

Rhode Island (Colony) Session Laws, 1757.
At the General Assembly [May 4, 1757 +].
[Newport, 1757.] pp. 6-19.
AAS copy.   8023

Rhode Island (Colony) Session Laws, 1757.
At the General Assembly [June 13, 1757 +].
[Newport, 1757.] pp. 20-37.
AAS copy.   8024

Rhode Island (Colony) Session Laws, 1757.
At the General Assembly [Aug. 10, 1757 +].
[Newport, 1757.] pp. 39-46.
Bongartz facsimile copy.   8025

Rhode Island (Colony) Session Laws, 1757.
At the General Assembly [Sept. 19, 1757 +].
[Newport, 1757.] pp. 47-64.
Bongartz facsimile copy.   8026

Rhode Island (Colony) Session Laws, 1757.
At the General Assembly [Oct. 1757].
[Newport, 1757.] pp. 65-83.
AAS copy.   8027

Rhode Island (Colony) Session Laws, 1758.
At the General Assembly [Feb. 14, 1758 +].
[Newport, 1758.] pp. 85-93.
AAS copy.   8246

Rhode Island (Colony) Session Laws, 1758.
At the General Assembly [Mar. 13, 1758 +].
[Newport, 1758.] pp. 93-114.
AAS copy.   8247

Rhode Island (Colony) Session Laws, 1758.
At the General Assembly [May 2, 1758 +].
[Newport, 1758.] 4 pp.
AAS copy.   8248

Rhode Island (Colony) Session Laws, 1758.
At the General Assembly [May 1758].
[Newport, 1758.] pp. 5-16.
AAS copy.   8249

Rhode Island (Colony) Session Laws, 1758.
At the General Assembly [June 12, 1758].
[Newport, 1758.] pp. 17-36.
AAS copy.   8250

Rhode Island (Colony) Session Laws, 1758.
At the General Assembly [Aug. 21, 1758 +].
[Newport, 1758.] pp. 35-49 irreg.
AAS copy.   8251

Rhode Island (Colony) Session Laws, 1758.

At the General Assembly [Oct. 1758].
[Newport, 1758.] pp. 50-55.
AAS copy.   8252

Rhode Island (Colony) Session Laws,
1758.
At the General Assembly [Dec. 18, 1758
+].
[Newport, 1759.] pp. 56-68.
AAS copy.   8253

Rhode Island (Colony) Session Laws,
1759.
At the General Assembly [Feb. 26, 1759
+].
[Newport, 1759.] pp. 70-109.
AAS copy.   8478

Rhode Island (Colony) Session Laws,
1759.
At the General Assembly [May 1, 1759
+].
[Newport, 1759.] 5 pp.
AAS copy.   8479

Rhode Island (Colony) Session Laws,
1759.
At the General Assembly [May 2, 1759
+].
[Newport, 1759.] pp. 5-13.
AAS copy.   8480

Rhode Island (Colony) Session Laws,
1759.
At the General Assembly [June 11, 1759
+].
[Newport, 1759.] pp. 14-30.
AAS copy.   8481

Rhode Island (Colony) Session Laws,
1759.
At the General Assembly . . . holden. . . .
on Monday the Twentieth of August. . . .
Boston, Draper, [1759]. [15] pp.
RIHS copy.   41075

Rhode Island (Colony) Session Laws,
1759.
August, 1759. At the General Assembly.
Boston, Draper, 1759. [19] pp.
Bongartz facsimile copy.   8482

Rhode Island (Colony) Session Laws,
1759.
October 1759. At the General Assembly.
Boston, Edes & Gill, 1760. [23] pp.
AAS copy.   8720

Rhode Island (Colony) Session Laws,
1760.
February, 1760. At the General Assembly.
Newport, [1760]. [17] pp.
AAS copy.   8721

Rhode Island (Colony) Session Laws,
1760.
May, 1760. At the General Assembly
[May 6, 1760].
[Newport, 1760.] [4] pp.
AAS copy.   8722

Rhode Island (Colony) Session Laws,
1760.
May, 1760. At the General Assembly
[May 7, 1760 +].
[Newport, 1760.] pp. [5]-17.
AAS copy.   8723

Rhode Island (Colony) Session Laws,
1760.
June, 1760. At the General Assembly.
[Newport, 1760.] pp. [18]-29.
AAS copy.   8724

Rhode Island (Colony) Session Laws,
1760.
August, 1760. At the General Assembly.
[Newport, 1760.] pp. [30]-39.
AAS copy.   8725

Rhode Island (Colony) Session Laws,
1760.
October, 1760. At the General Assembly.
[Newport, 1760.] pp. [40]-46.
AAS copy.   8726

Rhode Island (Colony) Session Laws,
1760.
December, 1760. At the General
Assembly.
[Newport, 1761.] [5] pp.
AAS copy.   8989

Rhode Island (Colony) Session Laws,
1761.
February, 1761. At the General Assembly.
[Newport, 1761.] [19] pp.
JCB copy.   8990

Rhode Island (Colony) Session Laws,
1761.
March, 1761. At the General Assembly.
[Newport, 1761.] [10] pp.
JCB copy.   8991

Rhode Island (Colony) Session Laws,
1761.
May, 1761. At the General Assembly.
[Newport, 1761.] 7 pp.
JCB copy.   8992

Rhode Island (Colony) Session Laws,
1761.
At the General Assembly [June 15, 1761
+].
[Newport, 1761.] pp. 7-17.
JCB copy.   8993

Rhode Island (Colony) Session Laws,
1761.
June, 1761. At the General Assembly.
[Newport, 1761.] pp. 18-37.
JCB copy.   8994

Rhode Island (Colony) Session Laws,
1761.
September, 1761. At a General Assembly.
[Newport, 1761.] pp. 38-47.
JCB copy.   8995

Rhode Island (Colony) Session Laws,
1761.
October, 1761. At a General Assembly.
[Newport, 1761.] pp. 48-59.
JCB copy.   8996

Rhode Island (Colony) Session Laws,
1761.
October, 1761. At a General Assembly
[Pub. Nov. 9, 1761].
Newport, 1761. pp. 60-66.
JCB copy.   8997

Rhode Island (Colony) Session Laws,
1762.
February, 1762. At the General Assembly.
[Newport, 1762.] pp. 67-84.
AAS copy.   9251

Rhode Island (Colony) Session Laws,
1762.
March, 1762. At the General Assembly.
[Newport, 1762.] pp. 85-108.
AAS copy.   9252

Rhode Island (Colony) Session Laws,
1762.
May, 1762. At the General Assembly.
[Newport, 1762.] pp. 109-118 (119).
AAS copy.   9253

Rhode Island (Colony) Session Laws,
1762.
June, 1762. At the General Assembly.
[Newport, 1762.] pp. 120-138.
AAS copy.   9254

Rhode Island (Colony) Session Laws,
1762.
August, 1762. At the General Assembly.
[Newport, 1762.] pp. 139-180.
AAS copy.   9255

Rhode Island (Colony) Session Laws,
1762.
September, 1762. At the General
Assembly.
[Newport, 1762.] pp. 181-203.
AAS copy.   9256

Rhode Island (Colony) Session Laws,
1762.
October, 1762. At the General Assembly.
[Newport, 1762.] pp. 205-220.
AAS copy.   9257

Rhode Island (Colony) Session Laws,
1763.
February, 1763. At the General Assembly.
Newport, [1763]. pp. 221-236.
AAS copy.   9498

Rhode Island (Colony) Session Laws,
1763.
May, 1763. At the General Assembly.

Newport, [1763]. 10 pp.
AAS copy.   9499

Rhode Island (Colony) Session Laws,
1763.
June, 1763. At the General Assembly.
Newport, [1763]. pp. 11-47.
AAS copy.   9500

Rhode Island (Colony) Session Laws,
1763.
August, 1763. At the General Assembly.
Newport, [1763]. pp. 49-68.
AAS copy.   9501

Rhode Island (Colony) Session Laws,
1763.
October, 1763. At the General Assembly.
Newport, [1763]. pp. 69-93.
AAS copy.   9502

Rhode Island (Colony) Session Laws,
1764.
January, 1764. At the General Assembly.
[Newport, 1764.] pp. 95-97.
AAS copy.   9815

Rhode Island (Colony) Session Laws,
1764.
February, 1764. At the General Assembly.
Newport, [1764]. pp. 99-130.
AAS copy.   9816

Rhode Island (Colony) Session Laws,
1764.
May, 1764. At the General Assembly.
Newport, [1764]. 16 pp.
AAS copy.   9817

Rhode Island (Colony) Session Laws,
1764.
June, 1764. At the General Assembly.
[Newport, 1764.] pp. 17-29.
AAS copy.   9818

Rhode Island (Colony) Session Laws,
1764.
July, 1764. At the General Assembly.
[Newport, 1764.] pp. 31-36.
AAS copy.   9819

Rhode Island (Colony) Session Laws,
1764.
September, 1764. At the General
Assembly.
[Newport, 1764.] pp. 37-48.
AAS copy.   9820

Rhode Island (Colony) Session Laws,
1764.
October, 1764. At the General Assembly.
Newport, [1764]. pp. 49-66.
AAS copy.   9821

Rhode Island (Colony) Session Laws,
1764.
November, 1764. At the General
Assembly.
[Newport, 1764.] pp. 67-83.
AAS copy.   9822

Rhode Island (Colony) Session Laws,
1765.
February, 1765. At the General Assembly.
Newport, [1765]. pp. 85-107.
AAS copy.   10154

Rhode Island (Colony) Session Laws,
1765.
May, 1765. At the General Assembly.
Newport, [1765]. 12 pp.
AAS copy.   10155

Rhode Island (Colony) Session Laws,
1765.
June, 1765. At the General Assembly.
Newport, [1765]. pp. 13-41.
AAS copy.   10156

Rhode Island (Colony) Session Laws,
1765.
September, 1765. At the General
Assembly.
[Newport, 1765.] pp. 43-60.
AAS copy.   10157

Rhode Island (Colony) Session Laws,
1765.
October, 1765. At the General Assembly.
Newport, [1765]. pp. 61-69.
AAS copy.   10158

Rhode Island (Colony) Session Laws,
1766.
February, 1766. At the General Assembly.
Newport, [1766]. pp. 71-84.
AAS copy.   10474

Rhode Island (Colony) Session Laws,
1766.
May, 1766. At the General Assembly.
Newport, [1766]. 12 pp.
AAS copy.   10475

Rhode Island (Colony) Session Laws,
1766.
June, 1766. At the General Assembly.
Newport, [1766]. pp. 13-23.
AAS copy.   10476

Rhode Island (Colony) Session Laws,
1766.
September, 1766. At the General
Assembly.
Newport, [1766]. pp. 25-33.
AAS copy.   10477

Rhode Island (Colony) Session Laws,
1766.
October, 1766. At the General Assembly.
Newport, [1766]. pp. 35-47.
AAS copy.   10478

Rhode Island (Colony) Session Laws,
1766.
December, 1766. At the General
Assembly.
[Newport, 1766.] pp. 49-61.
AAS copy.   10479

Rhode Island (Colony) Session Laws,
1767.
February, 1767. At the General Assembly.
Newport, 1767. pp. 63-78.
AAS copy.   10750

Rhode Island (Colony) Session Laws,
1767.
May, 1767. At the General Assembly.
Newport, [1767]. 14 pp.
AAS copy.   10751

Rhode Island (Colony) Session Laws,
1767.
June, 1767. At the General Assembly.
Newport, [1767]. pp. 15-48.
AAS copy.   10752

Rhode Island (Colony) Session Laws,
1767.
August, 1767. At the General Assembly.
Newport, [1767]. pp. 49-58.
AAS copy.   10753

Rhode Island (Colony) Session Laws,
1767.
October, 1767. At the General Assembly.
Newport, [1767]. pp. 59-69.
AAS copy.   10754

Rhode Island (Colony) Session Laws,
1768.
February, 1768. At the General Assembly.
Newport, [1768]. pp. 71-78, 78-81.
AAS copy.   11054

Rhode Island (Colony) Session Laws,
1768.
May, 1768. At the General Assembly.
[Newport, 1768.] 11 pp.
AAS copy.   11055

Rhode Island (Colony) Session Laws,
1768.
June, 1768. At the General Assembly.
Newport, [1768]. pp. 13-31.
AAS copy.   11056

Rhode Island (Colony) Session Laws,
1768.
September, 1768. At the General
Assembly.
Newport, [1768]. pp. 33-49.
AAS copy.   11057

Rhode Island (Colony) Session Laws,
1768.
October, 1768. At the General Assembly.
Newport, [1768]. pp. 51-63.
AAS copy.   11058

Rhode Island (Colony) Session Laws,
1769.

February, 1769. At the General Assembly.
Newport, [1769]. pp. 64-94.
AAS copy.   11438

Rhode Island (Colony) Session Laws,
1769.
May, 1769. At the General Assembly.
Newport, [1769]. 19 pp.
AAS copy.   11439

Rhode Island (Colony) Session Laws,
1769.
June, 1769. At the General Assembly.
Newport, [1769]. pp. 21-42.
AAS copy.   11440

Rhode Island (Colony) Session Laws,
1769.
September, 1769. At the General
Assembly.
Newport, [1769]. pp. 45-58.
AAS copy.   11441

Rhode Island (Colony) Session Laws,
1769.
October, 1769. At the General Assembly.
Newport, [1769]. pp. 61-79.
AAS copy.   11442

Rhode Island (Colony) Session Laws,
1770.
February, 1770. At the General Assembly.
Newport, [1770]. pp. 81-101.
AAS copy.   11831

Rhode Island (Colony) Session Laws,
1770.
May 1770. At the General Assembly.
Newport, [1770]. 19 pp.
AAS copy.   11832

Rhode Island (Colony) Session Laws,
1770.
June, 1770. At the General Assembly.
Newport, [1770]. pp. 21-37.
AAS copy.   11833

Rhode Island (Colony) Session Laws,
1770.
September, 1770. At the General
Assembly.
Newport, [1770]. pp. 39-66.
AAS copy.   11834

Rhode Island (Colony) Session Laws,
1770.
October 1770. At the General Assembly.
Newport, [1770]. pp. 61-84, irreg.
AAS copy.   11835

Rhode Island (Colony) Session Laws,
1771.
May, 1771. At the General Assembly.
[Newport, 1771.] 26 pp.
AAS copy.   12211

Rhode Island (Colony) Session Laws,
1771.
June, 1771. At the General Assembly.
Newport, [1771]. pp. 27-46.
AAS copy.   12212

Rhode Island (Colony) Session Laws,
1771.
August, 1771. At the General Assembly.
Newport, [1771]. pp. 47-69.
AAS copy.   12213

Rhode Island (Colony) Session Laws,
1771.
October, 1771. At the General Assembly.
Newport, [1771]. pp. 71-86.
AAS copy.   12214

Rhode Island (Colony) Session Laws,
1772.
May, 1772. At the General-Assembly.
Newport, [1772]. 23 pp.
AAS copy.   12538

Rhode Island (Colony) Session Laws,
1772.
August, 1772. At the General Assembly.
Newport, [1772]. pp. 25-51.
Composite copy.   12539

Rhode Island (Colony) Session Laws,
1772.
October, 1772. At the General Assembly.
Newport, [1772]. pp. 53-74.
Composite copy.   12540

Rhode Island (Colony) Session Laws,
1772.
December, 1772. At the General
Assembly.
Newport, [1772]. pp. 77-88.
Composite copy.   12541

Rhode Island (Colony) Session Laws,
1773.
January, 1773. At the General Assembly.
Newport, [1773]. pp. 89-94.
AAS copy.   12974

Rhode Island (Colony) Session Laws,
1773.
May, 1773. At the General Assembly.
Newport, 1773. 27 pp.
AAS copy.   12975

Rhode Island (Colony) Session Laws,
1773.
August, 1773. At the General Assembly.
Newport, [1773]. pp. 29-71.
AAS copy.   12976

Rhode Island (Colony) Session Laws,
1773.
October, 1773. At the General Assembly.
Newport, [1773]. pp. 73-91.
AAS copy.   12977

Rhode Island (Colony) Session Laws,
1774.
May, 1774. At the General Assembly.
[Newport, 1774.] 23 pp.
AAS copy.   13567

Rhode Island (Colony) Session Laws,
1774.
June, 1774. At the General Assembly.
Newport, [1774]. pp. 25-55.
AAS copy.   13568

Rhode Island (Colony) Session Laws,
1774.
August, 1774. At the General Assembly.
Newport, [1774]. pp. 57-85.
AAS copy.   13569

Rhode Island (Colony) Session Laws,
1774.
October, 1774. At the General Assembly.
Newport, [1774]. pp. 87-124.
AAS copy.   13570

Rhode Island (Colony) Session Laws,
1774.
December, 1774. At the General
Assembly.
Newport, [1774]. pp. 125-157.
AAS copy.   13571

Rhode Island (Colony) Session Laws,
1775.
April, 1775. At the General Assembly.
[Providence, 1775.] pp. 159-169.
AAS copy.   14418

Rhode Island (Colony) Session Laws,
1775.
May, 1775. At the General Assembly.
Providence, [1775]. 24 pp.
AAS copy.   14419

Rhode Island (Colony) Session Laws,
1775.
June, 1775. At the General Assembly . . .
the Second Monday in June.
Providence, [1775]. pp. 25-69.
AAS copy.   14420

Rhode Island (Colony) Session Laws,
1775.
June, 1775. At the General Assembly . . .
Wednesday, the Twenty-Eighth Day of
June.
Providence, [1775]. pp. 71-84.
Bongartz facsimile copy.   14421

Rhode Island (Colony) Session Laws,
1775.
August, 1775. At the General Assembly.
[Providence, 1775.] pp. 85-112.
AAS copy.   14422

Rhode Island (Colony) Session Laws,
1775.
October, 1775. At the General Assembly.
Providence, [1775]. pp. 113-200.
AAS copy.   14423

Rhode Island. Commissioners for
Valuation.

Instructions for Assistant Assessors.
[Providence, 1798.] [2] pp.
AAS copy.   34452

[Rhode Island. Commissioners for
Valuation.
Instructions for Principal Assessors.
[Providence, 1798.] Broadside.
(No copy located.)   34451

Rhode Island. Convention, 1790.
The Bill of Rights. . . . March 6, 1790.
[Providence, 1790.] Broadside.
AAS copy.   22845

Rhode Island. Convention, 1790.
Rhode-Island and Providence Plantations
united to the Great American Family . . .
May 31, 1790.
[Providence], Carter, [1790]. Broadside.
AAS ph copy.   22847

Rhode Island. Council of War, 1777.
. . . In Council of War, April 8, 1777. This
Council having Received. . . .
[Providence, 1777.] Broadside.
RIHS copy.   43347

Rhode Island. Council of War, 1777.
. . . In Council of War, July 1, 1777.
Whereas Blankets. . . .
[Providence, 1777.] Broadside.
RIHS copy.   43348

Rhode Island. Council of War, 1778.
. . . In Council of War, January 4, 1778.
Resolved . . . Recruiting Instructions.
[Providence, 1778.] Broadside.
RIHS copy.   43531

Rhode Island. Council of War, 1778.
. . . In Council of War, June 4, 1778. The
General Assembly. . . .
[Providence, 1778.] Broadside.
RIHS copy.   16044

Rhode Island. Council of War, 1778.
. . . In Council of War, June 9, 1778. His
Excellency. . . .
[Providence, 1778.] Broadside.
RIHS copy.   16045

Rhode Island. Council of War, 1778.
. . . In Council of War, July 29, 1778.
Whereas . . . the Continental
Congress. . . .
[Providence, 1778.] Broadside.
BPL copy.   43532

Rhode Island. Council of War, 1778.
. . . In Council of War, August 2, 1778. It
is Voted. . . .
[Providence, 1778.] Broadside.
RIHS copy.   16046

Rhode Island. Council of War, 1778.
. . . In Council of War, August 17, 1778. It
Having Pleased. . . . [Providence, 1778.]
Broadside.
RIHS copy.   16047

Rhode Island. Council of War, 1778.
Orders of the Council of War . . . October
and December, 1778.
Providence, [1778]. 22 pp.
AAS copy.   16048

Rhode Island. Council of War, 1779.
. . . March 8, 1779. Resolved, That the
Following Orders be Given to the
Recruiting Officers. . . .
Providence, Carter, [1779.] Broadside.
AAS copy.   43685

Rhode Island. Council of War, 1779.
. . . In Council of War, March 11, 1779.
Resolved . . . Blankets.
Providence, [1779]. Broadside.
LOC copy.   16497

Rhode Island. Council of War, 1779.
In Council of War, March 12, 1779.
Providence, [1779]. Broadside.
LOC copy.   16498

Rhode Island. Council of War, 1779.
. . . In Council of War, October 2, 1779.
Resolved . . . Stockings.
[Providence, 1779.] Broadside.
LOC copy.   16499

Rhode Island. Council of War, 1779.

Resolves and Orders [Jan. 19 - Feb.,
1779].
Providence, [1779]. 12 pp.
AAS copy.   16496

Rhode Island. Council of War, 1781.
. . . In Council of War, June 16th, 1781.
Whereas it Appears. . . .
[Providence, 1781.] Broadside.
AAS copy.   17342

Rhode Island. Council of War, 1781.
. . . In Council of War, East-Greenwich,
Sept. 29, 1781. Whereas
Five Hundred Men. . . .
[Providence, 1781.] Broadside.
AAS copy.   17344

Rhode Island. Council of War, 1781.
. . . In Council of War, East-Greenwich,
Sept. 29, 1781. Whereas it Appears. . . .
Providence, [1781]. Broadside.
LOC copy.   17343

Rhode Island. Election Prox, 1776.
For the Preservation of the Liberties of
America. The Honorable Nicholas Cooke.
. . .
[Newport? 1776?] Broadside.
NHS copy.   43146

Rhode Island. Election Prox, 1777.
Defenders of American Rights.
[Providence? 1777.] Broadside.
(There are two printings.)
RIHS copy.   43349

Rhode Island. Election Prox, 1777.
For the Safety of the People.
[Providence, 1777.] Broadside.
RIHS copy.   43350

Rhode Island. Election Prox., 1778.
His Excellency William Greene, Esquire.
. . .
[Providence? 1778.] Broadside.
RIHS copy.   43533

Rhode Island. Election Prox., 1778.
Independence, Liberty, and Safety. The
Honorable William Bradford. . . .
[Providence], Carter, [1778?]. Broadside
RIHS copy.   43534

Rhode Island. Election Prox., 1779.
Freedom in Elections! His Excellency
William Greene. . . .
[Providence], Southwick & Wheeler,
[1779]. Broadside.
RIHS copy.   43686

Rhode Island. Election Prox, 1779.
His Excellency William Greene, Esq. . . .
[Providence], Carter, [1779]. Broadside.
RIHS copy.   43687

Rhode Island. Election Prox, 1779.
Let us and our Constituents Remain Free
from Slavery. His Excellency William
Greene. . . .
[Providence], Carter, [1779]. Broadside.
RIHS copy.   43688

Rhode Island. Election Prox, 1780.
A. D. 1780. The Happiness of the
Community. . . .
[Providence], Carter, [1780.] Broadside.
AAS copy.   43872

Rhode Island. Election Prox, 1780.
A. D. 1780. The Happiness of the
Community. . . .
[Providence], Carter, [1780]. Broadside.
RIHS copy.   43874

Rhode Island. Election Prox, 1780.
Friends to America and Gen. Washington.
[Providence? 1780.] Broadside.
AAS copy.   43873

Rhode Island. Election Prox, 1780.
Real Friends to Liberty, Washington. . . .
[Providence? 1780.] Broadside.
RIHS copy.   43875

Rhode Island. Election Prox, 1781.
Gentlemen Landholders, who pay a Heavy
Tax.
[Providence? 1781.] Broadside.
RIHS copy.   44038

Rhode Island. Election Prox, 1781.
His Excellency William Greene, Esq;

Governor. The Honorable Jabez Bowen,
Esq; Deputy Governor.
[Providence? 1781.] Broadside.
(Two printings are reproduced.)
RIHS copy.   44039

Rhode Island. Election Prox, 1781.
His Excellency William Greene, Esq;
Governor. The Honorable Jabez Bowen,
Esq; Dep. Governor.
[Providence], Carter, [1781]. Broadside.
AAS copy.   44040

Rhode Island. Election Prox, 1782.
His Excellency William Greene, Esquire,
Governor. Hon. Jabez Bowen, Esq; Dep.
Gov.
[Providence? 1782.] Broadside.
RIHS copy.   44251

Rhode Island. Election Prox, 1782.
Independent Landowners - The Friends of
the People. . . .
[Providence], Carter, [1782]. Broadside.
RIHS copy.   44252

Rhode Island. Election Prox, 1782.
Under Such Rulers we Hope for Justice!
[Providence], Wheeler, [1782].
Broadside.
RIHS copy.   44253

Rhode Island. Election Prox, 1783.
His Excellency William Greene, Esq;
Governor. The Honorable Jabez Bowen,
Esq; Dep. Governor.
[Providence], Carter, [1783]. Broadside.
RIHS copy.   44447

Rhode Island. Election Prox, 1784.
1784. His Excellency William Greene. . . .
Providence, Wheeler, [1784]. Broadside.
RIHS copy.   44595

Rhode Island. Election Prox., 1785.
1785. His Excellency William Greene.
Providence, Wheeler, [1785]. Broadside.
RIHS copy.   44785

Rhode Island. Election Prox, 1786.
To Relieve the Distressed. His Excellency
John Collins. . . .
[Providence? 1786] Broadside.
RIHS copy.   44958

Rhode Island. Election Prox, 1787.
Perseverance. His Excellency John
Collins. . . .
[Providence? 1787.] Broadside.
RIHS copy.   45151

Rhode Island. Election Prox, 1787.
1787. Landholders. His Excellency
William Bradford. . . .
[Providence? 1787.] Broadside.
AAS copy.   45152

Rhode Island. Election Prox, 1788.
The Governor's Prox. His Excellency,
John Collins. . . .
[Providence? 1788.] Broadside.
RIHS copy.   45349

Rhode Island. Election Prox, 1788.
Liberty and Property Secured by
Perseverance. His Excellency John
Collins.
[Providence? 1788.] Broadside.
RIHS copy.   45350

Rhode Island. Election Prox, 1789.
Convention Prox, 1789. Landholders!
[Providence], Wheeler, [1789].
Broadside.
RIHS copy.   45574

Rhode Island. Election Prox, 1789.
His Excellency John Collins, Esquire,
Governor.
[Providence], Wheeler, [1789].
Broadside.
NHS copy.   45575

Rhode Island. Election Prox, 1790.
Coalition Prox. His Excellency Arthur
Fenner. . . .
[Providence? 1790?] Broadside.
NHS copy.   45985

Rhode Island. Election Prox., 1790.
Country Prox, 1790. The Protectors of
their Country.

[Providence], Wheeler, [1790].
Broadside.
RIHS copy.   45986

Rhode Island. Election Prox, 1790.
An Opposer of Land-Taxes and High
Salaries. Benjamin Bourn.
[Providence? 1790?] Broadside.
RIHS copy.   45987

Rhode Island. Election Prox, 1790.
A Supporter of the Rights of Mankind. Job
Comstock.
[Providence? 1790.] Broadside.
RIHS copy.   45988

Rhode Island. Election Prox, 1790.
Uninfluenced by Party. . . . Benjamin
Bowen.
[Providence? 1790.] Broadside.
RIHS copy.   45989

Rhode Island. Election Prox, 1791.
1791. His Excellency Arthur Fenner.
[Providence], Wheeler, [1791].
Broadside.
RIHS copy.   46271

Rhode Island. Election Prox., 1792.
B. Bourn, First, Paul Mumford, Second,
Representatives in Congress.
[Providence? 1792.] Broadside.
RIHS copy.   46557

Rhode Island. Election Prox, 1792.
[Benjamin Bourn. First Representative.
Providence, 1792.]
(Alden 1281; no copy located.)   46558

Rhode Island. Election Prox. 1792.
A Friend of the Rights of Man, Francis
Malbone, Second Representative.
[Providence? 1792.] Broadside.
RIHS copy.   46560

Rhode Island. Election Prox, 1792.
Friends to the Rights of Man. Benjamin
Bourn, First. . . .
[Providence? 1792.] Broadside.
RIHS copy.   46559

Rhode Island. Election Prox, 1793.
1793. His Excellency Arthur Fenner, Esq.
Governor.
[Providence], Wheeler, [1793].
Broadside.
RIHS copy.   46865

Rhode Island. Election Prox, 1794.
Peleg Arnold, Esq; 1st Representative.
[Providence? 1794.] Broadside.
RIHS copy.   47200

Rhode Island. Election Prox, 1794.
1794. His Excellency Arthur Fenner, Esq.,
Governor. . . .
[Providence], Carter & Wilkinson,
[1794]. Broadside.
(For editions see Alden 1373.)
RIHS copy.   27616

Rhode Island. Election Prox, 1795.
1795. His Excellency Arthur Fenner.
[Providence], Carter & Wilkinson,
[1795]. Broadside.
RIHS copy.   47575

Rhode Island. Election ʀrox, 1796.
James Burrill, jun. Esq. 1st
Representative.
[Providence? 1796.] Broadside.
RIHS copy.   47893

Rhode Island. Election Prox, 1796.
Peleg Arnold, Esq; 1st Representative.
[Providence? 1796.] Broadside.
RIHS copy.   47894

Rhode Island. Election prox, 1796.
Representatives in Congress. Benjamin
Bourn. . . .
[Providence? 1796?] Broadside.
RIHS copy.   47895

Rhode Island. Election Prox, 1796.
1796. His Excellency Arthur Fenner, Esq.
[Providence], Carter & Wilkinson,
[1796]. Broadside.
AAS copy.   47896

Rhode Island. Election Prox, 1796.
Thomas Tillinghast, Esq. of
East-Greenwich.

[Providence? 1796.] Broadside.
RIHS copy.   47897

Rhode Island. Election Prox, 1797.
1797. His Excellency Arthur Fenner.
[Providence], Carter & Wilkinson,
[1797]. Broadside.
(Two states appear.)
RIHS copies.   48241

Rhode Island. Election Prox, 1798.
Christopher Grant Champlin, Second
Representative.
[Providence, 1798.] Broadside.
(Two states appear.)
RIHS copies.   48592

Rhode Island. Election Prox, 1798.
John Brown, Esq; 1st Representative. . . .
[Providence? 1798.] Broadside.
RIHS copy.   48593

Rhode Island. Election Prox, 1799.
1799. His Excellency Arthur Fenner. . . .
Samuel J. Potter, Esq.
[Providence], Carter & Wilkinson,
[1799]. Broadside.
RIHS copy.   36223

Rhode Island. Election Prox, 1799.
1799. His Excellency Arthur Fenner. . . .
The Honourable George Brown. . . .
[Providence], Carter, [1799]. Broadside.
RIHS copy.   36222

Rhode Island. Election Prox, 1799.
1799. John Brown, Esq. Governor.
[Newport], Farnsworth, [1799].
Broadside.
RIHS copy.   36224

Rhode Island. General Assembly, 1776.
[A Bill relating to procurement of specie.
Providence, Carter, 1776. Broadside.]
(Alden 659; no copy known.)   43147

Rhode Island. General Assembly, 1779.
[March 20, 1779. Attack on Rhode Island.
Providence, 1779. Broadside?]
(Alden 776; no copy located.)   43689

Rhode Island. General Assembly, 1780.
[A List of deputies to the February
Session.
Providence, Wheeler, 1780.] Broadside.
(Alden 827; no copy known.)   43888

Rhode Island. General Assembly, 1786.
An Act to Stimulate and give Efficacy to
the Paper Bills. . . . In General Assembly,
October Session, A.D. 1786.
Providence, Wheeler, 1786. Broadside.
AAS copy.   44959

Rhode Island. General Assembly, 1789.
The Following is a Copy of a Bill . . .
Postponed to the next Session. September
21, 1789.
Providence, Wheeler, [1789]. Broadside.
AAS copy.   22110

Rhode Island. General Assembly.
Committee on Memorial of the
Providence Association of Mechanicks
and Manufacturers.
To the Honorable General Assembly,
June Session, A.D. 1799.
Newport, Farnsworth, 1799. 12 pp.
AAS copy.   35434

Rhose Island. General Assembly. General
Committee, 1776.
. . . At a Meeting . . . the 11th Day of
December, A.D. 1776. Resolved. That all
the Troops. . . .
[Providence, 1776.] 20 pp.
AAS copy.   43148

Rhode Island. Governor, 1776.
By the Honorable Nicholas Cooke. . . . A
Proclamation Whereas it is the Duty. . . .
[Nov. 4, 1776.]
Providence, Carter, [1776]. Broadside.
RIHS copy.   43149

Rhode Island. Governor, 1776.
By the Honorable Nicholas Cooke, Esq:
Governour. . . . A Proclamation. Whereas
the . . . Continental Congress [Fast, May
17. Dated May 6, 1776].
Providence, Carter, [1776]. Broadside.
AAS ph. copy.   43150

[Rhode Island. Governor, 1776.
Handbill relating to appearance of hostile
fleet.
Providence, 1776.]
(Alden 642a; no copy located.)   43151

Rhode Island. Governor, 1777.
. . . Providence, July 21, 1777. . . . To all
Brigadiers. . . .
[Providence, 1777.] Broadside.
RIHS copy.   43351

Rhode Island. Governor, 1778.
By His Excellency William Greene. . . . A
Proclamation [Continental Thanksgiving,
Dec. 30. Dated Dec. 8, 1778].
RISL copy.   43535

Rhode Island. Governor, 1779.
By His Excellency [blank] Esquire. . . .
Insturctions to the Commanders of . . .
Letters of Marque [Dated 177-].
n. p., n. d. Broadside.
JCB copy.   43690

Rhode Island, Governor, 1779.
By His Excellency William Greene. . . . A
Proclamation [Continental Fast, May,
1779. Dated Apr. 7, 1779].
Providence, Southwick & Wheeler,
[1779]. Broadside.
AAS copy.   19432

Rhode Island. Governor, 1779.
By His Excellency William Greene. . . . A
Proclamation [Thanksgiving, Dec. 9.
Dated Nov. 17, 1779].
Providence, Carter, [1779]. Broadside.
RIHS copy.   19433

Rhode Island. Governor, 1781.
By His Excellency William Greene. . . . A
Proclamation [Thanksgiving, Dec. 13.
Dated Nov. 26, 1781].
Providence, [1781]. Broadside.
RISL copy.   17346

Rhode Island. Governor, 1782.
By His Excellency William Greene. . . . A
Proclamation. Whereas the . . . Congress
[Apr. 13, 1782].
Providence, Carter, [1782]. Broadside.
RIHS copy.   44254

Rhode Island. Governor, 1782.
[By William Greene, a proclamation,
Nov. 4, 1782.
Providence, Carter, 1782.] Broadside.
(No copy known.)   44255

Rhode Island. Governor, 1783.
[By William Greene, a proclamation,
Nov. 14, 1783.
Providence, Carter, 1783.] Broadside.
(Alden 954; no copy known.)   44449

Rhode Island. Governor, 1783.
[By William Greene, a proclamation,
Nov. 17, 1783.
Providence, Carter, 1783.]
(Alden 955; no copy known.)   44448

Rhode Island. Governor, 1784.
By William Greene, Esq. . . . A
Proclamation [Peace, Mar. 1, 1784].
Providence, Carter, [1784]. Broadside.
JCB copy.   18755

Rhode Island. Governor, 1785.
By His Excellency William Greene. . . . A
Proclamation. . . . Thanksgiving [Dec. 1.
Dated Nov. 10, 1785].
Providence, Carter, [1785]. Broadside.
AAS copy.   44786

Rhode Island. Governor, 1789.
[By His Excellency, John Collins. . . . A
Proclamation . . . Nov. 2, 1789.
Providence, Wheeler, 1789.] Broadside.
(Alden 1157; no copy known.)   45576

Rhode Island. Governor, 1790.
By His Excellency Arthur Fenner. . . . A
Proclamation . . . Constitution of the
United States. . . . [Dated June 14, 1790.]
Providence, Carter, [1790]. Broadside.
RIHS copy.   45990

Rhode Island. Governor, 1790.
By His Excellency Arthur Fenner, Esq.
. . . A Proclamation [Oath of Allegiance.
Dated June 14, 1790].

Providence, Carter, [1790]. Broadside.
AAS copy.   22844

Rhode Island. Governor, 1791.
[By His Excellency Arthur Fenner, a
proclamation dated Nov. 7, 1791.
Providence, Carter, 1791.] Broadside.
(Alden 1252; no copy known.)   46272

Rhode Island. Governor, 1792.
By His Excellency Arthur Fenner. . . . A
Proclamation . . . [Nov. 5, 1792].
[Providence], Carter, [1792]. Broadside.
RIHS copy.   46561

Rhode Island. Governor, 1793.
By His Excellency Arthur Fenner. . . . A
Proclamation [Nov. 4, 1793]. . . .
[Providence], Carter & Wilkinson,
[1793]. Broadside.
RIHS copy.   46866

Rhode Island. Governor, 1793.
By His Excellency Arthur Fenner. . . . A
Proclamation [Smallpox. Sept. 21, 1793].
[Providence], Carter, [1793]. Broadside.
JCB copy.   26076

Rhode Island. Governor, 1794.
[By His Excellency Arthur Fenner, a
proclamation, Apr. 7, 1794.
Providence, Carter & Wilkinson, 1794.
Broadside.]
(Alden 1376; no copy known.)   47201

Rhode Island. Governor, 1794.
By His Excellency Arthur Fenner. . . . A
Proclamation. . . . [Nov. 3, 1794].
Warren, Phillips, [1794]. Broadside.
RIHS copy.   47202

Rhode Island. Governor, 1795.
By His Excellency Arthur Fenner. . . . A
Proclamation [Nov. 6, 1795.]
Providence, Carter & Wilkinson, [1795].
Broadside.
RIHS copy.   47576

Rhode Island. Governor, 1795.
By His Excellency Arthur Fenner. . . . A
Proclamation. . . . Thanksgiving [Nov. 19.
Dated Nov. 6, 1795].
Warren, Carter & Wilkinson, [1795].
Broadside.
(Evans assumed the imprint.)
RIHS copy.   29404

Rhode Island. Governor, 1796.
By His Excellency Arthur Fenner. . . . A
Proclamation [Nov. 7, 1796].
Warren, Phillips, [1796]. Broadside.
(The only known copy is imperfect.)
RIHS copy.   47898

Rhode Island. Governor, 1796.
By His Excellency Arthur Fenner. . . . To
the Town-Clerk. . . . Benjamin Bowen . . .
Judge. . . . This Fourth Day of November,
A.D. 1796.
[Warren, 1796.] Broadside.
RIHS copy.   31096

Rhode Island. Governor, 1797.
By His Excellency Arthur Fenner. . . . A
Proclamation. . . . Thanksgiving [Nov. 30.
Dated Oct. 30, 1797].
Warren, Phillips, [1797]. Broadside.
RIHS copy.   32758

Rhode Island. Governor, 1797.
. . . To the Freemen of the State. . . .
Elisha R. Potter. . . . Twenty-Fourth Day
of July, A. D. 1797.
[Providence, 1797.] Broadside.
RIHS copy.   32759

Rhode Island. Governor, 1798.
By His Excellency Arthur Fenner. . . . A
Proclamation. . . . An Act Establishing
the Digest of Laws.
Providence, Carter & Wilkinson, [1798].
Broadside.
AAS copy.   34449

Rhode Island. Governor, 1798.
[By His Excellency Arthur Fenner, a
Proclamation, Nov. 5, 1798.
Newport, Farnsworth, 1798. Broadside?]
(Alden 1576; no copy known.)   48594

Rhode Island. Governor, 1799.
By His Excellency Arthur Fenner . . . a

Proclamation. . . . Thanksgiving [Nov. 28,
Dated Nov. 5, 1799.]
Providence, Carter, [1799]. Broadside.
AAS copy.   36216

Rhode Island. Governor, 1800.
By His Excellency Arthur Fenner. . . . A
Proclamation . . . Thanksgiving [Nov. 27.
Dated Nov. 3, 1800.]
[Newport, 1800.] Broadside.
RIHS copy.   38382

Rhode Island. Governor's Independent
Company of Light Infantry in the Town of
Providence.
The Charter and Bye-laws of the. . . .
[Providence], Wheeler, 1795. 7 pp.
RIHS copy.   29367

Rhode Island. Laws, Statutes, etc., 1776.
. . . At a Meeting of a Committee [Sept.
12, 1776. Battalion of Militia].
[Providence, 1776.] Broadside.
RIHS copy.   15059

Rhode Island. Laws, Statutes, etc., 1776.
At the General Assembly. . . . Be it
Enacted [Firearms. Jan. 1776].
Providence, [1776]. Broadside.
RIHS copy.   15055

Rhode Island. Laws, Statutes, etc., 1776.
At the General Assembly . . . the
Twenty-First Day of November. . . . Be it
Enacted . . . that One Regiment. . . .
Providence, Carter, [1776]. Broadside.
RIHS copy.   43152

Rhode Island. Laws, Statutes, etc., 1776.
At the General Assembly . . . the
Twenty-First Day of November. . . . It is
Voted and Resolved, that Each
Captain. . . .
Providence, Carter, [1776]. Broadside.
RIHS copy.   43153

Rhode Island. Laws, Statutes, etc., 1776.
. . . In General Assembly, March Session.
. . . An Act for Purchasing Two Thousand
Arms.
[Providence, 1776.] Broadside.
RIHS copy.   15058

Rhode Island. Laws, Statutes, etc., 1776.
. . . In General Assembly, May Session,
1776. An Act Repealing an Act. . . .
[Providence, 1776.] Broadside.
RIHS copy.   15056

Rhode Island. Laws, Statutes, etc., 1776.
. . . In General Assembly, June Session,
1776. An Act Permitting Inoculation.
[Providence, 1776.] Broadside.
RIHS copy.   15057

Rhode Island. Laws, Statutes, etc., 1776.
. . . In General Assembly, December 2d
Session, 1776. Whereas the Act . . .
Directing the Alarm List. . . .
[Providence, 1776.] Broadside.
RIHS copy.   43154

Rhode Island. Laws, Statutes, etc., 1776.
. . . In General Assembly, December
Session, A.D. 1776. It is Voted and
Resolved, that all Male Persons. . . .
[Providence, 1776.] Broadside.
RIHS copy.   43155

Rhode Island. Laws, Statutes, etc., 1776.
Rules and Regulations for the Forces.
Newport, Southwick, 1776. 23 pp.
AAS copy.   43156

Rhode Island. Laws, Statutes, etc., 1777.
. . . An Act to Prevent Monopolies.
Providence, [1777]. 8 pp.
NYPL copy.   15573

Rhode Island. Laws, Statutes, etc., 1777.
. . . In General Assembly, March Second
Session, 1777. An Act for Numbering all
Persons.
[Providence, 1777.] Broadside.
RIHS copy.   43353

Rhode Island. Laws, Statutes, etc., 1777.
. . . In General Assembly, March Second
Session, A.D. 1777. Resolved, That each
of the Three Divisions. . . .
[Providence, 1777.] Broadside.
RIHS copy.   43354

Rhode Island. Laws, Statutes, etc., 1777.
. . . In General Assembly, March Session,
A.D. 1777. This Assembly . . . do
Resolve. . . .
[Providence, 1777.] Broadside.
RIHS copy.   43352

Rhode Island. Laws, Statutes, etc., 1777.
. . . In General Assembly, March 26, 1777.
An Act [Tax of £16,000].
Providence, 1777. [2] pp.
AAS copy.   15574

Rhode Island. Laws, Statutes, etc., 1777.
. . . In General Assembly, April 19, 1777.
Be it Enacted. . . .
[Providence, 1777.] [2] pp.
JCB copy.   43355

Rhode Island. Laws, Statutes, etc., 1777.
. . . In General Assembly, April 21, 1777.
An Act in Addition to an Act.
[Providence, 1777.] Broadside.
AAS copy.   43356

Rhode Island. Laws, Statutes, etc., 1777.
. . . In General Assembly, April 21, 1777.
It is Voted. . . .
[Providence, 1777.] Broadside.
RIHS copy.   43357

Rhode Island. Laws, Statutes, etc., 1777.
. . .In General Assembly, May Session,
1777. This Assembly. . . . Voted. . . .
[Providence, 1777.] Broadside.
JCB copy.   43358

Rhode Island. Laws, Statutes, etc., 1777.
. . . In General Assembly, May Session,
1777. Whereas by an Act. . . .
[Providence, J. Carter, 1777.] Broadside.
RIHS copy.   43359

Rhode Island. Laws, Statutes, etc., 1777.
. . . In General Assembly, May 2nd
Session, 1777. An Act to Prevent
Monopoly.
[Providence, 1777.] 15 pp.
AAS copy.   43360

Rhode Island. Laws, Statutes, etc., 1777.
. . . In General Assembly, June Session,
1777. An Act Establishing and Regulating
Fees.
[Providence, 1777.] 7 pp.
AAS copy.   43361

Rhode Island. Laws, Statutes, etc., 1777.
. . . In General Assembly, July 9, 1777.
Resolved, that One of the Divisions. . . .
[Providence, 1777.] Broadside.
RIHS copy.   43362

Rhode Island. Laws, Statutes, etc., 1777.
. . . In General Assembly, August Session,
1777. It is Voted . . . that the Continental
Officers . . .
[Providence, 1777.] Broadside.
RIHS copy.   43363

Rhode Island. Laws, Statutes, etc., 1777.
. . . In General Assembly, August 23d,
1777. An Act Assessing . . . a . . . Tax of
Thirty-Two Thousand Pounds.
[Providence, 1777.] [2] pp.
CU copy.   43364

Rhode Island. Laws, Statutes, etc., 1777.
. . . In General Assembly, September
Session, A.D. 1777. Resolved, that One
Half of the Militia. . . .
[Providence, 1777.] Broadside.
RIHS copy.   43365

Rhode Island. Laws, Statutes, etc., 1777.
. . . In General Assembly, October
Session, A.D. 1777. Whereas, by a Resolve
. . . the Families of Officers. . . .
[Providence, 1777.] Broadside.
JCB copy.   43366

Rhode Island. Laws, Statutes, etc., 1777.
. . . In General Assembly, October
Session, A.D. 1777. Whereas, Owing to
Divers Causes. . . .
[Providence, 1777.] Broadside.
RISL copy.   43367

Rhode Island. Laws, Statutes, etc., 1777.
. . . In General Assembly, December 4,
1777. An Act Assessing . . . a . . . Tax of
Forty-Eight Thousand Pounds.

[Providence, 1777.] Broadside.
RISL copy.   43368

Rhode Island. Laws, Statutes, etc., 1778.
. . . Feb. Session, 1778. Whereas the
Fines. . . .
[Providence, 1778.] Broadside.
LOC copy.   16038

Rhode Island. Laws, Statutes, etc., 1778.
. . . In General Assembly, February 16,
1778. An Act Assessing . . . a . . . Tax of
Thirty-Two Thousand Pounds.
[Providence, 1778.] Broadside.
RISL copy.   43536

Rhode Island. Laws, Statutes, etc., 1778.
. . . In General Assembly. March Session,
A. D. 1778. An Act in Addition to, and
Amendment of, an Act . . . Assessing a
Tax.
[Providence, 1778.] Broadside.
JCB copy.   16040

Rhode Island. Laws, Statutes, etc., 1778.
. . . In General Assembly, March Session,
1778. It is Voted and Resolved, That the
Colonels. . . . [Dated Mar. 18, 1778.]
[Providence, 1778.] Broadside.
RIHS copy.   43537

Rhode Island. Laws, Statutes, etc., 1778.
. . . In General Assembly, March Session,
1778. Whereas the Most Honorable the
Continental Congress. . . .
[Providence, 1778.] Broadside.
RIHS copy.   16041

Rhode Island. Laws, Statutes, etc., 1778.
. . . In General Assembly, May Session,
A.D. 1778. Resolved, That it be
. . . Recommended to . . . General
Sullivan. . . .
[Providence, 1778.] Broadside.
RIHS copy.   43543

Rhode Island. Laws, Statutes, etc., 1778.
. . . In General Assembly, May Session,
1778. It is Voted and Resolved, That any
Person. . . .
[Providence, 1778.] Broadside.
RIHS copy.   43538

Rhode Island. Laws, Statutes, etc., 1778.
. . . In General Assembly, May Second
Session, A.D. 1778. Resolved, That a
Committee be Appointed. . . .
[Providence, 1778.] Broadside.
RIHS copy.   43540

Rhode Island. Laws, Statutes, etc., 1778.
. . . In General Assembly, May Second
Session, A.D. 1778. Resolved, That all
Persons. . . .
[Providence, 1778.] Broadside.
RIHS copy.   43541

Rhode Island. Laws, Statutes, etc., 1778.
. . . In General Assembly, May Second
Session, A.D. 1778. Resolved, that Eight
Hundred . . . Men. . . .
[Providence, 1778.] Broadside.
RIHS copy.   43542

Rhode Island. Laws, Statutes, etc., 1778.
. . . In General Assembly, May Second
Session, A.D. 1778. Resolved, That the
Act Permitting Inoculation. . . .
[Providence, 1778.] Broadside.
RIHS copy.   43544

Rhode Island. Laws, Statutes, etc., 1778.
. . . In General Assembly, May Second
Session, A.D. 1778. An Act for
Calling in. . . .
[Providence, 1778.] Broadside.
RIHS copy.   43539

Rhode Island. Laws, Statutes, etc., 1778.
. . . In General Assembly, June . . . 1778.
An Act for Assessing . . . a Tax of
Thirty-two Thousand Pounds.
[Providence, 1778.] Broadside.
RIHS copy.   16039

Rhode Island. Laws, Statutes, etc., 1779.
. . . In General Assembly, August Session,
1799. It is Voted and Resolved, That the
Inlistments of the Non-Commissioned
Officers. . . .
[Providence, 1779.] Broadside.
AAS copy.   43697

Rhode Island. Laws, Statutes, etc., 1778.
. . . In General Assembly September
Session, A.D. 1778. Whereas by Reason of
the late Expedition. . . .
[Providence, 1778.] Broadside.
JCB copy.   43545

Rhode Island. Laws, Statutes, etc., 1778.
[. . . In General Assembly, September
session, A.D. 1778. ? Whereas it has
happened. . . .
Providence, 1778? Broadside.]
(Alden 750; no copy known.)   43546

Rhode Island. Laws, Statutes, etc., 1778.
[. . . In General Assembly, October
session, A.D. 1778. An Act Assessing . . .
a . . . Tax of Thirty Thousand Pounds. . . .
Providence? 1778. Broadside?]
(Alden 751; no copy known.)   43547

Rhode Island. Laws, Statutes, etc., 1778.
. . . In General Assembly, Oct. Session,
A.D. 1778. An Act Establishing and
Regulating Fees.
[Providence, 1778.] 8 pp.
RIHS copy.   16042

Rhode Island. Laws, Statutes, etc., 1778.
. . . In General Assembly, Oct. Session,
A.D. 1778. An Act Establishing and
Regulating Fees.
[Providence, 1778.] 8 pp.
RISL copy.   43548

Rhode Island. Laws, Statutes, etc., 1778.
. . . In General Assembly, October
Session, A. D. 1778. An Act for Enquiring
into the Rateable Property. . . .
[Providence, 1778.] Broadside.
RIHS copy.   16043

Rhode Island. Laws, Statutes, etc., 1778.
. . . In General Assembly, October
Session, A.D. 1778. An Act for Enquiring
into the Rateable Property. . . .
[Providence, 1778.] Broadside.
RIHS copy.   43549

Rhode Island. Laws, Statutes, etc., 1778.
. . . In General Assembly, December
Session, 1778. Whereas Great
Difficulties. . . .
[Providence, 1778.] Broadside.
RIHS copy.   43550

Rhode Island. Laws, Statutes, etc., 1779.
[An act to raise the sum of one hundred
thousand pounds.
Providence, Carter, 1779.]
(Alden 798; no copy known.)   43691

Rhode Island. Laws, Statutes, etc., 1779.
. . . In General Assembly, February
Session, A.D. 1779. An Act [Tax.
£90,000].
Providence, [1779]. Broadside.
RIHS copy.   16494

Rhode Island. Laws, Statutes, etc., 1779.
. . . In General Assembly, February
Session, 1779. An Act for Enforcing an
Act . . . Obliging . . . Military Duty.
Providence, Carter, [1779]. Broadside.
(No copy located.)   43692

Rhode Island. Laws, Statutes, etc., 1779.
. . . In General Assembly. February
Session, 1779. An Act [Tax £60,000].
[Providence, 1779.] Broadside.
RIHS copy.   16495

Rhode Island. Laws, Statutes, etc., 1779.
. . . In General Assembly, May Session,
1779. Whereas it is Necessary . . .
Resolved, That no Miller. . . .
Providence, Carter, [1779]. Broadside.
AAS copy.   43693

Rhode Island. Laws, Statutes, etc., 1779.
. . . In General Assembly, June Session,
1779. An Act Assessing . . . a Tax of Sixty
Thousand Pounds.
Providence, Southwick & Wheeler,
[1779]. Broadside.
RIHS copy.   43694

Rhode Island. Laws, Statutes, etc., 1779.
. . . In General Assembly, June Session,
1779. An Act Assessing . . . a Tax of Two
Hundred and Twenty-Five Thousand
Pounds.

Providence, Carter, [1779]. Broadside.
RIHS copy.   43695

Rhode Island. Laws, Statutes, etc., 1779.
. . . In General Assembly, June Session,
1779. An Act for the Better Forming . . .
the Military.
Providence, Carter, [1779]. [2] pp.
RIHS copy.   43696

Rhode Island. Laws, Statutes, etc., 1779.
. . . In General Assembly, October
Session, 1779. An Act for the Better
Forming . . . the Military.
[Providence], Carter, [1779]. 2 pp.
RIHS copy.   43698

Rhode Island. Laws, Statutes, etc., 1779.
. . . In General Assembly, December
Session, A.D. 1779. An Act for Assessing
. . . a Rate or Tax of One Hundred and
Twenty Thousand Pounds.
[Providence, 1779.] Broadside.
RISL copy.   43700

Rhode Island. Laws, Statutes, etc., 1779.
. . . In General Assembly, December
Session, 1779. An Act Establishing and
Regulating Fees.
[Providence, 1779.] 8 pp.
BrU copy.   43699

Rhode Island. Laws, Statutes, etc., 1780.
"And whereas there is a very Large Sum
of Money due. . . ." The Preceeding is a
True Extract. . . . November Session,
1780.
[Providence], Wheeler, [1780?].
Broadside.
RIHS copy.   43878

Rhode Island. Laws, Statutes, etc., 1780.
. . . In General Assembly, February
Session, 1780. An Act for Assessing . . . a
Rate or Tax of One Hundred and Eighty
Thousand Pounds.
Providence, Carter, [1780]. Broadside.
RISL copy.   43876

Rhode Island. General Assembly, 1780.
. . . In General Assembly, February
Session, 1780. Whereas it will be
Necessary. . . .
[Providence], Carter, [1780]. Broadside.
RIHS copy.   43877

Rhode Island. Laws, Statutes, etc., 1780.
. . . In General Assembly, May Session,
1780. An Act [Tax of £180,000].
[Providence, 1780.] Broadside.
RIHS copy.   16970

Rhode Island. Laws, Statutes, etc., 1780.
. . . In General Assembly, June Session,
1780. An Act for Raising . . . Six Hundred
and Ten Men.
[Providence], Carter, [1780]. Broadside.
RIHS copy.   43879

Rhode Island. Laws, Statutes, etc., 1780.
. . . In General Assembly, July Session,
1780. An Act for Assessing and
Apportioning a Rate or Tax of Four
Hundred Thousand Pounds.
Providence, Carter, [1780]. Broadside.
RISL copy.   43880

Rhode Island. Laws, Statutes, etc., 1780.
. . . In General Assembly, July 2d Session,
1780: An Act for Proportioning . . .
Supplies.
[Providence, 1780.] Broadside.
RIHS copy.   16971

Rhode Island. Laws, Statutes, etc., 1780.
. . . In General Assembly, July 2d Session,
1780. An Act for Raising Six Hundred and
Thirty . . . Men.
[Providence, 1780.] Broadside.
RIHS copy.   16972

Rhode Island. Laws, Statutes, etc., 1780.
. . . In General Assembly, July Session,
1780. An Act to Prevent Certain
Persons. . . .
[Providence, Wheeler, [1780]. Broadside.
AAS copy.   43881

Rhode Island. Laws, Statutes, etc., 1780.
[. . . In General Assembly, July session,
1780. It is voted and resolved, that six
hundred and ten blankets. . . .

Providence, Wheeler, 1780.] Broadside.
(Alden 835; no copy known.) 43882

Rhode Island. Laws, Statutes, etc., 1780.
. . . In General Assembly, July Second
Session, 1780. An Act for Assessing . . .
a Rate of Ten Thousand Pounds.
Providence, Wheeler, [1780]. Broadside.
YC copy. 43883

Rhode Island. Laws, Statutes, etc., 1780.
. . . In General Assembly, July 2d Session,
1780. Whereas notwithstanding the
Provision. . . .
[Providence], Carter, [1780]. Broadside.
RIHS copy. 43884

Rhode Island. Laws, Statutes, etc., 1780.
. . . In General Assembly, July 7, 1780.
Whereas . . . Six Hundred and Ten
Effective Men. . . .
[Providence], Wheeler, [1780].
Broadside.
RIHS copy. 43885

Rhode Island. Laws, Statutes, etc., 1780.
. . . In General Assembly, November
Session, 1780. An Act for Assessing . . . a
Rate or Tax of One Million of Pounds.
[Providence], Wheeler, [1780].
Broadside.
RISL copy. 43886

Rhode Island. Laws, Statutes, etc., 1780.
. . . In General Assembly, November
Session, 1780. An Act for Granting . . . a
Tax of Sixteen Thousand Pounds.
[Providence], Wheeler, [1780].
Broadside.
RISL copy. 43887

Rhode Island. Laws, Statutes, etc., 1780.
. . . In General Assembly, November
Session, 1780. An Act for Filling up . . .
Quota.
Providence, Carter, [1780]. [2] pp.
RIHS copy. 16973

Rhode Island. Laws, Statutes, etc., 1781.
. . . In General Assembly, January
Session, 1781. An Act Proportioning to
the Several Towns. . . .
[Providence, 1781.] Broadside.
LOC copy. 17336

Rhode Island. Laws, Statutes, etc., 1781.
. . . In General Assembly, February
Session, 1781. An Act for Incorporating
and bringing into the Field. . . .
[Providence, 1781.] Broadside.
LOC copy. 17337

Rhode Island. Laws, Statutes, etc., 1781.
. . . In General Assembly, February
Session, 1781. Whereas by an Act . . .
Twelve Hundred Men. . . .
[Providence, 1781.] Broadside.
RIHS copy. 17345

Rhode Island. Laws, Statutes, etc., 1781.
. . . In General Assembly, March Session,
1781. Whereas by an Act . . .
Apportioning. . . .
[Providence], Wheeler, [1781].
Broadside.
(The only known copy is imperfect.)
RIHS copy. 44041

Rhode Island. Laws, Statutes, etc., 1781.
. . . In General Assembly, March Session,
1781. Whereas by an Act [Army Quota].
[Providence, 1781.] Broadside.
AAS copy. 19434

Rhode Island. Laws, Statutes, etc., 1781.
. . . In General Assembly. May Session,
1781. Whereas the Legislature. . . .
Providence, Carter, [1781]. Broadside.
RIHS copy. 44042

Rhode Island. Laws, Statutes, etc., 1781.
. . . In General Assembly, May Second
Session, 1781. An Act for Granting . . . a
Tax of Six Thousand Pounds.
Providence, Carter, [1781]. Broadside.
RISL copy. 44043

Rhode Island. Laws, Statutes, etc., 1781.
. . . In General Assembly, May Second
Session, 1781. An Act for Granting . . . a
Tax of Twenty Thousand Pounds.

Providence, Carter, [1781]. Broadside.
RISL copy. 44044

Rhode Island. Laws, Statutes, etc., 1781.
. . . In General Assembly, May Second
Session, 1781. An Act for Incorporating
and bringing into the Field.
[Providence, Carter, 1781.] Broadside.
AAS copy. 44045

Rhode Island. Laws, Statutes, etc., 1781.
. . . In General Assembly, July Session,
1781. An Act for Proportioning . . .
Supplies of Beef.
[Providence], Wheeler, [1781].
Broadside.
(Two varieties are reproduced.)
RIHS copy. 44046

Rhode Island. Laws, Statutes, etc., 1781.
. . . In General Assembly, July Session,
1781. Whereas Five Hundred Men. . . .
[Providence, Carter, 1781.] Broadside.
AAS copy. 44047

Rhode Island. Laws, Statutes, etc., 1781.
. . . In General Assembly, July Session,
1781. Whereas from the Neglect. . . .
[Providence, 1781.] Broadside.
RISL copy. 44048

Rhode Island. Laws, Statutes, etc., 1781.
. . . In General Assembly, July Session,
1781. Whereas the Council of War. . . .
Providence, Wheeler, [1781]. Broadside.
LOC copy. 17338

Rhode Island. Laws, Statutes, etc., 1781.
. . . In General Assembly, August Session,
1781. An Act for Incorporating and
bringing into the Field. . . .
[Providence, 1781.] Broadside.
LOC copy. 17339

Rhode Island. Laws, Statutes, etc., 1781.
. . . In General Assembly, August Session,
1781. An Act for Mitigating of Penalties.
Providence, Carter, [1781]. Broadside.
AAS copy. 44049

Rhode Island. Laws, Statutes, etc., 1781.
. . . In General Assembly, August Session,
A.D. 1781. An Act for Proportioning the
Supplies of Beef.
Providence, Wheeler, [1781]. Broadside.
LOC copy. 17340

Rhode Island. Laws, Statutes, etc., 1781.
. . . In General Assembly, August Session,
1781. Whereas it is Necessary. . . .
[Providence, Carter, 1781.] Broadside.
AAS copy. 44050

Rhode Island. Laws, Statutes, etc., 1781.
. . . In General Assembly, December
1781. An Act Proportioning the Quantity
. . . of Beef.
Providence, Carter, [1781]. Broadside.
RIHS copy. 17341

Rhode Island. Laws, Statutes, etc., 1782.
. . . In General Assembly, January
Session, 1782. An Act for Granting . . . A
Tax of Twelve Thousand Pounds.
Providence, Carter, [1782]. Broadside.
RIHS copy. 17698

Rhode Island. Laws, Statutes, etc., 1782.
. . . In General Assembly, January
Session, 1782. It is Voted, That an
Account of the Number of Families. . . .
[Providence, 1782.] Broadside.
RISL copy. 44257

Rhode Island. Laws, Statutes, etc., 1782.
. . . General Assembly, February Session,
A.D. 1782. An Act for Granting . . . a Tax
of Six Thousand Pounds.
Providence, Wheeler, [1782]. Broadside.
RISL copy. 44258

Rhode Island. Laws, Statutes, etc., 1782.
. . . In General Assembly, February
Session, 1782. An Act for Granting . . . a
Tax of Six Thousand Pounds.
Providence, Carter, [1782]. Broadside.
Westerly, R.I., Public Library copy. 44256

Rhode Island. Laws, Statutes, etc., 1782.
. . . In General Assembly, February
Session, 1782. An Act for . . .
Tow-Cloth. . . .

Providence, Wheeler, [1782]. Broadside.
RIHS copy. 17699

Rhode Island. Laws, Statutes, etc., 1782.
. . . In General Assembly, February
Session, 1782. Whereas great Frauds. . . .
[Providence, 1782.] Broadside.
LOC copy. 17700

Rhode Island. Laws, Statutes, etc., 1782.
. . . In General Assembly, March 1, 1782.
An Act for Raising Two Hundred and
Fifty-Nine Men.
Providence, Carter, [1782]. Broadside.
RIHS copy. 44259

Rhode Island. Laws, Statutes, etc., 1782.
. . . In General Assembly, June Session,
1782. An Act for Granting . . . a Tax on
Twelve Thousand Pounds.
[Providence, 1782.] Broadside.
Westerly, R.I., Public Library copy. 44260

Rhode Island. Laws, Statutes, etc., 1783.
. . . In General Assembly, February
Session, 1783. An Act Laying Certain
Duties.
Providence, Carter, [1783]. Broadside.
AAS copy. 18155

Rhode Island. Laws, Statutes, etc., 1783.
. . . In General Assembly, February
Session, A.D. 1783. An Act to Disqualify
Persons.
[Providence, 1783.] Broadside.
AAS copy. 44450

Rhode Island. Laws, Statutes, etc., 1783.
. . . In General Assembly, June Session,
1783. An Act for Granting . . . a Tax of
Twenty Thousand Pounds.
[Providence, 1783.] Broadside.
RIHS copy. 44451

Rhode Island. Laws, Statutes, etc., 1783.
. . . In General Assembly, June Session,
1783. An Act Laying an Impost.
Providence, Carter, [1783]. Broadside.
AAS copy. 18156

Rhode Island. Laws, Statutes, etc., 1783.
. . . In General Assembly, December
Session, A. D. 1783. Whereas the most
Honorable the Congress. . . .
Providence, Carter, [1783]. Broadside.
AAS copy. 18157

Rhode Island. Laws, Statutes, etc., 1784.
. . . In General Assembly, February
Session, A.D. 1784. An Act Repealing the
. . . Test-Act.
Providence, Wheeler, [1784]. Broadside.
RIHS copy. 44596

Rhode Island. Laws, Statutes, etc., 1784.
. . . In General Assembly, February
Session, 1784. Whereas the
General-Treasurer [6% Certificates].
Providence, Carter, [1784]. Broadside.
(Evans' entry came from the order to
print.)
LOC copy. 18753

Rhode Island, Laws, Statutes, etc., 1784.
. . . In General Assembly, June Session,
1784. An Act for Granting . . . Twenty
Thousand Pounds.
[Providence, 1784.] Broadside.
LOC copy. 18754

Rhode Island, Laws, Statutes, etc., 1785.
. . . In General Assembly, February
Session, 1785. Whereas Certain Classes
. . . .
Providence, Carter, [1785]. Broadside.
NHS copy. 44787

Rhode Island. Laws, Statutes, etc., 1785.
. . . In General Assembly, August Session,
A.D. 1785. An Act for Granting. . . .
[Providence, 1785.] Broadside.
RIHS copy. 44788

Rhode Island. Laws, Statutes, etc., 1786.
An Act for Granting and Apportioning a
Tax of Twenty Thousand Pounds.
[Providence, 1786.] Broadside.
RISL copy. 44960

Rhode Island. Laws, Statutes, etc., 1786.
An Act for Transferring Real Estates. . . .
December Session, A. D. 1786.

Providence, Wheeler, [1787?] Broadside.
JCB copy.   19958

Rhode Island. Laws, Statutes, etc., 1786.
. . . In General Assembly, Especially
Convened . . . August 22, A. D. 1786.
[Public Credit].
Providence, Carter, [1786]. Broadside.
RIHS copy.   19959

Rhode Island. Laws, Statutes, etc., 1786.
. . . In General Assembly, March Session,
A. D. 1786. An Act Laying Duties.
Providence, Carter, [1786]. [2] pp.
RIHS copy.   19957

Rhode Island. Laws, Statutes, etc., 1786.
[. . . In General Assembly, May session,
A.D. 1786, An Act for emitting one
hundred thousand pounds.
Providence, Wheeler, 1786.] Broadside.
(Alden 1054; no copy found.)   44961

Rhode Island. Laws, Statutes, etc., 1787.
. . . An Act for Granting and
Apportioning a Tax of Thirty Thousand
Pounds. . . .
[Providence], Wheeler, [1787]. Broadside.
LOC copy.   20686

Rhode Island. Laws, Statutes, etc., 1787.
. . . In General Assembly, March Session,
A.D. 1787. An Act for Granting . . . a Tax
of Twenty Thousand Pounds.
[Providence, 1787.] Broadside.
RIHS copy.   45154

Rhode Island. Laws, Statutes, etc., 1787.
. . . In General Assembly, March Session,
A. D., 1787. An Act for the more Equal
Representation. . . .
Providence, Wheeler, [1787]. Broadside.
AAS copy.   20687

Rhode Island. Laws, Statutes, etc., 1787.
. . . In General Assembly, March Session,
A.D. 1787. An Act to Prevent Bribery.
[Providence, 1787.] Broadside.
RIHS copy.   45155

Rhode Island. Laws, Statutes, etc., 1787.
. . . In General Assembly, September
Session, A.D. 1787. An Act for
Collecting. . . .
[Providence, Carter, 1787.] Broadside.
AAS copy.   45156

Rhode Island. Laws, Statutes, etc., 1787.
. . . In General Assembly, October
Session, 1787. An Act for the more
Effectively Punishing . . . Larcenies.
[Providence, 1787.] Broadside.
AAS copy.   45157

Rhode Island. Laws, Statutes, etc., 1787.
. . . In General Assembly, December
Session, A.D. 1786. An Act Laying Duties
of Excise.
Providence, Carter, [1787]. [2] pp.
RIHS copy.   45153

Rhode Island. Laws, Statutes, etc., 1787.
. . . To the Honorable the General
Assembly. . . . A Committee to Enquire
into the State of the Debts. . . . Read
March 17th. . . . and Concurred.
Providence, Wheeler, [1789]. Broadside.
RIHS copy.   45158

Rhode Island. Laws, Statutes, etc., 1788.
. . . In General Assembly, February
Session, A.D. 1788. An Act Submitting to
the Consideration of the Freemen . . . the
Report of the Convention.
Providence, Wheeler, [1788]. Broadside.
AAS copy.   21430

[Rhode Island. Laws, Statutes, etc., 1788.
. . . In General Assembly, February, 1788.
An Act Submitting to the Consideration
of the Freemen . . . the Report of the
Convention.
Providence, Wheeler, [1788].
Broadside.].
(This is a ghost of 21430, q.v.)   21429

Rhode Island. Laws, Statutes, etc., 1788.
. . . In General Assembly, June Session,
A.D. 1788. An Act for Granting. . . . a
Tax of Thirty Thousand Pounds.
Providence, Wheeler, [1788]. Broadside.
RIHS copy.   45351

Rhode Island. Laws, Statutes, etc., 1789.
. . . In General Assembly, September
Session, A.D. 1789. An Act for Levying
. . . Certain Duties.
Providence, Wheeler, [1789]. 22 pp.
RIHS copy.   45578

Rhode Island. Laws, Statutes, etc., 1788.
. . . In General Assembly, October
Session, 1788. Whereas His Excellency
George Clinton. . . .
Providence, Wheeler, [1788]. 3 pp.
RIHS copy.   21431

Rhode Island. Laws, Statutes, etc., 1789.
[An Act laying an embargo on grain.
Newport, Edes, 1789.] Broadside.
(Alden 1178; no copy known.)   45577

Rhode Island. Laws, Statutes, etc., 1789.
. . . In General Assembly, March Session,
A.D. 1789. An Act for Granting . . . a Tax
of Twenty Thousand Pounds.
Providence, Carter, [1789]. Broadside.
RIHS copy.   22107

Rhode Island. Laws, Statutes, etc., 1789.
. . . In General Assembly, October
Session, A.D. 1789. An Act for Repealing
Two Paragraphs. . . .
Providence, Carter, [1789]. 8 pp.
AAS copy.   22111

Rhode Island. Laws, Statutes, etc., 1789.
. . . In General Assembly, September
Session, 1789. An Act Levying . . .
Imposts.
Providence, Wheeler, [1789]. 22 pp.
NYPL copy.   22108

Rhode Island. Laws, Statutes, etc., 1789.
. . . In General Assembly, September
Session, A.D. 1789. An Act Relative to a
Convention.
[Providence], Carter, 1789. Broadside.
RIHS copy.   22109

Rhode Island. Laws, Statutes, etc., 1790.
. . . January Session, A. D. 1790. An Act
Calling for a Convention.
[Providence], Carter, [1790]. Broadside.
AAS copy.   22840

Rhode Island. Laws, Statutes, etc., 1790.
. . . June Session, A. D. 1790. An Act
Prescribing the Mode of Electing
Senators.
[Providence], Carter, [1790]. Broadside.
AAS copy.   22841

Rhode Island. Laws, Statutes, etc., 1790.
. . . June Session, 1790. An Act to
Incorporate . . . The Providence Society
for Promoting the Abolition of Slavery.
[Providence], Carter, [1790]. 4 pp.
RIHS copy.   22842

Rhode Island. Laws, Statutes, etc., 1790.
. . . September Session, A. D. 1790. It is
Voted and Resolved That a
Representative. . . .
[Providence], Carter, [1790]. Broadside.
RIHS copy.   22843

Rhode Island. Laws, Statutes, etc., 1791.
. . . In General Assembly, June Session,
1791. An Act for Granting and
Apportioning a Tax of Six Thousand
Pounds.
Providence, Carter, [1791]. Broadside.
AAS copy.   23737

Rhode Island. Laws, Statutes, etc., 1791.
. . . In General Assembly. October
Session, A. D. 1791. Whereas the President
and Directors of the Bank. . . .
[Providence], Carter, [1791]. Broadside.
AAS copy.   23738

Rhode Island. Laws, Statutes, etc., 1792.
. . . In General Assembly, June Session,
A. D. 1792. It is Voted and Resolved,
That Two Representatives. . . .
Providence, Wheeler, [1792]. Broadside.
AAS copy.   24737

Rhode Island. Laws, Statutes, etc., 1791.
. . . In General Assembly. October
Session, A. D. 1791. Whereas the
President and Directors of the Bank. . . .
[Providence], Carter, [1791]. Broadside.
AAS copy.   23738

Rhode Island. Laws, Statutes, etc., 1793.
An Act to Organize the Militia.
Providence, Wheeler, [1793]. 11 pp.
(Title assumed by Evans.)
AAS copy.   26075

Rhode Island. Laws, Statutes, etc., 1794.
. . . In General Assembly, June Session,
A. D. 1794. Resolve for Choosing
Representatives to Congress.
Warren, Phillips, [1794]. Broadside.
RIHS copy.   27614

Rhode Island. Laws, Statutes, etc., 1794.
. . . In General Assembly. October
Session, A. D. 1794. An Act for Granting
and Apportioning a Tax of Six Thousand
Pounds.
Warren, Phillips, [1794]. 4 pp.
AAS copy.   27615

Rhode Island. Laws, Statutes, etc., 1794.
. . . Providence, June 16th, 1794. The
Following are the Conditions. . . .
[Providence ? 1794.] Broadside.
RIHS copy.   27613

Rhode Island. Laws, Statutes, etc., 1795.
Charter of the Rhode-Island Bank. . . .
October Session, A.D. 1795.
[Newport? 1795.] 8 pp.
NHS copy.   47577

Rhode Island. Laws, Statutes, etc., 1795.
. . . In General Assembly. June Session,
A.D. 1795. An Act for Taking a General
Estimate.
Warren, Phillips, 1795. 1 + pp.
(The only known copy is imperfect.)
RIHS copy.   47578

[Rhode Island. Laws, Statutes, etc., 1795.
. . . In General Assembly, October
Session, A.D. 1795. An Act for Granting a
Charter to the United Library Company
in Gloucester.
Warren, R. I., Phillips, 1795.]
(No copy known; see Alden 1440.)   29403

Rhode Island. Laws, Statutes, etc., 1795.
Table of Fees. Established by the General
Assembly . . . in January, 1795.
Providence, Carter & Wilkinson, [1795].
12 pp.
JCB copy.   29405

Rhode Island. Laws, Statutes, etc., 1796.
. . . In General Assembly. June Session,
A. D. 1796. An Act for Granting and
Apportioning a Tax.
Warren, Phillips, 1796. 4 pp.
RIHS copy.   31094

Rhode Island. Laws, Statutes, etc., 1796.
. . . June Session, A. D. 1796. Be it
Enacted . . . that Two Representatives . . .
be Elected.
[Warren, 1796.] Broadside.
RIHS copy.   31093

Rhode Island. Laws. Statutes, etc., 1796.
. . . In General Assembly. October
Session, A.D. 1796. An Act Directing the
Mode of Choosing a Representative.
Providence, Carter & Wilkinson, 1796.
Broadside.
(Alden 1500; present location unknown.)
                                             47899

Rhode Island. Laws, Statutes, etc., 1797.
. . . In General Assembly. October
Session, A. D. 1797. An Act for
Furnishing the Quota of this State.
[Providence], Carter & Wilkinson,
[1797]. Broadside.
RIHS copy.   32755

Rhode Island. Laws, Statutes, etc., 1797.
. . . In General Assembly. October
Session, A.D. 1797. An Act for Granting
and Apportioning a Tax of Twenty
Thousand Dollars.
Warren, Phillips, [1797]. 3 pp.
RIHS copy.   32756

Rhode Island. Laws, Statutes, etc., 1798.
. . . In General Assembly, June Session,
A. D. 1798. An Act for Calling out the
Militia.
Newport, Barber, [1798]. Broadside.
RIHS copy.   34448

Rhode Island. Laws, Statutes, etc., 1798.

Rhode Island. Laws, Statutes, etc., 1798.
. . . In General Assembly. October
Session, A. D. 1798. An Act for
Granting and Apportioning a Tax of
Twenty Thousand Dollars.
[Newport, Farnsworth, 1798.] Broadside.
RIHS copy. 34450

Rhode Island. Laws, Statutes, etc., 1798.
The Public Laws of the State.
Providence, Carter & Wilkinson, 1798.
652 pp.
AAS copy. 34453

Rhode Island. Laws, Statutes, etc., 1798.
Public Laws of the State . . . Passed since
. . . January, A.D. 1798.
Newport, Farnsworths, [1798]. 16 pp.
(The pagination given by Evans carries
this series thru the 1813 supplement.)
AAS copy. 34454

Rhode Island. Laws, Statutes, etc., 1798.
[Public Laws]. . . . Acts Made and Passed
. . . February, A. D. 1799.
[Newport, 1799.] pp. 17-18.
AAS copy. 36221

[Rhode Island. Laws, Statutes, etc., 1799.
An Act to Incorporate Washington Lodge
No. 3, of Free and Accepted Masons in
. . . Warren.
Warren, Phillips, 1799. Broadside.]
(No copy located.) 36214

Rhode Island. Laws, Statutes, etc., 1799.
At the General Assembly . . . February A.
D., 1799. An Act to Incorporate the
Newport Insurance Company.
Newport, Farnsworth, [1799]. 10 pp.
(Also entered as 35910, q. v.) 36215

Rhode Island. Laws, Statutes, etc., 1799.
[Public Laws]. . . . An Act Directing the
Payment of the Salaries of the Judges of
the Supreme Judicial Court.
[Newport, 1799.] pp. 19-25.
AAS copy. 36225

Rhode Island. Laws, Statutes, etc., 1800.
[Public Laws]. . . . Acts Made and Passed
. . . in October, A. D. 1799.
[Newport, 1800.] pp. 27-38.
AAS copy. 38388

Rhode Island. Laws, Statutes, etc., 1800.
[Public Laws]. . . . Acts Made and Passed
. . . in May, A. D. 1800.
[Newport, 1800.] pp. 39-46.
AAS copy. 38389

Rhode Island. Laws, Statutes, etc., 1800.
[Public Laws]. . . . Acts Made and Passed
. . . in October, A. D. 1800.
[Newport, 1800.] pp. 47-49.
AAS copy. 38390

Rhode Island. Militia, 1777.
Return of the Second Battalion.
[Providence? 1777.] Broadside.
RIHS copy. 43369

Rhode Island. Militia, 1780.
I the Subscriber do hereby Solemnly
Engage and Inlist . . . November Session,
1780.
[Providence? 1780.] Broadside.
RIHS copy. 43889

Rhode Island. Militia, 1780.
We the Subscribers do hereby Solemnly
. . . Inlist Ourselves . . . July, 1780.
[Providence? 1780.] Broadside.
JCB copy. 43890

Rhode Island. Secretary, 1797.
. . . November 6, 1797. The Following are
the Allowances to be Made to the
Officers and Soldiers.
[Providence], Carter & Wilkinson,
[1797]. Broadside.
AAS copy. 32757

Rhode Island. Session Laws, 1776.
January, 1776. At the General Assembly.
Providence, [1776]. pp. 201-265.
AAS copy. 15043

Rhode Island. Session Laws, 1776.
February, 1776. At the General Assembly.
Providence, [1776]. pp. 267-289.
AAS copy. 15044

Rhode Island. Session Laws, 1776.
March, 1776. At the General Assembly.
Providence, [1776]. pp. 291-347.
AAS copy. 15045

Rhode Island. Session Laws, 1776.
May, 1776. At the General Assembly.
[Providence, 1776.] 53 pp.
AAS copy. 15046

Rhode Island. Session Laws, 1776.
June, 1776. At the General Assembly.
Providence, [1776]. pp. 55-123.
Composite copy. 15047

Rhode Island. Session Laws, 1776.
July, 1776. At the General Assembly.
[Providence, 1776.] pp. 125-146.
AAS copy. 15048

Rhode Island. Session Laws, 1776.
August, 1776. At the General Assembly.
Providence, [1776]. pp. 147-164.
AAS copy. 15049

Rhode Island. Session Laws, 1776.
September, 1776. At the General
Assembly.
Providence, [1776]. pp. 165-185.
AAS copy. 15050

Rhode Island. Session Laws, 1776.
October, 1776. At the General Assembly.
Rehoboth, [1776]. 37 pp.
AAS copy. 15051

Rhode Island. Session Laws, 1776.
November, 1776. At the General
Assembly.
Providence, [1776]. 14 pp.
AAS copy. 15052

Rhode Island. Session Laws, 1776.
December, 1776. At the General Assembly
[Dec. 12 +].
Providence, [1776]. 9 pp.
AAS copy. 15053

Rhode Island. Session Laws, 1776.
December, 1776. At the General Assembly
[Dec. 23 +].
Rehoboth, [1776]. 44 pp.
AAS copy. 15054

[Rhode Island. Session Laws, 1777.
January, 1777. At the General Assembly.
Rehoboth, 1777. 58 pp.]
(There was no January session.) 15559

Rhode Island. Session Laws, 1777.
February, 1777. At the General Assembly.
Providence, [1777]. 30 pp.
AAS copy. 15560

Rhode Island. Session Laws, 1777.
March, 1777. At the General Assembly.
Providence, [1777]. 22 pp.
AAS copy. 15561

Rhode Island. Session Laws, 1777.
March, 1777. (Second Session.) At the
General Assembly.
Rehoboth, [1777]. 31 pp.
AAS copy. 15562

Rhode Island. Session Laws, 1777.
April, 1777. At the General Assembly.
Providence, [1777]. 19 pp.
AAS copy. 15563

Rhode Island. Session Laws, 1777.
May, 1777. At the General Assembly . . .
at Providence.
Providence, [1777]. 14 pp.
AAS copy. 15564

Rhode Island. Session Laws, 1777.
May, 1777. At the General Assembly . . .
at South-Kingstown.
Providence, [1777]. 47 pp.
AAS copy. 15565

Rhode Island. Session Laws, 1777.
June, 1777. At the General Assembly.
Attleborough, [1777]. 35 pp.
AAS copy. 15566

Rhode Island. Session Laws, 1777.
July, 1777. At the General Assembly.
Providence, [1777]. 8 pp.
AAS copy. 15567

Rhode Island. Session Laws, 1777.

Rhode Island. Session Laws, 1777.
August, 1777. At the General Assembly.
Providence, [1777]. 22 pp.
AAS copy. 15568

Rhode Island. Session Laws, 1777.
September, 1777. At the General
Assembly.
Attleborough, [1777]. 10 pp.
AAS copy. 15569

Rhode Island. Session Laws, 1777.
October, 1777. At the General Assembly.
Attleborough, [1777]. 16 pp.
AAS copy. 15570

Rhode Island. Session Laws, 1777.
December, 1777. At the General Assembly
. . . at East-Greenwich.
Attleborough, [1777]. 36 pp.
AAS copy. 15571

Rhode Island. Session Laws, 1777.
December, 1777. At the General Assembly
. . . at Providence.
Providence, [1777]. 11 pp.
AAS copy. 15572

Rhode Island. Session Laws, 1778.
February, 1778. At the General Assembly.
Attleborough, [1778]. 37 pp.
AAS copy. 16030

Rhode Island. Session Laws, 1778.
March, 1778. At the General Assembly.
Attleborough, [1778]. 19 pp.
AAS copy. 16031

Rhode Island. Session Laws, 1778.
May, 1778. At the General Assembly.
Providence, [1778]. 23 pp.
AAS copy. 16032

Rhode Island. Session Laws, 1778.
May (Second Session) 1778. At the
General Assembly.
Attleborough [1778]. 18 pp.
AAS copy. 16033

Rhode Island. Session Laws, 1778.
June, 1778. At the General Assembly.
Attleborough, [1778]. 25 pp.
AAS copy. 16034

Rhode Island. Session Laws, 1778.
September, 1778. At the General
Assembly.
Attleborough, [1778]. 18 pp.
AAS copy. 16035

Rhode Island. Session Laws, 1778.
October, 1778. At the General Assembly.
Providence, [1778]. 56 pp.
AAS copy. 16036

Rhode Island. Session Laws, 1778.
December, 1778. At the General
Assembly.
Providence, [1778]. 18 pp.
AAS copy. 16037

Rhode Island. Session Laws, 1779.
January, 1779. At the General Assembly.
Providence, [1779]. 7 pp.
AAS copy. 16486

Rhode Island. Session Laws, 1779.
February, 1779. At the General Assembly.
Providence, [1779]. 36 pp.
AAS copy. 16487

Rhode Island. Session Laws, 1779.
May, 1779. At the General Assembly.
Providence, [1779]. 34 pp.
AAS copy. 16488

Rhode Island. Session Laws, 1779.
June, 1779. At the General Assembly.
Providence, [1779]. 27 pp.
AAS copy. 16489

Rhode Island. Session Laws, 1779.
August, 1779. At the General Assembly.
Providence, [1779]. 17 pp.
AAS copy. 16490

Rhode Island. Session Laws, 1779.
September, 1779. At the General
Assembly.
Providence, [1779]. 27 pp.
AAS copy. 16491

Rhode Island. Session Laws, 1779.
October, 1779. At the General Assembly.

Providence, [1779]. 42 pp.
AAS copy.   16492

Rhode Island. Session Laws, 1779.
December, 1779. At the General
Assembly.
Providence, [1779]. 31 pp.
AAS copy.   16493

Rhode Island. Session Laws, 1780.
February, 1780. At the General Assembly.
Providence, [1780]. 34 pp.
AAS copy.   16961

Rhode Island. Session Laws, 1780.
March, 1780. At the General Assembly.
Providence, [1780]. 7 pp.
AAS copy.   16962

Rhode Island. Session Laws, 1780.
May, 1780. At the General Assembly.
Providence, [1780]. 37 pp.
AAS copy.   16963

Rhode Island. Session Laws, 1780.
June, 1780. At the General Assembly.
Providence, [1780]. 28 pp.
AAS copy.   16964

Rhode Island. Session Laws, 1780.
July, 1780. At the General Assembly.
Providence, [1780]. 26 pp.
AAS copy.   16965

Rhode Island. Session Laws, 1780.
July (Second Session) 1780. At the
General Assembly.
Providence, [1780]. 58 pp.
AAS copy.   16966

Rhode Island. Session Laws, 1780.
September, 1780. At the General
Assembly.
Providence, [1780]. 28 pp.
AAS copy.   16967

Rhode Island. Session Laws, 1780.
October, 1780. At the General Assembly.
Providence, [1780]. 15 pp.
AAS copy.   16968

Rhode Island. Session Laws, 1780.
November, 1780. At the General
Assembly.
Providence, [1780]. 49 pp.
AAS copy.   16969

Rhode Island. Session Laws, 1781.
January 1781. At the General Assembly.
Providence, [1781]. 24 pp.
AAS copy.   17327

Rhode Island. Session Laws, 1781.
February, 1781. At the General Assembly.
Providence, [1781]. 16 pp.
AAS copy.   17328

Rhode Island. Session Laws, 1781.
March, 1781. At the General Assembly.
[Providence], Carter, [1781]. 67 pp.
AAS copy.   17329

Rhode Island. Session Laws, 1781.
May, 1781. At the General Assembly.
Providence, [1781]. 31 pp.
AAS copy.   17330

Rhode Island. Session Laws, 1781.
May, 1781. Second Session. At the
General Assembly.
Providence, [1781]. 64 pp.
AAS copy.   17331

Rhode Island. Session Laws, 1781.
July, 1781. At the General Assembly.
Providence, [1781]. 41 pp.
AAS copy.   17332

Rhode Island. Session Laws, 1781.
August, 1781. At the General Assembly.
Providence, [1781]. 43 pp.
AAS copy.   17333

Rhode Island. Session Laws, 1781.
October, 1781. At the General Assembly.
Providence, [1781]. 28 pp.
AAS copy.   17334

Rhode Island. Session Laws, 1781.
December, 1781. At the General
Assembly.
Providence, [1781]. 36 pp.
AAS copy.   17335

Rhode Island. Session Laws, 1782.
January, 1782. At the General Assembly.
Providence, Carter, [1782]. 51 pp.
AAS copy.   17691

Rhode Island. Session Laws, 1782.
February, 1782. At the General Assembly.
Providence, Wheeler, [1782]. 33 pp.
AAS copy.   17692

Rhode Island. Session Laws, 1782.
May, 1782. At the General Assembly.
Providence, Carter, [1782]. 18 pp.
AAS copy.   17693

Rhode Island. Session Laws, 1782.
June, 1782. At the General Assembly.
Providence, Carter, [1782]. 28 pp.
AAS copy.   17694

Rhode Island. Session Laws, 1782.
August, 1782. At the General Assembly.
Providence, Carter, [1782]. 27 pp.
AAS copy.   17695

Rhode Island. Session Laws, 1782.
October, 1782. At the General Assembly.
Providence, Carter, [1782]. 27 pp.
AAS copy.   17696

Rhode Island. Session Laws, 1782.
November, 1782. At the General
Assembly.
Providence, Carter, [1782]. 34 pp.
AAS copy.   17697

Rhode Island. Session Laws, 1783.
February, 1783. At the General Assembly.
[Providence, 1783.] 81 pp.
AAS copy.   18150

Rhode Island. Session Laws, 1783.
May, 1783. At the General Assembly.
Providence, Carter, [1783]. 31 pp.
AAS copy.   18151

Rhode Island. Session Laws, 1783.
June, 1783. At the General Assembly.
Providence, Carter, [1783]. 35 pp.
AAS copy.   18152

Rhode Island. Session Laws, 1783.
October, 1783. At the General Assembly.
[Providence, 1783.] 35 pp.
AAS copy.   18153

Rhode Island. Session Laws, 1783.
December, 1783. At the General
Assembly.
Providence, Carter, [1783]. 29 pp.
AAS copy.   18154

Rhode Island. Session Laws, 1784.
February, 1784. At the General
Assembly. . . .
Providence, Wheeler, [1784]. 30 pp.
AAS copy.   18748

Rhode Island. Session Laws, 1784.
May, 1784. At the General Assembly.
Providence, Carter, [1784]. 38 pp.
AAS copy.   18749

Rhode Island. Session Laws, 1784.
June, 1784. At the General Assembly.
Providence, Wheeler, [1784]. 38 pp.
AAS copy.   18750

Rhode Island. Session Laws, 1784.
August, 1784. At the General Assembly.
Providence, Carter, [1784]. 22 pp.
AAS copy.   18751

Rhode Island. Session Laws, 1784.
October, 1784. At the General Assembly.
Providence, Carter, [1783]. 30 pp.
AAS copy.   18752

Rhode Island. Session Laws, 1785.
February, 1785. At the General Assembly.
Providence, Carter, [1785]. 32 pp.
AAS copy.   19218

Rhode Island. Session Laws, 1785.
May, 1785. At the General Assembly.
Providence, Wheeler, [1785]. 37 pp.
AAS copy.   19219

Rhode Island. Session Laws, 1785.
June, 1785. At the General Assembly.
[Providence, 1785.] 26 pp.
AAS copy.   19220

Rhode Island. Session Laws, 1785.
August, 1785. At the General Assembly.
[Providence, 1785.] 20 pp.
AAS copy.   19221

Rhode Island. Session Laws, 1785.
October, 1785. At the General Assembly.
Providence, Carter, [1785]. 44 pp.
AAS copy.   19222

Rhode Island. Session Laws, 1786.
February, 1786. At the General Assembly.
[Providence, 1786.] 46 pp.
AAS copy.   19950

Rhode Island. Session Laws, 1786.
March, 1786. At the General Assembly.
Providence, Wheeler, [1786]. 39 pp.
AAS copy.   19951

Rhode Island. Session Laws, 1786.
May, 1786. At the General Assembly.
Providence, Carter, [1786]. 22 pp.
AAS copy.   19952

Rhode Island. Session Laws, 1786.
June, 1786. At the General Assembly.
Providence, Carter, [1786]. 20 pp.
AAS copy.   19953

Rhode Island. Session Laws, 1786.
August, 1786. At the General Assembly.
Providence, Wheeler, [1786]. 9 pp.
AAS copy.   19954

Rhode Island. Session Laws, 1786.
October, 1786. At the General Assembly.
Newport, [1786]. 8 pp.
AAS copy.   19955

Rhode Island. Session Laws, 1786.
October (2d Session) 1786. At the General
Assembly.
Providence, Carter, [1786]. 9 pp.
AAS copy.   19956

Rhode Island. Session Laws, 1786.
December, 1786. At the General
Assembly.
Newport, [1787]. 25 pp.
AAS copy.   20679

Rhode Island. Session Laws, 1787.
March, 1787. At the General Assembly.
Providence, Wheeler, [1787]. 22 pp.
AAS copy.   20680

Rhode Island. Session Laws, 1787.
May, 1787. At the General Assembly.
Providence, Wheeler, [1787]. 12 pp.
AAS copy.   20681

Rhode Island. Session Laws, 1787.
June, 1787. At the General Assembly.
[Newport, 1787.] 14 pp.
AAS copy.   20682

[Rhode Island. Session Laws, 1787.
August, 1787. At the General Assembly.
Providence, 1787.]
(There was no August session.)   20683

Rhode Island. Session Laws, 1787.
September, 1787. At the General
Assembly.
Providence, Carter, [1787]. 17 pp.
AAS copy.   20684

Rhode Island. Session Laws, 1787.
October, 1787. At the General Assembly.
[Providence, 1787.] 14 pp.
AAS copy.   20685

Rhode Island. Session Laws, 1788.
February, 1788. At the General Assembly.
[Newport, 1788.] 18 pp.
AAS copy.   21423

Rhode Island. Session Laws, 1788.
March, 1788. At the General Assembly.
[Newport, 1788.] 22 pp.
AAS copy.   21424

Rhode Island. Session Laws, 1788.
May, 1788. At the General Assembly.
Providence, Carter, [1788]. 20 pp.
AAS copy.   21425

Rhode Island. Session Laws, 1788.
June, 1788. At the General Assembly.
[Providence], Carter, [1788]. 34 pp.
AAS copy.   21426

Rhode Island. Session Laws, 1788.
October, 1788. At the General Assembly.
[Providence], Carter, [1788]. 20 pp.
AAS copy.   21427

Rhode Island. Session Laws, 1788.
December, 1788. At the General
Assembly.
[Providence, 1788.] 12 pp.
AAS copy.   21428

Rhode Island. Session Laws, 1789.
March, 1789. At the General Assembly.
[Providence], Carter, [1789]. 22 pp.
AAS copy.   22101

Rhode Island. Session Laws, 1789.
May, 1789. At the General Assembly.
[Newport, 1789.] 18 pp.
AAS copy.   22102

Rhode Island. Session Laws, 1789.
June, 1789. At the General Assembly.
[Providence, 1789.] 17 pp.
AAS copy.   22103

Rhode Island. Session Laws, 1789.
September, 1789. At the General
Assembly.
Providence, Wheeler, 1789. 28 pp.
AAS copy.   22104

Rhode Island. Session Laws, 1789.
October, 1789. At the General Assembly.
[Providence], Carter, [1789]. 18 pp.
AAS copy.   22105

Rhode Island. Session Laws, 1789.
October, 1789 (2d Session). At the
General Assembly.
[Providence], Carter, [1789]. 18 pp.
AAS copy.   22106

Rhode Island. Session Laws, 1790.
January, 1790. At the General Assembly.
[Providence], Carter, [1790]. 16 pp.
AAS copy.   22835

Rhode Island. Session Laws, 1790.
May, 1790. At the General Assembly.
[Providence], Carter, [1790]. 22 pp.
AAS copy.   22836

Rhode Island. Session Laws, 1790.
June, 1790. At the General Assembly.
[Providence, 1790.] 16 pp.
AAS copy.   22837

Rhode Island. Session Laws, 1790.
September, 1790. At the General
Assembly.
[Providence], Carter, [1791]. 20 pp.
AAS copy.   22838

Rhode Island. Session Laws, 1790.
October, 1790. At the General Assembly.
[Providence], Carter, [1791]. 20 pp.
AAS copy.   22839

Rhode Island. Session Laws, 1791.
February, 1791. At the General Assembly.
[Providence, 1791.] 28 pp.
AAS copy.   23733

Rhode Island. Session Laws, 1791.
May, 1791. At the General Assembly.
[Providence, 1792.] 27 pp.
AAS copy.   23734

Rhode Island. Session Laws, 1791.
June, 1791. At the General Assembly.
Providence, Wheeler, [1792]. 33 pp.
AAS copy.   23735

Rhode Island. Session Laws, 1791.
October, 1791. At the General Assembly.
[Providence], Carter, [1792]. 41 pp.
AAS copy.   23736

Rhode Island. Session Laws, 1792.
February, 1792. At the General Assembly.
Providence, Wheeler, [1792]. 40 pp.
AAS copy.   24732

Rhode Island. Session Laws, 1792.
May, 1792. At the General Assembly.
Providence, Wheeler, [1792]. 30 pp.
AAS copy.   24733

Rhode Island. Session Laws, 1792.
June, 1792. At the General Assembly.
[Providence], Carter, [1792]. 30 pp.
AAS copy.   24734

Rhode Island. Session Laws, 1792.
August, 1792. At the General Assembly.
Providence, Wheeler, [1792]. 18 pp.
AAS copy.   24735

Rhode Island. Session Laws, 1792.
October, 1792. At the General Assembly.
Providence, Wheeler, [1792]. 42 pp.
AAS copy.   24736

Rhode Island. Session Laws, 1793.
February, 1793. At the General Assembly.
Providence, Wheeler, [1793]. 21 pp.
AAS copy.   26071

Rhode Island. Session Laws, 1793.
May, 1793. At the General Assembly.
[Providence], Carter, [1793]. 28 pp.
AAS copy.   26072

Rhode Island. Session Laws, 1793.
June, 1793. At the General Assembly.
Providence, Wheeler, [1793]. 17 pp.
AAS copy.   26073

Rhode Island. Session Laws, 1793.
October, 1793. At the General Assembly.
Providence, Wheeler, [1793]. 21 pp.
AAS copy.   26074

Rhode Island. Session Laws, 1794.
February, 1794. At the General Assembly.
[Providence]. Carter & Wilkinson,
[1794]. 28 pp.
AAS copy.   27607

Rhode Island. Session Laws, 1794.
March, 1794. At the General Assembly.
[Providence], Carter & Wilkinson,
[1794]. 33 pp.
AAS copy.   27608

Rhode Island. Session Laws, 1794.
May, 1794. At the General Assembly.
Providence, Wheeler, [1794]. 33 pp.
AAS copy.   27609

Rhode Island. Session Laws, 1794.
June, 1794. At the General Assembly.
Warren, Phillips, [1794]. 35 pp.
AAS copy.   27610

Rhode Island. Session Laws, 1794.
October, 1794. At the General Assembly.
Warren, Phillips, [1795]. 36 pp.
AAS copy.   27611

Rhode Island. Session Laws, 1795.
January, 1795. At the General Assembly.
Warren, R. I., Phillips, [1795]. 44 pp.
AAS copy.   29400

Rhode Island. Session Laws, 1795.
May, 1795. At the General Assembly.
Warren, R. I., Phillips, [1795]. 26 pp.
AAS copy.   29401

Rhode Island. Session Laws, 1795.
June, 1795. At the General Assembly.
Warren, R. I., Phillips, 1795. 27 pp.
AAS copy.   29402

Rhode Island. Session Laws, 1795.
October, 1795. At the General Assembly.
Warren, Phillips, 1796. 32 pp.
AAS copy.   31088

Rhode Island. Session Laws, 1796.
February, 1796. At the General Assembly.
Warren, Phillips, 1796. 37 pp.
AAS copy.   31089

Rhode Island. Session Laws, 1796.
May, 1796. At the General Assembly.
[Warren, 1796.] 24 pp.
AAS copy.   31090

Rhode Island. Session Laws, 1796.
June, 1796. At the General Assembly.
Warren, Phillips, 1796. 29 pp.
AAS copy.   31091

Rhode Island. Session Laws, 1796.
October, 1796. At the General Assembly.
Warren, Phillips, [1796]. 23 pp.
AAS copy.   31092

Rhode Island. Session Laws, 1797.
February, 1797. At the General Assembly.
Warren, Phillips, [1797]. 42 pp.
AAS copy.   32751

Rhode Island. Session Laws, 1797.

May, 1797. At the General Assembly.
Warren, Phillips, [1797]. 27 pp.
AAS copy.   32752

Rhode Island. Session Laws, 1797.
June, 1797. At the General Assembly.
Warren, Phillips, [1797]. 20 pp.
AAS copy.   32753

Rhode Island. Session Laws, 1797.
October, 1797. At the General Assembly.
Warren, Phillips, [1797]. 32 pp.
AAS copy.   32754

Rhode Island. Session Laws, 1797.
December, 1797. At the General
Assembly.
Warren, Phillips, 1798. 12 pp.
AAS copy.   34444

Rhode Island. Session Laws, 1798.
January, 1798. At the General Assembly.
Warren, Phillips, 1798. 21 pp.
AAS copy.   34445

Rhode Island. Session Laws, 1798.
May, 1798. At the General Assembly.
Warren, Phillips, 1798. 31 pp.
AAS copy.   34446

Rhode Island. Session Laws, 1798.
June, 1798. At the General Assembly.
Providence, Wheeler, [1798]. 27 pp.
AAS copy.   34447

Rhode Island. Session Laws, 1798.
October, 1798. At the General Assembly.
Newport, Farnsworth, 1799. 26 pp.
AAS copy.   36220

Rhode Island. Session Laws, 1799.
February, 1799. At the General Assembly.
Newport, Farnsworth, [1799]. 21 pp.
AAS copy.   36217

Rhode Island. Session Laws, 1799.
May, 1799. At the General Assembly.
Newport, Farnsworth, [1799]. 22 pp.
AAS copy.   36218

Rhode Island. Session Laws, 1799.
June, 1799. At a General Assembly.
Newport, Farnsworth, [1799]. 16 pp.
AAS copy.   36219

Rhode Island. Session Laws, 1799.
October, 1799. At the General Assembly.
Newport, Farnsworth, [1800]. 29 pp.
AAS copy.   38384

Rhode Island. Session Laws, 1800.
February, 1800. At the General Assembly.
Newport, Farnsworth, [1800]. 32 pp.
AAS copy.   38385

Rhode Island. Session Laws, 1800.
May, 1800. At the General Assembly.
Newport, Farnsworth, [1800]. 23 pp.
AAS copy.   38386

Rhode Island. Session Laws, 1800.
June, 1800. At the General Assembly.
Newport, Farnsworth, [1800]. 32 , 3 pp.
BrU copy.   38387

Rhode Island. Treasurer, 1780.
. . . To the Sheriff of the County of
[blank] . . . Greeting. . . . [Nov. 1780.]
[Providence, 1780.] Broadside.
LOC copy.   43891

Rhode Island. Treasurer, 1782.
. . . To the Sheriff of the County of
[blank] or to his Deputy, Greeting. . . .
September, A. D. 1782.
[Providence, 1782.] Broadside.
AAS ph. copy.   44261

. . . . The Rhode-Island Almanack for . . .
1728. . . . By Poor Robin.
Newport, 1728. [16] pp.
LOC copy.   2952

. . . . The Rhode-Island Almanack, for . . .
1729. . . . By Poor Robin.
Newport, Franklin for Fleet, 1729. [16]
pp.
AAS copy.   3099

. . . . The Rhode-Island Almanack, for . . .
1730. . . . By Poor Robin.
Newport, Franklin, 1730. [16] pp.

(The only copy reported is defective.)
RIHS copy.   3211

.... The Rhode-Island Almanack, for ...
1732.... By Poor Robin.
Newport, Franklin, 1732. [16] pp.
AAS copy.   3472

.... The Rhode-Island Almanack for ...
1733.
Newport, 1733. [16] pp.
AAS copy.   3601

.... The Rhode-Island Almanack for ...
1734.
Newport, 1734. [16] pp.
AAS copy.   3720

.... The Rhode Island Almanack for ...
1735.
Newport, 1735. [16] pp.
AAS copy.   3957

.... The Rhode-Island Almanack for ...
1739.
Newport, 1739. [16] pp.
RIHS copy.   4307

.... The Rhode-Island Almanack for ...
1740.
Newport, 1740. [16] pp.
AAS copy.   4416

The Rhode-Island Almanack for ... 1741.
Newport, 1741. [16] pp.
AAS copy.   4592

The Rhode-Island Almanack ... for ...
1794.
Warren, Phillips. [22] pp.
RIHS copy.   46867

The Rhode-Island Almanac, for ... 1801.
Newport, Farnsworth. [24] pp.
(For the text see 38392.)
AAS copy.   38391

The Rhode-Island Almanac, for ... 1801.
Newport, Farnsworth for Richardson.
[24] pp.
LOC copy.   38393

The Rhode Island Almanac, for ... 1801.
Newport, Farnsworth, Great Allowance to
those who Purchase Quantities. [24] pp.
AAS copy.   38392

The Rhode Island Almanac, for ... 1801.
Newport, Wilder. [24] pp.
RIHS copy.   38394

Rhode Island Brigade, 1776-1780.
A Statement of the Claim of the....
Boston, Bumstead, 1798. 13 pp.
AAS copy.   34455

The Rhode-Island Calendar: or, an
Almanack, for ... 1798.... By Isaac
Bickerstaff [by Benjamin West,
1730-1813].
[Albany, N. Y.], for Todd of Providence
and Newport. [24] pp.
RIHS copy.   33202

Rhode Island College
See
Brown University

Rhodes, John, b. 1755.
The Surprising Adventures ... of....
New York, Cotton for Forman, 1798. 250
pp., irreg.
AAS copy.   34461

Rhodes, John, b. 1755.
The Surprising Adventures and Sufferings
of....
Newark, N. J., Pennington & Dodge for
Cotton, 1799. 268 pp.
AAS copy.   36228

Rhymer, Merlin, pseud.
The Virginia Almanack ... for ... 1769.
Williamsburg, Rind. [48] pp.
LOC copy.   11059

[Rhymes Relating to the Present Times.
Philadelphia, Dunlap, 1765.]
(Adv. Pa. Gazette, Jan. 17, 1765.)   10159

Rhys, Morgan John, 1760-1804.
The Good Samaritan.

Philadelphia, Lang & Ustick, 1796. 20 pp.
AAS copy.   31087

Ricard, N.   X.
Precis du Compte Rendu.
Philadelphia, Parent, 1795. 29 pp.
HSP copy.   47579

Rice, David, 1733-1816.
An Essay on Baptism.
Baltimore, Goddard, 1789. 82 pp.
AAS copy.   22115

Rice, David, 1733-1816.
A Lecture on the Divine Decrees.
Lexington, [Ky.], Bradford, 1791. 72 pp.
Presb. Hist. Soc. copy.   46273

[Rice, David], 1733-1816.
Slavery Inconsistent with Justice and
Good Policy. By Philanthropos.
Lexington, Bradford, 1792. 43 pp.
Presb. Hist. Soc.   24741

Rice, David, 1733-1816.
Slavery Inconsistent with Justice and
Good Policy.
Philadelphia, Hall for Dickins, 1792. 36
pp.
HC copy.   24742

Rice, H. & P., booksellers, Philadelphia.
Henry & Patrick Rice's Catalogue ... for
1796.
Philadelphia, H. & P. Rice, [1796]. 82 pp.
AAS copy.   47900

Rice, H. & P., firm, Philadelphia.
Henry & Patrick Rice's Catalogue of ...
Books ... for 1795.
Philadelphia, H. & P. Rice, [1795]. 72,
[2] pp.
HSP copy.   47580

Rice & Co., Philadelphia.
[Rice and Co's. Catalogue of Books.
Philadelphia, 1791?] 60 pp.
(Only known copy lacks tp.)
AAS copy.   46274

Rice and Co., Philadelphia.
Rice and Co. Book-sellers and Stationers
... have Imported....
[Philadelphia, 1789?] Broadside.
HSP copy.   45579

Rich, Elisha, 1740-1804?
(Hemmenway, Vt. Hist. Gaz., III, 955.)
The Number of the Beast.
Chelmsford, 1775. 29, [1] pp.
AAS copy.   14425

Rich, Elisha, 1740-1804?
A Poem on the Bloody Engagement ...
on Bunker's Hill.
Chelmsford, Coverly, 1775. Broadside.
(The copy reproduced is cropped.)
AAS copy.   14426

[Rich, Elisha], 1740-1804?
(A. M. Hemmenway, Vt. Hist. Gazetteer,
III, 955.)
A Poem on the late Distress of the Town
of Boston.
Chelmsford, 1776. Broadside.
AAS copy.   15061

Rich, Elisha, 1740-1804?
Poetical Dialogues.
Boston, Coverly, 1775. 36 pp.
AAS copy.   42934

[Rich, Elisha], 1740-1804?
Poetical Remarks upon the Fight at the
Boston Light-House.
[Chelmsford, 1775.] Broadside.
(This copy may be cropped.)
AAS copy.   14427

Rich, Elisha, 1740-1804?
A Sermon on Ecclesiastical Liberty.
Concord, Coverly, 1776. 40 pp.
LOC copy.   43157

[Rich, John, 1682-1761.
The Spirit of Contradiction.
Philadelphia, Steuart, 1762.]
(Adv. Pa. Journal, Dec. 30, 1762.)   9258

[A Rich Treasure at an Easy Rate.
Boston, 1683. 37 pp.]

(Title from addenda to S. F. Haven list.
For a later edition see Evans 9372.)   339

A Rich Treasure.... Third Edition.
Boston, Fowle, 1763. 32 pp.
AAS copy.   9372

Richard E. Lee's Letter, the Attorney
General's Opinion, and the Affidavits.
Richmond, Va., Jones, 1800. 32 pp.
AAS copy.   37811

Richard, Andrew.
On the Night following the First of
October ... Shop Broken up....
Norwich, Octob. 3d, 1737.
[New London? 1737.] Broadside.
BPL copy.   40127

Richard, Old Father
See
Poor Richard   38398

Richards, George, d. 1814.
The Accepted.
[Portsmouth], Peirce, 1800. 83 pp.
AAS copy.   38399

Richards, George, d. 1814.
The Cry of the Watchmen.
Portsmouth, Melcher, 1795. 46 pp.
AAS copy.   29410

[Richards, George], d. 1814.
The Declaration of Independence; a
Poem.
Boston, 1793. 24 pp.
AAS copy.   26084

[Richards, George], d. 1814.
Hymns Composed on the Death of Gen.
Washington; and sung, at the Universalist
Meeting-House, Portsmouth, N. H.,
January, 1800.
[Portsmouth], Peirce, [1800]. [8] pp.
LOC copy.   38400

Richards, George, d. 1814.
Operative and Speculative Masonry.
Boston, Russells, 1793. 11 pp.
HC copy.   26087

Richards, George, d. 1814.
An Oration on the Independence of the
United States.
Portsmouth, Melcher, 1795. 35 pp.
AAS copy.   29411

Richards, George, d. 1814.
The Political Passing Bell.
Boston, Thomas, 1789. 15 pp.
(There are at least two issues.)
AAS copy.   22116

Richards, George, d. 1814.
Solemn Dirge!
[Portsmouth, N.H.], Federal Observer,
[1799]. Broadside.
AAS copy.   36229

[Richardson, Mr.]
The History of Two Good Boys and Girls.
Boston, Coverly, 1793. Price 4 coppers. 16
pp.
(The only known copy is imperfect.)
AAS copy.   46868

[Richardson, Mr.]
The History of Two Good Boys and Girls.
Boston, Coverly, 1793. Price 5 coppers. 30
pp.
(The only known copy is imperfect.)
AAS copy.   46869

Richardson, Ebenezer, pseud.
The Life, and Humble Confession, of
Richardson, the Informer.
[Boston? 1772?] Broadside.
HSP copy.   42373

Richardson, Jacob, & Co. Newport, R.I.
Imported from London and Bristol....
[Newport, 1758?] Broadside.
RIHS copy.   45991

[Richardson, John], 1647-1696.
1670. An Almanack.
Cambridge, 1670. [16] pp.
AAS copy.   154

[Richardson, John], 1647-1696.
(Sibley, II, 210-213.)....
An Almanack ... for ... 1670.

Cambridge, 1670. [16] pp.
AAS copy. 154

[Richardson, John], 1647-1696.
(Sibley, II, 210-213.)
The Necessity of a Well Experienced
Souldiery.
Cambridge, 1679. [2], 15 pp.
BPL copy. 276

[Richardson, John], 1647-1696.
(Sibley, II, 210-213.)
The Necessity of a Well Experienced
Souldiery.
Boston, 1681. 16 pp.]
(This printing is known only from the S.
F. Haven list.) 307

Richardson, John, 1667-1753.
An Account of the Life of. . . .
Philadelphia, Crukshank, 1783. vi, 236,
[2] pp.
AAS copy. 18158

[Richardson, Joseph, 1755-1803.
The Fugitive; a Comedy.
Boston, Blake, 1795.]
(Imprint assumed by Evans from list of
"Plays for Sale" in 28447.) 29412

Richardson, Joseph, 1778-1871.
An Oration, Pronounced at Tewksbury.
Medford, Mass., 1800. 8 pp.
MFM copy. 38401

Richardson, Luther, 1774-1811.
An Oration, Pronounced July 4, 1800.
Boston, Russell, [1800]. 19 pp.
AAS copy. 38402

[Richardson, Samuel, 1689-1761.
The History of Clarissa Harlowe.
Philadelphia, Spotswood, 1786.]
(Ghost of a London ed. Adv. in Pa.
Herald, July 12, 1786.) 19961

Richardson, Samuel, 1689-1761.
Clarissa. . . . First Boston Edition.
Boston, Hall, 1795. 142, [4] pp.
AAS copy. 29413

[Richardson, Samuel, 1689-1761.
The History of Clarissa Harlowe.
Cooperstown, Phinney, 1796.]
(Imprint assumed by Evans from advs.)
31100

Richardson, Samuel, 1689-1761.
The History of Miss Clarissa Harlowe.
Philadelphia, 1798. 117 pp.
AAS copy. 34464

Richardson, Samuel, 1689-1761.
Clarissa.
Suffield, Ct., Farnsworths for Cookes,
1798. 138, [1] pp.
AAS copy. 34463

Richardson, Samuel, 1689-1761.
Clarissa. . . . Abridged.
New Haven, Ct., Morse, 1800. 138 pp.
AAS copy. 38403

[Richardson, Samuel, 1689-1761.
Pamela.
New York, Parker, 1744. 2 vol.]
(In the N. Y. Weekly Post Boy of Dec. 24,
1744, Parker adv. Pamela as "lately
reprinted;" but he had bought copies from
Franklin so they probably carried the
Philadelphia imprint.) 5485

[Richardson, Samuel, 1689-1761.
Pamela. . . . Fifth Edition.
Boston, Harrison, 1744.]
(Adv. "Just reprinted" in Boston
News-Letter, Sept. 13, 1744, but probably
London printing.) 5487

[Richardson, Samuel, 1689-1761.
Pamela.
Philadelphia, Franklin, 1744.]
(The printing and binding are mentioned
in Franklin's accounts. "Just published,"
Pa. Gazette, Jan. 1, 1745.) 5486

[Richardson, Samuel, 1689-1761.
Pamela.
Philadelphia, Spotswood, 1786.]
(Ghost of a London ed. Adv. in Pa.
Herald, July 12, 1786.) 19963

[Richardson, Samuel, 1689-1761.
The History of Pamela.
Philadelphia, Woodhouse, 1792?]
(Imprint assumed by Evans from adv. for
books "Lately published" in 24171.) 24744

[Richardson, Samuel], 1689-1761.
The Pleasing History of Pamela.
Boston, Hall, [1793?]. 96 pp.
AAS copy. 26088

Richardson, Samuel, 1689-1761.
The History of Pamela.
Philadelphia, Gibbons, 1794. 107 pp.
(The only known copy is imperfect.)
AAS copy. 47203

Richardson, Samuel, 1689-1761.
The History of Pamela. . . . First
Worcester Edition.
Worcester, Thomas, etc., 1794. [6],
168 pp., 6 plates.
AAS copy. 27622

Richardson, Samuel, 1689-1761.
The History of Pamela.
Lansingburgh, [N.Y.], Pratt, 1796. 146
pp., front.
AAS copy. 47901

Richardson, Samuel, 1689-1761.
The History of Pamela.
New York, Mott & Lyon, for Duyckinck,
1796. 144 pp.
AAS copy. 31101

Richardson, Samuel, 1689-1761.
The History of Pamela.
New York, Tiebout & O'Brien, 1796.
(Present location unknown.) 47902

Richardson, Samuel, 1689-1761.
The History of Pamela. . . . Abridged.
Boston, Hall, 1797. 142 pp.
AAS copy. 32763

Richardson, Samuel, 1689-1761.
The History of Pamela.
New York, Kirk for Davis, 1798. 90, [2]
pp.
AAS copy. 48595

Richardson, Samuel, 1689-1761.
The History of Pamela.
New York, Kirk for Judah, 1798. 90, [2]
pp.
(An imprint variant of 48595, q.v.) 48596

Richardson, Samuel, 1689-1761.
The History of Pamela.
New York, Kirk for Stephens, 1798. 90,
[2] pp.
(An imprint variant of 48595, q.v.) 48597

Richardson, Samuel, 1698-1761.
The History of Pamela.
New York, Kirk for Tiebout, 1798. 90, [2]
pp.
(An imprint variant of 48595, q. v. for
text.)
AAS copy. 48598

Richardson, Samuel, 1689-1761.
The History of Pamela.
Fairhaven, Vt., Spooner, 1799. 106 pp.
(The only copy located is imperfect.)
VtHS copy. 36231

Richardson, Samuel, 1689-1761.
The History of Pamela.
Norristown, Pa., Sower, 1799. 156 pp.
AAS copy. 36230

[Richardson, Samuel], 1689-1761.
The Paths of Virtue Delineated.
Philadelphia, Woodhouse, 1791. 135 pp.
1 photo plate.
Philadelphia Free Library copy. 23740

[Richardson, Samuel], 1689-1761.
The Paths of Virtue Delineated; or, The
History . . . of . . . Clarissa Harlowe.
Cooperstown, Phinney, 1795. 154.
[1] pp.
(Title and imprint assumed by Evans
from adv.)
AAS copy. 29414

[Richardson, Samuel, 1689-1761.
The History of Sir Charles Grandison.
Philadelphia, Spotswood, 1786.]
(Ghost of a London ed. Adv. in Pa.
Herald, July 12, 1786.) 19962

Richardson, Samuel, 1689-1761.
The History of Sir Charles Grandison.
. . . Tenth Edition.
Philadelphia, Carey, Stewart & Co.,
[1790]. 160 pp.
AAS copy. 22852

Richardson, Samuel, 1689-1761.
The History of Sir Charles Grandison.
. . . First Boston Edition.
Boston, Hall, 1794. 113, [3] pp.,
6 plates.
d'Alté Welch copy. 27623

Richardson, Samuel, 1689-1761.
The History of Sir Charles Grandison.
. . . Eleventh Edition.
Philadelphia, Carey for Folwell, 1794.
160 pp.
AAS copy. 29415

Richardson, Samuel, 1689-1761.
The History of Sir Charles Grandison.
Boston, West, 1796. 176 pp.
AAS copy. 47903

Richardson, Samuel, 1689-1761.
The History of Sir Charles Grandison
. . . Twelfth Edition.
New London, Springer, 1797. 156 pp.
(No copy located.) 48242

[Richardson, Samuel, 1689-1761.
The History of Sir Charles Grandison.
Abridged.
Suffield, Ct., Farnsworths, 1797.]
(Imprint assumed by Evans from
Farnsworth's adv.) 32764

Richardson, Samuel, 1689-1761.
The History of Sir Charles Grandison.
Suffield, Ct., Farnsworths for Cookes,
1798. 143 pp.
AAS copy. 34465

[Richardson, William], fl. 1753.
The Liberties of the Laity not Infringed.
Newport, 1753. 25, [1] pp.
AAS copy. 7111

Richardson, William, importer.
William Richardson Imports Directly. . . .
[Boston, 1800?] Broadside.
MHS copy. 37023

[Richardson, William], 1743-1814.
The Cacique of Ontario.
Stoningtonport, Ct., Trumbull, 1799.
24 pp.
AAS copy. 36232

Richardson, William, 1743-1814.
A Philosophical Analysis. . . . Fourth
Edition.
Philadelphia, Spotswood, 1788. [4],
262 pp.
AAS copy. 21433

[Richardson, William, 1743-1814.
A Philosophical Analysis and Illustration
of Shakespeare's Hamlet.
Boston, Spotswood, 1794.]
(Imprint assumed by Evans from advs.)
27624

Richardson & Walker, firm, Boston.
A General Assortment European & India
Goods.
[Boston, 1794?] Broadside.
EI copy. 47204

Richmond, Edward, 1767-1842.
A Sermon, Preached October 11th, 1797.
Amherst, N. H., Preston, 1798. 40 pp.
AAS copy. 34467

Richmond, Va., Theater, 1792.
By Authority. The Virginia Company
. . . August 3d, 1792.
[Richmond, 1792.] Broadside.
(Not located, 1968.) 46562

Richmond, April 17th, 1783. By a
Gentleman who Arrived last Night. . . .
Richmond, Hayes, [1783]. Broadside.
Duke Univ. copy. 44452

[Die Richtigkeit der Welt und des
Zeitlichen Lebens.
Germantown, Saur, 1774. 30 pp.]
(No copy located.) 42689

Ricketts, John Bill.

Rickett's Circus. . . . August the 4th,
1797.
[Albany, 1797.] Broadside.
NYPL facsim. copy.   48243

[Rickett's Circus.
Play-bill of Rickett's Circus, August 2,
1794.
[Philadelphia, 1794.] Broadside.]
(No copy located.)   27625

[Rickman, John.]
An Authentic Narrative of a Voyage to
the Pacific Ocean: Performed by
Captain Cook.
Philadelphia, Bell, 1783. pp. [2], [9]-96,·
99-299, [1].
AAS copy.   17921

Rickman, Thomas Clio, 1761-1834.
The Fallen Cottage.
Philadelphia, 1793. 24 pp.
AAS copy.   26089

Riddel, William, 1768-1849.
The Christian Doctrines Stated.
Wiscasset, Me., Hoskins, 1800. 28 pp.
AAS copy.   38406

Ridentem Dicere Verum Quid Vetat?
[New York, 1734.] Broadside.
NYPL copy.   3832

Ridgely-Carnan, Charles, 1762-1829.
To Harry Dorsey Gouch, Esquire. Sir, It
is impossible. . . . August 8, 1787.
Baltimore, Hayes, [1787]. [2] pp.
(No copy located.)   45159

Ridgely-Carnan, Charles, 1762-1829.
To the Electors of Baltimore County. . . .
September 7, 1784.
[Baltimore, 1784.] [2] pp.
MdHS copy.   18757

[Ridley, James], 1736-1765.
The Adventures of Urad.
Boston, Mein & Fleeming, 1767. [4],
58 pp.
AAS copy.   41762

Rigby, Edward, 1747-1821.
An Essay on the Uterine Haemorrhage.
. . . Third Edition.
Philadelphia, Dobson, 1786. iv, 84 pp.
AAS copy.   19964

Rigg, Edward.
The New American Latin Grammar.
New York, Smith & Cairns, 1784.
123 pp.
AAS copy.   18758

Rigg, Edward.
The New American Latin Grammar.
New York, Gaine, 1788. 123 pp.
AAS copy.   21434

[Rigg, Edward.
The New American Latin Grammar.
New York, Gaine, 1790.]
("Lately printed by Hugh Gaine," adv.
in 22469.)   22853

Rigg, Edward.
The New American Latin Grammar.
New York, Gaine, 1797. 141 pp.
AAS copy.   32766

Rigg, Elisha.
The True Principle.
Lancaster, Pa., Bailey & Dickson, 1793.
35 pp.
AAS copy.   26090

Riggs, Caleb S.
To the Free Electors of Kings County. . . .
New-York, 26th April, 1800.
n.p., n.d. Broadside.
LOC ph. copy.   38407

A Right Improvement of the Righteous
Judgments of God.
[Boston? 1743.] Broadside.
HEH copy.   40317

The Right of the Governor and Company,
of the Colony of Connecticut, to . . .
Lands . . . West of . . . New York.
Hartford, 1773. 47 pp.
AAS copy.   12978

A Right to the Lord's Supper [by

Experience Mayhew, 1673-1758].
Boston, Draper for Henchman, 1741. [2],
29, 2 pp.
NYPL copy.   4754

The Right to the Tonnage [by Daniel
Dulany, 1722-1797].
Annapolis, 1766. 40 pp.
LOC copy.   10288

The Right Way to Shake off a Viper. . . .
Second Impression [by Cotton Mather,
1663-1728].
Boston, Kneeland for Gerrish, 1720. [2],
xiv, 64 pp.
AAS copy.   2143

The Rights of Asses, A Poem.
America (Burlington, N.J.), 1793. 11 pp.
MHS copy.   26091

The Rights of Colonies Examined.
Published by Authority [by Stephen
Hopkins, 1707-1785].
Providence, 1765. 24 pp.
AAS copy.   10009

The Rights of Colonies Examined. - For
the Children. . . . [by Stephen Hopkins,
1707-1785].
Providence, 1765. 24 pp.
AAS copy.   10010

The Rights of Great Britain Asserted
against the Claims of America [by Sir
John Dalrymple, bart., 1726-1810].
Philadelphia, Bell, 1776. 92, [6] pp.
AAS copy.   14727

[The Rights of Great Britain Asserted
against the Claims of America. . . .
Second Edition [by Sir John Dalrymple,
bart., 1726-1810].
Philadelphia, Bell, 1776.]
(There appears to have been a second
edition, but no means of distinguishing
copies of it is known.)   14728

The Rights of Suffrage.
Hudson, Stoddard, 1792. 45 pp.
MHS copy.   24769

The Rights of the Drama.
Boston, 1792. 48 pp.
AAS copy.   24691

[Riley, George.]
The Beauties of the Creation.
Philadelphia, Young, 1792. 348 pp.
AAS copy.   24745

[Riley, George]
The Beauties of the Creation. . . . Second
American Edition.
Philadelphia, Young, 1796. 346, [2] pp.
AAS copy.   31105

Riley, George.
Beauties of the Creation.
Worcester, Thomas, 1798. xii, 274, [2] pp.
AAS copy.   34470

Rimius, Heinrich, -1759?
A Candid Narrative.
Philadelphia, Bradford, 1753. 112 pp.
HSP copy.   7112

[Ringewald, Barthol.
Neue Zeitung und Wahre Prophezeyung.
Ephrata, 1749.]
(Metzger 136. No copy located.)   40514

[Riouffe, Honoré], baron, 1764-1813.
Revolutionary Justice.
Philadelphia, Folwell for Davies, [1796].
180 pp.
AAS copy.   31106

Ripley, Ezra, 1751-1841.
The Design and Blessedness of the
Gospel.
Boston, Thomas & Andrews, 1712 (1792).
43 pp.
AAS copy.   24746

Ripley, Ezra, 1751-1841.
Love to our Neighbour.
Boston, Hall, 1800. 31 pp.
BA copy.   38410

Ripley, Ezra, 1751-1841.
A Sermon, Delivered at York.

Portsmouth, N. H., Peirce, 1798. 24 pp.
AAS copy.   34471

Ripley, Ezra, 1751-1841.
A Sermon Preached on the Completion of
a General Repair.
Boston, Edes, 1792. 52 pp.
AAS copy.   24747

Ripley, Hezekiah, 1743-1831.
A Sermon, Delivered at the Installation of
. . . William B. Ripley.
Norwich, Ct., Hubbard, [1798]. 30 pp.
JCB copy.   34472

Rippon, John, 1751-1836.
An Account of the London Missionary
Society.
Philadelphia, Lang & Ustick, 1796. 16 pp.,
printed wraps.
AAS copy.   31107

Rippon, John, 1751-1836.
A Selection of Hymns.
Elizabethtown, Kollock, 1792. ix, [19],
416, [24] pp.
(The only copy located lacks four pages.)
AAS copy.   24748

Rippon, John, 1751-1836.
A Selection of Hymns. . . . First American
Edition.
New York, Durell, 1792. xiii, [21], 588,
[27] pp.
AAS copy.   24749

The Rise and Continuance of the
Substitutes.
Philadelphia, Bell, 1777. [4], 18 pp.
LCP copy.   15575

[The Rise and Progress of Directory
Confluent.
Bennington, 1789.]
("Just published," Vt. Gazette, Feb. 23,
1789.)   22117

[Ritchie, Abraham.
Advertisement.
Philadelphia, 1774.]
(From Aitken's accounts.)   13574

[Ritchie, Elizabeth]
A Short Account of the last Sickness and
Death of . . . John Wesley.
Baltimore, Adamses, 1791. 12 pp.
JCB copy.   46275

[Rittenhouse, David], 1732-1796.
The Continental Almanack, for . . . 1780.
Philadelphia, Bailey. [36] pp.
HEH copy.   16500

[Rittenhouse, David], 1732-1796.
The Continental Almanac, for . . .
1781. . . . By Anthony Sharp.
Philadelphia, Bailey. [36] pp.
AAS copy.   16974

[Rittenhouse, David], 1732-1796.
The Continental Almanac, for . . .
1782. . . . By Anthony Sharp.
Philadelphia, Bailey. [36] pp.
AAS copy.   17348

[Rittenhouse, David], 1732-1796.
The Continental Almanac, for . . .
1783. . . . By Anthony Sharp.
Philadelphia, Bailey. [36] pp.
AAS copy.   17701

[Rittenhouse, David], 1732-1796.
The Continental Almanac, for . . .
1784. . . . By Anthony Sharp.
Philadelphia, Bailey. [36] pp.
LOC copy.   18159

[Rittenhouse, David], 1732-1796.
The Continental Almanac, for . . .
1785. . . . By Anthony Sharp.
Philadelphia, Bailey. [36] pp.
AAS copy.   18759

[Rittenhouse, David], 1732-1796.
The Continental Almanac, for . . .
1785. . . . By Anthony Sharp.
Philadelphia, Kline & Reynolds.]
(From an adv. apparently for 18759.)
18760

[Rittenhouse, David], 1732-1796.
The Continental Pocket Almanack for . . .
1781. By Anthony Sharp.

Philadelphia, Bailey. [24] pp.
NYPL copy.   16975

[Rittenhouse, David], 1732-1796.
The Continental Pocket Almanack for . . .
1782. By Anthony Sharp.
Philadelphia, Bailey.]
(Assumed from the sequence.)   17349

Rittenhouse, David, 1732-1796.
Father Abraham's Almanack, for . . .
1776. . . . By Abraham Weatherwise.
Philadelphia, Dunlap. 36 pp.
AAS copy.   14428

[Rittenhouse, David], 1732-1796.
Father Abraham's Almanack, for . . .
1777. . . . By Abraham Weatherwise.
Philadelphia, Dunlap. 36 pp.
AAS copy.   15062

[Rittenhouse, David], 1732-1796.
Father Abraham's Almanack, for . . .
1778. . . . By Abraham Weatherwise.
Lancaster, Dunlap. 36 pp.
(No complete copy located.)
AAS copy.   15576

[Rittenhouse, David], 1732-1796.
Father Abraham's Almanack, for . . .
1779. . . . By Abraham Weatherwise.
Philadelphia, Dunlap. [30] pp.
AAS copy.   16050

[Rittenhouse, David], 1732-1796.
Father Abraham's Almanack, for . . .
1780. . . . By Abraham Weatherwise.
Philadelphia, Dunlap. [32] pp.
HSP copy.   16501

[Rittenhouse, David], 1732-1796.
Father Abraham's Almanack, for . . .
1781. . . . By Abraham Weatherwise.
Philadelphia, Dunlap. [32] pp.
AAS copy.   16976

[Rittenhouse, David], 1732-1796.
Father Abraham's Almanack, for . . .
1782. . . . By Abraham Weatherwise.
Philadelphia, Kline. [32] pp.
AAS copy.   17350

[Rittenhouse, David], 1732-1796.
Father Abraham's Almanack, for . . .
1783. . . . By Abraham Weatherwise.
Philadelphia, Dunlap. [32] pp.
LOC copy.   17702

[Rittenhouse, David], 1732-1796.
Father Abraham's Almanack, for . . .
1784. . . . By Abraham Weatherwise.
Philadelphia, Dunlap. [40] pp.
AAS copy.   18160

[Rittenhouse, David], 1732-1796.
Father Abraham's New-England
Almanack, for . . . 1782. . . . By Abraham
Weatherwise.
Hartford, Webster. [24] pp.
CHS copy.   17352

[Rittenhouse, David], 1732-1796.
Father Abraham's Pocket Almanack, for
. . . 1776.
Philadelphia, Dunlap. [48] pp.
(The only copy located lacks the final
leaf.)
AAS copy.   14429

[Rittenhouse, David], 1732-1796.
Father Abraham's Pocket Almanack, for
. . . 1777.
Philadelphia, Dunlap. [24] pp.
AAS copy.   15063

[Rittenhouse, David], 1732-1796.
Father Abraham's Pocket Almanack, for
. . . 1778.
Lancaster, Dunlap. [29] pp.
AAS copy.   15577

[Rittenhouse, David], 1732-1796.
Father Abraham's Pocket Almanack, for
. . . 1779.
Philadelphia, Dunlap. [24] pp.
AAS copy.   16051

[Rittenhouse, David], 1732-1796.
Father Abraham's Pocket Almanack, for
. . . 1780.
Philadelphia, Dunlap. [24] pp.
HSP copy.   16502

[Rittenhouse, David], 1732-1796.
Father Abraham's Pocket Almanack for
. . . 1781.
Philadelphia, Dunlap.]
(The one reported copy cannot be
located.)   16977

[Rittenhouse, David], 1732-1796.
Father Abraham's Pocket Almanack for
. . . 1782.
Philadelphia, Dunlap.]
(Assumed from the sequence.)   17351

[Rittenhouse, David], 1732-1796.
Father Abraham's Pocket Almanac for
. . . 1784.
Philadelphia, Dunlap.]
(Assumed from the sequence.)   18161

[Rittenhouse, David], 1732-1796.
Father Abraham's Pocket Almanack for
. . . 1785.
Philadelphia, Dunlap.
(Assumed by Hildeburn from the
sequence.)   18762

[Rittenhouse, David], 1732-1796.
Der Gantz Verbesserte
Nord-Americanische Calender, auf das
1776ste Jahr. . . . Von Anthony Sharp.
Lancaster, Bailey. 36 pp.]
(No copy located.)   14430

[Rittenhouse, David], 1732-1796.
Der Gantz Neue Verbesserte
Nord-Americanische Calender, auf das
1777ste Jahr.
Lancaster, Bailey, 36 pp.]
(Copy formerly owned by A. K.
Hostetter.)   15064

[Rittenhouse, David], 1732-1796.
Der Gantz Neue Verbesserte Nord
Americanische Calender, des 1778sten
Jahres.
Lancaster, Bailey. [44] pp.
AAS copy.   15578

[Rittenhouse, David], 1732-1796.
Der Gantz Neue Verbesserte Nord
Americanische Calender, das 1778sten
Jahr. . . . Zweite Auflage.
Lancaster, Bailey. [44] pp.]
(No copy of a "zweite auflage" has been
found.)   16052

Rittenhouse, David, 1732-1796.
Der Gantz Neue Verbesserte
Nord-Americanische Calender, auf das
1779ste Jahr.
Lancaster, Bailey. [40] pp.
LOC copy.   16053

[Rittenhouse, David], 1732-1796.
[Der Gantz Neue Verbesserte
Nord-Americanische Calender, auf das
1780ste Jahr.
Lancaster, Bailey.]
(Known only by this fragment.)
AAS copy.   16503

Rittenhouse, David, 1732-1796.
Der Gantz Neue Verbesserte
Nord-Americanische Calender, auf das
1781ste Jahr.
Lancaster, Bailey. [34] pp.
AAS copy.   16978

[Rittenhouse, David], 1732-1796.
Der Gantz Neue Verbesserte
Nord-Americanische Calender, auf das
1782ste Jahr Christi.
Lancaster, Bailey. [36] pp.
(The only copy located lacks the first
leaf.)
AAS copy.   17353

[Rittenhouse, David], 1732-1796.
Der Gantz Neue Verbesserte
Nord-Americanische Calender, auf das
1783ste Jahr Christi. . . .
Lancaster, Bailey. [36] pp.
LOC copy.   17704

[Rittenhouse, David], 1732-1796.
Der Gantz Neue Verbesserte
Nord-Americanische Calender auf das
1784ste Jahr Christi. . . . Von Anthony
Sharp.
Lancaster, Bailey. [36] pp.
AAS copy.   18162

[Rittenhouse, David], 1732-1796.

Der Gantz Neue Verbesserte
Nord-Americanische Calender auf das
1785ste Jahr Christi.
Lancaster, Bailey. [36] pp.
LOC copy.   18763

[Rittenhouse, David, 1732-1796.
Der Gantz Neue Verbesserte
Nord-Americanische Calender. Auf das
1786ste Jahr Christi.
Lancaster, Bailey.]
(Assumed by Seidensticker from the
sequence.)   19223

[Rittenhouse, David], 1732-1796.
Der Gantz Neue Verbesserte
Nord-Americanische Calender auf das
1787ste Jahr. . . . Von Anthony Sharp.
Lancaster, Bailey. [36] pp.
AAS copy.   19965

[Rittenhouse, David], 1732-1796.
The Lancaster Almanack, for . . .
1776. . . . By Anthony Sharp.
Lancaster, Bailey. [32] pp.
(The two known copies are
incomplete.)
LOC copy.   14431

[Rittenhouse, David], 1732-1796.
The Lancaster Almanack for . . . 1777.
Lancaster, Bailey.]
(Assumed by Evans from the sequence.)
                                                15065

[Rittenhouse, David], 1732-1796.
The Lancaster Almanack, for . . .
1778. . . . By Anthony Sharp.
Lancaster, Bailey. [28] pp.
AAS copy.   15579

[Rittenhouse, David], 1732-1796.
The Lancaster Almanack, for 1779. . . . By
Anthony Sharp.
Lancaster, Bailey. [32] pp.
AAS copy.   16054

[Rittenhouse, David], 1732-1796.
The Lancaster Almanack for . . . 1780.
Lancaster, Bailey.]
(No copy located.)   16504

[Rittenhouse, David], 1732-1796.
The Lancaster Pocket Almanack, for . . .
1778. . . . By Anthony Sharp.
Lancaster, Bailey. [24] pp.
AAS copy.   15580

[Rittenhouse, David], 1732-1796.
The Lancaster Pocket Almanack for . . .
1779.
Lancaster, Bailey.]
(Assumed by Hildeburn from the
sequence.)   16055

[Rittenhouse, David], 1732-1796.
The Lancaster Pocket Alamanck for . . .
1780.
Lancaster, Bailey.]
(No copy located.)   16505

[Rittenhouse, David], 1732-1796.
[The Maryland, Virginia and
Pennsylvania Almanack for . . . 1780.
Baltimore, Goddard.]
(The only known copy is imperfect. See
Wheeler 80.)
MdHS copy.   16506

Rittenhouse, David, 1732-1796.
An Oration, Delivered February 24, 1775.
Philadelphia, Dunlap, 1775. 27 pp.
AAS copy.   14432

[Rittenhouse, David], 1732-1796.
The Universal Almanack, for . . . 1773.
Philadelphia, Humphreys. [28] pp.
LOC copy.   12542

[Rittenhouse, David], 1732-1796.
The Universal Almanack, for . . .
1773. . . . Second Edition.
Philadelphia, Humphreys, [1773].
[28] pp.]
(Adv. Pa. Packet, Feb. 15, 1773.)   12979

[Rittenhouse, David], 1732-1796.
The Universal Almanack, for . . . 1774.
Philadelphia, Humphreys. [36] pp.
AAS copy.   12980

Rittenhouse, David, 1732-1796.
The Universal Almanack, for . . . 1775.

Philadelphia, Humphreys. [34] pp.
HSP copy. 13577

Rittenhouse, David, 1732-1796.
The Universal Almanack, for . . . 1776.
Philadelphia, Humphreys. [36] pp.
HSP copy. 14433

Rittenhouse, David, 1732-1796.
The Universal Almanack, for . . . 1777.
Philadelphia, Humphreys. [36] pp.
AAS copy. 15066

Rittenhouse, David, 1732-1796.
The Virginia Almanack for . . . 1774.
Williamsburg, Rind. [48] pp.
LOC copy. 12981

Rittenhouse, David, 1732-1796.
The Virginia Almanack for . . . 1775.
Williamsburg, Pinkney for Rind. 24 pp.
(The only copy available is imperfect.)
VaHS copy. 13578

Rittenhouse, David, 1732-1796.
The Virginia Almanack for . . . 1776.
Williamsburg, Dixon & Hunter. [46] pp.
NYPL copy. 14434

Rittenhouse, David, 1732-1796.
The Virginia Almanack for . . . 1777.
Williamsburg, Dixon & Hunter. [32] pp.
AAS copy. 15067

Rittenhouse, David, 1732-1796.
The Virginia Almanack for . . . 1778.
Williamsburg, Dixon & Hunter. [24] pp.
AAS copy. 15581

Rittenhouse, David, 1732-1796.
The Virginia Almanack for . . . 1779.
Williamsburg, Dixon & Hunter. [24] pp.
VaHS copy. 16056

Rittenhouse, David, 1732-1796.
The Virginia Almanack for . . . 1779.
Williamsburg, Dixon & Nicolson. [24] pp.
AAS copy. 16057

[Rittenhouse, David], 1732-1796.
The Virginia Almanack for . . . 1780.
Williamsburg, Dixon & Nicolson. [24] pp.
AAS copy. 16507

[Rittenhouse, David], 1732-1796.
Weatherwise's Town and Country
Almanack, for . . . 1781. . . . By Abraham
Weatherwise.
Boston, M'Dougall. Front., [36] pp.
AAS copy. 16979

[Rittenhouse, David], 1732-1796.
The Second Edition. Weatherwise's Town
and Country Almanack for . . . 1781. . . .
By Abraham Weatherwise.
Boston, M'Dougall. Front., [36] pp.
(Except for the Title-page this edition is
the same as 16979.)
AAS copy. 16980

[Rittenhouse, David], 1732-1796.
Weatherwise's Town and Country
Almanack, for . . . 1782. . . . By Abraham
Weatherwise.
Boston, Coverly & Hodge. Front., [36]
pp.
AAS copy. 17354

[Rittenhouse, David], 1732-1796.
Weatherwise's Town and Country
Almanack, for . . . 1783. . . . By Abraham
Weatherwise.
Boston, Hodge. [24] pp., 1 plate.
AAS copy. 17705

[Rittenhouse, David], 1732-1796.
Weatherwise's Town and Country
Almanack, for . . . 1784. . . . By Abraham
Weatherwise.
Boston, Coverly. [24] pp.
AAS copy. 18163

[Rittenhouse, David], 1732-1796.
Weatherwise's Town and Country
Almanack, for . . . 1784. . . . By Abraham
Weatherwise.
Boston, Norman & White. [24] pp.
AAS copy. 18164

[Rittenhouse, David], 1732-1796.
Weatherwise's Town and Country
Almanack, for . . . 1785. . . . By Abraham
Weatherwise.

Boston, Weeden & Barrett. [24] pp.
AAS copy. 18764

[Rittenhouse, David], 1732-1796.
Weatherwise's Town and Country
Almanack, for . . . 1786. By Abraham
Weatherwise.
Boston, Griffith. [24] pp.
AAS copy. 19225

[Rittenhouse, David], 1732-1796.
Weatherwise's Town and Country
Almanack, for . . . 1786. . . . By Abraham
Weatherwise.
Boston, Norman. [24] pp.
AAS copy. 19224

[Ritzema, Johannes]
Aan den Eerwaarden.
Philadelphia, Miller, 1763. 38 pp.
HSP copy. 9504

[Rivington, James, 1724-1802.
(D.A.B.)
A Catalogue of Books for Sale by. . . .
Philadelphia, 1761.]
(Adv. Pa. Journal, Feb. 26, 1761.) 8998

Rivington, James, 1724-1802.
A Catalogue of Books Sold by Rivington
and Brown.
Philadelphia? 1762. [2], 88 pp.
HSP copy. 9259

[Rivington, James], 1724-1802.
Names of the Subscribers [to Churchill's
Poems].
[New York? 1768?] lvi pp.
AAS copy. 41875

Rivington, James, 1724-1802.
New-York, April 27, 1775. To the
Public. . . .
[New York, 1775.] Broadside.
LOC copy. 14435

Rivington, James, 1724-1802.
New-York, February 15, 1773. . . .
Proposes to Publish. . . .
[New York, 1773.] Broadside.
AAS ph. copy. 12982

Rivington, James, 1724-1802.
Supplication of J. R********. To His
Excellency Henry Laurens.
Philadelphia, Woodward, 1800. [8] pp.
HC copy. 38594

Rivington, James, 1724-1802.
To the Public. Having already. . . . June 3,
1775.
[New York, 1775.] Broadside.
LOC copy. 14436

Rivington, James, 1724-1802.
Whosoever would Purchase the English
Edition of . . . Captain Cook. . . . Mar. 16,
1774.
[New York, Rivington, 1774.] Broadside.
JCB copy. 42690

Rivington's Gentleman and Lady's Pocket
Almanack for . . . 1774.
New York, Rivington. 84 (i.e. 72) pp.
(All known copies lack pp. 37-48.)
AAS copy. 12738

Rivington's Gentleman and Lady's Pocket
Almanack, for . . . 1775.
New York, Rivington. 72 pp.
NYHS copy. 13229

Rivington's New Almanack . . . for . . .
1774.
New York, Rivington. [36] pp.
AAS copy. 12737

Rivington's New Almanack . . . for
. . . 1775.
New York, Rivington. [40] pp.
NYPL copy. 13230

[Rivington's New-York Pocket Almanack
for . . . 1782.
New York, Rivington.]
"(This Day is published," Royal Gazette,
Dec. 12, 1781.) 17355

Rivington's New-York Pocket Almanack,
for . . . 1783.
New York, Rivington. [24] pp.
AAS copy. 17706

A Roaster. . . . By Sim Sansculotte [by
John Swanwick, 1740-1798].
Philadelphia, Johnson, 1796. 21 pp.
AAS copy. 31256

Robbins, Ammi Ruhamah, 1740-1813.
The Empires and Dominions of this World
Hartford, Hudson & Goodwin, 1789. 39
pp.
AAS copy. 22118

Robbins, Ammi Ruhamah, 1740-1813.
(Weis, Colonial Clergy N. E.)
To Treat of Eternal Concerns.
New Haven, [1772]. 27 pp.
CHS copy. 12543

Robbins, Chandler, 1738-1799.
An Address, Delivered at Plymouth, on
the 24th Day of January, 1793.
Boston, Belknap & Hall, 1793. 20 pp.
AAS copy. 26102

Robbins, Chandler, 1738-1799.
(Weis, Colonial Clergy N. E.)
The Character of Dorcas.
Boston, 1771. 35 pp.
AAS copy. 12215

Robbins, Chandler, 1738-1799.
A Century Sermon, Preached at Kingston
. . . April 2d, 1794.
Boston, Belknap & Hall, 1794. 24 pp.
AAS copy. 27630

Robbins, Chandler, 1738-1799.
A Discourse Delivered before the
Humane Society.
Boston, Fleet, 1796. 36 pp.
AAS copy. 31110

Robbins, Chandler, 1738-1799.
(Weis, Colonial Clergy N. E.)
A Reply to some Essays.
Boston, Fleets, 1773. viii, 76 pp.
AAS copy. 12984

Robbins, Chandler, 1738-1799.
A Sermon Preached at Plymouth,
December 22, 1793.
Boston, Bumstead, 1794. 56 pp.
AAS copy. 27629

Robbins, Chandler, 1738-1799.
A Sermon Preached at Plymouth,
December 22, 1793.
Stockbridge, Andrews, 1796. 46 pp.
AAS copy. 31111

Robbins, Chandler, 1738-1799.
A Sermon, Preached at the General
Convention . . . May 29, 1794.
Boston, Hall, 1794. 31 pp.
AAS copy. 27631

Robbins, Chandler, 1738-1799.
A Sermon, Preached at the Ordination of
. . . Eliphalet Gillett.
Hallowell, Wait, Robinson & Baker, 1795.
31 pp.
AAS copy. 29423

Robbins, Chandler, 1738-1799.
A Sermon, Preached at the Ordination of
. . . Ward Cotton.
Worcester, Mass., Worcester for Thomas,
1797. 34 pp.
AAS copy. 32772

Robbins, Chandler, 1738-1799.
A Sermon. Preached before His
Excellency John Hancock.
Boston, Adams, 1791. 51 pp.
AAS copy. 23741

Robbins, Chandler, 1738-1799.
(Weis, Colonial Clergy N. E.)
Some Brief Remarks.
Boston, Fleets, 1774. [4], 27 pp.
AAS copy. 13581

Robbins, Chandler, 1738-1799.
(Weis, Colonial Clergy N. E.)
To Please Christ.
Boston, Leverett, 1772. 30 pp.
HC copy. 12544

Robbins, Chandler, 1738-1799.
(Weis, Colonial Clergy N. E.)
The Ways of God Vindicated.
Boston, Mein & Fleeming, 1767. 42 pp.
AAS copy. 10755

Robbins, Ephraim.
A Friendly Letter to the Rev. Mr.
Cumings.
Newburyport, Barrett, 1796. 19 pp.
AAS copy.   31112

Robbins, Nathaniel, 1726-1795.
(Weis, Colonial Clergy N. E.)
Jerusalem's Peace Wished.
Boston, Boyles, 1772. 23 pp.
AAS copy.   12545

Robbins, Nathaniel, 1726-1795.
(Weis, Colonial Clergy N. E.)
A Sermon Preached at the Ordinatin of
. . . Benjamin Wadsworth.
Boston, Fleets, 1773. 30 pp.
AAS copy.   12985

Robbins, Nathaniel, 1726-1795.
(Weis, Colonial Clergy N. E.)
A Sermon Preached at the Ordination of
. . . Peter Thacher.
Boston, Draper, 1771. 40 pp.
AAS copy.   12216

[Robbins, Philemon, 1709-1781.
(Sibley, VIII, 616-627.)
A Plain Narrative.
Boston, Kneeland & Green, 1743. 44 pp.]
(A ghost of 6063 arising from an error in
Haven.)   5281

Robbins, Philemon, 1709-1781.
(Sibley, VIII, 616-627.)
A Plain Narrative.
Boston, Kneeland & Green, 1747. 44 pp.
AAS copy.   6063

Robbins, Philemon, 1709-1781.
(Sibley, VIII, 616-627.)
A Sermon Preached at the Ordination of
. . . Ammi-Ruhamah Robbins.
New Haven, 1762. 20 pp.
JCB copy.   9260

Robbins, Philemon, 1709-1781.
(Sibley, VIII, 616-627.)
A Sermon Preached at the Ordination of
. . . Chandler Robbins.
Boston, Kneeland, 1760. [2], 22 pp.
AAS copy.   8727

Robbins, Robert, 1741-1804.
Divine Sovereignty.
Norwich, Bushnell, 1792. 67 pp.
AAS copy.   24750

Robbins, Thomas, 1777-1856.
An Oration, Occasioned by the Death of
. . . Washington.
Danbury, [Ct.], Douglas & Nichols,
[1800]. 16 pp.
MFM copy.   38411

[Robe, James], 1688-1753.
A Short Narrative of the Extraordinary
Work at Cambuslang.
Boston, Kneeland, 1742. 24 pp.
AAS copy.   5047

[Robe, James], 1688-1753.
(D. N. B.)
A Short Narrative of the Extraordinary
Work at Cambuslang.
Philadelphia, Bradford, 1742. 36, [3] pp.
AAS copy.   5046

Roberdeau, Isaac, 1763-1829.
An Oration; upon the Death of General
Washington.
Philadelphia, Woodward, 1800. 30 pp.
PPL copy.   38412

[Roberts, Daniel, 1658-1727.
(Joseph Smith, Friends' Books, II.)
Some Memoirs of the Life of John
Roberts.
Boston, 1751.]
(Entry from Sabin.)   6774

[Roberts, Daniel, 1658-1727.
Some Memoirs of the Life of John
Roberts. . . . Third Edition.
Philadelphia, Chattin, 1752. 60 pp.]
(Imprint assumed by Evans from an adv.
The one copy reported cannot be located.)
                                                6926

Roberts, Daniel, 1658-1727.
Some Memoirs of the Life of John
Roberts. . . . Fourth Edition.

Philadelphia, Chattin, 1753. 69 pp.
AAS copy.   7113

Roberts, Daniel, 1658-1727.
Some Memoirs of the Life of John
Roberts. . . . Fifth Edition.
Philadelphia, Miller and Der Kindern,
1766. 67 pp.
AAS copy.   10482

Roberts, Daniel, 1658-1727.
Some Memoirs of the Life of John
Roberts. . . . Sixth Edition.
Philadelphia, Crukshank, 1773. 57, [3] pp.
AAS copy.   12986

[Roberts, Daniel, 1658-1727.
Some Memoirs of the Life of John
Roberts.
Philadelphia, Crukshank, 1783.]
(Adv. in 18353.)   18166

Roberts, Daniel, 1658-1727.
Some Memoirs of the Life of John
Roberts. . . . Seventh Edition.
Philadelphia, Crukshank, 1790. 66, [6] pp.
AAS copy.   22855

Roberts, George, 1766-1827.
Strictures on a Sermon.
[Philadelphia], Tuckniss, 1794. 56 pp.
AAS copy.   27632

[Roberts, Thomas, fl. 1786.
Catalogue of Books and Stationary.
Charleston, Childs, Haswell & M'Iver for
Roberts, 1786.]
(Entry from an adv.)   19966

Roberts, William, 1767-1849.
Too High a Pitch.
Worcester, Thomas, 1798. 156 pp.
AAS copy.   34475

Robertson, Alexander, 1742-1784.
New-York, June 23, 1769. To the
Publick. . . .
[New York, 1769.] Broadside.
LOC copy.   11445

[Robertson, John], 1712-1776.
Tables of Difference of Latitude and
Departure.
Philadelphia, Crukshank, 1790. [1], 90 pp.
AAS copy.   22856

[Robertson, John], 1712-1776.
Tables of Difference of Latitude and
Departure.
Wilmington, Del., Bonsal & Niles for Jess,
1799. [1], 91, [3], 59, [1] pp.
AAS copy.   36236

Robertson, Joseph, 1726-1802.
A Clear and Practical System of
Punctuation: Abridged [by Thaddeus
Mason Harris].
Boston, Thomas & Andrews, 1792. pp.
[6], [11]-48.
AAS copy.   24751

Robertson, Joseph, 1726-1802.
A Clear and Practical System of
Punctuation.
Boston, Thomas & Andrews, 1797. 48 pp.
AAS copy.   31113

[Robertson, Joseph], 1726-1802.
An Essay on Punctuation.
Philadelphia, James, 1789. 144 pp.
AAS copy.   22119

Robertson, William, 1721-1793.
An Historical Disquisition Concerning the
Knowledge which the Ancients had of
India.
Philadelphia, Young, 1792. pp. [i]-viii,
[13]-420 pp.
AAS copy.   24752

Robertson, William, 1721-1793.
The History of America. . . . Vol. I [-II].
New York, Campbell, 1798. 512; 511, [33]
pp.
AAS copy.   34476

Robertson, William, 1721-1793.
The History of America, Books IX. and
X.
Philadelphia, Humphreys, 1799. 196, [2]
pp.
AAS copy.   36237

Robertson, William, 1721-1793.
The History of America, Books IX and X.
Walpole, N.H., Carlisle for Thomas &
Thomas, 1800. 192 pp.
AAS copy.   38413

Robertson, William, 1721-1793.
The History of the Reign of Charles the
Fifth.
America (Philadelphia, Bell), 1770. 3 vol.
[18], vi-viii, [2], 360, [14]; [16], 374;
[45], 351, [44] pp.
(Sets differ in the arrangement of the
unnumbered pages. The AAS has a set
with the Bell imprint.)
AAS copy.   11837

Robertson, William, 1721-1793.
The History of the Reign of Charles the
Fifth. . . . In Two Volumes.
Philadelphia, Bell, 1770. [2], 374, [39],
351, [45] pp.
AAS copy.   42164

[Robespierre, Maximilien Marie Isidore
de, 1758-1794.
A Report on the Institution of National
Morality and Festivals in French [May 8,
1794].
New York, Birdsall & Hyer, 1794.]
(Imprint assumed by Evans from an adv.)
                                               28697

Robie, Thomas, 1689-1729.
(Sibley, V, 450-455.)
[An Ephemeris of the Coelestial Motions
for 1709.
Boston, 1708].
(The one copy reported could not be
located.)   1370

Robie, Thomas, 1689-1729.
. . . An Ephemeris of the Coelestial
Motions . . . for . . . MDCCX.
Boston, 1710. [16] pp.
AAS copy.   1430

[Robie, Thomas, 1689-1729.
(Sibley, V, 450-455.)
An Almanack of the Coelestial Motions
. . . for . . . 1711.
Boston, 1711.]
(No copy of this year found.)   1485

Robie, Thomas, 1689-1729.
. . . An Almanack . . . for . . . 1712.
Boston, 1712. [16] pp.
AAS copy.   1526

[Robie, Thomas, 1689-1729.
. . . An Almanack . . . for . . . 1713.
Boston, 1713.]
(No copy found.)   1582

Robie, Thomas, 1689-1792.
. . . An Almanack . . . for . . . 1714.
Boston, Green. [16] pp.
AAS copy.   1646

[Robie, Thomas, 1689-1729.
(Sibley, V, 450-455.)
An Almanack of the Coelestial Motions
. . . for . . . 1715.
Boston, 1715.]
(Assumed from the sequence.)   1714

Robie, Thomas, 1689-1729.
MDCCXVI. An Almanack.
Boston, 1716. [16] pp.
AAS copy.   1777

Robie, Thomas, 1689-1729.
MDCCXVII. An Almanack.
Boston, 1717. [16] pp.
AAS copy.   1851

Robie, Thomas, 1689-1729.
(Sibley, V, 450-455.)
MDCCXVIII. An Almanack.
Boston, Fleet for Crump, [1717]. [16] pp.
(The unique copy is imperfect.)
JCB copy.   1926

Robie, Thomas, 1689-1729.
(Sibley, V, 450-455.)
MDCCXX. An Almanack.
Boston, 1720. [16] pp.
HC copy.   2071

[Robie, Thomas], 1689-1729.
(Sibley, V, 450-455.)
A Letter to a Certain Gentleman.

Boston, 1719. 8 pp.
BPL copy.   2171

Robie, Thomas, 1689-1729.
(Sibley, V, 450-455.)
A Sermon Preached in the College.
Boston, Kneeland, 1721. [2], iv, 18 pp.
AAS copy.   2288

Robin, Claude C., b. 1750.
New Travels Through North-America.
Philadelphia, Bell, 1783. 112 pp.
AAS copy.   18167

Robin, Claude C., b. 1750.
New Travels through North-America.
Boston, Powars & Willis for Battelle, 1784.
95 pp.
AAS copy.   18765

Robin Hood.
The Life and Death of.... in
Twenty-Four Songs.
Philadelphia, Stewart & Cochran, [1792?]
54 leaves.
(Rosenbach: Ch 160; present location
unknown.)   46563

Robin Hood.
The Life and Death of....
New York, 1800. 80 pp.
AAS copy.   37827

Robin Hood Society, New York.
Debates at the ... 19th of July, 1774.
New York, [1774]. 14 pp.
(Set differently from 13486.)
NYHS copy.   42691

Robin Hood Society, New York.
Debates at the ... 19th of July, 1774.
New York, [1774]. 14 pp.
LCP copy.   13486

Robinson, Sir Christopher, 1766-1833.
Reports of Cases ... in ...
Admiralty.... Volume the First.
Philadelphia, Humphreys, 1800. xii, [4],
332 pp.
AAS copy.   38414

Robinson, J.   , fl. 1792.
The Yorker's Stratagem.
New York, Swords, 1792. 34 pp.
HEH copy.   26103

Robinson, James, of Philadelphia.
Robinson's Philadelphia Register and City
Directory, for 1799.
Philadelphia, Bioren, 1799. pp. [1]-16,
[154], [17]-50.
LCP copy.   36238

Robinson, Nathaniel, fl. 1769.
Verses Composed by ... when he was in
Albany Gaol.
New London, Green, 1769. 36 pp.
(Trumbull Supplement 2571. No copy
located.)   42001

Robinson, Nathaniel, fl. 1768.
Verses upon Fourteen Different
Occasions.... Third Edition.
Boston, McAlpine, 1773. 24 pp.
AAS copy.   42492

[Robinson, Robert, 1735-1790.
Ecclesiastical Researches.
New York, Wayland, 1795.]
(Known only by the prospectus in the
N.Y. Ev. Post, Jan. 12, 1795.)   29424

Robison, John, 1739-1805.
Extracts from Professor Robison's
"Proofs of a Conspiracy."
Boston, Manning & Loring, 1799. 30 pp.
(Also entered as 35181, q. v.)   36239

Robison, John, 1739-1805.
Proofs of a Conspiracy.... The Third
Edition.
Philadelphia, Dobson and Cobbet, 1798.
pp. [1]-204, 197-391.
AAS copy.   34477

Robison, John, 1739-1805.
Proofs of a Conspiracy.... The Fourth
Edition.
New York, Forman, 1798. 399 pp.
AAS copy.   34478

[Robson, John C.]
A Scriptural View of the Rise of the

Heathen, Jewish, and Christian
Monarchies.
New York, Buell, 1797. 99, [1] pp.
AAS copy.   48244

[Robson, John C.
A Scriptural View of the Rise of the
Heathen.
New York, Buel, 1798.]
(Entry from the copyright records.) 34479

Roby, Joseph, 1724-1803.
(Sibley, XI, 165-168.)
A Sermon Delivered at Lynn on the
General Fast, May 3, 1781.
Boston, Fleets, 1781. 31 pp.
AAS copy.   17356

Roby, Joseph, 1724-1803.
A Sermon, Delivered at Lynn, on the
General Fast, April 17, 1794.
Portland, Wait, [1794]. 31 pp.
AAS copy.   27636

Roche, Edward, 1754-1821.
A Funeral Oration, on the Death of ...
Washington.
Wilmington, [Del.], Wilson, 1800. 15,
[1] pp.
HSP copy.   38415

[Rochambeau, Jean Baptiste Donatien de
Vimeur, Comte de], 1725-1807.
Relation, ou Journal des Opérations du
Corps Francais.
Philadelphia, Hampton, [1781]. 15 pp.
National Archives, Paris, copy.   44051

Rochambeau, Donatien Marie Joseph de
Vimeur, vicomte de, 1755-1813.
Réponse du Général Rochambeau.
Philadelphia, Parent, [1797]. [2], 10 pp.
JCB copy.   32773

Roche, Regina Marie (Dalton),
1764?-1845.
The Children of the Abbey.
New York, M. L. Davis for Caritat, 1798.
4 vol. in 2.
(Only known copy cannot be filmed.)
                                            48599

[Roche, Regina Marie (Dalton),
1764?-1845.
The Children of the Abbey.
Philadelphia, 1798. 4 vol. in 2.]
(Imprint assumed by Evans from adv.)
                                            34480

[Roche, Regina Maria (Dalton),
1764?-1845.
Children of the Abbey.
New York, Caritat, 1799. 4 vol. in 2.]
(Imprint assumed by Evans from adv.
"New Publications, printed for H.
Caritat," Weekly Museum, Feb.
26, 1799.)   36240

Roche, Regina Maria (Dalton),
1764?-1845.
The Children of the Abbey.... In Four
Volumes.
Philadelphia, Bioren for Campbell, 1800.
195; 208; 172; 184 pp.
AAS copy.   38416

[Roche, Mrs. Regina Maria (Dalton),
1764?-1845.
Clermont.
Philadelphia, 1798.]
(Imprint assumed by Evans from adv.)
                                            34481

[Rock, Edmund.
Essay, Poems and Letters.
Wiscasset, Me., Hoskins, 1797. 500 pp.
(Proposed but not printed.)   32774

Rockhill, John.
Forasmuch as the Judicious Readers....
[Philadelphia? 1755.] Broadside.
HEH copy.   40796

Rockhill, John.
The State of the Controversy....
[Philadelphia? 1755.] Broadside.
HEH copy.   40797

Rockingham, N. H. Town Meeting, July
29, 1779.
State of New Hampshire, Rockingham SS.
At a Public Town Meeting ... July 29th,
1779.

n.p., [1779]. Broadside.
NHHS copy.   43701

Rockwell, Samuel.
An Oration, Delivered at the Celebration
of American Independence.
Litchfield, Ct., Collier, [1797]. 16 pp.
NYPL copy.   32775

A Rod for the Fool's Back.
See
Webster, Noah.   38417

[Rodgers, John, 1773-1838.
A Glorious Victory Obtained by One of
our "Useless Frigates."
Baltimore, 1799. Broadside.]
(See Minick 537.)   36241

[Rodney, Caesar Augustus], 1772-1824.
The Oracle of Liberty.
Philadelphia, Hall, [1791]. 39 pp.
NYPL copy.   23742

Roemeling, Christian Anton.
C. A. Roemelings, Gewesenen Predigers.
Ephrata, 1792. pp. [12], [1]-466, [2],
23-96.
AAS copy.   24755

[Roemeling, Christian Anton.]
Der Wunderbare Bussfertige Beichvater.
Germantown, [1753]. 36 pp.
(No complete copy located.)
HSP copy.   6950

Rogers, Rev. James.
The Authority and Duty of Christ's
Ministers.
Charleston, S. C., MacIver, 1794. 27 pp.
LOC copy.   31114

Rogers, John, 1648-1721.
An Answer to a Book Intituled, The
Lords Day.
Boston, 1721. [2], 30 pp.
AAS copy.   39751

Rogers, John, 1648-1721.
(D. A. B.)
The Book of the Revelation of Jesus
Christ.
Boston, 1720. [2], 262 pp.
AAS copy.   2172

Rogers, John, 1648-1721.
An Epistle Sent from God.
New London, Rogers, 1718. 40 pp.
JCB copy.   39690

Rogers, John, 1648-1721.
An Epistle Sent from God.
New York, for Stanbury, 1757. 25 pp.
HC copy.   8028

Rogers, John, 1648-1721.
(D. A. B.)
An Epistle to the Churches of Christ call'd
Quakers.
[New York, 1705.] ix, 90 pp.
(All known copies are similarly imperfect
as though leaves were deliberately
canceled before binding.)
AAS copy.   1232

[Rogers, John, 1648-1721.
(D. A. B.)
An Impartial Relation.
[Philadelphia], 1701. [4], 15 pp.]
(Title from Hildeburn; no copy found.)
                                             1019

Rogers, John, 1648-1721.
(D. A. B.)
John Rogers a Servant of Jesus Christ....
Third Edition.
Newport, 1754. 76 pp.
(No complete copy located.)
YC copy.   7310

Rogers, John, 1648-1721.
John Rogers, a Servant of Jesus Christ, to
any of the Flock.... Fourth Edition.
Norwich, 1776. 36, 24 pp.
(This Evans entry includes two separate
tracts.)
YC copy.   15068

Rogers, John, 1648-1721.
A Mid-Night-Cry from the Temple of
God.
[New York, 1705.] [2], 179 pp.
AAS copy.   1233

Rogers, John, 1648-1721.
A Mid-Night-Cry. . . . Second Edition.
New London, [Green for] Bolles, [1722].
[2], 270 pp.
(The Evans entry came from Haven. See
also Bates, supplement.)
AAS copy.   3348

[Rogers, John, 1648-1721.
(D. A. B.)
Treatise Concerning the One only True
God.
New York, 1706.]
(Ghost of a section of Evans 1233.)   1278

Rogers, John, 1666-1745
(Sibley, III, 273-276.)
Death the Certain Wages of Sin.
Boston, 1701. [12], 153, [1] pp.
BPL copy.   1020

Rogers, John, 1666-1745.
(Sibley, III, 273-276.)
The Perfect and Upright Man.
Boston, Draper for Henchman, 1739. [4],
18, [2], 24 pp.
AAS copy.   4417

Rogers, John, 1666-1745.
(Sibley, III, 273-276.)
A Sermon Preached before His
Excellency.
Boston, 1706. [2], 54 pp.
AAS copy.   1279

Rogers, John, 1674-1753.
An Answer to a Book Lately put forth.
[New York, 1726]. [2], xii, 87 pp.
AAS copy.   2809

Rogers, John, 1674-1753.
An Answer to a small Pamphlet
Entituled A Monitory Letter.
[New York? 1726.] [4], 19 pp.
YC copy.   2810

Rogers, John, 1674-1753.
A Brief Account of some of the Late
Suffering.
[New London? 1726.] 29 pp.
AAS copy.   39855

Rogers, John, 1684-1755.
(Sibley, V, 292-294.)
The Nature and Necessity.
Boston, Gerrish, 1728. 78 pp.
MHS copy.   3100

Rogers, John, 1712-1789.
(Sibley, IX, 189-198.)
The Nature and Necessity of Spiritual
Conversion.
Boston, Green & Russell, 1757. 24 pp.
AAS copy.   8029

Rogers, John, 1712-1789.
(Sibley, IX, 189-198.)
Three Sermons.
Boston, Edes & Gill for Kneeland, 1756.
61 pp.
AAS copy.   7785

Rogers, John, 1724-1799
(James S. Rogers, James Rogers, pp. 69,
99-101.)
A Looking-Glass for the Presbyterians.
Providence, 1767. 36 pp.
RIHS copy.   10756

Rodgers, John, 1727-1811.
The Divine Goodness Displayed.
New York, Loudon, 1784. 42 pp.
AAS copy.   18766

Rodgers, John, 1727-1811.
The Faithful Servant Rewarded.
New York, Greenleaf, 1795. 38 pp.
AAS copy.   29425

Rodgers, John, 1727-1811.
Holiness the Nature and Design.
Hartford, 1780. 28 pp.
CHS copy.   16981

Rogers, Medad, 1750-1824.
An Address to the Living.
D[anbury, Douglas & Ely, 1792]. 12 pp.
BA copy.   24753

Rogers, Nathaniel, 1701-1775.
(Sibley, VI, 556-560.)
The Character.

Boston, Draper for Henchman, 1739. [2],
24 pp.
(Signatured with 4417, q.v.)   4418

Rogers, Nathaniel, 1701-1775.
(Sibley, VI, 556-560.)
The Character of the Godley.
Boston, Fleet, 1763. 32 pp.
AAS copy.   9505

Rogers, Nathaniel, 1701-1775.
The Office of Gospel Ministers.
Boston, Fleet, 1763. 41 pp.
AAS copy.   9506

[Rogers, Ransford]
A Collection of Essays, on a Variety of
Subjects.
Newark, N. J., Woods, 1797. pp. [1]-84,
[5]-28, [3]-24, [2], [7]-22, 1-8.
MJHS copy.   34482

[Rogers, Samuel], 1763-1855.
The Pleasures of Memory.
Boston, Manning & Loring, 1795. [4], 124
pp., 4 plates.
AAS copy.   29426

Rogers, Samuel, 1763-1855.
The Pleasures of Memory.
Wilmington, Del., Wilson, 1800. 39 pp.
AAS copy.   38418

[Rogers, Timothy, 1589-1650?
The Righteous Man's Evidence.
Cambridge, 1668.]
(No copy known. Advertised in Evans
119.)   129

Rogers, Timothy, 1589-1650?
The Righteous Man's Evidence.
West Springfield, Grey for Patten, 1797. 132,
[1] pp.
AAS copy.   32776

[Rogers, William, 1751-1824.
A Circular Letter on . . . Justification.
Philadelphia, 1785. 24 pp.]
(Assumed from the imprint of the English
ed., "Philadelphia, 1785. London,
reprinted.")   19226

Rogers, William, 1751-1824.
An Oration, Delivered July 4th, 1789.
Philadelphia, Dobson, 1789. 32 pp.
AAS copy.   22120

Rogers, William, 1751-1824.
The Prayer, Delivered . . . the 22d of
February.
Philadelphia, Ormrod, 1800. 12 pp.
AAS copy.   38419

Rogers, William, 1751-1824.
A Sermon, Occasioned by the Death of
. . . Oliver Hart.
Philadelphia, Lang & Ustick, 1796. 39, [1]
pp.
AAS copy.   31115

[Rogers & Barker, Charleston, S. C.]
Prices Current. Charleston.
[Charleston, 1795.] Broadside.
JCB copy.   29427

Rogers & Fowle, Boston.
Boston, Nov. 9, 1749. Whereas Mr. Moses
Dickinson hath. . . .
[Boston, 1749.] Broadside.
MHS copy.   40515

Rogerson, Robert, b. 1757.
(Harvard College Records.)
An Anthem, Sacred to the Memory of His
Excellency John Hancock.
Boston, Thomas & Andrews, 1793. 8 pp.
NYPL copy.   26104

[Rojas Zorrilla, Francisco de, 1607-1648.
The Point of Honor.
Philadelphia, 1795.]
(Evans' entry from an adv. The one
recorded copy cannot now be located.)
                                         29428

[Rokeby, Matthew Robinson-Morris], 2d
baron, 1713-1800.
Appendix to the Considerations on the
Measures.
Philadelphia, Towne, 1775. 19 pp.
LOC copy.   14439

[Rokeby, Matthew Robinson-Morris], 2d
baron, 1713-1800.
Considerations on the Measures Carrying
on. . . .
Boston, Edes & Gill, 1774. 64 pp.
AAS copy.   13582

[Rokeby, Matthew Robinson- Morris], 2d
baron, 1713-1800.
Considerations on the Measures Carrying
on. . . . [Half-title:] Fourth Edition.
Boston, Edes & Gill, 1774. 64 pp.
AAS copy.   13583

[Rokeby, Matthew Robinson-Morris], 2d
baron, 1713-1800.
Considerations on the Measures Carrying
on. . . . [Half-title:] Fifth Edition.
Boston, Edes & Gill, 1774. 64 pp.
AAS copy.   13584

[Rokeby, Matthew Robinson-Morris], 2d
baron, 1713-1800.
Considerations on the Measures Carrying
on. . . .
Hartford, 1774. 63 pp.
AAS copy.   13585

[Rokeby, Matthew Robinson-Morris], 2d
baron, 1713-1800.
Considerations on the Measures Carrying
on. . . .
New York, Holt, 1774. [2], 73 pp.
AAS copy.   13586

[Rokeby, Matthew Robinson-Morris], 2d
baron, 1713-1800.
Considerations on the Measures Carrying
on. . . .
Philadelphia, Towne, 1774. 60 pp.
AAS copy.   13587

[Rokeby, Matthew-Robinson Morris. 2d
baron, 1713-1800.
Considerations on the Measures Carrying
on.
Norwich, Robertsons & Trumbull, 1775.]
(Entry from an adv. in an unlocated issue
of the Norwich Packet.)   14438

Roland de la Platière, Marie Jeanne
(Philipon), 1754-1793.
An Appeal to Impartial Posterity. . . .
Vol. I [-II].
New York, Wilson for Van Hook, 1798.
202, 164; 202, 235 pp.
AAS copy.   34483

Rollin, Charles, 1661-1741.
The Life of Alexander the Great.
Providence, Wheeler for Todd, 1796. pp.
[8], [13]-257, [2].
AAS copy.   31116

[Rollinson, William], 1762-1842.
(No. 33, Smith-Street.) To the Inhabitants
of New-York. . . . May 13, 1790.
[New York, 1790.] Broadside.
NYHS copy.   22857

Romaine, William, 1714-1795.
(D. N. B.)
The Knowledge of Salvation. . . . Fourth
Edition.
Boston, Fowle & Draper, 1759. 28 pp.
AAS copy.   8484

[Romaine, William, 1714-1795.
The Knowledge of Salvation. . . . Seventh
Edition.
Philadelphia, Dunlap, 1759.]
(Adv. Pa. Gazette, Aug. 23, 1759.)   8485

[The Roman Catholic Primer.
Philadelphia, Spotswood, 1786.]
(See Parsons 55, 56. Evans' entry from
adv., "Sold by," in Pa. Herald, July 12,
1786.)   19967

Romans, Bernard, 1720?-1784?
Annals of the Troubles in the
Netherlands. . . . Volume I.
Hartford, 1778. [8], cxx, 160 pp.
AAS copy.   16059

Romans, Bernard, 1720?-1784?
Annals of the Troubles in the
Netherlands. . . . Volume II.
Hartford, Hudson & Goodwin, 1782. 243
pp.
AAS copy.   17707

Romans, Bernard, 1720?-1784?

Chart Containing Part of East Florida.
[New York, 1775.] 3 sheets.
LOC copy.   14441

[Romans, Bernard, 1720?-1784?
Chart, Containing the Peninsula of
Florida.
[New York, 1775.] 6 sheets.]
(No copy located.)   14442

Romans, Bernard, 1720?-1784?
A Concise Natural History of East and West
Florida.
New York, 1775. 4, viii, 342, [2], lxxxix,
[4] pp., front., dedication, 10 plates.
AAS copy.   14440

Romans, Bernard, 1720?-1784?
A Concise Natural History of East and
West-Florida.
New York, Aitken, 1776. [2], 4, 342 pp., 6
plates, folded table.
AAS copy.   15069

Romans, Bernard, 1720?-1784?
Philadelphia, July 12, 1773. It is Proposed
to Print, a . . . Map, from Boston. . . .
[Philadelphia, 1775.] Broadside.
LCP copy.   14443

Romans, Bernard, 1720?-1784?
Philadelphia, August 5, 1773. Proposals
for Printing . . . Three very Elegant and
Large Maps.
[Philadelphia, Bradfords, 1773.]
Broadside.
JCB copy.   42493

[Romans, Bernard, 1720?-1784?
Roman's Map of the State of Connecticut.
Norwich, Townsend, 1777.]
("Just published and to be sold by
Nathaniel Townsend," Norwich Packet,
Sept. 8, 1777.)   15585

Romans, Bernard, 1720?-1784?
To the Hon'l Jno. Hancock . . . this
Map. . . .
[Philadelphia, 1775.] Map.
LOC copy.   14444

[Romans, Bernard], 1720?-1784?
The Townships or Grants East of Lake
Champlain.
[New Haven, 1778.] Map.
HEH copy.   43551

The Romans in Greece [by Vittorio
Barzoni, 1768-1829].
Boston, Manning & Loring for Nancrede,
1799. 84 pp.
AAS copy.   35160

The Romans in Greece [by Vittorio
Barzoni, 1768-1829.]
Boston, Manning & Loring for Nancrede,
1799. 80, [4] pp.
(Also entered as 35160, q. v.)   36243

[Romayne, Jeremiah, 1768-1818.
The American Israel.
Catskill, Croswell, 1795.]
(Imprint assumed by Evans from adv.
"Just published, and to be sold at this
office," in Catskill Packet, July 25, 1795.)
     29429

Rome, George.
Copy of a Letter Returned. . . .
Narragansett, 22d. December, 1767.
n.p., [1767]. Broadside.
MHS copy.   41763

Romeyn, John Brodhead, 1777-1825.
A Funeral Oration, in Remembrance of
. . . Washington.
Poughkeepsie, N. Y., Woods, 1800. 12 pp.
NYPL copy.   38421

Roney, James.
Philadelphia, July 23, 1779. To the Public.
Fortunately we have Preserved. . . .
[Philadelphia, 1779.] Broadside.
LOC copy.   43680

[Roosen, Gerhard], 1612-1711.
Christliches Gemueths-Gespraech.
Ephrata, 1769. 168 pp.
AAS copy.   11446

[Roosen, Gerhard], 1612-1711.
Christliches Gemüths-Gespräch.

Germantown, Billmeyer, 1790. 241 pp.
AAS copy.   22858

Root, Erastus, 1773-1846.
An Introduction to Arithmetic.
Norwich, Hubbard, 1795. 105 pp.
AAS copy.   29430

Root, Erastus, 1773-1846.
An Introduction to Arithmetic. . . .
Second Edition.
Norwich, Ct., Hubbard, 1796. 105 pp.
AAS copy.   31119

[Root, Erastus, 1773-1846.
An Introduction to Arithmetic.
Portsmouth, N.H., 1798. 105 pp.]
(As attributed, an error in Karpinski.)
     48600

[Root, Erastus, 1773-1846.
An Introduction to Arithmetic.
Norwich, Ct., Hubbard, 1799.]
(Bates 2576.)   36244

Root, Jesse, 1737-1822.
Reports of Cases Adjudged. . . . Vol. I.
Hartford, Ct., Hudson & Goodwin, 1798.
[4], 584, [52] pp.
AAS copy.   34485

Roots, Benajah, 1725-1787.
(Weis, Colonial Clergy N. E.)
A Few brief Remarks.
Hartford, 1770. 23 pp.
CHS copy.   11838

Roots, Benajah, 1725-1787.
The True Church of Christ Described.
Bennington, Haswell & Russell, [1785]. 38
pp.
AAS copy.   44789

Roots, Peter Philanthropos, 1765-1828.
A Letter to the First Congregational
Paedobaptist Church.
Hartford, Hudson & Goodwin, [1794].
156 pp.
AAS copy.   27637

Rosanna, or the Cruel Lover.
Danbury, Douglas, 1794. 8 pp.
(Only known copy is imperfect.)
BrU copy.   47205

[Roscoe, William], 1753-1831?
Strictures on Mr Burke's Two Letters.
Philadelphia, Thompson, 1797. iv, 50 pp.
(Also entered as 31876, q. v.)   32778

Roscoe, William, 1753-1831?
The Wrongs of Africa: a Poem.
Philadelphia, James, 1788. 26 pp.
AAS copy.   21435

Roscommon, pseud.
To the Author of those Intelligencers.
New York, 1733. 10 pp.
NYPL copy.   3722

Rose, Aquila, 1695-1723.
(D. A. B.)
Poems on Several Occasions.
Philadelphia, 1740. 56 pp.
("Just Published," Pa. Gazette, Aug. 13,
1741.)
HC copy.   4593

Rose, Henry, fl. 1794.
An Inaugural Dissertation.
Philadelphia, Woodward, 1794. 30 pp.
AAS copy.   27638

Rose, Johannes.
Mineralisches Pferde-Pulver.
[Lancaster, 1800?] Broadside.
LCP copy.   49144

Rose, Johannes.
Sassafras-oel.
[Lancaster, Pa., 1792.] Broadside.
LCP copy.   46564

[The Rose of Sharon: Anthem.
Philadelphia, M'Culloch, 1788.]
("Lately published," Federal Gazette,
Apr. 8, 1788.)   21436

Rosencrantz, Herman, 1716-1770.
The Life and Confession of. . . .
Philadelphia, Chattin, [1770]. 10, [1] pp.
NYHS copy.   11839

[Roslin Castle. A Song.
Philadelphia, Towne, 1779.]
(Adv. Pa. Evening-Post, June 15, 1779.)
     16508

[Ross, David, b. 1750.
Address to the Citizens of Ann Arundel.
Annapolis, Greens, 1792.]
(The origin of this entry is unknown.)
     24756

Ross, James, 1744-1827.
A Plain, Short, Comprehensive, Practical
Latin Grammar.
Chambersburg, Pa., Harper, 1798. viii,
158, [1] pp.
AAS copy.   34486

Ross, James, 1744-1827.
A Practical, New Vocabulary Latin and
English.
Chambersburg, [Pa.], Snowden &
M'Corkle, 1798. iv, 68 pp.
AAS copy.   48601

[Ross, James, 1744-1827.
A Practical, new Vocabulary, Latin into
English.
Chambersburg, Pa., Snowdon &
M'Corkle, 1799.]
(Adv. as for sale.)   36245

Ross, Robert, 1726-1799.
The American Grammar. . . . Seventh
Edition.
Hartford, Patten, 1782. 199, [1] pp.
AAS copy.   17708

Ross, Robert, 1726-1799.
The American Latin Grammar. . . . Fifth
Edition.
New York, Parker for Noel, 1770. [2],
162, [4] pp.
AAS copy.   11840

[Ross, Robert, 1726-1799.
The American Latin Grammar.
Newburyport, Mycall, Water-Street,
[1780]. 112 pp.]
(The copy described by Evans is, from the
address given in the imprint, that again
described by him as 27650 from advs. in
the Impartial Herald.)   16983

Ross, Robert, 1726-1799.
The American Latin Grammar. . . . Fifth
Edition.
Providence, 1780. 112 pp.
AAS copy.   16982

[Ross, Robert], 1726-1799.
The American Latin Grammar. . . .
Eighth Edition.
Springfield, Gray, 1793. 117 pp.
AAS copy.   26105

Ross, Robert, 1726-1799.
The American Latin Grammar.
Newburyport, Mycall, [1794?]. 112 pp.
(Adv. as "just published" Jan. 2, 1795.)
AAS copy.   27640

[Ross, Robert], 1726-1799.
The American Latin Grammar.
Providence, Carter & Wilkinson, 1794. 136
pp.
AAS copy.   27639

[Ross, Robert], 1726-1799.
(Palmer, First Ch. Bridgeport, pp. 8-9.)
A Complete Introduction to the Latin
Tongue.
New York, Parker, 1752. viii, 101, [2] pp.
HSP copy.   6928

[Ross, Robert], 1726-1799.
(Palmer, First Ch. Bridgeport, pp. 8-9.)
A Complete Introduction to the Latin
Tongue. . . . Second Edition.
Woodbridge, 1760. [4], 109, [2] pp.
PrU copy.   8728

[Ross, Robert], 1726-1799.
A Complete Introduction to the Latin
Tongue. . . . Fourth Edition.
New York, Gaine, 1767. [2], 109, 2 pp.
LOC copy.   10758

Ross, Robert, 1726-1799.
The New American Spelling Book.
New Haven, Greens, [1785]. 119, 13 pp.
AAS copy.   19227

[Ross, Robert, 1726-1799.
The New American Spelling Book.
New Haven, Greens, 1786.]
("Just Published, and now selling by the
Printers hereof," Conn. Journal, Jan. 11,
1786.)   19968

Ross, Robert, 1726-1799.
[A new primer, or little boy and girls's
spelling-book.
Bennington, Haswell & Russell, 1784.]
(McCorison 78; no copy known.)   44598

[Ross, Robert, 1726-1799.
The New Primer, or Little Boy and Girls
Spelling Book.
Boston, Edes, 1788. [96?] pp.
(The unique copy is imperfect.)
BPL copy.   21437

[Ross, Robert, 1726-1799.
The New Primer, or Little Boy and Girl's
Spelling-Book.
Middletown, Woodward & Green, 1790.]
("Just Published," Middlesex Gazette,
Feb. 27, 1790.)   22859

Ross, Robert, 1726-1799.
(C. R. Palmer, First Church Bridgeport,
pp. 8-9.)
A Plain Address.
New Haven, [1762]. 213, [7] pp.
(Issued with 9120, q.v.)   9261

Ross, Robert, 1726-1799.
A Sermon, in which the Union of the
Colonies is Considered.
New York, Holt, 1776. 28 pp.
AAS copy.   15070

Ross, Robert, 1726-1799.
A Sermon, Preached at New Town,
December 8th, 1773.
New Haven, [1773]. 58 pp.
CHS copy.   12987

Ross, William Morrey, d. 1818.
A Chemico-Physiological Inaugural
Dissertation.
New York, Swords, 1795. [2], 58 pp.
AAS copy.   29431

Ross, Zephaniah.
A Defence of the Divinity . . . of Jesus
Christ.
Springfield, 1795. 23 pp.
AAS copy.   29432

Ross, Zephaniah.
An Oration upon the Gloomy Aspects of
the Times.
Springfield, 1795. viii, 28 pp.
AAS copy.   29433

Ross & Douglas, booksellers, Petersburg.
A Catalogue of Books, &c., now
Selling. . . .
Petersburg, [Va.], 1800. [4], 31 pp.
NCU copy.   38237

Rotheram, John, 1725-1789.
(D. N. B.)
An Essay on Faith. . . . Third Edition.
New York, Parker, 1767. viii, 126 pp.
AAS copy.   10759

Rou, Lewis, 1676?-1750.
A Collection of Papers.
New York, 1725. 34 pp.
NYPL copy.   2698

Rouelle, John.
A Complete Treatise on the Mineral
Waters of Virginia.
Philadelphia, Cist for Dobson, 1792. [8],
xix, [1], 68 pp.
AAS copy.   24757

[Rouget de Lisle, Claude Joseph],
1760-1836.
The Marseilles Hymn. In French and
English.
Philadelphia, Carr, [1793]. [3] pp.
(Evans took the title from an adv.)
LOC copy.   26107

[Rouget de Lisle, Claude Joseph],
1760-1836.
The Marseilles Hymn in French &
English.
Philadelphia, Carr, [1793]. [3] pp.
NYPL copy.   26106

[Rouget de Lisle, Claude Joseph],
1760-1836.
The Marseilles Hymn in French and
English.
New York, Gilfert, [1796]. 3 pp.
LOC copy.   47904

[Rouget de Lisle, Claude Joseph],
1760-1836.
The Marseilles Hymn.
Philadelphia, Willig, [c. 1796]. [2] pp.
LOC copy.   47581

[Round Hand Copies Engraved for the
Use of Schools.
Boston, West, 1794.]
(Entry from advs., probably for copies of
22567, q.v.)   27641

Rousby, Gezelena.
New-York, January 20, 1769. As Mr.
Jauncey. . . .
[New York, 1769.] Broadside.
LOC copy.   11448

Rousby, Gezelena.
To the Freeholders. . . . New-York,
January 20, 1769.
[New York, 1769.] Broadside.
LOC copy.   11447

Rouso D'Eres, Charles Dennis, b. 1761.
Memoirs of . . . a Native of Canada.
Exeter, Ranlet, 1800. 176 pp.
AAS copy.   38422

[Rousseau, Jean Jacques, 1712-1778.
The Confessions of. . . .
New York, 1796. 2 vol.]
(Imprint assumed by Evans from advs.)
          31121

Rousseau, Jean Jacques, 1712-1778.
A Dissertation on Political Economy.
Albany, Barber & Southwick, 1797. 72,
214, [2] pp., 1 plate.
AAS copy.   32780

Rousseau, Jean Jacques, 1712-1778.
Eloisa. . . . Vol. I [-III].
Philadelphia, Longcope, 1796. 274; 267;
259 pp.
AAS copy.   31122

[Rousseau, Jean Jacques, 1712-1778.
Letters of an Italian Nun.
Philadelphia, 1794.]
(Imprint assumed by Evans from "Just
Published" advs. by several booksellers.)
          27642

Rousseau, Jean Jacques, 1712-1778.
Letters of an Italian Nun. . . . Fifth
Edition.
Philadelphia, Carey, 1796. 130 pp.
AAS copy.   31123

Rousseau, Jean Jacques, 1712-1778.
Letters of an Italian Nun. . . . First
Worcester Edition.
Worcester, Thomas & Thomas, 1796. 196
pp., 1 plate.
AAS copy.   31124

Rousseau, John Baptiste Clement.
An Inaugural Dissertation on Absorption.
Philadelphia, Ormrod, 1800. 36 pp.
AAS copy.   38423

Roussel, -
M. Roussel, Dancing-Master. . . . June 12,
1782.
Baltimore, Goddard, [1782]. Broadside.
(No copy located.)   44262

Rowna, Archibald Hamilton, 1751-1834,
defendant.
Report of the Trial of Archibald Hamilton
Rowna.
New York, Tiebout & O'Brien, 1794. [2],
152, [1] pp., 1 plate.
AAS copy.   27643

Rowe, Elizabeth (Singer), 1674-1737.
Devout Exercises. . . . Fourth Edition.
Boston, Rogers and Fowle for Blanchard,
1742. 148, [4] pp.
AAS copy.   5048

[Rowe, Elizabeth (Singer), 1674-1737.
Devout Exercises.
Boston. Blanchard, 1743.]

("Just published," Boston Evening Post,
Feb. 14, 1743.)   5282

[Rowe, Elizabeth (Singer), 1674-1737.
Devout Exercises.
Philadelphia, Franklin, 1745.]
(Adv. Pa. Gazette, Oct. 31, 1745, but
probably an English ed.)   5684

Rowe, Elizabeth (Singer), 1674-1737.
(D. N. B.)
Devout Exercises.
Lancaster, 1754. 126, [4] pp.
(The unique copy is imperfect.)
HSP copy.   7311

Rowe, Elizabeth (Singer), 1674-1737.
Devout Exercises of the Heart.
Boston, Hall, 1790. 139, [2] pp.
AAS copy.   22860

Rowe, Elizabeth (Singer), 1674-1737.
Devout Exercises of the Heart.
Philadelphia, Aitken, 1791. 271 pp.
AAS copy.   23743

Rowe, Elizabeth (Singer), 1674-1737.
Devout Exercises of the Heart.
Philadelphia, Dobson, 1791. 205, [3] pp.
AAS copy.   23744

Rowe, Elizabeth (Singer), 1674-1737.
Devout Exercises of the Heart.
Philadelphia, Hall, 1792. 214, [9] pp.
AAS copy.   24759

Rowe, Elizabeth (Singer), 1674-1737.
Devout Exercises of the Heart.
Windsor, Spooner for Ralph, 1792. 155,
[1] pp.
AAS copy.   24758

Rowe, Elizabeth (Singer), 1674-1737.
Devout Exercises of the Heart.
Exeter, Lamson, 1794. 140, [2] pp.
AAS copy.   27644

Rowe, Elizabeth (Singer), 1674-1737.
Devout Exercises of the Heart.
New Haven, Morse, 1794. 167 pp.
AAS copy.   27645

Rowe, Elizabeth (Singer), 1674-1737.
Devout Exercises of the Heart.
New York, Tiebout & O'Brien for Nutter,
1794. 233 pp.
(The only known copy is imperfect.)
AAS copy.   47206

Rowe, Elizabeth (Singer), 1674-1737.
Devout Exercises of the Heart.
New York, Durell, 1795. 178, [2] pp.
AAS copy.   47582

Rowe, Elizabeth (Singer), 1674-1737.
Devourt Exercises of the Heart.
New York, Tiebout & O'Brien for
Mitchell, [1795?]. 233, [8] pp.
(Copy cannot be filmed.)   47583

Rowe, Elizabeth (Singer), 1674-1737.
Devout Exercises of the Heart.
Dedham, Mass., Heatons, 1796. 142, [2]
pp.
AAS copy.   31125

Rowe, Elizabeth (Singer), 1674-1737.
Devout Exercises of the Heart.
Northampton, Mass., A. Wright for D.
Wright, 1798. 158 pp.
JCB copy.   34487

Rowe, Elizabeth (Singer), 1674-1737.
Devout Exercises of the Heart.
Philadelphia, Tuckniss, 1798. 214, [10]
pp.
AAS copy.   34488

Rowe, Elizabeth (Singer), 1674-1737.
Devout Exercises of the Heart.
Hartford, Ct., Babcock, 1800. 180 pp.
AAS copy.   38424

Rowe, Elizabeth (Singer), 1674-1737.
Friendship in Death.
Boston, Rogers & Fowle, 1747. [8], 71 pp.
AAS copy.   6064

Rowe, Elizabeth (Singer), 1674-1737.
Friendship in Death.
Boston, Hodge, Green, and Norman,
1782. pp. [4], vi-xvi, [2], [17]-264.
AAS copy.   17709

Rowe, Elizabeth (Singer), 1674-1737.
Friendship in Death.
New York, Hodge, 1786. pp. [iii]-xvi, [2],
[17]-264.
AAS copy.   44962

[Rowe, Elizabeth (Singer), 1674-1737.
Friendship in Death.
Boston, Bumstead for Larkin, 1790.]
(Evans entry from an adv.)   22861

Rowe, Elizabeth (Singer), 1674-1737.
Friendship in Death.
Boston, Bumstead for West and Larkin,
1792. xxxix, 310 pp.
AAS copy.   24760

Rowe, Elizabeth (Singer), 1674-1737.
Friendship in Death.
New York, Tiebout & O'Brien for
Duyckinck, 1795. xii, 300 pp.
AAS copy.   29434

Rowe, Elizabeth (Singer), 1674-1737.
Friendship in Death.
New York, Tiebout & O'Brien for Gomez,
1795. xii, 300 pp.
AAS copy.   29435

[Rowe, Elizabeth (Singer)], 1674-1737.
The History of Joseph. A Poem.
Philadelphia, Franklin, 1739. 63 pp.
UOP copy.   4419

[Rowe, Elizabeth (Singer)], 1674-1737.
The History of Joseph. A Poem.
Boston, 1743.]
("Lately printed," Boston Evening Post,
Aug. 8, 1743.)   5283

[Rowe, Elizabeth (Singer)], 1674-1737.
(D. N. B.)
The History of Joseph; a Poem.
Philadelphia, Hall & Sellers, 1767. [2], 66
pp.
AAS copy.   10760

Rowe, Elizabeth (Singer), 1674-1737.
[The History of Joseph and his Brethren.
Philadelphia, Lawrence, 1773?] 16 pp.
(No copy known. Entry from bookseller's
cat.)   42494

[Rowe, Elizabeth (Singer)], 1674-1737.
History of Joseph; a Poem.
Hartford, Hudson & Goodwin, 1784.
59 pp.
NYPL copy.   18767

Rowe, Elizabeth (Singer), 1674-1737.
The History of Joseph. A Poem.
Philadelphia, Crukshank, 1787. [2], 60,
[2] pp.
(Evans assumed the date of imprint from
an adv. in 21164.)
AAS copy.   21438

Rowe, J.
Singing of Psalms.
[Boston?], 1722. [2], 14 pp.
AAS copy.   39775

[Rowe, Nicholas, 1674-1718.
Jane Shore: a Tragedy.
New York, Gaine, 1761.]
(Adv. N. Y. Mercury, July 20, 1761.) 8999

[Rowe, Theophilus], fl. 1737.
The Life of Mrs. Elizabeth Rowe.
Boston, Rogers & Fowle, 1747. 119 pp.
(Evans assumed the date of the imprint
from the date of the adv. The only copy
located is defective.)
AAS copy.   6232

Rowland, David Sherman, 1719-1794.
Catholicism: or, Christian Charity.
Providence, 1772. [2], 75 pp.
AAS copy.   12546

Rowland, David Sherman, 1719-1794.
(Weis, Colonial Clergy N. E.)
Divine Providence.
Providence, [1766]. [4], viii, 31 pp.
AAS copy.   10483

Rowland, David Sherman, 1719-1794.
The Faithful Servant of Christ Call'd.
New London, 1783. 39 pp.
AAS copy.   18168

Rowland, David Sherman, 1719-1794.
Heresy, Detected and Exposed.

Hartford, Hudson & Goodwin, [1781]. 63
pp.
AAS copy.   17357

Rowland, David Sherman, 1719-1794.
Historical Remarks.
Providence, [1779]. 35 pp.
AAS copy.   16509

Rowland, David Sherman, 1719-1794.
Ministerial Necessity.
Hartford, Watson, 1776. 45 pp.
AAS copy.   15071

Rowland, David Sherman, 1719-1794.
(Weis, Colonial Clergy N.E.)
Ministers of Christ.
Boston, Mecom, [1761]. 43 pp.
AAS copy.   9000

Rowland, John Hamilton.
A Sermon Preached before the
Convention of the Protestant Episcopal
Church, at New-Brunswick.
New York, Gaine, 1785. 20 pp.
NYHS copy.   19228

Rowland, William Frederick, 1761-1843.
A Sermon, Delivered in Presence of His
Excellency.
Exeter, Ranlet, 1796. 32 pp.
AAS copy.   31126

Rowlandson, Joseph, 1631-1678.
(Sibley, I, 311-321.)
The Possibility of Gods Forsaking a
People.
Boston, 1682. [6], 22 pp.
(The Huntington copy has a Cambridge
imprint. The errata on the BPL copy
shows that Evans 331 and 332 were issued
jointly with this.)
BPL copy.   330

Rowlandson, Joseph, 1631-1678.
The Possibility of Gods Forsaking a
People.
Cambridge, Green, 1682. [6], 22 pp.
(The only known copy is imperfect.)
HEH copy.   39221

Rowlandson, Mary (White), 1635?-1678?
A Narative of the Captivity.
Boston, Coverly, 1770. 48 pp.
LOC copy.   42165

Rowlandson, Mary (White), 1635?-1678?
(D. A. B.)
A Narrative of the Captivity.
Boston, Coverly, 1770. 60 pp.
(No complete copy is known.)
AAS copy.   11841

Rowlandson, Mary (White), 1635?-1678?
(D. A. B.)
A Narrative of the Captivity.
Boston, Coverly, 1771. 59, [1] pp.
AAS copy.   12217

Rowlandson, Mary (White), 1635?-1678?
A Narrative of the Captivity.
Boston, Boyle, 1773. 40 pp.
AAS copy.   12988

Rowlandson, Mary (White), 1635?-1678?
A Narrative of the Captivity.
New London, 1773. 48 pp.
(See Vail, Frontier, No. 621.)
NYHS copy.   13589

Rowlandson, Mary (White), 1635?-1678?
A Narrative of the Captivity.
Boston, Fleets, 1791. 40 pp.
BA copy.   23745

Rowlandson, Mary (White), 1635?-1678?
A Narrative of the Captivity, Sufferings
and Removes of. . . .
Boston, Hall, 1794. 57 pp.
AAS copy.   27646

Rowlandson, Mary (White),1635?-1678?
A Narrative of the Captivity . . . of. . . .
[Leominster, Mass.], Whitcomb, [1794].
56 pp.
AAS copy.   47207

Rowlandson, Mary (White), 1635?-1678?
A Narrative of the Captivity of. . . .
Amherst, N. H., Coverly, [1795]. 64 pp.
AAS copy.   29436

Rowlandson, Mary (White), 1635?-1678?

A Narrative of the Captivity, Sufferings
and Removes, of. . . .
Haverhill, N.H., Coverly, [1796]. 64 pp.
AAS copy.   31127

Rowlandson, Mary (White), 1635?-1678?
A Narrative of the Captivity.
Boston, Fleets, 1800. 36 pp.
(No copy located could be filmed.)   38425

[Rowlandson, Mary (White), 1635?-1678?
(D. A. B.)
The Soveraignty & Goodness of God.
Cambridge, 1682.]
(No copy of this edition known.)   331

Rowlandson, Mary (White), 1635?-1678?
The Soveraignty. . . . The Second
Addition.
Cambridge, 1682. [6], 73 pp.
BPL copy.   332

Rowlandson, Mary (White), 1635?-1678?
(D. A. B.)
The Sovereignty and Goodness of God.
Boston, Fleet for Phillips, 1720. 80 pp.
LOC copy.   2173

Rowlett, John.
[Rowlett's Tables of Dicount.
Philadelphia, 1800.]
(Imprint assumed from copyright, July 31,
1800, but no issue dated earlier than 1802
found.)   38426

Rowlett, John.
[Table of Discount or Interest.
Philadelphia, 1800.]
(Copyright Jan. 9, 1800.)   38427

[Rowson, Susanna (Haswell)], 1762-1824.
America, Commerce & Freedom. . . .
Composed by A. Reinagle.
Philadelphia, Carr, [1794]. [2] pp.
NYPL copy.   27647

[Rowson, Susanna (Haswell), 1762-1824.
America, Commerce and Freedom.
[Boston, 1795.] Broadside.]
(Boston printing assumed by Evans from
adv. Perhaps a ghost of 27647.)   29437

[Rowson, Susanna (Haswell), 1762-1824.
Americans in England.
Boston, 1796.]
(Entry from Sabin 73603. See Vail, p. 85.)
31128

[Rowson, Susanna (Haswell)?],
1762-1824.
Captain Truxton or Huzza! for the
Constellation.
New York, Hewitt for Carrs, [1799]. [2]
pp.
LOC copy.   36247

Rowson, Susanna (Haswell), 1762-1824.
Charlotte. In Two Volumes.
Philadelphia, Humphreys for Carey, 1794.
87, [1]; 83, [9] pp.
AAS copy.   27649

Rowson, Susanna (Haswell), 1762-1824.
Charlotte. . . . In Two Volumes.
Second Philadelphia Edition . . . Carey
. . . 1794. 169, [1] pp.
AAS copy.   27650

Rowson, Susanna (Haswell), 1762-1824.
Charlotte Temple. . . . Two Volumes in
One. . . . Third American Edition.
Philadelphia, Ustick for Carey, 1797. 204
pp.
AAS copy.   32781

[Rowson, Susanna (Haswell), 1762-1824.
The Fille de Chambre.
Baltimore, Angell for Keatinge, 1794.]
(Imprint assumed by Evans from advs.)
27652

Rowson, Susanna (Haswell), 1762-1824.
The Fille de Chambre.
Philadelphia, H. & P. Rice for J. Rice,
1794. 207, [1] pp.
AAS copy.   27651

Rowson, Susanna (Haswell), 1762-1824.
The Fille de Chambre.
Baltimore, [S. & J. Adams for] Clayland,
1795. 256 pp.
(An imprint variant of 47584, q. v.) 47585

Rowson, Susanna (Haswell), 1762-1824.
The Fille de Chambre.
Baltimore, S. & J. Adams for Keatinge,
1795. 256 pp.
AAS copy.　　　47584

[Rowson, Susanna (Haswell)?],
1762-1824.
Huzza for the Constellation.
Philadelphia, Carr for Carr and Hewitt,
[1799]. 3 pp.
LOC copy.　　　36247

[Rowson, Susanna (Haswell), 1762-1824.
In Vain the Verdure of Spring. The Music
Composed by Benjamin Carr.
Philadelphia, Willig, 1796.]
(Entry from advs.)　　　31129

Rowson, Susanna (Haswell), 1762-1824.
The Inquisitor. . . . First American
Edition.
Philadelphia, Gibbons, 1793. 3 vol. in 1.
202, [1] pp.
AAS copy.　　　26108

Rowson, Susanna (Haswell), 1762-1824.
The Inquisitor. . .. In Three Volumes.
Philadelphia, Carey, 1794. 246 pp.
AAS copy.　　　27653

Rowson, Susanna (Haswell), 1762-1824.
The Little Sailor Boy. A Ballad.
Philadelphia, Carr, [1798]. [2] pp.
AAS copy.　　　34489

Rowson, Susanna (Haswell), 1762-1824.
Mentoria. . . . In Two Volumes.
Philadelphia, Smith for Campbell, 1794.
pp. [2], [1]-v, [1], [9]-106, [2]; [1]-116,
[3].
NYPL copy.　　　27654

Rowson, Susanna (Haswell), 1762-1824.
New Song, Sung by Mr. Darley.
[Philadelphia], Carey, [1794]. Broadside.
HSP copy.　　　27648

Rowson, Susanna (Haswell), 1762-1824.
Reuben and Rachel.
Boston, Manning & Loring for West, etc.,
1798. iv, 364 pp.
AAS copy.　　　34490

Rowson, Susanna (Haswell), 1762-1824.
Slaves in Algiers.
Philadelphia, Wrigley & Berriman, 1794.
[4], ii, 72, [2] pp.
AAS copy.　　　27655

[Rowson, Susanna (Haswell), 1762-1824.
Slaves in Algiers.
Boston, 1796.]
(Imprint assumed by Evans from advs.)
　　　31130

[Rowson, Susanna (Haswell), 1762-1824.
The Standard of Liberty.
Baltimore, 1795.]
(See Vail, Rowson, p. 70.)　　　29438

Rowson, Susanna (Haswell), 1762-1824.
Trials of the Human Heart. . . . In Four
Volumes.
Philadelphia, Wrigley & Berriman for
Rice, etc., 1795. xx, 156,; 156; 154;
172 pp.
AAS copy.　　　29439

Rowson, Susanna (Haswell), 1762-1824.
Truxton's Victory.
[Boston, Thomas & Andrews, 1799.]
2 pp.
AAS copy.　　　36248

Rowson, Susanna (Haswell), 1762-1824.
The Volunteers. A Musical
Entertainment.
Philadelphia, [1795]. pp. [1], 4-20.
(The Evans description came from advs.)
LOC copy.　　　29440

Roxbury, Mass. First Precinct.
An Address of Freeholders of the First
Precinct.
[Boston, 1773?] Broadside.
(No copy located.)　　　42495

Roxbury, Mass. First Precinct.
Whereas the Great and General Court . . .
12th January, 1773.
[Boston, 1773.] Broadside.
AAS copy.　　　42496

Roxbury Charitable Society.
Whereas in a State of Civil Society. . . .
Boston, Russell, 1794. Broadside.
MHS copy.　　　47208

The Royal Alphabet or a Child's best
Instructor. . . . First Worcester Edition.
Worcester, Thomas, 1787. 31 pp.
AAS copy.　　　20688

The Royal Alphabet.
Boston, Hall, 1793. 30, [1] pp.
CU copy.　　　46870

The Royal Alphabet, or, Child's Best
Instructor.
Boston, Hall, [1795]. 30 pp.
NYPL facs. copy.　　　29441

[The Royal Alphabet; or, Child's Best
Instructor.
Hudson, N. Y., Stoddard, 1795.]
(Imprint assumed by Evans from Stoddard
adv.)　　　29442

The Royal Alphabet.
Boston, Hall, 1798.
(Not located, 1968.)　　　46802

The Royal Convert: or, the Force of
Truth.
Boston, Hall, 1793. 68, [1] pp.
BPL copy.　　　26022

The Royal Convert, or, The Force of
Truth.
Brookfield, Mass., Merriam, 1800. 124 pp.
AAS copy.　　　38428

The Royal Primer Improved.
Philadelphia, Chattin, 1753. [96] pp.
(See Rosenbach 40. Evans' entry came
from Chattin's advs. The unique copy at
PPL is too fragile to reproduce.)　　　7114

[The Royal Primer.
Boston, M'Alpine, 1767.]
(From an adv., probably for copies of the
English 1767 ed.)　　　10761

The Royal Primer.
Boston, Boyles, 1770. 52 + pp.
(Only located copy is imperfect.)
PrU copy.　　　42166

The Royal Primer.
Boston, Mcalpine, 1773. [56] pp.
(The only copy located is incomplete.)
HEH copy.　　　12989

The Royal Primer.
Worcester, Thomas, 1787. 72 pp.
(The Evans entry came from a sale
catalogue.)
AAS copy.　　　18768

[The Royal Primer; or, an Esay and
Pleasant Guide to the Art of Reading.
Boston, Hall, 1795].
(Imprint assumed by Evans from Hall's
adv.)　　　29443

The Royal Primer.
Boston, Hall, 1796. 69 pp.
AAS copy.　　　31131

A Rub from Snub [by John Swanwick,
1740-1798].
Philadelphia, 1795. 80 pp.
AAS copy.　　　29594

Rubens, Peter Paul, pseud.
The Picture Exhibition.
Worcester, Thomas, 1788. 112, [7] pp.
AAS copy.　　　21392

Ruble, Johannes Casperus, 1719-1797.
(Weis, Clergy of the Middle Colonies.)
An Answer to Several Church Meetings.
New York, M'Lean, 1784. 19 pp.
NYHS copy.　　　18769

Ruddiman, Thomas, 1674-1757.
The Rudiments of the Latin Tongue.
Philadelphia, Aitken, 1776. 126 pp.
HSP copy.　　　15072

[Ruddiman, Thomas, 1674-1757.
The Rudiments of the Latin Tongue.
Newbern, 1778.]
("Just published," N.C. Gazette, Aug. 28,
1778.)　　　16063

Ruddiman, Thomas, 1674-1757.
The Rudiments of the Latin Tongue.
Philadelphia, Young, Stewart, &
M'Culloch, 1786. [2], 130 pp.
AAS copy.　　　19969

Ruddiman, Thomas, 1674-1757.
The Rudiments of the Latin Tongue.
Philadelphia, Bioren for Campbell, 1798.
[2], 130 pp.
JCB copy.　　　34491

Ruddock, Samuel Abial.
A Geographical View of All the Post
Towns in the United States.
[Boston, 1796.] Broadside.
MHS copy.　　　31132

[Ruddock, Samuel Abial.
A Geographical View of all the Post
Towns in the United States. . . . Also, the
Latitude and Longitude. . . .
Boston, Hall, White, and West, 1796.
Broadside.]
("Just Published," Columbian Centinel,
July 6, 1796.)　　　31133

[Ruddock, Samuel Abial.
Valuable Tables, for the Use of American
Merchants and Traders.
Boston, Hall, 1795. Broadside.]
(Entry from the copyright notice; imprint
assumed by Evans.)　　　29444

[Ruddock, Samuel Abial.
Valuable Tables.
Brookfield, Waldo, 1795. Broadside.]
(Imprint assumed by Evans from adv.
"Just published, and to be sold at the
store," in Moral and Political Telegraph,
May 20, 1795.)　　　29445

[Ruddock, Samuel Abial.
Valuable Tables.
Greenfield, Dickman, 1795. Broadside.]
(Imprint assumed by Evans from adv.
"Just published, and for sale at
Dickman's," in Greenfield Gazette, July
30, 1795.)　　　29446

[Ruddock, Samuel Abial.]
Valuable Tables.
Keene, N.H., Sturtevant, 1795. Broadside.
AAS copy.　　　47586

[Ruddock, Samuel Abial.
Valuable Tables.
Stockbridge, Andrews, 1795. Broadside.]
(Imprint assumed by Evans from adv.
"For sale at the Printing Office." in Western
Star, Dec. 15, 1795.)　　　29447

[Ruddock, Samuel Abial.
Valuable Tables.
Walpole, N.H., Thomas & Carlisle, 1795.
Broadside.]
(Imprint assumed by Evans from adv.)
　　　29448

[Ruddock, Samuel Abial.]
(Authorship from copyright notice.)
Valuable Tables.
Worcester, Thomas, 1795. Broadside.
AAS copy.　　　29449

[Ruddock, Samuel Abial.
Valuable Tables.
Litchfield, Ct., Collier, 1796.]
(Imprint assumed by Evans from Collier's
adv. "For Sale," Jan. 4, 1797.)　　　31134

[Ruddock, Samuel Abial.
Valuable Tables.
Newfield, Ct., Beach & Jones, 1796.]
(Imprint assumed by Evans from adv.
"For sale at this office" in Am.
Telegraphe, June 29, 1796.)　　　31135

[Ruddock, Samuel Abial.
Valuable Tables.
Norwich, Ct., Trumbull, 1796. Broadside.]
(Imprint assumed by Evans from adv.
"Just printed and for sale at Trumbull's
Printing-Office," Sept. 15, 1796.)　　　31136

[Ruddock, Samuel Abial.
Valuable Tables.
Rutland, Vt., Kirkaldie for Williams,
1796.]
(Imprint assumed by Evans from adv.
"Just Published, and now ready for sale at
the Printing Office," Rutland Herald,
Sept. 19, 1796.)　　　31137

[Ruddock, Samuel Abial]
Valuable Tables.
Windsor, Vt., 1796. Broadside.
VtHS (Rugg) copy. 31138

[Ruddock, Samuel Abiel.
Valuable Tables.
Putney, Vt., Sturtevant, 1797.]
(Imprint assumed by Evans from
Sturtevant's adv.) 32782

The Rudiments of Latin Prosody [by
James Otis, 1725-1783].
Boston, Mecom, 1760. 60, 72 pp.
AAS copy. 8701

The Rudiments of Latin Syntax and
Prosody [by Belcher Noyes, 1746-1791].
Salem, Hall, 1783. 51 pp.
AAS copy. 18072

Rudiments of Law and Government,
Deduced from the Law of Nature.
Charleston, 1783. 56 pp.
AAS copy. 18171

[Rudiments of Law and Government,
Deduced from the Law of Nature.
Charleston, Childs, Haswell & M'Iver,
1786.]
(Apparently from an adv. for a remainder
of 18171, q.v.) 19970

Rudiments of Reason; or, the Young
Experimental Philosopher.
New York, Berry, Rogers & Berry, 1793. 3
vol. xvi, 163; [2], 186; [2], 204, [20] pp.
AAS copy. 26109

Rudiments of Taste, in a Series of Letters
[by Mrs. Peddle].
Philadelphia, Spotswood, 1790. iv, 140 pp.
AAS copy. 22756

Rudiments of Taste [by Mrs. Peddle].
Chambersburg, Pa., Dover & Harper for
Carey, 1797. 52 pp.
AAS copy. 32643

Rudiments of Taste, in a Series of Letters
[by Mrs. Peddle].
Litchfield, Ct., Collier, [1799].
142 pp.
YC copy. 36053

[Rudman, Andrew], 1668-1708.
Naogra Andeliga Wisor.
[Philadelphia, Jansen, 1700?] 8 pp.
JCB copy. 39368

Eine Ruffende Wächter Stimme [by
Johannes Hildebrand, 1679-1765].
Germantown, 1747. 159 pp.
HSP copy. 5965

Ruggles, Edward, fl. 1789-1800.
Plan of the City Marietta.
[New London, 1789.] Map.
(The artist was probably Edward Ruggles
(b. 1763) of Pomfret.)
AAS copy. 22121

[Ruggles, Samuel]
To the Free Electors of the County of
Suffolk. . . . February 26, 1791.
[Boston, 1791.] Broadside.
MHS copy. 46276

Ruggles, Thomas, 1704-1770.
(Weis, Colonial Clergy N. E.)
The Death of Great . . . Men.
New Haven, 1763. 30 pp.
AAS copy. 9508

Ruggles, Thomas, 1704-1770.
(Dexter, I, 286-288.)
Ministerial Faithfulness.
New London, 1747. [4], 79 pp.
AAS copy. 6065

Ruggles, Thomas, 1704-1770.
The Right Improvement of Life.
New London, 1747. [6], 30 pp.
CHS copy. 6066

Ruggles, Thomas, 1704-1770.
(Dexter, I, 286-288.)
The Usefulness and Expedience of
Souldiers.
New London, 1737. [4], 26 pp.
AAS copy. 4193

The Rule of a new Creature [by Edward
Reyner, 1600-1668].
Boston, 1682. 15 pp.
(Mass. Hist. Soc., Proceedings, XLVI,
259.)
PPL copy. 333

The Rule of Life.
Springfield, Mass., Ashley & Brewer,
1800. 192 pp.
AAS copy. 38429

The Rule of the New-Creature to be
Practiced Every Day.
[Boston, 1742.] 24 pp.
BPL copy. 5049

Rules for the Society of Negroes, 1693 [by
Cotton Mather, 1663-1728].
[Boston, 1714.] Broadside.
(For the datint of this broadside see T. J.
Holmes, Cotton Mather, III, 935-937.)
NYPL copy. 653

The Rules of a Visit [by Cotton Mather,
1663-1728].
Boston, 1705. 40 pp.
YC copy. 1221

Rules of Arithmetic: Containing all the
Useful Tables in Money, Weights and
Measures.
Philadelphia, Humphreys, 1796. [2], 27,
[1] pp.
Western Reserve Hist. Soc. copy. 31139

Rules of Trial: or Half-way Convenant
Examined.
New London, [Green], 1770. 15 pp.
CHS copy. 11842

The Rules of Work of the Carpenters, in
the Town of Boston.
[Charlestown, Mass.], 1800. 34 pp.
(Also entered as 37003, q. v.) 38430

Rules, Maxims, and Observations, for the
Government . . . of an Army.
Norwich, Trumbull, [1777]. 26 pp.
AAS copy. 15588

Rulhière, Claude Carloman de,
1734-1791.
A History, or Anecdotes of the
Revolution in Russia.
Boston, Manning & Loring, for Nancrede,
1798. 195, [3] pp., 1 plate.
AAS copy. 34492

The Ruling & Ordaining Power [by
Thomas Foxcroft, 1697-1769].
Boston, Gerrish, 1724. [2], 45 pp.
AAS copy. 2531

Rum, Sir Richard, pseud.
See Indictment.

Rumford, Sir Benjamin Thompson, count,
1753-1814.
Essays, Political, Economical, and
Philosophical. . . . Vol. I.
Boston, Manning & Loring for West, etc.,
1798. xxiv, 464 pp., 7 plates.
AAS copy. 34656

Rumford, Sir Benjamin Thompson,
Count, 1753-1814.
Essays, Political, Economical, and
Philosophical. . . . Vol. II.
Boston, Manning & Loring for West, etc.,
1799. [18], 496 pp., 6 plates.
AAS copy. 36251

Rumsey, James, 1743-1792.
The Explanations, and Annexed
Plates. . . .
Philadelphia, James, 1788. 8, [4] pp., 3
plates.
APS copy. 21439

[Rumsey, James, 1743-1792.
A Plan, Wherein the Power of Steam is
Fully Shewn.
[Winchester, 1788.] 20, [2] pp.]
(No copy of such an edition could be
located.) 21440

Rumsey, James, 1743-1792.
Proposals for Forming a Company, to
Enable James Rumsey to Carry into
Execution. . . . his Steam-boat.
[Philadelphia? 1788.] Broadside.
LOC copy. 45352

Rumsey, James, 1743-1792.
A Short Treatise on the Application of
Steam. . . . By James Rumsey, of Berkeley
County.
Philadelphia, James, 1788. 26 pp.
NYPL copy. 21441

Rumsey, James, 1743-1792.
A Short Treatise on the Application of
Steam. . . . By James Rumsey, of Berkeley
County, Virginia.
Philadelphia, James, 1788. 26 pp.
AAS copy. 21442

Rumsey, James, 1743-1792.
A Short Treatise on the Application of
Steam. . . . By James Rumsey, of Berkeley
County, Virginia.
Philadelphia, James, 1788. 25 pp.
HEH copy. 45353

Rural Felicity, or, The History of Tommy
and Sally [by Richard Johnson,
1734-1793].
Philadelphia, Bailey, 1793. 31 pp.
(Present location unknown.) 46792

Rural Felicity [by Richard Johnson,
1734-1793].
New York, Oram, 1796. 29, [1] pp.
d'Alté A. Welch copy. 47819

[Rural Felicity, or History of Tommy and
Sally.
Boston, Folsom, 1798.]
(Imprint assumed by Evans from adv. in
33750: "New Books . . . Printed and Sold
Wholesale and Retail, by John W.
Folsom.") 34493

Rural Felicity [by Richard Johnson,
1734-1793].
Charlestown, Lamson, 1798. 31 pp.
d'Alte A. Welch copy. 48489

Rural Oeconomy. . . . Second Edition [by
Arthur Young, 1741-1820].
Philadelphia, Humphreys, 1776. 245,
[1] pp.
HSP copy. 15226

Rural Economy. . . . Third Edition [by
Arthur Young, 1741-1820].
Burlington, Neale, 1792. 299, [1] pp.
AAS copy. 25061

The Rural Socrates [by Hans Caspar
Hirzel, 1725-1803].
Hallowell, Me., Edes, 1800. xii, [4], 203,
xiii pp.
AAS copy. 38923

Rush, Benjamin, 1745-1813.
An Account of the Bilious Remitting
Yellow Fever.
Philadelphia, Dobson, 1794. x, 363 pp.
AAS copy. 27658

Rush, Benjamin, 1745-1813.
An Account of the Bilious Remitting
Yellow Fever. . . . Second Edition.
Philadelphia, Dobson, 1794. x, 363 pp.
AAS copy. 27659

Rush, Benjamin, 1745-1813.
[An Account of the Causes of longevity.
Philadelphia, 1793.]
(Goodman p. 382. No copy known.) 46871

Rush, Benjamin, 1745-1813.
[An account of the climate of
Pennsylvania.
Philadelphia, 1789.]
(Goodman, p. 382; no copy located.)
45580

Rush, Benjamin, 1745-1813.
An Account of the Sugar Maple-Tree.
Philadelphia, Aitken, 1792. 16 pp.
JCB copy. 24761

[Rush, Benjamin], 1745-1813.
An Address to the Inhabitants of the
British Settlements in America, upon
Slave-Keeping.
Boston, Boyles for Langdon, 1773. [2],
30 pp.
AAS copy. 12991

[Rush, Benjamin], 1745-1813.
An Address to the Inhabitants of the
British Settlements in America, upon
Slave-Keeping.

New York, Hodge & Shober, 1773. 36 pp.
WLC copy.   12992

[Rush, Benjamin], 1745-1813.
An Address to the Inhabitants of the
British Settlements in America, upon
Slave-Keeping.
Philadelphia, Dunlap, 1773. [2], 30 pp.
AAS copy.   12990

[Rush, Benjamin], 1745-1813.
An Address to the Inhabitants of the
British Settlements, on the Slavery of the
Negroes. The Second Edition.
Philadelphia, Dunlap, 1773. [2], 28, [2],
54 pp.
HC copy.   12993

[Rush, Benjamin], 1745-1813.
An Address to the Inhabitants of the
British Settlements in America, upon
Slave-Keeping. . . . Second Edition.
Philadelphia, Dunlap, 1773. [2], 28, [2],
54 pp.
JCB copy.   12994

[Rush, Benjamin], 1745-1813.
An Address to the Inhabitants of the
British Colonies in America, upon
Slave-Keeping.
Norwich, Spooner, 1775. 24 pp.
BA copy.   14447

Rush, Benjamin, 1745-1813.
Considerations on the Injustice and
Impolicy of Punishing Murder by Death.
Philadelphia, Carey, 1792. 19 pp.
NYHS copy.   24762

[Rush, Benjamin], 1745-1813.
Considerations upon the Present
Test-Law.
Philadelphia, Hall & Sellers, 1784. 23 pp.
AAS copy.   18770

[Rush, Benjamin], 1745-1813.
Considerations upon the Present Test
Law. . . . Second Edition.
Philadelphia, Hall & Sellers, 1785. 23 pp.
NYPL copy.   19230

Rush, Benjamin, 1745-1813.
Directions. As soon as you are
Affected. . . . September 10, 1793.
[Philadelphia, 1793.] Broadside.
(Not located, 1968.)   46872

[Rush, Benjamin], 1745-1813.
Directions for Preserving the Health of
Soldiers.
n.p., [1777?] Broadside.
CHS copy.   43370

[Rush, Benjamin], 1745-1813.
Directions for Preserving the Health of
Soldiers.
[Philadelphia, 1777.] 14 pp.]
(This entry describes a fragment of
Cutbush, Observations, 1808, in the
NLM.)   16065

Rush, Benjamin, 1745-1813.
Directions for Preserving the Health of
Soldiers.
Lancaster, 1778. 8 pp.
AAS copy.   16064

Rush, Benjamin, 1745-1813.
Directions for the Use of the Mineral
Water and Cold Bath, at Harrogate.
Philadelphia, Steiner, 1786. 12 pp.
LCP copy.   19971

[Rush, Benjamin], 1745-1813.
An Enquiry into the Effects of Public
Punishments.
Philadelphia, James, 1787. 18 pp.
AAS copy.   20689

Rush, Benjamin, 1745-1813.
An Inquiry into the Effects of Spirituous
Liquors.
Philadelphia, Bradford, [1784?]. 11 pp.
NLM copy.   22865

Rush, Benjamin, 1745-1813.
An Enquiry into the Effects of Spirituous
Liquors.
Philadelphia, Bradford, [1786]. 11 pp.
National Library of Medicine copy. 44963

Rush, Benjamin, 1745-1813.
An Enquiry into the Effects of Spirituous

Liquors. . . . Second Edition.
Philadelphia, Dobson, [1787]. 16 pp.
HC copy.   20690

Rush, Benjamin, 1745-1813.
An Inquiry into the Effects of Spirituous
Liquors.
Boston, Thomas & Andrews, 1790. 12 pp.
AAS copy.   22864

Rush, Benjamin, 1745-1813.
An Enquiry into the Effects of Spirituous
Liquors . . . Third Edition.
Philadelphia, M'Culloch, 1791. 12 pp.
NLM copy.   46277

Rush, Benjamin, 1745-1813.
An Enquiry into the Origin of the late
Epidemic Fever.
Philadelphia, Carey, 1793. 15 pp.
National Library of Medicine copy.   26111

Rush, Benjamin, 1745-1813.
Essays, Literary, Moral & Philosophical.
Philadelphia, Bradfords, 1798. [8],
378 pp.
AAS copy.   34495

[Rush, Benjamin, 1745-1813.
An Eulogeum in Honor of . . . Dr. William
Cullen.
New York, Durell, 1790.]
(A ghost of 22862.)   22863

Rush, Benjamin, 1745-1813.
An Eulogium in Honor of . . . Dr. William
Cullen.
Philadelphia, Dobson, 1790. 30, [1] pp.
AAS copy.   22862

Rush, Benjamin, 1745-1813.
An Eulogium . . . of David Rittenhouse.
Philadelphia, Ormrod & Conrad for J.
Ormrod, [1796]. 46 pp.
AAS copy.   31143

Rush, Benjamin, 1745-1813.
Experiments and Observations on the
Mineral Waters.
Philadelphia, Humphreys, 1773. 30 pp.
AAS copy.   12995

[Rush, Benjamin], 1745-1813.
An Inquiry into the Natural History of
Medicine.
Philadelphia, Pritchard & Hall, 1789.
56 pp.]
(No copy of a separate printing of this
item could be found. The recorded copies
were the first part of 22123, q. v.)   22122

Rush, Benjamin, 1745-1813.
. . . Letter from Doctor Benjamin Rush
. . . to Mr. Finly of York County.
[Philadelphia? 1766?] [2] pp.
AAS copy.   41657

Rush, Benjamin, 1745-1813.
Medical Inquiries and Observations.
Philadelphia, Pritchard & Hall, 1789. 206,
39 pp.
AAS copy.   22123

Rush, Benjamin, 1745-1813.
Medical Inquiries and Observations. . . .
Volume II.
Philadelphia, Dobson, 1793. [4], iv, 321,
[2] pp.
AAS copy.   26112

Rush, Benjamin, 1745-1813.
Medical Inquiries and Observations. . . .
Volume I.
Philadelphia, Dobson, 1794. 338 pp.
AAS copy.   27660

Rush, Benjamin, 1745-1813.
Medical Inquiries and Observations. . . .
Volume IV.
Philadelphia, Dobson, 1796. pp. [1]-vii,
[2], viii-ix, [1], [1]-258.
AAS copy.   31144

Rush, Benjamin, 1745-1813.
Medical Inquiries and Observations. . . .
Volume II.
Philadelphia, Dobson, 1797. vii, [1], 322,
[2] pp.
LCP copy.   32784

Rush, Benjamin, 1745-1813.
Medical Inquiries and Observations. . . .
Volume V.

Philadelphia, Budd and Bartram for
Dobson, 1798. xii, 236 pp.
AAS copy.   34496

Rush, Benjamin, 1745-1813.
The New Method of Inoculating for the
Small Pox.
Philadelphia, Cist, 1781. 28 pp.
LOC copy.   17362

[Rush, Benjamin], 1745-1813.
The New Method of Innoculating for the
Small-Pox. . . . 20th of February, 1791. . . .
Third Edition.
Philadelphia, Hall, 1791. 26 pp.]
(A ghost of 46565.)   46278

Rush, Benjamin, 1745-1813.
The New Method of Inoculating for the
Small-pox. . . . Third Edition.
Philadelphia, Hall 1792. 26, [1] pp.
HSP copy.   46565

Rush, Benjamin, 1745-1813.
Observations on the Duties of a Physician.
Philadelphia, Prichard & Hall, 1789. 11
pp.
APS copy.   45581

Rush, Benjamin, 1745-1813.
Observations upon the Cause and Cure of
the Tetanus.
[Philadelphia, 1785.] 14 pp.
(This misbound copy is apparently the one
described by Evans.)
BM copy.   19231

Rush, Benjamin, 1745-1813.
Observations upon the Origin of . . .
Yellow Fever.
Philadelphia, Budd & Bartram for
Dobson, 1799. 28 pp.
AAS copy.   36253

[Rush, Benjamin], 1745-1813.
Observations upon the Present
Government of Pennsylvania.
Philadelphia, Steiner & Cist, 1777. 24 pp.
JCB copy.   15589

[Rush, Benjamin], 1745-1813.
Observations upon the Present
Government.
Philadelphia, Cist, 1783.]
(Adv. Pa. Gazette, Dec. 31. 1783.)   18172

Rush, Benjamin, 1745-1813.
An Oration, Delivered before the
American Philosophical Society . . . on
the 27th of February, 1786.
Philadelphia, Cist, 1786. [8], 40 pp.
AAS copy.   19972

[Rush, Benjamin], 1745-1813.
An Oration Delivered before the
American Philosophical Society . . . the
27th of February, 1786. . . . Second
Edition.
Philadelphia, Cist, 1786.]
(No copy located has the words "second
edition.")   19973

Rush, Benjamin, 1745-1813.
An Oration, Delivered February 4, 1774.
Philadelphia, Crukshank, [1774]. 118 pp.
LCP copy.   13592

[Rush, Benjamin], 1745-1813.
A Plan for the Establishment of Public
Schools.
Philadelphia, Dobson, 1786. 36 pp.
BA copy.   19974

Rush, Benjamin, 1745-1813.
A Report of an Action for a Libel,
Brought . . . against William Cobbett.
Philadelphia, Woodward, 1800. [70] pp.
(Also entered as 37103, q. v.)   38433

Rush, Benjamin, 1745-1813.
A Second Address to the Citizens of
Philadelphia.
Philadelphia, Budd & Bartram for
Dobson, 1799. 40 pp.
UOP copy.   36254

[Rush, Benjamin], 1745-1813.
Sermons to Gentlemen upon Temperance.
Philadelphia, Dunlap, 1772. 44 pp.
LOC copy.   12547

[Rush, Benjamin], 1745-1813.

Syllabus of a Course of Lectures on Chemistry.
Philadelphia, 1770.] 48 pp.
AAS facsimile copy.   42167

Rush, Benjamin, 1745-1813.
A Syllabus of a Course of Lectures on Chemistry.
Philadelphia, Aitken, [1774]. 40 pp.
(The unique original could not be reproduced.)   42692

Rush, Benjamin, 1745-1813.
A Syllabus of a Course of Lectures on Chemistry.
Philadelphia, Cist, 1783. 39 pp., 1 folded leaf.
APS copy.   18173

Rush, Benjamin, 1745-1813.
A Syllabus of a Course of Lectures.
Philadelphia, Hall, 1792. 8 pp.
AAS copy.   46566

Rush, Benjamin, 1745-1813.
A Syllabus of a Course of Lectures on . . . Medicine.
Philadelphia, Bradford, 1795. 15 pp.
LCP copy.   47587

Rush, Benjamin, 1745-1813.
A Syllabus of a Course of Lectures on . . . Medicine.
Philadelphia, Bradfords, 1798. 19 pp.
AAS copy.   34497

Rush, Benjamin, 1745-1813.
Syllabus of Lectures . . . of Natural Philosophy.
Philadelphia, Brown, 1787. vi pp.
LCP copy.   45160

Rush, Benjamin, 1745-1813.
Thoughts upon Female Education.
Boston, Hall, 1787. 30 pp.
AAS copy.   20692

Rush, Benjamin, 1745-1813.
Thoughts upon Female Education.
Philadelphia, Prichard & Hall, 1787. 32 pp.
AAS copy.   20691

Rush, Benjamin, 1745-1813.
Thoughts upon Female Education.
Boston, Folsom for Brewer, 1791. 24 pp.
(Also issued bound with 23790, q.v.) 23747

Rush, Benjamin, 1745-1813.
Thoughts upon the Amusements.
[Philadelphia, 1790.] 8 pp.
LCP copy.   22866

Rush, Benjamin, 1745-1813.
Three Lectures upon Animal Life.
Philadelphia, Budd & Bartram for Dobson, 1799. viii, 84 pp.
AAS copy.   36255

Rush, Jacob, 1746-1820.
An Address, Delivered July 8th, 1790.
Philadelphia, Young, 1791. 38 pp.
LCP copy.   23748

[Rush, Jacob, 1746-1820.
A Charge Delivered . . . 30th June, 1798.
Philadelphia, 1798.]
(Entry from Sabin 74249.)   34498

The Rush-Light.
(Omitted, as a periodical.)   38434

Rushton, Edward, 1756-1814.
[Expostulatory Letter to George Washington.
Lexington, 1792.]
(McMurtrie: Ky 19; no copy known.)
                                              46567

Rushton, Edward, 1756-1814.
Expostulatory Letter to George Washington.
Lexington, Ky., Bradford, 1797. 16 pp.
NYPL copy.   32785

Rushton, Edward, 1756-1814.
Expostulatory Letter to George Washington.
[New York? 1797.] Broadside.
NYPL copy.   32786

[Russ, D.
The Urian Harmony.

Philadelphia, M'Culloch, 1791. 76 + pp.]
(Adv. in Carlisle Gazette, Aug. 3, 1791.)
                                              23749

[Russell, Benjamin, 1761-1845.
A New Wonder of Wonders, or the Wonderful Appearance of a Devil and Ghost.
Boston, Russell, 1784.]
("This Day Published, Adorn'd with a striking Likeness of his Infernal Majesty, and the Ghost of a Departed Hero", Independent Chronicle, Feb. 19, 1784. See note in Evans under 18771.)   18771

[Russell, Daniel], 1642-1679.
(Sibley, II, 284-287.)
. . . An Almanack . . . for . . . 1671.
Cambridge, 1671. [16] pp.
AAS copy.   164

Russell, Edward, 1653-1727.
(D. N. B.)
Admiral Russel's Letter.
Boston, 1692. 4 pp.
HC copy.   629

Russell, Ezekiel, 1743-1796.
This Day is Published . . . Diana's Shrines.
[Boston? 1773?] Broadside.
AAS copy.   42497

[Russell, Ezekiel], 1743-1796.
. . . Elegy, &c. Fair Daughter of America.
[Boston, Russell, 1786.] Broadside.
AAS copy.   44964

Russell, John, & Co., Boston.
Prospectus of the Nightingale.
[Boston, 1796.] 12 pp.
AAS copy.   30907

Russell, John Miller, 1768-1840.
A Funeral Oration on . . . Washington.
Boston, Russell for Nancrede, 1800. 22 pp.
AAS copy.   38435

Russell, John Miller, 1768-1840.
An Oration Pronounced at Charlestown, July 4, 1797.
Charlestown, Mass., Lamson, [1797]. 16 pp.
AAS copy.   32790

Russell, John Miller, 1768-1840.
An Oration, Pronounced at Charlestown, July 4, 1797. . . . Second Edition.
Philadelphia, Cobbett, 1797. 15 pp.
MHS copy.   32791

Russell, John Miller, 1768-1840.
The Pastoral Songs of P. Virgil Maro.
Boston, Manning & Loring, 1799. 92 pp.
(Also entered as 36625, q. v.)   36256

Russell, John Miller, 1768-1840.
A Poem, on the Fourth of July, 1798.
Boston, Manning & Loring, 1798. 16 pp.
AAS copy.   34500

Russell, Jonathan, 1655-1711.
(Sibley, II, 455-457.)
A Plea for the Righteousness of God.
Boston, 1704. [2], 25 pp.
AAS copy.   1193

Russell, Jonathan, 1771-1832.
An Oration, Pronounced in the Baptist Meeting-House.
Providence, Wheeler, 1800. 23 pp.
AAS copy.   38436

Russell, Jonathan, 1771-1832.
An Oration, Pronounced July 4th, 1800.
Warren, R. I., Phillips, 1800. 38 pp.
AAS copy.   38437

[Russell, Jonathan], 1771-1832.
To the Freemen of Rhode-Island, &c.
[Providence, 1800.] 16 pp.
LOC copy.   38438

Russell, Jonathan, 1771-1832.
A Tribute to the Memory of Nathan Hayward.
Providence, Wheeler, 1790. 14 pp.
BA copy.   22867

Russell, Joseph, 1775-1861.
An Oration; Pronounced in Princeton.
Worcester, Mass., Thomas, 1799. 29 pp.
AAS copy.   36257

Russell, Joseph, 1775-1861.
A Sermon Preached at Princeton (Massachusetts) April 8th, 1798.
Boston, Rhoades & Laughton, 1798. 26 pp.
AAS copy.   34501

Russell, Noadiah, 1659-1713.
(Sibley, III, 216-222.)
. . . Cambridge Ephemeris. An Almanack . . . for . . . 1684.
Cambridge, 1684. [16] pp.
MHS copy.   376

Russell, Robert, of Wadhurst, Sussex.
A Sermon on the Unpardonable Sin. . . . Seventieth Edition.
Bennington, Vt., Haswell & Russell, 1789. 23 pp.
VtU (W) copy.   45582

Russell, Robert, of Wadhurst, Sussex.
Seven Sermons.
Boston, 1701. [4], 248 pp.
AAS copy.   1021

Russell, Robert, of Wadhurst, Sussex.
Seven Sermons. . . . Sixth Edition.
Boston, B. Green for Buttolph, 1705. [4], 185 pp.
AAS copy.   39433

Russell, Robert, of Wadhurst, Sussex.
Seven Sermons. . . . Sixth Edition.
Boston, Allen for Buttolph, 1709. 172 pp.
AAS copy.   39495

Russell, Robert, of Wadhurst, Sussex.
Seven Sermons. . . . Eleventh Edition.
Boston, Allen for Eliot, 1718. 178 pp.
AAS copy.   39691

Russell, Robert, of Wadhurst, Sussex.
Seven Sermons.
Boston, Butler, 1727. 202 pp.
BPL copy.   2953

[Russell, Robert, of Wadhurst, Sussex.
Seven Sermons.
Boston, 1728.]
(Title from Haven.)   3101

Russell, Robert, of Wadhurst, Sussex.
Seven Sermons. . . . Fifty-First Edition.
Philadelphia, Steuart, 1763. 164, [4] pp.
AAS copy.   41412

[Russell, Robert, of Wadhurst, Sussex.
Seven Sermons. . . . Fiftieth Edition.
New York, Gaine, 1766. [4], 141, [3] pp.]
(The unique copy at NYPL could not be filmed.)   10484

Russell, Robert, of Wadhurst, Sussex.
Seven Sermons. . . . Fifty-Second Edition.
Philadelphia, Dunlap, 1766. 172 pp.
HSP copy.   10485

Russell, Robert, of Wadhurst, Sussex.
Seven Interesting Sermons. . . . Fiftieth Edition.
Boston, M'Alpine, 1767. 146, [1] pp.
AAS copy.   10763

Russell, Robert, of Wadhurst, Sussex.
Seven Sermons. . . . Forty-Sixth Edition.
Portsmouth, 1767. [4], 148 pp.
AAS copy.   10762

Russell, Robert, of Wadhurst, Sussex.
Seven Sermons. . . . Fiftieth Edition.
Boston, Thomas, 1772. 168 pp.
AAS copy.   12548

Russell, Robert, of Wadhurst, Sussex.
Seven Sermons. . . . Fiftieth Edition.
Boston, Thomas for Langdon, [1772]. 168 pp.
(For the text see 12548.)
AAS copy.   12549

Russell, Robert, of Wadhurst, Sussex.
Seven Sermons. . . . Fifty-First Edition.
Boston, Boyle, 1774. 132 pp.
AAS copy.   13593

Russell, Robert, of Wadhurst, Sussex.
Seven Sermons.
Boston, Fleets, 1784. 158 pp.
AAS copy.   18772

Russell, Robert, of Wadhurst, Sussex.
Seven Sermons.

Philadelphia, Stewart, 1788. 119,
[1] pp.
AAS copy.   21443

Russell, Robert, of Wadhurst, Sussex.
Sermons, on Different Important Subjects.
Baltimore, Adamses for Weems, 1791.
112 pp.
AAS copy.   46279

Russell, Robert, of Wadhurst, Sussex.
Seven Sermons.
New York, Durell, 1791. 156 pp.
(The only known copy cannot be
reproduced.)
NYPL copy.   46280

[Russell, Robert, of Wadhurst, Sussex.
Seven Sermons.
Baltimore, Graham, 1792?]
(Imprint assumed by Evans from an adv.)
                                   24763

Russell, Robert, of Wadhurst, Sussex.
Seven Sermons. . . . New Edition.
New York, Campbell, 1793. pp. [1]-24,
37-120.
NYPL copy.   26114

Russell, Robert, of Wadhurst, Sussex.
Seven Sermons.
New York, Durell, 1793. 156 pp.
AAS copy.   26115

Russell, Robert, of Wadhurst, Sussex.
Seven Sermons. . . . Fifty-Second Edition.
New York, Gaine, 1793. 143, [1] pp.
AAS copy.   26113

[Russell, Robert, of Wadhurst, Sussex.
Seven Sermons.
Philadelphia, Carey, 1793.]
(A Carey ed. assumed by Evans from
advs.)   26116

Russell, Robert, of Wadhurst, Sussex.
Seven Sermons.
Philadelphia, Carey, 1795. 144 pp.
(An imprint variant of 47588 q. v.)
AAS copy.   47589

Russell, Robert, of Wadhurst, Sussex.
Seven Sermons. . . . Sixty-Second Edition.
Philadelphia, Folwell for Campbell, 1795.
84 pp.
AAS copy.   29452

Russell, Robert, of Wadhurst, Sussex.
Seven Sermons.
Philadelphia, H. & P. Rice, 1795.
144 pp.
AAS copy.   47588

Russell, Robert, of Wadhurst, Sussex.
Seven Sermons.
Leominster, Mass., Prentiss for Thomas,
1797. 152 pp.
AAS copy.   32787

[Russell, Robert, of Wadhurst, Sussex.
Seven Sermons.
Wilmington, Del., Brynberg, 1797.]
(Imprint assumed by Evans from
Brynberg's adv.)   32788

Russell, Robert, of Wadhurst, Sussex.
Seven Sermons.
New Haven, Bunce, 1798. 144 pp.
AAS copy.   34499

Russell, Robert, of Wadhurst, Sussex.
Seven Sermons.
Suffield, Gray for Divier, [1799?].
144 pp.
CHS copy.   48958

[Russell, Samuel, 1660-1731.
(Sibley, III, 236-238.)
Connecticut Election Sermon.
Boston, 1699.]

(There is no reason to think that this
sermon was ever printed.)   895

Russell, Samuel, 1693-1746.
(Dexter, I, 107-108.)
Man's Liableness to be Deceiv'd.
New London, 1742. [2], 52 pp.
AAS copy.   5050

Russell, Samuel, fl. 1795.
Statement of Snuff and Tobacco
Manufacturers. . . . Dec. 7, 1795.
[Philadelphia, 1795.] Broadside.
(Not located, 1968.)   47590

Russell, William, 1690-1761.
(Dexter, I, 90-91.)
The Decay of Love.
New London, 1731. [4], 48 pp.
AAS copy.   3473

Russell, William, 1690-1761.
The Duty of an Army of Professing
Christians.
New London, 1760. 22, [2] pp.
CHS copy.   8729

[Russell, William], 1741-1793.
The History of Modern Europe. . . . Vol. I
[-IV].
Philadelphia, Maxwell for Birch and
Small, 1800.
[40], 496; [32], 467; [36], 475; [40], 452
pp.
AAS copy.   38439

[Russell & Clap's Auction Room, Boston.
Catalogue of the Library of Benjamin
Lincoln, Jr.
Boston, 1788.]
(Evans, from a notice of the sale.) 21204

Russell & Clap's Auction Room, Boston.
On Tuesday Morning, 16th October . . .
will be sold . . . the following Collection of
Books. . . .
[Boston, 1792]. Broadside.
MHS copy.   46568

Russell's American Almanack, for . . .
1782 [by Benjamin West, 1730-1813].
Boston, Russell. [24] pp.
AAS copy.   17434

Russell's Newhampshire & Vermont
Almanack, for . . . 1793.
Concord, Russell. [24] pp.
AAS copy.   24764

Russell's Newhampshire & Vermont
Almanack, for . . . 1794.
Concord, N.H., Russell. [32] pp.
AAS copy.   26117

Ruston, Thomas.
[An Essay on Inoculation.
Philadelphia, Bradfords, 1767.]
("Just published," Pa. Journal, Sept. 3,
1767.)   41764

Rutgers, Elizabeth (Benson), plaintiff.
Arguments and Judgment of the Mayor's
Court of the City of New-York, in a Cause
between Elizabeth Rutgers and Joshua
Waddington.
New York, Loudon, 1784. 47 pp.
NYPL copy.   18773

Rutgers, H.G., & Co.
Catalogue of Books, for Sale . . .
December 1st.
New York, Collins, [1798]. Broadside.
NYPL copy.   48603

Rutgers, H. G., & Co.
Catalogue of Books, for Sale . . . January
12th.
[New York, 1799.] Broadside.
NYPL copy.   35946

[Rutgers, H. G., & Co.
A Large Assignment of Valuable Books,

per the Fair American. . . . Sold at their
Auction Room, New York, Apr. 26,
1799.] Broadside?]
(McKay 142F.)   35947

[Rutgers, H. G., & Co.
A Large Catalogue of Books, Comprising
a General Assortment, Handsomely
Bound. Feb. 9, 1799.]
(McKay 142B.)   35948

Rutgers University.
Charter of a College to be Erected in
New-Jersey, by the Name of Queen's
College.
New York, Holt, 1770. 8 pp.
NYPL facsim. copy.   42168

Ruth, William.
Twenty-Five Dollars Reward. . . . Aug. 19,
1799.
New Castle, S. & J. Adams, [1799].
Broadside.
LCP copy.   48959

Rutherforth, Thomas, 1712-1771.
Institutes of Natural Law. . . . Vol. I
[-II].
Whitehall, Pa., Young, 1799. pp. [2],
[1]-474; [10], [13]-654.
AAS copy.   36260

Rutland County, Vt. Citizens.
To the Representatives of the Freemen of
the United States of America; in Congress
Assembled. . . . January, 1799.
[Rutland, 1799.] Broadside.
AAS copy.   36434

Rutland County, Vt. Freemen.
To the Representatives of the Freemen of
the United States of America. . . .
January, 1799.
n. p., [1799]. Broadside.
(Also entered as 36434, q. v.)   36261

Rutty, John, 1698-1775.
(D. N. B.)
The Liberty of the Spirit.
Philadelphia, Franklin & Hall, 1759. 64
pp.
AAS copy.   8486

Ryan, James, fl. 1779.
A Pedantic Pedagogue.
[Baltimore, 1779.] Broadside.
AAS copy.   16513

[Rycaut, Sir Paul], 1628-1700.
The Counterfeit Messiah.
Keene, Sturtevant for Taylor, 1795.
36 pp.
JCB copy.   29454

[Rycaut, Sir Paul, 1628-1700.
The Counterfeit Messiah.
Putney, Vt., Sturtevant, 1797. 36 pp.]
(Adv. in The Argus, Mar. 30, 1797.)
Probably a remainder of 29454, q. v.)
                                   32793

Ryer, John, 1759-1793.
Narrative of the Life, and Dying Speech
of. . . .
Danbury, Douglas, 1793. 15 pp.
AAS copy.   46873

Ryer, John 1759-1793.
Narrative of the Life and Dying Speech of
. . . October 2d, 1793.
[Poughkeepsie?] for the Flying
Stationers, [1793]. 24 pp.
JCB copy.   26118

Ryther, John, 1634?-1681.
(D. N. B.)
[The Best Friend.
Boston, 1721.] 180 pp.
(The only known copy is defective.)
AAS copy.   2289

S

Sackett, Nathaniel.
A Memorial, &c. . . . [September 27, 1785].
New York, Kollock, 1785. 11, [1] pp., 1 map.
NYPL copy.   19232

Sacred Concert. . . . June 11, 1800.
n. p., n. d. Broadside.
(Also entered as 38108, q. v.)   38444

Sacred Dirges, Hymns, and Anthems [by Oliver Holden, 1765-1831].
Boston, Thomas & Andrews, [1800]. 24, 4 pp., printed wrappers.
AAS copy.   37635

The Sacred Minister: a New Poem [by Samuel Mather, 1706-1785].
Boston, Boyles, 1773. 22, [1] pp.
AAS copy.   12864

Sacred Music, to be Performed in St. Paul's Church.
[New York, 1799.] Broadside.
(Also entered under 35951, q. v.)   36264

Sacred to the Memory of Mr. Ebenezer Jenckes. . . . Died at . . . St. Thomas . . . April 26, 1799.
[Providence, R. I., 1799.] Broadside.
AAS copy.   36265

Sacred to the Memory of Mrs. Ann Brown. . . . June 16, 1798.
[Providence, 1796.] Broadside.
AAS ph. copy.   48604

The Sad Effects of Sin [Cotton Mather, 1663-1728].
Boston, 1713. [2], xiv, [4], 64, 34 pp.
AAS copy.   1626

The Sad Estate of the Unconverted.
Boston, Kneeland & Green, 1736. [4], 50 pp.
YC copy.   4076

[A Safe Conduct through the Territories of the Republic of Venus.
Philadelphia, 1795.]
(Entry from adv. "Just Published in Philadelphia" in N. Y. Ev. Post, Mar. 16, 1795.)   29458

Saffin, John, 1632-1710.
A Brief and Candid Answer.
Boston, 1701. [2], 12 + pp.
NYHS copy.   1022

Sage, Sylvester, 1765-1841.
A Sermon, Delivered at the Installation of Rev. Jesse Townsend.
Catskill, N. Y., Croswell, [1798].
24 pp.
AAS copy.   34507

Sagittarius's Letters [by John Mein, fl. 1760-1775].
Boston, 1775. [2], 127 pp.
AAS copy.   14255

[Saige, Joseph], 1735-1812.
The Manual of a Free Man.
Richmond, Va., Dixon, 1799. 108, [1] pp.
AAS copy.   35767

The Sailor Boy [by Prince Hoare, 1755-1834].
[Philadelphia, Carr, 1793]. [2] pp.
AAS copy.   25613

A Sailor Lov'd a Lass. Composed by S. Storace for the Cherokee [by James Cobb, 1756-1818].
Philadelphia, B. Carr for Street and J. Carr, [1796]. [2] pp.
AAS copy.   30203

The Sailor, who had Served in the Slave Trade.
New Bedford, [1798?]. Broadside.
AAS copy.   48605

The Sailor's Medley. A Collection of the Most Admired Sea and Other Songs.
Philadelphia, Carey, 1800. front., 72 pp.
BrU copy.   38447

The Sailours Companion and Counsellour [by Cotton Mather, 1663-1728].
Boston, 1709. [2], 62 pp.
AAS copy.   1406

St. Aivre, Mr.
Arrangement of the Performance . . . Second Exhibition.
[New York], Childs & Swaine, [1791].
Broadside.
NYHS copy.   46281

St. Andre, Jean Bon.
A Summary Journal of the Cruise.
Philadelphia, 1794. 32 pp.
LOC copy.   27664

St. Andrew's Society of Philadelphia.
The Constitution and Rules of. . . .
Philadelphia, Hall & Sellers, 1769.
19 pp.
UOP copy.   11416

St. Andrew's Society of Philadelphia.
The Constitution and Rules of. . . .
Philadelphia, Hall & Sellers, 1791. [2], ii, 12 pp.
HSP copy.   23698

St. Andrew's Society of the State of New York.
At a Quarterly Meeting . . . the 15th Day of May, 1794.
[New York, 1794.] Broadside.
(Not located, 1968.)   47209

St Andrew's Society of the State of New York.
Rules for the St. Andrew's Society in New-York.
New York, Gaine, 1770. 15 pp.
NYHS copy.   11777

St. Andrew's Society of the State of New York.
Rules for the St. Andrew's Society.
New York, M'Lean, 1785. 14, [2] pp.
NYHS copy.   19135

Saint Aubin, Stéphanie Félicité Ducrest de, comtesse de Genlis, 1746-1830.
Hagar in the Desert.
Newburyport, Mycall, [1790?]. 24 pp.
BrU copy.   22547

St. Augustine Church Lottery.
Scheme of a Lottery, for the Purpose of Completing. . . . May 15, 1799.
[Philadelphia, 1799.] Broadside.
HSP copy.   48960

St. Cecilia Society, New York.
Constitution and Bye Laws of the. . . .
Adopted 7th January 1797.

New York, Harrisson, 1797. 8 pp.
(Best copy available)
NYHS copy.   48245

St. Clair, Arthur, 1734-1818, defendant.
Proceedings of a General Court Martial.
Philadelphia, Hall & Sellers, 1778. 52 pp., map.
AAS copy.   16141

Saint Clair's Defeat.
The Fourth Day of November. . . .
n. p., 1791? Broadside.
(Not located, 1968.)   46282

. . . Saint George's Day. Verses.
[Philadelphia], Poulson, Apr. 23, 1780.
Broadside.
NYHS copy.   43892

St. Hubert; or, Mistaken Friendship.
District of Columbia, Wood, 1800.
36 pp.
NYPL copy.   38448

[St. John, Henry, Viscount Bolingbroke], 1678-1751.
The Freeholder's Political Catechism.
[Boston? 1757.] [2], 33 pp.
BA copy.   8030

[St. John, Henry, Viscount Bolingbroke], 1678-1751.
The Freeholder's Political Catechism.
New London, 1769. 23 pp.
LOC copy.   11450

[St. John, Henry, Viscount Bolingbroke], 1678-1751.
Letters on the Spirit of Patriotism.
Philadelphia, Franklin & Hall, 1749. 86, [2] pp.
LCP copy.   6412

[St. John, Henry, Viscount Bolingbroke, 1678-1751.
Letters on the Spirit of Patriotism.
New York, Parker & Weyman, 1756.]
(From an adv.)   7786

St. John, J. Hector, pseud.
Letters from an American Farmer [by Michel Guillaume St. Jean de Crèvecoeur, 1735-1813].
Philadelphia, Carey, 1793. 240 pp.
AAS copy.   25357

St. John, J. Hector, pseud.
Letters from an American Farmer [by Michel Guillaume St. Jean de Crèvecoeur, 1735-1813].
Philadelphia, 1798. 260 pp.
(Entry from Sabin 17496).   33582

St. John, Peter, 1726-1811.
The Death of Abel.
Danbury, Douglas, 1793. pp. [4], [13]-186, [2].
AAS copy.   26120

St. John, Peter, 1726-1811.
A Dialogue between Flesh and Spirit.
[New York? 1768?] Broadside.
NYPL copy.   41877

[St. John, Peter, 1726-1811.
Poetical Relation of the Capture of the Congregation.
Danbury? 1791?]
(Entry from Sabin.)   23750

[St. John, Samuel], fl. 1783.
American Taxation, or the Spirit of Seventy Six.

[Hartford? n.d.] Broadside.
(Dated 1783 by Evans, this is apparently much later printing.)
BPL copy. 18174

Saint John's College, Annapolis.
An Address of the Visitors and Governors of. . . .
Baltimore, Hayes, 1794. [2], 22 pp.
MdHS copy. 27666

St. John's College, Annapolis.
Annapolis, May 25, 1789. Sir [blank]
After a long Suspension. . . .
[Annapolis, 1789.] [2] pp.
EPFL copy. 45583

St. John's College, Annapolis.
The Following is the Draught of a Proposal Act. . . .
[Annapolis, 1785.] Broadside.
St. John's College copy. 44791

[Saint Jure, Jean Baptiste de], 1588-1675.
An Extract of the Life of Monsieur de Renty.
Philadelphia, Tuckniss for Dickins, 1795. 70, [2] pp.
AAS copy. 29459

[Saint-Lambert, Jean François, marquis de, 1716-1803.
The Story of Sarah Phillips.
Wiscasset, Me., Hoskins & Scott, 1797.]
(Imprint assumed by Evans from adv.
"Just Published, and for Sale at the Telegraph Office," Nov. 24, 1797.) 32794

Saint-Pierre, Jacques Henri Bernardin de, 1737-1814.
Beauties of the Studies of Nature.
New York, Davises for Caritat, 1799. 332, [3] pp.
AAS copy. 36266

Saint-Pierre, Jacques Henri Bernardin de, 1737-1814.
The Beautiful History of Paul and Virginia.
Exeter, Ranlet, 1798. 163, [3] pp.
AAS copy. 48606

Saint-Pierre, Jacques Henri Bernardin de, 1737-1814.
Botanical Harmony Delineated.
Worcester, [Thomas for] Nancrede, 1797. 179, [5] pp., 4 plates.
(Issued with and without the plates.)
AAS copy. 32795

Saint-Pierre, Jacques Henri Bernardin de, 1737-1814.
Indian Cottage.
New York, M'Farlane, 1800. [2], 114 pp.
AAS copy. 38449

Saint-Pierre, Jacques Henri Bernardin de, 1737-1814.
Paul and Mary.
Philadelphia, Spotswood, 1792. [2], 166, 79, [5] pp., 1 plate.
AAS copy. 27667

Saint-Pierre, Jacques Henri Bernardin de, 1737-1814.
Paul and Mary.
Salem, Carlton for Cushing & Carlton, 1795. 105 pp.
AAS copy. 29460

[Saint-Pierre, Jacques Henri Bernardin de, 1737-1814.
Paul et Virginie.
Boston, for Spotswood and Nancrede, 1796.]
(In 31148 the text is in French and English on opposite pages; 31150 is the English text only; there may have been a French ed., but Evans' entry was assumed from an adv. "for sale" in Polar Star, Nov. 23, 1796.) 31149

Saint-Pierre, Jacques Henri Bernardin de, 1737-1814.
Paul and Virginia.
Boston, for Spotswood and Nancrede, 1796. 264 pp., 3 plates.
AAS copy. 31150

Saint-Pierre, Jacques Henri Bernardin de, 1737-1814.
Paul et Virginie . . . [2 tomes].

Boston, for Spotswood and Nancrede, 1796. 291 pp. 1 plate; 241, [11] pp., 1 plate.
BPL copy. 31148

Saint-Pierre, Jacques Henri Bernardin de, 1737-1814.
Paul and Virginia.
Wrentham, Mass., Heatons for Goodale and Warriner, 1799. 180 pp.
AAS copy. 36267

Saint-Pierre, Jacques Henri Bernardin de, 1737-1814.
Paul and Virginia.
Baltimore, Bonsal & Niles, 1800. 201 pp.
AAS copy. 38450

Saint-Pierre, Jacques Henri Bernardin de, 1737-1814.
Studies of Nature. . . . in Three Volumes. Vol. I [-III].
Worcester, [Thomas for] Nancrede, 1797. pp. [2], [1]-iii, [1], [iii]-lxiii, [1], [1]-395, 2 plates; 496 pp., 3 plates; 488 pp.
AAS copy. 32796

[Saint-Pierre, Jacques Henri Bernardin de, 1737-1814.
Studies of Nature. . . . In Three Volumes, Vol. II.
Worcester, [Thomas for] Nancrede, 1798. 496 pp.]
(The copies located are copies of Vol. II of 32796.) 34508

Saint-Pierre, Jacques Henri Bernardin de, 1737-1814.
A Vindication of Divine Providence.
Worcester, for Nancrede, 1797. 2 vol. [2], 331 pp., 2 plates; 432 pp., 3 plates.
(There is a separate issue of vol. I without the folding plate and ending with the words "The End.")
AAS copy. 32797

Saint-Pierre, Jacques Henri Bernardin de, 1737-1814.
Voyages of Amasis.
Boston, Thomas & Andrews, 1795. pp. [i]-iii, pp. [4]-137 in pairs.
AAS copy. 29461

[St. Vellum, M.
A Collection of Country Dances.
Walpole, N. H., Thomas & Carlisle, 1795.]
(Imprint assumed by Evans from adv.
"For sale at this office" in N. H. Journal, Nov. 3, 1795.) 29462

[Salas Barbadillo, Alonso Jeronimo de], 1580?-1635.
The Lucky Idiot.
Worcester, Mass., 1797. 144 pp.
AAS copy. 32798

Salem, Mass. Amity Fire Club.
Articles of the . . . February 10, 1796.
Salem, Carlton, 1796. 12 pp.
EI copy. 31152

Salem, Mass. Committee of Arrangements, 1789.
. . . As the President of the United States will Honor this Town. . . . October 27, 1789.
[Salem, 1789.] Broadside.
(The only known copy could not be reproduced.) 45584

Salem, Mass. Committee on Prices, 1779.
List of Prices for the Town of Salem. . . . September 6th, 1779.
Danvers, [1779].] Broadside.
AAS copy. 16514

Salem, Mass., Committee on Washington Observance.
Tribute to the Memory of Washington. Order of Procession.
[Salem, Cushing, 1800.] Broadside.
AAS copy. 38452

Salem, Mass. First Church.
A Copy of the Church-Covenants.
Boston, 1680. [2], 8 pp.
AAS copy. 295

Salem, Mass. First Church.
A Faithful Narrative of the Proceedings of the Ecclesiastical Council . . . in 1734.
Boston, Henchman, 1735. [3], vi, 94 pp.
AAS copy. 3958

Salem, Mass. Hospital.
The Following Regulations are to be Observed . . . June 25, 1798.
[Salem, 1798.] Broadside.
EI copy. 48607

Salem, Mass. Hospital.
Rules for Regulating Salem Hospital.
[Salem, 1773.] 8 pp.
AAS copy. 42498

Salem, Mass. Marine Society.
Laws of the. . . . March 25, 1766. . . . To. . . . 1781.
[Salem, 1801.] [2] pp.
EI copy. 44052

Salem, Mass. Number Five Fire Club.
Toujours Prêt. Articles of the No. 5 Fire-Club. . . . Revised . . . 1791.
Salem, Cushing, [1791]. 15 pp.
(The only known copy could not be reproduced.)
EI copy. 46283

Salem, Mass. Old Fire Club.
Articles of the. . . .
Salem, Dabney & Cushing, 1789. 8 pp.
AAS copy. 22125

Salem, Mass. Ordinances, etc., 1789.
Rules, Orders, and By-laws. . . . Aug. 17, 1789.
[Salem, 1789.] [2] pp.
HC copy. 22124

Salem, Mass. Ordinances, etc., 1798.
Rules and Regulations to be Observed by the Companies. . . . May 7, 1798.
[Salem, 1798.] Broadside.
EI copy. 34509

Salem, Mass. Selectmen, 1777.
The Price Act. . . . February 1, 1777.
Salem, Russell, [1777]. Broadside.
L. W. Jenkins copy. 15590

Salem, Mass. Selectmen, 1782.
Salem, December 10, 1782. Gentlemen, A Bill has Passed the House. . . .
[Salem, 1782.] Broadside.
LOC copy. 44263

Salem, Mass. Selectmen, 1791.
Essex SS - To Either of the Constables. . . .
[Salem, 1791.] Broadside.
NYHS copy. 23751

Salem, Mass., Selectmen, 1800.
Salem, November 18, 1800. Whereas there are Several Noted Forestallers. . . .
n. p., n.d. Broadside.
EI copy. 38451

Salem, Mass. Social Fire Company.
Articles Agreed. . . . October 21, 1774.
Salem, Halls, [1774?]. 7 pp.
(No copy available for reproduction.)
EI copy. 42693

Salem, Mass. Social Library.
Bylaws and Regulations of the. . . .
[Salem, 1797.] 32 pp.
AAS copy. 32800

Salem, Mass. Theatre. Washington Hall.
Last Night of Performing this Season . . . June 14th.
[Salem, 1799.] Broadside.
HC (Theater Coll.) copy. 36269

Salem, Mass. Third Congregational Church.
Rev. Sir, Our Destitutute State. . . . March 6, 1775.
[Salem, 1775.] Broadside.
AAS copy. 42935

Salem, Mass. Town Clerk.
Salem, April 22, 1796. To the Selectmen of the Town. . . .
[Salem, 1796.] Broadside.
EI copy. 31306

Salem, Mass. Town Meeting, Apr. 22, 1796.
To the Honorable the House of Representatives of the United States. The Memorial of the Subscribers. . . .
Salem, Carlton, 1796. Broadside.
EI copy. 31151

Salem, Mass. Union Fire Club.
Rules and Orders . . . Instituted . . . the
13th Day of September, A.D. 1770.
[Salem, 1770?] Broadside.
(No copy available for reproduction.)
EI copy.   42169

Salem, Mass. Union Fire Club.
Rules and Orders. . . . Revised . . .
December, 1791.
Salem, Cushing, 1791. 8 pp.
AAS copy.   46284

Salem and Danvers Aqueduct.
Rules and Regulations of the Proprietors
of the. . . 1797.
[Salem, 1797.] Broadside.
(The only recorded copy cannot be
located.)   32799

Salem, April 22, 1796. To the Selectmen of
the Town of [blank].
[Salem, 1796.] Broadside.
EI copy.   47905

Salem Gazette. The Occasional Salem
Gazette. . . . April 28.
Salem, Russell, [1775]. Broadside.
(The unique copy described by Evans
cannot now be located.)   15073

Salem, Tuesday, July 19, 1775. . . . An
Address to the British Soldiery.
Salem, Russell, [1775]. Broadside.
MHS copy.   42936

Salem, Wednesday, January 18, 1769. . . .
The Addresses to His Majesty.
[Salem, 1769.] Broadside.
AAS copy.   42002

Salem: Wednesday, Nov. 1.
[Salem, 1775.] Broadside.
BPL copy.   14449

Salenka, Gabriel.
. . . Lately Arrived from Europe, has . . . a
Dog. . . .
[Philadelphia], Woodward, [1796].
Broadside.
AAS copy.   47906

[Saliment, George Edward, fl. 1791-1800.
Minuetts with Eight Variations.
New York & Philadelphia, Carr, 1796.]
(No separate printing known; see
Sonneck-Upton, p. 263.)   31154

Salisbury, S. and S., merchants.
Hard-Ware Goods. S. and S. Salisbury,
Continue Importing. . . .
[Boston, 176-?] Broadside.
AAS copy.   41105

Salisbury, S. and S., merchants.
Hard-Ware Goods. S. and S. Salisbury.
[Boston, 1773?] Broadside.
AAS copy.   42499

Salter, Richard, 1721-1787.
(Sibley X, 404-409.)
The Gospel-Ministry.
[Hartford] for Stilman of Sandisfield,
[1766]. 24 pp.
AAS copy.   10486

Salter, Richard, 1721-1787.
A Sermon, Preached before the General
Assembly.
New London, 1768. 42 pp.
AAS copy.   11062

Saltonstall, Gurdon, 1666-1724.
(Sibley, III, 277-286.)
A Sermon Preached before the General
Assembly.
Boston, 1697. 80 pp.
HC copy.   812

Saltonstall, Gurdon, 1666-1724.
The State of the Mohegan Fields . . . New
London, Feb. the 3d. 1714.
[New London? 1715.] Broadside.
CHS copy.   39633

Saltonstall, Winthrop, 1775-1802.
An Inaugural Dissertation on . . .
nitrogene.
New York, Swords, 1796. 68 pp.
AAS copy.   31155

Salus Populi.

[Boston? 1728?] Broadside.
NYPL ph. copy.   39897

[Salva Conducta.
Boston, 1699. 8 pp.]
(Title from Haven.)   896

Salvation for All Men, Illustrated [by
John Clarke, 1755-1798].
Boston, Fleets, 1782. [1], iii, 26 pp.
AAS copy.   17489

Salvation for All Men, Illustrated. . . .
Second Edition [by John Clarke,
1755-1798].
Boston, Fleets, 1782. [1], iii, 26 pp.
AAS copy.   17490

The Salvation of American Liberty. . . .
May 15, 1770.
[New York, 1770.] Broadside.
LCP copy.   11846

The Salvation of American Liberty. To
the Public. . . . May 15, 1779.
[New York, 1779.] Broadside.
NYHS copy.   43702

The Salvation of the Soul Considered [by
Cotton Mather, 1663-1728].
Boston, Green, 1720. [2], 22 pp.
YC copy.   2144

Salzmann, Christian Gotthilf, 1744-1811.
Elements of Morality.
Providence, Carter & Wilkinson, 1795.
306, [2] pp.
AAS copy.   29464

Salzmann, Christian Gotthilf, 1744-1811.
Elements of Morality. . . . Vol. I [-II].
Philadelphia, Hoff & Kammerer, 1796.
248 pp., 10 plates; 259, [3] pp., 10 plates.
AAS copy.   31156

Salzmann, Christian Gotthilf, 1744-1811.
Elements of Morality. . . . Third American
Edition.
Wilmington, Del., Johnson, 1796. 232 pp.
AAS copy.   31157

Samenspraak over de Klaghte der
Raritanders [by Cornelius Van
Santvoord].
New York, 1726. [4], 194, xiv, [1] pp.
HEH copy.   2812

Sammlung Geistlicher Lieder.
Lancaster, Pa., Dell, 1798. [12], 109, [4]
pp.
LCP copy.   33625

Sammlung von Erbaulichen Gesängen.
Salisbury, Coupee & Schlump, 1797. [2],
30 pp.
(No copy located, 1968).   48246

Samoual, Jean Baptiste.
Description of a Plantation.
[Boston? 1796.] 12 pp., 1 map.
AAS copy.   31158

Sampson, Ezra, 1749-1823.
The Beauties of the Bible.
Hudson, N. Y., Stoddard, 1800. 283, [4]
pp.
AAS copy.   38459

Sampson, Ezra, 1749-1823.
The Ceasing and Failing.
Boston, Gill, 1776. 42 pp.
AAS copy.   15075

Sampson, Ezra, 1749-1823.
A Discourse Delivered February 19, 1795.
Boston, Hall, [1795]. 21 pp.
AAS copy.   29465

Sampson, Ezra, 1749-1823.
A Sermon Preached at Roxbury-Camp.
Watertown, 1775. 25 pp.
AAS copy.   14450

Sampson, Ezra, 1749-1823.
A Sermon, on the Death of Miss Olive
Soule.
New Bedford, Spooner, 1797. 11 pp.
BM copy.   32802

Sanders, Charlotte.
The Little Family.
Haverhill, Mass., Moore & Stebbins for

West, 1799. 2 vol. in 1. 143; 140 pp.
AAS copy.   36274

Sanders, Daniel Clarke, 1768-1850.
A Discourse Pronounced at Burlington.
Burlington, Vt. Baker, 1800. 20 pp.
AAS copy.   38460

Sanders, Daniel Clarke, 1768-1850.
The Pleasures and Advantages of Friendly
Society.
Windsor, Hutchins, 1792. 16 pp.
AAS copy.   24768

Sanders, Daniel Clarke, 1768-1850.
A Sermon, on Occasion of the Death of
Mr. Martin Harmon.
Vergennes, Vt., Waites, 1798. 22 pp.
AAS copy.   34512

Sanders, Daniel Clarke, 1768-1850.
[A Sermon on the death of the wife of Dr.
Hoyt, New Haven, Vt., 1795.]
(McCorison 354; no copy known.)   47591

Sanders, Daniel Clarke, 1768-1850.
A Sermon, Preached before His
Excellency.
Vergennes, Vt., Waites, 1798. 26 pp.
BA copy.   34513

Sandeman, Robert, 1718-1771.
(D. A. B.)
Some Thoughts on Christianity.
Boston, M'Alpine and Fleeming, 1764.
54 pp.
AAS copy.   9824

[Sandeman, Robert, 1718-1771.
Three Letters on Theron and Aspasio:
Addressed to the Author of that Work.
Boston, 1764.]
(Apparently a ghost of the Edinburgh ed.)
     9825

[Sandford E. fl. 1793.
The Columbian Harmony. . . . By E.
Sandford and John Rhea.
Alexandria, printed for E. Sandford,
1793.]
("Just published," Columbian Mirror,
July 17, 1793.)   26131

Sandiford, Ralph, 1693-1733.
A Brief Examination.
[Philadelphia], 1729. [16], 74 pp.
HSP copy.   3212

Sandiford, Ralph, 1693-1733.
(Sabin, XVIII, 435.)
The Mystrey of Iniquity. . . . Second
Edition.
[Philadelphia], 1730. 111 pp.
HSP copy.   3349

[Sands, Benjamin.]
[Metamorphosis.
Philadelphia, 1788?]. 1 leaf folded 3
times.
PPL copy.   45354

[Sands, Benjamin]
[Metamorphosis.
Philadelphia, 1792?]
PrU copy.   46569

[Sands, Benjamin.]
Metamorphosis, oder eine Verwandlung
von Bildern.
[Philadelphia, 1792?] 16 pp.
LCP copy.   46570

[Sands, Benjamin.]
[Metamorphosis.
Philadelphia, 1798?] 1 leaf folded 3 times.
PrU copy.   48608

Sands, Comfort, and Co.
Fish-Kill, December 22, 1781. The
Subscribers Inform the Gentlemen of the
Army. . . .
[Fishkill, 1781.] Broadside.
HEH copy.   44053

Sanger, Jedediah.
An Answer to General Jonas Platt's
Address to the People of the County of
Oneida. . . . October 1800.
n. p., n. d. Broadside.
NYPL ph. copy.   38461

Sanger, Zedekiah, 1748-1820.

A Discourse, Delivered at the Ordination of . . . James Wilson.
Providence, Wheeler, 1793. 32 pp.
AAS copy. 26135

Sanger, Zedekiah, 1748-1820.
A Discourse, Delivered at the Ordination of . . . Nehemiah Thomas.
Providence, Wheeler, 1793. 32 pp.
JCB copy. 26134

Sanger, Zedekiah, 1748-1820.
A Sermon, Preached, Feb. 28, 1798.
Warren, R. I., Phillips, 1798. 30 pp.
AAS copy. 34514

Sanger, Zedekiah, 1748-1820.
A Sermon, Preached, March 12, 1794.
Worcester, Thomas, 1795. 32 pp.
JCB copy. 29468

Sanger, Zedekiah, 1748-1820.
A Sermon, Preached (November 21, 1792).
Providence, Wheeler, 1793. 27 pp.
AAS copy. 26136

Sans Souci. Alias Free and Easy.
Boston, Warden & Russell, 1785. 24 pp.
AAS copy. 19234

Sans Souci, Alias Free and Easy. . . .
Second Edition.
Boston, Warden & Russell, 1785. 24 pp.
AAS copy. 19235

Sargeant, Samuel, 1755-1818.
A Sermon, Delivered at the Introduction of . . . Nahum Sargeant.
Windsor, [Vt.], Hough & Spooner, 1788. 22 pp.
AAS copy. 45355

Sargent, Winthrop, 1753-1820.
May 28th, 1800. The Following Authenticated Copies. . . .
[Natchez, 1800.] [6] pp.
NA copy. 38463

Sargent, Winthrop, 1753-1820.
Papers Relative to Certain American Antiquities.
Philadelphia, Dobson, 1796. iv, 39 pp., 2 plates.
AAS copy. 30038

Sarjeant, Thomas.
An Easy and Compendious System of Short Hand.
Philadelphia, Dobson & Lang, 1789. 46, [2] pp., front. and 12 plates.
AAS copy. 21869

Sarjeant, Thomas.
An Easy and Compendious System of Short-Hand.
Philadelphia, Lang for Dobson, 1792. 21, [1] pp., portrait, 10 plates.
AAS copy. 24370

Sarjeant, Thomas.
An Easy and Compendious System of Short Hand.
(See also Gurney, Thomas, 1705-1770.)

Sarjeant, Thomas.
Elementary Principles of Arithmetic.
Philadelphia, Dobson & Lang and Pritchard, 1788. [4], 95, [1] pp.
AAS copy. 21445

[Sarjeant, Thomas.
The Federal Arithmetician.
Philadelphia, Dobson, 1790.]
("In a few days will be published," Independent Gazette, Nov. 27, 1790.) 22870

Sarjeant, Thomas.
The Federal Arithmetician.
Philadelphia, Dobson, 1793. 263, [1] pp., 5 folded plates.
AAS copy. 26137

Sarjeant, Thomas.
An Introduction to the Counting House.
Philadelphia, Dobson & Lang, 1789. 52 pp.
AAS copy. 22127

[Sarjeant, Thomas.
A Paradigm of Inflections.

Philadelphia, Dobson & Lang, 1788.]
(Entry from an adv. in 21869.) 21446

[Sarjeant, Thomas.
Select Arithmetical Exercises.
Philadelphia, Dobson, 1793.]
(Adv. as "Preparing for the Press" in 26137.) 26138

[Sarjeant, Thomas.
Select Arithmetical Tables.
Philadelphia, Dobson & Lang, 1788.]
(Entry from adv. in 21869.) 21447

[Sarjeant, Thomas.
Select Arithmetical Tables.
Philadelphia, 1789. Broadside.]
(Adv. in 21869, etc., "just published.") 22128

[Sarjeant, Thomas.
A Synopsis of Logaritmical Arithmetic.
Philadelphia, Dobson & Lang, 1788.]
("May be had," Federal Gazette, June 6, 1788.) 21448

[Sarjeant, Thomas.]
[Twenty Arithmetical Tables.
Philadelphia, Seddon, 1786. Broadside.]
("Just Published . . . sold by Thomas Seddon," Pa. Eve. Herald, Apr. 29, 1786.) 19977

Sasse, Bernhard Henrich, fl. 1775.
Geistliche Lieder.
Hagerstown, Md., Gruber, 1799. 36, [2], 42 pp.
AAS copy. 36276

Satan's Harbinger [by Caleb Pusey, 1650-1727].
Philadelphia, 1700. [3], 114, [1] pp.
HSP copy. 948

A Satyr on the Sweepers Courage.
Printed by John Clean in Sweepers Alley, 1774. 8 pp.
BrU copy. 13595

A Satyrical Description of Commencement. Calculated to the Meridian of Cambridge in New-England.
Boston, [1740?]. Broadside.
Chapin Library copy. 40209

[Saul an Apostle of Liberty.
New York, 1779. 21 pp.]
(Sabin 77161. No copy located.) 16515

[Sault, Richard], d. 1702.
(D. N. B.)
The Second Spira.
Boston, 1693. [16], 55 pp.
LOC copy. 681

[Sault, Richard], d. 1702.
The Second Spira. . . . Sixth Edition.
Boston, Fleet & Crump for Eliot, 1715. [11], [1]-37, 37-38, 1-22.
AAS copy. 39634

[Sault, Richard], - 1702.
(D. N. B.)
The Second Spira.
Boston, 1721.
(Probably the ghost of an English printing. Adv. "Sold by Benjamin Eliot" in 2302.) 2290

[Sault, Richard], d. 1702.
The Second Spira.
Newport, [R. I.], Southwick, 1768. 37 pp.
AAS copy. 41878

[Sault, Richard], d. 1702.
The Second Spira.
Boston, at the Heart and Crown, [1772?] 8 pp.
AAS copy. 42374

[Sault, Richard], d. 1702.
The Second Spira.
Hartford, [1773]. 31 pp.
(Evans was describing a defective copy. Adv. as just published, Conn. Courant, Sept. 21, 1773.)
CHS copy. 14448

Saunders, Daniel.
A Journal of the Travels and Sufferings of. . . .

Salem, Cushing, 1794. 128, 15 pp.
AAS copy. 27671

Saunders, Daniel.
A Journal of the Travels and Sufferings of. . . .
Leominster, Mass., Prentiss for Thomas, 1797. 104, 21 pp.
AAS copy. 32804

[Saunders, Edward Clark].
A Collection of Hymns, Selected from sundry Poets.
Windham, [Ct.], Byrne, 1791. 34, [1] pp.
YC copy. 46285

Saunders, Richard, pseud.
Idea of the English School [by Benjamin Franklin, 1706-1790].
[Philadelphia, Franklin & Hall, 1751.] 8 pp.
UOP copy. 6668

Saunders, Richard, pseud.
The New-Years Gift: or a Pocket Almanack, for . . . 1741 . . . [by Benjamin Franklin, 1706-1790].
Philadelphia, Franklin. 31 pp.
YC copy. 4512

Saunders, Richard, pseud.
A Pocket Almanack for the Year 1742. . . . [by Benjamin Franklin, 1706-1790].
Philadelphia, Franklin. [16] pp.
LOC copy. 4718

Saunders, Richard, pseud.
A Pocket Almanack for the Year 1743 [by Benjamin Franklin, 1706-1790].
Philadelphia, Franklin. [16] pp.
LOC copy. 4955

Saunders, Richard, pseud.
A Pocket Almanack for the Year 1744. . . . By R. Saunders [by Benjamin Franklin, 1706-1790].
Philadelphia, Franklin. [24] pp.
LOC copy. 5188

Saunders, Richard, pseud.
A Pocket Almanack for the Year 1745. . . . By R. Saunders [by Benjamin Franklin, 1706-1790].
Philadelphia, Franklin. [24] pp.
LOC copy. 5397

Saunders, Richard, pseud.
A Pocket Almanack for the Year 1746. . . . By R. Saunders [by Benjamin Franklin, 1706-1790].
Philadelphia, Franklin. [24] pp.
LOC copy. 5596

Saunders, Richard, pseud.
A Pocket Almanack for the Year 1747. . . . By R. Saunders [by Benjamin Franklin, 1706-1790].
Philadelphia, Franklin. [24] pp.
LOC copy. 5770

Saunders, Richard, pseud.
A Pocket Almanack for the Year 1748. . . . By R. Saunders [by Benjamin Franklin, 1706-1790].
Philadelphia, Franklin. [24] pp.
MHS copy. 5951

Saunders, Richard, pseud.
A Pocket Almanack for . . . 1749. . . . By R. Saunders [by Benjamin Franklin, 1706-1790].
Philadelphia, Franklin & Hall. [24] pp.
HSP copy. 6138

Saunders, Richard, pseud.
A Pocket Almanack for the Year 1750. . . . By R. Saunders [by Benjamin Franklin, 1706-1790].
Philadelphia, Franklin & Hall, [1749]. [24] pp.
LOC copy. 6319

Saunders, Richard, pseud.
A Pocket Almanack for the Year 1751. . . . By R. Saunders [by Benjamin Franklin, 1706-1790].
Philadelphia, Franklin & Hall. [24] pp.
AAS copy. 6501

Saunders, Richard, pseud.
A Pocket Almanack for the Year 1752. . . . By R. Saunders [by Benjamin Franklin, 1706-1790].

Philadelphia, Franklin & Hall. [24] pp.
AAS copy. 6669

Saunders, Richard, pseud.
A Pocket Almanack for the Year 1753.
. . . By R. Saunders [by Benjamin
Franklin, 1706-1790].
Philadelphia, Franklin & Hall. [24] pp.
AAS copy. 6844

Saunders, Richard, pseud.
A Pocket Almanack for the Year 1754.
. . . By R. Saunders [by Benjamin
Franklin, 1706-1790].
Philadelphia, Franklin & Hall. [24] pp.
AAS copy. 7002

Saunders, Richard, pseud.
A Pocket Almanack for the Year 1755.
. . . By Richard Saunders [by Benjamin
Franklin, 1706-1790].
Philadelphia, Franklin & Hall. [24] pp.
LOC copy. 7195

Saunders, Richard, pseud.
A Pocket Almanack for the Year 1756.
. . . By R. Saunders [by Benjamin
Franklin, 1706-1790].
Philadelphia, Franklin & Hall. [24] pp.
HSP copy. 7419

Saunders, Richard, pseud.
A Pocket Almanack for the Year 1757.
. . . By R. Saunders [by Benjamin
Franklin, 1706-1790].
Philadelphia, Franklin & Hall. [22] pp.
AAS copy. 7667

Saunders, Richard, pseud.
A Pocket Almanack for the Year 1758.
. . . by R. Saunders [By Benjamin
Franklin, 1706-1790].
Philadelphia, Franklin & Hall. [24] pp.
UOP copy. 7898

Saunders, Richard, pseud.
A Pocket Almanack for the Year 1759.
Philadelphia, Franklin & Hall. [24] pp.
(No complete copy found.)
AAS copy. 8254

Saunders, Richard, pseud.
A Pocket Almanack for the Year 1760.
Philadelphia, Franklin & Hall. [24] pp.
(The only copy located is incomplete.)
AAS copy. 8487

Saunders, Richard, pseud.
A Pocket Almanack for . . . 1761.
Philadelphia, Franklin & Hall. [24] pp.
UOP copy. 8731

Saunders, Richard, pseud.
A Pocket Almanack for the Year 1762.
Philadelphia, Franklin & Hall. [24] pp.
LOC copy. 9001

Saunders, Richard, pseud.
A Pocket Almanack for . . . 1763.
Philadelphia, Franklin & Hall. [24] pp.
UOP copy. 9262

Saunders, Richard, pseud.
A Pocket Almanack for . . . 1764.
Philadelphia, Franklin & Hall. [24] pp.
LOC copy. 9509

Saunders, Richard, pseud.
A Pocket Almanack for . . . 1765.
Philadelphia, Franklin & Hall. [24] pp.
AAS copy. 9826

Saunders, Richard, pseud.
A Pocket Almanack for the Year 1766.
Philadelphia, Franklin & Hall. [24] pp.
AAS copy. 10160

Saunders, Richard, pseud.
A Pocket Almanack for . . . 1767.
Philadelphia, Hall & Sellers. [24] pp.
AAS copy. 10487

Saunders, Richard, pseud.
A Pocket Almanack for . . . 1768.
Philadelphia, Hall & Sellers. [24] pp.
HSP copy. 10764

Saunders, Richard, pseud.
A Pocket Almanack for . . . 1769.
Philadelphia, Hall & Sellers. [24] pp.
LOC copy. 11063

Saunders, Richard, pseud.

A Pocket Almanack for . . . 1770.
Philadelphia, Hall & Sellers. [24] pp.
LOC copy. 11451

Saunders, Richard, pseud.
A Pocket Almanack for . . . 1771.
Philadelphia, Hall & Sellers. [24] pp.
AAS copy. 11847

[Saunders, Richard, pseud.
A Pocket Almanack for . . . 1772.
Philadelphia, Hall & Sellers.]
(Adv. Pa. Gazette, Oct. 10, 1771.) 12219

Saunders, Richard, pseud.
A Pocket Almanack for . . . 1773.
Philadelphia, Hall & Sellers. [24] pp.
LOC copy. 12550

Saunders, Richard, pseud.
A Pocket Almanack for . . . 1774.
Philadelphia, Hall & Sellers. [24] pp.
HSP copy. 12996

Saunders, Richard, pseud.
A Pocket Almanack for . . . 1775.
Philadelphia, Hall &Sellers. [24] pp.
AAS copy. 13596

Saunders, Richard, pseud.
A Pocket Almanack for . . . 1776.
Philadelphia, Hall & Sellers. [24] pp.
LOC copy. 14451

[Saunders, Richard, pseud.
A Pocket Almanack for . . . 1777.
Philadelphia, Hall & Sellers.]
(Assumed by Hildeburn from the
sequence.) 15076

[Saunders, Richard, pseud.
A Pocket Almanack for . . . 1778.
York, Hall & Sellers.]
(Entry from Hildeburn.) 15591

[Saunders, Richard, pseud.
A Pocket Alamanck for . . . 1779.
Philadelphia, Hall & Sellers.]
(Assumed by Hildeburn from the
sequence.) 16066

Saunders, Richard, pseud.
A Pocket Almanack for . . . 1780.
Philadelphia, Hall & Sellers. [24] pp.
AAS copy. 16516

[Saunders, Richard, pseud.
A Pocket Almanack for 1781.
Philadelphia, Hall & Sellers.]
(Assumed by Hildeburn from the
sequence.) 16987

[Saunders, Richard, pseud.
A Pocket Almanack for . . . 1782.
Philadelphia, Hall & Sellers.]
(Assumed from the sequence.) 17365

Saunders, Richard, pseud.
A Pocket Almanack for . . . 1783.
Philadelphia, Hall & Sellers. [24] pp.
LOC copy. 17715

[Saunders, Richard, pseud.
A Pocket Almanack for . . . 1784.
Philadelphia, Hall & Sellers.]
(Assumed from the sequence.) 18176

[Saunders, Richard, pseud.
A Pocket Almanack for . . . 1785.
Philadelphia, Hall & Sellers.]
(Assumed by Hildeburn from the
sequence.) 18777

Saunders, Richard, pseud.
Poor Richard, 1733 An Almanack. . . . [by
Benjamin Franklin, 1706-1790].
Philadelphia, Franklin. [24] pp.
Rosenbach copy. 2541

Saunders, Richard, pseud.
Poor Richard, 1733. . . . Second Edition
[by Benjamin Franklin, 1706-1790].
Philadelphia, Franklin, 1733. [24] pp.
APS copy. 3542

Saunders, Richard, pseud.
Poor Richard, 1733. . . . By Richard
Saunders. . . . Third Impression [by
Benjamin Franklin, 1706-1790].
Philadelphia, Franklin. [24] pp.
HSP copy. 3543

Saunders, Richard, pseud.

Poor Richard, 1734. . . . By Richard
Saunders [by Benjamin Franklin,
1706-1790].
Philadelphia, Franklin. [24] pp.
AAS copy. 3657

Saunders, Richard, pseud.
[Poor Richard, 1735. An Almanack. . . .
By Richard Saunders [by Benjamin
Franklin, 1706-1790].
Philadelphia, Franklin, [1734]. [24] pp.]
(No copy found.) 3770

Saunders, Richard, pseud.
Poor Richard, 1736. An Almanack. . . . By
Richard Saunders [by Benjamin Franklin,
1706-1790].
Philadelphia, Franklin. [24] pp.
AAS copy. 3903

Saunders, Richard, pseud.
Poor Richard, 1737. An Almanack. . . .
[by Benjamin Franklin, 1706-1790].
Philadelphia, Franklin. [24] pp.
AAS copy. 4017

Saunders, Richard, pseud.
Poor Richard, 1738. . . . [by Benjamin
Franklin, 1706-1790].
Philadelphia, Franklin. [24] pp.
NYPL copy. 4141

Saunders, Richard, pseud.
Poor Richard, 1739. . . . [by Benjamin
Franklin, 1706-1790].
Philadelphia, Franklin. [24] pp.
AAS copy. 4247

Saunders, Richard, pseud.
Poor Richard, 1740. An Almanack. . . .
[by Benjamin Franklin, 1706-1790].
Philadelphia, Franklin. [24] pp.
AAS copy. 4364

Saunders, Richard, pseud.
Poor Richard, 1741. An Almanack. . . .
[by Benjamin Franklin, 1706-1790].
Philadelphia, Franklin, 1741. [24] pp.
(No perfect copy could be located.)
UOP copy. 4513

Saunders, Richard, pseud.
Poor Richard, 1742. An Almanack . . . [by
Benjamin Franklin], 1706-1790.
Philadelphia, Franklin. [24] pp.
LCP copy. 4719

Saunders, Richard, pseud.
Poor Richard, 1743. An Almanack. . . .
[by Benjamin Franklin, 1706-1790.]
Philadelphia, Franklin. [24] pp.
UOP copy. 4956

Saunders, Richard, pseud.
Poor Richard, 1744. An Almanack . . . by
Richard Saunders [by Benjamin Franklin,
1706-1790].
Philadelphia, Franklin; Annapolis, Green.
[24] pp.
(The AAS has a copy without Green's
name in the imprint.)
HSP copy. 5189

Saunders, Richard, pseud.
Poor Richard, 1745. An Almanack. . . . By
Richard Saunders [by Benjamin Franklin,
1706-1790].
Philadelphia, Franklin. [24] pp.
AAS copy. 5398

Saunders, Richard, pseud.
Poor Richard, 1746. An Almanack. . . . By
Richard Saunders [by Benjamin Franklin,
1706-1790].
Philadelphia, Franklin. [24] pp.
AAS copy. 5597

Saunders, Richard, pseud.
Poor Richard, 1747. An Almanack. . . . By
Richard Saunders [by Benjamin Franklin,
1706-1790].
Philadelphia, Franklin. [24] pp.
NYPL copy. 5771

Saunders, Richard, pseud.
Poor Richard Improved: Being an
Almanack . . . for . . . 1748. . . . By
Richard Saunders [by Benjamin Franklin,
1706-1790].
Philadelphia, Franklin. [36] pp.
AAS copy. 5952

Saunders, Richard, pseud.

Poor Richard Improved . . . an Almanack
. . . for . . . 1749 . . . By Richard Saunders
[by Benjamin Franklin, 1706-1790].
Philadelphia, Franklin & Hall. [36] pp.
(This is the first issue, in which on the
March calendar the circumference of the
earth is given as 4000 miles; corrected in
second issue.)
AAS copy.   6139

Saunders, Richard, pseud.
Poor Richard Improved . . . an Almanack
. . . for . . . 1750. . . . By Richard Saunders
[by Benjamin Franklin, 1706-1790].
Philadelphia, Franklin & Hall. [36] pp.
UOP copy.   6320

Saunders, Richard, pseud.
Poor Richard Improved . . . an Almanack
. . . for . . . 1751. . . . By Richard Saunders
[by Benjamin Franklin, 1706-1790].
Philadelphia, Franklin & Hall. [36] pp.
AAS copy.   6502

Saunders, Richard, pseud.
Poor Richard Improved: Being an
Almanack . . . for . . . 1752. . . . By
Richard Saunders [by Benjamin Franklin,
1706-1790].
Philadelphia, Franklin & Hall. [36] pp.
AAS copy.   6670

Saunders, Richard, pseud.
Poor Richard Improved: Being an
Almanack . . . for . . . 1753. . . . By
Richard Saunders [by Benjamin Franklin,
1706-1790].
Philadelphia, Franklin & Hall. [36] pp.
AAS copy.   6845

Saunders, Richard, pseud.
Poor Richard Improved . . . an Almanack
. . . for . . . 1754. . . . By Richard Saunders
[by Benjamin Franklin, 1706-1790].
Philadelphia, Franklin & Hall. [36] pp.
AAS copy.   7003

Saunders, Richard, pseud.
Poor Richard Improved . . . an Almanack
. . . for . . . 1755. . . . By Richard Saunders
[by Benjamin Franklin, 1706-1790].
Philadelphia, Franklin & Hall. [36] pp.
AAS copy.   7196

Saunders, Richard, pseud.
Poor Richard Improved . . . an Almanack
. . . for . . . 1756. . . . By Richard Saunders
[by Benjamin Franklin, 1706-1790].
Philadelphia, Franklin & Hall. [36] pp.
AAS copy.   7420

Saunders, Richard, pseud.
Poor Richard Improved: Being an
Almanack . . . for . . . 1757. . . . By
Richard Saunders [by Benjamin Franklin,
1706-1790].
Philadelphia, Franklin & Hall. [36] pp.
AAS copy.   7668

Saunders, Richard, pseud.
Poor Richard Improved . . . An Almanack
. . . for . . . 1758. . . . By Richard Saunders
[by Benjamin Franklin, 1706-1790].
Philadelphia, Franklin & Hall. [36] pp.
AAS copy.   7899

Saunders, Richard, pseud.
Poor Richard Improved: Being an
Almanack . . . for . . . 1759.
Philadelphia, Franklin & Hall. [36] pp.
AAS copy.   8255

Saunders, Richard, pseud.
Poor Richard Improved: Being an
Almanack . . . for . . . 1760.
Philadelphia, Franklin & Hall. [36] pp.
AAS copy.   8488

Saunders, Richard, pseud.
Poor Richard Improved: being an
Almanack . . . for 1761.
Philadelphia, Franklin & Hall. [36] pp.
AAS copy.   8732

Saunders, Richard, pseud.
Poor Richard Improved . . . an Almanack
. . . for . . . 1762.
Philadelphia, Franklin & Hall. [36] pp.
NYPL copy.   9002

Saunders, Richard, pseud.
Poor Richard Improved: Being an
Almanack . . . for . . . 1763.

Philadelphia, Franklin & Hall. [36] pp.
NYPL copy.   9263

Saunders, Richard, pseud.
Poor Richard Improved: being an
Almanack . . . for . . . 1764.
Philadelphia, Franklin & Hall. [36] pp.
AAS copy.   9510

Saunders, Richard, pseud.
Poor Richard Improved: being an
Almanack . . . for . . . 1765.
Philadelphia, Franklin & Hall. [36] pp.
AAS copy.   9827

Saunders, Richard, pseud.
Poor Richard Improved: Being an
Almanack . . . for . . . 1766.
Philadelphia, Franklin & Hall. [36] pp.
AAS copy.   10161

Saunders, Richard, pseud.
Poor Richard Improved: Being an
Almanack . . . for . . . 1767.
Philadelphia, Hall & Sellers. [36] pp.
AAS copy.   10488

Saunders, Richard, pseud.
Poor Richard Improved: Being an
Almanack . . . for . . . 1768.
Philadelphia, Hall & Sellers. [36] pp.
AAS copy.   10765

Saunders, Richard, pseud.
Poor Richard Improved: Being an
Almanack . . . for . . . 1769.
Philadelphia, Hall & Sellers. [36] pp.
AAS copy.   11064

Saunders, Richard, pseud.
Poor Richard Improved: being an
Almanack . . . for . . . 1770.
Philadelphia, Hall & Sellers. [36] pp.
AAS copy.   11452

Saunders, Richard, pseud.
Poor Richard Improved: Being an
Almanack . . . for . . . 1771.
Philadelphia, Hall & Sellers. [36] pp.
AAS copy.   11848

Saunders, Richard, pseud.
Poor Richard Improved: being an
Almanack . . . for . . . 1772.
Philadelphia, Hall & Sellers. [36] pp.
AAS copy.   12220

Saunders, Richard, pseud.
Poor Richard Improved: being an
Almanack . . . for . . . 1773.
Philadelphia, Hall & Sellers. [36] pp.
AAS copy.   12551

Saunders, Richard, pseud.
Poor Richard Improved: being an
Almanack . . . for . . . 1774.
Philadelphia, Hall & Sellers. [36] pp.
AAS copy.   12997

Saunders, Richard, pseud.
Poor Richard Improved: being an
Almanack . . . for . . . 1775.
Philadelphia, Hall & Sellers. [36] pp.
AAS copy.   13597

Saunders, Richard, pseud.
Poor Richard Improved: being
an Almanack . . . for . . . 1776.
Philadelphia, Hall & Sellers. [32] pp.
HSP copy.   14452

Saunders, Richard, pseud.
Poor Richard Improved: being an
Almanack. . . . For . . . 1777.
Philadelphia, Hall & Sellers, [1776]. [34]
pp.
(The only copy located is imperfect.)
LOC copy.   15077

[Saunders, Richard, pseud.
Poor Richard Improved: being an
Almanack . . . for . . . 1778.
York, Hall & Sellers.]
(Entry from Hildeburn.)   15592

Saunders, Richard, pseud.
Poor Richard Improved: being an
Almanack . . . for . . . 1779.
Philadelphia, Hall & Sellers. [36] pp.
HSP copy.   16067

Saunders, Richard, pseud.
Poor Richard Improved: being an

Almanack . . . for . . . 1780.
Philadelphia, Hall & Sellers. [36] pp.
AAS copy.   16517

Saunders, Richard, pseud.
Poor Richard Improved: being an
Almanack . . . for . . . 1781.
Philadelphia, Hall & Sellers. [36] pp.
LOC copy.   16988

Saunders, Richard, pseud.
Poor Richard Improved: being an
Almanack . . . for . . . 1782.
Philadelphia, Hall & Sellers. [36] pp.
AAS copy.   17366

Saunders, Richard, pseud.
Poor Richard Improved: being an
Almanack . . . for . . . 1783.
Philadelphia, Hall & Sellers. [36] pp.
LOC copy.   17716

Saunders, Richard, pseud.
Poor Richard Improved: being an
Almanack . . . for . . . 1784.
Philadelphia, Hall & Sellers. [36] pp.
AAS copy.   18177

Saunders, Richard, pseud.
Poor Richard Improved: being an
Almanack . . . for . . . 1785.
Philadelphia, Hall &.Sellers. [32] pp.
AAS copy.   18778

Saunders, Richard, pseud.
Poor Richard Improved: being an
Almanack . . . for . . . 1786.
Philadelphia, Hall & Sellers. [36] pp.
AAS copy.   19236

Saunders, Richard, pseud.
Poor Richard Improved: being an
Almanack . . . for . . . 1787.
Philadelphia, Hall & Sellers. [36] pp.
AAS copy.   19978

Saunders, Richard, pseud.
Poor Richard Improved: Being
an Almanack . . . for . . . 1788.
Philadelphia, Hall & Sellers. [36] pp.
LOC copy.   20694

Saunders, Richard, pseud.
Poor Richard Improved: being an
Almanack . . . for . . . 1789.
Philadelphia, Hall & Sellers. [36] pp.
LOC copy.   21449

Saunders, Richard, pseud.
Poor Richard Improved: being an
Almanack . . . for . . . 1790.
Philadelphia, Hall & Sellers. [40] pp.
AAS copy.   22129

Saunders, Richard, pseud.
Poor Richard Improved: being an
Almanack . . . for . . . 1791.
Philadelphia, Hall & Sellers. [44] pp.
AAS copy.   22872

Saunders, Richard, pseud.
Poor Richard Improved: being an
Almanack . . . for . . . 1792.
Philadelphia, Hall & Sellers. [44] pp.
AAS copy.   23753

Saunders, Richard, pseud.
Poor Richard Improved: being an
Almanack . . . for . . . 1793.
Philadelphia, Hall & Sellers. [44] pp.
AAS copy.   24770

Saunders, Richard, pseud.
Poor Richard Improved: being an
Almanack . . . for . . . 1794.
Philadelphia, Hall & Sellers. [44] pp.
AAS copy.   26139

Saunders, Richard, pseud.
Poor Richard Improved: being an
Almanack . . . for . . . 1795.
Philadelphia, Hall & Sellers. [44] pp.
AAS copy.   27672

Saunders, Richard, pseud.
Poor Richard Improved: being an
Almanack . . . for . . . 1800.
Philadelphia, Hall & Sellers. [44] pp.
AAS copy.   36277

Saunders, Richard, pseud.
Poor Richard Improved: being an
Almanack . . . for . . . 1801.

Philadelphia, Hall & Sellers. [36] pp.
AAS copy.   38464

Saunders, Richard, pseud.
Poor Richard Revived. Being an
Astronomical Diary, or Almanack, for
1801.
Newfield, Ct., Beach. [24] pp.
CHS copy.   38465

Saunders, William, 1743-1817.
Observations on the Superior Efficacy of
the Red Peruvian Bark.
Boston, Hodge for Green, [1783]. 91, [5]
pp.
AAS copy.   18178

Saunders, William, 1743-1817.
A Treatise on the Structure . . . of the
Liver.
Boston, Pelham, 1797. xx, 231 pp.
AAS copy.   32805

[Savage, Edward, 1761-1817.
Liberty Giving Support to the Bald-Eagle.
Baltimore, Smith, 1796.]
(No copy located.)   31160

[Savage, Edward, 1761-1817.
Liberty in the Form of the Goddess of
Youth, Giving Support to the Bald-Eagle.
Philadelphia, 1796. Broadside.]
(No copy located.)   31159

Savage, Ezekiel, 1760-1837.
An Eulogy on . . . Washington.
Salem, Mass., Cushing, 1800. 23 pp.
AAS copy.   38466

Savage, Samuel Phillips.
To be Sold by Public Vendue on Wednesday
the First of December . . . at the House of
Capt. Nathaniel Little . . . in Kingston.
. . . Boston, October 26, 1773.
[Boston, 1773.] Broadside.
MHS copy.   42520

[Savannah, Ga.
At a Meeting of the Inhabitants . . . the 2d
Day of July, 1795.
[Savannah, Johnstons, 1795.] Broadside.]
(Not located. See Ga. Hist. Quar., XVIII,
60.)   29469

Savannah, Ga. Convention, July 27, 1774.
The Critical Situation to which the British
Colonies. . . . [Dated] July 14, 1774.
[Savannah, 1774.] Broadside.
PRO copy.   42694

Savannah, Ga. Convention, Aug. 10, 1774.
Resolutions Entered into at Savannah.
[Savannah, 1774.] Broadside.
PRO copy.   42695

Savannah, Ga. Dancing Assembly.
Rules and Regulations. . . . 19th
November, 1790.
[Savannah, 1790.] Broadside.
DeRGL copy.   22873

[Savannah, Ga. Ordinances, etc., 1797.
The Fire Ordinance and Patrol Law.]
("A few Copies of the Fire Ordinance and
Patrol Law may be had of the Printers."
Georgia Gazette, Dec. 1, 1797.)   32806

Savannah, Ga. Town Guard.
The Friends of Constitutional Liberty.
[Savannah, 1779.] Broadside.
(Copy not located.)   43703

Savery, William, 1750-1804.
Three Sermons Preached . . . July 19,
1796.
New York, Collins, 1797. 55 pp.
AAS copy.   32807

Saw Ye my Hero George.
[Boston? 1789?] Broadside.
HEH copy.   45585

Sawyer, Matthias Enoch.
An Inaugural Dissertation.
Philadelphia, Dobson, 1793. 30 pp.
National Library of Medicine copy. 26140

Say, Benjamin, 1755-1813.
An Annual Oration Pronounced before
the Humane Society.
Whitehall, Pa., Young, 1799. 50 pp.
AAS copy.   36278

Say, Benjamin, 1755-1813.
A Short Compilation of the . . . Life . . . of
Thomas Say.
Philadelphia, Budd & Bartram, 1796. 32
(i.e., 34), [2], 151 pp.
(The AAS has another copy with the error
in pagination corrected.)
AAS copy.   31161

Say, Thomas, 1709-1796.
A True and Wonderful Account of. . . .
[Philadelphia?], 1792. 8 pp.
HEH copy.   46571

Say, Thomas, 1709-1796.
The Visions of a Certain Thomas Say.
Philadelphia, Mentz, 1774. 23 pp.
LCP copy.   13598

Saybrook Bar Lottery.
Say-Brook Barr Lottery, to Raise the Sum
of Five Hundred and Thirty Seven
Pounds. . . . June 5, 1773.
[Hartford, 1773.] Broadside.
CHS copy.   42500

Sayre, Francis Bowes, 1766?-1798.
An Inaugural Dissertation.
Trenton, Collins, 1790. 24 pp.
National Library of Medicine copy. 22874

Sayre, James, 1745-1798.
A Candid Narrative.
Fairfield, 1788. 36, [2] pp.
AAS copy.   21450

Sayre, John, 1738-1784.
From the New-York Journal. Mr. Holt.
. . .
[Philadelphia, 1776?] 6 pp.
AAS copy.   15078

Sayre, John, 1738-1784.
(Weis, Clergy Middle Colonies.)
A Sermon Preached before the
Convention.
New York, Rivington, 1773. 30 pp.
NYHS copy.   12998

[Sayre, Stephen], 1736-1818.
(D. A. B.)
The Englishman Deceived; a Political
Piece.
New York, Holt, 1768. [2], ii, 40 pp.
NYPL copy.   11065

[Sayre, Stephen], 1736-1818.
The Englishman Deceived; a Political
Piece.
Salem, 1768. 38 pp.
AAS copy.   11066

[Sayre, Stephen, 1736-1818.
(D. A. B.)
Reasons for not Signing.
New York, 1762.)
(A ghost of 15078, q.v.)   9265

Sayre, Stephen, 1736-1818.
A Short Narrative of the Life and
Character of. . . .
n.p., [1794]. 8 pp.
RIHS copy.   27673

Scale of Depreciation, Agreeable to an
Act of the Commonwealth of
Massachusetts . . . January, 1777. . . .
February 27th, 1781.
[Boston, 1781.] Broadside.
AAS copy.   44055

Scale of Depreciation, Agreeable to an
Act of the Commonwealth of
Massachusetts . . . January, 1777. . . . to
the 1st of October, [1781].
[Boston, 1781.] Broadside.
AAS copy.   44056

Scale of Depreciation, Agreeable to an
Act of the (now) Commonwealth of
Massachusetts, Passed September 29,
1780.
[Boston, 1781.] Broadside.
AAS copy.   44054

Scales, William, 1742-1799.
(Weis, Colonial Clergy N. E.)
The Confusion of Babel.
America, 1780. 87 pp.
AAS copy.   16989

Scales, William, 1742-1799.
Priestcraft Exposed from its Foundation.

Danvers, Russell, 1781. 16 pp.
AAS copy.   44057

The Scare-Crow [by William Cobbett,
1762-1835].
Philadelphia, Cobbett, 1796. 23 pp.
AAS copy.   30231

The Scare-Crow. . . . Second Edition [by
William Cobbett, 1762-1835].
Philadelphia, 1796. 23 pp.
AAS copy.   30232

A Scene in the First Act of the New
Farce.
[Philadelphia, 1764.] 8 pp.
LCP copy.   9829

[Schabaelje, Jon Philipsen, 1585?-1656.
Die Wandlende Seel.
Germantown, 1763. 8, 463, 25 pp.]
(Zahn Cat. No. 2, lot 64; no copy located.)
                                             9511

Schabaelje, Jon Philipsen, 1585?-1656.
Die Wandlende Seel.
Germantown, Saur, 1767. [8], 463, [25]
pp.
AAS copy.   41765

Schabaelje, Jon Philipsen, 1585?-1656.
Die Wandlende Seel.
Germantown, 1768. [8], 463, [25] pp.
AAS copy.   11067

Schabaelje, Jon Philipsen, 1585?-1656.
Die Wandlende Seel. . . . Zweyte Auflage.
Germantown, 1771. [8], 463, [23] pp.
AAS copy.   12221

Schabaelje, Jon Philipsen, 1585?-1656.
Die Wandlende Seel.
Germantown, Leibert, 1794. [8], 463, [22]
pp.
AAS copy.   27674

[Schaffer, Francis C.
A Pocket Companion for the German
Flute, Boston, 1798.]
(Entry from the proposals published in
Columbian Centinel, Sept. 12, 1798.)
                                             34516

Scheel, Heinrich Otto von, 1745-1807.
A Treatise of Artillery.
Philadelphia, Fenno, 1800. [2], 154, 6, [1]
pp., 12 plates.
(No copy with the plates could be
located.)
AAS copy.   38467

A Scheme (by Striking Twenty Thousand
Pounds, Paper Money).
[New York, 1737.] 6 pp.
(Attributed by Evans to Bradford's press,
but the AAS copy was bound into
Zenger's Journal.)
AAS copy.   4194

A Scheme for the Revival of Christianity.
New York, Gaine, 1753. 20 pp.
NYHS copy.   7115

Scheme for the Settlement of a new
Colony to the Westward of Pennsylvania [by
Samuel Hazard].
[Philadelphia, 1755.] [2] pp.
CSL copy.   40750

Scheme for the Settlement of a New
Colony to the Westward of Pennsylvania.
. . . July 24th, 1755 [by Samuel Hazard].
[Philadelphia, 1755.] [2] pp.
(The only copy located is partly obscured
by silking.)
CSL copy.   40751

Scheme of a Lottery Authorized by Act of
Assembly, for the Sale of . . . Mr. Robert
Edge Pine. . . . November 21, 1789.
[Philadelphia, 1789.] Broadside.
NYHS copy.   45586

Scheme of a Lottery for Assisting to Pave
the Streets at Fell's Point. . . . March 16,
1789.
Baltimore, Goddard, [1789]. Broadside.
(No copy located.)   45587

Scheme of a Lottery, for Disposing of the
Following Houses, Plate, Furniture, &c.
&c.

[New York, 1773.] Broadside.
LCP copy.   13001

Scheme of a Lottery, for Disposing of the
Following Houses, viz. . . .
[New York, 1773.] Broadside.
LCP copy.   13000

Scheme of a Lottery, For Raising the sum
of Seven Hundred and Fifty Pounds.
[New York, 1773.] Broadside.
LCP copy.   13002

[Scheme of a Lottery to be Drawn at
Brookhaven.
[New York, 1757.] Broadside.]
(No copy found.)   8031

Scheme of a Lottery to Raise £10,000
Old-Tenor for . . . Fortifications for . . .
Rhode-Island.
[Providence? 1756.] Broadside.
HSP copy.   40862

Scheme of a Lottery to Raise 40,800
Dollars.
Newark, Woods, 1793. Broadside.
NYHS copy.   26141

Scheme of a Lottery to Raise the Sum of
Four Thousand Pounds. . . . March 8,
1791.
Elizabethtown, Kollock, [1791].
Broadside.
NYHS copy.   23754

Scheme of a Lottery to Raise 39,900
Dollars.
Newark, N. J., Woods, 1794. Broadside.
NJHS copy.   27675

A Scheme to Drive the French out of . . .
America.
Boston, Fowle, 1755. 20, [3] pp.
AAS copy.   7377

Schenck, William, 1770-1823.
An Attempt to Delineate the Character
. . . of . . . Noah Wetmore.
Sag-Harbor, Frothingham, [1796]. 27 pp.
LOC copy.   31162

[Schenectady, N.Y. Academy.
Rules and Regulations for: . . .
Albany, Barber & Southwick, 1793. 20
pp.]
(The source of this entry has not been
discovered.)   26142

Schenectady, N. Y. Charter.
Charter of the City of Schenectady.
Albany, Websters, [1798]. 34, [1] pp.
AAS copy.   34517

Schenectady, N. Y. Citizens, 1768.
A Brief State of the Case of Roger
Shermerhorn. . . .
[New York, 1768?] 6 pp.
NYPL copy.   41879

Schenectady, April 13th, 1799. In
Committee. . . . Sir, it is the Opinion of a
Great Many of the Respectable
Electors. . . .
[Schenectady? 1799.] Broadside.
NYHS copy.   36279

[Schiller, Johann Christoph Friedrich
von, 1759-1805.
Cabal and Love.
Philadelphia, 1795.]
(Imprint assumed by Evans from adv.)
   29470

[Schiller, Johann Christoph Friedrich
von, 1759-1805.
The Ghost-Seer.
Charleston, Young, 1796.]
(Probably a ghost of 31163. "Just arrived
from New York," City Gazette, Sept. 12,
1796.)   31164

Schiller, Johann Christoph Friedrich von,
1759-1805.
The Ghost-Seer.
New York, Swords, 1796. 120 pp.
AAS copy.   31163

Schiller, Johann Christoph Friedrich von,
1759-1805.
The Robbers.
New York, Campbell, 1793. 120 pp.
AAS copy.   26143

Schiller, Johann Christoph Friedrich von,
1759-1805.
The Robbers. . . . Second American
Edition.
New York, Campbell, 1795. 102 pp.
AAS copy.   29471

[Schneeberger, Andrew.
Das Raben-Geschrey.
[Ephrata, 1776.] 2 pp.]
(Entry from Hildeburn; no copy located.)
   15079

[Schneeberger, Andrew.
Wurde Abgesungen den 31sten August
1793.
Ephrata, 1793. Broadside.]
(The Evans entry is from Seidensticker,
p. 134.)   26144

[Schneeberger, Barbara.
Die Stimme der Turteltaube.
[Ephrata, 1776.] 2 pp.]
(Entry from Hildeburn; no copy found.)
   15080

[Schneider, Peter, fl. 1792.
Merkwürdige Prophezeyung eines
Einsiedlers.
[Ephrata?], 1792.]
(The origin of this entry is unknown.)
   24772

[Schneider, Peter, fl. 1792.
Merkwürdige Prophezeyung.
Ephrata, 1793.]
(Entry from Seidensticker, pp. 132, 137.)
   26145

[Schneider, Peter, fl. 1792.
Merkwürdige Prophezeyung.
Ephrata, Mayer, 1794. 22 pp.]
(Entry from Seidensticker, p. 137.)   27676

[Schneider, Peter, fl. 1792.
Merkwürdige Prophezeyung eines
Einsiedlers.
Ephrata, Mayer, 1796.]
(Entry from Seidensticker, who assumed
the imprint from an adv.)   31165

[Schneider, Peter, fl. 1792.
Merkwürdige Prophezegung.
Ephrata, Mayer, 1797.]
(Entry from Seidensticker, p. 146.)   32808

[Schnering, Henrich Rupert.
Gott Schüzet Stärket und Erhält uns
in Gefahren.
Baltimore, Saur, 1794.]
(See Minick, 261.)   27677

[Schoepf, Johann David, 1752-1800.
The American Herbal.
New York, 1795.]
("Ready for the Press," Ev. Post, Mar. 16,
1795.)   29472

Ein Schön Geistlich Lied.
Lancaster, Bailey, [1780]. Broadside.
HSP copy.   43893

Ein Schön Lied von dem
Schweizerischen Erz-Freyheitssohn
Wilhelm Thellen.
Philadelphia, Miller, 1768. [16] pp.
HSP copy.   11068

Ein Schön Weltlich Lied.
Philadelphia, Armbruester, 1764.
Broadside.
HSP copy.   9830

Schönberg, Matthias.
Die Zierde der Jugend.
Lancaster, Pa., Albrecht, 1796. [2], 58 pp.
AAS copy.   31683

Eine Schöne, Anmuthige und
Lebenswürdige Historia.
Lancaster, Bailey & Dickson, 1792. 52 pp.
LCP copy.   46572

[Eine Schöne Sammlung der Neuesten
Lieder.
Reading, Pa., Jungmann, 1797.]
(Entry from the copyright notice.)   32809

[The School for Love; or, Scheme to Gain
Her.
Philadelphia, 1790.]
(Evans entry from an adv.)   22875

The School for Scandal.
Philadelphia, Bradford, 1779. iv, [2], 46
pp.
JCB copy.   16518

The School for Wives. . . . Sixth Edition
[by Hugh Kelly, 1739-1777].
Philadelphia, Dunlap, 1774. pp. [8].
[i]-iv, xiii-101.
HSP copy.   13361

The School of Good Manners. . . . Fifth
Edition [by Eleazar Moody, d. 1720].
New London, [Ct.], Greens, 1754. [2], ii,
80 pp.
YC copy.   40702

The School of Good Manners [by Eleazer
Moody, d. 1720].
Boston, Boyle, 1775. 79, [1] pp.
(No perfect copy located.)
AAS copy.   42886

The School of Good Manners [by Eleazar
Moody, d. 1720].
Portland, 1786. 58 pp.
AAS copy.   19807

The School of Good Manners. Composed
for the Help of Parents [by Eleazar
Moody, d. 1720].
Hartford, Patten, 1787. 36 pp.
AAS copy.   20528

The School of Good Manners. Composed
for the Help of Parents. . . . Seventeenth
Edition [by Eleazar Moody, d. 1720].
Windsor, Spooner, 1793. 40 pp.
AAS copy.   25834

The School of Good Manners. Composed
for the Help of Parents [by Eleazar
Moody, d. 1720].
Boston, Edes, 1794. 92 pp.
(No good copy located.)
AAS copy.   27337

The School of Good Manners. Composed
for the Help of Parents [by Eleazar
Moody, d. 1720].
Boston, Edes and Clap, 1794. 92 pp.
(An imprint variant of 27337, q. v. for
text.)
AAS copy.   47116

The School of Good Manners [by Eleazar
Moody, d. 1720].
Troy, Gardner & Billings, 1795. [2], 94
pp.
JCB copy.   29094

The School of Good Manners [by Eleazar
Moody, d. 1720].
Boston, Manning & Loring, 1805. 95 pp.
(This was the ed. which Evans described
from an imperfect copy.)
AAS copy.   30808

The School of Virtue, a Novel, on a New
Plan.
Philadelphia, Spotswood, 1790. [2], ii,
197, [3]; 72 pp.
AAS copy.   22876

The School of Wisdom: or, American
Monitor.
Philadelphia, Carey, 1800. pp. [i]-xii,
[5]-304.
AAS copy.   37099

The School of Wisdom, or Repository of the
most Valuable Curiosities.
New Brunswick, Lawson & Dunham,
1787. [2], 206 pp.
BA copy.   20695

Ein Schreiben der Herrnhutischen
Gemeine.
[Germantown? 1743.]
(The unique copy in the S. W.
Pennypacker collection is not now to be
found.)   5284

Schreiben des Evangelisch-Lutherischen und
Reformirten Kirchen-Raths.
Philadelphia, Miller, 1775. 40 pp.
HSP copy.   14394

Schroeder, Johann Georg.
Merkwürdige Geschichte.
Ephrata, 1790. 48 pp.
HEH copy.   22877

Schröter, Johann Samuel.
The Conquest of Belgrade. A Sonata.
New York, Gilfert, 1795. 11 pp.
(Not located, 1968.)   47692

Schubart, Christian Friedrich Daniel.
Schubart's Klaglied.
[Philadelphia], Cist for Willig, etc.,
[1799?]. [2] pp.
LCP copy.   48961

Die Schule der Weisheit oder Theil in
Poesie.
[Ephrata], 1748.
(Metzger 131. No copy located.)   40478

Schule der Weisheit.
Germantown, 1750. 146 pp.
(The only copies located are imperfect.)
NYPL copy.   6602

Schultz, Benjamin.
An Oration Delivered before the
Mosheimian Society, on July 23d, 1795.
Philadelphia, Dobson, 1795. 14 pp.
APS copy.   47593

[Schultz, Christopher] 1718-1789.
Kurze Fragen ueber die Christliche
Glaubens-Lehre.
Philadelphia, Cist, 1784. [10], 140 pp.
AAS copy.   18779

Schuyler, Philip John, 1733-1804.
Friends and Fellow-Citizens! Your
Attention. . . . [Apr. 23, 1796.]
n. p., [1796.]
NYPL copy.   47907

Schuyler, Philip John, 1733-1804,
defendant.
Proceedings of a General Court Martial.
Philadelphia, Hall & Sellers, 1778. 62 pp.
NYPL copy.   16142

Schuyler, Philip John, 1733-1804.
Remarks on the Revenue, of the State.
Albany, Websters, 1796. 24 pp.
AAS copy.   31166

Schuyler, Philip John, 1733-1804.
To the Stockholders. . . . June 7, 1793.
[Albany? 1793] Broadside.
(Copy is imperfect.)
NYPL copy.   46874

Schuylkill and Susquehanna Canal
Navigation Co.
Canal Lottery. . . . May 18, 1795.
[Philadelphia, 1795.] Broadside.
HSP copy.   29473

Schuylkill and Susquehannah Canal
Navigation Co.
Canal Lottery, No. Two . . . April 20th,
1796.
[Philadelphia, 1796.] Broadside.
LCP copy.   31167

Schuylkill and Susquehanna Canal
Navigation Co.
Plan for Raising by Loan a Sum of Money
. . . till the End of the Present Year 1794.
[Philadelphia, 1794.] Broadside.
LOC copy.   47210

[Schuylkill and Susquehannah Canal
Navigation Co.
. . . To the Senate and House of
Representatives of . . . Pennsylvania.
[Philadelphia, 1794.] [2] pp.
(No copy located.)   27678

Schuylkill Permanent Bridge Co.,
Philadelphia.
An Act of the Legislature of Pennsylvania
and a Patent to. . . .
Philadelphia, Fenno, [1798]. 21 pp.
MHS copy.   34321

Schwache, doch Wahre Ausdrücke.
[Philadelphia], Steiner, [1790]. [4] pp.
AAS copy.   22878

[Schwenkfelder Church.]
Catechismus, oder Anfaenglicher
Christ-licher Glaubens-Lehrer.
Philadelphia, Miller, 1763. [4], 146 pp.
AAS copy.   9512

Scipio's Reflections on Monroe's View
[by Uriah Tracy, 1755-1807].

Boston, Wayne, 1798. [4], 140 pp.
AAS copy.   34676

Scituate, R. I. Ordinances, etc.
Scituate, August 27, 1794. . . . An Act for
Mending and Repairing the Highways.
Providence, Wheeler, [1794]. Broadside.
Newport Hist. Soc. copy.   27612

Scituate, R.I. Town Meeting, 1794.
Scituate, August 27, 1794. Whereas the
Honorable the General Assembly . . .
Providence, Wheeler, [1794.] Broadside.
NHS copy.   47211

Scot's Charitable Society, Boston.
Rules and Regulations. . . . Renewed 1786.
Boston, Young & Minns, 1800. 8 pp.
NYHS copy.   37018

Scots Society in New York.
Rules and Orders Agreed upon by the
Scots Society in New-York.
New York, Parker, 1744. Broadside.
NYHS copy.   5462

Scots Thistle Society of Philadelphia.
Constitution of the. . . . Instituted
November 30th, 1796.
Philadelphia, Bioren, 1799. 28 pp.
LCP copy.   36108

[Scott, Frances.
A True and Wonderful Narrative of the
Surprising Captivity of. . . . Third Edition.
Boston, 1788.]
(Vail 787. A ghost of E19979.)   45356

[Scott, Gustavus, 1753-1800.
(D. A. B.)
A Letter from . . . to James Lloyd
Chamberlaine.
Baltimore, 1778.]
("Will speedily be published": 15747.) 16068

[Scott, Helenus], 1760-1821.
The Adventures of an East-India Rupee.
Philadelphia, Bell, 1783. 64 pp.
LOC copy.   18179

Scott, Job, 1751-1793.
The Baptism of Christ.
Providence, Carter, 1793. vii, [1], 185 pp.
AAS copy.   26146

Scott, Job, 1751-1793.
Journal of the Life . . . of. . . .
New York, Collins, 1797. xii, [2], 360 pp.
AAS copy.   32810

Scott, Job, 1751-1793.
Journal of the Life . . . of. . . .
Wilmington, Bonsal & Niles, 1797. x, [2],
324 pp.
AAS copy.   32811

Scott, Job, 1751-1793.
Journal of. . . .
New York, Collins, 1798. xii, [2], 360 pp.
AAS copy.   34518

Scott, John.
War Inconsistent.
Philadelphia, Woodward, 1799. 26 pp.
AAS copy.   36281

Scott, John.
War Inconsistent with . . . Christ.
New Bedford, Shearman, 1800. 24 pp.
AAS copy.   38472

Scott, John Morin, c. 1730-1784.
The Following Affidavit. . . . 9th January,
1769.
[New York, 1769.] Broadside.
LOC copy.   11453

Scott, John Morin, c. 1730-1784.
To the Freeholders and Freemen of the
City and County of New-York. . . .
January 6, 1769.
[New York, 1769.] Broadside.
LOC copy.   11454

Scott, John Morin, c. 1730-1784.
To the Public. The Provincial Congress of
New-York Yesterday Passed a Resolve.
. . . June 9, 1776.
[New York, 1776.] Broadside.
NYHS copy.   43176

Scott, John Morin, c. 1730-1784.

Zur nach Right. . . . January den 11de,
1769.
[New York, 1769.] Broadside.
LOC copy.   11455

Scott, Joseph, geographer.
An Atlas of the United States.
Philadelphia, Baileys, Davis, and Rices,
1796. tp., 19 maps.
LOC copy.   47908

[Scott, Joseph, geographer.
The New and Universal Gazetteer.
Philadelphia, Baileys, 1798.]
(No copy located with this imprint.) 34519

Scott, Joseph, geographer.
The New and Universal Gazetteer. . . .
Vol. I [-II].
Philadelphia, Baileys, 1799. xxxviii, [410]
pp., 6 maps; [436] pp., 4 maps.
AAS copy.   36282

Scott, Joseph, geographer.
The New and Universal Gazetteer. . . . in
Four Volumes. Vol. III [-IV].
Philadelphia, Patterson & Cochran, 1800.
[446] pp., 4 maps; [516] pp., 11 maps, 1
table.
AAS copy.   38473

Scott, Joseph, geographer.
The United States Gazetteer.
Philadelphia, Bailey, 1795. vi, [287] pp.,
19 maps.
AAS copy.   29476

[Scott, Joseph, importer.
Joseph Scott, Jun. at his shop, No. 6,
Dock-Square, Boston. . . .
[Boston, 1796.] Broadside.]
(The only copy recorded is not to be
located.)   31168

Scott, Joseph Warren, 1778-1871.
An Oration, Delivered . . . July 4, 1798.
New Brunswick, N. J., Blauvelt, 1798. 16
pp.
AAS copy.   34520

[Scott, Sarah (Robinson)], 1723-1795.
The Man of Real Sensibility.
Philadelphia, Humphreys, 1774. [2], 84,
[1] pp.
AAS copy.   42696

[Scott, Sarah (Robinson), 1723-1795.
The Man of Real Sensibility.
Philadelphia, Woodhouse, 1787.]
("Just Published and to be Sold by," Ind.
Gazetteer, Apr. 4, 1787.)   20696

[Scott, Sarah (Robinson)], 1723-1795.
The Man of Real Sensibility.
Philadelphia, Kammerer, 1797. 92, [2] pp.
AAS copy.   32812

[Scott, Sarah (Robinson)], 1723-1795.
The Man of Real Sensibility.
[Leominster, Mass.], Whitcomb, [1800].
42 pp.
AAS copy.   49145

[Scott, Sarah (Robinson)], 1723-1795.
The Man of Real Sensibility.
Wilmington, Del., Bonsal & Niles, 1800.
72 pp.
LOC copy.   38474

Scott, Sarah (Robinson), 1723-1795.
The Man of Sensibility.
Philadelphia, J. Johnson, 1797. 92 pp.
(Not located, 1968.)   48257

Scott, Thomas, of Annapolis.
A Sermon, Preached at St. Peter's
Church.
Philadelphia, Stewart & Cochran, 1792. 19
pp.
AAS copy.   24773

Scott, Thomas, 1747-1821.
The Force of Truth. . . . Third Edition.
Philadelphia, Young, 1793. 132 pp.
AAS copy.   26147

Scott, Thomas, 1747-1821.
The Force of Truth. . . . Third Edition.
New London, Green, 1795. 136 pp.
BPL copy.   29475

Scott, Thomas, 1747-1821.
A Vindication of the Divine Inspiration.

New York, Forman for Davis, 1797. 202,
[2] pp.
AAS copy.   32813

Scott, William, b. 1726.
O Tempora! O Mores!
Norwich, 1774. 32 pp.
AAS copy.   13599

Scott, William, b. 1726.
O Tempora! O Mores!
Philadelphia, Towne, 1774. xii, 20 pp.
AAS copy.   13600

[Scott, William, 1750-1804.
An Introduction to the Reading and
Spelling of the English Tongue.
Philadelphia, Dobson, 1787.]
("Just Published," Pa. Gazette, Feb. 28,
1787.)   20697

[Scott, William, 1750-1804.
Scott's Lessons in Elocution.
Philadelphia, Dobson, 1786.]
(Entry from an adv. for "New Books" in
Pa. Gazette, Aug. 2, 1786.)   19980

Scott, William, 1750-1804.
Lessons in Elocution. . . . First American
Edition.
Philadelphia, Young, 1788. 396 pp.
AAS copy.   21451

Scott, William, 1750-1804.
Lessons in Elocution. . . . Second
American Edition.
Philadelphia, Young, 1790. 436 pp.
(The only copy located is very defective.)
HSP copy.   22879

Scott, William, 1750-1804.
Lessons in Elocution. . . . Third American
Edition.
Philadelphia, Young, 1791. pp. [5]-viii,
[13]-436 pp., 4 plates.
AAS copy.   46286

Scott, William, 1750-1804.
Lessons in Elocution. . . . Fifth American
Edition.
Philadelphia, Young, 1794. pp. [i]-viii,
[13]-48, [61]-436. 4 plates.
AAS copy.   27680

Scott, William, 1750-1804.
Lessons in Elocution. . . . First Hartford
Edition.
Hartford, Hudson & Goodwin, 1795. 406
pp., 4 plates.
AAS copy.   29477

Scott, William, 1750-1804.
Lessons in Elocution.
New Haven, Morse, 1795. pp. [6],
[13]-427.
(Only copy is imperfect.)
CHS copy.   47594

Scott, William, 1750-1804.
Lessons in Elocution. . . . Fourth
American Edition.
New York, Forman, 1796. 400 pp. (irreg.)
AAS copy.   47909

Scott, William, 1750-1804.
Lessons in Elocution. . . . Sixth American
. . . Edition.
Philadelphia, Young, 1796. pp. [1]-viii,
[13]-436.
(Best copy available.)
AAS copy.   47910

Scott, William, 1750-1804.
Lessons in Elocution. . . . Seventh
American Edition.
Wilmington, Del., Brynberg, 1797. 383 pp., 4
plates.
AAS copy.   32814

Scott, William, 1750-1804.
Lessons in Elocution . . . Sixth American
. . . Edition.
Phildelphia, Bioren, 1798. pp. [i]-viii,
[13]-48, 61-436, 4 plates.
AAS copy.   34521

Scott, William, 1750-1804.
Lessons in Elocution.
New Haven, Bunce, 1799. 322, [30] pp.
AAS copy.   36283

Scott, William, 1750-1804.
Lessons in Elocution. . . . To this Edition

are Prefixed, Elements of Gesture.
New York, Kirk, 1799. [2], 396 pp., 4
plates.
AAS copy.   36284

Scott, William, 1750-1804.
Lessons in Elocution. . . . The Eighth
American . . . Edition.
Whitehall, Pa., Young, 1799. pp. [i]-viii,
[13]-436; 4 plates.
AAS copy.   36285

Scott, William, 1750-1804.
Lessons in Elocution. . . . Eighth
American Edition.
Worcester, Mass., Mower & Greenleaf for
Thomas, 1800. pp. [i]-viii, [13]-436; 4
plates.
AAS copy.   38475

[Scottow, Joshua], 1618-1693.
A Narrative of the Planting.
Boston, 1694. [4], 75, [1] pp.
AAS copy.   709

[Scottow, Joshua], 1618-1693.
Old Mens Tears.
Boston, 1691. [6], 23, [1] pp.
BA copy.   576

[Scottow, Joshua], 1618-1693.
(D. N. B.)
Old Mens Tears.
Boston, 1715. 58 pp.
(The only copy located is badly defective.)
BPL copy.   1779

[Scottow, Joshua], 1618-1693.
(D. N. B.)
Old Men's Tears.
Boston, Gray, 1733. [4], 20 pp.
AAS copy.   3604

Scottow, Joshua, 1618-1693.
(D. N. B.)
Old Men's Tears.
Boston, Gookin, 1749. 23 pp.
HC copy.   6413

[Scottow, Joshua], 1618-1693.
Old Men's Tears.
New London, 1769. 22 pp.
AAS copy.   11457

[Scougal, Henry], 1650-1678.
[Das Leben Gottes.
Germantown, 1755.] [21], 77 pp.
(The only known copy is imperfect.)
HSP copy.   7565

[Scougal, Henry], 1650-1678.
(D. N. B.)
Das Leben Gottes.
Philadelphia, Franklin, 1756. [21], 78, [1]
pp.
AAS copy.   7787

[Scougal, Henry], 1650-1678.
The Life of God in the Soul of Man.
n. p., 1727. [10?], 106, 4 pp.
(The only recorded copy is imperfect.)
AAS copy.   39872

[Scougal, Henry], 1650-1678.
(D. N. B.)
The Life of God.
Boston, Rogers & Fowle for Foster, 1741.
88 pp.
(Evans took his description from Haven.)
AAS copy.   4797

[Scougal, Henry], 1650-1678.
The Life of God in the Soul of Man.
Boston, Rogers & Fowle for Henchman,
1741. 88 pp.
(An imprint variant of 4797, q. v.)   40258

[Scougal, Henry], 1650-1678.
The Life of God.
New York, Gaine, 1766. ix, [1], 158, iv
pp.
(The only copy available lacks last 4 pp.)
LOC copy.   10490

[Scougal, Henry], 1650-1678.
(D. N. B.)
The Life of God.
Philadelphia, Dunlap, 1766. xxiv, 196 pp.
AAS copy.   10489

Scougal, Henry, 1650-1678.
The Life of God in the Soul of Man.

Boston, Edes, 1789. xiii, [1] 88 pp.
AAS copy.   22131

Scougal, Henry, 1650-1678.
The Life of God.
Philadelphia, Ormrod & Conrad, 1795. pp.
[6], [9]-140, [1]-28.
AAS copy.   29478

[Scougal, Henry], 1650-1678.
(D. N. B.)
A Sermon Preach'd on the 25th of
December.
Boston, 1737. [4], 28 pp.
AAS copy.   4195

Scourge, Humphrey, pseud.
Tit for Tat.
[New York, 1758.] 4 pp.
HSP copy.   8256

4th Edition. The Scourge. Numb. I.
Boston, Thomas, [1771]. Broadside.
AAS copy.   42275

The Scourge. Numb. I [-II].
Boston, Thomas, 1771. 2 broadsides.
AAS copy.   12222

The Scourge of Fashion, a Poem, by
Phylanthus.
New York, Ming & Young, 1800. 23 pp.
AAS copy.   38476

The Scribler; being a Letter from a
Gentleman.
[Philadelphia], 1764. 24 pp.
NYPL copy.   9831

A Scriptural Comment on the Athanasian
Creed.
Philadelphia, Lang, [1791]. 16 pp.
BA copy.   23396

A Scriptural View of the Rise of the
Heathen, Jewish, and Christian
Monarchies [by John C. Robson].
New York, Buell, 1797. 99, [1] pp.
AAS copy.   48244

The Scripture-Bishop. Or the Divine
Right of Presbyterian Ordination [by
Jonathan Dickinson, 1688-1747].
Boston, Henchman, 1732. [4], ii, 58 pp.
AAS copy.   3528

The Scripture Bishop, or, The Divine
Right of Presbyterian Ordination . . .
Examined [by Arthur Browne,
1699-1773].
n.p., 1733. [4], 52 pp.
AAS copy.   3636

The Scripture-Bishop Vindicated [by
Jonathan Dickinson, 1688-1747].
Boston, Kneeland & Green for
Henchman, 1733. [2], 126, [2], 158 pp.
AAS copy.   3651

A Scripture-Catechism; or, the Principles
of the Christian Religion.
[Boston, 1750?] [2], 32 pp.
AAS copy.   6603

The Scripture Doctrine Concerning
Predestination [by John Wesley, 1703-
1791].
Boston, Fleet, 1746. 16 pp.
MHS copy.   5881

The Scripture Doctrine of Predestination,
Election, and Reprobation [by John Wesley,
1703-1791].
Stockbridge, Andrews, 1795. 25 pp.
JCB copy.   29479

Scripture Truths and Precepts [by Shippie
Townsend, 1722-1798].
Boston, Hall, 1791. 23 pp.
AAS copy.   23838

[The Scripture Warning and Signs of the
Last Times.
Portsmouth, N. H., Peirce, 1798.]
("This Day Published, and for sale by C.
Peirce," Oracle of the Day, Mar. 10,
1798.)   34522

Scudder, William, b. 1747.
The Journal of. . . .
n. p., 1794. 250 pp.
(The only known copy is imperfect.)
NYHS copy.   27681

[Scull, Nicholas?], 1687?-1761?
(Pa. Mag. Hist. Biog., XIV, 378-380.)
Kawanio Che Keeteru.
[Philadelphia], 1756. 16 pp.
HSP copy.   7788

[Scull, Nicholas?], 1687?-1761?
Kawanio Che Keeteru. . . . Second
Edition.
Philadelphia, Chattin, 1756.)
("This Day was published. . . . The
Second Edition," Pa. Gazette, Mar. 18,
1756.)   7789

[Scull, Nicholas, 1687?-1761?
A Plan of the City and Environs of
Philadelphia.
[Philadelphia, 1777.] Map.]
(Published at Nurnberg, 1778. See P. Lee
Phillips, Descriptive List of Maps and
Views of Philadelphia in the Library of
Congress, item 168.)   15593

Scull, Nicholas, 1687?-1761?
(Pa. Mag. Hist. Biog., XIV, 378-380.)
To the Honourable Thomas Penn . . . this
Map of the Improved Part of . . .
Pennsylvania. . . .
Philadelphia, engraved by Turner, printed
by Davis, 1759.
HSP copy.   8489

[Scull, Nicholas], 1687?-1761?
To the Mayor . . . of Philadelphia. This
Plan of the Improved Part of the City. . . .
[Philadelphia, 1762.] map.
HSP copy.   9267

Scull, William, fl. 1765.
(Pa. Mag. Hist. Biog., LIX, 277-278.)
To the Honorable Thomas Penn . . . Map
of the Province of Pennsylvania.
Philadelphia, Nevil, 1770. Map.
JCB copy.   11850

Seabury, Samuel, 1706-1764.
A Modest Reply.
New York, 1759. [2], 18 pp.
CHS copy.   8490

Seabury, Samuel, 1706-1764.
(Sibley, VII, 432-40.)
A Sermon Preach'd at New-London.
New London, 1742. [4], 22 pp.
JCB copy.   5051

[Seabury, Samuel], bp., 1729-1796.
An Address to the Ministers and
Congregations.
[New Haven], 1790. 55 pp.
AAS copy.   22880

[Seabury, Samuel], bp., 1729-1796.
An Address to the Ministers and
Congregations.
Boston, Manning & Loring, 1797. 56 pp.
NYPL copy.   32815

[Seabury, Samuel], bp., 1729-1796.
An Alarm to the Legislature of the
Province of New-York.
New York, Rivington, 1775. 13, [2] pp.
AAS copy.   14453

Seabury, Samuel, bp., 1729-1796.
Bishop Seabury's Second Charge.
New Haven, Greens, [1786]. 20 pp.
LOC copy.   19981

Seabury, Samuel, bp., 1729-1796.
The Communion-Office.
New London, Green, 1786. 23 pp.
LOC copy.   19982

[Seabury, Samuel], bp., 1729-1796.
The Congress Canvassed.
[New York], 1774. 27, [1] pp.
AAS copy.   13601

Seabury, Samuel, bp., 1729-1796.
A Discourse Delivered before an
Assembly of Free and Accepted Masons.
Norwich, Sterry, 1715 (i.e., 1795). 17 pp.
CHS copy.   29480

Seabury, Samuel, bp., 1729-1796.
A Discourse Delivered before the
Triennial Convention.
New York, Gaine, 1792. 27 pp.
AAS copy.   24774

Seabury, Samuel, bp., 1729-1796.

A Discourse Delivered in St. James'
Church.
New London, Green, 1795. 23 pp.
AAS copy.   29481

Seabury, Samuel, bp., 1729-1796.
A Discourse, Delivered in St. John's
Church.
Boston, Thomas & Andrews, 1791, 22 pp.
AAS copy.   23755

Seabury, Samuel, bp., 1729-1796.
A Discourse on Brotherly Love.
New York, Gaine, 1777. 20 pp.
NYHS copy.   15594

Seabury, Samuel, bp., 1729-1796.
A Discourse on II Tim. III, 16.
New York, Gaine, 1777. 23 pp.
GTS copy.   15595

Seabury, Samuel, bp., 1729-1796.
Discourses on Several Important Subjects.
New York, Swords, 1798. vii, [1], 279 pp.
AAS copy.   34523

Seabury, Samuel, bp., 1729-1796.
Discourses on Several Subjects.
New York, Swords for Rivington, 1793. 2
vol. x, 344; viii, 301 pp.
AAS copy.   26148

Seabury, Samuel, bp., 1729-1796.
The Duty of Considering our Ways.
New Haven, Greens, [1789]. 18 pp.
AAS copy.   22132

Seabury, Samuel, bp., 1729-1796.
An Earnest Persuasive to Frequent
Communion.
New Haven, Greens, 1789. 23 pp.
LOC copy.   22133

[Seabury, Samuel], bp., 1729-1796.
Free Thoughts, on the Proceedings of the
Continental Congress.
[New York], 1774. 24 pp.
AAS copy.   13602

[Seabury, Samuel], bp., 1729-1796.
Free Thoughts, on the Proceedings of the
Continental Congress.
[New York], Printed in the Year
M,DCC,LXXIV [by Rivington]. 31 pp.
AAS copy.   42697

[Seabury, Samuel], bp., 1729-1796.
Prayers. A Prayer for the Courts of
Justice.
n. p., [1795?] [4] pp.
Pierce W. Gaines copy.   47595

Seabury, Samuel, bp., 1729-1796.
St. Peter's Exhortation.
New York, Gaine, [1777]. 23 pp.
BA copy.   15596

Seabury, Samuel, bp., 1729-1796.
A Sermon Delivered before the Boston
Episcopal, Charitable Society.
Boston, Fleets, 1788. [4], 24, 6 pp.
AAS copy.   21452

Seabury, Samuel, bp., 1729-1796.
A Sermon, Preached before the Grand
Lodge.
New York, Robertsons, Mills, & Hicks,
1783. 23 pp.
NYHS copy.   18180

[Seabury, Samuel], bp., 1729-1796.
A View of the Controversy between
Great-Britain and her Colonies.
New York, Rivington, 1774. 37, [2] pp.
AAS copy.   13603

Seagrave, Robert, 1693-1760.
(D. N. B.)
Remarks upon the Bishop of London's
Pastoral Letter.
Philadelphia, Bradford, 1740. [2], 21 pp.
AAS copy.   4594

[Seagrave, Robert, 1693-1760.
The True Protestant.
Boston, 1748.]
(Title from Haven.)   6236

Seagrave, Robert, 1693-1760.
(D. N. B.)
The True Protestant.
Philadelphia, 1748. [4], 35, [1] pp.
AAS copy.   6235

Seaman, Valentine, 1770-1817.
An Account of the Epidemic Yellow
Fever.
New York, Hopkins, Webb & Co., 1796.
ix, 150 pp.
NLM copy.   31169

[Seaman, Valentine, 1770-1817.
An Account of the Epidemic Yellow
Fever.
New York, Hopkins, Webb & Co., 1797.
ix, 246 pp.]
(Entry from Sabin.)   32816

Seaman, Valentine, 1770-1817.
A Dissertation on the Mineral Waters of
Saratoga.
New York, Campbell, 1793. 40 pp.
AAS copy.   26149

Seaman, Valentine, 1770-1817.
An Inaugural Dissertation on Opium.
Philadelphia, Johnston & Justice, 1792. 32
pp.
AAS copy.   24775

Seaman, Valentine, 1770-1817.
The Midwives Monitor.
New York, Collins, 1800. 123 pp.
NYAM copy.   38477

[Seaman's Articles, with the Act Entitled,
"An Act for the Government and
Regulation of Seamen in the Merchants'
Service."
Savannah, Johnston, 1792?]
(Title and imprint assumed by Evans from
an adv.)   24913

The Seaman's Journal: being an Easy and
Correct Method of Keeping the Daily
Reckoning.
Sagg-Harbour, Frothingham, [179?]. tp.
and blank journal.
East Hampton Free Library copy. 45793

[The Seaman's Journal-Book.
Providence, Carter & Wilkinson, 1797.
[48] pp.]
(This log book is entirely in ms. No
printing occurs.)   48248

The Seaman's Journal: being an Easy and
Correct Method of Keeping the Daily
Reckoning.
New London, Springer for Green, 1798.
[90] pp.
AAS copy.   48609

[The Seaman's Journal: being an Easy
and Correct Method of Keeping the Daily
Reckoning.
New Haven, Beers, 1800. [78] pp.]
(No copy located.)   38478

The Seaman's Journal-Book.
Providence, R.I., Carter & Wilkinson,
1795. [157] pp.
AAS copy.   47596

The Seaman's Log Book.
Providence, Carter & Wilkinson, 1798. 96
leaves.
JCB copy.   48610

[Search after Happiness. . . . And Armine
and Elvira. . . . Second Edition.
Philadelphia, Humphreys, 1775.]
(Adv. Pa. Journal, Feb. 1, 1775.)   14263

The Search after Happies [by Hannah
More, 1745-1833].
Boston, Spotswood, 1796. 33, [3] pp.
AAS copy.   30815

The Search after Happiness [by Hannah
More, 1745-1833].
Boston, Spotswood, 1797. 33, [3] pp.
AAS copy.   48185

Searle, John, 1721-1787.
(Weis, Colonial Clergy, N.E.)
The Character and Reward.
Newburyport, 1778. lxvi pp.
BA copy.   16069

Searle, John, 1721-1787.
A Funeral Sermon Delivered at
Newbury-Port.
Boston, Fleets, 1771. 54 pp.
AAS copy.   42276

Searle, John, 1721-1787.

(Weis, Colonial Clergy N. E.)
A Funeral Sermon Delivered at
Newbury-Port, Dec. 30, 1770.
Boston, Fleets for Emerson, 1771. 54 pp.
AAS copy.   12223

Searle, John, 1721-1787.
(Weis, Colonial Clergy N. E.)
Revelation a Guide to Reason.
Boston, Fleets, 1773. 35 pp.
AAS copy.   13003

Sears, Isaac, c. 1730-1786.
(D. A. B.)
An Advertisement. . . . January 24th,
1769.
[New York, 1769.] Broadside.
LOC copy.   11458

Searson, John.
Art of Contentment.
Baltimore, Pechin, [1797?]. 225, [1] pp.
AAS copy.   31170

Searson, John.
Mount Vernon, a Poem.
Philadelphia, Folwell, [1800]. front., pp.
[2], [i]-vi, [9]-83, [1], [1]-4.
AAS copy.   38479

Searson, John.
Poems on Various Subjects.
Philadelphia, Snowden & M'Corkle, 1797.
94, [9] pp.
AAS copy.   32817

[Searson, John].
Seven Hints for all who will take Them.
[Philadelphia, 1770.] Broadside.
LCP copy.   11851

[Searson, John.]
Two Discourses Delivered in the Prison.
Philadelphia, Evitt, [1770]. 17 pp.
NYHS copy.   11852

A Seasonable Account of the Christian.
Philadelphia, 1700. 19 pp.
HSP copy.   950

A Seasonable Advertisement to the
Freeholders. . . .
New-York, January 12, 1769.
[New York, 1769.] Broadside.
LOC copy.   11459

[A Seasonable Advice to the Inhabitants
of the Province of Pennsylvania.
Philadelphia, 1729. 3 pp.]
(Hildeburn 379.)   3213

Seasonable Motives [by Nathaniel
Byfield, 1653-1733].
Philadelphia, 1689. [2] pp.
MHS copy.   463

A Seasonable Plea for Liberty of
Conscience [by Isaac Backus, 1724-1806].
Boston, Freeman, 1770. 48 pp.
AAS copy.   11556

A Seasonable Testimony to the Glorious
Doctrines [by Cotton Mather, 1663-1728].
Boston, 1702. 15 pp.
AAS copy.   1074

The Seasons. An Interlocutory Exercise
[by John Lovell, 1710-1778].
Boston, Fleet, 1765. 8 pp.
AAS copy.   10043

[Seccomb, John], 1708-1792.
(Sibley, VIII, 481-490.)
Father Abbey's Will.
n.d., n.p. Broadside.
(Evans assumes that the first broadside
printing was in 1731. This is highly
improbable. An example of one of the
many undated later editions is here
reproduced.)
AAS copy.   3474

[Seccomb, John], 1708-1792.
Father Ab--y's Will.
n.d., n.p. Broadside.
(See note under 3474.)
AAS copy.   3475

Seccomb, John, 1708-1792.
(Sibley, VIII, 481-490.)
A Sermon Occasioned by the Death of . . .
Abigail Belcher.

Boston, Fleets, 1772. 25, [2] pp.
AAS copy.   12555

[Seccomb, John, 1708-1792.
(Sibley, VIII, 481-490.)
Eine zu Halifax den 3ten July 1770
Gehaltene Predigt.
Philadelphia, Miller, 1770.]
(Adv. Pa. Staatsbote, Feb. 5, 1770.)   11853

[Seccombe, Joseph], 1706-1760.
(Sibley, IX, 87-96.)
Business and Diversion.
Boston, Kneeland & Green, 1743. 21, [1]
pp.
AAS copy.   5285

[Seccombe, Joseph], 1706-1760.
(Sibley, IX, 87-96.)
An Essay to Excite a Further Inquiry.
Boston, Kneeland & Green, 1741. [4], ii,
16, [1] pp.
AAS copy.   4798

[Seccombe, Joseph], 1706-1760.
On the Death of the Reverend Benjamin
Colman.
Boston, Rogers & Fowle, [1748]. 8 pp.
("This day is Published," Ind. Adv., Feb.
29, 1748.)
AAS copy.   5937

[Seccombe, Joseph], 1706-1760.
(Sibley, IX, 87-96.)
A Plain and Brief Rehersal.
Boston, Kneeland and Green, 1740. [4],
ii, 23, [1] pp.
AAS copy.   4595

Seccombe, Joseph, 1706-1760.
Reflections on Hypocrisy.
Boston, Kneeland & Green, 1741. [4], 18
pp.
AAS copy.   4799

[Seccombe, Joseph], 1706-1760.
(Sibley, IX, 87-96.)
Some Occasional Thoughts.
Boston, Kneeland & Green, 1742. [4], ii,
16 pp.
(Contemporary attribution in AAS and
other copies.)
AAS copy.   5052

[Seccombe, Joseph], 1706-1760.
A Specimen.
Boston, Kneeland & Green, 1743. [4], iv,
29 pp.
AAS copy.   5286

[Seccombe, Joseph], 1706-1760.
(Sibley, IX, 87-96.)
The Ways of Pleasure.
Boston, Mecom, [1762]. [2], 14 pp.
AAS copy.   9268

Sechs Neue Politische Lieder.
n. p., 1769. 8 pp.
LCP copy.   42003

[Secker, Thomas], 1693-1768.
(D. N. B.)
An Answer to Dr. Mayhew's
Observations.
Boston, Draper, Edes & Gill, & Fleet,
1764. 59 pp.
AAS copy.   9832

Secker, William, d. 1681?
A Wedding Ring.
[Boston], S. G. for B. H., 1690. [64] pp.
(The unique copy is imperfect.)
BPL copy.   39279

Secker, William, d. 1681.
A Wedding Ring.
Boston, T. G[reen] for Boone, 1705. 89,
[3] pp.
(For text see 39435.)
AAS copy.   39434

Secker, William, d. 1681.
A Wedding Ring.
Boston, T. G[reen], for Buttolph, 1705.
89, [3] pp.
PPL copy.   39435

Secker, William, - 1681?
(D. N. B.)
A Wedding Ring.
Boston, Draper, 1750. 28, [5] pp.
AAS copy.   6604

Secker, William, d. 1681?
(D. N. B.)
[A Wedding Ring.
Boston, Kneeland, 1773.] 89, [2] pp.
(The only copy located is imperfect.)
AAS copy.   13004

A Second Address to the Freemen. . . . by
Horatio Juvenal [by Richard Alsop,
1761-1815].
[Litchfield, 1790.] 10 pp.
CHS copy.   22599

A Second Address, to the Reverend Moses
C. Welch [by Zephaniah Swift, 1759-
1823].
Windham, Ct., Byrne, 1796. 43 pp.
AAS copy.   31259

A Second Dialogue, between a Minister
and his Parishioner [by Nathaniel
Taylor?, 1722-1800].
Hartford, 1769. 15 pp.
(This Dialogue is included in Vol. 3 of the
N.Y., 1812, ed., of the Works of Joseph
Bellamy.)
BA copy.   11490

The Second Edition of Lord Howes, &
General Howes Proclamation with Notes,
and Emendations. . . . Jan. 1, 1777.
[Norwich, Ct., 1777.] Broadside.
CHS copy.   43371

A Second Edition, (with Necessary
Improvements) . . . of the Lawfulness . . .
of Organs.
Philadelphia, Steuart, 1763. 16 pp.
(The title given by Evans comes from
Hildeburn, who was apparently following
an adv. for this piece.)
MHS copy.   9369

A Second Essay on Free Trade and
Finance [by Pelatiah Webster, 1726-1795].
Philadelphia, Bradford, 1779. 20 pp.
AAS copy.   16671

A Second Familiar Conference [by John
Beach, 1700-1782].
New York, Holt, 1765. [4], 41 pp.
AAS copy.   9910

[A Second Letter from a Gentleman in
the Country to his Friend in Town.
New York, 1757.]
(Source of entry not found.)   8032

A Second Letter from a Minister of the
Church of England [by Samuel Johnson,
1696-1772].
Boston, 1734. [4], 113, [1] pp.
AAS copy.   3784

A Second Letter from One in the Country,
to his Friend in Boston.
[Boston, 1729.] 2 pp.
HC copy.   3215

A Second Letter from Phocion [by
Alexander Hamilton, 1757-1804].
New York, Loudon, 1784. 43 pp.
AAS copy.   18516

A Second Letter to a Friend; Giving a
more Particular Narrative of the Defeat of
the French Army at Lake-George [by
Charles Chauncy, 1705-1787].
Boston, Edes & Gill, 1755. 16 pp.
AAS copy.   7382

A Second Letter to- -Merchant in London.
[Boston, 1741.] 16 pp.
BPL copy.   4800

A Second Letter to the Congregations.
Philadelphia, Steuart, 1761. 32 pp.
AAS copy.   9003

A Second Letter to the Reverend George
Whitefield. . . . From his Friend Publicola.
Charleston, Timothy, 1747. 16 pp.
(No copy located.)   40438

A Second Letter, to the Reverend Joseph
Bellamy [by Ebenezer Devotion,
1714-1771].
New Haven, [1770]. 19 pp.
AAS copy.   11631

A Second Letter to the Reverend Mr.
Whitefield. . . . By Canoncus.
Boston, Fleet, 1745. 8 pp.

(For authorship and date see BSA, XLV, 131.)
HC copy. 5153

The Second Part of South-Sea Stock [by John Higginson, 1675-1718].
Boston, Henchman, 1721. [2], 26 pp.
(Attributed to a John Higginson by Eames and by Heartman in Cat. of 600 Pamphlets [1920], p. 50. The AAS copy belonged to a son of Higginson's minister.)
AAS copy. 2291

The Second Spira [by Richard Sault, d. 1702].
Boston, 1693. [16], 55 pp.
LOC copy. 681

The Second Spira. . . . Sixth Edition [by Richard Sault, d. 1702].
Boston, Fleet & Crump for Eliot, 1715. [11], [1]-37, 37-38, 1-22.
AAS copy. 39634

The Second Spira [by Richard Sault, -1702].
Boston, 1721.]
(Probably the ghost of an English printing. Adv. "Sold by Benjamin Eliot" in 2302.) 2290

The Second Spira [by Richard Sault, d. 1702].
Newport, [R. I.], Southwick, 1768. 37 pp.
AAS copy. 41878

The Second Spira [by Richard Sault, d. 1702].
Boston, at the Heart and Crown, [1772?] 8 pp.
AAS copy. 42374

The Second Spira [by Richard Sault, d. 1702].
Boston, Mill-Bridge, [1773?]. 8 pp.
AAS copy. 42501

The Second Spira [by Richard Sault, d. 1702].
Hartford, [1773]. 31 pp.
(Evans was describing a defective copy. Adv. as just published, Conn. Courant, Sept. 21, 1773.)
CHS copy. 14448

A Second Treatise on Church-Government [by Ebenezer Chaplin, 1733-1822].
Boston, Boyle, 1773. 78, [1] pp.
AAS copy. 12715

The Secret History of Elizabeth.
Rutland, Vt., Williams, 1799. 80 pp.
AAS copy. 36286

The Secretary's Guide [by William Bradford, 1663-1752].
New York and Philadelphia, 1728. [10], 192 pp.
LOC copy. 2997

The Secretary's Guide. . . . Fourth Edition [by William Bradford, 1658-1752].
New York, 1729. [10], 192 pp.
HSP copy. 3139

The Secretary's Guide. . . . Fifth Edition [by William Bradford, 1663-1752].
Philadelphia, Bradford, 1737. [10], 248 pp.
HSP copy. 4127

The Security of Englishmens' Lives. . . .
Fourth Edition [by John Somers, baron, 1651-1716].
New York, Hodge & Shober for Noel & Hazard, 1773. 101, [3] pp.
AAS copy. 13024

The Security of the Rights of Citizens in the State of Connecticut Considered [by Zephaniah? Swift, 1759-1823].
Hartford, Hudson & Goodwin, 1792. 102 pp.
(Attribution to Swift on Pierce Gaines' copy.)
BA copy. 24776

[Sedaine, Michel Jean], 1719-1797.
The Deserter, a Comic-Opera, by C. Dibdin.
New York, Campbell, 1787. 31, [1] pp.
LCP copy. 20331

[Sedaine, Michel Jean], 1719-1797.
The Deserter, a Comic Opera, by C. Dibdin.
Philadelphia, Dobson, 1787.]
(From an adv. in Pa. Mercury, July 6, 1787, for copies of 20331.) 20332

[Sedaine, Michel Jean], 1719-1797.
The Deserter: A Comic Opera. . . . By C. Dibdin.
Boston, Blake, 1795. 32 pp.
AAS copy. 29482

[Sedaine, Michel Jean, 1719-1797.
The Deserter. A Musical Drama. By C. Dibdin.
Philadelphia, 1795.]
(Imprint assumed by Evans from adv.) 29483

[Sedaine, Michel Jean], 1719-1797.
The Deserter: a Comic Opera. . . . By C. Dibdin. . . . Second Boston Edition.
Boston, Blake, 1796. 32 pp.
AAS copy. 31171

[Sedgwick, John], 1742-1820.
An Impartial Narrative, of the Proceedings of Nine Ministers, in the Town of Cornwall.
Hartford, Hudson & Goodwin, 1783. 48 pp.
AAS copy. 18181

Sedgwick, Theodore, pseud.
The Honourable Mr. Sedgwick's Political Last Will.
From a Republican Press, 1800. 21 pp.
AAS copy. 37645

See Brother See. A Favorite Song [by Samuel Arnold, 1740-1802].
New York, Gilfert, [c. 1795]. [2] pp.
AAS copy. 29119

Seely, Bezaleel.
Chester, the 7th Day of April, 1780. D. Sir, At a Meeting. . . .
n.p., [1770]. Broadside.
NYHS copy. 43777

[Seguenot, Francois].
A Letter from a Romish Priest.
Boston, Henchman, 1729. [2], ii, 26 pp.
AAS copy. 3216

Ein sehr Geistreicher Spiegel [by Israel Eckerlin, b. 1705].
[Ephrata, 1745.] Broadside.
HSP facsim. copy. 40359

Seiner Königlichen Erhabensten Majestät.
[Philadelphia, 1764.] [2] pp.
HSP copy. 9833

Seip, Frederic.
An Inaugural Dissertation.
Philadelphia, Way & Groff, 1800. 27 pp.
AAS copy. 38481

Seixas, Gershom Mendez, 1745-1816.
A Discourse Delivered . . . the Ninth of May, 1798.
New York, Davis for Judah, 1798. 32 pp.
AAS copy. 34524

Seixas, Gershom Mendez, 1745-1816.
A Religious Discourse, Delivered . . . Nov. 26, 1789.
New York, M'Lean, 1789. 16 pp.
HSP copy. 22134

[Selby, William, d. 1800.
Apollo and the Muses.
Boston, 1790.]
(Publication proposed in Columbian Centinel, June 16, 1790.) 22881

[Selby, William, d. 1800.
Two Anthems, for Three and Four Voices.
Boston, [1790]. [2], 16 pp.]
(Sonneck-Upton, p. 28. Not now to be located.) 22882

Seldon, Andrew, 1762?-1825.
The Young Child's Easy Guide to . . . Spelling.
Burlington, Vt., Haswell, 1800. 142 pp.
(The only reported copy is now mislaid.) 38482

A Select Collection of Historical Tracts and Anecdotes.
Philadelphia, Mesplet, 1774. 191 pp.
BM copy. 13604

Select Essays: Containing: the Manner of Raising and Dressing Flax.
Philadelphia, Bell, 1777. [8], 159, [1] pp.
AAS copy. 15597

Select Essays, with Some Few Miscellaneous . . . Verses.
[Boston], 1714. 47 pp.
AAS copy. 1715

Select Fables of Esop and other Fabulists [by Robert Dodsley, 1703-1764].
Philadelphia, James, [1790?]. lx, 218, [24] pp.
(Evans' entry was from an adv., apparently for this ed. The only copy located is imperfect.)
AAS copy. 22300

[A Select Number of Plain Tunes [by Andrew Law, 1749-1821].
[Cheshire, Conn., 1794.] 16 pp.]
(No such ed. located.) 27208

Select Pamphlets. Containing, 1. Mirabeau's Observations. . . .
Philadelphia, Carey, 1795.
(Only the tp is reproduced because the pamphlets are printed individually.)
PSL copy. 29484

Select Pamphlets Respecting the Yellow Fever.
Philadelphia, Carey, [1799].
(The pamphlets are described and reproduced separately as 26736, 26837, 26873, 26747, 33742, 35335.) 36287

Select Pamphlets: viz. 1. Lessons to a Young Prince. . . .
Philadelphia, Carey, 1796. pp. [6], [9]-68, 5 plates; [1]-103, [9]; [1]-48; [1]-23; [1]-104, [i]-xix.
(The contents differed with Carey's pamphlet supply.)
AAS copy. 31172

Select Pamphlets: viz. 1. Political Progress of Britain. . . .
Philadelphia, Carey, 1796. [2], 120; 96; v, [1], 66; 14; 22; 166, 1 plate; 22, [2]; 28, [4] pp.
AAS copy. 31173

Select Pamphlets: viz. 1. Rights of Man.
Philadelphia, Carey, 1796. [2], 76; 87, [1]; 103; 71; 44; 13, [3]; 116; 24 pp.
AAS copy. 31174

Select Plays: Containing, 1. Wild Oats. . . .
Philadelphia, Carey, 1796. [2], 72; 72; 58, [2]; [4], 68 pp.
AAS copy. 31175

[Select Poems on Various Occasions, Chiefly American.
Boston, Hall, 1787. 2 vol.]
("At the same Place may be had," Mass. Gazette, July 17, 1787.) 20698

The Select Songster or a Collection of Elegant Songs [by Chauncey Langdon, 1763-1830].
New Haven, Bowen, 1786. 66 pp.
AAS copy. 19750

[Select Stories for the Instruction and Amusement of Youth.
Philadelphia, 1795.]
(Impring assumed by Evans from adv.) 29485

Select Stories, or Miscellaneous Epitome of Entertainment.
New York, Harrisson, 1798. [4], 252 pp., 1 plate.
AAS copy. 34525

Select Verses, for Little Masters and Misses.
New York, Durell, 1790. [26] pp.
UOC copy. 22883

Selectae e Profanis Scriptoribus Historiae [by Jean Heuzet, 1660?-1728].
Philadelphia, Dobson, 1787. xiii, [7], 320 pp.
AAS copy. 20227

Selectae e Veteri Testamento Historiae
[by Jean Heuzet, 1660?-1728].
Philadelphia, Pritchard & Hall for James,
1787. xi, [1], 154, [1] pp.
NYPL copy.   20226

Selectae e Veteri Testamento [by Jean
Heuzet, 1660?-1728].
Philadelphia, Bache, 1789. [4], 170, [6]
pp.
AAS copy.   21683

Selectae e Veteri Testamento [by Jean
Heuzet, 1660?-1728].
Philadelphia, Dobson, 1795. xxiii, [1],
285, [3] pp.
AAS copy.   28270

Selectae e Veteri Testamento [by Jean
Heuzet, 1660?-1728].
Philadelphia, Dobson, 1795. xxiii, [1],
285, [3] pp.
AAS copy.   28272

A Selection of Miscellaneous Pieces, in
Verse and Prose.
Philadelphia, Lawrence, 1792. [4], 80 pp.
AAS copy.   24777

A Selection of Orations and Eulogies . . .
of Gen. George Washington.
Amherst, N. H., Preston, 1800. 165, [2]
pp.
AAS copy.   36859

A Selection of Prayers and Hymns from
Various Authors.
Middletown, Dunning, 1799. vi, 30 pp.
CHS copy.   48962

A Selection of Sacred Harmony [by
Andrew Adgate, d. 1793].
Philadelphia, Young, 1788. [16], 84, [2]
pp.
LOC copy.   45213

[A Selection of Sacred Harmony:
Containing an Explanation of the Gamut.
Philadelphia, M'Culloch, 1788.]
("Just published," Federal Gazette, Mar,
15, 1788.)   21453

A Selection of Sacred Harmony,
Containing Lessons Explaining the
Gamut. . . .
Philadelphia, Young and M'Culloch, 1790.
[4], 132 pp.
AAS copy.   22884

A Selection of Sacred Harmony:
Containing Lessons, Explaining the
Gamut. . . . Fourth Edition.
Philadelphia, Young and M'Culloch, 1794.
[4], 132 pp.
AAS copy.   47212

A Selection of Sacred Harmony:
Containing Lessons Explaining the
Gamut.
Philadelphia, M'Culloch for Young, Mills
& Son, 1797. [4], 132 pp.
HEH copy.   32818

A Selection of the Patriotic Addresses, to
the President.
Boston, Folsom, 1798. 360 pp.
AAS copy.   33345

Sellar, Richard.
An Account of the Sufferings of . . .
Philadelphia, Crukshank, 1772. 26 pp.
AAS copy.   12556

The Selling of Joseph [Samuel Sewall,
1652-1730].
Boston, 1700. 3 pp.
MHS copy.   951

The Senators [by Thomas Hallie De la
Mayne, fl. 1718-1773].
Philadelphia, Goddard, 1772. 31 pp.
HC copy.   12372

Seneca, Lucius Annaeus.
Seneca's Morals.
Boston, Thomas & Andrews, 1792. xxiv,
383 pp., 4 plates.
AAS copy.   24778

[Seneca, Lucius Annaeus.
Senaca's Morals. . . . Second American
Edition.
Boston, Thomas & Andrews, 1794.]

(This entry is apparently a ghost of
27683.)   27682

Seneca, Lucius Annaeus.
Seneca's Morals.
Boston, for B. Larkin, White, Thomas &
Andrews, D. West, E. Larkin & J. West,
1794. xxiv, 336 pp., 4 plates.
AAS copy.   27683

Seneca, Lucius Annaeus.
Seneca's Morals, by Way of Abstract.
Boston, Bumsted for Thomas &
Andrews, etc., 1800. pp. [i]-xvi, [15]-372;
4 plates.
AAS copy.   37818

Seneca Nation.
Documents Relative to Indian Affairs. To
the Great Council. . . .
[New York], Clayton & Kingsland,
[1817]. 28 pp.
(Evans was misled as to date by the old
BA cat.)
AAS copy.   28886

Sensibility. A Drama in Two Parts.
Boston, Spotswood, 1798. [2], 50 pp., 1
plate.
(The only known copy is imperfect.)
HC copy.   34526

Sententiae Pueriles; or Sentences for
Children.
Philadelphia, Dunlap, 1761. 36 leaves.
(Rosenbach - Ch 46; no copy located.)
                                              41245

A Sentimental Journey through France
and Italy [by Laurence Sterne,
1713-1768].
[Boston, Mein & Fleeming], 1768. 66 (96),
98 pp.
HC copy.   41886

A Sentimental Journey through France
and Italy. . . . Two Volumes [in one]
[by Laurence Sterne, 1713-1768].
[Philadelphia], North-America, Bell,
1770. 123 pp.
AAS copy.   42175

A Sentimental Journey through France
and Italy [by Laurence Sterne,
1713-1768].
Philadelphia, Seddon, 1790. 156 pp.
AAS copy.   22909

A Sentimental Journey through France
and Italy [by Laurence Sterne,
1713-1768].
Norwich, Bushnell & Hubbard, 1792. 254
pp.
AAS copy.   24818

A Sentimental Journey through France
and Italy. . . . First Worcester Edition
[by Laurence Sterne, 1713-1768].
Worcester, Thomas, 1793. 172 pp., 1 plate.
AAS copy.   26210

A Sentimental Journey through France
and Italy [by Laurence Sterne,
1713-1768].
New York, for the Bookseller, 1795. 316
pp.
(The plates called for by Evans were
apparently not in the trade copies.)
AAS copy.   29565

A Sentimental Journal through France
and Italy [by Laurence Sterne,
1713-1768].
New York, Tiebout & O'Brien for Smith
& Reid, 1795. 316 pp., front.
WLC copy.   47611

A Sentimental Journey through France
and Italy [by Laurence Sterne,
1713-1768].
New York, Reid, 1796. 316 pp., front.
(An imprint variant of 29565, q. v. for
text.)
AAS copy.   47924

The Sentiments of a British American [by
Oxenbridge Thacher, 1720-1765].
Boston, Edes & Gill, 1764. 16 pp.
AAS copy.   9851

The Sentiments of a Foreigner, on the
Disputes [by Guillaume Thomas
François Raynal, 1713-1796].

Philadelphia, Humphreys, 1775. 27, [1]
pp.
AAS copy.   14417

The Sentiments of a Free and
Independent Elector. . . . January 26th,
1771.
[New York, 1771.] 4 pp.
NYPL copy.   12224

The Sentiments of a Principal Freeholder.
[New York, 1736.] 4 pp.
AAS copy.   4074

The Sentiments of an American Woman.
[Philadelphia], Dunlap, [1780]. [2] pp.
AAS copy.   16992

[Sentiments on Education Collected from
the best Writers.
New York, Gaine, 1778.]
(Adv. N. Y. Mercury, No. 1377.)   16070

Sentiments upon the Religion of Reason
and Nature.
Philadelphia, Bioren and Madan for
Stephens and Denoon & Condie, 1795. 108
pp.
AAS copy.   29486

Sentiments upon the Religion of Reason
and Nature. . . . Second Edition.
Philadelphia, Bioren & Madan for
Stephens and Denoon and Condie, 1795.
108 pp.
AAS copy.   29487

Sentiments upon the Religion of
Reason and Nature. . . . Third Edition.
Philadelphia, Bioren & Madan for
Stephens and Denoon and Condie, 1795.
108 pp.
AAS copy.   29488

Sergeant, John, 1710-1749.
(D. A. B.)
The Causes and Danger.
Boston, Eliot, 1743. 36 pp.
AAS copy.   5287

Sergeant, John, 1710-1749.
A Letter from the Revd. Mr. Sergeant.
Boston, Rogers & Fowle for Henchman,
1743. 16 pp.
AAS copy.   5288

[Sergeant, John], 1710-1749.
(D. A. B.)
A Morning Prayer.
[Boston, 1740?] 15, [1], 23 pp.
(See Pilling 3108.)
AAS copy.   4596

A Series of Letters on Courtship and
Marriage.
Elizabethtown, [N. J.], Kollock, 1796.
[2], 152 pp.
AAS copy.   47911

A Series of Letters on Courtship and
Marriage.
Elizabethtown, [N. J.], Kollock for Davis,
1796. [2], 152 pp.
(An imprint variant of 47911, q.v. for
text.)
AAS copy.   47912

A Series of Letters on Courtship and
Marriage.
Springfield, Mass., Stebbins for Davis,
[1798]. [2], 195 pp.
(No perfect copy located.)
AAS copy.   34527

A Serious Address to Godfathers and
Godmothers.
Windsor, Vt., Spooner, 1794. 20 pp.
AAS copy.   27684

A Serious Address, to such of the
Inhabitants of Pennsylvania. . . .
Philadelphia, 1764. 12 pp.
HSP copy.   9834

A Serious Address, to such of the
Inhabitants of Pennsylvania. . . .
Reprinted.
Philadelphia, Steuart, 1764. 8 pp.
Rosenbach Foundation copy.   9836

[A Serious Address, to such of the
Inhabitants of Pennsylvania. . . . Second
Edition.

Philadelphia, 1764. 12 pp.]
(There were two editions, but no copy
bearing the words "Second Edition" has
been found.)   9835

A Serious Address, to such of the
Inhabitants of Pennsylvania. . . . Fourth
Edition.
Philadelphia, Steuart, 1764. 8 pp.
LCP copy.   9837

A Serious Address to such of the People
Called Quakers. . . . [by Isaac Grey].
Philadelphia, Bell, 1778. [2], 41, [3] pp.
AAS copy.   15843

A Serious Address to such of the People
Called Quakers. . . . [by Isaac Grey].
Philadelphia, Bell, 1778. [6], 41, [3] pp.
LCP copy.   15844

A Serious Address to such of the People
Called Quakers. . . . Second Edition [by
Isaac Grey].
Philadelphia, Steiner & Cist, 1778. 48 pp.
AAS copy.   15845

A Serious Address to the Candid and
Impartial Members of the Methodist
Communion.
New York, 1792. 14 pp.
NYPL copy.   24779

A Serious Address to the Clergy; by a
Minister of the Church of England.
Boston, Fowle, 1756. 14, [1] pp.
AAS copy.   7765

A Serious Address to the Freeholders and
Other Inhabitants of . . . Pennsylvania
[Sept. 10, 1758].
New York, 1758. 16 pp.
NYPL copy.   8237

A Serious Address to the Inhabitants of
the Colony of New-York, Containing a
full and Minute Survey of the Boston-Port
Act.
New York, Holt, 1774. 14, [6] pp.
AAS copy.   13605

A Serious Address to the Rulers of
America [by David Cooper, 1725-1795].
(Friends' Hist. Assoc., Bull., XXVI,
45-48.)
Trenton, 1783. 22 pp.
BA copy.   17839

A Serious Address to those who
Unnecessarily Frequent the Tavern [by
Thomas Foxcroft, 1697-1769].
Boston, Gerrish, 1726. [4], iv, 30 pp.
AAS copy.   2780

Serious Advice to the Inhabitants of the
Northern-Colonies [by Archibald
Kennedy, 1685-1763].
New York, 1755. 20 pp.
(See Wroth, American Bookshelf, pp.
118-126.)
JCB copy.   7347

A Serious and Earnest Address to the
Gentry.
Boston, Rogers & Fowle, 1746. 16 pp.
AAS copy.   5861

[A Serious Call from the City to the
Country.
New York, Gaine, 1757.]
(Adv. N. Y. Mercury, June 6, 1757.) 8033

A Serious Call from the City to the
Country.
Portsmouth, 1757. 8 pp.
NYHS copy.   8034

A Serious Call from the City to the
Country.
Woodbridge, 1757. 8 pp.
NYPL copy.   8035

A Serious Call in Christian Love [by
Benjamin Holme, 1683-1749].
Philadelphia, Crukshank, [1784]. 58 pp.
AAS copy.   18529

A Serious Call in Christian Love [by
Benjamin Holme, 1683-1749].
New York, Gaine, 1791. 55 pp.
AAS copy.   46194

A Serious Call in Christian Love [by

Benjamin Holme, 1683-1749].
Philadelphia, Johnson, 1795. 55 pp.
AAS copy.   28850

A Serious Call to Baptized Children. The
Third Edition.
Boston, Kneeland, 1759. 22 pp.
LOC copy.   41076

A Serious-Comical Dialogue between the
Famous Dr. Seth Hudson and . . . Joshua
How.
Boston, Mecom, 1762. 28 + pp.
(The only known copy is defective.)
AAS copy.   41309

Serious Consideration on Absolute
Predestination [by John Wesley, 1703-
1791].
Boston, Fleet, 1743. 24 pp.
AAS copy.   5310

Serious Considerations on Several
Important Subjects [by Anthony Benezet,
1713-1784].
Philadelphia, Crukshank, 1778. 48 pp.
AAS copy.   15737

Serious Considerations on the Election of
a President [by William Linn, 1752-1808].
New York, Furman, 1800. 36 pp.
AAS copy.   37835

Serious Considerations on the Election of
a President [by William Linn, 1752-1808].
Trenton, N. J., Sherman, Mershon &
Thomas, 1800. 24 pp.
AAS copy.   37836

Serious Considerations on the Present
State of the Affairs of the Northern
Colonies [by Archibald Kennedy,
1685-1763].
New York, 1754. 24 pp.
AAS copy.   7223

[Serious Considerations on the Present
State of the Affairs of the Northern
Colonies [by Archibald Kennedy,
1685-1763].
Philadelphia, Franklin & Hall, 1754.]
(Adv. Pa. Gazette, May 23, 1754.)   7224

Serious Facts, Opposed to "Serious
Considerations."
n.p., October, 1800. 16 pp.
AAS copy.   38486

A Serious Letter to the Young People of
Boston [by Samuel Mather, 1706-1785].
Boston, Edes, 1783. 27 pp.
AAS copy.   18033

[A Serious Poem.
Concord, N.H., Russell, 1793?]
(Evans assumed imprint from adv. "To be
sold" in 25274.)   26150

Serious Reflections Affectionately
Recommended [by Anthony Benezet,
1713-1784].
[Philadelphia, 1778.] 4 pp.
(The LCP has three undated eds. of this
item.)
AAS copy.   15738

Serious Reflections on the Times. A
Poem.
Philadelphia, Chattin, 1757. 16 pp.
WC copy.   8036

[Serious Thoughts on Sudden Death.
Bennington, Haswell & Russell, 1787.]
(McCorison 131; no copy known.)   45161

[Serious Thoughts on the Present Troubles
in Massachusetts.
Bennington, Haswell & Russell, 1787.]
(McCorison 132; no copy known.)   45162

[Serjent, Abel.
An Humble Address.
New York, 1792.]
("This day is Published, by L. Jones,"
N.Y. Diary, Aug. 25, 1792.)   24780

[Serle, Ambrose, 1742-1812.
The Christian Parent.
New York, Loudon, 1791. vi, 158, [2] pp.
AAS copy.   23756

[Serle, Ambrose], 1742-1812.
The Christian Parent.

Philadelphia, Young, 1795. pp. [i]-vi, [2],
[13]-172.
AAS copy.   29489

[Serle, Ambrose], 1742-1812.
The Christian Remembrancer.
New York, Loudon, 1791. iv, 273, [9] pp.
AAS copy.   23757

[Serle, Ambrose], 1742-1812.
The Christian Remembrancer.
Philadelphia, Young, 1795. iv, 284 pp.
AAS copy.   29490

[Serle, Ambrose], 1742-1812.
The Christian Remembrancer . . . Second
American Edition.
Chambersburg, Pa., Snowden &
M'Corkle, 1799. iv, 272 pp.
AAS copy.   36288

[Serle, Ambrose], 1742-1812.
Horae Solitariae. . . . Vol. I.
Philadelphia, Patterson & Cochran,
[1799]. [2], 430 pp.
AAS copy.   36289

A Sermon for December 15, 1796 [by
James Freeman, 1759-1835].
Boston, Spotswood, 1796. 21 pp.
AAS copy.   30451

A Sermon in Praise of Swearing.
Boston, Brown, 1767. 23 pp.
AAS copy.   10766

[A Sermon in Praise of Swearing.
Salem, 1790.]
(Entry from an adv.)   22885

A Sermon, of a New Kind [by William
Hart, 1713-1784].
New Haven, [1769]. 28 pp.
AAS copy.   11286

[A Sermon on Luke VIII. 28.
New York, 1741.]
(A ghost of 4959 originating in the Haven
entry.)   4801

A Sermon on Luke, XIX, 10.
Wilmington, Brynberg & Andrews, 1792.
24 pp.
Del. Hist. Soc. copy.   25575

A Sermon on Natural Religion. By a
Natural Man.
Boston, Thomas, [1771]. 16 pp.
AAS copy.   12225

A Sermon on Regeneration and Grace [by
John Bissett, 1762?-1810?].
Baltimore, Goddard, 1788. 30 pp.
AAS copy.   20970

A Sermon on Tea.
Lancaster, [1774]. 8 pp.
LOC copy.   13606

[A sermon on tea.
Charleston, S. C., Crouch, 1774.]
("In the Press" S. C. Gazette, Aug. 30,
1774: "just published," ibid. Sept. 13.) 42698

A Sermon on the Evacuation of
Charlestown. By an Aethiopian.
Philadelphia, Woodhouse, 1783. 16 pp.
NYHS copy.   18182

[A Sermon on the Present Situation of
Affairs.
Philadelphia, Bradfords, 1772. 11 pp.]
(A ghost of the BA copy of 17717, q.v.) 12557

A Sermon, on the Present Situation of the
Affairs of America and Great-Britain.
Written by a Black.
Philadelphia, Bradford & Hall, 1782. 11
pp.
JCB copy.   17717

[A Sermon on the Resurrection of Our
Lord.
Philadelphia, 1742.]
(Adv. Am. Weekly Mercury, May 13, 1742.) 5053

A Sermon Preached at a Lecture in
Marlborough . . . July 9, 1734 [by
Benjamin Kent, 1708-1788].

Boston, 1734. [2], 24 pp.
AAS copy.   3785

A Sermon Preach'd at Cambridge, after
the Funeral of Mrs. Elizabeth Foxcroft
[by Thomas Foxcroft, 1697-1769].
Boston, Green for Gerrish, 1721. [4], iv,
55 pp.
AAS copy.   2218

A Sermon, Preached at Litchfield [by
Samuel Andrews, 1737-1818].
[New Haven], 1770. 15 pp.
YC copy.   11551

A Sermon Preached at Northampton [by
Timothy Dwight, 1752-1817].
Hartford, [1781]. 34 pp.
AAS copy.   17144

A Sermon Preach't at the Funeral of Mrs.
Elizabeth Riscarrick [by Samuel Myles,
1664-1728].
Boston, 1698. 29 pp.
(The only known copy is defective.)
AAS copy.   833

A Sermon, Preached at the Anniversary
Meeting of the Planter's Society . . .
August the 7th, 1769.
Charleston, 1769. 13 pp.
HC copy.   11460

A Sermon Preached at the
King's-Chappel [by James Honyman, c.
1675-1750].
Boston, 1733. [2], 14 pp.
AAS copy.   3669

A Sermon Preach'd on the 25th of
December [by Henry Scougal, 1650-1678].
Boston, 1737. [4], 28 pp.
AAS copy.   4195

A Sermon Preached upon Ezek. 20. 30, 31
[by Samuel Willard, 1640-1707].
Boston, 1679. [2], 13 pp.
BPL copy.   277

A Sermon to Swine [by Josiah Sherman,
1729-1789].
Litchfield, Collier, 1787. 40 pp.
LOC copy.   20707

[A Sermon to the Bucks and Hinds of
America.
Philadelphia, Spotswood, 1788.]
(There was reported to be a copy at the
Somerset County (Pa.) Archaeological
and Historical Society.)   21454

Sermons on Important Subjects.
Hartford, Hudson & Goodwin, 1797. [4],
516 pp.
AAS copy.   32820

Sermons on Sacramental Occasions by
Divers Ministers.
Boston, Draper for Henchman, 1739. [4],
vii, [1], 275 pp.
AAS copy.   4438

Sermons on the Death of the Reverend
Mr. Waldron.
[Boston, 1727.] 1 leaf.
(The half-title after which are bound
E2848, E2872, and E2971, q. v.)
AAS copy.   39873

Sermons on Various Important Doctrines
and Duties of the Christian Religion.
Northampton, Mass., Butler, 1799. 448,
[1] pp.
AAS copy.   35583

Sermons, or, Declarations [by Stephen
Crisp, 1628-1692].
Philadelphia, Dunlap, 1768. 71 pp.
AAS copy.   10868

Sermons to Asses [by James Murray,
1732-1782].
[Boston, Mein & Fleeming], 1768. 135 pp.
AAS copy.   41851

Sermons to Asses. The Third Edition [by
James Murray, 1732-1782].
Philadelphia, Dunlap, 1769. 114 pp.
AAS copy.   11347

Sermons to Asses. The Fourth Edition [by
James Murray, 1732-1782].

Philadelphia, Dunlap, 1769. 63, [1] pp.
BA copy.   11348

Sermons to Asses. The Fifth Edition [by
James Murray, 1732-1782].
Philadelphia, Dunlap, 1770. 63 pp.
AAS copy.   11751

Sermons to Children [by Rebecca
Wilkinson].
Philadelphia, Young, 1795. 159, [1] pp.
AAS copy.   47686

Sermons to Children [by Rebecca
Wilkinson].
Boston, Hall, 1797. 105, [1] pp.
AAS copy.   32821

Sermons to Children [by Rebecca
Wilkinson].
Pittsfield, Smith, 1799. 96 pp.
CHS copy.   48993

Sermons to Doctors in Divinity [by James
Murray, 1732-1782].
Philadelphia, Dunlap, 1773. viii, 144 pp.
AAS copy.   12875

Sermons to Ministers of State [by James
Murray, 1732-1782].
Philadelphia, Bell, 1783. 79, [1] pp.
AAS copy.   18039

Sermons to Gentlemen upon Temperance
[by Benjamin Rush, 1745-1813].
Philadelphia, Dunlap, 1772. 44 pp.
LOC copy.   12547

Sermons to the Rich and Studious.
Litchfield, Collier, [1791]. 71 pp.
JCB copy.   23758

A Servant of the Lord [by Cotton Mather,
1663-1728].
Boston, 1704. 48 pp.
CL copy.   1177

Servetus, Mordecai, pseud.
The Mystic's Plea. . . . [by Elhanan,
Winchester, 1751-1797].
Philadelphia, 1781. 16 pp.
AAS copy.   17439

[Service for the Pennsylvania German
congregations occasioned by the defeat of
Braddock.
n.p., 1755?] Broadside.
(Metzger 189; no copy located.)   40798

[Service Funèbre de Louis XVI.
Philadelphia, 1794.]
(The origin of this entry is unknown.)
                                                       27685

Sessions, Darius.
To the Freemen of the Colony of
Rhode-Island. . . . April 15, 1775.
[Providence, 1775.] Broadside.
JCB copy.   42937

[A Set of Tables, in One of which the
Federal Currencies. . . .
Boston, Thomas & Andrews, 1795.
Broadside.]
(Probably a ghost of 29449. Title from
adv. in Columbian Centinel, May, 1795.)
                                                       29491

Sethonia. A Tragedy [by Alexander Dow,
d. 1779].
Philadelphia, Sparhawk, 1774. [8], 63 pp.
HSP copy.   13255

Seton, William, 1746-1798.
New-York, June 1, 1793, My House of
Commerce. . . .
[New York, 1793.] Broadside.
NYHS copy.   26151

Seven Hints for all who will take Them
[by John Searson].
[Philadelphia, 1770.] Broadside.
LCP copy.   11851

Seven Hints for all who will Take Them:
by a Church of England-man.
n.p., [1770]. Broadside.
AAS ph. copy.   42170

Seven Rational Sermons [by Miss R.
Roberts, d. 1788].
Philadelphia, Bell, 1777. 77, [1] pp.
AAS copy.   15584

Seven Sages. English.
The History of the Seven Wise Masters, of
Rome.
Boston, White, 1794. 34 pp.
AAS copy.   27669

Seven Sages. English.
The History of the Seven Wise Masters of
Rome.
Worcester, 1794. 31 pp.
AAS copy.   27670

[Seven Sages. English.
History of the Seven Wise Masters of
Rome.
Boston, Spotswood, 1795.]
(Imprint assumed by Evans from
Spotswood's adv. "For Sale by the
Printer," as in 29492.)   29467

Seven Sages, English.
Roman Stories. . . . Thirty-Fourth
Edition.
New York, Gomez, 1795. 144 pp.
(The only copy located is imperfect.)
AAS copy.   29466

Seven Sages. English.
The History of the Seven Wise Masters of
Rome.
Philadelphia, H. & P. Rice for J. Rice,
1795. 100 pp.
AAS   copy.   47597

Seven Sages. English.
The History of the Seven Wise Masters of
Rome.
New York, Tiebout, 1797. 95 pp.
(The only known copy is imperfect.)
HC copy.   48249

[Seven Sages. English.
History of the Seven Wise Masters of
Rome.
Wilmington, Del., Brynberg, 1797.]
(Imprint assumed by Evans from
Brynberg's adv.)   32803

Seven Sages. English.
The History of the Seven Wise Masters of
Rome.
Philadelphia, 1798. 96 pp.
d'Alté A. Welch copy.   48611

Seven Sages. English.
Roman Histories. . . . Fiftieth Edition.
Wilmington, [Del.], Wilson, 1796. 103 pp.
(Not located, 1968.)   47913

Seven Wise Mistresses of Rome
See Howard, Thomas, fl. 1700?

[Seven Wise Mistresses of Rome.
Roman Stories; or, The History of
the. . . .
Concord, N.H., Russell & Davis, 1796.]
(Imprint assumed by Evans from adv.
"This Day is Published, and to be Sold at
this Office," July 28, 1796.)   31176

The Seventeenth Jewel . . . the Intended
State of Maine.
n.p., 1797. 35 pp.
AAS copy.   32269

A Seventh Essay on Free Trade and
Finance [by Pelatiah Webster, 1726-1795].
Philadelphia, Oswald, 1785. 38 pp.
AAS copy.   19367

Sever, Nicholas, 1680-1764.
(Sibley, V, 90-96.)
A Speech on the Occasion of Col.
Lothrop's Death.
Boston, Fowle, 1750. [4], 2, [2], 12 pp.
AAS copy.   6605

Sever, Thomas.
An Ode, on the Sudden Death of Mr.
Daniel Holt.
[Leominster? 1798.] Broadside.
AAS copy.   34528

Several Poems. . . . Third Edition [by
Anne (Dudley) Bradstreet, 1612?-1672].
[Boston], 1758. xiii, [1], 233 pp.
AAS copy.   8091

Several Texts of Scripture Adduced in
Support of Adult Baptism [by Richard
Lee, 1747-1823].
Rutland, for Lee, [1794]. 7, [1] pp.
AAS copy.   27687

Severals Relating to the Fund [by John Woodbridge, 1614-1695].
[Boston? 1682.] 8 + pp.
(The only known copy is incomplete.)
WL copy.   337

Sewall, Daniel, 1755-1842.
[An Astronomical Diary; or Almanack, for . . . 1781.
Portsmouth.]
(Adv. Portsmouth Gazette, Nov. 1780.)
                                           43894

Sewall, Daniel, 1755-1842.
An Astronomical Diary: or Almanack, for . . . 1783.
Portsmouth. [24] pp.
LOC copy.   17718

Sewall, Daniel, 1755-1842.
An Astronomical Diary; or Almanack, for . . . 1784.
Portsmouth. [24] pp.
AAS copy.   18183

Sewall, Daniel, 1755-1842.
An Astronomical Diary, or, Almanac, for . . . 1785.
Portsmouth, Gerrish. [24] pp.
NYHS copy.   18780

Sewall, Daniel, 1755-1842.
An Astronomical Diary, or Almanac, for . . . 1786.
Portsmouth, Melcher & Osborne, 1785. [24] pp.
NHHS copy.   19237

Sewall, Daniel, 1755-1842.
An Astronomical Diary, or Almanac, for . . . . 1787.
Portsmouth, Gerrish for Lamson & Ranlet. [24] pp.
AAS copy.   19983

[Sewall, Daniel], 1755-1842.
An Astronomical Diary . . . for . . . 1787.
Portsmouth, Gerrish, for Lamson & Ranlet. Second Edition. [24] pp.]
(No such "Second Edition" located.)
                                           44965

Sewall, Daniel, 1755-1842.
An Astronomical Diary, or Almanack, for . . . 1788.
Portsmouth, Gerrish. [24] pp.
AAS copy.   20699

Sewall, Daniel, 1755-1842.
An Astronomical Diary, or Almanack, for . . . 1789.
Portsmouth, Melcher, [1788]. [24] pp.
AAS copy.   21455

Sewall, Daniel, 1755-1842.
An Astronomical Diary, or Almanack, for . . . 1790.
Portsmouth, Melcher. [24] pp.
AAS copy.   22135

Sewall, Daniel, 1755-1842.
An Astronomical Diary, or Almanack, for . . . 1791.
Portsmouth, Melcher. [24] pp.
AAS copy.   22886

Sewall, Daniel, 1755-1842.
An Astronomical Diary, or Almanack, for . . . 1792.
Portsmouth, Melcher. [24] pp.
MHS copy.   23759

Sewall, Daniel, 1755-1842.
An Astronomical Diary, or Almanac, for . . . 1793.
Portsmouth, Melcher. [24] pp.
AAS copy.   24781

Sewall, Daniel, 1755-1842.
An Astronomical Diary, or Almanack, for . . . 1794.
Portsmouth, Melcher. [24] pp.
AAS copy.   26152

Sewall, Daniel, 1755-1842.
An Astronomical Diary, or Almanack, for . . . 1795.
Portsmouth, Melcher. [24] pp.
AAS copy.   27688

Sewall, Daniel, 1755-1842.
An Astronomical Diary, or Almanack, for . . . 1796.

Portsmouth, Melcher. [24] pp.
AAS copy.   29493

Sewall, Daniel, 1755-1842.
An Astronomical Diary, Almanac, for . . . 1797.
Portsmouth, N.H., Peirce. [24] pp.
AAS copy.   31177

Sewall, Daniel, 1755-1842.
An Astronomical Diary, or Almanc, for . . . 1798.
Portsmouth, N. H., Peirce. [24] pp.
AAS copy.   32822

Sewall, Daniel, 1755-1842.
An Astronomical Diary, or Almanac, for . . . 1799.
Portsmouth, N. H., Peirce. [24] pp.
AAS copy.   34529

Sewall, Daniel, 1755-1842.
An Astronomical Diary, or Almanac, for . . . 1800.
Portsmouth, N. H., Peirce. [24] pp.
AAS copy.   36292

Sewall, Daniel, 1755-1842.
An Astronomical Diary, or Almanac, for . . . 1801.
Portsmouth, N. H., Peirce. [24] pp.
NYPL copy.   38487

[Sewall, Daniel], 1755-1842.
Bickerstaff's Almanac, for . . . 1800.
Portsmouth, N. H., Peirce. [24] pp.
AAS copy.   36293

[Sewall, Daniel], 1755-1842.
Bickerstaff's Astronomical Diary, or, Almanack for . . . 1799.
Portsmouth, N. H., Peirce. [24] pp.
(The only copy reported cannot now be located.)   34530

[Sewall, Daniel], 1755-1842.
The Concord Calendar: or, New Hampshire Almanack, for . . . 1791. . . . .
By Elijah Bickerstaff.
Concord, Hough. [24] pp.
AAS copy.   22887

Sewall, Daniel, 1755-1842.
An Eulogy, Occasioned by the Death of . . . Washington.
Portsmouth, N. H., Peirce, 1800. 20 pp.
AAS copy.   38488

Sewall, Daniel, 1755-1842.
Weatherwises's Astronomical Diary, or Almanack, for . . . 1799.
Portsmouth, N. H., Peirce. [24] pp.
(Only this tp. located.)
AAS copy.   34531

[Sewall, David], 1735-1825.
(Sibley XIII, 638-645.)
An Astronomical Diary: or, An Almanack for . . . 1758.
Portsmouth, N. H., Fowle. [16] pp.
AAS copy.   40938

[Sewall, David], 1735-1825.
An Astronomical Diary; or, Almanack, for . . . 1767. . . . Calculated for the Meridian of Portsmouth. . . .
Portsmouth, Fowle for Appleton. [16] pp.
LOC copy.   10229

[Sewall, David, 1735-1825.
The New Hampshire Almanack for 1767.
Portsmouth, D. & R. Fowle.]
(Adv. Portsmouth Gazette, Dec. 5, 1766.)
                                           41658

[Sewall, Jonathan], 1728-1796.
The Americans Roused, in a Cure for the Spleen.
New York, Rivington, [1775]. 32 pp.
AAS copy.   14455

[Sewall, Jonathan], 1728-1796.
A Cure for the Spleen.
America (Boston), 1775. 32 pp.
JCB copy.   14454

Sewall, Jonathan Mitchell, 1748-1808.
Eulogy on the Late General Washington.
Portsmouth, N. H., Treadwell, [1800]. 28 pp.
AAS copy.   38489

[Sewall, Jonathan Mitchell], 1748-1808.

Gen. Washington, a New Favorite Song.
n.p., [1776]. Broadside.
AAS ph. copy.   43158

[Sewall, Jonathan Mitchell], 1748-1808.
A New Epilogue to Cato. Spoken at a late Performance.
n.p., [1777]. [2] pp.
AAS copy.   43372

[Sewall, Jonathan Mitchell], 1748-1808.
A New Song. To the Tune of the British Grenadiers.
n.p., [1776]. Broadside.
HSP copy.   14918

[Sewall, Jonathan Mitchell], 1748-1808.
An Oration; Delivered at Portsmouth, New-Hampshire, on the Fourth of July, 1788.
Portsmouth, Osborne, 1788. 23 pp.
AAS copy.   21456

[Sewall, Jonathan Mitchell], 1748-1808.
Verses Occasioned by Reading the Answer of the President.
Boston, 1797. 7 pp.
AAS copy.   32823

[Sewall, Jonathan Mitchell], 1748-1808.
A Versification of President Washington's . . . Farewell Address.
Portsmouth, N. H., Peirce, 1798. 54 pp.
AAS copy.   34532

[Sewall, Jonathan Mitchell, 1748-1808.
War and Washington. A Song.
Philadelphia, Towne, 1779. Broadside.]
(Adv. Pa. Evening-Post, Jan. 15, 1780.)
                                           16520

Sewall, Joseph, 1688-1769.
(Sibley, V, 376-393.)
All Flesh is Grass.
Boston, Kneeland & Green, 1741. [4], 24 pp.
AAS copy.   4802

Sewall, Joseph, 1688-1769.
Believers Invited to Come to Christ.
Boston, Green for Gerrish, 1716. [2], 17, [2] pp.
(Signatured continuous with 1852.)
AAS copy.   1853

Sewall, Joseph, 1688-1769.
(Sibley, V, 376-393.)
A Caveat against Covetousness.
Boston, Green for Gerrish, 1718. [2], 22 pp.
AAS copy.   1997

Sewall, Joseph, 1688-1769.
(Sibley, V, 376-393.)
The Certainty & Suddenness of Christ's Coming.
Boston, Green for Gerrish, 1716. [2], 19, [1] pp.
(Signatured with 1853.)
AAS copy.   1852

Sewall, Joseph, 1688-1769.
(Sibley, V, 376-393.)
The Character and Blessedness of the Upright.
Boston, 1717. [2], 48 pp.
(Issued bound with 1899.)
AAS copy.   1927

Sewall, Joseph, 1688-1769.
(Sibley, V, 376-393.)
The Character and Reward.
Boston, Kneenland, 1763. [4], 20, [2] pp.
AAS copy.   9513

Sewall, Joseph, 1688-1769.
(Sibley, V, 376-393.)
Christ Victorious.
Boston, Kneeland & Green, 1733. [8], 46 pp.
AAS copy.   3723

Sewall, Joseph, 1688-1769.
Desires that Joshua's Resolution may be Revived.
Boston, Green for Gerrish, 1716. [2], xii, 80 pp.
AAS copy.   1854

Sewall, Joseph, 1688-1769.
(Sibley, V, 376-393.)
The Duty, Character and Reward.

Boston, Kneeland, 1708. (i.e. 1758).
[4], 22, [2] pp.
AAS copy.   8257

Sewall, Joseph, 1688-1769.
(Sibley, V, 376-393.)
The Duty of a People.
Boston, Henchman, 1727. [4], 24 pp.
MHS copy.   2954

Sewall, Joseph, 1688-1769.
The Duty of a People. . . . Second Edition.
Boston, Henchman, 1727. [4], 28 pp.
AAS copy.   2955

Sewall, Joseph, 1688-1769.
The Duty of Every Man.
Boston, Green, 1727. [4], 23 pp.
AAS copy.   2956

Sewall, Joseph, 1688-1769.
(Sibley, V, 376-393.)
The First and Great Commandment.
Boston, Fleet for Henchman, 1742. 31 pp.
AAS copy.   5054

Sewall, Joseph, 1688-1769.
God's People must Enquire.
Boston, Fowle for Henchman, 1742. 30 pp.
AAS copy.   5055

Sewall, Joseph, 1688-1769.
(Sibley, V, 376-393.)
He that would keep God's
Commandments.
Boston, Green for Henchman, 1728. [2],
vi, 28 pp.
AAS copy.   3102

Sewall, Joseph, 1688-1769.
The Holy Spirit.
Boston, Henchman, 1728. [4], 32 pp.
AAS copy.   3103

Sewall, Joseph, 1688-1769.
The Holy Spirit.
Boston, Draper for Henchman, 1741. [2],
vi, 133, [1] pp.
AAS copy.   4803

Sewall, Joseph, 1688-1769.
Jehovah is the King.
Boston, Green for Henchman, 1727. [4],
25 pp.
AAS copy.   2957

Sewall, Joseph, 1688-1769.
(Sibley, V, 376-393.)
The Lamb Slain.
Boston, Henchman, 1745. 34 pp.
AAS copy.   5685

Sewall, Joseph, 1688-1769.
(Sibley, V, 376-393.)
Nineveh's Repentance.
Boston, Draper for Henchman, 1740. [6],
33 pp.
AAS copy.   4597

Sewall, Joseph, 1688-1769.
(Sibley, V, 376-393.)
The Orphan's best Legacy.
Boston, Green for Gerrish and
Henchman, 1730. [4], 33, [1] pp.
AAS copy.   3351

Sewall, Joseph, 1688-1769.
Precious Treasure in Earthen Vessels.
Boston, Green for Gerrish and
Henchman, 1717. [2], vi, 36 pp.
(Some copies issued bound with 1874.)
AAS copy.   1928

Sewall, Joseph, 1668-1769.
Repentance.
Boston, Henchman, 1727. [4], 55 pp.
AAS copy.   2958

Sewall, Joseph, 1688-1769.
(Sibley, V, 376-393.)
Rulers must be Just.
Boston, Green for Gerrish, 1724. [4], 69,
[1] pp.
AAS copy.   2583

Sewall, Joseph, 1688-1769.
The Second Commandment.
Boston, Fleet for Henchman, 1742. 30 pp.
AAS copy.   5056

Sewall, Joseph, 1688-1769.
(Sibley, V, 376-393.)

A Sermon Preached at the
Thursday-Lecture.
Boston, Draper and Edes & Gill. 33 pp.
AAS copy.   9269

Sewall, Joseph, 1688-1769.
(Sibley, V, 376-393.)
A Tender Heart.
Boston, Kneeland, 1756. [4], 22, [2], 30
pp.
AAS copy.   7790

Sewall, Joseph, 1688-1769.
The Thirsty Invited to Come.
Boston, Rogers & Fowle, 1742. 24 pp.
LOC copy.   5057

Sewall, Joseph, 1688-1769.
(Sibley, V, 376-393.)
When the Godly Cease.
Boston, Kneeland & Green for
Henchman, 1737. [2], 32, [2], 36, [2], 18,
[2], 9 pp.
AAS copy.   4196

[Sewall, Samuel], 1652-1730.
Early Piety Exemplified in Elizabeth
Butcher.
Boston, 1718.]
(No copy of this first edition has been
found. For authorship see Holmes, Cotton
Mather, I, 285.)   1973

[Sewall, Samuel], 1652-1730.
Early Piety Exemplified in Elizabeth
Butcher [2nd ed.].
Boston, 1719.]
(No copy is to be found of this edition
which is assumed from an entry in Judge
Sewall's diary. See Holmes, Cotton
Mather, I, 285.)   2038

[Sewall, Samuel], 1652-1730.
Early Piety; Exemplified in Elizabeth
Butcher. . . . Fourth Edition.
Boston, Draper for Harrison, 1741. [2],
iv, 17, [1] pp.
(For authorship see Holmes, Cotton
Mather, I, 285.)
AAS copy.   5008

[Sewall, Samuel], 1652-1730.
In Remembrance of Mr. Samuel Hirst . . .
January 14 1726, 7.
[Boston, 1727.] Broadside.
NYPL ph. copy.   39874

Sewall, Samuel, 1652-1730.
A Memorial Relating to the Kennebeck
Indians.
[Boston, 1721.] 3 pp.
MHS copy.   2292

[Sewall, Samuel], 1652-1730.
Mrs. Judith Hull.
[Boston, 1695.] [1] p.
(There are ten and twelve-line editions.
The one reproduced is known both as a
separate and as the last leaf of Evans 729.)
AAS copy.   738

Sewall, Samuel, 1652-1730.
Phaenomena Quaedam Apocalyptica.
Boston, 1697. [8], 60 pp.
AAS copy.   813

Sewall, Samuel, 1652-1730.
Phaenomena quaedam Apocalyptica. . . .
Second Edition.
Boston, Green for Eliot, Gerrish, &
Henchman, 1727. [8], 64, 24 pp.
AAS copy.   2959

Sewall, Samuel, 1652-1730.
Proposals Touching the Accomplishment.
Boston, 1713. [2], 12, [1] pp.
AAS copy.   1647

[Sewall, Samuel], 1652-1730.
The Selling of Joseph.
Boston, 1700. 3 pp.
MHS copy.   951

Sewall, Samuel, 1652-1730.
A Small Vial of Tears . . . from the
Funeral of John Winthrop.
[Boston? 1717.] Broadside.
MHS copy.   39670

Sewall, Samuel, 1652-1730.
Tuesday, November 25, 1707.
Boston, 1707. Broadside.

MHS photostat copy; original not found.
                                         1332

[Sewall, Samuel], 1652-1730.
Upon Mr. Samuel Willard . . . November
21, 1700.
[Boston, 1700.] Broadside.
(The AAS has two settings of this piece. It
was commonly used as an end paper in
Willard's sermons.)
MHS copy.   952

[Sewall, Samuel], 1652-1730.
Upon Mr. Samuel Willard. . . . November
21, 1700. [Second Edition, May 12, 1720.]
[Boston, 1720.] Broadside.
MHS copy.   39731

[Scwall, Samuel], 1652-1730.
Upon the Drying up that Ancient River,
the Merry-mak. . . . January 15, 1719, 20.
[Boston, 1721.] Broadside.
AAS ph. copy.   39752

Sewall, Samuel, 1652-1730.
Wednesday, January 1. 1701.
[Boston, 1701.] Broadside.
(The printing usually reproduced was the
last leaf of Evans 1647, q.v.)
AAS copy.   1023

Sewall, Stephen, 1702-1760.
(Sibley, VI, 561-567.)
The Character of . . . Judge Dudley.
[Boston, 1759.] 4 pp.
(This is an appendix to 8354, q.v.)   6778

[Sewall, Stephen], 1702-1760.
From the Boston Weekly News-Letter,
Feb. 7, 1751.
[Boston, 1751.] Broadside.
AAS copy.   6779

Sewall, Stephen, 1734-1804.
Carmina Sacra.
Worcester, Thomas, 1789. 8 pp.
AAS copy.   22136

[Sewall, Stephen], 1734-1804.
(D. A. B.)
An Hebrew Grammar.
Boston, Draper for Harvard, 1763. [2], v,
[1], 83 pp.
AAS copy.   9514

Sewall, Stephen, 1734-1804.
Oratio Funebris.
[Boston, 1769.] [2], 8 pp.
(A part of 11161, q.v.)   11461

Sewall, Stephen, 1734-1804.
An Oration Delivered May viii.
Boston, Fleets, 1779. 8 pp.
AAS copy.   16521

Sewall, Stephen, 1734-1804.
The Scripture Account of the Shechinah.
Boston, Blake, 1794. 27 pp.
AAS copy.   27689

Sewall, Stephen, 1734-1804.
The Scripture History.
Boston, Blakes, 1796. 30 pp.
AAS copy.   31178

Sewall's Sheet Almanac, for 1800.
Portsmouth, N. H., Peirce. Broadside.
(The only reported copy is stained and
mutilated.)
AAS copy.   36294

Seward, Anna, 1742-1809.
Louisa, a Poetical Novel. . . . Fifth
Edition.
New Haven, Morse, 1789. [8], 80, [4] pp.
AAS copy.   22137

Seward, Anna, 1742-1809.
(M. E. Ashmun, Singing Swan, p. 5.)
Monody on Major Andre.
New York, Rivington, 1781. iv, 35 pp.
Columbia University copy.   17368

Seward, Anna, 1742-1809.
Monody on Major Andre.
Philadelphia, Story, [1782?]. 56 pp.
(No complete copy located.)
MeHS copy.   17719

Seward, Anna, 1742-1809.
Monody on Major Andre.

New York, Harrison & Purdy for Allen,
1788. 48 pp.
LOC copy.   21458

Seward, Anna, 1742-1809.
Monody on Major Andre.
Philadelphia, Story, [1788?]. 56 pp.
(Evans' entry came from Sabin, who was
apparently describing an incomplete copy
of this ed.)
AAS copy.   21457

Seward, Anna, 1742-1809.
Monody on Major Andre.
Philadelphia, Story, [1790?]. 56 pp.
LOC copy.   22888

Seward, Anna, 1742-1809.
Monody on the Unfortunate Major
Andre. . . . Second New-York Edition.
New York, Allen, 1792. 48 pp.
AAS copy.   24782

Seward, Anna, 1742-1809.
Monody on the Unfortunate Major Andre.
Hanover, N.H., Dunham, 1794. 48 pp.
AAS copy.   27690

Seward, Anna, 1742-1809.
Monody on Major Andre.
Boston, Spotswood and Wayne, 1798.
22 pp.
AAS copy.   34533

Seward, William, 1712-1782.
(Weis, Colonial Clergy N. E.)
Brotherly Love.
New Haven, [1771]. 63 pp.
AAS copy.   12226

Seward, William, 1712-1782.
(Weis, Colonial Clergy N. E.)
Due Consideration.
New Haven, 1772. 47 pp.
AAS copy.   12558

[Seward, William, gent.
Journal of a Voyage.
Boston, Henchman, 1740.]
(Apparently a ghost of the London edition
arising from Henchman's adv. The
London ed. is reproduced because of the
American interest of the title.)   4598

Sewel, Willem, 1653-1720.
(William Hull, Willem Sewel.)
The History of the Rise, Increase, and
Progress, of the . . . Quakers.
Philadelphia, Keimer, 1728. [12], 694,
[16] pp.
AAS copy.   3104

Sewel, Willem, 1653-1720.
The History of the Rise, Increase and
Progress, of the . . . Quakers. . . . Third
Edition.
Burlington, 1774. xii, 812, [16] pp.
AAS copy.   13607

[Sewel, Willem, 1653-1720.
The History of the Rise, Increase and
Progress, of the . . . Quakers. . . . Third
Edition.
Burlington, 1776. xii, 812, [16] pp.]
(A possible title-page variant of 13607,
q.v.)   15081

Seybert, Adam, 1773-1825.
An Inaugural Dissertation.
Philadelphia, Dobson, 1793. 78 pp.
AAS copy.   26153

The Shade of Alexander Pope [by Thomas
James Mathias, 1754?-1835].
Philadelphia, Maxwell for Dickens, 1800.
59, [4] pp.
(A part of 37937, q. v.)   37941

[Shadwell, Thomas, 1642?-1792.
Don Juan.
Boston, Blake, 1795.]
(The unique copy described by Evans is
not to be found, probably a ghost.) 29494

[Shakespeare, William, 1564-1616.
Catharine and Petruchio.
Philadelphia, Steuart, 1762.]
(From an adv.)   9270

Shakespeare, William, 1564-1616.
Hamlet.

Boston, Printed for David West . . . and
John West, [1794]. 72 pp.
AAS copy.   27692

[Shakespeare, William, 1564-1616.
King Lear.
New York, Gaine, 1761.]
(Adv. N. Y. Mercury, July 20, 1761.) 9004

Shakespeare, William, 1564-1616.
The Plays and Poems of. . . . Vol. I [-III].
Philadelphia, Bioren & Madan, 1795. [2],
xlviii, 384; 412; 432 pp., 1 plate.
AAS copy.   29496

Shakespeare, William, 1564-1616.
The Plays and Poems of. . . . Vol. IV
[-VIII].
Philadelphia, Bioren & Madan, 1796. 447;
392; 388; 452; 304, 128 pp.
AAS copy.   31180

[Shakespeare, William, 1564-1616.
The Tempest.
New York, Gaine, 1761.]
(Adv. N. Y. Mercury, July 20, 1761.) 9005

Shakespeare, William, 1564-1616.
Twelfth Night.
Boston, D. West and J. West, [1794]. 60
pp.
AAS copy.   27693

[Shakespeare, William, 1564-1616.
The Twins . . . Altered from
Shakespeare's Comedy of Errors. By
William Woods.
Philadelphia, Dobson, 1787.]
(Entry from an adv.)   20700

[Shakespeare's Jests, or the Jubilee
Jester.
New York, 1774.]
(Entry from Haven.)   13608

Shall the Free Men of Kentucky Secure
their Rights?
[Lexington? 1798.] Broadside.
LOC copy.   48612

Shall We Have a Convention? Citizens of
Kentucky.
[Lexington, 1798.] [2] pp.
LOC copy.   48613

[The Sham Beggar. A Farce.
Philadelphia, Steuart, 1762.]
(Pa. Journal, Dec. 30, 1762.)   9271

Shangar, Marcus.
A Letter to the Reverend John Tucker.
America (Boston), 1775. 17, [1] pp.
AAS copy.   14456

[Shannon & Poalk, auctioneers.
Auction of Very Select and Valuable
Books, Apr. 21, 1800.
Philadelphia, 1800.]
(McKay 143c.)   38256

[Shannon & Poalk, auctioneers.
A Quantity of Books, French and English,
May 12, 1800.
Philadelphia, 1800.]
(McKay 143F.)   38257

[Shannon & Poalk, auctioneers.
Scarce and Valuable Books, Aug. 27,
1800.
Philadelphia, 1800.]
(McKay 143i.)   38258

Shapleigh, Me., Proprietors.
This is to Give Notice. . . . York, Apr. 6,
1791.
[Portsmouth? 1791.] Broadside.
AAS copy.   24017

Sharp, Anthony, pseud.
The Continental Almanac, for . . .
1781. . . . [by David Rittenhouse,
1732-1796].
Philadelphia, Bailey. [36] pp.
AAS copy.   16974

Sharp, Anthony, pseud.
The Continental Almanac, for . . .
1782. . . . [by David Rittenhouse,
1732-1796].
Philadelphia, Bailey. [36] pp.
AAS copy.   17348

Sharp, Anthony, pseud.

The Continental Almanac, for . . .
1783. . . .
Philadelphia, Bailey. [36] pp.
AAS copy.   17701

Sharp, Anthony, pseud.
The Continental Almanac, for . . . 1784
[by David Rittenhouse, 1732-1796].
Philadelphia, Bailey. [36] pp.
LOC copy.   18159

Sharp, Anthony, pseud.
The Continental Almanac, for . . . 1785
[by David Rittenhouse, 1732-1796].
Philadelphia, Bailey. [36] pp.
AAS copy.   18759

[Sharp, Anthony, pseud.
The Continental Almanac, for . . . 1785
[by David Rittenhouse, 1732-1796].
Philadelphia, Kline & Reynolds.]
(From an adv. apparently for 18759.)
                                             18760

Sharp, Anthony, pseud.
The Continental Pocket Almanack for . . .
1781 [by David Rittenhouse, 1732-1796].
Philadelphia, Bailey. [24] pp.
NYPL copy.   16975

[Sharp, Anthony, pseud.
The Continental Pocket Almanack for . . .
1782 [by David Rittenhouse, 1732-1796].
Philadelphia, Bailey.]
(Assumed from the sequence.)   17349

[Sharp, Anthony, pseud.
Der Gantz neue Verbesserte
Nord-Americanische Calender, auf das
1776ste Jahr. . . . [by David Rittenhouse,
1732-1796].
Lancaster, Bailey. 36 pp.]
(No copy located.)   14430

Sharp, Anthony, pseud.
Der Gantz Neue Verbesserte
Nord-Americanische Calender auf das
1784ste Jahr Christi [by David
Rittenhouse, 1732-1796].
Lancaster, Bailey. [36] pp.
AAS copy.   18162

Sharp, Anthony, pseud.
Der Gantz Neue Verbesserte
Nord-Americanische Calender auf das
1787ste Jahr. . . . [by David Rittenhouse,
1732-1796].
Lancaster, Bailey. [36] pp.
AAS copy.   19965

Sharp, Anthony, pseud.
Der Gantz Neue Verbesserte
Nord-Americanische Calender, auf das
1789ste Jahr Christi.
Lancaster, Bailey. [36] pp.
AAS copy.   45357

Sharp, Anthony, pseud.
The Lancaster Almanack, for . . . 1775.
Lancaster, Bailey. [38] pp.
AAS copy.   13367

Sharp, Anthony, pseud.
The Lancaster Almanack, for . . . 1778 [by
David Rittenhouse, 1732-1796].
Lancaster, Bailey. [28] pp.
AAS copy.   15579

Sharp, Anthony, pseud.
The Lancaster Almanack, for 1779 [by
David Rittenhouse, 1732-1796].
Lancaster, Bailey. [32] pp.
AAS copy.   16054

Sharp, Anthony, pseud.
The Lancaster Pocket Almanack, for . . .
1778 [by David Rittenhouse, 1732-1796].
Lancaster, Bailey. [24] pp.
AAS copy.   15580

Sharp, Granville, 1735-1813.
(D. N. B.)
A Declaration of the People's Natural
Right.
Boston, Edes & Gill, 1774. 22 pp. 8 vo.
AAS copy.   13609

[Sharp, Granville, 1735-1813.
A Declaration of the People's Natural
Right.
Boston, Edes & Gill, 1774. 22 pp. 12 mo.]
(No copy of a 12 mo. ed. could be
located.)   13610

Sharp, Granville, 1735-1813.
A Declaration of the People's Natural
Right.
New York, Holt, 1774. 16 pp.
HC copy.   13611

Sharp, Granville, 1735-1813.
A Declaration of the People's Natural
Right.
Philadelphia, Dunlap, 1774. 21 pp.
LCP copy.   13613

Sharp, Granville, 1735-1813.
A Declaration of the People's Natural
Right.
Philadelphia, Towne, 1774. 21 pp.
LCP copy.   13612

Sharp, Granville, 1735-1813.
An Essay on Slavery.
Burlington, 1773. 28 pp.
AAS copy.   13005

Sharp, Granville, 1735-1813.
Letter from Granville Sharp.
Baltimore, Graham, Yundt & Patton, 1793.
11 pp.
NYPL copy.   26155

Sharp, Granville, 1735-1813.
Letter from Granville Sharp.
Baltimore, Yundt & Patton, 1793. 11 pp.
AAS copy.   26156

Sharp, Joshua.
Citizens and Farmer's Almanac, for . . .
1800.
Philadelphia, M'Culloch. [36] pp.
AAS copy.   36296

Sharp, Joshua.
Citizen's and Farmer's Almanac, for . . .
1801.
Philadelphia, M'Culloch. [40] pp.
LOC copy.   38491

[Sharp, Joshua.
The Columbian Almanac for . . . 1798.
Philadelphia? 36 pp.]
(Entry from an adv., perhaps for 32309.)
                                            32825

Sharp, Joshua.
Father Abraham's Almanac, for . . . 1801.
Philadelphia, Stewart. [40] pp.
AAS copy.   38492

Sharp, Joshua.
Father Tammany's Almanac, for . . . 1798.
Philadelphia, Young. [36] pp.
AAS copy.   32826

Sharp, Joshua.
Father Tammany's Almanac, for . . . 1801.
Philadelphia, Young, 1800. [36] pp.
(The only copy located is imperfect.)
BPL copy.   38493

[Sharp, Joshua.]
Poor Robin's Almanac for . . . 1799.
Philadelphia, M'Culloch. [32] pp.
AAS copy.   34535

Sharp, Joshua.
Father Tammany's Almanac, for . . . 1800.
Philadelphia, Hogan. [36] pp.
(The unique copy with this imprint cannot
be reproduced.)   36298

Sharp, Joshua.
Father Tammany's Almanac, for . . . 1800.
Philadelphia, Young. [36] pp.
(No perfect copy located.)
AAS copy.   36297

Sharp, Joshua.
The Pennsylvania Almanac, for . . . 1796.
Philadelphia, Carey. [36] pp.
HSP copy.   47598

Sharp, Joshua.
The Pennsylvania Almanac, for . . . 1796.
Philadelphia, Johnson. [36] pp.
AAS copy.   29497

Sharpe, John, fl. 1694-1717.
A Sermon Preached at Trinity Church in
New-York.
New York, 1706. [4], 20 pp.
NYPL copy.   1280

Shaveblock, Pasquin, pseud.
The Shaver's New Sermon.

Albany, M'Donald, 1796. 23 pp.
(Attributed to MacGowan because of his
use of the pseud. "Shaver," but by
internal evidence it must have been
written after his death.)
HEH copy.   30722

Shaveblock, Pasquin, pseud.
The Shaver's New Sermon.
New York, Hand and Garson, 1796. 23
pp.
AAS copy.   30723

Shaveblock, Pasquin, pseud.
The Shaver's New Sermon. . . . Sixth
Edition.
Philadelphia, Dobson for Griffiths &
Rhees, 1796. 16, 32 pp.
AAS copy.   30724

Shaw, John, 1708-1791.
(Sibley, VIII, 627-628.)
The Character of a Pastor.
Boston, Kneeland, 1753. [4], 35 pp.
AAS copy.   7116

Shaw, John, 1708-1791.
(Sibley, VIII, 627-628.)
Holding Forth.
Boston, Green & Russell, 1761. 32 pp.
AAS copy.   9006

Shaw, Josiah Crocker, 1767-1847.
An Oration, Delivered July 4th, 1798.
Newport, R. I., Farnsworths, 1798. 22 pp.
AAS copy.   34536

Shaw, Oakes, 1736-1807.
A Sermon Preached in Marshfield.
Boston, Edes & Gill, 1766. 36 pp.
BA copy.   10491

Shaw, R. G., & Co.
[A Very Valuable Collection of
Books. . . . Feb. 27, 1800.
Boston, 1800.]
(McKay 143A.)   37014

Shaw, R. G., & Co.
[Stock of New Books. . . . Dec. 9, 1800.
Boston, 1800.]
(McKay 143M.)   37012

Shaw, R. G., & Co.
[Valuable Books. . . . Dec. 24, 1800.
Boston, 1800.]
(McKay 143N.)   37013

[Shaw, Robert], fl. 1794.
The Gentleman's Amusement, A
Selection. . . .
Philadelphia, Carr, [1794]. 98 pp.
(For the bibliographical history of this see
Sonneck-Upton pp. 157-158. No complete
copy is known, and the other copy
detailed by Sonneck-Upton is not now to
be found.)
LOC copy.   27694

[Shaw, Robert, fl. 1794.
The Gentleman's Amusement. A Selection
of Solos. . . .
Philadelphia, New York, and Baltimore,
Carrs, [1796]. 77 pp.]
(This is reproduced as 27694, q. v.)   31182

Shaw, Robert, fl. 1794.
The Gentleman's Amusement, or
Companion for the German Flute.
Philadelphia, Carr, [1795]. pp. 27-42.
HSP copy.   29498

[Shaw, Robert, fl. 1794.
The Gentleman's Amusement, or
Companion for the German Flute.
Philadelphia, Carr, [1796]. pp. 44-76.]
(A part of 27694.)   31181

[Shaw, Robert G.
A Large, Valuable and Well Chosen
Assortment of Books. . . . Sept. 19,
1799.
Boston, 1799.]
(McKay 142 K.)   36299

[Shaw, Samuel, 1635-1696.
(D. N. B.)
The Angelical Life.
Boston, Rogers & Fowle, 1744. 180 pp.]
(Title from Haven.)   5488

[Shaw, Samuel, 1635-1696.
(D. N. B.)

Farewel Life.
[Boston], 1765. 173, [3] pp.]
(This entry apparently describes a
defective London ed.)   10163

[Shaw, Samuel], 1635-1696.
Immanuel.
Boston, Rogers & Fowle for Edwards,
1741. [2], 259 pp., irreg.
AAS copy.   4804

Shaw, Samuel, 1635-1696.
Immanuel. . . . Third Edition.
Boston, Rogers & Fowle for Edwards,
1744. 246 pp.
AAS copy.   5489

Shaw, Samuel, 1635-1696.
(D. N. B.)
The Voice of one Crying.
Boston, Rogers & Fowle for Edwards,
1746. 176 pp.
AAS copy.   5862

Shaw, William, 1741-1816.
The Resurrection of Good Men.
Boston, Hall, 1799. 24 pp.
AAS copy.   36300

Shaw, William, 1741-1816.
A Sermon, Preached November 14, 1787.
Boston, Freeman, 1788. 29 pp.
AAS copy.   21460

Shaw, William, 1741-1816.
A Sermon, Preached, October 3, 1792.
Boston, Thomas & Andrews, 1793. [2], 18
pp.
AAS copy.   26157

She Left Me Ah! for Gold - A Favorite
Song.
New York, Gilfert, [1796]. Broadside.
AAS copy.   31183

Shearman, John, d. 1764.
[Last words of. . . .]
Boston, Fowle, 1764. Broadside.
(Upper part of the only known copy is
missing.)
AAS copy.   41487

[Shebbeare, John?], 1709-1788.
(D. N. B.)
A Letter, from Batista Angeloni.
Carolina, for Merefield in Philadelphia,
[1764]. 8 pp.
HC copy.   9838

[Shebbeare, John ?], 1709-1788.
A Letter, from Batista Angeloni.
Ephrata, [1764]. 8 pp.
NYHS copy.   9839

Sheehan, Bryan, -1772.
Salem, January 16, 1774. An Account of
the Life of Bryan Sheehan.
Portsmouth, [1772]. Broadside.
(This is apparently the item described by
Evans from Hall's adv.)
HSP copy.   12559

[Sheehan, John, d. 1787.
Lamentation and Farewell.
Boston, Russell, 1787.]
(Entry from an adv.)   20701

Sheehan, John, d. 1787.
Life, Last Words and Dying Speech of
John Sheehan, who was Executed . . .
November Twenty-Second, 1787.
Boston, Russell. Broadside.
AAS copy.   20702

A Sheet Almanack for . . . 1797.
Boston, Fleet. Broadside.
AAS copy.   30431

[Sheffield, John Baker Holroyd], 1st Earl
of, 1735-1821.
Observations on the Commerce of the
American States.
Philadelphia, Bell, 1783. [2], 77 pp.
LOC copy.   17975

[Sheffield, John Baker Holroyd], 1st Earl
of, 1735-1821.
Observations on the Commerce of the
American States.
Philadelphia, Bell, 1783. [2], 77, [1] pp.
AAS copy.   17976

Sheldon, Elisha, defendant.

Proceedings of a General Court Martial
. . . at Fish-Kill, on the 25th Day of
October, 1780.
Hartford, Hudson & Goodwin, 1780.
16 pp.
CHS copy.   17048

Sheldon, W., of Norwich, Ct.
Cursory Remarks on the Laws Concerning
Usury.
Norwich, Trumbull, 1798. 63 pp.
AAS copy.   34537

Shepard, Jeremiah, 1648-1720.
(Sibley, II, 267-276.)
Early Offerings best Accepted.
Boston, 1712. [2], vi, 159 pp.
MHS copy.   1583

Shepard, Jeremiah, 1648-1720.
(Sibley, II, 267-276.)
An Ephemeris.
Cambridge, 1672. [16] pp.
AAS copy.   172

Shepard, Jeremiah, 1648-1720.
(Sibley, II, 267-276.)
God's Conduct of His Church.
Boston, 1715. [4], 34 pp.
HC copy.   1780

Shepard, Jeremiah, 1648-1720.
(Sibley, II, 267-276.)
A Sort of Believers Never Saved.
Boston, 1711. [2], iv, 72 pp.
AAS copy.   1527

Shepard, Samuel, 1739-1815.
An Answer to the Publications of
Messieurs Thurston, Woodman and Coe.
Exeter, Ranlet, 1793. 92, [1] pp.
AAS copy.   26158

Shepard, Samuel, 1739-1815.
The Principle of Universal Salvation.
Exeter, N. H., Ranlet, 1798. 36 pp.
AAS copy.   34538

Shepard, Samuel, 1739-1815.
A Scriptural Enquiry.
Exeter, Ranlet, 1794. 38 pp.
AAS copy.   27695

Shepard, Samuel, 1739-1815.
Three Letters.
Portsmouth, Osborne, 1791. 72 pp.
AAS copy.   23761

Shepard, Thomas, 1605-1649.
(D. A. B.)
The Church Membership.
Cambridge, 1663. [22], 26 pp.
AAS copy.   82

[Shepard, Thomas, 1605-1649.
(D. A. B.)
The Church-Membership of Children.
Cambridge, 1669.]
(Second edition of Evans 82. Known only
from S. F. Haven list.)   145

[Shepard, Thomas, 1605-1649.
The Church-Membership of Children.
Boston, 1762.]
(Entry from Haven.)   9272

Shepard, Thomas, 1605-1649.
The Church-Membership of Children.
New London, 1769. 39, [1] pp.
AAS copy.   11462

Shepard, Thomas, 1605-1649.
The Church-Membership of Children.
Hartford, 1786. 31 pp.
CHS copy.   19985

Shepard, Thomas, 1605-1649.
The Saints Jewel.
Boston, Allen for Boone, 1708. [2], 68 pp.
(The only known copy is imperfect.)
AAS copy.   39473

Shepard, Thomas, 1605-1649.
(D. A. B.)
The Saint's Jewel.
Boston, Gookin, 1743. 38, [1] pp.
AAS copy.   5289

Shepard, Thomas, 1605-1649.
(D. A. B.)
Sampwutteahae.
Cambridge, 1689. [4], 161 pp.
AAS copy.   497

Shepard, Thomas, 1605-1649.
A Short Catechism.
Cambridge, Green, 1654. [2], 60 pp.
AAS copy.   39167

Shepard, Thomas, 1605-1649.
(D. A. B.)
[The Sincere Convert.
Cambridge, 1664.] 190 pp.
(The unique copy is imperfect.)
AAS copy.   93

Shepard, Thomas, 1605-1649.
The Sincere Convert.
Boston, Draper for Henchman, 1735. [2],
162 + pp.
(The only known copy is defective.)
AAS copy.   40082

Shepard, Thomas, 1605-1649.
(D. A. B.)
The Sincere Convert. . . . Newly
Corrected.
Boston, Draper, 1742. [2], vi, [2], 165,
[1] pp.
AAS copy.   5058

[Shepard, Thomas, 1605-1649.]
The Sincere Convert.
New York, 1743.]
(Title from Hildeburn.)   5291

[Shepard, Thomas, 1605-1649.]
The Sincere Convert.
Philadelphia, 1743.]
(Adv. Pa. Journal, Aug. 8, 1743.)   5290

Shepard, Thomas, 1605-1649.
(D. A. B.)
The Sound Believer.
Boston, Draper for Henchman, 1736. [2],
ii, 281 pp.
AAS copy.   4077

Shepard, Thomas, 1605-1649.
The Sound Believer.
Boston, Green, Bushell & Allen, for
Henchman, 1742. [2], iv, 258 pp.
AAS copy.   5059

Shepard, Thomas, 1605-1649.
(D. A. B.)
Three Valuable Pieces.
Boston, Rogers & Fowle, 1747. [2], 7, [6],
53, [4], 27, [2], vi, 73, [2] pp.
AAS copy.   6067

[Shepard, Thomas, 1605-1649.
(D. A. B.)
Two Questions.
Boston, 1697. 15 pp.]
(The unique copy is mislaid.)   814

Shepard, Thomas, 1605-1649.
(D. A. B.)
Wine for Gospel Wantons.
Cambridge, 1668. 15 pp.
AAS copy.   130

[Shepard, Thomas], 1635-1677.
(Sibley, I, 327-335.)
. . . An Almanack for . . . 1656.
Cambridge, 1656. [16] pp.
AAS copy.   43

Shepard, Thomas, 1635-1677.
(Sibley, I, 327-335.)
Eye-Salve.
Cambridge, 1673. [4], 52 pp.
AAS copy.   182

Shepherd, Edward, 1766?-1826.
The Columbian Accountant.
New York, Swords, 1800. x, [2], 212 pp.
(The only copy located is imperfect.)
AAS copy.   38494

Shepherd, Job, pseud.
Poor Job, 1750. An Almanack.
Newport, Franklin. [24] pp.
HC copy.   6414

Shepherd, Job, pseud.
Poor Job, 1751. An Almanack.
Newport, Franklin. [24] pp.
AAS copy.   6606

Shepherd, Job, pseud.
Poor Job, 1752. An Almanack.
Newport, Franklin. [24] pp.
AAS copy.   6780

Shepherd, Job, pseud.

Poor Job, 1753. An Almanack.
Newport, Franklin. [24] pp.
AAS copy.   6929

Shepherd, Job, pseud.
Poor Job, 1754. An Almanack.
Newport, Franklin. [25] pp.
AAS copy.   7117

Shepherd, Job, pseud.
Poor Job, 1755. An Almanack.
Newport, Franklin. [24] pp.
AAS copy.   7313

Shepherd, Job, pseud.
Poor Job's Country and Townsman's
Almanack for . . . 1758.
Newport, Franklin. [16] pp.
AAS copy.   8037

. . . The Shepherd of Salisbury Plain.
Part I [by Hannah More, 1745-1833].
Philadelphia, Johnsons, [1800]. 36 pp.
AAS copy.   37128

. . . The Shepherd of Salibury Plain. Part
II [by Hannah More, 1745-1833].
Philadelphia, Johnsons, [1800]. 36 pp.
AAS copy.   37129

The Shepherd's Contemplation.
Philadelphia, Woodward, 1794. 8 pp.
LOC copy.   47213

Sherburne, Henry, 1741-1825.
The Oriental Philanthropist.
Portsmouth, N. H., Treadwell, 1800. 215,
[1] pp.
AAS copy.   38495

[Sheridan, Richard Brinsley Butler,
1751-1816.
The Critic: or a Tragedy Rehearsed.
Philadelphia, Dobson, 1787.]
(Entry from an adv.)   20703

[Sheridan, Richard Brinsley Butler,
1751-1816.
The Critic.
Boston, Spotswood, 1795.]
(Imprint assumed by Evans from adv.
"For sale" in 28597.)   29499

[Sheridan, Richard Brinsley Butler,
1751-1816.
The Duenna: a Comic Opera.
Philadelphia, Humphreys for Nutter in
New York, 1779.]
(No such ed. located.)   16522

[Sheridan, Richard Brinsley Butler,
1751-1816.
The Governess.
Boston, Spotswood, 1795.]
(Imprint assumed by Evans from adv.
"For sale" in 28597.)   29500

Sheridan, Richard Brinsley Butler,
1751-1816.
The Real and Genuine School for Scandal.
Philadelphia, Bell, 1782. 64 pp.
YC copy.   17720

Sheridan, Richard Brinsley Butler,
1751-1816.
The School for Scandal.
New York, Gaine, 1786. 86, [2] pp.
AAS copy.   19986

Sheridan, Richard Brinsley Butler,
1751-1816.
The School for Scandal.
Philadelphia, Prichard & Hall, 1789. 61,
[3] pp.
AAS copy.   22139

Sheridan, Richard Brinsley Butler,
1751-1816.
The School for Scandal.
Boston, Belknap & Hall, 1792. 96 pp.
AAS copy.   24785

Sheridan, Richard Brinsley Butler,
1751-1816.
. . . Song in The Stranger.
Philadelphia, B. Carr, etc., [c. 1797]. 2
leaves.
WLC copy.   48250

Sheridan, Thomas, 1719-1788.
A Complete Dictionary. . . . Fourth
Edition.

Philadelphia, Young, 1789. pp. [i,-viii,
[xiii]-lxxvi, [764].
AAS copy.   22140

Sheridan, Thomas, 1719-1788.
A Complete Dictionary.... Fifth Edition.
Philadelphia, Young, [1789.] pp. [i]-vi,
[xiii]-liv, [612].
AAS copy.   45588

Sheridan, Thomas, 1719-1788.
A Complete Dictionary.... Sixth Edition,
Carefully Revised ... by ... John
Andrews.
Philadelphia, Young, Mills & Son, 1796. 8,
[2], 60, [838] pp.
AAS copy.   31184

Sheridan, Thomas, 1719-1788.
A Complete Dictionary ... Sixth Edition.
Philadelphia, Young, Mills & Son, 1796. 8,
[2], 60, [838] pp.
(Text identical with 31884, q. v.)
AAS copy.   31185

Sheridan, Thomas, 1719-1788.
A Complete Dictionary.... Sixth Edition.
Philadelphia, Young, Mills & Son, 1796.
104, [887] pp.
AAS copy.   47914

Sheridan, Thomas, 1719-1788.
A Course of Lectures on Elocution.
Providence, Carter & Wilkinson, 1796. 156
pp.
AAS copy.   31186

Sheridan, Thomas, 1719-1788.
A Rhetorical Grammar of the English
Language.
Philadelphia, Bell and Bailey, 1783. xvi,
218, [2] pp.
AAS copy.   18184

Sheridan, Thomas, 1719-1788.
A Rhetorical Grammar.... Third
Edition.
Philadelphia, Young, 1789. [i]-viii,
[xiii]-lxxiii, [3] pp.
AAS copy.   45589

Sherlock, Richard, 1612-1689.
The Principles of the Holy Christian
Religion.... Ninth Edition.
New York, Bradford, 1704. [10], 56+ pp.
(The only recorded copy is imperfect.)
AAS copy.   39415

[Sherlock, Thomas], bp., 1678-1761.
(D. N. B.)
A Letter from the Lord Bishop of
London.
Boston, Draper, 1750. 15 pp.
AAS copy.   6607

Sherlock, Thomas, bp., 1678-1761.
A Letter ... to the Clergy and People of
London.
Williamsburg, Hunter, 1750. 20 pp.
(The unique original could not be
reproduced.)   40569

[Sherlock, Thomas], bp., 1678-1761.
(D. N. B.)
The Tryal of the Witnesses of the
Resurrection.
New London, 1754. 120 pp.
AAS copy.   7314

[Sherlock, Thomas], bp. 1678-1761.
The Trial of the Witnesses of the
Resurrection.
Philadelphia, Dobson, 1788. 143, [1] pp.
AAS copy.   21461

[Sherlock, Thomas], bp., 1678-1761.
The Trial of the Witnesses of the
Resurrection.
Philadelphia, Tuckniss, 1800. 128, 15 pp.
AAS copy.   38496

Sherlock, William, 1641?-1707.
A Practical Discourse Concerning Death.
Williamsburg, Parke, 1744. [8],
310 pp.
HEH copy.   40349

[Sherman, John], 1613-1685.
(Magnalia, Bk. 3, Pt. 2, Ch. 29.)
... An Almanack ... for ... 1674.
Cambridge, 1674. [16] pp.
HEH copy.   196

[Sherman, John], 1613-1685.
(Magnalia, Bk. 3, Pt. 2, Ch. 29.)
... An Almanack ... for ... 1676.
Cambridge, 1676. [16] pp.
AAS copy.   223

[Sherman, John], 1613-1685.
(Magnalia, Bk. 3, Pt. 2, Ch. 29.)
... An Almanack ... for ... 1677.
Cambridge, 1677. [16] pp.
AAS copy.   241

Sherman, Josiah, 1729-1789.
The Administrations of Parochial
Bishops.
Fairfield, Forgue & Bulkeley, 1789.
24 pp.
AAS copy.   22141

Sherman, Josiah, 1729-1789.
Christ the True Victim and Conqueror.
Litchfield, [1787]. 66 pp.
BA copy.   20704

Sherman, Josiah, 1729-1789.
(Weis, Colonial Clergy N. E.)
God in no Sense the Author of Sin.
Hartford, Hudson & Goodwin, 1784. 30
pp.
AAS copy.   18781

Sherman, Josiah, 1729-1789.
The History of Melchizedek.
Litchfield, [1787]. 28 pp.
(Dated from adv. in Litchfield Monitor,
Oct. 22, 1787.)
AAS copy.   19987

[Sherman, Josiah], 1729-1789.
The Nature of Moral Agency.
Litchfield, 1787.]
(Adv., Litchfield Monitor, Nov. 12, 1787.)
         20705

[Sherman, Josiah], 1729-1789.
Oracles of Reason.
Litchfield, [1787]. 40 pp.
VtU copy.   20706

[Sherman, Josiah], 1729-1789.
A Sermon to Swine.
Litchfield, Collier, 1787. 40 pp.
(This is 20706 with a different title.)
LOC copy.   20707

Sherman, Roger, 1721-1793.
(D. A. B.)
An Astronomical Diary ... for ... 1750.
Boston, Draper. [16] pp.
AAS copy.   6415

Sherman, Roger, 1721-1793.
An Almanack, for the Year ... 1750.
New York, De Foreest. [24] pp.
NYPL copy.   6416

Sherman, Roger, 1721-1793.
(D. A. B.)
An Astronomical Diary ... for ... 1751.
Boston, Draper. [16] pp.
AAS copy.   6608

Sherman, Roger, 1721-1793.
An Astronomical Diary, or an Almanack,
for the Year ... 1751.
New York, De Foreest. [24] pp.
LIHS copy.   6609

[Sherman, Roger], 1721-1793.
An Astronomical Diary ... for ... 1752.
Boston.]
(Assumed by Sabin from the sequence.)
         6782

Sherman, Roger, 1721-1793.
An Astronomical Diary ... for ... 1752.
New York, De Foreest. [26] pp.
AAS copy.   6781

[Sherman, Roger], 1721-1793.
An Astronomical Diary ... for ... 1753.
Boston, Fowle?]
(From an adv., probably for copies of
6930 or 6931.)   6932

Sherman, Roger, 1721-1793.
An Astronomical Diary ... for ... 1753.
New London, 1753. [16] pp.
AAS copy.   6931

Sherman, Roger, 1721-1793.
An Astronomical Diary.... for ... 1753.

New York, De Foreest. [24] pp.
NYPL copy.   6930

Sherman, Roger, 1721-1793.
An Astronomical Diary, or an Almanack
for ... 1754.
New London, 1754. [16] pp.
AAS copy.   7118

Sherman, Roger, 1721-1793.
An Astronomical Diary, or an Almanack,
for ... 1754.
New York, De Foreest. [22] pp.
(The unique copy is probably defective.)
NYPL copy.   7119

Sherman, Roger, 1721-1793.
An Astronomical Diary ... for ... 1755.
Boston, Fowle and the Booksellers. [16]
pp.
AAS copy.   7316

[Sherman, Roger, 1721-1793.
An Astronomical Diary ... for ... 1755.
New London, Green. [28] pp.]
(Assumed by Evans from the sequence.)
         7315

Sherman, Roger, 1721-1793.
The Connecticut Diary; or, an Almanack
for ... 1756.
New Haven, Parker. [16] pp.
AAS copy.   7566

Sherman, Roger, 1721-1793.
The Connecticut Diary: or, an Almanack,
for ... 1757.
New Haven, Parker. [16] pp.
AAS copy.   7791

Sherman, Roger, 1721-1793.
An Astronomical Diary ... for ... 1758.
New Haven, Parker. [16] pp.
CHS copy.   8038

Sherman, Roger, 1721-1793.
An Astronomical Diary, or an Almanack
for ... 1760.
Boston, for Henchman, Edwards, Dennis,
Winter, Leverett, and Webb. 1760. [24]
pp.
AAS copy.   8491

Sherman, Roger, 1721-1793.
An Almanack for the Year ... 1761.
Boston, Kneeland for Henchman,
Edwards, Dennis, Winter, Leverett, and
Webb, 1761. [16] pp.
AAS copy.   8734

[Sherman, Roger], 1721-1793.
A Caveat against Injustice.
New York, 1752. 15 pp.
LOC copy.   6933

[Sherman, Roger], 1721-1793.
Remarks on a Pamphlet, Entitled, "A
Dissertation on the Political Union....
[New Haven], 1784. 43 pp.
AAS copy.   18782

[Sherman, Roger], 1721-1793.
A Short Sermon on the Duty of Self
Examination.
New Haven, Morse, 1789. [2], 20 pp.
AAS copy.   45590

[Sherman, Thomas.]
[Divine Breathings.]
Boston, 1707. 80 pp.]
(No copy of this edition has been found.)
         1330

[Sherman, Thomas.]
Divine Breathings. ... Tenth Edition.
Boston, B. Green for Eliot, 1709. [4], 75,
[3] pp.
(The only known copy is imperfect.)
AAS copy.   39496

[Sherman, Thomas]
(LOC card.)
Divine Breathings: or, a Pious Soul
Thirsting.
Philadelphia, Gibbons, 1792. 104, [4] pp.
AAS copy.   24786

[Sherman, Thomas].
Divine Breathings: or, A Pious Soul
Thirsting after Christ. ... First Vermont
Edition.
Bennington, Haswell, 1795. 106, [2] pp.
VtHS copy.   29457

[Sherman, Thomas.]
Divine Breathings; or a Pious Soul
Thirsting. . . . Third Edition.
Elizabethtown, N. J., Kollock for Davis,
1797. 103 pp.
AAS copy. 32828

[Sherman, Thomas]
Divine Breathings: or, A Pious Soul
Thirsting after Christ. . . . First American
Edition.
Leominster, Mass., Prentiss for Thomas,
1799. 167, [7] pp.
AAS copy. 35412

[Shervington, William], -1763.
(W. Eames, Antigua Press, p. 5.)
The Antigonian and Bostonian Beauties.
Boston, Fowle, [1751 ?]. 8, 8 pp.
AAS copy. 7317

Sherwood, Samuel, 1730-1783.
The Church's Flight.
New York, Loudon, 1776. 54 pp.
AAS copy. 15082

Sherwood, Samuel, 1730-1783.
(Weis, Colonial Clergy N. E.)
A Sermon, Containing, Scriptural
Instructions.
New Haven, [1774]. 81, [1] pp.
AAS copy. 13614

Shewen, William, 1631?-1695.
(D. N. B.)
A Brief Testimony.
Philadelphia, 1701. 21 pp.
HSP copy. 1024

Shewen, William, 1631?-1695.
Counsel to the Christian-Traveller. . . .
Fifth Edition.
Lancaster, 1773. xv, [1], 95 pp.
AAS copy. 13006

Shewen, William, 1631?-1695.
Counsel to the Christian Traveller.
Salem, Cushing for Carlton, 1793. 119 pp.
AAS copy. 26159

[Shewen, William, 1631?-1695.
Good Advice to Youth.
Philadelphia, 1701].
(See Hildeburn. No copy found.) 1025

Shewing the Harmony of the Divine
Attributes.
[Boston, 1750?] Broadside.
MHS copy. 40532

Shield, William, 1748-1829.
Amidst the Illusions. A Favorite Song.
New York, Gilfert, [1795]. 3 pp.
LOC copy. 29501

Shield, William, 1748-1829.
The Cheering Rosary [by William Pearce].
Philadelphia, Carr, [1793]. [2] pp.
LOC copy. 25966

[Shield, William, 1748-1829.
Fame, let thy Trumpet Sound. A Song.
Philadelphia, Town, 1779.]
(Hildeburn 3877, from an adv.) 16523

Shield, William, 1748-1829.
The Heaving of the Lead. A Favorite Sea
Song [by William Pearce].
Philadelphia, Carr, [1793]. [2] pp.
AAS copy. 25967

Shield, William, 1748-1829.
How Can I Forget.
Carr, New York and Philadelphia. [2] pp.
(Evans entry was from advs.)
AAS copy. 29502

[Shield, William], 1748-1829.
Johnny and Mary.
New York, Hewitt, [1798?]. 1 leaf.
NYPL copy. 34539

Shield, William, 1748-1829.
Marian. Overture.
Philadelphia, Reinagle and Aitken,
[1789]. [2] pp.
LOC copy. 22142

[Shield, William, 1748-1829.
The Morning is Up.
New York, Hewitt, 1798.]
(No copy of a separate printing located.)
34540

Shield, William, 1748-1829.
Old Towler, a Favorite Hunting Song.
New York, Gilfert, [1796.] [2] pp.
NYPL copy. 47915

[Shield, William], 1748-1829.
The Streamlet.
New York, Hewitt, etc., [1797?]
Broadside.
NYPL copy. 48251

Shield, William, 1748-1829.
What are the Boasted Joys of Love.
Philadelphia, Carr, [1798]. [2] pp.
NYPL copy. 34541

[Shield, William], 1748-1829.
Whilst with Village Maids I Stray.
New York, Moller, [1797]. [2] pp.
LOC copy. 48252

[Shields, John.
Advertisement.
Philadelphia, 1784.]
(From Aitken's accounts.) 18783

[The Ship Revolution. Articles of
Agreement had . . . this 23rd day of
March.
Philadelphia, Dunlap, [1780]. Broadside.]
(Known from book catalogues.) 17369

Shipley, Jonathan, bp., 1714-1788.
A Sermon Preached before the
Incorporated Society . . . February 19,
1773.
Boston, Fleets, 1773. 17 pp.
AAS copy. 13009

Shipley, Jonathan, bp., 1714-1788.
A Sermon Preached before the
Incorporated Society . . . February 19,
1773.
New York, Hodge & Shober for Noel &
Hazard, 1773. 16 pp.
LOC copy. 13010

Shipley, Jonathan, bp., 1714-1788.
A Sermon Preached before the
Incorporated Society . . . February 19,
1773.
Newport, 1773. 16 pp.
AAS copy. 13011

Shipley, Jonathan, bp., 1714-1788.
A Sermon Preached before the
Incorporated Society . . . February 19,
1773.
Norwich, [1773]. 19 pp.
CHS copy. 13012

[Shipley, Jonathan, bp., 1714-1788.
A Sermon Preached before the
Incorporated Society . . . February 19,
1773.
Philadelphia, Aitken, 1773. 20 pp.]
(Entry apparently from an Aitken adv. for
13007.) 13008

Shipley, Jonathan, bp., 1714-1788.
A Sermon Preached before the
Incorporated Society . . . February 19,
1773.
Philadelphia, Bell for Woodhouse, 1773. [2],
20 pp.
AAS copy. 13007

[Shipley, Jonathan, bp., 1714-1788.
A Sermon Preached . . . February 19,
1773.
Newport, 1785. 17 pp.]
(Entry from Hammett.) 19238

Shipley, Jonathan, bp., 1714-1788.
A Speech Intended to have been Spoken.
Boston, Greenleaf, [1774]. 12 pp.
NYPL copy. 13615

[Shipley, Jonathan], bp., 1714-1788.
A Speech Intended to have been
Spoken. . . . Sixth Edition.
Boston, Edes & Gill, 1774. 24 pp.
AAS copy. 13616

[Shipley, Jonathan], bp., 1714-1788.
A Speech Intended to have been
Spoken. . . . Fifth Edition.
Hartford, 1774. 17 pp.
CHS copy. 13617

Shipley, Jonathan, bp., 1714-1788.
A Speech, Intended to have been
Spoken. . . . Fifth Edition.
Lancaster, 1774. 24 pp.
LCP copy. 13618

Shipley, Jonathan, bp., 1714-1788.
A Speech, Intended to have been Spoken.
New York, Holt, 1774. [4], 18 pp.
NYPL copy. 13619

[Shipley, Jonathan ,, bp., 1714-1788.
A Speech Intended to have been
Spoken. . . . Third Edition.
Philadelphia, Bradfords, 1774. vi, 29 pp.
AAS copy. 13620

Shipley, Jonathan, bp., 1714-1788.
A Speech Intended to have been Spoken.
Philadelphia, Towne, [1774]. 18 pp.
LCP copy. 13621

Shipley, Jonathan, bp., 1714-1788.
A Speech, Intended to have been Spoken.
Salem, Halls, [1774]. 16 pp.
AAS copy. 13623

Shipley, Jonathan, bp., 1714-1788.
A Speech Intenedd [!] to have been
Spoken.
Salem, Russell, 1774. 16 pp.
AAS copy. 13622

Shipley, Jonathan, bp., 1714-1788.
A Speech Intending to have been Spoken.
Williamsburg, Pinkney, 1774. 15 pp.
JCB copy. 42699

Shipley, Jonathan, bp., 1714-1788.
The Whole of the Celebrated Speech
of. . . .
Newport, 1774. 20 pp.
AAS copy. 13624

Shipley, Jonathan, bp., 1714-1788.
The Whole Speech of. . . .
[np., nd., 1774.] [2] pp.
NYPL copy. 13625

[The Shipmaster's Assistant and Owner's
Manual.
Salem, Cushing, 1797.]
(Imprint assumed by Evans from adv.
"For Sale by Thomas C. Cushing" in
Salem Gazette, Dec. 5, 1798.) 32829

[Shippen, John.
Observations on Novel-Reading.
Philadelphia, Bailey, 1794.]
(Imprint assumed by Evans from advs.)
27696

Shippen, John.
An Oration Delivered on the Anniversary
of the Scientific Society.
Philadelphia, Bailey, 1794. 23, [1] pp.
LCP copy. 27697

[Shippen, John].
The Story of Palemon and Eliza.
Harrisburg, Wyeth, 1796. 13, [1] pp.
AAS copy. 31187

The Shipwreck and Adventures of . . .
Pierre Viaud [by Jean Gaspard
Dubois-Fontanelle, 1737-1812].
Dover, N. H., Bragg, 1799. viii, 203 pp.
BA copy. 35425

[Shirley, James, 1596-1666.
The Gamester.
New York, Gaine, 1761.]
(Adv. N. Y. Mercury, July 20, 1761.) 9007

Shirley, William, 1694-1771.
(D. A. B.)
A Letter from William Shirley.
Boston, Draper for Henchman, [1746]. 31
pp.
AAS copy. 5863

Shirley, William, 1694-1771.
A Letter from William Shirley.
Boston, Rogers & Fowle for Blanchard,
1746. 16 pp.
AAS copy. 5864

Shirley, William, 1694-1771.
A Letter from William Shirley.
New York, [1747]. 20 pp.
JCB copy. 5865

[Shirley, William], 1694-1771.
Memoirs of the Principal Transactions of
the Last War. . . . Third Edition.

Boston, Green & Russell, 1758. pp. [i]-iv,
[9]-80.
AAS copy.   8258

Shirtliff, Roswell.
see
Shurtleff, Roswell.   38497

A Shocking Narrative of the Murder of
Mr. Joseph Porter, by Captain William
Corran.
Walpole, N.H., Thomas & Carlisle, 1795.
10 pp.
AAS copy.   47599

Shoemaker, Abraham.
The New-Jersey Almanack for . . . 1795.
Trenton, Collins. [44] pp.
AAS copy.   27698

Shoemaker, Abraham.
The New-Jersey Almanack for . . . 1796.
Trenton, Collins. [44] pp.
HSP copy.   29504

Shoemaker, Abraham.
The New-Jersey and New-York Almanac
. . . for . . . 1799.
Newark, N. J., Pennington & Dodge. [36]
pp.
HEH copy.   34542

Shoemaker, Abraham.
The New-Jersey and New-York Almanack
. . . for . . . 1799.
Newark, Pennington & Dodge. [36] pp.
HEH copy.   48614

Shoemaker, Abraham.
The New-Jersey and New-York Almanac,
for . . . 1800.
Newark, Day for Davis. [36] pp.
AAS copy.   36302

Shoemaker, Abraham.
The New-Jersey and New-York Almanac,
for . . . 1800.
Newark, Day for Parkhurst & Pennington.
[36] pp.
NYPL copy.   36303

[Shoemaker, Abraham.]
The New-Jersey and New-York Almanac,
for . . . 1800.
Newark, Halsey. [36] pp.]
(Copy at LOC not available for
reproduction.)   36304

Shoemaker, Abraham.
The New-Jersey and Pennsylvania
Almanac, for . . . 1799.
Trenton, N. J., Day. [36] pp.
NYHS copy.   34543

Shoemaker, Abraham.
The New-Jersey and Pennsylvania, for . . .
1800.
Trenton, Sherman, Mershon & Thomas.
[36] pp.
(Differs from 36305, q. v., only in wording
of imprint.)   36306

Shoemaker, Abraham.
The New-Jersey and Pennsylvania
Almanac, for . . . 1800.
Trenton, Sherman, Mershon & Thomas, at
their Office opposite the Indian-Queen
Tavern. [36] pp.
AAS copy.   36305

Shoemaker, Abraham.
The New-Jersey and Pennsylvania
Almanac, for . . . 1801.
Trenton, Sherman, Mershon & Thomas.
[36] pp.
NYHS copy.   38498

[Shoemaker, Abraham.]
The New Town and Country Almanac, for
. . . 1796.
New York, Shoemaker. [48] pp.
AAS copy.   29505

[Shoemaker, Abraham.]
Poulson's Town and Country Almanac,
for . . . 1795.
Philadelphia, Poulson. [44] pp.
AAS copy.   27699

[Shoemaker, Abraham.]
Poulson's Town and Country Almanac,
for . . . 1796.

Philadelphia, Poulson. [48] pp.
AAS copy.   29506

[Shoemaker, Abraham.]
Poulson's Town and Country Almanac,
for . . . 1797.
Philadelphia, Poulson. [48] pp.
AAS copy.   31189

[Shoemaker, Abraham.]
Poulson's Town and Country Almanac,
for . . . 1798.
Philadelphia, Poulson. [48] pp.
AAS copy.   32834

[Shoemaker, Abraham.]
Poulson's Town and Country Almanac,
for . . . 1799.
Philadelphia, Poulson. [48] pp.
AAS copy.   34544

[Shoemaker, Abraham.]
The Town and Country Almanac, for . . .
1799.
Philadelphia, Pearson. [44] pp.
(The only recorded copy is imperfect.)
HSP copy.   34545

[Shoemaker, Abraham.]
The Town and Country Almanack, for . . .
1800.
New York, Longworth & Wheeler. 36 pp.
(Also entered as 36441, q. v.)   36307

Shoemaker, Abraham.
The Town and Country Almanac, for . . .
1801.
New York, Longworth. [36] pp.
(The only copy located is imperfect.)
RU copy.   38499

Shoemaker, Abraham.
The United States Almanac, for . . . 1799.
Elizabethtown, Kollock for Dunham. [36]
pp.
LOC copy.   34547

Shoemaker, Abraham.
The United States Almanac, for . . . 1799.
Elizabethtown, N. J., Kollock for Judah.
[36] pp.
AAS copy.   34546

. . . The Shopkeeper Turned Sailor [by
Hannah More, 1745-1833].
Philadelphia, Johnsons, 1800. 35, [1] pp.
LCP copy.   37158

Short, Matthew, 1688-1731.
(Sibley, V, 394-396.)
A Thankful Memorial.
Boston, Kneeland and Green, 1729. [6],
33 pp.
AAS copy.   3217

Short, Thomas, 1690-1772.
(D. N. B.)
Medicina Britannica.
Philadelphia, Franklin & Hall, 1751. xx,
339, 40, 7 pp.
HSP copy.   6783

[Short, Thomas, 1690-1772.
Medicina Britannica.
Philadelphia, Franklin & Hall, 1765.]
(Sabin 80575; no copy known.)   41588

A Short Account of a Dreadful Thunder
Storm in Goshen.
n. p., n. d. Broadside.
CHS copy.   49146

A Short Account of Algiers [by Mathew
Carey, 1760-1839].
Philadelphia, Parker for Carey, 1794. [2],
46 pp., 1 map.
AAS copy.   26732

A Short Account of Algiers. . . . Second
Edition [by Mathew Carey, 1760-1839].
Philadelphia, Carey, 1794. 50, [2] pp., 1
map.
AAS copy.   26733

A Short Account of that Part of Africa,
Inhabited by the Negroes [by Anthony
Benezet, 1713-1784].
Philadelphia, 1762. 56 pp.
AAS copy.   9066

A Short Account of that Part of Africa,
Inhabited by the Negroes. . . . Second
Edition [by Anthony Benezet, 1713-1784].

Philadelphia, Dunlap, 1762. 80 pp.
AAS copy.   9067

A Short Account of the Death of a
Profligate Youth.
Springfield, [Mass.], Ashley, 1800. 12 pp.
AAS copy.   38500

A Short Account of the Life and
Character of John Campbell . . . to be
Executed this 29th of December, 1769.
[New York, 1769.] Broadside.
LCP copy.   11463

A Short Account of the Life and Death of
William Adams.
Philadelphia, Steiner, 1782. 34 pp.
AAS copy.   44264

A Short Account of the Plague [by Daniel
Defoe, 1661-1731].
New London, Green, 1793. 16 pp.
AAS copy.   25385

A Short Account of the Apostolic Rite of
Confirmation.
Albany, Websters, 1791. 19 pp.
NYPL copy.   23763

A Short Account of the Establishment of
the New See of Baltimore [by Charles
Plowden, 1743-1821].
Philadelphia, Carey, Stewart & Co., 1791.
20 pp.
Georgetown University copy.   23703

A Short Account of the Honourable
Emanuel Swedenborg.
Baltimore, Adams, 1792. [4], 23, [5] pp.
AAS copy.   24395

A Short Account of the last Sickness and
Death of . . . John Wesley [by Elizabeth
Ritchie].
Baltimore, Adamses, 1791. 12 pp.
JCB copy.   46275

A Short Account of the Sickness and
Death of John Wesley [by Thomas Taylor,
1738-1816].
Philadelphia, Johnson, 1791. 12 pp.
(The Evans entry came from an adv.)
HSP copy.   23822

A Short Account of the Sickness and
Death of the Rev. Mr. John Wesley.
Philadelphia, S. Johnston, 1791. 12 pp.
LCP copy.   46287

A Short Account of the State of Mendon
Third Parish.
Boston, 1773. 16 pp.
AAS copy.   12658

A Short Account of the Trouble and
Dangers our Forefathers met. . . .
Danvers, Russell, [1776].
(Anderson Galleries Cat. no. 1797, Jan.
2-22, 1924.)   43159

A Short Account of the Unhappy Death of
a Profligate Youth.
Baltimore, Graham for Hagerty, 1791. 12
pp.
AAS copy.   46288

A Short Address to the Voters of
Delaware. . . . Sept. 24, 1800.
[Dover? 1800.] 7 pp.
LOC copy.   49147

Short Advice to the Counties of
New-York [by Isaac? Wilkins], 1742-
1830].
New York, Rivington, 1774. 15 pp.
AAS copy.   13772

[A Short Almanac for the Year 1800.
New Brunswick, N. J., Blauvelt.]
(Title and imprint assumed by Evans from
adv.)   35215

[A Short and Accurate Account of all the
Various Sects.
Philadelphia, Denoon & Condie, 1795.]
(Entry from a prospectus in 29486;
probably not printed.)   29507

A Short and Easy Guide to Arithmetick,
Particularly Adapted to the Use of
Farmers and Tradesmen.
Boston, Hall, 1794. 64 pp.
HC copy.   27700

A Short and Practical Essay on Farming
[by John Lambert, fl. 1798].
Philadelphia, [1798]. 8 pp.
LCP copy. 33974

A Short and True Account of a Young
Youth.
Philadelphia, Armbruster, 1768. 8 pp.
LCP copy. 11069

[A Short, but Particular and Impartial,
Account of the Treatment of Slaves in . . .
Antigua.
Baltimore, Goddard & Angell, 1791.]
(The origin of this entry is unknown.)
23762

[A Short but Serious Address to the
Inhabitants of Pennsylvania.
Philadelphia, 1770.]
(Adv. Pa. Chronicle, Oct. 8, 1770.) 11854

[A Short Catechism for Young Children
to be Learnt before that of the
Assemblies.
Boston, 1738.]
("This day published," Boston Gazette,
July 24, 1738.) 4422

A Short Catechism, wherein the Chief
Principles of Religion are Taught [by
Benjamin Stinton, 1676-1718].
Boston, Fleets, 1766. 16 pp.
AAS copy. 10504

[A Short Compendium of English
Grammar. Collected from a Variety of
Authors.
Bennington, Haswell & Russell, 1786.]
(McCorison 120; no copy known.) 44966

[A Short Confession of Faith; Being the
Substance of all the Fundamentals.
Philadelphia, Bradford for White, 1734. 39
pp.]
(Said to have been in the Horatio Gates
Jones collection.) 3833

[A Short Confession of Faith, of the
Church of Christ, at Newport.
Philadelphia, 1731.]
((Probably a ghost of 3833 arising from a
misprint.) 3476

[Short Conversations.
Boston, Hall, 1795.]
(Imprint assumed by Evans from Hall's
adv. in 29599.) 29508

[Short Conversations, or an Esay Road to
the Temple of Fame.
Boston, Hall, 1793?]
(Imprint assumed by Evans from Hall's
advs.) 26161

Short Conversations; or, An Easy Road
[by Dorothy Kilner, 1755-1836].
Boston, Hall, 1794. 70 pp.
(Only known copy is imperfect.)
AAS copy. 47092

A Short Description of the State of
Tennessee [by Daniel Smith, 1748-1818].
Philadelphia, Lang & Ustick for Carey,
1796. 36 pp., 1 map.
AAS copy. 31199

A Short Description of the State of
Tennessee. . . . To which is Prefixed, the
Constitution of that State [by Daniel
Smith, 1748-1818].
Philadelphia, Lang & Ustick for Carey,
1796. 44 pp.
BA copy. 31200

A Short Description of the State of
Tennessee [by Daniel Smith, 1740-1818].
New York, Mott, 1797. 47 pp.
HEH copy. 48254

A Short Description of the Tennessee
Government [by Daniel Smith,
1748-1818].
Philadelphia, Carey, 1793. 20 pp., 1 map.
AAS copy. 26168

A Short Dialogue, between a Learned
Divine and a Beggar.
Norwich, 1795. 11, [1] pp.
CHS copy. 47600

A Short Dialogue, between a Learned
Divine and a Beggard.

Norwich, Ct., 1787. 8 pp.
(Trumbull Supplement 2608, no copy
known.) 45163

A Short Direction for an Unregenerate
Sinner.
New York, 1739. 24 pp.
HSP copy. 4421

A Short Discourse of a Life of Grace.
New York, W. Bradford, 1741. 100 pp.
HEH copy. 40259

A Short Discourse Shewing that our
Salvation [by Warham Mather, 1666-
1745].
[New London?], 1716. [4], 32 pp.
HC copy. 1839

A Short, Easy, and Comprehensive
Method of Prayer [by John Kelpius,
1673-1708].
Philadelphia, Miller, 1761. 36 pp.
NYHS copy. 8895

A Short, Easy, and Comprehensive
Method of Prayer. . . . Second Edition [by
John Kelpius, 1673-1708].
Germantown, 1763. 34 pp.
(The unique copy is imperfect.)
HSP copy. 9414

[Short-Hand Book.
Philadelphia, Keimer, 1728.]
(Adv. in 3071.) 3105

[Short-Hand Book. Second Impression.
Philadelphia, 1729.]
(Hildeburn 380.) 3218

A Short History of a Long Travel. . . .
Seventh Edition [by Stephen Crisp,
1628-1692].
Philadelphia, Bradford, 1751. 23 pp.
HSP copy. 6656

[A Short History of a Long Travel. . . .
Ninth Edition [by Stephen Crisp,
1628-1692].
Philadelphia, Chattin, 1752.]
(Adv. in 6959.) 6986

A Short History of a Long Travel. . . .
Tenth Edition [by Stephen Crisp,
1628-1692].
Philadelphia, Chattin, 1754. 23, [1] pp.
AAS copy. 7177

A Short History of a Long Travel [by
Stephen Crisp, 1628-1692].
Newport, Southwick, 1770. 22 pp.
RIHS copy. 42079

A Short History of a Long Travel. . . .
Eighth Edition [by Stephen Crisp,
1628-1692].
Philadelphia, Crukshank and Ferriss,
[1770]. 24 pp.
AAS copy. 11616

A Short History of a Long Travel [by
Stephen Crisp, 1628-1692].
Philadelpha, Crukshank, 1776. 24 pp.
AAS copy. 43016

A Short History of a Long Travel. . . .
Tenth Edition [by Stephen Crisp,
1628-1692].
Philadelphia, Crukshank, 1788. 24 pp.
LOC copy. 21031

A Short History of a Long Travel. . . .
Tenth Edition [by Stephen Crisp,
1628-1682].
Exeter, [N. H.], [1791?]. 34 + pp.
(The only known copy is imperfect.)
AAS copy. 46144

A Short History of a Long Travel [by
Stephen Crisp, 1628-1692].
Bennington, Haswell for Spencer, 1793. 35
pp.
AAS copy. 46720

A Short History of a Long Travel. . . .
Tenth Edition [by Stephen Crisp,
1628-1692].
Danbury, Douglas, 1794. 23 pp.
CHS copy. 47018

A Short History of a Long Travel [by
Stephen Crisp, 1628-1692].

New Bedford, Spooner for Davis & Taber,
1794. 24 pp.
AAS copy. 26831

A Short History of a Long Travel [by
Stephen Crisp, 1628-1692].
New Haven, 1797. 23 pp.
AAS copy. 32002

A Short History of Late Ecclesiastical
Oppressions in New-England and
Vermont [by John Cosens Ogden,
1751-1800].
Richmond, Va., Lyon, 1799. 19 pp.
AAS copy. 36006

[A Short History of Mr. Thomas
Thoroughgood.
Troy, Gardner, 1795.]
(Imprint assumed by Evans from adv. "for
sale" in The Recorder, Nov. 17, 1795.)
29509

A Short History of the Grand Rebellion in
Scotland.
[Boston], Gray, [1746]. Broadside.
NYPL copy. 5866

A Short History of the Late Ecclesiastical
Oppressions in New-England and
Vermont.
Richmond, Va., Lyon, 1799. 19 pp.
(Also entered as 36006, q. v.) 36308

A Short History of the Nature and
Consequences of Excise Laws [by James
Thomson Callender, 1758-1803].
Philadelphia, Printed for the Booksellers,
1795. 116 pp.
AAS copy. 28383

A Short History of the Nature and
Consequences of Excise Laws [by James
Thomson Callender, 1758-1803].
Philadelphia, for Stephens and Rivington,
1795. 116 pp.
LOC copy. 28384

A Short History of the Treatment that Dr.
Samuel Stearns hath met with.
[Worcester], 1786. 24 pp.
AAS copy. 20006

Short History of the Yellow Fever [by
Richard Folwell, 1768?-1814].
Philadelphia, Folwell, 1797. [1]-37, 46-64,
[8] pp.
LCP copy. 32138

Short History of the Yellow Fever. . . .
Second Edition [by Richard Folwell,
1768?-1814].
Philadelphia, Folwell, 1798. pp. [1]-37,
46-64, [16].
AAS copy. 33742

A Short Introduction to English Grammar
[by Robert Lowth, 1710-1787].
New York, Rogers & Berry, 1795. 144 pp.
JCB copy. 28990

A Short Introduction to Latin Grammar,
for the use of the University and Academy
of Pennsylvania [by James Davidson,
1732-1809].
Philadelphia, Cist, 1781. iv, 116 pp.
(The author's name appears on eds. 1804
et seq.)
AAS copy. 17370

A Short Introduction to Latin Grammar.
For the Use of the University . . . of
Pennsylvania. . . . Second Edition [by
James Davidson, 1732-1809].
Philadelphia, Cist, 1783. iv, 116 pp.
AAS copy. 18185

A Short Introduction to Latin Grammar,
for the Use of the University and
Academy of Pennsylvania. . . . Third
Edition [by James Davidson, 1732-1809].
Philadelphia, Cist, 1786. iv, 116 pp.
AAS copy. 19988

A Short Introduction to Latin Grammar,
for the use of the University and Academy
of Pennsylvania. . . . Fourth Edition [by
James Davidson, 1732-1809].
Philadelphia, Cist, 1789. iv, 116 pp.
AAS copy. 22143

A Short Introduction to Latin Grammar,
for the Use of the University and

Academy of Pennsylvania. . . . Fourth
Edition [by James Davidson, 1732-1809].
Boston, Folsom, 1790. v (iv), 127, [1] pp.
AAS copy.   22890

A Short Introduction to Latin Grammar,
for the Use of the University and
Academy of Pennsylvania. . . . Fifth
Edition [by James Davidson, 1732-
1809].
Boston, Folsom, 1792. 126, [1] pp.
AAS copy.   24787

A Short Introduction to Latin Grammar,
for the Use of the University and
Academy of Pennsylvania. . . . Sixth
Edition [by James Davidson, 1732-1809].
Exeter, Lamson, 1794. 108 pp.
AAS copy.   27701

A Short Introduction to Latin Grammar,
for the Use of the University and
Academy of Pennsylvania. . . . Fifth
Edition [by James Davidson, 1732-1809].
Philadelphia, Cist, 1797. iv, 116 pp.
AAS copy.   32835

A Short Introduction to Latin Grammar,
for the Use of the University and
Academy of Pennsylvania, Sixth Edition
[by James Davidson, 1732-1809].
Philadelphia, Cist, 1799. iv, 116 pp.
AAS copy.   36309

A Short Introduction to Latin Grammar,
for the Use of the University . . . of
Pennsylvania. . . . Seventh Edition [by
James Davidson, 1732-1809].
Wilmington, Del., Bonsal & Niles, 1800.
108 pp.
AAS copy.   38501

A Short Introduction to the Latin Tongue.
For Cheever eds. see author cards.

A Short Introduction to the Latin
Tongue. . . . Sixth Edition.
New York, 1749. [2], iv, 138 pp.
AAS copy.   6417

A Short Introduction to the Latin Tongue.
The Third Edition.
Philadelphia, Chattin for Williams of
Salem, 1755. 52 pp.
AAS copy.   7568

A Short Introduction to the Latin
Tongue. . . . Sixteenth Edition [by Ezekiel
Cheever, 1615-1708].
Boston, Knox, 1773. 72 pp.
(An imprint variant of 13013, q. v. for
text.)
AAS copy.   42424

A Short Narrative of the Claim, Title and
Right of the Heirs of . . . Samuel Allen.
[Boston, 1728.] 13 pp.
AAS copy.   3106

A Short Narrative of the Extraordinary
Work at Cambuslang [by James Robe,
1688-1753].
Boston, Kneeland, 1742. 24 pp.
AAS copy.   5047

A Short Narrative of the Extraordinary
Work at Cambuslang [by James Robe,
1688-1753].
Philadelphia, Bradford, 1742. 36, [3] pp.
AAS copy.   5046

Short Observations on Slavery [by
Anthony Benezet, 1713-1784].
[Philadelphia, 1781.] 12 pp.
AAS copy.   17096

Short Observations on Slavery,
Introductory to some Extracts from . . .
Raynal [by Anthony Benezet, 1713-1784].
Philadelphia, Story, [1785?]. 12 pp.
BPL copy.   44648

A Short Poem, on the Death of the Rev'd
Mr. George Whitefield. . . . Sept. 30th,
1770.
n.p., [1770]. Broadside.
HSP copy.   42171

A Short Relation Concerning a Dream
[by Samuel Clarke, b. 1721?].
Boston, Barclay, [1769]. 15 pp.
AAS copy.   11465

A Short Relation, Concerning a Dream
[by Samuel Clarke, b. 1721?].
New London, 1770. 12 pp.
BPL copy.   11857

A Short Relation Concerning a Dream
[by Samuel Clarke, b. 1721?].
Boston, [1785]. 16 pp.
AAS copy.   19402

A Short Reply to Mr. Stephen Hopkins's
Vindication. . . . April 10, 1755.
[Newport, 1755.] 6 pp.
BrU copy.   40799

A Short Reply to Mr. Whitefield's Letter.
Philadelphia, 1741. 62 pp.
BPL copy.   4085

A Short Review of the Political State of
Great-Britain [by Sir Nathaniel William
Wraxall, bart., 1751-1831].
Philadelphia, Dobson, 1787. 48 pp.
AAS copy.   20899

A Short Sermon on Self-Examination [by
Richard Baxter? 1615-1691].
New Haven, Morse, 1789. 20 pp.
(Evans took the title from the half title.)
AAS copy.   21670

A Short Sermon on the Duty of Self
Examination [by Roger Sherman,
1721-1793].
New Haven, Morse, 1789. [2], 20 pp.
AAS copy.   45590

A Short Sketch of the Evidence for the
Abolition of the Slave Trade [by William
Bell Crafton].
Philadelphia, Lawrence, 1792. 28, 16, [3]
pp.
AAS copy.   24233

A Short Sketch, of the Life of Mr. Lent
Munson [by Alexander Viets Griswold,
bp., 1766-1843].
Litchfield, Ct., Collier, [1797]. 8 pp.
BPL copy.   33827

A Short Specimen of Apostolick
Preaching [by James Relly, 1722?-1778].
Burlington, Collins, 1773. 19 pp.
HEH copy.   42488

A Short State of the Proceedings of the
Proprietors of East and West Jersey.
New York, Rivington, 1775. 23 pp.
HSP copy.   14285

[Short Stories for Young People. . . .
Second Windsor Edition.
Windsor, Vt., Mower, 1800. 27 pp.]
(A ghost of McCorison 873.)   38502

A Short System of Polite Learning [by
Daniel Joudon, 1767-1826].
Litchfield, Conn., Collier, 1797. 112 pp.
AAS copy.   32316

[A Short Treatise on Rice Machinery.
Charleston, 1786.]
(The origin of this entry is unknown.)
   19483

A Short Vindication of the Conduct of the
Referees.
[Boston, 1767.] 22 pp.
AAS copy.   10614

The Shorter Catechism.
See
Westminster Assembly of Divines. 38503

Shower, John, 1657-1715.
(D. N. B.)
Some Account of the Holy Life . . . of Mr.
Henry Gearing.
Boston, 1704. xxxiv, 134 pp.
AAS copy.   1194

[Shower, John], 1657-1715.
Some Account of the Holy Life . . . of Mr.
Henry Gearing.
Boston, Fleet for Phillips, etc., 1720. xxxv,
146 pp.
WLC copy.   2175

[Shower, John], 1657-1715.
The Tryal and Character of a real
Christian. . . . Fourth Edition.
New York, Bradford and DeForest, 1744.
[2], xxiv, 118 (i.e. 119) pp.
NYHS copy.   40350

[Shrubsole, William, 1729-1797.
Christian Memoirs.
Philadelphia, Neale & Kammerer, 1796.
400 pp.]
(The origin of this entry is unknown.)
   31190

Shultz, Benjamin.
An Inaugural Botanico-Medical
Dissertation.
Philadelphia, Dobson, 1795. [8], 55 pp., 1
folding plate.
AAS copy.   29510

Shultz, Benjamin.
An Oration Delivered before the
Mosheimian Society.
Philadelphia, Dobson, 1795. 14 pp.
AAS copy.   29511

Shumway, Nehemiah, 1761-1843.
The American Harmony, being a
Collection of the Most Approved Church
Music.
Philadelphia, M'Culloch, 1793. 212 pp.
(177-180 omitted in paging.)
AAS copy.   26162

[Shurtleff, James], 1745-1832.
A Concise Review of the Spirit.
[Augusta, Me.? 1798.] 47 pp.
AAS copy.   34548

[Shurtleff, James], 1745-1832.
The Substance of a Late Remarkable
Dream.
Hallowell, Me., Edes, 1800. 16 pp.
BrU copy.   38584

Shurtleff, Roswell, 1773-1861.
An Oration on . . . Washington.
Walpole, N. H., Carlisle for Thomas &
Thomas, 1800. 15 pp.
AAS copy.   38504

Shurtleff, William, 1689-1747.
(Sibley, V, 396-403.)
Distressing Dangers.
Boston, Green for Russell, 1727. [6], 50
pp.
AAS copy.   2960

Shurtleff, William, 1689-1747.
(Sibley, V, 396-403.)
The Faith and Prayer.
Boston, Draper for Henchman, 1740. [4],
iv, 30 pp.
AAS copy.   4599

Shurtleff, William, 1689-1747.
(Sibley, V, 396-403.)
Gospel Ministers.
Boston, Draper for Henchman, 1739. [4],
35 pp.
AAS copy.   4423

Shurtleff, William, 1689-1747.
(Sibley, V, 396-403.)
The Labour that Attends the
Gospel-Ministry.
Boston, Green for Russell, 1727. [6], 34
pp.
AAS copy.   2961

Shurtleff, William, 1689-1747.
(Sibley, V, 396-403.)
A Letter to Those of his Brethren.
Boston, Kneeland & Green, 1745. 23 pp.
AAS copy.   5686

Shurtleff, William, 1689-1747.
(Sibley, V, 396-403.)
The Obligations upon all Christians.
Boston, Fleet for Henchman, 1741. 27 pp.
AAS copy.   4806

[Shute, Daniel], 1722-1802.
(Sibley, XI.)
A Compendious and Plain Catechism.
Boston, Hall, 1794. 34 pp.
AAS copy.   27702

Shute, Daniel, 1722-1802.
A Sermon Delivered at the
Meeting-House . . . in Hingham.
Salem, Dabney & Cushing, 1787. 32 pp.
AAS copy.   20708

Shute, Daniel, 1722-1802.
(Sibley, XI.)
A Sermon Preached Before His
Excellency.
Boston, Draper, 1748 (1768). 70 pp.
AAS copy.   11071

Shute, Daniel, 1722-1802.
(Sibley, XI.)
A Sermon Preached to the . . . Artillery
Company.
Boston, Edes & Gill, 1767. 43 pp.
AAS copy.   10768

Shuttlesworth, Samuel, 1751-1834.
A Discourse Delivered in the Presence of
His Excellency.
Windsor, Hutchins, 1792. 16 pp.
AAS copy.   24788

The Siamese Tales.
Baltimore, Clayland & Dobbin for
Keatinge, [1797]. 178, [2] pp.
AAS copy.   32836

[Sibbes, Richard, 1577-1635.
Divine Meditations.
Philadelphia, Ustick, 1796.]
(Imprint assumed by Evans from adv.
"For sale," in 31115.)   31191

Sibbes, Richard, 1577-1635.
Divine Meditations and Holy
Contemplations.
Wilmington, Bonsal & Niles for Correy,
1797. 60 pp.
(Best copy available.)
LCP copy.   48253

Sibley, Solomon, 1769-1846.
An Oration, Delivered at Mendon.
Boston, Hall, 1796. 16 pp.
AAS copy.   31192

Sibyllae Americanae Genethliacum
Ludovico XVII.
Philadelphia, Towne, 1782. 16 pp.
LOC copy.   17721

[Sicard, Stephen, fl. 1788.
The New Constitution March.
Philadelphia, 1788.]
(Adv. in Philadelphia newspapers, Oct.,
1788.)   21462

Sicard, Stephen, fl. 1789.
The President of the United States'
March.
Philadelphia, M'Culloch, [1789?]
Broadside.
NYPL ph. copy.   45591

Siddons, Henry, 1774-1815.
The Sicilian Romance.
Philadelphia, Bradford, 1794. 36 pp.
AAS copy.   27703

[Siddons, Henry, 1774-1815.
The Sicilian Romance.
Boston, Blake, 1795.]
(Imprint assumed by Evans from adv. "for
sale" in 29115.)   29512

Sidney, Algernon, pseud.
No Convention. Friends, Fellow-Citizens.
[Lexington? 1798] 2 pp.
LOC copy.   48615

Sidrophel, Joseph, pseud.
An Astronomical Diary, or Almanack . . .
for . . . 1784.
Hartford, Webster. [14+] pp.
(The only known copy is imperfect.)
CHS copy.   44453

Ein '76 ger Lied.
n.p., [1785?]. Broadside.
HEH copy.   44792

Siegvolck, Paul, [pseud.].
The Everlasting Gospel. . . . By Paul
Siegvolck, [pseud.] [by Georg
Klein-Nicolai].
Germantown, 1753. viii, 152 pp.
AAS copy.   7033

Siegvolck, Paul, pseud.
Das von Jesu Christo . . . von Georg Paul
Siegvolck [by Georg Klein-Nicolai].
Germantown, 1768. [9], 175 pp.
AAS copy.   10942

Siegvolck, Georg Paul, pseud.
Das von Jesu Christo. . . . von Georg Paul
Siegvolck [by Georg Klein-Nicolai].
Germantown, 1769. [9], 175 pp.
AAS copy.   11304

Sierra Leone Company.

Substance of the Report Delivered . . .
March 27th, 1794.
Philadelphia, Dobson, 1795. 168 pp., 1
folding map.
AAS copy.   29513

Sierra Leone Company.
Substance of the Report of the Court of
Directors . . . the 26th of February, 1795.
Philadelphia, Dobson, 1795. 24 pp.
AAS copy.   29514

Sierra Leone Company.
Substance of the Reports Delivered . . . to
which is Prefixed Memoirs of Naimbanna.
Philadelphia, Dobson, 1799. 22, [2], 168,
24 pp., 1 map.
(The two reports are 29513 and 29514,
q. v.)
AAS copy.   36310

Sigfrid, Isaac.
Theological Theses.
New York, Brown, 1766. [12], 55, [3],
113, 4 pp.
AAS copy.   10493

Signatus [by Cotton Mather, 1663-1728].
Boston, Henchman, 1727. 40 pp.
AAS copy.   2918

The Silver Moon [by James Hook,
1746-1827].
Boston, von Hagen, [1798?] [2] pp.
JCB copy.   48475

Simes, Thomas.
The Military Guide. . . . In two Volumes.
Philadelphia, Humphreys, Bell, and
Aitken, 1776. [8], 384, [5] pp., 2 folding
plates; [192] pp., plate.
AAS copy.   15083

Simmons, Amelia.
American Cookery.
Hartford, Hudson & Goodwin, 1796. 47,
[1] pp.
AAS copy.   31193

Simmons, Amelia.
American Cookery. . . . Second Edition.
Albany, N. Y., Websters, [1796]. 64 pp.
(Adv. Albany Gazette, Oct. 31, 1796.)
AAS copy.   38503

Simmons, Amelia.
American Cookery.
Hartford, [Hudson & Goodwin for]
Butler, Northampton, 1798. 48 pp.
AAS copy.   34549

[Simmons, Amelia.
American Cookery. . . . Second Edition.
New York, Greenleaf, 1798.]
(Imprint assumed by Evans from adv.
"This Day Published, and for sale at
Greenleaf's . . . the Second Edition,"
Greenleaf's New Daily Adv., Jan. 20,
1798. The Hartford ed. was being adv.
Oct., 1798.)   34550

[Simmons, James], fl. 1793.
A Military Essay.
Charleston, Markland & M'Iver, 1793.
12 pp.
LOC copy.   26163

[Simmons, John], fl. 1794.
A New Pennsylvania Primer.
Philadelphia, 1794.]
(Entry from the copyright notice.)
                                             27704

[Simmons, Robert?]
These Times want Other. . . . It is a
Disagreeable Subject to Write upon
Informers.
New York, [1769]. Broadside.
LCP copy.   11466

Simons, Benjamin Benneau, 1776-1844.
A Funeral Oration . . . of Mrs.
Thomas Edwards.
Providence, Wheeler, [1795]. 10 pp.
AAS copy.   29515

Simons, James.
A New Principle of Tactics.
Charleston, S. C., Timothy & Mason,
1797. [2], 12 pp., 1 plate.
AAS copy.   32838

Simons, James.

A Rallying Point for All True Friends
to their Country.
[Charleston, S. C., 1800.] 16 pp.
MHS copy.   38506

[Simons, Menno], 1496-1559.
Ein Fundament und Klare Anweisung.
[Lancaster], Pa., 1794. [12], 675,
[5] pp.
AAS copy.   27310

The Simple Cobler of Aggawam [by
Nathaniel Ward, 1578-1652].
Boston, 1713. [4], 100 pp.
AAS copy.   1658

Simple Division.
Boston, White, [1787?] Broadside.
MHS copy.   45164

Simple Truth Vindicated [by Samuel
Pike, 1717?-1773].
Boston, Kneeland & Adams, 1771.
72 pp.
AAS copy.   12198

Simpson, William, chief justice.
The Practical Justice of . . . South-
Carolina.
Charleston, 1761. viii, 276 pp.
LOC copy.   9009

Sims, James, 1741-1820.
Observations on the Scarlatina
Anginosa.
Boston, Hall, 1796. 16 pp.
AAS copy.   31194

Sims, Stephen.
A Sober Reply . . . to a Paragraph in
Jonathan Edward's Discourse, Delivered
. . . Sept. 10th. 1741.
[New London? 1741.] Broadside.
LOC copy.   40260

Simsbury, Conn. First Congregational
Church.
The Result of an Ecclesiastical
Council . . . February 27, A.D. 1770.
[Hartford], 1770. 32 pp.
CHS copy.   11858

The Sin and Danger of Self-Love [by
Robert Cushman, d. 1625].
Boston, 1724. [2], vi, 24 pp.
AAS copy.   2519

Since then I'm Doom'd.
Philadelphia, Hupfeld, etc., [1798?].
Broadside.
(Copy not located.)   48616

[Sincere Piety Described [by Cotton
Mather, 1663-1728].
Boston, Kneeland for Edwards, 1719.]
24 pp.
(The two known copies are defective.)
NYPL copy.   2046

[The Sinfulness of Neglecting and
Profaning the Lord's Day.
Albany, Websters, 1789.]
("For sale," Albany Gazette, Dec. 10,
1789.)   22144

The Singular and Diverting Behaviour
of Doctor Marriot . . . on the 3d. of
June, 1774.
Philadelphia, Humphreys, 1774. 16 pp.
LCP copy.   13626

Sinners Invited to Come to Jesus.
Boston, Printed and Sold in Milk-Street,
1774. Broadside.
HSP copy.   42700

Sinners Invited to Come to Jesus.
Providence: Printed and Sold at the
Paper-Mills, [1774]. Broadside.
RIHS copy.   42701

Sion in Distress [by Benjamin Keach,
1640-1704].
Boston, 1683. [8], 128 pp.
AAS copy.   344

Sion in Distress [by Benjamin Keach,
1640-1704].
Boston, for Thomas Baker, 1683. [8],
128 pp.
(Differs from Evans 344 only in
imprint.)
HC copy.   345

Sir, At a late Meeting of the General
Committee Appointed to this City to
Promote the Election of Robert Yates. . . .
[New York? 1795.] Broadside.
Albany Institute copy.   47601

Sir, Our Adversaries in the Election. . . .
April 18, 1792.
[Albany, 1792.] Broadside.
(Also entered as 46372, q.v.)   46573

Sir [blank] You will Readily Discover
in the Writing, which M. the Abbe de la
Poterie has the Honor to Send you
[Mar. 3, 1789].
[Boston, 1789.] [1], 4 pp.
MHS copy.   45592

Sir, Your being a member of the Hon.
the Gen. Assembly. . . . [by Samuel
Stearns, 1747-1819].
[Providence, 1798.] Broadside.   34602

Siret, Louis Pierre, 1745-1797.
(LOC card.)
Elémens de la Langue Angloise.
Philadelphia, Bradford, 1792. pp. [24],
[11]-168.
BA copy.   24789

Siret, Louis Pierre, 1745-1797.
Elémens de la Langue Angloise.
Philadelphia, Bradford, 1794. pp. [1]-29,
[1], [11]-168.
AAS copy.   27705

[Sisson, George], 1683-1740.
An Answer, to Richard Harden's Reply.
Newport, 1730. [2], 83 pp.
QL copy.   3352

The Sister's Gift: or, the Naughty Boy
Reformed.
Worcester, Thomas, 1786. 31 pp.
AAS copy.   19989

The Sister's Gift: or, the Naughty Boy
Reformed. . . . Second Worcester Edition.
Worcester, Thomas for Andrews, 1789. 31
pp.
AAS copy.   22145

The Sister's Gift; or, The Naughty Boy
Reformed.
New York, 1790. 29, [1] pp.
AAS copy.   45992

[The Sister's Gift; or, The Naughty Boy
Reformed.
Boston, Hall, 1791. 28, [2] pp.]
(The origin of this entry is unknown.)
                                           23764

[The Sister's Gift, or The Naughty Boy
Reformed.
Boston, Hall, 1795.]
(A ghost of 29599 arising from Hall's adv.)
                                           29516

The Sister's Gift: or, The Naughty Boy
Reformed. . . . Third Worcester Edition.
Worcester, Mass., I. Thomas and I.
Thomas, Jr., for Thomas & Andrews, 1795.
31 pp.
AAS copy.   47602

Sister, Sarah.
By an Order from the Orphan's Court. . . .
January 23d, 1800.
[Philadelphia], Hall & Sellers, [1800].
Broadside.
(No copy could be located.)   38507

The Situation of Frederick-Town.
[Annapolis, 1748.] Broadside.
MdHS copy.   40479

Six Arguments against Chusing Joseph
Galloway.
[Philadelphia, 1766.] Broadside.
UOP copy.   10494

[Six Dialogues between Two Young
Ladies.
Boston, Fowle & Draper, 1760. 100 pp.]
(Imprint from adv., pagination from
Haven.)   8735

A Sixth Essay on Free Trade and Finance
[by Pelatiah Webster, 1726-1795].
Philadelphia, Bradford, 1783. 32 pp.
AAS copy.   18301

Sixth Massachusetts Turnpike
Corporation.
By Laws of the. . . .
Worcester, Mass., Mower & Greenleaf,
[1799]. 18, [2] pp.
AAS copy.   35803

A Sketch of the History of the War in
Europe.
New York, Kirk, 1798. 260 pp.
AAS copy.   34551

A Sketch of the Life of James Arminius.
Providence, Wheeler, 1793. 12 pp.
BrU copy.   26164

[A Sketch of the Times: or, The Cabinet
Display'd.
Baltimore, Dunlap, 1777.]
(Adv. Maryland Gazette, Jan. 21, 1777.)
                                           15598

Sketches of French and English Politicks
[by Richard Beresford, 1755-1803].
Charleston, S. C., Young, 1797. [2], 65
pp.
AAS copy.   31803

Sketches of the History, Genius,
Disposition . . . of the Fair Sex.
Philadelphia, Sansom, [1796?]. viii, 292
pp.
AAS copy.   31688

[Sketches of the History, Genius,
Disposition . . . of the Fair Sex.
Philadelphia, Sansom, [1800]. viii, 292
pp.]
(A ghost of 31688, dated from an adv.)
                                           38508

Sketches of the Life of Joseph Mountain
[by David Daggett, 1764-1851].
Hartford, Patten, [1790]. 14, [1] pp.
AAS copy.   45855

Sketches of the Life of Joseph Mountain
[by David Daggett, 1764-1851].
New Haven, Greens, 1790. 20 pp.
CHS copy.   22441

Sketches of the Life of Joseph Mountain
[by David Daggett, 1764-1851].
Norwich, Trumbull, [1790?]. 16 pp.
NYHS copy.   45856

Sketches on Rotations of Crops [by John
Beale Bordley, 1727-1804].
Printed for Cowan in Talboton, 1792.
[2], 47, errata slip.
MdHS copy.   46390

Sketches on Rotations of Crops [by John
Beale Bordley, 1727-1804].
Philadelphia, Cist, 1792. [2], 47 pp.,
errata slip.
BA copy.   24129

Sketches on Rotations of Crops [by John
Beale Bordley, 1727-1804].
Philadelphia, Cist, 1796. [2], 76 pp.
AAS copy.   30103

Sketches on Rotations of Crops [by John
Beale Bordley, 1727-1804].
Philadelphia, Cist, 1797. [2], 76 pp.
(Issued without the final 11 pages called
for by Evans.)
AAS copy.   31846

Skinner, Ichabod Lord, 1767-1852.
A Discourse on Music.
Hartford, Hudson & Goodwin, 1796. 18
pp.
AAS copy.   31195

Skinner, Ichabod Lord, 1767-1852.
A Farewell Discourse, Delivered at
North-Coventry.
Hartford, Ct., Hudson & Goodwin, 1799.
16 pp.
CHS copy.   36313

Skinner, Thomas, 1709-1762.
(Sibley, IX, 223-226.)
The Faithful Minister's Trials.
New London, 1751. [4], 49, [1] pp.
AAS copy.   6784

Skinner, Thomas, 1709-1762.
(Sibley, IX, 223-226.)
The Mourner Admonished.

Boston, Rogers & Fowle, 1746. 42, [1] pp.
HC copy.   5867

The Sky-Lark: or Gentlemen and Ladies'
Complete Songster.
Worcester, Thomas, 1795. 228 pp.
AAS copy.   29517

The Sky Lark: or Gentlemen & Ladies'
Complete Songster. . . . Second Edition.
Worcester, Thomas, 1797. 310, [2] pp.
(The title given by Evans comes from
advs.)
AAS copy.   32839

[Slack, Ann (Fisher)], 1719-1778.
The Pleasing Instructor, or Entertaining
Moralist.
Boston, Bumstead for B. Larkin & E.
Larkin, and D. West, 1795. 312, [3] pp.
AAS copy.   29518

Slater & Lord, firm.
Public Auction. On Tuesday next. . . .
February 13, 1796.
[New York? 1796.] Broadside.
(Not located, 1968.)   47916

Slator, Lionel.
Instructions for the Cultivating . . . of
Flax.
Boston, Kneeland & Green for
Henchman, 1735. iv, 45, [3], 39 pp.
AAS copy.   3959

Slavery Inconsistent with Justice and
Good Policy. By Philanthropos [by David
Rice, 1733-1816].
Lexington, Bradford, 1792. 43 pp.
Presb. Hist. Soc. copy.   24741

Slavery not Forbidden by Scripture [by
Richard Nisbet].
Philadelphia, 1773. [2], iii, [1], 30 pp.
AAS copy.   12903

Slender, Robert, pseud.
A Journey from Philadelphia to
New-York [by Philip Morin Freneau,
1752-1832].
Philadelphia, Bailey, 1787. 28 pp.
AAS copy.   20375

Slender, Robert, pseud.
Letters on Various Interesting and
Important Subjects. . . . [by Philip Morin
Freneau, 1752-1832].
Philadelphia, Hogan, 1799. 142, [1] pp.
AAS copy.   35516

Slygood, William, pseud.
The Universal Kalendar, and the
North-American Almanack, for . . . 1784
[by Samuel Stearns, 1747-1819].
[New York.] [24] pp.
(No perfect copy located.)   18196

Small, Abraham, 1764?-1829.
Sir, We have Taken the Liberty. . . . June,
1796.
[Philadelphia, 1796]. Broadside.
(Not located, 1968.)   47917

Small, Abraham, 1764?-1829.
Superb Family Bible. Proposals for
Printing. . . . June, 1796.
[Philadelphia, 1796.] [2] pp.
(Not located, 1968.)   47918

Small, Jacob.
[The prices of carpenters' work for
Baltimore.
Baltimore, 1796?]
(Minick 319; no copy known.)   47919

A Small Collection of Questions &
Answers, from Various Authors.
Litchfield, Ct., Collier, 1799. 15 pp.
Trinity College (Watkinson) copy.   36315

[A Small Collection of Sentimental
Extracts.
Bennington, Haswell, 1793?]
(Imprint assumed by Evans from adv.
"Just Published, And now ready for sale
at the Printing-Office," Vt. Gazette, Mar.
15, 1793.)   26165

A Small Sketch on Natural Philosophy.
Wilmington, Brynberg & Andrews, 1792.
24 pp.
(The unique copy is incorrectly paged.)
Del. Hist. Soc. copy.   25576

Smalley, John, 1734-1820.
(Weis, Colonial Clergy N. E.)
The Consistency of the Sinner's Inability.
Hartford, 1769. 71 pp.
AAS copy.   11467

Smalley, John, 1734-1820.
Eternal Salvation.
Hartford, Hudson & Goodwin, 1785. 29,
[1] pp.
AAS copy.   19245

Smalley, John, 1734-1820.
(Weis, Colonial Clergy N. E.)
The Inability of the Sinner.
Boston, Kneeland, 1772. 71 pp.
AAS copy.   12560

Smalley, John, 1734-1820.
The Law in all Respects Satisfied.
Hartford, Hudson & Goodwin, 1786. 32
pp.
AAS copy.   19991

Smalley, John, 1734-1820.
On the Evils of a Weak Government.
Hartford, Ct., Hudson & Goodwin, 1800.
51 pp.
AAS copy.   38509

Smalley, John, 1734-1820.
The Perfection of the Divine Law.
New Haven, Meigs, 1787. 25 pp.
AAS copy.   20710

Smart, Christopher, 1722-1771.
Hymns for the Amusement of Children.
Philadelphia, Spotswood, 1791. iv, 92 pp.
AAS copy.   23767

[Smart, Christopher, 1722-1771.
Hymns for the Instruction and
Amusement of Children.
Boston, Spotswood, 1795.]
(Imprint assumed by Evans from adv.
"may be had" in Columbian Centinel,
Jan. 4, 1795.)   29519

Smellie, William, 1697-1763.
An Abridgement of the Practice of
Midwifery.
Boston, Norman, [1786]. 56 pp., 39 plates.
AAS copy.   19992

Smellie, William, 1697-1763.
A Set of Anatomical Tables. . . . First
Worcester Edition.
Worcester, Thomas, 1793. 84 pp., 40 plates.
AAS copy.   26166

Smellie, William, 1740-1795.
The Philosophy of Natural History.
Philadelphia, Campbell, 1791. 490, [1] pp.
AAS copy.   23766

A Smile from the Youth that I Love.
Philadelphia, Willig, [1798?]. [2] pp.
JCB copy.   34552

Smith, Aaron, 1713-1781.
(Sibley, IX, 575-579.)
Some Temporal Advantages.
Boston, Kneeland, 1749. [4], 31, [1] pp.
AAS copy.   6418

Smith, Abraham L.
The Attack made on Mr. B.
Livingston. . . . October 7, 1785.
[New York, 1785.] Broadside.
NYHS copy.   44793

[Smith, Abraham L.
Statement Regarding an Assault on
Brockholst Livingston. . . . October 7,
1785.
[New York, 1785.] Broadside.]
(No copy located.)   19246

Smith, Adam, 1723-1790.
An Inquiry into the Nature and Causes of
the Wealth of Nations.
Philadelphia, Dobson, 1789. 3 vol. 412;
430; 387, [53] pp.
AAS copy.   22148

Smith, Adam, 1723-1790.
An Inquiry into the . . . Wealth of
Nations. . . . Vol. I- [-III].
Philadelphia, Dobson, 1796. 412; 430; 387,
[54] pp.
AAS copy.   31196

Smith, Amasa, 1756?-1847.

A Short Compendium of the Duty of
Artillerists.
Worcester, Mass., Thomas, 1800. 56 pp., 1
folding chart.
AAS copy.   38510

Smith, Benjamin, of South Carolina.
South-Carolina, May 11, 1780. Copy of an
intercepted Letter.
On Board the ship Palliser, printed by
Robertson, Macdonald & Cameron,
[1780]. Broadside.
(No copy located.)   43895

Smith, Caleb, 1723-1762.
(Dexter, I, 747-748.)
A Brief Account of. . . .
Woodbridge, 1763. [4], 60 pp.
NJHS copy.   9515

Smith, Caleb, 1723-1762.
(Dexter, I, 747-748.)
Diligence in the Work of God.
New York, Gaine, 1758. 39 pp.
NYHS copy.   8259

Smith, Caleb, 1723-1762.
The Various Branches of Ministerial
Duty.
Woodbridge, [N. J.], Parker, 1762. [2],
26 pp.
LOC copy.   41310

Smith, Charles, 1765-1836.
An Oration, Delivered at the Town of
Sunbury.
Philadelphia, Dobson, 1788. 29 pp.
AAS copy.   21463

Smith, Charles, 1768-1808.
The American War, from 1775-1783.
New York, Smith, 1797. 183 pp., 2 plates,
7 folding plans.
(The illustrations differ in reported
copies.)
AAS copy.   32842

[Smith, Charles], 1768-1808.
The American Gazetteer, or
Georgraphical Companion.
New York, Menut, 1797. [54], pp., 1 map.
AAS copy.   32841

Smith, Charles, 1768-1808.
The Gentleman's Political and
Commercial Pocket Almanac for 1801.
New York, 123 pp.
(The only recorded copy was lost in the
Albany fire.)   38511

Smith, Charles, 1768-1808.
The Gentleman's Political
Pocket-Almanack for . . . 1795.
New York, Allen. [2], 106 pp., 3 plates, 1
folding table.
AAS copy.   27707

Smith, Charles, 1768-1808.
The Gentleman's Political Pocket
Almanac for . . . 1796.
New York, Buel for Smith. 112 pp.
(Copy not located.)   47603

Smith, Charles, 1768-1808.
The Gentleman's Political
Pocket-Almanac for . . . 1796.
New York, Wayland & Davis for Smith. [2],
142 pp., 1 plate.
AAS copy.   29520

Smith, Charles, 1768-1808.
The Gentleman's Political Pocket
Almanac, for . . . 1797.
New York, Buel for Smith. 59, [1] pp., 2
plates.
AAS copy.   31197

Smith, Charles, 1768-1808.
Universal Georgraphy made Easy.
New York, Wayland & Davis for author and
L. Wayland, 1795. 192 pp., 7 maps.
AAS copy.   29521

[Smith, Charles Jeffery, 1740-1770.
(Weis, Colonial Clergy Va.)
An Address to the Inhabitants of . . .
Virginia.
Williamsburg, 1770.]
(From an adv.)   11860

Smith, Charles Jeffery, 1740-1770.
(Weis, Colonial Clergy Va.)

The Nature and Necessity of
Regeneration.
Woodbridge, 1765. xvi, 62 pp.
NYHS copy.   10164

Smith, Charlotte (Turner), 1749-1806.
D'Arcy. A Novel.
Philadelphia, Carey, 1796. 167 pp.
AAS copy.   31198

Smith, Charlotte (Turner), 1749-1806.
Elegiac Sonnets.
Philadelphia, Dobson, 1787. 36 pp.
AAS copy.   20711

Smith, Charlotte (Turner), 1749-1806.
Elegiac Sonnets. . . . Seventh Edition.
Boston, Spotswood, 1795. [8], 64 pp.
AAS copy.   29522

Smith, Charlotte (Turner), 1749-1806.
Elegiac Sonnets. . . . First Worcester
Edition.
Worcester, Thomas for Thomas &
Andrews, 1795. 126 pp., 5 plates.
(Also issued without plates and with
plates printed in colors.)
AAS copy.   29523

Smith, Charlotte (Turner), 1749-1806.
Montalbert. A Novel . . . Vol. 1.
Carlisle, Pa., Kline for Carey, [1795?].
[2], 270 pp.
(Vol. 2 was printed in 1800.)
LCP copy.   29524

Smith, Charlotte (Turner), 1749-1806.
Montalbert. A Novel. . . . In Two
Volumes.
Philadelphia, Snowden & McCorkle for
Carey, 1800. [2], 270; [2], 244 pp.
AAS copy.   38512

Smith, Charlotte (Turner), 1749-1806.
The Romance of Real Life.
Philadelphia, Carey, 1799. [2], 333, [1]
pp.
AAS copy.   36316

Smith, Charlotte (Turner), 1749-1806.
Rural Walks.
Philadelphia, Stephens, 1795. 199, [5] pp.
AAS copy.   29525

Smith, Chileab, 1742-1843.
An Answer to many Slanderous Reports.
Norwich, Robertson & Trumbull, 1774. 24
pp.
BM copy.   13628

[Smith, Cotton Mather, 1731-1806.
The Christian Edifice.
Hudson, Stoddard, 1786.]
("Just printed," Hudson Gazette, Sept., 7,
1786.)   19993

Smith, Cotton Mather, 1731-1806.
(Weis, Colonial Clergy N. E.)
A Good Minister of Jesus Christ.
Hartford, 1770. 30 pp.
AAS copy.   11861

Smith, Cotton Mather, 1731-1806.
(Weis, Colonial Clergy N. E.)
Jesus Christ, a Comforter.
Hartford, 1767. 24 pp.
CHS copy.   10769

Smith, Cotton Mather, 1731-1806.
A Sermon, Delivered at Stamford, on the
13th June, 1793.
Danbury, Douglas, 1793. 16 pp.
UTS copy.   26167

[Smith, Daniel], 1748-1818.
A Short Description of the State of
Tennessee.
Philadelphia, Lang & Ustick for Carey,
1796. 36 pp., 1 map.
AAS copy.   31199

[Smith, Daniel], 1748-1818.
A Short Description of the State of
Tennessee. . . . To which is Prefixed, the
Constitution of that State.
Philadelphia, Lang & Ustick for Carey,
1796. 44 pp.
BA copy.   31200

[Smith, Daniel], 1748-1818.
A Short Description of the State of
Tennessee.

New York, Mott, 1797. 47 pp.
HEH copy. 48254

[Smith, Daniel], 1748-1818.
A Short Description of the Tennassee
Government.
Philadelphia, Carey, 1793. 20 pp., 1 map.
AAS copy. 26168

Smith, Devereux.
To the People of Pennsylvania.
[Philadelphia, 1784] Broadside.
LCP copy. 18784

Smith, Ebenezer, b. 1756.
The Deceit and Unreasonableness of
Self-righteousness.
Boston, 1794. 28 pp.
AAS copy. 27708

Smith, Ebenezer, of Partridgefield.
Remarks on a Book.
Pittsfield, Mass., Allen, 1800. 12 pp.
CL copy. 38513

Smith, Edward Darrell, 1778-1819.
Inaugural Dissertation.
Philadelphia, Way & Groff, 1800. 54 pp.
AAS copy. 38514

[Smith, Elias], 1769-1846.
An Essay on the Fall of Angels and Men.
Wilmington, Brynberg & Andrews, 1792.
76 pp.
LOC copy. 26169

[Smith, Elias], 1769-1846.
An Essay on the Fall of Angels and Men.
Providence, Wheeler for Hunt, 1795. 50
pp.
RIHS copy. 29526

[Smith, Elias], 1769-1846.
An Essay on the Fall of Angels and Men.
Boston, Edes, 1796. 53, [1] pp.
NYHS copy. 31201

[Smith, Elias], 1769-1846.
An Essay on the Fall of Angels and Men.
Middletown, Ct., Woodward, 1796. 50 pp.
AAS copy. 31202

[Smith, Elihu Hubbard], 1771-1798.
Alcuin; a Dialogue.
New York, Swords, 1798. [4], 77, [7] pp.
(Six of the last seven pages are blank.)
NYHS copy. 34553

Smith, Elihu Hubbard, 1771-1798.
A Discourse, Delivered April 11, 1798.
New York, Swords, 1798. 30 pp.
AAS copy. 34554

Smith, Elihu Hubbard, 1771-1798.
Edwin and Angelina, or, The Banditti.
New York, Swords, 1797. 72 pp.
AAS copy. 32843

Smith, E(liza?).
The Compleat Housewife.
Williamsburg, 1742. [12], 228, [12] pp.
(The HEH copy has differences in the
adv. at end.)
AAS copy. 5061

[Smith, E(liza?)
The Compleat Housewife.
Williamsburg, 1752.]
(Adv. Mar. 22, May 29, 1752.) 6934

[Smith, E(liza?).
The Complete Housewife.
New York, Gaine, 1761.]
(Adv. N. Y. Mercury, no. 468.) 9010

[Smith, E(liza?).
The Compleat Housewife.
New York, Gaine, 1764.]
("Just published," N. Y. Mercury, Jan. 30,
1764.) 9840

Smith, Elizabeth, fl. 1773.
A Dialogue between Elizabeth Smith, and
John Sennet.
[Boston, 1773?] Broadside.
HSP copy. 42502

Smith, Ethan, 1762-1849.
A Farewell Sermon, Delivered at
Haverhill.
Peacham, Vt., Farley & Goss, 1800. 27 pp.
AAS copy. 38515

[Smith, Eunice, of Ashfield, Mass.
A Dialogue; or Discourse between Mary
and Martha.
Albany, Ellison, 1793. 16 pp.]
(Evans entry from Sabin 82541.) 26172

Smith, Eunice, of Ashfield, Mass.
A Dialogue or, Discourse between Mary
& Martha.
Boston, Russell, 1797. 16 pp.
AAS copy. 32844

Smith, Eunice, of Ashfield, Mass.
Practical Language Interpreted.
Boston, Russell for King, 1792. 24 pp.
AAS copy. 24791

Smith, Eunice, of Ashfield, Mass.
Practical Language Interpreted.
Exeter, Ranlet for Sleeper, 1792. 22 pp.
AAS copy. 46574

Smith, Eunice, of Ashfield, Mass.
Practical Language Interpreted.
Warren, Lee, [1792]. 24 pp.
JCB copy. 24792

Smith, Eunice, of Ashfield, Mass.
Practical Language Interpreted.
Stockbridge, R. Lee, 1793. 15 pp.
AAS copy. 26170

[Smith, Eunice, of Ashfield, Mass.
Practical Language Interpreted.
Dover, N. H., 1796. 23 pp.]
("For sale at this office," The Sun, May
18, 1796.) 31203

[Smith, Eunice], of Ashfield, Mass.
Some Arguments against
Worldy-Mindedness.
Boston, Russell for King, 1791. 16 pp.
AAS copy. 23767

Smith, Eunice, of Ashfield, Mass.
(Second Edition.) Some Arguments
against Worldly-Mindedness.
Boston, Russell, 1792. 16 pp.
AAS copy. 24795

[Smith, Eunice], of Ashfield, Mass.
Some Arguments against
Worldly-Mindedness.
Springfield, Gray, [1792]. 23 pp.
AAS copy. 24793

[Smith, Eunice], of Ashfield, Mass.
Some Arguments against
Worldly-Mindedness.
Warren, Lee, [1792]. 23 pp.
AAS copy. 24794

[Smith, Eunice, of Ashfield, Mass.
Some Arguments against
Worldly-Mindedness.
Stockbridge, Andrews for Lee, [1793]. 8
pp.]
(Evans entry from Sabin 82544.) 26171

[Smith, Eunice, of Ashfield, Mass.
Some Arguments against
Worldly-Mindedness.
Boston, Russell, 1794.]
(Imprint assumed by Evans from advs.)
27709

[Smith, Eunice], of Ashfield, Mass.
Some Arguments against
Worldly-Mindedness.
Rutland, Lee, 1795. 15 pp.
JCB copy. 47604

[Smith, Eunice], of Ashfield, Mass.
Some Arguments against Worldly
Mindedness.
Walpole, N. H., Thomas & Carlisle,
1795. 16 pp.
AAS copy. 29527

Smith, Eunice, of Ashfield, Mass.
Some Motives.
Greenfield, Mass., 1798. 24 pp.
Pocumtuck Valley Hist. Soc. copy. 34555

Smith, Eunice, of Ashfield, Mass.
Some of the Exercises of a Believing Soul.
Boston, Russell for King, 1792. 24 pp.
AAS copy. 46575

Smith, Francis, fl. 1783.
To Captain Alexander Patterson. . . . 15th
Nov. 1783.

[Trenton, 1783.] Broadside.
LCP copy. 18187

Smith, Grace.
The Dying Mothers Legacy.
Boston, T. Green, 1712. [2], 12 pp.
BPL copy. 39555

Smith, Henry, 1550-1591.
(D. N. B.)
The Examination of Usury.
[Boston], 1751. 23, [1] pp.
AAS copy. 6786

Smith, Hezekiah, 1737-1805.
The Doctrine of Believer's Baptism.
Boston, Freeman, 1766. [4], iv, 56 pp.
NYPL copy. 10496

Smith, Hezekiah, 1737-1805.
(Weis, Colonial Clergy N. E.)
A Second Reply to Mr. Jonathan Parsons.
Newport, 1769. 104 pp.
AAS copy. 11468

Smith, Hugh, 1736-1789.
Letters to Married Women. . . . First
American Edition.
Philadelphia, Carey, 1792. 167, [1] pp.
AAS copy. 24796

Smith, Hugh, 1736-1789.
Letters to Married Women.
Philadelphia, Lang & Ustick for Carey,
1796. 153 pp.
AAS copy. 31204

Smith, Isaac, 1736-1807.
A Charge, Delivered . . . the Seventh Day
of October, 1800.
n.p., n.d. Broadside.
NJHS copy. 38517

Smith, Isaac, 1744-1817.
A Sermon, Preached at the Instalment of
. . . Ethan Smith.
Concord, N. H., Hough for Mitchel, 1800.
55 pp.
AAS copy. 38516

Smith, Isaac, 1749-1829.
(Harvard College Records.)
A Sermon, Preached at Cambridge, May
5th, 1788.
Boston, Freeman, 1788. 19 pp.
AAS copy. 21464

[Smith, James], of Carolina.
(Memoirs of Mr. Law, London, 1721.)
Some Considerations on the
Consequences of the French Settling
Colonies on the Mississippi.
Boston, 1720. [4], 60 pp.]
(A ghost of the BPL copy of the London
ed.) 2176

Smith, James, 1737-1812.
An Account of the Remarkable
Occurrences in the Life and Travels
of. . . .
Lexington, Ky., Bradford, 1799. 88 pp.
NL copy. 36317

Smith, James, 1738-1812.
A Concise Economical Plan.
New York, Kirk, [1798?]. 16 pp.
NLM copy. 48617

Smith, James, 1738-1812.
Yellow Fever . . . Sept. 10, 1798.
[New York, 1798.] Broadside.
NYHS copy. 48618

Smith, Jeremiah, 1759-1842.
An Oration on the Death of . . .
Washington.
Exeter, Ranlet, 1800. 31 pp.
AAS copy. 38518

Smith, John, clockmaker.
The Curiosities of Common Water.
Philadelphia, 1723. 47 pp.
(The only known copy is imperfect.)
LOC copy. 2477

Smith, John, clockmaker.
The Curiosities of Common Water.
Boston, Edwards, 1725. 52 pp.
AAS copy. 2701

Smith, John, of Suffield, Ct.
An Oration, Pronounced July 4th, 1799.

Suffield, Gray, 1799. 15 pp.
AAS copy.   36318

[Smith, John], writer on agriculture.
The Husbandman's Magazine.
Boston, Allen for Boone, 1718. [4], 145,
[1] pp.
AAS copy.   39692

Smith, John, fl. 1675-1711.
An Essay on Universal Redemption.
Boston, Fleets, 1767. 71 pp.
AAS copy.   10770

Smith, John, 1681-1766.
A Narrative of Some Sufferings.
Philadelphia, Johnsons, 1800. 48 pp.
AAS copy.   38519

Smith, John, 1722-1771.
The Doctrine of Christianity.
Philadelphia, Franklin & Hall, 1748. iv,
56 pp.
HSP copy.   6239

Smith, John, 1722-1771.
The Doctrine of Christianity . . . .
Second Edition.
Philadelphia, Franklin & Hall, 1748. iv,
56 pp.
LCP copy.   6240

[Smith, John. d. 1773.
The Last Speech, Confession and Dying
Words of. . . .
Albany, Robertsons, 1773.]
(Title from the Hartford reprint.)   13019

Smith, John, d. 1773.
The Last Speech, Confession and Dying
Words of. . . .
Hartford, 1773. 8 pp.
NYPL copy.   13020

Smith, John, d. 1773.
The Last Speech, Confession and Dying
Words of. . . .
New Haven, [1773]. 8 pp.
YC copy.   13021

Smith, John, 1745-c. 1820.
(Weis, Colonial Clergy N.E.)
A Funeral Sermon, Occasioned by the
Death of Mrs. Mary Bowers.
Providence, Wheeler, 1793. 24 pp.
JCB copy.   26173

Smith, John, 1752-1809.
The Duty, Advantages, and Pleasure of
Public Worship.
Hanover, N. H., Dunham & True, 1795.
14 pp.
AAS copy.   29528

Smith, John, 1766-1831.
The Coming of the Son of Man.
Concord, N. H., Hough, 1797. 34 pp.
AAS copy.   32845

Smith, John, 1766-1831.
A Sermon, Preached in Salem, on the
Anniversary Thanksgiving.
Amherst, N. H., Preston, 1797. 32 pp.
AAS copy.   32846

Smith, John Blair, 1756-1799.
The Establishment of Christ's Kingdom.
Schenectady, Wyckoff, 1797. 42 pp.
NYHS copy.   32847

Smith, John Blair, 1756-1799.
Oratio Inauguralis . . . . Coll. Concordiae.
Schenectady, Wyckoff, 1796. 16 pp.
HEH copy.   31205

Smith, John Cotton, 1765-1845.
An Oration, Pronounced at Sharon.
Litchfield, Ct., Collier, [1798]. 23 pp.
AAS copy.   34556

[Smith, Joshua], d. 1731.
Divine Meditations and Prayers.
Boston, Kneeland & Green, 1744. [2],
iv. 170 pp.
NYPL copy.   5490

[Smith, Joshua], d. 1795.
Divine Hymns — or Spiritual Songs for
The Use of Religious Assemblies. . . .
Third Exeter Edition.
Exeter, Ranlet, 1791.]
(Adv. in Exeter, N. H. Gazetteer,
Oct. 14, 1791.)   23768

[Smith, Joshua, d. 1795.
Divine Hymns or Spiritual Songs for the
Use of Religious Assemblies.
Portsmouth, Melcher, 1791.]
("Just Published, by the Printer hereof,"
N. H. Gazette, Oct. 16, 1791.)   23769

Smith, Joshua, d. 1795.
Divine Hymns, or Spiritual Songs.
Exeter, Ranlet for Sleeper of Poplin,
1793. 192 pp.
AAS copy.   46875

Smith, Joshua, d. 1795.
Divine Hymns, or Spiritual Songs. . . .
Fifth Edition.
Danbury, Douglas, 1794. 180 pp.
(The only copy located is quite
imperfect.)
CHS copy.   47214

Smith, Joshua, d. 1795.
Divine Hymns, or, Spiritual Songs. . . .
Sixth Exeter Edition.
Exeter, [N. H.], Stearns & Winslow,
1794. 192 pp.
AAS copy.   47215

Smith, Joshua, d. 1795.
Divine Hymns, or Spiritual Songs.
Norwich, Conn., Hubbard, 1794. 192 pp.
AAS copy.   27710

[Smith, Joshua, d. 1795.
Divine Hymns, or Spiritual Songs. . . .
Second Norwich Edition.
Norwich, Hubbard, 1795.]
("Just published, and ready for sale by
the printers hereof," Weekly Register,
Feb. 10, 1796.)   29529

[Smith, Joshua, d. 1795.
Divine Hymns or Spiritual Songs.
Portsmouth, Melcher, 1795.]
(Imprint assumed by Evans from adv.
"Also lately published, and for sale,"
N.H. Gazette, Sept. 29, 1795.]   29530

[Smith, Joshua, d. 1795.
Divine Hymns, or Spiritual Songs. . . .
Sixth Edition.
Poughkeepsie, Douglas, 1796.]
(Imprint assumed by Evans from advs.)
   31206

[Smith, Joshua, d. 1795.
Divine Hymns, or Spiritual Songs. . . .
Seventh Exeter Edition.
Exeter, Ranlet, 1797.]
("Just published, and for sale at this
office," N. H. Spy, Feb. 25, 1797.)   32848

Smith, Joshua, d. 1795.
Divine Hymns, or Spiritual Songs.
New London, Springer for Springer &
Trumbull, 1797. 216 pp.
AAS copy.   32849

Smith, Joshua, d. 1795.
Divine Hymns, or Spiritual Songs. . . .
Eighth Edition.
Norwich, Ct., Storer, 1797. 216 pp.
AAS copy.   32850

Smith, Joshua, d. 1795.
Divine Hymns, or Spiritual Songs: for
the Use of Religious Assemblies. . . .
Ninth Edition.
Norwich, Ct., Steery, 1799. 214 pp.
AAS copy.   36319

Smith, Joshua, d. 1795.
Divine Hymns, or Spiritual Songs, for
the Use of Religious Assemblies. . . .
Latest and Largest Edition.
Portsmouth, N. H., Peirce, 1799. 168 pp.
HC copy.   36320

Smith, Joshua, d. 1795.
Divine Hymns, or Spiritual Songs. . . .
Seventh Edition.
Elizabethtown, Woods for Tiebout, 1800.
171 pp.
AAS copy.   38520

Smith, Joshua, d. 1795.
Divine Hymns, or Spiritual Songs.
New London, Ct., Springer, 1800. 192 pp.
(The only copy located is imperfect.)
NYHS copy.   38523

Smith, Joshua, d. 1795.
Divine Hymns, or Spiritual Songs.

New London, [Ct.], Springer for Green,
1800. 192 pp.
HEH copy.   38522

Smith, Joshua, d. 1795.
Divine Hymns, or Spiritual Songs.
Norwich, Ct., Trumbull, 1800. 187,
[5] pp.
(The only recorded copy is imperfect.)
WL copy.   38521

Smith, Josiah, 1704-1781.
The Broken Heart Relieved. . . . Second
Edition.
Charleston, [S. C.], Wells, 1773. 14 pp.
PrU copy.   42503

Smith, Josiah, 1704-1781.
(Sibley, VII, 569-585.)
The Burning of Sodom.
Boston, Fowle for Phillips, 1741. [8],
23 pp.
HC copy.   4808

Smith, Josiah, 1704-1781.
(Sibley, VII, 569-585.)
The Character and Duty.
Charleston, 1736. 29 pp.
NYPL copy.   4078

Smith, Josiah, 1704-1781.
(Sibley, VII, 569-585.)
The Character, Preaching, &c.
Boston, Rogers for Edwards and
Foster, 1740. [4], vi, 20, [1] pp.
AAS copy.   4600

Smith, Josiah, 1704-1781.
The Character, Preaching, &c.
Philadelphia, Franklin, 1740. 24 pp.
UOP copy.   4601

Smith, Josiah, 1704-1781.
The Character, Preaching, &c.
Charleston, 1765. [4], vi, 22 pp.
YC copy.   10165

Smith, Josiah, 1704-1781.
[A Christmas Sermon, Preach'd at
Charles-Town . . . December 25, 1739.
Charleston, 1740.]
(Adv. S. C. Gazette, Dec. 25, 1740.)   40210

Smith, Josiah, 1704-1781.
(Sibley, VII, 569-585.)
The Church of Ephesus Arraign'd.
Charleston, 1768. 43 pp.
AAS copy.   11072

Smith, Josiah, 1704-1781.
Death the End of All Men.
Charleston, [S. C.], Wells, 1771. 16 pp.
NYHS copy.   42277

Smith, Josiah, 1704-1781.
(Sibley, VII 569-585.)
A Discourse Delivered at Boston, on
July 11, 1726.
Boston, Gerrish and Hancock, 1726.
[4], iv, 22 pp.
AAS copy.   2813

Smith, Josiah, 1704-1781.
(Sibley, VII, 569-585.)
The Divine Right.
Boston, 1730. [2], 57 pp.
AAS copy.   3353

Smith, Josiah, 1704-1781.
(Sibley, VII, 569-585.)
The Doctrine and Glory.
Boston, 1742. [4], 19 pp.
BPL copy.   5062

Smith, Josiah, 1704-1781.
The Duty of Parents.
Boston, Henchman, 1730. [2], ii, 44 pp.
AAS copy.   3354

Smith, Josiah, 1704-1781.
(Sibley, VII, 569-585.)
A Funeral Discourse . . . to the Memory of
Mr. Joseph Moody.
Charleston, 1766. 15 pp.
MHS copy.   10497

Smith, Josiah, 1704-1781.
The Greatest Sufferers.
Boston, 1730. [2], ii, 21 pp.
AAS copy.   3355

Smith, Josiah, 1704-1781.
(Sibley, VII, 569-585.)
Humane Impositions.
Boston, Henchman, 1729. iii, 11 pp.
AAS copy.   3219

Smith, Josiah, 1704-1781.
(Sibley, VII, 569-585.)
Jesus Persecuted.
Boston, Kneeland & Green,
1745. 20, 22 pp.
AAS copy.   5687

[Smith, Josiah, 1704-1781.
(Sibley, VII, 569-585.)
Letters to the Rev. William Cooper.
Boston, 1743.]
(Title from Haven; apparently a ghost of
Smith's Four Letters, Edinburgh, 1743.)
                                             5292

Smith, Josiah, 1704-1781.
No new Thing to be Slander'd.
Boston, 1730. [2], 21, [1] pp.
AAS copy.   3356

Smith, Josiah, 1704-1781.
St. Paul's Victory and Triumph.
Charleston, [S. C.], Wells, 1774. 73 pp.
AAS copy.   42701a

Smith, Josiah, 1704-1781.
(Sibley, VII, 569-585.)
A Sermon Deliver'd at Charles-Town.
Boston, Kneeland & Green, 1739. [4],
16 pp.
HC copy.   4425

[Smith, Josiah, 1704-1781.
(Sibley, VII, 569-585.)
A Sermon on the Death of Rev. John
Thomas.
Charleston, 1771. 16 pp.]
(Entry from Haven.)   12228

Smith, Josiah, 1704-1781.
Sermon, Preached at Charlestown, South
Carolina. in . . . 1739 . . . Second Edition.
Charleston, Wells, 1773. 25 pp.
HEH copy.   42504

Smith, Josiah, 1704-1781.
(Sibley, VII, 569-585.)
A Sermon Preached in Boston, July 10th,
1726.
Boston, 1727. [4], 27 pp.
AAS copy.   2962

Smith, Josiah, 1704-1781.
(Sibley, VII, 569-585.)
Sermons on Several Important Subjects.
Boston, Edes & Gill, 1757. [2], viii, [4],
417 pp.
AAS copy.   8039

Smith, Josiah, 1704-1781.
Solomon's Caution.
Boston, Henchman, 1730. [2], 14 pp.
AAS copy.   3357

Smith, Josiah, 1704-1781.
(Sibley, VII, 569-585.)
Success a Great Proof.
Charleston, 1770. 14, [2] pp.
MHS copy.   11862

Smith, Josiah, 1704-1781.
The Young Man Warn'd.
Boston, Henchman, 1730. [2], 31, [2] pp.
AAS copy.   3358

Smith, Josiah, 1704-1781.
A Zeal of God.
Boston, Kneeland & Green, 1745.
(Signatured with 5687, q.v.)   5688

Smith, Matthew.
A Declaration and Remonstrance of the
Distressed and Bleeding Frontier.
[Philadelphia], 1764. 18 pp.
AAS copy.   9630

[Smith, Melancton], 1744-1798.
An Address to the People of the State of
New-York: Shewing the Necessity of
Making Amendments.
New York State, 1788. 26 pp.
AAS copy.   21465

[Smith Meriwether.]
Observations on the Fourth and Fifth
Articles of the Preliminaries for a Peace.

Richmond, Dixon & Holt, [1783]. 28 pp.
JCB copy.   44454

Smith, Michael, 1698-c. 1771.
(L. O. C.)
A Sermon Preached in Christ-Church.
Newbern, 1756. 19 pp.
HSP copy.   7792

Smith, Noah, 1756-1812.
A Speech Delivered at Bennington.
Hartford, 1779. 8 pp.
HC copy.   16525

Smith, Preserved, 1759-1834.
A Discourse, Delivered in Chester.
West Springfield, Gray, 1796. 22 pp.
AAS copy.   31207

Smith, Preserved, 1759-1834.
A Masonick Discourse.
Greenfield, Mass., Barker, 1798. 11 pp.
AAS copy.   34557

Smith, Robert, 1723-1793.
(Sprague, III, 172-175.)
The Detection Detected.
Lancaster, 1757. iv, 143 pp.
HSP copy.   8040

Smith, Robert, 1723-1793.
The Obligations of the Confederate States.
Philadelphia, Bailey, 1782. [4], 36 pp.
LOC copy.   17722

Smith, Robert, 1723-1793.
The Obligations of the Confederate States.
Baltimore, 1783. [4], 35 pp.
WLC copy.   18188

Smith, Robert, 1723-1793.
Philadelphia, January 5th, 1787. Sir, The
Subscriber. . . .
[Philadelphia, 1787.] Broadside.
LOC copy.   45165

Smith, Robert, 1723-1793.
(Sprague, III, 172-175.)
The Principles of Sin.
Philadelphia, Bradfords, 1767. 51 pp.
LOC copy.   10771

Smith, Robert, 1723-1793.
The Principles of Sin and Holiness.
Lancaster, Bailey & Dickson, 1793. 47 pp.
AAS copy.   26174

Smith, Robert, 1723-1793.
Three Sermons.
Lancaster, Bailey, 1791. [6], 25, [1], 20,
[1], 24, [1] pp.
Presb. Hist. Soc. copy.   23770

Smith, Robert, 1723-1793.
Three Sermons.
Carlisle, Kline, 1792. 68 pp.
AAS copy.   24797

Smith, Robert, 1723-1793.
A Wheel in the Middle of a Wheel.
Philadelphia, Dunlap, 1759. 57 pp.
LOC copy.   8492

Smith, Samuel, 1584-1662?
(D. N. B.)
The Great Assize.
Boston, 1727. [4], 194, 54 pp.
AAS copy.   2963

Smith, Samuel, 1720-1776.
(S. Smith, Hist. N. J., 1877 ed., pp. 3-4.)
The History of the Colony of
Nova-Caesaria.
Burlington, 1765. x, 573, [1] pp.
AAS copy.   10166

[Smith, Samuel], 1720-1776.
Necessary Truth: or Seasonable
Considerations.
Philadelphia, 1748. 16 pp.
HSP copy.   6241

Smith, Samuel, 1745-1799.
Last Words and Dying Speech of . . .
Concord, Mass., Bryant, and Boston,
Edes, [1799]. Broadside.
AAS copies.
(Two variant printings are reproduced.)
                                             36321

Smith, Samuel Harrison, 1772-1845.
(Circular). Philadelphia, February 20,
1796. Sir . . . I have Determined . . . a

Newspaper. . . . The New World.
[Philadelphia, Smith, 1796.] [3] pp.
HSP copy.   31208

Smith, Samuel Harrison, 1772-1845.
(Circular) Philadelphia, July 27, 1799. Sir.
. . .
[Philadelphia, 1799.] Broadside.
HSP copy.   36603

Smith, Samuel Harrison, 1772-1845.
Monthly Review. Samuel Harrison Smith,
Submits . . . the Re-publication of the
Monthly Review.
[Philadelphia, 1794.] 4 pp.
LCP copy.   27711

Smith, Samuel Harrison, 1772-1845.
Remarks on Education.
Philadelphia, Ormrod, 1798. 92 pp.
AAS copy.   34558

Smith, Samuel Stanhope, 1750-1819.
A Discourse Delivered on the 22d of
February, 1797.
Philadelphia, Ormrod & Conrad for
Ormrod, [1797]. pp. [1]-35, 40-41.
AAS copy.   32851

Smith, Samuel Stanhope, 1750-1819.
A Discourse on the Nature and
Reasonableness of Fasting.
Philadelphia, Young, 1795. 31, [1] pp.
AAS copy.   29531

Smith, Samuel Stanhope, 1750-1819.
The Divine Goodness to the United
States.
Philadelphia, Young, 1795. 38, [2] pp.
AAS copy.   29532

Smith, Samuel Stanhope, 1750-1819.
The Divine Goodness to the United
States. . . . Second Edition.
Philadelphia, Young, 1795. 38, [2] pp.
AAS copy.   29533

Smith, Samuel Stanhope, 1750-1819.
An Essay on the Causes of the Variety of
Complexion.
Philadelphia, Aitken, 1787. [4], 111, [1],
31 pp.
AAS copy.   20712

Smith, Samuel Stanhope, 1750-1819.
A Funeral Sermon, on . . . Richard
Stockton.
Trenton, 1781. 48 pp.
AAS copy.   17371

Smith, Samuel Stanhope, 1750-1819.
An Oration, upon the Death of . . .
Washington.
Trenton, N. J., Craft, 1800. 45, [1] pp.
AAS copy.   38524

Smith, Samuel Stanhope, 1750-1819.
An Oration, upon the Death of . . .
Washington. . . . Second Edition.
Trenton, [N. J.], Craft, 1800. 45, [1] pp.
BA copy.   38525

Smith, Samuel Stanhope, 1750-1819.
Sermons by. . . .
Newark, N. J., Halsey, 1799. viii, [2], 437,
[9] pp.
AAS copy.   36322

Smith, Samuel Stanhope, 1750-1819.
Three Discourses.
[Boston, 1791.] [2], 25, [1]; 24; 22 pp.
AAS copy.   23771

Smith, Samuel Stanhope, 1750-1819.
Three Discourses. . . . Second Edition.
Boston, Hall, 1791. 60 pp.
AAS copy.   23772

Smith, Samuel Stanhope, 1750-1819.
Three Discourses.
Lancaster, Dickson, 1792. 54, [1] pp.
AAS copy.   24798

Smith, Stephen, d. 1797.
Life, last Words and Dying Speech of. . . .
[Boston, 1797.] Broadside.
BPL copy.   32852

Smith, Theodore, fl. 1770-1810.
Three Duetts, for Two Performers on One
Harpsichord.
Philadelphia, Moller, [1793]. 13 pp.
NYPL copy.   27712

Smith, Thomas, 1702-1795.
(Sibley, VI, 400-410.)
The Great Duty of Gospel Ministers.
Boston, Kneeland, 1751. [4], 2, 63, [1]
pp.
AAS copy.　　　　　　　　　　　6787

Smith, Thomas, 1702-1795.
(Sibley, VI, 400-410.)
A Practical Discourse to Sea-Faring Men.
Boston, Boyles, 1771. 40 pp.
AAS copy.　　　　　　　　　　12229

Smith, Thomas Peters.
A Sketch of the Revolutions in Chemistry.
Philadelphia, S. H. Smith, 1798. 40 pp.
AAS copy.　　　　　　　　　　34559

Smith, Thomas-Laughton & Roger.
Charles-Town M[arch] to be Sold on
Wednesday the 29th Instant, a Cargo of
. . . Slaves.
[Charleston], Timothy, [176?].
Broadside.
AAS copy.　　　　　　　　　　42004

[Smith, Venture], 1729?-1805.
A Narrative of the Life and Adventures of
Venture.
New London, Holt, 1798. 32 pp.
CHS copy.　　　　　　　　　　34560

[Smith, William], of New York.
Advertisement. To all Farmers,
Desirous. . . .
[New York? 1770?] Broadside.
AAS ph. copy.　　　　　　　　42041

Smith, William, of New York.
New Lands to be Sold . . . in . . .
Queensborough.
[New York? 1770?] Broadside.
AAS ph. copy.　　　　　　　　42042

Smith, William, of New York.
To Farmers Inclining to Purchase new
Lands.
[New York? 1770?] Broadside.
AAS ph. copy.　　　　　　　　42043

[Smith, William], d. 1673.
Joyful Tidings to the Begotten of God.
Philadelphia, James, 1787. [2], 9 pp.
LCP copy.　　　　　　　　　　45166

Smith, William, 1697-1769.
(D. A. B.)
Mr. Smith's Opinion Humbly Offered.
New York, 1734. [2], 45 pp.
NYPL copy.　　　　　　　　　　3834

Smith, William, 1727-1803.
An Account of Washington College.
Philadelphia, Crukshank, 1784. 50 pp., 1
plate.
APS copy.　　　　　　　　　　18785

Smith William, 1727-1803.
An Address to the General Assembly.
Philadelphia, Aitken, 1788. 32 pp.
LCP copy.　　　　　　　　　　45358

[Smith, William], 1727-1803.
(D. A. B.)
An Answer to Mr. Franklin's Remarks.
Philadelphia, Bradford, 1764. 22 pp.
AAS copy.　　　　　　　　　　9841

[Smith, William], 1727-1803.
An Answer to Mr. Franklin's Remarks.
Philadelphia, Bradford, 1764. 22 pp.
(2nd ed. with 11 lines added on last page.)
NYPL copy.　　　　　　　　　9842

[Smith, William?], 1727-1803.
Antwort auf Hrn. Fraenklins
Anmerckungen.
[Germantown], 1765. 27 pp.
LOC copy.　　　　　　　　　　9904

[Smith, William], 1727-1803.
A Brief History of the Rise and Progress
of the Charitable Scheme.
Philadelphia, Franklin & Hall, 1755. [2],
18 pp.
HSP copy.　　　　　　　　　　7569

Smith, William, 1727-1803.
(D. A. B.)
A Charge, Delivered May 17, 1757.
Philadelphia, Franklin & Hall, 1757. 16
pp.
UOP copy.　　　　　　　　　　8041

Smith, William, 1727-1803.
The Christian Soldier's Duty.
Philadelphia, Chattin, 1757. [4], 38 pp.
AAS copy.　　　　　　　　　　8042

Smith, William, 1727-1803.
(D. A. B.)
A Discourse Concerning the Conversion
of the Heathen.
Philadelphia, Dunlap, 1760. [2], iii, [i],
53 pp.
NYPL copy.　　　　　　　　　8737

[Smith, William], 1727-1803.
Discourse Concerning the Conversion of
the Heathen Americans.
Philadelphia, Dunlap, 1790. iii, [1], 53
pp.]
(A ghost of 8737.)　　　　　　45993

Smith, William, 1727-1803.
Eulogium on Benjamin Franklin.
Philadelphia, Bache, 1792. [4], 40, v, [1]
pp.
AAS copy.　　　　　　　　　　24799

Smith, William, 1727-1803.
An Examination of the Connecticut
Claim.
Philadelphia, Crukshank, 1774. [2], 93, 32
pp., 1 folding map.
LCP copy.　　　　　　　　　　42702

[Smith, William], 1727-1803.
(D. A. B.)
An Examination of the Connecticut
Claim.
Philadelphia, Crukshank, 1774. [2], 94, 32
pp., map.
AAS copy.　　　　　　　　　　13629

Smith, William, 1727-1803.
A Funeral Address . . . Major-General
Mifflin.
[Lancaster, Pa.], Dicksons, [1800]. 19 pp.
HSP copy.　　　　　　　　　　38526

[Smith, William], 1727-1803.
A General Idea of the College of Mirania.
New York, Parker & Weyman, 1753. 86 pp.
BA copy.　　　　　　　　　　7121

Smith, William, 1727-1803.
(D. A. B.)
The Great Duty of Public Worship.
Philadelphia, Dunlap, 1761. x, 5-41 pp.
LCP copy.　　　　　　　　　　9011

[Smith, William], 1727-1803.
(D. A. B.)
An Historical Account of the Expedition
against the Ohio Indians.
Philadelphia, Bradford, 1765. [2], xiii, 71
pp., map, 2 plates.
NYPL copy.　　　　　　　　　10167

[Smith, William], 1727-1803.
An Historical Account of the Rise . . . of
the Canal Navigation in Pennsylvania.
Philadelphia, Poulson, 1795. [2], xvi, 80
pp., 1 map.
LCP copy.　　　　　　　　　　29474

[Smith, William], 1727-1803.
An Historical Account of the Rise . . . of
the Canal Navigation in Pennsylvania.
Philadelphia, Poulson, 1795. xvi, 77 pp.,
map.
AAS copy.　　　　　　　　　　47605

[Smith, William], 1727-1803.
Eine Kurtze Nachricht, von der
Christlichen und Liebreichen Anstalt.
Philadelphia, Armbruester, 1755. 16 pp.
HSP copy.　　　　　　　　　　7570

Smith, William, 1727-1803.
(D. A. B.)
The Last Summons.
Philadelphia, Steuart, 1762. 16 pp.
NYHS copy.　　　　　　　　　9274

Smith, William, 1727-1803.
A Letter on the Office and Duties of a
Protestant Ministry.
[Philadelphia], 1755.
(Curtis 555; no copy located.)　　40800

[Smith, William], 1727-1803.
Ode on the New-Year, 1753.
New York, Parker, [1753?]. 16 pp.
HEH copy.　　　　　　　　　　40670

Smith, William, 1727-1803.
(D. A. B.)
An Oration, Delivered, January 22, 1773.
Philadelphia, Dunlap, 1773. 15 pp.
HSP copy.　　　　　　　　　　13022

Smith, William, 1727-1803.
An Oration, in Memory of General
Montgomery.
New York, Anderson, 1776. 36 pp.
AAS copy.　　　　　　　　　　15085

Smith, William, 1727-1803.
An Oration in Memory of General
Montgomery.
Newport, 1776. [2], 30 pp.
NYPL copy.　　　　　　　　　15086

Smith, William, 1727-1803.
An Oration, in Memory of General
Montgomery.
Norwich, Robertsons & Trumbull, 1776.
22 pp.
AAS copy.　　　　　　　　　　15087

Smith, William, 1727-1803.
An Oration in Memory of General
Montgomery.
Philadelphia, Dunlap, 1776. [4], 44 pp.
AAS copy.　　　　　　　　　　15084

Smith, William, 1727-1803.
(D. A. B.)
Personal Affliction.
Philadelphia, Franklin & Hall, 1754. viii,
16, [1] pp.
UOP copy.　　　　　　　　　　7318

[Smith, William], 1727-1803.
A Poem on Visiting the Academy of
Philadelphia, 1753. 16 pp.
BA copy.　　　　　　　　　　7122

Smith, William, 1727-1803.
Proposals for Printing by
Subscription. . . .
Philadelphia, Bache, 1789. xxiii pp.
AAS copy.　　　　　　　　　　22150

[Smith, William], 1727-1803.
The Reverend Mr. Smith Vindicated.
[Philadelphia, 1756.] [2] pp.
LCP copy.　　　　　　　　　　7793

Smith, William, 1727-1803.
A Sermon, on Temporal and Spiritual
Salvation.
Philadelphia, Dobson, 1790. [4], 25, [3]
pp.
AAS copy.　　　　　　　　　　22891

Smith, William, 1727-1803.
A Sermon on the Present Situation.
Philadelphia, Humphreys, 1775. [4], iv, 32
pp.
AAS copy.　　　　　　　　　　14459

Smith, William, 1727-1803.
A Sermon on the Present Situation.
Wilmington, Del., 1775. 17 pp.
HSP copy.　　　　　　　　　　14460

Smith, William, 1727-1803.
A Sermon, Preached in Christ-Church,
Philadelphia, before the Provincial Grand
Master . . . the 24th of June, 1755.
Philadelphia, Franklin & Hall, [1755]. 24
pp.
APS copy.　　　　　　　　　　7571

Smith, William, 1727-1803.
A Sermon Preached in Christ-Church,
Philadelphia, (for the Benefit of the Poor).
. . .
Philadelphia, Dunlap, 1779. 35, [1] pp.
AAS copy.　　　　　　　　　　16526

[Smith, William], 1727-1803.
A Sermon Preached in Christ-Church,
Philadelphia (for the benefit of the Poor).
. . . December 28, 1778.
Philadelphia, Hall & Sellers, 1783. pp.
[147]-166.]
(An analytic of a larger work.)　　44455

Smith, William, 1727-1803.
A Sermon Preached in Christ-Church,
Philadelphia, on Friday, October 7th,
1785.
Philadelphia, Aitken, 1785. 40 pp.
AAS copy.　　　　　　　　　　19247

Smith, William, 1727-1803.
(D. A. B.)
Some Account of the Charitable
Corporation.
Philadelphia, Hall & Sellers, 1769. 48 pp.
AAS copy.   11469

Smith, William, 1727-1803.
(D. A. B.)
Some Account of the Charitable
Corporation. . . . Second Edition.
Philadelphia, Hall & Sellers, 1770. 56 pp.
AAS copy.   11863

[Smith, William], 1727-1803.
(D. A. B.)
Some Thoughts on Education.
New York, 1752. ix, 32 pp.
AAS copy.   6935

[Smith, William], 1727-1803.
The Speech of a Creek-Indians.
Boston, 1754.]
(No trace could be found of an American
printing. See Sabin 84673.)   7321

Smith, William, 1727-1803.
Two Sermons, Delivered in Christ
Church, Philadelphia, before the General
Convention.
Philadelphia, Dobson & Lang, 1789. 41,
[1], pp.
AAS copy.   22149

[Smith, William], 1728-1793.
(D. A. B.)
The Art of Pleading.
New York, Parker, 1751. 16 pp.
(For authorship see B. S. A., Papers,
XLIV, 306-307.)
NYHS copy.   6785

[Smith, William], 1728-1793.
The Candid Retrospect: or, the American
War Examined.
Charleston, Wells, 1780. 30 pp.
BM copy.   16728

[Smith, William], 1728-1793].
The Candid Retrospect; or the American
War Examined.
New York, 1780. 28 pp.
AAS copy.   16729

Smith, William, 1728-1793.
The History of the Province of
New-York. . . . Second Edition.
Philadelphia, Carey, 1792. 276 pp.
AAS copy.   24800

[Smith, William], 1728-1793.
(D. A. B.)
A Review of the Military Operations in
North-America.
New England (New Haven), 1758. 98 pp.
(For authorship see BSA, XLIV, 335.)
AAS copy.   8163

[Smith, William], 1728-1793.
(See Bib. Soc. Am., Papers, XLIV, 335.)
A Review of the Military Operations in
North-America.
New York, Robertsons, 1770. 170 pp.
AAS copy.   11701

[Smith, William], 1728-1793.
(D. A. B.)
Some Critical Observations upon a late
Poem, Entitled, The Breeches.
New York, 1750. 20 pp.
(See B.S.A., XLIV, 306.)
NYPL copy.   6611

Smith, William, 1754-1821.
The Christmas Dispute Revived.
Ballston, N. Y., Child for Lee, 1800. 12
pp.
AAS copy.   37794

Smith, William, 1754-1821.
Consolation from Homar.
Newport, Barber, 1789. [6], 64 pp.
AAS copy.   22046

Smith, William, 1754-1821.
Consolation from Homar.
Newburyport, Blunt, 1794. 60+ pp.
(The only known copy is imperfect.)
AAS copy.   47216

Smith, William, 1754-1821.
The Convict's Visitor.

Newport, Edes, [1791]. [2], ii, 85 pp.
MHS copy.   23776

Smith, William, 1754-1821.
A Discourse, at the Opening of the
Convention.
Providence, Carter, [1790]. 19, [1], xii
pp.
AAS copy.   22892

Smith, William, 1754-1821.
A Discourse, Delivered before the Grand
Lodge . . . on the 27th of June, 1791.
Providence, Wheeler, [1791]. 19 pp.
AAS copy.   23777

Smith, William, 1754-1821.
A Discourse Delivered in Christ's Church
at Norwich Landing.
Norwich, Trumbull, 1791. 26 pp.
AAS copy.   23778

Smith, William, 1754-1821.
A Discourse Delivered in St. John's
Church.
Providence, Carter, 1793. v, [1], 16 pp.
AAS copy.   26175

Smith, William, 1754-1821.
A Discourse, Delivered on the 18th of
October, 1797.
Newfield, Ct., Beach, [1798]. 20 pp.
BA copy.   34561

Smith, William, 1754-1821.
Doctor Smith's Answer.
Newfield, Ct., Beach, 1798. 144 pp.
AAS copy.   34562

Smith, William, 1754-1821.
A Letter from Conncecticut. . . .
November 16th, 1799.
[New Haven, 1799.] 4 pp.
Columbia Univ. copy.   36323

[Smith, William], 1754-1821.
The Masonic Burial-Office, as Observed
by the Grand Lodge of . . . Rhode Island.
Bennington, Haswell for Simans, [1799].
8 pp.
AAS copy.   36324

Smith, William, 1754-1821.
An Office of Induction, Adopted by the
Bishop . . . of Connecticut . . . Nov. 20th,
1799.
New Haven, Greens, [1799]. 8 pp.
Columbia Univ. copy.   36325

Smith, William Loughton, 1758-1812.
An Address from. . . .
Philadelphia, 1794. 32 pp.
AAS copy.   27713

[Smith, William Loughton], 1758-1812.
A Candid Examination of the Objections
to the Treaty.
Charleston, Young, 1795. 42 pp.
NYHS copy.   29534

Smith, William Loughton, 1758-1812.
A Comparative View of the Constitutions.
Philadelphia, Thompson, 1796. pp. [6],
[1]-4, 9-34; 6 folding tables.
AAS copy.   31209

Smith, William Loughton, 1758-1812.
A Dose for the Doctor. . . . November 25,
1788.
[Charleston, 1788.] Broadside.
HC copy.   45359

[Smith, William Loughton], 1758-1812.
The Eyes Opened, or The Carolinians
Convinced.
New York, Rivington, 1795. [2], 43, [3],
5 pp.
AAS copy.   29535

Smith, William Loughton, 1758-1812.
An Oration, Delivered in St. Philip's
Church.
Charleston, Young, [1796]. [4], 40 pp.
MHS copy.   31210

Smith, William Loughton, 1758-1812.
An Oration, Delivered in St. Philip's
Church. . . . Second Edition.
Charleston, Young, [1796]. [4], 40 pp.
MHS copy.   31211

[Smith, William Loughton], 1758-1812.

The Politicks and Views of a Certain
Party.
n.p., 1792. 36 pp.
AAS copy.   24801

[Smith, William Loughton], 1758-1812.
The Pretensions of Thomas Jefferson.
United States (Philadelphia), 1796. 64 pp.
AAS copy.   31212

[Smith, William Loughton], 1758-1812.
The Pretensions of Thomas Jefferson. . . .
Part the Second.
United States (Philadelphia), 1796. [2], 42
pp.
AAS copy.   31213

[Smith, William Loughton, 1758-1812.
The Pretensions of Thomas Jefferson.
Philadelphia, Cobbett, 1797.]
(Apparently a ghost of 31212. See Sabin
84829.)   32853

Smith, William Loughton, 1758-1812.
The Speech of Mr. Smith . . . in the
House. . . . December [23] 1794.
[Philadelphia, 1795.] 20 pp.
BA copy.   29536

Smith, William Loughton, 1758-1812.
The Speeches of Mr. Smith.
Philadelphia, Dobson, 1794. 75 pp., 1
folding table.
AAS copy.   27714

Smith, William Loughton, 1758-1812.
To the Citizens of Charleston District. . . .
Nov. 22.
[Charleston, 1788.] Broadside.
AAS ph. copy.   45360

Smith, William Moore, 1759-1821.
The Flowret. A Collection of Poems. . . .
Third Edition.
Baltimore, Story, 1799. 141, [2] pp., 1
plate.
LCP copy.   36326

Smith, William Moore, 1759-1821.
To the Claimants under the Sixth Article.
[Philadelphia, 1799.] 8 pp.
NYPL copy.   36327

[Smith, William Pitt], 1760-1796.
Observations on Conventions.
New York, Harrisson, 1793. 13 pp.
MHS copy.   26176

Smith, William Pitt, 1760-1796.
(N. Y. Gen. Biog. Record, X, 34.)
The Universalist.
New York, Childs, 1787. 305, [1] pp.
AAS copy.   20713

Smith, William Pitt, 1760-1796.
The Universalist.
New York, Childs, 1788. 305, [1] pp.
BA copy.   21466

Smith, William, & Co.
Agreement between William Smith . . . and
. . . Settlers Concerning 1,000,000 Acres of
Land in Nova Scotia.
[Philadelphia, 1765?] 4 pp.
(See Sabin 84583.)   8493

Smith & Bartlett, Boston.
Catalogue of Drugs and Medicines.
Boston, Manning & Loring, 1795. 22 pp.
LOC copy.   29537

Smith & Coit, firm, Hartford.
Hartford, 5th July, 1773. Just Imported.
. . .
[Hartford, 1773.] Broadside.
HEH copy.   42505

Smith, Moore, & Co.
At the Medical Pillar . . . Smith, Moore &
Co. have for Sale. . . .
New York, Loudon, [1784]. Broadside.
RU copy.   44599

Smith's Animadversions.
Philadelphia, 1742. 29 pp.
HSP copy.   5060

Smollett, Tobias George, 1721-1771.
The Adventures of Roderick Random.
Philadelphia, Carey, 1794. 2 vol. viii, 227,
[7]; [2], 255, [10] pp.
AAS copy.   27715

[Smollett, Tobias George], 1721-1771.
The History and Adventures of Peregrine
Pickle.
Leominster, Mass., Prentiss for Thomas,
1798. 104 pp.
AAS copy.   34563

Smollett, Tobias George, 1721-1771.
The History of England. . . . In Six
Volumes. . . . Vol. I [-II].
Philadelphia, Sweitzer for Campbell,
1796. 576 pp., 1 plate; 568 pp., 1 plate.
AAS copy.   31214

Smollett, Tobias George, 1721-1771.
The History of England. . . . In Six
Volumes. . . . Vol. III [-IV].
Philadelphia, Sweitzer for Campbell, 1797.
586 pp., 1 plate; 584 pp., 1 plate.
AAS copy.   32854

[Smollett, Tobias George], 1721-1771.
The History of England. . . . In Six
Volumes. . . . Vol. V.
Philadelphia, Folwell for Campbell, 1798.
511 pp., 1 plate.
AAS copy.   34564

[Smollett, Tobias George], 1721-1771.
The History of England. . . . In Six
Volumes. . . . Vol. VI.
Philadelphia, Bioren for Campbell, 1798.
[2], 452,59, [8] pp.
(No copy located has the plate called for
by Evans.)
AAS copy.   34565

[Smollett, Tobias George], 1721-1771.
The History of the British Empire.
Philadelphia, Folwell for Campbell, 1798.
475; 452, 59, [1] pp., 2 plates.
(There are also copies with the imprint of
Bioren. No copy located had the imprint
given by Evans.)
HC copy.   33879

[Smollett, Tobias George], 1721-1771.
A North Britain Extraordinary. . . . Third
Edition.
Philadelphia, Dunlap, 1769. 50 pp.
AAS copy.   11471

Smyth, Alexander, 1765-1830.
A Letter . . . to Francis Preston. . . . 10th
March, 1795.
[Richmond, 1795.] 14 pp.
VaU copy.   29538

[Smyth, Alexander, 1765-1830.
Letters . . . to Francis Preston.
Richmond, Va., Pleasants for Prichard &
Davidson, 1797.]
(Apparently a ghost arising from
booksellers' advs.)   32855

Smyth, Alexander, 1765-1830.
The Third and Last Letter.
[Richmond, Va.], 1796. 46 pp.
NYPL copy.   31215

Smyth, Edward.
A Dialogue between the Pulpit and
Reading-Desk.
Albany, Ellison, 1793. 164 pp.
AAS copy.   26177

[Smyth, Edward.
A Dialogue between the Pulpit and the
Reading-Desk.
Elizabethtown, Kollock, 1793?]
(Imprint assumed by Evans from
Kollock's advs.)   26178

Smyth, James Carmichael, 1741-1821.
The Effect of the Nitrous Vapour.
Philadelphia, Budd & Bartram for
Dobson, 1799. 174 pp., 1 folding table.
AAS copy.   36328

Smyth, John Ferdinand Dalziel,
1745-1811.
Capt. Smith, late of Maryland. . . .
[New York, Gaine, 1778.] 23 pp.
JCB copy.   16072

Snethen, Nicholas, 1769-1845.
A Reply to an Apology for Protesting.
Philadelphia, Tuckniss, 1800. 62 pp.
LOC copy.   38527

Snow, Joseph, 1715-1803.
A Friendly Address to the Inhabitants.
. . . December 19, 1794.

[Providence], Carter & Wilkinson, [1794].
Broadside.
RIHS copy.   27580

Snow, William.
The Fall of Man.
West Springfield, Mass., 1798. 12 pp.
NYHS copy.   34566

[Snowden, Nathaniel Randolph,
1770-1850.
A Free Mason Sermon.
Carlisle, Pa., Kline.]
("Just published," Kline's Gazette, Feb.
28, 1798.)   34567

[Snowden, Richard], d. 1825.
The American Revolution; Written in the
Style of Ancient History. . . . Vol. I.
Philadelphia, Jones, Hoff & Derrick,
1793. xii, 226 pp.
AAS copy.   26179

[Snowden, Richard], d. 1825.
The American Revolution; Written in the
Style of Ancient History. . . . Vol. II.
Philadelphia, Johnson, 1794. [12], 216 pp.
AAS copy.   27716

Snowden, Richard, d. 1825.
The American Revolution.
Baltimore, Pechin, [1802]. 360, 44 pp.
(See Sabin 85590 for date.)
AAS copy.   31216

[Snowden, Richard], d. 1825.
The Columbiad: or, A Poem on the
American War.
Philadelphia, Johnson, 1795. iv, 46 pp.
AAS copy.   29539

Snowden, Richard, d. 1825.
The Columbiad.
Baltimore, Pechin, [1802]. 44 pp.
(A part of 31216, q. v.)   31217

Snyder, G. W.
The Age of Reason Unreasonable.
Philadelphia, Cobbett, 1798. 213 pp.
LOC copy.   34568

So Dearly I Love Johnny O.
New York, Gilfert, [1796]. [2] pp.
JCB copy.   47920

A Sober Attention to the Scriptures of
Truth [by Shippie Townsend, 1722-1798].
Boston, Young & Etheridge, 1793. 24 pp.
AAS copy.   26180

Sober Considerations [by Cotton Mather,
1663-1728].
Boston, 1708. [2], 20 pp.
VaU copy.   1364

Sober Remarks on a Book Lately
Re-printed [by Edward Wigglesworth,
1693-1765].
Boston, Gerrish, 1724. [4], 78, [1] pp.
AAS copy.   2594

Sober Remarks on a Book Lately
Reprinted. . . . Second Edition [by
Edward Widdlesworth, 1693-1765].
Boston, Gerrish, 1724. [8], 126 pp.
AAS copy.   2595

A Sober Reply to a Mad Answer [by
Joshua Blanchard, fl. 1742-1807].
Boston, Rogers & Fowle, 1742. 16 pp.
AAS copy.   4897

Sober Sentiments [by Cotton Mather,
1663-1728].
Boston, Fleet, 1722. 37 pp.
AAS copy.   2360

Sobersides, Solomon, pseud.
Christmas Tales, for the Amusement.
Hudson, N. Y., Stoddard, 1794. 159, [1]
pp.
(The only known copy is imperfect.)
AAS copy.   47217

[Sobersides, Solomon, pseud.
Christmas Tales.
Hudson, N. Y., Stoddard, 1795.]
(Imprint assumed by Evans from
Stoddard's advs.)   29540

Sobersides, Solomon, pseud.
Christmas Tales.

Philadelphia, R. Johnson for B. & J.
Johnson, 1799. 144 pp.
(The only copy located is imperfect.)
                                             36329

Sobersides, Solomon, pseud.
A Pretty New-Year's Gift. . . . First
Worcester Edition.
Worcester, Thomas, 1786. 152, [4] pp.
AAS copy.   19995

Sobersides, Solomon, pseud.
A Pretty New-Year's Gift. . . . First
Worcester Edition.
Worcester, Thomas for Battelle, 1786. 152,
[4] pp.
(An imprint variant of 19995, q. v. for
text.)
AAS copy.   44967

Sobersides, Solomon, pseud.
A Pretty New Years Gift. . . . Second
Worcester Edition.
Worcester, Thomas & Thomas, 1796. 135,
[1] pp., printed wraps.
AAS copy.   31218

The Social Companion, and Songster's
Pocket Book.
Portsmouth, N. H., Larkin, 1799. 60 pp.
AAS copy.   36330

Socal Fire Club, Salem, Mass.
Articles of the . . . November 10, 1793.
Salem, Cushing, [1793]. [12] pp.
AAS copy.   26125

Social Harmony; or, The Cheerful
Songster's Companion.
New York, Campbell, 1795. 108 pp.
AAS copy.   29541

Social Library of the Town of Bath.
Rules and regulations for the. . . .
n. p., [1799]. Broadside.
(Also entered as 36250, q. v.)   36332

Social Society, Instituted at Schenectady,
June 28, 1798.
The Constitution of the. . . .
Schenectady, Stevenson, 1800. 15 pp.
NYPL copy.   38468

Society for Encouraging Industry and
Employing the Poor, Boston.
Advertisement. Boston, January 15, 1752.
[Boston, 1753.] Broadside.
MHS copy.   40671

Society for Encouraging Industry and
Employing the Poor, Boston.
At the Quarterly Meeting . . . May 8th,
1754. Voted, That there be a Dinner. . . .
Bring this Ticket with you.
Boston, July [blank] 1754.
[Boston, 1754.] Broadside.
AAS copy.   40717

Society for the Encouraging Industry and
Employing the Poor, Boston.
The Report of the Committee. . . .
February the 12th, 1752.
[Boston, 1753.] Broadside.
MHS copy.   40672

Society for Encouraging Industry and
Employing the Poor, Boston.
Whereas it is Found by Experience. . . .
Boston, 1754. 12 pp.
AAS copy.   7155

Society for Establishing Useful
Manufactures.
The Establishment of Manufactures. . . .
n. p., [179?]. 10 pp.
(No copy located.)   45794

Society for Establishing Useful
Manufactures.
Lottery, for Raising Six Thousand . . .
Dollars. . . . Patterson, November 24,
1795.
[Newark], Woods, [1795]. Broadside and
strip of tickets.
LOC copy.   47607

[Society for Establishing Useful
Manufactures.
Scheme of a Lottery to Raise 39,900
Dollars.
Newark, Woods, 1794. Broadside.]
(No copy located.)   27675

Society for Insuring Houses, Philadelphia.
The Deed of Settlement of the Society.
[Philadelphia, 1751.] 8 pp.
LOC copy.   6757

Society for Political Enquiries,
Philadelphia.
Rules and Regulations. . . . 9th February,
1787.
Philadelphia, Aitken, 1787. [2], 18 pp.
NYPL copy.   20645

Society for Promoting Domestic
Manufatures, Germantown.
The Constitution of the. . . .
Philadelphia, Oswald, 1790. 7 pp.
NYPL copy.   22534

Society for Promoting the Manufacture of
Sugar.
Constitution of the. . . .
Philadelphia, Aitken, 1793. 8 pp.
APS copy.   46876

Society for Propagating the Gospel among
the Indians and Others in North America.
A Brief Account of the Present State. . . .
[Boston, 1790.] 4 pp.
AAS copy.   22369

Society for Propagating the Gospel among
the Indians and Others in North America.
A Brief Account of the Present State . . .
of the Society.
[Boston, 1795.] 3 pp.
AAS copy.   28322

[Society for the Attainment of Useful
Knowledge.
Constitution of the. . . .
Philadelphia, Poulson, 1794. 12 pp.]
(Entry from Sabin 62251; no copy
located.)   27513

Society for the Encouragement of
Manufactures and the Useful Arts in
America. Philadelphia.
Philadelphia [blank] Sir, A Respectable
Body. . . .
[Philadelphia, 1788.] Broadside.
LOC copy.   45361

Society for the Information and Advice of
Immigrants.
. . . Boston, December 30, 1793. . . .
Articles.
[Boston, 1794?] Broadside.
(Not located, 1968.)   47218

Society for the Institution and Support of
First Day or Sunday Schools.
Sunday Schools. Whereas the good
Education of Youth. . . .
[Philadelphia, 1796.] Broadside.
LCP copy.   47921

Society for the Promotion of Useful Arts,
Albany, N. Y.
Transactions of the Society, Instituted in
the State of New-York, for the Promotion
of Agriculture, Arts, and Manufactures.
Part I.
New York, Childs & Swaine, 1792. xiii,
[3], 122 pp., 2 plates.
AAS copy.   24605

Society for the Promotion of Useful Arts,
Albany, N. Y.
Transactions of the Society, Instituted in
the State of New-York, for the Promotion
of Agriculture, Arts, and Manufactures.
Part II.
[New York], Childs & Swaine, 1794. 230,
[2] pp., 1 folding plate.
AAS copy.   27400

Society for the Promotion of Useful Arts,
Albany, N. Y.
Transactions of the Society Instituted in
the State of New-York, for the Promotion
of Agriculture, Arts, and Manufactures,
Part III.
Albany, Andrews, 1798. xli, 126, [3] pp.
NYHS copy.   34221

Society for the Promotion of Useful Arts,
Albany, N. Y.
Transactions of the Society for the
Promotion of Agriculture, Arts, and
Manufactures. Instituted in the State of
New-York.
Albany, Andrews, 1799. [6], 178 pp. 2
plates.

NYPL copy.   35935

[Society for the Propagation of the
Gospel in Foreign Parts.
Endeavours used by the Society . . . to
Instruct Negro Slaves in New York.
[New York?], 1730.]
(Sabin 54259. No copy found; probably
not American printing.)   3297

Society for the Relief of Distressed and
Decayed Pilots, their Widows and
Children.
Rules of the Society [Sept. 29,
1789.]
Philadelphia, Bradford, [1789].
Broadside.
HSP copy.   45593

Society for the Relief of Poor and
Distressed Masters of Ships, their Widows
and Children. Philadelphia.
An Act, for Incorporating the. . . .
Philadelphia, Tuckniss, 1800. 37 pp.
AAS copy.   38224

The Society for the Relief of Poor and
Distressed Masters of Ships, their Widows
and Children. Philadelphia.
Rules of the. . . .
Philadelphia, Bradford, 1787. pp. [4],
[i]-ii, [1]-2, 9-20.
AAS copy.   45167

Society for the Relief of Poor Widows
with Small Children.
Constitution of the Ladies Society,
Established in New York, for the Relief
of Poor Widows with Small Children.
New York, Oram, 1799. 38 pp.
AAS copy.   35952

Society for the Relief of Poor Widows
with Small Children.
Constitution of the Ladies Society,
Established in New-York, for the Relief
of Poor Widows with Small Children.
Second Edition.
New York, Oram, 1800. 64 pp.
NYPL copy.   38101

Society for the Relief of the Widows and
Orphans of the Clergy of the Protestant
Episcopal Church, in . . . South-Carolina.
Rules of the Society.
Charleston, Timothy, 1788. 28 pp.
AAS copy.   21410

Society for Useful Manufactures, New
Jersey.
Society for Useful Manufactures, No.
Be it Known that. . . .
New York, Gaine, [1791]. Broadside.
(The copy seen by Evans is now mislaid.)
                                             23799

[Society Instituted in Morris County,
N.J., for the Promotion of Learning and
Religion.
Petition and Representation of the. . . .
Newark, Woods, 1794.]
(The source of Evans' entry is unknown.)
                                             27350

The Society of St. George, in Maryland.
Rules and Constitution of. . . .
Baltimore, Hayes, 1799. 15 pp.
NYPL copy.   35148

Society of St. George, New York.
Rules of the Society of St. George.
New York, McLean, 1787. 15 pp.
NYHS copy.   20581

Society of the Cincinnati.
A Circular Letter . . . May 3, 1784.
Philadelphia, Oswald & Humphreys,
1784. 8 pp.
AAS copy.   18787

Society of the Cincinnati.
Proceedings of the . . . General-Meeting
. . . at Philadelphia, May, 1787.
Philadelphia, 1787. 17 pp.
BA copy.   20714

Society of the Cincinnati.
Proceedings . . . in General-Meeting
Convened at Philadelphia, May, 1790;
being the Third General-Meeting.
New York, Fenno, 1790. 7 pp.
LOC copy.   22893

Society of the Cincinnati.
Proceedings of the Cincinnati, by their
Delegates in an extra General-Meeting . . .
Philadelphia . . . May, 1791.
Philadelphia, Fenno, 1791. 6 pp.
CHS copy.   46289

Society of the Cincinnati.
Proceedings of the General Socielty . . .
May, 1800.
Philadelphia, Ormrod, 1800. 15 pp.
NYPL copy.   38528

Society of the Cincinnati. New Jersey.
A List of the Names of the Members . . .
in . . . New-Jersey.
n. p., [1791]. Broadside.
AAS copy.   46290

Society of the Cincinnati. New York
State.
Extract from the Proceedings . . . on the
4th of July, 1786.
New York, 1786. 20 pp.
LOC copy.   19996

Society of the Cincinnati. New York
State.
The Institution of the Society of the
Cincinnati.
New York, Loudon, 1784. 34 pp.
NYPL copy.   18788

Society of the Cincinnati. New York
State.
. . . The Members . . . will meet. . . . July
22, 1788.
[New York, 1788.] Broadside.
MHS copy.   45362

Society of the Cincinnati. New York
State.
New York, March 17, 1787. Sir, It not
being Convenient. . . .
[New York, 1787.] [i] p.
WLC copy.   45168

Society of the Cincinnati. Pennsylvania.
Proceedings of the Pennsylvania Society.
Philadelphia, Steele, 1785. Front., vii, 88
pp.
LOC copy.   19248

Society of the Cincinnati. South Carolina.
. . . Additional Rules . . . Ratified the 4th
Day of July, 1786.
Charleston, Bowen, Vandle & Andrews,
[1786]. Broadside.
LOC copy.   44968

[Society of the Cincinnati. South
Carolina.
Rules and Bye-Laws of the. . . .
Charleston, 1783.]
(Publication assumed from references in
the Aedanus Burke tracts.)   18189

Society of the Friendly Sons of St.
Patrick, New York.
Rules to be Observed by the Society.
New York, Gaine, 1786. 8 pp.
NYPL copy.   44969

Society of the Lying-In Hospital, New
York.
An Act to Incorporate the. . . .
Brooklyn, N. Y., Kirk, [1799]. 23 pp.
AAS copy.   35953

Society of the Lying-In Hospital, New
York.
Constitution of the. . . .
[New York], Furman, 1799. [1], 4 pp.
AAS copy.   35954

Society of the Sons of St. George,
Philadelphia.
Rules and Constitutions of. . . .
Philadelphia, Oswald, [1788]. 20 pp.
HSP copy.   21390

Society of the Sons of St. George,
Philadelphia.
Rules and Constitutions of the. . . .
Philadelphia, Cobbett, 1797. 25 pp.
LCP copy.   32683

Society of the United Brethren, for
Propagating the Gospel among the
Heathen, Bethlehem, Pa.
Stated Rules of the Society.
Philadelphia, Cist, [1788]. 15, [1], 4 pp.
AAS copy.   45363

Society of United Irishmen of Dublin.
Proceedings of the Society [1791-1794].
Philadelphia, Stephens, 1795. [10], 241
pp.
AAS copy.   28590

[The Solar System Displayed.
Philadelphia, Zeller, 1791.]
(Entry from an adv.)   23780

[A Soldier and his Lady. . . . A Song.
Philadelphia, Towne, 1779.]
(Adv. Pa. Evening-Post, Feb. 10, 1779.)
                                                 16527

A Solemn Address, to Christians &
Patriots [by Tunis Wortman, d. 1822].
New York, Denniston, 1800. 36 pp.
AAS copy.   39149

A Solemn Farewell to Levi Ames, being a
Poem Written a Few Days before his
Execution. . . . Oct. 21, 1772. [1773].
Boston, Draper, [1773]. Broadside.
HSP copy.   42506

A Soliloquy. Nulli Sincera Voluptas [by
William Livingston, 1723-1790].
[New York], 1770. 15 pp.
LCP copy.   11703

Solomon, Mr. & Mrs.
Mr. & Mrs. Solomon. Vocal Performers
from the Southward . . . April 22.
[Newburyport, 1794.] Broadside.
NYPL copy.   27717

Solomon, Samuel, 1780-1818.
A Guide to Health. . . . Fifty-Second
Edition.
Stockport, [England], Clarke for Bach of
N.Y., [1800]. 270 pp., plate.
LCP copy.   49148

Some Account of an Existing
Correspondence.
New York, Cobbett, 1800. 23 pp.
AAS copy.   38530

Some Account of Isaac Shoemaker.
[Philadelphia, 1779?] 8 pp.
AAS copy.   16528

Some Account of John Burns . . . and
Daniel Cronan, who were Executed . . .
the 12th of October 1789.
[Philadelphia, 1789.] Broadside.
HSP copy.   45594

Some Account of the Holy Life and Death
[by John Shower, 1657-1715].
Boston, 1704. xxxiv, 134 pp.
AAS copy.   1194

Some Account of the Holy Life . . . of Mr.
Henry Gearing [by John Shower,
1657-1715].
Boston, Fleet for Phillips, etc., 1720. xxxv,
146 pp.
WLC copy.   2175

Some Account of the Life and Death of
Matthew Lee, Executed . . . October 11,
1792.
Philadelphia, Johnston & Justice, 1793. 23
pp.
LOC copy.   46877

Some Account of the Life and Gospel
Labours, of William Reckitt . . . also . . .
of James Gough.
Philadelphia, Crukshank, 1783. [2], 164;
xxiv, 184 pp.
AAS copy.   18146

Some Account of the Life and Religious
Labours of Sarah Grubb [by Lindley
Murray, ed., 1745-1826].
Trenton, Collins, 1795. vi, 418 pp.
AAS copy.   28776

Some Account of the Life and Religious
Labours of Sarah Grubb [by Lindley
Murray, ed., 1745-1826].
Wilmington, Bonsal & Starr, 1795. 378,
[1] pp.
AAS copy.   28777

Some Account of the Pennsylvania
Hospital [by Benjamin Franklin,
1706-1790].

Philadelphia, Franklin & Hall, [1754]. 40
pp.
AAS copy.   7197

Some Advice to Governesses and
Teachers [by François de Salignac de la
Mothe Fénelon, 1651-1715].
Litchfield, Collier & Buel, 1795? 8 pp.
(The only known copy is imperfect.)
Forrest Bowe copy.   47417

Some Advice to Governesses and
Teachers [by François de Salignac de la
Mothe Fénelon, 1651-1715].
New York, Campbell for Lawrence, 1795.
8 pp.
NYPL copy.   47418

Some Advice to Governesses and
Teachers [by François de Salignac de la
Mothe Fénelon, abp., 1651-1715].
New York, Collins, 1799. 12 pp.
BA copy.   35476

Some Animadversions on a Reply to a
Letter from a Gentleman in New-York.
[New York] 1750. 16 pp.
(The HEH has an edition with the
incorrect imprint 1740.)
LCP copy.   6610

Some Arguments against
Worldly-Mindedness [by Eunice Smith]
of Ashfield, Mass.
Boston, Russell for King, 1791. 16 pp.
AAS copy.   23767

Some Arguments against
Worldly-Mindedness [by Eunice Smith of
Ashfield, Mass.]
Springfield, Gray, [1792]. 23 pp.
AAS copy.   24793

Some Arguments against
Worldly-Mindedness [by Eunice Smith,
of Ashfield, Mass.]
Warren, Lee, [1792]. 23 pp.
AAS copy.   24794

Some Arguments against
Worldly-Mindedness [by Eunice Smith, of
Ashfield, Mass.]
Rutland, Lee, 1795. 15 pp.
JCB copy.   47604

Some Arguments against Worldly
Mindedness [by Eunice Smith of Ashfield,
Mass.]
Walpole, N. H., Thomas & Carlisle, 1795. 16
pp.
AAS copy.   29527

Some Brief Remarks on the Nature of the
Gospel Ministry.
Baltimore, Goddard & Langworthy, 1785.
11 pp.
(No copy located.)   44794

Some Brief Remarks upon a Late Book
[by George Keith, 1638-1716].
New York, 1704. 20 pp.
JCB copy.   1163

Some Brief Remarks, upon a Letter to a
Gentleman.
Boston, Fleet, 1731. 12 pp.
BPL copy.   3477

Some by old Words. . . . July 25, 1772.
[Philadelphia, 1772.] Broadside.
LCP copy.   12561

[Some Chapters of the Book of Chronicles
of Isaac the Scribe.
New York, Holt, [1775]. 18 pp.]
(The unique copy could not be
reproduced.)   14461

Some Considerations against the Setting
up of a Market in this Town. . . . May
25th, 1733.
[Boston, 1733.] 4 pp.
BPL copy.   40029

[Some Considerations of, or a Brief Reply
to a Sermon.
Boston, Fleet, 1735.]
(Adv. Boston Evening Post, Nov. 10, 1735,
"speedily to be published.")   3960

Some Considerations on the Bills of
Credit [by Cotton Mather, 1663-1728].
Boston, 1691. 23 pp.

(For authorship see T. J. Holmes, Cotton
Mather, III, 998-1003.)
WL copy.   566

Some Considerations on the
Consequences of the French Settling
Colonies on the Mississippi [by James
Smith, of Carolina].
(A ghost of the BPL copy of the London
ed.)   2176

Some Considerations, Propounded to the
Several Sorts and Sects [by Jemima
Wilkinson, 1752-1819].
[Providence], 1779. 94 pp.
AAS copy.   19435

Some Considerations upon the Several
Sorts of Banks.
Boston, Fleet and Crump, 1716. 16 pp.
BPL copy.   1855

Some Consolatory Reflections . . .
Occasioned by the . . . Deaths of . . . the
Children of Capt. Joseph . . . Hinckley, of
Barnstable.
[Boston, 1733?] Broadside.
BPL copy.   40031

Some Critical Observations upon a late
Poem, Entitled The Breeches [by William
Smith, 1728-1793].
New York, 1750. 20 pp.
(See B.S.A., XLIV, 306 pp.)
NYPL copy.   6611

Some Deductions from the System
Promulgated [by Mrs. Judith (Sargent)
Stevens Murray, 1751-1820].
Norwich, Trumbull, 1782. 40 pp.
AAS copy.   17729

Some Deductions from the System
Promulgated [by Mrs. Judith (Sargent)
Stevens Murray, 1751-1820].
Portsmouth, 1782. 32 pp.
AAS copy.   17728

Some Difficulties Proposed for Solution
[by Noah Worcester, 1758-1837].
Newburyport, 1786. 61 pp.
AAS copy.   20158

Some Difficulties Proposed for Solution
[by Noah Worcester, 1758-1837].
Worcester, Worcester, 1793. 59 pp.
AAS copy.   26503

Some Doubts Respecting the Death,
Resurrection, and Ascension of Jesus. . . .
To which are Added, Reasons for
Scepticism. . . .
New York, Fellows, 1797. [4], 113 pp.
Buffalo & Erie County Public Library
copy.   34569

Some Excellent Verses for the Education
of Youth [by Nathaniel Crouch,
1632-1725?]
Boston, B. Green, 1708. 12 pp.
PPL copy.   39460

Some Excellent Verses on Admiral
Vernon's Taking the Forts.
[Boston, 1741.] Broadside.
NYPL copy.   4810

Some Extracts from an Ancient Dialogue
[by Eliphalet Williams, 1727-1803].
Hartford, Babcock, 1795. 16 pp.
AAS copy.   29543

Some Farraginous Remarks [by Joseph
Haynes, 1715-1801].
Concord, N. H., Russell for Haynes, 1793.
22, [1] pp.
AAS copy.   25593

Some few Remarks upon a Scandalous
Book.
Boston, 1701. 71, [1] pp.
AAS copy.   975

Some Fruits of Solitude. . . . Eighth
Edition [by William Penn, 1644-1718].
Newport, 1749. [12], 158, [7] pp.
AAS copy.   6392

Some Fugitive Thoughts on a Letter
Signed Freeman.
South Carolina, 1774. [2], 36 pp.
LOC copy.   13630

Some Funeral Verses Occasioned by the
Death of . . . Jonathan French . . .
February the 17th, 1720/21.
n. p. [1721]. Broadside.
NYHS copy.   39753

Some Important Observations,
Occasioned by . . . the Publick Fast [by
Stephen Johnson, 1724-1786].
Newport, 1766. [2], 61 pp.
AAS copy.   10346

Some Inquiries with Thoughts on
Religious Subjects.
[New York], 1757. [4], 27, [1] pp.
HSP copy.   40939

Some Meditations Concerning our
Honourable Gentlemen. . . . December 28,
1675 [by Wait Still Winthrop, 1643-1717].
New London, reprinted Apr. 4, 1721.
Broadside.
AAS ph. copy.   39758

Some Miscellaneous Observations on
Masonry.
Boston, Edes, 1798. 15 pp.
AAS copy.   34570

Some Miscellany Observations [by
Samuel Willard, 1640-1707].
Philadelphia, 1692. 16 pp.
YC copy.   631

Some Modern Directions for the Culture
of Silk.
Windham, [Byrne] for Starrs and
Eldridge, 1792. 38 pp.
(Evans assumed the imprint from an adv.)
HEH copy.   24802

Some Necessary Precautions, Worthy to
be Considered.
[Philadelphia, 1727?] Broadside.
APS copy.   2964

Some Necessary Remarks on the
Education of the Youth [by Anthony
Benezet, 1713-1784].
[Philadelphia, 1778?] 8 pp.
HSP copy.   15739

. . . Some New Thoughts for the New
Year.
Philadelphia, Johnsons, 1800. 36 pp.
AAS copy.   37169

Some Observations of Consequence.
[Philadelphia], 1768. 80 pp.
LOC copy.   11073

Some Observations on the Bill Intitled,
An Act for Granting to His Majesty an
Excise upon Wines.
Boston, 1754. [2], 12 pp.
AAS copy.   7319

Some Observations on the Charge Given
by the Honourable James De Lancey [by
Lewis Morris, 1671-1746].
New York, 1733/4. 18 pp.
NYPL copy.   3835

Some Observations on the Proceedings
against the Rev. Mr. Hemphill [by
Benjamin Franklin, 1706-1790].
Philadelphia, Franklin, 1735. 32 pp.
(The only known copy of this 1st ed. was
last reported in the possession of the late
James A. Williams of Philadelphia. The tp
is reproduced from the Freeman catalogue
of Dec. 13, 1937.)   3904

Some Observations on the Proceedings
against the Rev. Mr. Hemphill. . . .
Second Edition [by Benjamin Franklin,
1706-1790].
Philadelphia, Franklin, 1735. 32 pp.
AAS copy.   3905

Some Observations on the Reverend Mr.
Whitefield.
Boston, Henchman, 1740. 15 pp.
AAS copy.   4602

[Some Observations on the Reverend Mr.
Whitefield.
Philadelphia, 1740.]
(Adv. Pa. Gazette, June 19, 1740.)   4603

Some Observations on the Scheme
Projected for Emitting 60000l [by
Hugh Vans].

Boston, Kneeland and Green, 1738. [4],
25 pp.
AAS copy.   4308

Some Observations on the Situation,
Disposition, and Character of the Indian
Natives of this Continent [by Anthony
Benezet, 1713-1784].
Philadelphia, Crukshank, 1784. 59 pp.
AAS copy.   18356

Some Observations on the two Campaigns
against the Cherokee Indians. . . . In a
Second Letter from Philopatrios [by
Christopher Gadsden, 1724-1805].
Charleston, 1762. 88, [1] pp.
LCP copy.   9243

[Some Observations Relating to the
Establishment of Schools.
Philadelphia, 1789. 4 pp.]
(The origin of this entry is unknown.)
                                              22151

Some Observations Relating to the
Present Circumstances of the Province of
the Massachusetts-Bay.
Boston, Fowle, 1750. 20 pp.
AAS copy.   6612

Some Observations upon the French
Tongue [by Andrew Le Mercier,
1692-1763].
Boston, B. Green, 1724. [2], ii, 20 pp.
AAS copy.   39811

Some Occasional Thoughts [by Joseph
Seccomb, 1706-1760].
Boston, Kneeland & Green, 1742. [4], ii,
16 pp.
(Contemporary attribution in AAS and
other copies.)
AAS copy.   5052

[Some of the Dying Speeches and
Declarations of John Battes. . . .
Boston, Henchman, 1726.]
(Adv. Boston News-Letter, Nov. 3, 1726.)
                                               2814

Some of the Fundamental Truths [by
George Keith, 1638-1716].
[Philadelphia, 1692.] 15, [1] pp.
JCB copy.   604

Some Poetical Thoughts on the
Difficulties our Forefathers Endured.
[New Haven? 1776?] Broadside.
JCB copy.   43160

Some Proposals to Benefit the Province.
Boston, Eliot, 1720. 15 pp.
AAS copy.   2177

Some Queries, Concerning the Operation
of the Holy Spirit.
Philadelphia, Franklin, 1740? 16 pp.
LCP copy.   4604

Some Queries Intended to be Put to the
Rev. Dr. Witherspoon.
[Philadelphia? 1789?] 3 pp.
AAS copy.   45595

Some Reasons and Arguments [by
Benjamin Colman, 1673-1747].
Boston, Franklin for Gerrish and
Edwards, 1719. [2], 14 pp.
AAS copy.   2019

Some Reasons and Causes [by George
Keith, 1638-1716].
[Philadelphia, 1692.] 36 pp.
AAS copy.   606

Some Reasons that Influenced the
Governor [by Thomas Fitch, 1700-1774].
Hartford, [1766]. 14 pp.
AAS copy.   10297

Some Reflections on the Disputes between
New-York, New-Hampshire [by Thomas
Young, 1732-1777].
New Haven, 1764. 21, [2] pp.
NYPL copy.   9889

Some Reflections on the Law of
Bankruptcy.
New Haven, 1755. [2], 11 pp.
LOC copy.   7495

[Some] Remarkable Cities and Towns,
when Founded.

[Philadelphia? Carey? 1795?] [2] pp.
AAS copy.   47608

Some Remarkable Particulars [by William
Marshall, 1740?-1820].
Philadelphia, Hogan, 1799. 26, [2] pp.
LCP copy.   35771

Some Remarkable Proceedings in the
Assembly of Virginia Anno 1718.
[Philadelphia, 1725]. [4] pp.
APS copy.   2702

[Some Remarks on Abel Morgan's
Answer to Samuel Finley.]
(Adv. Pa. Gazette, Nov. 2, 1749.)   6419

[Some Remarks on Mr. Ebenezer
Kinnersley's two Letters.
Philadelphia, Franklin, 1740.]
(Adv. Pa. Gazette, Sept. 14, 1740. A
tentative title for 4542, q. v.)   4605

Some Remarks on Mr. President Clap's
History [by Thomas Darling, 1720-1789].
New Haven, 1757. 127 pp.
YC copy.   7881

Some Remarks on Mr. Worth's Appeal to
the Public.
Philadelphia, Aitken, 1790. 10 pp.
UTS copy.   45994

Some Remarks on Religion [by Hermon
Husbands, 1724-1795].
Philadelphia, Bradford, 1761. 38 pp.
LCP copy.   8885

Some Remarks on Silent Worship . . .
(from the London Review of December,
1791.)
[Connecticut? 1792?] Broadside.
(More probably printed around 1811.)
AAS copy.   46576

Some Remarks on the Great and Unusual
Darkness . . . May 19, 1780.
Danvers, 1780. 16 pp.
AAS copy.   16993

Some Remarks on the Memorial and
Remonstrance of the Corporation of
Trinity Church.
[New York, 1785.] 34 pp.
NYPL copy.   19249

Some Remarks on the Settlement of the
Line, and the Removal of the Courts from
Bristol to Taunton [in verse].
n. p., [1747?] Broadside.
RIHS copy.   40439

Some Remarks upon a late Pamphlet
Entitled. . . . [by John Graham,
1694-1774].
[Boston], 1733. [4], 44 pp.
AAS copy.   3660

Some Remarks upon a late Pamphlet
Signed. . . . [by Caleb Pusey, 1650-1727].
[Philadelphia, 1705.] 40 pp.
LOC copy.   1231

Some Remarks upon a Second Letter [by
John Graham, 1694-1774].
Boston, Henchman, 1736. [4], 128 pp.
YC copy.   4019

[Some Remarks upon the Times.
Philadelphia, 1741.]
(Adv. Pa. Gazette, June 11, 1741.)   4811

Some Remedies Proposed [by Francis
Rawle, c.1662-1727].
[Philadelphia], 1721. 20 pp.
LCP copy.   2287

Some Rude & Indigested Thoughts.
New London, 1730. [2], 12 pp.
BPL copy.   3359

Some Serious Thoughts on the Frowns of
Divine Providence in the Year 1764.
n. p., [1764?]. Broadside.
AAS copy.   41488

Some Seasonable Advice unto the Poor
[by Cotton Mather, 1663-1728].
[Boston, 1726.] 12 pp.
AAS copy.   2776

Some Seasonable Considerations [by

Gershom Bulkeley, 1636-1713].
New York, 1694. 62 pp.
HC copy.   688

Some Seasonable Enquiries Offered [by
Cotton Mather, 1663-1728].
[Boston], 1723. 12 pp.
AAS copy.   2459

Some Seasonable Observations and
Remarks upon the State of our
Controversy with Great Britain.
America (Boston), 1775. 14 pp.
AAS copy.   14462

Some Serious and Awful Considerations
[by Anthony Benezet, 1713-1784].
Philadelphia, Crukshank, [1769]. 48 pp.
AAS copy.   11175

Some Serious Thoughts on the Design of
Erecting a College in . . . New-York.
New York, 1749. [5], 9 pp.
CU copy.   6366

Some Short Account of the Life and
Character of . . . Joshua Eaton [by Eli
Forbes, 1726-1804].
Boston, Draper and Boyles, 1773. xxvii,
[1], 155 pp.
AAS copy.   12756

Some Short Observations made on the
Presbyterian Doctrine.
Philadelphia, 1721. 38 pp.
NYPL copy.   2293

[Some Short Observations made on the
Presbyterian Doctrine.
New London, 1724. 24 pp.]
(No copy of this title recorded by Evans
has been found. It is a reprint, if not a
ghost, of 2293.)   2584

Some Thoughts Occasioned by the
Earthquake . . . March 12th, 1761.
Portsmouth, Fowle, [1761]. 12 pp.
JCB copy.   41246

Some Thoughts on Education [by William
Smith, 1727-1803].
New York, 1752. ix, 32 pp.
AAS copy.   6935

Some Thoughts on Religion. By a Youth.
Providence, 1770. 24 pp.
AAS copy.   42172

[Some Thoughts on the Call of God.
[Boston? 1762.] 8 pp.]
(Origin of entry not found.)   9275

Some Thoughts on the Duration of the
Torments. . . .
Charleston, [S. C.], Wells for Edwards,
1759. [2], 37 pp.
LOC copy.   41077

Some Thoughts on the Gloomy Cloud that
Hangs over New-England.
Boston, 1792. 8 pp.
LOC copy.   24803

Some Thoughts on the Gloomy Cloud that
Hangs over New-England.
Boston, 1793. 8 pp.
AAS copy.   26181

[Some Thoughts upon the Names of the
Days of the Week.
Boston, 1771.]
(Adv. Mass. Gazette, Aug. 26, 1771.)
                                                 12230

[Some Transactions between the Indians
and Friends in Pennsylvania, in 1791 and
1792.
Philadelphia? 1792. 16 pp.
(Apparently a ghost of Sabin 60624.)
                                                 24333

Some truth, much wit. . . . The Humble
Confession . . . of Benjamin Towne [by
John Witherspoon, 1723-1794].
[Philadelphia, 1778.] 5, [1] pp.
HSP copy.   16173

[Somers, John Somers], baron, 1651-1716.
The Judgment of whole Kingdoms. . . .
Twelfth Edition.
Boston, Thomas for Langdon, [1773]. 144
pp.

(Date of publication from Thomas' copy.)
AAS copy.   13632

Somers, John Somers, baron, 1651-1716.
The Judgment of Whole Kingdoms. . . .
Eleventh Edition.
Philadelphia, Dunlap, 1773. 156, [1] pp.
AAS copy.   13023

Somers, John Somers, baron, 1651-1716.
The Judgment of whole Kingdoms.
New York, 1774.
(A copy was offered for sale but is not
now to be found.)   13633

Somers, John Somers, baron, 1651-1716.
The Judgment of whole Kingdoms. . . .
Twelfth Edition.
Newport, 1774. 156 pp.
AAS copy.   13631

[Somers, John Somers, baron, 1651-1716.
The Security of Englishmen's Lives.
Boston, 1720.]
(Title from Prince.)   2178

[Somers, John Somers], baron, 1651-1716.
The Security of Englishmen's Lives. . . .
Fourth Edition.
New York, Hodge & Shober for Noel &
Hazard, 1773. 101, [3] pp.
AAS copy.   13024

[Somerville & Noble.
Advertisement.
Philadelphia, 1775. Broadside.]
(From Aitken's records.)   14463

[Somerville & Nobel.
Prices Current.
Philadelphia, 1775. Broadside.]
(From Aitken's records.)   14464

A Son Excellence, Son Excellence le
Ministre Plenipotentiare de France.
[Philadelphia, 1779?] [4] pp.
LCP copy.   16177

[A Song Book. Containing upwards of
Forty of the Most Modern and Elegant
Songs.
Amherst, N. H., Preston, 1798.]
(Title and imprint assumed by Evans from
adv. "Just Published, by Samuel Preston,"
in Village Messenger, Jan. 20, 1798.)
                                                 34571

A Song, Composed by the British
Butchers, after the Fight at Bunker-Hill
on the 17th of June, 1775.
Boston, at the Bible and Heart, [1775].
Broadside.
NYHS copy.   42941

A Song, Composed by the British
Butchers, after the Fight at Bunker-Hill.
[Chelmsford? Coverly?, 1775?]
Broadside.
NYPL copy.   42940

A Song, Composed by the British
Soldiers, after the Battle at Bunker-Hill,
on the 17th of June, 1775.
n. p., [1775.] Broadside.
BPL copy.   42939

A Song Composed by the British Soldiers,
after the Battle at Bunker-Hill, on the
17th of June, 1775.
[Boston, 1775.] Broadside.
AAS copy.   14465

A Song Composed for the Fraternity of
Steuben Lodge, No. 18. . . . January 18,
1791 [by George Heartwell Spierin,
1787-1804].
[Goshen, 1791.] Broadside.
NYHS copy.   23784

Song, for the One Hundred and
Fifty-Third Anniversary of the . . .
Artillery Company. June, 1792.
[Boston, 1792.] Broadside.
HSP copy.   46577

[Song from The Jew and the Doctor.
Baltimore, Shaw, 1799.]
("Just published," Telegraphe, Dec. 4,
1799.)   48963

Song made on the Taking of General
Burgoyne.

n.p., [1777]. Broadside.
BPL copy.   15599

A Song Made upon the Election of New
Magistrates.
[New York, 1734.] Broadside.
NYPL copy.   3836

[Song of the Angels: from Luke, Chap. II:
Anthem.
Philadelphia, M'Culloch, 1788.]
("Just published," Federal Gazette, Dec.
11, 1788.)   21467

Song of Washington.
n. p., [1778?] Broadside.
HEH copy.   43552

. . . A Song on the Remarkable
Resurrection of above One Hundred and
Fifty Thousand Pounds Sterling [Apr. 2,
1750].
[Boston, Rogers & Fowle, 1750.]
Broadside.
EI copy.   40568

[A Song, on the Surrender of General
Burgoyne.
[Hartford, 1779.] Broadside.]
(Entry from adv. in Conn. Courant, Sept.
28, 1779, for "Burgoyne's Surrendery, a
Poem." See Sabin 86895. This is
apparently not the NYPL broadside.)
                                                 16529

A Song, on the Surrender of General
Burgoyne . . . October 17, 1777.
[Hartford? 1779?] Broadside.
NYPL copy.   43704

A Song, to the Tune of Hearts of Oak.
[New York, 1769.] Broadside.
LCP copy.   11472

Songs and Lullabies of the Good Old
Nurses. . . . First Worcester Edition.
Worcester, Mass., Thomas, 1799. 29,
[2] pp.
AAS copy.   36335

Songs, Composed for the Use and
Edification of Such as Love the Truth.
Providence, Waterman & Russell for
Pearce, [1768?]. 36 pp.
BrU copy.   41880

Songs, Duets, and Chorusses [by Samuel
Arnold, 1740-1802].
New York, Loudon, 1795. 16 pp.
NYPL copy.   29120

Songs for the Amusement of Children.
Middletown, Woodward, 1790. 31 pp.
BPL copy.   22894

Songs in the Comic Opera of Robin Hood
[by Leonard MacNally, 1752-1820].
[Philadelphia], Carey, 1794. 22 pp.
AAS copy.   27256

Songs. Naval and Military.
New York, Rivington, 1779. [2], xi, [1],
128 pp.
T.W. Streeter copy.   16530

[The Songs of Robin Hood.
New York, Parker, 1750.]
(From printer's adv.)   6613

The Songs of the Comic Opera Rosina [by
Frances (Moore) Brooke, 1724?-1789].
Philadelphia, Carey, 1794. 12 pp.
Grosvenor Library, Buffalo, copy.   26702

[The Songster's Magazine, Containing a
Choice Collection of the Most Approved
Songs.
Philadelphia, 1795.]
(Imprint assumed by Evans from advs.)
                                                 29542

Sonmans, Peter, of New Jersey.
To His Excellency John Lord Lovelace.
New York, 1709. 26 pp.
Bodleian copy.   1431

The Sons of Coke and Littleton. . . .
Engraved for Bickerstaff's Genuine
Boston Almanack, 1787 [by Benjamin West,
1730-1813].
[Boston, 1786.] [24] pp.
AAS copy.   20136

Sons of St. George, of Philadelphia.
Rules and Constitutions of. . . .
Philadelphia, Humphreys, 1772. 28 pp.
LCP copy.   12528

Sons of St. George, Philadelphia.
Rules and Constitutions of the Society of
Englishmen.
Philadelphia, Towne, 1774. 24 pp.
NYHS copy.   13544

Soren, John, b. 1759.
The Narrative of Mr. John Soren.
Boston, 1800. 54 pp.
AAS copy.   38531

Sorge, Rev. Mr.
An Authentic Account of the Barbarity of
the Russians.
Boston, Kneeland, 1759. 15, [1] pp.
(The pagination given by Evans is that of
the Fowle & Draper ed., also at AAS.)
AAS copy.   8494

Sorge, Rev. Mr.
Extracts of Two Letters.
Boston, Fowle & Draper, 1759. 23, [1] pp.
AAS copy.   41078

Sorlie, Sholto.
A Treatise on the New Sword Exercise.
Philadelphia, Cobbett, 1798. 24 pp.
HC copy.   34572

. . .Sorrowful Sam [by Sarah More,
1743?-1817].
Philadelphia, Johnsons, 1800. 36 pp.
AAS copy.   37137

The Sorrows of Werter [by Johann
Wolfgang von Goethe, 1749-1832].
New York, Wayland and Davis for L.
Wayland, 1795. 142, [1] pp.
(The only copy located is imperfect.)
AAS copy.   28753

The Sorrows of Werther [by Johann
Wolfgang von Goethe, 1749-1832].
New York, Bell, 1796. 142 pp.
(The only copy located could not be
filmed.)   30495

The Sorrows of Werter [by Johann
Wolfgang von Goethe, 1749-1832].
New York, Mott & Lyon for Gomez, 1796.
144 pp.
AAS copy.   30494

Sotweed Redivivus [by Ebenezer
Cooke?].
Annapolis, 1730. viii, 28 pp.
NYPL copy.   3266

The Soul upon the Wing [by Cotton Mather,
1663-1728].
Boston, Green, 1722. [4], 24, [1], vii, 67
pp.
AAS copy.   2361

A Soul Well-Anchored [by Cotton Mather,
1663-1728].
Boston, 1712. 24 pp.
JCB copy.   1558

The Souldier Told, what he Shall do [by
Cotton Mather, 1663-1728].
[Boston], 1707. 24 pp.
HC copy.   1315

South Carolina (Colony) 1736. Committee
Appointed to Examine into the
Proceedings of the People of Georgia.
Report of the Committee Appointed.
Charleston, 1736. 120 pp.
(LOC, JCB, and NYHS have a 1737 ed.
not in Evans.)
NYPL copy.   4082

South Carolina (Colony) Assembly, 1742.
Committee Appointed to Inquire into the
Causes of the Disappointment.
The Report of the Committee, of both
Houses [St. Augustine Expedition].
Charleston, 1742. 108, 52, [1] pp., map.
NYPL copy.   5063

South Carolina (Colony) Assembly, 1765.
. . . In the Commons House Assembly the
29th Day of November, 1765. . . . Several
late Acts of Parliament. . . .
Charleston, Timothy, [1765]. Broadside.
(No copy located.)   41589

South Carolina (Colony) Assembly, 1766.
. . . In the Commons House of Assembly,
the 28th Day of January, 1766. Ordered
. . . Printed. . . .
Charleston, Timothy, [1766]. [4] pp.
CHS copy.   41659

South Carolina (Colony) Assembly, 1766.
. . . In the Commons House of Assembly,
the 3d of February, 1766. Ordered, that
the Petition. . . .
Charleston, Timothy, [1766]. [8] pp.
CHS copy.   41660

South Carolina (colony) Assembly, 1775.
. . . The Actual Commencement of
Hostilities against this Continent. . . .
[Charleston? 1775]. Broadside.
NYPL copy.   42942

South Carolina (Colony) Auditor General,
1731.
Charlestown. . . . This is to give Notice
that James St. John . . . hath now Opened
his Office [Nov. 27, 1731].
Charleston, Whitmarsh, [1731].
Broadside.
NYPL facsim. copy.   39976

South Carolina (Colony) Council, 1731.
. . . At a Council held . . . October 19,
1731. . . . The Method and Form of
Granting Lands.
Charleston, Webb, [1731]. 6 pp.
PRO copy.   39977

South Carolina (Colony) Court of General
Sessions.
At a Court of the General Sessions.
Charleston, 1741. 39, [1] pp.
JCB copy.   4812

South Carolina (Colony) General
Assembly, 1737.
Report of the Committee, Appointed to
Examine into the Proceedings of . . .
Georgia.
Charleston, Timothy, 1737. 120 pp.
WLC copy.   401281

South Carolina (Colony) Governor, 1731.
. . . By His Excellency, Robert Johnson
. . . a Proclamation. . . . His Majesty's
Lands [Nov. 4, 1731].
[Charleston, 1731.] Broadside.
PRO copy.   39978

South Carolina (Colony) Governor, 1744.
By His Excellency James Glen. . . . A
Proclamation [Distemper. Aug. 3, 1744].
[Charleston, 1744.] Broadside.
NYPL copy.   5493

South Carolina (Colony) Governor, 1769.
. . . By His Excellency . . . Lord
Charles-Grenville Montagu. . . . A
Proclamation: Whereas the Present
General Assembly. . . . [Dated June 16,
1769].
Charleston [S. C.], Wells, [1769].
Broadside.
AAS copy.   42005

South Carolina (Colony) House Journals,
1766.
Votes of the Commons-House [Apr. 28 -
May 7, 1766].
Charleston, Timothy, 1766. [2], 14 pp.
APS copy.   41661

South Carolina (Colony) Laws, Statutes,
etc., 1732.
[The Quit-rent Roll Law.
Charleston, 1732.]
(McMurtrie, S. C. Imprints, 7.)   40004

South Carolina (Colony) Laws, Statutes,
etc., 1734.
[An Act for better settling and Regulating
of Pilots.
Charleston, Timothy, 1734]
(Adv. S. C. Gazette, Aug. 24, 1734; no
copy known.)   40061

South Carolina (Colony) Laws, Statutes,
etc., 1734.
[An Act for Regulating the Patrolls in this
Province.
Charleston, Timothy, 1734.]
(Adv. S. C. Gazette, June 29, 1734; no
copy known.)   40062

South Carolina (Colony) Laws, Statutes,

etc., 1734.
[An Art for the Better Regulating the
Militia.
Charleston, Timothy, 1734.]
(Adv. S. C. Gazette, June 22, 1734; no
copy known.)   40063

South Carolina (Colony) Laws, Statutes,
etc., 1735.
[Act for the Better Governing of Negroes.
Charleston, 1735.]
(Adv. S. C. Gazette, Apr. 19, 1735.) 40083

South Carolina (Colony) Laws, Statutes,
etc., 1736.
The Laws of the Province of South
Carolina.
Charleston, 1736. 2 vol. [6], xliv, [19],
473; [475]-619, [8], 59, [20], 17, [3] pp.
NYPL copy.   4080

South Carolina (Colony) Laws, Statutes,
etc., 1740.
[An Act for the Better Ordering and
Governing Negroes. . . . Passed May 10,
1740.
Charleston, 1740.
(Adv. S. C. Gazette, Nov. 13, 1740.) 40211

[South Carolina (Colony) Laws, Statutes,
etc., 1744.
An Act for the Relief of Insolvent
Debtors.
Charleston, 1744.]
(No copy found.)   5491

[South Carolina (Colony) Laws, Statutes,
etc., 1744.
An Act to Encourage the Destroying
Beasts of Prey.
Charleston, 1744.]
(No copy found.)   5492

South Carolina (Colony) Laws, Statutes,
etc., 1747.
. . . At a General Assembly . . . June, 1747
[tax act].
Charleston, Timothy, 1747. 23 pp.
LOC copy.   40442

South Carolina (Colony) Laws, Statutes,
etc., 1749.
The Tax Act. . . . At a General Assembly
[June 1, 1749]. . . .
Charleston, Timothy, 1749. [2], 25 pp.
LOC copy.   40517

South Carolina (Colony) Laws, Statutes,
etc., 1752.
. . . Acts Passed by the General Assembly
[Tax Act, May 1752].
Charleston, Timothy, 1752. 27 pp.
LOC copy.   40642

South Carolina (Colony) Laws, Statutes,
etc., 1754.
. . . At a General Assembly [May 11,
1754 +. Tax Act].
Charleston, Timothy, 1754. 27 pp.
LOC copy.   40719

South Carolina (Colony) Laws, Statutes,
etc., 1755.
. . . At a General Assembly . . . May, 1755
[Tax Act]. . . .
Charleston, Timothy, 1755. 31 pp.
LOC copy.   40801

South Carolina (Colony) Laws, Statutes,
etc., 1756.
. . . At a General Assembly . . . July, 1756
[tax Act]. . . .
Charleston, Timothy, 1746 (i.e. 1756). 27
pp.
LOC copy.   40863

South Carolina (Colony) Laws, Statutes,
etc., 1757.
. . . At a General Assembly . . . May 1757
[tax Act]. . . .
Charleston, Timothy, 1757. 27 pp.
LOC copy.   40940

South Carolina (Colony) Laws, Statutes,
etc., 1758.
. . . At a General Assembly . . . May, 1758
[tax act].
Charleston, Timothy, 1758. 35 pp.
LOC copy.   41011

South Carolina (Colony) Laws, Statutes,
etc., 1759.

. . . At a General Assembly . . . April, 1759 [taxes].
Charleston, Timothy, 1759. 28 pp.
LOC copy.   41097

South Carolina (Colony) Laws, Statutes, etc., 1760.
[Halftitle:] The Tax-Act, Passed the 31st Day of July, 1760.
Charleston, Timothy, 1760. [2], 29 pp.
LOC copy.   41169

South Carolina (Colony) Laws, Statutes, etc., 1760.
Acts of the General Assembly . . . Passed in the Year 1760.
Charleston, Timothy, 1760. [2], 56, [1] pp.
LOC copy.   41168

South Carolina (Colony) Laws, Statutes, etc., 1761.
Acts of the General Assembly . . . Passed in the Year 1761.
Charleston, Timothy, 1761. 25, [1] pp.
LOC copy.   41247

South Carolina (Colony) Laws, Statutes, etc., 1762.
An Act [Charleston Streets. Oct. 25, 1762].
Charleston, 1764. 4 + pp.
NYPL copy.   9843

South Carolina (Colony) Laws, Statutes, etc., 1762.
[Halftitle:] The Tax Act, Passed . . . May, 1762. . . .
Charleston, Timothy, 1762. [2], 30 pp.
LOC copy.   41311

South Carolina (Colony) Laws, Statutes, etc., 1764.
. . . At a General Assembly . . . October . . . 1764 [taxes].
Charleston, Timothy, 1764. 36 pp.
LOC copy.   41489

South Carolina (Colony) Laws, Statutes, etc., 1765.
At a General Assembly [Tax Act. Oct. 6, 1764].
Charleston, [1765]. 4 pp.
LOC copy.   10170

South Carolina (Colony) Laws, Statutes, etc., 1766.
The Tax-Act and Estimate, Passed the 22nd Day of July, 1766.
Charleston, 1766. [2], 30 pp.
LOC copy.   10498

South Carolina (Colony) Laws, Statutes, etc., 1767.
. . . At a General Assembly . . . Continued . . . to the Twenty-Eighth Day of May, 1767 [taxes].
Charleston, Timothy, 1768. 21 pp.
LOC copy.   41882

South Carolina (Colony) Laws, Statutes, etc., 1768.
An Act for Regulating and Ascertaining the Rates of Wharfage.
Charleston, Timothy, 1768. [2], 13 pp.
LOC copy.   41881

South Carolina (Colony) Provincial Congress, 1775.
Extracts from the Journals [Jan. 11-17, 1775].
Charleston, 1775. 45 pp.
LOC copy.   14466

South Carolina (Colony) Provincial Congress, 1775.
Extracts from the Journals [Nov. 1-29, 1775].
Charleston, 1776. [8], 165 pp.
LOC copy.   15090

South Carolina (Colony) Provincial Congress, 1776.
Extracts from the Journals [Feb. 1, 1776 +].
Charleston, 1776. 167 pp.
LOC copy.   15091

South Carolina (Colony) Session Laws, 1736.
Acts Passed by the General Assembly [May 29, 1736].

Charleston, 1736. 60 pp.
HSP copy.   4081

South Carolina (Colony) Session Laws, 1736.
Acts Passed by the General Assembly [Nov. 10, 1736-Apr. 11, 1738].
Charleston, Timothy, 1738. 144 pp.
LOC copy.   40175

South Carolina (Colony) Session Laws, 1737.
Acts Passed by the General Assembly [Mar. 5, 1736/7].
Charleston, 1737. pp. [2], 63-107.
HSP copy.   4199

South Carolina (Colony) Session Laws, 1740.
[Acts Passed by the General Assembly, May 1740-July 1742.
Charleston, 1742.] 139 pp.
(The only known copy lacks the tp.)
LOC copy.   40286

South Carolina (Colony) Session Laws, 1743.
Acts Passed . . . May . . . 1743.
Charleston, Timothy, 1743. 40 pp.
LOC copy.   40318

South Carolina (Colony) Session Laws, 1744.
Acts Passed [May, 1744].
Charleston, Timothy, 1744. 60 pp.
LOC copy.   40351

South Carolina (Colony) Session Laws, 1745.
Acts Passed by the General Assembly [Mar. 22, 1744/5-May 25, 1745].
Charleston, Timothy, 1745. 40 pp.
LOC copy.   40389

South Carolina (Colony) Session Laws, 1746.
Acts Passed [Jan. 3, 1745/6 +]. . . .
Charleston, Timothy, 1747. 43 pp.
LOC copy.   40440

South Carolina (Colony) Session Laws, 1747.
Acts Passed [June 13, 1747 +]. . . .
Charleston, Timothy, 1747. 60, [1] pp.
LOC copy.   40441

South Carolina (Colony) Session Laws, 1748.
Acts Passed [Feb. 17, 1746/7 +]
Charleston, Timothy, 1748. 7 pp.
LOC copy.   40480

South Carolina (Colony) Session Laws, 1748.
Acts Passed [In March, May, and June, 1748].
Charleston, Timothy, 1749. [2], 25 pp.
LOC copy.   40516

South Carolina (Colony) Session Laws, 1749.
Acts Passed [in June, 1749, and May, 1750.]
Charleston, Timothy, 1750. [2], 41, [1] pp.
LOC copy.   40570

South Carolina (Colony) Session Laws, 1751.
Acts Passed [Apr. 24, 1751 +].
Charleston, S.C., Timothy, 1751. 71, [1] pp.
HC-L copy.   40605

South Carolina (Colony) Session Laws, 1752.
Acts Passed . . . May, 1752.
Charleston, Timothy, 1753. [2], 36, [1] pp.
LOC copy.   40673

South Carolina (Colony) Session Laws, 1752.
Acts Passed . . . October, 1752.
Charleston, Timothy, 1753. 7 pp.
LOC copy.   40674

South Carolina (Colony) Session Laws, 1753.
Acts Passed [Apr. 21, 1753 +].
Charleston, Timothy, 1754. 19, [1] pp.
LOC copy.   40718

South Carolina (Colony) Session Laws, 1754.
Acts . . . at a Session [Nov. 12, 1754 Apr. 12, 1755].
Charleston, Timothy, 1755. 7 pp.
LOC copy.   40803

South Carolina (Colony) Session Laws, 1755.
Acts Passed . . . May, 1754.
Charleston, Timothy, 1755. 41, [2] pp.
LOC copy.   40802

South Carolina (Colony) Session Laws, 1755.
Acts Passed . . . in the Years 1755, 1756, 1757, and 1758.
Charleston, Timothy, 1759. 83, [1] pp.
LOC copy.   41080

South Carolina (Colony) Session Laws, 1759.
Acts . . . Passed . . . April, 1759.
Charleston, Timothy, 1759. 56 (i.e. 58), [1] pp.
LOC copy.   41081

South Carolina (Colony) Session Laws, 1760.
Acts of the General Assembly [Feb. 1760 +].
Charleston, 1760. 56, [1] pp.
NYPL copy.   8738

South Carolina (Colony) Session Laws, 1762.
Acts . . . Passed in the Year 1762.
Charleston, Timothy, 1762. [2], 49, [1] pp.
LOC copy.   41312

South Carolina (Colony) Session Laws, 1764.
Acts of the General Assembly [Jan. - Oct. 1764].
Charleston, Timothy, 1765. 34, [1] pp.
LOC copy.   10168

South Carolina (Colony) Session Laws, 1765.
Acts of the General Assembly [Jan. - Aug. 1765].
Charleston, 1765. 32 pp.
NYPL copy.   10169

South Carolona (Colony) Session Laws, 1768.
Acts of the General Assembly [Apr. 12, 1768 +].
Charleston, 1768. 84, [1] pp.
LOC copy.   11074

South Carolina (Colony) Session Laws, 1769.
Acts of the General Assembly . . . Passed in . . . 1769.
Charleston, S. C., Timothy, 1769. [3], 48, [1] pp.
LOC copy.   42006

South Carolina (Colony) Session Laws, 1769.
Acts of the General Assembly [Nov. 1769 - Apr. 1770].
Charleston, S.C., Bruce, 1770. [2], 48, [1] pp.
LOC copy.   42173

South Carolina (Colony) Session Laws, 1771.
Acts of the General Assembly . . . [January -] March, 1771.
Charleston, S. C., Bruce, 1771. [2], 17, [1] pp.
LOC copy.   42278

South Carolina. Commissioners of Forfeited Estates.
Advertisement. Will be Sold at Public Auction. . . . 10th September, 1783.
[Charleston, 1783.] Broadside.
HSP copy.   44456

South Carolina. Constitution, 1776.
South-Carolina. In a Congress [Nov. 1, 1775 +]. . . . A Constitution . . . Agreed to.
[Charleston, 1776.] 8 pp.
LOC copy.   15092

South Carolina. Constitution, 1790.
The Constitution of the State of South-Carolina.

[Charleston, 1790.] 8 pp.
JCB copy.   45995

South Carolina. Constitution, 1790.
The Constitution of the State of
South-Carolina.
Charleston, Timothy, 1790. 12 pp.
NYPL copy.   22896

South Carolina. Constitutional
Convention, 1788.
Ratification. Charleston, May 26, 1788.
[Charleston? 1788.] Broadside.
JCB copy.   45364

South Carolina. Court of General
Sessions.
... At the Courts ... of Cheraws and
Camden ... November, 1783.
[Charleston? 1783.] 4 pp.
MHS copy.   44457

South Carolina. Courts.
The Rules and Orders of the Courts of
Sessions.
New York, Swords, 1796. 48 pp.
NYHS copy.   31229

South Carolina. Courts.
[The Rules and Orders of the Courts of
Session ... July 1, 1800.
Charleston, 1800.]
("This day published," City Gazette, July
8, 1800.)   38535

South Carolina. General Assembly, 1777.
A Bill for Establishing the Constitution of
the State.
Charleston, Timothy, 1777. 23 pp.
(The incorrect date hitherto given for this
item arose from a typographical error in
the MB catalogue.)
BM copy.   20716

[South Carolina. General Assembly, 1793.
Report of a Committee ... on Report that
an Armed Force is Levying in this State.
Charleston, 1793. 11 pp.]
(Entry from Sabin; location given by
Evans an error.)   26183

South Carolina. General Assembly.
Committee of Ways and Means, 1785.
Second Report of Ways and Means.
[Charleston, 1785.] [6] pp., 16 tables.
LOC copy.   19253

South Carolina. General Assembly.
Committee of Ways and Means, 1786.
Second Report. ... February 15, 1786.
[Charleston, 1786.] [3] pp.
LOC copy.   44970

South Carolina. General Assembly. House
of Representatives, 1788.
Debates ... on the Constitution.
Charleston, Haswell, 1788. 55 pp.
LOC copy.   21470

[South Carolina. General Assembly.
House of Representatives, 1794.
Proceedings of the Legislature ...
Transmitted to the Senate, January 15,
1794.
Charleston, 1794.]
(The origin of this entry not identified.)
                                                 27721

South Carolina. General Assembly. House
of Representatives, 1799.
... November 29, 1799. Resolved, that 150
Copies of the Governor's Message ... be
Printed.
Columbia, Freneau & Paine, [1799]. [3]
pp.
LOC copy.   36337

South Carolina. General Assembly.
Senate, 1793.
... In the Senate December 21, 1793.
Resolved, That the Secretary of State be
Required not to Prepare any Grants of
Land. ...
[Charleston, 1793.] [2] pp.
LOC copy.   26184

South Carolina. Governor, 1780.
By His Excellency John Rutledge. ... A
Proclamation: Whereas the Enemy ...
[Mar. 2, 1780.]
[Charleston, 1780.] Broadside.
LOC copy.   43896

South Carolina. Governor, 1782.
... By His Excellency John Mathews. ...
A Proclamation. Whereas such Measures
only. ... [March 14, 1782.]
[Jacksonburgh, 1782.] 3 pp.
SCU copy.   44265

South Carolina. Governor, 1782.
The Speech of His Excellency John
Rutledge ... to the General Assembly ...
the 18th Day of January, 1782.
[Jacksonburgh, 1782.] 12 pp.
SCU copy.   44266

South Carolina. Governor, 1783.
By His Excellency Benjamin Guerard. ...
To [blank] Whereas in and by an
Ordinance. ... In the Year ... One
Thousand Seven Hundred and Eighty
[blank].
[Charleston, 1783?] Printed form.
AAS copy.   44458

South Carolina. Governor, 1785.
A Message from the Governor. ... 9th
February 1785.
[Charleston, 1785.] Broadside.
LOC copy.   19252

South Carolina. Laws, Statutes, etc., 1776.
An Act for the More Effectual Prevention
of the Desertion. ... Passed April 9th,
1776.
[Charleston, 1776.] 5 pp.
LOC copy.   43161

South Carolina. Laws, Statutes, etc., 1776.
An Act to Empower the Court of
Admiralty. ... Passed April 11th, 1776.
[Charleston, 1776.] 9 pp.
LOC copy.   43162

South Carolina. Laws, Statutes, etc., 1776.
An Act to Increase the Number of
Fire-Masters. ... Passed the 9th Day of
April, 1776.
[Charleston, 1776.] 4 pp.
LOC copy.   43163

South Carolina. Laws, Statutes, etc., 1776.
An Act to Prevent Sedition. ... Passed
April 11th, 1776.
[Charleston, 1776.] 7 pp.
LOC copy.   43164

South Carolina. Laws, Statutes, etc., 1776.
An Act to Punish those who Shall
Counterfeit. ... Passed the 9th Day of
April 1776.
[Charleston, 1776.] 4 pp.
LOC copy.   43165

South Carolina. Laws, Statutes, etc., 1776.
An Act to Revive and Continue. ...
Passed the 11th Day of April, 1776.
[Charleston, 1776.] 7 pp.
LOC copy.   43166

South Carolina. Laws, Statutes, etc., 1776.
An Ordinance for Altering the Time. ...
Passed April 11th, 1776.
[Charleston, 1776.] 5 pp.
LOC copy.   43167

South Carolina. Laws, Statutes, etc., 1776.
An Ordinance for Establishing an Oath of
Office. ... Passed the 6th Day of April,
1776.
[Charleston, 1776.] 4 pp.
LOC copy.   43168

South Carolina. Laws, Statutes, etc., 1776.
An Ordinance for Making Disposition of
Monies. ... Passed the 6th Day of April,
1776.
[Charleston, 1776.] 4 pp.
LOC copy.   43169

South Carolina. Laws, Statutes, etc., 1776.
An Ordinance to Ascertain the Duties. ...
Passed the 11th Day of April 1776.
[Charleston, 1776.] 4 pp.
LOC copy.   43170

South Carolina. Laws, Statutes, etc., 1776.
An Ordinance to Repeal Part of an
Ordinance. ... Passed the 9th Day of
April 1776.
[Charleston, 1776.] 4 pp.
LOC copy.   43171

South Carolina. Laws, Statutes, etc., 1777.

A Bill for Establishing the Constitution of
the State of South-Carolina.
Charleston, Timothy, 1777. 23 pp.
(Also entered as 20716, q. v.)   43373

South Carolina. Laws, Statutes, etc., 1777.
The Tax Act, Passed in January, 1777.
[Charleston, 1777.] [2], 13 pp.
LOC copy.   43374

South Carolina. Laws, Statutes, etc., 1778.
An Act for Establishing the Constitution.
Charleston, 1778. 15 pp.
LOC copy.   16073

South Carolina. Laws, Statutes, etc., 1779.
An Ordinance for Printing ... One
Million of Dollars.
[Charleston, 1779.] [2], 4 pp.
(Known only by this incomplete copy.)
LOC copy.   43705

South Carolina. Laws, Statutes, etc., 1779.
... At a General Assembly Begun and
Holden at Charlestown on Monday the
Fourth day of January [Tax].
[Charleston, 1779.] [2], 14 pp.
(The unique copy is in poor condition.)
HSP copy.   16531

South Carolina. Laws, Statutes, etc., 1782.
... An Act for Disposing of Certain
Estates.
[Halifax? 1782?] 8 pp.
JCB copy.   44267

South Carolina. Laws, Statutes, etc., 1782.
Extracts from an Act to Procure Recruits.
... February 26, 1782.
Jacksonburgh, Rogers, [1782]. 3 pp.
LOC copy.   44268

South Carolina. Laws, Statutes, etc., 1783.
An Act for Levying and Collecting
Certain Duties.
n.p., [1783]. 6 pp.
LOC copy.   44459

South Carolina. Laws, Statutes, etc., 1785.
An Act for Establishing County Courts.
... Mar. 17, 1785.
Charleston, Timothy, [1785]. [2], 35 pp.
NYPL copy.   44795

[South Carolina. Laws, Statutes, etc.,
1786.
An Act to Direct Executors.
Charleston, Timothy, 1786.]
(The origin of this entry has not been
found.)   19997

[South Carolina. Laws, Statutes, etc.,
1787.
The Installment Law.
Charleston, Childs, Haswell & M'Iver,
1787.]
(Entry from an adv.)   20717

South Carolina. Laws, Statutes, etc., 1790.
... An Ordinance, Prescribing ... the ...
Manner of Holding Elections.
[Charleston, 1790.] Broadside.
NYPL copy.   22898

South Carolina. Laws, Statutes, etc., 1790.
The Public Laws of the State of
South-Carolina.
Philadelphia, Aitken, 1790. lxxvii, [1],
504, 43, [59] pp.
AAS copy.   22897

South Carolina. Laws, Statutes, etc., 1794.
Laws and Regulations for the Militia.
Charleston, Timothy & Mason, 1794. 188,
[5] pp., 9 plates.
LOC copy.   27720

South Carolina. Laws, Statutes, etc., 1800.
... An Act to Prevent Negro Slaves ...
from being Brought into ... this State.
Charleston, M'Iver, [1800]. Broadside.
LOC copy.   38536

South Carolina. Laws, Statutes, etc., 1800.
At a General Assembly Begun ... the
Twenty-Fourth Day of November.
Charleston, M'Iver, [1800]. Broadside.
(Also entered as 38536, q. v.)   38534

South Carolina. Session Laws, 1776.
Acts ... Passed in September and
October, 1776.

Charleston, Timothy, [1776]. [2], 20, [1] pp.
LOC copy.   43172

South Carolina. Session Laws, 1777.
Acts of the General Assembly. . . . Passed the 22d and 23rd of August, 1777.
[Charleston, Timothy, 1777.] [2], 11, 4 pp.
LOC copy.   43375

South Carolina. Session Laws, 1778.
Acts and Ordinances . . . Passed in . . . 1778.
[Charleston, 1778.] [2], 4, 4, 12, 5, 3, 7, 1, 4, 4, 8, 2, 2, 7, 1, 4 pp.
LOC copy.   43553

South Carolina. Session Laws, 1779.
. . . At the General Assembly [Jan. 4 Feb. 13, 1779].
[Charleston, 1779.] 4 pp.
(No copy located.)   43706

South Carolina. Session Laws, 1782.
Acts Passed at a General Assembly [Jan. 8 - Feb. 26, 1782].
[Philadelphia], Dunlap, [1782]. 46 pp.
JCB copy.   17725

South Carolina. Session Laws, 1782.
Jacksonburgh March 1, 1782. . . .
Adjourned . . . Having Passed the Following . . . Laws . . .
Jacksonburgh, Rogers, 1782. 4 pp.
SCU copy.   44269

South Carolina. Session Laws. 1782.
Laws Enacted by the General Assembly. [Jan. 8 - Feb. 26, 1782.]
[Philadelphia? 1782.] 29 pp.
NYPL copy.   17724

South Carolina. Session Laws, 1783.
Acts and Ordinances of the General Assembly. [Jan. 6 - Nov. 17, 1783].
[Charleston, 1783.] [2], 74 pp., irreg.
NYPL copy.   18190

South Carolina. Session Laws, 1784.
Acts, Ordinances and Resolves . . . Passed in . . . 1784.
Charleston, Miller, 1784. 102, [2] pp., irreg.
JCB copy.   18789

South Carolina, Session Laws, 1785.
An Act to Establish a Medium [Sept. 20-Oct. 12, 1785].
[Charleston, 1785.] 14, [1], pp.
NYPL copy.   19251

South Carolina. Session Laws, 1785.
Acts, Ordinances, and Resolves . . . March, 1785.
Charleston, Timothy, 1785. [4], 35, 58, 16, 12, 12, 7, [2] pp.
JCB copy.   19250

South Carolina. Session Laws, 1786.
Acts, Ordinances, and Resolve . . . Passed in March, 1786.
Charleston, Bowen & Markland, 1786. [2], 71, [3] pp.
JCB copy.   19998

South Carolina. Session Laws, 1787.
Acts, Ordinances, and Resolves . . . Passed in March, 1787.
Charleston, Timothy, 1787. [2], 77, [2] pp.
LOC copy.   20715

South Carolina. Session Laws, 1788.
Acts and Ordinances . . . Passed in February, 1788.
Charleston, Timothy, 1788. [2], 34 pp.
NYPL copy.   21468

South Carolina. Session Laws, 1788.
Acts and Ordinances . . . Passed in October and November, 1788.
Charleston, Timothy, 1789. [2], 7 pp.
NYPL copy.   22152

South Carolina. Session Laws, 1789.
Acts, Ordinances, and Resolves . . . Passed in March, 1789.
Charleston, Timothy, [1789]. 62 pp.
NYPL copy.   22153

South Carolina. Session Laws, 1790.

Acts and Ordinances . . . Passed February 20th, 1790.
Charleston, Timothy, 1790. [2], 18 pp.
JCB copy.   22895

South Carolina. Session Laws, 1791.
Acts and Resolutions . . . Passed in February, 1791.
Charleston, Bowen, 1791. 98, [4] pp.
LOC copy.   23781

South Carolina. Session Laws, 1791.
Acts and Resolutions . . . Passed in December, 1791.
Charleston, Bowen, 1792. 60, [3] pp.
LOC copy.   24804

South Carolina. Session Laws, 1792.
Acts and Resolutions . . . December, 1792.
Charleston, 1793. 86 pp.
LOC copy.   26182

South Carolina. Session Laws, 1793.
Acts and Resolutions of the General Assembly . . . Passed in December, 1793.
Charleston, Timothy & Mason, 1794. [2], 44 pp.
(No copy located has the pagination given by Evans.)
LOC copy.   27718

South Carolina. Session Laws, 1794.
Acts and Resolutions of the General Assembly . . . Passed in April, 1794.
Charleston, Timothy & Mason, 1794. [2], 31 pp.
LOC copy.   27719

South Carolina. Session Laws, 1794.
Acts and Resolutions of the General Assembly. . . . Passed in December, MDCCXCIV.
Charleston, Young & Faust, 1795. 80, [3] pp.
HC copy.   34573

[South Carolina. Session Laws, 1794.
Acts and Resolutions of the General Assembly. . . . Passed in December, 1794.
Columbia, 1795. 80, [3] pp.]
(A duplicate of 29544, q. v.)   34574

South Carolina. Session Laws, 1795.
Acts and Resolutions of the General Assembly . . . from December 1794 [1795] to December, 1797.
Charleston, Faust, [1798]. 155, [1], 172, [10] pp.
MSL copy.   34575

South Carolina. Session Laws, 1795.
Acts and Resolutions of the General Assembly. . . . Passed in December, MDCCXCIV.
Columbia, Young & Faust, 1795. 80, [3] pp.
LOC copy.   29544

South Carolina. Session Laws, 1795.
Acts and Resolutions. . . . Passed in Nov. and Dec. 1795.
Charleston, Young & Faust, 1796. 59, [3]; 88, [2] pp.
MHS copy.   31219

South Carolina. Session Laws, 1796.
Acts and Resolutions of the General Assembly. . . . Passed in December, 1796.
Charleston, Young & Faust, 1797. pp. [59]-102, [2], [89]-132, [2] pp.
LOC copy.   32856

South Carolina. Session Laws, 1797.
Acts and Resolutions of the General Assembly. . . . Passed in December, 1797.
Charleston, Young for Faust, 1798. pp. [101]-155, [2]; [133]-172, [3].
LOC copy.   34576

South Carolina. Session Laws, 1798.
Acts and Resolutions. . . . Passed in December, 1798.
Charleston, Young & Faust, 1799. 44, [2], 46, [1] pp.
NYBA copy.   36336

South Carolina. Session Laws, 1798.
Acts and Resolutions of the General Assembly. . . . Passed in December, 1798.
The Second Edition.
Charleston, Freneau & Paine, 1800. pp. [2], 52-83.
LOC copy.   38532

South Carolina. Session Laws, 1798.
Acts and Resolutions of the General Assembly. . . . Passed in December, 1798.
The Second Edition.
Charleston, Freneau & Paine, 1800. pp. [1]-50, [2], 52-83, [1].
HC-L copy.   38532

South Carolina. Session Laws, 1799.
Acts and Resolutions of the General Assembly. . . . Passed in December, 1799.
Charleston, Freneau & Paine, 1800. 90 pp.
HC copy.   38533

South Carolina.
Charles-town, November 10th, 1774.
Gentlemen, The Delegates, who were sent by this Province to the . . . Congress at Philadelphia, being Returned, we take the Earliest Opportunity of Transmitting to you. . . .
[Charleston, 1774.] [2], 8 pp.
(Not available for filming.)
PPRF copy.   42703

[South Carolina Almanack for 1733.
Charleston, Whitmarsh.]
(McMurtrie, S. C. Imprints, 8.)   40032

[South-Carolina Almanack for 1738.
Charleston, Timothy.]
(Adv. S. C. Gazette, Oct. 29, 1737.)   40129

South-Carolina. An Account of Sundry Goods Imported, and . . . Exported . . . from the First of November 1738, to the First of November 1739.
Charleston, 1739. Broadside.
JCB copy.   4426

The South-Carolina & Georgia Almanac, for . . . 1789 [by John Tobler].
Charleston, Markland & M'Iver. [26] pp.
LOC copy.   21504

The South Carolina and Georgia Almanac, for . . . 1794 [by William Waring, pseud.].
Charleston, Markland & M'Iver. [32] pp.
(The only copy located is imperfect.)
AAS copy.   26422

The South-Carolina and Georgia Almanac, for . . . 1795 [by William Waring, pseud.].
Charleston, Markland & M'Iver. [36] pp.
MHS copy.   28025

The South-Carolina and Georgia Almanac, for . . . 1796.
Charleston, Markland & M'Iver. [36] pp.
AAS copy.   29545

The South-Carolina and Georgia Almanac, for . . . 1797.
Charleston, M'Iver. [36] pp.
SCHS copy.   31221

The South-Carolina and Georgia Almanac, for . . . 1798.
Charleston, Elliott. [41] pp.
(The only copy located is apparently incomplete.)
LOC copy.   32857

The South-Carolina & Georgia Almanac, for . . . 1799.
Charleston, Freneau & Paine. [48] pp.
NYHS copy.   34578

The South-Carolina & Georgia Almanac, for . . . 1799. . . . Second Edition.
Charleston, Freneau & Paine. [46] pp.
CLS copy.   36339

The South-Carolina & Georgia Almanac, for . . 1800.
Charleston, Freneau & Paine. [40] pp.
AAS copy.   36340

The South-Carolina & Georgia Almanac, for . . . 1800. . . . Second Edition.
Charleston, Freneau & Paine, [40] pp.
LOC copy.   36341

South Carolina Artillery. Charleston Ancient Battalion of Artillery. Rules of the. . . .
Charleston, Harrison, [1799]. 12 pp.
NYHS copy.   35293

The South-Carolina Justice of Peace [by

John Fauchereaud Grimké, 1752-1819].
Philadelphia, Aitken, 1778. viii, 510, [2]
pp.
(The AAS has also an interleaved three
vol. ed. with a title page for each volume.)
AAS copy.   21472

The South Carolina Justice of Peace [by
John Faucheraud Grimké, 1752-1819].
Philadelphia, Aitken, 1796. viii, 641, [2]
pp.
LOC copy.   30519

South Carolina Society, Charleston, S. C.
The Constitutional and Additional Rules.
... Fifth Edition.
Charleston, Timothy, 1770. iv, 4, 65 pp.
JCB copy.   42174

The South Carolina Society, Charleston,
S.C.
Information, to those who are Disposed to
Migrate to South-Carolina. ... March 26,
1795.
Charleston, 1795. Broadside.
AAS copy.   28411

The South Carolina Society, Charleston,
S.C.
Rules of the Incorporated South-Carolina
Society. ... Sixth Edition.
Charleston, S.C., Markland & M'Iver,
1795. 62 pp.
HC copy.   28410

South Carolina Society for Promoting and
Improving Agriculture.
Address and Rules of the. ...
Charleston, Timothy, 1785. 12 pp.
BA copy.   19254

South Carolina Society for Promoting and
Improving Agriculture.
Address and Rules ... and other Rural
Concerns.
Charleston, Freneau & Paine, 1798. 8 pp.
U. S. Dept. Agriculture copy.   34577

South Carolina Society for Promoting and
Improving Agriculture.
Letters and Observations on Agriculture.
[Charleston], Bowen, 1788. 32 pp.
BA copy.   21471

South-Carolina Yazoo Company.
An Extract from the Proceedings of the.
...
Charleston, Timothy, 1791. [10], 44, [2],
11, [2], 27, 13, [1] pp.
BA copy.   23783

South End Forever. North End Forever.
Extraordinary Verses on Pope-Night.
Sold by the Printers Boys in Boston,
[1768]. Broadside.
LOC copy.   41883

[Southeby, William, c.1650-c.1720.
(See Sabin 88264.)
An Anti Slavery Tract.
Philadelphia, 1715.]
(Hildeburn 135.)   1781

[Southeby, William, c.1650 - c.1720.
(See Sabin 88264.)
An Anti-Slavery Tract.
Philadelphia, 1717.]
(Hildeburn 144.)   1929

[Southeby, William, c.1650-c.1720.
A Testimony against Prophaneness in
Philadelphia.
Philadelphia, 1700.]
(See Hildeburn, I, 36.)   953

Southern Congress, Augusta, Georgia,
1763.
Journal of the Congress of the Four
Southern Governors ... with the Five
Nations ... at Augusta, 1763.
Charleston, 1764. [2], 45 pp.
NYPL copy.   9706

The Southern Stages Start from the
Baltimore Office. ...
Philadelphia, Oswald, [179?]. Broadside.
LOC copy.   45795

[The Southern States Ephemeris; or, the
North and South-Carolina and Georgia
Almanack for ... 1787.
Charleston, Bowen & Markland.]

("Just published," Columbia Herald, Nov.
6, 1786.)   20001

The Southern States Ephemeris: or, the
North and South-Carolina, and Georgia
Almanac, for ... 1788.
Charleston, Bowen, Vandle & Andrews.
[36] pp.
College of Charleston copy.   20720

[Southerne, Thomas, 1660-1746.
Oroonoko, or the Royal Slave.
Boston, Spotswood, 1794.]
(Imprint assumed by Evans from adv.
"May be had" in Columbian Centinel,
Aug. 27, 1794.)   27727

Southey, Robert, 1774-1843.
Joan of Arc, an Epic Poem.
Boston, Manning & Loring for Nancrede,
1798. 254 pp.
AAS copy.   34583

Southey, Robert, 1774-1843.
Joan of Arc, an Epic Poem.
Boston, Manning & Loring for Nancrede,
1798. 264 pp.
LCP copy.   34584

Southey, Robert, 1774-1843.
Joan of Arc, an Epic Poem.
Boston, Manning & Loring for Nancrede,
1798. 270 pp.
(Differs from 34583 only in the back
matter.)
AAS copy.   34585

[Southey, Robert, 1774-1843.
Joan of Arc, an Epic Poem.
Boston, Manning & Loring for Nancrede,
1798. 240 pp.]
(A ghost of 34585.)   34586

Southey, Robert, 1774-1843.
Poems.
Boston, Manning & Loring for Nancrede,
1799. 132 pp.
AAS copy.   36345

Southey, Robert, 1774-1843.
The Triumph of Woman, a Poem.
Philadelphia, Ormrod, 1798. 19 pp.
LCP copy.   48619

Southwark, Pa. Theater.
For the Benefit of Miss Storer [Mar. 30,
1770].
[Philadelphia, 1770.] Broadside.
HSP copy.   11867

Southwick, Remington, b. 1749.
The Columbian Calendar; or Almanac,
for ... 1801.
Dedham, [Mass.], Mann. [24] pp.
HSP copy.   38539

[Southwick, Solomon], 1731-1797.
Newport, April 17, 1783. Proposals for
Printing ... An Inquiry Concerning the
future Punishment.
[Newport, Southwick, 1783.] Broadside.
NYHS copy.   44460

The Sovereign Decrees of God [by Isaac
Backus, 1724-1806].
Boston, Kneeland for Freeman, 1773. 16
pp.
JCB copy.   12656

Sower, Christopher, 1693-1758.
(D. A. B.)
Ein Abgenöthigter Bericht.
Germantown, 1739.
(See Seidensticker, p. 12. Bought by
"Bru" at Pennypacker sale.)   4420

[Sower, Christopher], 1693-1758.
(D. A. B.)
Bekanntmachung.
[Germantown, 1741.] 2 pp.
HSP copy.   4796

[Sower, Christopher], 1693-1758.
Verschiedene Christliche Wahreiten.
Germantown, 1748. 32 pp.
HSP copy.   6233

[Sower, Christopher], 1693-1758.
Eine zu Dieser Zeit Höchst Nöthige
Warnung.
[Germantown, 1755]. [2] pp.
HSP copy.   7564

Sower, Christopher, 1721-1784.
Ein Einfältiges Reim-Gedichte.
[n. p., n. d., 1781.] 4 pp.
HSP copy.   17367

[Sower, Christopher], 1721-1784.
Eine Nuetzliche Anweisung.
Germantown, 1762. [2], 287, [5] pp.
AAS copy.   9264

[Sower, Christopher], 1721-1784.
Eine Nuetzliche Anweisung. ... Dritte
Auflage.
Germantown, 1772. [8], 262 pp.
AAS copy.   12552

[Sower, Christopher], 1721-1784.
Eine Nützliche Anweisung. ... Vierte
und Vermehrte Auflage.
Germantown, Leibert, 1792. [4], 282 pp.
AAS copy.   24771

Sower, Christopher, 1721-1784.
Wertheste Landes-Leute.
[Germantown, 1765.] [2] pp.
HSP copy.   10162

[Sower, Christopher], 1721-1784.
(D. A. B.)
Eine zu Dieser Zeit Höchstnöthige
Warnung.
[Germantown, 1764.] [2] pp.
HSP copy.   9828

[Sower, Christopher], 1754-1799.
Zuschrift an die Teutschen in
Pennsylvanien.
[New York, 1780.] 16 pp.
PRO copy.   43897

Sower, Samuel, 1767-1820.
Printing and Binding Done.
[Baltimore, 1797?] Broadside.
NYPL copy.   48255

Spain. Consejo de las Indias.
Traduction d'une Lettre de D. Joseph de
Galves. ... 6 Aoust 1778.
[New Orleans, 1778.] Broadside.
NYPL ph. copy.   43554

Spain. Legacion. United States.
A Letter to Timothy Pickering. ... July
11, 1797.
[Philadelphia, 1797.] 15 pp.
AAS copy.   32863

Spain. Sovereigns, etc., 1778.
Traduction d'une Lettre du Roi.
[New Orleans], Boudousquié, [1778].
[2] pp.
JCB copy.   43555

Spain. Sovereigns, etc., 1782.
Real Cedula, Concediendo Nuevas
Gracias para Formento del Comercio de
la Luisiana. 1782.
[New Orleans, 1782.] 15 pp.
Bancroft Library copy.   44270

Spalding, John, 1765?-1795.
Some Account of. ...
Philadelphia, Johnsons, 1799. 70 pp.
AAS copy.   36346

Spalding, Joshua, 1760-1825.
The Prayer of a True Penitent.
Salem, Dabney & Cushing, 1787. 24 pp.
HC copy.   20721

Spalding, Joshua, 1760-1825.
Sentiments Concerning the Coming ... of
Christ.
Salem, Cushing, 1796. [8], 273 pp.
AAS copy.   31225

Spalding, Josiah, 1751-1823.
The Duty and Importance of Calling.
Northampton, Mass., Butler, 1800. 40 pp.
AAS copy.   38541

Spalding, Josiah, 1751-1823.
A Sermon, on the Nature and Criminality.

Worcester, [1782]. 40 pp.
AAS copy.   18194

Spalding, Joshua, 1760-1825.
A Sermon, Preached at the Tabernacle.
Salem, [Mass.], Cushing, [1800]. 20 pp.
AAS copy.   38540

Spalding, Lyman, 1775-1821.

An Inaugural Dissertation.
Walpole, N. H., Carlisle, 1797. 30 pp.
AAS copy.   32864

Spalding, Lyman, 1775-1821.
A New Nomenclature of Chemistry.
Hanover, N. H., Davis, 1799. [7] pp.
HC copy.   36347

[Spangenberg, August Gottlieb, bp.,
1704-1792.
An Account of the Manner in which the
. . . United Brethren, Preach.
Philadelphia, Dobson, 1789.]
(Entry apparently from Dobson's adv. for
London 1788 ed.)   22155

Spangenberg, August Gottlieb, bp.,
1704-1792.
The Preaching of the Cross.
Philadelphia, Cist, 1793. [4], 54 pp.
AAS copy.   26196

Sparhawk, Ebenezer, 1738-1805.
A Discourse, Delivered January 18,
MDCCXCIV.
Worcester, Worcester, 1795. 22 pp.
AAS copy.   29553

Sparhawk, John.
Essentia Euphragiae.
[Philadelphia? 1770?] Broadside.
AAS copy.   42044

Sparhawk, John, 1730-1803.
A Catalogue of Books, &c. to be Sold
by. . . .
[Philadelphia, 1773?] 44 pp.
BrU copy.   42507

Sparhawk, John, 1730-1803.
A Table of the Several Chapters . . . of . . .
Dr. Tissot's
[Philadelphia, 1771.] Broadside.
AAS copy.   42279

Sparhawk, Thomas Stearns, 1770-1807.
An Oration, Delivered at Buckston.
Boston, Manning & Loring, 1798. 20 pp.
AAS copy.   34587

Spaulding, Mary, b. 1769.
A Remarkable Narrative of. . . .
Boston, Manning & Loring, 1795. 23 pp.
AAS copy.   29554

Spaulding, Mary, b. 1769.
A Remarkable Narrative of. . . .
Boston, Printed and Sold by the
Booksellers, 1795. 24 pp.
AAS copy.   29555

Specimen of a Surprizing Performance
Shortly to be Sent to the Press.
[Boston? 1762?] 8 pp.
AAS copy.   41313

[A Specimen of Divine Truths. A
Catechism.
New York, Holt for Low, 1765.]
("Just published, and to be sold by Peter
Low," N.Y. Gazette or Weekly Post-Boy,
Nov. 21, 1765.)   10174

A Specimen of the Confession of Faith.
Litchfield, [Ct.], 1800. 7 pp.
(Also entered as 37225, q. v.)   38542

A Specimen of the Harmony [by Joseph
Seccombe, 1706-1760].
Boston, Kneeland & Green, 1743. [4], iv,
29 pp.
AAS copy.   5286

A Specimen of the Unrelenting Cruelty of
Papists in France.
Boston, Draper, 1756. 20 pp.
LOC copy.   7795

Spectacle Nouveaux, par Messrs.
L'Egalité.
[Philadelphia, 1795.] Broadside.
LOC copy.   29162

A Speech, Deliver'd by an Indian Chief,
in Reply to a Sermon . . . by a Swedish
Missionary . . . at . . . Canastogoe.
[Philadelphia, 1715.] Broadside.
HSP copy.   39635a

The Speech Delivered from the Bench . . .
the 11 day of September, 1727 [by Isaac
Norris, 1671-1735].

[Philadelphia, 1727.] 3, [1] pp.
JCB copy.   2937

A Speech Intended to have been Spoken.
. . . Sixth Edition [by Jonathan Shipley,
bp., 1714-1788].
Boston, Edes & Gill, 1774. 24 pp.
AAS copy.   13616

A Speech Intended to have been Spoken.
. . . Fifth Edition [by Jonathan Shipley,
bp., 1714-1788].
Hartford, 1774. 17 pp.
CHS copy.   13617

A Speech Intended to have been Spoken.
. . . Third Edition [by Jonathan Shipley,
bp., 1714-1788].
Philadelphia, Bradfords, 1774. vi, 29 pp.
AAS copy.   13620

The Speech of a General Officer in the
House of Commons, February 20th, 1775
[by Sir John Burgoyne, 1722-1792].
[Boston? 1775?] 8 pp.
JCB copy.   42784

Speech of a Member of the General
Assembly [by Crean Brush, 1725?-1778].
New York, 1775. 12 pp.
AAS copy.   13848

[The Speech of a Creek-Indians [by
William Smith, 1727-1803].
Boston, 1754.]
(No trace could be found of an American
printing. See Sabin 84673.)   7321

The Speech of Death to Levi Ames. Who
was Executed . . . October 21, 1773.
[Boston, 1773.] Broadside.
MHS copy.   42508

The Speech of the Statue.
[New York, 1770.] Broadside.
LCP copy.   11868

The Speech of William Tr--n, Esq; who
was Executed on . . . the 18th of March,
1776.
[New York, 1776.] Broadside.
NYPL copy.   15095

A Speech said to have been Delivered
some time before the Close of the Last
Sessions [by Archibald Kennedy,
1685-1763].
[New York], 1755. 52 pp.
JCB copy.   7573

The Speeches in the Last Session of the
Present Parliament.
New York, Rivington, 1775. 72 pp.
BA copy.   14092

The Speeches of the Right Honourable
Mr. Pitt, General Conway. . . . [Stamp
Act. Jan. 14, 1766].
[Philadelphia, 1766.] [2] pp.
NYHS copy.   10463

[A Spelling Book.
Cambridge, 1643.]
(No copy known. See G. P. Winship,
Cambridge Press, p. 52.)   13

The Spelling-Book, and Child's Plaything.
New London, Green, 1769. 118 pp.
(The only known copy is imperfect.)
AAS copy.   42007

Spencer, Arthur.
To the Publick. . . . Surgeon's Mate. . . .
21st August, 1773.
[Boston, 1773.] Broadside.
AAS copy.   42509

[Spencer, Thomas], 1752-1840.
The New Vade Mecum; or, Young Clerk's
Magazine.
Lansingburgh, Tiffany for Spencer, 1794.
346 pp.
AAS copy.   27728

The Spendthrift Clapt Into Limbo.
[Philadelphia], 1800. 8 pp.
(Not located, 1968.)   49149

Ein Spiegel der Eheleute Nebst Schönen
Erinnerungen.
[Germantown], 1758. [2], 32 pp.
HSP copy.   8262

Ein Spiegel der Tauffe [by Henry Funck,
1760].
[Germantown], 1744. 94 pp.
HSP copy.   5400

Spiegel der Vollkommenheit.
Philadelphia, 1729. [2], 252 pp.
(Omitted as European printing.)
PSL copy.   39931

Spiegel für alle Menschen.
Philadelphia, Schweitzer, 1799. 80 pp.
(Also entered as 35202, q. v.)   36349

Spierin, George Heartwell, 1787-1804.
A Sermon, Delivered at Newburgh.
Goshen, Mandeville & Westcott, 1790.
[4], 11, [1] pp.
NYHS copy.   22900

[Spierin, George Heartwell], 1787-1804.
A Song Composed for the Fraternity of
Steuben Lodge, No. 18. . . . January 18,
1791.
[Goshen, 1791.] Broadside.
NYHS copy.   23784

Spiess, Christian Heinrich, 1755-1799.
The Mountain Cottager.
Philadelphia, Woodward for Hyndman,
1800. 228 pp.
AAS copy.   38544

Spindleshanks, Peter, pseud.
The Battle of the Two Taylors.
n. p., 1799. 12 pp.
AAS copy.   36350

The Spirit of Despotism [by Vicesimus
Knox, 1752-1821].
Philadelphia, Lang & Ustick, for Carey,
1795. x, 342 pp.
AAS copy.   28936

The Spirit of Despotism [by Vicesimus
Knox, 1752-1821].
Morristown, N. J., Mann, 1799. [10], 319
pp.
AAS copy.   35691

The Spirit of Liberty: or, Junius's Loyal
Address [by John Allen, fl. 1764.]
Boston, 1772.
(Adv. Boston Gazette, June 1, 1772.)
                             12501

The Spirit of Life Entring into the
Spiritually Dead [by Cotton Mather,
1663-1728].
Boston, 1707. 40 pp.
AAS copy.   1316

The Spirit of the Martyrs Revived [by
Ellis Hookes].
[New London?], 1750. [8], 283 pp.
HEH copy.   40543

Spiritual Food: or, Truth Displayed.
Philadelphia, Poulson, 1792. 72 pp.
AAS copy.   24807

[A Spiritual Journey Temporaliz'd.
New York, 1741.]
(Adv. N. Y. Weekly Journal, Dec. 14,
1741.)   4814

Spiritual Songs. . . . Sixteenth Edition [by
John Mason, 1646-1696].
Boston, Green, Bushell & Allen for
Henchman, 1743. [8], 151, [2] pp.
NYPL copy.   5235

Spiritual Songs. . . . Seventeenth Edition
[by John Mason, 1646-1694].
Boston, Z. Fowle, 1765. [8], 151 pp.
AAS copy.   41560

Spiritual Songs [by John Mason,
1646-1694.] [Seventeenth Edition.
New York, Gaine, 1771. [2], 152 pp.]
(The unique and badly defective copy
reproduced may be 11326.)
AAS copy.   12114

Spiritual Songs: or Songs of Praise, with
Penitential Cries. . . . Twentieth Edition
[by John Mason, 1646-1694].
Boston, Fleets, 1787. [4], 124 pp.
AAS copy.   20495

Spiritual Songs: or, Songs of Praise [by
John Mason, 1646-1694].

New York, Durell, [1790]. 199 pp.
AAS copy.   22649

[Spofford, Reginald], 1770-1827.
Ellen, the Richmond Primrose Girl.
Philadelphia and New York, B. Carr, etc.,
[1797?]. 2 pp.
AAS copy.   48256

[Spofford, Reginald], 1770-1827.
Ellen the Richmond Primrose Girl.
Boston, Von Hagen, [1798?]. [2] pp.
LOC copy.   48620

[Spofford, Reginald], 1770-1827.
Hark the Goddess Diana.
New York, Hewitt, etc., [1797?]. 3 pp.
AAS copy.   48257

The Spoiled Child. A Farce [by Prince
Hoare, 1755-1834].
Boston, Hall, 1796. 28 pp.
LOC copy.   30568

The Spoil'd Child. A Farce [by Prince
Hoare, 1755-1834].
Boston, Hall for Blake, 1796. 28, [3] pp.
AAS copy.   30569

Spooner, John Jones, 1757?-1799.
A Discourse . . . July 4th, 1794.
Petersburg, Va., Prentis, 1795. 20 pp.
AAS copy.   29556

Spooner, Judah Padock and Alden,
Publishers.
[Proposals for printing a newspaper.
Dresden, 1779.]
(McCorison 16; no copy known.)   43707

[Spooner's Almanac and Vermont
Register for 1797.
Fairhaven, Spooner, 1796.]
(McCorison 372; no copy known.)   47922

[Spooner's sheet almanac and register, for
1797.
Fairhaven, Spooner, 1796.]
(McCorison 373; no copy known.)   47923

Spooner's Vermont and Newyork
Almanack, for . . . 1800..
Bennington: Spooner. [24] pp.
YC copy.   48964

The Sportsman's Companion; or, an
Essay on Shooting.
New York, Robertsons, Mills & Hicks,
1783. 89, [2] pp.
(Evans assumed the imprint of this 1st ed.
from that of the 2nd ed.)
YC copy.   23785

The Sportsman's Companion or an Essay
on Shooting. . . . Second Edition.
Burlington, Neale, 1791. 89, [3] pp.
AAS copy.   23786

[The Sportsman's Companion or an Essay
on Shooting. . . . Third Edition.
Philadelphia, [1792].
(The unique copy reported cannot now be
located.)   24809

Spotswood, William, 1753?-1805.
Boston, 7th November, 1799. Proposals
for Publishing by Subscription . . .
Memoirs and Travels of . . . Count
Benjowsky.
[Boston, 1799.] Broadside.
AAS copy.   36170

Spotswood, William, 1753?-1805.
Boston, 20th April, 1795. . . . Prospectus
of a Belles Lettres Paper.
[Boston, 1795.] Broadside.
AAS copy.   47606

Spotswood, William, 1753?-1805.
William Spotswood's Catalogue of Books,
&c.
Boston, 1795. 68 pp.
MHS copy.   29558

Spotsylvania County, Va. Citizens.
An Address and Instructions . . . to James
Madison.
[Fredericksburg, 1795.] Broadside.
LOC copy.   29559

Sprigg, Richard.
The Theological Works of Richard Sprigg.

New York, Gaine, 1754. [6], 88 pp.
NYHS copy.   7322

Spring, Samuel, 1746-1819.
Christian Knowledge.
Newburyport, 1785. 46 pp.
AAS copy.   19257

Spring, Samuel, 1746-1819.
A Discourse, Delivered at the North
Church . . . November 7th, 1793.
Newburyport, Mycall, 1794. 40 pp.
AAS copy.   27730

Spring, Samuel, 1746-1819.
The Exemplary Pastor.
Windsor, Spooner, 1791. 39 pp.
AAS copy.   23787

[Spring, Samuel], 1746-1819.
A Friendly Dialogue, in Three Parts,
between Philalethes & Toletus.
Newburyport, 1784. 160, 32 pp.
AAS copy.   18792

Spring, Samuel, 1746-1819.
God the Author of Human Greatness.
Newburyport, Blunt, [1800]. 28 pp.
AAS copy.   38547

Spring, Samuel, 1746-1819.
Moral Disquisitions.
Newburyport, 1789. 252 pp.
AAS copy.   22156

Spring, Samuel, 1746-1819.
The Nature and Importance.
Newburyport, 1784. 64 pp.
AAS copy.   18793

Spring, Samuel, 1746-1819.
A Sermon Delivered at the North
Congregational Church.
Newburyport, 1778. 32 pp.
AAS copy.   16076

[Spring, Samuel, 1746-1819.
A Sermon on Family Prayer.
Newburyport, 1780.]
(Entry from Sprague, II, 87.)   16995

[Spring, Samuel, 1746-1819.
A Sermon on the Importance of Sinners.
Newburyport, 1780.]
(This is the half-title of 16997.)   16996

Spring, Samuel, 1746-1819.
A Sermon, Preached at the Ordination of
. . . Daniel Merril.
Newburyport, Blunt, 1794. 50 pp.
AAS copy.   27731

Spring, Samuel, 1746-1819.
A Sermon Preached at the Ordination of
. . . Pearson Thurston.
Dover, Ladd, 1792. 25 pp.
AAS copy.   24810

Spring, Samuel, 1746-1819.
The Substance of a Discourse Delivered at
Wesford.
Newburyport, 1780. 47, [1] pp.
AAS copy.   16997

Spring, Samuel, 1746-1819.
A Thanksgiving Sermon, Preached
November 29, 1798.
Newburyport, 1798. 26 pp.
AAS copy.   34590

Spring, Samuel, 1746-1819.
Three Sermons to Little Children.
Boston, Coverly, 1783. 65, [7] pp.
LOC copy.   18195

Spring, Samuel, 1746-1819.
Three Sermons to Little Children.
Newburyport, Mycall, 1783. 72, [11] pp.
(The only copy located is imperfect.)
AAS copy.   44461

Spring, Samuel, 1746-1819.
Three Sermons to Little Children.
New York, Durell, 1790. 95 pp.
AAS copy.   22901

Springfield, Mass. Library Company.
Catalogue of Books, belonging to the. . . .
[Springfield, Mass., Stebbins, 1796.] 7 pp.
Ct. Valley Hist. Soc. copy.   31227

Sprint, John.
The Bride-Womans Counseller.

Boston, Allen for Phillips, 1709. [4], 20
pp.
MHS copy.   39497

Sproat, James, 1722-1793.
(Dexter, I, 690-692.)
A Discourse, Occasioned by the Death of
. . . Whitefield.
Philadelphia, Bradfords, 1771. [2], 25 pp.
AAS copy.   12234

Spunkey, Simon, pseud.
A Poem, in two Cantos. . . . [by Samuel
Chipman, 1763-1839].
Vergennes, Vt., Chipman, 1799.]
(Entry from copyright and advs.)   35479

The Spunkiad: or Heroism Improved [by
John Woodworth?, 1768-1858].
Newburgh, N. Y., Denniston, 1798. 23 pp.
AAS copy.   35052

Spurrier, John.
The Practical Farmer.
Wilmington, Brynberg & Andrews, 1793.
pp. [2], [i]-x, [iii]-x, [1]-360, [i]-xv.
AAS copy.   26198

The Squabble; a Pastoral Eclogue. By
Agricola. With a Curious . . .
Frontispiece.
Philadelphia, Steuart, [1764]. 8 pp.
NYPL copy.   9565

The Squabble, a Pastoral Eclogue. By
Agricola. The Second Edition.
[Philadelphia], 1764. 8 pp.
HSP copy.   9564

Squibb, Robert.
The Gardener's Calendar.
Charleston, Wright, 1787. [8], 183,
[8] pp.
Duke Univ. copy.   20722

[Squibb, Robert.
The Gardener's Calender Improved.
Augusta, Ga., Smith, 1798.]
(Taken by Evans from proposals issued in
Southern Centinel, May 3, 1798.)   34592

Squire, Francis, 1682-1750.
An Answer to . . . the Independent Whig.
New York, Gaine, 1753. xii, 132 pp.
AAS copy.   7124

Stackhouse, Thomas, 1677-1752.
. . . Lehrbegriff der Ganzen Christlichen
Religion.
Philadelphia, Baisch, 1774. 7 vol.
(This work was printed in Germany. With
this imprint known only as vol. 1, 3, 5 and
6 at the AAS.)
AAS copy.   42704

[Stackhouse, Thomas, 1677-1752.
Lehrbegriff der Religion.
Philadelphia, 1794.]
(Imprint assumed by Evans from advs.)
     27732

Stafford, Cornelius William.
The Philadelphia Directory for 1797.
[Philadelphia], Woodward, 1797. [4],
203, [1], 76 pp., 1 folding map.
AAS copy.   32868

Stafford, Cornelius William.
The Philadelphia Directory for 1798.
[Philadelphia], Woodward, 1798. 166,
[2], 77, [2] pp.
AAS copy.   34593

Stafford, Cornelius William.
The Philadelphia Directory, for 1799.
[Philadelphia], Woodward, 1799. 159, 78,
[2] pp.
LCP copy.   36353

Stafford, Cornelus William.
The Philadelphia Directory, for 1800.
[Philadelphia], Woodward, 1800. 151,
[1], 80 pp.
AAS copy.   38549

Stafford, H., pseud.
An Astronomical Diary, Kalendar, or
Almanack for . . . 1793 [by Nehemiah
Strong, 1729-1807].
New Haven, Greens. [24] pp.
AAS copy.   24827

Stafford, H., pseud.

An Astronomical Diary, Calendar, or
Almanac, for . . . 1794 [by Nehemiah
Strong, 1729-1807].
New Haven, Greens. [24] pp.
AAS copy.   26232

Stafford, H., pseud.
An Astronomical Diary, Calendar, or
Almanac, for . . . 1795. . . . [by
Nehemiah Strong, 1729-1807].
New Haven, Greens, [24] pp.
AAS copy.   27755

Stafford, H., pseud.
An Astronomical Diary, Calendar, or
Almanack, for . . . 1796 [by Nehemiah
Strong, 1729-1807].
New Haven, Greens. [24] pp.
AAS copy.   29582

Stafford, H., pseud.
An Astronomical Diary, Calendar, or
Almanack, for . . . 1799 [by Nehemiah
Strong, 1729-1807].
New Haven, Greens. [24] pp.
AAS copy.   35618

Stafford, H., pseud.
An Astronomical Diary, Calendar, or
Almanack, for . . . 1800.
New Haven, Greens. [24] pp.
AAS copy.   36354

Stafford, H., pseud.
An Astronomical Diary, Calendar, or
Almanack, for . . . 1801.
New Haven, Greens. [24] pp.
AAS copy.   38550

Stafford, Hosea, pseud.
An Almanack, for . . . 1788 [by Nehemiah
Strong, 1729-1807].
New Haven, Greens. [24] pp.
AAS copy.   20733

Stafford, Hosea, pseud.
An Astronomical Diary, Kalendar, or
Almanack, for . . . 1789 [by Nehemiah
Strong, 1729-1807].
New Haven, Greens. [24] pp.
AAS copy.   21482

Stafford, Hosea, pseud.
An Astronomical Diary, Kalendar, or
Almanack for . . . 1790. . . . [by Nehemiah
Strong, 1729-1807].
New Haven, Greens. [24] pp.
AAS copy.   22170

Stafford, Hosea, pseud.
An Astronomical Ephemeris, Kalendar,
or Almanack, for 1776. . . . [by Nehemiah
Strong, 1729-1807].
New Haven, Greens. [20] pp.
AAS copy.   14479

Stafford, Hosea, pseud.
An Astronomical Ephemeris, Kalendar,
or Almanack, for . . . 1777. . . . [by
Nehemiah Strong, 1729-1807].
New Haven, Greens. [20] pp.
AAS copy.   15098

Stafford, Hosea, pseud.
Stafford's Almanac, for . . . 1778. . . . [by
Nehemiah Strong, 1729-1807].
New Haven, Greens. [24] pp.
AAS copy.   15609

Stafford, Hosea, pseud.
Stafford's Almanack, for . . . 1780. . . . [by
Nehemiah Strong, 1729-1807].
New Haven, Greens. [24] pp.
AAS copy.   16539

Stafford, Hosea, pseud.
Stafford's Almanack, for . . . 1781 [by
Nehemiah Strong, 1729-1807].
New Haven, Greens. [20] pp.
AAS copy.   17004

Stafford, Hosea, pseud.
Stafford's Almanac, for . . . 1782. . . . [by
Nehemiah Strong, 1729-1807].
New Haven, Greens. [20] pp.
AAS copy.   17374

Stafford, Hosea, pseud.
Stafford's Almanack, for . . . 1784 [by
Nehemiah Strong, 1729-1807].
New Haven, Green. [24] pp.
AAS copy.   18202

Stafford, Hosea, pseud.
Stafford's Almanac, for . . . 1785 [by
Nehemiah Strong, 1729-1807].
New Haven, Greens. [24] pp.
AAS copy.   18799

Stafford, Hosea, pseud.
Stafford's Almanack, for . . . 1786 [by
Nehemiah Strong, 1729-1807].
New Haven, Greens. [24] pp.
AAS copy.   19264

Stafford, Hosea, pseud.
Stafford's Almanack, for . . . 1787 [by
Nehemiah Strong, 1729-1807].
New Haven, Greens. [24] pp.
AAS copy.   20015

Stafford, Hosea, pseud.
Stafford's Connecticut Almanack, for . . .
1779. . . . [by Nehemiah Strong,
1729-1807].
New Haven, Greens. [20] pp.
AAS copy.   16088

Stafford, John Nathan, Jr.
An Almanack, for . . . 1799.
Litchfield, Ct., Collier. [24] pp.
Litchfield Hist. Soc. copy.   34594

Stafford, Joseph.
MDCCXXXVII. The Rhode-Island
Almanack.
Newport, 1737. [16] pp.
(The two known copies are imperfect. The
Evans title is an assumption.)
AAS copy.   4073

Stafford, Joseph.
MDCCXXXVIII. The Rhode-Island
Almanack.
Newport, 1738. [16] pp.
AAS copy.   4192

Stafford, Joseph.
An Almanack for the Year . . . 1739.
Boston, Fleet, 1739. [16] pp.
AAS copy.   4311

Stafford, Joseph.
An Almanack for the Year . . . 1740.
Boston, Fleet, 1740. [16] pp.
AAS copy.   4428

[Stafford, Joseph.
An Almanack for the Year . . . 1741.
Boston, Fleet, 1741. [16] pp.]
(Assumed by Evans from the sequence.)
     4607

[Stafford, Joseph.
An Almanack for the Year . . . 1742.
Boston. [16] pp.]
(Assumed by Evans from the sequence.)
     4815

[Stafford, Joseph.
An Almanack for the Year . . . 1743.
Boston, Fleet, 1743. [16] pp.]
(Assumed by Evans from the sequence; no
adv. found.)   5065

Stafford, Joseph.
An Almanack for the Year . . . 1744.
Boston, Green, Bushell & Allen, 1744.
[16] pp.
AAS copy.   5294

[Stafford, Joseph.
An Almanack for the Year . . . 1745.
Boston.]
(Assumed by Evans from the sequence;
not adv.)   5495

Stafford's Almanack, for . . . 1781. . . . By
Hosea Stafford [by Nehemiah Strong,
1729-1807].
New Haven, Greens. [20] pp.
AAS copy.   17004

Stafford's Almanack for . . . 1783 [by
Nehemiah Strong, 1729-1807].
New Haven, Greens. [24] pp.
AAS copy.   17732

Stafford's Almanack, for . . . 1786. By
Hosea Stafford [by Nehemiah Strong,
1729-1807].
New Haven, Greens. [24] pp.
AAS copy.   19264

Stafford's Almanack, for . . . 1791 [by
Nehemiah Strong, 1729-1807].

New Haven, Greens. [24] pp.
AAS copy.   22917

Stafford's Almanack, for . . . 1792 [by
Nehemiah Strong, 1729-1807].
New Haven, Greens. [24] pp.
AAS copy.   23809

Stafford's Almanack, for . . . 1797 [by
Nehemiah Strong, 1729-1807].
New Haven, Greens. [24] pp.
AAS copy.   31250

Stafford's Almanack, for . . . 1798.
New Haven, Greens. [24] pp.
AAS copy.   32892

Stamp Act Congress, New York, 1765.
Proceedings of the Congress at New-York.
Annapolis, 1766. 28 pp.
JCB copy.   10424

The Stamp-Act Repealed, the 8th of
February, 1766.
Hartford, April 11, 1766. . . .
[Hartford, 1766.] Broadside.
CHS copy.   41662

Stamp Duties. Any Certificate of
Naturalization.
Albany, N. Y., Barber & Southwick,
[1798]. Broadside.
MHS copy.   34877

Stancliff, John.
An Account of the Trial of Doctor Joseph
Priestly.
Philadelphia, Cist, 1784. 24 pp.
LOC copy.   18794

Stancliff, John.
[A Letter to Mr. James Moore.
Philadelphia, 1788?]
(Sabin 90149; no copy located.)   45365

Stancliff, John.
The Riddle of Riddles Unriddled.
Philadelphia, 1784. 27 pp.
LOC copy.   18795

Stancliff, John.
A Sermon, on the Death of . . .
Washington.
Mount Holly, [N. J.], Ustick, 1800. 23 pp.
NYPL copy.   38551

[Standfast, Richard.
Dialogue between a Blind Man and
Death.
Boston, 1773?] 16 pp.
(The only copy located is imperfect.)
CHS copy.   42510

[Standfast, Richard].
A Dialogue between a Blind-man and
Death.
Boston, Boyle, 1773. 16 pp.
AAS copy.   42511

[Standfast, Richard.
A Dialogue between a Blind man and
Death.
Boston, Russell for Plumer, [1790]. 16
pp.
(Entered again as 26199, q. v.)   22902

[Standfast, Richard.
A Dialogue between a Blind-man and
Death.
Boston, Russell for Grant, 1793. 16 pp.
(No copy located with this imprint.) 26200

Standfast, Richard.
A Dialogue between a Blind-man and
Death.
Boston, Russell for Plumer, [1793]. 16 pp.
BrU copy.   26199

[Standfast, Richard.
A Dialogue between a Blind Man and
Death.
Windsor, Vt., Spooner, 1794.]
(Imprint assumed by Evans from adv.
"For sale at this Office" in Spooner's
Vermont Journal, Oct. 20, 1794.)   27733

[Standfast, Richard.]
A Dialogue between a Blind Man and
Death.
Fairhaven, Vt., 1797. 8 pp.
HEH copy.   32869

Standfast, Richard.
[A Little Handful of Cordial Comforts.
Boston, 1690.] 45 pp.
(See Sabin 90160.)
BPL copy.   547

Standfast, Richard.
A New-Years-Gift.
Boston, T. Green for Buttolph, 1702.
50 + pp.
(The only known copy is defective.)
AAS copy.   39388

Standfast, Richard.
A New-Years-Gift. . . . Seventh Edition.
Boston, Kneeland & Green, 1733. [4], 31
pp.
BPL copy.   3725

Stanford, John, 1754-1834.
An Address Delivered at the Internment
of . . . Sarah Burger.
New York, Swordses for Burger, 1793. 10
pp.
AAS copy.   46878

Stanford, John, 1754-1834.
The Christian's Pocket Library, . . . Vol. I.
New York, Swords, 1796. iv, [2], 282, [2]
pp., 1 plate.
AAS copy.   31228

Stanford, John, 1754-1834.
. . . Christian's Pocket Library . . . Vol. II,
No. 1 [-6].
New York, Swords, 1800. Engraved tp.,
286, [2] pp.
NYHS copy.   38552

Stanford, John, 1754-1834.
A Collection of Evangelical Hymns.
New York, Swordses, 1793. 180 pp.
AAS copy.   46879

Stanford, John, 1754-1834.
A Collection of Hymns. In Three Parts.
New York, Swords, 1799.
(The only copy located could not be
reproduced.)   36355

Stanford, John, 1754-1834.
The Conversion of Juvenis.
New York, Swords, 1794. 46 pp.
AAS copy.   27734

Stanford, John, 1754-1834.
The Convert Instructed . . . of Baptism.
New York, T. & J. Swords, 1795. 65, [2]
pp.
AAS copy.   47609

Stanford, John, 1754-1834.
The Death of Euphemia Mitchell.
New York, Swords, 1792. 22, [1] pp.
AAS copy.   24811

Stanford, John, 1754-1834.
An Essay on the Law of God.
New York, Swords, 1791. 23 pp.
AAS copy.   23788

Stanford, John, 1754-1834.
The Goodness of God.
New York, Swords, 1799. 60 pp.
AAS copy.   36356

[Stanford, John, 1754-1834.
Hymns-for Youth.
New York, Swords, 1792?]
(Assumed by Evans from adv., "To be
sold" in 24811.)   24812

Stanford, John, 1754-1834.
A Lecture on the Excellence of the
Gospel.
New York, Swords, [1791]. 28 pp.
AAS copy.   23789

Stanford, John, 1754-1834.
Sacred Architecture.
New York, Swords, 1793. [2], 31, [2] pp.
AAS copy.   26201

Staniford, Daniel, 1766-1820.
The Art of Reading.
Boston, Russell for West, 1800. pp. [i]-viii,
[7]-234.
HC copy.   38554

Staniford, Daniel, 1766-1820.
A Short but Comprehensive Grammar.

Boston, Manning & Loring, 1797. 84 pp.
AAS copy.   32870

Staniford, Daniel, 1766-1820.
A Short but Comprehensive Grammar. '
. . . Second Edition.
Charlestown, [Mass.], Etheridge for
West, [1800]. 96 pp.
AAS copy.   38555

Stanly, John, 1774-1834.
To the Independent Electors of the Tenth
District North Carolina. . . . April 25,
1800.
[Newbern, 1800.] Broadside.
NYHS copy.   38556

Stanly, John Wright.
John Wright Stanley's Reply.
Philadelphia, 1769. 22, [1] pp.
NYHS copy.   11476

Stanly, John Wright.
Remarks on Scurrility. . . . September
26th, 1768.
Philadelphia, 1769. 8 pp.
JCB copy.   11477

Stanly, John Wright.
A State of the Accounts and Disputes.
Philadelphia, Miller, 1768. 20 pp.
LOC copy.   41884

Stanton, Daniel, 1708-1770.
A Journal of the Life . . . of. . . .
Philadelphia, Crukshank, 1772. xvii, [1],
184, 4, [1] pp.
AAS copy.   12565

Stanton, Phineas.
A Brief Historical View.
Norwich, Trumbull, 1777. 121, 47 pp.
CHS copy.   43376

[Stanton, Samuel.
Answer to Thomas Paine's Letter.
Philadelphia, 1797.]
(Evans' entry from the copyright record.)
                                                           32871

Stanton, William, fl. 1762.
Litchfield, August 2, 1762. Advertisement.
[Hartford? 1762.] Broadside.
CHS copy.   41314

Starke, Mariana, 1762-1838.
The Widow of Malabar.
Philadelphia, Story, [1791]. [8], 33, [3]
pp.
(Also issued bound in 24049, q.v.)   23791

Starke, Richard, d. 1772.
(Wm. & Mary College Quar., IV, 272; IX,
240.)
The Office and Authority of a Justice of
the Peace.
Williamsburg, Purdie & Dixon, 1774. [4],
356 pp.
AAS copy.   13637

The Starry Calculator; being an Almanac
for . . . 1799.
Chambersburg, Pa., Harper. [40] pp.
AAS copy.   34596

The Starry Calculator; being an Almanac
for . . . 1800.
Lancaster, Pa., Grimlers. [36] pp.
AAS copy.   36357

State of Facts. Shewing the Right of
Certain Companies to the Lands Lately
Purchased.
[Philadelphia], United States, 1795. 64
pp.
AAS copy.   28745

A State of Importations [by John Mein, fl.
1760-1775].
Boston, 1770. 87 pp.
(No copy located has the imprint given by
Evans.)
AAS copy.   11744

[The State of Massachusetts from the Best
Information, 1799.
New York.]
(The origin of this entry is unknown.)
                                                           35800

State of New Hampshire, in the Year . . .

One Thousand Seven Hundred and
Eighty-Four. . .
n. p., [c. 1786]. 16 pp.
JCB copy.   44971

State of New-York. Letter from a
Committee . . . to the Hon. Robert Yates.
. . . 23d February, 1789.
[Albany, 1789.] Broadside.
NYHS copy.   45596

[The State of Religion in New-England,
since the Rev. Mr. George Whitefield's
Arrival.
Boston, 1743.]
(Evans took his entry from an adv. which
did not contain the words "lately
published at Glasgow" which appear in
the adv. in the Boston Gazette, Feb. 15,
May 24, 1743.)   5233

State of the Case in Dispute.
New York, 1713. 8 pp.
(Neither copy reported could be found.)
                                                            1648

[State of the Embarrassments and
Difficulties the Trade Labors Under.
Boston, 1769. 24 pp.]
(Title from Haven.)   11478

A State of the Importations from
Great-Britain [by John Mein, fl.
1760-1775].
Boston, Mein & Fleeming, 1769. [4], 130
pp.
AAS copy.   11336

The State of the Lands said to be once
within the Bounds of the Charter of the
Colony of Connecticut.
New York, 1770. 16 pp.
BA copy.   11869

A State of the Trade Carried on with the
. . . Island of Hispaniola.
New York, Gaine, 1760. 15 pp.
JCB copy.   41170

The State of Trade in the Northern
Colonies [by Otis Little, 1712-1754].
Boston, Fleet, 1749. 43 pp.
AAS copy.   6346

A Statement, Explanatory of the
Resignation of the Officers of the
Regiment of Artillery. . . .
New York, Davis, 1797. 32 pp.
AAS copy.   32568

A Statement of the Cause of the M'Clary
Owners [by John Hale, 1762-1796].
Portsmouth, Melcher, 1795. 67 pp.
AAS copy.   28788

A Statement of the Measures
Contemplated against Samuel Bryan.
Philadelphia, Baileys, 1800. 62 pp.
AAS copy.   38557

A Statistical Table for the United States.
[Philadelphia, 1799.] Broadside.
NYPL copy.   36362

Staughton, William, 1770-1829.
A Discourse, Occasioned by the Sudden
Death of Three Young Persons.
Philadelphia, Ustick, 1797. 37 pp.
AAS copy.   32874

Staughton, William, 1770-1829.
Missionary-Encouragement.
Philadelphia, Ustick, 1798. 44 pp.
AAS copy.   34599

Staunton, Sir George Leonard, bart.,
1737-1801.
An Authentic Account of an Embassy . . .
to . . . China. . . . In Two Volumes.
Philadelphia, Bioren for Campbell, 1799.
xxiii, [1], 297 pp., 2 plates; 267, xxiv pp.,
6 plates, 1 folding table.
AAS copy.   36363

Staunton, September 3d, 1793.
Considering it the Duty of the People of
this District. . . .
[Staunton, 1793.] Broadside.
LOC copy.   26204

Stearns, Charles, 1753-1826.
Dramatic Dialogues for the Use of
Schools.

Leominster, Mass., Prentiss, 1798. 540 pp.
AAS copy.   34600

Stearns, Charles, 1753-1826.
The Ladies' Philosophy of Love.
Leominster, Mass., Prentiss, 1797. 76 pp.
AAS copy.   32876

Stearns, Charles, 1753-1826.
Principles of Religion and Morality.
Leominster, Mass., Prentiss, 1798. 79 pp.
AAS copy.   34601

Stearns, Charles, 1753-1826.
Principles of Religion.
Amherst, N. H., Preston, 1799. 72 pp.
AAS copy.   36364

Stearns, Charles, 1753-1826.
A Sermon: Preached at an Exhibition of
Sacred Musick.
Boston, Thomas & Andrews, 1792. 15 pp.
AAS copy.   24816

Stearns, Elisha.
An Eulogium on . . . Washington.
East Windsor, Ct., Pratt, 1800. 24 pp.
AAS copy.   38558

Stearns, Josiah, 1732-1788.
A Sermon Preached at Epping . . .
September 19, 1779.
Exeter, 1780. 40 pp.
AAS copy.   16998

Stearns, Josiah, 1732-1788.
A Sermon Preached at the Ordination of
. . . Nicolas Dudley.
Newburyport, 1778. 31 pp.
AAS copy.   16079

Stearns, Josiah, 1732-1788.
Sermons on the Divine Character.
Exeter, Ranlet, 1790. 64 pp.
AAS copy.   22905

Stearns, Josiah, 1732-1788.
Two Sermons, Preached at Epping.
Newburyport, 1777. 39 pp.
AAS copy.   15602

Stearns, Samuel, 1747-1819.
An Account of the Terrible Effects of the
Pestilential Infection.
Providence, for Child in Johnston, [1793].
[4], 8 pp.
AAS copy.   26206

Stearns, Samuel, 1747-1819.
An Account of the Terrible Effects of the
Pestilential Infection.
New York, 1794. 12 pp.
PPL copy.   27739

[Stearns, Samuel, 1747-1819.
The American Dispensatory.
New York, 1791.]
(Copyrighted but not printed.)   23794

Stearns, Samuel, 1747-1819.
The American Oracle.
New York, Hodge & Campbell, etc., 1791.
[8], 627, [1], xviii pp., 1 plate.
AAS copy.   23795

Stearns, Samuel, 1747-1819.
Dr. Stearns's Petition to His Excellency.
Worcester, Thomas, 1785. 12 pp.
AAS copy.   19260

[Stearns, Samuel, 1747-1819.
Dr. Stearn's Tour from London to Paris.
New Haven, Greens, 1791.]
("Just received, and to be Sold by the
Printers," Conn. Journal, Apr. 6, 1791.)
    23796

[Stearns, Samuel], 1747-1819.
(Appleton's Cyclopaedia of Am.
Biography.)
Edes & Gill's North-American Almanack
for . . . 1769.
Boston, Edes & Gill. Front., [16], 21, [3]
pp.
AAS copy.   11078

Stearns, Samuel, 1747-1819.
Edes & Gill's North-American Almanack
. . . for . . . 1770.
Boston, Edes & Gill and Fleets, 1770. [60]
pp.
MHS copy.   11479

Stearns, Samuel, 1747-1819.
The Free Mason's Calendar, and
Continental Almanac; for . . . 1793.
New York, Campbell. [72] pp.
AAS copy.   24817

[Stearns, Samuel, 1747-1819.
The Mystery of Animal Magnetism.
New Haven, Beers, 1791.]
(From advs. for the London ed.)   23797

Stearns, Samuel, 1747-1819.
The New-England Farmer's Almanack,
for . . . 1794.
Springfield, Hutchins. [24] pp.
AAS copy.   26207

Stearns, Samuel, 1747-1819.
The North-American Almanack . . . for
. . . 1776.
Boston, in Queen St. [16] pp.
AAS copy.   42943

Stearns, Samuel, 1747-1819.
The North-American's Almanack . . . for
. . . 1771.
Boston, Draper, Fleets, and Edes & Gill.
[24] pp.
(The Evans title is garbled from an adv.)
AAS copy.   11870

Stearns, Samuel, 1747-1819.
The North-American's Almanack . . . for
. . . 1772.
Boston, Draper, Fleets, and Edes & Gill.
[24] pp.
AAS copy.   12235

Stearns, Samuel, 1747-1819.
The North-American's Almanack . . . for
. . . 1774.
Boston, Edes & Gill and Fleets. [24] pp.
AAS copy.   13028

Stearns, Samuel, 1747-1819.
The North-American's Almanack . . . for
. . . 1775.
Boston, Edes & Gill and Fleets. [24] pp.
AAS copy.   13638

Stearns, Samuel, 1747-1819.
The North-American's Almanack . . . for
. . . 1776.
Worcester, Watertown, and Cambridge.
[24] pp.
AAS copy.   14473

Stearns, Samuel, 1747-1819.
The North American's Almanack, for
1777.
Worcester, Stearns & Bigelow. [24] pp.
(The AAS has a variant ed.)
AAS copy.   15096

Stearns, Samuel, 1747-1819.
(Appleton's Cyclopaedia of Am.
Biography.)
The North-American's Calendar and . . .
Almanack for . . . 1773.
Boston, Edes & Gill and Fleets. [24] pp.
AAS copy.   12566

[Stearns, Samuel], 1747-1819.
Second Edition of Edes & Gill's
North-American Almanack for . . . 1769.
Boston, Edes & Gill. [16], 21, [3] pp.,
front.
AAS copy.   41885

[Stearns, Samuel], 1747-1819.
Sir, Your being a member of the Hon. the
Gen. Assembly. . . .
[Providence, 1798.] Broadside.
RIHS copy.   34602

[Stearns, Samuel], 1747-1819.
Thomas's Massachusetts, Connecticut,
Rhode-Island, Newhampshire & Vermont
Almanack . . . for . . . 1789.
Worcester, Thomas. [48] pp.
(For compiler see Stearns to Thomas,
Mar. 3, 1788, in Thomas Mss., A.A.S.)
AAS copy.   21115

Stearns, Samuel, 1747-1819.
The Universal Kalendar, Comprehending
the Landman's and Seaman's Almanac,
for 1783.
[New York.] [24] pp.
AAS copy.   17727

[Stearns, Samuel], 1747-1819.
The Universal Kalendar, and the

North-American Almanack, for . . . 1784.
. . . by William Slygood.
[New York.] [24] pp.
(No perfect copy located.)
NYPL copy.   18196

Stearns, Samuel, 1747-1819.
The Universal Calendar, and The North
American Almanack, for . . . 1787.
Boston, Freeman. [24] pp.
AAS copy.   20007

Stearns, Samuel, 1747-1819.
The Universal Calendar, and the North
American Almanack, for . . . 1788.
Bennington, Haswell & Russell. [24] pp.
AAS copy.   20726

Stearns, Samuel, 1747-1819.
The Universal Calendar, and the
North-American's Almanack, for . . .
1788.
Boston, Edes & Son. [24] pp.
AAS copy.   20725

[Stearns, Samuel, 1747-1819.
The Universal Calendar, and North
American Almanack, for . . . 1788.
Norwich, Trumbull.]
(From an adv.)   20727

Stearns, Samuel, 1747-1819.
The Universal Calendar, and the North
American Almanack, for . . . 1789.
Bennington, Haswell & Russell. [24] pp.
AAS copy.   21476

Stearns, Samuel, 1747-1819.
The Universal Calendar, and the
North-American Almanack, for. . . . 1789.
Boston, Edes. [24] pp.
AAS copy.   45366

Stearns, Samuel, 1747-1819.
The Universal Calendar, and
Northamerican Almanack, for . . . 1790.
Bennington, Haswell & Russell. [24] pp.
AAS copy.   22162

Stearns, Samuel, 1747-1819.
The Universal Calendar: and North
American Almanack, for . . . 1791.
Bennington, Haswell. [24] pp.
AAS copy.   22906

Stearns, Samuel, 1747-1819.
The Universal Calendar, and North
American Almanack, for . . . 1791.
Boston, Edes. [28] pp.
AAS copy.   22907

Stearns, Samuel, 1747-1819.
The Universal Calendar, and the
North-American Almanac, for . . . 1792.
Boston, Edes. [24] pp.
AAS copy.   23798

Stearns, William, 1749-1783.
(Harvard records.)
A View of the Controversy.
Watertown, 1775. 33 pp.
AAS copy.   14474

Stebbing, Henry, 1687-1763.
[A Caution against Religious Delusions.
Charleston, 1740.]
(Adv. S. C. Gazette, Oct. 23, 1740.) 40212

Stebbins, Jonathan.
[An elegy on his wife.
New London? 1744?] 8 pp.
(The only known copy lacks tp.)
CHS copy.   40352

Stebbins, Jonathan.
An Elegy, on the Death of Mrs. Margaret
Stebbins.
Springfield, Stebbins & Russell, 1786. 8
pp.
AAS copy.   44972

Stebbins, Josiah, 1766-1829.
An Address to the Senior Class.
New Haven, Greens, [1796]. 23 pp.
AAS copy.   31234

[Stebbins, Luke], 1722-.
A Genealogy of the Family of Mr. Samuel
Stebbins.
Hartford, 1771. 24 pp.
AAS copy.   12236

Stedman, Steigel and Co.

. . . There are likewise to be Sold . . .
Plantations.
Lancaster, [Pa.], Bailey, [1773?]
Broadside.
(The only known copy is imperfect.)
HSP copy.   42512

Stedman, Steigel & Co.
There are likewise to be sold Several
Valuable Tracts of Land.
Lancaster, Bailey, [1774]. Broadside.
(The one copy recorded cannot be
located.) 42705

Steele, Eliphalet, 1742-1817.
A Discourse on Psalmody.
Utica, M'Lean, 1799. 15 pp.
HPL copy. 36365

Steele, John, 1710-1804.
The Shortness and Afflictions of Human
Life.
Boston, Edes, 1786. 27 pp.
AAS copy. 20008

Steele, Richard, 1629-1692.
An Antidote against Distractions.
New York, Parker & Weyman, 1754. [8],
128 pp.
AAS copy. 7323

Steele, Richard, 1629-1692.
(D. N. B.)
The Husbandmans Calling.
Boston, Green for Buttolph, 1713. [4],
viii, 282, [5] pp.
AAS copy. 1649

[Steele, Richard, 1629-1692.
The Religious Tradesman.
Newburyport, 1778. 180 pp.]
(Assumed by Evans from 16999.) 16080

[Steele, Richard], 1629-1692.
The Religious Tradesman, or, Plain and
Serious Hints.
Newburyport, [1780]. 180 pp.
AAS copy. 16999

[Steele, Richard], 1629-1692.
The Religious Tradesman, or, Plain and
Serious Hints.
Newburyport, Mycall for Titcomb &
Sawyer, [1790]. 180 pp.
(A duplicate of 16999, q. v.) 22831

Steele, Richard, 1672-1729.
(D. N. B.)
The Crisis.
Philadelphia, Keimer, 1725. viii, 44 pp.
HSP copy. 2703

[Steele, Richard, 1672-1729.
The Funeral.
New York, Gaine, 1761.]
(Adv. N. Y. Mercury, July 20, 1761.) 9014

[Steere, Richard], 1643-1721.
(Am. Antiq. Soc., Proc., LIII, 291-292.)
The Daniel Catcher.
[Boston], 1713. [2], 90 pp.
(For place of printing see G.E. Littlefield,
Early Mass. Press, II, 61.)
AAS copy. 1650

Steere, Richard, 1643-1721.
(Am. Antiq. Soc., Proc., LIII, 291-293.)
A Monumental Memorial.
Boston, 1684. [4], 12 pp.
MHS copy. 377

Steigel, Henry William, 1729-1785.
To be Sold by the Subscriber . . . the First
day of June.
Lancaster, [1774]. Broadside.
HSP copy. 13639

Steiner, Johann Conrad, 1707-1762.
(Steiner Memoir, pp. 12-19.)
Die Herrliche Erscheinung.
Philadelphia, Miller, 1763. [8], 478 pp.
AAS copy. 9518

Steiner, Johann Conrad, 1707-1762.
Schuldigstes Liebes-und Ehren-Denkmahl.
Philadelphia, Miller, [1761]. 31 pp.
(The unique copy is imperfect.)
HSP copy. 9015

[Steiner, Johann Conrad, 1707-1762.
Waechter-Stimm.

Germantown, 1752. 16 pp.]
(Ref. from Seidensticker.) 6937

Steinmetz, John.
To be Sold, by Public Vendue, at the
House of Mr. Daniel Barnitz at Hanover
. . . Land. . . . October 27, 1790.
Philadelphia, Steiner, [1790]. Broadside.
HSP copy. 46006

Stenson, William.
William Stenson . . . has for sale . . .
Liquors.
Baltimore, Goddard, [1784]. Broadside.
HEH copy. 44600

Stephen Van Rensselaer and John Frey
. . . have been Nominated. . . . March 31st,
1794.
[Albany? 1794.] Broadside.
(Not located, 1968.) 47219

Stephens, Joseph.
The Temple Rent in Twain.
Trenton, N. J., Day, 1797. 34, [1] pp.
LOC copy. 34603

[Stephens, Thomas], d. 1780.
Method and Plain Process for Making
Pot-Ash.
Boston, Edes & Gill, 1755.]
(Checked by J. H. Trumbull as "seen" but
no copy located.) 7575

[Stephens, Thomas], d. 1780.
The Method and Plain Process for Making
Pot-ash.
New York, Weyman, 1767.]
("To be Sold by W. Weyman," N. Y.
Gazette (Weyman), Mar. 2, 1767.) 10689

Stephens, Thomas, fl. 1794-1815.
A Catalogue of Books now Offered for
Sale.
Philadelphia, Wrigley & Berriman, 1794.
11 pp.
AAS copy. 27741

Stephens, Thomas, fl. 1794-1815.
A Catalogue of Prints and Paintings.
Philadelphia, Woodward, 1794. 8 pp.
(Present location unknown.) 47220

Stephens, Thomas, fl. 1794-1815.
Stephens's Catalogue of Books, &c. for
1795.
Philadelphia, [1795]. 84, [1] pp.
AAS copy. 47610

Stephens's Philadelphia Directory, for
1796.
Philadelphia, Woodward for Stephens. 19,
[1], 286, [2], 69, [3] pp., 1 map.
AAS copy. 31235

Sterett, Samuel.
To the Public. . . . December 31, 1788.
[Baltimore, 1788.] Broadside.
MdHS copy. 21478

Sterling, James, 1701-1763.
(Weis, Col. Clergy Md.)
A Sermon, Preached before His
Excellency.
Annapolis, 1755. 48 pp.
LOC copy. 7574

Sterling, William A.
The Child's Instructor.
Fairhaven, Vt., Spooner, 1796. 47, [1] pp.
VtHS (Rugg) copy. 31236

Sterne, Laurence, 1713-1768.
The Beauties of Sterne. . . . Tenth Edition.
Philadelphia, Spotswood, 1789. xii, 228
pp.
AAS copy. 22163

Sterne, Laurence, 1713-1768.
The Beauties of Sterne.
Philadelphia, Seddon, 1790. 191 pp.
AAS copy. 22908

[Sterne, Laurence, 1713-1768.
The Beauties of Sterne.
Philadelphia, Woodhouse, 1791.]
(Entry from adv. in 23440, "Lately
Published.") 23799

Sterne, Laurence, 1713-1768.

The Beauties of Sterne. . . . Eleventh
Edition.
Boston, Folsom, 1793. xii, 299, [1] pp.
AAS copy. 26208

Sterne, Laurence, 1713-1768.
The Beauties of Sterne. . . . Eleventh
Edition.
Boston, Folsom for Brewer, 1793. xii, 229,
[1] pp.
(This is identical with 26208 but for the
imprint.)
AAS copy. 26209

[Sterne, Laurence, 1713-1768.
The Koran.
Philadelphia, Bell, 1778. 2 vol.]
(Imprint assumed by Evans from adv. in
15918.) 16081

[Sterne, Laurence], 1713-1768.
Letters from Yorick to Eliza.
Philadelphia, Dunlap, 1773. 71 pp.
AAS copy. 13029

[Sterne, Laurence], 1713-1768.
Letters from Yorick to Eliza.
Burlington, Neale, 1792. 63 pp.
(The Evans entry was from an adv.)
AAS copy. 25325

[Sterne, Lawrence], 1713-1768.
Letters from Yorick to Eliza.
Burlington, [N.J.], Neale, 1792. 63 pp.
AAS copy. 46578

[Sterne, Laurence, 1713-1768.
Letters to his most Intimate Friends.
Philadelphia, Bell, 1778. 3 vol.]
(Imprint assumed by Evans from adv. in
15918.) 16082

[Sterne, Laurence], 1713-1768.
A Sentimental Journey through France
and Italy.
[Boston, Mein & Fleeming], 1768. 66,
(96), 98 pp.
HC copy. 41886

[Sterne, Laurence], 1713-1768.
A Sentimental Journey, through France
and Italy. . . . Two Volumes [in one].
[Philadelphia], North-America, Bell,
1770. 123 pp.
AAS copy. 42175

[Sterne, Laurence], 1713-1768.
A Sentimental Journey through France
and Italy.
Philadelphia, Seddon, 1790. 156 pp.
AAS copy. 22909

[Sterne, Laurence], 1713-1768.
A Sentimental Journey through France
and Italy.
Philadelphia, Woodhouse, 1791.]
(Entry from adv. in 23400, "Lately
Published.") 23800

[Sterne, Laurence], 1713-1768.
A Sentimental Journey through France
and Italy.
Norwich, Bushnell & Hubbard, 1792. 254
pp.
AAS copy. 24818

[Sterne, Laurence], 1713-1768.
A Sentimental Journey through France
and Italy. . . . First Worcester Edition.
Worcester, Thomas, 1793. 172 pp., 1 plate.
AAS copy. 26210

[Sterne, Laurence], 1713-1768.
A Sentimental Journey through France
and Italy.
New York, for the Bookseller, 1795. 316
pp.
(The plates called for by Evans were
apparently not in the trade copies.)
AAS copy. 29565

[Sterne, Laurence], 1713-1768.
A Sentimental Journey through France
and Italy.
New York, Tiebout & O'Brien for Smith
& Reid, 1795. 316 pp., front.
WLC copy. 47611

[Sterne, Laurence], 1713-1768.
A Sentimental Journey through France
and Italy.
New York, Reid, 1796. 316 pp., front.

(An imprint variant of 29565, q. v. for text.)
AAS copy.   47924

[Sterne, Laurence, 1713-1768.
The Sermons of Mr. Yorick.
Philadelphia, Humphreys, [1774]. 2 vol. 270; 257 pp.]
(These are vols. III and IV of 13640, q. v.)
                                             13641

Sterne, Laurence, 1713-1768.
The Whole Story of the Sorrows of Maria. . . . Second Edition.
Boston, 1793. 23 pp.
AAS copy.   46880

[Sterne, Laurence, 1713-1768.
The Whole Story of the Sorrows of Maria.
Salem, Dabney, 1793.]
(Imprint assumed by Evans from adv.
"Just published, and for Sale at Dabney's Book-Store," Salem Gazette, Sept. 3, 1793.)
                                             26211

Sterne, Laurence, 1713-1768.
The Works of. . . . In Five Volumes.
Philadelphia, Humphreys, 1774. Front., xiv, 370; 348; 270, [2]; 257; 250, [5] pp.
AAS copy.   13640

Sterne, Laurence, 1713-1768.
The Works of. . . . In Six Volumes.
Philadelphia, Humphreys, 1774. 5 vol.
(The same text of the "5 vol." ed., 13640, q. v., with different division into vols. No. "vol. 6" known.)
AAS copy.   42706

[Sterne, Laurence, 1713-1768.
Yorick's Sentimental Journey.
Philadelphia, Bell, 1771. 2 vol. in 1.]
(Adv. Pa. Gazette, June 6, 1771.)   12237

Sterry, Consider, 1761-1817.
The American Youth . . . a . . . Course of . . . Mathematics.
Providence, Wheeler, 1790. 387, [1] pp.
AAS copy.   22910

Sterry, Consider, 1761-1817.
A Complete Exercise Book.
Norwich, Conn., Sterry, 1795. 120, [1] pp.
AAS copy.   29566

Sterry, Consider, 1761-1817.
Proposals, for Printing by Subscription. . . .
[New London, 1788.] Broadside.
LOC copy.   45367

[Steuart, Andrew], -1769.
The Ass in the Lyon's Skin.
Philadelphia, Steuart, 1763. 8 pp.
LCP copy.   9519

Steuart, Andrew, -1769.
The Gentleman and Citizen's Pocket-Almanack. . . . For the Year 1762.
Philadelphia, Steuart. [48] pp.
HSP copy.   9016

Steuart, Andrew, -1769.
The Gentleman and Citizen's Pocket-Almanack. . . . For . . . 1763.
Philadelphia, Steuart. [48] pp.
HSP copy.   9278

Steuart, Andrew, -1769.
The Gentleman and Citizen's Pocket-Almanack. . . . For . . . 1764.
Philadelphia, Steuart. [48] pp.
LOC copy.   9520

Steuart, Andrew, -1769.
The Gentleman and Citizen's Pocket-Almanack. . . . for . . . 1765.
Philadelphia, Steuart. [48] pp.
AAS copy.   9847

Steuart, Andrew, -1769.
The Gentleman and Citizen's Pocket-Almanack . . . for . . . 1766.
Philadelphia, Steuart. [48] pp.
LOC copy.   10175

Steuart, Andrew, -1769.
The Gentleman and Citizen's Pocket-Almanack . . . for . . . 1767.
Philadelphia, Steuart. [48] pp.
AAS copy.   10502

Steuart, Andrew, -1769.

The Gentleman and Citizen's Pocket-Almanack. . . . For . . . 1768.
Philadelphia, Steuart. 1 folding leaf, [48] pp.
AAS copy.   10775

Steuart, Andrew, -1769.
The Gentleman and Citizen's Pocket Almanack. . . . For . . . 1769.
Philadelphia, Steuart. [48] pp.
HSP copy.   11079

Steuart, Andrew, -1769.
The Gentleman and Citizen's Pocket Almanack. . . . For . . . 1770.
Philadelphia, Magee for Steuart. [48] pp., 1 folding table.
AAS copy.   11480

[Steuart, Andrew, -1769.
The Gentleman and Citizen's Pocket Almanack. . . . For . . . 1770. . . . Second Edition.
Philadelphia, Magee for Steuart.]
(Title from Hildeburn.)   11481

Steuben, Friedrich Wilhelm Ludolf Gerhard Augustin, baron von, 1730-1794.
A Compend of Military Discipline for the Troops of New Hampshire.
Concord, Hough, 1794. 32 pp.
(The only copy located lacks the appendix called for on the tp.)
BM copy.   27370

Steuben, Friedrich Wilhelm Ludolf Gerhard Augustin, baron von, 1730-1794.
A Letter on the Subject of an Established Militia.
New York, M'Lean, 1784. [4], 16 pp.
AAS copy.   18796

Steuben, Friedrich Wilhelm Ludolf Gerhard Augustin von, 1730-1794.
A Letter on the Subject of an Established Militia.
New York, M'Lean, [1784]. [4], 16 pp.
AAS copy.   44601

Steuben, Friedrich Wilhelm Ludolf Gerhard Augustin, baron von, 1730-1794.
Regulations.
See
U.S. Inspector-General's Office.   38559

Stevens, Benjamin, 1721-1791.
(Sibley, X.)
The Gospel Ministry.
Portsmouth, 1765. [4], 42 pp.
AAS copy.   10176

Stevens, Benjamin, 1721-1791.
(Sibley, X.)
A Sermon Occasioned by the Death of Andrew Pepperell.
Boston, Fowle, 1752. 31 pp.
AAS copy.   6938

Stevens, Benjamin, 1721-1791.
(Sibley, X.)
A Sermon Occasioned by the Death of . . . Sir William Pepperrell.
Boston, Edes & Gill, 1759. vi, 24 pp.
AAS copy.   8497

Stevens, Benjamin, 1721-1791.
(Sibley, X.)
A Sermon Preached at Boston.
Boston, Draper, 1761. 72, [1] pp.
AAS copy.   9017

[Stevens, George Alexander], 1710-1784.
The Celebrated Lecture on Heads.
New York, Holt, 1767. 32 pp.
(The only known copy could not be reproduced.)   41766

Stevens, George Alexander], 1710-1784.
A New Lecture on Heads.
Boston, Knox, 1772. 56 pp.
AAS copy.   12568

[Stevens, George Alexander, 1710-1784.
The Celebrated Lecture on Heads.
Philadelphia, Dellap, [1772]. 28 pp.]
(A ghost of 20728, q. v.)   12567

Stevens, George Alexander, 1710-1784.
The Celebrated Lecture on Heads.
Philadelphia, Dellap, [1787]. 28 pp.
AAS copy.   20728

[Stevens, George Alexander, 1710-1784.

. . . Stevens' Celebrated Lectures on Heads.
Boston, 1794.]
(Imprint assumed by Evans from advs.)
                                             27742

Stevens, George Alexander, 1710-1784.
Songs, Comic, Satyrical, and Sentimental.
Philadelphia, Bell, 1778. 9, 12, 252 pp.
(Adv. in Pa. Ledger, Nov. 26, 1777.)
HC copy.   15603

Stevens, James Wilson.
An Historical and Geographical Account of Algiers.
Philadelphia, Hogan & M'Elroy, 1797. 304, [8] pp., 1 folding plate.
AAS copy.   32877

Stevens, James Wilson.
An Historical and Geographical Account of Algiers. . . . Second Edition.
Brooklyn, [N. Y.], Kirk for Brodie, 1800. front., 318, [6] pp.
AAS copy.   38560

[Stevens, John], 1749-1838.
Observations on Government, Including some Animadversions on Mr. Adams's Defence.
New York, Ross, 1787. 56 pp.
(Usually assigned to William Livingston, but the draft in Stevens' hand is at the Stevens Institute.)
LCP copy.   20465

Stevens, John, 1750-1799.
A Posthumous Publication, of some of the Writings of. . . .
Hartford, Ct., Hudson & Goodwin, 1799. 35 pp.
UTS copy.   36366

Stevens, John, 1750-1799.
The Valedictory Address. . . . Second Edition.
Hartford, [Ct.], Hudson & Goodwin, 1800. 24 pp.
AAS copy.   38561

Stevens, Joseph, 1682-1721.
(Sibley, V, 239-243.)
Another and Better Country.
Boston, Kneeland for Phillips, 1723. [2], xii, 116 pp.
AAS copy.   2478

Stevens, Simon, 1737-.
A Journal of Lieut. Simon Stevens.
Boston, Edes & Gill, 1760. 19 pp.
AAS copy.   8741

[Stevens, Simon, 1737-.
A Journal of Lieut. Simon Stevens.
New York, Parker, 1760.]
(From an adv.)   8742

Stevens, William, Revolutionary officer.
A System for the Discipline of the Artillery.
New York, Davis, 1797. pp. [1]-14, [13]-260, 24 plates.
AAS copy.   32878

Stevenson, Roger.
Military Instructions for Officers.
Philadelphia, Aitken, 1775. [8], vii, [1], 232, [4] pp., 12 plates.
AAS copy.   14475

Steward, Joseph, fl. 1759.
Poor Joseph. 1759. Being an Almanack.
Boston, Mecom. [24] pp.
AAS copy.   8263

[Steward, Joseph, fl. 1759.
Poor Joseph's Diary, for . . . 1760.
Boston.]
("Just Published," Boston Gazette, Dec. 17, 1759.)   8498

[Steward, Joseph, fl. 1759.
Poor Joseph's Almanack for the Year 1761.
Boston.]
(Assumed by Evans from the sequence.)
                                             8743

Stewart, Alexander,-1771.
(Weis, Colonial Clergy N. C.)
The Validity of Infant Baptism.
Newbern, 1758. 40 pp.
HC copy.   8264

Stewart, Dugald, 1753-1828.
Elements of the Philosophy of the Human
Mind.
Philadelphia, Young, 1793. pp. [i]-xi,
[1], [9]-500.
AAS copy. 26212

[Stewart, James Hood?
An Index to the Laws of Kentucky.
Lexington, Stewart, 1795.]
(Adv. Ky. Gazette, Mar. 7, 1795.) 28926

Stewart, Jesse.
Genuine French Creek Seneca Oil.
[Springfield, N. J.?, 1797?]. Broadside.
NYAM copy. 48258

Stewart, John, 1749-1822.
Prospectus of a Series of Lectures.
Philadelphia, Dobson, 1796. 16 pp.
AAS copy. 31237

[Stewart, John, 1749-1822.
The Revelation of Nature.
New York, Mott & Lyon, [1795]. 17, 21,
35, 41, 3, 12, 6, 2 pp.]
(Also entered as 31238, q. v.) 29567

[Stewart, John], 1749-1822.
The Revelation of Nature.
New York, Mott & Lyon, [1796]. xxxix,
[1], 104 pp.
AAS copy. 31238

Stewart, John, 1778-1797.
The Confession, Last Words, and Dying
Speech of. . . . Boston Jail, April 6, 1797.
[Boston, 1797.] Broadside.
Warren, Mass., Free Library copy. 32879

[Stewart, John, 1778-1797.
The Confession. Last Words, and Dying
Speech of. . . .
Harrington, Me., Edes, 1797.]
(Imprint assumed by Evans from adv. "To
be sold by the Printer hereof," Kennebeck
Intelligencer, May 5, 1797.) 32880

[Stewart, William M.
The Young Mason's Monitor.
New York, Harrison & Purdy, 1789.]
("Just published," N.Y. Weekly Museum,
Aug. 15 - Oct. 31, 1789.) 22164

[Stewart, William M.
The Young Mason's Monitor.
Portsmouth, Melcher, 5792 (1792). 62 pp.]
("Just published, and for sale by," N. H.
Gazette, Sept. 27, 1792.) 24819

Stewart and Jones, New York.
Stewart and Jones, on Murray's Wharf,
Have for Sale. . . .
New York, Gaine, [1793]. Broadside.
NYPL copy. 26213

Stickney, John, 1742-1826.
The Gentlemen and Lady's Musical
Companion.
Newburyport, [1774?]. [8], 212 pp.
AAS copy. 42045

Stickney, John, 1742-1826.
The Gentleman and Lady's Musical
Companion.
Newburyport, Bayley, 1774. 9, [3], 212 pp.
(None of the copies located by Evans
agrees with his entry.)
AAS copy. 13642

Stickney, John, 1742-1826.
The Gentleman and Lady's Musical
Companion.
Newburyport, Bayley for Boyle, etc., 1774.
9, [3], 212 pp.
HEH copy. 42707

[Stickney, John, 1742-1826.
The Gentleman and Ladies Musical
Companion.
Newburyport, Bayley for Larkin, 1783.]
(Adv. Salem Gazette, Dec. 4, 1783. There
is a fragment of what is apparently a copy
of this ed. in private hands.) 18197

Stiles, Abel, 1709-1783.
(Dexter, I, 488-490.)
Death God's Monitor.
Providence, 1768. 29 pp.
AAS copy. 11080

Stiles, Abel, 1709-1783.
(Dexter, I, 488-490.)

A Sermon, Preached at Rehoboth.
Providence, 1767. [2], 24 pp.
AAS copy. 10776

Stiles, Ezra, 1727-1795.
A Discourse on Saving Knowledge.
Newport, 1770. 48 pp.
AAS copy. 11871

Stiles, Ezra, 1727-1795.
A Discourse on the Christian Union.
Boston, Edes & Gill, 1761. 139 pp.
AAS copy. 9018

[Stiles, Ezra, 1727-1795.
A Discourse on the Christian Union.
Newport, 1762. 139 pp.]
(Apparently a ghost of 9018, q.v.) 9279

Stiles, Ezra, 1727-1795.
A Discourse on the Christian Union.
Brookfield, Mass., 1799. 163, [1] pp.
AAS copy. 36368

Stiles, Ezra, 1727-1795.
A Funeral Sermon, Delivered Thursday,
July 26, 1787.
New Haven, Greens, 1787. 34, [3] pp.
AAS copy. 20729

Stiles, Ezra, 1727-1795.
A History of Three of the Judges.
Hartford, Babcock, 1794. 357, [2] pp., 9
plates.
AAS copy. 27743

Stiles, Ezra, 1727-1795.
Oratio Funebris . . . Jonathan Law.
New London, 1751. [4], 12, [3] pp.
(Issued in black covers with 6651, but
separately signatured.)
AAS copy. 6789

Stiles, Ezra, 1727-1795.
Oratio Inauguralis.
Hartford, 1778. 40 pp.
AAS copy. 16083

Stiles, Ezra, 1727-1795.
A Sermon, Delivered at the Ordination of
. . . Henry Channing.
New London, 1787. 41 pp.
AAS copy. 20730

[Stiles, Ezra], 1727-1795.
To the Candid Public.
New London, Green, 1774. Broadside.
LOC copy. 42708

Stiles, Ezra, 1727-1795.
The United States Elevated.
New Haven, 1783. 99 pp.
AAS copy. 18198

Stiles, Ezra, 1727-1795.
The United States Elevated.
Worcester, Thomas, 1785. 172, [8] pp.
AAS copy. 19261

Stiles, Isaac, 1697-1760.
(Dexter, I, 264-267.)
The Character and Duty of Soldiers.
New Haven, 1755. [4], 28 pp.
AAS copy. 7576

Stiles, Isaac, 1697-1760.
(Dexter, I, 264-267.)
A Looking-Glass for Changlings.
New London, 1743. [4], 44 pp.
AAS copy. 5295

Stiles, Isaac, 1697-1760.
(Dexter, I, 264-267.)
A Prospect of the City of Jerusalem.
New London, 1742. [2], 59 pp.
AAS copy. 5066

Stiles, Isaac, 1697-1760.
A Sermon Preached by Isaac Stiles.
Newport, [1755]. [4], 33 pp.
AAS copy. 7577

Stillman, Samuel, 1738-1807.
Apostolic Preaching.
Boston, Edes, 1791. 75 pp.
AAS copy. 23801

Stillman, Samuel, 1738-1807.
Charity Considered.
Boston, Fleets, [1785]. 19 pp.
AAS copy. 19262

Stillman, Samuel, 1738-1807.
Death, the last Enemy.
Philadelphia, Crukshank, 1776. 28 pp.
AAS copy. 15097

Stillman, Samuel, 1738-1807.
(Weis, Colonial Clergy N. E.)
Four Sermons.
Boston, Russell, 1769. 87 pp.
AAS copy. 11482

Stillman, Samuel, 1738-1807.
A Good Minister of Jesus Christ.
Boston, Manning & Loring, 1797. 20 pp.
AAS copy. 32882

Stillman, Samuel, 1738-1807.
(Weis, Colonial Clergy N. E.)
Good News from a Far Country.
Boston, Kneeland & Adams for Freeman,
1766. 34 pp.
AAS copy. 10503

Stillman, Samuel, 1738-1807.
An Oration, Delivered July 4th, 1789.
Boston, Edes, 1789. 30 pp.
AAS copy. 22165

Stillman, Samuel, 1738-1807.
A Sermon, Occasioned by the Death of
. . . Washington.
Boston, Manning & Loring, [1800]. 26 pp.
AAS copy. 38563

Stillman, Samuel, 1738-1807.
(Weis, Colonial Clergy N. E.)
A Sermon Occasioned by the Decease of
Mrs. Mary Stillman.
Boston, Freeman, 1768. 31 pp.
AAS copy. 11081

Stillman, Samuel, 1738-1807.
A Sermon, Preached at Boston, April 25,
1799.
Boston, Manning & Loring, 1799. 23 pp.
AAS copy. 36369

Stillman, Samuel, 1738-1807.
A Sermon Preached before the Honorable
Council.
Boston, Fleets and Gill, 1779. 38 pp.
AAS copy. 16537

Stillman, Samuel, 1738-1807.
A Sermon, Preached May 31, 1791.
Providence, Carter, [1791]. 24, iv pp.
AAS copy. 23802

Stillman, Samuel, 1738-1807.
A Sermon Preached to the Ancient and
Honorable Artillery Company.
Boston, Edes & Gill, 1770. 32 pp.
AAS copy. 11872

Stillman, Samuel, 1738-1807.
The Substance of a Sermon Preached at
the Ordination of . . . Samuel Shepard.
Boston, Kneeland for Freeman, 1772. 33
pp.
BA copy. 12569

Stillman, Samuel, 1738-1807.
Thoughts on the French Revolution.
Boston, Manning & Loring, 1795. 27 pp.
AAS copy. 29569

Stillman, Samuel, 1738-1807.
(Weis, Colonial Clergy N. E.)
Two Sermons: the First from Psalm CII.
Boston, Kneeland for Freeman, 1773. 67
pp.
HC copy. 13030

Stillman, Samuel, 1738-1807.
Two Sermons: the First from Psalm
CII. . . . Second Edition.
Boston, Kneeland and Freeman, 1773. 67
pp.
AAS copy. 13031

Stillman, Samuel, 1738-1807.
Two Sermons: the First from Psalm
CII. . . . Second Edition.
Boston, Russell for Ellison, 1773. 31 pp.
AAS copy. 42513

Stillman, Samuel, 1738-1807.
Two Sermons: the First from Psalm
CII. . . . Fourth Edition.
Boston, Russell for Ellison, 1773. 31,
[1] pp.
AAS copy. 42514

Stillman, Samuel, 1738-1807.
(Weis, Colonial Clergy N. E.)
Young People.
Boston, Boyles, 1771. 31 pp.
(The AAS has another ed. lacking the title
"A Sermon" on p. 5.)
AAS copy.   12238

Stillman, Samuel, 1738-1807.
Young People Called upon to Consider.
Boston, Boyles, 1771. 31 pp.
AAS copy.   42280

Stilwell, Samuel, 1763-1848.
A Guide to Reason.
New York, Buel, 1794. 28 pp.
LOC copy.   27744

Stimson, Elisha.
The Mathamaticians Glory Astronomy
and New England Almanack for . . . 1774.
n.p., Printed for the Author, 1774. [22]
pp.
AAS copy.   42709

Stimulator [by Cotton Mather,
1663-1728].
New London, 1724. [2], 46 pp.
YC copy.   2559

Stinton, Benjamin, 1676-1718.
A Short Catechism. . . . Fourth Edition.
Boston, 1745. 16 pp.
AAS copy.   5691

[Stinton, Benjamin], 1676-1718.
(See 1730 and 1745 eds.)
A Short Catechism, wherein the Chief
Principles of Religion are Taught.
Boston, Fleets, 1766. 16 pp.
AAS copy.   10504

Stirling, John, M. A.
The Compendious System of Rhetoric.
Philadelphia, Prichard & Hall, 1789. 11
pp.
(The one recorded copy cannot now be
found.)   22166

Stirling, John, M. A.
A System of Rhetorick.
New York, Gaine, 1788. viii, 84 pp.
AAS copy.   21477

Stirredge, Elizabeth (Tayler), 1634-1706.
Strength in Weakness.
Philadelphia, Keimer, 1726. viii, [10],
159 pp.
AAS copy.   2815

Stith, William, 1707-1755.
(D. A. B.)
The History of . . . Virginia.
Williamsburg, 1747. viii, 331, v, 34 pp.
AAS copy.   6071

Stith, William, 1707-1755.
(D. A. B.)
The History of . . . Virginia.
London, 1753. viii, 331, v, 34 pp.
JCB copy.   7125

Stith, William, 1707-1755.
The Nature and Extent of Christ's
Redemption.
Williamsburg, 1753. 32 pp.
BA copy.   7126

Stith, William, 1707-1755.
(D. A. B.)
A Sermon, Preached before the General
Assembly.
Williamsburg, 1745/6. iv, 35 pp.
BA copy.   5869

Stith, William, 1707-1755.
(D. A. B.)
The Sinfulness . . . of Gaming.
Williamsburg, 1752. 27 pp.
HSP copy.   6939

Stock, John Edmonds, 1744-1835.
An Inaugural Essay.
Philadelphia, Gales, 1797. [i], iii, 43 pp.
AAS copy.   32883

Stoddard, Amos, 1762-1813.
A Masonic Address . . . June 24 . . . 5797.
Hallowell, Me., Robinson, 1797. 20 pp.
AAS copy.   32884

Stoddard, Amos, 1762-1813.

An Oration, Delivered before the Citizens
of Portland.
Portland, Me., 1799. 30 pp.
AAS copy.   36370

Stoddard, Amos, 1762-1813.
An Oration, Delivered in the Meeting
House.
Portland, Me., Baker & George, 1799. 14
pp.
AAS copy.   36371

Stoddard, Anthony, 1678-1760.
(Sibley, IV, 381-383.)
A Sermon Preached before the General
Assembly.
New London, 1716. [2], 28 pp.
AAS copy.   1856

Stoddard, Asa, 1771?-1794.
Composition of Asa Stoddard.
Middletown, Woodward, [1794?] 11 pp.
YC copy.   47221

Stoddard, Ashbel, 1763-1840.
Stoddard's Diary: or, the Columbia
Almanack for . . . 1787.
Hudson, Stoddard. [28] pp.
AAS copy.   20009

[Stoddard, Samuel, - 1762.
A Narrative of the Unhappy Life . . .
of. . .
Philadelphia, Steuart, 1762.]
(Adv. Pa. Gazette, Dec. 16, 1762.)   9197

Stoddard, Solomon, 1643-1729.
(Sibley, II, 111-122.)
An Answer to Some Cases of
Conscience.
Boston, Green for Gerrish, 1722. 15 pp.
AAS copy.   2387

Stoddard, Solomon, 1643-1729.
(Sibley, II, 111-122.)
An Appeal to the Learned.
Boston, 1709. [6], 98 pp.
AAS copy.   1433

Stoddard, Solomon, 1643-1729.
An Appeal to the Learned. . . . Second
Edition.
New York, Parker, 1751. [2], vi, 83 pp.
AAS copy.   40606

Stoddard, Solomon, 1643-1729.
(Sibley, II, 111-122.)
The Danger of Speedy Degeneracy.
Boston, 1705. 28, [3] pp.
AAS copy.   1234

Stoddard, Solomon, 1643-1729.
(Sibley, II, 111-122.)
The Defects of Preachers Reproved.
New London, 1724. [2], v, [1], 27 pp.
HC copy.   2585

Stoddard, Solomon, 1643-1729.
(Sibley, II, 111-122.)
The Defects of Preachers. . . . Second
Edition.
Boston, Kneeland & Green, 1747. [8], 18,
[1] pp.
AAS copy.   6072

[Stoddard, Solomon, 1643-1729.
The Defects of Preachers Reproved. . . .
Second Edition.
Boston, 1767.]
(Apparently a ghost of the 1747 ed. arising
from a typographical error in the AAS
cat. of 1836.)   10777

Stoddard, Solomon, 1643-1729.
(Sibley, II, 111-122.)
The Duty of Gospel-Ministers.
Boston, Phillips, 1718. [2], 25 pp.
AAS copy.   1998

Stoddard, Solomon, 1643-1729.
(Sibley, II, 111-122.)
The Efficacy of the Fear of Hell.
Boston, 1713. 208 pp.
YC copy.   1651

Stoddard, Solomon, 1643-1729.
(Sibley, II, 111-122.)
The Falseness of the Hopes of many
Professors.
Boston, 1708. [2], 28 pp.
JCB copy.   1371

Stoddard, Solomon, 1643-1729.
(Sibley, II, 111-122.)
Gods Frown in the Death of Usefull Men.
Boston, 1703. [2], 28 pp.
AAS copy.   1146

Stoddard, Solomon, 1643-1729.
(Sibley, II, 111-122.)
A Guide to Christ.
Boston, 1714. iii, xii, 10, 96 pp.
(No complete copy is reported.)
AAS copy.   1716

Stoddard, Solomon, 1643-1729.
(Sibley, II, 111-122.)
A Guide to Christ.
Boston, Draper for Henchman, 1735. [2],
viii, 8, 85, [1] pp.
AAS copy.   3962

Stoddard, Solomon, 1643-1729.
(Sibley, II, 111-122.)
A Guide to Christ.
Boston, Green for Henchman, 1742. [2],
ix, [9], 99 pp.
AAS copy.   5067

Stoddard, Solomon, 1643-1729.
A Guide to Christ. . . . Second Edition.
New York, Parker, 1751. xi, [9], 97, [2]
pp.
AAS copy.   40607

Stoddard, Solomon, 1643-1729.
The Inexcusableness.
Boston, 1708. [4], 28 pp.
AAS copy.   1372

Stoddard, Solomon, 1643-1729.
(Sibley, II, 111-122.)
The Nature of Saving Conversion. . . .
Second Edition.
Boston, for Sawyer, [1770]. [4], 130 pp.
AAS copy.   11873

Stoddard, Solomon, 1643-1729.
(Sibley, II, 111-122.)
The Necessity of Acknowledgment.
Boston, 1701. 34 pp.
YC copy.   1026

Stoddard, Solomon, 1643-1729.
The Presence of Christ with the Ministers.
Boston, Green, 1718. [2], 29, [1], 16 pp.
AAS copy.   1999

Stoddard, Solomon, 1643-1729.
(Sibley, II, 111-122.)
Question whether God is not Angry.
Boston, Green for Gerrish, 1723. 12 pp.
AAS copy.   2479

Stoddard, Solomon, 1643-1729.
(Sibley, II, 111-122.)
The Safety of Appearing.
Boston, 1687. [8], 351, [3] pp.
AAS copy.   434

Stoddard, Solomon, 1643-1729.
(Sibley, II, 111-122.)
The Safety of Appearing. . . . Second
Edition.
Boston, Henchman, 1729. [2], iv, 296, [2]
pp.
AAS copy.   3220

Stoddard, Solomon, 1643-1729.
The Safety of Appearing. . . . Third
Edition.
Boston, Henchman, 1742. [2], iv, 296, [1]
pp.
AAS copy.   5068

Stoddard, Solomon, 1643-1729.
Some Theological Conclusions.
[Boston? 1729?] Broadside.
AAS copy.   39932

[Stoddard, Solomon, 1643-1729.
The Sufficiency of one Good Sign.
Boston, 1703.]
(Title from Prince Ms. catalogue and from
adv. in 1234.)   1147

Stoddard, Solomon, 1643-1729.
(Sibley, II, 111-122.)
Those Taught by God the Father.
Boston, 1712. [2], 33 pp.
AAS copy.   1584

[Stoddard, Solomon, 1643-1729.
Those Taught by God the Father [second
edition].

Boston, 1712.]
(According to Sibley, II, 119, HC and
MHS both had copies of 1584 and a
"Second Edition, with some addition."
Apparently these 2d eds. were at
sometime discarded as duplicates.)   1585

Stoddard, Solomon, 1643-1729.
(Sibley, II, 111-122.)
Three Sermons Lately Preach'd at Boston.
Boston, Green for Henchman, 1717. [2],
118 pp.
AAS copy.   1930

Stoddard, Solomon, 1643-1729.
(Sibley, II, 111-122.)
A Treatise Concerning Conversion.
Boston, Franklin for Henchman. 1719.
[2], 143, [1] pp.
AAS copy.   2072

Stoddard, Solomon, 1643-1729.
(Sibley, II, 111-122.)
The Tryal of Assurance.
Boston, 1698. [2], 20 pp.
AAS copy.   853

Stoddard, Solomon, 1643-1729.
The Way for a People to Live Long in the
Land.
Boston, 1703. [2], 25 pp.
AAS copy.   1148

Stoddard, Solomon, 1643-1729.
The Way to know Sincerity and
Hypocrisy.
[Boston, 1719.] pp. [2], 117-143.
(This is the second title in 2072, q.v.) 2073

Stoddard's Diary: or the Columbian
Almanack, for . . . 1800. . . . By Andrew
Beers.
Hudson, N. Y., Stoddard. [36] pp.
(Reproduced as 35173, q. v.)   36372

Stokes, William, M.D., of Virginia.
Tentamen Medicum.
Philadelphia, Young, 1793. [2], 29 pp.
AAS copy.   26214

Stone, Eliab, 1737-1822.
A Discourse, Delivered at Reading.
February 22, 1800.
Boston, Manning & Loring, [1800]. 23 pp.
AAS copy.   38564

Stone, Eliab, 1737-1822.
A Discourse, Delivered at Reading, on the
Day of the National Fast.
Boston, Manning & Loring, 1799. 29 pp.
AAS copy.   36373

Stone, Eliab, 1737-1822.
(Weis, Colonial Clergy N. E.)
A Sermon at the Ordination of . . .
Ebenezer Hubbard.
Salem, Hall, 1783. 26 pp.
AAS copy.   18199

Stone, Eliab, 1737-1822.
A Sermon, Delivered August 20, 1793.
Boston, Hall, 1794. 30 pp.
AAS copy.   27745

Stone, Eliab, 1737-1822.
A Sermon, Preached in Cohasset.
Boston, Adams, 1798. 23 pp.
AAS copy.   34605

Stone, James, 1704-1742.
(Sibley, VII, 442-444.)
How Christ the Son Glorified God.
Boston, 1746. [2], ii, 16 pp.
HC copy.   5870

[Stone, John Hurford], 1763-1818.
Copies of Original Letters Recently
Written by Persons in Paris.
Philadelphia, Humphreys, 1798. 21, [3]
pp.
AAS copy.   34606

Stone, Joseph.
The Columbian Harmony.
[Boston, Thomas & Andrews, 1793.] viii,
112 pp.
(Imprint given by Evans was assumed
from advs.)
AAS copy.   26215

Stone, Nathan, 1708-1781.
(Sibley, VIII, 99-105.)
If Ministers Deny Christ.

Boston, Draper, 1765. [2], 41 pp.
AAS copy.   10177

Stone, Nathan, 1708-1781.
(Sibley, VIII, 99-105.)
Two Discourses Delivered at
Southborough.
Boston, Kneeland, 1761. [4], ii, 15, [1],
13 pp.
AAS copy.   9019

Stone, Nathan, 1737-1804.
The Duty of Worshiping God.
Boston, Manning & Loring, 1796. 17, [1],
14 pp.
AAS copy.   31240

Stone, Nathaniel, 1667-1755.
(Sibley, IV, 79-82.)
A Caution to Erring Christians.
[Boston, 1736?] 7 pp.
HC copy.   4312

Stone, Nathaniel, 1667-1755.
(Sibley, IV, 79-82.)
Concio ad Magistratum.
Boston, Green for Henchman, 1728. [4],
15 pp.
AAS copy.   3107

Stone, Nathaniel, 1667-1755.
(Sibley, IV, 79-82.)
A Lecture Sermon Asserting God's Right
Sovereignty.
Boston, 1720. [4], 12 pp.
BA copy.   2179

Stone, Nathaniel, 1667-1755.
(Sibley, IV, 79-82.)
On Account of Pleas of late Made.
[Boston, 1739.] 15 pp.
AAS copy.   4429

Stone, Nathaniel, 1667-1755.
Rulers are a Terror.
Boston, Green, 1720. [4], 22, [1] pp.
AAS copy.   2180

Stone, Nathaniel, 1667-1755.
(Sibley, IV, 79-82.)
Serious Reflections on late Publick
Concernments.
[Boston, 1734.] 8 pp.
HC copy.   3838

Stone, Nathaniel, 1667-1755.
(Sibley, IV, 79-82.)
A Very Brief Account.
Boston, Green, 1731. [2], 149 pp.
HC copy.   3478

Stone, Nathaniel, 1667-1755.
(Sibley, IV, 79-82.)
The Way to Attain Glory by Inheritance.
Boston, Crump for Gerrish, 1718. [2], ii,
92 pp.
(The two known copies are defective.)
CL copy.   2000

Stone, Samuel, 1602-1663.
(W. B. Sprague, Annals, I, 37-38.)
A Short Catechism.
Boston, 1684. 15 pp.
NYPL copy.   378

Stone, Samuel, 1602-1663.
A Short Catechism.
Boston, Green and Allen for Gibbons,
1699. 15 pp.
(The only recorded copy is defective.)
JCB copy.   39354

Stone, Samuel, 1602-1663.
(D. N. B.)
A Short Catechism.
Boston, 1720. [2], 13 pp.
WL copy.   2181

Stone, Timothy, 1742-1797.
The Nature, and Evil, of Selfishness.
Norwich, Green & Spooner, 1778. 32 pp.
AAS copy.   16084

Stone, Timothy, 1742-1797.
The Nature and Evil of Selfishness.
Norwich, Trumbull, 1778. 24 pp.
NYPL copy.   16085

Stone, Timothy, 1742-1797.
A Sermon Delivered at the Ordination of
. . . Lathrop Rockwell.
Norwich, Conn., Hubbard, 1794. 24 pp.
AAS copy.   27746

Stone, Timothy, 1742-1797.
A Sermon, Preached before His
Excellency Samuel Huntington.
Hartford, Hudson & Goodwin, 1792. 35
pp.
AAS copy.   24820

Stone, Timothy, 1742-1797.
Victory over Sin and Death.
Hartford, [1780]. 16 pp.
AAS copy.   17000

The Stone Cut out of the Mountain [by
Cotton Mather, 1663-1728].
[Boston]. 1716. [1], 13, 13 pp.
AAS copy.   1833

[Stonehouse, James, 1716-1795.
(D. N. B.)
Christ's Temptations.
Philadelphia, 1770.]
(Hildeburn, from an adv.)   11874

[Stonehouse, James, 1716-1795.
Universal Restitution.
Philadelphia, 1770.]
(Hildeburn, from an adv.)   11875

St - p! St-p! st-p! No: Tuesday-Morning,
December 17, 1765. The True-born Sons
of Liberty. . . .
[Boston, 1765.] Broadside.
MHS copy.   41590

Storace, Stephen, 1763-1796.
Ah can I Cease to Love Her.
Philadelphia, Carr, 1793. 1 p.
HSP copy.   26217

Storace, Stephen, 1763-1796.
Captivity. A Ballad.
[Philadelphia, Carr, 1793.] [2] pp.
AAS copy.   26218

Storace, Stephen, 1763-1796.
The Capture. A Favorite Song in the
Pirates [by James Cobb, 1756-1818].
Philadelphia, Carr, [1793]. 2 pp.
(No copy of the separate printing could be
located.)   25306

[Storace, Stephen], 1763-1796.
Fa la the Favorite Welch Air.
New York, Gilfert, [1797]. [2] pp.
LOC copy.   48259

Storace, Stephen, 1763-1796.
The Favorite Ballad of the Poor Black
Boy. . . . Composed by Storace.
Philadelphia, Carr, [1794]. [2] pp.
AAS copy.   27126

[Storace, Stephen], 1763-1796.
Lullaby a Favorite Song in The Pirates.
New York, Gilfert, [1795]. Broadside.
JCB copy.   47612

Storace, Stephen, 1763-1796.
The Much Admired Ballad of the Willow.
Philadelphia, Carr, and New York,
Hewitt, 1798. [2] pp.
NYPL copy.   34608

Storace, Stephen, 1763-1796.
No More his Fears Alarming.
[Philadelphia], Willig, [1795?]. [2] pp.
LOC copy.   47613

[Storace, Stephen], 1763-1796.
The Shipwreck'd Seaman's Ghost.
Philadelphia, Carr, 1793. [2] pp.]
(On examination the copies of the
"separate issue" listed in Sonneck-Upton,
p. 380, turn out to be identical with the
preceding item.)   26160

Storace, Stephen, 1763-1796.
Spirit of my Sainted Sire.
New York and Philadelphia, B. and J.
Carr, [c. 1795]. [3] pp.
NYPL copy.   47614

Storace, Stephen, 1763-1796.
Sweet Little Barbara. A Favorite Duett.
Philadelphia, B. Carr for J. Carr and
Hewitt, [1799]. 3 pp.
NL copy.   36375

[Storace, Stephen], 1763-1796.
Tho' You Think by this to Vex me. . . .
New York, Hewitt, etc., [1797?]. [2] pp.
NYPL copy.   48260

The Storekeeper's and Mechanic's Sheet
Almanac for . . . 1789.
Wilmington, Adams. Broadside.
(No copy located.) 45368

Storm, N., pseud.
The Town & Country Almanack, for . . .
1800.
Norwich, [Ct.], Trumbull. [24] pp.
AAS copy. 38566

[The Storm, or the American Syren:
being a Collection of the Newest and most
Approved Songs.
Williamsburg, Rind and Cumins, 1773.]
("Just Published," Va. Gazette, Feb. 11,
1773.) 13032

Storrs, John, 1735-1799.
A Sermon . . . at the Ordination of . . .
Richard Salter Storrs.
Springfield, 1786. 35 pp.
AAS copy. 20010

Story, Enoch, and Daniel Humphrey.
Philadelphia, January 14, 1775. Proposals
for Printing by Subscription . . . The
Pennsylvania Mercury.
[Philadelphia, 1775.] Broadside.
LOC ph copy. 14476

Story, Isaac, 1749-1816.
A Discourse, Delivered February 15,
1795.
Salem, Cushing, 1795. 29 pp.
AAS copy. 29571

Story, Isaac, 1749-1816.
The Love of Our Country Recommended.
Boston, Boyle, 1775. 23 pp.
NYPL copy. 13643

Story, Isaac, 1749-1816.
A Sermon, Preached August the 15th,
1798.
Salem, Cushing, 1798. 43 pp.
AAS copy. 34609

[Story, Isaac], 1774-1803.
All the World's a Stage.
Newburyport, Barrett, 1796. 15 pp.
AAS copy. 31242

[Story, Isaac], 1774-1803.
Consolatory Odes. . . . By Peter Quince.
New York, 1799.
(Sabin 92278 from NYSL cat. of 1855.)
36376

[Story, Isaac], 1774-1803.
Liberty, a Poem, Delivered on the Fourth
of July.
Newburyport, Barrett, 1795. 10 pp.
AAS copy. 29572

Story, Isaac, 1774-1803.
An Eulogy on . . . Washington.
Worcester, [Mass.], Thomas, 1800. 23 pp.
AAS copy. 38567

Story, Joseph, 1779-1845.
An Eulogy on . . . Washington.
Salem, [Mass.], Cushing, 1800. 24 pp.
AAS copy. 38568

Story, Joseph, 1779-1845.
The Power of Solitude. A Poem.
Boston, Russell, [1800]. 100 pp.
AAS copy. 38569

Story, Thomas, 1670?-1742.
The Means, Nature . . . and Effects of
True Faith.
Philadelphia, Gibbons, 1793. 35, [1] pp.
AAS copy. 46881

Story, Thomas, 1670?-1742.
(D. N. B.)
Two Discourses.
Providence, 1769. 43 pp.
AAS copy. 11483

A Story about Mary's Conversion [by
Richard Lee, 1747-1823].
Rutland, for Richard Lee, [1795]. 4 pp.
AAS copy. 47481

[A Story of a Very Remarkable Snake.
Hanover, N. H., Dunham & True, 1795.]
(Imprint assumed by Evans from ad. "For
Sale at this Office," Eagle, July 20, 1795.)
29573

[The Story of Amelia.
Windsor, Hutchins, 1792.]
(McCorison 235; no copy known.) 46579

The Story of Aeneas and Dido Burlesqued
[by Robert Wells].
Charleston, 1774. xvi, 94 pp.
(See Sabin 92337.)
NYPL copy. 13743

The Story of Joseph.
Philadelphia, Crukshank, 1797. 48 pp.
AAS copy. 48261

The Story of Joseph.
Philadelphia, Ustick, 1799. 39 pp.
AAS copy. 36377

. . . . The Story of Joseph and his
Brethren. Part I.
Philadelphia, Johnsons, 1800. 36 pp.
AAS copy. 37151

. . . . The Story of Joseph and his
Brethren. Part II.
Philadelphia, Johnson, 1800. 36 pp.
AAS copy. 37152

. . . . The Story of Joseph and his
Brethren. Part III.
Philadelphia, Johnson, 1800. 36 pp.
AAS copy. 37153

The Story of Palemon and Eliza [by John
Shippen].
Harrisburg, Wyeth, 1796. 13, [1] pp.
AAS copy. 31187

The Story of the Cruel Giant Barbarico.
Boston, Mein & Fleeming, 1768. 53, [1]
pp.
BPL copy. 11082

The Story of the Innocent Amelia.
Putney, Vt., for Hinds, 1799. 59 pp.
AAS copy. 36378

[The Story Teller, or Merry-Fellow's
Companion.
Boston, Spotswood, 1795.]
(Imprint assumed by Evans from
Spotswood's adv.) 29574

Stoughton, William, 1631-1701.
New-Englands True Interest.
Cambridge, 1670. 40 pp.
AAS copy. 156

Stoughton, William, 1631-1701.
(Sibley, I, 194-208.)
New-Englands True Interests.
Cambridge, 1670. [4], 38, [1] pp.
(To judge by the correction of the errata,
this is the second edition of Evans 156,
with which it agrees chiefly in having the
text on the last two pages reset.) 155

[Stout, Benjamin.]
Narrative of the Loss of the Ship
Hercules.
New York, Chevalier, [1798?]. liii, 113
pp.
AAS copy. 32886

[Stout, Benjamin.]
Narrative of the Loss of the Ship
Hercules.
Hudson, [N. Y.], Stoddard, 1800. 118 pp.
AAS copy. 38571

[Stout, Benjamin.]
Narrative of the Loss of the Ship
Hercules.
New Bedford, Shearman, 1800. 124 pp.
AAS copy. 38570

Stoutenburgh, Jacobus.
A Short Detail.
New York, Brown, 1764. 44 pp.
NYHS copy. 10178

Stover, William Lilly.
The Columbian Almanack . . . for . . .
Seventeen Hundred and Ninety-One.
Newport, Edes. [24] pp.
AAS copy. 22912

The Strait Gate [by Joshua Gee,
1698-1748].
Boston, Henchman, 1729. [2], 103 pp.
HC copy. 3167

[A Strange Account of the Rising and

Breaking of a Great Bubble.
Boston, 1691.]
(A ghost arising from Evans' confusion of
10778 with a reference to some other item,
perhaps 543.) 577

A Strange Account of the Rising and
Breaking of a Great Bubble.
Sagadahock (Boston), 1767. 22 pp.
HC copy. 10778

Strange and Remarkable Swanzey Vision
[by Samuel Clarke, 1721?-].
Salem, Russell, 1776. 8 pp.
JCB copy. 14680

The Strange and Wonderful Account of a
Dutch Hog.
[New York, 1791?] Broadside.
NYSL copy. 46291

A Strange and Wonderful Indian Dream.
[Boston, 1773.] 8 pp.
AAS copy. 12969

[Strange Relation of an Old Woman who
was Drowned.
New York, 1745.]
(Adv. N. Y. Evening Post, Nov. 4, 1745.)
5692

The Stranger's Assistant and School-Boy's
Instructor.
New York, Forman for Berry, Rogers &
Berry, 1795. 179, [1], ii pp., 4 folded
tables.
AAS copy. 29576

The Stranger's Assistant, being a
Collection of Short, Correct and Easy
Rules for Reducing Thirteen Different
Coins and Currencies into Each Other.
New York, Forman, [1795]. 125, [1] pp. 1
table.
JCB copy. 29575

The Streamlet [by William Shield,
1748-1829].
New York, Hewitt, etc., [1797?]
Broadside.
NYPL copy. 48251

Strebeck, George.
A Collection of Evangelical Hymns.
New York, Tiebout, 1797. 263, [1], 130
pp.
(Evans took the title from an adv. which
described the Liturgy as a part of this
work.)
AAS copy. 32567

Strebeck, George.
A Sermon on the Character of the
Virtuous Woman.
New York, 1800. 26 pp.
AAS copy. 38572

Strebeck, George.
A Sermon, Preached (by Courtesy). . . .
New York, Tiebout & O'Brien, 1796. 16
pp.
AAS copy. 31243

Street, Nicholas, 1730-1806.
The American States.
New Haven, [1777]. 34 pp.
LOC copy. 15604

[Street, Thomas George.]
Aura; or the Slave. A Poem.
Philadelphia, James, 1788. 23 pp.
AAS copy. 21479

[Stretch, L. M.
The Beauties of History. . . . Ninth
Edition.
Hartford, Patten, 1794. 2 vol.]
("In the Press of Nathaniel Patten," Am.
Mercury, Jan. 6, 1794.) 27751

[Stretch, L. M.
The Beauties of History.
Philadelphia, Campbell, 1794. 2 vol.]
(Imprint assumed by Evans from advs.)
27750

Stretch, L. M.
The Beauties of History. . . . Seventh
Edition.
Springfield, Gray, 1794. 2 vol. xxiv, 360;
xi, [1], 348 pp.
AAS copy. 27749

[Stretch, L. M.
The Beauties of History.
Hudson, Stoddard, 1795.]
(Imprint assumed by Evans from
Stoddard's adv.)   29577

Strict Congregational Churches in
Connecticut.
An Historical Narrative, and Declaration,
Shewing the Cause and Rise of the Strict
Congregational Churches.
Providence, 1781. 44 pp.
LOC copy.   17115

Strictures and Observations upon the
Three Executive Departments.
Printed in the United States of America,
M,DCC,XCII. 32 pp.
AAS copy.   24515

Strictures on a Pamphlet, Entitled, a
"Friendly Address. . . ." [by Charles Lee,
1731-1782].
Philadelphia, Bradfords, 1774. 15 pp.
LCP copy.   13372

Strictures on a Pamphlet, Entitled a
"Friendly Address. . . ." [by Charles Lee,
1731-1782].
Boston, Greenleaf, 1775. 20 pp.
AAS copy.   14151

Strictures on a Pamphlet, Entitled, "A
Friendly Address. . . ." [by Charles Lee,
1731-1782].
Boston, Thomas, 1775. 12 pp.
AAS copy.   14152

Strictures on a Pamphlet, Entitled, a
"Friendly Address. . . ." [by Charles Lee,
1731-1782].
New London, 1775. 16 pp.
AAS copy.   14154

Strictures on a Pamphlet, Entitled, a
"Friendly Address. . . ." [by Charles Lee,
1731-1782].
America [New York], 1774.]
(Entry from Sabin; no such ed. located.)
     13373

Strictures on a Pamphlet, Entitled "A
Friendly Address. . . ." [by Charles Lee,
1731-1782].
Newport, 1775. 15 pp.
JCB copy.   14155

Strictures on a Pamphlet, Entitled a
"Friendly Address. . . ." [by Charles Lee,
1731-1782].
Philadelphia, Bradfords, 1775. 25 pp.]
(No copy with this imprint located.) 14153

Strictures on a Pamphlet, Intituled, "A
Friendly Address. . . ." [by Charles Lee,
1731-1782].
Providence, Carter, 1775. 15 pp.
JCB copy.   42859

Strictures on a Pamphlet, Entitled, The
Case of George M'Intosh.
Savannah, 1777. 17 pp.
LOC copy.   15605

Strictures on Bishop Watson's "Apology
for the Bible" [by Joel Barlow, 1754-
1812].
New York, Fellows, 1796. [2], 48 pp.
LOC copy.   30027

Strictures on Female Education [by John
Bennett, curate of St. Mary's,
Manchester].
Norwich, Bushnell, [1792]. v, [1], 133 pp.
AAS copy.   24094

Strictures on Harvard University [by
William Austin, 1778-1841].
Boston, Folsom, 1798. 35 pp.
AAS copy.   33344

Strictures on Mr. Burke's Two Letters [by
Ralph Broome].
Philadelphia, Thompson, 1797. iv, 50 pp.
LOC copy.   31876

Strictures on Mr. Burke's Two Letters [by
William Roscoe, 1753-1831?].
Philadelphia, Thompson, 1797. iv, 50 pp.
(Also entered as 31876, q. v.)   32778

[The Strictures on the Friendly Address

Examined [by Henry Barry].
New London, 1775. 16 pp.]
(Entry from Haven.)   13864

The Strictures on the Friendly Address
Examined [by Henry Barry].
[New York], 1775. 14 pp.
AAS copy.   13863

The Strictures on the Friendly Address
Examined [by Henry Barry].
Philadelphia, 1775. 14 pp.
(According to Wilberforce Eames this
entry is a ghost of 13863.)   13865

Strictures on the Landed and Commercial
Interest of the United States, for 1786. By
Philaeni.
New York, Childs, [1786]. 20 pp.
NYHS copy.   19921

Strictures on the Love of Power in the
Prelacy [by Henry Purcell, d. 1802].
Charleston, Young, 1795. 68 pp.
LOC copy.   29374

Strictures on the Philadelphia Mischianza
[by Israel Mauduit, 1708-1787].
Philadelphia, Bailey, 1780. 22 pp.
LCP copy.   16868

Strictures on the Rev. Mr. Thatcher's
Pamphlet [by James Sullivan, 1744-1808].
Boston, 1784. 28, 2 pp.
AAS copy.   18800

Strictures on the Second Part of the Age
of Reason [by Bryan Fairfax, 8th baron
Fairfax, 1727-1802].
Georgetown, Va., Green, English & Co.,
1797. 91 pp.
NYPL copy.   32105

Strictures upon the Letter imputed to Mr.
Jefferson [by Tench Coxe, 1755-1824].
n.p., 1800. 12 pp.
LCP copy.   37265

Strictures upon the Observations of a
'Member of the Convention.'
New Hampshire, 1792. 15 pp.
BPL copy.   24823

Strong, Cyprian, 1743-1811.
Animadversions.
Hartford, Hudson & Goodwin, 1789.
56 pp.
AAS copy.   22168

Strong, Cyprian, 1743-1811.
Animadversions.
Concord, N.H., Russell, 1793. 56 pp.
AAS copy.   26227

Strong, Cyprian, 1743-1811.
The Christian System.
Hartford, Ct., Hudson & Goodwin, 1798.
26 pp.
AAS copy.   34610

Strong, Cyprian, 1743-1811.
A Discourse Delivered at Hebron.
Hartford, Ct., Hudson & Goodwin, 1799.
18 pp.
AAS copy.   36379

Strong, Cyprian, 1743-1811.
A Discourse, Delivered at the Interment
of . . . Ruth Sage.
Middletown, [Ct.], Woodward, [1793]. 16
pp.
AAS copy.   46882

Strong, Cyprian, 1743-1811.
A Discoure, Delivered at the Interment of
Mrs. Ruth Sage.
Middletown, Woodward, [1794]. 16 pp.
CHS copy.   47222

Strong, Cyprian, 1743-1811.
A Discourse on Acts II. 42.
Hartford, 1780. 46 pp.
AAS copy.   17001

Strong, Cyprian, 1743-1811.
A Discourse on Acts II. 42. . . . Second
Edition.
Hartford, Hudson & Goodwin, 1791. 56
pp.
AAS copy.   23804

Strong, Cyprian, 1743-1811.
God's Care of the New-England Colonies.

Hartford, [1777]. 31 pp.
HC copy.   15606

Strong, Cyprian, 1743-1811.
An Inquiry.
Hartford, Hudson & Goodwin, 1793. 103
pp.
AAS copy.   26228

Strong, Cyprian, 1743-1811.
The Kingdom is the Lord's.
Hartford, Ct., Hudson & Goodwin, 1799.
46 pp.
AAS copy.   36380

Strong, Cyprian, 1743-1811.
The Nature and Design of the Evangelical
Ministry.
Stockbridge, Andrews, 1795. 32 pp.
AAS copy.   29578

Strong, Cyprian, 1743-1811.
A Second Inquiry, into . . . Baptism.
Hartford, Hudson & Goodwin, 1796. 117,
[1] pp.
AAS copy.   31244

Strong, Cyprian, 1743-1811.
A Sermon Delivered at the Ordination of
. . . Zephaniah H. Smith.
Hartford, Hudson & Goodwin, 1786. 28
pp.
JCB copy.   20011

Strong, Cyprian, 1743-1811.
A Sermon, Preached at Chatham.
Middletown, [Ct.], Dunning, 1800. 20 pp.
CHS copy.   38574

Strong, Cyprian, 1743-1811.
A Sermon, Preached at Hartford.
Hartford, [Ct.], Hudson & Goodwin,
1800. 19 pp.
AAS copy.   38575

Strong, Jonathan, 1764-1814.
A Sermon, Delivered at the Ordination of
. . . Levi White.
Hartford, Ct., Hudson & Goodwin, 1798.
31 pp.
AAS copy.   34611

Strong, Jonathan, 1764-1814.
A Sermon Delivered on the Day of the
Annual Thanksgiving.
Boston, Young & Minns, [1795]. 27 pp.
AAS copy.   29579

Strong, Joseph, 1729-1803.
The Church of Christ one.
Norwich, Trumbull, 1783. 28, 26 pp.
AAS copy.   18200

Strong, Joseph, 1729-1803.
(Weis, Colonial Clergy N. E.)
The Duty of Singing.
New Haven, 1773. 28 pp.
AAS copy.   13033

Strong, Joseph, 1729-1803.
(Weis, Colonial Clergy N. E.)
The Importance of Duly Receiving.
New Haven, [1772]. 33 pp.
AAS copy.   12570

Strong, Joseph, 1729-1803.
The Office of the Ministers.
New Haven, 1775. 27 pp.
AAS copy.   14478

Strong, Joseph, 1729-1803.
(Weis, Colonial Clergy N. E.)
That Presbyterian Ministers. . . .
Hartford, 1768. 55 pp.
YC copy.   11083

Strong, Joseph, 1753-1834.
A Sermon, Preached at Norwich.
Norwich, [Ct.], Trumbull, 1800. 17 pp.
AAS copy.   38576

Strong, Joseph, 1753-1834.
A Sermon, Delivered at the Funeral of . . .
Samuel Huntington.
Hartford, Hudson & Goodwin, 1796. 19
pp.
AAS copy.   31245

Strong, Nathan, 1717-1795.
(Weis, Colonial Clergy N. E.)
A Sermon, Preached at the Ordination of
. . . Nathan Strong.

Hartford, [1774]. 36 pp.
LOC copy. 13644

Strong, Nathan, 1748-1816.
The Agency and Providence of God.
Hartford, 1780. 24 pp.
AAS copy. 17002

Strong, Nathan, 1748-1816.
A Discourse, Delivered on ... December
27, 1799.
Hartford, [Ct.], Hudson & Goodwin,
1800. 31 pp.
AAS copy. 38577

Strong, Nathan, 1748-1816.
The Doctrine of Eternal Misery.
Hartford, Hudson & Goodwin, 1796. 408
pp.
AAS copy. 31246

Strong, Nathan, 1748-1816.
The Hartford Selection of Hymns.
Hartford, Ct., Babcock, 1799. 333, [1] pp.
AAS copy. 36382

Strong, Nathan, 1748-1816.
Political Instruction from the Prophecies.
Hartford, Ct., Hudson & Goodwin, 1798.
30 pp.
AAS copy. 34612

Strong, Nathan, 1748-1816.
Political Instruction.
New York, Forman for Davis, 1799. 24
pp.
AAS copy. 36381

Strong, Nathan, 1748-1816.
The Reasons and Design of Public
Punishments.
Hartford, 1777. 18 pp.
AAS copy. 15607

Strong, Nathan, 1748-1816.
A Sermon, Delivered at the Funeral of
Mrs. Sarah Williams.
Hartford, [Ct.], Hudson & Goodwin,
1800. 15 pp.
AAS copy. 38578

Strong, Nathan, 1748-1816.
A Sermon, Delivered at the Ordination of
... Ichabod Lord Skinner.
Hartford, Hudson & Goodwin, 1794. 21
pp.
AAS copy. 27752

Strong, Nathan, 1748-1816.
A Sermon, Delivered in Presence of His
Excellency.
Hartford, Hudson & Goodwin, 1790. 32
pp.
AAS copy. 22913

Strong, Nathan, 1748-1816.
A Sermon, Preached at the Annual
Thanksgiving.
Hartford, Hudson & Goodwin, 1797. 16
pp.
AAS copy. 32887

Strong, Nathan, 1748-1816.
A Sermon, Preached at the Installation of
... David Huntington.
Middletown, Ct., Dunning, 1798. 24 pp.
AAS copy. 34613

Strong, Nathan, 1748-1816.
A Sermon, Preached in Hartford, June
10th, 1797.
Hartford, Babcock, 1797. 21 pp.
AAS copy. 32888

[Strong, Nathan, 1748-1816.
A Sermon, Preached in Hartford, June
10th, 1797.... Second Edition.
Hartford, Babcock, 1797. 21 pp.]
("The second edition," was adv. in Am.
Mercury, Aug. 28, 1797, but no copy
located carries those words.) 32889

Strong, Nathan, 1748-1816.
A Sermon, Preached March 18, 1778.
Norwich, Trumbull, 1778. 24 pp.
AAS copy. 16086

Strong, Nathan, 1748-1816.
A Sermon, Preached on the State Fast.
Hartford, Ct., Hudson & Goodwin, 1898.
20 pp.
AAS copy. 34614

Strong, Nathan, 1748-1816.
Sermons, on Various Subjects.... Vol. I.
Hartford, Ct., Hudson & Goodwin, 1798.
396 pp.
AAS copy. 34615

Strong, Nathan, 1748-1816.
Sermons, on Various Subjects.... Vol. II.
Hartford, Ct., Babcock for Cookes, 1800.
408 pp.
AAS copy. 38579

Strong, Nathan, 1748-1816.
A Thanksgiving Sermon.
Hartford, Ct., Hudson & Goodwin, 1800.
18 pp.
AAS copy. 38580

Strong, Nathaniel.
England's Perfect Schoolmaster....
Twelfth Edition.
Boston, Green for Buttolph, 1710. 128 pp.
Columbia University (Plimpton) copy.
1487

Strong, Nehemiah, 1729-1807.
See also under
Stafford, H., pseud. 38582

[Strong, Nehemiah], 1729-1807.
An Astronomical Ephemeris, Kalendar,
or Almanack, for 1776.... By Hosea
Stafford.
New Haven, Greens. [20] pp.
AAS copy. 14479

[Strong, Nehemiah], 1729-1807.
An Astronomical Ephemeris, Kalendar,
or Almanack, for ... 1777.... By Hosea
Stafford.
New Haven, Greens. [20] pp.
AAS copy. 15098

[Strong, Nehemiah], 1729-1807.
An Astronomical Ephemeris, Calendar,
or Almanack, for ... 1782.
Hartford, Hudson & Goodwin. [24] pp.
AAS copy. 17373

Strong, Nehemiah, 1729-1807.
An Astronomical Ephemeris, Calender,
or Almanack, for ... 1783.
Hartford, Hudson & Goodwin. [24] pp.
AAS copy. 17730

Strong, Nehemiah, 1729-1807.
An Astronomical Diary, or Almanack, for
... 1783.
Springfield, Babcock & Haswell. [24] pp.
AAS copy. 17731

Strong, Nehemiah, 1729-1807.
An Astronomical Ephemeris, Calender, or
Almanack, for ... 1784.
Hartford, Hudson & Goodwin. [24] pp.
AAS copy. 18201

Strong, Nehemiah, 1729-1807.
An Astronomical Ephemeris, Calendar, or
Almanack ... 1785.
Hartford, Hudson & Goodwin. [24] pp.
AAS copy. 18798

Strong, Nehemiah, 1729-1807.
An Astronomical Ephemeris, Calendar, or
Almanack, for ... 1786.
Hartford, Hudson & Goodwin. [24] pp.
AAS copy. 19263

Strong, Nehemiah, 1729-1807.
An Astronomical Diary, or Almanack for
... 1787.
Hartford, Babcock. [24] pp.
AAS copy. 20013

Strong, Nehemiah, 1729-1807.
An Astronomical Ephemeris, Calendar, or
Almanack, for ... 1787.
Hartford, Hudson & Goodwin. [24] pp.
AAS copy. 20014

Strong, Nehemiah, 1729-1807.
An Astronomical Diary, or Almanack, for
... 1787.
New Haven, Meigs & Dana. [24] pp.
(The only known copy is imperfect.)
BPL copy. 44973

Strong, Nehemiah, 1729-1807.
An Almanack, for the Year ... 1787.
Springfield, Stebbins & Russell. [24] pp.
AAS copy. 20012

Strong, Nehemiah, 1729-1807.
An Astronomical Diary, Kalender, or
Almanack, for ... 1788.
Hartford, Babcock. [22] pp.
(The AAS copy has different end matter.)
LOC copy. 20732

[Strong, Nehemiah], 1729-1807.
An Almanack, for ... 1788.... By Hosea
Stafford.
New Haven, Greens. [24] pp.
AAS copy. 20733

Strong, Nehemiah, 1729-1807.
An Astronomical Diary, Kalender, or
Almanack, for ... 1789.
Hartford, Babcock. [24] pp.
AAS copy. 21480

Strong, Nehemiah, 1729-1807.
An Astronomical Diary, Kalender, or
Almanack, for ... 1789.
Hartford, Patten. [24] pp.
LOC copy. 21481

Strong, Nehemiah, 1729-1807.
An Astronomical Diary, Kalender, or
Almanack, for ... 1789.
Hartford, Printed by Hudson & Goodwin.
[24] pp.
AAS copy. 45369

Strong, Nehemiah, 1729-1807.
An Astronomical Diary, Kalender, or
Almanack, for ... 1789.
Hartford, Reprinted by Hudson &
Goodwin. [24] pp.
CHS copy. 45370

[Strong, Nehemiah], 1729-1807.
An Astronomical Diary, Kalender, or
Almanack, for ... 1789.... By Hosea
Stafford.
New Haven, Greens. [24] pp.
AAS copy. 21482

Strong, Nehemiah, 1729-1807.
An Astronomical Diary, Kalender, or
Almanack, for ... 1789.
Northampton, Butler. [24] pp.
WLC copy. 21483

Strong, Nehemiah, 1729-1807.
An Astronomical Diary, Kalender, or
Almanack, for ... 1790.
Hartford, Babcock. [24] pp.
AAS copy. 22169

Strong, Nehemiah, 1729-1807.
An Almanack for ... 1790.
Hartford, Hudson & Goodwin. [24] pp.
CHS copy. 45597

[Strong, Nehemiah], 1729-1807.
An Astronomical Diary, Kalander or
Almanack for ... 1790.... By Hosea
Stafford.
New Haven, Greens. [24] pp.
AAS copy. 22170

Strong, Nehemiah, 1729-1807.
An Astronomical Diary, Kalender, or
Almanack, for ... 1791.
Hartford, Babcock. [24] pp.
AAS copy. 22915

Strong, Nehemiah, 1729-1807.
An Astronomical Diary, Kalender, or
Almanack, for ... 1791.
Hartford, Patten. [24] pp.
AAS copy. 22914

Strong, Nehemiah, 1729-1807.
An Astronomical Diary, Kalender, or
Almanack, for ... 1792.
Hartford, Babcock. [24] pp.
AAS copy. 23805

Strong, Nehemiah, 1729-1807.
An Astronomical Diary, Kalender, or
Almanack, for ... 1792.
Hartford, Patten. [24] pp.
AAS copy. 23806

Strong, Nehemiah, 1729-1807.
An Astronomical Diary, Calendar, or
Almanack, for ... 1792.
Litchfield, Collier. [24] pp.
AAS copy. 23807

Strong, Nehemiah, 1729-1807.
An Astronomical Diary, Kalender, or
Almanack, for ... 1793.

Hartford, Babcock. [24] pp.
LOC copy.   24825

Strong, Nehemiah, 1729-1807.
An Astronomical Diary, Calendar, or
Almanack, for . . . 1793.
Hartford, Patten. [24] pp.
AAS copy.   24824

Strong, Nehemiah, 1729-1807.
An Astronomical Diary, Kalendar, or,
Almanack, for . . . 1793.
Litchfield, Collier & Buel. [24] pp.
(The AAS has another ed. with different
text on the last leaf.)
AAS copy.   24826

[Strong, Nehemiah], 1729-1807.
An Astronomical Diary, Kalendar, or
Almanack for . . . 1793. . . . By H.
Stafford.
New Haven, Greens. [24] pp.
AAS copy.   24827

Strong, Nehemiah, 1729-1807.
An Astronomical Diary, Calendar, or
Almanack, for . . . 1794.
Hartford, Babcock. [24] pp.
AAS copy.   26229

[Strong, Nehemiah], 1729-1807.
An Astronomical Diary, Calendar, or,
Almanack, for . . . 1794.
Hartford, Babcock, for Patten.,]
(Imprint assumed by Evans from adv.
"Just Published by Nathaniel Patten . . .
Strong's Almanack," Am. Mercury, Nov.
4, 1793.)   26230

[Strong, Nehemiah], 1729-1807.
An Astronomical Diary, Calendar, or
Almanack, for . . . 1794. . . . By H.
Stafford.
New Haven, Greens. [24] pp.
AAS copy.   26232

Strong, Nehemiah, 1729-1807.
An Astronomical Diary, Calendar, or,
Almanack, for . . . 1794.
Springfield, Gray. [24] pp.
AAS copy.   26231

[Strong, Nehemiah, 1729-1807.
An Astronomical Diary, Kalendar, or
Almanack for . . . 1795.]
Hartford, Babcock.
(Title and imprint assumed by Evans from
adv. for "Almanacks.")   27753

[Strong, Nehemiah], 1729-1807.
An Astronomical Diary, Kalendar, or
Almanack for . . . 1795.
Hartford, Patten.]
(Assumed by Evans from adv. for
"Almanacks.")   27754

[Strong, Nehemiah], 1729-1807.
An Astronomical Diary, Calendar, or
Almanack, for . . . 1795. . . . By H.
Stafford.
New Haven, Greens. [24] pp.
AAS copy.   27755

[Strong, Nehemiah, 1729-1807.
An Astronomical Diary, Calendar, or
Almanack, for . . . 1795.
Springfield, Gray. [24] pp.]
(Imprint assumed by Evans from adv.
"Just Published and now ready for sale
by" in Hampshire and Berkshire
Chronicle.)   27756

Strong, Nehemiah, 1729-1807.
An Astronomical Diary, Calendar, or
Almanack for . . . 1796.
Hartford, Babcock. [24] pp.
AAS copy.   29580

[Strong, Nehemiah], 1729-1807.
An Astronomical Diary, Calendar, or
Almanack, for . . . 1796. . . . By H.
Stafford.
New Haven, Greens. [24] pp.
AAS copy.   29582

Strong, Nehemiah, 1729-1807.
An Astronomical Diary, Calendar, or
Almanack, for . . . 1797.
Hartford, Babcock. [24] pp.
AAS copy.   31247

Strong, Nehemiah, 1729-1807.
An Astronomical Diary, Calendar, or

Almanack, for . . . 1797. . . . By N. Strong.
Litchfield, Collier. [24] pp.
CHS copy.   47925

Strong, Nehemiah, 1729-1807.
Strong's Astronomical Diary, Calendar,
or, Almanack, for . . . 1797.
West Springfield, Gray. [24] pp.
AAS copy.   31248

Strong, Nehemiah, 1729-1807.
An Astronomical Diary, Calendar, or
Almanack, for . . . 1798.
Hartford, Babcock. [24] pp.
AAS copy.   32890

Strong, Nehemiah, 1729-1807.
An Astronomical Diary, Calendar, or
Almanack, for . . . 1799.
Hartford, [Ct.], Babcock. [24] pp.
YC copy.   34616

[Strong, Nehemiah], 1729-1807.
An Astronomical Diary, Calendar, or
Almanack, for . . . 1799 . . . By H.
Stafford.
New Haven, Greens. [24] pp.
AAS copy.   34618

Strong, Nehemiah, 1729-1807.
An Astronomical Diary, Calendar, or
Almanack, for . . . 1800.
Hartford, Ct., Babcock. [36] pp.
AAS copy.   36383

Strong, Nehemiah, 1729-1807.
Astronomy Improved.
New Haven, 1784. 52 pp., 2 plates.
AAS copy.   18797

[Strong, Nehemiah], 1729-1807.
The Connecticut Almanack, for . . . 1778.
Hartford, 1778. [16] pp.
AAS copy.   15608

Strong, Nehemiah, 1729-1807.
The Connecticut Almanack, for . . . 1779.
Hartford, Watson & Goodwin. [16] pp.
AAS copy.   16087

[Strong, Nehemiah], 1729-1807.
The Connecticut Almanack, for . . . 1780.
Hartford, Hudson & Goodwin. [24] pp.
AAS copy.   16538

Strong, Nehemiah, 1729-1807.
The Connecticut Almanack, for . . . 1781.
Hartford, Hudson & Goodwin. [24] pp.
(The AAS has variant issues.)
AAS copy.   17003

Strong, Nehemiah, 1729-1807.
The Connecticut Almanac, for . . . 1800.
Hartford, [Ct.], Dwier. 47 pp.
BPL copy.   36385

Strong, Nehemiah, 1729-1807.
The Connecticut, Massachusetts,
New-York, and Vermont Almanack, for
. . . 1795.
Litchfield, Collier & Buel. [24] pp.
AAS copy.   27757

Strong, Nehemiah, 1729-1807.
The Connecticut Pocket Almanac, for . . .
1800.
Hartford, Ct., John Babcock for E. & J.
Babcock. 47 pp.
AAS copy.   36384

Strong, Nehemiah, 1729-1807.
The Connecticut Pocket Almanack, for
. . . 1801.
Hartford, Ct., John Babcock for E. & J.
Babcock. 47 pp.
AAS copy.   38581

[Strong, Nehemiah], 1729-1807.
The Middlesex Almanack . . . for . . .
1791.
Middletown, Woodward. [24] pp.
CHS copy.   22916

[Strong, Nehemiah], 1729-1807.
The Middlesex Almanack . . . for . . .
1792.
Middletown, Woodward. [24] pp.
AAS copy.   23808

Strong, Nehemiah, 1729-1807.
The New-England Almanack, for . . .
1781.

Worcester, Haswell, [1780]. [24] pp.
AAS copy.   19436

[Strong, Nehemiah, 1729-1807.
Sheet Almanack for 1792.
New Haven, Greens. Broadside.]
(Assumed from advs. for sheet almanacs.)
                                               23810

[Strong, Nehemiah, 1729-1807.
Sheet Almanack for 1793.
Hartford, Babcock, 1792. Broadside.]
("This day published . . . Sheet
Almanacks," Am. Mercury, Sept. 24,
1792.)   24828

[Strong, Nehemiah, 1729-1807.
Sheet Almanack for 1794.
Hartford, Babcock. Broadside.]
(Assumed by Evans from advs. for
"Strong's Almanack.")   26233

[Strong, Nehemiah, 1729-1807.
Sheet Almanack for 1796.
Hartford, Babcock. Broadside.]
(Assumed by Evans from adv. "Sheet
almanacks for sale," Am. Mercury, Oct.
12, 1795.)   29581

[Strong, Nehemiah, 1729-1807.
Sheet Almanack for 1796.
New Haven, Greens. Broadside.]
(assumed by Evans from the Greens' advs.
for sheet almanacs.)   29583

[Strong, Nehemiah, 1729-1807.
Sheet Almanac for 1797.
Hartford, Babcock. Broadside.]
(Assumed for Evans from adv. "Sheet
Almanacs for Sale," Am. Mercury, Dec.
19, 1797.)   31249

[Strong, Nehemiah, 1729-1807.
Sheet Almanac for 1798.
Hartford, Babcock. Broadside.]
(Assumed by Evans from Babcock's advs.
for "sheet almanacs.")   32891

[Strong, Nehemiah, 1729-1807.
Sheet Almanac for 1798.
New Haven, Greens. Broadside.]
(Assumed by Evans from the Greens' adv.
for "sheet almanacs.")   32893

[Strong, Nehemiah, 1729-1807.
Sheet Almanac for 1799.
Hartford, Ct., Babcock. Broadside.]
(Assumed by Evans from advs. for "sheet
almanacks.")   34617

[Strong, Nehemiah], 1729-1807.
Sheet Almanac for 1800.
Hartford, Babcock. Broadside.]
(Adv. in Am. Mercury, Oct. 31, 1799.)
                                               36386

[Strong, Nehemiah], 1729-1807.
Stafford's Almanac, for . . . 1778. . . . By
Hosea Stafford.
New Haven, Greens. [24] pp.
AAS copy.   15609

[Strong, Nehemiah], 1729-1807.
Stafford's Almanac, for . . . 1780. . . . By
Hosea Stafford.
New Haven, Greens. [24] pp.
AAS copy.   16539

[Strong, Nehemiah], 1729-1807.
Stafford's Almanack, for 1781. . . . By
Hosea Stafford.
New Haven, Greens. [20] pp.
AAS copy.   17004

[Strong, Nehemiah], 1729-1807.
Stafford's Almanack, for . . . 1782. . . . By
Hosea Stafford.
New Haven, Greens. [20] pp.
AAS copy.   17374

[Strong, Nehemiah], 1729-1807.
Stafford's Almanack for . . . 1783. . . . By
Hosea Stafford.
New Haven, Greens. [24] pp.
AAS copy.   17732

[Strong, Nehemiah], 1729-1807.
Stafford's Almanack, for . . . 1784. . . . By
Hosea Stafford.
New Haven, Green, [24] pp.
AAS copy.   18202

[Strong, Nehemiah], 1729-1807.

Stafford's Almanac, for . . . 1785. . . . By
Hosea Stafford.
New Haven, Greens. [24] pp.
AAS copy.   18799

[Strong, Nehemiah], 1729-1807.
Stafford's Almanack, for . . . 1786. . . . By
Hosea Stafford.
New Haven, Greens. [24] pp.
AAS copy.   19264

[Strong, Nehemiah], 1729-1807.
Stafford's Almanack, for . . . 1787. . . . By
Hosea Stafford.
New Haven, Greens. [24] pp.
AAS copy.   20015

[Strong, Nehemiah], 1729-1807.
Stafford's Almanack, for . . . 1791.
New Haven, Greens. [24] pp.
AAS copy.   22917

[Strong, Nehemiah], 1729-1807.
Stafford's Almanack, for . . . 1792.
New Haven, Greens. [24] pp.
AAS copy.   23809

[Strong, Nehemiah], 1729-1807.
Stafford's Almanack, for . . . 1797.
New Haven, Greens. [24] pp.
AAS copy.   31250

[Strong, Nehemiah], 1729-1807.
Stafford's Almanack, for . . . 1798.
New Haven, Greens. [24] pp.
AAS copy.   32892

[Strong, Nehemiah], 1729-1807.
Stafford's Connecticut Almanack, for . . .
1779. . . . By Hosea Stafford.
New Haven, Greens. [20] pp.
AAS copy.   16088

Strong, Nehemiah, 1729-1807.
Strong's Almanack for . . . 1788.
New Haven, Meigs. [20] pp.
CHS copy.   20734

[Strong, Nehemiah], 1729-1807.
Strong's Almanack, for . . . 1796.
Springfield, Gray. [24] pp.
AAS copy.   29584

Strong's Almanack, for . . . 1796 [by
Nehemiah Strong, 1729-1807].
Springfield, Gray. [24] pp.
AAS copy.   29584

Strong's Astronomical Diary, Calendar
or, Almanack, for . . . 1798.
West Springfield, Gray. [28] pp.
AAS copy.   32894

Strong, Nehemiah, 1729-1807.
Strong's Connecticut and New-York
Almanack, for . . . 1794.
Litchfield, Collier & Buel. [24] pp.
CHS copy.   46883

[Strong, Nehemiah], 1729-1807.
Watson's Register, and Connecticut
Almanack . . . for 1775.
Hartford, Watson. [36] pp.
AAS copy.   13645

[Strong, Nehemiah], 1729-1807.
Watson's Register, and Connecticut
Almanack, for . . . 1776.
Hartford, Watson. [24] pp.
AAS copy.   14480

[Strong, Nehemiah], 1729-1807.
Watson's Connecticut Almanack, for . . .
1777.
Hartford, Watson. [24] pp.
AAS copy.   15099

[Strong, Simeon], 1735-1805.
A Paraphrase, on Eight Chapters of the
Prophet Isaiah.
Worcester, Thomas, 1795. 41 pp.
AAS copy.   28284

[Strother, John.
A Treatise on the Distillation of Ardent
Spirits.
Richmond, Va.?, 1796.]
(Entry from copyright record.)   31251

Stuart, David, of Wm. & Mary College.
An Oration, in Commemoration of the
Founders.

Williamsburg, Rind, 1772. 10 pp.
JCB copy.   12571

Stuart, James, M.D.
Directions for Medicine Chests. . . . May
9, 1795.
Philadelphia, Ormrod & Conrad, 1795. 8
pp.
(Austin 112; no copy located.)   47615

Stuart, James, M.D.
A Dissertation on the Salutary Effects of
Mercury.
Philadelphia, Bradfords, 1798. [12], 37
pp.
AAS copy.   34619

Stuart, William, fl. 1793.
An Oration, Delivered before the Uranian
Society.
New York, Swords, 1794. 23 pp.
AAS copy.   27758

Stubbs, Henry, 1606?-1678.
Conscience the Best Friend.
Boston, Green & Allen for Buttolph, 1699.
[6], 64 pp.
(The only known copy is imperfect.)
JCB copy.   39355

Stubbs, Henry, 1606?-1678.
(D. N. B.)
Conscience the Best Friend.
Boston, 1700. [20], 64 pp.
AAS copy.   954

Stubbs, Henry, 1606?-1678.
Conscience the Best Friend upon Earth.
Boston, 1714. [20], 62, [1] pp.
AAS copy.   1717

Studdiford, Peter, d. 1827.
A Funeral Sermon, on . . . Jacob R.
Hardenburgh.
New Brunswick, N. J., Blauvelt, 1791. 23
pp.
NYHS copy.   23811

---- Stulta est Clementia.
[Philadelphia, 1727.] 4 pp.
APS copy.   2965

Sturgeon, Robert.
A Trespass-Offering.
Boston, 1725. 4 pp.
HC copy.   2704

Sturm, Christoph Christian, 1740-1786.
Beauties of Nature Delineated.
Charlestown, Mass., Etheridge, 1800.
front., [2], 223, [1] pp.
AAS copy.   38583

[Styles, E.
Oration at Charlestown.
Westminster, Spooner & Green, 1782.
8 pp.]
(A ghost of 19437, q.v.)   17733

Styles, E.
An Oration, Delivered at the Rev. Mr.
Olcott's Church.
Westminster, Vt., 1782. 8 pp.
AAS copy.   19437

Subjects for Painters. By Peter Pindar [by
John Wolcot, 1738-1819].
Philadelphia, Spotswood, 1789.]
(Entry from an adv.)   22289

Subjects for Painters. By Peter Pindar [by
John Wolcot, 1728-1819].
Philadelphia, Spotswood, 1790. 59 pp.
LCP copy.   46105

The Subscribers to the Non-Importation
Agreement. . . . September 20, 1770.
[Philadelphia, 1770.] Broadside.
LOC copy.   11876

Subscription Paper for the Deputy
Commisary's Guide [by Elie Vallette].
[Annapolis, A. C. Green]. Broadside.
(No copy could be located.)   42738

The Substance, of a Council held at
Lancaster, August the 28th. 1764.
[Philadelphia], 1764. 19 pp.
NYPL copy.   9848

The Substance of a Late Remarkable
Dream [by James Shurtleff, 1745-1832].

Hallowell, Me., Edes, 1800. 16 pp.
BrU copy.   38584

The Substance of an Exercise, had this
Morning in Scurrility Hall [by Isaac
Hunt, 1742?-1809].
[Philadelphia], 1765. 6 pp.
NYPL copy.   10015

The Substance of Two Letters,
Concerning Communion.
Newport, 1768. 23 pp.
RIHS copy.   41887

Suffolk County, Mass. Convention, 1774.
At a Meeting of the Delegates of Every
Town and District [Sept. 6, 1774].
[Boston, 1774.] Broadside.
MHS copy.   13646

Suffolk County, Mass. Register of
Probate.
. . . December 12, 1715. Samuel Sewall,
Esq., Judge for the Probate of Wills. . . .
[Boston, 1715.] Broadside.
EI copy.   39635

Suffolk ss. At the Superior Court, &c.
August 1774. . . . We . . . Grand Jurors.
[Boston, 1774.] Broadside.
MHS copy.   13426

The Sugar Plumb. . . . First Worcester
Edition.
Worcester, Thomas, 1787. 123, [1] pp.
AAS copy.   20735

The Suicide. A Dialogue [by Thomas
Day, 1777-1855].
Litchfield, Ct., Collier, [1797]. 20 pp.
AAS copy.   32019

Sullivan, George, 1771-1838.
An Oration, Pronounced at Exeter.
Exeter, N. H., Ranlet, 1800. 16 pp.
AAS copy.   38585

[Sullivan, James], 1744-1808.
The Altar of Baal Thrown Down. . . . Par
Citoyen de Novion.
Boston, Adams & Larkin, 1795. 31 pp.
AAS copy.   29585

[Sullivan, James], 1744-1808.
The Altar of Baal Thrown Down. . . . Par
Citoyen de Novion [2nd Issue, without
halftitle and tail piece.]
Boston, Adams & Larkin, 1795. 31 pp.
NYPL copy.   29586

[Sullivan, James], 1744-1808.
The Altar of Baal Thrown Down. . . . By
Citoyen de Novion.
Philadelphia, 1795. 32 pp.
LCP copy.   29587

[Sullivan, James], 1744-1808.
The Altar of Baal Thrown Down. . . . Par
Citoyen de Novion.
Stockbridge, Andrews, 1795. 28 pp.
AAS copy.   29588

[Sullivan, James], 1744-1808.
Biographical Sketch of the Life &
Character of . . . Governor Hancock.
Boston, [1793]. 16 pp.
AAS copy.   26234

[Sullivan, James], 1744-1808.
Biographical Sketch of the Life &
Character of . . . Governor Hancock.
Boston, Coverly, [1793]. 11 pp.
MHS copy.   26235

Sullivan, James, 1744-1808.
The History of the District of Maine.
Boston, Thomas & Andrews, 1795. vii,
[1], 421 pp., 1 folding map.
AAS copy.   29589

[Sullivan, James], 1744-1808.
An Impartial Review of the Causes and
Principles of the French Revolution.
Boston, Edes, 1798. 101, [1] pp.
AAS copy.   34620

Sullivan, James, 1744-1808.
Observations upon the Government.
Boston, Hall, 1791. 55 pp.
AAS copy.   23812

[Sullivan, James], 1744-1808.
An Ode, Sung at the Lecture of the

Congregational Charitable Society, in
Boston, on the 12th of February, 1795. By
Mr. Rea.
[Boston, 1795.] Broadside.
MHS copy. 29590

[Sullivan, James], 1744-1808.
The Path to Riches.
Boston, Edes for Thomas & Andrews,
1792. 77 pp.
AAS copy. 24829

[Sullivan, James], 1744-1808.
Strictures on the Rev. Mr. Thatcher's
Pamphlet.
Boston, 1784. 28, 2 pp.
AAS copy. 18800

[Sullivan, James, 1744-1802.
Strictures upon the Rev. Mr. Thatcher's
Pamphlet.
Boston, Edes, 1785. 28, [2] pp.]
(This is a duplicate of 18800, q. v.) 19265

Sullivan, John, 1740-1795.
General Sullivan's Address.
Portsmouth, Gerrish, 1785. 8 pp.
MHS copy. 19266

Sullivan, John, 1740-1795.
Regulations for the . . . Troops of
New-Hampshire.
Portsmouth, Melcher & Osborne, 1785. 37
pp.
AAS copy. 19267

[Sullivan, William], 1774-1839.
The Demos in Council.
Boston, Cutler, 1799. 16 pp.
AAS copy. 35400

Sum of Testimonies of Truth [by John
Gerar William De Brahm, 1717-c. 1799].
[Philadelphia? 1795.] 7 pp.
DeRGL copy. 47397

Summary Arguments in Favor of
Episcopal Church Government.
Hanover, N. H., Dunham, 1794. 8 pp.
HEH copy. 27759

A Summary, Historical and Political. . . .
No. 1 [by William Douglass, 1691-1752].
Boston, Rogers & Fowle, 1747. 256 pp.
(This is the serial form of 6307, q.v.) 5936

A Summary View of the Courses of Crops
[by John Beale Bordley, 1727-1804].
Philadelphia, Cist, 1784. 22 pp.
AAS copy. 18373

A Summary View of the Rights of British
America [by Thomas Jefferson, pres.
U. S., 1743-1826].
Norfolk, [1774].
(Entry by Evans, apparently from a notice
in the [Norfolk] Virginia Gazette.) 13352

A Summary View of the Rights of British
America [by Thomas Jefferson, pres.
U. S., 1743-1826].
Philadelphia, Dunlap, 1774. 23 pp.
AAS copy. 13351

A Summary View of the Rights of British
America [by Thomas Jefferson, pres.
U. S., 1743-1826].
Williamsburg, Rind, [1774]. 23 pp.
LCP copy. 13350

Sumner, Charles Pinckney, 1776-1839.
The Compass.
Boston, Spotswood, [1795]. 12 pp.
AAS copy. 29591

Sumner, Charles Pinckney, 1776-1839.
Eulogy on the Illustrious George
Washington.
Dedham, [Mass.], Mann, 1800. 24 pp.
AAS copy. 38586

[Sumner, Clement, 1731-1795.
An Oration, Delivered . . . in Keene, on
June 24, A. L. 5790.
Keene, Griffith, [1790]. 22 pp.]
Sabin 93696 but no copy located.) 22918

Sumner, Joseph, 1740-1824.
Ministers Spiritual Builders.
Worcester, Thomas, 1791. 30 pp.
AAS copy. 23813

Sumner, Joseph, 1740-1824.

A Sermon, Preached at Shrewsbury.
Brookfield, Mass., Merriam, 1800. 26 pp.
AAS copy. 38587

Sun Fire Society, Boston.
Association and Articles . . . Instituted
. . . 8th May, 1765.
Boston, Weld & Greenough, 1794. 8,
[5] pp.
BPL copy. 26689

[Sundry Anthems. (Being Part of a
Proposed Collection.)]
("Just published," Pa. Gazette, Nov. 19,
1788.) 21484

Sundry, Letters and Petitions Addressed
to His Excellency James Garrard. . . .
September 4, 1799.
[Imprint trimmed off.] vi, 32 pp.
WisHS copy. 36389

Suplee, Nathan.
To the Electors of Pennsylvania. . . .
October 3d, 1799.
n.p., [1799]. 2 pp.
HSP copy. 36390

Supplement Extraordinary, June 10, 1773.
On Friday last the Chamber of
Commerce. . . .
[New York, 1773.] Broadside.
NYHS copy. 42515

Supplement Extraordinary to the
Independent Journal. Monday, July 28,
1788.
New York, M'Lean, [1788]. Broadside.
AAS ph. copy. 21172

Supplement to a Memoir [by Benjamin
Smith Barton, 1766-1815].
[Philadelphia, 1800.] 40 pp.
AAS copy. 36904

Supplement to the American Star, No. 5.
Culture of the Vine. . . . January 21,
1794.
[Philadelphia, 1794.] Broadside.
(Not located, 1968.) 47223

Supplement to the Encyclopaedia, or
Dictionary of Arts, Sciences, and
Miscellaneous Literature. In Three
Volumes.
Philadelphia, Dobson, 1803.
(More appropriately entered as Shaw
4162, q. v.) 38593

A Supplement to the Essay on Monies
[by John Beale Bordley, 1727-1804].
Philadelphia, Humphries, 1790. [2], 7 pp.
NYPL copy. 22368

Supplement to the Independent Chronicle.
Thursday, February 3, 1791.
Boston, Adams, [1791]. [4] pp.
AAS copy. 46292

Supplement to the New-York Gazetteer
No. 44.
Peace! . . . Philadelphia, March 24, 1783.
[Philadelphia, 1783.] Broadside.
NYHS copy. 44462

Supplement to the Pennsylvania Journal,
May 3, 1770.
[Numb. 1430. Watchman. No. V. . . .
April 21, 1770.
[Philadelphia, 1770.] [2] pp.
LCP copy. 11922

A Sure Guide to Hell. . . . Fourth Edition
[by Benjamin Bourn, fl. 1740].
Boston, Gookin, 1751. 63, [1] pp.
AAS copy. 6643

[A Sure Guide to Hell [by Benjamin
Bourn, fl. 1740].
New York, Parker, 1751.]
(From Bookseller's adv.) 6644

A Sure Guide to Hell. . . . Sixth Edition
[by Benjamin Bourn, fl. 1740].
New York, Holt, 1767.]
("Just publish'd," N.Y. Journal, Feb. 26,
1767.) 10568

A Surprising Account of the Life of the
late John Elwes, Esq. [by Edward
Topham, 1751-1820].
Philadelphia, Zeller, 1791. 71 pp.
PSL copy. 23837

The Surprizing Appearance of a Ghost,
with the Message he Brought.
Boston, Fowle & Draper, 1759. 23 pp.
HEH copy. 41082

Surr, Thomas Skinner, 1770-1847.
. . . George Barnwell. A New Novel.
Boston, Bumstead for Thomas &
Andrews, etc., 1800. 300 pp.
AAS copy. 38596

Surr, Thomas Skinner, 1770-1847.
George Barnwell, a Novel, in Two
Volumes.
Philadelphia, office of The True
American, 1800. [2], 167; [2], 185 pp.
(Present location unknown.) 49150

A Survey of Man, from the Cradle, to the
Grave.
New Haven, 1760. 16 pp.
MHS copy. 8744

[A Survey of Man, from the Cradle, to the
Grave.
Middletown, 1789.]
("To be sold at this office," Middlesex
Gazette, May 8, 1789.) 22171

[The Suspected Daughter, or Jealous
Father.
Boston, 1751.]
("This Day is Published. . . . To be sold at
the Bible and Crown. The Subscribers are
desir'd to send for their Books." Boston
Evening-Post, May 6, 1751.) 6790

Suspiria Vinctorum [by Cotton Mather,
1663-1728].
Boston, Fleet, 1726. [2], 22 pp.
AAS copy. 2777

Susquehanna Canal Co., Maryland.
At a Meeting of the Governor and
Directors . . . 28th May, 1795.
[n.p., 1795.] [2] pp.
HSP copy. 29032

The Susquehannah Title Stated [by
Barnabas Bidwell, 1763-1833].
Catskill, Croswell, 1796. 115 pp., 1 folding
insert.
AAS copy. 30091

Sutton, Mass.
The Inhabitants of the Town of Sutton, in
legal Town-Meeting Assembled, Jan. 27,
1777.
[Worcester, 1777.] Broadside.
MSL copy. 15610

Sutton, Mass. First Church, 1790.
The Covenant of the First Church. . . .
March 18, 1790.
n.p., [1790]. Broadside.
AAS copy. 45996

Swan, Abraham.
The British Architect.
Philadelphia, Bell for Norman, 1775. [5],
vi, 17, [2] pp., 60 plates.
AAS copy. 42944

Swan, Abraham.
The British Architect.
Boston, Folsom for Norman, 1794. 12 pp.,
60 plates.
AAS copy. 27761

Swan, Abraham.
A Collection of Designs in Architecture.
Philadelphia, Bell, 1775. viii pp., 10 plates.
NYPL copy. 14481

Swan, James, 1754-1830.
(D. A. B.)
A Dissuasion to Great-Britain.
Boston, Russell, [1772]. 70 pp.
AAS copy. 12572

Swan, James, 1754-1830.
(D. N. B.)
A Dissuasion to Great-Britain.
Boston, Greenleaf, 1773. 41 pp.
AAS copy. 13034

[Swan, James, 1754-1831.
On the Fisheries.
Boston, 1784.]
(Entry from Allibone.) 18801

[Swan, Timothy, 1758-1842.
The Federal Harmony.

Boston, Norman, 1785.]
(There is no proof that The Federal
Harmony was by Swan, and no 1785 ed.
has been found.)   19268

[Swan, Timothy?], 1758-1842.
The Federal Harmony.
Boston, Norman, [1788]. pp. 1-17, [1],
18-131.
(Evans' entry from an adv. This issue is
dated from publisher's address.)
AAS copy.   21485

[Swan, Timothy?], 1758-1842.
The Federal Harmony: in Three Parts.
Boston, Norman, 1790. 114 pp.
AAS copy.   22919

[Swan, Timothy?], 1758-1842.
The Federal Harmony.
Boston, Norman, 1792. 130 pp.
AAS copy.   24831

[Swan, Timothy?], 1758-1842.
The Federal Harmony.
Boston, Norman, 1793. 130 pp.
(Best copy available.)
LOC copy.   46884

[Swan, Timothy?, 1758-1842.
The Federal Harmony.
Boston, Norman, 1794. 100 pp.]
(Imprint assumed by Evans from adv.)
                                         27762

[Swanwick, John], 1740-1798.
British Honour and Humanity.
Philadelphia, Campbell, 1796. 58 pp.
AAS copy.   31255

Swanwick, John, 1740-1798.
(Circular.) Philadelphia, September 22,
1797. Sir. . . .
[Philadelphia, 1797.] 13 pp., 1 folding
table.
LOC copy.   32897

Swanwick, John, 1740-1798.
Poems on Several Occasions.
Philadelphia, Bailey, 1797. [4], 174 pp.
AAS copy.   32898

[Swanwick, John], 1740-1798.
A Roaster. . . . By Sim Sansculotte.
Philadelphia, Johnson, 1796. 21 pp.
AAS copy.   31256

[Swanwick, John], 1740-1798.
A Rub from Snub.
Philadelphia, 1795. 80 pp.
AAS copy.   29594

Swanwick, John, 1740-1798.
Thoughts on Education.
Philadelphia, Dobson, 1787. 36 pp.
JCB copy.   20736

Sweden, Treaties, etc.
By the United States in Congress
Assembled, a Proclamation. Whereas in
Pursuance of a Plenipotentiary
Commission Given on the 28th day of
September, 1782 [Made Sept. 25, 1783].
Philadelphia, Claypoole, [1783].
Broadside.
LOC copy.   18245

[Swedenborg, Emanuel, 1688-1772.
Aphorisms of Wisdom.
Boston, Folsom, 1792. 214 pp.
(A ghost of 26571, originating in the MHS
cat. of 1860.)
MHS copy.   24832

[Swedenborg, Emanuel], 1688-1772.
Aphorisms of Wisdom.
Boston, Folsom, 1794. 214 pp.
AAS copy.   26571

Swedenborg, Emanuel, 1688-1772.
Arcana Coelestia.
Boston, Belknap, 1794. 130 pp.
AAS copy.   27763

Swedenborg, Emanuel, 1688-1772.
The Delights of Wisdom.
Philadelphia, Baileys, 1796. pp. [i]-viii,
[v]-521, [3].
AAS copy.   31257

Swedenborg, Emanuel, 1688-1772.
The Doctrine of Life. . . . Third Edition.

Philadelphia, Bailey and Lang, 1792. 140
pp.
AAS copy.   24833

Swedenborg, Emanuel, 1688-1772.
The Doctrine of the New Jerusalem
Concerning the Lord.
Boston, Hall for Cazneau, 1795. 194, [2]
pp.
AAS copy.   29595

[Swedenborg, Emanuel], 1688-1772.
The Doctrine of the New Jerusalem
Concerning the Sacred Scripture.
Boston, Folsom, 1795. 186 pp.
AAS copy.   29596

Swedenborg, Emanuel, 1688-1772.
The Heavenly Doctrine of the New
Jerusalem.
Boston, Hall, 1794. 129, [1] pp.
AAS copy.   27764

[Swedenborg, Emanuel, 1688-1772.
Queries Concerning the Trinity.
Baltimore, Adams, 1792?]
(Entry from an adv.)   24834

Swedenborg, Emanuel, 1688-1772.
A Summary View of the Heavenly
Doctrines.
Philadelphia, Bailey, 1787. 80 pp.
AAS copy.   20737

Swedenborg, Emanuel, 1688-1772.
A Treatise on the Nature of Influx.
Boston, Thomas & Andrews, 1794. 174 pp.
AAS copy.   27765

Swedenborg, Emanuel, 1688-1772.
True Christian Religion. . . . Third
Edition.
Philadelphia, Bailey, 1789. 496 pp.
AAS copy.   22172

Swedenborg, Emanuel, 1688-1772.
True Christian Religion. . . . Third
Edition.
Philadelphia, Bailey, 1792. 478, [2] pp.
AAS copy.   24835

Swedenborg, Emanuel, 1688-1772.
The Wisdom of Angels.
Boston, Thomas & Andrews, 1794. xxiii,
[1], 358, [2] pp.
AAS copy.   27766

[Swedenborg, Emanuel, 1688-1772.
The Wisdom of Angels.
Boston, Thomas & Andrews, 1795.]
(Imprint assumed by Evans from adv.)
                                         29597

Swedenborg, Emanuel, 1688-1772.
The Wisdom of Angels.
Boston, Thomas & Andrews, 1796. 543 pp.
AAS copy.   31258

Swediour, Francois Xavier, 1748-1824.
Practical Observations on Venereal
Complaints. . . . Third Edition.
New York, Campbell, 1788. [4], 128 pp.
AAS copy.   21486

Sweet Amusement for Leisure Hours.
Exeter, Ranlet, 1797. 64 pp.
(The only copy located is imperfect.)
AAS copy.   34623

The Sweet Little Girl that I Love [by
James Hook, 1746-1827].
New York & Philadelphia, Carr, [1796].
[2] pp.
AAS copy.   30584

Sweet Passion of Love. Composed by Dr.
Arne [by Charles Dibdin, 1745-1814].
New York, Gilfert, [1795]. [1] pp.
AAS copy.   32041

[Sweet William of Plymouth [4 columns
of Verse].
[Boston], Sold at the Bible and Heart, in
Cornhill, [1783]. Broadside.]
(No copy of this ed. could be located.)
                                         19438

Sweeting, Whiting, d. 1791.
The Narrative of Whiting Sweeting . . .
Executed . . . the 26th August, 1791.
[Albany? 1791?] 54 pp.
(Best copy available.)
AAS copy.   46293

Sweeting, Whiting, d. 1791.
The Narrative of. . . .
Hartford, Hudson & Goodwin, [1791]. 36
pp.
AAS copy.   23815

Sweeting, Whiting, d. 1791.
The Narrative of. . . .
Lansingburgh, Tiffany, [1791]. 72 pp.
AAS copy.   23814

Sweeting, Whiting, d. 1791.
The Narrative of Whiting Sweeting.
Philadelphia, Lawrence, 1792. 72 pp.
Presbyterian Hist. Soc. copy.   24836

Sweeting, Whiting, d. 1791.
The Narrative of Whiting Sweeting.
Providence, Wheeler, [1792]. 64 pp.
(The Evans entry came from the adv. for
this ed.)
AAS copy.   24838

[Sweeting, Whiting, d. 1791.
The Narrative of Whiting Sweeting.
Wilmington, Brynberg & Andrews, 1792?]
(Entry from an adv., probably for copies
of 24836.)   24837

Sweeting, Whiting, d. 1791.
A Narrative of Whiting Sweeting.
Concord, N.H., Russell, 1793. 40 pp.
AAS copy.   26237

Sweeting, Whiting, d. 1791.
A Remarkable Narrative of Whiting
Sweeting.
Exeter, Ranlet, 1793. 40 pp.
AAS copy.   26238

Sweeting, Whiting, d. 1791.
A Remarkable Narrative of. . . . Second
Exeter Edition.
Exeter, Ranlet, 1794. 51, [1] pp.
AAS copy.   27768

Sweeting, Whiting, d. 1791.
The Narrative of. . . .
Providence, Wheeler, 1794. 59 pp.
BrU copy.   27767

[Sweeting, Whiting, d. 1791.
A Remarkable Narrative of. . . .
Salem, Cushing & Carlton, 1795.]
(Imprint assumed by Evans from an adv.)
                                         29598

Sweeting, Whiting, d. 1791.
A Remarkable Narrative of. . . . Fourth
Edition.
Dover, Bragg, 1796. 70 pp.
(Best copy available.)
HSP copy.   47926

Sweeting, Whiting, d. 1791.
The Narrative of Whiting Sweeting.
Windham, Vt., Huntington, 1797. 47 pp.
AAS copy.   32899

Swetland, Luke, 1729-1823.
A Very Remarkable Narrative of. . . .
Hartford, [178-?]. 16 pp.
(Best copy available.)
YC copy.   43753

Swieten, Gerard, freiherr van, 1700-1772.
The Diseases Incident to Armies.
Philadelphia, Bell, 1776. 164 pp.
AAS copy.   15100

Swieten, Gerard, freiherr van, 1700-1772.
The Diseases Incident to Armies.
Boston, Draper for McDougall, 1777.
167 pp.
MHS copy.   15611

Swift, John, 1679-1745.
A Funeral Discourse Deliver'd at
Marlborough.
Boston, Kneeland and Green, 1731. [4],
17, [5], 27.
AAS copy.   3479

Swift, John, 1679-1745.
(Sibley, IV, 387-390.)
A Sermon Preach'd at Boston.
Boston, Green for Hancock, 1732. [4], 25
pp.
AAS copy.   3607

Swift, John, 1714-1775.
(Sibley, IX, 333-336.)

A Sermon Delivered. . . . February 12, 1761.
Boston, Edes & Gill, 1761. 18 pp.
AAS copy.　　　　　　　　　9020

Swift, John, 1714-1775.
(Sibley, IX, 333-336.)
A Sermon Preached at the Ordination of
. . . Joseph Lee.
Boston, Kneeland & Adams, 1769. 26 pp.
AAS copy.　　　　　　　　　11486

Swift, Jonathan, 1667-1745.
The Adventures of Captain Gulliver.
Philadelphia, Young & M'Culloch, 1787.
128 pp.
(The only known copy is imperfect.)
PPL copy.　　　　　　　　　45170

Swift, Jonathan, 1667-1745.
The Adventures of Captain Gulliver.
Philadelphia, Young, 1791. 120 pp.
(Not located, 1968.)　　　　　46294

Swift, Jonathan, 1667-1745.
The Adventures of Captain Gulliver.
New York, Durell, [1793]. 16 + pp.
(The only copy recorded is incomplete.)
AAS copy.　　　　　　　　　26239

Swift, Jonathan, 1667-1745.
The Adventures of Captain Gulliver.
Boston, Hall, 1794. 119, [7] pp., 1 plate.
LOC copy.　　　　　　　　　29599

Swift, Jonathan, 1667-1745.
The Adventures of Captain Gulliver.
Philadelphia, Young, 1794. 159, [1] pp.
PrU copy.　　　　　　　　　47224

Swift, Jonathan, 1667-1745.
The Adventures of Capt. Gulliver.
Fairhaven, [1796?] 46 pp.
(Not located, 1968.)　　　　　47927

[Swift, Jonathan], 1667-1745.
A Discourse of the Contests.
[Boston], 1728. [4], 59 pp.
AAS copy.　　　　　　　　　3108

[Swift, Jonathan], 1667-1745.
The Journal of a Gaming Lady of Quality.
New York, Parker & Weyman, 1758.]
(From an adv.)　　　　　　　8265

Swift, Jonathan, 1667-1745.
A Sermon, on the Trinity.
Portland, Titcomb, 1792. 21 pp.
HEH copy.　　　　　　　　　46580

Swift, Jonathan, 1667-1745.
Three Sermons.
Williamsburg, Parks, 1747. 39 pp.
VaHS copy.　　　　　　　　40443

[Swift, Josiah]
Infant Baptism, Considered in a Letter,
1773.
Newport, [R. I.], Southwick, 1774. 16 pp.
RIHS copy.　　　　　　　　42710

Swift, Samuel, 1782-1875.
An Oration, Occasioned by the Death of
Mr. John Merrill.
Newburyport, March for Merrill, [1797].
11 pp.
(Evans' description was deduced from an
adv.)
AAS copy.　　　　　　　　　34624

Swift, Seth, 1749-1807.
The Work of the Gospel Ministry.
Bennington, Haswell, 1798. 28 (i.e. 29) pp.
AAS copy.　　　　　　　　　34625

[Swift, Zephaniah], 1759-1823.
An Address to the Rev. Moses C. Welch.
Windham, Conn., Byrne, 1794. 62 pp.
AAS copy.　　　　　　　　　27769

[Swift, Zephaniah], 1759-1823.
The Correspondent. Containing the
Publications in the Windham Herald. . . .
Windham, Byrne, 1793. 140 pp.
AAS copy.　　　　　　　　　26240

Swift, Zephaniah, 1759-1823.
An Oration on Domestic Slavery.
Hartford, Hudson & Goodwin, 1791.
23 pp.
AAS copy.　　　　　　　　　23816

[Swift, Zephaniah], 1759-1823.
A Second Address, to the Reverend Moses
C. Welch.
Windham, Ct., Byrne, 1796. 43 pp.
AAS copy.　　　　　　　　　31259

[Swift, Zephaniah?], 1759-1823.
The Security of the Rights of Citizens in
the State of Connecticut Considered.
Hartford, Hudson & Goodwin, 1792. 102
pp.
(Attribution to Swift on Pierce Gaines'
copy.)
BA copy.　　　　　　　　　24776

Swift, Zephaniah, 1759-1823.
A System of the Laws of . . .
Connecticut. . . . Volume I.
Windham, Byrne, 1795. vii (i.e., iv),
452 pp., 1 folding plate.
AAS copy.　　　　　　　　　29600

Swift, Zephaniah, 1759-1823.
A System of the Laws of . . .
Connecticut. . . . Volume II.
Windham, Ct., Byrne, 1796. v, [1], 479, [13]
pp.
(No copy located contains the plate called
for by Evans.)
AAS copy.　　　　　　　　　31260

Swinney, Lawrence.
For the New-York Gazette, Jan. 1, 1761.
To all Gentlemen in Town. . . .
[New York, 1761.] Broadside.
(No copy located.)　　　　　41248

Swinney, Lawrence.
Mr. Lawrence Sweeny, Esq; Vehicle
General of News. . . . this New-Year's
Morning . . . 1769. . . .
n.p., [1796]. Broadside.
AAS copy.　　　　　　　　　42008

Swinney, Lawrence.
New Year's Ode for the Year 1766.
[New York, 1766.] Broadside.
HSP copy.　　　　　　　　　41663

Swinney, Lawrence.
New-Year's Verses Made and Carried
about to the Customers of the New-York
Gazette by. . . .
[New York, 1767?]. Broadside.
NJHS copy.　　　　　　　　41767

Swords, T. & J., of New York.
New-York, July 5, 1790. Proposals for
Printing. . . . The Children's Friend.
[New York, 1790.] Broadside.
NYHS copy.　　　　　　　　22920

Swords, T. & J., of New York.
New-York, May 17, 1793. Proposals . . .
for Printing . . . the Posthumous Works of
Mrs. Ann Eliza Bleecker.
[New York, 1793.] Broadside.
NYHS copy.　　　　　　　　26241

Swords, T. & J., of New York.
New York, October 14, 1794. Proposals
. . . for Printing . . . Zoonomia.
[New York, 1794.] Broadside.
(Not located, 1968.)　　　　47225

Sydney, John, pseud.
According to my Promise.
[New York, 1734?]. 5 pp.
NYHS copy.　　　　　　　　3841

Sydney, John, pseud.
Nullum Tempus.
[New York, 1732.] [2] pp.
NYPL copy.　　　　　　　　3608

A Syllabical and Steganographical Table
[by P. R. Wouves].
Philadelphia, Bache, [1797]. [16] pp.
AAS copy.　　　　　　　　　33249

Syllabus of a Course of Lectures on
Chemistry [by Benjamin Rush,
1745-1813].
Philadelphia, 1770. 48 pp.
AAS facsimile copy.　　　　42167

Syllivan, Owen, pseud.
A Short Account of the Life of. . . .
Boston, Green & Russell, 1756. 12 pp.
AAS copy.　　　　　　　　　7796

Sylvan Letters; or, the Pleasures of a

Country Life [by George Wright, fl.
1770.
Philadelphia, Gibbons, 1793. 179 pp.
AAS copy.　　　　　　　　　26242

[Symmes, John Cleves, 1742-1814.
On the First Settlement of the Northwest
Territory.
Cincinnati, Maxwell, 1796.]
(No copy known.)　　　　　31261

Symmes, John Cleves, 1742-1814.
To the Respectable Public.
[Trenton, 1787.] 30 pp.
AAS copy.　　　　　　　　　20738

[Symmes, John Cleves, 1742-1814.
To the Respectable Public.
[Trenton, 1787.] 16 pp.]
(AAS copy acquired too late for
inclusion.)　　　　　　　　20739

Symmes, Thomas, 1678-1725.
(Sibley, IV, 411-417.)
A Discourse Concerning Prejudice.
Boston, Kneeland for Gerrish, 1722. [4],
iv, 21, [1] pp.
AAS copy.　　　　　　　　　2388

Symmes, Thomas, 1678-1725.
(Sibley, IV, 411-417.)
Good Soldiers Described, and Animated.
Boston, Kneeland for Gerrish and
Henchman, 1720. [2], iv, 37 pp.
AAS copy.　　　　　　　　　2182

Symmes, Thomas, 1678-1725.
Historical Memoirs of the late Fight at
Piggwacket. . . . Second Edition.
Boston, Green for Gerrish, 1725. [4], xii,
32 pp.
(There are copies with the word
"Piggwacket" in old English.)
AAS copy.　　　　　　　　　2706

Symmes, Thomas, 1678-1725.
The History of the Fight.
Fryeburg, Me., Russel, 1799. 60 pp.
AAS copy.　　　　　　　　　36392

Symmes, Thomas, 1678-1725.
(Sibley, IV, 411-417.)
Lovewell Lamented.
Boston, Green for Gerrish, 1725. [4], xii,
32 pp.
AAS copy.　　　　　　　　　2705

Symmes, Thomas, 1678-1725.
(Sibley, IV, 411-417.)
A Monitor for Delaying Sinners.
Boston, Green for Gerrish, 1719. [2], iv,
38 pp.
HC copy.　　　　　　　　　2074

Symmes, Thomas, 1678-1725.
An Ordination Sermon Preach'd at
Malden.
Boston, Franklin, 1722. [8], 28 pp.
AAS copy.　　　　　　　　　2389

Symmes, Thomas, 1678-1725.
(Sibley, IV, 411-417.)
The People's Interest.
Boston, Green for Gerrish, 1724. [2], vi,
35 pp.
AAS copy.　　　　　　　　　2586

[Symmes, Thomas], 1678-1725.
The Reasonableness of, Regular Singing.
Boston, Green for Gerrish, 1720. [2], 22
pp.
AAS copy.　　　　　　　　　2183

Symmes, Thomas, 1678-1725.
(Sibley, IV, 411-417.)
Utile Dulci.
Boston, Green for Gerrish, 1723. [2], ii,
59 pp.
MHS copy.　　　　　　　　2481

Symmes, William, 1728-1807.
The Duty and Advantages of Singing.
Danvers, 1779. 24 pp.
AAS copy.　　　　　　　　　16540

Symmes, William, 1728-1807.
A Sermon, Delivered at Andover.
Salem, 1769. 24 pp.
AAS copy.　　　　　　　　　11487

Symmes, William, 1728-1807.
A Sermon Preached before His Honor
Thomas Cushing.

Boston, Adams & Nourse, [1785]. 28 pp.
AAS copy.   19269

Symmes, William, 1762-1807.
An Oration, Delivered before the Citizens
of Portland.
Portland, Me., Baker, 1797. 19 pp.
AAS copy.   32900

Symmes, William, 1762-1807.
An Oration Delivered in the Meeting
House.
Portland, Baker, 5796 (1796). 16 pp.
AAS copy.   31262

[Symonds, Francis], of Danvers.
To the Printers in Essex.
[Salem, 1771.] [2] pp.
AAS copy.   42282

Synod of New York and Philadelphia.
A List of the Ministers & Congregations
belonging to the. . . .
[Philadelphia, 1777?] 6 + pp.
HSP copy.   43377

The Synod of New-York and Philadelphia
Vindicated [by John Blair, 1720-1771].

Philadelphia, Dunlap, 1754 (i.e. 1764). 50
pp.
AAS copy.   7151

[The Synod of New-York and
Philadelphia Vindicated.
Philadelphia, Dunlap, 1764.]
(A duplicate of entry 7151, q.v.)   9849

A Synopsis of Geography . . . for . . .
Grammar School in Wilmington.
Wilmington, [Del.], Adams, 1785. 58 pp.
AAS copy.   44796

The Syren; A Choice Collection of Sea,
Hunting and Other Songs.
Philadelphia, Carey, [1800]. front., 72 pp.
BrU copy.   38597

[The Syren; or, Musical Bouquet.
New York, Berry & Rogers, 1792?]
(Adv., "Just published" in 24146.)   24839

The Syren, or Vocal Enchantress.
Wilmington, Del., Bonsal & Niles, 1797.
38, 36, 24, 48, 30, [6] pp.
HC copy.   32901

A System of Chemistry; Comprehending
the History, Theory and Practice of the
Science.
Philadelphia, Dobson, 1791. 269 pp., 3
plates, 1 table.
LOC copy.   23817

A System of Exchange with almost all
Parts of the World [by Joseph James].
New York, Furman, 1800. pp. [i]-[iv],
[xiii]-180.
AAS copy.   37696

[A System of Mineralogy and Metallurgy.
Philadelphia, Dobson, 1795.]
("Published and for Sale by," adv. in
28190.)   29601

A System of Seamanship [by John Clerk,
1728-1812].
Philadelphia, Dobson, 1799. 192 pp., 8
folding plates.
AAS copy.   36393

The System of Short-Hand, Practiced by
Mr. Thomas Lloyd [by John Carey,
1756-1826].
Philadelphia, Rice, 1793. [2], 16 pp., 3
plates.
AAS copy.   25252

T

Taber, Joseph, 1731-1796?
An Address to the People Called Quakers.
Boston, Fleets, 1784. 67 pp.
AAS copy.   18802

[A Table Calculated to Shew in an Instant
the Contents (in Feet and Twelfth
Parts. . . .)
Boston, Allen, 1787.]
(Entry from an adv.)   20740

[A Table Calculated to Shew the Contents
(in Feet . . .) of any . . . Load of Wood.
Boston, 1771.]
(Adv. Mass. Gazette, July 18, 1771.) 12239

[A Table; Calculated to Shew the
Contents of any Sled or Cart Load of
Wood.
Boston, Edes, 1790.]
(Entry from an adv.)   22921

Table Exhibiting a Plan for the Reduction
of the Six per cent. Stock of the United
States. . . . December 27th, 1794.
[Philadelphia, 1794.] Broadside.
AAS copy.   27954

A Table for Receiving and Paying the
Gold Coins of Great Britain, and Portugal
. . . According to the Act of Congress . . .
Passed the 9th February, 1793.
[New York? 1793.] Broadside.
NYHS copy.   26366

A Table for the Ready Turning any Old
Tenor Sum, into Lawful Money.
Boston, 1750. [16] pp.
(For a criticism of this table see
Boston Evening-Post, Jan. 29, 1750.)
CHS copy.   6615

A Table for the Ready Turning any
Old Tenor Sum into Lawful Money. . . .
To which is Added Several Other
Useful Tables.
Boston, Bushell for Kneeland, 1750.
[16], 8 pp.
AAS copy.   6616

[A Table for Turning any Old Tenor Sum
into Lawful Money.
Boston, Rogers & Fowle, 1749.
Broadside.]
(Title from printers' adv.)   6422

[A Table for Understanding the Coins,
Weights and Measures, Mentioned in the
. . . old and New Testament.
Norwich, Trumbull, 1791.]
(A ghost arising from an adv. for
23986 in the Norwich Packet, Oct. 27,
1791.)   23818

[A Table of Interest at Six Per Cent.
Norwich, Trumbull, 1791.]
(A ghost arising from an adv. for 23986 in
the Norwich Packet, Oct. 27, 1791.)
                                             23819

[A Table of Interest on Lawful Money
Bills.
New London, 1757.]
(Adv. Conn. Gazette.)   8044

A Table of Simple Interest at 6 per
cent. for any Sum. . . . Haverhill,
July 10, 1765.
Boston, McAlpine & Fleeming, 1765.
Broadside.
(No copy located.)   41591

Table of the Kings and Queens.

Boston, Mein & Fleeming, [1767].
Broadside.
AAS copy.   10781

[A Table of the Value of Foreign
Gold . . . According to Act of
Congress.
Salem, Carleton, 1793?]
(Imprint assumed by Evans from adv.
"Just Published, and to be Sold by,"
in Salem Gazette, Sept. 3, 1793.)   26368

A Table of the Value of Lawful Money
Bills, in Old Tenor.
Newport, [1763]. Broadside.
(The wording of the title given by
Evans comes from an adv.)
JCB copy.   9521

A Table of the Value of the following
Lawful Money Bills, in Old Tenor.
Providence, Goddard, [1763?]
Broadside.
RIHS copy.   41413

A Table, Shewing how Provisions
Ought to be Sold when Dollars pass for
Six Shillings a-piece.
Boston, Fleet, [1750]. Broadside.
JCB copy.   40571

Tables, Shewing in Three Different
Views, the Comparative Value of the
Currency of the State of New York.
New York, Childs, 1795. [2], 33 pp.
AAS copy.   47616

Tables Shewing the Amount of any
Number of Dollars . . . in the
Currencies of all the United States.
[New England? 1781?] Broadside.
JCB copy.   44058

A Table Shewing the Distance from
one Post Town to Another. . . . May
1, 1789.
Philadelphia, Towne, [1789]. Broadside.
HSP copy.   45598

[A Table Shewing the Distance from
one Post Town to Another . . . May 1,
1790.
Philadelphia, Towne, [1790]. Broadside.]
(Source of entry not located.)   22922

A Table Shewing the Value of any
Number of Dollars.
[Philadelphia], Poulson, 1778. Broadside.
LOC copy.   43556

[A Table, Shewing the Value of 100
Dollars Deferred Stock.
Boston, West, 1798.]
(The only copy recorded cannot be
located.)   33574

[A Table to Bring Massachusetts
Currency into Dollars, Cents and Mills.
Boston, Edes, 1795.]
(Imprint assumed by Evans from adv.
"To be sold at the Printing Office,"
Boston Gazette, Oct. 5, 1795.)   29602

A Table to Bring Old Tenor into
Lawful Money at Twenty-Three and
One Third for One. . . . June, 1763.
Newport, [R. I.], Hall, [1764].
Broadside.
AAS copy.   41490

A Table to Bring Old Tenor into
Lawful Money, from Six Pence to Ten
Thousand Pounds.

Providence, Goddard, Jan. 1, 1764.
Broadside.
JCB copy.   41491

[Tables and Instructions to Reduce
Lawful Money to Federal.
Hallowell, Edes, 1796.]
(Imprint assumed by Evans from adv.
"Just published, and to be sold by the
Printer hereof," Kennebeck Intelligencer,
Jan. 2, 1796.)   31264

[Tables for Calculating Seamen's
Wages.
Boston, Edes, 1789.]
(Entry from an adv.)   22173

Tables of Difference of Latitude and
Departure [by John Robertson, 1712-
1776].
Philadelphia, Crukshank, 1790. [1],
90 pp.
AAS copy.   22856

Tables of Difference of Latitude and
Departure [by John Robertson, 1712-
1776].
Wilmington, Del., Bonsal & Niles for
Jess, 1799. [1], 91, [3], 59, [1 pp.
AAS copy.   36236

[Tables of Duties, Payable on Goods,
Imported into the United States . . .
after the 31st day of December, 1790.
Wilmington, Brynberg & Andrews,
1791.]
(Entry from an adv.)   23894

Tables, Shewing in Three Different
Views, the Comparative Value of the
Currency of the States of New
Hampshire. . . .
Portsmouth, N. H., Peirce, 1796. 39,
[1] pp.
NHSL copy.   31266

Die Täglichen Loosungen.
See
Moravians.

Taggart, Samuel, 1754-1825.
A Calm Impartial Inquiry.
Northampton, Butler, 1789. 123 pp.
AAS copy.   22174

Taggart, Samuel, 1754-1825.
A Discourse, Delivered at Colrain.
Greenfield, [Mass.], Dickman, 1800.
32 pp.
BA copy.   38599

Take Care!!! By an Act of the
Legislature, Passed at Princeton. . . .
n. p., [1789]. Broadside.
AAS ph. copy.   45599

Talbot, Catharine, 1721-1770.
Reflections on the Seven Days of the
week.
Newcastle, [Del.], Adamses, 1800.
36 pp.
AAS copy.   38601

Talbot, Robert.
A Catalogue of Medicines sold by
Mr. Robert Talbot at Burlington.
[Burlington? 1727?] Broadside.
NJHS copy.   39875

Talbot, Silas, 1751-1813.
Explanatory: Extract of a Letter from
Commodore Silas Talbot. . . . May
12th, 1800.

n. p., n. d. Broadside.
MHS copy. 38602

Tales of the Hermitage [by Mary (Hopkins) Pilkington, 1766-1839].
Philadelphia, Maxwell for Thackera, 1800. 158 pp.
EI copy. 38269

Tammany Society.
Sir, As all Nations have for Seven Centuries. . . .
[Philadelphia, Aitken, 1773.] Card.
LCP copy. 42516

Tammany Society, or Columbian Order.
Constitution Public, of the Society of St. Tammany.
New York, Greenleaf, 1789. 8 pp.
LOC copy. 22019

Tammany Society, or Columbian Order.
Constitutions of Tammany Society.
[New York, 1790.] 4 pp.
LOC copy. 45997

Tammany Society, or Columbian Order.
Constitutions of Tammany Society.
[New York], Harrisson, [1793]. 8 pp.
AAS copy. 46885

Tanguy de la Boissière, C. C., d. 1799.
Observations on the Dispatch.
Philadelphia, Moreau de Saint-Méry, 1797. 50 pp.
AAS copy. 32905

Tanguy de La Boissière, C. C., d. 1799.
Observations sur la Dépêche.
Philadelphia, Moreau de Saint-Méry, 1797. 50 pp.
AAS copy. 32904

Tanguy de la Boissière, C. C., d. 1799.
Philadelphia, 1794. Sir, A Stranger in your Country. . . .
[Philadelphia, 1794.] Broadside.
(No copy could be located.) 27770

Tansilla, Luigi, 1510?-1568.
The Nurse, a Poem.
New York, Furman for Gilbert, 1800. 30, 44, 34 pp.
AAS copy. 38604

Tans'ur, William, 1699?-1783.
The American Harmony. . . . Fifth Edition.
Newburyport, Bayley, 1769. 5, [1], 11, 96; [4], 96 pp.
AAS copy. 11489

Tans'ur, William, 1699?-1783.
The American Harmony. . . . Sixth Edition.
Newburyport, Bailey, 1771. pp. 1-5, [1], 1-96, [4], 1-96.
AAS copy. 12240

Tans'ur, William, 1699?-1783.
The American Harmony. . . . Seventh Edition.
Newburyport, Bailey, 1771. 5, [1], 10, [1], 7-8, [1], 96, [4], 96 pp.
(See Bib. Soc. Am., Papers, XLIX, 352.)
AAS copy. 12241

Tans'ur, William, 1699?-1783.
The American Harmony. . . . Eighth Edition.
Newburyport, 1773. 5, [1], 10, 7-8, 96, [4], 96 pp.
(Composite copy, imperfect.) 13035

Tans'ur, William, 1699?-1783.
The American Harmony. . . . Eighth Edition.
Newburyport, Bayley, 1774. 5, [1], 10, 7-8, 96; [4], 96 pp.
(No complete copy of this ed. located.)
AAS copy. 13647

[Tans'ur, William, 1699?-1783.
The Royal Melody Complete.
Boston, for McAlpine & Bayley, 1761?]
(Evans entry from an adv., but Boston News-Letter, June 11, 1761, says "Lately imported.") 9021

Tans'ur, William, 1699?-1783.
The Royal Melody Complete. . . . Third Edition.

Boston, M'Alpine, for Bayley and Williams, 1767. 13, [3], 14 [2], 96 pp.
(The Evans title came from an adv. For bib. see Bib. Soc. Am., Papers, XXXXIX, 345.)
AAS copy. 10782

Tans'ur, William, 1699?-1783.
(D. N. B.)
The Royal Melody Compleat. . . .
Fourth Edition.
[Boston], for Bayley at Newburyport, 1768. Front., [2], 13, [3], 14 pp., 112 plates.
(See Bib. Soc. Am., Papers, XXXXIX, 346.)
AAS copy. 11085

Taplin, William, d. 1807.
A Compendium of Practical . . . Farriery.
Philadelphia, Campbell, 1797. viii, 290, [6] pp., front.
(But for imprint and adv. leaf identical with 32906, q. v. for text.)
AAS copy. 48262

Taplin, William, d. 1807.
A Compendium of Practical . . . Farriery.
Wilmington, Del., Bonsal & Niles, for Campbell, 1797. viii, 290, [8] pp., 1 plate.
AAS copy. 32906

Taplin, William, d. 1807.
The Gentleman's Stable Directory. . . .
Twelfth Edition.
Philadelphia, Dobson, 1794. xvi, [4], 540 pp.
AAS copy. 27771

Tappan, David, 1752-1803.
The Beauty and Benefits of the Christian Church.
Boston, Hall, 1800. 46 pp.
AAS copy. 38605

Tappan, David, 1752-1803.
The Character and best Exercises.
Newburyport, 1782. 60 pp.
AAS copy. 17734

Tappan, David, 1752-1803.
The Character and Death of the Servant of God.
Newburyport, 1784. 50, 19 pp.
AAS copy. 18803

Tappan, David, 1752-1803.
Christian Thankfulness.
Boston, Hall, 1795. 40 pp.
AAS copy. 29604

Tappan, David, 1752-1803.
The Connexion between Faith in God. . . .
Portsmouth, Melcher, 1792. 29 pp.
AAS copy. 24840

Tappan, David, 1752-1803.
Copy of an Address.
Exeter, Stearns & Winslow, 1794. 11 pp.
AAS copy. 27772

[Tappan, David], 1752-1803.
Copy of the Address Delivered to the Students of Phillips' Academy, in Andover.
Exeter, Ranlet, 1791. [8] pp.
AAS copy. 23124

Tappan, David, 1752-1803.
A Discourse Delivered at the Third Parish in Newbury.
Salem, Hall, 1783. 19 pp.
AAS copy. 18203

Tappan, David, 1752-1803.
A Discourse Delivered in the Chapel of Harvard College, June 17, 1794.
Boston, Weld and Greenough, 1794. 16 pp.
AAS copy. 27773

Tappan, David, 1752-1803.
A Discourse Delivered in the Chapel of Harvard College, June 19, 1798.
Boston, Manning & Loring, 1798. 28 pp.
AAS copy. 34629

Tappan, David, 1752-1803.
A Discourse Delivered in the Chapel of Harvard College, September 16, 1794.
Boston, Weld & Greenough, 1794. 15 pp.
AAS copy. 27774

Tappan, David, 1752-1803.
A Discourse Delivered in the Chapel of Harvard College, November 17, 1795.
Boston, Folsom, 1795. 16 pp.
AAS copy. 29605

Tappan, David, 1752-1803.
A Discourse, Delivered to the Religious Society in Brattle-Street.
Boston, Hall, 1798. 31 pp.
AAS copy. 34627

Tappan, David, 1752-1803.
A Discourse Delivered to the Religious Society in Brattle-Street. . . . Second Edition.
Boston, Hall, 1798. 31 pp.
AAS copy. 34628

Tappan, David, 1752-1803.
A Discourse Delivered to the Students.
Boston, Manning & Loring, 1796. 20 pp.
AAS copy. 31267

Tappan, David, 1752-1803.
(Weis, Colonial Clergy N.E.)
The Duty of Private Christians.
Newburyport, 1778. viii, 56 pp.
AAS copy. 16089

Tappan, David, 1752-1803.
A Minister's Solemn Farewel.
Portsmouth, Melcher, 1793. 35 pp.
AAS copy. 26243

Tappan, David, 1752-1803.
The Question Answered.
Salem, Hall, 1783. 19 pp.
AAS copy. 18204

Tappan, David, 1752-1803.
A Sermon Delivered at Kennebunk.
Cambridge, [Mass.], Hilliard, 1800. 34 pp.
AAS copy. 38606

Tappan, David, 1752-1803.
A Sermon Delivered at the Ordination of . . . John Thornton Kirkland.
Boston, Belknap & Hall, 1794. 43 pp.
AAS copy. 27775

Tappan, David, 1752-1803.
A Sermon, Delivered at the Ordination of . . . Timothy Dickinson.
Boston, Thomas, 1789. 44 pp.
AAS copy. 22175

Tappan, David, 1752-1803.
A Sermon, Delivered at the Third Parish in Newbury.
Newburyport, Blunt & March, 1794. 25 pp.
AAS copy. 27776

Tappan, David, 1752-1803.
A Sermon, Delivered before the Annual Convention.
Boston, Hall, 1797. 34 pp.
AAS copy. 32907

Tappan, David, 1752-1803.
A Sermon, Delivered to the First Congregation in Cambridge . . . April 11, 1793.
Boston, Hall, 1793. 31 pp.
AAS copy. 26244

Tappan, David, 1752-1803.
A Sermon Preached before His Excellency.
Boston, Adams, 1792. 39 pp.
AAS copy. 24841

Tappan David, 1752-1803.
Two Friendly Letters.
Newburyport, 1785. 136 pp.
AAS copy. 19270

Tappen, Christopher.
To the Inhabitants of Ulster County. . . . April 16, 1793.
Kingston, Power & Copp. [1793].
Broadside.
Albany Institute copy. 46886

Tate, James.
Major est Veritas.
Savannah, Johnstons, 1790. [2], 16 pp.
BA copy. 22923

Tatham, William, 1752-1819.
Address to the Shareholders . . .

Interested in the Canals of Virginia.
Richmond, 1794.
(Sabin 94406; no copy located.)   47226

Tatham, William, 1752-1819.
The Political Economy of Inland
Navigation.
Philadelphia (i. e. London), 1799. xvi,
500, [3] pp.
(Only reported copy imperfect.)
APS copy.   36397

Tatham, William, 1752-1819.
Proposals for Publishing a . . . Map of
the Southern . . . United States.
. . . September, 1790.
[Richmond, 1790.] [2] pp.
JCB copy.   22924

Tatham, William 1752-1819.
A Topographical Analysis of . . .
Virginia, Compiled for the Years 1790-1.
[Philadelphia, 1791.] Broadside.
JCB copy.   23821

Tatham, William, 1752-1819.
A Topographical Analysis of . . .
Virginia, Compiled for the Years 1790-1.
Richmond, Nicolson, [1791]. Broadside.
HC copy.   23820

[Tauler, Johannes], 1290-1361.
(Jos. Thomas, Univ. Pron. Dict. Biog.)
The Plain Path to Christian Perfection.
Philadelphia, Crukshank, 1772. xi, [1],
124, 16 pp.
AAS copy.   12530

[Tauler, Johannes], 1290-1361.
The Plain Path to Christian Perfection.
Philadelphia, Crukshank, 1780, xi, [1],
91 pp.
AAS copy.   16953

[Taverner, William, -1731.
The Maid the Mistress.
New York, Gaine, 1761.]
(Adv. N. Y. Mercury, July 20, 1761.) 9022

Taxation of America. . . . While I
Rehearse my Story. . . .
n. p., [1779?]. Broadside.
(The one recorded copy cannot now be
located.)   42046

Tayler, Thomas, dissenting minister.
The Observation of the Lord's-Day.
Boston, Hall, 1792. 32 pp.
BA copy.   24842

Taylor, Abraham, fl. 1727-1740.
The Insufficience of Natural Religion.
Boston, Draper, 1755. [6], 33 pp.
AAS copy.   7578

[Taylor, Amos, 1748-1813?
American Babes Instructed.
Worcester, 1782.]
("Expected to be Published," pp. 20-21
in 17735.)   17736

Taylor, Amos, 1748-1813?
[The Genuine Experience, and dying
address, of Mrs. Dolly Taylor. Second
Edition.
Windsor, 1794?]
(McCorison 11; no copy known.)   47227

[Taylor, Amos], 1748-1813?
The Genuine Experience, and Dying
Address, of Mrs. Dolly Taylor.
. . . Third Edition.
Windsor, Vt., Spooner, 1795. 8 + pp.
(Known only by this fragment.)
AAS copy.   31268

[Taylor, Amos], 1748-1813?
The Genuine Experience, and Dying
Address, of Mrs. Dolly Taylor.
. . . Fourth Edition.
Bennington, for Taylor, 1796. 12 pp.
AAS copy.   31269

Taylor, Amos, 1748-1813?
Inestimable Lines of Poetry, by. . . .
[Keene, N.H., 1796.] Broadside.
VtHS copy.   47928

Taylor, Amos, 1748-1813?
A Narrative of the . . . Shakers.
Worcester, 1782. 23 pp.
AAS copy.   17735

[Taylor, Amos, 1748-1813?
Poems on the Rising Glory.
Worcester, 1782.]
("Expected to be Published," pp. 20-21
in 17735.)   17737

Taylor, Amos, 1748-1813?
[Poetical Specimens.
Windsor, 1794?]
(McCorison 13; no copy known.)   47228

Taylor, Amos, 1748-1813?
[Practical specimens of English
Education.
Putney, Sturtevant, 1797.]
(McCorison 454; no copy known.)   48263

[Taylor, Amos, 1748-1813?
The Religious Instructor.
Worcester, 1782.]
("Expected to be published," pp. 20-21
in 17735.)   17738

[Taylor, Amos, 1748-1813?
The Scholar's Primer.
Bennington, Haswell, 1796.]
("A new Publication, is now ready for
sale at the printing office," Vt. Gazette,
Sept. 9, 1796.)   31270

[Taylor, Christopher], d. 1686.
An Account of a Divine Visitation.
Philadelphia, Sansom, 1797. 60 pp.
AAS copy.   32908

[Taylor, Dorothy (Hutchins), 1755-1794.
The Genuine Experience, & Dying
Address of. . . .
Keene, Blake, 1794.]
(No copy of 1st or 2nd eds. known,
imprint conjectural.)   27778

[Taylor, Edward, 1741?-1797.
Werter to Charlotte. A Poem.
Baltimore, Hayes, 1787.]
(From an adv., apparently for 20741.)20742

[Taylor, Edward, 1741?-1797.
Werter to Charlotte; a Poem.
New York, Campbell, 1787.]
("This day published," N.Y. Gazetteer,
Apr. 5, 1787.)   20743

[Taylor, Edward], 1741?-1797.
Werter to Charlotte. A Poem.
[Philadelphia], Story, 1787. 40 pp.
AAS copy.   20741

Taylor, George.
To the Freeholders of the County of
Providence. . . . April 11, 1763.
[Providence, 1763.] Broadside.
JCB copy.   41414

Taylor, George Keith.
Substance of a Speech.
Richmond, Va., Pleasants, 1796. 36 pp.
VaSL copy.   31271

Taylor, Jacob, d. 1746.
[An Almanac for 1700.
Philadelphia, Janson.]
(Known only by this fragment.)
LCP copy.   39369

[Taylor, Jacob, d. 1746.
(Penn. Mag. Hist., IV, 433-442.)
An Almanack for . . . 1702.
Philadelphia, 1701.]
(No copy found.)   1027

[Taylor, Jacob, d. 1746.
An Almanack for . . . 1703.
Philadelphia, 1702.]
(No copy found.)   1095

[Taylor, Jacob, d. 1746.
An Almanack for . . . 1704.
Philadelphia, 1703.]
(No copy found.)   1149

Taylor, Jacob, d. 1746.
An Almanack for the Year 1705.
Philadelphia, [1704]. [32] pp.
APS copy.   1196

Taylor, Jacob, d. 1746.
Ephemeris Sideralis. A Mathematical
Almanack for . . . 1706.
Philadelphia [1705]. [32] pp.
APS copy.   1236

Taylor, Jacob, d. 1746.

Ephemeris Sideralis or an Almanack for
. . . 1707.
Philadelphia, Johnson. [32] pp.
LOC copy.   1281

Taylor, Jacob, d. 1746.
[An Almanack for the Year of Christian
Account 1708.
Philadelphia, 1707.]
(The one copy reported could not be
found.)   1333

[Taylor, Jacob, d. 1746.
An Almanack for the Year . . . 1709.
[Philadelphia, 1708.] [24] pp.
APS copy.   1373

[Taylor, Jacob, d. 1746.
An Almanack for 1710.
Philadelphia, 1709.]
(Title from Hildeburn.)   1434

Taylor, Jacob, d. 1746.
An Almanack for the Year . . . 1711.
Philadelphia, [1710]. [24] pp.
APS copy.   1488

Taylor, Jacob, d. 1746.
An Almanack for . . . 1712.
Philadelphia, 1711. [28] pp.
APS copy.   1528

[Taylor, Jacob, d. 1746.
An Almanack for . . . 1713.
Philadelphia, 1712.]
(Assumed from the sequence.)   1586

[Taylor, Jacob, d. 1746.
An Almanack for the Year . . . 1714.
Philadelphia, 1713.]
(No copy located.)   1652

[Taylor, Jacob, d. 1746.
An Almanack for 1715.
Philadelphia, 1714.]
(Title from Hildeburn.)   1718

[Taylor, Jacob, d. 1746.
An Almanack for the Year . . . 1716.
Philadelphia, [1715]. [48] pp.]
(Hildeburn 136.)   1782

[Taylor, Jacob, d. 1746.
An Almanack for the Year . . . 1717.
Philadelphia, 1716.]
(Hildeburn 139.)   1857

[Taylor, Jacob, d. 1746.
An Almanack for the Year . . . 1718.
Philadelphia, 1717.]
(Hildeburn 145.)   1931

[Taylor, Jacob], d. 1746.
An Almanack for . . . 1719.
Philadelphia, 1718. [34] pp.]
(No copy located with this imprint. Entry
apparently from an adv. for 2075.)   2001

[Taylor, Jacob], d. 1746.
An Almanack for . . . 1719.
Philadelphia, Bradford, 1719. [34] pp.
APS copy.   2075

[Taylor, Jacob], d. 1746.
An Almanack for the Year . . . 1720.
Philadelphia, Bradford, 1720. [24] pp.
APS copy.   2184

[Taylor, Jacob, d. 1746.
An Almanack for the Year . . . 1721.
Philadelphia, 1720.]
(Adv. Am. Weekly Mercury, Jan. 31,
1721.)   2185

[Taylor, Jacob, d. 1746.
An Almanack for the Year . . . 1722.
Philadelphia, 1721.]
(Hildeburn 175.)   2294

Taylor, Jacob, d. 1746.
An Ephemeris . . . for . . . 1723.
Philadelphia, [1722]. [32] pp.
APS copy.   2390

[Taylor, Jacob, d. 1746.
An Ephemeris . . . for . . . 1724.
Philadelphia, [1723]. [32] pp.]
(Assumed from the sequence.)   2483

[Taylor, Jacob, d. 1746.
An Ephemeris . . . for . . . 1725.
Philadelphia, [1724]. [32] pp.]
(Assumed from the sequence.)   2587

[Taylor, Jacob, d. 1746.
An Ephemeris . . . for . . . 1726.
Philadelphia, Bradford, 1725.]
(Assumed from the sequence.)   2707

Taylor, Jacob, d. 1746.
Taylor, 1726. A Compleat Ephemeris.
Philadelphia, Keimer, 1725. [48] pp.
LOC copy.   2708

[Taylor, Jacob, d. 1746.
An Almanack for . . . 1728.
Philadelphia, Keimer, 1727.]
(Hildeburn 317.)   2966

[Taylor, Jacob, d. 1746.
An Almanack for . . . 1729.
Philadelphia, 1728.]
(Hildeburn 352.)   3109

[Taylor, Jacob, d. 1746.
An Almanack for . . . 1730.
Philadelphia, Bradford, 1729.]
(Hildeburn, 381.)   3222

[Taylor, Jacob, d. 1746.
Pennsylvania, 1731. An Almanack.
Philadelphia, 1731.]
(Assumed from the sequence.)   3360

[Taylor, Jacob, d. 1746.
Pennsylvania, 1732. An Almanack.
Philadelphia, 1732.]
(Assumed from the sequence.)   3480

[Taylor, Jacob, d. 1746.
Pennsylvania, 1733. An Almanack.
Philadelphia, 1732.]
(Assumed from the sequence.)   3609

[Taylor, Jacob, d. 1746.
Pennsylvania, 1734. An Almanack.
Philadelphia, Bradford.]
(Adv. Pa. Gazette, Nov. 6, 1735.)   3726

[Taylor, Jacob, d. 1746.
Pennsylvania 1735. An Almanack.
Philadelphia, 1734.]
(Assumed from the sequence.)   3842

[Taylor, Jacob, d. 1746.
Pennsylvania, 1736. An Almanack.
Philadelphia, Bradford. [32] pp.]
(Adv. Pa. Gazette, Nov. 6, 1735.)   3963

[Taylor, Jacob, d. 1746.
Pennsylvania 1736. An Almanack for 1736.
Philadelphia, Franklin.]
(Assumed by Morrison.)   40084

Taylor, Jacob, d. 1746.
Pennsilvania, 1737. An Almanack.
Philadelphia, Bradford for Taylor. [32]
pp.
APS copy.   4084

Taylor, Jacob, d. 1746.
Pensilvania, 1738. An Almanack.
Philadelphia, Bradford for John Taylor.
[32] pp.
AAS copy.   4201

[Taylor, Jacob, d. 1746.
Pensilvania. 1739. An Almanack.
Philadelphia, Bradford.]
(Adv. Am. Weekly Mercury, Sept. 14, 1738.)   4313

Taylor, Jacob, d. 1746.
Pensilvania, 1740. An Almanack.
Philadelphia, Bradford. [32] pp.
APS copy.   4430

Taylor, Jacob, d. 1746.
Pensilvania, 1741. An Almanack.
Philadelphia, Bradford. [32] pp.
AAS copy.   4608

Taylor, Jacob, d. 1746.
Pensilvania, 1742. An Almanack.
Philadelphia, Bradford. [32] pp.
AAS copy.   4818

Taylor, Jacob, d. 1746.
Pensilvania. 1743. An Almanack.
Philadelphia, Warner. [32] pp.
AAS copy.   5069

Taylor, Jacob, d. 1746.
Pensilvania, 1744. An Almanack.
Philadelphia, Warner & Bradford.
[32] pp.
AAS copy.   5296

Taylor, Jacob, d. 1746.
Pennsylvania, 1745. An Almanack.
Philadelphia, Bradford. [32] pp.
AAS copy.   5496

Taylor, Jacob, d. 1746.
Pennsylvania, 1746. An Almanack.
Philadelphia, W. Bradford. [32] pp.
AAS copy.   5694

[Taylor, Jacob, d. 1746.
Pennsylvania. A Poem.
Philadelphia, 1728.]
(Probably a ghost of 7648.)   3110

Taylor, Jacob, d. 1746.
Tenebrae in   Or, The Eclip [ses].
[New York, 1698.] [48] pp.
(The only known copy is fragmentary.)
NYPL copy.   39332

[Taylor, James, of Newport, R. I.
Directions for Medicine Chests.
Newport, R. I., Barber, 1794.]
(The origin of this entry is unknown.)   27779

[Taylor, Jeremy, bp., 1613-1667.
(D. N. B.)
Contemplations of the State of Man.
Boston, 1721. 220 pp.]
(Title from Haven; apparently the ghost of
a London edition)   2295

Taylor, Jeremy, bp., 1613-1667.
Contemplations of the State of Man. . . .
Ninth Edition.
Boston, T. Fleet for Edwards, 1723. [6],
218 pp.
(But for imprint identical with 2471, q. v.)   39799

Taylor, Jeremy, bp., 1613-1667.
(D. N. B.)
Contemplations of the State of Man. . . .
Ninth Edition.
Boston, Fleet for Kneeland, 1723. [6], 218
pp.
BA copy.   2471

Taylor, Jeremy, bp., 1613-1667.
Contemplations of the State of Man. . . .
Ninth Edition.
Boston, T. Fleet for Eliot, 1723. [6], 218
pp.
(For text see 2471.)
AAS copy.   39800

Taylor, Jeremy, bp., 1613-1667.
The Life of Our Blessed Saviour.
Exeter, Ranlet for Larkin, 1794. 223, [4]
pp.
AAS copy.   27780

Taylor, Jeremy, bp., 1613-1667.
The Life of Our Blessed Saviour.
Greenfield, Mass., Dickman, 1796. 152 pp.
AAS copy.   31272

Taylor, Jeremy, bp., 1613-1667.
The Life of Our Blessed Saviour.
Newburyport, Blunt & March for Larkin,
1796. 248, [4] pp.
AAS copy.   31273

Taylor, Jeremy, bp., 1613-1667.
The Lives of the Holy Evangelists.
Leominster, Mass., Prentiss, 1797. 48 pp.
AAS copy.   32909

Taylor, Jeremy, bp., 1613-1667.
The Lives, Travels & Sufferings of the
Holy Evangelists.
[Leominster, Mass?], Whitcomb,
[1800?]. 48 pp.
AAS copy.   49151

[Taylor, John], 1580-1653.
The History of the New-Testament.
Boston, Mein & Fleeming, [1766?]. pp.
[153]-275.
(The second part of 41889, q. v. for text,
with a new tp.)
AAS copy.   41888

Taylor, John, 1580-1653.
Verbum Sempiternum. The Seventh
Edition.
New York, Printed for S. P., [1760?]. 275
pp.
PPL copy.   41171

Taylor, John, 1580-1653.

Verbum Sempiternum. The Third Edition.
Boston, Procter, [1765]. [280] pp.
AAS copy.   10179

[Taylor, John], 1580-1653.
Verbum Sempiternum. The Third Edition.
Boston, Mein & Fleeming, [1768?]. [2],
275 pp.
(No copy located.)   41889

Taylor, John, 1580-1653.
Verbum Sempiternum. The Seventh
Edition.
Philadelphia, Steuart, [1769?]. [286] pp.
PPL copy.   42009

Taylor, John, 1580-1653.
(D. N. B.)
Verbum Sempiternum. The Third Edition.
Providence, [c. 1774]. [280] pp.
(See Alden 566.)
HC copy.   11086

[Taylor, John], 1580-1653.
Verbum Sempiternum. The Twelvth
Edition.
Boston, 1786. vii, [1], iv, 148, vi, 107, [1],
iv, iv pp.
(No perfect copy located.)
AAS copy.   44974

Taylor, John, 1580-1653.
The Bible. The Eighth Edition.
Philadelphia, Johnson for Sower & Jones,
[1794]. 286 pp.
AAS copy.   26649

Taylor, John, 1580-1653.
The Bible. The Ninth Edition.
New England, [1799]. 274 pp.
PPL copy.   35190

[Taylor, John], 1694-1761.
The Value of a Child.
Philadelphia, Franklin & Hall, 1753. 30
pp.
LOC copy.   7128

Taylor, John, 1753-1824.
An Argument Respecting the
Constitutionality of the Carriage Tax.
Richmond, Davis, [1795]. 34 pp.
MHS copy.   29606

[Taylor, John], 1753-1824.
A Definition of Parties. . . . Philadelphia,
April 5th, 1794.
Philadelphia, Bailey, 1794. 16 pp.
JCB copy.   26861

[Taylor, John], 1753-1824.
An Enquiry into the Principles and
Tendency of Certain Public Measures.
Philadelphia, Dobson, 1794. iv, 92 pp.
AAS copy.   27782

[Taylor, John], 1753-1824.
An Examination of the late Proceedings in
Congress.
[Richmond, 1793.] 28 pp.
AAS copy.   26245

Taylor, John, 1762-1840.
An Oration, Delivered on the Anniversary
of Independence.
Greenfield, Dickman, 1796. 20 pp.
AAS copy.   31274

Taylor, John, 1762-1840.
A Sermon, Delivered on the Day of Public
Thanksgiving.
Greenfield, Mass., Barker, [1798]. 19 pp.
AAS copy.   34632

Taylor, Joseph, pseud.
God's Tender Mercy.
Boston, Russell, 1788. 16 pp.
AAS copy.   21487

Taylor, Joseph, pseud.
Narrative of the Revivication of. . . .
n.p., [1790]. 12 pp.
AAS copy.   45998

Taylor, Joseph, pseud.
A Remarkable and Extraordinary
Narrative of the Revivification of. . . .
Baltimore, Adamses for Isaacs, 1790.
8 pp.
AAS copy.   45999

Taylor, Joseph, pseud.
The Revivication of. . . . Sixth Edition.

America, for A. Nelson of Pownalboro,
[1788?] 16 pp.
AAS copy.   45371

[Taylor, Joseph, pseud.
The Wonderful Monitor.
Boston, 1787. 16 pp.]
(This is the cover-title of 21487, q.v.)
    21488

Taylor, Joshua, 1768-1861.
An Answer to the Rev. Jonathan Ward's
Brief Statement.
Hallowell, Me., Edes, 1800. [2], iii, [1],
76 pp.
NYPL copy.   38607

Taylor, Nathaniel, 1722-1800.
(Weis, Colonial Clergy N. E.)
The Office and Authority.
New Haven, 1765. 26 pp.
NYPL copy.   10180

Taylor, Nathaniel, 1722-1800.
(Weis, Colonial Clergy N. E.)
Praise due to God.
New Haven, [1762]. 28 pp.
CHS copy.   9282

[Taylor, Nathaniel?], 1722-1800.
A Second Dialogue, between a Minister
and his Parishioner.
Hartford, 1796. 15 pp.
(This Dialogue is included in Vol. 3 of the
N.Y., 1812, ed., of the Works of Joseph
Bellamy.)
BA copy.   11490

Taylor, Raynor, 1747-1825.
Amyntor, a Pastoral Song.
Philadelphia and New York, Carr, [c.
1795]. [2] pp.
AAS copy.   47617

[Taylor, Raynor, 1747-1825.
An Anthem, for Public or Private
Worship.
Philadelphia, Carr, 1794. 6 pp.]
(Adv. Baltimore Gazette, Dec. 26, 1793.)
    27783

Taylor, Raynor, 1747-1825.
Citizen Soldiers. A New Patriotic Song.
[Philadelphia, 1795?] Broadside.
LCP copy.   47618

[Taylor, Raynor, 1747-1825.
Divertimenti, or Familiar Lessons.
Philadelphia, 1797.]
(Adv. in Philadelphia newspapers in May,
1797.)   32910

Taylor, Raynor, 1747-1825.
An Easy and Familiar Lesson for Two
Performers.
Philadelphia and Baltimore, B. & I. Carr,
[179?] 3 pp.
LOC copy.   45796

Taylor, Raynor, 1747-1825.
Independent and Free.
[Philadelphia], Carr, [1796]. [2] pp.
LOC copy.   47929

Taylor, Raynor, 1747-1825.
The Lass of the Cot.
Philadelphia, Carr, etc., [1795]. [2] pp.
LOC copy.   29607

Taylor, Raynor, 1747-1825.
The Merry Piping Lad.
Philadelphia, Carr, [1795]. [2] pp.
LOC copy.   29608

Taylor, Raynor, 1747-1825.
Nancy of the Vale a Pastoral Ballad.
Philadelphia and New York, B. & I. Carr,
[1795]. [2] pp.
LOC copy.   47619

Taylor, Raynor, 1747-1825.
Nobody.
Philadelphia, B. Carr, [1798?]. [2] pp.
HEH copy.   48621

Taylor, Raynor, 1747-1825.
The President's March.
Philadelphia, Priest, [1795]. [2] pp.
BPL copy.   29609

Taylor, Raynor, 1747-1825.
Rustic Festivity.

Philadelphia, Carr, [1795]. [2] pp.
AAS copy.   29610

[Taylor, Raynor, 1747-1825.
Rustic Festivity. A New Song.
Philadelphia, Carr, [1798]. [2] pp.]
(Adv. as "republished" in Feb., 1798.
Perhaps identical with 29610.)   34633

Taylor, Raynor, 1747-1825.
Silvan the Shepherd Swain.
Philadelphia, B. Carr, etc., [1798]. [2]
pp.
LOC copy.   48622

Taylor, Raynor, 1747-1825.
Sonata for the Piano Forte.
Philadelphia, Carr, [1797]. 187 pp.
Sibley Music Lib., Eastman School of
Music, copy.   32911

[Taylor, Raynor, 1747-1825.
Summer, a Pastorale Song.
Philadelphia, Carr, 1798.]
(Adv. as "republished" Feb., 1798.)
    34634

Taylor, Raynor, 1747-1825.
Vive la Liberte.
Philadelphia, Carr, etc., 1795. [2] pp.
LOC copy.   29611

Taylor, Raynor, 1747-1825.
The Wand'ring Village Maid.
Philadelphia, Carr, etc., 1795. [2] pp.
LOC copy.   29612

[Taylor, Raynor], 1747-1825.
While the Morn is Inviting to Love.
Philadelphia, B. Carr, etc., [1797?]. [2]
pp.
LOC copy.   48264

Taylor, Raynor, 1747-1825.
The Wounded Soldier.
Philadelphia, Carr, [1794]. [2] pp.
UOP (Hopkinson Coll.) copy.   27784

[Taylor, Thomas], 1738-1816.
A Short Account of the Sickness and
Death of John Wesley.
Philadelphia, Johnson, 1791. 12 pp.
(The Evans entry came from an adv.)
HSP copy.   23822

[Taylor, Thomas], 1758-1835.
A Vindication of the Rights of Brutes.
Boston, 1795. 58 pp.
AAS copy.   29613

Taylor, Willett, d. 1811.
An Inaugural Dissertation.
New York, Swords, 1793. 28 pp.
AAS copy.   26246

Tea, Destroyed by Indians [Cut] Ye
Glorious Sons of Freedom.
[Boston? 1772.] Broadside.
(Ford 1635; no copy located.)   42375

Tea, Destroyed by Indians. Ye Glorious
Sons of Freedom. . . .
[Boston, 1773?] Broadside.
MHS copy.   42517

The Tea-Drinking Wife, to which is
Added The Tempest.
New York, for the Hawkers, 1797. 8 pp.
(The only known copy is imperfect.)
BrU copy.   48265

Tea-Table Dialogues [by Richard
Johnson, 1734-1793].
Philadelphia, James, 1789. 123 pp.
PrU copy.   45501

Tea-Table Dialogues [by Richard
Johnson, 1734-1793].
Philadelphia, Bailey, 1794. 144 pp.
(Copy too fragile to film.)   47086

Teall, Benjamin.
. . . Discourse, to his Scholars, after
Catechising.
New Haven, Greens, [1772]. 11, [1] pp.
CHS copy.   42376

Teall, Benjamin.
Benjamin Teall's Discourse, to his
Scholars.
New Haven, Greens, [1780?]. 12 pp.
(Best copy available.)
CHS copy.   43754

[T [eall], B [enjamin].
The Following Song Composed on the . . .
Death of Michael Griswould . . . in . . .
1771. . . .
[Boston? 1771]. Broadside.
HC copy.   42283

The Tear [by James Hook, 1746-1827].
New York & Philadelphia, Carr, [1796].
[2] pp.
JCB copy.   30585

Tears Dropt at the Funeral of . . . Mrs.
Elizabeth Hatch [By Joseph Metcalf,
1682-1723].
[Boston, 1710.] Broadside.
AAS copy.   39514

The Tears of America.
n. p., [1799]. Broadside.
AAS copy.   36399

Tell Truth and Shame Devil [by William
Dunlap, 1766-1839].
New York, Swords, 1797. [2], 45, [1] pp.
AAS copy.   32066

Telliamed; or the World Explain'd [by
Benoit de Maillet, 1656-1738].
Baltimore, Pechin for Porter, 1797. 268
pp.
AAS copy.   32414

Telltruth, Timothy, pseud.
The Collected Wisdom of Ages.
Philadelphia, Carey, 1799. 47 pp.
AAS copy.   36401

Temple, Samuel, 1770-1816.
A Concise Introduction to Practical
Arithmetic.
Boston, Hall, 1796. 116 pp.
AAS copy.   31276

Temple, Samuel, 1770-1816.
A Concise Introduction to Practical
Arithmetic.
Boston, Hall, 1798. 118 pp.
HC copy.   48623

The Temple of Wisdom [by Daniel Leeds,
ed., 1652-1720].
Philadelphia, Bradford, 1688. [8], 125,
[3], 86, [1] pp.
(The only available copies are imperfect.)
HSP copy.   447

The Temple Opening [by Cotton Mather,
1663-1728].
Boston, 1709. [2], 34 pp.
AAS copy.   1408

Temple Patrick Society, Carlisle, Pa.
A Debate Proposed in the. . . .
Philadelphia, Young for Knox and Miller,
1788. 23, [1] pp.
LCP copy.   45372

[Temple Patrick Society, Carlisle, Pa.
A Debate Proposed in the. . . .
Carlisle, 1792.]
(Entry apparently from a reference in the
Carlisle Gazette.)   24178

Templeton and Stewart, booksellers.
[A Large and Elegant Assortment of New
Books.
New York, 1771.]
(Adv. N. Y. Gazette, May 27, 1771.) 42284

[The Temporal Interest of North America
[by Joseph Morgan, 1671-1749?].
Philadelphia, Franklin, 1733.]
(Adv. in Pa. Gazette, Aug. 30, 1733. For
authorship see Sabin 94671.)   3691

Ten Broeck, Abraham.
In Committee. Albany, 4th March,
1795. . . .
[Albany, 1795.] Broadside.
NYPL copy.   28157

Ten Broek, Abraham.
. . . On the 13th instant, a Letter was
Received by . . . Albany, February 16,
1792.
Albany, Websters, [1792]. Broadside.
NYHS copy.   46581

Ten Minutes Advice to Every Gentleman
Going to Purchase a Horse [by William
Burdon].
Philadelphia, Crukshank for Aikman,

1775. [6], [1]-29, 36-49, [i]-70.
(The only known copy is imperfect.)
AAS copy.   42782

Ten Minutes Advice to Every Gentleman
going to Purchase a Horse [by William
Burdon].
Philadelphia, Crukshank, 1787. [6], 43,
[1], 70 pp.
AAS copy.   45171

The Ten Year's Almanack, or A Poetical
Attempt . . . Ending with the Year 1764
[by Joseph Fish, fl. 1765].
n.p., 1765. [1], 3, 60 pp.
NYPL ph. copy.   41538

Tench, Watkin, 1759?-1833.
A Narrative of the Expedition to
Botany-Bay.
New York, Swords, 1789. iv, [2], 64 pp.
AAS copy.   22176

[The Tenets of Union Discipline.
Baltimore? 1797.]
(Minick 397; no copy known.)   48266

Tennent, Gilbert, 1703-1764.
(D. A. B.)
All Things Come Alike to All.
Philadelphia, W. Bradford, 1745. 40 pp.
HSP copy.   5695

Tennent, Gilbert, 1703-1764.
(D. A. B.)
The Blessedness of Peace-Makers.
Philadelphia, Bradford, 1765. 50 pp.
AAS copy.   10181

Tennent, Gilbert, 1703-1764.
(D. A. B.)
Brotherly Love.
Philadelphia, Franklin & Hall, 1748.
36 pp.
LOC copy.   6243

Tennent, Gilbert, 1703-1764.
(D. A. B.)
The Danger of an Unconverted Ministry.
Philadelphia, Franklin, 1740. 31 pp.
LOC copy.   4609

Tennent, Gilbert, 1703-1764.
The Danger of an Unconverted
Ministry. . . . Second Edition.
Philadelphia, Franklin, 1740. 31 pp.
AHTS copy.   4610

Tennent, Gilbert, 1703-1764.
(D. A. B.)
The Danger of an Unconverted Ministry.
Boston, Rogers & Fowle, 1742. 20 pp.
AAS copy.   5070

[Tennent, Gilbert, 1703-1764.
The Danger of an Unconverted Ministry
[another impression].
Boston, Rogers & Fowle, 1742.]
(Evans' statement that there were two
impressions evidently had its origin in the
fact that there were two copies in the
Brinley library, sale nos. 3468 and 3469.)
     5071

Tennent, Gilbert, 1703-1764.
(D. A. B.)
The Danger of Forgetting God.
New York, 1735. 30 pp.
HSP copy.   3964

Tennent, Gilbert, 1703-1764.
The Danger of Spiritual Pride.
Philadelphia, W. Bradford, [1745]. 30, [1]
pp.
HSP copy.   5696

Tennent, Gilbert, 1703-1764.
A Discourse upon Christ's Kingly-Office.
Boston, Harrison, 1741. [2], iv, 25 pp.
(Evans' title appears to have come from
an adv. for this.)
AAS copy.   4822

[Tennent, Gilbert, 1703-1764.
A Discourse on Christ's Kingly-Office. . . .
Second Edition.
Boston, Harrison, 1741. 29 pp.]
(Haven says "2 editions.")　 4823

[Tennent, Gilbert, 1703-1764.
(D. A. B.)
Discourses on Several Important Subjects.

Boston, Rogers & Fowle, 1746.]
("Lately published," May 12, 1746.)   5871

Tennent, Gilbert, 1703-1764.
Discourses, on Several Subjects.
Philadelphia, W. Bradford, 1745. [4], 358,
[1] pp.
AAS copy.   5697

Tennent, Gilbert, 1703-1764.
(D. A. B.)
The Divine Government.
Philadelphia, Bradford, [1752]. 79 pp.
AAS copy.   6940

Tennent, Gilbert, 1703-1764.
(D. A. B.)
The Divinity of the Sacred Scriptures.
Boston, 1739. 27 pp.
(This is pp. 145-171 of 4438, q.v.)   4431

Tennent, Gilbert, 1703-1764.
The Duty of Self Examination.
Boston, 1739. 20 pp.
(This is pp. 125-144 of 4438, q.v.)   4432

Tennent, Gilbert, 1703-1764.
The Espousals.
New York, 1735. 66, [2] pp.
HSP copy.   3965

Tennent, Gilbert, 1703-1764.
(D. A. B.)
The Espousals.
Boston, Fleet for Henchman, 1741. 51 pp.
AAS copy.   4819

Tennent, Gilbert, 1703-1764.
[The Espousals.
Newport, R. I., 1741?] 64 pp.
(The only known copy lacks tp.)
Bradford Swan copy.   40261

Tennent, Gilbert, 1703-1764.
(D. A. B.)
The Examiner, Examined.
Philadelphia, Bradford, 1743. 146, [1] pp.
HSP copy.   5297

[Tennent, Gilbert, 1703-1764.
The Examiner, Examined.
Boston, 1743. 146, [1] pp.]
(This so-called Boston ed. is a defective
copy of 5297.)   5298

Tennent, Gilbert, 1703-1764.
A Funeral Sermon Occasion'd by the
Death of . . . John Rowland.
Philadelphia, W. Bradford, 1745. 72 pp.
HSP copy.   5698

Tennent, Gilbert, 1703-1764.
Die Gefahr.
Germantown, 1740. 45 pp.
HSP copy.   4611

Tennent, Gilbert, 1703-1764.
(D. A. B.)
The Good Mans Character.
Philadelphia, Bradford, [1756]. [2], 39
pp.
HSP copy.   7797

Tennent, Gilbert, 1703-1764.
The Happiness of Rewarding.
Philadelphia, Chattin, 1756. 32 pp.
LCP copy.   7798

Tennent, Gilbert, 1703-1764.
The Happiness of Rewarding. . . . Second
Edition.
Philadelphia, Chattin, 1756. 32 pp.
NYPL copy.   7799

Tennent, Gilbert, 1703-1764.
(D. A. B.)
Irenicum Ecclesiasticum.
Philadelphia, Bradford, 1749. vii, 141, [1]
pp.
AAS copy.   6423

Tennent, Gilbert, 1703-1764.
The Late Association for Defence,
Encouraged.
Philadelphia, Bradford, [1748]. [2], 46,
[1] pp.
HSP copy.   6244

Tennent, Gilbert, 1703-1764.
The Late Association for Defence,
Encourag'd. . . . Second Edition.
Philadelphia, Bradford, [1748]. 46 pp.
AHTS copy.   6245

Tennent, Gilbert, 1703-1764.
The Late Association for Defence Farther
Encourag'd.
Philadelphia, Bradford, [1748]. iv, 56 pp.
LCP copy.   6246

Tennent, Gilbert, 1703-1764.
The Late Association for Defence Farther
Encouraged.
Philadelphia, Franklin & Hall, 1748. iv,
183 pp.
NYPL copy.   6247

Tennent, Gilbert, 1703-1764.
The Legal Bow Bent.
Boston, 1739. 38 pp.
(This is pp. 173-210 of 4438, q.v.)   4433

Tennent, Gilbert, 1703-1764.
(D. A. B.)
Love to Christ.
Philadelphia, Bradford, 1744. 37, [1] pp.
HSP copy.   5497

Tennent, Gilbert, 1703-1764.
The Necessity of Holding Fast.
Boston, Kneeland & Green, 1743. [2], vi,
110, [2], 37, [3], 31 pp.
AAS copy.   5299

Tennent, Gilbert, 1703-1764.
The Necessity of Keeping the Soul.
Philadelphia, W. Bradford, [1745]. 24 pp.
HSP copy.   5699

Tennent, Gilbert, .1703-1764.
The Necessity of Praising God.
Philadelphia, W. Bradford, [1745]. 40 pp.
HSP copy.   5700

Tennent, Gilbert, 1703-1764.
The Necessity of Receiving the Truth in
Love.
New York, Zenger, 1735. 192 pp.
(Only known copy is defective.)
HEH copy.   40085

Tennent, Gilbert, 1703-1764.
The Necessity of Religious Violence.
New York, [1735]. [4], 44, [1] pp.
HSP copy.   3966

Tennent, Gilbert, 1703-1764.
The Necessity of Studying.
Philadelphia, Bradford, [1744]. 39 pp.
AAS copy.   5498

Tennent, Gilbert, 1703-1764.
The Necessity of Thankfulness.
Philadelphia, Bradford, 1744. 16 pp.
AAS copy.   5499

Tennent, Gilbert, 1703-1764.
(D. A. B.)
A Persuasive, to the Right Use of the
Passions.
Philadelphia, Dunlap, 1760. 43, [1] pp.
AAS copy.   8745

Tennent, Gilbert, 1703-1764.
The Preciousness of Christ.
Boston, 1739. 31 pp.
(This is pp. 243-274 of 4438, q.v.)   4434

Tennent, Gilbert, 1703-1764.
Remarks upon a Protestation.
Philadelphia, Franklin, 1741. 68 pp.
AAS copy.   4820

Tennent, Gilbert, 1703-1764.
The Righteousness of the Scribes.
Boston, Draper for Henchman, 1741. [4],
19 pp.
BA copy.   4821

Tennent, Gilbert, 1703-1764.
(D. A. B.)
A Sermon on I Chronicles xxix. 28.
Philadelphia, Dunlap, 1761. 27 pp.
AAS copy.   9023

Tennent, Gilbert, 1703-1764.
A Sermon Preach'd at Burlington . . .
November 23, 1749.
Philadelphia, Bradford, 1749. 28 pp.
AAS copy.   6424

Tennent, Gilbert, 1703-1764.
A Sermon Preach'd at Philadelphia,
January 7. 1747-8.
Philadelphia, Bradford, 1748. 34 pp.
AAS copy.   6248

Tennent, Gilbert, 1703-1764.
A Sermon Preach'd at Philadelphia, July
20. 1748.
Philadelphia, Bradford, 1749. 16 pp.
LOC copy.   6425

Tennent, Gilbert, 1703-1764.
A Sermon Preach'd in Greenwich.
Philadelphia, Bradford, [1746]. 42 pp.
HSP copy.   5872

[Tennent, Gilbert, 1703-1764.
A Sermon upon Justification.
Boston, 1741.]
("Just Published," Boston Weekly
New-Letter, Aug. 6, 1741.)   4826

Tennent, Gilbert, 1703-1764.
A Sermon upon Justification.
Philadelphia, Franklin, 1741. 29, [3] pp.
(The copy reproduced lacks a leaf of
advertising.)
AAS copy.   4824

[Tennent, Gilbert, 1703-1764.
A Sermon upon Justification. . . . Second
Edition.
Philadelphia, Franklin, 1741. 29, [3] pp.]
(Hildeburn says that there were two
editions.)   4825

Tennent, Gilbert, 1703-1764.
(D. A. B.)
Sermons on Important Subjects.
Philadelphia, Chattin, 1758. xxxviii, [3],
425 pp.
AAS copy.   8266

[Tennent, Gilbert, 1703-1764.
Sermons on Psalm XIV. 3. 4. 5. 7.
Boston, Draper, 1739.]
(This is a ghost of 4433 taken from
Haven.)   4436

Tennent, Gilbert, 1703-1764.
Several Discourses upon important
Subjects.
Philadelphia, W. Bradford, 1749. pp. [6],
5-40, [1]-27, [1]-10.
Presb. Hist. Soc. copy.   40518

Tennent, Gilbert, 1703-1764.
The Solemn Scene.
Boston, 1739. 31 pp.
(This is pp. 211-241 of 4438, q.v.)   4435

Tennent, Gilbert, 1703-1764.
A Solemn Warning.
Boston, Kneeland & Green for
Henchman, 1735. [2], xiii, [1], 205, [5],
xv, [1], 78 pp.
AAS copy.   3967

[Tennent, Gilbert, 1703-1764.
A Solemn Warning to the Secure World.
Philadelphia, 1740.]
(Adv. Am. Weekly Mercury, July 31,
1740.)   4612

Tennent, Gilbert, 1703-1764.
The Substance and Scope of Both
Testaments.
Philadelphia, Bradford, 1749. 27 pp.
AAS copy.   6426

Tennent, Gilbert, 1703-1764.
The Terrors of the Lord.
Philadelphia, Bradford, 1749. 10 pp.
LOC copy.   6427

Tennent, Gilbert, 1703-1764.
Twenty-Three Sermons.
Philadelphia, Bradford, 1744. [4], 465,
[3] pp.
AAS copy.   5500

Tennent, Gilbert, 1703-1764.
Two Sermons Preach'd at Burlington . . .
April 27th, 1749.
Philadelphia, Bradford, [1749]. 40 pp.
LOC copy.   6428

[Tennent, Gilbert, 1703-1764.
Two Sermons Preached at
New-Brunswick.
Boston, Harrison, 1742. 37 pp.]
(Apparently from a Harrison adv. of
5073.)   5072

[Tennent, Gilbert, 1703-1764.
Two Sermons Preached at
New-Brunswick.

Boston, Kneeland & Green, 1742. 37 pp.]
(Signatured with 5299, q.v.)   5073

Tennent, Gilbert, 1703-1764.
The Unsearchable Riches.
Boston, Draper for Henchman, 1739. vii,
[1], 59 pp.
(This is the first sermon in 4438, q.v.) 4437

Tennent, John, c.1700-c. 1760.
(D. A. B.)
An Essay on the Pleurisy.
Williamsburg, 1736. 46 pp.
MHS copy.   4085

Tennent, John, c. 1700-c. 1760.
An Essay on the Pleurisy.
Williamsburg, Parks, 1740. 36 pp.
APS copy.   40213

[Tennent, John, c. 1700-c.1760.
An Essay on Pleurisy.
New York, 1742. 46 pp.]
(Title from Haven; no copy located.) 5074

Tennent, John, c.1700-c.1760.
(D. A. B.)
Every Man his Own Doctor. . . . Second
Edition.
Williamsburg and Annapolis, 1734. 56 pp.
NYAM copy.   3843

[Tennent, John], c.1700-c.1760.
Every Man his Own Doctor. . . . Third
Edition.
Philadelphia, Franklin, 1734. 54 pp.
(No complete copy found.)
AAS copy.   3844

[Tennent, John], c.1700-c.1760.
Every Man his own Doctor. . . . Third
Edition.
Williamsburg and Annapolis, Parks, 1736.
69, [3] pp.
HSP copy.   40103

Tennent, John, c.1700-c.1760.
Every Man his own Doctor. . . . Fourth
Edition.
Philadelphia, Franklin, 1736. 56 pp.
HSP copy.   4086

[Tennent, John, c.1700-c.1760.
Every Man his Own Doctor.
Philadelphia, Franklin, 1737.]
("Just published. . . . Printed and Sold by
the Printer hereof," Pa. Gazette, Oct. 27,
1737.)   4202

[Tennent, John], c.1700-c.1760.
Every Man His Own Doctor.. . . . Fourth
Edition.
Williamsburgh, Hunter, 1751. 47, [1] pp.
AAS copy.   40608

Tennent, John, 1706-1732.
(Appleton's Cyclopaedia of Am. Biog.)
The Nature of Regeneration.
Boston, 1735. xv, [1], 78 pp.
(Signatured with 3967, q.v.)   3968

Tennent, William, 1705-1777.
Exhortations to Walk in Christ.
Boston, 1739. 22 pp.
(This is pp. 103-124 of 4438, q.v.)   4439

Tennent, William, 1705-1777.
A Sermon upon Matthew v. 23, 24.
New York, Parker, 1769. 20 pp.
LOC copy.   11491

Tennent, William, 1740-1777.
(Weis, Colonial Clergy N. E.)
An Address, Occasioned by the late
Invasion.
Philadelphia, Bradfords, 1774. 20 pp.
AAS copy.   13649

Tennent, William, 1740-1777.
(Sprague, III, 242-245.)
God's Sovereignty.
New York, Holt, 1765. [4], 20 pp.
AAS copy.   10182

Tennent, William, 1740-1777.
Mr. Tennent's Speech . . . Jan. 11, 1777.
Charleston, 1777. 28 pp.
LOC copy.   15612

Tennessee (Terr.) House Journals, 1794.
[Journal of the proceedings of the House
of Representatives, Aug. 25, 1794 +

Knoxville, Roulstone, 1794.]
(McMurtrie: Tenn. 6; no copy known.)
                                             47229

Tennessee. Constitution, 1796.
The Constitution of the State of
Tennessee.
[Knoxville? 1796.] pp. [3]-17.
HEH copy.   47930

Tennessee. Constitution, 1796.
The Constitution of the State of
Tennessee.
Knoxville, Roulstone, 1796. 16 pp.
NYPL copy.   31278

Tennessee. Constitution, 1796.
. . . The Constitution of the State of
Tennessee.
Philadelphia, Condie, 1796. 33, [3] pp.
AAS copy.   31279

Tennessee. Governor, 1796.
State of Tenesee. John Sevier, Esq.
Governor. . . . A Proclamation
[Convening General Assembly. Dated
July 11].
Knoxville, Roulstone, 1796.
(No copy located.)   31282

Tennessee. Governor, 1796.
. . . John Sevier, Governor . . . a
Proclamation. . . . This 10th Day of
August, 1796.
[Knoxville, 1796.] Broadside.
(No copy located.)   47931

Tennessee. Governor, 1798.
Knoxville 23d April 1798. Sir, So
Various. . . .
[Knoxville, 1798.] Broadside.
(No copy located.)   48624

[Tennessee. Governor, 1798.
A Proclamation, by His Excellency John
Sevier. . . . To Convene the General
Assembly [Dec. 3. Dated Oct. 15, 1798].
Knoxville, Roulstone, 1798. Broadside.]
(Broadside printing assumed by Evans.)
                                             34637

Tennessee. House Journals, 1796.
Journal of the House of Representatives.
. . . [Mar. 28-Apr. 23, 1796.]
Knoxville, Roulstone, 1796. 80 pp.
JCB copy.   31281

Tennessee. House Journals, 1796.
[Journal of the House of Representatives
begun July 30, 1796.
Knoxville, Roulstone, 1796.]
(Known only from the 1852 reprint.) 47932

Tennessee. Laws, Statutes, etc., 1800.
Laws Relative to Lands and Intestate
Estates.
Knoxville, Roulstone & Wilson, 1800.
86 pp.
JCB copy.   38612

Tennessee. Senate Journals, 1796.
[Journal of the Senate begun Mar. 28,
1796.
Knoxville, Roulstone, 1796.]
(Known from the 1852 reprint.)   47933

Tennessee. Senate Journals, 1796.
[Journal of the Senate begun July 30,
1796.
Knoxville, Roulstone, 1796.]
(Known from the 1852 reprint.)   47934

Tennessee. Session Laws, 1796.
Acts Passed at the First General
Assembly [Mar. 28 - Apr. 23, 1796].
Knoxville, Roulstone, 1796. 78 pp.
Composite copy.   31277

Tennessee. Session Laws, 1796.
Acts Passed at the Second Session of the
First General Assembly [July 30, 1796 +].
Knoxville, Roulstone, 1796. 13 pp.
HC-L copy.   47935

Tennessee. Session Laws, 1797.
Acts Passed at the First Session of the
Second General Assembly [Sept. 18 - Oct.
28, 1797.]
Knoxville, Roulstone, 1797. 120 pp.
LOC copy.   32913

Tennessee. Session Laws, 1799.
Acts Passed at the Second Session of the

Second General Assembly [Dec. 3, 1798-
Jan. 5, 1799].
Knoxville, Roulstone & Parrington, 1799.
70 pp.
LOC copy.   36403

Tennessee. Session Laws, 1799.
Acts Passed at the First Session of the
Third General Assembly [Sept. 16,
1799 +].
Knoxville, Roulstone & Wilson, 1799. 136
pp., irreg.
(No perfect copy located.)
LOC copy.   36402

Tennessee Company.
Notice is hereby Given. . . . This First
Day of January, 1791.
n.p., [1791]. Broadside.
Univ. of Calif., Berkeley, copy.   46295

The Tennessee Company.
The Tenesee Company to Messrs.
Strawbridge Jackson and Dexter. . . . 20th
of July, 1800.
[Philadelphia, 1800.] 23, [1] pp.
AAS copy.   38613

Tenney, Joseph.
The Gamut, or Scale of Music.
[Windsor], Spooner, 1795. 5 pp.
(Not located, 1968.)   47621

Tenny, Joseph.
A Brief Illustration of Infant Baptism.
Lansingburgh, 1794. 29 pp.
JCB copy.   27785

Terms, Conditions, and Circumstances
Touching Lands for Sale in the United
States.
[Philadelphia? 1798.] Broadside.
BM copy.   34882

Terra Beata [by Cotton Mather,
1663-1728].
Boston, Phillips, 1726. [2], 54 pp.
AAS copy.   2778

Territorial Company, Philadelphia, Pa.
Plan of Association of the Territorial
Company. Established April, 1795.
Philadelphia, Aitken, 1795. 21 pp.
LOC copy.   29550

Territory of the United States, South of the
River Ohio. Council Journals, 1794.
Journal of the Proceedings of the
Legislative Council [Aug. 25-Sept. 30,
1794.]
Knoxville, Roulstone, 1794. 39 pp.
AAS copy.   27726

Territory of the United States, South of
the River Ohio. Governor, 1794.
By William Blount, Governor. . . . A
Proclamation [Assembly]. . . . January
1st, 1794.
[Knoxville, 1794.] Broadside.
LOC copy.   27725

Territory of the United States, South of
the River Ohio. House Journals, 1795.
[Proceedings of the session at Knoxville,
June 28, 1795 +]
Knoxville, Roulstone, 1795.]
(Known only from 1852 reprint.)   47620

[Territory of the United States, South of
the River Ohio. Legislative Council
Journals, 1795.
Journal of the Proceedings of the
Legislative Council.
[June 29 - July 11, 1795].
(Probably not printed until 1852.)   29552

Territory of the United States, South of
the River Ohio. Session Laws, 1792.
Acts and Ordinances [June 11, 1792 -
Mar. 21, 1793].
[Knoxville, 1793.] viii pp.
(No perfect copy known.)
HC-L copy.   26195

Territory of the United States, South of
the River Ohio. Session Laws, 1794.
Acts Passed at the First Session of the
Territorial Assembly [Aug. 25 - Sept. 30,
1794].
Knoxville, Roulstone, 1794. viii, 101 pp.
LOC copy.   27724

Territory of the United States, South of

the River Ohio. Session Laws, 1795.
Acts Passed at the Second Session of the
First General Assembly [June 29 - July
11, 1795].
Knoxville, Roulstone, 1795. 31 pp.
LOC copy.   29551

[Tersteegen, Gerhard], 1697-1769.
Das Anhagen an Gott.
Germantown, 1764. [7], 56 pp.
HSP copy.   9850

[Tersteegen, Gerhard, 1697-1769.
Der Frommen Lotterie.
Germantown, 1744.] 381 cards.
NYPL copy.   5501

[Tersteegen, Gerhard, 1697-1769.
(J. Thomas, Univ. Pronouncing Dict.)
Der Frommen Lotterie.
[Germantown, Sower, 1751.]
(From printer's adv.)   6791

[Tersteegen, Gerhard], 1697-1769.
(J. Thomas, Univ. Pronouncing Dict.)
Geistliches Blumen-Gaertlein.
Germantown, 1747. 486, [6] pp.
AAS copy.   6073

[Tersteegen, Gerhard], 1697-1769.
Geistliches Blumen-Gaertlein.
Germantown, 1769. [12], 517, [29] pp.
AAS copy.   11492

[Tersteegen, Gerhard], 1697-1769.
Geistliches Blumen-Gaertlein.
Germantown, 1773. [12], 547 pp.
AAS copy.   13036

[Tersteegen, Gerhard], 1697-1769.
Geistliches Blumen-Gärtlein.
Germantown, Leibert, 1791. [12], 534, [7]
pp.
AAS copy.   23823

[Tersteegen, Gerhard], 1697-1769.
Geistliches Blumen-Gärtlein.
Germantown, Billmeyer, 1800. [12], 564,
[12] pp.
AAS copy.   38615

[Tersteegen, Gerhard, 1697-1769.
Glueckliche Genuegsamkeit.
Germantown, 1747.]
(Reichmann 88.)   6074

[Tersteegen, Gerhard], 1697-1769.
Die Kraft der Liebe Christi. . . . Zweyte
Auflage.
Philadelphia, Miller, 1772. 64 pp.
NYPL copy.   12573

Tersteegen, Gerhard, 1697-1769.
Vom Christlichen Gebrauch der Lieder.
Ephrata, 1792. 88 pp.
German Soc. of Pa. copy.   24843

[Tersteegen, Gerhard], 1697-1769.
(J. Thomas, Univ. Pronouncing Dict.)
Warnungs-Schreiben.
Germantown, 1748. 48 pp.
AAS copy.   6249

A Test of the Religious Principles of Mr.
Jefferson.
See
Jefferson, Thomas, pres. U. S., 1743-1826.
     38616-7

Testament de Mort d'Ogé, et Adresse de
Pinchiant aux Hommes de Couleur.
Philadelphia, Parent, [1793?]. [2], 28 pp.
JCB copy.   46887

Testart Freres & Cie.
A Philadelphie, 15 mai, 1794. . . .
[Philadelphia, 1794.] 2 leaves.
NYPL copy.   47230

A Testimony against Evil Customs.
Boston, Kneeland for Gerrish, 1719. 4 pp.
AAS copy.   2051

The Testimony and Advice of a Number
of Laymen.
[Boston, 1743.] 9, [1] pp.
AAS copy.   5300

The Testimony of an Association or Club
of Laymen.
Boston, Kneeland & Green, 1745. 8 pp.
AAS copy.   5701

A Testimony to the Order of the Gospel
[by John Higginson, 1616-1708].
Boston, 1701. 15 pp.
AAS copy.   978

Der Teutsche Pilgrim . . . einen
Sitten-Calender. . . . Auf das Jahr . . .
MDCCXXXI.
Philadelphia, A. Bradford. [32] pp.
Rosenbach Foundation copy.   3361

[Der Teutsche Pilgrim . . . Sitten-
Calender. Auf das Jahr . . . 1732.
Philadelphia, 1732.]
(Penn. Mag. Hist. Biog., VI, 370.)   3481

Der Teutsche Pilgrim . . . Sitten-Calender.
Auf das Jahr . . . MDCCXXXIII.
Philadelphia, A. Bradford. [32] pp.
Rosenbach Foundation copy.   3610

[Eine Teutsche und Englische Grammatic
[by - Koenig].
Germantown, 1747.]
(See Reichmann 83.)   6075

Teutschen Gesellschaft, Philadelphia.
See
German Society of Pennsylvania.

[Die Teutscher Kriegsartikel.
Philadelphia Franklin and Armbruester,
1757.]
(Curtis 609; no copy known.)   40942

[Thacher, Oxenbridge], 1719-1765.
Considerations on Lowering the Value of
Gold Coins.
[Boston, 1762.] 27 pp.
AAS copy.   9283

[Thacher, Oxenbridge?], 1719-1765.
(Sibley, X, 322-325)
Considerations on the Election of
Counsellors.
[Boston], 1761. 8 pp.
(For authorship see Boston Evening Post,
supplement, Dec. 1, 1766.)
AAS copy.   8827

[Thacher, Oxenbridge, 1719-1765.
The Sentiments of a British American.
Boston, Edes & Gill, 1764. 16 pp.
AAS copy.   9851

Thacher, Peter, 1651-1727.
(Sibley, II, 370-379.)
The Alsufficient Physician.
Boston, 1711. [2], 44 pp.
HC copy.   1529

Thacher, Peter, 1651-1727.
(Sibley, II, 370-379.)
Christ's Forgiveness of True Christians.
Boston, 1712. [2], 128 pp.
AAS copy.   1587

Thacher, Peter, 1651-1727.
(Sibley, II, 370-379.)
A Divine Riddle.
New London, 1723. [4], xi, [1], 62 pp.
BPL copy.   2484

[Thacher, Peter, 1651-1727.
(Sibley, II, 370-379.)
The Perpetual Covenant.
Boston, 1713.]
(Title from Prince list.)   1653

Thacher, Peter, 1651-1727.
(Sibley, II, 370-379.)
The Reverend Mr. Samuel Man, his
Funeral Sermon.
Boston, Kneeland for Gray, 1720. [2], x,
44, 39 pp.
AAS copy.   2076

Thacher, Peter, 1651-1727.
(Sibley, II, 370-379.)
The Saints' Victory.
Boston, 1696. 40 pp.
BPL copy.   774

Thacher, Peter, 1651-1727.
(Sibley, II, 370-379.)
The Signal and most Gracious Presence.
Boston, 1708.
(Issued signatures continuous with 1375,
q.v.)   1374

Thacher, Peter, 1651-1727.
Unbelief Detected and Condemned.

Boston, 1708. [12], 190 pp.
AAS copy. 1375

Thacher, Peter, 1677-1739.
A Brief Declaration of Mr. Peter Thacher
and Mr. John Webb.
Boston, Franklin for Henchman, 1720.
[2], 13 pp.
AAS copy. 2187

Thacher, Peter, 1677-1739.
(Sibley, IV, 303-308.)
Man's Frailty.
Boston, Kneeland and Green, 1730. [4],
31 pp.
AAS copy. 3362

[Thacher, Peter], 1677-1739.
(Sibley, IV, 303-308.)
A Vindication of the New-North-Church
in Boston.
Boston, Franklin for Henchman, 1720.
[2], 14 pp.
BA copy. 2186

Thacher, Peter, 1677-1739.
(Sibley, IV, 303-308.)
Wise and Good Civil Rulers.
Boston, Green for Gerrish, 1726. [4], 28
pp.
AAS copy. 2816

Thacher, Peter, 1688-1744.
(Sibley, V, 317-322.)
The Fear of God Restraining Men.
Boston, Boone, Gray, and Edwards, 1720.
[4], 20 pp.
BA copy. 2188

Thacher, Peter, 1716-1785.
(Sibley, X, 245.)
Prayer the Breath of a Good Man.
Providence, Carter, 1783. 27 pp.
AAS copy. 17739

Thacher, Peter, 1716-1785.
Select Discourses on Practical Subjects.
Leominster, Mass., Prentiss for Thacher,
1798. 114 pp.
AAS copy. 34638

Thacher, Peter, 1752-1802.
Brief Account of the Society for
Propagating the Gospel among the
Indians and Others in North-America. . . .
January, 1798.
[Boston, 1798.] 7 pp.
MHS copy. 34639

Thacher, Peter, 1752-1802.
The Nature and Effects of Christian
Sympathy.
Boston, Edes, 1794. 25 pp.
AAS copy. 27786

Thacher, Peter, 1752-1802.
Observations upon the Present State of
the Clergy.
Boston, Norman & White, 1783. 15 pp.
AAS copy. 18206

Thacher, Peter, 1752-1802.
An Oration Delivered at Watertown,
March 5, 1776.
Watertown, 1776. 15 pp.
AAS copy. 15101

Thacher, Peter, 1752-1802.
A Reply to the Strictures of Mr. J. S.
Boston, Norman, White & Freeman,
[1784]. 22 pp.
AAS copy. 18804

Thacher, Peter, 1752-1802.
The Rest which Remaineth.
Boston, Fleets, [1778]. 40 pp.
AAS copy. 16090

Thacher, Peter, 1752-1802.
A Sermon, Delivered at the First Church.
Boston, Hall, 1798. 27 pp.
AAS copy. 34642

Thacher, Peter, 1752-1802.
A Sermon, Occasioned by the Death of
. . . Washington.
Boston, Young & Minns, [1800]. [2], 21
pp.
AAS copy. 38618

Thacher, Peter, 1752-1802.
A Sermon, Preached at Charlestown,
February 29, 1788.

Boston, Allen, 1788. 21 pp.
AAS copy. 21489

Thacher, Peter, 1752-1802.
A Sermon, Preached at Charlestown, June
19, 1796.
Boston, Hall, 1796. 25, [1], 15, [1] pp.
AAS copy. 31283

Thacher, Peter, 1752-1802.
A Sermon, Preached at Dorchester, June
24, 1797.
Boston, Hall, 1797. 21, [1] pp.
AAS copy. 32914

Thacher, Peter, 1752-1802.
A Sermon, Preached at Exeter.
Exeter, Ranlet, [1790]. 44 pp.
AAS copy. 22925

Thacher, Peter, 1752-1802.
A Sermon, Preached at Lynn, August 13,
1794.
Boston, Hall, [1794]. 40 pp.
AAS copy. 27787

Thacher, Peter, 1752-1802.
A Sermon, Preached before the Ancient
and Honorable Artillery Company.
Boston, Manning and Loring, 1793. 27 pp.
AAS copy. 26249

Thacher, Peter, 1752-1802.
A Sermon, Preached in Boston, February
12, 1795.
Boston, Hall, 1795. 24 pp.
AAS copy. 29616

Thacher, Peter, 1752-1802.
A Sermon Preached June 12, 1799.
Boston, Young & Minns, [1799]. xviii pp.
AAS copy. 36405

Thacher, Peter, 1752-1802.
A Sermon, Preached October, 1788.
[Portland], Wait, [1788]. 26, [1] pp.
AAS copy. 21490

Thacher, Peter, 1752-1802.
A Sermon Preached to the Church and
Society in Brattle-Street.
Boston, Young & Minns, 1800. 18 pp.
AAS copy. 38619

Thacher, Peter, 1752-1802.
A Sermon, Preached to the Society in
Brattle-Street, Boston, April 17, 1796.
Boston, Sweetser, 1796. 32 pp.
AAS copy. 31284

Thacher, Peter, 1752-1802.
A Sermon Preached to the Society in
Brattle-Street, Boston, March 25th, 1798.
Boston, Rhoades & Laughton, 1798. 23 pp.
AAS copy. 34641

Thacher, Peter, 1752-1802.
A Sermon, Preached to the Society in
Brattle Street, Boston, Novembr 14, 1790.
Boston, Thomas & Andrews, 1791. 27 pp.
AAS copy. 23824

Thacher, Peter, 1752-1802.
A Sermon, Preached to the Society in
Brattle Street, Boston, November 14,
1790.
Boston, Thomas & Andrews, 1791. 31 pp.
AAS copy. 23825

Thacher, Peter, 1752-1802.
A Sermon, Preached to the Society in
Brattle Street, Boston, October 20, 1793.
Boston, Young, 1793. 30 pp.
AAS copy. 26248

Thacher, Peter, 1752-1802.
That the Punishment of the Finally
Impenitent. . . .
Salem, Hall, 1783. 51 pp.
AAS copy. 18207

[Thacher, Peter, 1752-1802.
To the Members of the Society for
Propagating the Gospel among the
Indians, and Others in North-America.
[Boston, 1798.] Broadside.]
(No copy located.) 34640

Thacher, Samuel.
An Oration, Pronounced July 4, 1796.
Boston, Hall, 1796. 24 pp.
AAS copy. 31285

Thacher, Thomas, 1620-1678.
(Magnalia, Bk. 3, Pt. 2, Ch. 26.)
A Brief Rule.
Boston, 1677. Broadside.
MHS copy. 242

Thacher, Thomas, 1620-1678.
(Sprague, I, 126-129.)
A Brief Rule to Guide the Common
People.
Boston, 1702. 8 pp.
HC copy. 1096

[Thacher, Thomas], 1620-1678.
A Brief Rule to Guide the Common
People . . . in the Small-Pox and Measels.
[Boston, 1721?]. 8 pp.
AML copy. 39754

Thacher, Thomas, 1620-1678.
(Magnalia, Bk. 3, Pt. 2, Ch. 26.)
A Fast of God's Chusing.
Boston, 1678. [6], 25 pp.
AAS copy. 258

Thacher, Thomas, 1756-1812.
A Discourse Delivered at Boston.
Boston, Fleets, 1800. 31 pp.
AAS copy. 38620

Thacher, Thomas, 1756-1812.
A Discourse, Delivered at Peterborough.
Amherst, N. H., Preston, 1800. 37 pp.
AAS copy. 38621

Thacher, Thomas, 1756-1812.
A Discourse, Delivered at the Third
Parish in Dedham, 19th February, 1795.
Boston, Fleet, 1795. 24 pp.
AAS copy. 29617

Thacher, Thomas, 1756-1812.
An Eulogy on George Washington.
Dedham, [Mass.], Mann, 1800. 22 pp.
AAS copy. 38622

Thacher, Thomas, 1756-1812.
A Sermon, Delivered at the Second
Church in Dedham, February 23d, 1784.
Boston, Edes, 1784. 22 pp.
AAS copy. 18805

Thacher, Thomas, 1756-1812.
A Sermon Preached at Milton.
Boston, Fleet, 1796. 26, [2], 28 pp.
(Issued with and without the attached
sermon by Mather.)
MHS copy. 31286

Thacher, Thomas, 1756-1812.
A Sermon, Preached in the Episcopal
Church.
Dedham, Mann & Adams, 1798. 30 pp.
AAS copy. 34645

Thacher, Thomas Cushing, 1771-1849.
An Eulogy on the Memory of . . .
Washington.
Boston, Manning & Loring, [1800]. 12 pp.
AAS copy. 38623

Thacher, Thomas Cushing, 1771-1849.
A Sermon, Preached at Lynn, December
11, 1795.
Boston, Hall, 1795. 22 pp.
AAS copy. 29618

Thacher, Thomas Cushing, 1771-1849.
A Sermon, Preached at Lynn, November
20th, 1794.
Boston, Hall, 1794. 24 pp.
AAS copy. 27788

[Thackera, James.
The Young Ladies' & Gentlemen's
Complete Drawing-Book.
Philadelphia, 1798.]
(Imprint assumed by Evans from adv.)
34643

The Thankful Christian [by Cotton
Mather, 1663-1728].
Boston, Green for Gerrish, 1717. [2], 43,
[1] pp.
BPL copy. 1907

[Tharp, Peter.]
An Elegy. On the Death of Capt.
Annanias Valentine . . . the 12th of
December, 1800.
[Kingston, N. Y., 1800.] Broadside.
(Reproduced as Shaw 438.)
AAS copy. 38624

Tharp, Peter.
An Elegy On the Death of Capt. Annanias
Valentine . . . the 12th of December, 1800.
Kingston, [N. Y.], Freer, [1800].
Broadside.
AAS copy. 38625

Tharp, Peter.
A New and Complete System of Federal
Arithmetic.
Newburgh, N. Y., Denniston, 1798. 138,
[2] pp.
AAS copy. 34644

That Jesus Christ is God by Nature
[by — Hanley].
Boston, Green & Russell, 1756. [2], vi, 83
pp.
AAS copy. 7800

Thaumatographia Christiana [by Cotton
Mather, 1663-1728].
Boston, 1701. 55 pp.
HC copy. 995

Thayer, Ebenezer, 1689-1733.
(Sibley, V, 455-457.)
Christ the Great Subject.
Goston, Kneeland for Gerrish and
Henchman, 1722. [2], iv, v, [1], 227, [3],
46 pp.
AAS copy. 2391

Thayer, Ebenezer, 1689-1733.
(Sibley, V, 455-457.)
Jerusalem Instructed & Warned.
Boston, Green for Gerrish, 1725. [4], 42
pp.
AAS copy. 2709

Thayer, Ebenezer, 1689-1733.
(Sibley, V, 455-457.)
Ministers of the Gospel.
Boston, Gerrish, 1727. [4], 30 pp.
AAS copy. 2967

Thayer, Ebenezer, 1734-1792.
Family Worship.
Newburyport, Blunt, 1799. 32 pp.
HEH copy. 36406

Thayer, Elihu, 1747-1812.
The Faithful Watchman.
Newburyport, Mycall, 1790. 37 pp.
AAS copy. 22926

Thayer, Elihu, 1747-1812.
A Funeral Discourse . . . at the Interment
of . . . Josiah Bartlett.
Exeter, Lamson, 1795. 20 pp.
AAS copy. 29619

Thayer, John, 1758-1815.
An Account of the Conversion of. . . .
Fifth Edition.
Baltimore, Goddard, 1788. 28 pp.
AAS copy. 21491

Thayer, John, 1758-1815.
An Account of the Conversion of . . .
John Thayer.
Wilmington, N.C., Bowen & Howard,
1789. 42 pp.
Sondley Reference Library, Asheville,
copy. 45600

Thayer, John, 1758-1815.
Controversy between . . . and the
Reverend George Lesslie.
Georgetown, Doyle, 1791. 37 pp.
(Incorrectly dated by Evans.)
Georgetown University copy. 26251

Thayer, John, 1758-1815.
Controversy between . . . and the Rev.
George Lesslie.
[Newburyport, 1793.] 167 pp.
AAS copy. 26250

Thayer, John, 1758-1815.
Controversy between the Rev. John
Thayer . . . and the Rev. George Leslie.
Philadelphia, Folwell, 1795. 32 pp.
UOP copy. 29620

Thayer, John, 1758-1815.
A Discourse, Delivered, at the Roman
Catholic Church in Boston, on the 9th of
May, 1798.
Boston, Hall, 1798. 31 pp.
AAS copy. 34646

Thayer, John, 1758-1815.

A Discourse, Delivered at the Roman
Catholic Church, in Boston, on the 9th of
May, 1798. . . . Second Edition.
Baltimore, Hanna, 1798. 31 pp.
MdHS copy. 48625

Thayer, John, 1758-1815.
A Discourse, Delivered at the Roman
Catholic Church in Boston, on the 9th of
May, 1798. . . . Second Edition.
Boston, Hall, 1798. 31 pp.
AAS copy. 34647

[Thayer, Nathaniel], 1769-1840.
Anthems and Hymns, to be Sung at the
Installation of the Reverend Mr. Emerson.
[Boston, 1799.] Broadside.
HSP copy. 36407

Thayer, Nathaniel, 1769-1840.
The Character of St. John the Baptist.
Leominster, Mass., Prentiss, 1797. 15 pp.
AAS copy. 32915

Thayer, Nathaniel, 1769-1840.
The Preaching and Practice of the
Apostles.
Portland, Me., Titcomb, 1799. 22 pp.
AAS copy. 36408

Thayer, Nathaniel, 1769-1840.
A Sermon, Delivered before the Ancient
and Honorable Artillery Company.
Boston, Manning & Loring, 1798. 20 pp.
AAS copy. 34648

Thayer, Nathaniel, 1769-1840.
A Sermon Delivered on the Day of
Fasting.
Boston, Belknap, 1795. 20 pp.
AAS copy. 29621

Thayer, Nathaniel, 1769-1840.
A Sermon, Preached at the Installation.
Boston, Hall, 1799. 30 pp.
AAS copy. 36409

Thayer, Nathaniel, 1769-1840.
A Sermon, Preached December 23.
Amherst, N. H., Biglow & Cushing, 1796.
19 pp.
AAS copy. 31287

Theatre.
[Boston, 1792.] 7 pp.
AAS copy. 24844

[The Theatre of Education, Consisting of
Entertaining Moral Instructions.
Philadelphia, Dobson, 1787.]
(Entry from an adv.) 20744

Theft and Murder! A Poem on the
Execution of Levi Ames.
[Boston], Sold near the Mill-Bridge,
[1773]. Broadside.
HC copy. 42518

Their Majesties Colony of Connecticut in
New-England Vindicated [by John Allyn,
d. 1696].
Boston, 1694. 43 pp.
AAS copy. 686

Then I fly to meet my Love a Favorite
Song.
New York, Gilfert, [1795]. pp. [6]-7.
JCB copy. 47622

Then Say my Sweet Girl can you love me.
. . . Sung by Mr. Barley [by James Hook,
1746-1827].
Philadelphia, Carr, [1794]. 4 pp.
AAS copy. 27789

Theobald, John.
Every Man his own Physician. . . . Tenth
Edition.
Boston, Cox & Berry, 1767. iv, [10], [1]
pp.
NLM copy. 10783

Theobald, John.
Every Man his own Physician. . . .
Seventh Edition.
Philadelphia, Jones, Hoff & Derrick,
1794. [12], 87 pp.
AAS copy. 27790

Theobald, John.
Every Man his own Physician. . . . Eighth
Edition.

Hartford, [Ct.], Babcock, 1800. 108 pp.
AAS copy. 38626

Theophilanthropy: or, The Spirit of
Genuine Religion.
Lancaster, Pa., 1799. 23 pp.
AAS copy. 26411

Theopolis Americana [by Cotton Mather,
1663-1728].
Boston, 1710. [4], 51, [2] pp.
AAS copy. 1469

Theory of Agency [by John Perkins,
1698-1781].
Boston, Perkins, 1771. 43 pp.
AAS copy. 12188

There is a Snake in the Grass!!! Citizens
of Kentucky. . . . August 15th, 1798.
[Lexington, 1798.] Broadside.
HEH copy. 34650

. . . There's not an Ear that is not
Deaf. . . . [Yearly Verses of the
American Weekly Mercury].
[Philadelphia, 1735.] Broadside.
AAS copy. 40086

Thermometrical Navigation [by Jonathan
Williams, 1750-1815].
Philadelphia, Aitken, 1799. xii, 98, [3]
pp., 1 folding chart.
LCP copy. 36722

These Presents Witnesses. . . . Reprinted
in October, 1750 [Newport, R.I.
Hand-in-Hand Fire-Club].
[Newport, 1750.] Broadside.
NYHS copy. 40559

These Times want Other. . . . It is a
Disagreeable Subject to Write upon
Informers [by Robert? Simmons].
New York, [1769]. Broadside.
LCP copy. 11466

Theses Concerning the Sabbath.
New London, Green, 1721. Broadside.
CHS copy. 39755

Things that Young People Should Think
upon [by Cotton Mather, 1663-1728].
Boston, 1700. 16 + pp.
(The unique copy is defective.)
AAS copy. 934

Things to be more Thought upon [by
Cotton Mather, 1663-1728].
Boston, 1713. 108 pp.
HC copy. 1628

The Third Book of Elegant Extracts for
the German Flute.
Philadelphia, Carr, [1798]. 32 pp.
(The title given by Evans came from
advs.)
LOC copy. 33667

A Third Extraordinary Budget.
[Boston, 1769.] 8 pp.
AAS copy. 11177

A Third Letter from a Minister [by
Samuel Johnson, 1696-1772].
Boston, 1737. [4], 20 pp.
(Authorship on authority of Schneider.)
AAS copy. 4148

Thirty Dollars Reward. Stolen out of the
Store of the Subscriber. . . . December 30,
1783 [altered to 1787].
[Worcester? 1787?] Broadside.
HEH copy. 44655

Thirty Important Cases [by Cotton
Mather, 1663-1728].
Boston, 1699. 78, [1] pp.
(The additional pages called for by Evans
were the Proposals separately printed in
1702. See T. J. Holmes, Cotton Mather,
II, 861-863.)
AAS copy. 878

This Indenture made [Mar. 25, 1731]. . . .
Between, the Proprietors of a Certain
Tract of Land . . . on the Western side of
Kenebunk-River, Adjoyning to the Inland
head of the Township of Wells . . . and
[blank].
[Boston, 1731.] [2] pp.
AAS copy. 39979

This is unto all Gentlemen who Shoes here. . . . Please to Remember my New-Years Box.
n. p., [1767] Broadside.
HSP copy.   41768

[This Night will be Performed at the Steps, Bottom of Long Wharf, a Comedy of Stripping the Bermudian Privatus.
[Boston, 1795.] Broadside.]
(The origin of this entry is unknown.)   29623

This Poem, Humbly Dedicated to Sir Q - C- o. . . .
[Philadelphia, 1765.] Broadside.
HSP copy.   10143

Tho' You Think by this to Vex me. . . .
[by Stephen Storace, 1763-1796].
New York, Hewitt, etc., [1797?]. [2] pp.
NYPL copy.   48260

Thomas à Kempis, 1380-1471.
The Christian Pattern.
Germantown, 1749. [2], 278 pp.
AAS copy.   6342

Thomas à Kempis, 1380-1471.
An Extract of the Christian's Pattern.
Philadelphia, Prichard & Hall for Dickins, 1789. 192 pp.
(The only known copy is imperfect.)
JCB copy.   45604

Thomas à Kempis, 1380-1471.
An Extract of the Christian's Pattern.
Philadelphia, Prichard & Hall and Dickins, 1790. 306, [10] pp.
(The only known copy is imperfect.)
NYHS copy.   46000

Thomas à Kempis, 1380-1471.
An Extract of the Christian's Pattern.
Philadelphia, Crukshank for Dickins, 1794. 306, [14] pp.
AAS copy.   27179

Thomas à Kempis, 1380-1471.
An Extract of the Christian's Pattern.
Philadelphia, Tuckniss for Dickins, 1798. 320 pp.
(The present location of the only recorded copy is unknown.)   48626

Thomas à Kempis, 1380-1471.
An Extract of the Christian's Pattern.
Philadelphia, Tuckniss for Cooper, 1800. 290, [2] pp.
(The only copy located is imperfect.)
RU copy.   37717

Thomas à Kempis, 1380-1471.
The Following of Christ. . . . Ninth Edition.
Philadelphia, J. Carey for M. Carey, 1800. 335 pp.
NYPL copy.   37718

[Thomas à Kempis, 1380-1471.
The Imitation of Christ.
Cambridge.]
(If a Cambridge edition was published, it was in 1669.)   114

Thomas à Kempis, 1380-1471.
Das Kleine A. B. C.
Germantown, 1742. Broadside.
HSP copy.   4982

Thomas à Kempis, 1380-1471.
Der Kleine Kempis. . . . Virte und Vermehrte Auflage.
Germantown, 1750. Front., 162 pp.
AAS copy.   6523

[Thomas à Kempis, 1380-1471.
Der Kleine Kempis. . . . Virte, und Verhmehrte Auflage.
Germantown, 1750. 162 pp., 1 plate.]
(A ghost of 6523, q.v.)   6698

Thomas à Kempis, 1380-1471.
Der Kleine Kempis. . . . Fuenfte und Vermehrte Auflage.
Germantown, 1773. Front., [10], 155 pp.
AAS copy.   12824

Thomas à Kempis, 1380-1471.
Der Kleine Kempis.
Germantown, 1788. [10], 155, [1], 12 pp.
AAS copy.   21183

Thomas à Kempis, 1380-1471.
Der Kleine Kempis.
Germantown, Leibert, 1795. [11], 180 pp.
AAS copy.   28920

Thomas à Kempis, 1380-1471.
Of the Imitation of Christ.
Philadelphia, Crukshank, 1783. 44, 211 pp.
AAS copy.   17992

[Thomas à Kempis, 1380-1471.
Of the Imitation of Christ.
Philadelphia, Crukshank for Dickins, 1791.]
(Entry from Dickins' advs.)   23480

Thomas à Kempis, 1380-1471.
The Soliloquy of the Soul.
Hartford, Ct., Babcock, 1800. 227, [1] pp.
AAS copy.   37719

[Thomas à Kempis, 1380-1471.
The Soliloquy of the Soul.
Philadelphia, Carey, 1800. 335 pp.]
(The reported copies of this ed. could not be located.)   37720

[Thomas à Kempis, 1380-1471.
Vier Buecher.
Germantown, 1749.]
(An unlaid ghost. See Reichmann III.)   6343

Thomas, Alexander, 1775?-1809.
The Orator's Assistant.
Worcester, Mass., Thomas, etc., 1797. 216 pp.
AAS copy.   32917

Thomas, Antoine Léonard, 1732-1785.
Essay on the Character . . . of Women.
Philadelphia, Aitken, 1774. 2 vol. v, [3], 124; [4], 129, [3] pp.
AAS copy.   13650

Thomas, David, 1732-c. 1815.
The Virginian Baptist.
Baltimore, Story, 1774. 68 pp.
(The only copy recorded is incomplete.)
Johns Hopkins copy.   13651

Thomas, David, 1732 - c. 1815.
The Novelty of Novelties Examined.
Philadelphia, 1782. [2], 37 pp.
AAS copy.   17740

Thomas, Elisha, d. 1788.
The Last Words of . . . on the 3d June, 1788.
n. p., [1788]. Broadside.
AAS copy.   45373

Thomas Elisha, d. 1788.
Life and Dying Speech of . . . June 3, 1788.
n. p., [1788]. Broadside.
NHHS copy.   45374

Thomas, Eliza, d. 1799.
A Vision; Tending to Edify.
[Stoningtonport], 1800. 15 pp.
NYSL copy.   38627

[Thomas, Sir George, bart.], 1695?-1774.
Octob. 20, 1740. My Lords.
[Philadelphia, 1740.] 8 pp.
HSP copy.   4613

Thomas, Isaiah, 1749-1831.
Catalogue of Books to be Sold by. . . . MDCCXXXVIII.
Worcester, Thomas, [1787]. 26, [1] pp.
AAS copy.   20745

Thomas, Isaiah, 1749-1831.
Catalogue of Books to be Sold. . . . November, MDCCXCII.
Worcester, Thomas & Worcester, [1792]. 42 pp.
AAS copy.   24845

Thomas, Isaiah, 1749-1831.
Catalogue of Books to be Sold. . . . October, MDCCXCVI.
Worcester, Thomas, Son & Thomas, [1796]. 47 pp.
AAS copy.   31290

Thomas, Isaiah, 1749-1831.
The Friends of Literature . . . American Editions . . . are now Selling. . . .
[Worcester, 1791.] [4] pp.
AAS copy.   46296

Thomas, Isaiah, 1749-1831.
Just Published, Embellished with Four Plates . . . The Massachusetts Calendar . . . for . . . 1772.
Boston, Thomas, [1771]. Broadside.
AAS copy.   42285

Thomas, Isaiah, 1749-1831.
Large Family Bible.
[Worcester, 1789.] [3] pp.
MHS copy.   21682

Thomas, Isaiah, 1749-1831.
Literary Proposal. . . . For Publishing . . . the Massachusetts Magazine.
[Boston], Thomas, 1788. 12, [4] pp.
AAS copy.   21492

[Thomas, Isaiah], 1749-1831.
New American Spelling Book.
Worcester, Thomas, 1785. 144 pp.
AAS copy.   19271

Thomas, Isaiah, 1749-1831.
An Oration: Delivered in Free Masons-Hall.
Worcester, 1781. 12 pp.
AAS copy.   17375

[Thomas, Isaiah, 1749-1831.
A Proposal for Printing . . . the Massachusetts Magazine.
Boston, Thomas, 1788. Broadside.]
(Apparently Evans assumed a broadside printing from a newspaper adv.)   21493

Thomas, Isaiah, 1749-1831.
Proposals for Printing by Subscription, Elements of General History.
[Worcester, Thomas, 1789.] [4] pp.
AAS copy.   45602

Thomas, Isaiah, 1749-1831.
A Specimen of . . . Printing Types.
Worcester, Thomas, 1785. 42 (50) leaves.
(We have reproduced the 2nd state which has 3 added leaves and several corrections. The AAS has also the first state.)
AAS copy.   19272

Thomas, Isaiah, 1749-1831.
This day was Published . . . Thomas's . . . Almanack, for . . . 1780.
[Worcester, 1779.] Broadside.
AAS copy.   19439

Thomas, Isaiah, 1749-1831.
Thomas and Andrew's Catalogue.
Boston, Thomas & Andrews, 1793. 60 pp.
AAS copy.   26252

Thomas, Isaiah, 1749-1831.
To Christians of every Denomination.
[Worcester, 1791.] [4] pp.
NYHS copy.   46297

Thomas, Isaiah, 1749-1831.
To the Customers for Thomas's Massachusetts Spy. . . . April 3d, 1786.
[Worcester, 1786.] Broadside.
AAS copy.   44975

Thomas, Isaiah, 1749-1831.
Worcester, January 12th, 1789. Proposals for Printing by Subscription A Disquisition on the Most Holy Deity.
[Worcester, 1789.] Broadside.
(No copy located.)   45603

Thomas, Isaiah, 1749-1831.
Worcester Massachusetts, Feb. 1, 1790. . . . An American Edition of the Bible.
[Worcester, 1790.] Broadside.
AAS ph. copy.   46001

Thomas, Isaiah, 1749-1831.
Worcester News-Paper — Free and Uninfluenced.
Proposals. . . . May 1782.
[Worcester, 1782.] Broadside.
AAS copy.   19440

Thomas, John Chew, 1764-1836.
Fairland, May 28th, 1800. Dear Sir. . . .
n. p., n. d. [2] pp.
LOC copy.   38629

Thomas, Philip Evans, 1738-1826.
Communications Interesting to the Public.
[Baltimore, 1789.] Broadside.
(The condition of the original is poor.)
LOC copy.   22177

Thomas, Robert Bailey, 1766-1846.
[No. I.] The Farmer's Almanack . . . for
. . . 1793.
Boston, Belknap & Hall. [48] pp.
AAS copy. 24847

Thomas, Robert Bailey, 1766-1846.
(No. II.) The Farmer's Almanack. . . . For
. . . 1794.
Boston, Belknap & Hall. [48] pp.
AAS copy. 26254

Thomas, Robert Bailey, 1766-1846.
(No. III.) The Farmer's Almanack. . . .
For . . . 1795.
Boston, Belknap for Smith. [48] pp.
AAS copy. 27792

Thomas, Robert Bailey, 1766-1846.
(No. IV.) Farmer's Almanack. . . . For
. . . 1796.
Boston, Belknap for Smith. [48] pp.
AAS copy. 29626

Thomas, Robert Bailey, 1766-1846.
No. V. The Farmer's Almanack . . . for
. . . 1797.
Boston, Manning & Loring for West, etc.
[48] pp.
AAS copy. 31294

Thomas, Robert Bailey, 1766-1846.
No. VI. The Farmer's Almanack . . . for
. . . 1798.
Boston, Manning & Loring for West, etc.
[48] pp.
AAS copy. 32922

Thomas, Robert Bailey, 1766-1846.
No. VII. The Farmer's Almanack . . . for
. . . 1799.
Boston, Manning & Loring for West. [48]
pp.
AAS copy. 34654

Thomas, Robert Bailey, 1766-1846.
No. VIII. The Farmer's Almanack . . . for
. . . 1800.
Boston, Manning & Loring for West. [48]
pp.
AAS copy. 36414

Thomas, Robert Bailey, 1766-1846.
No. IX. The Farmer's Almanack . . . for
. . . 1801.
Boston, Manning & Loring for West, etc.
[48] pp.
AAS copy. 38630

Thomas, Robert Bailey, 1766-1846.
Robert B. Thomas, Has for Sale at his
Book & Stationary Store, in Sterling. . . .
Leominster, Prentiss, 1796. [4] pp.
AAS copy. 31295

Thomas, Thomas.
The Pennsylvania Almanac. . . . For 1760.
Philadelphia, Dunlap. [32] pp.
AAS copy. 8502

[Thomas, Thomas
The Pennsylvania Almanac . . . for 1761.
Philadelphia, Dunlap.]
(Adv. Pa. Gazette, Sept. 25, 1760.) 8746

[Thomas, Thomas
The Pennsylvania Almanac . . . for 1762.
Philadelphia, Dunlap.]
(Adv. Pa. Gazette, Nov. 26, 1761.) 9024

Thomas, Thomas.
Thomas, 1762: being an Almanac . . . for
. . . 1762.
Philadelphia, Dunlap. [32] pp.
LOC copy. 41249

Thomas, Tristram, 1769-1847.
Disputatio Medica Inauguralis.
Philadelphia, Young, 1792. 24 pp.
National Library of Medicine copy. 24848

Thomas, William, fl. 1790.
Hodge's North-Carolina Almanack, for
. . . 1795.
Halifax, Hodge. [40] pp.
LOC copy. 27793

Thomas, William, fl. 1790.
Hodge's North-Carolina Almanack, for
. . . 1796.
Halifax, Hodge, [1795]. [48] pp.
HEH copy. 29627

Thomas, William, fl. 1790.
Hodge's North-Carolina Almanack, for
. . . 1797.
Halifax, N. C., Hodge. 48 pp.
AAS copy. 31296

Thomas, William, fl. 1790.
Hodge's North-Carolina Almanack, for
. . . 1798.
Halifax, N. C., Hodge. [48] pp.
NCU copy. 32923

Thomas, William, fl. 1790.
Hodge's North-Carolina Almanack, for
. . . 1799.
Halifax, Hodge. 48 pp.
AAS copy. 34655

Thomas, William, fl. 1790.
Hodge & Boylan's North-Carolina
Almanack, for . . . 1800.
Halifax, N. C., Hodge. 48 pp.
AAS copy. 36415

[Thomas, William, fl. 1790.
The North-Carolina Almanac for . . .
1790.
Fayetteville, Sibley & Howard.]
("Just published," N. C. Chronicle, Feb.
1, 1790.) 22179

Thomas & Andrews, Boston.
Catalogue of Books, (American Editions).
Boston, Thomas & Andrews, Feb. 1799.
36 pp.
AAS copy. 36416

Thomas & Andrews, Boston.
Proposal . . . for Printing . . . an Edition
of the Book of Common Prayer.
[Boston, 1789.] Broadside.
NYHS copy. 45605

Thomas & Andrews, Boston.
Proposal for Printing by Subscription, the
Life of Ezra Stiles. . . . July 18, 1797.
[Boston, 1797.] Broadside.
(Not located, 1968.) 48267

Thomas & Andrews, Boston.
Proposals for Printing by Subscription the
Second and Third Volumes of the History
of New-Hampshire. . . . December 21,
1790.
[Boston, 1790.] Broadside.
NYHS copy. 46002

Thomas and Sally [by Isaac Bickerstaffe,
1735?-1812?].
Philadelphia, Taylor, 1791. 24 pp.
LCP copy. 23204

Thomas, Andrews & Penniman, Albany,
N. Y.
American Publications. Catalogue of
Books for Sale.
[Albany, 1796.] Broadside.
NYHS copy. 31293

Thomas, Andrews & Penniman, Albany,
N. Y.
Catalogue of Books for Sale.
Albany, Andrews, [1798], 35 pp.
AAS copy. 32918

Thomas Gage's Proclamation
Versified. . . . June 30, 1775 [by John
Trumbull, 1750-1831].
[New York, 1775.] Broadside.
HSP copy. 14527

Thomas's Boston Almanack, for . . . 1775.
Boston, Thomas. Broadside.
AAS copy. 42711

Thomas's Massachusetts, Connecticut,
Rhode-island, Newhampshire & Vermont
Almanack . . . for . . . 1795 [by Ezra
Gleason, 1748?-1808?].
Worcester, Thomas, Price 9 dollars per
Gross. [48] pp.
(An imprint variant of 27052, q. v. for
text.)
AAS copy. 47063

Second Edition. Thomas's Massachusetts,
Connecticut, Rhodeisland, Newhampshire
& Vermont Almanack . . . for . . . 1795
[by Ezra Gleason, 1748-1808?].
Worcester, Thomas. [48] pp.
AAS copy. 27053

Thomas's Massachusetts,
New-Hampshire, and Connecticut
Almanack for . . . 1779 [by Ezra Gleason,
1748-1808?].
Worcester, Thomas. [24] pp.
AAS copy. 15813

Thomas's Massachusetts, New-Hampshire
and Connecticut Almanack for . . . 1780
[by Ezra Gleason, 1748-1808?].
Worcester, Thomas. [24] pp.
AAS copy. 16288

Thomas's Massachusetts New-Hampshire
and Connecticut Almanack, for . . . 1781
[by Ezra Gleason, 1748-1808?].
Worcester, Thomas. [24] pp.
AAS copy. 16786

Thomas's Massachusetts, Connecticut,
Rhode-Island, New-Hampshire and
Vermont Almanack for . . . 1782 [by Ezra
Gleason, 1748-1808?].
Worcester, Thomas. [37] pp.
AAS copy. 17174

Thomas's Massachusetts, Connecticut,
Rhode-Island, New-Hampshire and
Vermont Almanack, for . . . 1782. . . .
Second Edition [by Ezra Gleason,
1748-1808?].
Worcester, Thomas. [36] pp.
AAS copy. 17175

Thomas's Massachusetts, Connecticut,
Rhode-Island, New Hampshire and
Vermont Almanack, for . . . 1783 [by Ezra
Gleason, 1748-1808?].
Worcester, Thomas. [40] pp.
AAS copy. 17549

Thomas' Massachusetts, Connecticut,
Rhode Island, New-Hampshire and
Vermont Almanack . . . for . . . 1784 [by
Ezra Gleason, 1748-1808?].
Worcester, Thomas for Edes, Battelle, and
Green. [36] pp.
AAS copy. 17956

Thomas's Massachusetts, Connecticut,
Rhode-Island, New-Hampshire &
Vermont Almanack . . . for . . . 1785 [by
Benjamin West, 1730-1813].
Worcester, Thomas. [36] pp.
(Thomas' correspondence shows that West,
not Gleason, calculated this almanac.)
AAS copy. 18498

[Thomas's Massachusetts, Connecticut,
Rhode-Island, New-Hampshire &
Vermont Almanack . . . for . . . 1785. . . .
Second Edition [by Benjamin West,
1730-1813].
Worcester, Thomas. [36] pp.]
(There was a second printing of 18498, but
no way is known of distinguishing copies
of it.) 18499

Thomas's Massachusetts, Connecticut,
Rhode-Island, New-Hampshire &
Vermont Almanack . . . for . . . 1785. . . .
Third Edition [by Benjamin West,
1730-1813].
Worcester, Thomas. [36] pp.
AAS copy. 18500

Thomas's Massachusetts, Connecticut,
Rhode Island, New-Hampshire &
Vermont Almanack . . . for . . . 1786 [by
Benjamin West, 1730-1813].
Worcester, Thomas. 44 pp.
AAS copy. 19027

Thomas's Massachusetts, Connecticut,
Rhode-Island, New-Hampshire &
Vermont Almanack . . . for . . . 1787 [by
Ezra Gleason, 1748-1808?].
Worcester, Thomas. [48] pp.
AAS copy. 19686

Thomas's Massachusetts, Connecticut,
Rhode-Island, New-Hampshire and
Vermont Almanack . . . for . . . 1788 [by
Ezra Gleason, 1748-1808?].
Worcester, Thomas, [48] pp.
AAS copy. 20392

Thomas's Massachusetts, Connecticut,
Rhode-Island, Newhampshire & Vermont
Almanack . . . for . . . 1789 [by Samuel
Stearns, 1747-1819].
Worcester, Thomas. [48] pp.
(For compiler see Stearns to Thomas,

Mar. 3, 1788, in Thomas mss., A.A.S.)
AAS copy.   21115

Thomas's Massachusetts, Connecticut,
Rhode-Island, Newhampshire & Vermont
Almanack . . . for . . . 1790 [by Ezra
Gleason, 1748-1808?].
Worcester, Thomas. [48] pp.
AAS copy.   21857

Thomas's Massachusetts, Connecticut,
Rhode-Island, Newhampshire & Vermont
Almanack . . . for . . . 1791 [by Ezra
Gleason, 1748-1808?].
Worcester, Thomas. [48] pp.
AAS copy.   22537

Thomas's Massachusetts, Connecticut,
Rhode-Island, Newhampshire & Vermont
Almanack . . . for . . . 1792 [by Ezra
Gleason, 1748-1808?].
Worcester, Thomas. [48] pp.
AAS copy.   23414

Second Edition. Thomas's Massachusetts,
Connecticut, Rhodeisland, Newhampshire
& Vermont Almanack . . . for . . . 1792
[by Ezra Gleason, 1748-1808?]
Worcester, Thomas. [48] pp.
AAS copy.   23415

Thomas's Massachusetts, Connecticut,
Rhode-Island, Newhampshire & Vermont
Almanack . . . for . . . 1793 [by Ezra
Gleason, 1748-1808?].
Worcester, Thomas & Worcester. [48] pp.
AAS copy.   24358

Thomas's Massachusetts, Connecticut,
Rhode-island, Newhampshire & Vermont
Almanack . . . for . . . 1794 [by Ezra
Gleason, 1748-1808?].
Worcester, Thomas, etc. [48] pp.
AAS copy.   25547

Second Edition. Thomas's Massachusetts,
Connecticut, Rhodeisland, Newhampshire
& Vermont Almanack . . . for . . . 1794
[by Ezra Gleason, 1748-1808?].
Worcester, Thomas, etc. [44] pp.
NYPL copy.   25548

Thomas's Massachusetts, Connecticut,
Rhode-Island, Newhampshire & Vermont
Almanack . . . for . . . 1795 [by Ezra
Gleason, 1748-1808?].
Worcester, Thomas. Price 40s per Gross.
[48] pp.
AAS copy.   27052

Second Edition. Thomas's Massachusetts,
Connecticut, Rhodeisland, Newhampshire
& Vermont Almanack . . . for . . . 1795
[by Ezra Gleason, 1748-1808?].
Worcester, Thomas. [48] pp.
AAS copy.   27053

Thomas's Massachusetts, Connecticut,
Rhodeisland Newhampshire & Vermont
Almanack . . . for . . . 1796.
Worcester, Thomas. [48] pp.
AAS copy.   29624

Thomas's Massachusetts, Connecticut,
Rhode-Island, Newhampshire & Vermont
Almanack . . . for . . . 1797.
Worcester, Thomas. [48] pp.
AAS copy.   31291

Thomas's Massachusetts, Connecticut,
Rhode-island, Newhampshire & Vermont
Almanack . . . for . . . 1798.
Worcester, Mass., Thomas, etc. [48] pp.
AAS copy.   32919

Second Edition. Isaiah Thomas's
Massachusetts, Connecticut,
Rhode-island, Newhampshire & Vermont
Almanack . . . for . . . 1798.
Worcester, Mass., Thomas, etc. [48] pp.
AAS copy.   32920

Isaiah Thomas's Massachusetts,
Connecticut, Rhode-island.
Newhampshire & Vermont Almanack . . .
for . . . 1799.
Worcester, Thomas, for I. Thomas, Jr.,
etc. [48] pp.
AAS copy.   34652

Thomas's New-England Almanack . . . for
. . . 1775 [by Ezra Gleason, 1748-1808?].

Boston, Thomas. [24] pp.
AAS copy.   13299

Thomas's New-England Almanack . . . for
. . . 1775. . . . Second Edition [by Ezra
Gleason, 1748-1808?].
Boston, Thomas. [24] pp.
AAS copy.   13300

[Thome, Anastasia.
Ein Lob-Lied.
Ephrata, 1768.]
(Title from Seidensticker.)   11087

Thompson, Abraham.
Poems on the Most Solemn Subjects.
[New Haven, 1790.] 24 pp.
("This day is Published. . . . Printed for
the author; and sold by him at his home in
Broadway, New Haven," Conn. Journal,
Feb. 10, 1790.)
NYHS copy.   22928

Thompson, Andrew, b. 1771.
Andrew Thompson born February 2,
1770. . . . Andrew Thompson jun. born
July 23, 1794. . . . Providence March 20,
1796.
[Providence, 1796.] Broadside.
BrU copy.   47936

Thompson, Isaac.
Hinckley's Infallible Remedy for
Haemorrhoids.
[New London, 1790]. Broadside.
NYHS copy.   45797

[Thompson, Isaac], of Newcastle.
Happiness, a Characteristic Poem.
Philadelphia, 1774.]
("Just Published and to be Sold by
William Woodhouse," Dunlap's Pa. Packet,
Apr. 4, 1774.)   13652

[Thompson, John]
The Birth, Life and Character of Judas
Iscariot.
Amherst, N. H., Preston, 1797. 23 pp.
AAS copy.   32325

[Thompson, John]
The Birth, Life and Character of Judas
Iscariot.
Windsor, Vt., Spooner, [1796]. 19 pp.
VtHS (Rugg) copy.   30647

Thompson, John.
The Lost and Undone Son of Perdition.
Boston, [Z. Fowle], 1763. 20, [2] pp.
JCB copy.   41415

Thompson, John.
The Lost and Undone Son of Perdition.
Boston, 1765. 28 pp.
BPL copy.   10183

Thompson, John.
The Lost and Undone Son of Perdition.
Hartford, [1767?]. 15 pp.
CHS copy.   41769

Thompson, John.
The Lost and Undone Son of Perdition.
New London, Green, [1767?]. 23, [1] pp.
AAS copy.   41770

Thompson, John.
The Lost and Undone Son.
New London, 1767. 20 pp.
LOC copy.   10784

Thompson, John.
The Lost and Undone Son of Perdition.
Providence, [1769]. 20 pp.
(The unique copy is in poor condition.)
RIHS copy.   11493

Thompson, John.
The Lost and Undone Son.
Newport, 1770. 20 pp.
AAS copy.   11877

Thompson, John.
The Lost and Undone Son of Perdition.
Boston, Boyles, 1771. 15 pp.
AAS copy.   42286

Thompson, John.
The Lost and Undone Son of Perdition.
Norwich, [Ct.], Green & Spooner,
[1778?] 19 pp.
AAS copy.   43557

Thompson, John.
The Lost and Undone Son.
Danbury, Ely, [1790?] 16 pp.
CHS copy.   22929

Thompson, John.
The Lost and Undone Son.
n.p., 1794. 13 pp.
(Best copy available.)
NYPL copy.   47231

[Thompson, John.
The Lost and Undone Son of Perdition.
Amherst, N. H., Preston, 1797. 23 pp.]
(Ghost of 32325, q. v.)   32924

Thompson, John.
The Lost and Undone Son of Perdition.
[Leominster, Mass.], Whitcomb, [1800].
12 pp.
AAS copy.   49152

Thompson, Otis, 1776-1859.
A Funeral Oration . . . on . . . Eliab
Kingman.
Providence, Carter & Wilkinson, 1797. 14
pp.
AAS copy.   32925

Thompson, Otis, 1776-1859.
An Oration, Urging the Necessity of
Religion.
Providence, R. I., Carter & Wilkinson, 1798.
8 pp.
AAS copy.   34658

Thompson, Otis, 1776-1859.
A Poem, Delivered in the Chapel of
Rhode-Island College.
[Providence], Wheeler, [1798]. 8 pp.
AAS copy.   34659

Thompson, Otis, 1776-1859.
A Sermon, Preached on . . . January 26th,
1800.
Providence, [R. I.], Wheeler, 1800. 16 pp.
AAS copy.   38633

Thompson, Thomas W., 1766-1821.
An Oration, Pronounced the 4th Day of
July
Concord, N.H., Hough, 1799. 16 pp.
AAS copy.   36416

Thompson, William, of Baltimore.
The Baltimore Town and Fell's Point
Directory.
Baltimore, Pechin, [1796]. 99, [1] pp.
AAS copy.   31297

Thompson, William, of Boston.
To the Respectable Citizens of Boston.
William Thompson. . . . March 6, 1790.
[Boston, 1790.] Broadside.
AAS copy.   46003

[Thompson, William, of Nottingham.
The Child's Guide to the English Tongue.
Boston, 1716. 94 pp.
(From Prince catalogue.)   1858

Thompson & Small, firm, Philadelphia.
Superb Hot-Pressed Family Bible. . . .
January, 1798.
[Philadelphia, 1798.] Broadside.
HC copy.   48627

Thomson, Adam, -1767.
(H. A. Kelly, Dict. Am. Med. Biog.)
A Discourse on the Preparation of the
Body for the Small-Pox.
Philadelphia, Franklin & Hall, 1750. 24
pp.
AAS copy.   6617

[Thomson, Adam, -1767.
(H. A. Kelly, Dict. Am. Med. Biog.)
A Discourse on the Preparation of the
Body for the Small-Pox.
New York, Gaine, 1756.]
("Just published," N. Y. Mercury, No.
228.)   7801

Thomson, J.
Modern Practice of Farriery.
New York, Berry, Rogers & Berry,
[1793].
(No copy located.)   46888

Thomson, James, 1700-1748.
The Seasons.
n.p., 1764. xxviii, 206+ pp.

(The only known copy is defective.)
AAS copy.   41492

Thomson, James, 1700-1748.
The Seasons.
Philadelphia, Bell, 1777. Front., [8], 251
(253), [3] pp.
AAS copy.   15613

Thomson, James, 1700-1748.
The Seasons.
Philadelphia, Prichard & Hall, 1788. 196
pp.
AAS copy.   45375

Thomson, James, 1700-1748.
The Seasons.
Philadelphia, Rice, 1788. [4], vii, [1], 216
pp., 4 plates.
AAS copy.   21495

Thomson, James, 1700-1748.
The Seasons. . . . First American Edition.
Newburyport, Mycall, [1790]. 238 pp.
AAS copy.   22930

Thomson, James, 1700-1748.
The Seasons.
Philadelphia, Taylor for Campbell, 1790.
190 pp.
AAS copy.   22931

[Thomson, James, 1700-1748.
The Seasons.
Philadelphia, Woodhouse, 1791.]
(Entry based on an adv. for "American
editions" in 23178.)   23827

[Thomson, James, 1700-1748.
The Seasons.
Hartford, Babcock, 1792?]
(Entry from adv. "Just published, and to
be sold at this office," in Am. Mercury,
July 16, 1792.)   24849

[Thomson, James, 1700-1748.
The Seasons.
Newburyport, 1793.]
(Imprint assumed by Evans from adv.
"For Sale," in Essex Journal, June 5,
1793.)   26255

Thomson, James, 1700-1748.
The Seasons.
Philadelphia, Johnson, 1795. 194, [4] pp.
AAS copy.   29628

Thomson, James, 1700-1748.
The Seasons.
Philadelphia, Woodward, 1797. [4], xxiv,
200 pp., 4 plates.
AAS copy.   32927

Thomson, James, 1700-1748.
The Seasons.
Wrentham, Mass., Heaton, 1800. 168 pp.
AAS copy.   38634

[Thomson, James, 1700-1748.
Trancred and Sigismunda.
Boston, Spotswood, 1794.]
(Imprint assumed by Evans from adv.
"May be had" in Columbian Centinel,
Aug. 27, 1794.)   27794

Thomson, John, -1753.
(Sprague, III, 22.)
Doctrine of Convictions.
Philadelphia, Bradford, 1741. vii, 80 pp.
HSP copy.   4827

[Thomson, John], - 1753.
An Essay upon the Faith of Assurance.
Philadelphia, Franklin, 1740. 64 pp.
(No perfect copy located.)
YC copy.   40214

Thomson, John, - 1753.
(Sprague, III, 22.)
An Explication of the Shorter Catechism.
Williamsburg, 1749. xiv, 190, vi, 14 pp.
AAS copy.   6429

Thomson, John, - 1753.
The Government of the Church.
Philadelphia, Bradford, 1741. xiv, 130 pp.
HSP copy.   4828

[Thomson, John], - 1753.
(Sprague, III, 22.)
An Overture Presented to the Reverend
Synod.

[Philadelphia], 1729. 32 pp.
BPL copy.   3223

[Thomson, John], 1776-1799.
The Letters of Curtius.
Richmond, Va., Pleasants, 1798. 40 pp.
AAS copy.   34657

[Thomson, R., pseud?
A Tribute to the Swinish Multitude.
New York, Loudon, 1794.]
(Entry from the copyright notice of 29629,
q. v.)   27795

Thomson, R., pseud.?
A Tribute to the Swinish Multitude.
New York, Loudon, 1795. 96 pp.
AAS copy.   29629

Thorn, Stephen.
Haswell's Vermont Almanac, for . . . 1792.
Bennington, Haswell. [24] pp.
AAS copy.   23828

Thorn, Stephen.
Lyon's Vermont Calendar . . . for . . .
1794.
Rutland, Lyon. [16] pp.
LOC copy.   26256

[Thorn, Stephen.]
Lyon's Vermont Calendar . . . for . . .
1795. Calculated . . . by Samuel Mott.
Rutland, Lyon. 62 pp.
JCB copy.   27796

Thorn, Stephen.
Webster's Calendar; or, the Albany
Almanack, for . . . 1792.
Albany, Websters. [36] pp.
AAS copy.   23829

[Thorne, William, fl. 1763.
A New Set of Copies.
Philadelphia, Franklin & Hall, 1763.]
(Adv. Pa. Gazette, Nov. 3, 1763.)   9522

Thornton, Elisha.
An Almanack, for . . . 1788.
Newport, Edes. [24] pp.
AAS copy.   20747

Thornton, Elisha.
An Almanack, for . . . 1789.
Newport, Edes. [24] pp.
AAS copy.   21496

Thornton, Elisha.
An Almanack, for . . . 1790.
Newport, Edes. [24] pp.
AAS copy.   22180

Thornton, Elisha.
The New England Almanack . . . for . . .
1795.
Providence, Carter & Wilkinson. [24], 12
pp.
AAS copy.   27797

Thornton, Elisha.
The New-England Almanack . . . for . . .
1796.
Providence, Carter & Wilkinson. [24] pp.
AAS copy.   29630

Thornton, Elisha.
The New-England Almanack . . . for . . .
1797.
Providence, Carter & Wilkinson. [24] pp.
AAS copy.   31298

Thornton, Elisha.
The Rhode-Island Almanack, for . . .
1791.
Newport, Edes. [24] pp.
AAS copy.   22932

Thornton, Elisha.
The Rhode-Island Almanack, for . . .
1792.
Newport, Edes. [24] pp.
AAS copy.   23830

Thornton, Elisha.
The Rhode-Island Almanack, for . . .
1793.
Warren, Phillips. [24] pp.
AAS copy.   24850

Thornton, Elisha.
The Rhode-Island Almanack, for . . .
1793.

Warren, R.I., Phillips for Richardson.
[24] pp.
AAS copy.   46582

Thornton, Elisha.
The Rhode-Island Almanack . . . for . . .
1794.
Warren, R.I., Phillips for Richardson.
[24] pp.
AAS copy.   26257

[Thornton's sheet almanack for 1794.
Providence? 1794.] Broadside.
(Alden 1351; no copy known.)   47232

[Thornton, Elisha.
Thornton's Sheet Almanack for 1795.
Providence, Carter & Wilkinson, 1794.
Broadside.]
(Title and imprint assumed by Evans from
advs. for sheet almanacs.)   27798

[Thornton, Elisha.
Thornton's Sheet Almanack for 1796.
Providence, Carter & Wilkinson, 1795.
Broadside.]
("This day is published," Providence
Gazette, Jan. 10, 1795.)   29631

[Thornton, William], fl. 1753.
The Counterpoise: Being Thoughts on a
Militia.
New York, 1753.]
(Entry from Sabin, perhaps from an adv.
for copies of the London ed.)   7127

Thornton, William, 1759-1828.
(D.A.B.)
Prize Dissertation.
Philadelphia, Aitken, 1793. 110 pp., folded
table, errata.
LCP copy.   26258

Thoughts Concerning the Bank of North
America [by Tench Coxe, 1755-1824].
Philadelphia, 1787. 14 pp.
LOC copy.   20307

[Thoughts Concerning the Bank, with
some Facts Relating to such
Establishments [by Tench Coxe,
1755-1824].
Philadelphia, Humphreys, 1786.]
(Evans' assumed the imprint from advs.
The recorded copies are other eds.) 19591

[Thoughts Concerning the Nature of God.
Norwich, Conn., Trumbull, 1794.]
(Imprint assumed by Evans from adv.
"Just Published, and for sale at this
office," in Norwich Packet, July 31, 1794.)
                                             27799

The Thoughts of a Dying Man [by Cotton
Mather, 1663-1728].
Boston, 1697. 47, [1] pp.
AAS copy.   796

Thoughts on Agency [by John Perkins,
1698-1781].
New Haven, 1765. pp. [2], 5-27.
AAS copy.   10130

Thoughts on Christian Baptism, Deduced
from Scripture. By Observator.
New York, Durell, 1796. 27 pp.
AAS copy.   30923

[Thoughts on Conversation and Manners.
Augusta, Ga., Smith, 1797.]
(Imprint assumed by Evans from Smith's
adv.)   32928

Thoughts on Education [by James Burgh,
1714-1775].
Boston, Rogers & Fowle, 1749. 61, [2] pp.
AAS copy.   6294

Thoughts on General Safety. Addressed to
the Youth and Others. . . . By a Lover of
his Country.
Baltimore, Goddard, [1786]. Broadside.
EPFL copy.   44976

Thoughts on General Safety; Addressed to
the Youth and Others . . . Especially the
Inhabitants of Maryland.
[Baltimore, 1786.] 4 pp.
JCB copy.   44977

Thoughts on Government: Applicable to
the Present State [by John Adams, pres.
U.S., 1735-1826].

Boston, Gill, 1776. 16 pp.
AAS copy.   14640

Thoughts on Government: Applicable to
the Present State [by John Adams, pres.
U.S., 1735-1826].
Philadelphia, Dunlap, 1776. 28 pp.
AAS copy.   14639

Thoughts on Repentance [by William Duke,
1757-1840].
Baltimore, Goddard, 1789. 28 pp.
MdHS copy.   21803

Thoughts on the Christian Religion.
Boston, Hall, 1797. 14 pp.
AAS copy.   32929

Thoughts on the Doctrine of Universal
Salvation.
Philadelphia, Prichard & Hall, 1790. 24
pp.
JCB copy.   22934

Thoughts on the Entertainments of the
Stage.
Charleston, 1793. 20 pp.
LOC copy.   26259

[Thoughts on the Erection of the Theatre
in 1793.
Philadelphia, 1793.]
(The origin of this entry is unknown.)
                                             26260

Thoughts on the Examination and Trials
of Candidates [by Patrick Allison,
1740-1802]. (Sprague, III, 257-262.)
Parthenopoli (Philadelphia), 1766. 24 pp.
Presb. Hist. Soc. copy.   10223

Thoughts on the Five Per Cent.
Providence, Carter, 1782. 12 pp.
JCB copy.   17742

Thoughts on the Importance of the
Manners of the Great. . . . Fourth Edition
[by Hannah More, 1745-1833].
Philadelphia, Dobson, 1788. 81, [1] pp.
AAS copy.   21271

Thoughts on the Importance of the
Manners of the Great. . . . Eighth Edition
[by Hannah More, 1745-1833].
Philadelphia, Johnson, [1795]. 88 pp.
AAS copy.   29106

Thoughts on the Importance of the
Manners of the Great. . . . Fifth Edition
[by Hannah More, 1745-1833].
Worcester, Thomas, 1797. 84 pp.
AAS copy.   32503

Thoughts on the late Transactions
Respecting Falkland's Islands [by Samuel
Johnson, 1709-1784].
New York, Gaine, 1771. 48 pp.
AAS copy.   12088

Thoughts on the Lawfulness of War.
Philadelphia, Humphreys, 1796. 20 pp.
AAS copy.   31299

Thoughts on the Nature of War [by
Anthony Benezet, 1713-1784].
Philadelphia, Miller, 1766. 30 pp.
AAS copy.   10505

Thoughts on the Nature of War, &c. [by
Anthony Benezet, 1713-1784].
[Philadelphia, 1776?] 24 pp.
AAS copy.   14662

Thoughts on the State of the American
Indians [by Silas Wood, 1769-1847].
New York, Swords, 1794. 36 pp.
AAS copy.   28126

Thoughts, on the Subject of the Ensuing
Election. . . . April 1, 1800.
[Albany, N. Y.], Barber & Southwick,
[1800]. Broadside.
LOC ph. copy.   38635

Thoughts upon Several Passages of
Scripture [by Samuel Dexter, 1761-1816].
Worcester, Thomas, 1791. 60 pp.
AAS copy.   23324

Thoughts upon the Political Situation [by
Jonathan Jackson, 1743-1810].
Worcester, Thomas, 1788. 209 pp.
AAS copy.   21173

[Thoughts upon] the State of the Paper
Currency in New England.
Boston, 1743. 52 pp.
(The unique copy being imperfect, the
wording of the title is conjectural.)
MHS copy.   5302

[The Three Brothers, a Moral Tale.
Boston, Spotswood, 1795.]
(Imprint assumed by Evans from
Spotswood's adv. in 33153.)   32940

Three Curious Pieces. . . . By P. A. in
Boston.
Boston, Russell, 1782. 23, [1] pp.
AAS copy.   17447

Three Letters Addressed to the Public.
Philadelphia, Bradford, 1783. 28 pp.
AAS copy.   18219

Three Letters to Abraham Bishop [by
David Daggett, 1764-1851].
Bennington, Collier & Stockwell, [1800].
36 pp.
VtHS copy.   37282

Three Letters to Abraham Bishop [by
David Daggett, 1764-1851].
Hartford, Ct., Hudson & Goodwin, 1800.
36 pp.
AAS copy.   37281

Three Letters to Abraham Bishop [by
David Daggett, 1764-1851].
[New Haven, Greens, 1800.]
(Sabin 105939; no copy located.)   37283

Three Letters to the Reverend Mr. George
Whitefield.
Philadelphia, Bradford, [1739]. [2], 13
pp.
APS copy.   4354

Three New Marches.
Philadelphia, Willig, [1798?]. [2] pp.
(No copy located.)   34660

Three Practical Discourses.
Boston, Fleet & Crump for Henchman,
1715. 96 pp.
(The AAS has two variant imprints.)
BPL copy.   1746

Three Practical Discourses [by James
Janeway, 1636-1674].
Boston, Kneeland for Phillips, 1719. [2],
78 pp.
AAS copy.   39704

Three Practical Discourses.
Boston, Fleet for Buttolph, 1727. [2], 78
pp.
AAS copy.   2887

Three Sweet Hearts I Boast.
New York, Gilfert, [1797]. [2] pp.
AAS copy.   48268

Three Treatises, in which the
Fundamental Principle . . . of the . . .
Quakers . . . are . . . Declared.
Philadelphia, 1770. [8], 88, vii, [1], 111,
[1], 24, [4] pp.
(The AAS has another copy in
contemporary binding without the last 4
pp.)
AAS copy.   11661

Three Treatises, in which the
Fundamental Principle. . . .
Wilmington, 1783. [8], 88, vii, [1], 111, [1],
24 pp.
AAS copy.   18083

Throop, Benjamin, 1712-1785.
(Weis, Colonial Clergy N. E.)
Religion and Loyalty.
New London, 1758. 37 pp.
AAS copy.   8267

Throop, Benjamin, 1712-1785.
The Rest in Reserve for the Righteous.
New London, [Ct.], Green, 1759. 25 pp.
AAS copy.   41084

Throop, Benjamin, 1712-1785.
(Weis, Colonial Clergy N. E.)
A Thanksgiving Sermon.
New London, 1766. 16 pp.
LOC copy.   10506

Throop, William, 1720-1756.

(Dexter, 1, 749.)
A Sermon Occasion'd by . . . the Funeral
of Brinley Sylvester.
Boston, 1753. [4], 11 pp.
AAS copy.   7129

Thrum, Tam, pseud.
Look before Ye Loup.
Philadelphia, Dobson, 1798. [2], 40 pp.
LCP copy.   34661

Thumb, Tom, pseud.
The Famous Tommy Thumb's Little
Story-Book.
Boston, M'Alpine, 1768. 31 pp.
(The only known copy is imperfect.)
PrU copy.   41890

Thumb, Tom, pseud.
Tom Thumb's Folio. . . . Second
Worcester Edition.
Worcester, Thomas, 1794. 31 pp.
AAS copy.   27800

[Thumb, Tom, pseud.
Tom Thumb's Folio.
New York, 1796.]
(Imprint assumed by Evans from advs.)
                                             31300

Thumb, Tom, pseud.
Tom Thumb's Little Book.
Boston, Coverly, 1794. 16 pp.
AAS copy.   27801

Thumb, Tom, pseud.
Tom Thumb's Play-Book.
Providence, Waterman, 1768. 30, [2] pp.
AAS copy.   41891

Thurber, Benjamin.
Benjamin Thurber, at his Store. . . .
Providence, [1800?]. Broadside.
NYPL copy.   49153

[Thurber, Laban.
A Composition upon Several Divine
Subjects.
Norwich, Bushnell, 1792?]
("Is now in press," Norwich Weekly
Register, Dec. 20, 1791; "Is now ready,"
ibid., Jan. 10, 1792.)   24852

Thurber, Laban.
The Young Ladies' & Gentlemen's
Preceptor.
Warren, R. I., Phillips, 1797. 58 pp.
AAS copy.   32932

Thurber & Cahoon, Providence, R. I.
Just Imported from London, and Bristol.
[Providence, c. 1790.] Broadside.
(The only known copy is imperfect.)
YC copy.   46004

Thurber & Chandler, Providence.
Thurber & Chandler have for Sale. . . .
Providence, Wheeler, [c. 1790].
Broadside.
RIHS ph. copy.   46005

Thurford, Hugh, d. 1713.
The Grounds of a Holy Life. . . . Eleventh
Edition.
Philadelphia, Crukshank, 1788. viii, 123
pp.
AAS copy.   21509

Thurman, Ralph.
To the Inhabitants of the City and County
of New-York. . . . April 15, 1775.
[New York], Rivington, [1775].
Broadside.
LOC copy.   14484

Thursday last (25th May) Capt. Clark
Arrived here from England. . . .
[Boston], Mills & Hicks, [1775].
Broadside.
MHS copy.   42950

Thursday, September 20, 1770. At this
Juncture. . . .
[Philadelphia, 1770]. Broadside.
LOC copy.   11878

Thursday, Sept. 27, 1770. Many
Respectable Freeholders. . . .
[Philadelphia, 1770.] Broadside.
LOC copy.   11879

[Thurston, Benjamin], 1755-1804.
(Attribution by Sabin, based on date line.)

Address to the Public, Containing some
Remarks on the Present Political State.
Exeter, [1786]. 36 pp.
NYPL copy.   19470

[Thurston, Benjamin], 1755-1804.
An Address to the Public, Containing
some Remarks on the Present Political
State.
Exeter, [1787]. 36 pp.]
(A duplicate of 19470, q. v.)   20179

Thurston, Benjamin, 1755-1804.
A Discourse Delivered by Benjamin
Thurston.
Portsmouth, Melcher, 1789. 24 pp.
AAS copy.   22181

Thurston, Benjamin, 1755-1804.
Four Sermons.
Portsmouth, Osborne, 1791. 71 pp.
AAS copy.   23831

Thurston, Benjamin, 1755-1804.
A Sermon Delivered at Kittery.
Dover, N. H., Ladd, 1795. 22 pp.
AAS copy.   29637

Thurston, Benjamin, 1755-1804.
Two Sermons, Delivered by. . . .
Newburyport, Osborne, 1793. 19 pp.
AAS copy.   26261

Thurston, Benjamin, 1755-1804.
Two Sermons on the Divine Right of
Infant Baptism.
Exeter, Ranlet, 1792. 89 pp.
AAS copy.   24853

[The Tickler: Being a Series of Periodical
Papers.
New York, Hopkins, 1797.]
(Entry from the copyright record.)   32933

Tickletoby, Timothy, pseud.
The Impostor Detected [by Samuel Fisher
Bradford, 1776-1837].
Philadelphia, Bradford, 1796. 51, [1], 23
pp.
AAS copy.   30119

Tickletoby, Timothy, pseud.
The Impostor Detected. . . . Second
Edition [by Samuel Fisher Bradford,
1776-1837].
Philadelphia, Bradford, 1796. 51, [1],
23 pp.
LCP copy.   30120

[Ticknell, Richard, 1751-1793.
Anticipation. Containing the
Substance. . . .
New York, Rivington, 1779.]
("This Day will be Published." Royal
Gazette, Mar. 17, 1779.)   16544

[Ticknell, Richard, 1751-1793.
Anticipation. Containing the
Substance. . . . Sixth Edition.
Philadelphia, Bradford, 1779. [6], 33 pp.
LCP copy.   16543

Ticknor, Elisha, 1757-1821.
English Exercises.
Boston, Hall, [1792]. 60 pp.
AAS copy.   24854

Ticknor, Elisha, 1757-1821.
English Exercises. . . . Second Edition.
Boston, Belknap & Hall, 1793. 69 pp.
AAS copy.   26262

Ticknor, Elisha, 1757-1821.
English Exercises. . . . Third Edition.
Boston, Belknap, 1794. 72 pp.
AAS copy.   27802

Tiebout, John, 1772?-1826.
Proposals, for Publishing by Subscription.
A Narrative of the . . . Adventures of
Donald Campbell.
New York, Tiebout, 1799. 12 pp.
(No copy located.)   33488

[Tielke, Johann Gottlieb, 1731-1787.
Instructions for Officers who Wish to
Become Field Engineers.
New York, Smith, 1798.]
(Proposed but apparently not printed.)
                                              34663

Tiffany, Consider, 1733-1796.

Relation of the Melancholy Death of Six
Young Persons . . . June, 1767.
n.p., [1767]. Broadside.
CHS copy.   41771

Tilden, Stephen, 1690-1766.
Tilden's Miscellaneous Poems.
[New London ?], 1756. 30 pp.
MHS copy.   7802

[Tilden, Stephen, 1690-1766.
Tilden's Miscellaneous Poems. . . . Second
Edition.
New London, 1757.]
(Assumed by Evans from sequence of
editions.)   8045

Tilden, Stephen, 1690-1766.
Tilden's Miscellaneous Poems. . . . Third
Edition.
New London, [1758]. 58, [1] pp.
WL copy.   8268

[Tileston, Thomas.
Verses Dedicated to . . . John Foster.
Cambridge, 1681. Broadside.]
(Not found. See adv. in Evans 314 and text
in T. C. Simonds, Hist. So. Boston, pp.
34-39.)   308

Tillary, James, 1751-1818.
An Address, Delivered . . . on the Festival
of St. John the Baptist, June 24, 1788.
New York, Childs, 1788. 20 pp.
NYHS copy.   21497

Tillary, James, 1751-1818.
An Oration Delivered before the Society
of Black Friars.
New York, Childs & Swaine, 1789. 29 pp.
NYPL copy.   22182

Tillier, Rodolphe.
Memoire pour Rodolphe Tillier.
[New York], Parisot, [1800]. 18 pp.
JCB copy.   38637

Tillier, Rodolphe.
Translation of . . . Tillier's Justification.
Rome, [N. Y.], Waker, 1800. 16 pp.
LOC copy.   38638

Tillinghast, George, 1764-1829.
An Oration. . . . the Fourth Day of July,
A.D. 1794.
Providence, Carter & Wilkinson, [1794].
16 pp.
AAS copy.   27804

Tillinghast, John.
Thirty Dollars Reward. . . . Aug. 12, 1783.
Providence, Carter, [1783]. Broadside.
RIHS copy.   44463

Tillinghast, Pardon, 1622-1718.
(F. L. Weis, Colonial Clergy N. E.)
Water-Baptism Plainly Proved.
[Boston], 1689. [2], 17 pp.
AAS copy.   498

[Tillotson, Daniel.
Song on Vacation. . . . Yale College.
January 1, 1796.
[New Haven, 1796.] Broadside.]
(The origin of this entry is unknown.)
                                               31301

Tillotson, John, 1630-1694.
(D. A. B.)
The Usefulness of Consideration.
Philadelphia, W. Bradford, 1745. 20 pp.
LCP copy.   5702

Tilly, William.
Advertisement. Ran away . . . a Carolina
Indian Manservant. . . . June 14th 1697.
[Boston, 1697.] Broadside.
BPL copy.   39326

[Tilton, James], 1745-1822.
The Biographical History of Dionysius.
Philadelphia, 1788. 100 pp.
NYPL copy.   21498

Tilton, James, 1745-1822.
(D. A. B.)
Dissertatio Medica.
Philadelphia, Bradfords, 1771. [4], 23 pp.
NYPL copy.   12242

Time, Mark, pseud.
The New-York Almanack, for . . . 1774.

New York, Holt. 48 pp.
AAS copy.   42519

Time, Mark, pseud.
The Pennsylvania Almanack for 1789.
Philadelphia, Simons. [34] pp.
Bucks Co. Hist. Soc. copy.   21499

The Times A Poem [by Benjamin Church,
1734-1776].
[Boston, 1765.] 16 pp.
(Adv. by Fleet, Boston News-Letter, Oct.
31, 1765.)
AAS copy.   9930

The Times, Mankind. . . .
[New York, 1770.] 4 pp.
LCP copy.   11881

Timothy, Lewis, D. 1738.
[The Proposals, together with a Specimen
of the Laws of the Province.
Charleston, Timothy, 1734.]
(See McMurtrie, S.C. Imprints, 1731-40,
No. 12.)   40064

Tindal, Matthew, 1653?-1733.
Christianity as Old as the Creation.
Newburgh, N. Y., Denniston, 1798. 372
pp.
AAS copy.   34666

Tisdale, Joseph, 1736-1768.
The Speech of Joseph T - sd - e.
[Boston, 1767.] Broadside.
(No copy of the ed. described by Evans
could be located.)
AAS ph. copy.   10780

Tisdall, John.
Laws and Usages Respecting Bills of
Exchange.
Philadelphia, Bailey for Stephens, 1795.
iv, 55 pp.
AAS copy.   29640

Tissot, Samuel Auguste André David,
1728-1797.
Advice to the People . . . in Regard to
their Health.
London, (i.e. Boston, Mein & Fleeming),
1767. pp. [i]-xii, [6], [xiii]-xxiv, [1]-265;
[6], [1]-254.
Amherst College copy.   41772

Tissot, Samuel Auguste André David,
1728-1797.
Advice to the People. . . . Fourth Edition.
Philadelphia, Sparhawk, 1771. xviii, [4],
307 pp.
AAS copy.   12243

Tissot, Samuel Auguste André David,
1729-1797.
Advice to the People in General with
Regard to their Health.
Philadelphia, Sparhawk, 1771. xviii, [4],
307 pp.
HSP copy.   42287

[A Tit-bit for the Public; or, Memoirs of
an Antiquated Shaver.
Baltimore, Clayland & Dobbin, 1798.]
("On the all-glorious 4th of July, will be
published," Telegraphe, July 3, 1798.)
                                                34667

Tit for Tat; or, A Purge for a Pill. . . . By
Dick Retort [by William Cobbett,
1763-1835].
Philadelphia, [1796]. 34, 25 pp.
LOC copy.   30314

Tit for Tat; T'Other Side; or,
Bounce-About.
[Boston], Edes, [1782]. Broadside.
AAS copy.   44271

Titford, Isaac.
Wholesale Silk Ware-House.
[New York], M'Lean & Lang, [1798].
Broadside.
MHS copy.   48628

Tiverton, R.I. First Congregational
Church.
Scheme of a Lottery . . . May 20, 1785.
Providence, Wheeler, [1785]. Broadside.
JCB copy.   44797

To all Adherents to the British
Government. . . . August 15, 1783.

[New York], Morton and Horner, [1783].
Broadside.
NYHS copy.   44464

To all Christian People; more Especially
those who take the Connecticut Courant.
. . . January 1, 1794.
[Hartford, Hudson & Goodwin, 1794.]
Broadside.
CHS copy.   47233

To all Christian People; more especially
those who Take the Connecticut Courant.
. . . January 1, 1795.
[Hartford, 1795.] Broadside.
CHS copy.   47623

To all Farmers and Tradesmen, who want
good Settlements.
Philadelphia, Dunlap, 1772. Broadside.
LCP copy.   12574

To all his Kind Customers, the Boy who
Carries the Evening Post Wishes a Happy
New Year, 1769.
[Boston, 1769.] Broadside.
HSP copy.   42010

To all True Patriots and Real Lovers of
Liberty.
[Philadelphia, 1727.] 3 pp.
(The unique copy is mislaid.)   2968

To all true Whigs, and Particularly to such
as are Independent. . . . Sept. 28, 1775.
[New York, 1775.] Broadside.
LOC copy.   14485

To all whom these Presents may Concern.
Had I. . . .
New York, Bradford, 1713. 8 pp.
NYPL copy.   1641

To be Performed at the Brattle-Street
Church.
[Boston], Rhoades, [1800]. Broadside.
(Also entered as 37002, q. v.)   38641

To be Performed at the Old-South.
[Boston], Young & Minns, [1800].
Broadside.
(Also entered as 37011, q. v.)   38642

To be Sold by Public Auction On Tuesday
the Eighth of September [the Furniture of
Samuel Shoemaker].
Philadelphia, Dunlap, [1778]. Broadside.
LCP copy.   16092

To be Sold, on the 30th inst. if fair. . . .
Dumfries, March 1, 1791.
Alexandria, Hanson & Bond, [1791].
Broadside.
LOC copy.   46299

To be Sold, or Rented, Marlbro' Iron
Works.
[Winchester, Va.? 1791.] Broadside.
AAS copy.   46366

To Coll. Benjamin Fletcher.
[New York, 1693.] [3] pp.
PRO copy.   679

To D[octo]r R[o]g[er]s. Reverend Sir.
. . .
[New York, 1772.] Broadside.
NYHS copy.   12575

To F. H. Esq. [by Alexander Campbell, fl.
1726-1732].
[New York, 1732.] 4 pp.
NYPL copy.   3512

To His Excellency George Clinton. . . .
September 1, 1783.
[Fishkill, 1783.] Broadside.
JCB copy.   18210

To His Excellency the Governor, and the
Honourable Council of the State of
Maryland. The Address of the
Subscribers. . . .
[Annapolis, 1784.] Broadside.
LOC copy.   18582

To His Excellency William Burnet. . . .
Memorial of Evan Drummond.
[New York, 1724.] 6 pp.
NJSL copy.   2564

To His Excellency William Tryon, Esq;
Sir, As you have. . . .

[New York, 1775.] Broadside.
LOC copy.   14486

To Jacob Gibson. I Cannot but Consider
your Silence. . . . Sept. 22, 1798.
n. p., [1798]. Broadside.
LOC copy.   48629

[To John Cruger, James Jauncey. . . .
[New York, 1771.] Broadside.]
(This entry is a duplicate of 13121, q.v.)
                                              11968

To John Cruger, James Jauncey. . . .
[New York, 1774.] Broadside.
NYPL copy.   13121

To John De Noyellis, Esquire. . . . March
5th, 1772.
[New York, 1772.] [2] pp.
NYHS copy.   12337

To John M. S[cott], Esq. . . . July 23, 1774.
[New York, 1774.] 2 pp.
NYHS copy.   13653

To Luther Martin, and Robert Lemmon
. . . December 27, 1779.
[Baltimore, 1779.] [2] pp.
HC copy.   16225

To Messieurs Edward Payne & Henderson
Inches.
[Boston, 1769?] 14 pp.
AAS copy.   10626

To Messrs. Voter, Gracchus, Scaevola,
Keiling. . . . April 30, 1798.
[Lexington, 1798.] Broadside.
LOC copy.   48630

To Morris Morris.
[Philadelphia, 1728.] 2 pp.
LCP copy.   3111

To Mr. A. C. [by Francis Harrison, fl.
1732].
New York, 1732. 3 pp.
NYPL copy.   3547

To Mr. Isaac Low Veritas Presents his
Compliments. . . . March 16th, 1775.
[New York, 1775.] Broadside.
AAS ph. copy.   42945

To my Respected Friend I. N.
[Philadelphia, 1727.] 4 pp.
Rosenbach Foundation copy.   2889

To Perpetuate the Memory of Peace.
[Philadelphia, 1785.] 8 pp.
NYPL ph. copy.   44798

To Prevent Mistakes, the Fare of my
Carriage is Established. . . . [Sept. 23,
1789.]
[New York, 1789?] Broadside.
JCB copy.   45606

To Robert Jordan, and Others [by James
Logan, 1674 - 1751].
[Philadelphia, 1741.] 4 pp.
LCP copy.   4740

To Robert Lemmon, and Luther
Martin. . . . Nov. 17, 1779.
[Baltimore, 1779.] Broadside.
MdHS copy.   43708

To Satisfy the Impatience of the Public
. . . the Printing has been Desired. . . .
New York, Rivington, [1777]. Broadside.
NYHS copy.   43378

To the Advocates for Ministerial
Oppression.
[Philadelphia, 1773.] Broadside.
LCP copy.   12727

To the Agents of their High Mightinesses
the Dutch East-India Company. . . . 28th
October, 1773.
[New York, 1773.] Broadside.
NYHS copy.   13037

To the Americans in General, but to the
Citizens of South-Carolina in Particular.
n.p., [1780?] 11 pp.
(No copy located.)   43898

To the Associators of the City of
Philadelphia. A Considerable
Number. . . .

[Philadelphia, 1775.] Broadside.
LCP copy.   14487

To the Author of a Letter to Dr. Mather
[by Samuel Mather, 1706-1785].
Boston, Edes, 1783. 6 pp.
AAS copy.   18034

To the Candid Gentlemen and Ladies of
the City of New-York. [Signed,] A
Frenchman.
[New York, 1773.] Broadside.
LOC copy.   13038

To the Candid Public [by Ezra Stiles,
1727-1795].
New London, Green, 1774. Broadside.
LOC copy.   42708

To the Children of Light in this
Generation. It being Recommended to
Friends. . . . [by William Penn, 1644-
1718].
[Philadelphia, 1776.] 4 pp.
NYPL copy.   14968

To the Citizens of America, and
Especially those of Philadelphia. . . .
August 18, 1797.
[Philadelphia, 1797.] Broadside.
LOC copy.   48269

To the Citizens of America, who are
Creditors of the United States. . . . August
26, 1782.
[Philadelphia, 1782.] Broadside.
LOC copy.   17743

[To the Citizens of Annapolis. Jan. 13,
1775.
[Annapolis, 1775.] 2 pp.]
(The unique copy could not be filmed.)
                                              14489

To the Citizens of Annapolis. January 11,
1775.
[Annapolis, 1775.] Broadside.
LOC copy.   14488

To the Citizens of Burlington County.
n. p., [1800]. 16 pp.
LOC copy.   38643

To the Citizens of New-York. A Person
who Addresses you. . . . April 30, 1788.
[New York, 1788.] Broadside.
AAS ph. copy.   45376

To the Citizens of New-York. December
30, 1775.
[New York, 1775.] Broadside.
LOC copy.   14490

To the Citizens of New-York, Keep a
good Look-Out. . . . 29th April, 1788.
[New York, 1788.] Broadside.
LOC.copy.   21500

To the Citizens of New-York, on the
Present Critical Situation. . . .
[New York, 1774.] 2 pp.
NYPL copy.   13118

To the Citizens of New-York. The
Inhabitants of this City. . . . July 18, 1795.
[New York, 1795.] Broadside.
LOC copy.   47625

To the Citizens of New York. Your
Attention and Curiosity. . . . April 30,
1799.
[New York, 1799.] Broadside.
NYPL copy.   48965

To the Citizens of Pennsylvania.
[Philadelphia, 1799.] 16 pp.
(The only recorded copy cannot be
reproduced.)   36421

To the Citizens of Philadelphia. A Piece
Having been Published. . . .
[Philadelphia, 1771.] Broadside.
LCP copy.   12244

To the Citizens of Philadelphia. Fellow
Citizens. It is at all Times. . . . October 11,
1796.
[Philadelphia, 1796.] Broadside.
AAS copy.   47937

To the Citizens of the County of
Philadelphia. Friends and Fellow

Citizens. . . . The Election of James Ross.
. . .
[Philadelphia, 1799.] Broadside.
LOC copy.   36422

To the Citizens of the County of
Philadelphia. Friends and Fellow
Citizens. . . . James Ross.
[Philadelphia, 1800?]. Broadside.
(Also entered as 36422, q. v.)   38644

To the Citizens of Philadelphia. Friends,
Countrymen, Brethren. . . . [by William
Findley, 1741-1821].
[Philadelphia, 1787.] Broadside.
(The two originals are in poor condition.)
LOC copy.   20358

To the Citizens of the United States. . . .
New-York, March 8, 1800.
n. p., n. d. 6 pp.
LOC copy.   38645

[To the Citizens of Virginia. . . .
Richmond, July 7th, 1800.
Richmond, Pleasants, [1800]. Broadside.]
(Entry from Evans' note.)   38646

To the Commissioners and Assessors, of
Chester County, for the Year 1764.
[Philadelphia, 1764.] Broadside.
LCP copy.   9852

To the Commissioners Appointed by the
East-India Company, for the Sale of Tea.
[New York? 1773.] Broadside in three
columns.
NYPL ph. copy.   42521

To the Commissioners Appointed by the
East-India Company.
[Philadelphia, 1773.] Broadside.
LOC copy.   12999

To the Commissioners of Forfeitures of
the Western District . . . Whereas by an
Act . . . Passed the 4th of October, 1780. . . .
[New York, 1781?] Broadside.
LOC copy.   44059

To the Committee who Fitted out William
Kittletas.
[New York? 1798.] [2] pp.
NYPL copy.   34668

To the Committees of the Several Towns
and Counties of . . . North-Carolina,
Appointed for . . . Carrying into
Execution the Resolves of the Continental
Congress. . . . [Signed] William Hooper. . . .
June 19, 1775.
[Newbern, 1775.] [2] pp.
PRO copy.   42946

To the Congress. The Remonstrance of
the Subscribers. . . . 5th, 9 mo. 1777.
[Philadelphia], Bell, [1777]. Broadside.
HSP copy.   15499

To the Curious. A View of the Ancient
City of Jerusalem. . . . August 3, 1791.
[Boston, 1791.] Broadside.
MHS copy.   46300

To the Curious! To be Seen at [blank]
Two Camels. . . . [Aug. 4, 1789.]
[Salem? 1789?] Broadside.
(Located too late to be reproduced.)
                                             45607

To the Delaware Pilots A Ship Loaded
with Tea. . . . The Committee for Tarring
and Feathering.
[Philadelphia, 1773.] Broadside.
NYPL copy.   12941

To the Delaware Pilots. The Regard we
have. . . . December 7, 1773.
[Philadelphia, 1773.] Broadside.
NYPL copy.   12943

To the Delaware Pilots. We took the
Pleasure. . . . November 27, 1773.
[Philadelphia, 1773.] Broadside.
LCP copy.   12942

To the Detestable Author of a Scurrilous
Hand Bill. . . . June 9th, 1800.
[Albany, N. Y., 1800.] Broadside.
(No copy located.)   38647

To the Dissenting Electors of all
Denominations.

[New York, 1769.] Broadside.
LCP copy.   11494

To the Dis-United Inhabitants of the
Dis-United States. . . .
[New York, 1779.] [3] pp.
HSP copy.   16545

To the Editor of Porcupine's Gazette [by
Benjamin Griffith, fl. 1798].
n. p., [1798]. 8 pp.
(Copy cannot be reproduced.)   48461

To the Editor of the Providence Gazette.
The Enemies of Governor Fenner. . . .
November 6, 1785.
[Providence, c. 1795.] Broadside.
RIHS copy.   47626

[To the Electors and Freeholders of the
City of Philadelphia. Friends and
Fellow-Citizens. A Late law. . . .
[Philadelphia, 1774.] Broadside.]
(A duplicate of 15104, q.v.)   13654

To the Electors and Freeholders of the
City of Philadelphia. Friends and
Fellow Citizens, A Late Law. . . .
[Philadelphia, 1776.] Broadside.
LCP copy.   15104

To the Electors of a Representative to
Congress, for the First District. . . . A
Republican Elector.
[New York? 1799.] Broadside.
Albany Institute copy.   48966

[To the Electors of Dutchess County. At a
Meeting . . . 29th March, 1798.
Poughkeepsie, Power & Southwick,
[1798]. Broadside.]
(No copy located.)   34669

[To the Electors of Dutchess County. . . .
13 April, 1797.
Poughkeepsie, Power, 1797. Broadside.]
(No copy located.)   32936

To the Electors of Franklin County.
Fellow-Citizens. . . . May 1, 1798.
[Frankfort, 1798.] Broadside.
LOC copy.   48631

To the Electors of New-York.
January 6, 1776. . . .
[New York, 1776.] 2 pp.
NYHS copy.   15039

To the Electors of Pennsylvania. Take
your Choice! Thomas M'Kean - or -
James Ross.
[Philadelphia, 1799.] Broadside.
LOC copy.   36423

To the Electors of Pennsylvania. When a
Candidate. . . .
[Philadelphia, 1799.] 8 pp.
HSP copy.   36424

To the Electors of Pennsylvania. When the
Character of a Worthy Citizen. . . .
October 3d, 1799.
[Philadelphia, 1799.] 2 pp.
(Also entered as 36390, q. v.)   36425

To the Electors of Philadelphia
County. . . . Matthew Huston.
[Philadelphia, 1799.] 7 pp.
(The only recorded copy cannot be
reproduced.)   36426

To the Electors of the City and County of
New-York.
In an Address . . . by Alexander
Hamilton. . . . April 28, 1789.
[New York, 1789.] Broadside.
Albany Institute copy.   45608

To the Electors of the City of New York.
Fellow-Citizens. The Aristocratic
Prints. . . .
[New York, 1797.] Broadside.
NYHS ph. copy.   36427

To the Electors of the City of New-York.
Friends and Fellow-citizens. . . . Dec. 26,
1783.
New York, Loudon, [1783]. Broadside.
NYHS copy.   44465

To the Electors of the County of
Burlington.

Burlington, N. J., Neale, 1794. 16 pp.
(Parke-Bernet cat. 2094, item 317.)
                                             27807

To the Electors of the County of Dutchess
. . . Rinebeck, April 7, 1794.
[Poughkeepsie? 1794.] Broadside.
(Not located, 1968.)   47234

To the Electors of the District of
Long-Island. Fellow-Citizens. . . .
December 6, 1794.
[New York, 1794.] Broadside.
(Not located, 1968.)   47235

To the Electors of the Eastern District.
Fellow Citizens!
[New York? 1798.] Broadside.
NYHS copy.   48632

To the Electors of the Eastern District
Fellow Citizens!. . . . April 23, 1798.
[Albany, 1798.] Broadside.
NYPL copy.   33278

To the Electors of the Kennebec and
Somerset District.
[Augusta, Me., 1799.] Broadside.
AAS copy.   36428

To the Electors of the Southern District.
In Mr. Child's Paper. . . . April 28, 1789.
[New York, 1789.] Broadside.
Albany Institute copy.   45609

To the Electors of the Southern District.
In Mr. Child's Paper. . . . April 29, 1789.
[New York, 1789.] Broadside.
Albany Institute copy.   45610

. . . To the Electors of the State of
New-Jersey. Friends. . . . [August 25,
1792.]
[Norfolk, Va? 1792.] Broadside.
LOC copy.   46583

To the Electors of the State of New-York.
Fellow Citizens!
[Albany, 1795.] Broadside.
NYPL copy.   29641

To the Electors of the State of New-York.
Friends & Fellow-Citizens. A
Representative. . . . Albany, April 4, 1800.
n. p., [1800]. [2] pp.
LOC ph. copy.   38648

To the Electors of the State of New-York.
Friends and Fellow-Citizens. . . .
[New York? 1782?] Broadside.
NYHS copy.   44272

To the Electors of the State of New-York.
Friends and Fellow Citizens. . . . April 17,
1795.
[New York, 1795.] Broadside.
Albany Institute copy.   47627

To the Electors of the State of New-York.
Friends and Fellow Citizens, The
Impropriety. . . . April 23, 1795.
[New York, 1795.] Broadside.
Albany Institute copy.   47628

To the Electors of the State of New-York.
I Trust, Fellow Citizens, I may. . . .
[New York ? 1795.] Broadside.
LOC copy.   29642

To the Electors of the Tenth District of
the State of New-York. . . . Otsego, April
4, 1800.
n. p., n.d. Broadside.
LOC ph. copy.   38649

To the Electors of this City at Large.
Fellow-Citizens!. . . . December 23, 1783.
New York, Loudon, [1783]. Broadside.
NYHS copy.   44466

To the Farmers and Others, who Bring
Wheat to the City of New York for Sale. . . .
June 1st, 1798.
New York, Collins, [1798]. Broadside.
NYSL copy.   48633

To the Free Africans and other Free
People of Color in the United States. . . .
May 9, 1797.
Philadelphia, Poulson, [1797]. Broadside.
NYHS copy.   48270

To the Free and Independent Citizens of

Ulster County, and more Particularly . . .
Woodstock. . . . April, 1794.
n. p., [1794]. Broadside.
(Not located, 1968.) 47236

To the Free and Independent Electors of
the City and County of New York. . . .
April 28, 1789.
[New York, 1789.] Broadside.
NYHS copy. 45611

To the Free and Independent Electors of
the City of Philadelphia. Friends and
Fellow-Citizens [Nov. 5, 1776].
[Philadelphia, 1776.] Broadside.
LCP copy. 15028

To the Free and Independent Electors of
the County of Ulster. . . . Apr. 24, 1799.
[Catskill, 1799.] Broadside.
NYPL copy. 36430

To the Free & Independent Electors of the
State of New-York. Fellow-Citizens. A
Publication. . . .
[New York? 1791.] Broadside.
NYHS copy. 46301

To the Free and Independent Electors of
the State of New-York. Fellow Citizens!
In the Present. . . . April 19, 1798.
[New York, 1798.] Broadside.
LOC copy. 48634

To the Free and Independent Electors of
the State of New-York. Friends and
Fellow Citizens.
n. p., [1798]. Broadside.
Albany Institute copy. 48635

[To the Free and Independent Voters of
the City and County of Baltimore.
[Baltimore, 1798.] Broadside.]
(No copy located.) 34670

[To the Free and Loyal Inhabitants of the
City and Colony of New-York. Friends,
Fellow Citizens,
[New York, 1770.] Broadside.]
(Also entered as 13180, q. v.) 11588

To the Free and Loyal Inhabitants of the
City and Colony of New-York. Friends,
Fellow Citizens. . . .
[New York, 1774.] Broadside.
LOC copy. 13180

To the Free and Patriotic Inhabitants. . . .
May 31st, 1770.
[Philadelphia, 1770.] Broadside.
LCP copy. 11882

To the Free and Respectable Mechanicks,
and other Inhabitants of the City and
County of New-York. In this. . . . March
13, 1775.
[New York, 1775.] Broadside.
NYPL copy. 14491

To the Free Electors of the City of
New-York. Fellow-Citizens. . . .
April 30, 1794.
[New York, 1794.] Broadside.
(Not located, 1968.) 47237

To the Free Electors of the City of
New-York. Fellow Citizens, Your too
great Security. . . . April 29, 1790.
[New York, 1790.] Broadside.
NYHS copy. 22936

To the Free Electors of the County of
Suffolk. . . . February 26, 1791 [by Samuel
Ruggles].
[Boston, 1791.] Broadside.
MHS copy. 46276

To the Free Electors of the State of
New-York. Friends and Fellow-Citizens,
The Period. . . . February 23, 1795.
[New York, 1795.] Broadside.
AAS copy. 47629

To the Free, Virtuous, and Independent
Electors of Massachusetts.
[Boston, 1787.] Broadside.
MHS copy. 45172

To the Freeborn Citizens of New-York.
Gentlemen. . . . July 11, 1774.
[New York, 1774.] Broadside.
NYHS copy. 13655

To the Freeholders and Electors of the
City and County of Philadelphia.
Gentlemen. In a Supplement. . . . October
1st, 1764.
[Philadelphia, 1764.] 2 pp.
LCP copy. 9853

To the Freeholders and Electors of the
Province of Pennsylvania. Friends and
Countrymen. . . . [by James Biddle,
1731-1797].
[Philadelphia, 1765.] Broadside.
LCP copy. 9915

To the Freeholders & Freemen A Further
Information. . . . 2d of October 1727.
[Philadelphia, 1727.] 2 pp.
APS copy. 2969

To the Freeholders and Freemen, in
Pennsylvania. It is Certainly. . . . October
14, 1773.
[Philadelphia, 1773.] Broadside.
LCP copy. 13039

To the Freeholders and Freemen of
New-York. December 29, 1775.
[New York, 1775.] Broadside.
NYPL copy. 14492

[To the Freeholders and Freemen of the
City and County of New-York. As the last
Congress [Meeting, Mar. 6, 1775].
[New York, 1775.] Broadside.]
(The unique copy is mislaid.) 14317

To the Freeholders and Freemen of the
City, and County of New-York. Dear
Countrymen. . . .
[New York, 1774.] Broadside.
NYHS copy. 13689

To the Freeholders and Freemen of the
City and County of New-York.
Fellow-Citizens, As it is. . . .
[New York, 1775.] 2 pp.
NYPL copy. 14493

To the Freeholders and Freemen of the
City and County of New-York.
Gentlemen, Every good Citizen. . . .
January 19, 1769.
[New York, 1769.] Broadside.
LOC copy. 11456

To the Freeholders and Freemen of the
City and County of New-York.
Gentlemen, It was Doubtless Surprising.
. . . January 6, 1769.
[New York, 1769.] Broadside.
LOC copy. 11312

To the Freeholders & Freemen of the City
and County of New-York. Gentlemen,
Many Arts. . . . March 14th, 1775.
[New York, 1775.] Broadside.
NYPL copy. 14494

To the Freeholders, and Freemen, of the
City and County of New-York.
Gentlemen, The Important Advantages.
. . . January 4, 1770.
[New York, 1770.] Broadside.
LCP copy. 11883

To the Freeholders and Freemen, of the
City and County of New York.
Gentlemen, To pretend to prove. . . .
January 9th, 1769.
[New York, 1769.] Broadside.
LOC copy. 11229

To the Freeholders and Freemen of the
City and County of New-York, in
Communion with the Reformed Dutch
Church.
[New York, 1769.] Broadside.
NYPL copy. 11495

To the Freeholders and Freemen of the
City and County of New-York: the
Following Remarks [Feb. 15, 1768].
[New York, 1768.] [2] pp.
LCP copy. 11088

To the Freeholders and Freemen, of the
City and County of New-York. The
Querist, No. I.
[New York, 1769.] 2 pp.
LCP copy. 11431

To the Freeholders and Freemen, of the
City and County of New-York. The
Querist, No. II.
[New York, 1769.] 2 pp.
LCP copy. 11432

To the Freeholders and Freemen of the
City and County of New-York. This
Vindication. . . .
[New York, 1768.] 4 pp.
AAS copy. 41892

To the Freeholders and Freemen of the
City and County of New-York. Whereas. . . .
January 4, 1769.
[New York, 1769.] Broadside.
LOC copy. 11496

To the Freeholders and Freemen of the
City and County of New-York Wo unto
you. . . . New Jersey, February 19th, 1768.
[New York, 1768.] [2] pp.
NYPL copy. 11040

To the Free-Holders and Free-Men, of the
City, and Province of New-York:
Brethren, While. . . . November 13, 1773.
[New York, 1773.] [2] pp.
NYHS copy. 13040

To the Freeholders, and Freemen, of the
City and Province of New-York.
Gentlemen. . . .
[New York, 1769.] 2 pp.
LCP copy. 11497

To the Freeholders, and Freemen, of the
City and Province of New-York.
Gentlemen, the Method of Taking the
Suffrages. . . .
[New York, 1770?]. [2] pp.
(No copy could be located.) 42176

To the Freeholders and Freemen of the
City of New-York.
Fellow-Citizens. A Survey. . . . March
14th, 1775.
[New York, 1775.] 2 pp.
NYPL copy. 14495

To the Freeholders and Freemen of the
City of New-York. Fellow Citizens,
Several Members. . . . March 4, 1775.
[New York, 1775.] Broadside.
NYPL copy. 13809

To the Freeholders and Freemen, of the
City of New-York. Gentlemen, We beg
Leave. . . .
[New York, 1769.] Broadside.
LCP copy. 11234

To the Freeholders and other Electors for
the City and County of Philadelphia, and
Counties of Chester and Bucks.
[Philadelphia, 1764.] [2] pp.
UOP copy. 9854

To the Freeholders and other Electors of
Assembly-Men, for Pennsylvania.
[Philadelphia, 1765.] [2] pp.
LCP copy. 10184

To the Freeholders and Other Inhabitants
of the Town of Boston . . . March 1761
[by Silvester Gardiner, 1708-1786].
[Boston, 1761.] Broadside.
MHS copy. 8862

To the Freeholders, Freemen, and
Inhabitants, of the City and County of
New-York. Gentlemen, As a Report. . . .
[New York, 1775.] Broadside.
NYHS copy. 14496

To the Freeholders, Freemen, and
Inhabitants of the City and County of
New-York. Gentlemen: As the
Conduct. . . . Feb. 6, 1775.
[New York, 1775.] 2 pp.
LOC copy. 14497

To the Freeholders, Freemen, and
Inhabitants of the City of New-York; and
Particularly. . . .
[New York, 1774.] Broadside.
LOC copy. 13656

To the Freeholders, Merchants,
Tradesmen and Farmers, of the City and
County of Philad. . . . Gentlemen. . . .
Sept. 26, 1770.
[Philadelphia, 1770.] Broadside.
LCP copy. 11884

To the Freeholders of King's County, and the Other Counties in the Southern District. . . . March 18, 1789.
[New York, 1789.] 12 pp.
BPL copy.   45612

To the Free-Holders of New-Town. My Friends. . . . April 3d, 1775.
[New York, 1775.] Broadside.
LOC copy.   14498

To the Freeholders of New-York. To-day, Fellow-Citizens. . . . April, 29, 1789.
[New York, 1789.] Broadside.
Albany Institute copy.   45613

To the Freeholders of Prince William, Stafford, and Fairfax. Fellow Citizens. . . .
[Fredericksburg? 1796.] [4] pp.
LOC (Jefferson mss.) copy.   47938

To the Freeholders of the Congressional District of Henrico, &c.
[Richmond, 1798.] 6 pp.
(Not located, 1968.)   48636

[To the Freeholders of the County of Philadelphia.
[Philadelphia, 1757.] [2] pp.]
(Hildeburn 4632.)   8046

To the Freeholders of the District of Fairfax, Loudoun, and Prince-William.
[Richmond? 1794.] 22 pp.
VaU copy.   27808

To the Free-Holders of the Province of Pennsylvania. Friends and Countrymen, As the Time Approaches. . . .
[Philadelphia, 1742.] 4 pp.
HSP copy.   5075

To the Freeholders of the Province of Pennsylvania. Gentlemen. . . .
[Philadelphia, 1743?] 2 pp.
JCB copy.   40319

To the Freeholders of the Southern District. A Writer. . . . April 28, 1789.
[New York, 1789.] Broadside.
Albany Institute copy.   45614

To the Freeholders of the Southern District of the State of New-York. Gentlemen. . . . March 10, 1791.
[New York? 1791.] Broadside.
NYSL copy.   46303

To the Freeholders of the Southern District of the State of New-York. Gentlemen. . . . April 16, 1791.
[New York, 1791.] Broadside.
NYSL copy.   46302

To the Freeholders of the Town of Boston.
[Boston, 1760.] 4 pp.
MHS copy.   8747

To the Freeholders of the Town of Jamaica. My Fellow-Townsmen. . . . March, 28, 1775.
[New York, 1775.] Broadside.
LOC copy.   14499

To the Freeholders, to Prevent Mistakes.
[Philadelphia, 1727.] [2] pp.
APS copy.   2970

To the Freemen and Freeholders of New-York. Gentlemen. . . . Jan. 18, 1776.
[New York, 1776.] Broadside.
LOC copy.   15105

To the Freemen and Freeholders of the City and County of New-York. Friends and Fellow Citizens, From the Prudence. . . . March 4, 1774 [i.e. 1775].
[New York, 1775.] Broadside.
LOC copy.   14500

To the Freemen and Freeholders, of the City and County of New-York. Friends and Fellow-Citizens, When I. . . . September 23d, 1775.
[New York, 1775.] Broadside.
NYPL copy.   14501

To the Freemen and Freeholders of the City and County of New-York. John a Nokes. . . .
[New York, 1768.] Broadside.
LCP copy.   11089

To the Freemen and Freeholders of the City and County of New-York. The Author. . . .
[New York, 1768.] Broadside.
AAS copy.   11090

[To the Freemen and Freeholders of the City of New-York [Stamped Paper].
[New York, 1766.] Broadside.]
(No copy located.)   10507

To the Freemen and Freeholders of the East Ward of the City of New-York. Friends. . . .
[New York, 1776.] Broadside.
LOC copy.   15106

To the Freemen, Citizens of Philadelphia. The Preservation. . . . June 16, 1773.
[Philadelphia, 1773.] Broadside.
LCP copy.   12946

To the Freemen, Freeholders, and other Inhabitants of the City and County of New-York. Gentlemen. . . . July 16, 1774.
[New York, 1774.] [2] pp.
LOC copy.   13657

To the Freemen, Freeholders, and other Inhabitants of the City of New-York. My Friends. . . . Jan. 19th. 1775.
[New York, 1775.] Broadside.
NYHS copy.   14170

To the Freemen of America. My dear Countrymen. . . .
[Philadelphia, 1773.] Broadside.
LCP copy.   12873

To the Freemen of Baltimore-Town. . . . January 6, 1789.
[Baltimore, 1789.] Broadside.
MdHS copy.   22071

To the Freemen of Chatham County. Fellow Citizens, I have Addressed. . . .
[Savannah, 1795.] Broadside.
GHS copy.   29643

To the Freemen of Pennsylvania, and more Especially to those of . . . Philadelphia.
[Philadelphia, 1755?] Broadside.
HSP copy.   40805

To the Freemen of Pennsylvania. At Romae. . . .
[Philadelphia, 1772.] Broadside.
LCP copy.   12353

To the Freemen of Pennsylvania. By the Thirty-Fifth Section of the Constitution. . . .
[Philadelphia, 1779.] Broadside.
(No copy located.)   43709

To the Freeman of Pennsylvania. . . . Mentor.
[Philadelphia, 1792.] Broadside.
HSP copy.   46584

To the Freemen of Pennsylvania. My Countrymen and Fellow-Citizens. . . .
[Philadelphia, 1773.] Broadside.
NYPL copy.   12970

To the Freemen of Pennsylvania. Philadelphia, September 28, 1764.
[Philadelphia, 1764.] 2 pp.
LOC copy.   9855

To the Freemen of Pennsylvania. The Proposed Extension. . . . [Feb. 18, 1772] [by Thomas Mifflin, 1744-1800].
[Philadelphia, 1772.] Broadside.
HSP copy.   12465

To the Freemen of Rhode-Island, &c [by Jonathan Russell, 1771-1832].
[Providence, 1800.] 16 pp.
LOC copy.   38438

To the Freemen of the City of Philadelphia. . . . Oct. 9, 1792. Hambden.
[Philadelphia, 1792.] Broadside.
HSP copy.   46585

To the Freemen of the Colony of Rhode-Island. . . . April 11, 1758 [by Samuel Ward, 1725-1776].
[Newport, 1758.] 6 pp.
RIHS copy.   41017

To the Freemen of the Common Wealth of Pennsylvania. . . . June 18, 1777.
[Philadelphia, 1777.] Broadside.
LCP copy.   15614

To the Freemen of the Northern Liberties - Fellow-Citizens. . . . Brutus.
[Philadelphia, 1799.] Broadside.
LOC copy.   36429

To the Freemen of the State of Connecticut. . . . By Horatio Juvenal [by Richard Alsop, 1761-1815].
[Hartford, 1790.] 10 pp.
CHS copy.   22598

[To the Freemen of the State of Rhode-Island.
Providence, 1790. Broadside.]
(See Alden 1232.)   22937

To the Freemen of the State of Rhode-Island and Providence Plantations. . . . Newport, August 19, 1800.
n. p., n. d. Broadside.
LOC copy.   38652

To the Freemen of the State of Rhode-Island, &c. To the End. . . . Aug. 20, 1798.
[Providence, 1798.] Broadside.
RIHS copy.   34671

[To the Freemen of the Town of Providence.
Providence, Wheeler, [1796]. Broadside.]
(The origin of this entry is unknown.)   31303

[To the Freemen of this and the Neighbouring Towns. . . . Nov. 3, 1773.
Boston, 1773. Broadside.]
(Known only from ref. in Dartmouth Papers, II, 193.)   12691

To the Friend of his Country.
n.p., [1793]. Broadside.
BM copy.   26264

To the Friends of American Liberty. Gentlemen. . . . 4th March, 1775.
[New York, 1775.] Broadside.
NYPL copy.   14502

To the Friends of Freedom and Public Faith.
[Philadelphia? 1799.] 8 pp.
BPL copy.   36431

To the Friends of Israel Israel. . . . February 22, 1798.
[Philadelphia, 1798.] Broadside.
HSP copy.   34672

To the General Assembly. Gentlemen, As I am not Influenced. . . . March 14, 1772.
[New York, 1772.] [2] pp.
NYHS copy.   12576

To the General Assembly of Maryland. An Individual. . . . November 9, 1782.
Baltimore, Goddard, [1782]. [2] pp.
EPFL copy.   44273

To the General Assembly of Maryland. I have Carefully Revised. . . . [by Alexander Contee Hanson, 1749-1806].
[Annapolis, 1784.] [2] pp.
MdHS copy.   18518

[To the General Assembly of Maryland. . . . Prince George's County, 8th December, 1796.
[Annapolis, 1796.] Broadside.]
(No copy located.)   31056

To the General Assembly of Virginia. . . . Petitions. . . . District Court in Centerville.
[Alexandria? 1799?] Broadside.
VaSL copy.   48967

To the General Court of the Massachusetts, Assembled at Boston, Oct. 1780.
[Boston, 1780.] Broadside.
LOC copy.   17006

To the Generous Subscribers for the New-York Packet.
[New York, Loudons, 1788.] Broadside.
NYHS copy.   45377

To the Gentlemen, Freeholders and
Others in the County of Newcastle. . . .
[Wilmington, Del., 1774.] Broadside.
(No copy located.)			42712

To the Good People of Pennsylvania. . . .
January 5, 1773.
[Philadelphia, 1773.] 3 pp.
LCP copy.			12967

To the Honest and Industrious Mechanics
and Planters of Chatham County.
[Savannah, 1795.] Broadside.
GHS copy.			29644

To the Honest Electors of this Day. Be
cool, my Friends.
[Boston, 1785.] Broadside.
MHS copy.			44799

[To the Hon. the Speaker and House of
Delegates of Virginia; the Subscribing
Inhabitants of the County. . . . County
Courts.
[Richmond, 1793.] Broadside.]
(No copy located.)			26396

To the Honorable General Assembly, now
in Session, at New Haven. . . . Hartford,
October 10th, 1800.
n. p., n. d. [3] pp.
YC copy.			38653

To the Honorable the General Assembly
of the Commonwealth of Virginia. The
Petition of Sundry Freeholders and
Farmers of the County of [blank].
[Alexandria? 1799?] Broadside.
VaSL copy.			48968

To the Honorable the General Assembly
. . . of Connecticut. The Memorial of . . .
Black Men [by Isaac Hillard, b. 1737].
[n. p., 1797] 12 pp.
(This is apparently the item described by
Evans.)
LOC copy.			32252

To the Honorable the General Assembly
of . . . Connecticut, to be held . . . May,
1771.
[Hartford? 1771.] Broadside.
JCB copy.			42289

To the Honorable the General Assembly
of the Commonwealth of Virginia. A
Memorial and Remonstrance. . . .
[Richmond, 1785.] Broadside.
VaSL copy.			20108

To the Honorable the House of
Representatives of the United States. The
Memorial of the Subscribers, Merchants.
. . .
[Boston, 1796.] Broadside.
MHS copy.			31304

To the Honorable the Legislature of the
State of New York. . . . March 9, 1786.
[New York, 1786.] [2] pp.
AAS copy.			20024

To the Honorable the Legislature of the
United States. Being Informed. . . .
February, 1798.
n. p., [1798]. [2] pp.
LOC copy.			48637

To the Honorable the Representatives of
the Freemen of the Commonwealth of
Pennsylvania, in General Assembly
met. . . .
[Philadelphia, 1790.] Broadside.
LCP copy.			22938

To the Honorable the Senate and House
of Representatives of the United
States. . . . Petition. . . . Vessels of France.
n.p., [1800]. Broadside.
LOC copy.			38654

To the Honorable the Speaker and House
of Delegates for the State of Virginia.
[Alexandria? 1798.] Broadside.
VaSL copy.			48638

To the Honourable Adolph Philipse, Esq.
[New York, 1728.] 2, [3] pp.
NYPL copy.			3112

To the Honourable General Assembly . . .
The Memorial of Harry, Cuff, and Cato
[by Isaac Hillard, b. 1737].

n.p., [1797]. 12 pp.
(Copy not located.)			48142

To the Honourable House of
Representatives of this His Majesties
Province of New York [May 19, 1698].
New York, Bradford, 1698. 10 pp.
PRO copy.			852

To the Honourable Magistrate, and
Worthy Electorate of King's County . . .
New-York. January 23, 1776.
[New York, 1776.] Broadside.
NYHS copy.			43173

To the Honourable the General Assembly
of Maryland. The Petition of the
Subscribers. . . .
[Annapolis, 1785?] 4 pp.
(No copy located.)			44800

To the Honourable the Members of the
Senate . . . Justice and Humanity. . . .
February 22, 1786.
[Baltimore, 1786.] Broadside.
MdHS copy.			44978

To the Honourable the Speaker and
Members of both Houses of the General
Assembly of Virginia.
[Fredericksburg? 1795?] Broadside.
VaSL copy.			47630

To the Honourable the General Assembly
of . . . Connecticut, to be Convened . . .
October, 1771 [dated Sept. 5, 1771]. . . .
n.p., [1771]. Broadside.
HEH copy.			42288

To the Honourable the House of
Representatives of the United States. The
Memorial of the Subscribers, Citizens of
Massachusetts [April 28, 1796].
[Boston, 1796.] Broadside.
MHS copy.			31305

To the Honourable the Senate and House
of Representatives of . . . Pennsylvania. . . .
The Memorial . . . for . . . a Permanent
Bridge over the Schuylkill. . . . January 25,
1797.
[Philadelphia, 1797.] [2] pp.
HSP copy.			48271

To the Independent Citizens of Exeter.
Gentlemen, The Unhappy Contest. . . .
Dec. 15, 1777.
[Exeter, 1777.] Broadside.
AAS copy.			43379

[To the Independent Electors in the State
of New-York. The Time Approaches. . . .
[New York, 1792.] Broadside.]
(No broadside printing located. The text
is in The Diary; or, Loudon's Register,
New York, March 31, 1792, p. 2, columns
2-3.)			24857

To the Independent Electors of
Pennsylvania. . . . An American.
[Philadelphia, 1799.] 11 pp.
LCP copy.			36432

To the Independent Electors of
Pennsylvania. Citizens and Friends. . . .
A Federalist.
[Philadelphia, 1792.] Broadside.
HSP copy.			46586

To the Independent Electors, of the City
and County of Albany. At a Public . . .
Meeting of the Federalists. . . . March 14,
1788.
Albany, Webster, [1788]. Broadside.
NYHS copy.			45378

To the Independent Electors of the City
and County of Albany. . . . Mat. Visscher,
Clk. 15th March, 1788.
Albany, Webster, [1788]. Broadside.
NYHS copy.			45379

To the Independent Electors of the City of
New-York. There was a Time. . . . April
28, 1788.
[New York, 1788.] Broadside.
LOC copy.			21501

To the Independent Electors of the City of
New-York. To support the British
Nomination. . . . April 24th, 1798.
[New York, 1798.] Broadside.
NYHS copy.			48639

To the Independent Electors of the State
of New-York. Fellow Citizens, A
Numerous Meeting. . . . March 19, 1792.
[New York, 1792.] Broadside.
LOC copy.			24858

To the Independent Electors of the State
of New-York. Fellow Citizens, You will
be Shortly. . . . April 11, 1792.
[New York, 1792.] Broadside.
NYHS copy.			24859

To the Independent Freeholders and
Freemen, of this City and County. It
having been Industriously Propagated. . . .
Jan. 4, 1770.
[New York, 1770.] Broadside.
NYHS copy.			11677

. . . . To the Inhabitants of Anne-Arundel
County. [January 7, 1775]. . . .
[Annapolis, 1775.] 2 pp.
MdHS copy.			13816

To the Inhabitants of Germantown. Look
before you Leap!
[Philadelphia, 1798.] Broadside.
HSP copy.			48640

[To the Inhabitants of Germantown.
Whereas. . . . April the 27th, 1775.
[Germantown, 1775.] Broadside.]
(No copy located.)			14503

To the Inhabitants of King's County.
Friends. . . . 21st April, 1788.
New York, Childs, [1788]. [2] pp.
LOC copy.			21502

To the Inhabitants of King's County,
Friends and Fellow-Citizens. . . .
Flatbush, 28th April, 1788.
New York, Childs, [1788]. Broadside.
AAS ph. copy.			45380

To the Inhabitants of New-York, and all
the British Colonies. . . . 20th April, 1775.
[New York, 1775.] Broadside.
NYHS copy.			14504

To the Ihabitants of New-York. I am
much Alarmed. . . . 29th September, 1774.
[New York, 1774.] Broadside.
NYHS copy.			13342

To the Inhabitants of New-York. My dear
Friends. . . .
[New York, 1774.] Broadside.
LOC copy.			13658

To the Inhabitants of New-York. My
Fellow-Citizens, This City. . . . January
27, 1776.
[New York, 1776.] Broadside.
NYHS copy.			15107

To the Inhabitants of Pennsylvania. A
Very Dangerous Attempt. . . . October 13,
1773.
[Philadelphia, 1773.] Broadside.
HSP copy.			42522

To the Inhabitants of Pennsylvania.
Friends, Countrymen and Fellow Citizens,
A few days. . . .
[Philadelphia, 1782.] 7 pp.
LCP copy.			17744

To the Inhabitants of Philadelphia. To
Charge the Servants. . . .
[Philadelphia, 1771.] Broadside.
LCP copy.			12245

To the Inhabitants of South-Carolina. As
there is no Established Rule. . . . July 9,
1792.
[Charleston, 1792.] Broadside.
LCP copy.			46587

To the Inhabitants of the City and Colony
of New-York. Fathers. . . . June 30th,
1774.
[New York, 1774.] [2] pp.
NYHS copy.			13659

To the Inhabitants of the City and Colony
of New-York. From Mess. Bradford's
Paper of the 22d [June, 1774].
[New York, 1774.] Broadside.
LOC copy.			13660

[To the Inhabitants of the City and

County of New-York. Fellow Citizens, be
not Deceived.
[New York, 1769.] Broadside.]
(The unique copy could not be located.)
    11498

To the Inhabitants of the City and County
of New-York. Fellow Citizens, Be not
Deceived. . . .
[New York, 1776?] Broadside.
LOC copy.   43174

To the Inhabitants of the City and County
of New-York. Friends and Fellow-
Citizens, Notwithstanding. . . . April
13, 1775.
[New York, 1775.] Broadside.
NYPL copy.   14505

To the Inhabitants of the City and County
of New-York, Gentlemen. . . . June 5,
1774.
[New York, 1774.] Broadside.
NYHS copy.   13661

To the Inhabitants of the City and County
of New-York. Gentlemen, the Five
Deputies. . . . July 7th, 1774.
[New York, 1774.] Broadside.
NYHS copy.   42713

To the Inhabitants of the City and County
of New-York. Gentlemen. . . . July 12,
1774.
[New York, 1774.] Broadside.
NYPL copy.   13097

To the Inhabitants of the City and County
of New-York. My dear Countrymen. . . .
April 13, 1776.
[New York, 1776.] Broadside.
LOC copy.   15108

To the Inhabitants of the City and County
of New-York. My dear Countrymen. . . .
April 15, 1776.
[New York, 1776.] Broadside.
NYHS copy.   15109

To the Inhabitants of the City and County
of New-York. My Friends and
Countrymen. . . . April 16, 1776.
[New York, 1776.] Broadside.
NYPL copy.   15110

To the Inhabitants of the City and County
of New-York. The Wisest men. . . . March 4,
1775.
[New York, 1775.] 2 pp.
AAS ph. copy.   42947

To the Inhabitants of the City and County
of New-York. The Wisest Men. . . . March 4,
1775 [by Philip Livingston, 1716-1778].
[New York, 1775.] 2 pp.
NYPL copy.   14162

To the Inhabitants of the City and County
of Philadelphia. Gentlemen, you are
come. . . . July 14, 1770.
[Philadelphia, 1770.] Broadside.
LCP copy.   11885

To the Inhabitants of the City, County
and Province of New-York. . . . 11th
March, 1775.
New York, Holt, [1775]. 2 pp.
NYPL copy.   14506

To the Inhabitants of the City of
Philadelphia, and Parts Adjacent
[Soap-Boilers, Feb. 15, 1772].
[Philadelphia, 1772.] Broadside.
LCP copy.   12577

To the Inhabitants of the County of
Philadelphia. . . . A Dutch Man.
[Philadelphia, 1798.] Broadside.
HSP copy.   48641

To the Inhabitants of the District of
Schenectady. Our Antient and
Respectable Town. . . .
n.p., [c. 1788]. Broadside.
NYHS copy.   45381

To the Inhabitants of the Southern
District. Fellow-Citizens, The
Advocates. . . . April 25, 1789.
[New York, 1789.] Broadside.
Albany Institute copy.   45615

To the Inhabitants, Particularly the

Farmers and Planters of the State of
Maryland. . . . Feb. 1, 1785.
n.p., [1785]. Broadside.
(The only known copy is imperfect.)
LOC copy.   44801

To the Maid I Love Best. . . . Composed
by Mr. Hook [by William Upton].
[New York, 1798?] [2] pp.
(This is apparently the item described by
Evans from Gilfert's adv., which is also
responsible for the attribution of
authorship to Upton.)
AAS copy.   34912

To the Manufacturers and Mechanics of
Philadelphia, the Northern Liberties, and
District of Southwark. . . . June 8, 1774.
[Philadelphia, 1774.] Broadside.
LCP copy.   13664

To the Mayor . . . of Philadelphia. This
Plan of the Improved Part of the City. . . .
[by Nicholas Scull, 1687-1761].
[Philadelphia, 1762.] map.
HSP copy.   9267

To the Mechanicks and Free Electors of
the City and County of New-York. . . .
Dec. 23, 1783.
[New York], Loudon, [1783]. Broadside.
NYHS copy.   44467

To the Mechanics of the City of
New-York. . . . A Mechanic. April 28,
1789.
[New York, 1789.] Broadside.
Albany Institute copy.   45616

To the Members of the Free and Easy
Club.
[Savannah, 1795.] Broadside.
CHS copy.   29645

To the Members of the General Assembly
of Maryland. Gentlemen, Permit me. . . .
December 17, 1784 [by Alexander Contee
Hanson, 1749-1806].
[Annapolis, 1784.] [4] pp.
MdHS copy.   18519

To the Memory of that Faithful Minister
. . . Thomas Lightfoot, who fell Asleep . . .
November 4, 1725.
Philadelphia, Keimer, [1725]. Broadside.
NYHS copy.   39837

To the Memory of the late Dr.
Rittenhouse, this Poetical Effusion. . . .
[Philadelphia], Ormrod & Conrad,
[1796]. 4 pp.
LCP copy.   47939

To the Merchants and Manufacturers of
Great-Britain.
[Philadelphia, 1765.] [4] pp.
JCB copy.   10185

To the Merchants and other Inhabitants
of Pennsylvania.
That Baltimore. . . . Dec. 13, 1771.
[Philadelphia, 1771.] Broadside.
LCP copy.   12246

To the Merchants, and Traders, of the
City of Philadelphia.
Gentlemen, The Worthy. . . .
[Philadelphia, 1770.] Broadside.
LCP copy.   11886

To the Merchants Committee, the Dry
Goods Merchants, &c. . . . May 12, 1770.
[Philadelphia, 1770.] Broadside.
LCP copy.   11887

To the Militia of Pennsylvania. . . .
Nestor.
[Philadelphia, 1778.] Broadside.
LCP copy.   15919

To the Moderate and Independent
Electors of Dutchess. . . .
Poughkeepsie, Power, [1789?]. Broadside.
LOC copy.   45617

To the Non-Commissioned Officers and
Privates, of the Several Companies.
[Philadelphia, 1775.] [2] pp.
HSP copy.   14507

To the Patrons of the Columbia Magazine
this Map of Pennsylvania. . . .
[Philadelphia, Spotswood, 1790.] Map.

(This is apparently the map described by
Evans from an adv.)
AAS copy.   22804

To the Patrons of the Independent
Chronicle, their News-Carrier Presents.
. . . January 2, 1800.
[Boston, 1800.] Broadside.
AAS copy.   37686

To the Patrons of the Newburyport
Herald, &c. It is a Custom. . . .
[Newburyport, 1798.] Broadside.
EI copy.   34232

To the Patrons of the Salem Gazette [by
William Biglow, 1773-1844].
[Salem, 1798.] Broadside.
EI copy.   34511

To the People Called Freeholders and
Freemen, of the "Dirty Corporation"
[Feb. 21, 1772].
[New York, 1772.] Broadside.
LOC copy.   12578

To the People. Friends and Fellow
Citizens, When Partial Mischiefs. . . . 18th
June, 1792.
[New York? 1792.] Broadside.
NYHS copy.   46588

To the People of America. Stop. . . . Isaac
Wilkins. . . . May 4, 1775.
[New London, 1775.] Broadside.
LOC copy.   14509

To the People of Cecil. No I [-III].
Wilmington, [Del.], Wilson, [1800]. [2],
5; 8 pp.
LOC copy.   38655

To the People of Kentucky. . . . Franklin.
[Lexington, 1795.] Broadside.
LOC copy.   28706

To the People of Maryland, Gentlemen,
You have. . . . May 28, 1776.
[Baltimore, 1776.] Broadside.
MdHS copy.   15111

To the People of Maryland, Give me
Leave to Address you. . . . [by Luther
Martin? 1744-1826].
[Baltimore, 1779.] Broadside.
(The date given by Evans is a
typographical error.)
MdHS copy.   15112

To the People of New-Jersey. Friends. . . .
Sept. 30, 1800.
n. p., n. d. Broadside.
NJHS copy.   38656

To the People of New-York. Though the
Association. . . .
[New York, 1774]. Broadside.
NYPL copy.   13665

To the People of Pennsylvania. Friends
and Fellow-Citizens, The late Convention.
. . . [by Samuel Bryan, 1759-1821].
[Philadelphia, 1787.] Broadside.
AAS ph. copy.   20248

To the People of the District of Edenton.
[Edenton? 1788?] 13 pp.
VaU copy.   45382

[To the People of the State of New-York.
. . . A Citizen of Albany.
n. p., [1800]. 8 pp.]
(Entry from Evans' notes.)   38657

To the President and Council of
Philadelphia. The Remonstrance of the
Subscribers. . . . September 5th, 1777.
[Philadelphia], Bell, [1777]. 2 pp.
HSP copy.   15500

To the Printer of the Maryland Herald,
&c. [by Joseph Hopper Nicholson,
1770-1817].
[Easton? 1792.] 24 pp.
JCB copy.   29646

To the Printer. . . . Sir, It was a Custom
among the Lacedemonians. . . .
[Savannah, 1774.] Broadside.
GHS copy.   42714

To the Printer. Sir, this Minute came to
my Hands. . . . May 2d, 1739.

[Boston? 1739.] Broadside.
MHS copy.   40176

To the Printers in Essex [by Francis
Symonds, of Danvers].
[Salem, 1771.] [2] pp.
AAS copy.   42282

To the Printur of the Penselvaney
Kronical. [Oct. 1, 1772].
[Philadelphia, 1772.] Broadside.
LCP copy.   12579

To the Privates of the Several Battalions.
[Philadelphia, 1776.] 3 pp.
LCP copy.   15113

To the Provincial Congress. Gentlemen,
Whenever there is a Strong Probability....
[Boston, 1774.] Broadside.
NYPL copy.   13446

To the Public. A Few Days Ago.... April
17, 1798.
Hudson, N. Y., Stoddard, [1798]. [2] pp.
NYPL copy.   34674

To the Public.... A Friend to Truth.
Shawangunk, April 24, 1793.
n.p., [1793]. Broadside.
NYPL copy.   46889

To the Public. A Small Pamphlet....
[Boston, 1767?]. 18 pp.
AAS copy.   10627

To the Public All Lovers of Peace.... [by
John Dickinson, 1732-1808].
[Philadelphia, 1768.] 8 pp.
LOC copy.   11018

... To the Public. Although the Revenue
System.... A Republican, October 7,
1786.
Albany, C. R. Webster, [1786]. 16 pp.
BPL copy.   44979

To the Public. An Advertisement Having
Appeared.... May 17, 1774.
[New York, 1774.] Broadside.
LOC copy.   13669

To the Public. An Anonymous Letter....
July 25, 1768.
Philadelphia, Goddard, [1768].
Broadside.
HSP copy.   11019

To the Public. As it is Generally
Imagined.... 28th Dec. 1769.
[New York, 1769.] Broadside.
LOC copy.   11499

To the Public. As the Claim of Cornelius
C. Bogardus.... June 12th, 1775.
[New York, 1775.] [2] pp.
NYHS copy.   14510

To the Public. As the Election for
Members to Represent this State in
Congress.... January 4th, 1797.
[New Jersey, 1797.] Broadside.
LOC copy.   48272

To the Public. As the Merchants....
Sept. 14, 1774.
[New York, 1774.] Broadside.
NYHS copy.   13668

To the Public. Audi et Alteram
Partem.... Portsmouth New Hampshire,
April 19th, 1774.
[Boston? 1774.] [4] pp.
JCB copy.   42715

To the Public. By the following
Letters.... January 18, 1775.
[New York, 1775.] [2] pp.
AAS ph. copy.   42948

To the Public. By the Following
Letters.... Rembrancer. New-York,
January 18, 1775.
[New York, 1775.] 2 pp.
NYPL copy.   14314

To the Public. City of New-York, ss.
Personally appeared.... Thomas
Mesnard.... 30th of December, 1774.
[New York, 1774.] Broadside.
NYHS copy.   13666

To the Public. Civis Avows Himself to be
the Person....
[Philadelphia, 1773.] Broadside.
LCP copy.   42523

To the Public. Fellow-Citizens. Of all the
Extraordinary Performances.... Natchez,
November 15th, 1800.
n.p., n.d. Broadside.
MHS copy.   38658

To the Public. Fellow Citizens, Your
Sense and Humanity.... March 22, 1775.
[New York, 1775.] Broadside.
NYHS copy.   14513

To the Public. Few are Ignorant....
[New York, 1770.] [2] pp.
NYHS copy.   11890

[To the Public. Friends and Fellow
Citizens.... An Elector.
[New York, 1792.] [2] pp.]
(This item has not been identified or
located.)   26265

To the Public. Friends and Fellow-
Citizens, In Times of Election....
January 8, 1789.
[Baltimore, 1789.] Broadside.
LOC copy.   22222

To the Public. I Congratulate my
Countrymen on the ... Prospect of the
Repeal of the Stamp-Act.
[New York, 1765.] Broadside.
LCP copy.   41592

To the Public. I was Sorry to Observe....
April 21, 1786.
[Albany, 1786.] Broadside.
NYPL copy.   20025

To the Public. It is a Painful
Necessity.... August 2, 1790.
[Baltimore, 1790.] Broadside.
EPFL copy.   46007

To the Public. It may Appear Somewhat
Extraordinary.... [by John Cadwalader,
1747-1786].
[Annapolis? 1782?] 24 pp.
LCP copy.   44182

To the Public. "Loose thy neck...."
[Providence, 1792.] [2] pp.
AAS copy.   46589

To the Public. Many Citizens.... March
13, 1775.
[New York, 1775.] Broadside.
NYPL copy.   14511

To the Public. My Silence for Some Time
Past.... July 21, 1790.
[Baltimore, 1790.] Broadside.
EPFL copy.   46008

To the Public. New-York, August 13,
1771.
[New York, 1771.] Broadside.
NYHS copy.   12247

To the Public. Notwithstanding.... July
4, 1770.
[Philadelphia, 1770.] Broadside.
LCP copy.   11888

[To the Public. Pursuant to an Act of the
General Assembly.... Jan. 22, 1785.
[Richmond, 1785.] Broadside.]
(The unique copy is not now to be found.)
                                                   19274

[To the Public [Regarding a Publication
Signed "Plain Truth"].
[Philadelphia, 1776.] Broadside.]
(No copy located.)   14967

To the Public. Some Remarks on the
Proceedings of the Late Convention.
New Hampshire, 1791. 31 pp.
AAS copy.   23834

To the Public. That Great Britain will one
day fall.... January 9, 1770.
[New York, 1770.] 2 pp.
LOC copy.   11829

To the Public. The Advertisement....
October the 3d, 1770.
[Philadelphia, 1770.] Broadside.
LCP copy.   11823

To the Public. The *Crisis* being Deemed
... a Libel....
[New York, 1775.] Broadside.
LOC copy.   14512

To the Public. The Inhabitants of this City
are Desired.... March 8, 1770.
[New York, 1770.] Broadside.
LCP copy.   11889

To the Public. The late Detestation....
June 20, 1774.
[New York, 1774.] Broadside.
NYPL copy.   13670

To the Public. The long Expected Tea
Ship.... April 19, 1774.
[New York, 1774.] Broadside.
NYHS copy.   13671

To the Public. The Printer not being Able
to Publish Capt. Sweet's Answer....
April 19, 1774.
[Newport, 1774.] [2] pp.
JCB copy.   42716

To the Public. The Sense of the City....
April 21, 1774.
[New York, 1774.] Broadside.
NYHS copy.   13672

[To the Public. The Spirit of the
Times....
[New York, 1769.] Broadside.]
(Also entered as 13673, q. v.)   11500

To the Public. The Spirit of the
Times....
[New York, 1774.] Broadside.
NYHS copy.   13673

To the Public. The Undersigned.... Nov.
8, 1800.
[Natchez], Green, [1800]. Broadside.
LOC copy.   38659

To the Public. There has been a Design
Formed ... to send the Gospel to Guinea.
[Newport, 1776.] 8 pp.
AAS copy.   14803

To the Public. 'Tis Virtue only.... Pope.
[New York? 1780.] Broadside.
NYPL copy.   17007

To the Public. Various are the Plans....
January 15, 1772.
[Philadelphia, 1772.] Broadside.
LCP copy.   12580

To the Public. We the Undersigned....
Edward Heston.... Oct. 7th, 1799.
[Philadelphia? 1799.] Broadside.
LOC copy.   36433

To the Public. When Vice Prevails.... Jan.
28, 1772.
[New York, 1772.] Broadside.
LCP copy.   12336

To the Public. Whereas Advertisements....
December 28, 1769.
[New York, 1769.] Broadside.
LCP copy.   11501

To the Public. Whereas many
Misrepresentations [Pennsylvania Navy].
...
[Philadelphia, 1776.] Broadside.
LCP copy.   15114

To the Public. Whoever Seriously
Considers.... January 15th, 1770.
[New York, 1770.] Broadside.
NYHS copy.   11589

To the Publick. In Consequence of the
Unhappy Dispute at present Subsisting.
...
[Savannah, 1774.] Broadside.
GHS copy.   42717

To the Publick.... It must be an
Unpleasant Reflection to Every Lover of
Peace and Moderation.... August 3,
1774.
[Savannah, 1774.] Broadside.
GHS copy.   42718

To the Publick, New-York, November
16th, 1774.
[New-York, 1774.] Broadside.
NYPL copy.   13677

To the Publick. New-York, October 5, 1774.
[New York], Holt, [1774]. Broadside.
NYHS copy.   13674

To the Publick. New-York, October 27, 1774.
[New York, 1774.] Broadside.
NYHS copy.   13675

To the Publick. Stop him! . . . Nov. 21st.
[New York, 1774.] Broadside.
LOC copy.   13676

To the Publick. The Booksellers of the Town of Boston. . . .
Boston, [1759]. Broadside.
LOC copy.   8288

To the Publick. The Ship Lady Gage being Arrived . . . Dec. 15th, 1774.
[New York, 1774.] Broadside.
AAS ph. copy.   42719

To the Publick. We the Committee, who were Appointed. . . . March 24, 1775.
[New York, 1775.] Broadside.
LOC copy.   14514

To the Public. With Astonishment I Read. . . . Philalethes [by Robert Montfort].
[Savannah, 1789.] Broadside.
GHS copy.   21970

To the Real Patriots and Supporters of American Independence. . . . July 10, 1784.
[Philadelphia, 1784.] Broadside.
LCP copy.   44602

To the Real Patriots and Supporters of American Independence. . . .
Philadelphia, June 28, 1784.
[Philadelphia, 1784.] Broadside.
LCP copy.   18807

[To the Religious Society of Quakers [on the Evil Consequences of Drink].
[Philadelphia, 1788.] Broadside.]
(No copy located.)   21503

To the Representatives of the Freemen of the Commonwealth of Pennsylvania, in General Assembly met. Divers Freemen ["Free Quakers," Dec. 2, 1781].
[Philadelphia, 1781.] Broadside.
LCP copy.   17164

To the Representatives of the Freemen of the Commonwealth of Pennsylvania, in General Assembly met.
The Memorial . . . of Isaac Howell. . . .
[Philadelphia, 1782.] [4] pp.
(Presented to the House Aug. 21, 1782.)
LOC copy.   17165

To the Representatives of the Freemen of the Counties of Chester. . . . May 9, 1774.
[Philadelphia, 1774.] Broadside.
LCP copy.   13678

To the Representatives of the Free-men of the Province of Pennsilvania . . . the 10th. of the 3d. Moneth, 1692.
[Philadelphia, 1692.] 4 pp.
HSP copy.   628

To the Representatives of the Province of Pennsylvania now Met in this City.
[Philadelphia, 1774.] Broadside.
LCP copy.   42720

To the Republican Citizens of the State of Pennsylvania. Lancaster, Sept. 17, 1800.
. . .
n. p., n. d. 16 pp.
LCP copy.   38660

To the Republicans of Pennsylvania. . . .
August 7th, 1799.
[Philadelphia, 1799.] 7 pp.
(Not located, 1968.)   48969

To the Republicans of Pennsylvania. . . .
John Peter Muhlenberg. . . . 31st of August, 1799.
[Philadelphia, 1799.] 8 pp.
APS copy.   36435

To the Respectable Body of Gentlemen Nominated by the Publick. . . . September 29, 1774.

[New York, 1774.] Broadside.
NYPL copy.   13483

To the Respectable Inhabitants of the City of New-York. . . . 4th March, 1775.
[New York, 1775.] Broadside.
NYHS copy.   14515

To the Respectable Public. Have a Good End in View. . . . July 25, 1774.
[New York, 1774.] Broadside.
NYPL copy.   13679

To the Respectable Public. We Conceive. . . . July 20, 1774.
[New York, 1774.] Broadside.
NYHS copy.   13680

To the Respectable Publick. Certain Resolves. . . . July 20, 1774.
[New York, 1774.] Broadside.
NYHS copy.   13681

To the Reverend James Davenport [by Sarah (Parsons) Moorehead].
Boston, 1742. 8 pp.
BPL copy.   5011

To the Reverend Mr. Vesey.
[New York, 1732.] 4 pp.
NYPL copy.   3611

To the Reverend Mr. William Cooper.
[Boston, 1743.] 7 pp.
(The accompanying newspaper controversy was waged in the issues of January, 1742/3.)
AAS copy.   4950

To the Right Honourable, Mr. Harley, Wounded by Guiscard.
Boston, B. Green, 1711. Broadside.
BA copy.   39535

To the Senate and House of Representatives of the Commonwealth of Pennsylvania . . . Dec. 19th, 1793. The Address and Petition of Several Inhabitants. . . .
[Philadelphia], [1793.] Broadside.
HSP copy.   25987

To the Senate and House of Representatives of the United States. . . .
Providence, December 31, 1798.
[Providence, 1798?] 2 pp.
JCB copy.   48642

To the Senate and Representatives of the United States [by John Armstrong, 1758-1843].
[Poughkeepsie, 1798.] [2] pp.
NYPL copy.   33313

To the Several Battalions of Military Associators. . . . June 26, 1776.
[Philadelphia, 1776.] [2] pp.
LCP copy.   15115

To the Sons of Liberty in this City. . . .
February 3, 1770.
[New York, 1770.] Broadside.
LCP copy.   11891

To the Sons of Liberty of New-York. Fellow Citizens, It is the Peculiar Privilege. . . .
[New York, 1775.] Broadside.
NYHS copy.   14516

To the Speaker and Members of the House of Representatives of the United States of America in Congress Assembled: The Representation and Petition of the Subscribers. . . .
[Philadelphia? 1795.] Broadside.
HSP copy.   29647

To the Stockholders of the Bank of North-America, on the Subject of the Old and New Banks [by Pelatiah Webster, 1726-1795].
Philadelphia, Crukshank, 1791. 16 pp.
LCP copy.   23971

To the Supporters and Defenders of American Freedom . . . May 20, 1778 [by Alexander McDougall?, 1732-1786].
[Fishkill? 1778.] 12 pp.
(See Wroth Essays, p. 406.)
AAS copy.   16093

[To the Tenants of the Manor of

Rensselaerwyck. . . . A Tenant.
Albany? 1789.]
(No copy located.)   45618

To the Tories. . . . April 30 . . . 1776 by Arthur Donaldson, fl. 1776].
[Philadelphia, 1776.] Broadside.
HSP copy.   14739

To the Tradesmen, Farmers, and Other Inhabitants of the City and County of Philadelphia. . . . September 24, 1770.
[Philadelphia, 1770.] Broadside.
LCP copy.   11892

To the Tradesmen, Mechanics, &c. of the Province of Pennsylvania. . . . December 4, 1773.
[Philadelphia, 1773.] Broadside.
NYPL copy.   13041

To the Unbiassed & Independent Electors of the State of New-York. . . . April 7, 1789.
[New York, 1789.] Broadside.
Albany Institute copy.   45619

To the very Learned, Loquacious . . . Chairman. . . . March 4, 1775.
[New York, 1775.] Broadside.
NYPL copy.   14518

[To the Very Respectable and Humane Citizens of New-York. . . .
[New York, 1774.] Broadside.]
(The unique copy is mislaid.)   13144

To the Voters of Ann-Arundel County. . . . A Friend to Paper Money.
Elk-Ridge, September 23, 1786.
[Annapolis, 1786.] [2] pp.
MdHS copy.   44980

To the Voters of Anne-Arundel. . . .
September 26, 1792.
[Annapolis? 1792.] Broadside.
LOC copy.   46590

To the Voters of Baltimore County. If Men of Integrity. . . . September 25, 1787.
[Baltimore, 1787.] Broadside.
EPFL copy.   45173

To the Voters of Baltimore Town and County, Charges. . . . August 31, 1791.
Baltimore, Goddard & Angell, [1791]. Broadside.
EPFL copy.   46304

To the Voters of Maryland. On Monday next. . . . October 1, 1790.
[Baltimore, Goddard & Angell, 1790.] Broadside.
LOC copy.   22939

To the Voters of the City and County of Baltimore. Gentlemen, When the Extract. . . .
Baltimore, Yundt & Brown, [1798]. Broadside.
NYPL copy.   48643

To the Whig Mechanicks of the City and County of New-York. . . . Dec. 27, 1783.
[New York], State Printing-Office, [1783]. Broadside.
NYHS copy.   44468

To the Worthy and Industrious Mechanicks of this State. Fellow-Citizens!!!
New York, Loudon, [1783]. Broadside.
NYHS copy.   44469

To the Worthy Freeholders and Others, Inhabitants of the Province of Georgia.
Savannah, July 25, 1774.
[Savannah, 1774.] Broadside.
GHS copy.   42721

To the Worthy Freeholders and Others, Inhabitants of the Province of Georgia,
Savannah, July 30, 1774.
[Savannah, 1774.] Broadside.
GHS copy.   42722

To the Worthy Inhabitants of Baltimore-Town. At this Juncture. . . .
September 2, 1786.
[Baltimore, 1786.] Broadside.
EPFL copy.   44981

To the Worthy Inhabitants of New-York. Friends and Fellow-Citizens, As the

Hand-bill. . . . April 5, 1775.
[New York, 1775.] 2 pp.
NYPL copy.   14519

To the Worthy Inhabitants of New-York.
My dear Friends. . . .
[New York, 1773.] 4 pp.
NYPL copy.   13042

To the Worthy Inhabitants of the City and
County of New-York. Fellow
Countrymen. . . . July 9, 1774.
[New York, 1774.] Broadside.
NYHS copy.   13683

To the Worthy Inhabitants of the City and
County of New-York. My Fellow Citizens.
At this Interesting Crisis. . . .
[New York, 1774.] Broadside.
LOC copy.   13684

To the Worthy Inhabitants of the City of
New-York. Every good Citizen. . . .
[New York, 1773.] Broadside.
LOC copy.   12956

To the Worthy Inhabitants of the City of
New-York. My dear Fellow-Citizens. . . .
[New York, 1774.] Broadside.
NYHS copy.   13682

To the Worthy Inhabitants of the City of
New-York. No Subject. . . .
[New York, 1773.] [2] pp.
LOC copy.   12957

To the Worthy Inhabitants of the City of
New York. The Cause. . . .
[New York, 1773.] [2] pp.
NYHS copy.   12955

To the Worthy Inhabitants of the City of
New-York. . . . 16th September, 1774.
[New York, 1774.] Broadside.
NYHS copy.   13100

To the Worthy Supporters of the
Poughkeepsie Journal. . . . January 1,
1797.
[Poughkeepsie, 1797.] Broadside.
NYHS copy.   48273

To Their Excellencies Richard Viscount
Howe, Admiral, and William Howe, Esq;
General [by William Henry Drayton,
1742-1779].
[Charleston, 1776.] 8 pp.
AAS copy.   14742

To Walter Tolley, Benjamin Nicholson. . . .
[Baltimore, 1775.] Broadside.
MdHS copy.   14520

[Tobler, John.]
The Carolina and Georgia Almanack . . .
for . . . 1783.
Charleston, Keith & M'Iver. [24] pp.
LOC copy.   17745

[Tobler, John].
The Carolina and Georgia Almanack . . .
for . . . 1784.
[Charleston], for the Author. [20] pp.
AAS copy.   18211

Tobler, John.
The Georgia Almanack, for . . . 1771.
Charleston, for Johnston and Wells.
[32] pp.
NL copy.   11894

Tobler, John.
The Georgia and South-Carolina
Almanack, for . . . 1774.
Charleston, Wells for Johnston in Savannah.
[32] pp.
NYHS copy.   42524

Tobler, John.
The Georgia and South Carolina
Almanack, for . . . 1775.
Charleston, for Wells & J. Johnston in
Savannah. [32] pp.
AAS copy.   42723

Tobler, John.
The Georgia and South-Carolina
Almanack, for . . . 1775.
Charleston, Wells, for Johnston in
Savannah. [32] pp.
AAS copy.   13686

[Tobler, John.

Pennsylvania Town and Country Man's
Almanack for 1754.
Philadelphia, [32] pp.]
(No complete copy found.)
AAS copy.   40675

Tobler, John.
The Pennsylvania Town and
Country-Man's Almanack for . . . 1755.
Germantown, Sower; Philadelphia,
Marshall & Maule. [36] pp.
AAS copy.   7324

Tobler, John.
1756. The Pennsylvania Town and
Country-Man's Almanack.
Germantown and Philadelphia. [40] pp.
HSP copy.   7579

Tobler, John.
The Pennsylvania Town and
Country-Man's Almanack for . . . 1757.
Germantown, 1757. [40] pp.
AAS copy.   7803

Tobler, John.
1758. The Pennsylvania Town and
Country-Man's Almanack.
Germantown and Philadelphia. [40] pp.
HSP copy.   8047

Tobler, John.
1759. The Pennsylvania Town and
Country-Man's Almanack.
Germantown, Sower; Philadelphia,
Fussel, Marshall and Zane. [40] pp.
AAS copy.   8269

Tobler, John.
The Pennsylvania Town and
Country-Man's Almanack, for . . . 1760.
Germantown, Sower. [40] pp.
AAS copy.   8503

Tobler, John.
1761. The Pennsylvania Town and
Country-Man's Almanack.
Germantown, Sower for Fussel, Marshall,
and Zane. [40] pp., 1 plate.
AAS copy.   8748

Tobler, John.
The Pennsylvania Town and
Country-Man's Almanack, for . . . 1762.
Germantown, Sower for Fussel and Zane.
[40] pp.
AAS copy.   9025

Tobler, John.
1763. The Pennsylvania Town and
Country-Man's Almanack.
Germantown, Sower. [40] pp., plate.
AAS copy.   9284

Tobler, John.
The Pennsylvania Town and
Country-Man's Almanack, for. . . . 1764.
Germantown, Sower for Wilson and Zane.
[36] pp.
AAS copy.   41416

Tobler, John.
[The Pennsylvania Town and
Country-Man's Almanack for . . . 1764.
Wilmington, Adams. [40] pp.]
(The only copy located is defective.)
AAS copy.   9523

Tobler, John.
The Pennsylvania Town and Country
Man's Almanack, for . . . 1765.
Germantown, Sower for Wilson. [40] pp.
LCP copy.   41493

[Tobler, John.
The Pennsylvania Town and
Countryman's Almanack for . . . 1765.
Wilmington, Del., Adams.]
(Assumed by Hildeburn from the
sequence.)   9856

Tobler, John.
The Pennsylvania Town and
Country-Man's Almanack, for . . . 1766.
Germantown, Sower. [40] pp.
AAS copy.   10186

Tobler, John.
The Pennsylvania Town and
Country-Man's Almanack, for . . . 1767.
Wilmington, Adams, for Zane and Wilson.
[36] pp.

(The only copy located is defective.)
AAS copy.   10508

Tobler, John.
The Pennsylvania Town and
Country-man's Almanack, for . . . 1768.
Wilmington, Del., Adams, for Zane and
Wilson. [40] pp.
AAS copy.   10785

Tobler, John.
The Pennsylvania Town and
Country-Man's Almanack, for . . . 1769.
Wilmington, Del., Adams. [40] pp.
AAS copy.   11092

Tobler, John.
The Pennsylvania Town and
Country-man's Almanack, for . . . 1770.
Wilmington, Del., Adams. [40] pp.
AAS copy.   11502

Tobler, John.
The Pennsylvania Town and
Country-man's Almanack, for . . . 1771.
Wilmington, Del., Adams. [40] pp.
AAS copy.   11893

Tobler, John.
The Pennsylvania Town and
Country-man's Almanack, for . . . 1772.
Wilmington, Del., Adams. [40] pp.
AAS copy.   12248

Tobler, John.
The Pennsylvania Town and
Country-man's Almanack for . . . 1773.
Wilmington, Del., Adams. [36] pp.
(The only copy located lacks a leaf.)
AAS copy.   12581

Tobler, John.
The Pennsylvania Town and
Country-man's Almanack, for . . . 1774.
Wilmington, Del., Adams. [40] pp.
AAS copy.   13043

[Tobler, John.
The Pennsylvania Town and
Countryman's Almanack for . . . 1775.
Wilmington, Del., Adams.]
(Adv. Pa. Gazette, Oct. 12, 1774.)   13685

[Tobler, John.
The Pennsylvania Town and
Countryman's Almanack for . . . 1776.
Wilmington, Del., Adams.]
(Adv. Pa. Journal, Oct. 18, 1775.)   14521

Tobler, John.
The Pennsylvania Town and
Country-Man's Almanack, for . . . 1777.
Wilmington, Adams. [36] pp.
LOC copy.   15116

Tobler, John.
The South-Carolina Almanack, for . . .
1755.
Germantown, Saur for Viart in
Charleston. [24] pp.
NYHS copy.   40720

Tobler, John.
The South-Carolina Almanack for . . .
1756.
Germantown, [Pa.], Sower for Viart,
Charleston, [24] pp.
SCHS copy.   40804

Tobler, John.
The South-Carolina Almanack, for . . .
1757.
Germantown, [Pa.], Sower for Viart in
Charleston. [32] pp.
(The only known copy lacks a leaf.)
SCHS copy.   40864

Tobler, John.
The South-Carolina Almanack, for . . .
1758.
Germantown, Sower for Viart in
Charleston. [32] pp.
SCHS copy.   40941

Tobler, John.
The South-Carolina Almanack, for . . .
1759.
Charleston, Timothy. [32] pp.
SCHS copy.   41012

Tobler, John.
The South Carolina and Georgia
Almanack for . . . 1760.

Charleston, Timothy. [50] pp.
(The only known copy could not be
reproduced.)   41083

Tobler, John.
The South-Carolina and Georgia
Almanack, for . . . 1764.
Savannah, Johnston. [24] pp.
DeRGL copy.   41417

Tobler, John.
The South-Carolina & Georgia Almanack
for . . . 1765.
Charleston, Wells & Bruce. [32] pp.
LOC copy.   10187

Tobler, John.
The South Carolina & Georgia Almanack
for . . . 1766.
Charleston, Wells. [32] pp.
NYHS copy.   10188

Tobler, John.
The South-Carolina & Georgia Almanack
for . . . 1767.
Charleston, Wells. [32] pp.
NYPL ph. copy.   10509

Tobler, John.
The South-Carolina & Georgia Almanack,
for . . . 1768.
Charleston, Wells. [32] pp.
Composite copy.   10786

[Tobler, John.
The South-Carolina and Georgia
Almanack for . . . 1769.
Charleston, Wells.]
(Assumed from the sequence.)   11093

Tobler, John.
The South-Carolona and Georgia
Almanack, for . . . 1770.
Charleston, Wells. [32] pp.
NYHS copy.   11503

Tobler, John.
The South-Carolina and Georgia
Almanack, for . . . 1771.
Charleston, Wells and Johnston. [32] pp.
AAS copy.   42177

Tobler, John.
The South-Carolina and Georgia
Almanack, for . . . 1772.
Charleston, Wells, for Johnston in
Savannah. [32] pp.
LOC copy.   12249

[Tobler, John.
The South Carolina and Georgia
Almanack for . . . 1773.
Charleston, Wells.]
(Assumed from the sequence.)   12582

Tobler, John.
The Georgia and South-Carolina
Almanack, for the Year . . . 1774.
Charleston, Wells for Johnston. [32] pp.
NYHS copy.   13044

Tobler, John.
The South-Carolina and Georgia
Almanack, for . . . 1776.
Charleston, Wells, for Johnston in
Savannah. [32] pp.
NYPL ph. copy.   14522

Tobler, John.
The South-Carolina and Georgia
Almanack, for . . . 1777.
Charleston, Wells. [32] pp.
NYHS copy.   15117

Tobler, John.
The South-Carolina and Georgia
Almanack, for . . . 1778.
Charleston, Wells. [16] pp.
(The unique copy is imperfect.)
CLS copy.   15615

Tobler, John.
The South-Carolina and Georgia
Almanack, for . . . 1779.
Charleston, Wells. [32] pp.
NYPL copy.   16094

Tobler, John.
The South-Carolina and Georgia
Almanack, for . . . 1780.
Charleston, Wells. [20] pp.
NYPL ph. copy.   16548

Tobler, John.
The South-Carolina and Georgia
Almanack for . . . 1781.
Charleston, Wells. [36] pp.
LOC copy.   17008

[Tobler, John.
The South-Carolina and Georgia
Almanack . . . 1782.
Charlestown, Wells.]
(Assumed from the sequence.)   17377

Tobler, John.
The South-Carolina and Georgia
Almanack, for . . . 1784.
Charleston, Childs. [24] pp.
(No copy of a Timothy ed. and no perfect
copy found.)
AAS copy.   18212

Tobler, John.
The South-Carolina and Georgia
Almanack, for . . . 1785.
Charleston, Childs. [24] pp.
LOC copy.   18808

Tobler, John.
The South-Carolina and Georgia
Almanack, for . . . 1786.
Charleston, Childs, M'Iver & Co. [36] pp.
LOC copy.   19275

[Tobler, John.
The South-Carolina and Georgia
Almanack for . . . 1787.
Charleston, Childs, Haswell & M'Iver.]
(A duplicate of 19542, q. v.)   20026

[Tobler, John.]
The South-Carolina & Georgia Almanac,
for . . . 1789.
Charleston, Markland & M'Iver. [26] pp.
LOC copy.   21504

Tobler, John.
The South-Carolina and Georgia
Almanac, for . . . 1790.
Charleston, Markland & M'Iver. [40] pp.
AAS copy.   22186

Tabler, John.
The South-Carolina and Georgia
Almanac, for . . . 1791.
Charleston, Markland & M'Iver. [44] pp.
LOC copy.   22940

Tobler, John.
The South-Carolina and Georgia
Almanac, for . . . 1792.
Charleston, Markland & M'Iver. [36] pp.
LOC copy.   23835

Tobler, John.
The South-Carolina, North-Carolina, and
Georgia Almanack, for . . . 1792.
Charleston, Harrison. [36] pp.
(No complete copy located.)
AAS copy.   23836

Todd, Ambrose, 1764-1809.
Death and Mortality.
Hartford, Hudson & Goodwin, 1797. 16
pp.
AAS copy.   48274

Todd, John, 1719-1793.
An Humble Attempt.
Philadelphia, Steuart, 1763. 40 pp.
(In this copy the words "Propriety . . .
Psalms" are on a slip pasted over the
original wording "Necessity of
Evangelical and the Impropriety of Jewish
Psalms.")
AAS copy.   9524

Todd, Jonathan, 1713-1791.
(Dexter, I, 465-468.)
Be Followers.
[New London, 1743.] [4], 50 pp.
(The unique copy is defective.)
BrU copy.   5303

Todd, Jonathan, 1713-1791.
(Dexter, I, 465-468.)
Civil Rulers.
New London, 1749. [4], 79 pp.
AAS copy.   6430

[Todd, Jonathan], 1713-1791.
A Defence of the Doings of the . . . .
Consociation.
[New London], 1748. [2], 117, [1] pp.
MHS copy.   6250

Todd, Jonathan, 1713-1791.
(Dexter, I, 465-468.)
A Faithful Narrative.
New Haven, 1759. v, [1], 84, [1] pp.
AAS copy.   8504

Todd, Jonathan, 1713-1791.
The Good man Useful in Life.
New Haven, [1781]. 41 pp.
AAS copy.   17378

Todd, Jonathan, 1713-1791.
(Dexter, I, 465-468.)
Judgment and Mercy.
New Haven, [1770]. 52 pp.
AAS copy.   11895

Todd, Jonathan, 1713-1791.
The Peaceful and Happy End.
New Haven, [1782]. 36 pp.
AAS copy.   17746

Todd, Jonathan, 1713-1791.
(Dexter, I, 465-468.)
Public Mourning.
New London, 1756. 88 pp.
YC copy.   7804

Todd, Jonathan, 1713-1791.
A Reply to the Reverend Mr. Eells's
Serious Remarks.
New Haven, 1760. 74, 4, 59, iii pp.
AAS copy.   8749

Todd, Jonathan, 1713-1791.
The Soldier Waxing Strong.
New London, Green, 1747. [4], 46 pp.
CHS copy.   40444

Todd, Jonathan, 1713-1791.
The Vanity of Expectations.
New Haven, [1783]. 27 pp.
AAS copy.   18213

Todd, Jonathan, 1713-1791.
(Dexter, I, 465-468.)
The Young People Warned.
New London, 1741. [4], v, [3], 52 pp.
CHS copy.   4829

Todd, Joseph J.
[Catalogue of books in circulating library.
Providence, 1797.]
(Alden 1553; no copy known.)   48275

Todd, Timothy, 1758-1806.
An Ode for the Fourth of July 1799 . . .
Set to Music by the Rev. Chauncy Lee.
Hudson, [N. Y.], Fairman, [1799].
Broadside.
AAS copy.   36436

Todd, Timothy, 1758-1806.
An Oration, Delivered at Manchester.
Rutland, Kirkaldie for Williams, 1795. 13
pp.
AAS copy.   29649

Todd, William, fl. 1790.
An Oration, Delivered before the . . .
Masons.
Keene, Griffith, [1790]. 23 pp.
AAS copy.   22941

A Token for Children. That they may
Know to Avoid the Evil.
Boston, at the Heart and Crown, [1731?]
Broadside.
AAS copy.   39980

A Token for Mourners [by John Flavel,
1630?-1691].
Boston, T. Green for Eliot & Boone, 1707.
[10], 154 pp.
(The only known copy is imperfect.)
AAS copy.   39466

A Token for Mourners [by John Flavel,
1630?-1691].
Boston, Boone, 1725. [8], 124 pp.
LOC copy.   2635

[A Token for Youth. . . . Twenty-Fifth
Edition [by Mrs. Sarah Rede].
Boston, 1727.]
(Adv. Boston News-Letter, Feb. 9, 1727.)
     2886

A Token for Youth. . . . Twenty-Fifth
Edition [by Mrs. Sarah Rede].
Boston, 1729. [1], iii, 32 pp.
(The only known copy is imperfect.)
AAS copy.   39929

Toler, Henry.
The Faithful Minister's Work.
Philadelphia, Ormrod & Conrad, 1795. 80
pp.
AAS copy.   29650

Tolman, Thomas, 1756-1842.
An Oration, on the Death of . . .
Washington.
Peacham, Vt., Farley & Goss, 1800. 14 pp.
VtU copy.   38661

Tom Bolin: together with Collin and
Phebe. A Couple of Excellent New Songs.
[Boston], Sold next Liberty Pole, 1786.
[2] pp.
AAS copy.   44982

The Tom-Cod Catcher. On the Departure
of an Infamous B-r--t.
[Boston, 1769.] Broadside.
AAS copy.   42013

Tom Thumb's Folio, for Little Giants.
Boston, at the Bible and Heart, [178-?].
32 pp.
(Best copy available.)
AAS copy.   43755

Tom Thumb's Folio, or a New Play-Thing
for Little Boys and Girls.
Boston, N. Coverly, 1783. 32 pp.
AAS copy.   44470

Tom Thumb's Folio. . . . First Worcester
Edition.
Worcester, Thomas, 1787. 31 pp.
AAS copy.   20750

Tom Thumb's Folio.
Hartford, Patten, 1789. 29 pp.
(The only known copy is imperfect.)
CHS copy.   45620

Tom Thumb's Folio: or, A New
Threepenny Play Thing for Little Giants.
Boston, Hall, 1791. 31 pp.
CHS copy.   46305

Tom Thumb's Folio.
New York, Durell, 1793. 31 pp.
d'Alté A. Welch copy.   46890

Tom Thumb's Folio.
Boston, Hall, 1794. 28, [3] pp.
(Not located, 1968.)   47239

Tom Thumb's Folio.
Boston, Norman, [1794?] 29 pp.
AAS copy.   47238

[Tom Thumb's Folio.
Boston, Hall, 1795.]
(Adv. in 29599.)   29633

[Tom Thumb's Folio.
Hudson, N. Y., Stoddard, 1795.]
(Imprint assumed by Evans from
Stoddard's adv.)   29634

Tom Thumb's Folio.
New York, Oram, 1796. 30 pp.
(Best copy available.)
Brooklyn (N. Y.) Public Library copy.
                                             47940

[Tom Thumb's Little Book.
Boston, Hall, 1795.]
(Imprint assumed by Evans from Hall's
adv.)   29635

[Tom Thumb's Little Book.
Hudson, N. Y., Stoddard, 1795.]
(Imprint assumed by Evans from
Stoddard's adv.)   29636

Tom Thumb's New Riddle Book;
Containing a Variety of Entertaining
Riddles.
Boston, Folsom, 1798. 31 pp.
EI copy.   48644

Tom Thumb's Play-Book.
Boston, (Thomas for) Barclay, [1764].
31, [1] pp., printed covers.
AAS copy.   10189

Tom Thumb's Play-Book.
Boston, Kneeland & Adams, 1771. 31 pp.
(Apparently the imprint given by Evans
was his assumption from an adv.)
AAS copy.   12250

Tom Thumb's Play-Book.
Worcester, Thomas, 1786. 30, [1] pp.
AAS copy.   20021

Tom Thumb's Play-Book.
Worcester, Mass., Thomas, 1794. 30, [1]
pp.
(No perfect copy known.)
AAS copy.   47240

Tom Thumb's Play-Book, to Teach
Children their Letters.
Norwich, Hubbard, 1795. 32 pp.
CHS copy.   47631

Tom Thumb's Play-Book.
[?, 1798?] 31 pp.
(The only known copy is imperfect.)
AAS copy.   48645

Tommy Thumb's Song Book. . . . By
Nurse Lovechild. . . . First Worcester
Edition.
Worcester, Thomas, 1788. 59, [4] pp.
AAS copy.   21089

Tommy Thumb's Song Book. . . . By
Nurse Lovechild. . . . Second Worcester
Edition.
Worcester, Mass., Thomas, 1794. 59,
[4] pp.
AAS copy.   47241

[Tom Thumb's Song Book.
Boston, Hall, 1795.]
(Imprint assumed by Evans from Hall's
adv. in 29599.)   28987

Tomb, Samuel, 1766-1832.
The Duties of Gospel-Ministers.
Newburyport, Blunt, 1799. 34 pp.
AAS copy.   36437

Tomb, Samuel, 1766-1832.
An Oration on the Auspicious Birth . . . of
. . . Washington.
Newburyport, Blunt, 1800. 17, [3] pp.
AAS copy.   38662

The Tomb of James Molai [by Charles
Louis, Cadet de Gassicourt, 1769-1821].
Boston, Edes, 1797. 22 pp.
AAS copy.   31903

[Tomkins, John], 1663?-1706.
(D. N. B.)
A Brief Testimony to the Great Duty of
Prayer.
Boston, 1724. 80 pp.]
(No copy of this edition has been found.
For another see 2710.)   2588

Tomkins, John, 1663?-1706.
(D. N. B.)
A Brief Testimony. . . . Third Edition.
Philadelphia, Keimer, 1725. 78 pp.
AAS copy.   2710

Tompson, Benjamin, 1642-1714.
(Sibley, II, 103-111.)
A Funeral Tribute to . . . John Winthrope.
[Boston, 1676.] Broadside.
MHS copy.   224

Tompson, Benjamin, 1642-1714.
(Sibley, II, 103-111.)
The Grammarian's Funeral.
[Boston, 1708.] Broadside.
MHS copy.   1376

[Tompson, Benjamin], 1642-1714.
(Sibley, II, 103-111.)
A Neighbour's Tears.
[Boston, 1710.] Broadside.
MHS copy.   1489

[Tompson, Benjamin], 1642-1714.
New-Englands Crisis.
Boston, 1676. 31 pp.
(See H. J. Hall, Benjamin Tompson,
1924.)
HEH copy.   225

[Tompson, Edward], 1666-1705.
(Sibley, III, 306-310.)
An Elegiack Tribute to . . . Seaborn
Cotton.
[Boston, 1686.] Broadside.
MHS copy.   420

Tompson, Edward, 1666-1705.
(Sibley, III, 306-310.)
Heaven the Best Country.

Boston, 1712. [2], iv, 126 pp.
AAS copy.   1588

Tompson, Edward, 1666-1705.
(Sibley, III, 306-310.)
Heaven the Best Country. . . . Second
Impression.
Boston, 1715. [2], ii, 84 pp.
AAS copy.   1783

Tompson, John, 1740-1828.
The Question.
Dover, Ladd, 1793. 30 pp.
JCB copy.   26266

Tompson, William, 1697-1759.
(Sibley, VI, 284-286.)
The Duty of a People.
Boston, Kneeland & Green, 1743. 35, [2]
pp.
(Signatured to 5316, q.v.)   5301

Tontine Coffee-House, New York.
The Constitution and Nominations of
the. . . .
New York, 1796. [2], 47 pp.
AAS copy.   30886

A Tooth-full of Advice.
[New York, 1768.] Broadside.
LCP copy.   10833

Topham, Edward, 1751-1820.
The Life of John Elwes.
New York, Berry & Rogers, 1790. 95 pp.
LOC copy.   22942

[Topham, Edward], 1751-1820.
A Surprising Account of the Life of the
late John Elwes, Esq.
Philadelphia, Zeller, 1791. 71 pp.
PSL copy.   23837

[Toplady, Augustus Montague, 1740-1778.
Observations on the Divine Attributes.
York, Pa., Edie, 1793. 24 pp.]
(This is the first part of 26526, q.v.) 26267

[Torrey, John, fl. 1795.
Scriptural and Allegorical Poems.
New York, 1796.]
(Entry from copyright notice.)   31308

Torrey, Joseph, 1707-1791.
A Brief Representation of the Case
Depending between the Rev. Dr.
McSparren, Plaintiff, and the Rev. Mr.
Torrey, Defendant. . . . July 1739.
[Newport? 1739.] Broadside.
JCB copy.   40177

Torrey, Samuel, 1632-1707.
(F. L. Weis, Colonial Clergy.)
An Exhortation.
Cambridge, 1674. [8], 44 pp.
AAS copy.   197

Torrey, Samuel, 1632-1707.
(F. L. Weis, Colonial Clergy.)
Man's Extremity.
Boston, 1695. [4], 60 pp.
AAS copy.   739

Torrey, Samuel, 1632-1707.
(F. L. Weis, Colonial Clergy.)
A Plea for the Life of Dying Religion.
Boston, 1683. [8], 46, [1] pp.
AAS copy.   353

Torrey, William, 1608-1690.
(Chamberlain, Weymouth, Mass. IV,
677-678.)
A Brief Discourse.
Boston, Edes & Gill, 1757. [2], iv, iii, [1],
76 pp.
AAS copy.   8048

[Torrey, William, fl. 1799.
An Annual History of the Legislative
Proceedings of the State of New York. . . .
Vol. I.
New York, 1799.]
(Entry from the copyright.)   36438

The Tory Lie Detected!. . . . Edward
Livingston. . . . May 1, 1799.
[New York, 1799.] Broadside.
WLC copy.   36439

A Tory Medley [by Francis Hopkinson,
1737-1791].
[Philadelphia, 1780.] Broadside.

(See G. E. Hastings, Hopkinson, pp. 305-306.)
LCP copy.   15366

A Touch of the Times [by Samuel Keimer, 1688-1742].
Philadelphia, 1729.]
(Adv. Weekly Mercury, Apr. 24, 1729.)
                                           3174

A Touch on the Times. A New Song.
[Philadelphia? 1764?] 4 pp.
NYPL ph. copy.   41494

Touchstone, Geoffrey, pseud.
He wou'd be a Poet [by James Carey, d. 1801].
Philadelphia, 1796. 28 pp.
AAS copy.   30154

Touchstone, Geoffrey, pseud.
The House of Wisdom [by James Carey, d. 1801].
New York, 1798. 24 pp.
AAS copy.   33492

Touchstone, Geoffrey, pseud.
The House of Wisdom [by James Carey, d. 1801].
Philadelphia, 1798. 27 pp.
AAS copy.   33490

A Touch Stone for the Clergy. To Which is Added, A Poem, Wrote by a Clergyman in Virginia.
n.p. 1771. 16 pp.
BrU copy.   12251

A Touchstone for the Leading Partymen in the United States.
n. p., [1800]. 8 pp.
HC copy.   38663

Toulmin, Harry, 1766-1823.
A Description of Kentucky.
[London], 1792. 121, [3] pp., 1 map.
LOC copy.   26268

A Tour in Holland, in MDCCLXXXIV [by Elkanah Watson, 1758-1842].
Worcester, Thomas, 1790. 191 pp.
AAS copy.   23039

A Tour, through Upper and Lower Canada [by John Cosens Ogden, 1751-1800].
Litchfield, Ct., 1799. 119 pp.
AAS copy.   36007

A Tour, through Upper and Lower Canada [by John Cosens Ogden, 1751-1800].
Litchfield, Ct., 1799. 119 pp.
(Also entered as 36007, q. v.)   36440

Tousard, Louis de, 1749-1821.
Justification of Lewis Tousard.
Philadelphia, Humphreys, 1793. 33 pp.
BA copy.   26269

[Towgood, Michaiah], 1700-1792.
The Baptism of Infants a Reasonable Service.
Boston, Fleet, 1765. [2], iii, [1], 52 pp.
AAS copy.   10191

[Towgood, Michaiah, 1700-1792.
A Calm and Plain Answer to the Enquiry. . . .
Philadelphia, Humphreys, 1774.]
(Adv. Pa. Gazette, Feb. 2, 1774.)   13687

[Towgood, Michaiah], 1700-1792.
A Dissent from the Church of England. . . . Fourth Edition.
Boston, 1768. xi, [1], 324 pp.
AAS copy.   11094

[Towgood, Michaiah], 1700-1792.
The Dissenting Gentleman's Answer. . . . Fourth Edition.
New York, 1748. 64 pp.
AAS copy.   6251

[Towgood, Michaiah], 1700-1792.
The Dissenting Gentleman's Answer. . . . Fifth Edition.
Boston, Rogers & Fowle, 1748. 121, [6] pp.
AAS copy.   6252

Towgood, Michaiah], 1700-1792.

Recovery from Sickness. . . . Fourth Edition.
Boston, Fleets, 1768. 34, [1] pp.
AAS copy.   11905

[Towgood, Michaiah], 1700-1792.
Recovery from Sickness. . . . Fifth Edition.
Portsmouth, Peirce, 1794. 43 pp.
LOC copy.   27809

Town & Country Almanac . . . for . . . 1797.
Baltimore, Pechin for Hagerty and Thomas, Andrews & Butler. [36] pp.
LOC copy.   31309

The Town and Country Almanack, for . . . 1798. . . . By Isaac Bickerstaff [by Benjamin West, 1730-1815].
Norwich, Ct., Trumbull for Springer. [24] pp.
NYPL copy.   33203

The Town and Country Almanac, for . . . 1799 [by Abraham Shoemaker].
Philadelphia, Pearson. [44] pp.
(The only recorded copy is imperfect.)
HSP copy.   34545

The Town and Country Almanack, for . . . 1800.
New York, Longworth & Wheeler. 36 pp.
RU copy.   36441

The Town and Country Almanac, for . . . 1800.
Wilmington, Del., Bonsal & Niles. [48] pp.
AAS copy.   36442

Town & Country Almanac, (Revived) Calculated for Virginia, Pennsylvania, Delaware, Maryland and Kentucky - for . . . 1800.
Baltimore, Pechin for Thomas, Andrews & Butler. [36] pp.
MdHS copy.   36443

[The Town and Country Builders' Assistant.
Philadelphia, Johnson, 1794.]
(Imprint assumed by Evans from Johnson's adv. "Just Published," Gazette of the U.S., June 2, 1794.)   27810

The Town and Countryman's Almanack, for . . . 1788 [by William Waring, d. 1793].
Philadelphia, Crukshank. [44] pp.
LOC copy.   20855

A Town in its Truest Glory [by Cotton Mather, 1663-1728].
Boston, 1712. [2], 58 pp.
YC copy.   1560

Towne, Benjamin, d. 1793.
A Defence of Messers. Galloway and Wharton.
[Philadelphia, 1770.] Broadside.
LCP copy.   42178

Towne, Benjamin, d. 1793.
(D. A. B.)
To the Public. . . .
[Philadelphia, 1770.] 2 pp.
UOP copy.   11896

Townsend, Alderman.
Alderman Townsend's Speech in Defence of the Lord Mayor.
[Boston? 1771?] Broadside.
AAS copy.   42290

Townsend, David.
Principles and Observations.
Boston, Thomas & Andrews, 1793. 48 pp.
AAS copy.   26270

Townsend, Jonathan, 1697-1762.
(Sibley, VI, 150-153.)
Comfort for the Afflicted.
Boston, Fleet for Henchman, 1738. [4], v, [1], 22, 25 pp.
BPL copy.   4314

Townsend, Jonathan, 1697-1762.
An Exhortation.
[Boston], Belknap, 1729. [4], ii, 46 pp.
AAS copy.   3224

Townsend, Jonathan, 1697-1762.

God's Terrible Doings.
Boston, Kneeland & Green, 1746. 23 pp.
HC copy.   40416

Townsend, Jonathan, 1697-1762.
(Sibley, VI, 150-153.)
Ministers, and Other Christians.
Boston, Fowle for Winter, 1758. [2], 22 pp.
AAS copy.   8270

Townsend, Jonathan, 1721-1776.
(Sibley, XI.)
The Believing Gentile's Sure Title.
Boston, Green for Gookin, 1749. 24 pp.
AAS copy.   6431

Townsend, Jonathan, 1721-1776.
A Caveat against Strife.
Boston, Green for Gookin, 1749. 14 pp.
(Second part of 6308, q.v.)   6432

Townsend, Jonathan, 1721-1776.
(Sibley, XI.)
Sorrow Turned into Joy.
Boston, Kneeland, 1760. [4], 28 pp.
AAS copy.   8750

Townsend, Robert.
For Sale, the following Houses. . . .
Oyster-Bay, February 1, 1796.
[New York, 1796.] Broadside.
(Not located, 1968.)   47941

[Townsend, Shippie], 1722-1798.
An Attempt to Illustrate.
Boston, Mills and Hicks, 1773. 75 pp.
AAS copy.   12653

Townsend, Shippie, 1722-1798.
An Attention to the Scriptures.
Boston, Folsom, Hall & Clap, 1795. 24 pp.
AAS copy.   29651

Townsend, Shippie, 1722-1798.
The Gospel Considered.
Boston, Adams, 1792. 21 pp.
AAS copy.   24860

Townsend, Shippie, 1722-1798.
Gospel News.
Boston, Young & Minns, 1794. 376 pp.
AAS copy.   27811

[Townsend, Shippie], 1722-1798.
(G. B. Balch, Gen. Balch Families, pp. 47, 71.)
An Inquiry whether the Scriptures Enjoin. . . .
Boston, Kneeland & Adams for Bowes, 1768. 20 pp.
AAS copy.   11096

[Townsend, Shippie], 1722-1798.
The Master and Scholar Attending Catechising.
Boston, Edes, 1787. 16 pp.
AAS copy.   20520

Townsend, Shippie, 1722-1798.
Observations on the Religious Education of Children.
Boston, Edes for Hall, Folsom and West, 1797. 7 pp.
AAS copy.   32938

Townsend, Shippie, 1722-1798.
Peace and Joy.
Boston, Russell, 1788. 107, [1] pp.
AAS copy.   21505

Townsend, Shippie, 1722-1798.
A Practical Essay.
Boston, Adams & Nourse, 1783. 60 pp.
AAS copy.   18214

Townsend, Shippie, 1722-1798.
Repentance and Remission of Sins.
Boston, Warden & Russell for Battelle and Adams & Nourse, 1784. 24 pp.
AAS copy.   18809

[Townsend, Shippie], 1722-1798.
Scripture Truths and Precepts.
Boston, Hall, 1791. 23 pp.
AAS copy.   23838

[Townsend, Shippie], 1722-1798.
A Sober Attention to the Scriptures of Truth.
Boston, Young & Etheridge, 1793. 24 pp.
AAS copy.   26180

Townsend, Shippie, 1722-1798.
Some Remarks, on a Pamphlet.
Boston, Willis, 1783. 32 pp.
AAS copy. 18215

Townsend, Shippie, 1722-1798.
A View of a Most Magnificent
Singing-Choir.
Boston, Bumstead. 1793. 24 pp.
(No perfect copy located.)
WRHS copy. 29652

Townsend, Solomon, 1716-1796.
(Sibley, IX, 585-587.)
A Sermon, Preached in . . . Doctor Stiles's
Meeting.
Newport, 1771. 23 pp.
AAS copy. 12252

Townsend, Walter, fl. 1795.
Elegy, on the Death of Mr. Daniel Parish.
[n.p., 1795.] Broadside.
HEH copy. 29653

[A Tract against Water-Baptism.
Philadelphia? 1760.]
(Known only from the reply, 8937.) 8752

[Tracy, Uriah], 1755-1807.
Reflections on Monroe's View.
[Philadelphia, 1798.] 88 pp.
AAS copy. 34675

[Tracy, Uriah], 1755-1807.
Scipio's Reflections on Monroe's View.
Boston, Wayne, 1798. [4], 140 pp.
AAS copy. 34676

Trade and Commerce Inculcated.
[Boston], 1731. [2], 57, [1] pp.
MHS copy. 3387

A Tradesman's Address to his
Countrymen. . . . March 2, 1772.
[Philadelphia, 1772.] Broadside.
LCP copy. 12583

The Tradesmen's Protest against the
Proceedings of the Merchants. . . .
November 3, 1773.
[Boston], Russell, [1773]. Broadside.
MHS copy. 13046

[The Traditions of the Clergy.
Philadelphia, 1732.]
(Adv. in Penn. Gazette, Mar. 30, 1731/2.)
3618

The Tragedy of Louis Capet.
Boston, [Russell] for Plumer of
Newburyport, [1790]. Broadside.
(Evans' entry was from an adv.)
LOC copy. 22943

The Tragedy of Louis Capet. . . . Jan. 22,
1793.
[Boston, 1793.] Broadside.
EI copy. 26272

The Tragedy of Louis Capet. . . . Jan. 22,
1793.
[Boston, Russell] for Plummer of
Newburyport, [1793]. Broadside.
MHS copy. 26271

The Tragedy of Louis Capet. . . . Jan. 22,
1793.
Springfield, Gray, 1793. Broadside.
AAS copy. 26273

[The Tragedy of Louis XVI.
New York, Swords, 1793.]
(Imprint assumed by Evans from advs.)
26274

A Tragical Account of the Defeat of
Gen. St. Clair by the Savages.
[Boston? 1792?] Broadside.
NYHS copy. 46591

Traill, Robert.
To the Impartial Publick. . . . Portsmouth,
June 6th, 1769.
[Portsmouth, 1769.] [2] pp.
MHS copy. 42014

Trail, Robert, 1642-1716.
Thirteen Sermons.
Philadelphia, M'Culloch, 1796. pp.
[i]-viii, [13]-292, [4].
AAS copy. 31310

[The Traitor Detected, or, an

Examination of Mr. Randolph's
Vindication.
Baltimore, 1796.]
(The origin of this entry is unknown.)
31311

Translation of a Manuscript, Found on
Board a French Man of War.
Boston, 1759. 27 pp.
AAS copy. 8505

Transylvania Seminary.
We the Subscribers, for the Purpose of
Promoting . . . Knowledge. . . . [May,
1794].
[Lexington, Ky., 1794.] Broadside.
Presb. Hist.[Soc. copy. 47242

Ein Trauer Gedicht über eine Grausame
Mordthat.
Reading, Pa., Schneider für Bradley,
1799. 8 pp.
(No copy could be located.) 36444

Eine Trauergeschichte oder ein Neues
Lied.
n.p., [179?]. Broadside.
LCP copy. 45798

The Travellers; Exhibiting a Variety of
Characters.
New York, Oram, 1795. 30, [1] pp.
(Not seen since offered by N. R. Campbell
in 1915.) 29655

The Travellers; Exhibiting a Variety of
Characters Mounted upon . . . Animals.
New York, Durell for Kirk, 1800. 31 pp.
AAS copy. 38664

Travels before the Flood. . . . In Two
Volumes.
Carlisle, Pa., Kline for Loudon, 1797. iv,
164, 151 pp.
AAS copy. 32939

The Travels of Fancy: being a Political,
Historical, and Moral Account.
New Brunswick, N. J., Kollock & Arnett,
1784. 32 pp.
(Evans apparently took the imprint which
he gives from an adv. for this ed.)
NJHS copy. 18810

The Travels of Fourteen Englishmen [by
Nathaniel Crouch, 1632?-1725?].
Keene, Taylor, 1795. 20 pp.
AAS copy. 32004

Travels of Robinson Crusoe [by Daniel
Defoe, 1661?-1731].
Worcester, Thomas, 1786. 31, [1] pp.
AAS copy. 19599

Travels of Robinson Crusoe [by Daniel
Defoe, 1661?-1731].
Boston, Hall, 1798. 30 pp.
AAS copy. 33617

Travels of Robinson Crusoe. . . . First
Newport Edition [by Daniel Defoe,
1661?-1731].
Newport, R. I., Farnsworths, 1799. 26,
[2] pp.
AAS copy. 36445

See also Defoe, Daniel, 1661?-1731.

The Travels of the Imagination [by James
Murray, 1732-1782].
Philadelphia, Bell, 1778. 126, [2] pp.
HSP copy. 15918

Travis, Daniel.
. . . An Almanack . . . for 1707.
Boston, B. Green for Buttolph, 1707.
[24] pp.
AAS copy. 1334

Travis, Daniel.
. . . An Almanack . . . for . . . 1707.
Boston, B. Green for Phillips, 1707. [24]
pp.
MHS copy. 39457

Travis, Daniel.
. . . An Almanack . . . for . . . 1709.
Boston, 1709. [16] pp.
AAS copy. 1377

Travis, Daniel.
. . . An Almanack . . . for . . . 1710.
[New York], 1710. [16] pp.
AAS copy. 1435

Travis, Daniel.
. . . An Almanack . . . for . . . 1711.
Boston, Boone, 1711. [16], 4 pp.
AAS copy. 1490

Travis, Daniel.
. . . An Almanack . . . for . . . 1712.
Boston, 1712. [16] pp.
AAS copy. 1530

Travis, Daniel.
. . . An Almanack . . . for . . . 1713.
[New York], America, sold in Boston,
1713. [16] pp.
AAS copy. 39581

Travis, Daniel.
. . . An Almanack . . . for . . . 1713.
Boston, Boone, 1713. [16] pp.
AAS copy. 1589

[Travis, Daniel.
. . . An Almanack . . . for . . . 1714.
New York or Boston, 1714.]
(No copy found.) 1654

Travis, Daniel.
[MDCCXV. An Almanack.
Boston, 1715.] [16] pp.
(The only known copy is defective.)
AAS copy. 1719

Travis, Daniel.
MDCCXVI. An Almanack.
Boston, B. Green, 1716. [16] pp.
AAS copy. 39657

Travis, Daniel.
MDCCXVI. An Almanack.
New London and Boston, 1716. [16] pp.
(No copy of the New York edition listed
by Evans is known; possibly his entry is a
ghost of this imprint.)
AAS copy. 1784

Travis, Daniel.
MDCCXVII. An Almanack
Boston, B. Green, 1717. [16] pp.
AAS copy. 1859

Travis, Daniel.
MDCCXVIII. An Almanack.
Boston, 1718. [16] pp.
AAS copy. 1932

Travis, Daniel.
MDCCXIX. An Almanack.
Boston, Green, 1719. [16] pp.
AAS copy. 2002

Travis, Daniel.
MDCCXX. An Almanack.
Boston, Green, 1720. [16] pp.
AAS copy. 2077

Travis, Daniel.
MDCCXXI. An Almanack.
Boston, Green, 1721. [16] pp.
AAS copy. 2189

Travis, Daniel.
MDCCXXII. An Almanack.
Boston, Green, 1722. [16] pp.
AAS copy. 2296

Travis, Daniel.
MDCCXXII. An Almanack of Coelestial
Motions . . . for . . . 1722.
New London, Green, 1722. [16] pp.
(The unique original cannot be
reproduced.) 39776

Travis, Daniel.
MDCCXXIII. An Almanack.
Boston, Fleet, 1723. [16] pp.
AAS copy. 2392

[Travis, Daniel.
MDCCXXIV. An Almanack.
Boston, Fleet, 1723. [16] pp.]
(Assumed from the sequence.) 2486

A Treacle Fetch'd out of a Viper [by
Cotton Mather, 1663-1728].
Boston, 1707. [2], 32 pp.
VaU copy. 1317

Treat, Joseph, 1734-1797.
(The Treat Family, 1893, p. 253.)
A Thanksgiving Sermon.
New York, Gaine, 1762. [4], 12 pp.
NYPL copy. 9287

Treat, Richard, 1708-1778.
A Sermon Preach'd at the Ordination of
Mr. Daniel Lawrence.
Philadelphia, Bradford, 1747. 36 pp.
CHS copy.   6076

Treat, Robert, 1695-1770.
. . . An Almanack . . . for . . . 1723.
New London, 1723. [16] pp.
LOC copy.   2393

[Treat, Robert, 1695-1770.
(Dexter, I, 197.)
An Almanack . . . for . . . 1724.
New London, 1724. [16] pp.]
(Assumed from the sequence.)   2487

Treat, Robert, 1695-1770.
MDCCXXV. An Almanack . . . for 1725.
New London, 1725. [16] pp.
MHS copy.   2589

[Treat, Robert, 1695-1770.
An Almanack of the Coelestial Motions
. . . for 1726.
New London, 1726.]
(Assumed from the sequence.)   2711

Treat, Robert, 1695-1770.
MDCCXXVII. . . . An Almanack.
New London, 1727. [16] pp.
AAS copy.   2817

A Treatise Concerning Baptism [by John
Gratton, 1641-1712].
Boston, Franklin, 1726. [2], v, [1], 98 pp.
JCB copy.   39847

[A Treatise of Arithmetic [by John
Gough, 1721-1791].
Philadelphia, Young, 1792.]
(Imprint assumed by Evans from adv. in
25380 for books "published" by Young.)
                                                       25561

A Treatise of Military Exercise,
Calculated for the Use of the Americans
[by Lewis Nicola, 1717-1807].
Philadelphia, Styner & Cist, 1776. viii, 91,
[1] pp., 9 plates.
AAS copy.   14947

A Treatise on Church-Government in
Three Parts [by Ebenezer Chaplin,
1733-1822].
Boston, Boyles, 1773. 37, [3] pp.
AAS copy.   12714

A Treatise on Dress, Intended as a
Friendly and Seasonable Warning.
New Haven, 1783. 32 pp.
LOC copy.   18216

A Treatise on Silk Worms.
New York, Allen, 1793. 30, [2] pp.
NYHS copy.   26276

[Treatise on the Dismal Effects of Low
Spiritedness.
New York, 1765.]
("In the Press, and shortly will be
published," N. Y. Gazette, July 15,
1765.)   10192

A Treatise on the Gonorrhoea. By a
Surgeon of Norfolk, Virginia.
Norfolk, 1787. 32 + pp.
(No perfect copy known.)
LOC copy.   20752

A Treatise on the Nature and Subjects of
Christian Baptism [by Moses
Hemmenway, 1735-1811].
Philadelphia, Crukshank, 1790.
[2], 71 pp.
AAS copy.   22944

A Treatise on the Police of London [by
Patrick Colquhoun, 1745-1820].
Philadelphia, Sweitzer for Davies, 1798.
xii, [8], 342, xxiv pp., 1 folding table.
AAS copy.   33538

[A Treatise on Universal Redemption.
Wherein is Contained, many Scripture
Proofs.
Richmond, 1791.]
(JCB has copy lacking imprint but found
too late to include.)   23839

[A Treatise, Proving (a Posteriori) that
most of the Disorders Incident to the Fair
Sex, are Owing to Flatulencies.

Boston, Bushell, 1748.]
("Just published," Boston Evening-Post,
Mar. 14, 1748.)   6253

A Treatise Shewing the Need we Have.
Philadelphia, Armbruster, 1748. 26 pp.
BPL copy.   6254

The Treaty - Its Merits and Demerits
Fairly Discussed and Displayed.
[Boston, 1796.] 141 pp.
AAS copy.   31312

A Tree Planted by the Rivers of Water [by
Cotton Mather, 1663-1728].
Boston, 1704. [2], 69 pp.
AAS copy.   1178

Tremenda [by Cotton Mather, 1663-1728].
Boston, Green for Gray and Edwards,
1721. [2], 40, [1] pp.
AAS copy.   2251

Trenck, Friedrich, freiherr von der,
1726-1794.
The Life of Baron Frederic Trenck.
Philadelphia, Spotswood, 1789. Front., iv,
152; 159, [1] pp.
AAS copy.   22187

Trenck, Friedrich, freiherr von der,
1726-1794.
The Life of Baron Frederic Trenck.
Philadelphia, Spotswood, 1790. front.,
[4], 308 pp.
AAS copy.   46009

Trenck, Friedrich, freiherr von der,
1726-1794.
The Life of Baron Frederic Trenck.
Boston, Belknap & Young, 1792. 417 pp.,
1 plate.
AAS copy.   24861

Trenck, Frederick, freiherr von der,
1726-1794.
The Life of Baron Frederic Trenck.
Philadelphia, Woodhouse, 1792. 345, [1]
pp., 1 plate.
AAS copy.   24862

Trenck, Friedrich, freiherr von der,
1726-1794.
The Life of. . . .
Boston, Edes for Thomas & Andrews,
1793. 200 pp., 1 plate.
AAS copy.   26278

Trenck, Friedrich, freiherr von der,
1726-1794.
The Life of. . . . [4 vol. in 1.]
Boston, Greenough for Larkins, 1793. 107;
100; 92; 120 pp.
Composite set.   46891

Trenck, Friedrich, freiherr von der,
1726-1794.
The Life of. . . . Volume Fourth.
Boston, Larkins, 1793. 120 pp.
AAS copy.   26279

[Trenck, Friedrich, freiherr von der,
1726-1794.
The Life and Adventures of. . . .
Windsor, Vt., Spooner, 1793.]
(Imprint assumed by Evans from adv.
"For Sale, at the Book-Store under this
Office," Spooner's Vermont Journal, Mar.
25, 1793.)   26277

Trenck, Friedrich, freiherr von der,
1726-1794.
The Life of. . . .
Albany, Spencer, 1794. 345 pp., 1 plate.
AAS copy.   27812-3

Trenck, Friedrich, freiherr von der,
1726-1794.
The Life of. . . .
Philadelphia, Campbell, 1794. 256, 68 pp.,
1 plate.
AAS copy.   27814

Trenck, Friedrich, freiherr von der,
1726-1794.
The Life of Baron Frederick Trenck.
New York, Durell, 1796. 187 pp.
(Evans assumed the plate from other eds.)
AAS copy.   31313

Trenck, Friedrich, freiherr von der,
1726-1794.
The Life of Baron Frederic Trenck.

Philadelphia, Woodward, 1798. 394 pp.
HEH copy.   34678

Trenck, Friedrich, freiherr von der,
1726-1794.
The Life of Baron Frederick Trenck.
New York, Falconer, 1799. 144 pp.
NYPL copy.   36447

Trenck, Friedrich, freiherr von der,
1726-1794.
The Life of Baron Frederick Trenck.
Philadelphia, R. Johnson for B. & J.
Johnson, 1799. 198 pp., 1 plate.
AAS copy.   36446

Trent, Joseph.
An Inquiry into the Effects of Light.
Philadelphia, Way & Groff, 1800. 38 pp.
AAS copy.   38666

Trenton, N. J.
Order of the Funeral Procession . . . the
14th Day of January, 1800, in
Commemoration of . . . Washington.
n. p., n. d. Broadside.
NJHS copy.   38667

Trenton, N. J.
Verses, Composed and Sung . . . on the
. . . Funeral Eulogium in . . . Memory of
. . . Washington.
n. p., [1800]. Broadside.
HEH copy.   38668

Trenton, N. J. Library Company.
Laws and Regulations . . . May, 1797.
Trenton, Day, 1798. 18 pp.
NJHS copy.   34679

Trenton, N. J. Ordinances, etc.
Acts and Ordinances.
Trenton, Sherman, Mershon & Thomas,
1799. [2], 38 pp.
(Sold City Book Auction, Sept. 6, 1952.)
LOC ph copy.   36448

Trenton, June 5. By the Mail which
Arrived Last Evening we have Received
the Following. . . .
Trenton, Quequelle & Wilson, [1788].
Broadside.
NYPL copy.   21469

Le Tresor des Consolations.
New York, 1696. [5], 98 pp.
HSP copy.   775

[Treuhertzige Erinnerung und Warnung.
Philadelphia, Franklin & Armbruester,
1756.]
(Title from Seidensticker.)   7805

Treuhertzige Erinnerung [by Henry
Kemper].
Hannover, Stettinius, 1798. 110 pp.
LCP copy.   48493

Treuhertzige und Einfaeltige Anweisung.
Germantown, 1749. 40 pp.
HSP copy.   6433

[TrezIulneY,-.
A Letter to Washington.
Philadelphia, 1796. 48 pp.]
(A ghost of 31315, q. v.)   31314

The Trial of Abraham [by Christoph
Martin Wieland, 1733-1813].
[Boston], 1760. vi, 70, 4 pp.
(A variant of 41510; see Modern
Language Notes, Apr. 1930, pp. 246-247.)
                                                       41511

The Trial of Abraham [by Christoph
Martin Wieland, 1733-1813].
[Boston], 1764. vi, 70 pp.
AAS copy.   41510

The Trial of Abraham [by Christoph
Martin Wieland, 1733-1813].
Norwich, Trumbull, 1777. v, 60 pp.
NYPL copy.   15711

The Trial of Atticus before Justice Bean,
for a Rape.
Boston, Thomas, 1771. 55 pp.
NYPL copy.   42291

The Trial of Mr. Whitefield's Spirit [by
Samuel Weller, of Maidstone, Eng.].
Boston, Fleet, 1741. 46 pp.
AAS copy.   4837

The Trial of the Witnesses of the
Resurrection [by Thomas Sherlock,
1678-1761].
Philadelphia, Dobson, 1788. 143, [1] pp.
AAS copy.   21461

The Trial of Time - Presented by the
Carrier of the Connecticut Journal. . . .
January 1, 1800.
[New Haven, 1800.] Broadside.
LOC copy.   37240

The Trials of Eight Persons Indited for
Piracy.
Boston, Green for Edwards, 1718. [2], 25
pp.
MHS copy.   2003

The Trials of Five Persons for Piracy.
Boston, Fleet for Gerrish, 1726. 34 pp.
AAS copy.   2818

The Tribe of Asher [by Cotton Mather,
1663-1728].
Boston, 1717. [2], 34 pp.
BODL copy.   1908

Tribute to Caesar.
[Philadelphia, 1715?] [3], 29 pp.
(Attributed to Thomas Maule by Evans.
See Sabin, XXV, 476, and Essex Institute
Hist. Coll., LXXII, 42.)
HSP copy.   1572

A Tribute to the Memory of Catherine
Berrenger.
n. p., [1800]. Broadside.
AAS copy.   38670

Tribute to the Memory of Washington.
[Salem, 1799?] Broadside.
(Also entered as 38452, q. v.)   36449

A Tribute to Washington, for February
22d, 1800 [by John Lovett, 1761-1818].
Troy, Moffitt, 1800. 15 pp.
BrU copy.   37852

The Trifle-Hunter: or, The Adventures of
Prince Bonbennin.
Hartford, Babcock, 1798. 28, [3] pp.
AAS copy.   48646

The Trifle-Hunter. . . . First Newport
Edition.
Newport, R. I., Farnsworth, 1799. 29, [2]
pp.
AAS copy.   36450

Trimmer, Sarah (Kirby), 1741-1810.
An Easy Introduction to the Knowledge of
Nature.
Boston, Manning & Loring for West, 1796.
147, [1], 8 pp.
AAS copy.   31316

Trimmer, Sarah (Kirby), 1741-1810.
Fabulous Histories.
Philadelphia, Gibbons, 1794. 214 pp.
AAS copy.   27817

Trimmer, Sarah (Kirby), 1741-1810.
Fabulous Histories.
Baltimore, Keatinge, 1795. 214 pp.
(An imprint variant of 27817, q. v.)   47632

Trimmer, Sarah (Kirby), 1741-1810.
Fabulous Histories.
Philadelphia, J. Johnson, 1795. 214 pp.
(An imprint variant of 27817, q. v.)   47633

Trip, Tom, pseud.
Tommy Trip's History of the Beasts.
New York, Durell, 1800. 31 pp.
(Not located.)   49154

[Trip, Tom, pseud.
Tommy Trip's Pictures of Beasts and
Birds.
Boston, Hall, 1793.]
(Imprint assumed by Evans from Hall's
advs.)   26282

Triplett, Thomas.
An Inaugural Dissertation on Apoplexy.
Philadelphia, Way & Groff, 1798. 32 pp.
AAS copy.   34680

Tripp, John, 1761-1847.
The Bible the Word of God.
Boston, Bumstead, 1800. 62 pp.
BPL copy.   38672

Tripp, John, 1761-1847.
The Cherubims Explained.
Boston, Bumstead, 1795. 30, [1] pp.
AAS copy.   29657

The Tripple-Plea (by Samuel Keimer,
1688-1742].
Philadelphia, Keimer, [1723?] Broadside.
HEH copy.   39793

[Trisobio, Filippo.]
La Marmotte. Avec Accompagnement de
Harpe.
Philadelphia, Trisobio, [1797?] [2] pp.
NYPL copy.   48276

The Triumph of Infidelity [by Timothy
Dwight, 1752-1817].
Printed in the World, 1788. 24 pp.
AAS copy.   21066

The Triumph of Infidelity [by Timothy
Dwight, 1752-1817].
Printed in the World, 1788. 40 pp.
AAS copy.   21065

The Triumph of the Whigs: or, T'other
Congress Convened.
New York, Rivington, 1775. 8 pp.
NYHS copy.   14523

The Triumphant Christian.
Boston, Kneeland & Green, 1736. 42 pp.
AAS copy.   4087

The Triumphant Christian; or, Faith's
Victory. . . . Fifth Edition.
Boston, Kneeland, 1755. [2], 29 pp.
AAS copy.   7580

The Triumphant Christian. . . . Fifteenth
Edition.
New York, Farley, 1762. 40 pp.
NYPL copy.   41315

The Triumphant Christian: or, Faith's
Victory. . . . Sixth Edition.
Boston, Mills & Hicks, [1774]. 39 pp.
AAS copy.   13688

The Triumphant Christian: or Faith's
Victory. . . . Seventh Edition.
Hartford, [Ct.], Babcock, 1800. 36 pp.
CHS copy.   38673

The Triumphs of Faith Manifested to the
World. . . . [By] S. M.
[New London], Green, 1749. Broadside.
CHS copy.   40519

The Triumphs of Grace by [La Musse,
Marguerite de], 1665-1681.
Boston, Crump for Henchman, 1717. [2],
iii, 86 pp.
(The only copy located is imperfect.)
BPL copy.   1933

The Triumphs of Justice.
[Boston], 1732. [4], 27 pp.
AAS copy.   40005

The Triumphs of Love [by John Murdock,
1748-1834].
Philadelphia, Folwell, 1795. 83, [1] pp., 1
plate.
AAS copy.   29129

The Triumphs of Superstition: an Elegy
[by Thaddeus Mason Harris, 1768-1842].
Boston, Thomas & Andrews, 1790. 16 pp.
AAS copy.   22556

The Triumvirate of Pennsylvania.
[Philadelphia, 1725?] 4 pp.
LCP copy.   2712

[The Trooper's pocket companion.
Rutland, 1794.]
(McCorison 313; no copy known.)   47243

Trotter, Thomas, 1760-1832.
Observations on the Scurvy.
Philadelphia, Parker, 1793. 76 pp.
AAS copy.   26283

. . . . The Troubles of Life.
Philadelphia, Johnsons, 1800. 36 pp.
AAS copy.   37159

[Troy, N. Y. Convention.
Spirit of '76. At a numerous Meeting of
the Young Men of Troy . . . April 15,
1800.

n.p., n.d. Broadside.]
(Now dated 1809 by LOC.)   38545

Troy, N. Y. Library.
Laws and Catalogue of Troy Library. . . .
January 15th, 1800.
Troy, [Penniman for] Moffitt, 1800. 20
pp.
BA copy.   38674

Troy, Jan. 1, 1798. . . . The News-Lad's
Address, to the Readers of the Farmer's
Oracle [by Philip Morin Freneau,
1752-1832].
[Troy, 1798.] Broadside.
NYHS copy.   48444

A True Account of a Young Lady in
Boston, whose Father was Resolved she
should Marry a rich Frenchman.
Bennington, Vt., Haswell & Russell, 1790.
Broadside.
AAS copy.   46010

A True Account of the Loss of the Ship
Columbia.
Portsmouth, Mar. 28, 1792. Broadside.
NYHS copy.   24863

A True and Authentic History of His
Excellency George Washington [by
Jedidiah Morse, 1761-1836].
Philadelphia, Stewart, 1790. 23, [1] pp.
BA copy.   22933

A True and Exact History of the Jesuits.
Albany, Websters, 1790. 24 pp.
AAS copy.   46011

A True and Exact Relation [by
Winchilsea, Heneage Finch, 3d Earl of, d.
1689].
Cambridge, 1669. 18, [1] pp.
AAS copy.   139

A True and Faithful Narrative of the
Modes . . . [by William Goddard,
1740-1817].
Philadelphia, Goddard, 1771. 7 pp.
AAS copy.   12253

A True and Faithful Narrative of the
Proceedings of the House of Burgesses . . .
Feb. 5, 1739, 40.
[Boston, 1740?]. [2], 52 pp.
(Usually described as a Williamsburg
imprint, but the ornaments are from the
cases of Draper and Kneeland & Green.)
MHS copy.   4582

A True and Historical Narrative of the
Colony of Georgia.
Charleston, 1741. [2], xxiv, 176 pp.
NYPL copy.   4816

A True and Historical Narrative of the
Colony of Georgia.
Charleston, 1741. xviii, 118 pp.
(This edition was printed in London; see
De Renne cat.)
AAS copy.   4817

A True and Impartial State of the
Province of Pennsylvania.
Philadelphia, Dunlap, 1759. [2], v, [1],
3-173, [1], 34, [1] pp.
(The AAS has a variant issue. For
authorship see Sabin 60742.)
AAS copy.   8349

[A True and Particular Account
Contained in the Lives, Last Words and
Dying Confessions of . . . John Baptist
Collins, Emanuel Furtado, Augustus
Palacha.
Boston, Russell, 1794.]
(Title taken by Evans from adv. in 27563,
apparently for 27819.)   27818

A True and Particular Narrative of the
late Tremendous Tornado . . . July 1,
1792.
Boston, Russell, [1792]. Broadside.
NYHS copy.   24864

A True and Particular Relation of the
Dreadful Earthquake [by Pedro Lozano,
1697-1752].
Philadelphia, Franklin & Hall, 1749. 52
pp.
AAS copy.   6348

[A True and Particular Relation of the

Dreadful Earthquake [by Pedro Lozano, 1697-1752].
Boston, Fowle, [1750]. 8 pp.]
(From Sabin.)   6531

A True and Particular Relation of the
Dreadful Earthquake [by Pedro Lozano, 1697-1752],
Boston, Fowle, [1755?]. 8 pp.
AAS copy.   7453

A True and Wonderful Narrative of the
Surprising Captivity and Remarkable
Deliverance of Mrs. Frances Scott.
Boston, Russell, 1786. 24 pp.
MHS copy.   19979

A True and Wonderful Narrative of Two
Intire Particular Phoenomena.
Philadelphia, Armbruster, 1764. 4 pp.
JCB copy.   41495

The True Assistant Society of Hatters, of
the City of New-York.
Rules and Regulations, Adopted by the.
. . .
[New York, 1795.] 14 pp.
AAS copy.   47635

The True Assistant Society of Hatters, of
the City of New-York.
Rules and Regulations, Adopted by the.
. . .
[New York, 1795.] 14 pp.
AAS copy.   47635

True Copies of . . . The Agreement
between Lord Baltimore and Messieurs
Penn, dated 10 May 1732.
[Philadelphia, 1734?] 7, [1] pp.
(See Streeter, Americana, pp. 30-31.
Evans' entry is from an adv. in Pa.
Gazette, Feb. 3, 1736/7.)
LCP copy.   4182

A True Copy of a Genuine Letter, Sent
to the Archbishop of Canterbury.
New York, Steuart, 1761. 16 pp.
BA copy.   9027

A True Copy of a Genuine Letter Sent to
the Archbishop of Canterbury.
Boston, Edes & Gill, 1762. 15 pp.
AAS copy.   9288

True Copy of a Letter, from a Member of
St. P[au]l's.
[Philadelphia], 1764. 8 pp.
LCP copy.   9857

A True Copy of an Inimitable and
Incomprehensible Doggrel
[Philadelphia], Black-Beard (Steuart),
1763. Broadside.
LCP copy.   9525

A True Copy of the Oaths that are
Appointed. . . .
[Boston, 1693.] Broadside.
MA copy.   39306

A True Copy of Three Judgments [by
George Keith, 1638-1716].
[Philadelphia, 1692.] 1-9, 2-3, 12-13, 6-7,
[1] pp.
(William Smith gives author as Thomas
Budd.)
LOC copy.   608

A True Description of a Number of
Tyrannical Pedagogues.
[Boston], 1769. 8 pp.
AAS copy.   11210

The True Interest of America Impartially
Stated [by Charles Inglis, bp., 1734-1816].
Philadelphia, Humphreys, 1776. 71 pp.
AAS copy.   14809

The True Interest of America Impartially
Stated. . . . Second Edition [by Charles
Inglis, bp., 1734-1816].
Philadelphia, Humphreys, 1776. 71 pp.
AAS copy.   14810

The True Interest of the United States,
and Particularly of Pennsylvania [by
William Barton, 1755?-1817].
Philadelphia, Cist, 1786. [2], 31 pp.
NYPL copy.   19498

The True Means of Establishing Public

Happiness [by Timothy Dwight, 1752-1817].
New Haven, Greens for Beers, [1795].
[2], 40 pp.
AAS copy.   28610

A True Narrative of a most Stupendous
Trance and Vision . . . at Sharon . . .
January, 1789.
Printed for the booksellers, 1793. 12 pp.
AAS copy.   46892

The True Nature and Cause of the Tails of
Comets [by John Perkins, 1698-1781].
Boston, Edes & Gill, 1772. 8 pp.
AAS copy.   12517

True Pleasure, Chearfulness, and
Happiness.
Philadelphia, Bradfords, 1767. 22 pp.
JCB copy.   10787

The True Sons of Liberty and Supporters
of the Non-Importation Agreement.
[Boston, 1768.] Broadside.
MHS copy.   11097

The True State of Mr. Rou's Case [by
Lewis Rou, 1676?-1750].
New York, Bradford, 1726. 34 pp.
HSP copy.   2811

A True State of the Case of R[ebecca]
R[ichardson].
[Philadelphia, 1755.] 15 pp.
LCP copy.   7414

[A True State of the Establishment of the
Church of England in the Province.
Philadelphia, 1766.]
(Adv. Pa. Gazette, May 8, 1766.)   10510

[A True State of the Establishment of the
Church of England in this Province.
Philadelphia, 1737.]
(Adv. Pa. Gazette, July 21, 1737.)   4203

A True State of the Proceedings in the
Parliament of Great Britain [by Arthur
Lee, 1740-1792].
Philadelphia, Crukshank, 1774. 39 pp.
LCP copy.   13282

A True Survey & Report of the Road [by
Cotton Mather, 1663-1728].
Boston, 1712. [2], 46 pp.
AAS copy.   1561

Trueman, Roger, pseud.
The United States Almanack for . . . 1781.
Chatham, N. J., Kollock.
C. A. Philhower (of Westfield, N. J.) copy.
                                                   17009

Trueman, Roger, pseud.
The United States Almanack, for . . .
1783.
Chatham, Kollock. [36] pp.
AAS copy.   17747

Trueman, Timothy, pseud.
The Burlington Almanack for . . . 1771.
Burlington, Collins. [40] pp.
AAS copy.   11899

Trueman, Timothy, pseud.
New-Jersey. The Burlington Almanack,
for . . . 1772.
Burlington, Collins. [40] pp.
LOC copy.   12254

Trueman, Timothy, pseud.
New-Jersey. The Burlington Almanack for
. . . 1773.
Burlington, Collins. [40] pp.
AAS copy.   12584

Trueman, Timothy, pseud.
New-Jersey. The Burlington Almanack for
. . . 1774.
Burlington, Collins. [40] pp.
NYHS copy.   13048

Trueman, Timothy, pseud.
New-Jersey. The Burlington Almanack for
. . . 1775.
Burlington, Collins. [40] pp.
AAS copy.   13690

Trueman, Timothy, pseud.
New-Jersey. The Burlington Almanack for
. . . 1776.

Burlington, Collins. [40] pp.
LOC copy.   14524

Trueman, Timothy, pseud.
New-Jersey. The Burlington Almanack for
. . . 1777.
Burlington, Collins. [36] pp.
AAS copy.   15118

Trueman, Timothy, pseud.
New-Jersey. The Burlington Almanack for
. . . 1778.
Burlington, Collins. [36] pp.
AAS copy.   15617

Trueman, Timothy, pseud.
The New-Jersey Almanack for . . . 1779.
Trenton, Collins. [32] pp.
AAS copy.   16095

Trueman, Timothy, pseud.
The New-Jersey Almanac for . . . 1780.
Trenton, Collins. [36] pp.
AAS copy.   16549

Trueman, Timothy, pseud.
The New-Jersey Almanack for . . . 1781.
Trenton, Collins. [36] pp.
AAS copy.   17010

Trueman, Timothy, pseud.
The New-Jersey Almanack, for . . . 1782.
Trenton, Collins. [36] pp.
AAS copy.   17380

Trueman, Timothy, pseud.
The New-Jersey Almanack for . . . 1783.
Trenton, Collins. [36] pp.
AAS copy.   17748

Trueman, Timothy, pseud.
The New-Jersey Almanack for . . . 1784.
Trenton, Collins. [40] pp.
AAS copy.   18217

Trueman, Timothy, pseud.
The New-Jersey Almanack for . . . 1785.
Trenton, Collins. [40] pp.
AAS copy.   18811

Trueman, Timothy, pseud.
The New-Jersey Almanack for . . . 1786.
Trenton, Collins. [40] pp.
AAS copy.   19276

Trueman, Timothy, pseud.
The New-Jersey Almanack for . . . 1787.
Trenton, Collins. [40] pp.
AAS copy.   20034

Trueman, Timothy, pseud.
The New-Jersey Pocket Almanack for . . .
1781.
Trenton, Collins. [24] pp.
Trenton Public Library copy.   17011

Trueman, Timothy, pseud.
The New-Jersey Pocket Almanack for . . .
1782.
Trenton, Collins.
Rutgers University copy.   17381

[Truman, Mr., pseud.
Mr. Truman's Observations.
New York, 1736.]
(Adv. N. Y. Gazette, Feb. 3, 1735/6. This
is probably the same as 4088.)   4089

Truman, Thomas, 1752-1786.
An Oration: Delivered in Public. . . .
Providence, Carter, [1782]. [2], 14 pp.
AAS copy.   17749

Trumbull, Benjamin, 1735-1820.
An Appeal to the Public.
New Haven, Meigs, 1788. 53, [1] pp.
AAS copy.   21506

Trumbull, Benjamin, 1735-1820.
A Complete History of Connecticut. . . .
Vol. I.
Hartford, Hudson & Goodwin, 1797. xix,
[1], 587 pp., 1 map, 3 plates.
AAS copy.   32942

Trumbull, Benjamin, 1735-1820.
(Weis, Colonial Clergy N. E.)
A Discourse, Delivered at the
Anniversary Meeting.
New Haven, 1773. 38 pp.
AAS copy.   13049

Trumbull, Benjamin, 1735-1820.
God is to be Praised for the Glory.
New Haven, 1784. 37, [1] pp.
AAS copy. 18812

Trumbull, Benjamin, 1735-1820.
God is to be Praised for the Glory. . . .
Second Edition.
New Haven, [1784]. 28 pp.
AAS copy. 18813

Trumbull, Benjamin, 1735-1820.
Illustrations on the Counsel of God.
Springfield, 1783. 36 pp.
AAS copy. 18218

Trumbull, Benjamin, 1735-1820.
Illustrations on the Nature.
New London, Greens, 1791. 23 pp.
AAS copy. 23840

[Trumbull, Benjamin], 1735-1820.
(Weis, Colonial Clergy N. E.)
A Letter to an Honourable Gentleman of
the Council-Board.
New Haven, 1766. 26 pp.
HC copy. 10511

Trumbull, Benjamin, 1735-1820.
The Majesty and Mortality.
New Haven, [Ct.], Read & Morse, 1800.
31 pp.
AAS copy. 38679

Trumbull, Benjamin, 1735-1820.
A Plea, in Vindication.
New Haven, 1774. 102, [1] pp.
JCB copy. 13691

Trumbull, Benjamin, 1735-1820.
A Plea in Vindication.
New Haven, 1774. 160, [1] pp.
AAS copy. 13692

Trumbull, Benjamin, 1735-1820.
Proposals for Publishing by
Subscription. . . . A Complete History of
Connecticut.
[Hartford, 1796.] Broadside.
JCB copy. 31318

Trumbull, Benjamin, 1735-1820.
A Sermon, Delivered at the Installation of
. . . Alexander Gillet.
New Haven, Greens, 1793. [2], 20 pp.
CHS copy. 26287

Trumbull, Benjamin, 1735-1820.
A Sermon, Delivered at the Ordination of
. . . Aaron Woodward.
New Haven, Greens, 1794. 23 pp.
AAS copy. 27821

Trumbull, Benjamin, 1735-1820.
A Sermon, Delivered at the Ordination of
. . . Lemuel Tyler.
New Haven, Greens, 1793. [2], 20 pp.
AAS copy. 26285

Trumbull, Benjamin, 1735-1820.
A Sermon, Delivered at the Ordination of
. . . Reuben Moss.
New Haven, Greens, 1793. [2], 21 pp.
AAS copy. 26286

Trumbull, Benjamin, 1735-1820.
A Sermon, Delivered at the Ordination of
. . . Thomas Holt.
Worcester, Thomas, 1790. 36 pp.
AAS copy. 22945

Trumbull, Benjamin, 1735-1820.
Twelve Discourses.
Hartford, Ct., Hudson & Goodwin, 1799.
x, 305 pp.
AAS copy. 36455

[Trumbull, John], 1750-1831.
The Double Conspiracy, or Treason
Discovered.
[Hartford], 1783. 85, [2] pp.
AAS copy. 17918

[Trumbull, John], 1750-1831.
(D. A. B.)
An Elegy on the Times. . . . September 20,
A.D. 1774.
Boston, 1774.]
(Printed in a newspaper. Probably the first
separate printing was 14525, q.v.) 13693

[Trumbull, John], 1750-1831.

An Elegy on the Times: First Printed at
Boston.
New Haven, 1775. 15, [1] pp.
AAS copy. 14525

[Trumbull, John. 1750-1831.
(D. A. B.)
Epithalamium.
New Haven, 1769?]
(Separate publication of this poem was
assumed by Evans.) 11504

[Trumbull, John], 1750-1831.
An Essay on the Use and Advantages of
the Fine Arts.
New Haven, [1770]. 16 pp.
AAS copy. 11901

[Trumbull, John], 1750-1831.
M'Fingall: a Modern Epic Poem.
Philadelphia, Bradfords, 1775. [2], 40 pp.
AAS copy. 14528

[Trumbull, John], 1750-1831.
M'Fingal.
Hartford, Hudson & Goodwin, 1782. 100
pp.
AAS copy. 17750

[Trumbull, John], 1750-1831.
M'Fingal.
Hartford, Patten, 1782. 96 pp.
(For the text of this ed. see 17752.)
NYPL copy. 17751

[Trumbull, John], 1750-1831.
M'Fingal.
Hartford, Webster, 1782. 96 pp.
AAS copy. 17752

[Trumbull, John], 1750-1831.
M'Fingal.
Boston, Edes, 1785. 110 pp.
AAS copy. 19277

[Trumbull, John], 1750-1831.
M'Fingal.
Philadelphia, Carey, 1787. 125 pp.
AAS copy. 20754

Trumbull, John, 1750-1831.
M'Fingal.
Philadelphia, Carey, 1791. 95, [1] pp.
AAS copy. 23841

Trumbull, John, 1750-1831.
M'Fingal.
New York, Buel, 1795. vii, [1], 136 pp., 9
plates.
AAS copy. 29659

Trumbull, John, 1750-1831.
M'Fingal: a Modern Epic Poem.
Boston, Manning & Loring for Larkin,
1799. 141, [3] pp.
AAS copy. 36456

[Trumbull, John], 1750-1831.
A New Proclamation! By Thomas
Gage. . . .
[Hartford, 1775.] 8 pp.
LOC copy. 14526

[Trumbull, John], 1750-1831.
The Progress of Dulness.
[New Haven], 1772. 26 pp.
HC copy. 12585

[Trumbull, John], 1750-1831.
The Progress of Dulness, Part First. . . .
Second Edition.
[New Haven], 1773. 20 pp.
AAS copy. 13050

[Trumbull, John], 1750-1831.
The Progress of Dulness, Part Second.
[New Haven], 1773. 27, [1] pp.
AAS copy. 13051

[Trumbull, John], 1750-1831.
The Progress of Dulness. Part Third.
New Haven, 1773. 28 pp.
AAS copy. 13052

[Trumbull, John], 1750-1831.
The Progress of Dulness.
Exeter, Ranlet, 1794. 72 pp.
AAS copy. 27822

Trumbull, John, 1750-1831.
The Progress of Dulness.

Carlisle, Pa., Kline for Loudon, 1797. 72
pp.
BrU copy. 32943

[Trumbull, John], 1750-1831.
Thomas Gage's Proclamation
Versified. . . . June 30, 1775.
[New York, 1775.] Broadside.
HSP copy. 14527

Trumbull, John, 1756-1843.
New York, April 2, 1790. Proposals for
Publishing . . . The Death of Maj. Gen.
Warren. . . .
[New York], Fenno, [1790.] [2], 2, pp.
LOC copy. 22946

Trusdell, William.
New-York Mayor's Court. . . . Aug. 25,
1733.
[New York, 1733.] Broadside.
(No copy located.) 40033

Trustaff, Sir George Jeoffery, pseud.
A Foreigner's Scribble for Amusement.
New York, 1793. 20 pp.
NYHS copy. 26288

Truth Exploded; or, The Art of Lying and
Swearing, made Easy.
Hartford, 1796. 15 pp.
CHS copy. 47942

Truth is Great [by Isaac Backus,
1724-1806].
Boston, Freeman, [1781]. 36, 8 pp.
AAS copy. 17083

Truth Triumphant or, A Defence of the
Church of England.
New York, 1769. 64 pp.
AAS copy. 11505

Truth Will Out! [by Benjamin Franklin
Bache, 1769-1798].
[Philadelphia, 1798.] [4], 12 pp.
AAS copy. 33648

Truxtun, Thomas, 1755-1822.
Remarks Instructions, and Examples
Relating to the Latitude & Longitude.
Philadelphia, Dobson, 1794. pp. [3]-8,
[1]-74, [1]-31, [1], [i]-xxiii, 2 folded
plates.
AAS copy. 27823

The Tryal and Character of a real
Christian. . . . Fourth Edition [by John
Shower, 1657-1715].
New York, Bradford and Deforest, 1744.
[2], xxiv, 118 (i.e. 119) pp.
NYHS copy. 40350

The Tryal of the Witnesses of the
Resurrection [by Thomas Sherlock,
1678-1761]
New London, 1754. 120 pp.
AAS copy. 7314

The Tryals of Sixteen Persons for Piracy.
Boston, Edwards, 1726. 24, [1] pp.
AAS copy. 2819

The Tryed Professor [by Cotton Mather,
1663-1728].
Boston, Kneeland, 1719. 16 pp.
AAS copy. 2047

[Tryon, Thomas, 1634-1703.
(D. N. B.)
Some Memoirs of the Life of. . . .
Philadelphia, Dunlap, 1761.]
(Pa. Gazette, Sept. 10, 1761.) 9028

[Tryon, Thomas, 1634-1703.
(D. N. B.)
The Way to Health.
Philadelphia, Dunlap, 1758.]
(See Hildeburn 1609.) 8271

Tscherning, Valerius.
Catechismus, oder Kurzer Unterricht.
Philadelphia, Baird, 1786. [16], 392 pp.
AAS copy. 44983

Tubbs, Thomas.
Advertisement. Ran away . . . William
Haly. . . . Boston, March 22. 1753.
[Boston, 1753.] Broadside.
BPL copy. 40676

Tucke, John, 1702-1773.
The Ministers of Christ.

Portsmouth, Fowle, [1762]. 47 pp.
JCB copy.   41316

Tucker, Benjamin, 1734-1806.
To the Author of the Book, Entitled
"Letters and Remarks. . . ."
[Worcester, 1795.] 7 pp.
AAS copy.   29661

Tucker, John, 1719-1792.
(Sibley, XI.)
A Brief Account.
[Boston, 1767.] 12 pp.
AAS copy.   10788

Tucker, John, 1719-1792.
A Brief Account. . . . To which is
Annexed. . . .
Boston, Mein & Fleeming, [1767]. [2],
42, 14 pp.
AAS copy.   10789

Tucker, John, 1719-1792.
(Sibley, XI.)
The Example of Christ.
Boston, Kneeland, 1751. [4], 40 pp.
AAS copy.   6792

Tucker, John, 1719-1792.
(Sibley, XI.)
Four Sermons.
Boston, Kneeland, 1756. [4], viii, 99 pp.
AAS copy.   7806

Tucker, John, 1719-1792.
(Sibley, XI.)
God's Goodness.
Boston, Kneeland, 1757. [2], 23 pp.
AAS copy.   8049

Tucker, John, 1719-1792.
A Letter to the Rev. Mr. James Chandler.
Boston, Fleets, for Balch, 1767. 27 pp.
AAS copy.   10790

Tucker, John, 1719-1792.
(Sibley, XI.)
Ministers Considered.
Boston, Fleets, 1768. 28 pp.
AAS copy.   11098

Tucker, John, 1719-1792.
Ministers of the Gospel.
Boston, Fleets for Emerson, 1767. 36 pp.
AAS copy.   10791

[Tucker, John], 1719-1792.
Observations on the Doctrines.
Boston, Edes & Gill, 1757. 70 pp.
AAS copy.   8050

Tucker, John, 1719-1792.
(Sibley, XI.)
Remarks on a Discourse.
Boston, Mills & Hicks, 1774. 36 pp.
AAS copy.   13694

Tucker, John, 1719-1792.
Remarks on a Sermon of the Rev. Aaron
Hutchinson.
Boston, Fleets, for Balch, [1767]. 47 pp.
AAS copy.   10792

Tucker, John, 1719-1792.
Remarks on . . . James Chandler's Serious
Address.
Boston, Fleets, Emerson, and Balch,
1768. 43 pp.
AAS copy.   11099

Tucker, John, 1719-1792.
A Reply to the Rev. Mr. Chandler's
Answer.
Boston, Fleets, Emerson, and Balch, 1768.
55 pp.
AAS copy.   11100

Tucker, John, 1719-1792.
The Rev. Aaron Hutchinson's Reply.
Boston, Fleets, Emerson, and Balch, 1768.
40 pp.
AAS copy.   11101

Tucker, John, 1719-1792.
A Sermon, Delivered at Newbury-Port,
August 14th, 1788.
Newburyport, 1788. 52 pp.
AAS copy.   21507

Tucker, John, 1719-1792.
(Sibley, XI.)
A Sermon Preached at Cambridge.

Boston, Draper, 1771. 63 pp.
AAS copy.   12256

Tucker, John, 1719-1792.
(Sibley, XI.)
A Sermon Preached at the Ordination of
. . . Amos Moody.
Boston, Fleets, 1766. 34 pp.
AAS copy.   10512

Tucker, John, 1719-1792.
(Sibley, XI.)
The Two Following Sermons. . . .
Boston, Fleets for Emerson, 1769. 31 pp.
AAS copy.   11506

Tucker, John, 1719-1792.
The Validity of Presbyterian Ordination.
Boston, Fleets, [1778]. 32 pp.
AAS copy.   16096

Tucker, Josiah, 1712-1799.
The True Interest of Britain.
Philadelphia, Bell, 1776. 66, [6] pp.
AAS copy.   15119

Tucker, Josiah, 1712-1799.
The True Interest of Britain.
Philadelphia, Bell, 1776. 66, [6] pp.
JCB copy.   43177

[Tucker, Josiah, 1712-1799.]
The True Interest of Britain. . . . Second
Edition.
Philadelphia, Bell, 1776. 66, [6] pp.]
(No 2nd ed. has been distinguished.)
                                             15120

[Tucker, Nathaniel], 1750-1807.
The Bermudian. A Poem.
Williamsburg, Purdie & Dixon, 1774. [8], 15
pp.
AAS copy.   13695

Tucker, St. George, 1752-1827.
A Dissertation on Slavery.
Philadelphia, Carey, 1796. [6], [9]-106
pp.
AAS copy.   31319

Tucker, St. George, 1752-1827.
The Knight and Friars.
New York, [Oswald], 1786.
BrU - H copy.   20035

[Tucker, St. George], 1752-1827.
A Letter to a Member of Congress.
n. p., [1799]. 48 pp.
HC copy.   36457

[Tucker, St. George], 1752-1827.
A Letter, to the Rev. Jedediah Morse.
Richmond, Nicolson, 1795. 16 pp.
AAS copy.   29662

[Tucker, St. George], 1752-1827.
Liberty, a Poem on the Independence of
America.
Richmond, Davis, 1788. 20 pp.
JCB copy.   21508

[Tucker, St. George], 1752-1827.
The Probationary Odes of Jonathan
Pindar.
Philadelphia, Balch, 1796. [2], 103 pp.
LCP copy.   31320

[Tucker, St. George], 1752-1827.
Reflections on the Policy and Necessity of
Encouraging the Commerce . . . of the
United States.
New York, Loudons, 1786. 16 pp.
LCP copy.   20036

Tucker, St. George, 1752-1827.
To the Public. My Connection with Mr.
Richard Randolph. . . . May 5, 1793.
[Fredericksburg? 1793.] 1 p.
(Not located, 1968.)   46893

Tucker, Thomas Tudor, 1745-1828.
An Oration Delivered in St. Michael's
Church.
Charleston, Timothy & Mason, [1795].
27 pp.
MHS copy.   29663

Tucker, Thomas Tudor, 1745-1828.
To the Honorable the President and
Senate. . . .
n. p., [1795]. 3 pp.
LOC copy.   47634

Tucker & Thayer, firm, Boston.
Tucker & Thayer, No. 19 Cornhill,
Boston, import. . . .
[Boston, 1800?] Broadside.
(Two variants reproduced.)
EI copies.   49155

Tuckerman, Joseph, 1778-1840.
A Funeral Oration. . . . Washington.
Boston, Manning & Loring, [1800]. 24 pp.
AAS copy.   38680

Tudor, William, 1750-1819.
An Oration, Delivered March 5th, 1779.
Boston, Edes & Gill, 1779. 23 pp.
AAS copy.   16550

Tuesday Club, Annapolis, Md.
By Permission of . . . the President. . . .
July 15, 1755.
[Annapolis, 1755.] Broadside.
LOC copy.   40806

Tuesday Club, Annapolis, Md.
Sir, I hope that I shall have the Honour of
your Company. . . . December 2, 1755.
[Annapolis, Green, 1755.] Broadside.
LOC copy.   40807

Tufts, Cotton, 1731-1815.
An Oration, in Honour . . . of . . .
Washington.
Boston, Hall, 1800. 19 pp.
AAS copy.   38681

[Tufts, John], 1689-1750.
Anti-Ministerial Objections Considered.
Boston, Green for Gerrish, 1725. [2], 45
pp.
AAS copy.   2713

[Tufts, John], 1689-1750.
(Sibley, V, 457-461.)
A Collection of Thirty-Eight Psalm Tunes.
Boston, 1723.]
(See Music Lib. Assoc., Notes, XI,
47, and Boston News-Letter, Oct.
15, 1722, Jan. 28, Mar. 21, July 4, and
Nov. 21, 1723.)   2488

Tufts, John, 1689-1750.
(Sibley, V, 457-461.)
A Humble Call to Archippus.
Boston, Gerrish, 1729. [6], 25 pp.
AAS copy.   3225

[Tufts, John], 1689-1750.
(Sibley, V, 457-461.)
An Introduction to the Singing of Psalm
Tunes.
Boston, 1715.]
(See Music Lib. Assoc., Notes, XI, 46.)
                                              1785

Tufts, John, 1689-1750.
An Introduction to the Singing of Psalm
Tunes. . . . Fifth Edition.
Boston, Gerrish, 1726. [2], 9, [1] pp., 12
plates.
AAS copy.   39856

Tufts, John, 1689-1750.
An Introduction to the Singing of
Psalm-Tunes. . . . Seventh Edition.
Boston, Gerrish, 1728. [2], 9, [1] pp., 12
plates.
AAS copy.   39898

Tufts, John, 1689-1750.
An Introduction to the Singing of
Psalm-Tunes. . . . Eighth Edition.
Boston, Green, 1731. [2], 9, [1] pp., 12
plates.
MHS copy.   3482

Tufts, John, 1689-1750.
An Introduction to the Singing of
Psalm-tunes. . . . Ninth Edition.
Boston, 1736. [2], 8, [2] pp., 6 plates.
EI copy.   40104

Tufts, John, 1689-1750.
(Sibley, V, 457-461.)
An Introduction to the Singing of
Psalm-Tunes. . . . Tenth Edition.
Boston, Gerrish, 1738. [2], 7, [3] pp., 12
plates.
NYPL copy.   4315

Tufts, John, 1689-1750.
(Sibley, V, 457-461.)
An Introduction to the Singing of
Psalm-Tunes. . . . Eleventh Edition.

Boston, Gerrish, 1744. [1], 7, [3] pp., 12 plates.
AAS copy.   5502

[Tufts, John, 1689-1750.
(Sibley, V, 457-461.)
A Very Plain and Easy Introduction to the art of Singing.
Boston, Franklin for Gerrish, 1721. [4], 12 + pp.]
(Brinley 5885; bought by Forest. See Music Lib. Assoc., Notes, XI, 46-47.) 2297

Tufts, Joshua, 1716-1766.
(Sibley, X.)
The Believers most sure Freedom.
Portsmouth, Fowle, 1757. 16 pp.
AAS copy.   8051

[Tufts, Joshua, 1716-1766.
Portsmouth, in New-Hampshire, July 20, 1757.
[Portsmouth, 1757.]
(No copy located.)   8052

Die Tugenden und Würkungen des Arzney-Mittels.
[Lancaster, 179?] Broadside.
HSP copy.   45799

Tullar, Martin, 1753-1813.
The Virtues of a Prudent Wife.
Hanover, N. H., [1799]. 26, [2] pp.
AAS copy.   36458

Tulley, John, 1638-1701.
(Mass. Hist. Soc., Proc., 2nd. Ser., IV, 414-415.)
Tulley 1687. An Almanack.
Boston, 1687. [16] pp.
(See "John Tulley's Almanacks," Col. Soc. Mass., Publ., XIII, 207-223.)
AAS copy.   435

Tulley, John, 1638-1701.
Tulley 1688. An Almanack.
Boston, 1688. [2], 22 pp.
MHS copy.   454

Tulley, John, 1638-1701.
Tulley 1689. An Almanack.
Boston, 1689. [16] pp.
AAS copy.   499

Tulley, John, 1638-1701.
Tulley. 1690. An Almanack.
Boston, 1690. [16] pp.
AAS copy.   548

Tulley, John, 1638-1701.
Tulley. 1691. An Almanack.
Cambridge, 1691. [16] pp.
AAS copy.   578

Tulley, John, 1638-1701.
Tulley. 1692. An Almanack.
Cambridge, 1692. [16], 7, [1] pp.
AAS copy.   630

Tulley, John, 1638-1701.
Tulley 1693. An Almanack.
Boston, Harris, 1693. [26] pp.
(Issued with differing amounts of supplementary material at the end.)
AAS copy.   682

Tulley, John, 1638-1701.
Tulley 1693. An Almanack.
Boston, Harris for Phillips, 1693. [26] pp.
(Differs from Evans 682 only in imprint and words "Sold by Samuel Phillips" at end. The AAS has a mixed copy.)
MHS copy.   683

Tulley, John, 1638-1701.
Tulley, 1694. An Almanack.
Boston, 1694. [24] pp.
AAS ph. copy.   710

Tulley, John, 1638-1701.
Tulley, 1695. An Almanack.
Boston, 1695. [24] pp.
AAS copy.   740

Tulley, John, 1638-1701.
Tulley, 1696. An Almanack.
Boston, 1696. [16] pp.
AAS copy.   776

Tulley, John, 1638-1701.
Tulley, 1697. An Almanack.
Boston, 1697. [16] pp.
(There is a second issue in which the

reference to astrologers on p. [15] has been deleted.)
AAS copy.   815

Tulley, John, 1638-1701.
Tulley. 1698. An Almanack.
Boston, 1698. [16] pp.
AAS copy.   854

Tulley, John, 1638-1701.
Tulley, 1699. An Almanack.
Boston, 1699. [16] pp.
AAS copy.   897

Tulley, John, 1638-1701.
Tulley, 1700. An Almanack.
Boston, 1700. [16] pp.
AAS copy.   955

Tulley, John, 1638-1701.
Tulley, 1701. An Almanack for . . . 1701.
Boston, 1701. [16] pp.
AAS copy.   1028

Tulley, John, 1638-1701.
Tulley's Farewel 1702. An Almanack.
Boston, 1702. [16] pp.
AAS copy.   1097

Tulloh, Andrew.
To Farmers. Large Tracts. . . . September 23, 1800.
[Northumberland, Pa., 1800.] Broadside.
LCP copy.   49156

. . . Tumbling Feats, by the Two Surprising Youths. . . .
[New York], Louis Jones, [1792].
Broadside.
(The text is lost at the top.)
NYHS copy.   46592

Tunes in Three Parts, for the Several Metres of Dr. Watt's Version.
Philadelphia, Armbruster, 1763. 43, [1] pp.
(Only known copy is defective.)
HSP copy.   9526

Tunes in Three Parts, for the Several Metres in Dr. Watts's Version. . . . Second Edition.
Philadelphia, Armbruster, 1764. viii, 43, [1] pp.
HSP copy.   9858

Tunis. Treaties, etc., 1800.
Translation of the 11th, 12th, and 14th articles of the Treaty with Tunis.
[Philadelphia? 1800.] 2 pp.
LOC copy.   38911

Turell, Ebenezer, 1702-1778.
The Life and Character of . . . Benjamin Colman.
Boston, Rogers & Fowle, 1749. [20], 238, [1] pp.
(Imprint variant of 6434, q. v. for text.)   40520

Turell, Ebenezer, 1702-1778.
(Sibley, VI, 574-582.)
The Life and Character of . . . Benjamin Colman.
Boston, Rogers & Fowle and Edwards, 1749. [20], 238, [1] pp.
(AAS has a copy with variant tp.)
AAS copy.   6434

Turell, Ebenezer, 1702-1778.
The Life and Character of. . . . Benjamin Colman. . . . To which is Added, The Doctor's Discourse on the Parable of the Ten Virgins.
Boston, Rogers & Fowle and Edwards, 1749. [18], 238, [2], vi, 344 pp.
(For the text see 1602 and 6434.)
AAS copy.   40521

Turell, Ebenezer, 1702-1778.
(Sibley, VI, 574-582.)
Memoirs of the Life and Death of Jane Colman Turell.
Boston, Kneeland & Green for Edwards and Foster, 1735.
(Signatured with 3888, q.v. No copy of the separate printing mentioned by Allibone has been found.)   3969

Turell, Ebenezer, 1702-1778.
(Sibley, VI, 574-582.)
Ministers Should Carefully Avoid.

Boston, Draper for Edwards, 1740. 29 pp.
AAS copy.   4614

Turell, Ebenezer, 1702-1778.
(Sibley, VI, 574-582.)
Mr. Turell's Brief and Plain Exhortation.
Boston, Rogers & Fowle, 1748. 11 pp.
AAS copy.   6255

Turell, Ebenezer, 1702-1778.
(Sibley, VI, 574-582.)
Mr. Turell's Dialogue.
Boston, Rogers & Fowle, 1742. 18 pp.
AAS copy.   5076

Turell, Ebenezer, 1702-1778.
Mr. Turell's Dialogue. . . . Second Edition.
Boston, Rogers & Fowle, 1742. 24 pp.
BA copy.   5077

Turell, Ebenezer, 1702-1778.
Mr. Turell's Directions.
Boston, Rogers & Fowle, 1742. 15 pp.
AAS copy.   5078

[Turell, Ebenezer, 1702-1778.
Mr. Turell's Directions [Another Impression].
Boston, Rogers & Fowle, 1742. 15 pp.]
(A census of copies indicates that this 'other impression' is a confusion with the second edition, 5080.)   5079

Turell, Ebenezer, 1702-1778.
Mr. Turell's Direction. . . . Second Edition.
Boston, Rogers & Fowle, 1742. 15 pp.
AAS copy.   5080

Turell, Ebenezer, 1702-1778.
Mr. Turell's Direction. . . . Third Edition.
Boston, Rogers & Fowle, 1742. 15 pp.
NYHS copy.   5081

Turford, Hugh, d. 1713.
The Grounds of a Holy Life.
Philadelphia, Chattin for Buffin, 1753. 56 pp.
(Evans entry was from an adv.)
PSL copy.   7130

Turford, Hugh, d. 1713.
(D. N. B.)
The Grounds of a Holy Life. . . . Tenth Edition.
Philadelphia, Crukshank, 1772. viii, 123 pp.
AAS copy.   12586

Turford, Hugh, d. 1713.
The Grounds of a Holy Life. . . . Eleventh Edition.
Philadelphia, Crukshank, 1782. viii, 123 pp.
AAS copy.   17753

Turford, Hugh, d. 1713.
The Grounds of a Holy Life. . . . Twelfth Edition.
Hartford, [Ct.], Babcock, 1800. 120 pp.
AAS copy.   38682

The Turkish Fast, out of the Monthly Mercury, for December, 1697.
Boston, Green and Allen, May 13, 1698.
Broadside.
BPL copy.   39333

Turnbull, Robert James, 1775-1833.
A Visit to the Philadelphia Prison.
Philadelphia, Budd & Bartram, 1796. iv, 108 pp., 1 folded table.
AAS copy.   31321

[Turnbull, William, 1751-1822.
Advertisement, July 15, 1784.
Philadelphia, 1784. Broadside.]
(From Aitken's accounts.)   18814

[Turnbull, William, 1751-1822.
Advertisement, Sept., 1784.
Philadelphia, 1784. Broadside.]
(From Aitken's accounts.)   18815

[Turnbull, William, 1751-1822.
(O. D. Turnbull, William Turnbull, 3.)
Advertisement, Sept. 22, 1783.
Philadelphia, 1783.]
(From Aitken's accounts.)   18220

[Turnbull, William, 1751-1822.
Handbill, Sloop for Halifax.

Philadelphia, 1784. Broadside.]
(From Aitken's accounts.)   18816

Turner, Charles, 1732-1813.
Due Glory to be Given to God.
Boston, Fleets, 1783. 35 pp.
AAS copy.   18221

Turner, Charles, 1732-1813.
(Weis, Colonial Clergy N. E.)
General Directions.
Newport, 1762. 23 pp.
AAS copy.   9289

Turner, Charles, 1732-1813.
(Weis, Colonial Clergy N. E.)
Gospel Ministers.
Boston, Edes & Gill, 1770. 32 pp.
AAS copy.   11902

Turner, Charles, 1732-1813.
(Weis, Colonial Clergy N. E.)
A Sermon, Preached at Plymouth,
December 22d, 1773.
Boston, Greenleaf, 1774. 48 pp.
AAS copy.   13696

Turner, Charles, 1732-1813.
(Weis, Colonial Clergy N. E.)
A Sermon Preached before His
Excellency.
Boston, Draper, 1773. 45 pp.
AAS copy.   13053

Turner, George, fl. 1799.
Memoir on the Extraneous Fossils.
Philadelphia, Dobson, 1799. 11 pp.
LCP copy.   36459

Turner, James, d. 1759.
. . . Map of . . . Nova Scotia. . . . 2d
Edition.
Philadelphia, Hook, 1760. Map.
HEH copy.   41172

Turner, James, d. 1759.
. . . Map of the Province of Nova
Scotia. . . . 2d Edition.
Philadelphia, Aitken, 1776. Map.
LOC copy.   15121

Turner, John, & Co.
European and Indian Goods.
[New York], Morton & Horner, [1782?].
Broadside.
(Best copy available.)
NYHS copy.   43756

Turner, Nathaniel, 1771-1812.
A Funeral Oration . . . on . . . Benjamin
French.
Stockbridge, Andrews, 1797. 21 pp.
AAS copy.   32944

Turner, Richard, 1724?-1791.
An Introduction to Book Keeping. . . .
First American Edition.
Boston, Thomas & Andrews, 1794. 24,
[3], 9, 9, [3] pp.
AAS copy.   27824

Turner, Richard, 1753-1788.
An Abridgment of the Arts and Sciences.
New London, Springer, 1796. 167, [1] pp.
AAS copy.   31322

[Turner, Robert, fl. 1654-1665.
Botanoaotia.
Hartford, Patten, 1796.]
("As soon as 500 are subscribed for, it will
be put to press," Am. Mercury, July 18,
1796.)   31323

Turner, Thomas.
Meditations on the Uncertainty of Mans
Life.
Boston, B. Green, 1708. Broadside.
MHS copy.   39474

Twamley, Josiah.
Dairying Exemplified.
Providence, Carter & Wilkinson, 1796. 78,
[5] pp.
AAS copy.   31324

Tweedy, John.
A Catalogue of Druggs.
[Newport, 1760?] [28] pp.
AML copy.   8753

[Twelve Cents Worth of Wisdom.
Philadelphia, Curtis, 1795].

(Imprint assumed by Evans from advs.)
    28520

Twelve Cents Worth of Wit.
Philadelphia, Curtis, [1795]. 128 pp.
(No perfect copy located.)
AAS copy.   28521

[Twelve Cents Worth of Wit.
Philadelphia, Horgan, 1798.]
(Imprint assumed by Evans from adv.
"Just Published, and for sale by David
Horgan," in 33357.)   34684

Twenty-Four Fashionable Country
Dances for . . . 1799.
Boston, Norman, [1799]. [14] pp.
(The AAS copy has a different
arrangement of the plates.)
NYPL copy.   36460

A Twig of Birch for a Butting Calf.
New York, Buel, 1795. 46 pp.
AAS copy.   29665

A Twig of Birch for Billy's Breech.
Boston, Fleet, 1745. 13 pp.
(Attributed to John Cleaveland, but
incompatible with his views.)
AAS copy.   5563

Twilight's Orations.
Norfolk, Va., Willett & O'Connor, [1796.]
[2], 35 pp.
LCP copy.   31325

Twitcher, Titus.
Copy of a Letter from the New-Paltz. . . .
11th April, 1792.
[New York, 1792.] Broadside.
LOC copy.   46593

[Two Allegorical Poems, Entitled, Alonzo
. . . and, Amelia.
Baltimore, Angell, 1793.]
(Imprint assumed by Evans from adv. "to
be put to press" in Md. Journal, Sept. 29,
1793.)   26289

[The Two Congresses cut up [by Harrison
Gray, 1711?-1794].
Boston, Draper, 1774. 14 pp.]
(The imprint of the N. Y. ed. reads
"Boston printed.")   13697

The Two Congresses cut up [by Harrison
Gray, 1711?-1794].
New York, Rivington, [1775]. 14 pp.
(A reprint of 14074. Evans followed
Haven as to date of printing.)
NYPL copy.   13698

The Two Cousins [by Mrs. Pinchard].
Boston, Etheridge, 1796. 142 pp., 1 plate.
AAS copy.   31014

The Two Cousins [by Mrs. Pinchard].
New York, Tiebout, 1799. 130 pp.
(The only copy located is imperfect.)
AAS copy.   36120

[Two Curious and Important Letters from
Brutus to His Royal Highness Henry
Frederick.
Philadelphia, Evitt, 1770.]
(Entry from Hildeburn, following an adv.)
    11587

Two Discourses and a Prayer [by Samuel
Fothergill, 1715-1772].
Philadelphia, Steuart, [1767?]. 30 pp.
HSP copy.   10615

Two Discourses and a Prayer [by Samuel
Fothergill, 1715-1772].
New York, Parker, [1768?]. 23 pp.
(The only known copy has the imprint
date trimmed off.)
JCB copy.   41819

Two Discourses and a Prayer [by Samuel
Fothergill, 1715-1772].
New York, Parker, 1768. 27 pp.
AAS copy.   41820

Two Discourses and a Prayer [by Samuel
Fothergill, 1715-1772].
Newport, [1768]. 35 pp.
("Just published," Newport Mercury,
June 13, 1768.)
RIHS copy.   10616

Two Discourses Delivered in the Prison
[by John Searson].
Philadelphia, Evitt, [1770]. 17 pp.
NYHS copy.   11852

Two Discourses. On the Keeping of the
Commandments.
Philadelphia, Dobson & Lang, 1788. 62,
[2] pp.
AAS copy.   22146

Two Discourses. On the Keeping of the
Commandments.
New York, Patterson, 1789. pp. [1]-52,
[56]-57.
AAS copy.   22147

[Two Entertaining Stories for Young
Ladies.
Hudson, N. Y., Stoddard, 1795.]
(Imprint assumed by Evans from
Stoddard's advs.)   29666

Two Favorite New Songs at the American
Camp. Exhortation to the Freemen.
n. p., [1776?] Broadside.
HSP copy.   43178

Two Favorite Songs of the American
Camp. Exhortation to the Freemen of
America. . . .
[Boston, 1775?] Broadside.
HSP copy.   42949

Two Favorite Songs, made on the
Evacuation of the Town of Boston, by the
British Troops, on the 17th of March,
1776.
n. p., [1776?]. Broadside.
(The only reported copy could not be
located.)   43179

[Two] Favorite Songs made on the
Evacuation of the Town of Boston by the
Britons, March 17th, [1776].
[Boston? 1776?] Broadside.
JCB copy.   43180

Two Friends (Ship).
Proceedings of the Trial of the. . . .
Philadelphia, Ormrod & Conrad, 1795. pp.
[2], [i]-iii, [1], [3]-148.
AAS copy.   29667

The Two Interests Reconciled.
New York, 1726. 31 pp.
AAS copy.   3363

Two Letters. A Circular Letter. . . .
September 25, 1770.
[Philadelphia, 1770.] Broadside.
LOC copy.   11903

Two Letters from the Reverend Mr.
Williams & Wheelock.
Boston, Kneeland & Green, 1744. 31 pp.
AAS copy.   5523

[Two Letters to a Friend on the Present
Critical Conjuncture of Affairs in North
America [by Charles Chauncy,
1705-1787].
Boston? 1755. 54 pp.]
(This is a ghost of the London reprint of
7381 and 7382.)   7400

Two Letters to a Friend, on the Removal
of the Rev. Mr. J[ame]s S[proa]t [by
Andrew Ward of Guilford].
[New Haven?], 1769. 32 pp.
LOC copy.   11507

Two Lines of Un-accountable Characters
. . . near the Town of Taunton.
[Boston, 1714.] Broadside.
(No copy located.)   39603

[The Two Mothers; or the History of
Antigone and Phronissa.
Boston, 1759.]
("This Day Published," Boston Gazette,
Sept. 24, 1759.)   8506

Two New Songs: on the Disgraceful Flight
of the Ministerial Fleet and Army . . . on
March 17, 1776.
Boston, Bible & Heart, [1776?]
Broadside.
WLC copy.   43181

Two Poems. First, On a Soul Pleading
with God.
Norwich, 1775. 12 pp.

(Incorrect Evans entry is from Sabin 63614.)
LOC copy. 14409

Two Sermons Preached in Boston, March 5. 1723.
Boston, Kneeland for Edwards, 1723. [4], iv, 38, [2], ii, 36, [1] pp.
AAS copy. 2425

Two Songs for the Celebration of the 4th of July, 1799.
n.p., n.d. Broadside.
NYHS copy. 36462

Two Songs on the Brave General Montgomery, and Others, who fell . . .
Dec. 21, 1775.
Danvers, [1776.] Broadside.
(No copy available for reproduction.)
EI copy. 43182

Two Treatises, Containing Reasons why the People Called Quakers do not pay Tythes.
Philadelphia, Crukshank, 1771. [2], 10, 27 pp.
AAS copy. 12257

Two Unfortunate Concubines: or The History of Fair Rosamond . . . and Jane Shore.
Boston, White, 1796. 57+ pp.
(The only known copy is imperfect.)
AAS copy. 47943

Two very Circumstantial Accounts of the late Dreadful Earthquake at Lisbon.
Boston, Fowle, 1756. 16 pp.
AAS copy. 7653

[Two very Circumstantial Accounts of the late Dreadful Earthquake at Lisbon. . . . Second Edition. To which is Added an Account of the late Earthquake in Boston. Boston, Fowle, 1756. 32 pp.]
(From an adv.) 7654

. . . The Two Wealthy Farmers. . . . Part I [by Hannah More, 1745-1833].
Philadelphia, Johnsons, 1800. 36 pp.
AAS copy. 37132

. . . The Two Wealthy Farmers. . . . Part II [by Hannah More, 1745-1833].
Philadelphia, Johnsons, 1800. 36 pp.
AAS copy. 37133

. . . The Two Wealthy Farmers. . . . Part III [by Hannah More, 1745-1833].
Philadelphia, Johnsons, 1800. 36 pp.
AAS copy. 37134

. . . The Two Wealthy Farmers. . . . Part IV [by Hannah More, 1745-1833].

Philadelphia, Johnsons, 1800. 36 pp.
AAS copy. 37135

. . . The Two Wealthy Farmers. . . . Part V [by Hannah More, 1745-1833].
Philadelphia, Johnsons, 1800. 36 pp.
AAS copy. 37136

Tydings from Rome [by John Flavel, 1630?-1691].
[Cambridge], 1668. [2], 30 pp.
MHS copy. 131

Tyler, Andrew, 1719-1775.
(Sibley, X.)
The Terms of Christianity.
Boston, Edes & Gill, 1756. [2], 34 pp.
HC copy. 7807

Tyler, John, 1742-1823.
The Blessing of Peace.
Norwich, Trumbull, 1795. 20 pp.
AAS copy. 29668

Tyler, John, 1742-1823.
A Discourse Delivered in the City of New-London.
New London, Green, 1799. 21 pp.
HSP copy. 36463

Tyler, John, 1742-1823.
A Discourse, Delivered in the Meeting-House.
Norwich, Ct., Trumbull, 1799. 14 pp.
(The only recorded copy is mislaid.) 36464

Tyler, John, 1742-1823.
A Discourse, Delivered in the Meeting House of the First Society in Norwich.
Norwich, [Ct.], Trumbull, 1798. 27 pp.
AAS copy. 48647

Tyler, John, 1742-1823.
A Discourse Delivered in the New Meetinghouse.
Norwich, Ct., Sterry, 1796. 24, [1] pp.
LOC copy. 31327

Tyler, John, 1742-1823.
An Eulogy on the Life of . . . Washington.
Norwich, [Ct.], Hubbard, 1800. 32 pp.
AAS copy. 38683

Tyler, John, 1742-1823.
(Weis, Colonial Clergy N. E.)
The Sanctity of a Christian Temple.
Providence, 1761 (1771). [6], 36 pp.
AAS copy. 12258

[Tyler, John], 1742-1823.
Universal Damnation, and Salvation.
Boston, Edes, 1798. [2], 79 pp.
AAS copy. 34685

[Tyler, Royall], 1757-1826.

The Algerine Captive. . . . Volume I [-II].
Walpole, N. H., Carlisle, 1797. 214; 241 pp.
AAS copy. 32945

Tyler, Royall, 1757-1826.
A Christmas Hymn . . . Sung at Claremont, N. H., 1793.
[Windsor? 1794.] Broadside.
AAS ph. copy. 47244

[Tyler, Royall], 1757-1826.
The Contrast . . . by Thomas Wignell.
Philadelphia, Prichard & Hall, 1790.
Front., viii, [16], 79 pp.
AAS copy. 22948

Tyler, Royall, 1757-1826.
Convivial Song, Sung at Windsor.
[Windsor? 1799.] Broadside.
VtU copy. 48970

[Tyler, Royall, 1757-1826.
The Georgia Spec; or, Land in the Moon.
Boston, 1797.]
(Evans assumed the printing of Tyler's play.) 32946

Tyler, Royall, 1757-1826.
An Oration, Pronounced at Bennington.
Walpole, N. H., Carlisle for Thomas & Thomas, 1800. 16 pp.
AAS copy. 38684

[Tyler, Royall], 1757-1826.
The Origin of Evil, An Elegy.
Printed in the Year 1793. 8 pp.
AAS copy. 26290

Tyng, Dudley Atkins, 1760-1829.
An Address to the Ancient and Honorable Society of . . . Masons . . . 5786.
Newburyport, 1787. 16 pp.
AAS copy. 20210

Tyrannical Libertymen.
Hanover, N. H., 1795. 16 pp.
AAS copy. 29669

Tytler, James, 1747?-1805.
Paine's Second Part of the Age of Reason Answered.
Salem, Cushing, 1796. 107 pp.
AAS copy. 31328

Tytler, James, 1747?-1805.
The Rising of the Sun in the West.
Salem, Carlton, 1795. 24 pp.
MHS copy. 29670

Tytler, James, 1747?-1805.
A Treatise on the Plague.
Salem, Mass., Cushing for Macanulty, 1799. [4], 568, [1] pp.
AAS copy. 36465

u

Ulster Co., N.Y. Citizens, 1790.
Ulster County, April 16th, 1790. Sir, We
the Subscribers. . . .
[Goshen? 1790.] Broadside.
NYSL copy. 46012

Ulster Co. N. Y. Convention, Apr. 13,
1795.
Circular. Sir, A Number of your
Fellow-Citizens. . . . April 13, 1795.
[Kingston, 1795.] Broadside.
Albany Institute copy. 47636

Ulster Co., N. Y. Court of Common Pleas.
Rules. . . .
Goshen, Mandeville & Westcott, [1790].
Broadside.
NYPL ph. copy. 46013

An Unanswerable Answer to the Cavils.
New York, 1739. 4 pp.
PRO copy. 4440

The /Uncertainty/ of a/ Death-Bed
Repentance/. [by François de Salignac de
la Mothe Fenelon, 1651-1715].
[Germantown, 1756.] 16 pp.
(For authorship see BSA, XXXVI,
231-232.)
AAS copy. 7656

The Uncertainty of a/ Death-Bed/
Repentance/ [by François de Salignac de
la Mothe Fenelon, 1651-1715].
[Germantown, 1760?] 16 pp.
LCP copy. 8597

The Uncertainty of a Death-Bed
Repentance [by François de Salignac de
la Mothe Fenelon, 1651-1715].
[Germantown, 1766?]. 16 pp.
(Also entered as 8597, q. v.)
10296

Underwood, Michael, 1736-1820.
A Treatise on the Diseases of Children.
Philadelphia, Dobson, 1793. pp. [1]-xx,
[1]-404, 105-108.
AAS copy. 26291

[The Undutiful Daughter, or, The
Devonshire Wonder.
Keene, Blake, 1795.]
(Imprint assumed and title expanded by
Evans from Blake's adv.) 29671

[The Unequal Conflict. A Poem.
Carlisle, Kline, 1792?]
(Entry from adv. "to be Sold" in Carlisle
Gazette, May 2, 1792.) 24865

The Unerring Authority of the Catholic
Church [by Richard Challoner, bp.,
1691-1781].
Philadelphia, Lloyd, 1789. 203, [9] pp.
AAS copy. 21731

The Unfortunate Concubines; or, The
History of Fair Rosamond . . . and Jane
Shore.
Wilmington, [Del.], Brynberg, 1796.
140 pp.
AAS copy. 47944

The Unfortunate Hero; a Pindaric Ode
[by Benjamin Young Prime, 1733-1791].
New York, Parker & Weyman, 1758. 15
pp.
HEH copy. 41003

The Unfortunate Lovers: a Short,
Beautiful Poem.

Newport, Southwick, 1769. 8 pp.
MHS copy. 42015

Union, Activity and Freedom. . . . Dec.
18, 1769.
[New York, 1769.] Broadside.
LCP copy. 11508

Union Society, Newburyport, Mass.
Friendship in Adversity. Newbury Port.
Sir, the Union Society. . . .
[Newburyport, 1797.] Broadside.
EI copy. 32577

Union University, Schenectady.
Laws & Regulations for the Government
of Union-College.
Schenectady, Wyckoff, 1796. 20 pp.
(Not located, 1968.) 47945

[Union University, Schenectady.
Songs Sung at the First
Commencement. . . . May 3, 1797.
Schenectady, Wyckoff, 1797. Broadside.]
(Evans assumed the printing of this
broadside for the later custom.) 32947

Unitarianism; or, the Doctrine of the
Trinity Confuted.
Philadelphia, 1795. 46 pp.
AAS copy. 47638

United Company.
To the Honorable General Assembly of
the Colony of Connecticut . . . May 1776.
The Memorial . . .
[Norwich? 1776.] 8 pp.
JCB copy. 43183

United Illinois and Wabash Land
Companies.
An Account of the Proceedings of the
Illinois and Ouabache Land Companies.
Philadelphia, Young, 1796. [16], 55 pp.
AAS copy. 30618

United Illinois and Wabash Land
Companies.
Memorial of the Illinois and Wabach
Land Company. 13th January, 1797. . . .
Published by Order of the House.
Philadelphia, Folwell, [1797], 8, 8, 7, [1],
7 pp.
(See Sabin 84577.)
AAS copy. 32977

United Insurance Company.
We the Subscribers hereby Agree. . . .
February 1, 1796.
[New York, 1796.] Broadside.
(Not located, 1968.) 47946

United Society of House-Carpenters and
Joiners, of Lansingburgh and Troy.
Lansingburgh, 19th June, 1790. Rules and
Regulations.
[Lansingburgh? 1790.] Broadside.
NYSL copy. 46014

U. S.
Abstracts of the Goods, Wares and
Merchandise, Exported . . . to [30th Sept.
1794].
n.p., [1794]. Broadside.
(Only known copy cannot be reproduced.)
47245

U. S. Army. Continental Army, 1775.
Articles of Capitulation, Made and
Intered into between Richard
Montgomery . . . and the Citizens . . . of
Montreal.

[Baltimore], Dunlap, [1775]. Broadside.
AAS copy. 14540

U. S. Army. Continental Army, 1775.
By His Excellency George Washington,
Esquire, Commander in Chief of the
United Colonies of North-America. To
the Inhabitants of Canada.
[Philadelphia, 1775.] Broadside.
NYPL copy. 14542

U. S. Army. Continental Army, 1775.
Cambridge, 21st August, 1775. Wanted for
the Continental Army. . . .
[Cambridge, 1775.] Broadside.
MHS copy. 42951

U. S. Army. Continental Army, 1775.
Head-Quarters, Cambridge, 27th August,
1775. His Excellency. . . . New Cyder.
[Watertown, 1775.] Broadside.
BPL copy. 42952

U.S. Army. Continental Army, 1775.
Head-Quarters, Cambridge, November
1775. The Generals. . . .
[Cambridge? 1775.] Broadside.
LCP copy. 14556

U. S. Army. Continental Army, 1775.
Instructions for the Officers of the
Several Regiments of the Massachusetts-
Bay Forces. . . . 10th day of July 1775.
[Watertown, 1775.] Broadside.
MHS copy. 14243

U. S. Army, Continental Army, 1775.
Par son Excellence George Washington,
Commandant in Chef des Armees des
Provinces Unies de l'Amerique
Septentrionale. Aux Peuples de Canada.
[Philadelphia, 1775.] Broadside.
NYPL copy. 14543

U. S. Army. Continental Army, 1775.
A Return of Cloathing &c Wanting in Col.
[blank] Regiment, September [blank]
1775.
n. p., [1775]. Broadside.
MHS copy. 42953

U. S. Army. Continental Army, 1775.
A Return of the Regiment in the Service
of the United Colonies of North-America,
Commanded by Colonel [blank] July 1,
1775.
n. p., [1775]. Broadside.
AAS copy. 42955

U. S. Army. Continental Army, 1775.
A Return of the Regiment to the Service
of the United Colonies of North-America.
Commanded by Colonel [blank] July 1,
1775.
n. p., [1775]. Broadside.
MHS copy. 42954

U. S. Army. Continental Army, 1775.
We whose Names are hereunto Subscribed
. . . October the [blank] Annoq. Dom.
1775.
n. p., [1775]. Broadside.
AAS copy. 42956

[U. S. Army. Continental Army, 1776.
By His Excellency George Washington.
. . . A Proclamation [Bombardment of
N. Y. Aug. 16, 1776.]
New York, Holt, [1776]. Broadside.]
(No copy located.) 15153

U. S. Army. Continental Army, 1776.
By His Excellency George Washington.

. . . Whereas [Evacuation of Boston. Mar.
21, 1776].
[Watertown, 1776.] Broadside.
MHS copy.   15124

U. S. Army. Continental Army, 1776.
By His Excellency George Washington.
. . . Whereas the Ministerial Army. . . .
[Dated Mar. 21, 1776].
[Boston, 1776.] Broadside.
AAS facsim. copy.   43184

U. S. Army. Continental Army, 1776.
General Orders, Head-Quarters,
Philadelphia, Dec. 14, 1776. Colonel
Griffin. . . .
[Philadelphia, 1776.] Broadside.
HSP copy.   15182

U. S. Army. Continental Army, 1776.
Head-quarters, New-York, April 8th,
1776. The General, Informs the
Inhabitants, . . . Israel Putnam.
[New York, 1776.] Broadside.
NYPL copy.   43185

U. S. Army. Continental Army, 1776.
Head-Quarters, Philadelphia, Dec. 13th,
1776. The General has. . . .
[Philadelphia, 1776.] Broadside.
HSP copy.   15181

[U. S. Army. Continental Army, 1776.
I   have this day Voluntarily Enlisted
Myself as a Soldier in the American
Continental Army. . . .
[Philadelphia, 1776.] Broadside.]
(No copy located.)   15130

U. S. Army. Continental Army, 1776.
Instructions to the Officers Appointed to
Recruit [Nov. 21, 1776].
[Fishkill, 1776]. Broadside.
NYHS copy.   15184

U. S. Army. Continental Army, 1776.
To all Brave, Healthy, able Bodied, and
well Disposed Young Men.
[Philadelphia? 1776.] Broadside.
HSP copy.   15103

[U. S. Army. Continental Army, 1777.
Advertisement by General Mifflin, June 2,
1777.
Philadelphia. Broadside.]
(Entry from Aitken's accounts.)   15618

[U. S. Army. Continental Army, 1777.
Advertisement, for Returns, etc., by Maj.
Lewis Nichola, June 13, 1777.
Philadelphia, 1777. Broadside.]
(Entry from Aitken's records.)   15507

[U. S. Army. Continental Army, 1777.
Advertisement of General Weedon, Feb.
1777.
Philadelphia, 1777. Broadside.]
(Entry from Aitken's accounts.)   15645

U. S. Army. Continental Army, 1777.
Baltimore, September 13. We are
Favoured with the General Orders. . . .
Wilmington, September 5, 1777.
Baltimore, [1777]. Broadside.
NYPL copy.   15630

U. S. Army. Continental Army, 1777.
Bey Seiner Excellenz G. Waschington
[Grain. Dec. 20, 1777].
Lancaster, Bailey, [1777]. Broadside.
HSP copy.   15635

U. S. Army. Continental Army, 1777.
By His Excellency George Washington.
. . . I hereby Enjoin [Grain. Dec. 20,
1777].
Lancaster, Dunlap, [1777]. Broadside.
HSP copy.   15634

U. S. Army. Continental Army, 1777.
By His Excellency George Washington.
. . . Proclamation [Howe's Pardons. Jan.
25, 1777].
Baltimore, [1777]. Broadside.
LOC copy.   15633

U. S. Army. Continental Army, 1777.
By His Excellency George Washington.
. . . Proclamation [Howe's Pardons. Jan.
25, 1777].
Philadelphia, Bradfords, [1777].
Broadside.
LOC copy.   15632

U. S. Army. Continental Army, 1777.
By the Honorable Major-General
Putnam. . . . A Proclamation. Whereas
Some Soldiers . . . [Nov. 17, 1777.]
[Fishkill? 1777.] Broadside.
AAS ph. copy.   43380

U. S. Army. Continental Army, 1777.
Extract of a Letter from General Gates,
Dated. . . . November 25, 1777.
York, [Pa.], Hall & Sellers, 1777. [2] pp.
NYPL copy.   43381

[U. S. Army. Continental Army, 1777.
General Orders. Apr. 14, 1777.
Philadelphia, 1777. Broadside.]
(Entry from Aitken's accounts.)   15646

U. S. Army. Continental Army, 1777.
General Orders. Head Quarters. Morris
Town, January 22, 1777.
Philadelphia, Bradfords, [1777].
Broadside.
LCP copy.   15644

U. S. Army. Continental Army, 1777.
General Orders. Philadelphia, April 11,
1777.
[Philadelphia, 1777.] Broadside.
LCP copy.   15514

U. S. Army. Continental Army, 1777.
Good News from the Northern Army.
Boston, October 13th, 1777. . . . John
Glover, Major-General . . . Exeter, 1777.
[Exeter, 1777.] Broadside.
LOC copy.   43382

U. S. Army. Continental Army, 1777.
Good News from the Northern Army.
Boston, October 13, 1777. . . . John
Glover, Major-General. . . .
Portsmouth, [1777]. Broadside.
JCB copy.   43383

U. S. Army. Continental Army, 1777.
Head Quarters, August 25, 1777. Sir, A
Messenger. . . . Horatio Gates.
Philadelphia, Dunlap, [1777]. Broadside.
CHS copy.   43384

U. S. Army. Continental Army, 1777.
Head Quarters, Peeks-Kill, General
Orders for the Army under . . .
M'Dougall.
[Fishkill, 1777.] Broadside.
NYHS copy.   43385

[U. S. Army. Continental Army, 1777.
I   do Voluntarily Inlist Myself. . . .
Philadelphia, Dunlap, [1777]. Broadside.]
(No copy located.)   15682

U. S. Army. Continental Army, 1777.
Important and Fresh Intelligence. Exeter,
August 26th, 1777. . . . General Stark.
[Exeter, 1777.] [2] pp.
NL copy.   43386

[U. S. Army. Continental Army, 1777.
Philadelphia, May 1, 1777. Head Quarters.
General Orders.
[Philadelphia, 1777.] Broadside.]
(No copy located.)   15647

U. S. Army. Continental Army, 1777.
Recruiting Instructions for Thomas
Hartley. . . . G. Washington, Morristown,
January 12, 1777.
Baltimore, Goddard, [1777]. Broadside.
JCB copy.   43387

U. S. Army. Continental Army, 1777.
Standing Orders for the Garrison of
Philadelphia. . . . May 31, 1777.
[Philadelphia, 1777.] Broadside.
LCP copy.   15545

U. S. Army. Continental Army, 1778.
Advertisement. . . . Enoch Poor. . . .
January 21st, 1778. State of
New-Hampshire, February 17th, 1778.
[Exeter? 1778.] Broadside.
NHHS copy.   43505

U. S. Army. Continental Army, 1778.
Advertisement. . . . Soldiers . . . whose
Furloughs are Expired. . . . February 17th,
1778. . . . Exeter.
[Exeter? 1778.] Broadside.
NHHS copy.   43559

U. S. Army. Continental Army, 1778.

By the Hon. Major General, Arnold. . . .
A Proclamation [Military Law. June 19,
1778].
[Philadelphia, 1778.] Broadside.
LCP copy.   16108

[U. S. Army. Continental Army, 1778.
By the Hon. Major General Arnold. . . . A
Proclamation [Property. June 17, 1778].
[Philadelphia, 1778.] Broadside.]
(A ghost of 16108.)   16107

U. S. Army, Continental Army, 1778.
By the Honorable William Heath. . . . A
Proclamation [dated July 10, 1778].
[Boston, 1778.] Broadside.
MHS copy.   43560

U. S. Army. Continental Army, 1778.
Head Quarters, Peaks-Kill, General
Orders for the Army under the Command
of . . . M'Dougall.
[Poughkeepsie? 1778.] Broadside.
(Copy could not be located.)   43561

U. S. Army. Continental Army, 1778.
Rules and Articles for the Better
Government of the Troops.
Poughkeepsie, Holt, 1778. 26 pp.
(Anderson Galleries cat. 2016, no. 16;
present location unknown.)   43562

[U. S. Army. Continental Army, 1778.
Rules and Directions for the Better
Regulating the Military Hospital [Feb. 6,
1778].
[Philadelphia? 1778.] Broadside.]
(Ford 167. The unique copy seen by Evans
is mislaid.)   16143

U. S. Army. Continental Army, 1778.
Standing Orders for the Garrison of
Philadelphia, July 7, 1778.
[Philadelphia, 1778.] Broadside.
HSP copy.   43563

U. S. Army. Continental Army, 1778.
To the Inhabitants. . . . G. Washington.
. . . January 30, 1778.
Lancaster, [1778]. Broadside.
APS copy.   16144

U. S. Army. Continental Army, 1779.
. . . An Estimate of the Average Prices of
. . . Cloathing. . . . [Nov. 16, 1779.]
Philadelphia, Hayes, [1779] Broadside.
HEH copy.   43710

U. S. Army. Continental Army, 1779.
Whereas, Many Persons. . . . January 7,
1779.
Fishkill, [1779]. [2] pp.
LOC copy.   16645

U. S. Army. Continental Army, 1780.
L'Amour Paternel.
[Philadelphia, 1780.] Broadside.
NYPL copy.   17038

U. S. Army. Continental Army, 1780.
L'Amour Paternal . . . pour les Habitans
du Canada. . . . Signé La Fayette.
[Philadelphia, 1780.] Broadside.
BA copy.   43900

U. S. Army. Continental Army, 1780.
Boston, June 12, 1780. The Inhabitants of
the Town.
[Boston, 1780.] Broadside.
(No copy located.)   43901

U. S. Army. Continental Army, 1780.
By Horatio Gates. . . . A Proclamation.
The Patriotick Exertion. . . . [Aug. 4,
1780.]
n. p., [1780]. Broadside.
LOC copy.   43902

[U. S. Army. Continental Army, 1780.
By the Honourable Major General Baron
de Steuben [Dec. 20, 1780].
[Richmond, 1780.] Broadside.]
(The only copy recorded is mislaid.) 19441

U. S. Army. Continental Army, 1780.
By the Honourable Major General Baron
de Steuben [Dec. 20, 1780].
[Richmond, 1780.] Broadside.
AAS copy.   19441

U. S. Army. Continental Army, 1780.
Proceedings of a Board of General
Officers . . . Respecting Major John

Andre.... September 29, 1780.
Fishkill, Loudon, 1780. 23 pp.
PrU copy.   43903

U. S. Army. Continental Army, 1780.
Procedings of a Board of General Officers
... Respecting Major John André....
September 29, 1780.
New London, Green, 1780. 16+ pp.
(Trumbull's Supplement 2517; no copy
located.)   43904

U. S. Army. Continental Army, 1780.
Proceedings of a Board of General
Officers ... Respecting the Trial of Major
John Andre.... Sept. 29, 1780.
Norwich, Trumbull, 1780.
(Trumbull: Supplement 2518; no copy
located.)   43905

U. S. Army. Continental Army, 1780.
To the Medical Officers of the General
and Flying Hospitals.... January 20,
1780.
[Philadelphia, 1780.] Broadside.
(No copy located.)   43906

U. S. Army. Continental Army, 1781.
Orders for Regulating the Drawing and
Issuing of Provisions.
[Newburgh? 1781.] Broadside.
LOC copy.   44061

U. S. Army. Continental Army, 1783.
By His Excellency George Washington.
... The Bearer ... is hereby
Discharged ... [Fishkill, 1783.] [2] pp.
(There are several varieties of this form.)
LOC copy.   18230

U. S. Army. Continental Army, 1789.
(The Following is a Copy of the Memorial
Presented by the Officers of this State to
Congress. ...)
[Boston, 1789.] Broadside.
AAS ph. copy.   45621

U. S. Army. Continental Army, 1792.
(Circular.) Boston, (Massachusetts) Feb.
28, 1792. Sir, We have had the Honour to be
Appointed a Committee, by the Officers of
the Massachusetts Line....
[Boston, 1792.] Broadside.
NYHS copy.   24135

U. S. Army. Continental Army, 1792.
Circular Letter. From a Committee
Appointed by the Officers of the
Massachusetts Line....
[New York, 1792.] [3] pp.
LOC copy.   24136

U. S. Army. Continental Army, 1792.
Circular Letters from a Committee
Appointed by the Officers of the
Massachusetts Line of the Federal
Army.... February 28, 1792.
[New York? 1792.] Broadside.
AAS copy.   46594

U. S. Army, 1791.
Those Veterans, whose Services Entitled
them to Lands in the Western Territory.
... April 22, 1791.
[Boston? 1791.] Broadside.
MHS copy.   46298

U. S. Army, 1794.
To the Inhabitants of Certain Counties.
... November, 1794. Henry Lee.
[Pittsburgh, 1794.] Broadside.
LOC copy.   27978

U. S. Army, 1800.
Division Orders. January 14, 1800. After
the Recruits have been Instructed.... W.
Bentley, Lieut. Co. Comdt. 7th U. S. Regt.
[Richmond, 1800.] [3] pp.
LOC copy.   38729

U. S. Articles of Confederation.
Articles of Confederation.
[Philadelphia, July, 1776.] 8 pp.
LOC copy.   15148

U. S. Articles of Confederation.
Articles of Confederation.
[Philadelphia, August, 1776.] 6 pp.
(See Journals, LOC ed., VI, 1124.)
(The only copy located is in poor
condition.)
NHHS copy.   15149

[U. S. Articles of Confederation.
Articles of Confederation.
Annapolis, 1777. 8 pp.]
(No copy located; apparently a ghost.)
                                         15621

U. S. Articles of Confederation.
Articles of Confederation.
Annapolis, [1777]. 15 pp.
LOC copy.   15622

U. S. Articles of Confederation.
Articles of Confederation.
Boston, Gill, 1777. 16 pp.
AAS copy.   15623

U. S. Articles of Confederation.
Articles of Confederation.
Exeter, 1777. 8 pp.
AAS copy.   15624

[U. S. Articles of Confederation.
Articles de Confédération.
[Lancaster?], 1777. 16 pp.]
(The source of this entry has not been
located.)   15628

U. S. Articles of Confederation.
Articles of Confederation.
[Lancaster, 1777.] 6 pp.
NYPL ph. copy.   15620

U. S. Articles of Confederation.
Articles of Confederation.
Lancaster, 1777. 26 pp.
AAS copy.   15619

U. S. Articles of Confederation.
Articles of Confederation.
New London, 1777. 11 pp.
AAS copy.   15625

U. S. Articles of Confederation.
Articles of Confederation.
Newbern, 1777. 9 pp.
LOC copy.   15626

U. S. Articles of Confederation.
Articles of Confederation and Perpetual
Union.
[Providence, Carter, 1777.] 8 pp.
AAS copy.   43388

U. S. Articles of Confederation.
Articles of Confederation.
Williamsburg, Purdie, [1777]. [4] pp.
LOC copy.   15627

U. S. Articles of Confederation.
Artikel des Bundes.
Lancaster, 1778. 16 pp.
HSP copy.   16106

U. S. Articles of Confederation.
Articles of Confederation.
Williamsburg, Dixon & Hunter, 1778.
15 pp.
LOC copy.   16105

U. S. Attorney General.
See Dept. of Justice.

U. S. Board of Commissioners of the
Sinking Fund, 1793?
The Vice-President. ...
[Philadelphia? 1793?] 4 pp.
(Only known copy is imperfect.)
WLC copy.   46894

U. S. Board of Commissioners of the
Sinking Fund, 1793.
Report of the Board of Trustees of the
Sinking Fund. ... Published by Order of
the House.
[Philadelphia], Childs & Swaine, [1793].
29 pp.
AAS copy.   26364

U. S. Board of Commissioners of the
Sinking Fund, 1794.
Report of the Commissioners of the
Sinking Fund.
Philadelphia, Fenno, 1794. 8vo.]
(A description of 27894, q.v.)   27948

U. S. Board of Commissioners of the
Sinking Fund, 1795.
(Received the 18th December, 1795.)
Report of the Commissioners ... Stating
the Amount of their Purchases ... Since
... 1794. Published by Order of the
House.

[Philadelphia], Childs, [1796]. 14 pp.
AAS copy.   31462

U. S. Board of Commissioners of the
Sinking Fund, 1796.
Report of the Commissioners ... Stating
the Amount of their Purchases ... Since
... the 18th of December 1795. 16th
December, 1796. Ordered to lie on the
Table ... Published by Order of the
House.
[Philadelphia, 1796.] 6 pp.
AAS copy.   31463

U. S. Board of Commissioners of the
Sinking Fund, 1797.
Report of the Commissioners of the
Sinking Fund; Inclosing a Report to them,
from the Secretary of the Treasury. ...
5th December, 1797. ... Published by
Order of the House.
Philadelphia, Poulson & Young, 1797. 25
pp.
AAS copy.   33089

U. S. Board of the Commissioners of the
Sinking Fund, 1797.
Report of the Commissioners of the
Sinking Fund, Relative to the Sale of a
Part of the Capital Stock. ... 26th of
January 1797. ... Published by Order of
the House.
[Philadelphia, 1797.] 15 pp.
AAS copy.   33090

U. S. Board of Commissioners of the
Sinking Fund, 1798.
Report of the Commissioners of the
Sinking Fund, Inclosing a Report to
them. ... 17th December, 1798. Ordered
to lie on the Table. Published by Order of
the House. ...
Philadelphia, Way & Groff, [1798]. pp.
[1]-6, 1 folding table; pp. 9-11.
AAS copy.   34881

U. S. Board of Commissioners of the
Sinking Fund, 1799.
Report of the Commissioners. ... 11th
December, 1799. ... Printed by Order of
the House. ...
Philadelphia, Way & Groff, [1799]. 14 pp.
AAS copy.   36564

U. S. Board of Commissioners of the
Sinking Fund, 1800.
Report of the Commissioners of the
Sinking Fund, Inclosing a Report to
them. ... 28th of November, 1800.
Ordered to lie on the Table. Published by
Order of the House.
[Washington, 1800.] 9 pp., 1 folding table.
AAS copy.   38818

U. S. Board of Commissioners under
Article 6th of the Treaty between Great
Britain and the U. S., London, Nov. 19,
1794.
A Brief Statement of Opinions, Given by
the Board of Commissioners.
Philadelphia, Humphreys, 1800. viii, 72
pp.
(Also entered as 37428, q. v.)   38722

U. S. Board of Commissioners under
Article 6th of the Treaty between Great
Britain and the U.S., London, Nov. 19,
1794.
The Claims and Answer, in the Case of
William Cunningham & Co.
Philadelphia, Fenno, 1798. 12, [6], 72,
xix, [1]-36, 17, [1], 16 pp.
AAS copy.   34906

U. S. Board of Commissioners under
Article 6th of the Treaty between Great
Britain and the U. S., London, Nov. 19,
1794.
Sundry Resolutions and Proceedings.
Philadelphia, Aitken, 1799. 123 pp.
AAS copy.   36591

U. S. Board of Commissioners under
Article 6th of the Treaty between Great
Britain and the U. S., London, Nov. 19,
1794.
Sundry Resolutions of the. ...
Philadelphia, Humphreys, 1798. 18 pp.
HSP copy.   34907

[U. S. Board of Treasury, 1777.
Forms for Paying the Army, June, 1777.

Philadelphia, 1777.]
(Entry from Aitken's accounts.)   15631

U. S. Board of Treasury, 1777.
Treasury-Office, Philadelphia, September
6, 1777.
Additional Instructions.
[Philadelphia, 1777.] Broadside.
HSP copy.   43389

U. S. Board of Treasury, 1778.
Treasury Office, York-Town, April 15,
1778. . . .
n. p., [1778]. Broadside.
LOC copy.   43564

U. S. Board of Treasury, 1779.
Instructions . . . to the Respective
Commissioners. . . . January 12, 1779.
[Philadelphia, 1779.] Broadside.
NYPL copy.   43711

U. S. Board of Treasury, 1779.
Reports of the Board of Treasury,
Relative to Finance. (No. 1).
[Philadelphia, 1779.] 7 leaves.
LCP copy.   16633

U. S. Board of Treasury, 1779.
Table of the Sums Actually in Circulation.
Philadelphia, Claypoole, [1779]. 7 pp.
NJHS copy.   16635

U. S. Board of Treasury, 1779.
A Table of the First Year's Interest.
[Philadelphia, 1779.] 7 pp.
NJHS copy.   16634

U. S. Board of Treasury, 1779.
Treasury-Office, April 5th, 1779. Ordered,
that the Following Resolutions. . . .
[Philadelphia, 1779.] Broadside.
NYPL copy.   16642

U. S. Board of Treasury, 1779.
Treasury-Office, February 23d, 1779.
Ordered, That the Several
Commissioners. . . .
[Philadelphia, 1779.] Broadside.
NYPL copy.   16641

U. S. Board of Treasury, 1779.
Treasury Office, January 12, 1779. Sir, In
Pursuance. . . .
[Philadelphia, 1779.] Broadside.
NYPL copy.   16640

U. S. Board of Treasury, 1780.
Table for the Payment of Principal, and
Interest [June 28, 1780].
Philadelphia, Claypoole, 1780. 23 pp.
AAS copy.   17049

U. S. Board of Treasury, 1780.
Table for the Payment of the Second
Year's Interest.
Philadelphia, Claypoole, [1780]. 18 pp.
NJHS copy.   17050

U. S. Board of Treasury, 1785.
Board of Treasury, August 27, 1785. Since
the Resolve of Congress of the Sixth
July. . . .
[New York, 1785.] [27] pp.
LOC copy.   19280

U. S. Board of Treasury, 1785.
Board of Treasury, June 6, 1785. The
Board of Treasury to whom was Referred
the Petition of John Allen. . . .
[Philadelphia, 1785.] Broadside.
LOC copy.   44802

U. S. Board of Treasury, 1785.
The Board of Treasury, on the Motion of
. . . Mr. Howell, of the 8th July. . . .
[Philadelphia, 1785.] [2] pp.
LOC copy.   44803

U. S. Board of Treasury, 1785.
The Board of Treasury to whom was
Referred on the 7th July inst. . . .
[Philadelphia, 1785.] [2] pp.
LOC copy.   44804

U. S. Board of Treasury, 1786.
The Board of Treasury, to whom it was
Referred to Revise the System . . .
Report. . . . January 12, 1786.
[Philadelphia, 1786.] Broadside.
AAS copy.   44984

U. S. Board of Treasury, 1786.

The Board of Treasury to whom was
Referred their Letter of 29th of June . . .
Report. . . . July 19th, 1786.
[New York, 1786.].Broadside.
LOC copy.   20044

U. S. Board of Treasury, 1786.
Estimate of the Annual Expenditure of the
Civil Departments. . . . February 20, 1786.
[Philadelphia, 1786.] 13 pp.
LOC copy.   44985

[U. S. Board of Treasury, 1786.
That the Commissioners of the Board of
Treasury give Orders for the Continuation
of the Issue of Indents of Interest [Aug.
23, 1786]. . . .
[New York, 1786.] Broadside.]
(No copy located.)   20083

U. S. Board of Treasury, 1786.
Board of Treasury, April 8, 1786. Sir, We
do Ourselves the Honor. . . .
[New York, 1786.] 28 pp.
HC copy.   20042

U. S. Board of Treasury, 1786.
Board of Treasury, June 22, 1786. Sir, We
do ourselves the Honour. . . .
[New York, 1786.] [4] pp.
AAS copy.   20043

U. S. Board of Treasury, 1787.
The Board of Treasury to whom "It was
Referred. . . ." [Sept. 28, 1787].
[New York, 1787.] 14 pp.
NA copy.   20756

U. S. Board of Treasury, 1787.
The Board of Treasury to whom was
Referred a Motion. . . . April 16, 1787.
[New York, 1787.] Broadside.
LOC copy.   20755

U. S. Census Office. 1st Census, 1790.
Return of the Whole Number of Persons
within the Several Districts of the United
States.
Philadelphia, Childs & Swaine, 1791. 56
pp.
AAS copy.   23916

U. S. Census Office, 1st Census, 1790.
Return of the Whole Number of Persons . . .
Printed by Order of the House. . . .
Philadelphia, Gales, [1798]. 56 pp.
AAS copy.   34905

[U. S. Census Office. 1st Census, 1790.
Schedule of the Whole Number of Persons
within the Several Districts of the United
States, According to an Act. . . . October
31, 1791.
[Philadelphia, 1791.] Broadside.]
(No issue dated Oct. 31 could be located.)
          23917

U. S. Circuit Court (1st Circuit).
Declaration. Rhode-Island District Circuit
Court of the United States, June Term,
1798.
[Providence, 1798.] 8 pp.
RIHS copy.   34908

U. S. Circuit Court (3rd Circuit).
Copy of an Indictment. No. I [-II]. In the
Circuit Court of the United States.
[Philadelphia, 1799.] 4, 3 pp.
LOC copy.   36513

U. S. Circuit Court (5th Circuit).
The Case of Messrs. Brailsford and
Others. . . .
Savannah, Johnston, 1792. 36 pp.
NYHS copy.   24353

[U. S. Circuit Courts (District of North
Carolina).
. . . Hamiltons vs. Eaton. . . . June term,
1792.
[Newbern? 1792?] 83, [6] pp.]
(A part of 32426, q.v.)   46597

U. S. Commission under Article VI of
Jay's Treaty, 1794.
Commissioner's Office, Philadelphia, May
21, 1798.
[Philadelphia, 1798.] Broadside.
NYPL copy.   48648

U. S. Commissioners Appointed under the
Act to Provide for the Valuation of
Lands, Etc., Massachusetts.

Circular. Boston, November 9, 1799.
Sir. . . .
[Boston, 1799.] Broadside.
(Best copy available.)
MA copy.   48971

U. S. Commissioners Appointed under the
Act to Provide for the Valuation of
Lands, etc. Vermont.
Abstract of an Act to Provide for the
Valuation of Lands and Dwelling-Houses.
Vergennes, Vt., Waites, 1798. 35 pp.
HEH copy.   34708

U. S. Commissioners for Purchasing the
Public Debt, 1792.
Commissioner's Office. Receive of
Nathaniel Appleton. . . . 31st of March,
1792.
[Philadelphia? 1792] Broadside.
(Typical of a large class of documents
usually ommitted by Evans.)
Pierce W. Gaines copy.   46595

U. S. Commissioners for Purchasing the
Public Debt, 1792.
Report from the Commissioners. . . .
Published by Order of the House.
[Philadelphia], Childs & Swaine, [1792].
19 pp.
JCB copy.   24921

U. S. Commissioners for Purchasing the
Public Debt, 1792.
Report of the Commissioners . . . Stating
the Amount of Purchases and other
Proceedings Since their Report of the 16th
December, 1793.
[Philadelphia], Childs, [1794]. 23 pp.
AAS copy.   27947

U. S. Commissioners for the Relief of the
Refugees from the British Provinces.
Letter from the Commissioners. . . . 8th
May, 1800.
[Philadelphia, 1800.] 15 pp.
LCP copy.   49157

U. S. Commissioners for the Settlement of
the Accounts, 1793.
The Commissioners Appointed to Execute
the Several Acts of Congress. . . . June
29th, 1793.
[Philadelphia, 1793.] Broadside.
LOC copy.   46895

U. S. Commissioners for the Settlement of
the Accounts 1793.
Report of the Commissioners . . . Stating
Balances. Read 5th December, 1793.
[Philadelphia? 1794?] 4 pp.
WLC copy.   47246

U. S. Commissioners of the City of
Washington.
Letter . . . to the President. . . . 5th
December, 1799. (Published by Order of
the House. . . .).
[Philadelphia, 1799.] 9 pp., 2 folding
plates.
AAS copy.   36525

[U. S. Commissioners on the Accounts of
the States.
Report of the Commissioners. . . .
December 5, 1792.
[Philadelphia, 1792.] 4 pp.]
(Ed. assumed by Evans from 1803
printing.)   24922

U. S. Commissioners to Confer with the
Insurgents in the Western Counties of
Pennsylvania.
Report of the Commissioners.
Philadelphia, Childs & Swaine, 1794. 38,
[1] pp.
AAS copy.   27977

U. S. Commissioners to Examine and
Liquidate the Public Accounts, Northern
District.
Albany, Sept. 30, 1776.
[Albany, 1776.] Broadside.
NYHS copy.   43175

U. S. Commissioners to Execute Acts of
Congress to Provide for the Settlement of
Accounts between the United States and
the Individual States.
The Commissioners Appointed to . . .
Report [December 5, 1793].

[Philadelphia, Childs & Swaine, 1794.]
Broadside.
BA copy.   27949

U. S. Commissioners to Treat, Confer,
Determine and Conclude upon a Cartel
for the Exchange of Prisoners, 1779.
Report of the Commissioners.
Philadelphia, Claypoole, 1779. 20 pp.
AAS copy.   16631

U. S. Commissioners under the Act to
Provide for the Valuation of Lands and
Dwelling-Houses.
At a Meeting of the Board of
Commissioners, for the State of
Massachusetts, begun and held in Boston,
on the 24th Day of April, 1799.
[Boston, 1799.] Broadside.
MA copy.   36493

U. S. Commissioners under the Act to
Provide for the Valuation of Lands and
Dwelling-Houses.
At a Meeting . . . in the State of
Massachusetts, June, 1799.
[Boston, 1799.] Broadside.
MA copy.   36494

U. S. Commissioners under the Act to
Provide for the Valuation of Lands and
Dwelling-Houses.
Beverly, January 19, 1799. Circular. Sir,
As the Following. . . .
[Salem, 1799.] Broadside.
MHS copy.   35380

U. S. Commissioners under the Act to
Provide for the Valuation of Lands and
Dwelling-Houses.
To All to whom these Presents shall
Come. . . .
Vergennes, Vt., Waites, [1798].
Broadside.
VtHS copy.   34709

U. S. Committee on the Naval Force
Necessary for the Protection of the
Commerce of the United States against
the Algerian Corsairs.
Report of the. . . . January 2, 1794.
[Philadelphia, 1794.] 7 pp.
LOC copy.   27902

U. S. Comptroller of the Treasury, 1793.
(Circular) Treasury Department,
Comptroller's Office, April 27d, 1793.
[Philadelphia, 1793.] Broadside.
(No copy located.)   46896

U. S. Comptroller of the Treasury, 1793.
Explanations and Forms of Official
Documents.
[Philadelphia, 1793.] 15, [1]+ pp.
(The only known copy is imperfect.)
AAS copy.   46897

U. S. Comptroller of the Treasury, 1794.
Circular to the Collectors and Naval
Officers. . . . Aug. 1794.
[Philadelphia, 1794.] Broadside.
(No copy available for reproduction.)
                                            47247

U. S. Comptroller of the Treasury, 1794.
Circular to the Collectors and Naval
Officers. . . . June 19, 1794.
[Philadelphia, 1794. Broadside.
(No copy available for reproduction.)
                                            47248

U. S. Comptroller of the Treasury, 1794.
(Circular to the Collectors.) Treasury
Department, Comptroller's Office, April
[blank] 1794.
[Philadelphia, 1794.] Broadside.
(No copy available for reproduction.)
                                            47249

U. S. Comptroller of the Treasury, 1794.
Treasury Department, Comptroller's
Office June 26th, 1794. Circular to the
Collectors. . . .
[Philadelphia, 1794.] Broadside.
(No copy available for reproduction.)
                                            47250

U. S. Comptroller of the Treasury, 1796.
Treasury Department, Comptroller's
Office, September 26, 1796. (Circular to
Marshals.)
[Philadelphia, 1796.] [2] pp.
NYPL copy.   31461

U. S. Comptroller of the Treasury, 1799.
Circular to Collectors, Naval Officers
and Surveyors. . . . May 27, 1799.
[Philadelphia, 1799.] Broadside.
LOC copy.   36501

U. S. Comptroller of the Treasury, 1799.
Treasury Department, Comptroller's
Office. May 27, 1799.
[Philadelphia, 1799.] Broadside.
(Also entered as 36501, q. v.)   36594

U. S. Congress.
Journals of Congress: Containing their
Proceedings from September 5, 1774 to
[August 19, 1784]. . . . Volume I [-IX].
Philadelphia, Folwell, 1800. 289, [12];
480, [22]; 468, [16]; 537, [42]; 349, [34];
176, [22]; 396, [36]; 337, [16]; 227, [11],
29 pp.
AAS copy.   38750

U. S. Congress, 1791?
Amendments to the Act to Establish the
Post-Office and Post Roads.
[Philadelphia], Fenno, [1791?]. [4] pp.
NYHS copy.   46311

U. S. Congress, 1791?
Amendments to the Bill, entitled, "An Act
to Encourage the Recruiting Service. . . ."
[Philadelphia? 1791?] Broadside.
NYHS copy.   46312

U. S. 1st Congress, 1789-1791.
An Act Concerning Counsuls and Vice-
Consuls [Read the second time in the
Senate . . . Jany. 12th, 1791.]
Philadelphia, Brown, [1791]. 4 pp.
LOC copy.   46308

U. S. 1st Congress, 1789-1791.
. . . An Act Imposing Duties on the
Tonnage of Ships or Vessels. . . . 1790,
June the 24th - Read the Third Time.
[New York], Fenno, [1790], Broadside.
AAS copy.   22964

U. S. 1st Congress, 1789-1791.
An Act to Regulate Trade and Intercourse
with the Indian Tribes . . . 1790, June the
23d- Read the Third Time.
[New York], Fenno, [1790]. 2 pp.
LOC copy.   46015

U. S. 1st Congress, 1789-1791.
Amendments to Bill, entitled, "An Act
Repealing . . . the Duties . . . upon
Distilled Spirits. . . ."
[Philadelphia], Fenno, [1791]. 4 pp.
LOC copy.   46309

U. S. 1st Congress, 1789-1791.
Amendments to the Bill, Entitled "An Act
to Encourage the Recruiting Service. . . ."
[Philadelphia, 1791?] Broadside.
(Not located, 1968.)   46312

U. S. 1st Congress, 1789-1791.
A Bill Concerning the Navigation and
Trade.
[New York], Childs & Swaine, [1790].
Broadside.
LOC copy.   46016

U. S. 1st Congress, 1789-1791.
A Bill for the Government and Regulation
of Seamen.
[New York], Childs & Swaine, [1790]. 2
pp.
LOC copy.   46018

U. S. 1st Congress, 1789-1791.
A Bill Making Provision for the Debt.
[New York], Childs & Swaine, [1790]. 4
pp.
LOC copy.   46020

U. S. 1st Congress, 1789-1791.
A Bill, Repealing . . . the Duties
heretofore Laid upon Wines Imported.
[Philadelphia], Childs & Swaine, [1791].
[3] pp.
LOC copy.   46313

U. S. 1st Congress, 1789-1791.
A Bill to Amend the Act, Intituled "An
Act to Promote the Progress of the Useful
Arts."
Philadelphia, Childs & Swaine, [1790].
[3] pp.
LOC copy.   23848

U. S. 1st Congress, 1789-1791.
A Bill to Ascertain how far the Owners of
Ships. . . .
[Philadelphia, 1791.] Broadside.
LOC copy.   46314

U. S. 1st Congress, 1789-1791.
A Bill to Establish an Uniform Rule of
Naturalization.
New York, Greenleaf, [1790]. Broadside.
LOC copy.   46022

U. S. 1st Congress, 1789-1791.
A Bill to Establish an Uniform Rule of
Naturalization.
New York, Childs & Swaine, [1790].
Broadside.
LOC copy.   46021

[U. S. 1st Congress, 1789-1791.
A Bill to Promote the Progress of Science
and Useful Arts.
[New York, 1789.] 11 pp.]
(No copy located.)   22192

U. S. 1st Congress, 1789-1791.
A Bill to Promote the Progress of Useful
Arts.
New York, Childs & Swaine, [1790]. 4 pp.
LOC copy.   46023

U. S. 1st Congress, 1789-1791.
A Bill, to Regulate the Collection of
Duties, Imposed on Goods. . . .
[New York], Childs & Swaine, [1790]. 14
pp.
LOC copy.   46024

U. S. 1st Congress, 1789-1791.
A Bill to Regulate the Collection of
Duties on Imports.
[New York, 1790.] 68, [1] pp.
LOC copy.   46025

U. S. 1st Congress, 1789-1791. House.
The Committee Appointed to Examine
into and Report what Proceedings have
been had under the Act for . . . the
Protection of the Frontiers . . .
Report. . . .
[Philadelphia? 1791.] Broadside.
NYHS copy.   46306

U. S. 1st Congress, 1789-1791.
The Committee. Appointed to Examine
into the Measures Taken by Congress and
the State of Virginia. . . .
New York, Greenleaf, 1790. 6 pp.
NYPL copy.   22954

U. S. 1st Congress, 1789-1791.
The Committee Appointed to Report a
Plan . . . for the Payment of Interest.
[New York], Childs & Swaine, [1790].
[2] pp.
LOC copy.   46026

U. S. 1st Congress, 1789-1791.
The Congressional Register. . . . Volume
I.
New York, Harrisson & Purdy, 1789. 614,
[2] pp.
AAS copy.   22203

U. S. 1st Congress, 1789-1791.
The Congressional Register. . . . Volume
II.
New York, Hodge, Allen & Campbell,
1789. 449, [1], 185, [3], xiv, [2] pp.
AAS copy.   22204

U. S. 1st Congress, 1789-1791.
The Congressional Register. . . . Second
Edition. Volume II.
New York, Hodge, Allen & Campbell for
Lloyd, 1790. 449, (i.e., 471) pp.
NYPL copy.   22973

U. S. 1st Congress, 1789-1791.
The Congressional Register. . . . Volume
III.
New York, Hodge, Allen & Campbell, for
Lloyd, 1790. 502, [2] pp.
AAS copy.   22974

U. S. 1st Congress, 1789-1791.
The Congressional Register. . . . Volume
IV [Nos. i-v, with Acts Passed at the
Second Session, through No. xxxvii].
New York, Hodge, Allen & Campbell for
Lloyd, 1790.
(The best file located, that at NYPL, ends
with Vol. IV, No. 3, p. 152.)   22975

U. S. 1st Congress, 1789-1791.
. . . The Convention of a Number of
States. . . . Resolved . . . That the
Following Articles be Proposed . . . as
Amendments.
[Providence], Wheeler, [1789].
Broadside.
RIHS copy.   22202

U. S. 1st Congress, 1789-1791.
George Washington, President of the United
States. John Adams. . . .
[New York, 1789.] Broadside.
NYPL copy.   45622

U. S. 1st Congress, 1789-1791.
. . . In the House . . . 24th August, 1789.
Resolved . . . Amendments. . . . In Senate,
August 25, 1789.
New York, Greenleaf, [1789]. 3 pp.
LOC copy.   22201

[U. S. 1st Congress, 1789-1791.
Order of Congress on the Treasury for the
Payment of Arrears due to the troops of
Virginia and North-Carolina. . . . June 7,
1790.
[New York, 1790.] Broadside.]
(No copy located.)   22985

U. S. 1st Congress, 1789-1791.
Philadelphia, Wednesday, June 2.
Congress. . . .
[Philadelphia], Dunlap & Claypoole,
[1790]. Broadside.
AAS ph copy.   22986

U. S. 1st Congress, 1789-1791. House.
[An Act for punishment of certain crimes.
House printing of Senate Bill.
New York, 1789. 12? pp.]
(No copy known.)   45623

U. S. 1st Congress, 1789-1791. House.
An Act for the Establishment and Support
of Light-Houses. . . . Read the Third Time
and Passed.
New York, Greenleaf, [1789]. Broadside.
LOC copy.   45624

U. S. 1st Congress, 1789-1791. House.
[An Act for the temporary establishment
of the Post-Office. First House reading of
Senate Bill, Sept. 16.
New York, 1789. Broadside?]
(No copy found.)   45625

U. S. 1st Congress, 1789-1791. House.
An Act Imposing Duties on Tonnage . . .
1789. May 29. Read the Third Time.
New York, Greenleaf, 1789. Broadside.
LOC copy.   45626

U. S. 1st Congress, 1789-1791. House.
An Act making further Provision for the
Payment of the Debts. . . . 1790, July the
19th, Read the Third Time.
[New York], Fenno, [1790]. 2 pp.
LOC copy.   46027

U. S. 1st Congress, 1789-1791. House.
[An Act to allow Baron de Glaubech the
pay of a Captain. Read three times and
passed Sept. 29.
New York, 1789. Broadside.]
(No copy found.)   45627

U. S. 1st Congress, 1789-1791. House.
An Act to Establish an Executive
Department to be Denominated the
Department of War. . . . 1789, June 27. Read
the Third Time.
New York, Greenleaf, [1789]. Broadside.
AAS ph. copy.   45629

U. S. 1st Congress, 1789-1791. House.
An Act to Establish the Seat of
Government. . . . 1789. September the 22d.
(Passed the House.)
New York, Greenleaf, [1789]. Broadside.
LOC copy.   45630

U. S. 1st Congress, 1789-1791.
An Act to Establish the Treasury
Department. . . .1789, July 2.
New York, Greenleaf, [1789]. [2] pp.
LOC copy.   45631

U. S. 1st Congress, 1789-1791. House.
An Act to Provide for the Government of
the Territory, North-West of the . . .
Ohio. . . . 1789, July the 21st.

New York, Greenleaf, [1789]. Broadside.
LOC copy.   45632

U. S. 1st Congress, 1789-1791. House.
An Act to Provide more Effectually for
the Settlement of the Accounts. . . . 1790,
June the 22d - Read the Third Time.
[New York], Fenno, [1790]. 2 pp.
LOC copy.   46028

U. S. 1st Congress, 1789-1791. House.
An Act to Regulate the Collection of the
Duties Imposed by Law on the Tonnage
of Ships. . . . 1789. July 14th. (Read the
Third Time and Passed the House. . . .)
New York, Greenleaf, [1789]. 20 pp.
NA copy.   45633

U. S. 1st Congress, 1789-1791. House.
Additional Standing Rules and Orders.
[New York, 1789.] Broadside.
LOC copy.   45628

U. S. 1st Congress, 1789-1791. House.
Be it Enacted by the Senate and House
. . . that at Every Session. . . . 1789,
August the 10th.
[New York, 1789.] Broadside.
LOC copy.   45634

U. S. 1st Congress, 1789-1791. House.
[A Bill allowing certain compensation to
the Judges and Attorney General, House
Bill Sept. 17.
New York, 1789.]
(No copy known.)   45635

U. S. 1st Congress, 1789-1791. House.
[A Bill concerning the importation of
certain persons prior to 1808, House
reading Sept. 19.
New York, 1789.]
(No copy known.)   45636

U. S. 1st Congress, 1789-1791. House.
A Bill, Declaring the Officer, who in case
of Vacancies. . . . [Dec. 20, 1790].
[New York, 1790.] [2] pp.
NYPL ph. copy.   46017

U. S. 1st Congress, 1789-1791. House.
[A Bill establishing a Land Office in and
for the Western territory, read in the
House July 31 and ordered printed.
New York, 1789.]
(No copy known.)   45637

U. S. 1st Congress, 1789-1791. House.
[A Bill establishing the salaries of the
executive, read in the House Aug. 24.
Printed for Senate.
New York, 1789.]
(No copy known.)   45638

U. S. 1st Congress, 1789-1791. House.
[A Bill for allowing a compensation to the
President and Vice-President, read in
House, July 22, printed by order of the
Senate.
New York, 1789.]
(No copy known.)   45639

U. S. 1st Congress, 1789-1791. House.
[A Bill for amending part of "An Act to
Regulate the Collection of Duties on
Tonnage," read Sept. 17.
New York, 1789.]
(No copy known.)   45640

U. S. 1st Congress, 1789-1791. House.
[A Bill for collecting duties on imports,
read May 8 and ordered printed.
New York, 1789.]
(No copy known.)   45641

U. S. 1st Congress, 1789-1791. House.
[A Bill for laying a duty on imports, read
in House May 5, printed by Senate.
New York, 1789.]
(No copy known.)   45642

U. S. 1st Congress, 1789-1791. House.
[A bill for registering and clearing vessels,
read in House third time Aug. 3, ordered
printed by Senate.
New York, 1789. 14? pp.]
(No copy known.)   45644

U. S. 1st Congress, 1789-1791. House.
[A Bill for registering and clearing
vessels, read July 24 and ordered printed.
New York, 1789.]
(No copy known.)   45643

U. S. 1st Congress, 1789-1791. House.
A Bill for Registering and Clearing
Vessels. . . . 1789, August the 5th (Passed
the House. . . .)
New York, Greenleaf, [1789]. 14 pp.
NA copy.   45645

U. S. 1st Congress, 1789-1791. House.
[A Bill for suspending the operations of a
part of the "Act Imposing Duties on
Tonnage, read Sept. 9.
New York, 1789.]
(No copy known.)   45646

U. S. 1st Congress, 1789-1791. House.
[A Bill for the establishment and support
for lighthouses, read July 1 in House,
printed by Senate.
New York, 1789.]
(No copy known.)   45647

U. S. 1st Congress, 1789-1791. House.
[A Bill imposing duties on tonnage, read
in House May 25, printed by Senate.
New York, 1789.]
(No copy known.)   45648

U. S. 1st Congress, 1789-1791. House.
[A Bill making appropriations for the
service of the present year, read Sept. 21.
New York, 1789.]
(No copy known.)   45649

U. S. 1st Congress, 1789-1791. House.
A Bill Making Appropriations for the
Support of Government.
[New York], Childs & Swaine, [1790].
[2] pp.
LOC copy.   46019

U. S. 1st Congress, 1789-1791. House.
[A Bill making provision for the invalid
pensioners, read Sept. 18.
New York, 1789.]
(No copy known.)   45650

U. S. 1st Congress, 1789-1791. House.
[A Bill providing for the establishment of
hospitals for seamen, read Aug. 24.
New York, 1789.]
(No copy known.)   45651

U. S. 1st Congress, 1789-1791. House.
[A Bill providing for the expenses which
may attend negotiations with the Indians,
read Aug. 10.
New York, 1789.]
(No copy known.)   45652

U. S. 1st Congress, 1789-1791. House.
[A Bill to alter the time of the annual
meeting of Congress, read Sept. 21.
New York, 1789.]
(No copy known.)   45653

U. S. 1st Congress, 1789-1791. House.
[A Bill to establish an Executive
Department to be denominated the
Department of Foreign Affairs, read and
ordered printed June 2.
New York, 1789.]
(No copy known.)   45654

U. S. 1st Congress, 1789-1791. House.
[A Bill to establish an Executive
Department to be denominated the
Department of War, read in the House
June 2, ordered printed by Senate.
New York, 1789.]
(No copy known.)   45655

U. S. 1st Congress, 1789-1791. House.
[A Bill to establish an Executive
Department to be denominated the
Treasury Department, read in House June
2, printed in Senate.
New York, 1789.]
(No copy known.)   45656

U. S. 1st Congress, 1789-1791. House.
A Bill to Establish the Judicial Courts.
New York, Greenleaf, [1789]. 16 pp.
LOC copy.   45657

U. S. 1st Congress, 1789-1791. House.
[A Bill to establish the Judicial Courts, as
amended on the third reading.
New York, 1789.]
(No copy known.)   45658

U. S. 1st Congress, 1789-1791. House.
[A Bill to establish the seat of
government, read in House Sept. 14,

printed in Senate.
New York, 1789.]
(No copy known.) 45659

U. S. 1st Congress, 1789-1791. House.
[A Bill to explain and amend "An Act for
the Registering and Clearing
Vessells. . . ." Read Sept. 23.
New York, 1789.]
(No copy known.) 45660

U. S. 1st Congress, 1789-1791. House.
[A Bill to provide for the government of
the territory northwest of the Ohio, read
in House July 16, printed in Senate.
New York, 1789.]
(No copy known.) 45661

U. S. 1st Congress, 1789-1791. House.
[A Bill to provide for the safe-keeping of
the Acts, read and ordered printed Aug. 3.
New York, 1789.]
(No copy known.) 45662

U. S. 1st Congress, 1789-1791. House.
A Bill to Provide for the Settlement of the
Accounts between the United States. . . .
[New York], Childs & Swaine, [1789].
Broadside.
LOC copy. 45663

U. S. 1st Congress, 1789-1791. House.
[A Bill to recognize and adopt to the
Constitution the establishment of the
troops, read Sept. 17.
New York, 1789.]
(No copy known.) 45664

U. S. 1st Congress, 1789-1791. House.
[A Bill to regulate the collection of duties
imposed on goods imported, read and
ordered printed, May 24.
New York, 1789.]
(No copy known.) 45665

U. S. 1st Congress, 1789-1791. House.
[A Bill to regulate the collection of duties
imposed on goods imported, read and
ordered printed, June 29.
New York, 1789.]
(No copy known.) 45666

U. S. 1st Congress, 1789-1791. House.
[A Bill to regulate the taking the oath,
read Apr. 14.
New York, 1789.]
(No copy known.) 45667

U. S. 1st Congress, 1789-1791. House.
[A Bill to suspend part of "An Act to
Regulate the Collection of the Duties on
Tonnage. . . ." Read Aug. 28.
New York, 1789.]
(No copy known.) 45668

U. S. 1st Congress, 1789-1791. House.
The Committee of Elections, to whom was
Referred the Petition of Abraham Trigg
. . . Report.
[Philadelphia? 1791.] [2] pp.
NYHS copy. 46307

U. S. 1st Congress, 1789-1791. House.
In Congress at New-York, Monday the
9th of August, 1790. Sir, In Obedience to
a Resolution. . . .
[New York, 1790.] Broadside.
RISL copy. 22979

U. S. 1st Congress, 1789-1791. House.
In the House . . . April 7, 1789. Resolved,
That the Rules and Orders. . . .
[New York, 1789.] 3 pp.
(No copy located.) 45669

U. S. 1st Congress, 1789-1791. House.
. . . In the House . . . the 10th of July,
1789. . . . An Estimate of Supplies.
[New York, 1789.] 3 pp.
NYPL copy. 22199

U. S. 1st Congress, 1789-1791. House.
In the House . . . the third of March, 1791.
On Motion, Resolved that the
Consideration of the Amendments to the
Constitution. . . .
[Philadelphia, 1791.] [2] pp.
LOC copy. 23883

U. S. 1st Congress, 1789-1791. House.
. . . In the House . . . the 28th of July,
1789. Mr. Vining, from the
Committee. . . .

New York, Greenleaf, [1789]. 2 pp.
LOC copy. 22200

U. S. 1st Congress, 1789-1791. House.
Journal of the House [Mar. 4 - Sept. 29,
1789].
New York, Childs & Swaine, [1789].
177 pp.
AAS copy. 22208

[U. S. 1st Congress, 1789-1791. House.
Journal of the House [Mar. 4 - Sept. 29,
1789].
Richmond, Davis, [1790]. 145 pp.]
(No copy located.) 22980

U. S. 1st Congress, 1789-1791. House.
Journal of the House [Jan. 4 - Aug. 12,
1790].
New York, Childs & Swaine, 1790. 261 pp.
AAS copy. 22981

U. S. 1st Congress, 1789-1791. House.
Journal of the House [Jan. 4 - Aug. 11,
1790].
Richmond, Davis, 1791. 152 pp.
LOC copy. 23898

U. S. 1st Congress, 1789-1791. House.
Journal of the House [Dec. 6, 1790-Mar.
3, 1791].
Philadelphia, Childs & Swaine, 1791. 146
pp.
AAS copy. 23899

U. S. 1st Congress, 1789-1791. House.
To the Honorable the Speaker and the
Members of the House of Representatives
of the United States. The Petition of
James Jackson. . . . The Committee . . .
Respectfully Submit. . . .
[Philadelphia, 1791.] [2] pp.
LOC copy. 23904

U. S. 1st Congress, 1789-1791. Joint
Committee on Rules.
The Committee, Appointed to Confer with
the Committee of the Senate. . . .
[New York, 1789.] Broadside.
LOC copy. 45670

U. S. 1st Congress, 1789-1791. Joint
Committee on Rules.
[Joint rules for the enrollment of statutes,
July 27, 1789.
New York, Greenleaf, 1789.] Broadside.
(No copy known.) 45672

U. S. 1st Congress, 1789-1791. Joint
Committee on the Inauguration.
The Committee of Both Houses,
Appointed. . . . April 29th, 1789.
[New York, 1789.] Broadside.
AAS ph. copy. 45671

U. S. 1st Congress, 1789-1791. Senate.
An Act for Establishing the Salaries of the
Executive. . . .
[New York]. Greenleaf. [1789.]
Broadside.
LOC copy. 45673

U. S. 1st Congress, 1789-1791. Senate.
An Act for Laying a Duty on Goods. . . .
Read First Time in the Senate 18 May.
[New York, 1789.] [4] pp.
(Not located 1967).
LOC copy. 45674

U. S. 1st Congress, 1789-1791. Senate.
An Act for the Establishment and Support
of Light-Houses.
New York, Greenleaf, [1789]. Broadside.
LOC copy. 45678

U. S. 1st Congress, 1789-1791. Senate.
An Act for the Punishment of Certain
Crimes.
New York, Greenleaf, [1790]. 5 pp.
LOC copy. 45679

U. S. 1st Congress, 1789-1791. Senate.
An Act Supplementary to the Act for the
Establishment and Support of
Light-Houses.
[New York], Fenno, [1790]. Broadside.
LOC copy. 46058

U. S. 1st Congress, 1789-1791. Senate.
An Act to Establish Offices. . . . 1791,
February the 16th, - Passed the House.
[Philadelphia], Fenno, [1791.] 4 pp.
LOC copy. 46310

U. S. 1st Congress, 1789-1791. Senate.
An Act to Provide for the Safe Keeping
of the Acts [first Senate reading Aug. 31].
New York, Greenleaf, [1789.] [2] pp.
LOC copy. 45675

U. S. 1st Congress, 1789-1791. Senate.
[An Act to regulate processes in the
courts. Senate Bill read in the House first
and second times.
New York, 1789. 4? pp.
(No copy known.) 45676

U. S. 1st Congress, 1789-1791. Senate.
An Act to Regulate Processes in the
Courts. . . . In Senate . . . September 17,
1789.
New York, Greenleaf, [1789]. 4 pp.
LOC copy. 45677

U. S. 1st Congress, 1789-1791. Senate.
A Bill for Registering and Clearing
Vessels.
New York, Greenleaf, [1789]. 12 pp.
LOC copy. 45680

U. S. 1st Congress, 1789-1791. Senate.
A Bill for registering and clearing vessels,
Amendments 25-29, reported Aug. 17.
New York, Greenleaf, [1789]. 3 pp.
LOC copy. 45681

U. S. 1st Congress, 1789-1791. Senate.
[A Bill to amend the Constitution of the
United States, printing ordered by House
Sept. 14.
New York, 1789.]
(No copy known.) 45682

U. S. 1st Congress, 1789-1791. Senate.
A Bill to Establish the Judicial Courts.
New York, Greenleaf, [1789]. 12 pp.
LOC copy. 45683

U. S. 1st Congress, 1789-1791. Senate.
Journal of the First Session [Mar. 4 -
Sept. 29, 1789].
New York, Greenleaf, 1789. 172 pp.
AAS copy. 22207

U. S. 1st Congress, 1789-1791. Senate.
Journal of the Second Session of the
Senate [Jan. 4 - Aug. 12, 1790].
New York, Fenno, 1790. 224 pp.
AAS copy. 22982

U. S. 1st Congress, 1789-1791. Senate.
Journal of the Second Session of the
Senate [Jan. 4 - Aug. 12, 1790].
Richmond, Davis, 1791. 110 pp.
(The only copy located cannot be
reproduced.) 23900

U. S. 1st Congress, 1789-1791. Senate.
Journal of the Third Session of the Senate
[Dec. 6, 1790 - Mar. 3, 1791].
Philadelphia, Fenno, 1791. 203 pp.
AAS copy. 23901

U. S. 1st Congress, 1789-1791. Senate.
. . . July the 12th, 1790; The Committee
Appointed July the 2d. . . .
[Philadelphia], Fenno, [1790]. 2 pp.
LOC copy. 46029

U. S. 1st Congress, 1789-1791. Senate.
Rules for Conducting the Business of the
Senate.
n.p., [1790?]. 4 pp.
WLC copy. 46030

U. S. 2nd Congress, 1791-1793.
An Act Appointing Representatives
among the People. . . . 1791, November
the 24th - Read the Third Time.
[Philadelphia], Fenno, [1791]. Broadside.
LOC ph. copy. 46315

U. S. 2nd Congress, 1791-1793.
An Act for the Relief of Certain Widows.
. . . 1791, December the 1st. Read the Third
Time.
[Philadelphia], Fenno, [1791]. 2 pp.
LOC copy. 46316

U. S. 2nd Cong., 1791-1793.
An Act more Effectually to Provide for
the National Defence. . . . 1792. March the
6th, - Passed the House of
Representatives.
[Philadelphia], Fenno. [1792]. 7 pp.
NYPL ph. copy. 26296

U. S. 2nd Congress, 1791-1793.
An Alphabetical List of Senators [and members of the House] . . . First Session of the Second Congress.
[Philadelphia? 1792.] Broadside.
CHS copy.   46598

U. S. 2nd Congress, 1791-1793.
Amendments to the Bill, entitled, "An Act for Regulating Processes."
[Philadelphia], Fenno, [1792.] 3 pp.
LOC copy.   46599

U. S. 2nd Congress, 1791-1793.
Amendments to the Bill, entitled, "An Act more Effectually to Provide for the National Defence.
[Philadelphia], Fenno, [1792]. 2 pp.
LOC copy.   46600

U. S. 2nd Congress, 1791-1793.
Amendments to the Bill, entitled, "An Act to Ascertain and Regulate the Claims. . . .
[Philadelphia], Fenno, [1792]. Broadside.
(Not located, 1968.)   46601

U. S. 2nd Congress, 1791-1793.
A Bill Authorizing the Transfer of the Stock Standing to the Credit of Certain States.
[Philadelphia, 1793.] Broadside.
AAS copy.   26330

U. S. 2nd Congress, 1791-1793.
A Bill, Declaring the Officer, who . . . Shall Act as President. . . .
[Philadelphia, 1792.] [2] pp.
LOC ph. copy.   46602

U. S. 2nd Congress, 1791-1793.
A Bill Directing the Mode in which the Evidences of the Debt. . . .
[Philadelphia, 1792.] Broadside.
(No copy located.)   46603

U. S. 2nd Congress, 1791-1793.
A Bill for Regulating the Post-Office.
New York, Childs & Swaine, [1792]. 6 pp.
LOC copy.   46604

U. S. 2nd Congress, 1791-1793.
A Bill more Effectually to Provide for the National Defence.
[Philadelphia], Childs & Swaine, [1792]. 7 pp.
LOC copy.   46605

U. S. 2nd Congress, 1791-1793.
A Bill Providing for the Sale of Land . . . North-west of the River Ohio.
[Philadelphia, 1792.] Broadside.
(No copy located.)   46606

U. S. 2nd Congress, 1791-1793.
A Bill Providing for the Settlement of the Claims of Persons . . . Barred by the Limitations heretofore Established.
[New York], Childs & Swaine, [1792?]. Broadside.
WLC copy.   46607

U. S. 2nd Congress, 1791-1793.
A Bill to Establish the Post-Office.
[Philadelphia], Childs & Swaine, [1792]. 7 pp.
LOC copy.   46609

U. S. 2nd Congress, 1791-1793.
A Bill to Indemnify the Estate of the late Major-general Nathaniel Greene.
[Philadelphia, 1792.] Broadside.
LCP copy.   46610

U. S. 2nd Congress, 1791-1793.
The Committee to whom was Referred that Part of the President's Speech which Relates to the Transportation of Newspapers, Report. . . .
[Philadelphia, 1793.] [2] pp.
NYPL ph copy.   46899

U. S. 2nd Congress, 1791-1793.
The Committee to whom was Referred the Memorial of Arthur St. Clair, Report. . . .
[Philadelphia, 1793.] Broadside.
NYPL copy.   46898

U. S. 2nd Congress, 1791-1793.
The Committee to whom was Referred the Memorial of the Directors of the Ohio Company . . . Report. . . .
[Philadelphia, 1792.] 9 pp.
NYPL copy.   24872

U. S. 2nd Congress, 1791-1793.
George Washington, President. . . . Senators. . . . Representatives.
[Philadelphia? 1792?] Broadside.
CHS copy.   46611

U. S. 2nd Congress, 1791-1793.
Members of Congress.
[Philadelphia, 1792.] Broadside.
(No copy located.)   46612

U. S. 2nd Congress, 1791-1793.
Members of the Second Congress.
[New York, 1791.] Broadside.
AAS copy.   46317

U. S. 2nd Congress, 1791-1793. House.
An Act to Establish the Post-Office. . . . Sent to the Senate for Concurrence.
[Philadelphia], Fenno, [1792]. 7 pp.
LOC copy.   46613

U. S. 2nd Congress, 1791-1793. House.
A Bill for Placing on the Pension List, such Officers and Privates . . . as may be . . . Disabled [Feb. 15, 1793.]
[Philadelphia? 1793.] Broadside.
NYPL ph. copy.   46900

U. S. 2nd Congress, 1791-1793. House.
A Bill Respecting Fugitives from Justice. . . . Nov. 15, 1791.
[Philadelphia, 1791.] Broadside.
NYPL ph. copy.   46318

U. S. 2nd Congress, 1791-1793. House.
A Bill to Authorize a Loan in the Certificates.
n.p., [1792]. Broadside.
WLC copy.   46608

U. S. 2nd Congress, 1791-1793. House.
A Bill to Authorize a Loan in the . . . Notes of such States as shall have Balances due to them [Jan. 15, 1795].
[Philadelphia, 1793.] Broadside.
NYPL ph. copy.   46901

U. S. 2nd Congress, 1791-1793. House.
The Committee Appointed to Consider and Report whether and what Alterations are Necessary. . . . [Feb. 29, 1792.]
[Philadelphia, 1792.] [2] pp.
NYPL ph. copy.   46614

U. S. 2nd Congress, 1791-1793. House.
The Committee Appointed to take into Consideration, the Act for Establishing the Post-Office. . . . Report. . . .
[Philadelphia, 1792.] [2] pp.
LOC copy.   46615

U. S. 2nd Congress, 1791-1793. House.
The Committee, to whom was Referred the Petition of James Warington. . . .
[Philadelphia, 1792.] 3 pp.
LOC copy.   46617

U. S. 2nd Congress, 1791-1793. House.
The Committee to whom was Referred the Message of the President [on commerce] . . . the 14th instant . . . Report. . . .
[Philadelphia, 1792.] Broadside.
LOC copy.   46616

U. S. 2nd Congress, 1791-1793. House.
Estimate of the Expenditures for the Civil List . . . for the Year 1793. . . . Published by Order of the House.
[Philadelphia], Childs & Swaine, [1702]. 23 pp.
JCB copy.   24908

U. S. 2nd Congress, 1791-1793. House.
Journal of the House [Oct. 24, 1791 - May 8, 1792].
Philadelphia, Childs & Swaine, 1792. 245 pp.
AAS copy.   24910

U. S. 2nd Congress, 1791-1793. House.
Journal of the House . . . Second Session of the Second Congress [Nov. 5, 1792 - Mar. 2, 1793].
Philadelphia, Childs & Swaine, 1793. 267 (i.e. 167), [25] pp.
AAS copy.   26332

U. S. 2nd Congress, 1791-1793. House.
Proceedings in the House . . . Respecting the Contested Election for the Eastern District of . . . Georgia.

Philadelphia, Hall, 1792. pp. [1]-40, 45-71.
AAS copy.   24916

[U. S. 2nd Congress, 1791-1793. House.
Proceedings of the House . . . Respecting the Contested Election for the Eastern District of . . . Georgia.
New York, Loudon, 1792?].
(Evans' entry from an adv.)   24917

U. S. 2nd Congress, 1791-1793. House.
Resolved, that a Loan . . . be Opened at the Treasury.
[Philadelphia? 1792?] Broadside.
WLC copy.   46618

U. S. 2nd Congress, 1791-1793. House.
Committee to Enquire into the St. Clair Expedition.
. . . The 8th of May, 1792. Mr. Fitzsimons . . . Reported. . . .
[Philadelphia, 1792.] 13 pp.
NYPL copy.   24909

U. S. 2nd Congress, 1791-1793. Senate.
An Act Establishing a Mint.
[Philadelphia], Fenno, [1792]. 6 pp.
LOC copy.   24887

[U. S. 2nd Congress, 1791-1793. Senate.
. . . An Act Relative to the Election of a President.
[Philadelphia, Fenno, 1792.] 2 pp.]
(No printing of the Bill located.)   24879

U. S. 2nd Congress, 1791-1793. Senate.
An Act to Repeal Part of a Resolution of Congress of the Twenty-ninth of August, One thousand Seven Hundred and Eighty-Eight, 1793, February the 6th, Passed the House of Representatives.
[Philadelphia], Fenno, [1793]. Broadside.
LOC copy.   26302

U. S. 2nd Congress, 1791-1793. Senate.
Acts of Virginia, Maryland, and of the United States, respecting the District of Columbia.
[Philadelphia?], printed by Order of the U.S. Senate, [1792?]. 16 pp.
(Not located 1967.)
JCB copy.   46619

U. S. 2nd Congress, 1791-1793. Senate.
. . . In Senate, January 29, 1793. The Committee to whom was Referred the Motions . . . Relative to the Measures and Weights . . . Report. . . .
[Philadelphia], Fenno, [1793]. 3 pp.
(This is apparently the item described by Evans.)
AAS copy.   26348

U. S. 2nd Congress, 1791-1793. Senate.
. . . In Senate, May the 7th, 1792, ordered, That the Secretary of the Treasury. . . .
[New York? 1792.] Broadside.
NYHS copy.   46620

U. S. 2nd Congress, 1791-1793. Senate.
Journal of the Senate [Oct. 24, 1791 - May 8, 1792].
Philadelphia, Fenno, 1791. 228 pp.
AAS copy.   24911

U. S. 2nd Congress, 1791-1793. Senate.
Journal of the Senate . . . Second Session of the Second Congress [Nov. 5, 1792 - Mar. 2, 1793].
Philadelphia, Fenno, 1793. 100 pp.
AAS copy.   26333

[U. S. 2nd Congress, 1791-1793. Senate.
Committee on Post-Office.
Report of the Committee on Post-Office and Post Roads.
Philadelphia, Fenno, 1792. 2 pp.]
(No copy located.)   24923

[U. S. 2nd Congress, 1791-1793. Senate.
Committee on Weights and Measures.
The Committee to whom the Subject . . . was Referred. . . . April 4, 1792.
[Philadelphia], Fenno, [1792]. 2 pp.]
(Ghost of 24943, q. v.)   24871

U. S. 2nd Congress, 1791-1793. Senate.
Committee on Weights and Measures.
United States, In Senate, April 4, 1792.
The Committee to whom this Subject . . . was Referred. . . .
[Philadelphia], Fenno, [1792]. 2 pp.
NYPL copy.   24943

U. S. 3rd Congress, 1793-1795.
A Bill Authorizing the President . . . to
lay . . . Embargoes.
[Philadelphia, 1794.] Broadside.
LOC copy.   47251

U. S. 3rd Congress, 1793-1795.
A Bill Authorizing the Transfer of the
Stock Standing to the Credit of Certain
States.
[Philadelphia, 1795.] Broadside.
AAS copy.   29712

U. S. 3rd Congress, 1793-1795.
A Bill for the Ascertainment of Certain
Losses. . . .
[Philadelphia, 1795.] Broadside.
AAS copy.   29713

U. S. 3rd Congress, 1793-1795.
A Bill Making further Provision in Cases
of Drawbacks.
[Philadelphia, 1795.] [2] pp.
AAS copy.   29714

U. S. 3rd Congress, 1793-1795.
A Bill Relative to the Compensations of
Certain Officers. . . .
[Philadelphia, 1795.] [2] pp.
AAS copy.   29715

U. S. 3rd Congress, 1793-1795.
A Bill Supplementary to the Act "for
Enrolling and Licensing Ships. . . ."
[Philadelphia, 1795.] [2] pp.
AAS copy.   29717

U. S. 3rd Congress, 1793-1795.
A Bill Supplementary to the Act,
Intituled, "An Act to Provide more
Effectually for the Collections of the
Duties. . . ."
[Philadelphia, 1795.] [2] pp.
AAS copy.   29716

U. S. 3rd Congress, 1793-1795.
A Bill Supplementary to the Several Acts
Imposing Duties. . . .
[Philadelphia, 1795.] Broadside.
AAS copy.   29718

U. S. 3rd Congress, 1793-1795.
A Bill to Alter and Amend the Act . . .
Laying Certain Duties upon Snuff. . . .
[Philadelphia, 1795.] [4] pp.
LOC copy.   47639

U. S. 3rd Congress, 1793-1795.
A Bill to Amend the Act, Intituled, "An
Act to Establish an Uniform Rule of
Naturalization.
[Philadelphia, 1794.] Broadside.
AAS copy.   27899

U. S. 3rd Congress, 1793-1795.
A Bill to Establish an Uniform Rule of
Naturalization, and to Repeal the Act
heretofore Passed on that Subject.
[Philadelphia, 1795.] [2] pp.
AAS copy.   47640

U. S. 3rd Congress, 1793-1795.
A Bill to Establish an Uniform System of
Bankruptcy.
[Philadelphia], Childs & Swaine, [1794?]
13 pp.
WLC copy.   47252

U. S. 3rd Congress, 1793-1795.
A Bill to Establish Offices for the Purpose
of Granting Lands. . . .
[Philadelphia, 1795.] [3] pp.
AAS copy.   29719

U. S. 3rd Congress, 1793-1795.
The Committee, to whom it was Referred
to Report, "The Naval Force
Necessary. . . ." [Jan. 2, 1794].
[Philadelphia, 1794.] 7 pp.
LOC copy.   27902

U. S. 3rd Congress, 1793-1795.
The Committee to whom was Referred the
Several Petitions of the Quakers . . .
January, 1794.
[Philadelphia, 1794.], Broadside.
BA copy.   27904

U. S. 3rd Congress, 1793-1795.
The Committee to whom were Referred
Sundry Petitions . . . and also a Letter
from the Judges of the Circuit Court for
. . . North-Carolina.

[Philadelphia? 1793.] Broadside.
WLC copy.   46902

U. S. 3rd Congress, 1793-1795.
. . . February 10th, 1794. The Committee
of Elections. . . .
[Philadelphia], Fenno, [1794]. [4] pp.
(Not located, 1968.)   47275

U. S. 3rd Congress, 1793-1795.
. . . June 6th, 1794. The Committee to
which was Referred the Bill Intitled, "An
Act Providing for the Payment of a
Certain Sum of Money due to the French
Republic. . . . Report. . . .
[Philadelphia, 1794.] [2] pp.
AAS copy.   27897

U. S. 3rd Congress, 1793-1795.
List of Acts Passed at the First Session of
the Third Congress. No. 1. . . . 46.
[Philadelphia, 1794.] [2] pp.
AAS copy.   27885

U. S. 3rd Congress, 1793-1795.
List of Acts Passed at the First Session of
the Third Congress. No. 1. . . . 65.
[Philadelphia, 1794.] [2] pp.
AAS copy.   27884

U. S. 3rd Congress, 1793-1795.
A List of the Names and Places of Abode,
of the Members of the Senate and
House. . . . Philadelphia, Nov. 19, 1794.
[Philadelphia, 1794.] Broadside.
(Not located, 1968.)   47253

U. S. 3rd Congress, 1793-1795.
Report of the Committee Appointed to
Examine into the State of the Treasury
Department Made . . . the 22d Day of
May, 1794.
Philadelphia, Childs & Swaine, 1794. 86,
[2] pp.
AAS copy.   27909

U. S. 3rd Congress, 1793-1795.
Report of the Committee of Claims, on
the Petition of Gilbert Dench, Made the
29th of January, 1795.
[Philadelphia, 1795.] [1], 3 pp.
AAS copy.   29728

U. S. 3rd Congress, 1793-1795.
. . . Resolved by the Senate and House . . .
the following Article be Proposed . . . as
an Amendment to the Constitution. . . .
[Philadelphia, 1794.] Broadside.
JCB copy.,   47254

U. S. 3rd Congress, 1793-1795.
Resolved, that a Loan to the Amount of
the Balances . . . due from the United
States to the Individual States, be Opened.
[Philadelphia, 1793?] Broadside.
NYPL ph. copy.   46903

U. S. 3rd Congress, 1793-1795.
Resolved, that Provision Ought to be
Made . . . for the Sequestration of all the
Debts due . . . to the Subjects of the King.
n.p., [1794?] Broadside.
WLC copy.   47255

U. S. 3rd Congress, 1793-1795. House.
An Act Laying Additional Duties. . . .
Passed the House . . . May 17th, 1794.
[Philadelphia, 1794.] Broadside.
(Not located, 1968.)   47256

U. S. 3rd Congress, 1793-1795. House.
An Act to Regulate the Pay of the
Non-Commissioned Officers. . . .
December 12th, 1794. Passed the House.
[Philadelphia, 1794.] Broadside.
(Not located, 1968.)   47257

U. S. 3rd Congress, 1793-1795. House.
Amendments Proposed in the Committee
of the Whole House, to the Bill to Amend
the Act Intituled, "An Act to Establish an
Uniform Rule of Naturalization."
[Philadelphia, 1794.] Broadside.
AAS copy.   27898

[U. S. 3rd Congress, 1793-1795. House.
A Bill for the Ascertainment of Certain
Losses of the Officers of Government . . .
by the Insurgents.
[Philadelphia, 1794.] Broadside.
(The unique copy described by Evans
cannot now be located.)   27900

U. S. 3rd Congress, 1793-1795. House.
A Bill Laying Duties upon Carriages.
[Philadelphia, 1794.] [4] pp.
LOC copy.   47258

U. S. 3rd Congress, 1793-1795. House.
A Bill Making further Provision for
Securing. . . .
[Philadelphia], Childs & Swaine, [1794].
[2] pp.
LOC copy.   47259

U. S. 3rd Congress, 1793-1795. House.
A Bill Providing for Destroyed
Certificates [Dec. 27, 1793].
[Philadelphia, 1793.] Broadside.
NYPL ph. copy.   46904

U. S. 3rd Congress, 1793-1795. House.
A Bill Relative to Cessions of Jurisdiction
in . . . Lighthouses. . . . [Jan. 26, 1795.]
[Philadelphia, 1795.] Broadside.
WLC copy.   47641

U. S. 3rd Congress, 1793-1795. House.
A Bill to Provide for Organizing, Arming
and Disciplining the Militia.
Philadelphia, Childs, 1795. 16 pp.
AAS copy.   29720

U. S. 3rd Congress, 1793-1795. House.
The Committee Appointed to Enquire and
Report what Progress. . . .
[Philadelphia, 1795.] [2] pp.
WLC copy.   47642

U. S. 3rd Congress, 1793-1795. House.
The Committee Appointed to Enquire if
any or what Alterations Ought to be made
in the Act, passed the 7th Day of June,
1794.
n. p., [1794]. Broadside.
WLC copy.   47260

U. S. 3rd Congress, 1793-1795. House.
The Committee Appointed to Enquire,
whether any and what Alterations . . .
Virginia Line.
[Philadelphia, 1794.] Broadside.
LOC copy.   47261

U. S. 3rd Congress, 1793-1795. House.
The Committee Appointed to Enquire
whether any, or what further or other
Revenues are Necessary. . . .
n. p., [1794]. [4] pp.
WLC copy.   47262

U. S. 3rd Congress, 1793-1795. House.
The Committee Appointed to Examine
into and Report what Proceedings have
been Had . . . Frontiers . . . Report. . . .
[Philadelphia, 1795.] Broadside.
WLC copy.   47643

U. S. 3rd Congress, 1793-1795. House.
The Committee Appointed to Prepare and
Report a Plan for the Reduction of the
Public Debt. . . .
[Philadelphia, 1794.] [4] pp.
(Not located, 1968.)   47263

U. S. 3rd Congress, 1793-1795. House.
The Committee Appointed to Prepare and
Report such Standing Rules . . .
Report. . . . [January 7, 1794].
[Philadelphia, 1794.] [4] pp.
BA copy.   27903

U. S. 3rd Congress, 1793-1795. House.
The Committee, Directed to Report on
such of the Ports . . . Report. . . .
February 28, 1794.
[Philadelphia, Childs & Swaine, [1794]. 7
pp.
BA copy.   27905

U. S. 3rd Congress, 1793-1795. House.
The Committee of Claims to whom was
Referred the Petition of Joab Stafford,
Report. . . .
[Philadelphia, 1795.] [2] pp.
LOC copy.   47644

U. S. 3rd Congress, 1793-1795. House.
The Committee of Elections, to whom was
Referred the Petition of Henry
Latimer. . . .
[Philadelphia, 1794?] [2] pp.
NYPL ph. copy.   47264

U. S. 3rd Congress, 1793-1795. House.
The Committee to whom it was Referred

to Consider [light houses]. . . .
[Philadelphia, 1794?] Broadside.
LOC copy.   47265

U. S. 3rd Congress, 1793-1795. House.
The Committee, to whom it was Referred,
to Report the Means of Rendering the
Force. . . .
[Philadelphia, 1794.] Broadside.
LOC copy.   47266

U. S. 3rd Congress, 1793-1795. House.
The Committee, to whom it was Referred
to Report "The Naval Force
Necessary. . . ."
[Philadelphia? 1794]. 7 pp.
WLC copy.   47267

U. S. 3rd Congress, 1793-1795. House.
The Committee to whom was
Re-committed a Report on the Memorial
of Arthur St. Clair [Apr. 22, 1794].
[Philadelphia, 1794.] [3] pp.
BA copy.   27907

U. S. 3rd Congress, 1793-1795. House.
The Committee, to whom was Referred a
Petition of Sundry Inhabitants of the
County of, Washington. . . . May 16, 1794.
[Philadelphia, 1794.] [4] pp., 2 folding
charts.
BA copy.   27908

U. S. 3rd Congress, 1793-1795. House.
The Committee to whom was Referred
that Part of the President's Speech, which
Relates to the Improvement. . . .
[Philadelphia, 1794.] Broadside.
(Best copy available.)
LOC copy.   47268

U. S. 3rd Congress, 1793-1795. House.
The Committee to whom was Referred
that Part of the President's Speech which
Relates to the Policy of Idemnifying the
Sufferers by the Depredations of the
Insurgents.
[Philadelphia, 1794.] Broadside.
AAS copy.   27901

U. S. 3rd Congress, 1793-1795. House.
The Committee to whom was Referred the
Memorial of Arthur St. Clair, Report. . . .
[Philadelphia, 1795.] Broadside.
LOC copy.   47645

U. S. 3rd Congress, 1793-1795. House.
The Committee to whom was Referred the
Memorial of the Representatives of the
People of the Ohio, Report . . . [Apr. 8,
1794].
[Philadelphia, 1794.] Broadside.
LOC copy.   27906

U. S. 3rd Congress, 1793-1795. House.
The Committee to whom was Referred the
Message from the President . . . inclosing
. . . Letter from the Governor of North
Carolina.
[Philadelphia, 1794.] Broadside.
(No copy located.)   47270

U. S. 3rd Congress, 1793-1795. House.
The Committee to whom was Referred the
Petition of Colonel Lewis Dubois. . . .
[Philadelphia, 1794.] Broadside.
LOC copy.   47271

U. S. 3rd Congress, 1793-1795. House.
The Committee to whom was Referred the
Petition of William Denning. . . .
n.p., [1794]. Broadside.
WLC copy.   47272

U. S. 3rd Congress, 1793-1795. House.
The Committee to whom was Referred the
President's Message of the 30th of
January. . . .
[Philadelphia, 1794.] Broadside.
WLC copy.   47269

U. S. 3rd Congress, 1793-1795. House.
The Committee to whom was Referred,
the Remonstrance of the People West of
the Allegany Mountain. . . .
[Philadelphia, 1794] Broadside.
WLC copy.   47273

U. S. 3rd Congress, 1793-1795. House.
The Committee to whom were Referred
two Reports of the Secretary for the
Department of War. . . . 25th April, 1794.

[Philadelphia, 1794?] [2] pp.
(Not located, 1968.)   47274

U. S. 3rd Congress, 1793-1795. House.
In the House of Representatives, Monday,
February 24, 1794. Resolved, That a
Committee. . . .
[Philadelphia], Childs & Swaine, [1794].
6 pp.
LOC copy.   47276

U. S. 3rd Congress, 1793-1795. House.
Journal of the House . . . First Session of
the Third Congress [Dec. 2, 1793 - May
21, 1794].
Philadelphia, Childs & Swaine, 1793. 438,
[29] pp.
AAS copy.   27910

U. S. 3rd Congress, 1793-1795. House.
Journal of the House . . . Second Session
of the Third Congress [Nov. 3, 1794 -
Mar. 3, 1795].
Philadelphia, Childs & Swaine, 1794. 312,
[26] pp.
AAS copy.   29723

U. S. 3rd Congress, 1793-1795. House.
Mr. Hillhouse's Motion. 16th February.
[Philadelphia, 1795.] [4] pp.
NYPL copy.   47646

[U. S. 3rd Congress, 1793-1795. House.
Report of the Committee to Whom was
Referred the Message of the President of
the 17th. . . .
[Philadelphia, 1795.] Broadside.
(Apparently a ghost of Waters 680.) 29727

U. S. 3rd Congress, 1793-1795. House.
Resolved, That there be Raised, Armed
and Equipped, Fifteen Regiments [Mar.
12, 1794].
[Philadelphia, 1794.] Broadside.
LOC copy.   27896

U. S. 3rd Congress, 1793-1795. House.
Committee on the Mint.
Report on the State of the Mint. . . .
Published by Order of the House.
Philadelphia, Childs, 1795. 15 pp.
AAS copy.   29774

U. S. 3rd Congress, 1793-1795. Senate.
An Act Directing a Detachment from the
Militia. . . . Passed the House . . . April
23d, 1794.
[Philadelphia, 1794.] Broadside.
NYPL copy.   47277

U. S. 3rd Congress, 1793-1795. Senate.
An Act in Addition to the Act for the
Punishment of Certain Crimes. . . . [Mar.
14, 1794.]
[Philadelphia], Fenno, [1794]. [4] pp.
NYPL ph. copy.   47278

U. S. 3rd Congress, 1793-1795. Senate.
An Act in Addition to the Act for the
Punishment of Certain Crimes. . . . [June
2, 1794.]
[New York], Fenno, [1794]. [4] pp.
NYPL ph. copy.   47279

U. S. 3rd Congress, 1793-1795. Senate.
An Act in Alteration of the Act
Establishing a Mint. . . . [Feb. 18, 1794]
[Philadelphia], Fenno, [1794]. Broadside.
NYPL ph. copy.   47280

U. S. 3rd Congress, 1793-1795. Senate.
An Act to Regulate Proceedings in Cases
of Outlawry [Feb. 6, 1795].
[Philadelphia, 1795.] [4] pp.
NYPL copy.   47647

U. S. 3rd Congress, 1793-1795. Senate.
. . . February 10th, 1794. The Committee
of Elections. . . .
[Philadelphia], Fenno, [1794]. [4] pp.
NYHS copy.   47275

U. S. 3rd Congress, 1793-1795. Senate.
. . . April 4th, 1794. Ordered, That the
Three Letters. . . .
[Philadelphia, 1794.] 12 pp.
AAS copy.   27891

U. S. 3rd Congress, 1793-1795. Senate.
. . . December 5th, 1794. A Bill to Amend
and Explain the Twenty-Second Section.
[Philadelphia, 1794.] Broadside.
AAS copy.   27895

U. S. 3rd Congress, 1793-1795. Senate.
. . . January 9th, 1795. Ordered, That
Three Hundred Copies of the
Communication from the Minister of the
French Republic. . . .
[Philadelphia], Fenno, [1795]. 8 pp.
AAS copy.   29722

U. S. 3rd Congress, 1793-1795. Senate.
Journal of the Senate . . . First Session of
the Third Congress [Dec. 2, 1793-June 9,
1794].
Philadelphia, Fenno, 1793. 205 pp.
AAS copy.   27911

U. S. 3rd Congress, 1793-1795. Senate.
Journal of the Senate . . . Second Session
of the Third Congress [Nov. 3, 1794 -
Mar. 3, 1795].
Philadelphia, Fenno, 1794. 114, [12] pp.
AAS copy.   29724

U. S. 3rd Congress, 1793-1795. Senate.
. . . March the 26th, 1794. The Bill,
Entitled "An Act Limiting the Time for
Presenting Claims. . . ."
[Philadelphia, 1794.] Broadside.
AAS copy.   27890

U. S. 3rd Congress, 1793-1795. Senate.
. . . May 12th, 1794. On Motion, Ordered,
That the Memorial of Mr. Pinckney. . . .
[Philadelphia, 1794.] 32 pp.
AAS copy.   27892

U. S. 3rd Congress, 1793-1795. Senate.
. . . May the 23rd, 1794. Ordered, That the
Message from the President. . . .
[Philadelphia, 1794.] 11 pp.
AAS copy.   27893

U. S. 3rd Congress, 1793-1795. Senate.
. . . May the 29th, 1794. Ordered, that 300
Copies of the Report. . . .
[Philadelphia, 1794.] 4 pp., 2 folding
charts.
AAS copy.   27894

U. S. 4th Congress, 1795-1797.
An Act Directing Certain Experiments to
be made to Ascertain Uniform Standards
of Weights and Measures. . . . In Senate,
May the 31st, 1796.
[Philadelphia, 1796.] 8 pp.
AAS copy.   31334

U. S. 4th Congress, 1795-1797.
In the House . . . 4th of January, 1796. A
Message . . . was Received from the
President.
[Philadelphia, 1796.] 7 pp.
AAS copy.   31365

[U. S. 4th Congress, 1795-1797.
Report of the Committee to whom was
Referred the Resolutions of the Senate
Respecting the Southern and Western
Boundary of Georgia. 2 March, 1797.
[Philadelphia, 1797.]]
(A ghost of 32968, q. v.)   33036

U. S. 4th Congress, 1795-1797.
A List of the Names, and Places of
Abode, of the Members of the Senate, and
House.
[Philadelphia, 1795.] Broadside.
AAS copy.   29726

[U. S. 4th Congress, 1795-1797.
A List of the Names, and Places of
Abode, of the Members of the Senate, and
House.
[Philadelphia, 1796.] Broadside.]
(The located copies are actually 29726.)
                                             31357

U. S. 4th Congress, 1795-1797.
Mr. Maclay's Motion, 14th April 1796.
[Philadelphia, 1796.] [1] p.
AAS copy.   31361

U. S. 4th Congress, 1795-1797.
Mr. Samuel Smith's Motion, 4th January,
1796.
[Philadelphia, 1796.] [1] p.
AAS copy.   31362

U. S. 4th Congress, 1795-1797.
Report of the Committee Appointed the
Sixteenth of December last, to Enquire
into the Actual State of the
Fortifications. . . . 11th February 1797,

Committed. . . . Published by Order of the
House.
[Philadelphia, 1797.] 4 pp.
AAS copy.   32988

U. S. 4th Congress, 1795-1797. House.
An Act for Establishing Trading Houses
with the Indian Tribes. . . . 1796.
February the 1st, read the Third Time.
[Philadelphia, 1796.] 4 pp.
LOC copy.   47948

U. S. 4th Congress, 1795-1797. House.
An Act Laying Duties on Carriages. . . .
Passed the House . . . May 9, 1796.
[Philadelphia], Fenno, [1796]. 8 pp.
JCB copy.   47949

U. S. 4th Congress, 1795-1797. House.
An Act Relative to the Compensations . . .
Certain Officers Employed in the
Collection of Impost . . . Passed the
House . . . February 24, 1797.
[Philadelphia], Fenno, [1797]. [3] pp.
LOC copy.   32959

U. S. 4th Congress, 1795-1797. House.
A Bill for an Apportionment of
Representatives . . . to Compose the
House . . . after the 3d Day of March,
1797.
[Philadelphia], Childs & Swaine, [1797].
[3] pp.
LOC copy.   48277

U. S. 4th Congress, 1795-1797. House.
Debates of the House of Representatives
. . . with Respect to Treaties, and Upon
the Subject of the British Treaty.
Philadelphia, Bioren & Madan for Bache,
1796. [2], [1]-386, [3]-362.
(This was the original form of publication.
The two parts were later issued with the
"Part I" and "Part II" titlepages.)
AAS copy.   31351

[U. S. 4th Congress, 1795-1797. House.
Debates in the House of Representatives
. . . with Respect to Treaties, and upon the
Subject of the British Treaty.
Philadelphia, Bioren & Madan for Bache,
1796. 8 pp.]
(This is apparently a proof of the first
signature of 31351.)   31353

U. S. 4th Congress, 1795-1797. House.
Debates in the House of Representatives.
. . . Part II. Upon the . . . British Treaty.
Philadelphia, Bioren & Madan for Bache,
1796. 362 pp.
(This is the second part of 31351 for which
see text.)
AAS copy.   31352

U. S. 4th Congress, 1795-1797. House.
11th March, 1796, Committed to a
Committee of the Whole House Report.
. . . A Bill Authorizing a Loan for . . .
the City of Washington.
[Philadelphia, 1796.] 3 pp.
LOC copy.   31349

U. S. 4th Congress, 1795-1797. House.
14th March, 1796. . . . A Bill for the Relief
and Protection of American Seamen.
[Philadelphia, 1796.] 4 pp.
LOC copy.   31350

U. S. 4th Congress, 1795-1797. House.
Journal of the House . . . First Session of
the Fourth Congress [Dec. 7, 1795 - June
1, 1796].
Philadelphia, Childs, 1795. 537, [35] pp.,
irreg.
AAS copy.   31354

U. S. 4th Congress, 1795-1797. House.
Journal of the House . . . Second Session
of the Fourth Congress [Dec. 5, 1796 -
Mar. 3, 1797].
Philadelphia, Ross, 1796. 299, [28] pp.
AAS copy.   32969

U. S. 4th Congress, 1795-1797. House.
(Made the 4th of February, 1796, and
Committed. . . .) Report of the Committee
of Ways and Means . . . for the Public
Debt. Published by Order of the House.
[Philadelphia, 1796.] [3] pp.
AAS copy.   31379

U. S. 4th Congress, 1795-1797. House.
(Made the 4th of January, 1796. . . .)

Report of the Committee of Claims on the
Petition of John Baptist Dumon.
Published by Order of the House.
[Philadelphia, 1796.] 4 pp.
AAS copy.   31371

U. S. 4th Congress, 1795-1797. House.
(Made the 8th of February, 1796, and
Committed. . . .) Report of the Committee
of Commerce and Manufactures on the
Petitions of Israel Loring. . . . Published
by Order of the House.
[Philadelphia, 1796.] 6 pp.
AAS copy.   31380

U. S. 4th Congress, 1795-1797. House.
(Made the 11th of December, 1795.) The
Committee Appointed on the 7th
Instant. . . .
[Philadelphia, 1796.] 11 pp.
AAS copy.   31366

U. S. 4th Congress, 1795-1797. House.
(Made the 11th of January 1796. . . .)
Report of the Committee of Commerce
and Manufactures, on the Petition of John
Devereux. . . . Published by Order of the
House.
[Philadelphia, 1796.] 6 pp.
AAS copy.   31372

U. S. 4th Congress, 1795-1797. House.
(Made the 13th of January, 1796.) Report
of the Committee of Elections . . . on the
Memorial of John Richards.
[Philadelphia, 1796.] 6 pp.
AAS copy.   31373

U. S. 4th Congress, 1795-1797. House.
(Made the 14th of December, 1795.)
Report from the Committee. . . .
[Philadelphia], Childs, [1796]. 4 pp.
AAS copy.   31368

U. S. 4th Congress, 1795-1797. House.
(Made the 26th of January, 1796, and
Committed to . . . the Whole House. . . .)
Report of the Committee of Claims . . .
Respecting Officers and Soldiers. . . .
Published by Order of the House.
[Philadelphia, 1796.] 6 pp.
AAS copy.   31376

U. S. 4th Congress, 1795-1797. House.
(Made the 26th of January, 1796.) Report
of the Committee of Claims on the
Petition of John Griffin. Published by
Order of the House.
[Philadelphia, 1796.] 4 pp.
AAS copy.   31375

U. S. 4th Congress, 1795-1797. House.
(Made the 26th of January. . . .) Report of
the Committee of Claims, on the Petition
of Silas Clark. Published by Order of the
House.
[Philadelphia, 1796.] [3] pp.
AAS copy.   31374

U. S. 4th Congress, 1795-1797. House.
(Made the 29th of December, 1795.)
Report of the Committee . . . on the
Memorial of Parker, Hopkins and Meers.
Published by Order of the House.
[Philadelphia], Childs, [1796]. 4 pp.
AAS copy.   31370

U. S. 4th Congress, 1795-1797. House.
(Made the 29th of January, 1796, and
Committed. . . .) Report of the
Committee, Appointed to Enquire into the
Actual State of the Naval Equipment. . . .
Published by Order of the House.
[Philadelphia, 1796.] 5 pp.
AAS copy.   31378

U. S. 4th Congress, 1795-1797. House.
Memorial of the Illinois and Wabash Land
Company. 13th January 1797. . . . Published
by Order of the House.
[Philadelphia, 1797.] 8 pp.
AAS copy.   32976

U. S. 4th Congress, 1795-1797. House.
Mr. Blount's Motion, in the Committee of
the Whole House, on the Message from
the President. . . . Made 6th April, 1796.
[Philadelphia, 1796.] Broadside.
AAS copy.   31358

U. S. 4th Congress, 1795-1797. House.
Mr. Harper's Motion. 9th February 1797.

[Philadelphia, 1797.] 4 pp.
AAS copy.   32978

U. S. 4th Congress, 1795-1797. House.
Mr. Harper's Motion, 31st December,
1795.
[Philadelphia, 1796.] [1] pp.
AAS copy.   31359

U. S. 4th Congress, 1795-1797. House.
Mr. Kitchell's Motion, 1st April, 1796. . . .
Published by Order of the House.
[Philadelphia, 1796.] [3] pp.
AAS copy.   31360

U. S. 4th Congress, 1795-1797. House.
Mr. Samuel Smith's Motion. 7th May,
1796. . . . Published by Order of the
House.
[Philadelphia, 1796.] [1] p.
AAS copy.   31363

U. S. 4th Congress, 1795-1797. House.
Mr. William Smith's Motion, to Amend
the Constitution. . . . 6th January 1797.
Published by Order of the House.
[Philadelphia, 1797.] [3] pp.
AAS copy.   32979

U. S. 4th Congress, 1795-1797. House.
Papers, Relative to an Application to
Congress, for an Exclusive Right of
Searching for and Working Mines.
[Philadelphia], Smith, [1796]. 28 pp.
AAS copy.   31473

U. S. 4th Congress, 1795-1797. House.
Proceedings of the House . . . in the Case
of Robert Randall and Charles Whitney.
Published by Order of the House.
[Philadelphia, 1796.] 32 pp.
AAS copy.   31364

U. S. 4th Congress, 1795-1797. House.
Report of the Committee Appointed on
the Fifth Instant to Enquire into the . . .
Territory North West of the River Ohio. .
30th January 1797. Committed. . . .
Published by Order of the House.
[Philadelphia, 1797.] 7 pp.
AAS copy.   32987

U. S. 4th Congress, 1795-1797. House.
Report of the Committee Appointed to
Enquire if any, and what Alterations are
Necessary to be made in the Act to
Establish the Post-Office. . . . 4th April,
1796, Committee. . . . Published by Order
of the House.
[Philadelphia, 1796.] 8 pp.
AAS copy.   31387

U. S. 4th Congress, 1795-1797. House.
Report of the Committee Appointed to
Enquire into the Operation of the Act for
the Relief and Protection of American
Seamen. . . . 28th February 1797,
Committed. . . . Published by Order of the
House.
[Philadelphia, 1797.] 25 pp.
AAS copy.   32989

U. S. 4th Congress, 1795-1797. House.
Report of the Committee Appointed to
Enquire into the State of the Naval
Equipment. . . . 25th January, 1797.
Committed. . . . Published by Order of the
House.
[Philadelphia, 1797.] 6 pp.
AAS copy.   32986

U. S. 4th Congress, 1795-1797. House.
Report of the Committee Appointed to.
Enquire into the Truth of the Information,
that a Son of General LaFayette. . . . 26
April, 1796. Ordered to lie on the Table.
Published by Order of the House.
[Philadelphia, 1796.] 4 pp.
AAS copy.   31391

U. S. 4th Congress, 1795-1797. House.
Report of the Committee Appointed to
Enquire whether any, and what
Alterations Ought to be Made in the
Compensations Allowed by Law, to the
Officers of the United States. 9th January,
1797, Committed. . . . Published by Order
of the House.
[Philadelphia, 1797.] [3] pp.
AAS copy.   32984

U. S. 4th Congress, 1795-1797. House.
Report of the Committee Appointed to

Enquire whether any, and what
Alterations Ought to be made in the
Present Military. . . . 25th March, 1796,
Committed. . . . Published by Order of the
House.
[Philadelphia, 1796.] [3] pp.
AAS copy.　　　　31386

U. S. 4th Congress, 1795-1797. House.
Report of the Committee Appointed to
Enquire whether any, and what
Amendments may be Necessary in the Act
"To Ascertain and Fix the Military
Establishment. . . ." 13th January 1797,
Committed. . . . Published by Order of the
House.
[Philadelphia, 1797.] 4 pp.
AAS copy.　　　　32985

U. S. 4th Congress, 1795-1797. House.
Report of the Committee Appointed to
Prepare an Address to the President. . . .
12th December, 1796. Read. . . . Published
by Order of the House.
[Philadelphia, 1797.] 6 pp.
AAS copy.　　　　32983

U. S. 4th Congress, 1795-1797. House.
Report of the Committee Appointed to
take into Consideration the State of the
Fortifications. . . . 9th May, 1796.
Committed. . . . Published by Order of the
House.
[Philadelphia, 1796.] 4 pp.
AAS copy.　　　　31394

U. S. 4th Congress, 1795-1797. House.
Report of the Committee of Claims, on
the Memorial of Samuel G. Fowler. . . .
7th May, 1796. Committed. . . . Published
by Order of the House.
[Philadelphia, 1796.] 4 pp.
AAS copy.　　　　31393

U. S. 4th Congress, 1795-1797. House.
Report of the Committee of Claims, on
the Petition of Alexander Fowler. 17th
May, 1796. Committed.
[Philadelphia, 1796.] 5 pp.
AAS copy.　　　　31399

U. S. 4th Congress, 1795-1797. House.
Report of the Committee of Claims, on
the Petition of Anna Welsh. . . . 7th
February, 1797. . . . Published by Order of
the House.
[Philadelphia, 1797.] 6 pp.
AAS copy.　　　　33001

U. S. 4th Congress, 1795-1797. House.
Report of the Committee of Claims, on
the Petition of Benjamin Titcomb, 22d
December, 1795, Read. . . . 29th
December, 1795. Committed. . . .
Published by Order of the House.
[Philadelphia, 1796.] [3] pp.
AAS copy.　　　　31369

U. S. 4th Congress, 1795-1797. House.
Report of the Committee of Claims, on
the Petition of Catharine Greene. . . . 13th
May, 1796. Committed. . . . Published by
Order of the House.
[Philadelphia, 1796.] 6 pp.
AAS copy.　　　　31396

U. S. 4th Congress, 1795-1797. House.
Report of the Committee of Claims, on
the Petition of Comfort Sands. . . . 9th
February 1797. . . . Published by Order of
the House.
[Philadelphia, 1797.] 6 pp.
AAS copy.　　　　33002

U. S. 4th Congress, 1795-1797. House.
Report of the Committee of Claims on the
Petition of Edward St. Loe Livermore.
24th January, 1797, Committed. . . .
Published by Order of the House.
[Philadelphia, 1797.] 4 pp.
AAS copy.　　　　33000

U. S. 4th Congress, 1795-1797. House.
Report of the Committee of Claims, on
the Petition of Gilbert Dench. 4th January
1797, Committed. . . . Published by Order
of the House.
[Philadelphia, 1797.] 4 pp.
AAS copy.　　　　32995

U. S. 4th Congress, 1795-1797. House.
Report of the Committee of Claims, on

the Petition of Henry Hill. . . . 9th
December, 1796. Committed. . . .
Published by Order of the House.
[Philadelphia, 1797.] 4 pp.
AAS copy.　　　　32990

U. S. 4th Congress, 1795-1797. House.
Report of the Committee of Claims, on
the Petition of Henry Hill. 26th May,
1796. Committed. . . . Published by Order
of the House.
[Philadelphia, 1796.] 3 pp.
AAS copy.　　　　47950

U. S. 4th Congress, 1795-1797. House.
Report of the Committee of Claims, on
the Petition of James Ore. 12th January,
1797, Committed. . . . Published by Order
of the House.
[Philadelphia, 1796.] 4 pp.
AAS copy.　　　　32996

U. S. 4th Congress, 1795-1797. House.
Report of the Committee of Claims, on
the Petition of John Gibbons. . . . 22d
December 1796.
[Philadelphia, 1796.] 9 pp.
BA copy.　　　　32992

U. S. 4th Congress, 1795-1797. House.
Report of the Committee of Claims, on
the Petition of John Gibbons, 29th April
1796.
n.p., [1796]. 9 pp.
WLC copy.　　　　47951

U. S. 4th Congress, 1795-1797. House.
Report of the Committee of Claims, on
the Petition of Oliver Pollock. . . . 12th
January 1797, Committed. . . . Published
by Order of the House.
[Philadelphia, 1797.] 4 pp.
AAS copy.　　　　32997

U. S. 4th Congress, 1795-1797. House.
Report of the Committee of Claims, on
the Petition of Oliver Pollock. 26th May,
1796. Committed. . . . Published by Order
of the House.
[Philadelphia, 1796.] 4 pp.
AAS copy.　　　　31401

U. S. 4th Congress, 1795-1797. House.
Report of the Committee of Claims, on
the Petition of the Corporation of
Rhode-Island College. . . . 11th February
1797. . . . Published by Order of the
House.
[Philadelphia, 1797.] 4 pp.
AAS copy.　　　　33003

U. S. 4th Congress, 1795-1797. House.
Report of the Committee of Claims, on
the Petition of the Widow of the Late
Scolacuttow. . . . 17th January, 1797. . . .
Published by Order of the House.
[Philadelphia, 1797.] 4 pp.
AAS copy.　　　　32999

U. S. 4th Congress, 1795-1797. House.
Report of the Committee of Claims, on
the Petition of William Parsons. . . . 27th
December, 1796, Committed. . . .
Published by Order of the House.
[Philadelphia, 1797.] [3] pp.
AAS copy.　　　　32993

U. S. 4th Congress, 1795-1797. House.
Report of the Committee of Claims, on
the Petitions of Samuel Abbot and
Others. . . . 21st February, 1797,
Committed. . . .
[Philadelphia, 1797.] 4 pp.
AAS copy.　　　　33005

U. S. 4th Congress, 1795-1797. House.
Report of the Committee of Claims, to
whom it was Referred, on the 20th of
December last, to Enquire into . . . Acts
of Limitation. 24th February 1797. . . .
Published by Order of the House.
[Philadelphia, 1797.] 12 pp.
AAS copy.　　　　33006

U. S. 4th Congress, 1795-1797. House.
Report of the Committee of Claims, to
whom was Committed the Bill sent from
the Senate, Intituled, "An Act, Making an
Extra Allowance to Certain Clerks. . . .
17th May, 1796. Committed.
[Philadelphia, 1796.] 4 pp.
AAS copy.　　　　31398

U. S. 4th Congress, 1795-1797. House.
Report of the Committee of Claims, to
whom were Re-Committed the Petition of
Henry Hill. . . . 13th January, 1797,
Committed. . . . Published by Order of the
House.
[Philadelphia, 1797.] 6 pp.
AAS copy.　　　　32991

U. S. 4th Congress, 1795-1797. House.
Report of the Committee of Claims, to
whom were Referred, on the
Twenty-Fourth of December, 1795, Copies
of the Proceedings of the Accounting
Officers. . . . 29th December, 1796,
Committed.
[Philadelphia, 1797.] [3] pp.
AAS copy.　　　　32994

U. S. 4th Congress, 1795-1797. House.
Report of the Committee of Commerce
and Manufactures, on the Memorials of
Sundry Manufacturers of Chocolate 8th
February 1797. . . . Published by Order of
the House.
[Philadelphia, 1797.] 4 pp.
AAS copy.　　　　33010

U. S. 4th Congress, 1795-1797. House.
Report of the Committee of Commerce
and Manufactures, on the Memorials of
Sundry Manufacturers of Soap. . . . 23d
February, 1797. . . . Published by Order of
the House.
[Philadelphia, 1797.] 4 pp.
AAS copy.　　　　33011

U. S. 4th Congress, 1795-1797. House.
Report of the Committee of Commerce
and Manufactures, on the Petition of
North and Vezey. . . . 23d February
1797. . . . Published by Order of the
House.
[Philadelphia, 1797.] 4 pp.
AAS copy.　　　　33013

U. S. 4th Congress, 1795-1797. House.
Report of the Committee of Commerce
and Manufactures, on the Petition of
Samuel Legaré. . . . 27th December,
1796. . . . Published by Order of the
House.
[Philadelphia, 1797.] [3] pp.
AAS copy.　　　　33012

U. S. 4th Congress, 1795-1797. House.
Report of the Committee of Elections, to
whom was Recommitted the Petition of
Mathew Lyon. . . . 13th May, 1796.
Ordered to lie on the Table.
[Philadelphia, 1796.] [3] pp.
AAS copy.　　　　31397

U. S. 4th Congress, 1795-1797. House.
Report of the Committee of Elections to
whom was Referred the Petition of
Matthew Lyon. . . . 27th January, 1796,
Read. . . . 4th February, 1796, farther
Consideration Postponed. . . . Published
by Order of the House.
[Philadelphia, 1796.] 4 pp.
AAS copy.　　　　31377

U. S. 4th Congress, 1795-1797. House.
Report of the Committee of Elections, to
whom were Referred memorials of Joseph
Bradley Varnum. . . . 15th March, 1796,
Committed. . . . Published by Order of the
House.
[Philadelphia, 1796.] 4 pp.
AAS copy.　　　　31384

U. S. 4th Congress, 1795-1797. House.
Report of the Committee of Revisal and
Unfinished Business. . . . 9th December,
1796. . . . Published by Order of the
House.
[Philadelphia, 1797.] 8 pp.
AAS copy.　　　　33016

U. S. 4th Congress, 1795-1797. House.
Report of the Committee of Ways and
Means, on the Measures which Ought to
be Taken, Relative to the Balances. . . .
26th December, 1796. . . . Published by
Order of the House.
[Philadelphia, 1797.] 4 pp.
AAS copy.　　　　33019

U. S. 4th Congress, 1795-1797. House.
Report of the Committee of Ways and
Means, on the State of the Receipts and
Expenditures. . . . 17th March, 1796.

Committed. . . . Published by Order of the House.
[Philadelphia, 1796.] 11 pp.
AAS copy. 31385

U. S. 4th Congress, 1795-1797. House.
Report of the Committee of Ways and Means, Relative to Appropriations for the Military. . . . 18th May, 1796.
Committed. . . . Published by Order of the House.
[Philadelphia, 1796.] 12 pp.
AAS copy. 31400

U. S. 4th Congress, 1795-1797. House.
Report of the Committee of Ways and Means, to whom it was Referred to Enquire whether the Bank . . . 3d May, 1796. . . . Published by Order of the House.
[Philadelphia, 1796.] [3] pp.
AAS copy. 31392

U. S. 4th Congress, 1795-1797. House.
Reports of the Committee of Ways and Means, to whom it was Referred, to Take into Consideration, the Subject of further Revenues. . . 3d January 1797. . . .
Published by Order of the House.
[Philadelphia, 1797.] [3] pp.
AAS copy. 33020

U. S. 4th Congress, 1795-1797. House.
Report of the Committee of Ways and Means, to whom was Referred, a Resolution of the House, of the Tenth Instant. . . . 23d January, 1797. . . .
Published by Order of the House.
[Philadelphia, 1797.] 7 pp.
AAS copy. 33021

U. S. 4th Congress, 1795-1797. House.
Report of the Committee on the Memorial of the Commissioners . . . of a National University, 21st December 1796. . . .
Published by Order of the House.
[Philadelphia, 1797.] 6 pp.
AAS copy. 33029

U. S. 4th Congress, 1795-1797. House.
Report of the Committee on the Petition of Sundry Inhabitants of the Counties of St. Clair and Randolph. . . . 12th May 1796, Ordered to lie on the Table. 13th May 1796, Committed.
[Philadelphia, 1796.] 11 pp.
AAS copy. 31395

U. S. 4th Congress, 1795-1797. House.
Report of the Committee, to whom was Re-Committed, on the Fifth Ultimo, a Report of the Attorney-General. . . . 9th February, 1797. . . . Published by Order of the House.
[Philadelphia, 1797.] 10 pp.
AAS copy. 33025

U. S. 4th Congress, 1795-1797. House.
Report of the Committee, to whom was Re-Committed on the Sixteenth Instant, their Report. . . . 21 st February, 1797. . . .
Published by Order of the House.
[Philadelphia, 1797.] 6 pp.
AAS copy. 33026

U. S. 4th Congress, 1795-1797. House.
Report of the Committee, to whom was Referred, on the 13th Ultimo, the Memorial of the Illinois and Wabash Land Company. . . . 3d February, 1797. . . .
Published by Order of the House.
[Philadelphia, 1797.] 4 pp.
LOC copy. 33032

U. S. 4th Congress, 1795-1797. House.
Report of the Committee to whom was Referred, on the Twentieth of December last, a Letter from the Secretary of State. . . . 13th February 1797. . . .
Published by Order of the House.
[Philadelphia, 1797.] 6 pp.
AAS copy. 33034

U. S. 4th Congress, 1795-1797. House.
Report of the Committee to whom was Referred so much of the Speech of the President . . . as Relates to . . . Agriculture. 11th January 1797. . . .
Published by Order of the House.
[Philadelphia, 1797.] 8 pp.
AAS copy. 33031

U. S. 4th Congress, 1795-1797. House.

Report of the Committee, to whom was Referred the Memorial of Anna De Neufville. . . . 7th February 1797. . . .
Published by Orderof the House.
[Philadelphia, 1797.] [3] pp.
AAS copy. 33033

U. S. 4th Congress, 1795-1797. House.
Report of the Committee to whom was Referred the Message from the President . . . of the Second Ultimo. . . . 10th March, 1796, Committed . . . Published by Order of the House.
[Philadelphia, 1797.] 6 pp.
AAS copy. 31383

U. S. 4th Congress, 1795-1797. House.
Report of the Committee to whom were Re-Committed the Petition of Hugh Lawson White. . . . 17th January 1797. . . .
Published by Order of the House.
[Philadelphia, 1797.] 12 pp.
AAS copy. 33024

U. S. 4th Congress, 1795-1797. House.
Report of the Committee to whom were Referred so much of the Report of the Secretary of State . . . as Relate to Weights and Measures. 12th April, 1796.
Committed. . . . Published by Order of the House.
[Philadelphia, 1796.] 7 pp.
AAS copy. 31390

U. S. 4th Congress, 1795-1797. House.
Report on the Petition of John Car. . . .
5th January 1797. . . . Published by Order of the House.
[Philadelphia, 1797.] [3] pp.
AAS copy. 33030

U. S. 4th Congress, 1795-1797. House.
Reports of Committees, on the Petitions of Sundry Refugees. . . . 12th December 1796. . . . Published by Order of the House.
[Philadelphia, 1797.] 8 pp.
AAS copy. 33041

U. S. 4th Congress, 1795-1797. House.
Reports of Committees, on the Petitions of Sundry Refugees . . . [Feb. 17, 1796]. . . . Published by Order of the House.
[Philadelphia, 1796.] 8 pp.
AAS copy. 47952

U. S. 4th Congress, 1795-1797. House.
Standing Rules and Orders, of the House.
[Philadelphia], Childs, [1796]. 11 pp.
LOC copy. 31367

U. S. 4th Congress, 1795-1797. House.
12th April, 1796, Committed to a Committee of the Whole House. . . .
Report from the Committee, to whom were Referred the Message from the President.
[Philadelphia, 1796.] [1] p.
AAS copy. 31389

U. S. 4th Congress, 1795-1797. House.
23d February, 1796. Read and Committed. . . . Report of the Committee of Ways and Means, on . . . the Internal Revenues. . . . Published by Order of the House.
[Philadelphia, 1796.] 4 pp.
AAS copy. 31381

U. S. 4th Congress, 1795-1797. House.
25th February, 1796. Referred. . . . Report on the Legislative Provision Necessary for the Relief of American Seamen. . . .
Published by Order of the House.
[Philadelphia, 1796.] 4 pp.
AAS copy. 31382

U. S. 4th Congress, 1795-1797. Senate.
An Act Directing Certain Experiments to be made to Ascertain Certain Uniform Standards of Weights and Measures. . . .
Passed the House . . . May 19, 1796.
[Philadelphia], Fenno, [1796]. Broadside.
LOC copy. 31333

U. S. 4th Congress, 1795-1797. Senate.
An Act Making a Partial Appropriation for the Support of the Military Establishment for the Year One Thousand Seven Hundred and Ninety Six. . . .
Passed the House . . . March 7, 1796.
[Philadelphia], Fenno, [1796]. Broadside.
LOC copy. 31344

U. S. 4th Congress, 1795-1797. Senate.
In Senate of the United States, March 1st, 1797. Mr. Hillhouse. . . .
[Philadelphia, 1797.] 3 pp.
AAS copy. 32967

U. S. 4th Congress, 1795-1797. Senate.
In Senate of the United States, March 2d, 1797. The Committee to whom was Referred the Resolutions . . . Respecting the . . . Boundary of Georgia . . . Report. . . .
[Philadelphia, 1797.] 4 pp.
AAS copy. 32968

U. S. 4th Congress, 1795-1797. Senate.
In Senate of the United States, May 5, 1796. The Following Message. . . .
[Philadelphia, 1796.] 8 pp.
Pierce W. Gaines copy. 47953

U. S. 4th Congress, 1795-1797. Senate.
Journal of the Senate . . . First Session of the Fourth Congress [Dec. 7, 1795 - June 1, 1796].
Philadelphia, Fenno, 1795. 346, vi, xxi pp.
AAS copy. 31355

U. S. 4th Congress, 1795-1797. Senate.
Journal of the Senate . . . Second Session of the Fourth Congress [Dec. 5, 1796 - Mar. 3, 1797].
Philadelphia, Fenno, 1796. 175, [1], iv, 18 pp.
AAS copy. 32971

U. S. 4th Congress, 1795-1796. Senate.
Report of the Committee to whom was Referred the Message of the President . . . of the 8th of April, 1796.
[Philadelphia, 1796.] 5 pp.
AAS copy. 31388

U. S. 5th Congress, 1797-1799.
Amendments of the Senate to the Bill, Intituled "An Act for the More Effectual Collection of Certain Internal Revenues. . . ." (Published by Order of the House. . .).
[Philadelphia, 1798.] [3] pp.
AAS copy. 34693

U. S. 5th Congress, 1797-1799.
A Bill Authorizing the President . . . to Raise a Provincial Army.
[Philadelphia, Way & Groff, 1798]. 4 pp.
WLC copy. 48697

U. S. 5th Congress, 1797-1799.
A Bill Concerning Aliens.
n. p., [1798]. 3 pp.
WLC copy. 48649

U. S. 5th Congress, 1797-1799.
A Bill, Giving Eventual Authority to the President . . . to Augment the Army.
n.p., [1799]. 4 pp.
WLC copy. 48972

U. S. 5th Congress, 1797-1799.
A Bill supplementary to the Act, entitled, "An Act to Establish the Judicial Courts. . . ,"
n. p. [1798]. 2 pp.
WLC copy. 48650

U. S. 5th Congress, 1797-1799.
A Bill to Alter and Extend the Provisions of the Act entitled "An Act to Establish the Judicial Courts. . . ."
n.p., [1798]. 2 pp.
WLC copy. 48651

U. S. 5th Congress, 1797-1799.
A Bill to Establish an Uniform System of Bankruptcy.
[Philadelphia, Childs & Swaine, 1798.] 13 pp.
LOC copy. 48652

U. S. 5th Congress, 1797-1799.
A Bill to Establish an Uniform System of Bankruptcy.
[Philadelphia], Childs & Swaine, [1798].
13 pp.
LOC copy. 48653

U. S. 5th Congress, 1797-1799.
A Bill to Provide an Additional Armament for the . . . Protection of the Trade.
[Philadelphia, Way & Groff, 1798]. 3 pp.
WLC copy. 48654

U. S. 5th Congress, 1797-1799.
. . . Cap. XCVII. An Act for Carrying into
Execution the Treaty [July 4, 1797]. . . .
[Philadelphia], Duane, [1797]. 24 pp.
(Only known copy cannot be filmed.)
48279

U. S. 5th Congress, 1797-1799.
The Committee to whom was
Recommitted the Report of the
Committee. . . .
Philadelphia, Ross, 1799. Broadside.
(Not located, 1968.)   48973

U. S. 5th Congress, 1797-1799.
The Committee to whom was Referred the
Bill Authorizing the Acceptance, from the
State of Connecticut, of a Cession of the
Jurisdiction of the Territory West of
Pennsylvania [Feb. 15, 1799].
[Philadelphia, 1799]. pp. [3]-24.
(Also entered as 36579, q. v.)   38724

U. S. 5th Congress, 1797-1799.
In Committee, to whom was Referred the
Bill, Regulating Certain Proceedings. . . .
Amendments. . . .
[Philadelphia, Fenno, 1798.] 3 pp.
WLC copy.   48660

U. S. 5th Congress, 1797-1799.
The Debates, and Interesting Speeches in
the Fifth Congress of the U. States, at
their First Session.
Newburgh, N. Y., Denniston, 1797. 384
pp.
AAS copy.   32965

U. S. 5th Congress, 1797-1799.
Fifth Congress, Third Session. A List of
Acts Passed during the Session.
[Philadelphia? 1799.] [2] pp.
NYPL copy.   48974

U. S. 5th Congress, 1797-1799.
Fifth Congress - Third Session. A List of
the Names, and Places of Residence.
[Philadelphia, 1799?] Broadside.
AAS copy.   36516

U. S. 5th Congress, 1797-1799.
A List of the Names and Places of
Residence of the Members of the Senate
and House.
[Philadelphia, 1797.] Broadside.
AAS copy.   32975

U. S. 5th Congress, 1797-1799.
19th December, 1797. . . . A Bill to
Prescribe the Mode of taking Evidence in
Cases of Contested Elections.
[Philadelphia, 1797.] 3 pp.
WLC copy.   48281

U. S. 5th Congress, 1797-1799.
The Remonstrance and Petition of the
Legislature of . . . Tennessee to the
Senate.
[Philadelphia], Fenno, 1797. 12 pp.
AAS copy.   32980

U. S. 5th Congress, 1797-1799.
Report in Part, of the Committee of Ways
and Means, to whom was Referred, on the
11th of December last, a Letter and
Report from the Secretary of the
Treasury. . . . 1st January, 1798.
Committed. . . . (Published by Order of
the House. . . .)
[Philadelphia, 1798.] pp. [235]-238.
AAS copy.   48656

U. S. 5th Congress, 1797-1799.
Resolved by the Senate and House . . .
that the following Articles be
Proposed. . . . as Amendments.
[Philadelphia], Fenno, [1798.] Broadside.
WLC copy.   48657

U. S. 5th Congress, 1797-1799.
17th June, 1797. . . . A Bill to Prohibit
Citizens of the United States from
Entering into the Military . . . Service of
any Foreign Prince or State.
[Philadelphia, 1797.] 3 pp.
NYPL copy.   48278

U. S. 5th Congress, 1797-1799.
3d April, 1798. Read the first and Second
Time. . . . A Bill for Providing
Compensation for the Marshals.
[Philadelphia, 1798.] 9 pp.
WLC copy.   48689

U. S. 5th Congress, 1797-1799.
. . . 22d November, 1797. . . . A Bill for
the Relief of Refugees from . . .
Nova-Scotia.
[Philadelphia, 1797]. 2 pp.
WLC copy.   48280

U. S. 5th Congress, 1797-1799.
26th December, 1797. . . . A Bill
Supplementary to the . . . Act in Addition
to the Act for the Punishment of Certain
Crimes.
[Philadelphia, 1797.] 4 pp.
WLC copy.   48282

U. S. 5th Congress, 1797-1799. House.
An Act Providing for Salvage in cases of
Re-Capture.
[Philadelphia, 1799.] [3] pp.
LOC copy.   36473

U. S. 5th Congress, 1797-1799. House.
An Address in Answer to the Speech of
the President to Both Houses. . . .
Reported by a Select Committee Nov. 24,
1797. House of Representatives, Nov. 27,
1797, Ordered to be Committed.
Philadelphia, Gales, [1797]. 6 pp.
AAS copy.   32961

U. S. 5th Congress, 1797-1799. House.
Alterations to be made in the Bill,
Reported by the Post-Master General. . . .
7th February, 1799. (Published by Order
of the House. . . .).
[Philadelphia, 1799.] [3] pp.
AAS copy.   36489

U. S. 5th Congress, 1797-1799. House.
Amendment, Reported from the
Committee of the Whole House, to the Bill
in Addition to the Act, Intituled "An Act
for the Relief of American Seamen." 15th
February, 1798. Published by Order of the
House.
[Philadelphia], Ross, [1798.] 4 pp.
LOC copy.   34694

U. S. 5th Congress, 1797-1799. House.
Amendments Agreed to in the Committee
of the Whole House, to the Bill for
Establishing an Uniform System of
Bankruptcy. . . . (Published by Order of
the House. . . .).
[Philadelphia, 1799.] 7 pp.
LCP copy.   36490

U. S. 5th Congress, 1797-1799. House.
Amendments Proposed by Mr. Otis.
[Philadelphia], Gales, [1798]. 2 pp.
AAS copy.   34714

U. S. 5th Congress, 1797-1799. House.
A Bill Authorizing the President . . . to
Raise a Provisional Army.
[Philadelphia], Fenno, [1798]. 2 pp.
WLC copy.   48658

U. S. 5th Congress, 1797-1799. House.
15th March, 1798. . . . A Bill Making an
Appropriation for Completing the
Buildings . . . of . . . Washington.
n. p., [1798]. Broadside.
WLC copy.   48685

U. S. 5th Congress, 1797-1799. House.
A Bill for the Government of the Navy . . .
23d January, 1799. . . . (Published by
Order of the House. . . .).
[Philadelphia, 1799.] 18 pp.
AAS copy.   36496

U. S. 5th Congress, 1797-1799. House.
A Bill to Alter and Amend the Act,
entitled, "An Act to Establish the Judicial
Courts. . . ."
[Philadelphia, Way & Groff, 1798.] 7 pp.
WLC copy.   48659

U. S. 5th Congress, 1797-1799. House.
A Bill to Establish an Uniform System of
Bankruptcy throughout the United States.
8th February, 1798, Read the First and
Second Time, and Committed. . . .
(Published by Order of the House. . . .)
[Philadelphia, Gales, 1798.] 32 pp.
AAS copy.   34712

U. S. 5th Congress, 1797-1799. House.
A Bill to Establish an Uniform System of
Bankruptcy throughout the United States.
14th December, 1798. Read the First and
Second Time, and Committed. . . .

(Published by Order of the House. . . .)
[Philadelphia, 1798.] 32 pp.
AAS copy.   34713

U. S. 5th Congress, 1797-1799. House.
A Bill to Provide for Organizing, Arming
and Disciplining the Militia. . . . January
1st, 1798. Committed to a Committee.
Philadelphia, Gales, 1798. 18 pp.
AAS copy.   34715

U. S. 5th Congress, 1797-1799. House.
Committee Appointed to Enquire into the
Progress made in . . . Sale of the Lands
. . . Northwest of the River Ohio.
[Philadelphia, 1797.] 7 pp.
(No copy located.)   48283

U. S. 5th Congress, 1797-1799. House.
The Committee to whom was Referred the
Bill Authorizing the Acceptance, from the
State of Connecticut, of a Cession of . . .
Territory. . . .
[Philadelphia, 1799?] 24 pp.
(Also entered as 38724, q. v.)   36505

U. S. 5th Congress, 1797-1799. House.
Deposition of Gen. Elijah Clark . . . 27th
April, 1798, Ordered to lie on the Table.
[Philadelphia, 1798.] 8 pp.
AAS copy.   34786

U. S. 5th Congress, 1797-1799. House.
8th January, 1798. . . . A Bill in Addition
to the Act . . . for the Relief . . . of
American Seamen.
n. p., [1798]. 3 pp.
WLC copy.   48676

U. S. 5th Congress, 1797-1799. House.
15th January, 1798. . . . A Bill Providing
the Means of Intercourse between the
United States and Foreign Nations.
n.p., [1798]. 2 pp.
WLC copy.   48678

U. S. 5th Congress, 1797-1799. House.
14th February, 1798. . . . A Bill to Amend
the . . . Act Laying Duties on Stamped
Vellum.
[Philadelphia], Gales, [1798]. 3 pp.
WLC copy.   48681

U. S. 5th Congress, 1797-1799. House.
14th March, 1798. . . . A Bill for an
Additional Appropriation to Provide . . .
a Naval Armament. . . .
n.p., [1798]. Broadside.
WLC copy.   48684

U. S. 5th Congress, 1797-1799. House.
4th January, 1798. . . . A Bill to Prescribe
the Mode of Taking Evidence in . . .
Contested Elections.
n.p., [1798]. 4 pp.
WLC copy.   48675

U. S. 5th Congress, 1797-1799. House.
15th March, 1798. . . . A Bill Making an
Appropriation for Completing the
Buildings . . . of . . . Washington.
n. p., [1798]. Broadside.
WLC copy.   48685

U. S. 5th Congress, 1797-1799. House.
Further Report of the Committee,
Appointed on the Eighth July last, to
Prepare and Report Articles of
Impeachment against William Blount. . . .
25th January, 1798. (Committed. . . .)
[Philadelphia], Fenno, [1798]. 11 pp.
AAS copy.   34792

U. S. 5th Congress, 1797-1799. House.
Further Report from the Committee,
Appointed on the Eighth of July last, to
Prepare and Report Articles of
Impeachment against William Blount. . . .
[Philadelphia, 1798.] iv pp.
(No copy located has the pp. given by
Evans.)
LCP copy.   34793

[U. S. 5th Congress, 1797-1799. House.
Further Report from the Committee of
Impeachment against William Blount, 30
December, 1797.
[Philadelphia, 1798.]
(A ghost of 34793, q. v.)   34787

U. S. 5th Congress, 1797-1799. House.
Further Report of the Committee of
Revisal & Unfinished Business, on such of
the Laws . . . as are Near Expiring. 27th

December, 1798, Ordered to lie on the Table. (Published by Order of the House. . . .)
[Philadelphia, 1798.] 4 pp.
AAS copy. 34762

U. S. 5th Congress, 1797-1799. House. Further Report of the Committee of Revisal and Unfinished Business. . . . 24th December, 1799. . . . (Published by Order of the House. . . .)
[Philadelphia, 1799.] 8 pp.
AAS copy. 36518

U. S. 5th Congress, 1797-1799. House. Further Report of the Committee of Ways and Means, Instructed on the Fifth of December last, to Enquire what Alterations may be Necessary in the Act, Entitled an Act Laying Duties. . . . 14th February, 1798. Committed. . . . Published by Order of the House. . . .
[Philadelphia], Ross, [1798]. pp. [393]-403.
AAS copy. 34766

U. S. 5th Congress, 1797-1799. House. Further Report of the Managers Appointed to Conduct the Impeachment against William Blount. 20th December, 1798, Ordered to lie on the Table. (Published by Order of the House.)
[Philadelphia, 1798.] 4 pp.
AAS copy. 34790

U. S. 5th Congress, 1797-1799. House. Journal of the House . . . First Session of the Fifth Congress [May 15 - July 10, 1797].
Philadelphia, Ross, 1797. 140, [12] pp.
AAS copy. 32970

U. S. 5th Congress, 1797-1799. House. Journal of the House . . . Second Session of the Fifth Congress [Nov. 13, 1797 - July 16, 1798].
Philadelphia, Ross, 1797. 683, [53] pp.
AAS copy. 34719

U. S. 5th Congress, 1797-1799. House. A Journal of the Proceedings of the Third Session of the Fifth Congress [Dec. 3, 1798 - Mar. 2, 1799].
New London, Ct., Green, 1798-99. 549 pp.
AAS copy. 36520

U. S. 5th Congress, 1797-1799. House. Journal of the House . . . Third Session of the Fifth Congress [Dec. 3, 1798 - Mar. 2, 1799].
Philadelphia, Rose, 1798. 266, [24] pp.
AAS copy. 36519

U. S. 5th Congress, 1797-1799. House. . . . Letter from the Chevalier d'Yrujo. . . . 19th January, 1798.
[Philadelphia, 1798.] 4 pp.
AAS copy. 34788

U.S. 5th Congress, 1797-1799. House. Mr. Abiel Foster's Motion. . . . 16th February, 1799. . . . (Published by Order of the House. . . .).
[Philadelphia, 1799.] [3] pp.
AAS copy. 36559

U. S. 5th Congress, 1797-1799. House. Mr. Dwight Foster's Motion, June 6, 1798.
[Philadelphia, 1798.] Broadside.
AAS copy. 34721

U. S. 5th Congress, 1797-1799. House. Mr. Harper's Motion, 3d July, 1798.
[Philadelphia], Gales, [1798]. Broadside.
AAS copy. 34723

U. S. 5th Congress, 1797-1799. House. Mr. Harper's Motion. 5th June, 1798.
[Philadelphia, 1798.] [3] pp.
AAS copy. 34722

U. S. 5th Congress, 1797-1799. House. Mr. Harper's Motion, 6th July, 1798.
[Philadelphia, 1798.] 3 pp.
AAS copy. 34724

U. S. 5th Congress, 1797-1799. House. Mr. Harper's Motion, 12th December, 1798.
Philadelphia, Gales, [1798]. 4 pp.
AAS copy. 34725

U. S. 5th Congress, 1797-1799. House.

Mr. Harper's Motion. 24th November 1797.
[Philadelphia, 1797.] 2 pp.
NYPL copy. 48284

U. S. 5th Congress, 1797-1799. House. Mr. Sitgreaves's Motion, 22d May, 1798.
[Philadelphia], Gales, [1798]. Broadside.
AAS copy. 34726

U. S. 5th Congress, 1797-1799. House. 19th March, 1798. . . . A Bill to Revive . . . the Act Respecting the Compensation of Clerks.
n. p., [1798]. Broadside.
WLC copy. 48686

U. S. 5th Congress, 1797-1799. House. The Proceedings of the House . . . with Respect to the Petitions . . . for a Repeal of the Alien and Sedition Laws.
Philadelphia, Gales, 1799. 34 pp.
LOC copy. 36560

U. S. 5th Congress, 1797-1799. House. (Received and Read 19th May) Documents Referred to in the Presidents Speech to Both Houses. . . . Published by Order of the House.
Philadelphia, Ross, [1797]. 72, [1] pp.
AAS copy. 32966

U. S. 5th Congress, 1797-1799. House. Remonstrance and Petition of the Legislature of . . . Tennessee. . . . 20th December, 1797, Report Made. . . . Published by Order of the House.
[Philadelphia, 1797.] pp. [175]-201.
AAS copy. 32981

U. S. 5th Congress, 1797-1799. House. Report from the Committee Appointed to Consider the Amendments to the Bill for the Relief of the Refugees from . . . Canada . . . 27th February, 1798. Committed. . . . Printed by Order of the House. . . .
Philadelphia, Gales, [1798]. pp. [427]-434.
AAS copy. 34778

U. S. 5th Congress, 1797-1799. House. Report, in Part, from the Committee Appointed on so much of the President's Speech as Relates to the Protection of Commerce. . . . 1st May, 1798. Referred. . . . Printed by Order of the House.
Philadelphia, Gales, [1798.] pp. [515]-518.
AAS copy. 48661

U. S. 5th Congress, 1797-1799. House. Report in Part, of the Committee of Revisal and Unfinished Business. . . . 11th December, 1797. . . . Published by Order of the House.
[Philadelphia, 1797.] pp. [103]-106.
AAS copy. 33018

U. S. 5th Congress, 1797-1799. House. Report in Part, of the Committee to whom was Referred, on the 29th November last, so much of the President's Speech as Referred to the Protection of Commerce. . . . 8th March, 1798. Referred. . . . (Published by Order of the House. . . .)
[Philadelphia, 1798.] pp. [439]-455.
AAS copy. 34769

U. S. 5th Congress, 1797-1799. House. Report (in Part) of the Committee to whom was Referred so much of the President's Speech as Relates to the "Naval Establishment. . . ." 17th January, 1799, Committed. . . . (Published by Order of the House. . . .).
[Philadelphia, 1799.] 37 pp., 1 folding table.
AAS copy. 36563

U. S. 5th Congress, 1797-1799. House. Report of the Committee Appointed on the 4th of May last, to Enquire and Report . . . the Various Acts Establishing the Executive Departments. . . . 5th July, 1798. Committed. . . . (Published by Order of the House. . . .)
[Philadelphia, 1798.] pp. [551]-560.
AAS copy. 34777

U. S. 5th Congress, 1797-1799. House. Report of the Committee Appointed on

the Tenth Instant, to Prepare an Address to the President. . . . 12th December, 1798. Committed. . . . (Published by Order of the House. . . .)
[Philadelphia, 1798.] 6 pp.
AAS copy. 34776

U. S. 5th Congress, 1797-1799. House. Report of the Committee, Appointed on the Twenty-Fourth . . . "Act Regulating Foreign Coins. . . ." 11th December, 1797, Consideration Postponed. . . . Published by Order of the House.
[Philadelphia, 1797.] pp. [91]-94.
AAS copy. 32982

U. S. 5th Congress, 1797-1799. House. Report of the Committee Appointed on the 27th of March last, to Enquire into Alterations. . . . 25th April, 1798, Committed. . . . (Published by Order of the House. . . .)
[Philadelphia, 1798.] pp. [511]-514.
AAS copy. 34774

U. S. 5th Congress, 1797-1799. House. Reported of the Committee Appointed to Bring in a Bill for Making Further Provision for the Fortification of the Ports and Harbours. . . . June 10th, 1797.
[Philadelphia, 1797.] 8 pp.
LCP copy. 33028

U. S. 5th Congress, 1797-1799. House. Report of the Committee Appointed to Consider the Amendments to the Bill for the Relief of the Refugees. . . . 27th February, 1798.
Philadelphia, Gales, [1798?]. pp. [2], 429-434.
WLC copy. 48662

U. S. 5th Congress, 1797-1799. House. Report of the Committee Appointed to Inquire into the Operation of the Act for the Relief and Protection of American Seamen. . . . 22d November 1797, committed. . . . (Published by order of the House. . . .)
[Philadelphia, 1797.] pp. [17]-41.
AAS copy. 48285

U. S. 5th Congress, 1797-1799. House. Report of the Committee of Claims, on the Memorial of William Alexander . . . 4th January, 1798. Committed . . . (Published by Order of the House. . . .)
[Philadelphia, 1798.] [3] pp.
AAS copy. 34729

U. S. 5th Congress, 1797-1799. House. Report of the Committee of Claims, on the Memorials and Petitions of George P. Frost. . . . 19th March, 1798, Committed. . . . (Published by Order of the House. . . .)
[Philadelphia, 1798.] pp. [455]-458.
AAS copy. 34731

U. S. 5th Congress, 1797-1799. House. Report of the Committee of Claims, on the Memorials and Petitions of Thomas Cox. . . . 15th January, 1799. . . . [Published by Order of the House. . . .)
[Philadelphia, 1799.] 4 pp.
AAS copy. 36566

U. S. 5th Congress, 1797-1799. House. Report of the Committee of Claims, on the Petition of Anna Welsh. . . . 5th December, 1797, Committed. . . . (Published by Order of the House. . . .)
[Philadelphia, 1798.] pp. [63]-68.
AAS copy. 34749

[U. S. 5th Congress, 1797-1799. House. Report of the Committee of Claims, on the Petition of Comfort Sands. 20 December, 1798.
Philadelphia, 1798.]
(No copy located.) 34745

U. S. 5th Congress, 1797-1799. House. Report of the Committee of Claims, on the Petition of Comfort Sands. . . . 20th December 1797. committed. . . . [Philadelphia, 1797.] pp. [151]-156.
WLC copy. 48286

U. S. 5th Congress, 1797-1799. House. Report of the Committee of Claims, on the Petition of Edward St. Loe Livermore. . . . 8th December, 1797,

Committed. (Published by Order of the House).
[Philadelphia, 1797.] pp. [71]-74.
AAS copy. 48287

U. S. 5th Congress, 1797-1799. House. Report of the Committee of Claims, on the Petition of Sarah Alexander. . . . 2d January, 1798. Committed. . . . (Published by Order of the House. . . .)
[Philadelphia, 1798.] [3] pp.
AAS copy. 34734

U. S. 5th Congress, 1797-1799. House. Report of the Committee of Claims, on the Petition of Stephen Sayre, Presented the 29th March, 1796. . . . 25th January, 1799, Committed. . . . (Published by Order of the House. . . .).
[Philadelphia, 1799.] 14 pp.
AAS copy. 36567

U. S. 5th Congress, 1797-1799. House. Report of the Committee of Claims, on the Petition of the Corporation of Rhode-Island College. . . . 12th December, 1797. . . . Published by Order of the House.
[Philadelphia, 1797.] pp. [95]-101.
AAS copy. 33004

U. S. 5th Congress, 1797-1799. House. Report of the Committee of Claims, on the Petition of the Corporation of Rhode-Island College. . . . 12th December, 1797, Committed. . . . (Published by Order of the House. . . .)
[Philadelphia, 1798.] pp. [95]-101.
(Also entered as 33004, q. v.) 34744

U. S. 5th Congress, 1797-1799. House. Report of the Committee of Claims, on the Petition of Thomas Lewis. . . . 25th April, 1798. Committed. . . . (Published by Order of the House. . . .)
[Philadelphia, 1798.] [3] pp.
AAS copy. 34742

U. S. 5th Congress, 1797-1799. House. Report of the Committee of Claims, on the Petitions of Samuel Abbot and others. . . . 27th November, 1797, Committed.
[Philadelphia, 1797.] pp. [43] - 46.
WLC copy. 48288

U. S. 5th Congress, 1797-1799. House. Report of the Committee of Claims, to whom was Committed a Resolution of the House of the Sixteenth Instant . . . on the Expediency of Extending the Provisions of the Act in Addition to the Act for . . . the Frontiers . . . 29th January, 1798. . . . (Published by Order of the House. . . .).
[Philadelphia, 1798.] pp. [291]-294.
LCP copy. 34728

U. S. 5th Congress, 1797-1799. House. Report of the Committee of Claims, to whom was Re-committed, on the 5th of December last, the Petition of Henry Hull. . . . 14th February, 1798. Committed. . . . (Published by Order of the House)
[Philadelphia, 1798.] pp. [379]-394.
LCP copy. 34741

U. S. 5th Congress, 1797-1799. House. Report of the Committee of Claims, to whom was Recommitted, on the 24th Ultimo, the Petition of Comfort Sands. . . . 12th February, 1799, Committed. . . . (Published by Order of the House. . . .).
[Philadelphia, 1799.] 16 pp.
AAS copy. 36568

U. S. 5th Congress, 1797-1799. House. Report of the Committee of Claims, to whom were Recommitted the Petition of Henry Hill. . . . 22d November, 1797, Committed.
[Philadelphia, 1797.] pp. [43]-48.
WLC copy. 48289

U. S. 5th Congress, 1797-1799. House. Report of the Committee of Claims, to whom was referred, on the Fourth of January last, the Petition of Lucy Clark, 18th January, 1798, Committed. . . . (Published by Order of the House. . . .)
[Philadelphia, 1798.] pp. [279]-282.
AAS copy. 34737

U. S. 5th Congress, 1797-1799. House.

Report of the Committee of Claims, to whom was Referred, on the 4th Ultimo, the Petition of John Vaughan. 19th May, 1798. Committed. . . . (Published by Order of the House. . . .)
[Philadelphia, 1798.] pp. [539]-542.
AAS copy. 34746

U. S. 5th Congress, 1797-1799. House. Report of the Committee of Claims, to whom was Referred on the 7th Instant, the Petition of John Vaughan. . . . 21st February, 1799, Committed. . . . (Published by Order of the House. . . .).
[Philadelphia, 1799.] 4 pp.
AAS copy. 36569

U. S. 5th Congress, 1797-1799. House. Report of the Committee of Claims, to whom was Referred, on the 19th of February last, the Petition of Temple Elliot. 2d April, 1798. Committed. . . . (Published by Order of the House. . . .)
[Philadelphia, 1798.] pp. [487]-490.
AAS copy. 34738

U. S. 5th Congress, 1797-1799. House. Report of the Committee of Claims, to whom was Referred, on the 20th of December last, a Motion Relative to the Amendments Necessary to be Made in the Acts Respecting Invalid Pensioners. 26th March, 1798. Committed.
[Philadelphia, 1798.] pp. [463]-472.
AAS copy. 34727

U. S. 5th Congress, 1797-1799. House. Report of the Committee of Claims, to whom was Referred, on the 20th of December last, a Motion Relative to the Amendments. . . . 26th March, 1798. Committed.
[Philadelphia, 1798.] pp. [463]-472.
LOC copy. 48663

U. S. 5th Congress, 1797-1799. House. Report of the Committee on Claims, to whom was Referred on the 22d of December last, the Memorial of James Swan. 28th March, 1798, Committed. . . . (Published by Order of the House. . . .)
[Philadelphia, 1798.] pp. [475]-482.
AAS copy. 48664

U. S. 5th Congress, 1797-1799. House. Report of the Committee of Claims, to whom was Referred, on the 30th of March last, the Petition of Jonathan Haskell, 16th April, 1798, Committed. . . . (Published by Order of the House. . . .)
n. p., [1798]. pp. [2], 501-502.
AAS copy. 48665

U. S. 5th Congress, 1797-1799. House. Report of the Committee of Claims, to whom was Referred, on the 25th Ultimo, the Petition of John Baptiste Verdier. Committed. . . . (Published by Order of the House. . . .)
[Philadelphia, 1798.] 21 pp.
JCB copy. 34747

U. S. 5th Congress, 1797-1799. House. Report of the Committee of Claims, to whom was Referred, on the Twenty-First Ultimo, the Petition of John Carr, Presented the 21st of February, 1794. . . .
[Philadelphia, 1798.] pp. [275]-278.
(Also entered as 34736, q. v.) 34735

U. S. 5th Congress, 1797-1799. House. Report of the Committee of Claims, to whom was Referred, on the Twenty-First Ultimo, the Petition of John Carr, Presented the 21st of February, 1794, and the Report of a Committee thereon. . . . 17th January, 1798, Committed. . . . (Published by Order of the House. . . .)
[Philadelphia, 1798.] pp. [275]-278.
AAS copy. 34736

U. S. 5th Congress, 1797-1799. House. Report of the Committee of Claims, to whom was Referred, on the Twenty-First Ultimo, the Petition of John Carr. . . . 17th January, 1799, Committed. . . . (Published by Order of the House. . . .).
[Philadelphia, 1799.] 7 pp.
AAS copy. 36571

U. S. 5th Congress, 1797-1799. House. Report of the Committee of Claims, to whom was Referred, on the 24th of

January, and 11th of February, 1797. the Petition of John Nelson, and of Susannah Russell. . . . 23d January, 1798. Committee. . . . (Published by Order of the House. . . .)
[Philadelphia, 1798.] pp. [283]-290.
AAS copy. 34743

U. S. 5th Congress, 1797-1799. House. Report of the Committee of Claims, to whom was referred, on the 24th of November, 1797, the Petition of Benjamin Wells, 2d May, 1798, Committed. . . . (Published by Order of the House. . . .)
[Philadelphia, 1798.] pp. [523] - 526.
AAS copy. 34748

U. S. 5th Congress, 1797-1799. House. Report of the Committee of Claims, to whom was Referred on the 28th ult, the Petition of Moses White. . . . 4th February, 1799. Committed. . . .
[Philadelphia, 1799]. 5 pp.
AAS copy. 36572

U. S. 5th Congress, 1797-1799. House. Report of the Committee of Claims, to whom was Referred, on the 30th of March last, the Petition of Jonathan Haskell. . . . 24th December, 1798, Committed. . . . (Published by Order of the House. . . .)
[Philadelphia, 1798]. pp. [1]-4.
AAS copy. 34740

U. S. 5th Congress, 1797-1799. House. Report of the Committee of Claims, to whom was Referred, on the 30th of November last, the Petition of John Frank. 8th January, 1798, Committed. . . . (Published by Order of the House. . . .)
[Philadelphia, 1798.] pp. [255]-258.
AAS copy. 34739

U. S. 5th Congress, 1797-1799. House. Report of the Committee of Claims, to whom was Referred, on the Sixteenth Instant, the Memorial of James Perry. . . . 22d March, 1798, Committed. . . . (Published by Order of the House. . . .)
[Philadelphia, 1798.] pp. [459]-462.
AAS copy. 34733

U. S. 5th Congress, 1797-1799. House. Report of the Committee of Claims, to whom was Referred the Memorial of Alexander Macomb. . . . 30th January, 1798, Committed. . . . Published by Order of the House.
[Philadelphia], Ross, [1798]. pp. [311]-316, [1].
AAS copy. 34732

U. S. 5th Congress, 1797-1799. House. Report of the Committee of Claims, to whom were Referred the Memorials . . . of Joseph Ball. . . . 26th February, 1798, Committed. . . . (Published by Order of the House. . . .)
[Philadelphia, 1798.] pp. [419]-424.
AAS copy. 34730

U. S. 5th Congress, 1797-1799. House. Report of the Committee of Commerce & Manufactures, on the Petition of Pierre Joseph Flamend, in Behalf of Louis Le Guen. . . . 8th December, 1797, Committed. . . . (Published by Order of the House. . . .)
[Philadelphia, 1798.] pp. [75]-78.
AAS copy. 34755

U. S. 5th Congress, 1797-1799. House. Report of the Committee of Commerce & Manufactures, on the Petition of Peter Aupoix. 2d January, 1798, Committed. . . . (Published by Order of the House. . . .)
[Philadelphia, 1798.] pp. [491]-494.
AAS copy. 34750

U. S. 5th Congress, 1797-1799. House. Report of the Committee of Commerce & Manufactures, on the Petitions of Orchard Cook and Abiel Wood. . . . 29 December, 1797 . . . Committed. . . . (Published by Order of the House. . . .).
[Philadelphia, 1798.] pp. [223]-232.
BA copy. 34753

U. S. 5th Congress, 1797-1799. House. Report of the Committee of Commerce & Manufactures, to Whom was Referred, on the 25th of January last, the Petition of Gustavus and Hugh Colhoun. 18th April,

1798, Committed. . . . (Published by Order of the House. . . .)
[Philadelphia, 1798.] pp. [503]-508.
AAS copy.   34752

U. S. 5th Congress, 1797-1799. House.
Report of the Committee of Commerce & Manufactures, to whom was Referred, on the 21st of November last, the Petition of William Bell, 4th January, 1798, Committed. . . . (Published by Order of the House. . . .)
[Philadelphia, 1798.] pp. [247]-254.
AAS copy.   34751

U. S. 5th Congress, 1797-1799. House.
Report of the Committee of Commerce & Manufactures, to Whom was referred, on the Twenty-Fifth Ultimo, the Petition of James Heron. . . . 9th February, 1798, Committed. . . . (Published by Order of the House. . . .)
[Philadelphia, 1798.] pp. [435]-438.
AAS copy.   34756

U. S. 5th Congress, 1797-1799. House.
Report of the Committee of Commerce & Manufactures, to whom was Referred, on the 27th of December last, the Petition of Nathaniel Cutter. . . . 10th January, 1798, Committed. . . . (Published by Order of the House. . . .)
[Philadelphia, 1798.] [3] pp.
AAS copy.   34754

U. S. 5th Congress, 1797-1799. House.
Report of the Committee of Commerce and Manufactures, to whom was Referred the Petition of Reuben Smith. . . . 15th February, 1798. Committed. . . .
(Published by Order of the House. . . .)
[Philadelphia, 1798]. pp. [411]-414.
AAS copy.   48666

U. S. 5th Congress, 1797-1799. House.
Report of the Committee of Privileges.
Testimony . . . Relative to . . . Matthew Lyon. . . . 12 February, 1798.]
[Philadelphia, 1798.]
(No copy located; apparently a ghost of 34757.)   34758

U. S. 5th Congress, 1797-1799. House.
Report of the Committee of Privileges, to whom was Referred, on the Sixteenth Instant, a Motion for the Expulsion of Roger Griswold. . . . 20th February, 1798. Ordered to lie on the Table. (Published by Order of the House. . . .)
[Philadelphia, 1798.] 24 pp.
AAS copy.   34759

U. S. 5th Congress, 1797-1799. House.
Report of the Committee of Privileges, to whom was Referred, on the Thirtieth Ultimo, a Motion Relative to the "Expulsion from this House of Matthew Lyon. . . ." 2d February, 1798, Consideration Postponed. . . . (Published by Order of the House. . . .)
[Philadelphia, 1798.] 4 pp.
AAS copy.   34757

U. S. 5th Congress, 1797-1799. House.
Report of the Committee of Revisal and Unfinished Business, on Bills. . . . 11th December, 1798. . . . (Published by Order of the House. . . .)
[Philadelphia, 1798.] 10 pp.
AAS copy.   34761

U. S. 5th Congress, 1797-1799. House.
Report of the Committee of Revisal and Unfinished Business, to whom was Referred, on the 24th of March last, the Memorial of William Simmons. . . . 7th May, 1798. Committed. . . . (Published by Order of the House. . . .)
[Philadelphia, 1798.] pp. [535]-538.
AAS copy.   34763

U. S. 5th Congress, 1797-1799. House.
Report of the Committee of Revisal & Unfinished Business, to whom were Referred the Message of the President. . . . 31st January, 1798, Ordered to lie on the Table. (Published by Order of the House. . . .)
[Philadelphia, 1798.] pp. [319]-360.
AAS copy.   34764

U. S. 5th Congress, 1797-1799. House.
Report of the Committee of the House of

Representatives of the United States, Appointed to Prepare and Report Articles of Impeachment against William Blount. . . . Printed by Order of the House. . . .
[Philadelphia], Fenno, [1798]. [2], vi, 16, clx pp.
AAS copy.   34785

U. S. 5th Congress, 1797-1799. House.
Report of the Committee of Ways and Means, Instructed, by a Resolution of the Ninth Instant, "To Enquire into the Probable Annual Amount of the Duties. . . . " 21st January, 1799. . . .
(Published by Order of the House. . . .).
[Philadelphia, 1799.] 12 pp., 2 folded tables.
AAS copy.   36574

U. S. 5th Congress, 1797-1799. House.
Report of the Committee of Ways and Means, Instructed on the Ninth Instant, to Enquire and Report, by Bill or Otherwise. . . . 21st January, 1799, Committed. . . . (Published by Order of the House. . . .).
[Philadelphia, 1799.] 8 pp.
AAS copy.   36575

U. S. 5th Congress, 1797-1799. House.
Report of the Committee of Ways and Means, Instructed, on the Ninth Ultimo, to Enquire and Report . . . Regard the Entry of Stills. 14th February, 1798, Committed. . . . (Published by Order of the House. . . .)
[Philadelphia, 1798.] pp. [407]-410.
AAS copy.   34767

U. S. 5th Congress, 1797-1799. House.
Report of the Committee of Ways and Means, Instructed on the Sixth Ultimo, to Enquire whether any and what Additional Revenues will be Wanted for the Public Service. 2d May, 1798, Committed. . . .
(Published by Order of the House. . . .)
[Philadelphia, 1798.] 6, [11] pp.
AAS copy.   34765

U. S. 5th Congress, 1797-1799. House.
Report of the Committee on the Protection of Commerce. . . . 2d April, 1798. Referred. . . . (Published by Order of the House. . . .)
[Philadelphia, 1798.) pp. [483]-486.
AAS copy.   48667

U. S. 5th Congress, 1797-1799. House.
Report of the Committee to whom was Referred, on the Nineteenth Instant. . . . 22nd June, 1798, Committed. . . .
[Philadelphia, 1798.] 4 pp.
LOC copy.   48668

U. S. 5th Congress, 1797-1799. House.
Report of the Committee to whom was Referred on the 19th of December last, a Resolution. . . . 21st February, 1799, Committed. . . . (Published by Order of the House. . . .).
[Philadelphia, 1799.] 6 pp.
AAS copy.   36578

U. S. 5th Congress, 1797-1799. House.
Report of the Committee to whom was Referred, on the 23d ultimo . . . the Message from the President. . . . 8th March, 1798. Committed. . . .
[Philadelphia, 1798.] pp. [447]-454.
LOC copy.   48672

U. S. 5th Congress, 1797-1799. House.
Report of the Committee of Ways and Means, to whom was Referred, on the Twenty-Fifth Instant, the Petition of Sundry Distillers. . . . 28th January, 1799, Committed. . . . (Published by Order of the House. . . .).
[Philadelphia, 1799.] 4 pp.
AAS copy.   36576

U. S. 5th Congress, 1797-1798. House.
Report of the Committee, to whom was Referred, on the 29th of November last, so much of the President's Speech, as Relates to the Protection of Commerce. . . . 16th January 1798, Committed. . . .
(Published by Order of the House. . . .)
[Philadelphia, 1798.] pp. [263]-272.
AAS copy.   48673

U. S. 5th Congress, 1797-1799. House.
Report of the Committee to whom was

Referred, on the 30th of November last, A Representation and Remonstrance of the Legislature of . . . Georgia. . . . 3d May, 1798, Committed. . . . (Published by Order of the House. . . .).
[Philadelphia, 1798.] pp. [527]-530.
AAS copy.   48669

U. S. 5th Congress, 1797-1799. House.
Report of the Committee, to whom was Referred, on the 30th November last, the Memorial of the. . . . Quakers. . . . 28th January, 1798. Committed. . . .
(Published by Order of the House. . . .)
[Philadelphia, 1798.] pp. [295]-310.
AAS copy.   48670

U. S. 5th Congress, 1797-1798. House.
Report of the Committee to whom was Referred, on the 30th ultimo, the Bill . . . "An Act, Authorizing the President. . . ." 4th May 1798, Committed. . . . (Published by Order of the House. . . .).
[Philadelphia, 1798.] pp. [531]-534.
AAS copy.   48671

U. S. 5th Congress, 1797-1799. House.
Report of the Committee to whom was Referred, the Bill Authorizing the Acceptance from the State of Connecticut of a Cession of the Jurisdiction of the Territory West of · Pennsylvania. . . . February 15, 1799.
[Philadelphia, 1799.] [3]-24 pp.
(Apparently issued without tp.)
NYPL copy.   36579

U. S. 5th Congress, 1797-1799. House.
Report of the Committee to whom it was Referred to Prepare an Answer to the Speech of the President. . . . 19th May, 1797, Committed.
[Philadelphia], Gales, [1797]. pp. [1]-4, [4], 5-7.
AAS copy.   33037

U. S. 5th Congress, 1797-1799. House.
Report of the Committee, to whom was Recommitted, on the Sixth Instant, the Motion of the 24th Ultimo. . . . 15th December, 1797. . . . Published by Order of the House.
[Philadelphia, 1797.] pp. [107]-112.
AAS copy.   33027

U. S. 5th Congress, 1797-1799. House.
Report of the Committee to whom was Referred a Motion of the Sixth Instant, Relative to the Balances. . . . 7th July, 1798. Committed. . . . Printed by Order of the House. . . .
Philadelphia, Gales, [1798]. 3 pp.
AAS copy.   34775

U. S. 5th Congress, 1797-1799. House.
Report, from the Committee to whom was Referred, on the Third of April last, the Letter from Rufus Putnam. . . . 13th June, 1798. Committed. . . . Printed by Order of the House. . . .
Philadelphia, Gales, [1798]. pp. [551]-557.
AAS copy.   34779

U. S. 5th Congress, 1797-1799. House.
Report of the Committee to whom was Referred, on the 12th Instant, Certain Memorials and Petitions. . . . 21st February, 1799, Committed. . . .
(Published by Order of the House. . . .).
[Philadelphia, 1799.] 15 pp.
AAS copy.   36581

U. S. 5th Congress, 1797-1799. House.
Report of the Committee to whom it was Referred, on the 14th and 19th of February last, to Enquire . . . the Sale of the Lands North West of the River Ohio. . . . 13th June, 1798, Committed. . . .
(Published by Order of the House. . . .)
[Philadelphia, 1798.] pp. [547]-550.
AAS copy.   34780

U. S. 5th Congress, 1797-1799. House.
Report of the Committee to whom was Referred, on the Twentieth of December last, a Letter from the Secretary of State. . . . 8th December, 1797. . . .
Published by Order of the House.
[Philadelphia, 1797.] pp. [115]-120.
AAS copy.   33035

U. S. 5th Congress, 1797-1799. House.

Report from the Committee to whom was Referred, on the Twenty-Second Instant, the Memorial of Justine Adelaide Maxime DeGrasse. . . December 27, 1797. Committed. Philadelphia, Gales, [1797]. pp. [211]-222.
AAS copy.   33040

U. S. 5th Congress, 1797-1799. House. Report of the Committee to whom was Referred, on the 23d Ultimo, the Message from the President . . . Inclosing a Memorial. . . . 8th March, 1798, Committed. . . . (Published by Order of the House. . . .)
[Philadelphia, 1798.] pp. [447]-454.
AAS copy.   34782

U. S. 5th Congress, 1797-1799. House. Report from the Committee to whom was Referred on the Twenty-Third of January last, the Message from the President . . . Relative to . . . Persons Imprisoned for Debt. 26th February, 1798. Committed. . . . Printed by Order of the House. . . .
Philadelphia, Gales, [1798]. 3 pp.
AAS copy.   34773

U. S. 5th Congress, 1797-1799. House. Report of the Committee to whom was Referred, on the 29th of November last, so much of the President's Speech as Relates to the Protection of Commerce. . . . 9th April, 1798, Committed. . . . (Published by Order of the House. . . .)
[Philadelphia, 1798.] [3] pp.
AAS copy.   34770

U. S. 5th Congress, 1797-1799. House. Report of the Committee to whom was Referred, on the 29th of November last, so much of the President's Speech as Relates to the Protection of Commerce. . . . 22d May, 1798, Committed. . . . (Published by Order of the House. . . .)
[Philadelphia, 1798.] [3] pp.
AAS copy.   34771

U. S. 5th Congress, 1797-1799. House. Report from the Committee to whom was Referred, on the 29th of November last, so much of the President's Speech as Relates to the Reimbursement. . . . 14th February, 1798. Committed. . . . Printed by Order of the House. . . .
Philadelphia, Gales, [1798]. pp. [367]-376.
AAS copy.   34772

U. S. 5th Congress, 1797-1799. House. Report of the Committee to whom was Referred, on the Twenty-Ninth Ultimo, so much of the President's Speech, as Relates to the Protection of Commerce. . . . 26th December, 1797. . . Published by Order of the House.
[Philadelphia, 1797.] pp. [203]-209.
AAS copy.   33039

U. S. 5th Congress, 1797-1799. House. Report of the Committee to whom was Referred, on the 30th of November last, a Representation and Remonstrance of the Legislature of . . . Georgia. . . . 24th December, 1798, Committed. . . . (Published by Order of the House. . . .)
[Philadelphia, 1798.] 4 pp.
AAS copy.   34784

U. S. 5th Congress, 1797-1799. House. Report of the Committee of Claims, on the Petition of Oliver Pollock. . . . 18th December, 1797. . . . Published by Order of the House.
[Philadelphia, 1797.] pp. [147]-150.
AAS copy.   32998

U. S. 5th Congress, 1797-1799. House. Report of the Committee of Claims to whom was Referred, on the Fifth Instant, the Petition of Azor Bagley. 22d December, 1797. . . . Published by Order of the House.
[Philadelphia, 1797.] pp. [163]-174.
AAS copy.   33009

U. S. 5th Congress, 1797-1799. House. Report of the Committee of Claims, to whom it was Referred, on the 20th December last, to Enquire into . . . Acts of Limitation. . . . 6th December, 1797.

. . . Published by Order of the House.
[Philadelphia, 1797.] pp. [51]-62.
AAS copy.   33007

U. S. 5th Congress, 1797-1799. House. Report of the Committee of Claims, to whom was Referred, on the 25th Ultimo, the Petition of John Baptiste Verdier. Committed. . . . (Published by Order of the House. . . .)
[Philadelphia, 1798.] 21 pp.
JCB copy.   34747

U. S. 5th Congress, 1797-1799. House. Report of the Committee of Commerce and Manufactures, on the Petition of North and Vesey. . . . 22d November 1797. . . . Published by Order of the House.
[Philadelphia, 1797.] pp. [47]-50.
AAS copy.   33014

U. S. 5th Congress, 1797-1799. House. Report of the Committee of Commerce and Manufactures, on the Petitions of Orchard Cook and Abiel Wood. . . . 29th December, 1797. . . . Published by Order of the House.
[Philadelphia, 1797.] pp. [223]-232.
AAS copy.   33015

U. S. 5th Congress, 1797-1799. House. Report of the Committee of Revisal and Unfinished Business. . . . 20th November, 1797. . . . Published by Order of the House.
[Philadelphia, 1797.] 15 pp.
AAS copy.   33017

U. S. 5th Congress, 1797-1799. House. Report of the Committee of Ways and Means, Instructed to Enquire "Whether any . . . Alterations may be necessary in the Law Intituled "An Act Laying Duties on Stamped Vellum, Parchment, and Paper." 11th December, 1797. . . . Published by Order of the House.
[Philadelphia, 1797.] pp. [83]-88.
AAS copy.   33022

U. S. 5th Congress, 1797-1799. House. Report of the Committee of Ways and Means, on the Petition of William Tomlinson. . . . 18th December, 1797. . . . Published by Order of the House.
[Philadelphia, 1797.] pp. [143]-146.
AAS copy.   33023

U. S. 5th Congress, 1797-1799. House. Report of the Committee to whom was Referred the Remonstrance . . . of Tennessee. 20th December, 1797. . . . Published by Order of the House.
[Philadelphia, 1797.] pp. [159-162.]
AAS copy.   33038

U. S. 5th Congress, 1797-1799. House. Report on the Petition of John Carr. . . . 8th December, 1797. . . . Published by Order of the House.
[Philadelphia, 1797.] pp. [79]-82.
LCP copy.   33008

U. S. 5th Congress, 1797-1799. House. Report of the Committees in Congress to whom were Referred Certain Memorials and Petitions Complaining of the Acts of Congress, Concerning the Alien & Sedition Laws. . . .
Richmond, Va., Nicolson, 1799. 20 pp.
LOC copy.   36583

U. S. 5th Congress, 1797-1799. House. 7th March, 1798. . . . A Bill to Continue in Force . . . "An Act Prohibiting . . . the Exportation of Arms. . . ."
n. p., [1798]. Broadside.
WLC copy.   48683

U. S. 5th Congress, 1797-1799. House. 16th April, 1798. . . . A Bill to Enable the President . . . to Procure Cannon.
n. p., [1798]. 2 pp.
WLC copy.   48693

U. S. 5th Congress, 1797-1799. House. 6th April, 1798. A Bill for the Relief of sick and Disabled Seamen.
n. p., [1798]. 3 pp.
WLC copy.   48690

U. S. 5th Congress, 1797-1799. House. 6th July, 1798. Read the First and Second

Time, and Committed. . . . A Bill to Augment the Army.
[Philadelphia, 1798.] [3] pp.
(Copy not located.)   48695

U. S. 5th Congress, 1797-1799. House. Speech of Mr. Gallatin . . . on the Bill for Augmenting the Navy Establishment . . . February 11th, 1799.
[Philadelphia, 1799.] 12 pp.
(The one recorded copy cannot be located.)   36588

U. S. 5th Congress, 1797-1799. House. Standing Rules and Orders of the House. Philadelphia, Gales, 1797. 15 pp.
LCP copy.   33042

U. S. 5th Congress, 1797-1799. House. 10th April, 1798. Read the First and Second Time. . . . A Bill Supplementary to the Act Providing for the further Defence.
[Philadelphia, 1798.] 2 pp.
WLC copy.   48691

U. S. 5th Congress, 1797-1799. House. 10th January, 1798. . . . A Bill for the Relief of the Refugees from . . . Nova-Scotia.
n. p., [1798]. 2 pp.
WLC copy.   48677

U. S. 5th Congress, 1797-1799. House. The Testimony Given before a Committee of the Whole House . . . on the 5th, 6th and 8th of February, 1798.
[Philadelphia, 1798.] 16, [14] pp.
AAS copy.   34760

U. S. 5th Congress, 1797-1799. House. 3d January 1798, Read the First and Second Time. . . . A Bill Providing for the Payment of the Interest . . . to General Kosciusko.
n. p., [1798]. Broadside.
WLC copy.   48674

U. S. 5th Congress, 1797-1799. House. 13th April, 1798. Read the First and Second Time. . . . A Bill to Provide an Additional Regiment of Artillerists.
n. p., [1798]. Broadside.
WLC copy.   48692

U. S. 5th Congress, 1797-1799. House. 13 February, 1798. . . . A Bill in Addition to . . . an Act to Promote the. . . . Useful Arts.
n. p., [1798]. Broadside.
WLC copy.   48680

U. S. 5th Congress, 1797-1799. House. 13th December, 1798. . . . A Bill for the Erection of a Light-House.
[Philadelphia? 1798.] Broadside.
Pierce W. Gaines copy.   48679

U. S. 5th Congress, 1797-1799. House. 30th March, 1798, Read the First and Second Time. . . . a Bill making Appropriations for the Military Establishment.
n. p., [1798]. 3 pp.
WLC copy.   48688

U. S. 5th Congress, 1797-1799. House. 12th December, 1797. . . . A Bill for the Relief of the Representatives of William Carmichael.
[Philadelphia, 1797.] Broadside.
LOC copy.   32964

U. S. 5th Congress, 1797-1799. House. 28th February, 1799. . . . A Bill for the Relief of Sick and Disabled Seamen. . . .
n. p., [1798]. 3 pp.
WLC copy.   48682

U. S. 5th Congress, 1797-1799. House. 25th April, 1798. . . . A Bill Supplementary to . . . "An Act for the Relief of Persons Imprisoned for Debt."
n. p., [1798]. 2 pp.
WLC copy.   48694

U. S. 5th Congress, 1797-1799. House. 23d March, 1798 . . . A Bill Authorizing an Expenditure . . . for the Reimbursement of . . . consuls.
n. p., [1798]. Broadside.
WLC copy.   48687

U. S. 5th Congress, 1797-1799. Senate.

An Act Providing for the Enumeration of
the Inhabitants. . . . December 27th, 1798.
Passed by the House.
[Philadelphia], Fenno, [1799]. 6 pp.
LOC copy.   36474

U. S. 5th Congress, 1797-1799. Senate.
Amendment of the Senate to the Bill,
Intituled "An Act to Suspend the
Commercial Intercourse. . . ." (Published
by Order of the House. . . .)
n. p., [1798?] 2 leaves.
WLC copy.   48696

U. S. 5th Congress, 1797-1799. Senate.
Amendments of the Senate, to the Bill,
Intituled, "An Act for the Establishing
. . . the Marine Corps." (Printed by Order
of the House . . . .)
[Philadelphia, 1798.] 4 pp.
AAS copy.   34691

U. S. 5th Congress, 1797-1799. Senate.
Amendments of the Senate to the Bill,
Intituled, "An Act Making
Appropriations for the Military
Establishment". . . . 6th June, 1798,
Committed to a Committee of the Whole
House. . . . (Published by Order of the
House. . . .).
[Philadelphia, 1798.] 4 pp.
AAS copy.   34696

U. S. 5th Congress, 1797-1799. Senate.
Amendments of the Senate to the Bill
Intituled "An Act to Authorize the
Defence of the Merchant Vessels. . . ."
20th June, 1798, Committed. . . .
(Published by Order of the House. . . .).
[Philadelphia, 1798.] 4 pp.
AAS copy.   34698

U. S. 5th Congress, 1797-1799. Senate.
Amendments of the Senate, to the Bill,
Intituled, "An Act to Lay and Collect a
Direct Tax. . . . (Printed by Order of the
House. . . .)
[Philadelphia, 1798.] 4 pp.
AAS copy.   34702

U. S. 5th Congress, 1797-1799. Senate.
Amendments of the Senate, to the Bill,
Intituled, "An Act to Make a Further
Appropriation for the Additional Naval
Armament. (Printed by Order of the
House. . . .)
[Philadelphia, 1798.] [3] pp.
AAS copy.   34703

U. S. 5th Congress, 1797-1799. Senate.
A Bill Prohibiting for a Limited Time the
Exportation of Arms [June 8, 1797].
[Philadelphia], Fenno, [1797].
LOC copy.   32962

U. S. 5th Congress, 1797-1799. Senate.
A Bill Regulating Certain Proceedings in
Cases of Impeachment.
[Philadelphia, Fenno, 1798.] 2 pp.
WLC copy.   48698

U. S. 5th Congress, 1797-1799. Senate.
A Bill to Amend the Act . . . to Amend
and Repeal . . . "An Act to Ascertain and
Fix the Military Establishment. . . ."
[Philadelphia], Fenno, [1798]. Broadside.
WLC copy.   48699

U. S. 5th Congress, 1797-1799. Senate.
A Bill to Authorize the President . . . to
Cause to be Purchased . . . a Number of
Small Vessels.
[Philadelphia], Fenno, [1798]. Broadside.
WLC copy.   48700

U. S. 5th Congress, 1797-1799. Senate.
A Bill to Declare the Treaties betwixt the
United States and . . . France, void.
[Philadelphia], Way & Groff, [1798].
4 pp.
WLC copy.   48701

U. S. 5th Congress, 1797-1799. Senate.
A Bill to Enable the President . . . to
Purchase . . . Founderies.
[Philadelphia], Fenno, [1798]. Broadside.
WLC copy.   48702

U. S. 5th Congress, 1797-1799. Senate.
A Bill to Establish an Executive
Department.
[Philadelphia], Fenno, [1798]. 2 pp.
WLC copy.   48703

U. S. 5th Congress, 1797-1799. Senate.
A Bill to Extend to the District of
Tennessee, the Exception . . . for the
Collection of Duties.
[Philadelphia], Fenno, [1798]. Broadside.
WLC copy.   48704

U. S. 5th Congress, 1797-1799. Senate.
A Bill to Prevent Citizens of the United
States Privateering [June 9, 1797].
[Philadelphia], Fenno, [1797].
LOC copy.   32963

U. S. 5th Congress, 1797-1799. Senate.
The Committee, to whom was Referred
the Consideration of the Treaty. . . .
[New York], Fenno, [1798]. Broadside.
WLC copy.   48716

U. S. 5th Congress, 1797-1799. Senate.
The Committee, to whom was Referred
the Consideration of the Treaty. . . .
[Philadelphia, 1798.] Broadside.
LOC copy.   48717

U. S. 5th Congress, 1797-1799. Senate.
In Senate of the United States, July 6th,
1797. The Committee [on the
impeachment of William Blount]. . . .
[Philadelphia, 1797]. 5 pp.
LOC copy.   48290

U. S. 5th Congress, 1797-1799. Senate.
. . . In Senate, March 23d, 1798. The
Committee, to whom was Referred the
Petition of Joseph Nourse. . . .
[Philadelphia], Fenno, [1798]. 2 pp.
WLC copy.   48705

U. S. 5th Congress, 1797-1799. Senate.
. . . In Senate, March the 26th, 1798. A
Motion was made. . . .
[Philadelphia, 1798.] Broadside.
LOC copy.   48706

U. S. 5th Congress, 1797-1799. Senate.
. . . In Senate, March 28th, 1798. The
Committee Appointed. . . .
[Philadelphia], Way & Groff, [1798].
Broadside.
WLC copy.   48707

U. S. 5th Congress, 1797-1799. Senate.
. . . In Senate. March the 28th, 1798. The
Committee on the Bill supplementary to
. . . "An Act to Establish the Judicial
Courts. . . ."
[Philadelphia], Fenno, [1798]. 2 pp.
WLC copy.   48708

U. S. 5th Congress, 1797-1799. Senate.
. . . In Senate, April 11th, 1798. The
Committee to whom was Referred the
Bill. . . . Buildings. . . .
[Philadelphia], Fenno, [1798]. 2 pp.
WLC copy.   48709

U. S. 5th Congress, 1797-1799. Senate.
. . . In Senate, April the 20th, 1798. The
Committee to whom was Referred a Bill
. . . Oaths. . . .
[Philadelphia], Fenno, [1798]. Broadside.
WLC copy.   48710

U. S. 5th Congress, 1797-1799. Senate.
. . . In Senate, April 20th, 1798. The
Committee to whom was Referred the Act
. . . Stills. . . .
[Philadelphia], Fenno, [1798]. 12 pp.
WLC copy.   48711

U. S. 5th Congress, 1797-1799. Senate.
. . . In Senate, April the 25th, 1798. A
Motion was Made . . . Aliens. . . .
[Philadelphia], Fenno, [1798]. Broadside.
WLC copy.   48712

U. S. 5th Congress, 1797-1799. Senate.
. . . In Senate, April the 26th, 1798. A
Motion was made . . . Three Existing
Circuits. . . .
[Philadelphia], Fenno, [1798]. Broadside.
WLC copy.   48713

U. S. 5th Congress, 1797-1799. Senate.
Journal of the Senate . . . First Session
of the Fifth Congress [May 15 - July
10, 1797].
Philadelphia, Fenno, 1797. 115, [1],
xvii, [1], x pp.
LCP copy.   32972

U. S. 5th Congress, 1797-1799. Senate.

Journal of the Senate . . . Second Session
of the Fifth Congress [Nov. 13, 1797 - July
16, 1798].
Philadelphia, Fenno, [1798]. 501, [1], vii,
[1], 24 pp.
AAS copy.   34720

U. S. 5th Congress, 1797-1799. Senate.
Journal of the Senate . . . Third Session of
the Fifth Congress [Dec. 3, 1798 - Mar. 2,
1799].
Philadelphia, Fenno, 1799. 222, vi, xiv pp.
AAS copy.   36521

U. S. 5th Congress, 1797-1799. Senate.
Message from the Senate, Communicating
a Copy of the Plea, Filed by . . . William
Blount. 26th December, 1798,
Referred. . . . (Published by Order of the
House. . . .)
[Philadelphia, 1798.] 4 pp.
AAS copy.   34791

U. S. 5th Congress, 1797-1799. Senate.
(No. 1.) In Senate of the United States,
July 9th, 1798. The Committee to whom
was Referred a Bill, Entitled, "An Act for
the Relief of John Vaughan . . . "
Report. . . .
[Philadelphia, 1798.] 6 pp.
AAS copy.   34718

U. S. 5th Congress, 1797-1799. Senate.
Report, in Part, of the Committee,
Appointed on the 18th Instant, to
Consider what Rules are Necessary. . . .
20th December, 1798. Printed by Order of
the Senate.
Philadelphia, Way & Groff, [1798]. 4 pp.
AAS copy.   34789

U. S. 5th Congress, 1797-1799. Senate.
Report of the Committee Appointed to
Report the Proper Measures . . . William
Blount. . . .
[Philadelphia], Ross, [1798]. 6 pp.
NYPL copy.   48714

U. S. 5th Congress, 1797-1799. Senate.
Report of the Committee to whom was
Referred the Memorial and Petition of
Margaret Lapsley. Agreed to by the
Senate - March 19th, 1798. Published by
Order of the Senate. . . .
[Philadelphia], Way & Groff, [1798].
4 pp.
AAS copy.   34781

U. S. 5th Congress, 1797-1799. Senate.
Report of the Committee to whom was
Referred the Motion of the Seventeenth
January last, Respecting . . . Georgia.
Published by Order of the Senate. . . .
[Philadelphia], Ross, [1798]. 6 pp.
AAS copy.   34783

U. S. 5th Congress, 1797-1799. Senate.
Resolved, that the Duty or Trust Imposed
by the Constitution. . . .
[Philadelphia], Fenno, [1797]. 1 leaf.
WLC copy.   48715

U. S. 5th Congress, 1797-1799. Senate.
Rules for Conducting Business in the
Senate.
[Philadelphia, 1797.] 7 pp.
NYPL copy.   33043

U. S. 6th Congress, 1799-1801.
A Bill to Establish an Uniform Mode of
Drawing Jurors by Lot [Mar. 11, 1800].
[Philadelphia, 1800.] 10 pp.
AAS copy.   38715

U. S. 6th Congress, 1799-1801.
List of the Names, and Place of
Residence, of the Members of the Senate
and House.
[Philadelphia, 1799?] Broadside.
AAS copy.   36542

U. S. 6th Congress, 1799-1801. House.
An Act to Suspend in Part, an Act,
Entitled "An Act to Augment the
Army. . . ." Passed the House . . . January
24th, 1800.
[Philadelphia, 1800.] Broadside.
LOC copy.   38698

U. S. 6th Congress, 1799-1801. House.
Amendments, &c, Proposed by the House
. . . to the Amendments of the Senate, to
the Bill . . . "Mississippi Territory."

Printed by Order of the Senate. . . . April 28th, 1800.
[Philadelphia, 1800.] 4 pp.
LOC copy.   38707

U. S. 6th Congress, 1799-1801. House.
A Bill to Establish a Uniform System of Bankruptcy. . . . 6th January, 1800. Read the First and Second Time, and Ordered to be Committed. . . . Published by Order of the House.
[Philadelphia, 1800.] 35 pp.
AAS copy.   38716

U. S. 6th Congress, 1799-1801. House.
A Bill to Establish an Uniform System of Bankruptcy.
Baltimore, Campbell, Conrad & Co., 1800. 32 pp.
APS copy.   38717

U. S. 6th Congress, 1799-1801. House.
A Bill to Establish an Uniform System of Bankruptcy. . . . 30th January, 1800. . . (Published by Order of the House. . . .)
[Philadelphia, 1800.] 34, 2 pp.
AAS copy.   38718

U. S. 6th Congress, 1799-1801. House.
A Bill to Provide for the Better Establishment & Regulation of the Courts. . . . 11th March, 1800. . . . (Published by Order of the House. . . .)
[Philadelphia, 1800.] 44 pp.
AAS copy.   38720

U. S. 6th Congress, 1799-1801. House.
A Bill to Provide for the Execution of the Twenty-Seventh Article of the Treaty . . . with Great Britain. (As Amended . . . 2nd of April 1800].
[Philadelphia, 1800.] 3 pp.
NYHS copy.   49158

U. S. 6th Congress, 1799-1801. House.
A Bill to Provide for the More Convenient Organization of the Courts. . . . 1st April, 1800. Read. . . . (Published by Order of the House. . . .)
[Philadelphia, 1800.] 40 pp.
AAS copy.   38721

U. S. 6th Congress, 1799-1801. House.
The Committee to whom was Referred the Report of the Secretary of State, to whom was Referred the Memorial of Stephen Sayre, Report. . . .
[Philadelphia? 1800.] 6 pp.
(Pierce Gaines copy.)   38725

U. S. 6th Congress, 1799-1801. House.
11th February, 1800. Read the First and Second Time. . . . A Bill to Allow a Drawback. . . .
[Philadelphia, 1800.] Broadside.
LOC copy.   38730

U. S. 6th Congress, 1799-1801. House.
15th April, 1800. Read the First and Second Time. . . . A Bill in Addition to the Act intituled "An Act to Prohibit . . . the Slave Trade."
[Philadelphia, 1800.] 4 pp.
NYHS copy.   49160

U. S. 6th Congress, 1799-1801. House.
4th February, 1800. Read the First and Second Time. . . . A Bill to Continue in Force an Act Concerning Certain Fisheries.
[Philadelphia, 1800.] 2 pp.
LOC copy.   38732

U. S. 6th Congress, 1799-1801. House.
Further Report, (in Part) - of the Committee of Revisal and Unfinished Business. . . . What Laws have Expired. . . . 3th December, 1800. . . .
[Philadelphia, 1800.] 4 pp.
AAS copy.   38734

U. S. 6th Congress, 1799-1801. House.
Further Report, (in Part) - of the Committee, to whom was Re-committed on the 10th instant the Bill Directing the Erection of a Mausoleum. . . . 19th December, 1800.
[Washington? 1800.] [3] pp.
AAS copy.   38735

U. S. 6th Congress, 1799-1801. House.
Further Report, of the Committee of Revisal and Unfinished Business. 19th

December, 1800.
[Washington? 1800.] [3] pp.
AAS copy.   38736

U. S. 6th Congress, 1799-1801. House.
Journal of the House . . . First Session of the Sixth Congress.
Philadelphia, Ross, [1800]. 446, [32] pp.
AAS copy.   38748

U. S. 6th Congress, 1799-1801. House.
Letter from Arthur St. Clair. . . . Read the 14th. March 1800. . . . Printed by Order of the House.
Philadelphia, Poulson, 1800. 8 pp.
AAS copy.   38753

U. S. 6th Congress, 1799-1801. House.
Letter from Mr. Hornblower. . . . April 18th, 1800. Printed by Order of the House.
[Philadelphia, 1800.] 4 pp.
AAS copy.   38754

U. S. 6th Congress, 1797-1801. House.
Mr. Abiel Foster's Motion. . . . 4th February, 1800. . . . (Published by Order of the House. . . .)
[Philadelphia, 1800.] [3] pp.
AAS copy.   38786

U. S. 6th Congress, 1799-1801. House.
Mr. Bayard's Motion. 17th February, 1800. . . . (Published by Order of the House. . . .)
[Philadelphia, 1800.] [3] pp.
AAS copy.   38787

U. S. 6th Congress, 1799-1801. House.
Mr. Harper's Motion, 10th March, 1800. . . . (Published by Order of the House. . . .)
[Philadelphia, 1800.] 4 pp.
AAS copy.   38788

U. S. 6th Congress, 1799-1801. House.
Mr. Henry Lee's Motion, 10th March, 1800. . . . (Published by Order of the House. . . .)
[Philadelphia, 1800.] [3] pp.
AAS copy.   38789

U. S. 6th Congress, 1799-1801. House.
Mr. Livingston's Motion, 13th February, 1800. . . . (Published by Order of the House. . . .)
[Philadelphia, 1800.] [3] pp.
AAS copy.   38790

U. S. 6th Congress, 1799-1801. House.
Mr. Livingston's Motion. 20th February, 1800. . . . (Published by Order of the House. . . .)
[Philadelphia, 1800.] 4 pp.
AAS copy.   38791

U. S. 6th Congress, 1799-1801. House.
Mr. Marshall's Motion. Strike out [Apr. 25, 1800]. . . .
[Philadelphia, 1800.] Broadside.
AAS copy.   38792

U. S. 6th Congress, 1799-1801. House.
Mr. Nicholas's Motion, for Amending the Bill [Apr. 2, 1800]. . . . (Published by Order of the House. . . .)
[Philadelphia, 1800.] 4 pp.
AAS copy.   38793

U. S. 6th Congress, 1799-1801. House.
Mr. Nicholas's Motion, for Amending the Bill [Apr. 2, 1800]. . . . (With the Amendments of Mr. Marshall. . . .)
(Published by Order of the House. . . .)
[Philadelphia, 1800.] 4 pp.
AAS copy.   38794

U. S. 6th Congress, 1799-1801. House.
Mr. Nicholas's Motion. November 21, 1800. . . . Published by Order of the House.
[Washington? 1800.] [3] pp.
AAS copy.   38795

U. S. 6th Congress, 1799-1801. House.
Mr. Nicholas's Motion, 13th March, 1800. . . . (Published by Order of the House. . . .)
[Philadelphia, 1800.] [3] pp.
AAS copy.   38796

U. S. 6th Congress, 1799-1801. House.
Motion, Made in Committee of the

Whole. . . . November 25, 1800.
[Washington? 1800.] [1] p.
AAS copy.   38797

U. S. 6th Congress, 1799-1801. House.
Petition of Cato West. . . . 13th January, 1800. . . . (Published by Order of the House. . . .)
[Philadelphia, 1800.] [2], 27 pp.
AAS copy.   38799

U. S. 6th Congress, 1799-1801. House.
Report from the Committee of Revisal & Unfinished Business. . . . 23d January, 1800. . . . (Published by Order of the House. . . .)
[Philadelphia, 1800.] [4] pp.
AAS copy.   38809

U. S. 6th Congress, 1799-1801. House.
Report, From the Committee to whom was Referred, the Bill, Sent from the Senate, Intituled "An Act, for the Relief of Persons Imprisoned for Debt," 23d December, 1799. Committed. . . .
(Published by Order of the House. . . .).
[Philadelphia, 1799.] 4 pp.
AAS copy.   36562

U. S. 6th Congress, 1799-1801. House.
Report in Part, of the Committee Appointed on the 9th of December. . . . 11th March, 1800. . . . (Published by Order of the House. . . .)
[Philadelphia, 1800.] [3] pp.
AAS copy.   38811

U. S. 6th Congress, 1799-1801. House.
Report in Part, of the Committee Appointed on the 24th of December. . . . 18th February, 1800. . . . (Published by Order of the House. . . .)
[Philadelphia, 1800.] 5 pp.
AAS copy.   38812

U. S. 6th Congress, 1799-1801. House.
Report, in Part - of the Committee of Elections. . . . November 26, 1800. . . . Published by Order of the House.
[Washington? 1800.] 4 pp.
AAS copy.   38813

U. S. 6th Congress, 1799-1801. House.
Report in Part - of the Committee of Revisal and Unfinished Business. November 26, 1800. . . . Published by Order of the House.
[Washington, 1800.] 7 pp.
AAS copy.   38815

U. S. 6th Congress, 1799-1801. House.
Report in Part, of the Committee to whom were Referred on the 13th Ultimo, a Petition of Cato West. . . . 18th February, 1800. . . . (Published by Order of the House. . . .)
[Philadelphia, 1800.] 14 pp.
AAS copy.   38817

U. S. 6th Congress, 1799-1801. House.
Report (in Part) of the Committee to whom was Referred on the 28th . . . the Speech of the President. . . . 17th December, 1800. . . . Published by Order of the House.
[Washington, 1800.] [3] pp.
AAS copy.   38816

U. S. 6th Congress, 1799-1801. House.
Report of the Committee Appointed on the 5th Instant . . . the Great Copper Bed. 17th March, 1800. . . . (Published by Order of the House. . . .)
[Philadelphia, 1800.] 4 pp.
AAS copy.   38819

U. S. 6th Congress, 1799-1801. House.
Report of the Committee Appointed on the Fourth. . . . 6th December, 1799, Committed. . . .
[Philadelphia, Ross, 1799.] 7 pp.
AAS copy.   36565

U. S. 6th Congress, 1799-1801. House.
Report of the Committee Appointed on the 10th December . . . of the Territory North-West of the Ohio. . . . 3d March, 1800. . . . (Published by Order of the House. . . .)
[Philadelphia, 1800.] 4 pp.
AAS copy.   38820

U. S. 6th Congress, 1799-1801. House.

Report of the Committee, Appointed, on the Twentieth of March last, to Examine the . . . Public Debt. . . . 8th May, 1800. . . . Printed by Order of the House. [Philadelphia, 1800.] pp. [1]-11, 9 folded plates, [37]-39.
AAS copy.   38821

U. S. 6th Congress, 1799-1801. House. Report of the Committee Appointed on the 22nd Instant, to Prepare an Address. . . . 25th November 1800. . . . Published by Order of the House. [Washington, 1800.] 4 pp.
AAS copy.   38822

U. S. 6th Congress, 1799-1801. House. Report of the Committee, Appointed to Enquire into the Expendiency of Making further Provision. . . . 9th April. . . . (Published by Order of the House. . . .) [Philadelphia, 1800.] 4 pp.
AAS copy.   38823

U. S. 6th Congress, 1799-1801. House. Report of the Commiteee Appointed to Enquire into the Operation of the . . . Trading Houses. . . . 22d April, 1800. . . . Printed by Order of the House. . . . [Philadelphia, 1800.] 18 pp., 2 folded tables.
AAS copy.   38824

U. S. 6th Congress, 1799-1801. House. Report of the Committee of Claims Instructed on the 13th of January last . . . Loan-Office. . . . 28th March, 1800. . . . (Published by Order of the House. . . .) [Philadelphia, 1800.] 4 pp.
AAS copy.   38826

U. S. 6th Congress, 1799-1801. House. Report of the Committee of Claims, to whom was Referred, on the 6th of December last, the Petition of Seth Nelson. . . . 24th March, 1800. . . . (Published by Order of the House. . . .) [Philadelphia, 1800.] 5 pp.
AAS copy.   38827

U. S. 6th Congress, 1799-1801. House. Report of the Committee of Claims, to whom was Referred, on the 7th Instant, the Petition of John Vaughan. . . . 17th December, 1799, Committed. . . . (Published by Order of the House. . . .). [Philadelphia, 1799.] 4 pp.
AAS copy.   36570

U. S. 6th Congress, 1799-1801. House. Report of the Committee of Claims, to whom was Referred, on the 8th of January last, the Petition of Stephen Sayre. 4th March, 1800. . . . (Published by Order of the House. . . .) [Philadelphia, 1800.] 15 pp.
AAS copy.   38828

U. S. 6th Congress, 1799-1801. House. Report of the Committee of Claims, to whom was Referred, on the 8th of January last, the Petition of William Nicholas. 9th April, 1800. . . . (Published by Order of the House. . . .) [Philadelphia, 1800.] 4 pp.
AAS copy.   38829

U. S. 6th Congress, 1799-1801. House. Report of the Committee of Claims, to whom was Referred on the 8th of January last, the Petition of William Nicholas. . . . November 26, 1800. . . . Published by Order of the House. [Washington, 1800.] 6 pp.
AAS copy.   38830

U. S. 6th Congress, 1799-1801. House. Report of the Committee of Claims, to whom was Referred on the 9th of January last, the Memorial of David Jones. . . . 10th March, 1800. . . . Published by Order of the House. [Philadelphia, 1800.] 4 pp.
AAS copy.   38831

U. S. 6th Congress, 1799-1801. House. Report of the Committee of Claims, to whom was Referred, on the 10th of February last, the Petition of Amey Dardin. 18th March, 1800. . . . (Published by Order of the House. . . .) [Philadelphia, 1800.] 4 pp.
AAS copy.   38833

U. S. 6th Congress, 1799-1801. House. Report of the Committee of Claims, to whom was Referred, on the 10th of January last, the Petition of Tobias Rudolph. . . . 20th March, 1800. . . . (Published by Order of the House. . . .) [Philadelphia, 1800.] [3] pp.
AAS copy.   38832

U. S. 6th Congress, 1799-1801. House. Report of the Committee of Claims, to whom was Referred, on the 11th of December last, the Petition of Campbell Smith. 21st February, 1800. . . . (Published by Order of the House. . . .) [Philadelphia, 1800.] 12 pp.
AAS copy.   38834

U. S. 6th Congress, 1799-1801. House. Report of the Committee of Claims, to whom was Referred, on the 12th of December last, the Memorial of James Somervell. . . . 14th March, 1800. . . . (Published by Order of the House . . .) [Philadelphia, 1800.] 4 pp.
AAS copy.   38835

U. S. 6th Congress, 1799-1801. House. Report of the Committee of Claims, to whom was Referred, on the 13th instant, the Petition of Moses Gill. 19th February, 1800. . . . (Published by Order of the House. . . .) [Philadelphia, 1800.] 7, [1] pp.
AAS copy.   38836

U. S. 6th Congress, 1799-1801. House. Report of the Committee of Claims, to whom was Referred, on the 16th ultimo, the Petition of Oliver Pollock, 18th April, 1800. . . . Printed by Order of the House. . . .) [Philadelphia, 1800.] 6 pp.
AAS copy.   38837

U. S. 6th Congress, 1799-1800. House. Report of the Committee of Claims, to whom was Referred on the 17th ultimo, the Petition of Mary Wooster. . . . 28th April, 1800. . . . (Published by Order of the House. . . .) [Philadelphia, 1800.] 4 pp.
AAS copy.   38838

U. S. 6th Congress, 1799-1801. House. Report of the Committee of Claims, to whom was Referred, on the 18th February, 1800, the Petition of Thomas Johnson. 16th April, 1800. . . . (Published by Order of the House. . . .) [Philadelphia, 1800.] [3] pp.
AAS copy.   38839

U. S. 6th Congress, 1799-1801. House. Report, of the Committee of Claims, to whom was Referred on the 21st ultimo, the Petition . . . of Rhode-Island College. . . . 17th February, 1800. . . . (Published by Order of the House. . . .) [Philadelphia, 1800.] 4 pp.
AAS copy.   38840

U. S. 6th Congress, 1799-1801. House. Report of the Committee of Claims, to whom was Referred, on the 25th ultimo, the Petition of Jane Lynch. 26th April, 1800. . . . (Published by Order of the House. . . .) [Philadelphia, 1800.] [3] pp.
AAS copy.   38841

U. S. 6th Congress, 1799-1801. House. Report of the Committee of Claims, to whom was Referred, on the 25th ultimo, the Petition of John Baptiste Verdier. . . . (Published by Order of the House. . . .) [Philadelphia, 1800.] 21 pp.
AAS copy.   38842

U. S. 6th Congress, 1799-1801. House. Report of the Committee of Claims, to whom was Referred, on the 26th ultimo, the Petition of Gilbert Dench. 21st March, 1800. . . . (Published by Order of the House. . . .) [Philadelphia, 1800.] 4 pp.
AAS copy.   38843

U. S. 6th Congress, 1799-1801. House. Report of the Committee of Claims to whom was Referred, on the 27th of March last, the Memorial of Charles Pettit. . . .

29th April, 1800. . . . (Published by Order of the House. . . .) [Philadelphia, 1800.] 34 pp.
AAS copy.   38844

U. S. 6th Congress, 1799-1801. House. Report of the Committee of Claims, to whom was Referred, on the 28th of February last, the Petition of Ann Elliot. . . . (Published by Order of the House. . . .) [Philadelphia, 1800.] [3] pp.
AAS copy.   38845

U. S. 6th Congress, 1799-1801. House. Report of the Committee of Claims, to whom was Referred, on the 28th ultimo, the Petition of Moses White. . . . 15th January, 1800. . . . (Published by Order of the House. . . .) [Philadelphia, 1800.] 4 pp.
AAS copy.   38846

U. S. 6th Congress, 1799-1801. House. Report of the Committee, to whom was Referred, so much of the President's Speech, as Relates, to . . . the Judiciary. . . . 1st May, 1800. . . . Published by Order of the House. . . .) [Philadelphia, 1800.] 44 pp.
AAS copy.   38874

U. S. 6th Congress, 1799-1800. House. Report of the Committee of Claims, to whom was Referred the Petition of Benjamin Wells. . . . 21st April, 1800. . . . (Published by Order of the House. . . .) [Philadelphia, 1800.] 4 pp.
AAS copy.   38847

U. S. 6th Congress, 1799-1801. House. Report of the Committee of Claims, to whom were Referred, the Petitions of Benjamin Bird. . . . 22d April, 1800. . . . (Published by Order of the House. . . .) [Philadelphia, 1800.] 7 pp.
AAS copy.   38849

U. S. 6th Congress, 1799-1801. House. Report of the Committee of Claims, to whom were Referred, the Petitions of Temple Elliot. . . . 25th February, 1800. . . . (Published by Order of the House. . . .) [Philadelphia, 1800.] 4 pp.
AAS copy.   38850

U. S. 6th Congress, 1799-1801. House. Report of the Committee of Claims, to whom were Referred, the Several Petitions of Thomas Frothingham. . . . 11th March, 1800. . . . Published by Order of the House. . . . [Philadelphia, 1800.] 4 pp.
AAS copy.   38848

U. S. 6th Congress, 1799-1801. House. Report of the Committee of Commerce & Manufactures, Instructed on the 15th ultimo, to Enquire and Report. . . . 14th February, 1800. . . . (Published by Order of the House. . . .) [Philadelphia, 1800.] 7 pp.
AAS copy.   38851

U. S. 6th Congress, 1799-1801. House. Report of the Committee of Commerce and Manufactures, to whom was Referred on the 4th instant, the Petition of Robert Hooper. 9th December, 1800. [Washington, 1800.] 4 pp.
AAS copy.   38852

U. S. 6th Congress, 1799-1801. House. Report of the Committee of Commerce and Manufactures, to whom was Referred on the 5th instant, the Petition of Thomas Jenkins. . . . 9th December. . . . Published by Order of the House. [Washington, 1800.] 4 pp.
AAS copy.   38853

U. S. 6th Congress, 1799-1801. House. Report of the Committee of Commerce & Manufactures, to whom was Referred, on the 17th of December last, the Petition of Henry Stouffer. . . . 10th February, 1800. . . . (Published by Order of the House. . . .) [Philadelphia, 1800.] 16 pp.
AAS copy.   38854

U. S. 6th Congress, 1799-1801. House.

Report of the Committee of Commerce & Manufactures, to whom was Referred the Amendments Proposed. . . . 11th February, 1800. . . . (Published by Order of the House. . . .)
[Philadelphia, 1800.] 4 pp.
AAS copy.   38855

U. S. 6th Congress, 1799-1801. House. Report of the Committee of Revisal and Unfinished Business, on Bills . . . 10th December, 1799. . . . (Published by Order of the House. . . .).
[Philadelphia, 1799.] 6 pp.
AAS copy.   36573

[U. S. 6th Congress, 1799-1801. House. Report of the Committee of Revisal and Unfinished Business, to whom were Referred the Amendments to the Bill entitled "An Act to Provide for Mitigating . . . Forfeitures. . . ." [House Document, Jan. 25, 1800].
[Philadelphia, 1800.] 4 pp.]
(A ghost of 38809.)   38857

U. S. 6th Congress, 1799-1801. House. Report, of the Committee of Ways and Means, Instructed on the 17th instant to Enquire. . . . 31st December, 1800. . . . Published by Order of the House.
[Washington, 1800.] 4 pp.
AAS copy.   38858

U. S. 6th Congress, 1799-1801. House. Report of the Committee of Ways and Means, on Certain Appropriations for the Diplomatic Department. 5th May, 1800. . . . Printed by Order of the House.
[Philadelphia, 1800.] 21 pp.
AAS copy.   38859

U. S. 6th Congress, 1799-1801. House. Report of the Committee of Ways and Means, on Certain Appropriations for the Indian Department. 5th May, 1800. . . . Published by Order of the House.
[Philadelphia, 1800.] 12 pp.
AAS copy.   38860

U. S. 6th Congress, 1799-1801. House. Report of the Committee of Ways and Means, on the Subject of a Loan. . . .21st of February, 1800. . . . (Published by Order of the House. . . .)
[Philadelphia, 1800.] 24 pp.
AAS copy.   38861

U. S. 6th Congress, 1799-1801. House. Report of the Committee of Ways and Means, on the Subject of Further Revenue. 30th April, 1800. . . . (Published by Order of the House. . . .)
[Philadelphia, 1800.] 58 pp.
AAS copy.   38862

U. S. 6th Congress, 1799-1801. House. Report of the Committee to which was Referred the Bill sent from the Senate, Intituled "An Act Prescribing the Mode of Deciding Disputed Elections. . . ." 25th April, 1800. . . . (Published by Order of the House. . . .)
[Philadelphia, 1800.] 12 pp.
AAS copy.   38887

U. S. 6th Congress, 1799-1801. House. Report of the Committee to whom was Re-committed the Bill sent from the Senate, Intitled "An Act for the Relief of Persons Imprisoned for Debt," 30th December, 1799. . . . (Published by Order of the House. . . .)
[Philadelphia, 1799.] 4 pp.
LOC copy.   36577

U. S. 6th Congress, 1797-1801. House. Report of the Committee, to whom was Re-committed, the Report on the Petition of Cato West. . . . 13th March, 1800. . . .
[Philadelphia, 1800.] 4 pp.
AAS copy.   38863

U. S. 6th Congress, 1799-1800. House. Report of the Committee to whom was Referred, on the 4th instant, the Petition of Isaac Zane. 21st February, 1800. . . . (Published by Order of the House. . . .)
[Philadelphia, 1800.] 3 pp.
AAS copy.   38864

U. S. 6th Congress, 1799-1801. House. Report of the Committee, to Whom was

Referred, on the 7th ultimo, the Memorial of Matthew Patterson. . . . 8th April, 1800. . . . (Published by Order of the House. . . .)
[Philadelphia, 1800.] 6 pp.
AAS copy.   38865

U. S. 6th Congress, 1799-1801. House. Report of the Committee to whom was Referred, on the 7th ultimo, the Memorial of Matthew Patterson. . . . 23d December 1800. . . . Published by Order of the House.
[Washington, 1800.] 7 pp.
AAS copy.   38866

U. S. 6th Congress, 1799-1801. House. Report of the Committee to whom was Referred on the 7th ultimo, the Petition of William Hill. . . . 4th April, 1800. . . . (Published by Order of the House. . . .)
[Philadelphia, 1800.] 7 pp.
AAS copy.   38867

U. S. 6th Congress, 1799-1801. House. Report of the Committee to whom was Referred, on the 13th ultimo, the Petition of William Tazewell, 9th April, 1800. . . . (Published by Order of the House. . . .)
[Philadelphia, 1800.] 9 pp.
AAS copy.   38868

U. S. 6th Congress, 1799-1801. House. Report of the Committee, to whom was Referred, on the 14th instant, the Message of the President. . . . 20th January, 1800. . . . (Published by Order of the House. . . .)
[Philadelphia, 1800.] 28 pp.
AAS copy.   38869

U. S. 6th Congress, 1799-1801. House. Report of the Committee to whom was Referred, on the 18th instant, the Petition of John Mountjoy, 21st February, 1800. . . . (Published by Order of the House. . . .)
[Philadelphia, 1800.] 4 pp.
AAS copy.   38870

U. S. 6th Congress, 1799-1801. House. Report of the Committee to whom was Referred on the 21st February last, the Petition of Sundry Inhabitants of Mount-Pleasant. . . . 11th March, 1800. . . . (Published by Order of the House. . . .)
[Philadelphia, 1800.] 4 pp.
AAS copy.   38871

U. S. 6th Congress, 1799-1801. House. Report of the Committee to whom was Referred on the 21st of February last, the Petition of Sundry Inhabitants of Mount-Pleasant. . . . 14th March, 1800. . . . (Published by Order of the House. . . .)
[Philadelphia, 1800.] 4 pp.
AAS copy.   38872

U. S. 6th Congress, 1799-1801. House. Report of the Committee, to whom were Referred, on the 24th of December . . . Several Petitions. . . 2d April, 1800. . . . (Published by Order of the House. . . .)
[Philadelphia, 1800.] 17 pp.
AAS copy.   38897

U. S. 6th Congress, 1799-1801. House. Report of the Committee to whom was Referred, on the 26th, ultimo, the Consideration of the Expediency of Accepting . . . Jurisdiction . . . West of Pennsylvania. . . 21st March, 1800. . . . Published by Order of the House. . . .
[Philadelphia, 1800.] 31 pp.
LCP copy.   38873

U. S. 6th Congress, 1799-1801. House. Report of the Committee, to whom was Referred, so much of the President's Speech, as Relates to . . . the Judiciary. . . . 1st May, 1800. . . . Published by Order of the House. . . .
[Philadelphia, 1800.] 44 pp.
AAS copy.   38874

U. S. 6th Congress, 1799-1801. House. Report of the Committee to whom was Referred, so much of the Speech of the President . . . as Relates to . . . National Defence. . . . 13th January, 1800. . . . (Published by Order of the House. . . .)

[Philadelphia, 1800.] 4, [2] pp.
AAS copy.   38876

[U. S. 6th Congress, 1799-1801. House. Report of the Committee to whom was Referred, the Bill, sent from the Senate, Intituled "An Act, for Relief of Persons Imprisoned for Debt." 23d December, 1799. . . . (Published by Order of the House. . . .).
[Philadelphia, 1799.] 4 pp.]
(A ghost of 36562, q. v.)   36580

U. S. 6th Congress, 1799-1801. House. Report of the Committee to whom was Referred, the Report of the Secretary of War. . . . 9th May, 1800. . . . Published by Order of the House.
[Philadelphia, 1800.] 5 pp.
LCP copy.   38895

U. S. 6th Congress, 1799-1801. House. Report of the Committee to whom were Referred, Sundry Petitions. . . . 16th April, 1800. . . . (Published by Order of the House. . . .)
[Philadelphia, 1800.] 11 pp.
AAS copy.   38898

U. S. 6th Congress, 1799-1801. House. Report of the Secretary of the Navy on the Petition of Sundry French Officers. . . . 27th December, 1799. . . . (Published by Order of the House. . . .).
[Philadelphia, 1799?]. 4 (i.e. 3) pp.
AAS copy.   36582

U. S. 6th Congress, 1799-1801. House. Report of the Secretary of the Navy on the Petition of Sundry French Officers . . . 27th December, 1799. . . . (Published by Order of the House. . . .)
[Philadelphia, 1800?] 4 pp.
(Also entered as 36582, q. v.)   38900

U. S. 6th Congress, 1799-1801. House. Report on the Petition of Abraham Bell. . . . 2d April, 1800. . . . (Published by Order of the House. . . .)
[Philadelphia, 1800.] [3] pp.
AAS copy.   38901

U. S. 6th Congress, 1799-1801. House. Report to the Committee Appointed to Enquire whether . . . lands . . . North-West of the Ohio. 19th February, 1800. . . . (Published by Order of the House. . . .)
[Philadelphia, 1800.] [3] pp.
AAS copy.   38825

U. S. 6th Congress, 1799-1801. House. Rules and Orders of the House. Philadelphia, Oswald, 1799. 22 pp.
HSP copy.   48975

U. S. 6th Congress, 1799-1801. House. 2d December, 1800. Read the First and Second Time. . . . A Bill, Directing the Erection of a Mausoleum to George Washington.
[Washington, 1800.] Broadside.
HEH copy.   38907

U. S. 6th Congress, 1799-1801. House. 16th December, 1799. Read the First and Second Time, and Committed to a Committee of the whole House, on Thursday next, a Bill Providing for the Enumeration of the Inhabitants. . . .
[Philadelphia, 1799.] 7 pp.
LOC copy.   36586

U. S. 6th Congress, 1799-1801. House. 16 December, 1799. Read the First and Second Time, and Committed to a Committee of the whole House on Thursday next. A Bill Providing for Salvage. . . .
[Philadelphia, 1799.] 3 pp.
LOC copy.   36585

U. S. 6th Congress, 1799-1801. House. 16th December, 1799. Read the First and Second Time, and Committed to a Committee of the whole House on Wednesday Next. A Bill for the Preservation of Peace with the Indian Tribes.
[Philadelphia, 1799.] 2 pp.
LOC copy.   36587

U. S. 6th Congress, 1799-1801. House. Standing Rules and Orders of the House.

Philadelphia, Oswald, 1799. 22 pp.
AAS copy.   36590

U. S. 6th Congress, 1799-1801. House.
3d March, 1800. Read the First and
Second Time.... A Bill to Enable the
President ... to Borrow Money....
[Philadelphia? 1800.] 2 pp.
JCB copy.   49159

U. S. 6th Congress, 1799-1801. House.
13th February, 1800. Read the First and
Second Time.... A Bill more Effectually
to Provide for the National Defence.
[Philadelphia, 1800.] 10 pp.
AAS copy.   38909

U. S. 6th Congress, 1799-1801. House.
31st March, 1800. Read the First and
Second Time.... An Act Prescribing the
Mode of Deciding Disputed Elections of
President and Vice-President.
[Philadelphia, 1800.] 6 pp.
NYPL copy.   49162

U. S. 6th Congress, 1799-1801. House.
26th March, 1800. Read the First and
Second Time.... A Bill Making
Appropriation for the Support of
Government for ... 1800.
[Philadelphia, 1800.] 9 pp.
NYHS copy.   49161

U. S. 6th Congress, 1799-1801. Senate.
An Address and Remonstrance of the
Legislature of the State of Georgia
[Senate Doc., Dec. 31, 1800].
[Washington, 1800.] 18 pp.
AAS copy.   38705

U. S. 6th Congress, 1799-1801. Senate.
Amendment, Proposed by Mr. Bingham.
... In Senate ... February 28th, 1800.
[Philadelphia, 1800.] 4 pp.
AAS copy.   38706

U. S. 6th Congress, 1799-1801. Senate.
Amendments of the Senate, to the Bill
Entitled, "An Act Supplemental to the
Act, Entitled, An Act for an Amicable
Settlement of ... Mississippi Territory."
17th April, 1800.
[Philadelphia, 1800.] 4 pp.
AAS copy.   38708

U. S. 6th Congress, 1799-1801. Senate.
Amendments of the Senate, to the Bill,
Entituled, "An Act to Amend the Act
Intituled, An Act Providing for the Sale of
Lands ... North-west of the Ohio. ..."
23d April, 1800.
[Philadelphia, 1800.] 8 pp.
LOC copy.   38709

U. S. 6th Congress, 1799-1801. Senate.
Amendments of the Senate to the Bill
Intituled An Act in Addition to the Act,
Intitled "An Act Regulating Grants of
Land. ..." 21st February, 1800. ...
Published by Order of the House.
[Philadelphia, 1800.] 6 pp.
AAS copy.   38710

U. S. 6th Congress, 1799-1801. Senate.
Amendments of the Senate to the Bill,
Intituled "An Act Providing for Salvage.
... 31st January, 1800. Referred to the
Committee of Commerce and
Manufactures. Published by Order of the
House.
[Philadelphia, 1800.] 6 pp.
AAS copy.   38711

U. S. 6th Congress, 1799-1801. Senate.
Amendments of the Senate to the Bill
intituled "An Act Providing for the
Enumeration of the Inhabitants. ... 6th
February, 1800. ... (Published by Order
of the House. ...)
[Philadelphia, 1800.] 4 pp.
NYPL copy.   49163

U. S. 6th Congress, 1799-1801. Senate.
Amendments of the Senate to the Bill,
Intituled, An Act to Divide the Territory
... Northwest of the Ohio. ... 22d April,
1800. Referred....
[Philadelphia, 1800.] 4 pp.
AAS copy.   38712

U. S. 6th Congress, 1799-1800. Senate.
Amendments Proposed to the Bill,
Entitled, "An Act in Addition to the Act,

Entitled "An Act Regulating Grants of
Land. ..." [In Senate, February 20th,
1800.]
[Philadelphia, 1800.] 4 pp.
AAS copy.   38713

U. S. 6th Congress, 1799-1801. Senate.
... April 29th, 1800. A Motion was made
... that a Committee ... Enquire into ...
the Expenditure of Public Money....
[Philadelphia, 1800.] Broadside.
LOC copy.   38746

U. S. 6th Congress, 1799-1801. Senate.
A Bill to Establish an Uniform System of
Bankruptcy.... Printed by Order of the
Senate.... 11th March, 1800.
[Philadelphia, 1800.] 39 pp.
AAS copy.   38719

U. S. 6th Congress, 1799-1801. Senate.
... A Bill to Repeal an Act, Entitled, "An
Act for the Punishment of Certain
Crimes. ..."
[Washington?], Duane, [1800?].
Broadside.
LOC copy.   38737

U. S. 6th Congress, 1799-1801. Senate.
... February 7th, 1800. The Committee,
to whom was Referred the Bill, Passed by
the House of Representatives, Entitled,
"An Act to Suspend, in Part, an Act,
Entitled An Act to Augment the Army.
..." Report. ...
[Philadelphia, 1800.] Broadside.
NYHS copy.   38740

U. S. 6th Congress, 1799-1801. Senate.
... February 26th, 1800. A Motion was
Made that ... the Committee of
Privileges ... Enquire, who is the Editor
of ... the General Advertiser.
[Philadelphia, 1800.] Broadside.
LCP copy.   38741

U. S. 6th Congress, 1799-1801. Senate.
... February 26th, 1800. The Following
Motion was Made. ...
[Philadelphia, 1800.] [1] p.
AAS copy.   38742

U. S. 6th Congress, 1799-1801. Senate.
Further Report in Part, of the Committee
of Privileges, on the Form of Proceedings
in the Case of William Duane.... March
25th, 1800.
[Philadelphia, 1800.] 4 pp.
AAS copy.   38733

U. S. 6th Congress, 1799-1801. Senate.
... January 16th, 1800. The Committee to
whom was Referred the Bill, Entitled,
"An Act Providing for Salvage. ..."
[Philadelphia, 1800.] 3 pp.
AAS copy.   38738

U. S. 6th Congress, 1799-1801. Senate.
... January 23d, 1800. Ordered, That the
Memorial of the Connecticut Academy of.
Arts and Sciences. ...
[Philadelphia, 1800.] 7 pp.
AAS copy.   38739

U. S. 6th Congress, 1799-1801. Senate.
Journal of the Senate ... First Session of
the Sixth Congress.
Philadelphia, Fenno, 1799. 336, [2], xx
pp.
AAS copy.   38749

U. S. 6th Congress, 1799-1801. Senate.
... March 5th, 1800. The Committee, to
whom was Referred the Bill. ...
[Philadelphia, 1798.] [1] p.
AAS copy.   38743

U. S. 6th Congress, 1799-1801. Senate.
... March 6th, 1800. Resolved, That the
Committee of Privileges be....
[Philadelphia, 1800.] Broadside.
LCP copy.   38744

U. S. 6th Congress, 1799-1801. Senate.
... March 14th, 1800. The Committee, to
whom was Referred.
[Philadelphia, 1800.] 7 pp.
AAS copy.   38745

U. S. 6th Congress, 1799-1801. Senate.
... May 8th, 1800. The Joint Committee
of both Houses.... Equestrian Statue of
General Washington.

[Philadelphia, 1800.] [1] p.
AAS copy.   38747

U. S. 6th Congress, 1799-1801. Senate.
Printed by Order of the Senate ... May
1st, 1800. A Bill Supplementary to the
Act, Entitled, "An Act to Establish
theTreasury Department. ..."
[Philadelphia, 1800.] Broadside.
LOC copy.   38803

U. S. 6th Congress, 1799-1801. Senate.
Printed by Order of the Senate ... May
9th, 1800. An Act to Permit, in Certain
Cases, the Bringing of Slaves into
Mississippi Territory.
[Philadelphia, 1800.] Broadside.
LOC copy.   38804

U. S. 6th Congress, 1799-1801. Senate.
Report, in Part, of the Committee of
Privileges [Mar. 22, 1800]. ... Printed by
Order of the Senate.
[Philadelphia, 1800.] 4 pp.
AAS copy.   38814

U. S. 6th Congress, 1799-1801. Senate.
Report of the Committee of Privileges on
the Measures.... 19th of February. ...
Printed by order of the Senate [Mar. 14,
1800].
[Philadelphia, 1800.] 7 pp.
AAS copy.   38856

U. S. 6th Congress, 1799-1801. Senate.
Report of the Committee to whom was
Referred so much of the Presidents
Speech as Relates to the Exercise of the
Local Powers. ...Printed by Order of the
Senate.... December 17th, 1800.
[Washington, 1800.] 4 pp.
AAS copy.   38875

U. S. 6th Congress, 1799-1801. Senate.
Report of the Committee, to whom was
Referred the Bill, Authorizing Seth
Harding. ... Printed by Order of the
Senate.... March 31st, 1800.
[Philadelphia, 1800.] 4 pp.
AAS copy.   38877

U. S. 6th Congress, 1799-1801. Senate.
Report of the Committee, to whom was
Referred the Bill, Entitled "An Act in
Addition to the Act, Entitled An Act
Regulating the Grants of Land
Appropriated ... for the Society of the
United Brethren [Feb. 17, 1800].
[Philadelphia, 1800.] 7 pp.
AAS copy.   38878

U. S. 6th Congress, 1799-1801. Senate.
Report of the Committee, to Whom was
Referred the Bill, Entitled, "An Act
Providing for the Enumeration of the
Inhabitants.... Printed by Order of the
Senate ... [Jan. 21, 1800].
[Philadelphia, 1800.] 6 pp.
LOC copy.   38879

U. S. 6th Congress, 1799-1801. Senate.
Report of the Committee, to whom was
Referred the Bill, entitled "An Act ...
Providing for the Sale of the Lands of the
United States. ..." Printed by Order of
the Senate ... April 19th, 1800.
[Philadelphia, 1800.] 8 pp.
NYPL copy.   49164

U. S. 6th Congress, 1799-1801. Senate.
Report of the Committee to whom was
Referred the Bill Entitled "An Act to
Alter and Establish Sundry Post
Roads.... April 4th, 1800.
[Philadelphia, 1800.] 6 pp.
WLC copy.   38881

U. S. 6th Congress, 1799-1801. Senate.
Report of the Committee, to whom was
Referred the Bill, Entitled "An Act
Supplemental to the Act, Entitled an Act
for an Amicable Settlement of the Limits
with the State of Georgia. ... Printed by
Order of the Senate. ... April 9th, 1800.
[Philadelphia, 1800.] 4 pp.
AAS copy.   38880

U. S. 6th Congress, 1799-1801. Senate.
Report of the Committee, to whom was
Referred the Bill, Entitled "An Act to
Divide the Territory ... North-west of the
Ohio ... [Apr. 16, 1800].

[Philadelphia, 1800.] 4 pp.
AAS copy.   38882

U. S. 6th Congress, 1799-1801. Senate.
Report of the Committee, to whom was
Referred the Bill, Entitled "An Act to
Extend the Privilege of Obtaining
Patents. . . ." Printed by Order of the
Senate. . . . March 28th, 1800.
[Philadelphia, 1800.] 4 pp.
AAS copy.   38883

U. S. 6th Congress, 1799-1801. Senate.
Report of the Committee, to whom was
Referred the Bill, Entitled "An Act to
make further Provision for the Removal
. . . of the Government. . . . Printed by
Order of the Senate. . . . April 12th, 1800.
[Philadelphia, 1800.] [3] pp.
AAS copy.   38884

U. S. 6th Congress, 1799-1801. Senate.
Report of the Committee, to whom was
Referred the Bill for the Relief of Ithamer
Canfield [Feb. 17, 1800].
[Philadelphia, 1800.] 4 pp.
LOC copy.   38885

U. S. 6th Congress, 1799-1801. Senate.
Report of the Committee to whom was
Referred the Bill, from the House of
Representatives, Entitled "An Act to
Authorize the Sale . . . of Lands. . . .
Printed by Order of the Senate . . . April
28th, 1800.
[Philadelphia, 1800.] 4 pp.
AAS copy.   38886

U. S. 6th Congress, 1799-1801. Senate.
Report of the Committee, to whom was
Referred the Bill, Supplementary to the
Laws . . . fixing the Compensations. . . .
Printed by Order of the Senate. . . . April
22d, 1800.
[Philadelphia, 1800.] [3] pp.
AAS copy.   38888

U. S. 6th Congress, 1799-1801. Senate.
Report of the Committee, to whom was
Referred the Bill, to Amend an Act,
Entitled "An Act to Establish the Judicial
Courts. . . ." Printed by Order of the
Senate . . . April 28th, 1800.
[Philadelphia, 1800.] 2 pp.
NYPL copy.   38889

U. S. 6th Congress, 1799-1801. Senate.
Report of the Committee, to whom was
Referred the Bill to Establish a General
Stamp-office. Printed by Order of the
Senate. . . . April 2d, 1800.
[Philadelphia, 1800.] [3] pp.
AAS copy.   38890

U. S. 6th Congress, 1799-1801. Senate.
Report of the Committee, to whom was
Referred the Bill, "To Establish the
District of Kennebunk. . . ." Printed by
Order of the Senate . . . April 28th, 1800.
[Philadelphia, 1800.] 4 pp.
AAS copy.   38891

U. S. 6th Congress, 1799-1801. Senate.
Report of the Committee, to whom was
Referred the Letter of John
Henderson. . . . Printed by Order of the
Senate. . . . April 7th, 1800.
[Philadelphia, 1800.] [3] pp.
AAS copy.   38892

U. S. 6th Congress, 1799-1801. Senate.
Report of the Committee, to whom was
Referred the Memorial of Daniel Smith
[Jan. 23, 1800]. Printed by Order of the
Senate.
[Philadelphia, 1800.] 8 pp.
AAS copy.   38893

U. S. 6th Congress, 1799-1801. Senate.
Report of the Committee, to whom was
Referred the Petition, of Thomas
Burling. . . . Printed by Order of the
Senate. . . . April 7th, 1800.
[Philadelphia, 1800.] [3] pp.
AAS copy.   38894

U. S. 6th Congress, 1799-1801. Senate.
Report of the Committee to whom was
Referred the Resolution Authorising an
Enquiry. . . . Printed by Order of the
Senate. . . . May 9th, 1800.
[Philadelphia, 1800.] 13 pp.
AAS copy.   38896

U. S. 6th Congress, 1799-1801. Senate.
Report of the Committee, to whom were
Referred the Petitions of Joseph
Russel. . . . Printed by Order of the Senate
. . . [Mar. 17, 1800].
[Philadelphia, 1800.] 7 pp.
AAS copy.   38899

U. S. 6th Congress, 1799-1801. Senate.
Rules for Conducting Business in the
Senate [Nov. 1800].
[Washington, 1800.] 7 pp.
AAS copy.   38905

U. S. Constitution.
Amendments Proposed.
Boston, Adams, 1790. 8 pp.
AAS copy.   22953

U. S. Constitution.
Congress of the United States. . . . The
Conventions of a Number of States . . .
Amendments. . . .
[Philadelphia, Childs & Swaine, 1792.] 11
pp.
LOC copy.   46596

U. S. Constitution.
De Constitutie, Eenpariglyk. . . .
Albany, 1788. 32 pp.
LOC copy.   21522

U. S. Constitution.
Constitution and Frame of Government.
New Brunswick, 1787. 16 pp.
NYPL copy.   20793

U. S. Constitution.
The Constitution and Laws of the United
States.
Portsmouth, Osborne, 1790. 157 pp.
AAS copy.   22951

U. S. Constitution.
The Constitution, as Formed for the
United States . . . with the Resolves . . . of
the Assembly of Pennsylvania Thereon.
Philadelphia, Bradford, 1787. 16 pp.
NYPL copy.   20794

U. S. Constitution.
Die Constitution der Vereinigten Staaten
von America . . . 1787.
Hagerstown, Gruber, 1799. 22 pp.
UOP copy.   36506

U. S. Constitution.
Constitution of the United States of
America.
n. p., [1787?]. [2] pp., in double columns.
RIHS copy.   45175

[U. S. Constitution.
The Constitution of the United States.
[Hartford, 1787.] 8 pp.]
(A ghost of 21523, q. v.)   20802

U. S. Constitution.
The Constitution of the United States.
New Haven, Meigs, 1787. Broadside.
CSL copy.   20795

U. S. Constitution.
The Constitution of the United States.
Philadelphia, Young & M'Culloch, 1787.
12 pp.
NYHS copy.   45174

U. S. Constitution.
The Constitution of the United States.
Portsmouth, Melcher, [1787]. Broadside.
BPL copy.   20796

U. S. Constitution.
The Constitution of the United States.
Portsmouth, Melcher, 1787. 16 pp.
NYPL copy.   20797

U. S. Constitution.
The Constitution of the United States.
Trenton, 1787. 16 pp.
LOC copy.   20798

U. S. Constitution.
The Constitution of the United States
[with the Conn. Ratification, Jan. 9,
1788].
[Hartford, 1788.] 8 pp.
NYPL copy.   21523

U. S. Constitution.
The New Constitution of the United
States.

Hartford, Patten, 1789. [36] pp.
CHS copy.   45685

U. S. Constitution.
The Constitution of the United States.
Portsmouth, Melcher, 1789. 40 pp.
HEH copy.   45686

U. S. Constitution.
[Constitution of the United States of
America.]
[Newport, Edes, 1790.] [3] pp.
(This is apparently the second leaf of an
unique copy of an issue of 22849. See
Alden 1233.)
AAS copy.   22848

U. S. Constitution.
Constitution of the United States of
America.
[Newport, 1790.] Broadside. [3] pp.
AAS copy.   22849

[U. S. Constitution.
Constitution of the United States of
America.
Providence, Carter, 1790. [3] pp.]
(Only known copy owned by E. Morrill in
1943.)   22976

U. S. Constitution.
The Constitution of the United States of
America.
Windsor, Spooner, 1790. 23 pp.
AAS copy.   22977

U. S. Constitution.
The Constitution of the United States.
Philadelphia, Fenno, 1791. 24 pp.
AAS copy.   23888

[U. S. Constitution.
The Constitution of the United States.
Boston, Adams, 1793?].
(Ordered printed, by the General Court.)
26331

U. S. Constitution.
Constitution of the United States of
America.
Philadelphia, Stephens, 1795. 22 pp.
(The only copy located is imperfect.)
JCB copy.   29729

U. S. Constitution.
The Constitution of the United States.
Bennington, Vt., Haswell, 1798. 23 pp.
AAS copy.   34794

U. S. Constitution.
Constitution of the United States.
Newark, N. J., Pennington & Dodge,
1798. 40 pp.
AAS copy.   34795

U. S. Constitution.
The Constitution of the United States.
Newport, R. I., Farnsworths, 1798. 22 pp.
Newport Hist. Soc. copy.   34796

U. S. Constitution.
The Constitution of the United States of
America.
Baltimore, Warner & Hanna for Herty,
1799. 34 pp.
(The only known copy cannot be
reproduced.)   36510

[U. S. Constitution.
The Constitution of the United States.
Hagerstown, Md., 1799.]
("Just published," Md. Herald, May 27,
1799.)   36511

U. S. Constitution.
The Constitution of the United States of
America. To which is Prefixed, the
Constitution of the State of Tennessee.
Knoxville, Roulstone & Parrington, 1799.
30 pp.
NYBA copy.   36404

U. S. Constitution.
The Constitution of the United States.
Lexington, [Ky.], Bradford, 1799. lxvi pp.
(Only known copy lacks title page.)
U. of Chi. copy.   48976

U. S. Constitution.
The Constitution of the United States of
America.
New London, Ct., Green, 1799. 16 pp.
NYPL copy.   36507

U. S. Constitution.
The Constitution of the United States of
America.
Philadelphia, Fenno, 1799. 48 pp.
HC copy.   36509

U. S. Constitution.
The Constitution of the United States of
America. . . . (Published by Order of the
House of Representatives.)
Philadelphia, Oswald, 1799. 27 pp.
AAS copy.   36508

U. S. Constitution.
The Constitution or Frame of
Government, for the United States.
Boston, Adams & Nourse, 1787. 32 pp.
(AAS has another issue with "Wilson"
corrected to "Morris" on p. 24.)
AAS copy.   20801

U. S. Constitution.
The Constitution, or Frame of
Government, for the United States.
Boston, Fleets, [1787]. 16 pp.
LOC copy.   20799

U. S. Constitution.
The Constitution or Frame of
Government, for the United States.
Boston, Fleets, [1787]. 20 pp.
HC copy.   20800

U. S. Constitution.
The Constitution or Frame of
Government.
Boston, Fleets, [1788]. 23 pp.
LOC copy.   45385

U. S. Constitution.
The Constitution, Proposed for the
Government of the United States.
Philadelphia, Hall & Sellers, 1787. 24 pp.
NYPL copy.   20803

U. S. Constitution.
Die Constitution, so wie. . . .
Albany, Webster, 1788. 24 pp.
NYSL copy.   45386

[U. S. Constitution.
The Federal Constitution.
Richmond, Davis, [1787]. 11 pp.]
(No copy located.)   20804

U. S. Constitution.
Federal Convention. We, the People. . . .
[Boston], Edes, [1787]. [2] pp.
MHS copy.   20809

[U. S. Constitution.
Federal Constitution; with the
Amendments (with Constitutions of
Vermont, Georgia and Kentucky. . . .)
Philadelphia, 1796.]
(Title and imprint assumed by Evans from
advs.)   31405

U. S. Constitution.
The Foederal Constitution, being the
Result of the Important Deliberations.
[New York, 1787.] 18 pp.
LOC copy.   20805

U.S . Constitution.
New Constitution of the United States.
n.p., [1789?] [2] pp.
CHS copy.   45684

U. S. Constitution.
The Pennsylvania Packet . . . September
19, 1787.
[Philadelphia, 1787.] 4 pp.
LOC copy.   20819

U. S. Constitution.
Plan of the Federal Convention.
Richmond, Dixon, [1787]. 16 pp.
NYPL copy.   20806

U. S. Constitution.
[Plan of the Federal Government.
Wilmington, Del., Craig, 1789.]
(Adv. Del. Gazette, Oct. 31, 1789.)   45687

U. S. Constitution.
A Plan of the New Federal Government.
Baltimore, Goddard, [1787]. [2] pp., text
in 3 columns.
JCB copy.   45176

U. S. Constitution.
Proceedings of the Foederal Convention.

Philadelphia, Bradford, 1787. 15 pp.
LOC copy.   20808

U. S. Constitution.
Result of the Deliberations of the Federal
Convention. Convened at Philadelphia,
in the year 1787.
[New York, 1787.] 12 pp.
LOC copy.   20810

[U. S. Constitution.
Results of the Deliberations of the
Federal Convention. In Convention, Sept.
17, 1787.
[Philadelphia, 1787.] 16 pp.]
(The only copy reported is mislaid.) 20811

U. S. Constitution.
Supplement to the Independent Journal,
Saturday, September 22, 1787.
[New York, 1787.] 4 pp.
LOC copy.   20812

U. S. Constitution.
Supplement to the Norfolk and
Portsmouth Journal. Friday, September
28, 1787.
Norfolk, M'Lean, [1787]. [4] pp.
LOC copy.   20813

U. S. Constitution.
Verfahren der Vereinigten Convention.
Frederick Town, [1787]. 18 pp.
NYPL copy.   20814

U. S. Constitution.
Verfahren der Verinigten Convention.
Germantown, Billmeyer, [1787?]. 16 pp.
LOC copy.   45177

U. S. Constitution.
We, the People of the United States. . . .
Wilmington, Craig, [1787]. [3] pp.
LCP copy.   45179

[U. S. Constitution.
We, the People of the United States, in
Order to form. . . .
Alexandria, Richards, [1787]. 3 pp.]
(A garbled entry, source unknown.) 20820

U. S. Constitution.
We the People of the United States, in
Order to form. . . .
Hartford, Patten, 1787. 16 pp.
LOC copy.   20821

U. S. Constitution.
We the People of the United States, in
Order to Form. . . .
[Philadelphia, 1787.] 4 pp.
JCB copy.   20817

U. S. Constitution.
We, the People of the United States. . . .
[Philadelphia], Dunlap & Claypoole,
[1787]. 4 pp.
(No copy located.)   45178

U. S. Constitution.
We, the People of the United States, in
Order to form. . . .
[Philadelphia], Dunlap & Claypoole,
[1787]. 6 pp.
LOC copy.   20818

U. S. Constitution.
We, the People of the United States, in
Order to form. . . .
Providence, Carter, [1787]. [2] pp.
RIHS copy.   20822

U. S. Constitutional Convention, 1787.
Articles Agreed upon by the Foederal
Convention . . . September 17, 1787.
New York, M'Lean, [1787]. 4 pp.
NYHS copy.   20791

U. S. Constitutional Convention, 1787.
Artykelen, die Geaccordeerd zyn by de
Foedderale Conventie.
Albany, Babcock, [1787]. 4 pp.
Williams College copy.   20792

U. S. Constitutional Convention, 1787.
Postscript to the Carlisle Gazette,
Wednesday, Sept. 26, 1787.
[Carlisle, 1787.] Broadside.
LOC copy.   20807

U. S. Constitutional Convention, 1787.
Proceedings of the Federal Convention.

Boston, Fleets, [1787]. 16 pp.
AAS copy.   45180

U. S. Constitutional Convention, 1787.
Proceedings of the Foederal Convention.
[Providence], Carter, [1787]. [2] pp.
RIHS copy.   45182

U. S. Constitutional Convention, 1787.
We the People of the States of
New-Hampshire. . . . [Aug. 6, 1787].
[Philadelphia, 1787.] 7 leaves.
LOC copy.   20815

U.S. Constitutional Convention, 1787.
We, the People of the United States [Sept.
13, 1787].
[Philadelphia, 1787.] 4 leaves.
LOC ph copy.   20816

U. S. Continental Congress. Marine
Committee.
Warrant. The Marine Committee . . . to
Equip . . . the Fleet. . . .
[Philadelphia? 1776.] Broadside.
JCB copy.   43195

[U. S. Continental Congress, 1774.
The Articles of Association. . . . In
Congress . . . October 20, 1774.
New Haven, [1774]. 4 pp.]
(No copy located.)   13705

U. S. Continental Congress, 1774.
The Association, Agreed upon by the
Grand American Congress. . . . October
20, 1774.
Boston, Edes & Gill, [1774]. Broadside.
AAS copy.   42724

U. S. Continental Congress, 1774.
The Association Entered into by the
American Continental Congress. . . .
October 20, 1774.
[Philadelphia, 1774.] Broadside.
LOC copy.   42725

U. S. Continental Congress, 1774.
The Association, &c. . . . In Congress . . .
October 20, 1774.
[Philadelphia, 1774.] 9 pp.
AAS ph. copy.   13703

U. S. Continental Congress, 1774.
The Association, &c. . . . In Congress . . .
October 20, 1774.
[Philadelphia, 1774.] 11 pp.
NYPL copy.   13704

U. S. Continental Congress, 1774.
Auszüge aus den Stimmungen.
Philadelphia, Miller, 1774. 76 pp.
JCB copy.   13735

U. S. Continental Congress, 1774.
Auszüge aus den Stimmungen . . . und
die Schlüsse der im Jenner 1775.
Philadelphia, Muller, 1775. 66 pp.
LOC copy.   42957

U. S. Continental Congress, 1774.
Extracts from the Votes and Proceedings
of the American Continental Congress
[Oct. 14-20, 1774].
n. p., [1774?] [2], 16 pp.
JCB copy.   42726

U. S. Continental Congress, 1774.
[Extracts from the Votes and Proceedings
of the American Continental Congress
held . . . the 5th of September 1774.]
Albany, Robertsons, 1774. 12, 8, 33, 11, 5
pp.
(The only recorded copy is defective.)
AAS copy.   42727

[U. S. Continental Congress, 1774.
Extracts from the Votes and Proceedings
of the American Continental Congress,
held . . . the 5th of September, 1774.
Containing the Bill of Rights. . . .
Annapolis, 1774. 44 pp.]
(A ghost of 13716, q.v.)   13727

U. S. Continental Congress, 1774.
Extracts from the Votes and Proceedings
of the American Continental Congress,
held . . . the 5th of September, 1774.
Containing the Bill of Rights. . . .
Annapolis, 1774. [4], 44 pp.
NYPL copy.   13716

U. S. Continental Congress, 1774.

Extracts from the Votes and Proceedings of the American Continental Congress, held . . . the 5th of September, 1774. Containing the Bill of Rights. . . .
Boston, Boyle and Mills & Hicks, 1774. 43 pp.
AAS copy. 13717

U. S. Continental Congress, 1774.
Extracts from the Votes and Proceedings of the American Continental Congress, held . . . the 5th of September, 1774. Containing the Bill of Rights. . . .
Boston, Boyle and Mills & Hicks, 1774. 52 pp.
AAS copy. 13728

U. S. Continental Congress, 1774.
Extracts from the Votes and Proceedings of the American Continental Congress, held . . . the 5th of September, 1774. Containing the Bill of Rights. . . .
Boston, Boyle, Mills & Hicks, and Cox & Berry, 1774. 43 pp.
AAS copy. 13718

U. S. Continental Congress, 1774.
Extracts from the Votes and Proceedings of the American Continental Congress, held . . . the 5th of September, 1774.
Boston, Edes & Gill and Fleets, 1774. 40 pp.
AAS copy. 42728

U. S. Continental Congress, 1774.
Extracts from the Votes and Proceedings of the American Continental Congress, held . . . the 5th of September 1774. Containing the Bill of Rights. . . .
Boston, Edes & Gill and Fleets, 1774. 49 pp.
AAS copy. 13719

U. S. Continental Congress, 1774.
Extracts from the Votes and Proceedings of the American Continental Congress, held . . . the 5th of September, 1774. Containing the Bill of Rights. . . .
Boston, Edes & Gill and Fleets, 1774. 56 pp.
AAS copy. 13729

U. S. Continental Congress, 1774.
Extracts from the Votes and Proceedings of the American Continental Congress, held . . . the 5th of September, 1774.
Boston, Edes & Gill, Fleets, 1774. 41 pp.
AAS copy. 42729

U. S. Continental Congress, 1774.
Extracts from the Votes and Proceedings of the American Continental Congress, held . . . the 5th of September, 1774. Containing the Bill of Rights. . . .
Hartford, [1774]. 48 pp.
AAS copy. 13720

[U. S. Continental Congress, 1774.
Extracts from the Votes and Proceedings of the American Continental Congress, held . . . the 5th of September, 1774. Containing the Bill of Rights. . . .
Hartford, [1774]. 48 pp.]
(A duplicate of 13720, q.v.) 13730

U. S. Continental Congress, 1774.
Extracts from the Votes and Proceedings of the American Continental Congress, held . . . the Fifth of September, 1774.
Lancaster, [Pa.] Herbert, 1774. 14 pp.
AAS copy. 42730

U. S. Continental Congress, 1774.
Extracts from the Votes and Proceedings of the American Continental Congress, held . . . the 5th of September 1774. Containing the Bill of Rights. . . .
New London, 1774. 16 pp.
AAS copy. 13731

U. S. Continental Congress, 1774.
Extracts from the Votes and Proceedings of the American Continental Congress, held . . . the 5th of September, 1774. Containing, the Bill of Rights. . . .
New London, 1774. 70 pp.
AAS copy. 13732

U. S. Continental Congress, 1774.
Extracts from the Votes and Proceedings of the American Continental Congress, held . . . 5th September, 1774. Containing the Bill of Rights. . . .

New York, Gaine, 1774. 59 pp.
NYHS copy. 13721

U. S. Continental Congress, 1774.
Extracts from the Votes and Proceedings of the American Continental Congress, held . . . the 5th of September, 1774. Containing the Bill of Rights. . . .
New York, Holt, [1774]. 25, 7 pp.
(No copy of the Holt ed. of these Extracts could be found. The second title, here filmed, is separately signatured.)
NYHS copy. 13733

U. S. Continental Congress, 1774.
Extracts from the Votes and Proceedings of the American Continental Congress, held . . . Sept. 5, 1774. Containing, the Bill of Rights. . . .
New York, Rivington, 1774. 36 pp.
NYHS copy. 13736

U. S. Continental Congress, 1774.
[Extracts from the votes and proceedings of the American Continental Congress, held the 5th Septembr, 1774.
Newbern, Davis, 1775.]
(Adv. N. C. Gazette, Feb. 24, 1775.) 42960

U. S. Continental Congress, 1774.
Extracts from the Votes and Proceedings of the American Continental Congress, held . . . the 5th of September, 1774. Containing the Bill of Rights. . . .
Newport, 1774. 59 pp.
AAS copy. 13722

U. S. Continental Congress, 1774.
Extracts from the Votes and Proceedings of the American Continental Congress, held . . . the fifth day of September, 1774. Containing, the Bill of Rights. . . .
Norwich, 1774. 41 pp.
AAS copy. 13723

[U. S. Continental Congress, 1774.
Extracts from the Votes and Proceedings of the Continental Congress, held . . . on the Fifth day of September, M,DCC,LXXIV. Containing, the Bill of Rights. . . . The Second Norwich Edition.
Norwich, 1774.]
(Copies formerly in the possession of Wilberforce Eames and G. P. Winship not now to be located.) 13734

U. S. Continental Congress, 1774.
Extracts from the Votes and Proceedings of the American Continental Congress, held . . . the 5th of September, 1774. Containing the Bill of Rights. . . .
[Philadelphia, Bradfords, 1774. [4], 23, [1], 50 pp.
LCP copy. 13726

U. S. Continental Congress, 1774.
Extracts from the Votes and Proceedings of the American Continental Congress, held . . . the 5th of September 1774. Containing an Association. . . .
Philadelphia, Bradfords, Oct. 24, 1774. [2], 11, 36 pp.
NYPL copy. 13713

U. S. Continental Congress, 1774.
Extracts from the Votes and Proceedings of the American Continental Congress, held . . . the 5th of September 1774. Containing the Bill of Rights. . . .
Philadelphia, Bradfords, Oct. 27, 1774. [4], 12, 11, [1], 36 pp.
NYPL copy. 13714

U. S. Continental Congress, 1774.
Extracts from the Votes and Proceedings of the American Continental Congress, held . . . the 5th of September 1774. Containing the Bill of Rights. . . .
Philadelphia, Bradfords, Oct. 27, 1774. [4], 23, 36 pp.
NYPL copy. 13715

U. S. Continental Congress, 1774.
Extracts from the Votes and Proceedings of the American Continental Congress, held . . . on the fifth day of September, 1774. Containing, the Bill of Rights. . . .
Providence, 1774. 50 pp.
AAS copy. 13724

U. S. Continental Congress, 1774.
Extracts from the Votes and Proceedings of the American Continental Congress,

held . . . the 5th of September, 1774.
Williamsburg, Purdie & Dixon, 1774. 47, [1] pp.
LOC copy. 13725

U. S. Continental Congress, 1774.
The Following Extract from the Votes and Proceedings of the American Continental Congress, we are Induced to Publish thus. . . .
[Boston? 1774.] 8 pp.
NYHS copy. 13710

U. S. Continental Congress, 1774.
The Following Extracts from the Votes. . . . In Congress . . . October 20, 1774.
Boston, Edes & Gill, [1774]. Broadside.
MHS copy. 13709

U. S. Continental Congress, 1774.
The Following Extracts from the Votes. . . . In Congress . . . October, 20, 1774.
Boston, Fleets, [1774]. Broadside.
AAS copy. 13708

U. S. Continental Congress, 1774.
The Following Extracts from the Votes. . . . In Congress . . . October 20, 1774.
New Haven, [1774]. [2] pp.
LOC copy. 13711

U. S. Continental Congress, 1774.
The Following Extracts from the Votes. . . . In Congress . . . October 20, 1774.
Newport, 1774. 8 pp.
JCB copy. 13712

U. S. Continental Congress, 1774.
Grand American Congress. . . .
[Resolution of Oct. 8-11, 1774.]
Salem, Halls, [1774]. Broadside.
LOC copy. 42731

U. S. Continental Congress, 1774.
Journal [Sept. 5 - Oct. 26, 1774].
New York, Gaine, 1774. 104, [4] pp.
LOC copy. 13739

U. S. Continental Congress, 1774.
Journal [Sept. 5 - Oct. 26, 1774].
Philadelphia, Bradfords, 1774. [4], 132 pp.
AAS copy. 13737

U. S. Continental Congress, 1774.
Journal [Sept. 5 - Oct. 26, 1774].
Philadelphia, Bradfords, 1774. [4], 144 pp.
LCP copy. 13738

U. S. Continental Congress, 1774.
A Letter to the Inhabitants of the Province of Quebec.
Philadelphia, Bradfords, 1774. pp. [2], 37-50.
APS copy. 42732

U. S. Continental Congress, 1774.
Lettre Adressée aux Habitans de . . . Quebec.
Philadelphia, Mesplet, 1774. [2],18 pp.
AAS copy. 13740

U. S. Continental Congress, 1774.
The 9th Article of the Association of the late Continental Congress. . . . Salem, Dec. 3, 1774.
[Salem, 1774.] Broadside.
EI copy. 13706

U. S. Continental Congress, 1774.
The Petition of the Grand American Continental Congress.
Boston, [1774]. 8 pp.
AAS copy. 13741

U. S. Continental Congress, 1774.
Philadelphia. In Congress Thursday, September 22, 1774. Resolved. . . .
[Philadelphia, 1774.] Broadside.
LOC copy. 42733

U.S. Continental Congress, 1774.
Philadelphia. In Congress, Thursday, September 22, 1774. Resolved. . . .
[Philadelphia], Bradfords, [1774].
Broadside.
MHS copy. 13702

U. S. Continental Congress, 1774.
Proceedings of the General Congress . . .
September 1774. . . . In the Congress,
Saturday, Sept. 17, 1774.
New York, Holt, [1774]. [2] pp.
NYPL copy.   13701

U. S. Continental Congress, 1774.
. . . Proceedings. . . . September 5 . . .
October 20, 1774.
Portsmouth, [1774]. Broadside.
LOC ph. copy.   42734

U. S. Continental Congress, 1774.
Proceedings of the Grand American
Continental Congress at Philadelphia,
September 5, 1774.
Portsmouth, Fowle, [1774]. [2] pp.
AAS copy.   42735

U. S. Continental Congress, 1774.
To the People of Great-Britain . . .
September 5th, 1774.
[Philadelphia, 1774.] 36 pp.
(Issued under common title-page with
13714, q.v.)   13707

U. S. Continental Congress, 1774.
To the Printer of the Pennsylvania Packet.
Sir, Please to Insert . . . the following
Extracts from the Minutes of
Congress. . . . Sept. 17, 1774.
[Philadelphia, 1774.] Broadside.
(No copy located.)   42736

U. S. Continental Congress, 1775.
An Address from the Delegates of the
Twelve United Colonies, to the People of
England. . . . July 8, 1775.
Newport, 1775. 15 pp.
AAS copy.   14535

[U. S. Continental Congress, 1775.
An Address of the Twelve United
Colonies of North-America, by their
Representatives in Congress, to the People
of Ireland.
New York, 1775. 10 pp.]
(Entry from Haven.)   14537

[U. S. Continental Congress, 1775.
The Address of the Twelve United
Colonies, by their Delegates in Congress,
to the Inhabitants of Great-Britain; and
also, their Address to the Inhabitants of
Ireland.
New York, Rivington, 1775.]
(From an adv., probably for the two
separate tracts.)   14539

U. S. Continental Congress, 1775.
An Address of the Twelve United
Colonies of North-America, by their
Representatives in Congress, to the People
of Ireland.
Norwich, Robertsons & Trumbull, 1775.
16 pp.
(No perfect copy located.)
CHS copy.   14538

U. S. Continental Congress, 1775.
An Address of the Twelve United
Colonies of North-America, by their
Representatives in Congress, to the People
of Ireland. . . . July 28, 1775.
Philadelphia, Bradfords, 1775. [2], 10 pp.
AAS copy.   14536

[U. S. Continental Congress, 1775.
Affidavits and Depositions, Relative to
the Commencement of the late Hostilities.
[Philadelphia, 1775.] Broadside.]
(No copy located.)   14183

U. S. Continental Congress, 1775.
The Answer of the Congress to the King's
Proclamation.
[New York? 1775.] Broadside.
NYPL copy.   14568

U. S. Continental Congress, 1775.
A Declaration by the Representatives of
the United Colonies of North-America,
now met in General Congress at
Philadelphia, seting forth the Causes and
Necessity of their taking up Arms. . . .
July 6th, 1775.
New York, Holt, [1775]. [2] pp.
NYHS copy.   14546

U. S. Continental Congress, 1775.
A Declaration by the Representatives of
the United Colonies of North-America.

now met in the General Congress at
Philadelphia, Seting forth the Causes and
Necessity of their taking up Arms [July 6,
1775].
New York, Holt, 1775. 2 pp.
NYPL copy.   14545

U. S. Continental Congress, 1775.
A Declaration by the Representatives of
the United Colonies of North-America,
now met in General Congress, at
Philadelphia; Setting forth the Causes and
Necessity of their taking up Arms [June!
6, 1775].
Newport, 1775. 11 pp.
AAS copy.   14547

U. S. Continental Congress, 1775.
A Declaration by the Representatives of
the United Colonies of North-America,
now met in General Congress at
Philadelphia, Seting forth the Causes and
Necessity of their taking up Arms [July 6,
1775].
Philadelphia, Bradfords, 1775. [2], 13 pp.
AAS copy.   14544

U. S. Continental Congress, 1775.
A Declaration by the Representatives of
the United Colonies of North-America,
now met in General Congress at
Philadelphia, Setting forth the Causes and
Necessity of taking up Arms [July 6,
1775].
Portsmouth, [1775]. [2] pp.
AAS copy.   14550

[U. S. Continental Congress, 1775.
A Declaration by the Representatives of
the United Colonies of North America,
now met in General Congress at
Philadelphia, Setting forth the Causes and
Necessity of their taking up Arms. . . .
July 6, 1775.
Providence, [1775]. Broadside.]
(There was a copy in the possession of Dr.
Rosenbach.)   14548

U. S. Continental Congress, 1775.
A Declaration by the Representatives of
the United Colonies of North-America.
Salem, Russell, 1775. 8 pp.
AAS copy.   42959

U. S. Continental Congress, 1775.
A Declaration by the Representatives of
the United Colonies of North-America,
now met in General Congress at
Philadelphia, Setting forth the Causes and
Necessity of their taking up Arms [July 6,
1775].
Watertown, 1775. 15 pp.
AAS copy.   14549

U. S. Continental Congress, 1775.
A Declaration of the Representatives of
the United Colonies of North-America.
Newburyport, 1775. 8 pp.
AAS copy.   42958

U. S. Continental Congress, 1775.
An die Einwohner von Irland.
Philadelphia, Miller, 1775. 16 pp.
HSP copy.   14574

U. S. Continental Congress, 1775.
Extract of a Letter from General
Montgomery, Dated Camp before St.
John's, October 20, 1775. . . .
[Philadelphia, 1775.] [2] pp.
LOC copy.   14541

U. S. Continental Congress, 1775.
Extracts from the Votes and Proceedings
of the American Continental Congress,
held at Philadelphia, 10th May, 1775.
New York, Anderson, 1775. [4], 192 pp.
AAS copy.   14572

[U. S. Continental Congress, 1775.
Extracts from the Votes and Proceedings
of the American Continental Congress,
held at Philadelphia on the 5th of
September, 1774.
New York, Holt, [1775]. 96 pp.]
(The unique copy is mislaid.)   14553

U. S. Continental Congress, 1775.
Extracts from the Votes and Proceedings
of the American Continental Congress,
held at Philadelphia, September 5, 1774.
Philadelphia, Bradfords, 1775. 80 pp.
NYPL copy.   14551

U. S. Continental Congress, 1775.
Extracts from the Proceedings of the
American Continental Congress, held at
Philadelphia, on the Tenth day of May,
1775.
Providence, [1775]. 22 pp.
NYPL copy.   14573

U. S. Continental Congress, 1775.
The Humble Petition of the Twelve
United Colonies . . . to the King.
Philadelphia, Bradfords, 1775. 8 pp.
JCB copy.   42961

[U. S. Continental Congress, 1775.
In Congress, Monday, June 12, 1775. As
the Great Governor . . . [Fast, July 20,
1775].
n. p., [1775]. Broadside.]
(No printed copy located.)   42962

U. S. Continental Congress, 1775.
In Congress, Monday, June 12, 1775. As
the Great Governor . . . [Fast, July 20,
1775].
Philadelphia, Bradfords, [1775].
Broadside.
(No complete copy located.)
NA copy.   14563

U. S. Continental Congress, 1775.
In Congress, Monday, June 12, 1775. As
the Great Governor . . . [Fast, July 20,
1775].
Watertown, [1775]. Broadside.
AAS copy.   14565

U. S. Continental Congress, 1775.
In Congress, Thursday, June 22, 1775.
Resolved, That a Sum not Exceeding Two
Millions. . . .
n. p., [1775]. Broadside.
LOC copy.   42963

[U. S. Continental Congress, 1775.
In Congress, Friday, November 3, 1775.
The Congress Taking into Consideration.

[Philadelphia, 1775.] Broadside.]
(Perhaps not printed.)   14566

U. S. Continental Congress, 1775.
In Congress, December 6, 1775. We the
Delegates. . . .
[Philadelphia], Dunlap, [1775].
Broadside.
AAS copy.   14567

U. S. Continental Congress, 1775.
Journal of the Proceedings of the
Congress, held at Philadelphia, May 10,
1775.
New York, Gaine, 1775. iv, 140 pp.
NYPL copy.   14571

U. S. Continental Congress, 1775.
Journal of the Proceedings of the
Congress, held at Philadelphia, May 10,
1775.
Philadelphia, Bradfords, 1775. [4], iv, 239
pp.
AAS copy.   14569

U. S. Continental Congress, 1775.
Journal of the Proceedings of the
Congress . . . May 10, 1775.
Wilmington, 1776. 110 pp.
HC copy.   15144

U. S. Continental Congress, 1775.
Lettre Addressée aux Habitans.
[Philadelphia, 1775.] 7 pp.
LOC copy.   14575

U. S. Continental Congress, 1775.
A List of the Delegates who Attended the
Congress, held at Philadelphia, May 10,
1775.
[Philadelphia, 1775.] Broadside.
NYPL copy.   14576

[U. S. Continental Congress, 1775.
The Petition of the American Continental
Congress, to the King.
Boston, Thomas, 1775.]
(Adv. in Mass. Spy, Mar. 9, 1775,
probably for 13741, or 14555.)   14554

[U. S. Continental Congress, 1775.
The Petition of the Grand American
Continental Congress, to the King's Most
Excellent Majesty.

Boston, [1775]. 8 pp.]
(The same as 13741, q.v.)   14555

U. S. Continental Congress, 1775.
Philadelphia. In Congress, Monday, May
15, 1775. The City and County of
New-York. . . .
[Philadelphia? 1775.] Broadside.
LOC copy.   14560

U. S. Continental Congress, 1775.
Philadelphia, in Congress, June 12, 1775.
A Proclamation for a Continental Public
Fast. . . .
[Philadelphia, 1775.] Broadside.
MHS copy.   42964

U. S. Continental Congress, 1775.
Philadelphia, June 15. In Congress, June
12, 1775. [Fast, July 20, 1775].
[Philadelphia], Dunlap, [1775].
Broadside.
LCP copy.   14564

U. S. Continental Congress, 1775.
Philadelphia. In Congress, December 6,
1775. We the Delegates. . . .
[Philadelphia? 1775.] Broadside.
NYPL facsim. copy.   42965

U. S. Continental Congress, 1775.
Philadelphia, September 29, 1775. The
Following Letters now Published by Order
of the Honourable Continental Congress.
. . .
[Philadelphia, 1775.] Broadside.
BPL copy.   14558

U. S. Continental Congress, 1775.
Rules and Articles, for the Better
Government of the Troops. . . . June 30,
1775.
[Baltimore, 1775.] [2] pp.
MdHS copy.   14578

U. S. Continental Congress, 1775.
Rules and Articles, for the Better
Government of the Troops Raised.
New York, Gaine, 1775. 16 pp.
LOC copy.   14579

U. S. Continental Congress, 1775.
Rules and Articles, for the Better
Government of the Troops [June 30,
1775].
Philadelphia, Bradfords, 1775. 16 pp.
AAS copy.   14577

U. S. Continental Congress, 1775.
Rules and Articles for the Better
Government of the Troops Raised [Nov.
7, 1775].
Philadelphia, Bradfords, 1775. 16 pp.
LOC copy.   14581

U. S. Continental Congress, 1775.
Rules and Articles, for the better
Government of the Troops Raised.
Watertown, 1775. 16 pp.
BA copy.   14580

U. S. Continental Congress, 1775.
Rules for the Regulation of the Navy of
the United Colonies.
Philadelphia, Bradford, 1775. 8 pp.
YC copy.   14582

U. S. Continental Congress, 1775.
The Several Assemblies of New-Jersey,
Pennsylvania and Virginia. . . . July 31,
1775.
[Philadelphia, 1775.] 8 pp.
HC copy.   14583

U. S. Continental Congress, 1775.
Several Methods of Making Salt-Petre.
Philadelphia, Bradfords, 1775. 12 pp.
NYPL copy.   14584

U.S. Continental Congress, 1775.
Several Methods of Making Salt-Petre.
. . . And an Appendix, by Doctor William
Whiting.
Watertown, 1775. 20 pp.
AAS copy.   14585

U. S. Continental Congress, 1775.
The Twelve United Colonies, by their
Delegates in Congress, to the Inhabitants
of Great-Britain. . . . July 8, 1775.
New York, Holt, [1775]. 2 pp.
NYPL copy.   14534

U. S. Continental Congress, 1775.
The Twelve United Colonies, by their
Delegates in Congress; to the Inhabitants
of Great-Britain. . . . July 8, 1775.
[Philadelphia, 1775.] 8 pp.
AAS copy.   14532

U. S. Continental Congress, 1775.
The Twelve United Colonies, by their
Delegates in Congress, to the Inhabitants
of Great-Britain.
Philadelphia, Bradfords, 1775. 16 pp.
JCB copy.   14533

U. S. Continental Congress, 1775.
The Twelve United Colonies, by their
Delegates in Congress; to the Inhabitants
of Great-Britain. . . . July 8th, 1775.
Portsmouth, 1775. [2] pp.
NHHS copy.   42966

[U. S. Continental Congress, 1775.
Whereas the Government of Great Britain
hath Prohibited the Exportation of Arms.
. . .
Philadelphia, 1775.]
(Ordered printed.)   14588

U. S. Continental Congress, 1775.
The Whole Proceedings of the American
Continental Congress, held at
Philadelphia on the 5th of September,
1774.
New York, Holt, 1775. [4], 96 pp.
NYHS copy.   14552

U. S. Continental Congress, 1776.
At a Conference of the Delegates. . . . July
5, 1776.
[Philadelphia, 1776.] Broadside.
LOC copy.   15150

U. S. Continental Congress, 1776.
Aux Habitants de la Province du Canada.
. . . 24 Janvier 1776.
[Philadelphia], Mesplet & Berger, [1776].
Broadside.
LCP copy.   15123

U. S. Continental Congress, 1776.
Baltimore, Dec. 31, 1776. This Morning.
. . .
Baltimore, [1776]. Broadside.
MdHS copy.   15152

[U. S. Continental Congress, 1776.
Extract, from the Journal of the
Proceedings [Quebec. Oct. 26, 1774].
[Philadelphia, 1776.] [6] pp.]
(Uusally found after p. 96 of 15089, q.v.)
          15125

U. S. Continental Congress, 1776.
Extracts from the Journals of Congress.
Philadelphia, Dunlap, 1776. [2], 45 pp.
AAS copy.   15154

U. S. Continental Congress, 1776.
Extracts of Letters, &c.
Charleston, 1776. 23 pp.
NYPL copy.   15126

U. S. Continental Congress, 1776.
Extracts of Letters, &c. Published by
Order of Congress.
Charleston, Timothy, 1776. 25 pp.
(Copy not located.)
S.C. Hist. Comm. copy.   43187

U. S. Continental Congress, 1776.
General Post-Office, Philadelphia, May 1,
1776. . . . In Congress . . . April 16, 1776.
[Baltimore? 1776.] Broadside.
NYPL copy.   15127

U. S. Continental Congress, 1776.
I   do Acknowledge the United
States of America. . . .
[Philadelphia, 1776.] Broadside.
LOC copy.   15183

U. S. Continental Congress, 1776.
In Congress. January 17, 1776. Resolved,
That the Colonels . . .
[Philadelphia, 1776.] Broadside.
NYPL photostat copy.   15128

U. S. Continental Congress, 1776.
In Congress, January 30, 1776. Resolved,
That it be Recommended to the Several
Assemblies in New-England. . . .
[Watertown? 1776.] Broadside.
MHS copy.   43188

U. S. Continental Congress, 1776.
In Congress. March 6, 1776. Resolved,
That any Goods. . . .
[Philadelphia, 1776.] Broadside.
NYHS copy.   15131

U. S. Continental Congress, 1776.
In Congress, Saturday, March 16, 1776. In
Times of Impending Calamity. . . .
New London, [1776]. Broadside.
LOC copy.   15134

U. S. Continental Congress, 1776.
In Congress, Saturday, March 16, 1776. In
Times of Impending Calamity. . . .
Philadelphia, Dunlap, [1776]. Broadside.
LCP copy.   15132

U. S. Continental Congress, 1776.
In Congress March 23, 1776. Whereas the
Petition. . . .
[Watertown, 1776.] Broadside.
MHS copy.   15136

U. S. Continental Congress, 1776.
In Congress, March 23, 1776. Whereas the
Petitions. . . .
Philadelphia, Dunlap, [1776]. Broadside.
LCP copy.   15135

U. S. Continental Congress, 1776.
In Congress, Wednesday, April 3, 1776.
Instructions. . . .
[Philadelphia, 1776.] Broadside.
LOC copy.   15137

U. S. Continental Congress, 1776.
In Congress, Wednesday, April 3, 1776.
Instructions to the Commanders. . . .
[Philadelphia? 1776] Broadside.
JCB copy.   43190

[U. S. Continental Congress, 1776.
In Congress April 3, 1776. Resolved, That
Blank Commissions. . . .
[Philadelphia, 1776.] Broadside.]
(No copy with this wording has been
located, but there are several variant
issues.)   15139

U. S. Continental Congress, 1776.
In Congress, April 3, 1776. Resolved, That
every Person. . . .
[Philadelphia, 1776.] Broadside.
LOC copy.   15138

[U. S. Continental Congress, 1776.
In Congress, May 6, 1776 [Instructions to
Commanders of American Vessels].
[Philadelphia, 1776.] Broadside.]
(No copy located.)   15140

U. S. Continental Congress, 1776.
In Congress, May 15, 1776. Whereas His
Britannic Majesty. . . .
Philadelphia, Dunlap, [1776]. Broadside.
NYPL copy.   15141

[U. S. Continental Congress, 1776.
In Congress, May 21, 1776 [Resolutions
Regarding Treatment of Prisoners on
Prizes].
[Watertown, 1776.] Broadside.]
(No such Mass. printing could be located.)
          15143

U. S. Continental Congress, 1776.
In Congress, May 21, 1776. Resolved,
That all Persons. . . .
[Philadelphia, 1776.] Broadside.
LOC copy.   15142

U. S. Continental Congress, 1776.
In Congress, July 19, 1776. Resolved, That
it be Earnestly Recommended. . . .
[Philadelphia, 1776.] [3] pp.
LOC copy.   15165

U. S. Continental Congress, 1776.
In Congress, July 19, 1776. Resolved, That
a Copy of the Circular Letters. . . .
[Boston? 1776.] Broadside.
MHS copy.   43189

U. S. Continental Congress, 1776.
In Congress, August 28, 1776. Resolved,
That there be. . . .
[Philadelphia, 1776.] Broadside.
LOC copy.   15166

U. S. Continental Congress, 1776.
In Congress, September 16, 1776.
Resolved, That Eighty-Eight. . . .

[Philadelphia, 1776.] Broadside.
NYPL copy.   15167

U. S. Continental Congress, 1776.
In Congress, October 3d, 1776. Resolved,
That Five Millions. . . .
Hartford, Watson & Goodwin. Broadside.
NYHS copy.   15170

U. S. Continental Congress, 1776.
In Congress, October 3d, 1776. Resolved,
That Five Millions. . . .
[Philadelphia], Dunlap, [1776].
Broadside.
LCP copy.   15169

[U. S. Continental Congress, 1776.
In Congress, October 29th, 1776. . . .
October 30th.
Philadelphia, Dunlap, 1776. Broadside.]
(The only recorded copy is mislaid.) 15171

U. S. Continental Congress, 1776.
In Congress, November 23, 1776.
Resolved, That a Committee. . . .
[Philadelphia, 1776.] Broadside.
LOC copy.   15172

U. S. Continental Congress, 1776.
In Congress. December 11, 1776. Whereas,
the just war. . . .
Baltimore, [1776]. Broadside.
NYPL copy.   15175

U. S. Continental Congress, 1776.
In Congress. December 11, 1776. Whereas,
the just War. . . . [Fast, Jan. 29].
Hartford, [1776]. Broadside.
CHS copy.   15176

U. S. Continental Congress, 1776.
In Congress. December 23, 1776. Resolved
that . . . Persons Entrusted with Money.
. . .
Baltimore, [1776]. Broadside.
NYPL copy.   15177

U. S. Continental Congress, 1776.
Congress, December 27, 1776. Resolved,
That the Council of Safety of
Pennsylvania. . . . In Council of Safety,
Philadelphia, January 1, 1777.
Philadelphia, Dunlap, [1777]. Broadside.
HSP copy.   43390

U. S. Continental Congress, 1776.
In Congress. December 30, 1776. It
Appearing. . . .
Baltimore, [1776], Broadside.
LOC copy.   15178

U. S. Continental Congress, 1776.
In Congress. December 31, 1776.
Resolved, That any Restrictions . . . upon
the Exportation of Staves. . . .
Baltimore, Dunlap, [1776]. Broadside.
MdHS copy.   15179

U. S. Continental Congress, 1776.
In Congress. The Delegates of the United
Colonies. . . . [Form of Army
Commission].
[Philadelphia, 1776.] Broadside.
LCP copy.   15129

U. S. Continental Congress, 1776.
In Congress. The Delegates of the United
States [Form of Naval Commission].
[Philadelphia, 1776.] Broadside.
BPL copy.   15180

U. S. Army. Continental Army, 1776.
Instructions to the Officers Appointed to
Recruit in New York.
Fishkill, Loudon, 1776. Broadside.
NYHS copy.   43186

U. S. Continental Congress, 1776.
Journals of Congress. Containing the
Proceedings from January 1, 1776, to
January 1, 1777. . . . Volume II.
York, Dunlap, 1778. [2], 520, xxvii pp.
AAS copy.   16137

U. S. Continental Congress, 1776.
Journal of the Congress . . . Continued.
Philadelphia, Bradfords, 1776. [4], 218
pp.
LOC copy.   15186

U. S. Continental Congress, 1776.
Journals of Congress. Wednesday, August
14, 1776.

[Philadelphia, 1776.] [2] pp.
LOC copy.   15185

U. S. Continental Congress, 1776.
The Journals of the Proceedings of
Congress [Jan 11 - Apr. 29, 1776].
Philadelphia, Aitken, 1776. [2], 93, [3],
237 pp.
(Most copies lack the 2nd and 3rd
title-pages.)
AAS copy.   15145

U. S. Continental Congress, 1776.
Philadelphia, July 4th, 1776. Gentlemen,
The Congress this Morning. . . .
[Philadelphia, 1776.] Broadside.
LOC copy.   43191

U. S. Continental Congress, 1776.
Philadelphia, September 17. The
Following. . . .
[Philadelphia, 1776.] Broadside.
NYPL copy.   15168

U. S. Continental Congress, 1776.
A Proclamation for a Continental Fast. In
Congress, Saturday, March 16, 1776.
[Philadelphia? 1776.] Broadside.
JCB copy.   43192

U. S. Continental Congress, 1776.
Die Repräsentanten der Vereinigten
Staaten. . . . den 10ten December, 1776.
[Philadelphia, 1776.] Broadside.
HSP copy.   15174

U. S. Continental Congress, 1776.
The Representatives of the United States.
. . . December 10, 1776.
[Philadelphia, 1776.] Broadside.
AAS copy.   15173

[U. S. Continental Congress, 1776.
Resolutions Adopted at a Conference. . . .
the 5th Day of July, 1776.
[Philadelphia, 1776.] Broadside.]
(See Journals, LOC ed., VI, 1123.)   15151

U. S. Continental Congress, 1776.
Resolves of the Honourable Continental
Congress. Published . . . for the City and
County of Albany.
[Albany, 1776.] Broadside.
NYHS copy.   43193

U. S. Continental Congress, 1776.
Rules and Articles for the Better
Government of the Troops.
Fishkill, Loudon, 1776. 31 pp.
YC copy.   43194

U. S. Continental Congress, 1776.
Rules and Articles for the Better
Government of the Troops.
Hartford, Watson, 1777. 26 + pp.
(The only known copy is imperfect.)
AAS copy.   43391

U. S. Continental Congress, 1776.
The Rules and Articles of War. . . .
Extracted from the Journals of Congress,
for the Year 1776.
Baltimore, Edwards, 1794. 28 pp.
MdHS copy.   27974

U. S. Continental Congress, 1776.
There shall be a Firm, Inviolable, and
Universal Peace. . . .
[Philadelphia, 1776.] 5 pp.
NA copy.   15191

U. S. Continental Congress, 1776.
To the Inhabitants of the Colony of
New-York. . . . Jan. 9, 1776.
[New York, 1776.] 7 pp.
NYPL copy.   15146

U. S. Continental Congress, 1776.
The Tory Act. Published . . . Jan. 2, 1776.
[Philadelphia, 1776.] Broadside.
LOC copy.   15147

U. S. Continental Congress, 1777.
Bey Dem Congres, den 8ten October,
1777.
[Philadelphia? 1777?] Broadside.
JCB copy.   43392

U. S. Continental Congress, 1777.
Copy of a Letter from the Rev. Mr.
Samuel Kirkland.
York, Hall & Sellers, 1777. Broadside.
NYPL copy.   15642

U. S. Continental Congress, 1777.
Extract of a Letter from General Gates
. . . October 18, 1777. . . . In Congress,
Nov. 1, 1777.
Burlington, Collins, [1777]. Broadside.
(No copy located.)   43393

U. S. Continental Congress, 1777.
Extract of a Letter from General Gates
. . . October 18, 1777. . . . In Congress,
Nov. 1. . . . Thanksgiving.
Lancaster, Bailey, [1777]. [2] pp.
HSP copy.   43394

U. S. Continental Congress, 1777.
Extract uit de Dag-Registers.
Philadelphia, Dunlap, 1777. 48 pp.
JCB copy.   15643

U. S. Continental Congress, 1777.
Great Encouragement for Seamen. . . .
March 29, 1777.
Danvers, [1777]. Broadside.
EI copy.   15648

U. S. Continental Congress, 1777.
In Congress, February 15, 1777. Resolved
[Prices].
Baltimore, [1777]. Broadside.
NYPL copy.   15653

[U. S. Continental Congress, 1777.
In Congress, February 24, 1777.
Baltimore, [1777]. Broadside.]
(Origin of entry unknown.)   15654

[U. S. Continental Congress, 1777.
In Congress. February 25, 1777
[Desertions].
Philadelphia, Dunlap, 1777. Broadside.]
(Ordered printed.)   15655

U. S. Continental Congress, 1777.
In Congress. Baltimore, February 26th,
1777 [Rate of Interest].
Baltimore, [1777]. Broadside.
NYPL copy.   15656

U. S. Continental Congress, 1777.
In Congress, April 1 [-10], 1777. For the
Better Regulating the Pay of the Army.
[Philadelphia], Dunlap, [1777].
Broadside.
MHS copy.   15658

U. S. Continental Congress, 1777.
In Congress, April 4, 1777. Resolved, 1.
That there be one Commissary-General.
. . .
Philadelphia, Dunlap, [1777]. Broadside.
(No copy located.)   43395

U. S. Continental Congress, 1777.
In Congress, April 4 [-10], 1777.
Resolved [Musters].
[Philadelphia], Dunlap, [1777].
Broadside.
MHS copy.   15659

U. S. Continental Congress, 1777.
In Congress, April 7, 1777. Resolved
[Hospital Service].
[Philadelphia], Dunlap, [1777]. [2] pp.
AAS copy.   15660

[U. S. Continental Congress, 1777.
In Congress, April 7, 1777 [Hospital].
[Philadelphia], Hall & Sellers, 1779.
Broadside.]
(Ford 160; no copy located.)   16574

U. S. Continental Congress, 1777.
In Congress, April 11, 1777. Resolved
[Provisions].
[Philadelphia], Dunlap, [1777].
Broadside.
LCP copy.   15661

U. S. Continental Congress, 1777.
In Congress, April 14, 1777. Resolved,
That from and after the Publication
hereof. . . .
[Philadelphia], Dunlap, [1777].
Broadside.
(Heartman: Cradle 231; no copy located.)
                                              43396

U. S. Continental Congress, 1777.
In Congress, April 14, 1777. Resolved,
That from and after the Publication
hereof [Better Government of Troops].
Philadelphia, Dunlap, [1777]. Broadside.
AAS copy.   15662

U. S. Continental Congress, 1777.
In Congress, April 14th, 1777. Resolved,
That it be Recommended to the
Executive. . . .
[Philadelphia, 1777.] Broadside.
LOC copy.   15664

U. S. Continental Congress, 1777.
In Congress, April 14, 1777. Resolved,
That it be Recommended to the
Executive. . . . April 29, Resolved. . . .
Philadelphia, Dunlap, [1777]. Broadside.
LOC copy.   15665

[U. S. Continental Congress, 1777.
In Congress, April 14, 1777. Resolved,
That it is the Duty of Congress. . . .
[Philadelphia], Dunlap, [1777].
Broadside.]
(No copy located.)   15666

[U. S. Continental Congress, 1777.
In Congress, April 14, 1777 [Revision of
Rules and Articles of War].
[Philadelphia, 1777.] 2 pp.]
(Offered for sale 1941; not now to be
found.)   15663

U. S. Continental Congress, 1777.
In Congress, April 14, 1777. Whereas the
State of Pennsylvania. . . .
[Philadelphia], Dunlap, [1777].
Broadside.
LOC copy.   15667

U. S. Continental Congress, 1777.
In Congress, April 29, 1777. Resolved,
That it be Recommended. . . .
Philadelphia, Dunlap, [1777]. Broadside.
AAS copy.   15668

U. S. Continental Congress, 1777.
In Congress, May 12, 1777. Resolved,
That all Post-Masters. . . .
[Philadelphia, 1777.] Broadside.
LOC copy.   15669

U. S. Continental Congress, 1777.
In Congress, May 14, 1777. Resolved,
That the Quarter-Master General. . . .
Philadelphia, Dunlap, [1777]. [2] pp.
AAS copy.   15670

[U. S. Continental Congress, 1777.
In Congress, May 14, 1777. Resolved,
That the Quarter-Master General. . . .
Fishkill, [1777]. [2] pp.]
(No copy located.)   15671

U. S. Continental Congress, 1777.
In Congress, June 10, 1777. Resolved,
That for Supplying the Army. . . .
Philadelphia, Dunlap, [1777]. 4 pp.
NYPL copy.   15672

U. S. Continental Congress, 1777.
In Congress, June, 10, 1777. Resolved, 1.
That for Supplying the Army. . . .
[Poughkeepsie, Holt, 1777]. 4 pp.
YC copy.   43397

U. S. Continental Congress, 1777.
In Congress, June 20, 1777. Resolved,
That a Suitable Person. . . . October 11,
1777. Resolved, That the Commissary of
Hides. . . .
Yorktown, [Pa.], Hall & Sellers, [1777].
Broadside.
HSP copy.   43398

U. S. Continental Congress, 1777.
In Congress, June 10, 1777. Resolved,
That to Supply the Army. . . .
Yorktown, Hall & Sellers, [1778?]. 4 pp.
APS copy.   43565

U. S. Continental Congress, 1777.
In Congress. Monday 30th June, 1777.
[New Connecticut].
Philadelphia, Steiner & Cist, [1777].
Broadside.
NYHS copy.   15673

[U. S. Continental Congress, 1777.
In Congress, August 6, 1777. The
Committee of Treasury. . . .
[Philadelphia, 1777.] Broadside.]
(No copy located.)   15674

U. S. Continental Congress, 1777.
In Congress, September 6, 1777. The
Committee on the Treasury. . . .

Philadelphia, Dunlap, [1777]. Broadside.
LOC copy.   15675

U. S. Continental Congress, 1777.
In Congress, October 4, 1777. Congress
Resumed. . . .
Poughkeepsie, Holt, [1777]. Broadside.
NYSL copy.   43399

U. S. Continental Congress, 1777.
In Congress, October 8th, 1777. Whereas it
is of Essential Consequence. . . .
Lancaster, Bailey, [1777]. Broadside.
(From Am. Art Assoc. Cat., Apr. 22,
1919, item 53.)   43400

[U. S. Continental Congress, 1777.
In Congress, October 8, 1777.
Philadelphia, 1777. Broadside.]
(Ordered printed; Ford 180.)   15677

[U. S. Continental Congress, 1777.
In Congress, October 12, 1775. . . .
September 6, 1777. . . . Extracts from the
Minutes [Recruiting].
[Philadelphia, 1777.] Broadside.]
(No copy located.)   15676

[U. S. Continental Congress, 1777.
In Congress, November 1, 1777.
Forasmuch [Thanksgiving, Dec. 18].
[York, 1777.] Broadside.]
(No copy of this edition located.)   15678

U. S. Continental Congress, 1777.
In Congress, November 22, 1777.
Pursued. . . .
[Providence, 1777.] Broadside.
RIHS copy.   43401

U. S. Continental Congress, 1777.
In Congress. The Delegates of the United
States [Form of Officers' Commission].
[Philadelphia, 1777.] Broadside.
Reproduced from Henkels cat. 738 (May,
1895).   15681

U. S. Continental Congress, 1777.
Intelligence from Red-Bank. . . . October
23d 1777.
Lancaster, Bailey, [1777]. Broadside.
JCB copy.   43402

U. S. Continental Congress, 1777.
Journals of Congress. Containing the
Proceedings from Sept. 5. 1774. to Jan. 1.
1776. . . . Volume I.
Philadelphia, Aitken, 1777. [2], 310, [12]
pp.
AAS copy.   15683

U. S. Continental Congress, 1777.
Journals of Congress. Containing the
Proceedings of the Year, 1776. . . .
Volume II.
Philadelphia, Aitken, 1777. [2], 513,
[22] pp.
AAS copy.   15684

[U. S. Continental Congress, 1777.
Journals of Congress. Containing the
Proceedings from January 1, 1776, to
January 1, 1777. . . . Volume II.
York, Dunlap, 1777. [2], 520, xxvii pp.]
(The copy described by Evans was
correctly entered as 16137.)   15685

U. S. Continental Congress, 1777.
Journals of Congress, Containing the
Proceedings from January 1st, 1777, to
January 1st, 1778. . . . Volume III.
Philadelphia, Dunlap, [1778]. 603, [1],
xxii, [12] pp.
(Reissued with a new title page by
Patterson of N. Y. in 1788. See Evans
21527.)
AAS copy.   16138

U. S. Continental Congress, 1777.
Journals of Congress Containing the
Proceedings from January 1, 1777, to
January 1, 1778. . . . Volume III.
New York, Patterson, [1788]. 603, [1],
xxii pp.
AAS copy.   21527

U. S. Continental Congress, 1777.
Philadelphia, August 22, 1777. By an
Express. . . .
[Philadelphia], Dunlap, [1777].
Broadside.
LOC copy.   15686

[U. S. Continental Congress, 1777.
Proclamation. Sintenmal der König. . . .
Nov. 16, 1777.
[Fishkill, 1777.] Broadside.]
(No copy located.)   15687

U. S. Continental Congress, 1778.
An Address of the Congress to the
Inhabitants of the United States. . . . May
9, 1778.
Baltimore, Dunlap, [1778]. Broadside.
EPFL copy.   43566

U. S. Continental Congress, 1778.
An Address of the Congress. . . . May 9,
1778.
Boston, Powars & Willis, [1778].
Broadside.
AAS copy.   16099

U. S. Continental Congress, 1778.
[An Address] of the Congress to the
Inhabitants of the United States. . . . May
9, 1778.
Boston, White & Adams, [1778].
Broadside.
(The only known copy is defective.)
AAS copy.   43567

U. S. Continental Congress, 1778.
An Address of the Congress to the
Inhabitants of the United-States of
America. . . . May 9th, 1778.
Exeter, 1778. Broadside.
MHS copy.   16100

U. S. Continental Congress, 1778.
An Address of the Congress. . . . May 9,
1778.
Hartford, [1778]. Broadside.
CHS copy.   16101

U. S. Continental Congress, 1778.
Address of the Congress. . . . May 9, 1778.
Lancaster, [1778]. Broadside.
LCP copy.   16102

U. S. Continental Congress, 1778.
An Address of the Congress. . . . May 9,
1778.
Providence, [1778]. Broadside.
RIHS copy.   16103

U. S. Continental Congress, 1778.
An Address of the Congress. . . . May 9,
1778.
Williamsburg, Purdie, [1778]. [2] pp.
LOC copy.   16104

U. S. Continental Congress, 1778.
An Address of Congress. . . . May 9, 1778.
York, [1778]. Broadside.
LOC copy.   16097

U. S. Continental Congress, 1778.
By the Congress. . . . Manifesto. These
United States, having been Driven to
Hostilities [Oct. 30, 1778].
[Philadelphia, 1778.] Broadside.
LOC copy.   16132

U. S. Continental Congress, 1778.
Congress Having Resolved to Raise a
Corps . . . to be Commanded by General
Count Pulaski.
[Philadelphia? 1778.] Broadside.
VaSL copy.   16109

U. S. Continental Congress, 1778.
The Deluded Tools of the Enemy. . . .
February 27, 1778.
n.p., [1778]. Broadside.
NA copy.   16110

U. S. Continental Congress, 1778.
The Following Paper is Reprinted in
New-York by Authority. . . . By the
Congress. . . . Manifesto.
[New York, 1778.] [4] pp.
WLC copy.   16133

U. S. Continental Congress, 1778.
The Following State of Facts. . . .
[Philadelphia, 1778?] Broadside.
AAS copy.   43568

U. S. Continental Congress, 1778.
Friends and Countrymen, Three Years
have now Passed Away. . . . May 9, 1778.
[Annapolis, 1778.] Broadside.
MdHS copy.   16098

U. S. Continental Congress, 1778.

I do that I will Faithfully. . . .
[Philadelphia, 1778.] Broadside.
LOC copy. 16114

U. S. Continental Congress, 1778.
Important Intelligence. . . . Baltimore,
May 4th.
[Baltimore], Dunlap, [1778]. Broadside.
MdHS copy. 16111

U. S. Continental Congress, 1778.
In Congress, February 3, 1778. Resolved,
That Every Officer. . . .
[Philadelphia? 1778.] Broadside.
LOC copy. 16113

U. S. Continental Congress, 1778.
In Congress, February 5, 1778. Resolved
that the Captain. . . . February 9.
[Philadelphia, 1778.] [2] pp.
JCB copy. 43569

U. S. Continental Congress, 1778.
In Congress, February 5, 1778. Resolved,
That the Captain. . . . February 9.
Resolved. . . .
[Philadelphia? 1778.] [2] pp.
AAS copy. 16115

U. S. Continental Congress, 1778.
In Congress, February 6, 1778. For the
Better Regulating the Hospitals. . . .
[Philadelphia, 1778.] Broadside.
LOC copy. 43570

U. S. Continental Congress, 1778.
In Congress, February 11, 1778. Resolved,
That there Shall be. . . .
[Philadelphia, 1778.] Broadside.
LOC copy. 43571

U. S. Continental Congress, 1778.
In Congress, February 27, 1778. Resolved,
That a Company of Bakers. . . .
n. p., [1778]. Broadside.
LOC copy. 43572

U. S. Continental Congress, 1778.
In Congress, March 2, 1778. Whereas, it is
Essential. . . .
[Philadelphia, 1778.] Broadside.
LOC copy. 16116

U. S. Continental Congress, 1778.
In Congress, March 13, 1778. Congress
Resumed the Consideration. . . .
[York, Pa., 1778.] Broadside.
MHS copy. 43573

U. S. Continental Congress, 1778.
In Congress, April 14th, 1778. Resolved,
That the Commissary General. . . . April
16th.
[Philadelphia, 1778.] Broadside.
NYHS copy. 43574

U. S. Continental Congress, 1778.
In Congress 16th April, 1778. Resolved,
That Nothing Contained. . . . 1st
September.
Philadelphia, Dunlap, [1778]. Broadside.
LCP copy. 43575

U. S. Continental Congress, 1778.
In Congress, April 23, 1778. Whereas
Persuasion. . . .
York, Hall & Sellers, [1778]. Broadside.
NYHS copy. 16119

U. S. Continental Congress, 1778.
In Congress, May 2, 1778. Resolved, That
the Managers of the Lottery. . . .
[Philadelphia? 1778.] Broadside.
LCP copy. 16120

U. S. Continental Congress, 1778.
In Congress, May 6, 1778. Whereas
Congress have Received. . . .
[Philadelphia, 1778.] Broadside.
AAS copy. 43576

U. S. Continental Congress, 1778.
In Congress, May 14, 1777. Resolved,
That the Quarter-Master. . . .
Fishkill, [1778]. [2] pp.
LOC copy. 16123

U. S. Continental Congress, 1778.
In Congress, May 18, 1778. Resolved,
That Bills of Exchange. . . . [With
Treasury transmittal of Aug. 4, 1778.]
[Philadelphia, Dunlap, 1778.] [3] pp.
CHS copy. 16124

U. S. Continental Congress, 1778.
In Congress, May 22, 1778 [Resolution,
Prisoners].
York, [1778]. Broadside.
LOC copy. 16125

U. S. Continental Congress, 1778.
In Congress, May 27, 1778. Establishment
of the American Army. . . . June 2, 1778.
York, [1778]. [2] pp.
APS copy. 16126

U. S. Continental Congress, 1778.
In Congress, June 6, 1778. Resolved, That
the Resolution. . . .
York, [1778]. Broadside.
JCB copy. 16127

U. S. Continental Congress, 1778.
In Congress, June 9, 1778. Whereas
Doubts have Arisen. . . .
Yorktown, Hall & Sellers, [1778].
Broadside.
NYHS copy. 43577

U. S. Continental Congress, 1778.
In Congress, July 20, 1778. The
Committee . . . Ebenezer Hazard.
[Philadelphia, 1778.] Broadside.
MHS copy. 43578

U. S. Continental Congress, 1778.
In Congress, July 25, 1778. 1. Resolved,
that the Expedition. . . .
[Philadelphia, 1778.] Broadside.
LOC copy. 43579

[U. S. Continental Congress, 1778.
In Congress, August 14, 1778 [Supplying
Enemy with food].
[Philadelphia], Hall & Sellers, 1779.
Broadside.]
(Ford 223; no copy located.) 16580

U. S. Continental Congress, 1778.
In Congress, August 26, 1776. Whereas, in
the Course. . . . In Congress, September
25, 1778.
[Philadelphia, 1778.] Broadside.
JCB copy. 16128

U. S. Continental Congress, 1778.
In Congress, September 26, 1778.
Resolved, That a House. . . .
[Philadelphia, 1778.] Broadside.
JCB copy. 16130

U. S. Continental Congress, 1778.
In Congress, October 8, 1778. Resolved
that all Limitations. . . .
Philadelphia, Dunlap, [1778]. Broadside.
NHHS copy. 16131

U. S. Continental Congress, 1778.
In Congress. November 24, 1778.
Congress took into Consideration. . . .
[Philadelphia, 1778.] Broadside.
AAS copy. 16136

U. S. Continental Congress, 1778.
In Congress, December 19, 1777. Whereas
Sir William Howe. . . . In Congress, January
21, 1778.
[Philadelphia? 1778.] [2] pp.
AAS copy. 16112

U. S. Continental Congress, 1778.
Mr. Dunlap, Be Pleased to Print. . . .
Henry Laurence, President. . . . July 4,
1778.
Philadelphia, Dunlap, [1778]. Broadside.
(No copy located.) 43580

U. S. Continental Congress, 1778.
Paris, May 18, 1778. Gentlemen, Certain
Intelligence. . . . Read in Congress, July 8,
1778.
[Philadelphia, 1778.] Broadside.
NYHS copy. 43581

U. S. Continental Congress, 1778.
A Proclamation [American Armed
Vessels. May 9, 1778].
Lancaster, [1778]. Broadside.
LCP copy. 16121

U. S. Continental Congress, 1778.
A Proclamation [American Armed
Vessels. May 9, 1778].
York, Dunlap, [1778]. Broadside.
NYPL copy. 16122

[U. S. Continental Congress, 1778.

A Proclamation for a General Fast [Apr.
22]. . . . In Congress, March 7th, 1778.
[Philadelphia, 1778.] Broadside.]
(No copy of such an edition could be
located.) 16117

U. S. Continental Congress, 1778.
A Proclamation. It Having Pleased
Almighty God. . . . Massachusetts . . .
December 5th, 1778 [declaring Dec. 13 a
day of Continental thanksgiving].
[Boston? 1778.] Broadside.
(No copy located.) 43582

[U. S. Continental Congress, 1778.
A Proclamation [Thanksgiving, Dec. 30.
Dated Nov. 17, 1778].
Philadelphia, Dunlap, 1778. Broadside.]
(No copy of such a printing has been
located.) 16134

U. S. Continental Congress, 1778.
A Proclamation. Whereas Congress. . . .
[American Armed Vessels. May 9, 1778].
NYPL copy. 16122

U. S. Continental Congress, 1778.
York-Town. In Congress, May 6, 1778.
Whereas Congress . . . Treaty of Amity.
. . .
Annapolis, Green, [1778]. Broadside.
(Copy not located.) 43583

U. S. Continental Congress, 1778.
Your Committee, to whom was Referred
to Consider and Report on the Currency
[September 19, 1778].
[Philadelphia, 1778.] Broadside.
NA copy. 16129

U. S. Continental Congress, 1779.
A Circular Letter from the Congress.
Boston, [1779]. 15 pp.
AAS copy. 16559

U. S. Continental Congress, 1779.
A Circular Letter from the Congress.
New London, [1779]. 19 pp.
LOC copy. 16560

U. S. Continental Congress, 1779.
A Circular Letter from the Congress.
Philadelphia, Claypoole, [1779]. 12 pp.
AAS copy. 16558

U. S. Continental Congress, 1779.
A Circular Letter from the Congress. . . .
Sept. 13, 1779.
Philadelphia, Dunlap, [1779]. 12 pp.
WLC copy. 43712

U. S. Continental Congress, 1779.
A Circular Letter from the Congress.
Poughkeepsie, [1779]. 8 pp.
LOC copy. 16561

U. S. Continental Congress, 1779.
Description of Counterfeit Bills.
[Philadelphia, 1779.] Broadside.
LOC copy. 16562

U. S. Continental Congress, 1779.
An Estimate of the Average Price in
December, 1778. . . . August 25, 1779.
[Philadelphia, 1779.] Broadside.
LOC copy. 16563

U. S. Continental Congress, 1779.
In Congress, January 2, 1779. Whereas . . .
Counterfeits have Appeared. . . .
Philadelphia, Dunlap, [1779]. Broadside.
JCB copy. 16564

U. S. Continental Congress, 1779.
In Congress, January 9, 1779 [Prisoners].
Philadelphia, Dunlap, [1779]. Broadside.
LOC copy. 16565

U. S. Continental Congress, 1779.
In Congress, January 13, 1779. We Cannot
Review. . . .
Philadelphia, Dunlap, [1779]. [2] pp.
AAS copy. 16566

U. S. Continental Congress, 1779.
In Congress, March 2, 1779. The Board of
War. . . .
[Philadelphia], Hall & Sellers, 1779.
Broadside.
NHHS copy. 16567

U. S. Continental Congress, 1779.
In Congress, March 5, 1779. Resolved,

That the . . . Certificates. . . .
[Philadelphia], Hall & Sellers, [1779].
Broadside.
NHHS copy.   16568

U. S. Continental Congress, 1779.
In Congress, March 6, 1779. Resolved,
That . . . Admiralty. . . .
Philadelphia, Claypoole, [1779].
Broadside.
NHHS copy.   16569

U. S. Continental Congress, 1779.
In Congress, March 15, 1779. Resolved,
That all . . . Light Dragoons. . . .
[Philadelphia], Hall & Sellers, [1779].
Broadside.
NHHS copy.   16570

U. S. Continental Congress, 1779.
In Congress, March 16, 1779. Whereas
Discontent. . . .
[Philadelphia], Hall & Sellers, [1779].
Broadside.
MHS copy.   43716

U. S. Continental Congress, 1779.
In Congress, March 23, 1779, Ordinance
for Regulating the Cloathing.
n.p., [1779]. Broadside.
NHHS copy.   16573

U. S. Continental Congress, 1779.
In Congress, March 23, 1779, Ordinance
for Regulating the Cloathing. . . .
Philadelphia, Claypool, [1779].
Broadside.
LOC copy.   16571

[U. S. Continental Congress, 1779.
In Congress, March 23, 1779 [Cloathing].
[Philadelphia], Hall & Sellers, [1779]. 2
pp.]
(Ford 211. No copy could be located.)
                                          16572

U. S. Continental Congress, 1779.
In Congress, April 14, 1779 [Enemy
Lines].
Philadelphia, Hall & Sellers, [1779].
Broadside.
LOC copy.   16575

U. S. Continental Congress, 1779.
In Congress, May 22, 1779
[Supernumerary Officers].
Philadelphia, Claypoole, [1779].
Broadside.
LOC copy.   16576

U. S. Continental Congress, 1779.
In Congress, Friday, June 11, 1779.
Resolved, That Twenty Millions of
Dollars. . . .
Wilmington, Adams, [1779]. Broadside.
LOC copy.   43715

U. S. Continental Congress, 1779.
In Congress, June 29, 1779. As Congress.
. . . [$20,000,000 loan].
Philadelphia, Claypoole, [1779].
Broadside.
MHS copy.   16577

U. S. Continental Congress, 1779.
In Congress, July 30, 1779. Ordinance for
Establishing a Board of Treasury.
[Philadelphia, 1779.] Broadside.
LOC copy.   16579

U. S. Continental Congress, 1779.
In Congress, August 14, 1778. Resolved,
That the Resolution . . . Medical
Affairs. . . .
[Philadelphia], Hall & Sellers, 1779.
Broadside.
NYAM copy.   43713

U. S. Continental Congress, 1779.
In Congress, August 16, 1779. Resolved,
That the Clothier General. . . .
Philadelphia, Claypool, [1779].
Broadside.
CHS copy.   43714

U. S. Continental Congress, 1779.
In Congress, October 8, 1778. Resolved,
That all Limitations of Prices of Gold and
Silver. . . . January 14, 1779.
Philadelphia, Dunlap, [1779]. Broadside.
NYPL copy.   16581

[U. S. Continental Congress, 1779.

In Congress, October 28, 1779 [Leather].
[Philadelphia, 1779.] Broadside.]
(Not in Ford; no copy found.)   16582

U. S. Continental Congress, 1779.
In Congress, November 25th, 1779. Whereas
Congress. . . . November 26th, 1779. . . .
Philadelphia, Claypoole, [1779].
Broadside.
(The only copy located is in bad
condition.)
Williams College copy.   16583

U. S. Continental Congress, 1778.
Journals of Congress, Containing the
Proceedings from January 1st, 1778, to
January 1st, 1779. . . . Volume IV.
Philadelphia, Claypoole, [1779]. [2], 748,
[2], lxxxix, [5] pp.
AAS copy.   16584

U. S. Continental Congress, 1779.
Journals of Congress. Containing the
Proceedings from January 1, 1779, to
January 1, 1780. . . . Volume V.
Philadelphia, Claypoole, 1782. 464, [15],
lxxiv pp.
MHS copy.   17766

U. S. Continental Congress, 1779.
Journals of Congress [Jan. 1 - Feb. 1,
1779].
Philadelphia, Claypoole, 1779. 12 pp.
HSP copy.   16585

U. S. Continental Congress, 1779.
Journals of Congress [Feb. 1 - Mar. 1,
1779].
Philadelphia, Claypoole, [1779]. 50 pp.
LOC copy.   16586

U. S. Continental Congress, 1779.
Journals of Congress [Mar. 1 - 30, 1779].
Philadelphia, Claypoole, [1779]. 56 pp.
LOC copy.   16587

U. S. Continental Congress, 1779.
Journals of Congress [Mar. 31 - Apr. 10,
1779].
Philadelphia, Claypoole, [1779]. 24 pp.
LOC copy.   16588

U. S. Continental Congress, 1779.
Journals of Congress [Apr. 12 - 17, 1779].
Philadelphia, Claypoole, [1779]. 19 pp.
LOC copy.   16589

U. S. Continental Congress, 1779.
Journals of Congress [Apr. 19 - 24, 1779].
Philadelphia, Claypoole, [1779]. 24 pp.
LOC copy.   16590

U. S. Continental Congress, 1779.
Journals of Congress [Apr. 24 - May 3,
1779].
Philadelphia, Claypoole, [1779]. 16 pp.
LOC copy.   16591

U. S. Continental Congress, 1779.
Journals of Congress [May 1 - 10, 1779].
Philadelphia, Claypoole, [1779]. 15 pp.
LOC copy.   16592

U. S. Continental Congress, 1779.
Journals of Congress [May 10 - 15, 1779].
Philadelphia, Claypoole, [1779]. 14 pp.
LOC copy.   16593

U. S. Continental Congress, 1779.
Journals of Congress [May 17 - 22, 1779].
Philadelphia, Claypoole, [1779]. 24 pp.
LOC copy.   16594

U. S. Continental Congress, 1779.
Journals of Congress [May 24 - 29, 1779].
Philadelphia, Claypoole, [1779]. 20 pp.
LOC copy.   16595

U. S. Continental Congress, 1779.
Journals of Congress [May 31 - June 5,
1779].
Philadelphia, Claypoole, [1779]. 15 pp.
LOC copy.   16596

U. S. Continental Congress, 1779.
Journals of Congress [June 7 - 12, 1779].
Philadelphia, Claypoole, [1779]. 19 pp.
LOC copy.   16597

U. S. Continental Congress, 1779.
Journals of Congress [June 14 - 19, 1779].
Philadelphia, Claypoole, [1779]. 10 pp.
LOC copy.   16598

U. S. Continental Congress, 1779.
Journals of Congress [June 21 - 26, 1779].
Philadelphia, Claypoole, [1779]. 13 pp.
LOC copy.   16599

U. S. Continental Congress, 1779.
Journals of Congress [June 28 - July 3,
1779].
Philadelphia, Claypoole, [1779]. 15 pp.
LOC copy.   16600

U. S. Continental Congress, 1779.
Journals of Congress [July 5 - 12, 1779].
Philadelphia, Claypoole, [1779]. 9 pp.
LOC copy.   16601

U. S. Continental Congress, 1779.
Journals of Congress [July 12-17, 1779].
Philadelphia, Claypoole, [1779]. 10 pp.
LOC copy.   16602

U. S. Continental Congress, 1779.
Journals of Congress [July 19-24, 1779].
Philadelphia, Claypoole, [1779]. 14 pp.
LOC copy.   16603

U. S. Continental Congress, 1779.
Journals of Congress [July 26 - 31, 1779].
Philadelphia, Claypoole, [1779]. 16 pp.
LOC copy.   16604

U. S. Continental Congress, 1779.
Journals of Congress [Aug. 2 - 7, 1779].
Philadelphia, Claypoole, [1779]. 11 pp.
LOC copy.   16605

U. S. Continental Congress, 1779.
Journals of Congress [Aug. 9 - 14, 1779].
Philadelphia, Claypoole, [1779]. 10 pp.
LOC copy.   16606

U. S. Continental Congress, 1779.
Journals of Congress [Aug. 16 - 21, 1779].
Philadelphia, Claypoole, [1779]. 13 pp.
LOC copy.   16607

U. S. Continental Congress, 1779.
Journals of Congress [Aug. 23 - 28, 1779].
Philadelphia, Claypoole, [1779]. 14 pp.
AAS copy.   16608

U. S. Continental Congress, 1779.
Journals of Congress [Aug. 30 - Sept. 4,
1779].
Philadelphia, Claypoole, [1779]. 12 pp.
LOC copy.   16609

U. S. Continental Congress, 1779.
Journals of Congress [Sept. 6 - 11, 1779].
Philadelphia, Claypoole, [1779]. 10 pp.
LOC copy.   16610

U. S. Continental Congress, 1779.
Journals of Congress [Sept. 13 - 18, 1779].
Philadelphia, Claypoole, [1779]. 22 pp.
LOC copy.   16611

U. S. Continental Congress, 1779.
Journals of Congress [Sept. 20 - 25, 1779].
Philadelphia, Claypoole, [1779]. 9 pp.
LOC copy.   16612

U. S. Continental Congress, 1779.
Journals of Congress [Sept. 26 - Oct. 2,
1779].
Philadelphia, Claypoole, [1779]. 11 pp.
LOC copy.   16613

U. S. Continental Congress, 1779.
Journals of Congress [Oct. 4 - 9, 1779].
Philadelphia, Claypoole, [1779]. 11 pp.
LOC copy.   16614

U. S. Continental Congress, 1779.
Journals of Congress [Oct. 11 - 16, 1779].
Philadelphia, Claypoole, [1779]. 8 pp.
LOC copy.   16615

U. S. Continental Congress, 1779.
Journals of Congress [Oct. 18 - 23, 1779].
Philadelphia, Claypoole, [1779]. 12 pp.
LOC copy.   16616

U. S. Continental Congress, 1779.
Journals of Congress [Oct. 25 - 30, 1779].
Philadelphia, Claypoole, [1779]. 13 pp.
LOC copy.   16617

U. S. Continental Congress, 1779.
Journals of Congress [Nov. 1 - 6, 1779].
Philadelphia, Claypoole, [1779]. 7 pp.
LOC copy.   16618

U. S. Continental Congress, 1779.
Journals of Congress [Nov. 8 - 12, 1779].
Philadelphia, Claypoole, [1779]. 11 pp.
LOC copy. 16619

U. S. Continental Congress, 1779.
Journals of Congress [Nov. 15 - 20, 1779].
Philadelphia, Claypoole, [1779]. 19 pp.
LOC copy. 16620

U. S. Continental Congress, 1779.
Journals of Congress [Nov. 22 - 27, 1779].
Philadelphia, Claypoole, [1779]. 15 pp.
LOC copy. 16621

U. S. Continental Congress, 1779.
Journals of Congress [Nov. 29 - Dec. 4, 1779].
Philadelphia, Claypoole, [1779]. 12 pp.
LOC copy. 16622

U. S. Continental Congress, 1779.
Journals of the Congress [Dec. 6 - 11, 1779].
Philadelphia, Claypoole, [1779]. 10 pp.
LOC copy. 16623

U. S. Continental Congress, 1779.
Journals of Congress [Dec. 13 - 18, 1779].
Philadelphia, Claypoole, [1779]. 12 pp.
AAS copy. 16624

U. S. Continental Congress, 1779.
Journals of Congress [Dec. 20 - 31, 1779].
Philadelphia, Claypoole, [1780]. 16 pp.
NYPL copy. 17025

U. S. Continental Congress, 1779.
Observations on the American
Revolution.
Philadelphia, Steiner & Cist, 1779. [4], 122 pp.
AAS copy. 16625

U. S. Continental Congress, 1779.
Proclamation [Fast, First Thursday in May. Dated Mar. 20, 1779].
Philadelphia, Hall & Sellers, [1779].
Broadside.
LOC copy. 16552

[U. S. Continental Congress, 1779.
Report of a Committee Appointed to
Propose a Plan for Maritime Courts of
Appeal.
Philadelphia, 1779.]
(Ordered printed Oct. 29, 1779.) 16630

U. S. Continental Congress, 1779.
Report of the Committee for Regulating
Departments, &c.
[Philadelphia, 1779.] [4] pp.
NA copy. 16632

U. S. Continental Congress, 1779.
Supplement to the Maryland Gazette. . . .
June 4, 1779. To the Inhabitants of the
United States. . . . [May 26, 1779]
[Annapolis, 1779.] [2] pp.
HEH copy. 43717

U. S. Continental Congress, 1779.
To the Inhabitants of the United States.
. . . The Present Situations. . . .
Annapolis, Greens, [1779]. Broadside.
(No copy located.) 43718

U. S. Continental Congress, 1779.
To the Inhabitants of the United States of
America. Friends and Countrymen. The
Present Situation [May 26, 1779.
Hartford, June 9].
[Hartford, 1779.] Broadside.
CHS copy. 43611

U. S. Continental Congress, 1779.
To the Inhabitants of the United States of
America. Friends and Countrymen. The
Present Situation [May 26, 1779].
Philadelphia, Claypoole, [1779]. [2] pp.
LCP copy. 16636

U. S. Continental Congress, 1779.
To the Inhabitants of the United States of
America. Friends and Countrymen, The
Present Situation. . . .
Providence, Carter, [1779]. [2] pp.
AAS copy. 19442

[U. S. Continental Congress, 1779.
Whereas it Becomes us. . . . Resolved.
That it be Recommended to the Several
States to Appoint . . . the 9th day of

December next . . . Thanksgiving.
[Philadelphia, 1779.] Broadside.]
(No copy could be located.) 16554

[U. S. Continental Congress, 1780.
By the United States in Congress
Assembled. A Proclamation [Fast, Apr.
26. Dated Mar. 11, 1780].
[Philadelphia, 1780.] Broadside.]
(No Philadelphia broadside printing of
this proclamation has been found.) 17013

[U. S. Continental Congress, 1780.
By the United States in Congress
Assembled. A Proclamation [Sept. 1, 1780].
Philadelphia, 1780. Broadside.]
(Ford 335; no copy located.) 17016

[U. S. Continental Congress, 1780.
By the United States in Congress
Assembled. A Proclamation
[Thanksgiving Dec. 7. Dated
Oct. 18, 1780].
Philadelphia, 1780. Broadside.]
(A Philadelphia broadside printing was
assumed by Evans from the Exeter
printing, which he saw.) 17017

[U. S. Continental Congress, 1780.
Extract from the Journal of Congress,
August 26, 1780.
[Philadelphia, 1780.] 2 pp.]
(No such item could be located.) 17019

U. S. Continental Congress, 1780.
In Congress, February 25, 1780. Resolved,
That the Several States. . . .
[Philadelphia, 1780.] 4 pp.
NYPL copy. 17020

U. S. Continental Congress, 1780.
In Congress, May 2, 1780.
Instructions. . . .
[Philadelphia, 1780.] [2] pp.
LOC copy. 17021

U. S. Continental Congress, 1780.
In Congress, June 28th, 1780. Whereas
Congress. . . .
[Philadelphia, 1780.] Broadside.
NYPL copy. 17022

U. S. Continental Congress, 1780.
In Congress, October 3d, 1780. Resolved,
That the Regular Army. . . .
Philadelphia, Claypoole, [1780].
Broadside.
HSP copy. 17023

U. S. Continental Congress, 1780.
In Congress, October 30, 1780
[Resolutions on the Southern Army].
Philadelphia, Claypoole, [1780].
Broadside.]
(Reported by Ford from a copy in a
private library.) 17024

U. S. Continental Congress, 1780.
Journals of Congress . . . from January
1st, 1779. . . . Volume V.
Philadelphia, Claypool, [1780?]. 64+ pp.
(The only known copy cannot be
reproduced.) 43907

[U. S. Continental Congress, 1780.
Journals of Congress, January, 1780.
[Philadelphia, 1780.] 38 pp.]
(The Evans entry apparently describes a
later Claypoole ed. which lacked tp.) 17026

[U. S. Continental Congress, 1780.
Journals of Congress, for February, 1780.
[Philadelphia, 1780.] pp. 41 - 73.]
(No copy of this issue could be
reproduced.) 17027

U. S. Continental Congress, 1780.
Journals of Congress, for March, 1780.
[Philadelphia, 1780.] pp. 75 - 106.
LOC copy. 17028

U. S. Continental Congress, 1780.
Journals of Congress, for April, 1780.
[Philadelphia, 1780.] pp. 106-131.
LOC copy. 17029

[U. S. Continental Congress, 1780.
Journals of Congress, for May, 1780.
[Philadelphia, 1780.] pp. 132-162.]
(No copy of this issue could be
reproduced.) 17030

U. S. Continental Congress, 1780.
Journals of Congress, for June, 1780.
[Philadelphia, 1780.] pp. 164 - 198.
LOC copy. 17031

U. S. Continental Congress, 1780.
Journals of Congress, for July, 1780.
[Philadelphia, 1780.] pp. 199 - 237.
LOC copy. 17032

U. S. Continental Congress, 1780.
Journals of Congress, for August, 1780.
[Philadelphia, 1780.] pp. 239-274.
LOC copy. 17033

U. S. Continental Congress, 1780.
Journals of Congress, for September, 1780.
[Philadelphia, 1780.] pp. 275-314.
LOC copy. 17034

U. S. Continental Congress, 1780.
Journals of Congress, for October, 1780.
[Philadelphia, 1780.] pp. 315-349.
LOC copy. 17035

U. S. Continental Congress, 1780.
Journals of Congress, for November, 1780.
[Philadelphia, 1780.] pp. 351-384.
LOC copy. 17036

U. S. Continental Congress, 1780.
Journals of Congress, for December, 1780.
[Philadelphia, 1780.] pp. 385-403, irreg.
LOC copy. 17037

U. S. Continental Congress, 1780.
Journals of Congress, from January 1st,
1780, to January 1st, 1781.
Philadelphia, Claypoole, [1781]. 403,
xxxviii, [3] pp.
LCP copy. 17392

U. S. Continental Congress, 1780.
Observations on the American
Revolution.
Providence, 1780. 126 pp.
AAS copy. 17039

U. S. Continental Congress, 1780.
Plan for Conducting the Hospital
Department.
Philadelphia, Claypoole, [1780]. 8 pp.
AAS copy. 17040

U. S. Continental Congress, 1780.
Plan for Conducting the Inspector's
Department.
Philadelphia, Claypoole, [1780]. 8 pp.
NYPL copy. 17041

U. S. Continental Congress, 1780.
Plan for Conducting the Quartermaster
General's Department . . . July 15th, 1780.
Philadelphia, Claypoole, 1780. 16 pp.
AAS copy. 43908

U. S. Continental Congress, 1780.
Plan for Conducting the Quartermaster
General's Department . . . July 15th, 1780.
Philadelphia, Claypoole, [1780]. 15 pp.
(The AAS has also a 16 pp. ed.)
AAS copy. 17042

U. S. Continental Congress, 1780.
Resolutions, Acts and Orders of Congress,
for the Year 1780. Volume VI.
[Philadelphia], Dunlap, [1786]. 257, [1],
xliii pp.
AAS copy. 20079

U. S. Continental Congress, 1781.
[An Address] of the Continental Congress
to the Inhabitants of the United States.
Boston, White & Adams, [1781].
Broadside.
(Reproduced as 43567.) 44062

U. S. Continental Congress, 1781.
By a Gentleman from Philadelphia we are
Favour'd with the Pennsylvania Packet of
the 18th. . . . Published by Order of
Congress.
[Philadelphia], Opposite the Court-
House, [1781]. Broadside.
(Reproduced from Am. Art Assoc. Cat.,
Feb. 8, 1917, item 85.) 44063

U. S. Continental Congress, 1781.
By the United States in Congress
Assembled. A Proclamation [Continental
Thanksgiving, Dec. 13]. . . . State of
New-Hampshire. . . . November 16, 1781.

[Exeter, 1781]. Broadside.
BPL copy.   17389

U. S. Continental Congress, 1781.
By the United States in Congress
Assembled, A Proclamation [Fast, May 3.
Dated Lebanon, Apr. 6, 1781].
New London, [1781]. Broadside.
YC copy.   17124

U. S. Continental Congress, 1781.
By the United States in Congress
Assembled, April 7, 1781. Be it
Ordained. . . .
[Philadelphia, 1781.] Broadside.
NYPL copy.   17384

U. S. Continental Congress, 1781.
By the United States in Congress
Assembled, August 7th, 1781, Whereas the
States of New-Hampshire and New
York. . . .
Exeter, 1781. Broadside.
NHHS copy.   44064

[U. S. Continental Congress, 1781.
By the United States in Congress
Assembled, March 3, 1781 [Prisoners].
[Philadelphia, 1781.] [2] pp.]
(Ford 356, but no copy located.)   17383

U. S. Continental Congress, 1781.
By the United States in Congress
Assembled. Proclamation [Fast, May 3,
Dated Boston, Apr. 11, 1781].
[Boston, 1781.] Broadside.
AAS copy.   17386

[U. S. Continental Congress, 1781.
By the United States in Congress
Assembled. Proclamation [Fast, May 3.
Dated Mar. 20, 1781].
[Philadelphia, 1781.] Broadside.]
(Assumed by Evans from 17386; no copy
of Philadelphia printing located.)   17385

[U. S. Continental Congress, 1781.
By the United States in Congress
Assembled. A Proclamation
[Thanksgiving, Dec. 13. Dated Oct. 26,
1781].
[Philadelphia, 1781.] Broadside.]
(Assumed by Evans from 17389; no copy
of Philadelphia printing located.)   17388

U. S. Continental Congress, 1781.
(Circular.) Philadelphia, February 8, 1781.
Sir, Your Excellency. . . .
Providence, Carter, [1781]. Broadside.
RISL copy.   44065

U. S. Continental Congress, 1781.
The Constitutions of the Several
Independent States of America.
Philadelphia, Bailey, 1781. [2], 226.
MHS copy.   17390

U. S. Continental Congress, 1781.
Cornwallis Retreating! Philadelphia,
April 7, 1781.
[Boston], Willis, [1781]. Broadside.
NYPL copy.   17391

U. S. Continental Congress, 1781.
Journals of Congress . . . for the Year
1781. . . . Volume VII.
New York, Patterson, 1787. 552, [17],
lxxix pp.
AAS copy.   20773

U. S. Continental Congress, 1781.
Journals of the Continental Congress. . . .
For the Year 1781. . . . Volume VII.
Philadelphia, Claypoole, 1781. 522, [4],
lxxix pp.
AAS copy.   17767

U. S. Continental Congress, 1781.
An Ordinance, Ascertaining what
Captures on Water Shall Be Lawful [Dec. 4,
1781].
Philadelphia, Claypoole, [1781].
Broadside.
HC copy.   17393

U. S. Continental Congress, 1781.
An Ordinance, Relative to the Capture
and Condemnation of Prizes [Mar. 27,
1781].
Philadelphia, Claypoole, [1781].
Broadside.
LOC copy.   17394

U. S. Continental Congress, 1781.
An Ordinance, Relative to the Capture
and Condemnation of Prizes. . . . [Mar 27,
1781.]
[Philadelphia? 1781?] Broadside.
LOC copy.   44066

[U. S. Continental Congress, 1781.
Resolved, That it be Recommended to the
Several States . . . a Duty of Five per cent.
[Philadelphia, 1781.] Broadside.]
(Ford 355; no copy located.)   17396

[U. S. Continental Congress, 1781.
Rules and Articles for the Better
Government of the Troops Raised.
Philadelphia, 1781. 36 pp.]
(Ford 302, Sabin 74060, but no copy
located.)   17397

U. S. Continental Congress, 1781.
The United States in Congress Assembled.
September 7, 1781. The following Form of
the Exequation. . . .
[Philadelphia? 1781.] [2] pp.
NYPL copy.   44067

U. S. Continental Congress, 1782.
By the United States in Congress
Assembled, January 3, 1782 [Hospitals].
[Philadelphia, 1782.] Broadside.
LOC ph. copy.   17755

U. S. Continental Congress, 1782.
By the United States, in Congress
Assembled, January 10, 1782. Plan for
Conducting the Inspector's Department.
[Philadelphia, 1782.] Broadside.
AAS copy.   17756

[U. S. Continental Congress, 1782.
By the United States in Congress
Assembled. February 20, 1782 [Exchange
of Prisoners].
[Philadelphia, 1782.] Broadside.]
(Not in Ford; no copy located.)   17757

U. S. Continental Congress, 1782.
By the United States in Congress
Assembled. February 20, 1782. Whereas it
has become. . . .
[Philadelphia, 1782.] Broadside.
NYPL copy.   17758

U. S. Continental Congress, 1782.
[By the United States in Congress
Assembled, February 23, 1782. . . .
Cornwallis.
Philadelphia, Claypoole, 1782.]
Broadside.
(No copy known.)   44275

U. S. Continental Congress, 1782.
By the United States in Congress
Assembled, April 22, 1782. . . . A System
on which Provisions are to be Issued.
[Philadelphia, 1782.] [2] pp.
LOC copy.   44277

U. S. Continental Congress, 1782.
By the United States in Congress
Assembled, July 23d, 1782. Resolved, That
in Conducting. . . .
[Philadelphia, 1782.] Broadside.
LOC copy.   44276

U. S. Continental Congress, 1782.
By the United States in Congress
Assembled, August 7, 1782. Resolved,
That the Secretary at War. . . .
[Philadelphia, 1782.] Broadside.
AAS copy.   17759

U. S. Continental Congress, 1782.
By the United States, in Congress
Assembled, September 4th, 1782. On the
Report of a Grand Committee. . . .
[Philadelphia, 1782.] Broadside.
LOC copy.   17760

[U. S. Continental Congress, 1782.
By the United States in Congress
Assembled. October 4th, 1782. Whereas by
the Articles of Confederation. . . .
[Philadelphia, 1782.] Broadside.]
(No copy located.)   17761

U. S. Continental Congress, 1782.
By the United States in Congress
Assembled. Proclamation [Thanksgiving,
Nov. 28. Dated Oct. 11, 1782].
[Philadelphia, 1782.] Broadside.

(The copy described by Evans cannot now
be located.)   17762

U. S. Continental Congress, 1782.
An Ordinance, for Amending an
Ordinance, Ascertaining what Captures
on Water shall be Lawful [Jan. 8, 1782].
[Philadelphia, 1782.] Broadside.
LOC copy.   17769

U. S. Continental Congress, 1782.
An Ordinance for Further Amending the
Ordinance, Ascertaining what Captures
on Water shall be Lawful. [Feb. 26, 1782].
[Philadelphia, 1782.] Broadside.
MHS copy.   17770

U. S. Continental Congress, 1782.
An Ordinance for the Better Distribution
of Prizes [July 10, 1782].
[Philadelphia, 1782.] Broadside.
JCB copy.   17771

U. S. Continental Congress, 1782.
Regulations for the Quarter Master
General's Department. . . . October 23,
1782.
[Philadelphia, 1782.] Broadside.
JCB copy.   17775

U. S. Continental Congress, 1783.
Address and Recommendations to the
States.
Boston, 1783. 62 pp.
AAS copy.   18225

U. S. Continental Congress, 1783.
Address and Recommendations to the
States.
Philadelphia, Claypoole, 1783. 14, [1], 9,
[2], 3, 6, 5, 4, 20 pp.
AAS copy.   18223

U. S. Continental Congress, 1783.
Address and Recommendations to the
States.
Philadelphia, Claypoole, 1783. 14, [1], 9,
[2], 3, 6, 5, 4, 26 pp.
AAS copy.   18224

U. S. Continental Congress, 1783.
Address and Recommendations to the
States.
Trenton, 1783. 56 pp.
HEH copy.   18228

U. S. Continental Congress, 1783.
Addresses and Recommendations to the
States.
Hartford, Hudson & Goodwin, 1783. 50,
[31] pp., 1 folding table.
AAS copy.   18226

U. S. Continental Congress, 1783.
Addresses and Recommendations to the
States.
Richmond, 1783. 60+ pp.
LOC copy.   18227

U. S. Continental Congress, 1783.
By His Excellency Elias Boudinot. . . . A
Proclamation [Mutiny. June 24, 1783].
Philadelphia, Claypoole, [1783].
Broadside.
LOC copy.   18229

U. S. Continental Congress, 1783.
By the United States of America in
Congress Assembled. A Proclamation,
Declaring the Cessation of Arms [Apr.
11. Dated at Exeter Apr. 24, 1783].
Exeter, [1783.] Broadside.
(The unique original is in poor condition.)
NHHS copy.   18240

U. S. Continental Congress, 1783.
By the United States in Congress
Assembled. A Proclamation, Declaring
the Cessation of Arms [dated Apr. 11,
1783].
Philadelphia, Claypoole, [1783].
Broadside.
LCP copy.   44471

U. S. Continental Congress, 1783.
By the United States of America in
Congress Assembled. A Proclamation,
Declaring the Cessation of Arms [Apr.
11, 1783].
Philadelphia, Claypoole, [1783].
Broadside.
NYPL facsimile copy.   18238

U. S. Continental Congress, 1783.
By the United States of America, in
Congress Assembled. A Proclamation,
Declaring the Cessation of Arms [Apr.
11, 1783].
Providence, Carter, [1783]. Broadside.
RIHS copy.   18241

U. S. Continental Congress, 1783.
By the United States of America in
Congress Assembled. A Proclamation,
Declaring the Cessation of Arms [Apr.
11, 1783].
Richmond, [1783]. Broadside.
LOC copy.   18242

[U. S. Continental Congress, 1783.
By the United States of America in
Congress Assembled. A Proclamation,
Declaring the Cessation of Arms [Apr.
11. Dated at Newcastle, Apr. 15, 1783].
[Wilmington, 1783.] Broadside.]
(no copy located.)   18243

U. S. Continental Congress, 1783.
By the United States in Congress
Assembled, a Proclamation [Indian
Lands. Sept. 22, 1783].
Philadelphia, Claypoole, [1783].
Broadside.
LCP copy.   18244

[U. S. Continental Congress, 1783.
By the United States in Congress
Assembled. A Proclamation
[Thanksgiving, Dec. 11. Dated Oct. 18,
1783].
Philadelphia, 1783. Broadside.]
(Evans assumed a Philadelphia printing
from 18248.)   18247

[U. S. Continental Congress, 1783.
By the United States in Congress
Assembled, A Proclamation [Treaty of
Paris, Sept. 3, 1783].
Annapolis, 1783. Broadside.
(Not in Ford, origin of entry unknown.)
                                    18249

U. S. Continental Congress, 1783.
By the United States in Congress
Assembled, a Proclamation [treaty with
Sweden].
Baltimore, Hayes & Killen, [1783].
Broadside.
LCP copy.   44473

U. S. Continental Congress, 1783.
By the United States in Congress
Assembled, February 17, 1783. Whereas
by the Eighth Article....
[Philadelphia, 1783.] [3] pp.
LOC copy.   18232

U. S. Continental Congress, 1783.
By the United States of America, in
Congress Assembled, March 22d, 1783
[half pay].
[Philadelphia? 1783.] Broadside.
JCB copy.   44474

U. S. Continental Congress, 1784.
By the United States in Congress
Assembled. April 23, 1784. Resolved, That
so much of the Territory.... May 20,
1785.
Hartford, Hudson & Goodwin, [1785].
[4] pp.
CHS copy.   44805

U. S. Continental Congress, 1783.
By the United States in Congress
Assembled. November 1, 1783. The
Committee....
[Philadelphia, 1783.] [2] pp.
AAS copy.   18246

U. S. Continental Congress, 1783.
The Committee, Consisting of Mr. Duane,
Mr. Peters.... [Indian Treaty, Oct. 15,
1783].
[Philadelphia, 1783.] Broadside.
(Printer's copy.)
NL copy.   44475

U. S. Continental Congress, 1783.
The Committee Consisting of Mr. Duane
... and Mr. A. Lee, to whom were
Referred....
[Philadelphia, 1783.] Broadside.
NA copy.   18263

U. S. Continental Congress, 1783.

The Committee, Consisting of Mr. Duane
... and Mr. Lee, to whom were
Referred....
[Philadelphia, 1783.] Broadside.
LOC copy.   18262

U. S. Continental Congress, 1783.
The Committee, to whom were Referred
the Act of the Legislature of Virginia.
[Philadelphia, 1783.] Broadside.
NYPL copy.   18264

U. S. Continental Congress, 1783.
Journal of the United States in Congress
Assembled.... Volume VIII Nov., 1782
- Nov., 1783].
Philadelphia, Claypoole, 1783. 483, [1],
xxxvi pp.
AAS copy.   18266

U. S. Continental Congress, 1783.
Journal of the United States in Congress
Assembled [Nov. 3, 1783 - June 3,
1784].... Volume IX.
Philadelphia, Dunlap, [1784]. 317, xviii.
(The copy reproduced was issued without
the index.)
AAS copy.   18840

U. S. Continental Congress, 1783.
March 18, 1783. Resolved, That it be
Recommended....
[Philadelphia, 1783.] [4] pp.
NA copy.   18268

U. S. Continental Congress, 1783.
An Ordinance to Amend an Ordinance,
Entitled "an Ordinance for Establishing
Courts for the Trial of Piracies" [Mar. 4,
1783].
[New York, 1783.] Broadside.
JCB copy.   20075

U. S. Continental Congress, 1783.
Resolved, That it be Recommended to the
Several States.... a Duty of Five Per
Centum.
[Philadelphia, 1783.] [2] pp.
NA copy.   18269

U. S. Continental Congress, 1783.
Table for the Payment of Principal and
Interest of Loans, Agreeable to the
Resolutions of Congress, of the
Twenty-Eighth day of June, 1780.
Philadelphia, Aitken, 1783. 24 pp.
NYPL copy.   18271

U. S. Continental Congress, 1783.
Tables for the Payment of Principal and
Interest of Loans, Agreeable to the
Resolutions of Congress of the
Twenty-Eighth day of June, 1780.
Philadelphia, Bradford, 1783. [36] pp.
HSP copy.   18272

U. S. Continental Congress, 1784.
By the United States in Congress
Assembled, January 14, 1784. Resolved
Unanimously ... British Subjects....
[Annapolis, 1784.] Broadside.
AAS copy.   44603

U. S. Continental Congress, 1784.
By the United States in Congress
Assembled, March 23, 1784. On the
Report of the Committee of
Qualifications....
[Annapolis, 1784.] Broadside.
NYPL copy.   18824

U. S. Continental Congress, 1784.
By the United States in Congress
Assembled, April 30, 1784. The Trust....
[Annapolis, 1784.] Broadside.
LOC copy.   18825

U. S. Continental Congress, 1784.
By the United States in Congress
Assembled. June 3, 1784. On the
Report....
[Annapolis, 1784.] Broadside.
LOC copy.   18826

U. S. Continental Congress, 1784.
By the United States in Congress
Assembled, November 1, 1783. The
Committee.... April 19, 1784....
[Annapolis, 1784.] [2] pp.
LOC copy.   18827

U. S. Continental Congress, 1784.
The Committee Appointed to Prepare a

Plan for the Temporary Government of
the Western Territory.
[Annapolis, 1784.] Broadside.
HSP copy.   18829

U. S. Continental Congress, 1784.
The Committee Consisting of [blank] to
whom was Referred a Motion [on
certificates]....
[Annapolis? 1784?] Broadside.
NYPL copy.   44604

U. S. Continental Congress, 1784.
The Committee Consisting of Mr.
Beresford ... Indian Affairs....
[Annapolis, 1784.] [3] pp.
(Evans is in error in attributing this to
Jefferson.)
LOC copy.   18830

[U. S. Continental Congress, 1784.
The Committee Consisting of Mr.
M'Henry ... Invalids.
[Annapolis, 1784.] Broadside.]
(No copy located.)   18831

U. S. Continental Congress, 1784.
The Committee Consisting of Mr. Mercer
... Frontier Posts.
[Annapolis, 1784.] Broadside.
NA copy.   18832

[U. S. Continental Congress, 1784.
The Committee Consisting of Mr. Spaight
... Finance.
[Annapolis, 1784.] Broadside.]
(Duplicate of 18826, q. v.)   18833

[U. S. Continental Congress, 1784.
The Committee to whom was
Recommended the Report of a plan for a
Temporary Government of the Western
Territory, have Agreed to the Following
Resolutions....
[Annapolis, 1784.] Broadside.]
(This is a ghost of 18835.)   18834

U. S. Continental Congress, 1784.
The Committee to whom was
Recommitted the Report of a plan for a
Temporary Government of the Western
Territory, have Agreed to the Following
Resolution....
[Annapolis, 1784.] Broadside.
HSP copy.   18835

U. S. Continental Congress, 1784.
The Committee to whom was Referred
Sundry Letters and Papers Relative to
Commercial Matters.
[Annapolis, 1784.] Broadside.
LOC copy.   18836

U. S. Continental Congress, 1784.
The Grand Committee Consisting
of   Appointed ... National Debt....
[Annapolis, 1784.] Broadside.
LOC copy.   18837

U. S. Continental Congress, 1784.
The Grand Committee Consiting of Mr.
Stone ... Penobscot....
[Annapolis, 1784.] Broadside.
LOC copy.   18838

U. S. Continental Congress, 1784.
The Grand Committee to whom was
Referred a Letter of the governor of
Massachusetts, of the 28th of October,
1783.
[Annapolis, 1784.] Broadside.
AAS copy.   18839

U. S. Continental Congress, 1784.
Journal of the Committee of the States
[June - Aug., 1784].
[Philadelphia], Dunlap, 1784. 47 pp.
AAS copy.   18841

U. S. Continental Congress, 1784.
An Ordinance for Ascertaining the Mode
of Locating and Disposing of Lands in the
Western Territory.
[Annapolis, 1784.] [4] pp.
LOC copy.   18842

U. S. Continental Congress, 1784.
A Statement of the National Debt....
April 27, 1784.
Richmond, Dunlap & Hayes, [1784]. 12
pp.
LOC copy.   18844

U. S. Continental Congress, 1784.
The United States in Congress Assembled,
April 27, 1784. Congress Resumed the
Consideration of the Report of the Grand
Committee . . . on the National Debt.
[Philadelphia? 1784.] 4 pp.
AAS copy.   44606

U. S. Continental Congress, 1784.
The United States in Congress Assembled,
April 27, 1784. Congress . . . National
Debt.
[Annapolis, 1784.] Broadside.
(For the 4 p. ed. see Supplement.)
LOC copy.   18845

U. S. Continental Congress, 1784.
The United States, in Congress
Assembled, April 27, 1784. Congress . . .
National Debt.
Boston, Adams & Nourse, 1784. 12 pp.
AAS copy.   18846

U. S. Continental Congress, 1785.
By the United States in Congress
Assembled. February 23, 1785.
Resolved. . . .
[New York, 1785.] Broadside.
NYPL copy.   19281

U. S. Continental Congress, 1785.
By the United States in Congress
Assembled. March 17th, 1785. Whereas it
must Conduce. . . .
[Philadelphia, 1785.] Broadside.
LOC copy.   44806

U. S. Continental Congress, 1785.
By the United States in Congress
Assembled. March 31, 1785. An
Ordinance. . . .
[New York, 1785.] Broadside.
AAS copy.   19282

U. S. Continental Congress, 1785.
By the United States in Congress
Assembled. April 23, 1784. Resolved, That
so much of the Territory. . . .
[New York, 1785.] [4] pp.
AAS copy.   19283

U. S. Continental Congress, 1785.
By the United States in Congress
Assembled. June 7, 1785. Resolved, That
it be. . . .
[New York, 1785.] [2] pp.
NYPL copy.   19284

U. S. Continental Congress, 1785.
By the United States in Congress
Assembled. July 27, 1785. Resolved, That
the Secretary. . . .
[New York, 1785.] Broadside.
AAS copy.   19285

U. S. Continental Congress, 1785.
By the United States in Congress
Assembled, August 17, 1785. . . .
[New York, 1785.] Broadside.
LOC copy.   19286

U. S. Continental Congress, 1785.
By the United States in Congress
Assembled, September 27, 1785. The
Report. . . .
[New York, 1785.] [3] pp.
AAS copy.   19287

U. S. Continental Congress, 1785.
By the United States in Congress
Assembled, September 30, 1785. Resolved,
That it Shall be the Duty. . . .
[New York, 1785.] [2] pp.
AAS copy.   19289

[U. S. Continental Congress, 1785.
By the United States in Congress
Assembled, September 30, 1785. Resolved,
[That the Commissioners. . . .].
[New York, 1785.] [2] pp.]
(This is a duplicate of 19289, q. v.) 19288

[U. S. Continental Congress, 1785.
By the United States in Congress
Assembled, October 3, 1785. . . . Loan
Officers.
[New York, 1785.] Broadside.]
(Not in Ford.)   19290

U. S. Continental Congress, 1785.
By the United States in Congress
Assembled, October 12, 1785. Where as it
is Indispensably. . . .

[New York, 1785.] Broadside.
NYPL copy.   19291

U. S. Continental Congress, 1785.
By the United States in Congress
Assembled, November 2, 1785. On a
Report. . . .
[New York, 1785.] Broadside.
NYPL copy.   19292

U. S. Continental Congress, 1785.
The Committee Appointed to Revise the
System of the War-Office. . . .
[New York? 1785.] Broadside.
NYHS copy.   44807

U. S. Continental Congress. 1785.
The Committee Consisting of   to
Whom was Referred a Motion of Mr.
King . . . Resolve of the Congress of the
23d Day of April, 1784.
[New York, 1785.] Broadside.
LOC copy.   19296

U. S. Continental Congress, 1785.
The Committee Consisting of   to
whom was Referred the Motion of Mr.
Monroe, Submit. . . . [July 13, 1785].
[New York, 1785.] Broadside.
LOC copy.   19301

[U. S. Continental Congress, 1785.
The Committee Consisting of   to
whom were Referred a Letter. . . . March
18, 1785.
[New York, 1785.] Broadside.]
(The unique copy seen by Evans is not
now to be found.)   19300

U. S. Continental Congress, 1785.
The Committee Consisting of [blank] to
whom was Referred a Motion. . . .
[New York, 1785.] Broadside.
LOC copy.   44808

U. S. Continental Congress, 1785.
The Committee Consisting of Mr. Gerry,
Mr. Ellery and Mr. Wilson, to whom was
Referred a Petition . . . of Mr. Oliver
Pollock. . . .
[Philadelphia, 1785.] Broadside.
LOC copy.   44809

U. S. Continental Congress, 1785.
The Committee Consisting of Mr. Gerry,
Mr. Williamson, and Mr. Hardy, to whom
were Referred a Motion.
[New York, 1785.] Broadside.
LOC copy.   19293

U. S. Continental Congress, 1785.
The Committee Consisting of Mr. Hardy,
Mr. Houston, Mr. Read, Mr. Williamson,
and Mr. Holten. . . .
[New York, 1785.] Broadside.
LOC copy.   19294

U. S. Continental Congress, 1785.
The Committee Consisting of Mr. Howell,
Mr. Monroe, Mr. Pinckney, Mr. R. R.
Livingston and Mr. Gardner. . . .
[New York, 1785.] Broadside.
LOC copy.   19295

U. S. Continental Congress, 1785.
The Committee Consisting of Mr.
M'Henry, Mr. Dick and Mr. Williamson,
to whom was Referred a Motion . . .
Respecting Invalids.
[New York, 1785.] Broadside.
LOC copy.   19297

U. S. Continental Congress, 1785.
The Committee Consisting of Mr.
M'Henry, Mr. Read. . . .
[New York, 1785.] Broadside.
LOC copy.   19298

U. S. Continental Congress, 1785.
The Committee Consisting of Mr.
Pinckney, Mr. R.R. Livingston . . . to
whom were Referred a Letter. . . .
[Philadelphia, 1785.] Broadside.
LOC copy.   44810

U. S. Continental Congress, 1785.
The Committee Consisting of Mr.
Williamson, Mr. Stewart and Mr. Hardy,
to whom were Referred a Letter.
[New York, 1785.] Broadside.
LOC copy.   19299

U. S. Continental Congress, 1785.

The Committee of Qualifications Report,
That the Confederation . . . until January
5, 1783.
[Philadelphia, 1785.] Broadside.
(Also entered as 44812, q. v.)   44811

U. S. Continental Congress, 1785.
The Committee of Qualifications Report,
That the Confederation was Ratified. . . .
n.p., [1785]. Broadside.
RIHS copy.   44812

U. S. Continental Congress, 1785.
The Committee to whom was Referred a
Motion of Mr. R. R. Livingston and two
Motions of Mr. Monroe. . . .
[New York, 1785.] Broadside.
LOC copy.   19303

U. S. Continental Congress, 1785.
The Committee to whom were Referred a
Letter from Baron de Steuben . . .
February 5, 1785. . . .
[New York, 1785.] [2] pp.
LOC copy.   19302

U. S. Continental Congress, 1785.
The Committee to whom was Referred the
Letter of the Commissioners . . . to form
Treaties with Indian Tribes. . . .
[New York, 1785]. [2] pp.
LOC copy.   19304

U. S. Continental Congress, 1785.
The Committee to whom was Referred the
Memorial of Mr. P. Landais, Report. . . .
[New York, 1785.] Broadside.
LOC copy.   19305

U. S. Continental Congress, 1785.
The Committee to whom were Referred a
Letter of the [blank] of December from
the Honorable Cyrus Griffin.
[Philadelphia, 1785.] Broadside.
AAS copy.   44813

U. S. Continental Congress, 1785.
The Committee to whom were Referred
the Petition of . . . Kaskaskies. . . .
[Philadelphia, 1785.] Broadside.
LOC copy.   44814

U. S. Continental Congress, 1785.
The Grand Committee, Consisting
of   to whom was Referred a
Motion of Mr. Monroe, for Repealing. . . .
[New York, 1785.] [2] pp.
AAS copy.   19313

U. S. Continental Congress, 1785.
The Grand Committee Consisting of Mr.
Foster. . . .
[New York, 1785.] Broadside.
LOC copy.   19307

U. S. Continental Congress, 1785.
The Grand Committee Consisting of Mr.
Howell. . . . [March 31, 1785].
[New York, 1785.] Broadside.
AAS copy.   19308

[U. S. Continental Congress, 1785.
The Grand Committee Consisting of Mr.
Stone. . . . [February, 1785].
[New York, 1785.] Broadside.]
(The copy reported by Evans can not now
be located.)   19312

U. S. Continental Congress, 1785.
The Grand Committee, to whom was
Recommitted a Report, on the Subject of
Supplies for the year One Thousand Seven
Hundred and Eighty-Five. . . . [July 18,
1785].
[New York, 1785.] Broadside.
LOC copy.   19309

U. S. Continental Congress, 1785.
The Grand Committee to whom was
Recommitted a Report on the Subject of
Supplies for the year One Thousand Seven
Hundred and Ehighty-Five [sic]. . . .
[September, 1785].
[New York, 1785.] Broadside.
LOC copy.   19310

U. S. Continental Congress, 1785.
The Grand Committee, to whom was
Recommitted a Report on the Subject of
Supplies for the year One Thousand Seven
Hundred and Eighty-Five. . . . [Sept. 27,
1785].

[New York, 1785.] Broadside.
LOC copy.   19311

[U. S. Continental Congress, 1785.
The Grand Committee, to whom was
Referred a Letter from the Superintendant
of Finance. . . . [April 15, 1785].
[New York, 1785.] Broadside.]
(No copy located.)   19314

[U. S. Continental Congress, 1785.
Journal of the United States in Congress
Assembled: Containing the Proceedings
from . . . November, 1784. [to Apr. 13,
1785].
[Philadelphia], Dunlap, 1785. 120 pp.]
(A part of 19316 q. v.)   19315

U. S. Continental Congress, 1785.
Journal of the United States in Congress
Assembled: Containing the Proceedings
from . . . November, 1784 [to Nov. 4,
1785].
[Philadelphia], Dunlap, 1785. 368, xxvi
pp.
MHS copy.   19316

U. S. Continental Congress, 1785.
Motion of Mr. Gerry, Seconded by Mr.
Howell.
[Philadelphia, 1785.] Broadside.
LOC copy.   44815

U. S. Continental Congress, 1785.
An Ordinance for Ascertaining the Mode
of Disposing of Lands in the Western
Territory.
[Philadelphia, 1785.] [2] pp.
LOC copy.   44818

U. S. Continental Congress, 1785.
Proclamation. By the United States in
Congress Assembled [Counterfeits. Feb.
2, 1785].
[New York, 1785.] Broadside.
LOC copy.   19327

U. S. Continental Congress, 1785.
Propositions Respecting the Coinage.
[New York, 1785.] [12] pp.
AAS copy.   19328

U. S. Continental Congress, 1785.
A State of the Representation in Congress
. . . Pursuant to the Act of the 17th
August, 1785.
[New York, 1785.] Broadside.
NYPL copy.   19332

U. S. Continental Congress, 1785.
That upon the Supplies Furnished by
Impressment. . . .
[New York, 1785.] Broadside.
LOC copy.   44816

U. S. Continental Congress, 1785.
War-Office, April, 25, 1785. Sir, On the
Memorial of Captain Jesse Grant. . . . The
Committee. . . .
[New York, 1785.] Broadside.
AAS copy.   19334

U. S. Continental Congress, 1785.
War Office. September 12th, 1785. The
Secretary. . . . The Committee. . . .
[New York, 1785.] Broadside.
AAS copy.   19335

U. S. Continental Congress, 1785.
Whereas Doubts have Arose with some of
the Commissioners . . . [Dec. 30, 1785].
[Philadelphia, 1786.] Broadside.
LOC copy.   44986

U. S. Continental Congress, 1786.
An Act for Raising a Further Sum of
Money for the Protection of the Frontiers.
. . . Approved, May second, 1792.
[Philadelphia, 1792.] Broadside.
LOC copy.   20038

U. S. Continental Congress, 1786.
An Address from the United States in
Congress Assembled to the Legislatures.
[New-York, 1786.] [3] pp.
NYPL copy.   20039

U. S. Continental Congress, 1786.
[Address from the United States in
Congress assembled to the Legislatures.
Philadelphia, Dunlap, 1786.]
(Ford: Bib. Notes 553; no copy known.)
                                              44987

U. S. Continental Congress, 1786.
By the United States in Congress
Assembled. January 2, 1786. Ordered,
That the Secretary . . . Report the Number
of States which have Complied. . . . Jan. 4,
1786 . . . the Secretary Reports. . . .
[New York, 1786.] [3] pp.
LOC copy.   20045

U. S. Continental Congress, 1786.
By the United States in Congress
Assembled. Wednesday, May 31, 1786. . . .
Articles of War.
[New York, 1786.] 8 pp.
JCB copy.   44989

[U. S. Continental Congress, 1786.
By the United States in Congress
Assembled, June 27, 1786 [Court of
Appeals].
[New York, 1786.] Broadside.]
(The unique copy in NYSL was lost in the
Albany fire.)   20046

U. S. Continental Congress, 1786.
By the United States in Congress
Assembled, July 14th, 1786 [Delegates].
[New York, 1786.] Broadside.
LOC copy.   20047

U. S. Continental Congress, 1786.
By the United States in Congress
Assembled. August 2, 1786. Resolved,
That for the Services. . . .
[New York, 1786.] [2] pp.
LOC copy.   20048

U. S. Continental Congress, 1786.
By the United States in Congress
Assembled. August 7, 1786. An Ordinance
for the Regulation of Indian Affairs.
[New York, 1786.] [2] pp.
LOC copy.   20049

U. S. Continental Congress, 1786.
By the United States in Congress
Assembled. August 8, 1786. On a
Report. . . .
[New York, 1786.] Broadside.
LOC copy.   20050

U. S. Continental Congress, 1786.
By the United States in Congress
Assembled. September 18, 1786. The
Committee, Consisting of Mr.
Pickney. . . .
[New York, 1786.] Broadside.
LOC copy.   20051

U. S. Continental Congress, 1786.
By the United States, in Congress
Assembled. October 10, 1786. The
Committee Consisting of Mr. Pettit. . . .
[Philadelphia, 1786.] Broadside.
HSP copy.   44988

U. S. Continental Congress, 1786.
By the United States in Congress
Assembled. October 20, 1786. The
Committee Consisting of Mr. Pettit. . . .
[New York, 1786.] Broadside.
LOC copy.   20052

[U. S. Continental Congress, 1786.
By the United States in Congress
Assembled, October 23, 1786. The
Committee Consisting of Mr. Pinckney.

[New York, 1786.] Broadside.]
(Ford 431; not now to be located.)   20053

U. S. Continental Congress, 1786.
The Committee Consisting of Mr.
Johnson, Mr. King . . . to whom was
Referred a Letter . . . of the 16th [August,
1786].
[New York, 1786.] Broadside.
LOC copy.   20057

U. S. Continental Congress, 1786.
The Committee Consisting of Mr.
Johnson, Mr. Pinckney and Mr. Pettit.
[Philadelphia, 1786.] Broadside.
LOC copy.   44990

U. S. Continental Congress, 1786.
The Committee, Consisting of Mr.
Johnson, Mr. Pinckney . . . to Prepare a
Plan of a Temporary Government.
[New York, 1786.] [2] pp.
LOC copy.   20058

U. S. Continental Congress, 1786.

The Committee Consisting of Mr. King,
Mr. Johnson. . . . to whom was Referred
an Act. . . .
[Philadelphia, 1786.] Broadside.
LOC copy.   44991

U. S. Continental Congress, 1786.
The Committee, Consisting of Mr. King,
Mr. Pinckney . . . the System of General
Revenue, Recommended by Congress on
the 18th of April, 1783. . . .
[New York, 1786.] [2] pp.
LOC copy.   20085

U. S. Continental Congress, 1786.
The Committee, Consisting of Mr.
Pinckney, Mr. Dane . . . on Revising the
System . . . for the Settlement of
Accounts. . . .
[New York, 1786.] Broadside.
AAS copy.   20059

U. S. Continental Congress, 1786.
The Committee Consisting of Mr.
Pinckney, Mr. King, Mr. Johnson, Mr.
Grayson and M. Hinchman. . . .
[Philadelphia, 1786.] Broadside.
(No copy located.)   44992

U. S. Continental Congress, 1786.
The Committee Consisting of Mr.
Pinckney, Mr. Monroe . . . Appointed to
form an Ordinance. . . .
[New York, 1786.] [2] pp.
LOC copy.   20060

U. S. Continental Congress, 1786.
The Committee Consisting of Mr. St.
Clair, Mr. Lee . . . to whom was Referred
a Report of the Secretary of War. . . .
[New York, 1786.] [4] pp.
LOC copy.   20061

U. S. Continental Congress, 1786.
The Committee, Consisting of Mr. Smith,
Mr. Long . . . to whom was Committed a
Motion of Mr. King. . . .
[New York, 1786.] Broadside.
LOC copy.   20062

U. S. Continental Congress, 1786.
The Committee to whom a motion of Mr.
Dane was Referred for Considering.
[Philadelphia, 1786.] [2] pp.
LOC copy.   44993

U. S. Continental Congress, 1786.
The Committee to whom was Referred a
Motion of the Delegates of the State of
Connecticut. . . .
[New York, 1786.] Broadside.
AAS copy.   20063

U. S. Continental Congress, 1786.
The Committee to whom was Referred to
the Letter of Governor Henry, Report. . . .
[Philadelphia, 1786.] Broadside.
LOC copy.   44994

U. S. Continental Congress, 1786.
The Grand Committee, Consisting
of _____ to whom was Referred a Motion
of Mr. Monroe. . . .
[New York, 1786.] [2] pp.
LOC copy.   20067

U. S. Continental Congress, 1786.
The Grand Committee, Consisting of
[blank] to whom were . . . Referred a
Motion of Mr. Monroe, Respecting . . .
Western Lands.
[Philadelphia, 1786.] Broadside.
LOC copy.   44995

U. S. Continental Congress, 1786.
The Grand Committee, Consisting of Mr.
Livermore, Mr. Dane . . . Appointed to
Report such Amendments. . . .
[Philadelphia, 1786.] [2] pp.
LOC copy.   44996

U. S. Continental Congress, 1786.
The Grand Committee, Consisting of Mr.
Johnson, Mr. Pinckney . . . to whom were
Referred a Motion of Mr. Monroe, upon
the Subject of the Western Territory.
[Philadelphia, 1786.] Broadside.
LOC copy.   44997

U. S. Continental Congress, 1786.
Impressed, with a Sense of the Sacred
Trust. . . .
[Philadelphia, 1786.] Broadside.
LOC copy.   44998

U. S. Continental Congress, 1786.
Journal of the United States in Congress
Assembled: Containing the Proceedings
from . . . November, 1786, to . . .
November, 1787. Vol. XII.
[New York], 1787. 255, [10] pp.
AAS copy.   20772

U. S. Continental Congress, 1786.
Journal of the United States in Congress
Assembled [Nov. 3, 1785 - Nov. 3, 1786].
. . . Volume XII.
[Philadelphia, Dunlap, [1786]. 267, [1],
xvi pp.
AAS copy.   20068

U. S. Continental Congress, 1786.
Motion of Mr. Dane. Resolved, That the
Geographer. . . . [Western Territory. May 3,
1786].
[New York, 1786.] Broadside.
LOC copy.   20070

U. S. Continental Congress, 1786.
A Motion of Mr. Dane, That a Committee
of Five be Appointed. . . . February 27,
1786.
[New York, 1786.] [2] pp.
LOC copy.   20069

U. S. Continental Congress, 1786.
An Ordinance, &c. [Indian Affairs, July
26, 1786].
[New York, 1786.] Broadside.
LOC copy.   20071

U. S. Continental Congress, 1786.
An Ordinance for Establishing a Board, to
Liquidate . . . all Accounts [Oct. 13,
1786].
[New York, 1786.] Broadside.
LOC copy.   20072

U. S. Continental Congress, 1786.
An Ordinance for the Establishment of
the Mint. . . . September 20, 1786.
[New York, 1786.] [2] pp.
LOC copy.   20073

U. S. Continental Congress, 1786.
An Ordinance for the Establishment of
the Mint [Oct. 16, 1786].
[New York, 1786.] Broadside.
LOC copy.   20074

U. S. Continental Congress, 1786.
The Report of a Committee, Appointed to
Consider whether any and what Measures
[Apr. 18, 1783]. . . .
[New York, 1786.] Broadside.
LOC copy.   20078

U. S. Continental Congress, 1786.
[Resolved, that the Court of Appeals . . .
the sloop Chester. . . .
Philadelphia, Dunlap, 1786.]
(Ford: Bib. Notes 545; no copy known.)
                                             44999

U. S. Continental Congress, 1786.
United States in Congress Assembled.
February 15, 1786. The Committee
Consisting of Mr. King, Mr. Pinckney . . .
Report. . . .
[New York, 1786.] [2] pp.
LOC copy.   20084

U. S. Continental Congress, 1786.
United States in Congress Assembled,
March 3, 1786. The Committee Consisting
of Mr. Kean, Mr. Gorham. . . .
[New York, 1786.] Broadside.
AAS copy.   20086

U. S. Continental Congress, 1786.
Whereas Doubts have Arose with some of
the Commissioners Appointed . . . the
20th of February, 1782. . . .
[Philadelphia, 1786?] Broadside.
(No copy located.)   45000

U. S. Continental Congress, 1786.
Your Committee beg Leave to Report. . . .
[New York, 1786.] Broadside.
LOC copy.   20091

U. S. Continental Congress, 1787.
By the United States in Congress
Assembled, March 23, 1787 [Civil List].
[New York, 1787.] [2] pp.
AAS copy.   20757

U. S. Continental Congress, 1787.

By the United States in Congress
Assembled, April 21st, 1787 [Copper
Coinage].
[New York, 1787.] Broadside.
LOC copy.   20758

[U. S. Continental Congress, 1787.
By the United States in Congress
Assembled, April 21st, 1787 [Western
Lands].
[New York, 1787.] Broadside.]
(Apparently a ghost of Ford 440.)   20759

U. S. Continental Congress, 1787.
By the United States in Congress
Assembled. May 3, 1787 [Report of Board
of Treasury].
[New York, 1787.] Broadside.
LOC ph. copy.   20760

U. S. Continental Congress, 1787.
By the United States in Congress
Assembled, May 7, 1787. An Ordinance
for Settling the Accounts. . . .
[New York, 1787.] Broadside.
AAS copy.   20761

U. S. Continental Congress, 1787.
By the United States in Congress
Assembled. October 3, 1787 [Frontier
Troops].
[New York, 1787.] Broadside.
LOC copy.   20762

U. S. Continental Congress, 1787.
By the United States in Congress
Assembled. October 11, 1787 [Report of
the Board of Treasury].
[New York, 1787.] [2] pp.
AAS copy.   20763

U. S. Continental Congress, 1787.
The Committee Consisting of   to
whom was Referred the Memorial of
Samuel Holden Parsons [July 10, 1787].
[New York, 1787.] Broadside.
LOC copy.   20765

U. S. Continental Congress, 1787.
The Committee, Consisting of Mr.
Carrington, Mr. Varnum . . . to whom was
Referred a Motion of Mr. Carrington for
Revising the Ordinance. . . .
[New York, 1787.] Broadside.
NA copy.   20766

U. S. Continental Congress, 1787.
The Committee, Consisting of Mr. Dane,
Mr. Clark . . . to Consider . . . the Civil
Department. . . .
[New York, 1787.] Broadside.
NA copy.   20767

U. S. Continental Congress, 1787.
The Committee, Consisting of Mr. Dane,
Mr. Hawkins . . . to whom were Referred
the Report of the Secretary of War [Oct. 12,
1787].
[New York, 1787.] Broadside.
NA copy.   20768

[U. S. Continental Congress. 1787.
The Committee Consisting of Mr.
Johnson, Mr. Pinckney . . . Appointed to
Prepare a Plan [Apr. 26, 1787].
[New York, 1787.] Broadside.]
(No copy located.)   20769

U. S. Continental Congress, 1787.
The Committee Consisting of Mr.
Kearney, Mr. Carrington . . . to whom
was Referred the Report of the Secretary
of War [Aug. 3, 1787].
[New York, 1787.] [4] pp.
LOC copy.   20770

U. S. Continental Congress, 1787.
An Ordinance for the Government of the
Territory . . . Northwest of the River Ohio
[second reading].
[Philadelphia, Dunlap, 1787.] [2] pp.
LOC copy.   45181

U. S. Continental Congress, 1787.
Schedule of the Requisitions on the
Several States. . . . 1782 . . . 1786 [January
1, 1787].
[New York, 1787.] Broadside.
LOC copy.   20784

[U. S. Continental Congress, 1787.
Schedule of Requisitions on the Several
States [for 1787. Dated Sept. 25].

[New York, 1787.] Broadside.]
(Ford 448. No copy located.)   20785

U. S. Continental Congress, 1787.
A State of the Representatives in
Congress for the Month of. . . . Pursuant
to the Act of 17 August, 1785.
[New York, 1787.] Broadside.
LOC copy.   20787

U. S. Continental Congress, 1787.
We the People of the United States [Printed
for the N. Y. Convention].
[Poughkeepsie, 1788.] 20 pp.
NYPL ph. copy.   21524

U. S. Continental Congress, 1787.
United States in Congress Assembled,
April 13, 1787. The Following Letter. . . .
[New York, 1787.] [3] pp.
LOC copy.   20776

U. S. Continental Congress, 1788.
By the United States in Congress
Assembled. February 12, 1788. On the
Report. . . .
[New York, 1788.] Broadside?
(No copy located.)   45387

U. S. Continental Congress, 1788.
By the United States in Congress
Assembled, June 11, 1788. On the Report
of a Committee, Consisting of Mr. Dane,
Mr. Hamilton. . . .
[New York, 1788.] Broadside.
LOC copy.   21512

U. S. Continental Congress, 1788.
By the United States in Congress
Assembled, June 20, 1788. The Committee
. . . on the Missisippi [sic].
[New York, 1788.] Broadside.
NYPL copy.   21514

U. S. Continental Congress, 1788.
By the United States in Congress
Assembled. July 9, 1788. A Supplement to
an Ordinance Entitled "An Ordinance for
. . . the Western Territory."
[New York, 1788.] Broadside.
NYPL copy.   21515

U. S. Continental Congress, 1788.
By the United States in Congress
Assembled, Wednesday, August 20, 1788.
The Committee, Consisting of Mr. Clark,
Mr. Dane, Mr. Williamson. . . .
[New York, 1788.] [2] pp.
AAS copy.   21516

U. S. Continental Congress, 1788.
By the United States in Congress
Assembled, September 13, 1788. Whereas
the Convention. . . .
[New York, 1788.] Broadside.
LOC copy.   21518

U. S. Continental Congress, 1787.
The United States in Congress Assembled,
Friday, September 28, 1787.
Philadelphia, Dunlap & Claypoole,
[1787]. Broadside.
LOC copy.   20790

U. S. Continental Congress, 1788.
By the United States in Congress
Assembled, a Proclamation [Cherokee
lands. Sept. 1, 1788].
[New York, 1788.] Broadside.
NYPL copy.   21517

U. S. Continental Congress, 1788.
The Committee, Consisting of [blank] to
whom was Referred the Memorial of
George Morgan . . . on the River
Mississippi. . . .
[New York, 1788.] Broadside.
NYPL copy.   21513

U. S. Continental Congress, 1788.
The Committee Consisting of [Blank] to
whom was Referred the Report of the
Board of Treasury [Aug. 20, 1788.]
[New York, 1788.] [4] pp.
LOC copy.   21519

U. S. Continental Congress, 1788.
The Committee Consisting of Mr.
Carrington, Mr. Edwards . . . to whom
were Referred the Ratifications. . . .
[New York, 1788.] Broadside.
LOC copy.   21520

U. S. Continental Congress, 1788.
The Committee, Consisting of Mr.
Wadsworth, Mr. Irwine . . . to whom was
Referred the Petition of the French [May
5, 1788].
[New York, 1788.] Broadside.
LOC copy.   21521

U. S. Continental Congress, 1788.
Journal of the United States in Congress
Assembled: Containing the Proceedings
from . . . November, 1787. To . . .
November, 1788. Volume XIII.
[Philadelphia], Dunlap, [1788]. 170, [2],
xcviii, xi pp.
AAS copy.   21526

U. S. Continental Congress, 1788.
United States in Congress Assembled.
May 22d, 1788. The Committee Consisting
of Mr. Dane, Mr. Williamson. . . .
[New York, 1788.] Broadside.
NYPL copy.   21534

U. S. Declaration of Independence.
In Congress, July 4, 1776. A Declaration.
n. p., [1776]. Broadside.
(2 columns, 70 lines in first; Walsh 5.)
NYHS copy.   43196

U. S. Declaration of Independence.
In Congress, July 4, 1776. A Declaration.
n. p., [1776]. Broadside, 2 columns.
LCP copy.   15157

U. S. Declaration of Independence.
In Congress, July 4, 1776. A Declaration.
n. p., [1776]. Broadside.
(2 columns, 65 lines in first; Walsh 6.)
Mrs. Joseph Carson copy.   43197

U. S. Declaration of Independence.
In Congress, July 4, 1776. A Declaration.
n. p., [1776]. Broadside.
(2 columns, with line of 65 type ornaments
between; Walsh 11.)
BPL copy.   43198

U. S. Declaration of Independence.
In Congress, July 4, 1776. Declaration.
n. p., [1776]. Broadside.
(2 columns, with 58 lines in the first;
Walsh 14.)
AAS copy.   43199

U. S. Declaration of Independence.
In Congress, July 4, 1776. Declaration.
n. p., [1776]. [2] pp.
(Walsh 16; no copy located.)   43200

U. S. Declaration of Independence.
In Congress, July 4, 1776. A Declaration.
[Boston, 1776.] Broadside, 2 columns.
MHS copy.   15162

U. S. Declaration of Independence.
In Congress, July 4, 1776. A Declaration.
Boston, Gill, Powars & Willis, [1776].
Broadside.
MHS copy.   15161

U. S. Declaration of Independence.
In Congress, July 4, 1776. Declaration.
[Exeter, 1776.] Broadside.
(Walsh 15.)
AAS ph. copy.   43201

U. S. Declaration of Independence.
In Congress, July 4, 1776. A Declaration.
[London? 1776?] Broadside.
(Engraved oval portrait of John Hancock.)
JCB copy.   43202

U. S. Declaration of Independence.
In Congress, July 4, 1776. A Declaration.
New York, Gaine, [1776]. Broadside.
NYHS copy.   43203

U. S. Declaration of Independence.
White-Plains, July 9, 1776. In Convention.
New York, Holt, [1776]. Broadside.
NYPL copy.   15158

U. S. Declaration of Independence.
In Congress, July 4, 1776. A Declaration.
Newport, [1776]. Broadside.
RIHS copy.   15160

U. S. Declaration of Independence.
In Congress, July 4, 1776. A Declaration.
Newport, June 13, 1776. Broadside.
AAS copy.   15159

U. S. Declaration of Independence.
In Congress, July 4, 1776. A Declaration.
Philadelphia, Dunlap, [1776]. Broadside.
MHS copy.   15155

U. S. Declaration of Independence.
In Congress, July 4, 1776. A Declaration.
[Philadelphia], Dunlap, [1776].
Broadside.
APS copy.   15156

U. S. Declaration of Independence.
In Congress, July 4, 1776. A Declaration.
[Salem?, 1776]. Broadside, 4 columns.
EI copy.   15164

U. S. Declaration of Independence.
In Congress, July 4, 1776. A Declaration.
Salem, Russell, [1776]. Broadside.
AAS copy.   15163

U. S. Declaration of Independence.
In Congress, July 4, 1776. . . . In Congress,
January 18, 1777. . . .
Baltimore, [1777]. Broadside.
NYPL copy.   15650

U. S. Declaration of Independence.
The Declaration of Independence and
Constitution of the United States, to
which is Prefixed the Constitution of the
State of New-York.
New York, Buel, 1796. 37 pp.
AAS copy.   31404

U. S. Declaration of Independence.
The Declaration of American
Independence.
Richmond, Va., Jones & Dixon, 1799. 40
pp.
VaU copy.   36514

U. S. Dept. of Foreign Affairs, 1785.
Office for Foreign Affairs, 13th May,
1785. The Secretary. . . .
[New York, 1785.] Broadside.
AAS copy.   19318

U. S. Dept. of Foreign Affairs, 1785.
Office for Foreign Affairs, July 4, 1785.
The Secretary. . . .
[New York, 1785.] 9 pp.
NYPL copy.   19319

U. S. Dept. of Foreign Affairs, 1785.
Office for Foreign Affairs, September 19,
1785. The Secretary. . . .
[New York, 1785.] Broadside.
AAS copy.   19320

U. S. Dept. of Foreign Affairs, 1785.
Office for Foreign Affairs, 29th
September, 1785. The Secretary. . . .
[New York, 1785.] [4] pp.
LOC copy.   19321

U. S. Dept. of Foreign Affairs, 1785.
Office for Foreign Affairs, 7th October,
1785. The Secretary. . . .
[New York, 1785.] Broadside.
LOC copy.   19322

U. S. Dept. of Foreign Affairs, 1785.
Office for Foreign Affairs, October 13,
1785. The Secretary. . . .
[New York, 1785.] Broadside.
LOC copy.   19324

U. S. Dept. of Foreign Affairs, 1785.
Office for Foreign Affairs, 20th October,
1785. The Secretary. . . .
[New York, 1785.] [3] pp.
LOC copy.   19325

U. S. Dept. of Foreign Affairs, 1785.
The Secretary of the United States for the
Department of Foreign Affairs, to whom
was Referred. . . .
[New York, 1785.] [2] pp.
LOC copy.   19323

U. S. Dept. of Foreign Affairs, 1785.
State of the Duties Payable by Vessels
of the United States. . . .
New York, Childs, [1785]. 19 pp.
LOC copy.   19331

U. S. Dept. of Foreign Affairs, 1787.
Office for Foreign Affairs. 6th April, 1787
[Treaty with Gt. Brit.].
[New York, 1787.] [2] pp.
LOC copy.   20775

U. S. Dept. of Justice, 1790.
Report of the Attorney-General. Read in
the House of Representatives, December
31, 1790.
[Philadelphia], Childs & Swaine, [1791].
[2], 34 pp.
AAS copy.   23908

U. S. Dept. of Justice, 1790.
Report of the Attorney-General. Read in
the House of Representatives, December
31, 1790 [Second Edition].
[Philadelphia], Childs & Swaine, [1791].
[2], 32 pp.
AAS copy.   23909

U. S. Dept. of Justice, 1790.
Richmond, March 26, 1790. It Having
Been Provided. . . . Edward Carrington,
Marshall.
[Richmond, 1790.] Broadside.
LOC copy.   22999

U. S. Dept. of Justice, 1794.
No. I. Philadelphia, February 7th, 1794.
Sir, I have Considered. . . .
[Philadelphia, 1794.] Broadside.
(No copy located.)   47281

U. S. Dept. of Justice, 1794.
No. II. Philadelphia, March 14th, 1794.
Sir, I have. . . .
[Philadelphia, 1794.] Broadside.
(No copy located.)   47282

U. S. Dept. of Justice, 1795.
Report of the Attorney General, of Fees
and Regulations . . . in the Courts. . . .
Published by Order of the House.
Philadelphia, Childs, [1795]. 21 pp.
AAS copy.   29761

U. S. Dept. of Justice, 1796.
Letter from the Attorney General,
Accompanying his Report on the Petition
of Sundry Inhabitants of the County of St.
Clair. . . . 10th May, 1796. . . . Published
by Order of the House.
[Philadelphia, 1796.] 8 pp.
AAS copy.   31429

U. S. Dept. of Justice, 1796.
Letter from the Attorney-General,
Accompanying his Report on the
Resolution of the Eighth Ultimo. . . . 5th
May, 1796, Committed. . . . 22d December
1796, Committed. . . . Published by Order
of the House.
[Philadelphia, 1796.] 6 pp.
AAS copy.   31430

U. S. Dept. of Justice, 1796.
(Made the 26th January, 1796.) Letter and
Report of the Attorney General, to whom
was Referred the Petition of James
Mackey. Published by Order of the House.
[Philadelphia, 1796.] 8 pp.
AAS copy.   31428

U. S. Dept. of Justice, 1796.
Report of the Attorney General to to [!]
Congress; Containing a Collection of
Charters. . . . Printed by Order of the
Senate.
Philadelphia, Fenno, 1796. 171 pp.
AAS copy.   31431

U. S. Dept. of Justice, 1797.
Letter from the Attorney-General
Accompanying his Report on the Petition
of Fanny Forsyth. . . . 13th January 1797.
. . . Published by Order of the House.
[Philadelphia, 1797.] 7 pp.
AAS copy.   33062

U. S. Dept. of Justice, 1797.
Letter from the Attorney General,
Inclosing his Report on the Memorial of
John Hobby . . . 27th February, 1797. . . .
Published by Order of the House.
[Philadelphia, 1797.] [4] pp.
AAS copy.   33061

U. S. Dept. of State, 1790.
Report of the Secretary of State, on the
Subject of Establishing a Uniformity in
the Weights, Measures and Coins.
New York, Childs & Swaine, 1790. 21 pp.
LOC copy.   22994

U. S. Dept. of State, 1790.
Report of the Secretary of State, on the
Subject of Establishing a Uniformity in

the Weights, Measures and Coins.
New York, Childs & Swaine, 1790. pp.
[1]-21, [1], 21-22.
LOC copy.   22995

U. S. Dept. of State, 1790.
Report of the Secretary of State, on the
Subject of Establishing a Uniformity in
the Weights, Measures and Coins.
New York, Childs & Swaine, 1790. 22 pp.
LOC copy.   22996

U. S. Dept. of State, 1790.
Report of the Secretary of State, on the
Subject of Establishing a Uniformity in
the Weights, Measures and Coins.
New York, Childs & Swaine, 1790. 49 pp.
AAS copy.   22997

U. S. Dept. of State, 1790.
Report of the Secretary of State, on the
Subject of Establishing a Uniformity in
the Weights, Measures and Coins.
New York, Childs & Swaine, 1790 (1791).
52, [1] pp.
BA copy.   23910

U. S. Dept. of State, 1790.
The Secretary of State, to whom was
Referred . . . the Letter of John H.
Mitchell. . . . April 14, 1790.
[New York, 1790.] [2] pp.
LOC copy.   23001

U. S. Dept. of State, 1791.
Report of the Secretary of State, on the
Subject of the Cod and Whale Fisheries
. . . February 1, 1791.
Philadelphia, Childs & Swaine, 1791. 28
pp.
AAS copy.   23911

U. S. Dept. of State, 1791.
Report of the Secretary of State, on the
Subject of the Cod and Whale Fisheries.
. . . February 1st, 1791. Published by Order
of the Senate.
Philadelphia, Fenno, 1791. 34 pp., 3
charts.
NYPL copy.   23912

U. S. Dept. of State, 1791.
Report of the Secretary of State, to the
President of the United States, of the
Quantity and Situation of the Lands not
Claimed by the Indians. . . . November 10,
1791.
[Philadelphia, 1791.] 8 pp.
AAS copy.   23913

[U. S. Dept. of State, 1791.
Report on Privileges and Restrictions on
the Commerce of the United States, in
Foreign Countries. . . . February 14, 1791.
Philadelphia, Childs & Swaine, 1791.]
(Apparently a ghost of 26339.)   23915

U. S. Dept. of State, 1791.
The Secretary of State, to whom was
Referred, by the House of Representatives
of the United States, the Petition of Jacob
Isaack. . . . November 21st, 1791.
[Philadelphia, 1791.] Broadside.
LCP copy.   23919

U. S. Dept. of State, 1792.
Report of the Secretary of State, on the
Subject of the Cod and Whale Fisheries
. . . Feb. 1, 1791.
Philadelphia, Childs & Swaine, 1792.
45 pp.
LOC copy.   24924

U. S. Dept. of State, 1793.
A Message . . . Relative to France and
Great Britain, Delivered December 5,
1793.
Philadelphia, Childs & Swaine, 1793. 102,
[2], 116, 32 pp.
(No copy located has the pagination given
by Evans.)
AAS copy.   26334

U. S. Dept. of State, 1793.
Philadelphia, January 8th, 1793. Sir, I
have the Honor to . . . Report . . . the
Assays . . . on the Gold and Silver Coins.
. . .
[Philadelphia, 1793.] [2] pp.
JCB copy.   26338

U. S. Dept. of State, 1793.
Philadelphia, January 8th, 1793. Sir, I

have the Honor. . . .
[Philadelphia, 1793.] 2 leaves.
LOC copy.   46905

U. S. Dept. of State, 1793.
Report of the Secretary of State, on the
Privileges and Restrictions on the
Commerce of the United States in Foreign
Countries.
Philadelphia, Childs & Swaine, 1793. 20
pp.
AAS copy.   26339

U. S. Dept. of State, 1794.
A Letter and Instructions from Sir
William Scott. . . . 22nd Nov. 1794.
[Philadelphia, 1794.] 8 pp.
LCP copy.   47283

U. S. Dept. of State, 1794.
Letter from the Secretary of State,
Accompanying an Address from the
Representatives of the French People. . . .
April 22d, 1794.
[Philadelphia, 1794.] [2] pp.
AAS copy.   27926

U. S. Dept. of State, 1794.
A Message of the President . . . Enclosing
Three Letters from the Minister
Plenipotentiary. . . . Published by Order of
the House [Apr. 4, 1794].
Philadelphia, Childs & Swaine, 1794. 15
pp.
AAS copy.   27916

[U. S. Dept. of State, 1794.
A Message from the President. . . .
Transmitting a Copy of a Letter from the
Minister Plenipotentiary of his Britannic,
in Answer to a Letter. . . . May 23, 1794.
Philadelphia, Childs & Swaine, 1794.]
(A description of 27893, q.v.)   27915

U. S. Dept. of State, 1794.
A Message from the President . . .
Transmitting a Letter from the Secretary
of State to the Minister Plenipotentiary of
his Britannic Majesty, with an enclosure
. . . Dated 22d May, 1794. Published by
order of the House.
Philadelphia, Childs & Swaine, 1794. 20
pp.
AAS copy.   27914

U. S. Dept. of State, 1794.
A Message of the President . . .
Transmitting a Report of the Secretary of
State of such Laws. . . . Published by
Order of the House [Dec. 30, 1794].
Philadelphia, Childs & Swaine, 1794. 12
pp.
AAS copy.   27918

U. S. Dept. of State, 1794.
A Message of the President . . .
Transmitting a Report of the Secretary of
State upon the Several Complaints. . . .
Published by Order of the House [Mar. 5,
1794].
Philadelphia, Childs & Swaine, 1794. 8 pp.
AAS copy.   27917

U. S. Dept. of State, 1794.
A Message from the President.
Transmitting Certain Documents Relative
to Hostile Threats. . . . Published by
Order of the House [May 20, 1794].
Philadelphia, Childs & Swaine, 1794. 24
pp.
AAS copy.   27913

U. S. Dept. of State, 1794.
Philadelphia, January 21st, 1794. Sir, In
Pursuance of an Instruction. . . .
[Philadelphia, 1794.] [2] pp.
LOC copy.   27927

U. S. Dept. of State, 1794.
Philadelphia, Saturday, 7th June, 1794.
Sir, Having in Conformity. . . .
[Philadelphia, 1794.] 16 pp.
AAS copy.   27924

U. S. Dept. of State, 1794.
Rule as to the Sailing of Vessels of War of
the Belligerent Nations from the United
States. . . . June 18th, 1794.
[Philadelphia, 1794.] Broadside.
AAS copy.   27929

[U. S. Dept. of State, 1794.
The Secretary of the United States for the

Department of Foreign Affairs . . .
Reports. . . .
[Philadelphia, 1794.] 62 pp.]
(No copy located.)   27929

U. S. Dept. of State, 1795.
Letter from the Secretary of State,
Enclosing the Reports of the Late and
Present Director of the Mint. . . . 14th
December, 1795. Committed.
Philadelphia, Baileys, 1795. 14 pp.
AAS copy.   31433

U. S. Dept. of State, 1796.
Department of State, April 16, 1796. The
Secretary of State Requests. . . .
[Philadelphia? 1796.] 13 pp.
(Not located, 1968.)   47954

U. S. Dept. of State, 1796.
Letter from the Secretary of State,
Inclosing the Estimates. . . . 7th April,
1796. Committed. . . . Published by Order
of the House.
[Philadelphia, 1796.] 11 pp.
AAS copy.   31432

U. S. Dept. of State, 1797.
Congress of the United States. In Senate,
January the 20th, 1797. The Following
Message from the President of the
United States, was Read, Communicating
the Copy of a Letter from the Secretary
. . . to the Minister . . . to . . . France.
[Philadelphia, 1797.] 104 pp.
AAS copy.   33050

U. S. Dept. of State, 1797.
A Letter from Mr. Pickering, Secretary of
State, to Mr. Pinckney.
Richmond, Va., Nicolson, [1797]. 93 pp.
VaSL copy.   33064

U. S. Dept. of State, 1797.
A Letter from Mr. Pickering, Secretary
. . . of State . . . to Mr. Pinckney.
Stockbridge, Mass., Rosseter & Willard,
1797. 98, [6] pp.
(No copy located.)   33065

U. S. Dept. of State, 1797.
Letter from Mr. Pickering, Secretary of
State, to the Chevalier de Yrujo. . . .
August 8th, 1797.
[Trenton, N. J., 1797.] 37 pp.
AAS copy.   33067

U. S. Dept. of State, 1797.
Letter from the Secretary of State
Inclosing a Report of the Director of the
Mint. . . . 8th December, 1797. . . .
Published by Order of the House.
[Philadelphia, 1797.] pp. [123]-141.
AAS copy.   33068

U. S. Dept. of State, 1797.
Letter from the Secretary of State to
Charles C. Pinckney. . . . 15th of
November, 1796.
New York, Hopkins, Webb & Co., 1797.
54 pp.
NYHS copy.   33063

U. S. Dept. of State, 1797.
Message from the President of the United
States Transmitting a Report . . . from the
Secretary of State, of the Depredations
Committed on the Commerce of the
United States. . . . June 22, 1797. . . .
Published by Order of the House.
Philadelphia, Ross, [1797]. 10, [148] pp.
AAS copy.   33053

U. S. Dept. of State, 1797.
Message from the President of the United
States, Transmitting a Report . . . from
the Secretary of State Relative to . . . the
Boundary Line between the United States
and East and West-Florida. June 12th,
1797. . . . Published by Order of the House.
[Philadelphia, 1797.] 36 pp.
AAS copy.   33052

U. S. Dept. of State, 1797.
Report of the Secretary of State, on the
Memorial of Antonia Carmichael. . . . 23d
February, 1797. . . . Published by Order of
the House.
[Philadelphia, 1797.] 8 pp.
AAS copy.   33069

U. S. Dept. of State, 1797.
Report of the Secretary of State, on the

Memorial of Antonia Carmichael. . . . 22d November, 1797. . . . Published by Order of the House.
[Philadelphia, 1797.] 8 pp.
AAS copy. 33070

U. S. Dept. of State, 1797.
Report of the Secretary of State on the Memorial of Sundry Citizens. . . . 27th February, 1797. . . . Published by Order of the House.
[Philadelphia, 1797.] 9, [57] pp.
AAS copy. 33071

U. S. Dept. of State, 1798.
. . . 1st September, 1798. Sir, Annexed is a Copy. . . .
[Philadelphia? 1798.] Broadside.
NYHS copy. 48718

U. S. Dept. of State, 1798.
. . . Instructions for the Private Armed Vessels of the United States.
[Philadelphia, 1798.] 8 pp.
AAS copy. 34695

U. S. Dept. of State, 1798.
Instructions to Charles Cotesworth Pinckney, John Marshall and Elbridge Gerry.
Philadelphia, Cobbett, 1798. 15, 71 pp.
AAS copy. 48719

U. S. Dept. of State, 1798.
Instructions to Charles Cotesworth Pinckney, John Marshall and Elbridge Gerry.
Philadelphia, Way & Groff, 1798. 20 pp.
AAS copy. 34837

U. S. Dept. of State, 1798.
Instructions to the Envoys Extraordinary. . . . Published by the Secretary of State . . . 22d June, 1798.
Philadelphia, Ross, [1798]. 131 pp.
(There is another issue with "Philadelphia" in large caps.)
AAS copy. 34838

[U. S. Dept. of State, 1798.
A Letter from Mr. Pickering, Secretary of State, to Mr. Pinckney.
Richmond, Va., Nicolson, [1798]. 93 pp.]
(A ghost of 33064, q. v.) 34840

U. S. Dept. of State, 1798.
Letter from the Secretary of State, Accompanying a Report and Abstract of all the Returns of Registered American Seamen. . . . 1st March, 1798. Referred. . . . Published by Order of the House. . . .
Philadelphia, Way & Groff, [1798]. 55 pp.
AAS copy. 34841

[U. S. Dept. of State, 1798.
Passport & Roll d'Equipage.
Newburyport, March, 1797.]
(Imprint assumed from adv.
"Just printed" in Independent Herald, July 27, 1797.) 34843

[U. S. Dept. of State, 1798.
Passport and Roll of Equipage . . . 6th of February, 1798.
[Philadelphia? 1798.] Broadside.]
(No copy located.) 34842

[U. S. Dept. of State, 1798.
Passport and Roll of Equipage.
Portland, Me., Rand, 1798.]
(Impring assumed by Evans from adv.
"For sale at this office" in Oriental Trumpet, Jan. 4, 1798.) 34844

[U. S. Dept. of State, 1798.
Passport and Roll of Equipage.
Wiscasset, Hoskins & Scott, 1798.]
(Imprint assumed by Evans from adv.
"Just Published, and for Sale at this Office," Wiscasset Telegraph, Jan. 12, 1798.) 34846

[U. S. Dept. of State, 1798.
Role d'Equipage.
Wilmington, Del., Smyth, 1798.]
(Imprint assumed by Evans from adv.) 34845

U. S. Dept. of State, 1798.
Verhaltungsbefehle an Charles Cotesworth Pinckney.
Philadelphia, Sweetzer, 1798. 19 pp.
(The pagination given by Evans is that for

34818, bound next to it.)
APS copy. 34839

[U. S. Dept. of State, 1799.
Copies of the Communications Relative to our Affairs with France, with a Report of the Secretary of State, Submitted to Congress January, 1799.
[Philadelphia, 1799.] 168 pp.]
(This item recorded by Evans has not been identified.) 36512

U. S. Dept. of State, 1799.
Letter from the Secretary of State, Accompanying his Report on the Claim of John Brown Cutting. . . . 27th February, 1799. Read. . . . Printed by Order of the House. . . .).
Philadelphia, Way & Groff, [1799]. 23 pp.
AAS copy. 36531

U. S. Dept. of State, 1799.
Letter from the Secretary of State Inclosing Abstracts of all the Returns. . . . 10th December, 1799. . . .
[Philadelphia], [1799]. 20, 16 pp., 8 folded tables.
AAS copy. 36532

U. S. Dept. of State, 1799.
Message from the President . . . Accompanying a Report of the Secretary of State . . . 18th January, 1799.
n. p., n. d. 16 pp.
AAS copy. 36548

U. S. Dept. of State, 1799.
Message from the President . . . Accompanying a Report of the Secretary of State. . . . 21st January, 1799. . . . Published by Order of the House. . . .
Philadelphia, Fenno, 1798 [!]. [2], 45 pp.
AAS copy. 36546

U. S. Dept. of State, 1799.
Message from the President . . . Accompanying a Report of the Secretary of State. . . . 21st January, 1799. . . . Published by Order of the House. . . .
Philadelphia, Fenno, 1799. [2], 45, [2] pp.
AAS copy. 36547

U. S. Dept. of State, 1799.
Standing Instructions to Consuls. . . . [24 Jany. 1800].
[Philadelphia, 1799?] [2] pp.
MHS copy. 48977

U. S. Dept. of State, 1799.
To the President of the United States, the Secretary of State Respectfully Submits . . . January 18, 1799.
[Philadelphia, 1799.] 45, [2] pp.
(This is 36547 without the tipped-on message of transmittal.)
AAS copy. 36592

U. S. Dept. of State, 1800.
Letter from the Secretary of State, Inclosing Abstracts . . . of Registered Seamen. . . . 12th December, 1800. . . . Published by Order of the House.
[Washington? 1800.] 16 (i.e. 15) pp., 1 folding table.
AAS copy. 38756

U. S. Dept. of State, 1800.
Letter from the Secretary of State, Inclosing his Report . . . of the Twenty-Eighth Ultimo. 1st April, 1800. . . . (Published by Order of the House. . . .)
[Philadelphia, 1800.] 6 pp.
AAS copy. 38757

U. S. Dept. of State, 1800.
. . . Philadelphia, April 30, 1800. Sir, I Inclose. . . .
[Philadelphia, 1800.] 15 pp.
AAS copy. 38727

U. S. Inspector General's Office, 1776
see
U. S. Laws, Statutes, etc., 1776

[U. S. Inspector-General's Office, 1779.
Regulations for the Order and Discipline of the Troops.
Hartford, Hudson & Goodwin, [1779]. 138, [6] pp., 8 plates.]
(A ghost of 17774.) 16628

U. S. Inspector-General's Office, 1779.
Regulations for the Order and Discipline of the Troops.
Philadelphia, Steiner & Cist, 1779. 154, [9] pp., 8 plates.
AAS copy. 16627

U. S. Inspector-General's Office, 1781.
Regulations for the Order and Discipline of the Troops of the United States.
Boston, Fleets, 1781. 110+ pp.
(The only known copy is imperfect.)
AAS copy. 44068

U. S. Inspector-General's Office, 1782.
Regulations for the Order and Discipline of the Troops of the United States.
Boston, Fleets, 1782. 112 pp.
Boston Univ. copy. 44278

U. S. Inspector-General's Office, 1782.
Regulations for the Order and Discipline of the Troops.
Hartford, Hudson & Goodwin, [1782]. 89, [7] pp., 8 plates.
AAS copy. 17774

U. S. Inspector-General's Office, 1782.
Regulations for the Order and Discipline of the Troops of the United States. Part I.
Hartford, Hudson & Goodwin, [1782?] 138, [6] pp., 8 folding plates.
(The only known copy could not be reproduced.) 44279

U. S. Inspector-General's Office, 1782.
Regulations &. . . . Of the Arms. . . .
[Philadelphia, 1782.] 77, [1], iv pp., 8 plates.
HSP copy. 17773

[U. S. Inspector-General's Office, 1783.
Regulations for the Order and Discipline of the Troops.
Boston, Fleet, 1784.]
(Title from an adv.) 18843

U. S. Inspector-General's Office, 1783.
Regulations for the Order and Discipline of the Troops.
Hartford, Patten, [1783]. 107, [1] pp. 8 folding plates.
AAS copy. 18267

U. S. Inspector-General's Office, 1785.
Regulations for the Order and Discipline of the Troops.
Philadelphia, Cist, 1785. [4], 151, [8] pp., 8 plates.
(No perfect copy located.)
NYPL copy. 19329

U. S. Inspector-General's Office, 1786.
Regulations for the Order and Discipline of the Troops. Part I.
Philadelphia, Oswald, 1786. 143 pp.
National Library of Medicine copy. 20077

U. S. Inspector-General's Office, 1787.
Regulations for the Order and Discipline of the Troops of the United States. . . .
Boston, Fleets, 1787. 112 pp.
(The Evans entry is from an adv.)
AAS copy. 20782

U. S. Inspector-General's Office, 1787.
Regulations for the Order and Discipline of the Troops of the United States.
Hartford, Hudson & Goodwin, [1787].
138, [6] pp., 8 plates.
(The title given by Evans came from adv. in the Conn. Courant, Mar. 19, 1787. The only copy located is incomplete.)
AAS copy. 20780

U. S. Inspector-General's Office, 1787.
Regulations for the Order and Discipline of the Troops of the United States. . . .
Fifth Edition Revised and Rendered Conformable to the New York Establishment.
New York, Greenleaf, 1787. 80 pp, 1 plate.
NYPL copy. 20781

U. S. Inspector-General's Office, 1787.
[Rules and Articles for the government of the troops as of May 31, 1786.
New York, Swaine, 1787.]
(No copy known.) 45184

U. S. Inspector-General's Office, 1787.
Rules and Articles for the Better Government of the Troops.

Richmond, Davis, 1787. 22 pp.
VaHS copy.   45183

[U. S. Inspector-General's Office, 1788.
Baron Steuben's Regulations.
Salem, Dabney & Cushing, 1788.]
("To be sold," Salem Mercury, May 6,
1788; "for sale," ibid, Aug. 26.)   21531

U. S. Inspector-General's Office, 1788.
Regulations for the Order and Discipline
of the Troops of the United States. . . .
First Worcester Edition.
Worcester, Thomas, 1788. 96 pp., 2
folding plates.
AAS copy.   21530

[U. S. Inspector-General's Office, 1790.
Regulations for the Order and Discipline
of the Troops of the United States.
Boston, Fleets, 1790.]
(Entry from an adv.)   22990

[U. S. Inspector-General's Office, 1790.
Regulations for the Order and Discipline
of the Troops of the United States.
Fayetteville, Howard & Roulstone for
Sibley, 1790. 72 pp.]
(Weeks, p. 70; not now to be found.) 22991

[U. S. Inspector-General's Office, 1790.
Regulations for the Order and Discipline
of the Troops of the United States.
New York, Gaine, 1790.]
("Just published," N. Y. Journal, Apr. 22,
1790.)   22992

U. S. Inspector-General's Office, 1791.
Regulations for the Order and Discipline
of the Troops of the United States.
Providence, Wheeler, 1791. 115 pp.,
1 plate.
RIHS copy.   23907

U. S. Inspector-General's Office, 1792.
Regulations for the Order and Discipline
of the Troops.
Hartford, Patten, 1792. 95, [1] pp., 8
plates.
AAS copy.   24919

[U. S. Inspector-General's Office, 1792.
Regulations for the Order and Discipline
of the Troops.
Windsor, Vt., Spooner, 1792. 91 pp.]
(This entry originated with Gilman.)
                                              24920

U. S. Inspector-General's Office, 1792.
Rules and Articles for the Better
Government of the Troops.
n. p., [1792?]. [4], 64 pp.
(Not located, 1968.)   46621

U. S. Inspector-General's Office, 1793.
Regeln fur die Ordnung und Disciplin
der Truppen.
Philadelphia, Cist, 1793. 84, [4], 31 pp., 8
plates.
LCP copy.   26361

U. S. Inspector-General's Office, 1793.
Regulations for the Order and Discipline
of the Troops.
Boston, Folsom for Norman, 1793. 91, [1]
pp., 8 plates.
AAS copy.   26356

[U. S. Inspector-General's Office, 1793.
Regulations for the Order and Discipline
of the Troops.
New Brunswick, Arnett & Blauvelt,
1793?]
(Imprint assumed by Evans from advs.)
                                              26357

U. S. Inspector-General's Office, 1793.
Regulations for the Order and Discipline
of the Troops. . . . Part 1.
Philadelphia, Oswald, 1793. 48 pp.
AAS copy.   26358

[U. S. Inspector-General's Office, 1793.
Regulations for the Order and Discipline
of the Troops.
Savannah, Johnstons, 1793?]
(Imprint assumed by Evans from adv. "A
Few Copies . . . to be sold at the Printing
Office," Ga. Gazette, Jan. 2, 1793.) 26359

U. S. Inspector-General's Office, 1793.
Regulations for the Order and Discipline
of the Troops.

Windsor, Vt., Spooner, 1793. 91 pp., 2
plates.
VtHS copy.   26360

U. S. Inspector-General's Office, 1794.
Regulations for the Order and Discipline
of the Troops of the United States.
Baltimore, Keatinge, 1794. 153, [8] pp., 8
plates.
AAS copy.   27957

U. S. Inspector-General's Office, 1794.
Regulations for the Order and Discipline
of the Volunteer Army.
Baltimore, Adamses for Keatinge, 1794.
36 pp.
APS copy.   47285

U. S. Inspector-General's Office, 1794.
Regulations for the Order and Discipline
of the Troops of the United States.
[Bennington], Vt., Haswell, 1794. 94,
[4] pp., 8 numbered plates.
AAS copy.   27959

U. S. Inspector-General's Office, 1794.
Regulations for the Order and Discipline
of the Troops of the United States.
Boston, Thomas & Andrews, 1794. 153,
[3], 34 pp., 8 plates.
AAS copy.   27960

U. S. Inspector-General's Office, 1794.
Regulations for the Order and Discipline
of the Troops of the United States.
Boston, W..West and J. West, 1794. 153,
[5], 34 pp. 8 plates.
BA copy.   27961

U. S. Inspector-General's Office, 1794.
Regulations for the Order and Discipline
of the Troops of the United States . . . and
the Militia Act of Massachusetts . . . 1793.
Boston, for West and West, 1794. 153, [3],
34 pp. 8 plates.
HEH copy.   47284

U. S. Inspector-General's Office, 1794.
Regulations for the Order and Discipline
of the Troops of the United States. . . . An
the Militia Law of South-Carolina.
Charleston, Young, 1794. 40, [1], 73, 15,
[5] pp., 8 plates.
LOC copy.   27964

U. S. Inspector-General's Office, 1794.
Regulations for the Order and Discipline
of the Troops of the United States . . . and
the Act for Forming . . . the Militia in
New Hampshire.
Exeter, Ranlet, 1794. 91 pp., 8 plates.
(The "third title" called for by Evans is a
part of 27961.)
AAS copy.   27963

U. S. Inspector-General's Office, 1794.
Regulations for the Order and Discipline
of the Troops of the United States.
Exeter, Ranlet for Thomas & Andrews,
1794. 91 pp., 8 plates.
AAS copy.   27962

U. S. Inspector-General's Office, 1794.
Regulations for the Order and Discipline
of the Troops of the United States.
[Halifax, N. C.], Hodge & Wills, 1794.
[4], 73, [7], 62 pp., 8 plates.
AAS copy.   27965

U. S. Inspector-General's Office, 1794.
Regulations for the Order and Discipline
of the Troops of the United States.
New York, Greenleaf, 1794. 95, [5] pp., 8
plates.
AAS copy.   27967

[U. S. Inspector-General's Office, 1794.
Regulations for the Order and Discipline
of·the Troops of the United States.
Newbern, N. C., Martin, 1794.]
(Apparently a ghost of 27965.)   27968

U. S. Inspector-General's Office, 1794.
Regulations for the Order and Discipline
of the Troops of the United States.
Philadelphia, Cist, 1794. [4], 73, [5] pp.,
8 plates.
AAS copy.   27969

U. S. Inspector-General's Office, 1794.
Regulations for the Order and Discipline
of the Troops of the United States [with]

Laws for Regulating the Militia of . . .
New-Jersey.
Philadelphia, Cist, 1794. [4], 73, [5], 39
pp., 8 plates.
AAS copy.   27970

U. S. Inspector-General's Office, 1794.
Regulations for the Order and Discipline
of the Troops of the United States . . . and
the Laws for . . . Militia of . . .
New-Hampshire.
Portsmouth, Melcher, 1794. xxxvi, 153,
[3] pp., 8 plates.
AAS copy.   27972

[U. S. Inspector-General's Office, 1794.
Regulations for the Order and Discipline
of the Volunteer Army of the United
States. . . . With Instructions for the
Exercise of the Light Horse.
Wilmington, Del., Adams, 1794.]
("Just Published by the Printers hereof,"
Delaware and Eastern Shore Adv., Nov.
15, 1794.)   27973

U. S. Inspector-General's Office, 1794.
Rules and Articles for the Better
Government of the Troops.
Philadelphia, Steiner & Kammerer, 1794.
62 pp.
BA copy.   27975

[U. S. Adjutant-General's Office, 1794.
Rules and Regulations for the Militia.
Charleston, Timothy & Mason, 1794.]
(A ghost of 27720, q. v.)   27976

[U. S. Inspector-General's Office, 1794.
Steuben's Manual Exercise (Abridged for
the Accommodation of Non-
Commissioned Officers.
Hartford, Babcock, 1794.]
(Imprint assumed by Evans from adv.
"For Sale by John Babcock" in Am.
Mercury, Aug. 25, 1794.)   27966

[U. S. Inspector-General's Office, 1794.
Steuben's Military Exercise.
Philadelphia, Oswald, 1794.]
(Imprint assumed by Evans from adv.
"For Sale at Oswald's" in Independent
Gazetteer, Jan. 14, 1794.)   27971

[U. S. Inspector-General's Office, 1794.
Steuben's Regulations. . . . First Maryland
Edition.
Baltimore, Edwards, 1794.]
(The origin of this entry is unknown.)
                                              27958

U. S. Inspector-General's Office, 1795.
Regulations for the Order and Discipline
of the Troops of the United States. . . .
Part I.
Philadelphia, Cist, 1795. [4], 151, [8] pp.,
8 folded plates.
AAS copy.   29778

[U. S. Inspector-General's Office, 1795.
Regulations for the Order and Discipline
of the Volunteer Army of the United
States.
Wilmington, Del., Adams, 1795.]
(Imprint assumed by Evans from adv.
"Just Published by the Printers hereof,"
Del. & Eastern Shore Adv., Dec. 20,
1794.)   29779

[U. S. Inspector-General's Office, 1796.
Regulations for the Order and Discipline
of the Troops of the United States.
New London, Green, 1796.]
(Imprint assumed by Evans from an adv.
"To be sold by" in Conn. Gazette, May
26, 1796.)   31469

[U. S. Inspector-General's Office, 1796.
Regulations for the Order and Discipline
of the Troops of the United States.
Providence, 1796.]
(Imprint assumed by Evans from a
bookseller's adv.)   31470

[U. S. Inspector-General's Office, 1796.
Steuben's Military Discipline.
Baltimore, 1796.]
(Imprint assumed by Evans from an adv.)
                                              31471

[U. S. Inspector-General's Office, 1796.
Steuben's Military Discipline.
Edenton, N. C., 1796.]

(Imprint assumed by Evans from an adv.)
31472

U. S. Inspector-General's Office, 1798.
Regulations for the Order and Discipline
of the Troops of the United States.
New York, Gaine, 1798. [4], 73, 15, 4 pp.,
8 folded plates.
NYHS copy.   34898

U. S. Inspector-General's Office, 1798.
Regulations for the Order and Discipline
of the Troops of the United States.
Philadelphia, Cist, 1798. [4], 151, [8] pp.,
1 folded plate.
VaSL copy.   34899

U. S. Inspector-General's Office, 1798.
Regulations for the Order and Discipline
of the Troops of the United States. . . .
[Together with] An Act for the
Regulation of the Militia of the
Commonwealth.
[Philadelphia, Cist, 1798.]
(No such copy found.)   34900

U. S. Inspector-General's Office, 1798.
Regulations for the Order and Discipline
of the Troops of the United States.
Philadelphia, Young, 1798. [4], 73, [5]
pp., 10 folded plates.
AAS copy.   34901

U. S. Inspector-General's Office, 1798.
Scheme of the Review, for the 13th
November, 1798.
[Philadelphia, 1798.] Broadside.
LOC copy.   48720

[U. S. Inspector-General's Office, 1798.
Steuben's Manual Exercise.
Hartford, Ct., Babcock, 1798.]
(Imprint assumed by Evans from adv.
"For sale" in Amer. Mercury, June 14,
1798.)   34896

[U. S. Inspector-General's Office, 1798.
Steuben's Manual Exercises.
Frankfort? Ky., Hunter & Beaumont,
1798.]
("Just Published by Hunter & Beaumont."
Palladium, Nov. 7, 1799.)   34895

[U. S. Inspector-General's Office, 1798.
Steuben's Military Regulations, with
Eight Plates.
New York, Greenleaf, 1798.]
(Imprint assumed by Evans from adv.)
34897

U. S. Inspector-General's Office, 1800.
Regulations for the Order and Discipline
of the Troops.
Philadelphia, Cist, 1800. [4], 151, [8] pp.,
8 folded plates.
AAS copy.   38806

U. S. Inspector of the Revenue, 1791.
Explanations and Instructions Concerning
the Act, Entitled, "An Act Repealing . . .
Duties . . . upon Distilled Spirits . . .
Passed . . . the 2d of March, 1791.
[Philadelphia, 1791.] 23 pp.
NYPL copy.   23897

U. S. Laws, Statutes, etc., 1776.
Règlement Militaire.
Philadelphia, Mesplet & Berger, 1776. 39
pp.
LCP copy.   15190

U. S. Laws, Statutes, etc., 1776.
Rules and Articles for the Better
Government of the Troops.
[Boston, 1776.] 25 pp.
HC copy.   15188

U. S. Laws, Statutes, etc., 1776.
Rules and Articles for the Better
Government of the Troops.
Fishkill, 1776. 31 pp.
NYHS copy.   15189

U. S. Laws, Statutes, etc., 1776.
Rules and Articles for the Better
Government of the Troops.
Philadelphia, Dunlap, 1776. 36 pp.
AAS copy.   15187

U. S. Laws, Statutes, etc., 1776.
Rules and Articles for the Better
Government of the Troops.

Philadelphia, 1782. 39 pp.
AAS copy.   17776

U. S. Laws, Statutes, etc., 1777.
Rules and Articles for the Better
Government of the Troops.
Boston, Edes, 1777. 31, [1], 2 pp.
AAS copy.   15689

U. S. Laws, Statutes, etc., 1783.
An Ordinance, to Amend an Ordinance,
Entitled, "An Ordinance for Establishing
Courts. . . ." [Mar. 4, 1783.]
[Philadelphia, 1783.] Broadside.
JCB copy.   44476

U. S. Laws, Statutes, etc., 1785.
An Ordinance for Ascertaining the mode
of Disposing of Lands in the Western
Territory.
[New York, 1785.] Broadside.
LOC copy.   19326

U. S. Laws, Statutes, etc., 1785.
An Ordinance for Ascertaining the Mode
of Disposing of Lands in the Western
Territory.
[Philadelphia, 1785.] Broadside.
(No copy located.)   44817

U. S. Laws, Statutes, etc., 1785.
An Ordinance for Ascertaining the Mode
of Disposing of Lands in the Western
Territory.
[Philadelphia, 1785.] [2] pp.
LOC copy.   44818

U. S. Laws, Statutes, etc., 1786.
An Ordinance for Establishing a Board to
Liquidate. . . .
[Philadelphia, 1786.] Broadside.
LOC copy.   45001

U. S. Laws, Statutes, etc., 1787.
An Ordinance for the Government of the
Territory . . . North-West of the River Ohio.
[July 13, 1787].
[New York, 1787.] [2] pp.
WLC copy.   20779

U. S. Laws, Statutes, etc., 1787.
An Ordinance for the Government of the
Western Territory. [May 9, 1787].
[New York, 1787.] [2] pp.
LOC copy.   20778

U. S. Laws, Statutes, etc., 1787.
An Ordinance for Regulating the Post
Office [June, 1787].
[New York, 1787.] Broadside.]
(Ford 442; not now to be located.) 20777

U. S. Laws, Statutes, etc., 1787.
A Supplement to an Ordinance Entitled,
"An Ordinance for Ascertaining of the
Mode of Disposing of Lands in the
Western Territory."
[New York, 1787.] [2] pp.
LOC copy.   20788

[U. S. Laws, Statutes, etc., 1788.
An Act for the Punishment of Certain
Crimes.
New York, Greenleaf, [1788]. 5, [1] pp.]
(Apparently a ghost of an Act of 1789.)
21510

[U. S. Laws, Statutes, etc., 1788.
An Act to Establish the Judicial Courts.
New York, Greenleaf, [1788]. 12 pp.]
(Apparently a ghost of a later Federal
Act.)   21511

U. S. Laws, Statutes, etc., 1788.
A Supplement to an Ordinance Entitled,
"An Ordinance for Ascertaining the Mode
of Disposing of Lands [Mar. 19, 1788].
[New York, 1788.] [2] pp.
NYPL copy.   21533

U. S. Laws, Statutes, etc., 1789 (1st Cong.)
Acts Passed at the First Congress.
Philadelphia, Childs, 1795. 434, [48] pp.
NYPL copy.   29674

U. S. Laws, Statutes, etc., 1789 (1st
Cong.].
Laws of the United States of America;
Comprising the Acts of the First Congress
and the Treaties.
Exeter, Ranlet, 1792. pp. [159]-700.
(This is a continuation of 22951, q. v.)
NHHS copy.   24914

U. S. Laws, Statutes, etc., 1789 (1st Cong.
1st sess.)
. . . An Act for Allowing a Compensation
to the President and Vice-President. . . .
Approved, September the 24th, 1789.
[New York, 1789.] Broadside.
NYPL copy.   45688

U. S. Laws, Statutes, etc., 1789 (1st Cong.,
1st sess.)
. . . An Act for Allowing Certain
Compensation to the Judges . . . and to
the Attorney General. . . . Approved,
September the 23d, 1789.
[New York, 1789.] Broadside.
NYPL copy.   45689

U. S. Laws, Statutes, etc., 1789 (1st Cong.
1st sess.)
. . . An Act for Allowing Compensation to
the members of the Senate and House. . . .
Approved, September the 22d, 1789.
[New York, 1789.] 2 pp.
NYPL copy.   45690

U. S. Laws, Statutes, etc., 1789 (1st Cong.,
1st sess.)
. . . An Act for Establishing an Executive
Department . . . the Department of
Foreign Affairs. . . . Approved, July 27,
1789.
[New York, 1789.] Broadside.
NYPL copy.   45691

U. S. Laws, Statutes, etc., 1789 (1st Cong.,
1st sess.)
. . . An Act for Establishing the Salaries
of the Executive Officers. . . . Approved
September the 11th, 1789.
[New York, Childs & Swaine, 1789].
Broadside.
NYPL copy.   45692

U. S. Laws, Statutes, etc., 1789 (1st Cong.,
1st sess.)
. . . An Act for Laying a Duty on Goods.
. . . July 4, 1789.
[New York], Childs & Swaine, [1789]. 3
pp.
NYPL copy.   22193

U. S. Laws, Statutes, etc., 1789 (1st Cong.,
1st sess.)
. . . An Act for Laying a Duty on Goods,
Wares and Merchandizes. . . . Approved,
July 4, 1789.
[New York, 1789.] 3 pp.
NYPL copy.   45693

U. S. Laws, Statutes, etc., 1789 (1st Cong.
1st sess.)
. . . An Act for Laying a Duty on Goods,
Wares, and Merchandises, Imported.
Richmond, [Va.], Davis, [1789]. 2 pp.
AAS copy.   45694

U. S. Laws, Statutes, etc., 1789 (1st Cong.
1st sess.)
. . . An Act for Registering and Clearing
Vessels.
New York, Childs & Swaine, 1789. 12 pp.
WLC copy.   45695

U. S. Laws, Statutes, etc., 1789 (1st Cong.,
1st sess.)
. . . An Act for Registering and Clearing
Vessels. . . . September the 1st, 1789.
[New York, 1789.] 12 pp.
NYPL copy.   45696

U. S. Laws, Statutes, etc., 1789 (1st Cong.,
1st sess.)
. . . An Act for Settling the Accounts
between the United States and Individual
States. . . . August the 5th 1789.
[New York, 1789.] Broadside.
NYPL copy.   45697

U. S. Laws, Statutes, etc., 1789 (1st Cong.,
1st sess.)
. . . An Act for the Establishment and
Support of Lighthouses. . . . August the
7th, 1789.
[New York, 1789.] Broadside.
NYPL copy.   45698

U. S. Laws, Statutes, etc., 1789 (1st Cong.,
1st sess.)
. . . An Act for the Temporary
Establishment of the Post-Office. . . .
September 22d, 1789.
[New York, 1789.] Broadside.
NYPL copy.   45699

U. S. Laws, Statutes, etc., 1789 (1st Cong.,
1st sess.)
. . . An Act Imposing Duties on Tonnage.
. . . July 20, 1789.
[New York, 1789.] Broadside.
NYPL copy. 45700

U. S. Laws, Statutes, etc., 1789 (1st Cong.
1st sess.)
. . . An Act making Appropriations for the
Service of the Present Year. . . .
September the 29th, 1789.
[New York, 1789.] 2 pp.
AAS copy. 45701

U. S. Laws, Statutes, etc., 1789 (1st Cong.,
1st sess.)
An Act Providing for the Actual
Enumeration. . . .
New York, Greenleaf, [1789]. 4 pp.
LOC copy. 45702

U. S. Laws, Statutes, etc., 1789 (1st Cong.,
1st sess.)
. . . An Act Providing for the Expences
which may Attend Negociations . . . with
the Indian Tribes. . . . August the 20th,
1789.
[New York, 1789.] Broadside.
AAS copy. 22196

U. S. Laws, Statutes, etc., 1789 (1st Cong.
1st sess.)
. . . An Act Providing for the Expenses
which may attend Negociations . . . with
the Indian Tribes. . . . Approved August
the 20th, 1789.
[New York, 1789]. Broadside.
NYPL copy. 45703

U. S. Laws, Statutes, etc., 1789 (1st Cong.,
1st sess.)
. . . An Act Providing for the Payment of
the Invalid Pensioners. . . . Approved,
September 29th, 1789.
[New York, 1789.] Broadside.
NYPL copy. 45704

U. S. Laws, Statutes, etc., 1789 (1st Cong.,
1st sess.)
. . . An Act Providing for the Payment of
the Invalid Pensioners. . . . October 13,
1789.
[New York, 1789.] Broadside.
LOC copy. 22197

U. S. Laws, Statutes, etc., 1789 (1st Cong.,
1st sess.)
. . . An Act to Allow the Baron de
Glaubeck the Pay of a Captain. . . .
Approved September the 29th, 1789.
[New York, 1789.] Broadside.
NYPL copy. 45705

U. S. Laws, Statutes, etc., 1789 (1st Cong.,
1st sess.)
. . . An Act to Alter the Time for the next
Meeting of Congress. . . . Approved,
September the 29th, 1789.
[New York, 1789.] Broadside.
NYPL copy. 45706

U. S. Laws, Statutes, etc., 1789 (1st Cong.,
1st sess.)
. . . An Act to Establish . . . the
Department of War. . . . August the 7th,
1789.
[New York, 1789.] Broadside.
AAS copy. 22194

U. S. Laws, Statutes, etc., 1789 (1st Cong.,
1st sess.)
. . . An Act to Establish the Judicial
Courts. . . . Approved, September the
24th, 1789.
[New York, 1789.] 12 pp.
NYPL copy. 45707

U. S. Laws, Statutes, etc., 1789 (1st Cong.
1st sess.)
. . . An Act to Establish the Treasury
Department. . . . Approved, September
the 2d, 1789.
[New York, 1789.] 2 pp.
NYPL copy. 45708

U. S. Laws, Statutes, etc., 1789 (1st Cong.,
1st sess.)
. . . An Act to Explain and Amend an Act
. . . for Registering. . . . Approved,
September the 29th, 1789.
New York, Childs & Swaine, [1789].

Broadside.
NYPL copy. 45709

U. S. Laws, Statutes, etc., 1789 (1st Cong.,
1st sess.)
. . . An Act to Provide for the
Government of the Territory North-West
of the River Ohio. . . . August the 7th, 1789.
[New York, 1789.] Broadside.
AAS copy. 22195

U. S. Laws, Statutes, etc., 1789 (1st Cong.,
1st sess.)
. . . An Act to Provide for the
Safe-Keeping of the Acts, Records, and
Seal. . . . Approved, September the 15th,
1789.
[New York, 1789.] [2] pp.
NYPL copy. 45711

U. S. Laws, Statutes, etc., 1789 (1st Cong.
1st sess.)
. . . An Act to Recognize and Adapt to the
Constitution . . . the Troops. . . .
Approved, September the 29th, 1789.
[New York, 1789.] Broadside.
NYPL copy. 45712

U. S. Laws, Statutes, etc., 1789 (1st Cong.,
1st sess.)
. . . An Act to Regulate Processes in the
Courts. . . . Approved, September the
29th, 1789.
[New York, 1789.] Broadside.
NYPL copy. 45714

U. S. Laws, Statutes, etc., 1789 (1st Cong.,
1st sess.)
. . . An Act to Regulate the Collection of
the Duties.
New York, Childs & Swaine, 1789. 22 pp.
(The only copy located is imperfect.)
AAS copy. 22198

U. S. Laws, Statutes,etc., 1789 (1st Cong.
1st sess.)
. . . An Act to Regulate the Collection of
the Duties . . . on . . . Tonnage . . . and on
Goods. . . . Approved, July 31, 1789.
[New York, 1789.] 21 pp.
NYPL copy. 45713

U. S. Laws, Statutes, etc., 1789 (1st Cong.,
1st sess.)
. . . An Act to Regulate the Time and
Manner of Administering Certain Oaths.
. . . Approved, June 1, 1789.
[New York, 1789.] [2] pp.
NYPL copy. 45715

U. S. Laws, Statutes, etc., 1789 (1st Cong.
1st sess.)
. . . An Act to Suspend Part of an Act . . .
to Regulate the Collection of the Duties.
. . . Approved, September the 16th, 1789.
[New York, Childs & Swaine, 1789].
Broadside.
NYPL copy. 45716

U. S. Laws, Statutes, etc., 1789 (1st
Cong., 1st-3rd sess.).
Acts Passed [Mar. 4, 1789 - Mar. 3, 1791].
Hartford, Hudson & Goodwin, 1791. [10],
327 pp.
AAS copy. 23843

U. S. Laws, Statutes, etc., 1789 (1st Cong.,
1st sess.)
Acts Passed . . . at the First Session of the
First Congress.
Hartford, Hudson & Goodwin, 1791. pp.
[10], [3]-327.
WLC copy. 46319

U. S. Laws, Statutes, etc., 1789 (1st Cong.,
1st sess.)
Acts Passed [Mar. 4 - Sept. 29, 1789].
New Haven, Greens, [1789]. 81, [1] pp.
NYPL copy. 22191

U. S. Laws, Statutes, etc., 1789 (1st Cong.,
1st sess.)
Acts Passed [Mar. 4 - Sept. 29, 1789].
New York, Childs & Swaine, [1789]. 105
pp.
AAS copy. 22189

[U. S. Laws, Statutes, etc., 1789 (1st
Cong., 1st sess.).
Acts Passed [Mar. 4 - Sept. 29, 1789].
New York, Childs & Swaine, [1790?]. 93,
[1] pp.]

(This is a copy of 22189, q.v., without the
Index.) 22949

U. S. Laws, Statutes, etc., 1789 (1st Cong.,
1st sess.)
Acts Passed [Mar. 4 - Sept. 29, 1789].
New York, Hodge, Allen & Campbell,
1789. pp. [i]-xxi, [25]-185, [2], i-xiv, [2].
LCP copy. 22190

U. S. Laws, Statutes, etc., 1789 (1st Cong.,
1st sess.)
Acts Passed [Mar. 4 - Sept. 29, 1789].
Philadelphia, Childs & Swaine, [1791].
93, [2] pp.
LOC copy. 23842

U. S. Laws, Statutes, etc., 1789 (1st Cong.,
1st sess.)
Acts Passed at the First Session of the
Congress.
Philadelphia, Childs & Swaine, 1791. 157,
[1] pp.
APS copy. 46320

U. S. Laws, Statutes, etc., 1789 (1st Cong.,
1st sess.)
Acts Passed [Mar. 4 - Sept. 29, 1789].
Richmond, Davis, [1790]. 79, [1] pp.
NYPL copy. 22950

U. S. Laws, Statutes, etc., 1789 (1st Cong.
1st sess.)
Acts Passed at the First Session of the
Congress . . . M,DCC,LXXXIX. . . .
Volume 1.
Philadelphia, Stephens, 1794. 376, [45]
pp.
JCB copy. 27825

U. S. Laws, Statutes, etc., 1789 (1st Cong.)
Acts Passed at the First [-third] Session
of Congress. . . . Volume I.
Philadelphia, Oswald, 1793. 375, [46] pp.
WLC copy. 46908

U. S. Laws, Statutes, etc., 1789 (1st Cong.,
1st sess.)
The Convention of a Number of the
States. . . . Resolved by the Senate and
House. . . .
[New York, 1789.] 2 pp.
LOC copy. 45717

U. S. Laws, Statutes, etc., 1789 (1st Cong.
1st sess.)
Impost and Tonnage Laws . . . and a
Table of Fees. . . . Approved, July 20,
1789.
Philadelphia, Humphreys, [1789].
Broadside.
LCP copy. 45718

U. S. Laws, Statutes, etc., 1789 (1st Cong.
1st sess.)
In Council, June 23, 1789. . . . An Act to
Regulate the Time and Manner of
Administering Certain Oaths. . . .
Approved June 1, 1789.
[Richmond? 1789.] [2] pp.
VaU copy. 45719

U. S. Laws, Statutes, etc., 1789 (1st Cong.,
1st sess.)
. . . Resolved . . . that it be Recommended
to the Several States . . . Goals. . . .
Approved, September the 23d, 1789.
[New York, 1789.] Broadside.
NYPL copy. 45721

U. S. Laws, Statutes, etc., 1789 (1st Cong.,
1st sess.)
. . . Resolved, That it shall be the Duty of
the Secretary of State, to Procure . . .
Statutes of the Several States. . . .
Approved, September the 23d, 1789.
[New York, 1789.] Broadside.
NYPL copy. 45722

U. S. Laws, Statutes, etc., 1789 (1st Cong.,
1st sess.)
. . . Resolved . . . that John White. . . .
Approved, September the 29th, 1789.
[New York, 1789.] Broadside.
NYPL copy. 45720

U. S. Laws, Statutes, etc., 1789 (1st Cong.,
1st sess.)
. . . Resolved, That the Survey Directed by
Congress in their Act of June the Sixth.
. . . Approved, August 26th, 1789.
[New York, 1789.] Broadside.
NYPL copy. 45723

U. S. Laws, Statutes, etc., 1790.
Laws of the United States, being a
Supplement to the Congressional Register.
New York, Hodge, Allen & Campbell,
1790. pp. [143]-185, [2], [i]-xiv, [2].
HEH copy.   46072

U. S. Laws, Statutes, etc., 1790 (1st Cong.
2nd sess.).
. . . An Act Authorizing the Secretary of
the Treasury to Finish the Light-House,
on Portland-Head. . . . August the Tenth,
1790.
[New York, Childs & Swaine, 1790.]
Broadside.
LOC copy.   22955

U. S. Laws, Statutes, etc., 1790 (1st Cong.,
2nd sess.)
An Act Declaring the Consent of
Congress. . . . In Senate . . . January 5,
1790.
[New York], Fenno, [1790]. Broadside.
LOC copy.   46031

U. S. Laws, Statutes, etc., 1790 (1st Cong.
2nd sess.)
. . . An Act for Establishing the
Temporary and Permanent Seat of the
Government. . . . Approved, July the
sixteenth, 1790.
[New York], Childs & Swaine, [1790].
Broadside.
AAS copy.   46032

U. S. Laws, Statutes, etc., 1790 (1st Cong.,
2nd sess.)
. . . An Act for Finally Adjusting and
Satisfying the Claims. . . . Approved, June
the 4th, 1790.
[New York], Childs & Swaine, [1790].
Broadside.
LOC copy.   46033

U. S. Laws, Statutes, etc., 1790 (1st Cong.,
2nd sess.)
. . . An Act for Giving Effect to an Act,
intituled, "An Act Providing for the
Ennumeration of the Inhabitants of . . ."
Rhode Island. . . . Approved, July the
fifth, 1790.
[New York], Childs & Swaine, [1790].
Broadside.
RIHS copy.   46034

U. S. Laws, Statutes, etc., 1790 (1st Cong.,
2nd sess.).
. . . An Act for Giving Effect to the
Several Acts there-in Mentioned, in
Respect to the State of North-Carolina.
. . . Approved, February the 8th, 1790.
[New York, 1790.] [2] pp.
JCB copy.   22956

U. S. Laws, Statutes, etc., 1790 (1st Cong.
2nd sess.)
. . . An Act for Giving Effect to the
Several Acts . . . in Respect to . . .
North-Carolina.
New York, Childs & Swaine, [1790]. [2]
pp.
LOC copy.   46035

U. S. Laws, Statutes, etc., 1790 (1st Cong.,
2nd sess.)
. . . An Act for Giving Effect to the
Several Acts therein Mentioned, in
Respect to the State of Rhode-Island.
[New York, 1790.] [2] pp.
LOC copy.   22957

U. S. Laws, Statutes, etc., 1790 (1st Cong.,
2nd sess.).
. . . An Act for Providing for Holding a
Treaty or Treaties to Establish Peace with
Certain Indian Tribes. . . . Approved, July
the twenty-second, 1790.
[New York, 1790.] Broadside.
LOC copy.   22966

U. S. Laws, Statutes, etc., 1790 (1st Cong.
2nd sess.).
. . . An Act for Regulating the Military
Establishment. . . . Approved, April 30th,
1790.
[New York], Childs & Swaine, [1790]. 3
pp.
LOC copy.   22958

U. S. Laws, Statutes, etc., 1790 (1st Cong.,
2nd sess.)
An Act for Regulating the Military
Establishment.

[New York], Fenno, [1790]. 3 pp.
LOC copy.   46036

U. S. Laws, Statutes, etc., 1790 (1st Cong.,
2nd sess.)
An Act for the Encouragement of
Learning.
[New York], Fenno, [1790]. 2 pp.
LOC copy.   46037

U. S. Laws, Statutes, etc., 1790 (1st Cong.
2nd sess.)
. . . An Act for the Encouragement of
Learning. . . . Approved, May the 31st,
1790.
[New York, 1790.] [2] pp.
LOC copy.   46038

U. S. Laws, Statutes, etc., 1790 (1st Cong.
1st sess.).
. . . An Act for the Government &
Regulation of Seamen in the Merchant
Service. . . . Approved July 20th, 1790.
Boston, Fleet, [1791]. [2] pp.
(This is apparently the copy seen by
Evans; there were several eds.)
AAS copy.   23849

U. S. Laws, Statutes, etc., 1790 (1st Cong.,
2nd sess.).
. . . An Act for the Government and
Regulation of Seamen in the Merchants
Service. . . . Approved, July the
Twentieth, 1790.
[New York, 1790.] 4 pp.
(The AAS has 5 printings of this Act in
broadside form with ships' articles on the
reverse.)
LOC copy.   22959

U. S. Laws, Statutes, etc., 1790 (1st Cong.
2nd sess.)
An Act for the Government and
Regulation of Seamen.
Warren, R. I., Phillips, 1792. 16 pp.
AAS copy.   24866

U. S. Laws, Statutes, etc., 1790 (1st Cong.
2nd sess.).
. . . An Act for the Government of the
Territory of the United States, South of
the River Ohio. . . . Approved, May
twenty-sixth, 1790.
[New York], Childs & Swaine, [1790].
Broadside.
AAS copy.   22960

U. S. Laws, Statutes, etc., 1790 (1st Cong.
2nd sess.)
. . . An Act for the Government of the
Territory. . . . Approved, May
twenty-sixth, 1790.
[New York], Childs & Swaine, [1790].
Broadside.
LOC copy.   46039

U. S. Laws, Statutes, etc., 1790 (1st Cong.
2nd sess.)
An Act for the Government of the
Territory . . . South of the River Ohio.
[Philadelphia], Fenno, [1790]. Broadside.
LOC copy.   46040

U. S. Laws, Statutes, etc., 1790 (1st Cong.
2nd sess.)
. . . An Act for the Punishment. . . .
Approved, April 30th, 1790.
[New York], Childs & Swaine, [1790]. 7
pp.
LOC copy.   46041

U. S. Laws, Statutes, etc., 1790 (1st Cong.
2nd sess.)
. . . An Act for the Relief of Disabled
Soldiers. . . . Approved, August the
eleventh, 1790.
[New York, 1790.] [3] pp.
LOC copy.   46042

U. S. Laws, Statutes, etc., 1790 (1st Cong.,
2nd sess.).
. . . An Act for the Relief of John Stewart
and John Davidson.
[New York, 1790.] Broadside.
LOC copy.   22961

U. S. Laws, Statutes, etc., 1790 (1st Cong.
2nd sess.)
. . . An Act further to Provide for the
Payment. . . . Approved, July the 16th,
1790.
[New York, 1790.] Broadside.
LOC copy.   46043

U. S. Laws, Statutes, etc., 1790 (1st Cong.,
2nd sess.).
. . . An Act Further to Suspend Part of an
Act, Entituled, "An Act to Regulate the
Collection of the Duties. . . ." Approved,
the 15th of April, 1790.
[New York], Childs & Swaine, [1790].
Broadside.
LOC copy.   22962

U. S. Laws, Statutes, etc., 1790 (1st Cong.,
2nd sess.).
. . . An Act Imposing Duties on the
Tonnage of Ships or Vessels. . . .
Approved, July the Twentieth, 1790.
[New York, 1790.] Broadside.
LOC copy.   22963

U. S. Laws, Statutes, etc., 1790 (1st Cong.
2nd sess.)
. . . An Act Making Appropriations for
the Support of Government. . . .
Approved, March 26th, 1790.
[New York, 1790.] [2] pp.
WLC copy.   46044

U. S. Laws, Statutes, etc., 1790 (1st Cong.
2nd sess.)
. . . An Act Making Certain
Appropriations therein Mentioned. . . .
Approved, August the twelfth, 1790.
[New York, 1790.] Broadside.
HC copy.   46045

U. S. Laws, Statutes, etc., 1790 (1st Cong.
2nd sess.)
. . . An Act Making further Provision for
the Payment. . . . Approved, August the
tenth, 1790.
[New York], Childs & Swaine, [1790]. 4
pp.
LOC copy.   46046

U. S. Laws, Statutes, etc., 1790 (1st Cong.,
2nd sess.).
. . . An Act Making further Provisions for
the Payment of the Debts of the United
States. . . . Approved, August the tenth,
1790.
[New York], Childs & Swaine, [1790]. 4
pp.
AAS copy.   22965

U. S. Laws, Statutes, etc., 1790 (1st Cong.
2nd sess.)
An Act Making Provision for the Debt.
[New York, 1790.] 4 pp.
LOC copy.   46047

U. S. Laws, Statutes, etc., 1790 (1st Cong.
2nd sess.)
. . . An Act Making Provision for the
Debt. . . . Approved, August the fourth,
1790.
[New York, 1790.] 7 pp.
LOC copy.   46048

U. S. Laws, Statutes, etc., 1790 (1st Cong.
2nd sess.)
An Act Making Provision for the Debt.
[New York], Fenno, [1790]. 4 pp.
LOC copy.   46049

U. S. Laws, Statutes, etc., 1790 (1st Cong.
2nd sess.)
. . . An Act Making Provision for the
Reduction. . . . Approved, August the
twelfth, 1790.
[New York, 1790.] [2] pp.
LOC copy.   46050

U. S. Laws, Statutes, etc., 1790 (1st Cong.
2nd sess.)
. . . An Act Providing for Holding a
Treaty. . . . Approved, July the
twenty-second, 1790.
[New York], Childs & Swaine, [1790].
Broadside.
LOC copy.   46051

U. S. Laws, Statutes, etc., 1790 (1st Cong.
2nd sess.)
An Act Providing for the Actual
Enumeration of the Inhabitants.
New York, Greenleaf, [1790]. 4 pp.
LOC copy.   46052

U. S. Laws, Statutes, etc., 1790 (1st Cong.
2nd sess.)
. . . An Act Providing for the
Enumeration of the Inhabitants. . . .
[Mar. 1, 1790.]

New York, Childs & Swaine, 1790. 3 pp.
HEH copy.   46053

U. S. Laws, Statutes, etc., 1790 (1st Cong.
2nd sess.)
An Act Providing for the Means of
Intercourse. . . .
[New York], Fenno, [1790]. Broadside.
LOC copy.   46054

U. S. Laws, Statutes, etc., 1790 (1st Cong.
2nd sess.)
. . . An Act Providing the Means. . . .
Approved, July the first, 1790.
[New York, 1790.] Broadside.
HEH copy.   46055

U. S. Laws, Statutes, etc., 1790 (1st Cong.
2nd sess.)
. . . An Act Supplemental to the Act for
Establishing the Salaries. . . . Approved
June the fourth, 1790.
[New York, 1790.] Broadside.
LOC copy.   46056

U. S. Laws, Statutes, etc., 1790 (1st Cong.
2nd sess.)
An Act, Supplemental to the Act for
Establishing the Salaries.
[Philadelphia], Fenno, [1790]. Broadside.
LOC copy.   46057

U. S. Laws, Statutes, etc., 1790 (1st Cong.
2nd sess.)
An Act, Supplementory to the Act,
entitled, "An Act Making further
Provision for the Payment of the Debts.
. . ." Approved 27th December, 1790.
[New York, 1790.] Broadside.
AAS copy.   46059

U. S. Laws, Statutes, etc., 1790 (1st Cong.
2nd sess.)
An Act to Allow Compensation to John
Ely.
[Philadelphia], Fenno, [1790]. Broadside.
LOC copy.   46060

U. S. Laws, Statutes, etc., 1790 (1st Cong.
2nd sess.)
. . . An Act to Alter the Times. . . .
Approved, August the eleventh, 1790.
[New York, 1790.] Broadside.
LOC copy.   46061

U. S. Laws, Statutes, etc., 1790 (1st Cong.,
2nd sess.).
. . . An Act to Amend the Act for the
Establishment and Support of
Light-Houses. . . . Approved, July the
twenty-second, 1790.
[New York, 1790.] Broadside.
LOC copy.   22967

U. S. Laws, Statutes, etc., 1790 (1st Cong.
2nd sess.)
. . . An Act to Authorize the Purchase of a
Tract of Land for the Use of the United
States. . . . Approved, July the fifth, 1790.
[New York], Childs & Swaine, [1790].
Broadside.
AAS copy.   46062

U. S. Laws, Statutes, etc., 1790 (1st Cong.
2nd sess.)
. . . An Act to Continue in force for a
Limited Time an Act . . . for the
Temporary Establishment of the
Post-Office. . . . Approved, August the
fourth, 1790.
[New York, 1790.] Broadside.
AAS copy.   46063

U. S. Laws, Statutes, etc., 1790 (1st Cong.
2nd sess.)
An Act to Describe the Mode in which the
Public Acts. . . .
[Philadelphia], Fenno, [1790]. Broadside.
LOC copy.   46064

U. S. Laws, Statutes, etc., 1790 (1st Cong.
2nd sess.)
. . . An Act to Enable the Officers . . . of
the Virginia Line. . . . Approved, August
the tenth, 1790.
[New York, 1790.] [2] pp.
LOC copy.   46065

U. S. Laws, Statutes, etc., 1790 (1st Cong.,
2nd sess.).
. . . An Act to Prescribe the Mode in
which the Public Acts. . . . Approved,
May twenty-sixth, 1790.

[New York, 1790.] Broadside.
NYPL copy.   22968

U. S. Laws, Statutes, etc., 1790 (1st Cong.
2nd sess.)
An Act to Prevent Bringing Goods. . . .
[Philadelphia], Fenno, [1790]. 2 pp.
LOC copy.   46066

U. S. Laws, Statutes, etc., 1790 (1st Cong.
2nd sess.)
An Act to Promote the Progress of Useful
Arts.
[Philadelphia], Fenno [1790]. 3 pp.
LOC copy.   46067

U. S. Laws, Statutes, etc., 1790 (1st Cong.
2nd sess.)
An Act to Provide for Mitigating. . . .
[Philadelphia], Fenno, [1790]. Broadside.
LOC copy.   46068

U. S. Laws, Statutes, etc., 1790 (1st Cong.,
2nd sess.).
. . . An Act to Provide for the Settlement
of Accounts. . . . Approved, August 5,
1790.
[New York, 1790.] [2] pp.
LOC copy.   22969

U. S. Laws, Statutes, etc., 1790 (1st.
Cong., 2nd sess.).
. . . An Act to Provide more Effectually
for the Collecting of the Duties. . . .
Approved August the fourth, 1790.
[New York], Childs & Swaine, [1790.] 41
pp.
LOC copy.   22970

[U. S. Laws, Statutes, etc., 1790 (1st
Cong., 2nd sess.).
. . . An Act to Regulate the Collection of
the Duties.
Savannah, Johnstone, 1790.]
(From an adv.)   22971

U. S. Laws, Statutes, etc., 1790 (1st Cong.,
2nd sess.).
. . . An Act to Regulate Trade and
Intercourse with the Indian Tribes. . . .
Approved, July the twenty-second, 1790.
[New York, 1790.] [2] pp.
LOC copy.   22972

U. S. Laws, Statutes, etc., 1790 (1st Cong.
2nd sess.)
. . . An Act to Satisfy the Claims of John
M'Cord. . . . Approved, July the first,
1790.
[New York, 1790.] Broadside.
LOC copy.   46069

U. S. Laws, Statutes, etc., 1790 (1st Cong.,
2nd sess.).
Acts Passed [Jan. 4 - Aug. 12, 1790].
New York, Childs & Swaine, [1790]. 226,
[2] pp.
BA copy.   22952

U. S. Laws, Statutes, etc., 1790 (1st Cong.,
2nd sess.)
Acts Passed at the Second Session.
Philadelphia, Childs & Swaine, 1791. 414
pp.
APS copy.   46324

U. S. Laws, Statutes, etc., 1790 (1st Cong.
2nd sess.).
Acts Passed [Jan. 4 - Aug. 12, 1790].
Richmond, Davis, [1791]. 112, [2] pp.
NYPL copy.   23844

U. S. Laws, Statutes, etc., 1790 (1st Cong.
2nd sess.)
Acts Passed [Jan. 4-Aug. 12, 1790].
Wilmington, Andrews & Brynberg, 1790. 120
pp.
(The only recorded copy could not be
reproduced.)   46070

U. S. Laws, Statutes, etc., 1790 (1st Cong.
2nd sess.)
[Certain Laws Interesting to gentlemen
concerned in the revenue, navigation, and
commerce.
Baltimore, Goddard & Angell, 1790.]
("Just published," Washington Spy, Dec. 23,
1790.)   46071

[U. S. Laws, Statutes, etc., 1790 (1st
Cong. 2nd sess.).
Laws for the Better Regulating Seamen in
the Merchants' Service.

Norfolk, Baxter & Wilson, 1792?]
(Imprint assumed by Evans from an adv.)
      24912

U. S. Laws, Statutes, etc., 1790 (1st Cong.
2nd sess.)
An Ordinance for Regulating the
Post-Office.
[New York, 1790.] [4] pp.
LOC copy.   46073

U. S. Laws, Statutes, etc., 1790 (1st Cong.
2nd sess.)
. . . Resolved . . . that all Surveys. . . .
Approved, August the twelfth, 1790.
[New York, 1790.] Broadside.
LOC copy.   46074

U. S. Laws, Statutes, etc., 1790 (1st Cong.
2nd sess.)
. . . Resolved . . . That the Clerks in the
Office of the Commissioner of Army
Accounts. . . . Approved, August the
Second, 1790.
[New York, 1790.] Broadside.
LOC copy.   46075

U. S. Laws, Statutes, etc., 1790 (1st Cong.
3rd sess.)
. . . An Act Supplementary to the Act,
Intitled, "An Act Making further
Provisions for the Payment of the Debts
of the United States. . . . Approved
December twenty-seventh, 1790.
[Philadelphia? 1791.] Broadside.
NYPL copy.   23867

U. S. Laws, Statutes, etc., 1790 (1st Cong.
3rd sess.)
Acts Passed [Dec. 6, 1790 - Mar. 3, 1791].
Philadelphia, Childs & Swaine, [1791].
pp. [225] - [286].
(Issued without the supplementary
material found bound in some copies.)
AAS copy.   23845

U. S. Laws, Statutes, etc., 1790 (1st Cong.,
3rd sess.)
Acts Passed [Dec. 6, 1790 - Mar. 3, 1791].
Richmond, Dixon, [1791]. 41, [1] pp.
NYPL copy.   23846

U. S. Laws, Statutes, etc., 1790 (1st Cong.,
3rd sess.)
Acts Passed at the Third Session.
Philadelphia, Childs & Swaine, 1791. 120,
[57] pp.
APS copy.   46326

[U. S. Laws, Statutes, etc., 1790 (1st
Cong. 3rd sess.)
Rules and Articles for the Better
Government of the Troops.
Philadelphia, 1790. 39 pp.]
(Entry from Sabin 74064. The Rules were
approved by Washington, Mar. 3, 1791.)
      23000

U. S. Laws, Statutes, etc., 1791.
An Act Concerning Consuls and
Vice-Consuls.
n. p., [1791]. [3] pp.
LOC copy.   46321

U. S. Laws, Statutes, etc., 1791.
[An Act repealing . . . duties . . . upon
distilled spirits.
Baltimore, Goddard & Angell, 1791.]
(Minick 41; no copy known.) 46322

U. S. Laws, Statutes, etc., 1791.
An Act to Incorporate the Subscribers to
the Bank of ----.
[Philadelphia], Fenno, [1791]. 7 pp.
LOC copy.   46323

U. S. Laws, Statutes, etc., 1791.
Laws of the United States of America.
Volume I.
New York, Childs & Swaine, [1791]. pp.
[1]-[viii], [5]-592.
AAS copy.   23902

U. S. Laws, Statutes, etc., 1791.
Laws of the United States of America. . . .
Volume I.
Philadelphia, Brown, 1791. [4], 490, [24]
pp.
AAS copy.   23903

U. S. Laws, Statutes, etc., 1791.
Rules and Articles for the Better
Government of the Troops.

[Philadelphia, 1791.] 44 pp.
AAS copy.   23918

U. S. Laws, Statutes, etc., 1791 (1st Cong.
3rd sess.).
. . . An Act Declaring the Consent of
Congress, that a New State be Formed . . .
by the Name of . . . Kentucky. . . .
Approved, February the fourth, 1791.
[Philadelphia, 1791.] Broadside.
NYPL copy.   23850

U. S. Laws, Statutes, etc., 1791 (1st Cong.
3rd sess.).
. . . An Act Declaring the Consent of
Congress to a Certain Act of the State of
Maryland. . . . Approved, February 9,
1791.
[Philadelphia, 1791.] Broadside.
AAS copy.   23851

U. S. Laws, Statutes, etc., 1791 (1st Cong.
3rd sess.).
. . . An Act Fixing the Time for the next
Annual Meeting of Congress. . . .
Approved, March the second, 1791.
[Philadelphia, 1791.] Broadside.
AAS copy.   23852

U. S. Laws, Statutes, etc., 1791 (1st Cong.
3rd sess.).
. . . An Act for the Admission of the State
of Vermont. . . . Approved, February the
eighteenth, 1791.
[Philadelphia, 1791.] Broadside.
NYPL copy.   23856

U. S. Laws, Statutes, etc., 1791 (1st Cong.
3rd sess.).
. . . An Act for Granting Lands to the
Inhabitants and Settlers at Vincennes. . . .
Approved, March the third, 1791.
[Philadelphia, 1791.] [2] pp.
NYPL copy.   23853

U. S. Laws, Statutes, etc., 1791 (1st Cong.
3rd sess.).
. . . An Act for Making Compensations to
the Commissioners of Loans. . . .
Approved, March the third, 1791.
[Philadelphia, 1791.] Broadside.
AAS copy.   23854

U. S. Laws, Statutes, etc., 1791 (1st Cong.
3rd sess.).
. . . An Act for Raising and Adding
another Regiment. . . . Approved, March
the third, 1791.
[Philadelphia, 1791.] [4] pp.
AAS copy.   23855

U. S. Laws, Statutes, etc., 1791 (1st Cong.
3rd sess.).
. . . An Act Giving Effect to the Laws of
the United States within the State of
Vermont. . . . . Approved, March the
second, 1791.
[Philadelphia, 1791.] [2] pp.
AAS copy.   23857

U. S. Laws, Statutes, etc., 1791 (1st Cong.
3rd sess.).
. . . An Act in Addition to an Act,
Intitled, "An Act for Establishing the
Salaries of the Executive Officers. . . .
Approved, March the third, 1791.
[Philadelphia, 1791.] Broadside.
AAS copy.   23858

U. S. Laws, Statutes, etc., 1791 (1st Cong.
3rd sess.).
. . . An Act Making an Appropriation for
the Purpose therein Mentioned. . . .
Approved, March the third, 1791.
[Philadelphia, 1791.] Broadside.
AAS copy.   23859

U. S. Laws, Statutes, etc., 1791 (1st Cong.
3rd sess.).
. . . An Act Making Appropriations for
the Support of Government. . . .
Approved, February the 11th, 1791.
[Philadelphia, 1791.] Broadside.
AAS copy.   23860

U. S. Laws, Statutes,.etc., 1791 (1st Cong.
3rd sess.).
. . . An Act Making further Provision for
the Collection of the Duties. . . .
Approved, March the third, 1791.
[Philadelphia, 1791.] [3] pp.
AAS copy.   23861

U. S. Laws, Statutes, etc., 1791 (1st Cong.
3rd sess.).
. . . An Act Providing Compensations for
the Officers of the Judicial Courts. . . .
Approved, March the third, 1791.
[Philadelphia, 1791.] [2] pp.
AAS copy.   23862

U. S. Laws, Statutes, etc., 1791 (1st Cong.
3rd sess.).
. . . An Act Regulating the Number of
Representatives to be Chosen by the
States of Kentucky and Vermont. . . .
Approved, February the twenty-fifth,
1791.
[Philadelphia, 1791.] Broadside.
AAS copy.   23863

U. S. Laws, Statutes, etc., 1791 (1st Cong.
3rd sess.).
. . . An Act Relative to the Rix-Dollar of
Denmark. . . . Approved, March the third,
1791.
[Philadelphia, 1791.] Broadside.
AAS copy.   23864

U. S. Laws, Statutes, etc., 1791 (1st Cong.,
3rd sess.)
An Act Repealing, after the last Day of
June next, the Duties heretofore Laid
upon Distilled Spirits. . . . Approved
March the Third, 1791.
[Philadelphia? 1791.] [3] pp.
AAS copy.   46325

U. S. Laws, Statutes, etc., 1791 (1st Cong.
3rd sess.).
. . . An Act Repealing, after the Last Day
of June next, the Duties . . . upon Distilled
Spirits. . . . Approved, March the third,
1791.
[Philadelphia, 1791.] 16 pp.
NYPL copy.   23865

U. S. Laws, Statutes, etc., 1791 (1st Cong.
3rd sess.).
An Act Repealing . . . the Duties
heretofore Laid upon Distilled Spirits.
[Philadelphia], Fenno, [1791]. 24 pp.
LOC copy.   46327

U. S. Laws, Statutes, etc., 1791 (1st Cong.
3rd sess.).
. . . An Act Supplemental to the Act
"Establishing the Treasury Department".
. . . Approved, March the third, 1791.
[Philadelphia, 1791.] Broadside.
AAS copy.   23866

U. S. Laws, Statutes, etc., 1791 (1st Cong.
3rd sess.).
. . . An Act Supplementary to the Act,
Intitled, "An Act to Incorporate the
Subscribers to the Bank of the United
States". . . . Approved, March the second,
1791.
[Philadelphia, 1791.] Broadside.
AAS copy.   23876

U. S. Laws, Statutes, etc., 1791 (1st Cong.
3rd sess.).
. . . An Act Supplementary to the Act,
Making Provision for the Reduction of the
Public Debt. . . . Approved, March the
third, 1791.
[Philadelphia, 1791.] Broadside.
AAS copy.   23868

U. S. Laws, Statutes, etc., 1791 (1st Cong.
3rd sess.).
. . . An Act to Amend "An Act, for
Establishing the Temporary and
Permanent Seat of the Government. . . ."
Approved, March the third, 1791.
[Philadelphia, 1791.] Broadside.
AAS copy.   23869

U. S. Laws, Statutes, etc., 1791 (1st Cong.,
3rd sess.)
. . . An Act to Continue an Act . . .
declaring the Assent of Congress.-. . .
Approved, February the ninth, 1791.
[Philadelphia, 1791.] Broadside.
LOC copy.   46328

U. S. Laws, Statutes, etc., 1791 (1st Cong.
3rd sess.).
. . . An Act to Continue an Act, Intitled
"An Act Declaring the Assent of Congress
. . .". . . . Approved, January the tenth,
1791.

[Philadelphia, 1791.] Broadside.
AAS copy.   23870

U. S. Laws, Statutes, etc., 1791 (1st Cong.
3rd sess.)
. . . An Act to Continue in Force for a
Limited Time, an Act, Intitled "An Act
for the Temporary Establishment of the
Post-Office. . . . Approved: March the
third, 1791.
[Philadelphia, 1791.] Broadside.
NYPL copy.   23871

U. S. Laws, Statutes, etc., 1791 (1st Cong.
3rd sess.)
. . . An Act to Continue in Force, for a
Limited Time, an Act Passed at the First
Session of Congress, Intitled, "An Act to
Regulate Processes in the Courts of the
United States. . . . Approved, February
the eighteenth, 1791.
[Philadelphia, 1791.] Broadside.
AAS copy.   23872

U. S. Laws, Statutes, etc., 1791 (1st Cong.
3rd sess.)
. . . An Act to Continue in Force the Act
therein Mentioned, and to make further
Provision for the Payment of Pensions.
. . . Approved, March the third, 1791.
[Philadelphia, 1791.] Broadside.
AAS copy.   23873

U. S. Laws, Statutes, etc., 1791 (1st Cong.
3rd sess.)
. . . An Act to Explain and Amend an Act,
Intitled "An Act Making further
Provision for the Payment of the Debts of
the United States". . . . Approved, March
the second, 1791.
[Philadelphia, 1791.] Broadside.
AAS copy.   23874

U. S. Laws, Statutes, etc., 1791 (1st Cong.
3rd sess.)
. . . An Act to Incorporate the Subscribers
to the Bank of the United States. . . .
Approved February the twenty-fiifth,
1791.
[Philadelphia, 1791.] 7 pp.
NYPL copy.   23875

U. S. Laws, Statutes, etc., 1791 (1st Cong.
3rd sess.)
. . . An Act to Provide for the Unlading of
Ships. . . . Approved, January the Seventh,
1791.
[Philadelphia, 1791.] Broadside.
AAS copy.   23877

U. S. Laws, Statutes, etc., 1791 (1st Cong.
3rd sess.)
. . . An Act to Provide for the Unloading
of Ships . . . in Cases of Obstruction by
Ice. . . . Approved, January the Seventh,
1791.
[Philadelphia, 1791.] Broadside.
LOC copy.   46329

[U. S. Laws, Statutes, etc., 1791 (1st
Cong. 3rd sess.)
The Excise Laws, or, "An Act Repealing
after the last day of June next, the Duties
. . . upon Distilled Spirits.
Philadelphia, Dobson, 1791.]
(No such printing located.)   23896

U. S. Laws, Statutes, etc., 1791 (1st Cong.
3rd sess.)
. . . Resolved . . . that a Mint shall be
Established. . . . Approved, March the
third, 1791.
[Philadelphia, 1791.] Broadside.
AAS copy.   23880

U. S. Laws, Statutes, etc., 1791 (1st Cong.
3rd sess.)
. . . Resolved . . . that Andrew Brown, or
any other Printer. . . . Approved,
February the eighteenth, 1791.
[Philadelphia, 1791.] Broadside.
AAS copy.   23878

U. S. Laws, Statutes, etc., 1791 (1st Cong,
3rd sess.)
. . . Resolved . . . that the President of the
United States be, and he hereby is
Requested, to Cause an Estimate . . .
lands . . . Ohio. . . . Approved, March the
third, 1791.
[Philadelphia, 1791.] Broadside.
AAS copy.   23882

U. S. Laws, Statutes, etc., 1791 (1st Cong. 3rd sess.)
. . . Resolved . . . that the President of the United States be Requested to be Communicated to the National Assembly. . . . Approved, March the second, 1791.
[Philadelphia, 1791.] Broadside.
AAS copy.   23879

U. S. Laws, Statutes, etc., 1791 (1st Cong. 3rd sess.)
. . . Whereas Congress did, by a Resolution of the twenty-third day of September . . . Resolved . . . Jail. . . . March the third, 1791.
[Philadelphia, 1791.] Broadside.
AAS copy.   23881

U. S. Laws, Statutes, etc., 1791 (2nd Cong.).
Acts Passed [Oct. 24, 1791 - Mar. 2, 1793].
Philadelphia, Childs & Swaine, [1793].
291, ii, [25] pp. 8 vo.
AAS copy.   26295

U. S. Laws, Statutes, etc., 1791 (2nd Cong.).
Acts Passed at the First [-second] Session of the Second Congress. . . . Volume II.
Philadelphia, Oswald, 1793. 380, [26] pp.
WLC copy.   46909

U. S. Laws, Statutes, etc., 1791 (2nd Cong.)
Acts Passed at the Second Congress.
Philadelphia, Childs, 1795. 406, [24] pp.
AAS copy.   29675

U. S. Laws, Statutes, etc., 1792 (2d Cong. 1st sess.).
. . . An Act for Raising a farther sum of Money for the Protection of the Frontiers. . . . Approved May second, 1792.
[Philadelphia, 1792.] [4] pp.
NYPL copy.   24890

U. S. Laws, Statutes, etc., 1792 (2nd Cong. 1st sess.)
. . . An Act Authorizing the Grant . . . of Certain Lands to the Ohio Company. . . . Approved April twenty-first, 1792.
[Philadelphia, Childs & Swaine, 1792.] [2] pp.
NYPL copy.   46621a

U. S. Laws, Statutes, etc., 1792 (2nd Cong. 1st sess.)
. . . An Act, Concerning Consuls and Vice Consuls [Apr. 14, 1792].
[Philadelphia, 1792.] 3 pp.
NYPL copy.   46622

U. S. Laws, Statutes, etc., 1792 (2nd Cong. 1st sess.)
An Act Concerning the Duties on Spirits . . . 1792, May the 2d - Passed the House.
[Philadelphia], Fenno, [1792]. 5 pp.
LOC copy.   46623

U. S. Laws, Statutes, etc., 1792 (2nd Cong. 1st sess.)
An Act Concerning the Duties on Spirits . . . Approved, May eighth, 1792.
[Philadelphia, 1792.] 5 pp.
LCP copy.   46624

U. S. Laws, Statutes, etc., 1792 (2nd Cong. 1st sess.)
. . . An Act for Altering the Times of Holding the Circuit Courts [Apr. 13, 1792].
[Philadelphia, 1792.] [2] pp.
NYPL copy.   46625

U. S. Laws, Statutes, etc., 1792 (2nd Cong. 1st sess.)
. . . An Act for Apportioning Representatives [Apr. 14, 1792].
[Philadelphia, 1792.] Broadside.
NYPL copy.   46626

U. S. Laws, Statutes, etc., 1792 (2nd Cong. 1st sess.).
. . . An Act for Ascertaining the Bounds of a Tract of Land Purchased by John Cleves Symmes [Apr. 12, 1792].
[Philadelphia, 1792.] Broadside.
NYPL copy.   46627

U. S. Laws, Statutes, etc., 1792 (2nd Cong. 1st sess.).

. . . An Act for Finishing the Light-house . . . at the Mouth of Cape Fear River [Apr. 2, 1792].
[Philadelphia, 1792.] Broadside.
NYPL copy.   46628

U. S. Laws, Statutes, etc., 1792 (2nd Cong. 1st sess.).
. . . An Act for Fixing the Compensations of the Doorkeepers [Apr. 12, 1792].
[Philadelphia, 1792.] Broadside.
NYPL copy.   46629

U. S. Laws, Statutes, etc., 1792. (2nd Cong. 1st sess.)
An Act for Regulating Processes in the Courts. . . .
[Philadelphia], Fenno, [1792]. 3 pp.
(No copy located.)   46630

U. S. Laws, Statutes, etc., 1791 (2nd Cong. 1st sess.)
. . . An Act for the Relief of David Cook. . . . Approved, December sixteenth, 1791.
[Philadelphia], Childs & Swaine, [1791]. Broadside.
NYPL copy.   23884

U. S. Laws, Statutes, etc., 1791 (2nd cong., 1st sess.)
. . . An Act for the Relief of David Cook and Thomas Campbell.
[Philadelphia, 1791.] Broadside.
LOC copy.   46330

U. S. Laws, Statutes, etc., 1791 (2nd Cong. 1st sess.)
. . . An Act Granting further Time for Making Return of the Enumeration of the Inhabitants . . . of South-Carolina. . . . Approved November the eighth, 1791.
[Philadelphia, 1791.] Broadside.
NYPL copy.   23885

U. S. Laws, Statutes, etc., 1791 (2nd Cong. 1st sess.)
. . . An Act Making Appropriations for the Support of Government. . . . Approved, December twenty-third, 1791.
[Philadelphia], Childs & Swaine, [1791]. [3] pp.
NYPL copy.   23886

U. S. Laws, Statutes, etc., 1791 (2nd Cong., 1st sess.)
. . . An Act Making Appropriations for the Support of Government. . . . Approved, December Twenty-Third, 1791.
[Philadelphia, 1791?]
(Not located, 1968.)   46331

U. S. Laws, Statutes, etc., 1792 (2nd Cong. 1st sess.)
An Act more Effectually to Provide for the National Defence . . . 1792, March the 6th - Passed the House.
[Philadelphia], Fenno, [1792]. 7 pp.
(No copy located.)   46631

U. S. Laws, Statutes, etc., 1792 (2nd Cong. 1st sess.).
[An Act more Effectually to Provide for the National Defence by Establishing an Uniform Militia.
Lexington, Ky., Bradford, 1792.]
(McMurtrie: Ky 20; no copy known.)   46632

U. S. Laws, Statutes, etc., 1792 (2nd Cong. 1st sess.).
An Act Relative to the Compensations to Certain Officers . . . 1792, May the 2d.
[Philadelphia], Fenno, [1792]. 2 pp.
LOC copy.   46633

U. S. Laws, Statutes, etc., 1792 (2nd Cong. 1st sess.)
. . . An Act Supplementary to the Act for the Establishment and Support of Light Houses [Apr. 12, 1792].
[Philadelphia, 1793.] Broadside.
(Not located, 1968.)   46634

U. S. Laws, Statutes, etc., 1792 (2nd Cong. 1st sess.)
An Act to Ascertain and Regulate the Claims of Half Pay . . . 26th of January, 1792.
[Philadelphia], Fenno, [1792]. 3 pp.
(No copy located.)   46635

U. S. Laws, Statutes, etc., 1792 (2nd Cong. 1st sess.).

. . . An Act to Compensate the Corporation of . . . the Academy of Wilmington [Apr. 13, 1792].
[Philadelphia, 1792.] Broadside.
NYPL copy.   46636

U. S. Laws, Statutes, etc., 1792 (2nd Cong. 1st sess.).
. . . An Act to Compensate the Services of the late Colonel George Gibson. . . . Approved, May eighth, 1792.
[Philadelphia, 1792.] Broadside.
LOC copy.   46637

U. S. Laws, Statutes, etc., 1792 (2nd Cong. 1st sess.).
An Act to Erect a Light-house on Montaugh Point.
[Philadelphia], Fenno, [1792]. Broadside.
LOC copy.   46638

U. S. Laws, Statutes, etc., 1792 (2nd Cong. 1st sess.).
. . . An Act to Erect a Light-House on Montok Point [Apr. 12, 1792].
[Philadelphia, 1792.] Broadside.
NYPL copy.   46639

U. S. Laws, Statutes, etc., 1792 (2nd Cong. 1st sess.).
. . . An Act to Establish the Post-Office. . . . Approved, February the twentieth, 1792.
[Philadelphia, 1792.] 6 pp.
LOC copy.   46640

U. S. Laws, Statutes, etc., 1792 (2nd Cong. 1st sess.).
[An Act to Provide for Calling forth the Militia.
Lexington, Ky., Bradford, 1792.]
(McMurtrie: Ky 21; no copy known.)   46641

U. S. Laws, Statutes, etc., 1791 (2nd Cong. 1st sess.)
Acts Passed [Oct. 24, 1791 - May 8, 1792].
Philadelphia, Brown, 1792. pp. [5], 8-114, [i]-xvi, [3].
AAS copy.   24869

U. S. Laws, Statutes, etc., 1791 (2nd Cong. 1st sess.)
Acts Passed [Oct. 24, 1791 - May 8, 1792].
Philadelphia, Childs & Swaine, [1792]. 175, [iii] pp.
AAS copy.   24868

U. S. Laws, Statutes, etc., 1791 (2nd Cong. 1st sess.)
Acts Passed [Oct. 24, 1791 - May 8, 1792].
Richmond, Davis, 1792. 74, x pp.
LOC copy.   24870

U. S. Laws, Statutes, etc., 1791 (2nd Cong. 1st sess.)
Acts Passed at the First Session of the Second Congress . . . M,DCC,XCI. . . . Volume II.
Philadelphia, Stephens, 1794. 380, [26] pp.
JCB copy.   27826

[U. S. Laws, Statutes, etc., 1792.
An Act to Explain and Amend an Act, Entitled, "An Act to Enable the Officers and Soldiers of the Virginia Line. . . ."
Philadelphia, Fenno, [1792]. 2 pp.]
(No copy of such a printing has been located.)   24867

U. S. Laws, Statutes, etc., 1792.
Duties Payable on Goods . . . Imported.
New York, Allen, 1792. [2], 26 pp.
(No copy located.)   46642

U. S. Laws, Statutes, etc., 1792 (2d Cong. 1st sess.).
. . . An Act Authorizing the Grant and Conveyance of Certain Lands to John Cleves Symmes. . . . Approved, May fifth, 1792.
[Philadelphia, 1792.] Broadside.
NYPL copy.   24891

U. S. Laws, Statutes, etc., 1792 (2nd Cong. 1st sess.)
. . . An Act Concerning Certain Fisheries of the United States. . . . Approved February sixteenth, 1792.
[Philadelphia, 1792.] [3] pp.
NYPL copy.   24875

U. S. Laws, Statutes, etc., 1792 (2nd Cong. 1st sess.).
. . . An Act Concerning Duties on Spirits. . . . Approved, May eighth, 1792.
[Philadelphia, 1792.] [4] pp.
NYPL copy.   24894

U. S. Laws, Statutes, etc., 1792 (2d Cong. 1st sess.).
. . . An Act Concerning the Claim of John Brown Cutting. . . . Approved, May eighth, 1792.
[Philadelphia, 1792.] Broadside.
NYPL copy.   24893

U. S. Laws, Statutes, etc., 1792 (2d Cong. 1st sess.).
. . . An Act Declaring the Consent of Congress to a Certain Act of the State of Maryland. . . . Approved, March the nineteenth, 1792.
[Philadelphia, 1792.] Broadside.
NYPL copy.   24881

U. S. Laws, Statutes, etc., 1792 (2d Cong. 1st sess.).
. . . An Act Establishing a Mint. . . . Approved, April the second, 1792.
[Philadelphia, 1792.] 5 pp.
NYPL copy.   24886

U. S. Laws, Statutes, etc., 1792 (2d Cong. 1st sess.).
. . . An Act for Carrying into Effect a Contract between the United States and the State of Pennsylvania. . . . Approved, January the third, 1792.
[Philadelphia, 1792.] Broadside.
NYPL copy.   24873

U. S. Laws, Statutes, etc., 1792 (2nd Cong. 1st sess.).
. . . An Act for Making Compensations to the Commissioners of Loans. . . . Approved, May eighth, 1792.
[Philadelphia, 1792.] Broadside.
NYPL copy.   24895

U. S. Laws, Statutes, etc., 1792 (2d Cong. 1st sess.).
. . . An Act for Making Farther and More Effectual Provision for the Protection of the Frontiers. . . . Approved March the fifth, 1792.
[Philadelphia], Childs & Swaine, [1792]. [3] pp.
NYPL copy.   24880

U. S. Laws, Statutes, etc., 1792 (2d Cong. 1st sess.).
. . . An Act for Regulating Processes in the Courts. . . . Approved, May eighth, 1792.
[Philadelphia, 1792.] [4] pp.
NYPL copy.   24896

U. S. Laws, Statutes, etc., 1792 (2nd Cong. 1st sess.).
. . . An Act for the Relief of Certain Widows. . . . Approved, March the twenty-seventh, 1792.
[Philadelphia, 1792.] [2] pp.
NYPL copy.   24883

U. S. Laws, Statutes, etc., 1792 (2d Cong, 1st sess.).
. . . An Act Making Alterations in the Treasury and War Departments. . . . Approved, May eighth, 1792.
[Philadelphia, 1792.] 2 pp.
NYPL copy.   24897

U.S. Laws, Statutes, etc., 1792 (2d Cong., 1st sess.).
. . . An Act Making Certain Appropriations. . . . Approved May eighth, 1792.
[Philadelphia, 1792.] [2] pp.
NYPL copy.   24898

U.S. Laws, Statutes, etc., 1792 (2nd Cong. 1st sess.).
. . . An Act more Effectually to Provide for the National Defence. . . . Approved May eighth, 1792.
[Philadelphia, 1792.] [3] pp.
NYPL copy.   24899

U. S. Laws, Statutes, etc., 1792 (2d Cong. 1st sess.).
. . . An Act Providing for the Settlement of Claims. . . . Approved, March the twenty-seventh, 1792.

[Philadelphia, 1792.] Broadside.
NYPL copy.   24884

U.S. Laws, Statutes, etc., 1792 (2nd Cong. 1st sess.).
. . . An Act Relative to the Compensations to Certain Officers. . . . Approved May eighth, 1792.
[Philadelphia, 1792.] Broadside.
NYPL copy.   24900

U. S. Laws, Statutes, etc., 1792 (2d Cong. 1st sess.).
. . . An Act Relative to the Election of a President. . . . Approved, March the first, 1792.
[Philadelphia], Childs & Swaine, [1792]. [2] pp.
NYPL copy.   24878

U. S. Laws, Statutes, etc., 1792 (2nd Cong. 1st sess.).
. . . An Act Respecting the Government of the Territories. . . . Approved, May eighth, 1792.
[Philadelphia, 1792.] Broadside.
NYPL copy.   24902

U. S. Laws, Statutes, etc., 1792 (2d Cong. 1st sess.)
. . . An Act Supplemental to the Act for Making Farther and More Effectual Provision for the Protection of the Frontiers. . . . Approved March the twenty eighth, 1792.
[Philadelphia, 1792.] Broadside.
NYPL copy.   24885

U. S. Laws, Statutes, etc., 1792 (2nd Cong. 1st sess.).
. . . An Act Supplementary to the Act for Making Provision for the Debt. . . . Approved May eighth, 1792.
[Philadelphia, 1792.] [3] pp.
NYPL copy.   24901

U. S. Laws, Statutes, etc., 1792. (2d Cong. 1st sess.).
. . . An Act to Alter the Time for the next Annual Meeting of Congress. . . . Approved May fifth, 1792.
[Philadelphia, 1792.] Broadside.
NYPL copy.   24892

U. S. Laws, Statutes, etc., 1792 (2nd Cong. 1st sess.).
. . . An Act to Continue in Force the Act, Intituled, "An Act to Provide for Mitigating or Remitting the Penalties. . . ." Approved, May eighth, 1792.
[Philadelphia, 1792.] Broadside.
NYPL copy.   24903

U. S. Laws, Statutes, etc., 1792 (2d Cong. 1st sess).
. . . An Act to Establish the Post-Office. . . . Approved February the twentieth, 1792.
[Philadelphia, 1792.] 8 pp.
NYPL copy.   24876

U. S. Laws, Statutes, etc., 1792 (2d Cong. 1st sess.).
An Act to Establish the Post-Office. . . . 1792, January the 10th - Passed the House.
[Philadelphia], Fenno. 10 pp.
LOC copy.   24877

U. S. Laws, Statutes, etc., 1792 (2d Cong. 1st sess.).
. . . An Act to Extend the Time Limited for Settling the Accounts of the United States with the Individual States. . . . Approved, January twenty-third, 1792.
[Philadelphia, 1792.] Broadside.
NYPL copy.   24874

U. S. Laws, Statutes, etc., 1792 (2d Cong. 1st sess.).
. . . An Act to Indemnify the Estate of the Late Major General Nathaniel Green. . . . Approved, April twenty-seventh, 1792.
[Philadelphia, 1792.] Broadside.
NYPL copy.   24888

U. S. Laws, Statutes, etc., 1792 (2nd Cong. 1st sess.).
. . . An Act to Provide for a Copper Coinage. . . . Approved, May eighth, 1792. Broadside.
NYPL copy.   24904

U. S. Laws, Statutes, etc., 1792 (2d Cong. 1st sess.).
. . . An Act to Provide for Calling forth the Militia. . . . Approved, May second, 1792.
[Philadelphia, 1792.] 2 pp.
NYPL copy.   24889

U. S. Laws, Statutes, etc., 1792 (2d Cong. 1st sess.).
. . . An Act to Provide for the Settlement of the Claims of Widows and Orphans. . . . Approved, March the twenty-third, 1792.
[Philadelphia, 1792.] [2] pp.
NYPL copy.   24882

U. S. Laws, Statutes, etc., 1792. (2nd Cong. 2nd sess.)
. . . An Act Concerning the Registering and Recording of Ships or Vessels. . . . Approved, thirty-first of December 1792.
[Philadelphia], Childs & Swaine, [1793]. 12 pp.
AAS copy.   26298

U. S. Laws, Statutes, etc., 1792 (2nd Cong. 2nd sess.).
Acts Passed [Nov. 5, 1792 - Mar. 2, 1793]. Philadelphia, Childs & Swaine, [1793]. pp. [175-291. fol.
U.S. Law Library copy.   26293

U.S. Laws, Statutes, etc., 1792 (2nd Cong. 2nd sess.).
Acts Passed [Nov. 5, 1792 - Mar. 2, 1793]. Richmond, Davis, 1793. 52, [1] pp.
NYPL copy.   26294

[U.S. Laws, Statutes, etc., 1793.
An Act more Effectually to Provide for the National Defence.
Augusta, Smith, 1793.]
(Imprint assumed by Evans from advs.)   26297

U.S. Laws, Statutes, etc., 1793 (2nd Cong. 2nd sess.).
. . . An Act for Enrolling and Licensing Ships. . . . Approved, eighteenth of February, 1793.
[Philadelphia, 1793.] 13 pp.
AAS copy.   26307

U.S. Laws, Statutes, etc., 1793 (2nd Cong. 2nd sess.).
. . . An Act for Extending the Time for Receiving on Loan. . . . Approved, March second 1793.
[Philadelphia, 1793.] Broadside.
AAS copy.   26320

U.S. Laws, Statutes, etc., 1793 (2nd Cong. 2nd sess.).
. . . An Act for Repealing the Several Impost Laws. . . . Approved, February twenty seventh 1793.
[Philadelphia, 1793.] Broadside.
(Printed on the sheet with 26314, q.v.)   26313

U.S. Laws, Statutes, etc., 1793 (2nd Cong. 2nd sess.).
. . . An Act for the Relief of Elijah Bostwick. . . . Approved March second 1792.
[Philadelphia, 1792.] [2] pp.
AAS copy.   26321

U.S. Laws, Statutes, etc., 1793 (2nd Cong. 2nd sess.).
. . . An Act in Addition to, and in Alteration of the Act, Entitled, "An Act to Extend the Time Limited for Settling the Accounts of the United States. . . . Approved, February twenty seventh, 1793.
[Philadelphia, 1793.] [2] pp.
AAS copy.   26314

U.S. Laws, Statutes, etc., 1793 (2nd Cong. 2nd sess.).
. . . An Act in Addition to the Act, Entitled, "An Act to Establish the Judicial Courts. . . ." Approved, March second, 1793.
[Philadelphia, 1793.] [2] pp.
AAS copy.   26329

U.S. Laws, Statutes, etc., 1793 (2nd Cong. 2nd sess.).
. . . An Act Making Addition to the Compensation of Certain Public Officers. . . . Approved, March second, 1793.
[Philadelphia, 1793.] Broadside.

(Found only on sheet with 26321, q.v.)
26322

U.S. Laws, Statutes, etc., 1793 (2nd Cong. 2nd sess.).
. . . An Act Making an Appropriation to Defray the Expense of a Treaty with the Indians North West of the Ohio. . . .
Approved March second 1793.
[Philadelphia, 1793.] Broadside.
(Found only on sheet with 26321, q.v.)
26323

U.S. Laws, Statutes, etc., 1793 (2nd Cong. 2nd sess.).
. . . An Act Making Appropriations for the Support of Government. . . .
Approved, February twenty eighth, 1793.
[Philadelphia, 1793.] [4] pp.
AAS copy.   26316

U.S. Laws, Statutes, etc., 1793 (2nd Cong. 2nd sess.).
. . . An Act Making Certain Appropriations therein Mentioned. . . .
Approved, March second, 1793.
[Philadelphia, 1793.] [2] pp.
AAS copy.   26324

U.S. Laws, Statutes, etc., 1793 (2nd Cong. 2nd sess.).
. . . An Act Making Provision for the Persons therein Mentioned. . . .
Approved, February twenty seventh, 1793.
[Philadelphia, 1793.] Broadside.
(Found only on sheet with 26314, q.v.)
26315

U.S. Laws, Statutes, etc., 1793 (2nd Congress. 2nd sess.).
. . . An Act Providing Compensation to the President. . . . Approved February eighteenth - twenty-second. 1793.
[Philadelphia, 1792.] [2] pp.
AAS copy.   26308

U.S. Laws, Statutes, etc., 1793 (2nd Cong. 2nd sess.).
. . . An Act Providing for the Payment of the First Instalment due on a Loan Made of the Bank of the United States. . . .
Approved, March second, 1793.
(Found only on sheet with 26321, q.v.)
26325

U.S. Laws, Statutes, etc., 1793 (2nd Cong. 2nd sess.).
. . . An Act Regulating Foreign Coins. . . .
Approved, February ninth, 1793.
[Philadelphia, 1793.] Broadside.
AAS copy.   26303

U. S. Laws, Statutes, etc., 1793 (2nd Cong. 2nd sess.).
. . . An Act Relative to Claims. . . .
Approved, February twelfth, 1793.
[Philadelphia, 1793.] Broadside.
AAS copy.   26305

U.S. Laws, Statutes, etc., 1793 (2nd Cong. 2nd sess.).
. . . An Act Respecting Fugitives from Justice. . . . Approved, February twelfth, 1793.
[Philadelphia, 1793.] Broadside.
AAS copy.   26306

U.S. Laws, Statutes, etc., 1793 (2nd Cong. 2nd sess.).
. . . An Act Supplementary to the Act, Entitled, "An Act to Provide more Effectually for the Collection of the Duties. . . ." Approved, March second, 1793.
[Philadelphia, 1793.] [2] pp.
AAS copy.   26327

U.S. Laws, Statutes, etc., 1793 (2nd Cong. 2nd sess.).
. . . An Act Supplementary to the Act for the Establishment and Support of Light-Houses. . . . Approved, March second 1793.
[Philadelphia, 1793.] [2] pp.
AAS copy.   26326

U.S. Laws, Statutes, etc., 1793 (2nd Cong. 2nd sess.).
. . . An Act to Alter the Times and Places of Holding the Circuit Courts. . . .
Approved, March second, 1793.
[Philadelphia, 1793.] [2] pp.
AAS copy.   26328

U.S. Laws, Statutes, etc., 1793 (2nd Cong. 2nd sess.).
. . . An Act to Amend an Act, Intituled "An Act Establishing a Mint."
[Philadelphia], Childs & Swaine, [1793].
Broadside.
AAS copy.   26299

U.S. Laws, Statutes, etc., 1793 (2nd Cong. 2nd sess.).
. . . An Act to Ascertain the Fees in Admiralty Proceedings. . . . Approved, March first, 1793.
[Philadelphia, 1793.] [2] pp.
AAS copy.   26318

U.S. Laws, Statutes, etc., 1793 (2nd Cong. 2nd sess.).
. . . An Act to Authorize the Adjustment of a Claim of Joseph Henderson. . . .
Approved, February twenty second 1793.
[Philadelphia, 1793.] Broadside.
(Found only on sheet with 26308, q.v.)
26311

U.S. Laws, Statutes, etc., 1793. (2nd Cong. 2nd sess.).
. . . An Act to Authorize the Comptroller of the Treasury to Settle the Account of Thomas Wishart. . . . Approved February twenty second 1793.
[Philadelphia, 1793.] Broadside.
(Found only on the sheet with 26308, q.v.)
26312

U. S. Laws, Statutes, etc., 1793 (2nd Cong. 2nd sess.).
An Act to Authorize the Settlement of the Accounts of Lewis Garanger. . . . 1793, January 2d.
[Philadelphia], Fenno, [1793]. Broadside.
LOC copy.   46906

U.S. Laws, Statutes, etc., 1793 (2nd Cong. 2nd sess.).
An Act to Continue in Force . . . and to Amend the Act . . . Providing the Means of Intercourse. . . . 1793, January the 18th.
[Philadelphia], Fenno, [1793]. Broadside.
LOC copy.   46907

U.S. Laws, Statutes, etc., 1793 (2nd Cong. 2nd sess.).
. . . An Act to Continue in Force for a Limited Time, and to Amend the Act, Intituled "An Act to Provide the Means of Intercourse between the United States, and Foreign Nations. . . . Approved, February 9th 1793.
[Philadelphia, 1793.] Broadside.
AAS copy.   26304

U.S. Laws, Statutes, etc., 1793 (2nd Cong. 2nd sess.).
. . . An Act to Promote the Progress of the Useful Arts. . . . Approved, February twenty-first, 1793.
[Philadelphia, 1793.] [3] pp.
AAS copy.   26309

U.S. Laws, Statutes, etc., 1793 (2nd Cong. 2nd sess.).
. . . An Act to Provide for the Allowance of Interest. . . . Approved, January fourteenth, 1792.
[Philadelphia], Childs & Swaine, [1793].
Broadside.
AAS copy.   26300

U.S. Laws, Statutes, etc., 1793 (2nd Cong. 2nd sess.).
. . . An Act to Regulate the Claims to Invalid Pensions. . . . Approved, February twenty eighth 1793.
[Philadelphia, 1793.] [2] pp.
AAS copy.   26317

[U. S. Laws, Statutes, etc., 1793 (2d Cong. 2d sess.).
. . . An Act to Regulate the Claims to Invalid Pensions. . . . Approved, January 28, 1793.
[Philadelphia, 1793.] [2] pp.]
(The copies located by Evans were 26317, of which it is apparently a ghost.)   26301

U.S. Laws, Statutes, etc., 1793 (2nd sess.).
. . . An Act to Regulate Trade and Intercourse with the Indian Tribes. . . .
Approved March first 1793.
[Philadelphia, 1793.] [3] pp.
AAS copy.   26319

U. S. Laws, Statutes, etc., 1793 (2nd Cong. 2nd sess.).
. . . An Act to Repeal Part of a Resolution of Congress of the Twenty Ninth of August, 1788, Respecting the Inhabitants of Post Saint Vincents. . . . Approved, February twenty first, 1793.
[Philadelphia, 1793.] Broadside.
(Found only on the sheet with 26308, q.v.)
26310

U. S. Laws, Statutes, etc., 1793 (3rd Cong.)
Acts Passed at the Third Congress.
Philadelphia, Childs, 1795. pp. [1]-144, [i]-iii, [1], [145]-260, [i]-iv, [24].
AAS copy.   29676

U. S. Laws, Statutes, etc., 1793 (3rd Cong. 1st sess.).
Acts Passed at the Third Congress . . . First Session.
[Hartford, 1794.] pp. [487]-570.
HEH copy.   47290

U. S. Laws, Statutes, etc., 1793 (3rd Cong. 1st sess.).
Acts Passed at the Third Congress.
Philadelphia, Childs and Swaine, 1794.
144, iii pp.
AAS copy.   27827

[U. S. Laws, Statutes, etc., 1794.
The Laws for Regulating the Militia of the United States.
Baltimore, Angell, for Fisher & Cole, 1794.]
(Imprint assumed by Evans from adv. "This day is published," in Md. Journal, Sept. 22, 1794.)   27956

U. S. Laws, Statutes, etc., 1794 (3rd Cong.)
Acts Passed at the Third Congress.
Richmond, Davis, [1795]. pp. [55]-108, [2].
VaSL copy.   29678

U. S. Laws, Statutes, etc., 1794 (3rd Cong. 1st sess.).
. . . An Act Allowing Lieutenant Colonel Tousard an Equivalent for his Pension. . . . Approved - April the Thirteenth, 1794.
[Philadelphia, 1794.] Broadside.
JCB copy.   27848

U. S. Laws, Statutes, etc., 1794 (3rd Cong. 1st sess.)
. . . An Act Allowing to Major-General La Fayette his Pay. . . . Approved, March the Twenty-Seventh, 1794.
[Philadelphia, 1794.] Broadside.
(Printed on sheet with 27879.)
JCB copy.   27841

U. S. Laws, Statutes, etc., 1794 (3rd Cong. 1st sess.)
. . . An Act Authorizing a Loan of One Million of Dollars. . . . Approved - March the Twentieth, 1794.
[Philadelphia, 1794.] Broadside.
JCB copy.   27836

U. S. Laws, Statutes, etc., 1794 (3rd Cong. 1st sess.)
. . . An Act Authorizing a Settlement of Certain Expenses of the Commissioners of Loans. . . . Approved - June the Fifth 1794. . . . An Act Allowing Additional Compensation to the Principal Clerks. . . . Approved - June the Seventh 1794.
[Philadelphia, 1794.] Broadside.
AAS copy.   27866

U. S. Laws, Statutes, etc., 1794 (3rd Cong. 1st sess.)
. . . An Act Concerning Invalids. . . . An Act for the Relief of Nicholas Rich. . . .
Approved - June the Seventh 1794.
[Philadelphia, 1794.] Broadside.
AAS copy.   27874

U. S. Laws, Statutes, etc., 1794 (3rd Cong. 1st sess.)
. . . An Act Directing a Detachment from the Militia. . . . Approved -May the Ninth 1794.
[Philadelphia, 1794.] Broadside.
AAS copy.   27852

U. S. Laws, Statutes, etc., 1794 (3rd Cong. 1st sess.)

. . . An Act Directing a Detachment . . .
Approved - May the Ninth, 1794.
[Philadelphia, 1794.] Broadside.
LOC copy.   47286

U. S. Laws, Statutes, etc., 1794 (3rd Cong.
1st sess.)
. . . An Act for Erecting a Lighthouse on
the Island of Seguin. . . . An Act further
to Authorize the Adjournment of Circuit
Courts. . . . May the Nineteenth 1794.
[Philadelphia, 1794.] Broadside.
AAS copy.   27855

U. S. Laws, Statutes, etc., 1794 (3rd Cong.
1st sess.)
. . . An Act for Extending the Benefit of a
Drawback. . . . Approved - June the
Fourth, 1794.
[Philadelphia, 1794.] Broadside.
AAS copy.   27862

U. S. Laws, Statutes, etc., 1794 (3rd Cong.
1st sess.)
. . . An Act for the Relief of Stephen
Paranque. . . . Approved -
April the Second, 1794.
[Philadelphia, 1794.] Broadside.
JCB copy.   27843

U. S. Laws, Statutes, etc., 1794 (3rd Cong.
1st sess.)
. . . An Act for the Relief of Thomas
Jenkins and Sons. . . . Approved -
February the Nineteenth, 1794.
[Philadelphia, 1794.] Broadside.
NYPL copy.   27831

U. S. Laws, Statutes, etc., 1794 (3rd Cong.
1st sess.)
. . . An Act for the Remission of the
Duties Arising on the Tonnage of Sundry
French Vessels. . . . Approved - March the
Seventh, 1794.
[Philadelphia, 1794.] Broadside.
JCB copy.   27833

U. S. Laws, Statutes, etc., 1794 (3rd Cong.
1st sess.)
. . . An Act for the Remission of the
Duties on Eleven Hogsheads of Coffee.
. . . An Act Supplementary to "An Act to
Provide for the Defence of Certain Ports".
. . . Approved - May the Ninth, 1794.
[Philadelphia, 1794.] Broadside.
AAS copy.   27851

U. S. Laws, Statutes, etc., 1794 (3rd Cong.
1st sess.)
An Act for Transferring, for a Limited
Time, the Jurisdiction of Suits. . . .
Approved - April the Third, 1794.
[Philadelphia, 1794.] Broadside.
JCB copy.   27844

U. S. Laws, Statutes, etc., 1794 (3rd Cong.
1st sess.)
. . . An Act further Extending the Time
for Receiving on Loan the Domestic Debt.
. . . An Act to Compensate Arthur St.
Clair. . . . Approved - May the Thirty
First 1794.
[Philadelphia, 1794.] Broadside.
AAS copy.   27858

U. S. Laws, Statutes, etc., 1794 (3rd Cong.
1st sess.)
. . . An Act in Addition to the "Act for
Making Further and More Effectual
Provision for the Protection of the
Frontiers". . . . Approved - June the
Seventh 1794.
[Philadelphia, 1794.] Broadside.
AAS copy.   27871

U. S. Laws, Statutes, etc., 1794 (3rd Cong.
1st sess.)
. . . An Act in Addition to the Act for the
Punishment of Certain Crimes. . . .
Approved - June the Fifth 1794.
[Philadelphia, 1794.] [3] pp.
AAS copy.   27869

U. S. Laws, Statutes, etc., 1794 (3rd Cong.
1st sess.)
. . . An Act in Alteration of the Act
Establishing a Mint. . . . Approved, March
the Third, 1794.
[Philadelphia, 1794.] Broadside.
JCB copy.   27832

U. S. Laws, Statutes, etc., 1794 (3rd Cong.
1st sess.)

. . . An Act Laying Additional Duties on
Goods. . . . Approved - June the Seventh
1794.
[Philadelphia, 1794.] [2] pp.
AAS copy.   27872

U. S. Laws, Statutes, etc., 1794 (3rd Cong.
1st sess.)
. . . An Act Laying Certain Duties upon
Snuff. . . . Approved - June the Fifth 1794.
[Philadelphia, 1794.] 6 pp.
AAS copy.   27870

U. S. Laws, Statutes, etc., 1794 (3rd Cong.
1st sess.)
. . . An Act Laying Duties on Licenses.
. . . Approved - June the Fifth 1794.
[Philadelphia, 1794.] [3] pp.
AAS copy.   27867

U. S. Laws, Statutes, etc., 1794 (3rd Cong.
1st sess.)
. . . An Act Laying Duties on Property
Sold at Auction. . . . Approved - June the
Ninth 1794.
[Philadelphia, 1794.] [4] pp.
AAS copy.   27878

U. S. Laws, Statutes, etc., 1794 (3rd Cong.
1st sess.)
. . . An Act Laying Duties upon Carriages.
. . . Approved - June the Fifth 1794.
[Philadelphia, 1794.] [3] pp.
AAS copy.   27864

U. S. Laws, Statutes, etc., 1794 (3rd Cong.
1st sess.)
. . . An Act Laying Duties upon Carriages.
. . . Approved, June the Fifth, 1794.
[Philadelphia, 1794.] 37 pp.
JCB copy.   47287

U. S. Laws, Statutes, etc., 1794 (3rd Cong.
1st sess.)
. . . An Act Limiting the Time for
Presenting Claims. . . . Approved - April
the Twenty First 1794.
[Philadelphia, 1794.] Broadside.
AAS copy.   27847

U. S. Laws, Statutes, etc., 1794 (3rd Cong.
1st sess.)
. . . An Act Making an Alteration in the
Flag of the United States. . . . Approved,
January the Thirteenth, 1794.
[Philadelphia, 1794.] Broadside.
NYPL copy.   27830

U. S. Laws, Statutes, etc., 1794 (3rd Cong.
1st sess.)
. . . An Act Making Appropriation for the
Support of Government. . . . Approved,
March the Fourteenth, 1794.
[Philadelphia, 1794.] [3] pp.
JCB copy.   27834

U. S. Laws, Statutes, etc., 1794 (3rd
Cong., 1st sess.)
. . . An Act Making Appropriations for
the Support of Government. . . . Approved
- March the Fourteenth 1794.
[Philadelphia, 1794.] [3] pp.
AAS copy.   47288

U. S. Laws, Statutes, etc., 1794 (3rd Cong.
1st sess.)
. . . An Act Making Appropriations for
the Support of the Military Establishment.
. . . Approved, March the Twenty-First,
1794.
[Philadelphia, 1794.] [2] pp.
JCB copy.   27838

U. S. Laws, Statutes, etc., 1794 (3rd Cong.
1st sess.)
. . . An Act Making further Provision for
Securing and Collecting the Duties. . . .
Approved - June the Fifth 1794.
[Philadelphia, 1794.] [4] pp.
AAS copy.   27868

U. S. Laws, Statutes, etc., 1794. (3rd
Cong. 1st sess.)
. . . An Act Making further Provision for
the Expenses Attending the Intercourse of
the United States with Foreign Nations.
. . . Approved - March the Twentieth,
1794.
[Philadelphia, 1794.] Broadside.
JCB copy.   27835

U. S. Laws, Statutes, etc., 1794 (3rd Cong.
1st sess.)

. . . An Act Making Provision for the
Payment of the Interest on the Balances
due to Certain States. . . . Approved - May
the Thirty-First, 1794.
[Philadelphia, 1794.] Broadside.
AAS copy.   27859

[U. S. Laws, Statutes, etc., 1794 (3rd
Cong. 1st sess.)
An Act of the Congress . . . Passed June 7,
1794 "Laying Additional Duties on
Goods"
Boston, Adams & Larkin, 1794.]
(Imprint assumed by Evans from adv.)
                                            27873

U. S. Laws, Statutes, etc., 1794 (3rd Cong.
1st sess.)
. . . An Act Prohibiting for a Limited
Time the Exportation of Arms and
Ammunition. . . . Approved - May the
Twenty-Second 1794.
[Philadelphia, 1794.] Broadside.
AAS copy.   27856

U. S. Laws, Statutes, etc., 1794.
An Act Prohibiting for a Limited Time
the Exportation of Arms.
[Philadelphia, 1794.] Broadside.
LOC copy.   47289

U. S. Laws, Statutes, etc., 1794 (3rd Cong.
1st sess.)
. . . An Act Providing for the Payment of
Certain Expenses Incurred by Fulwar
Skipwith. . . . An Act for the Relief of
Reuben Smith. . . . Approved - May the
nineteenth 1794.
[Philadelphia, 1794.] Broadside.
AAS copy.   27854

U. S. Laws, Statutes, etc., 1794 (3rd Cong.
1st sess.)
. . . An Act Providing for the Payment of
the Second Instalment. . . . Approved -
June the Fourth 1794.
[Philadelphia, 1794.] Broadside.
AAS copy.   27861

U. S. Laws, Statutes, etc., 1794 (3rd Cong.
1st sess.)
. . . An Act Providing for the Raising and
Organizing a Corps of Artillerists. . . .
Approved - May the Ninth 1794.
[Philadelphia, 1794.] Broadside.
AAS copy.   27850

U. S. Laws, Statutes, etc., 1794 (3rd Cong.
1st sess.)
. . . An Act Providing for the Relief of
Such of the Inhabitants of Saint Domingo.
. . . Approved, February the Twelfth,
1794.
[Philadelphia, 1794.] Broadside.
NYPL copy.   27829

U. S. Laws, Statutes, etc., 1794 (3rd Cong.
1st sess.)
. . . An Act to Amend the Act Intituled
"An Act to Enable the Officers. . . ."
Approved - June the Ninth 1794. . . . An
Act Making Appropriations. . . .
Approved - June the Ninth 1794.
[Philadelphia, 1794.] [2] pp.
AAS copy.   27877

U. S. Laws, Statutes, etc., 1794 (3rd Cong.
1st sess.)
. . . An Act Supplementary to the Act
Intituled "Act to Promote the Progress of
Useful Arts. . . ." Approved - June the
Seventh 1794. . . . An Act Making Certain
Alterations in the Act for Establishing the
Judicial Courts. . . . Approved - June the
Ninth 1794.
[Philadelphia, 1794.] [2] pp.
AAS copy.   27875

U. S. Laws, Statutes, etc., 1794 (3rd Cong.
1st sess.)
. . . An Act to Authorize Ephraim
Kimberly. . . . An Act for the Relief of
Leffert Lefferts. . . . Approved - April the
Eighteenth 1794.
[Philadelphia, 1794.] Broadside.
AAS copy.   27846a

U. S. Laws, Statutes, etc., 1794 (3rd Cong.
1st sess.)
. . . An Act to Authorize the President of
the United States in Certain Cases, to
Alter the Plan for Holding a Session of

Congress. . . . Approved April the Third, 1794.
[Philadelphia, 1794.] Broadside.
JCB copy. 27845

U. S. Laws, Statutes, etc., 1794 (3rd Cong. 1st sess.)
. . . An Act to Authorize the President of the United States to Lay, Regulate and Revoke Embargoes. . . . An Act to Authorize the Settlement of the Account of Lewis Dubois. . . . Approved - June the Fourth 1794.
[Philadelphia, 1794.] Broadside.
AAS copy. 27860

U. S. Laws, Statutes, etc., 1794 (3rd Cong. 1st sess.)
. . . An Act to Authorize the President . . . to Cause to be Purchased . . . Gallies. . . . Approved - June the Fifth 1794. . . . An Act to Make Provision for the Widow . . . of Robert Forsyth. . . . Approved - June the Seventh 1794.
[Philadelphia, 1794.] Broadside.
AAS copy. 27865

U. S. Laws, Statutes, etc., 1794 (3rd Cong. 1st sess.)
. . . An Act to Continue in Force for a Limited Time, the Act Supplementary to the Act for the Establishment and Support of Light Houses. . . . Approved - June the Seventh 1794. . . . An Act Declaring the Consent of Congress. . . . June the Ninth 1794.
[Philadelphia, 1794.] Broadside.
AAS copy. 27876

U. S. Laws, Statutes, etc., 1794 (3rd Cong. 1st sess.)
. . . An Act to Continue in Force the Act for the Relief of Persons Imprisoned for Debt. . . . An Act to Alter the Time for the Next Annual Meeting of Congress. . . . Approved - May the Thirtieth 1794.
[Philadelphia, 1794.] Broadside.
AAS copy. 27857

U. S. Laws, Statutes, etc., 1794 (3rd Cong. 1st sess.)
. . . An Act to Erect a Lighthouse on the Head-land of Cape Hatteras. . . . Approved - May the Thirteenth 1794.
[Philadelphia, 1794.] Broadside.
AAS copy. 27853

U. S. Laws, Statutes, etc., 1794 (3rd Cong. 1st sess.)
. . . An Act to Establish the Post-Office. . . . Approved - May the eighth, 1794.
[Philadelphia, 1794.] 11 pp.
AAS copy. 27849

U. S. Laws, Statutes, etc., 1794 (3rd Cong. 1st sess.)
. . . An Act to Extend the Term of Credit for Teas. . . . An Act for the Relief of John Robbe. . . . Approved - June the Fourth 1794.
[Philadelphia, 1794.] Broadside.
AAS copy. 27863

U. S. Laws, Statutes, etc., 1794 (3rd Cong. 1st sess.)
. . . An Act to Prohibit the Carrying on the Slave-Trade. . . . Approved, March the Twenty-Second, 1794.
[Philadelphia, 1794.] [2] pp.
JCB copy. 27839

U. S. Laws, Statutes, etc., 1794 (3rd Cong. 1st sess.)
. . . An Act to Provide a Naval Armament. . . . Approved, March the Twenty-Seventh, 1794.] [2] pp.
[Philadelphia, 1794.] Broadside.
JCB copy. 27840

U. S. Laws, Statutes, etc., 1794 (3rd Cong. 1st sess.)
. . . An Act to Provide for Placing Buoys. . . . Approved - April the Fifth 1794.
[Philadelphia, 1794.] Broadside.
AAS copy. 27846

U. S. Laws, Statutes, etc., 1794 (3rd Cong. 1st sess.)
. . . An Act to Provide for the Defence of Certain Parts. . . . Approved, March the Twentieth, 1794.
[Philadelphia, 1794.] Broadside.
RIHS copy. 27837

U. S. Laws, Statutes, etc., 1794 (3rd Cong. 1st sess.)
. . . An Act to Provide for the Erecting and Repairing Present Arsenals. . . . Approved - April the Second, 1794.
[Philadelphia, 1794.] Broadside.
JCB copy. 27842

U. S. Laws, Statutes, etc., 1793 (3rd Cong. 1st sess.)
Acts Passed at the Third Congress.
Richmond, Davis, [1794]. 60 pp.
VaSL copy. 27828

U. S. Laws, Statutes, etc., 1794 (3rd Cong. 1st sess.)
In Congress, March 26, 1794. Resolved . . . that an Embargo be Laid. . . .
Approved - March the Twenty-Sixth 1794.
[Philadelphia, 1794.] Broadside.
LOC copy. 47291

U. S. Laws, Statutes, etc., 1794. (3rd Cong. 1st sess.)
In Congress, March 26, 1794. Resolved . . . that an Embargo be Laid. . . .
Approved - March the Twenty-Sixth, 1794. . . . Reprinted in Salem, March 30, 1794.
[Salem, 1794.] Broadside.
EI copy. 47292

U. S. Laws, Statutes, etc., 1794 (3rd Cong. 1st sess.)
. . . Resolved by the Senate and House of Representatives . . . that during the Continuance of the Present Embargo. . . . Approved - April the Second 1794.
[Philadelphia, 1794.] Broadside.
WLC copy. 47293

[U. S. Laws, Statutes, etc., 1794 (3rd Cong. 1st sess.)
. . . Resolved [Defining the Embargo Resolution].
[Philadelphia, 1794.] Broadside.]
(Apparently a ghost of 27835, q. v.) 27880

U. S. Laws, Statutes, etc., 1794 (3rd Cong. 1st sess.)
. . . Resolved by the Senate and Representatives . . . That an Embargo be laid. . . . Approved - March the Twenty-Sixth, 1794.
[Philadelphia, 1794.] Broadside.
(Printed on sheet with 27841.)
JCB copy. 27879

U. S. Laws, Statutes, etc., 1794 (3rd Cong. 1st sess.)
. . . Resolved by the Senate and House of Representatives . . . That the Present Embargo be Continued. . . . Approved - April the Eighteenth 1794.
[Philadelphia, 1794.] Broadside.
AAS copy. 27881

U. S. Laws, Statutes, etc., 1794 (3rd Cong. 1st sess.)
. . . Resolved by the Senate and House of Representatives . . . That the President of the United States be Authorized to Direct Clearances. . . . Approved - May the Seventh 1794.
[Philadelphia, 1794.] Broadside.
AAS copy. 27882

U. S. Laws, Statutes, etc., 1794 (3rd Cong. 1st sess.)
. . . Resolved by the Senate and House of Representatives . . . That the Secretary for the Department of War, be, and he is hereby Directed to make out an Exact List. . . . That it shall be the Duty of the Respective Clerks of the Several District Courts. . . . Approved - June the Ninth 1794.
[Philadelphia, 1794.] Broadside.
AAS copy. 27883

U. S. Laws, Statutes, etc., 1794 (3rd Cong. 1st sess.)
Whereas, the Injuries which have been Suffered . . . Resolved, that . . . all Commercial Intercourse be Prohibited.
n. p., [1794] Broadside.
WLC copy. 47294

U. S. Laws, Statutes, etc., 1794 (3rd Cong. 2nd sess.)
Acts Passed at the Second Session of the Third Congress.
Philadelphia, Childs, 1795. pp. [143]-260, iv.
HEH copy. 47653

U. S. Laws, Statutes, etc., 1795 (3rd Cong. 2nd sess.)
. . . An Act Authorizing the Payment of Four Thousand Dollars. . . . Approved, February the twenty seventh, 1795.
[Philadelphia, 1795.] Broadside.
HEH copy. 47648

U. S. Laws, Statutes, etc., 1795. (3rd Cong. 2nd sess.)
An Act Authorizing the Transfer of the Stock Standing to the Credit of Certain States. . . . Approved, January the second, 1795.
[Philadelphia, 1795.] Broadside.
(Copy not located.) 47649

U. S. Laws, Statutes, etc., 1794 (3rd Cong. 2nd sess.)
. . . An Act Extending the Privilege of Franking to James White. . . . Approved, December the Third, 1794.
[Philadelphia, 1794.] Broadside.
NYPL copy. 27887

U. S. Laws, Statutes, etc., 1795 (3rd Cong. 2nd sess.)
. . . An Act for the More General Promulgation of the Laws. . . .
[Philadelphia, 1795.] Broadside.
NYPL copy. 47650

U. S. Laws, Statutes, etc., 1795 (3rd Cong. 2nd sess.)
. . . An Act in Addition to the Act entitled, "An Act to Regulate the Pay of the Non-Commissioned Officers. . . . Approved, January the Twenty-Ninth, 1795.
[Philadelphia, 1795.] Broadside.
NYPL copy. 47651

U. S. Laws, Statutes, etc., 1795 (3rd Cong. 2nd sess.)
An Act of the President . . . Making Provision for the Compensation of the Officers of the Revenue in . . . Ohio and Tennessee [Jan. 28, 1795].
[Philadelphia, 1795.] Broadside.
HEH copy. 47652

U. S. Laws, Statutes, etc., 1794 (3rd Cong. 2nd sess.)
. . . An Act to Amend and Explain the Twenty-Second Section of "The Act Establishing the Judicial Courts,". . . . Approved, December the Twelfth, 1794.
[Philadelphia, 1794.] Broadside.
NYPL copy. 27888

U. S. Laws, Statutes, etc., 1794 (3rd Cong. 2nd sess.)
. . . An Act to Authorize the Officers of the Treasury to Audit . . . the Account of . . . Edward Blanchard. . . . An Act Authorizing a Loan of Two Million of Dollars. . . . Approved, December the Eighteenth, 1794.
[Philadelphia, 1794.] Broadside.
NYPL copy. 27889

U. S. Laws, Statutes, etc., 1794. (3rd Cong. 2nd sess.)
. . . An Act to Authorize the President to Call Out and Station a Corps of Militia, in . . . Pennsylvania. . . . Approved, November the Twenty-Ninth, 1794.
[Philadelphia, 1794.] Broadside.
NYPL copy. 27886

U. S. Laws, Statutes, etc., 1794 (3rd Cong. 2nd sess.)
Acts Passed at the Second Session of the Third Congress.
Philadelphia, Childs, 1795. pp. [143]-260, [i], iv, [24] pp.
LOC copy. 29677

U. S. Laws, Statutes, etc., 1795.
Acts Passed at the First [-Second] Session of the Fourth Congress.
Philadelphia, Dobson, 1797. pp. [261]-316, 325-455, [495]-566, [120].
NYPL copy. 48291

U. S. Laws, Statutes, etc., 1795.
A Bill to Provide for Organizing, Arming, and Disciplining the Militia. . . .
Published by Order of the General Court of New-Hampshire.
Hanover, Dunham & True, 1795. 16 pp.
AAS copy. 29721

U. S. Laws, Statutes, etc., 1795.
Laws of the United States. . . . Volume I.
Boston, Adams & Larkin, 1795. pp. [1]-8,
5-8, 13, 519.
AAS copy. 29725

[U. S. Laws, Statutes, etc., 1795 (3rd
Cong. 2nd sess.)
. . . An Act Establishing the Pay and
Rations of the Militia. . . .
[Philadelphia, 1795.] Broadside.]
(No such printing located.) 29679

U. S. Laws, Statutes, etc., 1795 (3rd Cong.
2nd sess.)
. . . An Act Supplementary to the Act,
Intituled, "An Act to Provide more
Effectually for the Collection of the
Duties. . . ." Approved, February the
Twenty-Sixth, 1795.
[Philadelphia, 1795.] [4] pp.
LOC copy. 29698

U. S. Laws, Statutes, etc., 1795 (3rd Cong.
2nd sess.)
. . . An Act Supplementary to the Several
Acts imposing Duties . . . Approved,
January the Twenty Ninth, 1795.
[Philadelphia, 1795.] [2] pp.
LOC copy. 29699

U. S. Laws, Statutes, etc., 1795 (3rd Cong.
2nd sess.)
. . . An Act for Continuing and Regulating
the Military Establishment. . . . Approved,
March the third, 1795.
[Philadelphia, 1795.] [4] pp.
LOC copy. 29680

U. S. Laws, Statutes, etc., 1795 (3rd Cong.
2nd sess.)
. . . An Act for Reviving Certain Suits. . . .
Approved, January the Twenty Eighth,
1795.
[Philadelphia, 1795.] Broadside.
LOC copy. 29681

U. S. Laws, Statutes, etc., 1795 (3rd Cong.
2nd sess.)
. . . An Act for the More Effective
Recovery of Debts. . . . Approved, March
the Third, 1795.
[Philadelphia, 1795.] [2] pp.
LOC copy. 29682

U. S. Laws, Statutes, etc., 1795 (3rd Cong.
2nd sess.)
. . . An Act for the Relief of Peter
Covenhoven. . . . Approved, January the
first, 1795.
[Philadelphia, 1795.] Broadside.
LOC copy. 29683

U. S. Laws, Statutes, etc., 1795 (3rd Cong.
2nd sess.)
. . . An Act for the Relief of William
Seymour. . . . Approved, March the
Second, 1795.
[Philadelphia, 1795.] Broadside.
LOC copy. 29685

U. S. Laws, Statutes, etc., 1795 (3rd Cong.
2nd sess.)
. . . An Act for the Reimbursement of a
Loan. . . . Approved, February the Twenty
First, 1795.
[Philadelphia, 1795.] Broadside.
LOC copy. 29686

U. S. Laws, Statutes, etc., 1795 (3rd Cong.
2nd sess.)
. . . An Act for the remission of Tonnage
Duties. . . . Approved, January the
Twenty Eighth, 1795.
[Philadelphia, 1795.] Broadside.
LOC copy. 29684

U. S. Laws, Statutes, etc., 1795 (3rd Cong.
2nd sess.)
. . . An Act further Extending the Time
for Receiving on Loan the Domestic Debt.
. . . Approved, January the
Twenty-Eighth, 1795.
[Philadelphia, 1795.] Broadside.
LOC copy. 29687

U. S. Laws, Statutes, etc., 1795 (3rd Cong.
2nd sess.)
. . . An Act Making Appropriations for
the Support of Government. . . .
Approved, January the Second, 1795.
[Philadelphia, 1795.] [3] pp.
LOC copy. 29688

U. S. Laws, Statutes, etc., 1795 (3rd Cong.
2nd sess.)
. . . An Act Making Appropriations for
the Support of the Military Establishment.
. . . Approved, Thirty First Decr., 1794.
[Philadelphia, 1795.] Broadside.
LOC copy. 29689

U. S. Laws, Statutes, etc., 1795 (3rd Cong.
2nd sess.)
. . . An Act Making further Appropriations
for the Military and Naval Establishments.
. . . Approved, March the Third, 1795.
[Philadelphia, 1795.] [2] pp.
LOC copy. 29690

U. S. Laws, Statutes, etc., 1795 (3rd Cong.
2nd sess.)
. . . An Act Making further Provision for
the Support of Public Credit. . . .
Approved, March the Third, 1795.
[Philadelphia], Fenno, [1795]. [6] pp.
LOC copy. 29691

U. S. Laws, Statutes, etc., 1795 (3rd Cong.
2nd sess.)
. . . An Act Making further Provision in
Cases of Drawbacks. . . . Approved,
January the Twenty Ninth, 1795.
[Philadelphia, 1795.] [3] pp.
LOC copy. 29692

U. S. Laws, Statutes, etc., 1795 (3rd Cong.
2nd sess.)
. . . An Act Providing for the Payment of
Certain Instalments. . . . Approved
January the Eighth, 1795.
[Philadelphia, 1795.] Broadside.
LOC copy. 29693

U. S. Laws, Statutes, etc., 1795 (3rd Cong.
2nd sess.)
. . . An Act Relative to the Compensations
of Certain Officers. . . . Approved,
February the Fourteenth, 1795.
[Philadelphia, 1795.] [2] pp.
LOC copy. 29694

U. S. Laws, Statutes, etc., 1795 (3rd Cong.
2nd sess.)
. . . An Act Relative to the Passing of
Coastal Vessels between Long Island and
Rhode Island. . . . Approved, March the
Second, 1795.
[Philadelphia, 1795.] Broadside.
LOC copy. 29695

U. S. Laws, Statutes, etc., 1795 (3rd Cong.
2nd sess.)
. . . An Act Supplementary to the Act
Concerning Invalids. . . . Approved,
February the Twenty First, 1795.
[Philadelphia, 1795.] Broadside.
LOC copy. 29696

U. S. Laws, Statutes, etc., 1795. (3rd
Cong. 2nd sess.)
. . . An Act Supplementary to the Act,
Intituled, "An Act Establishing a Mint.
. . ." Approved, March the Third, 1795.
[Philadelphia, 1795.] [2] pp.
LOC copy. 29697

U. S. Laws, Statutes, etc., 1795 (3rd Cong.
2nd sess.)
. . . An Act to Alter and Amend the Act,
Intituled "An Act Laying Certain Duties
upon Snuff and Refined Sugar. . . ."
Approved, March the Third, 1795.
[Philadelphia, 1795.] [4] pp.
LOC copy. 29700

U. S. Laws, Statutes, etc., 1795 (3rd Cong.
2nd sess.)
. . . An Act to Amend the Act, Entitled,
"An Act to Establish the Post-Office. . . ."
Approved, February the Twenty Fifth,
1795.
[Philadelphia, 1795.] [2] pp.
LOC copy. 29701

U. S. Laws, Statutes, etc., 1795 (3rd Cong.
2nd sess.)
. . . An Act to Authorize a Grant of Lands
to the French Inhabitants of Galliopolis.
. . . Approved, March the Third, 1795.
[Philadelphia, 1795.] [2] pp.
LOC copy. 29702

U. S. Laws, Statutes, etc., 1795 (3rd Cong.
2nd sess.)
. . . An Act to Authorize the Allowance of
Drawback on Part of the Cargo of the

Ship Enterprise. . . . Approved, February
the Thirteenth, 1795.
[Philadelphia, 1795.] Broadside.
LOC copy. 29703

U. S. Laws, Statutes, etc., 1795 (3rd Cong.
2nd sess.)
. . . An Act to Continue in Force for a
Limited Time the Acts therein Mentioned.
. . . Approved, March the Second, 1795.
[Philadelphia, 1795.] Broadside.
LOC copy. 29704

U. S. Laws, Statutes, etc., 1795 (3rd Cong.
2nd sess.)
. . . An Act to Continue in Force the Act
"for Ascertaining the Fees. . . ."
Approved, February the Twenty-Fifth,
1795.
[Philadelphia, 1795.] Broadside.
LOC copy. 29705

U. S. Laws, Statutes, etc., 1795 (3rd Cong.
2nd sess.)
. . . An Act to Establish a Uniform Rule
of Naturalization. . . . Approved January
the Twenty-Ninth, 1795.
[Philadelphia, 1795.] [2] pp.
LOC copy. 29706

U. S. Laws, Statutes, etc., 1795 (3rd Cong.
2nd sess.)
. . . An Act to Establish the Office of
Purveyor of Public Supplies. . . .
Approved, February the Twenty-Third,
1795.
[Philadelphia, 1795.] Broadside.
LOC copy. 29707

U. S. Laws, Statutes, etc., 1795 (3rd Cong.
2nd sess.)
. . . An Act to Provide for Calling forth
the Militia. . . . Approved, February the
Twenty-Eighth, 1795.
[Philadelphia, 1795.] [2] pp.
LOC copy. 29708

U. S. Laws, Statutes, etc., 1795 (3rd Cong.
2nd sess.)
. . . An Act to Provide some Present
Relief. . . . Approved February the
Twenty Seventh, 1795.
[Philadelphia, 1795.] Broadside.
LOC copy. 29709

U. S. Laws, Statutes, etc., 1795 (3rd Cong.
2nd sess.)
. . . An Act to Regulate the Compensation
of Clerks. . . . Approved March the Third,
1795.
[Philadelphia, 1795.] Broadside.
LOC copy. 29710

U. S. Laws, Statutes, etc., 1795 (3rd Cong.
2nd sess.)
. . . An Act to Regulate the Pay of the
Non-Commissioned Officers. . . .
Approved, January the Second, 1795.
[Philadelphia, 1795.] [2] pp.
LOC copy. 29711

U. S. Laws, Statutes, etc., 1795 (3rd Cong.
2nd sess.)
Duties Payable by Law on all
Goods Imported . . . after the Last Day of
March 1795.
[Philadelphia, 1795.] 15 pp.
(Copy cannot be reproduced.) 47654

U. S. Laws, Statutes, etc., 1795 (4th
Cong., 1st sess.).
Acts Passed at the First Session of the
Fourth Congress.
Philadelphia, Childs, 1796. 137, [3], 46, iv
pp.
AAS copy. 31331

U. S. Laws, Statutes, etc., 1795 (4th
Cong., 1st sess.).
Acts Passed at the First Session of the
Fourth Congress.
Richmond, Va., Davis. 55, 13, [1] pp.
VaSL copy. 31332

U. S. Laws, Statutes, etc., 1796.
The Laws of the United States. . . . In
Three Volumes. Vol. I [-II].
Philadelphia, Folwell, 1796. 494, [1];
576 pp.
AAS copy. 31356

U. S. Laws, Statutes, etc., 1796.
The Laws of the United States of

America. In Three Volumes. Vol. III.
Philadelphia, Folwell, 1796. 477, [131] pp.
AAS copy.   32973

U. S. Laws, Statutes, etc., 1796 (4th Cong.
1st sess.)
. . . An Act Authorising and Directing the
Secretary of War to Place Certain Persons
. . . on the Pension List. . . . Approved
Apr. 20, 1796.
[Philadelphia, 1796.] 5 pp.
(No copy available for reproduction.)
      47955

U. S. Laws, Statutes, etc., 1796 (4th Cong.
1st sess.)
. . . An Act Authorizing the Erection of a
Light-House on Baker's Island.
[Philadelphia, 1796?] Broadside.
WLC copy.   47956

U. S. Laws, Statutes, etc., 1796 (4th Cong.
1st sess.)
. . . An Act Authorizing the Erection of a
Light-House on Cape Cod.
n. p., [1796?] 2 pp.
WLC copy.   47957

U. S. Laws, Statutes, etc., 1796 (4th Cong.
1st sess.)
. . . An Act for Allowing Compensation to
the Members of the Senate, and House.
. . . Approved March the Tenth 1796.
[Philadelphia, 1796.] 2 pp.
LOC copy.   47958

U. S. Laws, Statutes, etc., 1796 (4th Cong.
1st sess.)
. . . An Act for Establishing Trading
Houses with the Indian Tribes [Apr. 18,
1796].
[Philadelphia, 1796.] 3 pp.
JCB copy.   47959

U. S. Laws, Statutes, etc., 1796 (4th Cong.
1st sess.)
. . . An Act for Laying Duties on
Carriages. . . . Approved - May the
Twenty-Eighth, 1796.
[Philadelphia, 1796.] 4 pp.
Pierce W. Gaines copy.   47960

U. S. Laws, Statutes, etc., 1796.
An Act for the Government and
Regulation of Seamen.
New London, Springer, [1796?] [2] pp.
CHS copy.   47961

U. S. Laws, Statutes, etc., 1796 (4th Cong.
1st sess.)
. . . An Act for the Relief of Benjamin
Strother [Feb. 26, 1796].
[Philadelphia, 1796.] Broadside.
(No copy available for reproduction.)
      47962

U. S. Laws, Statutes, etc., 1796 (4th Cong.
1st sess.)
. . . An Act for the Relief of Certain
Officers. . . . Approved - March the
Twenty-Third 1796.
[Philadelphia, 1796.] 2 pp.
WLC copy.   47963

U. S. Laws, Statutes, etc., 1796 (4th Cong.
1st sess.)
An Act for the Relief of Israel Loring. . . .
Approved - March the Tenth, 1796.
[Philadelphia, 1796.] Broadside.
LOC copy.   47964

U. S. Laws, Statutes, etc., 1796 (4th Cong.
1st sess.)
An Act for the Relief of Persons
Imprisoned for Debts. . . . Approved -
May the Twenty-Eighth, 1796.
[Philadelphia, 1796.] Broadside.
(Copy not located.)   47965

U. S. Laws, Statutes, etc., 1796 (4th Cong.
1st sess.)
. . . An Act further Extending the Time
for Receiving on Loan the Domestic Debt.
. . . [Feb. 19, 1796.]
[Philadelphia, 1796.] Broadside.
(No copy available for reproduction.)
      47966

U. S. Laws, Statutes, etc., 1796 (4th Cong.
1st sess.)
. . . An Act in Addition to . . . "An Act
Making further Provision for the . . .

Redemption of the Public Debt". . . .
[Apr. 28, 1796.]
[Philadelphia, 1796.] 2 pp.
WLC copy.   47967

U. S. Laws, Statutes, etc., 1796 (4th Cong.
1st sess.)
. . . An Act Making Appropriations. . . .
Approved - February the Fifth, 1796.
[Philadelphia, 1796.] 4 pp.
LOC copy.   47968

U. S. Laws, Statutes, etc., 1796 (4th
Cong., 1st sess.)
. . . An Act Making an Appropriation
towards defraying. . . . Approved - May
the Sixth, 1796.
[Philadelphia, 1796.] 2 pp.
LOC copy.   47969

U. S. Laws, Statutes, etc., 1796 (4th Cong.
1st sess.)
. . . An Act Making Certain Provisions in
Regard to the Circuit Court for . . .
North-Carolina. . . . Approved - March
the Thirty-First 1796.
[Philadelphia, 1796.] 2 pp.
WLC copy.   47970

U. S. Laws, Statutes, etc., 1796 (4th Cong.
1st sess.)
. . . An Act Making further Provision for
the Expenses Attending the Intercourse
. . . with Foreign Nations. . . . Approved -
May the Thirtieth 1796.
[Philadelphia, 1796.] 2 pp.
WLC copy.   47971

U. S. Laws, Statutes, etc., 1796 (4th Cong.
1st sess.)
An Act Passed at the First Session of the
Fourth Congress.
Detroit, M'Call, 1796. [2], 16 pp.
AAS facsim. copy.   47972

U. S. Laws, Statutes, etc., 1796 (4th Cong.
1st sess.)
. . . An Act Providing for the Sale of the
Lands . . . North-West of the River Ohio.
. . . Approved - May the Eighteenth, 1796.
[Philadelphia, 1796.] 4 pp.
WLC copy.   47973

U. S. Laws, Statutes, etc., 1796. (4th
Cong. 1st sess.)
. . . An Act Regulating the Grants of
Land. . . . Approved - June the First 1796.
[Philadelphia, 1796.] 4 pp.
LOC copy.   47974

U. S. Laws, Statutes, etc., 1796 (4th Cong.
1st sess.)
. . . An Act Supplementary to . . . "An Act
to Provide a Naval Armament." Approved
- April the Twentieth 1796.
[Philadelphia, 1796.] Broadside.
WLC copy.   47975

U. S. Laws, Statutes, etc., 1796 (4th Cong.
1st sess.)
. . . An Act to Ascertain and Fix the
Military Establishment. . . . Approved -
May the Thirtieth 1796.
[Philadelphia, 1796.] 4 pp.
JCB copy.   47976

U. S. Laws, Statutes, etc., 1796 (4th Cong.
1st sess.)
. . . An Act to Continue in Force . . . the
Appointment of a Health Officer. . . .
Approved May the Twelfth, 1796.
[Philadelphia, 1796.] 3 pp.
(No copy available for reproduction.)
      47977

U. S. Laws, Statutes, etc., 1796 (4th Cong.
1st sess.)
. . . An Act to Regulate the Compensation
of Clerks. . . . Approved - May the
Thirtieth 1796.
[Philadelphia, 1796.] 4 pp.
WLC copy.   47978

U. S. Laws, Statutes, etc., 1796 (4th
Cong., 1st sess.).
. . . An Act for Laying Duties on
Carriages. . . . Approved - May the
Twenty-Eighth, 1796.
[Philadelphia, 1796.] 8 pp.
NYPL copy.   31335

U. S. Laws, Statutes, etc., 1796 (4th
Cong., 1st sess.).

. . . An Act for the Relief and Protection
of American Seamen. . . . Approved - May
Twenty-Eighth, 1796.
[Philadelphia, 1796.] 2 pp.
LOC copy.   31336

U. S. Laws, Statutes, etc., 1796 (4th
Cong., 1st sess.).
. . . An Act in Addition to an Act,
Intituled "An Act Supplementary to the
Act, Intituled, "An Act to Provide more
Effectually for the Collection of the Duties
on Goods. . . ." Approved May the
Twenty-Seventh, 1796.
[Philadelphia, 1796.] 2 pp.
LOC copy.   31341

U. S. Laws, Statutes, etc., 1796 (4th
Cong., 1st sess.)
. . . An Act Making further
Appropriations for the Year One
Thousand Seven Hundred and Ninety Six.
. . Approved - June the First 1796. [and
four other Acts.]
[Philadelphia, 1796.] 4 pp.
JCB copy.   31342

U. S. Laws, Statutes, etc., 1796 (4th
Cong., 1st sess.)
. . . An Act Making further Provision
Relative to the Revenue Cutters. . . .
Approved - May Sixth, 1796.
[Philadelphia, 1796.] 2 pp.
LOC copy.   31343

U. S. Laws, Statutes, etc., 1796 (4th
Cong., 1st sess.).
. . . An Act Providing Passports for the
Ships and Vessels of the United States.
. . . Approved-June the First, 1796.
Philadelphia, Childs, 1796. [2] pp.
LOC copy.   31345

U. S. Laws, Statutes, etc., 1796 (4th
Cong., 1st sess.)
. . . An Act Relative to Quarantine. . . .
Approved - May the twenty-seventh, 1796
[and three other Acts.]
[Philadelphia, 1796.] 3 pp.
JCB copy.   31346

U. S. Laws, Statutes, etc., 1796 (4th
Cong., 1st sess.).
. . . An Act to Regulate the Trade and
Intercourse with the Indian Tribes. . . .
Approved - May the Nineteenth, 1796.
[Philadelphia, 1796.] 6 pp.
LOC copy.   31347

U. S. Laws, Statutes, etc., 1796 (4th
Cong., 1st sess.)
. . . An Act to Suspend, in Part, the Act
Intituled "An Act to Alter the Act, Intitled
"An Act Laying Certain Duties upon
Snuff. . . ." Approved - June the First,
1796.
[Philadelphia, 1796.] 2 pp.
LOC copy.   31348

U. S. Laws, Statutes, etc., 1796 (4th
Cong., 1st sess.).
District of Salem and Beverly. Extract
from an Act . . . Entitled "An Act for the
Relief and Protection of American
Seamen."
[Salem, 1796.] Broadside.
EI copy.   31339

U. S. Laws, Statutes, etc., 1796. (4th
Cong. 1st sess.)
Extract from an Act, for the Relief and
Protection of American Seamen.
n. p., [1796]. Broadside.
AAS copy.   47979

U. S. Laws, Statutes, etc., 1796 (4th
Cong., 1st sess.)
Extract from the Act of Congress, Passed
the 28th Day of May, 1796, entitled "An
Act for the Relief and Protection of
American Seamen" [35 lines].
[Providence? 1796.] Broadside.
JCB copy.   31337

U. S. Laws, Statutes, etc., 1796 (4th
Cong., 1st sess.).
Extract from the Act of Congress, Passed
the 28th of May, 1796, entitled "An Act
for the Relief and Protection of American
Seamen" [24 lines].
[Providence? 1796.] Broadside.
AAS copy.   31338

U. S. Laws, Statutes, etc., 1796 (4th Cong., 1st sess.).
An Extract of the Act, Entitled "An Act for the Relief and Protection of American Seamen".... Approved - May the Twenty-Eighth, 1796.
Baltimore, Hayes, [1796]. Broadside.
LOC copy. 31340

U. S. Laws, Statutes, etc., 1796. (4th Cong. 2nd sess.)
Acts Passed at the Second Session of the Fourth Congress [Dec. 5, 1796 - Mar. 3, 1797.]
Richmond, Va., Davis, 1797. pp. [55]-84.
NYPL copy. 32950

U. S. Laws, Statutes, etc., 1797.
Duties, imposed . . . on all Stamped Vellum . . . from the 31st Day of December, 1797.
[New York], Hopkins, [1798?]
Broadside.
(Not located, 1968.) 48728

U. S. Laws, Statutes, etc., 1797.
The Laws of the United States of America, Containing the Acts of the Fourth Congress.
Philadelphia, Folwell, 1797. 306, [9] pp.
AAS copy. 32974

U. S. Laws, Statutes, etc., 1797 (4th Cong. 2nd sess.)
An Act Repealing in Part "The Act Concerning the Duties on Spirits. . . ."
Approved March 3d, 1797.
[Philadelphia, 1797.] [2] pp.
LOC copy. 32960

U. S. Laws, Statutes, etc., 1797 (4th Cong. 2nd sess.)
Duties Payable by Law, on all Goods . . . Imported . . . after the last Day of June, 1797.
[Philadelphia, 1797.] 20 pp.
LOC copy. 48294

U. S. Laws, Statutes, etc., 1797 (5th Cong. 1st sess.)
An Act Authorizing a Detachment from the Militia. . . . Approved, June 24th, 1797.
[Philadelphia, 1797.] Broadside.
LOC copy. 32953

U. S. Laws, Statutes, etc., 1797 (5th Cong. 1st sess.)
. . . An Act in Addition to an Act, Intituled "An Act . . . Registering . . . Ships." Approved June 27th, 1797.
[Philadelphia, 1797.] [2] pp.
LOC copy. 32954

U. S. Laws, Statutes, etc., 1797 (5th Cong. 1st sess.)
An Act Laying Duties on Stamped Vellum. . . . Approved . . . July 8, 1797.
Walpole, N. H., Carlisle, 1797. 20 pp.
LOC copy. 32957

U. S. Laws, Statutes, etc., 1797 (5th Cong. 1st sess.)
An Act Laying Duties on Stamped Vellum. . . . Approved July sixth, 1797.
[Philadelphia, 1797.] pp. 22-35.
HSP copy. 48292

[U. S. Laws, Statutes, etc., 1797 (5th Cong. 1st sess.)
An Act Laying Duties upon Stamped Vellum, Parchment, and Paper. Passed July 9, 1797.
[Alexandria, 1797.] Broadside.]
(No copy located.) 32955

[U. S. Laws, Statutes, etc., 1797 (5th Cong. 1st sess.)
. . . An Act Prohibiting Exportation of Arms. . . . Approved, June Fourteen, 1797.
[Philadelphia, 1797.] Broadside.]
(No copy located.) 32958

U. S. Laws, Statutes, etc., 1797 (5th Cong. 1st sess.)
An Act to Provide for the further Defence of the Ports. . . . June 23d, 1797. Approved.
[Philadelphia, 1797.] Broadside.
CHS copy. 48293

U. S. Laws, Statutes, etc., 1797 (5th Cong. 1st sess.)
Acts Passed at the First Session of the Fifth Congress (May 15 - July 10, 1797).
Philadelphia, Folwell, [1797]. 50 pp.
AAS copy. 32952

U. S. Laws, Statutes, etc., 1797 (5th Cong. 1st sess.)
Acts Passed at the First Session of the Fifth Congress [May 15 - July 10, 1797].
Philadelphia, Ross, 1797. 46, [2] pp.
AAS copy. 32951

U. S. Laws, Statutes, etc., 1797 (5th Cong. 1st sess.)
Acts passed at the First Session of the Fifth Congress.
Richmond, Va., Davis, 1798. 18, [1] pp.
AAS copy. 34687

U. S. Laws, Statutes, etc., 1797 (5th Cong. 1st sess.)
Stamp Act. An Act Laying Duties . . . Approved-July 6, 1797.
New York, Oram [1797]. Broadside.
LOC copy. 32956

U. S. Laws, Statutes, etc., 1797 (5th Cong. 2nd sess.)
Acts Passed at the Second Session of the Fifth Congress.
Philadelphia, Folwell, [1798]. pp. [49]-240, [i]-vii, [1]
AAS copy. 34688

U. S. Laws, Statutes, etc., 1797 (5th Cong. 2nd sess.)
Acts Passed at the Second Session of the Fifth Congress.
Richmond, Va., Davis, 1798. 84, iv pp.
VaSL copy. 34689

U. S. Laws, Statutes, etc., 1798 (5th Cong. 2nd sess.)
An Act to Regulate and Fix the Compensation of the Officers . . . Collecting the Internal Revenue . . . Approved July 11, 1798.
[Philadelphia, 1798.] 7 pp.
LCP copy. 48727

U. S. Laws, Statutes, etc., 1798 (5th Cong. 2nd sess.)
23d April, 1798. . . . An Act to Establish an Executive Department.
n. p., [1798]. 2 pp.
WLC copy. 48721

U. S. Laws, Statutes, etc., 1798 (5th Cong. 2nd sess.)
30th April, 1798 An Act, to Authorize the President . . . to Cause to be Purchased . . . a Number of Small Vessels.
n. p., [1798]. Broadside.
WLC copy. 48722

[U. S. Laws, Statutes, etc., 1798.
An Act More Effectually to Protect the Commerce and Coasts of the United States.
[Philadelphia, 1798.] Broadside.]
(No copy located.) 34697

[U. S. Laws, Statutes, etc., 1798.
An Authentic Copy of the American Stamp Act.
New London, Ct., Holt, 1798.]
("To.-morrow will be Published," The Bee, Jan. 17, 1798; "For sale," ibid, Jan. 31.) 34875

U. S. Laws, Statutes, etc., 1798.
Extracts from the Revenue Laws.
Lexington, Ky., Bradford, 1798. 26 pp.
LOC copy. 34717

U. S. Laws, Statutes, etc., 1798.
Extracts from the Internal Revenue Laws . . . for the Use of the Officers of the Revenue, within the District of New York.
New York, Jones, [1798]. [2], 88 pp.
NYPL copy. 34716

U. S. Laws, Statutes, etc., 1798.
Marine Rules and Regulations.
[Philadelphia], Fenno, 1798. 56, [6] pp.
AAS copy. 34893

U. S. Laws, Statutes, etc., 1798.
The Post-Office Law, with Instructions.

Philadelphia, Cist, [1798]. 99, [8] pp.
LOC copy. 34904

U. S. Laws, Statutes, etc., 1798.
The Several Acts Relative to Stamp Duties.
Washington, Ky., Hunter & Beaumont, 1798. 20 pp.
(Imprint assumed by Evans from adv.)
AAS copy. 34876

[U. S. Laws, Statutes, etc., 1798.
The Stamp Duties.
Lexington, Ky., Bradford, 1798.]
(Imprint assumed by Evans from for sale adv. in Ky. Gazette, Sept. 26, 1798.) 34878

[U. S. Laws, Statutes, etc., 1798.
A Table or List of the Different Rates of Stamp Duties upon Stamped Paper.
Newburyport, March, 1798. Broadside.]
(Title and imprint assumed by Evans from adv.) 34879

[U. S. Laws, Statutes, etc., 1798.
A Table or List of the Different Rates of Stamp Duties upon Stamped Paper.
Salem, Cushing, 1798.]
(Imprint assumed by Evans from adv. "Just Published, and for Sale at this Office," Salem Gazette, July 31, 1798.) 34880

U. S. Laws, Statutes, etc., 1798 (5th Cong.)
The Laws of the United States of America. In Four Volumes. Vol. IV.
Philadelphia, Folwell, 1798. pp. [1]-240, i-vii, [241]-561, [1], [1]-26, [i]-iv, [48] pp.
LOC copy. 36523

U. S. Laws, Statutes, etc., 1798 (5th Cong.).
The Laws of the United States of America, Vol. IV.
Philadelphia, M'Culloch for Carey, 1799. pp. [1]-240, i-vii, [241]-561, [1]-26, [i]-iv, [48] pp.
HEH copy. 36524

U. S. Laws, Statutes, etc., 1798 (5th Cong., 2nd sess.)
. . . An Act Concerning Aliens. . . . Approved, June 22d, 1798.
[Philadelphia, 1798.] Broadside.
LOC copy. 34690

U. S. Laws, Statutes, etc., 1798 (5th Cong., 2nd sess.)
An Act for the Government and Regulation of Seamen in the Merchants' Service.
Baltimore, Pechin, [1798]. [2] pp.
(No copy of this printing located.) 34692

U. S. Laws, Statutes, etc., 1798 (5th Cong. 2nd sess.)
An Act Laying Duties on Stamped Vellum. . . . Approved - February 28, 1798. 20 pp.
LCP copy. 48723

U. S. Laws, Statutes, etc., 1798. (5th Cong. 2nd sess.)
An Act making an Appropriation for Completing the Buildings . . . of Washington.
n. p., [1798]. Broadside.
WLC copy. 48724

U. S. Laws, Statutes, etc., 1798 (5th Cong. 2nd sess.)
An Act Supplementary to, and to Amend the Act, Intituled, "An Act to establish an Uniform Rule of Naturalization. . . ."
Approved - June 18, 1798.
[Philadelphia, 1798.] [2] pp.
LOC copy. 34700

U. S. Laws, Statutes, etc., 1798 (5th Cong. 2nd sess.)
An Act to Continue . . . an Act Prohibiting . . . Exportation of Arms. . . . Approved, April 7, 1798.
[Philadelphia, 1798.] Broadside.
LOC copy. 34699

U. S. Laws, Statutes, etc., 1798 (5th Cong. 2nd sess.)
An Act, to Lay and Collect a Direct-Tax.

[Philadelphia, 1798.] 15 pp.
LOC copy.   48725

U. S. Laws, Statutes, etc., 1798 (5th Cong.
2nd sess.)
An Act to Provide for the Valuation of
Lands and Dwelling Houses.
[Boston, 1798.] pp. [i]-22, [2], [25]-35; 2
folding tables.
AAS copy.   34704

U. S. Laws, Statutes, etc., 1798 (5th Cong.
2nd sess.)
An Act to Provide for the Valuation of
Lands and Dwelling-Houses.
[Hartford, Hudson & Goodwin, 1798.] 19
pp.
AAS copy.   48726

U. S. Laws, Statutes, etc., 1798 (5th Cong.
2nd sess.)
An Act Supplementary to, and to Amend
the Act, Intituled, "An Act to Establish an
Uniform Rule of Naturalization. . . ."
Approved - June 18, 1798.
[Philadelphia, 1798.] [2] pp.
LOC copy.   34700

U. S. Laws, Statutes, etc., 1798 (5th Cong.
2nd sess.)
An Act to Suspend Commercial
Intercourse between the United States and
France, Approved June 13th, 1798.
[Philadelphia, 1798.] 2, 2 pp.
LOC copy.   34710

U. S. Laws, Statutes, etc., 1798 (5th Cong.
2nd sess.)
Extract from an Act, Entitled, "An Act to
Provide for the Valuation of Land and
Dwelling-Houses.
[Philadelphia? 1798.] 15 pp.
NL copy.   34705

U. S. Laws, Statutes, etc., 1798 (5th Cong.
2nd sess.)
Federal System of Direct Taxation,
Enacted by Congress . . . July 9, 1798.
Hudson, N. Y., Stoddard, [1798].66 pp.
NYPL copy.   34701

U. S. Laws, Statutes, etc., 1798 (5th Cong.
2nd Sess.).
Acts Passed at the Second Session of the
Fifth Congress.
Philadelphia, Bioren for Dobson, 1800.
pp. [2], [51]-240, i-vii.
NYPL copy.   49166

U. S. Laws, Statutes, etc., 1798 (5th Cong.
2nd sess.)
Notice to Mariners. We Publish for the
. . . Coasting Trade the following Extracts
from the Act of 16th July, 1798. . . .
[Philadelphia], Hogan & Thompson,
[1798?] Broadside.
(Copy not located.)   48729

U. S. Laws, Statutes, etc., 1798 (5th Cong.
3rd sess.)
Acts Passed at the Third Session of the
Fifth Congress.
Halifax, N. C., Hodge, [1799]. 123, [1]
pp.
AAS copy.   36480

U. S. Laws, Statutes, etc., 1798 (5th Cong.
3rd sess.)
Acts Passed at the Third Session of the
Fifth Congress.
Lexington, Ky., Bradford, 1799. 136 pp.
(The unique copy is imperfect.)
University of Louisville copy.   36481

U. S. Laws, Statutes, etc., 1798 (5th Cong.
3rd sess.)
Acts Passed at the Third Session of the
Fifth Congress.
[Philadelphia, 1799.] pp. [240]-561,
[1]-26, [i]-iv, [48] pp.
AAS copy.   36479

U. S. Laws, Statutes, etc., 1798 (5th Cong.
3rd sess.).
Acts Passed at the Third Session of the
Fifth Congress.
[Philadelphia, 1799.] pp. [240]-561, [1],
[1]-26, [i]-iv, [48].
(A minor variant of 36479, which see for
the text.)
AAS copy.   36483

U. S. Laws, Statutes, etc., 1798 (5th Cong.
3rd sess.)
Acts Passed at the Third Session of the
Fifth Congress.
Pittsburgh, Pa., Scull, [1799]. 168 pp.
(The only copy located could not be
filmed.)   36484

U. S. Laws, Statutes, etc., 1798 (5th Cong.
3rd sess.)
Acts Passed at the Third Session of the
Fifth Congress.
Portland, Me., Jenks, 1799. 202, [2] pp.
AAS copy.   36485

U. S. Laws, Statutes, etc., 1798 (5th Cong.
3rd sess.)
Acts Passed at the Third Session of the
Fifth Congress.
Providence, R. I., Carter, 1799. 202, [2]
pp.
BrU copy.   36486

U. S. Laws, Statutes, etc., 1798 (5th Cong.
3rd sess.).
Acts Passed at the Third Session of the
Fifth Congress.
Richmond, Va., Jones, 1799: 140, 4, 15 pp.
VaU copy.   36487

[U. S. Laws, Statutes, etc., 1798 (5th
Cong. 3rd sess.).
Acts Passed at the Third Session of the
Fifth Congress.
Rutland, Vt., Williams, 1799. 202, [2] pp.]
(Entry from Gilman.)   36488

U. S. Laws, Statutes, etc., 1799.
Marine Rules and Regulations.
Boston, Manning & Loring for Clap, 1799.
64 pp.
BPL copy.   36544

U. S. Laws, Statutes, etc., 1799 (5th Cong.
3rd sess.).
An Act for the Better Organizing of the
Troops of the United States. . . .
Approved - March 3, 1799.
[Philadelphia, 1799.] 22 pp.
JCB copy.   36470

U. S. Laws, Statutes, etc., 1799 (5th Cong.
3rd sess.).
An Act for the Government of the Navy.
. . . Approved March 2d, 1799.
[Philadelphia, 1799.] 16 pp.
NYHS copy.   36471

[U. S. Laws, Statutes, etc., 1799 (5th Cong.
3rd sess.).
. . . An Act further to Suspend Intercourse
with France. Approved February 9, 1798.
n. p., [1799]. Broadside.]
(Entry from Evans' notes.)   36522

U. S. Laws, Statutes, etc., 1799 (5th Cong.
3rd sess.).
An Act in Addition to "An Act for the
Relief of Sick and Disabled Seamen". . . .
Approved - March 2, 1799.
[Philadelphia? 1799.] Broadside.
LOC copy.   36472

U. S. Laws, Statutes, etc., 1799 (5th Cong.
3rd sess.)
An Act Respecting Quarantines. . . .
Approved February 25, 1799.
n. p., [1799]. [2] pp.
LOC copy.   36475

U. S. Laws, Statutes, etc., 1799 (5th Cong.
3rd sess.).
An Act to Establish the Post-Office. . . .
Approved, March 2, 1799.
[Philadelphia, 1799.] 23 pp.
LOC copy.   36476

U. S. Laws, Statutes, etc., 1799 (5th Cong.
3rd sess.)
An Act to Regulate the Collection of
Duties. . . . Passed March 2, 1799.
[Charleston, S.C., 1799.] 76 pp.
HC copy.   36478

U. S. Laws, Statutes, etc., 1799 (5th Cong.
3rd sess.).
An Act to Regulate the Collection of
Duties. . . . Approved - March 2, 1799.
Philadelphia, Ross, [1799]. 171, [1], 12
pp.
AAS copy.   36477

U. S. Laws, Statutes, etc., 1798 (5th Cong.
3rd sess.).
Acts Passed at the Third Session of the
Fifth Congress.
New London, Ct., Green, 1799. [2], 188
pp.
AAS copy.   36482

U. S. Laws, Statutes, etc., 1798. (5th
Cong. 3rd sess.)
Acts Passed at the Third Session of the
Fifth Congress.
Pittsburgh, Pa., Scull, [1799]. 168 pp.
(Neither reported copy of this printing
could be located.)   36484

U. S. Laws, Statutes, etc., 1800 (6th Cong.
1st sess.)
An Act for the Better Government of the
Navy.
[Philadelphia? 1800.] 23 pp.
AAS copy.   38692

U. S. Laws, Statutes, etc., 1800 (6th Cong.
1st sess.)
An Act Further to Suspend the
Commercial Intercourse between the
United States and France. . . . Approved
. . . February 27th, 1800.
[Philadelphia, 1800.] 3 pp.
LOC copy.   38693

U. S. Laws, Statutes, etc., 1800 (6th Cong.
1st sess.)
An Act, to Amend an Act, Intituled, An
Act for Appointing Electors. . . . Passed,
January 20th, 1800.
[Philadelphia, 1800.] [2] pp.
LOC copy.   38694

U. S. Laws, Statutes, etc., 1800 (6th Cong.
1st sess.)
An Act to Amend the Act, Intituled "An
Act Providing for the Sale of the Lands
. . . North-West of the Ohio". . . . May 10,
A. D. 1800.
[Philadelphia, 1800.] Broadside.
(The only recorded copy is mislaid.) 38695

U. S. Laws, Statutes, etc., 1800 (6th Cong.
1st sess.)
An Act to Enlarge the Powers of
Surveyors of the Revenue. . . . Approved,
May 13, A. D. 1800.
[Philadelphia, 1800.] 4 pp.
AAS copy.   38696

U. S. Laws, Statutes, etc., 1800 (6th Cong.
1st sess.).
An Act to Establish a General
Stamp-Office. . . . Approved, April 23,
A.D. 1800.
Washington, Way & Groff, [1800]. 8 pp.
NYPL copy.   49165

U. S. Laws, Statutes, etc., (6th Cong. 1st
sess.)
An Act to Establish an Uniform System of
Bankruptcy. . . . April 4, 1800.
Philadelphia, Maxwell for Dickins, 1800.
33 pp.
AAS copy.   38697

U. S. Laws, Statutes, etc., 1800 (6th Cong.
1st sess.)
Acts Passed at the First Session of the
Sixth Congress.
Halifax, [N. C.], Hodge, [1800]. 28 pp.
AAS copy.   38701

U. S. Laws, Statutes, etc., 1800 (6th Cong.
1st sess.)
Acts Passed at the First Session of the
Sixth Congress.
[Philadelphia, 1800.] 223, [1], vii pp.
AAS copy.   38700

U. S. Laws, Statutes, etc., 1800 (6th Cong.
1st sess.)
Acts Passed at the First Session of the
Sixth Congress.
Philadelphia, Folwell, [1800]. 352, iv,
[22] pp.
(Found only as Vol. V of the Laws of the
United States, Washington, D.C., Smith,
1801; and Philadelphia, Carey, 1803;
reproduced as S5321.)   38699

U. S. Laws, Statutes, etc., 1800 (6th Cong.
1st sess.)
Acts Passed at the First Session of the
Sixth Congress.

Portland, [Me.], Jenks, 1800. 223, [1], vii pp.
(Only copy located is imperfect.)
AAS copy.   38702

U. S. Laws, Statutes, etc., 1800 (6th Cong., 1st sess.)
Acts Passed at the First Session of the Sixth Congress.
Richmond, [Va.], Jones, 1800. 106, [2] pp.
VaU copy.   38703

[U. S. Laws, Statutes, etc., 1800 (6th Cong. 1st sess.)
Acts Passed at the First Session of the 6th Congress.
Rutland, Vt., Williams, 1800. 223, vii pp.].
(Entry from Gilman. Known only by one sheet bound in Rutland Herald, Apr. 7, 1800, at AAS.)   38704

U. S. Laws, Statutes, etc., 1800 (6th Cong. 1st sess.)
A Law to Establish an Uniform System of Bankruptcy.
Newport, [R. I.], Barber, [1800]. 18 pp.
RIHS copy.   38751

U. S. Laws, Statutes, etc., 1800 (6th Cong. 1st sess.)
A Law to Establish an Uniform System of Bankruptcy, throughout the United States.
Passed the Fifth Day of April, 1800.
New York, Campbell, [1800]. 44 pp.
CHS copy.   49167

U. S. Laws, Statutes, etc., 1800 (6th Cong. 1st sess.)
National Bankrupt Law.
[Philadelphia? 1800?] 33 pp.
AAS copy.   38798

U. S. Laws, Statutes, etc., 1800 (6th Cong. 1st sess.)
Rules and Articles for the Better Government of the Troops.
Lancaster, [Pa.], Hutter, [1800]. 56 pp.
LOC copy.   38904

U. S. Laws, Statutes, etc., 1800. (6th Cong., 1st sess.)
Rules and Articles for the Better Government of the Troops.
Washington, Way & Groff, 1800. 92 pp.
AAS copy.   38903

U. S. Marine Corps.
[Reward of $10.00 for the Apprehension of a Deserter from the Marine Barracks at Fredericktown. Aug. 28, 1800.
Fredericktown, Bartgis, 1800. Broadside.]
(Minick 590.)   38902

U. S. Marine Office, 1783.
[To all captains . . . I do hereby recall all armed vessels . . . Robert Morris. . . .
April 14, 1783.
Providence, Carter, 1783.] Circular.
(Alden 967; no copy known.)   44477

U. S. Mint, 1796.
Orders and Directions for Conducting the Mint. . . . November 2, 1795.
Philadelphia, Fenno, 1796. 36 pp.
LCP copy.   31465

U. S. Mint, 1797.
Letter from the Director of the Mint. . . . December 19, 1797. . . . Printed by Order of the House.
Philadelphia, Gales, [1797]. 8 pp.
AAS copy.   33091

U. S. Mint, 1797.
Letter from the Secretary of State, inclosing a Report of the Director of the Mint. . . . 20th December, 1796.
[Philadelphia, 1797?] 19 pp.
AAS copy.   48295

U. S. Mint, 1798.
To all whom it may Concern. . . . July 12, 1798.
[Philadelphia, 1798. 2 pp.
AAS copy.   34883

U. S. Mint, 1799.
Message from the President. . . . Inclosing a Report to Him from the Director of the Mint . . . during . . . 1798. . . . 31st January, 1799. . . . Published by Order of the House.

[Philadelphia], 1799.] 7 pp.
AAS copy.   36555

U. S. Naval Board, 1775.
Naval Pay List. . . . Extract from the Minutes.
[Philadelphia? 1775?] Broadside.
JCB copy.   42967

[U. S. Naval Board, 1777.
Advertisement for Seamen, Feb. 17, 1777.
Philadelphia, 1777. Broadside.]
(Entry from Aitken's accounts.)   15637

[U. S. Naval Board, 1777.
For the Encouragement of the Navy, Aug. 11, 1777.
Philadelphia, 1777. Broadside.]
(Entry from Aitken's accounts.)   15638

[U. S. Naval Board, 1777.
Letters and Orders Feb. 26, 1777.
Philadelphia, 1777. Broadside.]
(Entry from Aitken's accounts.)   15639

[U. S. Naval Board, 1777.
Resolve of the Marine Committee. Apr. 1, 1777.
Philadelphia, 1777. Broadside.]
(Entry from Aitken's account.)   15640

[U. S. Naval Board, 1777.
Rules and Regulations. Apr. 12, 1777.
Philadelphia, 1777. Broadside.]
(Aitken's accounts.)   15641

U. S. Navy Dept., 1799.
Letter from the Secretary of the Navy Accompanying Sundry Statements. . . . 26th December, 1798. Referred. . . . Published by Order of the House. . . .
Philadelphia, Gales, [1799]. 30 pp., 1 folded table.
AAS copy.   36528

U. S. Navy Dept., 1799.
Letter from the Secretary of the Navy, to the Chairman of the Committee, Appointed on . . . the President's Speech. 12th February, 1799, Committed. . . . (Published by Order of the House. . . .).
n. p., [1799]. 4 pp.
AAS copy.   36529

U. S. Navy Dept., 1799.
Letter from the Secretary of the Navy, to the Chairman of the Committee, on the Naval Establishment. . . . Presented . . . 2d of January, 1799. (Published by Order of the House. . . .).
n. p., [1799]. 16 pp.
AAS copy.   36530

U. S. Navy Dept., 1800.
Letter and Report of the Secretary of the Navy. . . . 20th March 1800.
[Philadelphia, 1800.] 8 pp.
AAS copy.   38752

U. S. Navy Dept., 1800.
Letter from the Secretary of the Navy, Transmitting a Report of . . . Pensions. . . . 2d December, 1800. . . . Published by Order of the House.
[Washington? 1800.] 6 pp.
AAS copy.   38758

U. S. Office of Finance, 1781.
. . . Philadelphia, 12th December, 1781.
Proposals will be Received. . . .
[Philadelphia, 1781.] Broadside.
LOC copy.   44069

[U. S. Office of Finance, 1782.
Office of Finance, October 10, 1782
[Rations Contractors]
[Philadelphia, 1782.] Broadside.].
(Ford 387; no copy located.)   17768

U. S. Office of Finance, 1785.
A Statement of the Accounts of the United States of America, during the Administration of the Superintendant of Finance . . . 1781 . . . 1784.
Philadelphia, Aitken, 1785. x, [211] pp.
AAS copy.   19333

U. S. Post Office Dept., 1775.
Directions to the Deputy Post-Masters.
[Philadelphia, 1775.] Broadside.
HSP copy.   14587

U. S. Post Office Dept., 1775.

Tables of the Post of all Single Letters.
[Philadelphia, 1775.] Broadside.
NA copy.   14586

[U. S. Post-Office Dept., 1782.
General Post-Office, October 24th, 1782.
Extract from an Ordinance. . . .
[Philadelphia, 1782.] Broadside.]
(Ford 390; no copy located.)   17764

U. S. Post-Office Dept., 1790.
General Post-Office, New-York, January 20, 1790. Sir, In Obedience. . . .
[New York, 1790.] 7 pp.
LOC copy.   22978

[U. S. Post-Office Dept., 1792.
A Table of the Post-Offices in the United States; with their Distance from Philadelphia.
[Philadelphia, 1792.]
(Evans' entry was from an adv., and the imprint was assumed.)   24935

U. S. Post-Office Dept., 1796.
Table of Post-Offices. . . . November 15, 1796.
[Philadelphia, 1796.] Broadside.
MHS copy.   47980

U. S. Post-Office Dept., 1798.
Letter from the Assistant Post-Master-General. . . . 26th March, 1798. Referred. . . .
Philadelphia, Way & Groff, [1798].
[24] pp.
AAS copy.   34903

U. S. Post-Office Dept., 1799.
Letter from the Post-Master-General. . . . 8th January, 1799, Referred. . . .
(Published by Order of the House. . . .).
[Philadelphia, 1799.] 48 pp.
AAS copy.   36526

U. S. Post Office Dept., 1800.
The Post-Office Law, with Instructions. . . . 1800.
Washington, Cist, [1800]. [2], 64 pp.
LCP copy.   38801

U. S. Post Office Department, 1800.
Table of Post Offices and Rates of Postage of Single Letters for Post Offices in Massachusetts.
[Dated:] Philadelphia, April 14, 1800.
Broadside.
AAS copy.   38908

U. S. President, 1789.
By the President of the United States. . . . A Proclamation [Thanksgiving, Nov. 26. Dated Oct. 3, 1789.].
[New York, Childs & Swaine, 1789.]
Broadside.
LOC ph copy.   22211

U. S. President, 1789.
By the President. . . . A Proclamation. . . . Whereas a Treaty between the United States, and . . . Indians. . . .
[New York, 1789.] Broadside.
(Not located.)
HSP copy.   45724

U. S. President, 1789.
By the President. . . . A Proclamation. Whereas . . . Arthur St. Clair . . . Treaty . . . at Fort-Harmar [Dated Sept. 29, 1789.]
n.p., [1789]. 8 pp.
AAS ph. copy.   45725

U. S. President, 1789.
Speech of His Excellency . . . to both Houses. . . . April 30, 1789.
[Albany], Webster, [1789]. Broadside.
AAS ph copy.   22212

U. S. President, 1789.
Speech of His Excellency . . . to the Honorable Congress, upon his Introduction to Office. New York, May 1.
[Newport, 1789.] Broadside.
RIHS copy.   45726

U. S. President, 1789.
Speech of His Excellency . . . upon his Introduction to Office. New York, May 1.
[New York, 1789.] Broadside.
NYHS copy.   45727

U. S. President, 1790.

Proclamation of the President of the
Treaty with the Creek Indians. New York.
August 14, 1790.
New York, Childs & Swaine, 1790.
Broadside.
AAS copy.   22989

U. S. President, 1790.
Speech of the President of the United
States, to both Houses of Congress . . .
Dec. 8, 1790.
[Philadelphia], Fenno, [1790]. Broadside.
HSP copy.   46076

U. S. President, 1791.
By the President . . . A Proclamation
[limits of the District of Columbia, Jan.
24, 1791].
[Philadelphia, 1791.] Broadside.
(Not located, 1968.)   46332

U. S. President, 1791.
By the President . . . a Proclamation
[treaty with the Cherokees, Nov. 11,
1791].
[Philadelphia, 1791.] Broadside.
(Not located, 1968.)   46333

U. S. President, 1791.
Speech of the President of the United
States, to both Houses of Congress;
October 25, 1791.
Philadelphia, Fenno, [1791]. [2] pp.
AAS copy.   23921

U. S. President, 1792.
By the President of the United States. A
Proclamation. Whereas Certain Violent . . .
Proceedings. . . . [Dated Sept. 15, 1792.]
(Reproduced from Henkels cat. 1463, item
253.)   46643

U. S. President, 1792.
Extract from an Act of the President . . .
Dated the Fourth Day of August 1792. . . .
Distilled Spirits.
[Philadelphia? 1792?] Broadside.
NYPL copy.   46644

U. S. President, 1792.
Speech of the President of the United
States to both Houses of Congress, Nov.
6, 1792.
[Philadelphia, 1792.] Broadside.
AAS copy.   24934

U. S. President, 1792.
Terms and Conditions . . . Buildings . . .
of Washington. . . . Terms of Sale [Oct. 8,
1792].
[Philadelphia? 1792.] Broadside.
(No copy located.)   46645

U. S. President, 1792.
United States, November the 22d, 1792.
Gentlemen of the Senate, and of the
House. . . .
[Philadelphia], Childs & Swaine, [1792].
7 pp.
LOC copy.   24945

U. S. President, 1792.
United States. To All to whom these
Presents Come - Greetings. Whereas John
Bailey. . . . February 23d, 1792.
[Philadelphia, 1792.] Broadside.
(Not located, 1968.)   46646

[U. S. President, 1793.
By the President. . . . A Proclamation
[Duplaine. Dated Oct. 10, 1793].
[Philadelphia, 1793.] Broadside.
(No copy located.)   26337

[U. S. President, 1793.
The Correspondence of Mr. Jefferson, Mr.
Genet, &c as Delivered in the Message of
the President . . . 5th December, 1793.
New York, Childs, 1794. 102 pp.]
(No copy located.)   27925

U. S. President, 1793.
Fellow Citizens of the Senate, and of the
House. . . . December 3, 1793.
[Philadelphia, 1793.] Broadside.
NYHS copy.   46910

U.S. President, 1793.
Proclamation. By the President. . . .
Whereas it appears, that a State of War
Exists.
[Boston], Argus, [1793]. Broadside.
AAS copy.   26336

U. S. President, 1793.
Speech of the President . . . to both
Houses of Congress, December 3, 1793.
[Philadelphia, 1793.] Broadside.
JCB copy.   46911

U. S. President, 1793.
Speech of the President . . . to both
Houses of Congress. Fellow-Citizens. . . .
December 3d, 1793.
[Philadelphia, 1793.] [4] pp.
WLC copy.   46912

[U. S. President, 1793.
22d April, 1793. By the President. . . . A
Proclamation. Whereas it Appears that a
State of War Exists.
[Philadelphia, 1793.] Broadside.
(No copy located has the wording given by
Evans.)   26335

[U. S. President, 1794.
By the President. . . . Proclamation.
Whereas from a Hope . . . [Sept. 25,
1794].
[Philadelphia, 1794.] Broadside.]
(No copy located.)   27912

U. S. President, 1794.
In Congress, March 26, 1794. Resolved
. . . that an Embargo be Laid. . . .
Approved - March the Twenty-Sixth, 1794
. . . By direction of the President. . . .
[Philadelphia, 1794.] Broadside.
(Not located, 1968.)   47295

U. S. President, 1794.
The Secretary of the Treasury. Sir, I
cannot Charge my Memory. . . . April 8th,
1794.
[Philadelphia, 1794.] Broadside.
LOC copy.   27919

U. S. President, 1794.
Speech of the President of the United
States to both Houses of Congress. . . .
November the 19th, 1794.
[Philadelphia, 1794.] [4] pp.
AAS copy.   27923

U. S. President, 1794.
United States, 15th January, 1794.
Gentlemen of the Senate, and of the
House of Representatives. I Lay before
you. . . .
[Philadelphia, 1794.] 11 pp.
AAS copy.   27920

U. S. President, 1794.
United States, 16th January, 1794.
Gentlemen of the Senate, and of the
House of Representatives, I Transmit. . . .
[Philadelphia, 1794.] 26 (i.e., 36) pp.
AAS copy.   27921

U. S. President, 1794.
United States, 22d of January, 1794.
Gentlemen of the Senate and of the House
of Representatives, I Forward. . . .
[Philadelphia, 1794.] 4 pp.
AAS copy.   27922

U. S. President, 1795.
By Authority. By the President . . . a
Proclamation. . . . A Day of Public
Thanksgiving [Feb. 19. Dated Jan. 1,
1795.]
[Boston, 1795.] Broadside.
AAS copy.   29731

U. S. President, 1795.
By the President . . . a Proclamation. . . .
A Day of Public Thanksgiving [Feb. 19.
Dated Jan. 1, 1795].
[Philadelphia, 1795.] Broadside.
MHS copy.   29730

U. S. President, 1795.
By the President . . . a Proclamation. . . .
A Day of Public Thanksgiving [Feb. 19.
Dated Jan. 1, 1795].
Providence, Carter & Wilkinson, [1795].
Broadside.
AAS copy.   29733

[U. S. President, 1795.
By the President. . . . A Proclamation. . . .
Commissioners . . . to Confer with the
Citizens of the Western Counties [Dated
July 10, 1795].
[Philadelphia, 1795.] Broadside.]
(No copy located.)   29734

U. S. President, 1795.
A Message of the President of the United
States to Congress, Relative to France and
Great Britain: Delivered, December 5,
1793. . . . Published by Order of the
House.
Philadelphia, Carey, 1795. pp. [1]-132,
[4], [1], 159, [1]-11, [1]-28, 19-26, 4.
HSP copy.   29735

U. S. President, 1795.
A Message of the President of the United
States to Congress, Relative to France and
Great Britain; Delivered December 5,
1793. Published by Order of the House.
Philadelphia, Carey, 1795. 132, [4], 159,
[1] pp.
AAS copy.   29736

U. S. President, 1795.
Official Letters. . . . Vol. I [-II].
Boston, Manning & Loring for Hall, etc.,
1795. 340; 356 pp.
(Apparently issued without the portrait
called for by Evans.)
AAS copy.   29737

U. S. President, 1795.
Philadelphia, Dec. 8, 1795. This day,
Precisely at 12 o'clock, The President . . .
met both Houses . . . and Addressed them
in the following Speech. . . .
[Philadelphia, 1795.] Broadside.
AAS copy.   29741

U. S. President, 1795.
President's Message. Philadelphia, March
31. . . . January 30.
[Newport? 1795.] Broadside.
RIHS copy.   47655

U. S. President, 1795.
The Proceedings of the Executive of the
United States, Respecting the Insurgents,
1794.
Philadelphia, Fenno, 1795. 130 pp.
AAS copy.   29738

U. S. President, 1795.
Speech of the President . . . 8th of
December, 1795.
[Philadelphia, 1795.] 7 pp.
AAS copy.   29739

U. S. President, 1795.
Speech of the President . . . to both
Houses of Congress. December 8, 1795.
[Philadelphia, 1795.] Broadside.
AAS copy.   29740

U.S. President, 1795.
State of Connecticut January 23, 1795. . . .
By the President of the United States . . .
a Proclamation. . . . A Day of Public
Thanksgiving [Feb. 19. Dated Jan. 1,
1795.].
[Hartford, 1795.] Broadside.
CHS copy.   29732

U. S. President, 1796.
By George Washington, President of the
United States of America; a
Proclamation, Whereas a Treaty of Amity.
. . . Done . . . the 29th Day of February.
[Philadelphia, 1796.] 30 pp.
AAS copy.   31412

U. S. President, 1796.
A Collection of the Speeches of the
President.
Boston, Manning & Loring for Cotton,
1796. 282, [1] pp.
AAS copy.   31402

U. S. President, 1796.
From the Office of the Pennsylvania Daily
Advertiser. . . . April 1. The Following . . .
Message from the President [Mar. 30,
1796]. . . .
[Philadelphia, 1796.] Broadside.
HEH copy.   47981

U. S. President, 1796.
George Washington, President of the United
States of America. To all to whom these
Presents Shall come,-Greeting: Whereas
a Treaty . . . Algiers. . . . Done . . . the
Seventh Day of March.
[Philadelphia, 1796.] 8 pp.
AAS copy.   31409

U. S. President, 1796.
Message from the President of the United

States, accompanying a Copy of the
Treaty concluded between the United
States and . . . Algiers. 8th March, 1796,
Read. . . . 9th March, 1796, Committed. . . .
Published by Order of the House.
[Philadelphia, 1796.] 11 pp.
AAS copy.   31408

U. S. President, 1796.
Message from the President of the United
States, Accompanying a Copy of the
Treaty of Amity . . . Great Britain. 1st
March, 1796, Read, and . . . Committed to
the. . . . Whole House.
[Philadelphia, 1796.] 32 pp.
AAS copy.   31411

U. S. President, 1796.
Message from the President of the United
States, Accompanying a Copy of the
Treaty of Friendship . . . Spain.
29th March, 1796, Referred. . . . Published
by Order of the House. 19 pp.
AAS copy.   31418

U. S. President, 1796.
Message from the President of the United
States, Accompanying a Memorial of the
Commissioner. . . . 8th January, 1796,
Referred. . . . 25th January, 1796, Report
Made. . . . Published by Order of the
House.
[Philadelphia, 1796.] 13 pp.
AAS copy.   31406

U. S. President, 1796.
Message from the President of the United
States, Accompanying the Translation of a
Letter from the Minister of the French
Republic. . . . 25th March 1796, Ordered
to lie on the Table. Published by Order of
the House.
[Philadelphia, 1796.] 4 pp.
AAS copy.   31421

U. S. President, 1796.
Message from the President of the United
States, Assigning the Reasons which
Forbid his Compliance. . . . 30th March,
1796, Ordered to lie on the Table.
Published by Order of the House.
[Philadelphia, 1796.] 6 pp.
AAS copy.   31417

U. S. President, 1796.
Official Letters to the Honourable
American Congress. . . . Vol. I [-II].
Second Boston Edition.
Boston, Manning & Loring, for S. Hall,
etc., 1796. 340 pp., 1 plate; 356 pp.
AAS copy.   31422

U. S. President, 1796.
Official Letters to the Honorable
American Congress. . . . Vol. I [-II].
New York, Campbell, 1796. 296; [2], 311
pp.
AAS copy.   31423

U. S. President, 1796.
The President's Message. On the Treaty
Papers. Centinel-Office, April 7, 1796. . . .
[Signed] March 30, 1796.
[Boston, 1796.] Broadside.
AAS copy.   31416

U. S. President, 1796.
The President's Message. On the Treaty
Papers Gentlemen of the House. . . .
March 30, 1796.
[Boston], Martin, [1796]. Broadside.
AAS copy.   31415

U. S. President, 1796.
The President's Message, on the Treaty
Papers. Herald-Office, April 8, 1796.
[Newburyport, 1796.] Broadside.
BPL copy.   47982

U. S. President, 1796.
President's Message. Philadelphia, March
31. The Following is a Copy. . . .
[Philadelphia, 1796.] Broadside.
AAS copy.   31420

U. S. President, 1796.
President's Speech. American Congress.
House of Representatives, Wednesday,
December 7.
[Newport, 1796.] Broadside.
LOC copy.   31427

U. S. President, 1796.

Received the 13th of January, 1796.)
Message from the President. . . .
Published by Order of the House.
[Philadelphia, 1796.] 11 pp.
AAS copy.   31407

U. S. President, 1796.
Speech of the President of the United
States, to both Houses of Congress.
December 7, 1796.
[Philadelphia? 1796.] Broadside.
AAS copy.   31426

U. S. President, 1796.
Speech of the President of the United
States, to both Houses of Congress,
December 7, 1796.
Philadelphia, Ormrod & Conrad for J.
Ormrod, 1796. 12 pp.
LOC copy.   31425

U. S. President, 1796.
Speech of the President of the United
States, to both Houses of Congress, on
Wednesday, December 7, 1796.
Philadelphia, 1796. [2], 9 pp.
AAS copy.   31424

U. S. President, 1796.
Talk of the President . . . to his Beloved
Men of the Cherokee Nation [Aug. 29,
1796].
[Philadelphia, 1796.] Broadside.
AAS ph. copy.   47983

[U. S. President, 1797.
By the President. . . . A Proclamation
[National Fast, May 9, 1797.]
[Philadelphia, 1797.] Broadside.]
(No copy of such a printing located.)
                                                 33046

U. S. President, 1797.
By the President of the United States of
America. A Proclamation. Whereas the
Constitution. . . . [Signed Mar. 25, 1797].
[Philadelphia, 1797.] Broadside.
LOC copy.   33047

U. S. President, 1797.
Confidential Message from the President
. . . Inclosing Sundry Documents from the
Departments of State and War. . . . July 3,
1797. . . . Published by Order of the
House.
Philadelphia, Ross, [1797]. 8, [24], 23 pp.
AAS copy.   33054

U. S. President, 1797.
From the Mercury-Office. President's
Speech. Mercury Office, Nov. 29.
[Boston, Young & Minns, 1797.]
Broadside.
MHS copy.   33060

U. S. President, 1797.
Message Confidentiel du President . . .
Refermant Plusieurs Documents des
Departemens de l'Etat et de la Guerre . . .
3 Julliet 1797. . . . Publié par Ordre de la
Chambre des Représentans.
Philadelphia, Ross, [1797]. 85 pp.
LOC copy.   33055

U. S. President, 1797.
Message from the President of the United
States, Accompanying an Official
Statement of the Expenditure, to the End
of the Year 1796. . . . 16th February 1797.
. . . Published by Order of the House.
[Philadelphia, 1797.] 8 pp.
AAS copy.   33051

U. S. President, 1797.
A Message from the President of the
United States of America, to Congress;
Relative to the French Republic;
Delivered January 19, 1797. . . . Published
by Order of the House.
Philadelphia, Ross, [1797]. pp. [1]-24,
24-55, 57-92, [1]-22.
AAS copy.   33048

[U. S. President, 1797.
Message of the President of the United
States Relative to the Affair of William
Blount: and the Report of a Committee of
Congress Containing the Evidence
Relative thereto. Proceedings on
Impeachment.
[Philadelphia], July 5, 1797. 182 pp.]
(Apparently a garbled entry originating in
Poore.)   34798

U. S. President, 1797.
A Message from the President of the
United States of America, to Congress;
Relative to the French Republic;
Delivered January 19, 1797. . . . Published
by Order of the House.
Philadelphia, Ross, [1797]. pp. [1]-24,
24-55, 57-92, [56], [1]-16, [380], 1-207,
[12].
AAS copy.   33049

U. S. President, 1797.
The President's Message of January 19,
1797.
Albany, Websters, 1797. 44 pp.
NYSL copy.   48296

[U. S. President, 1797.
The Speech of the President of the United
States to both Houses of Congress, May
16, 1797.
n. p., [1797]. Broadside.]
(No such printing located.)   33057

U. S. President, 1797.
Speech of the President of the United
States, to both Houses of Congress . . .
May 16th, 1797.
[Philadelphia, 1797.] 12 pp.
AAS copy.   33056

U. S. President, 1797.
The Speech of the President of the United
States to both Houses of Congress . . .
Nov. 23, 1797. House of Representatives,
Nov. 23, 1797, Ordered to be Committed.
Philadelphia, Gales, [1797]. 8 pp.
AAS copy.   33058

U. S. President, 1797.
Speech of the President of the United
States to both Houses of Congress,
November 23, 1797.
[Philadelphia, 1797.] Broadside.
AAS copy.   33059

U. S. President, 1798.
America and France. The Intire Message
of the President.
Boston, Russel, [1798]. 71 pp.
AAS copy.   34815

U. S. President, 1798.
Bericht des Presidenten der Vereinigten
Staaten an die Beiden Häuser des
Congresses vom 3ten April, 1798.
Philadelphia, Schweitzer, 1798. 54 pp.
LOC copy.   34818

U. S. President, 1798.
By the President of the United States of
America . . . Fasting and Prayer [May 9.
Dated Mar. 23, 1798].
[Philadelphia, 1798.] Broadside.
AAS copy.   34797

U. S. President, 1798.
House of Representatives . . . March 19
[Message Concerning the Dispatches from
the Envoys Extraordinary of the United
States to the French Republic].
[Philadelphia, 1798.] 2 pp.
LOC copy.   34810

[U. S. President, 1798.
In Senate of the United States. April 5th,
1798.
[Philadelphia, 1798.] 71 pp.
(This is a copy of 34812, q. v., lacking the
first leaf.)   34813

[U. S. President, 1798.
Memorial from the Envoys at Paris . . .
Communicated by the President to
Congress, May 4th, 1798.
Carlisle, Pa., Kline, 1798.]
(Assumed by Evans from adv. in Carlisle
Gazette, July 4, 1798.)   34820

U. S. President, 1798.
Message from the President of the United
States, Accompanying a Communication,
No. 8 from the Envoys. . . . 18th June,
1798. Ordered to lie on the Table. Printed
by Order of the House. . . .
Philadelphia, Gales, [1798]. pp. [1]-48,
41-56, 65-72.
AAS copy.   34824

U. S. President, 1798.
Message from the President of the United
States, Accompanying a Report from the
Secretary of State, and Copies of Acts. . . .

17th January, 1798, Referred.
. . .(Published by Order of the House. . . .)
[Philadelphia, 1798.] 12 pp.
AAS copy.   34799

U. S. President, 1798.
Message from the President of the United
States Accompanying a Report Made to
him by the Secretary of State, Exhibiting a
Statement of the Losses. . . . 19th
February, 1798. Ordered to lie on the
Table. (Published by Order of the House.
. . .)
[Philadelphia, 1798.] 11 pp., 1 folding
table.
AAS copy.   34805

U. S. President, 1798.
Message from the President of the United
States, Accompanying a Report to him
from the Secretary of State, also an
Account of the Expenditures for . . .
Claims. . . . 20th February, 1798, Ordered
to lie on the Table. Published by Order of
the House. . . .
[Philadelphia], Ross, [1798]. [7] pp.
AAS copy.   34806

U. S. President, 1798.
Message from the President of the United
States, Accompanying a Report to him
From the Secretary of State, and Sundry
Documents Relative to . . .
Mississippi. . . . 23d January, 1798.
Ordered to lie on the Table. Published by
Order of the House. . . .
Philadelphia, Ross, [1798]. 91 pp.
AAS copy.   34801

U. S. President, 1798.
Message from the President of the United
States, Accompanying a Representation
from the Judge of the District of
Pennsylvania. . . . January 18th, 1798.
Committed. . . . Printed by Order of the
House. . . .
Philadelphia, Gales, [1798]. 8 pp.
AAS copy.   34800

U. S. President, 1798.
Message from the President of the United
States, Accompanying Copies of Two Acts
of the Parliament. . . . 2d February, 1798.
Referred. . . . Published by Order of the
House. . . .
[Philadelphia, 1798.] 29 pp.
AAS copy.   34802

U. S. President, 1798.
Message from the President of the United
States, Accompanying the
Communications from the Envoys
Extraordinary to the French Republic,
Received since the Fourth of May last. 5th
June, 1798 - Ordered to lie on the Table.
Printed by Order of the House.
Philadelphia, Way & Groff, [1798]. 17 pp.
AAS copy.   34822

U. S. President, 1798.
Message from the President of the United
States, Inclosing a Letter, and Sundry
Documents, from the Governor of . . .
Pennsylvania. . . . 27th June, 1798.
Committed. . . . Printed by Order of the
House. . . .
Philadelphia, Gales, [1798]. 8 pp.
AAS copy.   34826

U. S. President, 1798.
Message from the President of the
United States, Inclosing a Letter to him
from the Governor of South Carolina. . . .
February 5th, 1798. Referred. . . . Printed
by Order of the House. . . .
Philadelphia, Gales, [1798]. 22 pp.
AAS copy.   34803

U. S. President, 1798.
Message from the President of the United
States, Inclosing a Memorial of the
Commissioners. . . . of the City of
Washington. 23rd February, 1798. Printed
by Order of the House. . . .
Philadelphia, Gales, [1798]. 14 pp.
AAS copy.   34807

U. S. President, 1798.
The Message of the President . . . of 5th
March, 1798.
Philadelphia, Way & Groff, [1798]. 8 pp.
WLC copy.   48731

U. S. President, 1798.
The Message of the President of the
United States, of 5th March, 1798. . . .
Printed by Order of the Senate. . . .
Philadelphia, Way & Groff, [1798]. 8 pp.
AAS copy.   34809

U. S. President, 1798.
Message of the President of the United
States to Both Houses of Congress. June
5th, 1798.
[Philadelphia, 1798.] 15 pp.
AAS copy.   34821

U. S. President, 1798.
Message of the President of the United
States, to Both Houses of Congress. June
18, 1798.
[Philadelphia, 1798.] 72 pp.
AAS copy.   34823

U. S. President, 1798.
Message of the President of the United
States, to Both Houses of Congress June
21st, 1798.
[Philadelphia, 1798.] 8 pp.
AAS copy.   34825

U. S. President, 1798.
Message of the President of the United
States, to Both Houses of Congress. May
4th, 1798.
[Philadelphia, 1798.] 72 pp.
AAS copy.   34819

U. S. President, 1798.
Message from the President of the United
States, Transmitting an Official Statement
of the Expenditure. . . . 13th February,
1798. Read, and Ordered to lie on the
table. . . . Printed by Order of the
House. . . .
Philadelphia, Gales, [1798]. 7 pp.
AAS copy.   34804

[U. S. President, 1798.
Message from the President of the United
States. . . . Tunis. . . . 23 February, 1798.
[Philadelphia, 1798.] 8 pp.]
(No such document has been located.)
                                         34808

U. S. President, 1798.
Message of the President of the United
States to both Houses of Congress. April
Third, M,DCC,XCVIII.
[Newark, N.J., Newark Gazette Office,
1798]. 80 pp.
(Only copy cannot be reproduced.)   48730

U. S. President, 1798.
Message of the President of the United
States to Both Houses of Congress. April
3d, 1798.
[Philadelphia, 1798.] 71 pp.
AAS copy.   34812

U. S. President, 1798.
Message of the President of the United
States to Both Houses of Congress, April
3d, 1798.
Philadelphia, Dobson & Ormrod, 1798. 60
pp.
LOC copy.   34814

U. S. President, 1798.
Newburyport Herald-Office, December 17,
1798. . . . The President's Speech.
[Newburyport], March, [1798].
Broadside.
NYHS copy.   34834

U. S. President, 1798.
Postscript to the Mercury. Tuesday noon,
March 27.
[Boston, 1798.] Broadside.
AAS copy.   34811

U. S. President, 1798.
The President's Address, to Both Houses
of Congress, Philadelphia, Dec. 8.
[Richmond], Davis, [1798]. Broadside.
LOC copy.   48732

U. S. President, 1798.
President's Answer to the Inhabitants of
Providence.
[Providence], Carter & Wilkinson,
[1798]. Broadside.
RIHS copy.   34836

U. S. President, 1798.
President's Speech. By an Arrival this

Morning. . . . December 8.
[Newport], Farnsworths, [1798].
Broadside.
RIHS copy.   48733

U. S. President, 1798.
President's Speech. Providence, Saturday
Evening, December 15, 1798.
[Providence], Carter & Wilkinson,
[1798]. Broadside.
RIHS copy.   34833

U. S. President, 1798.
The President's Speech to Both Houses of
Congress. We Felicitate. . . . December 8,
1798.
Portsmouth, N. H., Peirce, [1798].
Broadside.
AAS copy.   34835

U. S. President, 1798.
Speech of the President of the United
States, to both Houses of Congress,
December 8th, 1798.
[Philadelphia, 1798.] Broadside.
AAS copy.   34832

U. S. President, 1798.
Speech of the President of the United
States to Both Houses of Congress . . .
Delivered the Eighth of December, 1798.
8th December, 1798. Committed. . . .
Published by Order of the House.
Philadelphia, Gales, [1798]. 8 pp.
AAS copy.   34831

U. S. President, 1799.
By the President of the United States of
America. A Proclamation. . . . That . . .
the 25th Day of April next be Observed
. . . as a Day of . . . Fasting [Dated Mar.
6, 1799].
[Philadelphia, 1799.] Broadside.
AAS copy.   36497

U. S. President, etc., 1799.
By the President of the United States of
America, a Proclamation. Whereas by Act
of Congress. . . . Entitled "An Act further
to Suspend the Commercial
Intercourse. . . ." [Dated June 26, 1799.]
[Philadelphia, 1799.] Broadside.
LOC copy.   36498

U. S. President, 1799.
By the President of the United States of
America. A Proclamation. Whereas by an
Act of the Congress . . . Passed the Ninth
Day of February last. . . . Given . . . this
17th Day of July, A. D. 1792.
[Philadelphia, 1799.] Broadside.
LOC copy.   36499

[U. S. President, 1799.
By the President of the United States of
America. Whereas the
Congress of the United States "In Honour
of the Memory of Gen. George
Washington. . . ."
[Philadelphia, 1799.] Broadside.]
(Entry from Evans' record.)   36500

U. S. President, 1799.
Message from the President of the United
States, Accompanying an Extract of a
Letter. . . . 28th January, 1799. . . .
Philadelphia, Fenno, 1799. 8 pp.
AAS copy.   36545

U. S. President, 1799.
Message from the President of the United
States Accompanying his Annual Account
of the Application of Grants made. . . .
1798. 8th January, 1799. . . . Published by
Order of the House.
Philadelphia, Gales, [1799]. 7 pp.
AAS copy.   36550

U. S. President, 1799.
Message from the President . . .
Accompanying Sundry Papers Relative to
Impressment. . . . 8th January, 1799. . . .
Published by Order of the House. . . .
Philadelphia, Gales, [1799]. 8 pp.
AAS copy.   36553

U. S. President, 1799.
Message from the President . . .
Accompanying Sundry Papers Relative to
the Affairs of . . . the French Republic.
18th January, 1799. Published by Order of
the House. . . .

[Philadelphia, 1799.] 123 pp.
AAS copy.   36551

U. S. President, 1799.
Message from the President . . .
Accompanying Sundry Papers Relative to
the Affairs of . . . the French Republic.
22d January, 1799. Published by Order of
the Senate.
[Philadelphia, 1799.] 123 pp.
AAS copy.   36552

U. S. President, 1799.
Message from the President . . .
Communicating to the House . . .
Information . . . Mentioned in his
Message of the 28th of January.
Philadelphia, Fenno, [1799]. 6 pp.
AAS copy.   36554

U. S. President, 1799.
Message from the President . . .
Transmitting a Statement of the
Vessels. . . . March 2d, 1799.
[Philadelphia, 1799.] Broadside.
AAS copy.   36556

U. S. President, 1799.
Message from the President . . .
Transmitting Certain Documents. . . . 5th
December, 1799. . . . (Published by Order
of the House. . . .).
[Philadelphia, 1799.] 42 pp.
AAS copy.   36557

U. S. President, 1799.
Speech of the President of the United
States to both Houses of Congress. 3d
December, 1799.
[Philadelphia], Ross, [1799]. 7 pp.
AAS copy.   36589

U. S. President, 1800.
An Account of Louisiana, being an
Abstract of Documents.
Philadelphia, Conrad, etc., 1800. 50 pp.
NYSL copy.   36753

U. S. President, 1800.
Message from the President of the United
States, Accompanying an Account of the
Application of Grants. . . . 20th January,
1800. . . . (Published by Order of the
House. . . .)
[Philadelphia, 1800.] 3 pp.
AAS copy.   38778

U. S. President, 1800.
Message from the President of the United
States, Accompanying a Report of the
Secretary of State. . . . 23d January,
1800. . . . (Published by Order of the
House. . . .)
[Philadelphia, 1800.] 8 pp.
AAS copy.   38779

U. S. President, 1800.
Message from the President of the United
States, Transmitting a Report of the
Secretary of State. . . . 7th February,
1800. . . . (Published by Order of the
House. . . .)
[Philadelphia, 1800.] 8 pp.
AAS copy.   38782

U. S. President, 1800.
Message from the President of the United
States, Transmitting a Report from the
Secretary of War. . . . A Return of the
Officers. . . . Printed by Order of the
Senate. . . . April 17th, 1800.
[Philadelphia, 1800.] 28 pp.
AAS copy.   38781

U. S. President, 1800.
Message from the President of the United
States, Transmitting a Report of the
Secretary of War, on . . . our Military
System. . . . 13th January, 1800. . . .
Printed by Order of the House.
[Philadelphia, 1800.] 41 pp.
AAS copy.   38783

U. S. President, 1800.
Message from the President of the United
States, Transmitting an Original Letter
from Mrs. Washington. . . . 8th January,
1800. . . . (Published by Order of the
House. . . .).
[Philadelphia, 1800.] [3] pp.
AAS copy.   38780

U. S. President, 1800.
Message from the President of the United
States, Transmitting Sundry Statements
Relative to the Mint. . . . 8th January,
1800. . . . Printed by Order of the
House. . . .
Philadelphia, Way & Groff, [1800].
7 pp.
AAS copy.   38784

[U. S. President, 1800.
Message from the President of the United
States, Transmitting two Reports; one
from the Acting Secretary of War, the
Other from the Secretary of the
Treasury. . . .
n.p., n.d. 34 pp.]
(Entry from an Evans note.)   38785

U. S. President, 1800.
President's Speech! On Saturday the 22d
November. . . .
[Wilmington, Del., 1800.] Broadside.
DHS copy.   38802

[U.S. President, 1800.
A Proclamation, by the President of the
United States. Whereas the Congress. . . .
to Testify their Grief for the Death of . . .
Washington. . . . At Philadelphia, the
Sixth Day of January . . . One Thousand
Eight Hundred.
[Philadelphia, 1800.] Broadside.]
(Evans note; no copy located.)   38805

U. S. President, 1800.
Speech of the President of the United
States, to both Houses of Congress. 22d
November, 1800. . . . Published by Order
of the House.
[Washington, 1800.] 7 pp.
AAS copy.   38906

U. S. Register of the Treasury, 1782.
A General View of Receipts and
Expenditures . . . to the 31st December,
1781. . . . November 18, 1782.
[Philadelphia, 1782.] Broadside.
AAS copy.   17765

U. S. Register of the Treasury, 1783.
A State of the Receipts and Expenditures
. . . from . . . January, 1783.
[Philadelphia, 1783.] Broadside.
LOC copy.   18270

U. S. Register of the Treasury, 1785.
General Account of Receipts and
Expenditures of the United States . . .
1784 . . . 1785.
[New York, 1785.] Broadside.
JCB copy.   44819

U. S. Register of the Treasury, 1786.
Dr. State of New-Hampshire.
[New York, 1786.] 82 pp.
BA copy.   20037

U. S. Register of the Treasury, 1786.
. . . General Account of Receipts and
Expenditures of the United States . . .
from 1st November, 1785, to 30th June,
1786.
[New York, 1786.] Broadside.
AAS copy.   20066

U. S. Register of the Treasury, 1786.
Schedule of Requisitions on the Several
States. . . . July 1, 1786.
[New York, 1786.] Broadside.
AAS copy.   20081

U. S. Register of the Treasury, 1786.
Schedule of the French and Dutch Loans.
[New York, 1786.] [2] pp.
AAS copy.   20082

[U. S. Register of the Treasury, 1788.
Schedule of the Requisitions on the
Several States . . . 1782 . . . 1787.
[New York, 1788.] Broadside.]
(Ford 457; not now to be located.)   21532

U. S. Register of the Treasury, 1789.
A General Statement of the Foreign
Loans.
[New York, 1789.] [3] pp.
NYPL copy.   22206

[U. S. Register of the Treasury, 1790.
Report of the Register of the Treasury, to
the House of Representatives, on the

Accounts of Robert Morris . . . 1781 . . .
1784 [Mar. 4, 1790].
[New York, 1790.] 2 pp.]
(No copy located.)   22993

U. S. Register of the Treasury, 1791.
Statements of the Receipts and
Expenditures of Public Moneys during the
Administration of the Finances by Robert
Morris, Esquire, late Superintendant, with
Other Extracts and Accounts from the
Public Records, made out by the Register
of the Treasury, by Direction of A
Committee of the House . . . the 19th
March 1790 [Feb. 16, 1791].
[Philadelphia, 1791.] 36, 4, 14 pp.
AAS copy.   23922

U. S. Register of the Treasury, 1793.
Statement of the Purchase of the Public
Stock by the Agents to the Trustees
Named in the Act of the Reduction of the
Public Debt to the 1st of August,
December 13, 1793.
[Philadelphia, 1793.] Broadside.
NYHS copy.   46913

U. S. Register of the Treasury, 1793.
Statement of the Purchases of Public
Stock by the Agents to the Trustees
Named in the Act for the Reduction of the
Public Debt to the 16th December, 1793.
[Philadelphia, 1793.] Broadside.
NYHS copy.   46914

U. S. Register of the Treasury, 1796.
(Received the 14th December, 1795.)
Sundry Estimates and Statements Relative
to Appropriations for . . . 1796. . . .
Published by Order of the House.
[Philadelphia, 1796.] 29 pp.
AAS copy.   31460

U. S. Register of the Treasury, 1800.
An Account of the Receipts and
Expenditures of the United States, for the
Year 1799. . . . In Pursuance of the
Standing Order of the House.
Washington, D.C., [1800]. 74, [12] pp.
and folding tables.
AAS copy.   38689

U. S. Register of the Treasury, 1800.
An Account of the Receipts and
Expenditures of the United States, for the
Year 1799. . . . Published by Order of the
House.
Washington, D. C., Way & Groff, [1800].
pp. [1]-8, [17]-74, 2 folded tables, [8], 2
folded tables.
AAS copy.   38690

[U. S. Superintendent of Finance, 1781.
Plan for Establishing a National Bank.
Providence, 1781. 11 pp.]
(Sabin 50866. "This day published,"
Amer. Journal, June 20, 1781.)   17395

U. S. Superintendent of Indian Affairs.
Southern District.
Pursuant to an Ordinance of Congress the
7th August, 1786. . . . Richard Winn.
Charleston, Markland & M'Iver, [1786].
Broadside.
(No copy located.)   45002

U. S. Supreme Court, 1793.
A Case Decided . . . in February, 1793.
Boston, Adams & Larkin, 1793. 80 pp.
AAS copy.   25371

U. S. Supreme Court, 1793.
A Case Decided . . . in February, 1793.
Philadelphia, Dobson, 1793. [2], 120, [1]
pp.
AAS copy.   25370

U. S. Treasurer, 1793.
The Treasurer of the United States'
Accounts of Payments and Receipts . . . to
the thirty-first Day of December, 1792.
[Philadelphia], Childs & Swaine, [1793].
23 pp.
BA copy.   46915

U. S. Treasurer, 1794.
Accounts of the Treasurer of the United
States of Payments and Receipts of Public
Monies . . . on Account of the War
Department . . . to the 30th of September,
1794. Published by Order of the House.
[Philadelphia]. Childs, [1794]. 46 pp.
AAS copy.   27932

U. S. Treasurer, 1794.
The Treasurer of the United States'
Accounts . . . also, the War Department
Accounts . . . to [Dec. 31, 1793]. . . .
[Philadelphia], Childs & Swaine, [1794].
60 pp.
LOC copy.   47296

U. S. Treasurer, 1794.
The Treasurer of the United States'
Accounts . . . Ending . . . March 1794.
Also the War Department Accounts . . . to
March 1794.
[Philadelphia], Childs & Swaine, [1794].
51 pp.
WLC copy.   47297

U. S. Treasurer, 1795.
Accounts of the Treasurer of the United
States, of Payments and Receipts . . .
Ending the Thirtieth Day of September
1794.
[Philadelphia], Childs, [1795]. 31, 16 pp.
(Not located, 1968.)   47656

U. S. Treasurer, 1796.
Accounts of the Treasurer of the United
States, of Payments and Receipts of
Public Monies, Commencing the First of
January, and Ending the Thirty-First of
December, 1795. . . . Published by Order
of the House.
[Philadelphia, 1796.] 148 pp.
AAS copy.   31435

U. S. Treasurer, 1797.
Accounts of the Treasurer of the United
States, of Payments and Receipts of
Public Monies . . . 1796.
[Philadelphia, 1797. [2], [1]-16, [3]-154
pp.
AAS copy.   33074

U. S. Treasurer, 1797.
Accounts of the Treasurer of the United
States, of Payments and Receipts of
Public Monies . . . Ending . . . December,
1797. . . . (Published by Order of the
House. . . .)
[Philadelphia, 1798.] 143 pp.
AAS copy.   34848

U. S. Treasurer, 1798.
Treasury of the United States, December
20th, 1798. Sir. . . .
[Philadelphia, 1798.] 83 pp.
AAS copy.   34885

U. S. Treasurer, 1799.
Accounts of the Treasurer of the United
States, of Payments and Receipts of
Public Monies . . . 1798. . . . Printed by
Order of the House.
[Philadelphia? 1799.] 15 pp.
AAS copy.   36469

U. S. Treasurer, 1799.
Treasury United States. December 6th,
1799. Sir, My Specie, War and Navy
Accounts. . . .
[Philadelphia, 1799.] 41 pp.
(The one recorded copy cannot be
reproduced.)   36596

U. S. Treasurer, 1799.
Treasury of the United States, February
11, 1799. Sir My Account of the Receipts
and Expenditures . . . for the Quarter
Ending the 30th September. . . .
[Philadelphia, 1799.] 27 pp.
HEH copy.   36541

U. S. Treasurer, 1799.
Treasury of the United States, February
11th, 1799. Sir, My Account of
Receipts. . . .
[Philadelphia, 1799.] 27 pp.
(Also entered as 36541, q. v.)   36595

U. S. Treasurer, 1800.
Accounts of the Treasurer of the United
States, of his Receipts and Expenditures
. . . for the Quarter Ending the 30th of
June last. 8th December, 1800. Ordered to
lie on the Table. Published by Order of
the House.
[Washington, D. C., 1800.] 143 pp.
AAS copy.   38691

U. S. Treasury Dept., 1789.
. . . September 19, 1789. The Secretary . . .
Reports. . . . Estimate of the Expenditure.

New York, Greenleaf, [1789]. 26 pp.
AAS copy.   22213

[U. S. Treasury Dept., 1789.
This Indenture made [for Loan
Certificates].
[New York, 1789.] Broadside.]
(The copy reported by Evans cannot now
be located.)   22205

U. S. Treasury Dept., 1790.
Report of the Secretary of the Treasury to
the House of Representatives, Relative to
a Provision for the Support of the Public
Credit.
New York, Childs & Swaine, 1790. 51 pp.
AAS copy.   22998

U. S. Treasury Dept., 1790.
Treasury Department, March 1, 1790.
Pursuant to the Act. . . .
New York, Childs & Swaine, [1790]. 10
pp.
LOC copy.   23002

U. S. Treasury Dept., 1790.
Treasury Department, March 4, 1790. In
Obedience to the Order. . . .
[New York, 1790.] 3 pp.
AAS copy.   23003

U. S. Treasury Dept., 1790.
Treasury department, July 20th, 1790. In
Obedience to the Order. . . .
[New York], Childs & Swaine, [1790]. 4
pp.
NYPL copy.   23004

U. S. Treasury Dept., 1790.
Treasury Department, December 13, 1790.
In Obedience to the Order . . . the said
Secretary further Respectfully
Reports. . . .
[New York], Childs & Swaine, [1790]. 22
pp.
AAS copy.   23006

U. S. Treasury Dept., 1790.
Treasury Department, December 13, 1790.
In Obedience to the Order . . . the said
Secretary Respectfully Reports. . . .
[New York], Childs & Swaine, [1790]. 7
pp.
AAS copy.   23005

[U. S. Treasury Dept., 1791.
Letter from the Treasurer of the United
States with Accounts of Receipts and
Expenditures of Public Moneys from July
11 to Sept. 30, 1791.
Philadelphia, Childs & Swaine, [1791]. 52
pp.]
(No copy located.)   23924

U. S. Treasury Dept., 1791.
Pursuant to the Order of the House . . . of
the 18th of January, 1791 . . . the . . .
Secretary . . . Submits the Following
Report. . . . April 5, 1792.
[Philadelphia, 1792.] [4] pp.
AAS copy.   24918

U. S. Treasury Dept., 1791.
Report of the Secretary of the Treasury of
the United States on the Subject of
Manufactures. . . . December 5, 1791.
[Philadelphia], Childs & Swaine, [1791].
[4], 58 pp.
AAS copy.   23914

U. S. Treasury Dept., 1791.
The Secretary of the Treasury Having
Attentively Considered the Subject
Referred to him by the Order of the
House of Representatives of the Fifteenth
Day of April last. . . . [Jan. 28, 1791.]
[Philadelphia], Childs & Swaine, [1791].
22 pp.
AAS copy.   23920

U. S. Treasury Dept., 1791.
Statement of the Purchases of Public
Stock by the Agents to the Trustees [Nov.
4, 1791].
[Philadelphia, 1791.] Broadside.
WLC copy.   46334

U. S. Treasury Dept., 1791.
The Treasurer of the United States'
Accounts of Payments and Receipts of
Public Monies, from 1st October, 1790, to
30th June, 1791. Presented to the House
. . . 26th October, 1791.

[Philadelphia], Childs & Swaine, [1791].
52 pp.
AAS copy.   23923

U. S. Treasury Dept., 1791.
Treasury Department, January 6, 1791.
Sir, I have the Honor to Inform you. . . .
[Philadelphia, 1791.] [3] pp., 1 table.
AAS copy.   23926

U. S. Treasury Dept., 1791.
Treasury Department, January 6, 1791. Sir
I have the Honor to Transmit. . . .
Estimates.
[Philadelphia, 1791.] 12 pp.
AAS copy.   23925

U. S. Treasury Dept., 1791.
Treasury Department, February 15, 1791.
Sir, I do Myself the Honor. . . .
[Philadelphia, 1791.] [4] pp.
LOC copy.   23927

U. S. Treasury Dept., 1791.
Treasury Department, May 13th, 1791
(Circular). Sir, I find Instances. . . .
[Philadelphia, 1791.] 1 p.
AAS copy.   46335

U. S. Treasury Dept., 1791.
Treasury Department, September 21,
1791. (Circular) Sir, It being
necessary. . . .
[Philadelphia, 1791]. 1 p.
AAS copy.   46336

U. S. Treasury Dept., 1791.
Treasury of the United States. December
5th, 1791. Sir, Permit me. . . .
[Philadelphia, 1791.] 14 pp.
LOC copy.   23928

U. S. Treasury Dept., 1792.
Abstract of Goods . . . Exported . . . 1790,
to . . . 1791.
n.p., [1792]. [5] pp.
WLC copy.   46647

U. S. Treasury Dept., 1792.
(Circular to the Collectors of the
Customs.) Treasury Department, October
25, 1792.
[Philadelphia, 1792.] Broadside.
AAS copy.   46648

U. S. Treasury Dept., 1792.
(Circular) Treasury Department,
February 6, 1792.
[Philadelphia, 1792.] Broadside.
AAS copy.   46649

U. S. Treasury Dept., 1792.
(Circular.) Treasury Department, July 20,
1792.
[Philadelphia, 1792.] [2] pp.
AAS copy.   46650

U. S. Treasury Dept., 1792.
(Circular.) Treasury Department, August
6, 1792.
[Philadelphia, 1792.] Broadside.
AAS copy.   46651

U. S. Treasury Dept., 1792.
(Circular) Treasury Department, August
27th, 1792.
[Philadelphia, 1792.] Broadside.
NYPL copy.   46652

U. S. Treasury Dept., 1792.
(Circular) Treasury Department, August
31st, 1792.
[Philadelphia, 1792.] [2] pp.
AAS copy.   46653

U. S. Treasury Dept., 1792.
(Circular) Treasury Department, October
12, 1792.
[Philadelphia, 1792.] Broadside.
AAS copy.   46654

U. S. Treasury Dept., 1792.
Estimate of the Expenditures for the Civil
List . . . for the Year 1792.
[Philadelphia], Childs & Swaine, [1791].
20 pp.
NYPL copy.   23895

U. S. Treasury Dept., 1792.
Report of the Secretary of the Treasury,
on the Act for Laying Duties on Spirits.

&c. Read in the House . . . March 6th,
1792.
[Philadelphia], Childs & Swaine, [1792].
20 pp.
AAS copy.   24925

U. S. Treasury Dept., 1792.
Report of the Secretary of the Treasury on
the Petition of Catharine Greene. Read in
the House . . . December 26, 1791.
[Philadelphia], Childs & Swaine, [1792].
35 pp.
AAS copy.   24936

U. S. Treasury Dept., 1792.
Report of the Secretary of the Treasury,
on the Subject of the Public Debt.
Presented to the House . . . February 7th,
1792.
[Philadelphia], Childs & Swaine, [1792].
15 pp.
AAS copy.   24926

U. S. Treasury Dept., 1792.
Report of the Secretary of the Treasury
Respecting the Redemption of the Public
Debt. . . . Published by Order of the
House. . . .
[Philadelphia], Childs & Swaine, [1792].
[4], 10 pp.
AAS copy.   24927

U. S. Treasury Dept., 1792.
Return of the Duties on Imports . . .
Transmitted to the House . . . by the
Secretary of the Treasury, March 28, 1792.
[Philadelphia], Childs & Swaine, [1792].
[2], 9 pp., chart.
NYPL copy.   24928

[U. S. Treasury Dept., 1792.
The Secretary of the Treasury, Pursuant
to a Resolution of the House . . . of the
8th Instant. . . . March 16.
[Philadelphia], Childs & Swaine, [1792].
8 pp.]
(This is a ghost of 24940, q.v.)   24929

U. S. Treasury Dept., 1792.
The Secretary of the Treasury to whom
the House of Representatives were Pleased
to Refer the Several Petitions . . .
respectfully submits the Following
Report. . . . April 16, 1792.
[Philadelphia, 1792.] [3] pp.
AAS copy.   24930

U. S. Treasury Dept., 1792.
The Secretary of the Treasury, to whom
was Referred the Several Petitions in the
List hereunto Annexed Specified
Respectfully makes the following
Report. . . . November 19, 1792.
[Philadelphia, 1792.] [2] pp.
AAS copy.   24931

U. S. Treasury Dept., 1792.
The Secretary of the Treasury, to whom
were Referred by the House of
Representatives, the Several Petitions . . .
Makes the following Report. . . . April 18,
1792.
[Philadelphia], Childs & Swaine, [1792].
11 pp.
AAS copy.   24932

U. S. Treasury Dept., 1792.
The Secretary of the Treasury to whom
were Referred Certain Papers Concerning
a Marine Hospital. . . . April 17th, 1792.
[Philadelphia, 1792.] Broadside.
NYPL copy.   24933

[U. S. Treasury Dept., 1792.
The Treasurer of the United States.
Accounts of Payments and Receipts of
Public Monies . . . [Jan. 1 - Sept. 20,
1792]. Presented to the House . . .
November 6, 1792.
[Philadelphia, 1792.] 67 pp.]
(Also entered as 26352, q.v.)   24939

U. S. Treasury Dept., 1792.
Treasury Department, January 23, 1792.
Sir, I have the Honor [Budget].
[Philadelphia, 1792.] [4] pp.
AAS copy.   24937

U. S. Treasury Dept., 1792.
Treasury of the United States. February
28th, 1792. Sir, My Specie Account. . . .
[Philadelphia, 1792.] 11 pp.
AAS copy.   24938

U. S. Treasury Dept., 1792.
Treasury Department, March 16, 1792.
The Secretary of the Treasury, Pursuant
to a Resolution. . . .
[Philadelphia], Childs & Swaine, [1792].
8 pp.
AAS copy.   24940

U. S. Treasury Dept., 1792.
Treasury Department, April 16th, 1792.
Sir, I have the Honor to Transmit
herewith a Report. . . .
[Philadelphia, 1792.] [2] pp.
AAS copy.   24941

U. S. Treasury Dept., 1792.
Treasury Department September 15th,
1792.
[Philadelphia, 1792.] Broadside.
AAS copy.   46655

U. S. Treasury Dept., 1792.
Treasury department, Dec. 7th, 1792. Sir,
I have the Honor herewith to Transmit
Certain Statements. . . .
[Philadelphia, 1792.] 8 pp.
AAS copy.   24942

U. S. Treasury Dept., 1793.
Abstract of Goods, Wares and
Merchandize Exported from . . . the 1st of
October, 1791, to the 30th September,
1792. . . . Published by Order of the
House.
[Philadelphia], Childs & Swaine, [1793].
[4] pp., 5 folded tables.
AAS copy.   26340

U. S. Treasury Dept., 1793.
An Account of the Receipts and
Expenditures of the United States
Commencing with the Establishment of
the Treasury Department. . . . Published
by Order of the House.
Philadelphia, Childs & Swaine, 1793. 61
pp., 1 folding plate.
AAS copy.   26341

U. S. Treasury Dept., 1793.
Circular to the Collectors of Customs.
Philadelphia, August 4, 1793. . . .
[Philadelphia, 1793.] [3] pp.
LOC copy.   26342

U. S. Treasury Dept., 1793.
(Circular) Treasury Department, January
22d, 1793. Enclosed is an Act. . . .
[Philadelphia, 1793.] Broadside.
(Left side wanting; only known copy.)
AAS copy.   46917

U. S. Treasury Dept., 1793.
(Circular) Treasury Department, March
13, 1793. Sir, Proof has been Filed. . . .
[Philadelphia, 1793.] Broadside.
AAS copy.   46918

U. S. Treasury Dept., 1793.
(Circular.) Treasury Department, March
29th, 1793. Sir, A Question. . . .
[Philadelphia, 1793.] Broadside.
AAS copy.   46919

U. S. Treasury Dept., 1793.
(Circular) Treasury Department, April 12,
1793, Sir, The Collectors. . . .
[Philadelphia, 1793.] Broadside.
Pierce Gaines copy.   46920

U. S. Treasury Dept., 1793.
(Circular.) Treasury Department, April
29th, 1793. Sir, It having been. . . .
[Philadelphia, 1793.] Broadside.
AAS copy.   46921

U. S. Treasury Department, 1793.
(Circular.) Treasury Department, May 30,
1793. Sir, It being the Opinion. . . .
[Philadelphia, 1793.] Broadside.
AAS copy.   46922

U. S. Treasury Dept., 1793.
(Circular.) Treasury Department, August
22, 1793. Sir, Though it was not
Expressly. . . .
[Philadelphia, 1793.] Broadside.
AAS copy.   46923

U. S. Treasury Dept., 1793.
Communications from the Secretary of the
Treasury, to the House of Representatives.
. . . Printed Aggreeably to a Resolution of

the House, of the 2d of March, 1793.
Philadelphia, Fenno, [1793]. 65 pp.,
1 folded table.
AAS copy.   26343

U. S. Treasury Dept., 1793.
General State of the Revenue on Domestic
Distilled Spirits . . . House . . . Order of
the 8th of May 1792 [Transmitted Mar. 2,
1793].
[Philadelphia], Childs & Swaine, [1793].
[4] pp., 1 folding plate.
AAS copy.   26344

[U. S. Treasury Dept., 1793.
General Statement of Appropriations and
Expenditures of the United States,
December, 1792.
[Philadelphia, 1793.] Broadside.]
(No copy located.)   26345

[U. S. Treasury Dept?, 1793.
A List of Names of Persons to whom
Military Patents have Issued out of the
Secretary's office.
[Philadelphia, 1793.] 25 pp.]
(No copy located.)   26354

U. S. Treasury Dept., 1793.
Report of the Secretary of the Treasury,
Relative to the Loans. . . . Published by
Order of the House [Feb. 13, 1793].
[Philadelphia], Childs & Swaine, [1793].
22 pp.
(The copy described by Evans had other
material bound with it.)
AAS copy.   26347

U. S. Treasury Dept., 1793.
Sundry Estimates and Statements Relative
to Appropriations for the Service of the
Year 1794.
[Philadelphia, 1794]. 29 (i.e. 26) pp.
LOC copy.   26349

U. S. Treasury Dept., 1793.
Sundry Statements, by the Secretary of the
Treasury. In Conformity with the
Resolution of the House of
Representatives of the 23d of January,
1793.
[Philadelphia], Childs & Swaine, [1793].
31 pp.
AAS copy.   26351

U. S. Treasury Dept., 1793.
Sundry Statements made by the Secretary
of the Treasury . . . 23d of January,
1793.
[Philadelphia, 1793.] [4] pp.
(Not located, 1968.)   46924

U. S. Treasury Dept., 1793.
Sundry Statements Respecting the Several
Foreign Loans. . . . Published by Order of
the House.
[Philadelphia], Childs & Swaine, [1793].
6 pp.
AAS copy.   26350

U. S. Treasury Dept., 1793.
The Treasurer of the United States,
Accounts of Payments and Receipts of
Public Monies . . . to the 30th of
September, 1792. Presented to the House
of Representatives November 6, 1792.
[Philadelphia, 1793.] 67 pp.
AAS copy.   26352

U. S. Treasury Dept., 1793.
Treasury Department [   ] 1793. Sir,
It Appears that the Summary. . . .
[Philadelphia, 1793.] Broadside.
Pierce W. Gaines copy.   46916

U. S. Treasury Dept., 1793.
Treasury Department, January 10th, 1793.
Sir, The Resolution. . . .
[Philadelphia, 1793.] [2] pp.
AAS copy.   46925

U. S. Treasury Dept., 1793.
Treasury Department. February [13]
1793. Sir, In Obedience. . . .
[Philadelphia, 1793.] 6 pp.
AAS copy.   46926

U. S. Treasury Dept., 1793.
Treasury Department. February 19th,
1793. Sir, The last Letter. . . .
[Philadelphia, 1793.] 22 pp., 1 folding
table.

(This seems to be the item described by Evans under this no.)
AAS copy.   26346

U. S. Treasury Dept., 1793.
Treasury Department, February 14th, 1793. Sir, I have the Honor. . . .
[Philadelphia, 1793.] [2] pp.
AAS copy.   46927

U. S. Treasury Dept., 1794.
An Account of the Receipts and Expenditures of the United States for the Year 1792. . . . Published by Order of the House.
Philadelphia, Fenno, 1794. 59 pp.
AAS copy.   27930

U. S. Treasury Dept., 1794.
An Account of the Receipts and Expenditures of the United States for the Year 1793. . . . Published by Order of the House.
Philadelphia, Fenno, 1794. 65, [12] pp.
AAS copy.   27931

[U. S. Treasury Dept., 1794.
Circular of Instructions Relative to Licenses Given to Vessels. August 29, 1794.
Philadelphia, 1794. [2] pp.]
(Apparently a description of a circular similar to 27940.)   27942

[U. S. Treasury Dept., 1794.
Circular Relative to Captured and Condemned American Vessels. August 14, 1794.
Philadelphia, 1794. Broadside.]
(A description of a circular similar to 27940.)   27941

[U. S. Treasury Dept., 1794.
Circular to Collectors Relative to Equipment of Armed Vessels. October 6, 1794.
Philadelphia, 1794. Broadside.]
(A description of a circular similar to 27940.)   27943

U. S. Treasury Dept., 1794.
(Circular.) Treasury Department, [January 10th] 1794. Sir, A Provisory Arrangement. . . .
[Philadelphia, 1794.] Broadside.
(This is evidently the item described by Evans.)
AAS copy.   27939

U. S. Treasury Dept., 1794.
(Circular) Treasury Department April 18, 1794. Sir. . . .
[Philadelphia, 1794.] Broadside.
AAS copy.   47298

U. S. Treasury Dept., 1794.
(Circular) Treasury Department, April 23d 1794. . . . Our Treaty with Sweden.
[Philadelphia? 1794] Broadside.
WLC copy.   47299

U. S. Treasury Dept., 1794.
(Circular) Treasury Department June 17th. 1794. Sir, I Send you herewith an Act. . . .
[Philadelphia, 1794.] Broadside.
AAS copy.   27940

U. S. Treasury Dept., 1794.
(Circular) Treasury Department, [Nov. 29] 1794. Sir, I Have to Request. . . .
[Philadelphia, 1794.] Broadside.
AAS copy.   27944

U. S. Treasury Dept., 1794.
(Circular) Treasury Department, [Nov. 29], 1794. Sir, I have to Request. . . .
[Philadelphia, 1794.] Broadside.
AAS copy.   47300

U. S. Treasury Dept., 1794.
Principles and Course of Proceeding . . . Monies Borrowed Abroad. . . . April 1, 1794.
[Philadelphia, 1794.] Broadside.
AAS copy.   47301

U. S. Treasury Dept., 1794.
Query, Stated by the Secretary. . . . 24th March, 1794.
[Philadelphia, 1794.] Broadside.
LOC copy.   47302

U. S. Treasury Dept., 1794.
Report of the Secretary of the Treasury Respecting the Tonnage of Vessels [Jan. 7, 1794].
[Philadelphia], Childs & Swaine, [1794]. [4] pp., 2 tables.
AAS copy.   27946

U. S. Treasury Dept., 1794.
Statements Exhibiting the Periods at which Monies were Received for the Sale of Bills on Amsterdam.
[Philadelphia], Childs & Swaine, [1794]. 2 leaves.
WLC copy.   47303

U. S. Treasury Dept., 1794.
Statements in Relation to the Foreign and Domestic Debt. . . . Prepared at the Treasury, for the Committee Appointed to Examine into the State of the Treasury Department. . . . Published by Order of the Committee [May 22, 1794].
[Philadelphia], Childs & Swaine, [1794]. [55] pp.
BA copy.   27950

U. S. Treasury Dept., 1794.
A Summary Statement Exhibiting the Receipts into the Treasury. . . .
[Philadelphia], Childs & Swaine, [1794]. 12 pp.
AAS copy.   27951

U. S. Treasury Dept., 1794.
A Summary Statement of the Receipts and Expenditures of the United States . . . Published by Order of the House.
[Philadelphia], Childs & Swaine, [1794]. [17] pp.
AAS copy.   27952

U. S. Treasury Dept., 1794.
Sundry Estimates and Statements Relative to Appropriations for the Service of the Year 1795. . . . Published by Order of the House.
[Philadelphia], Childs, [1794] 36 pp.
AAS copy.   27953

U. S. Treasury Dept., 1794.
Treasury Department, February 5th, 1794. Sir; I have the Honor to Transmit. . . .
[Philadelphia, 1794.] [3] pp.
LOC copy.   47305

U. S. Treasury Dept., 1794.
Treasury Department, April 25, 1794. Sir, I have the Honor to Transmit. . . .
[Philadelphia, 1794.] [4] pp.
LOC copy.   47304

U. S. Treasury Dept., 1794.
Treasury Department, June 2d, 1794. Sir, I Have the Honor to Transmit. . . .
[Philadelphia, 1794.] [4] pp.
AAS copy.   27945

U. S. Treasury Dept., 1794.
Treasury Department. Revenue Office [blank] 1794. A Note of the General Dimensions of the Heavy Cannon. . . .
[Philadelphia, 1794.] Broadside.
LOC copy.   47306

U. S. Treasury Dept., 1795.
Abstract of Goods, Wares, and Merchandize, Exported from the United States . . . 1793 . . . 1794. Published by Order of the House.
Philadelphia, Childs, 1795. 12 pp.
AAS copy.   29762

U. S. Treasury Dept., 1795.
An Account of the Receipts and Expenditures of the United States for . . . 1794. . . . Published by Order of the House.
Philadelphia, Fenno, 1795. 87, [32] pp.
AAS copy.   29763

[U. S. Treasury Dept., 1795.
Circular of Instructions to Collectors. . . . March 16, 1795.
[Philadelphia, 1795.] 3 pp.]
(No copy located.)   29764

[U. S. Treasury Dept., 1795.
Circular Relative to Entries of Dutiable Goods. . . . March 28, 1795.
[Philadelphia, 1795.] Broadside.]
(No copy located.)   29765

U. S. Treasury Dept., 1795.
(Circular) To the Collectors and Naval Officers. Treasury Depart, March [blank] 1795.
[Philadelphia, 1795.] [8] pp.
(The one recorded copy is not available.)   47657

U. S. Treasury Dept., 1795.
Circular to the Collectors and Naval Officers. Treasury Department, March 18th, 1795.
[Philadelphia, 1795.] Broadside.
(The only known copy is not available.)   47658

U. S. Treasury Dept., 1795.
Circular. Treasury Department, Register's Office, 2d March, 1795.
[Philadelphia, 1795.] [2] pp.
JCB copy.   29775

U. S. Treasury Dept., 1795.
For the Information of the Merchants Concerned in the Exportation of Merchandize Entitled to a Drawback. . . .
[Philadelphia, 1795.] 8 pp., 1 folded table.
LOC copy.   29766

U. S. Treasury Dept., 1795.
For the Information of the Merchants Concerned in the Exportation of Merchandize Entitled to a Drawback. . . .
[Philadelphia], Smith, [1795.]. 8 pp.
LOC copy.   29767

U. S. Treasury Dept., 1795.
For the Information of the Merchants, Concerned in . . . Exportation.
[Providence], Wheeler, [1795]. 8 pp.
RIHS copy.   29769

[U. S. Treasury Dept., 1795.
For the Information of the Merchants Concerned in the Exportation of Merchandize Entitled to a Drawback.
Salem, Carlton, 1795. 8 pp.]
(The unique copy could not be located.)   29768

[U. S. Treasury Dept., 1795.
Letter from the Secretary of the Treasury, to the Chairman of the Committee of Ways and Means. . . . January 4, 1795.
Philadelphia, 1795.]
(A ghost of 31447, q. v.)   29770

U. S. Treasury Dept., 1795.
Proceedings of the Accounting Officers of the Treasury. . . . Accompanying a Letter from the Secretary . . . Received the 24th December 1795. Published by Order of the House.
[Philadelphia], Childs, [1795]. 31 pp.
AAS copy.   29771

U. S. Treasury Dept., 1795.
(Received the 17th of December, 1795) Treasury of the United States, December 16, 1795. Sir, my specie Accounts. . . .
n. p., [1795?] 16 pp.
WLC copy.   47659

U. S. Treasury Dept., 1795.
Report of the Secretary of the Treasury, for the Improvement and Better Management of the Revenues . . . Read in the House . . . the Second February, 1795, and Published by their Order.
Philadelphia, Childs, 1795. 11 pp.
AAS copy.   29773

U. S. Treasury Dept., 1795.
Report of the Secretary of the Treasury, Read in the House . . . January 19th, 1795. . . . Printed by Order of the House.
[Philadelphia], Fenno, 1795. 90 pp., 10 folded tables.
AAS copy.   29772

U. S. Treasury Dept., 1795.
Sir, It is Necessary that I should Inform you that John Kean . . . has Resigned.
[Philadelphia, 1795.] Broadside.
(The only known copy is not available.)   47660

U. S. Treasury Dept., 1795.
Treasury Department. January 21st, 1795. In Consequence of the Resolution of the House. . . .
[Philadelphia, 1795.] Broadside.
JCB copy.   47661

U. S. Treasury Dept., 1796.
. . . Account of Fines, Penalties, and
Forfeitures. . . . January 1, 1796.
[Boston?], 1796. Broadside.
MHS copy.   47984

U. S. Treasury Dept., 1796.
An Account of the Receipts and
Expenditures of the United States, for the
Year 1795. . . . Published by Order of the
House.
Philadelphia, Fenno, 1796. 83, [18] pp.
AAS copy.   31434

[U. S. Treasury Dept., 1796.
Circular Directing Returns of Exports to
be made to the Register of the Treasury.
July 22, 1796.
Philadelphia, Ross, 1796. Broadside.]
(The origin of this entry is unknown.)
                                             31439

[U. S. Treasury Dept., 1796.
Circular of Instructions Relative to Bonds
to Secure Payment of Duties. November
17, 1796.
Philadelphia, Ross, 1796. Broadside.]
(The origin of this entry is unknown.)
                                             31442

[U. S. Treasury Dept., 1796.
Circular of Instructions Relative to
Passports for Ships and Vessels of the
United States. August 15, 1796.
Philadelphia, Ross, 1796. Broadside.]
(The origin of this entry is unknown.)
                                             31440

[U. S. Treasury Dept., 1796.
Circular of Instructions Relative to the
Shipment of American Seamen. June 19,
1796.
Philadelphia, Ross, 1796. [2] pp.
(The origin of this entry is unknown.)
                                             31437

[U. S. Treasury Dept., 1796.
Circular of Instructions to Collectors
Relative to Return of Exports. September
8, 1796.
Philadelphia, Ross, 1796. [2] pp.]
(The origin of this entry is unknown.)
                                             31441

[U. S. Treasury Dept., 1796.
Circular Relating to Relief and Protection
of American Seamen and Proof of
Citizenship. July 19, 1796.
Philadelphia, Ross, 1796. [2] pp.]
(The origin of this entry is unknown.)
                                             31438

[U. S. Treasury Dept., 1796.
Circular Relating to the Cargoes of
Prize-Vessels. November 26, 1796.
Philadelphia, Ross, 1796. [2] pp.]
(The origin of this entry is unknown.)
                                             31443

[U. S. Treasury Dept., 1796.
Circular Relative to Vessels and Property
Captured by Privateers. June 30, 1796.
Philadelphia, Ross, 1796. Broadside.]
(The origin of this entry has not been
discovered.)   31436

U. S. Treasury Dept., 1796.
(Circular.) Supervisor's Office, District of
New-York June 30th, 1796.
Gentlemen. . . .
[New York, 1796.] [2] pp.
NYPL copy.   47986

U. S. Treasury Dept., 1796.
(Circular) Supervisor's Office, New-York,
June 1, 1796. Sir. . . .
[New York, 1796.] [2] pp.
NYPL copy.   47987

U. S. Treasury Dept., 1796.
Circular to the Collectors and Naval
Officers. . . . June 3rd, 1796.
[Philadelphia, 1796.] [2] pp.
(No copy available for reproduction.)
                                             47985

U. S. Treasury Dept., 1796.
District of Rhode-Island. Duties on
Carriages.
[Providence? 1796?] Broadside.
AAS copy.   47988

U. S. Treasury Dept., 1796.

An Estimate for an Appropriation of
Monies, for the Services of the Year
1796. . . . Received 14th of December,
1795. Published by Order of the House.
[Philadelphia, 1796.] 29 pp.
AAS copy.   31444

U. S. Treasury Dept., 1796.
Extracts from Circular Letters. . . .
Selected June 1796.
Philadelphia, Fenno, [1796]. 70 pp.
LOC copy.   47989

[U. S. Treasury Dept., 1796.
Instructions Relative to Forms to be used
by Receivers of Public Moneys.
Philadelphia, 1796.]
(Assumed by Evans from legislation.)
                                             31445

U. S. Treasury Dept., 1796.
Letter and Report of the Secretary of the
Treasury, on the Memorial of Sundry
Merchants of the City of Philadelphia,
16th March, 1796, Committed. . . .
Published by Order of the House.
[Philadelphia, 1796.] [4] pp.
AAS copy.   31454

U. S. Treasury Dept., 1796.
Letter and Report of the Secretary of the
Treasury, on the Petitions of Hopley
Yeaton. . . . 15th March, 1796, Ordered to
lie on the Table. 16th March, 1796.
Committed. . . . Published by Order of the
House.
[Philadelphia, 1796.] 7 pp.
AAS copy.   31453

U. S. Treasury Dept., 1796.
Letter from the Secretary of the Treasury
Accompanying a Plan for . . . Collecting
Direct Taxes. . . . 14th December,
1796-Ordered to lie on the Table.
Published by Order of the House.
[Philadelphia, 1796?] 68, [1] pp., 11
tables.
HEH copy.   47990

U. S. Treasury Dept., 1796.
Letter from the Secretary of the Treasury,
Accompanying a Report and Estimates of
the Sums Necessary to be Appropriated
for the Service of the Year 1797. . . . 16th
December, 1796, Ordered to lie on the
Table.
[Philadelphia, 1796.] 33 pp.
AAS copy.   31446

U. S. Treasury Dept., 1796.
Letter from the Secretary of the Treasury,
Accompanying a Statement of Goods,
Wares and Merchandize, Exported from
. . . October 1794, to . . . September
1795. . . . 12th May, 1796. Ordered to lie
on the Table. Published by Order of the
House. . . .
[Philadelphia, 1796.] 11 pp.
AAS copy.   31457

U. S. Treasury Dept., 1796.
Letter from the Secretary of the Treasury,
Accompanying an Abstract of the Official
Emoluments and Expenditures of the
Officers of the Customs, for the Year
1795. . . . 4th April, 1796. Referred.
[Philadelphia, 1796.] 12 pp.
AAS copy.   31455

U. S. Treasury Dept., 1796.
Letter from the Secretary of the Treasury
. . . Accompanying an Estimate of the
Receipts and Expenditures . . . for . . .
1796. 18th May, 1796. Published by Order
of the House.
[Philadelphia, 1796.] 4, [2] pp.
LOC copy.   31458

U. S. Treasury Dept., 1796.
Letter from the Secretary of the Treasury
Accompanying Sundry Statements, made
in Pursuance of the Resolutions of the 2d
of March, 1795. . . . 7th March, 1796.
Read and Ordered to be on the Table.
(Published by Order of the House. . . .)
[Philadelphia, 1796.] 40 pp., 2 folding
tables.
AAS copy.   31451

U. S. Treasury Dept., 1796.
Letter from the Secretary of the Treasury,
to the Chairman of the Committee of

Ways and Means, Accompanying an
Estimate. . . . 18th May 1796.
n. p., [1796?] [7] pp.
WLC copy.   47991

U. S. Treasury Dept., 1796.
Letter from the Secretary of the Treasury,
to the Chairman of the Committee of
Ways and Means. Published by Order of
the House of Representatives, the 12th of
March, 1796.
[Philadelphia, 1796.] 4 pp.
LOC copy.   31452

U. S. Treasury Dept., 1796.
. . . Letter from the Secretary of the
Treasury to the Chairman of the
Committee of the Ways and Means
Relative to Certain Additional Provisions
[Presented to the House the 3d of
February, 1796.]
[Philadelphia, 1796.] 6 pp.
AAS copy.   47992

U. S. Treasury Dept., 1796.
Letter from the Secretary of the Treasury
to the Chairman of the Committee of
Ways and Means, Relative to an
Inaccuracy . . . in the . . . Receipts and
Expenditures for 1794. Published by Order
of the House 18th April.
[Philadelphia, 1796.] 6 pp.
AAS copy.   31456

U. S. Treasury Dept., 1796.
(Presented to the House the 4th of
January, 1796.) Letter of the Secretary of
the Treasury, to the Chairman of the
Committee of Ways and Means.
[Philadelphia, 1796.] 16 pp.
LOC copy.   31447

U. S. Treasury Dept., 1796.
(Presented to the House, the 19th of
January, 1796.) A Statement, Shewing the
final Liquidation of the French Loans.
[Philadelphia, 1796.] Broadside.
AAS copy.   31459

U. S. Treasury Dept., 1796.
(Presented to the House the 3d of
February, 1796.) Letter from the Secretary
of the Treasury, Relative to Addition of
Provisions for the Execution of the Act
Making further Provisions for the Support
of Public Credit.
[Philadelphia, 1796.] 6 pp.
NYPL copy.   31450

U. S. Treasury Dept., 1796.
(Received January 25th, 1796.) Letter
from the Secretary of the Treasury
Accompanying a Return of the Exports of
the United States [October 1, 1790-
September 30, 1795].
[Philadelphia, 1796.] [6] pp.
LOC copy.   31449

U. S. Treasury Dept., 1796.
(Received the 25th of January, 1796.)
Letter from the Secretary of the Treasury,
Accompanying a Report and Statements
made in Pursuance of Two Resolutions of
the House. . . . 18th of January, 1796.
[Philadelphia, 1796.] 25 pp.
LOC copy.   31448

U. S. Treasury Dept., 1796.
A Statement of the Aggregate of the
Appropriations . . . for the War
Department . . . to the 1st January, 1796.
[n. p.], [1796]. 19 pp.
WLC copy.   47993

U. S. Treasury Dept., 1796.
Treasury Department, August 8, 1796.
Public Notice is Hereby Given . . . Lands
. . . north west of the River Ohio. . . .
[Philadelphia, 1796.] 2 pp.
AAS copy.   47994

U. S. Treasury Dept., 1797-1799.
Circular to Collectors, Naval Officers, and
Surveyors. . . . July 4, 1797.
[Philadelphia, 1797.] Broadside.
(Best copy available.)
WLC copy.   48298

U. S. Treasury Dept., 1797.
Account of Receipts and Expenditures of
the United States . . . April, 1796 . . .
March, 1797. Published by Order of the
House.

[Philadelphia, 1797.] 15 pp.
AAS copy.   33073

U. S. Treasury Dept., 1797.
An Account of the Receipts and
Expenditures of the United States for the
Year 1796. . . . Published by Order of the
House.
Philadelphia, Fenno, [1797]. [4], 85, [12],
irreg., including 5 folding charts.
AAS copy.   48297

U. S. Treasury Dept., 1797.
An Account of the Receipts and
Expenditures of the United States, for the
Year 1797. . . . Published by Order of the
House. . . .
Philadelphia, Fenno, [1798]. 76, [16] pp.
and folding plates.
AAS copy.   34847

U. S. Treasury Dept., 1797.
(Circular to the Collectors of the
Customs.) Treasury Department. April
8th, 1797. . . .
[Philadelphia, 1797.] Broadside.
(The only recorded copy is not available.)
                                             48299

U. S. Treasury Dept., 1797.
Circular to the Collectors of the Customs
and Supervisors of the Revenue. . . .
November 28th, 1797.
[Philadelphia, 1797.] Broadside.
(The only known copy is not available.)
                                             48300

U. S. Treasury Dept., 1797.
(Circular.) Treasury Department, March
1797. Sir. . . .
[Philadelphia, 1797.] Broadside.
(The one reported copy is not available.)
                                             48301

U. S. Treasury Department, 1797.
(Circular) Treasury Department, June
16th, 1797. Sir. . . .
[Philadelphia, 1797.] Broadside.
(The only recorded copy is not available.)
                                             48302

U. S. Treasury Dept., 1797.
(Circular) Treasury Department, July 6th,
1797. Sir. . . .
[Philadelphia, 1797.] Broadside.
(The only recorded copy is not available.)
                                             48303

U. S. Treasury Dept., 1797.
Information to Distillers District of
Maryland, Supervisor's Office, May 1st,
1797.
Baltimore, Clayland and Dobbin, [1797].
Broadside.
(No copy located.)   48304

U. S. Treasury Dept., 1798.
The Following Schedule and Estimate. . . .
May 17th 1798.
[Philadelphia, 1798.] 2, [1] pp.
AAS copy.   48734

U. S. Treasury Dept., 1797.
Letter and Report of the Secretary of the
Treasury, Accompanied with Sundry
Statements Relative to the Military and
Naval Establishments . . . in Pursuance of
Three Resolutions of the House of
Representatives of the 3d of March, 1797
. . . 7th February, 1798 . . . Referred.
[Philadelphia], Ross, [1798]. [56] pp.
LOC copy.   34852

U. S. Treasury Dept., 1797.
Letter from the Secretary of the
Treasury, Accompanied with his Report
and Estimates . . . for . . . 1798. . . . 11th
December, 1797. . . . Published by Order of
the House.
Philadelphia, Poulson & Young, 1797. 47
pp.
AAS copy.   33075

U. S. Treasury Dept., 1797.
Letter from the Secretary of the Treasury,
Accompanying a Plan for Laying and
Collecting Direct Taxes. . . . 14th
December, 1796. . . . Published by Order
of the House.
[Philadelphia, 1797.] 68, [9] pp. 9 folding
charts.
AAS copy.   33076

U. S. Treasury Dept., 1797.
Letter from the Secretary of the Treasury,
Accompanying a Report and Sundry
Statements. . . . 16th February 1797. . . .
Published by Order of the House.
[Philadelphia, 1797.] 20 pp.
AAS copy.   33077

U. S. Treasury Dept., 1797.
Letter from the Secretary of the Treasury,
Accompanying a Report from the
Commissioners of the City of
Washington. . . . 17th December 1797. . . .
Published by Order of the House.
[Philadelphia], Ross, [1797]. 8 pp., 2
folding tables.
AAS copy.   33078

U. S. Treasury Dept., 1797.
Letter from the Secretary of the Treasury,
Accompanying a Statement Exhibiting the
Amount of Drawbacks Paid. . . . 16th
December 1796. . . . Published by Order of
the House.
[Philadelphia, 1797.] [3] pp., 1 folded
table.
AAS copy.   33079

U. S. Treasury Dept., 1797.
Letter from the Secretary of the Treasury,
Accompanying a Statement of Goods,
Wares and Merchandize, Exported. . . .
9th February, 1797. . . . Published by
Order of the House.
[Philadelphia, 1797.] 10 pp.
AAS copy.   33080

U. S. Treasury Dept., 1797.
Letter from the Secretary of the Treasury,
Accompanying an Abstract of the Official
Emoluments and Expenditures of the
Officers of the Customs for . . . 1796. . . .
17th February, 1797. . . . Published by
Order of the House.
[Philadelphia, 1797.] [10] pp.
AAS copy.   33081

U. S. Treasury Dept., 1797.
Letter from the Secretary of the Treasury,
Accompanying his Report and two
Estimates of the Secretary at War . . .
19th January 1797. . . . Published by Order
of the House.
[Philadelphia, 1797.] 7 pp.
AAS copy.   33082

U. S. Treasury Dept., 1797.
Letter from the Secretary at War. . . . 15th
February, 1797. . . . Published by Order of
the House.
[Philadelphia, 1797.] 4 pp.
AAS copy.   33083

U. S. Treasury Dept., 1797.
Letter from the Secretary of the Treasury,
Accompanying Sundry Statements in
Relation to the Annual Expenditures of
the War Department. . . . 12th December,
1796. . . . Published by Order of the
House.
[Philadelphia, 1797.] 7, [3], 15, [1], 19
pp., 2 folded tables.
AAS copy.   33084

U. S. Treasury Dept., 1797.
Letter from the Secretary of the Treasury,
Transmitting a Copy of a Letter from the
Commissioners of the City of
Washington. . . . 3d of June, 1797. . . .
Published by Order of the House.
[Philadelphia, 1797.] 10 pp.
AAS copy.   33085

U. S. Treasury Dept., 1797.
Letter from the Secretary of the Treasury,
Transmitting a Report and Sundry
Statements Exhibiting a View of the
Debts. . . . 29th December, 1796. . . .
Published by Order of the House.
[Philadelphia, 1797.] 39 pp.
AAS copy.   33087

U. S. Treasury Dept., 1797.
Letter from the Secretary of the Treasury,
Transmitting a Report, together with an
Estimate for a Supplementary
Appropriation, for the Services of the
Year 1797. . . . Published by Order of the
House.
[Philadelphia, 1797.] 8 pp.
AAS copy.   33088

U. S. Treasury Dept., 1797.

Letter from the Secretary of the Treasury
Transmitting the Copy of a Letter from
the Commissioners Appointed under the
Act "For Establishing the Temporary and
Permanent Seat of the Government" . . .
29th December, 1796.
[Philadelphia, 1796.] 26 pp., 1 folded
table.
AAS copy.   33086

U. S. Treasury Dept., 1797.
Proceedings of the Accounting Officers of
the Treasury. . . . 29th December, 1796,
Committed. . . . Published by Order of the
House.
[Philadelphia, 1797?] 31 pp.
AAS copy.   48305

U. S. Treasury Dept., 1798.
Abstract of the Stamp Law. . . . March 1,
1798.
[Philadelphia, 1798.] Broadside.
HSP copy.   34874

[U. S. Treasury Dept., 1798.
Articles of Agreement made on the
Fourth day of September, One Thousand
Seven Hundred and Ninety-Eight Between
Oliver Wolcott, Secretary of the Treasury
and And. Welton.
[Philadelphia, 1798.] [2] pp.]
(No copy located.)   34849

[U. S. Treasury Dept., 1798.
Circular to the Collector of Customs. . . .
March 21, 1798.
[Philadelphia, 1798.] Broadside.]
(No copy located.)   34850

U. S. Treasury Dept., 1798.
Extract from the Instructions to the
Assessors Appointed under the Act,
Entitled, "An Act to Provide for the
Valuation of Lands."
[Philadelphia, 1798.] Broadside.
HSP copy.   34706

U. S. Treasury Dept., 1798.
Letter and Report of the Secretary of the
Treasury, Accompanying a Plan, for
Regulating the Collection of Duties. . . .
25th January, 1798, Referred. . . .
(Published by Order of the House. . . .)
[Philadelphia, 1798.] 158 pp.; 1 folding
table.
AAS copy.   34856

U. S. Treasury Dept., 1798.
Letter from the Secretary of the Treasury,
Accompanying a Letter to him from the
Comptroller of the Treasury. . . . 20th
March, 1798, Referred. . . . Published by
Order of the House. . . .
[Philadelphia], Ross, [1798]. [8] pp., 2
folded tables.
AAS copy.   34860

U. S. Treasury Dept., 1798.
Letter from the Secretary of the Treasury,
Accompanying a Report and Estimate of
an Appropriation of Monies for . . .
Clerks. . . . 28th May, 1798. Ordered to lie
on the Table (Published by Order of the
House. . . .)
[Philadelphia, 1798.] 4 pp.
AAS copy.   34861

U. S. Treasury Dept., 1798.
Letter from the Secretary of the Treasury,
Accompanying a Report and Statement of
the Sums Necessary to . . . the Navy. . . .
11th July, 1798. Referred. . . . Printed by
Order of the House. . . .
Philadelphia, Gales, [1798]. 7 pp.
AAS copy.   34862

U. S. Treasury Dept., 1798.
Letter from the Secretary of the Treasury,
Accompanying a Report of the Late
Commissioner of the Revenue. . . . 23d
February, 1798. Ordered to lie on the
Table. (Published by Order of the
House. . . .)
[Philadelphia], Oswald, [1798]. [2], 12
pp., 24 tables.
LCP copy.   34858

U. S. Treasury Dept., 1798.
Letter from the Secretary of the Treasury,
Accompanying a Statement Exhibiting
the Amount of Drawbacks. . . . 9th
February, 1798, Ordered to lie on the

Table. Published by Order of the House. . . .
[Philadelphia], Ross, [1798]. [3] pp., 1 folded table.
AAS copy.   34863

U. S. Treasury Dept., 1798.
Letter from the Secretary of the Treasury, Accompanying a Statement of the Several Existing Contracts. . . . 30th March, 1798.- Ordered to lie on the Table. Published by Order of the House. . . .
Philadelphia, Way & Groff, [1798]. 6 pp.
AAS copy.   34864

U. S. Treasury Dept., 1798.
Letter from the Secretary of the Treasury, Accompanying his Report on the Memorial of Sundry Merchants. . . . 13th April, 1798, Committed. . . . (Published by Order of the House. . . .)
[Philadelphia, 1798.] 8 pp.
AAS copy.   34866

U. S. Treasury Dept., 1798.
Letter from the Secretary of the Treasury, Accompanying his Report on the Petitions of Sundry Inhabitants of . . . Newport. . . . 6th February 1798. Referred. . . .
(Published by Order of the House. . . .)
[Philadelphia, 1798.] 4 pp.
AAS copy.   34857

U. S. Treasury Dept., 1798.
Letter from the Secretary of the Treasury, Accompanying his Report Respecting . . . Foreign Coins. . . . 11th January, 1798. Referred. . . . Published by Order of the House. . . .
[Philadelphia], Ross, [1798]. pp. [4], [4]-6.
AAS copy.   34855

U. S. Treasury Dept., 1798.
Letter from the Secretary of the Treasury, Accompanying Sundry Statements, Exhibiting the Amount of Duties. . . . 13th December, 1798. - Ordered to lie on the Table. Published by Order of the House. . . .
Philadelphia, Way & Groff, [1798]. 12 pp.
AAS copy.   34871

U. S. Treasury Dept., 1798.
Letter from the Secretary of the Treasury, Accompanying the Copy of a Letter from the Commissioners of the City of Washington. . . . 11th December, 1798. Ordered to lie on the Table.
Philadelphia, Fenno, 1798. [7] pp.
AAS copy.   34870

U. S. Treasury Dept., 1798.
Letter from the Secretary of the Treasury, Accompanying two Statements, Marked A & B, Exhibiting the Tonnage of Shipping. . . . 6th April, 1798. - Ordered to lie on the Table. . . . Published by Order of the House. . . .
Philadelphia, Way & Groff, [1798]. [7] pp.
AAS copy.   34865

U. S. Treasury Dept., 1798.
Letter from the Secretary of the Treasury, Inclosing a Report and Estimates. . . . 24th December, 1798. Referred. . . . Published by Order of the House. . . .
Philadelphia, Way & Groff, [1798]. 110 pp.
AAS copy.   34872

U..S. Treasury Dept., 1798.
Letter from the Secretary of the Treasury, Inclosing his Report on the Petition of Jonathan Jackson. . . . 18th April, 1798. Ordered to lie on the Table. Printed by Order of the House. . . .
Philadelphia, Gales, [1798]. 16 pp.
AAS copy.   34867

U. S. Treasury Dept., 1798.
Letter from the Secretary of the Treasury, to the Chairman of the Committee of Ways & Means. . . . 25th May, 1798. Referred. . . . (Published by Order of the House. . . .)
[Philadelphia, 1798.] 8 pp.
AAS copy.   34868

U. S. Treasury Dept., 1798.
Letter from the Secretary of the Treasury, Transmitting a Copy of a Letter from the

Commissioners. . . . 29th May, 1798, Ordered to lie on the Table. . . .
(Published by Order of the House. . . .)
[Philadelphia, 1798.] 40 pp., 1 folding table.
AAS copy.   34869

U. S. Treasury Dept., 1798.
Letter from the Secretary of the Treasury, Transmitting a Statement of Goods, Wares & Merchandize, Exported. . . . 6th March, 1798. Ordered to lie on the Table (Published by Order of the House. . . .)
[Philadelphia], Oswald, [1798]. [4] pp. 1 table.
LCP copy.   34859

U. S. Treasury Dept., 1798.
Letter from the Secretary of the Treasury, Transmitting Statements of Goods, Wares and Merchandize, Imported . . . 8th January, 1798. Ordered to lie on the Table. Published by Order of the House. . . .
[Philadelphia], Ross, [1798. (3) pp., 2 folded tables.
AAS copy.   34854

U. S. Treasury Dept., 1798.
Letters from the Secretary of the Treasury, Accompanying his Report, made in Pursuance of a Resolution of the House . . . 14th of December last. January 8th, 1798. Referred. . . . Printed by Order of the House. . . .
Philadelphia, Gales, [1798]. 8 pp.
AAS copy.   34853

U. S. Treasury Dept., 1798.
Massachusetts District. Supervisor's Office. Boston, May 31st, 1798. A Table or List of the Different Rates of Stamp Duties.
[Boston, 1798.] Broadside.
EI copy.   34079

U. S. Treasury Dept., 1798.
(N.) Form of a Collector's Half-Yearly Abstract. . . . January 20th, 1798.
n. p., [1798]. Broadside.
(Not located, 1968.)   48735

U. S. Treasury Dept., 1798.
Report of the Secretary of the Treasury, made in Pursuance of a Resolution of the House, of the 22d Instant,. . . . Dec. 28, 1797. Committed. . . .
Philadelphia, Gales, [1798]. 8 pp.
AAS copy.   34873

[U. S. Treasury Dept., 1798.
Return of Seamen . . . of Monies . . . Register of White Persons.
[Boston, 1798.] 4 pp.]
(No copy located.)   34851

U. S. Treasury Dept., 1798.
Statement of the Purchases of Public Stock.
[Philadelphia? 1798.] Folding table.
WLC copy.   48736

U. S. Treasury Dept., 1798.
Treasury Department, February 15, 1798. (Circular.)
[Philadelphia, 1798.] Broadside.
(The one reported copy cannot be located.)   48737

U. S. Treasury Dept., 1798.
Treasury Department, February 24, 1798. Circular.
[Philadelphia, 1798.] Broadside.
(The one recorded copy cannot be located.)   48738

U. S. Treasury Dept., 1798.
Treasury Department, March 1, 1798. Public Notice.
[Philadelphia, 1798.] Broadside.
(Not located, 1968.)   48739

U. S. Treasury Dept., 1798.
Treasury Department, Trenton, September 8th, 1798 (Circular).
[Trenton, N. J., 1798.] [2] pp.
LOC copy.   34884

U. S. Treasury Dept., 1799.
Abstract of Cases Transmitted.
[Philadelphia? 1799.] [1] p., 7 folded tables.
(Also entered as 38687, q. v.)   36467

U. S. Treasury Dept., 1799.
An Account of the Receipts and Expenditures of the United States, for the Year 1798. . . . Published by Order of the House.
Philadelphia, Fenno, [1799]. pp. [7]-78, [12]; 12 folding tables.
AAS copy.   36468

U. S. Treasury Dept., 1799.
Circular to Collectors, Naval Officers and Surveyors. . . . 23d February, 1799.
[Philadelphia, 1799.] [3] pp.
(Only copy cannot be reproduced.) 48978

U. S. Treasury Dept., 1799.
(Circular to Commissioners of Loans.). . . . June 1st, 1799.
[Philadelphia, 1799.] [2] pp.
LCP copy.   48979

U. S. Treasury Dept., 1799.
(Circular.) Treasury Department, March 30th, 1799.
[Philadelphia, 1799.] [2] pp.
MHS copy.   36502

U. S. Treasury Dept., 1799.
District of Connecticut. To [blank] Surveyor of the Revenue. . . .
n.p., [1799?]. [2] leaves.
CHS copy.   48980

U. S. Treasury Dept., 1799.
Letter from the Secretary, Inclosing Sundry Statements. . . . January 31st, 1799. . . . Published by Order of the House. . . .
[Philadelphia], Way & Groff, [1799]. [6] pp., 5 folded tables.
AAS copy.   36527

U. S. Treasury Dept., 1799.
Letter from the Secretary of the Treasury, Accompanied with a Report and Estimates. . . . 18th of December, 1799. Referred. . . . Published by Order of the House. . . .
Philadelphia, Poulson, 1799. 117 pp.
AAS copy.   36533

U. S. Treasury Dept., 1799.
Letter from the Secretary of the Treasury, Inclosing a Letter from the Comptroller. . . . 16th February, 1799. . . . Published by Order of the House.
[Philadelphia], Ross, [1799]. [7] pp., 2 folded tables.
AAS copy.   36534

U. S. Treasury Dept., 1799.
Letter from the Secretary of the Treasury, Inclosing a Statement of the Tonnage of the Shipping. . . . 7th February, 1799. . . . (Published by Order of the House. . . .).
[Philadelphia], Oswald, [1799]. [3] pp., 1 folded table.
AAS copy.   36535

U. S. Treasury Dept., 1799.
Letter from the Secretary of the Treasury, to the Chairman of the Committee of Ways & Means. . . . (Published by Order of the House. . . .).
[Philadelphia, 1799.] 39 pp.
AAS copy.   36536

U. S. Treasury Dept., 1799.
Letter from the Secretary of the Treasury, Transmitting a Statement of Goods. . . . 7th February, 1799. . . . Published by Order of the House. . . .
[Philadelphia], Ross, [1799]. [3] pp., 1 folded table.
AAS copy.   36537

U. S. Treasury Dept., 1799.
Letter from the Secretary of the Treasury, Transmitting a Statement of the Official Emoluments. . . . 1st March, 1799. (Published by Order of the House. . . .).
[Philadelphia], Oswald, [1799]. [4] pp., 6 folded tables.
AAS copy.   36538

U. S. Treasury Dept., 1799.
Letter from the Secretary of the Treasury, Transmitting Copies of Two Letters. . . . 5th December, 1799.
[Philadelphia], Ross, [1799]. 18 pp., 4 folded tables.
AAS copy.   36539

U. S. Treasury Dept., 1799.
Letter from the Secretary of the Treasury,
Transmitting Two Statements. . . . 30th
January, 1799. Published by Order of the
House. . . .
[Philadelphia], Ross, [1799]. [4] pp., 2
folded tables.
AAS copy.   36540

U. S. Treasury Dept., 1799.
Supervisor's Office, Massachusetts
District, Boston, December [blank] 1799.
Sir [blank].
[Boston? 1799.] 1 leaf.
AAS copy.   48981

U. S. Treasury Dept., 1799.
To the Inhabitants of the [blank]
Collection District. . . . 14 July 1798.
n.p., [1799]. Broadside.
Pierce W. Gaines copy.   48982

U. S. Treasury Dept., 1799.
Treasury Department, February 12th,
1799. Circular to Collectors. . . .
[Philadelphia, 1799.] [2] pp.
LCP copy.   48983

U. S. Treasury Dept., 1799.
Treasury Department, June 26th, 1799.
Circular to the Collectors. . . .
[Philadelphia, 1799.] Broadside.
(No copy available.)   48984

U. S. Treasury Dept., 1799.
Treasury Department. August 1, 1799.
Circular to the Collectors. . . .
[Philadelphia, 1799.] Broadside.
(No copy available.)   48985

U. S. Treasury Dept., 1800.
Abstract of Cases Transmitted to the
Secretary of the Treasury.
[Philadelphia, 1840.] [2] pp., 7 folded
plates.
AAS copy.   38687

U. S. Treasury Dept., 1800.
Accompanying the Report of the
Committee of Claims, on the Petition of
Oliver Pollock. Made the 18th of April,
1800.
n. d., n. p. 6 pp.
AAS copy.   38688

U. S. Treasury Dept., 1800.
(Circular.) District of Connecticut,
Supervisor's-Office, August 26th, 1800.
[Hartford? 1800.] Broadside.
CHS copy.   49168

U. S. Treasury Dept., 1800.
(Circular.) Supervisor's Office,
Providence, May 5th, 1800.
[Providence? 1800.] [3] pp.
NHS copy.   49169

U. S. Treasury Dept., 1800.
Circular to the Collectors of the Customs.
Treasury Department, Washington, Sept.
27, 1800.
[Washington, 1800.] 2 pp.
LCP copy.   49170

U. S. Treasury Dept., 1800.
Connecticut, Supervisor's-Office, March
[blank] 1800.
[Hartford? 1800.] Broadside.
CHS copy.   49171

U. S. Treasury Dept., 1800.
Exports of the United States . . . to . . .
September 1799. . . . February 7th. 1800.
[Philadelphia? 1800.] fold. tabl.
WLC copy.   49172

U. S. Treasury Dept., 1800.
Extracts of Letters Received by J. Jackson
. . . from the Treasury Department. . . .
10th March, 1800.
[Boston, 1800.] [3] pp.
AAS copy.   38731

U. S. Treasury Dept., 1800.
Form C. District of Massachusetts. To
[blank] Surveyor of the Revenue. . . . In
Pursuance . . . "An Act to lay and Collect
A Direct Tax. . . ."
[Boston, 1800.] [2] pp.
AAS copy.   49173

U. S. Treasury Dept., 1800.
Letter from the Secretary of the Treasury,

Accompanied with a Report and
Estimates. . . . 11th December, 1800. . . .
Published by Order of the House.
[Washington? 1800]. pp. [1], [1]-6, 8-99.
AAS copy.   38759

U. S. Treasury Dept., 1800.
Letter from the Secretary of the Treasury
Accompanying a Report of the
Commissioner of the Revenue. . . .
December 22, 1800. . . . Published by
Order of the House.
[Washington? 1800.] [12] pp., 16 folded
tables.
AAS copy.   38760

U. S. Treasury Dept., 1800.
Letter from the Secretary of the Treasury,
Accompanying Copies of Two Letters
from the Commissioners of the City of
Washington. . . . 12th December, 1800. . . .
Published by Order of the House.
Washington? 1800.] 16 pp.
AAS copy.   38761

U. S. Treasury Dept., 1800.
Letter from the Secretary of the Treasury
Accompanying his Report on the Petition
of Benjamin Wells. . . . 2nd April, 1800.
Referred to the Committee of Claims.
[Philadelphia, 1800.] 21 pp.
AAS copy.   38762

U. S. Treasury Dept., 1800.
Letter from the Secretary of the Treasury,
Accompanying his Reports on the
Memorial of David Jones. . . . 25th
March, 1800. . . (Published by Order of
the House. . . .)
[Philadelphia, 1800.] 13 pp.
AAS copy.   38763

U. S. Treasury Dept., 1800.
Letter from the Secretary of the Treasury
to the Chairman of the Committee of
Ways and Means. . . . 10th April,
1800. . . . (Published by Order of the
House. . . .)
[Philadelphia, 1800.] 7 pp.
AAS copy.   38764

U. S. Treasury Dept., 1800.
Letter from the Secretary of the Treasury,
Transmitting a Letter from the
Comptroller, Accompanied with an
Abstract. . . . 10th March, 1800. . . .
Printed by Order of the House.
[Philadelphia, 1800.] pp. [4], 6 folded
tables, [11] - 17.
AAS copy.   38765

U. S. Treasury Dept., 1800.
Letter from the Secretary of the Treasury,
Transmitting a Letter from the
Comptroller of the Treasury. . . . 25th
April, 1800. . . . Printed by Order of the
House.
[Philadelphia, 1800.] pp. [4], 3 folded
tables, [2], 4 folded tables, [2], 3 folded
tables.
AAS copy.   38766

U. S. Treasury Dept., 1800.
Letter from the Secretary of the Treasury,
Transmitting a Report. . . . 5th February,
1800. . . . Printed by Order of the House.
[Philadelphia, 1800.] pp. 8, 8 folded
tables, 25-30, 1 table.
AAS copy.   38767

U. S. Treasury Dept., 1800.
Letter from the Secretary of the Treasury,
Transmitting a Statement Exhibiting the
Amount of Duty on Salt. . . . Published
by Order of the Senate. . . . April 3d, 1800.
[Philadelphia, 1800.] [3] pp., 1 folded
table.
AAS copy.   38768

U. S. Treasury Dept., 1800.
Letter from the Secretary of the Treasury,
Transmitting a Statement, Exhibiting the
Tonnage of the Shipping. . . . April 12th,
1800. . . . (Published by Order of the
House. . . .
[Philadelphia, 1800.] [3] pp., 1 folded
table.
AAS copy.   38769

U. S. Treasury Dept., 1800.
Letter from the Secretary of the Treasury,
Transmitting a Statement of the Goods,
Wares and Merchandize Exported. . . .

February 10th, 1800. . . . Printed by Order
of the House.
Philadelphia, Poulson, 1800. [3] pp., 1
folded table.
AAS copy.   38770

U. S. Treasury Dept., 1800.
Letter from the Secretary of the Treasury,
Transmitting Two Statements, Exhibiting
the Amount of Duties. . . . February 10th,
1800. . . . Printed by Order of the House.
Philadelphia, Poulson, 1800. [3] pp., 2
folded tables.
AAS copy.   38771

U. S. Treasury Dept., 1800.
Letter from the Secretary of the Treasury
Transmitting Two Statements; one
Exhibiting the Value . . . of the Goods . . .
Imported. . . . 3d. March, 1800.-Ordered
to lie on the Table - Printed by Order of
the House.
Philadelphia, Poulson, Mar. 12, 1800. [4]
pp., 2 folded tables.
AAS copy.   38772

U. S. Treasury Dept., 1800.
Report, &c. The Secretary of War. . . .
February 15th, 1800.
[Philadelphia, 1800.] 3 pp.
AAS copy.   38808

U. S. Treasury Dept., 1800.
Report from the Secretary of the
Treasury, Accompanying an Estimate. . . .
April 24th, 1800.
[Philadelphia, 1800.] [3] pp.
AAS copy.   38810

U. S. Treasury Dept., 1800.
A Statement Exhibiting the Amount of
Drawback . . . 1796 . . . 1798.
[Philadelphia? 1800.] fold. table.
WLC copy.   49174

U. S. Treasury Dept., 1800.
Supervisor's Office, Massachusetts
District, Boston. March 24, 1800.
[Boston, 1800.] [3] pp.
AAS copy.   49175

U. S. Treasury Dept., 1800.
Supervisor's Office, Massachusetts
District, Boston, October 24, 1800.
[Boston, 1800.] [2] pp.
AAS copy.   49176

U. S. Treasury Office, 1777.
In Congress, Baltimore, January 14th,
1777. . . . Treasury-Office, Baltimore,
January 30, 1777. . . .
Baltimore, [1777]. Broadside.
LOC copy.   15652

U. S. Treasury Office, 1777.
In Congress, March 25, 1777. . . .
Treasury-Office, Philadelphia, March 25,
1777.
[Philadelphia, 1777.] Broadside.
NYPL copy.   15657

U. S. Treasury Office, 1779.
Treasury-Office, March 12, 1779. Ordered,
That the Several Commissioners. . . .
[Philadelphia, 1779.] Broadside.
CHS copy.   43719

U. S. Treasury Office, 1779.
Treasury-Office, Philadelphia, February 5,
1779.
[Philadelphia, 1779.] Broadside.
CHS copy.   43720

U. S. Treaties, etc., 1778.
The Articles, Published by Congress, of a
Treaty . . . Executed at Paris.
Lancaster, Dunlap, [1778]. 12, [17] pp.
LCP copy.   16145

U. S. Treaties, etc., 1778.
Treaties between the Thirteen United
States . . . and His Most Christian
Majesty.
n.p., [1778?] Broadside.
NYHS copy.   43585

[U. S. Treaties, etc., 1778.
Treaties of Amity, and Commerce. . . .
Newbern, 1778.]
("Immediately published here," N. C.
Gazette, May 29, 1778.)   16148

U. S. Treaties, etc., 1778.

Treaties of Amity and Commerce. . . .
Philadelphia, Dunlap, 1778. pp. [2], 10,
[2], 11-34.
AAS copy.   16146

U. S. Treaties, etc. 1778.
Treaties of Amity and Commerce. . . .
Philadelphia, Dunlap, 1778. 34 pp.
NYPL copy.   16147

U. S. Treaties, etc., 1779.
Treaties of Amity and Commerce . . .
between His Most Christian Majesty and
the Thirteen United States.
Hartford, 1779. 32 pp.
NYPL copy.   16643

U. S. Treaties, etc., 1779.
The Treaties of Amity and Commerce . . .
between His Most Christian Majesty and
the Thirteen United States.
Norwich, Trumbull, 1779. 24 pp.
CHS copy.   16644

U. S. Treaties, etc., 1782.
By the United States in Congress
Assembled. A Proclamation. . . . Done at
the Hague, the 8th Day of October, 1782.
n.p., [1782]. Broadside.
NYHS copy.   44280

U. S. Treaties, etc., 1783.
Boston, April 7, 1783. By the Ship
Astrea. . . .
[Boston], Russell, [1783]. Broadside.
BPL copy.   17851

U. S. Treaties, etc., 1783.
By the United States in Congress
Assembled, a Proclamation [Treaty of
Paris, Jan. 14, 1784].
Annapolis, Dunlap, [1784]. Broadside.
LOC   copy.   18819

U. S. Treaties, etc., 1783.
Declaration of the American Ministers.
Providence, April 7, 1783.
Providence, Carter, [1783]. Broadside.
RIHS copy.   44478

[U. S. Treaties, etc., 1783.
The Definitive Treaty between Great
Britain, and the United States, Signed at
Paris, the 3rd day of September 1783.
[Annapolis], 1783. 22 pp.]
(Not in Ford; no copy located.)   18250

U. S. Treaties, etc., 1783.
Definitive Treaty, London, September 30.
Baltimore, [1783]. Broadside.
MdHS copy.   18251

U. S. Treaties, etc., 1783.
Definitive Treaty. Sunday Evening
Arrived the Lord Hyde Packet.
New York, Ross, 1783. Broadside.
NYPL ph. copy.   44480

U. S. Treaties, etc., 1783.
Definitive Treaty of Peace. Providence,
December 1, 1783.
Providence, Carter, [1783]. Broadside.
AAS ph. copy.   44479

[U. S. Treaties, etc., 1783.
Der Difinitive Friedens-Tractat zwischen
Gross-Brittanien und den Vereinigten
Staaten.
[Lancaster, 1783.] Broadside.]
(Title from Hildeburn.)   18254

U. S. Treaties, etc., 1783.
The Following is a Correct Transcript of
the Treaty between France and the United
States. . . . 22d of January . . . 1783.
[Philadelphia, 1783.] Broadside.
NYHS copy.   44481

U. S. Treaties, etc., 1783.
A General Peace! New-York, March 26.
Salem, Hall, [1783]. Broadside.
(The only recorded copy could not be
reproduced.)   44482

U. S. Treaties, etc., 1783.
A General Peace. Providence, March 31,
1783.
Providence, Carter, [1783]. Broadside.
RIHS copy.   44483

[U. S. Treaties, etc., 1783.
New-York, March 24, 1783. The

Following is Copied from a Handbill. . . .
New York, 1783. Broadside.]
(No copy located; assumed by Evans from
18237.)   18236

U. S. Treaties, etc., 1783.
New-York, March 27, 1783. The
Following is Copied from a Handbill. . . .
Portsmouth, [1783]. Broadside.
LOC copy.   18237

U. S. Treaties, etc., 1783.
New-York, November 26. . . . The
Definitive Treaty, between Great-Britain
and the United States. . . .
Baltimore, [1783]. Broadside.
AAS copy.   18252

U. S. Treaties, etc., 1783.
New-York, November 26. . . . The
Definitive Treaty, between Great-Britain
and the United States. . . .
Philadelphia, Claypoole, [1783].
Broadside.
LOC copy.   18253

U. S. Treaties, etc., 1783.
Peace, Liberty and Independence.
Philadelphia, March 24, 1783.
Baltimore, Goddard, 1783. Broadside.
LOC copy.   18235

U. S. Treaties, etc., 1783.
Philadelphia, March 19, Articles Agreed
upon.
[Philadelphia? 1783.] Broadside.
MHS copy.   44484

U. S. Treaties, etc., 1783.
Philadelphia, March 24, 1783, His Most
Christian Majesty's Cutter the
Triumph. . . .
[Philadelphia], Claypoole, [1783].
Broadside.
MHS copy.   18234

U. S. Treaties, etc., 1783.
Salem, April 5. By the Ship Astrea.
Salem, Hall, [1783]. Broadside.
BPL copy.   44485

[U. S. Treaties, etc., 1783.
State of Rhode-Island and Providence
Plantations. A Proclamation [Peace of
Paris].
Providence, Carter, [1784]. Broadside.]
(A duplicate of 18755, q. v.)   18823

U. S. Treaties, etc., 1783.
Supplement to the Pennsylvania Packet.
Wednesday, April 9, 1783. . . . The
Preliminary Articles of Peace.
Philadelphia, Claypoole, [1783].
Broadside.
WLC copy.   44486

U. S. Treaties, etc., 1783.
The United States in Congress Assembled,
To all who shall these Presents Greetings:
Whereas in and by our Commission
[Treaty. Apr. 15, 1783].
[Philadelphia, 1783.] Broadside.
LOC copy.   18233

U. S. Treaties, etc., 1784.
Articles of a Treaty, Concluded at Fort
Stanwix.
[Trenton, 1784.] [2] pp.
NYPL copy.   18817

U. S. Treaties, etc., 1785.
Articles of a Treaty, Concluded at Fort
M'Intosh.
[New York, 1785.] [2] pp.
NYPL copy.   19278

U. S. Treaties, etc., 1785.
Articles of a Treaty, Concluded at
Hopewell.
[New York, 1785.] [3] pp.
(Found too late for inclusion.)
SC Archives (201/26/4) copy.   19279

U. S. Treaties, etc., 1786.
Articles of a Treaty Concluded at
Hopewell . . . [Jan. 10, 1786, with the]
Chickasaw.
[Philadelphia, 1786.] 4 pp.
(No copy located.)   45003

U. S. Treaties, etc., 1786.
Articles of a Treaty, Concluded at the
Mouth of the Great Miami [Jan. 31, 1786]

. . . between the . . . United States . . . and
the . . . Shawanoe.
[New York, 1786.] Broadside.
LOC copy.   20041

U. S. Treaties, etc., 1786.
Articles of a Treaty, Concluded at the
Mouth of the Great Miami . . . [Jan. 31,
1786, with the] Shawnee.
[Philadelphia, 1786.] Broadside.
LOC copy.   45004

U. S. Treaties, etc., 1786.
Supplement to the Daily Advertiser,
Tuesday, June 6, 1786. . . . A Treaty . . .
between . . . Prussia, and the United
States.
[New York, 1786.] Broadside.
LOC copy.   20088

U. S. Treaties, etc., 1786.
Treaty of Amity and Commerce between
the United States . . . and . . . Prussia.
[New York?], 1786. 35 pp.
JCB copy.   20089

[U. S. Treaties, etc., 1786.
The United States in Congress
Assembled: To all whom these Presents
shall come Greeting. Treaty . . . between
the United States . . . and . . . the King of
Prussia.
[New York, 1786.] Broadside.]
(No copy located.)   20087

U. S. Treaties, etc., 1787.
The United States of America, in
Congress Assembled, To all who shall see
these Presents. . . .
[New York, 1787.] [3] pp.
LOC copy.   20789

U. S. Treaties, etc., 1788.
. . . 1784. Convention . . . for the Purpose
of Determining . . . the Functions . . . of
their Respective Consuls.
[New York, 1788.] 10 pp.
LOC copies.   21525

U. S. Treaties, etc., 1793.
Extract from the Treaty of Amity and
Commerce between the United States . . .
and His Most Christian Majesty. . . .
Article 25.
[Philadelphia, 1793.] Broadside.
(No copy located.)   46928

U. S. Treaties, etc., 1794.
Treaty with Great Britain.
Mercury-Office, Saturday, July 4.
[Boston, 1794.] Broadside.
AAS copy.   47307

U. S. Treaties, etc., 1795.
for other eds. see
Gt. Brit. Treaties, etc., 1795
and
France. Treaties, etc., 1795

U. S. Treaties, etc., 1795.
George Washington, President. . . . To all
to whom These Presents Shall come -
Greeting. . . . A Treaty of Peace, between
the United States . . . and the Tribes of
Indians called the Wyandots. . . .
[Philadelphia, 1795.] 8 pp.
AAS copy.   29742

U. S. Treaties, etc., 1795.
(Authentic.) Treaty of Amity.
Albany, Websters, 1795. 32 pp.
NYSL copy.   47662

U. S. Treaties, etc., 1795.
George Washington, President. . . . To all
to whom These Presents Shall come:
Greeting. . . . "Articles with the
Cherokee. . . ."
[Philadelphia, 1795.] 7 pp.
HSP copy.   47663

U. S. Treaties, etc., 1795.
Important State Papers; Containing the
Treaties Existing between the United
States and Foriegn Powers.
New York, 1795. 92 pp.
NYPL copy.   29760

U. S. Treaties, etc., 1795.
Treaties between the United States and
Great-Britain and the United States and
France.

West Springfield, Davison, 1795.
AAS copy.　　　　　　29759

U. S. Treaties, etc., 1795.
Treaties of Alliance, Amity & Commerce
between the United States . . . and the
French.
Charleston, Beleurgey, 1795. [4], 40, iv
pp.
(The only copy of this ed. located is too
fragile to film.)　　　　　　29758

U. S. Treaties, etc., 1796.
At A Treaty, held at the City of New
York, with . . . "The Seven Nations of
Canada."
[New York? 1796?] 3 pp.
NYPL copy.　　　　　　47996

U. S. Treaties, etc., 1796.
By George Washington, President . . . a
Proclamation Whereas a Treaty of
Amity. . . .
[Philadelphia, 1796.] 30 pp.
Pierce W. Gaines copy.　　　　　　47995

U. S. Treaties, etc., 1796.
A Treaty between the United States and
His Catholic Majesty, 27th October, 1795.
[Philadelphia], Fenno, 1796. 19 pp.
NYHS copy.　　　　　　31419

U. S. Treaties, etc., 1797.
Treaties of Amity and Commerce.
Boston, Hall, 1797. 71 pp.
AAS copy.　　　　　　33045

Gt. Brit. Treaties, etc., 1796.
Treaty of Amity, Commerce &
Navigation, between his Britannic
Majesty and the United States . . . as
Published in the Philadelphia Gazette . . .
the 1st of March, 1796.
Philadelphia, Ormrod & Conrad, 1796. 45
pp.
LOC copy.　　　　　　31414

[U. S. Treaties, et., 1796.
The Treaty of Commerce and Navigation
between America and Great Britain. With
the Observations of two Respectable
Writers.
Boston, Russell, 1796.]
(Apparently a ghost of 31312.)　　　　　　31413

U. S. Treaties, etc., 1796.
A Treaty of Peace and Friendship, made
and Concluded between the President . . .
and . . . the Creek Nation [June 29,
1796]. . . .
[New York? 1796.] 4 pp.
NYPL copy.　　　　　　47997

U. S. Treaties, etc., 1797.
Treaty of Peace and Friendship between
the United States . . . and Tripoli. . . .
Signed . . . the 3d Day of January 1797.
[Philadelphia, 1797.] 7 pp.
WLC copy.　　　　　　48306

U. S. Treaties, etc., 1798.
At a Treaty held with the Oneida Nation
. . . on the First Day of June . . . One
Thousand Seven Hundred and
Ninety-Eight.
[Philadelphia, 1798?] 3 pp.
LOC copy.　　　　　　36495

U. S. Treaties, etc., 1798.
Treaty of Peace and Friendship, between
the United States . . . and . . . Tunis.
[Philadelphia, 1798.] 11 pp.
WLC copy.　　　　　　48740

U. S. Treaties, etc., 1799.
Articles of a Treaty between the United
States of America and the Cherokee
Indians.
Philadelphia, Fenno, [1799]. 8 pp.
LOC copy.　　　　　　36491

U. S. Treaties, etc., 1799.
Supplement to the North-Carolina
Journal, No. 390. Articles of a Treaty
between the United States of America and
the Cherokee Indians.
[Halifax, N. C., 1799.] pp. 121-123, [1].
NL copy.　　　　　　36492

[U. S. Treaties, etc., 1800.
Articles of Agreement of the Convention
of Amity and Commerce between the
United States and France.

New York, Dec. 20, 1800. Broadside.]
(Entry from Evans.)　　　　　　38714

U. S. Treaties, etc., 1800.
[Treaty between the French Republic and
the United States.
Baltimore, 1800.]
(Minick 586; no copy known.)　　　　　　49177

U. S. War Dept., 1776.
War-Office, November 14th, 1776. To the
Associators. . . .
[Philadelphia], Dunlap, [1776].
Broadside.
LOC copy.　　　　　　15192

U. S. War Dept., 1786.
A Plan for the General Arrangement of
the Militia [Mar. 18, 1786].
[New York, 1786.] 34 pp.
LOC copy.　　　　　　20076

U. S. War Dept., 1786.
War-Office, April 25, 1785. Sir, On the
Memorial of Captain Jesse Grant. . . .
[New York, 1786.] Broadside.
LOC copy.　　　　　　20090

U. S. War Dept., 1787.
Instructions to　　　Superintendent of
Indian Affairs [Feb. 3, 1787].
[New York, 1787.] Broadside.
LOC copy.　　　　　　20771

[U. S. War Dept., 1787.
The Secretary of the United States for the
Department of War . . . Reports. . . . July
20, 1787.
[New York, 1787.] [2] pp.]
(Ford 446; not now to be located.)　　　20786

U. S. War Dept., 1788.
[The Secretary of the United States for
the Department of War to whom was
Referred his Letter . . . of the 16 of
April. . . .
New York, 1788.]
(Ford 574; no copy known.)　　　　　　45389

[U. S. War Dept., 1790.
A Plan for the General Arrangement of
the Militia. . . . Published by Order of the
House.
New York, Childs & Swaine, 1790. [4], 3
pp.]
(A garbled entry for 22988 and 22958.)
　　　　　　22987

U. S. War Dept., 1790.
A Plan for the General Arrangement of
the Militia. . . . Published by Order of the
House [Jan. 18, 1790].
New York, Childs & Swaine, 1790. 26 pp.
AAS copy.　　　　　　22988

U. S. War Dept., 1790.
War-Office, January 18, 1790. Sir . . . the
Militia.
[New York, 1790.] Broadside.
AAS copy.　　　　　　46077

U. S. War Dept., 1790.
War Office of the United States.
Information . . . to . . . Pensioners [Jan.
28, 1790].
[New York, 1790.] Broadside.
HSP copy.　　　　　　46078

U. S. War Dept., 1792.
United States, January the 16th, 1792. As
the Circumstances which have engaged the
United States in the Present Indian
War. . . .
Philadelphia, Claypoole, [1792].
Broadside.
NYHS copy.　　　　　　24944

[U. S. War Dept., 1792.
War Department. August 6, 1792.
Information is hereby Given to all the
Military Invalids. . . .
[Philadelphia, 1792.] Broadside.]
(No copy located.)　　　　　　24946

U. S. War Dept., 1793.
Report of the Secretary of War on
Forty-Seven Petitions. [February 8],
1793.
[Philadelphia], Childs & Swaine, [1793].
11 pp.
LOC copy.　　　　　　26362

U. S. War Dept., 1793.

Report of the Secretary of War on
Thirty-Five Petitions. [February 27],
1793.
[Philadelphia], Childs & Swaine, [1793].
11, [1] pp.
LOC copy.　　　　　　26363

U. S. War Dept., 1794.
Department of War, December 10, 1794.
Sir, In Obedience. . . .
[Philadelphia, 1794?] 4 pp.
JCB copy.　　　　　　47308

U. S. War Dept., 1794.
Report of the Secretary of War on Sixty
Petitions. 1794. Published by Order of the
House. . . .12 March, 1794.
[Philadelphia] Childs & Swaine, [1794.]
22 pp.
BA copy.　　　　　　27955

[U. S. War Dept., 1794.
War Department. May 19, 1794. To the
Governor of Rhode Island.
[Philadelphia, 1794.] Broadside.]
(No copy located.)　　　　　　27979

U. S. War Dept., 1795.
Department of War, January 26th, 1795.
Sir. . . . Report of the Secretary of War.
[Philadelphia, 1795.] [2] pp.
AAS copy.　　　　　　47664

U. S. War Dept., 1795.
(Received the 14th December, 1795.)
Letter from the Secretary of War. . . .
Published by Order of the House.
[Philadelphia, 1796.] 22 pp.
AAS copy.　　　　　　31466

U. S. War Dept., 1795.
United States December 30th, 1794.
Gentlemen. . . . I lay before you a Report
made to me by the Secretary of War. . . .
[Philadelphia, 1795.] 7 pp.
AAS copy.　　　　　　29776

U. S. War Dept., 1796.
Letter and Reports of the Secretary of
War, to the Committee Appointed to
Enquire into the Naval Equipment. . . .
Published by Order of the House . . . 2d
March, 1796.
[Philadelphia, 1796.] 11 pp.
AAS copy.　　　　　　31467

U. S. War Dept., 1796.
(Received the 20th of January 1796.)
Report from the Department of War,
Relative to the Fortifications. . . .
Published by Order of the House.
[Philadelphia, 1796.] 9 pp.
AAS copy.　　　　　　31468

[U. S. War Dept., 1797.
Letter from the Secretary of War,
Relative to Expense of Building and
Equipping Certain Vessels of War. 2
January, 1797.
Philadelphia, 1797.]
(A ghost of 33094, q. v.)　　　　　　33093

U. S. War Dept., 1797.
Letter from the Secretary of War,
Inclosing his Report on the Petition of
Hugh Lawson White. 26th December,
1796. Read and Ordered to be Committed.
[Philadelphia, 1797.] 8 pp.
AAS copy.　　　　　　33092

[U. S. War Dept., 1797.
Letter from the Secretary of War,
Relative to Expense of Building and
Equipping Certain Vessels of War. 2
January, 1797.
Philadelphia, 1797.]
(A ghost of 33094, q. v.)　　　　　　33093

U. S. War Department, 1797.
Letter from the Secretary at War, to the
Chairman of the Committee on the Naval
Equipment. . . . 25th January, 1797. . . .
Published by Order of the House.
[Philadelphia, 1797.] 11 pp., 1 folded
sheet.
AAS copy.　　　　　　33094

U. S. War Dept., 1797.
Letter from the Secretary at War,
Transmitting an Explanatory Letter. . . .
20th February, 1797. . . . Printed by Order
of the House.

[Philadelphia, 1797.] 8 pp.
AAS copy. 33095

U. S. War Dept., 1797.
Letter from the Secretary of War,
Transmitting Sundry Statements Relative
to the Frigates. . . . June 17th, 1797.
Philadelphia, Poulson, 1797. 7, [3] pp., 1
folding table.
AAS copy. 33096

U. S. War Dept., 1797.
19th June, 1797. Committed to a
Committee of the Whole House, this Day.
Report of the Secretary of War. Published
by Order of the House.
[Philadelphia, 1797.] [4] pp.
AAS copy. 33098

U. S. War Dept., 1797.
Regulations to be Observed in the
Delivery and Distribution of Fuel. . . .
Twenty-Sixth day of December, A.D.
1797.
[Philadelphia, 1797.] Broadside.
LOC copy. 33097

U. S. War Dept., 1797.
Report of the Secretary of War, on the
Petition on Monsieur Poirey. . . . 5th
January, 1797. Published by Order of the
House.
[Philadelphia, 1797.] [4] pp.
AAS copy. 33099

U. S. War Dept., 1797.
Uniform for the Navy of the United
States. . . . August 24, 1797.
[Philadelphia, 1797.] Broadside.
AAS copy. 33100

U. S. War Dept., 1798.
Letter from the Secretary at War,
Accompanying a Report and Sundry
Statements. . . . 23d April, 1798.
Referred. . . . Printed by Order of the
House. . . .
Philadelphia, Gales, [1798]. 15 pp.
AAS copy. 34891

U. S. War Dept., 1798.
Letter from the Secretary of War,
Accompanying his Report Relative to the
Running of a Line. . . . January 5th, 1798.
Committed. . . . Printed by Order of the
House. . . .
Philadelphia, Gales, [1798]. 18 pp.
AAS copy. 34886

U. S. War Dept., 1798.
Letter from the Secretary of War,
Inclosing a Report and Sundry
Statements. . . . 16th April, 1798.
Committed. . . . Published by Order of the
House. . . .
Philadelphia, Way & Groff, [1798]. 32 pp.
AAS copy. 34890

U. S. War Dept., 1798.
Letter from the Secretary of War,
Inclosing a Statement of the Number of
Cannon. . . . 12th April, 1798, - Ordered to
lie on the Table. Published by Order of
the House. . . .
Philadelphia, Way & Groff, [1798]. 7 pp.
AAS copy. 34889

U. S. War Dept., 1798.
Letter from the Secretary of War,
Inclosing his Report on the Petition of
Stephen Cantrill. . . . 5th April, 1798.
Committed. . . . Printed by Order of the
House. . . .
Philadelphia, Gales, [1798]. 24 pp.
AAS copy. 34887

U. S. War Dept., 1798.
Letter from the Secretary at War, to the
Chairman of the Committee, Appointed
on the 15th of January last. . . . 1st May,
1798. Ordered to lie on the Table. Printed
by Order of the House. . . .
[Philadelphia], Ross, [1798]. 54 pp., 1
folded table.
LCP copy. 34892

U. S. War Dept., 1798.
Letter from the Secretary of War, to the
Chairman of the Committee on . . . the
President's Speech. . . . 11th April, 1798.
Committed. . . . (Published by Order of
the House. . . .)

[Philadelphia, 1798.] 16 pp.
AAS copy. 34888

U. S. War Dept., 1798.
Regulations Respecting Extra-Allowances
to Officers. . . . [December 19, 1798].
[Philadelphia? 1798?] Broadside.
Pierce W. Gaines copy. 48741

U. S. War Dept., 1798.
Rules and Regulations Respecting the
Recruiting Service.
[Philadelphia, 1798.] 14, [3] pp., 1
folding table.
BA copy. 34894

U. S. War Dept., 1798.
Rules and Regulations Respecting the
Recruiting Service.
[Philadelphia, 1798.] 14 pp., 3 blank
forms, the last dated 1798.
LOC copy. 34902

U. S. War Dept., 1798.
To Volunteer Companies. . . . November
1st, 1798.
[Philadelphia, 1798.] Broadside.
LOC copy. 48742

U. S. War Dept., 1799.
Message from the President . . .
Accompanying a Report to him, from the
Secretary of War. . . . 31st December,
1798. Referred. . . . (Published by Order of
the House. . . .).
[Philadelphia, 1799.] 27 pp.
AAS copy. 36549

U. S. War Dept., 1799.
Rules and Regulations Respecting the
Recruiting Service.
[Philadelphia, 1799.] 14, [4] pp., 2 blank
forms, latter dated 1799.
NYPL copy. 36584

U. S. War Dept., 1799.
Uniform for the Army of the United
States. . . . This 9th Day of January, 1799.
[Philadelphia, 1799.] Broadside.
LOC copy. 36598

U. S. War Dept., 1800.
Letter from the Secretary at War.
Accompanying a Report Exhibiting the
Expenses of the National Armory. . . . 7th
January, 1800. . . . (Published by Order of
the House. . . .)
[Philadelphia, 1800.] 8 pp.
AAS copy. 38755

U. S. War Dept., 1800.
Letter from the Secretary of War,
Accompanying his Report on the Petition
of John Armstrong. . . . 21st March,
1800. . . . Printed by Order of the House.
[Philadelphia, 1800.] 8 pp.
AAS copy. 38773

U. S. War Dept., 1800.
Letter from the Secretary of War,
Accompanying his Report on the Petitions
of William Milton. . . . 14th March,
1800. . . . Printed by Order of the House.
[Philadelphia, 1800.] 41 pp.
AAS copy. 38774

U. S. War Dept., 1800.
Letter from the Secretary of War, and the
Secretary and Comptroller . . . on the
Claim of Seth Harding. . . . 17th February,
1800. . . . (Published by Order of the
House. . . .)
[Philadelphia, 1800.] 7 pp.
AAS copy. 38775

U. S. War Dept., 1800.
Letter from the Secretary of War, to the
Chairman of the Committee . . . on . . .
the Speech of the President. . . . 13th
February, 1800. . . .
[Philadelphia, 1800.] 13 pp.
AAS copy. 38776

U. S. War Dept., 1800.
Philadelphia, December 21, 1799.
Major-General Hamilton has Received
thro' the Secretary of War the Following
Order. . . . The Death of Washington. . . .
Newport, January 1, 1800.
[Newport, 1800.] Broadside.
HEH copy. 38800

U. S. War Dept., 1800.

Regulations Respecting Certain Supplies
. . . Philadelphia, this First Day of March,
A. D. 1800.
[Philadelphia, 1800.] Broadside.
LCP copy. 38807

The United States Almanack, for . . .
1780.
Chatham, [N. J.], Kollock. [32] pp.
NJHS copy. 43721

The United States Almanack for . . . 1781.
Chatham, N. J., Kollock. [32] pp.
Chatham, N. J., Hist. Soc. copy. 17009

The United States Almanac, for . . .
1785. . . .
By Anthony Sharp [by David
Rittenhouse, 1732-1796].
New York, Kollock. [36] pp.
AAS copy. 44597

The United States Almanac . . . for . . .
1798.
Wilmington, Del., Adams. [24] pp.
AAS copy. 33101

The United States Almanac, for . . . 1800.
Elizabeth, N.J., Kollock for Dunham.
[36] pp.
HEH copy. 36599

The United States Almanac, for . . . 1801.
Reading, [Pa.], Jungman & Brickmann.
[40] pp.
AAS copy. 38912

[United States and New Hampshire
register for 1796.
Dover, Bragg, 1795.]
(Not seen since the Stickney sale, Mar. 22,
1910.) 47665

United States Bank.
For the Information of Persons
Transacting Business. . . . December 1,
1784.
[Philadelphia], Hall & Sellers, [1784].
Broadside.
LOC copy. 44607

The United States Calendar, and
Gentleman's Complete Pocket-
Companion, for . . . 1801.
New York, Furman & Loudon for Fenno,
1800. [120] pp.
HC copy. 38913

United States Court Kalendar, and
Gentleman's Complete Pocket-
Companion, for . . . 1800.
New York, Cobbett. [134] pp.
NYHS copy. 36601

[The United States Court Kalendar, and
Gentleman's Complete Pocket-
Companion, for 1800.
New York, Furman & Loudon for Fenner.
[134] pp.]
(A Ghost of the Cobbett ed., for which see
36601.) 38913

United States Lottery.
United States Lottery; 1776. The Scheme
is. . . .
Philadelphia, Bradfords, [1776].
Broadside.
JCB copy. 43204

United States Lottery.
A List of the Fortunate Numbers in the
First Class.
[York], Hall & Sellers, [1778]. [2], 55
pp.
NYPL copy. 16150

United States Lottery.
A List of the Fortunate Numbers in the
Second Class.
Philadelphia, Dunlap, 1779. 54 pp.
HSP copy. 16646

United States Lottery.
A List of the Fortunate Numbers in the
Third Class.
Philadelphia, Hall & Sellers, 1780. [2], 57
pp.
HSP copy. 17051

United States Lottery.
A List of the Fortunate Numbers in the
Fourth Class.

[Philadelphia], Hall & Sellers, [1782]. 83, [1] pp.
HSP copy.   17398

United States Lottery.
United States Lottery No. [   ] Class the First. This Ticket. . . .
[Philadelphia, 1776.] Broadside.
LOC copy.   15194

United States Lottery.
United States Lottery; 1776 the Scheme is. . . .
Philadelphia, Bradfords, [1776].
Broadside.
JCB copy.   15193

United States Lottery.
United States Lottery. The Scheme.
Philadelphia, Dunlap, [1779]. Broadside.
LOC copy.   16647

United States Lottery.
United States Lottery; the Scheme is. . . .
Philadelphia, Dunlap, [1778]. Broadside.
LCP copy.   16149

United States of America, December 23d, 1796. To the Senate and the House.
[Philadelphia? 1796?] [3] pp.
(Not located, 1968.)   47947

The United States Register, for the Year 1794.
Philadelphia, Stewart & Cochran and M'Culloch, 1794. 202 pp.
AAS copy.   27983

The United States Register, for the Year 1795.
Philadelphia, Carey, 1794. 195, [1] pp.
AAS copy.   27984

The Universal Almanack, for . . . 1773 [by David Rittenhouse, 1732-1796].
Philadelphia, Humphreys. [28] pp.
LOC copy.   12542

[The Universal Almanack, for . . . 1773. . . Second Edition [by David Rittenhouse, 1732-1796].
Philadelphia, Humphreys, [1773]. [28] pp.
(Adv. Pa. Packet, Feb. 15, 1773.)   12979

The Universal Almanack, for . . . 1774 [by David Rittenhouse, 1732-1796].
Philadelphia, Humphreys. [36] pp.
AAS copy.   12980

Universal Damnation, and Salvation [by John Tyler, 1742-1823].
Boston, Edes, 1798. [2], 79 pp.
AAS copy.   34685

[The Universal Dream-Book.
Wilmington, Del., Brynberg, 1797.]
(Imprint assumed by Evans from advs.)   33103

The Universal Interpreter of Dreams.
Baltimore, Keatinge, 1795. 208 pp.
NYPL copy.   28635

The Universal Interpreter of Dreams and Visions.
Philadelphia, Stewart & Cochran, 1797. 120 pp.
AAS copy.   48307

The Universal Kalendar, and the North-American Almanack, for . . . 1784. . . . by William Slygood [by Samuel Stearns, 1747-1819].
[New York.] [24] pp.
(No perfect copy located.)
NYPL copy.   18196

The Universal Peace-Maker.
Philadelphia, Armbruster, 1764. 15 pp.
JCB copy.   9797

[The Universal Pocket Almanack for . . . 1757.
New York, Parker & Weyman.]
("Just Published," Nov. 1, 1756.)   7723

[The Universal Right of Suffrage is in Danger from the Bryan's Station Ticket.
[Kentucky, 1799.] Broadside.]
(The one reported copy cannot be located.)   36604

The Universal Tontine.
[Articles of Association.]
[Philadelphia, 1792.] [2], 21 pp.
(No copy located.)   24950

[The Universal Spelling Book.
Philadelphia, Carey, 1793?]
(Imprint assumed by Evans from advs.)   26371

[Universal Spelling-Book.
Wilmington, Del., Brynberg, 1797.]
(Imprint assumed by Evans from Brynberg's adv.)   33105

Universalism Contrary to Scripture.
New London, Green, 1794. 117, [3] pp.
AAS copy.   27985

Universalist Church of America. General Convention, 1790.
Articles of Faith . . . Adopted . . . in Philadelphia, on the 25th of May, 1790.
Philadelphia, Dobson, 1790. 16 pp.
LCP copy.   23009

Universalist Church of America. General Convention, 1791.
Evangelical Psalms, Hymns, and Spiritual Songs.
Philadelphia, Dobson, 1792. [2], 222, [1], viii pp.
AAS copy.   24951

Universalist Church of America. General Convention, 1793.
General Convenation, at Oxford, Massachusetts, September 4, 1793.
[Boston, 1793.] [2] pp.
AAS copy.   26372

Universalist Church of America. General Convention, 1795.
Circular. The Ministers . . . at Bennington, Vermont, September 16th, 1795.
[Bennington? 1795.]
(The one recorded copy could not be found.)   47666

Universalist Church of America. Milford Convention, 1797.
The Elders and Messengers . . . September 20, 1797.
[Boston, 1797.] [2] pp.
AAS copy.   33106

[The Universe, a Miscellany, or Moral View of the Intellectual World.
Philadelphia, 1782.]
(Prospectus in Freeman's Journal, Oct. 2, 1782.)   17777

Unpartheyische Gedancken [by Henry Melchior Muhlenberg, 1711-1787].
[Germantown, 1752.] 4 pp.
HSP copy.   6890

Upham, Timothy, 1748-1811.
A Discourse, Delivered . . . in Deerfield.
Concord, N. H., Hough, 1794. 19 pp.
AAS copy.   27986

[Unitie our Dutie.
Cambridge, 1646.]
(Probably a ghost. See G. P. Winship, Cambridge Press, pp. 89-90.)   19

The Unmasked Nabob of Hancock County. . . .
Portsmouth, N. H., Peirce, 1796. 24 pp.
AAS copy.   31477

Eine Unterweisung von der Rechtigkeit des Menschlichen Lebens.
[Ephrata, 1760?] Broadside.
LCP copy.   41173

Upham, Timothy, 1748-1811.
A Sermon Delivered before the Columbian Lodge.
Portsmouth, Melcher, 1793. 23 pp.
AAS copy.   26373

Upon Mr. Samuel Willard . . . November 21, 1700 [by Samuel Sewall, 1652-1730].
[Boston, 1700.] Broadside.
(The AAS has two settings of this piece. It was commonly used as an end paper in Willard's sermons.)
MHS copy.   952

Upon Mr. Samuel Willard. . . . November

21, 1700 [Second Edition, May 12, 1720]
[by Samuel Sewall, 1652-1720].
[Boston, 1720.] Broadside.
MHS copy.   39731

Upon the Death of the Virtuous and Religious Mrs. Lydia Minot . . . Interred January 27, 1667.
[Cambridge, Mass., 1668.] Broadside.
MHS copy.   39178

Upon the Drying up that Ancient River, the Merrymak. . . . January 15, 1719, 20 [by Samuel Sewall, 1652-1730].
[Boston, 1721.] Broadside.
AAS ph. copy.   39752

Upon the Enlargement of the Infamous Ebenezer Richardson.
[Salem, 1772?] Broadside.
(No copy available for reproduction.)
EI copy.   42377

Upon the 24th of May, 1743 . . . between Messrs. Penns . . . and Lord Baltimore. . . .
[Philadelphia? 1743.] Broadside.
HSP copy.   40320

[The Upright Lives of the Heathen [by Charles Woolverton].
Philadelphia, Bradford, [1740]. 16 pp.]
(Title from Hildeburn.)   4660

Upsher, Thomas.
(The Friend, XVII, 29, 36.)
To Friends in Ireland.
Philadelphia, 1700. 22 pp.
HEH copy.   956

[Upton, William].
To the Maid I Love Best. . . . Composed by Mr. Hook.
[New York, 1798?] [2] pp.
(This is apparently the item described by Evans from Gilfert's adv., which is also responsible for the attribution of authorship to Upton.)
AAS copy.   34912

[Uranian Society, Philadelphia.
The First Uranian Concert. . . . April 12, 1787. Syllabus. . . .
Philadelphia, Oswald, 1787.]
(The program was printed for subscribers and reprinted in the Pa. Gazette, Apr. 11, 1787.)   20646

Uranian Society, Philadelphia.
Introductory Lessons. . . . Jan. 1, 1785.
[Philadelphia, 1785.] [4], 4, 20.
LOC copy.   19194

[Uranian Society, Philadelphia.
Introductory Lessons . . . for Promoting the Knowledge of Vocal Music.
Philadelphia, Aitken, 1786.]
(Entry from an adv., perhaps for 19194.)   19920

Urrutia, Manuel Joseph de.
Ynstruccion del Modo de Substanciar, y Determinar las Caucas . . . óbra Hecha por el Doctor. . . . [Dated Nov. 25, 1769.]
[New Orleans, 1769.] 51 pp.
(The only recorded copy could not be located.)
Archive General des Indias, Seville, copy. 42016

Urstandliche [by Johann Conrad Beissel, 1690-1768].
Ephrata, 1745. [8], 294 pp.
(See Seidensticker, pp. 24-25.)
AAS copy.   5538

Ury, John, d. 1741.
The Defence of John Ury.
[Philadelphia, 1741.] [2] pp.
AAS copy.   40262

Ury, John, d. 1741.
The Dying Speech of John Ury, who was Executed . . . the 29th of August, 1741.
[Philadelphia, 1741.] [2] pp.
AAS copy.   40263

[Useful and Correct Money Tables, Exhibiting the Amount of any Number of Dollars from 1 to 2000. . . .
Charleston, Burd & Haswell, 1786.]
(Entry from an adv.)   20093

A Useful and Necessary Companion.
Boston, Boone, 1708. [4], 84 pp.
RF copy.   39475

A Useful Essay, being a Concise Account
of the Excellency of the Common Prayer.
Hanover, [N.H.], Dunham, 1793. 11 pp.
HC copy.   46929

Useful Miscellanies [by William Dover].
Philadelphia, Chattin, 1753. 96, [1] pp.
AAS copy.   6993

Useful Remarks. An Essay upon
Remarkables [by Cotton Mather,
1663-1728].
New London, 1723. [2], 45 pp.
AAS copy.   2451

Useful Tables. 1st. A Table Shewing the
Value of any Number of Dollars &
Cents. . . .
Worcester, Hutchins for Brazer, April

27th, 1795. Broadside.
AAS copy.   47667

[Useful Tables, whereby the Money of
England is Reduced into Money of
Portugal.
Philadelphia, Hall & Sellers, 1771.]
(Adv. Pa. Gazette, Mar. 7, 1771.)   12262

Uss, Francis, 1761-1789.
The Narrative of the Life . . . Executed
. . . 31st of July, 1789.
[Poughkeepsie?], 8 pp.
(The only known copy is imperfect.)
NYPL copy.   45728

[Ussher, George Neville.
The Elements of English Grammar.
Portsmouth, Melcher, 1790.]
("Just Published," N. H. Gazette, July 2,
1790. In the N. H. Journal, Sept. 2, the
advertisement was revised to read that
Ussher's Rhetoric is affixed to the
Elements Of English Grammar.)   23010

Ussher, George Neville.
The Elements of English Grammar. . . .
Second American Edition.
Exeter, Ranlet, 1796. 110, [1] pp.
AAS copy.   31480

Ussher, James, 1581-1656.
[Immanuel, or the Mystery of the
Incarnation.
Williamsburg, Parks, 1736.]
(Wroth, Wm. Parks 81.)   40105

Utilia [by Cotton Mather, 1663-1728].
Boston, Fleet & Crump for Gerrish, 1716.
[8], 288 pp.
(Differs only in imprint from 1834, q. v.)
                                    39654

Utilia [by Cotton Mather, 1663-1728].
Boston, Fleet & Crump for Henchman,
1716. [8], 288 pp.
AAS copy.   1834

V

The Vade Mecum for America [by Thomas Prince, 1687-1758].
Boston, Kneeland and Green for Henchman and Hancock, 1731. [2], iv, [2], 220 pp.
AAS copy.   3470

The Vade Mecum for America [by Thomas Prince, 1687-1758].
Boston, Kneeland and Green for Henchman, 1732. [2], iv, [2], 220 pp.
AAS copy.   3598

Vade Mecum: or, the Dealers Pocket Companion.
Boston, Fleets, 1772. [2], ii, [36] pp.
JCB copy.   12360

[Vaill, Joseph], 1751-1838.
An Address to a Deist.
New London, Springer, 1796. 12 pp.
AAS copy.   29951

Vaill, Joseph, 1751-1838.
Noah's Flood: a Poem.
New London, Green, 1796. 28 pp.
AAS copy.   31481

[Vaill, Joseph, 1751-1838.
Noah's Flood: a Poem.
Hartford, Hudson & Goodwin, 1797.]
(Apparently a ghost of 31481 arising from 1797 adv.)   33109

A Valedicion, for New-Year's Day. 1763.
[Boston, 1763.] Broadside.
MHS copy.   9487

A Valedictory Address to the Young Gentlemen, who Commenced Bachelors of Arts, at Yale-College, July 25th, 1776 [by Timothy Dwight, 1752-1817].
New Haven, [1776]. 22 pp.
AAS copy.   14747

A Valedictory Oration, Pronounced at the Commencement Held at Nassau-Hall . . . 1759.
New York, Gaine, 1759. 10 pp.
BA copy.   8508

[Valentine, John], d. 1724.
The Postscript. Sir . . . Deadham, 1720.
[Boston, 1720.] 3 pp.
LOC copy.   39732

Valentine, John, d. 1724.
(T. W. Valentine, Valentines in America, pp. 110-115.)
To the Honourable. His Majesty's Justices.
[Boston, 1720.] 20 pp.
AAS copy.   2151

Valentine and Orson.
The Renowned History of Valentine and Orson.
Haverhill, Edes, 1794. 100 pp.
AAS copy.   27605

Valentine and Orson.
The Renowned History of. . . .
New York, Forman for Gomez, 1794.
(Present location unknown.)   47309

[Valentine and Orson.
The Renowned History of Valentine and Orson.
Exeter, Lamson, 1795.]
(Imprint assumed by Evans from Lamson's adv.)   29783

[Valentine and Orson.
The History of Valentine and Orson.

Salem, Cushing & Carlton, 1795.]
(Imprint assumed by Evans from Cushing's adv.)   29782

[Valentine and Orson.
The History of Valentine and Orson.
Wilmington, Del., Brynberg, 1797.]
(Imprint assumed by Evans from Brynberg's adv.)   33110

Valentine and Orson.
The Renowned History of. . . .
Hartford, Ct., Babcock, 1800. 141, [2] pp.
AAS copy.   38368

[Valentine's Gift, with an Account of Old Zigzag.
Philadelphia, Spotswood, 1786.]
(Ghost of a London ed. Adv. in Pa. Herald, July 12, 1783.)   20094

Valerius [by Cotton Mather, 1663-1728].
Boston, Fleet for Gerrish, 1723. 24 pp.
HC copy.   2460

Vallette, Elie.
The Deputy Commissary's Guide.
Annapolis, 1774. [2], iv, 248, [11] pp., plate.
AAS copy.   13742

Vallette, Elie.
Now Ready for the Press . . . the Deputy Commissary's Guide.
[Annapolis, A. C. Green, 1774.]
Broadside.
(Not available for filming.)
MdHS copy.   42737

[Vallette, Elie]
Subscription Paper for the Deputy Commisary's Guide.
[Annapolis, A.C. Green]. Broadside.
(No copy could be located.)   42738

The Valley of Hinnom [by Cotton Mather, 1663-1728].
Boston, Allen for Starke, 1717. [2], 49, [1], 6 pp.
MHS copy.   1910

[A Valuable Collection of Books in Different Departments of Literature and Science.
Philadelphia, 1796.]
(The origin of this entry has not been located.)   31482

Valuable Secrets Concerning Arts and Trades.
Norwich, Hubbard, 1795. [2], xxii. 240 pp.
AAS copy.   29243

Valuable Secrets, Concerning Arts and Trades. . . . Third American Edition.
Boston, Bumstead, 1798. 264 pp.
AAS copy.   34913

Valuable Tables [by Samuel Abial Ruddock].
Keene, N.H., Sturtevant, 1795. Broadside.
AAS copy.   47586

Valuable Tables [by Samuel Abial Ruddock].
Worcester, Thomas, 1795. Broadside.
AAS copy.   29449

Valuable Tables [by Samuel Abial Ruddock].
Windsor, Vt., 1796. Broadside.
VtHS (Rugg) copy.   31138

The Value of a Child [by John Taylor, 1694-1761].
Philadelphia, Franklin & Hall, 1753. 30 pp.
LOC copy.   7128

Value of Foreign Gold, in Dollars and Cents, and in £ s. d.
Salem, Cushing, [1790?]. Broadside.
MHS copy.   46079

Value of Foreign Gold, in Dollars and Cents, and in £ s.d.
Salem, [Mass.], Cushing, [1791].
Broadside.
AAS copy.   46337

[Vanbrugh, Sir John, 1664-1726.
The Confederacy. A Comedy.
Philadelphia, 1794.]
(Imprint assumed by Evans from adv.)   29784

Vanbrugh, Sir John, 1664-1726.
The Provoked Husband.
Boston, D. West and J. West, [1794]. 79 pp.
AAS copy.   27987

[Vanbrugh, John, 1664-1726.
The Provoked Wife.
New York, Gaine, 1761.]
(Adv. N. Y. Mercury, July 20, 1761.)   9029

Van Buskirk, Lawrence, 1775-1797.
Six Sermons.
New York, Kirk, 1797. viii, 123 pp.
LCP copy.   33111

[Van Campen, Moses], b. 1757.
A Narrative of the Capture of Certain Americans, at Westmoreland.
Hartford, [1780?] Front., 24 pp.
LOC copy.   18273

Van Courtlandt, Stephanus, 1643-1700.
A Journal . . . to Albany.
New York, Bradford, 1693. 15 pp.
Bibl. Nationale copy.   39307

Vancouver Charles, fl. 1785-1813.
A General Compendium; of . . . Natural Philosophy.
Philadelphia, 1785. viii, 48 pp., 1 plate.
NYPL copy.   19337

[Van Cuelen, Jacobus]
The Delaware Almanac . . . for . . . 1789.
Wilmington, Craig. [24] pp.
(The only copy located is very imperfect.)
AAS copy.   21536

[Van Cuelen, Jacobus.]
The Delaware Almanac . . . for . . . 1790.
Wilmington, Craig. [26] pp.
AAS copy.   22215

Van Cuelen, Jacobus.
The Delaware Almanac . . . for . . . 1791.
Wilmington, Andrews, Craig & Brynberg. [26] pp.
LOC copy.   23011

Van Cuelen, Jacobus.
The Federal Almanac, for . . . 1790.
Wilmington, Craig. [36] pp.
AAS copy.   45729

Van Dam, Rip, 1662-1736.
The Arguments of the Council.
New York, 1733. [2], 63 pp.
NYPL copy.   3727

Van Dam, Rip, 1662-1736.

Copy of a Letter from Rip Van Dam. . . .
April 26th, 1736.
[New York, 1736.] 4 pp., irreg.
NYPL copy. 4090

Van Dam, Rip, 1662-1736.
Farther Proceedings Concerning the Case
of Rip Van Dam.
[New York, 1734.] pp. 65-[68].
NYPL copy. 3845

Van Dam, Rip, 1662-1736.
Heads of Articles of Complaint by Rip
Van Dam, Esq; Against His Excellency
William Cosby.
Boston, 1734. 28 pp.
NYPL copy. 3847

Van Dam, Rip, 1662-1736.
Heads of Articles of Complaint, made by
Rip Van Dam, Esq; on Thursday, the 30th
of May, 1734.
[New York, 1734.] pp. 69-71.
NYPL copy. 3846

[Van Dam, Rip, 1662-1736.
Protestation.
New York, 1736.]
(This title is the adv. for 4093.) 4092

Van Dam, Rip, 1662-1736.
Sir; Whereas on the 10th Day of March.
[New York, 1736.] Broadside.
NYPL copy. 4091

Van Dam, Rip, 1662-1736.
To All to Whom these Presents Shall
Come.
[New York, 1736.] pp. 69-73.
NYPL copy. 4093

Vanden Broek, Reinier John.
Address Delivered at the Consecration.
New York, Oram, 1796. 19 pp.
AAS copy. 47998

Van Der Kemp, Francis Adrian,
1752-1829.
Speech of . . . at a Meeting, the First of
June.
Whitestown, Easton, 1795. 19 pp.
BA copy. 29785

Vandike, John, pseud.
A Narrative of the Captivity of John
Vandike.
Hanover, 1799. 32 pp.
(The one recorded copy cannot be
reproduced.) 36608

Van Driessen, Petrus
De Aanbiddelyke Wegen Gods.
New York, 1726. [10], 79, [2] pp.
NYPL copy. 2820

Van Driessen, Petrus.
The Adorable Ways of God.
New York, 1726. [10], 75 pp., irreg.
NYPL copy. 2821

Van Driessen, Petrus
De Heerlykheit.
New York, 1730. [6], xx, 444.
NYHS copy. 3364

[Van Horne, David], 1746-1801.
Instructions for the Cavalry, of the State
of New-York.
Albany, Websters, 1798. 70, iii pp.
(The only known copy is imperfect.)
NYPL copy. 34914

Van Horne, Frederick.
A Sermon . . . before the Brethren of
Solomon's Lodge.
[Poughkeepsie], Power & Southwick,
[1798]. 10 pp.
NYHS copy. 34915

[Van Lier, -]
The Power of Grace Illustrated.
Philadelphia, Neale & Kammerer, 1796.
142 pp.
(An imprint variant of 30194, q. v. for
text.)
AAS copy. 48000

[Van Lier, -]
The Power of Grace Illustrated.
Philadelphia, Neale & Kammerer for
Condie, 1796. 142 pp.

(An imprint variant of 30194, q. v. for
text.)
AAS copy. 48001

[Van Lier, -]
The Power of Grace Illustrated.
Philadelphia, Neale & Kammerer for
Denoon, 1796. 142 pp.
AAS copy. 30194

[Van Lier, -]
The Power of Grace Illustrated.
Philadelphia, for Denoon, 1796. 142 pp.
(An imprint variant of 30194, q. v. for
text.) 47999

Van Ness, John Peter, 1770-1847.
An Oration, Composed and Delivered
by. . . .
Albany, Webster, [1788].
("This day published," Albany Journal,
Feb. 2, 1788.)
HEH copy. 21537

Van Pelt, Peter J., 1778-1861.
An Oration, in Consequence of the Death
of . . . Washington.
Brooklyn, [N. Y.], Kirk, 1800. 24 pp.
AAS copy. 38921

Van Rensselaer, Stephen, 1764-1839.
To the Inhabitants Residing in the Manor
of Rensselaerwyck. . . . April 27, 1789.
[Albany? 1789.]
(The one reported copy cannot be
located.) 45730

The Vanity of the Life of Man. . . . By R.
B. [by Nathaniel Crouch, 1632?-1725?].
Boston, Kneeland & Green, 1733. 30 pp.
(No copy could be located.) 40016

The Vanity of the Life of Man. . . . Fourth
Edition [by Nathaniel Crouch,
1632?-1725?].
New London, 1769. 24 pp.
AAS copy. 11227

The Vanity of the World, a Poem.
n.p., [179?]. Broadside.
NYPL ph. copy. 45800

The Vanity of War and Riches. . . . A
Poem.
n.p., [1770?[. Broadside.
NYPL copy. 42047

[Vans, Hugh.]
(M.H.S., Proc., XLIII, 441-447.)
An Inquiry into the Nature and Uses of
Money.
Boston, Kneeland & Green, 1740. [2], 78
pp.
AAS copy. 4533

[Vans, Hugh.]
(A. M. Davis, Colonial Currency
Reprints, III, 477-478.)
Some Observations on the Scheme
Projected for Emitting 60000l.
Boston, Kneeland and Green, 1738. [4],
25 pp.
AAS copy. 4308

Vansant, John.
To the Public. Philadelphia Gaol, the 12th
of the 10th Month, 1772.
[Philadelphia, 1772.] 2 pp.
LCP copy. 12589

[Van Santvoord, Cornelius]
Samenspraak over de Klaghte der
Raritanders.
New York, 1726. [4], 194, xiv, [1] pp.
HEH copy. 2812

Van Shermain, Theodorus, pseud.
A Vision of Hell [by Jacob Green,
1722-1790].
New Haven, 1770. 24 pp.
(The Evans entry is apparently a
typographical error for this copy.)
NYHS copy. 14792

Van Shermain, Theodorus, pseud.
A Vision of Hell. . . . [by Jacob Green,
1722-1790].
Amherst, N. H., Preston, 1797. 24 pp.
AAS copy. 32206

Van Solingen, Henry M.
An Inaugural Dissertation.

New York, Swords, 1792. 32 pp.
AAS copy. 24953

[Vanuxem, -
Circular Letter in French, Sept. 24, 1777.
Philadelphia, 1777. Broadside.]
(Entry from Aitken's accounts.) 15690

Van Vleck, Abraham H.
To the Public. . . . August 4th, 1775.
[New York, 1775.] Broadside.
NYPL copy. 14589

Van Vlierden, Petrus.
Handleidinge Tot eene Hervormde
Geloovs-Belydenis.
Kingston, N. J., Copp & Frier, 1794. 32
pp.
HEH copy. 27988

Van Vlierden, Petrus.
Het lot Van Lichaam.
Catskill, Croswell, 1794. [4], 30, [1] pp.
(The title given by Evans is from an adv.)
NYHS copy. 27989

[Van Wagenen, Hubert.
The Descending of Christ into Hell.
New York, 1794.]
(The origin of this entry is unknown.) 27990

[Vardill, John], 1749-1811.
Candid Remarks on Dr. Witherspoon's
Address.
Philadelphia, 1772. [2], 59, [2] pp.
(This is not the same text as Vardill's
newspaper attack, but it is ascribed to him
in a contemporary hand in the NYSL
copy.)
AAS copy. 12346

Varick. The Worst Card in the Federal
Pack.
[New York, 179?]. Cartoon.
(No copy located.) 45801

Various Extracts on the Foederal
Government.
Richmond, Davis, [1787]. [2], 64 pp.
NCU copy. 20824

Varlo, Charles, 1725-1795?
A New System of Husbandry.
Philadelphia, 1785. 2 vol. pp. [18], i-iv,
17-364, 1 folding plate; 368 pp.
(Front matter varies in different copies.)
AAS copy. 19338

Varnum, James Mitchell, 1748-1789.
The Case, Trevett against Weeden.
Providence, Carter, 1787. iv, 60 pp.
AAS copy. 20825

Varnum, James Mitchell, 1748-1789.
An Oration, Delivered at Marietta, July 4,
1788.
Newport, 1788. 14 pp.
AAS copy. 21538

Varnum, James Mitchell, 1748-1789.
An Oration: Delivered before a Lodge of
. . . Masons.
Providence, R. I., Carter, [1779]. 11 pp.
AAS copy. 43722

Varnum, James Mitchell, 1748-1789.
An Oration: Delivered in the Episcopal
Church.
Providence, Carter, [1783]. 10 pp.
AAS copy. 44281

Varnum, Joseph Bradley, 1751-1821.
An Address . . . to the . . . Massachusetts
Militia.
Cambridge, [Mass.], Hilliard, 1800. 26
pp.
AAS copy. 38922

[Vas, Petrus.
Korte Schets.
New York, 1730.]
(The unique copy could not be found.) 3365

Vattel, Emmerich de, 1714-1767.
The Law of Nations.
New York, Berry and Rogers, 1787. lxxiv,
728 pp.
AAS copy. 45185

Vattel, Emmerich de, 1714-1767.
The Law of Nations.

New York, Campbell, 1796. 563 pp.
AAS copy.   31483

A Vaudevil, sung by the Characters. . . .
[Boston, 1776.] Broadside.
MHS copy.   15195

Vaughan, John, 1775-1807.
Observations on Animal Electricity.
Wilmington, Del., Smyth, 1797. 32 pp.
AAS copy.   33112

Vaughan, John, 1775-1807.
The Valedictory Lecture.
Wilmington, [Del.], Wilson, 1800. 36 pp.
YC copy.   38924

[Vaughan, William?] 1751-1835.
The Catechism of Man.
Philadelphia, Humphreys for Carey, 1794.
[2], 34 pp.
AAS copy.   27991

Vaux, George.
Advertisement. Whereas an
Advertisement. . . . March 31st. 1733.
[Boston, 1733.] Broadside.
BPL copy.   40034

[The Vendue, or Six Month's Credit. A
New Song.
Poughkeepsie, 1796.]
("Just published, and for sale by N.
Power, and the Posts," Poughkeepsie
Journal, Oct. 26, 1796.)   31484

Venema, Pieter
Arithmetica.
New York, 1730. [5], 120 pp.
NYHS copy.   3366

Venning, Ralph, 1621-1674.
(D. N. B.)
Milk and Honey. . . . Tenth Edition.
Boston, 1708. [8], 86 pp.
BPL copy.   1378

Veracitas's last Tribute. . . . April 2, 1772
[Philadelphia, 1772.] [2] pp.
HSP copy.   12590

The Veracity and Equity.
Boston, Fleet, 1723. 16 pp.
AAS copy.   2480

Verba Opportuna [by Cotton Mather,
1663-1728].
Boston, 1715. 46, [2] pp.
CL copy.   1766

Verba Vivifica [by Cotton Mather,
1663-1728].
Boston, 1714. [2], 37 pp.
CL copy.   1700

[Verbessere A-B-C- oder Namenbuecher.
Philadelphia, Miller, 1766.]
(Adv. Phila. Staatsbote, Mar. 17, 1766.)
                                                   10514

[Der Verbesserte Hoch-Deutsche
Americanische Land und Staats Calender.
Auf das Jahr . . . 1785.
Frederick Town, Bartgis.
Franklin & Marshall College copy.   18851

[Der Verbesserte Hoch-Deutsche
Americanische Land und Staats Calender.
Auf das Jahr . . . 1786.
Frederick Town, Bartgis.]
(Assumed by Seidensticker from the
sequence.)   19339

[Der Verbesserte Hoch-Deutsche
Americanische Land und Staats Calender.
Auf das Jahr . . . 1787.
Frederick Town, Bartgis.]
(Entry from Seidensticker, p. 117.)   20095

[Der Verbesserte Hoch-Deutsche
Americanische Land und Staats Calender
auf das Jahr . . . 1788.
Frederick Town, Bartgis.]
(Assumed by Seidensticker from the
sequence.)   20826

[Der Verbesserte Hoch-Deutsche
Americanische Land und Staats Calender
auf das Jahr . . . 1789.
Frederick Town, Md., Bartgis.]
(Assumed by Seidensticker from the
sequence.)   21539

[Der Verbesserte Hoch-Deutsche
Americanische Land und Staats Calender.
Auf das Jahr . . . 1790.
Fredericktown, Bartgis.]
(Assumed by Seidensticker.)   22216

[Der Verbesserte Hoch-Deutsche
Americanische Land und Staats Calender.
Auf das Jahr . . . 1791.
Frederick Town, Bartgis.]
(Entry from Seidensticker.)   23012

[Der Verbesserte Hoch-Deutsche
Americanische Land und Staats Calender.
Auf das Jahr . . . 1792.
Frederick Town, Bartgis.]
(Publication assumed by Seidensticker.)
                                                   23932

[Der Verbesserte Hoch-Deutsche
Americanische Land und Staats Calender.
Auf das Jahr . . . 1793.
Frederick Town, Md., Bartgis.]
(Assumed from Bartgis' adv. for "English
and German almanacks.")   24954

[Der Verbesserte Hoch-Deutsche
Americanische Land und Staats Calender.
Auf das Jahr . . . 1794.
Frederick Town, Md., Bartgis.]
(Entry from Seidensticker.)   26374

[Der Verbesserte Hoch-Deutsche
Americanische Land und Staats Calender
Auf das Jahr . . . 1795.
Frederick Town, Bartgis.]
(Entry taken by Evans from
Seidensticker.)   27992

Der Verbessert Hoch-Deutsch-
Americanischer Land und Staats-Calender.
Auf das 1796ste Jahr Christi.
Frederickstown, Bartgis, 1795. [28] pp.
(The only copy located is imperfect.)
Enoch Pratt Free Library copy.   29786

[Der Verbesserte Hoch Deutsche
Americanische Land and Staats Calender.
Auf das Jahr . . . 1797.
Frederick Town, Md., Bartgis.]
(Title and imprint assumed from adv. in
Bartgis's Federal Gazette, Dec. 22, 1796.)
                                                   31485

[Der Verbesserte Hoch Deutsche
Americanische Land und Staats Calendar.
Auf das Jahr . . . 1798.]
Frederick Town, Bartgis.]
(Assumed by Seidensticker from the
sequence.)   33113

[Der Verbesserte Hoch Deutsche
Americanische Land und Staats Calender
auf das Jahr 1799.
Fredericktown, Md., Bartgis.]
(Evans took the entry from Seidensticker,
p. 149.)   34916

Verbum Sempiternum
See
John Taylor, 1580-1653.

Der Vereinigten Staaten Calender, auf das
Jahr . . . 1798.
Philadelphia, Kammerer. [34] pp.
(No perfect copy located.)
AAS copy.   33114

Der Vereinigten Staaten Calender auf
das Jahr . . . 1799.
Philadelphia, Kämmerer. [38] pp.
HSP copy.   34917

Der Vereinigten Staaten Calender, auf das
Jahr . . . 1800.
Philadelphia, Kämmerer & Helmbold.
[42] pp.
HSP copy.   36610

Der Vereinigten Staaten Calender, auf das
Jahr . . . 1801.
Philadelphia, Helmbold & Geyer. [42] pp.
HSP copy.   38925

[Vergilius Maro, Publius.
M. Martel's Literal Translation of the
Works of Virgil.
New York, 1797.]
(Entry from the copyright record.) 33125

Vergilius Maro, Publius.
The Pastoral Songs of. . . .

Boston, Manning & Loring, 1799. [4], 92
pp.
AAS copy.   36625

Vergilius Maro, Publius.
The Works of Virgil.
Worcester, Mass., Worcester for West,
1796. 673, [1] pp.
AAS copy.   31496

[Das Vergnügte Leben eines Einsamen,
Namens Jorgel.
[Ephrata, 1788.] Broadside.?]
(Attributed by Seidensticker to HSP, but
not located.)   21544

[Verhandlungen des Coetus von
Pennsylvanien.
Philadelphia, 1748.]
(See Hildeburn 4625.)   6257

[Verhandlungen des Coetus von
Pennsylvanien.
Philadelphia, Franklin & Armbruester,
1757.]
(See Hildeburn 1567.)   8053

Veritt, Paul
To my Friends in Pensilvania.
[Philadelphia, 1738?] 3 pp.
LCP copy.   4316

Verkoop van de Onderstaande
Onbebouwde Loten Landen.
Philadelphia, Bailey, [1785?]. Broadside.
(No copy located.)   44820

Vermont.
[Handbook for apprehending a prisoner.
Windsor, Hutchins, 1791.]
(McCorison 200; no copy known.)   46338

Vermont. Census.
Schedule, Containing the Number of
Inhabitants.
n.p., [1790?] Broadside.
VtHS copy.   46080

Vermont. Census, 1791.
Schedule, containing the Number of
Inhabitants in each Town. . . . Total
85,539.
Windsor, [Vt.], Spooner, [1791].
Broadside.
(Not located, 1968.)   46339

Vermont. Constitution, 1778.
The Constitution of the State of Vermont.
Hartford, [1778]. 24 pp.
AAS copy.   16151

Vermont. Constitution, 1785.
The Constitution of the State of Vermont.
Windsor, 1785. 44 pp.
AAS copy.   19343

Vermont. Constitution, 1786.
The Constitution of Vermont. . . . Revised
. . . June, 1786.
Windsor, 1786. 30 pp.
VtU copy.   20096

Vermont. Constitution, 1792.
The Constitution of Vermont, as Revised
. . . by the Council of Censors . . .
October, 1792.
Rutland, Haswell, [1792]. 14 pp.
(The unique copy is imperfect.)
VtSL copy.   24956

Vermont. Constitution, 1793.
The Constitution of Vermont.
Windsor, Vt., Spooner, 1793. 29 pp.
AAS copy.   26378

Vermont. Convention, 1779.
To the Inhabitants of the Town of
[blank]. . . . April 23s, 1779.
[Portsmouth, 1779.] Broadside.
Plainfield, N. H., Town Clerk's Copy.
                                                   43723

Vermont. Council, 1779.
. . . In Council, Windsor, 7th June, 1779.
Resolved, That the Captain-General's
Orders. . . .
[Dresden, 1779.] Broadside.
LCP copy.   16653

Vermont. Council of Censors, 1786.
The Proceedings of the Council of
Censors.

Windsor, 1786. 28 pp.
AAS copy.   20098

Vermont. Council of Censors, 1792.
Proceedings of the Council of Censors . . .
at Rutland . . . in the Year 1792.
Rutland, Haswell, 1792. 80 pp.
AAS copy.   24958

Vermont. Council of Censors, 1800.
An Address of the Council of Censors.
Bennington, Vt., Haswell, 1800. 32, [1]
pp.
AAS copy.   38928

Vermont. Council of Safety, 1777.
Providence, Aug. 21. The Following. . . .
In Council of Safety, Bennington, August
16, 1777. . . .
[Providence, 1777.] Broadside.
LOC copy.   43403

Vermont. General Assembly, 1778.
Outlines of a Plan . . . October, A.D. 1778,
to be Pursued for the Establishment of the
State.
[Dresden, 1778.] Broadside.
(Copy not located.)   43586

Vermont. General Assembly, 1779.
[Letters.
Dresden, Spooners, 1779.]
(McCorison 20; no copy known.)   43724

Vermont. General Assembly, 1779.
A Public Defence.
Dresden, 1779. 56, 4 pp.
HC copy.   16391

Vermont. General Assembly, 1781.
[Claim to the New Hampshire Grants.
Westminster, Spooner & Green, 1781.
Broadside.]
(McCorison 38; no copy known.)   44070

Vermont. General Assembly, 1781.
Proceedings of Grand Committee of the
Legislature . . . at Charlestown . . .
October, 1781.
Exeter, 1782. 4 pp.
AAS copy.   17779

Vermont. General Assembly, 1781.
. . . Windsor, Feb. 12th, 1781. Agreeable
to the Order of the day. . . .
[Westminster, 1781.] 2 pp.
HEH photostat copy.   17405

Vermont. General Assembly, 1784.
[Doings of the Assembly for the
consideration of the People.
Bennington, Haswell & Russell, 1784.] 4
pp.
(McCorison 79; no copy known.)   44609

[Vermont. General Assembly, 1793.
Extract from the Journals and
Proceedings, in Grand Committee, at
Rutland, October 1792.
[Rutland, Haswell, 1793.] Broadside.]
(The origin of this entry is unknown.)
                                             26380

Vermont. General Assembly, 1795.
A List of Arrearages of Taxes . . . on the
15th Day of September, A. D. 1795.
Rutland, [1795]. 13 pp.
LOC copy.   29790

Vermont. General Assembly Journals,
1784.
A Journal of the Proceedings of the
General Assembly . . . February, 1784.
Windsor, 1784. 64 pp.
LOC copy.   18853

Vermont. General Assembly Journals,
1784.
A Journal of the Proceedings of the
General Assembly . . . October, 1784.
Windsor, 1785. 57 pp.
AAS copy.   18854

Vermont. General Assembly Journals,
1785.
A Journal of the Proceedings of the
General Assembly . . . at Norwich . . .
June 1785.
Windsor, 1785. 52 pp.
AAS copy.   19344

Vermont. General Assembly Journals,
1785.

A Journal of the Proceedings of the
General Assembly . . . October, 1785.
Windsor, Hough & Spooner, 1786. 80 pp.
(No perfect copy is known. Evans' entry
was from Gilman.)
LOC copy.   19345

Vermont. General Assembly Journals,
1786.
A Journal of the Proceedings of the
General Assembly [Oct. 12-31, 1786].
Windsor, 1786. 128 pp.
(No perfect copy known.)
VtU copy.   20097

Vermont. General Assembly Journals,
1787.
A Journal of the Proceedings of the
General Assembly . . . February, 1787.
Windsor, 1787. 63 pp.
VtSL copy.   20831

Vermont. General Assembly Journals,
1788.
A Journal of the Proceedings of the
General Assembly . . . October, 1788.
Windsor, 1789. 50 pp.
VtSL copy.   21541

Vermont. General Assembly Journals,
1789.
A Journal . . . at Westminster . . .
October, 1789.
Windsor, Spooner, 1790. 67 pp.
AAS copy.   22218

Vermont. General Assembly Journals,
1790.
A Journal . . . at Castleton . . . October,
1790.
Windsor, Spooner, 1791. 54 pp.
AAS copy.   23937

Vermont. General Assembly Journals,
1791.
A Journal . . . at Bennington, January,
1791.
Bennington, Haswell, 1791. 85 pp.
AAS copy.   23938

Vermont. General Assembly Journals,
1791.
A Journal . . . at Windsor, October 13th,
1791.
Windsor, Spooner, [1792]. 49 pp.
LOC copy.   24957

Vermont. General Assembly Journals,
1792.
A Journal . . . at Rutland, in October,
1792.
Rutland, Haswell, [1793]. 114 pp.
AAS copy.   26379

Vermont. General Assembly Journals,
1793.
A Journal . . . at Windsor in October, One
Thousand Seven Hundred and
Ninety-Three.
Windsor, Spooner, 1794. 205 pp.
AAS copy.   27995

Vermont. General Assembly Journals,
1794.
A Journal . . . at Rutland in October One
Thousand Seven Hundred and
Ninety-Four.
Bennington, Haswell, [1795]. 229 pp.
AAS copy.   29789

Vermont. General Assembly Journals,
1795.
A Journal . . . at Windsor, October
Eighth, One Thousand Seven Hundred
and Ninety-Five.
Rutland, [1796]. 170 pp.
AAS copy.   31488

Vermont. General Assembly Journals,
1797.
A Journal of the Proceedings of the
General Assembly . . . at Rutland . . .
October Thirteenth, One Thousand Seven
Hundred and Ninety-Six.
Bennington, Haswell, 1797. 184 pp.
AAS copy.   33119

Vermont. General Assembly Journals,
1797.
A Journal of the Proceedings of the
General Assembly . . . at Windsor,
October . . . One Thousand, Seven
Hundred and Ninety Seven.

Bennington, Haswell for Williams, 1798.
287 pp.
VtSL copy.   34923

Vermont. General Assembly Journals,
1798.
Journal of the General Assembly . . . at
. . . Vergennes, October . . .
M,DCC,XVIII.
Bennington, Haswell, [1798]. 300 pp.
AAS copy.   34924

Vermont. General Assembly Journals,
1799.
A Journal . . . at Windsor, October Tenth,
One Thousand Seven Hundred and
Ninety-Nine.
Rutland, Vt., 1799. 157 (i.e. 158) pp.
AAS copy.   36616

Vermont. Governor, 1778.
By His Excellency Thomas
Chittenden. . . . A Proclamation. Amid
the many . . . [Thanksgiving, Nov. 26;
dated Oct. 18, 1778].
[Hanover, N.H., 1778.] Broadside.
DC copy.   43587

Vermont. Governor, 1779.
By His Excellency Thomas
Chittenden. . . . A Proclamation
[Allegiance. June 3, 1779].
[Dresden], Padock & Spooner, [1779].
Broadside.
MHS ph. copy.   16652

Vermont. Governor, 1779.
By His Excellency Thomas
Chittenden. . . . A Proclamation [Laws.
Feb. 23, 1779].
[Dresden, 1779.] Broadside.
VtSL copy.   16651

Vermont. Governor, 1779.
[Proclamation for a Fast Day, April 1779.
Dresden, 1779.] Broadside.
(McCorison 25; no copy known.)   43725

Vermont. Governor, 1780.
[Thanksgiving proclamation for 1780.
Westminster, Spooner & Green, 1780.]
Broadside.
(McCorison 32; no copy known.)   43909

Vermont. Governor, 1781.
By His Excellency Thomas
Chittenden. . . . A Proclamation
[Boundary. July 18, 1781].
[Westminster, 1781.] Broadside.
NYSL copy.   17403

Vermont. Governor, 1781.
By His Excellency Thomas Chittenden . . .
a Proclamation [Thanksgiving, Dec. 6.
Dated Oct. 27, 1781].
[Westminster, 1781.] Broadside.
AAS copy.   17404

Vermont. Governor, 1781.
[Fast Day proclamation for April, 1781.
Westminster, Spooner & Green, 1781.
Broadside.]
(Known from printers' bill only.)   44071

[Vermont. Governor, 1783.
By His Excellency Tho. Chittenden . . . a
Proclamation [Thanksgiving, Nov. 13,
Dated Oct. 16, 1783].
Windsor, 1783. Broadside.]
(Broadside publication assumed by Evans;
wording from Vermont Journal, Oct. 23,
1783.)   18277

Vermont. Governor, 1784.
By His Excellency Thomas
Chittenden. . . . A Proclamation. As
Public Praise . . . a Day of Public
Thanksgiving [Dec. 2. Dated Oct. 18,
1784].
[Windsor? 1784.] Broadside.
AAS ph. copy.   44610

Vermont. Governor, 1784.
[Fast Day proclamation.
Bennington, Haswell & Russell, 1784.]
(McCorison 81; no copy known.)   44611

Vermont. Governor, 1785.
By His Excellency Thomas
Chittenden. . . . A Proclamation [Fast,
Apr. 27. Dated Mar. 24, 1785].

[Windsor, 1785.] Broadside.
Brattleboro Pub. Library copy.   44821

Vermont. Governor, 1785.
[Thanksgiving Day proclamation for
Nov., 1785.
Windsor, Hough & Spooner, 1785.]
Broadside.
(McCorison 103; no copy known.)   44822

Vermont. Governor, 1786.
[Fast day proclamation.
Bennington, Haswell & Russell, 1786.]
Broadside.
(McCorison 125; no copy known.)   45005

Vermont. Governor, 1787.
By His Excellency Thomas Chittenden . . .
a Proclamation. . . . Daniel Sharp [Dated
Feb. 27, 1787].
Windsor, 1787. Broadside.
(The only known copy is at present
mislaid.)   20829

Vermont. Governor, 1787.
By His Excellency Thomas
Chittenden. . . . Whereas the
State-Laws. . . . Given . . . this 20th day of
October, One Thousand Seven Hundred
and Eighty-Seven. . . .
[Windsor, 1787.] Broadside.
VtU ph. copy.   20830

[Vermont. Governor, 1787.
Regulations for the Order and Discipline
of the Troops of . . . Vermont.
Bennington, 1787.]
("Just Published," Vt. Journal, Apr. 9,
1787.)   20832

Vermont. Governor, 1788.
By His Excellency, Thomas
Chittenden. . . . A Proclamation. . . .
Thanksgiving [Nov. 27].
[Bennington, 1788.] Broadside.
(McCorison 153. No copy located.)   45390

Vermont. Governor, 1788.
[Fast day Proclamation.
Bennington, Haswell & Russell, 1788.]
Broadside.
(McCorison 152; no copy located.)   45391

Vermont. Governor, 1789.
By His Excellency Moses Robinson. . . . A
Proclamation . . . Public Thanksgiving
[Nov. 26. Dated Oct. 17, 1789].
[Windsor, 1789.] Broadside.
NYHS copy.   45731

Vermont. Governor, 1789.
[Fast Day proclamation.
Bennington, Haswell & Russell, 1789.]
Broadside.
(McCorison 171; no copy known.)   45732

Vermont. Governor, 1790.
By His Excellency Moses Robinson. . . . A
Proclamation [Fast, Apr. 28. Dated Mar.
31, 1790].
[Bennington, 1790.] Broadside.
NYHS copy.   23014

Vermont. Governor, 1791.
By His Excellency Thomas
Chittenden. . . . A Proclamation [Fast,
Apr. 27. Dated Jan. 27, 1791].
[Bennington, 1791.] Broadside.
NYHS copy.   23936

Vermont. Governor, 1791.
By His Excellency Thomas Chittenden . . .
a Proclamation [Thanksgiving, Dec. 1.
Dated Oct. 20, 1791].
Windsor, Spooner, [1791]. Broadside.
NYHS copy.   23935

Vermont. Governor, 1792.
[Fast day proclamation.
Bennington, Haswell, 1792. Broadside.]
(McCorison 240; no copy known.)   46656

Vermont. Governor, 1792.
[Thanksgiving day proclamation.
Bennington, Haswell, 1792. Broadside.]
(McCorison 241; no copy known.)   46657

Vermont. Governor, 1793.
By His Excellency Thomas Chittenden . . .
a Proclamation [Fast, Apr. 10. Dated
Mar. 10, 1793].

[Rutland, 1793.] Broadside.
NYHS copy.   26377

Vermont. Governor, 1794.
By His Excellency Thomas Chittenden . . .
[Fast, Apr. 9, Dated Jan. 24, 1794].
Bennington, Haswell, [1794]. Broadside.
AAS copy.   27994

Vermont. Governor, 1794.
General Orders. State of Vermont,
Rutland, June 21st, 1794.
[Bennington? 1794.] Broadside.
(Copy not located.)   47310

Vermont. Governor, 1794.
[Thanksgiving day proclamation, Oct.
1794.
Windsor, Spooner, 1794. Broadside.]
(McCorison 317; no copy known.)   47311

[Vermont. Governor, 1795.
By His Excellency Thomas
Chittenden. . . . a Proclamation. . . .
Public Thanksgiving [Dec. 3. Dated Oct.
15, 1795].
[Windsor, Spooner, 1795.] Broadside.]
(Broadside printing assumed by Evans.)
          29788

[Vermont. Governor, 1796.
By His Excellency Thomas
Chittenden. . . . A Proclamation . . .
Thanksgiving [Dec. 1. Dated Oct. 27,
1796.]
[Rutland, 1796.] Broadside.]
(The origin of this entry is unknown.)
          31487

[Vermont. Governor, 1797.
By His Excellency Isaac Tichenor. . . . A
Proclamation . . . Thanksgiving [Dec. 7.
Dated Oct. 24, 1797].
[Windsor, 1797.] Broadside.]
(Evans assumed a broadside printing.)
          33121

[Vermont. Governor, 1797.
By His Excellency Thomas
Chittenden. . . . A Proclamation . . . a Day
of Public Humiliation, Fasting & Prayer
[Apr. 19. Dated Mar. 10, 1797.].
[Burlington, 1797.] Broadside.]
(Evans assumed a broadside printing.)
          33120

Vermont. Governor, 1798.
By His Excellency Isaac Tichenor. . . . A
Proclamation [Fast, Apr. 18. Dated Mar.
16, 1798].
[Rutland, 1798.] Broadside.
(The unique copy is mislaid.)   34921

Vermont. Governor, 1798.
By Isaac Tichenor, Governor. . . . A
Proclamation. . . . Thanksgiving [Dec. 6.
Dated Oct. 29, 1798].
Vergennes, Waites, [1798]. Broadside.
VtU copy.   34922

Vermont. Governor, 1798.
General Orders. . . . January 2, 1798.
Rutland, Fay, [1798]. Broadside.
(Not located, 1968.)   48743

Vermont. Governor, 1798.
Speech of His Excellency Governor
Tichenor to the Council and House. . . .
October 12, 1798.
[Vergennes, 1798.] Broadside.
Dartmouth College copy.   48744

Vermont. Governor, 1799.
[Fast day proclamation.
? 1799.] Broadside.
(McCorison 548; no copy known.)   48986

Vermont. Governor, 1799.
Speech of His Excellency Governor
Tichenor. . . . 12th October, 1799.
Windsor, Vt., [1799]. Broadside.
Dartmouth College copy.   36615

[Vermont. Governor, 1800.
By His Excellency Isaac Tichenor. . . . A
Proclamation for a Day of Solemn Fasting
[Apr. 23. Dated Mar. 19, 1800.]
n.p., n.d., Broadside.]
(Broadside printing assumed by Evans
from newspaper printing.)   38929

Vermont. Laws, Statutes, etc., 1779.
Acts and Laws of the State of Vermont.

[Dresden], 1779. [2], 12, 110 pp.
AAS copy.   16649

Vermont. Laws, Statutes, etc., 1779.
[Scheme of a lottery, passed Feb. 24,
1779.
Dresden, Spooners, 1779.]
(McCorison 18; no copy known.)   43726

Vermont. Laws, Statutes, etc., 1780.
. . . Acts and Laws, Passed . . . at
Bennington, October 1780.
[Westminster, Spooner & Green, 1780.
[6] pp.
VtU ph. copy.   43910

Vermont. Laws, Statutes, etc., 1781.
An Act for Levying a Tax of Six-Pence on
the Pound. . . . 27th October 1781.
Westminster, Spooner, [1781]. Broadside.
AAS copy.   44072

Vermont. Laws, Statutes, etc., 1781.
[An act for procuring provision for the
troops.
Westminster, Spooner, 1781. Broadside.]
(Sabin 99085; no copy known.)   44073

Vermont. Laws, Statutes, etc., 1781.
[An act regulating the militia passed
February, 1781.
Westminster, Spooner & Green, 1781.]
(McCorison 43; no copy known.)   44074

Vermont. Laws, Statutes, etc., 1782.
. . . An Act for the Purpose of Raising
Three Hundred Able-bodied Effective
Men. . . . Passed Feb. 1782.
[Westminster, 1782.] [2] pp.
AAS copy.   44283

Vermont. Laws, Statutes, etc., 1783.
An Act Directing the Treasurer to Issue
State Notes.
Bennington, Vt., Haswell & Russell, 1783.
[3] pp.
AAS copy.   44487

Vermont. Laws, Statutes, etc., 1784.
An Act for the Limitation of Actions. . . .
March 20, 1784.
[Windsor, 1784.] Broadside.
AAS copy.   44612

Vermont. Laws, Statutes, etc., 1784.
An Act Regulating the Choice of a
Council of Censors.
[Windsor, 1784.] [2] pp.
VtU copy.   44613

Vermont. Laws, Statutes, etc., 1784.
. . . An Act to Enable Persons who have
made Improvements on Lands. . . .
[Windsor, 1784.] [3] pp.
VtU copy.   44614

Vermont. Laws, Statutes, etc., 1784.
. . . Bennington, March 1, 1784. An Act to
Enable Persons who have . . . made
Improvements on Lands. . . .
[Windsor, 1784.] [2] pp.
NYPL ph. copy.   44616

Vermont. Laws, Statutes, etc., 1784.
. . . Bennington, March 1, 1784. Extract
from a Proposed Act for the Limitation of
Actions.
[Windsor, 1784.] Broadside.
VtU copy.   44617

Vermont. Laws, Statutes, etc., 1785.
. . . An Act for the Purpose of Levying the
Taxes . . . Passed . . . 16th June.
[Windsor? 1785.] Broadside.
(McCorison 106; no copy located.)   44823

Vermont. Laws, Statutes, etc., 1787.
An Act Regulating the Militia.
[Windsor, Hough & Spooner, 1787.] 16
pp.
VtSL copy.   45186

Vermont. Laws, Statutes, etc., 1791.
An Act Regulating the Choice of a
Council of Censors.
Windsor, Spooner, 1791. Broadside.
LOC copy.   46340

Vermont. Laws, Statutes, etc., 1791.
Statutes of the State of Vermont.
Bennington, Haswell, 1791. [1], 315, [7]
pp.
AAS copy.   23939

Vermont. Laws, Statutes, etc., 1793.
An Act for Regulating and Governing the
Militia.
Windsor, Vt., Spooner, 1793. 29 pp.
VtHS copy.   26375

Vermont. Laws, Statutes, etc., 1796.
An Act Dividing the State into Districts.
Rutland, 1796. 15 pp.
VtSL copy.   48002

[Vermont. Laws, Statutes, etc., 1797.
An Act Assessing a Tax of One Cent on
each Acre. . . . Passed November 10th,
1797.
[Bennington, 1797.] [2] pp.]
(No copy of such a printing located.)
    33115

Vermont. Laws, Statutes, etc., 1797.
An Act for Regulating and Governing the
Militia. . . . March 10th, 1797.
Bennington, 1797. 58 pp.
VtU copy.   33116

Vermont. Laws, Statutes, etc., 1798.
An Act Establishing Fees.
Vergennes, Waites, 1798. 15 pp.
VtU copy.   34919

Vermont. Laws, Statutes, etc., 1798.
Laws of the State of Vermont.
Rutland, Fay, 1798. pp. [405]-621,
[1]-205, [2].
AAS copy.   34925

Vermont. Legislature, 1796.
A List of Arrearages of Taxes, Due from
the Several Towns . . . on the 21st Day of
October, A. D. 1796.
Rutland, Vt., [1796]. 11 pp.
LOC copy.   31489

Vermont. Legislature, 1799.
. . . In General Assembly, Windsor,
November 5th, 1799. Resolved, That the
Senators and Representatives of this State
. . . Propose . . . the following
Amendments to the Constitution of the
United States. . . . In Council . . .
Concurred.
[Windsor, 1799.] Broadside.
AAS copy.   36617

Vermont. Memorial Meeting.
The Illustrious and Beloved George
Washington.
(See 36419.)   36612

Vermont. Session Laws, 1779.
Acts and Laws [June 2, 1779].
[Dresden, 1779]. pp. 111-112.
NYPL ph. copy.   16650

Vermont. Session Laws, 1779.
Acts and Laws [Oct. 1779 - Mar. 1780].
Hartford, 1780. [7] pp.
AAS ph. copy.   17052

Vermont. Session Laws, 1779.
[Votes of the Assembly February session,
1779.
Dresden, 1779.]
(No copy known.)   43727

[Vermont. Session Laws, 1780.
Acts and Laws . . . March 8th, A. D. 1780.
Hartford, 1780. 5 pp.]
(This is a part of 17052, q.v.)   17053

Vermont. Session Laws, 1780.
Acts and Laws . . . Passed Oct. 1780 [
June 1781].
[Westminster, 1781.] [16] pp.
(This is apparently the item described by
Evans.)
AAS copy.   17054

Vermont. Session Laws, 1780.
. . . Acts and Laws, Passed . . . October,
1780.
[Westminster, 1781.] pp. 125-128.
VtSL copy.   44076

Vermont. Session Laws, 1781.
Acts and Laws . . . February 1781.
Westminster, [1781]. [11] pp.
VtSL copy.   17399

Vermont. Session Laws, 1781.
[Acts and Laws . . . April 1781.

Westminster, Spooner & Green, 1781.] 2
pp.
(McCorison 46; no copy known.)   44075

Vermont. Session Laws, 1781.
Acts and Laws . . . April 1781.
[Westminster], 1781. [4] pp.
AAS copy.   17400

Vermont. Sesson Laws, 1781.
Acts and Laws . . . June 1781.
[Westminster, 1781.] [12] pp.
AAS copy.   17401

Vermont. Session Laws, 1781.
Acts and Laws . . . October 1781.
[Westminster, 1781.] [4] pp.
AAS copy.   17402

[Vermont, Session Laws, 1782.
Acts and Laws . . . January, 1782.
Westminster, Spooner & Green, 1782.]
(Printing assumed by Evans.)   17778

Vermont. Session Laws, 1782.
Acts and Laws [Feb. 15, 1782 - Feb. 27,
1783.
Windsor, Hough & Spooner, 1783. 12 pp.
AAS copy.   44488

Vermont. Session Laws, 1782.
Revised Laws [June 21 - Oct. 24, 1782].
[Bennington, 1783.] 38 pp.
AAS copy.   18276

Vermont. Session Laws, 1783.
Acts and Laws. . . . Passed by the General
Assembly . . . at . . . Windsor, February
1783.
[Windsor, 1783.] [6] pp.
AAS copy.   18274

Vermont. Session Laws, 1783.
Acts and Laws. . . . Passed by the General
Assembly . . . at Westminster, October,
1783.
Windsor, 1784. 10 pp.
AAS copy.   18275

Vermont. Session Laws, 1783.
Acts and Laws [Oct. 17 - 23, 1783].
Windsor, Vt., Hough & Spooner, 1784.
pp. 39-46.
AAS copy.   44615

Vermont. Session Laws, 1784.
Acts and Laws, Passed . . . in February &
March, 1784.
Windsor, 1784. 15 pp.
AAS copy.   18852

Vermont. Session Laws, 1784.
Acts and Laws [Mar. 3 - 9, 1784].
Windsor, Vt., Hough & Spooner, 1784.
pp. 49-54.
AAS copy.   44618

Vermont. Session Laws, 1784.
. . . Acts and Laws, Passed by the General
Assembly . . . at Rutland, in October,
1784.
Windsor, 1785. 12 pp.
AAS ph. copy.   19340

Vermont. Session Laws, 1785.
Acts and Laws, Passed by the General
Assembly. . . . at Windsor, in October,
1784.
[Windsor, 1785.] 9 pp.
AAS ph. copy.   19342

Vermont. Session Laws, 1785.
Acts and Laws . . . Passed . . . at Norwich,
in June, 1785.
Windsor, 1785. 7 pp.
VtU copy.   19341

Vermont. Session Laws, 1786.
Acts and Laws . . . Passed . . . in October,
1786.
Bennington, Haswell & Russell, 1786. [12]
pp.
AAS copy.   45006

Vermont. Session Laws, 1786.
Acts and Laws . . . Passed . . . in October,
1786.
[Windsor, 1786.] 20 pp.
AAS copy.   45007

Vermont. Session Laws, 1787.
Statutes . . . Passed . . . in February and
March, 1787.

Windsor, 1787. 171 pp.
AAS copy.   20827

Vermont. Session Laws, 1787.
Acts and Laws. . . . Passed . . . October,
1787.
[Windsor, 1787.] 16 pp.
AAS copy.   20828

Vermont. Session Laws, 1788.
Acts and Laws. . . . October, 1788.
[Windsor, 1788.] 28 pp.
AAS copy.   21540

Vermont. Session Laws, 1789.
Acts and Laws. . . . October, 1789.
[Windsor, 1789.] 19 pp.
AAS copy.   22217

Vermont. Session Laws, 1790.
Acts and Laws. . . . October, 1790.
[Windsor, 1790.] 11 pp.
AAS copy.   23013

Vermont. Session Laws, 1791.
Acts and Laws . . . January, 1791.
Bennington, Haswell, [1791]. 28 pp.
AAS copy.   23933

Vermont. Session Laws, 1791.
Acts and Laws . . . 1791.
Windsor, Spooner, [1791]. 43 pp.
AAS copy.   23934

Vermont. Session Laws, 1792.
Acts and Laws, Passed . . . in October,
1792.
Rutland, Haswell, [1792]. 95 pp.
AAS copy.   24955

Vermont. Session Laws, 1793.
Act and Laws Passed . . . October [1793].
Windsor, Vt., Spooner, 1793. 70 pp.
AAS copy.   26376

Vermont. Session Laws, 1794.
Acts and Laws Passed . . . October, 1794.
Bennington, Haswell, [1794]. 171 pp.
AAS copy.   27993

Vermont. Session Laws, 1795.
Acts and Laws, Passed . . . October 1795.
[Bennington, Haswell, 1796.] 77, [6] pp.
(Issued as a continuation of 23939.)
AAS copy.   48003

Vermont. Session Laws, 1795.
Acts and Laws, Passed . . . October, One
Thousand Seven Hundred and
Ninety-Five.
Rutland, [1795]. 166 pp.
AAS copy.   29787

Vermont. Session Laws, 1796.
Acts and Laws, Passed . . . October, One
Thousand Seven Hundred and Ninety-Six.
Bennington, Haswell, 1796. 185 pp.
AAS copy.   31486

Vermont. Session Laws, 1797.
Acts and Laws . . . February, A.D. One
Thousand Seven Hundred and
Ninety-Seven.
Bennington, Haswell, 1797. 100 pp.
LOC copy.   33117

Vermont. Session Laws, 1797.
Acts and Laws . . . October, One
Thousand Seven Hundred and
Ninety-Seven.
Rutland, Fay, 1797. [2], 110 pp.
LOC copy.   33118

[Vermont. Session Laws, 1797.
Acts and Laws . . . October, One
Thousand Seven Hundred and
Ninty-Seven.
Rutland, Fay, 1798. 110 pp.]
(A ghost of 33118, q. v.)   34920

Vermont. Session Laws, 1798.
Acts and Laws Passed . . . October One
Thousand Seven Hundred and Ninety
Eight.
Bennington, Haswell, 1799. 141, [4] pp.
AAS copy.   36613

Vermont. Session Laws, 1799.
Acts and Laws, Passed . . . October, A. D.
One Thousand Seven Hundred &
Ninety-Nine.
Rutland, Vt., [1799]. 133 pp.
AAS copy.   36614

Vermont. Session, 1800.
Acts and Laws Passed . . . October,
M,DCCC.
[Bennington], Haswell, [1800]. 159 pp.
AAS copy. 38927

Vermont. State's Attorney.
The Several States' Attorneys in
Account. . . . October 25th, 1796.
[Rutland, 1796.] Broadside.
(Not located, 1968.) 48004

Vermont. Supreme Executive Council,
1783.
A Copy of a Remonstrance of the Council.
Hartford, Hudson & Goodwin, 1783. 20
pp.
AAS copy. 18278

Vermont. Treasurer, 1782.
The Treasurer's Address to the
Legislature, in June last. . . . August 15,
1781.
Westminster, Spooner, 1782. 12 pp.
NYPL ph. copy. 44284

Vermont. Treasurer, 1783.
The Treasurer takes this Method . . . May
27, 1783.
[Windsor? 1783.] Broadside.
NYHS copy. 44489

Vermont. Treasurer, 1790.
. . . To [blank] Constable of [blank] in
the County of Windham. . . . October,
1790.
n.p., [1790]. Broadside.
VtHS copy. 46081

Vermont. Treasurer, 1794.
. . . To [blank] First Constable of the
County of [blank]. . . . Rutland . . . 1794.
[Rutland? 1794.] Broadside.
(Not located, 1968.) 47312

[Vermont. Treasurer, 1796.
The State of Vermont, in Account Current
with the Hon. Samuel Mattocks as
Treasurer, from September 15, 1795, to
September 15th, 1796.
[Rutland, 1796.] Broadside.]
(The origin of this entry is unknown.)
31490

Vermont. Treasurer, 1799.
State of Vermont, Treasurer's Office, June
2, 1799. To the Sheriff of the County of
[blank].
[Rutland? 1799.] Broadside.
(Not located, 1968.) 48987

Vermont. Treasurer, 1800.
General List . . . for the Year 1800. . . .
Middlebury, Oct. 29, 1800.
n.p., n.d. [11] pp.
(The only reported copy is not now to be
found.) 38930

Vermont. Treaties, etc., 1781.
Articles of Union . . . February 1781.
[Westminster, Spooner & Green, 1781.] 3
pp.
Plainfield, N.H., Town Clerk copy. 44077

Vermont. University.
. . . The Subscribers for Building a College
at Burlington. . . . Burlington, September
20th, 1800.
n.p., n.d. Broadside.
VtU copy. 38933

The Vermont Almanack, for . . . 1793.
Vermont, Haswell, in Bennington and
Rutland. [24] pp.
(Only copy is imperfect.)
AAS copy. 46658

The Vermont Almanac, and Register, for
. . . 1795 [by Levi Hackley].
Windsor, Spooner. [60] pp.
AAS copy. 27079

The Vermont Almanac . . . for . . . 1796
[by Samuel Williams, 1743-1817].
Vermont, Kirkaldie. [54] pp.
(No perfect copy located.)
AAS copy. 29895

The Vermont Almanac and Register, for
. . . 1797 [by Samuel Williams,
1743-1817].
Rutland, Vt. [60] pp.
NYHS copy. 31637

The Vermont Almanac, for . . . 1797.
Rutland, Vt., [Hutchins]. [24] pp.
VtU copy. 48005

The Vermont Almanac for . . . 1798 [by
Samuel Williams, 1743-1817].
Rutland. [36] pp.
(The only copy located is imperfect.)
AAS copy. 33228

The Vermont Almanac . . . for . . . 1799
[by Samuel Williams, 1743-1817].
Rutland, Walker. [44] pp.
VtSL copy. 35031

The Vermont Almanac and Register, for
. . . 1800 [by Samuel Williams,
1743-1817].
Rutland, Vt. [36] pp.
AAS copy. 36723

Vermont Convention, 1774.
The Proceedings of the Convention . . . of
the New-Hampshire Settlers.
Hartford, Watson, 1775. 17 pp.
VtSL copy. 42968

Vermont Gazette.
Bennington, March 24, 1800. Sir, The
Establishment of the Press. . . .
[Bennington, 1800.] Broadside.
(Not located, 1968.) 49178

Vermont Gazette.
To the Republicans of the Western
District. . . . Feb. 13, 1800.
[Bennington, 1800.] Broadside.
(Not located, 1968.) 49179

[Vermont Gazetteer.
Westminster, Spooner, 1782.]
(McCorison 55; no copy known.) 44282

[The Vermont Primer, or Young Child's
Guide to the English Language.
Bennington, 1785.]
(McCorison 108; no copy known.) 44824

Vermonters Unmasked [by Charles
Phelps, 1715-1789].
[Albany, 1782.] 12 pp.
VtU copy. 17674

[Vernon, Edward, 1684-1757.
(D. N. B.)
The Genuine Speech.
Boston, Kneeland & Green, 1741.]
("Just published," Boston Gazette, Nov.
3, 1741.) 4830

Verplanck, Isaac.
Advertisement. . . . Albany, Sept. 2, 1772.
[Albany, 1772.] Broadside.
NYPL ph. copy. 42379

[Verschiedene Alte und Neuere
Geschichten.
Germantown, 1744.]
(Seidensticker, p. 24.) 5503

[Verschiedene Alter und Neuere
Geschichten. . . . Zweite Auflage.
Germantown, 1748.]
(Adv. by Sower May 16, 1748.) 6258

Verschiedene alte und neuere
Geschichten.
Germantown, 1755. 201 pp.
AAS copy. 7582

Verschiedene Alter und Neuere
Geschichten.
Chestnuthill, Saur, 1792. 168 pp.
PSL copy. 24961

Verschiedene Christliche Wahreiten [by
Christopher Sower, 1693-1758].
Germantown, 1748. 32 pp.
HSP copy. 6233

Verschiedene Sympathetische und
Geheime Kunst-Stücke.
Offenbach am Mayn [Reading, Pa.?],
Gedruckt in der Calender-Fabrike, 1790.
16 pp.
(Only known copy is imperfect.)
LCP copy. 46802

A Verse, Occasioned by Seeing the
North-Spinning, in Boston.
Boston, 1769. Broadside.
MHS copy. 42017

A Verse Occasioned by the Late Horrid
Massacre in King-Street. You True Sons
of Liberty. . . .
[Boston, 1770?] Broadside.
MHS ph. copy. 42179

Verses Addressed by the Carrier to the
Subscribers of the New-York Morning
Post. . . . January 1, 1790.
[New York, 1790.] Broadside.
NYHS copy. 46083

[Verses Addressed to Mr. Elisha Thomas.
Portsmouth, Osborne, 1788.]
(Entry from an adv.) 21545

Verses, Composed and Sung at Trenton.
n.p., [1800]. Broadside.
(Also entered as 38668, q. v.) 38934

Verses, Composed by a Young Lady, on
the Death of Mrs. Clarissa
Huntington. . . . July 11th, 1796.
[Hartford, 1796.] Broadside.
CHS copy. 48006

Verses, Composed on the Death of Eight
Young Men . . . April 28th, 1790.
[Newburyport? 1790.] Broadside.
AAS copy. 46084

Verses for the New-Year, 1787, by the
Boy who Carries about the Newport
Mercury.
[Newport, 1785.] Broadside.
RIHS copy. 45187

[Verses for the New Year 1788, for the
Benefit of the Persons who carry the
Pennsylvania Packet.
[Philadelphia, 1788.] Broadside.]
(The unique copy located by Evans is not
now to be found.) 21380

Verses for the New Year's Day, 1789.
Addressed to the Customers of the
Connecticut Courant.
[Hartford, 1789.] Broadside.
NYHS copy. 45733

Verses for the Year 1789, Addressed to
the Subscribers for the Daily Advertiser.
[New York, 1789.] Broadside.
NYPL copy. 45734

Verses for the Year 1790. Addressed to
the Generous Subscribers of the
New-York Weekly Museum.
[New York, 1790.] Broadside.
AAS copy. 46085

Verses Made on the Sudden Death of Six
Young Women . . . July 23, 1782.
n.p., n.d. Broadside.
AAS copy. 19443

Verses made on the Sudden Death of Six
Young Women . . . Drowned July 13,
1782.
Newport, Barber, [1782?]. Broadside.
(The only known copy is mutilated.)
Providence Public Library copy. 44285

Verses made on the Sudden Death of Six
Young Women . . . July 13, 1782.
[Newport], Farnsworths, [1798?]
Broadside.
RIHS copy. 48745

Verses Occasioned by Reading the
Answer of the President [by Jonathan
Mitchell Sewall, 1748-1808].
Boston, 1797. 7 pp.
AAS copy. 32823

The Verses of the News-Carrier, of the
Daily Advertiser . . . on the New Year,
1790.
[New York, 1790.] Broadside.
NYHS copy. 46086

Verses of the Post, to the Generous
Subscribers for the Poughkeepsie
Advertiser. . . . January 1st, 1787.
n.p., n.d. Broadside.
AAS copy. 45188

Verses of the Printer's Boy [of the
Maryland Gazette]. . . . January 1, 1786.
[Baltimore, 1786.] Broadside.
NYPL copy. 45008

The Verses of the Printer's Boy that

Carries about the Pennsylvania Journal, 1743/4.
[Philadelphia, Bradford, 1744.]
Broadside.
HSP copy.   5478

Verses, of the Printers Lads, who Carry the Pennsylvania Gazette. . . . Ode on the New-Year. January 1, 1768.
[Philadelphia, 1768.] Broadside.
LCP copy.   11031

Verses on Doctor Mayhew's Book [by John Aplin].
Providence, 1763. 19 pp.
AAS copy.   9327

Verses, on the New Year, 1787. Humbly Addressed by the Lads who Distribute the Independent Gazetteer. . . . Philadelphia, January 1, 1787.
[Philadelphia, 1787.] Broadside.
AAS copy.   45189

Verses on the New-Year, January 2, 1792. Addressed to the Pennsylvania Mercury.
[Philadelphia, 1792.] Broadside.
NYHS copy.   46659

. . . . Verses on the Sudden and Awful Death of Mrs. Rebecca Giles . . . the 17th Day of June, 1773 [Dated Salem, July 25, 1773].
[Salem, 1773.] Broadside.
AAS copy.   42525

Verses, Written on the Death of Mr. Benjamin Tubbs, of Hebron - Who Died . . . January 15th, 1799.
n.p., n.d. Broadside.
NYPL copy.   36621

A Versification of President Washington's . . . Farewell Address [by Jonathan Mitchell Sewall, 1748-1808].
Portsmouth, N.H., Peirce, 1798. 54 pp.
AAS copy.   34532

Die Verstossung der Französischen Freyheit und Gleichheit.
Lancaster, Albrecht, 1798. 36 pp.
LCP copy.   48746

Very Important. Office of the Philadelphia Gazette. June 18, 1798.
[Philadelphia, 1798.] Broadside.
(The unique copy is mislaid.)   34363

A Very Needful Caution [by Cotton Mather, 1663-1728].
Boston, 1707. 60 pp.
AAS copy.   1318

A Very Surprising Narrative.
See
Panther, Abraham.   38935

Vesey, William, 1674-1746.
(Sibley, IV, 173-179.)
A Sermon Preached in Trinity Church.
New York, 1709. 22 pp.
NYHS copy.   1436

The Vial Poured upon the Sea [by Cotton Mather, 1663-1728].
Boston, Fleet for Belknap, 1726. [2], 51 pp.
MHS copy.   2779

Viaud, Pierre.
The Surprizing yet Real and True Voyages . . . of . . . Pierre Viaud [by Jean Gaspard Dubois-Fontanelle, 1737-1812].
Philadelphia, Bell, 1774. [1], xii, 144, [4], 108, [2] pp.
(The AAS has another copy with the plate printed in red.)
AAS copy.   13257

The Vicar of Wakefield [by Oliver Goldsmith, 1728-1774].
Philadelphia, Mentz, 1772. 2 vol. in 1. 180 pp.
AAS copy.   12405

The Vicar of Wakefield [by Oliver Goldsmith, 1728-1774].
Newburyport, [1780]. 156 pp.
AAS copy.   16787

The Vicar of Wakefield. . . . Vol I [-II]
[by Oliver Goldsmith, 1728-1774].

Norwich, [Ct.], Bushnell, 1791. 344 pp.
AAS copy.   46184

The Vicar of Wakefield. . . . In Two Volumes [by Oliver Goldsmith, 1728-1774].
Philadelphia, Young, 1791. 140; 134, [2] pp.
AAS copy.   23417

The Vicar of Wakefield [by Oliver Goldsmith, 1728-1774].
Providence, Wheeler, 1792. 226 pp.
AAS copy.   24361

The Vicar of Wakefield. . . . Two Volumes [in one] [by Oliver Goldsmith, 1728-1774].
Philadelphia, Young, 1795. 140, 134, [2] pp.
AAS copy.   28759

The Vicar of Wakefield. . .. Two Volumes [in one] [by Oliver Goldsmith, 1728-1774].
Worcester, Thomas, 1795. 267 pp.
AAS copy.   28758

Vice in its Proper Shape. . . . First Worcester Edition.
Worcester, Thomas, 1789. 128 pp.
AAS copy.   22221

[Victor, H. B.
The Compleat Instructor for the Violin. . . .
Philadelphia, 1778.]
("Just published," Pa. Ledger, Apr. 4, 1778.)   16152

Victorina [by Cotton Mather, 1663-1728].
Boston, Green for Henchman, 1717. [2], viii, 86 pp.
AAS copy.   1911

Viets, Roger, 1738-1811.
A Sermon, on the Duty of Attending. . . .
Hartford, Hudson & Goodwin, 1789. 43 pp.
AAS copy.   22223

Viets, Roger, 1738-1811.
A Serious Address and Farewell.
Hartford, Hudson & Goodwin, 1787. 12 pp.
BPL copy.   20835

Viets, Roger, 1738-1811.
A Sermon, Preached before the . . . Masons.
Hartford, [Ct.], Hudson & Goodwin, 1800. 12 pp.
CHS copy.   38936

Viets, Roger, 1738-1811.
A Sermon, Preached in St. Peter's Church.
Hartford, [Ct.], Hudson & Goodwin, 1800. 15 pp.
CHS copy.   38937

Viets, Roger, 1738-1811.
A Sermon, Preached in St. Andrew's.
Hartford, Hudson & Goodwin, 1787. 15 pp.
BPL copy.   20836

A View of a Christian Church [by Jacob Green, 1722-1790].
Chatham, 1781. viii, 62 pp.
PrU copy.   17553

[A View of the Administration of the Federal Government.
Washington, Ky., Hunter & Beaumont, 1798.]
(Imprint assumed by Evans from adv.
"Just published by the Printers hereof," Frankfort Palladium, Sept. 18, 1798.)   34928

A View of the Calumnies Lately Spread.
[Philadelphia, 1729.] 4 pp.
APS copy.   3227

A View of the Calvinistic Clubs in the United States [by John Cosens Ogden, 1751-1800].
[Litchfield, Ct., 1799?] 23 pp.
AAS copy.   36008

A View of the Controversy between Great-Britain and her Colonies [by

Samuel Seabury, bp., 1729-1796].
New York, Rivington, 1774. 37, [2] pp.
AAS copy.   13603

A View of the New England Illuminati [by John Cosens Ogden, 1751-1800].
Philadelphia, Carey, 1799. 20 pp.
APS copy.   36009

A View of the New-England Illuminati. . . . Second Edition [by John Cosens Ogden, 1751-1800].
Philadelphia, Carey, 1799. 20 pp.
AAS copy.   36010

A View of the Principles, Operations and Probable Effects of the Funding System of Pennsylvania.
Philadelphia, Aitken, 1788. 23 pp.
JCB copy.   21546

A View of the Proposed Constitution of the United States [by John Nicholson, 1760?-1800].
Philadelphia, Aitken, 1787. 37 pp.
BA copy.   20591

[A View of the Quarterly Diminution of the Funded Six Per Cent Stocks of the United States.
Boston, Russell, 1796.]
(Imprint assumed by Evans from advs.)   31493

A View of the Scandals Lately Spread.
[Philadelphia, 1729 ?] 4 pp.
APS copy.   3228

A View of the Title to Indiana [by Samuel Wharton, 1732-1800].
[Philadelphia, 1775.] 24 pp.
PrU copy.   42983

View of the Title to Indiana [by Samuel Wharton, 1732-1800].
Philadelphia, Styner & Cist, 1776. 46 pp.
AAS copy.   15219

Vigilantius [by Cotton Mather, 1663-1728].
Boston, 1706. [2], 38 pp.
VaU copy.   1265

Vigilius [by Cotton Mather, 1663-1728].
Boston, Franklin, 1719. [2], 14 pp.
AAS copy.   2048

[The Village Harmony, or Youth's Assistant to Sacred Music.
Exeter, Ranlet, 1795.]
(Offered C. W. Unger, List 980, Item 49.)   29793

The Village Harmony, or Youth's Assistant to Sacred Music. . . . Second Edition.
Exeter, Ranlet, 1796. 187, [1] pp.
(The only copy known is defective.)
BrU copy.   31494

[The Village Harmony, or Youth's Assistant to Sacred Musick. . . . Third Edition.
Exeter, Ranlet, 1797.]
(Assumed by Evans from the sequence of editions.)   33123

The Village Harmony: or, Youth's Assistant to Sacred Music. . . . Fourth Edition.
Exeter, Ranlet, 1798. [2], 201, [1] pp.
AAS copy.   34930

The Village Harmony: or, Youth's Assistant to Sacred Music. . . . Fifth Edition.
Exeter, Ranlet, 1800. [2], 205, [1] pp.
AAS copy.   38938

[The Village Holiday. Song.
New York, Gilfert, 1795.]
(See Sonneck-Upton, p. 443.)   29794

The Village Merchant: a Poem [by Philip Morin Freneau, 1752-1832].
Philadelphia, Hoff & Derrick, 1794. 16 pp.
AAS copy.   27019

The Village Orphan: a Tale for Youth.
Philadelphia, Thompson for Thackara, 1800. [2], 152 pp.
AAS copy.   38940

[The Village Recruit. Song.
New York, Gilfert, 1798.]
(Imprint assumed by Evans from adv.
"just published.")   34932

The Village Wedding.
Boston, Spotswood, [179?]. front. 22, 28
pp.
LOC copy.   45802

[Villiers, R.
Richmond Garden, a Poem.
Richmond, 1788?]
(Adv. in State Gazette of N. C., Apr. 16,
1789.)   21547

Vinal, William, 1718-1781.
(Sibley, X.)
A Sermon on the Accursed Thing.
Newport, 1755. 25 pp.
LOC copy.   7583

Vinall, John, 1736-1823.
The Preceptor's Assistant.
Boston, Edes for Thomas & Andrews,
1792. 288 pp.
AAS copy.   24962

[Vincent, Nathaniel, 1639?-1697.
The Day of Grace.
Boston, 1722. 160 pp.]
(Probably a ghost of 3114, q.v.)   2395

[Vincent, Nathaniel, 1639?-1697.
(D. N. B.)
The Day of Grace.
Boston, 1725. 143 pp.]
(A Haven entry which has never been
verified.)   2714

Vincent, Nathaniel, 1639?-1697.
(D. N. B.)
The Day of Grace.
Boston, Butler, 1728. [4], 156 pp.
AAS copy.   3114

Vincent, Nathaniel, 1639?-1697.
A Discourse on Forgiveness.
Boston, 1722. [4], 36, [1] pp.
AAS copy.   2394

Vincent, Nathaniel, 1639?-1697.
The Spirit of Prayer. . . . Sixth Edition.
Boston, Green for Boone, 1702. 215 pp.
BA copy.   1098

Vincent, Thomas, 1634-1678.
Christ's Certain and Sudden Appearance.
Boston, Green for Harris, 1690. [4], 220
pp.
(The unique copy is in poor condition.)
AAS copy.   39280

Vincent, Thomas, 1634-1678.
Christ's Certain and Sudden Appearance.
. . . Tenth Edition.
Boston, Allen for Gray, 1718. [4], 266 pp.
AAS copy.   39693

[Vincent, Thomas, 1634-1678.
(D. N. B.)
Christ's Certain and Sudden Appearance.
Philadelphia, Franklin, 1740.]
(Adv. in 4633.)   4615

Vincent, Thomas, 1634-1678.
(D. N. B.)
Companion for Communicants.
Boston, Gray, 1730. [2], 34 pp.
AAS copy.   3367

Vincent, Thomas, 1634-1678.
(D. N. B.)
An Explicatory Catechism.
Boston, 1711. [8], 327, [1], 4 pp.
AAS copy.   1531

Vincent, Thomas, 1634-1678.
(D. N. B.)
Explicatory Catechism.
Boston, Henchman, Phillips, and
Hancock, 1729. [2], viii, 315 pp.
AAS copy.   3229

[Vincent, Thomas], 1634-1678.
Gods Terrible Voice.
Cambridge, [Mass.], Green, 1667. 31 pp.
HC copy.   39174

[Vincent, Thomas], 1634-1678.
(D. N. B.)
God's Terrible Voice.

Cambridge, 1668. 31 pp.
AAS copy.   132

Vincent, Thomas, 1634-1678.
God's Terrible Voice.
New London, Green, 1770. 28 pp.
LOC copy.   11908

Vincent, Thomas, 1634-1678.
God's Terrible Voice.
New London, Seth White, 1770. 28 pp.
(A tp. variant of 11908, q. v. for text.)
CHS copy.   42179a

[Vincent, Thomas, 1634-1678.
God's Terrible Voice in the City.
Windham, Byrne, 1790. 48 pp.]
(Entry from the defective Brinley copy;
ed. uncertain.)   23942

Vincent, Thomas, 1634-1678.
[God's Terrible Voice in the City.
Windham, Byrne, 1795.] 46 pp.
(The only known copy lacks the tp.)
CHS copy.   29795

Vincent, Thomas, 1634-1678.
The True Christian's Love.
Boston, Draper for Henchman, 1739. [6],
220 pp.
(Both known copies are poor.)
AAS copy.   40178

A Vindication of an Association.
Portsmouth, Fowle, 1758. 39, [1] pp.
AAS copy.   8272

The Vindication. Of James Alexander.
New York, 1733. [2], 20 pp.
NYPL copy.   3848

A Vindication of Mr. Randolph's
Resignation [by Edmund Randolph,
1753-1813].
Philadelphia, Smith, 1795. 103 pp.
AAS copy.   29385

A Vindication of Mr. Randolph's
Resignation [by Edmund Randolph,
1753-1813].
Philadelphia, Smith, 1795. 103, [2] pp.
AAS copy.   29384

A Vindication of New-England [by
Increase Mather, 1639-1723].
[Boston, 1690?] [2], 27 pp.
(Attributed to Charles Morton by Holmes,
Increase Mather, II, 615, 635; but the text
makes this questionable.)
AAS copy.   452

A Vindication of the Appendix to the
Sober Remarks [by Thomas Foxcraft,
1697-1769].
Boston, Green, 1725. [4], 59 pp.
AAS copy.   2636

A Vindication of the Bank of Credit.
[Boston], 1714. [2], 20, 22 pp.
AAS copy.   1685

A Vindication of the Bishop of Landaff's
Sermon [by Charles Inglis, 1734-1816].
New York, Holt, 1768. viii, 82 pp.
AAS copy.   10934

A Vindication of the British Colonies [by
James Otis, 1725-1783].
Boston, Edes & Gill, 1765. 32 pp.
AAS copy.   10117

A Vindication of the Conduct and
Character of John Adams.
New York, Totten for Longworth and
Burtsell, 1800. 24 pp.
AAS copy.   38941

A Vindication of the Conduct of Thomas
Jefferson. . . . Richmond, April 12th, 1800.
[Richmond, 1800.] [7] pp.
(A part of 38943, q. v.)   38942

A Vindication of the Divine Authority.
[Boston, 1716?] [2], 28 pp.
(Holmes, Increase Mather, II, 615-618.)
AAS copy.   957

A Vindication of the General Ticket Law.
Richmond, [Va.], Pleasants, 1800. 23,
[1], 7 pp.
LOC copy.   38943

A Vindication of the Ministers of Boston.

Boston, Green for Gerrish, 1722. [2], 14
pp.
AAS copy.   2396

A Vindication of the New-North-Church
in Boston [by Peter Thacher, 1677-1739].
Boston, Franklin for Henchman, 1720.
[2], 14 pp.
BA copy.   2186

A Vindication of the Religious Society
Called Quakers.
Mount-Holly, [N. J.] Ustick, 1800. 8 pp.
(Also entered as 37475, q. v.)   38944

A Vindication of the Remarks of one in
the Country [by Edward Wigglesworth,
1693-1765].
Boston, Kneeland for Henchman, 1720. 20
pp.
AAS copy.   2190

A Vindication of the Reverend
Commission.
Philadelphia, Bradford, 1735. [2], 63 pp.
YC copy.   3971

A Vindication of the Reverend Mr.
George Whitefield.
Boston, Fleet, 1745. 15 pp.
AAS copy.   5704

A Vindication of the Rights of Brutes [by
Thomas Taylor, 1758-1835].
Boston, 1795. 58 pp.
AAS copy.   29613

[A Vindication of the Rights of Election.
New York, Inslee & Car, 1771.]
(From an adv.)   12263

A Vindication of Thomas Jefferson [by
DeWitt Clinton, 1769-1828].
New York, Denniston, 1800. 47 pp.
AAS copy.   37195

Vining, Ebenezer.
A Funeral Sermon.
Conway, Mass., Leonards, 1798. 11 pp.
AAS copy.   34933

Vining, John, 1758-1802.
Eulogium. . . . In Commemoration of . . .
Washington.
Philadelphia, Ormrod, 1800. 20 pp.
AAS copy.   38946

Vining, John, 1758-1802.
Eulogium. . . . In Commemoration of . . .
Washington.
Philadelphia, Ormrod, 1800. 32 pp.
(No copy of such an ed. found.)   38947

Virginia (Colony) Association, 1770.
The Association Entered into. . . . 22nd of
June, 1770.
[Williamsburg, 1770.] Broadside.
LOC copy.   11911

Virginia (Colony) Committee of
Correspondence, 1775.
Williamsburg, Saturday, April 29, 1775.
Late last night. . . .
[Williamsburg], Purdie, [1775]. [2] pp.
LOC copy.   14602

Virginia (Colony) Committee of Safety,
1775.
Williamsburg, October 26. Whereas Lord
Dunmore. . . .
Baltimore, Dunlap, [1775]. Broadside.
(No copy could be located.)   42969

Virginia (Colony) Convention, Aug. 1,
1774.
At a Very Full Meeting of Delegates. . . .
[Williamsburg, 1774.] Broadside.
LOC ph. copy.   42739

Virginia (Colony) Convention, Aug. 1-6,
1774.
Instructions for the Deputies Appointed
to Meet in General Congress.
[Williamsburg, 1774?] 4 pp.
(A ghost of E13057, q. v.)   42529

Virginia (Colony) Convention, March 20,
1775.
At a Convention of Delegates for the
Counties . . . at . . . Richmond . . . the 20th
of March, 1775.
Williamsburg, Purdie, [1775]. 4 pp.
LOC copy.   14590

Virginia (Colony) Convention, March 20, 1775.
Journal of the Proceedings.
Williamsburg, Dixon & Hunter, 1775. 28 pp.
NYPL copy. 14594

Virginia (Colony) Convention, March 20, 1775.
The Proceedings of the Convention . . . at Richmond . . . on the 20th of March 1775.
Williamsburg, Purdie, [1775]. [2], 20 pp.
JCB copy. 14597

Virginia (Colony) Convention, July 17, 1775.
Ordinances Passed at a Convention held at . . . Richmond.
Williamsburg, Purdie, [1775]. 51 pp.
NYPL copy. 14595

Virginia (Colony) Convention, July 17, 1775.
The Proceedings of the Convention . . . at Richmond . . . the 17th of July, 1775.
Williamsburg, Purdie, [1775]. 59 pp.
NYPL copy. 14598

Virginia (Colony) Convention, December 1, 1775.
Ordinances Passed at a Convention held in . . . Williamsburg.
Williamsburg, Purdie, [1775]. 34 pp.
NYPL copy. 14596

Virginia (Colony) Council, 1734.
The Humble Address of the Council [in reply to Lt. Gov. Gooch's Speech of Aug. 22, 1734].
[Williamsburg, Parks, 1734.] [2] pp.
LOC ph. copy. 40065

Virginia (Colony) Council, 1736.
The Humble Address of the Council.
[Williamsburg, 1736.] [2] pp.
LOC ph. copy. 40106

Virginia (Colony) Council, 1738.
To . . . William Gooch . . . the Humble Address of the Council . . . the 4th Day of November, 1738.
[Williamsburg, Parks, 1738.] [2] pp.
LOC ph. copy. 40151

Virginia (Colony) Council, 1740.
The Humble Address of the Council [in reply to the Lt.-Gov.'s address of May 22, 1740] Sir, We His Majesty's most Dutiful. . . .
[Williamsburg, 1740.] [2] pp.
LOC ph. copy. 40215

Virginia (Colony) Council, 1740.
The Humble Address of the Council [in reply to the Lieutenant-Governor's speech of Aug. 21, 1740].
[Williamsburg, 1740.] [2] pp.
LOC copy. 40216

Virginia (Colony) Council, 1742.
The Humble Address of the Council [in reply to Gooch's address of May 6, 1742].
[Williamsburg, 1742.] [2] pp.
LOC copy. 40287

Virginia (Colony) Council, 1744.
The Humble Address of the Council [in reply to Gooch's speech of Sept. 4, 1744].
[Williamsburg, 1744.] 2 pp.
LOC ph. copy. 40353

Virginia (Colony) Council, 1746.
To the Honourable William Gooch . . . the Humble Address of the Council [replying to his Speech of Feb. 20, 1745/6].
[Williamsburg, 1746.] [2] pp.
LOC ph. copy. 41417

Virginia (Colony) Council, 1747.
To the Honourable William Gooch . . . the Humble Address of the Council [in reply to his speech of Mar. 30, 1747].
[Williamsburg, 1747.] 2 pp.
LOC ph. copy. 40445

Virginia (Colony) Council 1748.
To . . . William Gooch . . . the Humble Address of the Council [to his Speech of Oct. 27, 1748].
[Williamsburg, 1748.] [2] pp.
(No copy at present available.) 40481

Virginia (Colony) Council, 1750.
. . . Thomas Lee . . . Commander in Chief. . . . Whereas Low Jackson . . . is Charged with Coming . . . [Aug. 15, 1750].
[Williamsburg, 1750.] Broadside.
HEH copy. 40572

Virginia (Colony) Council, 1754.
February 16th, 1754. To the Honourable Robert Dinwiddie.
[Williamsburg, Hunter, 1754.] Broadside.
HSP copy. 40721

Virginia (Colony) Council, 1757.
April 16th, 1757. To . . . Robert Dinwiddie . . . the Humble Address of the Council. . . .
[Williamsburg, 1757.] Broadside.
HEH copy. 40943

Virginia (Colony) Council, 1757.
September 22d, 1756. To the Honorable Robert Dinwiddie. . . .
[Williamsburg, 1756.] [2] pp.
HEH copy. 40865

Virginia (Colony) Council, 1758.
September 18, 1758. To . . . Francis Fauquier.
[Williamsburg, 1758.] Broadside.
LOC ph. copy. 41013

Virginia (Colony) Council, 1759.
February 24th, 1759. To . . . Francis Fauquier . . . the Humble Address of the Council.
[Williamsburg, 1759.] Broadside.
LOC ph. copy. 41085

Virginia (Colony) Council, 1762.
April 1, 1762. To . . . Francis Fauquier . . . the Humble Address of the Council.
[Williamsburg, Royle, 1762.] Broadside.
LOC ph. copy. 41318

Virginia (Colony) Council, 1763.
May 20, 1763. To . . . Francis Fauquier . . . the Humble Address of the Council. . . .
[Williamsburg, 1763.] Broadside.
LOC ph. copy. 41418

Virginia (Colony) Council, 1764.
January 14, 1764. To . . . Francis Fauquier . . . the Humble Address.
[Williamsburg, 1764.] Broadside.
LOC ph. copy. 41496

Virginia (Colony) Council, 1764.
October 31, 1764. To . . . Francis Fauquier . . . the Humble Address of the Council.
[Williamsburg, 1764.] Broadside.
LOC ph. copy. 41497

Virginia (Colony) Council, 1766.
November 7, 1766. To . . . . Francis Fauquier . . . the Humble Address of the Council.
[Williamsburg, 1766.] Broadside.
LOC ph. copy. 41665

Virginia (Colony) Council, 1770.
. . . By the Honourable William Nelson. . . . A Proclamation. Whereas by the Death of . . . Baron de Botetourt. . . .
[Williamsburg, 1770.] Broadside.
(Not available for reproduction.)
College of William and Mary copy. 42180

Virginia (Colony) Council, 1771.
To the Honourable William Nelson. . . . The Address of the Council [July 12, 1771].
[Williamsburg, 1771.] 2 pp.
LOC ph. copy. 42292

Virginia (Colony) Council, 1772.
To His Excellency the Right Honourable John Earl of Dunmore [Feb. 10, 1772].
[Williamsburg, 1772.] Broadside.
LOC ph. copy. 42380

Virginia (Colony) Council, 1773.
To His Excellency . . . John Earl of Dunmore . . . the Humble Address of the Council [answering his speech of Mar. 5, 1773].
[Williamsburg, 1773.] Broadside.
LOC ph. copy. 42526

Virginia (Colony) Council. 1774.

To His Excellency . . . John Earl of Dunmore . . . the Humble Address of the Council [in reply to his speech of May 6, 1774].
[Williamsburg, 1774.] Broadside.
LOC ph. copy. 42740

Virginia (Colony) Council, 1775.
To all the Good People of Virginia.
[Williamsburg, 1775.] Broadside.
LOC ph. copy. 42970

Virginia (Colony) Council, 1775.
To His Excellency the Right Hon. John Earl of Dunmore . . . the Humble Address of the Council [in reply to his address of June 1, 1775].
[Williamsburg, 1775.] Broadside.
LOC ph. copy. 42971

Virginia (Colony) General Assembly, 1718.
Some Remarkable Proceedings in the Assembly . . . 1718.
[Philadelphia? 1718?] [4] pp.
PRO copy. 39694

Virginia (Colony) General Assembly, 1772.
Saturday, the 28th of March. . . . A Bill for the more Easy . . . Administration of Justice.
[Williamsburg, 1772.] 6 pp.
(Only known copy imperfect.)
LOC ph. copy. 42381

Virginia (Colony) General Assembly, 1773.
Instructions for the Deputies Appointed to meet in General Congress.
[Williamsburg, 1773.] 4 pp.
LCP copy. 13057

Virginia (Colony) General Assembly.
House of Burgesses, 1732.
The Humble Address of the House . . . to . . . William Gooch. . . . May 20, 1732.
[Williamsburg, 1732.] [2] pp.
PRO copy. 40007

Virginia (Colony) General Asembly.
House of Burgesses, 1738.
To . . . William Gooch. . . . The Humble Address of the . . . Burgesses . . . the 6th Day of November, 1738.
[Williamsburg, Parks, 1738.] [2] pp.
LOC copy. 40153

Virginia (Colony) General Assembly.
House of Burgesses, 1740.
The Humble Address of the Burgesses, met in Assembly [in reply to Gooch's speech of Aug. 21, 1740].
[Williamsburg, 1740.] [2] pp.
LOC ph. copy. 40220

Virginia (Colony) General Assembly.
House of Burgesses, 1742.
The Humble Address of the House. . . . Sir, We his Majesty's most Dutiful. . . . [in reply to Gooch's address of May 6, 1742].
[Williamsburg, 1742.] [2] pp.
LOC copy. 40289

Virginia (Colony) General Assembly.
House of Burgesses, 1744.
The Humble Address of the House [in answer to Gooch's Speech of Sept. 4, 1744].
[Williamsburg, 1744.] 2 pp.
LOC ph. copy. 40355

Virginia (Colony) General Assembly.
House of Burgesses, 1747.
To the Honourable Sir William Gooch . . . the Humble Address of the House [in reply to his speech of Apr. 1, 1747].
[Williamsburg, Parks, 1747.] 2 pp.
LOC ph. copy. 40446

Virginia (Colony) General Assembly.
House of Burgesses, 1748.
To the Honourable Sir William Gooch . . . the Humble Address of the House [replying to his speech of Oct. 27, 1748.]
[Williamsburg, 1748.] Broadside.
LOC ph. copy. 40485

Virginia (Colony) General Assembly.
House of Burgesses, 1757.
April 18th, 1757. To . . . Robert

Dinwiddie . . . the Humble Address of the House.
[Williamsburg, 1757.] Broadside.
HEH copy.   40994

Virginia (Colony) General Assembly.
House of Burgesses, 1758.
September 28, 1758. To . . . Francis Fauquier. . . .
[Williamsburg, 1758.] Broadside.
(Sabin 99924; no copy located.)   41014

Virginia (Colony) General Assembly.
House of Burgesses, 1759.
February 27th, 1759. To the Honorable Francis Fauquier . . . The Humble Address of the House.
[Williamsburg, 1759.] Broadside.
LOC ph. copy.   41088

Virginia (Colony) General Assembly.
House of Burgesses, 1759.
March 6th, 1759. To the Honorable Francis Fauquier . . . the Humble Address of the House.
[Williamsburg, 1759.] Broadside.
LOC ph. copy.   41089

Virginia (Colony) General Assembly.
House of Burgesses, 1762.
April 1, 1762. To the Honourable Francis Fauquier . . . the Humble Address of the House. . . .
[Williamsburg, Royle, 1762.] Broadside.
LOC ph. copy.   41320

Virginia (Colony) General Assembly.
House of Burgesses, 1763.
May 21, 1763. To the Honourable Francis Fauquier . . . the Humble Address of the House.
[Williamsburg, 1763.] [2] pp.
LOC ph. copy.   41420

Virginia (Colony) General Assembly.
House of Burgesses, 1764.
January 16, 1764. To the Honourable Francis Fauquier . . . the Humble Address of the House.
[Williamsburg, 1764.] Broadside.
LOC ph. copy.   41500

Virginia (Colony) General Assembly.
House of Burgesses, 1764.
January 19, 1764. To the Honourable Francis Fauquier . . . the Humble Address of the House.
[Williamsburg, 1764.] Broadside.
LOC ph. copy.   41501

Virginia (Colony) General Assembly.
House of Burgesses, 1764.
November 2, 1764. To the Honorable Francis Fauquier . . . the Humble Address of the House.
[Williamsburg, 1764.] Broadside.
LOC ph. copy.   41502

Virginia (Colony) General Assembly.
House of Burgesses, 1766.
November 14, 1766. To the Honourable Francis Fauquier . . . the Humble Address of the House. . . .
[Williamsburg, 1766.] [2] pp.
LOC ph. copy.   41669

Virginia (Colony) General Assembly.
House of Burgesses, 1768.
To His Excellency the Right Honourable Norborne, Baron de Botetourt . . . the Humble Address of the House.
[Williamsburg, 1768.] Broadside.
(No copy located.)   41893

Virginia (Colony) General Assembly.
House of Burgesses, 1769.
Resolves of the House of Burgesses, Passed the 16th of May, 1769.
Williamsburg, Rind, [1769]. Broadside.
VaSL copy.   11512

Virginia (Colony) General Assembly.
House of Burgesses, 1769.
To His Excellency the . . . Baron de Botetourt. . . . The Humble Address of the House [May 10, 1769].
[Williamsburg, 1769.] Broadside.
LOC ph. copy.   42018

Virginia (Colony) General Assembly.
House of Burgesses, 1769.
Williamsburg, Wednesday, the 17th May, 1769.

Williamsburg, [1769]. [3] pp.
LOC copy.   11513

Virginia (Colony) General Assembly.
House of Burgesses, 1772.
To His Excellency . . . John Earl of Dunmore . . . the Humble Address of the House [Feb. 11, 1772].
[Williamsburg, 1772.] Broadside.
LOC ph. copy.   42383

Virginia (Colony) General Assembly.
House of Burgesses, 1774.
Tuesday, the 24th of May, 14 Geo. III. 1774.
[Williamsburg, 1774.] Broadside.
NYPL copy.   13746

Virginia (Colony) General Assembly.
House of Burgesses, 1775.
The Proceedings of the House . . . Convened . . . June, 1775.
Williamsburg, Purdie, [1775]. 48 pp.
LOC copy.   14599

Virginia (Colony) Governor, 1732.
The Speech of the Honourable William Gooch . . . to the General Assembly [May 18, 1732].
Williamsburg, Parks, 1732. [4] pp.
PRO copy.   40006

Virginia (Colony) Governor, 1734.
The Speech of the Honourable William Gooch . . . the 22d Day of August . . . 1734.
Williamsburg, Parks, 1734. [4] pp.
(One page missing from the only known copy.)
LOC ph. copy.   40066

Virginia (Colony) Governor, 1736.
The Speech of the Honourable William Gooch. . . . I Cannot but Congratulate my self. . . .
[Williamsburg, Parks, 1736.] [2] pp.
PRO copy.   40107

Virginia (Colony) Governor, 1738.
The Speech of . . . William Gooch [Nov. 4, 1738].
[Williamsburg, Parks, 1738.] [2] pp.
LOC ph. copy.   40152

Virginia (Colony) Governor, 1740.
The Speech of the Honourable William Gooch. . . . As I am Entrusted [May 22, 1740]. . . .
[Williamsburg, 1740.] [2] pp.
LOC ph. copy.   40217

Virginia (Colony) Governor, 1740.
The Speech of the Honourable William Gooch [Aug. 21, 1740].
[Williamsburg, 1740.] Broadside.
LOC ph. copy.   40218

Virginia (Colony) Governor, 1742.
The Speech of . . . William Gooch. . . . Gentlemen . . . the Care and Concern of Societies. . . .
[Williamsburg, 1742.] [2] pp.
LOC ph. copy.   40288

Virginia (Colony) Governor, 1744.
The Speech of the Honourable William Gooch [Sept. 4, 1744].
Williamsburg, Parks, 1744. 4 pp.
LOC ph. copy.   40354

Virginia (Colony) Governor, 1748.
The Speech of the Honourable William Gooch [Mar. 30, 1747].
Williamsburg, Parks, 1748. 4 pp.
PRO copy.   40483

Virginia (Colony) Governor, 1748.
The Speech of the Honorable Sir William Gooch. . . . Tho there is not any Thing. . . . [Oct. 27, 1748].
[Williamsburg, 1748.] pp. 3-4, [4].
PRO copy.   40484

Virginia (Colony) Governor, 1759.
The Speech, of a Gentleman of the Council . . . [Mar. 5, 1759].
[Williamsburg, 1759.] Broadside.
LOC copy.   41086

Virginia (Colony) Governor, 1759.
The Speech of the Honorable Francis Fauquier . . . to the General Assembly [Sept. 14, 1759]. . . .

Williamsburg, Hunter, 1759. 4 pp.
LOC ph. copy.   41087

Virginia (Colony) Governor, 1762.
The Speech of the Honourable Francis Fauquier . . . to the General-Assembly . . . the 2d of November 1762.
Williamsburg, Royle, 1762. 4 pp.
LOC copy.   41319

Virginia (Colony) Governor, 1763.
The Speech of the Honourable Francis Fauquier to the General Assembly . . . the 19th of May, 1763.
Williamsburg, Royle, 1763. 4 pp.
LOC ph. copy.   41419

Virginia (Colony) Governor, 1764.
The Speech of the Honourable Francis Fauquier . . . to the General-Assembly . . . January, 1764.
Williamsburg, Royle, 1764. 4 pp.
MHS copy.   41498

Virginia (Colony) Governor, 1764.
The Speech of the Honourable Francis Fauquier . . . to the General Assembly . . . October, 1764.
Williamsburg, Royle, 1764. 4 pp.
LOC ph. copy.   41499

Virginia (Colony) Governor, 1765.
. . . By the Hon. Francis Fauquier. . . . A Proclamation. Whereas a Party of Cherokees. . . . [Dated May 13, 1765.]
[Williamsburg, 1765.] Broadside.
LOC ph. copy.   41593

Virginia (Colony) Governor, 1766.
The Speech of the Honourable Francis Fauquier . . . to the General Assembly, Summoned to be held . . . the 6th of November.
Williamsburg, Purdie & Dixon, 1766. 4 pp.
LOC ph. copy.   41666

Virginia (Colony) Governor, 1766.
The Speech of the Honourable Francis Fauquier . . . to the General Assembly, Summoned to be held . . . the 6th Day of November.
Williamsburg, Rind, [1766]. Broadside.
LOC ph. copy.   41667

Virginia (Colony) Governor, 1769.
. . . By His Excellency the Right Honourable Norborne Baron de Botetourt. . . . A Proclamation. Whereas I have Received Information. . . . [Oct. 19, 1769.]
[Williamsburg, 1769.] Broadside.
LOC ph. copy.   42019

Virginia (Colony) Governor, 1769.
The Speech of His Excellency. . . . Norborne Baron de Botetourt . . . the 7th Day of November, 1769.
[Williamsburg, 1769.] Broadside.
LOC ph. copy.   42020

Virginia (Colony) Governor, 1772.
The Speech of His Excellency . . . John Earl of Dunmore . . . the 10th Day of February, 1772.
[Williamsburg, 1772.] Broadside.
LOC ph. copy.   42382

Virginia (Colony) Governor, 1773.
The Speech of His Excellency the Right Honourable John Earl of Dunmore . . . the 4th Day of March, 1773.
[Williamsburg, 1773.] Broadside.
LOC ph. copy.   42527

[Virginia (Colony) Governor, 1774.
By His Excellency the . . . Earl of Dunmore. . . . A Proclamation [Prorogation].
[Williamsburg, 1774.] Broadside.]
(Assumed by Evans from the printing in the Journal.)   13745

Virginia (Colony) Governor, 1774.
The Speech of His Excellency the Right Honourable John Earl of Dunmore . . . the 5th of May, 1774.
[Williamsburg, 1774.] Broadside.
LOC copy.   42741

Virginia (Colony) Governor, 1774.
Whereas I have Reason to Apprehend . . .

this 25th Day of April, 1774.
[Williamsburg, 1774.] Broadside.
LOC ph. copy.   42742

Virginia (Colony) Governor, 1775.
At a Council Held at the Palace May 2,
1775.
[Williamsburg], Pinkney, [1775].
Broadside.
PRO copy.   42972

Virginia (Colony) Governor, 1775.
By His Excellency the Right Hon. John
Earl of Dunmore. . . . A Proclamation
[Grants. May 8, 1775].
[Williamsburg, 1775.] Broadside.
NYPL copy.   14591

Virginia (Colony) Governor, 1775.
By His Excellency the Right Honourable
John Earl of Dunmore. . . . A
Proclamation [Martial Law. Nov. 7,
1775].
[Norfolk, 1775.] Broadside.
LOC ph. copy.   14592

Virginia (Colony) Governor, 1775.
By His Excellency the Right Honourable
John Earl of Dunmore. . . . A
Proclamation. Virginia. . . . Given . . . this
21st Day of March.
[Williamsburg, 1775.] Broadside.
LOC copy.   42974

Virginia (Colony) Governor, 1775.
By His Excellency the Right Honourable
John Earl of Dunmore. . . . A
Proclamation. Virginia. . . . Given . . . this
28th Day of March.
[Williamsburg, 1775.] Broadside.
LOC ph. copy.   42975

Virginia (Colony) Governor, 1775.
By His Excellency the Right Hon. John
Earl of Dunmore. . . . A Proclamation.
Virginia . . . Whereas . . . Patrick Henry
. . . Given . . . this 6th Day of May, 1775.
[Williamsburg, 1775.] Broadside.
PRO copy.   42976

Virginia (Colony) Governor, 1775.
The Governour's Answer to the
Joint-Address. . . . June 10, 1775.
[Williamsburg, 1775.] [2] pp.
LOC copy.   14593

Virginia (Colony) Governor, 1775.
Speech of His Excellency the Right
Honourable John Earl of Dunmore . . .
the 1st of June, 1775.
Williamsburg, Purdie, [1775]. [2] pp.
LOC copy.   14601

[Virginia (Colony) Governor, 1776.]
By His Excellency the Right Honorable
John Earl of Dunmore. . . . A
Proclamation [Martial Law. Nov. 7].
[Off Norfolk, 1776.] Broadside.]
(A duplicate of 14592, q.v.)   15196

Virginia (Colony) House Journals, 1732.
The Journal of the House of Burgesses.
[May 18, - July 1, 1732].
Williamsburg, Parks, 1732. [2], 60 pp.
PRO copy.   3612

Virginia (Colony) House Journals, 1734.
Journal of the House of Burgesses [Aug.
22-Oct. 4, 1734].
[Williamsburg, Parks, 1734. 74 pp.
(No copy at present available.)   40067

Virginia (Colony) House Journals, 1736.
The Journal of the House of Burgesses
[Aug. 5, 1736 +].
Williamsburg, 1736. [4], 86 pp.
Mrs. Geo. P. Coleman copy.   4095

Virginia (Colony) House Journals, 1738.
The Journal of the House of Burgesses
[Nov. 1, 1738 +].
Williamsburg, 1738. [4], 78 pp.
Mrs. Geo. P. Coleman copy.   4318

Virginia (Colony) House Journals, 1740.
The Journal of the House [May 22, 1740
+].
Williamsburg, 1740. [2], 51 pp., irreg.
LOC copy.   4618

Virginia (Colony) House Journals, 1740.
The Journals of the House of Burgesses
[Aug. 21, 1740 +].

Williamsburg, 1740. 7 pp.
Mrs. Geo. P. Coleman copy.   4619

Virginia (Colony) House Journals, 1742.
The Journal of the House of Burgesses
[May 6, 1742 +].
Williamsburg, 1742. [6], 78 pp.
(The only copy located is imperfect.)
LOC copy.   5083

Virginia (Colony) House Journals, 1744.
The Journal of the House of Burgesses
[Sept. 4 - Oct. 25, 1744].
Williamsburg, 1744. [2], 86 pp.
VaSL copy.   5504

Virginia (Colony) House Journals, 1746.
The Journal of the House of Burgesses
[Feb. 20 - Apr. 12, 1746].
Williamsburg, Parks, 1746. [2], 82 pp.
PRO copy.   5873

Virginia (Colony) House Journals, 1746.
The Journal of the House of Burgesses
[July 11-16, 1746].
Williamsburg, 1746. [2], 8 pp.
Coleman copy.   5874

Virginia (Colony) House Journals, 1747.
The Journal of the House of Burgesses
[Mar. 30 - Apr. 18, 1747].
[Williamsburg, 1747.] 19 pp.
Coleman copy.   6077

Virginia (Colony) House Journal, 1748.
The Journal: of the House of Burgesses
[Oct. 27, 1748 - May 11, 1749].
Williamsburg, 1748. [2], 4, [2], 5-181 pp.
(No perfect copy known.)
Composite copy.   6435

Virginia (Colony) House Journals, 1752.
The Journal of the House of Burgesses
[Feb. 27 - Apr. 20, 1752].
Williamsburg, 1752. [2], 124 pp.
LOC copy.   6943

Virginia (Colony) House Journals, 1753.
The Journal of the House of Burgesses
[Nov. 1 - Dec. 19, 1753].
Williamsburg, 1753. [1], 2, [1], 88 pp.
NYPL copy.   7131

Virginia (Colony) House Journals, 1754.
The Journal of the House of Burgesses
[Feb. 14-23, 1754].
Williamsburg, 1754. pp. 3, 2-14.
VaSL copy.   7325

Virginia (Colony) House Journals, 1754.
The Journal of the House of Burgesses
[Aug. 22 - Sept. 5, 1754].
[Williamsburg, 1754]. 22 pp.
LOC copy.   7326

Virginia (Colony) House Journals, 1754.
The Journal of the House of Burgesses
[Oct. 17 - Nov. 2, 1754].
Williamsburg, [1754]. [2], 24 pp.
VaSL copy.   7327

Virginia (Colony) House Journals, 1755.
The Journal of the House of Burgesses
[May 1 - July 9, 1755].
Williamsburg, 1755. 83 pp.
LOC copy.   7584

Virginia (Colony) House Journals, 1755.
The Journal of the House of Burgesses
[Aug. 5-23, 1755].
Williamsburg, 1755. [2], 24 pp.
LOC copy.   7585

Virginia (Colony) House Journals, 1755.
The Journal of the House of Burgesses
[Oct. 27 - Nov. 8, 1755].
Williamsburg, 1755. 16 pp.
LOC copy.   7586

Virginia (Colony) House Journals, 1756.
The Journal of the House of Burgesses
[Mar. 25 - May 5, 1756].
[Williamsburg, 1756.] 78 pp.
LOC copy.   7810

Virginia (Colony) House Journals, 1756.
The Journal of the House of Burgesses
[Sept. 20-28, 1756].
[Williamsburg, 1756.] 12 pp.
LOC copy.   7811

Virginia (Colony) House Journals, 1757.

The Journal of the House of Burgesses
[Apr. 14 - June 8, 1757].
Williamsburg, 1757. [2], 101 pp.
NYPL copy.   8055

Virginia (Colony) House Journals, 1758.
The Journal of the House of Burgesses
[Mar. 30 - Apr. 12, 1758].
Williamsburg, 1758. [2], 15 pp.
VaSL copy.   8274

Virginia (Colony) House Journals, 1758.
The Journal of the House of Burgesses
[Sept. 14 - Oct. 12, 1758].
Williamsburg, 1758. 57 pp.
G. P. Coleman copy.   8275

Virginia (Colony) House Journals, 1758.
The Journal of the House of Burgesses
[Nov. 9-11, 1758].
Williamsburg, 1758. 4 pp.
G. P. Coleman copy.   8276

Virginia (Colony) House Journals, 1759.
The Journal of the House of Burgesses
[Feb. 22 - Apr. 14, 1759].
Williamsburg, 1759. 94 pp.
LOC copy.   8511

Virginia (Colony) House Journals, 1759.
The Journal of the House of Burgesses
[Nov. 1-21, 1759].
[Williamsburg, 1759.] 26 pp.
LOC copy.   8512

Virginia (Colony) House Journals, 1760.
The Journal of the House of Burgesses
[Mar. 4-14, 1760].
Williamsburg, 1760. [2], 14 pp.
NYPL copy.   8757

Virginia (Colony) House Journals, 1760.
The Journal of the House of Burgesses
[May 19-24, 1760].
Williamsburg, 1760. 13 pp.
NYPL copy.   8758

Virginia (Colony) House Journals, 1760.
The Journal of the House of Burgesses
[Oct. 6, 1760 - Apr. 10, 1761].
Williamsburg, 1761. 99 pp.
LOC copy.   9032

Virginia (Colony) House Journals, 1761.
The Journal of the House of Burgesses
[Nov. 3-14, 1761].
Williamsburg, 1761. 28 pp.
VaSL copy.   9033

Virginia (Colony) House Journal, 1762.
The Journal of the House of Burgesses
[Jan. 14-21, 1762].
[Williamsburg, 1762.] pp. 3-14.
VaSL copy.   9293

Virginia (Colony) House Journals, 1762.
The Journal of the House of Burgesses
[Mar. 30 - Apr. 7, 1762].
[Williamsburg, 1762.] pp. 3-16.
VaSL copy.   9294

Virginia (Colony) House Journals, 1762.
Journal of the House of Burgesses [Nov. 2
Dec. 23, 1762].
[Williamsburg, 1762.] pp. 3-116, irreg.
VaSL copy.   9295

Virginia (Colony) House Journals, 1763.
The Journal of the House of Burgesses
[May 19-31, 1763].
[Williamsburg, 1763.] 31 pp.
LOC copy.   9530

Virginia (Colony) House Journals, 1764.
The Journal of the House of Burgesses
[Jan. 12-21, 1764].
[Williamsburg, 1764.] pp. 3-25.
VaSL copy.   9861

Virginia (Colony) House Journals, 1765.
The Journal of the House of Burgesses
[Oct. 30 - Dec. 13, 1764; May 1 - June 1,
1765].
[Williamsburg, 1765.] pp. 3-154.
VaSL copy.   10193

Virginia (Colony) House Journals, 1766.
Journal of the House [Nov. 6 - Dec. 16,
1766].
[Williamsburg, 1766.] 77 pp.
(No complete copy located.)
VaSL copy.   41668

Virginia (Colony) House Journals, 1767.
The Journal of the House [Mar. 12-Apr. 11, 1767].
[Williamsburg, 1767.] pp. 78-136.
VaSL copy.   41774

Virginia (Colony) House Journals, 1768.
[Journal of the House for Mar. 31-Apr. 16, 1768.
Williamsburg, Rind, 1768.]
("Just published," Rind's Gazette, June 9, 1768.)   41894

Virginia (Colony) House Journals, 1769.
Journal of the House of Burgesses. . . .
Begun . . . the Eighth Day of May . . . 1769.
Williamsburg, Rind, 1769. 42 pp.
LOC copy.   42021

Virginia (Colony) House Journal, 1769.
Journal of the House of Burgesses [Nov. 7, 1769 - June 28, 1770].
Williamsburg, 1770. 271 pp.
VaSL copy.   11910

Virginia (Colony) House Journals, 1771.
Journal of the House [July 11-20, 1771.]
Williamsburg, Rind, 1771. 24 pp.
(The only known copy lacks tp.)
VaSL copy.   42293

Virginia (Colony) House Journal, 1772.
Journal of the House of Burgesses [Feb. 10 - Apr. 11, 1772].
Williamsburg, Rind, 1772. 164 pp.
NYPL copy.   12592

Virginia (Colony) House Journals, 1773.
Journal of the House of Burgesses [Mar. 4-15, 1773].
Williamsburg, Rind, [1773]. 31 pp.
LOC copy.   13058

Virginia (Colony) House Journal, 1774.
Journal of the House of Burgesses [May 5 26, 1774].
Williamsburg, Rind, 1774. 75 pp.
(The unique copy has a number of imperfect pages.)
LOC copy.   13749

Virginia (Colony) House Journal, 1775.
Journal of the House of Burgesses . . . June . . . 1775.
[Williamsburg, 1775.] [4] pp.
NYPL ph. copy.   42977

Virginia (Colony) House of Burgesses, 1773.
By the Upper House . . . October 28, 1773.
[Williamsburg, 1773.] Broadside.
LOC copy.   42528

Virginia (Colony) House of Burgesses, 1773.
To His Excellency . . . John Earl of Dunmore . . . the Humble Address [in answer to his speech of Mar. 13, 1773].
[Williamsburg, 1773.] Broadside.
LOC ph. copy.   42530

Virginia (Colony) House of Burgesses, 1774.
To . . . John Earl of Dunmore . . . the Humble Address of the House [in reply to his address of May 6, 1774].
[Williamsburg, 1774.] Broadside.
(Reported by LOC to be same as 42740.)
                                    42743

[Virginia (Colony) Laws, Statutes, etc., 1730.
All the Public Acts.
Williamsburg, 1730.]
(See Wroth, William Parks, p. 45.)   3369

[Virginia (Colony) Laws, Statutes, etc., 1730.
The New Virginia Tobacco-Law.
Williamsburg, 1730.]
(See Wroth, William Parks, p. 45.)   3371

Virginia (Colony) Laws, Statutes, etc., 1732.
. . . An Act to Enable the Masters of Ships. . . .
[Williamsburg, 1732.] [2] pp.
PRO copy.   40009

Virginia (Colony) Laws, Statutes, etc., 1733.
A Collection of all the Acts of Assembly.

Williamsburg, 1733. [6], 628 pp.
Composite copy.   3728

Virginia (Colony) Laws, Statutes, etc., 1737.
An Exact Abridgment of all of the Public Acts.
Williamsburg, 1737. xlvii, [1], 345, [82] pp.
AAS copy.   4204

Virginia (Colony) Laws, Statutes, etc., 1739.
A Continuation of the Abridgment of all the Public Acts.
Williamsburg, 1739. pp. vi, [2], 347-376, [28].
NYPL copy.   4441

Virginia (Colony) Laws, Statutes, etc., 1752.
The Acts of Assembly, now in Force.
Williamsburg, 1752. [6], vi, 455, [1] pp.
AAS copy.   6941

Virginia (Colony) Laws, Statutes, etc., 1753.
Acts of Assembly, now in Force. . . . 1748.
[Williamsburg, 1753?] 58 pp.
VaSL copy.   40677

Virginia (Colony) Laws, Statutes, etc., 1769.
The Acts of Assembly now in Force.
Williamsburg, 1769. [2], 577 pp.
AAS copy.   11511

Virginia (Colony) Lieutenant Governor, 1748.
By the Honourable Sir William Gooch . . . a Proclamation, Proroguing the General Assembly [to Sept. 1, dated Aug. 26, 1748.]
[Williamsburg, 1748.] Broadside.
VaHS copy.   40482

Virginia (Colony) Lieutenant Governor, 1754.
. . . By . . . Robert Dinwiddie. . . . A Proclamation, for Encouraging Men to Enlist [Feb. 19, 1754].
[Williamsburg, 1754.] Broadside.
HEH copy.   40722

Virginia (Colony) Lieutenant Governor, 1754.
September 5th, 1754. The Speech of the Honourable Robert Dinwiddie. . . .
[Williamsburg, Hunter, 1754.] 2 pp.
HSP copy.   40723

Virginia (Colony) Lieutenant Governor, 1754.
The Speech of the Honourable Robert Dinwiddie . . . to the General Assembly.
Williamsburg, Hunter, 1754. 4 pp.
HSP copy.   40724

Virginia (Colony) Lieutenant Governor, 1755.
The Speech of the Honorable Robert Dinwiddie . . . to the General Assembly . . . May . . . 1755.
Williamsburg, Hunter, 1755. 4 pp.
LOC copy.   40808

Virginia (Colony) Lieutenant Governor, 1756.
The Speech of . . . Robert Dinwiddie . . . to the General Assembly.
Williamsburg, Hunter, 1756. 4 pp.
HEH copy.   40866

Virginia (Colony) Lieutenant Governor, 1757.
The Speech of . . . Robert Dinwiddie . . . the 14th of April, 1757.
Williamsburg, Hunter, 1757. 4 pp.
HEH copy.   40945

Virginia (Colony) Lieutenant Governor, 1758.
The Speech of the Honorable Francis Fauquier. . . . To the General Assembly [Sept. 14, 1758].
[Williamsburg, 1758.] 4 pp.
LOC copy.   8277

Virginia (Colony) Planters, 1733.
The Case of the Planters of Tobacco.
[Williamsburg, 1732.] 4 pp.
(No copy located.)   40008

[Virginia (Colony) Session Laws, 1680.
The Laws of Virginia for 1680.
Williamsburg, 1682.]
(No copy known. See Executive Journals of the Council of Virginia, I (1925), p. 493.)   334

Virginia (Colony) Session Laws, 1732.
Acts of Assembly Passed [May 18 - July 1, 1732]. . . . being the Third Session.
Williamsburg, 1732. [2], 44 pp.
PRO copy.   40010

Virginia (Colony) Session Laws, 1734.
At a General Assembly [Aug. 22, 1734 +].
[Williamsburg, 1734.] 51 pp.
NYPL copy.   3849

Virginia (Colony) Session Laws, 1736.
At a General Assembly [Aug. 5, 1736 +].
[Williamsburg, 1736.] 48 pp.
NYPL copy.   4094

Virginia (Colony) Session Laws, 1738.
At a General Assembly [Nov. 1, 1738 +].
[Williamsburg, 1738.] 52 pp.
NYPL copy.   4317

Virginia (Colony) Session Laws, 1740.
At a General Assembly [May 22, 1740 +].
[Williamsburg, 1740.] 21 pp.
LOC copy.   4616

Virginia (Colony) Session Laws, 1740.
At a General Assembly [Aug. 21, 1740 +].
[Williamsburg, 1740.] 2 pp.
VaSL copy.   4617

Virginia (Colony) Session Laws, 1742.
. . . At a General Assembly, begun . . . the Sixth Day of May . . . 1742. . . .
[Williamsburg, 1742.] 58 pp.
VaSL copy.   40290

Virginia (Colony) Session Laws, 1744.
Acts of Assembly Passed [Sept. 4, 1744].
Williamsburg, Parks, 1744. [2], 58 pp.
VaSL copy.   40356

Virginia (Colony) Session Laws, 1746.
Acts of Assembly, Passed . . . February. . . . 1745/6].
Williamsburg, Parks, 1746. [2], 55 pp.
VaSL copy.   40419

Virginia (Colony) Session Laws, 1746.
. . . At a General Assembly . . . Fourth Session [July 11-16, 1746.] [4] pp.
VaSL copy.   40420

Virginia (Colony) Session Laws, 1747.
. . . At a General Assembly [Mar. 30 - Apr. 18, 1747] . . . being the Fifth Session.
[Williamsburg, Parks, 1747.] [4] pp.
(No copy at present available.)   40447

Virginia (Colony) Session Laws, 1748.
. . . At a General Assembly [Oct. 27, 1748-May 11, 1749].
[Williamsburg, 1749.] 40+ pp.
(The only known copy is imperfect.)
VaSL copy.   40522

Virginia (Colony) Session Laws, 1752.
At a General Assembly [Feb. 27, 1752 +].
[Williamsburg, 1752.] 47, [1] pp.
AAS copy.   6942

Virginia (Colony) Session Laws, 1753.
Acts of Assembly . . . Second Session [Nov. 1, 1753 +].
Williamsburg, Hunter, 1754. [2], 46 pp.
VaSL copy.   40725

Virginia (Colony) Session Laws, 1754.
. . . At a General Assembly . . . Third Session [Feb. 14, 1754 +].
[Williamsburg, 1754.] 4 pp.
VaSL copy.   40726

Virginia (Colony) Session Laws, 1754.
. . . At a General Assembly . . . Fourth Session [Aug. 22, 1754 +].
[Williamsburg, 1754.] 6 pp.
VaSL copy.   40727

Virginia (Colony) Session Laws, 1754.
. . . At the General Assembly . . . Fifth Session [Oct. 17, 1754].
[Williamsburg, 1754.] 11 pp.
HEH copy.   40728

Virginia (Colony) Session Laws, 1755.
... At a General Assembly ... May ...
1755 ... being the Sixth Session. ...
[Williamsburg, 1755.] 35 pp.
VaSL copy.   40809

Virginia (Colony) Session Laws, 1755.
... At a General Assembly ... August
... 1755 ... being the Seventh
Session. ...
[Williamsburg, 1755.] 22 pp.
VaSL copy.   40810

Virginia (Colony) Session Laws, 1755.
... At a General Assembly ... October
... 1755. ... Being the Eighth
Session. ...
[Williamsburg, 1755.] 8 pp.
VaSL copy.   40811

Virginia (Colony) Session Laws, 1756.
At a General Assembly [Mar. 25, 1756
+].
[Williamsburg, 1756.] 28 pp.
NYPL copy.   7808

Virginia (Colony) Session Laws, 1756.
At a General Assembly [Sept. 20, 1756
+].
[Williamsburg, 1756.] 4 pp.
NYPL copy.   7809

Virginia (Colony) Session Laws, 1757.
At a General Assembly [Apr. 14, 1757
+].
[Williamsburg, 1757.] 48 pp.
NYPL copy.   8054

Virginia (Colony) Session Laws, 1758.
... At a General Assembly. ... March
... 1758; being the Fourth Session.
[Williamsburg, 1758.] 5 pp.
VaSL copy.   41015

Virginia (Colony) Session Laws, 1758.
... At a General Assembly ... September
... 1758; being the First Session.
[Williamsburg, 1758.] 34 pp.
VaSL copy.   41016

Virginia (Colony) Session Laws, 1758.
... At a General Assembly ... September
... 1758 ... being the Second Session.
[Williamsburg, 1758.] 2 pp.
NYPL copy.   8273

Virginia (Colony) Session Laws, 1759.
At a General Assembly [Feb. 22, 1759
+].
[Williamsburg, 1759.] 36 pp.
NYPL copy.   8509

Virginia (Colony) Session Laws, 1759.
At a General Assembly [Nov. 1, 1759 +].
[Williamsburg, 1759.] 8 pp.
NYPL copy.   8510

Virginia (Colony) Session Laws, 1760.
At a General-Assembly [Mar. 4, 1760 +].
[Williamsburg, 1760.] 6 pp.
NYPL copy.   8754

Virginia (Colony) Session Laws, 1760.
At a General-Assembly [May 19, 1760].
[Williamsburg, 1760.] 6 pp.
NYPL copy.   8755

Virginia (Colony) Session Laws, 1760.
At a General-Assembly [Oct. 6, 1760 +].
[Williamsburg, 1760.] 7 pp.
NYPL copy.   8756

Virginia (Colony) Session Laws, 1761.
At a General Assembly [Mar. 5, 1761 +].
[Williamsburg, 1761.] pp. 9-50.
NYPL copy.   9030

Virginia (Colony) Session Laws, 1761.
At a General Assembly [May 26, 1761
+].
[Williamsburg, 1761.] 14 pp.
NYPL copy.   9031

Virginia (Colony) Session Laws, 1762.
At a General-Assembly [Jan. 14, 1762
+].
[Williamsburg, 1762.] 2 pp.
NYPL copy.   9290

Virginia (Colony) Session Laws, 1762.
At a General-Assembly [Mar. 30, 1762
+].

[Williamsburg, 1762.] 10 pp.
NYPL copy.   9291

Virginia (Colony) Session Laws, 1762.
At a General-Assembly [Nov. 2, 1762 +].
[Williamsburg, 1762.] 52 pp.
NYPL copy.   9292

Virginia (Colony) Session Laws, 1763.
... At a General Assembly ... May, 1763
... being the Fifth Session.
[Williamsburg, 1763.] 9 pp.
NYPL copy.   41421

Virginia (Colony) Session Laws, 1764.
... At a General-Assembly ... January,
1764 ... being the Sixth Session.
[Williamsburg, 1764.] 10 pp.
LOC copy.   41503

Virginia (Colony) Session Laws, 1764.
... At a General Assembly ... October,
1764 ... being the Seventh Session.
[Williamsburg, 1765.] 73 pp.
NYPL copy.   41594

Virginia (Colony) Session Laws, 1766.
At a General Assembly [Nov. 6, 1766 +].
Williamsburg, 1766. 58 pp.
NYPL copy.   10515

[Virginia (Colony) Session Laws, 1768.
Acts of the General Assembly [Mar. 31,
1768 +].
Williamsburg, 1768.]
(Probably not printed.)   11105

Virginia (Colony) Session Laws, 1769.
Acts of the General Assembly [Nov. 7,
1769 - June 28, 1770].
Williamsburg, 1770. [2], 83 pp.
VaSL copy.   11909

Virginia (Colony) Session Laws, 1771.
Acts of the General Assembly [July 11,
1771].
Williamsburg, Rind, 1771. [2], 8 pp.
AAS copy.   12265

Virginia (Colony) Session Laws, 1772.
Acts of the General Assembly [Feb. 10,
1772 +].
Williamsburg, Rind, 1771. [2], 51 pp.
AAS copy.   12264

Virginia (Colony) Session Laws, 1772.
Acts of the General Assembly [Feb.
10-Apr. 11, 1772].
Williamsburg, Rind, 1772. [2], 59 pp.
LOC copy.   42384

Virginia (Colony) Session Laws, 1772.
Acts of the General Assembly [Feb. 10 -
Apr. 11, 1772].
Williamsburg, Rind, 1771 (1772). [2], 49,
[2] pp.
(The NYPL has a second issue with 59 pp.
and date corrected.)
NYPL copy.   12591

Virginia (Colony) Session Laws, 1773.
... At a General Assembly [Mar. 4, 1773
+].
[Williamsburg, 1773.] 16 pp.
VaSL copy.   13056

Virginia (Colony) Treaties, etc., 1756.
A Treaty Held with the Catawba.
Williamsburg, 1756. xiv, 25 pp.
BA copy.   7689

Virginia.
A List of Balances Due from the Several
Counties for Taxes from 1782 to ... 1790.
Richmond, Dixon, 1790. 4 pp.
LCP copy.   23020

Virginia. Adjutant General's Office.
To the Worshipful County Court. ... The
last General Assembly Having Authorized
me ... to Raise as many Additional
Companies of Artillery and Troops of
Cavalry. ... February 12th, 1796.
[Richmond, 1796.] Broadside.
LOC copy.   31505

Virginia. Auditor of Public Accounts,
1787.
List of Pensioners for the Year 1786. ...
January 30, 1787.
[Richmond, 1787.] [2] pp.
(No perfect copy located.)
LOC copy.   45190

Virginia. Auditor of Public Accounts,
1787.
List of Pensioners for the Year 1787. ...
30th November, 1787.
[Richmond, 1787.] [2] pp.
LOC copy.   45191

Virginia. Auditor of Public Accounts,
1788.
A List of Pensioners, for the Year 1788.
[Richmond, 1788.] Broadside.
AAS copy.   45392

Virginia. Auditors of Public Accounts,
1790.
A List of the Pensioners ... for ... 1789.
... January 1, 1790.
[Richmond, 1790.] Broadside.
NYPL copy.   46087

Virginia. Auditor of Public Accounts,
1792.
List of Pensioners Paid by the State of
Virginia, for the Year 1791.
[Richmond, 1792.] Broadside.
LOC copy.   26393

Virginia. Auditor of Public Accounts,
1792.
List of Pensioners Continued by the ...
Executive for the Year 1792.
[Richmond, 1793.] Broadside.
LOC copy.   26394

[Virginia. Auditor of Public Accounts,
1793.
A List of Pensioners, Provided for by
Congress. ...
[Richmond, 1793?] Broadside.]
(No copy located.)   26395

Virginia. Auditor of Public Accounts,
1794.
List of Pensioners Continued by the
Honorable the Executive from the Year
1793.
[Richmond, 1794.] Broadside.
LOC copy.   28004

Virginia. Auditor of Public Accounts,
1795.
(Circular.) Richmond, Supervisor's Office,
December 31st, 1795. Gentlemen. ... The
Inspectors of Surveys.
[Richmond, 1795.] Broadside.
LOC copy.   29802

Virginia. Auditor of Public Accounts,
1795.
List of Pensioners, Continued by the
Honorable the Executive, for the Year
One Thousand Seven Hundred and
Ninety-four.
[Richmond, 1795.] Broadside.
LOC copy.   29801

Virginia. Auditor of Public Accounts,
1795.
List of Pensioners Continued by the ...
Executive, for the Year 1795.
[Richmond, 1796.] Broadside.
LOC copy.   31504

Virginia. Auditor of Public Accounts,
1796.
List of Pensioners Continued by the
Honorable the Executive for the Year
1796.
[Richmond, 1797.] Broadside.
LOC copy.   33130

Virginia. Auditor of Public Accounts,
1797.
List of Pensioners Continued by the
Honorable the Executive, for the Year
1797.
[Richmond, Davis, 1798.] Broadside.
LOC copy.   34940

Virginia. Auditor of Public Accounts,
1798.
List of Pensioners, Continued by the
Honorable the Executive, for the Year
1798.
[Richmond, 1799.] Broadside.
NYPL copy.   36644

Virginia. Auditor of Public Accounts,
1800.
List of Pensioners Continued by the
Honourable the Executive, for the Year
1799.

[Richmond, 1800.] Broadside.
NYPL copy.   38958

[Virginia. Board of War and Ordinance,
1779.
. . . Williamsburg, August 17, 1779. The
Defenceless . . . Situation. . . .
[Williamsburg, 1779.] Broadside.]
(No copy located.)   16656

[Virginia. Census, 1800.
Arrangements of . . . Virginia, for . . .
Taking the Second Census.
[Winchester, Bowen, 1800.] Broadside.]
(Entry from Evans' notes.)   38949

Virginia. Citizens, 1792.
To the Honorable the Legislature. . . . The
Memorial of Sundry Merchants . . . for the
Establishment of a Bank.
[Richmond? 1792?] Broadside.
EI copy.   46660

Virginia, Citizens, 1800.
To the Honorable Speaker, and the Rest
of the Honorable Members. . . . Sundry
Inhabitants of the County of [blank]. . . .
[Alexandria? 1800?] Broadside.
VaSL copy.   49180

Virginia. Convention, Dec. 1, 1775.
The Proceedings of the Convention
[- Jan. 20, 1776].
Williamsburg, Purdie, [1776]. [4], 106
pp.
NYPL copy.   15197

Virginia. Convention, 1776.
The Following Declaration. . . .
[Williamsburg, 1776.] [2] pp.
VaHS copy.   43205

Virginia. Convention, 1776.
Friday, June 14, 1776. Prostscript. No. 72.
[Williamsburg, 1776.] [4] pp.
LOC copy.   43206

Virginia. Convention, 1776.
In a General Convention. . . . The Sixth
Day of May.
[Williamsburg, 1776.] [2] pp.
LCP copy.   43207

Virginia. Convention, May 6, 1776.
In Convention. Saturday, March 25,
1775. . . . July 3, 1776. An Ordinance.
[Williamsburg, 1776.] [2] pp.
LOC copy.   15201

Virginia. Convention, May 6, 1776.
In Convention. Present 112 Members.
Wednesday, May 15, 1776.
[Williamsburg, 1776.] Broadside.
MA copy.   15200

Virginia. Convention, May 6, 1776.
Ordinances Passed at a General
Convention.
Williamsburg, Purdie, [1776]. 44 pp.
VaSL copy.   15199

Virginia. Convention, May 6, 1776.
The Proceedings of the Convention
[- July 5, 1776].
Williamsburg, Purdie, [1776]. 185 pp.
NYPL copy.   15198

Virginia. Convention, 1788.
Debates and Other Proceedings.
Petersburg, 1788. 194 pp.
AAS copy.   21551

Virginia. Convention, 1788.
Debates and Other Proceedings. . . .
Volume II [- III].
Petersburg, Prentice, 1789. 195; 228 pp.
AAS copy.   22225

Virginia. Convention, 1788.
Journal of the Convention in Virginia.
[Richmond], Davis, [1788]. 42 pp.
NYPL copy.   21555

Virginia. Convention, 1788.
Poughkeepsie, July 2d, 1788. Just Arrived
by Express The Ratification. . . . of
Virginia.
[Poughkeepsie, 1788.] Broadside.
AAS ph. copy.   45393

Virginia. Convention, 1788.
Richmond, State of Virginia. In

Convention, Wednesday, the 25th of June,
1788.
Richmond, Davis, [1788]. 3 pp.
LOC copy.   21552

Virginia. Convention, 1788.
Richmond, State of Virginia. In
Convention, Wednesday, the 25th of June,
1788. . . . Friday the 27th. . . .
Richmond, Davis, [1788]. 4 pp.
LOC copy.   21553

Virginia. Convention, 1788.
Supplement to the Independent Journal,
New-York, July 2, 1788.
New York, M'Leans, [1788]. Broadside.
NYPL copy.   21559

Virginia. Council, 1776.
Williamsburg, Aug. 20, 1776. Sir. . . .
[Williamsburg, 1776.] Broadside.
LOC copy.   43208

Virginia. Council, 1779.
In Council, June 16, 1779. The Board
Proceeded. . . .
Williamsburg, Dixon & Nicolson, [1779].
Broadside.
LOC copy.   16657

Virginia. Council, 1779.
War Office, Williamsburg, November 11,
1779. The Appointment of a Clothier. . . .
In Council, November 15, 1779.
[Williamsburg, 1779.] Broadside.
LOC copy.   16663

Virginia. Council, 1781.
In Council, April 12, 1781. Sir, Having
Received an Application. . . .
n.p., [1781]. Broadside.
LOC copy.   44079

Virginia. Council, 1781.
In Council, January 19, 1781. Sir, The
Invasion. . . .
[Richmond, 1781.] Broadside.
LOC copy.   17410

Virginia. Council, 1781.
In Council, March 26, 1781. Sir, I
Inclose. . . .
[Richmond, 1781.] Broadside.
LOC copy.   17411

Virginia. Council, 1781.
In Council, March 30, 1781. Sir. The Act
of October 1780. . . .
[Richmond, 1781.] Broadside.
LOC copy.   44078

Virginia. Council, 1785.
Council Chamber, October 20, 1785.
Gentlemen, The Act. . . .
[Richmond, 1785.] Broadside.
(The only known copy is imperfect.)
LOC copy.   44825

Virginia. Council, 1786.
In Council, December 27, 1786. The
Board. . . .
[Richmond, 1786?] Broadside.
(No copy located.)   45009

Virginia. Council, 1786.
In Council February 20, 1786.
Gentlemen. . . .
[Richmond, 1786.] Broadside.
LOC copy.   45010

Virginia. Council, 1786.
To Prevent Impositions, the Board in
Council, Dec. 4, 1786. . . .
[Richmond, 1786.] Broadside.
LOC copy.   45011

Virginia. Council, 1787.
In Council, December 20, 1787. The
Board Proceeded. . . .
[Richmond? 1787.] Broadside.
(No copy located.)   45193

Virginia. Council, 1787.
In Council, January 29, 1787. Gentlemen,
The Executive. . . .
[Richmond, 1787.] Broadside.
LOC copy.   45192

Virginia. Council, 1788.
In Council, May 20, 1788. Gentlemen, I
beg leave. . . .
[Richmond, 1788.] Broadside.
LOC copy..   45394

Virginia. Executive Council, 1788.
In Council, 29th Dec. 1788. Sir, In the
Settlement. . . .
[Richmond, 1788.] Broadside.
LOC copy.   21554

Virginia. Executive Council, 1797.
In Council, January 16th, 1797.
Gentlemen, The Executive. . . .
[Richmond, 1797.] Broadside.
LOC copy.   33127

Virginia. Executive Council, 1798.
(Circular.) In Council, 8th of January,
1798. Gentlemen. . . .
[Richmond, Davis, 1798.] Broadside.
LOC copy.   34938

Virginia. General Assembly, 1776.
A Plan of Government. Laid before the
. . . House.
[Williamsburg, 1776.] [2] pp.
LOC copy.   43209

Virginia. General Assembly, 1779.
A Bill for Establishing Religious
Freedom, Printed for the Consideration of
the People.
[Richmond, 1779?] Broadside.
BPL copy.   19350

[Virginia. General Assembly, 1784.
The Articles of Confederation.
Richmond, [1784]. 35 pp.]
(Authorized, 1784; printed 1785. See
19349.)   18818

Virginia. General Assembly, 1784.
The Articles of Confederation.
Richmond, Dixon & Holt, [1785]. 25 pp.
AAS copy.   19349

Virginia. General Assembly, 1784.
Report of the Committee of Revisors.
Richmond, Dixon & Holt, 1784. 6, 90 pp.
LOC copy.   18863

Virginia. General Assembly, 1785.
In the House of Delegates. November 14,
1785. Whereas the Relative Situation. . . .
[Richmond, 1785.] Broadside.
NYPL copy.   19352

Virginia. General Assembly, 1785.
In the House of Delegates, Thursday, the
30th of December, 1784. . . .
[Richmond, 1785.] [4] pp.
VaU copy.   44826

Virginia. General Assembly, 1786.
. . . In the House of Delegates, January
13, 1786. Resolved . . . Bills of
Exchange. . . . Agreed to by the Senate.
[Richmond, 1786.] Broadside.
AAS copy.   45012

[Virginia. General Assembly, 1786.
In the House of Delegates. Tuesday, the
1st of November, 1786 [Paper Money].
[Richmond, 1786.] Broadside.]
(Unique copy described by Evans not now
to be located.)   20105

Virginia. General Assembly, 1787.
In the House of Delegates, Thursday, the
25th of October, 1787. . . . October 31st,
Agreed to by the Senate.
[Richmond, 1787.] Broadside.
AAS copy.   20839

Virginia. General Assembly, 1787.
Resolved Unanimously that the Common
Right of Navigating the Mississippi. . . .
[Richmond, 1787.] Broadside.
(No copy known.)   45194

Virginia. General Assembly, 1788.
. . . Friday, the 20th November, 1788.
Resolved, That an Application be made
. . . to the Congress. . . .
[Richmond, 1788.] Broadside.
AAS ph. copy.   45395

Virginia. General Assembly, 1788.
. . . Friday, the 20th November, 1788. Sir,
The Freemen. . . .
[Richmond? 1788.] Broadside.
AAS ph. copy.   45396

Virginia. General Assembly, 1792.
Draughts of such Bills, as have been
Prepared by the Committee. . . .

Transmitted to the Executive on the
Twenty-Sixth of March. . . . Vol. I.
Richmond, Davis, 1792. [2], 194 pp.
VaSL copy.   24964

Virginia. General Assembly, 1792.
Draughts of such Bills, as have been
Prepared by the Committee. . . .
Transmitted to the Executive on the
Eighteenth of August. . . . Vol. II.
Richmond, Davis, 1792. 90 pp.
VaSL copy.   24965

Virginia. General Assembly, 1793.
. . . In the House of Delegates, Thursday,
28th November, 1793. Resolved, That a
State cannot . . . be made a
Defendant. . . . 1793, December 3d,
Agreed to by the Senate.
[Richmond, 1793.] Broadside.
AAS copy.   26391

Virginia. General Assembly, 1798.
Instructions from the . . . to Stephens
Thompson Mason.
[Richmond, Davis, 1798?]. [2] pp.
AAS copy.   34939

Virginia. General Assembly, 1799.
An Address of the Fifty-Eight Federal
Members of the Virginia Legislature.
Augusta, Me., Edes, 1799. 39 pp.
BA copy.   36631

Virginia. General Assembly, 1799.
Address of the Fifty-Eight Federal
Members of the Virginia Legislature.
[Philadelphia, 1799.] 12 pp.
(The one recorded copy of this ed. cannot
be reproduced.)   36632

[Virginia. General Assembly, 1799.
Address of the General Assembly to the
People of the Commonwealth.
Richmond, 1799.]
(Entry from Swem 7922.)   36633

Virginia. General Assembly, 1799.
The Address of the Legislature of Virginia
to the People.
[Norfolk], Printed for the Constitutional
Society. March 28, 1799. 26 pp.
(The one recorded copy of this ed. cannot
be reproduced.)   36634

Virginia. General Assembly, 1799.
The Address of the Minority of the
Virginia Legislature.
Albany, Andrews, [1799]. 20 pp.
NYHS copy.   36636

Virginia. General Assembly, 1799.
The Address of the Minority of the
Legislature of Virginia.
Petersburg, Prentis, 1799. 16 pp.
Duke University copy.   36637

Virginia. General Assembly, 1799.
An Address of the Minority of the
Virginia Legislature.
[Richmond, 1799.] 16 pp.
AAS copy.   36635

Virginia. General Assembly, 1799.
The Awful Crisis which has Arrived.
Richmond, Nicholson, [1799]. [4] pp.
LOC copy.   36638

Virginia. General Assembly, 1799.
The Communications of the Several
States, on the Resolutions of the
Legislature of Virginia.
Richmond, [1799]. 20 pp.
LOC copy.   36639

Virginia. General Assembly, 1799.
The Declaration of American
Independence. . . . Proceedings of the
Legislature.
Richmond, Jones & Dixon, 1799. 40 pp.
WLC copy.   36640

Virginia. General Assembly, 1799.
In the House of Delegates, Friday,
January 11, 1799. . . . January 16th, 1799,
Agreed to by the Senate.
[Richmond, 1799.] Broadside.
LOC copy.   36641

[Virginia. General Assembly, 1799.
Report of the Committee on the State of
the Business in the High Court of
Chancery.

Richmond. 1799.]
(Swem 7963.)   36646

[Virginia. General Assembly, 1799.
Resolutions that the General Assembly
. . . will Cooperate with the Authorities
of the United States. . . . Jan. 10, 1799.
Richmond. 1799.]
(Swem 7916.)   36647

Virginia. General Assembly, 1800.
A Bill to Amend an Act Entituled An Act
for Equalizing the Land Tax.
[Richmond, 1800.] 2 pp.
LOC copy.   38951

Virginia. General Assembly, 1800.
A Bill Concerning the High Court of
Chancery.
[Richmond, 1800.] 2 pp.
LOC copy.   38950

Virginia. General Assembly, 1800.
Communications from Several States . . .
Respecting the Alien and Sedition Laws.
Richmond, Jones, [1800]. 104 pp.
LOC copy.   38952

Virginia. General Assembly, 1800.
Instructions from the . . . to Stephens
Thompson Mason. . . .
[Richmond, Davis, 1800?] [2] pp.
(Also entered as 34939, q. v.)   38953

Virginia. General Assembly, 1800.
Proceedings of the Virginia Assembly on
the Answers of Sundry States.
Albany, [N. Y.], Barber & Southwick,
1800. pp. [1]-48, [50]-57.
AAS copy.   38959

Virginia. General Assembly, 1800.
Proceedings of the Virginia Assembly, on
the Answers of Sundry States.
Philadelphia, Carey, 1800. 59, [1] pp.
AAS copy.   38960

Virginia. General Assembly, 1800.
Richmond, January 30, 1800. Dear Sir,
The Legislature of this State . . . Deemed
it Expedient to Prescribe a Mode of
Choosing Electors. . . .
n.p., n.d. Broadside.
LOC copy.   38962

Virginia. General Assembly. House of
Delegates, 1779.
A Bill, Entitled, An Act for the Relief of
Certain Nonjurors. . . . March 22, 1779.
[Williamsburg, 1779.] 2 pp.
LCP copy.   43729

Virginia, General Assembly. House of
Delegates, 1784.
In the House of Delegates, Friday, the
24th of December, 1784. A Motion . . .
Christian Religion.
[Richmond, 1784.] [2] pp.
(Not located 1967.)
LOC copy.   44619

Virginia. General Assembly. House of
Delegates, 1784.
In the House of Delegates, Friday, the
24th of December, 1784. A Motion . . .
Christian Religion.
[Richmond, 1784.] [2] pp.
LOC copy.   44619

Virginia. General Assembly. House of
Delegates, 1784.
In the House of Delegates, Tuesday the
28th of December, 1784. Mr. Ronald
Reported. . . .
[Richmond, 1784.] 4 pp.
LOC copy.   44620

Virginia. General Assembly. House of
Delegates, 1786.
In the House of Delegates, Wednesday,
the 29th of November, 1786.
[Richmond, 1787.] Broadside.
LOC copy.   20838

Virginia. General Assembly. House of
Delegates, 1788.
In the House of Delegates, Monday, the
7th of January, 1788. On a Motion
made. . . .
[Richmond, 1788.] [3] pp.
NYPL ph. copy.   45397

Virginia. General Assembly. House of

Delegates, 1789.
In the House of Delegates. December 15,
1789. . . . The Executive. . . .
[Richmond, 1789.] Broadside.
LOC copy.   45735

Virginia. General Assembly. House of
Delegates, 1795.
In the House of Delegates, Saturday,
December 12, 1795.
[Richmond, 1795.] Broadside.
NYPL copy.   29798

Virginia. General Assembly. House of
Delegates, 1796.
. . . In the House of Delegates, Tuesday,
December the 13th, 1796. Ordered That
the Public Printer. . . .
[Richmond, 1796.] Broadside.
LOC copy.   31501

Virginia. General Assembly. House of
Delegates, 1798.
Debates in the House . . . upon . . . the
Alien and Sedition Laws.
Richmond, Nicholson, 1818 (i.e. 1798).
189, [2] pp.
LCP copy.   34935

[Virginia. General Assembly. House of
Delegates, 1798.
. . . In the House of Delegates, Tuesday,
December the 13th, 1798 [Constitutional
Convention].
[Richmond, 1798.] Broadside.]
(No copy located.)   34941

Virginia. General Assembly. House of
Delegates, 1798.
Virginia to wit, In the House of
Delegates, Friday, December 21st, 1798.
[Richmond, 1798.] [2] pp.
LOC copy.   34942

Virginia. General Assembly. House of
Delegates, 1798.
Virginia Resolutions of 1798.
[Richmond? 1798?] [39] pp.
HC copy.   48747

Virginia. General Assembly. House of
Delegates, 1800.
Report of the Committee to whom was
Committed the Proceedings of Sundry of
the other States. [Jan. 7, 1800].
Richmond, [1800]. 71 pp.
VaU copy.   38961

Virginia. General Assembly. Senate, 1787.
By the Senate, January 20, 1787. Ordered,
that the Printer. . . .
[Richmond, 1787.] [3] pp.
LOC copy.   45195

Virginia. Governor, 1777.
Williamsburg, December 13, 1777. The
Following Resolutions. . . .
[Williamsburg, 1777.] Broadside.
(Copy not located.)
Wis. Hist. Soc. copy.   43404

Virginia. Governor, 1778.
Williamsburg, April 12, 1779. Sir, The
Season is now Come. . . .
[Williamsburg, 1778.] Broadside.
(Copy not located.)   43588

Virginia. Governor, 1778.
Williamsburg, August 6, 1778. Sir, By the
Resolution of Congress. . . .
[Williamsburg, 1778.] Broadside.
LOC copy.   43589

Virginia. Governor, 1779.
Williamsburg, June 18, 1779. Sir, You are
Desired. . . .
[Williamsburg, 1779.] Broadside.
(No copy located.)   43728

Virginia. Governor, 1781.
By His Excellency Thomas Jefferson. . . .
I Have thought fit . . . to Issue this my
Proclamation . . . This 19th Day of
January.
[Richmond, 1781.] Broadside.
WLC copy.   44080

Virginia. Governor, 1787.
Virginia, to witt: By His Excellency
Edmund Randolph. . . . A Proclamation.
Whereas . . . George Rogers Clarke. . . .
Dated Feb. 28, 1787.]

[Richmond, 1787.] Broadside.
(No copy located.)   45196

Virginia. Governor, 1791.
By the Governor of the Commonwealth of
Virginia. . . . A Proclamation. Whereas it
is Represented [Samuel Brady, May 3,
1791].
Richmond, 1791. Broadside.
HSP copy.   46341

Virginia. Governor, 1792.
By the Governor . . . a Proclamation.
Whereas the Public Interest. . . . The 7th
Day of June, 1792.
[Richmond, 1792.] Broadside.
LOC copy.   46661

Virginia. Governor, 1792.
Richmond, July 6, 1792. Gentlemen. . . .
[Richmond, 1792.] Broadside.
LOC copy.   46662

Virginia. Governor, 1793.
By the Governor . . . a Proclamation. The
President. . . . [May 13, 1793.]
[Richmond, 1793.] Broadside.
LOC ph. copy.   46930

Virginia. Governor, 1793.
By the Governor . . . a Proclamation.
Whereas . . . the Plague. . . . 17th Day of
September . . . 1793.
[Richmond, 1793.] Broadside.
(Not located, 1968.)   46931

Virginia. Governor, 1794.
By the Governor . . . a Proclamation.
Whereas . . . Banditti. . . . [Aug. 20,
1794.]
[Richmond, 1794.] Broadside.
(Copy not located.)   47313

Virginia. Governor, 1794.
(Circular.) Richmond, January 25, 1794.
Gentlemen, It is Essentially
Necessary. . . .
[Richmond, 1794.] Broadside.
LOC copy.   28000

Virginia. Governor, 1794.
(Circular.) Richmond, January 25, 1794.
Gentlemen. It is Essentially. . . .
[Richmond, 1794.] Broadside.
LOC copy.   47315

Virginia. Governor, 1794.
Council Chamber, January 25, 1794. Sir,
The Annexed Resolution. . . .
[Richmond, 1794.] Broadside.
LOC copy.   28001

Virginia. Governor, 1794.
General Orders . . . July 19, 1794.
[Richmond, 1794.] Broadside.
HEH copy.   47316

Virginia. Governor, 1794.
Militia Orders.
[Richmond, 1794.] Broadside.
HEH copy.   47317

Virginia. Governor, 1794.
Richmond, December 16, 1794. Sir, When
the Citizens. . . .
[Richmond, 1794.] Broadside.
(Copy not located.)   47318

Virginia. Governor, 1795.
By the Governor. . . . A Proclamation. . . .
[May 21, 1795].
[Richmond, 1795.] Broadside.
VaSL copy.   47668

[Virginia. Governor, 1800.
A Letter from Governor Monroe, Several
Documents. . . . Dec. 30, 1800.
Richmond, 1800.]
(Swem 8004.)   38957

Virginia. Governor, 1800.
A Letter from Governor Monroe, to the
General Assembly.
Richmond, Jones, 1800. 16 pp.
YC copy.   38956

Virginia. High Court of Chancery, 1785.
. . . At a High Court of Chancery held in
Richmond, the 8th Day of May 1785.
[Richmond? 1785?] Broadside.
(The only recorded copy cannot be
located.)   44827

Virginia. High Court of Chancery, 1798.
. . . March 16, 1798. Between Robert
Pleasants . . . and Mary Logan. . . .
[Richmond, 1800.] 18 pp.
LCP copy.   38963

Virginia. House Journals, 1776.
Journal of the House of Delegates. . . .
Anno Domini, 1776.
Williamsburg, Purdie, [1776]. 145 pp.
NYPL copy.   15204

Virginia. House Journals, 1777.
Journal of the House of Delegates [May 5
- June 28, 1777].
Williamsburg, Purdie, [1777]. 150 pp.
NYPL copy.   15696

Virginia. House Journals, 1777.
Journal of the House of Delegates [Oct.
20, 1777- Jan. 24, 1778].
Williamsburg, Purdie, [1778]. [2], 143
pp.
NYPL copy.   16155

Virginia. House Journals, 1778.
Journal of the House of Delegates [May 4
- June 1, 1778].
Williamsburg, Purdie, [1778]. 50 pp.
VaSL copy.   16156

[Virginia. House Journals, 1778.
Journal of the House of Delegates [Oct. 5
- Dec. 19, 1778].
Williamsburg, 1779.]
(No copy located.)   16658

Virginia. House Journals, 1779.
Journal of the House of Delegates [May 3
- June 26, 1779].
Williamsburg, Clarkson & Davis, [1779].
78 pp.
LOC copy.   16659

Virginia. House Journals, 1779.
Journal of the House of Delegates. . . .
Anno Domini, 1779 [Oct. 4- Dec. 24,
1779].
Williamsburg, Clarkson & Davis, [1780].
132 pp.
HEH copy.   17056

Virginia. House Journals, 1780.
Journal of the House of Delegates [May 1
- July 14, 1780].
Richmond, [1780]. 88 pp.
LOC copy.   17057

Virginia. House Journals, 1780.
Journal of the House of Delegates [Oct.
16, 1780 - Jan. 2, 1781].
[Richmond, 1781.] 120 pp.]
(Not printed until 1827.)   17414

[Virginia. House Journals, 1781.
Journal of the House of Delegates [Mar.
1, 1781 +].
Richmond, 1781.]
(No copy of 1781 printing located.)   17415

Virginia. House Journals, 1781.
Journal of the House of Delegates [May 7
- June 23, 1781].
Charlottesville, [1781]. 52 pp.
LOC copy.   17416

[Virginia. House Journals, 1781.
Journal of the House of Delegates [Oct. 1,
1781 - Jan. 5, 1782].
Richmond, 1782.]
(No copy of a 1782 printing located.) 17783

[Virginia. House Journals, 1782.
Journal of the House of Delegates [May 6
- June 14, 1782].
Richmond, 1782.]
(No copy of a 1782 printing located.) 17784

[Virginia. House Journals, 1782.
Journal of the House of Delegates [May
5- June 28, 1782].
Richmond, 1783.]
(Probably not printed until 1828.)   18285

[Virginia. House Journals, 1782.
Journal of the House of Delegates [Oct.
21 - Dec. 28, 1782].
Richmond, 1783.]
(Probably not printed until 1828.)   18284

Virginia. House Journals, 1783.

Journal of the House of Delegates [Oct.
20 - Dec. 22, 1783].
[Richmond, 1784.] 156 pp.
LOC copy.   18859

Virginia. House Journals, 1784.
Journal of the House of Delegates [May 3
- June 30, 1784].
[Richmond, 1784.] 123 pp.
VaSL copy.   18860

Virginia. House Journals, 1784.
Journal of the House of Delegates [Oct.
18, 1784 - Jan. 7, 1785].
[Richmond, 1785.] 104 pp.
LOC copy.   19353

Virginia. House Journals, 1785.
Journal of the House of Delegates [Oct.
17, 1785 - Jan. 21, 1786].
[Richmond, 1786.] 153 pp.
LOC copy.   20106

Virginia. House Journals, 1786.
Journal of the House of Delegates [Oct.
16, 1786 - Jan. 11, 1787].
Richmond, Dixon & Holt, [1787]. 157 pp.
VaSL copy.   20840

Virginia. House Journals, 1787.
Journal of the House of Delegates [Oct.
15, 1787 - Jan. 8, 1788].
[Richmond, 1788.] 111 pp.
VaSL copy.   21556

[Virginia. House Journals, 1788.
Journal of the House of Delegates [June
23 - 30, 1788].
Richmond, 1788.]
(Not printed until 1828.)   21557

Virginia. House Journals, 1788.
Journal of the House of Delegates [Oct.
20 - Dec. 30, 1788].
Richmond, Dixon, [1789]. 92 pp.
VaSL copy.   22226

Virginia. House Journals, 1789.
Extract from the Journal of . . . the 8th of
December, 1789.
[Richmond, 1789.] [2] pp.
LOC copy.   45736

Virginia. House Journals, 1789.
Journal of the House of Delegates [Oct.
19 - Dec. 19, 1789].
Richmond, Dixon, [1790]. 120 pp.
VaSL copy.   23018

Virginia. House Journals, 1790.
Journal of the House of Delegates [Oct.
18 - Dec. 29, 1790].
Richmond, Dixon, [1791]. 169 pp.
VaSL copy.   23944

Virginia. House Journals, 1791.
Journal of the House of Delegates [Oct.
17 - Dec. 20, 1791].
Richmond, Davis, 1791. 147 pp.
VaSL copy.   24966

Virginia. House Journals, 1792.
Journal of the House of Delegates [Oct. 1
- Dec. 28, 1792].
Richmond, Davis, 1792. 226 pp.
VaSL copy.   26390

Virginia. House Journals, 1793.
Journal of the House of Delegates [Oct.
21 - Dec. 12, 1793].
Richmond, Davis, 1793. 132 pp.
(Errors in paging appear in all copies. The
text of this seems to be complete.)
VaSL copy.   28002

Virginia. House Journals, 1794.
Journal of the House of Delegates [Nov.
11 - Dec. 27, 1794.].
Richmond, Davis, 1794. 127 pp.
VaSL copy.   29799

Virginia. House Journals, 1795.
Journal of the House of Delegates [Nov.
10-Dec. 29, 1795].
Richmond, Davis, 1795. 138 pp.
(No perfect copy located.)
Composite copy.   31502

Virginia. House Journals, 1796.
Journal of the House of Delegates [Nov. 8
- Dec. 27, 1796].
Richmond, Davis, 1796. 102 pp.
(The unique original cannot now be

located. NYPL has a photostat which
cannot be reproduced.)   33128

Virginia. House Journals, 1797.
Journal of the House of Delegates [Dec.
4, 1797-Jan. 19, 1798].
Richmond, Va., Davis, 1797. 115 pp.
VaSL copy.   34936

Virginia. House Journals, 1798.
Journal of the House of Delegates [Dec.
3, 1798-Jan. 26, 1799].
Richmond, Jones & Dixon, 1798. 104 pp.
VaSL copy.   36642

Virginia. House Journals, 1799.
Journal of the House of Delegates [Dec.
2, 1799-Jan. 28, 1800].
Richmond, Jones, 1799. 105 pp.
VaSL copy.   38954

[Virginia. Laws, Statutes, etc., 1776.
An Act to Oblige the Free Male
Inhabitants.
Williamsburg, Purdie, [1776]. 2 pp.
(A duplicate of 15693, q.v.)   15202

Virginia. Laws, Statutes, etc., 1777.
An Act for Raising Volunteers.
[Williamsburg, 1777.] [2] pp.
LOC copy.   15691

Virginia. Laws, Statutes, etc., 1777.
An Act for the more Speedily Completing
the Quota of Troops.
[Williamsburg, 1777.] 3 pp.
LOC copy.   15692

Virginia. Laws, Statutes, etc., 1777.
An Act to Oblige the Free Male
Inhabitants of this State . . . to give
Assurance of Allegiance.
Williamsburg, Purdie, [1777]. [2] pp.
NYPL copy.   15693

Virginia. Laws, Statutes, etc., 1780.
An Act for Speedily Recruiting the Quota.
[Richmond? 1780.] [2] pp.
LOC copy.   43911

Virginia. Laws, Statutes, etc., 1780.
An Act more Effectually to Prevent and
Punish Desertion.
[Williamsburg, 1780.] [2] pp.
LOC copy.   43912

Virginia. Laws, Statutes, etc., 1781.
An Act for Enlisting Soldiers. . . . June 21,
1781.
Charlottesville, Dunlap & Hayes, [1781].
Broadside.
LOC copy.   44081

Virginia. Laws, Statutes, etc., 1781.
An Act for Recruiting this State's Quota.
[Richmond? 1781.] 4 pp.
LOC copy.   44082

Virginia. Laws, Statutes, etc., 1781.
An Act for Supplying the Army.
[Richmond? 1781.] [2] pp.
LOC copy.   44083

[Virginia. Laws, Statutes, 1782.
An Act, for Ascertaining Certain Taxes.
Richmond, [1782]. 7 pp.]
(Perhaps misdated by Evans; no such item
now to be found.)   17780

[Virginia. Laws, Statutes, etc., 1784.
An Act for Opening and Extending the
Navigation of Potomack River.
Alexandria, [1784]. 4 pp.]
(The copy described by Evans is not now
to be found.)   20103

Virginia. Laws, Statutes, etc., 1784.
An Act to Authorize the Congress. . . .
[Richmond, 1784.] Broadside.
LOC copy.   18857

[Virginia. Laws, Statutes, etc., 1784.
Acts of Assembly, Printed since the
Revised Code. viz. For the Years 1784 and
1785.
Richmond, Nicolson, 1793.]
(The origin of this entry is unknown, but
probably an adv. for 26387.)   26386

Virginia. Laws, Statutes, etc., 1784.
Acts of General Assembly, for Clearing
and Improving the Navigation of James
River.

Richmond, Nicolson, [1793]. 28 pp.
AAS copy.   26387

Virginia. Laws, Statutes, etc., 1785.
A Collection of all such Public Acts . . .
Passed Since the year 1768, as are now in
Force.
Richmond, Nicolson & Prentis, 1785. 235
pp.
AAS copy.   19351

Virginia. Laws, Statutes, etc., 1786.
An Act Concerning the Erection of . . .
Kentucky into an Independent State. . . .
Jan. 6, 1786.
[Richmond?] 1786.] Broadside.
WLC facsim. copy.   45013

Virginia. Laws, Statutes, etc., 1786.
An Act for Appointing Deputies . . to a
Convention . . . for . . . Revising the
Foederal Constitution. . . . November 23,
1786.
[Richmond, 1786.] Broadside.
AAS copy.   20101

Virginia. Laws, Statutes, etc., 1786.
An Act for Establishing Religious
Freedom, Passed . . . 1786.
[Richmond, 1786.] 7 pp.
LOC copy.   20102

Virginia. Laws, Statutes, etc., 1786.
An Act to Enable the Citizens . . . to
Discharge Certain Taxes.
[Richmond, 1786.] Broadside.
LOC copy.   45014

Virginia. Laws, Statutes, etc., 1787.
Virginia, to wit. . . . An Act Concerning
the Convention to be held in June next.
Passed December 12th, 1787.
[Richmond, 1787.] Broadside.
AAS copy.   20842

Virginia. Laws, Statutes, etc., 1788.
An Act Concerning the Erection of
Kentucky into an Independent State [Dec.
29, 1788].
[Richmond, 1788.] Broadside.
(Best copy available.)
WisHS copy.   45398

Virginia. Laws, Statutes, etc., 1788.
An Act Directing the Mode of Proceeding
under Certain Executions. . . . January 4,
1785.
[Richmond? 1788.] Broadside.
(Best copy available.)
Duke University copy.   45399

Virginia. Laws, Statutes, etc., 1788.
An Act to Amend the Several Acts
Respecting the Militia. . . . January 1,
1788.
[Richmond, 1788.] Broadside.
(No copy located.)   45400

Virginia. Laws, Statutes, etc., 1788.
In the House of Delegates, the 25th of
December, 1788. Resolved, That the
Executive . . . In Council, December 29,
1788.
[Richmond, 1788.] Broadside.
LOC copy.   45402

Virginia. Laws, Statutes, etc., 1792.
[An Act concerning the erection of the
district of Kentucky into an independent
State.
Lexington, Bradford, 1792.] Broadside.
(No copy located.)   46663

Virginia. Laws, Statutes, etc., 1792.
Certain Acts of the General Assembly . . .
Passed . . . the First Day of October . . .
One Thousand Seven Hundred and
Ninety-Two, the Operation whereof was
Suspended.
Richmond, Davis, 1794. 119 pp.
VaSL copy.   27998

[Virginia. Laws, Statutes, etc., 1793.
Certain Acts . . . for Regulating the
Militia.
Richmond, Davis, [1793].]
(Title and imprint assumed by Evans from
advs.)   26389

Virginia. Laws, Statutes, etc., 1793.
Richmond, January [   ] 1793. . . . An
Act for the Regulating the Militia. . . .

[Richmond, 1793.] Broadside.
HSP copy.   46932

Virginia. Laws, Statutes, etc., 1794.
An Act for Regulating Pilot's Fees.
[Richmond? 1784?] Broadside.
(The only known copy is mutilated.)
LOC copy.   44621

Virginia. Laws, Statutes, etc., 1794.
A Collection of all such Acts of the
General Assembly . . . as are now in
Force.
Richmond, Davis, 1794. 380 pp.
AAS copy.   27999

Virginia. Laws, Statutes, etc., 1796.
Abridgment of the Public Permanent
Laws.
Richmond, Davis, 1796. [2], 385 pp.
LOC copy.   31497

Virginia. Laws, Statutes, etc., 1796.
An Act to Amend the Penal Laws.
[Richmond, 1796?] 16 pp.
(No copy available.)   48007

[Virginia. Laws, Statutes, etc., 1796.
Acts . . . for Regulating Pilots.
Norfolk, Va., Willett & O'Connor, 1796.]
("May be had at the Herald Office,"
Norfolk Herald, June 23, 1796.)   31500

Virginia. Laws, Statutes, etc., 1796.
Acts of the Commonwealth of Virginia,
for Regulating the Militia; together with
the Acts of the Congress.
Richmond, Davis, 1796. 36, 26 pp.
LOC copy.   31498

[Virginia. Laws, Statutes, etc., 1799.
An Act Concerning Elections.
Richmond, 1799.]
(Printing assumed from House Journal,
Dec. 8, 1799.)   36626

[Virginia. Laws, Statutes, 1799.
An Act Imposing Certain Taxes on Law
Process.
Richmond, 1799.]
(Printing assumed by Swem from House
Journal, Jan. 25, 1799. See Council
Journal, Feb. 6, 1799.)   36627

[Virginia. Laws, Statutes, etc., 1799.
An Act Laying Taxes for the Support of
Government.
Richmond, 1799.]
(Printing assumed by Swem from House
Journal, Jan. 25, 1799. See Council
Journal, Feb. 6, 1799.)   36628

Virginia. Laws, Statutes, etc., 1799.
Militia Law. . . . Passed January 23, 1799.
[Richmond, 1799.] [2] pp.
LOC copy.   36645

Virginia. Lieutenant Governor, 1790.
In Council, January 21, 1790. Gentlemen,
A List of the Pensioners. . . .
[Richmond, 1790.] Broadside.
NYPL copy.   46088

Virginia. Lieutenant Governor, 1794.
By the Lieutenant Governor . . . a
Proclamation. Whereas I have Received
Information . . . Contagious Disease. . . .
[Aug. 2, 1794.]
[Richmond, 1794.] Broadside.
HEH copy.   47314

Virginia. Militia, 1776.
[Continental and Provincial Articles of
War.
Williamsburg, Purdie, 1776.]
(cf. Purdie's Virginia Gazette, Aug. 30,
1776.)   43210

Virginia. Senate Journals, 1776.
Journal of the Senate. Anno Domini,
1776.
Williamsburg, Purdie, [1776]. 65 pp.
NYPL copy.   15205

Virginia. Senate Journals, 1777.
Journal of the Senate [May 5 - June 28,
1777].
Williamsburg, Purdie, [1777]. 50 pp.
(The unique copy is incomplete.)
NYPL copy.   15697

Virginia. Senate Journals, 1777.

Journal of the Senate [Oct. 21, 1777 - Jan. 24, 1778].
Williamsburg, Dixon & Hunter, 1777. 58 pp.
NYPL copy. 16157

Virginia. Senate Journals, 1778.
Journal of the Senate [May 4 - June 1, 1778].
Williamsburg, Dixon & Hunter, 1778. 20 pp.
LOC copy. 16660

Virginia. Senate Journals, 1778.
Journal of the Senate [May 4 - June 1, 1778].
Williamsburg, Dixon & Hunter, 1778. 20 pp.
JCB copy. 43590

Virginia. Senate Journals, 1778.
Journal of the Senate [Oct. 5 - Dec. 19, 1778].
Williamsburg, Dixon & Nicholson, 1779. 60 pp.
LOC copy. 16661

Virginia. Senate Journals, 1779.
Journal of the Senate [May 3 - June 26, 1779].
Williamsburg, Dixon & Nicolson, 1779. 59 pp.
LOC copy. 16662

Virginia. Senate Journals, 1779.
Journal of the Senate [Oct. 4 - Dec. 24, 1779].
Williamsburg, Clarkson & Davis, [1780]. 76 pp.
LOC copy. 17058

[Virginia. Senate Journals, 1780.
Journal of the Senate [May 1 - July 14, 1780].
Richmond, 1780.]
(No copy found.) 17059

[Virginia. Senate Journals, 1780.
Journal of the Senate [Oct. 16, 1780 - Jan. 2, 1781.]
Richmond, 1781.]
(No copy located.) 17412

[Virginia. Senate Journals, 1781.
Journal of the Senate [Mar. 1-22, 1781].
Richmond, 1781.]
(No copy located.) 17413

[Virginia. Senate Journals, 1781.
Journal of the Senate [Oct. 1, 1781 - Jan. 5, 1782].
Richmond, 1782.]
(No copy located.) 17785

[Virginia. Senate Journals, 1782.
Journal of the Senate [May 6 - June 14, 1782].
Richmond, 1782.]
(No copy located.) 17786

[Virginia. Senate Journals, 1782.
Journal of the Senate [Oct. 21 - Dec. 28, 1782].
Richmond, 1783.
(Probably not printed.) 19345

[Virginia. Senate Journals, 1783.
Journal of the Senate. [May 5 - June 28, 1783].
Richmond, 1783.]
(Probably not printed.) 18287

Virginia. Senate Journals, 1783.
Journal of the Senate [Oct. 20 - Dec. 22, 1783].
Richmond, Nicolson & Prentis, [1784]. 55 pp.
LOC copy. 18861

[Virginia. Senate Journals, 1784.
Journal of the Senate [May 3 - June 30, 1784].
Richmond, 1784.]
(Probably not printed.) 18862

[Virginia. Senate Journals, 1784.
Journal of the Senate [Oct. 18, 1784 - Jan. 7, 1785].
Richmond, 1785.]
(Probably not printed.) 19354

[Virginia. Senate Journals, 1785.

Journal of the Senate [Oct. 17, 1785 - Jan 21, 1786].
Richmond, 1786.]
(Evans assumed this ed. from the 1827 printing, and the recorded copies are actually that ed.) 20107

[Virginia. Senate Journals, 1786.
Journal of the Senate [Oct. 16, 1786 - Jan. 11, 1787].
Richmond, 1787.]
(Not printed until 1828.) 20841

[Virginia. Senate Journals, 1787.
Journal of the Senate [Oct. 15, 1787 - Jan. 8, 1788].
Richmond, 1788.]
(Not printed until 1828.) 21558

[Virginia. Senate Journals, 1788.
Journal of the Senate [June 23 - Dec. 30, 1788].
Richmond, Dixon, 1789.]
(This was not printed until 1828.) 22227

[Virginia. Senate Journals, 1789.
Journal of the Senate [Oct 19 - Dec. 19, 1789].
Richmond, 1790.]
(Not printed until 1828.) 23019

[Virginia. Senate Journals, 1790.
Journal of the Senate [Oct. 18 - Dec. 28, 1790].
Richmond, 1791.]
(Apparently not printed until 1828.) 23945

Virginia. Senate Journals, 1791.
Journal of the Senate. . . . October Session . . . 1791.
Richmond, Nicolson, 1791. 72 pp.
LOC copy. 24967

[Virginia. Senate Journals, 1792.
Journal of the Senate [Oct. 1 - Dec. 28, 1792].
Richmond, 1793.]
(Not printed.) 26392

Virginia. Senate Journals, 1793.
[Journal of the Senate, Oct. 21 - Dec. 13, 1793.
Richmond, Nicholson, 1794.] 50+ pp.
(The only known copy is badly defective.)
LOC copy. 28003

[Virginia. Senate Journals, 1794.
Journal of the Senate [Nov. 11 - Dec. 27, 1794.]
Richmond, 1795.]
(Apparently not printed.) 29800

[Virginia. Senate Journals, 1795.
Journal of the Senate [Nov. 10 - Dec. 29, 1795].
Richmond, Nicolson, 1796.]
(Not printed.) 31503

[Virginia. Senate Journals, 1796.
Journal of the Senate [Nov. 8 - Dec. 27, 1796].
Richmond, Nicolson, 1797.]
(Copy at Wm. & Mary found too late.) 33129

[Virginia. Senate Journals, 1797.
Journal of the Senate [Dec. 4, 1797 - Jan. 25, 1798].
Richmond, Nicolson, 1798.]
(Copy at Wm. & Mary found too late.) 34937

[Virginia. Senate Journals, 1798.
Journal of the Senate [Dec. 3, 1798 - Jan. 26, 1799].
Richmond, Nicolson, 1798.]
(Copy at Wm. & Mary found too late.) 36643

[Virginia. Senate Journals, 1799.
Journal of the Senate [Dec. 2, 1799- Jan. 28, 1800].
Richmond, Nicolson, 1799.]
(Swem 7954; no copy found.) 38955

Virginia. Session Laws, 1776.
At a General Assembly [Oct. 7, 1776 +].
Williamsburg, Purdie, [1776]. 56 pp.
VaSL copy. 15203

Virginia. Session Laws, 1777.
At a General Assembly [May 5, 1777 +].

Williamsburg, Purdie, [1777]. [2], 34 pp.
NYPL copy. 15694

Virginia. Session Laws, 1777.
At a General Assembly [Oct. 20, 1777 +].
Williamsburg, Purdie, [1777]. [2], 40 pp.
NYPL copy. 15695

Virginia. Session Laws, 1778.
At a General Assembly [May 4, 1778 +].
Williamsburg, Purdie, [1778]. 14 pp.
NYPL copy. 16153

Virginia. Session Laws, 1778.
At a General Assembly [Oct. 5, 1778 +].
Williamsburg, Purdie, [1778]. 46 pp.
NYPL copy. 16154

Virginia. Session Laws, 1779.
Acts Passed at a General Assembly [May 3 - June 26, 1779].
Williamsburg, Dixon & Nicolson, [1779]. 57 pp.
LOC copy. 16654

Virginia. Session Laws, 1779.
Acts Passed at a General Assembly [Oct. 4 - Dec. 24, 1779].
Williamsburg, Dixon & Nicolson, [1779]. 48 pp.
(No good copy located.)
VaSL copy. 16655

Virginia. Session Laws, 1780.
Acts Passed at a General Assembly [May 1 - July 14, 1780].
Richmond, [1780]. 46 pp.
NYPL copy. 17055

Virginia. Session Laws, 1780.
Acts Passed at a General Assembly [Oct. 16, 1780 - Jan. 2, 1781].
Richmond, [1781]. 34 pp.
LOC copy. 17407

Virginia. Session Laws, 1781.
Acts Passed at a General Assembly [Mar. 1, 1781 +].
Richmond, [1781]. 8, [1] pp.
VaSL copy. 17408

Virginia. Session Laws, 1781.
Acts Passed at a General Assembly [May 7 - June 23, 1781].
Charlottesville, [1781]. 18, [1] pp.
NYPL copy. 17409

Virginia. Session Laws, 1781.
Acts Passed at a General Assembly [Nov. 5, 1781-Jan. 5, 1782].
Richmond, [1782]. 32 pp.
VaSL copy. 17781

Virginia. Session Laws, 1782.
Acts Passed at a General Assembly [May 6-June 14, 1782].
Richmond, [1782]. 38 pp.
VaSL copy. 17782

Virginia. Session Laws, 1782.
Acts Passed at a General Assembly [Oct. 21 - Dec. 28, 1782].
Richmond, Dunlap & Hayes, [1783]. 32 pp.
VaSL copy. 18281

Virginia. Session Laws, 1783.
Acts Passed at a General Assembly [May 5 - June 28, 1783].
Richmond, [1783]. 45, [1] pp.
VaSL copy. 18282

Virginia. Session Laws, 1783.
Acts Passed at a General Assembly [Oct. 20 - Dec. 22, 1783].
Richmond, [1783]. 26 pp.
VaSL copy. 18283

Virginia. Session Laws, 1784.
Acts Passed at a General Assembly [May 3 - June 30, 1784].
Richmond, [1784]. 23 pp.
VaSL copy. 18858

Virginia. Session Laws, 1784.
Acts Passed [Oct. 18, 1784 - Jan. 7, 1785].
Richmond, Dunlap & Hayes, [1785]. [2], 31 pp.
VaSL copy. 19348

Virginia. Session Laws, 1785.
Acts Passed at a General Assembly [Oct.

17, 1785 - Jan. 21, 1786].
Richmond, Dunlap & Hayes, [1786]. [2],
73 pp.
VaSL copy. 20104

Virginia. Session Laws, 1786.
Acts Passed [Oct. 16, 1786+].
Richmond, Dixon, Holt, Nicholson, and
Davies, [1787]. 56, [1] pp.
VaSL copy. 20837

Virginia. Session Laws, 1787.
Acts Passed [Oct. 15, 1787 - Jan. 8, 1788].
Richmond, David & Nicolson, [1788]. 47,
[1] pp.
LOC copy. 21548

Virginia. Session Laws, 1787.
Acts Passed [Oct. 15, 1787 - Jan. 8, 1788].
Richmond, Dixon, Davis, & Nicolson. 47,
[2] pp.
LOC copy. 21549

Virginia. Session Laws, 1788.
Acts Passed [June 23 - 30, 1788].
[Richmond, 1788]. Broadside.
LOC copy. 21550

Virginia. Session Laws, 1788.
Acts Passed at a General Asembly [Oct.
20 - Dec. 30, 1788].
Richmond, Dixon, Davis & Nicholson,
[1789]. 49, [1] pp.
LOC copy. 22224

Virginia. Session Laws, 1789.
Acts Passed at a General Assembly [Oct.
19 - Dec. 19, 1789].
Richmond, Dixon, [1790]. 50 pp.
AAS copy. 23017

Virginia. Session Laws, 1790.
Acts Passed at a General Assembly [Oct.
18 - Dec. 29, 1790].
Richmond, Dixon, [1791]. 66 pp.
AAS copy. 23943

Virginia. Session Laws, 1791.
Acts Passed at a General Assembly [Oct.
17 - Dec. 20, 1791].
Richmond, Davis, 1791. 44 pp.
VaSL copy. 24963

Virginia. Session Laws, 1792.
Acts Passed at a General Assembly [Oct.]
- Dec. 28, 1792].
Richmond, Davis, 1793. 123 pp.
VaSL copy. 26388

Virginia. Session Laws, 1793.
Acts Passed at a General Assembly [Oct.
21 - Dec. 12, 1793].
Richmond, Davis, 1794. 56 pp.
VaSL copy. 27997

Virginia. Session Laws, 1794.
Acts Passed at a General Assembly [Nov.
11 - Dec. 28, 1794].
Richmond, Davis, 1795. 39 pp.
VaSL copy. 29796

Virginia. Session Laws, 1794.
Akten, welche in der General-Assembly
der Republick Virginien Passert worden
sind.
Philadelphia, Cist, 1795. 152 pp.
VaSL copy. 29797

Virginia. Session Laws, 1795.
Acts Passed at a General Assembly [Nov.
10-Dec. 28, 1795].
Richmond, Davis, 1796. 59 pp.
VaSL copy. 31499

Virginia. Session Laws, 1796.
Acts Passed [Nov. 8 - Dec. 29, 1796].
Richmond, Davis, 1797. 48 pp.
VaSL copy. 33126

Virginia. Session Laws, 1797.
Acts Passed at a General Assembly [Dec.
4, 1797-Jan. 25, 1798].
Richmond, Davis, 1798. 51 pp.
VaSL copy. 34934

Virginia. Session Laws, 1798.
Acts Passed at a General Assembly [Dec.
3, 1798+].
Richmond, Dixons, 1799. 36 pp.
VaSL copy. 36629

Virginia. Session Laws, 1799.
Acts Passed at a General Assembly [Dec.

2, 1799-Jan. 28, 1800.]
Richmond, Jones, 1800. 35 pp.
VaSL copy. 38948

Virginia. Treasurer, 1787.
State of the Public Taxes, Payable for . . .
1786.
[Richmond, 1787.] Broadside.
NYPL copy. 45197

Virginia. Treasury Office, 1786.
Revenue Taxes. . . . October 30, 1786.
[Richmond, 1786.] [2] pp.
LOC copy. 45015

Virginia. War Office, 1779.
War Office (Williamsburg) August 17,
1779. Sir. . . .
[Williamsburg, 1779.] Broadside.
NYHS copy. 43730

[The Virginia Almanac for 1741.
Williamsburg, Parks.] [32] pp.
(The only known copy cannot be
reproduced.) 40221

[The Virginia Almanack for 1743.
Williamsburg, 1742.] [32] pp.
(No copy located.) 40291

[The Virginia Almanac for 1744.
Williamsburg, Parks.] [18+] pp.
(The only known copy cannot be
reproduced.) 40321

[The Virginia Almanack, for 1746.
Williamsburg, Parks.]
(Adv. Va. Gazette, Oct. 10, 1745.) 40390

The Virbinia Almanack, for . . . 1748.
Williamsburg, Parks. [32] pp.
(No perfect copy known.)
Colonial Williamsburg copy. 40448

The Virginia Almanack, for . . . 1749.
Williamsburg, Park. [32] pp.
(The only known copy is imperfect.)
HEH copy. 40486

The Virginia Almanack, for . . . 1750.
Williamsburg, Parks. [32] pp.
(No perfect copy known.)
Colonial Williamsburg copy. 40523

The Virginia Almanack, for . . . 1751.
Williamsburg, Hunter. [32] pp.
VaHS copy. 40573

The Virginia Almanack, for the Year . . .
1752 [by Theophilus Grew, -1759].
Williamsburg, Hunter. [32] pp.
LOC copy. 6688

The Virginia Almanack, for the Year . . .
1753 [by Theophilus Grew, -1759].
Williamsburg, Hunter. [32] pp.
LOC copy. 6851

The Virginia Almanack, for . . . 1754 [by
Theophilus Grew, -1759].
Williamsburg, Hunter. [32] pp.
LOC copy. 7013

The Virginia Almanack, for the Year . . .
1755 [by Theophilus Grew, -1759].
Williamsburg, Hunter. [32] pp.
LOC copy. 7207

The Virginia Almanack, for the Year . . .
1756. . . . By Theophilus Wreg [by
Theophilus Grew, -1759].
Williamsburg, Hunter. [32] pp.
VaHS copy. 7428

The Virginia Almanack, for the Year . . .
1757. . . . By Theophilus Wreg [by
Theophilus Grew, -1759].
Williamsburg, Hunter. [24] pp.
VaHS copy. 7679

The Virginia Almanack, for the Year . . .
1758. . . . By Theophilus Wreg [by
Theophilus Grew, -1759].
Williamsburg, Hunter. [32] pp.
HEH copy. 7908

The Virginia Almanack, for the Year . . .
1759. . . . By Theophilus Wreg [by
Theophilus Grew, -1759].
Williamsburg, Hunter. [32] pp.
(The only known copy is incomplete.)
VaHS copy. 8145

[The Virginia Almanack, for the Year . . .
1760. . . . By Theophilus Wreg [by
Theophilus Grew, -1759].
Williamsburg, Hunter. [32] pp.]
(No copy located.) 8359

The Virginia Almanack for . . . 1761. . . .
By Theophilus Wreg [by Theophilus
Grew, -1759].
Williamsburg, Hunter. [36] pp.
LOC copy. 8610

The Virginia Almanack for . . . 1762. . . .
By Theophilus Wreg [by Theophilus
Grew, -1759].
Williamsburg, Royle. [32] pp.
LOC copy. 8868

[The Virginia Almanack, for . . . 1763. . . .
By Theophilus Wreg [by Theophilus
Grew, -1759].
Williamsburg, Royle.]
(Assumed from the sequence.) 9130

The Virginia Almanac, for . . . 1764. . . .
By Theophilus Wreg [by Theophilus
Grew, -1759].
Williamsburg, Royle. [48] pp.
WLC copy. 9399

The Virginia Almanack, for . . . 1765. . . .
By Theophilus Wreg [by Theophilus
Grew, -1759].
Williamsburg, Royle. [48] pp.
LOC copy. 9684

The Virginia Almanack for . . . 1766. . . .
By Theophilus Wreg [by Theophilus
Grew, -1759].
Williamsburg, Purdie. [24] pp.
LOC copy. 9995

The Virginia Almanack for the Year . . .
1768.
Williamsburg, Purdie & Dixon. [40] pp.
LOC copy. 10779

The Virginia Almanack for . . . 1769.
Williamsburg, Purdie & Dixon. [44] pp.
LOC copy. 11084

The Virginia Almanack for . . . 1770.
Williamsburg, Purdie & Dixon. [40] pp.
LOC copy. 11488

The Virginia Almanack for . . . 1770.
Williamsburg, Rind. [36] pp.
LOC copy. 11514

The Virginia Almanack for . . . 1771.
Williamsburg, Purdie & Dixon. [48] pp.
LOC copy. 11913

The Virginia Almanack for . . . 1771.
Williamsburg, Rind. [32] pp.
VaHS copy. 11912

The Virginia Almanack for . . . 1772.
Williamsburg, Purdie & Dixon. [48] pp.
LOC copy. 12267

The Virginia Almanack for . . . 1772.
Williamsburg, Rind. [32] pp.
AAS copy. 12266

The Virginia Almanack for . . . 1773.
Williamsburg, Purdie & Dixon. [36] pp.
VaHS copy. 12593

The Virginia Almanack for . . . 1773.
Williamsburg, Rind. [36] pp.
LOC copy. 42385

The Virginia Almanack for . . . 1774.
Williamsburg, Purdie & Dixon. [48] pp.
AAS copy. 13059

The Virginia Almanack for . . . 1775.
Williamsburg, Dixon & Hunter. [48] pp.
AAS copy. 13579

The Virginia Almanack for . . . 1775. . . .
By David Rittenhouse.
Williamsburg, Pinkney for Rind. 24 pp.
(The only copy available is imperfect.)
VaHS copy. 13578

The Virginia Almanack for . . . 1776. . . .
By David Rittenhouse.
Williamsburg, Dixon & Hunter. [92] pp.
NYPL copy. 14434

The Virginia Almanack for . . . 1777. . . .
By David Rittenhouse.
Williamsburg, Dixon & Hunter. [32] pp.
AAS copy.   15067

The Virginia Almanack for . . . 1778. . . .
By David Rittenhouse.
Williamsburg, Dixon & Hunter. [26] pp.
AAS copy.   15581

The Virginia Almanack for . . . 1779. . . .
By David Rittenhouse.
Williamsburg, Dixon & Hunter. [24] pp.
VaHS copy.   16056

The Virginia Almanack for . . . 1779. . . .
By David Rittenhouse.
Williamsburg, Dixon & Nicolson. [24] pp.
AAS copy.   16057

The Virginia Almanack for . . . 1780 [by
David Rittenhouse, 1732-1796].
Williamsburg, Dixon & Nicolson. [24] pp.
AAS copy.   16507

The Virginia Almanack for . . . 1781. . . .
By Robert Andrews.
Richmond, Dixon & Nicolson. [24] pp.
AAS copy.   16698

The Virginia Almanack for . . . 1782. . . .
By Robert Andrews.
Richmond, Dixon & Nicolson. [24] pp.
AAS copy.   17080

The Virginia Almanack for . . . 1783. . . .
By Robert Andrews.
Richmond, Nicolson & Prentis. [24] pp.
LOC copy.   17458

The Virginia Almanack for . . . 1784. . . .
By Robert Andrews.
Richmond, Dixon & Holt. [24] pp.
AAS copy.   17817

The Virginia Almanack, for . . . 1784. . . .
By Robert Andrews.
Richmond, Nicolson & Prentis. [24] pp.
VaSL copy.   17816

[The Virginia Almanac for 1785.
Richmond? [20+] pp.]
(Also entered as E18330, q. v.)   44622

The Virginia Almanack, for . . . 1785. . . .
By Robert Andrews.
Richmond, Dixon & Holt. [32] pp.
AAS copy.   18330

The Virginia Almanack for . . . 1786. . . .
By Robert Andrews.
Richmond, Dixon & Holt. [24] pp.
VaHS copy.   18912

The Virginia Almanack, for . . . 1786. . . .
By Robert Andrews.
Richmond, Nicolson. [24] pp.
AAS copy.   18911

[The Virginia Almanack for . . . 1787.
Petersburg, Hunter & Prentis.]
(Origin of entry unknown.)   20110

The Virginia Almanack, for . . . 1787 [by
Robert Andrews, d. 1804].
Richmond, Davis. [36] pp.
VaSL copy.   19743

[The Virginia Almanack, for . . . 1788.
Richmond, Dixon.]
("Just published," Va. Gazette Oct. 25,
1787. Probably 20199 or 20200.)   20843

[The Virginia Almanack for . . . 1790.
Norfolk, Prentis & Baxter.]
(Assumed by Evans from the sequence.)   22228

[The Virginia Almanack for . . . 1790.
Petersburg, Pleasants. [36] pp.]
(No such ed. known.)   45737

[The Virginia Almanac; or The
Winchester Ephemeris for 1790.
Winchester, Bowen.]
(Adv. Winchester Centinal, Nov. 11,
1789.)   45738

The Virginia Almanack, for . . . 1792.
Petersburg, Prentis. [32] pp.
AAS copy.   46342

[The Virginia Almanack for . . . 1793.

Norfolk, Baxter & Wilson.]
(The origin of this entry is unknown.)
                                             24968

The Virginia Almanack, for . . . 1793.
Petersburg, Prentis. [36] pp.
NYPL copy.   24969

The Virginia Almanack, for . . . 1793.
Richmond, Carey. [32] pp.
VaHS copy.   24970

The Virginia Almanac for . . . 1794.
Winchester, Bowen. [24] pp.
(The only known copy is imperfect.)
AAS copy.   46933

[The Virginia Almanac, for . . . 1795.
Winchester, Bowen.]
(The origin of this entry is unknown.)
                                             28005

[The Virginia Almanac, for . . . 1796.
Winchester, Bowen.]
(The origin of this entry is unknown.)
                                             29804

The Virginia Almanack, for . . . 1797 [by
Robert Andrews, d. 1804].
Richmond, Nicolson. [48] pp.
AAS copy.   29991

[The Virginia Almanac for the Year . . .
1797. By the North Mountain Philosopher.
Winchester, Bowen.]
(No copy located.)   31506

The Virginia Almanack, for . . . 1798 [by
Robert Andrews, d. 1804].
Richmond, Nicolson. [38] pp.
VaSL copy.   31737

The Virginia Almanac, for . . . 1798.
Winchester, Bowen. [38] pp.
AAS copy.   33131

The Virginia Almanack for . . . 1799.
Leesburg, Bartgis & Silliman. [36] pp.
(Not located, 1968.)   48748

The Virginia Almanack . . . for . . . 1799.
Petersburg, Prentis. [32] pp.
AAS copy.   48749

The Virginia Almanac, for . . . 1799.
Winchester, Bowen. [36] pp.
AAS copy.   34943

The Virginia Almanac, for . . . 1800.
Fredericksburg, Green for Weems. [36]
pp.
AAS copy.   36650

The Virginia Almanac, for . . . 1800.
Lynchburg, Carter. [32] pp.
(Copy not available for reproduction.)
                                             48988

[The Virginia Almanac, for . . . 1800.
Richmond, Nicolson.] 62 pp.
(The one recorded copy lacks tp.)
VaSL copy.   36649

The Virginia and Farmer's Almanac, for
. . . 1793.
Winchester, Bowen. [32] pp.
AAS copy.   24971

[The Virginia and Maryland Almanack.
. . . For . . . 1730 by John Warner.
Annapolis, 1729.]
(Adv. Md. Gazette, Oct. 28, 1729.)   3374

[The Virginia and Maryland Almanack.
. . . For . . . 1731 by John Warner.
Annapolis, 1730.]
(Adv. Md. Gazette, Oct. 20, 1730.)   3375

[The Virginia and North Carolina
Almanack for 1789.
Petersburg?]
(Adv. Va. Gazette & Petersburg
Intelligencer, Nov. 27, 1788.)   45401

[The Virginia and N. Carolina Almanack
for 1797.
Norfolk, Willett & O'Connor.]
(No copy located.)   31507

[The Virginia & N. Carolina Almanac,
for . . . 1798.
Norfolk, Willett & O'Connor.]
(Entry from advs.)   33132

The Virginia & North Carolina Almanac,
for . . . 1800.
Fredericksburg, Green for Weems. [36]
pp.
AAS copy.   36651

The Virginia Gazette, and Agricultural
Repository.
Dumfries, Fierer & Fosdick. Newspaper.
(Omitted as a serial.)   46664

The Virginia Gazette, and Agricultural
Repository.
Dumfries, Fierer & Fosdick, [1791].
Newspaper.
(Omitted as a serial.)   46343

[The Virginia Miscellany, Consisting of
new Poems.
Williamsburg, 1731.]
(Probably not printed. See Wroth, Parks,
p. 46.)   3483

[Virginia Revived, or, A Plan to Bring in
Cash.
Williamsburg, Rind, 1769?]
("will be published," Rind's Va. Gazette,
Mar. 16, 1769.)   42022

Virginia. sc. I do hereby Certify that
George Mercer . . . Declared before
me. . . .
[Williamsburg, 1765?] Broadside.
LOC ph. copy.   41595

The Virginia Society for Promoting the
Abolition of Slavery.
The Constitution of. . . .
[Richmond, 1795.] Broadside.
HSP copy.   29803

The Virgin's Advice: or the Oxfordshire
Tragedy.
Newport, [1729 ?]. 8 pp.
RIHS copy.   3368

Virtue and Vice: or the History of Charles
Careful. . . . First Worcester Edition.
Worcester, Thomas, 1787. 61, [2] pp.
AAS copy.   20851

Virtue and Vice: or, The History of
Charles Careful, and Harry Heedless.
Boston, Hall, 1792. 61, [2] pp.
AAS copy.   46665

[Virtue and Vice; or the History of
Charles Careful.
Boston, Hall, 1793.]
(Imprint assumed by Evans from Hall
advs.)   26409

Virtue and Vice: or, The History of
Charles Careful.
Boston, Hall, 1795. 61 pp.
LOC copy.   29818

Virtue and Vice: or the History of Charles
Careful. . . . Second Worcester Edition.
Worcester, Thomases, 1796. 61, [2] pp.,
printed wraps.
AAS copy.   31514

Virtue and Vice: or the History of Charles
Careful. . . . Third Worcester Edition.
Worcester, Thomas, 1800. 61, [2] pp.
AAS copy.   38968

Virtue in a Cottage, or, a Mirror for
Children, Displayed in the History of
Sally Bark.
Hartford, Babcock, 1795. 31 pp.
AAS copy.   47669

The Virtues of Society [by Sarah
Wentworth (Apthorp) Morton,
1759-1816].
Boston, Manning & Loring, 1799. 46 pp.
AAS copy.   35844

The Virtuous, Faithful and Loving Wife's
Garland.
[Boston], 1795. Broadside.
EI copy.   29819

A Vision Concerning the Mischievous
Seperation. . . . [by George Keith,
1638-1716].
Philadelphia, 1692. 7 pp.
YC copy.   610

The Vision of Divine Mystery.

[Boston], 1732. 87 pp.
HC copy.   3613

A Vision of Hell [by Jacob Green, 1722-1790].
New London, [1770]. 35 pp.
AAS copy.   11674

A Vision of Hell . . . by Theodorus Van Shermain [by Jacob Green, 1722-1790].
New Haven, 1770. 24 pp.
NYHS copy.   42104

A Vision of Hell. . . . By Theodorus van Shemain [by Jacob Green, 1722-1790].
Boston, Boyle, 1773. 20 pp.
AAS copy.   12798

A Vision of Hell. . . . by Theodorus Van Shemain [by Jacob Green, 1722-1790].
Springfield, [Mass.], Gray, 1793. 23 pp.
AAS copy.   46766

A Vision of Hell. . . . By Theodorus von Shemain [by Jacob Green, 1722-1790].
Amherst, N. H., Preston, 1797. 24 pp.
AAS copy.   32206

A Vision of the Printer's Boy. The Carrier of the American Mercury. . . . Hartford, January 1, 1789.
[Hartford, 1789.] Broadside.
NYHS copy.   21645

Visions, for the Entertainment and Instruction of Young Minds [by Nathaniel Cotton, 1705-1788].
Exeter, Ranlet, 1794. 121, [2] pp.
(Imprint assumed by Evans from adv. in 29386.)
AAS copy.   28482

Visit for a Week [by Lucy Peacock, fl. 1786-1816].
Philadelphia, Ormrod & Conrad, 1796. [4], 275, [11] pp., 1 plate.
AAS copy.   30966

Vital Christianity: a Brief Essay [by Cotton Mather, 1663-1728].
Philadelphia, Keimer for Phillips and Peter, 1725. [4], 30, [1] pp.
(For authorship see Holmes, Cotton Mather, III, 1184-1185.)
MHS copy.   2700

Vital Christianity: a Brief Essay [by Cotton Mather, 1663-1728].
Philadelphia, Harry, 1730. [6], 26 pp.
(For authorship see Holmes, Cotton Mather, III, 1184-1185.)
HSP copy.   3350

[Vital Spark: Anthem.
Philadelphia, M'Culloch, 1788.]
("Lately Published," Federal Gazette, Apr. 8, 1788.)   21567

Vivian, Thomas, d. 1793.
Three Instructive Dialogues. . . . Tenth Edition.
Baltimore, Graham, 1791. 31 pp.
AAS copy.   23952

Vivian, Thomas, d. 1793.
Three Dialogues.
Bennington, Haswell, 1797. 24 pp.
HEH copy.   33139

[Vizcardo y Guzmán, Juan Pablo], 1748-1798.
Lettre aux Espagnols - Americains.
A Philadelphie, MDCCXCXIX. [2], 41 pp.
WLC copy.   36658

[The Vocal Charmer.
Philadelphia, Spotswood, 1793?]
(A ghost of 22400 resulting from Evans' misreading of the adv. in Dunlap's Am. Daily Advertiser, Jan. 19, 1793.)   26410

The Vocal Companion, Being a Choice Collection of the most Approved Songs.
Philadelphia, Carey, 1796. 196 pp., 1 plate.
AAS copy.   31515

[The Vocal Magazine of New Songs.
Philadelphia, 1783?]
(Sonneck-Upton, p. 445; no copy known.)   44490

[The Vocal Muse: or Ladies Songster.

[Philadelphia], Dobson & Young and Kammerer, 1792.]
(Entry from adv. "just published" in Dunlap's Am. Daily Adv., Oct. 5, 1792.)   24978

The Vocal Remembrancer; being a Choice Selection of the Most Admired Songs.
Philadelphia, Spotswood, 1790. viii, 184 pp.
AAS copy.   23028

[The Vocal Remembrancer: being a Choice Selection of the most Admired Songs.
Philadelphia, Spotswood, 1793?]
(Imprint assumed by Evans from Spotswood's advs. for "new books.")   26411

[Vogler, Gerard]
The Request.
New York and Philadelphia, B. Carr; Baltimore, J. Carr, [1796]. Broadside.
AAS copy.   48008

A Voice from Heaven [by Cotton Mather, 1663-1728].
Boston, Kneeland, 1719. 16 pp.
JCB copy.   2049

A Voice from the Tombs.
New York, Parker, 1762. 12 pp.
(The only known copy could not be reproduced.)   41321

The Voice of God in a Tempest [by Cotton Mather, 1663-1728].
Boston, Kneeland, 1723. [4], 19 pp.
AAS copy.   2461

[The Voice of God to Christless Unregenerate Sinners.
Boston, Gray and Butler, 1730. [2], 46 pp.]
(The unique copy could not be found; possibly a catalogue ghost.)   3372

The Voice of God to the People [by David Austin, 1760-1831].
Elizabethtown, Kollock, 1796. 154 pp.
LOC copy.   30006

The Voice of the People.
[Boston, 1754.] 8 pp.
MHS copy.   7329

The Voice of the Prophets [by David McGregore, 1710-1777].
[Hartford? 1776.] 15 pp.
CHS copy.   43055

The Voice of the Prophets Considered in a Discourse or Sermon.
n.p., 1776. 15 pp.
AAS copy.   43211

The Voice of Warning, to Christians [by John Mitchell Mason, 1770-1829].
New York, Hopkins, 1800. 40 pp.
AAS copy.   37904

[Volck, Alexander.
Das Entdeckte Geheimnuess.
Philadelphia, Boehm, 1748. [8], 124 + pp.]
(No copy located.)   6437

Vollstaendiges Marlburger Gesang-Buch.
See
Marlburger Gesang-Buch.

[Volney, Constantin François Chasseboeuf, comte de], 1757-1820.
Common Sense: or Natural Ideas Opposed to Supernatural.
New York, 1795. 203, [1] pp.
(All located copies have the derogatory statement about priests cut out of p. 137.)
AAS copy.   29820

[Volney, Constantin François Chasseboeuf, comte de, 1757-1820.
Common Sense: or, Natural Ideas Opposed to Supernatural.
Philadelphia, 1795. 204 pp.]
(A ghost of 29820.)   29821

[Volney, Constantin François Chasseboeuf, comte de, 1757-1820.
Elements of the Study of History.
Philadelphia, 1795.]

(Evans' entry from copyright notice. The one reported copy cannot now be located.)   29822

Volney, Constantin François Chasseboeuf, comte de, 1757-1820.
The Law of Nature.
Philadelphia, Bailey for Stephens, 1796. viii, [4], 161 pp., 1 plate.
LCP copy.   31516

Volney, Constantin François Chasseboeuf, comte de, 1757-1820.
The Law of Nature.
Philadelphia, 1797. 56 pp.
AAS copy.   33141

[Volney, Constantin François Chasseboeuf, comte de, 1757-1820.
The Ruins or Meditations on the Revolutions of Empires.
Philadelphia, 1795.]
(Evans' entry from copyright notice. The one recorded copy cannot now be located.)   29823

Volney, Constantin François Chasseboeuf, comte de, 1757-1820.
The Ruins.
New York, Davis, 1796. 305 pp., 2 plates, 1 map.
AAS copy.   31517

Volney, Constantin François Chasseboeuf, comte de, 1757-1820.
The Ruins.
Philadelphia, Lyon, 1799. xxiv, 406, 45 pp., 2 plates, 1 map.
AAS copy.   36661

[Volney, Constantin François Chasseboeuf, comte de, 1757-1820.
Travels through Syria and Egypt.
Philadelphia, 1795.]
(Proposed but not published.)   29824

Volney, Constantin François Chasseboeuf, comte de, 1757-1820.
Travels through Egypt and Syria.
New York, Tiebout, 1798. [2], 256; 297, [5] pp.
(An imprint variant of 34949, q. v. for text.)
AAS copy.   48750

Volney, Constantin François Chasseboeuf, comte de, 1757-1820.
Travels through Egypt and Syria. In Two Volumes.
New York, Tiebout for Duyckinck, 1798. [2], 256; 297, [5] pp.
(Evans guessed at the imprint.)
JCB copy.   34949

Volney, Constantin François Chasseboeuf, comte de, 1757-1820.
Volney's Answer to Doctor Priestley.
Philadelphia, 1797. 15 pp.
LCP copy.   33140

Voltaire, Francois Marie Arouet de, 1694-1778.
The Man Worth Forty Crowns.
Philadelphia, Bell, 1778. 116, [4] pp.
AAS copy.   16161

Voltaire, Francois Marie Arouet de, 1694-1778.
Miscellanies.
Philadelphia, Bell, 1778. [4], 130, [2], 129, 128 pp.
AAS copy.   16162

[Voltaire, François Marie Arouet de], 1694-1778.
The Philosophical Dictionary, for the Pocket.
Catskill, Croswell for Fellows and Duyckinck, 1796. [10], 336 pp.
AAS copy.   31518

The Volunteer Laureate: or Fall of Peter Pindar.
New York, Mott & Lyon for Smith, 1796. 23 pp.
JCB copy.   29997

[The Volunteer Songster, or Vocal Remembrances for 1799.
Baltimore, 1799.]
(Imprint assumed by Minick from adv. "For sale" in Telegraphe, Jan. 29, 1799.)   36662

[The Volunteer's March; being a Full and True Account of the Bloody Fight . . . at Pigwocket.
Boston, Franklin, 1725.] Broadside.
(Adv. N. E. Courant, May 31, 1725.) 39838

[Vom Cometen.
Germantown, 1746. Broadside.]
(Title from adv.)   5876

Von der Richtigkeit des Menschlichen Lebens.
[Ephrata, 1765?] Broadside.
LCP copy.   41596

[Vorschlag zur Errichtung einer Deutschen Schule [by Nicolaus Ludwig Zinzendorf, 1700-1760].
[Germantown, 1742.] Broadside.]
(Reprinted Fresenius Nachrichten, III, 740.)   5109

Vorspiel der Neuen-Welt.
Philadelphia, Franklin, 1732. 200 pp.
HSP copy.   3503

Vose, Solomon, 1768-1809.
A Masonick Charge: Delivered at Greenfield.
Greenfield, Mass., Barker, 1798. 11 pp.
AAS copy.   34950

The Voters New Catechism.
[New York, 1768.] Broadside.
AAS ph. copy.   11108

Vox Populi. Liberty, Property, and No Stamps. The News-Boy Who Carries the Boston Evening Post. . . .
[Boston, 1766?] Broadside.
HSP copy.   41670

A Voyage to Boston. A Poem [by Philip Morin Freneau, 1752-1832].
New York, Anderson, [1775]. 24 pp.
NYHS copy.   14043

A Voyage to Boston. A Poem [by Philip Morin Freneau, 1752-1832].
Philadelphia, Woodhouse, 1775. 24 pp.
AAS copy.   14044

[A Voyage to the Moon, by Count D'Artois.
Bennington, 1786.]
("Just published," Vt. Gazette, June 6, 1786.)   20117

[The Voyages and Adventures of Captain Robert Boyle [by William Rufus Chetwood, d. 1766].
Boston, Folsom, 1790.]
(Entry apparently from adv. for a London ed.)   22402

The Voyages and Adventures of Captain Robert Boyle [by William Rufus Chetwood, d. 1766].
Boston, Folsom, 1792. 249, [2] pp.
AAS copy.   46409

The Voyages and Adventures of Captain Robert Boyle [by William Rufus Chetwood, d. 1766].
Greenfield, Dickman for Thomas & Andrews and West, 1794. 244 pp.
AAS copy.   26766

The Voyages and Adventures of Captain Robert Boyle [by William Rufus Chetwood, d. 1766].
Cooperstown, Phinney for Spencers & Webb, 1796. 264 pp.
AAS copy.   30188

The Voyages and Adventures of Captain Robert Boyle [by William Rufus Chetwood, d. 1766].
Walpole, N. H., Carlisle for Thomas & Thomas, 1799. 244 pp.
AAS copy.   35299

Le Vrai Patron des Saines Paroles [by Cotton Mather, 1663-1728].
[Boston, 1704.] 15 pp.
BPL copy.   1179

W

Waarschouwing Tegens Zeker Boekje.
New York, 1736. [2], 32 pp.
(The only copy located is incomplete.)
NYHS copy.   4097

Waddell, William, fl. 1776.
To the Freeholders. . . . Sept. 23, [1776].
New York, Gaine, [1776]. Broadside.
LOC copy.   15211

Wadsworth, Benjamin, 1670-1737.
Acquaintance with God Yields Peace.
Boston, J. Allen for Henchman, 1717. [2],
31, [1] pp.
JCB copy.   39671

[Wadsworth, Benjamin, 1670-1737.
(Sibley, IV, 83-91.)
Advice to Children.
Boston, 1719.]
(Adv. Boston News-Letter, Apr. 27, 1719.)
                                              2078

Wadsworth, Benjamin, 1670-1737.
(Sibley, IV, 83-91.)
Assembling at the House of God.
Boston, 1711. 24 pp.
MHS copy.   1532

Wadsworth, Benjamin, 1670-1737.
The Benefits of a Good, and the Mischiefs
of an Evil, Conscience.
Boston, Green for Eliot, 1719. [2], ii, 213,
[7] pp.
AAS copy.   2079

Wadsworth, Benjamin, 1670-1737.
(Sibley, IV, 83-91.)
The Blameless Christian.
Boston, 1707. [4], 55 pp.
AAS copy.   1335

Wadsworth, Benjamin, 1670-1737.
(Sibley, IV, 83-91.)
The Bonds of Baptism.
Boston, 1717. [4], 31 pp.
HC copy.   1934

Wadsworth, Benjamin, 1670-1737.
(Sibley, IV, 83-91.)
Christian Advice to the Sick and Well.
Boston, 1714. [4], 107 pp.
AAS copy.   1720

Wadsworth, Benjamin, 1670-1737.
Christian Advice to the Sick and Well.
Boston, Allen for Buttolph, 1714. [4], 107
pp.
(The only known copy is imperfect.)
MHS copy.   39604

Wadsworth, Benjamin, 1670-1737.
(Sibley, IV, 83-91.)
Christ's fan in His Hand.
Boston, Kneeland for Eliot, 1722. [4], 28
pp.
AAS copy.   2397

Wadsworth, Benjamin, 1670-1737.
The Churches Shall Know.
Boston, Allen for Boone, [1717]. [2], 34
pp.
(Issued under common halftitle with 1913,
q. v.)   1935

Wadsworth, Benjamin, 1670-1737.
(Sibley, IV, 83-91.)
Considerations to Prevent Murmurings.
Boston, 1706. [4], 25 pp.
(Printed signatures continuous with Evans
1286, q.v.)   1282

Wadsworth, Benjamin, 1670-1737.
(Sibley, IV, 83-91.)

Constant Preparedness for Death.
Boston, Green for Eliot, 1718. [2], 27,
[3] pp.
AAS copy.   2004

Wadsworth, Benjamin, 1670-1737.
The Danger of Hypocrisy.
Boston, 1711. [2], 43, [1] pp.
AAS copy.   1533

Wadsworth, Benjamin, 1670-1737.
Death is Certain.
Boston, Allen for Boone, 1710. [6], 21 pp.
MHS copy.   1492

Wadsworth, Benjamin, 1670-1737.
(Sibley, IV, 83-91.)
A Dialogue Between a Minister and his
Neighbour.
Boston, Kneeland for Eliot, 1724. [2], iv,
102 pp.
AAS copy.   2590

Wadsworth, Benjamin, 1670-1737.
(Sibley, IV, 83-91.)
A Dialogue between a Minister and his
Neighbour.
Boston, Kneeland for Adams, 1772. 123,
[1], 4 pp.
AAS copy.   12597

Wadsworth, Benjamin, 1670-1737.
(Sibley, IV, 83-91.)
Early Seeking of God.
Boston, 1715. [2], 52 pp.
AAS copy.   1786

Wadsworth, Benjamin, 1670-1737.
An Essay, for the Charitable Spreading of
the Gospel.
Boston, Green for Eliot, 1718. [2], 36 pp.
AAS copy.   2005

Wadsworth, Benjamin, 1670-1737.
An Essay on the Decalogue.
Boston, Green for Eliot and Gerrish,
1719. [2], iv, 133, [1] pp.
AAS copy.   2080

[Wadsworth, Benjamin, 1670-1737.
(Sibley, IV, 83-91.)
An Essay on the Decalogue.
Boston, 1721.]
(Title from Haven who took it from an
undated adv. in 2302; a ghost of 2080,
q.v.)   2298

Wadsworth, Benjamin, 1670-1737.
(Sibley, IV, 83-91.)
An Essay to do Good.
Boston, 1710. 44 pp.
AAS copy.   1491

Wadsworth, Benjamin, 1670-1737.
(Sibley, IV, 83-91.)
Exhortations to Early Piety.
Boston, 1702. 87 pp.
MHS copy.   1099

Wadsworth, Benjamin, 1670-1737.
The Faithful Reprover.
Boston, 1711. [2], 70 pp.
MHS copy.   1534

Wadsworth, Benjamin, 1670-1737.
Faithful Warnings.
Boston, Green for Eliot, 1722. [4], 24 pp.
AAS copy.   2398

Wadsworth, Benjamin, 1670-1737.
Fervent Zeal Against Flagrant
Wickedness.

Boston, Green for Eliot, 1718. [2], 31, [1]
pp.
AAS copy.   2006

Wadsworth, Benjamin, 1670-1737.
Five Sermons.
Boston, Allen for Buttolph, 1714. xi, [1],
168 pp.
AAS copy.   1721

Wadsworth, Benjamin, 1670-1737.
Five Sermons.
Boston, Allen for Eliot, 1714. xi, [1], 168
pp.
(Differs only in imprint from 1721, q. v.)
                                              39605

[Wadsworth, Benjamin, 1670-1737.
Five Sermons.
Boston, 1721.]
(From Haven who took it from an
undated adv. in 2302; a ghost of 1721,
q.v.)   2299

Wadsworth, Benjamin, 1670-1737.
(Sibley, IV, 83-91.)
Fraud and Injustice Detected.
Boston, 1712. [2], 29 pp.
AAS copy.   1590

Wadsworth, Benjamin, 1670-1737.
(Sibley, IV, 83-91.)
Good Souldiers a Great Blessing.
Boston, 1700. 28 pp.
AAS copy.   958

Wadsworth, Benjamin, 1670-1737.
The Gospel not Opposed.
Boston, Green for Eliot, 1719. [2], 46 pp.
AAS copy.   2081

Wadsworth, Benjamin, 1670-1737.
(Sibley, IV, 83-91.)
The Great and Last Day of Judgment.
Boston, 1709. [10], 132 pp.
AAS copy.   1437

[Wadsworth, Benjamin, 1670-1737.
(Sibley, IV, 83-91.)
The Great and Last Day of Judgment.
Boston, 1713. 168 pp.]
(Title from Haven, but the one copy
located was a mutilated specimen of the
1709 ed.)   1655

Wadsworth, Benjamin, 1670-1737.
A Guide for the Doubting.
Boston, 1711. [4], 277, [5] pp.
(Evans took his description from Haven,
who apparently saw a copy lacking pages
at both ends.)
AAS copy.   1787

Wadsworth, Benjamin, 1670-1737.
A Guide for the Doubting. . . . Second
Impression.
Boston, Green for Buttolph, 1715. [4],
202, [8] pp.
(The AAS has also an issue with the
imprint of Green for Phillips.)
AAS copy.   1788

Wadsworth, Benjamin, 1670-1737.
A Guide for the Doubting. . . . Second
Impression.
Boston, B. Green for Phillips, 1715. [4],
202, [8] pp.
(For the text see 1788.)
AAS copy.   39636

Wadsworth, Benjamin, 1670-1737.
(Sibley, IV, 83-91.)
A Guide for the Doubting. . . . Third
Impression.

Boston, Kneeland for Buttolph, 1720. [4],
254, [5] pp.
AAS copy.   2191

Wadsworth, Benjamin, 1670-1737.
(Sibley, IV, 83-91.)
Hearty Submission and Resignation.
Boston, B. Green, 1716. [2], ii, 123 pp.
BPL copy.   1860

[Wadsworth, Benjamin, 1670-1737.
Hearty Submission and Resignation.
Boston, 1720.]
(Haven took this title from an undated
adv. in 2302; it is a ghost of 1860, q. v.)
                                           2192

Wadsworth, Benjamin, 1670-1737.
An Help to get Knowledge.
Boston, 1714. [2], ix, [1], 176, [4] pp.
AAS copy.   1722

Wadsworth, Benjamin, 1670-1737.
The Highest Dwelling with the Lowest.
Boston, 1711. [2], 46 pp.
AAS copy.   1535

Wadsworth, Benjamin, 1670-1737.
The Imitation of Christ.
Boston, 1722. [4], 25, [1] pp.
AAS copy.   2399

Wadsworth, Benjamin, 1670-1737.
Invitations to the Gospel Feast.
Boston, B. Green for Buttolph, 1715. [2],
ii, 193, [6] pp.
(For the text see 1789.)
AAS copy.   39637

Wadsworth, Benjamin, 1670-1737.
Invitations to the Gospel Feast.
Boston, Green for Eliot, 1715. [2], ii, 193,
[6] pp.
(AAS has issues with imprint of Buttolph
and Phillips.)
MHS copy.   1789

Wadsworth, Benjamin, 1670-1737.
Invitations to the Gospel Feast.
Boston, B. Green for Phillips, 1715. [2],
ii, 193, [6] pp.
(For the text see 1789.)
AAS copy.   39638

Wadsworth, Benjamin, 1670-1737.
(Sibley, IV, 83-91.)
It's Honourable.
Boston, Green for Eliot, 1725. [2], 20 pp.
AAS copy.   2715

Wadsworth, Benjamin, 1670-1737.
King William Lamented in America.
Boston, 1702. [2], 30 pp.
AAS copy.   1100

Wadsworth, Benjamin, 1670-1737.
A Letter of Wholesome Counsels.
[Boston, 1709.] 33 pp.
(The only reported copy is imperfect.)
BPL copy.   1438

[Wadsworth, Benjamin, 1670-1737.
Letter to a Friend on . . . Baptism.
Boston, 1709.]
(Title from the Prince catalogue; no copy
seen in modern times.)   1439

[Wadsworth, Benjamin?, 1670-1737.
Letter to those Towns or Villages.
Boston, 1709.]
(Title from Prince catalogue; no copy seen
in modern times.)   1440

Wadsworth, Benjamin, 1670-1737.
The Lord Jesus.
Boston, Starkey, 1721. [2], 34 pp.
(Common half-title and signatured with
2253, q.v.)
AAS copy.   2300

Wadsworth, Benjamin, 1670-1737.
The Lord's Day, Proved to be the
Christian Sabbath.
Boston, Green for Eliot, 1720. [2], iv, 63,
[1] pp.
AAS copy.   2193

Wadsworth, Benjamin, 1670-1737.
Man's Present State.
Boston, 1715. [2], 22 pp.
AAS copy.   1792

Wadsworth, Benjamin, 1670-1737.

Men Self-Condemned.
Boston, 1706. [4], 88, [2] pp.
AAS copy.   1283

Wadsworth, Benjamin, 1670-1737.
Ministers Naturally Caring for Souls.
Boston, 1715. [2], 28 pp.
LOC copy.   1790

Wadsworth, Benjamin, 1670-1737.
(Sibley, IV, 83-91.)
Mutual Love and Peace among Christians.
Boston, 1701. [2], 30 pp.
AAS copy.   1029

Wadsworth, Benjamin, 1670-1737.
Now or Never the Time to be Saved. . . .
Second Impression.
Boston, B. Green for Buttolph, 1707. vi,
40 pp.
MHS copy.   39458

Wadsworth, Benjamin, 1670-1737.
(Sibley, IV, 83-91.)
Public Worship a Christian Duty.
Boston, 1704. 92 + pp.
(The only copy located is imperfect.)
LOC copy.   1197

[Wadsworth, Benjamin, 1670-1737.
Restraints, Merciful and Wonderful.
Boston, 1713.]
(Title from Haven. Perhaps a ghost of one
of the sermons printed in Evans 1721.)
                                           1656

Wadsworth, Benjamin, 1670-1737.
Rulers Feeding & Guiding their People.
Boston, B. Green, 1716. [2], 67 pp.
AAS copy.   1861

Wadsworth, Benjamin, 1670-1737.
The Saint's Prayer.
Boston, 1715. [2], 64 pp.
HC copy.   1791

Wadsworth, Benjamin, 1670-1737.
The Sin of Pride.
Boston, B. Green for Eliot, 1718. [2], 32
pp.
BPL copy.   39695

Wadsworth, Benjamin, 1670-1737.
Some Considerations about Baptism.
Boston, Green for Eliot, 1719. [2], ii, 80
pp.
AAS copy.   2082

Wadsworth, Benjamin, 1670-1737.
Surviving Servants of God.
Boston, Green for Gerrish, 1724. [4], 24,
[2], 25, [3], 36 pp.
AAS copy.   2591

Wadsworth, Benjamin, 1670-1737.
True Piety the Best Policy.
Boston, 1722. [2], 25, [1] pp.
MHS copy.   2400

[Wadsworth, Benjamin, 1670-1737.
Twelve Sermons on Various Subjects.
Boston, 1721 [2], iv, 258 pp.]
(From Haven, who took it from an
undated adv. in 2302; a ghost of 1936,
q.v.)   2301

Wadsworth, Benjamin, 1670-1737.
Twelve Single Sermons.
Boston, 1717. [2], iv, 258 pp.
AAS copy.   1936

Wadsworth, Benjamin, 1670-1737.
Unchast Practices Procure Divine
Judgments.
Boston, Green for Buttolph and Eliot,
1716. [2], 34 pp.
MHS copy.   1862

Wadsworth, Benjamin, 1670-1737.
Vicious Courses.
Boston, Allen, 1719. [2], 32 pp.
LOC copy.   2083

Wadsworth, Benjamin, 1670-1737.
(Sibley, IV, 83-91.)
Vicious Courses.
Boston, Rogers & Fowle, 1744. 31 pp.
AAS copy.   5506

Wadsworth, Benjamin, 1669-1737.
The Way of Life Opened.

Boston, B. Green for Phillips, 1712. [2],
ii, 148, [4] pp.
AAS copy.   39556

Wadsworth, Benjamin, 1670-1737.
The Well-Ordered Family.
Boston, 1712. [4], 121, [5] pp.
AAS copy.   1591

Wadsworth, Benjamin, 1670-1737.
The Well-Ordered Family. . . . Second
Edition.
Boston, 1719. [4], 121, [5] pp.
(No complete copy was found.)
AAS copy.   2084

Wadsworth, Benjamin, 1750-1826.
America Invoked to Praise the Lord.
Salem, Cushing, 1795. 31 pp.
AAS copy.   29825

Wadsworth, Benjamin, 1750-1826.
An Eulogy on the Excellent Character of
. . . Washington.
Salem, Cushing, 1800. 32 pp.
AAS copy.   38972

Wadsworth, Benjamin, 1750-1826.
(Weis, Colonial Clergy N. E.)
A Sermon, Preached at the Ordination
of . . . Josiah Badcock.
Salem, Hall, 1783. 36 pp.
AAS copy.   17789

Wadsworth, Benjamin, 1750-1826.
Social Thanksgiving a Pleasant Duty.
Salem, Cushing, [1796]. 38 pp., errata
slip.
AAS copy.   31519

Wadsworth, Daniel, 1704-1747.
(Dexter, I, 340-341.)
Christ's Presence.
New London, 1740. [2], 28 pp.
CHS copy.   4621

Wadsworth, Ebenezer.
To His Excellency William Shirley. . . .
The Representation and Petition of . . .
[May, 1754].
[Boston, 1754.] Broadside.
MA copy.   40729

The Wages of Sin . . . a Poem; Occasioned
by the Untimely Death of Richard Wilson,
who was Executed . . . the 19th of
October, 1732.
Boston, [1732]. Broadside.
NYHS copy.   40012

[A Waggon Load of Money.
Philadelphia, Spotswood, 1786.]
(Ghost of a London ed. Adv. in Pa.
Herald, July 12, 1786.)   20118

Wagner, Tobias, d. 1775.
M. Tobias Wagners Abschieds-Rede.
Ephrata, 1759. 39 pp.
HSP copy.   8514

Ein Wahafftiger Bericht.
[Germantown], 1752. 46, 40 pp.
(Evans lists under the title of the second
part.)
AAS copy.   6847

[Die Wahre Brantwein Berennerung.
York, Pa., Mayer, 1797.]
(A duplicate of 33851, q. v.)   33142

[Wahre und Wahrscheinliche
Begebenheiten.
Philadelphia, 1766].
(Seidensticker, p. 76.)   10517

[Ein Wahrhafter und Besonderer Bericht
von . . . Richard Merrels.
Reading, Pa., Jungmann, 1797.]
Adv. Neue Unpartheyische Readinger
Zeiting, Dec. 27, 1797.)   48308

Wahrheit und Guter Rath.
Philadelphia, Cist, 1783. 35 pp.
HSP copy.   18291

Wait, Thomas Baker, 1762-1830.
Proposals, for Publishing . . . a . . .
Volume, on Husbandry. Portland . . . May
10, 1787.
[Portland, 1787.] Broadside.
JCB copy.   45198

Wait's York, Cumberland and Lincoln

Almanack, for . . . 1792 [by Nathaniel
Low, 1740-1808].
Portland, Wait. [36] pp.
AAS copy.   23512

Wait's York, Cumberland and Lincoln
Almanack, for . . . 1794 [by Nathaniel
Low, 1740-1808].
Portland, Wait. [36] pp.
AAS copy.   25733

Wait's York, Cumberland and Lincoln
Almanack, for . . . 1795 [by Nathaniel
Low, 1740-1808].
Portland, Wait. [36] pp.
AAS copy.   27237

Wait's York, Cumberland and Lincoln
Almanack, for . . . 1796 [by Nathaniel
Low, 1740-1808].
Portland, Wait. [36] pp.
AAS copy.   28989

Wake, Baldwin, fl. 1774.
To Samuel Allinson. . . . December 17,
1774.
[Burlington, 1774.] Broadside.
LCP copy.   13753

Wakefield, Gilbert, 1756-1801.
An Examination of the Age of Reason.
Boston, West, 1794. 36 pp.
AAS copy.   28016

Wakefield, Gilbert, 1756-1801.
An Examination of the Age of Reason.
New York, Forman and Davis, 1794. 55
pp.
AAS copy.   28017

Wakefield, Gilbert, 1756-1801.
An Examination of the Age of Reason.
New York, Forman for Fellows, 1794. 55
pp.
AAS copy.   28018

Wakefield, Gilbert, 1756-1801.
An Examination of the Age of Reason.
Worcester, Thomas, 1794. 40 pp.
AAS copy.   28019

[Wakefield, Gilbert, 1756-1801.
A Plain Account of the Ordinance of
Baptism. . . . Fourth Edition.
Norwich, Trumbull, 1793.]
(Subscriptions solicited and Trumbull
named as publisher in Norwich Packet,
Mar. 21, 1793. "Just published," ibid Sept.
12.)   26412

Wakefield, Priscilla (Bell), 1751-1832.
Mental Improvement.
New Bedford, Shearman for Greene, 1799.
264 pp.
AAS copy.   36664

Wakeman, Samuel, 1635-1692.
(F. L. Weis, Colonial Clergy.)
Sound Repentance.
Boston, 1685. [8], 44 pp.
NYPL copy.   398

Wakeman, Samuel, 1635-1692.
(F. L. Weis, Colonial Clergy.)
A Young Man's Legacy.
Cambridge, 1673. 45 pp.
HEH copy.   183

Walden, Isaac, fl. 1762.
A Narrative of the Travels of. . . .
[New London], 1773. 12 pp.
NYPL copy.   13062

Waldo, Albigence, 1750-1794.
An Oration; Delivered in . . . Colchester.
Hartford, Babcock, [1784]. 18 pp.
AAS copy.   18868

Waldo, Joseph & Daniel, Merchants.
Imported from London & Sold by
Wholesale or Retail. . . .
[Boston, 1748.] Broadside.
MHS ph. copy.   40487

Waldo, Samuel, 1696-1759.
Boston, May 22d, 1735. Whereas since my
Return from St. George's River. . . .
[Boston, 1735.] 2 pp.
JCB copy.   40087

Waldo, Samuel, 1696-1759.
A Defence of the Title.

[Boston, 1736. 41 pp.
AAS copy.   4098

Waldo, Samuel, 1696-1759.
Samuel Waldo of Boston, merchant . . .
hereby notifies all Persons. . . . 3d March,
1734.
[Boston, 1735.] Broadside.
LOC copy.   40088

Waldo, Samuel, 1696-1759.
Whereas it is Industriously Reported. . . .
7th. May 1734.
[Boston, 1734.] Broadside.
BPL copy.   40068

Wales, Ebenezer, 1696-1774.
(C. M. Carter, John Redington, pp. 51-52,
54-57.)
The Counsels and Directions of. . . .
New London, 1774. 15, [1] pp.
NYHS copy.   13754

Wales, Samuel, 1748-1794.
The Dangers of our National Prosperity.
Hartford, Barlow & Babcock, 1785. 38 pp.
AAS copy.   19359

A Walk and Conversation, between a
Fond Father and his Little Son.
Norwich, Trumbull, 1794.
(Goodspeed's cat. 168, no. 323.)   28020

Walker, George, 1772-1847.
The Vagabond. A Novel.
Boston, Russell for West & Greenleaf and
J. West, 1800. xii, 228 pp.
AAS copy.   38973

Walker, James, merchant.
James Walker . . . is now Selling. . . .
New York, Harrison & Purdy, [1790].
Broadside.
LOC copy.   46089

Walker, James, fl. 1797.
An Inquiry into the Causes of Sterility.
Philadelphia, Oswald, 1797. 22 pp.
AAS copy.   33143

Walker, James L., fl. 1792.
Painting in General.
Baltimore, Edwards, [1792]. Broadside.
LOC copy.   24979

[Walker, Jeremiah, d. 1793.
The Fourfold Foundation of Calvinism.
Portsmouth, Melcher, 1793?]
(Imprint assumed by Evans from adv.
"Just Published and for Sale by," in N.H.
Gazette, July 9, 1793.)   26413

Walker, Jeremiah, d. 1793.
The Fourfold Foundation of Calvinism.
Richmond, Dixon, 1791. viii, 48 pp.
LOC copy.   23953

Walker, Patrick, 1666?-1745?
The Great Scots Prophet . . . Alexander
Peden.
Philadelphia, Chattin, [1758]. 32 pp.
LOC copy.   8279

[Walker, Patrick], 1666?-1745?
The Life and Prophecies of . . . Alexander
Peden.
Newburyport, A. Walker, 1798. 59 pp.
(Not located, 1968.)   48751

Walker, Robert, 1716-1783.
Sermons on Practical Subjects. . . . Third
Edition.
Philadelphia, Crukshank for Aitken, 1772.
iv, 295, [1] pp.
AAS copy.   12598

Walker, Robert, 1716-1783.
Sermons on Practical Subjects.
Philadelphia, Aitken, 1790. iv, 295, [1]
pp.
AAS copy.   23029

Walker, Robert, 1716-1783.
Sermons on Practical Subjects. . . . Vol. I.
Albany, M'Donald, 1796. [2], iv, [4], 285
pp.
AAS copy.   31520

Walker, Robert, 1716-1783.
Sermons on Practical Subjects. . . . In Two
Volumes. Vol. II.
Albany, M'Donald, 1797. vii, [1], 278 pp.
AAS copy.   33144

Walker, Thomas, 1749-1817, defendant.
The Whole Proceedings on the Trial of
Indictment.
Philadelphia, Woodward for Smith, 1794.
104, xix pp.
AAS copy.   27076

Walker, Timothy, 1705-1782.
(Sibley, VII, 603-614.)
Those who have the form of Godliness.
Salem, 1772. 30 pp.
AAS copy.   12599

Walker, Timothy, 1705-1782.
(Sibley, VII, 603-614.)
The Way to Try.
Boston, Green, Bushell & Allen for Eliot,
1743. 29 pp.
AAS copy.   5306

[Walker, Timothy], 1737-1822.
An Address to the Inhabitants of the New
Hampshire Grants. . . . July 18, 1778.
Dresden? 1778.]
(First printed from a ms. copy in the
Records of the Governor and Council of
Vermont, V, 521-525, and N. H. State
Papers, X, 268-271.)   16163

Walker, Timothy P.
The Flaming Sword.
Norwich, Ct., 1799. 12 pp.
CHS copy.   36665

Wall, George, fl. 1788.
A Description . . . of . . . the
Trigonometer.
Philadelphia, Poulson, 1788. 32 pp., 1
plate.
BA copy.   21568

Wall, Rachel, d. 1789.
Life, Last Words and Dying Confession,
of Rachel Wall.
[Boston, 1789.] Broadside.
AAS copy.   22235

Wallace, James.
A Short Treatise of the Virtues of Dr.
Bateman's Pectoral Drops. . . . To be sold
only by James Wallace.
New York, Zenger, [1731]. 4, 36 pp.
NYAM copy.   39981

Wallace, James Westwood, d. 1838.
An Inaugural Physiological Dissertation.
Philadelphia, Dobson, 1793. [6], 34 pp.
AAS copy.   26414

Wallace, Jonathan.
Carlisle, October, 1798.
Fellow-Citizens. . . .
[Carlisle, Kline, 1798.] Broadside.
HSP copy.   34951

Walley, Thomas, 1618-1679.
(See Magnalia, Bk. 3, Pt. 4, Ch. 6.)
Balm in Gilead.
Cambridge, 1669. [3], 20 pp.
LOC copy.   146

Walley, Thomas, 1618-1679.
(Magnalia, Bk. 3, Pt. 4, Ch. 6.)
Balm in Gilead.
Cambridge, 1670. [4], 20 pp.
AAS copy.   157

Wallin, Benjamin, 1711-1782.
(Allibone.)
Evangelical Hymns and Songs.
Boston, Edes & Gill, 1762. 155 pp.
NYPL copy.   9297

Walling, William.
Wonderful Providence of God.
Boston, Skinner, 1730. 16 pp.
JCB copy.   3373

The Wallingford Case Stated.
New Haven, 1761. 8 pp.
AAS copy.   9035

Wallis, George, lawyer.
From the United States Chronicle,
Thursday, February 19, 1784.
Providence, Wheeler, [1784]. Broadside.
RIHS copy.   44623

Wallis, George, 1740-1802.
The Art of Preventing Diseases.
New York, Campbell, 1794. 571 pp.
AAS copy.   28021

Wallis, James, orator.
The Bible Defended.
Halifax, [N. C.], Hodge, 1798. 115 pp.
Presb. Hist. .Soc. copy.   48309

Wallis, James, orator.
An Oration on the Death of . . .
Washington.
Raleigh, [N. C.], Gales, 1800. 16 pp.
NYPL copy.   38974

Walpole, George, 3rd earl of Orford,
1730-1791.
Rise, Cynthia, Rise. A Favorite Sonnet.
Written by the Earl of Orford. Composed
by Mr. Hook.
[Philadelphia, Carr, 1793.] [3] pp.
(Evans entry came from advs. in Daily
Am. Advertiser, Dec., 1793.)
LOC copy.   26092

Walpole, N.H. Convention, 1780.
At a Convention . . . 15th Day of
November.
n. p., [1780]. Broadside.
NHHS copy.   43913

Walsh, Thomas, 1730-1759.
The Great Salvation.
Wilmington, [Del.] Adams, 1770. 20 pp.
HEH copy.   42181

Walsh, Thomas, 1730-1759.
The Whole Armour of God.
Wilmington, [Del.], Adams, 1770. 28 pp.
HEH copy.   42182

Walsh, Thomas, 1730-1759.
The Whole Armour of God.
New York, Kirk, 1798. 36 pp.
(The only copy recorded cannot be
reproduced.)   34952

Walter, Nathaniel, 1711-1776.
(Sibley, VIII, 630-634.)
The Character of a Christian Hero.
Boston, Draper for Henchman, 1746. 22
pp.
AAS copy.   5877

Walter, Nathaniel, 1711-1776.
(Sibley, VIII, 630-634.)
The Character of a True Patriot.
Boston, Henchman, 1745. 20 pp.
AAS copy.   5706

Walter, Nathaniel, 1711-1776.
(Sibley, VIII, 630-634.)
An Heavenly and God-like Zeal.
Boston, Rogers for Eliot, 1742. 40 pp.
AAS copy.   5085

Walter, Nathaniel, 1711-1776.
The Thoughts of the Heart.
Boston, Rogers & Fowle for Proctor,
1741. 31 pp.
(An imprint variant of 4832, q. v. for text.)
AAS copy.   40264

Walter, Nathaniel, 1711-1776.
(Sibley, VIII, 630-634.)
The Thoughts of the Heart.
Boston, Rogers & Fowle for Procter [sic.]
and Dennis, 1741. 31 pp.
(The AAS has a copy without Dennis'
name in the imprint.)
AAS copy.   4832

Walter, Nehemiah, 1663-1750.
(Sibley, III, 294-301.)
The Body of Death Anatomized.
Boston, B. Green for S. Phillips, 1707.
[2], 26 pp.
AAS copy.   1336

[Walter, Nehemiah, 1663-1750.
The Body of Death Anatomized [another
impression].
Boston, B. Green, 1707.]
(Apparently an incomplete description of
a copy of 1336.)   1337

Walter, Nehemiah, 1663-1750.
(Sibley, III, 294-301.)
The Body of Death. . . . Second Edition.
Boston, Draper for Proctor, 1736. [4], 26
pp.
AAS copy.   4099

Walter, Nehemiah, 1663-1750.
(Sibley, III, 294-301.)
A Discourse Concerning the
Wonderfulness of Christ.

Boston, 1713. [2], vi, [6], 240 pp.
AAS copy.   1657

Walter, Nehemiah, 1663-1750.
(Sibley, III, 294-301.)
Discourses on the Whole LVth Chapter of
Isaiah.
Boston, Fowle for Henchman, 1755. [2],
xxvi, [4], 512 pp.
AAS copy.   7588

Walter, Nehemiah, 1663-1750.
An Elegiack Verse, on the Death of . . .
Elijah Corlet . . . Feb. 24, 1687.
[Boston? 1687?] Broadside.
HC copy.   39244

Walter, Nehemiah, 1663-1750.
(Sibley, III, 294-301.)
Faithfulness in the Ministry.
Boston, Kneeland for Gerrish, 1723. [4],
26 pp.
AAS copy.   2489

[Walter, Nehemiah, 1663-1750.
(Sibley, III, 294-301.)
The Man of War: a Sermon Preached to
the Artillery Company at Boston.
Boston, B. Green for B. Eliot, 1711.]
(Title from adv. on last page of 1537.)
     1536

Walter Nehemiah, 1663-1750.
(Sibley, III, 294-301.)
A Plain Discourse on Vain Thoughts.
Boston, 1721. [2], 149, [5] pp.
AAS copy.   2302

Walter, Nehemiah, 1663-1750.
(Sibley, III, 294-301.)
Practical Discourses.
Boston, Kneeland and Green for Gerrish
and Henchman, 1726. [4], 176 pp.
AAS copy.   2822

[Walter, Nehemiah, 1663-1750.
(Sibley, III, 294-301.)
Sermons.
Boston, 1722. 230 pp.]
(Title from Haven; a ghost of 7588.) 2401

Walter, Nehemiah, 1663-1750.
(Sibley, III, 294-301.)
Unfruitful Hearers.
Boston, 1696. 67 pp.
HC copy.   777

Walter, Nehemiah, 1663-1750.
(Sibley, III, 294-301.)
Unfruitful Hearers. . . . Re-printed.
Boston, Draper for Henchman, 1754. [2],
v, [1], 68 pp.
AAS copy.   7330

[Walter, Thomas], 1696-1725.
(Sibley, VI, 18-24.)
A Choice Dialogue.
Boston, Boone, Gray, and Edwards, 1720.
[2], xxi, [1], 79, [3] pp.
HC copy.   2194

[Walter, Thomas], 1696-1725.
(Sibley, VI, 18-24.)
An Essay upon that Paradox, Infallibility
may Sometimes Mistake.
Boston, Henchman, 1724. [2], 120, [1]
pp.
(The AAS has another issue with a less
caustic final paragraph of text and a
shorter Errata.)
AAS copy.   2592

Walter, Thomas, 1696-1725.
(Sibley, VI, 18-24.)
The Grounds and Rules of Musick.
Boston, 1721. iv, 24, [32] pp.
(See Am. Antiq. Soc., Proc., XLII,
235-246.)
NYPL copy.   2303

Walter, Thomas, 1696-1725.
(Sibley, VI, 18-24.)
The Grounds and Rules of Musick.
Boston, 1723. iv, 25, [32] pp.
(See Am. Antiq. Soc., Proc., XLII,
238-239.)
HC copy.   2490

Walter, Thomas, 1696-1725.
The Grounds and Rules of Musick. . . .
Third Edition.

Boston, Draper for Gerrish, 1740. [2], iv,
40, 12, 16.
HC copy.   4622

Walter, Thomas, 1696-1725.
(Sibley, VI, 18-24.)
The Grounds and Rules of Musick.
Boston, Gerrish, 1746. [2], iii, [1], 25 pp.,
16 plates.
AAS copy.   5878

Walter, Thomas, 1696-1725.
(Sibley, VI, 18-24.)
The Grounds and Rules of Musick.
Boston, Mecom, for Johnston, [1760].
[2], iv, 25 pp., 23 plates.
AAS copy.   8760

Walter, Thomas, 1696-1725.
The Grounds and Rules of Musick.
Boston, Johnston, 1764. [1], 25 pp., 24
plates.
AAS copy.   41504

[Walter, Thomas], 1696-1725.
The Little-Compton Scourge. . . . By
Zechariah Touchstone. . . . Aug. 10, 1721.
Boston, J. Franklin, [1721]. Broadside.
NYPL ph. copy.   39756

Walter, Thomas, 1696-1725.
The Scriptures the only Rule of Faith.
Boston, Green for Henchman, 1723. [4],
ii, 45 pp.
AAS copy.   2491

Walter, Thomas, 1696-1725.
(Sibley, VI, 18-24.)
The Sweet Psalmist of Israel.
Boston, Franklin for Gerrish, 1722. [6],
28 pp.
NYPL copy.   2402

Walter, Thomas, 1696-1725.
The Sweet Psalmist of Israel.
Boston, Franklin for Fleet, 1722. [8], 28
pp.
BA copy.   2403

Walter, William, 1737-1800.
A Discourse Delivered before the
Humane Society.
Boston, Fleets, 1798. 48 pp.
AAS copy.   34953

[Waltersdorf, Ernst Gottlieb], 1725-1761.
Fliegender Brief Evangelischer Worte.
Lancaster, 1794. [20], 218 pp.
AAS copy.   26981

[Walton, George], 1740-1804.
Observations upon the Effects.
Philadelphia, Aitken, 1781. 10 pp., 1
folded leaf.
AAS copy.   17419

[Walton, John, of Norwich].
An Account of the Surprizing Events of
Providence, which Hapned at the Raising
of a Bridge in Norwich, June 28th 1728.
New London, Green, 1728. 10 pp.
CHS copy.   2981

Walton, John, 1694-1764.
(Dexter, II, 232-235.)
An Essay on Fevers.
Boston, Fleet, 1732. 16, 8 pp.
YC copy.   3614

Walton, John, 1694-1764.
The Religion of Jesus.
Boston, 1736. [2], 28 pp.
(No copy found with imprint given by
Evans.)
BPL copy.   4100

Walton, John, 1694-1764.
Remarks on, or, an Examination of Mr.
Bulkly's Account.
Newport, 1731. [4], 112 pp.
BPL copy.   3484

Walton, John, 1694-1764.
A Vindication of the True Christian
Baptism.
Boston, 1738. [4], 98, [1] pp.
AAS copy.   4320

[Walton, William], 1740-1824.
A Narrative of the Captivity . . . of
Benjamin Gilbert.
Philadelphia, Crukshank, 1784. 96 pp.
AAS copy.   18497

[The Wandering Jew. Or the Shoemaker
of Jerusalem.
New London, [1760]. 8 pp.]
(In Brinley 9066.)　　　　　　　　8761

The Wandering Young Gentlewoman.
[Philadelphia], Stewart, 1764.
JCB ph. of tp. only.　　　　　　41505

The Wandering Young Gentlewoman, or
Cat-Skin's Garland.
Printed in the Year 1793. [8] pp.
(The only known copy is imperfect.)
AAS copy.　　　　　　　　　　46934

Wante, Charles Etienne Pierre.
Memoire Relatif . . . de St. Domingue.
Baltimore, Adams, 1793. 30 pp.
JCB copy.　　　　　　　　　　26415

Wanton, Joseph, 1705-1780.
Observations and Reflections on the
Present State of . . . Rhode-Island.
[Newport, 1763.] 4 pp.
RIHS copy.　　　　　　　　　41422

Wanton, Joseph, 1705-1780.
. . . To the Freemen and
Freeholders. . . . You were Pleased last
Year . . . to Place me in the Chief
Seat. . . . April 9, 1770.
[Newport, 1770.] Broadside.
(No perfect copy known.)
JCB copy.　　　　　　　　　42183

Wanton, Joseph, 1705-1780.
To the Freemen of the Colony of
Rhode-Island. . . . April 12, 1775.
[Newport, 1775.] Broadside.
RIHS copy.　　　　　　　　42978

Wanton, Joseph, 1731-1780.
(Sibley XIII, 143-148.)
Postscript to the Newport Mercury. To
the Freemen of the Town of Newport.
[Newport, 1774.] 3 pp.
(The only known copy is mutilated.)
BrU copy.　　　　　　　　　42744

Wanton, William, 1670-1733.
A True Representative of the Conduct of
. . . Richard Ward. . . . 3d Jan. 1733.
[Newport, 1733.] Broadside.
RIHS copy.　　　　　　　　40035

[The Wanton Wife. A Ballad.
Keene, Blake, 1795.]
(Imprint assumed by Evans from Blake's
adv.)　　　　　　　　　　　29826

War, Temporal and Spiritual, Considered.
[Boston, 1762.] 16 pp.
BrU copy.　　　　　　　　　9298

War with the Devil [by Benjamin Keach,
1640-1704].
[New York, 1707.] [6], 177 pp.
PPL copy.　　　　　　　　　1207

[The Warbling Songster, or Cure for
Dulness.
Philadelphia, 1795.]
(Imprint assumed by Evans from adv.)
　　　　　　　　　　　　　29827

[Ward, Andrew], of Guilford.
Two Letters to a Friend, on the Removal
of the Rev. Mr. J[ame]s S[proa]t.
[New Haven?], 1769. 32 pp.
LOC copy.　　　　　　　　11507

[Ward, Benjamin M.
An Essay on Religion.
Baltimore, Adams, 1790.]
(The origin of this entry is unknown.)
　　　　　　　　　　　　　23030

[Ward, Edward, 1667-1731.
(D. N. B.)
Female Policy Detected.
Boston, Eliot, 1742. 200 pp.]
(Probably a ghost of a London printing.)
　　　　　　　　　　　　　5086

[Ward, Edward], 1667-1731.
Female Policy Detected.
Boston, 1786. 22, [2] pp.
AAS copy.　　　　　　　　20119

Ward, Edward, 1667-1731.
Female Policy Detected.
New York, Gomez, 1794. 143 pp.
AAS copy.　　　　　　　　28022

Ward, Edward, 1667-1731.
Female Policy Detected.
Boston, Edes, 1793?]
(Imprint assumed by Evans from Edes'
advs.)　　　　　　　　　　26416

[Ward, Edward], 1667-1731.
Female Policy Detected.
Haverhill, Edes, 1795. 88 pp.
AAS copy.　　　　　　　　29828

[Ward, Edward, 1667-1731.
Female Policy Detected.
Philadelphia, Campbell, 1795.]
(Imprint assumed by Evans from adv.
"Books printed for Robert Campbell" in
28755.)　　　　　　　　　29829

[Ward, Edward, 1667-1731.
Female Policy Detected.
New York, 1798.]
(Imprint assumed by Evans from advs.)
　　　　　　　　　　　　34954

Ward, Edward, 1667-1731.
Female Policy Detected.
New York, 1800. 70 pp.
(The only copy reported is defective.)
AAS copy.　　　　　　　　38975

[Ward, Edward, 1667-1731.
(D. N. B.)
Nuptial Dialogues.
Boston, Fowle, 1753.]
(From adv. in 7145, probably for London
ed.)　　　　　　　　　　　7133

Ward, Ephraim, 1741-1818.
Fidelity Approved.
Brookfield, Mass., Merriam, 1800. 26, [1]
pp.
AAS copy.　　　　　　　　38976

Ward, Henry, 1732-1797.
Peter Mumford, Post-Rider, doth, upon
Oath, Declare. . . . August 9th, 1764.
[Newport, 1764.] Broadside.
LCP copy.　　　　　　　　41506

Ward, Henry, 1732-1797.
Providence, Saturday Afternoon, April 11,
1789. Gentlemen. . . .
[Providence, 1789.] Broadside.
BrU copy.　　　　　　　　22237

Ward, Jonathan, 1769-1860.
A Brief Statement . . . of the Weslean
Methodists.
Hallowell, Me., Edes, 1799. 32 pp.
AAS copy.　　　　　　　　36666

Ward, Joseph.
American Lands, and Funds. . . .
Land-office in Boston, April, 1784.
Boston, Russell, [1784]. Broadside.
JCB copy.　　　　　　　　44503

[Ward, Nathaniel], 1578-1652.
The Simple Cobler of Aggawam.
Boston, 1713. [4], 100 pp.
AAS copy.　　　　　　　　1658

Ward, Richard.
Just Imported, in the last Ships. . . .
[Salem, 1788?] Broadside.
JCB copy.　　　　　　　　45403

Ward, Richard, 1689-1763.
The Remonstrance of. . . . February 7,
1737.
[Newport, R. I., 1737.] 4 pp.
RIHS copy.　　　　　　　　40130

Ward, Samuel, 1725-1776.
Newport, April 7, 1767. To Enable the
Freemen. . . .
[Newport, 1767.] [2] pp.
Westerly Public Library copy.　　41775

[Ward, Samuel], 1725-1776.
To the Freemen of the Colony of
Rhode-Island. . . . April 11, 1758.
[Newport, 1758.] 6 pp.
RIHS copy.　　　　　　　　41017

Ward, Samuel, 1725-1776.
(D. A. B.)
To the Hon. Stephen Hopkins, Esq. . . .
12th April, 1757.
[Newport, 1757.] 4 pp.
AAS copy.　　　　　　　　8057

Ward, Samuel, 1725-1776.

To the Public. . . . 10th April, 1764.
[Newport, 1764.] 4 pp.
AAS copy.　　　　　　　　41507

Ward, Samuel, 1725-1776.
To the Public. . . . April 16, 1764.
[Newport, 1764.] [2] pp.
AAS copy.　　　　　　　　41508

Ward, Thomas, 1652-1708.
(D. N. B.)
A Demonstration of the Uninterrupted
Succession.
[Philadelphia], 1766. 47 pp.
LCP copy.　　　　　　　　10518

Ware, Henry, 1764-1845.
The Continuance of Peace.
Boston, Hall, 1795. 31 pp.
AAS copy.　　　　　　　　29830

Ware, Henry, 1764-1845.
A Sermon, Occasioned by the Death of
George Washington.
Boston, Hall, 1800. 27 pp.
AAS copy.　　　　　　　　38977

Wareham Social Library, Wareham,
Mass.
Catalogue of Books . . . 1798.
New Bedford, Spooner, 1798. 7 pp.
AAS copy.　　　　　　　　34955

Wareing, Elijah.
On the Death of John Wagstaffe.
Philadelphia, Steuart, 1760. Broadside.
HSP copy.　　　　　　　　8762

Ein Warhofftiger Bericht.
[Germantown, Pa., 1742.] 46 pp.
(Reproduced as a part of 4884, q. v.) 40292

Waring, Thomas.
Charleston, October 14, 1794. Dear Sir,
As I Propose to Offer myself a
Candidate. . . .
[Charleston, 1794.] [1] leaf.
AAS copy.　　　　　　　　47319

Waring, William, d. 1793.
The Burlington Almanac, for . . . 1791.
Burlington, Neale & Lawrence. [36] pp.
AAS copy.　　　　　　　　22384

[Waring, William, d. 1793.
A Journal for Lunar Observations.
Philadelphia, 1791.]
(Entry taken from the copyright notice.)
　　　　　　　　　　　　23954

Waring, William, d. 1793.
The New-Jersey Almanack for . . . 1788.
Trenton, Collins. [52] pp.
(The AAS has two issues.)
AAS copy.　　　　　　　　20852

Waring, William, d. 1793.
The New-Jersey Almanack for . . . 1789.
Trenton, Collins. [40] pp.
AAS copy.　　　　　　　　21569

Waring, William, d. 1793.
The New-Jersey Almanack for . . . 1790.
Trenton, Collins. [40] pp.
AAS copy.　　　　　　　　22238

Waring, William, d. 1793.
The New-Jersey Almanack for . . . 1791.
Trenton, Collins. [40] pp.
AAS copy.　　　　　　　　23031

Waring, William, d. 1793.
The New-Jersey Almanack for . . . 1792.
Trenton, Collins. [44] pp.
AAS copy.　　　　　　　　23955

Waring, William, d. 1793.
The New-Jersey Almanack for . . . 1793.
Trenton, Collins. [44] pp.
AAS copy.　　　　　　　　24980

[Waring, William], d. 1793.
(Watson, Annals of Philadelphia, I, 290.)
Poor Will's Almanack, for . . . 1787.
Philadelphia, Crukshank. [44] pp.
AAS copy.　　　　　　　　20120

Waring, William, d. 1793.
Poor Will's Almanack, for . . . 1788.
Philadelphia, Crukshank. [44] pp.
AAS copy.　　　　　　　　20853

Waring, William, d. 1793.

Poor Will's Almanack, for . . . 1789.
Philadelphia, Crukshank. [40] pp.
(No complete copy found.)
AAS copy.   21570

Waring, William, d. 1793.
Poor Will's Almanack, for . . . 1790.
Philadelphia, Crukshank. [44] pp.
AAS copy.   22239

Waring, William, d. 1793.
Poor Will's Almanack, for . . . 1791.
Philadelphia, Crukshank. [44] pp.
AAS copy.   23032

Waring, William, d. 1793.
Poor Will's Almanack, for . . . 1792.
Philadelphia, Crukshank, [48] pp.
AAS copy.   23956

Waring, William, d. 1793.
Poor Will's Almanack, for . . . 1793.
Philadelphia, Crukshank. [48] pp.
AAS copy.   24981

[Waring, William], d. 1793.
Poor Will's Pocket Almanack, for . . .
1787.
Philadelphia, Crukshank. [32] pp.
AAS copy.   20121

[Waring, William], d. 1793.
Poor Will's Pocket Almanack, for . . .
1788.
Philadelphia, Crukshank. [32] pp.
AAS copy.   20854

[Waring, William], d. 1793.
Poor Will's Pocket Almanack, for . . .
1789.
Philadelphia, Crukshank. [32] pp.
AAS copy.   21571

[Waring, William], d. 1793.
Poor Will's Pocket Almanack, for . . .
1790.
Philadelphia, Crukshank. [40] pp.
AAS copy.   22240

[Waring, William], d. 1793.
Poor Will's Pocket Almanack, for . . .
1791.
Philadelphia, Crukshank. [40] pp.
AAS copy.   23033

[Waring, William], d. 1793.
Poor Will's Pocket Almanack, for . . .
1792.
Philadelphia, Crukshank. [44] pp.
AAS copy.   23957

[Waring, William], d. 1793.
Poor Will's Pocket Almanack, for . . .
1793.
Philadelphia, Crukshank. [42] pp.
AAS copy.   24982

Waring, William, d. 1793.
Poulson's Town and Country Almanack,
for . . . 1789.
Philadelphia, Poulson. [40] pp.
AAS copy.   21572

Waring, William, d. 1793.
Poulson's Town and Country Almanac,
for . . . 1790.
Philadelphia, Poulson. [36] pp.
AAS copy.   22241

Waring, William, d. 1793.
Poulson's Town and Country Almanac,
for . . . 1791.
Philadelphia, Poulson. [36] pp.
AAS copy.   23034

Waring, William, d. 1793.
Poulson's Town and Country Almanac,
for . . . 1792.
Philadelphia, Poulson. [36] pp.
AAS copy.   23958

[Waring, William], d. 1793.
Poulson's Town and Country Almanac,
for . . . 1793.
Philadelphia, Poulson. [40] pp.
LOC copy.   24983

[Waring, William] d. 1793.
Poulson's Town and Country Almanac,
for . . . 1793. . . . Second Edition.
Philadelphia, Poulson. [40] pp.
AAS copy.   46666

Waring, William, d. 1793.
The South-Carolina and Georgia
Almanac, for . . . 1793.
Charleston, Markland & M'Iver. [40] pp.
LOC copy.   24984

[Waring, William], d. 1793.
The Town and Countryman's Almanack,
for . . . 1788.
Philadelphia, Crukshank. [44] pp.
LOC copy.   20855

Waring, William, pseud.
Poor Will's Almanack, for . . . 1794.
Philadelphia, Crukshank. [48] pp.
AAS copy.   26418

[Waring, William], pseud.
Poor Will's Almanack for . . . 1795.
Philadelphia, Crukshank. [44] pp.
HSP copy.   28023

Waring, William, pseud.
Poor Will's Pocket Almanack, for . . .
1794.
Philadelphia, Crukshank. [44] pp.
AAS copy.   26419

[Waring, William], pseud.
Poor Will's Pocket Almanack, for . . .
1795.
Philadelphia, Crukshank. [48] pp.
AAS copy.   28024

Waring, William, pseud.
The New-Jersey Almanack for . . . 1794.
Trenton, Collins. [48] pp.
PrU copy.   26417

Waring, William, pseud.
. . . Poulson's Town and Country
Almanac, for . . . 1793 ["Second
Edition"].
Philadelphia, Poulson. [40] pp.
AAS copy.   26420

Waring, William, pseud.
Poulson's Town and Country Almanac,
for . . . 1794.
Philadelphia, Poulson. [44] pp.
AAS copy.   26421

[Waring, William], pseud.
The South Carolina and Georgia
Almanac, for . . . 1794.
Charleston, Markland & M'Iver. [32] pp.
(The only copy located is imperfect.)
AAS copy.   26422

[Waring, William], pseud.
The South Carolina and Georgia
Almanac, for . . . 1795.
Charleston, Markland & M'Iver. [36] pp.
MHS copy.   28025

Warner, Effingham, 1778?-1793.
Select Pieces on Religious Subjects.
New York, Oram, 1796. [2], 104 pp.
AAS copy.   31521

Warner, George James.
Means for the Preservation of Public
Liberty.
New York, Greenleaf and Judah, 1797.
[2], 22 pp.
AAS copy.   33145

Warner, John.
[An Almanack for 1729.
Annapolis, Parks, 1728.]
(Wroth 48.)   39899

[Warner, John.
(Wroth, William Parks, p. 41.)
The Virginia and Maryland Alamack. . . .
For . . . 1730.
Annapolis, 1729.]
(Adv. Md. Gazette, Oct. 28, 1729.)   3374

[Warner, John.
The Virginia and Maryland Almanack.
. . . For . . . 1731.
Annapolis, 1730.]
(Adv. Md. Gazette, Oct. 20, 1730.)   3375

Warner, John.
The Virginia and Maryland Almanack.
. . . For . . . 1732.
[Williamsburg], Parks. [22] pp.
(The only known copy is imperfect.)
JCB copy.   40011

Warner, John.

[Warner's Almanack, for 1737.
Williamsburg, Parks.]
(Adv. Va. Gazette, Nov. 26, 1736.)   40108

Warner, John.
[Warner's Almanack, for 1738.
Williamsburg, Parks.]
(Adv. Va. Gazette, Nov. 25, 1737.)   40131

Warner, John.
[Warner's Almanack, for 1739.
Williamsburg, Parks.]
(Adv. Va. Gazette, Dec. 22, 1738.)   40154

Warner, John.
[Warner's Almanack, for 1740.
Williamsburg, Parks.]
(Adv. Va. Gazette, Nov. 23, 1739.)   40179

Warner, John.
Warner's Almanack . . . for . . . 1742.
Williamsburg, Parks, [1741]. [26] pp.
LOC copy.   40265

A Warning Piece. A Poetical Thought.
[Salem, 1780.] Broadside.
HC copy.   17062

[A Warning Piece to all Clergymen.
New York, 1744.]
(Adv. N.Y. Evening Post, Dec. 24, 1744.)
       5507

A Warning to Disobedient Youth: being a
Relation Concerning a Certain Henry
Webb.
Carlisle, Kiteley, 1788. 8 pp.
BPL copy.   45404

A Warning to the Flocks [by Cotton
Mather, 1663-1728].
Boston, 1700. 79, [1] pp.
AAS copy.   935

A Warning to Young & Old: in the
Execution of William Wieser . . . 21st of
November, 1754.
n. p., n. d. Broadside.
AAS facsim. copy.   40730

Eine Warnung an Erweckte Seelen von
einen Mitglied der Reformirten Kirche.
Philadelphia, Steiner, 1783. 52 pp.
LCP copy.   44491

Warnungs-Schreiben [by Gerhard
Tersteegen, 1697-1769].
Germantown, 1748. 48 pp.
AAS copy.   6249

Warren, Isaac, fl. 1775.
The Heavens. . . . An Astronomical
Diary: or, Almanack for 1775.
Woburn [Mass.], 1775. [20] pp.
AAS copy.   42979

Warren, Isaac, fl. 1775.
The North American's Almanack, for . . .
1777.
Worcester, Stearns & Bigelow. [24] pp.
AAS copy.   15212

Warren, John, 1753-1815.
An Eulogy on the Honourable Thomas
Russell.
Boston, Sweetser, 1796. 31, [1], 3 pp.
AAS copy.   31522

[Warren, John], 1753-1815.
A Monody on the Death of the Hon.
Thomas Russell, . . . May 4, 1796.
[Boston, 1796.] Broadside.
LOC copy.   48009

Warren, John, 1753-1815.
An Oration, Delivered July 4th, 1783.
Boston, Gill, [1783]. 32 pp.
AAS copy.   18292

Warren, Joseph, 1741-1775.
(D. A. B.)
An Oration, Delivered March 5th, 1772.
Boston, Edes & Gill, 1772. 18 pp.
AAS copy.   12600

Warren, Joseph, 1741-1775.
An Oration, Delivered March 5th,
1772. . . . Second Edition.
Boston, Edes & Gill, 1772. 18 pp.
JCB copy.   12601

Warren, Joseph, 1741-1775.
(D. A. B.)

An Oration; Delivered March Sixth, 1775.
Boston, Edes & Gill and Greenleaf, 1775.
23 pp.
AAS copy.   14608

Warren, Joseph, 1741-1775.
An Oration Delivered March the 6th,
1775.
New York, Anderson, 1775. 16 pp.
NYPL copy.   14609

Warren, Joseph, 1741-1775.
An Oration Delivered March 6, 1775.
Newport, 1775. 22 pp.
AAS copy.   14610

Warren, Lemuel, 1733-1812.
(Foster, Descendants of Arthur Warren,
pp. 42-43.)
Warren's New England Almanack, for . . .
1775.
Norwich, Robertsons & Trumbull. [36]
pp.
AAS copy.   13755

Warren, Lemuel, 1733-1812.
Warren Revived: An Astronomical
Diary: or Almanack, for . . . 1783.
Norwich, Trumbull. [24] pp.
AAS copy.   44286

[Warren, Mercy (Otis)], 1728-1814.
The Adulateur. A Tragedy.
Boston, 1773. 32 pp.
AAS copy.   13063

[Warren, Mercy (Otis)], 1728-1814.
The Blockheads: or, the Affrighted
Officers.
Boston, 1776. 19, [2] pp.
AAS copy.   15213

[Warren, Mercy (Otis)], 1728-1814.
The Group, a Farce.
New York, Anderson, [1775]. 15 pp.
NYPL copy.   14612

[Warren, Mercy (Otis)], 1728-1814.
The Group, a Farce.
Philadelphia, Humphreys, 1775. 16 pp.
NYPL copy.   14613

[Warren, Mercy (Otis)], 1728-1814.
. . . The Group, as Lately Acted.
Boston, Edes & Gill, 1775. 22 pp.
AAS copy.   14611

[Warren, Mercy (Otis)], 1728-1814.
The Motley Assembly, a Farce.
Boston, Coverly in Newbury-Street, 1779.
15 pp.
(The AAS has a copy with the imprint of
Coverly in Marlborough-Street.)
AAS copy.   16668

[Warren, Mercy (Otis)], 1728-1814.
Observations on the new Constitution,
and on the Federal and State Conventions.
[Boston, 1788.] 19 pp.
AAS copy.   21111

[Warren, Mercy (Otis)], 1728-1814.
Observations on the New Constitution
and on the Federal and State Conventions.
New York, 1788. 22 pp.
AAS copy.   21112

Warren, Mercy (Otis), 1728-1814.
Poems, Dramatic and Miscellaneous.
Boston, Thomas & Andrews, 1790. 252 pp.
AAS copy.   23035

Warren, Moses, d. 1829.
A Sermon Preached at the Funeral of
Abdiel Loomis, who Departed this Life
June 29th, 1800.
Springfield, Mass., Brewer, [1806?]. 12
pp.
CVHS copy.   38978

Warren Insurance Co., Warren, R. I.
The Charter of the. . . .
Warren, Phillips, 1800. 16 pp.
BrU copy.   38980

Warren, R. I. Church Lottery.
Scheme of a Lottery. . . . November 28,
1794.
Warren, Phillips, [1794]. Broadside.
JCB copy.   28026

Warren, R. I. Library Society.
The Charter and By-Laws for the. . . .

Warren, R. I., Phillips, 1799. 31 pp.
AAS copy.   36668

Warren, R. I. Schools.
An Address of a School-Master . . . at an
Exhibition.
Warren, R. I., Phillips, 1799. 7 pp.
NYHS copy.   36667

Warrington, Thomas, fl. 1749-1770.
The Love of God.
Williamsburg, [Va.], Hunter, 1753. 24 pp.
JCB copy.   40678

Washburn, Azel, 1764-1841.
The Duty of Magnifying the Work of the
Lord.
Hanover, [N. H.], Davis, 1800. 25, [1]
pp.
AAS copy.   38981

Washburn, Azel, 1764-1841.
Two Discourses, Delivered in the College
Chapel.
Hanover, N. H., Dunham & True, 1795.
30, [1] pp.
AAS copy.   29833

Washington, Bushrod, 1762-1829.
Reports of Cases Argued . . . in . . .
Virginia . . . Vol. I.
Richmond, Nicolson, 1798. [8], 392, [32]
pp.
AAS copy.   34958

Washington, Bushrod, 1762-1829.
Report of Cases Argued . . . in . . .
Virginia. . . . Vol. II.
Richmond, Nicolson, 1799. [1], vii, [1],
302, [2], 19 pp.
AAS copy.   36670

Washington, George, 1732-1799.
Works are listed alphabetically by actual
title, instead of being grouped by subject,
such as Farewell Address.

Washington, George, pseud.
Letters from George Washington, to
Several of his Friends in the Year 1776.
[Philadelphia?], 1778. pp. [2], [1]-48,
48-52.
(The only known copy cannot be
reproduced.)   43591

Washington, George, pres. U.S.,
1732-1799.
The Address, and Resignation of . . . Geo.
Washington. . . . Second Lansingburgh
Edition.
Lansingburgh, Pratt, 1796. 24 pp.
AAS copy.   48011

Washington, George, pres. U.S.,
1732-1799.
The Address, and Resignation of . . . Geo.
Washington.
Lansingburgh, Pratt, 1796. 26 pp.
(Not located, 1968.)   48010

[Washington, George, pres. U. S.,
1732-1799.
Address and Resignation.
Troy, N. Y., Pratt, 1799.]
(Imprint assumed by Evans from Pratt's
adv.)   33150

Washington, George, pres. U. S.,
1732-1799.
An Address by George Washington,
President of the United States, to his
Fellow-Citizens, on Declining being
Considered as a Candidate.
Norwich, Ct., Hubbard, 1796. 34 pp.
AAS copy.   31540

Washington, George, pres. U.S.,
1732-1799.
Address from the President to the People
. . . Announcing his Intentions of
Retiring.
Petersburg, Prentis, [1796]. pp. [3]-16.
(Best copy available.)
Jones Mem. Lib., Lynchburg, Va., copy.
                                             48012

Washington, George, pres. U.S.,
1732-1799.
Address of George Washington on
Declining being Considered a Candidate.
n.p., 1796. 22 pp.
(The unique copy described by Evans is
not now to be found.)   31529

Washington, George, pres. U.S.,
1732-1799.
Address of George Washington. . .
Preparatory to his Declination.
Wilmington, Wilson, 1796. 23 pp.
(Not available for reproduction.)
Wilmington Free Inst. copy.   48013

[Washington, George, pres. U. S.,
1732-1799.
The Address of George Washington,
President of the United States, to his
Fellow-Citizens, on Declining being
Considered a Candidate.
Norwich, Ct., Trumbull, 1796.]
(Apparently a ghost arising from
Trumbull's adv. for 31540.)   31541

Washington, George, pres. U. S.,
1732-1789.
Address of George Washington, President
of the United States, to his Fellow
Citizens, on his Declining being
Considered a Candidate.
Exeter, [N. H.], Ranlet, 1800. 36 pp.
HC copy.   38982

Washington, George, pres. U.S.,
1732-1799.
Address of George Washington, President
of the United States to the People of
America . . . 19th September, 1796. On
Apprizing them, that he Declined.
Bennington, Haswell, 1796. 45 pp.
AAS copy.   31528

Washington, George, pres. U.S.,
1732-1799.
Address of George Washington, President
. . . to the People of the United States.
Baltimore, Jackson for G. & H.S.
Keatinge, 1796. 36 pp.
Johns Hopkins Univ. copy.   48014

Washington, George, pres. U.S.,
1732-1799.
Address of George Washington, to the
People of the United States, Announcing
his Resolution to Retire.
Providence, Carter & Wilkinson, 1796. 22
pp.
RIHS copy.   31550

Washington, George, pres. U.S.,
1732-1799.
Address of George Washington, to the
People of the United States Preparatory
to his Declination.
Baltimore, Keatinge, 1796. 23 pp.
BPL copy.   31527

Washington, George, pres. U.S.,
1732-1799.
The Address of His Excellency George
Washington, President of the United
States of America, to the People of the
said States: on his Declining to be a
Candidate for the Office of President.
Albany, Barber & Southwick, 1796. 22,
(i.e. 23) pp.
NYHS copy.   31525

[Washington, George, pres. U.S.,
1732-1799.
The Address of Resignation of our
Worthy President.
Poughkeepsie, Power, 1796.]
(Imprint assumed by Evans from adv.
"for sale at this office," Poughkeepsie
Journal, Oct. 26, 1796.)   31549

Washington, George, pres. U. S.,
1732-1799.
Address of the late General George
Washington to the Citizens of the United
States, on Declining a Re-Election.
Hartford, [Ct.], Hudson & Goodwin,
[1800?].
Broadside.
AAS copy.   38983

Washington, George, pres. U. S.,
1732-1799.
The Address of the late George
Washington, when President, to the
People of the United States, on Declining
being Considered a Candidate.
[Charlestown, Mass., 1800.] 24 pp.
AAS copy.   38986

Washington, George, pres. U. S.,
1732-1799.

The Address of the late George
Washington, when President, to the
People of the United States, on Declining
being Considered a Candidate.
[Charlestown, Mass., 1800.] 30 pp.
AAS copy.   38985

Washington, George, pres. U. S.,
1732-1799.
The Address of the late George
Washington, when President, to the
People of the United States, on Declining
being Considered a Candidate.
Salem, [Mass.], Cushing, 1800. 32 pp.
AAS copy.   38984

Washington, George, pres., U.S.,
1732-1799.
Address of the President to the People.
New York, Tiebout, 1796. 36 pp.
AAS copy.   31536

Washington, George, pres. U. S.,
1732-1799.
An Address of the President to the People
of the United States on his Declining
being Considered a Candidate.
Charleston, S. C., Timothy & Mason,
1796.
PrU copy.   31533

Washington, George, pres. U.S.,
1732-1799.
An Address to the People of the United
States [Sept. 17, 1796]. . . .
Exeter, Ranlet, 1796. 8 pp.
HEH copy.   48015

Washington, George, pres. U.S.,
1732-1799.
An Address to the People of the United
States.
Newcastle, Del., Adamses, 1796. 21 pp.
LOC copy.   31534

Washington, George, pres. U.S.,
1732-1799.
An Address to the People of the United
States.
Chambersburg, Dover & Harper, 1796. 19
pp.
NYPL copy.   31532

Washington, George, pres. U. S.,
1732-1799.
America's Legacy.
Hudson, N. Y., 1797. 200 pp.
AAS copy.   33148

Washington, George, pres. U. S.,
1732-1799.
America's Legacy: Containing General
Washington's Farewell Orders to the
Armies. . . .
Charleston, [S. C.], Young, 1800. 58 pp.
LOC copy.   38987

Washington, George, pres. U.S.,
1732-1799.
A Circular Letter, from His Excellency
George Washington, Commander in Chief
of the Armies of the United States of
America; Addressed to the Governors of
the Several States, on his Resigning the
Command.
Philadelphia, Smith, [1783]. 51, [1] pp.
LOC copy.   18261

Washington, George, pres. U.S.,
1732-1799.
A Circular Letter from His Excellency,
George Washington, Commander-in-Chief
of the Armies of the United States of
America: Occasioned by his
Determination to Resign.
Newport, 1783. 12 pp.
JCB copy.   18260

Washington, George, pres. U.S.,
1732-1799.
A Circular Letter from His Excellency
General Washington, to the Several
States, Called his Legacy.
Annapolis, Green, [1783]. [2], 27 pp.
MdHS copy.   18257

[Washington, George, pres. U.S.,
1732-1799.
The Circular Letter from His Excellency
. . . Commander in Chief . . . to the
Governors . . . on his Resigning the
Command.

New York, Oswald, 1786.]
("Now in the Press. . . . Sold by . . . Mr.
Oswald," Pa. Herald, Nov. 15, 1786.)
      20054

[Washington, George, pres. U.S.,
1732-1799.
The Circular Letter from His Excellency
. . . Commander in Chief . . . to the
Governors . . . on his Resigning the
Command.
Philadelphia, Bailey, 1786.]
("Now in the Press," Pa. Herald, Nov. 15,
1786.)   20055

Washington, George, pres. U.S.,
1732-1799.
A Circular Letter of His Excellency . . .
Commander in Chief.
Philadelphia, Smith, [1787]. 51, [1] pp.
HEH copy.   20764

[Washington, George, pres. U.S.,
1732-1799.
Columbia's Legacy; or, Washington's
Farewell Address.
[Newburyport, 1796.] pp. [8 - 50, [1].]
(A ghost of 38988 arising from the
defective copy in NYPL.)   31538

Washington, George, pres. U. S.,
1732-1799.
Columbia's Legacy: or, Washington's
Farewell Address.
Newburyport, March, 1800. 50, [1] pp.
AAS copy.   38988

Washington, George, pres. U.S.,
1732-1799.
Columbia's Legacy; or, Washington's
Valedictory Advice.
Philadelphia, Sweitzer & Ormrod, 1796.
89 pp.
LOC copy.   31545

Washington, George, pres. U.S.,
1732-1799.
Extract of a Letter. . . . June 15, 1788.
[Philadelphia, 1788?] [2] pp.
(Not located.)
LCP copy.   45405

Washington, George, pres. U.S.,
1732-1799.
The Farewell Address.
Philadelphia, Sweitzer for Carey, 1800. 46
pp.
AAS copy.   38989

Washington, George, pres. U.S.,
1732-1799.
General Washington's Resignation. . . .
December 23d, 1783.
[Newburyport], Mycall, 1784. Broadside.
JCB copy.   44624

Washington, George, pres. U.S.,
1732-1799.
George Washington to the People of the
United States.
Philadelphia, Maxwell for Dickins &
Maxwell, 1800. frontis., [2], 40 pp.
AAS copy.   38990

Washington, George, pres. U. S.,
1732-1799.
General Washington's Letter, Declaring
his Acceptance of the Command of the
Armies of the United States. In Senate,
July 18, 1798.
[Philadelphia], Published for General
Information, [1798]. Broadside.
AAS copy.   34829

Washington, George, pres. U.S.,
1732-1799.
General Washington's Resignation and
Address, in a Circular Letter to the
Honorable the President of the State of
New-Hampshire.
Exeter, 1783. 16 pp.
AAS copy.   18258

Washington, George, pres. U.S.,
1732-1799.
George Washington's Resignation.
Windsor, Vt., Spooner, 1796. 23 pp.
AAS copy.   31552

Washington, George, pres. U.S.,
1732-1799.
His Excellency General Washington's

Last Legacy. . . . June 11, 1783.
[Philadelphia? 1783.] Broadside.
AAS copy.   44492

Washington, George, pres. U.S.,
1732-1799.
Interesting. By Capt. Earl Arrived. . . .
[Newport], Companion Office, [1798].
Broadside.
(Only copy is imperfect.)
RIHS copy.   48752

Washington, George, pres. U.S.,
1732-1799.
The Journal of Major George
Washington.
Williamsburg, 1754. 28 pp.
Colonial Williamsburg copy.   7331

[Washington, George, pres. U. S.,
1732-1799.
July 18, 1798. Gentlemen of the Senate.
. . . John Adams.
Philadelphia, Fenno, 1798. 4 pp.]
(No copy could be located.)   34828

Washington, George, pres. U.S.,
1732-1799.
The Last Official Address, of His
Excellency General Washington, to the
Legislatures of the United States.
Hartford, Hudson & Goodwin, 1783. 48
pp.
AAS copy.   18259

Washington, George, pres. U. S.,
1732-1799.
The Last Will and Testament of Gen.
George Washington.
Boston, Russell and Manning & Loring,
1800. 24 pp.
AAS copy.   38991

Washington, George, pres. U. S.,
1732-1799.
The Last Will and Testament of General
George Washington.
Philadelphia, Maxwell for Dickins, 1800.
26 pp.
AAS copy.   38992

Washington, George, pres. U. S.,
1732-1799.
The Last Will and Testament of Gen.
George Washington.
Portland, [Me.], Jenks, 1800. 24 pp.
BPL copy.   38993

Washington, George, pres. U. S.,
1732-1799.
The Last Will and Testament, of General
George Washington.
Worcester, [Mass.], Thomas, 1800. 23 pp.
AAS copy.   38994

Washington, George, pres. U.S.,
1732-1799.
Legacies of Washington.
Trenton, [N. J.], Sherman, Mershon &
Thomas, 1800. 283 pp., 1 plate.
AAS copy.   38995

Washington, George, pres. U.S.,
1732-1799.
The Legacy of the Father of his Country.
Stockbridge, Andrews, 1796. 26 pp.
LOC copy.   31551

Washington, George, pres. U.S.,
1732-1799.
The Legacy of the Father of his Country.
Address of George Washington, on
Declining being Considered a Candidate.
n. p., [1796?]. pp. [1]-4, 25-40, printed
wraps.
AAS copy.   48016

Washington, George, pres. U.S.,
1732-1799.
The Legacy of the Father of his Country.
Address . . . on Declining being
Considered a Candidate.
Boston, Russell for West, 1796. 43 pp.
AAS copy.   31530

Washington, George, pres. U. S.,
1732-1799.
The Legacy of the Father of his Country.
Northampton, Mass., Butler, 1797. 24 pp.
AAS copy.   33149

Washington, George, pres. U.S.,
1732-1799.

The Legacy of the Father of his Country.
[Charlestown? 1800.] 22 pp.
(No copy located.)   49181

Washington, George, pres. U. S.,
1732-1799.
A Letter from His Excellency . . . to . . .
Benjamin Harrison.
Richmond, Nicolson & Prentis, 1783. 16
pp.
WLC copy.   44493

[Washington, George, pres. U. S.,
1732-1799.
Message of the President of the United
States, Transmitting a Letter from
General Washington. . . . July 17th, 1798.
[Philadelphia, 1798.] [2] pp.]
(No copy located.)   34827

Washington, George, pres. U. S.,
1732-1799.
Mount Vernon, April 2, 1784. The
Subscriber would Lease. . . .
Alexandria, Richards, [1784]. Broadside.
NYPL copy.   44625

Washington, George, pres. U. S.,
1732-1799.
Mount Vernon, July 15, 1773. The
Subscriber, having Obtained Patents. . . .
[Williamsburg? 1773.] Broadside.
InU copy.   42532

Washington, George, pres. U. S.,
1732-1799.
Official Letters to the Honorable
American Congress. . . . Vol. II.
New York, Rivington and Campbell, 1796.
[2], 311 pp.
AAS copy.   48017

Washington, George, pres. U. S.,
1732-1799.
President Washington's Resignation and
Address.
Newburyport, Barrett, 1796. 19 pp.
AAS copy.   31537

Washington, George, pres. U. S.,
1732-1799.
President Washington's Resignation &
Address.
Portsmouth, [N. H.], Melcher, 1800. 22
pp.
AAS copy.   38996

Washington, George, pres. U. S.,
1732-1799.
The President's Address . . . on his
Declining another Election.
Amherst, N. H., Cushing, [1796]. 35 pp.
JCB copy.   31526

Washington, George, pres. U. S.,
1732-1799.
The President's Address to the Citizens of
the United States in Consequence of his
Resignation.
[Richmond, 1796.] [20] pp.
(Not located, 1968.)   48018

Washington, George, pres. U. S.,
1732-1799.
The President's Address, to the Peopde
[sic].
n.p., [1796]. 24 pp.
(The only copy located is incomplete.)
LOC copy.   31548

[Washington, George, pres. U. S.,
1732-1799.
The President's Address to the People.
Boston, Sweetser, 1796.]
(Imprint assumed by Evans from adv.
"This Day is published" in Federal
Orrery, Oct. 3, 1796.)   31531

Washington, George, pres. U. S.,
1732-1799.
[The President's Address to the people of
the United States.
Elizabeth (Hager's) Town, 1796.]
(Adv. Washington Spy, Oct. 12, 1796.)
                                               48019

Washington, George, pres. U. S.,
1732-1799.
The President's Address to the People . . .
Announcing his Design of Retiring.
Philadelphia, 1796. 16 pp.
LOC copy.   31546

Washington, George, pres. U.S.,
1732-1799.
The President's Address to the People . . .
Announcing his Intention of Retiring.
Philadelphia, Ormrod & Conrad for
Ormrod, 1796. 23 pp.
LCP copy.   31543

Washington, George, pres. U.S.,
1732-1799.
The President's Address to the People . . .
Announcing his Intention of Retiring. . . .
Ormrod's Second Edition.
Philadelphia, Ormrod & Conrad for
Ormrod, 1796. 23 pp.
NYPL copy.   31544

Washington, George, pres. U.S.,
1732-1799.
The President's Address to the People . . .
September 17, 1796.
Philadelphia, Young, Mills & Son, 1796.
28 pp.
AAS copy.   31547

Washington, George, pres. U.S.,
1732-1799.
The President's Address to the People . . .
17th September, 1796.
[Philadelphia, 1796.] 16 pp.
NYPL copy.   31542

Washington, George, pres. U.S.,
1732-1799.
The President's Address, to the People of
the United States.
[Reading, Pa.], Schneider, [1796]. 18 pp.
NYPL copy.   48020

Washington, George, pres. U.S.,
1732-1799.
Resignation of His Excellency, George
Washington, President of the United
States; and his Address to the Citizens . . .
September 17th, 1796.
New York, Oram, [1796]. 26 pp.
JCB copy.   31535

Washington, George, pres. U.S.,
1732-1799.
Selections from the Correspondence
of. . . .
Charlestown, [Mass.], Etheridge, 1800.
79, [1] pp.
AAS copy.   38997

Washington, George, pres. U.S.,
1732-1799.
Senate of the United States, July 18,
1798. . . . The Letter Received this
Morning from General Washington. . . .
[Philadelphia, 1798.] 4 pp.
WLC copy.   48753

Washington, George, pres. U.S.,
1732-1799.
To the Editor of the United States
Gazette. . . . 3d March, 1797. . . . Certain
Forged Letters. . . .
[Philadelphia, 1797.] Broadside.
AAS copy.   33072

Washington, George, pres. U.S.,
1732-1799.
To the People of the United States. . . .
17th September, 1796.
Newport, R. I., Barber, [1796]. [2] pp.
AAS copy.   31539

Washington, George, pres. U. S.,
1732-1799.
Washington's Letter, Declaring his
Acceptance of the Command. . . . July 13,
1798.
[Boston], Russell, [1798]. Broadside.
EI copy.   34830

Washington, George, pres. U.S.,
1732-1799.
Washington's Monuments of Patriotism.
Philadelphia, Baileys for Ormrod, 1800.
338, 44 pp., 1 plate.
AAS copy.   39021

Washington, George, pres. U.S.,
1732-1799.
Washington's Political Legacies.
Boston, Russell & West, 1800. 208, xiv pp.
AAS copy.   38998

Washington, George, pres. U. S.,
1732-1799.
Washington's Political Legacies.

New York, Forman, 1800. 292, [8] pp.
AAS copy.   38999

Washington, George, pres. U. S.,
1732-1799.
The Will of Gen. George Washington.
Stonington-Port, Ct., Trumbull for Crary,
1800. 35 pp.
AAS copy.   39006

Washington, George, pres. U. S.,
1732-1799.
The Will of General George Washington.
Alexandria, 1800. 32 pp.
AAS copy.   39000

Washington, George, pres. U. S.,
1732-1799.
The Will of General George Washington.
Baltimore, Dobbin, 1800. 26 pp.
AAS copy.   39001

Washington, George, pres. U. S.,
1732-1799.
The Will of General George Washington.
[Charleston, S. C.], Freneau & Paine,
[1800]. 16 pp.
NYPL copy.   39005

Washington, George, pres. U.S.,
1732-1799.
[The Will of General George Washington.
Elizabethtown, Grieves, 1800.]
("In the press," Md. Herald, Feb. 27,
1800.)   49182

Washington, George, pres. U. S.,
1732-1799.
The Will of General George Washington.
Frederick Town, Bartgis, [1800]. 26 pp.
HEH copy.   39007

[Washington, George, pres. U. S.,
1732-1799.
The Will of General George Washington.
Georgetown, S. C., Burd, 1800. 19 pp.]
(No copy located.)   39002

Washington, George, pres. U. S.,
1732-1799.
The Will of General George Washington.
Hudson, [N. Y.], Stoddard, 1800. 47 pp.
HEH copy.   39004

Washington, George, pres. U. S.,
1732-1799.
The Will of Gen. George Washington.
New York, Furman, 1800. 23, [1] pp.
NYHS copy.   39004

Washington, Martha (Custis).
Lady Washington's Lamentation.
Boston, Coverly, [1800]. Broadside.
(Also entered as 37770, q. v.)   39008

The Washington Almanac, for . . . 1801.
Baltimore, Keatinge, 1801. [32] pp.
(The only recorded copy is imperfect.)
LOC copy.   39011

Washington, D.C. Theater, 1800.
. . . On Monday Evening, Sept. 1st 1800
. . . The Secret.
[Washington, 1800.] Broadside.
LOC copy.   49183

Washington, D. C. Theater, 1800.
On Friday Evening, Aug. 29th, 1800.
[Washington], Way & Groff, [1800].
Broadside.
(Reproduced from the Month at
Goodspeed's, Sept. 1935, p. 21.)   39009

Washington College.
To the Inhabitants of the Eastern Shore.
. . . Gentlemen, By the foregoing Act for
Founding a College. . . .
[Annapolis? 1782.] Broadside.
(No copy located.)   44287

Washington Hotel Lottery.
List of the Fortunate Numbers, Drawn in
the. . . .
Boston, Young & Minns, 1794. [20] pp.
(The title given by Evans was assumed
from the adv. in the Independent
Chronicle, May 29, 1794.)
NEHGS copy.   28029

Washington Hotel Lottery.
A List of the Prizes . . . Drawn . . .
October 29, 1793.

[Boston, 1793.] Broadside.
BPL copy. 26430

Washington Insurance Co., Providence, R.I.
Charter of the. . . .
[Providence], Wheeler, 1800. 12 pp.
AAS copy. 38344

The Washingtoniana.
Baltimore, Sower, 1800. frontis., pp.
[i]-viii, [7]-258, 271-98, [6].
AAS copy. 39018

The Washingtoniana.
Baltimore, Sower, 1800. frontis., pps. [i]-
vii, [7]-258, 271-98, [7].
(This differs from 39018 only in the list of
subscribers.) 39019

Washingtoniana: a Collection of Papers.
Petersburgh, Va., Ross & Douglas, 1800.
xvi, 95, [1] pp.
AAS copy. 39017

Washingtons Ankunft in Elisium.
Lancaster, [Pa.], Hütter, 1800. 36 pp.
LOC copy. 39020

Washington's March [and] The New
President's March.
New York, B. Carr, [1796]. Broadside.
(Title and imprint assumed by Evans from
adv. in N. Y. American Minerva, Feb. 23,
1796.)
HEH copy. 31553

Washington's March [and] Washington's
March at the Battle of Trenton.
Philadelphia, Willig, [1796]. Broadside.
AAS copy. 31555

Washington's March. As Performed at the
New Theatre, Philadelphia.
[Philadelphia], Willig, [1795?]. [2] pp.
HEH copy. 29834

A Watch for a Wise Man's Observation.
Boston, 1699. Broadside.
MHS copy. 898

The Watchman, No. I. . . . The Dangerous
Unconstitutional Innovations. . . .
February 8, 1770.
[New York, 1770.] [2] pp.
NYHS copy. 11916

The Watchman, No. II. . . . It is a Truth.
. . . Feb. 17, 1770.
[New York, 1770.] Broadside.
LCP copy. 11917

The Watchman, No. III. Homines. . . .
March 10, 1770.
[New York, 1770.] [2] pp.
LCP copy. 11919

The New-York Journal, &c. No. 1424. The
Watchman, No. III. . . . March 10, 1770.
[New York, 1770.] [2] pp.
LCP copy. 11918

The Watchman, No. IV. . . . All
Intelligent Beings. . . . March 29, 1770.
[New York, 1770.] [2] pp.
LCP copy. 11920

The Watchman, No. V. . . . When a
Kingdom. . . . April 21, 1770.
[New York, 1770.] [2] pp.
LOC copy. 11921

The Watchman's Alarm to Lord N - h [by
John Allen, fl. 1764].
Salem, Russell, 1774. 32 pp.
(Apparently Evans guessed at the
imprint.)
NYHS copy. 13757

The Watch-Tower. Numb. LIII. . . .
January 16, 1756 [by William Livingston,
1723-1790].
[New York, Gaine, 1756]. Broadside.
NYHS copy. 7698

Waterhouse, Benjamin, 1754-1846.
Heads of a Course of Lectures.
Providence, Wheeler, [1788?] Broadside.
RIHS copy. 45406

Waterhouse, Benjamin, 1754-1846.
Heads of a Course of Lectures . . . in
Natural History.

[Providence, Wheeler, c. 1794].
Broadside.
HC copy. 43758

Waterhouse, Benjamin, 1754-1846.
On the Principle of Vitality.
Boston, Fleets, 1790. [4], 24, [4] pp.
AAS copy. 23038

Waterhouse, Benjamin, 1754-1846.
A Prospect of Exterminating the
Small-Pox.
Cambridge, [Mass.], Hilliard, 1800. 40
pp.
NLM copy. 39022

Waterhouse, Benjamin, 1754-1846.
The Rise, Progress, and Present State of
Medicine.
Boston, Fleets, 1792. xii, 31 pp.
AAS copy. 24987

Waterhouse, Benjamin, 1754-1846.
A Synopsis of a Course of Lectures.
Boston, Adams & Nourse, 1786. x, 44 pp.
AAS copy. 20123

[Waterhouse, Samuel.]
Jem-mi-bul-le-ro. . . . Presented by the
Boys that Carries about the . . . New-York
Gazette . . . 1766.
[New York, 1766.] Broadside.
LCP copy. 10426

[Waterhouse, Samuel.]
Proposals for Printing by Subscription the
History of Adjutant Trowel.
[Boston, 1766.] 8 pp.
BA copy. 10519

[Waterhouse, Samuel.]
(D.A.B. article on Thomas Pownall.)
Proposals for Printing by Subscription.
The History of . . . Sir Thomas Brazen.
[Boston], 1760. 18, [1] pp.
AAS copy. 8763

Waterland, Daniel, 1683-1740.
Regeneration Stated and Explained.
New York, Gaine, 1793. 43 pp.
(Printed with 25837, q.v.)
26432

Waterman, Elijah, 1769-1825.
An Oration, Delivered before the Society
of the Cincinnati.
Hartford, Hudson & Goodwin, 1794. 20
pp.
AAS copy. 28031

Waterman, Foster, 1768-1843.
(Harvard College records.)
The Child's Instructor, being an Original
Spelling Book. . . . Vol. I [-II].
Boston, Thomas & Andrews, 1793. 2 vol.
36; 192 pp.
AAS copy. 26433

[Waterman, Foster, 1768-1843.
The Child's Instructor. Being an Original
Spelling Book.
Boston, Thomas & Andrews, 1794.]
(Imprint assumed by Evans from adv.
"Just Published" in Columbian Centinel,
Mar. 15, 1794.) 28032

Waterman, Nehemiah, d. 1802.
An Oration, Delivered at Bozrah.
Windham, [Ct.], Byrne, 1800. 16 pp.
CHS copy. 39023

Waterman, Simon, 1737-1813.
Death Chosen Rather than Life.
Hartford, Hudson & Goodwin, 1788. 32·
pp.
AAS copy. 21574

Waters, Anthony.
The Fine Bay Horse True Briton. . . .
[New York, 1763.] Broadside.
NYPL copy. 41340

Waters, Nicholas Baker, 1764-1796.
Tentamen Medicum Inaugurale.
Philadelphia, Young, 1788. 23 pp.
LCP copy. 21575

Waters, Samuel, 1750-1828.
Meditations on Abraham's Conduct.
Worcester, Thomas, 1793. 24 pp.
AAS copy. 26434

Watertown, Mass. Council of Churches,
1723.

A True and Genuine Account of the
Result.
Boston, Fleet, [1723]. [4], 28 pp.
AAS copy. 2492

Watervliet, N. Y. Freeholders.
At a Meeting of . . . Freeholders of
Watervliet, Bern and Bethlehem, Held at
. . . Albany, on the 18th Day of April,
1799.
[Albany, 1799.] Broadside.
NYSL copy. 36672

Watkins, John.
An Essay on the End of the World.
Worcester, Thomas, 1795. 36 pp.
AAS copy. 29838

Watkins, John Watkin.
(Columbia Univ. records.)
An Oration Delivered November 10, 1791.
New York, M'Lean, 1792. 15 pp.
NYHS copy. 26435

Watkins, Robert.
An Examination of the Executive
Proceeding. . . .
Augusta, [Ga.], Smith, 1799. 30 pp.
NYHS copy. 36673

Watkinson, Edward.
An Essay upon OEconomy. The Fourth
Edition.
New York, 1765. 35 pp.
AAS copy. 10197

Watkinson, Edward.
An Essay upon OEconomy. The Fourth
Edition.
Newport, 1765. 35 pp.
LOC copy. 10196

[Watkinson, Edward.
An Essay upon OEconomy. The Fourth
Edition.
Philadelphia, 1765. 35 pp.]
(The copies located are fragments with
supposititious titlepages.) 10198

Watkinson, Edward.
An Essay upon Oeconomy. The Fourth
Edition.
Providence, Goddard, 1765. 35 pp.
RIHS copy. 41597

Watkinson, Edward.
An Essay upon OEconomy. The Fourth
Edition.
Woodbridge, 1765. 35 pp.
(The unique copy is incomplete.)
MHS copy. 10199

Watson, Charles C.
Charles C. Watson, Taylor and
Habit-maker. . . . March 28, 1792.
[Philadelphia], Johnston & Justice,
[1792]. Broadside.
LOC copy. 46667

[Watson, Elkanah, 1758-1842.
Land for sale. . . . March 15, 1796.
Albany, Barber & Southwick, [1796].
Broadside.
(No copy located.) 31560

[Watson, Elkanah], 1758-1842.
A Tour in Holland, in MDCCLXXXIV.
Worcester, Thomas, 1790. 191 pp.
AAS copy. 23039

Watson, Richard, bp., 1737-1816.
An Address to the People of Great
Britain.
New York, Buel for Davis, 1798. 24 pp.
AAS copy. 34961

Watson, Richard, bp., 1737-1816.
An Address to the People of Great
Britain.
Philadelphia, Cobbett, 1798. 40 pp.
AAS copy. 34962

Watson, Richard, bp., 1737-1816.
An Address to Young Persons after
Confirmation.
Boston, Spotswood and Nichols, 1797.
102, [2] pp.
AAS copy. 33153

Watson, Richard, bp., 1737-1816.
An Apology for Christianity.

Providence, Carter & Wilkinson, 1794.
viii, 155 pp.
AAS copy. 28033

Watson, Richard, bp., 1737-1816.
An Apology for Christianity.
New Brunswick, Blauvelt, 1796. x, 136 pp.
AAS copy. 31561

Watson, Richard, bp., 1737-1816.
An Apology for Christianity.
Philadelphia, Carey, 1796. 56 pp.
AAS copy. 31562

Watson, Richard, bp., 1737-1816.
An Apology for Christianity. . . . Third
American Edition.
Schenectady, Wyckoff, 1796. 144 pp.
AAS copy. 31563

Watson, Richard, bp., 1737-1816.
An Apology for the Bible.
Albany, Barber & Southwick, 1796. pp.
[1]-168, 161-172, 187-192.
AAS copy. 31564

Watson, Richard, bp., 1737-1816.
An Apology for the Bible.
Boston, Manning & Loring for White,
1796. 168 pp.
AAS copy. 31565

Watson, Richard, bp., 1737-1816.
An Apology for the Bible.
Lancaster, Pa., Hamilton and Dicksons,
1796. 118 pp.
AAS copy. 31566

Watson, Richard, bp., 1737-1816.
An Apology for the Bible.
New Brunswick, Blauvelt, 1796. [2], 201,
[12] pp.
AAS copy. 31567

Watson, Richard, bp., 1737-1816.
An Apology for the Bible.
New York, Buel, 1796. iv, 252 pp.
AAS copy. 31568

Watson, Richard, bp., 1737-1816.
An Apology for the Bible.
New York, Swords, 1796. 178, [1] pp.
AAS copy. 31569

Watson, Richard, bp., 1737-1816.
An Apology for the Bible.
Newburgh, Denniston, 1796. 232 pp.
AAS copy. 31570

Watson, Richard, bp., 1737-1816.
An Apology for the Bible.
Philadelphia, Carey, 1796. [2], 80 pp.
AAS copy. 31571

Watson, Richard, bp., 1737-1816.
An Apology for the Bible. . . . Second
Philadelphia Edition.
Philadelphia, Carey, 1796. [2], 80 pp.
AAS copy. 31572

Watson, Richard, bp., 1737-1816.
An Apology for the Bible.
Philadelphia, Woodward for Young, 1796.
206 pp.
(Evans confuses two editions.)
AAS copy. 31573

Watson, Richard, bp., 1737-1816.
An Apology for the Bible.
Chambersburg, Pa., Dover & Harper for
Riddle & Lane, 1797. [2], 80 pp.
AAS copy. 33154

Watson, Richard, bp., 1737-1816.
An Aplogy for the Bible.
Lexington, Ky., Bradford, 1797. 94, [2]
pp.
NYPL copy. 33155

Watson, Richard, bp., 1737-1816.
An Apology for the Bible.
Litchfield, Ct., Collier, 1797. 230 pp.
AAS copy. 33156

Watson, Richard, bp., 1737-1816.
An Apology for the Bible.
Newbern, Martin for Shute & Hatch,
1797. 77 pp.
NCU copy. 48311

Watson, Richard, bp., 1737-1816.
An Apology for the Bible.

Philadelphia, Carey, 1797. [2], 80 pp.
JCB copy. 33157

Watson, Richard, bp., 1737-1816.
Christian Panoply.
Shepherd's Town, Va., Rootes &
Blagrove, 1797. 332 pp.
AAS copy. 33158

Watson, Robert, of Georgia.
A Digest of the Laws of the State of
Georgia.
Philadelphia, Aitken, 1800. vi, [2], 837,
[29] pp.
(Also entered as 37505, q. v.) 39024

Watson, Thomas, -1686.
Light in Darkness.
Boston, Green & Russell, 1757. 22 pp.
LOC copy. 8058

[Watson, Thomas, -1686.
(D. N. B.)
A Sermon Explaining the Fourth
Commandment.
Wilmington, Del., 1772.]
(From an unlocated adv.) 12603

Watson, William, barrister at law.
A Treatise of the Law of Partnership.
Albany, Websters for Spencer, etc., 1795.
368 pp.
AAS copy. 29839

Watson's Connecticut Almanack, for . . .
1777 [by Nehemiah Strong, 1729-1807].
Hartford, Watson. [24] pp.
AAS copy. 15099

Watson's Register, and Connecticut
Almanack, for . . . 1776 [by Nehemiah
Strong, 1729-1807].
Hartford, Watson. [24] pp.
AAS copy. 14480

Watt, Robert, d. 1794, defendant.
The Trials at Large of Robert Watt and
David Downie.
New York, Tiebout & O'Brien, 1794. 88
pp.
AAS copy. 27815

Watt, Robert, d. 1794, defendant.
The Trials at Large of Robert Watt and
David Downie.
Philadelphia, M'Kenzie and Wrigley &
Berriman, 1794. 41 pp.
MHS copy. 27816

[Watt, Thomas.
Watt's Complete Spelling Book. Tenth
Edition.
Philadelphia, Bradfords, 1771.]
(Adv. Pa. Journal, Mar. 7, 1771.) 12271

Watters, James, d. 1798.
A New Periodical Publication. . . . The
Weekly Magazine. . . . 13th of December,
1797.
[Philadelphia, 1797.] Broadside.
HSP copy. 48310

Watters, James, d. 1798.
A New Periodical Publication. . . . 13th of
December, 1797.
[Philadelphia, 1797.] Broadside.
HSP copy. 33159

Watters, James, d. 1798.
Sir, Being on the Point. . . . December
18th, 1797.
[Philadelphia, 1797.] Broadside.
HSP copy. 33160

Watts, Isaac, 1674-1748.
Appendix, Containing a Number of
Hymns.
Boston, Leverett, 1760. 84, [1] pp., 16
plates.
AAS copy. 41174

Watts, Isaac, 1674-1748.
The Beauties of the Late Rev. Dr. Isaac
Watts.
Elizabethtown, Kollock, 1796. [2], 229,
[5] pp.
AAS copy. 31574

Watts, Isaac, 1674-1748.
The Beauties of the Late . . . Dr. Isaac
Watts.

Newburyport Blunt for Carey, 1797. 239
pp.
AAS copy. 33161

[Watts, Isaac, 1674-1748.
Catechisms.
Boston, Rogers & Fowle for Blanchard,
1747.]
(Title from an adv.) 6079

Watts, Isaac, 1674-1748.
The Final Set of Catechisms. . . . Twelfth
Edition.
Boston, S. Kneeland, 1762. 16 pp.
(The only copy located could not be
reproduced.) 41322

Watts, Isaac, 1674-1748.
The Child's Catechism.
Norwich, Trumbull, 1788. 31 pp.
(No copy located.) 45407

Watts, Isaac, 1674-1748.
Doctor Watts's First Catechism.
Boston, Hall, [1795]. 7, [1] pp.
AAS copy. 29842

Watts, Isaac, 1674-1748.
Dr. Watts' Plain and Easy Catechisms.
Exeter, Ranlet, 1791. 36 pp.
AAS copy. 23961

Watts, Isaac, 1674-1748.
Dr. Watts' Plain and Easy Catechisms.
Exeter, Ranlet, 1792. 96 pp.
AAS copy. 24992

Watts, Isaac, 1674-1748.
A Catechism for Children.
Windham, [Ct.], Byrne, 1795. 47 pp.
AAS copy. 47670

[Watts, Isaac, 1674-1748.
Dr Watts' Catechisms and Prayers, for
Children and Youth.
Charleston, S. C., Young, 1796.]
(Imprint assumed by Evans from
Young's advs.) 31576

Watts, Isaac, 1674-1748.
Dr. Watts's Catechism for Little
Children.
Windham, Ct., Byrne, 1796.
(The unique copy could not be
reproduced.) 31575

Watts, Isaac, 1674-1748.
Dr. Watts's Plain and Easy Catechisms.
Newburyport, Blunt, 1797. 156 pp.
AAS copy. 33167

Watts, Isaac, 1674-1748.
A Catechism for Children.
Windham, Ct., Byrne, 1798. 46 pp.
AAS copy. 34963

Watts, Isaac, 1674-1748.
Christian Discipline.
Boston, Mecom, [1759]. 26, [2] pp.
AAS copy. 8515

Watts, Isaac, 1674-1748.
Christmas Anthem.
Worcester, Mass., Thomas, 1795. 8 pp.
AAS copy. 47671

Watts, Isaac, 1674-1748.
A Comprehensive Abridgment of Dr.
Watts's Lyric Poems. . . . By Solomon
Howe.
Northampton, Mass., Wright, etc., 1798.
48, 16 pp.
(The AAS has a variant issue.)
AAS copy. 34964

[Watts, Isaac, 1674-1748.
(D. N. B.)
Directions for the Better Government.
Boston, 1729.]
(Adv. Boston News-Letter, Oct. 30,
1729.) 3230

Watts, Isaac, 1674-1748.
A Discourse on the Way of Instruction.
Boston, Rogers & Fowle, 1748. ix, [1],
62, 18, [2] pp.
(The only copy located is imperfect.
Imprint reconstructed from adv.)
AAS copy. 6260

Watts, Isaac, 1674-1748.
Discourses on the Love of God.

Philadelphia, Woodward, 1799. 224 pp.
AAS copy. 36674

[Watts, Isaac, 1674-1748.
(D. N. B.)
Divine Songs Attempted in easy
Language.
Boston, 1719.]
(No copy could be located.) 2085

Watts, Isaac, 1674-1748.
Divine Songs Attempted in Easy
Language. . . . Seventh Edition.
Boston, Kneeland & Green for
Henchman, 1730. [2], iv, 42 pp.
(The only copy located is imperfect.)
AAS copy. 39960

[Watts, Isaac, 1674-1748.
Divine Songs Attempted in Easy
Language for the Use of Children. . . .
Eighth Edition.
Philadelphia, Franklin, 1737.]
(Adv. Pa. Gazette, Mar. 24, 1736/7.)
4206

Watts, Isaac, 1674-1748.
[Divine Songs. . . . The Ninth Edition?
Boston, 1740?]
(Known only by this defective copy.)
AAS copy. 40222

[Watts, Isaac, 1674-1748.
Divine Songs Attempted in Easy
Language for the Use of Children.
New York, 1744.]
(Title from adv. in N. Y. Weekly Post-
Boy.) 5508

[Watts, Isaac, 1674-1748.
Divine Songs.
New York, 1747.]
("There is now in the Press," N. Y.
Evening-Post, Jan. 26, 1746/7.) 6080

[Watts, Isaac, 1674-1748.
Divine Songs Attempted in Easy
Language for the Use of Children. . . .
Eleventh Edition.
Philadelphia, Franklin & Hall, 1749.]
("Lately published," Pa. Gazette, Jan. 16,
1749/50.) 6438

Watts, Isaac, 1674-1748.
Divine Songs. . . . Twelfth Edition.
Philadelphia, Franklin & Hall, 1750. vi,
41 pp.
HSP copy. 40574

[Watts, Isaac, 1674-1748.
Divine Songs.
New York, Gaine, 1753.]
("Just published, and to be sold by the
Printer," N. Y. Mercury, Dec. 3, 1753.)
7134

[Watts, Isaac, 1674-1748.
Divine Songs.
Philadelphia, Chattin, 1757.]
(Adv. Pa. Gazette, June 16, 1757.) 8059

Watts, Isaac, 1674-1748.
Divine Songs. . . . Eleventh Edition.
Boston, Fowle & Draper, 1759. [2], iv,
48 pp.
(The only known copy is imperfect.)
AAS copy. 41090

[Watts, Isaac, 1674-1748.
Divine Songs.
New York, Gaine, 1760.]
(Adv. N. Y. Mercury No. 467.) 8765

[Watts, Isaac, 1674-1748.
Divine Songs.
Philadelphia, Dunlap for Noel, 1760.]
(From adv.) 8764

Watts, Isaac, 1674-1748.
Divine Songs. . . . Fifteenth Edition.
Portsmouth, N. H., D. & R. Fowle, 1764.
32 pp.
AAS copy. 41509

Watts, Isaac, 1674-1748.
Divine Songs. . . . Fifteenth Edition.
Boston, D. & J. Kneeland for Leverett,
1765. 36 pp.
AAS copy. 41598

[Watts, Isaac, 1674-1748.
Divine Songs. . . . Fourteenth Edition.

Boston, Perkins, 1771. 47 pp.]
(Entry from Haven.) 12272

Watts, Isaac, 1674-1748.
Divine Songs. . . . Sixteenth Edition.
New London, Green, 177 [2?].
35, [1] pp.
(The only known copy is imperfect.)
YC copy. 42386

Watts, Isaac, 1674-1748.
Divine Songs. . . . Fifteenth Edition.
Boston, Bowes, 1773. v, 42 pp.
(The only known copy is imperfect.)
AAS copy. 42533

Watts, Isaac, 1674-1748.
Divine Songs. . . . Fifteenth Edition.
Boston, T. & S. Fleet, 1773. [2], 44,
[1] pp.
AAS copy. 42534

Watts, Isaac, 1674-1748.
Divine Songs. . . . Fifteenth Edition.
Boston, Leverett, 1773. pp. [i]-v, [1]-7,
9-42.
AAS copy. 42535

Watts, Isaac, 1674-1748.
[Divine and Moral Songs.
Newport, 1773.] [2], iv, 52 + pp.
(The unique copy is defective.)
Providence Public Library copy. 13066

Watts, Isaac, 1674-1748.
Divine Songs. . . . Sixteenth Edition.
Philadelphia, Crukshank for Aitken,
[1773]. Front., 29, [1] pp.
AAS copy. 13065

Watts, Isaac, 1674-1748.
Divine Songs. . . . Fourteenth Edition.
Boston, Greenleaf's Printing Office, 1774.
44 pp.
PPL copy. 42745

Watts, Isaac, 1674-1748.
Divine Songs. . . . Fourteenth Edition.
Boston, Barclay, 1775. 48, [1] pp.
CL copy. 42980

Watts, Isaac, 1674-1748.
Divine Songs. . . . Fourteenth Edition.
Boston, Coverly, 1775. 47, [1] pp.
AAS copy. 42981

Watts, Isaac, 1674-1748.
Divine Songs. . . . Seventeenth Edition.
Norwich, Green & Spooner, 1777. 36 pp.
Gillett Griffin copy. 43405

Watts, Isaac, 1674-1748.
Divine Songs.
Boston, Coverly, [1778]. 48 pp.
(The only known copy is very defective.)
AAS copy. 43592

Watts, Isaac, 1674-1748.
Divine Songs.
Boston, Coverly, 1778. 48 pp.
AAS copy. 43593

Watts, Isaac, 1674-1748.
Divine Songs. . . . Twentieth Edition.
[Imprint cut off; 1780?] 46 pp.
AAS copy. 43914

[Watts, Isaac, 1674-1748.
Divine Songs for the use of Children.
Philadelphia, Aitken, 1781.]
(Mentioned in 17312.) 17421

Watts, Isaac, 1674-1748.
Divine Songs.
Hartford, Hudson & Goodwin, 1783.
60 pp.
(The only known copy is imperfect.)
AAS copy. 44494

Watts, Isaac, 1674-1748.
Divine Songs Attempted in Easy
Language.
Norwich, Trumbull, 1783.
CHS copy. 18294

Watts, Isaac, 1674-1748.
Divine Songs. . . . Twenty-Fifth Edition.
Hartford, Webster, [1784?] 47 pp.
CHS copy. 44626

Watts, Isaac, 1674-1748.
Divine Songs.

Newburyport, Mycall, 1784. 54 pp.
AAS copy. 44627

Watts, Isaac, 1674-1748.
Divine Songs. . . . Seventeenth Edition.
Philadelphia, Crukshank, 1784. 24 pp.
AAS copy. 44628

Watts, Isaac, 1674-1748.
Divine Songs. . . . Seventy Eighth
Edition.
Bennington, Vt., Haswell & Russell,
1785. 24 pp.
(The only known copy is imperfect.)
AAS copy. 44828

[Watts, Isaac, 1674-1748.
Watts' Divine Songs for Children.
Charlestown, 1787.]
(From a bookseller's adv. in Boston
Gazette, Jan. 22, 1787, for the London
ed.) 20857

Watts, Isaac, 1674-1748.
Divine Songs: in Easy Language.
Springfield, [Mass.], 1788. 31, [1] pp.,
printed wrappers.
AAS copy. 45408

Watts, Isaac, 1674-1748.
Divine and Moral Songs for Children.
Worcester, Thomas, 1788. 118 pp.
AAS copy. 21576

Watts, Isaac, 1674-1748.
Divine Songs, Attempted in Easy
Language.
New Haven, Meigs, 1789. 8 pp.
CHS copy. 45739

Watts, Isaac, 1674-1748.
Divine Songs.
Springfield, 1789. 31 pp.
d'Alte A. Welch copy. 22244

[Watts, Isaac, 1674-1748.
Divine and Moral Songs.
Bennington, 1790.]
("Just published," Vt. Gazette, Apr. 5,
1790.) 23040

Watts, Isaac, 1674-1748.
Divine and Moral Songs.
Boston, Hall, 1790. 71, [3] pp.
YC copy. 46090

Watts, Isaac, 1674-1748.
Divine Songs Attempted in Easy
Language.
Middletown, [Ct.], Woodward, 1790.
32 pp.
AAS copy. 46091

Watts, Isaac, 1674-1748.
Divine Songs, Attempted in Easy
Language.
New Haven, Morse, 1790. 66 pp.,
printed wraps.
AAS copy. 46092

Watts, Isaac, 1674-1748.
Divine Songs.
Boston, Hall, 1792. 71, [3] pp.
(Not located, 1968.) 46669

Watts, Isaac, 1674-1748.
Divine Songs.
Boston, Fleet, 1793. 46 pp.
(Evans assumed a Hall imprint from the
adv. in 25606.)
HC copy. 26436

Watts, Isaac, 1674-1748.
Divine Songs.
Exeter, Ranlet, 1793. 96 pp.
AAS copy. 26437

Watts, Isaac, 1674-1748.
Divine Songs.
Newburyport, Osborne, 1793. 48 pp.
AAS copy. 26438

Watts, Isaac, 1674-1748.
Divine Songs. . . . Sixty-Fourth Edition.
Boston, Coverly, 1794. 40 pp.
(No better copy available.)
AAS copy. 47320

Watts, Isaac, 1674-1748.
Divine Songs.
Canaan, Phinney, 1794. 36 pp.
HEH copy. 47321

Watts, Isaac, 1674-1748.
Divine Songs Attempted in Easy
Language for the Use of Children.
Hartford, Babcock, 1794. 31 pp.
(The title given by Evans was based on an
adv. in the Am. Mercury, Jan. 6, 1794.)
AAS copy.　　　　　　　　　　28034

Watts, Isaac, 1674-1748.
Divine Songs Attempted in Easy
Language, for the Use of Children.
Keene, N.H., Blake, 1794.
(Heartman's Cat. 101 (Apr. 5, 1920), no.
192.)　　　　　　　　　　　　28035

Watts, Isaac, 1674-1748.
Divine Songs Attempted in Easy
Language.
Bennington, Haswell, 1795. 35 pp.
WLC copy.　　　　　　　　　　29840

Watts, Isaac, 1674-1748.
Divine Songs, Attempted in Easy
Language.
Dover, Bragg, 1795. 34 pp.
AAS copy.　　　　　　　　　　29841

Watts, Isaac, 1674-1748.
Divine Songs Attempted in Easy
Language.
Hartford, [Ct.], Babcock, 1795. 31 pp.
AAS copy.　　　　　　　　　　47672

Watts, Isaac, 1674-1748.
Divine and Moral Songs.
Boston, Hall, 1796. 70 pp., 1 plate.
AAS copy.　　　　　　　　　　31577

Watts, Isaac, 1674-1748.
Divine Songs, Attempted in Easy
Languages. . . . Third Dover Edition.
[Dover, N.H.], Bragg, 1796. 32 + pp.
(The only known copy is imperfect.)
HC copy.　　　　　　　　　　48021

Watts, Isaac, 1674-1748.
Divine and Moral Songs.
Leominster, Prentiss, 1796. 72 pp.
AAS copy.　　　　　　　　　　31578

Watts, Isaac, 1674-1748.
Divine Songs: in Easy Language.
New London, Springer, 1796. 28 pp.,
front.
CHS copy.　　　　　　　　　　48022

Watts, Isaac, 1674-1748.
Divine Songs, Attempted in Easy
Language, for the Use of Children. . . .
Sixty-Fourth Edition.
Haverhill, N. H., Coverly, 1797. 36 pp.
NYPL copy.　　　　　　　　　33162

Watts, Isaac, 1674-1748.
Divine and Moral Songs. . . . Second
Leominster Edition.
Leominster, Prentiss, 1797. 48 + pp.
(The only known copy is imperfect.)
AAS copy.　　　　　　　　　　48313

Watts, Isaac, 1674-1748.
Divine Songs.
New Haven, Bunce, 1797. 72 pp.
YC copy.　　　　　　　　　　48312

Watts, Isaac, 1674-1748.
Divine Songs, Attempted in Easy
Language, for the Use of Children.
Newark, N. J., Pennington & Dodge for
Davis, 1797. 72 pp.
AAS copy.　　　　　　　　　　33163

[Watts, Isaac, 1674-1748.
Divine Songs, Attempted in Easy
Language, for the Use of Children.
Rutland, Vt., Fay, 1797.]
(Imprint assumed by Evans from adv. in
Rutland Herald, Aug. 21, 1797.)　　33164

Watts, Isaac, 1674-1748.
Divine Songs, Attempted in Easy
Language.
Boston, Edes, 1798. 47 pp.
AAS copy.　　　　　　　　　　34965

Watts, Isaac, 1674-1748.
Divine Songs Attempted in Easy
Language.
Hartford, Babcock, 1798. 70 pp.
CHS copy.　　　　　　　　　　48754

Watts, Isaac, 1674-1748.
Divine and Moral Songs.

Boston, Hall, 1799. 70 pp., irreg., 1 plate.
AAS copy.　　　　　　　　　　36675

Watts, Isaac, 1674-1748.
Divine Songs, Attempted in Easy
Language.
Medford, Mass., Coverly, 1799. 30 pp.
AAS copy.　　　　　　　　　　36677

Watts, Isaac, 1674-1748.
Divine Songs Attempted in Easy
Language. . . . Ninety Fifth Edition.
Boston, Coverly, [1800?]. 36 pp.
AAS copy.　　　　　　　　　　49184

Watts, Isaac, 1674-1748.
Divine and Moral Songs.
Catskill, Croswells for Chittenden at
Hudson, [1800?] 36 pp.
d'Alte A. Welch copy.　　　　　49185

Watts, Isaac, 1674-1748.
Divine Songs, Attempted in Easy
Language.
New Haven, Read & Morse, 1800. front.,
64 pp.
BPL copy.　　　　　　　　　　39026

Watts, Isaac, 1684-1748.
Divine Songs Attempted in Easy
Language.
Philadelphia, M'Culloch, 1800. 31 pp.
(Not located, 1968.)　　　　　　49186

Watts, Isaac, 1674-1748.
Divine Songs, Attempted in Easy
Language.
Salem, [Mass.], J. Cushing for T. C.
Cushing, 1800. 48 pp.
AAS copy.　　　　　　　　　　39025

Watts, Isaac, 1674-1748.
Divine Hymns, in Verse, for Children.
Baltimore, Corbet, 1799. 70 pp.
AAS copy.　　　　　　　　　　36676

Watts, Isaac, 1674-1748.
The Doctrine of the Passions.
Elizabethtown, Kollock, for Hodge, 1795.
[2], vi, 210, [5] pp.
AAS copy.　　　　　　　　　　29843

Watts, Isaac, 1674-1748.
The End of Time.
Boston, Kneeland & Green, 1740. 45, [2]
pp.
AAS copy.　　　　　　　　　　4623

[Watts, Isaac], 1674-1748.
An Essay toward the Proof of a Separate
State of Souls. . . . Second Edition.
Boston, Rogers & Fowle, 1748. pp.
[9]-189.
AAS copy.　　　　　　　　　　40488

Watts, Isaac, 1674-1748.
The First Set of Catechisms. . . . Ninth
Edition.
Boston, Blanchard, 1745. 16 pp.
AAS copy.　　　　　　　　　　40391

Watts, Isaac, 1674-1748.
The First Set of Catechisms. . . . Seventh
Edition.
Boston, Rogers & Fowle, 1748. 18, [2] pp.
(Signatured with 6260, q.v.)　　　6262

Watts, Isaac, 1674-1748.
The First Set of Catechisms. . . . Eleventh
Edition.
Boston, Kneeland, 1753. 16 pp.
MHS copy.　　　　　　　　　　7135

[Watts, Isaac, 1674-1748.
The First and Second Catechism.
New York, Holt, 1765.]
(From an adv.)　　　　　　　　10200

Watts, Isaac, 1674-1748.
The First Set of Catechisms. . . . Eighth
Edition.
Boston, Kneeland & Adams, 1770. 16 pp.
LOC copy.　　　　　　　　　　11923

Watts, Isaac, 1674-1748.
The First Set of Catechisms. . . . Twelfth
Edition.
Boston, Boyle, 1773. 15 pp.
AAS copy.　　　　　　　　　　13067

Watts, Isaac, 1674-1748.
First Set of Catechisms. . . . Eighth
Edition.

Portsmouth, Melcher & Osborne, 1785. 36,
26, 34 pp.
DC copy.　　　　　　　　　　44829

Watts, Isaac, 1674-1748.
The First Catechism. . . . To which is
Added, the Second Catechism.
Norwich, Trumbull, 1788.
CHS copy.　　　　　　　　　　21577

Watts, Isaac, 1674-1748.
The First Catechism. . . . To which is
added, The Second Catechism.
West Springfield, [Mass.], Davison,
[1796?] [24] pp.
AAS copy.　　　　　　　　　　48023

[Watts, Isaac, 1674-1748.
Five Tracts on Various Subjects.
Boston, Rogers & Fowle, 1749.]
(From printers' adv. It is doubtful that
there was a volume with this title.)　6439

Watts, Isaac, 1674-1748.
The Glory of Christ as God-Man.
Boston, Manning & Loring for West,
1795. 287 pp.
AAS copy.　　　　　　　　　　29844

Watts, Isaac, 1674-1748.
A Guide to Prayer. . . . Eighth Edition.
Boston, Draper for Henchman, 1739. [2],
x, 228, [4] pp.
BPL copy.　　　　　　　　　　4443

[Watts, Isaac, 1674-1748.
A Guide to Prayer.
Boston, Rogers & Fowle, 1746.]
(Title from an adv.)　　　　　　5879

Watts, Isaac, 1674-1748.
A Guide to Prayer.
Elizabethtown, N. J., Kollock, 1797. pp.
[2], [i]-ix, [1], [3]-235, [4].
AAS copy.　　　　　　　　　　33165

Watts, Isaac, 1674-1748.
The Historical Catechism for Children.
Windham, Byrne, 1797. 70 pp.
CHS copy.　　　　　　　　　　48314

Watts, Isaac, 1674-1748.
Honey out of the Rock.
Boston, Fleet & Crump for Gerrish, 1715.
24 pp.
HEH copy.　　　　　　　　　　39639

[Watts, Isaac, 1674-1748.
Horae Lyricae.
Philadelphia, Franklin, 1741.]
("Shortly will be reprinted," Pa. Gazette,
Nov. 26, 1741.)　　　　　　　　4833

Watts, Isaac, 1674-1748.
Horace Lyricae. . . . Ninth Edition.
Boston, Rogers & Fowle and Blanchard,
1748. [2], xxiii, [11], 248, [4] pp.
AAS copy.　　　　　　　　　　6263

Watts, Isaac, 1674-1748.
Horae Lyricae. . . . Tenth Edition.
New York, Parker, 1750. xxii, [12], 265,
[5] pp.
AAS copy.　　　　　　　　　　6620

[Watts, Isaac, 1674-1748.
Horae Lyricae.
Boston, Fowle & Draper, 1762.]
(The only reported copy could not be
located.)　　　　　　　　　　9300

Watts, Isaac, 1674-1748.
Horae Lyricae. . . . Tenth Edition.
New York, Gaine, 1762. xxiii, [1], 212,
[4] pp.
AAS copy.　　　　　　　　　　9299

Watts, Isaac, 1674-1748.
Horae Lyricae. . . . Twelvth Edition.
Boston, Kneeland for Leverett, 1772. xxii,
[10], 250, [4] pp.
(No copy found with imprint given by
Evans, who took his entry from an adv.
AAS has another issue with the imprint of
Kneeland for Bowes.)
AAS copy.　　　　　　　　　　12604

Watts, Isaac, 1674-1748.
Horae Lyricae. . . . Twelvth Edition.
Boston, D. Kneeland for Bowes, 1772.
xxii, [10], 250 pp.

(An imprint variant of 12604, q. v. for text.)
AAS copy.   42387

[Watts, Isaac, 1674-1748.
Horae Lyricae.
Philadelphia, Bell, 1777.]
(Adv. Pa. Gazette, Jan. 5, 1778.)   15702

Watts, Isaac, 1674-1748.
Horae Lyricae.
Philadelphia, Aitken, 1781. 267, [7] pp.
AAS copy.   17422

Watts, Isaac, 1674-1748.
Horae Lyricae.
Boston, Hall, 1790. xxxviii, 252 pp.
(An imprint variant of 23041, q.v. for text.)
AAS copy.   46093

Watts, Isaac, 1674-1748.
Horae Lyricae.
Boston, Hall for Larkin, etc., 1790. xxxviii, 252 pp.
AAS copy.   23041

[Watts, Isaac, 1674-1748.
Horae Lyricae. . . . Tenth Edition, Corrected.
New York, Gaine, 1792.]
(Imprint assumed by Evans from Gaine's advs.)   24988

Watts, Isaac, 1674-1748.
Horae Lyricae.
Philadelphia, Aitken, 1792. 277 pp.
AAS copy.   24989

Watts, Isaac, 1674-1748.
Horae Lyricae.
Elizabethtown, Kollock, 1793. 219 pp.
AAS copy.   26439

Watts, Isaac, 1674-1748.
Horae Lyricae.
Exeter, Ranlet for Thomas & Andrews, 1795. 204 pp.
AAS copy.   29845

Watts, Isaac, 1674-1748.
Horae Lyricae.
Windham, Ct., Byrne, 1798. 208 pp.
AAS copy.   34966

Watts, Isaac, 1674-1748.
[Hymns and Spiritual Songs. . . . Seventh Edition.
Boston, 1720?] 360 pp.
(The only known copy is defective.)
MHS copy.   39733

Watts, Isaac, 1674-1748.
Hymns and Spiritual Songs. . . . Fifteenth Edition.
Philadelphia, Franklin, 1741. xii, [2], 274, [12] pp.
NL copy.   40266

Watts, Isaac, 1674-1748.
Hymns and Spiritual Songs. . . . Sixteenth Edition.
Boston, Rogers & Fowle for Henchman, 1742. xii, 317, [18] pp.
BPL copy.   40293

[Watts, Isaac, 1674-1748.
Hymns and Spiritual Songs.
Philadelphia, Franklin, 1742.]
(Adv. Pa. Gazette, Sept. 23, 1742.)   5087

[Watts, Isaac, 1674-1748.
Hymns and Spiritual Songs.
Boston, Harrison, 1743.]
("This day published," Boston Evening Post, Jan. 31, 1743.)   5307

[Watts, Isaac, 1674-1748.
Hymns and Spiritual Songs.
New York, Gaine, 1752. xii, 291, xvi pp.]
(No copy located.)   6945

Watts, Isaac, 1674-1748.
Hymns and Spiritual Songs. . . .
Eighteenth Edition.
New York, Gaine, 1761. xii, 291, xiv, [8] pp.
(No copy with the final leaf of adv. could be found.)
AAS copy.   9036

Watts, Isaac, 1674-1748.

Hymns and Spiritual Songs. . . . Twentieth Edition.
Boston, Fowle & Draper, 1762. xxiv, 312, 8 pp., 8 plates.
AAS copy.   41323

Watts, Isaac, 1674-1748.
Hymns and Spiritual Songs. . . .
Twenty-First Edition.
Boston, [M'Alpine] for Mein, 1766. xxiv, 264 + pp.
(The only known copy is defective.)
BPL copy.   41671

Watts, Isaac, 1674-1748.
Hymns and Spiritual Songs . . .
Twenty-First Edition.
Boston, Kneeland & Adams for Perkins, 1767. xxiv, 312 pp., 22 plates.
AAS copy.   41776

Watts, Isaac, 1674-1748.
Hymns and Spiritual Songs. . . . Twentieth Edition.
Philadelphia, Hall & Sellers, 1767. xiii, 281, [4] pp.
(No complete copy known.)
Composite copy.   10797

Watts, Isaac, 1674-1748.
Hymns and Spiritual Songs. . . .
Twenty-Second Edition.
Boston, Mein & Fleeming, 1769. xxiii, [1], 284 pp.
AAS copy.   11520

Watts, Isaac, 1674-1748.
Hymns and Spiritual Songs. . . .
Twenty-Second Edition.
Boston, D. Kneeland for Bowes, 1771. xxiv, 312 pp.
(An imprint variant of 12273, q. v. for text.)
AAS copy.   42294

Watts, Isaac, 1674-1748.
Hymns and Spiritual Songs. . . .
Twenty-Second Edition.
Boston, D. Kneeland for Perkins, 1771. xxiv, 312 pp.
(An imprint variant of 12273, q. v. for text.)
AAS copy.   42295

Watts, Isaac, 1674-1748.
Hymns and Spiritual Songs. . . .
Twenty-Second Edition.
Boston, Knox, 1771. xxiv, 312 pp.
AAS copy.   12273

Watts, Isaac, 1674-1748.
Hymns and Spiritual Songs.
Philadelphia, Dunlap, 1771. xxvi, 326, [2] pp.
JCB copy.   42296

Watts, Isaac, 1674-1748.
Hymns and Spiritual Songs.
New York, Gaine, 1771. xxvi, 328, [4] pp.
AAS copy.   12274

Watts, Isaac, 1674-1748.
Hymns and Spiritual Songs. . . .
Twenty-Second Edition.
Boston, Fleeming, 1772. 244 pp.
HC copy.   12605

Watts, Isaac, 1674-1748.
Hymns and Spiritual Songs. . . .
Twenty-Seventh Edition.
Boston, Fleets, 1772. [2], viii, [12], 263 pp.
AAS copy.   12606

[Watts, Isaac, 1674-1748.
Hymns and Spiritual Songs.
Boston, Kneeland & Davis, 1773.]
(Entry from an adv.)   13068

Watts, Isaac, 1674-1748.
Hymns and Spiritual Songs. . . . Thirty Seventh Edition.
Boston, Boyle, 1774. 237, [2] pp.
AAS copy.   42746

[Watts, Isaac, 1674-1748.
Hymns and Spiritual Songs.
Philadelphia, Hall & Sellers, 1778.]
(Adv. Pa. Gazette, Jan. 5, 1778.)   16165

Watts, Isaac, 1674-1748.
Hymns and Spiritual Songs. . . .
Twenty-Fourth Edition.

Philadelphia, Hall & Sellers, 1772. xxiii, [i], 281, [4] pp.
AAS copy.   42388

Watts, Isaac, 1674-1748.
Hymns and Spiritual Songs.
Hartford, Webster, 1781. 299, [1] pp.
(The only copy located is imperfect.)
CHS copy.   44084

Watts, Isaac, 1674-1748.
Hymns and Spiritual Songs.
Providence, 1781. 281, xi pp.
AAS copy.   17423

Watts, Isaac, 1674-1748.
Hymns and Spiritual Songs. . . .
Thirty-Ninth Edition.
Boston, Fleets, 1782. [2], 248, [26] pp.
AAS copy.   19444

Watts, Isaac, 1674-1748.
Hymns and Spiritual Songs.
Newburyport, Mycall for Leverett and Larkin, 1782. 264, xii pp.
AAS copy.   17791

Watts, Isaac, 1674-1748.
Hymns and Spiritual Songs.
Worcester, Mass., Thomas, 1786. pp. [2], 123-224, [1].
(The second part of 19509, q. v. for text, issued with this tp.)
AAS copy.   45016

Watts, Isaac, 1674-1748.
Hymns and Spiritual Songs.
Philadelphia, Crukshank, 1787. [2], 298 pp.
Hartford Seminary Foundation copy.   20858

Watts, Isaac, 1674-1748.
Hymns and Spiritual Songs.
Boston, Norman, 1789. 232, [8] pp.
AAS copy.   22245

Watts, Isaac, 1674-1748.
Hymns and Spiritual Songs.
New York, Gaine, 1789. [2], 277, [4] pp.
(Too fragile to copy.)   45740

[Watts, Isaac, 1674-1748.
Hymns and Spiritual Songs.
Boston, Bumstead, 1790. 276 pp.]
(Ghost of 1791 ed.)   46094

[Watts, Isaac, 1674-1748.
Hymns and Spiritual Songs.
Philadelphia, Campbell, 1790.]
(Entry from an unlocated adv.)   23042

Watts, Isaac, 1674-1748.
Hymns and Spiritual Songs.
Boston, Bumstead for D. West, E. Larkin and B. Larkin, 1791. 276 pp.
AAS copy.   46344

Watts, Isaac, 1674-1748.
Hymns and Spiritual Songs.
New York, Berry & Rogers and Reid, 1792. 272 pp.
AAS copy.   24990

Watts, Isaac, 1674-1748.
Hymns and Spiritual Songs.
New York, Durell, 1792. xiv, 274 pp.
AAS copy.   24991

Watts, Isaac, 1674-1748.
Hymns and Spiritual Songs.
New York, Hodge & Campbell, 1792. 286, [2] pp.
AAS copy.   46670

Watts, Isaac, 1674-1748.
Hymns and Spiritual Songs.
Philadelphia, Spotswood, 1793. 246, x pp.
(Not located, 1968.)   46935

Watts, Isaac, 1674-1748.
Hymns and Spiritual Songs.
Wilmington, Del., Brynberg & Andrews, 1793. 284 pp.
(No copy located.)   46936

Watts, Isaac, 1674-1748.
Hymns and Spiritual Songs.
Salem, Cushing & Carlton, 1794. 246, [18] pp.
AAS copy.   28036

Watts, Isaac, 1674-1748.

Hymns and Spiritual Songs.
New York, Campbell, 1795. 312 pp.
AAS copy.   47672a

Watts, Issac, 1674-1748.
Hymns and Spiritual Songs.
Newburyport, Mycall for Thomas, Larkin
and West, [c. 1795]. 26+ pp.
(The only known copy is defective.)
LCP copy.   47673

Watts, Isaac, 1674-1748.
Hymns and Spiritual Songs.
Wilmington, [Del.], Brynberg, 1796. 242,
[10] pp.
AAS copy.   48024

Watts, Isaac, 1674-1748.
Hymns and Spiritual Songs.
Elizabethtown, Kollock, 1797. [2], 286 pp.
AAS copy.   48315

Watts, Isaac, 1674-1748.
Hymns and Spiritual Songs.
Albany, Websters, 1800. 247, [17] pp.
(The only copy located is imperfect.)
AAS copy.   39027

Watts, Isaac, 1674-1748.
Hymns and Spiritual Songs.
New York, Durell, 1800. 254, [13] pp.
(Both copies located are imperfect.)
AAS copy.   39028

Watts, Isaac, 1674-1748.
Hymns and Spiritual Songs.
New York, Durell for Arden, 1800. 254,
[13] pp.
(Differs only in imprint from 39028, q. v.
for text.)
AAS copy.   39029

Watts, Isaac, 1674-1748.
The Improvement of the Mind.
Exeter, Lamson & Odiorne for West,
1793. ix, [1], 200, [2], 130 pp.
AAS copy.   26440

Watts, Isaac, 1674-1748.
Logick. . . . Sixteenth Edition.
Philadelphia, Dobson, 1789. pp. [i]-x,
[13]-348.
AAS copy.   22246

Watts, Isaac, 1674-1748.
Logic. . . . Second American Edition.
Newburyport, Barrett for Thomas &
Andrews, 1796. 285 pp.
AAS copy.   31579

Watts, Isaac, 1674-1748.
Miscellaneous Thoughts. . . . First
American Edition.
Elizabethtown, Kollock, 1796. 240, [3] pp.
AAS copy.   31580

Watts, Isaac, 1674-1748.
Orthodoxy and Charity United. . . .
Second Edition.
Boston, Rogers & Fowle, 1749. [2], xii,
[2], 280 pp.
AAS copy.   6440

[Watts, Isaac, 1674-1748.
Orthodoxy and Charity United. . . .
Second Edition.
Boston, Rogers & Fowle for Blanchard
and Amory, 1749. [2], xii, [2], 280 pp.]
(No copy with this variation of imprint
located.)   6441

Watts, Isaac, 1674-1748.
A Preservative from the Sins.
Philadelphia, Franklin, 1744. 58, [1] pp.
UOP copy.   5509

[Watts, Isaac, 1674-1748.
A Preservative.
Boston, Blanchard, 1745.]
("Just published," Boston Gazette, Aug.
20, 1745. For another ed. see 6264.)   5707

Watts, Isaac, 1674-1748.
A Preservative from the Sins. . . . Fifth
Edition.
Boston, Rogers & Fowle, 1748. 69, [3] pp.
AAS copy.   6264

[Watts, Isaac, 1674-1748.
A Preservative from the Sins and Follies.
Boston, Blanchard, 1755.]
(From an adv.)   7589

Watts, Isaac, 1674-1748.
A Preservative from the Sins and Follies.
. . . Fourth Edition.
Boston, Fowle, 1765. 46, [1] pp.
AAS copy.   10201

[Watts, Isaac, 1674-1748.
A Preservative from the Sins . . . of
Childhood.
Boston, Hall, 1789.]
(Entry from an adv.)   22247

Watts, Isaac, 1674-1748.
The Psalms of David, Imitated. . . .
Seventh Edition.
Philadelphia, Franklin and Meredith for
Godfrey, 1729. viii, 318, [26] pp., irreg.
HSP copy.   3135

Watts, Isaac, 1674-1748.
[The Psalms of David, put in Verse.
Philadelphia, Franklin, 1740.]
(Curtis 173; Hildeburn 667; no copy
known.)   40223

Watts, Isaac, 1674-1748.
The Psalms of David, Imitated. . . .
Thirteenth Edition.
Boston, Rogers & Fowle for Edwards,
1741. [2], vi, 319, [17] pp.
LOC copy.   4672

[Watts, Isaac, 1674-1748.
The Psalms of David, Imitated.
Philadelphia, Franklin, 1741.]
(Adv. Pa. Gazette, Aug. 20, 1741.)   4673

[Watts, Isaac, 1674-1748.
The Psalms of David, Imitated. . . .
Fifteenth Edition.
Boston, Edwards, 1743.]
("Just published," Boston Gazette, Jan.
18, 1743.)   5129

Watts, Isaac, 1674-1748.
The Psalms of David, Imitated. . . .
Eighteenth Edition.
Boston, Rogers & Fowle for Edwards,
1749. vii, [1], 318, [7] pp.
AAS copy.   40524

Watts, Isaac, 1674-1748.
The Psalms of David, Imitated. . . .
Sixteenth Edition.
Philadelphia, Chattin, Muir, Schippius
and Noel, [1753?]. [4], 320, [30] pp.
(The only copy located is defective.)
HSP copy.   6965

[Watts, Isaac, 1674-1748.
The Psalm of David, Imitated.
New York, Gaine, 1754.]
("Just published, and to be sold by the
Printer hereof," N.Y. Mercury, Mar. 23,
1754.)   7150

[Watts, Isaac, 1674-1748.
The Psalms of David Imitated.
New York, Gaine, 1756.]
(From an adv.)   7620

[Watts, Isaac, 1674-1748.
The Psalms of David Imitated. . . .
Seventeenth Edition.
Philadelphia, Chattin, 1757.]
(Adv. Pa. Gazette, May 26, 1757.)   7847

Watts, Isaac, 1674-1748.
The Psalms of David, Imitated. . . .
Nineteenth Edition.
New York, Noel, 1758. [8], 320, [24] pp.
(Only known copy is imperfect.)
AAS copy.   41018

Watts, Isaac, 1674-1748.
The Psalms of David Imitated.
Boston, Kneeland for Leverett, 1759. vi,
304, [25] pp.
AAS copy.   41091

Watts, Isaac, 1674-1748.
The Psalms of David Imitated.
New York, Gaine, 1760.
(A copy was offered for sale in 1932.) 8545

Watts, Isaac, 1674-1748.
The Psalms of David, Imitated.
Philadelphia, Dunlap, 1760. viii, 308, [26]
pp.
HSP copy.   8546

Watts, Isaac, 1674-1748.
The Psalms of David, Imitated.

Philadelphia, Dunlap for Noel, 1760. viii,
308, 28 pp., 12 leaves.
HSP copy.   41175

Watts, Isaac, 1674-1748.
The Psalms of David, Imitated. . . .
Twentieth Edition.
Woodbridge, 1760. vi, 282, [24] pp.
HSP copy.   8547

Watts, Isaac, 1674-1748.
The Psalms of David, Imitated. . . .
Twenty third Edition.
Boston, Kneeland, 1761. vi, 304, [25] pp.
(The AAS has an issue with the names of
Wharton and Bowes in the imprint.)
AAS copy.   8797

Watts, Isaac, 1674-1748.
The Psalms of David, Imitated. . . .
Twentythird Edition.
Boston, D. & J. Kneeland for Wharton &
Bowes, 1761.
(Except for back matter an imprint
variant of E8797, q. v. for text.)
AAS copy.   41250

[Watts, Isaac], 1674-1748.
The Psalms of David, Imitated.
New York, for Garrat & Noel, [1761?].
[2], 99 pp.
NYPL copy.   8798

Watts, Isaac, 1674-1748.
The Psalms of David, Imitated. . . .
Twentieth Edition.
Portsmouth, [N. H.], Fowle, 1762. vii,
[1], 336 pp.
AAS copy.   41324

Watts, Isaac, 1674-1748.
The Psalms of David Imitated. . . .
Twentyfourth Edition.
Boston, D. & J. Kneeland, 1763. 304 pp.
(No such imprint located. See 9346.) 41423

Watts, Isaac, 1674-1748.
The Psalms of David, Imitated. . . .
Twenty-fourth Edition.
Boston, D. & J. Kneeland for Wharton &
Bowes, 1763. [2], 304, [23] pp.
(A tp. variant of 9346, q. v.)   41424

Watts, Isaac, 1674-1748.
The Psalms of David Imitated. . . .
Twentyfourth Edition.
Boston, Kneeland for Edwards, 1763. vi,
304, [25] pp.
(No copy located with imprint given by
Evans. The AAS has a Kneeland for
Leverett issue.)
BPL copy.   9346

Watts, Isaac, 1674-1748.
The Psalms of David Imitated. . . .
Twenty-First Edition.
Boston, M'Alpine, 1766. 328, 8 pp., 16
plates.
AAS copy.   41672

Watts, Isaac, 1674-1748.
The Psalms of David, Imitated. . . .
Twenty-First Edition.
Boston, M'Alpine for Rand, 1766. 328 pp.
(Identical with 41672, q. v., except for
imprint and the fact that it was issued
without the back matter.)
AAS copy.   41673

[Watts, Isaac, 1674-1748.
The Plalms of David, Imitated. . . .
Twenty-Seventh Edition.
Philadelphia, Hall and Sellers, 1766. vi,
282, [24] pp.]
(No copy of this ed. located.)   10242

Watts, Isaac, 1674-1748.
The Psalms of David, Imitated.
[Boston], Kneeland & Adams for
Leverett, 1767. 304 pp.
(A tp. variant of 10559, q. v.)   41777

Watts, Isaac, 1674-1748.
The Psalms of David, Imitated. . . .
Twenty-Fifth Edition.
Boston, Kneeland & Adams for Wharton
& Bowes, 1767. vi, 304, [25] pp.
AAS copy.   10559

[Watts, Isaac, 1674-1748.
The Psalms of David, Imitated. . . .
Twenty Fifth Edition.
Boston, Perkins, 1767. 304, 312, 22 pp.]

(No copy located with this imprint
variant.)   10560

Watts, Isaac, 1674-1748.
The Psalms of David Imitated. . . .
Twenty-Sixth Edition.
Boston, Mein & Fleeming, 1768. xxx, 346,
[2] pp.
AAS copy.   10836

Watts, Isaac, 1674-1748.
The Psalms of David Imitated. . . .
Twenty-Sixth Edition.
Boston, Mein & Fleeming for Appleton,
1768. xxx, 346, [2] pp.
(An imprint variant of 10876, q. v. for
text.)   41895

Watts, Isaac, 1674-1748.
The Psalms of David Imitated. . . .
Twenty-Sixth Edition.
Boston, Kneeland for Bowes, 1770. xxxi,
[1], 372 pp.
(The only copy located lacks a few pages
at the end.)
AAS copy.   11571

Watts, Isaac, 1674-1748.
The Psalms of David Imitated. . . .
Twenty-Sixth Edition.
Boston, Kneeland for Leverett, 1770. xxxi,
[1], 372 pp.
BPL copy.   42184

Watts, Isaac, 1674-1748.
The Psalms of David Imitated. . . .
Twenty-Seventh Edition.
Boston, Fleets, 1771. xxiv, 298, [20] pp.
(The AAS has issues with the imprints of
McAlpine and Perkins.)
AAS copy.   11992

Watts, Isaac, 1674-1748.
The Psalms of David, Imitated. . . .
Twenty-Fifth Edition.
Boston, M'Alpine, 1771. 328 pp.
(An imprint variant of 42298, q. v. for
text.)
AAS copy.   42297

Watts, Isaac, 1674-1748.
The Psalms of David, Imitated. . . .
Twenty-Fifth Edition.
Boston, [M'Alpine for] Perkins, 1771. 328
pp.
AAS copy.   42298

Watts, Isaac, 1674-1748.
The Psalms of David, Imitated. . . .
Twenty-Seventh Edition.
Boston, Mein, 1771. xxiv, 298, [20] pp.
(An imprint variant of 11992, q. v.)   42299

[Watts, Isaac, 1674-1748.
The Psalms of David, Imitated. . . .
Twenty-Seventh Edition.
Boston, Hodgson, 1772.]
(Imprint assumed by Evans from adv. No
copy located.)   12324

Watts, Isaac, 1674-1748.
The Psalms of David; Imitated. . . .
Thirty-First Edition.
Boston, Perkins, 1772. 299 pp.
AAS copy.   12325

Watts, Isaac, 1674-1748.
The Psalms of David, Imitated.
New York, Gaine, 1772. viii, 317, [25] pp.
AAS copy.   12326

Watts, Isaac, 1674-1748.
The Psalms of David, Imitated. . . .
Thirty-Seventh Edition.
Boston, Ellison, 1773. [1], xxx, 356 pp.
(The only known copy is imperfect.)
AAS copy.   42537

Watts, Isaac, 1674-1748.
The Psalms of David Imitated.
Boston, Kneeland and Davis for Leverett,
1773. viii, 318, [22] pp.
(Evans assumed his imprint from an adv.
which was apparently for this ed., of
which no perfect copy is known. There
were several other Boston eds. in 1773
which will be reproduced in the
supplement.)
AAS copy.   12679

Watts, Isaac, 1674-1748.
The Psalms of David, Imitated. . . .
Twenty-Seventh Edition.

Boston, M'Alpine, 1773. 312 pp.
JCB copy.   42536

Watts, Isaac, 1674-1748.
The Psalms of David, Imitated. . . .
Thirty-Seventh Edition.
Boston, Mills & Hicks, 1773. 299 pp.
AAS copy.   42538

Watts, Isaac, 1674-1748.
The Psalms of David Imitated.
Norwich, 1773. 394 pp.
AAS copy.   12680

Watts, Isaac, 1674-1748.
The Psalms of David, Imitated. . . .
Thirtieth Edition.
Philadelphia, Hall & Sellers, 1773. vi,
282, [24] pp.
LCP copy.   12681

Watts, Isaac, 1674-1748.
The Psalms of David, Imitated. . . . Thirty
Seventh Edition.
Boston, Boyles, 1774. 299 pp.
AAS copy.   42747

Watts, Isaac, 1674-1748.
The Psalms of David, Imitated.
Norwich, Robertsons & Trumbull, 1774.
300, [12] pp.
LOC copy.   13152

[Watts, Isaac, 1674-1748.
The Psalms of David Imitated.
Boston, 1775.]
(Entry from an adv.)   13836

[Watts, Isaac, 1674-1748.
The Psalms of David, Imitated.
Philadelphia, Hall & Sellers, 1778.]
(Adv. Pa. Gazette, Jan. 5, 1778.)   15742

Watts, Isaac, 1674-1748.
The Psalms of David Imitated.
Hartford, 1780. 337, [10] pp.
AAS copy.   16714

[Watts, Isaac, 1674-1748.
The Psalms of David, Imitated.
Hartford, Webster, 1781. 337, [10] pp.]
(No such ed. located.)   44085

Watts, Isaac, 1674-1748.
The Psalms of David, Imitated. . . . The
Fortieth Edition.
Newburyport, 1781. 325, [11], 14, [3] pp.
AAS copy.   17098

[Watts, Isaac, 1674-1748.
The Psalms of David, Imitated. . . . The
Fortieth Edition [with the Hymns and
Spiritual Songs].
Newburyport, 1781. 325, [11], 264, xii
pp.]
(The copy described by Evans consists of
copies of 17098 and 17791 bound
together.)   17099

Watts, Isaac, 1674-1748.
The Psalms of David, Imitated.
Philadelphia, Aitken, 1781. 252 pp.
(Some copies have Laws' Select-Tunes
bound at the end; see 17098.)
AAS copy.   17097

Watts, Isaac, 1674-1748.
The Psalms of David, Imitated. . . .
Forty-First Edition.
Providence, Wheeler, 1781. 325, [11] pp.
(The "Second Title" given by Evans is
17423.)
R.I.Hist.Soc. copy.   19399

Watts, Isaac, 1674-1748.
The Psalms of David, Imitated. . . .
Thirty-Ninth Edition.
Boston, Fleets, 1782. pp. [26], [3]-300.
AAS copy.   44288

[Watts, Isaac, 1674-1748.
The Psalms of David Imitated.
Providence, 1782.]
(Probably a ghost arising from an adv. for
an earlier ed.)   17475

Watts, Isaac, 1674-1748.
The Psalms of David Imitated.
Chatham, 1783. 292 pp.
(The only copy located cannot be
reproduced.)   17844

Watts, Isaac, 1674-1748.

The Psalms of David, Imitated.
Hartford, Patten, 1784. 323, [1 +] pp.
(No located copy had a complete index.)
AAS copy.   18357

Watts, Isaac, 1674-1748.
The Psalms of David, Imitated. . . .
Forty-Fifth Edition.
Boston, Norman & Bowen, 1785. [2], 224,
179, [4], 16 pp.
AAS copy.   18930

Watts, Isaac, 1674-1748.
The Psalms of David, Imitated. . . . First
Worcester Edition.
Worcester, Thomas, 1786. 151, [1] pp.
AAS copy.   19508

Watts, Isaac, 1674-1748.
The Psalms of David, Imitated.
Worcester, Thomas, 1786. 224, [1] pp.
AAS copy.   19509

Watts, Isaac, 1674-1748.
The Psalms of David, Imitated.
Boston, Edes for Boyle, Larkin, and
White, 1787. 296, [10], 252, xi pp.
AAS copy.   20232

Watts, Isaac, 1674-1748.
The Psalms of David, Imitated.
Boston, Fleets, 1787. [24], 302, [2], viii,
256, [27] pp.
AAS copy.   20231

Watts, Isaac, 1674-1748.
The Psalms of David, Imitated.
Boston, Folsom, 1789. 317, [11], 265, xii
pp.
(The imprint given by Evans is that of the
"second part," which is really a separate
work.)
Congregational Library copy.   21687

Watts, Isaac, 1674-1748.
The Psalms of David.
Boston, Norman, [1789]. 276, [8] pp.
AAS copy.   45741

Watts, Isaac, 1674-1748.
The Psalms of David. Imitated.
Boston, Bumstead for West and E. Larkin,
1791. 320 pp.
AAS copy.   46345

Watts, Isaac, 1674-1748.
The Psalms of David. Imitated.
Boston, Folsom, 1791. 300, 276 pp.
(Imprint variant of 23193, q. v. for text.)
AAS copy.   46346

Watts, Isaac, 1674-1748.
The Psalms of David. Imitated.
Boston, Folsom for West, etc., 1791. 300,
252 pp.
AAS copy.   23193

Watts, Isaac, 1674-1748.
The Psalms of David. Imitated.
Boston, Norman, 1791. 232, [24] pp.
(Only this imperfect copy located.)
AAS copy.   46347

Watts, Issac, 1674-1748.
The Psalms of David Imitated.
Boston, Thomas & Andrews, 1791. 227,
[1] pp.
AAS copy.   23192

Watts, Isaac, 1674-1748.
The Psalms of David, Imitated.
Boston, Bumstead for Boyle and West,
1792. 582 pp.
AAS copy.   24105

Watts, Isaac, 1674-1748.
The Psalms of David, Imitated.
Newburyport, Mycall for Thomas &
Andrews and Larkin, [1792]. 288, 246,
[18] pp.
AAS copy.   24106

Watts, Isaac, 1674-1748.
The Psalms of David, Imitated.
Boston, Bumstead for White and Larkin,
1793. 574 pp.
AAS copy.   46937

Watts, Isaac, 1674-1748.
The Psalms of David. Imitated.
Carlisle, Bushnell, 1793. 272, 240 pp.
(Only the tp. can be reproduced.)
NYPL copy.   25182

Watts, Isaac, 1674-1748.
The Psalms of David, Imitated.
Exeter, Ranlet, 1793. 483, [9] pp.
AAS copy.   25181

[Watts, Isaac, 1674-1748.
The Psalms of David, Imitated.
New York, 1793?]
(Imprint assumed by Evans from
bookseller's adv.)   25183

Watts, Isaac, 1674-1748.
The Psalms of David, Imitated.
Norwich, Bushnell & Hubbard for Larkin,
[1793]. 309, [11], 246, [10] pp.
AAS copy.   25184

Watts, Isaac, 1674-1748.
The Psalms of David, Imitated.
Norwich, [Ct.], Bushnell & Hubbard for
Larkin of Boston, [1793]. 309, [12], 246,
[8] pp.
AAS copy.   46938

Watts, Isaac, 1674-1748.
The Psalms of David, Imitated.
Salem, Cushing for Carlton, 1793. 288 pp.
(Evans' entry is based on advs. His second
title is 28036.)
AAS copy.   25185

Watts, Isaac, 1674-1748.
The Psalms of David, Imitated.
Boston, Bumstead, 1794. 316 pp.
(Only this poor copy could be
reproduced.)
AAS copy.   26655

Watts, Isaac, 1674-1748.
The Psalms of David, Imitated.
Boston, Folsom, 1794. 272, 240, [1] pp.
(The only copy located is defective.)
AAS copy.   26656

Watts, Isaac, 1674-1748.
The Psalms of David, Imitated.
Exeter, Lamson for Thomas & Andrews
and West, 1794. [2], 576 pp.
AAS copy.   26657

Watts, Isaac, 1674-1748.
The Psalms of David, Imitated.
Haverhill, Ladd & Bragg for Atwood,
1794. 255, [9] pp.
(For the Hymns described by Evans as
part of this item see supplement.)
AAS copy.   26658

Watts, Isaac, 1674-1748.
The Psalms of David, Imitated.
Boston, Bumstead, 1795. 595, [1] pp.
AAS copy.   28279

[Watts, Isaac, 1674-1748.
The Psalms of David, Imitated.
Brookfield, Waldo, 1795.]
(Imprint assumed by Evans from Waldo's
advs.)   28280

Watts, Isaac, 1674-1748.
The Psalms of David, Imitated.
Salem, Cushing & Carlton, 1795. 288 pp.
(Evans' Second Title is 28036, q. v.)
AAS copy.   28281

Watts, Isaac, 1674-1748.
The Psalms of David, Imitated.
Boston, Bumstead, 1796. 595 pp.
AAS copy.   30072

Watts, Isaac, 1674-1748.
The Psalms of David, Imitated.
Boston, Bumstead, 1798. pp. [5]-595.
AAS copy.   33413

Watts, Isaac, 1674-1748.
The Psalms of David, Imitated.
Boston, Bumstead, 1799. 595 pp.
AAS copy.   35192

Watts, Isaac, 1674-1748.
The Psalms of David, Imitated.
Brookfield, Mass., E. Merriam for G.
Merriam, etc., [1800?] pp. [11], [3]-288,
[1]-245, [9].
MHS copy.   35193

Watts, Isaac, 1674-1748.
The Psalms of David, Imitated.
Brookfield, Mass., E. Merriam for G.
Merriam, etc., [1799?] pp. [11], [3]-288,
[1]-245, [9].

(Differs from 35193 only in second tp.
imprint variant; see Evans XII, 267.)
                                             35194

[Watts, Isaac, 1674-1748.
The Psalms of David, Imitated.
Hartford, 1799.]
(Imprint assumed by Evans from adv.)
                                             35195

Watts, Isaac, 1674-1748.
The Psalms of David, Imitated.
Northampton, Mass., Butler, 1799. 233 pp.
AAS copy.   35196

Watts, Isaac, 1674-1748.
Psalms, Carefully Suited to the Christian
Worship.
Philadelphia, Campbell, 1799. 292, [10]
pp.
AAS copy.   35191

[Watts, Isaac, 1674-1748.
Dr. Watts's Imitation of the Psalms of
David.
New York, Durell, 1800. 304 pp.]
(This imprint was assumed from the fact
that copies of the Psalms were bound with
copies of the Hymns with this imprint.
Those located lack tp., however.)   36951

Watts, Isaac, 1674-1748.
Dr. Watts's Imitation of the Psalms of
David.
New York, Durell for Arden, 1800. 304
pp.
AAS copy.   36950

Watts, Isaac, 1674-1748.
[The Psalms of David, Imitated.
Albany, Websters, 1800.] 323, [1] pp.
(The only copy located is imperfect.)
AAS copy.   39030

Watts, Isaac, 1674-1748.
Reliquiae Juveniles..... First American
Edition.
Portsmouth, Peirce for Blake, 1796. xii,
304 pp.
AAS copy.   31581

[Watts, Isaac, 1674-1748.
The Second Sett of Catechisms.
Boston, Blanchard, 1745.]
(The First Set, of which the AAS has a
copy, was adv. in Dec., 1745.)   5708

Watts, Isaac, 1674-1748.
The Second Sett of Catechisms. . . .
Seventh Edition.
Boston, Rogers & Fowle, 1748. 67, [1] pp.
AAS copy.   6265

Watts, Isaac, 1674-1748.
Select Songs for Children.
New York, Harrisson, 1794. 68, [3] pp.
(Only copy cannot be reproduced.) 47323

Watts, Isaac, 1674-1748.
Sermons on Various Subjects. . . . Seventh
Edition.
Boston, Rogers & Fowle and Blanchard,
1746. front., [2], xxii, [2], 740, [3] pp.
AAS copy.   5880

Watts, Isaac, 1674-1748.
A Short View of the Whole Scripture
History.
Carlisle, Pa., Kline, 1797. [2], 298 pp.
AAS copy.   33166

Watts, Isaac, 1674-1748.
A Wonderful Dream.
Sold at the Printing-Office in Hartford,
[1766]. 12 pp.
AAS copy.   41676

Watts, Isaac, 1674-1748.
A Wonderful Dream
Printed and Sold in New London, [1766].
12 pp.
(Adv. Feb. 7, 1766.)
CHS copy.   11924

Watts, Isaac, 1674-1748.
A Wonderful Dream.
Sold in the Printing-Office in
New-London, [1766?]. 12 pp.
NYPL ph. copy.   41675

Watts, Isaac, 1674-1748.
A Wonderful Dream [with cuts].

Printed and Sold in New London [1766?].
12 pp.
AAS copy.   41674

[Watts, Isaac, 1674-1748.
A Wonderful Dream.
Albany, Websters, 1789. 11, [1] pp.]
(The source of this entry is unknown.)
                                             22248

Watts, Isaac, 1674-1748.
A Wonderful Dream.
Windham, [Ct.], [1790?]. 12 pp.
CHS copy.   46095

Watts, Isaac, 1674-1748.
A Wonderful Dream.
Middletown, Bow, 1792. [16] pp.
YC copy.   46671

Watts, Isaac, 1674-1748.
A Wonderful Dream.
New Haven, Morse, 1792. 11 pp.
AAS copy.   46672

Watts, Isaac, 1674-1748.
A Wonderful Dream.
Danbury, Douglas for Crawford, 1794. 12
pp.
CHS copy.   47322

Watts, Isaac, 1674-1748.
A Wonderful Dream.
Leominster, Mass., 1800. 12 pp.
AAS copy.   39031

Watts, Isaac, 1674-1748.
The World to Come.
Boston, Rogers & Fowle, 1748. 189; 192,
[4] pp.
AAS copy.   6261

Watts, Isaac, 1674-1748.
The Young Child's Catechism.
New Haven, Greens, [1777?]. 24 pp.
AAS copy.   43406

Watts, Isaac, 1674-1748.
The Young Child's Catechism.
Hartford, Hudson & Goodwin, 1792. 14
pp.
AAS copy.   24993

[Watts, John, 1661-1702.
A Baptist Catechism.
Philadelphia, 1700.]
(For author and title see Hildeburn, I,
36.)   959

Watts, Washington.
An Inquiry into the Causes . . . of the
Yellow Fever.
Philadelphia, Ormrod, 1799. 42 pp.
LCP copy.   36678

[The Waves were Hush'd, the Sky Serene.
Song.
New York, Gilfert, 1798.]
(Title and imprint assumed by Evans from
Gilfert's adv.)   34967

The Waxen Doll, The Morning Air, The
Primroses, and The Tempest of War.
[Boston, 1720?] Broadside.
HEH copy.   39734

Way, Nicholas, c. 1750-1797.
Dissertatio Medica.
Philadelphia, Miller, 1771. [4], 19 pp.
LOC copy.   12275

Way & Groff, Philadelphia.
Proposals . . . for Printing . . . Count
Rumford's Essays.
[Philadelphia, 1797.] Broadside.
LCP copy.   48316

The Way of Truth Laid out. . . . Second
Edition [by Cotton Mather, 1663-1728].
Boston, Kneeland for Henchman, 1721.
[2], 8, 95, [4] pp.
JCB copy.   2254

[The Way to a Blessed Estate.
Cambridge, 1667.]
(Known only from S. Green's list of his
publications.)   117

The Way to be Happy in a Miserable
World. . . . Sixth Edition.
New York, Loudon, 1791. 23, [1] pp.
NYPL copy.   46348

The Way to be Happy in a Miserable
World. The Sixth Edition.
Norwich, Ct., Trumbull, 1796. 23 pp.
CHS copy.   31582

The Way to Get Married.... Composed
by Mr. Hook [by James C. Cross, d.
1810?].
New York, Gilfert, [1797]. [2] pp.
(This is apparently the item described by
Evans from an adv.)
AAS copy.   33583

... The Way to Plenty [by Hannah More,
1745-1833].
Philadelphia, Johnsons, 1800. 36 pp.
AAS copy.   37139

The Way to Wealth [by Benjamin
Franklin, 1706-1790].
Philadelphia, Franklin, 1758 (i.e., Hall &
Sellers, 1773). 16 pp.
(Only these ph. can now be located.) 42440

The Way Worn Traveller.... Composed
by Dr. Arnold [by George Colman,
1762-1836].
Philadelphia, Carr, 1794. 3 pp.
AAS copy.   26783

Wayne, Caleb Parry, 1776-1849.
Boston, April 2, 1798. Proposals ... for
Publishing ... the History of Sir Charles
Grandison.
[Boston, 1798.] Broadside.
MHS copy.   34466

Ways and Means [by Francis Rawle,
1662-1727].
Philadelphia, Keimer, 1725. 65, [7] pp.
Composite copy.   2697

The Ways of Pleasure [by Joseph
Seccombe, 1706-1760].
Boston, Mecom, [1762]. [2], 14 pp.
AAS copy.   9268

[We His Majesty's most Dutiful and
Loyal Subjects, the late
Representatives.... 27th of May, 1774.
[Williamsburg, 1774.] Broadside.]
(A variant entry for 13747.)   13748

We Observe in One of the South-Carolina
Newspapers an Advertisement, Dated the
19th of June, 1770....
[Savannah, 1770.] Broadside.
PRO copy.   42185

[We, the Shopkeepers of Philadelphia....
(German ed.)
Philadelphia, Miller, 1770.] Broadside.]
(Described by Hildeburn as the copy in
the S. W. Pennypacker coll.)   11926

We, the Shopkeepers of Philadelphia....
April 9th, 1770.
Philadelphia, Miller, [1770]. Broadside.
LOC copy.   11925

We the Subscribers do hereby Severally
Enlist into the Service of the
United Colonies.... Dated this day
of   A.D. 1776.
[Watertown, 1776.] Broadside.
MA copy.   14882

We the Subscribers, Inhabitants of the
Town of.... June, 1774.
[Boston, 1774.] Broadside.
(For another printing see 13427.)
AAS copy.   13163

We the Subscribers, Inhabitants of the
Town of.... June, 1774.
[Boston, 1774.] Broadside.
(For another printing see 13163.)
AAS copy.   13427

We the Subscribers, Inhabitants of the
Town of [blank] Having Taken into
serious Consideration ... the Liberties of
North-America....
[Portsmouth? 1774.] 1 leaf.
NHHS copy.   42748

We the Subscribers, Owners, and
Possessors of Wharf in this City ... [Feb.
7, 1762].
[Philadelphia? 1762.] Broadside.
HSP copy.   41326

[We, the Underwritten, Having

Associated for the Purpose of Handing
down to Posterity those Pure and Sacred
Principles of Liberty. . . .
[Richmond, 1784.] Broadside.]
(No copy located.)   18864

We whose Names are Under Written, do
hereby Severally Inlist Ourselves into the
Service of the United American
Colonies. . . . July, 1776.
[Watertown, 1776.] Broadside.
EI copy.   14883

A Weaned Christian [by Cotton Mather,
1663-1728].
Boston, 1704. 42, [1] pp.
AAS copy.   1180

The Weakness of Brutus Exposed [by
Pelatiah Webster, 1726-1795].
Philadelphia, Sparhawk, 1787. 23 pp.
AAS copy.   20872

Weatherwise, Abraham, pseud.
An Almanack, for . . . 1788.
Boston, Folsom. [24] pp.
AAS copy.   45199

Weatherwise, Abraham, pseud.
An Almanack, for . . . 1788.
Portsmouth, Melcher. [24] pp.
AAS copy.   20859

Weatherwise, Abraham, pseud.
An Almanack ... for ... 1801.
Portsmouth, [N. H.], Treadwell, [24] pp.
NHHS copy.   39032

Weatherwise, A., pseud.
An Astronomical Diary: or Almanack, for
... 1796.
Boston, for Larkin, etc. Bumstead's
Edition. [24] pp.
AAS copy.   29846

Weatherwise, Abraham, pseud.
The Astronomical Repository ... for ...
1800.
Boston, Edes. [24] pp.
AAS copy.   36679

Weatherwise, Abraham, pseud.
The Book of Knowledge.
New York, 1793. 34, [1] pp.
(Only this imperfect copy exists.)
AAS copy.   46939

Weatherwise, Abraham, pseud.
Father Abraham's Almanack ... for ...
1759.
New York, Gaine. [40] pp., front.,
portrait, plan.
AAS copy.   8282

[Weatherwise, Abraham, pseud.
Father Abraham's Almanack ... for ...
1759.
Philadelphia, Dunlap, for Noel. [40] pp.,
plan.]
(No copy with this variety of imprint has
been found.)   8281

Weatherwise, Abraham, pseud.
Father Abraham's Almanack ... for ...
1759.
Philadelphia, Dunlap. [40] pp., front.,
fold. port., plan.
(Three line imprint. No perfect copy
known.)
AAS copy.   41019

Weatherwise, Abraham, pseud.
Father Abraham's Almanack ... for ...
1759.
Philadelphia, Dunlap. [40] pp., front.,
portrait, plan.
(Four line imprint.)
AAS copy.   8280

Weatherwise, Abraham, pseud.
Father Abraham's Almanac ... for ...
1760.
Philadelphia, Dunlap. [48] pp.
AAS copy.   8516

Weatherwise, Abraham, pseud.
Father Abraham's Almanac ... for ...
1762.
Philadelphia, Dunlap. front., [38] pp.
AAS copy.   9037

Weatherwise, Abraham, pseud.

Father Abraham's Almanac ... for ...
1763.
Philadelphia, Dunlap. [40] pp.
LOC copy.   9301

Weatherwise, Abraham, pseud.
Father Abraham's Almanack ... for ...
1764.
Philadelphia, Dunlap. [40] pp.
LOC copy.   9533

Weatherwise, Abraham, pseud.
Father Abraham's Almanack. . . . For . . .
1765.
Philadelphia, Dunlap. front., [34] pp.
AAS copy.   9864

Weatherwise, Abraham, pseud.
Father Abraham's Almanack ... for ...
1766.
Philadelphia, Dunlap. [39] pp.
AAS copy.   10203

Weatherwise, Abraham, pseud.
Father Abraham's Almanack ... for ...
1767.
Philadelphia, Dunlap. front., [36] pp.
AAS copy.   10520

Weatherwise, Abraham, pseud.
Father Abraham's Almanack ... for 1768.
Philadelphia, Dunlap. [40] pp.
(The only copy located is imperfect.)
AAS copy.   10799

Weatherwise, Abraham, pseud.
Father Abraham's Almanack, for ...
1769.
Philadelphia, Dunlap. [36] pp.
AAS copy.   11110

Weatherwise, Abraham, pseud.
Father Abraham's Almanack, for ...
1770.
Philadelphia, Dunlap. [32] pp.
AAS copy.   11521

Weatherwise, Abraham, pseud.
Father Abraham's Almanack, for ...
1771.
Philadelphia, Dunlap. [36] pp.
AAS copy.   11927

Weatherwise, Abraham, pseud.
Father Abraham's Almanack, for ...
1772.
Philadelphia, Dunlap. [36] pp.
AAS copy.   12276

Weatherwise, Abraham, pseud.
Father Abraham's Almanack, for ...
1773.
Philadelphia, Dunlap. 36 pp.
AAS copy.   12607

Weatherwise, Abraham, pseud.
Father Abraham's Almanack, for ...
1774.
Philadelphia, Dunlap. 36 pp.
AAS copy.   13069

Weatherwise, Abraham, pseud.
Father Abraham's Almanack, for ...
1775.
Philadelphia, Dunlap. 36 pp.
AAS copy.   13575

Weatherwise, Abraham, pseud.
The Federal Almanack, for ... 1791.
Boston, White & Cambridge. [24] pp.
AAS copy.   23043

Weatherwise, Abraham, pseud.
Father Abraham's Almanack ... Fitted
for the Latitude of Nevis. For the Year
... 1759.
Philadelphia, Dunlap. [40] pp., fold.
port., plan.
HEH copy.   40958

Weatherwise, Abraham, pseud.
Father Abraham's Almanack, for ...
1777. ... [by David Rittenhouse,
1732-1796].
Philadelphia, Dunlap. 36 pp.
AAS copy.   15062

Weatherwise, Abraham, pseud.
Father Abraham's Almanack, for ...
1778. ... [by David Rittenhouse,
1732-1796].

Lancaster, Dunlap. 36 pp.
(No complete copy located.)
AAS copy.   15576

Weatherwise, Abraham, pseud.
Father Abraham's Almanack, for . . . 1779
[by David Rittenhouse, 1732-1796].
Philadelphia, Dunlap. [30] pp.
AAS copy.   16050

Weatherwise, Abraham, pseud.
Father Abraham's Almanack, for . . .
1780. . . . [by David Rittenhouse,
1732-1796].
Philadelphia, Dunlap. [32] pp.
HSP copy.   16501

Weatherwise, Abraham, pseud.
Father Abraham's Almanack, for . . .
1781. . . . [by David Rittenhouse,
1732-1796].
Philadelphia, Dunlap. [32] pp.
AAS copy.   16976

Weatherwise, Abraham, pseud.
Father Abraham's Almanack, for . . .
1782 . . . [by David Rittenhouse,
1732-1796].
Philadelphia, Kline. [32] pp.
AAS copy.   17350

Weatherwise, Abraham, pseud.
Father Abraham's Almanack, for . . .
1783. . . .
Philadelphia, Dunlap. [32] pp.
LOC copy.   17702

Weatherwise, Abraham, pseud.
Father Abraham's Almanack, for . . . 1784
[by David Rittenhouse, 1732-1796].
Philadelphia, Dunlap. [40] pp.
AAS copy.   18160

Weatherwise, Abraham, pseud.
Father Abraham's New-England
Almanack, for . . . 1782. . . . [by David
Rittenhouse, 1732-1796].
Hartford, Webster. [24] pp.
CHS copy.   17352

[Weatherwise, Abraham, pseud.
Father Abraham's Speech.
New Haven, 1770? 16 pp.]
(This is the same as 10619, q.v.)   11929

Weatherwise, Abraham, pseud.
The Massachusetts Almanack, for . . .
1791.
Boston, Mills & Doyle for Hovey.
Broadside.
NYHS copy.   23044

Weatherwise, Abraham, pseud.
The Massachusetts and New Hampshire
Almanack, for . . . 1792.
Boston, White & Cambridge. [24] pp.
AAS copy.   23962

Weatherwise, Abraham, pseud.
The Massachusetts and New-Hampshire
Almanack, for . . . 1793.
Boston, White & Cambridge. [24] pp.
AAS copy.   24994

Weatherwise, Abraham, pseud.
The Massachusetts, New-Hampshire,
Rhode-Island, Connecticut, and Vermont
Almanack, for . . . 1794.
Boston, [Coverly]. [24] pp.
AAS copy.   26441

Weatherwise, Abraham, pseud.
Mr. Weatherwise's Pocket-Almanac . . .
for 1760.
Philadelphia, Dunlap. [30] pp., 2 folding
plates.
AAS copy.   8517

Weatherwise, Abraham, pseud.
Mr. Weatherwise's Pocket-Almanac . . .
for 1761.
Philadelphia, Dunlap. [24] pp.
LOC copy.   8766

Weatherwise, A., pseud.
Mr. Weatherwise's Pocket-Almanac, [on
an Entire New Plan.] For 1761.
Philadelphia, Dunlap. [24] pp.
AAS copy.   41176

Weatherwise, Abraham, pseud.
Mr. Weatherwise's Pocket-Almanac. . . .
For 1762.

Philadelphia, Dunlap. [24] pp.
HSP copy.   9038

Weatherwise, A., pseud.
Mr. Weatherwise's Pocket-Almanac . . .
for 1763.
Philadelphia, Dunlap. [24] pp.
AAS copy.   41325

Weatherwise, Abraham, pseud.
The New-England Callendar: or
Almanack, for . . . 1793.
Boston, Coverly. [24] pp.
AAS copy.   24995

Weatherwise, Abraham, pseud.
The New-England Town and Country
Almanack . . . for . . . 1769.
Providence, Goddard & Carter. [32] pp.
(The entry given by Evans is an error.)
AAS copy.   11113

Weatherwise, Abraham, pseud.
The New-Hampshire Calendar: or an
Almanack, for . . . 1795.
Newburyport, Blunt & March. [24] pp.
AAS copy.   28038

Weatherwise, Abraham, pseud.
The New-York Almanack, for . . . 1796.
Albany, Websters. [36] pp.
(Too fragile to copy.)   47674

Weatherwise, Abraham, pseud.
The New-York Almanack, for . . . 1796.
Whitestown, Easton. [24] pp.
AAS copy.   47675

Weatherwise, Abraham, pseud.
The Town and Country Almanack, for
. . . 1787.
Boston, Folsom. [24] pp.
AAS copy.   45017

Weatherwise, Abraham, pseud.
The Town and Country Almanack, for . . .
1790.
Boston, White & Cambridge, [24] pp.
AAS copy.   22249

Weatherwise, Abraham, pseud.
The Town and Country Almanack, for . . .
1798.
Boston, White. [24] pp.
(The only copy located is imperfect.)
AAS copy.   33168

Weatherwise, Abraham, pseud.
The Town and Country Almanack, for . . .
1801.
Boston, Larkins, etc. [24] pp.
AAS copy.   39033

Weatherwise, Abraham, pseud.
Weatherwise's Town and Country
Almanack, for . . . 1781. . . . [by David
Rittenhouse, 1732-1796].
Boston, M'Dougall. Front., [36] pp.
AAS copy.   16979

Weatherwise, Abraham, pseud.
The Second Edition. Weatherwise's Town
and Country Almanack for . . . 1781. . . .
[by David Rittenhouse, 1732-1796].
Boston, M'Dougall. Front., [36] pp.
(Except for the title page, this edition is
the same as 16979.)
AAS copy.   16980

Weatherwise, Abraham, pseud.
Weatherwise's Town and Country
Almanack, for . . . 1782 [by David
Rittenhouse, 1732-1796].
Boston, Coverly & Hodge. Front., [36]
pp.
AAS copy.   17354

Weatherwise, Abraham, pseud.
Weatherwises's Town and Country
Almanack, for . . . 1783. . . .
Boston, Hodge. [24] pp., 1 plate.
AAS copy.   17705

Weatherwise, Abraham, pseud.
Weatherwise's Town and Country
Almanack, for . . . 1782. . . . [by David
Rittenhouse, 1732-1796].
Boston, Coverly & Hodge. Front., [36]
pp.
AAS copy.   17354

Weatherwise, Abraham, pseud.
Weatherwise's Town and Country

Almanack, for . . . 1784 [by David
Rittenhouse, 1732-1796].
Boston, Coverly. [24] pp.
AAS copy.   18163

Weatherwise, Abraham, pseud.
Weatherwise's Town and Country
Almanack, for . . . 1784 [by David
Rittenhouse, 1732-1796].
Boston, Norman & White. [24] pp.
AAS copy.   18164

Weatherwise, Abraham, pseud.
Weatherwise's Town and Country
Almanack, for . . . 1785 [by David
Rittenhouse, 1732-1796].
Boston, Weeden & Barrett. [24] pp.
AAS copy.   18764

Weatherwise, Abraham, pseud.
Weatherwise's Town and Country
Almanack, for . . . 1786 [by David
Rittenhouse, 1732-1796].
Boston, Griffith. [24] pp.
AAS copy.   19225

Weatherwise, Abraham, pseud.
Weatherwise's Town and Country
Almanack, for . . . 1786 [by David
Rittenhouse, 1732-1796].
Boston, Norman. [24] pp.
AAS copy.   19224

Weatherwise, Abraham, pseud.
Weatherwise's Town and Country
Almanack, for . . . 1787.
Boston, Griffith. [24] pp.
AAS copy.   20126

Weatherwise, Abraham, pseud.
Weatherwise's Town and Country
Almanack, for . . . 1787.
Boston, Norman. [24] pp.
AAS copy.   20125

Weatherwise, Abraham, pseud.
Weatherwise's Town and Country
Almanack, for . . . 1790.
Boston, Folsom. [24] pp.
MHS copy.   22250

Weatherwise, Anthony, pseud.
The Farmer's Calendar; or, Fry and
Southwick's Almanack, for . . . 1798.
Albany, N. Y., Fry & Southwick. [34] pp.
(The two known copies have identical
mutilations.)
Newport Hist. Soc.   33172

Weatherwise, J. pseud.
The Farmer's Almanack, for . . . 1799.
Norwich, Ct., J. Trumbull and S.
Trumbull. [24] pp.
AAS copy.   34968

Weatherwise, J., pseud.
The Farmer's Almanack, for . . . 1800.
Norwich, Ct., Trumbull. [24] pp.
AAS copy.   36680

Weatherwise's Almanack, for . . . 1787.
Portland, Wait. [24] pp.
AAS copy.   20124

Weatherwise's Almanack, for . . . 1789.
Boston, Freeman. [24] pp.
AAS copy.   21579

Weatherwise's Almanack for . . . 1790.
Portsmouth, Osborne. [24] pp.
AAS copy.   22251

Weatherwise's Almanack, for . . . 1792.
Printed for, and Sold by Most of the
Shopkeepers. [24] pp.
(Not located, 1968.)   46349

Weatherwise's Almanack, for the Year
. . . 1794.
[Portsmouth, Melcher.] [24] pp.
LOC copy.   26442

Weatherwise's Almanack for . . . 1795.
Boston, for the Booksellers. [24] pp.
AAS copy.   28037

Weatherwise's Almanack, for . . . 1797.
Boston, Boyle, etc. [24] pp.
AAS copy.   31583

Weatherwise's Almanack, for . . . 1798.
Boston, B. Larkin, etc. [24] pp.
MHS copy.   33169

Weatherwise's Almanack, for . . . 1798.
Exeter, N. H. [24] pp.
LOC copy.   33170

Weatherwise's Almanac, for . . . 1800.
[Portsmouth, N. H.], Peirce for the
Booksellers in Boston, Salem,
Newburyport, Portsmouth. [4], 12, [8]
pp.
AAS copy.   36681

Weatherwise's Almanac, for the Year of
Christian Aera, 1801.
Printed for . . . the Booksellers in
Boston. . . . [Portsmouth, N. H., Peirce.]
[24] pp.
AAS copy.   39034

Weatherwise's Boston Almanack, for . . .
1786.
Plymouth, Coverly. [24] pp.
(No copy located.)
LOC copy.   44830

Weatherwise's Federal Almanack, for . . .
1788.
Boston, Norman. [24] pp.
AAS copy.   20860

Weatherwise's Federal Almanack, for . . .
1789.
Boston, Norman. [24] pp.
AAS copy.   21580

Weatherwise's Federal Almanack for . . .
1790.
Boston, Norman. Broadside.
AAS copy.   22252

Weatherwise's Genuine Almanack, for . . .
1790.
Exeter, Ranlet. [24] pp.
AAS copy.   22253

Weatherwise's Genuine Almanack, for . . .
1793.
[Portsmouth], for the shopkeepers. [24]
pp.
LOC copy.   46673

Weatherwise's Genuine Almanack, for . . .
1798.
Boston, Russell. [24] pp.
AAS copy.   33171

Weatherwise's Genuine Massachusetts,
New-Hampshire, Vermont, Rhode-Island,
and Connecticut Almanack, for . . . 1792.
Boston, Coverly. [24] pp.
AAS copy.   23963

Weatherwise's Genuine Massachusetts,
Rhodeisland and Connecticut Almanack,
for . . . 1791.
Boston, Coverly. [24] pp.
AAS copy.   23045

Weatherwise's Genuine Massachusetts,
Rhodeisland and Connecticut Almanack,
for . . . 1791.
Boston, Printed for the Booksellers. [24]
pp.
AAS copy.   23046

Weatherwise's Massachusetts,
Connecticut, Rhodeisland,
Newhampshire and Vermont Almanack,
for . . . 1799.
Medford, Mass., Coverly. [24] pp.
AAS copy.   34969

Weatherwise's Massachusetts,
Connecticut, Rhodeisland, Newhampshire
and Vermont Almanack, for . . . 1799.
Salem, Coverly. [24] pp.
(But for cover identical with 34969, q. v.)
AAS copy.   34970

Weatherwise's Newhampshire,
Massachusetts and Vermont Almanack,
for . . . 1791.
Exeter, Ranlet. [24] pp.
AAS copy.   23047

Weatherwise's Plymouth Almanack, for
. . . 1786.
Plymouth, Coverly. [24] pp.
AAS copy.   44831

[Weatherwise's sheet almanac for 1791.]
(Adv. Strafford Recorder, Oct. 28, 1790.)
                                             46096

Weatherwise's Town and Country
Almanack, for . . . 1782. . . . By Abraham
Weatherwise [by David Rittenhouse,
1732-1796].
Boston, Coverly & Hodge. Front., [36]
pp.
AAS copy.   17354

Weatherwise's Town and Country
Almanack, for . . . 1786.
Boston, Freeman. [24] pp.
(Only copy located is defective.)
AAS copy.   44832

[Weatherwise's Town and Country
Almanack for . . . 1789.
Boston, White & Cambridge?]
(Assumed from the sequence.)   21581

Weatherwise's Town and Country
Almanack, for . . . 1791.
Boston, Printed for the Booksellers. [24]
pp.
AAS copy.   23048

Weatherwise's Town and Country
Almanack, for . . . 1791.
Boston, Folsom. [24] pp.
AAS copy.   23049

Weatherwise's Town and Country
Almanack, for . . . 1792.
Boston, Folsom. [24] pp.
AAS copy.   23964

Webb, Benjamin, 1695-1746.
(Sibley, VI, 112.)
The Present Scope.
Boston, 1733. [4], 25 pp.
LOC copy.   3729

Webb, Conrade, 1778-1842.
Union Considered as the only Safety.
Providence, Wheeler, 1798. 19 pp.
AAS copy.   34971

Webb, Elizabeth.
Einige Glaubens-Bekentnisse.
Philadelphia, Cist, 1783. 55 pp.
AAS copy.   18296

Webb, Elizabeth.
Einige Glaubens-Bekentnisse.
Philadelphia, Cist, 1798. 48 pp.
AAS copy.   34972

Webb, Elizabeth.
A Letter from . . . to Anthony William
Boehm.
Philadelphia, Crukshank, 1781. 44 pp.
AAS copy.   17424

Webb, Elizabeth.
A Letter from . . . to Anthony William
Boehm.
Philadelphia, Crukshank, 1783. 44 pp.
AAS copy.   18295

Webb, Elizabeth.
A Letter from . . . to Anthony William
Boehm. . . , Third Edition
Philadelphia, Tuckniss, 1798. 44 pp.
LOC copy.   34973

Webb, George, b. 1708?
Batchelors-Hall.
Philadelphia, 1731. 12 pp.
APS copy.   3485

Webb, George, of New-Kent, Va.
The Office and Authority of a Justice of
Peace.
Williamsburg, 1736. x, 364, [4] pp.
AAS copy.   4101

Webb, John, 1687-1750.
(Sibley, V, 463-471.)
The Believer's Redemption.
Newport, 1728. [4], 55 pp.
BPL copy.   3115

Webb, John, 1687-1750.
(Sibley, V, 463-471.)
A Brief Discourse at the Ordination of a
Deacon.
Boston, Green for Henchman and
Phillips, 1731. [2], 20 pp.
AAS copy.   3486

Webb, John, 1687-1750.
(Sibley, V, 463-471.)
Christ's Suit to the Sinner.

Boston, Kneeland & Green, 1741. [4], 43
pp.
AAS copy.   4834

Webb, John, 1687-1750.
(Sibley, V, 463-471.)
The Duty of a Degenerate People.
Boston, Kneeland and Green, 1734. [4],
41 pp.
AAS copy.   3850

Webb, John, 1687-1750.
The Duty of Ministers.
Boston, Gerrish, Kneeland, Belknap, and
Love, 1727. [4], 22 pp. 8 vo.
AAS copy.   2971

[Webb, John, 1687-1750.
The Duty of Ministers.
Boston, 1727. 12 mo.]
(A ghost of 2971 arising from the Haven
entry.)   2972

Webb, John, 1687-1750.
(Sibley, V, 463-471.)
The Duty of Survivers.
Boston, Draper for Henchman and Eliot,
1739. [4], 36 pp.
AAS copy.   4444

Webb, John, 1687-1750.
(Sibley, V, 463-471.)
The Government of Christ.
Boston, Draper, 1738. [4], 39 pp.
AAS copy.   4321

Webb, John, 1687-1750.
The Great Concern of New-England.
Boston, Fleet, 1730 (1731). [4], 36 pp.
AAS copy.   3487

Webb, John, 1687-1750.
The Greatness of Sin Improv'd.
Boston, Kneeland & Green, 1734. [4], 29,
[9] pp.
AAS copy.   3851

Webb, John, 1687-1750.
(Sibley, V, 463-471.)
Practical Discourses.
Boston, Draper for Henchman, 1726. [2],
v, [1], 350 pp.
AAS copy.   2823

Webb, John, 1687-1750.
A Seasonable Warning.
Boston, 1726. [4], 29, [1] pp.
BA copy.   2824

Webb, John, 1687-1750.
A Seasonable Warning. . . . Second
Edition.
Boston, Gerrish, 1726. [2], 31, [1] pp.
MHS copy.   2825

Webb, John, 1687-1750.
(Sibley, V, 463-471.)
A Sermon, Preached at the Thursday
Lecture.
Boston, Green, 1722. [4], 27 pp.
AAS copy.   2404

Webb, John, 1687-1750.
(Sibley, V, 463-471.)
Some Plain and Necessary Directions.
Boston, Gray, 1729. [2], iv, 170 pp.
AAS copy.   3231

Webb, John, 1687-1750.
Some Plain and Necessary Directions. . . .
Second Edition.
Boston, Rogers & Fowle for Eliot, 1741.
[8], 166, [2] pp.
AAS copy.   4835

Webb, John, 1687-1750
Vows Made unto God.
Boston, 1728. [4], 41 pp.
BPL copy.   3116

Webb, John, 1687-1750.
The Young-Mans Duty Explained.
Boston, Kneeland for Henchman, 1718.
[4], ii, 34 pp.
HC copy.   2007

Webb, John, 1687-1750.
The Young-man's Duty, Explained.
Boston, Kneeland, 1725. [2], ii, 33 pp.
LOC copy.   2716

Webb, Thomas, c.1724-1796.
(D. A. B.)
A Military Treatise.
Philadelphia, Dunlap, 1759. [2], xiii, [1],
111 pp., 2 folded plates.
BA copy.					8518

[Webb, Thomas Smith], 1771-1819.
The Freemason's Monitor.
Albany, N. Y., Spencer & Webb, 1797.
[12], 284 pp.
AAS copy.				33173

Webb, William, fl. 1798.
An Inaugural Dissertation on the Colic.
Philadelphia, Ormrod, 1798. 27 pp.
AAS copy.				34974

[Webbe, John]
(F. L. Mott, Hist. Am. Magazines, I,
passim.)
A Discourse Concerning Paper Money.
Philadelphia, Bradford, [1743]. 11 pp.
HSP copy.				5308

Webbe, Samuel, 1740-1816.
The Mansion of Peace.
New York, Hewitt, [1797?] [2] pp.
NYPL copy.				48317

Webbe, Samuel, 1740-1816.
The Mansion of Peace.
Philadelphia, Willig, [1797?] [2] pp.
NYPL copy.				48318

Webster, Alexander, 1707-1784.
(D. N. B.)
Divine Influence.
Boston, Kneeland & Green, 1743. [2], 41
pp.
AAS copy.				5309

[Webster, Charles Richard], 1762-1834.
The Clerk's Magazine.
Albany, N. Y., Websters, [1800?]. [4],
310, [6] pp.
AAS copy.				37192

Webster, Charles R. & George, firm.
Printing-Office, State Street, Albany, July
20, 1791. Proposals . . . Thomas Paine.
[Albany, N.Y., 1791.] Broadside.
CHS copy.				46350

Webster, Daniel, 1782-1852.
An Oration Pronounced at Hanover.
Hanover, [N. H.], Davis, 1800. 15 pp.
AAS copy.				39035

Webster, Jacob.
Jacob Webster, of Windsor, in
Connecticut, being Taken Blind, did
thereupon Compose the following Verses.
A. D. 1756.
n.p., n.d. Broadside.
AAS copy.				40867

[Webster, Noah, 1758-1843.
An American Selection of Lessons in
Reading and Speaking.
Hartford, Hudson & Goodwin, 1785.]
(A ghost arising from a typographical
error.)					19365

Webster, Noah, 1758-1843.
An American Selection of Lessons in
Reading and Speaking. . . . Third Edition.
Philadelphia, Young & M'Culloch, 1787.
372 pp.
(Issued with and without a portrait of
Washington.)
AAS copy.				20862

Webster, Noah, 1758-1843.
An American Selection of Lessons in
Reading and Speaking. . . . Fourth
Edition.
Hartford, Hudson & Goodwin, 1788. 204
pp.
(The only copy available is imperfect.)
AAS copy.				21582

Webster, Noah, 1758-1843.
An American Selection of Lessons in
Reading and Speaking. . . . Fifth Edition.
Hartford, Hudson & Goodwin, 1789. 202
pp.
LOC copy.				22255

Webster, Noah, 1758-1843.
An American Selection of Lessons in
Reading and Speaking. . . . Sixth Edition.

Newport, Edes, 1789. 204, 6, 12 pp.
AAS copy.				22256

Webster, Noah, 1758-1843.
An American Selection of Lessons in
Reading and Speaking. . . . Thomas and
Andrews's First Edition.
Boston, Thomas and Andrews, 1790. 239,
[1] pp.
AAS copy.				23050

Webster, Noah, 1758-1843.
An American Selection of Lessons in
Reading and Speaking. . . . Sixth Edition.
Hartford, Hudson & Goodwin, 1790. 202
pp.
CHS copy.				46097

Webster, Noah, 1758-1843.
An American Selection of Lessons in
Reading and Speaking. . . . Thomas and
Andrews's Second Edition.
Boston, Thomas & Andrews, 1792. 239,
[1] pp.
AAS copy.				24997

Webster, Noah, 1758-1843.
An American Selection of Lessons in
Reading and Speaking. . . . Seventh
Connecticut Edition.
Hartford, Hudson & Goodwin, 1792. 252
pp.
(This edition was issued without the
frontispiece portrait.)
AAS copy.				24998

Webster, Noah, 1758-1843.
An American Selection of Lessons in
Reading and Speaking. . . . Eighth
Connecticut Edition.
Hartford, Hudson & Goodwin, 1793. 252
pp.
AAS copy.				26445

Webster, Noah, 1758-1843.
An American Selection of Lessons in
Reading and Speaking. . . . Thomas and
Andrews's Third Edition.
Boston, Thomas & Andrews, 1793. 239,
[1] pp.
AAS copy.				26443

Webster, Noah, 1758-1843.
An American Selection of Lessons in
Reading and Speaking. . . . Thomas and
Andrews' Fourth Edition.
Boston, Thomas & Andrews, 1793. 239,
[1] pp.
AAS copy.				26444

Webster, Noah, 1758-1843.
An American Selection of Lessons in
Reading and Speaking. . . . First Edition
by Geo. Bunce & Co.
New York, Bunce, 1794. 239 pp.
(Issued also with adv. matter bound in.)
AAS copy.				28040

Webster, Noah, 1758-1843.
An American Selection of Lessons in
Reading and Speaking. . . . Thomas and
Andrew's Fifth Edition.
Boston, Thomas & Andrews, 1794. 239,
[1] pp.
AAS copy.				28041

Webster, Noah, 1758-1843.
An American Selection of Lessons in
Reading and Speaking. . . . Ninth
Connecticut Edition.
Hartford, Hudson & Goodwin, 1794. 252
pp.
AAS copy.				28039

Webster, Noah, 1758-1843.
An American Selection of Lessons, in
Reading and Speaking. . . . First Albany
Edition.
Albany, Websters, [1795]. 239, [1] pp.
HC copy.				29847

Webster, Noah, 1758-1843.
An American Selection of Lessons in
Reading and Speaking. . . . Second
Edition by Geo. Bunce & Co.
New York, Bunce, 1795. 239 pp., irreg.
CHS copy.				29849

Webster, Noah, 1758-1843.
An American Selection of Lessons in
Reading and Speaking. . . . The Tenth
Edition.

Hartford, Hudson & Goodwin, [1796?].
261, [2] pp.
AAS copy.				29848

Webster, Noah, 1758-1843.
An American Selection of Lessons, in
Reading and Speaking. . . . Second Albany
Edition.
Albany, Websters, 1796. 239, [1] pp.
NYSL copy.				31584

Webster, Noah, 1758-1843.
An American Selection of Lessons in
Reading and Speaking. . . . Thomas and
Andrews' Sixth Edition.
Boston, Thomas & Andrews, 1796. 239,
[1] pp.
AAS copy.				31585

Webster, Noah, 1758-1843.
An American Selection of Lessons in
Reading and Speaking. . . . Thomas and
Andrews' Seventh Edition.
Boston, Thomas & Andrews, 1796. 240 pp.
AAS copy.				31586

Webster, Noah, 1758-1843.
An American Selection of Lessons in
Reading and Speaking. . . . Thomas and
Andrews' Eighth Edition.
Boston, Thomas & Andrews, 1796. 240 pp.
AAS copy.				31587

Webster, Noah, 1758-1843.
An American Selection of Lessons in
Reading and Speaking. . . . Thomas and
Andrews' Ninth Edition.
Boston, Thomas & Andrews, 1796. 240 pp.
AAS copy.				31588

Webster, Noah, 1758-1843.
An American Selection of Lessons in
Reading and Speaking. . . . The Eleventh
Edition.
Hartford, Hudson & Goodwin, [1796].
261, [2] pp.
NYPL copy.				31589

Webster, Noah, 1758-1843.
An American Selection of Lessons, in
Reading and Speaking. . . . Third Albany
Edition.
Albany, Websters, 1797. 236, [4] pp.
AAS copy.				33174

Webster, Noah, 1758-1843.
An American Selection of Lessons in
Reading and Speaking. . . . Thomas and
Andrews' Ninth Edition.
Boston, Thomas & Andrews, 1797. 240 pp.
AAS copy.				33175

Webster, Noah, 1758-1843.
An American Selection of Lessons in
Reading and Speaking. . . . Thomas and
Andrews' Tenth Edition.
Boston, Thomas & Andrews . . . Sold . . .
by said Thomas, etc., 1797.
(Text identical with 33175, q. v.)
AAS copy.				33176

Webster, Noah, 1758-1843.
An American Selection of Lessons in
Reading and Speaking. . . . Thomas and
Andrews' Tenth Edition.
Boston, Thomas & Andrews . . . sold . . .
by Thomas Son & Thomas, 1797. 240 pp.
(Text identical with 33175, q. v.)
AAS copy.				33177

Webster, Noah, 1758-1843.
An American Selection of Lessons in
Reading and Speaking. . . . Thomas &
Andrews, Eleventh Edition.
Boston, Thomas & Andrews, etc., 1797.
240 pp.
(Text identical with 33175, q. v.)
AAS copy.				33178

Webster, Noah, 1758-1843.
An American Selection of Lessons in
Reading and Speaking. . . . Twelfth
Edition.
Hartford, Hudson & Goodwin, [1797].
261, [2] pp.
AAS copy.				33179

Webster, Noah, 1758-1843.
An American Selection of Lessons in
Reading and Speaking. . . . Thirteenth
Edition.

Hartford, Hudson & Goodwin, [1798?].
240 pp.
AAS copy.   34975

Webster, Noah, 1758-1843.
An American Selection of Lessons in
Reading and Speaking. . . . Thomas and
Andrews' Eleventh Edition.
Boston, Thomas & Andrews, 1799. 240 pp.
AAS copy.   36682

Webster, Noah, 1758-1843.
An American Selection of Lessons in
Reading and Speaking. . . . Fourteenth
Edition.
Hartford, Ct., Hudson & Goodwin,
[1799?]. 240 pp.
AAS copy.   36683

Webster, Noah, 1758-1843.
An American Selection of Lessons in
Reading and Speaking. . . . Twelvth
Edition.
New York, Duyckinck, etc., 1799. 261, [2]
pp.
NYSL copy.   48989

Webster, Noah, 1758-1843.
An American Selection of Lessons in
Reading and Speaking. . . . Third Albany
Edition.
Albany [N. Y.], Websters, 1800. 236, [4]
pp.
NYPL copy.   39038

Webster, Noah, 1758-1843.
An American Selection of Lessons, in
Reading and Speaking. . . . The Fourth
Albany Edition.
Albany, [N. Y.], Websters, 1800. 236, [3]
pp.
HEH copy.   39039

Webster, Noah, 1758-1843.
An American Selection of Lessons in
Reading and Speaking. . . . Thomas and
Andrews' Eleventh Edition.
Boston, Thomas & Andrews, etc., 1800.
240 pp.
AAS copy.   39036

Webster, Noah, 1758-1843.
An American Selection of Lessons in
Reading and Speaking. . . . Thomas and
Andrews' Twelfth Edition.
Boston, Thomas & Andrews, etc., 1800.
240 pp.
(But for front matter identical with 39036,
q. v.)
AAS copy.   39037

Webster, Noah, 1758-1843.
An American Selection of Lessons in
Reading and Speaking. . . . Fifteenth
Edition.
Hartford, Hudson & Goodwin, [1800],
240 pp.
(The copy reproduced is imperfect.)
AAS copy.   49187

Webster, Noah, 1758-1843.
An American Selection of Lessons in
Reading and Speaking.
New York, Waites for Duyckinck, 1800.
261, [7] pp.
AAS copy.   49188

Webster, Noah, 1758-1843.
[The American Spelling Book.
Bennington, Haswell & Russell, 1787.]
(McCorison 140; no copy known.)   45200

[Webster, Noah, 1758-1843.
The American Spelling-Book. . . . Sixth
Edition.
Hartford, Hudson & Goodwin, 1787.]
(A duplicate of 20868.)   20863

[Webster, Noah, 1758-1843.
The American Spelling-Book. . . . Seventh
Edition.
Philadelphia, Young & M'Cullock, 1787.]
("Just Published, and to be Sold by Young
& M'Cullock," Pa. Gazette, Aug. 24,
1787.)   20864

Webster, Noah, 1758-1843.
[The American Spelling Book.
Bennington, 1788.]
(Skeel-Carpenter 13; no copy located.)
    45409

Webster, Noah, 1758-1843.

[The American Spelling Book.
Boston, Folsom, 1788.]
(Skeel-Carpenter 14; no copy located.)
    45410

Webster, Noah, 1758-1843.
The American Spelling Book . . . Eleventh
Edition.
Hartford, Hudson & Goodwin, [1788?]
153 pp.
JCB copy.   45413

Webster, Noah, 1758-1843.
The American Spelling Book. . . . Eighth
Edition.
Philadelphia, Young, 1788.
(No copy located; Skeel-Carpenter 8.)
    45411

Webster, Noah, 1758-1843.
[The American Spelling Book. . . . Ninth
Edition.
New York, Campbell, 1788.]
(Skeel-Carpenter 9; no copy known.)
    45412

[Webster, Noah, 1758-1843.
The American Spelling-Book. . . . Tenth
Edition.
Philadelphia, Young, 1788.]
(Adv. in 21043.)   21584

[Webster, Noah, 1758-1843.
The American Spelling-Book. . . .
Eleventh Edition.
Philadelphia, Young, 1788.]
(Adv. Conn. Gazette, Jan. 23, 1789.) 21585

Webster, Noah, 1758-1843.
[The American Spelling Book.
Bennington, Haswell & Russell, 1789.]
(Skeel-Carpenter 15; no copy known.)
    45742

Webster, Noah, 1758-1843.
The American Spelling Book. . . . Thomas
and Andrews' First Edition.
Boston, Thomas & Andrews, 1789. 144 pp.
AAS copy.   22257

Webster, Noah, 1758-1843.
The American Spelling Book. . . . Eighth
Connecticut Edition.
Hartford, Hudson & Goodwin, [1789].
153 pp.
(Evans' entry was constructed from advs.
The unique copy could not be
reproduced.)   23051

Webster, Noah, 1758-1843.
[The American Spelling Book. . . . Twelfth
Edition.
New York, Campbell, 1789.]
(Skeel-Carpenter 18; no copy known.)
    45743

Webster, Noah, 1758-1843.
[The American Spelling Book. . . .
Twelfth Edition.
Philadelphia, 1789.]
(Skeel-Carpenter 19; no copy known.)
    45744

Webster, Noah, 1758-1843.
The American Spelling Book. . . . Twelfth
Edition.
Providence, Carter, 1789. 146+ pp.
(The only known copy is imperfect.)
AAS copy.   45745

Webster, Noah, 1758-1843.
The American Spelling Book. . . . Fourth
Vermont Edition.
Bennington, Haswell, [1790?] 96+ pp.
(The only copy located is imperfect.)
AAS copy.   46098

Webster, Noah, 1758-1843.
The American Spelling Book. . . . Thomas
& Andrews's Second Edition.
Boston, Thomas & Andrews, 1790. 144 pp.
LOC copy.   23052

Webster, Noah, 1758-1843.
[The American Spelling Book.
Hartford, Hudson & Goodwin, 1790.]
(Skeel-Carpenter 23; no copy known.)
    46099

[Webster, Noah, 1758-1843.
The American Spelling Book. . . . Thomas
and Andrew's Third Edition.

Boston, Thomas & Andrews, 1791.]
(Adv. Columbian Centinel, Apr. 9, 1791.)
    23965

Webster, Noah, 1758-1843.
The American Spelling Book . . . Tenth
Connecticut Edition.
Hartford, Hudson & Goodwin, [1791?]
153 pp.
(No better copy available.)
CHS copy.   46351

Webster, Noah, 1758-1843.
The American Spelling Book. . . . Thomas
& Andrews's Fourth Edition.
Boston, Thomas & Andrews, 1792. 144 pp.
BM copy.   24999

Webster, Noah, 1758-1843.
The American Spelling Book. . . .
Eleventh Connecticut Edition.
Hartford, Hudson & Goodwin, [1792?]
153 pp.
(The only known copy is imperfect.)
Stanford, Cal., Univ. copy.   46674

Webster, Noah, 1758-1843.
The American Spelling-Book. . . . The
Fourteenth Edition.
New York, Campbell, 1792. 144 pp.
(The only known copy is imperfect.)
CSL copy.   25000

Webster, Noah, 1758-1843.
The American Spelling Book. . . . Thomas
& Andrews' Fifth Edition.
Boston, Thomas & Andrews, 1793. 144 pp.
PPL copy.   46940

Webster, Noah, 1758-1843.
The American Spelling Book. . . . Thomas
& Andrews' Eighth Edition.
Boston, 1793. 144 pp.
(The only known copy cannot be
reproduced.)   46942

Webster, Noah, 1758-1843.
The American Spelling Book. . . . Thomas
& Andrew's Sixth Edition.
Boston, Thomas & Andrews, 1793. pp.
[6]-144.
AAS copy.   46941

Webster, Noah, 1758-1843.
The American Spelling Book. . . . Twelfth
Connecticut Edition.
Hartford, Hudson & Goodwin, [1793].
153 pp.
CSL copy.   26446

[Webster, Noah, 1758-1843.
The American Spelling Book. . . .
Thirteenth Connecticut Edition.
Hartford, Hudson & Goodwin, 1793.]
(Not adv. by publishers. Assumed by
Evans from sequence.)   26447

Webster, Noah, 1758-1843.
[The American Spelling Book. . . .
Fifteenth Edition.
New York, Campbell, 1793.]
(Skeel-Carpenter 33; no copy known.)
    46943

Webster, Noah, 1758-1843.
The American Spelling Book. . . . Eighth
Vermont Edition.
Bennington, Haswell, 1794. 156 pp.
(The only known copy is imperfect.)
WRHS copy.   47324

Webster, Noah, 1758-1843.
The American Spelling Book. . . . The
Fourteenth Connecticut Edition.
Hartford, Hudson & Goodwin, [1794?].
YC copy.   28044

Webster, Noah, 1758-1843.
The American Spelling Book.
Albany, Websters, 1794.
("This day printed," Albany Gazette,
Nov. 3, 1794.)   28042

Webster, Noah, 1758-1843.
The American Spelling Book. . . . The
Fifteenth Connecticut Edition.
Hartford, Hudson & Goodwin, [1794].
164 pp.
NL copy.   28045

Webster, Noah, 1758-1843.
The American Spelling Book. . . . Thomas
& Andrews' Ninth Edition.

Boston, Thomas & Andrews, 1794. 156 pp.
AAS copy. 28043

[Webster, Noah, 1758-1843.
The American Spelling Book. . . . Thomas
& Andrews' Tenth Edition.
Boston, Thomas & Andrews, 1794. 156
pp., 1 plate.]
(No copy of the 10th ed. located.) 29852

Webster, Noah, 1758-1843.
The American Spelling Book.
New York, Bunce, 1794.
(See Skeel-Carpenter, p. 23.) 28046

Webster, Noah, 1758-1843.
The American Spelling Book. . . .
Sixteenth Connecticut Edition.
Hartford, Hudson & Goodwin, [1795].
164 pp.
LOC copy. 29850

[Webster, Noah, 1758-1843.
The American Spelling Book. . . . Thomas
& Andrews' Eleventh Edition.
Boston, Thomas & Andrews, 1795. 156
pp., 1 plate.]
(No copy of an 11th ed. located.) 29853

Webster, Noah, 1758-1843.
The American Spelling Book. . . . Thomas
& Andrews' Twelfth Edition.
Boston, Thomas & Andrews, 1795. 156
pp., 1 plate.
(No perfect copy located.)
BPL copy. 29854

Webster, Noah, 1758-1843.
The American Spelling Book. . . .
Seventeenth Connecticut Edition.
Hartford, Hudson & Goodwin, [1795?].
164 pp.
Trinity College (Watkinson) copy. 29851

Webster, Noah, 1758-1843.
The American Spelling Book. . . . IXth
Vermont Edition.
Bennington, Haswell, 1796. pp. [8],
[13]-167.
Sheldon Art Museum, Middlebury, Vt.
48025

[Webster, Noah, 1758-1843.
The American Spelling Book. . . . Thomas
& Andrews' Thirteenth Edition.
Boston, Thomas & Andrews, 1796. 156 pp.
(No copy of this edition located.) 31590

[Webster, Noah, 1758-1843.
The American Spelling Book. . . . Thomas
& Andrews' Fourteenth Edition.
Boston, Thomas & Andrews, 1796. 156
pp.]
(No copy located.) 31591

Webster, Noah, 1758-1843.
The American Spelling Book. . . . The
Eighteenth Connecticut Edition.
Hartford, Hudson & Goodwin, [1796].
165, [1] pp.
NYPL copy. 31592

[Webster, Noah, 1758-1843.
The American Spelling Book. . . . Thomas
& Andrews' Fifteenth Edition.
Boston, Thomas & Andrews, 1797. 156
pp.]
(No copy located.) 33180

[Webster, Noah, 1758-1843.
The American Spelling Book. . . . Thomas
& Andrews' Sixteenth Edition.
Boston, Thomas & Andrews, 1797. 150
pp.]
(No copy located.) 33181

Webster, Noah, 1758-1843.
The American Spelling Book. . . .
Nineteenth Edition.
New York, Davis for Allen, etc., 1797.
165, [1] pp.
(Entry from Albert A. Beeber Cat. 1927.
p. 19.) 33183

Webster, Noah, 1758-1843.
The American Spelling-Book. . . . Thomas
& Andrews' Seventeenth Edition.
Boston, Thomas & Andrews, etc., 1798.
156, [3] pp.
AAS copy. 34976

Webster, Noah, 1758-1843.

The American Spelling Book. . . . Thomas
& Andrews' Eighteenth Edition.
Boston, Thomas & Andrews, etc., 1798.
156 pp.
AAS copy. 34977

[Webster, Noah, 1758-1843.
The American Spelling Book. . . . Thomas
& Andrews' Nineteenth Edition.
Boston, Thomas & Andrews, etc., 1798.
156, [2] pp.
(No copy located.) 34978

Webster, Noah, 1758-1843.
The American Spelling Book. . . .
Nineteenth Connecticut Edition.
Hartford, Hudson & Goodwin, [1798].
165, [1] pp.
(No perfect copy located.)
AAS copy. 33182

[Webster, Noah, 1758-1843.
The American Spelling Book. . . . The
Twentieth Connecticut Edition.
Hartford, Hudson & Goodwin, [1798].
165, 1 pp.
(No copy located. See Skeel-Carpenter,
56.) 34979

Webster, Noah, 1758-1843.
The American Spelling Book. . . . XVth
Vermont Edition.
Bennington, Pomeroy, 1799. 164 pp.
AAS copy. 48990

Webster, Noah, 1758-1843.
The American Spelling Book. . . . Thomas
& Andrews' Twentieth Edition.
Boston, Thomas & Andrews, 1799. 156 pp.
AAS copy. 36684

[Webster, Noah, 1758-1843.
The American Spelling Book. . . . Thomas
& Andrews' Twenty-First Edition.
Boston, Thomas & Andrews, 1799.]
(No copy of this ed. located.) 36685

Webster, Noah, 1758-1843.
The American Spelling Book. . . .
Twenty-First Connecticut Edition.
Hartford, [Ct.], Hudson & Goodwin,
[1799]. 165, [1] pp.
NYHS copy. 36686

Webster, Noah, 1758-1843.
The American Spelling Book. . . . Third
Albany Edition.
Albany, [N. Y.], Websters, [1800]. 168
pp.
NYPL copy. 39041

Webster, Noah, 1758-1843.
The American Spelling Book. . . . Thomas
& Andrews' Twenty-Second Edition.
Boston, Thomas & Andrews, 1800. 156 pp.
AAS copy. 39040

Webster, Noah, 1758-1843.
The American Spelling Book. . . .
Twenty-Second Connecticut Edition.
Hartford, [Ct.], Hudson & Goodwin,
[1800]. 165, [1] pp.
(The unique original cannot be filmed.)
NYPL copy. 39042

[Webster, Noah, 1758-1843.
The Art of Speaking.
Albany, Websters, 1788.]
("Now selling," Albany Gazette, Dec. 26,
1788.) 21583

[Webster, Noah], 1758-1843.
Attention! or, new Thoughts on a Serious
Subject.
Hartford, Hudson & Goodwin, 1789. 18
pp.
NYPL copy. 22258

Webster, Noah, 1758-1843.
A Brief History of Epidemic . . .
Diseases. . . . Vol. I- [II].
Hartford, Ct., Hudson & Goodwin, 1799.
pp. [i]-xii, [9]-348; [4], [1]-352.
AAS copy. 36687

Webster, Noah, 1758 - 1843.
Circular. To the Clergymen. . . . May 7,
1798.
[New Haven, 1798.] Broadside.
NYPL copy. 34985

Webster, Noah, 1758-1843.
(Circular) To the Physicians of

Philadelphia. . . . Oct. 31, 1795.
[New York, 1795.] Broadside.
LCP copy. 47676

Webster, Noah, 1758-1843.
A Collection of Essays.
Boston, Thomas & Andrews, 1790. xvi,
414 pp.
AAS copy. 23053

Webster, Noah, 1758-1843.
A Collection of Papers on . . . Bilious
Fevers.
New York, Hopkins, Webb & Co., 1796.
pp. [i]-x, [i]-ix, [1], [1]-52, [2],
[53]-246.
AAS copy. 31593

Webster, Noah, 1758-1843.
Dissertations on the English Language.
Boston, Thomas, 1789. 410 pp.
AAS copy. 22259

Webster, Noah, 1758-1843.
Effects of Slavery.
Hartford, Hudson & Goodwin, 1793. 56
pp.
AAS copy. 26448

[Webster, Noah], 1758-1843.
The Farmer's Catechism.
Canaan, N. Y., Phinney, 1795.
(Known only by this tp ph. See
Skeel-Carpenter 533.)
AAS copy. 29855

[Webster, Noah, 1758-1843.
A Grammatical Institute.
Philadelphia, Young, 1780. 220 pp.]
(Title assumed by Evans from advs. See A
Plain and Comprehensive Grammar.)
22260

[Webster, Noah, 1758-1843.
The First Part of the Grammatical
Institute . . . Abridged; for the use of
Small Children.
Philadelphia, Dobson, 1786.]
(Entry from an adv. for "New Books" in
Pa. Gazette, Aug. 2, 1786.) 20128

[Webster, Noah, 1758-1843.
A Grammatical Institute.
Philadelphia, Young, 1789. 220 pp.]
(Imprint assumed by Evans from advs.)
22260

Webster, Noah, 1758-1843.
A Grammatical Institute. . . . Part I.
Hartford, Hudson & Goodwin, [1783].
119, [1] pp.
AAS copy. 18297

[Webster, Noah, 1758-1843.
A Grammatical Institute. . . . Part I. . . .
Second Edition.
Hartford, Hudson & Goodwin, 1784].
(No copy with words "Second Edition"
found.) 18298

Webster, Noah, 1758-1843.
A Grammatical Institute. . . . Part I. . . .
Third Edition.
Hartford, Hudson & Goodwin, 1784. 138
pp.
HC copy. 18870

Webster, Noah, 1758-1843.
A Grammatical Institute. . . . Part I. . . .
Fourth Edition.
Hartford, Hudson & Goodwin, 1785. 138
pp.
JCB copy. 19361

Webster, Noah, 1758-1843.
A Grammatical Institute. . . . Part I.
Boston, Edes, [1786?] 134+pp.
(The only known copy could not be
reproduced.) 45018

Webster, Noah, 1758-1843.
A Grammatical Institute. . . . Part II.
Hartford, Hudson & Goodwin, 1784. 139
pp.
AAS copy. 18871

Webster, Noah, 1758-1843.
A Grammatical Institute. . . . Sixth
Edition.
Hartford, Hudson & Goodwin, 1787. 138
pp.
(No copy available for reproduction.)
45201

Webster, Noah, 1758-1843.
A Grammatical Institute.... Part II.
Hartford, Barlow & Babcock, 1785. 139
pp.
AAS copy.   19363

Webster, Noah, 1758-1843.
A Grammatical Institute.... Part II.
Hartford, Hudson & Goodwin, 1785. 139
pp.
LOC copy.   19362

Webster, Noah, 1758-1843.
A Grammatical Institute.... Part II....
Fourth Edition.
Hartford, Hudson & Goodwin, [1787].
129 pp.
AAS copy.   20866

[Webster, Noah, 1758-1843.
A Grammatical Institute.... Part II....
Fifth Edition.
Hartford, Hudson & Goodwin, 1787.]
(Assumed from the sequence of editions.)
                                             20867

[Webster, Noah, 1758-1843.
A Grammatical Institute.... Part II....
Sixth Edition.
Hartford, Hudson & Goodwin, 1787.]
(No copy of this ed. located.)   20868

Webster, Noah, 1758-1843.
A Grammatical Institute.... Part II....
Third Edition, Revised.
Philadelphia, Young & M'Cullock, 1787.
132 pp.
AAS copy.   20869

Webster, Noah, 1758-1843.
A Grammatical Institute.... Part
Second.... Thomas and Andrews's First
Edition.
Boston, Thomas & Andrews, 1790. 125 pp.
AAS copy.   23054

[Webster, Noah, 1758-1843.
A Grammatical Institute.... Part
Second.... First Connecticut Edition.
Hartford, Hudson & Goodwin, 1790.]
(Imprint assumed by Evans from Conn.
Courant advs. for "all parts.")   23055

[Webster, Noah, 1758-1843.
A Grammatical Institute.... Part
Second.... Second Connecticut Edition.
Hartford, Hudson & Goodwin, 1791.]
(See Skeel & Carpenter, 23.)   23966

Webster, Noah, 1758-1843.
A Grammatical Institute.... Part
Second.... Thomas and Andrews's
Second Edition.
Boston, Thomas & Andrews, 1792. 120 pp.
AAS copy.   25001

Webster, Noah, 1758-1843.
A Grammatical Institute.... Part
Second.... Third Connecticut Edition.
Hartford, Hudson & Goodwin, 1792. 131
pp.
AAS copy.   25002

Webster, Noah, 1758-1843.
A Grammatical Institute.... Part
Second.... Thomas and Andrews' Third
Edition.
Boston, Thomas & Andrews, 1794. 116 pp.
(Also issued with advs. at end.)
AAS copy.   28047

Webster, Noah, 1758-1843.
A Grammatical Institute.... Part
Second.... The Fourth Connecticut
Edition.
Hartford, Hudson & Godwin, [1794]. 129
pp.
AAS copy.   28048

Webster, Noah, 1758-1843.
A Grammatical Institute.... Part
Second.
Albany, Websters, 1796. 115 pp.
LOC copy.   31594

Webster, Noah, 1758-1843.
A Grammatical Institute.... Part
Second.... Thomas and Andrews' Fourth
Edition.
Boston, Thomas & Andrews, 1796. 116 pp.
AAS copy.   31595

Webster, Noah, 1758-1843.

A Grammatical Institute.... Part
Second.... Fifth Connecticut Edition.
Hartford, Hudson & Goodwin, 1796. 136
pp.
AAS copy.   31596

Webster, Noah, 1758-1843.
A Grammatical Institute.... Part
Second.... Thomas and Andrews' Fifth
Edition.
Boston, Thomas & Andrews, etc., 1797.
116 pp.
AAS copy.   33184

Webster, Noah, 1758-1843.
A Grammatical Institute.... Part
Second.
New York, Wilsons for Duyckinck, 1798.
119, [1] pp.
AAS copy.   34980

Webster, Noah, 1758-1843.
A Grammatical Institute.... Part
Second.... Thomas & Andrews' Sixth
Edition.
Boston, Thomas & Andrews, etc., 1800.
116 pp.
AAS copy.   39044

Webster, Noah, 1758-1843.
A Grammatical Institute.... Part
Second.... Sixth Connecticut Edition.
Hartford, Hudson & Goodwin, 1800. 131
pp.
CHS copy.   39043

Webster, Noah, 1758-1843.
A Grammatical Institute.... Part III.
Hartford, Barlow & Babcock, 1785. 186
pp.
AAS copy.   19364

Webster, Noah, 1758-1843.
A Gramatical Institute.... Part III....
Second Edition.
Hartford, Hudson & Goodwin, [1785?].
188 pp.
JCB copy.   44833

Webster, Noah, 1758-1846.
A Grammatical Institute.... Part III....
Second Edition.
Hartford, Hudson & Goodwin, [1786].
188 pp.
AAS copy.   45019

Webster, Noah, 1758-1843.
An Introduction to English Grammar.
Philadelphia, Young, 1788. 36 pp.
AAS copy.   45414

[Webster, Noah], 1758-1843.
A Letter to General Hamilton,
Occasioned by his Letter to President
Adams.
[New York, 1800.] 8 pp.
AAS copy.   39045

[Webster, Noah], 1758-1843.
A Letter to General Hamilton,
Occasioned by his Letter to President
Adams.
New York, Belden, 1800. 15 pp.
MHS copy.   39047

[Webster, Noah], 1758-1843.
A Letter to General Hamilton,
Occasioned by his Letter to President
Adams.
[Philadelphia, 1800.] pp. [3]-10.
AAS copy.   39046

[Webster, Noah], 1758-1843.
A Letter to General Hamilton,
Occasioned by his Letter to President
Adams.
Salem, Mass., Cushing, 1800. 29 pp.]
(A ghost of 38153.)   39048

Webster, Noah, 1758-1843.
A Letter to the Governors, Instructors
and Trustees.
New York, Hopkins, 1798. 36 pp.
AAS copy.   34981

Webster, Noah, 1758-1843.
The Little Reader's Assistant.
Hartford, Babcock, 1790. 48, 80, 13 pp.
NYPL copy.   23056

Webster, Noah, 1758-1843.
The Little Reader's Assistant.... Second
Edition.

Hartford, Babcock, 1791. 141 pp.
AAS copy.   23967

Webster, Noah, 1758-1843.
The Little Reader's Assistant.... Third
Edition.
Northampton, Butler, 1791. 137 pp.
Composite copy.   23968

[Webster, Noah, 1758-1843.
The Little Reader's Assistant.
Hartford, Babcock, 1793?]
(Imprint assumed by Evans from advs.
"For sale at this Office" and "Just
Published" in Am. Mercury, Oct. 21 and
Dec. 23, 1793.)   26449

[Webster, Noah, 1758-1843.
The Little Reader's Assistant.
Hartford, Ct., Babcock, 1798.]
(Imprint assumed by Evans from
Babcock's adv.)   34982

Webster, Noah, 1758-1843.
The Little Reader's Assistant.... Fourth
Edition.
Northampton, Mass., Butler, 1798. 138 pp.
AAS copy.   34983

[Webster, Noah], 1758-1843.
The New-England Primer, Amended.
New York, Patterson, 1789. [72] pp.
CHS copy.   45746

[Webster, Noah], 1758-1843.
An Oration, "On the Extent and Power of
Political Delusion."
Bennington, Stockwell, [1800]. 15 pp.
(This is the caption title of 39055, q. v.)
                                             39049

Webster, Noah, 1758-1843.
An Oration Pronounced before the
Citizens of New-Haven.
New Haven, Greens, [1798]. 16 pp.
AAS copy.   34984

Webster, Noah, 1758-1843.
A Plain and Comprehensive Grammar.
Philadelphia, Young, 1789. pp. [1]-4,
[9]-220.
AAS copy.   45747

[Webster, Noah], 1758-1843.
The Prompter; or a Commentary on
Common Sayings.
Hartford, Hudson & Goodwin, 1791. 94
pp.
HC copy.   23969

[Webster, Noah], 1758-1843.
The Prompter.
Albany, Websters, 1792. 92 pp.]
(See Skeel-Carpenter, 653.)   25003

[Webster, Noah], 1758-1843.
The Prompter; or a Commentary on
Common Sayings.
Boston, Thomas & Andrews, 1792. 96 pp.
AAS copy.   25004

[Webster, Noah], 1758-1843.
The Prompter; or a Commentary on
Common Sayings.
New London, Green, 1792.]
("For sale," Conn. Gazette, Aug. 16,
1792.)   25005

[Webster, Noah], 1758-1843.
The Prompter; or a Commentary on
Common Sayings.
Philadelphia, Cist, 1792.]
(See Skeel-Carpenter, 657.)   25006

[Webster, Noah], 1758-1843.
The Prompter; or a Commentary on
Common Sayings.
Boston, Thomas & Andrews, 1793. 96 pp.
AAS copy.   26451

[Webster, Noah], 1758-1843.
The Prompter; a Commentary on
Common Sayings.... Fourth Edition.
New York, Bunce, 1793. 96 pp.
AAS copy.   26450

[Webster, Noah], 1758-1843.
The Prompter; or, a Commentary on
Common Sayings.
Newark, N. J., Woods, 1793. 56 pp.
NYHS copy.   26452

[Webster, Noah], 1758-1843.
The Prompter.
Boston, Folsom, 1794. 96 pp.
CHS copy.   28050

[Webster, Noah], 1758-1843.
The Prompter; or a Commentary on
Common Sayings.
Boston, Thomas & Andrews, 1794. 84 pp.
AAS copy.   28049

[Webster, Noah, 1758-1843.
The Prompter; a Commentary on
Common Sayings.
New York, Bunce, 1794.]
(Imprint assumed from adv.
"Just Published, and for sale, by George
Bunce," in Am. Minerva, Sept. 25, 1794.)
                                             28051

[Webster, Noah, 1758-1843.
The Prompter; a Commentary on
Common Sayings.
Philadelphia, Carey, 1794.]
(See Skeel-Carpenter 664. Imprint
assumed by Evans from adv. "Just
Published, and for sale by M. Carey,"
Gazette of the U. S., Feb. 4, 1794.) 28052

[Webster, Noah, 1758-1843.
The Prompter.
Leominster, Prentiss, 1795.]
(Apparently a ghost of one of the later
eds.)   29856

[Webster, Noah], 1758-1843.
The Prompter; or, a Commentary on
Common Sayings.
New York, Campbell, 1795. 108 pp.
AAS copy.   47677

[Webster, Noah], 1758-1843.
The Prompter; or a Commentary on
Common Sayings.
Leominster, Prentiss, 1796. 44 pp.
AAS copy.   31597

[Webster, Noah], 1758-1843.
The Prompter; or a Commentary on
Common Sayings.
New York, Bunce, 1796.]
(Imprint assumed by Evans from adv.
"now published" in American Minerva,
Jan. 11, 1796.)   31598

[Webster, Noah], 1758-1843.
The Prompter; or a Commentary on
Common Sayings.
Philadelphia, Carey, 1796. 95 pp.
AAS copy.   31599

[Webster, Noah], 1758-1843.
The Prompter; or a Commentary on
Common Sayings.
Boston, Thomas & Andrews, 1797. 84 pp.
AAS copy.   33185

[Webster, Noah], 1758-1843.
The Prompter; or a Commentary on
Common Sayings. . . . Second Leominster
Edition.
[Leominster], Prentiss, 1797. 91, [2] pp.
(This copy in original covers never had
the final 7 pp. called for by Evans.)
AAS copy.   33186

[Webster, Noah], 1758-1843.
The Prompter; or a Commentary on
Common Sayings.
New Brunswick, N.J., Blauvelt, 1797. 84
pp.
(No perfect copy located.)
NYPL copy.   33187

[Webster, Noah], 1758-1843.
The Prompter.
n.p., 1798. 88 pp.
(No copy located.)   48755

Webster, Noah, 1758-1843.
The Prompter.
Chambersburg, Harper for Carey, 1798. 85
pp.
(Not located, 1968.)   48756

[Webster, Noah], 1758-1843.
The Prompter; or a Commentary on
Common Sayings.
Printed for, and sold by the Book-Sellers,
Dec. 1799. 72 pp.
AAS copy.   36688

[Webster, Noah], 1758-1843.
The Prompter: or, a Commentary on
Common Saying. . . . Third Albany
Edition.
Albany, Webster, 1800. 95, [1] pp.
AAS copy.   39050

[Webster, Noah], 1758-1843.
The Prompter; or a Commentary on
Common Sayings.
Alexandria, Westcotts, 1800. 102 pp.
LOC copy.   39051

[Webster, Noah], 1758-1843.
The Prompter: to which is Added The
Whistle.
Burlington, N. J., Neale, 1792. 50 pp.
Rutgers University copy.   25007

[Webster, Noah], 1758-1843.
The Revolution in France.
New York, Bunce, 1794. 72 pp.
AAS copy.   28053

[Webster, Noah], 1758-1843.
A Rod for the Fool's Back.
n.p., [1800]. 11 pp.
YC copy.   39054

[Webster, Noah], 1758-1843.
A Rod for the Fool's Back.
n.p., 1800. 12 pp.
YC copy.   39053

[Webster, Noah], 1758-1843.
. . . A Rod for the Fool's Back.
Bennington, Stockwell, [1800]. 15 pp.
AAS copy.   39055

[Webster, Noah], 1758-1843.
A Rod for the Fool's Back.
New Haven, Read & Morse, 1800. 10 pp.
YC copy.   39052

[Webster, Noah, 1758-1843.
Rudiments of English Grammar.
Albany, Websters, 1790.]
("This day published," Albany Gazette,
Mar. 22, 1790.)   23058

[Webster, Noah], 1758-1843.
Rudiments of English Grammar.]
Boston, Russell for Guild, 1790.]
("This day published," Mass. Centinel,
Apr. 3, 1790; see Skeel-Carpenter 447.)
                                             23059

Webster, Noah, 1758-1843.
Rudiments of English Grammar.
Hartford, Babcock, 1790. 80 pp.
AAS copy.   23057

Webster, Noah, 1758-1843.
Sketches of American Policy.
Hartford, Hudson & Goodwin, 1785. 48
pp.
HC copy.   19366

Webster, Noah, 1758-1843.
A Syllabus of Mr. Webster's Lectures . . .
June 15, 1786.
[New Haven, 1786.] Broadside.
YC copy.   45020

Webster, Noah, 1758-1843.
Ten Letters to Dr. Joseph Priestly.
New Haven, Read & Morse, 1800. 29 pp.
AAS copy.   39056

Webster, Noah, 1758-1843.
To the Public. It is a Subject. . . . May 7th,
1794.
[New York, Bunce, 1794.] Broadside.
NYPL copy.   47325

Webster, Noah, 1758-1843.
To the Public. . . . To Accommodate
Country Readers. . . .
[New York, 1794.] Broadside.
(Same as 47325, q.v.)   47326

[Webster, Pelatiah], 1726-1795.
An Address to the Stockholders of the
Bank of North America, on the Subject of
the Old and New Banks.
Philadelphia, Crukshank, 1791. 8 pp.]
(Apparently a ghost of 23971.)   23970

[Webster, Pelatiah], 1726-1795.
A Dissertation on the Political Union and
Constitution of the Thirteen United
States.

Hartford, Hudson & Goodwin, 1783. 30
pp.
AAS copy.   18300

[Webster, Pelatiah], 1726-1795.
A Dissertation on the Political Union and
Constitution of the Thirteen United
States.
Philadelphia, Bradford, 1783. 47 pp.
AAS copy.   18299

[Webster, Pelatiah, 1726-1795.
An Essay in the Principles.
[Philadelphia], Aitken, 1787. 52 pp.]
(Also entered as 20306, q. v.)   20870

[Webster, Pelatiah], 1726-1795.
An Essay on Credit, in which the Doctrine
of Banks is Considered.
Philadelphia, Oswald, 1786. 42 pp.
AAS copy.   20129

[Webster, Pelatiah], 1726-1795.
An Essay on the Seat of the Federal
Government.
Philadelphia, Bailey, 1789. [2], 34 pp.
AAS copy.   22262

[Webster, Pelatiah], 1726-1795.
A Fifth Essay on Free Trade.
Philadelphia, Bailey, 1780. 23 pp.
AAS copy.   17065

[Webster, Pelatiah], 1726-1795.
A Fourth Essay on Free Trade.
Philadelphia, Hall & Sellers, 1780. 16 pp.
AAS copy.   17064

[Webster, Pelatiah], 1726-1795.
A Plea for the Poor Soldiers.
New Haven, 1790. 33 pp.
BA copy.   23061

[Webster, Pelatiah], 1726-1795.
A Plea for the Poor Soldiers.
Philadelphia, Bailey, 1790. 39 pp.
AAS copy.   23060

Webster, Pelatiah, 1726-1795.
Political Essays.
Philadelphia, Crukshank, 1791. viii, 504
pp.
AAS copy.   23972

[Webster, Pelatiah], 1726-1795.
Reasons for Repealing the Act of the
Legislative of Pennsylvania, of September
13, 1785.
Philadelphia, Oswald, 1786. 8 pp.
AAS copy.   20130

[Webster, Pelatiah], 1726-1795.
Remarks on the Address of Sixteen
Members of the Assembly of
Pennsylvania.
Philadelphia, Oswald, 1787. 28 pp.
AAS copy.   20871

[Webster, Pelatiah], 1726-1795.
A Second Essay on Free Trade and
Finance.
Philadelphia, Bradford, 1779. 20 pp.
AAS copy.   16671

[Webster, Pelatiah], 1726-1795.
A Seventh Essay on Free Trade and
Finance.
Philadelphia, Oswald, 1785. 38 pp.
AAS copy.   19367

[Webster, Pelatiah], 1726-1795.
A Sixth Essay on Free Trade and Finance.
Philadelphia, Bradford, 1783. 32 pp.
AAS copy.   18301

[Webster, Pelatiah], 1726-1795.
To the Stockholders of the Bank of
North-America, on the Subject of the Old
and New Banks.
Philadelphia, Crukshank, 1791. 16 pp.
LCP copy.   23971

[Webster, Pelatiah], 1726-1795.
The Weakness of Brutus Exposed.
Philadelphia, Sparhawk, 1787. 23 pp.
AAS copy.   20872

Webster, Samuel, 1718-1796.
The Blessedness of Those who Die in the
Lord.
Boston, Edes, 1793. 23 pp.
AAS copy.   26453

Webster, Samuel, 1718-1796.
An Elegy, [to the] Memory of Mason and
Alpheus . . . Hale . . . July 3, 1790.
n.p., [1790]. Broadside.
(Known only by this fragment.)
AAS copy.   46100

Webster, Samuel, 1718-1796.
(Sibley, X.)
Justification.
Boston, Edes & Gill, 1765. 35 pp.
AAS copy.   10204

Webster, Samuel, 1718-1796.
(Sibley, X.)
Ministers Labourers.
Salem, 1772. 40 pp.
AAS copy.   12609

Webster, Samuel, 1718-1796.
(Sibley, X.)
The Misery and Duty.
Boston, Edes & Gill, 1774. 31 pp.
AAS copy.   13758

Webster, Samuel, 1718-1796.
The Nature and Importance. . . .
Newburyport, Mycall, 1784. 32 pp.
AAS copy.   44629

Webster, Samuel, 1718-1796.
(Sibley, X.)
A Sermon Preached before the Honorable
Council.
Boston, Edes & Gill, 1777. 44 pp.
AAS copy.   15703

Webster, Samuel, 1718-1796.
Soldiers, and Others.
Boston, Edes & Gill, 1756. 16 (i.e. 22) pp.
AAS copy.   7813

Webster, Samuel, 1718-1796.
The Sufficiency and Excellency.
Newburyport, Blunt, 1794. 23 pp.
AAS copy.   28054

[Webster, Samuel], 1718-1796.
(Sibley, X.)
A Winter Evening's Conversation.
Boston, Green & Russell, 1757. 30, [2] pp.
AAS copy.   8060

[Webster, Samuel], 1718-1796.
A Winter Evening's Conversation.
New Haven, 1757. 26, v pp.
AAS copy.   8061

[Webster, Samuel], 1718-1796.
(Sibley, X.)
The Winter Evening Conversation
Vindicated.
Boston, Edes & Gill, [1759]. 126 pp.
(Imprint date following inscriptions in
two presentation copies.)
AAS copy.   8283

Webster, Samuel, 1718-1796.
(Sibley, X.)
Young Children.
Salem, 1773. 54 pp.
AAS copy.   13071

Webster, Samuel, 1718-1796.
(Sibley, X.)
Young Children and Infants. . . . Third
Edition.
Boston, Fleets, 1780. 35 pp.
AAS copy.   17066

Webster, Samuel, 1718-1796.
Young Children and Infants.
Boston, Fleets, 1780. 36 pp.
AAS copy.   43915

Webster, Samuel, 1743-1777.
Rabshakeh's Proposals.
Boston, Edes & Gill, 1775. 30 pp.
AAS copy.   14615

[Webster, Zephaniah, 1759-1798.
Webster's New-England Almanack for . . .
1789.
Springfield, Webster.]
(Entry from an adv.)   21586

Webster's New-England Almanack, for
. . . 1788.
Springfield, Mass., Webster. [26] pp.
AAS copy.   45202

Webster's New-York Almanack, for . . .
1784.

New York, Charles Webster. [26] pp.
(Not located.)
LOC copy.   44495

The Wedding: an Epic Poem.
n.p., [1796]. [8] pp.
AAS copy.   31600

The Wedding Day [by James Hook,
1746-1827].
Boston, von Hagen, etc., [1799?]. [2] pp.
AAS copy.   48888

Weeds, Enos.
The American Orthographer. . . . Book I.
Danbury, Douglas & Nichols, [1798]. 60
pp.
JCB copy.   34986

Weed, Enos.
The American Orthographer. Book II.
Danbury, Douglas & Nichols, 1798. 36 pp.
AAS copy.   34987

[Weed, Enos.
The American Orthographer. Book III.
Danbury, Douglas & Nichols, 1798.]
(Evans' entry was from an adv. or
prospectus.)   34988

Weeden, Job.
Job Weeden, Salem News-Boy, begs
Leave to Present the Following Lines. . . .
Jan. 1, 1772.
n. p., n. d. Broadside.
AAS copy.   42389

Weeden, Job.
On the Commencement of the Year 1769,
Job Weeden, Salem News-Boy . . . Carries
the Essex Gazette.
[Salem, 1769.] Broadside.
HSP copy.   42023

Weedon, J.
A Set of Round Hand Copies.
Boston, Hill, [1797]. [16] leaves.
AAS copy.   33188

De Weegshale de Garade Gods [by
Bernardus Freeman, 1660-1743].
Amsterdam, 1721.
(Omitted as foreign printing.)   2219

Weekes, George, 1689-1772.
(Josiah Paine, Harwich, pp. 406-407.)
Ebenezer.
Boston, [1728]. [2], 30, 24 pp.
MHS copy.   3117

Weeks, Levi, defendant.
Report of the Trial of. . . .
New York, Furman, 1800. 98 pp.
AAS copy.   38372

[The Weeks Preparation. . . . (Also) The
Church of England-man's Private
Devotions.
Annapolis, 1729.]
(Wroth 59; no copy known.)   39933

Weems, Mason Locke, 1759-1825.
A History, of the Life . . . of . . .
Washington.
Georgetown, Green & English, [1800].
[4], 80 pp.
HSP copy.   39061

Weems, Mason Locke, 1759-1825.
A History of the Life . . . of . . .
Washington. . . . Second Edition.
Philadelphia, Bioren, [1800?]. [2], 82 pp.,
1 plate.
AAS copy.   39062

Weems, Mason Locke, 1759-1825.
A History of the Life . . . of . . .
Washington. . . . Third Edition.
Philadelphia, Bioren, [1800?] 84 pp., 1
plate.
(Issued with and without the portrait
frontispiece.)
AAS copy.   39063

Weems, Mason Locke, 1759-1825.
Hymen's Recruiting-Serjeant.
Philadelphia, Maxwell, 1800. front., 19,
[1] pp.
NYPL copy.   39064

[Weems, Mason Locke], 1759-1825.
The Life and Memorable Actions of
George Washington.

[Baltimore], Keatinge, [1800]. 96 pp.,
irreg.
HSP copy.   39065

Weems, Mason Locke, 1759-1825.
The Lover's Almanac, No. I.
Fredericksburg, Green for Weems. [48]
pp.
Colonial Williamsburg copy.   34996

Weems, Mason Locke, 1759-1825.
The Philanthropist; or, A Good Twelve
Cents Worth of Political Love Powder.
n. p., [1799]. [2], 30 pp.
(The only known copy is imperfect.)
MdHS copy.   36694

Weems, Mason Locke, 1759-1825.
The Philanthropist; or A Good Twelve
Cents Worth of Political Love Powder.
n. p., J. May, 1799. 31 pp.
NYSL copy.   36696

[Weems, Mason Locke, 1759-1825.
The Philanthropist; or, A Good Twelve
Cents Worth of Political Love Powder.
Alexandria, Westcots, 1799. 30 pp.]
(Apparently a ghost arising from an adv.)
                                             36695

Weems, Mason Locke, 1759-1825.
The Philanthropist; or a Good Twenty-Five
Cents Worth of Political Love Powder.
Charleston, [S. C.], Young, [1799]. 31 pp.
SCHS copy.   36698

Weems, Mason Locke, 1759-1825.
The Philanthropist; or, A Good
Twenty-Five Cents Worth of Political
Love Powder.
Dumfries, [1799]. 30 pp., 1 leaf insert.
AAS copy.   36697

[Der Weg der Gottseligkeit.
Germantown, 1771.]
(Printed in the Geistliches Magazien, II,
83-128. Seidensticker, p. 84, implies a
separate printing, but none has been
located.)   12278

Die Wege und Werke Gottes in der Seele.
Chestnuthill, Saur, 1792. 59 pp.
AAS copy.   25010

Weichenhan, Erasmus, d. 1594.
Christliche Betrachtungen.
Germantown, Billmeyer, 1791. [8], 785,
[3] pp.
AAS copy.   23975

Weihnachts-Lieder, Gebäter . . . für
die Kinder.
Reading, Jungmann & Gruber, 1793.
(Present location unknown.)   46944

Weiser, Johann Conrad, 1696-1760.
Translation of a German Letter.
[Philadelphia, 1757.] 7 pp.
UOP copy.   8062

Weiser, Johann Conrad, 1696-1760.
(D. A. B.)
Ein Wohl-gemeindter.
[Philadelphia, 1741.] [2] pp.
HSP copy.   4836

Weiss, Georg Michael, 1700-1763.
Der in der Americanischen Wildnusz.
Philadelphia, Bradford, 1729. v, 29 pp.
LOC copy.   3233

[Weiss, Ludwig?], 1717-1796.
Getreue Warnung gegen Lockvoegel.
Philadelphia, 1764. 15 pp.
NYPL copy.   9865

Welch, Moses Cook, 1754-1824.
The Addressor Addressed.
Norwich, Ct., Hubbard, 1796. 36 pp.
AAS copy.   31607

Welch, Moses Cook, 1754-1824.
An Eulogy . . . at the Funeral of Dea.
Benjamin Chaplin.
Norwich, Ct., Hubbard, 1796. 10 pp.
AAS copy.   31608

Welch, Moses Cook, 1754-1824.
The Glorious Resurrection of the Saints.
Windham, Conn., Byrne, 1794. 24 pp.
AAS copy.   28057

[Welch, Moses Cook], 1754-1824.

The Hope of Immortality.
Norwich, Trumbull, 1789. 21 pp.
UTS copy. 22263

Welch, Moses Cook, 1754-1824.
A Reply to the Correspondent.
Norwich, Conn., Hubbard, 1794. 64 pp.
AAS copy. 28058

Welch, Moses Cook, 1754-1824.
A Sermon, Preached at the Funeral of
Mrs. Peggy Pond.
Hartford, [Ct.], Hudson & Goodwin,
1800. 27 pp.
AAS copy. 39066

Welch, William, -1754.
The Last Speech and Dying Words.
[Boston, 1754.] Broadside.
MHS copy. 7333

Weld, Edmund, 1631-1668.
A Dialogue between Death, Soul, Body
and Jesus Christ.
Boston, Z. Fowle, 1763. Broadside.
AAS copy. 41425

Weld, Edmund, 1631-1668.
A Dialogue between Death, the Soul,
Body, World and Jesus Christ.
Boston, Russell for Howe of Ringe,
[1787]. Broadside.
AAS copy. 45203

Weld, Edmund, 1631-1668.
A Funeral Elegy by Way of Dialogue.
Boston, Kneeland, [1720?]. Broadside.
NYHS copy. 39715

Weld, Edmund, 1631-1668.
A Funeral Elegy by Way of Dialogue.
Boston, Kneeland, [175?]. Broadside.
NYHS copy. 40533

Weld, Edmund, 1631-1668.
A Funeral Elegy, by Way of Dialogue;
between Death, Soul, Body, World, and
Jesus Christ.
n. p., [1752?]. Broadside.
HSP copy. 40643

Weld, Edmund, 1631-1668.
A Funeral Elegy.
Boston, D. & J. Kneeland for J. Winter,
[1760?]. Broadside.
LOC copy. 41178

Weld, Edmund, 1631-1668.
(Sibley I, 220.)
A Funeral Elegy by way of Dialogue;
between Death, Soul, Body and Jesus
Christ.
Boston, S. Kneeland, [1760?]. Broadside.
NYHS copy. 41177

Weld, Edmund, 1631-1668.
A Funeral Elegy by the Way of a
Dialogue.
Springfield, Mass., at the Chronicle
Printing Office, [1787 ?]. Broadside.
NYHS copy. 45204

Weld, Edmund, 1631-1668.
A Funeral Elegy by Way of Dialogue.
Springfield, Mass., Chronicle Printing
Office, [1790]. Broadside.
NYHS copy. 46101

Weld, Ezra, 1736-1816.
A Discourse, Delivered April 25, 1799.
Boston, Manning & Loring, 1799. 31 pp.
AAS copy. 36699

Weld, Ezra, 1736-1816.
A Funeral Address.
Boston, Hall, 1798. 14 pp.
BA copy. 34997

Weld, Ezra, 1736-1816.
A Sermon, Delivered October 17, 1792.
Windham, Byrne, 1793. 35 pp.
AAS copy. 26456

Weld, Ezra, 1736-1816.
A Sermon, on Christian Union.
Boston, Weld & Greenough, 1794. 30 pp.
AAS copy. 28059

Weld, Ezra, 1736-1816.
A Sermon, Preached at a Singing Lecture.
Springfield, Weld, 1789. 28 pp.
AAS copy. 22264

Weld, Ezra, 1736-1816.
(Weis, Colonial Clergy N. E.)
A Sermon, Preached at the Ordination of
. . . Samuel Niles.
Boston, Thomas, 1772. 48 pp.
AAS copy. 12610

Weld, Ezra, 1736-1816.
A Sermon, Preached September 23, 1772.
Boston, Russell, [1772]. 37 pp.
AAS copy. 12611

W[elfare], M[ichael]
The Naked Truth.
[Philadelphia], 1729. 11 pp.
HSP facsim. copy. 39934

[Weller, Samuel], of Maidstone, Eng.
The Trial of Mr. Whitefield's Spirit.
Boston, Fleet, 1741. 46 pp.
AAS copy. 4837

Welles, Arnold, 1761-1827.
An Address, to the Members of the
Massachusetts Charitable Fire Society . . .
June 2, 1797.
Boston, Etheridge, 1797. 26, [1] pp.
AAS copy. 33195

[Welles, Noah?], 1718-1776.
(Weis, Colonial Clergy N. E.)
Animadversions, Critical and Candid.
New York, Mecom, 1763. 22, [1] pp.
AAS copy. 9534

Welles, Noah, 1718-1776.
(Weis, Colonial Clergy N. E.)
A Discourse Delivered at Fairfield.
New York, Holt, 1774. 27 pp.
AAS copy. 13759

Welles, Noah, 1718-1776.
The Divine Right of Presbyterian
Ordination.
New York, Holt, 1763. 78 pp.
AAS copy. 9535

Welles, Noah, 1718-1776.
(D. A. B.)
Patriotism Described.
New London, Green, 1764. 30 pp.
AAS copy. 9866

[Welles, Noah], 1718-1776.
(D. A. B.)
The Real Advantages which Ministers and
People may Enjoy.
[New Haven], 1762. 47 pp.
AAS copy. 9302

Welles, Noah, 1718-1776.
(Weis, Colonial Clergy N. E.)
A Vindication of . . . Presbyterian
Ordination.
New Haven, 1767. 159 pp.
AAS copy. 10800

Welles, Noah, 1718-1776.
A Vindication of . . . Presbyterian
Ordination.
Litchfield, Ct., Collier, [1796]. 189 pp.
AAS copy. 31609

Wells, Amos.
The Equal Rights of Man.
Norwich, [Ct.], Sterry, 1800. 13 pp.
AAS copy. 39067

Wells, Elizabeth, fl. 1793.
Some Melancholy and Heart-felt
Reflections.
[Newport, 1793.] Broadside.
RIHS copy. 26457

Wells, John, 1770-1823.
An Oration, Delivered on the Fourth of
July, 1798.
New York, M'Lean & Lang, 1798. 22 pp.
AAS copy. 34998

[Wells, Richard.]
(See Sabin 102599.)
A Few Political Reflections Submitted to
the Consideration of the British Colonies.
Philadelphia, Dunlap, 1774. 86 pp.
LCP copy. 13760

[Wells, Richard.]
(See Sabin 102599.)
The Middle Line.
Philadelphia, Crukshank, 1775. 48 pp.
LOC copy. 14616

Wells, Robert, 1728?-1794.
Charlestown, February 3d, 1768. The Sale
of Negroes. . . .
[Charleston, 1768.] Broadside.
AAS copy. 41896

[Wells, Robert], 1728?-1794.
The Story of Aeneas and Dido
Burlesqued.
Charleston, 1774. xvi, 94 pp.
(See Sabin 92337.)
NYPL copy. 13743

[Wells, Robert], 1728?-1794.
The Story of Aeneas and Dido
Burlesqued.
Philadelphia, 1774.]
("To be sold," Dunlap's Pa. Packet, Mar.
21, 1774.) 13744

[Wells, William, 1744-1827.
A Sermon, Delivered at Putney.
Putney, Vt., Sturtevant, [1797]. 12 pp.]
(A ghost of 34999 arising from a
prospectus.) 33196

Wells, William, 1744-1827.
A Sermon, Delivered at Putney.
Putney, Vt., Sturtevant, [1798]. 12 pp.
AAS copy. 34999

[Wells, William, 1744-1827.
A Sermon, Delivered by the Rev. William
Wells, at the Interment of Mrs. Pardon
Taylor and Edward Palmer.
Putney, Vt., Sturtevant, 1797.]
(Apparently a ghost of 35000.) 33197

Wells, William, 1744-1827.
A Sermon, Preached at Brattleborough.
Brattleborough, 1798. 20 pp.
AAS copy. 35000

Wells's Register together with an
Almanack . . . by George Andrews . . . for
. . . 1769.
Charleston, Wells. [66] pp.
AAS copy. 11111

[Wells's Register of the Southern British
American Colonies for . . . 1770.
Charleston, Wells.]
(Assumed from the sequence.) 11523

[Wells's Register of the Southern British
American Colonies for . . . 1771.
Charleston, Wells.]
(Assumed by Evans from the sequence.) 11930

[Wells's Register of the Southern British
American Colonies for . . . 1772.
Charleston, Wells.]
(Assumed by Evans from the sequence.) 12279

[Wells's Register of the Southern British
American Colonies for . . . 1773.
Charleston, Wells.]
(Assumed by Evans from the sequence.) 12612

Wells's Register: together with an
Almanack . . . for . . . 1774.
Charlestown, [S. C.], Wells. 96 pp.
(The only copy located is imperfect.)
SCHS copy. 13072

Wells's Register: Together with an
Almanack . . . for . . . 1775. . . . The
Thirteenth Edition.
Charleston, Wells. [2], 140 pp.
AAS copy. 13761

[Wells's Register of the Southern British
American Colonies for . . . 1776.
Charleston, Wells.]
(Assumed by Evans from the sequence.) 14617

Welsh, Thomas, 1751-1831.
(Burrage, Mass. Med. Soc., 32-33.)
An Oration, Delivered March 5th, 1783.
Boston, Gill, [1783]. 18 pp.
AAS copy. 18302

Welsh Society of Pennsylvania.
Constitution and Rules of the. . . .
Mount Holly, Ustick, 1799. 12 pp.
HSP copy. 36072

Welsteed, William, 1696-1753.
(Sibley, VI, 153-158.)

The Dignity and Duty.
Boston, Kneeland, 1751. [4], 59 pp.
AAS copy.   6793

[Welton, Richard, 1671?-1726.
(D. N. B.)
The Farewell Sermon.
Philadelphia, 1726.]
(Adv. Am. Weekly Mercury, Feb. 15,
1726.)   2826

Welwood, Andrew.
Meditations.
Boston, Rogers & Fowle for McAlpine,
1744. 279, [4] pp.
AAS copy.   5510

Wenham, Mass.
The Price Act. . . . March 14, 1777.
Danvers, [1777]. Broadside.
EI copy.   15704

Werden, Peter, 1728-1808.
Letters to a Friend.
Lansingburgh, N. Y., Wands, 1796. 64 pp.
AAS copy.   31610

Werter and Charlotte [by Johann
Wolfgang von Goethe, 1749-1832].
Boston, Thomas & Andrews, 1798. 284 pp.
AAS copy.   33803

Werter to Charlotte. A Poem [by Edward
Taylor, 1741?-1797].
[Philadelphia], Story, 1787. 40 pp.
AAS copy.   20741

Wesley, Charles, 1707-1788.
An Elegy on the late . . . George
Whitefield.
Philadelphia, Johnston & Justice for
Glendinning, 1792. 16 pp.
AAS copy.   26458

Wesley, Charles, 1707-1788.
An Epistle to the Reverend Mr. George
Whitefield.
Baltimore, Adams, 1790. 7 pp.
NYPL copy.   23064

Wesley, Charles, 1707-1788.
An Epistle to the Reverend Mr. George
Whitefield.
Philadelphia, Johnston & Justice, 1793.
6 pp.
AAS copy.   26459

[Wesley, Charles], 1707-1788.
A Funeral Hymn, Composed by . . .
George Whitefield. . . . Ah! Lovely
Appearance of Death!
n. p., [1770?] Broadside.
AAS copy.   42186

[Wesley, Charles], 1707-1788.
A Funeral Hymn, Composed by . . .
George Whitefield. . . . Ah! Lovely
Appearance of Death!
[Boston], Green & Russell, [1770?].
Broadside.
NHHS copy.   42187

[Wesley, Charles], 1707-1788.
A Funeral Hymn, Composed by . . .
George Whitefield. . . . Ah! Lovely
Appearance of Death!
Portsmouth, Fowles, [1770]. Broadside.
NHHS copy.   42188

[Wesley, Charles], 1707-1788.
A Hymn, Composed by the Reverend Mr.
Whitefield, to be Sung over his own
Corps. Taken from the Original, May 1,
1764.
n. p., [1770]. Broadside.
HSP copy.   42190

[Wesley, Charles], 1707-1788.
Hymns for those that Seek.
Philadelphia, Steiner, 1781. 65, [2] pp.
HSP copy.   17425

Wesley, Charles, 1707-1788.
A Sermon Preached . . . April 4, 1742. . . .
Nineteenth Edition.
Wilmington, [Del.], Adams, 1770. 12 pp.
HEH copy.   42191

Wesley, Charles, 1707-1788.
To the Reverend Mr. George
Whitefield. . . . A Poem.
Boston, [1774?] Broadside.
Bostonian Society copy.   42048

Wesley, John, 1703-1791.
The Character of a Methodist.
Philadelphia, Johnston & Justice for
Glendinning, 1793. 12 pp.
AAS copy.   26460

[Wesley, John], 1703-1791.
A Collection of Psalms and Hymns.
Charleston, 1737. 73 pp.
NYPL copy.   4207

Wesley, John, 1703-1791.
A Collection of Psalms and Hymns.
Philadelphia, Steiner, 1781. 144, [4] pp.
HSP copy.   17427

Wesley, John, 1703-1791.
A Dialogue between a Predestinarian and
his Friend. . . . Fourth Edition.
New Haven, 1770. 12 pp.
AAS copy.   11931

Wesley, John, 1703-1791.
A Dialogue between a Predestinarian and
his Friend. . . . Fifth Edition.
Newport, Southwick, 1774. 15 pp.
AAS copy.   42749

Wesley, John, 1703-1791.
A Dialogue, between a Predestinarian,
and his Friend.
Boston, MDVIIXCVI (1796). 11 pp.
NYPL copy.   31611

Wesley, John, 1703-1791.
Explanatory Notes upon the New
Testament. . . . Volume the First. . . .
First American Edition.
Philadelphia, Crukshank for Dickins,
1791. 416 pp.
AAS copy.   23976

Wesley, John, 1703-1791.
Explanatory Notes upon the New
Testament. . . . Volume the Second.
Philadelphia, Cist for Dickins, 1791. 348
pp.
HEH copy.   46352

Wesley, John, 1703-1791.
Explanatory Notes upon the New
Testament. . . . Volume the Third.
Philadelphia, Prichard & Hall for Dickins,
1791. 342, [4] pp.
(Best copy available.)
NYPL copy.   46353

[Wesley, John], 1703-1791.
Explanatory Notes upon the New
Testament. . . . Volume the Second [
Third]. The First American Edition.
Philadelphia, Crukshank, 1792.]
(Imprint assumed by Evans from an adv.,
probably for 1791 ed.)   25011

Wesley, John, 1703-1791.
An Extract of the Rev. Mr. John Wesley's
Journals. Volume I.
Philadelphia, Tuckniss for Dickins, 1795.
[2], 316, [2] pp.
AAS copy.   29861

Wesley, John, 1703-1791.
The Extraordinary Case of Elizabeth
Hobson.
Philadelphia, Johnston & Justice for
Glendinning, 1792. 17 pp.
AAS copy.   25012

Wesley, John, 1703-1791.
Free Grace.
Boston, Fleet, 1741. 32 pp.
BPL copy.   4840

[Wesley, John, 1703-1791.
Free Grace.
Philadelphia, Franklin, 1741. 32 pp.]
(Adv. Pa. Gazette, Oct. 29, 1741.)   4839

Wesley, John, 1703-1791.
Free Grace.
Philadelphia, Pleadwell, 1740/1. 32 pp.
HSP copy.   4838

Wesley, John, 1703-1791.
Hymns and Sacred Poems.
Philadelphia, Bradford, 1740. vii, [5], 237
pp.
HSP copy.   4624

Wesley, John, 1703-1791.
[Hymns and Spiritual Songs. . . . Fourth
Edition.

Philadelphia, 1756.] [4] pp.
(The only known copy is imperfect.)
HC copy.   40868

Wesley, John, 1703-1791.
Hymns and Spiritual Songs. . . .
Fourteenth Edition.
Philadelphia, Dunlap, 1770. 132, [4], 4 pp.
HSP copy.   42192

[Wesley, John], 1703-1791.
Hymns and Spiritual Songs.
Philadelphia, Steiner, 1770. iv, 132, [4]
pp.]
(No such ed. located.)   42193

Wesley, John, 1703-1791.
Hymns and Spiritual Songs.
Philadelphia, Steiner, 1781. 136, [4] pp.
HSP copy.   17426

Wesley, John, 1703-1791.
Hymns for the Nativity.
Philadelphia, Dunlap, 1769. 24 pp.
HSP copy.   42024

Wesley, John, 1703-1791.
A Most Tragical Series of Remarkable
Judgments.
Exeter, Ranlet, 1795. 12 pp.
NYHS copy.   29862

Wesley, John, 1703-1791.
(D. N. B.)
Primitive Physick. . . . Twelfth Edition.
Philadelphia, Steuart, 1764. 80, [8] pp.
AML copy.   9867

[Wesley, John, 1703-1791.
Primitive Physick. . . . Thirteenth Edition.
New York, 1769.]
("Just Published, And Sold at the
Printing-Office," N. Y. Journal, Apr. 27,
1769.)   11524

Wesley, John, 1703-1791.
Primative Physick. . . . Fourteenth
Edition.
Philadelphia, Crukshank, 1770. 83, [2] pp.
AML copy.   11932

[Wesley, John], 1703-1791.
Primitive Physic.
Philadelphia, Crukshank, 1773.]
(Adv. Pa. Journal, Aug. 14, 1773.)   13073

[Wesley, John], 1703-1791.
Primitive Physic.
Philadelphia, Crukshank, 1788.]
(Entry from adv. for "American editions"
in 21164.)   21588

Wesley, John, 1703-1791.
Primative Physic. . . . Sixteenth Edition.
Trenton, 1788. 125 pp.
AAS copy.   21589

Wesley, John, 1703-1791.
Primitive Physic.
Philadelphia, Prichard & Hall for Dickins,
1789. 196 pp.
AAS copy.   22265

Wesley, John, 1703-1791.
Primitive Physic. . . . Twenty-Second
Edition.
Philadelphia, Hall for Dickins, 1791. 191
pp.
AAS copy.   23977

Wesley, John, 1703-1791.
Reasons against a Separation.
[London, 1791.] 8 pp.
NYPL copy.   23978

Wesley, John, 1703-1791.
The Saints' Everlasting Rest. . . .
Extracted from the Works of Mr. Richard
Baxter, by. . . .
Philadelphia, Tuckniss, 1800. 399, [1] pp.
(Also entered as 36910, q. v.)   39069

[Wesley, John], 1703-1791.
The Scripture Doctrine Concerning
Predestination.
Boston, Fleet, 1746. 16 pp.
MHS copy.   5881

[Wesley, John], 1703-1791.
The Scripture Doctrine of Predestination,
Election, and Reprobation.
Stockbridge, Andrews, 1795. 25 pp.
JCB copy.   29479

[Wesley, John], 1703-1791.
Serious Consideration on Absolute
Predestination.
Boston, Fleet, 1743. 24 pp.
AAS copy.　　　　　　　　　　5310

Wesley, John, 1703-1791.
A Sermon on the Death of . . . George
Whitfield.
Boston, Fleeming, 1771. 24 pp.
AAS copy.　　　　　　　　　　12280

Wesley, John, 1703-1791.
A Sermon on the Death of . . . Whitefield.
New York, Holt, 1771. 28 pp.
AAS copy.　　　　　　　　　　42300

Wesley, John, 1703-1791.
A Sermon Preached on the Occasion of
the Death of . . . John Fletcher.
Springfield, Mass., Stebbins, 1797. 16 pp.
AAS copy.　　　　　　　　　　33198

Wesley, John, 1703-1791.
Sermons on Several Occasions. . . . Vol. I
[-II].
Philadelphia, Crukshank for Dickins,
1794. [4], 291; 296, [3] pp.
(The imprint given by Evans is that of
Vol. II.)
AAS copy.　　　　　　　　　　28060

Wesley, John, 1703-1791.
Sermons on Several Occasions. . . . Vol.
III.
Philadelphia, Tuckniss, 1800. 263, [1] pp.
AAS copy.　　　　　　　　　　39068

Wesley, John, 1703-1791.
A Short Account of the Life and Death of
. . . John Fletcher.
New York, Durell, 1795. 225 pp.
AAS copy.　　　　　　　　　　29863

Wesley, John, 1703-1791.
Thoughts upon Slavery.
Philadelphia, Crukshank, 1774. 83 pp.
AAS copy.　　　　　　　　　　13762

Wesley, John, 1703-1791.
Thoughts upon Slavery.
Philadelphia, Story, 1784. 87 pp.
(No copy located.)　　　　　　　44630

[Wesley, John, 1703-1791.
Thoughts upon Slavery.
Philadelphia, Hall for Dickins, 1792.]
(Imprint assumed by Evans from an adv.)
　　　　　　　　　　　　　　25014

Wesley, John, 1703-1791.
The Works of. . . . Volume I.
Philadelphia, Steiner, 1783. pp. [v]-296,
[4].
AAS copy.　　　　　　　　　　44496

Wesley, John, 1703-1791.
The Works of. . . . Volume III.
Philadelphia, Steiner, 1783. 296, [4] pp.
LCP copy.　　　　　　　　　　44497

West, Benjamin, 1730-1813.
　West contributed to a greater or less
degree to some 200 almanacs, and some of
these were plagiarized. Here are entered
under his name those which bear it, and
the anonymous editions traditionally
attributed to him. All anonymous editions
are entered under title also.

West, Benjamin, 1730-1813.
An Account of the Observation of Venus.
Providence, 1769. [6], 22 pp.
AAS copy.　　　　　　　　　　11525

West, Benjamin, 1730-1813.
(D. A. B.)
An Almanack, for the Year . . . 1763.
Providence, Goddard. [24] pp.
AAS copy.　　　　　　　　　　9303

[West, Benjamin], 1730-1813.
An Almanack, for . . . 1784. . . . By Isaac
Bickerstaff.
Springfield, Babcock. [24] pp.
AAS copy.　　　　　　　　　　18303

[West, Benjamin], 1730-1813.
An Almanack, for . . . 1786. . . . By Isaac
Bickerstaff.
Hartford, Patten. [24] pp.
AAS copy.　　　　　　　　　　19369

[West, Benjamin], 1730-1813.
An Almanack, for . . . 1786. . . . By Isaac
Bickerstaff.
Springfield, Stebbens & Russell. [24] pp.
AAS copy.　　　　　　　　　　19370

[West, Benjamin, 1730-1813.
An Almanack, for . . . 1787.
Hartford, Patten.]
(A duplicate of 20132, q. v.)　　　20133

[West, Benjamin], 1730-1813.
An Almanack, for the Year . . . 1787. . . .
By Isaac Bickerstaff.
Hartford, Patten. [24] pp.
AAS copy.　　　　　　　　　　20132

[West, Benjamin], 1730-1813.
An Almanack, for . . . 1795. . . . By Isaac
Bickerstaff.
Boston, Hall. [24] pp.
AAS copy.　　　　　　　　　　28061

[West, Benjamin], 1730-1813.
An Almanack, for . . . 1796. . . . By Isaac
Bickerstaff.
Boston, Etheridge for Blake. [24] pp.
AAS copy.　　　　　　　　　　29864

[West, Benjamin], 1730-1813.
An Astronomical Diary, Kalender, or
Almanack, for . . . 1788. . . . By Isaac
Bickerstaff.
Hartford, Hudson & Goodwin. [24] pp.
AAS copy.　　　　　　　　　　20874

[West, Benjamin], 1730-1813.
An Astronomical Diary, Kalender, or
Almanack, for . . . 1789. . . . By Isaac
Bickerstaff.
Hartford, Patten. [24] pp.
AAS copy.　　　　　　　　　　21590

[West, Benjamin], 1730-1813.
An Astronomical Diary, Kalendar, or
Almanack, for . . . 1790. . . . By Isaac
Bickerstaff.
Hartford, Patten. [24] pp.
AAS copy.　　　　　　　　　　22266

[West, Benjamin], 1730-1813.
An Astronomical Diary, Kalendar, or
Almanack, for . . . 1791. . . . By Isaac
Bickerstaff.
Hartford, Patten. [24] pp.
(The AAS has variant issues.)
AAS copy.　　　　　　　　　　23065

[West, Benjamin], 1730-1813.
An Astronomical Diary, Kalendar, or
Almanack, for . . . 1793. . . . By Isaac
Bickerstaff.
Hartford, Patten. [24] pp.
AAS copy.　　　　　　　　　　25015

[West, Benjamin], 1730-1813.
An Astronomical Diary, or Almanck, for
. . . 1785. . . . By Isaac Bickerstaff.
Hartford, Barlow & Babcock. [24] pp.
AAS copy.　　　　　　　　　　18873

[West, Benjamin], 1730-1813.
An Astronomical Diary: or, an
Almanack, for . . . 1785. . . . By Isaac
Bickerstaff.
Springfield, Brooks & Russel. [24] pp.
AAS copy.　　　　　　　　　　18874

[West, Benjamin], 1730-1813.
An Astronomical Diary: or Almanack, for
. . . 1795. . . . By Isaac Bickerstaff.
Hartford, Babcock. [24] pp.
AAS copy.　　　　　　　　　　28062

[West, Benjamin], 1730-1813.
An Astronomical Diary: or Almanack, for
. . . 1796. . . . By Isaac Bickerstaff.
Boston, B. Larkin, etc., Bumstead's
Edition. [24] pp.
AAS copy.　　　　　　　　　　29865

[West, Benjamin], 1730-1813.
An Astronomical Diary: or Almanack, for
. . . 1797. . . . By Isaac Bickerstaff.
Boston, Boyle, etc. [24] pp.
AAS copy.　　　　　　　　　　31613

[West, Benjamin], 1730-1813.
An Astronomical Diary or Almanack, for
. . . 1797. . . . By Isaac Bickerstaff.

Dover, N. H. [24] pp.
AAS copy.　　　　　　　　　　31612

[West, Benjamin], 1730-1813.
Bickerstaff, Isaac, pseud.
An Astronomical Diary, Kalendar, or
Almanack, for . . . 1790.
Hartford, [Ct.], Babcock. [24] pp.
AAS copy.　　　　　　　　　　45431

[West, Benjamin], 1730-1813.
Bickerstaff's Almanack, for . . . 1788.
Norwich, Trumbull. [24] pp.
AAS copy.　　　　　　　　　　20875

[West, Benjamin], 1730-1813.
Bickerstaff's Almanack, for . . . 1789.
Boston, Freeman. [24] pp.
(The only copy located lacks a leaf.)
AAS copy.　　　　　　　　　　21591

[West, Benjamin], 1730-1813.
Bickerstaff's Boston Almanack, for . . .
1768.
Boston, Mein & Fleeming. [44] pp.
AAS copy.　　　　　　　　　　10801

[West, Benjamin], 1730-1813.
Bickerstaff's Boston Almanack, for . . .
1769.
Boston, Mein & Fleeming. [44] pp.
AAS copy.　　　　　　　　　　11112

[West, Benjamin], 1730-1813.
Bickerstaff's Boston Almanack, for . . .
1769. . . . Second Edition.
Boston, Mein & Fleeming. [44] pp.
AAS copy.　　　　　　　　　　41898

[West, Benjamin], 1730-1813.
Bickerstaff's Boston Almanack. For . . .
1773.
Boston, Fleeming. [40] pp.
AAS copy.　　　　　　　　　　12613

[West, Benjamin], 1730-1813.
Bickerstaff's Boston Almanack, for . . .
1774.
Boston, Mills & Hicks. Front., 32 pp.
AAS copy.　　　　　　　　　　13074

[West, Benjamin], 1730-1813.
Bickerstaff's Boston Almanack, for . . .
1775.
Boston, Mills & Hicks. 32 pp.
AAS copy.　　　　　　　　　　13763

West, Benjamin, 1730-1813.
Bickerstaff's Boston Almanack, for . . .
1778.
Danvers, Russell. [24] pp.
AAS copy.　　　　　　　　　　15705

West, Benjamin, 1730-1813.
Bickerstaff's Boston Almanack, for . . .
1779.
Danvers, Russell. [24] pp.
AAS copy.　　　　　　　　　　16166

[West, Benjamin], 1730-1813.
Bickerstaff's Boston Almanack, for . . .
1782.
Boston, Russell. [24] pp.
NYPL copy.　　　　　　　　　17428

[West, Benjamin], 1730-1813.
Bickerstaff's Boston Almanack, for . . .
1783.
Boston, Russell. [24] pp.
AAS copy.　　　　　　　　　　17792

[West, Benjamin], 1730-1813.
Second Edition. Bickerstaff's Boston
Almanack, for . . . 1783.
Boston, Russell. [24] pp.
AAS copy.　　　　　　　　　　19445

[West, Benjamin], 1730-1813.
Bickerstaff's Boston Almanack, for . . .
1783.
Boston, Russell. [24] pp.
AAS copy.　　　　　　　　　　17792

[West, Benjamin], 1730-1813.
Bickerstaff's Boston Almanack, for . . .
1784.
Boston, Russell and Adams & Nourse,
1784. [24] pp.
AAS copy.　　　　　　　　　　18304

[West, Benjamin], 1730-1813.
Bickerstaff's Boston Almanack, for . . .
1785.
Boston, Folsom. [24] pp.
AAS copy.   18875

[West, Benjamin], 1730-1813.
Bickerstaff's Boston Almanack, for . . .
1785.
Boston, Russell and Vicker. [24] pp.
AAS copy.   18876

[West, Benjamin], 1730-1813.
Bickerstaff's Boston Almanack, for . . .
1785. . . . Second Edition.
Boston, Russell. [24] pp.
(The only reported copy of this ed. is
incomplete.)
AAS copy.   18877

[West, Benjamin], 1730-1813.
Bickerstaff's Boston Almanack for . . .
1785. . . . Third Edition.
Boston, Russell. [20] pp.
AAS copy.   18878

[West, Benjamin], 1730-1813.
Bickerstaff's Boston Almanack for . . .
1788.
Newburyport, Mycall. [24] pp.
AAS copy.   20876

[West, Benjamin], 1730-1813.
Bickerstaff's Boston Almanack . . . for
1789.
Boston, Russell. [24] pp.
AAS copy.   21592

[West, Benjamin], 1730-1813.
Bickerstaff's Boston Almanack, for . . .
1790.
Boston, for the booksellers. [20] pp.
AAS copy.   22267

[West, Benjamin], 1730-1813.
Bickerstaff's Boston Almanack . . . for . . .
1788. . . . Fourth Edition.
Boston, Russell. [24] pp.
AAS copy.   45040

[West, Benjamin], 1730-1813.
Bickerstaff's Boston Almanack, or the
Federal Calendar, for . . . 1788.
Boston, Russell. [24] pp.
LOC copy.   20877

[West, Benjamin, 1730-1813.
Bickerstaff's Boston Almanack, or the
Federal Calendar, for . . . 1788. . . .
Second Editon.
Boston, Russell. [24] pp.]
(Assumed from the sequence of editions.)
        20878

[West, Benjamin], 1730-1813.
Bickerstaff's Boston Almanack, or, the
Federal Calendar, for . . . 1788. . . . Third
Edition.
Boston, Russell. [24] pp.
AAS copy.   20879

[West, Benjamin], 1730-1813.
Bickerstaff's Boston Almanack, or,
Federal Calendar, for 1790.
[Boston], Russell. [24] pp.
AAS copy.   22268

[West, Benjamin], 1730-1813.
Bickerstaff's Boston Almanack, or
Federal Callender, for 1790. . . . Second
Edition.
[Boston], Russell. [24] pp.]
(Evans assumed a 2nd ed. from the fact
that there was a 3rd; it may not have been
so marked.)   22269

[West, Benjamin], 1730-1813.
Bickerstaff's Boston Almanack, or
Federal Calendar, for 1790. . . . Third
Edition.
[Boston], Russell. [24] pp.
AAS copy.   22270

[West, Benjamin], 1730-1813.
Bickerstaff's Boston Almanack . . . for
1791.
[Boston], Russell. [24] pp.
AAS copy.   23066

[West, Benjamin], 1730-1813.
Bickerstaff's Connecticut Almanack, for
. . . 1791.

Norwich, Trumbull. [24] pp.
AAS copy.   23068

[West, Benjamin], 1730-1813.
Bickerstaff's Genuine Almanack, for . . .
1787.
Boston, Cambridge. [24] pp.
AAS copy.   20134

[West, Benjamin], 1730-1813.
Bickerstaff's Genuine Almanack for . . .
1789.
Norwich, Trumbull. [24] pp.
AAS copy.   21593

[West, Benjamin], 1730-1813.
Bickerstaff's Genuine Almanack, for . . .
1791.
Boston, Bumstead. [24] pp.
AAS copy.   23069

[West, Benjamin], 1730-1813.
Bickerstaff's Genuine Almanack, for . . .
1792.
Boston: Printed for and Sold by the
Booksellers. [24] pp.
AAS copy.   23979

[West, Benjamin, 1730-1813.
Bickerstaff's Genuine Almanack for . . .
1792.
Boston: Printed and sold by the
Shop-keepers in Town and Country.]
(Evans' entry from an adv. There are two
issues which he does not list, but they do
not have this imprint.)   23980

[West, Benjamin], 1730-1813.
Bickerstaff's Genuine Almanack, for . . .
1796.
Boston, White. [24] pp.
(The only copy recorded lacks two leaves
at the end.)
AAS copy.   29866

[West, Benjamin, 1730-1813.
Bickerstaff's Genuine Almanack, for . . .
1797.
Boston, White. [24] pp.]
(Assumed by Evans from the sequence.)
        31615

[West, Benjamin], 1730-1813.
Bickerstaff's Genuine Almanack, for . . .
1798.
Boston, Russell. [24] pp.
AAS copy.   33199

[West, Benjamin], 1730-1813.
Bickerstaff's Genuine Almanack, for . . .
1798.
Boston, White. [24] pp.
AAS copy.   33200

[West, Benjamin, 1730-1813.
Bickerstaff's Genuine and Correct
Almanack, for . . . 1787.
Boston, Russell.]
(Entry from an adv. in the Independent
Chronicle, Nov. 16, 1786, apparently for
copies of 20136, q. v.)   20135

[West, Benjamin], 1730-1813.
Bickerstaff's Genuine Boston Almanack,
for . . . 1786.
Boston, Russell, [1785]. [24] pp.
AAS copy.   19372

[West, Benjamin], 1730-1813.
Bickerstaff's Genuine Boston Almanack
. . . for 1791.
[Boston], Russell. [24] pp.
AAS copy.   45832

[West, Benjamin], 1730-1813.
Bickerstaff's Genuine Boston Almanack
. . . for 1791. . . . Third Edition.
[Boston], Russell. [24] pp.
AAS copy.   45883

[West, Benjamin], 1730-1813.
Bickerstaff's Genuine Boston Almanack
. . . for 1791. . . . Sixth Edition.
[Boston], Russell. [24] pp.
AAS copy.   23067

[West, Benjamin], 1730-1813.
Bickerstaff's Genuine Boston Almanack,
or, Federal Calendar, for 1792.
[Boston], Russell. [24] pp.
AAS copy.   23982

[West, Benjamin], 1730-1813.

Bickerstaff's Genuine Boston Almanack,
or, Federal Calendar for . . . 1792. . . .
Second Edition.
[Boston], Russell. [24] pp.
AAS copy.   23983

[West, Benjamin], 1730-1813.
Bickerstaff's Genuine Boston Almanack
. . . for 1793.
[Boston], Russell. [24] pp.
AAS copy.   25016

[West, Benjamin], 1730-1813.
Bickerstaff's Genuine Boston Almanack
. . . for 1793. . . . Second Edition.
[Boston], Russell. [24] pp.
(The only copy located is imperfect.)
NYPL copy.   25017

[West, Benjamin], 1730-1813.
Bickerstaff's Genuine Massachusetts,
New-Hampshire, Vermont, Rhode-Island,
and Connecticutt Almanack, for . . . 1792.
Boston, Covely (sic.), 1792. [24] pp.
AAS copy.   23984

[West, Benjamin], 1730-1813.
Bickerstaff's Genuine Massachusetts,
New-Hampshire, Vermont, Rhode-Island,
and Connecticutt Almanack, for . . . 1792.
Boston, Coverly, 1792. [24] pp.
LOC copy.   23985

[West, Benjamin], 1730-1813.
Bickerstaff's Genuine Massachusetts,
New-Hampshire, Vermont, Rhode-Island,
and Connecticut Almanack, for . . . 1793.
Boston, Coverly.]
(Assumed by Evans as a continuation of
23985.)   25018

[West, Benjamin], 1730-1813.
Bickerstaff's Genuine Massachusetts,
Rhodeisland and Connecticut Almanack,
for . . . 1791.
Boston, for the Booksellers. [24] pp.
(The AAS has two variant issues.)
AAS copy.   23070

[West, Benjamin, 1730-1813.
Bickerstaff's Genuine Massachusetts,
Rhode-Island, and Connecticut Almanack
. . . for 1795.
Boston, Coverly?]
(Although this title was adv. it is
apparently a ghost of one of the other
Bickerstaffs.)   28064

[West, Benjamin], 1730-1813.
Bickerstaff's Improved Almanack, for . . .
1785.
Norwich, Trumbull. [24] pp.
AAS copy.   18879

[West, Benjamin], 1730-1813.
Bickerstaff's Improved: being an
Almanack, for . . . 1790.
Norwich, Trumbull. [24] pp.
AAS copy.   22271

[West, Benjamin], 1730-1813.
Bickerstaff's Massachusetts, Connecticut,
Rhodeisland, Newhampshire and
Vermont Almanack, for . . . 1799.
Salem, Coverly. [24] pp.
AAS copy.   35001

[West, Benjamin], 1730-1813.
Bickerstaff's New-England Almanack, for
. . . 1776.
Norwich, Robertsons & Trumbull. [24]
pp.
AAS copy.   14618

[West, Benjamin], 1730-1813.
Bickerstaff's New-England Almanack, for
. . . 1777.
Norwich, Trumbull, [1776]. [24] pp.
AAS copy.   15215

[West, Benjamin], 1730-1813.
Bickerstaff's New-England Almanack, for
. . . 1778.
Norwich, Trumbull. [24] pp.
AAS copy.   15706

[West, Benjamin], 1730-1813.
Bickerstaff's New-England Almanack, for
. . . 1779.
Norwich, Trumbull. [24] pp.
AAS copy.   16167

[West, Benjamin], 1730-1813.

Bickerstaff's New-England Almanack, for
. . . 1780.
Norwich, Trumbull. [22] pp.
AAS copy. 16672

[West, Benjamin], 1730-1813.
Bickerstaff's New-England Almanack, for
. . . 1781.
Norwich, Trumbull. [24] pp.
AAS copy. 17067

[West, Benjamin], 1730-1813.
Bickerstaff's New-England Almanack . . .
for . . . 1781. . . . By Isaac Bickerstaff.
Providence, Carter. [32] pp.
AAS copy. 19446

[West, Benjamin], 1730-1813.
Bickerstaff's New-England Almanack, for
. . . 1782.
Hartford, Patten. [24] pp.
CHS copy. 17429

[West, Benjamin], 1730-1813.
Bickerstaff's New-England Almanack, for
. . . 1782.
Norwich, Trumbull. [22] pp.
AAS copy. 17430

[West, Benjamin], 1730-1813.
Bickerstaff's New-England Almanack, for
. . . 1783.
Hartford, Patten.]
(Assumed from the sequence.) 17794

[West, Benjamin], 1730-1813.
Bickerstaff's New-England Almanack, for
. . . 1783.
Norwich, Trumbull. [28] pp.
AAS copy. 17793

[West, Benjamin], 1730-1813.
Bickerstaff's New-England Almanack, for
. . . 1784.
Norwich, Trumbull. [32] pp.
AAS copy. 18305

[West, Benjamin], 1730-1813.
Bickerstaff's New-England Almanack, for
. . . 1785.
Hartford, Patten. [24] pp.
AAS copy. 44513

[West, Benjamin], 1730-1813.
The New-England Almanack, for 1786,
[by Isaac Bickerstaff, pseud.]
Hartford, Elisha Babcock. [24] pp.
CHS copy. 44651

[West, Benjamin], 1730-1813.
The New-England Almanack . . . for . . .
1786. . . . [by Isaac Bickerstaff, pseud.]
Hartford, Barlow & Babcock. [24] pp.
AAS copy. 44650

[West, Benjamin], 1730-1813.
Bickerstaff's New-England Almanack, for
. . . 1786.
Norwich, Trumbull. [24] pp.
AAS copy. 19373

[West, Benjamin], 1730-1813.
Bickerstaff's New-England Almanack, for
. . . 1787.
Norwich, Trumbull. [28] pp.
(The AAS has two issues.)
AAS copy. 20137

[West, Benjamin], 1730-1813.
Bickerstaff's New-England Almanack, for
. . . 1792.
Norwich, Trumbull. [20] pp.
AAS copy. 23986

[West, Benjamin], 1730-1813.
Bickerstaff's New-England Almanack, for
. . . 1793.
Norwich, Trumbull. [24] pp.
AAS copy. 25024

[West, Benjamin], 1730-1813.
Bickerstaff's New-England Almanack for
. . . 1794.
Norwich, Trumbull. [24] pp.
AAS copy. 26461

[West, Benjamin], 1730-1813.
Bickerstaff's New-England Almanack, for
. . . 1796.
Springfield, Gray. [24] pp.
(The only copy located is badly defective.)
AAS copy. 29867

[West, Benjamin], 1730-1813.
Bickerstaff's New-York Almanack, for . . .
1778.
Norwich, Trumbull for Loudon at
Fishkill. [24] pp.
LOC copy. 15707

[West, Benjamin], 1730-1813.
Bickerstaff's New-York Almanack, for . . .
1779.
New York, Mills & Hicks. [24] pp.
(Evans' entry was apparently from an adv.
for this ed.)
LOC copy. 16673

[West, Benjamin], 1730-1813.
Bickerstaff's Sheet Almanack for . . .
1794.
Norwich, 1793. Broadside.]
(Printing assumed by Evans from advs. for
sheet almanacs.) 26462

[West, Benjamin], 1730-1813.
The Federal Almanack, for . . . 1792.
Boston: Printed for and Sold by the
Booksellers. [24] pp.
AAS copy. 23981

[West, Benjamin], 1730-1813.
The Federal Almanack, for . . . 1795. . . .
By Isaac Bickerstaff.
Boston, White. [24] pp.
NYHS copy. 28065

[West, Benjamin], 1730-1813.
The Federal Almanack, for . . . 1797.
Boston, Boyle etc. [24] pp.
AAS copy. 31614

[West, Benjamin], 1730-1813.
The Massachusetts, Connecticut,
Newhampshire, Rhode-Island, and
Vermont Almanack, for . . . 1793. . . . By
Isaac Bickerstaff.
Boston, Coverly. [24] pp.
AAS copy. 25019

[West, Benjamin], 1730-1813.
The Massachusetts, Connecticut,
Newhampshire, Rhode-Island, and
Vermont Almanack, for . . . 1793. . . . By
Isaac Bickerstaff.
Boston, Coverly for Gardner. [24] pp.
AAS copy. 25020

[West, Benjamin], 1730-1813.
The Massachusetts, Connecticut,
Newhampshire, Rhode-Island, and
Vermont Almanack, for . . . 1793. . . . By
Isaac Bickerstaff.
Boston, Clapp. [24] pp.]
(No copy with this imprint could be
located.) 25021

[West, Benjamin], 1730-1813.
The Massachusetts, New-Hampshire,
Rhode-Island, Connecticut, and Vermont
Almanack, for . . . 1794. . . . By Isaac
Bickerstaff.
Boston, [Coverly]. [24] pp.
AAS copy. 26463

West, Benjamin, 1730-1813.
The New-England Almanack, for . . .
1764.
Providence, Goddard. [24] pp.
AAS copy. 9536

West, Benjamin, 1730-1813.
The New-England Almanack . . . for . . .
1765.
Providence, Goddard. [24] pp.
AAS copy. 9868

West, Benjamin, 1730-1813.
(D. A. B.)
The New-England Almanack . . . for . . .
1766.
Providence, Goddard. [24] pp.
AAS copy. 10205

West, Benjamin, 1730-1813.
The New-England Almanack . . . for . . .
1767.
Boston, Printers and Booksellers. [24] pp.
AAS copy. 41677

West, Benjamin, 1730-1813.
The New-England Almanack . . . for . . .
1767.
Providence, Goddard. [24] pp.
AAS copy. 10521

West, Benjamin, 1730-1813.
The New-England Almanack . . . for . . .
1768.
Providence, Goddard and Carter. [24] pp.
AAS copy. 10802

West, Benjamin, 1730-1813.
The New-England Almanack . . . for . . .
1769.
Boston, Mein and Fleeming for West.
[24] pp.
AAS copy. 11114

West, Benjamin, 1730-1813.
The New-England Almanack . . . for . . .
1770.
Providence, Carter. [32] pp.
AAS copy. 11527

West, Benjamin, 1730-1813.
The New-England Almanack . . . for . . .
1771.
Providence, Carter. [24] pp.
AAS copy. 11934

West, Benjamin, 1730-1813.
The New-England Almanack . . . for . . .
1772.
Newport, Campbell. [24] pp.
RIHS copy. 12283

West, Benjamin, 1730-1813.
The New-England Almanack . . . for . . .
1772.
Providence, Carter. [24] pp.
AAS copy. 12282

West, Benjamin, 1730-1813.
The New-England Almanack . . . for . . .
1773.
Providence, Carter. [32] pp.
AAS copy. 12614

West, Benjamin, 1730-1813.
The New-England Almanack . . . for . . .
1774.
Providence, Carter. [24] pp.
AAS copy. 13075

West, Benjamin, 1730-1813.
The New-England Almanack . . . for . . .
1775.
Providence, Carter. [24] pp.
AAS copy. 13764

West, Benjamin, 1730-1813.
The New-England Almanack . . . for . . .
1776.
Providence, Carter. [32] pp.
AAS copy. 14619

West, Benjamin, 1730-1813.
The New-England Almanack . . . for . . .
1777.
Providence, Carter. [24] pp.
AAS copy. 15216

West, Benjamin, 1730-1813.
The New-England Almanack . . . for . . .
1778.
Providence, Carter. [24] pp.
AAS copy. 15708

West, Benjamin, 1730-1813.
The New-England Almanack . . . for . . .
1779.
Providence, Carter. [24] pp.
AAS copy. 16168

West, Benjamin, 1730-1813.
The New-England Almanack . . . for . . .
1780.
Providence, Carter. [36] pp.
AAS copy. 16674

West, Benjamin, 1730-1813.
The New-England Almanack . . . for . . .
1781.
Providence, Carter. [32] pp.
AAS copy. 17068

[West, Benjamin], 1730-1813.
The New-England Almanack, for . . .
1782. By Isaac Bickerstaff.
Providence, Carter. [24] pp.
AAS copy. 17431

[West, Benjamin], 1730-1813.
The New-England Almanack . . . for . . .
1783. . . . By Isaac Bickerstaff.
Providence, Carter. [24] pp.
AAS copy. 17795

[West, Benjamin], 1730-1813.
The New-England Almanack . . . for 1784.
. . . By Isaac Bickerstaff.
Providence, Carter. [24] pp.
AAS copy.   18306

[West, Benjamin], 1730-1813.
The New-England Almanack . . . for . . .
1785. . . . By Isaac Bickerstaff.
Providence, Carter. [24] pp.
AAS copy.   18880

[West, Benjamin], 1730-1813.
The New-England Almanack . . . for . . .
1786. . . . By Isaac Bickerstaff.
Providence, Carter. [24] pp.
AAS copy.   19375

[West, Benjamin], 1730-1813.
The New-England Almanack . . . for . . .
1787. . . . By Isaac Bickerstaff.
Providence, Carter. [24] pp.
AAS copy.   20138

[West, Benjamin], 1730-1813.
The New-England Almanack, or Lady's
and Gentleman's Diary, for . . . 1788. . . .
By Isaac Bickerstaff.
Providence, Carter. [24] pp.
AAS copy.   20880

[West, Benjamin], 1730-1813.
The New-England Almanack . . . for . . .
1789. . . . By Isaac Bickerstaff.
Providence, Carter. [24] pp.
AAS copy.   21594

[West, Benjamin], 1730-1813.
The New-England Almanack . . . for . . .
1790. . . . By Isaac Bickerstaff.
Providence, Carter. [24] pp.
AAS copy.   22272

[West, Benjamin], 1730-1813.
The New-England Almanack . . . for . . .
1791. . . . By Isaac Bickerstaff.
Providence, Carter. [24] pp.
AAS copy.   23071

[West, Benjamin], 1730-1813.
The New-England Almanack . . . for . . .
1791. . . . By Isaac Bickerstaff.
Providence, Carter for Richardson. [24]
pp.]
(No copy with this imprint located.) 23072

[West, Benjamin], 1730-1813.
The New-England Almanack, or, Lady's
and Gentleman's Diary, for . . . 1792. . . .
By Isaac Bickerstaff.
Providence, Carter. [24] pp.
AAS copy.   23987

[West, Benjamin], 1730-1813.
The New-England Almanack, or, Lady's
and Gentleman's Diary, for . . . 1792. By
Isaac Bickerstaff.
Providence, Carter for Richardson.]
(Evans assumed the imprint from an adv.)
    23988

[West, Benjamin], 1730-1813.
The New-England Almanack . . . for . . .
1793. . . . By Isaac Bickerstaff.
Providence, Carter. [24] pp.
AAS copy.   25022

[West, Benjamin], 1730-1813.
The New-England Almanack . . . for . . .
1793. By Isaac Bickerstaff.
Providence, Carter for Richardson. [24]
pp.]
(Imprint assumed by Evans from
Richardson advs.)   25023

[West, Benjamin], 1730-1813.
The New-England Almanack . . . for . . .
1794. . . . By Isaac Bickerstaff.
Providence, Carter. [24] pp.
RIHS copy.   26464

[West, Benjamin], 1730-1813.
The New-England Almanack . . . for . . .
1794. . . . By Isaac Bickerstaff.
Providence, Carter & Wilkinson. [24] pp.
AAS copy.   26465

[West, Benjamin], 1730-1813.
The New-England Almanack . . . for . . .
1795. . . . By Isaac Bickerstaff.
Providence, Carter & Wilkinson. [24] pp.

(For the second title called for by Evans
see 27797.)
AAS copy.   28066

[West, Benjamin], 1730-1813.
The New-England Almanack . . . for . . .
1796. . . . By Isaac Bickerstaff.
Providence, Carter & Wilkinson. [24] pp.
AAS copy.   29868

[West, Benjamin], 1730-1813.
The New-England Almanack . . . for . . .
1798. . . . By Isaac Bickerstaff.
Providence, Carter & Wilkinson. [24] pp.
AAS copy.   33201

[West, Benjamin], 1730-1813.
The New-England Almanack . . . for . . .
1799. . . . By Isaac Bickerstaff.
Providence, Carter & Wilkinson. [24] pp.
AAS copy.   35002

[West, Benjamin], 1730-1813.
The New-England Almanack . . . for . . .
1800. . . . By Isaac Bickerstaff.
Providence, R. I., Carter. [24] pp.
AAS copy.   36700

[West, Benjamin], 1730-1813.
The New-England Almanack . . . for . . .
1801. . . . By Isaac Bickerstaff.
Providence, R. I., Carter. [24] pp.
AAS copy.   36962

[West, Benjamin], 1730-1813.
The New-England Callendar: or
Almanack, for . . . 1793. By Isaac
Bickerstaff.
Boston, Coverly. [24] pp.
AAS copy.   25026

[West, Benjamin], 1730-1813.
The New-England Calendar: or, the
Boston Almanack, for . . . 1786. . . . By
Copernicus Partridge.
Boston, Battelle. [24] pp.
AAS copy.   19376

[West, Benjamin, 1730-1813.
New-England Sheet Almanack for . . .
1789.
Norwich, Trumbull. Broadside.]
(Assumed from an adv.)   21595

West, Benjamin, 1730-1813.
The North American Calendar . . . for . . .
1781.
Providence, Wheeler for Barber. [24] pp.
AAS copy.   17069

West, Benjamin, 1730-1813.
The North-American Calendar . . . for . . .
1782.
Providence, Wheeler. [40] pp.
AAS copy.   17432

[West, Benjamin, 1730-1813.
The North-American Calendar . . . for . . .
1782.
Providence, Wheeler for Barber.]
(An imprint variant of 17432, apparently
assumed by Evans from Barber's adv.)
    17433

West, Benjamin, 1730-1813.
The North-American Calendar . . . for . . .
1783.
Providence, Wheeler. [32] pp.
AAS copy.   17796

West, Benjamin, 1730-1813.
The North-American Calendar . . . 1783.
Providence, Wheeler for Barber. [32] pp.
AAS copy.   17797

West, Benjamin, 1730-1813.
The North-American Calendar, or, The
Rhode-Island Almanack, for . . . 1784.
Newport, R. I., Southwick. [24] pp.
AAS copy.   44498

West, Benjamin, 1730-1813.
The North-American Calendar, or, the
Rhode-Island Almanack, for . . . 1784.
Newport, Wheeler. [24] pp.
AAS copy.   18309

West, Benjamin, 1730-1813.
The North-American Calendar: or, the
Rhode-Island Almanack, for . . . 1784.
Providence, Wheeler. [24] pp.
AAS copy.   18308

West, Benjamin, 1730-1813.
The North-American Calendar, or the
Rhode-Island Almanack, for . . . 1784.
Providence, Wheeler for Reilly, Thurber &
Chandler. [24] pp.
AAS copy.   18307

West, Benjamin, 1730-1813.
The North-American Calendar: or, the
Rhode-Island Almanack, for . . . 1785.
Providence, Wheeler. [36] pp.
(The AAS has two printings.)
AAS copy.   18881

[West, Benjamin], 1730-1813.
The North-American Calendar: or, the
Rhode-Island Almanack, for . . . 1786.
Providence, Wheeler. [24] pp.
(The AAS has two issues.)
AAS copy.   19377

[West, Benjamin], 1730-1813.
The North-American Calendar: or, the
Rhode-Island Almanack, for . . . 1786. . . .
Second Edition. By Copernicus Partridge.
Providence, Wheeler. [24] pp.
AAS copy.   19378

West, Benjamin, 1730-1813.
The North-American Calendar: or, the
Rhode-Island Almanack, for . . . 1787.
Providence, Wheeler. [24] pp.
(The AAS has four issues.)
AAS copy.   20139

[West, Benjamin], 1730-1813.
The North-American Calendar: or, the
Rhode-Island Almanack, for . . . 1788.
Providence, Wheeler. [24] pp.
AAS copy.   20881

[West, Benjamin], 1730-1813.
The North & South Carolina and Georgia
Almanack, for . . . 1786.
Charleston, S. C., Timothy. 20 pp.
(A duplicate of 19145, q. v.)   20140

[West, Benjamin], 1730-1813.
The Rhode-Island Calendar: or, an
Almanack, for . . . 1798. . . . By Isaac
Bickerstaff.
[Albany, N. Y.], for Todd of Providence
and Newport. [24] pp.
RIHS copy.   33202

West, Benjamin, 1730-1813.
The Rhode-Island Sheet Almanack, for
. . . 1787.
[Providence, Wheeler.] Broadside.
(Reproduced from a poor photostat
because the original is mislaid.)
RIHS copy.   20141

[West, Benjamin], 1730-1813.
The Rhode Island Sheet Almanack for
1789.
Providence, Wheeler. Broadside.]
.(Assumed from an adv. for almanacs.)
    21596

West, Benjamin, 1730-1813.
Russell's American Almanack, for . . .
1780.
Danvers, Russell. [24] pp.
AAS copy.   16675

West, Benjamin, 1730-1813.
Russell's American Almanack, for . . .
1781.
Danvers, Russell. [24] pp.
AAS copy.   17070

[West, Benjamin], 1730-1813.
Russell's American Almanack, for . . .
1782.
Boston, Russell. [24] pp.
AAS copy.   17434

[West, Benjamin], 1730-1813.
A Sheet Almanack for 1793.
Norwich, Trumbull. Broadside.]
(Assumed by Evans from Trumbull's advs.
for sheet almanacs.)   25025

[West, Benjamin], 1730-1813.
Sheet Almanack for 1794.
Providence, Carter & Wilkinson.
Broadside.]
(Imprint assumed by Evans from advs. for
sheet almanacs.)   26466

[West, Benjamin], 1730-1813.
Sheet Almanac for 1795.

Hartford, Babcock, 1794.]
(Assumed by Evans from Babcock's adv.
for "almanacs.")   28063

[West, Benjamin], 1730-1813.
Sheet Almanack for 1796.
Norwich, Trumbull, 1795. Broadside.]
(Taken by Evans from Trumbull's adv. for
sheet almanacs.)   29870

[West, Benjamin], 1730-1813.
The Sons of Coke and Littleton. . . .
Engraved for Bickerstaff's Genuine
Boston Almanack, 1787.
[Boston, 1786.] [24] pp.
AAS copy.   20136

West, Benjamin, 1730-1813.
The South-Carolina Almanack . . . for . . .
1775.
Charleston, Crouch [24] pp.
AAS copy.   42750

[West, Benjamin], 1730-1813.
Thomas's Massachusetts, Connecticut,
Rhode-Island, New-Hampshire &
Vermont Almanack . . . for . . . 1785.
Worcester, Thomas. [36] pp.
(Thomas' correspondence shows that West,
not Gleason, calculated this almanac.)
AAS copy.   18498

[West, Benjamin], 1730-1813.
Thomas's Massachusetts, Connecticut,
Rhode-Island, New-Hampshire &
Vermont Almanack . . . for . . . 1785. . . .
Second Edition.
Worcester, Thomas. [36] pp.]
(There was a second printing of 18498, but
no way is known of distinguishing copies
of it.)   18499

[West, Benjamin], 1730-1813.
Thomas's Massachusetts, Connecticut,
Rhode-Island, New-Hampshire &
Vermont Almanack . . . for . . . 1785. . . .
Third Edition.
Worcester, Thomas. [36] pp.
AAS copy.   18500

[West, Benjamin], 1730-1813.
Thomas's Massachusetts, Connecticut,
Rhode Island, New-Hampshire &
Vermont Almanack . . . for . . . 1786.
Worcester, Thomas. 44 pp.
AAS copy.   19027

[West, Benjamin], 1730-1813.
. . . Thomas's Massachusetts, Connecticut
. . . Almanack . . . for . . . 1787 ["second
edition"].
Worcester, Thomas. [48] pp.
(Not located.)
LOC copy.   45021

[West, Benjamin], 1730-1813.
Town & Country Almanack, for . . . 1795.
. . . By Isaac Bickerstaff.
Norwich, Conn., Trumbull. [24] pp.
AAS copy.   28067

[West, Benjamin], 1730-1813.
Town & Country Almanack, for . . . 1796.
. . . By Isaac Bickerstaff.
Norwich, Trumbull. [36] pp.
AAS copy.   29869

[West, Benjamin], 1730-1813.
The Town and Country Almanack, for . . .
1797. . . . By Isaac Bickerstaff.
Norwich, Conn., Trumbull. [48] pp.
AAS copy.   31616

[West, Benjamin], 1730-1813.
The Town and Country Almanack, for . . .
1798. . . . By Isaac Bickerstaff.
Norwich, Ct., Trumbull for Springer. [24]
pp.
NYPL copy.   33203

[West, Benjamin], 1730-1813.
The Town and Country Almanack, for . . .
1799. . . . By Isaac Bickerstaff.
Norwich, Ct., Trumbull. [24] pp.
(Assumed by Evans from the sequence.)
                                                    35003

[West, Benjamin], 1730-1813.
Webster's Calendar; or the Albany
Almanack, for . . . 1796. . . . By Isaac
Bickerstaff.

Albany, Webster, for Webster & Street.
[48] pp.
AAS copy.   29871

[West, Benjamin], 1730-1813.
Webster's Calendar; or the Albany
Almanack, for . . . 1797. . . . By Isaac
Bickerstaff.
Albany, Websters. [36] pp.
AAS copy.   31617

[West, Benjamin], 1730-1813.
West's Almanack, for . . . 1776.
Providence, Carter. Broadside.
AAS copy.   14620

[West's Sheet Almanack, for 1771.
Providence, Carter.]
(Alden 434.)   42194

[West, Benjamin], 1730-1813.
West's Sheet Almanack for 1772.
Providence, Carter, 1771.] Broadside.
("Just published," Nov. 9, 1771; Alden
465.)   42301

[West, Benjamin], 1730-1813.
Wheeler's North-American Calendar, and
Rhode-Island Almanack, for . . . 1788.
Providence, Wheeler. [24] pp.
AAS copy.   20882

[West, Benjamin], 1730-1813.
Wheeler's North-American Calendar . . .
for . . . 1789.
Providence, Wheeler. [24] pp.
AAS copy.   21597

[West, Benjamin], 1730-1813.
Wheeler's North-American Calendar, or
an Almanack, for . . . 1790.
Providence, Wheeler. [36] pp.
AAS copy.   22273

[West, Benjamin], 1730-1813.
Wheeler's North-American Calendar, or
an Almanack, for . . . 1791.
Providence, Wheeler. [24] pp.
AAS copy.   23073

[West, Benjamin], 1730-1813.
Wheeler's North-American Calendar, or
an Almanack, for . . . 1792.
Providence, Wheeler. [24] pp.
AAS copy.   23989

[West, Benjamin], 1730-1813.
Wheeler's North-American Calendar, or
an Almanack, for . . . 1793. . . .
Providence, Wheeler. [24] pp.
AAS copy.   25027

[West, Benjamin], 1730-1813.
Wheeler's North-American Calendar, or
an Almanack, for . . . 1794.
Providence, Wheeler. [24] pp.
AAS copy.   26467

[West, Benjamin], 1730-1813.
Wheeler's North-American Calendar, or
an Almanack, for . . . 1795.
Providence, Wheeler. [24] pp.
(For eds. see Alden 1352.)
AAS copy.   28068

[West, Benjamin], 1730-1813.
Wheeler's North-American Calendar, or
an Almanack, for . . . 1796.
Providence, Wheeler. [20] pp.
AAS copy.   29872

[West, Benjamin], 1730-1813.
Wheeler's North-American Calendar, or
an Almanack, for 1797.
Providence, Wheeler. [24] pp.
AAS copy.   31618

[West, Benjamin], 1730-1813.
Wheeler's North American Calendar, or
an Almanack, for . . . 1798.
Providence, Wheeler, [24] pp.
AAS copy.   33204

[West, Benjamin, 1730-1813.
Wheeler's North-American Calendar, or
an Almanack for . . . 1799.
Providence, Wheeler. [24] pp.]
(Assumed by Evans from the sequence.)
                                                    35004

[West, Benjamin], 1730-1813.
Wheeler's Sheet Almanack, for . . . 1788.

Providence, Wheeler. Broadside.
(See Alden 1111.)
NYHS copy.   20883

West, Benjamin, ex-Shaker.
Scriptural Cautions.
Hartford, Webster, 1783. 15 pp.
CHS copy.   18310

West, David, 1765-1810.
Catalogue of Books, Printed and
Published in America.
Boston, West, 1799.. 36 pp.
EI copy.   36701

West, David, 1765-1810.
David West's Catalogue of Books.
Boston, West, 1793. 60 pp.
AAS copy.   26468

[West, Gilbert, 1703-1756.
(D. N. B.)
A Defence of the Christian Revelation.
Boston, Rogers & Fowle, 1749.]
(Title from booksellers' adv.)   6442

West, John, 1770-1827.
A Catalogue of Books Published in
America, and for Sale at the Bookstore
of. . . .
Boston, Etheridge, 1797. 36 pp.
AAS copy.   33205

West, John, 1770-1827.
A Catalogue of Books; Published in
America.
Boston, West, 1799. 36 pp.
(Possibly a ghost of 33205; the one
recorded copy could not be located.) 36702

West, Moses.
A Treatise Concerning Marriage.
[Philadelphia, Bradford, 1730.] 39 pp.
(Adv. Am. Weekly Mercury, June 25,
1730.)
AAS copy.   3377

West, Moses.
A Treatise Concerning Marriage.
Philadelphia, Bradford, [1738 ?]. 39 pp.
AAS copy.   4322

West, Samuel, 1730-1807.
An Anniversary Sermon.
Boston, Draper & Folsom, 1778. 79 pp.
AAS copy.   16169

West, Samuel, 1730-1807.
An Anniversary Sermon, Preached at
Plymouth.
Boston, Draper & Folsom, [1778]. 79 pp.
AAS copy.   43594

West, Samuel, 1730-1807.
(Weis, Colonial Clergy N. E.)
Christ the Grand Subject.
Boston, Kneeland, 1764. [4], 28 pp.
AAS copy.   9869

West, Samuel, 1730-1807.
Essays on Liberty.
Boston, Hall, 1793. 54 pp.
AAS copy.   26469

West, Samuel, 1730-1807.
Essays on Liberty. . . . Part First.
New Bedford, Spooner, 1795. 48 pp.
AAS copy.   29873

West, Samuel, 1730-1807.
Essays on Liberty. . . . Part Second.
New Bedford, Spooner, 1795. 96 pp.
AAS copy.   29874

West, Samuel, 1730-1807.
A Sermon Preached before the Honorable
Council.
Boston, Gill, 1776. 70 pp.
AAS copy.   15217

West, Samuel, 1730-1807.
A Sermon, Preached December 3, 1788.
Salem, Dabney & Cushing, 1789. 28 pp.
JCB copy.   22274

West, Samuel, 1738-1808.
The Christian Soldier.
Boston, Manning & Loring, 1794. 19 pp.
AAS copy.   28069

West, Samuel, 1738-1808.
Greatness the Result of Goodness.

Boston, Manning & Loring, [1800]. 40 pp.
AAS copy.   39070

West, Samuel, 1738-1808.
A Sermon, Delivered at Boston, March
12th, 1789.
Boston, Thomas, 1789. 31 pp.
AAS copy.   22275

West, Samuel, 1738-1808.
A Sermon, Delivered upon the late
National Thanksgiving.
Boston, Etheridge, 1795. 20 pp.
AAS copy.   29875

West, Samuel, 1738-1808.
A Sermon Preached at Dedham, Second
Church.
Boston, Edes, 1785. 23 pp.
AAS copy.   19379

West, Samuel, 1738-1808.
(Weis, Colonial Clergy N. E.)
A Sermon Preached at the Ordination of
. . . Jonathan Newell.
Boston, Edes & Gill, 1775. 31 pp.
AAS copy.   14621

West, Samuel, 1738-1808.
A Sermon, Preached before His
Excellency James Bowdoin . . . May 31,
1786.
Boston, Adams & Nourse, [1786]. 32 pp.
AAS copy.   20142

West, Samuel, 1738-1808.
Two Discourses Delivered at Needham.
Boston, Edes, 1785. 39 pp.
AAS copy.   19380

West, Stephen, 1735-1819.
A Dissertation on Infant-Baptism.
Hartford, Hudson & Goodwin, 1798. 106
pp.
AAS copy.   35006

West, Stephen, 1735-1819.
The Duty and Obligation of Christians.
Hartford, 1779. 23 pp.
AAS copy.   16676

West, Stephen, 1735-1819.
(Weis, Colonial Clergy N. E.)
An Essay on Moral Agency.
New Haven, [1772]. 255, [5] pp.
AAS copy.   12615

West, Stephen, 1735-1819.
An Essay on Moral Agency.
Salem, Cushing, 1794. 252, 61, [1] pp.
AAS copy.   28070

West, Stephen, 1735-1819.
Grace a Necessary Qualification.
Stockbridge, Andrews, 1795. 27 pp.
AAS copy.   29876

West, Stephen, 1735-1819.
The Impotency of Sinners.
Hartford, [1777]. 39 pp.
(Adv. as just published, Conn. Courant,
Dec. 2, 1777.)
AAS copy.   12616

West, Stephen, 1735-1819.
An Inquiry into the Ground and Import of
Infant Baptism.
Stockbridge, Andrews, 1794. 120 pp.
AAS copy.   28071

West, Stephen, 1735-1819.
The Scripture Doctrine of Atonement.
New Haven, Meigs, Bowen & Dana, 1785.
xii, 164, [1] pp.
AAS copy.   19381

West, Stephen, 1735-1819.
A Sermon, Preached in Lenox . . .
December 6, 1787.
Hudson, N. Y., Stoddard, 1788. 22 pp.
NYHS copy.   21599

West, Stephen, 1735-1819.
A Sermon; Preached in Lenox . . .
December, 6th, 1787.
Pittsfield, Russell, 1787. 12 pp.
CHS copy.   21598

West, Stephen, 1735-1819.
A Vindication . . . of the Church in
Stockbridge.
Hartford, 1780. 99 pp.
AAS copy.   17071

West, William, of Scituate, R.I.
Scheme of a Lottery. . . . 7th Day of
January, 1786.
[Providence? 1786.] Broadside.
RIHS copy.   45022

West Boston Bridge Company.
Concise View of the Facts, &c.
[Boston, 1800.] pp. [2]-8.
MHS copy.   37021

Westcott, James D.
An Oration, Commemorative of the
Declaration of American Independence.
Philadelphia, Young, 1794. 16 pp.
HSP copy.   47327

[The Western Almanac, for . . . 1797.
Carlisle, Pa., Loudon for Kline.]
(Adv. Carlisle Gazette, Oct. 19, 1796.)
      35007

The Western Almanac, for . . . 1798.
Carlisle, Pa., Loudon for Kline. [36] pp.
AAS copy.   35008

[Western Almanac, for . . . 1799.
Carlisle, Kline.]
(Adv. Carlisle Gazette, Oct. 24, 1798.)
      35009

[The Western Almanack, for . . . 1800.
Pittsburgh?]
(Adv. in Pittsburgh Gazette, Nov. 16,
1799.)   36703

Western and Northern Inland Lock
Navigation Companies.
Report of the Directors.
New York, Forman, 1796. 20 pp.
AAS copy.   31623

The Western Calendar: or, An Almanack
for . . . 1799.
Washington, Pa., Colerick. [36] pp.
(The only copy located is imperfect.)
AAS copy.   48757

The Western Calendar: or, An Almanack
for . . . 1801.
Pittsburgh, Scull. [36] pp.
AAS copy.   39071

The Western Ephemeris, for . . . 1796.
Pittsburgh, Scull. [44] pp.
AAS copy.   47678

Western Inland Lock Navigation Co.
At a Meeting of the Board of Directors. . . .
February 12, 1798.
[Albany, 1798.] Broadside.
NYPL copy.   35011

Western Inland Lock Navigation Co.
. . . The Directors . . . have Determined to
Construct a Canal. . . . January 18th, 1796.
[New York, 1796.] Broadside.
NYPL copy.   31621

Western Inland Lock Navigation Co.
Rates of Toll. The Directors. . . . March 1,
1797.
Albany, Websters, [1797]. Broadside.
NYPL copy.   33207

Western Inland Lock Navigation Co.
Rates of Toll to be Received at
Fort-Schuyler. . . . August 18, 1797.
[Albany, 1797.] Broadside.
NYPL copy.   33208

Western Inland Lock Navigation Co.
Report of the Directors. . . . 16th
February, 1798.
Albany, Websters, [1798]. 32 pp.
AAS copy.   35012

Westford, Mass.
Know all Men by These Presents, That
we, John Abbot. . . .
[Boston, 1794.] Broadside.
LOC copy.   28075

[Westminster Assembly of Divines.
The Assembly's Catechism.
Cambridge, 1668.]
(No copy known. Title from S. Green's
list.)   133

[Westminster Assembly of Divines.
The Assembly's Catechism with Notes.
. . . By the late I. Watts. . . . Fifth Edition.

Philadelphia, Franklin & Hall, 1748.]
(Title from adv.)   6266

Westminster Assembly of Divines.
The Assembly's Catechism with Notes.
. . . By I. Watts. . . . Sixth Edition.
Boston, Rogers & Fowle, 1748. 38, [2] pp.
AAS copy.   6267

[Westminster Assembly of Divines.
The Assembly's Catechism.
Lancaster, 1754.]
(Adv. in 7311.)   7336

Westminster Assembly of Divines.
The Assembly's Catechism.
Stockbridge, Andrews, 1795. 31 pp.
AAS copy.   29879

[Westminster Assembly of Divines.
The Assembly's Shorter Catechism
Explained.
Philadelphia, 1767.]
(Adv. Pa. Journal, May 21, 1767.)   10611

Westminster Assembly of Divines.
The Assembly's Shorter Catechism.
Philadelphia, Young, 1788. vi, 282, [10]
pp.
(The imprint given by Evans was assumed
from an adv. No perfect copy located.)
Presbyterian Hist. Soc. copy.   21600

Westminster Assembly of Divines.
A Catechism for Youth.
Philadelphia, Aitken, 1783. 172 pp.
LOC copy.   18311

Westminster Assembly of Divines.
The Confession of Faith, together with the
Larger Catechism.
Boston, Kneeland for Henchman, 1723.
[2], 161, [1] pp.
AAS copy.   2493

Westminster Assembly of Divines.
The Confession of Faith.
Philadelphia, Franklin, 1745. 567, [24] pp.
HSP copy.   5709

Westminster Assembly of Divines.
The Larger Catechism.
Boston, Draper for McAlpine, 1745. 88
pp.
AAS copy.   40392

[Westminster Assembly of Divines.
The Larger Catechism.
Boston, 1750.]
("Just Re-printed, And Sold opposite the
Prison," Boston Gazette, Aug. 21, 1750.)
      6621

[Westminster Assembly of Divines.
The Larger Catechism.
Lancaster, 1754.]
(Adv. in 7311.)   7334

Westminster Assembly of Divines.
The Larger Catechism.
Boston, Fowle & Draper, 1762. 41 pp.
AAS copy.   9304

[Westminster Assembly of Divines.
The Larger Catechism.
Philadelphia, Steuart, 1762.]
(Adv. Pa. Gazette, Dec. 20, 1762.)   9305

Westminster Assembly of Divines.
The Larger Catechism.
Boston, Mills and Hicks, 1773. 47 pp.
AAS copy.   42539

Westminster Assembly of Divines.
The Larger Catechism.
Philadelphia, Aitken, 1775. 40 pp.
AAS copy.   42982

Westminster Assembly of Divines.
The Larger Catechism.
Philadelphia, Campbell, 1794. 48 pp.
AAS copy.   28076

[Westminster Assembly of Divines.
The Shorter Catechism.
Cambridge, 1665.]
(No copy known.)   105

Westminster Assembly of Divines.
The Shorter Catechism.
Cambridge, Green for Phillips, 1682. [2],
16+ pp.

(The only known copy is imperfect.)
HEH copy.   39222

[Westminster Assembly of Divines.
The Shorter Catechism.
Boston, 1683. [2], 54 pp.]
(There was a copy in the library of Fisher
Howe, Jr., of Chestnut Hill.)   354

Westminster Assembly of Divines.
The Shorter Catechism.
Cambridge, Green, 1689. [2], 28 pp.
(No copy located.)   39270

Westminster Assembly of Divines.
The Shorter Catechism.
[Boston], 1691. 31, [3] pp.
BPL copy.   579

Westminister Assembly of Divines.
The Shorter Catechism.
Boston, 1698. [2], 46 pp.
AAS copy.   855

Westminster Assembly of Divines.
The Shorter Catechism.
Boston, Green & Allen for Phillips, 1699.
24? pp.
(The only known copy is imperfect.)
AAS copy.   39356

Westminster Assembly of Divines.
The Shorter Catechism.
Boston, Green & Allen for Buttolph, 1701.
[2], 46 pp.
BPL copy.   39377

Westminster Assembly of Divines.
The Shorter Catechism.
Boston, Rogers for Henchman, 1728. [2],
46 pp.
HEH copy.   39900

Westminister Assembly of Divines.
The Shorter Catechism.
Boston, Gerrish, 1729. 24 pp.
(No perfect copy found.)
AAS copy.   3234

Westminster Assembly of Divines.
The Shorter Catechism.
Boston, Fleet, 1731. 24 pp.
BPL copy.   39982

Westminster Assembly of Divines.
The Shorter Catechism.
Boston, Kneeland & Green for Hancock,
1733. [2], 46 pp.
(The only known copy is imperfect.)
AAS copy.   40036

[Westminister Assembly of Divines.
The Shorter Catechism.
Philadelphia, Franklin, 1734.]
(Adv. in Pa. Gazette, Mar. 21, 1733/4.)
3973

Westminster Assembly of Divines.
The Shorter Catechism.
Boston, Kneeland & Green, 1737. 23, [1]
pp.
JCB copy.   40132

Westminster Assembly of Divines.
The Shorter Catechism.
Boston, Kneeland & Green, 1739. 18 pp.
NYPL copy.   4445

Westminster Assembly of Divines.
The Shorter Catechism.
Boston, Draper, 1740. [2], 46 pp.
AAS copy.   4625

Westminster Assembly of Divines.
The Shorter Catechism.
New London, 1746. [43] pp.
LOC copy.   5882

[Westminster Assembly of Divines.
The Shorter Catechism.
Philadelphia, Franklin & Hall, 1749.]
("Just published, and to be sold by the
printers hereof," Pa. Gazette, June 22,
1749.)   6443

Westminster Assembly of Divines.
The Shorter Catechism.
Boston, Fleet, 1751. 24 pp.
(The only copy located is imperfect.)
BPL copy.   6795

Westminster Assembly of Divines.

The Shorter Catechism of the Reverend
Assembly.
Lancaster, 1754.]
(Adv. in 7311.)   7335

Westminster Assembly of Divines.
The Shorter Catechism.
New London, [Ct.], Green, 1754. [24] pp.
JCB copy.   40731

[Westminster Assembly of Divines.
The Shorter Catechism, Agreed Upon.
New York, Gaine, 1754.]
("Just published, and to be sold by the
Printer hereof," N. Y. Mercury, June 17,
1754.)   7337

Westminster Assembly of Divines.
The Shorter Catechism.
Boston, Green & Russell, 1757. 46 pp.
AAS copy.   8063

Westminster Assembly of Divines.
The Shorter Catechism.
Boston, Fleet, 1759. 23, [1] pp.
AAS copy.   8519

Westminster Assembly of Divines.
The Shorter Catechism.
Philadelphia, Bradford, 1760. 48 pp.
AAS copy.   8767

Westminster Assembly of Divines.
The Shorter Catechism.
Boston, 1762. 24 pp.
NYPL copy.   41327

Westminster Assembly of Divines.
The Shorter Catechism.
Boston, Kneeland, 1762. [2], 48, [1] pp.
PPL copy.   9306

[Westminster Assemly of Divines.
The Shorter Catechism.
Philadelphia, Steuart, 1762.]
(Adv. Pa. Gazette, Dec. 20, 1762.)   9307

Westminster Assembly of Divines.
The Shorter Catechism.
Boston, Fleet, 1765. 23, [1] pp.
AAS copy.   10206

Westminster Assembly of Divines.
The Shorter Catechism.
Boston, Perkins, 1768. 33 pp.
LOC copy.   11115

Westminster Assembly of Divines.
The Shorter Catechism.
New London, Green, 1769. 34+ pp.
(The only known copy is imperfect.)
CHS copy.   42025

[Westminster Assembly of Divines.
The Shorter Catechism.
Philadelphia, Aitkin, 1770.]
(No copy found.)   11935

Westminster Assembly of Divines.
The Shorter Catechism.
Norwich, [Ct.], Green & Spooner, 1777.
32 pp.
AAS copy.   43407

Westminster Assembly of Divines.
The Shorter Catechism.
Baltimore, 1782. 28 pp.
MdHS copy.   17799

Westminster Assembly of Divines.
The Shorter Catechism.
Hartford, Patten, 1782. 38 pp.
CHS copy.   17798

Westminster Assembly of Divines.
The Shorter Catechism.
New Haven, Meigs & Dana, 1786. 30 pp.
AAS copy.   20143

[Westminster Assembly of Divines.
The Shorter Catechism.
Bennington, Haswell and Russell, 1790.]
("Just published," Vt. Gazette, Apr. 26,
1790.)   23076

Westminster Assembly of Divines.
The Shorter Catechism.
New York, MacGill, 1791. 104+ pp.
(The only known copy is imperfect.)
AAS copy.   46354

Westminster Assembly of Divines.
[The Shorter Catechism.

Albany, 1792.] 35, [1] pp.
(The only known copy is badly defective.)
AAS copy.   25030

Westminster Assembly of Divines.
The Shorter Catechism.
Lansingburgh, Tiffany, 1795. 71 pp.
(The only copy located is defective.)
AAS copy.   29880

Westminster Assembly of Divines.
The Shorter Catechism.
Newburyport, Blunt, 1797. 58 pp.
AAS copy.   33211

[Westminster Assembly of Divines.
The Shorter Catechism.
Troy, Pratt, 1797.]
(Imprint assumed by Evans from adv.
"For sale at this Office," Farmers Oracle,
Aug. 22, 1797.)   33212

Westminster Assembly of Divines.
The Shorter Catechism.
Castine, Me., Waters, 1800. 66 pp.
AAS copy.   39079

[Westminster Assembly of Divines.
The Westminster Assembly's Shorter
Catechism, Explained. . . . By E. and R.
Erskine. . . .
Philadelphia, Campbell, 1794.]
(Imprint assumed by Evans from
Campbell advs.)   28077

[Weston, Edward], 1703-1770.
(D. N. B.)
The Englishman Directed.
Boston, Rogers & Fowle, 1748. 77, [2] pp.
AAS copy.   6268

Weston, Isaac, fl., 1783.
The Massachusetts Almanack, for . . .
1783.
Salem, Hall. [24] pp.
AAS copy.   17800

Weston, William, 1752?-1833.
Report . . . on . . . the Water of the River
Bronx.
[New York], Furman, 1799. 16 pp.
AAS copy.   36709

West's Almanack, for . . . 1776 [by
Benjamin West, 1730-1813].
Providence, Carter, Broadside.
AAS copy.   14620

Wetenhall, Edward, bp., 1636-1713.
Graecae Grammaticae.
Philadelphia, Humphreys, 1776. [4], 93
pp.
AAS copy.   15218

[Wetenhall, Edward, bp., 1636-1713.
Graecae Grammaticae Institutio.
Philadelphia, Young, 1786.]
(Entry from an adv.   20144

Wetenhall, Edward, bp., 1636-1713.
Graecae Grammaticae.
Philadelphia, Spotswood, etc., 1789. 97
pp.
AAS copy.   22277

Wetenhall, Edward, bp., 1636-1713.
A Short Introduction to Grammar.
Philadelphia, Steuart, 1762. iv, 137, [4]
pp.
HSP copy.   9309

Wetenhall, Edward, bp., 1636-1713.
A Short Introduction to Grammar.
Philadelphia, Humphreys, 1773. v, [1],
145 pp.
AAS copy.   13080

Wetenhall, Edward, bp., 1636-1713.
A Short Introduction to Grammar. . . .
Third Edition.
Philadelphia, Crukshank, 1779. v, 145 pp.
LOC copy.   43731

Wetherill, Samuel, 1736-1816.
An Apology for the Religious Society,
Called Free Quakers.
Philadelphia, Folwell, [1798?]. 37 pp.
AAS copy.   35015

Wetherill, Samuel, 1736-1816.
A Confutation of the Doctrines of
Antinomianism.

Philadelphia, Lang, 1790. 48 pp.
LCP copy.   23077

Wetherill, Samuel, 1736-1816.
The Divinity of Jesus Christ.
Philadelphia, Bailey & Lang, 1792. 68, [1]
pp.
AAS copy.   25031

Wetherill, Samuel, 1736-1816.
The Grounds and Reason of Incarnation.
Philadelphia, Bailey & Lang, 1791. 66, [1]
pp.
HEH copy.   23993

Wetherill, Samuel, 1736-1816.
The Grounds and Reason of the
Incarnation.
Philadelphia, Bailey & Lang, 1791. 66, [2]
pp.
HEH copy.   46355

[Wetherill, Samuel], 1736-1816.
Some Observations on the Doctrines of
John Murray.
Philadelphia, Bailey & Crukshank, 1790.]
(Probably from a descriptive adv. for
23077.)   23078

Wethersfield, Conn. Union Library
Society.
Constitution and By-laws of the. . . .
Hartford, Hudson & Goodwin, 1784. 19
pp.
CHS copy.   18882

Wetmore, Izrahiah, 1728-1798.
The Important Duties.
New Haven, Morse, 1791. 22 pp.
AAS copy.   23994

Wetmore, Izrahiah, 1728-1798.
A Sermon Preached before the Honorable
General Assembly . . . May 13th, 1773.
[New London, 1773.] 40 pp.
AAS copy.   13076

Wetmore, Izrahiah, 1728-1798.
(Weis, Colonial Clergy N. E.)
A Sermon, Preached before the . . .
General Assembly . . . May 13th, 1773.
Norwich, Spooner for Ransom, 1775. 31
pp.
JCB copy.   14622

[Wetmore, James], 1695-1760.
(Dexter, I, 133-138.)
Eleutherius Enervatus.
New York, 1733. 115 pp.
YC copy.   3731

[Wetmore, James], 1695-1760.
(Dexter, I, 133-138.)
A Letter from a Minister of the Church of
England.
New York, Zenger [1730]. 28 pp.
(Evans, following Sabin, gives a
description of this item in place of its
title.)
NYHS copy.   3378

[Wetmore, James,] 1695-1760.
(Dexter, I, 133-138.)
A Letter from a Minister.
New York, [1732?]. 28 pp.]
(A ghost of 3378, q.v.)   3615

[Wetmore, James, 1695-1760.
A Letter Occasioned by Mr. Dickinson's
Remarks.
Boston, Fleet, 1744. 40 pp.]
(Title from an adv., possibly for N.Y. ed.)
                                             5514

Wetmore, James, 1695-1760.
A Letter Occasioned by Mr. Dickinson's
Remarks.
New York, 1744. 40, [1] pp., irreg.
BA copy.   5513

Wetmore, James, 1695-1760.
(Dexter, I, 133-138.)
Quakerism.
New York, [1731]. [4], xi, [1], 69, [2]
pp.
AAS copy.   3489

Wetmore, James, 1695-1760.
(Dexter, I, 133-138.)
A Vindication of the Professors.
Boston, Rogers & Fowle, 1747. 43, [2] pp.
AAS copy.   6081

Wetmore, Robert Griffith, 1774-1803.
Address to the Episcopal Congregations.
Catskill, Croswell, [1798]. 31 pp.
NYHS copy.   35016

Wetmore, Robert Griffith, 1774-1803.
A Feeble Attempt.
Albany, [N. Y.], Websters, 1800. 22 pp.
JCB copy.   39080

[Wetmore, Robert Griffith, 1774-1803.
Observations on Masonry.
New York, 1800.]
(Entry from copyright.)   39082

Wetmore, Robert Griffith, 1774-1803.
An Oration, Occasioned by the Death of
. . . Washington.
Copperstown, Phinney, 1800. 23 pp.
HEH copy.   39081

Wetmore, Robert William.
To the Honourable General Assembly.
[New Haven, 1798.] Broadside.
AAS copy.   35017

Wetmore, Timothy Fletcher, 1764-1799.
An Inaugural Dissertation.
New York, Swords, 1795. 42, [1] pp.
AAS copy.   29881

Wetmore, William, 1749-1830.
An Oration on the Death of . . .
Washington.
Castine, Waters, [1800]. 30 pp.
AAS copy.   39083

Weylie, John V.
A Funeral Sermon, in Commemoration of
. . . Washington.
[Frederick, Md.? 1800.] 18 pp.
PPL copy.   39084

Whalley, Thomas Sedgwick, 1746-1828.
Edwy and Edilda, a Tale.
Albany, [N. Y.], Andrews, 1800. 175 pp.,
6 plates.
AAS copy.   39085

Wharton, Charles Henry, 1748-1833.
An Elegy to the Memory of Mrs. Mary
Wharton.
[Philadelphia], Ormrod, [1798]. 7 pp.
LCP copy.   35018

Wharton, Charles Henry, 1748-1833.
[A letter to the Roman Catholics of the
city of Worcester.
Annapolis, Green, 1784.] pp. 51-56.
(Known only by this fragment.)
JCB copy.   44631

[Wharton, Charles Henry], 1748-1833.
A Letter to the Roman Catholics of the
City of Worcester.
Philadelphia, Aitken, 1784. 40 pp.
AAS copy.   18883

[Wharton, Charles Henry], 1748-1833.
A Poetical Epistle to His Excellency
George Washington.
Philadelphia, Kline, 1781. 10 pp.
LCP copy.   17435

[Wharton, Charles Henry], 1748-1833.
A Poetical Epistle to His Excellency
George Washington.
Providence, 1781. Front., 24 pp.
AAS copy.   17436

[Wharton, Charles Henry], 1748-1833.
A Poetical Epistle, to His Excellency
George Washington.
Springfield, 1782. 18 pp.
AAS copy.   17801

[Wharton, Charles Henry], 1748-1833.
A Reply to An Address to the Roman
Catholics of the United States.
Philadelphia, Cist, 1785. 97, [1], 9, [1]
pp.
AAS copy.   19382

Wharton, Charles Henry, 1748-1833.
A Sermon on the Relations of the
Christian Ministry.
Philadelphia, Aitken, 1785. 24 pp.
AAS copy.   19383

Wharton, Charles Henry, 1748-1833.
A Short and Candid Enquiry.

Wilmington, Brynberg & Andrews, 1791.
48 pp.
LCP copy.   23995

Wharton, Charles Henry, 1748-1833.
A Short and Candid Enquiry.
Philadelphia, Ormrod & Conrad, 1796. 59,
[1] pp.
AAS copy.   31625

[Wharton, Samuel], 1732-1800.
Plain Facts: being an Examination into
the Rights of Indian Nations.
Philadelphia, Aitken, 1781. 164, [1] pp.
MHS copy.   17437

[Wharton, Samuel], 1732-1800.
View of the Title to Indiana.
[Philadelphia? 1775.] 24 pp.
PrU copy.   42983

[Wharton, Samuel], 1732-1800.
View of the Title of Indiana.
Philadelphia, Styner & Cist, 1776. 46 pp.
AAS copy.   15219

[Wharton, Samuel], 1732-1800.
View of the Title to Indiana.
Williamsburg, Dixon & Nicholson, 1779. 8
pp.
JCB copy.   43732

What is our Situation? [by Joseph
Hopkinson, 1770-1842].
[Philadelphia, 1798.] 40 pp.
AAS copy.   33904

What is Sauce for a Goose is also Sauce
for a Gander [by Hugh Williamson,
1735-1819].
Philadelphia, 1764. 8 pp.
JCB copy.   9879

What Should be most of all Tho't upon
[by Cotton Mather, 1663-1728].
Boston, 1713. [2], ii, 42, [1] pp.
HC copy.   1629

What think ye of the Congress now [by
Thomas Bradbury Chandler].
New York, Rivington, 1775. 48, 4 pp.
AAS copy.   13866

Wheating, W.
. . . . Woods's Town and Country
Almanac . . . for . . . 1792.
Newark, N. J., Woods. [40] pp.
NJHS copy.   23997

Wheatley, Phillis, afterward Phillis Peters,
1753?-1784.
An Elegiac Poem, on . . . George
Whitefield.
[Boston], Russell and Boyles, [1770].
Broadside.
LCP copy.   11812

Wheatley, Phillis, afterward Phillis Peters,
1753?-1784.
An Elegiac Poem, on . . . George
Whitefield.
Boston, Russell and Boyles, [1770]. 8 pp.
NYPL copy.   11813

[Wheatley, Phillis, afterward Phillis
Peters, 1753?-1784.
An Elegiac Poem . . . Mr. Whitefield.
New York, Inslee & Car, 1770.]
(Adv. N. Y. Gazette & Post Boy, Oct. 30,
1770.)   11814

[Wheatley, Phillis, afterward Phillis
Peters, 1753?-1784.
An Elegiac Poem, on . . . Geo. Whitefield.
Philadelphia, Goddard, 1770.]
(Adv. Pa. Chronicle, Oct. 29, 1770.) 11815

Wheatley, Phillis, afterward Phillis Peters,
1753?-1784.
An Elegiac Poem, on the Death of . . .
George Whitefield.
[Newport, Southwick, 1770]. Broadside.
HSP copy.   42195

Wheatley, Phillis, afterward Phillis Peters,
1753?-1784.
An Elegiac Poem. On the Death of . . .
George Whitefield.
Newport, Southwick, [1770?] 8 pp.
NHS copy.   42196

Wheatley, Phillis, afterward Phillis Peters,
1753?-1784.

An Elegiac Poem Sacred to the Memory
of . . . George Whitefield.
Boston, Fowle, 1770. 8 pp.
(The one recorded copy cannot now be
located.)   42197

Wheatley, Phillis, afterward Phillis Peters,
1753?-1784.
An Elegy, Sacred to the Memory of . . .
Samuel Cooper.
Boston, Russell, 1784. 8 pp.
AAS copy.   18726

Wheatley, Phillis, afterward Phillis Peters,
1753?-1784.
An Elegy, to Miss Mary Moorhead. . . .
December 15, 1773.
[Boston], M'Alpine, [1773]. Broadside.
MHS copy.   42540

Wheatley, Phillis, afterward Phillis Peters,
1753?-1784.
Liberty and Peace, a Poem.
Boston, Warden & Russell, 1784. 4 pp.
AAS copy.   18727

Wheatley, Phyllis, afterward Phillis
Peters, 1753?-1784.
An Ode, on the Birth Day of Pompey
Stockbridge.
n.p., n.d. Broadside.
(Porter 267; present location unknown.)
                                                        49189

Wheatley, Phillis, afterward Phillis Peters,
1753?-1784.
Phillis's Poem on the Death of Mr.
Whitefield.
[Boston, 1770.] Broadside.
AAS copy.   42198

Wheatley, Phillis, afterward Phillis Peters,
1753?-1784.
[Poems. 1st American ed.
Albany, 1779.]
(McMurtrie: Albany 10.)   43733

Wheatley, Phillis, afterward Phillis Peters,
1753?-1784.
Poems on Various Subjects.
Philadelphia, Crukshank, 1786. 66, [2] pp.
AAS copy.   19913

Wheatley, Phillis, afterward Phillis Peters,
1753?-1784.
Poems on Various Subjects.
Philadelphia, James, 1787. 55, [3] pp.
AAS copy.   45205

Wheatley, Phillis, afterward Phillis Peters,
1753?-1784.
Poems on Various Subjects.
Philadelphia, Crukshank, 1789. 66, [2] pp.
AAS copy.   45748

Wheatley, Phillis, afterward Phillis Peters.
1753?-1784.
Poems on Various Subjects.
Albany, Barber & Southwick for Spencer,
1793. 89, [3] pp.
AAS copy.   25983

Wheatley, Phillis, afterward Phillis Peters,
1753?-1784.
To Mrs. Leonard, on the Death of her
Husband.
[Boston, 1771.] Broadside.
HSP copy.   42302

Wheatley, Phillis, afterward Phillis Peters,
1753?-1784.
To the Hon'ble Thomas Hubbard. . . .
January 2, 1773.
[Boston, 1773.] Broadside.
HSP copy.   42541

Wheatley, Phillis, afterward Phillis Peters,
1753?-1784.
To the Rev. Mr. Pitkin. . . . June 16th,
1772.
[Boston, 1772.] Broadside.
LOC copy.   12518

Wheaton, George, 1728-1803.
(Bost. Transcript, Apr. 12, 1911).
An Astronomical Diary . . . for . . . 1753.
By George Wheten.
Boston, Fowle. pp. [16], 17-24.
AAS copy.   6946

Wheaton, George, 1728-1803.
An Astronomical Diary, or, An Almanack
for . . . 1754.

Boston, Fowle. [16] pp.
BPL copy.   40679

[Wheaton, George, 1728-1803.
An Astronomical Diary, or An Almanack
for . . . 1755.
Boston, Fowle. [16] pp.]
(The only known copy lacks tp.)
AAS copy.   40732

Wheaton, George, 1728-1803.
An Astronomical Diary; or, an Almanack
for . . . 1757.
Boston, Edes & Gill. [16] pp.
AAS copy.   40869

Wheaton, Hannah.
The Author . . . Now Casts her Mite. . . .
[Boston, 1799.] Broadside.
HEH copy.   36710

Wheaton, Hannah.
An Independent Ode, Dedicated to the
Illustrious President.
[Boston?, 1795.] Broadside.
NYHS copy.   28885

Wheaton, Hannah.
A New-Year's Ode. While Gabriel
Strikes.
[New York? 1795]. Broadside.
NYHS copy.   47679

Wheaton, Hannah.
A New Year's Wish. Now Fair Aurora
[January, 1795].
[n.p., 1795.] Broadside.
NYHS copy.   29882

Wheaton, Hannah.
A New Year's Wish. The Author's being
Absent. . . . December, 1793.
[Philadelphia? 1793.] Broadside.
AAS copy.   46945

[Wheaton, Hannah.
On Taking an Affectionate Farewell.
[Boston, 1799.] Broadside.]
(Evans; Ford; no copy located.)   36711

[Wheaton, Hannah.
Poem on Washington.
n.p., 1800.]
(A ghost of 28885, Wegelin 442.)   39086

Wheaton, Jesse.
Wheaton's Jaundice Bitters.
n. p., [1799?]. Broadside.
AAS copy.   48991

Wheaton, Levi, 1761-1851.
An Oration, Delivered to the Society of
Black Friars, November 10, 1796.
New York, M'Lean & Lang, 1797. 22 pp.
LOC copy.   33213

Wheeler, Bennett, 1756-1806.
Proposals for Printing . . . The United
States Chronicle. . . . November 26, 1783.
[Providence, 1783.] Broadside.
AAS ph. copy.   44499

Wheeler, Bennett, 1756-1806.
The Young Mason's Monitor.
Providence, 5791 (1791). 46, [1] pp.
RIHS copy.   23996

Wheeler, Mercy, b. 1706.
An Address to Young People.
Boston, 1733. vi, 9, [1] pp.
BPL copy.   3732

Wheeler, Thomas,-1676.
(Wheeler Family in America, pp. 1-12.)
A Thankfull Remembrance.
Cambridge, 1676. [6], 14, 32 pp.
AAS copy.   226

Wheeler's North-American Calendar, and
Rhode-Island Almanack, for . . . 1788 [by
Benjamin West, 1730-1813].
Providence, Wheeler. [24] pp.
AAS copy.   20882

Wheeler's North-American Calendar . . .
for . . . 1789 [by Benjamin West,
1730-1813].
Providence, Wheeler. [24] pp.
AAS copy.   21597

Wheeler's North-American Calendar, or
an Almanack, for . . . 1790 [by Benjamin
West, 1730-1813].

Providence, Wheeler. [36] pp.
AAS copy.   22273

Wheeler's North-American Calendar, or
an Almanack, for . . . 1791 [by Benjamin
West, 1730-1813].
Providence, Wheeler. [24] pp.
AAS copy.   23073

Wheeler's North-American Calendar, or
an Almanack, for . . . 1792 [by Benjamin
West, 1730-1813].
Providence, Wheeler. [24] pp.
AAS copy.   23989

Wheeler's North-American Calendar, or
an Almanack, for . . . 1793. . . . [by
Benjamin West, 1730-1813].
Providence, Wheeler. [24] pp.
AAS copy.   25027

Wheeler's North-American Calendar, or
an Almanack, for . . . 1794 [by Benjamin
West, 1730-1813].
Providence, Wheeler. [24]pp.
AAS copy.   26467

Wheeler's North-American Calendar, or
an Almanack, for . . . 1795 [by Benjamin
West, 1730-1813].
Providence, Wheeler. [24] pp.
(For eds. see Alden 1352.)
AAS copy.   28068

Wheeler's North-American Calendar, or
an Almanack, for . . . 1796 [by Benjamin
West, 1730-1813].
Providence, Wheeler. [20] pp.
AAS copy.   29872

Wheeler's North-American Calendar, or
an Almanack, for 1797 [by Benjamin
West, 1730-1813].
Providence, Wheeler. [24] pp.
AAS copy.   31618

Wheeler's North American Calendar, or
an Almanack, for . . . 1798 [by Benjamin
West, 1730-1813].
Providence, Wheeler. [24] pp.
AAS copy.   33204

[Wheeler's North-American Calendar, or
an Almanack for . . . 1799.
Providence, Wheeler. [24] pp.]
(Assumed by Evans from the sequence.)
                                                        35004

Wheeler's Sheet Almanack, for . . . 1788
[by Benjamin West, 1730-1813].
Providence, Wheeler. Broadside.
(See Alden 1111.)
NYHS copy.   20883

Wheelock, Eleazar, 1711-1779.
A Continuation of the Narrative.
Boston, Draper, 1765. 25 pp.
(The first issue lacks the final leaf.)
AAS copy.   10207

Wheelock, Eleazar, 1711-1779.
A Continuation of the Narrative.
[Hartford], 1771. 61 pp.
(We have reproduced a copy of the 2nd
issue with errata on p. 61. AAS has also
1st issue.)
AAS copy.   12284

Wheelock, Eleazar, 1711-1779.
A Continuation of the Narrative of the
Indian Charity School.
[Portsmouth], New Hampshire, 1772. 40
pp.
AAS copy.   42390

Wheelock, Eleazar, 1711-1779.
A Continuation of the Narrative of the
Indian Charity School [Sept. 26, 1772 -
Oct. 15, 1773].
Hartford, 1773. 68 pp.
AAS copy.   13077

Wheelock, Eleazar, 1711-1779.
A Continuation of the Narrative of the
Indian Charity School.
[Portsmouth], New Hampshire, 1773. 40
pp.
AAS copy.   42542

Wheelock, Eleazar, 1711-1779.
A Continuation of the Narrative of the
Indian Charity-School.

Hartford, 1775. 54 pp.
AAS copy.   14623

Wheelock, Eleazar, 1711-1779.
Liberty of Conscience.
Hartford, Watson, [1776]. 31 pp.
AAS copy.   15220

Wheelock, Eleazar, 1711-1779.
A Plain and Faithful Narrative.
Boston, Draper, 1763. 55 pp.
(The AAS has an earlier state with the
word "ledge" omitted from line 1, p. viii.)
AAS copy.   9537

Wheelock, Eleazar, 1711-1779.
The Preaching of Christ.
Boston, Kneeland, 1761. [4], 26 pp.
AAS copy.   9039

Wheelock, John, d. 1817.
A Concise Narrative of my
Proceedings. . . . September 3, 1777.
[Fishkill, 1777.] Broadside.
DC copy.   43408

Wheelock, John, 1754-1817.
(G. T. Chapman, Alumni of Dartmouth,
pp. 2-3.)
An Essay on . . . Painting, Music and
Poetry.
Hartford, [1774]. 15 pp.
AAS copy.   13765

Wheelwright, Tomothy, pseud.
King's County, the 12th of September,
1734.
[New York, 1734.] 3 pp.
NYPL copy.   3853

Wheland, William.
A Narrative of the Horrid Murder &
Piracy.
[Philadelphia], Folwell, [1800]. 16 pp.
AAS copy.   39087

Whelpley, Samuel, 1766-1817.
Animadversions on Mr. Day's Sermon.
Danbury, Douglas & Ely, 1792. 62, [1] pp.
CHS copy.   25032

[Whelpley, Samuel, 1766-1817.
Animadversions on Mr. Paine's Age of
Reason.
Troy, Gardner & Billings, 1795.]
(Entry from the prospectus in The
Recorder, June 16, 1795.)   29883

[When America First at Heaven's
Command. A Song.
Philadelphia, 1779. Broadside.]
(Adv. Pa. Evening-Post, Feb. 10, 1779.)
                                    16678

When First this Humble Roof I Knew [by
Sir John Burgoyne, 1722-1792].
[New York, Carr, 1796.] 1 leaf.
(The unique copy is mislaid.)   30140

When Lucy was Kind [by James Hook,
1746-1827].
Philadelphia & New York, Carr, [1796].
[2] pp.
YC copy.   30586

When on the Ocean [by Samuel Arnold,
1740-1802].
New York, Gilfert, [1799?]. [2] pp.
AAS copy.   48777

When Pensive I Thought on My Love [by
George Colman, 1762-1836].
New York, Gilfert, [1799?]. [2] pp.
AAS copy.   33537

When Rural Lads and Lasses Gay.
New York, Gilfert, [c. 1795]. [2] pp.
LOC copy.   47680

When Seated with Sal [by William Reeve,
1757-1815].
Philadelphia, etc., Carr, [1795]. [2] pp.
AAS copy.   28503

[When the Cares of the Day. A Song.
Philadelphia, 1779. Broadside.]
(Adv. Pa. Evening-Post, Feb. 10, 1779.)
                                    16679

When the Hollow Drum. In the
Mountaineers [by George Colman,
1762-1836].

Philadelphia, etc., Carr, [1797]. [3] pp.
NYPL copy.   31954

When the Mind is in Tune. Sung by Miss
Broadhurst.
New York, Philadelphia, and Baltimore,
Carr. [2] pp.
HSP copy.   33214

When William at Eve [by Frances
(Moore) Brooke, 1724-1789].
New York, Gilfert, [1797]. Broadside.
NYPL copy.   31873

Where are Ye all now?
[Baltimore, 1784.] Broadside.
MdHS copy.   18884

Whereas a Great Number of People have
Express'd a Desire. . . .
[Boston, 1774.] Broadside.
LOC copy.   13767

Whereas a Paper, Signed Philo
Patriae. . . .
[New York, 1769.] Broadside.
LCP copy.   11230

Whereas a Report Prevails in this
City. . . . New-York, January 23, 1769.
[New York, 1769.] Broadside.
LCP copy.   11433

Whereas an Association. . . . December,
1773.
[New York, 1773.] Broadside.
NYHS copy.   13078

Whereas in the late Examination before
the Honourable House of Assembly. . . .
This 16th Day of January, 1769.
[New York, 1769.] 2 pp.
LCP copy.   11529

Whereas it is Pretended by an
Advertisement Dated the 6th of January,
1769. . . .
[New York, 1769.] Broadside.
LOC copy.   11528

Whereas it is the Prevailing Rage of the
Present Times . . . to form
Associations. . . .
n. p., [1775]. Broadside.
MHS copy.   42984

Wheten, George, see also Wheaton,
George, 1728-1803.
An Astronomical Diary . . . for . . . 1753.
Boston, Fowle. pp. [16], 17-24.
AAS copy.   6946

Whig Society.
At a Meeting . . . the 3d of May, 1784.
[New York, 1784.] Broadside.
NYHS copy.   44632

While Gasping Freedom Wails her Future
Fate. . . .
[Boston, 1768.] Broadside.
MHS copy.   41899

Whilst with Village Maids I Stray [by
William Shield, 1748-1829].
New York, Moller, [1797]. [2] pp.
LOC copy.   48252

A Whip for the American Whig by
Timothy Tickle, Esqr.
[New York, 1769.] [2] pp.
(No copy located.)   42026

Whipple, Enoch, 1755-c. 1840.
The Importance of Early Piety.
Gilmanton, N. H., Russel, [1799]. 13 pp.
NYHS copy.   36712

Whipple, Levi.
I Levi Whipple, of Cranston. . . . April
13th, 1767.
[Providence, 1767.] Broadside.
JCB copy.   41778

Whitaker, Benjamin, fl. 1700-1751.
(Records of Court of Chancery of S. C., p.
185.)
At a Court of the General Sessions.
Charleston, 1741. 39 pp.
JCB copy.   4812

Whitaker, Nathaniel, 1730-1795.
(D. A. B.)
An Antidote against Toryism.

Newburyport, 1777. [2], 34 pp.
AAS copy.   15709

Whitaker, Nathaniel, 1730-1795.
A Brief History of the Settlement of the
Third Church.
Salem, Hall, 1784. 32 pp.
AAS copy.   18885

Whitaker, Nathaniel, 1730-1795.
A Confutation of Two Tracts.
Boston, Thomas, 1774. 98 pp.
AAS copy.   13768

Whitaker, Nathaniel, 1730-1795.
A Funeral Sermon on . . . George
Whitefield.
Salem, [1770]. 38 pp.
AAS copy.   11937

Whitaker, Nathaniel, 1730-1795.
A Sermon Preached at the Ordination of
. . . Isaac Foster.
Hartford, Green, 1765. 64 pp.
HC (M.B. Jones) copy.   41599

Whitaker, Nathaniel, 1730-1795.
The Mutual Care.
Salem, Hall, 1785. 34 pp.
AAS copy.   19384

Whitaker, Nathaniel, 1730-1795.
The Reward of Toryism.
Newburyport, 1783. 32 pp.
AAS copy.   18312

[Whitaker, Nathaniel, 1730-1795.]
The Trial of the Spirits.
Providence, Goddard, 1662 (1762). vi,
34 pp.
NYPL copy.   9308

Whitaker, Nathaniel, 1730-1795.
Two Sermons: on the Doctrine of
Reconciliation.
Salem, 1770. 167, [1] pp.
AAS copy.   11938

[Whitcomb, Chapman], 1765-1833.
A Concise View of Antient and Modern
Religion.
[Leominster, Mass?], Whitcomb, [1800].
12 pp.
AAS copy.   49190

Whitcomb, Chapman, 1765-1833.
Miscellaneous Poems.
Worcester, 1795. 12 pp.
AAS copy.   29884

Whitcomb, Chapman, 1765-1833.
Miscellaneous Poems.
Rutland, 1795. 12 pp.
(The only copy is imperfect.)
HC copy.   47681

[Whitcomb, Chapman], 1765-1833.
A Poem, on Religious Ignorance.
n.p., for the Purchaser, 1795. Broadside.
AAS copy.   47682

[Whitcomb, Chapman], 1765-1833.
A Poem, on Religious Ignorance.
Boston, 1795. 4 pp.
AAS copy.   29332

[Whitcomb, Chapman], 1765-1833.
A Poem, on Religious Ignorance, Pride
and Avarice.
[Leominster, Mass? 1800?] Broadside.
AAS copy.   49191

White, Alexander, 1761?-1784.
The Life, Last Words, and Dying
Speeches of. . . .
[Boston], Russell, [1784]. Broadside.
(Not found 1967.)
RF copy.   44633

White, Alexander, 1761?-1784.
A Narrative of the Life and Conversion
of. . . .
Boston, Powars & Willis, [1784]. 23 pp.
AAS copy.   18886

White, Anthony Walton, 1750-1803.
The Military System for the New-Jersey
Cavalry.
New Brunswick, Arnett, 1793. [2], 80, [4]
pp., 1 folding table.
AAS copy.   26474

White, Charles, 1728-1813.

A Treatise on the Management of
Pregnant . . . Women.
Worcester, Thomas, 1793. pp. [2], vii-328;
2 plates.
AAS copy.   26475

White, Daniel.
The True Reason for Mr. Daniel White
and Mr. Thomas Byles Disposing of their
Interest.
Newport, Franklin, 1728. Broadside.
RIHS copy.   39901

White, Daniel Appleton, 1776-1861.
A Eulogy on George Washington.
Haverhill, [Mass.], Moore, 1800. 18 pp.
MHS copy.   39088

[White, Ebenezer], 1709-1779.
(Weis, Colonial Clergy N. E.)
A Brief Narrative of the Proceedings of
the Eastern Association.
New Haven, 1764. 31, [1] pp.
AAS copy.   9871

White, Elizabeth, d. 1660.
Experience of God's Gracious Dealing.
Boston, Kneeland & Green, 1741. [2], 21
pp.
BPL copy.   4841

White, Francis.
The Philadelphia Directory.
Philadelphia, Young Stewart &
M'Culloch, 1785. [4], 98, [2] pp.
AAS copy.   19385

White, Henry, fl. 1775.
To the Public. . . . The 29th day of April,
1775.
[New York, 1775.] Broadside.
NYPL copy.   14624

White, James, 1755?-1824.
A Catalogue of Books . . . for Sale.
Boston, [1798]. 48 pp.
AAS copy.   33215

White, James, 1755?-1824.
For Sale . . . a Large Collection of Books.
[Boston, 1800?] Broadside.
(No copy located.)   49192

White, John, 1677-1760.
(Sibley, IV, 421-424.)
The Gospel Treasure.
Boston, Boone, 1725. [4], 40, [2] pp.
AAS copy.   2717

White, John, 1677-1760.
(Sibley, IV, 421-424.)
New England's Lamentations.
Boston, Fleet, 1734. [4], 2, 5, [1], 42, 10,
[2], 15 pp.
AAS copy.   3854

White, John, 1677-1760.
New-England's Lamentations. . . . Second
Edition.
Boston, Fleet, 1734. [4], 2, 4, 42, 10, [2],
15 pp.
AAS copy.   3855

White, John, 1677-1760.
(Sibley, IV, 421-424.)
Secret Prayer Inculcated.
Boston, Green for Henchman, 1719. [2],
iv, 50 pp.
AAS copy.   2086

White, John, baker.
To the Honourable . . . General Court.
[Boston, 1771?] 3 pp.
AAS copy.   42303

[White, John, of Cambridge Univ.
Three Letters from a Gentleman.
Boston, Rogers & Fowle, 1749.]
(Title from booksellers' adv.)   6444

White, Joseph, 1745-1814.
Sermons, Preached before the University
of Oxford.
Boston, Greenough for Larkin, 1793. 269,
[1], lvii pp.
AAS copy.   26476

White, Stephen, 1718-1794.
(Weis, Colonial Clergy N. E.)
Civil Rulers.
New London, 1763. 39 pp.
AAS copy.   9538

White, Stephen, 1718-1794.
Death Dissolves.
Hartford, 1779. 17 pp.
AAS copy.   16680

[White, William], bp., 1748-1836.
The Case of the Episcopal Churches in the
United States Considered.
Philadelphia, Claypoole, 1782. 35 pp.
AAS copy.   17802

White William, bp., 1748-1836.
The Character of the Evangelist St. John.
Philadelphia, Hall & Sellers, 1785. 24, [3]
pp.
AAS copy.   44834

White, William, bp., 1748-1836.
A Sermon, Delivered in Christ-Church, on
the 21st day of June, 1786.
Philadelphia, Hall & Sellers, 1786. [2], 31
pp.
AAS copy.   20145

White, William, bp., 1748-1836.
A Sermon, on the due Celebration of . . .
Thanksgiving.
Philadelphia, Hall & Sellers, 1786. 18 pp.
AAS copy.   20146

White, William, bp., 1748-1836.
A Sermon on the Duty of Civil Obedience.
Philadelphia, Ormrod, 1799. 26 pp.
AAS copy.   36713

White, William, bp., 1748-1836.
A Sermon, on the Reciprocal Influence.
Philadelphia, Ormrod & Conrad, 1795. 36
pp.
AAS copy.   29885

White, William Charles, 1777-1818.
Orlando: or Parental Persecution.
Boston, Russell for Blakes, 1797. 64 pp., 1
plate.
BrU copy.   33216

Whitefield, George, 1714-1770.
Abraham's Offering up his son Isaac.
Philadelphia, Bradford, [174-?]. 30 pp.
(The only known copy cannot be
reproduced.)   40186

[Whitefield, George, 1714-1770.
An Account of the Money he Received.
Boston, Kneeland & Green, Edwards &
Eliot, 1741. 44 pp.]
("Sold by," New England Weekly Journal,
June 9, 1741. Ghost of London ed.) 4842

[Whitefield, George, 1714-1770.
An Account of the Money Received.
Philadelphia, 1741.]
("To be sold," Pa. Gazette, Dec. 3, 1741.)
                                          4843

Whitefield, George, 1714-1770.
The Almost Christian.
Boston, Fleet for Harrison, 1739. 22, [1]
pp.
BPL copy.   4446

Whitefield, George, 1714-1770.
An Answer to the First and Second Part.
Boston, Rogers & Fowle, 1744 [/5]. [4],
16, 14, 24 pp.
AAS copy.   5515

[Whitefield, George, 1714-1770.
An Answer to the First and Second Part
[Another Impression].
Boston, Rogers & Fowle, 1744. [4], 16, 14,
24 pp.]
(Assumed by Evans from the statement
that this tract went through three
impressions; if so they have not been
distinguished.)   5516

[Whitefield, George, 1714-1770.
An Answer to the First and Second Part
[Another Impression].
Boston, Rogers & Fowle, 1744. [4], 16, 14,
24 pp.]
(See note under 5516.)   5517

Whitefield, George, 1714-1770.
A Brief Account of the Occasion.
Boston, Rogers & Fowle, 1744. 15 pp.,
irreg.
AAS copy.   5518

Whitefield, George, 1714-1770.

A Brief Account of some Lent . . .
Processions.
Boston, Fowle and Edes & Gill, 1755. 19
pp.
AAS copy.   7590

[Whitefield, George, 1714-1770.
A Brief Account of some Lent . . .
Processions.
Philadelphia, Chattin, 1755.]
(Adv. Pa. Gazette, Dec. 25, 1755.)   7591

Whitefield, George, 1714-1770.
A Brief General Account, of the First
Part of the Life of . . . Whitefield.
Philadelphia, [Bradfords, 1741]. [2], iii,
57 pp.
HSP copy.   40267

Whitefield, George, 1714-1770.
A Brief and General Account.
Boston, Draper for Henchman, 1740. [2],
ii, 54, [1] pp.
AAS copy.   4629

Whitefield, George, 1714-1770.
A Brief and General Account.
Boston, Kneeland & Green, Edwards &
Eliot, 1740. [4], 48 pp.
NYPL copy.   4628

Whitefield, George, 1714-1770.
A Brief and General Account.
Philadelphia, Bradford, 1740. [2] iii, 57
pp.
HSP copy.   4627

Whitefield, George, 1714-1770.
A Brief and General Account.
Philadelphia, Franklin, 1740. [2], iii, 66
pp.
LCP copy.   4626

Whitefield, George, 1714-1770.
A Brief and General Account.
Boston, Kneeland & Green, Edwards &
Eliot, 1741. [4], 48 pp.
NYPL copy.   4844

Whitefield, George, 1714-1770.
Britain's Mercies.
Philadelphia, Bradford, 1746. 27 pp.
HSP copy.   5883

Whitefield, George, 1714-1770.
Britain's Mercies. . . . Second Edition.
Boston, Kneeland & Green, 1746. 22 pp.
AAS copy.   5884

[Whitefield, George], 1714-1770.
Christmas well Kept.
[Boston], Kneeland & Green, 1739. 11 pp.
AAS copy.   4447

[Whitefield, George, 1714-1770.
Christmas Well Kept.
Boston, 1772.]
(Entry from Haven.)   12617

[Whitefield, George, 1714-1770.
A Collection of Hymns for Social
Worship.
Philadelphia, Bradford, 1765.]
(Adv. Pa. Journal, May 9, 1765.)   10209

[Whitefield, George, 1714-1770.
A Collection of Hymns. . . . Thirteenth
Edition.
New York, Parker for Noel, 1768.]
("Just published. . . . Printed for Garrat
Noel," N.Y. Journal, Jan. 18, 1768.) 11116

Whitefield, George, 1714-1770.
A Collection of Hymns. . . . Thirteenth
Edition.
Philadelphia, Hall, 1768. xi, [1], 182 pp.
HSP copy.   41900

Whitefield, George, 1714-1770.
A Continuation of the Journal of a
Voyage from Gibraltar to Savannah. . . .
Sixth Edition.
Boston, Fleet for Harrison, 1740. 46, [1]
pp.
(Evans' erroneous title probably comes
from an ntp copy at HC.)
AAS copy.   4632

[Whitefield, George, 1714-1770.
A Continuation of the Reverend Mr.
Whitefield's Journal During the Time he
was Detained in England. . . . Also, A
Continuation . . . from his Embarking. . . .

Boston, Harrison, 1740.]
("Just published," Boston Evening Post, Oct. 27, 1740.)   4635

Whitefield, George, 1714-1770.
A Continuation of the Reverend Mr. Whitefield's Journal During the Time he was Detained in England. . . . Vol. II.
Philadelphia, Franklin, 1740. 205, [5] pp.
AAS copy.   4633

Whitefield, George, 1714-1770.
A Continuation of the Reverend Mr. Whitefield's Journal from a few Days after his Arrival at Georgia.
Philadelphia, Franklin, 1740. 96 pp.
LCP copy.   4636

Whitefield, George, 1714-1770.
A Continuation of the Reverend Mr. Whitefield's Journal, from a few Days after his Arrival at Savannah.
Philadelphia, Franklin, 1741. 126 pp.
LCP copy.   4846

Whitefield, George, 1714-1770.
A Continuation of the Reverend Mr. Whitefield's Journal, from his Arrival at Savannah, May 7.
Boston, Rogers & Fowle, Edwards & Eliot, 1741. 54, [1] pp.
AAS copy.   4855

Whitefield, George, 1714-1770.
A Continuation of the Reverend Mr. Whitefield's Journal from his Embarking after the Embargo.
Philadelphia, Franklin, 1740. 145, [4] pp.
HC copy.   4634

[Whitefield, George, 1714-1770.
A Continuation of the Reverend Mr. Whitefield's Journal from his Leaving New-England; his Travels through New-York.
Boston, 1741. 47 pp.]
(Apparently an incorrect description of a copy of 4851.)   4852

Whitefield, George, 1714-1770.
A Continuation of the Reverend Mr. Whitefield's Journal from his Leaving New-England, October, 1740.
Boston, Rogers for Edwards & Eliot, 1741. 47, [1] pp.
JCB copy.   4851

Whitefield, George, 1714-1770.
A Continuation of the Reverend Mr. Whitefield's Journal from his Leaving Stanford.
Boston, Kneeland & Green, 1741. 40 pp.
JCB copy.   4853

[Whitefield, George, 1714-1770.
A Continuation of the Revered Mr. Whitefield's Journal, from his Leaving Stanford.
Philadelphia, Franklin, 1741.]
("To be sold," Pa. Gazette, Nov. 5, 1741.)   4854

Whitefield, George, 1714-1770.
A Continuation of the Reverend Mr. Whitefield's Journal from Savannah.
Boston, Fowle for Kneeland & Green, 1741. 96 pp.
AAS copy.   4848

[Whitefield, George, 1714-1770.
A Continuation of the Reverend Mr. Whitefield's Journal from Savannah.
Boston, Kneeland & Green for Edwards & Eliot, 1741. 96 pp.]
("In a few days will be published," Boston Ev. Post, Mar. 30, 1741.)   4849

Whitefield, George, 1714-1770.
A Continuation of the Reverend Mr. Whitefield's Journal from Savannah.
Boston, Rogers for Edwards and Eliot, 1741. 96 pp.
(Except for the imprint, identical with 4848.)
AAS copy.   4847

[Whitefield, George, 1714-1770.
A Continuation of the Reverend Mr. Whitefield's Journal from Savannah.
Philadelphia, Franklin, 1741.]
(Apparently a ghost arising from an adv. for 4846.)   4850

Whitefield, George, 1714-1770.
Directions how to Hear Sermons. . . . Third Edition.
Boston, Rogers & Fowle, and Eliot, 1740. 15 pp.
AAS copy.   4637

[Whitefield, George, 1714-1770.
Directions how to hear Sermons.
Philadelphia, Bradford, 1740.]
(Adv. Am. Weekly Mercury, Apr. 17, 1740.)   4638

Whitefield, George, 1714-1770.
The Doctrine of Election Defended.
Windham, Byrne, [1791]. 28 pp.
NYPL copy.   23998

Whitefield, George, 1714-1770.
The Duty and Interest of Early Piety.
Boston, Kneeland & Green, and Harrison, 1739. [4], 15 pp.
HEH copy.   4448

Whitefield, George, 1714-1770.
Eighteen Sermons.
Newburyport, Blunt, 1797. [8], 368, [6] pp.
AAS copy.   33217

Whitefield, George, 1714-1770.
An Expostulatory Letter. . . . Third Edition.
Philadelphia, Bradford, 1753. 15 pp.
LOC copy.   7136

Whitefield, George, 1714-1770.
Fifteen Sermons.
New York, Gaine, 1794. 324 pp.
AAS copy.   28078

Whitefield, George, 1714-1770.
Fifteen Sermons.
Philadelphia, Carey, 1794. 324 pp.
AAS copy.   28079

Whitefield, George, 1714-1770.
Five Sermons on the Following Subjects. . . .
Philadelphia, Franklin, 1746. xii, [2], 169 pp.
JCB copy.   5885

[Whitefield, George, 1714-1770.
Five Sermons, viz. . . .
Philadelphia, Bradford, 1740.]
(Evans took his title from Haven, whose entry has no imprint date.)   4639

[Whitefield, George], 1714-1770.
Free Grace Indeed!
Boston, Rogers & Fowle for Edwards & Eliot, 1741. 39 pp.
LOC copy.   4857

Whitefield, George, 1714-1770.
A Further Account of God's Dealings.
Boston, Rogers & Fowle, 1746. [2], 38 pp.
HC copy.   5887

Whitefield, George, 1714-1770.
A Further Account of God's Dealings.
Philadelphia, Bradford, 1746. 64, [1] pp., folding sheet.
AAS copy.   5886

Whitefield, George, 1714-1770.
The Great Duty of Family Religion.
Boston, Fleet for Harrison, 1739. 23 pp.
AAS copy.   4450

Whitefield, George, 1714-1770.
The Heinous Sin of Drunkenness.
Philadelphia, Bradfords, [1740]. 18 pp.
(Adv. Am Weekly Mercury, Apr. 17, 1740.)
PSL copy.   4640

Whitefield, George, 1714-1770.
Hymn, Composed by the late Reverend Mr. George Whitefield.
[Boston], Russell, 1790. Broadside.
AAS copy.   23079

Whitefield, George, 1714-1770.
The Indwelling of the Spirit.
Boston, Kneeland & Green, 1739. 23 pp.
AAS copy.   4451

[Whitefield, George, 1714-1770.
The Indwelling of the Spirit.
Philadelphia, Bradford, 1740.]

(Adv. Am. Weekly Mercury, Mar. 11, 1739/40.)   4641

Whitefield, George, 1714-1770.
[The Indwelling of the Spirit.
Williamsburg, 1740.]
(Wroth, Wm. Parks, 114.)   40224

Whitefield, George, 1714-1770.
The Indwelling of the Spirit. . . . Fifth Edition.
Boston, Rogers for Henchman, 1741. 22, [1] pp.
NYPL copy.   4858

[Whitefield, George, 1714-1770.
Intercession Every Christian's Duty.
New York, 1739.]
(Adv. N.Y. Weekly Journal, Jan. 7, 1739/40. A Boston ed. is adv. in 4449.)   4452

[Whitefield, George, 1714-1770.
Journal, from London to Gilbraltar.
Boston, Harrison, 1741.]
("Now in press," Boston Ev. Post, Jan. 5, 1741; possibly a ghost of 4631.)   4845

Whitefield, George, 1714-1770.
A Journal of a Voyage from Gilbraltar to Georgia.
Philadelphia, Franklin, 1739. 252 pp.
(The AAS and HSP have copies with the first title-page dated 1740.)
UOP copy.   4453

Whitefield, George, 1714-1770.
A Journal of a Voyage from Gilbralter to Georgia.
Philadelphia, Franklin, 1740. 252 pp.
AAS copy.   40225

[Whitefield, George, 1714-1770.
A Journal of a Voyage from London to Gilbraltar.
Boston, 1739.]
(Haven says that there was a Boston reprint of the London, 1738, ed.)   4454

Whitefield, George, 1714-1770.
A Journal of a Voyage from London to Gibraltar. . . . Sixth Edition.
Boston, Fleet for Harrison, 1740. 54, [1] pp.
MHS copy.   4631

Whitefield, George, 1714-1770.
A Journal of a Voyage from London to Gilbraltar. . . . Sixth Edition.
Philadelphia, Franklin, 1740. 64 pp.
LCP copy.   4630

Whitefield, George, 1714-1770.
The Knowledge of Jesus Christ.
Providence, Carter, 1793. 14 pp.
AAS copy.   26477

Whitefield, George, 1714-1770.
The Last Will, and Testament, of. . . .
Boston, 1771. vii pp.
(Despite the imprint, Evans apparently describing this copy.)
BPL copy.   12285

Whitefield, George, 1714-1770.
[A Letter from the Rev. Mr. George Whitefield to a Friend in London, Concerning Archbishop Tillotson.
Charleston, S. C., 1740.]
(Adv. S. C. Gazette, Apr. 11, 1740.)   40227

Whitefield, George, 1714-1770.
A Letter from the Reverend Mr. Whitefield to a Friend in London.
Philadelphia, Franklin, 1740. 8 pp.
YC copy.   4643

Whitefield, George, 1714-1770.
A Letter from the Reverend Mr. Whitefield, to a Reverend Divine in Boston; Giving a Short Account of his late Visit to Bermuda.
Philadelphia, Franklin & Hall, 1748. 7 pp.
AAS copy.   6269

Whitefield, George, 1714-1770.
A Letter from the Reverend Mr. Whitefield to some Church Members.
Boston, Kneeland & Green, Edwards & Eliot, 1740. 13 pp.
AAS copy.   4644

Whitefield, George, 1714-1770.
A Letter from the Reverend Mr.
Whitefield to some Church Members.
New York, 1740.]
(Title from Haven, probably a ghost of the
reprint in 4588.) 4645

Whitefield, George, 1714-1770.
A Letter from the Reverend Mr.
Whitefield, to some Church Members.
Philadelphia, Franklin, [1740]. 8 pp.
HSP copy. 4646

Whitefield, George, 1714-1770.
A Letter from the Reverend Mr.
Whitefield to some Church Members. . . .
Third Edition.
Charleston, 1741. 8 pp.
BM copy. 4859

Whitefield, George, 1714-1770.
A Letter from the Reverend Mr.
Whitefield, to the Religious Societies
Lately form'd in England and Wales.
Philadelphia, Bradford, [1739]. 19 pp.
LCP copy. 4455

Whitefield, George, 1714-1770.
A Letter from the Reverend Mr. George
Whitefield, to the Reverend Mr. John
Wesley.
Boston, Rogers for Kneeland & Green and
Edwards & Eliot, 1740. 31, [1] pp.
AAS copy. 4647

Whitefield, George, 1714-1770.
A Letter from the Reverend Mr. George
Whitefield, to the Reverend Mr. John
Wesley.
Philadelphia, Franklin, 1741. 24 pp.
UOP copy. 4856

Whitefield, George, 1714-1770.
A Letter from the Reverend Mr. George
Whitefield, to the Reverend Mr. John
Wesley.
Lansingburgh, 1789. 24 pp.
AAS copy. 22278

Whitefield, George, 1714-1770.
A Letter from the Rev. Mr. Whitefield
from Georgia, to a Friend in London.
Charleston, 1740. 11 pp.
BM copy. 4642

Whitefield, George, 1714-1770.
A Letter to His Excellency Governor
Wright.
Charleston, 1768. 28 pp.
(Evans in correcting Haven misdated this
ed.)
NYPL copy. 10803

Whitefield, George, 1714-1770.
A Letter to the Reverend Dr. Chauncy.
Boston, Kneeland & Green, 1745. [2], 14
pp.
AAS copy. 5710

Whitefield, George, 1714-1770.
A Letter to the Reverend Dr. Chauncy.
Philadelphia, W. Bradford, 1745. 32 pp.
NYPL copy. 5711

Whitefield, George, 1714-1770.
A Letter to the Reverend Dr. Durell.
Boston, Fleets, 1768. 39 pp.
AAS copy. 11117

Whitefield, George, 1714-1770.
A Letter to the Rev. the President . . . of
Harvard-College.
Boston, Kneeland & Green, 1745. 22 pp.
AAS copy. 5712

Whitefield, George, 1714-1770.
The Lord our Righteousness.
Boston, Kneeland & Green, 1742. 28 pp.
AAS copy. 5090

Whitefield, George, 1714-1770.
The Marks of the New Birth. . . . Sixth
Edition.
New York, 1739. 28 pp.
(There is an adv. for a Philadelphia ed. in
Am. Weekly Mercury, Nov. 29, 1739.)
LOC copy. 4456

Whitefield, George, 1714-1770.
The Marks of the New-Birth.
Boston, Rogers & Fowle, 1740. 16 pp.
AAS copy. 40228

Whitefield, George, 1714-1770.

The Marks of the new Birth. . . . Fifth
Edition.
Philadelphia, Bradfords, [1742?]. 24 pp.
HSP copy. 40294

Whitefield, George, 1714-1770.
The Marriage of Cana.
Philadelphia, Bradford, 1742. 40 pp.
AAS copy. 5091

Whitefield, George, 1714-1770.
The Necessity and Benefits.
Boston, Rogers & Fowle, 1740. 24 pp.
(Evans' title was quite certainly an error
for this.)
LOC copy. 4648

Whitefield, George, 1714-1770.
Nine Sermons. . . . Second Edition.
Boston, Kneeland & Green, 1743. [2], ii,
iii, [1], 220 pp.
JCB copy. 5311

Whitefield, George, 1714-1770.
Observations on Some Fatal Mistakes.
Philadelphia, Bradford, 1763. 24 pp.
LCP copy. 9539

Whitefield, George, 1714-1770.
Observations on some Fatal Mistakes.
Boston, Draper, 1764. 24 pp.
AAS copy. 9872

[Whitefield, George, 1714-1770.
Observations on some Fatal Mistakes.
Philadelphia, Bradford, 1764. 24 pp.]
(All reported copies are Boston eds.
Apparently a ghost originating in Haven.)
9873

Whitefield, George, 1714-1770.
The Prodigal Son.
Boston, Kneeland & Green, 1742. 20 pp.
YC copy. 5089

Whitefield, George, 1714-1770.
The Prodigal Son.
Boston, Rogers & Fowle, 1742. 16 pp.
NYHS copy. 40295

Whitefield, George, 1714-1770.
The Rev. Mr. Whitefield's Answer. To the
Bishop of London's last Pastoral Letter.
New York, 1739. [2], 21 pp.
LOC copy. 4457

Whitefield, George, 1714-1770.
The Rev. Mr. Whitefield's Answer to the
Bishop of London's last Pastoral Letter.
Philadelphia, Bradfords, [1739]. 16 pp.
HEH copy. 40180

[Whitefield, George, 1714-1770.
A Sermon Entituled, The Wise and
Foolish Virgins.
Philadelphia, Bradford, 1740.]
(Apparently a ghost of one of the other
printings.) 4649

Whitefield, George, 1714-1770.
A Sermon, on Luke 8th, 18.
[Windham, Byrne], 1792. 16 pp.
AAS copy. 25033

Whitefield, George, 1714-1770.
A Sermon on Regeneration. . . . Second
Edition.
Boston, Fleet for Harrison, 1739. 23 pp.
NYPL copy. 4459

Whitefield, George, 1714-1770.
A Sermon on Self-Denial.
Boston, Fleet for Harrison, 1739. 23 pp.
AAS copy. 4449

Whitefield, George, 1714-1770.
A Sermon on the Eternity of
Hell-Torments.
Boston, Rogers & Fowle, 1740. 16 pp.
AAS copy. 40229

Whitefield, George, 1714-1770.
Sermons on Various Important Subjects.
Boston, Rogers & Fowle for Henchman,
1741. [12], 383 pp.
NYHS copy. 4860

Whitefield, George, 1714-1770.
Sermons on Various Subjects. In two
Volumes.
Philadelphia, Franklin, 1740. iv, 223; iv,
224 pp.
HSP copy. 4650

Whitefield, George, 1714-1770.
A Short Address to Persons of all
Denominations.
New York, Gaine, 1756. 8 pp.
LOC copy. 40870

Whitefield, George, 1714-1770.
A Short Address to Persons of all
Denominations. . . . Third Edition.
Philadelphia, Franklin & Hall, 1756. 16
pp.
UOP copy. 7815

Whitefield, George, 1714-1770.
A Short Address to Persons of all
Denominations. . . . Fourth Edition.
Boston, Green & Russell, 1756. 16 pp.
AAS copy. 7816

Whitefield, George, 1714-1770.
A Short Address to Persons of all
Denominations. . . . Fifth Edition.
Boston, Edes & Gill, 1756. 16 pp.
AAS copy. 7817

Whitefield, George, 1714-1770.
A Short Address to Persons of all
Denominations. . . . Sixth Edition.
Boston, Fowle, 1756. 13, [1] pp.
BA copy. 7818

Whitefield, George, 1714-1770.
Some Remarks on a Pamphlet.
Philadelphia, Bradford, 1749. 46 pp.
AAS copy. 6445

Whitefield, George, 1714-1770.
Some Remarks on a Pamphlet.
Boston, 1749. 32 pp.
(Evans' description was a combination of
an adv. and a defective copy.)
AAS copy. 6446

Whitefield, George, 1714-1770.
Some Remarks upon a late Charge.
Boston, Rogers & Fowle, 1745. 23 pp.
AAS copy. 5713

[Whitefield, George, 1714-1770.
Some Remarks on a Late Pamphlet.
Boston, Kneeland & Green, 1743. 26 pp.]
(Evans was apparently in error in
assuming that this first edition was
American printing. The second edition,
5313, was adv. "Just published" in the
Boston Gazette, Feb. 22, 1743.) 5312

Whitefield, George, 1714-1770.
Some Remarks on a late Pamphlet. . . .
Second Edition.
Boston, Kneeland & Green, 1743. 26, [1]
pp.
AAS copy. 5313

Whitefield, George, 1714-1770.
Ten Sermons.
Newburyport, Blunt & March for Thomas
& Andrews, etc., 1795. 217, [6] pp.
AAS copy. 29886

Whitefield, George, 1714-1770.
Ten Sermons.
Portsmouth, N. H., Peirce & Larkin, 1797.
206 pp.
AAS copy. 33218

Whitefield, George, 1714-1770.
Three Letters from the Reverend Mr. G.
Whitefield.
Philadelphia, Franklin, 1740. 16 pp.
AAS copy. 4651

Whitefield, George, 1714-1770.
A True Copy of the Last Will and
Testament of. . . .
n.p., [1770?] Broadside.
HSP copy. 42199

Whitefield, George, 1714-1770.
A True Copy of the last Will and
Testament of the. . . .
Boston, Coverly, 1771. Broadside.
AAS copy. 42304

[Whitefield, George, 1714-1770.
The Two First Parts of his Life.
Philadelphia, Bradford, 1765.]
(From an adv.) 10210

Whitefield, George, 1714-1770.
Two Funeral Hymns, Composed by . . .
George Whitefield. . . . who Departed . . .
the Thirtieth of September, 1770.

[Boston], Russell & Boyles, [1770].
Broadside.
MHS copy.   42200

Whitefield, George, 1714-1770.
Two Sermons. The Almost Christian. . . .
Elizabethtown, N. J., Kollock, 1794. 39
pp.
AAS copy.   28080

Whitefield, George, 1714-1770.
Von Georg Weitfields Predigten, Der
Erste Theil.
Germantown, 1740. 18 pp.
HSP copy.   4653

Whitefield, George, 1714-1770.
Von Georg Weitfields Predigten, der
Zweyte Theil.
Germantown, 1740. 76 pp.
HSP copy.   4654

[Whitefield, George, 1714-1770.
Von Georg Weitfields Predigten. Der
Dritte Theil.
Germantown, 1740.]
(Adv. in 4528.)   4655

[Whitefield, George, 1714-1770.
Voorbidding ein eider Christen's Plicht,
en de Wyze. . . .
New York and Philadelphia, 1740.]
(Title from Haven; looks suspiciously like
a scrambled adv.)   4657

[Whitefield, George, 1714-1770.
Voorbidding een eider Christen's Plicht,
Vertoont. . . .
New York, 1740.]
(Adv. N. Y. Weekly Journal, Mar. 3,
1739/40.)   4656

Whitefield, George, 1714-1770.
What Think ye of Christ?
Philadelphia, Bradford, [1739]. 28 pp.
HSP copy.   4458

Whitefield, George, 1714-1770.
What Think Ye of Christ?
Boston, Fowle for Henchman, 1741. 30 pp.
MHS copy.   4861

Whitefield, George, 1714-1770.
The Wise and Foolish Virgins.
Philadelphia, Bradfords, [1739]. 27 pp.
HSP copy.   40181

[Whitefield, George, 1714-1770.
Worldly Business.
Philadelphia, Bradford, 1740.]
(Adv. Am. Weekly Mercury.)   4652

Whitefield, George, 1714-1770.
De Wyze en Dwooze Maagden.
New York, Zenger for Goelet, [1740?]. 44
pp.
(The only known copy cannot be
reproduced.)   40230

Whitefield, George, pseud.
A Funeral Hymn, Composed by . . .
George Whitefield. . . . Ah! Lovely
Appearance of Death!
n.p., [1770?] Broadside.
AAS copy.   42186

Whitefield, George, pseud.
A Funeral Hymn, Composed by George
Whitefield. . . . Ah! Lovely Appearance of
Death!
[Boston], Green & Russell, [1770?]
Broadside.
NHHS copy.   42187

Whitefield, George, pseud.
A Funeral Hymn, Composed by . . .
George Whitefield. . . . Ah! Lovely
Appearance of Death!
Portsmouth, Fowles, [1770]. Broadside.
NHHS copy.   42188

Whitefield, George, pseud.
A Hymn, composed by the Reverend Mr.
Whitefield, to be sung over his own Corps.
Taken from the Original May 1, 1764.
n.p., [1770]. Broadside.
HSP copy.   42190

Whitefield, Nathaniel.
Whitefield's Almanack for . . . 1760.
Newport, R. I., Franklin. [24] pp.
AAS copy.   41092

[Whitefield, and Tennent.
Boston, Henchman, 1741.]
(Title from Haven and an unlocated adv.)
                                             4862

Whitehead, George, 1636-1723.
(D. N. B.)
A Christian Epistle.
Philadelphia, 1691. 15 pp.
HSP copy.   580

[Whitehead, John, 1740-1804.
A Discourse Delivered at the New
Chapel.
Philadelphia, Crukshank for Dickins,
1791.]
(A first ed. assumed by Evans from
24000.)   23999

Whitehead, John, 1740-1804.
A Discourse Delivered at the New
Chapel. . . . Second American Edition.
Philadelphia, Crukshank for Dickins,
1791. 69, [3] pp.
AAS copy.   24000

Whitehead, John, 1740-1804.
A Discourse Delivered at the New
Chapel.
Philadelphia, Hall, 1791. 69, [2] pp.
(Best copy available.)
LCP copy.   46356

Whitelaw, James, 1748-1829.
A Correct Map of the State of Vermont.
[Rutland], 1796. Map.
AAS copy.   31626

Whitelaw, James, 1748-1829.
A Map of the State of Vermont . . . 1793.
[Boston, 1793?] Map.
AAS copy.   26478

Whitelaw, James, 1748-1829.
Ryegate, (Vermont) October 27th, 1795.
Proposals for Publishing . . . a Correct
Map of . . . Vermont.
[Ryegate, Vt., 1796.] Broadside.
LOC copy.   29887

The Whiteoak Anthum.
[Philadelphia, 1765.] Broadside.
LCP copy.   10211

Wither my Love. A Favorite Song [by
James Cobb, 1756-1818].
Philadelphia, Carr, [1793]. [2] pp.
AAS copy.   25309

Whiting, John, 1635-1689.
(Sibley, I, 343-347.)
The Way of Israels Welfare.
Boston, 1686. [8], 38 pp.
AAS copy.   421

Whiting, Samuel, 1597-1679.
(S. E. Morison, Founding, pp. 406-407.)
Abraham's Humble Intercession.
Cambridge, 1666. [8], 349, [1] pp.
LOC copy.   111

Whiting, Samuel, 1597-1679.
(S. E. Morison, Founding, pp. 406-407.)
A Discourse of the last Judgment.
Cambridge, 1664. [14], 160 pp.
LOC copy.   94

[Whiting, Samuel, 1597-1679
(C. Mather, Magnalia, Bk. 3, Ch. 28.)
Oratio, quam Comitijs Cantabrigiensibus.
[Cambridge?] 1649. 16 pp.]
(Not American printing.)   29

Whiting, Samuel, 1597-1679.
(S. E. Morison. Founding p. 406-407.)
Oratio, quam Comitijs Cantabrigiensibus.
Boston, 1709. 16 pp.
HC copy.   1441

Whiting, Samuel, 1670-1725.
A Sermon, Preached at Windham.
New London, [Ct.], Byrne, 1800. 35 pp.
(Also entered as 36755, q. v.)   39090

Whiting, Samuel, 1744-1819.
An Oration . . . at Sheffield, July 4th,
1796.
Stockbridge, Andrews, 1796. 17 pp.
AAS copy.   31628

Whiting, Samuel, 1744-1819.
Samuel Whiting, next door to the

Court-House, Great-Barrington . . . Dry
Goods.
New York, Morton, [1789?]. Broadside.
NYHS copy.   45749

Whiting, Samuel, 1750-1819.
A Discourse, Delivered before His
Honour.
Rutland, Vt., Jay, 1797. 23 pp.
AAS copy.   33220

Whiting, Samuel, 1750-1819, attributed
author.
A Sermon, Preached at Windham, A.D.
1721 [by Eliphalet Adams, 1677-1753].
Windham, Ct., Byrne, 1800. 35 pp.
AAS copy.   36755

Whiting, Thurston, 1752-1829.
A Discourse Delivered in the Meeting
House in Pownall-borough.
Wiscasset, Hoskin & Scott, 1798. 27 pp.
JCB copy.   35021

Whiting, Thurston, 1752-1829.
An Oration, Delivered in the Baptist
Meeting House, in Thomaston.
Hallowell, Robinson, [1798]. 21 pp.
JCB copy.   35022

[Whiting, William], 1730-1792.
(Am. Antiq. Soc., Proc., LXVI, 119-166.)
An Address to the Inhabitants of the
County of Berkshire.
Hartford, [1778]. 28 pp.
AAS copy.   15717

Whitman, Benjamin, 1768-1840.
An Index to the Laws of Massachusetts.
Worcester, Thomas, Son & Thomas, 1797.
152 pp.
AAS copy.   33221

Whitman, Benjamin, 1768-1840.
An Oration, Delivered at Taunton.
New Bedford, Spooner, 1798. 18 pp.
AAS copy.   35023

Whitman, Elnathan, 1709-1777.
(Weis, Colonial Clergy N. E.)
Able and Faithful Ministers.
Norwich, 1773. 29, [1] pp.
AAS copy.   13079

Whitman, Elnathan, 1709-1777.
(Dexter, I, 343-344.)
The Character and Qualifications.
New London, 1745. [4], 40 pp.
AAS copy.   5714

Whitman, Elnathan, 1709-1777.
(Weis, Colonial Clergy N. E.)
The Death of Good Men.
Hartford, 1771. 19 pp.
CHS copy.   12286

Whitman, Kilborn, 1765-1835.
An Oration, Pronounced at Bridgewater.
Boston, Etheridge, 1798. 39 pp.
AAS copy.   35024

Whitman, Kilborn, 1765-1835.
A Sermon, Delivered June 10th, 1795.
Hallowell Hook, Wait & Baker, 1796. 36
pp.
AAS copy.   31629

Whitman, Levi, 1748-1838.
Jesus Christ the Resurrection.
Boston, Freeman, 1786. 22 pp.
HC copy.   20147

Whitman, Levi, 1748-1838.
A Sermon, Preached at Wellfleet, March
9, 1800.
Boston, Manning & Loring, 1800. 20 pp.
AAS copy.   39091

Whitman, Levi, 1748-1838.
A Sermon, Preached October 6, 1786.
Boston, Freeman, 1787. 20 pp.
AAS copy.   20885

[Whitman, Levi, 1748-1838.
Twenty Sermons, for the Use of Seamen.
Boston, Belknap, 1795.]
(Entry from the prospectus.)   29888

Whitman, Samuel, 1676-1751.
(Sibley, IV, 315-317.)
A Discourse of God's Omniscience.
New London, 1733. [4], 26 pp.
AAS copy.   3733

Whitman, Samuel, 1676-1751.
(Sibley, IV, 315-317.)
The Happiness of the Godly.
New London, 1727. [4], 27 pp.
AAS copy.   2974

Whitman, Samuel, 1676-1751.
(Sibley, IV, 315-317.)
Practical Godliness.
New London, 1714. [2], 44 pp.
AAS copy.   1723

Whitman, Samuel, 1751-1826.
A Dissertation on the Origin of Evil.
Northampton, Mass., Butler, 1797. 31 pp.
AAS copy.   33222

Whitman, Samuel, 1751-1826.
The Doctrine of Christ.
Northampton, Butler, 1790. 36 pp.
AAS copy.   23080

Whitman, Samuel, 1751-1826.
God the Author of Spiritual Life.
Northampton, Butler, 1794. 29 pp.
AAS copy.   28082

Whitman, Samuel, 1751-1826.
The Nature and Design of the Baptism of
Christ.
Northampton, Mass., Butler, 1800. 31 pp.
AAS copy.   39092

Whitman, Samuel, 1751-1826.
The Perfection of the Divine Constitution.
Northampton, Butler, 1793. 45, [1] pp.
AAS copy.   26480

Whitman, Samuel, 1751-1826.
Two Sermons.
Northampton, Butler, 1792. 43 pp.
AAS copy.   25034

Whitney, Eli, 1765-1825.
An Oration on the Death of Mr. Robert
Grant.
New Haven, Greens, [1792]. 15 pp.
AAS copy.   25035

Whitney, Josiah, 1731-1824.
(Weis, Colonial Clergy N. E.)
The Christian Minister.
Boston, Kneeland, 1763. [4], 25 pp.
AAS copy.   9540

Whitney, Josiah, 1731-1824.
The Essential Requisities.
Hartford, Babcock, 1788. 40 pp.
AAS copy.   21601

Whitney, Josiah, 1731-1824.
A Sermon, Addressed to a Military
Company.
Windham, [Ct.], Byrne, 1800. 15 pp.
MHS copy.   39093

Whitney, Josiah, 1731-1824.
A Sermon, Occasioned by the Death of
. . . Israel Putnam.
Windham, Byrne, [1790]. 28 pp.
AAS copy.   23081

Whitney, Josiah, 1731-1824.
A Sermon, Occasioned by the Death of
the Rev. Noadiah Russel.
Providence, Carter & Wilkinson, 1796. 27
pp.
AAS copy.   31630

Whitney, Peter, 1744-1816.
American Independence Vindicated.
Boston, Draper, 1777. 55 pp.
AAS copy.   15710

Whitney, Peter, 1744-1816.
Christ's Ambassadors.
Boston, Young & Minns, 1800. 26 pp.
AAS copy.   39094

Whitney, Peter, 1744-1816.
The Duty of Praising the Works of God.
Worcester, Thomas, Son & Thomas, 1796.
23 pp.
AAS copy.   31631

Whitney, Peter, 1744-1816.
The History of the County of Worcester.
Worcester, Thomas, 1793. 339 pp., 1 map.
AAS copy.   26481

Whitney, Peter, 1744-1816.
(Weis, Colonial Clergy N. E.)
The Transgression of a Land.

Boston, Boyle, 1774. 71 pp.
AAS copy.   13769

Whitney, Peter, 1744-1816.
Weeping and Mourning.
Brookfield, Mass., Merriam, 1800. 28 pp.
AAS copy.   39095

Whitney, Phineas, 1740-1819.
A Sermon, Delivered January 1st, 1800.
Boston, Manning & Loring, 1800. 32 pp.
AAS copy.   39096

[The Whitsuntide Gift.
Philadelphia, Spotswood, 1786.]
(Ghost of a London ed. Adv. in Pa.
Herald, July 12, 1786.)   20148

[Whittaker, James, 1751-1787.
A Concise Statement of the Principles of
the Only True Church.
[Worcester, Thomas? 1785.] 18 pp.]
(A ghost of 22664 and 23082, arising
apparently from a defective copy.)   19386

[Whittaker, James, 1751-1787.
A Concise Statement.
Bennington, Haswell & Russell, 1790. 24
pp.]
(Also entered as 22664, q.v.)   23082

Whittelsey, Chauncey, 1717-1787.
A Brief Discourse Deliver'd at
North-Haven.
New Haven, [1760]. 51 pp.
CHS copy.   8768

Whittelsey, Chauncey, 1717-1787.
(Weis, Colonial Clergy N. E.)
A Discourse Occasioned by the Death . . .
of Mrs. Mary Clap.
New Haven, [1769]. 24 pp.
AAS copy.   11530

Whittelsey, Chauncey, 1717-1787.
The Importance of Religion.
New Haven, 1778. 23 pp.
AAS copy.   16170

Whittelsey, Chauncey, 1717-1787.
(Weis, Colonial Clergy N. E.)
A Sermon Occasioned by the Death of
Mrs. Abigail Noyes.
New Haven, [1768]. 32 pp.
AAS copy.   11118

Whittelsey, Chauncey, 1717-1787.
(Dexter, I, 613-616.)
A Sermon Preach'd at New-Haven.
New London, 1744. [8], 34, [1] pp.
AAS copy.   5519

Whittelsey, Chauncey, 1717-1787.
A Sermon, Preach'd June 22d, 1769.
New Haven, [1769]. 31 pp.
AAS copy.   11531

Whittelsey, Samuel, 1686-1752.
A Publick Spirit.
New London, 1731. [4], 45 pp.
AAS copy.   3490

Whittelsey, Samuel, 1686-1752.
(Dexter, I, 41-44.)
The Regards Due.
Boston, 1730. [4], 34 pp.
AAS copy.   3379

Whittelsey, Samuel, 1686-1752.
(Dexter, I, 41-44.)
A Sermon Preach'd at the Ordination of
Mr. Samuel Whittelsey, jun.
Boston, Draper for Eliot, 1739. [4], 32 pp.
AAS copy.   4460

Whittelsey, Samuel, 1686-1752.
The Woful Condition.
Boston, Kneeland and Green for Gerrish,
1731. [8], 23 pp.
AAS copy.   3491

Whittemore, Joseph.
Joseph Whittemore, Presents the
Following Address to his Friends,
Patrons, and Customers, Wishing them
. . . a Happy New-Year.
Boston, January 1, 1796. Broadside.
HSP copy.   31632

Whittemore, Joseph.
Joseph Whittemore, presents. . . . January
1, 1798.

[Boston, 1798.] Broadside.
AAS copy.   35025

Whittemore, Joseph.
To his Friends and Customers. . . .
January 1, 1795.
[Boston, 1795.] Broadside.
AAS copy.   47683

Whittemore, Joseph.
To the Generous Patrons of. . . .
[Boston, 1797.] Broadside.
HSP copy.   33223

[Whittemore, Nathaniel], 1673-1754.
. . . An Almanack for . . . MDCCV.
Boston, B. Green for Phillips, 1705. [16]
pp.
AAS copy.   39436

[Whittemore, Nathaniel], 1673-1754.
. . . An Almanack for . . . MDCCVI.
Boston, 1706. [16] pp.
(Evans omits the first of this series, that
for 1705, with imprint dated 1705.)
AAS copy.   1237

[Whittemore, Nathaniel], 1673-1754.
. . . An Almanack for . . . 1707.
Boston, 1707. [16] pp.
AAS copy.   1284

[Whittemore, Nathaniel, 1673-1754.
. . . An Almanack for . . . 1708.
Boston, 1708. [16] pp.]
(No copy found.)   1338

[Whittemore, Nathaniel], 1673-1754.
. . . An Almanack for . . . 1713.
America [Boston], 1713. [16] pp.
AAS copy.   39582

[Whittemore, Nathaniel], 1673-1754.
The Farmers Almanack for . . . 1714.
America . . . Boone . . . in Boston, 1714.
[16] pp.
AAS copy.   39606

[Whittemore, Nathaniel], 1673-1754.
The Farmers Almanack (Corrected &
Amended) . . . 1714.
Boston, Bookseller's Shops, 1714. [16] pp.
(The AAS has also the uncorrected
edition.)
AAS copy.   1724

[Whittemore, Nathaniel], 1673-1754.
. . . An Almanack for . . . 1715.
America [Boston], 1715. [16] pp.
AAS copy.   39640

[Whittemore, Nathaniel], 1673-1754.
(C. Hudson, Lexington, II, 754.)
. . . An Almanack for . . . 1716.
America [Boston], 1716. [16] pp.
AAS copy.   1793

[Whittemore, Nathaniel], 1673-1754.
(C. Hudson, Lexington, II, 754.)
. . . An Almanack for . . . 1717.
American [Boston], 1717. [16] pp.
AAS copy.   1863

[Whittemore, Nathaniel], 1673-1754.
(C. Hudson, Lexington, II, 754.)
. . . An Almanack for . . . 1718.
America [Boston], 1718. [16] pp.
AAS copy.   1937

Whittemore, Nathaniel, 1673-1754.
(C. Hudson, Lexington, II, 754.)
. . . An Almanack for . . . 1719.
Boston, Fleet, 1719. [16] pp.
AAS copy.   2008

Whittemore, Nathaniel, 1673-1754.
(C. Hudson, Lexington, II, 754.)
. . . An Almanack for . . . 1720.
Boston, Fleet, 1720. [16] pp.
AAS copy.   2087

Whittemore, Nathaniel, 1673-1754.
(C. Hudson, Lexington, II, 754.)
An Almanack for the Year . . . 1721.
Boston, Fleet, 1721. [16] pp.
AAS copy.   2195

Whittemore, Nathaniel, 1673-1754.
. . . An Almanack for the Year . . . 1722.
Boston, 1722. [16] pp.
AAS copy.   2304

Whittemore, Nathaniel, 1673-1754.

An Almanack for the Year . . . 1723.
Boston, Fleet, 1723. [16] pp.
AAS copy.   2405

Whittemore, Nathaniel, 1673-1754.
An Almanack for the Year . . . 1724. . . .
By N. Wittemore.
Boston, J. Allen, 1724. [16] pp.
AAS copy.   39819

Whittemore, Nathaniel, 1673-1754.
An Almanack for the Year . . . 1724.
Boston, Green, 1724. [16] pp.
(The AAS has also the Allen edition, and
the BPL the Fleet edition.)
AAS copy.   2494

Whittemore, Nathaniel, 1673-1754.
An Almanack. For the Year . . . 1725.
Boston, for the Booksellers, 1725. [16] pp.
AAS copy.   2593

Whittemore, Nathaniel, 1673-1754.
An Almanack for the Year . . . 1726.
Boston, Boone, 1726. [16] pp.
AAS copy.   2718

Whittemore, Nathaniel, 1673-1754.
A New Almanack for the Year . . . 1727.
Boston, Boone, 1727. [16] pp.
AAS copy.   2827

Whittemore, Nathaniel, 1673-1754.
An Almanack for the Year . . . 1728.
Boston, Boone, 1728. [16] pp.
AAS copy.   2975

Whittemore, Nathaniel, 1673-1754.
An Almanack or Diary, for . . . 1729.
Boston, 1729. [16] pp.
AAS copy.   3119

[Whittemore, Nathaniel, 1673-1754.
The Farmer's Almanack for . . . 1730.
Boston, 1729.]
(Assumed by Evans from the sequence.)
   3235

[Whittemore, Nathaniel, 1673-1754.
An Almanack or Diary, for . . . 1731.
Boston, 1731.]
(Assumed by Evans from the sequence.)
   3380

[Whittemore, Nathaniel, 1673-1754.
An Almanack for the Year . . . 1732.
Boston, 1732. [16] pp.]
(Assumed by Evans from the sequence.)
   3492

[Whittemore, Nathaniel, 1673-1754.
An Almanack for the Year . . . 1733.
Boston, 1733.]
(Assumed by Evans from the sequence.)
   3617

[Whittemore, Nathaniel, 1673-1754.
An Almanack for the Year . . . 1734.
Boston, 1734.]
(Assumed by Evans from the sequence.)
   3734

[Whittemore, Nathaniel, 1673-1754.
An Almanack for the Year . . . 1735.
Boston, 1735. [16] pp.]
(Evans described a defective copy of
another almanac.)   3856

[Whittemore, Nathaniel, 1673-1754.
An Almanack for the Year . . . 1736.
Boston, 1736. [16] pp.]
(No copy found.)   3974

[Whittemore, Nathaniel, 1673-1754.
An Almanack for the Year . . . 1737.
Boston, 1736.]
(Assumed by Evans from the sequence.)
   4102

Whittemore, Nathaniel, 1673-1754.
Whittemore Revived. An Almanack for
. . . 1738.
Boston, Fleet, 1738. [16] pp.
AAS copy.   4208

[Whittemore, Nathaniel, 1673-1754.
An Almanack for the Year . . . 1739.
Boston, 1739. [16] pp.]
(No copy located.)   4323

Whittemore, Nathaniel, 1673-1754.
Whittemore Continued. Being an
Almanack for . . . 1740.

Boston, Fleet, 1740. [16] pp.
AAS copy.   4461

[Whittemore, Nathaniel, 1673-1754.
An Almanack for the Year . . . 1741.
Boston, 1741.]
(Assumed by Evans from the sequence.)
   4658

Whittington and his Cat, 1770.
The Famous and Remarkable History
of. . . .
Boston, sold at the Heart & Crown,
[1770?]. 16 pp.
BPL copy.   42049

Whittington and his Cat, 1780.
The Famous and Remarkable History of
Sir Richard Whittington.
Boston, at the Bible & Heart, [1780?]. 16
pp.
(Not located.)   43917

Whittington and his Cat, 1788.
The Famous History of Whittington and
his Cat.
Hartford, Patten, 1788. Front., 28 pp.
AAS copy.   21602

Whittington and his Cat, 1790.
The Famous History of Whittington and
his Cat.
Middletown, Woodward, 1790. 27 pp.
CHS copy.   23083

Whittington and his Cat, 1791.
The Famous History of Whittington and
his Cat.
New York, Durell, [1791?]. [30] pp.
(Not located, 1968.)   46357

Whittington and his Cat, 1794.
The Famous History of Sir Richard
Whittington.
Baltimore, Fisher, 1794. 31 pp.
AAS copy.   47328

[Whittington and his Cat, 1794.
The Remarkable History of. . . .
Portsmouth, N.H., Peirce, 1794.]
("This Day Printed, In a Pamphlet, And
to be Sold at this Office," Oracle of the
Day, Oct. 25, 1794.)   28083

Whittington and his Cat, 1795.
The Famous History of. . . .
Newfield, [Ct.], Beach & Jones, [1795].
27, [1] pp.
AAS copy.   47684

[Whittington and his Cat, 1796.
The Famous History of Sir Richard
Whittington.
Dover, N.H., Bragg, 1796.]
(Imprint assumed by Evans from adv.
"For sale at this office," The Sun, May 18,
1796.)   31633

Whittington and his Cat, 1800.
The Famous History of. . . .
New York, Durell for Duyckinck, 1800. 31
pp.
(An imprint variant of 37395, q.v.)   49193

Whittington and his Cat, 1800.
The Famous History of. . . .
New York, Durell for Harrison, 1800. 31
pp.
AAS copy.   37395

Whittington and his Cat, 1800.
The Famous History of. . . .
New York, Durell for Stephens, 1800.
(An imprint variant of 37395, q.v.)   49194

Whitwell, Benjamin, 1772-1825.
An Eulogy, on . . . Washington.
Hallowell, Me., Edes, 1800. 18 pp.
BA copy.   39097

Whitwell, Samuel, d. 1791.
An Oration Delivered to the Society of the
Cincinnati . . . July 4, 1789.
Boston, Russell, 1789. 20 pp.
AAS copy.   22279

Whitwell, William, 1737-1781.
A Discourse Delivered to the First
Church.
Salem, [1770]. 31 pp.
AAS copy.   11940

Whitwell, William, 1737-1781.

(Weis, Colonial Clergy N. E.)
A Discourse, Occasioned by the loss of a
Number of Vessels.
Salem, 1770. 21 pp.
AAS copy.   11939

Whoever has Candidly Traced the Rapid
Growth of These Colonies. . . .
[Boston, 1774.] Broadside.
MHS copy.   13770

Whoever has Candidly Traced the Rapid
Growth of these Colonies. . . .
[Boston, 1775?] Broadside.
MHS copy.   42985

The Whole Duty of Man [by Richard
Allestree, 1619-1681].
Williamsburg, 1746. xx, 303 pp.
LOC copy.   5888

The Whole Duty of Woman. . . . Second
Edition [by William Kenrick, 1725-1779].
Boston, Fowle & Draper, 1761. 44 + pp.
(The only known copy is imperfect.)
AAS copy.   41206

[The Whole Duty of Woman [by William
Kenrick, 1725-1779].
New London, 1761.]
(Adv. in N. L. Gazette, July, 1761. but
possibly for the Boston ed., of which there
is a copy at AAS.)   8896

[The Whole Duty of Woman [by William
Kenrick, 1725-1779].
Boston, Fowle & Draper, 1762. 100 pp.]
(Imprint from adv., pagination from
Haven never verified.)   9152

The Whole Duty of Woman [by William
Kenrick, 1725-1779].
Philadelphia, Crukshank, 1788. 62, [10]
pp.
LCP copy.   21184

The Whole Duty of Woman. . . . Sixth
Edition [by William Kenrick, 1725-1779].
Boston, Hall, 1790. 61, [1] pp.
AAS copy.   22601

The Whole Duty of Woman. . . . Eighth
Edition [by William Kenrick, 1725-1779].
Boston, Hall, 1793. 56 pp.
AAS copy.   25686

The Whole Duty of Woman. . . .
Fourteenth Edition [by William Kenrick,
1725-1779].
Concord, [N.H.], Hough, 1793. 35 pp.
(The only known copy is in poor
condition)
AAS copy.   46794

The Whole Duty of Woman. . . .
Fourteenth Edition [by William Kenrick,
1725-1779].
Danbury, Douglas, 1793. 34, [2] pp.
CHS copy.   46795

The Whole Duty of Woman. . . . Ninth
Edition [by William Kenrick, 1725-1779].
Boston, Hall, 1794. 56 pp.
AAS copy.   27181

The Whole Duty of Woman [by William
Kenrick, 1725-1779].
Exeter, Stearns & Winslow, 1794. 56 pp.
AAS copy.   27182

The Whole Duty of Woman [by William
Kenrick, 1725-1779].
Walpole, N. H., Carlisle, 1797. 68 pp.
AAS copy.   32335

The Whole Duty of Woman [by William
Kenrick, 1725-1779].
Litchfield, Ct., Collier, [1798]. 106 pp.
(The one recorded copy is lost.)   33948

The Whole Duty of Woman [by William
Kenrick, 1725-1779].
Philadelphia, Ormrod, 1798. 157 pp.
AAS copy.   33949

Wholesome Words [by Cotton Mather,
1663-1728].
Boston, 1713. [2], 24 pp.
AAS copy.   1630

Wickham, John, 1763-1839.
The Substance of an Argument . . . in. . . .
The United States vs. Hylton.

Richmond, Davis, [1795]. 15 pp.
MHS copy.　　　　　29889

Widder, Philip.
Er. Ehrw. Hrn. Philip Widders.
Philadelphia, Miller, 1764.]
(Adv. Phil. Staatsbote, Sept. 10, 1764.)
　　　　　9874

[Eine Widerlegung des Freyen Willins.
Ephrata, 1788.]
(Origin of entry unknown.)　　　　　21603

. . . . The Widowed Mourner [by John
Gardiner, 1737-1793].
[Boston, 1791.] [8] pp.
AAS copy.　　　　　23400

The Widowed Mourner [by John
Gardiner, 1737-1793].
[Boston, 1791.] 7, [1] pp.
AAS copy.　　　　　46179

Wieland, Christoph Martin, 1733-1813.
Socrates out of his Senses. . . . Vol. I
[-II].
Newburgh, N. Y., Denniston for Fellows,
1797. xvii, [1], 105; [3], 119 pp.
AAS copy.　　　　　33224

[Wieland, Christoph Martin], 1733-1813.
The Trial of Abraham.
[Boston], 1760. vi, 70, 4 pp.
(A variant of 41510; see Modern
Language Notes, Apr. 1930, pp. 246-247.)
　　　　　41511

[Wieland, Christoph Martin], 1733-1813.
The Trial of Abraham.
[Boston], 1764. vi, 70 pp.
AAS copy.　　　　　41510

[Wieland, Christoph Martin], 1733-1813.
The Trial of Abraham.
Norwich, Trumbull, 1777. v, 60 pp.
NYPL copy.　　　　　15711

Wieland [by Charles Brockden Brown,
1771-1810].
New York, Swords for Caritat, 1798. [4],
298 pp.
AAS copy.　　　　　33461

Wigglesworth, A.
An Extract from an Eulogium on . . .
Washington.
Albany, [N. Y.], Barber & Southworth,
1800. 7 pp.
AAS copy.　　　　　39098

Wigglesworth, Edward, 1693-1765.
(Sibley, V, 546-555.)
The Blessedness of the Dead.
Boston, Gerrish, 1731. [4], iv, 23, [5], 24
pp.
AAS copy.　　　　　3493

Wigglesworth, Edward, 1693-1765.
(Sibley, V, 546-555.)
A Discourse Concerning the Duration.
Boston, Henchman, 1729. [4], 19 pp.
AAS copy.　　　　　3236

Wigglesworth, Edward, 1693-1765.
(Sibley, V, 546-555.)
The Doctrine of Reprobation.
Boston, Draper and Fleet, 1763. 48 pp.
AAS copy.　　　　　9541

Wigglesworth, Edward, 1693-1765.
(Sibley, V, 546-555.)
An Enquiry into the Truth.
Boston, Draper for Henchman, 1738. [8],
90 pp.
AAS copy.　　　　　4324

Wigglesworth, Edward, 1693-1765.
(Sibley, V, 546-555.)
A Faithful Servant.
Boston, Henchman, 1737. [2], 18 pp.
(Signatured with 4196, q.v.)　　　　　4209

[Wigglesworth, Edward], 1693-1765.
(Sibley, V, 546-555.)
A Letter from one in the Country to his
Friend in Boston, Containing some
Remarks upon a late Pamphlet, Entituled,
The Distressed State of the Town of
Boston.
Boston, Franklin for Henchman, 1720.
[2], 22 pp.
BPL copy.　　　　　2128

Wigglesworth, Edward, 1693-1765.
(Sibley, V, 546-555.)
A Letter to the Reverend Mr. George
Whitefield.
Boston, Fleet, 1745. 61, [2], 5 pp.
AAS copy.　　　　　5715

[Wigglesworth, Edward], 1693-1765.
(Sibley, V, 546-555.)
A Project for the Emission of an Hundred
Thousand Pounds.
Boston, Kneeland for Edwards, 1720. 16
pp.
AAS copy.　　　　　2168

Wigglesworth, Edward, 1693-1765.
(Sibley, V, 546-555.)
A Seasonable Caveat.
Boston, Henchman, 1735. [4], 33, [1] pp.
AAS copy.　　　　　3975

[Wigglesworth, Edward], 1693-1765.
(Sibley, V, 546-555.)
Sober Remarks on a Book Lately
Re-printed.
Boston, Gerrish, 1724. [4], 78, [1] pp.
AAS copy.　　　　　2594

[Wigglesworth, Edward], 1693-1765.
(Sibley, V, 546-555.)
Sober Remarks on a Book Lately
Reprinted. . . . Second Edition.
Boston, Gerrish, 1724. [8], 126 pp.
AAS copy.　　　　　2595

Wigglesworth, Edward, 1693-1765.
(Sibley, V, 546-555.)
Some Distinguishing Characters.
Boston, Fleet, 1754. 34 pp.
AAS copy.　　　　　7338

Wigglesworth, Edward, 1693-1765.
(Sibley, V, 546-555.)
Some Evidences of the Divine Inspiration.
Boston, Fowle for Henchman, 1755. 26,
[1] pp.
AAS copy.　　　　　7592

Wigglesworth, Edward, 1693-1765.
(Sibley, V, 546-555.)
Some Thoughts.
Boston, Draper, 1757. 31 pp.
AAS copy.　　　　　8064

Wigglesworth, Edward, 1693-1765.
(Sibley, V, 546-555.)
The Sovereignty of God.
Boston, Rogers & Fowle, 1741. 35, [1] pp.
AAS copy.　　　　　4863

[Wigglesworth, Edward], 1693-1765.
(Sibley, V, 546-555.)
A Vindication of the Remarks of one in
the Country.
Boston, Kneeland for Henchman, 1720. 20
pp.
AAS copy.　　　　　2190

Wigglesworth, Edward, 1732-1794.
The Authority of Tradition.
Boston, Fleets, 1778. 39 pp.
AAS copy.　　　　　16171

Wigglesworth, Edward, 1732-1794.
Calculations on American Population.
Boston, Boyle, 1774. 24 pp.
AAS copy.　　　　　14625

Wigglesworth, Edward, 1732-1794.
The Hope of Immortality.
Boston, Fleets, 1779. 24, iii pp.
AAS copy.　　　　　16681

[Wigglesworth, Michael, 1631-1705.
(D. A. B.)
The Day of Doom.
Cambridge, 1662.]
(No copy of this first edition known.)　　71

Wigglesworth, Michael, 1631-1705.
(D. A. B.)
The Day of Doom.
[Cambridge, 1666.] [4], 78 (i.e. 98) pp.
(No perfect copy known.)
MHS copy.　　　　　112

[Wigglesworth, Michael, 1631-1705.
The Day of Doom.
Cambridge, [Mass.], S.G. and M.J. for
Usher, 1670.]
(No copy located.)　　　　　39180

[Wigglesworth, Michael, 1631-1705.
(D. A. B.)

Day of Doom.
Cambridge, 1683.]
(Probably a ghost of a London edition.
See Am. Antiq. Soc. Proc., XXXIX,
79-80.)　　　　　355

Wigglesworth, Michael, 1631-1705.
(D. A. B.)
The Day of Doom.
Boston, 1701. [12], 80 pp.
AAS copy.　　　　　1030

Wigglesworth, Michael, 1631-1705.
The Day of Doom. . . . Sixth Edition.
Boston, Allen for Boone, 1715. pp.
[3] -12, 1-82.
(For text see 1794.)
AAS copy.　　　　　39641

Wigglesworth, Michael, 1631-1705.
The Day of Doom. . . . Sixth Edition.
Boston, Allen for Buttolph, 1715. 82 pp.
HEH copy.　　　　　39642

Wigglesworth, Michael, 1631-1705.
(D. A. B.)
The Day of Doom. . . . Sixth Edition.
Boston, Allen for Eliot, 1715. 12, 82 pp.
(AAS has also a copy with the imprint
Allen for Boone, and HEH, Allen for
Buttolph.)
AAS copy.　　　　　1794

[Wigglesworth, Michael, 1631-1705.
(D. A. B.)
The Day of Doom. . . . Seventh Edition.
Boston, Fleet, 1751. 104 pp.
AAS copy.　　　　　6796

Wigglesworth, Michael, 1631-1705.
The Day of Doom.
Norwich, [Ct.], Spooner, 1774. 36 pp.
AAS copy.　　　　　42751

Wigglesworth, Michael, 1631-1705.
The Day of Doom.
Norwich, [Ct.], Green & Spooner, 1777.
36 pp.
AAS copy.　　　　　43409

[Wigglesworth, Michael, 1631-1705.
(D. A. B.)
Massachusetts Election Sermon, May 12,
1686.
Boston, 1686.]
(Not printed.)　　　　　422

Wigglesworth, Michael, 1631-1705.
(Sibley, I, 259-286.)
Meat out of the Eater.
Cambridge, 1670. 208 pp.
YC copy.　　　　　158

Wigglesworth, Michael, 1631-1705.
(D. A. B.)
Meat out of the Eater.
Boston, 1689. 208 pp.
BPL copy.　　　　　500

[Wigglesworth, Michael, 1631-1705.
(D. A. B.)
Meat out of the Eater.
Boston, 1706.]
(Title from adv., "to be sold," Boston
News Letter, July 15, 1706.)　　　　　1285

Wigglesworth, Michael, 1631-1705.
Meat out of the Eater. . . . Fifth Edition.
Boston, Allen for Boone, 1717. 143 pp.
(For text see 1938.)
AAS copy.　　　　　39672

Wigglesworth, Michael, 1631-1705.
Meat out of the Eater. . . . Fifth Edition.
Boston, Allen for Buttolph, 1717. 143 pp.
(For text see 1938.)
AAS copy.　　　　　39673

Wigglesworth, Michael, 1631-1705.
(D. A. B.)
Meat out of the Eater. . . . The Fifth
Edition.
Boston, Allen for Elliot, 1717. 143 pp.
(Known also with imprints of Allen for
Buttolph, Fleet, Boone, and Henchman.)
AAS copy.　　　　　1938

Wigglesworth, Michael, 1631-1705.
Meat out of the Eater. . . . Fifth Edition.
Boston, Allen for Fleet, 1717. 143 pp.
(For text see 1938.)
AAS copy.　　　　　39674

Wigglesworth, Michael, 1631-1705.
Meat out of the Eater. . . . Fifth Edition.
Boston, Allen for Henchman, 1717. 143
pp.
(But for imprint identical with 1938, q.v.)
                                         39675

Wigglesworth, Michael, 1631-1705.
Meat out of the Eater. . . . Fifth Edition.
Boston, Allen for Starke, 1717. 143 pp.
(For text see 1938.)
MHS copy.   39676

[Wigglesworth, Michael, 1631-1705.
(D.A.B.)
Meat out of the Eater. . . . Sixth Edition.
Boston, 1721. 144 pp.]
(Title obtained by Haven from adv. in
3202 which did not give date or edition of
copy offered.)   2305

Wigglesworth, Michael, 1631-1705.
Meat out of the Eater. . . . Sixth Edition.
New London, 1770. 140 pp.
(The AAS has parts of 2 issues.)
BPL copy.   11941

Wigglesworth, Samuel, 1689-1768.
(Sibley, V, 406-412.)
The Blessedness of Such as Trust in
Christ.
Boston, Kneeland, 1755. [4], 28, [2], 29
pp.
AAS copy.   7593

Wigglesworth, Samuel, 1689-1768.
(Sibley, V, 406-412.)
An Essay for Reviving Religion.
Boston, Kneeland for Henchman, 1733.
[4], 36 pp.
AAS copy.   3735

Wigglesworth, Samuel, 1689-1768.
(Sibley, V, 406-412.)
The Excellency of the Gospel-Message.
Boston, Henchman, 1727. [4], 28 pp.
AAS copy.   2976

Wigglesworth, Samuel, 1689-1768.
God's Promise.
Boston, Kneeland, 1755. [2], 29 pp.
(The second part of 7593, q.v.)   7594

Wigglesworth, Samuel, 1689-1768.
(Sibley, V, 406-412.)
The Pleasures of Religion.
Boston, 1728. [4], iv, 34 pp.
BA copy.   3120

Wigglesworth, Samuel, 1689-1768.
A Religious Fear.
Boston, Henchman and Hancock, 1728.
[4], iii, [1], 42 pp.
AAS copy.   3121

[Wigglesworth, Samuel, 1689-1768.
A Sermon, at the Ordination of John
Warren.
Boston, 1733.]
(Evans obtained this title from Sprague, I,
146; it was probably not printed.)   3736

Wigglesworth, Samuel, 1689-1768.
(Sibley, V, 406-412.)
A View of the Inestimable Treasure.
Boston, Kneeland & Green, 1746. 24 pp.
AAS copy.   5889

Wight, Elnathan, 1715-1761.
Ministers Ambassadors.
Boston, Edes & Gill, 1755. 25, [4] pp.
(The only reported copy is imperfect.)
NYHS copy.   7595

Wight, Henry, 1753-1837.
A Sermon, Delivered, October 9, 1793.
Warren, R. I., Phillips, 1794. 24 pp.
AAS copy.   28084

Wightman, Valentine, 1681-1747.
(Whitman, George Wightman, pp. 31-35.)
The Excellency of Faith.
New London, 1739. [2], 27 pp.
(The title given by Evans was from a
mutilated copy.)
JCB copy.   4462

[Wightman, Valentine, 1681-1747.
(Whitman, George Wightman, pp. 31-35.)
Infant Baptism.
New London, 1729 ?]
(Assumed by Evans from references in the
controversy with John Bulkley.)   3237

Wightman, Valentine, 1681-1747.
(Whitman, George Wightman, pp. 31-35.)
A Letter to the Elders.
[Boston ? 1725.] 16 pp.
MHS copy.   2719

[Wightman, Valentine, 1681-1747.
(Whitman, George Wightman, pp. 31-35.)
Some Brief Remarks.
Newport, 1731.]
(This title is Trumbull's revision of an
adv. in the New England Weekly Journal,
Oct. 4, 1731.)   3494

Wightman, Valentine, 1681-1747.
Some Brief Remarks on a Book.
Newport, Franklin, 1732. [2], ii, 40 pp.
(The only known copy is imperfect.)
CHS copy.   40013

Wignell, Thomas, pseud.
The Contrast . . . [by Royall Tyler,
1757-1826].
Philadelphia, Prichard & Hall, 1790.
Front., viii, [16], 79 pp.
AAS copy.   22948

Wijnpersse, Dionysius van de, 1724-1808.
A Proof of the True and Eternal Godhead.
Philadelphia, Young, 1796. pp. [i]-v, [1],
[13]-198 pp.
AAS copy.   31666

Wikoff, Isaac.
An Address to my Fellow Citizens. . . .
July 11, 1771.
[Philadelphia, 1771.] Broadside.
LCP copy.   12287

Wikoff, Isaac.
To the Public. . . . October 26, 1771.
[Philadelphia, 1771.] [4] pp.
LCP copy.   12288

[Wilberforce, pseud.
To the Freemen of Kentucky.
[Lexington, 1795.] [2] pp.
(The origin of this entry is unknown.)
                                         29890

Wilberforce, William, 1759-1833.
A Practical View.
Philadelphia, Ormrod, 1798. 343, [13] pp.
AAS copy.   35026

Wilberforce, William, 1759-1833.
A Practical View. . . . Second American
Edition.
Boston, Manning & Loring for Larkin,
Davis, and Hudson & Goodwin, 1799. 300
pp.
AAS copy.   36716

Wilberforce, William, 1759-1833.
A Practical View. . . . Second American
Edition.
Boston, Manning & Loring for Larkin,
1799. 300 pp.
(An imprint variant of 36716, q. v. for
text.)
AAS copy.   48992

[Wilcox, Thomas], 1549-1608.
(D. N. B.)
A Guide to Eternal Glory.
Boston, 1702. 108 pp.
(Possibly the author was Thomas
Wilcocks, 1622 -.)
AAS copy.   1101

[Wilcocks, Thomas], b. 1622.
A Choice Drop of Honey.
Cambridge, 1668.]
(Known only from S. Green's list of his
publications.)   118

[Wilcocks, Thomas], b. 1622.
A Choice Drop of Honey.
Boston, 1734.]
(Evans obtained this title from the Brinley
catalogue which described a copy lacking
the tp. It was probably 4864.)   3857

[Wilcocks, Thomas], b. 1622.
A Choice Drop of Honey. . . . Seventh
Edition.
Boston, Rogers for Proctor, 1741. 23 pp.
AAS copy.   4864

Wilcocks, Thomas, b. 1622.
A Choice Drop of Honey. . . . Eighth
Edition.

Boston, Fowle, for Kneeland & Green,
1741. 23 pp.
(Evans was in error as to the imprint of
the copy which he described.)
BPL copy.   4865

[Wilcocks, Thomas], b. 1622.
A Choice Drop of Honey. . . . Ninth
Edition.
Boston, 1741.]
(Assumed by Evans from the sequence.)
                                          4866

Wilcocks, Thomas, b. 1622.
A Choice Drop of Honey. . . . Tenth
Edition.
Boston, Draper for Henchman, 1741. [2],
ii, 20 pp.
CHS copy.   4867

Wilcocks, Thomas, b. 1622.
A Choice Drop of Honey. . . . Tenth
Edition.
Boston, Henchman, 1743. 24 pp.
BA copy.   5314

[Wilcocks, Thomas], b. 1622.
A Choice drop of Honey.
Newport, 1770. 23 pp.
RIHS copy.   11942

W[ilcox], T[homas], b. 1622.
A Choice Drop of Honey. . . . Seventh
Edition.
New London, Green, 1772. 24 pp.
(No copy located.)   42391

W[ilcocks], T[homas], b. 1622.
A Choice Drop of Honey.
Newport, R. I., Hunter, 1772. 23 pp.
AAS copy.   42392

Wilcocks, Thomas, b. 1622.
A Choice Drop of Honey.
Philadelphia, Miller, 1774. 32 pp.
HSP copy.   42752

Wilcocks, Thomas, b. 1622.
A Choice Drop of Honey.
Carlisle, [Pa.], Kline & Reynolds, 1790.
[2], 22 pp.
AAS copy.   46103

[Wilcocks, Thomas, b. 1622.
A Choice Drop of Honey.
Wilmington, Del., Adams, 1794.]
(Imprint assumed by Evans from adv.
"Just published by the Printer hereof,"
Delaware & Eastern Shore Adv., May 31,
1794.)   28085

[Wilcocks, Thomas], b. 1622.
A Guide to Eternal Glory.
Boston, Kneeland, 1757. 170 pp.
(No complete copy located.)
MHS copy.   8065

[Wilcocks, Thomas], b. 1622.
A Guide to Eternal Glory.
New York, Noel, 1759.]
("Lately published," N. Y. Gazette, May
14, 1759.)   8521

Wilcocks, Thomas, b. 1622.
Thoma Wilcocks Köstlicher
Honig-Tropfen.
Philadelphia, Miller, 1774. viii, 32 pp.
AAS copy.   13771

[Wilcocks, Thomas], b. 1622.
A Choice Drop of Honey. . . . Forty-Fifth
Edition.
Baltimore, Adamses, 1793. 24 pp.
HSP copy.   46946

[Wilcocks, Thomas], b. 1622.
A Choice Drop of Honey.
Walpole, N.H., Lee, 1795. 20 pp.
CHS copy.   47685

Wild, Daniel.
[A Large, and Well Assorted Collection
of Books. . . . May 29, 1800.
Boston, 1800.]
(McKay 143G.)   37006

Wild, Daniel.
[A Small, but Very Valuable Collection of
New Books. . . . July 2, 1800.
Boston, 1800.]
(McKay 143H.)   37007

Wild, Daniel.

[A Large and General Assortment of New and Valuable Books . . . Oct. 23, 1800.
Boston, 1800.]
(McKay 143K.)   37004

Wild, Daniel.
[A Large and General Assortment of Valuable Books. . . . Nov. 15, 1800.
Boston, 1800.]
(McKay 143L.)   37005

Wilde, Samuel Sumner, 1771-1855.
An Oration, Delivered at Pownallborough.
Wiscasset, Me., Hoskins, 1799. 20 pp.
AAS copy.   36717

Wilde, Samuel Sumner, 1771-1855.
An Oration, Delivered at Thomaston, July 4th, 1797.
Hallowell, Robinson, 1797. 15 pp.
AAS copy.   33225

Wilder, John, 1758-1836.
(Chapman, Alumni of Dartmouth, p. 35.)
The Blessedness of Departed Saints.
Providence, Wheeler, [1790]. 30 pp.
AAS copy.   23084

Wilder, John, 1758-1836.
A Discourse, Delivered May 9, 1798.
Wrentham, Mass., Heatons, 1798. 27 pp.
AAS copy.   35027

[The Wiles of Popery.
Boston, Fleet, 1745.]
("Just published," Boston Evening Post, Apr. 22, 1745.)   5716

[Wilkes, John, 1727-1797.
The North Britain. No. 1, and 2. New York, 1769.]
(Revision of a Haven entry; certainly a ghost. Perhaps reflecting a section of 11119.)   11532

[Wilkes, John, 1727-1797.
The North Briton, No. 45.
Boston, 1763.]
(Title from Haven, probably reflecting the reprint in 9543.)   9545

Wilkes, John, 1727-1797.
A Speech in the House of Commons.
Poughkeepsie, Holt, 1779. 8 pp.
(Eberstadt Cat. 163, no. 53.)   16682

Wilkes, John, 1727-1797.
[The Works of. . . .]
New York, Gaine, 1769.
(This American ed. is known only by this 34 p. fragment. See adv. in N. Y. Gazette; and Weekly Mercury, May 29, 1769.)
NYPL copy.   11119

Wilkins, Henry, 1767-1847.
The Family Adviser.
Philadelphia, Hall for Dickins, 1793. 97, [3], 103, [11] pp.
AAS copy.   26482

Wilkins, Henry, 1767-1847.
The Family Adviser. . . . Second Edition.
Philadelphia, Tuckniss for Dickins, 1795. 98, [2], 103, [11] pp.
AAS copy.   29891

Wilkins, Henry, 1767-1847.
An Inaugural Dissertation.
Philadelphia, Hall, 1793. 16 pp.
NLM copy.   26483

[Wilkins, Henry], 1767-1847.
An Original Essay on Animal Motion.
Philadelphia, 1792. 33 pp.
LCP copy.   25036

[Wilkins, Isaac, 1742-1830.
The Republican Dissected.
New York, Rivington, 1775.]
(Adv. N. Y. Gazetteer, Apr. 13, 1775.)   14626

[Wilkins, Isaac?], 1742-1830.
(Appleton's Cyclopaedia Am. Biog.)
Short Advice to the Counties of New-York.
New York, Rivington, 1774. 15 pp.
AAS copy.   13772

Wilkins, John, 1614-1672.
(D. N. B.)
A Discourse Concerning the Beauty of Providence.

Boston, Eliot, 1718. x, 80, [4] pp.
(The only known copy is defective.)
AAS copy.   2009

Wilkins, John, 1614-1672.
(D. N. B.)
A Discourse Concerning the Beauty of Providence. . . . Fifth Edition.
Boston, Kneeland for Eliot, 1720. [2], x, 80 pp.
AAS copy.   2196

Wilkins, Richard, of Boston, bookseller.
Advertisement. It has been Thought Proper. . . .
[Boston, 1690?] Broadside.
HC copy.   39281

[Wilkinson, Edward], 1727?-1809.
Wisdom, a Poem.
Philadelphia, James, 1787. 16 pp.
AAS copy.   20886

[Wilkinson, Edward, 1727?-1809.
Wisdom, a Poem.
Hudson, Stoddard, 1788.]
("Just published at this office," Hudson Gazette, July 8, 1788.)   21606

[Wilkinson, Edward], 1727?-1809.
Wisdom, a Poem.
Newport, [1788]. 16 pp.
AAS copy.   21605

[Wilkinson, Edward], 1727?-1809.
Wisdom, a Poem.
Philadelphia, James, 1788. 19 pp.
LCP copy.   45415

[Wilkinson, Edward, 1727?-1809.
Wisdom, a Poem.
Catskill Landing, Crosswell, 1792.]
(Entry from adv. "May be had at this Office" in Catskill Packet, Aug. 6, 1792.)
                                 25037

[Wilkinson, Edward], 1727?-1809.
Wisdom, a Poem.
Litchfield, [Ct.], Collier & Buel, 1792. 20 pp.
AAS copy.   46675

[Wilkinson, Edward], 1727?-1809.
Wisdom. A Poem.
Haverhill, Edes, 1794. 16 pp.
Haverhill Public Library copy.   28086

[Wilkinson, Edward], 1727?-1809.
Wisdom, a Poem.
New York, Collins, 1797. 21 pp.
AAS copy.   48319

[Wilkinson, Edward], 1727?-1809.
Wisdom: a Poem.
Litchfield, Ct., 1798. 24 pp.
CHS copy.   35029

Wilkinson, Eliab.
The New-England Calendar . . . for . . . 1800.
Warren, R. I., Phillips. [24] pp.
AAS copy.   36720

Wilkinson, Eliab.
The New-England Calendar . . . for . . . 1800.
[Warren, R. I., Phillips for] Richardson. [24] pp.
AAS copy.   36721

[Wilkinson, Jemima], 1752-1819.
Some Considerations, Propounded to the Several Sorts and Sects.
[Providence], 1779. 94 pp.
AAS copy.   19435

[Wilkinson, Jemima, 1752-1819.
(D. A. B.)
The Universal Friends' Advice.
Philadelphia, Bailey, 1784.]
(See Sabin 1043. Adv. Freeman's Journal, Nov. 24, 1784.)   18849

[Wilkinson, Rebecca.]
Sermons to Children.
Philadelphia, Young, 1795. 159, [1] pp.
AAS copy.   47686

[Wilkinson, Rebecca.]
Sermons to Children.
Boston, Hall, 1797. 105, [1] pp.
AAS copy.   32821

[Wilkinson, Rebecca].
Sermons to Children.
Pittsfield, Smith, 1799. 96 pp.
CHS copy.   48993

[Wilkinson, Thomas, 1751-1836.
An Appeal to England.
Dover, N.H., Bragg, 1794.]
(Imprint assumed by Evans from adv. "Just published, and for sale by Eliphalet Ladd," The Phenix, Aug. 9, 1794. None of the books in this adv. is known with Ladd's imprint.)   28087

Wilkinson, William, 1760-1852.
The Federal Calculator.
Providence, Carter & Wilkinson, 1795. 64 pp.
AAS copy.   29892

The Will of a Father Submitted to [by Cotton Mather, 1663-1728].
Boston, 1713. 40 pp.
AAS copy.   1631

Willard, John, 1733-1807.
A Sermon Preached at the Ordination of Mr. John Willard.
Middletown, [1786]. 46 pp.
AAS copy.   19721

Willard, Joseph, 1738-1804.
An Address in Latin. . . . Of . . . Washington.
[Charlestown], Etheridge, 1800. 31 pp.
AAS copy.   39101

Willard, Joseph, 1738-1804.
An Address in Latin. . . . Of . . . Washington.
[Charlestown, Mass.] Etheridge, 1800. 44 pp.
AAS copy.   39100

[Willard, Joseph], 1738-1804.
(D. A. B.)
Ames's Almanack Revived . . . for . . . 1766 . . . By a Late Student at Harvard-College.
Boston, Draper, etc. [24] pp.
AAS copy.   10212

Willard, Joseph, 1738-1804.
A Sermon, Delivered May 13, 1790.
Boston, Hall, 1790. 31 pp.
AAS copy.   23085

Willard, Joseph, 1738-1804.
A Sermon, Delivered October 16, 1793.
Boston, Hall, 1794. 47 pp.
AAS copy.   28088

Willard, Joseph, 1738-1804.
A Sermon, Preached May 11, 1785.
Salem, Hall, 1785. 54 pp.
AAS copy.   19387

Willard, Joseph, 1738-1804.
A Thanksgiving Sermon Delivered at Boston.
Boston, Fleets, 1784. 39 pp.
AAS copy.   18887

Willard, Joseph, 1741-1828.
(Weis, Colonial Clergy N. E.)
The Duty of the Good and Faithful Soldier.
Boston, Fleets, 1781. 23 pp.
AAS copy.   17438

Willard, Samuel, 1640-1707.
(Sibley, II, 13-36.)
The Barren Fig Trees Doom.
Boston, 1691. [6], 300 pp.
AAS copy.   581

Willard, Samuel, 1640-1707.
(Sibley, II, 13-36.)
The Best Priviledge.
Boston, 1701. [2], 30 pp.
MHS copy.   1031

Willard, Samuel, 1640-1707.
Brief Directions to a Young Scholar.
Boston, Draper for Hancock, 1735. [4], iv, 7 pp.
AAS copy.   3976

Willard, Samuel, 1640-1707.
(Sibley, II, 13-16.)
A Brief Discourse of Justification.
Boston, 1686. [6], 168 pp.
AAS copy.   423

[Willard, Samuel], 1640-1707.
(Sibley, II, 13-36.)
A Brief Reply to Mr. George Kieth.
Boston, 1703. [2], 66 pp.
AAS copy.   1150

Willard, Samuel, 1640-1707.
(Sibley, II, 13-36.)
The Character of a Good Ruler.
Boston, 1694. [6], 31 pp.
AAS copy.   711

Willard, Samuel, 1640-1707.
The Checkered State of the Gospel
Church.
Boston, 1701. 64 pp.
AAS copy.   1032

Willard, Samuel, 1640-1707.
The Child's Portion.
Boston, 1684. [8], 227 pp.
AAS copy.   380

Willard, Samuel, 1640-1707.
The Christians Exercise.
Boston, 1701. [4], 268 pp.
AAS copy.   1033

[Willard, Samuel, 1640-1707.
(Sibley, II, 13-36.)
The Christians Exercise.
Boston, 1721. [4], 268 pp.]
(Title taken by Haven from adv. in 3202
for what was probably a remainder of
1033. Evans took the pagination from the
first edition.)   2306

Willard, Samuel, 1640-1707.
(Sibley, II, 13-36.)
A Compleat Body of Divinity.
Boston, Green and Kneeland for Eliot and
Henchman, 1726. [2], iv, 3, [3], 914, [1]
pp. Port.
AAS copy.   2828

Willard, Samuel, 1640-1707.
(Sibley, II, 13-36.)
Covenant-keeping.
Boston, 1682. [12], 150 pp.
(The pagination as given by Evans
includes no. 281 which was issued bound
with this copy.)
AAS copy.   335

Willard, Samuel, 1640-1707.
The Danger of Taking God's Name in
Vain.
Boston, 1691. [2], 30 pp.
AAS copy.   582

Willard, Samuel, 1640-1707.
(Sibley, II, 13-36.).
The Doctrine of the Covenant.
Boston, 1693. [8], 165 pp.
AAS copy.   684

Willard, Samuel, 1640-1707.
(Sibley, II, 13-36.)
The Duty of a People.
Boston, 1680. [2], 13 pp.
AAS copy.   296

Willard, Samuel, 1640-1707.
The Fear of an Oath.
Boston, 1701. 29, [2] pp.
AAS copy.   1034

Willard, Samuel, 1640-1707.
The Fiery Tryal.
Boston, 1682. [4], 20 pp.
AAS copy.   336

Willard, Samuel, 1640-1707.
(Sibley, II, 13-36.)
The Fountain Opened.
Boston, 1700. [4], 208, [2] pp.
(The AAS has another issue with the
name of Benj. Eliot in the imprint.)
AAS copy.   960

Willard, Samuel, 1640-1707.
(Sibley, II, 13-36.)
The Fountain Opened . . . Second Edition.
Boston, Green, 1722. [2], 40 pp.
AAS copy.   2406

Willard, Samuel, 1640-1707.
The Fountain Opened.
Boston, Green for Eliot, Gerrish, &
Henchman, 1727. 24 pp.
(Signatured with 2959, q.v.)   2977

Willard, Samuel, 1640-1707.
(Sibley, II, 13-36.)
The Heart Garrisoned.
Cambridge, 1676. [2], 21 pp.
LOC copy.   227

Willard, Samuel, 1640-1707.
Heavenly Merchandize.
Boston, 1686. [6], 171, [2] pp.
BPL copy.   424

Willard, Samuel, 1640-1707.
(Sibley, II, 13-36.)
The High Esteem . . . John Hull.
Boston, 1683. [2], 20 pp.
AAS copy.   356

Willard, Samuel, 1640-1707.
(Sibley, II, 13-36.)
Impenitent Sinners.
Boston, 1698. [8], 52 pp.
(The unique copy is imperfect.)
LOC copy.   856

Willard, Samuel, 1640-1707.
(Sibley, II, 13-36.)
Israel's True Safety.
Boston, 1704. [2], 34, [2], 44, [6] pp.
AAS copy.   1198

Willard, Samuel, 1640-1707.
(Sibley, II, 13-36.)
The Just Man's Prerogative.
Boston, 1706. [4], 28, [4], 25 pp.
AAS copy.   1286

Willard, Samuel, 1640-1707.
The Law Established by the Gospel.
Boston, 1694. 39 pp.
AAS copy.   712

Willard, Samuel, 1640-1707.
Love's Pedigree.
Boston, 1700. 28 pp.
AAS copy.   961

Willard, Samuel, 1640-1707.
The Man of War.
Boston, Green & Allen for Eliot, 1699. 30,
[1] pp.
AAS copy.   900

Willard, Samuel, 1640-1707.
(Sibley, II, 13-36.)
The Man of War.
Boston, Green & Allen for Perry, 1699. 30,
[1] pp.
(This differs from 900 only in the
imprint.)
MHS copy.   899

Willard, Samuel, 1640-1707.
(Sibley, II, 13-36.)
Mercy Magnified.
Boston, 1684. [8], 391, [1] pp.
YC copy.   379

Willard, Samuel, 1640-1707.
Morality not to be Relied on.
Boston, 1700. 28 pp.
AAS copy.   962

Willard, Samuel, 1640-1707.
The Mourners Cordial.
Boston, 1691. 4, 137, [1] pp.
AAS copy.   583

Willard, Samuel, 1640-1707.
(Sibley, II, 13-36.)
Ne Sutor Ultra Crepidam.
Boston, 1681. [8], 27 pp.
AAS copy.   309

Willard, Samuel, 1640-1707.
The Peril of the Times Displayed.
Boston, 1700. 168 pp.
AAS copy.   963

Willard, Samuel, 1640-1707.
Prognostics of Impending Calamities.
Boston, 1701. 32 pp.
AAS copy.   1035

Willard, Samuel, 1640-1707.
Promise-Keeping.
Boston, 1691. [2], 28 pp.
AAS copy.   584

Willard, Samuel, 1640-1707.
Reformation of the Great Duty.
Boston, 1694. 76 pp.
AAS copy.   713

Willard, Samuel, 1640-1707.
A Remedy against Despair.
Boston, 1700. 70 pp.
BPL copy.   964

Willard, Samuel, 1640-1707.
Rules for the Discerning.
Boston, 1693. [2], 30 pp.
AAS copy.   685

[Willard, Samuel], 1640-1707.
(Sibley, II, 13-36.)
A Sermon Preached upon Ezek. 20. 30, 31.
Boston, 1679. [2], 13 pp.
BPL copy.   277

Willard, Samuel, 1640-1707.
The Sinfulness.
[Boston], 1691. [2], 29 pp.
AAS copy.   585

Willard, Samuel, 1640-1707.
(Sibley, II, 13-36.)
Some Brief Sacramental Meditations.
Boston, 1711. [2], vi, 257, [5] pp.
AAS copy.   1537

Willard, Samuel, 1640-1707.
Some Brief Sacramental Meditations. . . .
Second Edition.
Boston, Green, Bushell & Allen for
Henchman, 1743. [2], vi, 216, [4] pp.
AAS copy.   5315

[Willard, Samuel], 1640-1707.
(Sibley, II, 13-36.)
Some Miscellany Observations.
Philadelphia, 1692. 16 pp.
YC copy.   631

Willard, Samuel, 1640-1707.
Spiritual Desertions Discovered.
Boston, 1699. 144 pp.
AAS copy.   901

[Willard, Samuel, 1640-1707.
(Sibley, II, 13-36.)
Spiritual Desertions Discovered.
Boston, 1713. 160 pp.]
(A reprint of 901. Adv. by B. Eliot in
Evans 1665.)   1659

Willard, Samuel, 1640-1707.
Spiritual Desertions Discovered.
Boston, Eliot, 1741. 144 pp.
(The unique copy, owned by the AAS, is
mislaid. For another edition see 901.)   4868

Willard, Samuel, 1640-1707.
The Truly Blessed Man.
Boston, 1700. 652, [3] pp.
AAS copy.   965

Willard, Samuel, 1640-1707.
(Sibley, II, 13-36.)
Useful Instructions.
Cambridge, 1673. [4], 80 pp.
AAS copy.   184

Willard, Samuel, 1640-1707.
Walking with God.
Boston, 1701. 56 pp.
AAS copy.   1036

Willard, Samuel, 1705-1741.
(Sibley, VII, 281-287.)
The Minister of God Approved.
Boston, Kneeland & Green, 1743. xvi, 60,
35, [2] pp.
AAS copy.   5316

Willcocks, Henry.
Proposals for Printing . . . The Virginia
Gazette. . . . January 1, 1787.
[Winchester, 1787.] Broadside.
AAS copy.   45207

Willett, Marinus, 1740-1830.
Hartford, August 21, 1777. The Following
is a Narrative. . . .
[Hartford, 1777.] Broadside.
NYPL copy.   43410

William and Mary College.
The Charter, and Statutes.
Williamsburg, Parks, 1736. 121, [2] pp.
JCB copy.   40109

William and Mary College.
The Charter of the College of William &
Mary.

Richmond, Va., Nicolson, 1800. 77 pp.
AAS copy.   37204

William and Mary College.
The Charter, Transfer and Statutes.
Williamsburg, 1758. 164 pp.
NYPL copy.   8284

William and Mary College.
Statutes of the University.
Richmond, Davis, 1792. 16 pp.
VaSL copy.   25038

William and Mary College.
William & Mary College, March 20,
1770. . . . On the 15th of August . . . the
Medals will be Publickly Presented. . . .
[Williamsburg, 1770.] Broadside.
LOC copy.   42201

[William Augustus, Duke of Cumberland,
1721-1765.
Address of the Duke of Cumberland.
Boston, Fleet, 1746.]
("This day published," Boston Ev. Post,
Apr. 21, 1746.)   5891

William Crotty. To which are Added,
Five Other New Songs.
[Philadelphia], Stewart, [176?]. 8 pp.
PrU copy.   41106

William Goddard's Pennsylvania,
Delaware, Maryland, and Virginia
Almanack . . . for . . . 1785 [by Andrew
Ellicott, 1754-1820].
Baltimore, Goddard for Richards. [44]
pp.
AAS copy.   18457

William Jackson, an Importer.
[Boston, 1768.] Broadside.
MHS copy.   11120

William of the Ferry [by James Hook,
1746-1827].
Philadelphia & New York, [1796]. [2] pp.
AAS copy.   30587

William Reily's Courtship, Trial, and
Marriage.
[Baltimore? 1798?]. 12 pp.
MdHS copy.   48758

William Riley's Courtship to Collian
Band.
Suffield, [Ct.], 1800. 8 pp.
NL copy.   39103

William Story jun. was Married to Miss
Bathsheba Gray December 6th, 1778. . . .
Ipswich, May 14, 1791.
[Salem? 1791.] Broadside.
(The only known copy could not be
reproduced.)
EI copy.   46358

Williams, Abraham, 1727-1784.
(Weis, Colonial Clergy N. E.)
A Sermon Preached at the Ordination of
. . . Timothy Hilliard.
Boston, Draper and Fleets, 1771. 31 pp.
AAS copy.   12289

Williams, Abraham, 1727-1784.
(Weis, Colonial Clergy N. E.)
A Sermon on James V. 9.
Boston, Drapers, 1766. 29 pp.
AAS copy.   10522

Williams, Abraham, 1727-1784.
(Weis, Colonial Clergy N. E.)
A Sermon Preach'd at Boston.
Boston, Kneeland, 1762. [4], 28 pp.
AAS copy.   9310

Williams, Benjamin, 1754-1814.
Newbern, October 6th, 1794. Dear Sir. . . .
[Newbern, 1794.] Broadside.
HSP copy.   28089

[Williams, David], 1738-1816.
Lessons to a Young Prince. . . . Sixth
Edition.
New York, Childs & Swain for Berry &
Rogers, 1791. pp. [5]-56, 49-68; 5 plates.
AAS copy.   24001

[Williams, David, 1738-1816.
Lessons to a Young Prince.
Philadelphia, Carey, Stewart & Co.,
1791.]

(Entry apparently from an adv. for copies
of 24001.)   24002

[Williams, Edward.
The Five Strange Wonders of the
World. . . . Which was Written on
Purpose to make . . . New England Merry.
Boston, Fleet, 1734.]
("In a few Days will be published,"
Weekly Rehearsal, Sept. 2, 1734. "Just
Published," ibid., Sept. 23.)   3858

Williams, Eleazer, 1688-1742.
(Sibley, V, 471-474.)
An Essay to Prove.
New London, 1723. [2], 54 pp.
AAS copy.   2945

Williams, Eleazer, 1688-1742.
Sensible Sinners.
New London, 1735. [2], vi, 58 pp.
AAS copy.   3977

Williams, Eliphalet, 1727-1803.
(Weis, Col. Clergy N. E.)
The Duty of a People.
New London, 1756. 71 pp.
AAS copy.   7819

Williams, Eliphalet, 1727-1803.
(Weis, Colonial Clergy N. E.)
God's Wonderful Goodness.
New London, Green, 1760. 31 pp.
AAS copy.   8769

Williams, Eliphalet, 1727-1803.
(Weis, Colonial Clergy N. E.)
The Ruler's Duty.
Hartford, 1770. [2], 33 pp.
AAS copy.   11943

Williams, Eliphalet, 1727-1803.
(Weis, Colonial Clergy N. E.)
A Sermon, Preached in the Audience of
the General Assembly.
Hartford, [1769]. 44 pp.
AAS copy.   11533

[Williams, Eliphalet], 1727-1803.
Some Extracts from an Ancient Dialogue.
Hartford, Babcock, 1795. 16 pp.
AAS copy.   29543

Williams, Elisha, 1694-1755.
(Sibley, V 588-598.)
Death the Advantage.
New London, 1728. [4], 42 pp.
AAS copy.   3122

Williams, Elisha, 1694-1755.
Divine Grace Illustrious.
New London, 1728. [4], 47 pp.
AAS copy.   3123

[Williams, Elisha], 1694-1755.
(Sibley, V, 588-598.)
The Essential Rights.
Boston, Kneeland & Green, 1744. [2], 66
pp.
(HC, JCB, & NYPL have copies of an
issue with only 7 lines of errata on the last
page.)
AAS copy.   5520

Williams, Helen Maria, 1762-1827.
Letters Containing a Sketch of the Politics
of France.
Philadelphia, for Carey, Young, Dobson,
Rices, and Ormrod, 1796. 283 pp.
AAS copy.   31634

Williams, Helen Maria, 1762-1827.
Letters Containing a Sketch of the Scenes
which Passed in . . . France.
Philadelphia, Snowden & M'Corkle, 1796.
160 pp.
AAS copy.   31635

Williams, Helen Maria, 1762-1827.
Letters from France. . . . Vol. II.
Boston, Thomas & Andrews, West, and
Larkin, 1792. [4], 138 pp.
AAS copy.   25039

[Williams, Helen Maria, 1762-1827.
Letters from France.
New York, Allen, 1793. 4 vols. in 2.]
(A ghost resulting from an error in the
printed BA catalogue.)   26484

Williams, Helen Maria, 1762-1827.
Letters on the French Revolution. . . .
First American Edition.

Boston, Belknap & Young, 1791. 137 pp.
AAS copy.   24003

Williams, Helen Maria, 1762-1827.
Letters from France. . . . Second
American Edition.
New York, Allen, 1794. 4 vol. in 2. [2],
219; [4], 276 pp.
AAS copy.   28090

Williams, Helen Maria, 1762-1827.
Memoirs of Mons. and Madame du F.
Boston, 1794. 47 pp.
(Imprint given by Evans was assumed
from advs.)
AAS copy.   28091

[Williams, Helen Maria], 1762-1827.
A Residence in France.
Elizabethtown, N. J., Kollock for Davis,
1798. 517 pp.
AAS copy.   35030

[Williams, John], 1636?-1709.
A Brief Discourse Concerning the
Lawfulness.
Boston, 1712. [4], 35 pp.
AAS copy.   1592

Williams, John, 1664-1729.
(Sibley, III, 249-262.)
God in the Camp.
Boston, 1707. [2], 22 pp.
AAS copy.   1339

Williams, John, 1664-1729.
The Redeemed Captive.
Boston, 1707. [6], 104 pp.
AAS copy.   1340

Williams, John, 1664-1729.
(Sibley, III, 249-262.)
The Redeemed Captive. . . . Second
Edition.
Boston, Fleet, 1720. [6], 98 pp.
NYPL copy.   2197

Williams, John, 1664-1729.
(Sibley, III, 249-262.)
The Redeemed Captive. . . . Third
Edition.
Boston, Kneeland, 1758. [4], iv, 104 pp.
BA copy.   8285

Williams, John, 1664-1729.
(Sibley, III, 249-262.)
The Redeemed Captive. . . . Fourth
Edition.
New London, [1773]. 79 pp.
AAS copy.   13081

Williams, John, 1664-1729.
(Sibley, III, 249-262.)
The Redeemed Captive. . . . Fifth Edition.
Boston, Boyle, 1774. 70, [1] pp.
AAS copy.   13773

Williams, John, 1664-1729.
The Redeemed Captive. . . . Fifth Edition.
New London, [1776]. 72 pp.
NL copy.   15221

Williams, John, 1664-1729.
The Redeemed Captive. . . . Fourth
Edition.
Greenfield, Dickman, 1793. [2], iii, [1],
154 pp.
AAS copy.   26485

Williams, John, 1664-1729.
The Redeemed Captive Returning.
Boston, Hall, 1795. 132 pp.
AAS copy.   29893

Williams, John, 1664-1729.
The Redeemed Captive. . . . Sixth Edition.
Greenfield, Mass., Dickman, 1800. 248 pp.
AAS copy.   39104

Williams, John, 1664-1729.
(Sibley, III, 249-262.)
A Serious Word.
Boston, Green, 1729. [2], 60 pp.
HC copy.   3238

Williams, John, 1664-1729.
Several Arguments. . . . Second Edition.
Boston, J. Franklin, 1721. [4], 20 pp.
HC copy.   39757

Williams, John, 1664-1729.
(Sibley, III, 249-262.)
Warning to the Unclean.

Boston, 1699. 64 pp.
NYHS copy.   902

[Williams, John], 1761-1818.
The Curate of Elmwood. A Tale.
Boston, Russell, 1800. 82 pp.
LOC copy.   39105

[Williams, John], 1761-1818.
A Dirge, or Sepulchral Service . . . of . . .
Washington.
[Boston, Thomas & Andrews, 1800.] 4 pp.
AAS copy.   39106

Williams, John, of Boston.
An Answer to a late Pamphlet.
Boston, Franklin, 1722. [4], 20 pp.
AAS copy.   2407

Williams, John, of Boston.
Several Arguments.
Boston, Franklin, 1721. [4], 20 pp.
(See G. L. Kittredge, Introduction to I.
Mather, Several Reasons, 1921 ed.)
MHS copy.   2307

Williams, John Foster, 1743-1814.
Capt. J. F. Williams' Apparatus for
Extracting Fresh Water from Salt Water.
Boston, Russell, [1793]. [2] pp.
NYPL copy.   46947

Williams, John Mascoll?, 1741-1827.
Letters to the late Incorporated Baptist
Church in Haverhill.
Printed in the year 1793, for the author. 20
pp.
AAS copy.   26486

Williams, John Mascoll, 1741-1827?
A Mistake in the Contents of the Second
Chapter.
Haverhill, Mass., Edes, 1795. 18 pp.
AAS copy.   29894

Williams, Jonathan, 1750-1815.
Memoir on the use of the
Thermometer. . . . Extracted from the
Third Volume of . . . Transactions.
Philadelphia, Aitken, 1792. [79] - 100, 1
map.
BM copy.   25040

Williams, Nathan, 1735-1829.
The Blessedness of the Dead.
Hartford, Hudson & Goodwin, 1796. 28
pp.
AAS copy.   31636

Williams, Nathan, 1735-1829.
Carefully to Observe.
Hartford, Hudson & Goodwin, 1793. 22,
[1] pp.
AAS copy.   26487

Williams, Nathan, 1735-1829.
Circumspection in our Walk.
Norwich, [Ct.], Sterry, 1795. 16 pp.
AAS copy.   47687

Williams, Nathan, 1735-1829.
An Enquiry Concerning . . . Baptism.
Hartford, Hudson & Goodwin, 1788. 86
pp.
AAS copy.   21607

Williams, Nathan, 1735-1829.
An Enquiry Concerning . . . Baptism.
Boston, Thomas & Andrews, 1792. 70 pp.
MHS copy.   25041

Williams, Nathan, 1735-1829.
An Enquiry Concerning . . . Baptism. . . .
Second Edition.
Boston, Thomas & Andrews, 1792. 70 pp.
AAS copy.   25042

Williams, Nathan, 1735-1829.
No Cause nor Need of Pain in Heaven.
New Haven, Morse, 1794. 30 pp.
AAS copy.   28092

Williams, Nathan, 1735-1829.
Order and Harmony.
Hartford, Hudson & Goodwin, 1793. 31
pp.
AAS copy.   26488

Williams, Nathan, 1735-1829.
A Sermon, Preached in the Audience of
the General Assembly.
Hartford, 1780. 38 pp.
AAS copy.   17072

Williams, Nathaniel, 1675-1738.
(Sibley, IV, 182-186.)
The Method of Practice in the Small-Pox.
Boston, Kneeland, 1752. [4], 16 pp.
(The plate called for by Evans was an
extra illustration in one of the SGO
copies.)
AAS copy.   6947

Williams, Nehemiah, 1749-1796.
Twenty Four Sermons.
Worcester, Mass., Worcester, 1797. 339
pp.
AAS copy.   33227

[Williams, Otho Holland.]
Congress. The Residence Law. . . .
October 26, 1790.
[Hagerstown? 1790.] Broadside.
(No copy located.)   46102

Williams, Renwick, defendant.
Trial of. . . .
New York, Marschalk, 1791. 55 pp.
(The only known copy cannot be
reproduced.)
HSP copy.   46359

[Williams, Renwick, defendant.
The Trial of. . . . Taken in Short Hand by
Edward Hodgson.
New York, Greenleaf for Marshalk,
1791.]
("This day is Published," N. Y. Journal,
April 16, 1791.)   23445

[Williams, Roger], 1604?-1683.
An Answer to a Letter sent from Mr.
Coddington. . . .
[Boston, 1678.] 10 pp.
RIHS copy.   39211

[Williams, Roger], 1604?-1683.
George Fox Digg'd out.
Boston, 1676. [8], 208, 119 pp, irreg.
AAS copy.   228

Williams, Samuel, 1743-1817.
A Discourse Delivered before His
Excellency.
Rutland, Vt., Lyon, 1794. 34 (i.e. 35) pp.
AAS copy.   28093

Williams, Samuel, 1743-1817.
(Weis, Colonial Clergy N. E.)
A Discourse on the Love of Our Country.
Salem, Halls, 1775. 29 pp.
AAS copy.   14627

Williams, Samuel, 1743-1817.
The Evidence of Personal Christianity.
Rutland, Haswell, 1792. 32 pp.
AAS copy.   25043

Williams, Samuel, 1743-1817.
The Influence of Christianity.
Boston, Boyle, 1780. 32 pp.
AAS copy.   17073

Williams, Samuel, 1743-1817.
The Love of Our Country.
Rutland, Haswell, 1792. 28 pp.
NYHS copy.   25044

Williams, Samuel, 1743-1817.
The Natural and Civil History of
Vermont.
Walpole, Thomas & Carlisle, 1794. 416
pp., 1 map.
AAS copy.   28094

Williams, Samuel, 1743-1817.
(Weis, Colonial Clergy N. E.)
Regeneration the most Important
Concern.
Boston, Fleets, 1766. 53 pp.
AAS copy.   10523

Williams, Samuel, 1743-1817.
(Weis, Colonial Clergy N. E.)
A Sermon, Preached January 13, 1773.
Salem, 1773. 40 pp.
AAS copy.   13082

[Williams, Samuel, 1743-1817.
The Vermont Almanac and Register, for
. . . 1795.
Rutland, Kirkaldie.].
(A ghost of 27079. Evans assumed the
imprint from adv. "Just Published,
And now ready for sale at this Office"
in Rutland Herald, Dec. 8, 1794.)   28095

[Williams, Samuel], 1743-1817.
The Vermont Almanac . . . for . . . 1796.
Vermont, Kirkaldie. [54] pp.
(No perfect copy located.)
AAS copy.   29895

[Williams, Samuel], 1743-1817.
The Vermont Almanac and Register, for
. . . 1797.
Rutland, Vt. [60] pp.
NYHS copy.   31637

[Williams, Samuel], 1743-1817.
The Vermont Almanac for . . . 1798.
Rutland. [36] pp.
(The only copy located is imperfect.)
AAS copy.   33228

[Williams, Samuel], 1743-1817.
The Vermont Almanac . . . for . . . 1799.
Rutland, Walker. [44] pp.
VtSL copy.   35031

[Williams, Samuel], 1743-1817.
The Vermont Almanac and Register, for
. . . 1800.
Rutland, Vt. [36] pp.
AAS copy.   36723

Williams, Simon Finley, 1764-1800.
An Oration, Delivered on the Fourth of
July, 1796.
Dover, N. H., Bragg, 1796. 24 pp.
AAS copy.   31638

Williams, Simon Finley, 1764-1800.
A Sermon Delivered at the Interment of
Miss Sally Philbrick.
Concord, N.H., Russell & Davis, 1795. 24
pp.
AAS copy.   47688

Williams, Simon Finley, 1764-1800.
Two Sermons, Delivered at the First
Parish.
Newburyport, Mycall, 1791. [4], 54 pp.
AAS copy.   46360

Williams, Solomon, 1700-1776.
(Sibley, VI, 352-361.)
The Business, Scope and End.
New London, 1746. [4], 42 pp.
NYPL copy.   5892

Williams, Solomon, 1700-1776.
Christ, the King.
Boston, Rogers & Fowle for Henchman,
1744. [4], 151 pp.
AAS copy.   5521

Williams, Solomon, 1700-1776.
(Sibley, VI, 352-361.)
The Comfort and Blessedness.
New London, 1742. [4], 38, [1] pp.
AAS copy.   5092

Williams, Solomon, 1700-1776.
The Duty of Christian Soldiers.
New London, 1755. [4], 35 pp.
NYHS copy.   7596

Williams, Solomon, 1700-1776.
(Sibley, VI, 352-361.)
The Duty of Christians.
Norwich, 1773. 40 pp.
AAS copy.   13083

Williams, Solomon, 1700-1776.
(Sibley, VI, 352-361.)
A Firm and Immoveable Courage.
New London, 1741. [4], 44 pp.
AAS copy.   4869

Williams, Solomon, 1700-1776.
(Sibley, VI, 352-361.)
The Frailty.
Boston, Draper, 1740. [4], 31 pp.
AAS copy.   4659

Williams, Solomon, 1700-1776.
(Sibley, VI, 352-361.)
The Glorious Reward.
Boston, Eliot, 1730. [4], 27 pp.
AAS copy.   3381

Williams, Solomon, 1700-1776.
The Greatness and Sovereignty of God.
Norwich, Trumbull, 1777. 28 pp.
AAS copy.   15712

Williams, Solomon, 1700-1776.
The Ministers of the Gospel.

New London, 1744. [2], 53 pp.
AAS copy.   5522

Williams, Solomon, 1700-1776.
The More Excellent Way.
New London, 1742. [4], ii, 39, [2] pp.
AAS copy.   5093

Williams, Solomon, 1700-1776.
The Power and Efficacy of the Prayers.
Boston, Kneeland & Green, 1742. [4], 28
pp.
AAS copy.   5094

Williams, Solomon, 1700-1776.
(Sibley, VI, 352-361.)
The Relations of God's People to Him.
New London, 1760. 28 pp.
AAS copy.   8770

Williams, Solomon, 1700- 1776.
(Sibley, VI, 352-361.)
The Sad Tendency of Divisions.
Newport, [1751]. 29 pp.
LOC copy.   6797

Williams, Solomon, 1700-1776.
(Sibley, VI, 352-361.)
The Servants of the Lord.
Boston, Kneeland & Green, 1743. [4], 22
pp.
AAS copy.   5317

Williams, Solomon, 1700-1776.
The Surprizing Variety.
New London, 1742. [4], 44 pp.
AAS copy.   5095

Williams, Solomon, 1700-1776.
The True State of the Question.
Boston, Kneeland, 1751. [2], vi, 144 pp.
AAS copy.   6798

Williams, Solomon, 1700-1776.
(Sibley, VI, 352-361.)
The Vanity of Human Life.
Boston, Kneeland, 1754. [4], 19 pp.
AAS copy.   7339

Williams, Solomon, 1700-1776.
A Vindication of the Gospel-Doctrine.
Boston, Rogers & Fowle, 1746. 95 pp.
AAS copy.   5893

Williams, Solomon, 1700-1776.
The Word of God.
Boston, Green, 1754. 25 pp.
AAS copy.   7340

Williams, Solomon, 1752-1834.
Jesus Christ the Physician.
Norwich, Green & Spooner, 1778. 32 pp.
AAS copy.   16172

Williams, Stephen, 1693-1782.
(Sibley, VI, 25-35.)
Drawing near to God.
Boston, Kneeland, 1772. 43 pp.
AAS copy.   12618

[Williams, Thomas], Calvinist preacher.
The Age of Credulity.
Philadelphia, Lang & Ustick for Ustick,
1796. 45, [3] pp.
AAS copy.   31639

[Williams, Thomas], Calvinist preacher.
The Age of Infidelity.
Boston, Manning & Loring for West,
1794. 47 pp.
AAS copy.   28096

[Williams, Thomas], Calvinist preacher.
The Age of Infidelity.
New York, Birdsall, 1794. 62 (i.e. 52) pp.
AAS copy.   28097

[Williams, Thomas], Calvinist preacher.
The Age of Infidelity.
New York, Buel for Fellows, 1794. 59, [1]
pp.
Pierce W. Gaines copy.   47329

[Williams, Thomas], Calvinist preacher.
The Age of Infidelity.
New York, Buel for Fellows, 1794. 59 pp.
(Not located, 1968.)   47330

[Williams, Thomas], Calvinist preacher.
The Age of Infidelity.
Philadelphia, Ustick, 1794. 70 pp.
AAS copy.   28099

[Williams, Thomas], Calvinist preacher.
The Age of Infidelity.
Salem, Cushing & Carleton, 1794.]
(Imprint assumed by Evans from adv.
"Just Published, and for sale," Salem
Gazette, Nov. 18, 1794.)   28098

[Williams, Thomas], Calvinist preacher.
The Age of Infidelity. . . . Third Edition.
Worcester, Thomas, 1794. 60 pp.
AAS copy.   28100

Williams, Thomas, Calvinist preacher.
The Age of Infidelity.
New York, Buel for Fellows, 1795. 59, [1]
pp.
NYPL copy.   29896

[Williams, Thomas], Calvinist preacher.
The Age of Infidelity. Part II.
Philadelphia, Lang & Ustick, 1796. pp.
[i]-iv, [2], [5]-67.
AAS copy.   31640

Williams, W.
First Principles of Geography.
Charleston, S. C., Bowen, 1798. [4], 11
pp., 3 plates, 1 table.
LOC copy.   35032

Williams, William, 1665-1741.
Cambridge Ephemeris. An Almanack . . .
for . . . 1685.
Cambridge, Green, 1685. [16] pp.
AAS copy.   399

Williams, William, 1665-1741.
Cambridge Ephemeris. An Almanack . . .
for . . . 1685.
Cambridge, Green for Phillips, 1685. [16]
pp.
YC copy.   400

[Williams, William], 1665-1741.
Cambridge Ephemeris. An Almanack . . .
for . . . 1687.
Cambridge, 1687. [16] pp.
MHS copy.   436

Williams, William, 1665-1741.
(Sibley, III, 263-269.)
The Danger of not Reforming.
Boston, 1707. [2], 30 pp.
AAS copy.   1341

Williams, William, 1665-1741.
(Sibley, III, 263-269.)
The Death of a Prophet.
Boston, Green for Henchman,
Phillips and Hancock, 1729. [4], 28 pp.
AAS copy.   3239

Williams, William, 1665-1741.
(Sibley, III, 263-269.)
Directions to such as are Concern'd. . . .
Second Edition.
Boston, Kneeland & Green, 1738. [2], 23
pp.
(No complete copy located.)
BA copy.   4325

Williams, William, 1665-1741.
(Sibley, III, 263-269.)
The Duty and Interest of a People.
Boston, Kneeland and Green, 1736. [2],
viii, 120, [2], 38, 19 pp.
AAS copy.   4103

Williams, William, 1665-1741.
(Sibley, III, 263-269.)
An Essay to Prove the Interest of the
Children.
Boston, 1727. [4], viii, 42 pp.
AAS copy.   2978

Williams, William, 1665-1741.
(Sibley, III, 263-269.)
The Great Concern of Christians.
Boston, Kneeland, 1723. [4], 28 pp.
AAS copy.   2496

Williams, William, 1665-1741.
(Sibley, III, 263-269.)
The Great Duty of Ministers.
Boston, Kneeland and Green for Gerrish
and Henchman, 1726. [4], 28 pp.
AAS copy.   2829

Williams, William, 1665-1741.
(Sibley, III, 263-269.)
The Great Salvation Revealed.
Boston, Crump for Gerrish and

Henchman, 1717. [2], vii, [1], 195, [1], 8
pp.
AAS copy.   1939

Williams, William, 1665-1741.
(Sibley, III, 263-269.)
The Honour of Christ.
Boston, Green, 1728. [2], 22 pp.
NYPL copy.   3124

Williams, William, 1665-1741.
A Painful Ministry.
Boston, Green, 1717. [2], 25 pp.
AAS copy.   1940

Williams, William, 1665-1741.
(Sibley, III, 263-269.)
A Plea for God.
Boston, Green for Henchman, 1719. [4],
42 pp.
AAS copy.   2088

[Williams, William, 1665-1741.
Several Sermons on Heb. xi. 7 and Prov.
ii, 1-6.
Boston, 1729.]
(A ghost of 3125, by William Williams,
1688-1760, arising from the adv. in the
New-England Weekly Journal, Feb. 3,
1729.)   3240

Williams, William, 1665-1741.
(Sibley, III, 263-269.)
The Work of Ministers.
Boston, 1733. [4], 26 pp.
AAS copy.   3737

Williams, William, 1688-1760.
(Sibley, V, 295-300.)
Christ Living in the Saints.
Boston, Rogers & Fowle, 1743. 31 pp.
AAS copy.   5318

Williams, William, 1688-1760.
(Sibley, V, 295-300.)
A Discourse on Saving Faith.
Boston, Kneeland & Green and Eliot,
1741. [2], 50 pp.
(Issued as the third part of 4703, q.v.)
                                             4870

[Williams, William], 1688-1760.
(Sibley, V, 295-300.)
The Divine Promises.
Boston, Draper for Gookin, 1746. 32 pp.
AAS copy.   5894

Williams, William, 1688-1760.
(Sibley, V, 295-300.)
Divine Warnings.
Boston, Gerrish, 1728. [2], xii, 132, [2], 4
pp.
AAS copy.   3125

Williams, William, 1688-1760.
(Sibley, V, 295-300.)
The Duty of Parents.
Boston, Green for Gerrish, 1721. [2], viii,
60, [2], 22 pp.
AAS copy.   2308

Williams, William, 1688-1760.
God the Strength of Rulers.
Boston, Kneeland, 1741. [4], 52 pp.
AAS copy.   4871

Williams, William, 1688-1760.
(Sibley, V, 295-300.)
Martial Wisdom.
Boston, Fleet for Henchman, 1737. [4], 31
pp.
AAS copy.   4210

Williams, William, 1688-1760.
The Obligations of Baptism.
Boston, Green for Gerrish, 1721. [2], 22
pp.
(Signatures continuous with 2308, q.v.)
                                             2309

Williams, William, 1688-1760.
(Sibley, V, 295-300.)
The Office.
Boston, Kneeland and Green, 1729. [4],
34 pp.
AAS copy.   3241

Williams, William, 1688-1760.
(Sibley, V, 295-300.)
The Serious Consideration.
Boston, Fleet, 1738. 23 pp.
AAS copy.   4326

Williams, William, 1731-1811.
Advertisement. Any Gun-smith or
Lock-maker, within the County of
Windham. . . . June 1st, 1775.
[New London? 1775.] Broadside.
CHS copy.   42760

Williams, William, 1765-1811.
Take Notice. To be Sold at Auction in
Billerica. . . . May 27th, 1800.
[Boston? 1800.] Broadside.
(Not located, 1968.)   49195

Williams College.
Commencement . . . September 6, 1797.
The Order of the Exercises.
[Bennington], Merrill, [1797]. Broadside.
WC copy.   33229

Williams College.
Commencement at Williams College,
September 5, 1798. The Order of the
Exercises.
Stockbridge, Rosseter, [1798]. Broadside.
(Not located, 1968.)   48759

Williams College.
Commencement at Williams College,
September 4, 1799. Order of Exercises.
Pittsfield, Mass., Smith. Broadside.
Williams College copy.   36726

Williams College.
Commencement . . . September 3, 1800.
Order of Exercises.
Stockbridge, Mass. [1800]. Broadside.
Williams College copy.   39108

Williams College. Alumni Catalogue,
1799.
Catalogus, Senatus Academici. . . .
Pittsfield, Mass., Smith, 1799. Broadside.
MHS copy.   36725

Williams College. Laws, 1795.
The Laws of Williams College.
Stockbridge, Andrews, 1795. 42 pp.
JCB copy.   29898

Williams College. Library.
A Catalogue of Books.
Bennington, Haswell, 1794. 16 pp.
Williams College copy.   28101

Williams College. Student Catalogue,
1795.
Catalogue of the Students . . . October,
MDCCXCV.
Albany, Webster, [1795]. Broadside.
Williams College copy.   29897

Williams College. Student Catalogue,
1796.
Catalogue of the Students . . . October,
1796.
Stockbridge, [1796]. Broadside.
AAS ph. copy.   48026

Williams College. Student Catalogue,
1797.
Catalogue of Students in Williams
College, October, 1797.
Stockbridge, Rosseter & Willard, [1797].
Broadside.
WC copy.   48320

Williams College. Student Catalogue,
1798.
Catalogue of Students . . . Nov. 1798.
Pittsfield, Holly & Smith, [1798].
Broadside.
(Not located, 1968.)   48760

Williams College. Student Catalogue,
1799.
Catalogue of Students . . . Nov. 1799.
Pittsfield, Mass., Smith, [1799].
Broadside.
MHS copy.   36724

Williams College. Student Catalogue,
1800.
Catalogue of Students in Williams
College, November, 1800.
[Pittsfield, Mass., 1800.] Broadside.
AAS copy.   39107

Williamsburg, Va. Citizens.
Wednesday, July 14, 1779. Williamsburg
to wit. . . .
[Williamsburg, 1779.] [2] pp.
LOC copy.   16683

[Williamsburg, May 1. Several Copies of
the Following Bills. . . .
Williamsburg, Purdie, [1777]. 2 pp.]
(No copy located.)   15354

Williamsburg, May 31, 1774. Gentlemen,
Last Sunday Morning Several Letters. . . .
[Williamsburg, 1774.] 1 leaf.
LOC copy.   42753

[Williamsburg, Saturday, April 29, 1775.
Late last Night. . . .
Williamsburg, Purdie, [1775].
Broadside.]
(A dup. of 14602, q.v.)   14628

Williamsburg (Virginia) Sept. 9. The
Shocking account of Damage done by the
Rains. . . .
[Baltimore], Dunlap, [1775]. Broadside.
(No copy could be located.)   42986

[Williamson, Charles], 1757-1808.
Description of the Genesee Country.
Albany, N. Y., Andrews, 1798. 37 pp., 2
maps, 1 plate.
AAS copy.   35033

[Williamson, Charles], 1757-1808.
Description of the Settlement of the
Genesee Country.
New York, Swords, 1799. 63 pp., 1 folding
map.
AAS copy.   36727

Williamson, Charles, 1757-1808.
The Legislature at their last Session. . . .
[July 4, 1797.]
[Albany, 1797.] Broadside.
NYPL copy.   33230

[Williamson, Hugh], 1735-1819.
Letters from Sylvius to the Freemen.
New York, Carroll & Patterson, 1787.
[2], 34 pp.
NYHS copy.   20887

[Williamson, Hugh], 1735-1819.
(D. A. B.)
The Plain Dealer: or, a few Remarks upon
Quaker-Politicks.
Philadelphia, 1764. 19 pp.
NYPL copy.   9875

[Williamson, Hugh], 1735-1819.
The Plain Dealer; Numb. I.
Philadelphia, Steuart, [1764]. 16 pp.
NYHS copy.   9876

[Williamson, Hugh], 1735-1819.
The Plain Dealer: Numb. II.
Philadelphia, 1764. 16 pp.
NYPL copy.   9877

[Williamson, Hugh, 1735-1819.
The Plain Dealer: or, Remarks on Quaker
Politics. . . . Numb. III.
Philadelphia, 1764. 24 pp.
NYPL copy.   9878

[Williamson, Hugh, 1735-1819.
The Plea of the Colonies.
Philadelphia, Bell, 1777. Front., [8], 38,
[2] pp.
NYPL copy.   15713

[Williamson, Hugh], 1735-1819.
What is Sauce for a Goose is also Sauce
for a Gander.
Philadelphia, 1764. 8 pp.
JCB copy.   9879

Williamson, John Brown, d. 1802.
Preservation; or, The Hovel of the Rocks.
Charleston, [S. C.], Cox, 1800. vii, [1], 75
pp.
AAS copy.   39110

Williamson, Matthias Hampton.
An Inaugural Dissertation.
Philadelphia, Johnston & Justice, 1793. 36
pp.
NLM copy.   26489

Williamson, Peter, 1730-1799.
Sufferings of. . . .
Stockbridge, [Mass.], 1796. 15 pp.
AAS copy.   48027

[Williamson, T. G.
The Hobbies, a Favorite Song.
Boston, Thomas & Andrews, 1797.]
(Adv. in newspapers.)   33231

Willich, Anthony Florian Madinger.
Lectures on Diet and Regimen. . . . Vol.
I - [-II].
Boston, Manning & Loring, 1800. pp.
[i]-xxxii, [1]-304; [2], [13]-334.
AAS copy.   39111

Willich, Anthony Florian Madinger.
Lectures on Diet and Regimen. . . . Two
Volumes Abridged in One.
Boston, Manning & Loring for Nancrede,
1800. xxiv, 381, [3] pp.
LCP copy.   39112

Willich, Anthony Florian Madinger.
Proposals for Printing by Subscription
Lectures on Diet and Regimen.
[Boston, 1799?] 7 pp.
Countway Library copy.   48994

[Willis, John, fl. 1775.
Advertisement.
Philadelphia, 1775. Broadside.]
(From Aitken's records.)   14629

[Willis, George, M.D.
The Art of Preventing Diseases.
New York, 1797.]
(The origin of this entry is unknown.)   33232

[Willis, Hannah.
Surprizing Account of the Captivity of
. . .
Stonington Port, Trumbull, 1799. 15, [1]
pp.
(Entry from Bates 2658.)   36391

Willis, John, fl. 1795.
An Inaugural Dissertation on . . .
Vegetable Astringents.
Philadelphia, McKenzie, 1795. 36 pp.
NLM copy.   29899

Willis, Lydia (Fish), 1709-1767.
Madam Willis's Letters.
Boston, Coverly, 1788. 47 pp.
AAS copy.   21608

Willis, Lydia (Fish), 1709-1767.
Rachel's Sepulchre.
[Boston? Coverly? 1767?] 39 pp.
AAS copy.   41779

Willison, John, 1680-1750.
The Afflicted Man's Companion.
Philadelphia, Young, 1788. pp. [i]-x,
[13]-230.
AAS copy.   21610

Willison, John, 1680-1750.
The Afflicted Man's Companion.
Boston, Greenough for Larkin, 1795. 270,
[6] pp.
AAS copy.   29900

Willison, John, 1680-1750.
The Afflicted Man's Companion.
Wilmington, Del., Johnson, 1796. 272 pp.
AAS copy.   31641

[Willison, John, 1680-1750.
An Explanation of the Assembly's Shorter
Catechism.
Philadelphia, Young, 1791.]
(Entry from adv. for "American Editions,
to be sold," in 23178.)   24004

Willison, John, 1680-1750.
Looking unto Jesus.
Boston, Gray, 1731. [2], 34 pp.
AAS copy.   39983

Willison, John, 1680-1750.
Looking unto Jesus.
Boston, Gray, 1733. [2], 28 pp.
(The only known copy is imperfect.)
AAS copy.   40037

Willison, John, 1680-1750.
Looking unto Jesus.
Boston, Kneeland & Green, 1741. [2], 32,
[2] pp.
(The only known copy is in poor
condition.)
AAS copy.   40268

Willison, John, 1680-1750.
Looking to Jesus.
Boston, Gray, 1743. [2], 34 pp.
(An imprint variant of 5319, q. v.)   40322

Willison, John, 1680-1750.

Looking to Jesus.
Boston, Henchman, 1743. [2], 34 pp.
BA copy.   5319

Willison, John, 1680-1750.
Looking to Jesus.
Boston, Kneeland, 1759. [2], 46 pp.
AAS copy.   41093

[Willison, John], 1680-1750.
(D. N. B.)
The Mother's Catechism for the Young
Child.
Boston, 1729.]
(Title from adv. This is possibly the work
of the same title by Richard Baxter,
1615-1691.)   3192

[Willison, John, 1680-1750.
The Mother's Catechism.
Philadelphia, Bailey, 1783.]
(Adv. Freeman's Journal, July 30, 1783.)
                                                 18313

Willison, John, 1680-1750.
The Mother's Catechism. . . . Second
Edition.
Philadelphia, Steele, 1785. 48 pp.
JCB copy.   44835

[Willison, John, 1680-1750.
The Mother's Catechism.
New York, Greenleaf, 1787.]
("This Day Published. And to be Sold at
this Printing-Office," N. Y. Journal, May
31, 1787.)   20888

[Willison, John, 1680-1750.
The Mother's Catechism.
New York, Campbell, 1788.]
("This day published," N. Y. Journal,
Jan. 9, 1788.)   21611

[Willison, John, 1680-1750.
The Mother's Catechism.
Philadelphia, Bailey, 1788.]
("Lately published," Federal Gazette,
Dec. 10, 1788.)   21612

[Willison, John, 1680-1750.
The Mother's Catechism.
Lansingburgh, 1789.]
("Just published," Federal Herald, Jan.
19, 1789.)   22281

[Willison, John, 1680-1750.
The Mother's Catechism.
Carlisle, Kline, 1791.]
(Adv. Carlisle Gazette, Jan. 25, 1792.)
                                                 24005

[Willison, John, 1680-1750.
The Mother's Catechism.
New Brunswick, N.J., Blauvelt, 1794.]
(Imprint assumed by Evans from
Blauvelt's advs.)   28102

[Willison, John, 1680-1750.
The Mother's Catechism.
Philadelphia, Campbell, 1794.]
(Imprint assumed by Evans from
Campbell's advs.)   28103

Willison, John, 1680-1750.
The Mother's Catechism.
Harrisburgh, Wyeth for Loudon, 1795. 24
pp.
AAS copy.   29901

[Willison, John], 1680-1750.
The Mother's Catechism, Containing
Short and Easy Questions. . . . Sixth
Edition.
Trenton, Day, 1795. 35 pp.
NYHS copy.   29902

[Willison, John, 1680-1750.
The Mother's Catechism.
Trenton, N. J., Day, 1798.]
(Imprint assumed by Evans from Day's
adv.)   35034

Willison, John, 1680-1750.
Sacramental Meditations.
Newburyport, Robinson for West, 1794. x,
[2], 288 pp.
AAS copy.   28104

Willison, John, 1680-1750.
Sacramental Meditations.
Philadelphia, M'Culloch and Carey, 1794.
288 (i.e. 287) pp.
AAS copy.   28105

[Willison, John, 1680-1750.
(D. N. B.)
Scripture Songs.
Philadelphia, 1772.]
(Entry from Aitken's records.)   12619

Willison, John, 1680-1750.
Some Dying Words of the late. . . .
Boston, Z. Fowle, [1756]. 8 pp.
AAS copy.   40871

Willison, John, 1680-1750.
A Treatise Concerning the
Sanctification. . . .
Philadelphia, Young, 1788. pp. [1]-xvi,
[25]-315, [1].
AAS copy.   21613

[Willison, John, 1680-1750.
(D. N. B.)
The Young Communicant's Catechism.
Wilmington, Del., 1765.]
(Adv. Pa. Gazette, Apr. 18, 1765.)   10213

Williston, Noah, 1734-1811.
A Sermon, Preached at the Ordination of
. . . David Howe Williston.
Hanover, N.H., Dunham, 1794. 37 pp.,
errata note.
AAS copy.   28106

Williston, Seth, 1770-1851.
An Address to Parents.
Suffield, Ct., Gray, 1799. 96 pp.
AAS copy.   36728

Williston, Seth, 1770-1851.
The Agency of God.
Geneva, N. Y., E. Eaton for Eaton,
Walker & Co., [1800]. 24 pp.
AAS copy.   39113

Willock, John, mariner.
The Voyages and Adventures of. . . .
Philadelphia, Hogan & M'Elroy for
Gibson, 1798. pp. [vii]-xi, [1], [13]-283,
[1]-8; 1 plate.
AAS copy.   35035

Willock, John, mariner.
The Voyages and Adventures of. . . .
Philadelphia, Hogan & M'Elroy, 1798. pp.
[vii]-xi, [13]-283, [1]-8, 1 plate.
(An imprint variant of 35035, q. v.)   48761

Willock, Thomas.
For Sale by the Subscriber. . . . 19th June,
1787.
[Norfolk], M'Lean, [1787]. Broadside.
HEH copy.   45208

Willsford, John, of Burlington, N. J.
(Joseph Smith, Friends' Books, II,
943-944.)
A Brief Exhortation.
[Philadelphia, 1691.] 11 pp.
FL copy.   586

[Willsford, John, of Burlington, N. J.
An Epistle for General Service.
Philadelphia, 1690.]
(No copy found. See Sabin 104545.)   549

Wilmer, James Jones, 1749-1814.
An Address to the Citizens of the United
States.
Baltimore, Pechin, [1796]. 16 pp.
BA copy.   31642

Wilmer, James Jones, 1749-1814.
Consolation.
Philadelphia, Woodward, 1794. 80 pp.
AAS copy.   28107

[Wilmer, James Jones, 1749-1814.
Consummation.
Baltimore, Angell, 1793.]
(Subscriptions solicited Md. Journal, Feb.
26, 1793.)   26490

Wilmer, James Jones, 1749-1814.
Memoirs by James Wilmer.
Baltimore, Adams, 1792. 16 pp.
BA copy.   25045

Wilmer, James Jones, 1749-1814.
A Sermon, on the Doctrine of the
New-Jerusalem Church.
Baltimore, Goddard & Angell, 1792. 23
pp.
BA copy.   25046

Wilmer, James Jones, 1749-1814.

Support under Trials.
Wilmington, Adams, 1795. 48 pp.
LCP copy.   29903

Wilmington, Del., Academy.
Draught of a Plan of Education for the
Wilmington Academy.
Wilmington, Adams, 1786. 8 pp.
JCB copy.   20149

[Wilmington, Del. Library Company.
An Act to Incorporate the. . . .
Wilmington, 1788.]
(The source of this entry is unknown.)
                                                 21046

Wilmington, Del. Library Company.
A Catalogue of Books.
Wilmington, Brynberg & Andrews, 1789.
19 pp.
HEH copy.   45750

Wilmington Mercury. Printed
Occasionally. . . . Sept. 23, 1798.
[Wilmington, Del., 1798.] Broadside.
NYPL copy.   35036

Wilmington, N.C. Committee of
Correspondence, 1774.
Gentlemen, At this Conjuncture of British
Politics. . . .
[Wilmington, 1774.] Broadside.
PRO copy.   42754

Wilmington, N. C. Inhabitants, 1774.
At a General Meeting of the Inhabitants.
. . . July 21st, 1774.
[Wilmington, 1774.] Broadside.
PRO copy.   42755

The Wilmingtoniad, or a Touch at the
Times.
Wilmington, [Del.], Wilson, [1800]. 19
pp.
(No copy could be reproduced.)   39115

Wilson, Daniel, 1749-1774.
The Life and Confession of. . . .
[Providence? 1774.] Broadside.
AAS copy.   13774

Wilson, Goodridge.
An Inaugural Dissertation on Absorption.
Philadelphia, Oswald, 1797. [2], 25 pp.
NLM copy.   33233

[Wilson, James, 1742-1798.
An Address to the Citizens of
Philadelphia.
Philadelphia, 1784.]
(The origin of this entry is unknown.)
                                                 18888

Wilson, James, 1742-1798.
A Charge Delivered . . . to the Grand Jury
. . . the 23d day of May, 1791.
Richmond, Davis, 1791. 29 pp.
LOC copy.   24006

[Wilson, James], 1742-1798.
Considerations on the Bank of
North-America.
Philadelphia, Hall & Sellers, 1785. 35 pp.
AAS copy.   19388

[Wilson, James], 1742-1798.
Considerations on the Nature and the
Extent of the Legislative Authority of the
British Parliament.
Philadelphia, Bradfords, 1774. iv, 35 pp.
AAS copy.   13775

Wilson, James, 1742-1798.
An Introductory Lecture to a Course of
Law Lectures.
Philadelphia, Dobson, 1791. 96 pp.
LCP copy.   24007

Wilson, James, 1742-1798.
The Substance of a Speech.
Philadelphia, Bradford, 1787. 10, [2] pp.
AAS copy.   20889

Wilson, James, 1751-1799.
Peace: a Sermon.
New York, 1788. 21 pp.
NYHS copy.   21614

Wilson, James, 1751-1799.
The Utility of the Scriptures.
Alexandria, D. C., Thomas & Westcott,
1798. 61 pp.
AAS copy.   35037

Wilson, James, 1760-1839.
Apostolic Church Government.
Providence, Wheeler, 1798. xii, [4], 234,
[1] pp.
AAS copy.   35038

Wilson, James, 1760-1839.
An Oration, Delivered before the
Providence Association of Mechanics.
Providence, Wheeler, 1794. 27, [5] pp.
AAS copy.   28108

[Wilson, James, 1760-1839.
The Second Edition of an Oration.
Providence, Wheeler, 1794.]
(The 2nd ed. was apparently identical with
the 1st., 28108.)   28109

Wilson, James, 1760-1839.
The Proceedings of Seven Gentlemen.
[Providence], Wheeler, [1793]. 4 pp.
AAS copy.   26491

Wilson, James, 1760-1839.
Substance of a Discourse; on . . .
Washington.
Providence, Wheeler, 1800. 16 pp.
BrU copy.   39116

Wilson, John, c.1591-1667.
(D. A. B.)
A Copy of Verses . . . on . . . Joseph
Brisco.
[Cambridge, 1657.] Broadside.
(The typography makes it unlikely that
this is Cambridge Press printing, but see
S. A. Green, Ten Fac-simile
Reproductions, p. 30.)
MHS copy.   48

Wilson, John, c.1591-1667.
A Seasonable Watch-Word.
Cambridge, 1677. [4], 10 pp.
LOC copy.   243

Wilson, John, c.1591-1667.
(D. A. B.)
A Song of Deliverance.
Boston, 1680. [8], 44 pp.
NYPL copy.   297

Wilson, John, d. 1835.
(U. of Pa. Alumni Cat.)
An Inaugural Experimental Dissertation.
Philadelphia, Lang & Ustick, 1796. 25 pp.
AAS copy.   31644

[Wilson, Rachel.
A Discourse, Delivered on Saturday.
New York, 1769.]
("Just Published," N. Y. Journal, Nov. 9,
1769.)   11534

Wilson, Rachel.
A Discourse, Delivered on Saturday.
Newport, 1769. 24 pp.
AAS copy.   11535

Wilson, Rachel.
A Discourse, Delivered on Saturday.
Dover, N. H., Ladd, 1792. 22 pp.
YC copy.   25047

[Wilson, Samuel, 1701-1750.
A Scripture Manual. . . . Third Edition.
Philadelphia, Armbruster, 1763.]
(From an adv.)   9546

Wilson, Samuel, 1702-1750.
A Scripture Manual. . . . Fourth Edition.
Newport, 1772. 31 pp.
AAS copy.   12620

Wilson, Samuel, 1702-1750.
A Scripture-Manuel. . . . Tenth Edition.
Elizabethtown, Kollock, 1793. 22 pp.
AAS copy.   46948

Wilson, Samuel, 1702-1750.
A Scripture-Manual.
Philadelphia, Lang & Ustick, 1795. 48 pp.
UTS copy.   29905

Wilson, Samuel, fl. 1800.
The Kentucky English Grammar.
Lexington, Bradford, 1797. 71 pp.
KyU ph copy.   35039

Wily, John.
A Treatise on the Propagation of Sheep.
Williamsburg, 1765. 52 pp.
BA copy.   10214

Winch, Silas, 1744-1834.
The Age of Superstition.
Boston, Fleet, 1795. 20 pp.
AAS copy.   29906

Winchell, Jacob, b. 1739.
A Short Treatise, in Favour of the
Baptists.
Hartford, [Ct.], Watson, [1773]. 27 pp.
AAS copy.   42543

[Winchell, John], d. 1794.
A Few Neglected Scriptures.
Hudson, [N. Y.], Stoddard, 1789. 22 + pp.
(The only copy located is imperfect.)
AAS ph. copy.   45751

Winchester, Elhanan, 1751-1797.
An Attempt to Collect the Scripture
Passages in Favour of the Universal
Restoration.
Providence, Wheeler, 1786. viii, 64 pp.
LOC copy.   20150

[Winchester, Elhanan, 1751-1797.
(D. A. B.)
Collection of Psalms, Hymns and Poems.
Boston, 1772.]
(Assumed by Evans from the title of
13084.)   12621

[Winchester, Elhanan, 1751-1797.
Collection of Hymns.
Philadelphia, Story, 1787.]
(Entry from an adv.)   20890

Winchester, Elhanan, 1751-1797.
A Course of Lectures, on the
Prophecies. . . . Vol. I.
Norwich, Trumbull & Sterry, 1794. pp. [i]
- v, [1], [3]-302, [i]-iv, [1].
AAS copy.   28110

Winchester, Elhanan, 1751-1797.
A Course of Lectures. . . . Vol. II.
Norwich, Hubbard for Trumbull, 1795.
258 pp.
AAS copy.   29907

Winchester, Elhanan, 1751-1797.
A Course of Lectures on the Prophecies.
Walpole, [N. H.], Carlisle for Thomas &
Thomas, 1800. frontis., 524; 525 pp., 1
folding map.
(Three varieties of the frontispiece,
engraved by Robinson, Purvis, or
Doolittle.)
AAS copy.   39117

Winchester, Elhanan, 1751-1797.
A Discourse Delivered before the . . .
Masons . . . at Norwich . . . the 24 of
June . . . 1795.
Norwich, Sterry, 1795. 13, [1] pp.
HC-A copy.   29908

Winchester, Elhanan, 1751-1797.
The Divinity of Christ.
[Philadelphia, 1784.] 39 pp.
AAS copy.   18889

Winchester, Elhanan, 1751-1797.
The Divinity of Christ.
[Boston, 1786.] 25 pp.
AAS copy.   20151

[Winchester, Elhanan, 1751-1797.
The Divinity of Christ.
[Philadelphia, 1794.] 25 pp.]
(A ghost of 20151.)   28111

Winchester, Elhanan, 1751-1797.
An Elegy on the Death of . . . John
Wesley.
Philadelphia, Johnson & Justice, 1792. 11
pp.
HSP copy.   25048

Winchester, Elhanan, 1751-1797.
The Execution Hymn, Composed on Levi
Ames . . . Executed . . . the 21st of
October, 1773.
[Boston], Russell, [1773]. Broadside.
MHS copy.   42544

Winchester, Elhanan, 1751-1797.
The Face of Moses Unveiled.
Philadelphia, Story, 1787. 54, [2] pp.
AAS copy.   20891

Winchester, Elhanan, 1751-1797.
[The face of Moses unveiled.
Newbern? 1791.]
(McMurtrie, N.C. 174.)   46361

[Winchester, Elhanan, 1751-1797.
Four Discourses, Entitled, The Face of
Moses. . . . Philadelphia, 1786.]
(Entry from an adv. for 20891 and other
Winchester tracts.)   20152

Winchester, Elhanan, 1751-1797.
The Gospel of Christ.
Philadelphia, Towne, 1783. 140 pp.
AAS copy.   18314

[Winchester, Elhanan, 1751-1797.
The Gospel of Christ.
Philadelphia, 1793.]
(Imprint assumed by Evans from advs.)
                                             26492

[Winchester, Elhanan], 1751-1797.
The Mystic's Plea. . . . By Mordecai
Servetus.
Philadelphia, 1781. 16 pp.
AAS copy.   17439

Winchester, Elhanan, 1751-1797.
(Weis, Colonial Clergy N. E.)
A New Book of Poems.
Boston, Thomas, 1773. 72 pp.
AAS copy.   13084

Winchester, Elhanan, 1751-1797.
The Outcasts Comforted.
Philadelphia, 1782. 18 pp.
HEH copy.   17803

Winchester, Elhanan, 1751-1797.
A Plain Political Catechism.
Greenfield, Mass., Dickman, 1796. 107 pp.
AAS copy.   31645

Winchester, Elhanan, 1751-1797.
A Plain Political Catechism.
Philadelphia, Folwell, 1796. 96 pp.
AAS copy.   31646

Winchester, Elhanan, 1751-1797.
Remarks upon a Pamphlet Intitled "An
Address from the Baptist Church. . . ."
Philadelphia, Towne, 1781. 28 pp.
HSP copy.   17440

Winchester, Elhanan, 1751-1797.
The Seed of the Woman.
Philadelphia, 1781. 58 pp.
AAS copy.   17441

Winchester, Elhanan, 1751-1797.
Ten Letters Addressed to Mr. Paine.
Boston, Folsom, 1794. [2], 125, [1] pp.
AAS copy.   28112

Winchester, Elhanan, 1751-1797.
Ten Letters Addressed to Mr. Paine. . . .
Second Edition.
New York, Campbell, 1795. 100 pp.
AAS copy.   29909

[Winchester, Elhanan, 1751-1797.
Thirteen Hymns.
Baltimore, 1776.]
(Assumed by Evans from 15223.)   15222

Winchester, Elhanan, 1751-1797.
Thirteen Hymns. . . . Second Edition.
Baltimore, 1776. 20 pp.
BA copy.   15223

Winchester, Elhanan, 1751-1797.
The Three Woe Trumpets.
Boston, Folsom, 1794. 79 pp.
AAS copy.   28113

Winchester, Elhanan, 1751-1797.
The Three Woe Trumpets.
Brookfield, [Mass.], Merriam, 1800. 87
pp.
NYPL copy.   39118

Winchester, Elhanan, 1751-1797.
Two Lectures on the Prophecies.
Norwich, Trumbull, 1792. 77, [1] pp.
JCB copy.   25049

Winchester, Elhanan, 1751-1797.
The Universal Restoration.
Philadelphia, Dobson, 1792. lvi, 220 pp.
AAS copy.   25050

Winchester, Elhanan, 1751-1797.
The Universal Restoration.
Hudson, Stoddard, 1793. 204 pp.
AAS copy.   26493

[Winchester, Elhanan, 1751-1797.

[Philadelphia? 1750?] Broadside.
LOC copy.   40575

Wirt, William, 1772-1834.
An Oration Delivered in Richmond.
Richmond, [Va.], Jones, 1800. 19 pp.
JCB copy.   39124

Wisdom, a Poem [by Edward Wilkinson, 1727?-1809].
Philadelphia, James, 1787. 16 pp.
AAS copy.   20886

Wisdon, a Poem [by Edward Wilkinson, 1727?-1809].
Newport [1788]. 16 pp.
AAS copy.   21605

Wisdom, a Poem [by Edward Wilkinson, 1727?-1809].
Philadelphia, James, 1788. 19 pp.
LCP copy.   45415

Wisdom, a Poem [by Edward Wilkinson, 1727?-1809].
Litchfield, [Ct.], Collier & Buel, 1792. 20 pp.
AAS copy.   46675

Wisdom. A Poem[by Edward Wilkinson, 1727?-1809].
Haverhill, Edes, 1794. 16 pp.
Haverhill Public Library copy.   28086

Wisdom, a Poem [by Edward Wilkinson, 1727?-1809].
New York, Collins, 1797. 21 pp.
AAS copy.   48319

Wisdom: a Poem [by Edward Wilkinson, 1727?-1809].
Litchfield, Ct., 1798. 24 pp.
CHS copy.   35029

Wisdom in Miniature: or the Young Gentleman and Lady's Magazine - (No. 1.)
Hartford, Babcock, 1796. 30, [1] pp.
AAS copy.   31650

Wisdom in Miniature: or The Young Gentleman and Lady's Magazine.
Hartford, Ct., Babcock, 1798. 30, [1] pp.
AAS copy.   35045

Wisdom in Miniature: or the Young Gentleman and Lady's Magazine.
Hartford, [Ct.], Babcock, 1800. 30 pp.
LOC copy.   39125

Wisdom in Miniature; or The Young Gentleman and Lady's Pleasing Instructor. . . . First Worcester Edition.
Worcester, Thomas, 1795. 222 pp., 1 plate.
AAS copy.   29914

Wisdom in Miniature: or the Young Gentleman and Lady's Pleasing Instructor. . . . Second Worcester Edition.
Worcester, Thomas, Son & Thomas, 1796. 192 pp., 1 plate.
AAS copy.   31651

Wisdom in Miniature: or the Young Gentleman and Lady's Pleasing Instructor. . . . Third Edition.
Brooklyn, [N. Y.], Kirk, 1800. 208 pp.
NYHS copy.   39126

The Wisdom of Crop the Conjuror. . . . First Worcester Edition.
Worcester, Thomas, 1786. 43, [4] pp.
AAS copy.   20153

The Wisdom of Crop the Conjurer. . . . Second Worcester Edition.
Worcester, Thomas, 1794. 59, [4] pp.
AAS copy.   28117

Wise, Jeremiah, 1679-1756.
(Sibley, IV, 550-553.)
A Funeral Sermon.
Boston, Henchman, 1725. [2], 34 pp.
MHS copy.   2720

Wise, Jeremiah, 1679-1756.
(Sibley, IV, 550-553.)
Prayer for a Succession.
Boston, Fleet for Hancock, 1731. 63 pp.
HC copy.   3495

Wise Jeremiah, 1679-1756.
(Sibley, IV, 550-553.)

Rulers the Ministers of God.
Boston, Fleet for Hancock, 1729. 54, [1] pp.
AAS copy.   3242

Wise, Jeremiah, 1679-1756.
A Sermon Shewing the Suitableness . . . of Prayer.
Boston, Allen for Boone, 1717. [8], 40 pp.
LOC copy.   39677

[Wise, John], 1652-1725.
The Churches Quarrel Espoused.
New York, 1713. 152 pp.
HSP copy.   1660

Wise, John, 1652-1725.
The Churches Quarrel Espoused. . . . Second Edition.
Boston, 1715. [4], 116 pp.
AAS copy.   1795

[Wise, John], 1652-1725.
The Freeholder's Address to the Honourable House. . . . March 15, 1720.
Boston, J. Franklin for Gray, [1721?]. 7 pp.
BPL copy.   39759

[Wise, John], 1652-1725.
A Friendly Check, from a Kind Relation.
[Boston, 1721.] 7 pp.
BPL copy.   2310

Wise, John, 1652-1725.
A Vindication of the Government of New-England Churches.
Boston, Allen for Boone, 1717. 105, [1], 12 pp.
AAS copy.   1941

Wise, John, 1652-1725.
A Vindication of the Government of New-England Churches.
Boston, Boyles, 1772. 80, 96, 68, [1] pp.
AAS copy.   12625

Wise, John, 1652-1725.
A Vindication of the Government of New-England Churches.
Boston, Boyles, 1772. 271, [13] pp.
AAS copy.   12626

[Wise, John], 1652-1725.
A Word of Comfort to a Melancholy Country.
Boston, 1721. [4], 58 pp.
AAS copy.   2311

Wiseman, Billy, pseud.
Puzzling Cap: a Choice Collection of Riddles.
New York, Durell for Law, 1800. 31 pp.
d'Alte A. Welch copy.   39127

Wister, Johannes, 1708-1789.
Bekanntmachung!
[Germantown, 1764.] [4] pp.
HSP copy.   9880

Wisewell, Ichabod.
Upon the Death of . . . Samuel Arnold . . . September 1.
[Boston? 1693]. Broadside.
AAS ph copy.   39308

The Witch [by William Reeve, 1757-1815].
New York, Gilfert, [1797]. [2] pp.
AAS copy.   48239

[Witherspoon, John], 1723-1794.
Address to the Inhabitants of Jamaica.
Philadelphia, Bradfords, 1772. 27 pp.
JCB copy.   12627

Witherspoon, John, 1723-1794.
Christian Magnanimity.
Princeton, N. J., 1787. iv, 44 pp.
AAS copy.   20893

Witherspoon, John, 1723-1794.
The Dominion of Providence.
Philadelphia, Aitken, 1776. [4], 78, [1] pp.
AAS copy.   15224

Witherspoon, John, 1723-1794.
Ecclesiastical Characteristics. . . . Seventh Edition.
Philadelphia, Bradfords, 1767. 60 pp.
AAS copy.   10804

[Witherspoon, John, 1723-1794.
Essay on Money, as a Medium of Commerce.
Charleston, Timothy, 1786.]
("Just published," State Gazette of S. C., Sept. 28, 1786.)   20155

[Witherspoon, John], 1723-1794.
Essay on Money, as a Medium of Commerce.
Philadelphia, Young, Stewart, & M'Culloch, 1786. [4], 60 pp.
AAS copy.   20154

[Witherspoon, John, 1723-1794.
An Essay on Money.
New York, Loudons, 1787.]
("Just Published," N. Y. Packet, Jan. 16, 1787.)   20894

[Witherspoon, John, 1723-1794.
A Letter from a Blacksmith.
Newburyport, Mycall, [1785]. 72 pp.]
(A ghost of 20417, q. v.)   19389

[Witherspoon, John, 1723-1794.
Practical Discourses.
Philadelphia, Bradfords, 1770.]
(Adv. Pa. Journal, June 21, 1770, probably for copies of Edinburgh 1768 ed.)   11944

[Witherspoon, John], 1723-1794.
Recantation of Benjamin Towne.
[Fishkill? 1778?] [5] pp.
AAS copy.   43595

Witherspoon, John, 1723-1794.
A Series of Letters on Education.
New York, Buel, 1797. 108 pp.
HC copy.   33236

Witherspoon, John, 1723-1794.
A Sermon on the Religious Education of Children.
Elizabethtown, Kollock, 1789. 24 pp.
AAS copy.   22284

[Witherspoon, John, 1723-1794.
A Sermon on the Religious Education of Children.
New York, M'Lean, etc., 1789.]
(Entry apparently from an adv. for 22284.)   22285

[Witherspoon, John, 1723-1794.
A Sermon on the Religious Education of Children.
Putney, Vt., Sturtevant, 1797.]
(Advs. Argus, Feb. 12, 1798.)   33237

[Witherspoon, John], 1723-1794.
Some truth, much wit. . . . The Humble Confession . . . of Benjamin Towne.
[Philadelphia, 1778.] 5, [1] pp.
HSP copy.   16173

Witherspoon, John, 1723-1794.
The Works of. . . .
Philadelphia, Woodward, 1800. pp. [1]-36, [4], 37-604; [1]-632; [4], 9-611, [12].
AAS copy.   39128

[The Wits of Westminister.
Philadelphia, Dunlap, 1773.]
(Adv. Pa. Packet, July 12, 1773.)   13085

Witsius, Herman, 1636-1708.
The Oeconomy of the Convenant. . . . Volume I [-III].
New York, Forman for Lee & Stokes, 1798. 460, [4]; iv, 448; iv, 455 pp.
AAS copy.   35046

Witter, Ezra, 1768-1833.
Resignation to the Afflictive Dispensations.
Springfield, Mass., Ashby, 1799. 11 pp.
(A part of 35134, q. v.)   36734

The Witty and Entertaining Exploits of George Buchanan.
New York, Reid, 1789. 36 pp.
AAS copy.   45752

A Wo and a Warning.
[Philadelphia, 1765.] Broadside.
HSP copy.   10216

Wo des Verächters Netz. . . .
Philadelphia, den 19ten May 1766.
[Philadelphia, 1766.] Broadside.
(No copy located.)   41680

Woburn, Mass. First Church.
Some Brief Remarks upon the Result of a
Council . . . Jan. 9, 1746.
[Boston, 1747.] 8 pp.
AAS copy.　　　　　　　　　　　　6069

[Ein Wohl Eingerichtetes Deutsches
A.B.C.
Germantown, Billmeyer, 1790.]
(Entry from copyright record.)　　24008

[Ein Wohl Eingerichtetes Deutsches
A.B.C.
Germantown, Billmeyer, 1791.]
(Entry from copyright record.)　　24009

Ein wohl Eingerichtetes Deutsches A B C.
Germantown, Billmeyer, 1792. Front., xiv,
120 pp.
AAS copy.　　　　　　　　　　　　25051

[Ein Wohl Eingerichtetes Deutsches
A B C.
Germantown, Billmeyer, 1794.]
(Imprint apparently assumed by Evans
from Billmeyer adv.)　　　　　　28118

Ein Wohl Eingerichtetes Deutsches
A B C.
Germantown, Billmeyer, 1796. xiv, 120
pp., 1 plate.
AAS copy.　　　　　　　　　　　　31652

Wohl-Eingerichtetes Vieh-Arzney-Buch.
Philadelphia, Miller, 1771. [10], 184 pp.
AAS copy.　　　　　　　　　　　　12292

Der Wohlerfahrne Baum-Gärtner.
Lebanon, Pa., Schnee, [1799]. [2], 16 pp.
HSP copy.　　　　　　　　　　　　36735

[Wohlfahrt, Michael, 1684-1741.
(Pa. Mag. Hist. Biog., XIV, 388.)
Die Weissheit Gottes.
Philadelphia, Franklin and Wuster, 1737.]
(See Hildeburn 568.)　　　　　　4211

[Wohlfahrt, Michael, 1684-1741.
The Wisdom of God.
Philadelphia, Franklin, 1737.]
(See Hildeburn 569.)　　　　　　4212

[Wolcot, John], 1738-1819.
Expostulary Odes. By Peter Pindar.
Philadelphia, Spotswood, 1789.]
(Entry from an adv.)　　　　　　22287

[Wolcot, John], 1738-1819.
Hair Powder: a Plaintive Epistle . . . by
Peter Pindar.
New York, Smith, 1795. [2], 20, [1] pp.
AAS copy.　　　　　　　　　　　29915

[Wolcot, John], 1738-1819.
Instructions to a Celebrated Laureat. . . .
By Peter Pindar, Esq. . . . The Eighth
Edition.
New York, 1788. 27 pp.
NYPL copy.　　　　　　　　　　21615

[Wolcot, John], 1738-1819.
The Lousiad.
Philadelphia, Humphreys, 1786. 16 pp.
AAS copy.　　　　　　　　　　　20156

[Wolcot, John], 1738-1819.
The Lousiad. . . . By Peter Pindar.
Philadelphia, Spotswood, 1789. 48 pp.
AAS copy.　　　　　　　　　　　22286

[Wolcot, John, 1738-1819.
Peter Pindar's new Gypsy Song.
Composed by Thomas Wright.
Philadelphia, Carr, 1793.]
(Adv. in Dec. newspapers.)　　　26495

[Wolcot, John], 1738-1819.
Pindariana; or Peter's Portfolio.
Philadelphia, Bache, 1794. x, 242 pp.
AAS copy.　　　　　　　　　　　28119

[Wolcot, John], 1738-1819.
The Poetical Works of Peter Pindar.
Philadelphia, Spotswood, 1789. ix, [1],
314 pp.
AAS copy.　　　　　　　　　　　22288

[Wolcot, John], 1738-1819.
The Poetical Works of Peter Pindar.
Newburyport, Mycall for Boyle, [1790?].
viii, 314 pp.
AAS copy.　　　　　　　　　　　23087

[Wolcot, John], 1738-1819.
The Poetical Works of Peter Pindar. . . .
Vol. II.
Philadelphia, Spotswood and Rice, 1790.
pp. [191]-402.
AAS copy.　　　　　　　　　　　23088

[Wolcot, John], 1738-1819.
The Poetical Works of Peter Pindar. . . .
Vol. I [- II].
Philadelphia, Spotswood & Rice, 1792.
viii, 307, [1]; iv, 324 pp.
AAS copy.　　　　　　　　　　　25052

[Wolcot, John], 1738-1819.
The Poetical Works of Peter Pindar.
Philadelphia, Spotswood, 1794. 2 vol. viii,
307, [1]; vi, 447 (i.e., 427) pp.
AAS copy.　　　　　　　　　　　28120

[Wolcot, John, 1738-1819.
The Poetical Works of Peter Pindar.
Cincinnati, Freeman, 1797. 2 vol.]
(Entry from proposals.)　　　　33238

[Wolcot, John], 1738-1819.
Subjects for Painters. By Peter Pindar.
Philadelphia, Spotswood, 1789.]
(Entry from an adv.)　　　　　　22289

[Wolcot, John], 1738-1819.
Subjects for Painters. By Peter Pindar.
Philadelphia, Spotswood, 1790. 59 pp.
LCP copy.　　　　　　　　　　　46105

[Wolcot, John], 1738-1819.
The Works of Peter Pinder. . . . In Three
Volumes.
New York, Wayland, 1793. 3 vol., 490 pp.
(Only vol. 1-2 known.)
HEH copy.　　　　　　　　　　　46950

Wolcott, Roger, 1679-1767.
(D. A. B.)
A Letter to the Reverend Mr. Noah
Hobart.
Boston, Green & Russell, 1761. 24 pp.
AAS copy.　　　　　　　　　　　9041

Wolcott, Roger, 1679-1767.
(D. A. B.)
Poetical Meditations.
New London, 1725. [4], lvi, ii, 78, [4] pp.
AAS copy.　　　　　　　　　　　2722

[Wolcott, William, 1753-1825.
A Devout Wish.
Hartford, Webster, [1781]. Broadside.]
(No copy located.)　　　　　　17442

[Wolcott, William], 1753-1825.
Grateful Reflections on the Divine
Goodness.
Hartford, [1779]. 60 pp.
AAS copy.　　　　　　　　　　　16684

Wolfe, James, 1727-1759.
General Wolfe's Instructions.
Philadelphia, Bell, 1778. 142, [2] pp.
AAS copy.　　　　　　　　　　　16174

Wollstonecraft, Mary, 1759-1797.
An Historical and Moral View of the . . .
French Revolution. . . . Volume I.
Philadelphia, Dobson, 1795. xv, [1], 380
pp.
(No copy of Vol. II located.)
AAS copy.　　　　　　　　　　　29916

Wollstonecraft, Mary, 1759-1797.
Letters Written during a Short Residence
in Sweden.
Wilmington, Del., Wilson & Johnson,
1796. 218, [6], 12 pp.
AAS copy.　　　　　　　　　　　31653

Wollstonecraft, Mary, 1759-1797.
A Vindication of the Rights of Woman.
Boston, Edes for Thomas & Andrews,
1792. 340 pp.
AAS copy.　　　　　　　　　　　25054

Wollstonecraft, Mary, 1759-1797.
A Vindication of the Rights of Woman.
Philadelphia, Gibbons, 1792. 274, [2] pp.
AAS copy.　　　　　　　　　　　25053

Wolstenholme, Daniel.
To the Public. As Mr. Allen. . . . [Dated
Nov. 9, 1768.]
[Annapolis, 1768.] Broadside.
MdHS copy.　　　　　　　　　　41901

Women Invited to War.
Boston, Edes, 1787. 35, [1] pp.
AAS copy.　　　　　　　　　　　20895

The Wonder of Nature. . . . Being a
Strange Account of one Hen. T'Kent.
Boston, B. Green, 1702. 8 pp.
BPL copy.　　　　　　　　　　　39389

[The Wonder of Wonders! or, the
Wonderful Appearance of an Angel.
New York, Anderson, [1774]. 24 pp.]
(Title from an adv., pagination from
Haven.)　　　　　　　　　　　　13780

A Wonderful Account of a Little Girl . . .
in the Town of Jericho.
[Windsor, Vt.], 1800. 12 pp.
VtHS (Rugg) copy.　　　　　　39129

A Wonderful Account of the Conversion
of Two Young Girls.
Windsor, Vt., Spooner, 1795. 12 pp.
(Evans' entry is apparently a ghost of this
ed. arising from an adv. in the Rutland
Herald, Aug. 21, 1797.)
NHSL copy.　　　　　　　　　　33239

[A Wonderful Account of the Death and
Burial of the Old Hermit.
Boston, Russell, 1786. Broadside.]
(Entry from 19532, referring apparently to
20175.)　　　　　　　　　　　　20157

. . . The Wonderful Advantages of
Adventuring in the Lottery!!!
Philadelphia, Johnsons, 1800. 36 pp.
AAS copy.　　　　　　　　　　　37131

The Wonderful Appearance of an Angel,
Devil & Ghost.
Boston, Boyle, 1774. 31 pp.
AAS copy.　　　　　　　　　　　13779

A Wonderful Discovery of a Hermit! Who
Lived Upwards of 200 Years [by James
Buckland, fl. 1785].
n. p., [1786?]. Broadside.
PrU copy.　　　　　　　　　　　44863

A Wonderful Discovery of a Hermit [by
James Buckland, fl. 1785].
[Boston, 1786.] Broadside.
AAS copy.　　　　　　　　　　　19532

A Wonderful Discovery of an Old Hermit
[by James Buckland, fl. 1785].
Norwich, Trumbull, 1786. 8 pp.
AAS copy.　　　　　　　　　　　19531

A Wonderful Discovery of a Hermit, who
Lived Upwards of 200 Years [by James
Buckland, fl. 1785].
Springfield, 1786. 12 pp.
AAS copy.　　　　　　　　　　　44864

A Wonderful Discovery of a Hermit [by
James Buckland, fl. 1775].
Hartford, 1787. 12 pp.
AAS copy.　　　　　　　　　　　45047

A Wonderful Discovery of an Old Hermit
[by James Buckland, fl. 1775].
Windham, 1792. 11 pp.
LOC copy.　　　　　　　　　　　24154

A Wonderful Dream [by B. Nicoll].
[New York, 1770.] 2 pp.
NYPL copy.　　　　　　　　　　11791

The Wonderful Escape, or Sagacity
Outwitted: a Curious Story.
Boston, White, 1796. 22 pp.
(Present location unknown.)　　48028

The Wonderful Life . . . of . . . Robinson
Crusoe [by Daniel Defoe, 1661?-1731].
New York, Gaine, 1774. 138, [4] pp.
AAS copy.　　　　　　　　　　　42582

The Wonderful Life . . . of . . . Robinson
Crusoe [by Daniel Defoe, 1661?-1731].
New York, Gaine, 1777.]
(From an adv.)　　　　　　　　15283

The Wonderful Life and Adventures of
Robinson Crusoe [by Daniel Defoe,
1661?-1731].
Hartford, Ct., Babcock, 1800. 31 pp.
AAS copy.　　　　　　　　　　　37305

The Wonderful Life and most Surprising
Adventures of Robinson Crusoe of York

[by Daniel Defoe, 1661?-1731].
New York, Durell, [1793]. 148 pp.
d'Alte Welch copy.   25386

The Wonderful Life, and Most Surprising
Adventures, of . . . Robinson Crusoe
[by Daniel Defoe, 1661?-1731].
New York, Tiebout, 1800. 134 pp.
AAS copy.   37306

The Wonderful Life and Surprising
Adventures of Robinson Crusoe [by
Daniel Defoe, 1661?-1731].
Boston, White & Cambridge, 1792. 72 pp.
AAS copy.   24253

The Wonderful Life, and Surprising
Adventures . . . of . . . Robinson Crusoe
[by Daniel Defoe, 1661?-1731].
Boston, Hall, 1794. 116 pp.
CHS copy.   26865

[The Wonderful Life, and Surprising
Adventures of . . . Robinson Crusoe [by
Daniel Defoe, 1661?-1731].
Philadelphia, Carey, 1794.]
(Imprint assumed by Evans from advs.)
                                             26866

The Wonderful Life and Most Surprising
Adventures of . . . Robinson Crusoe [by
Daniel Defoe, 1661?-1731].
New York, Hurtin for Duyckinck, 1795.
143 pp.
AAS copy.   28555

The Wonderful Life and Surprising
Adventures of Robinson Crusoe [by
Daniel Defoe, 1661?-1731].
Philadelphia, M'Culloch, 1800. 144 pp.
(The only recorded copy cannot be
reproduced.)   37307

The Wonderful Narrative.
Boston, Rogers & Fowle, 1742. 108, [1]
pp.
(For question of authorship see BSA,
XLV, 127-128.)
AAS copy.   4915

[A Wonderful Visit from the Dead.
Windsor, Vt., Spooner, 1797.]
(Imprint assumed by Evans from adv.
"For Sale at this Office," Vt. Journal,
Mar. 17, 1797.)   33240

[The Wonders of the Invisible World.
New London, Ct., Holt, 1798.]
(Imprint assumed by Evans from adv.
"For Sale at this Office," The Bee, Jan.
31, 1798.)   35047

Wood, Abraham, 1752-1804.
Divine Songs, Extracted from Mr. J.
Hart's Hymns.
Boston, Thomas, 1789. 32 pp.
AAS copy.   21877

Wood, Abraham, 1752-1804.
A Funeral Elegy on the Death of . . .
Washington.
Boston, Thomas & Andrews, 1800. 8 pp.
AAS copy.   39131

Wood, Abraham, 1752-1804.
A Hymn on Peace.
[Worcester, 1784?]. [16] pp.
BPL copy.   18890

Wood, Amos, 1760-1798.
A Sermon Preached before His
Excellency.
Portsmouth, Melcher, 1794. 36 pp.
AAS copy.   28124

Wood, Benjamin, 1772-1849.
The Obligation of Ministers.
Worcester, Mass., Worcester for Thomas,
1797. 40 pp.
AAS copy.   33241

Wood, Benjamin, 1772-1849.
A Sermon, Delivered at Upton, August
8th, 1800.
Worcester, Mass., Greenleaf, 1800. 22 pp.
AAS copy.   39132

Wood, John, master of the Episcopal
Charity School, New York.
Mentor, or the American Teacher's
Assistant.
New York, Buel, 1795. [4], 374, [4] pp.
(The AAS has an almost identical issue

with the words "copy-right secured" on p.
374.)
AAS copy.   29917

[Wood, John, of Vt.
By Permission of the Legislature. . . . A
Lottery. . . . March 9, 1797.
[Rutland, 1797.] Broadside.]
(Broadside printing assumed from adv.
Rutland Herald, Mar. 13, 1797.)   33242

Wood, John, of Vt.
Capt. John Wood's Lottery, Assigned to
Col. Mathew Lyon.
[Rutland, Vt., 1798?] Broadside.
AAS copy.   35048

[Wood, John, of Vt.
To the Public. Being Engaged in a
Lottery. . . . September 28th, 1797.
[Rutland, 1797.] Broadside.]
(Broadside printing assumed by Evans
from adv. Rutland Herald, Oct. 8, 1797.)
                                             33243

[Wood, Sally Sayward (Barrell)],
1759-1855.
Julia, and the Illuminated Baron.
Portsmouth, N. H., Peirce, 1800. 288 pp.
AAS copy.   39134

Wood, Samuel, 1752-1836.
A Discourse, Delivered at Boscawen.
Concord, [N. H.], Hough, 1800. 15 pp.
LOC copy.   39133

Wood, Samuel, 1752-1836.
A Discourse, Delivered at the Ordination
of . . . Benjamin Wood.
Worcester, Mass., Worcester for Thomas,
1797. 31 pp.
AAS copy.   33244

Wood, Samuel, 1752-1836.
The Leading Truths of Revealed Religion.
Worcester, Worcester, 1794. 40 pp.
AAS copy.   28125

[Wood, Samuel], 1752-1836.
An Oration on Early Education.
Dresden, Spooner, 1779. 14 pp.
(Best copy available.)
DC copy.   43734

Wood, Silas, 1769-1847.
Letters Addressed to the Electors.
New York, Swords, 1800. 22 pp.
NYHS copy.   39135

[Wood, Silas], 1769-1847.
Thoughts on the State of the American
Indians.
New York, Swords, 1794. 36 pp.
AAS copy.   28126

Wood, Wilkes, 1770-1843.
(Weston, Hist. Middleboro, pp. 229-330.)
An Oration, Pronounced before the
Philosophical Society.
New Bedford, Spooner, 1795. 11 pp.
AAS copy.   29918

Wood, William, fl. 1629-1635.
New-England's Prospect. . . . Third
Edition.
Boston, Fleet and Green & Russell, 1764.
[2], xviii, 128 pp.
AAS copy.   9884

The Wood Robin.
Boston, von Hagen, [1800?]. Broadside.
JCB copy.   49196

Woodbridge, Ashbel, 1704-1758.
(Dexter, I, 309-310.)
A Sermon Delivered before the General
Assembly.
New London, 1753. [4], 44 pp.
AAS copy.   7137

Woodbridge, Benjamin, 1712-1785.
(Dexter, I, 656-657.)
The Blessed State of the Dead.
New London, 1751. [4], 79 pp.
CHS copy.   6799

Woodbridge, Benjamin, 1712-1785.
The Death of Godly and Faithful Men.
New Haven, 1756. [2], 32 pp.
CHS copy.   7821

[Woodbridge, John], 1614-1695.
F. L. Weis, Colonial Clergy.)

Severals Relating to the Fund.
[Boston? 1682.] 8+ pp.
(The only known copy is incomplete.)
WL copy.   337

Woodbridge, Samuel, 1683-1746.
Obedience to the Divine Law.
New London, 1724. [4], 28 pp.
HC copy.   2596

Woodbridge, Timothy, 1656-1732.
(Weis, Colonial Clergy N. E.)
The Duty of God's Professing People.
New London, 1727. [2], iv, 16 pp.
MHS copy.   2979

Woodbridge, Timothy, 1656-1732.
Jesus Christ doth Actually Reign.
New London, Green, 1727. [4], 33 pp.
BPL copy.   2980

Woodbridge, William, 1755-1836.
A Plain and Concise Grammar.
Middletown, [Ct.], Dunning, 1800. 84 pp.
CU copy.   39136

Woodbridge, William, 1755-1836.
A Plain and Concise View of the System
of Education.
Middletown, Ct., Dunning, 1799. 8 pp.
NYPL copy.   36736

Woodbridge, William, 1755-1836.
The Plain Spelling Book.
Middletown, [Ct.], Dunning, 1800. 143,
[1] pp.
HC copy.   39137

Woodbridge, William, 1755-1836.
A Sermon Delivered at Middlefield.
Middletown, [Ct.], Dunning, 1800. 14, [1]
pp.
AAS copy.   39138

Woodbridge, William, 1755-1836.
A Sermon on the Care of the Soul.
Middletown, Ct., Dunning, 1798. 40 pp.
AAS copy.   35049

Woodhouse, James, 1770-1809.
An Inaugural Dissertation.
Philadelphia, Woodhouse, [1792]. 34 pp.
AAS copy.   25055

Woodhouse, James, 1770-1809.
Observations on the Combination.
Philadelphia, Jones, Hoff & Derrick,
1793. 20 pp.
AAS copy.   26496

Woodhouse, James, 1770-1809.
The Young Chemist's Pocket Companion.
Philadelphia, Oswald, 1797. 56, [2] pp.
AAS copy.   33245

[Woodhouse, William, 1740?-1795.
Catalogue of new and old Books for Sale
by. . . .
Philadelphia, 1772.]
(Adv. Pa. Chronicle, Sept. 19, 1772.)
                                             12629

Woodhouse, William, 1740?-1795.
Philadelphia, March 11, 1771. To be
Published and Sold. . . . A Pennsylvania
Sailor's Letters.
[Philadelphia, 1771.] Broadside.
HSP copy.   12106

Woodhull, John, 1744-1824.
A Sermon, for the Day of Publick
Thanksgiving.
Trenton, Collins, 1790. 24 pp.
AAS copy.   23089

[The Wood-Lark, or] a Choice Collection
of . . . English Songs.
Philadelphia, Bradford, [1765?]. [2], ii,
xiv, 190, 194 pp.
LCP copy.   41600

Woodman, Joseph, 1748-1807.
A Discourse; Delivered by the Particular
Desire of the Military Society.
Concord, N. H., Russell & Davis, 1794. 16
pp.
Presb. Hist. Soc. copy.   28127

Woodman, Joseph, 1748-1807.
A Sermon, on Christian Candour.
Concord, N. H., Hough, 1792. 30 pp.
AAS copy.   25056

Woodruff, Hezekiah North, 1763-1833.
The Life and Character of a Gospel
Minister.
Boston, Edes, 1795. 31 pp.
AAS copy. 29919

Woodruff, Hezekiah North, 1763-1833.
A Sermon, Occasioned by the Death of
. . . Washington.
Stonington-Port, Trumbull for Smiths,
1800. 16 pp.
AAS copy. 39139

Woodruff, Hezekiah S., 1754-1844.
To the Publick. . . . Were All Men
Faithful. . . .
[Trenton, 1779.] Broadside.
NYAM copy. 43735

Woodruff, Merit N., 1780-1799.
Devotional Harmony.
n. p., [1800?]. 60 pp.
AAS copy. 39140

Woods, John, b. 1765?
Proposals for Publishing . . . The Rural
Magazine.
[Newark, 1797?] Broadside.
NYHS copy. 48321

Woods, Leonard, 1774-1854.
A Contrast between the Effects of
Religion.
Boston, Russell, 1799. 20 pp.
AAS copy. 36737

Woods, Leonard, 1774-1854.
Envy Wishes, then Believes.
Leominster, Mass., Prentiss, 1796. 16 pp.
AAS copy. 31654

Woods, Leonard, 1774-1854.
Two Sermons on Profane Swearing.
Newburyport, March, 1799. 39 pp.
AAS copy. 36738

[Woods's Town and Country Almanac . . .
for . . . 1793.
Newark, Woods.]
(Entry from Nelson, who had not seen a
copy.) 25058

Woodstock, Pa.
Charter of the Town of Woodstock.
Martinsburg, Willis, [1791]. Broadside.
LOC copy. 46362

[Woodward, Hezekiah], 1590-1675.
A Few Drops of Choice Honey.
Exeter, Ranlet, 1794. 26 (i.e., 48) pp.
AAS copy. 26970

Woodward, Israel Beard, 1767-1810.
American Liberty and Independence.
Litchfield, Ct., [1798]. 26 pp.
AAS copy. 35050

Woodward, John, 1671-1747.
(Sibley, IV, 186-188.)
Civil Rulers are God's Ministers.
Boston, 1712. [2], 46 pp.
AAS copy. 1593

Woodward, John, fl. 1797.
The Noted Stud Horse. . . . May, 1797.
[New London], Green's Press, [1797].
Broadside.
CHS copy. 48322

[Woodward, Josiah], 1660-1712.
The Baseness and Perniciousness of the
Sin of Slandering.
Boston, Boyles, 1769. 24 pp.
AAS copy. 11518

Woodward, Josiah, 1660-1712.
A Disswasive from the Sin of
Drunkenness.
Lancaster, [Pa.], Dunlap, 1755. 22, [1]
pp.
HEH copy. 40813

Woodward, Josiah, 1660-1712.
An Earnest Persuasive.
Lancaster, [Pa.], Dunlap, 1755. 14, [1]
pp.
HSP copy. 40814

Woodward, Josiah, 1660-1712.
Fair Warnings. . . . Fourth Edition.
Boston, Rogers for Phillips, 1729. [12],
142 pp.
AAS copy. 3243

Woodward, Josiah, 1660-1712.
A Kind Caution to Profane Swearers.
Newport, 1768. 15 pp.
RIHS copy. 11123

[Woodward, Josiah, 1660-1712.
A Kind Caution to Profane Swearers.
Boston, 1770. 13 pp.]
(Entry from Haven; no copy since
located.) 11947

Woodward, Josiah, 1660-1712.
The Young Man's Monitor.
Philadelphia, Miller, 1767. 60 pp.
HSP copy. 41780

Woodward, Samuel, 1727-1782.
(Weis, Colonial Clergy N. E.)
The Help of the Lord.
Boston, Gill, 1779. 29 pp.
AAS copy. 16685

Woodward, Samuel, 1727-1782.
(Weis, Colonial Clergy N. E.)
The Office, Duties, and Qualifications.
Boston, Mecom, 1760. 31 pp.
AAS copy. 8771

Woodward, Samuel, 1727-1782.
(Weis, Colonial Clergy N. E.)
A Sermon Preached at the Ordination of
. . . John Marsh.
New Haven, 1774. 30 pp.
AAS copy. 13781

Woodward, Samuel, 1727-1782.
A Sermon Preached October 9, 1760.
Boston, Mecom, [1760]. 30 pp.
AAS copy. 8772

Woodward, Samuel, 1727-1782.
(Weis, Colonial Clergy N. E.)
Submission to the Providence of God.
Boston, Fleets, 1783. [4], ii, 18 pp.
AAS copy. 18315

Woodward, William Henry, 1774-1818.
An Oration, Delivered at Hanover.
Hanover, N. H., True, [1798]. 15 pp.
JCB copy. 35051

Woodward, William Henry, 1774-1818.
An Oration, Pronounced at Hanover.
Hanover, N. H., Davis, 1800. 17 pp.
AAS copy. 39141

[Woodworth, John]?, 1768-1858.
The Spunkiad: or Heroism Improved.
Newburgh, N. Y., Denniston, 1798. 23 pp.
AAS copy. 35052

Woollen Manufactory Lottery.
Scheme of a Lottery. . . . Hartford, Feb.
17, 1791.
[Hartford, 1791.] Broadside.
CHS copy. 46363

Woolman, John, 1720-1772.
(D. A. B.)
Considerations on Keeping Negroes. . . .
Part Second.
Philadelphia, Franklin & Hall, 1762. 52
pp.
AAS copy. 9314

Woolman, John, 1720-1772.
Considerations on Pure Wisdom.
Philadelphia, Hall & Sellers, 1768. 28 pp.
AAS copy. 11124

Woolman, John, 1720-1772.
(D. A. B.)
Considerations on the true Harmony of
Mankind.
Philadelphia, Crukshank, 1770. 33 pp.
AAS copy. 11948

Woolman, John, 1720-1772.
An Epistle to the Quarterly and Monthly
Meetings of Friends.
[Burlington, 1772.] 16 pp.
AAS copy. 12630

Woolman, John, 1720-1772.
An Extract from John Woolman's
Journal.
[Philadelphia, 1770.] 7 pp.
LCP copy. 11949

[Woolman, John, 1720-1772.
(D. A. B.)
A First Book for Children. . . . Third
Edition.

Philadelphia, Crukshank and Ferriss,
[1769]. 16? pp.]
(Entry from Haven.) 11538

[Woolman, John, 1720-1772.
A Journal of the Life . . . of. . . .
Philadelphia, Crukshank, 1790.]
(Entry from an adv.) 23090

[Woolman, John, 1720-1772.
A First Book for Children, A.B.C.D.&.
Wilmington, Del., Brynberg, 1797.]
(Imprint assumed by Evans from
Brynberg's adv.) 33248

Woolman, John, 1720-1772.
(D. A. B.)
Some Considerations on the Keeping of
Negroes.
Philadelphia, Chattin, 1754. [6], 24, [2]
pp.
HSP copy. 7341

Woolman, John, 1720-1772.
The Works of. . . . In two Parts.
Philadelphia, Crukshank, 1774. xiv, [2],
436 pp.
AAS copy. 13782

Woolman, John, 1720-1772.
(D. N. B.)
The Works of. . . . Second Edition.
Philadelphia, Crukshank, 1775. xiv, [2],
432 pp.
AAS copy. 14631

Woolman, John, 1720-1772.
The Works of. . . . Third Edition.
Philadelphia, Johnsons, 1800. 448 pp.
AAS copy. 39142

[Woolsey, Melancthon Lloyd, 1758-1819.
Address Delivered at Platsburg.
Lansingburgh, 1800.]
(Sabin 105214.) 39143

Woolston, Thomas, 1670-1733.
(D. N. B.)
A Free Gift to the Clergy.
Philadelphia, 1724. 52 pp.
(The unique copy is imperfect.)
JH copy. 2597

Woolverton, Charles.
Christ the Eternal Word.
Philadelphia, Franklin, 1738. 40 pp.
UOP copy. 4327

[Woolverton, Charles.
The Spirit's Teaching. . . . Second
Edition.
Philadelphia, Franklin and Meredith,
1729.]
(Adv. Pa. Gazette, Nov. 27, 1729.) 3244

[Woolverton, Charles.]
The Upright Lives of the Heathen.
Philadelphia, Bradford, [1740]. 16 pp.]
(Title from Hildeburn.) 4660

Woolworth, Aaron, 1763-1821.
The Evil of Lying: a Sermon.
Sagg-Harbour, Frothingham, 1793. 15 pp.
Presb. Hist. Soc. copy. 46951

Wooster, David, 1711-1777.
New-York, Aug. 29, 1775. Fresh News.

[New York, 1775.] Broadside.
BPL copy. 14343

Wooten, James.
[A Sermon Preached at the Opening of St.
Anne's Church . . . the 24th of September,
1704.
Annapolis, Reading, 1704.]
(Wroth 14. No copy known.) 39416

Worcester, Francis, 1698-1783.
A Bridle for Sinners. . . . Second Edition.
Boston, 1760. 35 pp.
(No perfect copy found.)
BPL copy. 41179

Worcester, Francis, 1698-1783.
(Weis, Colonial Clergy N. E.)
A Bridle for Sinners. . . . Third Edition.
Boston, Fowle for Chapin, 1763. 44 pp.
(The only copy located is badly worn.)
AAS copy. 9548

Worcester, Francis, 1698-1783.
Bridle for Sinners. . . . Fourth Edition.

Boston, Russell for Lazell, 1782. 32 pp.
(No perfect copy located.)
AAS copy.   17804

[Worcester, Francis, 1698-1783.
Rise, Travils, and Triumph.
Boston, 1763. 150 pp.]
(Title from Haven.)   9549

Worcester, Francis, 1698-1783.
(Weis, Colonial Clergy N. E.)
Sabbath-Profanity.
Boston, Mecom, 1760. 40 pp.
LOC copy.   8773

[Worcester, Leonard], 1767-1846.
Letters and Remarks.
Worcester, Worcester, 1795. 36 pp.
AAS copy.   29921

Worcester, Leonard, 1767-1846.
An Oration, Pronounced at Peacham.
Peacham, Vt., Farley & Goss, 1800. 20 pp.
AAS copy.   39144

Worcester, Noah, 1758-1837.
A Candid Discussion.
Worcester, Worcester, 1794. 103 pp.
AAS copy.   28130

Worcester, Noah, 1758-1837.
An Election Sermon, Delivered at
Concord.
Concord, [N. H.], Russell, [1800]. 28 pp.
AAS copy.   39145

Worcester, Noah, 1758-1837.
A Familiar Dialogue.
Worcester, Worcester, 1793. 45 pp.
AAS copy.   26502

Worcester, Noah, 1758-1837.
A Friendly Letter to . . . Thomas Baldwin.
Concord, N.H., Hough, 1791. 48 pp.
AAS copy.   24011

Worcester, Noah, 1758-1837.
The Gospel-Ministry Illustrated.
Newburyport, Mycall for Hoyt, [1791]. 34
pp.
AAS copy.   24012

Worcester, Noah, 1758-1837.
Impartial Inquiries.
Worcester, Worcester, 1794. 28 pp.
AAS copy.   28131

Worcester, Noah, 1758-1837.
The Natural Teacher. . . . Second Edition.
Concord, N. H., Hough, 1798. 59 pp.
NYPL copy.   35053

[Worcester, Noah], 1758-1837.
A Polemic Essay.
Newark, [N. J.], Pennington & Dodge,
1799. 42 pp.
NYHS copy.   36739

Worcester, Noah, 1758-1837.
A Sermon Delivered at Haverhill.
Haverhill, N. H., Coverly, 1796. 33 pp.
AAS copy.   31657

Worcester, Noah, 1758-1837.
A Sermon, on the Creation.
Worcester, Worcester, 1794. 23 pp.
AAS copy.   28132

[Worcester, Noah], 1758-1837.
Some Difficulties Proposed for Solution.
Newburyport, 1786. 61 pp.
AAS copy.   20158

[Worcester, Noah], 1758-1837.
Some Difficulties Proposed for Solution.
Worcester, Worcester, 1793. 59 pp.
AAS copy.   26503

Worcester, Samuel, 1770-1821.
An Oration: Delivered, at the Colby
Chapel.
Hanover, Dunham & True, 1795. 12 pp.
AAS copy.   29922

Worcester, Samuel, 1770-1821.
An Oration, Pronounced at Newipswich.
Amherst, N. H., Cushing, 1796. 24 pp.
AAS copy.   31658

Worcester, Samuel, 1770-1821.
An Oration, Sacred to the Memory of . . .
Washington.

Leominster, Mass., Adams & Wilder,
1800. 21 pp.
(A variant setting of the tp. is
reproduced.)
AAS copies.   39146

Worcester, Samuel, 1770-1821.
Six Sermons, on . . . Future Punishment.
Worcester, Mass., Greenleaf, 1800. 156
pp.
AAS copy.   39147

Worcester, Thomas, 1768-1831.
A Dialogue.
Concord, N.H., Hough, 1794. 24 pp.
AAS copy.   28133

Worcester, Thomas, 1768-1831.
An Oration, Delivered at Salisbury.
Concord, N. H., Davis, 1798. 16 pp.
(Evans guessed at the imprint.)
BPL copy.   35054

Worcester, Thomas, 1768-1831.
A Sacred Ode, on the Sudden Death of
Lieut. Emerson.
[Boston], Printed next Liberty Pole, 1791.
Broadside.
(Not located, 1968.)   46364

Worcester, Thomas, 1768-1831.
The Solemnity of Marriage Illustrated.
Concord, N. H., Hough, 1798. 26 pp.
AAS copy.   35055

Worcester, Thomas, 1768-1831.
A Thanksgiving Sermon. Delivered
November 12, 1795.
Newburyport, Mycall, 1796. 31 pp.
AAS copy.   31659

Worcester, Mass.
House Lots for Sale. . . . December 24th,
1784.
Worcester, Thomas, 1785. Broadside.
AAS copy.   19390

Worcester, Mass. Committee of
Correspondence.
In Committee Chamber, Worcester, Nov.
18, 1776.
[Worcester, 1776.] Broadside.
AAS copy.   43213

Worcester, Mass. Convention, Jan. 17,
1775.
[At a Convention of Committees for the
County of Worcester]. . . . Resolved, That
it be Recommended. . . .
[Boston, 1775.] Broadside.
(The only known copy is imperfect.)
AAS copy.   42987

Worcester, Mass. Convention, Jan. 17,
1775.
At a Convention of Committees for the
County of Worcester. . . . Whereas Isaac
Jones of Weston. . . .
[Boston, 1775.] Broadside.
AAS copy.   42988

Worcester, Mass. Convention, 1779.
Proceedings . . . on the 3d Day of August,
1779.
[Worcester, 1779.] Broadside.
AAS copy.   43736

Worcester, Mass. Worcester Associate
Library Company.
Rules and Regulations.
Worcester, Worcester, 1793. 12 pp.
AAS copy.   26506

Worcester, Mass. Worcester Fire Society.
Articles containing the Rules and
Regulations.
Worcester, Thomas, 1793. 10 pp.
AAS copy.   26507

Worcester, Mass., Worcester Fire Society.
Articles: Containing the Rules and
Regulations. . . . Revised . . . January,
1798.
Worcester, Thomas, 1798. 12 pp.
AAS copy.   35056

Worcester County Convention.
. . . In Convention. Tuesday, April 9,
1782.
Worcester, 1782. Broadside.
AAS copy.   19447

Worcester County, Mass. Committee of
Correspondence, 1774.
Worcester, June 13th, 1774. Gentlemen.
Many Persons in this County. . . .
[Boston, 1775.] Broadside.
AAS copy.   42756

Worcester County, Mass. Sheriff.
Two Hundred Dollars Reward. . . .
Nathan Davis. . . . October 25, 1778.
[Worcester, 1778.] Broadside.
AAS copy.   43596

Worcester, January 3d, 1793. We the
Subscribers. . . .
[Worcester, 1793.] Broadside.   26504

Worcester, January 4th, 1793. (Circular.)
Sir, The General Court. . . .
[Worcester, 1793.] Broadside.
AAS copy.   26505

A Word in Season. Fellow Citizens. . . .
[New York, 1736.] [2] pp.
AAS copy.   4104

A Word in Season to all Protestants.
Philadelphia, Armbruster, [1763]. 7 pp.
HSP copy.   9550

A Word of Advice. Beware my good
Friends.
[New York, 1768.] Broadside.
NYPL copy.   11125

A Word of Advice. Mark well the
Barretor!
[New York, 1768.] Broadside.
NYPL copy.   11126

A Word of Advice, to such as are Settling
new Plantations.
Boston, Fleet for Henchman, 1739. 15 pp.
HC copy.   4463

A Word of Comfort to a Melancholy
Country [by John Wise, 1652-1725].
Boston, 1721. [4], 58 pp.
AAS copy.   2311

A Word of Counsel and Warning.
Providence, 1771. 23 pp.
(The only known copy is imperfect.)
RIHS copy.   42306

A Word of Counsel and Warning, to all
who are Rejectors. . . . Second Edition [by
Samuel Bixby?, 1755-1848].
Worcester, 1779. 31 pp.
AAS copy.   16207

A Word or Two More from the Obscure
and Remote Person. . . . April 7th, 1729.
[Boston, 1729.] 2 pp.
BA copy.   39935

Words for a Funeral Anthem. . . . At the
Funeral of the Reverend Dr. Samuel
Cooper . . . Jan. 2, 1784.
[Boston, 1784.] Broadside.
AAS copy.   44634

Words of Consolation to Mr. Robert
Stetson. . . . November 7th, 1718 [by
Nathaniel Pitcher, 1685-1723].
[Boston, 1718.] Broadside.
EI copy.   39689

The Words of Moses, Blot me I Pray thee
out [by Andrew Lee, 1745-1832].
Norwich, Trumbull, 1787. 24 pp.
AAS copy.   20453

The Words of Understanding [by Cotton
Mather, 1663-1728].
Boston, Kneeland for Edwards, 1724. [2],
105, [1] pp.
AAS copy.   2562

The Work and Contention of Heaven [by
Ralph Erskine, 1685-1752].
n. p., [1740]. 4 pp.
AAS copy.   40190

Work Within-Doors [by Cotton Mather,
1663-1728].
Boston, 1709. 40 pp.
AAS copy.   1409

Workman, Benjamin.
The American Accountant.

Philadelphia, M'Culloch for Young, 1789.
pp. [4], [13]-224.
AAS copy. 22290

Workman, Benjamin.
The American Accountant. . . . Second
Edition.
Philadelphia, Young, 1793. pp. [4],
[13]-220, [1]-3, [1].
AAS copy. 26508

Workman, Benjamin.
The American Accountant. . . . Third
Edition.
Philadelphia, Young, 1796. pp. [4],
[13]-220, 4.
AAS copy. 31660

Workman, Benjamin.
The Columbian Almanack, for . . . 1790.
Philadelphia, Stewart. [40] pp.
AAS copy. 21743

[Workman, Benjamin.
Elements of Geography.
Philadelphia, M'Culloch, 1789.]
(Entry from an adv.) 22291

Workman, Benjamin.
Elements of Geography. . . . In Six
Sections. . . . Second Edition.
Philadelphia, M'Culloch, 1790. 124 pp., 2
maps, 1 plate.
(No copy located has the map of the
world.)
American Geographical Soc. copy. 23091

Workman, Benjamin.
Elements of Geography. . . . In Seven
Sections. . . . Third Edition.
Philadelphia, M'Culloch, 1790. 148 pp., 8
maps.
AAS copy. 23092

[Workman, Benjamin.
Elements of Geography. . . . In Seven
Sections.
Philadelphia, M'Culloch, 1791.]
(Entry from copyright record.) 24013

Workman, Benjamin.
Elements of Geography. . . . Fourth
Edition.
Philadelphia, M'Culloch, 1793. 180 pp., 7
maps, 1 plate.
UOP copy. 26509

Workman, Benjamin.
Elements of Geography. . . . Fifth Edition.
Philadelphia, M'Culloch, 1795. 180 pp., 7
maps.
HC copy. 29924

Workman, Benjamin.
Elements of Geography. . . . Sixth Edition.
Philadelphia, M'Culloch, 1796. 180 pp., 7
maps, 1 plate.
(No copy located contains the map which
should be opp. p. 83.)
AAS copy. 31661

Workman, Benjamin.
Elements of Geography. . . . Seventh
Edition.
Philadelphia, M'Culloch, 1799. 180 pp., 7
maps.
AAS copy. 36740

[Workman, Benjamin].
Father Tammany's Almanac, for . . . 1786.
Philadelphia, Young, Stewart &
M'Culloch. [38] pp.
LOC copy. 19391

[Workman, Benjamin.]
Father Tammany's Almanac, for . . . 1787.
Philadelphia, Young & M'Culloch. [36]
pp.
AAS copy. 20160

Workman, Benjamin.
Father Tammany's Almanack, for . . .
1788.
Philadelphia, Young & M'Culloch. [36]
pp.
AAS copy. 20897

[Workman, Benjamin]
Father Tammany's Almanac, for . . . 1789.
Philadelphia, Young. [36] pp.
LOC copy. 21617

[Workman, Benjamin.

Father Tammany's Almanack. For . . .
1790.
Philadelphia, M'Culloch.]
(Adv. Federal Gazette, Oct. 9, 1789.)
22292

Workman, Benjamin.
Father Tammany's Almanac, for . . . 1791.
Philadelphia, Young. [40] pp.
AAS copy. 23093

[Workman, Benjamin.]
Father Tammany's Almanac, for . . . 1792.
Philadelphia, M'Culloch. [36] pp.
VaSL copy. 24014

[Workman, Benjamin.]
Father Tammany's Almanac, for . . . 1793.
Philadelphia, M'Culloch. [36] pp.
LOC copy. 25059

[Workman, Benjamin.]
Father Tammany's Almanac, for . . . 1793.
Philadelphia, Young. [36] pp.
AAS copy. 46668

[Workman, Benjamin.]
Father Tammany's Almanac for . . . 1794.
Philadelphia, M'Culloch.]
(Printing assumed by Evans from the
sequence.) 26510

[Workman, Benjamin.]
Father Tammany's Almanac for 1795.
Philadelphia, M'Culloch.]
(Entry constructed by Evans from
M'Culloch's advs.) 28135

Workman, Benjamin.
Father Tammany's Almanac, for . . . 1796.
Philadelphia, Young. [32] pp.
(No perfect copy located.)
AAS copy. 29925

[Workman, Benjamin]
Father Tammany's Almanac, for . . . 1799.
Philadelphia, M'Culloch. [28?] pp.
(No complete copy located.)
AAS copy. 35057

[Workman, Benjamin.
Father Tammany's Pocket Almanac for
. . . 1787.
Philadelphia, Young & M'Culloch.]
(Assumed from the sequence. Not adv.
with 20160.) 20161

Workman, Benjamin.
The Federal Almanac, for . . . 1790.
Philadelphia, Young. [36] pp.
AAS copy. 22293

Workman, Benjamin.
Gauging Epitomized.
Philadelphia, Young, 1788. [4], 120 pp.
AAS copy. 21618

[Workman, Benjamin.]
The Pennsylvania, Delaware, Maryland,
and Virginia Almanack . . . for . . . 1788.
Baltimore, Goddard, [48] pp.
MdHS copy. 20898

[Workman, Benjamin.]
The Pennsylvania, Delaware, Maryland,
and Virginia Almanack . . . for . . . 1789.
Baltimore, Goddard. [48] pp.
MdHS copy. 21619

[Workman, Benjamin].
The Pennsylvania, Delaware, Maryland
and Virginia Almanack . . . for . . . 1790.
Baltimore, Goddard & Angell. [48] pp.
LOC copy. 22294

[Workman, Benjamin.]
The Pennsylvania, Delaware, Maryland,
and Virginia Almanack . . . for . . . 1791.
Baltimore, Goddard and Angell. 46 pp.
AAS copy. 23094

Workman, Benjamin.
A Treatise of Arithmetic. . . . Second
Edition.
Philadelphia, Young, 1796. pp. [i]-vi, [2],
[13]-376.
(Also entered as 30503, q. v.) 31663

Workman, Benjamin.
The Virginia Almanack, for . . . 1790.
Richmond, Davis. [48] pp.
AAS copy. 22295

The Works of Peter Pinder. . . . In Three
Volumes [by John Wolcot, 1738-1819].
New York, Wayland, 1793. 3 vol., 490 pp.
(Only vol. 1-2 known.)
HEH copy. 46950

The Works of Peter Pindar, Esq. [by John
Wolcot, 1738-1819].
New York, Allen, 1794. 2 vol. viii, 316; iv,
329 pp.
AAS copy. 28121

The Works of Peter Porcupine. Fourth
Edition [by William Cobbett, 1762-1835].
Philadelphia, Bradford, 1796. [2], 88; vi,
66, vii, [1], 66, [2]; [8], 111; 71 pp.
LOC copy. 30234

The World Alarm'd [by Cotton Mather,
1663-1728].
Boston, Green for Gerrish, 1721. [2], 16,
[2] pp.
AAS copy. 2255

The World Displayed; or, a Curious
Collection of Voyages and Travels. . . .
Vol. I [-V].
Philadelphia, Dobelbower, Key and
Simpson, 1795. [4], 504 pp., 6 plates; [4],
456 pp., 7 plates; [4], 487 pp., 6 plates;
[4], 464 pp., 5 plates; [4], 485 pp., 6
plates.
(There are some irregularities of
pagination.)
AAS copy. 29926

The World Displayed; or, a Curious
Collection of Voyages and Travels. . . .
Vol. VI [- VIII].
Philadelphia, Dobelbower, Key &
Simpson, 1796. [4], 464 pp., 6 plates; [2],
510 pp., 6 plates; [4], 446, 26 pp., 6 plates,
1 map.
AAS copy. 31664

The World in a String, or Money Toss'd
in a Basket.
Bennington, Haswell & Russell, 1790.
12 pp.
(Evans saw an imperfect copy.)
AAS copy. 26511

The World Turned Upside Down or the
Comical Metamorphoses.
Boston, M'Dougall, [1780?]. 64 pp.
(The only known copy is very imperfect.)
Oberlin College copy. 43918

The World Turned Upside Down or The
Comical Metamorphoses.
Boston, Norman, [179?]. [2], 64, [1] pp.
CHS copy. 45805

[The World Turned Upside Down, or the
Folly of Man.
Philadelphia, 1779.]
(Entry taken by Hildeburn from an adv.,
the location of which he did not record.)
16686

The Worlds Vanity.
New London, Green, [1752?]. Broadside.
CHS copy. 40644

Ein Wort für Allerley Sünder die Busse
Bedürffin.
Philadelphia, Armbruster, 1754. 96 pp.,
irreg.
HSP copy. 40733

Worthington, William, 1695-1756.
(Dexter, I, 156-158.)
The Duty of Rulers.
New London, 1744. [4], 43 pp.
AAS copy. 5524

[Worthy, James].
The Child's Plain Pathway to Eternal
Life.
New London, Green, 1765. 8 pp.
JCB copy. 41528

[Worthy, James.
The Child's Plain Pathway.
Hudson, 1786.]
("Just published," Hudson Gazette, Sept.
14, 1786.) 20162

[Worthy, James.]
The Child's Plain Path-way to Eternal
Life.
Newburyport, 1793. 12 pp.
AAS copy. 26512

Worthy Example of a Married Daughter:
who fed her Father with her own Milk.
Boston, at the Bible & Heart, [176-?].
Broadside.
NYPL copy.   41107

A Worthy Example of a Virtuous Wife.
Boston, Russell for Hallowell, 1794.
Broadside.
AAS copy.   28136

Wortman, Tunis, d. 1822.
An Oration on the Influence of Social
Institution.
New York, Van Alen, 1796. 31 pp.
AAS copy.   31665

[Wortman, Tunis], d. 1822.
A Solemn Address, to Christians &
Patriots.
New York, Denniston, 1800. 26 pp.
AAS copy.   39149

Wortman, Tunis, d. 1822.
A Treatise, Concerning Political Enquiry.
New York, Forman, 1800. 296 pp.
AAS copy.   39150

[Wouves, P. R.]
A Syllabical and Steganographical Table.
Philadelphia, Bache, [1797]. [16] pp.
AAS copy.   33249

[Wraxall, Sir Nathaniel William], bart.,
1751-1831.
A Short Review of the Political State of
Great-Britain.
Philadelphia, Dobson, 1787. 48 pp.
AAS copy.   20899

Wreg, Theophilus, pseud.
The Virginia Almanack, for the Year . . .
1756. . . . By Theophilus Wreg [by
Theophilus Grew, -1759].
Williamsburg, Hunter. [32] pp.
VaHS copy.   7428

Wreg, Theophilus, pseud.
The Virginia Almanack, for the Year . . .
1757. . . . By Theophilus Wreg [by
Theophilus Grew, -1759].
Williamsburg, Hunter. [24] pp.
VaHS copy.   7679

Wreg, Theophilus, pseud.
The Virginia Almanack, for the Year . . .
1758. . . . By Theophilus Wreg [by
Theophilus Grew, -1759].
Williamsburg, Hunter. [32] pp.
HEH copy.   7908

Wreg, Theophilus, pseud.
The Virginia Almanack, for the Year . . .
1759. . . . By Theophilus Wreg [by
Theophilus Grew, -1759].
Williamsburg, Hunter. [32] pp.
(The only known copy is incomplete.)
VaHS copy.   8145

[Wreg, Theophilus, pseud.
The Virginia Almanack, for the Year . . .
1760. . . . By Theophilus Wreg [by
Theophilus Grew, -1759].
Williamsburg, Hunter. [32] pp.]
(No copy located.)   8359

Wreg, Theophilus, pseud.
The Virginia Almanack for . . . 1761. . . .
By Theophilus Wreg.
Williamsburg, Hunter. [36] pp.
LOC copy.   8610

Wreg, Theophilus, pseud.
The Virginia Almanack for . . . 1762. . . .
By Theophilus Wreg.
Williamsburg, Royle. [32] pp.
LOC copy.   8868

Wreg, Theophilus, pseud.
The Virginia Almanack, for . . . 1763.
Williamsburg, Royle.
(Assumed from the sequence.)   9130

Wreg, Theophilus, pseud.
The Virginia Almanack, for . . . 1764.
Williamsburg, Royle. [48] pp.
WLC copy.   9399

Wreg, Theophilus, pseud.
The Virginia Almanack, for . . . 1765.
Williamsburg, Royle. [48] pp.
LOC copy.   9684

Wreg, Theophilus, pseud.
The Virginia Almanack for . . . 1766.
Williamsburg, Purdie. [24] pp.
LOC copy.   9995

Wreg, Theophilus, pseud.
(D. A. B.)
The Virginia Almanack, for . . . . 1767.
Williamsburg, Purdie. [32] pp.
HEH copy.   10327

Wreg, Theophilus, pseud.
The Virginia Almanack for . . . 1767.
Williamsburg, Purdie & Dixon. [24] pp.
(The only recorded copy lacks a leaf.)
HEH copy.   41679

Wren, Roger, pseud.
Sentiments of the Humours.
Boston, 1763. 20, [1] pp.
AAS copy.   9551

The Wretched Slave [by Jean Francois
Lesueur, 1760-1837].
New York, Gilfert for Von Hagen,
[1797]. [2] pp.
JCB copy.   32374

The Wretched Slave. Sung in the new
Opera of Paul and Virginia.
New York, Gilfert for Von Hagen,
[1800?]. [2] pp.
(Also reproduced as 32374, q. v.)   39151

Wright, Eliphalet, 1729-1784.
The Difference between those Called the
Standing Churches. . . .
Norwich, [Ct.], Trumbull, MDCC,LXXV
(1778). 24 pp.
CHS copy.   43597

Wright, Eliphalet, 1729-1784.
A People ripe for an Harvest.
Norwich, Trumbull, [1776]. 20 pp.
CHS copy.   15225

Wright, George (author of the "Rural
Christian.").
The Gentleman's Miscellany.
Exeter, Ranlet for Clap, etc., 1797. 216 pp.
AAS copy.   33250

Wright, George (author of the "Rural
Christian.").
The Lady's Miscellany.
Boston, for Clap, etc., 1797. 225, [3] pp.
AAS copy.   33251

[Wright, George], fl. 1770.
Sylvan Letters; or, the Pleasures of a
Country Life.
Philadelphia, Gibbons, 1793. 179 pp.
AAS copy.   26242

Wright, John, 1667-1748?
The Speech of John Wright.
[Philadelphia, 1741.] 4 pp.
HSP copy.   4872

Wright, John, fl. ca. 1720-1730.
Spiritual Songs for Children. . . . Fourth
Edition.
Boston, Z. Fowle, 1764.] 64 pp.
AAS copy.   41512

Wright, John, fl. 1720-1730.
Spiritual Songs for Children. . . . Seventh
Edition.
Boston, 1784. 47 pp.
(No better copy located.)
AAS copy.   44635

Wright, Paul, d. 1785.
The New and Complete Life of . . . Christ.
Philadelphia, Dunning & Hyer, 1795. 407,
[3] pp., 25 plates.
AAS copy.   29927

Wright, Paul, d. 1785.
The New and Complete Life of . . . Christ.
New York, Birdsall & Menut, 1795. 427, 3
pp., 30 plates, 1 map.
AAS copy.   29928

[Wright, Peter, fl. 1775.
Advertisement.
Philadelphia, 1775. Broadside.]
(From Aitken's records.)   14632

[Wright, S., & Co., Charleston, S. C.
A Catalogue of New Books.

Charleston, Childs, M'Iver & Co. for
Wright, 1786.]
(Entry from an adv.)   20163

Wright, Samuel, 1683-1746.
A Treatise of Being Born Again. . . .
Sixteenth Edition.
Boston, Draper for Henchman, 1738. [4],
viii, 168 pp.
BPL copy.   4328

Wright, Samuel, 1683-1746.
(D. N. B.)
A Treatise of being Born Again. . . .
Seventeenth Edition.
Boston, Draper for Henchman, 1742. [2],
viii, 168 pp.
AAS copy.   5096

[Wrighten, Mrs.]
Young Willy for Me.
New York, Hewitt for Carr, [1797]. [2]
pp.
HSP copy.   33252

The Writing Scholar's Assistant.
Worcester, Thomas, 1785. [24] leaves.
AAS copy.   19392

[The Writings of a Pretended Prophet.
Rutland, Vt., Williams, 1796. 12 pp.]
(Imprint assumed by Evans from later
eds.)   30821

[The Writings of a Pretended Prophet.
Rutland, Vt., Williams & Fay, 1797.]
(Imprint assumed by Evans from adv. in
Rutland Herald, May 8, 1796.)   32506

The Writings of Laco [by Stephen
Higginson, 1743-1828].
Boston, 1789. 39 pp.
AAS copy.   21886

Wudrian, Valentin, 1584-1625.
M. Valentin Wudrians Seel.
Ephrata, 1762. [10], 465, [3] pp.
AAS copy.   9315

Das Wunder ohne Massen.
Philadelphia, Miller, 1761. 16 pp.
AAS copy.   9042

Der Wunderbare Bussfertige Beichvater
[by Christian Anton Roemeling].
Germantown, [1753]. 36 pp.
(No complete copy located.)
HSP copy.   6950

[Die Wunderbare Geschichte von
Ambrose Gwinnett [by Isaac Bickerstaffe,
1735?-1812?].
Philadelphia, Cist, 1784.]
(Hildeburn, from an adv.)   18507

Die Wunderbare Lebensbeschreibung . . .
des . . . Robinson Crusoe [by Daniel
Defoe, 1661?-1731].
Philadelphia, Cist, 1788. Front., [2], 154
pp.
AAS copy.   21045

Die Wunderthätige Kraft.
Philadelphia, Miller, 1761. 16 pp.
HSP copy.   9043

Wyche, William.
An Essay on the Theory and Practice of
Fines.
New York, Swords for Rivington, 1794.
78, [1] pp.
AAS copy.   28137

Wyche, William.
An Examination of the Examiners
Examined.
New York, Wayland & Davis, 1795. 44,
[2] pp.
The imprint given by Evans was assumed
from an adv. in Ev. Post, Jan. 2, 1795.)   29929

Wyche, William.
Party Spirit.
New York, Swords, 1794. 23 pp.
AAS copy.   28138

Wyche, William.
A Treatise on the Practice of the Supreme
Court.
New York, Swords, 1794. xvi, 355, [3] pp.
NYPL copy.   28139

Wyche, William.
A Treatise on the Practice of the Supreme
Court. . . . Second Edition.
New York, Swords, 1794. xvi, 355, [4] pp.
AAS copy.   28140

[Wynne, John Huddlestone], 1743-1788.
Choice Emblems.
Philadelphia, Crukshank, 1790. xii, 166
pp.
AAS copy.   22854

[Wyoming, Pa.
Petition to the General Assembly of
Connecticut. [May 7, 1771].
[New York, 1771.] Broadside.]
(Apparently from an unidentified adv.)
                                             12293

[Wythe, George], 1726-1806.

Case upon the Statute for Distribution.
Richmond, Nicolson, 1796. 38 pp.
AAS copy.   31672

Wythe, George, 1726-1806.
Decisions of Cases in Virginia.
Richmond, Nicolson, 1795. 165, [2] pp.
VaSL copy.   29930

[Wythe, George], 1726-1806.
A Report of the Case between Field and
Harrison.
Richmond, Nicolson, 1796. 32 pp.
VaSL copy.   31667

[Wythe, George], 1726-1806.
[Report of the Case] Between Joseph
Wilkins . . . and John Taylor.
[Richmond, 1796.] 30, [1] pp.
LOC copy.   31670

[Wythe, George], 1726-1806.
[Report of the Case] Between, William
Fowler and Susanna his Wife, Plaintiffs
and Lucy Saunders.
[Richmond, 1796.] 28 pp.
LOC copy.   31668

[Wythe, George], 1726-1806.
[Report of the Case] Between William
Yates and Sarah his Wife . . . and
Abraham Salle. . . .
[Richmond, 1796.] 30, [1] pp.
(No complete copy located.)
LOC copy.   31671

[Wythe, George], 1726-1806.
[Report of the Case of] Love against
Donelson and Hodgson.
[Richmond, 1796.] 34 pp.
LOC copy.   31669

Y

Yale-College Subject to the General
Assembly [by Samuel Whittelsey Dana,
1760-1830].
New Haven, 1784. 44 pp.
AAS copy.   18434

Yale University.
The Declaration of the Rector and Tutors
. . . against . . . Whitefield.
Boston, Fleet, 1745. 14, [1] pp.
AAS copy.   5719

Yale University.
Freshman Laws.
New Haven, Bowen, [1786?] Broadside.
NYPL facsim. copy.   45023

[Yale University.
The Judgment of the Rector and Tutors.
Boston, Fleet, 1745.]
("This day is published," Boston Evening
Post, Apr. 15, 1745.)   5721

Yale University.
The Judgment of the Rector and Tutors.
New London, 1745. [2], 10 pp.
AAS copy.   5720

[Yale University.
Proceedings of the Council at Ordination
of Abiel Holmes.
[New Haven, 1785.] 16 pp.
(This item is the last 16 pp. of 20407, q. v.)
                                    19394

Yale University.
Scheme of the Exhibitions at the Public
Commencement . . . September 14, 1796.
[New Haven, 1796.] Broadside.
YC copy.   35060

Yale University.
Scheme of the Exercises at the Public
Commencement . . . September 13th, 1797.
[New Haven], Greens, [1797]. Broadside.
YC copy.   35061

Yale University.
Scheme of the Exercises at the Public
Commencement . . . September 13th, 1797.
[New Haven], Greens, [1797]. Broadside.
CHS copy.   48323

Yale University.
Scheme of the Exhibitions at the Public
Commencements . . . September 12th
1798.
[New Haven, 1798.] Broadside.
YC copy.   35062

Yale University.
Scheme of the Exercises at the Public
Commencement. . . . Sept. 11, 1799.
[New Haven, 1799.] Broadside.
YC copy.   36743

Yale University.
Scheme of the Exhibitions at the Public
Commencement . . . September 10, 1800.
[New Haven], Greens, [1800]. Broadside.
YC copy.   39154

Yale University.
Two Dialogues . . . Delivered in a
Quarter-Day . . . March 28, 1776.
Hartford, Watson, 1776. 31 pp.
AAS copy.   43214

Yale University. Alumni Catalogue, 1724.
Catalogus Eorum qui . . . ab Anno 1702,
ad Annum 1724. Alicujus Gradus
Laurea Donati Sunt.
New London, 1724. Broadside.
MHS copy.   2598

[Yale University. Alumni Catalogue,
1730.
Catalogus Eorum qui . . . ab Anno 1702,
ad Annum 1730, Alicujus Gradus Laurea
Donati sunt.
[New London, 1730.] Broadside.]
(No copy found.)   3382

Yale University. Alumni Catalogue, 1733.
Catalogus . . . ab Anno 1702, ad Annus
1733.
New London, 1733. Broadside.
YC copy.   3738

[Yale University. Alumni Catalogue,
1736.
Catalogus . . . ab Anno 1702, ad Annum
1736.
New London, 1736. Broadside.]
(No copy found.)   4105

Yale University. Alumni Catalogue, 1739.
Catalogus . . . ab Anno 1702, ad Annum
1739.
New London, 1739. Broadside.
MHS copy.   4464

Yale University. Alumni Catalogue, 1742.
Catalogus . . . ab Anno 1702, ad Annum
1742.
New London, 1742. Broadside.
YC copy.   5097

Yale University. Alumni Catalogue, 1745.
Catalogus . . . ab Anno 1702, ad Annum
1745.
[New London, 1745.] Broadside.
YC copy.   5718

Yale University. Alumni Catalogue, 1748.
Catalogus . . . ab Anno 1702, ad Annum
1748.
New London, 1748. Broadside.
YC photostat copy.   6270

Yale University. Alumni Catalogue, 1751.
Catalogus . . . ab Anno 1702, ad Annum
1751.
New London, 1751. Broadside.
YC copy.   6800

Yale University. Alumni Catalogue, 1754.
Catalogus . . . ab Anno 1702, ad Annum
1754.
New London, 1754. Broadside.
YC photostat copy.   7342

Yale University. Alumni Catalogue, 1757.
Catalogus eorum qui . . . ab Anno 1702,
ad Annum 1757. . . . Alicujus Gradus
Laurea Donati Sunt.
New Haven, 1757. Broadside.
AAS copy.   8066

Yale University. Alumni Catalogue, 1760.
Catalogus Eorum qui . . . ab Anno 1702,
ad Annum 1760, Alicujus Gradus Laurea
Donati Sunt.
New Haven, 1760. Broadside.
YC copy.   8774

Yale University. Alumni Catalogue, 1763.
Catalogus eorum qui . . . ab Anno 1702,
ad Annum 1763. Alicujus Gradus
Laurea Donati Sunt.
New Haven, 1763. Broadside.
YC copy.   9552

Yale University. Alumni Catalogue, 1766.
Catalogus Eorum qui . . . ab Anno 1702,
ad Annum 1766. Alicujus Gradus
Laurea Donati Sunt.
[New Haven, 1766.] Broadside.
YC copy.   10526

Yale University. Alumni Catalogue, 1769.
Catalogus eorum qui . . . ab Anno 1702,
ad Annum 1769. Alicujus Gradus Laurea
Donati Sunt.
[New Haven, 1769.] Broadside.
YC copy.   11539

Yale University. Alumni Catalogue, 1772.
Catalogus eorum qui . . . ab Anno 1702,
ad Annum 1772, Alicujus Gradus Laurea
Donati sunt.
[New Haven, 1772.] Broadside.
MHS copy.   12631

Yale University. Alumni Catalogue, 1775.
Catalogus eorum qui . . . ab Anno 1702 ad
Annum 1775, alicujus Gradus Laurea
Donati sunt.
[New Haven, 1775.] Broadside.
AAS copy.   14633

Yale University. Alumni Catalogue, 1778.
Catalogus eorum qui . . . ab Anno
MDCCII and Annum MDCCLXVIII
alicujus Gradus Laurea Donati sunt.
New Haven, 1778. 22 pp.
AAS copy.   16175

Yale University. Alumni Catalogue, 1781.
Catalogus Accademiae . . .
M.DCC.LXXXI.
Hartford, Hudson & Goodwin, 1781. 33
pp.
AAS copy.   17443

Yale University. Alumni Catalogue, 1784.
Catalogus Senatus Academici.
New Haven, 1784. 31 pp.
AAS copy.   18891

Yale University. Alumni Catalogue, 1787.
Catalogus Senatus Academici.
New Haven, Meigs, [1787]. 32 pp.
AAS copy.   20901

Yale University. Alumni Catalogue, 1790.
Catalogus Senatus Academici. . . .
New Haven, Greens, [1790]. 34 pp.
YC copy.   23095

Yale University. Alumni Catalogue, 1793.
Catalogus Senatus Academici. . . .
New Haven, Greens, [1793]. 36 pp.
AAS copy.   26518

Yale University. Alumni Catalogue, 1796.
Catalogus Senatus Academici. . . .
New Haven, Greens, [1796]. 36 pp.
AAS copy.   31674

Yale University. Alumni Catalogue, 1799.
Catalogus Senatus Academici. . . .
New Haven, Greens, [1799]. 38 pp.
HC copy.   36742

Yale University. Laws.
Collegii Yalensis . . . Statuta.
New London, 1748. [4], 20 pp.
AAS copy.   6271

Yale University. Laws.
Collegii Yalensis . . . Statuta.
New Haven, 1755. [4], 22, [1] pp.
MHS copy.   7599

Yale University. Laws.
Collegii Yalensis . . . Statua.
New Haven, 1759. [4], 25, [1] pp.
AAS copy.   8523

Yale University. Laws.
Collegii Yalensis . . . Statuta.
New Haven, 1764. [8], 24 pp.
YC copy.   9885

Yale University. Laws.
The Laws of Yale-College.
New Haven, 1774. 27 pp.
AAS copy.   13783

Yale University. Laws.
The Laws of Yale-College.
New Haven, Meigs, 1787. 36 pp.
AAS copy.   20902

Yale University. Laws.
The Laws of Yale-College . . . Enacted . . .
1795.
New Haven, Greens, [1795]. 40 pp.
AAS copy.   29931

Yale University. Laws.
The Laws of Yale-College . . . Enacted . . .
1795.
New Haven, Greens, 1800. 40 pp.
AAS copy.   39153

Yale University. Library.
A Catalogue of the Library of
Yale-College.
New London, 1743. [4], 44, [4] pp.
AAS copy.   5320

Yale University. Library.
A Catalogue of Books in the Library.
New Haven, 1755. [2], ii, 40, [3] pp.
AAS copy.   7598

Yale University. Library.
Catalogue of Books.
[New Haven], Greens, 1791. 50, [2] pp.
AAS copy.   24015

Yale University. Quaestiones, 1740.
Quaestiones. . . . MDCCXL.
[New London, 1740.] Broadside.
YC copy.   4662

[Yale University, Quaestiones, 1741.
Quaestiones. . . . MDCCXLI.
[New London, 1741.] Broadside.]
(No copy known.)   4874

Yale University. Quaestiones, 1742.
Quaestiones. . . . MDCCXLII.
[New London, 1742.] Broadside.
YC copy.   5099

Yale University. Quaestiones, 1743.
Quaestiones. . . . MDCCXLIII.
[New London, 1743.] Broadside.
YC copy.   5322

Yale University. Quaestiones, 1744.
Quaestions. . . . MDCCXLIV.
[New London, 1744.] Broadside.
YC copy.   5526

[Yale University. Quaestiones, 1745.
Quaestiones. . . . MDCCXLV.
[New London, 1745.] Broadside.]
(No copy located.)   5723

Yale University. Quaestiones, 1746.
Quaestiones. . . . MDCCXLVI.
[New London, 1746.] Broadside.
YC copy.   5896

Yale University. Quaestiones, 1747.
Quaestiones. . . . MDCCXLII.
[New London, 1747.] Broadside.
AAS copy.   6086

Yale University. Quaestiones, 1748.
Quaestiones. . . . MDCCXLVIII.
[New London, 1748.] Broadside.
YC copy.   6273

Yale University. Quaestiones, 1749.
Quaestiones. . . . MDCCXLIX.
[New London, 1749.] Broadside.
AAS copy.   6448

Yale University. Quaestiones, 1750.
Quaestiones. . . . MDCCL.
[New London, 1750.] Broadside.
AAS copy.   6623

Yale University. Quaestiones, 1751.
Quaestiones. . . . MDCCLI.
[New London, 1751.] Broadside.
HC copy.   6802

Yale University. Quaestiones, 1752.
Quaestiones. . . . MDCCLII.
[New London, 1752.] Broadside.
YC copy.   6949

Yale University. Quaestiones, 1753.
Quaestiones. . . . MDCCLIII.
[New London, 1753.] Broadside.
YC copy.   7139

Yale University. Quaestiones, 1754.
Quaestiones. . . . MDCCLIV.
[New London, 1754.] Broadside.
YC copy.   7344

[Yale University. Quaestiones, 1755.
Quaestiones. . . . MDCCLV.
[New Haven, 1755.] Broadside.]
(No copy located.)   7601

Yale University. Quaestiones, 1756.
Quaestiones. . . . MDCCLVI.
[New Haven, 1756.] Broadside.
LOC copy.   7823

Yale University. Quaestiones, 1757.
Quaestiones. . . . MDCCLVII.
[New Haven, 1757.] Broadside.
YC copy.   8068

[Yale University. Quaestiones, 1758.
Quaestiones. . . . MDCCLVIII.
[New Haven, 1758.] Broadside.]
(No copy located.)   8287

[Yale University. Quaestiones, 1759.
Quaestiones. . . . MDCCLIX.
[New Haven, 1759.] Broadside.]
(No copy known.)   8525

Yale University. Quaestiones, 1760.
Quaestiones. . . . MDCCLX.
[New Haven, 1760.] Broadside.
YC copy.   8776

Yale University. Quaestiones, 1761.
Quaestiones. . . . MDCLXI.
[New Haven, 1761.] Broadside.
YC copy.   9045

Yale University. Quaestiones, 1762.
Quaestiones. . . . MDCCLXII.
[New Haven, 1762.] Broadside.
YC copy.   9316

Yale University. Quaestiones, 1763.
Quaestiones. . . . MDCCLXIII.
[New Haven, 1763.] Broadside.
YC copy.   9553

Yale University. Quaestiones, 1764.
Quaestiones. . . . MDCC,LXIV.
[New Haven, 1764.] Broadside.
YC copy.   9886

Yale University. Quaestiones, 1765.
Quaestiones. . . . MDCCLXV.
[New Haven, 1765.] Broadside.
YC copy.   10219

Yale University. Quaestiones, 1766.
Quaestiones. . . . MDCCLXVI.
[New Haven, 1766.] Broadside.
YC copy.   10527

Yale University. Quaestiones, 1767.
Quaestiones. . . . MDCCLXVII.
[New Haven, 1767.] Broadside.
YC copy.   10806

Yale University. Quaestiones, 1768.
Quaestiones. . . . M,DCC,LXVIII.
[New Haven, 1768.] Broadside.
YC copy.   11127

Yale University. Quaestiones, 1769.
Quaestiones. . . . M,DCC,LXIX.
[New Haven, 1769.] Broadside.
YC copy.   11540

[Yale University. Quaestiones, 1770.
Quaestiones. . . . M,DCC,LXX.
(New Haven, 1770.) Broadside.]
(No copy located.)   11950

Yale University. Quaestiones, 1771.
Quaestiones. . . . M,DCC,LXXI.
[New Haven, 1771.] Broadside.
YC copy.   12294

Yale University. Quaestiones, 1772.
Quaestiones. . . . M,DCC,LXXII.
[New Haven, 1772.] Broadside.
YC copy.   12632

Yale University. Quaestiones, 1773.
Quaestiones. . . . M, DCC, LXXIII.

[New Haven, 1773.] Broadside.
MHS copy.   13087

Yale University. Quaestiones, 1774.
Quaestiones . . . MDCCLXXIV.
[New Haven, 1774.] Broadside.
YC copy.   13784

Yale University. Quaestiones, 1781.
Quaestiones. . . . M,DCC,LXXXI.
Hartford, Hudson & Goodwin, [1781].
Broadside.
AAS copy.   17446

Yale University. Quaestiones, 1782.
Quaestiones. . . . MDCCLXXXII.
New Haven, [1782]. Broadside.
MHS copy.   17806

Yale University. Quaestiones, 1783.
Quaestiones. . . . MDCCLXXXIII.
New Haven, Greens, [1783]. Broadside.
YC copy.   18317

Yale University. Quaestiones, 1784.
Quaestiones . . . M.DCC.LXXXIV.
New Haven, Meigs, Bowen & Dana,
[1784]. Broadside.
YC copy.   18893

Yale University. Quaestiones, 1785.
Quaestiones. . . . MDCCLXXXV.
New Haven, Meigs, Bowen & Dana,
[1785]. Broadside.
YC copy.   19395

Yale University. Quaestiones, 1786.
Quaestiones. . . . M.DCC.LXXXVI.
[New Haven], Meigs & Dana, [1786].
Broadside.
YC copy.   20167

Yale University. Quaestiones. 1787.
Quaestiones. . . . M.DCC.LXXXVII.
[New Haven, 1787.] Broadside.
NYPL copy.   20903

Yale University. Quaestiones, 1788.
Quaestiones. . . . M.DCC.LXXXVIII.
New Haven, Meigs, [1788]. Broadside.
YC copy.   21622

Yale University. Quaestiones, 1789.
Quaestiones. . . . M.DCC.LXXXIX.
[New Haven, 1789.] Broadside.
YC copy.   22297

[Yale University. Quaestiones, 1790.
Quaestiones . . . M.DCC.XC.
[New Haven, 1790.] Broadside.]
(This series apparently discontinued with
the preceding issue.)   23097

Yale University. Student Catalogue, 1778.
Catalogus Recentium. . . .
M,DCC,LXXVIII.
[New Haven, 1778.] Broadside.
YC copy.   43598

Yale University. Student Catalogue, 1780.
Catalogus Recentium in Collegio Yalensi,
M.DCC.LXXX.
[New Haven, 1780.] Broadside.
AAS copy.   17075

Yale University. Student Catalogue, 1781.
Catalogus Recentium . . . MDCCLXXXI.
[Hartford, Hudson & Goodwin, 1781.]
Broadside.
MHS copy.   17444

Yale University. Student Catalogue, 1782.
Catalogus Recentium, in Collegio-Yalensi,
M,DCC,LXXXII.
[New Haven? 1782.] Broadside.
AAS copy.   44289

Yale University. Student Catalogue, 1784.
Catalogus Recentum . . . M,DCC,
LXXXIV.
New Haven, Meigs, Bowen & Dana,
[1784]. Broadside.
YC copy.   44636

Yale University. Student Catalogue, 1796.
Catalogue of the Members of
Yale-College, 1796.
[New Haven, 1796.] Broadside.
NL copy.   31673

Yale University. Student Catalogue, 1797.
Catalogue of the Members of
Yale-College, 1797.

[New Haven], Greens, [1797]. Broadside.
YC copy.   35058

Yale University. Student Catalogue, 1797.
Catalogue of the Members of
Yale-College, 1797.
[New Haven], Greens, [1797]. Broadside.
YC copy.   48324

Yale University. Student Catalogue, 1798.
Catalogue of the Members of Yale-College
. . . November, 1798.
[New Haven, 1798.] Broadside.
YC copy.   35059

Yale University. Student Catalogue, 1799.
Catalogue of the Members of Yale College
. . . November, 1799.
[New Haven, 1799.] Broadside.
YC copy.   36741

Yale University. Student Catalogue, 1800.
Catalogue of the Members of Yale College
. . . November, M,DCCC.
New Haven, Read & Morse, [1800].
Broadside.
AAS copy.   39152

Yale University. Student Catalogue,
Freshmen, 1794.
Catalogue Recentium . . . Admissorum.
[New Haven, 1794.] Broadside.
YC copy.   28141

Yale University. Student Catalogue,
Juniors, 1794.
Catalogue of the Junior Class . . .
M,DCC,XCIV.
New Haven, Morse, [1794]. Broadside.
YC copy.   47331

Yale University. Student Catalogue,
Sophomore, 1794.
Catalogues Classis Sophimorum . . .
MDCCXCIV.
[New Haven, 1794.] Broadside.
YC copy.   47332

Yale University. Student Catalogue.
Sophomore, 1795.
Catalogue of the Sophomore Class. . . .
1795.
[New Haven, 1795.] Broadside.
YC copy.   47691

Yale University. Theses, 1718.
Honoratissimo . . . Gurdono Saltonstall
. . . Theses Hasce. . . . MDCCXVIII.
New London, Green, 1718. Broadside.
MHS copy.   39696

Yale University. Theses, 1728.
Praeclarissimo . . . D. Josepho
Tallcott. . . . Theses . . . Die Undesimo
Septembris, MDCCXXVIII.
New London, Green, [1728]. Broadside.
AAS copy.   39902

Yale University. Theses, 1730.
Praeclarissimo. . . . Joseph Talcott.
[New London, 1730.] Broadside.
MHS copy.   3383

[Yale University. Theses, 1731.
Praeclarissimo . . . Josepho Tallcott.
New London, 1731. Broadside.]
(No copy found.)   3496

[Yale University. Theses, 1732.
Praeclarissimo . . . Josepho Tallcott.
New London, 1732. Broadside,]
(No copy known.)   3619

Yale University. Theses, 1733.
Praeclarissimo . . . Josepho Tallcott.
New Haven, 1733. Broadside.
YC copy.   3739

[Yale University. Theses, 1734.
Praeclarissimo . . . Josepho Tallcott.
New London, 1734. Broadside.]
(No copy of the theses for this year has
been found.)   3859

Yale University. Theses, 1735.
Praeclarissimo . . . Josepho Tallcott.
New London, 1735. Broadside.
AAS copy.   3978

[Yale University. Theses, 1736.
Praeclarissimo . . . Josepho Tallcott.
New London, 1736. Broadside.]
(No copy found.)   4106

Yale University. Theses, 1737.
Praeclarissimo. . . . MDCCXXXVII.
New London, [1737]. Broadside.
YC copy.   4213

Yalé University. Theses, 1738.
Praeclarissimo . . . Josepho Tallcott.
New London, 1738. Broadside.
AAS copy.   4329

Yale University. Theses, 1739.
Praeclarissimo. . . . MDCCXXXIX.
[New London, 1739.] Broadside.
YC copy.   4465

Yale University. Theses, 1740.
Praeclarissimo. . . . MDCCXL.
[New London, 1740.] Broadside.
YC copy.   4661

[Yale University. Theses, 1741.
Praeclarissimo. . . . MDCCXLI.
[New London, 1741.] Broadside.]
(No copy known.)   4873

Yale University. Theses, 1742.
[Praeclarissimo. . . . MDCCXLII.
[New London], 1742.] Broadside.
YC copy.   5098

Yale University. Theses, 1743.
Praeclarissimo. . . . MDCCXLIII.
[New London], 1743. Broadside.
YC copy.   5321

Yale University. Theses, 1744.
Praeclarissimo. . . . Jonathan Law.
New Haven (New London), 1744.
Broadside.
YC copy.   5525

Yale University. Theses, 1745.
Praeclarissimo . . . Jonathan Law.
New Haven (New London), 1745.
Broadside.
YC copy.   5722

Yale University. Theses, 1746.
Praeclarissimo . . . Jonathan Law.
New Haven (New London), 1746.
Broadside.
YC copy.   5895

Yale University. Theses, 1747.
Praeclarissimo . . . Jonathan Law.
New Haven (i.e. New London), 1747.
Broadside.
AAS copy.   6085

[Yale University. Theses, 1748.
Praeclarissimo . . . Jonathan Law.
New Haven (i.e. New London), 1748.
Broadside.]
(No copy found.)   6272

Yale University. Theses, 1749.
Praeclarissimo. . . . Jonathan Law.
New Haven (i.e. New London), 1749.
Broadside.
AAS copy.   6447

Yale University. Theses, 1750.
Praeclarissimo. . . . Jonathan Law.
New Haven (i.e. New London), 1750.
Broadside.
AAS copy.   6622

Yale University. Theses, 1751.
Praeclarissimo . . . Rogero Wolcott.
New Haven (i.e. New London), 1751.
Broadside.
YC copy.   6801

Yale University. Theses, 1752.
Praeclarissimo . . . Rogero Wolcott.
New Haven (i.e. New London), 1752.
Broadside.
AAS copy.   6948

Yale University. Theses, 1753.
Praeclarissimo . . . Rogero Wolcott.
New Haven (i.e. New London), 1753.
Broadside.
YC copy.   7138

Yale University. Theses, 1754.
Praeclarissimo . . . Thomae Fitch.
New Haven (New London), 1754.
Broadside.
YC copy.   7343

Yale University. Theses, 1755.
Praeclarissimo . . . Thomae Fitch.

New Haven, 1755. Broadside.
YC copy.   7600

Yale University. Theses, 1756.
Praeclarissimo . . . Thomae Fitch.
New Haven, 1756. Broadside.
YC copy.   7822

Yale University. Theses, 1757.
Praeclarissimo . . . Thomae Fitch.
New Haven, 1757. Broadside.
YC copy.   8067

Yale University. Theses, 1758.
Praeclarissimo . . . Thomae Fitch.
New Haven, 1758. Broadside.
YC copy.   8286

Yale University. Theses, 1759.
Praeclarissimo . . . Thomae Fitch.
New Haven, 1759. Broadside.
YC copy.   8524

Yale University. Theses, 1760.
Praeclarissimo . . . Thomae Fitch.
New Haven, 1760. Broadside.
YC copy.   8775

[Yale University. Theses, 1761.
Praeclarissimo . . . Thomae Fitch.
New Haven, 1761. Broadside.]
(No copy known.)   9044

Yale University. Theses, 1762.
Viro Praestantissimo . . . Thomae Fitch.
[New Haven], 1762. Broadside.
YC copy.   9317

Yale University. Theses, 1763.
Viro Praestantissimo . . . Thomae Fitch.
New Haven, 1763. Broadside.
YC copy.   9554

Yale University. Theses, 1764.
Viro Praestantissimo . . . Thomae Fitch.
New Haven, 1764. Broadside.
YC copy.   9887

Yale University. Theses, 1765.
Viro Praestantissimo . . . Thomae Fitch.
New Haven, 1765. Broadside.
AAS copy.   10220

Yale University. Theses, 1766.
Viro Praestantissimo.
New Haven, 1766. Broadside.
AAS copy.   10528

Yale University. Theses, 1767.
Viro Praestantissimo . . . Gulielmo Pitkin.
New Haven, 1767. Broadside.
YC copy.   10807

Yale University. Theses, 1768.
Viro Praestantissimo . . . Gulielmo Pitkin.
New Haven, 1768. Broadside.
YC copy.   11128

Yale University. Theses, 1769.
Viro Praestantissimo . . . Gulielmo Pitkin.
New Haven, 1769. Broadside.
YC copy.   11541

Yale University. Theses, 1770.
Viro Praestantissimo . . . Gulielmo Pitkin.
New Haven, 1770. Broadside.
AAS copy.   11951

Yale University. Theses, 1771.
Viro Praestantissimo . . . Gulielmo Pitkin.
New Haven, 1771. Broadside.
YC copy.   12295

Yale University. Theses, 1772.
Viro Praestantissimo . . . Gulielmo Pitkin.
New Haven, 1772. Broadside.
YC copy.   12633

Yale University. Theses, 1773.
Viro Praestantissimo . . . Gulielmo Pitkin.
New Haven, 1773. Broadside.
AAS copy.   13088

Yale University. Theses, 1774.
Viro Praestantissimo. . . . Jonathan
Trumbull.
New Haven, 1774. Broadside.
AAS copy.   13785

Yale University. Theses, 1781.
Illustrissimo et Literaturà. . . . Jonathani
Trumbull.

Hartford, Hudson & Goodwin, [1781.]
Broadside.
AAS copy.   17445

Yale University. Theses, 1782.
Illustrissimo et Literatura . . . Jonathani
Trumbull.
[New Haven, 1782.] Broadside.
AAS copy.   17805

Yale University. Theses, 1783.
Illustrissimo. . . . MDCCLXXXIII.
[New Haven, 1783.] Broadside.
AAS copy.   18316

Yale University. Theses, 1784.
Illustrissimo Pietate.
[New Haven], Meigs, Bowen & Dana,
[1784]. Broadside.
YC copy.   18892

Yale University. Theses, 1785.
Illustrissimo Matthaeo Griswold. . . .
M.DCC.LXXV.
New Haven, Meigs, Bowen & Dana,
[1785]. Broadside.
YC copy.   19393

Yale University. Theses, 1786.
Illustrissimo Samueli Huntington. . . .
M.DCC.LXXXVI.
[New Haven], Meigs & Dana, [1786].
Broadside.
AAS copy.   20166

Yale University. Theses, 1787.
Illustrissimo Samueli Huntington.
New Haven, Meigs, 1787. Broadside.
YC copy.   20900

Yale University. Theses, 1788.
Illustrissimo Samueli Huntington.
New Haven, Meigs, 1788. Broadside.
YC copy.   21621

Yale University. Theses, 1789.
Illustrissimo Samueli Huntington. . . .
New Haven, 1789. Broadside.
YC copy.   22296

Yale University. Theses, 1790.
Illustrissimo Samueli Huntington. . . .
New Haven, Greens, 1790. Broadside.
YC copy.   23096

Yale University. Theses, 1791.
Illustrissimo Samueli Huntington. . . .
M,DCC,XCI.
[New Haven], Greens, [1791]. Broadside.
HC copy.   24016

Yale University. Theses, 1792.
Illustrissimo Samueli Huntington. . . .
M,DCC,XCII.
New Haven, Greens, [1792]. Broadside.
YC photo. copy.   25060

Yale University. Theses, 1793.
Illustrissimo Samueli Huntington. . . .
New Haven, Greens, 1793. Broadside.
AAS copy.   26519

[Yale University. Theses, 1794.
Illustrissimo Samueli Huntington. . . .
New Haven, Greens, 1794. Broadside.]
(No copy located.)   28142

Yale University. Theses, 1795.
Illustrissimo Samuel Huntington. . . .
M,DCC,XCV.
[New Haven], Greens. Broadside.
AAS copy.   29932

[Yale University. Theses, 1796.
Illustrissimo Olivero Wolcott. . . .
New Haven, Greens, 1796. Broadside.]
(Printing ssumed by Evans from the
sequence.)   31675

Yale University. Theses, 1797.
Illustrissimo Olivero Wolcott.
[New Haven], Greens, [1797]. Broadside.
AAS copy.   33253

[Yankee Doodle. A New Federal Song.
Philadelphia, 1798].
(Evans' entry from an adv., possibly for
33902.)   35063

Yankee Doodle An Original American
Air.
Philadelphia, New York, and Baltimore,

Carrs, [1796]. 4 pp.
PPL (Keffer) copy.   31676

A Yankee Song. Father and I went down
to Camp. . . .
[Salem], Sold at the Bible and Heart,
[1793]. Broadside.
EI copy.   25139

Yarico to Inkle, an Epistle.
Springfield, [Mass.] Babcock, 1784. 24 pp.
AAS copy.   44637

Yarico to Inkle, an Epistle.
Hartford, Babcock, 1792. 19 pp.
AAS copy.   46677

Yarico to Inkle, An Epistle.
Marblehead, 1792. 31 pp.
(Authorship attributed to Isaac Story
because of tradition that he printed this
ed. during his college vacation. However,
there is a London 1736 ed.)
AAS copy.   24822

[Yarico to Inkle, An Epistle.
Boston, Edes, 1794.)
(Imprint assumed by Evans from adv. "To
be sold by the Printers hereof," Boston
Gazette, Jan. 20, 1794.)   27748

The Yarmouth Tragedy; or, Jemmy and
Nancy's Garland.
Worcester, Mass., 1787. 8 pp.
AAS copy.   45209

. . . . Yarrimore. An Indian Ballad.
Philadelphia, Carr, [1794]. [2] pp.
NYPL (Shapiro) copy.   28143

Yarrow, Thomas.
An Oration Delivered at Mount-Pleasant.
Mount Pleasant, N. Y., Durell, 1798. 16 pp.
BA copy.   35065

[Yates, Abraham], 1724-1796.
Political Papers, Addressed to the
Advocates for a Congressional Revenue.
New York, Kollock, 1786. 20 pp.
NYPL copy.   20168

Yates, Abraham, 1724-1796.
Resolutions and Extracts from the
Journals of the Hon. the Congress.
Albany, Webster, 1786. 31 pp.
NYHS copy.   20080

Yates, Peter Waldron, 1747-1826.
An Address Delivered . . . Schenectady,
December 27, 1783.
Albany, Balentine, 1784. 30 pp.
BA copy.   18894

Yates, Peter Waldron, 1747-1826.
An Oration, on the Death of George
Washington.
Albany, [N. Y.], Barber & Southwick,
1800. 16 pp.
BPL copy.   39155

Yates, William, fl. 1797.
A View of the Science of Life.
Whitehall, Pa., Young, 1797. pp. [8],
[i]-iii, 16, 232.
AAS copy.   33254

[Ye Fair Married Dames. A Song.
Philadelphia, 1779.]
(Hildeburn from an adv. which has not
been rediscovered.)   16687

A Year and a Life well Concluded [by
Cotton Mather, 1663-1728].
Boston, Kneeland for Gray, 1719/20. 24
pp.
YC copy.   2146

A Yearly Tax of 140,000 Dollars! A Few
Plain Facts. . . . April 30, 1799.
[New York, 1799.] Broadside.
NYHS copy.   48995

The Yearly Verses of the Printer's Lad
who Carrieth about the New-York Weekly
Post-Boy [Dated in ms. Jan. 1745].
[New York, Parker, 1745.] Broadside.
NYPL ph. copy.   40393

The Yearly Verses of the Printer's Lad,
who Carrieth about the Pennsylvania
Gazette. . . . Jan. 1, 1739.

[Philadelphia, Franklin, 1739.]
Broadside.
AAS copy.   40182

The Yearly Verses of the Printer's Lad,
who Carrieth about the Pennsylvania
Gazette. . . . January 1, 1740.
[Philadelphia, Franklin, 1740.]
Broadside.
AAS copy.   40269

The Yearly Verses of the Printer's Lad,
who Carrieth about the Pennsylvania
Gazette. . . . Jan. 1, 1741.
[Philadelphia, Franklin 1741.] Broadside.
(Bound with the issue of Jan. 1, 1740/1.)
AAS copy.   40296

[The Yearly Verses of the Printer's Lad,
who Carrieth about the Pennsylvania
Gazette. . . . Jan. 1741 [/2].
Philadelphia, 1742. Broadside.]
(No copy located.)   5036

The Yearly Verses of the Printer's Lads,
who Carry the Pennsylvania Gazette. . . .
January 1. 1743.
[Philadelphia, 1743.] Broadside.
AAS copy.   5274

Yearsley, Ann, 1756-1806.
The Royal Captives. . . . Volume I [-II].
Philadelphia, Campbell, 1795. iv, 128, 122
pp.
AAS copy.   29933

Yearsley, Ann, 1756-1806.
The Royal Captives.
Philadelphia, Woodward, 1795. [8], 273
pp.
AAS copy.   29934

Yeatman, Charleton.
The Mariner's Guide.
Philadelphia, Bioren, 1798. [2], 21 pp.
(The only recorded copy cannot be
located.)   35066

. . . Yellow Fever. . . . [by John Beale
Bordley, 1727-1804].
[Philadelphia, 1794.] 11 pp.
(Prefatory note: "A few copies more, with
notes, are struck off.")
LCP copy.   26684

Yesterday Arrived an Express from our
Army in Canada, New-York, November
13, 1775.
New York, Holt, [1775]. Broadside.
NYHS copy.   14634

York, Pa. Town Meeting, 1779.
York, 18th June, 1779. At a Meeting. . . .
Lancaster, Bailey, [1779]. [4] pp.
NYHS copy.   43737

York Academy.
The Order for Morning and Evening
Prayers, as used in. . . .
Philadelphia, Young, Stewart, and
M'Culloch, 1786. 23 pp.
(The only reported copy cannot be
located.)   45024

Yorke, Samuel, auctioneer.
Drugs & Medicines. . . . Will be Sold. . . .
May 26th, 1800.
[Philadelphia], Humphreys, [1800].
Broadside.
AAS copy.   38255

[The Yorkshire Wonder.
New York, De Foreest, 1747.]
("Just published, and to be sold by the
Printer hereof," N. Y. Evening Post, Apr.
27, 1747.)   6087

Youle, Joseph, d. 1795.
A Inaugural Dissertation on Respiration.
New York, Swords, 1793. 39 pp.
AAS copy.   26520

[Young, Arthur, 1741-1820.
Notes on Farming.
Hudson, Stoddard, 1794.]
(Imprint assumed by Evans from
Stoddard's advs.)   28144

[Young, Arthur], 1741-1820.
Rural Oeconomy. . . . Second Edition.
Philadelphia, Humphreys, 1776. 245, [1]
pp.
HSP copy.   15226

Young, Edward, 1683-1765.
The Complaint; or Night-Thoughts.
Philadelphia, Bell, 1777. [10], 357, [3] pp.
AAS copy.   15714

[Young, Edward], 1683-1765.
The Complaint: or, Night-Thoughts.
Philadelphia, Prichard & Hall, 1787. [2],
300 pp.
AAS copy.   20904

Young, Edward, 1683-1765.
The Complaint: or Night-Thoughts.
Newburyport, Mycall, [1789?] 408 pp.
(Adv. in Benj. Guild Cat. of 1789.)
AAS copy.   23098

Young, Edward, 1683-1765.
The Complaint: or, Night-Thoughts.
Philadelphia, Taylor, 1791. 303 pp.
(Evans took his entry from an adv. and
assumed the imprint.)
AAS copy.   24018

[Young, Edward], 1683-1765.
The Complaint: or, Night-Thoughts.
Philadelphia, Woodhouse, 1791.]
(Evans entry from an adv.)   24019

Young, Edward, 1683-1765.
The Complaint: or, Night-Thoughts.
Philadelphia, Young, 1791. 303 pp.
AAS copy.   46365

Young, Edward, 1683-1765.
The Complaint: or, Night-Thoughts.
New York, Tiebout for Bell, 1796. xii, 266
pp., 1 plate.
AAS copy.   31677

Young, Edward, 1683-1765.
The Complaint: or, Night-Thoughts.
New York, Tiebout for Reid, etc., 1796.
xii, 266 pp., 1 plate.
AAS copy.   31678

[Young, Edward], 1683-1765.
The Complaint: or, Night-Thoughts.
Philadelphia, Woodward for Stafford,
1798. x, 266 pp., 2 plates.
AAS copy.   35067

[Young, Edward], 1683-1765.
The Complaint; or, Night-Thoughts.
Philadelphia, H. & P. Rice and J. Rice,
1800. frontis., x, 266 pp.]
(Neither of the recorded copies could be
located.)   39157

[Young, Edward], 1683-1765.
Devout Thoughts of the Retired Penitent.
Portsmouth, Peirce, 1795.]
(Imprint assumed by Evans from adv.
"This Day Published, and to be sold by
the Printer hereof," Oracle of the Day,
Apr. 28, 1795.)   29936

Young, Edward, 1683-1765.
Nocte Cogitata.
Caroloppidi (Charlestown), 1786. 21 pp.
AAS copy.   20170

[Young, Edward], 1683-1765.
A Poem on the Day of Judgment.
New York, Parker & Weyman and Noel,
1753.]
("Just published," N. Y. Mercury, Oct.
29, 1753.)   7141

Young, Edward, 1683-1765.
A Poem on the last Day. . . . Sixth
Edition.
Boston, Fowle, 1753. 54 pp.
AAS copy.   7140

Young, Edward, 1683-1765.
The Last Day.
Philadelphia, Dobson, 1786. 40 pp.
NYPL copy.   20169

[Young, Edward], 1683-1765.
The Last Day.
Salem, Cushing, 1790.]
(Entry from an adv.)   23099

Young, Edward, 1683-1765.
The Last Day. A Poem.
Elizabethtown, Kollock for Davis, 1797.
39 pp.
AAS copy.   48325

Young, Edward, 1683-1765.
A Poem on the Last Day.

Boston, Hall, 1793. pp. [6], [11] - 58.
AAS copy.   26521

Young, Edward, 1683-1765.
A Poem on the Last Day.
Boston, Hall, 1795. pp. [6], [11]-58.
AAS copy.   29937

[Young, Edward], 1683-1765.
Resignation. In Two Parts.
Philadelphia, Bradford, 1764. 74 pp.
AAS copy.   9888

Young, Edward, 1683-1765.
Resignation.
Philadelphia, James, 1777. 54 pp.
JCB copy.   43411

Young, Edward, 1683-1765.
Resignation.
Philadelphia, Story, 1785. 48 pp.
AAS copy.   44836

[Young, Edward], 1683-1765.
Resignation.
Philadelphia, Story, 1786.]
("Also for Sale, just published," Pa. Eve.
Herald, Jan. 18, 1786.)   20171

Young, Edward, 1683-1765.
Resignation.
Philadelphia, Johnson, 1791. 72 pp.
BM copy.   24020

Young, Edward, 1683-1765.
Resignation.
Worcester, Thomas for Thomas, 1795. 48
pp.
AAS copy.   29939

Young, Edward, 1683-1765.
Resignation.
Worcester, Mass., Thomas, 1799. 55, [1]
pp.
AAS copy.   36746

[Young, Edward], 1683-1765.
The Revenge.
New York, Gaine, 1761.]
(Imprint assumed by Evans from adv. in
N. Y. Mercury, July 20, 1761.)   9046

Young, Edward, 1683-1765.
The Revenge: a Tragedy.
Boston, West and West, [1794]. 60, [1]
pp.
AAS copy.   28145

[Young, James, of Baltimore.
The Baltimore Directory.
Baltimore, 1786.]
(Proposed in Maryland Gazette, Oct. 31,
1786.)   20172

Young, John, D.D., minister at Hawick,
Scotland.
Essays on the Following Interesting
Subjects.
Philadelphia, Humphreys, 1798. [2], 148,
[3] pp.
AAS copy.   35068

Young, John, d. 1797.
Narrative of the Life, Last Dying Speech
& Confession of. . . .
[New York, 1797.] 8 pp.
NYHS copy.   33255

[Young, John, of New Hampshire.
A Free and Natural Inquiry.
Portsmouth? 1796.]
(Entry from copyright notice.)   31679

Young, John, of New Hampshire.
The Poor Man's Companion.
Newbury, Vt., Coverly, [1796]. 100, [1]
pp.
VtHS (Rugg) copy.   31680

Young, John, of Philadelphia.
Young's Vocal and Instrumental Musical
Miscellany. . . . [No. 1-8].
Philadelphia, Carey, [1793]. 63 pp.
LOC copy.   26522

Young, Joseph, 1733-1814.
Calvinism and Universalism.
New York, Campbell, 1793. xx, 124 pp.
AAS copy.   26523

Young, Joseph, 1733-1814.
A New Physical System of Astronomy.

New York, Hopkins, [1800]. 188, [1] pp.,
diagrams, plates.
AAS copy.   39158

Young, Robert, c.1750-1779.
The Dying Criminal: a Poem.
New-London, [1779]. Broadside.
HEH copy.   43739

Young, Robert, c.1750-1779.
The Dying Criminal: a Poem.
[Worcester, 1779.] Broadside.
AAS ph. copy.   43738

Young, Robert, c. 1750-1779.
The Last Words and Dying Speech of. . . .
New London, [1779]. Broadside.
(The Evans entry is from an adv. for two
broadsides; for the Poem see the
Supplement.)
HEH copy.   16688

Young, Robert, c. 1750-1779.
The Last Words and Dying Speech of. . . .
Worcester, [1779]. Broadside.
AAS copy.   19448

Young, Thomas, 1732-1777.
In Congress, May 15, 1776. Whereas His
Britannic Majesty. . . .
[Philadelphia, 1777.] Broadside.
(JCB Annual Report, 1935-1936, pp.
28-29.)
JCB copy.   15649

[Young, Thomas], 1732-1777.
(D. A. B.)
A Poem Sacred to the Memory of James
Wolfe.
New Haven, [1761]. 19 pp.
(Dated from adv. in Conn. Gazette, Sept.
12, 1761.)
LOC copy.   8471

[Young, Thomas], 1732-1777.
(D. A. B.)
Some Reflections on the Disputes between
New-York, New-Hampshire.
New Haven, 1764. 21, [2] pp.
NYPL copy.   9889

Young, William, 1755-1829.
Books for Sale. . . . 1792.
[Philadelphia, Young, 1792.] 12 pp.
LOC copy.   25062

Young, William, 1755-1829.
Brown's Dictionary of the Bible.
Proposals.
[Philadelphia, Young, 1792.] Broadside.
JCB copy.   46678

Young, William, 1755-1829.
Current Price of Paper for sale by. . . .
[Philadelphia, 1798.] Broadside.
AAS copy.   48762

Young, William, 1755-1829.
William Young's Catalogue for 1787.
Philadelphia, Young & M'Culloch,
[1786]. [2], 30 pp.
AAS copy.   20173

[Young, William P.
Catalogue of Books.
Charleston, Young, 1796.]
(No copy known.)   31681

Young, William P.
The Palladium of Knowledge; or, the
Carolinian and Georgian Almanac, for
. . . 1788.
Charleston, Wright. [38] pp.
LOC copy.   20905

Young, William P.
The Palladium of Knowledge: or, The
Carolina and Georgia Almanac, for . . .
1796.
Charleston, Young. [48] pp.
LOC copy.   29940

[Young, William P.
The Palladium of Knowledge: or, The
Carolina and Georgia Almanac, for . . .
1796. . . . Second Edition.
Charleston, Young. [48] pp.]
(This Day is Published, S.C. Gazette,
Nov. 27, 1795.)   29941

[Young, William P.
The Palladium of Knowledge: or, The
Carolina and Georgia Almanac, for . . .

1796. . . . Third Edition.
Charleston, Young.]
(Adv. in Dec., 1795.)   29942

[Young, William P.]
Palladium of Knowledge: or, the Carolina and Georgia Almanac, for . . . 1797.
Charleston, Young. [50] pp.
AAS copy.   31682

[Young, William P.]
Palladium of Knowledge: or, the Carolina and Georgia Almanac, for . . . 1798.
Charleston, Young. [48] pp.
AAS copy.   33256

Young, William P.
Palladium of Knowledge: or, The Carolina and Georgia Almanac, for . . . 1799.
Charleston, Young. [48] pp.
NYPL copy.   35069

[Young & Minns] Boston.
Proposal, for Printing by Subscription, in One Volume Octavo, Gospel News.
[Boston, Young & Minns, 1794.]
Broadside.
AAS copy.   47333

Young & Old Remember Death. . . . March 20th, 1770 [by Samuel Buell, 1716-1798].
New London, 1770. Broadside.]
(No copy located.)   11591

The Young Clerk's Guide.
Boston, B. Green for Buttolph, 1708. [2], 188 pp.
(The only known copy is imperfect.)
MHS copy.   39476

The Young Clerk's Magazine: or, English Law-Repository. . . . Fifth Edition.
Philadelphia, Dunlap & Crukshank, 1774. [4], 303 pp.
AAS copy.   13786

The Young Clerk's Magazine. . . . Sixth Edition.
Philadelphia, Crukshank, 1788. [4], 299, [7] pp.
AAS copy.   21623

The Young Clerk's Magazine. . . . Seventh Edition.
Philadelphia, Crukshank, 1792. [4], 299, [7] pp.
AAS copy.   25063

The Young Clerk's Magazine: or, English Law-Repository. . . . Eighth Edition.
Philadelphia, Crukshank, 1795. [4], 299, [7] pp.
AAS copy.   29944

[The Young Clerk's Vade Mecum. . . . Seventh Edition.
Philadelphia, Bradfords, 1771.]
(Adv. Pa. Journal, Feb. 14, 1771.)   12296

The Young Clerk's Vade Mecum: or, Compleat Law-Tutor.
New York, Gaine, 1776. [12], 236, iv, 86, [10] pp.
AAS copy.   15227

[The Young Clerk's Vade Mecum.
New York, Gaine, 1787.]
("Just Published," N. Y. Gazetteer, Apr. 12, 1787.)   20906

The Young Convert's First Experiences.
[Boston], Printed and Sold near Liberty-Pole, [1795]. Broadside.
AAS copy.   29943

The Young Gentleman's Parental Monitor.
Hartford, Patten, 1792. [8], 148 pp., 1 plate.
AAS copy.   25064

[The Young Gentleman's Parental Monitor.
New York, Loudon, 1792?]
(Entry from adv. "This day . . . published and sold by the Printer hereof," N. Y. Diary, Aug. 25, 1792.)   25065

The Young Gentlemen and Ladies' Accidence.

Worcester, Thomas & Worcester, 1792. 53 pp.
(Evans' entry was from an adv.)
AAS copy.   25066

Young Jemmy is a Pleasing Youth. A Favorite Song.
Boston, von Hagen, [1799]. [2] pp.
BPL copy.   36747

[The Young Ladies and Gentlemen's Spelling Book.
Providence, R. I., Carter & Wilkinson, 1797.]
(A ghost of 31709 arising from advs.)   33257

The Young Lady's Accidence; or a Short and Easy Introduction to English Grammar [by Caleb Bingham, 1757-1819].
Boston, Greenleaf & Freeman, 1785. 45 pp.
AAS copy.   18934

The Young Lady's Accidence. . . . Third Edition [by Caleb Bingham, 1757-1819].
Boston, Thomas, 1789. 57 pp.
(Evans assumed the imprint from an adv.)
AAS copy.   21692

The young Lady's Parental Monitor.
Hartford, Patten, 1792. 164 pp.
AAS copy.   25067

[The Young Lady's Parental Monitor.
New London, Greens, 1792.]
("In the press," Conn. Gazette, May 31, 1792; "Just published," ibid. July 26.)   25068

[The Young Lady's Parental Monitor.
New York, Loudon, 1792?]
(Entry from adv. "This day . . . published and sold by the Printer hereof," N. Y. Diary, Aug. 25, 1792.)   25069

The Young Man's Companion. . . . Second Edition.
New York, Bradfords, 1710. [15], 226 pp.
(No perfect copy located.)
AAS copy.   39517

The Young Man's Companion. . . . Third Edition.
Philadelphia, A. Bradford, 1718. [16], 264 (?) pp.
(The only known copy is imperfect.)
NYPL copy.   39697

The Young Man's Dream: together with the Young Maiden's Dream.
Boston, Bible & Heart, [178-]. Broadside.
NYPL copy.   43759

The Young Man's Magazine, Containing the Substance of Moral Philosophy.
Philadelphia, Story, 1784. 35 pp.
AAS copy.   18895

[The Young Man's Magazine.
Philadelphia, Dobson, 1786.]
(From an adv. in Pa. Gazette, Apr. 19, 1786, apparently for a remainder of 18895, q. v.)   20174

[The Young Man's Monitor.
Cambridge, 1668.]
(Title from S. Green's list.)   134

The Young Mans Preservative [by Cotton Mather, 1663-1728].
Boston, 1701. 72 pp.
AAS copy.   997

The Young Misses Magazine.
Philadelphia, Young, 1800. 2 vol.
(Also entered as 38324, q. v.)   39159

The Young Misses Magazine. . . . Vol. I - II [by Marie Le Prince de Beaumont, 1711-1789].
Whitehall, Pa., Young, 1800. 341, [1]; 324 pp.
Composite copy.   38324

[The Young Nurses Magazine. Containing Dialogues between a Governess and Several Young Ladies.
Philadelphia, Dobson, 1787. 4 vol. in 2.]
(Entry from an adv.)   20907

The Young Quaker, a Comedy [by John

O'Keeffe, 1747-1833].
Philadelphia, Bradford, 1794. 62, [2] pp.
AAS copy.   27448

Young Secretary's Guide.
see
Hill, Thomas (i.e. John)

. . . Young Simon in his Lovely Sue [by Samuel Arnold, 1740-1802].
New York, Gilfert, [c. 1795]. [2] pp.
JCB copy.   29121

Young Willy for Me [by Mrs. Wrighten].
New York, Hewitt for Carr, [1797]. [2] pp.
HSP copy.   33252

Youth in its Brightest Glory [by Cotton Mather, 1663-1728].
Boston, 1709. 36 pp.
HC copy.   1410

Youth Under a Good Conduct [by Cotton Mather, 1663-1728].
Boston, 1704. 44 pp.
BA copy.   1181

The Youthful Jester, or Repository of Wit [by Richard Johnson, 1734-1793].
Baltimore, Warner & Hanna, 1800. 108 pp.
AAS copy.   39160

[The Youth's Assistant: and, the Farmer's Friend.
Concord, N. H., Russell, 1793?]
(Imprint assumed by Evans from adv. "This day Published, and for Sale" in the Mirror, Jan. 7, 1793.)   26524

Youth's Friendly Monitor. . . . Third Edition [by James Burgh, 1714-1775].
Hartford, Patten, 1787. 60 pp.
AAS copy.   20256

Youth's Friendly Monitor. . . . Fourth American Edition [by James Burgh, 1714-1775].
Worcester, Thomas, 1797. 84 pp.
AAS copy.   48083

[The Youth's Instructor in the English Tongue.
Boston, 1731.]
(Item not identified; apparently from an adv.)   3411

[The Youth's Instructor in the English Tongue.
Boston, Henchman, 1750. Front., [4], 130 pp.]
(No copy located.)   6485

The Youth's Instructor.
Boston, Fowle for Edwards and Leverett, 1752. 192 pp.
(The only recorded copy is mislaid.) 40645

The Youth's Instructor in the English Tongue.
Boston, Green & Russell for Henchman, 1757. 159 pp.
(The only copy located is imperfect.)
AAS copy.   7884

The Youth's Instructor in the English Tongue.
Boston, D. & J. Kneeland for Leverett, 1760. 149, [1] pp.
BPL copy.   41180

The Youth's Instructor in the English Tongue.
Boston, S. Kneeland, 1760. 149, [1] pp.
(The only copy located is incomplete; pagination from the Libbie copy.)
AAS copy.   8582

The Youth's Instructor in the English Tongue: or the Art of Spelling.
Boston, Fleets, 1761. 146, [1] pp.
AAS copy.   41252

The Youth's Instructor in the English Tongue.
Boston, Kneeland & Adams, 1767. 159 pp.
LOC copy.   10603

The Youth's Instructor in the English Tongue: or the Art of Spelling Improved.
Boston, M'Alpine, 1767. 148 + pp.